To Jim

With

his five

Coaching at St John's

from

WISDEN

CRICKETERS' ALMANACK

2010

Zak

Robbie

Sayd Berry

Archielock

Alfie

James

SW.

Finlay

Thanks

Keatley

Frank

E May

EDITED BY SCYLD BERRY

WISDEN

CRICKETERS' ALMANACK

2010

147th EDITION

John Wisden & Co

JOHN WISDEN & CO
An imprint of A&C Black Publishers Ltd
36 Soho Square, London W1D 3QY

Reader feedback: almanack@wisden.com

www.wisden.com

WISDEN CRICKETERS' ALMANACK
Editor **Scyld Berry**
Deputy editors **Hugh Chevallier, Steven Lynch** and **Harriet Monkhouse**
Consultant editor **Matthew Engel**
Production co-ordinator **Peter Bather**
Chief statistician **Philip Bailey**
Design consultant **Peter Ward**
Proofreader **Charles Barr**
Database and typesetting **Stephen Cubitt**
Publisher **Charlotte Atyeo**
Consultant publisher **Christopher Lane**

Typeset in Times New Roman and Univers by David Lewis XML Associates Bungay NR35 1JB
Printed in the UK by CPI William Clowes Ltd Beccles NR34 7TL

A CIP catalogue record for this book is available from the British Library

"Wisden" and its woodcut device are registered trademarks of John Wisden & Co

EDITIONS

Cased ISBN 978-1-408124-66-6 £45
Soft cover ISBN 978-1-408124-64-2 £45
Large format ISBN 978-1-408124-65-9 £55
Leatherbound ISBN 978-1-408130-69-8 £260

A Taste of Wisden 2010

"All Sangakkara could think about was that he and his team-mates
were now held hostage: 'Standing still next to the roundabout we
were sitting ducks for the 12 gunmen.'"
The terrorist attack on Lahore, page 27

* * *

"In 2009 Sehwag broke Test cricket's sound barrier
by scoring at more than a run a ball."
The Leading Cricketer in the World, page 80

* * *

"From shambles to Shangri-La, all in the space of 12 months."
Vic Marks on the England team in 2009, page 430

* * *

"It was like following a weekend at Silvio Berlusconi's villa with
a tea dance at E. W. Swanton's."
The 2009 County Championship, page 566

* * *

"'I began the day crying, I ended it crying,
but we won a World Cup in between.'"
Women's World Cup, page 1008

* * *

"Now we had a situation where England and their
administrators simply could not bring themselves to accept an
umpiring decision – a regrettable development."
Mike Atherton on South Africa v England, page 1297

* * *

"'It was the best railway journey I ever made,' he began, and in
the next 600 words this much-loved reporter, who has been a
professional journalist man and boy, supplied the most evocative
essay of the year."
Michael Henderson on Cricket in the Media, page 1625

* * *

"The authorities struggle for a definition of the Spirit of Cricket.
Perhaps the best answer is David Shepherd."
Obituaries, page 1681

6

LIST OF CONTRIBUTORS

Tanya Aldred
David Rayvern Allen
Michael Armstrong-James
Chris Aspin
Mike Atherton
Philip August
Charlie Austin
Colin Bateman
Edward Bevan
Ian Bishop
Paul Bolton
Lawrence Booth
Stephen Brenkley
Daniel Brettig
Colin Bryden
Ian Callender
Don Cameron
Stephen Chalke
Ian Chappell
Simon Cleaves
Malcolm Conn
Paul Coupar
Tony Cozier
John Curtis
Geoffrey Dean
Ralph Dellor
Norman de Mesquita
William Dick
Philip Eden
Paul Edwards
Peter English
John Etheridge
Stephen Fay
Duncan Fletcher
Andy Flower
David Foot

Warwick Franks
Haydn Gill
Nagraj Gollapudi
Gideon Haigh
David Hardy
Norman Harris
Douglas Henderson
Michael Henderson
Paul Hiscock
Richard Hobson
Grenville Holland
Nick Hoult
Steve James
Paul Jones
Abid Ali Kazi
Patrick Kidd
Jarrod Kimber
Stephen Lamb
Justin Langer
Richard Latham
David Llewellyn
Will Luke
Lynn McConnell
Andrew McGlashan
Neil Manthorp
Vic Marks
Christopher Martin-Jenkins
Robin Martin-Jenkins
Alison Mitchell
R. Mohan
Benjamin Moorehead
Gerald Mortimer
Tony Munro
Paul Newman
Michael Parkinson
Mark Pennell

Sarah Potter
Neil Priscott
Qamar Ahmed
Andrew Radd
Charles Randall
Andrew Renshaw
Jenny Roesler
Graham Russell
Chloe Saltau
Osman Samiuddin
Faraz Sarwat
Neville Scott
Shahid Hashmi
Ravi Shastri
Utpal Shuvro
Mehluli Sibanda
Rob Smyth
Andrew Stevenson
Fraser Stewart
Andrew Strauss
Alec Swann
Pat Symes
Bruce Talbot
Ivo Tennant
Sa'adi Thawfeeq
John Townsend
Anand Vasu
Michael Vockins
David Warner
Paul Weaver
Tim Wellock
John Westerby
Simon Wilde
Martin Williamson
Andy Wilson
Dean Wilson

Photographers are credited as appropriate. Special thanks to Patrick Eagar, Graham Morris and Philip Brown.

Cartoons by Nick Newman.

Round the World Contributors to the Round the World section are listed after their articles.

The editor also acknowledges with gratitude assistance from the following: Robin Abrahams, David Baggett, Derek Barnard, Trevor Bedells, Benedict Bermange, Keith Booth, Mike Brearley, Gordon Burling, Marion Collin, Brian Croudy, Prakash Dahatonde, Nigel Davies, Frank Duckworth, Gulu Ezekiel, M. L. Fernando, Ric Finlay, David Frith, Keith Gerrish, Ghulam Mustafa Khan, Richard Gillard, Nicholas Goldman, Michael Hatt, Jonathan Hungin, Brian Hunt, David Kendix, Rajesh Kumar, Dr Tony Lewis, Nirav Malavi, Mahendra Mapagunaratne, Ian Marshall, Roy Morgan, Francis Payne, Bryce Payton, Andrew Samson, Mike Smith, Mark Stickings, Richard Walker, John Ward, Charlie Wat, James Watson, Alan West, Alan Williams and Graeme Wright.

The production of *Wisden* would not be possible without the support and co-operation of many other cricket officials, county scorers, writers and lovers of the game. To them all, many thanks.

PREFACE

Wisden, in the 147 years of its existence, has reported on many significant events beyond the cricket field. None of them, however, has had such a direct and violent impact upon the game as the terrorist attack in Pakistan last year on Sri Lanka's cricket team. Seven of their players were wounded. It was thanks to some outstanding bravery, and fortune, that not one of them was killed, although eight other people were.

One responsibility of this edition, therefore, has been to reconstruct that dreadful March day when cricket lost its innocence – while hoping that a terrorist attack on a cricket team will never be attempted again, and fearing that it probably will. The sport upon the field is becoming ever more adventurous; but safeguarding cricketers, following the horror in Lahore, has to err on the side of caution now.

The one good purpose which violence serves is to remind the unscathed of how lucky they are: in this case, of what a beautifully peaceful place a cricket field normally is. We only appreciate the game fully when the outside world intrudes. The same reminder came during the two World Wars. In the England of 70 years ago there was no first-class cricket – full stop. Before all the survivors pass away, Stephen Chalke has discovered how English cricket managed to endure six whole summers of war, and recounts the story superbly in one of our features.

As ever, the great privilege of editing *Wisden* is being able to ask anyone to write for it, confident that refusals are rare, almost unknown. Drawing on all these correspondents and contributors from around the world, *Wisden* is the sum of our collective experience. I am proud to say I cannot think of any human activity which records itself, and thus perpetuates and strengthens itself, as *Wisden* chronicles cricket.

Turning this collective experience into book form is the work of three deputy editors: Hugh Chevallier, Steven Lynch and Harriet Monkhouse. Their devotion – through rites of passage like births and deaths, new typesetters and computer systems – goes far beyond the call of duty to superhuman proportions in January and February; and Peter Bather ensures the handsome lay-out. Admiration should be directed, not at celebrity, but at those who are the finest in their field.

This year we welcome new typesetters, DLXML, to the Wisden team, and thank Mike Smith, who so ably set this almanack for more than two decades. Christopher Lane and Philip Bailey are the other indispensable players.

My gratitude also goes to the *Sunday Telegraph*, for allowing me to combine editing *Wisden* with being their cricket correspondent, thereby enabling me to report to you from the front line; and to my wonderful wife and children.

SCYLD BERRY
Bristol, March 2010

CONTENTS

Part One – Comment

Part Two – Records and Registers

Part Three – English and European Cricket

STATISTICS

INTERNATIONAL CRICKET IN ENGLAND

LV= COUNTY CHAMPIONSHIP

ONE-DAY COUNTY COMPETITIONS

OTHER ENGLISH CRICKET

Contents

EUROPEAN CRICKET

Part Four – Overseas Cricket

CRICKET IN AUSTRALIA

CRICKET IN BANGLADESH

CRICKET IN INDIA

CRICKET IN NEW ZEALAND

CRICKET IN PAKISTAN

CRICKET IN SOUTH AFRICA

CRICKET IN SRI LANKA

CRICKET IN THE WEST INDIES

CRICKET IN ZIMBABWE

OTHER OVERSEAS INTERNATIONAL CRICKET

OTHER OVERSEAS CRICKET

Part Five – Law and Administration

Part Six – The Wisden Review

Part Seven – The Almanack

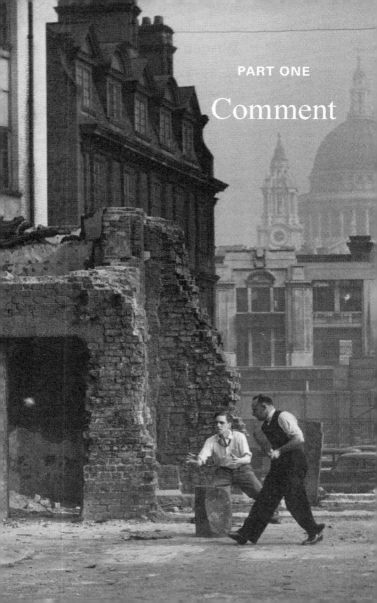

PART ONE

Comment

Wisden Honours

THE LEADING CRICKETER IN THE WORLD

Virender Sehwag (page 80)

The Leading Cricketer in the World is chosen by the editor of *Wisden* in consultation with some of the world's most experienced cricket writers and commentators. The selection is based on a player's class and form shown in all cricket during the calendar year, and is guided by statistics rather than governed by them. There is no limit to how many times a player may be chosen. A list of past winners can also be found on page 80; a notional list, backdated to 1900, appeared on page 35 of *Wisden 2007*.

FIVE CRICKETERS OF THE YEAR

Stuart Broad (page 82)   Michael Clarke (page 85)
Graham Onions (page 87)   Matt Prior (page 89)
Graeme Swann (page 91)

The Five Cricketers of the Year are chosen by the editor of *Wisden*, and represent a tradition that dates back to 1889, making this the oldest individual award in cricket. Excellence in (or influence on) the previous English summer are the major criteria for inclusion in the Five. No one can be chosen more than once. A list of past winners can be found on page 425.

THE WISDEN TEST XI

The *Wisden* Test XI, based solely on performances in Test cricket during the previous calendar year, is selected by a panel of three experienced cricket writers and commentators – all former Test cricketers – from different parts of the world; the editor of *Wisden* has the deciding vote where necessary. The *Wisden* Test XI (see page 93) was first introduced in *Wisden 2009*.

YOUNG WISDEN SCHOOLS CRICKETER OF THE YEAR

Jos Buttler (page 935)

The Schools Cricketer of the Year, based on first-team performances during the previous English summer, is chosen by *Wisden's* schools correspondent in consultation with the editor of *Wisden* and other experienced observers of schools cricket. The winner's school must be in the UK, play cricket to a standard approved by *Wisden's* schools correspondent and provide reports to this almanack.

WISDEN BOOK OF THE YEAR

Harold Larwood by Duncan Hamilton (page 1615)

The *Wisden* Book of the Year is selected by *Wisden's* guest book reviewer; all cricket books published in the previous calendar year and submitted to *Wisden* for possible review are eligible. A list of past winners can be found on page 1616.

Full details of past winners of all these honours can be found at www.wisden.com.

NOTES BY THE EDITOR

An Indian businessman arrived at the India Office in London more than a century ago, seeking permission to start the first steel industry in his own country. Jamshedji Tata was graciously given permission, but only after the Viceroy of India had declared that he would eat his hat if Tata succeeded in producing one ingot of steel. As the Allied war effort in Asia was later to depend on the steel made in the city named after its founder, Jamshedpur, it was just as well for most of us – if not for the viceregal digestion – that Tata did succeed.

Indian businessmen have now taken over the English invention of Twenty20 cricket, just as Jamshedji's descendants, the Tata Steel Group, have bought up what was British Steel. Last year the second Indian Premier League was staged in South Africa, relocated there with a speed and efficiency previously unknown to cricket, and the inaugural Champions League – the first tournament for domestic Twenty20 winners, and some runners-up – was staged in India. While the International Cricket Council repeatedly stated that Test cricket is the highest form of the sport, they organised a second World Twenty20, and seem to be turning it into an almost annual event.

The England and Wales Cricket Board announced before the start of last season that the 2009 Pro40 would be the final 40-over competition, and that it would be replaced by an all-singing and all-dancing Twenty20, so that county cricket would have not one but two 20-over tournaments per summer. Later, the ECB worked out that the sums did not add up, reverted to one 20-over tournament, and abolished the domestic 50-over competition instead. There was no catching the Twenty20 boat once it had sailed east.

England regain the Ashes

Of England captains, only Len Hutton in 1953 and Stanley Jackson in 1905 have done as much as Andrew Strauss accomplished to regain the Ashes during an exhilarating summer: David Gower could be added to this roll of honour, but Australia were at their lowest ebb in 1985. All of these four captains were the leading run-scorers on either side. Their examples created an admirably resilient team spirit among their players. Lower-order batting is one key indicator of a team's morale, and in 2009 England's not only scored more runs, they scored them far more quickly than Australia's. In consequence, England had time to win the two Tests they dominated, whereas Australia had time to win only one.

Strauss, like Jackson, was lucky overall, apart from losing the services of his best batsman, Kevin Pietersen, after the Second Test. Strauss won four tosses, Jackson five, Hutton none at all. Strauss was lucky too in that Brett Lee broke down on the eve of the First Test, after running through England Lions at Worcester with a spell of reverse swing the like of which was not seen again all summer. Lee's combination of fast yorkers and bouncers would not have been to the taste of England's lower order. Moreover, in his absence, Australia had nobody with the experience of English conditions, or the personality, to lead their attack (their four main bowlers in Cardiff were all playing their first Test in this country). Mitchell Johnson was always capable of a magical delivery – whether his bouncer, which all of England's right-hand batsmen found very difficult to play, or the odd ball which swung – but he did not have the confident persona of a strike-bowler.

Strauss was lucky again in that the Australians were knocked out of the ICC World Twenty20 by West Indies and Sri Lanka. Two warm-up games in a month did not give their bowlers sufficient opportunity to adjust fully to the Dukes balls, now used in Tests only in England. Even so, Strauss and his team deserve great acclaim, especially as he had been in the job for no more than six months, his counterpart Ricky Ponting for five and a half years.

The natural order over the last century is pretty clear: in Australia, Australia win almost twice as many Tests as England; in England, the sides are well matched; and normally England need a great fast bowler to tip the balance, wherever the series is staged. Strauss had the benefit of two superlative *spells* of fast bowling, by Andrew Flintoff at Lord's and by Stuart Broad at The Oval. But the most succinct explanation of this conundrum – how on earth did England win when they averaged 34.15 runs per wicket against Australia's 40.64, the biggest disparity that has ever been overturned in any Test series – has to be this: Strauss's batting and captaincy, and the team spirit which he and the new coach Andy Flower created. (If it is thought that I have been swayed by ghosting Strauss's book on the Ashes, I would point out that our reviewer of the series, Christopher Martin-Jenkins, reaches the same conclusion; and Strauss won the Compton–Miller medal as player of the series.)

One particular judgment stands out. Strauss was widely criticised in the media for not making Australia follow on at Lord's, as would have happened in the old days (when there were rest days and no back-to-back Tests). But had Australia batted at anything like their normal rate on that sunny third day at Lord's, against tired bowling, England could easily have been set 200 in the fourth innings, or more. Overall, Strauss was criticised as too defensive, yet his team took six Australian wickets in one session, seven in another, and eight in another. It is worth noting that Hutton, and Peter May in 1956 when he retained the Ashes, were even more criticised by the English media, for being even more defensive.

Same result, much less impact

The 2009 series was the best – the most deliciously fluctuating – Ashes series since 1981, with one exception. But it did not excite the public imagination to anything like the same extent as the one of 2005. Four causes were widely identified. One was that fewer great cricketers were involved in 2009: only one, Ponting, unequivocally deserved this title, although he was not treated as such by the sections of crowds that booed him. Secondly, the suspense was not so intense because England had been waiting only two and a half years to regain the Ashes, not half a generation as in 2005. Thirdly, although there was so very little between the teams, the Tests themselves were not close, except for Edgbaston, and that was ruined by rain.

Fourthly, and perhaps most importantly, the 2009 Ashes series had a television audience of one quarter of what it had been at the equivalent stages in 2005. It was not on free-to-air television – and, a few months afterwards, a committee chaired by David Davies recommended to the UK government that home Ashes series should be available, owing to their "national resonance", for all to see. This has to be right: the creation of role models is essential for the health of English cricket. Sights such as Flintoff's spell on the fifth morning at Lord's, or Broad's at The Oval, or Strauss's sangfroid in both innings on the turning pitch which was conveniently provided for that game, or Graeme Swann's exuberance whether batting or bowling spin, are seeds which have to be sown if the sport is to prosper.

Sophia so good

Cardiff lived up to the honour of becoming the 100th Test venue by staging the opening Test faultlessly at Sophia Gardens. The friendly spirit of all officials was widely appreciated, and the setting hailed as a delight to the eye. For England's cricketers, who had seldom played in Glamorgan, it was something of a neutral venue: several admitted to being uncommonly nervous as the series began, and there was no familiar setting to soothe them. Also, the pitch was a Welsh one, suited to the off-cutters of a Don Shepherd or Steve Barwick. But England's miraculous escape – the longest partnership by any Test No. 10 and 11 to achieve a draw – made the Ashes opener a success overall. Not that the United Kingdom needs any more Test grounds. Fewer venues with greater capacities would make prices more affordable, compared with £70 and upwards for one day of the Ashes. What England does need is one large stadium for Twenty20 cricket, and the ECB's reluctance to negotiate seriously for the use after 2012 of the Olympic Stadium, at something like full capacity, and in an area of London without a cricket ground, has been deeply regrettable.

Gibson's greatest challenge

England's good housekeeping in the Ashes, compared to Australia's profligacy with wides and no-balls, is illustrated in our review of the series. Later, in South Africa, they bowled only four no-balls in four Tests: an issue which had bedevilled England had gone away. Ottis Gibson, their bowling coach, can take much of the credit, not for waving a magic wand, but for supervising practice day after day, making sure that England's bowlers always had an umpire standing in the nets, and breaking the bad habit.

If anybody can talk enough sense to bring West Indies' administrators and players together, it will be Gibson in his new role as their head coach. The very existence of the West Indies cricket team – rather than separate entities such as Jamaica or Trinidad & Tobago – will be in doubt if there is another players' strike to follow the one last year, when their first team missed the Champions Trophy and their home series against Bangladesh. As Chris Gayle takes bowling apart, he reminds us that West Indian cricket at its exuberant best has a style like no other.

Where there isn't a will...

If the Football Association reduced the length of Premiership matches to 72 minutes, supporters would naturally claim that the chances of England winning the World Cup had been diminished. If the Rugby Football Union reduced professional club games to 64 minutes, the effect upon the national team would be criticised as injurious. Yet, somehow, the ECB have got away with abolishing the domestic 50-over competition: no limited-overs match henceforth between counties will be longer than 40 overs per side.

"If at first you don't succeed, try, try and try again" is a fine maxim – though not, as the joke goes, for sky-divers. But England's administrators have changed it into: "If at first you don't succeed, give up." The facts are:

	World Cup	Champions Trophy	World Twenty20	Total
Australia	4	2	0	6
West Indies	2	1	0	3
India	1	$1/2$	1	$2^1/_2$
Pakistan	1	0	1	2
Sri Lanka	1	$1/2$	0	$1^1/_2$
New Zealand......	0	1	0	1
South Africa	0	1	0	1
England..........	**0**	**0**	**0**	**0**

In other words, England remain the only Full Member of the ICC (excluding the two most recent additions, Bangladesh and Zimbabwe) never to have won a global tournament, in 17 attempts. And the official response has been to alter the domestic structure in such a way as to reduce England's chances of winning the World Cup in future. Is this right, or ethically defensible? Should it not be the duty of every national sporting body to do what it can to enable the national team to win, for nothing will do more to popularise this sport than winning? I would also argue that it is the duty of national government to ensure that winning, not the maximisation of income, is the priority of a national sporting body.

When Lord MacLaurin was chairman of the ECB, their mission statement was for England to be the best in the world: to be No. 1 in Test and one-day cricket. Not any more: this has all been watered down into being "successful". Before we move on, however, we should record that five first-class counties had the interests of the national team at heart and acknowledged the hand which feeds each of them over £2m a year. The other 13 counties ignored the recommendation of the ECB's own cricket committee that 50-over cricket should be preserved, voted for a 40-over competition, and then had their majority verdict endorsed by the full board of the ECB, which is designed to rubber-stamp the first-class counties' interests.

The official rationale was that 40-over cricket was more popular with county members than 50-over cricket. Of course it was: one was played in summer, the other in spring. Snail-racing and toenail-clipping are likely to attract more spectators than a lukewarm 50-over game in April – which is when the Friends Provident Trophy was fated to start – between two counties playing the day after they have finished a four-day match. At the end of last April three counties played a Championship game from Wednesday to Saturday *and* a 50-over match on Sunday *and* another 50-over match on Monday, with much travelling in between. When the members of the Professional Cricketers' Association voted last summer, it was not surprising that over 82% expressed the belief that the domestic game should mirror international cricket; and 89% said they did not have faith in the ECB's leadership.

There is nothing wrong with a 50-over match played between two relatively fresh and skilled sides on a true pitch. The essential ingredients are genuine pace, high-class spin, and batsmen trying to bat through an innings to make hundreds. Such was the standard of 40-over county cricket last season that the death bowling for Warwickshire and Worcestershire was done by Jonathan Trott and Daryl Mitchell, bowling gentle medium-pace. No wonder the two counties in the inaugural Champions League were embarrassed, and only one county cricketer (Eoin Morgan) was bought in the IPL auction of 2010. Only two one-day hundreds were scored for England last year; and the habit will be acquired with even greater difficulty in 40-over county cricket, unless the bowling becomes ever more dire. The ICC regulation that a ball must be changed after 34 overs in a one-day international, as it starts to reverse-swing, will be another novelty to which England's future 50-over players will be forced to adjust.

Taylor-made to succeed

Winning World Cups and the World Twenty20 is not something to which England Women are strangers, and they must be congratulated on doing both in the space of a few months. Organising the women's tournament alongside the knockout stages of the men's World Twenty20 last summer was a fine initiative by the ICC; and it allowed television viewers to see the exceptional skill of Claire Taylor. In England's semi-final against Australia at The Oval, *Wisden's* first female Cricketer of the Year gave a perfect demonstration of run-chasing by scoring 76 not out from 53 balls. The ECB deserve credit, in this case, for giving England's women cricketers exactly what they need to be the best of their kind. Where there is an official will, there is a way to win.

Pandora's abdominal protector

As with every human invention, both good and ill have resulted from India's virtual takeover and vigorous commercialisation of Twenty20 cricket. For good, the parameters of batting and fielding have been extended, increasing the game's delights. Bowling has been less improved: at least that seemed to be the case at Centurion last November when England were hit by South Africa's opening pair of Graeme Smith and Loots Bosman for 170 runs. What used to take a couple of sessions in a Test match, or even a whole day in the 1950s, was scored from 13 overs.

During the World Twenty20 in England, Sri Lanka's Tillekeratne Dilshan popularised the stroke whereby he went down on his back knee and helped the ball over his left shoulder or straight over his head. Some called it the "Dilscoop", but it would be wrong to credit him with the stroke's invention. In 1933, when batting for the West Indians at Lord's, Learie Constantine scooped over his head for six a full toss from MCC's pace bowler Maurice Allom, and there are earlier references too. Australia's wicketkeeper either side of the First World War, Hanson Carter, who in his day-job was an undertaker, might have got the idea for his shovel shot from grave-digging. After the introduction of the helmet, the stroke became less fraught with physical danger and was occasionally used.

Let Dilshan be truly honoured for his bravery during the terrorist attack on the Sri Lankan team bus in Lahore, when a cricket team was directly targeted for the first time, and the sport became no longer an escape from daily life but part of it. Dilshan's heroic role in piloting the team bus to safety is described in the article following these Notes.

Another good to come out of Twenty20 is that the boundaries of fielding have been extended, literally. Several international fielders have now palmed the ball up inside the rope to stop it going for six, been carried over the boundary by their momentum, then returned to the field of play to complete the catch. As described in our introduction to the Laws (page 1499), MCC now intend to amend one of them, without spoiling either the fun or the breathtakingly gymnastic skills Twenty20 has mothered. The change is designed to stop a fielder back-pedalling beyond the boundary before leaping into the air and palming the ball back inside the rope.

Where there's an ill…

It was neither good nor ill, merely silly of the IPL's commissioner, Lalit Modi, to claim: "The quality of cricket that is played in the IPL is by far the best in the cricket matches that I have seen or for that matter anybody else has seen." One expects a businessman to talk up the value of his product, especially during a global recession. Far more disturbing was the Indian board's reprimand of their highly estimable coach, Gary Kirsten, for making perfectly valid criticisms of the IPL. Almost half of each franchise team consists of uncapped young Indian players, which is a commendable initiative, and it is obvious that the standard of the IPL is below that of international cricket.

For staging the second IPL in South Africa without any surveillance by the Anti-Corruption and Security Unit, "cricket paid a price", according to the ICC. Shortly afterwards "a number of approaches" were made to various cricketers to fix matches in the World Twenty20 in England. It is a matter of faith whether we believe the ACSU's claim that all of the approaches made to players were reported to them. The growth of Twenty20 has attracted many people not interested in the traditional formats and, in these straitened times, not all will have the good of the game at heart. Tim May, chief executive of the international players' union FICA, said: "Twenty20 is just ripe for corruption – the shorter the game, the more influence each particular incident can have. So I think it opens up a great deal of opportunities for the bookmakers to try and corrupt players." And a corrupt cricketer will take the contagion back to the country from which he comes.

Umpiring after Shep

David Shepherd died last year. If Dickie Bird was the most famous of all umpires, Shep was the most loved. Even the most frustrated fast bowler, who had just had his appeal rejected, could see from his rueful, emollient, smile that Shep understood the game's tribulations and sympathised. It was perhaps as well, though, that he had retired before the ICC introduced their system of referrals and reviews.

Four Test series trialled referrals, an immensely complicated system whereby a team could refer a decision by the two on-field umpires to the third umpire, with a maximum of three unsuccessful referrals per innings. Then came the Umpire Decision Review System, with a limit of two unsuccessful reviews per innings. This was an improvement, if only because anything had to be better than its predecessor, but it was still the source of conflict – notably when Graeme Smith was given not out in the Johannesburg Test against England. And, while players openly questioned the umpires' decisions, spectators in the ground had to twiddle their thumbs, not having the faintest idea what was going on.

Fashions change. It has become polite to turn your back on a person, if he or she is entering a PIN number. It is now considered sensible to dispense with a third man, however many edges fly for four: it is no coincidence that last year saw the second-fastest rate of scoring ever known in Test cricket. But questioning the umpire's decision must never become a fashion: it will have damaging long-term consequences for all levels of the game. What may start as fun – a club bowler or fielder making the shape of a T when he disagrees with a decision – will become a whole process of insidious undermining.

I remain with the ex-Sir Allen Stanford on this one, although not, I trust, in other respects. The system of consultation that he trialled in his Twenty20 matches in Antigua is the best seen so far. Technology needs to be incorporated on an increasing scale: if the best three or four umpires, such as Simon Taufel and Aleem Dar, officiated in all Test matches, I think everyone would be happy simply to have line-decisions settled by technology, and for the rest accept umpires' very occasional human errors. But the standard dips alarmingly after this elite handful, so technology such as Hawk-Eye, Hot Spot, and the Snickometer, must be used at the highest level.

It would be best if the three umpires arrived at a decision together, through consultation, as in the Stanford tournament, and without any questioning by the players. There is enough on a captain's plate already without the decision of whether or not to use a review becoming a major, match-turning issue. It is also illogical that justice should be rationed: after two unsuccessful reviews, a team can suffer a gross miscarriage without any recourse.

And maybe the three umpires should take it in turns, so that each does one session per day in front of the television and two in the middle. But let the ICC do their experiments outside Test series. The last year of umpiring trials –

while earnest and well-intentioned – damaged the image of the game, and of the ICC itself, because any organisation which keeps on tinkering and making new announcements loses respect.

Value for money

Lest it be thought I have been too critical in these pages of the ECB, let me bring the reader's attention to the good which they do. They have spread out an umbrella under which staff and many, many volunteers do invaluable work for club or school cricket. In addition to promoting women's cricket in the way it should be, during 2009 the ECB have:

- donated £2m to *Chance to Shine*
- made grants (so much more useful than loans) of over £2m to recreational clubs
- donated £400,000 to Lord's Taverners
- given more than £3m to the 38 county boards to spend on their development operations
- spent another £3m on development managers and officers, and on age-group and Minor Counties cricket
- spent over £800,000 on subsidising and administering coaching programmes for everyone below elite Level 4
- had to cough up £650,000 a year on child protection, in the form of Criminal Records Bureau checks. (Ludicrously, the government insist that even a regular club scorer now has to have a CRB check. A child cannot go into the scorer's box and ask for his or her stats without this bureaucracy.)

Personally, I would like to see a little less of the development budget going on coaching and a little more in providing decent playing facilities. While covering England's one-day series in South Africa, I visited the Galashwe township in Kimberley, where Loots Bosman grew up and learned his cricket at a club called Yorkshire, and another township club in Port Elizabeth, called Gelvandale, again with very few resources, which has produced three Test players in Ashwell Prince, Alviro Petersen and Wayne Parnell. What children need if they are to play cricket are sunshine, space, a true surface of some kind (it doesn't have to be turf initially: Prince and Petersen grew up playing for one street against another), and a bat and a taped tennis ball. These are inexpensive items, if not always easy to obtain. Coaching comes later; and role models are necessary too. Bosman, I should add, is still the only indigenous African batsman to have represented South Africa.

Add up all the ECB's sums and you can just about allow their claim that they invest 20% of their total cricket expenditure on development. What should be debated is how the rest of their net income – mostly generated by the England team through broadcasting deals – is spent. Well over half of it goes in distribution fees to the counties, only for them to do what is sometimes not in the national interest. If the first-class counties accept over £2m a year each, as they do, they should feel obliged in return to raise standards by reducing the amount they play and to mirror international formats.

Less stress for Strauss

It is nothing less than outrageous that the England team is flogged into the ground primarily to subsidise the counties. One by one, the England players last year – after climbing the summit of their Test match profession by defeating Australia – fell off their perches. In the one-day series alone, James Anderson, Stuart Broad and Paul Collingwood, three of the pillars of England's one-day side, had to be rested; and Anderson picked up a knee injury that dogged him the whole winter. It was indefensible to schedule a flight to Belfast the day after the Ashes, and for England to be forced to play ten limited-overs games in the four following weeks, then stuck on the plane next day for the Champions Trophy.

Restraint, not rotation, is the answer. It was fine to rest Anderson for England's tour of Bangladesh, and consistent with English cricket's tradition of allowing fast bowlers to miss a tour. Otherwise, the 11 best cricketers must take the field, in a mentally and physically fit state. (It is surely no coincidence that Australia have fallen from grace at the same time that their programme has been increased almost to England proportions.) To field an England side packed with replacements, because the main players are exhausted, would be to defraud spectators, viewers, broadcasters, and the game itself.

It was an eloquent condemnation of the ECB's scheduling, and their failure to implement a key recommendation of the 2007 Schofield Report which they themselves commissioned, when Strauss felt unable to lead England on their tour of Bangladesh. All England's modern captains have been stressed out by the job, but it happened to Strauss after a single year. He and Andy Flower had rapidly become as fine a pairing as Michael Vaughan or Nasser Hussain with Duncan Fletcher. Strauss had led England to the Ashes, and a shared Test series in South Africa, and had regenerated their 50-over side. When England played without him, they lost a 20-over game against the Netherlands at Lord's. Strauss and his players deserve better treatment from their employers.

Test of champions

Calls for a Test championship play-off have grown louder, but a fair and workable plan has yet to be proposed. If every one, two or four years, the top two countries meet in a one-off final, far too much weight could fall on the toss. The best team can be decided only by a full Test series. This is why they were invented.

Until a workable way is devised, it is up to administrators to organise the Test programme far more coherently – if they truly want the format to survive. India played South Africa, in India, in a three-Test series in 2008 and again in a two-Test series less than two years later in early 2010. This is lamentable: far better to stage one series of five Tests, identify the stronger side in all conditions and, over two months, engage the attention of the whole cricket world. Instead, India and South Africa decided the top place in the world Test rankings – in India's favour – on the inadequate basis of two games.

This summer will offer a taste of what a Test championship play-off would be like, when Pakistan meet Australia at Lord's and Headingley: the first neutral Tests in England since 1912, when Australia met South Africa in a triangular series. One hopes the weather is kinder than it was then. The ECB are right to help Pakistan's national cricket team survive in exile, but the world should provide for Pakistan's future at the same time. As land prices are not at their most expensive, perhaps now is the time to buy an out-of-town venue which can be built like a fortress for security – much like Mohali, on the outskirts of Chandigarh, where England played in December 2008.

If the ICC move to India, we might as well say ta, ta

The ICC are set to move their headquarters from Dubai. If they relocate to India, cricket will be compromised. Were the ICC to be based in New Delhi or Mumbai, the power-base of their next president Sharad Pawar, the staff would become predominantly Indian as the main current administrators would find it too difficult to relocate their families there, and the organisation would cease to reflect the attitudes and values of all its members. The sport would become as much of a hostage to India and their ambitions as it was to England and Australia when the headquarters were at Lord's. Cricket, like any other organism, needs diversity to evolve, rather than Indianisation. It is not a business, or an industry like steel, to be taken over.

THE TERRORIST ATTACK IN LAHORE

When cricket lost its innocence

Nagraj Gollapudi and Scyld Berry

Mahela Jayawardene, Sri Lanka's captain, was finding it difficult to reach his wife on her mobile phone. Already on that Tuesday morning he had tried her twice, but on both occasions the call went straight to voicemail. It was his ritual on tour to call Christina as soon as he boarded the team bus, and it was no different after he had walked out of the Pearl Continental hotel in Lahore and joined the rest of the Sri Lankan cricketers waiting to go to the Gaddafi Stadium.

At about 8.20 a.m., the convoy – comprising a white minivan for the ICC match officials, security vehicles, policemen on motorbikes, a fire engine and an ambulance, as well as the Sri Lankans' team bus, although not the Pakistanis' – turned left out of the hotel, did a U-turn, then drove alongside a canal in the residential district of Gulberg. "All the roads were supposedly blocked off," Chris Broad, the match referee who was travelling in the minivan, remembers. "But we saw the occasional tuk-tuk and motorbike on the roads, so they weren't really clear."

The atmosphere in the Sri Lankans' air-conditioned bus on March 3, 2009, the third day of the Lahore Test, was no different to any other morning. Some players had opted to draw down the window blinds; some, like Jayawardene, who always sits in the left corner at the back of the bus, preferred to watch the outside scenes, as he tried again to call Christina. There was a bit of banter. Some players listened to music on their iPods, others phoned their loved ones back home.

Paul Farbrace, Sri Lanka's assistant coach, was pondering how to bowl Pakistan out twice in the next three days. Farbrace sat three seats back on the front left-hand side, behind the new mystery spinner Ajantha Mendis, of whom he had high hopes, with the opening batsman Tharanga Paranavitana behind him. Kumar Sangakkara and Thilan Samaraweera, who had scored a double-century in the first two days of the game, were sitting further back and talking about how to give Jayawardene a victory in his last Test as captain before he stood down to focus on his batting.

Suddenly, as the convoy approached the Liberty Roundabout, Jayawardene heard sharp, crackling noises – and Tillekeratne Dilshan screaming in Sinhalese to his team-mates to get down below the seats. Jayawardene realised they were being shot at and inadvertently dropped his phone on the floor.

"There is a 30-second clip still on Christina's voicemail of the attacks and surrounding noise," Jayawardene says. "Including the players screaming inside the bus."

The first noises that Farbrace heard were like popcorn exploding loudly. He also heard shouts from the back of the bus – Jayawardene had been wounded. "I got hit on the right ankle, and later it was reported it was shrapnel," Jayawardene says. But a bullet had grazed him, his sock was soaked in blood, and he could not feel his right foot any more.

Farbrace heard shouts of "Get down, get down!" from Dilshan. "I had absolutely no idea that we were being attacked by terrorists. I just thought there was something going on in the street," he says, shock in his voice still, months later.

For defence, Farbrace tried to wrap himself around the seat in front. Mendis then fell down in front of him, with shrapnel in his head and back. "Just then I felt something hit my right arm, and a piece of metal was sticking out of my arm with blood everywhere," Farbrace recollects.

Sangakkara, who had just been immersed in his conversation with Samaraweera, dared to raise his head to get a glimpse of what exactly was happening – and brushed with death: "For some reason I moved my head to get a better view and a split second later I felt a bullet fizz past my ear into the vacant seat."

The bus had been brought to a halt as it reached the roundabout. The terrorists' first bullets were bang on target: they killed five security men in a leading vehicle, then punctured the front tyres of the Sri Lankan bus, forcing the driver Mohammad Khalil to abandon the wheel. Muttiah Muralitharan, Sri Lanka's world-record-breaking spinner, recalls: "After about 30 seconds the bus came to a halt, and the bullets were raining on the coach. Fortunately, being a 60-seater bus, there was loads of space and most of us dived into the aisle."

A poor-quality image taken from video footage shows the proximity of two gunmen to the minivan in which the match officials are trapped. To the left – and providing some shelter from other terrorists – is an ambulance.

Sri Lanka's cricket team were now a stationary target. Paranavitana was hit in the chest and fell down instantly. "I thought he was finished," was Samaraweera's initial reaction. "His shirt was full of blood." Next instant Samaraweera himself thought something had hit his left leg. He felt it and there was blood on his hands. A bullet had pierced the inside of his thigh, a hand's length from the knee.

Others, like Sri Lanka's coach Trevor Bayliss, were lucky. The window beside which he sat had three bullet holes at chest height. "Had Trevor not got down he would've been shot three times," Farbrace says. "It was remarkable only one bullet actually went into somebody, and it was Thilan Samaraweera."

All Sangakkara could think about was that he and his team-mates were now held hostage in the middle of a big city centre: "Standing still next to the roundabout we were sitting ducks for the 12 gunmen."

And, as the awful minutes passed, the occupants of the bus could do nothing but wait, trapped. "The only thought that passed my mind was when I'm going to be hit next," Jayawardene says. Farbrace never feared he would die, but admits he was thinking: "Please don't hit me again." Muralitharan recalls: "I thought, 'If I die, it does not matter, but we have to get the bus moving.'"

Outside, the noise was getting louder. Initially, it was only bullets being sprayed at the convoy. Now there were explosions, as the players cowered under the seats. So many windows had been shattered that street dust had seeped through the cracks and holes and was now clouding the view. "We only found out afterwards that a rocket launcher just missed us as we began moving and turned for the stadium gates, the rocket blowing up an electricity pylon," Sangakkara says. "Khalil saw a hand grenade tossed at us that failed to explode."

Muralitharan thinks the experience of nearly three decades of civil war back home gave the Sri Lankans a small understanding of how to survive. "The players reacted instinctively and naturally, diving right down on to the floor of the bus rather than on the seats," he says. "Had we panicked, staying on seats or trying to run, we might have been killed."

Nobody can precisely say for how long the bus served as a firing range. What is known is that the terrorists' first strike came soon after 8.30 a.m.; and, as the minutes ticked by, two heroes emerged. The first was Dilshan, who was sitting at the front. The seating in the bus was such that, on entering, you took a couple of steps up before turning right, with the driver, Khalil, to your left. Climbing a further three steps took you into the main seating area. So Dilshan was in a higher, and better, position than the driver to see what was happening outside, but only if he put himself in mortal danger by sticking his head up. Yet that is what he did; then he directed the driver to start moving the bus.

"Dilshan's voice will stay with me for ever," Farbrace says. "He was shouting to the bus driver to 'Reverse! Reverse!' as he had seen the terrorists ahead of us. The driver was under fire from the gunmen but Dilshan, who was sitting at the front behind the driver, kept lifting his head and looking through the window to see where the terrorists' fire was coming from and guiding the driver. The driver was trying to hide under the steering wheel almost, and Dilshan was navigating him."

If Dilshan wins the bravery medal from Farbrace, Sangakkara confers that honour on the driver. "The truth is we owe our lives to the courageous Mohammad Khalil – I will for ever be grateful to him. The tyres of the bus had been shot out, and he was in grave personal danger, exposed to gunfire at the front of the bus. But he was hell-bent on getting us to safety and, somehow, he got that bus moving again. Had Khalil not acted with such courage and presence of mind, most of us would have been killed."

Khalil crashed past the iron barricades to the Gaddafi, less than half a kilometre from the Liberty Roundabout. When the bus stopped next, the players did not yet realise they were at the ground. Only when people outside

The Sri Lankan team bus at the Gaddafi Stadium.

started to shout "Get out!" did the players scramble from the bus and help their injured team-mates into the dressing-room.

"As we moved towards the stadium, Tharanga [Paranavitana] announced he was hit as he sat up holding his chest. He collapsed on to his seat, and I feared the worst," Sangakkara recollects. Muralitharan says: "Blood was pouring down the aisle. I thought he was going to die and we were screaming for an ambulance to take him and Thilan." Incredibly, the bullet had hit Paranavitana's sternum at such an angle that it had not penetrated.

Samaraweera realised he could not stand up, and sought the help of Chamara Kapugedera, who lifted him from the bus to the dressing-room, where the players pulled the door shut behind them. They could still hear gunshots in the distance – the Sri Lankan team were now safe, or at least safer, but the minivan holding the umpires and match officials remained stranded at the Liberty Roundabout.

Jayawardene remembers the shooting continuing for quite some time after they had reached the dressing-room. "We could still hear the shots, and then realised it was the umpires' van that was being shot at. I'm still surprised how the officials escaped, as their vehicle was much smaller and less secure."

At breakfast in the Pearl Continental that morning, Pakistan's captain Younis Khan had walked up to the table where Ahsan Raza, the fourth umpire, was sitting to inform him that his team would start for the ground 15 minutes later than usual. On the first two days of the Lahore Test, both teams had started for the ground at the same time, followed by the match officials' minibus. But on this Tuesday morning, Younis said his team were very tired after spending much of the First Test in Karachi, and almost two days in Lahore, under the unrelenting sun. In Karachi, the teams and officials had set off at different times, but Younis thought he had better obtain permission here.

Raza recalls Chris Broad, the match referee, being seated at his table when Younis approached. Broad remembers only that he had been chatting to Danish Kaneria and Kamran Akmal on the next table, and was happy to have some company when Raza joined him – especially as Broad wanted to buy a "good hockey stick" for his nephew and had asked Raza, who comes from Lahore, for help. Broad doesn't recollect any conversation with Younis. "When we boarded the minibus, I remember thinking: 'Why aren't the Pakistanis here?' I didn't see their bus at all. My understanding is that when the shooting started, they were on their way somewhere behind us. Then they were told to turn back to the hotel. I don't know."

Abdul Sami Khan, liaison officer for the match officials, had told Broad and Raza that their 12-seater vehicle was ready to depart for the Gaddafi. The other four officials were on-field umpires Simon Taufel and Steve Davis, the third umpire Nadeem Ghauri, and Peter Manuel, the ICC's regional manager of Pakistani and Sri Lankan umpires. Sami sat alongside the driver; behind them, Raza sat on the left-hand side, paired with Broad to his right; Davis and Ghauri were behind them, with Taufel and Manuel in the back row.

As they approached the Liberty Roundabout, behind the Sri Lankan team bus, policemen in light-blue uniforms were stopping the traffic. "Peter Manuel said afterwards that he saw cars coming out in front of these policemen," Broad says. "When we were about two-thirds of the way round the round-about, I heard a popping sound, and Raza told us to get down on the floor of the bus."

Bullets began ripping through the match officials' van: about 85 bullet holes were later counted, according to Raza. He lay in what might have been the safest place in the vehicle, curled up in the tiny hollow square by the sliding door. "Broad was screaming and shouting various things in his shocked state," Raza remembers. He was worried that with his 6ft 4in frame Broad was an easy target for the terrorists.

B. K. Bangash, AP/PA

The terrorists' weapons are put in display on Lahore.

Broad admits he was terrified, never having heard the sound of real gunshots before. The closest he had come was in 2006: "I had been in a hotel in Colombo, and having lunch with Billy Bowden, when a bomb went off – the Tamil Tigers had tried to kill the Pakistan High Commissioner in Sri Lanka. Billy thought it was a thunderstorm, but I said immediately it was a bomb. The South African players flew home straight away."

Raza says that, like Sangakkara, he lifted his head up – to try and calm Broad down – and was immediately struck by two bullets. The first one pierced his right lung while the second one burst open his liver. "I felt as if a fireball had exploded inside me," he says.

The pain became unbearable. Raza started to recite the *kalima*, an Islamic prayer. He felt his heart was sinking, and his breathing slowed down. Words spurted out of his mouth as he pleaded: "Water, I need water, Chris. Please, Chris!"

"In the bus we were stationary for ten to twelve minutes," Broad says, "and three-quarters of the way through Ahsan Raza was hit, and all this blood gushed very quickly out of his back and this stream was rushing on to the step of the bus. I arced up and tried to put my hand on his back to stop the flow." Like the Sri Lankans, Broad was lucky. "If my head had been four inches higher when the bullet had been fired I would have copped it."

Zafar Khan, the minivan driver, was shot in his heart and killed instantly. The liaison officer Sami, also at the front, was hit in the shoulder. Someone was needed to drive the van to safety. Despite Broad's best attempts, blood just kept coming out of Raza's torn body.

"Then the van door opened and a chap in black got in with a pistol, and for a moment we all thought – this is it. He jumped over me and on to a seat to get away from the shooting," Broad remembers. "I don't think we were the major target, so the terrorists wandered off into the side streets." Broad's fear was that, if this intruder started to shoot, the terrorists would target the van again.

Broad credits the dead Zafar for having pulled up the van beside the stationary ambulance, which had stopped on the roundabout to their left. "We saw the ambulance later at the ground and the whole of the left-hand side had bullets in it, and the tyres were shot out. So there had been a lot of firing from the left side, and if the ambulance had not been there we would have taken those bullets. Our driver was a hero for pulling up alongside it and giving us some cover."

As the firing quietened down, Broad remembers Nadeem Ghauri put his head up above the seats and looked out of the windows – the glass was no longer there because it had been shot out. "He said, 'They've gone'. Then another chap in black – we found out later they were from the elite force – dragged the dead driver out of his seat and on to the road and drove us towards the Gaddafi." All this time the side door of the van was still ajar, and none of the passengers had got up off the floor.

When they came to the barricades outside the stadium, there was a lot of shouting because the alarmed troops manning them were ready to open fire at anyone approaching. "We heard metal being dragged across the road, and the bus veered round one barricade and another, then stopped outside the stadium.

Nir Elias, Reuters

Tillekeratne Dilshan carries his daughter on his return to Colombo, the day after the attack.

The side door opened and Ahsan was just dragged out of the van on to the dusty road. He had been blocking the doorway and had to be moved, but I remember thinking – why does he have to be dragged out like this?" Broad wonders, still.

"We ran into the umpires' room at the stadium, and the relief was something I'd never known before – tears, swearing, hugs. Everyone realised it had been one of the most terrifying moments of our lives," Broad says.

In the Sri Lankan dressing-room, meanwhile, the frayed nerves, hurt bodies and numb minds had not yet settled down. Some players retreated into various corners trying to find a free space for themselves to understand what had happened. Some were instantly on the phone; others stared into oblivion. Tears started streaming from some players as they tried to explain the happenings to their families back in Sri Lanka.

Then the steadily settling calm was destroyed by desperate Pakistan Cricket Board officials, security personnel and paramedics who had rushed to the ground along with ambulances. "There was a lot of panic, a lot of anger as people came in and started to mention the names of certain terrorist groups. We were adamant not to get back into the ambulance when the paramedics suggested we go to the hospital. I refused to go back on the road," Farbrace says. "What we needed was help and support, not commotion."

The security officials did not know what to do. Players were screaming for doctors. In the ensuing mêlée, someone suggested they had to calm down. Furious, Jayawardene almost hit the man who suggested it, as he took him by the scruff of his collar and shouted at him to shut up and get a paramedic for two players bleeding profusely. "We were in a state of shock – and this guy was asking us to be patient!" he says, raising the pitch of his voice.

By then Jayawardene had finally contacted his wife Christina. He called her as soon as he entered the dressing-room. Mercifully, she had still not listened to her messages on voicemail.

Ambulances eventually arrived. Paranavitana and Samaraweera were rushed to hospital. But as more people started entering the dressing-room the players feared the terrorists could still come back. So they asked everyone to vacate the room, and only when it was ascertained that an official was genuine was he allowed to enter.

A television in the dressing-room was replaying footage of the shooting, which allowed the Sri Lankans to view their miraculous escape. But they were alarmed at the media reporting their whereabouts. "When the media was reporting that the players were safe inside the ground, the players were shocked, as that would help the terrorists to rush to the ground," Jayawardene says.

The Sri Lankan president, Mahinda Rajapakse, called Jayawardene, telling him that he was sending a charter plane straight from Colombo. Hotel staff at the Pearl Continental were told to pack the players' bags, and after a few hours the party were airlifted by helicopter from the ground to Lahore airport. As captain, Jayawardene did not want to leave Samaraweera and Paranavitana behind. Only when the doctors in Lahore gave the pair an all-clear did the team board the flight.

Sri Lanka were not supposed to be in Pakistan in 2009. Originally, India were scheduled to tour Pakistan for a Test series, but they had pulled out in the aftermath of the terrorist attacks in Mumbai which had been spread over the last dreadful days of November 2008. So the Sri Lankan board had agreed to fill the breach. Their players, obviously, had some apprehensions.

"After the Indians pulled out, and the Australians too refused to tour Pakistan, we were a bit concerned when our administrators accepted the tour," Jayawardene says. "So we actually questioned the board about the security conditions. They assured us that the Pakistan government had promised us VVIP security, so with those assurances we went ahead with the tour."

Everyone felt there was a stark difference in security when the action shifted after the Karachi Test to Lahore. "We went to the ODIs and were comfortable with the security around us in both Karachi and Lahore," Jayawardene says. "But when we went back for the Test series we felt the security wasn't what it had been during the ODI in Lahore. We questioned that, but people in the know-how and the authorities explained it was fine. We accepted their word at face value because we were no security experts."

In fact, a move by Pakistan's Supreme Court had created a power vacuum in Punjab and the provincial capital Lahore. The national opposition leader Nawaz Sharif had been barred from elected office, and his brother Shahbaz,

Eranga Jayawardena, AP/PA

Kumar Sangakkara and Mohammad Khalil embrace. Khalil was in Colombo in April to be officially thanked for his bravery.

head of the Punjab government, was also ousted. Pakistan's president Asif Ali Zardari took charge of the province and immediately made changes to key posts in the police and security departments. Nawaz Sharif held Zardari's move to topple his brother opened up the possibility for the attack.

The intensity of this attack by terrorists – whose identity, to date, remains unproven – can be gauged from what they left behind: a large weapons cache including anti-personnel mines and two unexploded car bombs, a total of eight people killed, and about 20 injured, including eight members of the Sri Lankan touring party. One of the dead was a traffic policeman, Tanvir Iqbal, who had specifically asked to be on duty at the roundabout so he could see the cricketers.

"All the talk that no one would target cricketers seems so hollow now. Far from being untouchable, we are now prize targets for extremists. That's an uncomfortable reality we have to come to terms with," adds Sangakkara, now Sri Lanka's captain.

What still angers the players is that they could never see their 12 masked assailants, who had arrived from nowhere and launched this unprecedented attack on a cricket team. "Now you think about it you feel crazy," Jayawardene reflects. "We couldn't do anything about it, that was the sad part. There was no way for us to run, no way for us to hide, but stay on the floor. We couldn't react. We couldn't hit back at them. That was a desperate situation. We had no choices." Sportsmen, normally, do not accept defeat lying down.

Wounds started to heal once the participants reached home. The Sri Lankan board appointed counsellors to help their players heal psychologically. The ICC also told the umpires and Broad to seek counselling, after they had been flown to Abu Dhabi that night and driven to the ICC's headquarters in Dubai.

Pakistani doctors told Raza it would take him at least 18 months to recover, after 80 stitches were inserted on one side of his body and he lost the use of the lung that had been punctured by a bullet. Yet he returned to stand in a senior game two and a half months after being shot. Raza never allowed his willpower to desert him: once 20 pints of blood had been transfused into his body, he knew he would stand on his feet soon. But he can no longer sit in public places where people smoke, nor can he tolerate strong perfumes. He thanks Broad for risking his life and using his presence of mind to try and stop the flow of blood.

Broad met the Sri Lankans again in September 2009 in Colombo, where he was the match referee during a tri-series: "I chatted to one or two of their players, but didn't go into it in too much detail. I was so pleased to see all of them – especially Samaraweera who was the most badly injured – back playing again," he says.

During the Ahmedabad Test in India in late 2009, while travelling back to the team hotel, Samaraweera heard a firecracker flying past the team bus. He jumped out of his seat, and Sangakkara had to hold him tight. Samaraweera, who, in spite of his experiences, had a prolific year otherwise as the leading run-scorer in Test cricket, is now just happy to be alive. He has kept the bullet, which the doctors who operated on him in Colombo gave to his wife Erandathi, saying it was a lucky bullet as it had failed to reach the bone a few centimetres away.

"I think I will keep it all my life," Samaraweera says with a big smile. "At the moment it is a terrible thing, but with time it may be something like a lucky thing which I can look at and think about in the future."

Of the day when cricket lost its innocence, and his final Test as Sri Lanka's captain, Jayawardene has a unique memory – or so it is to be hoped. "It was not the ideal one, but it was a great farewell for a captain. Once you go through all this, everything else becomes immaterial."

THE ASHES, 2009

How we won the Ashes

ANDREW STRAUSS

Plenty has been – and will continue to be – written about the 2009 Ashes. Journalists and supporters alike have been surprised and even shocked by what exactly went on. How can a team go from being trounced by an innings in the Fourth Test to a historic victory in the deciding match that started little more than a week later? How could a team who scored far more centuries, as well as having the three top wicket-takers in the series, end up losing? Much of the series defied logic, and that is what makes cricket such an alluring game.

I am supposed to be shedding some light on how England won the Ashes in 2009. If Australia were statistically so superior, how were we able to defeat them? I would like to say that there was a great masterplan, generated in the months before the series, using all the latest technology and scientific dissection of the Australian players, which allowed us to find weaknesses that other teams had not been able to decipher. I would like to say that there were huge tactical victories, where my knowledge of the local conditions allowed me to outfox Ricky Ponting, my opposite number, and in doing so lay the foundations of our victory. The truth is that neither of these played a significant part. I do believe, however, that as a side we made some important progress, both before the series and during it, which ultimately allowed us to step on to that podium at The Oval and receive the Ashes urn.

Patrick Eagar

Leader of men: Andrew Strauss calls a team meeting on the fourth evening of the Lord's Test.

An Ashes series is the pinnacle for any English cricketer. We know that we are judged more on our performances against Australia than against any other country, and we also know that our country takes more than a passing interest in our performance against the "old enemy". It would be wrong, therefore, not to treat an Ashes series differently from any other. Steve Bull, the England psychologist, talks about athletes having to get their heads around the fact that the Olympics are not like any other meeting. They have to prepare themselves differently; if they are not careful, the pressure of the Olympics is likely to jump up and consume the athlete at the most important moment.

With that in mind, we did spend more time than usual preparing for the series. Just as Australia had Justin Langer's dossier on our players, so we had one on theirs. We also tried to include in at least some of our preparation all those players who were likely to play a part in the Ashes. It was vitally important that we all knew how we were going to deal with unforeseen circumstances that might crop up during the season. How were we going to cope with the media? How should we react to sledging? What type of cricket were we looking to play? We needed answers to these questions and countless others before the Tests started. And quietly, over a series of dinners with the players in the preceding months, the answers became apparent.

I do still maintain, however, that the planning aspect was not important. It might have been if we had not planned at all, since we would have been at a huge disadvantage. But by planning properly, we simply made sure we were taking part on a level playing field: Australia had done their homework too.

So, were individual performances responsible for our victory? Well, yes and no. We would have lost at Cardiff if it hadn't been for Paul Collingwood's dogged resistance, continued by James Anderson and Monty Panesar in the final overs. We certainly wouldn't have won the Lord's Test if I hadn't got a century in the first innings, and Andrew Flintoff hadn't got five wickets in the fourth. In the decider at The Oval, we would have struggled to bowl Australia out cheaply if Stuart Broad hadn't produced an inspirational spell of bowling at just the right time; we wouldn't have been in such a comfortable position going into the final two days without Jonathan Trott's fairytale century on debut; and we certainly needed Graeme Swann's eight-wicket haul to finish them off. There is a huge individual element to the game of cricket, and without players having the ability and will to put in match-defining performances, victories would seldom be achievable.

But while the media love to create heroes from Ashes victories, and villains from defeats, I think it is entirely wrong to single out individuals as being responsible for England winning the Ashes. To win a five-Test series, there is no doubt that you need every single member of the side to contribute. What about Graham Onions taking two wickets with the first two balls of the second day at Edgbaston? What about Matt Prior's counter-attacking batting at No. 6 throughout the series? What about James Anderson's priceless wickets at Lord's and Edgbaston? Players are selected to perform, and if they don't perform collectively, you won't win.

So if our victory cannot be attributed to tactical acumen, superior planning, or inspired individual performances, what can it be attributed to?

Statement of intent: Strauss comes down the wicket at Lord's and slams the ball so hard he dislocates Nathan Hauritz's finger.

I believe the answer lies somewhere in what people like to call the unity, or spine, of the team. It is hard to go into this side of the story without descending very quickly into what cricketers like to call "psycho-babble", the sort of language you hear in self-help or motivational books, so I will attempt to keep this clear and concise.

As a side we went through a huge amount of upheaval in the 12 months before the Ashes series. First, we lost our long-term captain, Michael Vaughan, during the previous summer, leaving a rather large hole to fill in a short space of time. Shortly afterwards, the team had the huge opportunities and even larger pitfalls of the Stanford 20/20 to contend with. By the end of the year, we were confronted with the Mumbai bombings, and their effect on us as individuals and cricketers. At the start of 2009, English cricket was again in turmoil with the new captain, Kevin Pietersen, and the coach, Peter Moores, being relieved of their positions.

On the surface, it looked as if these occurrences would be the perfect way to ensure that we wouldn't win the Ashes series less than eight months down the line. However, I believe strongly that shared experiences, the type of which don't happen every day, are actually what bring teams together. Which club side doesn't at some point look back to its worst defeat, and laugh about it? Which batsman doesn't look back at his most horrific run of form and realise how much he learned from it? It was the same with this England team. We needed some stability, which Andy Flower and myself tried to bring in as

ASHES 2009 REFLECTIONS

The coach's view

Andy Flower

The excitement and interest surrounding an Ashes series was no surprise. Every cricketer in the world recognises the special relationship between England and Australia. They may not have been first-hand, but I'd had my own experiences. In 2005, while still playing at Essex, I had been caught up in the exhilaration expressed by a nation watching one of the greatest series of all time. I saw what it meant. I took note. Just as I did Down Under in 2006-07 when working with the National Academy players in Perth for six weeks.

I knew all about the Ashes and their special vicissitudes. And I also knew we could win in 2009. Obviously I didn't know we would, but there were a couple of major reasons why I felt some quiet confidence beforehand. First was the make-up of the respective teams. We were likely to play five bowlers, Australia only four. I thought it would be interesting to see which theory would come out on top.

And that led into a second reason – the absence of the great Shane Warne from the Australian line-up. I now felt the spinning option was an area we could exploit, and actually thought we might have played two spinners on more than the single occasion we did in Cardiff.

As it was, the saving of that first Test in Wales was a key moment. A draw there was as good as a win. We felt that the momentum was with us as we went to Lord's still deadlocked at 0–0 in the series rather than 1–0 down.

And then at Lord's, skipper Andrew Strauss played the innings of the series with his 161. That set up victory and preceded the first of three Australian first-innings collapses in the series: three excellent efforts from our bowlers that handed us three opportunities for victory. We took two – failing only at Edgbaston – and that was enough to win the series. We dominated three Tests and so deserved to win the series in my opinion.

Were there worries after losing so badly at Leeds? Some, yes, but this England side are quite good at dealing with such situations – testimony to Strauss's remarkable strength as a leader. We went to The Oval for the final Test knowing there was as much pressure on the Australians – so fearful of another series loss in England – as on us. We avoided distractions, and just concentrated on our skills. And it paid off.

It was some feeling afterwards. Sadly, the hectic schedule left little time for proper celebration. But winning the Ashes as a coach is certainly up there with any achievement I've managed in the game. Not that I am sated in any way. There are still greater things out there to be achieved.

quickly as possible. We needed some honesty about where we were as a side, and how hard we needed to work to go forward. Above all, though, we needed as a group to use our experiences to bring us closer together, and I am absolutely certain we did: that was the critical factor.

How were we able to overturn the humiliating defeat at Headingley? Because we had been there several times in the recent past – like the Jamaica Test – and learned from them. How were we able to win a series in which we scored fewer hundreds and took fewer wickets than Australia? Because we had become accustomed to relying on each other to get us out of sticky situations. If the top order failed, we could rely on Prior, Swann and Broad to eke out some valuable runs. If Anderson wasn't taking wickets, we could rely on Swann or Broad. If Flintoff or Pietersen was unable to play, we knew we could make up for that loss. It is very powerful to have that belief in a side, especially as that belief generally comes from repeated success over a long period of time. We didn't have that luxury.

Many people will look back at the Ashes of 2009 and say that the quality of cricket was not as high as in 2005, or that the public's imagination was not captured quite to the same extent. I don't think it matters. The Ashes series is about the cricket teams of two proud nations doing battle to the utmost of their ability, hoping to make their supporters proud. In that sense, this series was no different from any other, and it is for that reason we will remember the Ashes of 2009 so fondly.

Andrew Strauss has played 71 Tests for England, 21 as captain, winning eight and losing three.

THE ASHES, 2009

A particularly Australian mongrel

MICHAEL PARKINSON

At the age of 12 Ricky Ponting scored four centuries in a week in a junior cricket competition in his native Tasmania. Kookaburra gave him a bat contract, which at the time might have seemed like a publicity stunt but nowadays, 23 years later, appears to have been a remarkable example of inspired judgment.

Today Ricky Ponting is regarded as one of the greatest batsmen of them all. No Australian has scored more runs in Test cricket; only two other batsmen – Sachin Tendulkar and Brian Lara – have scored more Test runs; only Tendulkar has scored more Test centuries.

He is the third-highest scorer in one-day cricket behind Tendulkar and Sanath Jayasuriya. He has captained Australia to the highest number of consecutive wins in Test cricket, equalling Steve Waugh's run of 16. He has been on the winning side in more Test matches as player and captain than anyone else: 95 winning Test matches as a player, 44 as captain. His batting average is 55.67.

When Rodney Marsh saw him aged 15 at the Australian Cricket Academy, he said he was the best young batsman he had seen. He watched him hook a bumper from a senior fast bowler and said to his assistant: "This kid will play for Australia."

Marsh said that the thing that convinced him Ponting was special was his balance, a gift defining the player's athleticism both as a batsman and fielder. One of the most graceful and satisfying sights in cricket is to see the finish of Ponting's pull shot – body leaning back, bat high in follow-through. It demonstrates that style is innate, and given only to the blessed few.

If you watch Ponting field – quick feet, fast reflex – you understand what Marsh observed as remarkable two decades ago. Watch his golf swing and you would conclude this is an athlete incapable of an awkward and uncoordinated movement.

And yet, for all his gifts, the young Ponting's early years as a professional cricketer were far from seamless, and not without incident. There was the odd blip on the way from schoolboy legend in Tasmania to captain of Australia. When he was first selected for his country, aged 20, his gifts as a cricketer were soon threatened by a capacity for silly misdemeanour which came to a head in 1999, when Ponting was involved in an incident at an all-night bar in Sydney. He was punched by a security guard, causing one and a half black eyes, and the unforgettable comment that he had failed to duck a bouncer.

Ponting faced the media, admitted he had a problem with drink, apologised and promised to do something about it. The media didn't buy it. One commentator called it "a sad and unconvincing performance", remarking "you could take the boy out of Tasmania but not Tassie out of the boy".

Getting the balance right: Ricky Ponting pulls for four during his century at Cardiff, and relaxes with daughter Emmy after the innings victory at Leeds.

Another said Ponting seemed "set on self-destruction" and likened him to George Best.

That comparison would have been legitimate only if Ponting had been an alcoholic like Best. He wasn't. He was a daft drunk with a low tolerance of alcohol, but a long way from being a soak. His choice was to balance his talent against his weakness, and decide which to give up. It sounds easy though, of course, it wasn't. But it tells you everything about Ponting's intelligence and resolve that he turned a potentially disastrous incident into a triumph. From that moment, he began to establish himself not simply as a great player but by developing into a class act as a captain and as a man.

It hasn't been a voyage on calm seas with a following wind. If you want that kind of tranquil life then don't become captain of Australia. It was John Howard, when Prime Minister of Australia, who told me that he merely held the second most important job in the land. He was only half joking.

The Australian media, gorged on a decade when their country not only dominated world cricket but redefined the way Test cricket is played, quickly sought a scapegoat when Australia twice lost the Ashes in England. Ponting's response was a single-minded dedication to the business of scoring runs and winning matches: six weeks after the Ashes he had led his team to a 6–1 one-day win over England and to the Champions Trophy. His greatest asset is to be his own man, seemingly unaffected by the boo boys, like those who jeered him during the Ashes series, to their shame. His greatest delight is in proving his critics wrong.

Before the Third Test against Pakistan in Hobart, there were those who reckoned that his batting might be showing signs of decline, that he ought to consider moving from No. 3 to a less vulnerable position. In spite of an injured and painful arm which he didn't whinge about, or even mention in his defence, he went back to his native Tasmania and scored a double-century. What made it even more praiseworthy was that, before his innings came to full and glorious flower, the early part was uncertain and uncomfortable. But then Ponting has always been a particularly Australian mongrel, an unflinching cross between battler and maestro.

If the media sometimes have doubts about Ponting, those who play with and against him – particularly the Poms – have no reservation about his dedication to the business of winning.

During the last Ashes series he was fielding close in when Matt Prior hit a ball hard into the ground; it flew up and hit Ponting in the mouth. Being a decent bloke and seeing blood on his opponent's countenance, Prior enquired: "Are you all right, mate?" – whereupon Ponting told him to mind his own business, or words to that effect. (In fact, he gave Prior an instruction using only two words, the second of which was "off".)

On the other hand, at the conclusion of the Ashes, having had by general consent an unlucky series, he won over everyone, even those who had taunted and cursed him during the tour, with his honesty and refusal to make excuses.

Off the field, Ponting has worked for five years raising funds for the Children's Cancer Institute of Australia. He was introduced by Phil Kearns, the former Wallabies rugby captain, and admits that what he saw changed his life. Nowadays he and his wife Rianna have their own charity – the Ponting Foundation – and I for one can attest from personal experience that the Pontings are formidable and persuasive fund-raisers. Indeed when Ponting says that the best part of playing cricket for Australia is that it gave him a chance to understand the problems and needs of children with cancer, you cannot doubt his sincerity.

Ricky Ponting is a true Australian working-class hero, a great cricketer and a good bloke. He is 35 and, if he heeds the whispers from the wings, ought to be planning a graceful exit. Instead he has his sights set on unfinished business. He is looking beyond the next Ashes in Australia to the series after that in England in 2013.

Just before the Ashes in 2009, Ponting was asked if he'd be back again in four years. "I think I'd need a wheelchair if I'm still playing then," he said. After The Oval, with the Ashes lost, he said to himself: "I need to do this again, to get it right, to beat them on their own turf."

That is his ambition. Only a fool would bet against him.

This is a man who is familiar with the road to redemption.

Sir Michael Parkinson is a journalist, author and broadcaster.

THE ASHES, 2009

Glazed, not gimlet-eyed...

GIDEON HAIGH

There is always something special about an Ashes summer. The summer of 2009 was so special as to be disturbing. The Ashes introduced to cricket the concept of the five-Test series; it has become the final fastness against its phasing out. England have not played a country over five Tests apart from Australia since 2004-05 (ignoring the ten-ball Test in Antigua); Australia have not played a country over five Tests apart from England since 2000-01. Thus were two teams stretched in ways quite unfamiliar to them, like teenagers being expected to graduate from SMS to iambic pentameters – and it showed.

The wins were conquests. The losses were capitulations. The batting collapses were ruinous and utter. The bowling collapses – see Mitchell Johnson at Lord's, Monty Panesar at Cardiff – were complete. Have teams played more contrasting consecutive Tests than Headingley and The Oval? Have teams struggled as much with putting consecutive deliveries in the same place?

One phenomenon that received a long-overdue debunking was the ever-popular concept of momentum: the notion that success inevitably begets further success. Australia had all the momentum coming into the Second and Fifth Tests, and it availed them nought. England mowed Australia down in the Third Test, then were mown down twice in two and a half days in the Fourth. Momentum is classically defined as the product of mass times velocity; in 2009, it was revealed in cricket to be the sum of the past juals cliché.

Stretched over two months, the effect was of the slow unfolding of very abrupt events, like an Ingmar Bergman film remade in the style of *The West Wing*. It was often fascinating; it was also, sometimes, not very good or of a particularly high standard. It revealed, too, just how much cricket has lost in the gradual eclipse of the five-Test format. You genuinely *did* see teams and individuals in every circumstance, lifted by luck, taxed by trials, and feel as though you had come to know them better – that, indeed, they had also come to know themselves more completely.

For the Australians, even though they held the trophy, the series presented perhaps the greater demands, in adapting not merely to England's unfamiliar conditions, but also to the Ashes' unique duration. They arrived off the back of one-day series in South Africa and the Gulf; they played some bad Twenty20 cricket, then had two weeks in the nets in Leicester. How often do cricketers have no games for a fortnight? How often do they spend that fortnight in the home of Showaddywaddy and Gaye Bykers on Acid? How many interviews and press conferences can they give explaining that they are "looking forward to the challenge"? The Australians were forced to find out.

"We were really happy with the way the people in Leicester looked after us," says Ricky Ponting in his *Captain's Diary 2009*, and... er... that's it for

Cracking... Mitchell Johnson follows the ball to the Lord's boundary as Alastair Cook square-cuts.

the Australians' longest stay in any city during the year. Not that one was expecting an account of a visit to the Abbey Pumping Station or a salute to the excellence of Walkers crisps, but it is a kind of comment: the modern cricketer is fully alive only when fully involved playing. And the longer the tour, the more broadly spaced the games, the greater the need for self-regulation, for self-direction, for the individual to find a balance between discipline and relaxation, exertion and rest.

The Australians did not make the same mistake as in 2005, in programming games outside the Tests of a derisory two days – no more than glorified net sessions. Again, though, there was a sense of time killed rather than used to advantage between the big events. The old-fashioned tour involving proper first-class matches against states, counties and provinces is a thing of the past, we are told, for economic reasons. Yet the ideal structure to succeed it, abetting competition for places among players, providing an opportunity to retrieve form and confidence and to rehearse match conditions, has never really been found. On this longest of tours, the effect was even more pronounced than usual: the gaps between Tests were first and foremost about rest for those playing, and then and only then for giving Andrew McDonald something to write about on his postcards home.

Like an army campaigning far from home, its supply lines stretched, Australia also had multiple centres of authority. There was a captain and a vice-captain. There was a coach and his staff. There was a duty selector liaising with colleagues back in Australia. Only the last had a vote in choosing the teams. This is a recent arrangement and so far, as sportsmen these days are wont to mangle the expression, the proof is in the pudding. It is not at all clear how individuals 12,000 miles away and at least 13 years out of international cricket are better equipped to choose teams than those on the spot.

Not that Australian players can complain overmuch; it was they who traded away involvement in selection on tour, thanks to the residue of Steve Waugh's decisions to exclude Shane Warne from the St John's

Fidgety boys hearing the swish of a cane

Test of 1999 and Michael Slater from the Oval Test of 2001. Waugh and Warne in particular were never on quite the same terms thereafter. To borrow William Safire's description of Richard Nixon and George Meany, they were "diametrically allied": "That is, they respected and admired each other and did not like or trust each other."

Quite how the decisions of the selectors from their far remove to exclude Phillip Hughes at Edgbaston and Nathan Hauritz at The Oval inflected the series can only be conjectural. But Ponting's matter-of-fact comment in mid-November that he should be a selector, and that he had told Cricket Australia just that, suggested misgivings about the process that had grown rather than diminished since the Ashes.

When Australia plunged into the series at Cardiff, there seemed no holding them. The spirit they had bottled recently in South Africa was obvious. It was startling, however, with memories of the constant pressure and event of 2005 still fresh, to watch international cricket of such low intensity as on the fourth day, as Australia coasted towards a declaration against bowlers and fielders so devoid of energy and ambition. All teams look shabby under the cosh, of course, but some look shabbier than others: England here looked a great deal poorer than Australia in similar circumstances, awaiting a declaration, as at Lord's. Marcus North was there capable of a brilliant direct-hit run-out, to dismiss Matt Prior, almost from the backward-point boundary; England awaited Ponting's move at Sophia Gardens like fidgety boys sent to the headmaster's office hearing the swish of a cane.

Then, on the last afternoon, Australia faltered, as both sides would throughout the series, releasing the pressure so assiduously built. Ponting had come to the series excited by his team's feat in overcoming South Africa on their home pitches; he owed loyalty, he felt, to the players who had delivered for him there; he relied on two in the game's closing stages, Johnson and North. Neither broke through, nor looked like doing so. Ben Hilfenhaus, despite four top-order wickets, was granted just 12 of the last day's 98 overs.

If this was a glimpse of Australia's limitations, the first session at Lord's revealed them in stark relief. In his book, Ponting paints a dainty but disturbing picture of his young players' preparation: "I could hear the excitement in their voices and see an almost glazed look in their eyes when they first looked out over the ground they've dreamt about playing a Test on since they first thought about playing for Australia." Australian eyes at Lord's are meant to be gimlet not glazed; on the other hand, perhaps the only way to watch was between one's fingers, as Andrew Strauss and Alastair Cook hit 22 boundaries before lunch.

When a team has played so badly, there is always the nagging sense, among themselves and their opponents, that a repeat is possible, maybe even probable, especially over cricket's maximum course. It was Australia's batsmen rather than their bowlers that plumbed the depths from then, but in hindsight it was the first two hours of the Second Test that was a touchstone for England over the long, ensuing summer.

The institution of the five-Test series is due its next revival at the end of this year when England trip to Australia, and it is hard to know what to expect after the English prodigies of 2005, the Australian pageant of 2006-07, and the alternating predicaments of 2009. Which is, of course, exactly as one would wish it.

Gideon Haigh is the author of The Ultimate Test, *on the 2009 Ashes series.*

THE STRUCTURE OF COUNTY CRICKET

Pitching for change

JUSTIN LANGER

Contrary to some people's opinions, I am a great admirer of English cricket and in particular the county system. There is no doubt there are areas that could be tweaked and improved to ensure a steadier flow of young players ready to step up to the next level, but overall county cricket is potentially a steady platform from which English cricket can benefit.

Selective coverage of my so-called leaked dossier last summer suggested I was biting the hand that fed me for seven wonderful seasons of county cricket. In fact, that could not be further from the truth. My suggestions to the Australian coach Tim Nielsen, who is also a close friend, were simply observations I have made over the years playing county cricket and also playing in many Ashes battles.

It would be very naive to suggest this sort of thing doesn't go on every day of the week to ensure a professional advantage over your opposition. International, first-class and even club cricketers canvass as much information as they can in an attempt to expose any weaknesses in their opponents' armoury. I suppose my mistake was that my views were inked in paper, and therefore became a perceived commodity for some journalists and critics.

In many ways I was amazed by the amount of discussion caused by my thoughts, but I was also shocked by the criticism aimed at me after England regained the Ashes at The Oval. Just another arrogant Australian so-and-so, I guess, who has egg on his face now that England again hold the urn.

This may of course be the case, but those critics should be aware of the support I gained from some of the most recognised names involved with English cricket. Through phone calls, text messages and emails they all contacted me to support my views, except maybe my opinion that James Anderson's body language tends to deteriorate when things don't go his way. People can throw as many stones as they like, but it would be naive if they thought English cricket was all rainbows and butterflies because they beat Australia 2–1 on home soil.

Either way, those who have listened to or read my views in the past would know it is not my style to criticise publicly any fellow player, because I respect how hard the game is. Equally, I make no apology for trying to help Australia retain the Ashes because, as much as I love what England has offered me in the way of memories and friendships, I am always going to be a red-blooded Australian who wants to see Australia beat England in any Ashes contest. Surely Englishmen everywhere wouldn't want it any other way. Isn't that the brilliance and fun of the Australia–England rivalry over the years?

Only two years ago I raised a few eyebrows in Australia when I suggested the first division of the County Championship was as good as any domestic cricket I had played in the world. Having spent a career boasting about the

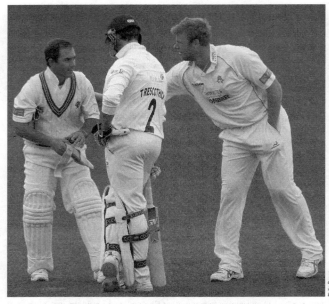

Under fire: Andrew Flintoff checks Justin Langer is unharmed after hitting him on the arm in the Lancashire–Somerset match of April 2008, the game that led Langer to praise the intensity of county cricket at its best.

standard of the Sheffield Shield and its positive effect as a nursery for Australia's success, I was similarly excited about the intensity of the first division during the 2008 summer. I felt, and still feel, that a young player excelling in it is much closer to being ready for international cricket than had been the case.

In the first game of that season Marcus Trescothick and I faced Andrew Flintoff, James Anderson, Sajid Mahmood and Glen Chapple on a fast wicket at Old Trafford. Marcus and I might have been wearing a green helmet with an Australian coat of arms above its peak, such was the fire of the contest. For us both, it felt as though we were back playing Test cricket: a playground we were both missing, for different reasons. Although we were wearing maroon Somerset helmets, the intensity of the match was outstanding.

Admittedly, such illustrious company doesn't come together all that often in a county fixture, but on those cold April days the scene was set for a tough summer in the first division. In the ideal world more contests like those would occur throughout a county season, but the reality of international cricket these days ensures such games are the exception rather than the rule.

Ironically, one of the problems facing international cricket today has long affected the counties. There is a danger that, if the international game isn't careful, it will become a glorified form of county cricket, where players have so little time to find any balance in their lives that injury, fatigue and a reduced standard of play will become the norm. The difference between county and international cricket is that county players have to endure the zombie mentality of cricket saturation for only six months of the year, while international players have to fight it for 12 months, year in year out.

Don't most people want to see a high level of competition and performance from the best sportsmen rather than a high volume of games between players who are physically and mentally worn out? Cricketers at both levels would prefer to play less, so that they perform at their best more often, but then they, like the administrators, also know that more play means more money.

In this, the quandary for the game lies.

In essence, the major issue for the English game is the extraordinary amount of cricket. For years, I believed that the quantity of games played by the counties created the opportunity to develop some of the toughest cricketers in the world. In order to shine consistently on the conveyor belt that is county cricket, a player must have an enormous mental and physical capacity. He must also be technically sound, hungry and determined for success, and willing to step out of the comfortable surrounds of being a day-to-day county pro.

Unfortunately this view, while theoretically viable, is flawed, because very few players take up this option of using the system to develop their natural abilities to the highest degree. Instead of it producing a constant flow of battle-hardened young players ready for the international circuit, most young cricketers get worn out and develop poor habits and attitudes towards training and playing, and therefore any pursuit of excellence quickly disappears.

Those who do excel are often written off as bullies who feed off the weak county system; and while this must be frustrating for them, players such as Graeme Hick, Mark Ramprakash and Marcus Trescothick are shining lights to be admired rather than admonished. For years I have heard it said that such players, Trescothick aside, never excelled at the next level. But my strong view is that in different circumstances both Hick and Ramprakash had all the attributes to succeed as Test cricketers.

Throughout my time at Somerset I was intrigued by the way the club was able to develop. There is an old saying that "if nothing changes, nothing changes". Somerset had a choice three years ago. They could stay on the same course of mediocrity and remain the whipping boys of the county circuit – or they could dare to be bold and make real changes. Some were quite a radical departure, but the proof is there: by changing attitudes and encouraging a path of constant improvement in all aspects of the club, the rewards and positive outcomes will follow.

While Somerset still have not won the County Championship, the overall improvement over the last three years has been excellent. Led by coach Andy Hurry, whose background in the Royal Marines had given him the skills to

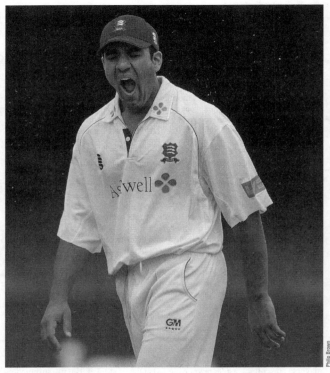

Fit to drop: a weary Ravi Bopara in the field for Essex v Middlesex in August 2009.

implement a new level of work ethic, discipline and focus, Somerset have shown that the pain of discipline in all areas is nothing like the pain of disappointment. For a number of years the outcomes had been so mediocre that the pain of disappointment became a strong motivator to make a change.

In order to make change, though, you need to have vision. If I were in charge of English cricket I would have a clear idea of where I would want the system to head in the next decade and beyond.

Firstly, I would look at ways of cutting down the amount of cricket. At one stage last season Somerset played something like 15 out of 17 days at the back end of the summer. Between games there was travel, sometimes long, on a team coach, followed by a sleep in a new bed in a different hotel, followed by another day's play in different colours of clothing at a different cricket ground. One day, it is a first-class game, the next it is a 50-, 40- or 20-over game. I know old stagers will say the modern-day cricketer just needs to harden up and that it was even harder in their day, but common sense suggests that such abysmal preparation cannot be good for the standard of the game or its players.

I know there isn't a player or coach who would deny that more rest and preparation time would be beneficial all round. Balance at the crease is the most essential component of technical success for a batsman or bowler: balance in life is equally important for a person. A county player simply has no balance in his life: it is cricket, cricket and more cricket, and frankly this is not a healthy system.

Bonus points aren't a great concept either. There are far too many draws, and again this can't be healthy because the emphasis often shifts from winning a game outright to securing enough bonus points to stave off relegation, or scrape over the line for promotion. Throughout my tenure as the Somerset captain I tried to instil a belief in the players that winning games was a sure-fire way of gaining promotion and staving off relegation. There is greatness in boldness, as has been shown by Durham, who must be applauded for their professionalism and ability to win games outright over the last two years.

Unfortunately, the bonus-point problem is magnified by the third major issue in county cricket, and that is the standard of pitches. English pitches are not poor in a conventional way: it is just that they are so good that they should often be marked as poor because it is so difficult to take the 20 wickets required to win a game. Even as a top-order batsman I am of the firm view that pitches must be equally weighted for both batsmen and bowlers. This certainly isn't the case at most venues across the country. I have sympathy for groundsmen because they are like the players: the quantity of cricket makes it virtually impossible for them to prepare and produce great pitches day in day out.

If all county games were staged on pitches like the ones Somerset encountered in Durham last season, then the current bonus-point system would work quite well. At Riverside, conditions were bowler-friendly but those who applied themselves scored very satisfying runs. Like stand-out county cricketers, Durham's pitch is rare, and most other pitches are simply too flat for the present points system to be beneficial. Better a simple system that rewards first-innings lead and victories only.

Change is tough. But in order to rejuvenate the county system and ensure that the England Test (and one-day) team make the 2005 and 2009 Ashes triumphs regular occurrences, then maybe the short-term pain of such change would be worth looking at. There is an opportunity to use the strengths of the county system to England's advantage, but unless there is some bold and courageous vision, followed by action, then the same results will occur at all levels because "if nothing changes, nothing changes".

Justin Langer played 105 Tests for Australia, and captained Somerset from 2007 to 2009. In all, he appeared in 360 first-class matches, hitting 28,382 runs at an average of 50.23.

HOW ENGLISH CRICKET SURVIVED
THE SECOND WORLD WAR

"We were prisoners no longer"

STEPHEN CHALKE

The news on Thursday August 24, 1939 was ominous: German threats against the Polish city of Danzig, a treaty between Hitler and Stalin, an Emergency Powers Act passing through parliament. Yet county cricket was playing on: in the words of Neville Cardus, "a haven of peace in an unruly world".

"We didn't know a great deal about what was happening," Northamptonshire's Dennis Brookes recalled, years later. "We read what Chamberlain was saying, but even then we didn't think there was going to be a war." That afternoon at Northampton, the Lancashire captain Lionel Lister was waiting to bat. He received a message from his Territorial Army unit, unbuckled his pads and departed. "It was then we realised there was something afoot."

Wednesday August 30 was the last day of sunshine. At Lord's, as the members in the Long Room clapped a Bill Edrich century, a man was removing the bust of W. G. Grace to safety.

By Friday, with children already being evacuated from the cities, county cricket was confined to one venue: Hove, where Yorkshire agreed to play out the last day of Jim Parks's benefit match. In an eerie atmosphere they dismissed Sussex for 33, won by nine wickets and set off in a hired charabanc through blacked-out towns and villages. "The farther we got from Brighton," Len Hutton wrote, "the deeper was our conviction that we would be lucky if we ever played cricket again."

The summer was over: for Hutton, only 23 years old and already holding the world record Test score; for Hedley Verity, the great slow left-armer, seven wickets for nine runs on that last day; for Sussex's Jack Holmes, no longer to captain England in that winter's Tests in India; for the in-form Edrich of Middlesex; and for Northamptonshire's gentle skipper Robert Nelson, who on Thursday evening had slipped away from Taunton ahead of his team. All went their separate ways.

On Sunday morning, 21 years after the Armistice that concluded "the war to end all wars", Prime Minister Chamberlain announced that the country was once more at war with Germany.

In the First World War little cricket had been played. Lord Hawke, president of MCC and Yorkshire, set the tone, striking from future consideration any Yorkshire cricketer who did not volunteer. At The Oval the Surrey secretary, asked about the nets, replied: "They'll be up, but I don't expect our fellows will use them much. They'll be afraid of being jeered at by the men in the tram cars."

The Bradford League caused controversy by not disbanding, but by 1917 the mood had changed. "The nation had by then readjusted its life to the state of war," *Wisden* recorded, "and no objection was felt to an attempt to stage some exhibition matches in the cause of charity." In a one-day game at Lord's, 7,000 spectators saw an England Army XI, led by Captain P. F. Warner, defeat an Australian Army XI.

By 1939 Warner, now Sir Pelham, was 65 years old. When the MCC secretary and assistant secretary volunteered for service, he became deputy assistant secretary, determined that cricket would continue to fly the flag at Lord's.

Some saw cricket as a distraction – Surrey's Errol Holmes said it felt "rather like going on a picnic when your home was on fire" – but many recognised its potential to raise morale. As *The Cricketer* put it, "It takes people out of themselves, and if we are a fortress let us have some fun inside the fortress so long as it does not conflict with military exigencies."

There was no question of the counties staging more than occasional one- or two-day matches. The players were dispersed about the country, and several of the county grounds found themselves put to other uses. For the Whit bank holiday of 1940 Nottinghamshire played a two-day game against Derbyshire, both teams near full strength, but it was not the serious affair it had been 12 months earlier. When Derbyshire's Bill Copson failed to arrive, one of the umpires batted in his place.

At Lord's, a programme of charity matches emerged as the summer progressed. The first, in early May, was between the City of London Police and the London Fire Service. The police brought a band, the fire service displayed 48 of its engines, and in bright sunshine a crowd of 1,600 gathered.

Warner planned a great two-day match for the Whit holiday, Over-30s versus Under-30s, featuring 22 of England's best cricketers. Then Germany invaded Holland and Belgium, and the serving cricketers were summoned. The match was cancelled.

Hundreds of thousands of British troops escaped from the beaches of Dunkirk, Paris fell and Britain stood alone, awaiting attack.

The former England captain Gubby Allen was at the Air Component base in Folkestone, where the Dunkirk evacuation was co-ordinated. His brief diary reveals how his life then went on:

4 June	Air Component disbanded
7 June	Saw *Gone with the Wind*
8 June	Eton Ramblers v XL Club at Lord's – took nine for 23
10 June	Italy declares war
14 June	Paris captured
15 June	Sandhurst v MCC, stay Percy Chapman at Worplesdon
17 June	France asks for Armistice

The leagues in the Midlands and North continued, though as in the First War the Bradford League stood out, the only one still to pay its professionals. With each team allowed four professionals, and with military duties causing much coming and going, more than 100 first-class cricketers appeared in Bradford during the war, 36 of them Test cricketers. The most popular was Learie Constantine, the electrifying West Indian all-rounder.

In the South, two new clubs were formed in 1940: London Counties and the British Empire XI. London Counties emerged from a meeting in Andrew

Sandham's cricket school in south London. Its primary purpose was "to augment the depleted income" of professional cricketers; they played clubs around outer London, and Jack Hobbs was their president. The club's philosophy, never to let up against weaker opposition, led to some one-sided contests, but much money was raised, some of it passed on to local charities. Travel was difficult; some players came from night duties in the police or fire service, but – as Somerset's Frank Lee put it – "it augmented our meagre salaries and prevented us from going rusty."

The British Empire XI began in early May with a hastily arranged match, played for a barrel of beer, against Rosslyn Park. It was a great success, and by the end of the summer they had played 37 games. The brainchild of the 19-year-old Desmond Donnelly, it was a more idealistic venture than London

Counties. They played as amateurs, aimed to entertain, raised money for the Red Cross and St John's Ambulance, and hoped to create international fellowship by picking sides that drew from all the cricket-playing countries. Donnelly, fresh from public school on the Isle of Wight, was a tea-planter's son, and he listed himself as D. L. Donnelly (Assam). Other regulars included Bertie Clarke, the West Indian leg-spinner and medical student, Ray Smith, the Essex all-rounder and farmer, and Robert Nelson, the Northamptonshire captain, an officer in the Royal Marines. Pelham Warner became president, and four times that summer they played at Lord's.

Donnelly enlisted in the RAF the following year. After the war he took his idealism into politics, standing in the 1945 election for the Common Wealth party and then

Bertie Clarke: 665 wickets in six summers in the British Empire XI.

serving for 20 years from 1950 as an independently minded Labour MP. But arguably the British Empire XI was his greatest achievement. In the six years of war it played 243 matches, raising £15,000 for charity.

Trevor Bailey, the leading schoolboy cricketer of the early war years, played occasionally, and he recalls "the sessions in the bar after matches, the girls who liked cricketers, and the autograph hunters. I can't remember any of the games, just the fun." The person who made the biggest impression on Bailey was Bertie Clarke: "the first black West Indian whom I got to know really well. I was fascinated by his enthusiasm, ability and unfailing cheerfulness."

In August, while the Battle of Britain raged in the skies over south-east England, cricket continued at Lord's. Playing for Sir Pelham Warner's XI, Essex's Reg Taylor, freshly decorated with the Distinguished Flying Cross, was cheered all the way to the wicket, bowled for nought and cheered all the way back again. "It is hard," Warner wrote, "to remember any cricketer receiving a greater reception."

On Saturday September 7, with the German blitzkrieg intensifying, air-raid sirens seemed to have ended the day's play at Lord's. Then an all-clear brought the players back, and the last four wickets fell in seven balls. In the evening, Warner stood at the top of the pavilion, watching the fires blazing in the London docks. Sirens, gunfire, shell-splinters, smoke: there would be no more cricket that summer.

Wisden called it "a strange and dramatic end", though – with its offices suffering extensive damage – the almanack did not appear till December 1941, 15 months later. Less than half the size of its predecessor, it nevertheless followed tradition and listed the fixtures for 1941.

The county clubs encouraged members to pay their subscriptions and, with little expenditure, most of them reported small annual profits. Yet no maintenance work was undertaken, and the scars of war were ever more visible. At Edgbaston several hundred seats were taken to local air-raid shelters, the scorebox damaged, and the "Shed", where players took lunch, destroyed. At Old Trafford there was extensive damage to pavilion and stands, as well as a bomb crater in the middle of the ground.

The Oval spent the war first as a barrage-balloon site, then an assault course; then a prisoner-of-war cage was erected. There was damage to the Surrey Tavern and to the terrace in front of the Long Room. The secretary worked from his home in Wimbledon, organising teams to play around the county, but it was hard to keep track of the players. He would have wanted the young Bedser twins, but at the start of June 1940 they were on the Belgian border.

Bramall Lane, Sheffield, 1940: "enough to break a man's heart", the head groundsman said.

"We got issued with a Colt revolver and six rounds of ammunition," Sir Alec recalls. "That was all we had when the Germans came." The twins ran across a cornfield as the planes approached, dived for cover and felt the spray of shots between them. "It was all over in seconds. You thought, 'Thank God for that,' and just got on with it."

In the rush to the coast, they were stranded on a roadside when a van pulled up. The driver was a Surrey member from Wimbledon. "We can't leave you two behind," he called out.

Others were not lucky: Robert Nelson died that October in an air raid on his marine unit in Kent; Ken Farnes, the England fast bowler, was killed in a plane crash in Oxfordshire; Gerry Chalk, the Kent captain, was shot down over France; and Maurice Turnbull, Glamorgan's secretary and captain, was killed while trying to halt advancing tanks in Normandy.

In July 1943 Hedley Verity, a professional cricketer who had risen to the rank of captain in the Green Howards, was shot while leading his men against German fire in Sicily. At Lord's, on the Saturday following the announcement of his death, his Yorkshire captain Brian Sellers stepped out to toss for the Army against the National Police. In his blazer pocket he found a note from 1939, from the scorer at Hove: "6–1–9–7" – Verity's last bowling figures.

Bill Edrich was a bomber pilot, flying low-level missions into Germany and winning the DFC. One Saturday his squadron, stationed in Norfolk, was due to play at Massingham Hall, but they were called away in the morning to attack German ships near the Dutch coast. Two of their planes were shot down and, before taking the field that afternoon, replacement cricketers had to be found.

"It was a hard and exciting game," he wrote. "But every now and then one's mind would flicker off to the briefing, and to joking with a pal whose broken body was now washing in the long, cold tides, and one saw again his machine cartwheeling down, flaming from nose to tail. Then a ball would roll fast along the green English turf, and in the distance the village clock would strike and the mellow echoes would ring through the lazy air of that perfect summer afternoon."

His younger brother Geoff spent three years as a prisoner of the Japanese. Even in the Far East his battalion had sports equipment, and in Singapore, on their occasional rest days, they staged cricket matches, complete with typed scorecards. Edrich scored centuries in three such games, then at Changi he played in the famous "Tests", beating Ben Barnett's Australians 2–1.

"We were prisoners no longer," he said. "It was a Test match between England and Australia. We forgot everything else."

They were moved to Thailand, and there was no more cricket: only long days of work, meagre rations, dysentery and cholera. "We were in tents on bamboo slats. I looked out one morning, and I saw this boy from the 5th Norfolks. He was a skeleton. I thought, 'How's he walking?' You had to have a bit of luck, and will power. A lot of the boys died of a broken heart. They couldn't see the end. There was one march, when we moved camp, maybe 20 miles, when some of us were ready to pack in. And if you dropped out, that was it – you got a bayonet through you from the guards. But 'Keep going,' my friend said. You had to have one or two decent chaps with you to get through."

A break from the serious business: gunners of the Surrey and Sussex Yeomanry in Italy, 1944.

More troops were posted overseas. Cricket was played in the relative luxury of the Gezira club in Egypt, where a young Jim Laker learned to bowl off-spin on the matting, and Wally Hammond, passing through, hit two centuries. With victory in the Desert War, makeshift pitches sprang up all over North Africa.

Cricket was also played in the Pentangular tournament in Bombay, where by 1944 the Europeans included Denis Compton, Joe Hardstaff and the young Reg Simpson. The Bedsers played twice on a hastily created ground in Italy, where they persuaded their Surrey team-mate Arthur McIntyre to become a wicketkeeper. Also in Italy, in a prisoner-of-war camp, Bill Bowes and Freddie Brown played with improvised balls till the Red Cross sent supplies.

And cricket was played in Afghanistan and Uganda, in Iraq and Sierra Leone, in the moat of a Polish castle, on the lava-strewn rock-like ground of Reykjavik and on the beach at Salerno. One officer in the Middle East described how his men carried everywhere a rolled-up cricket mat: "On several occasions we've played an innings during an evening, then finished the match on the following day on the same mat – perhaps 200 miles away." Wherever there were British servicemen, it seemed, there was some sort of cricket.

In the spring of 1941, Double British Summer Time was introduced, and Lord's often extended play till 7.30. For servicemen in uniform, entry was

A narrow miss: the doodlebug that almost hit Lord's, July 1944.

free: "The gates of the temple," declared the *Manchester Guardian*, "are open nowadays to all who serve their country." Civilians, meanwhile, could "forget the war for sixpence".

Father Time was dislodged by a barrage balloon cable, the Pavilion bell was rung only for air-raid warnings, and the scorecard carried information about local shelters: "Spectators are advised not to loiter in the streets." The RAF based an air-crew reception centre at the ground, forcing the two teams to change out of the same dressing-room, and on Saturdays the members' lunch room became a makeshift replacement for the shattered local synagogue.

No bomb ever landed on the field of play at Lord's – unlike Folkestone where in 1942 a fielding soldier was killed – but in July 1944 a flying-bomb cut out overhead, causing the players to throw themselves on the ground. The bomb exploded in Regent's Park and, when two balls later Jack Robertson hit Bob Wyatt for six, the large crowd burst into song:

> There'll always be an England, and England shall be free,
> If England means as much to you, as England means to me.

Most fixtures were one-day contests, though no one considered limiting the overs. One team would bat, then declare; if the second team overtook them, their innings would go on until the close. If both were out before then, a second innings would be started. Captains, on winning the toss, tended to field.

In June 1941 at Lord's, in front of 15,000 spectators, the Army and RAF played a six-and-a-half-hour match in which 98 eight-ball overs were bowled and 523 runs scored. Kent's Les Ames, in his first game of the summer, hit a century that included three sixes into the Pavilion. It was, according to Robertson-Glasgow, "not first-class cricket, but it was first-class fun."

A new audience was gathering. At the Varsity Match the spectators around the Tavern jeered the Cambridge team's brand new caps, considering the expense "a failure to take the war seriously". Then in July, when Frank Lee opened for London Counties, *The Times* reported that "he was not considered by a section of the crowd to be sufficiently exuberant; apparently it is considered that only the 'hit or miss' technique is suitable to one-day cricket."

Such cricket continued through 1942 and 1943. Edgbaston shook off its wounds sufficiently to stage a cricket week in 1942. The Minister of Labour, Ernest Bevin, thought it would lift the spirits of local munitions workers, and in six frantic weeks the ground was restored from its desolation. For August bank holiday 1943, Lord's staged a two-day match between England and the Dominions. Admission was now a shilling for all, and over 38,000 paid. They were treated to 940 runs and a thrilling England victory minutes from time.

Two new teams were created in 1944: a Royal Australian Air Force XI, featuring a young Keith Miller, and a West of England XI, formed by the Gloucester club cricketer George Elliott, and consisting mainly of county cricketers stationed in the west. In that summer of D-Day and the liberation of Paris, Elliott's task of raising teams was never-ending: "Either a bowler was posted overseas or a batsman to the North of Scotland. More phone calls, taxis, crowded trains, and one more player, hot and sometimes bad-tempered, was propelled on to the field almost too tired and bewildered to hold up his bat."

When after the war Leicestershire advertised for a new secretary, one to sort out the loss of their home ground in Aylestone Road, Elliott's skills in crisis management won him the job.

The war in Europe ended in May 1945, and five three-day Victory Tests between England and Australia were staged. They were not official Tests – too many cricketers were still elsewhere – but the cricket was dynamic, and a total of 367,000 people watched the 15 days. It was the first first-class cricket in England since 1939.

Three of the Tests were played at Lord's, the others at the war-ravaged grounds of Bramall Lane and Old Trafford. For the Manchester game, Lancashire employed German prisoners of war at three farthings an hour to repair and paint the ground.

The fifth Test at Old Trafford took place the week after Victory in Japan. The sight of packed Manchester omnibuses labelled "Cricket Ground" and gates closed at mid-day added to the general euphoria. When Bill Edrich hit the winning runs, levelling the series at 2–2, *The Times* declared it "as good a game of cricket as the heart of man could throb for."

Bill's brother Geoff, down to six stone, was now in Japan, and he woke one morning to find his guards all gone. The war was over at last, and he arrived back in England in November, gradually rebuilding his strength with pints of ale. In the years of county cricket that followed, he was a great team man, he never lacked courage, and he walked when he was out. He was haunted at times, but the lessons of his war never left him.

Getty Images

Dismantling the prison cage at The Oval, 1945: the groundsman would soon walk miles across the Gravesend marshes, looking for weed-free turf.

Many cricketers had had easy wars as physical training instructors, but others – such as Trevor Bailey driving past lines of emaciated prisoners at Belsen – had seen sights that would never leave them. They had lost important cricket years but, as Alec Bedser says, "The war made men of us. It toughened us up. After that I was never nervous when I played cricket."

Sir Home Gordon in *The Cricketer* noticed a greater acceptance of umpires' decisions: "I have seen a few shocking verdicts, but none of the pre-war disgruntlement on returning to the pavilion." He attributed this to "the widespread inoculation of obedience and discipline." "You had a better attitude," Bedser says. "You learned just to get on with things. You didn't ask questions."

The war did raise questions, however, not least in social attitudes. In 1943 Learie Constantine booked into the Imperial Hotel, Russell Square, but on arrival he was called "a nigger" and told that his presence would be unacceptable to their American guests. He took the hotel to the High Court and won his case. Then in August 1945, the only black man in the side, he captained the Dominions against England at Lord's. It could not have happened in 1939.

Wisden questioned the sustainability of the amateur–professional divide. By the late 1930s, it argued, few of the county captains were genuine amateurs, and those few were "survivors of an almost lost society". The war accelerated the demise of that society, and by 1952 England had a professional captain, Len Hutton. "If someone who had risen from the ranks was good enough to lead an army regiment in the field of battle," he wrote, "professional cricketers could be good enough to lead England in the field of sport."

Questions were raised about the shape post-war cricket should take, with MCC setting up a special committee in late 1942. Rival entertainments, such as cinemas and ice-rinks, were growing in popularity, and there was a view that the county game would need an injection of cricket's wartime spirit. There were calls for a one-day knockout cup, for Sunday play, for "natural pitches", for a two-day, one-innings county championship. The committee voted in favour of the one-day cup but, with the problem of the drawn game unresolved, the idea was shelved. The 1939 experiment with eight-ball overs was dropped; otherwise the first-class summer of 1946 differed in only minor respects from that of 1939.

There were few new players when the counties once more took the field. Somerset and Glamorgan had an average age of 38, Surrey and Yorkshire 36. "Once the initial freshness had worn off," Frank Lee wrote, "we found it all far more strenuous than we anticipated." "I was always hungry," Bill Edrich said. "I had to renew a lot of cricket gear so the coupon situation soon grew difficult."

Lancashire appealed for £100,000 to create a modern Old Trafford with a capacity of 40,000, but donations fell well short of even half that sum. Surrey relaid its entire field with tens of thousands of turfs brought from Gravesend marshes, employing shilling-an-hour volunteers from the local flats. There was little money even to heat the pavilion, but the county could not bring itself to accept a proposal to host greyhound racing.

The next summer, 1947, was a golden one, the hottest since 1911, and the crowds that flocked to the grounds, crowds who lived with bombsites and ration books, were uplifted by the devil-may-care batting of Denis Compton and Bill Edrich.

Brian Castor was secretary of Surrey. A prisoner of war under the Japanese, he wanted nothing more than to return to the England of the 1930s. Yet in his heart, when he surveyed the packed Oval that summer, he knew the reality: "It won't always be like this," he said.

English cricket would soon need to adapt. For now it was proud to have survived the war.

Stephen Chalke is an author, publisher, and captain of Winsley Third XI.

Limited-edition reprints of the 1940-45 editions of Wisden *are available from Willows Publishing (see page 1631).*

THE TEA INTERVAL

This little social heaven

IVO TENNANT

For some years now, the first-class umpires in England have grown increasingly restive over the fact that they are last to leave the field and first back on to it when the intervals end all too soon. For them, tea is a break not of 20 minutes but effectively 15, insufficient time to put their feet up, let alone have a second cup of Darjeeling.

Last summer the sticking point was the Pro40. The 25 members of the First-Class Umpires Association under the chairmanship of Peter Willey – and which administrator would dare disagree with him? – lobbied the ECB for an additional ten minutes for tea. After all, there was no lunch break in these matches. The umpires were, in part, successful: in the Clydesdale Bank 40 this season the interval will be extended to 25 minutes.

The aristocratic convention of afternoon tea is said to have entered English society around 1840, thanks to the peckishness of the Duchess of Bedford. But the tea interval, perhaps surprisingly, did not originate in English cricket at all. One reason for this was that tea – the drink – was not favoured by athletes of the 19th century. So there was no afternoon break in county matches, and umpires were expected to exert sufficient bladder control. A scorecard of the fixture between Nottinghamshire and England in 1845 indicates that there was just one, very Dickensian, stoppage for a repast. "The ordinary" was a meal in the middle of the day, which was held on cricket grounds at two o'clock.

No, the tea interval was a gift from the Australians, perhaps in return for convicts and the game of cricket itself. The interval occurred in Australia from 1881-82 because of the heat, and would last between 30 and 45 minutes, which doubtless pleased every umpire. When Warwick Armstrong brought his Australian touring party of 1921, the "Big Ship" insisted on tea intervals as well as much else besides.

Before then, according to references in *The Cricketer*, the tea interval seems to have been either a moveable or a non-existent feast. Few mentions are made in any records, although there is evidence that administrators tried to prevent a second interval taking place during a day's play in England in 1903. It was also proposed at this time to "enliven" county matches by the introduction of bands, leading to debate over whether these should perform during play.

The convention of tea seems to have gradually spread. In a long article in *The Times* in 1909, "A Correspondent" (E. B. Osborn) wrote: "There is no denying that the tea interval, which was unknown to our cricket-playing forefathers, is a bad quarter of an hour for the spectators. Veterans regard this new fashion as a symptom of 'slackness' on the part of the present generation of cricketers. No constant incumbent of the hard and abbreviated benches at Lord's or The Oval can help noticing that the crowd, individually and sometimes collectively, resents the loss of time involved and is injured in its temperament, if not in its temper."

Osborn then posed the pertinent question: is afternoon tea a necessity for the modern Englishman? He conceded that it was a "stimulus" to mental exertion and that in country-house and village matches it provided an opportunity to meet and talk with visitors who had driven to watch the game. "For all one knows, marriages may be made in this little social heaven of the tea interval." In the Colonies, he concluded, tea was often drunk at all three meals, and hence it would be inhuman to deprive touring Australians of it. "Let our guests boil the 'billy', metaphorically speaking, at 4.30 p.m."

Fielding captains in England came to relish the tea interval not because of the food or drink, but on account of the disruption to the concentration of batsmen and a wicket often falling upon resumption of play. The ten-minute interval between innings was regulated in 1910 but this, of course, could fall before or after teatime. It could be added to the quarter of an hour for tea if an innings concluded when this was due to be taken, leading to shouts of "Loafers!" directed at players at Lord's in 1909. Much later, in the 1950s, tea was extended to 20 minutes' duration.

Willey himself had been reconciled to no alteration in the ECB regulations. There was a prevailing view that spectators would not want the hours of play extended even further on a day (most days) of sluggish over-rates. Twenty minutes, surely, was sufficient time for a cuppa and a selection from one of the

Lining up for a cup: spectators during the Victory Test between England and Australia at Lord's in July 1945 form an orderly queue at the tea interval.

culinary outlets at county grounds? Time enough to go to the Gents, update the scorecard and visit the museum.

Umpires, however, had the support of last year's chairman of the ECB's cricket committee, Jack Simmons. For, as everybody in the game knows, "Flat Jack" likes his tea (and his lunch and dinner). "I was very sympathetic to them, and of course we had to consider their concerns," Simmons said. "I was aware they had less time off the field than the players. I thought extending the intervals would suit the county chief executives, as spectators would have more time to eat at their bars and restaurants and be less inclined to bring sandwiches. We are in the entertainment industry. I was fortunate to be invited into a box at Manchester City and we were given a buffet before the match, pie and gravy at half-time, and cake and a glass of wine at the end. I was hungry and ate the lot."

The professional cricketer of 2010 is still served cucumber sandwiches at Lord's, along with smoked salmon and ham. And, although fruit juice, mineral water and isotonic energy drinks are provided as alternatives to tea, there are still cakes: fruit, ginger, carrot and Victorian sponge, if not cup cakes. Their comforting appearance defies the belief that all change in the game is for the worse.

LAHORE, TUESDAY, MARCH 3, 2009: Video footage of two of the terrorists who ambushed the Sri Lankan Test team and match officials; the players are later airlifted from the Gaddafi Stadium.

Matthew Impey, PA Photos

ENTERTAINMENT FROM START TO FINISH: England's Stuart Broad fails to run out Edgar Schiferli, and the Netherlands gain a famous victory on the opening night of the World Twenty20. Supporters in Karachi watch Pakistan defeat Sri Lanka in the final.

Shakil Adil, AP/PA

Graham Morris

AND FOR MY NEXT TRICK... Sri Lanka's Angelo Mathews, behind the boundary but off the ground, saves six by parrying the ball back into play during the World Twenty20. Timing his leap to perfection, Warwickshire's Jonathan Trott catches Sussex's Ed Joyce in his pocket.

Michael Regan, Getty Images

FIVE CRICKETERS OF THE YEAR: Stuart Broad.

FIVE CRICKETERS OF THE YEAR: Michael Clarke.

FIVE CRICKETERS OF THE YEAR: Graham Onions.

FIVE CRICKETERS OF THE YEAR: Graeme Swann.

FIVE CRICKETERS OF THE YEAR: Matt Prior.

Graham Morris

WHEN 40-OVER CRICKET WAS FUN

From church to Chappell

T ANYA A LDRED

It is the late 1960s and free love abounds. Not, however, at Lord's. Cricket is wretched and miserable. Crowds are down, counties are depressed, some nearly bankrupt, and all around people are finding other, more entertaining ways to spend their time.

Is there a way out? Perhaps. The Rothmans Cavaliers have been pottering around the country on Sunday afternoons for a few years. A sort of world XI consisting mostly of old players, they pull in full houses, and BBC2, almost wherever they go. The Test and County Cricket Board look over and lick their lips, and in 1969 the Sunday League is born – a 40-over competition to be played on Sunday afternoons, starting late enough to digest the roast dinner and placate the keep-the-Sabbath-special lobby, and finishing early enough for the children to get to bed and for the TV schedules. It is, Norman Preston writes in *Wisden 1970*, an "instant success".

In the beginning, not too many players take it seriously. Peter Walker of Glamorgan, who went on to host the BBC coverage for many years, remembers: "In my early career we were still playing the same game W. G. Grace had played. It took us a long time to get the hang of it; the players used to call it baseball, we were very sceptical."

But not all counties felt the same. Lancashire, through the wise eyes of Jack Bond, saw in this new competition an opportunity. "A lot of people were treating it as a bit of a joke, like they would do with the Twenty20 when it first came in, but we didn't," says Bond. "We said, 'Right, we've been brought up in league cricket, we've got to give it a go, not just from a batting and bowling point of view but fielding too.'

"The only trouble was, after a while, the lads were thinking more of playing on a Sunday than they were of the Championship games and, to be honest, I was as well. I would give people a bowl in the Championship to keep them ticking over for the Sunday."

Alan Ealham, in his fourth season of playing for Kent in 1969, shared the sentiment. "We were a young side, and the Sunday League was fun; it suited our way of playing, which was different from the Colin Cowdrey way of playing. When we went back to the Championship on a Monday it could be a bit flat."

The competition gave the counties another reason for being. A club that had no chance in the Championship, and that had been knocked out of the Gillette Cup early, now had something to play for. And the crowds that first year were huge, ridiculous numbers: 5,500 at Lydney to watch Gloucestershire v Sussex; 8,000 at Ilford for Essex v Middlesex; and nearly 8,000 at the United Services Ground for Hampshire against Essex, the biggest crowd anyone could

Taking the game to the people: the BBC's David Vine interviews Leicestershire's Ray Illingworth and Tony Lewis of Glamorgan at Llandudno in June 1969.

remember at Portsmouth. Nearly 10,000 turned up to watch Lancashire and Glamorgan at Southport; 12,000 at Old Trafford to watch Hampshire – and so on, all through the season.

"Members weren't keen originally, but then we started winning," says Bond. "They used to turn up to watch us field, with Clive Lloyd and David Hughes, one at cover and one at extra cover, and Harry Pilling on the boundary throwing it in flat.

"My benefit game was a John Player game and we had 20,000 people in the ground. Many's the time we had ten or fifteen coaches leaving at five in the morning to see us play in South Wales.

"Yorkshire hated the flipping game. Brian Close said that it was a waste of time and this, that and the other, but suddenly they realised it was a spectator sport. All cricket should be a spectator sport.

"People started enjoying it again. It was a family day, they could bring their kids and sit on the grass, all the way round, even in front of the pavilion."

There was a different atmosphere, too. There were no cheerleaders, no high-decibel blasts of pop music, but there were John Player girls who handed out cigarettes. And where at the Championship there would have been applause, here there was chanting, of a well-behaved sort. And just the sense of a game being alive.

David Green, then a swashbuckling batsman for Gloucestershire, says: "I remember against Yorkshire at the Wagon Works there were 8,000 spectators, and only 1,500 could have seen anything – there were two rows of benches and the rest were milling around. They were 138 for six needing 13 off 16 balls, and they didn't make it. I was just running back to the tin shed and this bloke came up, grabbed me by the arm and said, 'That was the best game I've ever seen!' It was crap really, but players respond to that huge excitement."

Ealham too remembers the difference in the atmosphere on a Sunday. "At Kent we were very lucky to have a good membership, 11,000 or so. But during Championship games it would be mostly retired people sitting quietly. There would be silence as the bowler ran up to bowl, and if someone hit a four there would be a ripple of applause. In the Sunday League, there would be clapping and cheering from when the bowler ran in – you had club players watching, shouting, a certain football element. It suited our style."

And who wouldn't have warmed to the overseas players trying their hand at this new game (the qualification rules had been relaxed in 1968)? Barry Richards, Greg Chappell, Garry Sobers, Majid Khan, Asif Iqbal, Mike Procter, Clive Lloyd, and so the list went on. Chappell was the first to score a century in this format. It was an industrial-sized banquet of tasty treats.

Peter Walker remembers something special from Barry Richards one Sunday in 1970: "He was a bit of a prima donna. We were the opposition, the cameras came, and he demolished us, got a hundred, took the applause, bowed to the cameras and hit the next ball up in the air. I've never seen anyone toy with the ball like that."

Visiting royalty: Somerset's Australian Greg Chappell joins in the fun at Northlands Road, Southampton, in August 1969; Hampshire's Bob Stephenson admires.

In the 1971 *Wisden*, Jim Laker wrote a piece under the title "Thrills of Sunday Cricket". Laker was not prone to undue bouts of excitement – but even he couldn't help himself. "If one takes into account the fact that BBC2 is still available only to a certain section of the cricketing public," he wrote, "and that a Sunday afternoon on a warm summer day offers too many alternatives, it is really incredible to believe that 1,250,000 people watched the Roses match on August 30, 1970."

But they did. And 27,000, plus turnstile-jumpers, were actually at Old Trafford to watch Bond receive the trophy. Laker described "the vast crowd complete with rattles, scarves, banners and even a representation of shaved heads and bovver boots".

One of the ideas of the competition was that it would bring cricket to the people, and the list of outgrounds reads like a gazetteer of a forgotten, if not quite idyllic, land: Burton-on-Trent, Buxton, Harlow, Leyton, Purfleet, Ebbw Vale, Llandudno, Neath, Lydney, Bournemouth, Blackheath, Folkestone, Maidstone, Peterborough, Brislington, Glastonbury, Torquay, Weston-super-Mare, Yeovil, Leatherhead, Sutton, Nuneaton, Dudley, Kidderminster, Stourbridge, Harrogate, Huddersfield, Hull, Sheffield.

"We'd all played club cricket as kids and were used to the facilities. A change of venue all added to the atmosphere," says Green. "No one likes to look a fool, but there was an element of light-heartedness to it. I felt we responded to the enthusiasm of the crowd; there was much more response than on a wet Tuesday or Wednesday. And if you cocked up you didn't sacrifice your first-class average."

The new game changed players too. "Stuart Leary, the South African, found he could hit sixes," says Ealham, "and he was always picking up the Sunday paper, asking where he was in the six-hitting table. I think it helped a lot of players lose their inhibitions, though it may have ruined one or two. The restricted run-up messed up a few bowlers, too, though it was all right for us because we had Derek Underwood."

To start with, the scores were low, that first year. Despite *Wisden* raving about the "feverish tempo", only 15 totals over 200 were made, and 160 would normally win a game. The pitches were helpful to the bowlers, and batsmen were happy to defend.

Sometimes, they took it to extremes. Somerset and Essex met on July 27 at Johnson Park, Yeovil, a ground with drainage problems. After eight overs of medium-pace, the spinners came on: the off-spinner and Somerset captain Brian Langford bowled almost exclusively to Essex opener Brian Ward. Eight overs later he finished with figures of 8–8–0–0. Ward explained afterwards to Stephen Chalke: "I thought I'd play him out."

And in his seven home games in '69, Derek Shackleton bowled 56 overs for 127, notching up 11 maidens and eight wickets. Not too bad for a 45-year-old medium-pacer.

David Green has similar memories. "Mike P[rocter] and David Smith were our opening bowlers," he says. "We had two slips and a gully, a recognisably orthodox field till the last ten overs. Lever and Shuttleworth used to fire away as if they were in the Championship. The fielding was very 1900s; there was not too much diving around – people were not rubbing heads against concrete steps."

The strictures of the 21st century were a while away too, at least in Gloucestershire. "Saturday night out was sacrosanct," says Green. "It was not like having to play a Championship match the next day. I would put on a couple of sweaters and sweat like a badger for a couple of overs in the nets on the Sunday and be fine. We either travelled by coach or four to a car. On a Sunday night we'd have half a shandy with the opposition – there was a great freemasonry."

But times were changing. Already in 1972 a further competition had been added, the Benson & Hedges Cup. And the game, if it didn't grow stale, became more formulaic. "Gradually, sides started having more defensive fields," says Walker, "and the game started to become very predictable with a slow start, a blitz at the end, and a recovery from a slow start or a throw-your-bat session in the middle."

The League went on to be played over 45 and 50 overs too, under 14 different names. The BBC lost interest after a while, and Sunday afternoon cricket was swallowed up by *Sunday Grandstand*. The number of overseas players was limited, and the Sunday League became the Tuesday, Thursday and any-day-you-fancy league. For

The lion's den: Worcestershire's Glenn Turner fields beside some partisan Kent supporters, Canterbury, 1972.

Walker, the *coup de grâce* was two divisions. This year it will be three groups.

But nothing can take away the fun and sheer randomness of those early years: from Fred Trueman's debut for Derbyshire (four overs for six became eight overs for 35), to Yorkshire and Glamorgan batting to the accompaniment of dummy bombing raids from the military tattoo on an adjoining field. And the outstanding memory should go to Jack Bond, who collected Lancashire's first outright trophy for 35 years at Nuneaton, in 1969: "It was a two o'clock start," he says, "and we had so many supporters come down they were out of pies by one." Some supporters, some fun, some game.

WHEN 50-OVER CRICKET WAS ABOLISHED

Bizarre and short-sighted

DUNCAN FLETCHER

It is an age-old lament. It is also an age-old neglect. Nothing is ever done about the glaringly obvious fact that county cricketers play too much cricket. And especially the fact that they play too much one-day cricket. It has to be the major reason why England have never won a global one-day trophy.

Not only do they play too much, they also play it at the wrong time. Generally games are tagged on to the end of four-day Championship matches, when players are tired, and sometimes from long hours of travelling as well as playing. There is no time to think and reflect, no time to rest, no time to practise. So there is little intensity. How can there be, when the players have just finished a four-day game? It is not their fault. Their minds become trained to be complacent, relying on the subconscious to muddle their way through. By the middle of the season they are burnt out and on autopilot. The mediocrity is manifested in the little things – like the running between the wickets and, especially, the fielding. It is all too easy to leave the big jobs (scoring hundreds, bowling at the death) to the overseas pro.

Too often, matches are played at the start of the summer when the pitches are too spicy. It is little wonder that England have struggled to produce power-hitters for the powerplay overs. You just cannot do that on the pitches provided. You produce batsmen very good square of the wicket, but rarely able to hit straight over the top. In international cricket your top three all need to be able to hit high down the ground. They obviously cannot do that all the time, but they do need to have that ability.

In county cricket there is no time for specific one-day nets or middle practices. The practices before a four-day match will centre on that format. The one-day stuff will only become relevant on the morning of the game. That is too late.

And even when there is time, more often than not the nets are not suitable. The groundstaff simply do not have the requisite opportunity to prepare the sort of flat surfaces on which batsmen can play lots of audacious shots. Instead, the net surfaces are like early-season pitches that seam and jag around, and batsmen find themselves just surviving. I have to say I have a lot of sympathy for the groundstaff in this regard. They just have too much to do. If only more counties were like Leicestershire, where a member of the groundstaff is placed solely in charge of the nets, which I believe are still the best in the country.

The ECB's decision to scrap 50-over cricket for the 2010 domestic season is bizarre and short-sighted. Maybe they are cleverly gazing into the future and seeing that all international one-day cricket will soon be of a 40-over duration, and so are taking a gamble on playing 40-over stuff now. But I doubt it. It is all to do with the finances, and not the standard of the cricket.

South Africa will suffer similarly. Their reduction to 40 overs in domestic cricket is a mistake too. Previously they played matches over 45 overs, and I thought that was just about close enough to replicate international cricket of 50 overs. South Africa had not won the World Cup but they had shown up well enough in the 50-over format.

But was this shorter domestic game a problem all along? Recently South Africa seem to have struggled in batting for the full 50 overs. Maybe the accumulated experience of playing a slightly shorter game is having its effects. It will now only get worse. Modifications in cricket always take time to show their true effects. Take the umpire referral system. You cannot expect it to be perfect straight away.

Ten overs is a lot of cricket. We have seen how much can happen in games where an innings lasts just 20 overs. Well, a lot can happen in ten, too. There is a skill to building constant momentum throughout a 50-over innings so that you still have wickets in hand at the end to make a charge. The advent of the batting powerplay has made it even more

Adapt and prosper: Warwickshire have increasingly turned to the medium-pace of Jonathan Trott at the end of a one-day innings.

imperative to play the full 50 overs so that real scenarios are repeated time and time again, rather than have shorter powerplays squashed into a shorter game.

If county cricket is to provide cricketers of sufficient grounding and experience, it needs to schedule its various formats in sealed-off blocks. It is good that it is now down to three competitions, but the amount of cricket to be played within them is not so good. You need to play a block of Championship cricket, then a block of one-day (50, not 40 overs) cricket, then the Twenty20 Cup in its entirety. Then, say, another block of one-day games, then a block of Championship cricket at the end.

I know how difficult the scheduling must be, and I am not for one minute suggesting a reduction in the number of counties (unless they are becoming an unsustainable financial drain), but county cricket desperately needs these windows so that its players can specialise and master the skills required. They simply cannot do that at the moment, and it is producing a lot of mediocre cricketers. They could be so much better.

Between 1999 and 2007, Duncan Fletcher coached England in 166 one-day internationals. The results were 75 wins, 82 defeats, two ties and seven no-results.

THE PLIGHT OF THE COUNTY REPORTER

An endangered species

GERALD MORTIMER

A remark made by Jeff Brown has stayed with me for years. He was one of those who set out with Durham when they gained first-class status in 1992 and, for five years, serviced the four titles in Newcastle: morning, evening, Saturday Pink and Sunday. There was plenty to keep him busy but, by the time he left to join Tyne Tees Television, Jeff said: "I had never before realised that a job could be so much fun."

The Durham contingent, of whom only Tim Wellock soldiers on, found a welcome in what was effectively a closed society. They were the 18th county, and not all the other teams had journalists covering them at home and away. But everybody knew everybody else, and each season's meetings were little reunions.

"I had covered some Minor Counties cricket with Durham," said Brown, "and was often the only one present, unless Mike Berry decided to take in a particular game. I had also done football and was used to cliques keeping stories to themselves. The thing that struck us when we set out in the Championship was how open everybody was – that and the endless chatter. There was so much laughter, but it never seemed to affect anybody's ability to do the job.

"Last summer, I looked in at the Riverside to watch Durham polish off Warwickshire. The press facilities are now very luxurious, but there were only five people there. It was more like entering a library." This, of course, was to watch the county champions making a good fist of defending their title. In Brown's time, they were scrapping at the other end of the table, but the press boxes were vibrant.

More than ever, it appears to be a lost world. During the winter of 2008-09, there were disturbing reports of old friends either being forced to reapply for their jobs or facing redundancy. Even those not in that predicament wondered how much cricket they would see. The local paper reporter was an endangered species, along with evening newspapers themselves, and those who survived were looking over their shoulders in case a company accountant was assessing their industry. Mark Eklid, my successor at the *Derby Telegraph*, was kept on the road by sponsorship from Specsavers. It seemed an irresistible topic for dressing-room humour but, somehow, he escaped.

Not only local papers were affected. The most alarming rumour of the winter concerned the *Daily Telegraph*, a paper that many first bought because of its comprehensive coverage of county cricket. Once freelances were on the *Telegraph* list, they were guaranteed work for the summer and knew their commitments for weeks ahead. Other journalists begged a look at the programme to see who would be at their next match, whether it was a day of

Scarborough in the late 1980s. *Standing:* Derek Hodgson (*Independent*), Terry Brindle (formerly *Yorkshire Post*), David Hopps (*Yorkshire Post*), Martin Searby (*Sheffield Star*). *Middle row:* unknown, Doug Ibbotson (*Daily Telegraph*), Dick Streeton (*The Times*). *Front row:* John Callaghan (*Yorkshire Evening Post*), Robert Mills (*Hull Daily Mail*).

laughter with David Green, the urbane company of Doug Ibbotson, Dicky Rutnagur announcing how well he was writing, or many others, very few of whom provoked an anticipatory groan.

The threat of cutbacks turned out to be true. Almost all that appeared in the *Telegraph* in the early weeks of the season was minuscule agency reports under names that were either fictitious or of people who were not present. At a stroke and with a minimum of notice, a group of gifted freelances became former cricket journalists.

The shrinkage became more dramatic in 2009, but it had been in progress for many years. Queen's Park, Chesterfield, was always a favoured venue and, when I began in 1970, it was wise to be there promptly to claim a seat. The tabloid papers all had northern cricket correspondents, based in the Manchester offices. Especially for matches between Derbyshire and Yorkshire, we were certain to see Derek Hodgson, Peter Johnson, John Sadler and Howard Booth, master of the expenses sheet, in addition to the broadsheet writers. Booth was credited with one of the most imaginative claims: "reversing mileage for the year", as compensation for the times he backed out of his drive to go to work.

Between Test matches, the leading correspondents were at county games, so we knew John Woodcock, John Arlott, Alex Bannister, Crawford White and, especially if the match was at Canterbury, Jim Swanton as colleagues rather than remote figures with little time to spare from the international circuit. When Clive Rice returned to Nottinghamshire as coach in 1999, one of his first questions at the start of the season was about the lack of numbers in the Trent Bridge press box.

For more than 30 years, latterly on a freelance basis, David Warner followed Yorkshire for the *Bradford Telegraph & Argus*. Known as Plum, for reasons that need no explanation in *Wisden*, he is a great observer and raconteur. His special subject was the legendary Yorkshire freelance Dick Williamson. Plum's tales are so vivid that even those who never met Williamson came to feel they knew him well.

"There was a greater certainty in my early days," Plum told me. "When September arrived, we looked forward to the following April. There was no reason to think it was anything other than a permanent job. We also knew where we were, and there was a rhythm to the season.

"Some anecdotes were aired endlessly but people were too polite to say they'd heard them 20 times. The old tales were expected, and prompts would be supplied. When four-day cricket and two divisions came in, we went for years without seeing a particular county or the people who followed it. Sadly, there are now fewer opportunities for young journalists."

One side-effect of the four-day game was to diminish county cricket in Sunday papers. With Saturday starts, all shades of the Sunday market could guarantee material for their summer sports pages but, once longer games were arranged starting on Wednesday, there was no certainty of any action. This led to the demise of a species known as "Sunday burglars". These were one-day-a-week writers, using the weekend to supplement income from other jobs and, while a few were charming, many turned up with no knowledge of what had happened in the rest of the week. Regulars were subjected to a barrage of questions from people who then expected priority on the telephones: particularly irksome at outgrounds. They were not popular and were occasionally given a hard time.

The spread of mobile phones was another blow to local freelances, cutting income from the hire of landlines. Martin Searby, then following Yorkshire, was an early entrant in that field with an instrument that resembled a car battery, in weight as well as appearance. Unfortunately, many of the blind spots of the embryo network coincided with cricket grounds. "British Telecom: their finger on the button? My hands round their throat," he growled in exasperation during a radio broadcast.

Means of communication began to change in the 1980s with the appearance of the Tandy, the forerunner of more sophisticated laptops. The typewriter was gently phased out, although not all had previously embraced them. Jim Kilburn's elegant prose for the *Yorkshire Post* was always handwritten, the final full stop coinciding with the last ball of the day before the sheets of paper were handed to a telephonist.

Eating habits hardly changed. Most people brought their own but none matched the style of Eric Hill's double-decker salad box as he sat in his little annexe to the Taunton box. On one bitterly cold day at Bramall Lane, a volunteer went to buy fish and chips. With the windows firmly closed, the smell lingered, and Kilburn, returning from his lunchtime stroll, was appalled. Tobacco smoke soon took over, there being no shortage of addicts. The habit among many was to take a lunchtime pint or two, either in the ground or

Gerald Mortimer, cricket correspondent of the *Derby Evening Telegraph* for 32 years.

a convenient pub. That was an established part of the relaxed, convivial atmosphere.

John May, who spent a decade following Hampshire, now lectures in sports journalism at a Southampton university. He succeeded the gentlemanly but incurably vague David Kenny, the subject of almost as many stories as Williamson. In the cramped old press box at the back of Derby's dilapidated Grandstand, we observed a respectful silence when May made his first contact with Shane Warne, who was joining Hampshire the following season. He rang the Australians' hotel in Sri Lanka and was put straight through: no worries then about illegal bookmakers in the subcontinent. "He was the biggest name in world cricket, but was as good as gold," May recalled. "When we went to meet him at Heathrow at the start of the following season, he said he had to keep a few things for his column in *The Times*, but would be happy to talk to the locals at the end of every day. All players were pleased to have a rapport, but now clubs are starting to employ press officers to make everything more formal.

"I was fortunate in that I travelled with Mike Neasom. He was from the rival paper in Portsmouth but was willing to take this young cub under his wing and, very gently, show him how to behave in press boxes. Newcomers had to establish their credentials before they were fully accepted but, after being told where to tread gently, I encountered no hostility. The evening paper people were like the infantry, slogging through the running copy while the nationals waited to be given their wordage around teatime, then doing overnight pieces and digging out quotes – and, of course, being a source of local knowledge to answer all the questions. Even then, I began to wonder if we were a last, privileged generation. No part of my working life was as enjoyable, and it brought me into contact with many I still regard as friends."

As well as being one of the *Daily Telegraph's* correspondents for around 30 years, Mike Beddow is the freelance covering Warwickshire and Worcestershire. In his early days, copy for the Press Association (PA) and the Exchange Telegraph (Extel) with half-hourly scores for Joint Services gave freelances the basis of their income. On top of that, they hired out telephones and provided coverage for national and local newspapers, television stations and local radio. "I used to have two pieces a day for *The Sun*, as an example," Beddow said. "Demand varied between matches, but it was possible to make a good living. It is very difficult now, and perhaps the most significant change is the value of PA copy. When papers sent their own men or made a specific order, PA reports had a limited airing. Now they are often the only source of information. I fear 2009 may have marked the end of serious coverage of county cricket, because everybody is cutting back. Perhaps that is due to the recession, but it is also an attitude of mind, and I wonder if there is any way back."

It is almost as if the England and Wales Cricket Board are in league with newspaper proprietors. The ECB continue to stress the importance of the Championship, but the way four-day fixtures were fitted into odd corners in 2009 hardly bore out their claim. Newspapers follow the elite events. It happens in winter with blanket coverage of the Premier League and scant notice of the 72 clubs in the Football League. The summer emphasis is on Test cricket, with five or six reporters present to find different angles. It is hard to imagine that Swanton would have accepted this challenge to his omniscience. Many of the main correspondents are former Test players for whom county cricket became a chore in the days before central contracts. Now they concentrate their attentions on international cricket and, although that is a consuming job, Christopher Martin-Jenkins always found time to espouse the county game when he was *The Times's* correspondent. Any professional sport needs publicity, and many of county cricket's virtues go unheralded.

Frank Keating hailed David Foot as the monarch of county cricket reporters. At a lunch to celebrate Foot's 80th birthday, it was revealed that, when he returned home after covering cricket, his wife Anne did not ask who had made runs or taken wickets. Her question was always: "Was it a good box?" Footy loves the jokes, the familiarity of old friends and the ambience of cricket. I hope he never has to say he was the only one in attendance.

Gerald Mortimer first contributed to Wisden *in 1983, and is the longest-serving of the 18 county correspondents.*

THE CRICKET PHOTOGRAPH OF THE YEAR

Capturing cricket's future

In its millennium edition, Wisden invited Patrick Eagar, the doyen of cricket photography, to select the defining images of the 20th century, one from each decade. The ten photographs that appear in *Wisden 2000* give an immediate and fascinating glimpse into cricket history, from George Beldam's unforgettable image of Victor Trumper to an extraordinary salmon-leap of a catch by Jonty Rhodes.

Wisden, in partnership with MCC, is now launching an annual Cricket Photograph of the Year competition. The winning images will be chosen by a panel of independent expert judges appointed by Wisden and MCC and free of outside influence. The judges will draw up a shortlist from which they will select a winner and two runners-up. The chosen images will best capture the joy, drama, spirit or essence of cricket, wherever in the world it is played, watched or experienced.

Each year, starting in the 2011 edition, the winning photographs will be included in *Wisden's* colour section. All the shortlisted entries will be exhibited at Lord's, and there will be prizes for the winning photographers.

The competition is open to all photographers – amateur and professional – throughout the world. The only stipulations are that entries must, in one way or another, have a cricket theme, and have been taken during 2010. Beyond that, there is no restriction whatever. Photographs may be from the beach, village green, maidan, street, stadium, snowfield – anywhere. Put simply, Wisden and MCC invite submissions of the most outstanding images of cricket captured in 2010.

Had such a competition existed for the past 100 years, the range of images built up within the pages of *Wisden* would have formed a compelling archive of the game's ever-changing face. Those editing *Wisden 2111* should be lucky enough to have just such an archive.

For full details, visit: www.lords.org/photooftheyear.

1900s: Victor Trumper

1990s: Jonty Rhodes

THE WISDEN CITY CUP

A fast track to the top

Scyld Berry

Launching the inaugural Wisden City Cup last summer was an attempt – one of many, of course – to revive cricket in Britain's inner cities. Where it differed from other projects, schemes and initiatives was that it offered a fast-track opportunity to the top.

It seemed consistent with the values of John Wisden. Back in mid-Victorian times he promoted matches and tours in addition to playing, making and selling sports equipment, and publishing an almanack.

The template was simple. Divide a city into four geographical areas; let the four teams play each other twice each in 20-over games on midweek evenings; hire good, accessible, club grounds (in inner cities they are in such short supply that many youngsters who cannot afford to belong to a club are condemned to mediocre pitches and facilities, if any); and let players between the ages of 16 and 25 (with two exceptions) play – with a pink ball, which stands out as the evening darkens, with or without sightscreens. Then have a meal together afterwards, so that each game is a social occasion as well as a sporting one.

Our inaugural year saw Middlesex pilot the scheme, brilliantly, under their chief development officer Phil Knappett. When Angus Fraser had first played for Middlesex in the 1980s, there were five players of Afro-Caribbean origin at the club. When he took over as the county's director of cricket in January 2009, they had none, and only one Asian, Owais Shah, even though half of some of the county's age-group teams are Asian. Middlesex's professional cricketers were predominantly white middle-class, reflecting the decline of cricket in our inner cities; and Fraser was ready to do something about it.

London, north of the Thames, was divided into West, North-West, North-East and East. A county match at Hornsey in 1959 was about as close as Middlesex had come to Tower Hamlets and Brick Lane, where there are thousands upon thousands of people from Bangladesh who are hungry for the sport. Yet there is not one grass pitch in East London for them to play on.

Trials were held, open to anyone, though there was little point in those already playing for a premier league club turning up. At one of those trials, held in Hackney's Victoria Park, a 22-year-old ran in. A fortnight later Maaz Haffeji was bowling against the Australians in the nets at Lord's, and he is now one of two WCC players training with Middlesex. Only then did I fully realise how damaging it is to have no live cricket on free-to-air television: he had never been able to see how fast bowlers use the crease.

The generous competition sponsors were the Foundation for Sport and the Arts, who enabled us to hire the grounds at Hornsey, Southgate, Brondesbury and Eastcote, and to provide food and colourful kit. Each team had its sponsor: Barclays, The Times, Freshfields and W. H. Ireland. The London Mayor's

Fund put up match awards worth £100 for each qualifying game, and £250 for the final. Brit Insurance provided £1,000 in batting and bowling prizes. Wisden put up £1,000 in fielding prizes (the best fielder in each match was awarded three points, the second-best two, the third one). Even the last qualifying game, the only dead match, had intensity because of the prizes and opportunities on offer.

London West – Barclays Eagles – set the pace by winning the first four of their six qualifying games. They selected their coach, the recent Middlesex all-rounder Chris Peploe, although a coach could bat no higher than No. 7, and Shaftab Khalid, still the only *doosra* bowler produced by county cricket, who toured India with England A in 2004. But while these two former first-class players were the stars, they did not dominate, such was the overall standard. North-West – WHI Nomads – lost their first four games, then won their last two. To decide the other finalists, the second game between the North-East (Freshfields Flyers) and East (The Times Tigers) was the crunch, and East squeezed through after winning both head-to-heads. Mostly but not exclusively of Bangladeshi origin, half of the East team had not played regularly on grass before; they were learning fast.

In the final at Hornsey, The Times Tigers made 129 for seven. After a powerful start, Barclays Eagles collapsed on a wearing late-August pitch against the Tigers' spinners. The scenes, on a reduced scale, were reminiscent of England winning at The Oval a few days before. Is any community in Britain keener on cricket now than the Bangladeshis of London's East End? Well, perhaps Afghan refugees who have come to this country; and this summer, Middlesex are organising a junior WCC competition as well, to which any 14- to 16-year-olds will have access, except for those who already have an opportunity to perform.

Finally, the representative match, a real showcase: a WCC XI, drawn from the four teams, played a Middlesex XI at Southgate, again a Twenty20 game. Amateurs v Professionals. Half the Middlesex team were Academy players, but half had played for the first team – and the WCC XI won, with several wickets and balls to spare. Which only goes to show what talent there is in Britain outside the traditional club and county structures; and what fun can be had, and what multiracial harmony achieved, in promoting it.

Wisden City Cup	*Played*	*Won*	*Lost*	*Points*
West	6	4	2	8
East	6	3	3	6
North-East	6	3	3	6
North-West	6	2	4	4

Leading run-scorer Mylo Wilkin, 225 runs at 45.00.
Leading wicket-taker M. R. Qureshi, 11 wickets at 8.36.
Leading fielder Farokh Chodhry (11 points).

The Wisden City Cup seeks a variety of sponsors to help achieve its aim of expanding beyond London to other British cities. For all details, visit www.wisdencitycup.com.

THE LEADING CRICKETER IN THE WORLD, 2009

Virender Sehwag

SCYLD BERRY

Several strong candidates advanced their case to be the Leading Cricketer in the World in 2009. None, however, made such an impact as to displace the incumbent, Virender Sehwag, India's 31-year-old opening batsman, who extended the sport's traditional boundaries further still. He scored more quickly than any specialist batsman in Tests or one-day internationals. Last year he broke Test cricket's sound barrier by scoring at more than a run a ball.

Australia's former captain Ian Chappell, in as good a position to judge as anybody alive, directly compared Sehwag to Sir Donald Bradman: they have the fastest scoring-rate among players of their generation, and are the only men to have exceeded 290 three times in Tests. Chappell called Sehwag "the greatest destroyer since the U-boat", and dismissed the accusation that he prospered only in home conditions by pointing out that he averaged almost 50 abroad.

Sehwag raised the bar even higher than in 2008, when he had scored at a strike-rate of 85 runs per 100 balls in Tests, and 120 in one-day internationals. In 2009 he did not play so much, after injuring his right shoulder during the second IPL, and for much of the year the giant rested. It was no coincidence that, in his absence, India were knocked out in the early stages of both the World Twenty20 and the Champions Trophy. He still played in all of India's Test matches in 2009 – a three-Test series in New Zealand and another at home to Sri Lanka – and, in steering them to No. 1 in the Test rankings for the first time, Sehwag averaged 70, with a strike-rate of 108.9.

Adam Gilchrist had set a new standard with his strike-rate of 81.9 while averaging 47 in Tests, but he did so almost entirely from the relative comfort of No. 7 in one of the greatest Test teams of all. Sehwag has taken on the opposition from the first ball of India's innings, shredding their confidence with his strokeplay, demoralising them as no Test batsman has done since Bradman, who scored at 61.2 per 100 balls. In one-day internationals in 2009 Sehwag had a strike-rate of 136.5 – again, far higher than any batsman of substance has achieved over a lengthy period – while averaging 45.

"The feat of the year", as Chappell called it, came when Test cricket returned to the Brabourne Stadium in Mumbai last December. Sri Lanka scored 366 for eight on the opening day as they attempted, in the last match of the series, to overturn India's 1–0 lead. Next morning they continued to 393 all out; 79 overs remained in the day. Few would have thought of winning the game from this position, rather than settling for a draw. Sehwag did. By the close of the second day he had scored 284 not out from 239 balls with 40 fours and seven sixes – and Sri Lanka are Asia's best fielding side.

By dispiriting bowlers Sehwag has made batting so much easier for team-mates. Rangana Herath made a fine comeback last year as Sri Lanka's left-arm spinner, yet, when he came on to bowl, Sehwag went down the pitch to drive his second ball for six. Herath's fellow spinner was Muttiah Muralitharan, his captain Kumar Sangakkara – a candidate himself to be the Leading Cricketer in the World. But Sehwag still surged to the second-fastest Test double-hundred ever recorded, from only 168 balls. Those of us who saw the fastest – Nathan Astle's from 153 balls against England – would vouch that Christchurch's drop-in pitch played as flawlessly as an artificial one.

Sehwag, not surprisingly, could not continue in the same vein next morning and was dismissed for 293 from 254 balls. But by then India had taken a first-innings lead, and Sehwag had given his team so much time that even though Sri Lanka made more than 300 in their second innings as well, India won by an innings early on the fifth day, and took the series 2–0 to claim top spot.

While Sehwag was batting at the Brabourne, South Africa and England were preparing for a one-day international in Durban, and a television in Kingsmead's pavilion was switched on silently while the captains did their press conferences. Both Graeme Smith and Andrew Strauss kept looking at the distant screen to watch Sehwag. One definition of genius is doing what nobody else can: and in 2009 Sehwag batted like nobody else has ever done for any length of time.

Sehwag learned to bat on a driveway of smooth concrete beside his house on the outskirts of Delhi, with a younger brother and neighbours to bowl taped tennis balls quickly. If he had an identical twin, who batted at the same rate as Viru in 2009, India would score 600 in a day of 90 overs. Test cricket has been threatened by the greater excitement that is perceived in 50-over and 20-over cricket; it will not be if more batsmen emulate Sehwag, as he pushes back the parameters and scores at the same rate in Tests as others do in Twenty20.

Strauss was nominated by several correspondents who were consulted about this award. Besides leading England's improvement in Test cricket to regain the Ashes, and squaring the four-Test series in South Africa, he also resurrected England's 50-over cricket. But England under Strauss lost a Test series in the West Indies, which none of the main Test-playing countries had done for six years, although allowance has to be made for the fact that the captain had no say in his squad's selection after his hurried appointment; and, in one-day cricket, England were hammered 7–1 by Australia during the year.

Tillekeratne Dilshan was the other main nominee. His case rests more on limited-overs than on Test cricket: if we deduct the Chittagong Test, in which he scored two hundreds, he averaged 52.80 last year, and did not make the Wisden Test XI as he gained only one of the three selectors' votes. Superb in his hand–eye co-ordination, Dilshan came ever closer to Sehwag in his approach as he was promoted to open the batting for Sri Lanka in all three formats, without ever surpassing the trendsetter. He scored more runs in Twenty20 internationals than anybody else last year (471), although none in the World Twenty20 final at Lord's. He can be credited with popularising the scoop on bended knee over the shoulder, but not its invention.

Sehwag has to be first on the team-sheet to represent the World, whatever the game's format. He would take on the Martians, however hostile and alien their attack, disrupting their lines and wavelengths; and, if he succeeded, as he normally does, he would make life so much easier for those who followed.

FIVE CRICKETERS OF THE YEAR

The Five Cricketers of the Year represent a tradition that dates back in Wisden *to 1889, making this the oldest individual award in cricket. The Five are picked by the editor, and the selection is based, primarily but not exclusively, on the players' influence on the previous English season. No one can be chosen more than once. Since 2004,* Wisden *has also chosen a Leading Cricketer in the World. Scyld Berry's article on Virender Sehwag appears on pages 80–81.*

A list of past Cricketers of the Year appears on pages 426–428.

Stuart Broad

PAUL NEWMAN

It was with his devastating, series-winning, career-defining bowling spell at The Oval that Stuart Broad made an indelible mark on Ashes history; but it was in the previous, chastening Test at Headingley that he helped shift the momentum that was swinging Australia's way.

When England, still leading the series 1–0, staggered to the end of the second day of the Fourth Test, they were teetering at 82 for five in their second innings, still 261 behind Australia and heading for the most comprehensive defeat. What happened next not only irritated Australia but played no small part in England regaining their self-esteem for the decider.

"It was typical Andy Flower," says Broad. "He gathered those of us still to bat on the Sunday morning and said 'I don't care how you do it. You can leave every ball, block every ball or hit every ball for four, but go out there and show some fight. We must leave this ground with something to show for our efforts.' Matty Prior started it by going after them and they started to get a bit frustrated.

"Then Graeme Swann came in. I always enjoy batting with him, because we hit the ball in different areas but score at a decent pace, and we just got a bit of momentum going. It was a good laugh, the crowd got behind us and the atmosphere was fantastic. We clawed a little bit back and it gave us a lot of confidence."

In an eighth-wicket stand of 108 in 12.3 overs, Broad scored 61 to follow career-best figures of six for 91. He might not have been selected had Andrew Flintoff been fit. It did not stop Australia levelling the series with an innings victory, but some pride had been restored and foundations laid for what was to come in Kennington.

STUART CHRISTOPHER JOHN BROAD was born in Nottingham on June 24, 1986, to former England batsman Chris and mother Carole, "the most positive person you will ever meet," according to her son. "Mum texted me that Sunday morning at Headingley to say 'get a hundred runs ahead and then take a few early wickets and you could be back in the match'." She was hoping for a repeat of the 1981 partnership there between Ian Botham and Graham Dilley that went into folklore.

Broad was always destined to be a cricketer, from the times when he would get his sister Gemma, later analyst for the England one-day and women's teams, to throw a ball at him in the garden, and he would play on the Trent Bridge outfield with Philip Robinson, son of his dad's opening partner Tim. Yet it was at hockey that he initially thrived, before a growth spurt and a spell in Victoria, Australia, with Hoppers Crossing transformed him from an opening batsman into a bowler. He earned his first-class debut with Leicestershire in 2005, before his 19th birthday.

"Up until I was 16 I just turned my arm over with the keeper stood up, trying to bowl maidens and swinging it nicely," says Broad. "My most successful sport then was hockey, where I had trials with England. I was a goalie. I was short then and pretty fearless, but it came to an end when I was hit by a fierce shot in the leg. I was 17 and getting more serious about cricket."

Cricket was in his genes, and he was also influenced by Frank Hayes and David Steele, his coaches at Oakham School. Broad's paternal grandfather would take him to Lord's once a year to watch England. "We would get up at 5.30 a.m. to get the bus then the train to London," says Broad. "There was the one time (in 1997) when Glenn McGrath was virtually unplayable. There was another when I saw Jimmy Anderson playing against South Africa. I was a little kid and he was bowling for England, and he's only four years older than me!

"I was a regular viewer on television too. I was watching with my grandparents when Andrew Caddick took four wickets in an over at Headingley against West Indies, and Darren Gough was another favourite. I was always a big fan of seeing wickets fall. Watching someone get a five-for was much better for me than seeing a batsman get a hundred."

After his one-day international debut against Pakistan in 2006, Broad was selected for the squad against India at Lord's in 2007, but overlooked in favour of Chris Tremlett. His Test debut had to wait until the following winter and the bowler's graveyard of the Sinhalese Sports Club in Colombo. Since then, progress has been sustained and rapid.

Another breakthrough came in 2008, when Broad worked with Ottis Gibson at England's academy in Loughborough and was told that a bowling action remodelled by Kevin Shine was not working. "Ottis told me I was too chest-on, so I went back to how I used to be," says Broad. "I stood still for three months when I was trying to change too much. I wouldn't blame Kevin Shine, he was trying to look after my body. At the end of the day he made a suggestion and I took it on."

This progress culminated in Broad becoming perhaps the first really tall England bowler to swing the ball both ways at 90mph, a heady mix that proved too much for Ricky Ponting and his team at The Oval. A 12-over spell of five for 37 included four for eight in 21 balls. His freshness for the big moment had undoubtedly been helped by his mature decision not to go to the Indian Premier League earlier in 2009.

"The Oval has given me a lot of confidence for what I can achieve," says Broad. "There have been times in my Test career where I haven't been sure where to go, whether to be an economical bowler or try to bowl bouncers and knock someone's head off. The thing about The Oval was that I bowled the way that suits me best, trying to hit the top of off stump using a bit of variation."

Broad's manner will be familiar to anyone who watched his ultra-competitive father play for England, before the poacher became an ICC referee. "I always look at my attitude as competitiveness and a passion for the game, but there are times when it can bubble over, like with dad, and that's something I'm working to control," says Broad. "My dad was a bowler in a batsman's body, because he was so fiery, and I think as a bowler I have to be like that. There is nothing worse than seeing a bowler with no spirit or fight."

It is unlikely to be a failing of which he is ever accused.

Michael Clarke

MALCOLM CONN

There was a time when Michael Clarke was viewed even by some of his team-mates as a bit of a glory boy. Richly talented and with an impeccable pedigree, this kid was along for the ride – the only 20-something in a team of hard-nosed 30-somethings who ruled the world, a Generation Y in a group of uncompromising streetfighters. Even when he was made vice-captain after Adam Gilchrist retired early in 2008, Gilchrist was one of those warning that Clarke should not assume he would be Australia's next captain. Was he tough enough when it counted? He has been answering in the affirmative almost ever since.

In 2009, Clarke reinforced his status as one of Australia's premier batsmen, but was gutted when a string of sterling performances came to nothing. It was no consolation that he was Australia's leading run-scorer in the Ashes, with 448 runs at 64; he failed twice at The Oval, where England won easily to claim the series 2–1. Clarke had dominated the first four Tests with two centuries, a 93 and an 83, and was in line for the Compton–Miller medal for the series' best player. That was until the man who rightly beat him for the honour, England captain Andrew Strauss, completely out-batted him and out-thought him at The Oval, with a catch at short cover in the first innings and a spectacular run-out in the second. "The game always finds a way of biting you on the backside," Clarke observed later.

MICHAEL JOHN CLARKE was born on April 2, 1981, in Liverpool, a nondescript suburb amid the vast urban sprawl of Sydney's working-class west. The second child and only son of Les and Debbie Clarke, Michael is not sure when he first played cricket. "Like any six-year-old you want to be like your father," says Clarke. "Cricket and rugby league were his two sports, so they were my two sports." He has memories of playing in the morning and watching his father play in the afternoon, sitting around in whites hoping to be called on as twelfth man. Les once owned a brick truck and was a milkman, but the career change which set his son on the path to sporting glory came when the family bought an indoor cricket centre. It became a second home for seven-year-old Michael.

For his senior Grade debut, as a tiny 16-year-old, he was picked as a left-arm spinner and No. 8 batsman. At 18, he captained Australia Under-19 and signed his first New South Wales contract. Turning up to training, he couldn't quite believe he was sharing the same space as Steve and Mark Waugh, Glenn McGrath, and his idol Michael Slater.

Clarke's NSW upbringing is widely assumed to be the reason for his light feet and desire to advance against spinners. The Sydney Cricket Ground has been Australia's Mecca for spin in recent decades, with Stuart MacGill, Nathan Hauritz and Beau Casson all changing states to exploit its turning surface. However, Clarke claims his nimble movement came much earlier, from the decade he spent in his father's cricket centre. "Indoor cricket had something to do with it, because every time you hit the ball you had to run to the halfway line," he says. "If you can take a couple of steps down the wicket you're halfway there. Certainly that's had more of an impact than the SCG, because I played like that as a kid.

"The strength of my batting against spin is the cut shot, so trying to get down the wicket allows me to push back off my front leg to play the cut, which scores me a lot of runs. I reckon I score more runs against spin off the back foot than the front foot, but because I try and go down the wicket it can force the bowler to drop a little shorter."

Clarke never had trouble making sacrifices for his cricket. While his mates were out partying on a Friday night he would often be practising at the centre, believing his party was a cricket match the following day. But it was all a bit of a lark. He was picked on potential for Australia's one-day side in January 2003, and toured India in 2004-05, aged 23, believing he would be the reserve batsman to Brad Hodge. Instead, Clarke was stunned to learn he would be making his debut in the First Test at Bangalore.

"I was in next, I was listening to my iPod and thinking 'if I get a duck here I don't really care.' I'd just received my baggy green off Warnie and I was that excited, I was loving every minute of it." He didn't make a duck. Over the next two days, Clarke made a seemingly effortless 151, and he finished the series with an average of 57. Little more than a month later his first home Test, against New Zealand in Brisbane, produced 141. How much fun was this?

Everyone wanted a piece of him. There was enormous media attention, while sponsorships and endorsements came thick and fast. Mates were always ringing for tickets. He loved his self-image: Michael Clarke the entertainer. "I wanted everyone to like me, to love the way I played – just the way I loved watching the way Slats [Slater] batted." A year later, he had failed to make another hundred and was dropped from the Test side.

It became the defining moment of his cricket career. "I was shattered. I flew home and cried with my dad for hours on the couch," recalled Clarke. "He said very clearly, 'Mate, you can stay here, you can be upset, there's a shoulder here to cry on for as long as you want, or you can go the other way, get back into the nets, train your backside off and get back into the team.' That week after I got dropped had an impact on where I sit as a person as well as a cricketer. There are major things that happen in your life which change your thinking, and that's the biggest challenge I've faced in cricket.

"I know my game better. My shot selection has improved out of sight, my disciplines off the field have improved enormously. Cricket always comes first now in regard to endorsements or sponsors. My preparation is always my No. 1 focus. Before I was dropped, I didn't know how to prepare."

Pre-axing, Clarke averaged 37 in 20 Tests, including those two hundreds. From his return in 2006 to the end of January 2010, he averaged 57 with 11 centuries, raising the question of when, not if, he will succeed Ricky Ponting. And the first part of the answer came in October 2009 when, aged 28, he was appointed Australia's Twenty20 captain.

Graham Onions

Tim Wellock

After two years flirting with England's second team, Graham Onions could not even get into Durham's side at the end of the 2008 season. His team-mate Mark Davies had nosed ahead of him on to the England Lions tours of India and New Zealand. But working hard at home proved the catalyst for Onions's transformation.

"Not being part of the celebrations when Durham won their first title down at Canterbury really hurt," he says. "I got very frustrated and, after being in the England set-up a year earlier, not hearing from them hurt as well. I had to prove I could take my game to the next level, so I trained really hard over the winter. I had struggled in 2008 after a six-week lay-off with a heel injury, and it wasn't the first time a season had tailed off for me. I was determined it wouldn't happen again."

A year later, he had been a leading figure in Durham retaining the County Championship; taken his first 20 Test wickets during the summer, helping to regain the Ashes; usurped a central contract from colleague Steve Harmison; and toured South Africa with the Test and one-day squads, saving two Tests with some never-say-die batting from No. 11.

Onions burst from the 2009 traps with a series of long, accurate spells. By midsummer, he had taken 40 Championship wickets in five games, either side of his Test debut. It was at Taunton that he heard of his Test selection against West Indies; he celebrated with six for 31 as Somerset succumbed for 69. Returning from Test duty, he claimed seven for 38 against Warwickshire at Edgbaston, where he would later dismiss Shane Watson and Mike Hussey with the first two balls of the second day of the Ashes Test. Onions played three matches against Australia before being omitted for the Oval decider. But his two-in-two prompted pop singer Lily Allen to profess her love for him.

His Test debut at Lord's in early May had inauspicious beginnings. After a golden duck, he had his first ball pulled for four, and conceded 22 runs in his first four overs. But his fifth was a maiden, and in the sixth he had Lendl Simmons caught at first slip, Jerome Taylor by the wicketkeeper and Sulieman Benn at third slip. Denesh Ramdin was lbw in his seventh over, and last man Lionel Baker in his tenth. In a single spell, he had taken five for 38.

England's demands meant there were to be only two more appearances for Durham, but his electrifying start had already propelled them towards their second successive title. His 45 Championship wickets came at 15.28.

GRAHAM ONIONS was born in Gateshead on September 9, 1982, and it was at the town's nearby leisure centre, rather than St Thomas More RC School in Blaydon, that he took the opportunity to try several sports. Given his natural whippiness, he shone at badminton – he was selected for England Under-15 – but it was at Gateshead Fell Cricket Club that his real talent began to emerge.

"I also used to play in the street at home," he says. "We had one neighbour who used to confiscate the tennis balls which went in his garden, but one Christmas he gave me about 30 back. There was a boy three doors along who used to get migraines, and if he couldn't come out I'd be devastated. I'd be back at his door two hours later to see if he was better."

There was no cricketing background in the family, but Onions, who has an elder sister, says of his parents, Richard and Maureen: "I owe everything to them for the support they have given me. I still live near them with my girlfriend, Emma, and we're a very close family. I'm very passionate about my roots, and I think the passion for the area within the Durham team is a major reason for their success." As he developed into a lean, 6ft 2in pace bowler, he was spotted by Durham coach Geoff Cook, and made his Second Eleven debut aged 18. He had the choice of a contract or a university sports science course, but he had already decided he wanted to be a professional cricketer.

Onions has become a fine length bowler – at the Loughborough academy he was told that 50–55% of Test wickets fall to balls pitching about six steps in front of the batsman – who dismissed seven of his 20 Test victims in the 2009 season lbw, but there have been a few hiccoughs.

"I used to be fourth seamer, and when I was brought on I would try too hard," he says. "I remember being thrown the ball at an important stage of a game at Scarborough, and Phil Jaques hit me for four successive fours. I was thinking 'I'm not sure I can do this.' But Dale Benkenstein was a huge influence as captain, and you have to learn from all those experiences. Otherwise I could not have done what I did in my first season of Test cricket. I often went for 15 to 20 runs in my first three overs, but always came back strongly."

Onions acknowledges a big debt to Ottis Gibson, with whom he shared the new ball for Durham in 2006 – a huge stride forward after his final three games of the previous season yielded one for 198 in 39 overs. "I worked hard with Ottis in his England role to develop an inswinger. My stock ball is slightly back of a length, hitting the seam, but I bowl the inswinger slightly fuller and it's a big wicket-taker, especially against tailenders. I share Ottis's belief that you have to test the batsman from the very first ball. As a fast bowler, you're going to bowl a limited amount of overs, so I treat every ball as though it's my last. If you take wickets early it gets you on a roll and gets the team going, so I'm a lot more focused than I used to be in my preparations." Gibson, in turn, described the man who became England's opening bowler in South Africa as "a very quick learner".

"Two wickets with the first two balls of the day in an Ashes Test was something I wouldn't even dream about," Onions says. "I can't claim to have bowled Mike Hussey first ball because I had spotted a weakness. When he played with us at Durham, he was the nicest man you could meet, but he also came in and changed the club. It's such a great honour and a challenge to play Test cricket against people like him. I don't feel I'm anywhere near the finished article and I have a massive desire to keep on improving."

No comfort zone, then, for the first bowler since Tony Lock and Jim Laker in 1956 to enjoy the rare double of helping his county to retain the Championship and his country to win the Ashes.

Matt Prior

ROBIN MARTIN-JENKINS

Many people's abiding image of the 2009 Ashes will be Graeme Swann wheeling away into the covers having taken the final wicket at The Oval. Or perhaps Andrew Flintoff genuflecting at Lord's. Or could it be something more obscure, something almost lost in the commotion of the final day? As Marcus North executed an expansive sweep against Swann, the ball gripped the dusty soil and ripped past his bat to be caught by England's wicketkeeper, who glanced down at North's back foot and, with a swivel of the hips, whipped off the bails with his right hand. North half-looked round, guiltily, to see his foot on the line. There was no need for the third umpire. Matt Prior was already dancing a jig of joy as his team-mates poured over him.

The dismissal was not the most important of the day; by then, England would have regained the Ashes anyway. But it stood out for two reasons. It represented an immense talent finally fulfilled, in a cricketer with a huge work ethic who has always been desperate to succeed. And among the pile of Ashes coverage there have been only fragments of comment about Prior's glovework; like a good football referee, his best work went unnoticed.

His stumping at The Oval crowned a year that began with the birth of his first child. Prior comfortably out-kept the vaunted Brad Haddin, was England's second-highest run-scorer in the Ashes, with a Gilchrist-like strike-rate of 82, and established himself as the first-choice keeper in all three formats. "It was crazy, like nothing I've ever played in before," Prior says of the Ashes. "More so for the off-pitch goings-on than for what happened on the field. I did a press conference at Lord's and I've never seen so many people and cameras crammed into one room. It was quite daunting. I started to be recognised in public for the first time."

MATTHEW JAMES PRIOR was born in Johannesburg on February 26, 1982, to a South African mother and an English father. His early childhood was relatively serene; from the age of eight he played cricket at King Edward VII (the school of Gary Player and Graeme Smith) where he says the aim was winning. "We didn't play for enjoyment. The enjoyment came when we won. It was only when I came here that I experienced the idea that sport is more about taking part."

Here, of course, is England, to which his family uprooted when he was 11. Before long, his parents separated and his mother developed breast cancer. It was a challenging time for a young boy trying to establish an identity in a new country, but Prior says it put his sporting life into perspective. "You can sometimes feel it's the end of the world if you don't score runs, but I've always known things could be a lot worse."

It was five years before he felt settled, and a sports scholarship to Brighton College helped. He was mentored by former Sussex bowler John Spencer. "John was a great help," he recalls. "He taught me the value of putting my work in before I was allowed to play games." Prior helped to make the college one of the strongest school sides in the country. "It was on a tour of India in 1997-98 that he really showed how much a cut above the rest of the talented team he was," Spencer remembers. "He played the classy Indian spinners superbly, scoring six fifties and 205 not out."

His performances were noted by the county, whose cricket manager, Peter Moores, saw enough in the raw, slightly cocky schoolboy to thrust Prior into Sussex's first team in 2001. On his first-class debut at Worcester, he hooked a fired-up Andy Bichel and gave as good as he got in the inevitable verbals. His batting partner, James Kirtley, suggested in a few stern words that, in the interests of their safety, it wasn't the best idea for a 19-year-old debutant to wind up the Australian fast bowler.

The hundreds followed in time, as did talk that Prior could be the answer to England's keeping problems. Moores, now England coach, and his fellow selectors thought so, and handed him a Test debut against West Indies at Lord's in 2007. Cynics (and fans of Chris Read and James Foster) who muttered about nepotism were silenced when Prior became the first England wicketkeeper to score a century on debut. A brilliant innings it was too, taking on the short ball with glee and cover-driving anything overpitched with an élan that had commentators purring. He averaged nearly 65 in that series and, despite not making any significant contributions against India later in the summer, he was the natural first-choice keeper for the tour of Sri Lanka, where, again, he was one of England's most successful batsmen.

But despite the runs and the solidity he brought to the lower middle order, his keeping began to suffer under the relentless scrutiny of TV cameras. There were expensive drops off Ryan Sidebottom against India and Sri Lanka, and a worrying propensity to leak byes. Also, Prior's combative attitude and constant chatter began to grate. He was heavily implicated at Trent Bridge when Zaheer

Khan complained that England were trying to put him off by throwing jelly beans on the pitch, though Prior has always denied being the culprit.

The selectors replaced him with his former Sussex team-mate, Tim Ambrose, for the tour of New Zealand. The irony was plain: Ambrose had moved to Warwickshire two years earlier, frustrated that a regular place was being barred by Prior. "I knew I only had myself to blame for being dropped," Prior says. "And I knew there was no magic solution – I just had to keep working hard and I might get another go."

He was recalled for the one-day series with South Africa in August 2008, and toured India that winter. Shortly afterwards Moores, a former keeper himself, parted company with England, which might have left Prior short of a sympathetic ear. "Pete was a massive influence on my career," Prior says. "I met him as a 13-year-old, when I volunteered to keep in a coaching session. He made the next hour the best fun I'd ever had in sport, and from then on I was hooked."

But the ECB's academy director, Dave Parsons, put Prior in touch with former England keeper Bruce French, and they quickly bonded. There was clearly much work still to do on Prior's technique. In the Caribbean in March, he had his first keeping world record: most byes in a Test by a specialist wicketkeeper (52).

"Speed is everything with keeping," French says. "I quickly noticed with Matt that, while he was powerful, he was slow to the ball. His hands were actually really good, but his lack of footwork meant he wasn't getting them, and his head, in behind the ball. The way he kept in the Ashes was magnificent. But it was the result of a huge amount of effort."

Graeme Swann

ALEC SWANN

The celebrations may have been overexuberant, but they were perfectly understandable. When a well-flighted off-break found Mike Hussey's inside edge and thigh pad before ending up in Alastair Cook's hands at short leg, Graeme Swann could be forgiven for going over the top. Once it became apparent that the surface at The Oval bore an uncanny resemblance to a sandpit, the onus was on him to perform, and four days later he had delivered. That wicket confirmed the prize which English cricket craves most – the climax of a heady year for Swann, who rose from a supporting tourist to the country's No. 1 spinner.

GRAEME PETER SWANN was born in Northampton on March 24, 1979. His early childhood was spent playing any sport possible on the Old Northamptonians' ground – the ideal place for two sport-crazy kids to wear themselves out – where their father played in the Northamptonshire County League as a combative batsman. The two grass nets were given a thorough workout every other weekend: the younger brother had to do most of the bowling at his elder sibling, and found it easier to get the ball down the other end if he bowled spin.

This gave way to junior club cricket at Horton House, supervised by Ted Gascoyne, and later his sons David and Sam. Success as an all-rounder for the Northants Cricket Association and Northants Schools resulted in a step up to the Midlands and England Under-14 and Under-15 teams. In 1997-98, Swann helped England win the Under-19 World Cup in South Africa, with a frugal spell against Australia and an unbeaten batting cameo against New Zealand in the final.

A contract at his home county followed, and Swann rapidly advanced to the senior England tour of South Africa in 1999-2000. But well-documented indiscretions – such as missing the team bus – meant a solitary one-day international and a return to the county ranks. A few years on, his career was turning sour. Moving to Nottinghamshire in 2005 proved a turning point, just as it had for his friend Ryan Sidebottom.

Far from the obvious choice for a spinner, Trent Bridge was Swann's destination for the simple fact that he was tolerated and appreciated. "I was told they wanted players who played hard but enjoyed themselves, and that was music to my ears. I should have left Northampton earlier, but it means I appreciate what I've got now a lot more." Familiarity does indeed breed contempt, and contempt was what Swann had discovered for the set-up at Wantage Road.

But the expectation that spinners were there to win games on the spin-friendly surfaces at Northampton would stand him in good stead at his new home, where consistent performances caught the eye of England's new coach, Peter Moores. His eagerness to be involved in everything from the off – whether emptying his brother's bag over the floor after a suicidal single in a Sunday friendly was turned down, or running down the pitch first ball to get off a pair – is Swann's dominant characteristic, as a sportsman and as a person. Naturally restless, he had no need for an excess of patience to be successful at Northampton. The one trait spinners need in abundance has come on in leaps and bounds since his move up the M1.

It was in Sri Lanka in October 2007 that Swann's potential resurfaced. His integral part in England's unexpected one-day series victory did not bring an immediate elevation to Test level, but it did show an ability to perform. A handful of decent efforts the following summer put him in line for a Test debut in Chennai in December 2008. Even for such an extrovert, doubts were floating around: "I'd played a few one-day games, so I knew I was capable of getting these players out. The difference with Test cricket is the whole rhythm; it's a case of seeing whether you fit in." He did fit in, instantly, dismissing Gautam Gambhir and Rahul Dravid in his first over. By January 2010, he had struck in the first over of a Test spell 17 times, the mark of a spinner who rips the ball so much that he is always cutting his middle finger, and who bowls an attacking line.

Competent performances in India were not enough to oust Monty Panesar from England's next Test side, in Jamaica, but a twist of fate in Antigua, where an unfit pitch forced a transfer from North Sound to St John's, provided an opportunity that Swann grasped eagerly.

"I wanted a bowl in the nets, I bowled at Andrew [Strauss] and bowled well. I was told not to do anything that night and to prepare as if I was going to play. As it turned out, it was pivotal to what has happened since. It was a chance to bowl on pretty flat wickets where I'd get a lot of bowling – and against a few left-handers who I enjoy bowling at." When Swann reached 50 Test wickets at Centurion in December 2009, he had dismissed a higher percentage of left-handers – 66% – than anyone had ever done in their first 50. The new umpiring review system has encouraged finger spinners, but has not been an unqualified blessing.

Nineteen wickets in the West Indies, and seven more in the return series at home, secured his place for the Ashes. A poor performance with the ball in Cardiff, due to a mix of nerves and overexcitement, was offset by a pair of innings which underlined one reason why Swann has risen to prominence. ("If I hadn't scored a few I might not have played at Lord's.")

Cricket has a habit of revealing an individual's personality, and Swann's batting shows his. The upbeat extrovert comes through in his try-and-be-damned approach. "Batting so low in the order, I'm given licence to do pretty much what I want. When I started, it was my bowling that was more of a reflection of me, but that's changed over the past few years."

Crucial wickets at Lord's, a morale-boosting 62 at Headingley and eight vital wickets on the Oval dustbowl were his main contributions to the Ashes triumph, and encapsulated Swann's strengths. The ability to put a poor performance to one side – a skill many fail to master – and move on to the next challenge explains why he has had such a career-defining year, taking 54 Test wickets, more than anybody bar Mitchell Johnson.

It is a difference in mindset that emphasises the position he now finds himself in. "Eighteen months ago, I was hoping to go to India as the second spinner. Now I look at where we're touring and who I'm going to get the chance to bowl at." And his well-earned success will do little to calm the exuberance that defines him.

THE WISDEN TEST XI

Team of the year

SCYLD BERRY

The Wisden Test XI of 2009 was chosen with no fundamental disagreements among the selectors, although some countries played too little Test cricket to supply much evidence of individual worth. There was an unhealthy lack of contact between West and East: New Zealand were the only non-Asian country to complete a Test series against an Asian one in 2009 (excluding Bangladesh's victories over a below-strength West Indies). Direct comparisons were therefore more difficult in the absence of head-to-head confrontations.

Our Test XI consists of the eleven cricketers who received either two or three votes from the panel of three selectors, all of them prominent commentators. This year they were the West Indian fast bowler Ian Bishop; Ian Chappell, who captained Australia in the 1970s; and the former Indian all-rounder Ravi Shastri.

Four members of the Wisden Test XI were unanimous choices: Kumar Sangakkara, although his position in the batting order was the subject of dispute; Mahendra Singh Dhoni, the wicketkeeper, captain and No. 7, like last year; Mitchell Johnson, the one unanimous selection among the world's fast bowlers; and Graeme Swann, unopposed as the first-choice spinner, a fine achievement for one who was virtually a newcomer to Test cricket.

Bishop, always on the look-out for new talent, did not select the sometimes injured **Virender Sehwag** to open for the Wisden Test XI, which is based more on form than the Leading Cricketer of the World, where class dictates. But the others did. Shastri defines Sehwag as "simply the most destructive opener"; to Chappell, Sehwag is "the type of player who keeps opposing captains awake at night, and he produced the feat of the year in scoring 284 off 79 overs against Sri Lanka in Mumbai."

Andrew Strauss was selected by Bishop and Chappell as the second opening batsman, but not by Shastri, who preferred Gautam Gambhir. Chappell notes that Strauss in 2009 enhanced his reputation as a batsman and skipper; Bishop says he led England with "distinction", and his team depended on his batting and captaincy, while observing that Chris Gayle and Simon Katich had been "very impressive" too. As for Graeme Smith, he enjoyed a wonderful year in 2008, and at the start of 2010, but not in between.

As **Gautam Gambhir** – who got two votes, like Sehwag and Strauss – is a fine player of spin, he is the opener who has to drop down to No. 3, in the opinion of the convenor, the editor. Shastri believes Gambhir is the finest player of spin among all contemporary openers: this was demonstrated not least when India had to follow on in New Zealand and Gambhir batted India to safety over ten hours in scoring 137 against Daniel Vettori. He hit four centuries in his nine Test innings in 2009.

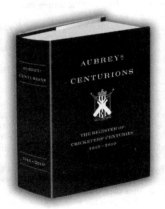

Sachin Tendulkar still holds on to the No. 4 position, in the eyes of Bishop and Shastri. In fact Shastri, who has probably seen more of Tendulkar's batting – as team-mate and commentator – than anybody, thinks he is better than ever: "His hunger hasn't diminished after 20 years in the game, and he seems to have more time for his shots than a few years ago." Tendulkar, he says, is "more relaxed" too, or at least he gives the impression that the pressure on him affects him less.

Kumar Sangakkara, the only unanimous choice among the batsmen, was No. 3 in the eyes of Bishop – who thinks the Sri Lankan is "a class act the world over" – and of Chappell, who rates Sangakkara "an ideal No. 3 who can recover a poor start or counter-attack". Somebody, however, has to drop down and Shastri, who had opted for Ricky Ponting as his No. 3, voted for Sangakkara as his No. 5, just ahead of Mahela Jayawardene, "one of the best timers on a slow wicket of all time". Sangakkara has had relatively more success outside Asia than his team-mate, and can act as reserve wicketkeeper.

A superb leader who can look after egos

Although his normal position is No. 4, **Jacques Kallis** has to give way to Tendulkar and drop to No. 6. There, as Shastri says, "Kallis's technique can counter the second new ball, and his hunger – like Sachin's – has not diminished, and he is batting more aggressively." Chappell, who would have had Kallis at No. 4, calls him "one of the most underrated quiet achievers in the game". Chappell would also have had Tillekeratne Dilshan, as "perhaps the most improved performer of the year. He has benefited from a promotion to the top of Sri Lanka's order but in this side he could move things along quickly at No. 6."

Mahendra Singh Dhoni, the unanimous choice as captain and keeper, led India to No. 1 in the Test rankings last year, for the first time. Indeed, by the end of 2009 Dhoni had yet to lose a Test match, let alone a series while in charge. "A man who handles multiple roles with aplomb and always seems to make runs when they are needed," Chappell calls him. Shastri, who has watched him so often, observes that Dhoni "is a superb leader of men as he can look after egos".

Although he was wayward in the Ashes series, shunning the limelight and the new ball, the fast left-handed **Mitchell Johnson** was still the one unanimous selection among the world's pace bowlers. "By sheer numbers he is the leading fast bowler of the year," Bishop notes: Johnson took 63 Test wickets in his 13 Tests. "At times he is inaccurate and inconsistent, but even during those periods he still takes wickets," says Chappell, "and he has the great attribute of taking wickets in groups."

Graeme Swann was unanimously selected as the specialist spinner, supplanting Harbhajan Singh from last year's XI. Shastri, a former spinner himself, said that playing so much 50- and 20-over cricket during the year made Harbhajan lose his flight and pitch too short. He admires Swann's attitude: "He is aggressive and likes the big stage, and he is improving all the time." Chappell remarks that Swann "would challenge Dilshan as the year's biggest improver. A wicket-taking spinner with good flight and variation who thinks aggressively in all departments of the game." For good measure, as Bishop says, Swann is "a valuable lower-order batsman".

Bishop, the fast-bowling expert on the panel, went for **Peter Siddle**'s "durability and aggression over the year, which has been impressive for a relatively young international player". Chappell was tempted to give the West Indian newcomer Kemar Roach a spot, but settled for Siddle because he "is strong, relentless and always gives everything he's got". Shastri opted for Dale Steyn, but the South African was too often below par in 2009, and as the Wisden Test XI pays heed to form, Siddle with 45 Test wickets beats Steyn with 22 at an average of 32.

James Anderson takes the final position on the strength of the votes of Bishop and Shastri: and he would take the new ball with Siddle, allowing Johnson to be more comfortable as first change. According to Bishop: "Ben Hilfenhaus has grown and carried himself admirably in 2009. However, I feel Anderson as England's leader in the bowling department has moved to the top of his game." Shastri, who considered Mohammad Asif but thought he had not bowled quite enough, went for Anderson as "a match-winner in overcast conditions".

THE WISDEN TEST XI OF 2009

V. Sehwag (*India*)
A. J. Strauss (*England*)
G. Gambhir (*India*)
S. R. Tendulkar (*India*)
K. C. Sangakkara (*Sri Lanka*)
J. H. Kallis (*South Africa*)
*†M. S. Dhoni (*India*)
M. G. Johnson (*Australia*)
G. P. Swann (*England*)
P. M. Siddle (*Australia*)
J. M. Anderson (*England*)

The 2009 team shows seven changes from the inaugural Wisden Test XI of 2008 (see *Wisden 2009*, page 91), which was: V. Sehwag, G. C. Smith, R. T. Ponting, S. R. Tendulkar, K. P. Pietersen, S. Chanderpaul, *†M. S. Dhoni, Harbhajan Singh, M. G. Johnson, D. W. Steyn, Zaheer Khan.

The leading Test averages for 2009 can be found on page 999.

THE LEADING CRICKETER IN THE WORLD: Virender Sehwag.

FROM TINY ACORNS… Man of the Match Maruf Chowdhury of The Times Tigers is watched by Mylo Wilkin of Barclays Eagles during the final of the Wisden City Cup (see page 78).

Christopher Lee

Patrick Eagar

SUCH STUFF AS DREAMS ARE MADE ON… England Women, captained by Charlotte Edwards, carried all before them in 2009, winning the World Cup (*above left*) and World Twenty20, after Claire Taylor and Beth Morgan steered them to a tense semi-final victory over Australia. It was almost as good for the Afghani men, who qualified for the third World Twenty20, in the Caribbean in April.

ICC

Philip Brown

SEIZING THE MOMENT (1): Philip Brown won the Veuve Clicquot England Cricket photography award for his shot of Ravi Bopara being hit by a Fidel Edwards bouncer during the Barbados Test, in February 2009.

Gareth Copley, PA Photos

SEIZING THE MOMENT (2): Gareth Copley won the Sports Action award in the World Press Photo contest for his image of Jonathan Trott being run out in the Fifth Ashes Test, at The Oval. See page 77 for the launch of a photographic competition open to all.

REVENGE IS TWEET: During the Roses Twenty20 game at Leeds, Jacques Rudolph killed a pigeon with his throw; umpire Peter Willey tends to an injured pigeon, also hit by the ball, during a Championship match at Lord's. But at Canterbury the game between the Australians and England Lions was delayed after this gull made off with a bail.

Philip Brown

NOT ANOTHER BORE DRAW! Four times in less than a year, England were involved in Tests drawn with the last pair holding on for dear life. At Antigua in February (*above*), West Indies survived, but elsewhere it was England who did the thwarting: at Cardiff in the Ashes (*below*), and twice during the winter tour of South Africa (Centurion, *opposite top*, and Cape Town, *opposite below*).

Patrick Eagar

GOLDEN GRAEME: Alastair Cook catches Mike Hussey off Graeme Swann – and the Ashes are England's.

PART TWO

Records
and
Registers

FEATURES OF 2009

In the past, *Wisden* has run separate lists of the statistical features of the English and overseas seasons (eg 2007 and 2006-07). These have now been combined in a single list of statistical features of the calendar year. Because the section now covers the calendar year, some of the features listed occurred in matches reported in *Wisden 2009* and some will be reported in *Wisden 2011*; these items are indicated by [W09] or [W11].

Double-Hundreds (79)

	Mins	Balls	4s	6s		
390†	838	648	53	1	S. C. Cook	Lions v Warriors at East London.[W11]
344*	414	351	43	6	M. W. Goodwin	Sussex v Somerset at Taunton.
313	760	568	27	4	Younis Khan	Pakistan v Sri Lanka (First Test) at Karachi.
312	473	333	44	7	Sunny Singh	Haryana v Madhya Pradesh at Indore. [W11]
309*	458	322	38	4	R. G. Sharma	Mumbai v Gujarat at Mumbai. [W11]
303*	461	338	35	4	J. C. Hildreth	Somerset v Warwickshire at Taunton.
302*	647	488	34	1	Rafatullah Mohmand	WAPDA v Sui Southern Gas at Sheikhupura. [W11]
301	635	459	27	0	Wasim Jaffer	Mumbai v Saurashtra at Chennai.
298	497	380	54	1	D. K. H. Mitchell	Worcestershire v Somerset at Taunton.
296*	443	294	35	2	Fawad Alam	National Bank v Customs at Karachi.
293	366	254	40	7	V. Sehwag	India v Sri Lanka (Third Test) at Mumbai.
291	698	452	30	2	R. R. Sarwan	West Indies v England (Fourth Test) at Bridgetown.
289	523	393	36	0	Aamer Sajjad	WAPDA v Sui Southern Gas at Sheikhupura. [W11]
284	432	327	39	4	‡Misbah-ul-Haq	Sui Northern Gas v Lahore Shalimar at Lahore. [W11]
282	574	381	26	8	L. M. P. Simmons	West Indies A v England XI at Basseterre.
275	610	435	27	1	‡D. P. M. D. Jayawardene	Sri Lanka v India (First Test) at Ahmedabad.
274	489	380	39	1	M. R. Ramprakash	Surrey v Leicestershire at The Oval.
270*	467	339	24	4	R. W. T. Key	Kent v Glamorgan at Cardiff.
270		472	23	3	A. D. Mathews	Basnahira North v Kandurata at Colombo.
265*		365	27	3	W. U. Tharanga	Ruhuna v Basnahira South at Colombo.
265*	464	382	23	2	A. M. Rahane	Mumbai v Hyderabad at Hyderabad. [W11]
261	469	394	33	3	B. J. Hodge	Victoria v Queensland at Melbourne.
257	567	422	40	1	A. Mukund	Tamil Nadu v Hyderabad at Hyderabad. [W11]
256	603	483	43	2	J. A. Raval	Auckland v Central Districts at Auckland.
254*	511	368	35	1	‡M. J. Di Venuto	Durham v Sussex at Chester-le-Street.
254*	572	394	34	4	Khalid Latif	Karachi Blues v Peshawar at Rawalpindi. [W11]
254	554	356	28	8	A. G. Prince	Warriors v Titans at Centurion.
250	671	476	20	5	‡S. Badrinath	Tamil Nadu v Mumbai at Mumbai. [W11]
247	393	310	23	7	‡Misbah-ul-Haq	Sui Southern Gas v Sui Southern Gas at Sheikhupura.
245*	393	286	36	1	P. J. Ingram	Central Districts v Wellington at Wellington. [W11]
241	712	556	27	0	Khurram Manzoor	PIA v KRL at Karachi. [W11]
240	286	218	35	4	R. O. Hinds	Barbados v Leeward Islands at Philipsburg.
240	531	423	32	0	‡D. P. M. D. Jayawardene	Sri Lanka v Pakistan (First Test) at Karachi.
234		194	23	12	H. G. J. M. Kulatunga	Colts v Ragama at Colombo.
231	454	318	31	0	‡T. T. Samaraweera	Sri Lanka v Pakistan (First Test) at Karachi.
231	450	403	22	4	‡R. S. Morton	Leeward Islands v Combined Campuses & Colleges at Charlestown.
230*	328	219	25	6	Naved Ashraf	Rawalpindi v Hyderabad at Islamabad. [W11]
230	360	274	28	4	Zeeshan Mushtaq	Islamabad v Quetta at Islamabad.
229*	370	318	29	2	Ijaz Ahmed	Faisalabad v Quetta at Faisalabad.
225	429	324	33	1	E. J. M. Cowan	Tasmania v South Australia at Hobart. [W11]
224	638	413	23	2	S. Dhawan	Delhi v Baroda at Vadodara. [W11]
223	443	342	23	4	J. O. Troughton	Warwickshire v Hampshire at Birmingham.
222*	492	362	18	1	Rameez Alam	Multan v Peshawar at Multan. [W11]
222	410	329	31	1	‡C. J. L. Rogers	Derbyshire v Essex at Derby.
221	454	361	28	3	Zeeshan Butt	Faisalabad v Abbottabad at Sargodha. [W11]
220*	567	400	27	0	L. J. Woodcock	Wellington v Central Districts at Wellington. [W11]
219*	545	353	27	1	M. L. Love	Queensland v New South Wales at Brisbane.

Mins	Balls	4s	6s		
219	387	325	37	0	M. J. Lumb . . . . Hampshire v Nottinghamshire at Nottingham.
219	371	274	31	0	‡M. J. Di Venuto . . . . Durham v Nottinghamshire at Chester-le-Street.
219		259	27	0	W. G. R. K. Alwis . . Saracens v Colombo at Colombo. [W11]
215	331	247	31	4	‡V. Sibanda . . . . Mid West Rhinos v Mountaineers at Mutare. [W11]
214	414	338	32	0	‡T. T. Samaraweera . . Sri Lanka v Pakistan (Second Test) at Lahore.
212		325	18	4	D. S. Smith . . . . Windward Islands v Guyana at St George's.
211	425	324	26	3	A. McGrath . . . . Yorkshire v Warwickshire at Birmingham.
211		382	23	1	N. A. N. N. Perera . . Burgher v Seeduwa Raddoluwa at Colombo. [W11]
210	448	300	31	2	‡R. S. Morton . . . . Leeward Islands v Barbados at Crab Hill.
209	416	320	26	1	‡V. Sibanda . . . . Zimbabwe XI v Kenya at Kwekwe.
208	339	277	27	1	‡C. J. L. Rogers . . . . . Derbyshire v Kent at Derby.
208	348	255	34	0	D. I. Stevens . . . . Kent v Middlesex at Uxbridge.
207*	420	329	21	2	J. W. A. Taylor . . . . . Leicestershire v Surrey at The Oval.
207*	485	367	15	4	M. Klinger . . . . South Australia v Victoria at Melbourne. [W11]
206*	576	326	23	2	V. S. Solanki . . . . Worcestershire v Yorkshire at Leeds.
205		304	22	2	D. M. G. S. Dissanayake Bloomfield v Badureliya at Colombo. [W11]
204*	553	427	27	2	U. Afzaal . . . . Surrey v Northamptonshire at Northampton.
204*	443	309	22	1	C. A. Pujara . . . . Saurashtra v Maharashtra at Rajkot. [W11]
204	515	396	23	4	O. J. Phillips . . . . Combined Campuses & Colleges v Leeward Islands at Charlestown.
204	357	270	28	1	M. A. Carberry . . . . . Hampshire v Warwickshire at Southampton.
203	550	395	25	2	H. G. Kuhn . . . . Titans v Warriors at Centurion.
203	418	295	21	4	D. J. Vilas . . . . Lions v Titans at Johannesburg.
202*	284	233	21	0	Faisal Khan . . . . Sialkot v Peshawar at Sialkot. [W11]
202	362	226	24	0	Salman Butt . . . . National Bank v ZTBL at Lahore.
202	335	253	34	1	Ashar Zaidi . . . . Islamabad v Sialkot at Sialkot. [W11]
201*	502	382	25	0	S. Chanderpaul . . . . . . Durham v Worcestershire at Worcester.
201	489	328	24	1	J. D. Ryder . . . . New Zealand v India (Second Test) at Napier.
201	398	293	20	2	R. S. Bopara . . . . Essex v Surrey at Colchester.
200*	439	338	16	2	Faisal Iqbal . . . . PIA v Sui Southern Gas at Karachi.
200*	467	327	20	3	Fahad Iqbal . . . . PIA v ZTBL at Faisalabad.
200*	360	259	30	1	Adnan Raees . . . . Abbottabad v Peshawar at Abbottabad. [W11]
200	349	259	24	4	‡S. Badrinath . . . . South Zone v North Zone at Rajkot.

† *National record.*
‡ *Badrinath, Di Venuto, Jayawardene, Misbah-ul-Haq, Morton, Rogers, Samaraweera and Sibanda each scored two double-hundreds.*

Hundred on First-Class Debut

112	A. Ashok . . . . Cambridge University v Oxford University at Cambridge.
109	C. Barron . . . . KwaZulu-Natal Inland v Griqualand West at Pietermaritzburg. [W11]
116*	V. Bhalla . . . . Punjab v Hyderabad at Mohali. [W11]
101*	U. J. Birkenstock . . . . . . Boland v Griqualand West at Paarl. [W11]
152	J. S. Gatting . . . . Sussex v Cambridge UCCE at Cambridge.
102	M. D. U. S. Jayasundera . . Navy v Sebastianites at Moratuwa. [W11]
102	R. J. McCone . . . . Canterbury v Otago at Christchurch.
105	J. Maudzi . . . . Mountaineers v Mid West Rhinos at Mutare. [W11]
130 and 100*	Noor Ali . . . . Afghanistan v Zimbabwe XI at Mutare.
106	S. Prasad . . . . Jharkhand v Goa at Dhanbad. [W11]
142*	S. J. Rhodes . . . . Wellington v Otago at Queenstown. [W11]
135	Sharjeel Khan . . . . Hyderabad v Islamabad at Islamabad. [W11]

Most Hundreds in Successive Innings

Four

V. Sibanda (Zimbabwe XI/Mid West Rhinos) . . . . 209 and 116* v Kenya at Kwekwe.
107 and 101* v Southern Rocks at Masvingo. [W11]

Three

R. S. Bopara (England)	104	v West Indies (Fourth Test) at Bridgetown.
	143	v West Indies (First Test) at Lord's.
	108	v West Indies (Second Test) at Chester-le-Street.
D. S. Jadhav (Assam).............	114	v Tripura at Guwahati. [W11]
	111	v Vidarbha at Guwahati. [W11]
	165*	v Andhra at Guwahati. [W11]
A. N. Petersen (Lions)	129 and 105*	v Titans at Johannesburg.
	128	v Eagles at Kimberley. [W11]
J. J. Pienaar (Easterns)	154	v Namibia at Windhoek. [W11]
	112 and 135	v South Western Districts at Oudtshoorn. [W11]
T. T. Samaraweera (Sinhalese/Sri Lanka).	154*	v Moors at Colombo.
	140	v Tamil Union at Colombo.
	231	v Pakistan (First Test) at Karachi.

Hundred in Each Innings of a Match

N. J. Dexter........	146	118	Middlesex v Kent at Uxbridge.
T. M. Dilshan	162	143	Sri Lanka v Bangladesh (Second Test) at Chittagong. [W09]
P. J. Hughes	115	160	Australia v South Africa (Second Test) at Durban.
Jahangir Mirza	135*	101*	WAPDA v Customs at Sialkot.
K. D. Karthik	153	103	South Zone v Central Zone at Bangalore.
Khalid Latif	123	105*	Karachi Whites v Lahore Shalimar at Muridke.
J. G. Myburgh.......	199	101*	Canterbury v Central Districts at New Plymouth.
Noor Ali	130	100*	Afghanistan v Zimbabwe XI at Mutare (*on first-class debut*).
A. N. Petersen......	129	105*	Lions v Titans at Johannesburg.
J. J. Pienaar.......	112	135	Easterns v South Western Districts at Oudtshoorn. [W11]
A. M. Rahane	143	101*	Mumbai v Haryana at Rohtak. [W11]
R. G. Sharma	141	108	Mumbai v Uttar Pradesh at Hyderabad.
V. Sibanda	209	116*	Zimbabwe XI v Kenya at Kwekwe.
V. Sibanda	107	101*	Mid West Rhinos v Southern Rocks at Masvingo. [W11]
T. Taibu	172	120	Zimbabwe XI v Afghanistan at Mutare.
S. O. Tikolo	158	169	Kenya v Canada at King City.
M. E. Trescothick	108	107*	Somerset v Warwickshire at Birmingham.

Carrying Bat through Completed Innings

Bismillah Khan	63*	Quetta (106) v Multan at Okara. [W11]
C. H. Gayle	165*	West Indies (317) v Australia (Second Test) at Adelaide.
J. M. How	190*	New Zealand A (430) v England Lions at Queenstown.
Imran Ali..................	90*	Faisalabad (188) v Multan at Faisalabad. [W11]
Imran Farhat	117*	Pakistan (223) v New Zealand (Third Test) at Napier.
D. S. Jadhav	165*	Assam (327) v Andhra at Guwahati. [W11]
Khalid Latif................	254*	Karachi Blues (458) v Peshawar at Rawalpindi. [W11]
Khurram Manzoor............	86*	PIA (215) v National Bank at Karachi.
J. F. Mostert	105*	North West (244) v Western Province at Cape Town.
S. A. Northeast.............	128*	Kent (265) v Gloucestershire at Bristol.
Saeed Anwar...............	122*	KRL (241) v Habib Bank at Karachi.
F. Takarusenga	65*	Westerns (145) v Centrals at Harare.
Taufeeq Umar	100*	Habib Bank (195) v Karachi Blues at Karachi. [W11]
W. U. Tharanga	265*	Ruhuna (450) v Basnahira South at Colombo.
Zohaib Khan	114*	ZTBL (270) v Sui Northern Gas at Gujranwala. [W11]

Most Sixes in an Innings

12	H. G. J. M. Kulatunga (234)...............	Colts v Ragama at Colombo.
9	D. N. A. Athulathmudali (153).............	Chilaw Marians v Colts at Colombo. [W11]
9	C. S. Baugh (129).......................	Jamaica v Trinidad & Tobago at St Elizabeth.
9	K. P. S. P. Karunanayake (172)	Sinhalese v Badureliya at Colombo. [W11]
9	P. D. Trego (103*).......................	Somerset v Yorkshire at Taunton.

Four Sixes off Consecutive Balls

4   A. B. de Villiers off A. B. McDonald ....   South Africa v Australia (Third Test) at Cape Town.

Most Runs in Boundaries

	4s	6s		
222	54	1	D. K. H. Mitchell (298)	Worcestershire v Somerset at Taunton.
218	53	1	S. C. Cook (390)	Lions v Warriors at East London. [W11]
218	44	7	Sunny Singh (312)	Haryana v Madhya Pradesh at Indore. [W11]
208	43	6	M. W. Goodwin (344*)	Sussex v Somerset at Taunton.
202	40	7	V. Sehwag (293)	India v Sri Lanka (Third Test) at Mumbai.

Longest Innings

Mins		
838	S. C. Cook (390)	Lions v Warriors at East London. [W11]
821	S. S. Shukla (178*)	Uttar Pradesh v Tamil Nadu at Nagpur.
760	Younis Khan (313)	Pakistan v Sri Lanka (First Test) at Karachi.
712	Khurram Manzoor (241)	PIA v KRL at Karachi. [W11]
698	R. R. Sarwan (291)	West Indies v England (Fourth Test) at Bridgetown.
671	S. Badrinath (250)	Tamil Nadu v Mumbai at Mumbai. [W11]
647	Rafatullah Mohmand (302*)	WAPDA v Sui Southern Gas at Sheikhupura. [W11]
643	G. Gambhir (137)	India v New Zealand (Second Test) at Napier.
638	S. Dhawan (224)	Delhi v Baroda at Vadodara. [W11]
635	Wasim Jaffer (301)	Mumbai v Saurashtra at Chennai.
610	D. P. M. D. Jayawardene (275)	Sri Lanka v India (First Test) at Ahmedabad.
606	J. A. Rudolph (198)	Yorkshire v Worcestershire at Leeds.
603	J. A. Raval (256)	Auckland v Central Districts at Auckland.

An Hour without Scoring

P. J. Horton ....   Lancashire v Somerset at Manchester (65 mins on 28*).
Saqib Maqsood ....   Lahore Ravi v Rawalpindi at Lahore (63 mins on 0*).

Unusual Dismissals

Obstructing the Field
Riaz Kail (30) ....   Abbottabad v Quetta at Abbottabad. [W11]

Stumped by a Substitute
D. A. Stiff (25). ....   Somerset v Hampshire at Taunton.

First-Wicket Partnership of 100 in Each Innings

149	103	Noor Ali/Ahmed Shah, Afghanistan v Zimbabwe XI at Mutare.
207	100*	W. U. Tharanga/K. Y. de Silva, Nondescripts v Colombo at Colombo. [W11]
109	117	J. T. Smuts/M. L. Price, Eastern Province v Griqualand West at Port Elizabeth. [W11]

Highest Wicket Partnerships

First Wicket

428†   P. J. Ingram/J. M. How, Central Districts v Wellington at Wellington. [W11]
315   G. P. Rees/M. J. Cosgrove, Glamorgan v Surrey at The Oval.
314   M. J. Di Venuto/K. J. Coetzer, Durham v Nottinghamshire at Chester-le-Street.
285   Nasir Jamshed/Umar Amin, National Bank v WAPDA at Mirpur.
261   M. A. Carberry/J. H. K. Adams, Hampshire v Warwickshire at Southampton.
257   Afaq Raheem/Inam-ul-Haq, ZTBL v Lahore Shalimar at Lahore.

Second Wicket

580§   Rafatullah Mohmand/Aamer Sajjad, WAPDA v Sui Southern Gas at Sheikhupura. [W11]
284   K. B. Pawan/G. Satish, Karnataka v Maharashtra at Pune. [W11]
262   A. B. Barath/L. M. P. Simmons, West Indies A v England XI at Basseterre.
258   S. O. Kukreja/A. M. Rahane, Mumbai v Hyderabad at Hyderabad. [W11]

Third Wicket

404   M. R. Ramprakash/S. J. Walters, Surrey v Leicestershire at The Oval.
346   J. J. Sayers/A. McGrath, Yorkshire v Warwickshire at Birmingham.
330   S. R. Waters/S. O. Tikolo, Kenya v Canada at King City.
317   V. S. Solanki/M. M. Ali, Worcestershire v Yorkshire at Leeds.
314   H. H. Dippenaar/H. D. Ackerman, Leicestershire v Surrey at Leicester.
312   S. Badrinath/R. Dravid, South Zone v North Zone at Rajkot.
309   G. O. Jones/M. van Jaarsveld, Kent v Glamorgan at Canterbury.
306   S. B. Haig/N. T. Broom, Otago v Central Districts at Napier. [W11]
284*   Faisal Khan/Mohammad Ayub, Sialkot v Peshawar at Sialkot. [W11]
283*   N. T. Paranavitana/T. T. Samaraweera, Sinhalese v Moors at Colombo.
264*   D. Elgar/H. H. Dippenaar, Eagles v Lions at Kimberley. [W11]
259   M. H. W. Papps/P. G. Fulton, Canterbury v Northern Districts at Christchurch.
259   A. Mukund/S. Badrinath, Tamil Nadu v Hyderabad at Hyderabad. [W11]
255   A. J. A. Gray/M. D. Walters, Western Province v Free State at Bloemfontein.
252   Asad Shafiq/Wajihuddin, Karachi Blues v Hyderabad at Mirpur Khas. [W11]

Fourth Wicket

437†   D. P. M. D. Jayawardene/T. T. Samaraweera, Sri Lanka v Pakistan (First Test) at Karachi.
363   M. W. Goodwin/C. D. Hopkinson, Sussex v Somerset at Taunton.
342   S. H. Marathe/R. G. Sharma, Mumbai v Gujarat at Mumbai. [W11]
293   Mohammad Hafeez/Misbah-ul-Haq, Sui Northern Gas v Sui Southern Gas at Sheikhupura.
283   Usman Tariq/Naved Yasin, Multan v Peshawar at Multan.
280   Rameez Alam/Naved Yasin, Multan v Peshawar at Multan. [W11]
279   Zahid Mansoor/Usman Saeed, Rawalpindi v Hyderabad at Hyderabad.
273   R. Dravid/M. K. Pandey, Karnataka v Uttar Pradesh at Meerut. [W11]
272*   C. A. Pujara/R. A. Jadeja, Saurashtra v Maharashtra at Rajkot. [W11]
272   S. S. Shukla/Parvinder Singh, Uttar Pradesh v Tamil Nadu at Nagpur.
271   L. R. P. L. Taylor/J. D. Ryder, New Zealand v India (Second Test) at Napier.
266   P. A. Patel/B. D. Thaker, Gujarat v Mumbai at Mumbai. [W11]
263   Imran Javed/Naumanullah, National Bank v KRL at Rawalpindi. [W11]
258   Usman Arshad/Ijaz Ahmed, Faisalabad v Peshawar at Sargodha.
257   C. A. Ingram/S. R. Adair, Eastern Province v KwaZulu-Natal at Port Elizabeth.
256   M. Manhas/R. Bhatia, Delhi v Maharashtra at Delhi. [W11]
250   D. M. Bravo/K. A. Pollard, Trinidad & Tobago v Barbados at Pointe-à-Pierre.

Fifth Wicket

479†   Misbah-ul-Haq/Usman Arshad, Sui Northern Gas v Lahore Shalimar at Lahore. [W11]
353   H. G. J. M. Kulatunga/A. R. S. Silva, Colts v Ragama at Colombo.
335   J. O. Troughton/T. R. Ambrose, Warwickshire v Hampshire at Birmingham.
318*   J. C. Hildreth/C. Kieswetter, Somerset v Warwickshire at Taunton.
302   Zeeshan Butt/Ijaz Ahmed, Faisalabad v Abbottabad at Sargodha. [W11]
273   Haris Sohail/Mohammad Ayub, Sialkot v Peshawar at Peshawar.

Sixth Wicket

365†   S. C. Cook/T. L. Tsolekile, Lions v Warriors at East London. [W11]
351   D. P. M. D. Jayawardene/H. A. P. W. Jayawardene, Sri Lanka v India (First Test) at Ahmedabad.
329   S. Badrinath/C. Ganapathy, Tamil Nadu v Mumbai at Mumbai. [W11]
268   R. A. White/A. J. Hall, Northamptonshire v Leicestershire at Northampton.
261   R. R. Sarwan/D. Ramdin, West Indies v England (Fourth Test) at Bridgetown.
253   Bilal Khilji/Ali Azmat, WAPDA v Customs at Islamabad. [W11]

270 runs were put on by A. Rawat, S. Rana and J. Sharma for Haryana's sixth wicket v Tripura at Rohtak[W11]; Rawat retired hurt after 234 runs had been added.

Seventh Wicket

205*   G. R. Hay/B. J. Diamanti, Central Districts v Canterbury at Rangiora.
193   A. K. Perera/W. C. A. Ganegama, Nondescripts v Army at Colombo. [W11]
186   J. D. Ryder/D. L. Vettori, New Zealand v India (First Test) at Hamilton.
175   W. G. R. K. Alwis/M. D. Randika, Saracens v Colombo at Colombo. [W11]

Eighth Wicket

222*   I. J. L. Trott/C. R. Woakes, Warwickshire v Hampshire at Southampton.
195   J. W. A. Taylor/J. K. H. Naik, Leicestershire v Derbyshire at Leicester.
192   A. U. Rashid/A. Shahzad, Yorkshire v Hampshire at Basingstoke.
181   Saad Nasim/Mohammd Saeed, Lahore Shalimar v Karachi Whites at Lahore. [W11]
178   P. de Bruyn/Q. Friend, Dolphins v Lions at Potchefstroom.
170   Fahad Iqbal/Ali Imran, PIA v ZTBL at Faisalabad.
167   C. F. K. van Wyk/R. J. McCone, Canterbury v Otago at Christchurch.
167   Humayun Farhat/Mohammad Aslam, Habib Bank v Customs at Islamabad. [W11]
163   O. J. Khanwilkar/R. R. Powar, Mumbai v Punjab at Chandigarh. [W11]
161   V. Sibanda/R. W. Chakabva, Zimbabwe XI v Kenya at Kwekwe.
160   E. Chigumbura/R. W. Price, Northerns v Westerns at Harare.
157   A. Shahzad/D. J. Wainwright, Yorkshire v Sussex at Hove.
152   M. A. Ealham/L. J. Fletcher, Nottinghamshire v Hampshire at Southampton.

Ninth Wicket

233   I. J. L. Trott/J. S. Patel, Warwickshire v Yorkshire at Birmingham.
225   L. J. Woodcock/M. J. Tugaga, Wellington v Central Districts at Wellington. [W11]
197   R. D. B. Croft/A. J. Shantry, Glamorgan v Leicestershire at Colwyn Bay.
158   Zulqarnain Haider/Rehan Riaz, ZTBL v Customs at Islamabad. [W11]
150   Azeem Rafiq/M. J. Hoggard, Yorkshire v Worcestershire at Worcester.

Tenth Wicket

122   K. R. N. U. Perera/S. H. M. Silva, Badureliya v Saracens at Panadura. [W11]
115   R. C. C. Canning/P. S. E. Sandri, Cape Cobras v Titans at Paarl.
114   J. Sharma/S. Badhwar, Haryana v Andhra at Anantapur. [W11]
110   A. Maregwede/H. Matanga, Southern Rocks v Mountaineers at Mutare. [W11]
109   R. J. M. G. M. Rupasinghe/S. D. C. Malinga, Tamil Union v Colombo at Colombo.
104   L. Meyer/J. Theron, Warriors v Eagles at Bloemfontein.

† *National record.*   § *World record.*

Most Wickets in an Innings

10-143	Zulfiqar Babar	Multan v Islamabad at Multan. [W11]
9-35	Yasir Arafat	KRL v Sui Southern Gas at Rawalpindi.
9-42	Rashid Latif	Rawalpindi v Islamabad at Islamabad. [W11]
9-47	S. C. D. Boralessa	Colombo v Moors at Colombo. [W11]
9-109	S. Randiv	Bloomfield v Army at Colombo. [W11]
8-20	G. Wallace	Jamaica v Leeward Islands at Basseterre.
8-27	Mohammad Rameez	Rawalpindi v Peshawar at Islamabad. [W11]
8-27	T. G. Southee	Northern Districts v Wellington at Hamilton. [W11]
8-32	R. Vinay Kumar	Karnataka v Delhi at Delhi. [W11]
8-41	N. O. Miller	Jamaica v Combined Campuses & Colleges at Bridgetown.

8-46	Mohammad Rameez	Rawalpindi v Multan at Multan. [W11]
8-50	S. Randiv	Bloomfield v Chilaw Marians at Katunayake. [W11]
8-53	Tanvir Ahmed	Karachi Blues v Abbottabad at Abbottabad. [W11]
8-54	Sohail Tanvir	KRL v PIA at Mirpur.
8-59	Danish Kaneria	Habib Bank v Sui Southern Gas at Karachi.
8-59	S. Prasanna	Army v Bloomfield at Panagoda.
8-66	J. C. Tredwell	Kent v Glamorgan at Canterbury.
8-66	D. Hettiarachchi	Chilaw Marians v Bloomfield at Katunayake. [W11]
8-68	W. R. D. Wimaladarma	Saracens v Army at Panagoda. [W11]
8-84	P. R. George	South Australia v Tasmania at Hobart. [W11]
8-98	S. M. Fallah	Maharashtra v Baroda at Pune. [W11]
8-107	W. R. D. Wimaladarma	Saracens v Tamil Union at Colombo. [W11]
8-111	S. C. D. Boralessa	Colombo v Badureliya at Colombo. [W11]
8-116	Danish Kaneria	Essex v Leicestershire at Chelmsford.
8-117	S. M. Senanayake	Sinhalese v Nondescripts at Colombo. [W11]
8-123	S. Prasanna	Army v Sinhalese at Colombo. [W11]
8-128	Mohammad Naved	Lahore Shalimar v WAPDA at Lahore.

Most Wickets in a Match

15-174	Sohail Tanvir	KRL v PIA at Mirpur.
13-81	Danish Kaneria	Habib Bank v Sui Southern Gas at Karachi.
13-116	Mohammad Rameez	Rawalpindi v Peshawar at Islamabad. [W11]
13-119	S. Randiv	Bloomfield v Chilaw Marians at Katunayake. [W11]
13-122	S. C. D. Boralessa	Colombo v Moors at Colombo. [W11]
13-132	Mohammad Rameez	Rawalpindi v Multan at Multan. [W11]
13-138	D. Hettiarachchi	Chilaw Marians v Bloomfield at Katunayake. [W11]
13-139	Tanvir Ahmed	Karachi Blues v Abbottabad at Abbottabad. [W11]
13-187	S. Randiv	Bloomfield v Army at Colombo. [W11]
13-225	T. M. U. S. Karunaratne	Seeduwa Raddoluwa v Singha at Colombo. [W11]
13-226	D. Hettiarachchi	Chilaw Marians v Badureliya at Katunayake. [W11]
13-259	W. R. D. Wimaladarma	Saracens v Tamil Union at Colombo. [W11]
12-70	S. Weerakoon	Colts v Bloomfield at Colombo.
12-73	D. S. Lucas	Northamptonshire v Gloucestershire at Cheltenham.
12-91	M. Morkel	Titans v Eagles at Bloemfontein.
12-95	S. Prasanna	Army v Bloomfield at Panagoda.
12-98	Rizwan Akbar	Rawalpindi v Multan at Islamabad.
12-112	R. M. G. K. Sirisoma	Lankan v Navy at Welisara. [W11]
12-117	Zahoor Khan	Faisalabad v Karachi Blues at Sargodha.
12-147	Abdur Rauf	Multan v Peshawar at Multan.
12-166	Kashif Daud	ZTBL v Habib Bank at Islamabad. [W11]
12-168	Zulfiqar Babar	Multan v Islamabad at Multan. [W11]
12-196	Imran Tahir	Easterns v Boland at Benoni. [W11]
12-203	Danish Kaneria	Essex v Leicestershire at Chelmsford.

Outstanding Innings Analyses

3–1–3–5	E. O'Reilly	Gauteng v Easterns at Johannesburg.
4–0–4–5	Junaid Khan	KRL v Customs at Mirpur.
5.2–3–2–4	M. N. R. Cooray	Panadura v Sebastianites at Panadura. [W11]

Hat-Tricks (10)

Abdur Rauf	Multan v Peshawar at Multan.
R. Cameron	Gauteng v Griqualand West at Johannesburg.
Danish Kaneria	Essex v Derbyshire at Derby.
D. M. G. S. Dissanayake	Basnahira North v Kandurata at Colombo.
J. E. C. Franklin	Gloucestershire v Derbyshire at Cheltenham.
D. Hettiarachchi	Chilaw Marians v Tamil Union at Colombo. [W11]
M. J. Hoggard	Yorkshire v Sussex at Hove.
N. C. K. Liyanage	Singha v Sebastianites at Colombo. [W11]
M. J. McClenaghan	Central Districts v Canterbury at Rangiora.
Zohaib Shera	Karachi Whites v National Bank at Karachi (*on first-class debut*). [W11]

Hundred and Hat-Trick

J. E. C. Franklin . . . .   Gloucestershire v Derbyshire at Cheltenham.

Match Double (100 runs and 10 wickets)

S. Randiv . . . .   112, 48*; 4-78, 9-109   Bloomfield v Army at Colombo. [W11]

Most Wicketkeeping Dismissals in an Innings

8 ct†	A. Z. M. Dyili	Eastern Province v Free State at Port Elizabeth. [W11]
7 ct	P. Bisht	Delhi v Baroda at Vadodara. [W11]
7 ct	P. A. Browne	Barbados v Windward Islands at Bridgetown.
5 ct, 2 st . .	S. M. Fernando	Air Force v Seeduwa Raddoluwa at Colombo. [W11]
7 ct	Sarfraz Ahmed	PIA v Habib Bank at Karachi.
6 ct	Ahmed Said	WAPDA v Lahore Shalimar at Lahore. [W11]
6 ct	Amin-ur-Rehman	National Bank v Sui Southern Gas at Faisalabad. [W11]
6 ct	Amir Khan	Uttar Pradesh v Tamil Nadu at Nagpur.
6 ct	M. S. Bisla	Jammu and Kashmir v Andhra at Anantapur. [W11]
6 ct	W. Bossenger	Griqualand West v Border at East London. [W11]
6 ct	G. L. Brophy	Yorkshire v Durham at Chester-le-Street.
6 ct	S. M. Davies	Worcestershire v Nottinghamshire at Worcester.
6 ct	M. S. Dhoni	India v New Zealand (Third Test) at Wellington.
6 ct	Farhan Asghar	Lahore Ravi v Quetta at Lahore. [W11]
6 ct	J. S. Foster	Essex v Glamorgan at Cardiff.
6 ct	C. D. Hartley	Queensland v New South Wales at Brisbane.
6 ct	Javed Mansoor	Karachi Blues v Abbottabad at Abbottabad. [W11]
6 ct	C. Kieswetter	Somerset v Lancashire at Taunton.
6 ct	P. D. McGlashan	Northern Districts v Central Districts at Whangarei (1st inns). [W11]
6 ct	P. D. McGlashan	Northern Districts v Central Districts at Whangarei (2nd inns). [W11]
6 ct	T. J. New	Leicestershire v Derbyshire at Derby.
6 ct	T. Ngulube	Matabeleland Tuskers v Southern Rocks at Masvingo. [W11]
5 ct, 1 st . .	N. V. Ojha	Central Zone v South Zone at Bangalore.
5 ct, 1 st . .	T. D. Paine	Tasmania v Victoria at Hobart.
5 ct, 1 st . .	Sarfraz Ahmed	Pakistan A v Sri Lanka A at Dambulla.
6 ct	Sarfraz Ahmed	PIA v WAPDA at Lahore. [W11]
6 ct	Shahbaz Butt	Lahore Ravi v Hyderabad at Lahore. [W11]
6 ct	D. J. Vilas	Lions v Warriors at Port Elizabeth.

† *National record.*

Most Wicketkeeping Dismissals in a Match

12 ct†	P. D. McGlashan	Northern Districts v Central Districts at Whangarei. [W11]
10 ct	Ahmed Said	WAPDA v Lahore Shalimar at Lahore. [W11]
10 ct	P. A. Browne	Barbados v Windward Islands at Bridgetown.
10 ct	A. Z. M. Dyili	Eastern Province v Free State at Port Elizabeth. [W11]
10 ct	C. D. Hartley	Queensland v New South Wales at Brisbane.
10 ct	Sarfraz Ahmed	PIA v WAPDA at Lahore. [W11]
10 ct	M. N. van Wyk	Eagles v Lions at Johannesburg.
10 ct	D. J. Vilas	Lions v Warriors at Port Elizabeth.
9 ct	Amin-ur-Rehman	National Bank v Sui Southern Gas at Faisalabad. [W11]
9 ct	B. G. Barnes	KwaZulu-Natal v KwaZulu-Natal Inland at Pietermaritzburg. [W11]
9 ct	P. Bisht	Delhi v Baroda at Vadodara. [W11]
9 ct	W. Bossenger	Griqualand West v Border at East London. [W11]
9 ct	J. S. Foster	Essex v Gloucestershire at Bristol.
7 ct, 2 st . .	M. J. Harris	Gauteng v Boland at Paarl.
9 ct	Javed Mansoor	Karachi Blues v Abbottabad at Abbottabad. [W11]
8 ct, 1 st . .	B. B. McCullum	New Zealand v Pakistan (Third Test) at Napier.
9 ct	A. A. Mulla	Canada v Scotland at Aberdeen.

8 ct, 1 st .	Sarfraz Ahmed	Pakistan A v Sri Lanka A at Dambulla.
9 ct	M. S. Wade	Victoria v New South Wales at Melbourne.
9 ct	Zulfiqar Jan	KRL v Habib Bank at Karachi. [W11]

† *National record.*

Five Catches in an Innings in the Field

M. D. Bell	Wellington v Northern Districts at Hamilton. [W11]
D. M. Bravo	Trinidad & Tobago v Jamaica at St Elizabeth.
J. M. Brodie	Wellington v Otago at Wellington.
S. I. de Saram	Ragama v Moors at Colombo. [W11]
H. H. Gibbs	Cape Cobras v Eagles at Cape Town.
Naumanullah	National Bank v ZTBL at Lahore.
A. C. Voges	Western Australia v Queensland at Brisbane.
Wajahatullah Wasti . .	ZTBL v Lahore Shalimar at Lahore. [W11]

Seven Catches in a Match in the Field

J. M. Kemp	Cape Cobras v Eagles at Cape Town. [W11]
S. D. Robson	Middlesex v Glamorgan at Swansea.
A. C. Voges	Western Australia v Queensland at Brisbane.
Wajahatullah Wasti . .	ZTBL v Lahore Shalimar at Lahore. [W11]

No Byes Conceded in Total of 500 or More

C. D. Hartley§	Queensland v Victoria (806-8 dec) at Melbourne.
H. A. P. W. Jayawardene . .	Sri Lanka v India (726-9 dec) (Third Test) at Mumbai.
J. A. Simpson	Middlesex v Kent (652-7 dec) at Uxbridge.
Kamran Akmal	Pakistan v Sri Lanka (644-7 dec) (First Test) at Karachi.
M. V. Boucher	South Africa v England (574-9 dec) (Second Test) at Durban.
M. N. van Wyk	Eagles v Cape Cobras (573-8 dec) at Bloemfontein. [W11]
R. H. Motwani	Maharashtra v Karnataka (553-4 dec) at Pune. [W11]
U. Kaul	North Zone v South Zone (548) at Rajkot.
D. L. R. Smith	New South Wales v Queensland (547-7 dec) at Brisbane.
Kashif Hayat	Peshawar v Multan (538-6 dec) at Multan. [W11]
Kashif Hayat	Peshawar v Sialkot (522-2 dec) at Sialkot. [W11]
T. D. Paine	Tasmania v New South Wales (521-4 dec) at Newcastle.
S. M. Davies	Worcestershire v Yorkshire (516) at Worcester.
J. S. Foster	Essex v Kent (512-9 dec) at Chelmsford.
A. Maregwede	Southern Rocks v Mashonaland Eagles (512-8 dec) at Masvingo. [W11]
D. W. A. N. D. Vitharana .	Badureliya v Sinhalese (506) at Colombo. [W11]
V. R. Samant	Mumbai v Tamil Nadu (501) at Mumbai. [W11]

§ *World record.*

Highest Innings Totals

806-8 dec	Victoria v Queensland at Melbourne.
785	Tamil Nadu v Hyderabad at Hyderabad. [W11]
765-6 dec	Pakistan v Sri Lanka (First Test) at Karachi.
760-7 dec	Sri Lanka v India (First Test) at Ahmedabad.
749-9 dec	West Indies v England (Fourth Test) at Bridgetown.
742-5 dec	Sussex v Somerset at Taunton.
726-9 dec	India v Sri Lanka (Third Test) at Mumbai.
702-8 dec	Glamorgan v Surrey at The Oval.
690-9	Lions v Warriors at East London. [W11]
674-6 dec	Australia v England (First Test) at Cardiff.
672-4 dec	Somerset v Warwickshire at Taunton.
671-2	WAPDA v Sui Southern Gas at Sheikhupura. [W11]
662-5 dec	Auckland v Central Districts at Auckland.
654-8 dec	Hampshire v Nottinghamshire at Nottingham.

652-7 dec	Kent v Middlesex at Uxbridge.
651	South Africa v Australia (Third Test) at Cape Town.
650-9 dec	Saurashtra v Bengal at Kolkata. [W11]
648-5 dec	Durham v Nottinghamshire at Chester-le-Street.
648-6 dec	Mumbai v Gujarat at Mumbai. [W11]
644-7 dec	Sri Lanka v Pakistan (First Test) at Karachi.
643-9 dec	Victoria v South Australia at Adelaide. [W11]
642	India v Sri Lanka (Second Test) at Kanpur.
637-6 dec	Mumbai v Saurashtra at Chennai.
634-8 dec	Durham v Worcestershire at Worcester.
630-8 dec	Warwickshire v Hampshire at Birmingham.
627	National Bank v Customs at Karachi.
620-7 dec	Kent v Surrey at The Oval.
620-9 dec	Sussex v Worcestershire at Worcester.
619-9 dec	New Zealand v India (Second Test) at Napier.
617-7 dec	Queensland v West Indians at Brisbane.
609-6 dec	Sui Northern Gas v Lahore Shalimar at Lahore. [W11]
608-4 dec	Surrey v Leicestershire at The Oval.
606	Sri Lanka v Pakistan (Second Test) at Lahore.
605-9 dec	Islamabad v Quetta at Islamabad.
600-6 dec	England v West Indies (Fourth Test) at Bridgetown.
600-8 dec	Yorkshire v Warwickshire at Birmingham.
600-8 dec	Northamptonshire v Leicestershire at Northampton.

Lowest Innings Totals

41	Quetta v Rawalpindi at Islamabad.
51	Quetta v Peshawar at Peshawar.
51	England v West Indies (First Test) at Kingston.
57	Police v Sebastianites at Colombo.
59	Bangladesh Cricket Board Academy v Zimbabweans at Bogra.
62†	Quetta v Peshawar at Islamabad. [W11]
62	Uttar Pradesh v Bengal at Kanpur. [W11]
66	Peshawar v Karachi Blues at Rawalpindi. [W11]
66	Habib Bank v Karachi Blues at Karachi. [W11]
69	Somerset v Durham at Taunton.
69	Sebastianites v Air Force at Moratuwa. [W11]
69	Badureliya v Chilaw Marians at Katunayake. [W11]
73	KwaZulu-Natal v Northerns at Durban. [W11]
74	Cape Cobras v Warriors at East London.
75	Leeward Islands v Windward Islands at Gros Islet.

† *One batsman absent hurt.*

Highest Fourth-Innings Totals

479-6	Somerset v Yorkshire at Taunton (set 476).
450-7	Central Districts v Canterbury at New Plymouth (set 448).
445-1	Central Districts v Wellington at Wellington (set 443). [W11]
407-6	Quetta v Karachi Blues at Karachi (set 495). [W11]
406	Australia v England (Second Test) at Lord's (set 522).
403	South Zone v West Zone at Chennai (set 678).

Match Aggregate of 1,500 Runs

1,628 for 17	England (600-6 dec and 279-2 dec) v West Indies (749-9 dec) (Fourth Test) at Bridgetown.
1,606 for 31	Yorkshire (438 and 363-5 dec) v Somerset (326 and 479-6) at Taunton.
1,598 for 21	India (426 and 412-4) v Sri Lanka (760-7 dec) (First Test) at Ahmedabad.
1,590 for 35	Islamabad (438 and 382-8 dec) v Hyderabad (466 and 304-7) at Islamabad. [W11]
1,553 for 18	Sri Lanka (644-7 dec and 144-5) v Pakistan (765-6 dec) (First Test) at Karachi.

Lowest Match Aggregate

85 for 11§   Quetta (forfeit and 41) v Rawalpindi (forfeit and 44-1) at Islamabad.

§ *World record.*

Matches Dominated by Batting (1,200 runs at 80 runs per wicket)

1,224 for 9 (136.00)	Leicestershire (593-5 dec and 23-0) v Surrey (608-4 dec) at The Oval.
1,263 for 11 (114.81)	Sussex (742-5 dec) v Somerset (521-6) at Taunton.
1,628 for 17 (95.76)	England (600-6 dec and 279-2 dec) v West Indies (749-9 dec) (Fourth Test) at Bridgetown.
1,553 for 18 (86.27)	Sri Lanka (644-7 dec and 144-5) v Pakistan (765-6 dec) (First Test) at Karachi.
1,280 for 15 (85.33)	Warwickshire (500 and 108-1) v Somerset (672-4 dec) at Taunton.
1,200 for 15 (80.00)	Peshawar (295 and 383-3) v Sialkot (522-2 dec) at Sialkot. [W11]

Win Losing Only One Wicket

Quetta (forfeit and 41) v Rawalpindi (forfeit and 44-1) at Islamabad.

Four Individual Hundreds in an Innings

Victoria (806-8 dec) v Queensland at Melbourne.
Easterns (541-9 dec) v Westerns at Harare.
Australia (674-6 dec) v England (First Test) at Cardiff.
Kent (620-7 dec) v Surrey at The Oval.
Durham (648-5 dec) v Nottinghamshire at Chester-le-Street.
Glamorgan (702-8 dec) v Surrey at The Oval.

Six Individual Fifties in an Innings

Victoria (806-8 dec) v Queensland at Melbourne.
Warwickshire (428) v Sussex at Hove.
Somerset (523-8) v Worcestershire at Taunton.
India (726-9 dec) v Sri Lanka (Third Test) at Mumbai.
Pakistan (455) v New Zealand (Third Test) at Napier.
Tamil Nadu (785) v Hyderabad at Hyderabad. [W11]

Large Margin of Victory

Islamabad (605-9 dec) beat Quetta (94 and 96) at Islamabad by an innings and 415 runs.
Sri Lanka (384 and 447-6 dec) beat Bangladesh (208 and 158) (Second Test) at Chittagong by 465 runs. [W09]
Islamabad (182 and 419) beat Abbottabad (100 and 81) at Islamabad by 420 runs. [W11]
South Zone (548 and 319-3 dec) beat North Zone (300 and 156) at Rajkot by 411 runs.

Win after Following On

Essex (370 and 155) lost to Kent (205 and 512-9 dec) at Chelmsford by 192 runs.
Peshawar (263 and 77) lost to Rawalpindi (81 and 334) at Islamabad by 75 runs. [W11]

Eleven Bowlers in an Innings

Dolphins v Cape Cobras (329-2) at Durban. [W11]

Most Extras in an Innings

b	l-b	w	n-b	pen	
74	35	12	11	16		West Indies (544) v England (Fifth Test) at Port-of-Spain.
63	32	3	22	6		KRL (352-5 dec) v Sui Southern Gas at Rawalpindi. [W11]
62	19	24	9	10		South Africa (651) v Australia (Third Test) at Cape Town.
62	13	11	12	26		Durham (543) v Somerset at Taunton.
61	20	5	8	28		England (569-6 dec) v West Indies (Second Test) at Chester-le-Street.
61	18	13	4	26		Karachi Whites (486) v National Bank at Karachi. [W11]
60	23	11	5	16	5	Abbottabad (429) v Hyderabad at Hyderabad.
59	9	17	14	19		Lahore Ravi (348) v Hyderabad at Lahore. [W11]
57	16	21	5	10	5	Glamorgan (566) v Leicestershire at Colwyn Bay.
56	6	16	1	33		Trinidad & Tobago (505) v Barbados at Pointe-à-Pierre.
56	24	19	11	2		Warwickshire (500) v Somerset at Taunton.
56	14	11	8	23		Karachi Whites (520-8 dec) v Lahore Shalimar at Lahore. [W11]
54	22	14	1	17		Karachi Blues (552-7 dec) v Hyderabad at Mirpur Khas. [W11]
53	11	6	8	28		Leicestershire (403-9 dec) v Kent at Leicester.
53	20	18	9	6		Karnataka (488) v Baroda at Vadodara. [W11]
53	18	22	6	7		Habib Bank (353) v National Bank at Lahore. [W11]
52	7	22	8	15		Warriors (484) v Eagles at Bloemfontein.
51	1	18	2	30		Derbyshire (326) v Essex at Chelmsford.
51	18	16	3	14		Yorkshire (524) v Hampshire at Basingstoke.
51	3	12	8	28		Abbottabad (238) v Karachi Blues at Abbottabad. [W11]
51	9	1	32	9		Mumbai (648-6 dec) v Gujarat at Mumbai. [W11]
50	6	13	1	30		Essex (370) v Kent at Chelmsford.
50	5	8	14	23		Karachi Whites (404) v Sui Northern Gas at Karachi. [W11]

Career Aggregate Milestones

20,000 runs.........	R. T. Ponting.
15,000 runs.........	A. D. Brown, S. C. Ganguly, M. E. Trescothick, M. van Jaarsveld.
10,000 runs.........	I. R. Bell, P. D. Collingwood, S. I. de Saram, H. H. Dippenaar, S. I. Fernando, D. J. Hussey, Misbah-ul-Haq, M. J. North, N. Pothas, A. G. Prince, J. A. Rudolph, T. T. Samaraweera, M. J. Walker, R. P. A. H. Wickremaratne.
500 wickets	Naved-ul-Hasan, G. P. Swann, S. Weerakoon, Zaheer Khan.
500 dismissals	Kamran Akmal.

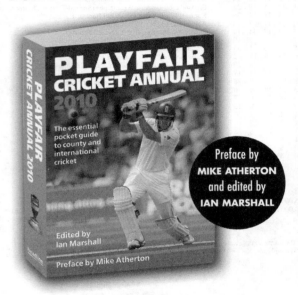

RECORDS

COMPILED BY PHILIP BAILEY

This section covers
- first-class records to December 31, 2009 (pages 117–155).
- List A one-day records to December 31, 2009 (pages 156–158).
- List A Twenty20 records to December 31, 2009 (pages 159–160).
- Test records to January 27, 2010, the end of the Bangladesh v India series (pages 161–202).
- Test records series by series (pages 203–290).
- one-day international records to December 31, 2009 (pages 291–301).
- World Cup records (pages 301–305).
- Twenty20 international records to December 31, 2009 (pages 306–308).
- miscellaneous other records to December 31, 2009 (pages 308–312).
- women's Test and one-day international records to December 31, 2009 (pages 312–315).

The sequence
- Test series records begin with those involving England, arranged in the order their opponents entered Test cricket (Australia, South Africa, West Indies, New Zealand, India, Pakistan, Sri Lanka, Zimbabwe, Bangladesh). Next come all remaining series involving Australia, then South Africa – and so on until Zimbabwe v Bangladesh records appear on pages 287–288.

Notes
- Unless otherwise stated, all records apply only to first-class cricket. This is considered to have started in 1815, after the Napoleonic War.
- mid-year seasons taking place outside England are given simply as 2002, 2003, etc.
- (E), (A), (SA), (WI), (NZ), (I), (P), (SL), (Z) or (B) indicates the nationality of a player or the country in which a record was made.
- in career records, dates in italic indicate seasons embracing two different years (i.e. non-English seasons). In these cases, only the first year is given, e.g. *2008* for 2008-09.

See also
- up-to-date Test records on www.cricinfo.com and at www.cricketarchive.co.uk/Archive/Records/Tests/index.html.
- Features of 2009 (pages 98–109).

CONTENTS

FIRST-CLASS RECORDS

BATTING RECORDS

BOWLING RECORDS

ALL-ROUND RECORDS

WICKETKEEPING RECORDS

FIELDING RECORDS

TEAM RECORDS

LIST A ONE-DAY RECORDS

LIST A TWENTY20 RECORDS

TEST RECORDS

BATTING RECORDS

BOWLING RECORDS

ALL-ROUND RECORDS

WICKETKEEPING RECORDS

FIELDING RECORDS

TEAM RECORDS

PLAYERS

UMPIRES

TEST SERIES

ONE-DAY INTERNATIONAL RECORDS

TWENTY20 INTERNATIONAL RECORDS

MISCELLANEOUS RECORDS

WOMEN'S TEST AND ONE-DAY INTERNATIONAL RECORDS

FIRST-CLASS RECORDS

BATTING RECORDS

HIGHEST INDIVIDUAL INNINGS

In the history of first-class cricket, there have been **176** individual scores of 300 or more:

501*	B. C. Lara	Warwickshire v Durham at Birmingham	1994
499	Hanif Mohammad	Karachi v Bahawalpur at Karachi	1958-59
452*	D. G. Bradman	NSW v Queensland at Sydney	1929-30
443*	B. B. Nimbalkar	Maharashtra v Kathiawar at Poona	1948-49
437	W. H. Ponsford	Victoria v Queensland at Melbourne	1927-28
429	W. H. Ponsford	Victoria v Tasmania at Melbourne	1922-23
428	Aftab Baloch	Sind v Baluchistan at Karachi	1973-74
424	A. C. MacLaren	Lancashire v Somerset at Taunton	1895
405*	G. A. Hick	Worcestershire v Somerset at Taunton	1988
400*	B. C. Lara	West Indies v England at St John's	2003-04
394	Naved Latif	Sargodha v Gujranwala at Gujranwala	2000-01
390	**S. C. Cook**	**Lions v Warriors at East London**	**2009-10**
385	B. Sutcliffe	Otago v Canterbury at Christchurch	1952-53
383	C. W. Gregory	NSW v Queensland at Brisbane	1906-07
380	M. L. Hayden	Australia v Zimbabwe at Perth	2003-04
377	S. V. Manjrekar	Bombay v Hyderabad at Bombay	1990-91
375	B. C. Lara	West Indies v England at St John's	1993-94
374	D. P. M. D. Jayawardene	Sri Lanka v South Africa at Colombo	2006
369	D. G. Bradman	South Australia v Tasmania at Adelaide	1935-36
366	N. H. Fairbrother	Lancashire v Surrey at The Oval	1990
366	M. V. Sridhar	Hyderabad v Andhra at Secunderabad	1993-94
365*	C. Hill	South Australia v NSW at Adelaide	1900-01
365*	G. S. Sobers	West Indies v Pakistan at Kingston	1957-58
364	L. Hutton	England v Australia at The Oval	1938
359*	V. M. Merchant	Bombay v Maharashtra at Bombay	1943-44
359	R. B. Simpson	NSW v Queensland at Brisbane	1963-64
357*	R. Abel	Surrey v Somerset at The Oval	1899
357	D. G. Bradman	South Australia v Victoria at Melbourne	1935-36
356	B. A. Richards	South Australia v Western Australia at Perth	1970-71
355*	G. R. Marsh	Western Australia v South Australia at Perth	1989-90
355	B. Sutcliffe	Otago v Auckland at Dunedin	1949-50
353	V. V. S. Laxman	Hyderabad v Karnataka at Bangalore	1999-2000
352	W. H. Ponsford	Victoria v NSW at Melbourne	1926-27
350	Rashid Israr	Habib Bank v National Bank at Lahore	1976-77
345	C. G. Macartney	Australians v Nottinghamshire at Nottingham	1921
344*	G. A. Headley	Jamaica v Lord Tennyson's XI at Kingston	1931-32
344*	**M. W. Goodwin**	**Sussex v Somerset at Taunton**	**2009**
344	W. G. Grace	MCC v Kent at Canterbury	1876
343*	P. A. Perrin	Essex v Derbyshire at Chesterfield	1904
342	J. L. Langer	Somerset v Surrey at Guildford	2006
341	G. H. Hirst	Yorkshire v Leicestershire at Leicester	1905
341	C. M. Spearman	Gloucestershire v Middlesex at Gloucester	2004
340*	D. G. Bradman	NSW v Victoria at Sydney	1928-29
340	S. M. Gavaskar	Bombay v Bengal at Bombay	1981-82
340	S. T. Jayasuriya	Sri Lanka v India at Colombo	1997-98
339	D. S. Lehmann	Yorkshire v Durham at Leeds	2006
338*	R. C. Blunt	Otago v Canterbury at Christchurch	1931-32
338	W. W. Read	Surrey v Oxford University at The Oval	1888
337*	Pervez Akhtar	Railways v Dera Ismail Khan at Lahore	1964-65
337*	D. J. Cullinan	Transvaal v Northern Transvaal at Johannesburg	1993-94
337	Hanif Mohammad	Pakistan v West Indies at Bridgetown	1957-58
336*	W. R. Hammond	England v New Zealand at Auckland	1932-33

336	W. H. Ponsford	Victoria v South Australia at Melbourne	1927-28
335*	M. W. Goodwin	Sussex v Leicestershire at Hove	2003
334*	M. A. Taylor	Australia v Pakistan at Peshawar	1998-99
334	D. G. Bradman	Australia v England at Leeds	1930
333	K. S. Duleepsinhji	Sussex v Northamptonshire at Hove	1930
333	G. A. Gooch	England v India at Lord's	1990
332	W. H. Ashdown	Kent v Essex at Brentwood	1934
331*	J. D. Robertson	Middlesex v Worcestershire at Worcester	1949
331*	M. E. K. Hussey	Northamptonshire v Somerset at Taunton	2003
329*	M. E. K. Hussey	Northamptonshire v Essex at Northampton	2001
329	Inzamam-ul-Haq	Pakistan v New Zealand at Lahore	2002
325*	H. L. Hendry	Victoria v New Zealanders at Melbourne	1925-26
325	A. Sandham	England v West Indies at Kingston	1929-30
325	C. L. Badcock	South Australia v Victoria at Adelaide	1935-36
324*	D. M. Jones	Victoria v South Australia at Melbourne	1994-95
324	J. B. Stollmeyer	Trinidad v British Guiana at Port-of-Spain	1946-47
324	Waheed Mirza	Karachi Whites v Quetta at Karachi	1976-77
323	A. L. Wadekar	Bombay v Mysore at Bombay	1966-67
323	D. Gandhi	Bengal v Assam at Gauhati	1998-99
322*	M. B. Loye	Northamptonshire v Glamorgan at Northampton	1998
322	E. Paynter	Lancashire v Sussex at Hove	1937
322	I. V. A. Richards	Somerset v Warwickshire at Taunton	1985
321	W. L. Murdoch	NSW v Victoria at Sydney	1881-82
320	R. Lamba	North Zone v West Zone at Bhilai	1987-88
319	Gul Mahomed	Baroda v Holkar at Baroda	1946-47
319	C. J. L. Rogers	Northamptonshire v Gloucestershire at Northampton	2006
319	V. Sehwag	India v South Africa at Chennai	2007-08
318*	W. G. Grace	Gloucestershire v Yorkshire at Cheltenham	1876
317	W. R. Hammond	Gloucestershire v Nottinghamshire at Gloucester	1936
317	K. R. Rutherford	New Zealanders v D. B. Close's XI at Scarborough	1986
317	C. H. Gayle	West Indies v South Africa at St John's	2004-05
316*	J. B. Hobbs	Surrey v Middlesex at Lord's	1926
316*	V. S. Hazare	Maharashtra v Baroda at Poona	1939-40
316	R. H. Moore	Hampshire v Warwickshire at Bournemouth	1937
315*	T. W. Hayward	Surrey v Lancashire at The Oval	1898
315*	P. Holmes	Yorkshire v Middlesex at Lord's	1925
315*	A. F. Kippax	NSW v Queensland at Sydney	1927-28
315*	G. A. Hick	Worcestershire v Durham at Worcester	2002
315	M. A. Wagh	Warwickshire v Middlesex at Lord's	2001
315	J. L. Langer	Somerset v Middlesex at Taunton	2007
314*	C. L. Walcott	Barbados v Trinidad at Port-of-Spain	1945-46
314*	Wasim Jaffer	Mumbai v Saurashtra at Rajkot	1996-97
313*	S. J. Cook	Somerset v Glamorgan at Cardiff	1990
313*	Raqibul Hasan	Barisal v Sylhet at Fatullah	2006-07
313	H. Sutcliffe	Yorkshire v Essex at Leyton	1932
313	W. V. Raman‡	Tamil Nadu v Goa at Panjim	1988-89
313	**Younis Khan**	**Pakistan v Sri Lanka at Karachi**	**2008-09**
312*	W. W. Keeton	Nottinghamshire v Middlesex at The Oval†	1939
312*	J. M. Brearley	MCC Under-25 v North Zone at Peshawar	1966-67
312	R. Lamba	Delhi v Himachal Pradesh at Delhi	1994-95
312	J. E. R. Gallian	Lancashire v Derbyshire at Manchester	1996
312	**Sunny Singh**	**Haryana v Madhya Pradesh at Indore**	**2009-10**
311*	G. M. Turner	Worcestershire v Warwickshire at Worcester	1982
311*	J. P. Crawley	Hampshire v Nottinghamshire at Southampton	2005
311	J. T. Brown	Yorkshire v Sussex at Sheffield	1897
311	R. B. Simpson	Australia v England at Manchester	1964
311	Javed Miandad	Karachi Whites v National Bank at Karachi	1974-75
311	G. C. Smith	Somerset v Leicestershire at Taunton	2005
310*	J. H. Edrich	England v New Zealand at Leeds	1965
310*	M. E. K. Hussey	Northamptonshire v Gloucestershire at Bristol	2002

310	H. Gimblett	Somerset v Sussex at Eastbourne	1948
309*	S. P. James	Glamorgan v Sussex at Colwyn Bay	2000
309*	H. D. Ackerman	Leicestershire v Glamorgan at Cardiff	2006
309*	**R. G. Sharma**	**Mumbai v Gujarat at Mumbai**	**2009-10**
309	V. S. Hazare	The Rest v Hindus at Bombay	1943-44
309	V. Sehwag	India v Pakistan at Multan	2003-04
308*	F. M. M. Worrell	Barbados v Trinidad at Bridgetown	1943-44
308*	D. Mongia	Punjab v Jammu and Kashmir at Jullundur	2000-01
307*	T. N. Lazard	Boland v W. Province at Worcester, Cape Province . . .	1993-94
307	M. C. Cowdrey	MCC v South Australia at Adelaide.	1962-63
307	R. M. Cowper	Australia v England at Melbourne	1965-66
306*	A. Ducat	Surrey v Oxford University at The Oval	1919
306*	E. A. B. Rowan	Transvaal v Natal at Johannesburg.	1939-40
306*	D. W. Hookes	South Australia v Tasmania at Adelaide	1986-87
306*	S. R. Nair	Kerala v Services at Palakkad	2007-08
306	M. H. Richardson	New Zealanders v Zimbabwe A at Kwekwe	2000-01
306	S. M. Katich	New South Wales v Queensland at Sydney	2007-08
305*	F. E. Woolley	MCC v Tasmania at Hobart	1911-12
305*	F. R. Foster	Warwickshire v Worcestershire at Dudley	1914
305*	W. H. Ashdown	Kent v Derbyshire at Dover	1935
305*	P. Dharmani	Punjab v Jammu and Kashmir at Ludhiana	1999-2000
304*	A. W. Nourse	Natal v Transvaal at Johannesburg.	1919-20
304*	P. H. Tarilton	Barbados v Trinidad at Bridgetown	1919-20
304*	E. D. Weekes	West Indians v Cambridge University at Cambridge. . .	1950
304	R. M. Poore	Hampshire v Somerset at Taunton	1899
304	D. G. Bradman	Australia v England at Leeds	1934
303*	W. W. Armstrong	Australians v Somerset at Bath.	1905
303*	Mushtaq Mohammad	Karachi Blues v Karachi University at Karachi	1967-68
303*	Abdul Azeem	Hyderabad v Tamil Nadu at Hyderabad.	1986-87
303*	S. Chanderpaul	Guyana v Jamaica at Kingston	1995-96
303*	G. A. Hick	Worcestershire v Hampshire at Southampton	1997
303*	D. J. Sales	Northamptonshire v Essex at Northampton	1999
303*	N. V. Knight	Warwickshire v Middlesex at Lord's	2004
303*	**J. C. Hildreth**	**Somerset v Warwickshire at Taunton**	**2009**
302*	P. Holmes	Yorkshire v Hampshire at Portsmouth	1920
302*	W. R. Hammond	Gloucestershire v Glamorgan at Bristol	1934
302*	Arjan Kripal Singh‡	Tamil Nadu v Goa at Panjim	1988-89
302*	B. J. Hodge	Leicestershire v Nottinghamshire at Nottingham.	2003
302*	C. A. Pujara	Saurashtra v Orissa at Rajkot	2008-09
302*	**Rafatullah Mohmand**	**WAPDA v Sui Southern Gas at Sheikhupura**	**2009-10**
302	W. R. Hammond	Gloucestershire v Glamorgan at Newport	1939
302	L. G. Rowe	West Indies v England at Bridgetown	1973-74
301*	E. H. Hendren	Middlesex v Worcestershire at Dudley	1933
301*	V. V. S. Laxman	Hyderabad v Bihar at Jamshedpur	1997-98
301*	P. G. Fulton	Canterbury v Auckland at Christchurch.	2002-03
301*	J. P. Crawley	Hampshire v Nottinghamshire at Nottingham	2004
301*	D. S. Lehmann	South Australia v Western Australia at Adelaide.	2005-06
301*	M. R. Ramprakash	Surrey v Northamptonshire at The Oval	2006
301	W. G. Grace	Gloucestershire v Sussex at Bristol	1896
301	**Wasim Jaffer**	**Mumbai v Saurashtra at Chennai**.	**2008-09**
300*	V. T. Trumper	Australians v Sussex at Hove	1899
300*	F. B. Watson	Lancashire v Surrey at Manchester	1928
300*	Imtiaz Ahmed	PM's XI v Commonwealth XI at Bombay	1950-51
300*	G. K. Khoda	Central Zone v South Zone at Panaji	2000-01
300*	M. L. Love	Queensland v Victoria at Melbourne (Junction Oval) . .	2003-04
300*	Shoaib Khan	Peshawar v Quetta at Peshawar	2003-04
300*	Bazid Khan	Rawalpindi v Hyderabad at Hyderabad	2004-05
300*	S. S. Das	Orissa v Jammu and Kashmir at Cuttack	2006-07
300*	A. Mukund	Tamil Nadu v Maharashtra at Nasik.	2008-09
300	J. T. Brown	Yorkshire v Derbyshire at Chesterfield	1898

300	D. C. S. Compton	MCC v N. E. Transvaal at Benoni	1948-49
300	R. Subba Row	Northamptonshire v Surrey at The Oval	1958
300	Ramiz Raja	Allied Bank v Habib Bank at Lahore	1994-95
300	Yasir Hameed	NWFP v Baluchistan at Peshawar	2007-08

† *Played at The Oval because Lord's was required for Eton v Harrow.*

‡ *W. V. Raman and Arjan Kripal Singh scored triple-hundreds in the same innings, a unique occurrence.*

Bold type denotes innings played since January 1, 2009.

DOUBLE-HUNDRED ON DEBUT

227	T. Marsden	Sheffield & Leicester v Nottingham at Sheffield	1826
207	N. F. Callaway†	New South Wales v Queensland at Sydney	1914-15
240	W. F. E. Marx	Transvaal v Griqualand West at Johannesburg	1920-21
200*	A. Maynard	Trinidad v MCC at Port-of-Spain	1934-35
232*	S. J. E. Loxton	Victoria v Queensland at Melbourne	1946-47
215*	G. H. G. Doggart	Cambridge University v Lancashire at Cambridge	1948
202	J. Hallebone	Victoria v Tasmania at Melbourne	1951-52
230	G. R. Viswanath	Mysore v Andhra at Vijayawada	1967-68
260	A. A. Muzumdar	Bombay v Haryana at Faridabad	1993-94
209*	A. Pandey	Madhya Pradesh v Uttar Pradesh at Bhilai	1995-96
210*	D. J. Sales	Northants v Worcestershire at Kidderminster	1996
200*	M. J. Powell	Glamorgan v Oxford University at Oxford	1997

† *In his only first-class innings. He was killed in action in France in 1917.*

TWO SEPARATE HUNDREDS ON DEBUT

148	and 111	A. R. Morris	New South Wales v Queensland at Sydney	1940-41
152	and 102*	N. J. Contractor	Gujarat v Baroda at Baroda	1952-53
132*	and 110	Aamer Malik	Lahore A v Railways at Lahore	1979-80
130	**and 100***	**Noor Ali**	**Afghanistan v Zimbabwe XI at Mutare**	**2009**

TWO DOUBLE-HUNDREDS IN A MATCH

| A. E. Fagg | 244 | 202* | Kent v Essex at Colchester | 1938 |

TRIPLE-HUNDRED AND HUNDRED IN A MATCH

| G. A. Gooch | 333 | 123 | England v India at Lord's | 1990 |

DOUBLE-HUNDRED AND HUNDRED IN A MATCH

In addition to Fagg and Gooch, there have been **54** further instances of a batsman scoring a double-hundred and a hundred in the same first-class match. The most recent are:

Mohammad Ramzan	205	102*	Faisalabad v Sargodha at Faisalabad	2000-01
M. W. Goodwin	115	203*	Sussex v Nottinghamshire at Nottingham	2001
D. P. Fulton	208*	104*	Kent v Somerset at Canterbury	2001
B. C. Lara	221	130	West Indies v Sri Lanka at Colombo	2001-02
Minhazul Abedin	210	110	Chittagong v Dhaka at Mymensingh	2001-02
A. T. Rayudu	210	159*	Hyderabad v Andhra at Secunderabad	2002-03
H. H. Kanitkar	112	207*	Maharashtra v Services at Aurangabad	2003-04
M. J. Horne	118	209*	Auckland v Northern Districts at Auckland	2003-04
S. A. Newman	117	219	Surrey v Glamorgan at The Oval	2005
P. A. Jaques	240	117	Australia A v India A at Cairns	2006

C. J. L. Rogers	128	222*	Northamptonshire v Somerset at Taunton....	2006
M. W. Goodwin	119	205*	Sussex v Surrey at Hove	2007
Younis Khan	106	202*	Yorkshire v Hampshire at Southampton.....	2007
V. Sibanda	**209**	**116***	**Zimbabwe XI v Kenya at Kwekwe**	**2009-10**

Notes: Zaheer Abbas achieved the feat four times, for Gloucestershire between 1976 and 1981, and was not out in all eight innings. M. R. Hallam did it twice for Leicestershire, in 1959 and 1961; N. R. Taylor twice for Kent, in 1990 and 1991; and G. A. Gooch did it for England in 1990 (see above) and Essex in 1994.

Bold type denotes innings played since January 1, 2009.

TWO SEPARATE HUNDREDS IN A MATCH MOST TIMES

R. T. Ponting	8	M. R. Ramprakash	6	M. L. Hayden	5
Zaheer Abbas	8	G. M. Turner	6	G. A. Hick	5
W. R. Hammond	7	C. B. Fry	5		
J. B. Hobbs	6	G. A. Gooch	5		

Current players only:

| S. G. Law | 4 | **A. N. Petersen** | **3** | M. van Jaarsveld | 3 |
| J. P. Crawley | 4 | C. J. L. Rogers | 3 | | |

Notes: W. Lambert scored 107 and 157 for Sussex v Epsom at Lord's in 1817, and it was not until W. G. Grace made 130 and 102* for South of the Thames v North of the Thames at Canterbury in 1868 that the feat was repeated.

Bold type denotes the latest instance occurred since January 1, 2009.

FIVE HUNDREDS OR MORE IN SUCCESSION

D. G. Bradman (1938-39)	6	B. C. Lara (1993-94/1994)	5
C. B. Fry (1901)	6	P. A. Patel (2007/2007-08)	5
M. J. Procter (1970-71)	6	E. D. Weekes (1955-56)	5
M. E. K. Hussey (2003)	5		

Notes: Bradman also scored four hundreds in succession twice, in 1931-32 and 1948/1948-49; W. R. Hammond did it in 1936-37 and 1945/1946, and H. Sutcliffe in 1931 and 1939.

Current players only:

S. Badrinath (2007/2007-08)	4	S. R. Tendulkar (1994-95)	4
Ijaz Ahmed, jun. (1994-95)	4	Yasir Hameed (2002-03/2003)	4
V. Sibanda (2009-10)	**4**	Younis Khan (1999-2000)	4

Notes: T. W. Hayward (Surrey v Nottinghamshire and Leicestershire), D. W. Hookes (South Australia v Queensland and New South Wales) and V. Sibanda (Zimbabwe XI v Kenya and Mid West v Southern Rocks) are the only players to score two hundreds in each of two successive matches. Hayward scored his in six days, June 4-9, 1906.

The most fifties in consecutive innings is ten – by E. Tyldesley in 1926, by D. G. Bradman in the 1947-48 and 1948 seasons and by R. S. Kaluwitharana in 1994-95.

Bold type denotes innings played since January 1, 2009.

MOST HUNDREDS IN A SEASON

D. C. S. Compton (1947)	18	W. R. Hammond (1937)	13
J. B. Hobbs (1925)	16	T. W. Hayward (1906)	13
W. R. Hammond (1938)	15	E. H. Hendren (1923)	13
H. Sutcliffe (1932)	14	E. H. Hendren (1927)	13
G. Boycott (1971)	13	E. H. Hendren (1928)	13
D. G. Bradman (1938)	13	C. P. Mead (1928)	13
C. B. Fry (1901)	13	H. Sutcliffe (1928)	13
W. R. Hammond (1933)	13	H. Sutcliffe (1931)	13

Since 1969 (excluding G. Boycott – above)

G. A. Gooch (1990)	12	M. R. Ramprakash (1995)	10
S. J. Cook (1991)	11	M. R. Ramprakash (2007)	10
Zaheer Abbas (1976)	11	G. M. Turner (1970)	10
G. A. Hick (1988)	10	Zaheer Abbas (1981)	10
H. Morris (1990)	10		

Note: The most achieved outside England is eight by D. G. Bradman in Australia (1947-48), D. C. S. Compton (1948-49), R. N. Harvey and A. R. Morris (both 1949-50) in South Africa, M. D. Crowe in New Zealand (1986-87), Asif Mujtaba in Pakistan (1995-96), V. V. S. Laxman in India (1999-2000), M. G. Bevan in Australia (2004-05) and **V. Sibanda in Zimbabwe (2009-10)**.

Bold type denotes performances in the calendar year 2009-10.

MOST DOUBLE-HUNDREDS IN A SEASON

D. G. Bradman (1930)	6	W. R. Hammond (1933)	4
K. S. Ranjitsinhji (1900)	5	W. R. Hammond (1934)	4
E. D. Weekes (1950)	5	E. H. Hendren (1929-30)	4
Arun Lal (1986-87)	4	V. M. Merchant (1944-45)	4
C. B. Fry (1901)	4	G. M. Turner (1971-72)	4

Current players only:

A. Chopra (2007-08)	3	D. S. Jadhav (2003-04)	3
R. Dravid (2003-04)	3	P. A. Jaques (2006)	3
B. J. Hodge (2004)	3	M. R. Ramprakash (1995)	3
M. E. K. Hussey (2001)	3		

Note: R. Dravid scored his three double-hundreds in three different countries; P. A. Jaques scored his in two.

MOST DOUBLE-HUNDREDS IN A CAREER

D. G. Bradman	37	B. C. Lara	13	A. Sandham	11
W. R. Hammond	36	C. P. Mead	13	G. Boycott	10
E. H. Hendren	22	W. H. Ponsford	13	M. W. Gatting	10
H. Sutcliffe	17	J. T. Tyldesley	13	S. M. Gavaskar	10
C. B. Fry	16	P. Holmes	12	J. Hardstaff, jun	10
G. A. Hick	16	Javed Miandad	12	V. S. Hazare	10
J. B. Hobbs	16	**J. L. Langer**	**12**	**B. J. Hodge**	**10**
M. R. Ramprakash	**15**	R. B. Simpson	12	I. V. A. Richards	10
C. G. Greenidge	14	J. W. Hearne	11	A. Shrewsbury	10
K. S. Ranjitsinhji	14	L. Hutton	11	R. T. Simpson	10
G. A. Gooch	13	D. S. Lehmann	11	G. M. Turner	10
W. G. Grace	13	V. M. Merchant	11	Zaheer Abbas	10

Bold type denotes those who played in the calendar year 2009.

MOST HUNDREDS IN A CAREER

(50 or more)

		Total	Total Inns	100th 100 Season	Inns	400+	300+	200+
1	J. B. Hobbs	197	1,315	1923	821	0	1	16
2	E. H. Hendren	170	1,300	1928-29	740	0	1	22
3	W. R. Hammond	167	1,005	1935	680	0	4	36
4	C. P. Mead	153	1,340	1927	892	0	0	13
5	G. Boycott	151	1,014	1977	645	0	0	10
6	H. Sutcliffe	149	1,088	1932	700	0	1	17
7	F. E. Woolley	145	1,532	1929	1,031	0	1	9

		Total	Total Inns	100th 100 Season	Inns	400+	300+	200+
8	G. A. Hick	136	871	1998	574	1	3	16
9	L. Hutton	129	814	1951	619	0	1	11
10	G. A. Gooch	128	990	1992-93	820	0	1	13
11	W. G. Grace	126	1,493	1895	1,113	0	3	13
12	D. C. S. Compton	123	839	1952	552	0	1	9
13	T. W. Graveney	122	1,223	1964	940	0	0	7
14	D. G. Bradman	117	338	1947-48	295	1	6	37
15	I. V. A. Richards	114	796	1988-89	658	0	1	10
16	**M. R. Ramprakash**	**108**	**701**	**2008**	**676**	**0**	**1**	**15**
	Zaheer Abbas	108	768	1982-83	658	0	0	10
18	A. Sandham	107	1,000	1935	871	0	1	11
	M. C. Cowdrey	107	1,130	1973	1,035	0	1	3
20	T. W. Hayward	104	1,138	1913	1,076	0	1	8
21	G. M. Turner	103	792	1982	779	0	1	10
	J. H. Edrich	103	979	1977	945	0	1	4
23	L. E. G. Ames	102	951	1950	916	0	0	9
	E. Tyldesley	102	961	1934	919	0	0	7
	D. L. Amiss	102	1,139	1986	1,081	0	0	3

Notes: In the above table, 200+, 300+ and 400+ include all scores above those figures.

E. H. Hendren, D. G. Bradman and I. V. A. Richards scored their 100th hundreds in Australia; G. A. Gooch scored his in India. His record includes his century in South Africa in 1981-82, which is no longer accepted by the ICC. Zaheer Abbas scored his 100th in Pakistan. Zaheer Abbas and G. Boycott did so in Test matches.

J. W. Hearne	96	Mushtaq Mohammad	72	G. H. Hirst	60
C. B. Fry	94	J. O'Connor	72	R. B. Simpson	60
M. W. Gatting	94	**R. T. Ponting**	**72**	P. F. Warner	60
C. G. Greenidge	92	W. G. Quaife	72	I. M. Chappell	59
A. J. Lamb	89	K. S. Ranjitsinhji	72	**M. W. Goodwin**	**59**
A. I. Kallicharran	87	D. Brookes	71	A. L. Hassett	59
W. J. Edrich	86	M. D. Crowe	71	W. Larkins	59
R. B. Kanhai	86	A. C. Russell	71	M. P. Maynard	59
J. L. Langer	**86**	A. R. Border	70	A. Shrewsbury	59
G. S. Sobers	86	**S. R. Tendulkar**	**70**	J. G. Wright	59
J. T. Tyldesley	86	D. Denton	69	**R. Dravid**	**58**
P. B. H. May	85	C. L. Hooper	69	A. E. Fagg	58
R. E. S. Wyatt	85	M. J. K. Smith	69	P. H. Parfitt	58
J. Hardstaff, jun	83	M. G. Bevan	68	W. Rhodes	58
D. S. Lehmann	82	D. C. Boon	68	P. N. Kirsten	57
S. M. Gavaskar	81	R. E. Marshall	68	L. B. Fishlock	56
M. E. Waugh	81	R. N. Harvey	67	A. Jones	56
Javed Miandad	80	P. Holmes	67	C. A. Milton	56
M. Leyland	80	J. D. Robertson	67	C. W. J. Athey	55
B. A. Richards	80	P. A. Perrin	66	C. Hallows	55
M. L. Hayden	**79**	K. C. Wessels	66	Hanif Mohammad	55
S. G. Law	**79**	B. C. Lara	65	D. M. Jones	55
C. H. Lloyd	79	S. J. Cook	64	D. B. Vengsarkar	55
S. R. Waugh	79	T. M. Moody	64	W. Watson	55
K. F. Barrington	76	R. G. Pollock	64	M. A. Atherton	54
J. G. Langridge	76	R. T. Simpson	64	M. Azharuddin	54
C. Washbrook	76	K. W. R. Fletcher	63	**J. P. Crawley**	**54**
H. T. W. Hardinge	75	R. T. Robinson	63	D. J. Insole	54
R. Abel	74	G. Gunn	62	W. W. Keeton	54
G. S. Chappell	74	K. J. Barnett	61	W. Bardsley	53
D. Kenyon	74	D. L. Haynes	61	B. F. Davison	53
K. S. McEwan	74	R. A. Smith	61	A. E. Dipper	53
Majid Khan	73	V. S. Hazare	60	**M. J. Di Venuto**	**53**

D. I. Gower	53	D. W. Randall	52	G. Cox, jun	50
G. L. Jessop	53	**S. Chanderpaul**	**51**	H. E. Dollery	50
H. Morris	53	J. Cox	51	K. S. Duleepsinhji	50
James Seymour	53	E. R. Dexter	51	M. T. G. Elliott	50
Shafiq Ahmad	53	**B. J. Hodge**	**51**	H. Gimblett	50
E. H. Bowley	52	**M. E. K. Hussey**	**51**	W. M. Lawry	50
D. B. Close	52	**V. V. S. Laxman**	**51**	Sadiq Mohammad	50
A. Ducat	52	J. M. Parks	51	F. B. Watson	50
N. Hussain	52	W. W. Whysall	51		
J. E. Morris	52	B. C. Broad	50		

Bold type denotes those who played in the calendar year 2009.

Other Current Players

In addition to the above, the following who played in 2009 have scored 30 or more hundreds.

J. H. Kallis	49	Wasim Jaffer	39	S. C. Ganguly	32
S. M. Katich	48	M. A. Butcher	38	Misbah-ul-Haq	32
M. van Jaarsveld	48	J. E. R. Gallian	38	U. Afzaal	31
A. D. Brown	45	K. P. Pietersen	38	G. Gambhir	31
M. L. Love	45	O. A. Shah	37	H. H. Gibbs	31
D. P. M. D. Jayawardene	44	D. J. Hussey	36	N. D. McKenzie	31
M. P. Vaughan	42	P. A. Jaques	36	V. Sehwag	31
R. W. T. Key	41	A. J. Strauss	35	Zahoor Elahi	31
M. B. Loye	41	J. A. Rudolph	34	T. M. Dilshan	30
C. J. L. Rogers	41	Younis Khan	34	D. L. Hemp	30
H. D. Ackerman	40	D. M. Benkenstein	33	T. T. Samaraweera	30
B. F. Smith	40	H. H. Dippenaar	33	R. R. Sarwan	30
A. Symonds	40	Hasan Raza	33	C. M. Spearman	30
M. E. Trescothick	39	Ijaz Ahmed	33	S. Sriram	30

MOST RUNS IN A SEASON

	Season	I	NO	R	HS	100s	Avge
D. C. S. Compton	1947	50	8	3,816	246	18	90.85
W. J. Edrich	1947	52	8	3,539	267*	12	80.43
T. W. Hayward	1906	61	8	3,518	219	13	66.37
L. Hutton	1949	56	6	3,429	269*	12	68.58
F. E. Woolley	1928	59	4	3,352	198	12	60.94
H. Sutcliffe	1932	52	7	3,336	313	14	74.13
W. R. Hammond	1933	54	5	3,323	264	13	67.81
E. H. Hendren	1928	54	7	3,311	209*	13	70.44
R. Abel	1901	68	8	3,309	247	7	55.15

Notes: 3,000 in a season has been surpassed on 19 other occasions (a full list can be found in *Wisden* 1999 and earlier editions). W. R. Hammond, E. H. Hendren and H. Sutcliffe are the only players to achieve the feat three times. K. S. Ranjitsinhji was the first batsman to reach 3,000 in a season, with 3,159 in 1899. M. J. K. Smith (3,245 in 1959) and W. E. Alley (3,019 in 1961) are the only players except those listed above to have reached 3,000 since World War II.

W. G. Grace scored 2,739 runs in 1871 – the first batsman to reach 2,000 runs in a season. He made ten hundreds including two double-hundreds, with an average of 78.25 in all first-class matches.

The highest aggregate in a season since the reduction of County Championship matches in 1969 is 2,755 by S. J. Cook (42 innings) in 1991, and the last batsman to achieve 2,000 was M. R. Ramprakash (2,026 in 2007).

2,000 RUNS IN A SEASON MOST TIMES

J. B. Hobbs	17	F. E. Woolley	13	C. P. Mead	11
E. H. Hendren	15	W. R. Hammond	12	T. W. Hayward	10
H. Sutcliffe	15	J. G. Langridge	11		

Note: Since the reduction of County Championship matches in 1969, G. A. Gooch is the only batsman to have reached 2,000 runs in a season five times.

1,000 RUNS IN A SEASON MOST TIMES

Includes overseas tours and seasons

W. G. Grace............ 28	A. Jones.............. 23	G. Gunn.............. 20
F. E. Woolley 28	T. W. Graveney........ 22	T. W. Hayward 20
M. C. Cowdrey 27	W. R. Hammond 22	G. A. Hick 20
C. P. Mead............ 27	D. Denton 21	James Langridge 20
G. Boycott............ 26	J. H. Edrich 21	J. M. Parks........... 20
J. B. Hobbs 26	G. A. Gooch 21	A. Sandham........... 20
E. H. Hendren 25	W. Rhodes............ 21	M. J. K. Smith 20
D. L. Amiss........... 24	D. B. Close 20	C. Washbrook 20
W. G. Quaife 24	K. W. R. Fletcher 20	
H. Sutcliffe 24	M. W. Gatting 20	

Notes: F. E. Woolley reached 1,000 runs in 28 consecutive seasons (1907–1938), C. P. Mead in 27 (1906–1936).

Outside England, 1,000 runs in a season has been reached most times by D. G. Bradman (in 12 seasons in Australia).

Three batsmen have scored 1,000 runs in a season in each of four different countries: G. S. Sobers in West Indies, England, India and Australia; M. C. Cowdrey and G. Boycott in England, South Africa, West Indies and Australia.

HIGHEST AGGREGATES OUTSIDE ENGLAND

	Season	I	NO	R	HS	100s	Avge
In Australia D. G. Bradman.............	1928-29	24	6	1,690	340*	7	93.88
In South Africa J. R. Reid.................	1961-62	30	2	1,915	203	7	68.39
In West Indies E. H. Hendren	1929-30	18	5	1,765	254*	6	135.76
In New Zealand M. D. Crowe	1986-87	21	3	1,676	175*	8	93.11
In India C. G. Borde	1964-65	28	3	1,604	168	6	64.16
In Pakistan Saadat Ali	1983-84	27	1	1,649	208	4	63.42
In Sri Lanka R. P. Arnold...............	1995-96	24	3	1,475	217*	5	70.23
In Zimbabwe **V. Sibanda**	**2009-10***	**15**	**2**	**1,215**	**215**	**8**	**93.46**
In Bangladesh Minhazul Abedin...........	2001-02	15	1	1,012	210	3	72.28

Note: In more than one country, the following aggregates of over 2,000 runs have been recorded:

M. Amarnath (P/I/WI).......	1982-83	34	6	2,234	207	9	79.78
J. R. Reid (SA/A/NZ)	1961-62	40	2	2,188	203	7	57.57
S. M. Gavaskar (I/P)	1978-79	30	6	2,121	205	10	88.37
R. B. Simpson (I/P/A/WI)	1964-65	34	4	2,063	201	8	68.76
M. H. Richardson (Z/SA/NZ) .	2000-01	34	3	2,030	306	4	65.48

* *Incomplete season.*

Bold type denotes performances in the calendar year 2009.

LEADING BATSMEN IN AN ENGLISH SEASON

(Qualification: 8 completed innings)

Season	Leading scorer	Runs	Avge	Top of averages	Runs	Avge
1946	D. C. S. Compton	2,403	61.61	W. R. Hammond......	1,783	84.90
1947	D. C. S. Compton	3,816	90.85	D. C. S. Compton	3,816	90.85
1948	L. Hutton............	2,654	64.73	D. G. Bradman	2,428	89.92
1949	L. Hutton............	3,429	68.58	J. Hardstaff..........	2,251	72.61
1950	R. T. Simpson	2,576	62.82	E. D. Weekes	2,310	79.65
1951	J. D. Robertson	2,917	56.09	P. B. H. May	2,339	68.79
1952	L. Hutton............	2,567	61.11	D. S. Sheppard	2,262	64.62
1953	W. J. Edrich	2,557	47.35	R. N. Harvey........	2,040	65.80
1954	D. Kenyon...........	2,636	51.68	D. C. S. Compton	1,524	58.61
1955	D. J. Insole	2,427	42.57	D. J. McGlew	1,871	58.46
1956	T. W. Graveney......	2,397	49.93	K. Mackay	1,103	52.52
1957	T. W. Graveney......	2,361	49.18	P. B. H. May	2,347	61.76
1958	P. B. H. May	2,231	63.74	P. B. H. May........	2,231	63.74
1959	M. J. K. Smith.......	3,245	57.94	V. L. Manjrekar	755	68.63
1960	M. J. K. Smith.......	2,551	45.55	R. Subba Row.......	1,503	55.66
1961	W. E. Alley	3,019	56.96	W. M. Lawry.......	2,019	61.18
1962	J. H. Edrich	2,482	51.70	R. T. Simpson........	867	54.18
1963	J. B. Bolus..........	2,190	41.32	G. S. Sobers	1,333	47.60
1964	T. W. Graveney......	2,385	54.20	K. F. Barrington	1,872	62.40
1965	J. H. Edrich	2,319	62.67	M. C. Cowdrey......	2,093	63.42
1966	A. R. Lewis........	2,198	41.47	G. S. Sobers	1,349	61.31
1967	C. A. Milton	2,089	46.42	K. F. Barrington	2,059	68.63
1968	B. A. Richards.......	2,395	47.90	G. Boycott	1,487	64.65
1969	J. H. Edrich	2,238	69.93	J. H. Edrich.........	2,238	69.93
1970	G. M. Turner........	2,379	61.00	G. S. Sobers	1,742	75.73
1971	G. Boycott..........	2,503	100.12	G. Boycott..........	2,503	100.12
1972	Majid Khan	2,074	61.00	G. Boycott	1,230	72.35
1973	G. M. Turner........	2,416	67.11	G. M. Turner.......	2,416	67.11
1974	R. T. Virgin........	1,936	56.94	C. H. Lloyd........	1,458	63.39
1975	G. Boycott..........	1,915	73.65	R. B. Kanhai	1,073	82.53
1976	Zaheer Abbas	2,554	75.11	Zaheer Abbas	2,554	75.11
1977	I. V. A. Richards.....	2,161	65.48	G. Boycott	1,701	68.04
1978	D. L. Amiss........	2,030	53.42	C. E. B. Rice.......	1,871	66.82
1979	K. C. Wessels	1,800	52.94	G. Boycott	1,538	102.53
1980	P. N. Kirsten	1,895	63.16	A. J. Lamb	1,797	66.55
1981	Zaheer Abbas	2,306	88.69	Zaheer Abbas	2,306	88.69
1982	A. I. Kallicharran ...	2,120	66.25	G. M. Turner.......	1,171	90.07
1983	K. S. McEwan.......	2,176	64.00	I. V. A. Richards......	1,204	75.25
1984	G. A. Gooch	2,559	67.34	C. G. Greenidge	1,069	82.23
1985	G. A. Gooch	2,208	71.22	I. V. A. Richards.....	1,836	76.50
1986	C. G. Greenidge	2,035	67.83	C. G. Greenidge	2,035	67.83
1987	G. A. Hick	1,879	52.19	M. D. Crowe........	1,627	67.79
1988	G. A. Hick..........	2,713	77.51	R. A. Harper........	622	77.75
1989	S. J. Cook	2,241	60.56	D. M. Jones........	1,510	88.82
1990	G. A. Gooch	2,746	101.70	G. A. Gooch	2,746	101.70
1991	S. J. Cook	2,755	81.02	C. L. Hooper.......	1,501	93.81
1992	{ P. D. Bowler	2,044	65.93	Salim Malik	1,184	78.93
	M. A. Roseberry	2,044	56.77			
1993	G. A. Gooch	2,023	63.21	D. C. Boon	1,437	75.63
1994	B. C. Lara	2,066	89.82	J. D. Carr	1,543	90.76
1995	M. R. Ramprakash ...	2,258	77.86	M. R. Ramprakash	2,258	77.86
1996	G. A. Gooch	1,944	67.03	S. C. Ganguly........	762	95.25
1997	S. P. James	1,775	68.26	G. A. Hick	1,524	69.27
1998	J. P. Crawley	1,851	74.04	J. P. Crawley	1,851	74.04
1999	S. G. Law	1,833	73.32	S. G. Law	1,833	73.32
2000	D. S. Lehmann	1,477	67.13	M. G. Bevan	1,124	74.93

Season	Leading scorer	Runs	Avge	Top of averages	Runs	Avge
2001	M. E. K. Hussey	2,055	79.03	D. R. Martyn.........	942	104.66
2002	I. J. Ward...........	1,759	62.82	R. Dravid	773	96.62
2003	S. G. Law	1,820	91.00	S. G. Law	1,820	91.00
2004	R. W. T. Key.......	1,896	79.00	R. W. T. Key	1,896	79.00
2005	O. A. Shah..........	1,728	66.46	M. E. K. Hussey	1,074	76.71
2006	M. R. Ramprakash ...	2,278	103.54	M. R. Ramprakash	2,278	103.54
2007	M. R. Ramprakash ...	2,026	101.30	M. R. Ramprakash	2,026	101.30
2008	S. C. Moore.........	1,451	55.80	T. Frost.............	1,003	83.58
2009	**M. E. Trescothick** ...	**1,817**	**75.70**	**M. R. Ramprakash** ...	**1,350**	**90.00**

Notes: The highest average recorded in an English season was 115.66 (2,429 runs, 26 innings) by D. G. Bradman in 1938.

In 1953, W. A. Johnston averaged 102.00 from 17 innings, 16 not out.

MOST RUNS

Dates in italics denote the first half of an overseas season; i.e. *1945* denotes the 1945-46 season.

		Career	R	I	NO	HS	100s	Avge
1	J. B. Hobbs.........	1905–1934	61,237	1,315	106	316*	197	50.65
2	F. E. Woolley.......	1906–1938	58,969	1,532	85	305*	145	40.75
3	E. H. Hendren.......	1907–1938	57,611	1,300	166	301*	170	50.80
4	C. P. Mead	1905–1936	55,061	1,340	185	280*	153	47.67
5	W. G. Grace	1865–1908	54,896	1,493	105	344	126	39.55
6	W. R. Hammond	1920–1951	50,551	1,005	104	336*	167	56.10
7	H. Sutcliffe........	1919–1945	50,138	1,088	123	313	149	51.95
8	G. Boycott	1962–1986	48,426	1,014	162	261*	151	56.83
9	T. W. Graveney	1948–*1971*	47,793	1,223	159	258	122	44.91
10	G. A. Gooch........	1973–2000	44,846	990	75	333	128	49.01
11	T. W. Hayward.......	1893–1914	43,551	1,138	96	315*	104	41.79
12	D. L. Amiss	1960–1987	43,423	1,139	126	262*	102	42.86
13	M. C. Cowdrey......	1950–1976	42,719	1,130	134	307	107	42.89
14	A. Sandham	1911–*1937*	41,284	1,000	79	325	107	44.82
15	G. A. Hick	*1983*–2008	41,112	871	84	405*	136	52.23
16	L. Hutton	1934–1960	40,140	814	91	364	129	55.51
17	M. J. K. Smith	1951–1975	39,832	1,091	139	204	69	41.84
18	W. Rhodes	1898–1930	39,802	1,528	237	267*	58	30.83
19	J. H. Edrich........	1956–1978	39,790	979	104	310*	103	45.47
20	R. E. S. Wyatt......	1923–1957	39,405	1,141	157	232	85	40.04
21	D. C. S. Compton ...	1936–1964	38,942	839	88	300	123	51.85
22	E. Tyldesley........	1909–1936	38,874	961	106	256*	102	45.46
23	J. T. Tyldesley	1895–1923	37,897	994	62	295*	86	40.66
24	K. W. R. Fletcher...	1962–1988	37,665	1,167	170	228*	63	37.77
25	C. G. Greenidge	1970–1992	37,354	889	75	273*	92	45.88
26	J. W. Hearne........	1909–1936	37,252	1,025	116	285*	96	40.98
27	L. E. G. Ames.......	1926–1951	37,248	951	95	295	102	43.51
28	D. Kenyon	1946–1967	37,002	1,159	59	259	74	33.63
29	W. J. Edrich........	1934–1958	36,965	964	92	267*	86	42.39
30	J. M. Parks	1949–1976	36,673	1,227	172	205*	51	34.76
31	M. W. Gatting	1975–1998	36,549	861	123	258	94	49.52
32	D. Denton..........	1894–1920	36,479	1,163	70	221	69	33.37
33	G. H. Hirst	1891–1929	36,323	1,215	151	341	60	34.13
34	I. V. A. Richards	*1971*–1993	36,212	796	63	322	114	49.40
35	A. Jones	1957–1983	36,049	1,168	72	204*	56	32.89
36	W. G. Quaife	1894–1928	36,012	1,203	185	255*	72	35.37
37	R. E. Marshall	*1945*–1972	35,725	1,053	59	228*	68	35.94

		Career	R	I	NO	HS	100s	Avge
38	G. Gunn	1902–1932	35,208	1,061	82	220	62	35.96
39	D. B. Close	1949–1986	34,994	1,225	173	198	52	33.26
40	Zaheer Abbas	*1965–1986*	34,843	768	92	274	108	51.54
41	J. G. Langridge	1928–1955	34,380	984	66	250*	76	37.45
42	G. M. Turner	*1964–1982*	34,346	792	101	311*	103	49.70
43	C. Washbrook	1933–1964	34,101	906	107	251*	76	42.67
44	M. Leyland	1920–1948	33,660	932	101	263	80	40.50
45	H. T. W. Hardinge	1902–1933	33,519	1,021	103	263*	75	36.51
46	**M. R. Ramprakash**	**1987–2009**	**33,244**	**701**	**89**	**301***	**108**	**54.32**
47	R. Abel	1881–1904	33,124	1,007	73	357*	74	35.46
48	A. I. Kallicharran	*1966–1990*	32,650	834	86	243*	87	43.64
49	A. J. Lamb	*1972–1995*	32,502	772	108	294	89	48.94
50	C. A. Milton	1948–1974	32,150	1,078	125	170	56	33.73
51	J. D. Robertson	1937–1959	31,914	897	46	331*	67	37.50
52	J. Hardstaff, jun	1930–1955	31,847	812	94	266	83	44.35
53	James Langridge	1924–1953	31,716	1,058	157	167	42	35.20
54	K. F. Barrington	1953–1968	31,714	831	136	256	76	45.63
55	C. H. Lloyd	*1963–1986*	31,232	730	96	242*	79	49.26
56	Mushtaq Mohammad	*1956–1985*	31,091	843	104	303*	72	42.07
57	C. B. Fry	*1892–1921*	30,886	658	43	258*	94	50.22
58	D. Brookes	1934–1959	30,874	925	70	257	71	36.10
59	P. Holmes	1913–1935	30,573	810	84	315*	67	42.11
60	R. T. Simpson	*1944*–1963	30,546	852	55	259	64	38.32
61 {	L. G. Berry	1924–1951	30,225	1,056	57	232	45	30.25
	K. G. Suttle	1949–1971	30,225	1,064	92	204*	49	31.09
63	P. A. Perrin	1896–1928	29,709	918	91	343*	66	35.92
64	R. B. Kanhai	*1954–1981*	29,250	675	83	256	86	49.40
65	P. F. Warner	1894–1929	29,028	875	75	244	60	36.28
66	J. O'Connor	1921–1939	28,764	903	79	248	72	34.90
67	Javed Miandad	*1973–1993*	28,647	631	95	311	80	53.44
68	T. E. Bailey	1945–1967	28,641	1,072	215	205	28	33.42
69	K. J. Barnett	1979–2002	28,593	784	76	239*	61	40.38
70	D. W. Randall	1972–1993	28,456	827	81	237	52	38.14
71	**J. L. Langer**	**1991–2009**	**28,382**	**622**	**57**	**342**	**86**	**50.23**
72	E. H. Bowley	1912–1934	28,378	859	47	283	52	34.94
73	B. A. Richards	*1964–1982*	28,358	576	58	356	80	54.74
74	G. S. Sobers	*1952–1974*	28,315	609	93	365*	86	54.87
75	A. E. Dipper	1908–1932	28,075	865	69	252*	53	35.27
76	D. G. Bradman	*1927–1948*	28,067	338	43	452*	117	95.14
77	J. H. Hampshire	1961–1984	28,059	924	112	183*	43	34.55
78	P. B. H. May	1948–1963	27,592	618	77	285*	85	51.00
79	R. T. Robinson	1978–1999	27,571	739	85	220*	63	42.15
80	B. F. Davison	*1967–1987*	27,453	766	79	189	53	39.96
81	Majid Khan	*1961–1984*	27,444	700	62	241	73	43.01
82	A. C. Russell	1908–1930	27,358	717	59	273	71	41.57
83	E. G. Hayes	1896–1926	27,318	896	48	276	48	32.21
84	A. E. Fagg	1932–1957	27,291	803	46	269*	58	36.05
85	James Seymour	1900–1926	27,237	911	62	218*	53	32.08
86	W. Larkins	1972–1995	27,142	842	54	252	59	34.44
87	A. R. Border	*1976–1995*	27,131	625	97	205	70	51.38
88	**S. G. Law**	**1988–2009**	**27,080**	**601**	**65**	**263**	**79**	**50.52**
89	P. H. Parfitt	1956–*1973*	26,924	845	104	200*	58	36.33
90	M. E. Waugh	1985–2003	26,855	591	75	229*	81	52.04
91	G. L. Jessop	1894–1914	26,698	855	37	286	53	32.63
92	K. S. McEwan	*1972–1991*	26,628	705	67	218	74	41.73
93	D. E. Davies	1924–1954	26,564	1,032	80	287*	32	27.90
94	A. Shrewsbury	1875–1902	26,505	813	90	267	59	36.65
95	M. J. Stewart	1954–1972	26,492	898	93	227*	49	32.90
96	C. T. Radley	1964–1987	26,441	880	134	200	46	35.44

		Career	R	I	NO	HS	100s	Avge
97	D. I. Gower.........	1975–1993	26,339	727	70	228	53	40.08
98	C. E. B. Rice........	1969–1993	26,331	766	123	246	48	40.95
99	A. J. Stewart........	1981–2003	26,165	734	81	271*	48	40.06
100	R. A. Smith........	1980–2003	26,155	717	87	209*	61	41.51

Bold type denotes those who played in the calendar year 2009.

Note: Some works of reference provide career figures which differ from those in this list, owing to the exclusion or inclusion of matches recognised or not recognised as first-class by *Wisden*.

Other Current Players with 20,000 Runs

	Career	R	I	NO	HS	100s	Avge
M. L. Hayden...........	1991–2008	24,603	515	47	380	79	52.57
J. P. Crawley	1990–2009	24,361	584	60	311*	54	46.49
M. J. Di Venuto	1991–2009	22,751	528	38	254*	54	46.43
S. R. Tendulkar	1988–2009	21,859	416	44	248*	70	58.76
R. Dravid	1990–2009	21,419	442	60	270	58	56.07
R. T. Ponting	1992–2009	20,397	407	54	257	72	57.78

HIGHEST CAREER AVERAGE

(Qualification: 10,000 runs)

Avge		Career	I	NO	R	HS	100s
95.14	D. G. Bradman	1927–1948	338	43	28,067	452*	117
71.22	V. M. Merchant	1929–1951	229	43	13,248	359*	44
67.46	Ajay Sharma	1984–2000	166	16	10,120	259*	38
65.18	W. H. Ponsford	1920–1934	235	23	13,819	437	47
64.99	W. M. Woodfull	1921–1934	245	39	13,388	284	49
58.76	**S. R. Tendulkar**	**1988–2009**	**416**	**44**	**21,859**	**248***	**70**
58.24	A. L. Hassett	1932–1953	322	32	16,890	232	59
58.19	V. S. Hazare	1934–1966	365	45	18,621	316*	60
57.83	D. S. Lehmann	1987–2007	479	33	25,795	339	82
57.78	**R. T. Ponting**	**1992–2009**	**407**	**54**	**20,397**	**257**	**72**
57.32	M. G. Bevan	1989–2006	400	66	19,147	216	68
57.22	A. F. Kippax	1918–1935	256	33	12,762	315*	43
56.83	G. Boycott	1962–1986	1,014	162	48,426	261*	151
56.55	C. L. Walcott	1941–1963	238	29	11,820	314*	40
56.37	K. S. Ranjitsinhji	1893–1920	500	62	24,692	285*	72
56.22	R. B. Simpson	1952–1977	436	62	21,029	359	60
56.10	W. R. Hammond	1920–1951	1,005	104	50,551	336*	167
56.07	**R. Dravid**	**1990–2009**	**442**	**60**	**21,419**	**270**	**58**
56.02	M. D. Crowe	1979–1995	412	62	19,608	299	71
55.51	L. Hutton	1934–1960	814	91	40,140	364	129
55.34	E. D. Weekes	1944–1964	241	24	12,010	304*	36
55.11	S. V. Manjrekar	1984–1997	217	31	10,252	377	31
55.06	**D. J. Hussey**	**2002–2009**	**211**	**21**	**10,462**	**275**	**36**
54.87	G. S. Sobers	1952–1974	609	93	28,315	365*	86
54.74	B. A. Richards	1964–1982	576	58	28,358	356	80
54.67	R. G. Pollock	1960–1986	437	54	20,940	274	64
54.56	**S. M. Katich**	**1996–2009**	**364**	**45**	**17,405**	**306**	**48**
54.32	**M. R. Ramprakash**	**1987–2009**	**701**	**89**	**33,244**	**301***	**108**
54.24	F. M. M. Worrell	1941–1964	326	49	15,025	308*	39
54.05	A. Flower	1986–2006	372	69	16,379	271*	49

Note: G. A. Headley (1927–1954) scored 9,921 runs, average 69.86.

Bold type denotes those who played in the calendar year 2009.

FASTEST FIFTIES

Minutes

11	C. I. J. Smith (66)	Middlesex v Gloucestershire at Bristol	1938
13	Khalid Mahmood (56)	Gujranwala v Sargodha at Gujranwala.	2000-01
14	S. J. Pegler (50)	South Africans v Tasmania at Launceston	1910-11
14	F. T. Mann (53)	Middlesex v Nottinghamshire at Lord's.	1921
14	H. B. Cameron (56)	Transvaal v Orange Free State at Johannesburg.	1934-35
14	C. I. J. Smith (52)	Middlesex v Kent at Maidstone	1935

Note: The number of balls taken to achieve fifties was rarely recorded until recently. C. I. J. Smith's two fifties (above) may have taken only 12 balls each. Khalid Mahmood reached his fifty in 15 balls.

Fifties scored in contrived circumstances and with the bowlers' compliance are excluded from the above list, including the fastest of them all, in 8 minutes (13 balls) by C. C. Inman, Leicestershire v Nottinghamshire at Nottingham, 1965, and 10 minutes by G. Chapple, Lancashire v Glamorgan at Manchester, 1993.

FASTEST HUNDREDS

Minutes

35	P. G. H. Fender (113*)	Surrey v Northamptonshire at Northampton	1920
40	G. L. Jessop (101)	Gloucestershire v Yorkshire at Harrogate	1897
40	Ahsan-ul-Haq (100*)	Muslims v Sikhs at Lahore.	1923-24
42	G. L. Jessop (191)	Gentlemen of South v Players of South at Hastings .	1907
43	A. H. Hornby (106)	Lancashire v Somerset at Manchester	1905
43	D. W. Hookes (107)	South Australia v Victoria at Adelaide.	1982-83
44	R. N. S. Hobbs (100)	Essex v Australians at Chelmsford.	1975

Notes: The fastest recorded authentic hundred in terms of balls received was scored off 34 balls by D. W. Hookes (above). Research of the scorebook has shown that P. G. H. Fender scored his hundred from between 40 and 46 balls. He contributed 113 to an unfinished sixth-wicket partnership of 171 in 42 minutes with H. A. Peach.

E. B. Alletson (Nottinghamshire) scored 189 out of 227 runs in 90 minutes against Sussex at Hove in 1911. It has been estimated that his last 139 runs took 37 minutes.

Hundreds scored in contrived circumstances and with the bowlers' compliance are excluded, including the fastest of them all, in 21 minutes (27 balls) by G. Chapple, Lancashire v Glamorgan at Manchester, 1993, 24 minutes (27 balls) by M. L. Pettini, Essex v Leicestershire at Leicester, 2006, and 26 minutes (36 balls) by T. M. Moody, Warwickshire v Glamorgan at Swansea, 1990.

FASTEST DOUBLE-HUNDREDS

Minutes

113	R. J. Shastri (200*)	Bombay v Baroda at Bombay	1984-85
120	G. L. Jessop (286)	Gloucestershire v Sussex at Hove	1903
120	C. H. Lloyd (201*)	West Indians v Glamorgan at Swansea	1976
130	G. L. Jessop (234)	Gloucestershire v Somerset at Bristol	1905
131	V. T. Trumper (293)	Australians v Canterbury at Christchurch	1913-14

FASTEST TRIPLE-HUNDREDS

Minutes

181	D. C. S. Compton (300)	MCC v North Eastern Transvaal at Benoni	1948-49
205	F. E. Woolley (305*)	MCC v Tasmania at Hobart	1911-12
205	C. G. Macartney (345)	Australians v Nottinghamshire at Nottingham.	1921
213	D. G. Bradman (369)	South Australia v Tasmania at Adelaide	1935-36

MOST RUNS IN A DAY BY ONE BATSMAN

390*	B. C. Lara	Warwickshire v Durham at Birmingham..........	1994
345	C. G. Macartney	Australians v Nottinghamshire at Nottingham......	1921
334	W. H. Ponsford	Victoria v New South Wales at Melbourne........	1926-27
333	K. S. Duleepsinhji	Sussex v Northamptonshire at Hove...........	1930
331*	J. D. Robertson	Middlesex v Worcestershire at Worcester.........	1949
325*	B. A. Richards	South Australia v Western Australia at Perth.......	1970-71

Note: These scores do not necessarily represent the complete innings. See pages 117–120.

There have been another 13 instances of a batsman scoring 300 runs in a day (see *Wisden 2003*, pages 278–279, for full list).

LONGEST INNINGS

Hrs	Mins			
16	55	R. Nayyar (271)	Himachal Pradesh v Jammu and Kashmir at Chamba.......................	1999-2000
16	10	Hanif Mohammad (337)	Pakistan v West Indies at Bridgetown.....	1957-58
		Hanif believes he batted 16 hours 39 minutes.		
14	38	G. Kirsten (275)	South Africa v England at Durban.......	1999-2000
13	**58**	**S. C. Cook (390)**	**Lions v Warriors at East London......**	**2009-10**
13	**41**	**S. S. Shukla (178*)**	**Uttar Pradesh v Tamil Nadu at Nagpur .**	**2008-09**
13	19	S. T. Jayasuriya (340)	Sri Lanka v India at Colombo...........	1997-98
13	17	L. Hutton (364)	England v Australia at The Oval.........	1938

Bold type denotes innings played since January 1, 2009.

1,000 RUNS IN MAY

	Runs	Avge
W. G. Grace, May 9 to May 30, 1895 (22 days)	1,016	112.88
Grace was 46 years old.		
W. R. Hammond, May 7 to May 31, 1927 (25 days)	1,042	74.42
Hammond scored his 1,000th run on May 28, thus equalling Grace's record of 22 days.		
C. Hallows, May 5 to May 31, 1928 (27 days)	1,000	125.00

1,000 RUNS IN APRIL AND MAY

	Runs	Avge
T. W. Hayward, April 16 to May 31, 1900	1,074	97.63
D. G. Bradman, April 30 to May 31, 1930	1,001	143.00
On April 30 Bradman was 75 not out.		
D. G. Bradman, April 30 to May 31, 1938	1,056	150.85
Bradman scored 258 on April 30, and his 1,000th run on May 27.		
W. J. Edrich, April 30 to May 31, 1938	1,010	84.16
Edrich was 21 not out on April 30. All his runs were scored at Lord's.		
G. M. Turner, April 24 to May 31, 1973	1,018	78.30
G. A. Hick, April 17 to May 29, 1988	1,019	101.90
Hick scored a record 410 runs in April, and his 1,000th run on May 28.		

MOST RUNS SCORED OFF AN OVER

(All instances refer to six-ball overs)

36	G. S. Sobers	off M. A. Nash, Nottinghamshire v Glamorgan at Swansea (six sixes)..	1968
36	R. J. Shastri	off Tilak Raj, Bombay v Baroda at Bombay (six sixes)......	1984-85
34	E. B. Alletson	off E. H. Killick, Nottinghamshire v Sussex at Hove (46604446; including two no-balls)............................	1911
34	F. C. Hayes	off M. A. Nash, Lancashire v Glamorgan at Swansea (646666)	1977

34†	A. Flintoff	off A. J. Tudor, Lancashire v Surrey at Manchester (64444660; including two no-balls)	1998
34	C. M. Spearman	off S. J. P. Moreton, Gloucestershire v Oxford UCCE at Oxford (666646)	2005
		This was Moreton's first over in first-class cricket.	
32	I. T. Botham	off I. R. Snook, England XI v Central Districts at Palmerston North (466466)	1983-84
32	P. W. G. Parker	off A. I. Kallicharran, Sussex v Warwickshire at Birmingham (466664)	1982
32	I. R. Redpath	off N. Rosendorff, Australians v Orange Free State at Bloemfontein (666464)	1969-70
32	C. C. Smart	off G. Hill, Glamorgan v Hampshire at Cardiff (664664)	1935
32	Khalid Mahmood	off Naved Latif, Gujranwala v Sargodha at Gujranwala (666662)	2000-01

† Altogether 38 runs were scored off this over, the two no-balls counting for two extra runs each under ECB regulations.

Notes: The following instances have been excluded because of the bowlers' compliance: 34 – M. P. Maynard off S. A. Marsh, Glamorgan v Kent at Swansea, 1992; 34 – G. Chapple off P. A. Cottey, Lancashire v Glamorgan at Manchester, 1993; 34 – F. B. Touzel off F. J. J. Viljoen, Western Province B v Griqualand West at Kimberley, 1993-94. Chapple scored a further 32 off Cottey's next over.

There were 35 runs off an over received by A. T. Reinholds off H. T. Davis, Auckland v Wellington at Auckland 1995-96, but this included 16 extras and only 19 off the bat.

In a match against KwaZulu-Natal at Stellenbosch in 2006-07, W. E. September (Boland) conceded 34 in an over: 27 to M. Bekker, six to K. Smit, plus one no-ball.

In a match against Canterbury at Christchurch in 1989-90, R. H. Vance (Wellington) deliberately conceded 77 runs in an over of full tosses which contained 17 no-balls and, owing to the umpire's understandable miscalculation, only five legitimate deliveries.

The greatest number of runs scored off an eight-ball over is 34 (40446664) by R. M. Edwards off M. C. Carew, Governor-General's XI v West Indians at Auckland, 1968-69.

MOST SIXES IN AN INNINGS

16	A. Symonds (254*)	Gloucestershire v Glamorgan at Abergavenny	1995
15	J. R. Reid (296)	Wellington v Northern Districts at Wellington	1962-63
14	Shakti Singh (128)	Himachal Pradesh v Haryana at Dharmsala	1990-91
14	D. J. Hussey (275)	Nottinghamshire v Essex at Nottingham	2007
13	Majid Khan (147*)	Pakistanis v Glamorgan at Swansea	1967
13	C. G. Greenidge (273*)	D. H. Robins' XI v Pakistanis at Eastbourne	1974
13	C. G. Greenidge (259)	Hampshire v Sussex at Southampton	1975
13	G. W. Humpage (254)	Warwickshire v Lancashire at Southport	1982
13	R. J. Shastri (200*)	Bombay v Baroda at Bombay	1984-85
12	Gulfraz Khan (207)	Railways v Universities at Lahore	1976-77
12	I. T. Botham (138*)	Somerset v Warwickshire at Birmingham	1985
12	R. A. Harper (234)	Northamptonshire v Gloucestershire at Northampton	1986
12	D. M. Jones (248)	Australians v Warwickshire at Birmingham	1989
12	U. N. K. Fernando (160)	Sinhalese SC v Sebastianites C and AC at Colombo	1990-91
12	D. N. Patel (204)	Auckland v Northern Districts at Auckland	1991-92
12	W. V. Raman (206)	Tamil Nadu v Kerala at Madras	1991-92
12	G. D. Lloyd (241)	Lancashire v Essex at Chelmsford	1996
12	Wasim Akram (257*)	Pakistan v Zimbabwe at Sheikhupura	1996-97
12	S. I. de Saram (188)	Ragama v Badureliya at Colombo	2007-08
12	K. J. O'Brien (171*)	Ireland v Kenya at Nairobi	2008
12	**H. G. J. M. Kulatunga (234)**	**Colts v Ragama at Colombo**	**2008-09**

Note: F. B. Touzel (128*) hit 13 sixes for Western Province B v Griqualand West in contrived circumstances at Kimberley in 1993-94.

Bold type denotes performances in the calendar year 2009.

MOST SIXES IN A MATCH

20	A. Symonds (254*, 76)	Gloucestershire v Glamorgan at Abergavenny	1995
17	W. J. Stewart (155, 125)	Warwickshire v Lancashire at Blackpool..............	1959

MOST SIXES IN A SEASON

80	I. T. Botham	1985	49	I. V. A. Richards	1985
66	A. W. Wellard................	1935	48	A. W. Carr..................	1925
57	A. W. Wellard................	1936	48	J. H. Edrich	1965
57	A. W. Wellard................	1938	48	A. Symonds.................	1995
51	A. W. Wellard................	1933			

MOST BOUNDARIES IN AN INNINGS

	4s/6s			
72	62/10	B. C. Lara (501*)	Warwickshire v Durham at Birmingham ..	1994
68	68/–	P. A. Perrin (343*)	Essex v Derbyshire at Chesterfield........	1904
65	64/1	A. C. MacLaren (424)	Lancashire v Somerset at Taunton	1895
64	64/–	Hanif Mohammad (499)	Karachi v Bahawalpur at Karachi	1958-59
57	52/5	J. H. Edrich (310*)	England v New Zealand at Leeds........	1965
57	52/5	Naved Latif (394)	Sargodha v Gujranwala at Gujranwala....	2000-01
55	55/–	C. W. Gregory (383)	NSW v Queensland at Brisbane	1906-07
55	53/2	G. R. Marsh (355*)	W. Australia v S. Australia at Perth	1989-90
55	51/3†	S. V. Manjrekar (377)	Bombay v Hyderabad at Bombay	1990-91
55	52/3	D. S. Lehmann (339)	Yorkshire v Durham at Leeds	2006
55	**54/1**	**D. K. H. Mitchell (298)**	**Worcestershire v Somerset at Taunton .**	**2009**
54	53/1	G. H. Hirst (341)	Yorkshire v Leicestershire at Leicester ...	1905
54	**53/1**	**S. C. Cook (390)**	**Lions v Warriors at East London ......**	**2009-10**
53	53/–	A. W. Nourse (304*)	Natal v Transvaal at Johannesburg.......	1919-20
53	45/8	K. R. Rutherford (317)	New Zealanders v D. B. Close's XI at Scarborough.....................	1986
53	51/2	V. V. S. Laxman (353)	Hyderabad v Karnataka at Bangalore.....	1999-2000
53	52/1	M. W. Goodwin (335*)	Sussex v Leicestershire at Hove.........	2003
52	47/5	N. H. Fairbrother (366)	Lancashire v Surrey at The Oval	1990
52	50/2	C. J. L. Rogers (319)	Northamptonshire v Gloucestershire at Northampton....................	2006
51	51/–	W. G. Grace (344)	MCC v Kent at Canterbury	1876
51	47/4	C. G. Macartney (345)	Australians v Notts at Nottingham.......	1921
51	50/1	B. B. Nimbalkar (443*)	Maharashtra v Kathiawar at Poona	1948-49
51	49/2	G. A. Hick (315*)	Worcestershire v Durham at Worcester ...	2002
51	50/1	Salman Butt (290)	Punjab v Federal Areas at Lahore	2007-08
51	**44/7**	**Sunny Singh (312)**	**Haryana v Madhya Pradesh at Indore .**	**2009-10**
50	47/–‡	A. Ducat (306*)	Surrey v Oxford U. at The Oval.........	1919
50	46/4	D. G. Bradman (369)	S. Australia v Tasmania at Adelaide	1935-36
50	35/15	J. R. Reid (296)	Wellington v N. Districts at Wellington...	1962-63
50	42/8	I. V. A. Richards (322)	Somerset v Warwickshire at Taunton.....	1985
50	50/–	Shoaib Khan (300*)	Peshawar v Quetta at Peshawar	2003-04

† *Plus one five.*
‡ *Plus three fives.*

Bold type denotes performances in the calendar year 2009.

PARTNERSHIPS OVER 500

624	for 3rd	K. C. Sangakkara (287) and D. P. M. D. Jayawardene (374), Sri Lanka v South Africa at Colombo	2006
580	**for 2nd**	**Rafatullah Mohmand (302*) and Aamer Sajjad (289), WAPDA v Sui Southern Gas at Sheikhupura**	**2009-10**
577	for 4th	V. S. Hazare (288) and Gul Mahomed (319), Baroda v Holkar at Baroda .	1946-47
576	for 2nd	S. T. Jayasuriya (340) and R. S. Mahanama (225), Sri Lanka v India at Colombo	1997-98
574*	for 4th	F. M. M. Worrell (255*) and C. L. Walcott (314*), Barbados v Trinidad at Port-of-Spain	1945-46
561	for 1st	Waheed Mirza (324) and Mansoor Akhtar (224*), Karachi Whites v Quetta at Karachi	1976-77
555	for 1st	P. Holmes (224*) and H. Sutcliffe (313), Yorkshire v Essex at Leyton ...	1932
554	for 1st	J. T. Brown (300) and J. Tunnicliffe (243), Yorkshire v Derbyshire at Chesterfield	1898
520*	for 5th	C. A. Pujara (302*) and R. A. Jadeja (232*), Saurashtra v Orissa at Rajkot	2008-09
502*	for 4th	F. M. M. Worrell (308*) and J. D. C. Goddard (218*), Barbados v Trinidad at Bridgetown	1943-44

HIGHEST PARTNERSHIPS FOR EACH WICKET

The following lists include all stands above 400; otherwise the top ten for each wicket.

First Wicket

561	Waheed Mirza and Mansoor Akhtar, Karachi Whites v Quetta at Karachi	1976-77
555	P. Holmes and H. Sutcliffe, Yorkshire v Essex at Leyton	1932
554	J. T. Brown and J. Tunnicliffe, Yorkshire v Derbyshire at Chesterfield........	1898
490	E. H. Bowley and J. G. Langridge, Sussex v Middlesex at Hove.............	1933
464	R. Sehgal and R. Lamba, Delhi v Himachal Pradesh at Delhi	1994-95
462	M. Vijay and A. Mukund, Tamil Nadu v Maharashtra at Nasik..............	2008-09
459	Wasim Jaffer and S. K. Kulkarni, Mumbai v Saurashtra at Rajkot	1996-97
456	E. R. Mayne and W. H. Ponsford, Victoria v Queensland at Melbourne	1923-24
451*	S. Desai and R. M. H. Binny, Karnataka v Kerala at Chikmagalur	1977-78
431	M. R. J. Veletta and G. R. Marsh, Western Australia v South Australia at Perth .	1989-90
428	J. B. Hobbs and A. Sandham, Surrey v Oxford University at The Oval.......	1926
428	**P. J. Ingram and J. M. How, Central Districts v Wellington at Wellington** .	**2009-10**
425*	L. V. Garrick and C. H. Gayle, Jamaica v West Indies B at Montego Bay	2000-01
424	I. J. Siedle and J. F. W. Nicolson, Natal v Orange Free State at Bloemfontein ..	1926-27
421	S. M. Gavaskar and G. A. Parkar, Bombay v Bengal at Bombay.............	1981-82
418	Kamal Najamuddin and Khalid Alvi, Karachi v Railways at Karachi	1980-81
415	N. D. McKenzie and G. C. Smith, South Africa v Bangladesh at Chittagong	2007-08
413	V. Mankad and Pankaj Roy, India v New Zealand at Madras	1955-56
410	V. Sehwag and R. Dravid, India v Pakistan at Lahore	2005-06
406*	D. J. Bicknell and G. E. Welton, Notts v Warwickshire at Birmingham	2000
405	C. P. S. Chauhan and M. S. Gupte, Maharashtra v Vidarbha at Poona	1972-73
403	Rizwan-uz-Zaman and Shoaib Mohammad, PIA v Hyderabad at Hyderabad ...	1999-2000

Second Wicket

580	**Rafatullah Mohmand and Aamer Sajjad, WAPDA v Sui Southern Gas at Sheikhupura**	**2009-10**
576	S. T. Jayasuriya and R. S. Mahanama, Sri Lanka v India at Colombo.........	1997-98
475	Zahir Alam and L. S. Rajput, Assam v Tripura at Gauhati..................	1991-92
465*	J. A. Jameson and R. B. Kanhai, Warwicks v Gloucestershire at Birmingham. .	1974
455	K. V. Bhandarkar and B. B. Nimbalkar, Maharashtra v Kathiawar at Poona....	1948-49
451	W. H. Ponsford and D. G. Bradman, Australia v England at The Oval........	1934
446	C. C. Hunte and G. S. Sobers, West Indies v Pakistan at Kingston	1957-58

441	C. C. Bradfield and J. D. C. Bryant, E. Province v North West at Potchefstroom	2002-03
438	M. S. Atapattu and K. C. Sangakkara, Sri Lanka v Zimbabwe at Bulawayo	2003-04
431	Yasir Hameed and Asad Shafiq, NWFP v Baluchistan at Peshawar.	2007-08
429*	J. G. Dewes and G. H. G. Doggart, Cambridge U. v Essex at Cambridge	1949
426	Arshad Pervez and Mohsin Khan, Habib Bank v Income Tax at Lahore	1977-78
417	K. J. Barnett and T. A. Tweats, Derbyshire v Yorkshire at Derby	1997
415	A. Jadeja and S. V. Manjrekar, Indians v Bowl XI at Springs	1992-93
403	G. A. Gooch and P. J. Prichard, Essex v Leicestershire at Chelmsford	1990

Third Wicket

624	K. C. Sangakkara and D. P. M. D. Jayawardene, Sri Lanka v South Africa at Colombo	2006
467	A. H. Jones and M. D. Crowe, New Zealand v Sri Lanka at Wellington	1990-91
459	C. J. L. Rogers and M. J. North, Western Australia v Victoria at Perth	2006-07
456	Khalid Irtiza and Aslam Ali, United Bank v Multan at Karachi.	1975-76
451	Mudassar Nazar and Javed Miandad, Pakistan v India at Hyderabad.	1982-83
445	P. E. Whitelaw and W. N. Carson, Auckland v Otago at Dunedin.	1936-37
438*	G. A. Hick and T. M. Moody, Worcestershire v Hampshire at Southampton . . .	1997
436*	D. L. Maddy and B. J. Hodge, Leics v Loughborough UCCE at Leicester	2003
436	S. S. Das and S. S. Raul, Orissa v Bengal at Baripada.	2001-02
434	J. B. Stollmeyer and G. E. Gomez, Trinidad v British Guiana at Port-of-Spain .	1946-47
429*	J. A. Rudolph and H. H. Dippenaar, South Africa v Bangladesh at Chittagong .	2003
424*	W. J. Edrich and D. C. S. Compton, Middlesex v Somerset at Lord's.	1948
417	G. A. Hick and B. F. Smith, Worcestershire v Gloucestershire at Worcester. . . .	2004
413	D. J. Bicknell and D. M. Ward, Surrey v Kent at Canterbury	1990
410*	R. S. Modi and L. Amarnath, India in England v The Rest at Calcutta	1946-47
409	V. V. S. Laxman and R. Dravid, South Zone v West Zone at Surat.	2000-01
408	S. Oberoi and D. R. Fox, Oxford U. v Cambridge U. at Cambridge	2005
406*	R. S. Gavaskar and S. J. Kalyani, Bengal v Tripura at Agartala.	1999-2000
405	A. Jadeja and A. S. Kaypee, Haryana v Services at Faridabad.	1991-92
404	**M. R. Ramprakash and S. J. Walters, Surrey v Leicestershire at The Oval.**	**2009**
403	M. R. Ramprakash and M. A. Butcher, Surrey v Sussex at Hove	2007

Fourth Wicket

577	V. S. Hazare and Gul Mahomed, Baroda v Holkar at Baroda	1946-47
574*	C. L. Walcott and F. M. M. Worrell, Barbados v Trinidad at Port-of-Spain	1945-46
502*	F. M. M. Worrell and J. D. C. Goddard, Barbados v Trinidad at Bridgetown . . .	1943-44
470	A. I. Kallicharran and G. W. Humpage, Warwicks v Lancs at Southport	1982
462*	D. W. Hookes and W. B. Phillips, South Australia v Tasmania at Adelaide	1986-87
448	R. Abel and T. W. Hayward, Surrey v Yorkshire at The Oval.	1899
437	**D. P. M. D. Jayawardene and T. T. Samaraweera, Sri Lanka v Pakistan at Karachi.**	**2008-09**
436	S. Abbas Ali and P. K. Dwevedi, Madhya Pradesh v Railways at Indore	1997-98
425*	A. Dale and I. V. A. Richards, Glamorgan v Middlesex at Cardiff	1993
424	I. S. Lee and S. O. Quin, Victoria v Tasmania at Melbourne	1933-34
411	P. B. H. May and M. C. Cowdrey, England v West Indies at Birmingham	1957
410	G. Abraham and P. Balan Pandit, Kerala v Andhra at Palghat.	1959-60
402	W. Watson and T. W. Graveney, MCC v British Guiana at Georgetown	1953-54
402	R. B. Kanhai and K. Ibadulla, Warwicks v Notts at Nottingham	1968

Fifth Wicket

520*	C. A. Pujara and R. A. Jadeja, Saurashtra v Orissa at Rajkot.	2008-09
479	**Misbah-ul-Haq and Usman Arshad, Sui Northern Gas v Lahore Shalimar at Lahore**	**2009-10**
464*	M. E. Waugh and S. R. Waugh, New South Wales v Western Australia at Perth	1990-91
420	Mohammad Ashraful and Marshall Ayub, Dhaka v Chittagong at Chittagong . .	2006-07
410*	A. Chopra and S. Badrinath, India A v South Africa A at Delhi	2007-08
405	S. G. Barnes and D. G. Bradman, Australia v England at Sydney	1946-47

401	M. B. Loye and D. Ripley, Northamptonshire v Glamorgan at Northampton ...	1998
397	W. Bardsley and C. Kelleway, New South Wales v South Australia at Sydney...	1920-21
393	E. G. Arnold and W. B. Burns, Worcestershire v Warwickshire at Birmingham.	1909
391	A. Malhotra and S. Dogra, Delhi v Services at Delhi......................	1995-96

Sixth Wicket

487*	G. A. Headley and C. C. Passailaigue, Jamaica v Lord Tennyson's XI at Kingston..	1931-32
428	W. W. Armstrong and M. A. Noble, Australians v Sussex at Hove...........	1902
411	R. M. Poore and E. G. Wynyard, Hampshire v Somerset at Taunton..........	1899
376	R. Subba Row and A. Lightfoot, Northamptonshire v Surrey at The Oval	1958
372*	K. P. Pietersen and J. E. Morris, Nottinghamshire v Derbyshire at Derby......	2001
371	V. M. Merchant and R. S. Modi, Bombay v Maharashtra at Bombay..........	1943-44
365	B. C. Lara and R. D. Jacobs, West Indians v Australia A at Hobart...........	2000-01
365	**S. C. Cook and T. L. Tsolekile, Lions v Warriors at East London.**	**2009-10**
356	W. V. Raman and A. Kripal Singh, Tamil Nadu v Goa at Panjim.............	1988-89
353	Salah-ud-Din and Zaheer Abbas, Karachi v East Pakistan at Karachi	1968-69

Seventh Wicket

460	Bhupinder Singh, jun. and P. Dharmani, Punjab v Delhi at Delhi.............	1994-95
347	D. St E. Atkinson and C. C. Depeiza, West Indies v Australia at Bridgetown...	1954-55
344	K. S. Ranjitsinhji and W. Newham, Sussex v Essex at Leyton	1902
340	K. J. Key and H. Philipson, Oxford University v Middlesex at Chiswick Park ..	1887
336	F. C. W. Newman and C. R. N. Maxwell, Sir J. Cahn's XI v Leicestershire at Nottingham......................................	1935
335	C. W. Andrews and E. C. Bensted, Queensland v New South Wales at Sydney .	1934-35
325	G. Brown and C. H. Abercrombie, Hampshire v Essex at Leyton	1913
323	E. H. Hendren and L. F. Townsend, MCC v Barbados at Bridgetown..........	1929-30
315	D. M. Benkenstein and O. D. Gibson, Durham v Yorkshire at Leeds	2006
308	Waqar Hassan and Imtiaz Ahmed, Pakistan v New Zealand at Lahore	1955-56

Eighth Wicket

433	A. Sims and V. T. Trumper, A. Sims' Aust. XI v Canterbury at Christchurch...	1913-14
313	Wasim Akram and Saqlain Mushtaq, Pakistan v Zimbabwe at Sheikhupura....	1996-97
292	R. Peel and Lord Hawke, Yorkshire v Warwickshire at Birmingham	1896
291	R. S. C. Martin-Jenkins and M. J. G. Davis, Sussex v Somerset at Taunton	2002
270	V. T. Trumper and E. P. Barbour, New South Wales v Victoria at Sydney......	1912-13
268	S. Sriram and M. R. Srinivas, Tamil Nadu v Punjab at Mohali	2002-03
263	D. R. Wilcox and R. M. Taylor, Essex v Warwickshire at Southend..........	1946
257	N. Pothas and A. J. Bichel, Hampshire v Gloucestershire at Cheltenham	2005
256	S. P. Fleming and J. E. C. Franklin, New Zealand v S. Africa at Cape Town ...	2005-06
255	E. A. V. Williams and E. A. Martindale, Barbados v Trinidad at Bridgetown...	1935-36

Ninth Wicket

283	A. Warren and J. Chapman, Derbyshire v Warwickshire at Blackwell	1910
268	J. B. Commins and N. Boje, South Africa A v Mashonaland at Harare........	1994-95
251	J. W. H. T. Douglas and S. N. Hare, Essex v Derbyshire at Leyton...........	1921
249*†	A. S. Srivastava and K. Seth, Madhya Pradesh v Vidarbha at Indore	2000-01
246	T. T. Bresnan and N. Gillespie, Yorkshire v Surrey at The Oval	2007
245	V. S. Hazare and N. D. Nagarwalla, Maharashtra v Baroda at Poona	1939-40
244*	Arshad Ayub and M. V. Ramanamurthy, Hyderabad v Bihar at Hyderabad	1986-87
239	H. B. Cave and I. B. Leggat, Central Districts v Otago at Dunedin	1952-53
233	**I. J. L. Trott and J. S. Patel, Warwickshire v Yorkshire at Birmingham** ...	**2009**
232	C. Hill and E. Walkley, South Australia v New South Wales at Adelaide	1900-01

† *276 unbeaten runs were scored for this wicket in two separate partnerships; after Srivastava retired hurt, Seth and N. D. Hirwani added 27.*

Tenth Wicket

307	A. F. Kippax and J. E. H. Hooker, New South Wales v Victoria at Melbourne . .	1928-29
249	C. T. Sarwate and S. N. Banerjee, Indians v Surrey at The Oval	1946
239	Aqeel Arshad and Ali Raza, Lahore Whites v Hyderabad at Lahore	2004-05
235	F. E. Woolley and A. Fielder, Kent v Worcestershire at Stourbridge.	1909
233	Ajay Sharma and Maninder Singh, Delhi v Bombay at Bombay	1991-92
230	R. W. Nicholls and W. Roche, Middlesex v Kent at Lord's	1899
228	R. Illingworth and K. Higgs, Leicestershire v Northamptonshire at Leicester . . .	1977
219	D. J. Thornely and S. C. G. MacGill, New South Wales v Western Australia at Sydney	2004-05
218	F. H. Vigar and T. P. B. Smith, Essex v Derbyshire at Chesterfield.	1947
214	N. V. Knight and A. Richardson, Warwickshire v Hampshire at Birmingham . .	2002

Note: There have been only 11 last-wicket stands of 200 or more, the 11th being 211 by M. Ellis and T. J. Hastings for Victoria v South Australia at Melbourne in 1902-03.

Bold type denotes partnerships in the calendar year 2009.

UNUSUAL DISMISSALS

Handled the Ball

There have been **55** instances in first-class cricket. The most recent are:

G. A. Gooch	England v Australia at Manchester.	1993
A. C. Waller	Mashonaland CD v Mashonaland Under-24 at Harare	1994-95
K. M. Krikken	Derbyshire v Indians at Derby	1996
A. Badenhorst	Eastern Province B v North West at Fochville.	1998-99
S. R. Waugh	Australia v India at Chennai.	2000-01
M. P. Vaughan	England v India at Bangalore.	2001-02
Tushar Imran	Bangladesh A v Jamaica at Spanish Town.	2001-02
Al Sahariar	Dhaka v Chittagong at Dhaka	2003-04
Junaid Zia	Rawalpindi v Lahore at Lahore	2003-04
D. J. Watson	Dolphins v Eagles at Bloemfontein	2004-05
M. Zondeki	Cape Cobras v Eagles at Bloemfontein	2006-07
L. N. Mosena	Free State v Limpopo at Bloemfontein	2006-07

Obstructing the Field

There have been **22** instances in first-class cricket. T. Straw of Worcestershire was given out for obstruction v Warwickshire in both 1899 and 1901. The last occurrence in England involved K. Ibadulla of Warwickshire v Hampshire at Coventry in 1963. The most recent are:

Arshad Ali	Sukkur v Quetta at Quetta	1983-84
H. R. Wasu	Vidarbha v Rajasthan at Akola.	1984-85
Khalid Javed	Railways v Lahore at Lahore	1985-86
C. Binduhewa	Singha SC v Sinhalese SC at Colombo	1990-91
S. J. Kalyani	Bengal v Orissa at Calcutta	1994-95
R. C. Rupasinghe	Rio v Kurunegala Youth at Colombo.	2001-02
K. N. S. Fernando	Lankan v Army at Welisara	2006-07
H. R. Jadhav	Baroda v Uttar Pradesh at Baroda	2006-07
Riaz Kail	**Abbottabad v Quetta at Abbottabad**	**2009-10**

Bold type denotes dismissals since January 1, 2009.

Hit the Ball Twice

There have been **21** instances in first-class cricket. The last occurrence in England involved J. H. King of Leicestershire v Surrey at The Oval in 1906. The most recent are:

Aziz Malik	Lahore Division v Faisalabad at Sialkot.	1984-85
Javed Mohammad	Multan v Karachi Whites at Sahiwal	1986-87
Shahid Pervez	Jammu and Kashmir v Punjab at Srinagar	1986-87
Ali Naqvi	PNSC v National Bank at Faisalabad.	1998-99
A. George	Tamil Nadu v Maharashtra at Pune	1998-99
Maqsood Raza	Lahore Division v PNSC at Sheikhupura.	1999-2000
D. Mahajan	Jammu and Kashmir v Bihar at Jammu	2005-06

Timed Out

There have been **four** instances in first-class cricket:

A. Jordaan	Eastern Province v Transvaal at Port Elizabeth (SACB match). . . .	1987-88
H. Yadav	Tripura v Orissa at Cuttack.	1997-98
V. C. Drakes	Border v Free State at East London	2002-03
A. J. Harris	Nottinghamshire v Durham UCCE at Nottingham.	2003

BOWLING RECORDS

TEN WICKETS IN AN INNINGS

In the history of first-class cricket, there have been **80** instances of a bowler taking all ten wickets in an innings:

	O	M	R		
E. Hinkly (Kent)				v England at Lord's.	1848
*J. Wisden (North)				v South at Lord's.	1850
V. E. Walker (England)	43	17	74	v Surrey at The Oval.	1859
V. E. Walker (Middlesex).	44.2	5	104	v Lancashire at Manchester	1865
G. Wootton (All England)	31.3	9	54	v Yorkshire at Sheffield	1865
W. Hickton (Lancashire).	36.2	19	46	v Hampshire at Manchester	1870
S. E. Butler (Oxford).	24.1	11	38	v Cambridge at Lord's	1871
James Lillywhite (South)	60.2	22	129	v North at Canterbury	1872
A. Shaw (MCC)	36.2	8	73	v North at Lord's.	1874
E. Barratt (Players)	29	11	43	v Australians at The Oval	1878
G. Giffen (Australian XI)	26	10	66	v The Rest at Sydney	1883-84
W. G. Grace (MCC)	36.2	17	49	v Oxford University at Oxford . . .	1886
G. Burton (Middlesex)	52.3	25	59	v Surrey at The Oval.	1888
†A. E. Moss (Canterbury).	21.3	10	28	v Wellington at Christchurch	1889-90
S. M. J. Woods (Cambridge U.) . .	31	6	69	v Thornton's XI at Cambridge . . .	1890
T. Richardson (Surrey)	15.3	3	45	v Essex at The Oval	1894
H. Pickett (Essex)	27	11	32	v Leicestershire at Leyton	1895
E. J. Tyler (Somerset)	34.3	15	49	v Surrey at Taunton.	1895
W. P. Howell (Australians).	23.2	14	28	v Surrey at The Oval.	1899
C. H. G. Bland (Sussex)	25.2	10	48	v Kent at Tonbridge	1899
J. Briggs (Lancashire).	28.5	7	55	v Worcestershire at Manchester . .	1900
A. E. Trott (Middlesex).	14.2	5	42	v Somerset at Taunton	1900
A. Fielder (Players).	24.5	1	90	v Gentlemen at Lord's	1906
E. G. Dennett (Gloucestershire) . .	19.4	7	40	v Essex at Bristol	1906
A. E. E. Vogler (E. Province)	12	2	26	v Griqualand W. at Johannesburg. .	1906-07
C. Blythe (Kent)	16	7	30	v Northants at Northampton	1907
J. B. King (Philadelphia).	18.1	7	53	v Ireland at Haverford‡.	1909
A. Drake (Yorkshire)	8.5	0	35	v Somerset at Weston-s-Mare. . . .	1914
W. Bestwick (Derbyshire)	19	2	40	v Glamorgan at Cardiff.	1921
A. A. Mailey (Australians).	28.4	5	66	v Gloucestershire at Cheltenham. .	1921
C. W. L. Parker (Glos.).	40.3	13	79	v Somerset at Bristol.	1921
T. Rushby (Surrey)	17.5	4	43	v Somerset at Taunton	1921

	O	M	R		
J. C. White (Somerset)	42.2	11	76	v Worcestershire at Worcester	1921
G. C. Collins (Kent)	19.3	4	65	v Nottinghamshire at Dover	1922
H. Howell (Warwickshire)	25.1	5	51	v Yorkshire at Birmingham	1923
A. S. Kennedy (Players)	22.4	10	37	v Gentlemen at The Oval	1927
G. O. B. Allen (Middlesex)	25.3	10	40	v Lancashire at Lord's	1929
A. P. Freeman (Kent)	42	9	131	v Lancashire at Maidstone	1929
G. Geary (Leicestershire)	16.2	8	18	v Glamorgan at Pontypridd	1929
C. V. Grimmett (Australians)	22.3	8	37	v Yorkshire at Sheffield	1930
A. P. Freeman (Kent)	30.4	8	53	v Essex at Southend	1930
H. Verity (Yorkshire)	18.4	6	36	v Warwickshire at Leeds	1931
A. P. Freeman (Kent)	36.1	9	79	v Lancashire at Manchester	1931
V. W. C. Jupp (Northants)	39	6	127	v Kent at Tunbridge Wells	1932
H. Verity (Yorkshire)	19.4	16	10	v Nottinghamshire at Leeds	1932
T. W. Wall (South Australia)	12.4	2	36	v New South Wales at Sydney	1932-33
T. B. Mitchell (Derbyshire)	19.1	4	64	v Leicestershire at Leicester	1935
J. Mercer (Glamorgan)	26	10	51	v Worcestershire at Worcester	1936
T. W. J. Goddard (Glos.)	28.4	4	113	v Worcestershire at Cheltenham	1937
T. F. Smailes (Yorkshire)	17.1	5	47	v Derbyshire at Sheffield	1939
E. A. Watts (Surrey)	24.1	8	67	v Warwickshire at Birmingham	1939
*W. E. Hollies (Warwickshire)	20.4	4	49	v Notts at Birmingham	1946
J. M. Sims (East)	18.4	2	90	v West at Kingston	1948
T. E. Bailey (Essex)	39.4	9	90	v Lancashire at Clacton	1949
J. K. Graveney (Glos.)	18.4	2	66	v Derbyshire at Chesterfield	1949
R. Berry (Lancashire)	36.2	9	102	v Worcestershire at Blackpool	1953
S. P. Gupte (President's XI)	24.2	7	78	v Combined XI at Bombay	1954-55
J. C. Laker (Surrey)	46	18	88	v Australians at The Oval	1956
J. C. Laker (England)	51.2	23	53	v Australia at Manchester	1956
G. A. R. Lock (Surrey)	29.1	18	54	v Kent at Blackheath	1956
K. Smales (Nottinghamshire)	41.3	20	66	v Gloucestershire at Stroud	1956
P. M. Chatterjee (Bengal)	19	11	20	v Assam at Jorhat	1956-57
J. D. Bannister (Warwickshire)	23.3	11	41	v Comb. Services at Birmingham§	1959
A. J. G. Pearson (Cambridge U.)	30.3	8	78	v Leics at Loughborough	1961
N. I. Thomson (Sussex)	34.2	19	49	v Warwickshire at Worthing	1964
P. J. Allan (Queensland)	15.6	3	61	v Victoria at Melbourne	1965-66
I. J. Brayshaw (W. Australia)	17.6	4	44	v Victoria at Perth	1967-68
Shahid Mahmood (Karachi Whites)	25	5	58	v Khairpur at Karachi	1969-70
E. E. Hemmings (International XI)	49.3	14	175	v West Indies XI at Kingston	1982-83
P. Sunderam (Rajasthan)	22	5	78	v Vidarbha at Jodhpur	1985-86
S. T. Jefferies (W. Province)	22.5	7	59	v Orange Free State at Cape Town	1987-88
Imran Adil (Bahawalpur)	22.5	3	92	v Faisalabad at Faisalabad	1989-90
G. P. Wickremasinghe (Sinhalese)	19.2	5	41	v Kalutara at Colombo	1991-92
R. L. Johnson (Middlesex)	18.5	6	45	v Derbyshire at Derby	1994
Naeem Akhtar (Rawalpindi B)	21.3	10	28	v Peshawar at Peshawar	1995-96
A. Kumble (India)	26.3	9	74	v Pakistan at Delhi	1998-99
D. S. Mohanty (East Zone)	19	5	46	v South Zone at Agartala	2000-01
O. D. Gibson (Durham)	17.3	1	47	v Hampshire at Chester-le-Street	2007
M. W. Olivier (Warriors)	26.3	4	65	v Eagles at Bloemfontein	2007-08
Zulfiqar Babar (Multan)	**39.4**	**3**	**143**	**v Islamabad at Multan**	**2009-10**

Note: In addition, the following instances were achieved in 12-a-side matches:

	O	M	R		
E. M. Grace (MCC)	32.2	7	69	v Gents of Kent at Canterbury	1862
W. G. Grace (MCC)	46.1	15	92	v Kent at Canterbury	1873
†D. C. S. Hinds (A. B. St Hill's XII)	19.1	6	36	v Trinidad at Port-of-Spain	1900-01

* J. Wisden and W. E. Hollies achieved the feat without the direct assistance of a fielder. Wisden's ten were all bowled; Hollies bowled seven and had three lbw.

† On debut in first-class cricket.   ‡ Pennsylvania.   § Mitchells & Butlers Ground.

Bold type denotes performances in the calendar year 2009.

OUTSTANDING BOWLING ANALYSES

	O	M	R	W		
H. Verity (Yorkshire)	19.4	16	10	10	v Nottinghamshire at Leeds . . .	1932
G. Elliott (Victoria)	19	17	2	9	v Tasmania at Launceston	1857-58
Ahad Khan (Railways)	6.3	4	7	9	v Dera Ismail Khan at Lahore .	1964-65
J. C. Laker (England)	14	12	2	8	v The Rest at Bradford.	1950
D. Shackleton (Hampshire)	11.1	7	4	8	v Somerset at Weston-s-Mare .	1955
E. Peate (Yorkshire)	16	11	5	8	v Surrey at Holbeck	1883
K. M. Dabengwa (Westerns) . . .	4.4	3	1	7	v Northerns at Harare.	2006-07
F. R. Spofforth (Australians) . . .	8.3	6	3	7	v England XI at Birmingham .	1884
W. A. Henderson (NE Transvaal)	9.3	7	4	7	v OFS at Bloemfontein	1937-38
Rajinder Goel (Haryana)	7	4	4	7	v Jammu and Kashmir at Chandigarh.	1977-78
N. W. Bracken (NSW)	7	5	4	7	v South Australia at Sydney. . .	2004-05
V. I. Smith (South Africans) . . .	4.5	3	1	6	v Derbyshire at Derby	1947
S. Cosstick (Victoria)	21.1	20	1	6	v Tasmania at Melbourne	1868-69
Israr Ali (Bahawalpur).	11	10	1	6	v Dacca U. at Bahawalpur	1957-58
A. D. Pougher (MCC)	3	3	0	5	v Australians at Lord's.	1896
G. R. Cox (Sussex)	6	6	0	5	v Somerset at Weston-s-Mare .	1921
R. K. Tyldesley (Lancashire). . .	5	5	0	5	v Leicestershire at Manchester	1924
P. T. Mills (Gloucestershire) . . .	6.4	6	0	5	v Somerset at Bristol	1928

MOST WICKETS IN A MATCH

19-90	J. C. Laker	England v Australia at Manchester	1956
17-48†	C. Blythe	Kent v Northamptonshire at Northampton.	1907
17-50	C. T. B. Turner	Australians v England XI at Hastings	1888
17-54	W. P. Howell	Australians v Western Province at Cape Town	1902-03
17-56	C. W. L. Parker	Gloucestershire v Essex at Gloucester.	1925
17-67	A. P. Freeman	Kent v Sussex at Hove	1922
17-89	W. G. Grace	Gloucestershire v Nottinghamshire at Cheltenham . . .	1877
17-89	F. C. L. Matthews	Nottinghamshire v Northants at Nottingham	1923
17-91	H. Dean	Lancashire v Yorkshire at Liverpool	1913
17-91†	H. Verity	Yorkshire v Essex at Leyton	1933
17-92	A. P. Freeman	Kent v Warwickshire at Folkestone	1932
17-103	W. Mycroft	Derbyshire v Hampshire at Southampton	1876
17-106	G. R. Cox	Sussex v Warwickshire at Horsham.	1926
17-106†	T. W. J. Goddard	Gloucestershire v Kent at Bristol	1939
17-119	W. Mead	Essex v Hampshire at Southampton	1895
17-137	W. Brearley	Lancashire v Somerset at Manchester	1905
17-137	J. M. Davison	Canada v USA at Fort Lauderdale	2004
17-159	S. F. Barnes	England v South Africa at Johannesburg	1913-14
17-201	G. Giffen	South Australia v Victoria at Adelaide	1885-86
17-212	J. C. Clay	Glamorgan v Worcestershire at Swansea.	1937

† *Achieved in a single day.*

Note: H. Arkwright took 18-96 for MCC v Gentlemen of Kent in a 12-a-side match at Canterbury in 1861.

There have been 57 instances of a bowler taking 16 wickets in an 11-a-side match, the most recent being 16-189 by Sohail Khan for Sui Southern Gas v WAPDA at Karachi, 2007-08.

FOUR WICKETS WITH CONSECUTIVE BALLS

There have been **35** instances in first-class cricket. R. J. Crisp achieved the feat twice, for Western Province in 1931-32 and 1933-34. A. E. Trott took four in four balls and another hat-trick in the same innings for Middlesex v Somerset in 1907, his benefit match. Occurrences since the Second World War:

F. Ridgway	Kent v Derbyshire at Folkestone	1951
A. K. Walker‡	Nottinghamshire v Leicestershire at Leicester	1956
D. Robins†	South Australia v New South Wales at Adelaide..............	1965-66
S. N. Mohol	President's XI v Combined XI at Poona	1965-66
P. I. Pocock	Surrey v Sussex at Eastbourne	1972
S. S. Saini†	Delhi v Himachal Pradesh at Delhi	1988-89
D. Dias	W. Province (Suburbs) v Central Province at Colombo.........	1990-91
Ali Gauhar	Karachi Blues v United Bank at Peshawar...................	1994-95
K. D. James§	Hampshire v Indians at Southampton	1996
G. P. Butcher	Surrey v Derbyshire at The Oval	2000
Fazl-e-Akbar	PIA v Habib Bank at Lahore	2001-02
C. M. Willoughby	Cape Cobras v Dolphins at Durban	2005-06

† *Not all in the same innings.*
‡ *Having bowled Firth with the last ball of the first innings, Walker achieved a unique feat by dismissing Lester, Tompkin and Smithson with the first three balls of the second.*
§ *James also scored a century, a unique double.*

Notes: In their match with England at The Oval in 1863, Surrey lost four wickets in the course of a four-ball over from G. Bennett.

Sussex lost five wickets in the course of the final (six-ball) over of their match with Surrey at Eastbourne in 1972. P. I. Pocock, who had taken three wickets in his previous over, captured four more, taking in all seven wickets with 11 balls, a feat unique in first-class matches. (The eighth wicket fell to a run-out.)

HAT-TRICKS

Double Hat-Trick

Besides Trott's performance, which is mentioned in the preceding section, the following instances are recorded of players having performed the hat-trick twice in the same match, Rao doing so in the same innings.

A. Shaw	Nottinghamshire v Gloucestershire at Nottingham	1884
T. J. Matthews	Australia v South Africa at Manchester	1912
C. W. L. Parker	Gloucestershire v Middlesex at Bristol	1924
R. O. Jenkins	Worcestershire v Surrey at Worcester	1949
J. S. Rao	Services v Northern Punjab at Amritsar.....................	1963-64
Amin Lakhani	Combined XI v Indians at Multan	1978-79

Five Wickets in Six Balls

W. H. Copson	Derbyshire v Warwickshire at Derby........................	1937
W. A. Henderson	N.E. Transvaal v Orange Free State at Bloemfontein	1937-38
P. I. Pocock	Surrey v Sussex at Eastbourne	1972
Yasir Arafat	Rawalpindi v Faisalabad at Rawalpindi......................	2004-05

Yasir Arafat's five wickets were spread across two innings and interrupted only by a no-ball.

Most Hat-Tricks

D. V. P. Wright	7	V. W. C. Jupp	5	Fazl-e-Akbar	4
T. W. J. Goddard........	6	A. E. G. Rhodes.........	5	A. P. Freeman	4
C. W. L. Parker	6	F. A. Tarrant	5	J. T. Hearne	4
S. Haigh...............	5	R. G. Barlow	4	J. C. Laker.............	4

Records and Registers

G. A. R. Lock 4	M. J. Procter 4	F. S. Trueman 4
G. G. Macaulay 4	T. Richardson 4	
T. G. Matthews 4	F. R. Spofforth 4	

Current players only:

D. G. Cork 2	M. J. Hoggard 2	P. D. R. L. Perera 2
J. E. C. Franklin 2	G. J-P. Kruger 2	Saqlain Mushtaq 2
P. V. Gandhe 2	J. D. Lewry 2	C. M. Willoughby 2
S. J. Harmison 2	M. Ntini 2	

Hat-Trick on Debut

There have been **17** instances in first-class cricket. Occurrences since the Second World War:

J. C. Treanor	New South Wales v Queensland at Brisbane	1954-55
V. B. Ranjane	Maharashtra v Saurashtra at Poona	1956-57
Arshad Khan	Dacca University v East Pakistan B at Dacca	1957-58
N. Fredrick	Ceylon v Madras at Colombo	1963-64
J. S. Rao	Services v Jammu and Kashmir at Delhi	1963-64
Mehboodullah	Uttar Pradesh v Madhya Pradesh at Lucknow	1971-72
R. O. Estwick	Barbados v Guyana at Bridgetown	1982-83
S. A. Ankola	Maharashtra v Gujarat at Poona	1988-89
J. Srinath	Karnataka v Hyderabad at Secunderabad	1989-90
S. P. Mukherjee	Bengal v Hyderabad at Secunderabad	1989-90
S. M. Harwood	Victoria v Tasmania at Melbourne	2002-03
P. Connell	Ireland v Netherlands at Rotterdam	2008
Zohaib Shera	**Karachi Whites v National Bank at Karachi**	**2009-10**

Notes: R. R. Phillips (Border) took a hat-trick in his first over in first-class cricket (v Eastern Province at Port Elizabeth, 1939-40) having previously played in four matches without bowling.

J. S. Rao took two more hat-tricks in his next match.

Bold type denotes performances in the calendar year 2009.

250 WICKETS IN A SEASON

	Season	O	M	R	W	Avge
A. P. Freeman	1928	1,976.1	423	5,489	304	18.05
A. P. Freeman	1933	2,039	651	4,549	298	15.26
T. Richardson	1895‡	1,690.1	463	4,170	290	14.37
C. T. B. Turner	1888†	2,427.2	1,127	3,307	283	11.68
A. P. Freeman	1931	1,618	360	4,307	276	15.60
A. P. Freeman	1930	1,914.3	472	4,632	275	16.84
T. Richardson	1897‡	1,603.4	495	3,945	273	14.45
A. P. Freeman	1929	1,670.5	381	4,879	267	18.27
W. Rhodes	1900	1,553	455	3,606	261	13.81
J. T. Hearne	1896‡	2,003.1	818	3,670	257	14.28
A. P. Freeman	1932	1,565.5	404	4,149	253	16.39
W. Rhodes	1901	1,565	505	3,797	251	15.12

† *Indicates 4-ball overs.*   ‡ *5-ball overs.*

Notes: In four consecutive seasons (1928-31), A. P. Freeman took 1,122 wickets, and in eight consecutive seasons (1928-35), 2,090 wickets. In each of these eight seasons he took over 200 wickets.

T. Richardson took 1,005 wickets in four consecutive seasons (1894-97).

The earliest date by which any bowler has taken 100 wickets in an English season is June 12, achieved by J. T. Hearne in 1896 and C. W. L. Parker in 1931, when A. P. Freeman did it on June 13.

200 WICKETS IN A SEASON MOST TIMES

A. P. Freeman	8	J. T. Hearne	3	T. Richardson	3
C. W. L. Parker	5	G. A. Lohmann	3	M. W. Tate	3
T. W. J. Goddard	4	W. Rhodes	3	H. Verity	3

Notes: A. P. Freeman reached 200 wickets in eight successive seasons – 1928 to 1935 – including 304 in 1928.

The last bowler to reach 200 wickets in a season was G. A. R. Lock (212 in 1957).

100 WICKETS IN A SEASON MOST TIMES

(Includes overseas tours and seasons)

W. Rhodes	23	C. W. L. Parker	16	G. H. Hirst	15
D. Shackleton	20	R. T. D. Perks	16	A. S. Kennedy	15
A. P. Freeman	17	F. J. Titmus	16		
T. W. J. Goddard	16	J. T. Hearne	15		

Notes: D. Shackleton reached 100 wickets in 20 successive seasons – 1949 to 1968.

Since the reduction of County Championship matches in 1969, D. L. Underwood (five times) and J. K. Lever (four times) are the only bowlers to have reached 100 wickets in a season more than twice. The highest aggregate in a season since 1969 is 134 by M. D. Marshall in 1982.

100 WICKETS IN A SEASON OUTSIDE ENGLAND

W		Season	Country	R	Avge
116	M. W. Tate	1926-27	India/Ceylon	1,599	13.78
113	Kabir Khan	1998-99	Pakistan	1,706	15.09
107	Ijaz Faqih	1985-86	Pakistan	1,719	16.06
106	C. T. B. Turner	1887-88	Australia	1,441	13.59
106	R. Benaud	1957-58	South Africa	2,056	19.39
105	Murtaza Hussain	1995-96	Pakistan	1,882	17.92
104	S. F. Barnes	1913-14	South Africa	1,117	10.74
104	Sajjad Akbar	1989-90	Pakistan	2,328	22.38
103	Abdul Qadir	1982-83	Pakistan	2,367	22.98

LEADING BOWLERS IN AN ENGLISH SEASON

(Qualification: 10 wickets in 10 innings)

Season	Leading wicket-taker	Wkts	Avge	Top of averages	Wkts	Avge
1946	W. E. Hollies	184	15.60	A. Booth	111	11.61
1947	T. W. J. Goddard	238	17.30	J. C. Clay	65	16.44
1948	J. E. Walsh	174	19.56	J. C. Clay	41	14.17
1949	R. O. Jenkins	183	21.19	T. W. J. Goddard	160	19.18
1950	R. Tattersall	193	13.59	R. Tattersall	193	13.59
1951	R. Appleyard	200	14.14	R. Appleyard	200	14.14
1952	J. H. Wardle	177	19.54	F. S. Trueman	61	13.78
1953	B. Dooland	172	16.58	C. J. Knott	38	13.71
1954	B. Dooland	196	15.48	J. B. Statham	92	14.13
1955	G. A. R. Lock	216	14.49	R. Appleyard	85	13.01
1956	D. J. Shepherd	177	15.36	G. A. R. Lock	155	12.46
1957	G. A. R. Lock	212	12.02	G. A. R. Lock	212	12.02
1958	G. A. R. Lock	170	12.08	H. L. Jackson	143	10.99
1959	D. Shackleton	148	21.55	J. B. Statham	139	15.01
1960	F. S. Trueman	175	13.98	J. B. Statham	135	12.31
1961	J. A. Flavell	171	17.79	J. A. Flavell	171	17.79
1962	D. Shackleton	172	20.15	C. Cook	58	17.13
1963	D. Shackleton	146	16.75	C. C. Griffith	119	12.83
1964	D. Shackleton	142	20.40	J. A. Standen	64	13.00

Season	Leading wicket-taker	Wkts	Avge	Top of averages	Wkts	Avge
1965	D. Shackleton	144	16.08	H. J. Rhodes	119	11.04
1966	D. L. Underwood	157	13.80	D. L. Underwood	157	13.80
1967	T. W. Cartwright	147	15.52	D. L. Underwood	136	12.39
1968	R. Illingworth	131	14.36	O. S. Wheatley	82	12.95
1969	R. M. H. Cottam	109	21.04	A. Ward	69	14.82
1970	D. J. Shepherd	106	19.16	Majid Khan	11	18.81
1971	L. R. Gibbs	131	18.89	G. G. Arnold	83	17.12
1972	T. W. Cartwright B. Stead	98 98	18.64 20.38	I. M. Chappell	10	10.60
1973	B. S. Bedi	105	17.94	T. W. Cartwright	89	15.84
1974	A. M. E. Roberts	119	13.62	A. M. E. Roberts	119	13.62
1975	P. G. Lee	112	18.45	A. M. E. Roberts	57	15.80
1976	G. A. Cope	93	24.13	M. A. Holding	55	14.38
1977	M. J. Procter	109	18.04	R. A. Woolmer	19	15.21
1978	D. L. Underwood	110	14.49	D. L. Underwood	110	14.49
1979	D. L. Underwood J. K. Lever	106 106	14.85 17.30	J. Garner	55	13.83
1980	R. D. Jackman	121	15.40	J. Garner	49	13.93
1981	R. J. Hadlee	105	14.89	R. J. Hadlee	105	14.89
1982	M. D. Marshall	134	15.73	R. J. Hadlee	61	14.57
1983	J. K. Lever D. L. Underwood	106 106	16.28 19.28	Imran Khan	12	7.16
1984	R. J. Hadlee	117	14.05	R. J. Hadlee	117	14.05
1985	N. V. Radford	101	24.68	R. M. Ellison	65	17.20
1986	C. A. Walsh	118	18.17	M. D. Marshall	100	15.08
1987	N. V. Radford	109	20.81	R. J. Hadlee	97	12.64
1988	F. D. Stephenson	125	18.31	M. D. Marshall	42	13.16
1989	D. R. Pringle S. L. Watkin	94 94	18.64 25.09	T. M. Alderman	70	15.64
1990	N. A. Foster	94	26.61	I. R. Bishop	59	19.05
1991	Waqar Younis	113	14.65	Waqar Younis	113	14.65
1992	C. A. Walsh	92	15.96	C. A. Walsh	92	15.96
1993	S. L. Watkin	92	22.80	Wasim Akram	59	19.27
1994	M. M. Patel	90	22.86	C. E. L. Ambrose	77	14.45
1995	A. Kumble	105	20.40	A. A. Donald	89	16.07
1996	C. A. Walsh	85	16.84	C. E. L. Ambrose	43	16.67
1997	A. M. Smith	83	17.63	A. A. Donald	60	15.63
1998	C. A. Walsh	106	17.31	V. J. Wells	36	14.27
1999	A. Sheriyar	92	24.70	Saqlain Mushtaq	58	11.37
2000	G. D. McGrath	80	13.21	C. A. Walsh	40	11.42
2001	R. J. Kirtley	75	23.32	G. D. McGrath	40	15.60
2002	M. J. Saggers K. J. Dean	83 83	21.51 23.50	C. P. Schofield	18	18.38
2003	Mushtaq Ahmed	103	24.65	Shoaib Akhtar	34	17.05
2004	Mushtaq Ahmed	84	27.59	D. S. Lehmann	15	17.40
2005	S. K. Warne	87	22.50	M. Muralitharan	36	15.00
2006	Mushtaq Ahmed	102	19.91	Naved-ul-Hasan	35	16.71
2007	Mushtaq Ahmed	90	25.66	Harbhajan Singh	37	18.54
2008	J. A. Tomlinson	67	24.76	M. Davies	41	14.63
2009	**Danish Kaneria**	**75**	**23.69**	**G. Onions**	**69**	**19.95**

1,500 WICKETS

Dates in italics denote the first half of an overseas season; i.e. *1970* denotes the 1970-71 season.

		Career	W	R	Avge
1	W. Rhodes	1898–1930	4,187	69,993	16.71
2	A. P. Freeman	1914–1936	3,776	69,577	18.42
3	C. W. L. Parker	1903–1935	3,278	63,817	19.46
4	J. T. Hearne	1888–1923	3,061	54,352	17.75

		Career	W	R	Avge
5	T. W. J. Goddard	1922–1952	2,979	59,116	19.84
6	W. G. Grace	1865–1908	2,876	51,545	17.92
7	A. S. Kennedy	1907–1936	2,874	61,034	21.23
8	D. Shackleton	1948–1969	2,857	53,303	18.65
9	G. A. R. Lock	1946–1970	2,844	54,709	19.23
10	F. J. Titmus	1949–1982	2,830	63,313	22.37
11	M. W. Tate	1912–1937	2,784	50,571	18.16
12	G. H. Hirst	1891–1929	2,739	51,282	18.72
13	C. Blythe	1899–1914	2,506	42,136	16.81
14	D. L. Underwood	1963–1987	2,465	49,993	20.28
15	W. E. Astill	1906–1939	2,431	57,783	23.76
16	J. C. White	1909–1937	2,356	43,759	18.57
17	W. E. Hollies	1932–1957	2,323	48,656	20.94
18	F. S. Trueman	1949–1969	2,304	42,154	18.29
19	J. B. Statham	1950–1968	2,260	36,999	16.37
20	R. T. D. Perks	1930–1955	2,233	53,770	24.07
21	J. Briggs	1879–1900	2,221	35,431	15.95
22	D. J. Shepherd	1950–1972	2,218	47,302	21.32
23	E. G. Dennett	1903–1926	2,147	42,571	19.82
24	T. Richardson	1892–1905	2,104	38,794	18.43
25	T. E. Bailey	1945–1967	2,082	48,170	23.13
26	R. Illingworth	1951–1983	2,072	42,023	20.28
27 {	N. Gifford	1960–1988	2,068	48,731	23.56
	F. E. Woolley	1906–1938	2,068	41,066	19.85
29	G. Geary	1912–1938	2,063	41,339	20.03
30	D. V. P. Wright	1932–1957	2,056	49,307	23.98
31	J. A. Newman	1906–1930	2,032	51,111	25.15
32	†A. Shaw	1864–1897	2,027	24,580	12.12
33	S. Haigh	1895–1913	2,012	32,091	15.94
34	H. Verity	1930–1939	1,956	29,146	14.90
35	W. Attewell	1881–1900	1,951	29,896	15.32
36	J. C. Laker	1946–1964	1,944	35,791	18.41
37	A. V. Bedser	1939–1960	1,924	39,279	20.41
38	W. Mead	1892–1913	1,916	36,388	18.99
39	A. E. Relf	1900–1921	1,897	39,724	20.94
40	P. G. H. Fender	1910–1936	1,894	47,458	25.05
41	J. W. H. T. Douglas	1901–1930	1,893	44,159	23.32
42	J. H. Wardle	1946–1967	1,846	35,027	18.97
43	G. R. Cox	1895–1928	1,843	42,136	22.86
44	G. A. Lohmann	1884–1897	1,841	25,295	13.73
45	J. W. Hearne	1909–1936	1,839	44,926	24.42
46	G. G. Macaulay	1920–1935	1,837	32,440	17.65
47	M. S. Nichols	1924–1939	1,833	39,666	21.63
48 {	J. B. Mortimore	1950–1975	1,807	41,904	23.18
	C. A. Walsh	1981–2000	1,807	39,233	21.71
50	C. Cook	1946–1964	1,782	36,578	20.52
51	R. Peel	1882–1899	1,752	28,442	16.23
52	H. L. Jackson	1947–1963	1,733	30,101	17.36
53	J. K. Lever	1967–1989	1,722	41,772	24.25
54	T. P. B. Smith	1929–1952	1,697	45,059	26.55
55	J. Southerton	1854–1879	1,681	24,290	14.44
56	A. E. Trott	1892–1911	1,674	35,317	21.09
57	A. W. Mold	1889–1901	1,673	26,010	15.54
58	T. G. Wass	1896–1920	1,666	34,092	20.46
59	V. W. C. Jupp	1909–1938	1,658	38,166	23.01
60	C. Gladwin	1939–1958	1,653	30,265	18.30
61	M. D. Marshall	1977–1995	1,651	31,548	19.10
62	W. E. Bowes	1928–1947	1,639	27,470	16.76
63	A. W. Wellard	1927–1950	1,614	39,302	24.35
64	J. E. Emburey	1973–1997	1,608	41,958	26.09

		Career	W	R	Avge
65	P. I. Pocock	1964–1986	1,607	42,648	26.53
66	N. I. Thomson	1952–1972	1,597	32,867	20.58
67 {	J. Mercer	1919–1947	1,591	37,210	23.38
	G. J. Thompson	1897–1922	1,591	30,058	18.89
69	J. M. Sims	1929–1953	1,581	39,401	24.92
70 {	T. Emmett	1866–1888	1,571	21,314	13.56
	Intikhab Alam	*1957–1982*	1,571	43,474	27.67
72	B. S. Bedi	*1961–1981*	1,560	33,843	21.69
73	W. Voce	1927–1952	1,558	35,961	23.08
74	A. R. Gover	1928–1948	1,555	36,753	23.63
75 {	T. W. Cartwright	1952–1977	1,536	29,357	19.11
	K. Higgs	1958–1986	1,536	36,267	23.61
77	James Langridge	1924–1953	1,530	34,524	22.56
78	J. A. Flavell	1949–1967	1,529	32,847	21.48
79	E. E. Hemmings	1966–1995	1,515	44,403	29.30
80 {	C. F. Root	1910–1933	1,512	31,933	21.11
	F. A. Tarrant	*1898–1936*	1,512	26,450	17.49
82	R. K. Tyldesley	1919–1935	1,509	25,980	17.21

† *The figures for A. Shaw exclude one wicket for which no analysis is available.*

Note: Some works of reference provide career figures which differ from those in this list, owing to the exclusion or inclusion of matches recognised or not recognised as first-class by *Wisden*.

Current Players with 1,000 Wickets

	Career	W	R	Avge
M. Muralitharan	1989–2009	1,366	26,806	19.62
A. R. Caddick	1991–2009	1,180	31,387	26.59
R. D. B. Croft	1989–2009	1,107	39,190	35.40

ALL-ROUND RECORDS

REMARKABLE ALL-ROUND MATCHES

V. E. Walker	20*	108	10-74	4-17	England v Surrey at The Oval	1859
W. G. Grace	104			2-60	10-49	MCC v Oxford University at Oxford .	1886
G. Giffen	271		9-96	7-70	South Australia v Victoria at Adelaide	1891-92
B. J. T. Bosanquet	103	100*	3-75	8-53	Middlesex v Sussex at Lord's	1905
G. H. Hirst	111	117*	6-70	5-45	Yorkshire v Somerset at Bath	1906
F. D. Stephenson	111	117	4-105	7-117	Notts v Yorkshire at Nottingham	1988

Note: E. M. Grace, for MCC v Gentlemen of Kent in a 12-a-side match at Canterbury in 1862, scored 192* and took 5-77 and 10-69.

HUNDRED AND HAT-TRICK

G. Giffen, Australians v Lancashire at Manchester	1884
W. E. Roller, Surrey v Sussex at The Oval. *Unique instance of 200 and hat-trick*	1885
W. B. Burns, Worcestershire v Gloucestershire at Worcester	1913
V. W. C. Jupp, Sussex v Essex at Colchester	1921
R. E. S. Wyatt, MCC v Ceylonese at Colombo	1926-27
L. N. Constantine, West Indians v Northamptonshire at Northampton	1928
D. E. Davies, Glamorgan v Leicestershire at Leicester	1937
V. M. Merchant, Dr C. R. Pereira's XI v Sir Homi Mehta's XI at Bombay	1946-47
M. J. Procter, Gloucestershire v Essex at Westcliff-on-Sea	1972
M. J. Procter, Gloucestershire v Leicestershire at Bristol	1979
K. D. James, Hampshire v Indians at Southampton. *Unique instance of 100 and four wickets in four balls*	1996
J. E. C. Franklin, Gloucestershire v Derbyshire at Cheltenham	**2009**

Bold type denotes performances in the calendar year 2009.

THE DOUBLE

The double was traditionally regarded as 1,000 runs and 100 wickets in an English season. The feat became exceptionally rare after the reduction of County Championship matches in 1969.

Remarkable Seasons

	Season	R	W		Season	R	W
G. H. Hirst	1906	2,385	208	J. H. Parks	1937	3,003	101

1,000 Runs and 100 Wickets

W. Rhodes 16		W. G. Grace 8		F. J. Titmus 8
G. H. Hirst 14		M. S. Nichols 8		F. E. Woolley 7
V. W. C. Jupp 10		A. E. Relf 8		G. E. Tribe 7
W. E. Astill 9		F. A. Tarrant 8		
T. E. Bailey 8		M. W. Tate . . . . 8†		

† *M. W. Tate also scored 1,193 runs and took 116 wickets on the 1926-27 MCC tour of India and Ceylon.*

Note: R. J. Hadlee (1984) and F. D. Stephenson (1988) are the only players to perform the feat since the reduction of County Championship matches in 1969. A complete list of those performing the feat before then may be found on page 202 of the 1982 *Wisden*. T. E. Bailey (1959) was the last player to achieve 2,000 runs and 100 wickets in a season; M. W. Tate (1925) the last to reach 1,000 runs and 200 wickets. Full lists may be found in *Wisdens* up to 2003.

Wicketkeeper's Double

The only wicketkeepers to achieve 1,000 runs and 100 dismissals in a season were L. E. G. Ames (1928, 1929 and 1932, when he scored 2,482 runs) and J. T. Murray (1957).

WICKETKEEPING RECORDS

MOST DISMISSALS IN AN INNINGS

9 (8ct, 1st)	Tahir Rashid	Habib Bank v PACO at Gujranwala	1992-93
9 (7ct, 2st)	W. R. James*	Matabeleland v Mashonaland CD at Bulawayo	1995-96
8 (all ct)	A. T. W. Grout	Queensland v Western Australia at Brisbane	1959-60
8 (all ct)†	D. E. East	Essex v Somerset at Taunton	1985
8 (all ct)	S. A. Marsh‡	Kent v Middlesex at Lord's	1991
8 (6ct, 2st)	T. J. Zoehrer	Australians v Surrey at The Oval	1993
8 (7ct, 1st)	D. S. Berry	Victoria v South Australia at Melbourne	1996-97
8 (7ct, 1st)	Y. S. S. Mendis	Bloomfield v Kurunegala Youth at Colombo	2000-01
8 (7ct, 1st)	S. Nath§	Assam v Tripura at Guwahati	2001-02
8 (all ct)	J. N. Batty¶	Surrey v Kent at The Oval	2004
8 (all ct)	Golam Mabud	Sylhet v Dhaka at Dhaka.	2005-06
8 (all ct)	**A. Z. M. Dyili**	**Eastern Province v Free State at Port Elizabeth**	**2009-10**

There have been **82** further instances of seven dismissals in an innings. R. W. Taylor achieved the feat three times, and S. A. Marsh, K. J. Piper and Wasim Bari twice. One of Marsh's two instances was of eight dismissals – see above. A fuller list can be found in *Wisdens* before 2004. The most recent occurrences are:

7 (all ct)	R. D. Jacobs	West Indies v Australia at Melbourne.	2000-01
7 (all ct)	N. D. Burns	Leicestershire v Somerset at Leicester	2001
7 (all ct)	R. J. Turner	Somerset v Northamptonshire at Taunton.	2001
7 (all ct)	W. A. Seccombe	Queensland v New South Wales at Brisbane	2001-02
7 (all ct)	M. G. Croy	Otago v Auckland at Auckland.	2001-02
7 (all ct)	Wasim Ahmed	Dadu v PWD at Karachi	2002-03
7 (all ct)	S. G. Clingeleffer	Tasmania v Western Australia at Perth.	2003-04
7 (6ct, 1st)	C. O. Browne	Barbados v Jamaica at Kingston	2003-04

7 (all ct)	Adnan Akmal	Lahore Blues v Karachi Blues at Karachi	2004-05
7 (all ct)	G. J. Hopkins	New Zealand A v South Africa A at Centurion . . .	2004-05
7 (all ct)	Mohammad Kashif	Rawalpindi v Multan at Multan	2004-05
7 (all ct)	T. L. Tsolekile	Western Province Boland v Dolphins at Durban . .	2004-05
7 (all ct)	M. S. Dhoni	East Zone v Central Zone at Gwalior	2004-05
7 (all ct)	Shahin Hossain	Barisal v Rajshahi at Rajshahi.	2004-05
7 (all ct)	G. J. Hopkins	New Zealand A v Sri Lanka A at Kandy	2005-06
7 (all ct)	D. H. Yagnik	Rajasthan v Saurashtra at Rajkot.	2005-06
7 (all ct)	N. Pothas	Hampshire v Lancashire at Manchester	2006
7 (6ct, 1st)	Shahin Hossain	Barisal v Dhaka at Dhaka	2006-07
7 (all ct)	B. B. J. Griggs	Central Districts v Northern Districts at Hamilton .	2007-08
7 (all ct)	C. D. Hartley	Queensland v New South Wales at Brisbane	2007-08
7 (all ct)	L. D. Sutton	Lancashire v Yorkshire at Leeds.	2008
7 (all ct)	Jamal Anwar	Federal Areas v Punjab at Islamabad	2008-09
7 (all ct)	Kamran Akmal	National Bank v Habib Bank at Karachi.	2008-09
7 (all ct)	**Sarfraz Ahmed**	**PIA v Habib Bank at Karachi**	**2008-09**
7 (all ct)	**P. A. Browne**	**Barbados v Windward Islands at Bridgetown** . .	**2008-09**
7 (all ct)	**P. Bisht**	**Delhi v Baroda at Vadodara**.	**2009-10**
7 (5ct, 2st)	**S. M. Fernando**	**Air Force v Seeduwa Raddoluwa at Colombo** . .	**2009-10**

* *W. R. James also scored 99 and 99 not out.*   † *The first eight wickets to fall.*
‡ *S. A. Marsh also scored 108 not out.*   § *On his only first-class appearance.*
¶ *J. N. Batty also scored 129.*

Bold type denotes performances in the calendar year 2009.

WICKETKEEPERS' HAT-TRICKS

W. H. Brain, Gloucestershire v Somerset at Cheltenham, 1893 – three stumpings off successive balls
   from C. L. Townsend.
G. O. Dawkes, Derbyshire v Worcestershire at Kidderminster, 1958 – three catches off successive
   balls from H. L. Jackson.
R. C. Russell, Gloucestershire v Surrey at The Oval, 1986 – three catches off successive balls from
   C. A. Walsh and D. V. Lawrence (2).

MOST DISMISSALS IN A MATCH

13 (11ct, 2st)	W. R. James*	Matabeleland v Mashonaland CD at Bulawayo. . . .	1995-96
12 (8ct, 4st)	E. Pooley	Surrey v Sussex at The Oval	1868
12 (9ct, 3st)	D. Tallon	Queensland v New South Wales at Sydney.	1938-39
12 (9ct, 3st)	H. B. Taber	New South Wales v South Australia at Adelaide. . .	1968-69
12 (all ct)	**P. D. McGlashan**	**Northern Districts v Central Districts at**	
		Whangarei	**2009-10**
11 (all ct)	A. Long	Surrey v Sussex at Hove	1964
11 (all ct)	R. W. Marsh	Western Australia v Victoria at Perth	1975-76
11 (all ct)	D. L. Bairstow	Yorkshire v Derbyshire at Scarborough.	1982
11 (all ct)	W. K. Hegg	Lancashire v Derbyshire at Chesterfield	1989
11 (all ct)	A. J. Stewart	Surrey v Leicestershire at Leicester.	1989
11 (all ct)	T. J. Nielsen	South Australia v Western Australia at Perth.	1990-91
11 (10ct, 1st)	I. A. Healy	Australians v N. Transvaal at Verwoerdburg.	1993-94
11 (10ct, 1st)	K. J. Piper	Warwickshire v Derbyshire at Chesterfield	1994
11 (all ct)	D. S. Berry	Victoria v Pakistanis at Melbourne	1995-96
11 (10ct, 1st)	W. A. Seccombe	Queensland v Western Australia at Brisbane.	1995-96
11 (all ct)	R. C. Russell	England v South Africa (2nd Test) at Johannesburg	1995-96
11 (10ct, 1st)	D. S. Berry	Victoria v South Australia at Melbourne	1996-97
11 (all ct)	Wasim Yousufi	Peshawar v Bahawalpur at Peshawar.	1997-98
11 (all ct)	Aamer Iqbal	Pakistan Customs v Karachi Whites at Karachi. . . .	1999-2000
11 (10ct, 1st)	S. Nath†	Assam v Tripura at Guwahati	2001-02
11 (all ct)	Wasim Ahmed	Dadu v PWD at Karachi	2002-03

11 (7ct, 4st)	J. N. Batty	Surrey v Lancashire at Manchester	2004
11 (7ct, 4st)	M. S. Dhoni	India A v Zimbabwe Select XI at Harare	2004
11 (all ct)	Adnan Akmal	Lahore Blues v Karachi Blues at Karachi	2004-05
11 (9ct, 2st)	M. S. Bisla	Himachal Pradesh v Saurashtra at Dharmasala	2004-05

* *W. R. James also scored 99 and 99 not out.*   † *On his only first-class appearance.*

Bold type denotes performances in the calendar year 2009.

100 DISMISSALS IN A SEASON

128 (79ct, 49st)	L. E. G. Ames 1929	104 (82ct, 22st)	J. T. Murray 1957
122 (70ct, 52st)	L. E. G. Ames 1928	102 (69ct, 33st)	F. H. Huish 1913
110 (63ct, 47st)	H. Yarnold 1949	102 (95ct, 7st)	J. T. Murray 1960
107 (77ct, 30st)	G. Duckworth 1928	101 (62ct, 39st)	F. H. Huish 1911
107 (96ct, 11st)	J. G. Binks 1960	101 (85ct, 16st)	R. Booth 1960
104 (40ct, 64st)	L. E. G. Ames 1932	100 (91ct, 9st)	R. Booth 1964

Note: L. E. G. Ames achieved the two highest stumping totals in a season: 64 in 1932, and 52 in 1928.

1,000 DISMISSALS

Dates in italics denote the first half of an overseas season; i.e. *1914* denotes the 1914-15 season.

			Career	*M*	*Ct*	*St*
1	R. W. Taylor	1,649	1960–1988	639	1,473	176
2	J. T. Murray	1,527	1952–1975	635	1,270	257
3	H. Strudwick	1,497	1902–1927	675	1,242	255
4	A. P. E. Knott	1,344	1964–1985	511	1,211	133
5	R. C. Russell	1,320	1981–2004	465	1,192	128
6	F. H. Huish	1,310	1895–1914	497	933	377
7	B. Taylor	1,294	1949–1973	572	1,083	211
8	S. J. Rhodes	1,263	1981–2004	440	1,139	124
9	D. Hunter	1,253	1889–1909	548	906	347
10	H. R. Butt	1,228	1890–1912	550	953	275
11	J. H. Board	1,207	1891–*1914*	525	852	355
12	H. Elliott	1,206	1920–1947	532	904	302
13	J. M. Parks	1,181	1949–1976	739	1,088	93
14	R. Booth	1,126	1951–1970	468	948	178
15	L. E. G. Ames	1,121	1926–1951	593	703	418†
16	D. L. Bairstow	1,099	1970–1990	459	961	138
17	G. Duckworth	1,096	1923–1947	504	753	343
18	H. W. Stephenson	1,082	1948–1964	462	748	334
19	J. G. Binks	1,071	1955–1975	502	895	176
20	T. G. Evans	1,066	1939–1969	465	816	250
21	A. Long	1,046	1960–1980	452	922	124
22	G. O. Dawkes	1,043	1937–1961	482	895	148
23	R. W. Tolchard	1,037	1965–1983	483	912	125
24	W. L. Cornford	1,017	1921–1947	496	675	342

† *Record.*

Current Players with 500 Dismissals

		Career	*M*	*Ct*	*St*
952	P. A. Nixon	1989–2009	335	885	67
683	C. M. W. Read	*1997*–2009	190	647	36
676	M. V. Boucher	*1995*–2009	222	640	36
604	N. Pothas	*1993*–2009	201	559	45
564	J. N. Batty	1994–2009	191	500	64
533	Kamran Akmal	*1997*–2009	145	489	44

FIELDING RECORDS

excluding wicketkeepers

MOST CATCHES IN AN INNINGS

7	M. J. Stewart	Surrey v Northamptonshire at Northampton	1957
7	A. S. Brown	Gloucestershire v Nottinghamshire at Nottingham	1966

MOST CATCHES IN A MATCH

10	W. R. Hammond†	Gloucestershire v Surrey at Cheltenham	1928
8	W. B. Burns	Worcestershire v Yorkshire at Bradford	1907
8	F. G. Travers	Europeans v Parsees at Bombay	1923-24
8	A. H. Bakewell	Northamptonshire v Essex at Leyton.	1928
8	W. R. Hammond	Gloucestershire v Worcestershire at Cheltenham	1932
8	K. J. Grieves	Lancashire v Sussex at Manchester.	1951
8	C. A. Milton	Gloucestershire v Sussex at Hove	1952
8	G. A. R. Lock	Surrey v Warwickshire at The Oval	1957
8	J. M. Prodger	Kent v Gloucestershire at Cheltenham	1961
8	P. M. Walker	Glamorgan v Derbyshire at Swansea.	1970
8	Masood Anwar	Rawalpindi v Lahore Division at Rawalpindi	1983-84
8	M. C. J. Ball	Gloucestershire v Yorkshire at Cheltenham	1994
8	J. D. Carr	Middlesex v Warwickshire at Birmingham.	1995
8	G. A. Hick	Worcestershire v Essex at Chelmsford	2005
8	A. P. McLaren	Eagles v Lions at Johannesburg.	2007-08

† *Hammond also scored a hundred in each innings.*

MOST CATCHES IN A SEASON

78	W. R. Hammond	1928		69	P. M. Walker.	1960
77	M. J. Stewart	1957		66	J. Tunnicliffe.	1895
73	P. M. Walker.	1961		65	W. R. Hammond	1925
71	P. J. Sharpe	1962		65	P. M. Walker.	1959
70	J. Tunnicliffe.	1901		65	D. W. Richardson	1961
69	J. G. Langridge	1955				

Note: The most catches by a fielder since the reduction of County Championship matches in 1969 is 49 by C. J. Tavaré in 1978.

750 CATCHES

Dates in italics denote the first half of an overseas season; i.e. *1970* denotes the 1970-71 season.

		Career	*M*			*Career*	*M*
1,018	F. E. Woolley	1906–1938	979	784	J. G. Langridge . . .	1928–1955	574
887	W. G. Grace	1865–1908	879	764	W. Rhodes	1898–1930	1,107
830	G. A. R. Lock	1946–*1970*	654	758	C. A. Milton	1948–1974	620
819	W. R. Hammond .	1920–1951	634	754	E. H. Hendren. . . .	1907–1938	833
813	D. B. Close	1949–1986	786				

Note: The most catches by a current player is 408 by S. G. Law (*1988–2009*).

TEAM RECORDS

HIGHEST INNINGS TOTALS

1,107	Victoria v New South Wales at Melbourne	1926-27
1,059	Victoria v Tasmania at Melbourne	1922-23
952-6 dec	Sri Lanka v India at Colombo................................	1997-98
951-7 dec	Sind v Baluchistan at Karachi...............................	1973-74
944-6 dec	Hyderabad v Andhra at Secunderabad	1993-94
918	New South Wales v South Australia at Sydney	1900-01
912-8 dec	Holkar v Mysore at Indore	1945-46
912-6 dec†	Tamil Nadu v Goa at Panjim	1988-89
910-6 dec	Railways v Dera Ismail Khan at Lahore.......................	1964-65
903-7 dec	England v Australia at The Oval.............................	1938
900-6 dec	Queensland v Victoria at Brisbane	2005-06
887	Yorkshire v Warwickshire at Birmingham......................	1896
868†	North Zone v West Zone at Bhilai	1987-88
863	Lancashire v Surrey at The Oval	1990
855-6 dec†	Bombay v Hyderabad at Bombay.............................	1990-91
850-7 dec	Somerset v Middlesex at Taunton	2007
849	England v West Indies at Kingston...........................	1929-30
843	Australians v Oxford & Cambridge U P & P at Portsmouth	1893
839	New South Wales v Tasmania at Sydney.......................	1898-99
826-4	Maharashtra v Kathiawar at Poona...........................	1948-49
824	Lahore Greens v Bahawalpur at Lahore.......................	1965-66
821-7 dec	South Australia v Queensland at Adelaide	1939-40
815	New South Wales v Victoria at Sydney	1908-09
811	Surrey v Somerset at The Oval..............................	1899
810-4 dec	Warwickshire v Durham at Birmingham.......................	1994
807	New South Wales v South Australia at Adelaide	1899-1900
806-8 dec	**Victoria v Queensland at Melbourne**	**2008-09**
805	New South Wales v Victoria at Melbourne	1905-06
803-4 dec	Kent v Essex at Brentwood.................................	1934
803	Non-Smokers v Smokers at East Melbourne	1886-87
802-8 dec	Karachi Blues v Lahore City at Peshawar	1994-95
802	New South Wales v South Australia at Sydney	1920-21
801-8 dec	Derbyshire v Somerset at Taunton	2007
801	Lancashire v Somerset at Taunton	1895
798	Maharashtra v Northern India at Poona	1940-41
793	Victoria v Queensland at Melbourne	1927-28
791-6 dec	Karnataka v Bengal at Calcutta	1990-91
791	Nottinghamshire v Essex at Chelmsford.......................	2007
790-3 dec	West Indies v Pakistan at Kingston	1957-58
786	New South Wales v South Australia at Adelaide	1922-23
785	**Tamil Nadu v Hyderabad at Hyderabad**	**2009-10**
784	Baroda v Holkar at Baroda	1946-47
783-8 dec	Hyderabad v Bihar at Secunderabad..........................	1986-87
781-7 dec	Northamptonshire v Nottinghamshire at Northampton	1995
781	Lancashire v Warwickshire at Birmingham	2003
780-8	Punjab v Delhi at Delhi	1994-95
777	Canterbury v Otago at Christchurch..........................	1996-97
775	New South Wales v Victoria at Sydney	1881-82

† *Tamil Nadu's total of 912-6 dec included 52 penalty runs from their opponents' failure to meet the required bowling rate. North Zone's total of 868 included 68, and Bombay's total of 855-6 dec included 48.*

Note: The highest total in a team's second innings is 770 by New South Wales v South Australia at Adelaide in 1920-21.

Bold type denotes performances in the calendar year 2009.

HIGHEST FOURTH-INNINGS TOTALS

654-5	England v South Africa at Durban	1938-39
	After being set 696 to win. The match was left drawn on the tenth day.	
604	Maharashtra (*set 959 to win*) v Bombay at Poona........................	1948-49
576-8	Trinidad (*set 672 to win*) v Barbados at Port-of-Spain	1945-46
572	New South Wales (*set 593 to win*) v South Australia at Sydney............	1907-08
529-9	Combined XI (*set 579 to win*) v South Africans at Perth	1963-64
518	Victoria (*set 753 to win*) v Queensland at Brisbane	1926-27
513-9	Central Province (*won*) v Southern Province at Kandy....................	2003-04
507-7	Cambridge University (*won*) v MCC and Ground at Lord's...............	1896
506-6	South Australia (*won*) v Queensland at Adelaide	1991-92
503-4	South Zone (*won*) v England A at Gurgaon	2003-04
502-6	Middlesex (*won*) v Nottinghamshire at Nottingham......................	1925
502-8	Players (*won*) v Gentlemen at Lord's	1900
500-7	South African Universities (*won*) v Western Province at Stellenbosch	1978-79

MOST RUNS IN A DAY (ONE SIDE)

721	Australians (721) v Essex at Southend (1st day)...........................	1948
651	West Indians (651-2) v Leicestershire at Leicester (1st day)	1950
649	New South Wales (649-7) v Otago at Dunedin (2nd day)	1923-24
645	Surrey (645-4) v Hampshire at The Oval (1st day).........................	1909
644	Oxford U. (644-8) v H. D. G. Leveson Gower's XI at Eastbourne (1st day) ...	1921
640	Lancashire (640-8) v Sussex at Hove (1st day)...........................	1937
636	Free Foresters (636-7) v Cambridge U. at Cambridge (1st day).............	1938
625	Gloucestershire (625-6) v Worcestershire at Dudley (2nd day)	1934

MOST RUNS IN A DAY (BOTH SIDES)

(excluding the above)

685	North (169-8 and 255-7), South (261-8 dec) at Blackpool (2nd day)........	1961
666	Surrey (607-4), Northamptonshire (59-2) at Northampton (2nd day)........	1920
665	Rest of South Africa (339), Transvaal (326) at Johannesburg (1st day).......	1911-12
663	Middlesex (503-4), Leicestershire (160-2) at Leicester (2nd day)	1947
661	Border (201), Griqualand West (460) at Kimberley (1st day)...............	1920-21
649	Hampshire (570-8), Somerset (79-3) at Taunton (2nd day)	1901

HIGHEST AGGREGATES IN A MATCH

Runs	Wkts		
2,376	37	Maharashtra v Bombay at Poona	1948-49
2,078	40	Bombay v Holkar at Bombay	1944-45
1,981	35	South Africa v England at Durban	1938-39
1,945	18	Canterbury v Wellington at Christchurch.....................	1994-95
1,929	39	New South Wales v South Australia at Sydney	1925-26
1,911	34	New South Wales v Victoria at Sydney	1908-09
1,905	40	Otago v Wellington at Dunedin	1923-24

In Britain

Runs	Wkts		
1,815	28	Somerset v Surrey at Taunton...........................	2002
1,808	20	Sussex v Essex at Hove...............................	1993
1,795	34	Somerset v Northamptonshire at Taunton................	2001
1,723	31	England v Australia at Leeds..........................	1948
1,706	23	Hampshire v Warwickshire at Southampton..............	1997
1,683	14	Middlesex v Glamorgan at Southgate...................	2005
1,665	33	Warwickshire v Yorkshire at Birmingham..............	2002
1,659	13	Somerset v Middlesex at Taunton......................	2007
1,655	25	Derbyshire v Nottinghamshire at Derby................	2001
1,650	19	Surrey v Lancashire at The Oval......................	1990

LOWEST INNINGS TOTALS

12†	Oxford University v MCC and Ground at Oxford	1877
12	Northamptonshire v Gloucestershire at Gloucester...............	1907
13	Auckland v Canterbury at Auckland........................	1877-78
13	Nottinghamshire v Yorkshire at Nottingham	1901
14	Surrey v Essex at Chelmsford	1983
15	MCC v Surrey at Lord's	1839
15†	Victoria v MCC at Melbourne..........................	1903-04
15†	Northamptonshire v Yorkshire at Northampton	1908
15	Hampshire v Warwickshire at Birmingham	1922
	Following on, Hampshire scored 521 and won by 155 runs.	
16	MCC and Ground v Surrey at Lord's	1872
16	Derbyshire v Nottinghamshire at Nottingham...............	1879
16	Surrey v Nottinghamshire at The Oval	1880
16	Warwickshire v Kent at Tonbridge	1913
16	Trinidad v Barbados at Bridgetown	1942-43
16	Border v Natal at East London (first innings)	1959-60
17	Gentlemen of Kent v Gentlemen of England at Lord's.......	1850
17	Gloucestershire v Australians at Cheltenham	1896
18	The Bs v England at Lord's..............................	1831
18†	Kent v Sussex at Gravesend	1867
18	Tasmania v Victoria at Melbourne	1868-69
18†	Australians v MCC and Ground at Lord's..................	1896
18	Border v Natal at East London (second innings).............	1959-60
19	Sussex v Surrey at Godalming	1830
19†	Sussex v Nottinghamshire at Hove	1873
19	MCC and Ground v Australians at Lord's.................	1878
19	Wellington v Nelson at Nelson	1885-86
19	Matabeleland v Mashonaland at Harare	2000-01

† *One man absent.*

Note: At Lord's in 1810, The Bs, with one man absent, were dismissed by England for 6.

LOWEST TOTALS IN A MATCH

34	(16 and 18) Border v Natal at East London....................	1959-60
42	(27 and 15) Northamptonshire v Yorkshire at Northampton.............	1908

Note: Northamptonshire batted one man short in each innings.

LOWEST AGGREGATE IN A COMPLETED MATCH

Runs	Wkts		
85	11†	**Quetta v Rawalpindi at Islamabad**	**2008-09**
105	31	MCC v Australians at Lord's................................	1878

† *Both teams forfeited their first innings.*

Note: The lowest aggregate in a match in which the losing team was bowled out twice since 1900 is 157 for 22 wickets, Surrey v Worcestershire at The Oval, 1954.

Bold type denotes performances in the calendar year 2009.

LARGEST VICTORIES

Largest Innings Victories

Inns and 851 runs	Railways (910-6 dec) v Dera Ismail Khan at Lahore	1964-65
Inns and 666 runs	Victoria (1,059) v Tasmania at Melbourne	1922-23
Inns and 656 runs	Victoria (1,107) v New South Wales at Melbourne.............	1926-27
Inns and 605 runs	New South Wales (918) v South Australia at Sydney	1900-01
Inns and 579 runs	England (903-7 dec) v Australia at The Oval.................	1938
Inns and 575 runs	Sind (951-7 dec) v Baluchistan at Karachi...................	1973-74
Inns and 527 runs	New South Wales (713) v South Australia at Adelaide	1908-09
Inns and 517 runs	Australians (675) v Nottinghamshire at Nottingham	1921

Largest Victories by Runs Margin

685 runs	New South Wales (235 and 761-8 dec) v Queensland at Sydney ..	1929-30
675 runs	England (521 and 342-8 dec) v Australia at Brisbane	1928-29
638 runs	New South Wales (304 and 770) v South Australia at Adelaide ...	1920-21
609 runs	Muslim Commercial Bank (575 and 282-0 dec) v WAPDA at Lahore......................................	1977-78
585 runs	Sargodha (336 and 416) v Lahore Municipal Corporation at Faisalabad..	1978-79
573 runs	Sinhalese (395-7 dec and 350-2 dec) v Sebastianites at Colombo..	1990-91
571 runs	Victoria (304 and 649) v South Australia at Adelaide	1926-27
562 runs	Australia (701 and 327) v England at The Oval.................	1934
556 runs	Nondescripts (397-8 dec and 313-6 dec) v Matara at Colombo....	1998-99

Victory Without Losing a Wicket

Lancashire (166-0 dec and 66-0) beat Leicestershire by ten wickets at Manchester......	1956
Karachi A (277-0 dec) beat Sind A by an innings and 77 runs at Karachi	1957-58
Railways (236-0 dec and 16-0) beat Jammu and Kashmir by ten wickets at Srinagar	1960-61
Karnataka (451-0 dec) beat Kerala by an innings and 186 runs at Chikmagalur.........	1977-78

Notes: There have been **29** wins by an innings and 400 runs or more, the most recent being **an innings and 415 runs by Islamabad v Quetta at Islamabad in 2008-09.**

There have been **18** wins by 500 runs or more, the most recent being 533 runs by Chilaw Marians v Rio at Colombo in 2001-02.

There have been **32** wins by a team losing only one wicket, the most recent being by **Rawalpindi v Quetta at Islamabad in 2008-09.**

Bold type denotes performances in the calendar year 2009.

TIED MATCHES

Since 1948, a tie has been recognised only when the scores are level with all the wickets down in the fourth innings. There have been **32** instances since then, including two Tests (see Test record section); Sussex have featured in five of those, Essex and Kent in four each.

The most recent instances are:

Bahawalpur v Peshawar at Bahawalpur	1988-89
Wellington v Canterbury at Wellington	1988-89
Sussex v Kent at Hove	1991
Nottinghamshire v Worcestershire at Nottingham	1993
Somerset v West Indies A at Taunton	†2002
Warwickshire v Essex at Birmingham	2003
Worcestershire v Zimbabweans at Worcester	2003

† *Somerset (453) made the highest total to tie a first-class match.*

MATCHES COMPLETED ON FIRST DAY

(Since 1946)

Derbyshire v Somerset at Chesterfield, June 11	1947
Lancashire v Sussex at Manchester, July 12	1950
Surrey v Warwickshire at The Oval, May 16	1953
Somerset v Lancashire at Bath, June 6 (H. F. T. Buse's benefit)	1953
Kent v Worcestershire at Tunbridge Wells, June 15	1960

SHORTEST COMPLETED MATCHES

Balls

Balls		
121	**Quetta (forfeit and 41) v Rawalpindi (forfeit and 44-1) at Islamabad**	**2008-09**
350	Somerset (35 and 44) v Middlesex (86) at Lord's	1899
352	Victoria (82 and 57) v Tasmania (104 and 37-7) at Launceston	1850-51
372	Victoria (80 and 50) v Tasmania (97 and 35-2) at Launceston	1853-54
419*	England XI (82 and 26) v Australians (76 and 33-6) at Aston	1884
425	Derbyshire (180-0 dec and forfeit) v Northamptonshire (forfeit and 181-2) at Northampton	1992
432	Victoria (78 and 67) v Tasmania (51 and 25) at Hobart	1857-58
435	Northamptonshire (4-0 dec and 86) v Yorkshire (4-0 dec and 88-5) at Bradford	1931
442*	Wellington (31 and 48) v Nelson (73 and 7-1) at Nelson	1887-88
445	Glamorgan (272-1 dec and forfeit) v Lancashire (forfeit and 51) at Liverpool	1997
450	Bengal Governor's XI (33 and 59) v Maharaja of Cooch-Behar's XI (138) at Calcutta	1917-18

* *Match completed on first day.*

Bold type denotes performances in the calendar year 2009.

LIST A ONE-DAY RECORDS

List A is a concept intended to provide an approximate equivalent in one-day cricket of first-class status. It was introduced by the Association of Cricket Statisticians and Historians and is now recognised by the ICC, with a separate category for Twenty20 cricket. Further details are available at www.acscricket.com/ListA/Description.html. List A games comprise:

(a) One-day internationals.
(b) Other international matches (e.g. A-team internationals).
(c) Premier domestic one-day tournaments in Test-playing countries.
(d) Official tourist matches against the main first-class teams (e.g. counties, states, provinces and national Board XIs).

The following matches are excluded:

(a) Matches originally scheduled as less than 40 overs per side (e.g. Twenty20 games).
(b) World Cup warm-up games.
(c) Tourist matches against teams outside the major domestic competitions (e.g. universities).
(d) Festival games and pre-season friendlies.

Note: This section covers one-day cricket to December 31, 2009.

BATTING RECORDS

HIGHEST INDIVIDUAL INNINGS

268	A. D. Brown	Surrey v Glamorgan at The Oval	2002
222*	R. G. Pollock	Eastern Province v Border at East London	1974-75
207	Mohammad Ali	Pakistan Customs v DHA at Sialkot.	2004-05
206	A. I. Kallicharran	Warwickshire v Oxfordshire at Birmingham	1984
204*	**Khalid Latif**	**Karachi Dolphins v Quetta Bears at Karachi**	**2008-09**
203	A. D. Brown	Surrey v Hampshire at Guildford	1997
202*	A. Barrow	Natal v SA African XI at Durban.	1975-76
201*	R. S. Bopara	Essex v Leicestershire at Leicester.	2008
201	V. J. Wells	Leicestershire v Berkshire at Leicester.	1996

MOST RUNS

	Career	M	I	NO	R	HS	100s	Avge
G. A. Gooch	1973–1997	614	601	48	22,211	198*	44	40.16
G. A. Hick	*1983–2008*	651	630	96	22,059	172*	40	41.30
S. R. Tendulkar	*1989–2009*	527	514	54	20,946	186*	56	45.53
I. V. A. Richards	1973–1993	500	466	61	16,995	189*	26	41.96
C. G. Greenidge	1970–1992	440	436	33	16,349	186*	33	40.56
A. J. Lamb	1972–1995	484	463	63	15,658	132*	19	39.14
D. L. Haynes	1976–1996	419	416	44	15,651	152*	28	42.07
K. J. Barnett	1979–2005	527	500	54	15,564	136	17	34.89
S. T. Jayasuriya	*1989–2009*	539	524	25	15,532	189	31	31.12
S. C. Ganguly	*1989–2008*	426	410	42	15,278	183	31	41.51
M. G. Bevan	*1989–2006*	427	385	124	15,103	157*	13	57.86
R. Dravid	*1992–2009*	442	409	55	15,041	153	21	42.48

HIGHEST PARTNERSHIP FOR EACH WICKET

326*	for 1st	Ghulam Ali and Sohail Jaffer, PIA v ADBP at Sialkot	2000-01
331	for 2nd	S. R. Tendulkar and R. Dravid, India v New Zealand at Hyderabad . . .	1999-2000
309*	for 3rd	T. S. Curtis and T. M. Moody, Worcestershire v Surrey at The Oval . .	1994
275*	for 4th	M. Azharuddin and A. Jadeja, India v Zimbabwe at Cuttack	1997-98
267*	for 5th	Minhazul Abedin and Khaled Mahmud, Bangladeshis v Bahawalpur at Karachi	1997-98
226	for 6th	N. J. Llong and M. V. Fleming, Kent v Cheshire at Bowdon	1999
203*	for 7th	S. H. T. Kandamby and H. M. R. K. B. Herath, Sri Lanka A v South Africa A at Benoni	2008-09
203	for 8th	Shahid Iqbal and Haaris Ayaz, Karachi Whites v Hyderabad at Karachi	1998-99
155	for 9th	C. M. W. Read and A. J. Harris, Notts v Durham at Nottingham	2006
106*	for 10th	I. V. A. Richards and M. A. Holding, West Indies v England at Manchester.	1984

BOWLING RECORDS

BEST BOWLING ANALYSES

8-15	R. L. Sanghvi	Delhi v Himachal Pradesh at Una	1997-98
8-19	W. P. U. J. C. Vaas	Sri Lanka v Zimbabwe at Colombo	2001-02
8-20*	D. T. Kottehewa	Nondescripts v Ragama at Colombo	2007-08
8-21	M. A. Holding	Derbyshire v Sussex at Hove	1988
8-26	K. D. Boyce	Essex v Lancashire at Manchester	1971
8-30	G. D. R. Eranga	Burgher v Army at Colombo	2007-08
8-31	D. L. Underwood	Kent v Scotland at Edinburgh	1987
8-43	S. W. Tait	South Australia v Tasmania at Adelaide	2003-04
8-66	S. R. G. Francis	Somerset v Derbyshire at Derby	2004

* *Including two hat-tricks.*

MOST WICKETS

	Career	M	B	R	W	BB	4W/i	Avge
Wasim Akram.	1984–2003	594	29,719	19,303	881	5-10	46	21.91
A. A. Donald.	1985–2003	458	22,856	14,942	684	6-15	38	21.84
Waqar Younis.	1988–2003	412	19,841	15,098	675	7-36	44	22.36
J. K. Lever	1968–1990	481	23,208	13,278	674	5-8	34	19.70
J. E. Emburey	1975–2000	536	26,399	16,811	647	5-23	26	25.98
M. Muralitharan. . . .	**1991–2009**	**425**	**22,365**	**14,316**	**641**	**7-30**	**28**	**22.33**
I. T. Botham	1973–1993	470	22,899	15,264	612	5-27	18	24.94

WICKETKEEPING AND FIELDING RECORDS

MOST DISMISSALS IN AN INNINGS

8	(all ct)	D. J. S. Taylor	Somerset v Combined Universities at Taunton . . .	1982
8	(5ct, 3st)	S. J. Palframan	Boland v Easterns at Paarl	1997-98
8	(all ct)	D. J. Pipe	Worcestershire v Hertfordshire at Hertford	2001
7	(6ct, 1st)	R. W. Taylor	Derbyshire v Lancashire at Manchester	1975
7	(4ct, 3st)	Rizwan Umar	Sargodha v Bahawalpur at Sargodha	1991-92
7	(all ct)	A. J. Stewart	Surrey v Glamorgan at Swansea.	1994
7	(all ct)	I. Mitchell	Border v Western Province at East London	1998-99
7	(6ct, 1st)	M. K. P. B. Kularatne	Galle v Colts at Colombo	2001-02
7	**(5ct, 2st)**	**T. R. Ambrose**	**Warwickshire v Middlesex at Birmingham . . . .**	**2009**
7	**(3ct, 4st)**	**W. A. S. Niroshan**	**Chilaw Marians v Saracens at Katunayake . . . .**	**2009-10**

MOST CATCHES IN AN INNINGS IN THE FIELD

5	V. J. Marks	Combined Universities v Kent at Oxford	1976
5	J. M. Rice	Hampshire v Warwickshire at Southampton	1978
5	A. J. Kourie	Transvaal v Western Province at Johannesburg	1979-80
5	J. N. Rhodes	South Africa v West Indies at Bombay	1993-94
5	J. W. Wilson	Otago v Auckland at Dunedin	1993-94
5	K. C. Jackson	Boland v Natal at Durban	1995-96
5	Mohammad Ramzan	PNSC v PIA at Karachi	1998-99
5	Amit Sharma	Punjab v Jammu and Kashmir at Ludhiana	1999-2000
5	B. E. Young	South Australia v Tasmania at Launceston	2001-02
5	Hasnain Raza	Bahawalpur v Pakistan Customs at Karachi	2002-03
5	D. J. Sales	Northamptonshire v Essex at Northampton	2007
5	L. N. Mosena	Free State v North West at Bloemfontein	2007-08

TEAM RECORDS

HIGHEST INNINGS TOTALS

496-4	(50 overs)	Surrey v Gloucestershire at The Oval	2007
443-9	(50 overs)	Sri Lanka v Netherlands at Amstelveen	2006
438-5	(50 overs)	Surrey v Glamorgan at The Oval	2002
438-9	(49.5 overs)	South Africa v Australia at Johannesburg..................	2005-06
434-4	(50 overs)	Australia v South Africa at Johannesburg..................	2005-06
429	(49.5 overs)	Glamorgan v Surrey at The Oval	2002
424-5	(50 overs)	Buckinghamshire v Suffolk at Dinton......................	2002
418-5	(50 overs)	South Africa v Zimbabwe at Potchefstroom	2006-07
414-7	**(50 overs)**	**India v Sri Lanka at Rajkot**	**2009-10**
413-4	(60 overs)	Somerset v Devon at Torquay	1990
413-5	(50 overs)	India v Bermuda at Port-of-Spain	2006-07
412-4	(50 overs)	United Arab Emirates v Argentina at Windhoek	2007-08
411-6	(50 overs)	Yorkshire v Devon at Exmouth..........................	2004
411-8	**(50 overs)**	**Sri Lanka v India at Rajkot**	**2009-10**
410-5	**(50 overs)**	**Canterbury v Otago at Timaru**	**2009-10**
409-6	(50 overs)	Trinidad & Tobago v North Windward Islands at Kingston....	2001-02
408-4	(50 overs)	KRL v Sialkot at Sialkot................................	2002-03
406-5	(60 overs)	Leicestershire v Berkshire at Leicester	1996
405-4	(50 overs)	Queensland v Western Australia at Brisbane	2003-04
404-3	(60 overs)	Worcestershire v Devon at Worcester......................	1987
403-3	**(50 overs)**	**Somerset v Scotland at Taunton**	**2009**
402-2	(50 overs)	New Zealand v Ireland at Aberdeen	2008
401-7	(50 overs)	Gloucestershire v Buckinghamshire at Wing	2003

LOWEST INNINGS TOTALS

18	(14.3 overs)	West Indies Under-19 v Barbados at Blairmont	2007-08
23	(19.4 overs)	Middlesex v Yorkshire at Leeds	1974
30	(20.4 overs)	Chittagong v Sylhet at Dhaka	2002-03
31	(13.5 overs)	Border v South Western Districts at East London...........	2007-08
34	(21.1 overs)	Saurashtra v Mumbai at Mumbai	1999-2000
35	(18 overs)	Zimbabwe v Sri Lanka at Harare	2003-04
36	(25.4 overs)	Leicestershire v Sussex at Leicester	1973
36	(18.4 overs)	Canada v Sri Lanka at Paarl	2002-03
38	(15.4 overs)	Zimbabwe v Sri Lanka at Colombo	2001-02
39	(26.4 overs)	Ireland v Sussex at Hove	1985
39	(15.2 overs)	Cape Cobras v Eagles at Paarl *(one man absent)*	2008-09

Bold type denotes performances in the calendar year 2009 or, in career figures, players who appeared in that year.

LIST A TWENTY20 RECORDS

Note: This section covers Twenty20 cricket to December 31, 2009.

BATTING RECORDS

HIGHEST INDIVIDUAL INNINGS

158*	B. B. McCullum	Kolkata Knight Riders v Bangalore Royal Challengers at Bangalore	2007-08
152*	G. R. Napier	Essex v Sussex at Chelmsford	2008
141*	C. L. White	Somerset v Worcestershire at Worcester	2006
124*	**M. J. Lumb**	**Hampshire v Essex at Southampton**	**2009**
117*	A. Symonds	Deccan Chargers v Rajasthan Royals at Hyderabad	2007-08
117	C. H. Gayle	West Indies v South Africa at Johannesburg	2007-08
116*	G. A. Hick	Worcestershire v Northamptonshire at Luton	2004
116*	I. J. Thomas	Glamorgan v Somerset at Taunton.......................	2004
116*	C. L. White	Somerset v Gloucestershire at Taunton.	2006
116*	M. E. K. Hussey	Chennai Superstars v Kings XI Punjab at Mohali.	2007-08
115	Imran Farhat	Lahore Eagles v Multan Tigers at Karachi	2005-06
115	S. E. Marsh	Kings XI Punjab v Rajasthan Royals at Mohali	2007-08

MOST RUNS

	Career	M	I	NO	R	HS	100s	Avge
B. J. Hodge	2003–2009	74	71	11	2,366	106	1	39.43
D. J. Hussey	2004–2009	84	81	13	2,113	100*	1	31.07
G. C. Smith	2003–2009	62	62	6	1,856	105	1	33.14
H. D. Ackerman ..	2003–2009	55	55	7	1,811	87	0	37.72
B. B. McCullum ..	2004–2009	67	67	7	1,787	158*	1	29.78
J-P. Duminy	2003–2009	67	64	15	1,720	99*	0	35.10
I. J. L. Trott	2003–2009	61	56	14	1,708	86*	0	40.66
S. T. Jayasuriya ..	2004–2009	65	65	4	1,604	114*	1	26.29
M. van Jaarsveld .	2003–2009	80	71	10	1,573	76*	0	25.78
H. H. Gibbs......	2003–2009	69	67	6	1,526	98	0	25.01
K. C. Sangakkara	2004–2009	53	50	4	1,506	94	0	32.73

HIGHEST PARTNERSHIP FOR EACH WICKET

175	for 1st	V. S. Solanki and G. A. Hick, Worcs v Northants at Kidderminster	2007
186	for 2nd	J. L. Langern and C. L. White, Somerset v Gloucestershire at Taunton ..	2006
162	**for 3rd**	**Abdul Razzaq and Nasir Jamshed, Lahore Lions v Quetta Bears at Lahore**	**2009**
140*	**for 4th** {	**N. L. McCullum and A. D. Mascarenhas, Otago v Canterbury at Dunedin** .... **E. Chigumbura and C. Zhuwawo, Northerns v Centrals at Bulawayo**	**2008-09** **2009**
149	for 5th	Y. V. Takawale and S. V. Bahutule, Maharashtra v Gujarat at Mumbai .	2006-07
104	for 6th	D. J. Hussey and W. P. Saha, Kolkata Knight Riders v Kings XI Punjab at Mohali.	2007-08
91	for 7th	P. D. Collingwood and M. H. Yardy, England v West Indies at The Oval	2007
78	for 8th	R. S. A. Palliyaguruge and J. G. N. Priyantha, Saracens v Chilaw Marians at Colombo	2006-07
59*	for 9th	G. Chapple and P. J. Martin, Lancashire v Leicestershire at Leicester ...	2003
59	for 10th	H. H. Streak and J. E. Anyon, Warwickshire v Worcs at Birmingham...	2005

BOWLING RECORDS

BEST BOWLING ANALYSES

6-14	Sohail Tanvir	Rajasthan Royals v Chennai Superstars at Jaipur..........	2007-08
6-15	S. R. Abeywardene	Panadura v Air Force at Colombo	2005-06
6-21	A. J. Hall	Northamptonshire v Worcestershire at Northampton.......	2008
6-24	T. J. Murtagh	Surrey v Middlesex at Lord's...........................	2005
6-25	Irfanuddin	Karachi Dolphins v Sialkot Stallions at Karachi	2005-06
6-25	M. G. Dighton	Tasmania v Queensland at Toowoomba.................	2006-07

MOST WICKETS

	Career	M	B	R	W	BB	4W/i	Avge
T. Henderson	2003–2009	75	1,614	1,937	84	4-29	1	23.05
Umar Gul	2004–2009	46	1,004	1,078	78	5-6	7	13.82
Yasir Arafat	2005–2009	59	1,189	1,541	78	4-17	4	19.75
J. A. Morkel	2003–2009	90	1,546	2,036	78	4-30	2	26.10
A. D. Mascarenhas	2003–2009	63	1,261	1,501	76	5-14	2	19.75
A. J. Hall	2003–2009	52	1,076	1,353	71	6-21	3	19.05
G. R. Napier	2003–2009	55	1,143	1,386	70	4-10	1	19.80
C. M. Willoughby.	2003–2009	65	1,439	1,691	70	4-9	3	24.15

WICKETKEEPING AND FIELDING RECORDS

MOST DISMISSALS IN AN INNINGS

7 (all ct)	E. F. M. U. Fernando Lankan v Moors at Colombo	2005-06

MOST CATCHES IN AN INNINGS IN THE FIELD

Twelve fielders have made four catches in an innings in the field. They are B. G. Drew, **G. D. Elliott**, I. Khan, Nauman Ali, A. N. Petersen, D. Pretorius, M. Pushpakumara, D. J. Sales, J. N. Shah, W. R. Smith, S. R. Tendulkar and M. K. Tiwary.

TEAM RECORDS

HIGHEST INNINGS TOTALS

260-6	(20 overs)	Sri Lanka v Kenya at Johannesburg......................	2007-08
250-3	(20 overs)	Somerset v Gloucestershire at Taunton	2006
245-4	(20 overs)	Nondescripts v Air Force at Colombo	2005-06
242-3	(20 overs)	Essex v Sussex at Chelmsford	2008
241-6	**(20 overs)**	**South Africa v England at Centurion.....................**	**2009-10**
240-5	(20 overs)	Chennai Superstars v Kings XI Punjab at Mohali	2007-08

LOWEST INNINGS TOTALS

30	**(11.1 overs)**	**Tripura v Jharkhand at Dhanbad.........................**	**2009-10**
47	(14.3 overs)	Titans v Eagles at Centurion.............................	2003-04
58	**(15.1 overs)**	**Rajasthan Royals v Royal Challengers Bangalore at Cape Town**	**2008-09**
59	(12.1 overs)	Army v Sinhalese at Colombo	2006-07
65	(13.4 overs)	Warriors v Eagles at Port Elizabeth	2005-06

Bold type denotes performances in the calendar year 2009 or, in career figures, players who appeared in that year.

TEST RECORDS

Note: This section covers all Tests up to January 27, 2010.

BATTING RECORDS

HIGHEST INDIVIDUAL INNINGS

400*	B. C. Lara.............	West Indies v England at St John's............	2003-04
380	M. L. Hayden..........	Australia v Zimbabwe at Perth.................	2003-04
375	B. C. Lara.............	West Indies v England at St John's............	1993-94
374	D. P. M. D. Jayawardene .	Sri Lanka v South Africa at Colombo (SSC).....	2006
365*	G. S. Sobers...........	West Indies v Pakistan at Kingston	1957-58
364	L. Hutton	England v Australia at The Oval	1938
340	S. T. Jayasuriya	Sri Lanka v India at Colombo (RPS)...........	1997-98
337	Hanif Mohammad........	Pakistan v West Indies at Bridgetown	1957-58
336*	W. R. Hammond........	England v New Zealand at Auckland	1932-33
334*	M. A. Taylor...........	Australia v Pakistan at Peshawar..............	1998-99
334	D. G. Bradman.........	Australia v England at Leeds	1930
333	G. A. Gooch	England v India at Lord's.....................	1990
329	Inzamam-ul-Haq........	Pakistan v New Zealand at Lahore	2002
325	A. Sandham	England v West Indies at Kingston	1929-30
319	V. Sehwag	India v South Africa at Chennai...............	2007-08
317	C. H. Gayle...........	West Indies v South Africa at St John's.........	2004-05
313	**Younis Khan**	**Pakistan v Sri Lanka at Karachi**	**2008-09**
311	R. B. Simpson..........	Australia v England at Manchester	1964
310*	J. H. Edrich...........	England v New Zealand at Leeds	1965
309	V. Sehwag	India v Pakistan at Multan	2003-04
307	R. M. Cowper..........	Australia v England at Melbourne	1965-66
304	D. G. Bradman.........	Australia v England at Leeds	1934
302	L. G. Rowe	West Indies v England at Bridgetown	1973-74
299*	D. G. Bradman.........	Australia v South Africa at Adelaide	1931-32
299	M. D. Crowe..........	New Zealand v Sri Lanka at Wellington	1990-91
293	**V. Sehwag**	**India v Sri Lanka at Mumbai (BS)**...........	**2009-10**
291	I. V. A. Richards.......	West Indies v England at The Oval	1976
291	**R. R. Sarwan**.........	**West Indies v England at Bridgetown**	**2008-09**
287	R. E. Foster...........	England v Australia at Sydney................	1903-04
287	K. C. Sangakkara	Sri Lanka v South Africa at Colombo (SSC).....	2006
285*	P. B. H. May...........	England v West Indies at Birmingham	1957
281	V. V. S. Laxman........	India v Australia at Kolkata	2000-01
280*	Javed Miandad	Pakistan v India at Hyderabad	1982-83
278	D. C. S. Compton	England v Pakistan at Nottingham..............	1954
277	B. C. Lara.............	West Indies v Australia at Sydney	1992-93
277	G. C. Smith...........	South Africa v England at Birmingham.........	2003
275*	D. J. Cullinan	South Africa v New Zealand at Auckland	1998-99
275	G. Kirsten	South Africa v England at Durban.............	1999-2000
275	**D. P. M. D. Jayawardene**	**Sri Lanka v India at Ahmedabad**	**2009-10**
274*	S. P. Fleming	New Zealand v Sri Lanka at Colombo (PSS).....	2003
274	R. G. Pollock	South Africa v Australia at Durban	1969-70
274	Zaheer Abbas	Pakistan v England at Birmingham	1971
271	Javed Miandad	Pakistan v New Zealand at Auckland	1988-89
270*	G. A. Headley..........	West Indies v England at Kingston	1934-35
270	D. G. Bradman	Australia v England at Melbourne	1936-37
270	R. Dravid	India v Pakistan at Rawalpindi................	2003-04
270	K. C. Sangakkara	Sri Lanka v Zimbabwe at Bulawayo	2003-04
268	G. N. Yallop...........	Australia v Pakistan at Melbourne	1983-84
267*	B. A. Young	New Zealand v Sri Lanka at Dunedin	1996-97

267	P. A. de Silva	Sri Lanka v New Zealand at Wellington	1990-91
267	Younis Khan	Pakistan v India at Bangalore	2004-05
266	W. H. Ponsford	Australia v England at The Oval	1934
266	D. L. Houghton	Zimbabwe v Sri Lanka at Bulawayo	1994-95
262*	D. L. Amiss	England v West Indies at Kingston	1973-74
262	S. P. Fleming	New Zealand v South Africa at Cape Town	2005-06
261*	R. R. Sarwan	West Indies v Bangladesh at Kingston	2003-04
261	F. M. M. Worrell	West Indies v England at Nottingham	1950
260	C. C. Hunte	West Indies v Pakistan at Kingston	1957-58
260	Javed Miandad	Pakistan v England at The Oval	1987
259	G. M. Turner	New Zealand v West Indies at Georgetown	1971-72
259	G. C. Smith	South Africa v England at Lord's	2003
258	T. W. Graveney	England v West Indies at Nottingham	1957
258	S. M. Nurse	West Indies v New Zealand at Christchurch	1968-69
257*	Wasim Akram	Pakistan v Zimbabwe at Sheikhupura	1996-97
257	R. T. Ponting	Australia v India at Melbourne	2003-04
256	R. B. Kanhai	West Indies v India at Calcutta	1958-59
256	K. F. Barrington	England v Australia at Manchester	1964
255*	D. J. McGlew	South Africa v New Zealand at Wellington	1952-53
254	D. G. Bradman	Australia v England at Lord's	1930
254	V. Sehwag	India v Pakistan at Lahore	2005-06
253	S. T. Jayasuriya	Sri Lanka v Pakistan at Faisalabad	2004-05
251	W. R. Hammond	England v Australia at Sydney	1928-29
250	K. D. Walters	Australia v New Zealand at Christchurch	1976-77
250	S. F. A. F. Bacchus	West Indies v India at Kanpur	1978-79
250	J. L. Langer	Australia v England at Melbourne	2002-03

Note: The highest individual innings for Bangladesh is 158* by Mohammad Ashraful against India at Chittagong in 2004-05.

Bold type denotes innings played since January 1, 2009.

HUNDRED ON TEST DEBUT

C. Bannerman (165*)	Australia v England at Melbourne	1876-77
W. G. Grace (152)	England v Australia at The Oval	1880
H. Graham (107)	Australia v England at Lord's	1893
†K. S. Ranjitsinhji (154*)	England v Australia at Manchester	1896
†P. F. Warner (132*)	England v South Africa at Johannesburg	1898-99
†R. A. Duff (104)	Australia v England at Melbourne	1901-02
§R. E. Foster (287)	England v Australia at Sydney	1903-04
G. Gunn (119)	England v Australia at Sydney	1907-08
†R. J. Hartigan (116)	Australia v England at Adelaide	1907-08
†H. L. Collins (104)	Australia v England at Sydney	1920-21
W. H. Ponsford (110)	Australia v England at Sydney	1924-25
A. A. Jackson (164)	Australia v England at Adelaide	1928-29
†G. A. Headley (176)	West Indies v England at Bridgetown	1929-30
J. E. Mills (117)	New Zealand v England at Wellington	1929-30
Nawab of Pataudi sen. (102)	England v Australia at Sydney	1932-33
B. H. Valentine (136)	England v India at Bombay	1933-34
†L. Amarnath (118)	India v England at Bombay	1933-34
†P. A. Gibb (106)	England v South Africa at Johannesburg	1938-39
S. C. Griffith (140)	England v West Indies at Port-of-Spain	1947-48
A. G. Ganteaume (112)	West Indies v England at Port-of-Spain	1947-48
†J. W. Burke (101*)	Australia v England at Adelaide	1950-51

P. B. H. May (138)	England v South Africa at Leeds	1951
R. H. Shodhan (110)	India v Pakistan at Calcutta	1952-53
B. H. Pairaudeau (115)	West Indies v India at Port-of-Spain	1952-53
†O. G. Smith (104)	West Indies v Australia at Kingston	1954-55
A. G. Kripal Singh (100*)	India v New Zealand at Hyderabad	1955-56
C. C. Hunte (142)	West Indies v Pakistan at Bridgetown	1957-58
C. A. Milton (104*)	England v New Zealand at Leeds	1958
†A. A. Baig (112)	India v England at Manchester	1959
Hanumant Singh (105)	India v England at Delhi	1963-64
Khalid Ibadulla (166)	Pakistan v Australia at Karachi	1964-65
B. R. Taylor (105)	New Zealand v India at Calcutta	1964-65
K. D. Walters (155)	Australia v England at Brisbane	1965-66
J. H. Hampshire (107)	England v West Indies at Lord's	1969
†G. R. Viswanath (137)	India v Australia at Kanpur	1969-70
G. S. Chappell (108)	Australia v England at Perth	1970-71
‡§L. G. Rowe (214, 100*)	West Indies v New Zealand at Kingston	1971-72
A. I. Kallicharran (100*)	West Indies v New Zealand at Georgetown	1971-72
R. E. Redmond (107)	New Zealand v Pakistan at Auckland	1972-73
†F. C. Hayes (106*)	England v West Indies at The Oval	1973
‡C. G. Greenidge (107)	West Indies v India at Bangalore	1974-75
†L. Baichan (105*)	West Indies v Pakistan at Lahore	1974-75
G. J. Cosier (109)	Australia v West Indies at Melbourne	1975-76
S. Amarnath (124)	India v New Zealand at Auckland	1975-76
Javed Miandad (163)	Pakistan v New Zealand at Lahore	1976-77
†A. B. Williams (100)	West Indies v Australia at Georgetown	1977-78
†D. M. Wellham (103)	Australia v England at The Oval	1981
†Salim Malik (100*)	Pakistan v Sri Lanka at Karachi	1981-82
K. C. Wessels (162)	Australia v England at Brisbane	1982-83
W. B. Phillips (159)	Australia v Pakistan at Perth	1983-84
¶M. Azharuddin (110)	India v England at Calcutta	1984-85
D. S. B. P. Kuruppu (201*)	Sri Lanka v New Zealand at Colombo (CCC)	1986-87
†M. J. Greatbatch (107*)	New Zealand v England at Auckland	1987-88
M. E. Waugh (138)	Australia v England at Adelaide	1990-91
A. C. Hudson (163)	South Africa v West Indies at Bridgetown	1991-92
R. S. Kaluwitharana (132*)	Sri Lanka v Australia at Colombo (SSC)	1992-93
D. L. Houghton (121)	Zimbabwe v India at Harare	1992-93
P. K. Amre (103)	India v South Africa at Durban	1992-93
†G. P. Thorpe (114*)	England v Australia at Nottingham	1993
G. S. Blewett (102*)	Australia v England at Adelaide	1994-95
S. C. Ganguly (131)	India v England at Lord's	1996
†Mohammad Wasim (109*)	Pakistan v New Zealand at Lahore	1996-97
Ali Naqvi (115)	Pakistan v South Africa at Rawalpindi	1997-98
Azhar Mahmood (128*)	Pakistan v South Africa at Rawalpindi	1997-98
M. S. Sinclair (214)	New Zealand v West Indies at Wellington	1999-2000
†Younis Khan (107)	Pakistan v Sri Lanka at Rawalpindi	1999-2000
Aminul Islam (145)	Bangladesh v India at Dhaka	2000-01
†H. Masakadza (119)	Zimbabwe v West Indies at Harare	2001
T. T. Samaraweera (103*)	Sri Lanka v India at Colombo (SSC)	2001
Taufeeq Umar (104)	Pakistan v Bangladesh at Multan	2001-02
†Mohammad Ashraful (114)	Bangladesh v Sri Lanka at Colombo (SSC)	2001-02
V. Sehwag (105)	India v South Africa at Bloemfontein.	2001-02
L. Vincent (104)	New Zealand v Australia at Perth	2001-02
S. B. Styris (107)	New Zealand v West Indies at St George's	2002
J. A. Rudolph (222*)	South Africa v Bangladesh at Chittagong	2003
‡Yasir Hameed (170, 105)	Pakistan v Bangladesh at Karachi	2003
†D. R. Smith (105*)	West Indies v South Africa at Cape Town	2003-04
A. J. Strauss (112)	England v New Zealand at Lord's	2004
M. J. Clarke (151)	Australia v India at Bangalore	2004-05
†A. N. Cook (104*)	England v India at Nagpur	2005-06
M. J. Prior (126*)	England v West Indies at Lord's	2007
M. J. North (117)	**Australia v South Africa at Johannesburg**	**2008-09**

†Fawad Alam (168)	Pakistan v Sri Lanka at Colombo (PSS).	**2009**
†I. J. L. Trott (119)	England v Australia at The Oval	**2009**
Umar Akmal (129)	Pakistan v New Zealand at Dunedin.	2009-10
†A. B. Barath (104)	West Indies v Australia at Brisbane	2009-10

† *In his second innings of the match.*
‡ *L. G. Rowe and Yasir Hameed are the only batsmen to score a hundred in each innings on debut.*
§ *R. E. Foster (287, 19) and L. G. Rowe (214, 100*) are the only batsmen to score 300 runs in their debut Tests.*
¶ *M. Azharuddin is the only batsman to score hundreds in each of his first three Tests.*

Notes: L. Amarnath and S. Amarnath were father and son.
Ali Naqvi and Azhar Mahmood achieved the feat in the same innings.
Only Bannerman, Houghton and Aminul Islam scored hundreds in their country's first Test.

Bold type denotes innings played since January 1, 2009.

TRIPLE-HUNDRED AND HUNDRED IN A TEST

G. A. Gooch (England) . . . . 333 and 123 v India at Lord's 1990

The only instance in first-class cricket. M. A. Taylor (Australia) scored 334 and 92 v Pakistan at Peshawar in 1998-99.*

DOUBLE-HUNDRED AND HUNDRED IN A TEST

K. D. Walters (Australia).	242 and 103 v West Indies at Sydney	1968-69
S. M. Gavaskar (India).	124 and 220 v West Indies at Port-of-Spain	1970-71
†L. G. Rowe (West Indies)	214 and 100* v New Zealand at Kingston	1971-72
G. S. Chappell (Australia)	247* and 133 v New Zealand at Wellington.	1973-74
B. C. Lara (West Indies)	221 and 130 v Sri Lanka at Colombo (SSC).	2001-02

† *On Test debut.*

TWO SEPARATE HUNDREDS IN A TEST

S. M. Gavaskar (I).	3	C. G. Greenidge (WI) . .	1	**Mohammad Yousuf (P)**	**1**
R. T. Ponting (A)	**3**	A. P. Gurusinha (SL). . .	1	J. Moroney (A)	1
A. R. Border (A)	2†	W. R. Hammond (E). . .	1	A. R. Morris (A)	1
G. S. Chappell (A).	2	Hanif Mohammad (P) . .	1	E. Paynter (E)	1
P. A. de Silva (SL)	2‡	V. S. Hazare (I)	1	L. G. Rowe (WI)	1¶
R. Dravid (I).	**2**	G. P. Howarth (NZ). . . .	1	A. C. Russell (E).	1
M. L. Hayden (A)	**2**	**P. J. Hughes (A).**	**1**	R. B. Simpson (A).	1
G. A. Headley (WI)	2	Inzamam-ul-Haq (P) . . .	1	G. S. Sobers (WI)	1
H. Sutcliffe (E)	2	Javed Miandad (P).	1	A. J. Stewart (E)	1
C. L. Walcott (WI)	2§	A. H. Jones (NZ)	1	**A. J. Strauss (E).**	**1**
W. Bardsley (A)	1	D. M. Jones (A).	1	M. E. Trescothick (E) . .	1
D. G. Bradman (A)	1	**J. H. Kallis (SA).**	**1**	G. M. Turner (NZ)	1
I. M. Chappell (A).	1	R. B. Kanhai (WI)	1	M. P. Vaughan (E)	1
D. C. S. Compton (E) . .	1	G. Kirsten (SA)	1	Wajahatullah Wasti (P) .	1
T. M. Dilshan (SL).	**1**	B. C. Lara (WI)	1	K. D. Walters (A)	1
A. Flower (Z)	1	A. Melville (SA)	1	S. R. Waugh (A)	1
G. W. Flower (Z).	1	L. R. D. Mendis (SL). . .	1	E. D. Weekes (WI)	1
G. A. Gooch (E)	1	B. Mitchell (SA)	1	Yasir Hameed (P)	1¶

† *A. R. Border scored 150* and 153 against Pakistan in 1979-80 to become the first to score 150 in each innings of a Test match.*
‡ *P. A. de Silva scored 138* and 103* against Pakistan in 1996-97 to become the first to score two not-out hundreds in a Test match.*
§ *C. L. Walcott scored twin hundreds twice in one series, against Australia in 1954-55.*
¶ *L. G. Rowe's and Yasir Hameed's two hundreds were on Test debut.*

Bold type denotes those who have played Test cricket since January 1, 2009.

MOST DOUBLE-HUNDREDS

D. G. Bradman (A)	12	**K. C. Sangakkara (SL)**	**6**	C. G. Greenidge (WI)	4
B. C. Lara (WI)	9	**V. Sehwag (I)**	**6**	L. Hutton (E)	4
W. R. Hammond (E)	7	**R. Dravid (I)**	**5**	**Mohammad Yousuf (P)**	**4**
M. S. Atapattu (SL)	6	**R. T. Ponting (A)**	**5**	**G. C. Smith (SA)**	**4**
Javed Miandad (P)	6	G. S. Chappell (A)	4	**S. R. Tendulkar (I)**	**4**
D. P. M. D. Jayawardene (SL)	**6**	S. M. Gavaskar (I)	4	Zaheer Abbas (P)	4

Bold type denotes those who have played Test cricket since January 1, 2009.

MOST HUNDREDS

S. R. Tendulkar (I)	**45**	M. C. Cowdrey (E)	22	D. C. S. Compton (E)	17
R. T. Ponting (A)	**39**	W. R. Hammond (E)	22	M. D. Crowe (NZ)	17
S. M. Gavaskar (I)	34	D. C. Boon (A)	21	A. C. Gilchrist (A)	17
B. C. Lara (WI)	34	**S. Chanderpaul (WI)**	**21**	**V. Sehwag (I)**	**17**
J. H. Kallis (SA)	**33**	R. N. Harvey (A)	21	D. B. Vengsarkar (I)	17
S. R. Waugh (A)	32	G. Kirsten (SA)	21	M. S. Atapattu (SL)	16
M. L. Hayden (A)	**30**	**K. C. Sangakkara (SL)**	**21**	M. A. Atherton (E)	16
D. G. Bradman (A)	29	K. F. Barrington (E)	20	S. C. Ganguly (I)	16
R. Dravid (I)	**29**	P. A. de Silva (SL)	20	**K. P. Pietersen (E)**	**16**
A. R. Border (A)	27	G. A. Gooch (E)	20	R. B. Richardson (WI)	16
D. P. M. D. Jayawardene (SL)	**27**	**G. C. Smith (SA)**	**20**	H. Sutcliffe (E)	16
G. S. Sobers (WI)	26	M. E. Waugh (A)	20	G. P. Thorpe (E)	16
Inzamam-ul-Haq (P)	25	C. G. Greenidge (WI)	19	**Younis Khan (P)**	**16**
G. S. Chappell (A)	24	L. Hutton (E)	19	J. B. Hobbs (E)	15
Mohammad Yousuf (P)	**24**	C. H. Lloyd (WI)	19	R. B. Kanhai (WI)	15
I. V. A. Richards (WI)	24	M. A. Taylor (A)	19	Salim Malik (P)	15
Javed Miandad (P)	23	D. I. Gower (E)	18	**R. R. Sarwan (WI)**	**15**
J. L. Langer (A)	23	D. L. Haynes (WI)	18	A. J. Stewart (E)	15
M. Azharuddin (I)	22	**A. J. Strauss (E)**	**18**	C. L. Walcott (WI)	15
G. Boycott (E)	22	M. P. Vaughan (E)	18	K. D. Walters (A)	15
				E. D. Weekes (WI)	15

Note: The most hundreds for Zimbabwe is 12 by A. Flower, and the most for Bangladesh is **5** by **Mohammad Ashraful**.

Bold type denotes those who have played Test cricket since January 1, 2009.

MOST HUNDREDS AGAINST ONE TEAM

D. G. Bradman	19	Australia v England	G. S. Sobers	10	West Indies v England
S. M. Gavaskar	13	India v West Indies	**S. R. Tendulkar**	**10**	**India v Australia**
J. B. Hobbs	12	England v Australia	S. R. Waugh	10	Australia v England

MOST DUCKS

C. A. Walsh (WI)	43	M. Dillon (WI)	26	**S. J. Harmison (E)**	**21**
G. D. McGrath (A)	35	**Danish Kaneria (P)**	**25**	**M. Ntini (SA)**	**21**
S. K. Warne (A)	34	D. K. Morrison (NZ)	24	Waqar Younis (P)	21
M. Muralitharan (SL)	**33**	B. S. Chandrasekhar (I)	23	M. A. Atherton (E)	20
C. S. Martin (NZ)	**27**	M. S. Atapattu (SL)	22	B. S. Bedi (I)	20
C. E. L. Ambrose (WI)	26	S. R. Waugh (A)	22		

Bold type denotes those who have played Test cricket since January 1, 2009.

CARRYING BAT THROUGH TEST INNINGS

(Figures in brackets show team's total)

A. B. Tancred	26*	(47)	South Africa v England at Cape Town	1888-89
J. E. Barrett	67*	(176)†	Australia v England at Lord's	1890
R. Abel	132*	(307)	England v Australia at Sydney	1891-92
P. F. Warner	132*	(237)†	England v South Africa at Johannesburg	1898-99
W. W. Armstrong	159*	(309)	Australia v South Africa at Johannesburg	1902-03
J. W. Zulch	43*	(103)	South Africa v England at Cape Town	1909-10
W. Bardsley	193*	(383)	Australia v England at Lord's	1926
W. M. Woodfull	30*	(66)§	Australia v England at Brisbane	1928-29
W. M. Woodfull	73*	(193)‡	Australia v England at Adelaide	1932-33
W. A. Brown	206*	(422)	Australia v England at Lord's	1938
L. Hutton	202*	(344)	England v West Indies at The Oval	1950
L. Hutton	156*	(272)	England v Australia at Adelaide	1950-51
Nazar Mohammad¶	124*	(331)	Pakistan v India at Lucknow	1952-53
F. M. M. Worrell	191*	(372)	West Indies v England at Nottingham	1957
T. L. Goddard	56*	(99)	South Africa v Australia at Cape Town	1957-58
D. J. McGlew	127*	(292)	South Africa v New Zealand at Durban	1961-62
C. C. Hunte	60*	(131)	West Indies v Australia at Port-of-Spain	1964-65
G. M. Turner	43*	(131)	New Zealand v England at Lord's	1969
W. M. Lawry	49*	(107)	Australia v India at Delhi	1969-70
W. M. Lawry	60*	(116)‡	Australia v England at Sydney	1970-71
G. M. Turner	223*	(386)	New Zealand v West Indies at Kingston	1971-72
I. R. Redpath	159*	(346)	Australia v New Zealand at Auckland	1973-74
G. Boycott	99*	(215)	England v Australia at Perth	1979-80
S. M. Gavaskar	127*	(286)	India v Pakistan at Faisalabad	1982-83
Mudassar Nazar¶	152*	(323)	Pakistan v India at Lahore	1982-83
S. Wettimuny	63*	(144)	Sri Lanka v New Zealand at Christchurch	1982-83
D. C. Boon	58*	(103)	Australia v New Zealand at Auckland	1985-86
D. L. Haynes	88*	(211)	West Indies v Pakistan at Karachi	1986-87
G. A. Gooch	154*	(252)	England v West Indies at Leeds	1991
D. L. Haynes	75*	(176)	West Indies v England at The Oval	1991
A. J. Stewart	69*	(175)	England v Pakistan at Lord's	1992
D. L. Haynes	143*	(382)	West Indies v Pakistan at Port-of-Spain	1992-93
M. H. Dekker	68*	(187)	Zimbabwe v Pakistan at Rawalpindi	1993-94
M. A. Atherton	94*	(228)	England v New Zealand at Christchurch	1996-97
G. Kirsten	100*	(239)	South Africa v Pakistan at Faisalabad	1997-98
M. A. Taylor	169*	(350)	Australia v South Africa at Adelaide	1997-98
G. W. Flower	156*	(321)	Zimbabwe v Pakistan at Bulawayo	1997-98
Saeed Anwar	188*	(316)	Pakistan v India at Calcutta	1998-99
M. S. Atapattu	216*	(428)	Sri Lanka v Zimbabwe at Bulawayo	1999-2000
R. P. Arnold	104*	(231)	Sri Lanka v Zimbabwe at Harare	1999-2000
Javed Omar	85*	(168)†‡	Bangladesh v Zimbabwe at Bulawayo	2000-01
V. Sehwag	201*	(329)	India v Sri Lanka at Galle	2008
S. M. Katich	131*	(268)	Australia v New Zealand at Brisbane	2008-09
C. H. Gayle	**165***	**(317)**	**West Indies v Australia at Adelaide**	**2009-10**
Imran Farhat	**117***	**(223)**	**Pakistan v New Zealand at Napier**	**2009-10**

† *On debut*   ‡*One man absent.*   § *Two men absent.*   ¶ *Father and son.*

Notes: G. M. Turner (223*) holds the record for the highest score by a player carrying his bat through a Test innings. He is also the youngest player to do so, being 22 years 63 days old when he first achieved the feat (1969).

D. L. Haynes, who is alone in achieving this feat on three occasions, also opened the batting and was last man out in each innings for West Indies v New Zealand at Dunedin, 1979-80.

Bold type denotes innings played since January 1, 2009.

750 RUNS IN A SERIES

	T	I	NO	R	HS	100s	Avge		
D. G. Bradman	5	7	0	974	334	4	139.14	A v E	1930
W. R. Hammond...	5	9	1	905	251	4	113.12	E v A	1928-29
M. A. Taylor......	6	11	1	839	219	2	83.90	A v E	1989
R. N. Harvey......	5	9	0	834	205	4	92.66	A v SA	1952-53
I. V. A. Richards..	4	7	0	829	291	3	118.42	WI v E	1976
C. L. Walcott	5	10	0	827	155	5	82.70	WI v A	1954-55
G. S. Sobers	5	8	2	824	365*	3	137.33	WI v P	1957-58
D. G. Bradman	5	9	0	810	270	3	90.00	A v E	1936-37
D. G. Bradman	5	5	1	806	299*	4	201.50	A v SA	1931-32
B. C. Lara........	5	8	0	798	375	2	99.75	WI v E	1993-94
E. D. Weekes	5	7	0	779	194	4	111.28	WI v I	1948-49
†S. M. Gavaskar....	4	8	3	774	220	4	154.80	I v WI	1970-71
B. C. Lara........	6	10	1	765	179	3	85.00	WI v E	1995
Mudassar Nazar ...	6	8	2	761	231	4	126.83	P v I	1982-83
D. G. Bradman	5	8	0	758	304	2	94.75	A v E	1934
D. C. S. Compton..	5	8	0	753	208	4	94.12	E v SA	1947
‡G. A. Gooch	3	6	0	752	333	3	125.33	E v I	1990

† *Gavaskar's aggregate was achieved in his first Test series.*
‡ *G. A. Gooch is alone in scoring 1,000 runs in Test cricket during an English season with 1,058 runs in 11 innings against New Zealand and India in 1990.*

MOST RUNS IN A CALENDAR YEAR

	T	I	NO	R	HS	100s	Avge	Year
Mohammad Yousuf (P)......	11	19	1	1,788	202	9	99.33	2006
I. V. A. Richards (WI).......	11	19	0	1,710	291	7	90.00	1976
G. C. Smith (SA)............	15	25	2	1,656	232	6	72.00	2008
S. M. Gavaskar (I)...........	18	27	1	1,555	221	5	59.80	1979
R. T. Ponting (A)............	15	28	5	1,544	207	6	67.13	2005
R. T. Ponting (A)............	11	18	3	1,503	257	6	100.20	2003
J. L. Langer (A).............	14	27	0	1,481	215	5	54.85	2004
M. P. Vaughan (E)...........	14	26	2	1,481	197	6	61.70	2002
V. Sehwag (I)...............	14	27	1	1,462	319	3	56.23	2008

Notes: M. Amarnath reached 1,000 runs in 1983 on May 3.
  The only batsman to score 1,000 runs in a year before World War II was C. Hill of Australia: 1,061 in 1902.
  M. L. Hayden (Australia) scored 1,000 runs in each year from 2001 to 2005.

MOST RUNS

1 S. R. Tendulkar (India)	13,234
2 B. C. Lara (West Indies/World) ..	11,953
3 R. T. Ponting (Australia)	11,859
4 R. Dravid (India/World).......	11,372
5 A. R. Border (Australia)	11,174
6 S. R. Waugh (Australia)	10,927
7 J. H. Kallis (South Africa/World) .	10,640
8 S. M. Gavaskar (India)	10,122
9 D. P. M. D. Jayawardene (SL)....	9,120
10 G. A. Gooch (England)........	8,900
11 Javed Miandad (Pakistan).......	8,832
12 Inzamam-ul-Haq (Pakistan/World) .	8,830
13 S. Chanderpaul (West Indies) ..	8,669
14 M. L. Hayden (Australia)......	8,625
15 I. V. A. Richards (West Indies)...	8,540
16 A. J. Stewart (England).........	8,463
17 D. I. Gower (England)	8,231
18 G. Boycott (England)	8,114
19 G. S. Sobers (West Indies)	8,032
20 M. E. Waugh (Australia).......	8,029
21 M. A. Atherton (England).......	7,728
22 J. L. Langer (Australia).........	7,696
23 M. C. Cowdrey (England).......	7,624
24 C. G. Greenidge (West Indies) ...	7,558
25 K. C. Sangakkara (Sri Lanka)..	7,549
26 M. A. Taylor (Australia)	7,525
27 C. H. Lloyd (West Indies).......	7,515
28 D. L. Haynes (West Indies)......	7,487
29 Mohammad Yousuf (Pakistan) .	7,431
30 D. C. Boon (Australia)	7,422

31 G. Kirsten (South Africa)   7,289
32 W. R. Hammond (England)   7,249
33 S. C. Ganguly (India)   7,212
34 S. P. Fleming (New Zealand)   7,172
35 G. S. Chappell (Australia).   7,110
36 D. G. Bradman (Australia)   6,996

Bold type denotes those who have played Test cricket since January 1, 2009.

MOST RUNS FOR EACH COUNTRY

ENGLAND

		T	I	NO	R	HS	100s	Avge
1	G. A. Gooch	118	215	6	8,900	333	20	42.58
2	A. J. Stewart	133	235	21	8,463	190	15	39.54
3	D. I. Gower	117	204	18	8,231	215	18	44.25
4	G. Boycott	108	193	23	8,114	246*	22	47.72
5	M. A. Atherton	115	212	7	7,728	185*	16	37.69
6	M. C. Cowdrey	114	188	15	7,624	182	22	44.06
7	W. R. Hammond	85	140	16	7,249	336*	22	58.45
8	L. Hutton	79	138	15	6,971	364	19	56.67
9	K. F. Barrington	82	131	15	6,806	256	20	58.67
10	G. P. Thorpe	100	179	28	6,744	200*	16	44.66
11	M. E. Trescothick	76	143	10	5,825	219	14	43.79
12	D. C. S. Compton	78	131	15	5,807	278	17	50.06
13	N. Hussain	96	171	16	5,764	207	14	37.18
14	M. P. Vaughan	82	147	9	5,719	197	18	41.44
15	**A. J. Strauss**	**71**	**130**	**5**	**5,436**	**177**	**18**	**43.48**
16	J. B. Hobbs	61	102	7	5,410	211	15	56.94
17	I. T. Botham	102	161	6	5,200	208	14	33.54
18	J. H. Edrich	77	127	9	5,138	310*	12	43.54
19	T. W. Graveney	79	123	13	4,882	258	11	44.38
20	**K. P. Pietersen**	**58**	**104**	**4**	**4,824**	**226**	**16**	**48.24**
21	A. J. Lamb	79	139	10	4,656	142	14	36.09
22	H. Sutcliffe	54	84	9	4,555	194	16	60.73
23	P. B. H. May	66	106	9	4,537	285*	13	46.77
24	E. R. Dexter	62	102	8	4,502	205	9	47.89
25	M. W. Gatting	79	138	14	4,409	207	10	35.55
26	A. P. E. Knott	95	149	15	4,389	135	5	32.75
27	M. A. Butcher	71	131	7	4,288	173*	8	34.58
28	R. A. Smith	62	112	15	4,236	175	9	43.67

AUSTRALIA

		T	I	NO	R	HS	100s	Avge
1	**R. T. Ponting**	**142**	**240**	**27**	**11,859**	**257**	**39**	**55.67**
2	A. R. Border	156	265	44	11,174	205	27	50.56
3	S. R. Waugh	168	260	46	10,927	200	32	51.06
4	**M. L. Hayden**	**103**	**184**	**14**	**8,625**	**380**	**30**	**50.73**
5	M. E. Waugh	128	209	17	8,029	153*	20	41.81
6	J. L. Langer	105	182	12	7,696	250	23	45.27
7	M. A. Taylor	104	186	13	7,525	334*	19	43.49
8	D. C. Boon	107	190	20	7,422	200	21	43.65
9	G. S. Chappell	87	151	19	7,110	247*	24	53.86
10	D. G. Bradman	52	80	10	6,996	334	29	99.94
11	R. N. Harvey	79	137	10	6,149	205	21	48.41
12	A. C. Gilchrist	96	137	20	5,570	204*	17	47.60
13	K. D. Walters	74	125	14	5,357	250	15	48.26
14	I. M. Chappell	75	136	10	5,345	196	14	42.42
15	M. J. Slater	74	131	7	5,312	219	14	42.83
16	W. M. Lawry	67	123	12	5,234	210	13	47.15
17	R. B. Simpson	62	111	7	4,869	311	10	46.81
18	I. R. Redpath	66	120	11	4,737	171	8	43.45

		T	I	NO	R	HS	100s	Avge
19	K. J. Hughes	70	124	6	4,415	213	9	37.41
20	D. R. Martyn	67	109	14	4,406	165	13	46.37
21	I. A. Healy	119	182	23	4,356	161*	4	27.39
22	**M. J. Clarke**	**58**	**94**	**12**	**4,116**	**166**	**13**	**50.19**

SOUTH AFRICA

		T	I	NO	R	HS	100s	Avge
1	**J. H. Kallis**	134†	**226**	32	**10,557**	**189***	**33**	**54.41**
2	G. Kirsten	101	176	15	7,289	275	21	45.27
3	**R. R. Smith**	**80†**	**140**	**9**	**6,757**	**277**	**20**	**51.58**
4	H. H. Gibbs	90	154	7	6,167	228	14	41.95
5	**M. V. Boucher**	**129†**	**183**	**22**	**5,012**	**125**	**5**	**31.13**
6	D. J. Cullinan	70	115	12	4,554	275*	14	44.21

† *J. H. Kallis also scored 44 and 39*, G. C. Smith 12 and 0, and M. V. Boucher 0 and 17 for the ICC World XI v Australia in the Super Series Test of 2005-06.*

WEST INDIES

		T	I	NO	R	HS	100s	Avge
1	B. C. Lara	130†	230	6	11,912	400*	34	53.17
2	**S. Chanderpaul**	**123**	**210**	**32**	**8,669**	**203***	**21**	**48.70**
3	I. V. A. Richards	121	182	12	8,540	291	24	50.23
4	G. S. Sobers	93	160	21	8,032	365*	26	57.78
5	C. G. Greenidge	108	185	16	7,558	226	19	44.72
6	C. H. Lloyd	110	175	14	7,515	242*	19	46.67
7	D. L. Haynes	116	202	25	7,487	184	18	42.29
8	R. B. Kanhai	79	137	6	6,227	256	15	47.53
9	R. B. Richardson	86	146	12	5,949	194	16	44.39
10	**C. H. Gayle**	**85**	**150**	**6**	**5,848**	**317**	**12**	**40.61**
11	C. L. Hooper	102	173	15	5,762	233	13	36.46
12	**R. R. Sarwan**	**83**	**146**	**8**	**5,759**	**291**	**15**	**41.73**
13	E. D. Weekes	48	81	5	4,455	207	15	58.61
14	A. I. Kallicharran	66	109	10	4,399	187	12	44.43
15	R. C. Fredericks	59	109	7	4,334	169	8	42.49

† *B. C. Lara also scored 5 and 36 for the ICC World XI v Australia in the Super Series Test of 2005-06.*

NEW ZEALAND

		T	I	NO	R	HS	100s	Avge
1	S. P. Fleming	111	189	10	7,172	274*	9	40.06
2	M. D. Crowe	77	131	11	5,444	299	17	45.36
3	J. G. Wright	82	148	7	5,334	185	12	37.82
4	N. J. Astle	81	137	10	4,702	222	11	37.02

INDIA

		T	I	NO	R	HS	100s	Avge
1	S. R. Tendulkar	164	268	29	13,234	248*	45	55.37
2	R. Dravid	138†	238	28	11,372	270	29	54.15
3	S. M. Gavaskar	125	214	16	10,122	236*	34	51.12
4	S. C. Ganguly	113	188	17	7,212	239	16	42.17
5	V. V. S. Laxman	109	180	27	6,993	281	14	45.70
6	D. B. Vengsarkar	116	185	22	6,868	166	17	42.13
7	V. Sehwag	73†	125	5	6,318	319	17	52.65
8	M. Azharuddin	99	147	9	6,215	199	22	45.03
9	G. R. Viswanath	91	155	10	6,080	222	14	41.93
10	Kapil Dev	131	184	15	5,248	163	8	31.05
11	M. Amarnath	69	113	10	4,378	138	11	42.50

† *R. Dravid also scored 0 and 23, and V. Sehwag also scored 76 and 7, for the ICC World XI v Australia in the Super Series Test of 2005-06.*

PAKISTAN

		T	I	NO	R	HS	100s	Avge
1	Javed Miandad	124	189	21	8,832	280*	23	52.57
2	Inzamam-ul-Haq	119†	198	22	8,829	329	25	50.16
3	Mohammad Yousuf	88	152	12	7,431	223	24	53.07
4	Salim Malik	103	154	22	5,768	237	15	43.69
5	Younis Khan	63	112	7	5,260	313	16	50.09
6	Zaheer Abbas	78	124	11	5,062	274	12	44.79
7	Mudassar Nazar	76	116	8	4,114	231	10	38.09
8	Saeed Anwar	55	91	2	4,052	188*	11	45.52

† *Inzamam-ul-Haq also scored 1 and 0 for the ICC World XI v Australia in the Super Series Test of 2005-06.*

SRI LANKA

		T	I	NO	R	HS	100s	Avge
1	D. P. M. D. Jayawardene .	110	182	13	9,120	374	27	53.96
2	K. C. Sangakkara	88	147	10	7,549	287	21	55.10
3	S. T. Jayasuriya	110	188	14	6,973	340	14	40.07
4	P. A. de Silva	93	159	11	6,361	267	20	42.97
5	M. S. Atapattu	90	156	15	5,502	249	16	39.02
6	A. Ranatunga	93	155	12	5,105	135*	4	35.69
7	H. P. Tillekeratne	83	131	25	4,545	204*	11	42.87

ZIMBABWE

		T	I	NO	R	HS	100s	Avge
1	A. Flower	63	112	19	4,794	232*	12	51.54

BANGLADESH

No player has scored 4,000 Test runs for Bangladesh. The highest total is:

	T	I	NO	R	HS	100s	Avge
Habibul Bashar	50	99	1	3,026	113	3	30.87

Bold type denotes those who have played Test cricket since January 1, 2009.

CAREER AVERAGE OVER 50

(Qualification: 20 innings)

Avge		T	I	NO	R	HS	100s
99.94	D. G. Bradman (A).............	52	80	10	6,996	334	29
60.97	R. G. Pollock (SA)............	23	41	4	2,256	274	7
60.83	G. A. Headley (WI)	22	40	4	2,190	270*	10
60.73	H. Sutcliffe (E).............	54	84	9	4,555	194	16
59.23	E. Paynter (E)...............	20	31	5	1,540	243	4
58.67	K. F. Barrington (E).........	82	131	15	6,806	256	20
58.61	E. D. Weekes (WI)...........	48	81	5	4,455	207	15
58.45	W. R. Hammond (E)	85	140	16	7,249	336*	22
57.78	G. S. Sobers (WI)...........	93	160	21	8,032	365*	26
57.50	**G. Gambhir (I)**	**29**	**52**	**4**	**2,760**	**206**	**9**
56.94	J. B. Hobbs (E).............	61	102	7	5,410	211	15
56.68	C. L. Walcott (WI)..........	44	74	7	3,798	220	15
56.67	L. Hutton (E)	79	138	15	6,971	364	19
55.67	**R. T. Ponting (A)**	**142**	**240**	**27**	**11,859**	**257**	**39**
55.37	**S. R. Tendulkar (I)**..........	**164**	**268**	**29**	**13,234**	**248***	**45**
55.10	**K. C. Sangakkara (SL)**........	**88**	**147**	**10**	**7,549**	**287**	**21**
55.00	E. Tyldesley (E).............	14	20	2	990	122	3
54.56	**J. H. Kallis (SA/World)**	**135**	**228**	**33**	**10,640**	**189***	**33**
54.20	C. A. Davis (WI)............	15	29	5	1,301	183	4
54.20	V. G. Kambli (I).............	17	21	1	1,084	227	4
53.96	**D. P. M. D. Jayawardene (SL)**...	**110**	**182**	**13**	**9,120**	**374**	**27**
53.86	G. S. Chappell (A)...........	87	151	19	7,110	247*	24
53.81	A. D. Nourse (SA)...........	34	62	7	2,960	231	9
53.75	**R. Dravid (I/World)**..........	**139**	**240**	**28**	**11,395**	**270**	**29**
53.07	**Mohammad Yousuf (P)**........	**88**	**152**	**12**	**7,431**	**223**	**24**
53.04	**M. E. K. Hussey (A)**	**48**	**83**	**11**	**3,819**	**182**	**11**
52.88	B. C. Lara (WI/World)........	131	232	6	11,953	400*	34
52.57	Javed Miandad (P)	124	189	21	8,832	280*	23
52.46	**V. Sehwag (I/World)**	**74**	**127**	**5**	**6,401**	**319**	**17**
51.62	J. Ryder (A)	20	32	5	1,394	201*	3
51.54	A. Flower (Z)................	63	112	19	4,794	232*	12
51.14	**T. T. Samaraweera (SL)**	**57**	**90**	**13**	**3,938**	**231**	**11**
51.12	S. M. Gavaskar (I)	125	214	16	10,122	236*	34
51.06	S. R. Waugh (A)............	168	260	46	10,927	200	32
50.89	**G. C. Smith (SA/World)**........	**81**	**142**	**9**	**6,769**	**277**	**20**
50.73	**M. L. Hayden (A)**	**103**	**184**	**14**	**8,625**	**380**	**30**
50.56	A. R. Border (A)	156	265	44	11,174	205	27
50.23	I. V. A. Richards (WI)........	121	182	12	8,540	291	24
50.19	**M. J. Clarke (A)**	**58**	**94**	**12**	**4,116**	**166**	**13**
50.09	**Younis Khan (P)**............	**63**	**112**	**7**	**5,260**	**313**	**16**
50.06	D. C. S. Compton (E)..........	78	131	15	5,807	278	17

Bold type denotes those who have played Test cricket since January 1, 2009.

HIGHEST PERCENTAGE OF TEAM'S RUNS OVER TEST CAREER

(Qualification: 20 Tests)

	Tests	Runs	Team Runs	% of Team Runs
D. G. Bradman (Australia)........	52	6,996	28,810	24.28
G. A. Headley (West Indies)	22	2,190	10,239	21.38
B. C. Lara (West Indies)..........	131	11,953	63,328	18.87
L. Hutton (England)..............	79	6,971	38,440	18.13
J. B. Hobbs (England)	61	5,410	30,211	17.90
A. D. Nourse (South Africa)	34	2,960	16,659	17.76

	Tests	Runs	Team Runs	% of Team Runs
E. D. Weekes (West Indies).......	48	4,455	25,667	17.35
B. Mitchell (South Africa)........	42	3,471	20,175	17.20
H. Sutcliffe (England)	54	4,555	26,604	17.12
B. Sutcliffe (New Zealand)	42	2,727	16,158	16.87

The percentage shows the proportion of a team's runs scored by that player in all Tests in which he played, including team runs in innings in which he did not bat.

FASTEST FIFTIES

Minutes

27	Mohammad Ashraful	Bangladesh v India at Mirpur	2007
28	J. T. Brown	England v Australia at Melbourne	1894-95
29	S. A. Durani	India v England at Kanpur	1963-64
30	E. A. V. Williams	West Indies v England at Bridgetown.......	1947-48
30	B. R. Taylor	New Zealand v West Indies at Auckland	1968-69
31	W. J. O'Reilly..............	Australia v South Africa at Johannesburg....	1935-36
32	R. Benaud	Australia v West Indies at Kingston	1954-55
32	W. J. Cronje	South Africa v Sri Lanka at Centurion	1997-98

The fastest fifties in terms of balls received (where recorded) are:

Balls

24	J. H. Kallis	South Africa v Zimbabwe at Cape Town	2004-05
26	Shahid Afridi..............	Pakistan v India at Bangalore	2004-05
26	Mohammad Ashraful	Bangladesh v India at Mirpur	2007
27	Yousuf Youhana	Pakistan v South Africa at Cape Town	2002-03
28	E. A. V. Williams	West Indies v England at Bridgetown.......	1947-48
28	I. T. Botham	England v India at Delhi	1981-82
29	B. Yardley.................	Australia v West Indies at Bridgetown	1977-78
29	T. G. Southee	New Zealand v England at Napier	2007-08
30	Kapil Dev	India v Pakistan at Karachi	1982-83
30	**T. M. Dilshan**..............	**Sri Lanka v New Zealand at Galle**........	**2009**
31	A. Ranatunga	Sri Lanka v India at Kanpur	1986-87
31	W. J. Cronje	South Africa v Sri Lanka at Centurion	1997-98
32	I. V. A. Richards...........	West Indies v India at Kingston	1982-83
32	I. T. Botham	England v New Zealand at The Oval	1986
32	V. Sehwag.................	India v England at Chennai...............	2008-09
32	**Umar Akmal**	**Pakistan v New Zealand at Wellington**	**2009-10**

Bold type denotes performances since January 1, 2009.

FASTEST HUNDREDS

Minutes

70	J. M. Gregory	Australia v South Africa at Johannesburg....	1921-22
75	G. L. Jessop................	England v Australia at The Oval...........	1902
78	R. Benaud	Australia v West Indies at Kingston	1954-55
80	J. H. Sinclair	South Africa v Australia at Cape Town	1902-03
81	I. V. A. Richards...........	West Indies v England at St John's.........	1985-86
86	B. R. Taylor	New Zealand v West Indies at Auckland	1968-69

The fastest hundreds in terms of balls received (where recorded) are:

Balls

56	I. V. A. Richards	West Indies v England at St John's	1985-86
57	A. C. Gilchrist	Australia v England at Perth	2006-07
67	J. M. Gregory	Australia v South Africa at Johannesburg	1921-22
69	S. Chanderpaul	West Indies v Australia at Georgetown	2002-03
70	**C. H. Gayle**	**West Indies v Australia at Perth**	**2009-10**
71	R. C. Fredericks	West Indies v Australia at Perth	1975-76
74	Majid Khan	Pakistan v New Zealand at Karachi	1976-77
74	Kapil Dev	India v Sri Lanka at Kanpur	1986-87
74	M. Azharuddin	India v South Africa at Calcutta	1996-97
76	G. L. Jessop	England v Australia at The Oval	1902

Bold type denotes performances since January 1, 2009.

FASTEST DOUBLE-HUNDREDS

Minutes

214	D. G. Bradman	Australia v England at Leeds	1930
217	N. J. Astle	New Zealand v England at Christchurch	2001-02
223	S. J. McCabe	Australia v England at Nottingham	1938
226	V. T. Trumper	Australia v South Africa at Adelaide	1910-11
234	D. G. Bradman	Australia v England at Lord's	1930
240	W. R. Hammond	England v New Zealand at Auckland	1932-33
241	S. E. Gregory	Australia v England at Sydney	1894-95
245	D. C. S. Compton	England v Pakistan at Nottingham	1954

The fastest double-hundreds in terms of balls received (where recorded) are:

Balls

153	N. J. Astle	New Zealand v England at Christchurch	2001-02
168	**V. Sehwag**	**India v Sri Lanka at Mumbai (BS)**	**2009-10**
182	V. Sehwag	India v Pakistan at Lahore	2005-06
194	V. Sehwag	India v South Africa at Chennai	2007-08
211	H. H. Gibbs	South Africa v Pakistan at Cape Town	2002-03
212	A. C. Gilchrist	Australia v South Africa at Johannesburg	2001-02
220	I. T. Botham	England v India at The Oval	1982
222	V. Sehwag	India v Pakistan at Multan	2003-04
227	V. Sehwag	India v Sri Lanka at Galle	2008
229	P. A. de Silva	Sri Lanka v Bangladesh at Colombo (PSS)	2002

Bold type denotes performances since January 1, 2009.

FASTEST TRIPLE-HUNDREDS

Minutes

288	W. R. Hammond	England v New Zealand at Auckland	1932-33
336	D. G. Bradman	Australia v England at Leeds	1930

The fastest triple-hundred in terms of balls received (where recorded) is:

Balls

278	V. Sehwag	India v South Africa at Chennai	2007-08

MOST RUNS SCORED OFF AN OVER

28	B. C. Lara (466444)	off R. J. Peterson	WI v SA at Johannesburg . .	2003-04
27	Shahid Afridi (666621)	off Harbhajan Singh	P v I at Lahore	2005-06
26	C. D. McMillan (444464)	off Younis Khan	NZ v P at Hamilton	2000-01
26	B. C. Lara (406664)	off Danish Kaneria	WI v P at Multan	2006-07
26	**M. G. Johnson (446066)**	**off P. L. Harris**	**A v SA at Johannesburg . .**	**2009-10**

Bold type denotes performances since January 1, 2009.

MOST RUNS IN A DAY

309	D. G. Bradman	Australia v England at Leeds	1930
295	W. R. Hammond	England v New Zealand at Auckland	1932-33
273	D. C. S. Compton	England v Pakistan at Nottingham	1954
271	D. G. Bradman	Australia v England at Leeds	1934

MOST SIXES IN A CAREER

A. C. Gilchrist (A)	100		J. H. Kallis (SA/World)	**69**
B. C. Lara (WI)	88		**R. T. Ponting (A)**	**69**
C. L. Cairns (NZ)	87		I. T. Botham (E)	67
I. V. A. Richards (WI)	84		C. G. Greenidge (WI)	67
A. Flintoff (E/World)	**82**		**C. H. Gayle (WI)**	**65**
M. L. Hayden (A)	**82**		C. L. Hooper (WI)	63
V. Sehwag (I/World)	**76**		Kapil Dev (I)	61
C. H. Lloyd (WI)	70			

Bold type denotes those who have played Test cricket since January 1, 2009.

SLOWEST INDIVIDUAL BATTING

0	in 101 minutes G. I. Allott, New Zealand v South Africa at Auckland	1998-99
4*	in 110 minutes Abdul Razzaq, Pakistan v Australia at Melbourne	2004-05
7	in 123 minutes G. Miller, England v Australia at Melbourne	1978-79
9	in 132 minutes R. K. Chauhan, India v Sri Lanka at Ahmedabad	1993-94
10*	in 133 minutes T. G. Evans, England v Australia at Adelaide	1946-47
12	in 140 minutes R. Dravid, India v England at The Oval	2007
14*	in 165 minutes D. K. Morrison, New Zealand v England at Auckland	1996-97
18	in 194 minutes W. R. Playle, New Zealand v England at Leeds	1958
19*	in 217 minutes M. D. Crowe, New Zealand v Sri Lanka at Colombo (SSC)	1983-84
25	in 242 minutes D. K. Morrison, New Zealand v Pakistan at Faisalabad	1990-91
29*	in 277 minutes R. C. Russell, England v South Africa at Johannesburg	1995-96
35	in 332 minutes C. J. Tavaré, England v India at Madras	1981-82
60	in 390 minutes D. N. Sardesai, India v West Indies at Bridgetown	1961-62
62	in 408 minutes Ramiz Raja, Pakistan v West Indies at Karachi	1986-87
68	in 458 minutes T. E. Bailey, England v Australia at Brisbane	1958-59
99	in 505 minutes M. L. Jaisimha, India v Pakistan at Kanpur	1960-61
105	in 575 minutes D. J. McGlew, South Africa v Australia at Durban	1957-58
114	in 591 minutes Mudassar Nazar, Pakistan v England at Lahore	1977-78
146*	in 655 minutes M. J. Greatbatch, New Zealand v Australia at Perth	1989-90
163	in 720 minutes Shoaib Mohammad, Pakistan v New Zealand at Wellington	1988-89
201*	in 777 minutes D. S. B. P. Kuruppu, Sri Lanka v New Zealand at Colombo	
	(CCC)	1986-87
275	in 878 minutes G. Kirsten, South Africa v England at Durban	1999-2000
337	in 970 minutes Hanif Mohammad, Pakistan v West Indies at Bridgetown	1957-58

SLOWEST HUNDREDS

557 minutes	Mudassar Nazar, Pakistan v England at Lahore....................	1977-78
545 minutes	D. J. McGlew, South Africa v Australia at Durban	1957-58
535 minutes	A. P. Gurusinha, Sri Lanka v Zimbabwe at Harare	1994-95
516 minutes	J. J. Crowe, New Zealand v Sri Lanka at Colombo (CCC)	1986-87
500 minutes	S. V. Manjrekar, India v Zimbabwe at Harare......................	1992-93
488 minutes	P. E. Richardson, England v South Africa at Johannesburg...........	1956-57

Notes: The slowest hundred for any Test in England is 458 minutes (329 balls) by K. W. R. Fletcher, England v Pakistan, The Oval, 1974.

The slowest double-hundred in a Test was scored in 777 minutes (548 balls) by D. S. B. P. Kuruppu for Sri Lanka v New Zealand at Colombo (CCC), 1986-87, on his debut.

PARTNERSHIPS OVER 400

624	for 3rd	K. C. Sangakkara (287)/D. P. M. D. Jayawardene (374)....................	SL v SA	Colombo (SSC)	2006
576	for 2nd	S. T. Jayasuriya (340)/R. S. Mahanama (225)	SL v I	Colombo (RPS)	1997-98
467	for 3rd	A. H. Jones (186)/M. D. Crowe (299)......	NZ v SL	Wellington	1990-91
451	for 2nd	W. H. Ponsford (266)/D. G. Bradman (244) .	A v E	The Oval	1934
451	for 3rd	Mudassar Nazar (231)/Javed Miandad (280*)	P v I	Hyderabad	1982-83
446	for 2nd	C. C. Hunte (260)/G. S. Sobers (365*)	WI v P	Kingston	1957-58
438	for 2nd	M. S. Atapattu (249)/K. C. Sangakkara (270)	SL v Z	Bulawayo	2003-04
437	**for 4th**	**D. P. M. D. Jayawardene (240)/** **T. T. Samaraweera (231)**..............	**SL v P**	**Karachi**	**2008-09**
429*	for 3rd	J. A. Rudolph (222*)/H. H. Dippenaar (177*)	SA v B	Chittagong	2003
415	for 1st	N. D. McKenzie (226)/G. C. Smith (232) ...	SA v B	Chittagong	2007-08
413	for 1st	V. Mankad (231)/Pankaj Roy (173)........	I v NZ	Madras	1955-56
411	for 4th	P. B. H. May (285*)/M. C. Cowdrey (154)..	E v WI	Birmingham	1957
410	for 1st	V. Sehwag (254)/R. Dravid (128*)	I v P	Lahore	2005-06
405	for 5th	S. G. Barnes (234)/D. G. Bradman (234)....	A v E	Sydney	1946-47

Notes: 415 runs were added for the third wicket for India v England at Madras in 1981-82 by D. B. Vengsarkar (retired hurt), G. R. Viswanath and Yashpal Sharma. 408 runs were added for the first wicket for India v Bangladesh at Mirpur in 2007 by K. D. Karthik (retired hurt), Wasim Jaffer (retired hurt), R. Dravid and S. R. Tendulkar.

Bold type denotes partnerships since January 1, 2009.

HIGHEST PARTNERSHIPS FOR EACH WICKET

The following lists include all stands above 300; otherwise the top ten for each wicket.

First Wicket

415	N. D. McKenzie (226)/G. C. Smith (232).........	SA v B	Chittagong	2007-08
413	V. Mankad (231)/Pankaj Roy (173)	I v NZ	Madras	1955-56
410	V. Sehwag (254)/R. Dravid (128*)	I v P	Lahore	2005-06
387	G. M. Turner (259)/T. W. Jarvis (182)	NZ v WI	Georgetown	1971-72
382	W. M. Lawry (210)/R. B. Simpson (201)..........	A v WI	Bridgetown	1964-65
368	G. C. Smith (151)/H. H. Gibbs (228)	SA v P	Cape Town	2002-03
359	L. Hutton (158)/C. Washbrook (195)	E v SA	Johannesburg	1948-49
338	G. C. Smith (277)/H. H. Gibbs (179)	SA v E	Birmingham	2003
335	M. S. Atapattu (207*)/S. T. Jayasuriya (188)	SL v P	Kandy	2000
329	G. R. Marsh (138)/M. A. Taylor (219)	A v E	Nottingham	1989
323	J. B. Hobbs (178)/W. Rhodes (179)	E v A	Melbourne	1911-12
301	G. C. Smith (139)/H. H. Gibbs (192)	SA v WI	Centurion	2003-04

Second Wicket

576	S. T. Jayasuriya (340)/R. S. Mahanama (225)	SL v I	Colombo (RPS)	1997-98
451	W. H. Ponsford (266)/D. G. Bradman (244)......	A v E	The Oval	1934
446	C. C. Hunte (260)/G. S. Sobers (365*)...........	WI v P	Kingston	1957-58
438	M. S. Atapattu (249)/K. C. Sangakkara (270)......	SL v Z	Bulawayo	2003-04
382	L. Hutton (364)/M. Leyland (187)	E v A	The Oval	1938
369	J. H. Edrich (310*)/K. F. Barrington (163).......	E v NZ	Leeds	1965
351	G. A. Gooch (196)/D. I. Gower (157)............	E v A	The Oval	1985
344*	S. M. Gavaskar (182*)/D. B. Vengsarkar (157*) ...	I v WI	Calcutta	1978-79
331	R. T. Robinson (148)/D. I. Gower (215).........	E v A	Birmingham	1985
331	C. H. Gayle (317)/R. R. Sarwan (127)	WI v SA	St John's	2004-05
315*	H. H. Gibbs (211*)/J. H. Kallis (148*).........	SA v NZ	Christchurch	1998-99
314	G. Gambhir (179)/R. Dravid (136)	I v E	Mohali	2008-09
301	A. R. Morris (182)/D. G. Bradman (173*)	A v E	Leeds	1948

Third Wicket

624	K. C. Sangakkara (287)/			
	D. P. M. D. Jayawardene (374)	SL v SA	Colombo (SSC)	2006-0000
467	A. H. Jones (186)/M. D. Crowe (299)...........	NZ v SL	Wellington	1990-91
451	Mudassar Nazar (231)/Javed Miandad (280*)	P v I	Hyderabad	1982-83
429*	J. A. Rudolph (222*)/H. H. Dippenaar (177*)	SA v B	Chittagong	2003
397	Qasim Omar (206)/Javed Miandad (203*)	P v SL	Faisalabad	1985-86
370	W. J. Edrich (189)/D. C. S. Compton (208)......	E v SA	Lord's	1947
363	Younis Khan (163)/Mohammad Yousuf (192)	P v E	Leeds	2006
352*‡	Ijaz Ahmed, sen. (211)/Inzamam-ul-Haq (200*) ...	P v SL	Dhaka	1998-99
341	E. J. Barlow (201)/R. G. Pollock (175)...........	SA v A	Adelaide	1963-64
338	E. D. Weekes (206)/F. M. M. Worrell (167).......	WI v E	Port-of-Spain	1953-54
336	V. Sehwag (309)/S. R. Tendulkar (194*)	I v P	Multan	2003-04
330	H. M. Amla (176*)/J. H. Kallis (186)...........	SA v NZ	Johannesburg	2007-08
324	Younis Khan (267)/Inzamam-ul-Haq (184)	P v I	Bangalore	2004-05
323	Aamir Sohail (160)/Inzamam-ul-Haq (177)	P v WI	Rawalpindi	1997-98
319	A. Melville (189)/A. D. Nourse (149)...........	SA v E	Nottingham	1947
319	Younis Khan (199)/Mohammad Yousuf (173)......	P v I	Lahore	2005-06
316†	G. R. Viswanath (222)/Yashpal Sharma (140)	I v E	Madras	1981-82
315	R. T. Ponting (206)/D. S. Lehmann (160).........	A v WI	Port-of-Spain	2002-03
311	K. C. Sangakkara (222*)/D. P. M. D. Jayawardene (165)	SL v B	Kandy	2007
308	R. B. Richardson (154)/I. V. A. Richards (178)	WI v A	St John's	1983-84
308	G. A. Gooch (333)/A. J. Lamb (139)	E v I	Lord's	1990
303	I. V. A. Richards (232)/A. I. Kallicharran (97)....	WI v E	Nottingham	1976
303	M. A. Atherton (135)/R. A. Smith (175)..........	E v WI	St John's	1993-94

† *415 runs were scored for this wicket in two separate partnerships; D. B. Vengsarkar retired hurt when he and Viswanath had added 99 runs.*

‡ *366 runs were scored for this wicket in two separate partnerships; Inzamam retired ill when he and Ijaz had added 352 runs.*

Fourth Wicket

437	**D. P. M. D. Jayawardene (240)/**			
	T. T. Samaraweera (231)	**SL v P**	**Karachi**	**2008-09**
411	P. B. H. May (285*)/M. C. Cowdrey (154)	E v WI	Birmingham	1957
399	G. S. Sobers (226)/F. M. M. Worrell (197*).......	WI v E	Bridgetown	1959-60
388	W. H. Ponsford (181)/D. G. Bradman (304).......	A v E	Leeds	1934
353	S. R. Tendulkar (241*)/V. V. S. Laxman (178)	I v A	Sydney	2003-04
352	**R. T. Ponting (209)/M. J. Clarke (166)**	**A v P**	**Hobart**	**2009-10**
350	Mushtaq Mohammad (201)/Asif Iqbal (175)	P v NZ	Dunedin	1972-73
336	W. M. Lawry (151)/K. D. Walters (242)	A v WI	Sydney	1968-69
322	Javed Miandad (153*)/Salim Malik (165)	P v E	Birmingham	1992
320	J. N. Gillespie (201*)/M. E. K. Hussey (182).....	A v B	Chittagong	2005-06
310	P. D. Collingwood (206)/K. P. Pietersen (158).....	E v A	Adelaide	2006-07

Fifth Wicket

405	S. G. Barnes (234)/D. G. Bradman (234)	A v E	Sydney	1946-47
385	S. R. Waugh (160)/G. S. Blewett (214)	A v SA	Johannesburg	1996-97
376	V. V. S. Laxman (281)/R. Dravid (180)	I v A	Kolkata	2000-01
332*	A. R. Border (200*)/S. R. Waugh (157*)	A v E	Leeds	1993
327	J. L. Langer (144)/R. T. Ponting (197)	A v P	Perth	1999-2000
322†	B. C. Lara (213)/J. C. Adams (94)	WI v A	Kingston	1998-99
303	R. Dravid (233)/V. V. S. Laxman (148)	I v A	Adelaide	2003-04
300	S. C. Ganguly (239)/Yuvraj Singh (169)	I v P	Bangalore	2007-08
293	C. L. Hooper (233)/S. Chanderpaul (140).	WI v I	Georgetown	2001-02
281	Javed Miandad (163)/Asif Iqbal (166)	P v NZ	Lahore	1976-77
281	S. R. Waugh (199)/R. T. Ponting (104)	A v WI	Bridgetown	1998-99

† *344 runs were scored for this wicket in two separate partnerships; P. T. Collins retired hurt when he and Lara had added 22 runs.*

Sixth Wicket

351	D. P. M. D. Jayawardene (275)/ H. A. P. W. Jayawardene (154*)	SL v I	**Ahmedabad**	**2009-10**
346	J. H. Fingleton (136)/D. G. Bradman (270)	A v E	Melbourne	1936-37
317	D. R. Martyn (133)/A. C. Gilchrist (204*)	A v SA	Johannesburg	2001-02
298*	D. B. Vengsarkar (164*)/R. J. Shastri (121*)	I v A	Bombay	1986-87
282*	B. C. Lara (400*)/R. D. Jacobs (107*)	WI v E	St John's	2003-04
281	G. P. Thorpe (200*)/A. Flintoff (137).	E v NZ	Christchurch	2001-02
279	M. L. Hayden (153)/A. Symonds (156)	A v E	Melbourne	2006-07
274*	G. S. Sobers (163*)/D. A. J. Holford (105*)	WI v E	Lord's	1966
272	M. Azharuddin (199)/Kapil Dev (163)	I v SL	Kanpur	1986-87
271	A. G. Prince (162*)/M. V. Boucher (117)	SA v B	Centurion	2008-09

Seventh Wicket

347	D. St E. Atkinson (219)/C. C. Depeiza (122)	WI v A	Bridgetown	1954-55
308	Waqar Hassan (189)/Imtiaz Ahmed (209)	P v NZ	Lahore	1955-56
248	Yousuf Youhana (203)/Saqlain Mushtaq (101*)	P v NZ	Christchurch	2000-01
246	D. J. McGlew (255*)/A. R. A. Murray (109)	SA v NZ	Wellington	1952-53
235	R. J. Shastri (142)/S. M. H. Kirmani (102).	I v E	Bombay	1984-85
225	C. L. Cairns (158)/J. D. P. Oram (90).	NZ v SA	Auckland	2003-04
223*	H. A. P. W. Jayawardene (120*)/ W. P. U. J. C. Vaas (100*)	SL v B	Colombo (SSC)	2007
221	D. T. Lindsay (182)/P. L. van der Merwe (76)	SA v A	Johannesburg	1966-67
217	K. D. Walters (250)/G. J. Gilmour (101)	A v NZ	Christchurch	1976-77
217	V. V. S. Laxman (130)/A. Ratra (115*)	I v WI	St John's	2001-02

Eighth Wicket

313	Wasim Akram (257*)/Saqlain Mushtaq (79)	P v Z	Sheikhupura	1996-97
256	S. P. Fleming (262)/J. E. C. Franklin (122*)	NZ v SA	Cape Town	2005-06
253	N. J. Astle (156*)/A. C. Parore (110)	NZ v A	Perth	2001-02
246	L. E. G. Ames (137)/G. O. B. Allen (122)	E v NZ	Lord's	1931
243	R. J. Hartigan (116)/C. Hill (160).	A v E	Adelaide	1907-08
217	T. W. Graveney (165)/J. T. Murray (112).	E v WI	The Oval	1966
173	C. E. Pellew (116)/J. M. Gregory (100)	A v E	Melbourne	1920-21
170	D. P. M. D. Jayawardene (237)/ W. P. U. J. C. Vaas (69)	SL v SA	Galle	2004
168	R. Illingworth (107)/P. Lever (88*)	E v I	Manchester	1971
168	H. H. Streak (127*)/A. M. Blignaut (91)	Z v WI	Harare	2003-04

Ninth Wicket

195	M. V. Boucher (78)/P. L. Symcox (108)	SA v P	Johannesburg	1997-98
190	Asif Iqbal (146)/Intikhab Alam (51)	P v E	The Oval	1967
180	J-P. Duminy (166)/D. W. Steyn (76)	SA v A	Melbourne	2008-09
163*	M. C. Cowdrey (128*)/A. C. Smith (69*)	E v NZ	Wellington	1962-63
161	C. H. Lloyd (161*)/A. M. E. Roberts (68)	WI v I	Calcutta	1983-84
161	Zaheer Abbas (82*)/Sarfraz Nawaz (90)	P v E	Lahore	1983-84
154	S. E. Gregory (201)/J. McC. Blackham (74)	A v E	Sydney	1894-95
151	W. H. Scotton (90)/W. W. Read (117)	E v A	The Oval	1884
150	E. A. E. Baptiste (87*)/M. A. Holding (69)	WI v E	Birmingham	1984
149	P. G. Joshi (52*)/R. B. Desai (85)	I v P	Bombay	1960-61

Tenth Wicket

151	B. F. Hastings (110)/R. O. Collinge (68*)	NZ v P	Auckland	1972-73
151	Azhar Mahmood (128*)/Mushtaq Ahmed (59)	P v SA	Rawalpindi	1997-98
133	Wasim Raja (71)/Wasim Bari (60*)	P v WI	Bridgetown	1976-77
133	S. R. Tendulkar (248*)/Zaheer Khan (75)	I v B	Dhaka	2004-05
130	R. E. Foster (287)/W. Rhodes (40*)	E v A	Sydney	1903-04
128	K. Higgs (63)/J. A. Snow (59*)	E v WI	The Oval	1966
127	J. M. Taylor (108)/A. A. Mailey (46*)	A v E	Sydney	1924-25
124	J. G. Bracewell (83*)/S. L. Boock (37)	NZ v A	Sydney	1985-86
120	R. A. Duff (104)/W. W. Armstrong (45*)	A v E	Melbourne	1901-02
118	N. J. Astle (222)/C. L. Cairns (23*)	NZ v E	Christchurch	2001-02

Bold type denotes partnerships since January 1, 2009.

HIGHEST PARTNERSHIPS FOR EACH COUNTRY

ENGLAND

359	for 1st	L. Hutton (158)/C. Washbrook (195)	v SA	Johannesburg	1948-49
382	for 2nd	L. Hutton (364)/M. Leyland (187)	v A	The Oval	1938
370	for 3rd	W. J. Edrich (189)/D. C. S. Compton (208) . . .	v SA	Lord's	1947
411	for 4th	P. B. H. May (285*)/M. C. Cowdrey (154) . . .	v WI	Birmingham	1957
254	for 5th	K. W. R. Fletcher (113)/A. W. Greig (148) . . .	v I	Bombay	1972-73
281	for 6th	G. P. Thorpe (200*)/A. Flintoff (137)	v NZ	Christchurch	2001-02
197	for 7th	M. J. K. Smith (96)/J. M. Parks (101*)	v WI	Port-of-Spain	1959-60
246	for 8th	L. E. G. Ames (137)/G. O. B. Allen (122)	v WI	Lord's	1931
163*	for 9th	M. C. Cowdrey (128*)/A. C. Smith (69*)	v NZ	Wellington	1962-63
130	for 10th	R. E. Foster (287)/W. Rhodes (40*)	v A	Sydney	1903-04

AUSTRALIA

382	for 1st	W. M. Lawry (210)/R. B. Simpson (201)	v WI	Bridgetown	1964-65
451	for 2nd	W. H. Ponsford (266)/D. G. Bradman (244) . . .	v E	The Oval	1934
315	for 3rd	R. T. Ponting (206)/D. S. Lehmann (160)	v WI	Port-of-Spain	2002-03
388	for 4th	W. H. Ponsford (181)/D. G. Bradman (304) . . .	v E	Leeds	1934
405	for 5th	S. G. Barnes (234)/D. G. Bradman (234)	v E	Sydney	1946-47
346	for 6th	J. H. Fingleton (136)/D. G. Bradman (270) . . .	v E	Melbourne	1936-37
217	for 7th	K. D. Walters (250)/G. J. Gilmour (101)	v NZ	Christchurch	1976-77
243	for 8th	R. J. Hartigan (116)/C. Hill (160)	v E	Adelaide	1907-08
154	for 9th	S. E. Gregory (201)/J. McC. Blackham (74) . .	v E	Sydney	1894-95
127	for 10th	J. M. Taylor (108)/A. A. Mailey (46*)	v E	Sydney	1924-25

SOUTH AFRICA

415	for 1st	N. D. McKenzie (226)/G. C. Smith (232).....	v B	Chittagong	2007-08
315*	for 2nd	H. H. Gibbs (211*)/J. H. Kallis (148*).......	v NZ	Christchurch	1998-99
429*	for 3rd	J. A. Rudolph (222*)/H. H. Dippenaar (177*) .	v B	Chittagong	2003
249	for 4th	J. H. Kallis (177)/G. Kirsten (137)	v WI	Durban	2003-04
267	for 5th	J. H. Kallis (147)/A. G. Prince (131)	v WI	St John's	2004-05
271	for 6th	A. G. Prince (162*)/M. V. Boucher (117)	v B	Centurion	2008-09
246	for 7th	D. J. McGlew (255*)/A. R. A. Murray (109) ..	v NZ	Wellington	1952-53
150	for 8th {	N. D. McKenzie (103)/S. M. Pollock (111) ...	v SL	Centurion	2000-01
		G. Kirsten (130)/M. Zondeki (59)..........	v E	Leeds	2003
195	for 9th	M. V. Boucher (78)/P. L. Symcox (108)	v P	Johannesburg	1997-98
103	for 10th	H. G. Owen-Smith (129)/A. J. Bell (26*).....	v E	Leeds	1929

WEST INDIES

298	for 1st	C. G. Greenidge (149)/D. L. Haynes (167)....	v E	St John's	1989-90
446	for 2nd	C. C. Hunte (260)/G. S. Sobers (365*).......	v P	Kingston	1957-58
338	for 3rd	E. D. Weekes (206)/F. M. M. Worrell (167)...	v E	Port-of-Spain	1953-54
399	for 4th	G. S. Sobers (226)/F. M. M. Worrell (197*)...	v E	Bridgetown	1959-60
322	for 5th†	B. C. Lara (213)/J. C. Adams (94)	v A	Kingston	1998-99
282*	for 6th	B. C. Lara (400*)/R. D. Jacobs (107*).......	v E	St John's	2003-04
347	for 7th	D. St E. Atkinson (219)/C. C. Depeiza (122)..	v A	Bridgetown	1954-55
148	for 8th	J. C. Adams (101*)/F. A. Rose (69)	v Z	Kingston	1999-2000
161	for 9th	C. H. Lloyd (161*)/A. M. E. Roberts (68)	v I	Calcutta	1983-84
106	for 10th	C. L. Hooper (178*)/C. A. Walsh (30).......	v P	St John's	1992-93

† *344 runs were added between the fall of the 4th and 5th wickets: P. T. Collins retired hurt when he and Lara had added 22 runs.*

NEW ZEALAND

387	for 1st	G. M. Turner (259)/T. W. Jarvis (182)	v WI	Georgetown	1971-72
241	for 2nd	J. G. Wright (116)/A. H. Jones (143)	v E	Wellington	1991-92
467	for 3rd	A. H. Jones (186)/M. D. Crowe (299)	v SL	Wellington	1990-91
271	**for 4th**	**L. R. P. L. Taylor (151)/J. D. Ryder (201)** ..	**v I**	**Napier**	**2008-09**
222	for 5th	N. J. Astle (141)/C. D. McMillan (142)	v Z	Wellington	2000-01
246*	for 6th	J. J. Crowe (120*)/R. J. Hadlee (107*).......	v SL	Colombo (CCC)	1986-87
225	for 7th	C. L. Cairns (158)/J. D. P. Oram (90)........	v SA	Auckland	2003-04
256	for 8th	S. P. Fleming (262)/J. E. C. Franklin (122*) ..	v SA	Cape Town	2005-06
136	for 9th	I. D. S. Smith (173)/M. C. Snedden (22)	v I	Auckland	1989-90
151	for 10th	B. F. Hastings (110)/R. O. Collinge (68*)	v P	Auckland	1972-73

INDIA

413	for 1st	V. Mankad (231)/Pankaj Roy (173)	v NZ	Madras	1955-56
344*	for 2nd	S. M. Gavaskar (182*)/D. B. Vengsarkar (157*) .	v WI	Calcutta	1978-79
336	for 3rd†	V. Sehwag (309)/S. R. Tendulkar (194*).....	v P	Multan	2003-04
353	for 4th	S. R. Tendulkar (241*)/V. V. S. Laxman (178) ..	v A	Sydney	2003-04
376	for 5th	V. V. S. Laxman (281)/R. Dravid (180)......	v A	Kolkata	2000-01
298*	for 6th	D. B. Vengsarkar (164*)/R. J. Shastri (121*)..	v A	Bombay	1986-87
235	for 7th	R. J. Shastri (142)/S. M. H. Kirmani (102).....	v E	Bombay	1984-85
161	for 8th	A. Kumble (88)/M. Azharuddin (109)	v SA	Calcutta	1996-97
149	for 9th	P. G. Joshi (52*)/R. B. Desai (85)	v P	Bombay	1960-61
133	for 10th	S. R. Tendulkar (248*)/Zaheer Khan (75)	v B	Dhaka	2004-05

†*415 runs were scored for India's 3rd wicket v England at Madras in 1981-82, in two partnerships: D. B. Vengsarkar and G. R. Viswanath put on 99 before Vengsarkar retired hurt, then Viswanath and Yashpal Sharma added a further 316.*

PAKISTAN

298	for 1st	Aamir Sohail (160)/Ijaz Ahmed, sen. (151) . . .	v WI	Karachi	1997-98
291	for 2nd	Zaheer Abbas (274)/Mushtaq Mohammad (100)	v E	Birmingham	1971
451	for 3rd	Mudassar Nazar (231)/Javed Miandad (280*) .	v I	Hyderabad	1982-83
350	for 4th	Mushtaq Mohammad (201)/Asif Iqbal (175) . .	v NZ	Dunedin	1972-73
281	for 5th	Javed Miandad (163)/Asif Iqbal (166)	v NZ	Lahore	1976-77
269	for 6th	Mohammad Yousuf (223)/Kamran Akmal (154)	v E	Lahore	2005-06
308	for 7th	Waqar Hassan (189)/Imtiaz Ahmed (209) . . .	v NZ	Lahore	1955-56
313	for 8th	Wasim Akram (257*)/Saqlain Mushtaq (79) . .	v Z	Sheikhupura	1996-97
190	for 9th	Asif Iqbal (146)/Intikhab Alam (51).	v E	The Oval	1967
151	for 10th	Azhar Mahmood (128*)/Mushtaq Ahmed (59)	v SA	Rawalpindi	1997-98

SRI LANKA

335	for 1st	M. S. Atapattu (207*)/S. T. Jayasuriya (188). .	v P	Kandy	2000
576	for 2nd	S. T. Jayasuriya (340)/R. S. Mahanama (225) .	v I	Colombo (RPS)	1997-98
624	for 3rd	K. C. Sangakkara (287)/			
		D. P. M. D. Jayawardene (374).	v SA	Colombo (SSC)	2006
437	**for 4th**	**D. P. M. D. Jayawardene (240)/**			
		T. T. Samaraweera (231)	**v P**	**Karachi**	**2008-09**
280	for 5th	T. T. Samaraweera (138)/T. M. Dilshan (168) .	v B	Colombo (PSS)	2005-06
351	**for 6th**	**D. P. M. D. Jayawardene (275)/**			
		H. A. P. W. Jayawardene (154*)	**v I**	**Ahmedabad**	**2009-10**
223*	for 7th	H. A. P. W. Jayawardene (120*)/			
		W. P. U. J. C. Vaas (100*)	v B	Colombo (SSC)	2007
170	for 8th	D. P. M. D. Jayawardene (237)/			
		W. P. U. J. C. Vaas (69)	v SA	Galle	2004
105	for 9th	W. P. U. J. C. Vaas (50*)/			
		K. M. D. N. Kulasekara (64).	v E	Lord's	2006
79	for 10th	W. P. U. J. C. Vaas (68*)/M. Muralitharan (43)	v A	Kandy	2003-04

ZIMBABWE

164	for 1st	D. D. Ebrahim (71)/A. D. R. Campbell (103) .	v WI	Bulawayo	2001
135	for 2nd	M. H. Dekker (68*)/A. D. R. Campbell (75) . .	v P	Rawalpindi	1993-94
194	for 3rd	A. D. R. Campbell (99)/D. L. Houghton (142).	v SL	Harare	1994-95
269	for 4th	G. W. Flower (201*)/A. Flower (156)	v P	Harare	1994-95
277*	for 5th	M. W. Goodwin (166*)/A. Flower (100*)	v P	Bulawayo	1997-98
165	for 6th	D. L. Houghton (121)/A. Flower (59).	v I	Harare	1992-93
154	for 7th	H. H. Streak (83*)/A. M. Blignaut (92)	v WI	Harare	2001
168	for 8th	H. H. Streak (127*)/A. M. Blignaut (91)	v WI	Harare	2003-04
87	for 9th	P. A. Strang (106*)/B. C. Strang (42).	v P	Sheikhupura	1996-97
97*	for 10th	A. Flower (183*)/H. K. Olonga (11)	v I	Delhi	2000-01

BANGLADESH

161	for 1st	Tamim Iqbal (84)/Junaid Siddique (74)	v NZ	Dunedin (Univ)	2007-08
200	**for 2nd**	**Tamim Iqbal (151)/Junaid Siddique (55)** . . .	**v I**	**Mirpur**	**2009-10**
130	for 3rd	Javed Omar (119)/Mohammad Ashraful (77) .	v P	Peshawar	2003
120	for 4th	Habibul Bashar (77)/Manjural Islam Rana (35)	v WI	Kingston	2003-04
144	for 5th	Mehrab Hossain (83)/Mushfiqur Rahim (79) . .	v NZ	Chittagong	2008-09
191	for 6th	Mohammad Ashraful (129*)/			
		Mushfiqur Rahim (80).	v SL	Colombo (PSS)	2007
111	for 7th	Shakib Al Hasan (96)/Mushfiqur Rahim (61) . .	v SL	Mirpur	2008-09
87	for 8th	Mohammad Ashraful (81)/			
		Mohammad Rafique (111)	v WI	Gros Islet, St Lucia	2003-04
77	for 9th	Mashrafe bin Mortaza (79)/			
		Shahadat Hossain (31)	v I	Chittagong	2007
69	for 10th	Mohammad Rafique (65)/			
		Shahadat Hossain (3*)	v A	Chittagong	2005-06

Bold type denotes partnerships since January 1, 2009.

UNUSUAL DISMISSALS

Handled the Ball

W. R. Endean	South Africa v England at Cape Town	1956-57
A. M. J. Hilditch	Australia v Pakistan at Perth	1978-79
Mohsin Khan	Pakistan v Australia at Karachi	1982-83
D. L. Haynes	West Indies v India at Bombay	1983-84
G. A. Gooch	England v Australia at Manchester	1993
S. R. Waugh	Australia v India at Chennai	2000-01
M. P. Vaughan	England v India at Bangalore	2001-02

Obstructing the Field

L. Hutton	England v South Africa at The Oval.	1951

Note: There have been no cases of Hit the Ball Twice or Timed Out in Test cricket.

BOWLING RECORDS

MOST WICKETS IN AN INNINGS

10-53	J. C. Laker	England v Australia at Manchester.	1956
10-74	A. Kumble	India v Pakistan at Delhi.	1998-99
9-28	G. A. Lohmann	England v South Africa at Johannesburg	1895-96
9-37	J. C. Laker	England v Australia at Manchester.	1956
9-51	M. Muralitharan.	Sri Lanka v Zimbabwe at Kandy	2001-02
9-52	R. J. Hadlee	New Zealand v Australia at Brisbane	1985-86
9-56	Abdul Qadir.	Pakistan v England at Lahore	1987-88
9-57	D. E. Malcolm.	England v South Africa at The Oval.	1994
9-65	M. Muralitharan.	Sri Lanka v England at The Oval	1998
9-69	J. M. Patel	India v Australia at Kanpur	1959-60
9-83	Kapil Dev	India v West Indies at Ahmedabad.	1983-84
9-86	Sarfraz Nawaz	Pakistan v Australia at Melbourne	1978-79
9-95	J. M. Noreiga.	West Indies v India at Port-of-Spain.	1970-71
9-102	S. P. Gupte.	India v West Indies at Kanpur	1958-59
9-103	S. F. Barnes	England v South Africa at Johannesburg	1913-14
9-113	H. J. Tayfield	South Africa v England at Johannesburg	1956-57
9-121	A. A. Mailey	Australia v England at Melbourne	1920-21
8-7	G. A. Lohmann	England v South Africa at Port Elizabeth.	1895-96
8-11	J. Briggs.	England v South Africa at Cape Town	1888-89
8-24	G. D. McGrath.	Australia v Pakistan at Perth	2004-05
8-29	S. F. Barnes	England v South Africa at The Oval.	1912
8-29	C. E. H. Croft	West Indies v Pakistan at Port-of-Spain	1976-77
8-31	F. Laver	Australia v England at Manchester.	1909
8-31	F. S. Trueman	England v India at Manchester.	1952
8-34	I. T. Botham	England v Pakistan at Lord's	1978
8-35	G. A. Lohmann	England v Australia at Sydney	1886-87
8-38	L. R. Gibbs	West Indies v India at Bridgetown	1961-62
8-38	G. D. McGrath.	Australia v England at Lord's.	1997
8-43†	A. E. Trott	Australia v England at Adelaide	1894-95
8-43	H. Verity	England v Australia at Lord's.	1934
8-43	R. G. D. Willis.	England v Australia at Leeds	1981
8-45	C. E. L. Ambrose.	West Indies v England at Bridgetown	1989-90
8-46	M. Muralitharan.	Sri Lanka v West Indies at Kandy	2005
8-51	D. L. Underwood.	England v Pakistan at Lord's	1974
8-52	V. Mankad.	India v Pakistan at Delhi.	1952-53
8-53	G. B. Lawrence	South Africa v New Zealand at Johannesburg	1961-62
8-53†	R. A. L. Massie.	Australia v England at Lord's.	1972
8-53	A. R. C. Fraser.	England v West Indies at Port-of-Spain	1997-98

8-55	V. Mankad	India v England at Madras	1951-52
8-56	S. F. Barnes	England v South Africa at Johannesburg	1913-14
8-58	G. A. Lohmann	England v Australia at Sydney	1891-92
8-58	Imran Khan	Pakistan v Sri Lanka at Lahore	1981-82
8-59	C. Blythe	England v South Africa at Leeds	1907
8-59	A. A. Mallett	Australia v Pakistan at Adelaide	1972-73
8-60	Imran Khan	Pakistan v India at Karachi	1982-83
8-61†	N. D. Hirwani	India v West Indies at Madras	1987-88
8-61	M. G. Johnson	Australia v South Africa at Perth	2008-09
8-64†	L. Klusener	South Africa v India at Calcutta	1996-97
8-65	H. Trumble	Australia v England at The Oval	1902
8-68	W. Rhodes	England v Australia at Melbourne	1903-04
8-69	H. J. Tayfield	South Africa v England at Durban	1956-57
8-69	Sikander Bakht	Pakistan v India at Delhi	1979-80
8-70	S. J. Snooke	South Africa v England at Johannesburg	1905-06
8-70	M. Muralitharan	Sri Lanka v England at Nottingham	2006
8-71	G. D. McKenzie	Australia v West Indies at Melbourne	1968-69
8-71	S. K. Warne	Australia v England at Brisbane	1994-95
8-71	A. A. Donald	South Africa v Zimbabwe at Harare	1995-96
8-72	S. Venkataraghavan	India v New Zealand at Delhi	1964-65
8-75†	N. D. Hirwani	India v West Indies at Madras	1987-88
8-75	A. R. C. Fraser	England v West Indies at Bridgetown	1993-94
8-76	E. A. S. Prasanna	India v New Zealand at Auckland	1975-76
8-79	B. S. Chandrasekhar	India v England at Delhi	1972-73
8-81	L. C. Braund	England v Australia at Melbourne	1903-04
8-83	J. R. Ratnayeke	Sri Lanka v Pakistan at Sialkot	1985-86
8-84†	R. A. L. Massie	Australia v England at Lord's	1972
8-84	Harbhajan Singh	India v Australia at Chennai	2000-01
8-85	Kapil Dev	India v Pakistan at Lahore	1982-83
8-86	A. W. Greig	England v West Indies at Port-of-Spain	1973-74
8-86	J. Srinath	India v Pakistan at Calcutta	1998-99
8-87	M. G. Hughes	Australia v West Indies at Perth	1988-89
8-87	M. Muralitharan	Sri Lanka v India at Colombo (SSC)	2001
8-92	M. A. Holding	West Indies v England at The Oval	1976
8-94	T. Richardson	England v Australia at Sydney	1897-98
8-97	C. J. McDermott	Australia v England at Perth	1990-91
8-103	I. T. Botham	England v West Indies at Lord's	1984
8-104†	A. L. Valentine	West Indies v England at Manchester	1950
8-106	Kapil Dev	India v Australia at Adelaide	1985-86
8-107	B. J. T. Bosanquet	England v Australia at Nottingham	1905
8-107	N. A. Foster	England v Pakistan at Leeds	1987
8-108	S. C. G. MacGill	Australia v Bangladesh at Fatullah	2005-06
8-109	P. A. Strang	Zimbabwe v New Zealand at Bulawayo	2000-01
8-112	G. F. Lawson	Australia v West Indies at Adelaide	1984-85
8-126	J. C. White	England v Australia at Adelaide	1928-29
8-141	C. J. McDermott	Australia v England at Manchester	1985
8-141	A. Kumble	India v Australia at Sydney	2003-04
8-143	M. H. N. Walker	Australia v England at Melbourne	1974-75
8-164	Saqlain Mushtaq	Pakistan v England at Lahore	2000-01
8-215†	J. J. Krejza	Australia v India at Nagpur	2008-09

† *On Test debut.*

Note: The best for Bangladesh is 7-36 by Shakib Al Hasan against New Zealand at Chittagong in 2008-09.

OUTSTANDING BOWLING ANALYSES

	O	M	R	W		
J. C. Laker (E)	51.2	23	53	10	v Australia at Manchester	1956
A. Kumble (I)	26.3	9	74	10	v Pakistan at Delhi	1998-99
G. A. Lohmann (E)	14.2	6	28	9	v South Africa at Johannesburg	1895-96
J. C. Laker (E)	16.4	4	37	9	v Australia at Manchester	1956

	O	M	R	W		
G. A. Lohmann (E)	9.4	5	7	8	v South Africa at Port Elizabeth	1895-96
J. Briggs (E)	14.2	5	11	8	v South Africa at Cape Town	1888-89
S. J. Harmison (E)	12.3	8	12	7	v West Indies at Kingston	2003-04
J. Briggs (E)	19.1	11	17	7	v South Africa at Cape Town	1888-89
M. A. Noble (A)	7.4	2	17	7	v England at Melbourne	1901-02
W. Rhodes (E)	11	3	17	7	v Australia at Birmingham	1902
J. J. C. Lawson (WI)	6.5	4	3	6	v Bangladesh at Dhaka	2002-03
A. E. R. Gilligan (E)	6.3	4	7	6	v South Africa at Birmingham	1924
M. J. Clarke (A)	6.2	0	9	6	v India at Mumbai.	2004-05
S. Haigh (E)	11.4	6	11	6	v South Africa at Cape Town	1898-99
Shoaib Akhtar (P)	8.2	4	11	6	v New Zealand at Lahore	2002
D. L. Underwood (E)	11.6	7	12	6	v New Zealand at Christchurch.	1970-71
S. L. V. Raju (I)	17.5	13	12	6	v Sri Lanka at Chandigarh	1990-91
H. J. Tayfield (SA)	14	7	13	6	v New Zealand at Johannesburg	1953-54
C. T. B. Turner (A)	18	11	15	6	v England at Sydney	1886-87
M. H. N. Walker (A)	16	8	15	6	v Pakistan at Sydney	1972-73
E. R. H. Toshack (A)	2.3	1	2	5	v India at Brisbane	1947-48
H. Ironmonger (A)	7.2	5	6	5	v South Africa at Melbourne.	1931-32
T. B. A. May (A)	6.5	3	9	5	v West Indies at Adelaide	1992-93
Pervez Sajjad (P)	12	8	5	4	v New Zealand at Rawalpindi.	1964-65
K. Higgs (E)	9	7	5	4	v New Zealand at Christchurch.	1965-66
P. H. Edmonds (E)	8	6	6	4	v Pakistan at Lord's	1978
J. C. White (E)	6.3	2	7	4	v Australia at Brisbane	1928-29
J. H. Wardle (E)	5	2	7	4	v Australia at Manchester	1953
R. Appleyard (E)	6	3	7	4	v New Zealand at Auckland	1954-55
R. Benaud (A)	3.4	3	0	3	v India at Delhi	1959-60

WICKET WITH FIRST BALL IN TEST CRICKET

	Batsman dismissed			
A. Coningham	A. C. MacLaren	A v E	Melbourne	1894-95
W. M. Bradley	F. Laver	E v A	Manchester	1899
E. G. Arnold	V. T. Trumper	E v A	Sydney	1903-04
G. G. Macaulay	G. A. L. Hearne	E v SA	Cape Town	1922-23
M. W. Tate	M. J. Susskind	E v SA	Birmingham	1924
M. Henderson	E. W. Dawson	NZ v E	Christchurch	1929-30
H. D. Smith	E. Paynter	NZ v E	Christchurch	1932-33
T. F. Johnson	W. W. Keeton	WI v E	The Oval.	1939
R. Howorth	D. V. Dyer	E v SA	The Oval.	1947
Intikhab Alam	C. C. McDonald	P v A.	Karachi	1959-60
R. K. Illingworth	P. V. Simmons	E v WI	Nottingham	1991
N. M. Kulkarni	M. S. Atapattu	I v SL	Colombo (RPS)	1997-98
M. K. G. C. P. Lakshitha	Mohammad Ashraful	SL v B	Colombo (SSC)	2002

HAT-TRICKS

F. R. Spofforth	Australia v England at Melbourne	1878-79
W. Bates	England v Australia at Melbourne	1882-83
J. Briggs	England v Australia at Sydney	1891-92
G. A. Lohmann	England v South Africa at Port Elizabeth.	1895-96
J. T. Hearne	England v Australia at Leeds	1899
H. Trumble	Australia v England at Melbourne	1901-02
H. Trumble	Australia v England at Melbourne	1903-04
T. J. Matthews† . . . . T. J. Matthews.	} Australia v South Africa at Manchester	1912
M. J. C. Allom‡.	England v New Zealand at Christchurch	1929-30

T. W. J. Goddard	England v South Africa at Johannesburg	1938-39
P. J. Loader	England v West Indies at Leeds	1957
L. F. Kline	Australia v South Africa at Cape Town	1957-58
W. W. Hall	West Indies v Pakistan at Lahore	1958-59
G. M. Griffin	South Africa v England at Lord's	1960
L. R. Gibbs	West Indies v Australia at Adelaide	1960-61
P. J. Petherick‡	New Zealand v Pakistan at Lahore	1976-77
C. A. Walsh§	West Indies v Australia at Brisbane	1988-89
M. G. Hughes§	Australia v West Indies at Perth	1988-89
D. W. Fleming‡	Australia v Pakistan at Rawalpindi	1994-95
S. K. Warne	Australia v England at Melbourne	1994-95
D. G. Cork	England v West Indies at Manchester	1995
D. Gough	England v Australia at Sydney	1998-99
Wasim Akram¶	Pakistan v Sri Lanka at Lahore	1998-99
Wasim Akram¶	Pakistan v Sri Lanka at Dhaka	1998-99
D. N. T. Zoysa‖	Sri Lanka v Zimbabwe at Harare	1999-2000
Abdul Razzaq	Pakistan v Sri Lanka at Galle	2000
G. D. McGrath	Australia v West Indies at Perth	2000-01
Harbhajan Singh	India v Australia at Kolkata	2000-01
Mohammad Sami	Pakistan v Sri Lanka at Lahore	2001-02
J. J. C. Lawson§	West Indies v Australia at Bridgetown	2002-03
Alok Kapali	Bangladesh v Pakistan at Peshawar	2003
A. M. Blignaut	Zimbabwe v Bangladesh at Harare	2003-04
M. J. Hoggard	England v West Indies at Bridgetown	2003-04
J. E. C. Franklin	New Zealand v Bangladesh at Dhaka	2004-05
I. K. Pathan‖	India v Pakistan at Karachi	2005-06
R. J. Sidebottom	England v New Zealand at Hamilton	2007-08

† *T. J. Matthews did the hat-trick in each innings of the same match.*
‡ *On Test debut.*
§ *Not all in the same innings.*
¶ *Wasim Akram did the hat-trick in successive matches.*
‖ *D. N. T. Zoysa did the hat-trick in the match's second over; I. K. Pathan in the match's first over.*

FOUR WICKETS IN FIVE BALLS

M. J. C. Allom	England v New Zealand at Christchurch	1929-30
	On debut, in his eighth over: W-WWW	
C. M. Old	England v Pakistan at Birmingham	1978
	Sequence interrupted by a no-ball: WW-WW	
Wasim Akram	Pakistan v West Indies at Lahore (*WW-WW*)	1990-91

MOST WICKETS IN A TEST

19-90	J. C. Laker	England v Australia at Manchester	1956
17-159	S. F. Barnes	England v South Africa at Johannesburg	1913-14
16-136†	N. D. Hirwani	India v West Indies at Madras	1987-88
16-137†	R. A. L. Massie	Australia v England at Lord's	1972
16-220	M. Muralitharan	Sri Lanka v England at The Oval	1998
15-28	J. Briggs	England v South Africa at Cape Town	1888-89
15-45	G. A. Lohmann	England v South Africa at Port Elizabeth	1895-96
15-99	C. Blythe	England v South Africa at Leeds	1907
15-104	H. Verity	England v Australia at Lord's	1934
15-123	R. J. Hadlee	New Zealand v Australia at Brisbane	1985-86
15-124	W. Rhodes	England v Australia at Melbourne	1903-04
15-217	Harbhajan Singh	India v Australia at Chennai	2000-01

14-90	F. R. Spofforth	Australia v England at The Oval	1882
14-99	A. V. Bedser	England v Australia at Nottingham	1953
14-102	W. Bates	England v Australia at Melbourne	1882-83
14-116	Imran Khan	Pakistan v Sri Lanka at Lahore	1981-82
14-124	J. M. Patel	India v Australia at Kanpur	1959-60
14-144	S. F. Barnes	England v South Africa at Durban	1913-14
14-149	M. A. Holding	West Indies v England at The Oval	1976
14-149	A. Kumble	India v Pakistan at Delhi	1998-99
14-191	W. P. U. J. C. Vaas	Sri Lanka v West Indies at Colombo (SSC)	2001-02
14-199	C. V. Grimmett	Australia v South Africa at Adelaide	1931-32

† *On Test debut.*

Note: The best for South Africa is 13-132 by M. Ntini against West Indies at Port-of-Spain, 2004-05, for Zimbabwe 11-255 by A. G. Huckle against New Zealand at Bulawayo, 1997-98, and for Bangladesh 12-200 by Enamul Haque, jun. against Zimbabwe at Dhaka, 2004-05.

MOST BALLS BOWLED IN A TEST

S. Ramadhin (West Indies) sent down 774 balls in 129 overs against England at Birmingham, 1957. It was the most delivered by any bowler in a Test, beating H. Verity's 766 for England against South Africa at Durban, 1938-39. In this match Ramadhin also bowled the most balls (588) in a Test or first-class innings, since equalled by Arshad Ayub, Hyderabad v Madhya Pradesh at Secunderabad, 1991-92.

MOST WICKETS IN A SERIES

	T	R	W	Avge		
S. F. Barnes	4	536	49	10.93	England v South Africa	1913-14
J. C. Laker	5	442	46	9.60	England v Australia	1956
C. V. Grimmett	5	642	44	14.59	Australia v South Africa	1935-36
T. M. Alderman	6	893	42	21.26	Australia v England	1981
R. M. Hogg	6	527	41	12.85	Australia v England	1978-79
T. M. Alderman	6	712	41	17.36	Australia v England	1989
Imran Khan	6	558	40	13.95	Pakistan v India	1982-83
S. K. Warne	5	797	40	19.92	Australia v England	2005
A. V. Bedser	5	682	39	17.48	England v Australia	1953
D. K. Lillee	6	870	39	22.30	Australia v England	1981
M. W. Tate	5	881	38	23.18	England v Australia	1924-25
W. J. Whitty	5	632	37	17.08	Australia v South Africa	1910-11
H. J. Tayfield	5	636	37	17.18	South Africa v England	1956-57
A. E. E. Vogler	5	783	36	21.75	South Africa v England	1909-10
A. A. Mailey	5	946	36	26.27	Australia v England	1920-21
G. D. McGrath	6	701	36	19.47	Australia v England	1997
G. A. Lohmann	3	203	35	5.80	England v South Africa	1895-96
B. S. Chandrasekhar	5	662	35	18.91	India v England	1972-73
M. D. Marshall	5	443	35	12.65	West Indies v England	1988

Notes: The most for New Zealand is 33 by R. J. Hadlee against Australia in 1985-86, for Sri Lanka 30 by M. Muralitharan against Zimbabwe in 2001-02, for Zimbabwe 22 by H. H. Streak against Pakistan in 1994-95 (all in three Tests), and for Bangladesh 18 by Enamul Haque, jun. against Zimbabwe in 2004-05 (two Tests).

75 WICKETS IN A CALENDAR YEAR

	T	R	W	Avge	5W/i	10W/m	Year
S. K. Warne (A)	15	2,114	96	22.02	6	2	2005
M. Muralitharan (SL)	11	1,521	90	16.89	9	5	2006
D. K. Lillee (A)	13	1,781	85	20.95	5	2	1981
A. A. Donald (SA)	14	1,571	80	19.63	7	–	1998
M. Muralitharan (SL)	12	1,699	80	21.23	7	4	2001
J. Garner (WI)	15	1,604	77	20.83	4	–	1984
Kapil Dev (I)	18	1,739	75	23.18	5	1	1983
M. Muralitharan (SL)	10	1,463	75	19.50	7	3	2000

MOST WICKETS

1	**M. Muralitharan (SL/World)**	**792**
2	S. K. Warne (Australia)	708
3	A. Kumble (India)	619
4	G. D. McGrath (Australia)	563
5	C. A. Walsh (West Indies)	519
6	Kapil Dev (India)	434
7	R. J. Hadlee (New Zealand)	431
8	S. M. Pollock (South Africa)	421
9	Wasim Akram (Pakistan)	414
10	C. E. L. Ambrose (West Indies)	405
11	**M. Ntini (South Africa)**	**390**
12	I. T. Botham (England)	383
13	M. D. Marshall (West Indies)	376
14	Waqar Younis (Pakistan)	373
15	Imran Khan (Pakistan)	362

16	{ D. K. Lillee (Australia)	355
	{ **W. P. U. J. C. Vaas (Sri Lanka)**	**355**
18	**Harbhajan Singh (India)**	**345**
19	A. A. Donald (South Africa)	330
20	R. G. D. Willis (England)	325
21	**D. L. Vettori (New Zealand/World)**	**313**
22	B. Lee (Australia)	310
23	L. R. Gibbs (West Indies)	309
24	F. S. Trueman (England)	307
25	D. L. Underwood (England)	297
26	C. J. McDermott (Australia)	291
27	B. S. Bedi (India)	266
28	**J. H. Kallis (South Africa/World)**	**260**
29	{ J. Garner (West Indies)	259
	{ J. N. Gillespie (Australia)	259

Bold type denotes those who have played Test cricket since January 1, 2009.

MOST WICKETS FOR EACH COUNTRY

ENGLAND

		T	Balls	R	W	Avge	5W/i	10W/m
1	I. T. Botham	102	21,815	10,878	383	28.40	27	4
2	R. G. D. Willis	90	17,357	8,190	325	25.20	16	–
3	F. S. Trueman	67	15,178	6,625	307	21.57	17	3
4	D. L. Underwood	86	21,862	7,674	297	25.83	17	6
5	J. B. Statham	70	16,056	6,261	252	24.84	9	1
6	M. J. Hoggard	67	13,909	7,564	248	30.50	7	1
7	A. V. Bedser	51	15,918	5,876	236	24.89	15	5
8	A. R. Caddick	62	13,558	6,999	234	29.91	13	1
9	D. Gough	58	11,821	6,503	229	28.39	9	–
10	**S. J. Harmison**	**62†**	**13,192**	**7,091**	**222**	**31.94**	**8**	**1**
11	**A. Flintoff**	**78†**	**14,747**	**7,303**	**219**	**33.34**	**3**	**–**
12	J. A. Snow	49	12,021	5,387	202	26.66	8	1
13	J. C. Laker	46	12,027	4,101	193	21.24	9	3
14	S. F. Barnes	27	7,873	3,106	189	16.43	24	7
15	A. R. C. Fraser	46	10,876	4,836	177	27.32	13	2
16	G. A. R. Lock	49	13,147	4,451	174	25.58	9	3
17	**J. M. Anderson**	**46**	**9,430**	**5,431**	**156**	**34.81**	**8**	**–**
18	M. W. Tate	39	12,523	4,055	155	26.16	7	1
19	F. J. Titmus	53	15,118	4,931	153	32.22	7	–

† A. Flintoff also took 4-59 and 3-48, and S. J. Harmison also took 1-60 and 3-41, for the ICC World XI v Australia in the Super Series Test of 2005-06.

AUSTRALIA

		T	Balls	R	W	Avge	5W/i	10W/m
1	S. K. Warne	145	40,705	17,995	708	25.41	37	10
2	G. D. McGrath	124	29,248	12,186	563	21.64	29	3
3	D. K. Lillee	70	18,467	8,493	355	23.92	23	7
4	B. Lee	76	16,531	9,554	310	30.81	10	–
5	C. J. McDermott	71	16,586	8,332	291	28.63	14	2
6	J. N. Gillespie	71	14,234	6,770	259	26.13	8	–
7	R. Benaud	63	19,108	6,704	248	27.03	16	1
8	G. D. McKenzie	60	17,681	7,328	246	29.78	16	3
9	R. R. Lindwall	61	13,650	5,251	228	23.03	12	–
10	C. V. Grimmett	37	14,513	5,231	216	24.21	21	7
11	M. G. Hughes	53	12,285	6,017	212	28.38	7	1
12	S. C. G. MacGill	44	11,237	6,038	208	29.02	12	2
13	J. R. Thomson	51	10,535	5,601	200	28.00	8	–
14	A. K. Davidson	44	11,587	3,819	186	20.53	14	2
15	G. F. Lawson	46	11,118	5,501	180	30.56	11	2
16 {	K. R. Miller	55	10,461	3,906	170	22.97	7	1
{	T. M. Alderman	41	10,181	4,616	170	27.15	14	1
18	W. A. Johnston	40	11,048	3,826	160	23.91	7	–

SOUTH AFRICA

		T	Balls	R	W	Avge	5W/i	10W/m
1	S. M. Pollock	108	24,353	9,733	421	23.11	16	1
2	**M. Ntini**	101	**20,834**	**11,242**	390	**28.82**	18	4
3	A. A. Donald	72	15,519	7,344	330	22.25	20	3
4	**J. H. Kallis**	134†	**17,310**	**8,126**	259	**31.37**	5	–
5	**D. W. Steyn**	36	**7,389**	**4,386**	185	**23.70**	12	3
6	H. J. Tayfield	37	13,568	4,405	170	25.91	14	2

† *J. H. Kallis also took 0-35 and 1-3 for the ICC World XI v Australia in the Super Series Test of 2005-06.*

WEST INDIES

		T	Balls	R	W	Avge	5W/i	10W/m
1	C. A. Walsh	132	30,019	12,688	519	24.44	22	3
2	C. E. L. Ambrose	98	22,103	8,501	405	20.99	22	3
3	M. D. Marshall	81	17,584	7,876	376	20.94	22	4
4	L. R. Gibbs	79	27,115	8,989	309	29.09	18	2
5	J. Garner	58	13,169	5,433	259	20.97	7	–
6	M. A. Holding	60	12,680	5,898	249	23.68	13	2
7	G. S. Sobers	93	21,599	7,999	235	34.03	6	–
8	A. M. E. Roberts	47	11,135	5,174	202	25.61	11	2
9	W. W. Hall	48	10,421	5,066	192	26.38	9	1
10	I. R. Bishop	43	8,407	3,909	161	24.27	6	–
11	S. Ramadhin	43	13,939	4,579	158	28.98	10	1

NEW ZEALAND

		T	Balls	R	W	Avge	5W/i	10W/m
1	R. J. Hadlee	86	21,918	9,611	431	22.29	36	9
2	**D. L. Vettori**	96†	**23,875**	**10,409**	312	**33.36**	18	3
3	C. L. Cairns	62	11,698	6,410	218	29.40	13	1
4	**C. S. Martin**	53	**10,475**	**5,917**	176	**33.61**	8	1
5	D. K. Morrison	48	10,064	5,549	160	34.68	10	–

† *D. L. Vettori also took 1-73 and 0-38 for the ICC World XI v Australia in the Super Series Test of 2005-06.*

INDIA

		T	Balls	R	W	Avge	5W/i	10W/m
1	A. Kumble	132	40,850	18,355	619	29.65	35	8
2	Kapil Dev	131	27,740	12,867	434	29.64	23	2
3	**Harbhajan Singh**	**81**	**22,690**	**10,696**	**345**	**31.00**	**23**	**5**
4	B. S. Bedi	67	21,364	7,637	266	28.71	14	1
5	B. S. Chandrasekhar	58	15,963	7,199	242	29.74	16	2
6	J. Srinath	67	15,104	7,196	236	30.49	10	1
7	**Zaheer Khan**	**70**	**14,063**	**7,765**	**235**	**33.04**	**9**	**1**
8	E. A. S. Prasanna	49	14,353	5,742	189	30.38	10	2
9	V. Mankad	44	14,686	5,236	162	32.32	8	2
10	S. Venkataraghavan	57	14,877	5,634	156	36.11	3	1
11	R. J. Shastri	80	15,751	6,185	151	40.96	2	–

PAKISTAN

		T	Balls	R	W	Avge	5W/i	10W/m
1	Wasim Akram	104	22,627	9,779	414	23.62	25	5
2	Waqar Younis	87	16,224	8,788	373	23.56	22	5
3	Imran Khan	88	19,458	8,258	362	22.81	23	6
4	**Danish Kaneria**	**58**	**17,157**	**8,705**	**254**	**34.27**	**15**	**2**
5	Abdul Qadir	67	17,126	7,742	236	32.80	15	5
6	Saqlain Mushtaq	49	14,070	6,206	208	29.83	13	3
7	Mushtaq Ahmed	52	12,532	6,100	185	32.97	10	3
8	Shoaib Akhtar	46	8,143	4,574	178	25.69	12	2
9	Sarfraz Nawaz	55	13,927	5,798	177	32.75	4	1
10	Iqbal Qasim	50	13,019	4,807	171	28.11	8	2

SRI LANKA

		T	Balls	R	W	Avge	5W/i	10W/m
1	**M. Muralitharan**	**131†**	**43,345**	**17,832**	**787**	**22.65**	**66**	**22**
2	**W. P. U. J. C. Vaas**	**111**	**23,438**	**10,501**	**355**	**29.58**	**12**	**2**

† *M. Muralitharan also took 2-102 and 3-55 for the ICC World XI v Australia in the Super Series Test of 2005-06.*

ZIMBABWE

		T	Balls	R	W	Avge	5W/i	10W/m
1	H. H. Streak	65	13,559	6,079	216	28.14	7	–

BANGLADESH

No player has taken 150 Test wickets for Bangladesh. The highest total is:

	T	Balls	R	W	Avge	5W/i	10W/m
Mohammad Rafique	33	8,744	4,076	100	40.76	7	–

Bold type denotes those who have played Test cricket since January 1, 2009.

BEST CAREER AVERAGES

(Qualification: 75 wickets)

Avge		T	W	Avge		T	W
10.75	G. A. Lohmann (E)	18	112	18.63	C. Blythe (E)	19	100
16.43	S. F. Barnes (E)	27	189	20.39	J. H. Wardle (E)	28	102
16.53	C. T. B. Turner (A)	17	101	20.53	A. K. Davidson (A)	44	186
16.98	R. Peel (E)	20	101	20.94	M. D. Marshall (WI)	81	376
17.75	J. Briggs (E)	33	118	20.97	J. Garner (WI)	58	259
18.41	F. R. Spofforth (A)	18	94	20.99	C. E. L. Ambrose (WI)	98	405
18.56	F. H. Tyson (E)	17	76				

BEST CAREER STRIKE-RATES

(Balls per wicket. Qualification: 75 wickets)

SR		T	W	SR		T	W
34.19	G. A. Lohmann (E)	18	112	45.42	F. H. Tyson (E)	17	76
38.75	**S. E. Bond (NZ)**	**18**	**87**	45.46	C. Blythe (E)	19	100
39.94	**D. W. Steyn (SA)**	**36**	**185**	45.74	Shoaib Akhtar (P)	46	178
41.65	S. F. Barnes (E)	27	189	46.76	M. D. Marshall (WI)	81	376
43.49	Waqar Younis (P)	87	373	47.02	A. A. Donald (SA)	72	330
44.52	F. R. Spofforth (A)	18	94	**47.03**	**Mohammad Asif (P)**	**17**	**83**
45.12	J. V. Saunders (A)	14	79	49.32	C. E. H. Croft (WI)	27	125
45.18	J. Briggs (E)	33	118	49.43	F. S. Trueman (E)	67	307

Bold type denotes those who have played Test cricket since January 1, 2009.

BEST CAREER ECONOMY-RATES

(Runs per six balls. Qualification: 75 wickets)

ER		T	W	ER		T	W
1.64	T. L. Goddard (SA)	41	123	1.94	W. J. O'Reilly (A)	27	144
1.67	R. G. Nadkarni (I)	41	88	1.94	H. J. Tayfield (SA)	37	170
1.88	H. Verity (E)	40	144	1.95	A. L. Valentine (WI)	36	139
1.88	G. A. Lohmann (E)	18	112	1.95	F. J. Titmus (E)	53	153
1.89	J. H. Wardle (E)	28	102	1.97	S. Ramadhin (WI)	43	158
1.91	R. Illingworth (E)	61	122	1.97	R. Peel (E)	20	101
1.93	C. T. B. Turner (A)	17	101	1.97	A. K. Davidson (A)	44	186
1.94	M. W. Tate (E)	39	155	1.98	L. R. Gibbs (WI)	79	309

HIGHEST PERCENTAGE OF TEAM'S WICKETS OVER TEST CAREER

(Qualification: 20 Tests)

	Tests	Wkts	Team Wkts	% of Team Wkts
M. Muralitharan (Sri Lanka/World)	**132**	**792**	**2,050**	**38.63**
S. F. Barnes (England).	27	189	494	38.25
R. J. Hadlee (New Zealand).	86	431	1,255	34.34
C. V. Grimmett (Australia)	37	216	636	33.96
Fazal Mahmood (Pakistan)	34	139	410	33.90
W. J. O'Reilly (Australia)	27	144	446	32.28
S. P. Gupte (India)	36	149	470	31.70
Mohammad Rafique (Bangladesh).	33	100	328	30.48
A. V. Bedser (England)	51	236	777	30.37

Note: Excluding the Super Series Test, Muralitharan has taken 787 out of 2,030 wickets in his 131 Tests for Sri Lanka, a percentage of 38.76.

The percentage shows the proportion of a team's wickets taken by that player in all Tests in which he played, including team wickets in innings in which he did not bowl.

Bold type denotes those who have played Test cricket since January 1, 2009.

ALL-ROUND RECORDS

HUNDRED AND FIVE WICKETS IN AN INNINGS

England
A. W. Greig	148	6-164	v West Indies	Bridgetown	1973-74
I. T. Botham	103	5-73	v New Zealand	Christchurch	1977-78
I. T. Botham	108	8-34	v Pakistan	Lord's	1978
I. T. Botham	114	6-58, 7-48	v India	Bombay	1979-80
I. T. Botham	149*	6-95	v Australia	Leeds	1981
I. T. Botham	138	5-59	v New Zealand	Wellington	1983-84

Australia
C. Kelleway	114	5-33	v South Africa	Manchester	1912
J. M. Gregory	100	7-69	v England	Melbourne	1920-21
K. R. Miller	109	6-107	v West Indies	Kingston	1954-55
R. Benaud	100	5-84	v South Africa	Johannesburg	1957-58

South Africa
J. H. Sinclair	106	6-26	v England	Cape Town	1898-99
G. A. Faulkner	123	5-120	v England	Johannesburg	1909-10
J. H. Kallis	110	5-90	v West Indies	Cape Town	1998-99
J. H. Kallis	139*	5-21	v Bangladesh	Potchefstroom	2002-03

West Indies
D. St E. Atkinson	219	5-56	v Australia	Bridgetown	1954-55
O. G. Smith	100	5-90	v India	Delhi	1958-59
G. S. Sobers	104	5-63	v India	Kingston	1961-62
G. S. Sobers	174	5-41	v England	Leeds	1966

New Zealand
B. R. Taylor†	105	5-86	v India	Calcutta	1964-65

India
V. Mankad	184	5-196	v England	Lord's	1952
P. R. Umrigar	172*	5-107	v West Indies	Port-of-Spain	1961-62

Pakistan
Mushtaq Mohammad	201	5-49	v New Zealand	Dunedin	1972-73
Mushtaq Mohammad	121	5-28	v West Indies	Port-of-Spain	1976-77
Imran Khan	117	6-98, 5-82	v India	Faisalabad	1982-83
Wasim Akram	123	5-100	v Australia	Adelaide	1989-90

Zimbabwe
P. A. Strang	106*	5-212	v Pakistan	Sheikhupura	1996-97

† *On debut.*

HUNDRED AND FIVE DISMISSALS IN AN INNINGS

D. T. Lindsay	182	6ct	SA v A............	Johannesburg........	1966-67
I. D. S. Smith	113*	4ct, 1st	NZ v E............	Auckland...........	1983-84
S. A. R. Silva	111	5ct	SL v I.............	Colombo (PSS)	1985-86
A. C. Gilchrist	133	4ct, 1st	A v E	Sydney.............	2002-03

100 RUNS AND TEN WICKETS IN A TEST

A. K. Davidson	44 80	5-135 6-87 }	A v WI.........	Brisbane...........	1960-61
I. T. Botham	114	6-58 7-48 }	E v I..........	Bombay	1979-80
Imran Khan	117	6-98 5-82 }	P v I..........	Faisalabad.........	1982-83

2,000 RUNS AND 200 WICKETS

	Tests	Runs	Wkts	Tests for 1,000/100 Double
R. Benaud (Australia)	63	2,201	248	32
†I. T. Botham (England)	102	5,200	383	21
C. L. Cairns (New Zealand).............	62	3,320	218	33
A. Flintoff (England/World)	**79**	**3,845**	**226**	**43**
R. J. Hadlee (New Zealand).............	86	3,124	431	28
Imran Khan (Pakistan).................	88	3,807	362	30
†**J. H. Kallis (South Africa/World)**.......	**135**	**10,640**	**260**	**53**
Kapil Dev (India).....................	131	5,248	434	25
A. Kumble (India)....................	132	2,506	619	56
S. M. Pollock (South Africa)............	108	3,781	421	26
†G. S. Sobers (West Indies).............	93	8,032	235	48
W. P. U. J. C. Vaas (Sri Lanka)	**111**	**3,089**	**355**	**47**
D. L. Vettori (New Zealand/World)	**97**	**3,779**	**313**	**47**
S. K. Warne (Australia)	145	3,154	708	58
Wasim Akram (Pakistan)................	104	2,898	414	45

Note: H. H. Streak scored 1,990 runs and took 216 wickets in 65 Tests for Zimbabwe.

Bold type denotes those who have played Test cricket since January 1, 2009.

† *J. H. Kallis has also taken 152 catches, S. K. Warne 125, I. T. Botham 120 and G. S. Sobers 109. These four and C. L. Hooper (5,762 runs, 114 wickets and 115 catches for West Indies) are the only players to have achieved the treble of 1,000 runs, 100 wickets and 100 catches in Test cricket.*

WICKETKEEPING RECORDS

MOST DISMISSALS IN AN INNINGS

7 (all ct)	Wasim Bari...........	Pakistan v New Zealand at Auckland	1978-79
7 (all ct)	R. W. Taylor..........	England v India at Bombay..............	1979-80
7 (all ct)	I. D. S. Smith	New Zealand v Sri Lanka at Hamilton	1990-91
7 (all ct)	R. D. Jacobs	West Indies v Australia at Melbourne	2000-01
6 (all ct)	A. T. W. Grout	Australia v South Africa at Johannesburg ...	1957-58
6 (all ct)	D. T. Lindsay	South Africa v Australia at Johannesburg ...	1966-67
6 (all ct)	J. T. Murray	England v India at Lord's	1967
6 (5ct, 1st)	S. M. H. Kirmani	India v New Zealand at Christchurch	1975-76
6 (all ct)	R. W. Marsh	Australia v England at Brisbane	1982-83
6 (all ct)	S. A. R. Silva	Sri Lanka v India at Colombo (SSC).......	1985-86
6 (all ct)	R. C. Russell..........	England v Australia at Melbourne.........	1990-91

6 (all ct)	R. C. Russell............	England v South Africa at Johannesburg ...	1995-96
6 (all ct)	I. A. Healy	Australia v England at Birmingham	1997
6 (all ct)	A. J. Stewart..........	England v Australia at Manchester	1997
6 (all ct)	M. V. Boucher	South Africa v Pakistan at Port Elizabeth ...	1997-98
6 (all ct)	Rashid Latif	Pakistan v Zimbabwe at Bulawayo	1997-98
6 (all ct)	M. V. Boucher	South Africa v Sri Lanka at Cape Town	1997-98
6 (5ct, 1st)	†C. M. W. Read	England v New Zealand at Birmingham	1999
6 (all ct)	M. V. Boucher	South Africa v Zimbabwe at Centurion.....	2004-05
6 (all ct)	G. O. Jones...........	England v Bangladesh at Chester-le-Street..	2005
6 (all ct)	C. M. W. Read	England v Australia at Melbourne.........	2006-07
6 (5ct, 1st)	C. M. W. Read	England v Australia at Sydney	2006-07
6 (all ct)	**M. S. Dhoni ....**	**India v New Zealand at Wellington ......**	**2008-09**

† *On debut.*

Bold type denotes performances since January 1, 2009.

MOST STUMPINGS IN AN INNINGS

| 5 | K. S. More............... | India v West Indies at Madras .... | 1987-88 |

MOST DISMISSALS IN A TEST

11 (all ct)	R. C. Russell..........	England v South Africa at Johannesburg ...	1995-96
10 (all ct)	R. W. Taylor..........	England v India at Bombay...............	1979-80
10 (all ct)	A. C. Gilchrist	Australia v New Zealand at Hamilton......	1999-2000
9 (8ct, 1st)	G. R. A. Langley	Australia v England at Lord's	1956
9 (all ct)	D. A. Murray	West Indies v Australia at Melbourne......	1981-82
9 (all ct)	R. W. Marsh..........	Australia v England at Brisbane	1982-83
9 (all ct)	S. A. R. Silva	Sri Lanka v India at Colombo (SSC)......	1985-86
9 (8ct, 1st)	S. A. R. Silva	Sri Lanka v India at Colombo (PSS)......	1985-86
9 (all ct)	D. J. Richardson	South Africa v India at Port Elizabeth.....	1992-93
9 (all ct)	Rashid Latif	Pakistan v New Zealand at Auckland	1993-94
9 (all ct)	I. A. Healy	Australia v England at Brisbane	1994-95
9 (all ct)	C. O. Browne	West Indies v England at Nottingham......	1995
9 (7ct, 2st)	R. C. Russell..........	England v South Africa at Port Elizabeth ...	1995-96
9 (8ct, 1st)	M. V. Boucher	South Africa v Pakistan at Port Elizabeth ...	1997-98
9 (8ct, 1st)	R. D. Jacobs	West Indies v Australia at Melbourne......	2000-01
9 (all ct)	Kamran Akmal........	Pakistan v West Indies at Kingston........	2004-05
9 (all ct)	G. O. Jones	England v Bangladesh at Chester-le-Street..	2005
9 (8ct, 1st)	A. C. Gilchrist	Australia v England at Sydney	2006-07
9 (8ct, 1st)	**B. B. McCullum ......**	**New Zealand v Pakistan at Napier.......**	**2009-10**
9 (all ct)	**B. J. Haddin ....**	**Australia v Pakistan at Sydney...........**	**2009-10**

Notes: S. A. R. Silva made 18 dismissals in two successive Tests.

The most stumpings in a match is 6 by K. S. More for India v West Indies at Madras in 1987-88.

J. J. Kelly (8ct) for Australia v England in 1901-02 and L. E. G. Ames (6ct, 2st) for England v West Indies in 1933 were the only wicketkeepers to make eight dismissals in a Test before World War II.

Bold type denotes performances since January 1, 2009.

MOST DISMISSALS IN A SERIES

(Played in 5 Tests unless otherwise stated)

28 (all ct)	R. W. Marsh..........	Australia v England.....................	1982-83
27 (25ct, 2st)	R. C. Russell..........	England v South Africa...................	1995-96
27 (25ct, 2st)	I. A. Healy	Australia v England (6 Tests)	1997
26 (23ct, 3st)	J. H. B. Waite	South Africa v New Zealand.............	1961-62
26 (all ct)	R. W. Marsh..........	Australia v West Indies (6 Tests).........	1975-76
26 (21ct, 5st)	I. A. Healy	Australia v England (6 Tests)	1993
26 (25ct, 1st)	M. V. Boucher	South Africa v England.................	1998

26 (24ct, 2st)	A. C. Gilchrist	Australia v England....................	2001
26 (24ct, 2st)	A. C. Gilchrist	Australia v England....................	2006-07
25 (23ct, 2st)	I. A. Healy	Australia v England....................	1994-95
25 (23ct, 2st)	A. C. Gilchrist	Australia v England....................	2002-03
25 (all ct)	A. C. Gilchrist	Australia v India	2007-08

Notes: S. A. R. Silva made 22 dismissals (21ct, 1st) in three Tests for Sri Lanka v India in 1985-86.

H. Strudwick, with 21 (15ct, 6st) for England v South Africa in 1913-14, was the only wicketkeeper to make as many as 20 dismissals in a series before World War II.

150 DISMISSALS

			T	*Ct*	*St*
1	**M. V. Boucher (South Africa/World)**		**491**	**130**	**469**	**22**
2	A. C. Gilchrist (Australia)........................		416	96	379	37
3	I. A. Healy (Australia)...........................		395	119	366	29
4	R. W. Marsh (Australia)		355	96	343	12
5	P. J. L. Dujon (West Indies)		270	79	265	5
6	A. P. E. Knott (England).........................		269	95	250	19
7	A. J. Stewart (England)..........................		241	82	227	14
8	Wasim Bari (Pakistan)		228	81	201	27
9	{ T. G. Evans (England)...........................		219	91	173	46
	{ R. D. Jacobs (West Indies)		219	65	207	12
11	A. C. Parore (New Zealand)		201	67	194	7
12	S. M. H. Kirmani (India).........................		198	88	160	38
13	D. L. Murray (West Indies).......................		189	62	181	8
14	A. T. W. Grout (Australia)		187	51	163	24
15	**Kamran Akmal (Pakistan)**.....................		**181**	**48**	**159**	**22**
16	I. D. S. Smith (New Zealand)		176	63	168	8
17	R. W. Taylor (England)..........................		174	57	167	7
18	R. C. Russell (England)..........................		165	54	153	12
19	**B. B. McCullum (New Zealand)**.................		**163**	**49**	**153**	**10**
20	D. J. Richardson (South Africa)		152	42	150	2
21	{ **K. C. Sangakkara (Sri Lanka)**....................		**151**	**48**	**131**	**20**
	{ A. Flower (Zimbabwe)		151	55	142	9

Notes: The record for P. J. L. Dujon excludes two catches taken in two Tests when not keeping wicket; A. J. Stewart's record likewise excludes 36 catches taken in 51 Tests, A. C. Parore's three in 11 Tests, B. B. McCullum's one catch in one Test, and A. Flower's nine in eight Tests. K. C. Sangakkara's record excludes 26 catches taken in 40 matches when not keeping wicket but includes two catches taken as wicketkeeper in a match where he took over when the designated keeper was injured.

Excluding the Super Series Test, **M. V. Boucher** has made **489** dismissals (467 ct, 22 st in 129 Tests) for South Africa, a national record. The most wicketkeeping dismissals for Bangladesh is 87 (Khaled Mashud 78 ct, 9 st in 44 Tests).

W. A. Oldfield made 52 stumpings, a Test record, in 54 Tests for Australia; he also took 78 catches.

Bold type denotes those who have played Test cricket since January 1, 2009.

FIELDING RECORDS

(Excluding wicketkeepers)

MOST CATCHES IN AN INNINGS

5	V. Y. Richardson	Australia v South Africa at Durban	1935-36
5	Yajurvindra Singh	India v England at Bangalore	1976-77
5	M. Azharuddin.................	India v Pakistan at Karachi	1989-90
5	K. Srikkanth..................	India v Australia at Perth	1991-92
5	S. P. Fleming	New Zealand v Zimbabwe at Harare	1997-98

MOST CATCHES IN A TEST

7	G. S. Chappell	Australia v England at Perth.	1974-75
7	Yajurvindra Singh	India v England at Bangalore.	1976-77
7	H. P. Tillekeratne.	Sri Lanka v New Zealand at Colombo (SSC) . .	1992-93
7	S. P. Fleming	New Zealand v Zimbabwe at Harare	1997-98
7	M. L. Hayden.	Australia v Sri Lanka at Galle	2003-04

Note: There have been **25** instances of players taking six catches in a Test, the most recent being A. N. Cook for England v New Zealand at Hamilton, 2007-08.

MOST CATCHES IN A SERIES

(Played in 5 Tests unless otherwise stated)

15	J. M. Gregory.	Australia v England	1920-21
14	G. S. Chappell	Australia v England (6 Tests).	1974-75
13	R. B. Simpson	Australia v South Africa.	1957-58
13	R. B. Simpson	Australia v West Indies	1960-61
13	B. C. Lara.	West Indies v England (6 Tests).	1997-98
13	R. Dravid	India v Australia (4 Tests)	2004-05

100 CATCHES

Ct	T		Ct	T	
193	**139†**	**R. Dravid (India/World)**	120	114	M. C. Cowdrey (England)
181	128	M. E. Waugh (Australia)	115	102	C. L. Hooper (West Indies)
171	111	S. P. Fleming (New Zealand)	**114**	**109**	**V. V. S. Laxman (India)**
164	131†	B. C. Lara (West Indies/World)	112	168	S. R. Waugh (Australia)
164	**142**	**R. T. Ponting (Australia)**	111	81†	**G. C. Smith (SA/World)**
157	104	M. A. Taylor (Australia)	110	62	R. B. Simpson (Australia)
156	156	A. R. Border (Australia)	110	85	W. R. Hammond (England)
152	**110**	**D. P. M. D. Jayawardene (SL)**	109	93	G. S. Sobers (West Indies)
152	**135†**	**J. H. Kallis (SA/World)**	108	125	S. M. Gavaskar (India)
128	**103**	**M. L. Hayden (Australia)**	105	75	I. M. Chappell (Australia)
125	145	S. K. Warne (Australia)	105	99	M. Azharuddin (India)
122	87	G. S. Chappell (Australia)	105	100	G. P. Thorpe (England)
122	121	I. V. A. Richards (West Indies)	**104**	**164**	**S. R. Tendulkar (India)**
120	102	I. T. Botham (England)	103	118	G. A. Gooch (England)

† *Excluding the Super Series Test, Dravid has made 192 catches in 138 Tests for India, Lara 164 in 130 Tests for West Indies, and Kallis 148 in 134 Tests for South Africa, all national records. G. C. Smith has made 108 catches in 80 Tests for South Africa.*

Note: The most catches in the field for other countries are Pakistan 93 in 124 Tests (Javed Miandad); Zimbabwe 60 in 60 Tests (A. D. R. Campbell); Bangladesh **23** in 52 Tests (**Mohammad Ashraful**).

Bold type denotes those who have played Test cricket since January 1, 2009.

TEAM RECORDS

HIGHEST INNINGS TOTALS

952-6 dec	Sri Lanka v India at Colombo (RPS)	1997-98
903-7 dec	England v Australia at The Oval.	1938
849	England v West Indies at Kingston.	1929-30
790-3 dec	West Indies v Pakistan at Kingston.	1957-58
765-6 dec	**Pakistan v Sri Lanka at Karachi . . . .**	**2008-09**
760-7 dec	**Sri Lanka v India at Ahmedabad . . . .**	**2009-10**
758-8 dec	Australia v West Indies at Kingston	1954-55

756-5 dec	Sri Lanka v South Africa at Colombo (SSC)	2006
751-5 dec	West Indies v England at St John's.	2003-04
749-9 dec	**West Indies v England at Bridgetown**	**2008-09**
747	West Indies v South Africa at St John's	2004-05
735-6 dec	Australia v Zimbabwe at Perth	2003-04
729-6 dec	Australia v England at Lord's	1930
726-9 dec	**India v Sri Lanka at Mumbai (BS)**	**2009-10**
713-3 dec	Sri Lanka v Zimbabwe at Bulawayo.	2003-04
708	Pakistan v England at The Oval	1987
705-7 dec	India v Australia at Sydney	2003-04
701	Australia v England at The Oval	1934
699-5	Pakistan v India at Lahore.	1989-90
695	Australia v England at The Oval.	1930
692-8 dec	West Indies v England at The Oval.	1995
687-8 dec	West Indies v England at The Oval.	1976
682-6 dec	South Africa v England at Lord's	2003
681-8 dec	West Indies v England at Port-of-Spain	1953-54

The highest innings for the countries not mentioned above are:

671-4	New Zealand v Sri Lanka at Wellington.	1990-91
563-9 dec	Zimbabwe v West Indies at Harare.	2001
488	Bangladesh v Zimbabwe at Chittagong	2004-05

Bold type denotes performances since January 1, 2009.

HIGHEST FOURTH-INNINGS TOTALS

To win

418-7	West Indies (needing 418) v Australia at St John's.	2002-03
414-4	South Africa (needing 414) v Australia at Perth	2008-09
406-4	India (needing 403) v West Indies at Port-of-Spain	1975-76
404-3	Australia (needing 404) v England at Leeds	1948
369-6	Australia (needing 369) v Pakistan at Hobart	1999-2000
362-7	Australia (needing 359) v West Indies at Georgetown	1977-78
352-9	Sri Lanka (needing 352) v South Africa at Colombo (PSS)	2006
348-5	West Indies (needing 345) v New Zealand at Auckland.	1968-69
344-1	West Indies (needing 342) v England at Lord's	1984

To tie

347	India v Australia at Madras	1986-87

To draw

654-5	England (needing 696 to win) v South Africa at Durban	1938-39
429-8	India (needing 438 to win) v England at The Oval	1979
423-7	South Africa (needing 451 to win) v England at The Oval.	1947
408-5	West Indies (needing 836 to win) v England at Kingston.	1929-30

To lose

451	New Zealand (lost by 98 runs) v England at Christchurch	2001-02
445	India (lost by 47 runs) v Australia at Adelaide	1977-78
440	New Zealand (lost by 38 runs) v England at Nottingham.	1973
431	New Zealand (lost by 121 runs) v England at Napier	2007-08
417	England (lost by 45 runs) v Australia at Melbourne	1976-77

413	Bangladesh (lost by 107 runs) v Sri Lanka at Mirpur....................	2008-09
411	England (lost by 193 runs) v Australia at Sydney.......................	1924-25
410	Sri Lanka (lost by 96 runs) v Australia at Hobart......................	2007-08
406	**Australia (lost by 115 runs) v England at Lord's**	**2009**
402	Australia (lost by 103 runs) v England at Manchester	1981

Bold type denotes performances since January 1, 2009.

MOST RUNS IN A DAY (BOTH SIDES)

588	England (398-6), India (190-0) at Manchester (2nd day).................	1936
522	England (503-2), South Africa (19-0) at Lord's (2nd day)...............	1924
509	Sri Lanka (509-9) v Bangladesh at Colombo (PSS) (2nd day).............	2002
508	England (221-2), South Africa (287-6) at The Oval (3rd day).............	1935

MOST RUNS IN A DAY (ONE SIDE)

509	Sri Lanka (509-9) v Bangladesh at Colombo (PSS) (2nd day).............	2002
503	England (503-2) v South Africa at Lord's (2nd day)	1924
494	Australia (494-6) v South Africa at Sydney (1st day)...................	1910-11
475	Australia (475-2) v England at The Oval (1st day)......................	1934
471	England (471-8) v India at The Oval (1st day)	1936
458	Australia (458-3) v England at Leeds (1st day)........................	1930
455	Australia (455-1) v England at Leeds (2nd day)........................	1934
452	New Zealand (452-9 dec) v Zimbabwe at Harare (1st day)	2005-06
450	Australia (450) v South Africa at Johannesburg (1st day)	1921-22

MOST WICKETS IN A DAY

27	England (18-3 to 53 all out and 62) v Australia (60) at Lord's (2nd day)......	1888
25	Australia (112 and 48-5) v England (61) at Melbourne (1st day)...........	1901-02

HIGHEST AGGREGATES IN A TEST

Runs	Wkts			Days played
1,981	35	South Africa v England at Durban	1938-39	10†
1,815	34	West Indies v England at Kingston.............	1929-30	9‡
1,764	39	Australia v West Indies at Adelaide	1968-69	5
1,753	40	Australia v England at Adelaide	1920-21	6
1,747	25	Australia v India at Sydney....................	2003-04	5
1,723	31	England v Australia at Leeds	1948	5
1,702	28	Pakistan v India at Faisalabad.................	2005-06	5

† No play on one day. *‡ No play on two days.*

LOWEST INNINGS TOTALS

26	New Zealand v England at Auckland	1954-55
30	South Africa v England at Port Elizabeth	1895-96
30	South Africa v England at Birmingham	1924
35	South Africa v England at Cape Town	1898-99
36	Australia v England at Birmingham	1902
36	South Africa v Australia at Melbourne	1931-32
42	Australia v England at Sydney	1887-88
42	New Zealand v Australia at Wellington	1945-46
42†	India v England at Lord's	1974
43	South Africa v England at Cape Town	1888-89
44	Australia v England at The Oval	1896
45	England v Australia at Sydney	1886-87
45	South Africa v Australia at Melbourne	1931-32
46	England v West Indies at Port-of-Spain	1993-94
47	South Africa v England at Cape Town	1888-89
47	New Zealand v England at Lord's	1958
47	West Indies v England at Kingston	2003-04

The lowest innings for the countries not mentioned above are:

53†	Pakistan v Australia at Sharjah	2002-03
54	Zimbabwe v South Africa at Cape Town	2004-05
62	Bangladesh v Sri Lanka at Colombo (PSS).	2007
71	Sri Lanka v Pakistan at Kandy	1994-95

† *Batted one man short.*

FEWEST RUNS IN A FULL DAY'S PLAY

95	Australia (80), Pakistan (15-2) at Karachi (1st day, 5½ hours)	1956-57
104	Pakistan (0-0 to 104-5) v Australia at Karachi (4th day, 5½ hours).	1959-60
106	England (92-2 to 198) v Australia at Brisbane (4th day, 5 hours).	1958-59
	England were dismissed five minutes before the close of play, leaving no time for Australia to start their second innings.	
111	South Africa (48-2 to 130-6 dec), India (29-1) at Cape Town (5th day, 5½ hours).	1992-93
112	Australia (138-6 to 187), Pakistan (63-1) at Karachi (4th day, 5½ hours)	1956-57
115	Australia (116-7 to 165 and 66-5 after following on) v Pakistan at Karachi (4th day, 5½ hours)	1988-89
117	India (117-5) v Australia at Madras (1st day, 5½ hours)	1956-57
117	New Zealand (6-0 to 123-4) v Sri Lanka at Colombo (SSC) (5th day, 5¾ hours).	1983-84

In England

151	England (175-2 to 289), New Zealand (37-7) at Lord's (3rd day, 6 hours)	1978
158	England (211-2 to 369-9) v South Africa at Manchester (5th day, 6 hours)....	1998
159	Pakistan (208-4 to 350), England (17-1) at Leeds (3rd day, 6 hours).	1971

LOWEST AGGREGATES IN A COMPLETED TEST

Runs	Wkts			Days played
234	29	Australia v South Africa at Melbourne	1931-32	3†
291	40	England v Australia at Lord's	1888	2
295	28	New Zealand v Australia at Wellington	1945-46	2
309	29	West Indies v England at Bridgetown.............	1934-35	3
323	30	England v Australia at Manchester	1888	2

† *No play on one day.*

LARGEST VICTORIES

Largest Innings Victories

Inns & 579 runs	England (903-7 dec) v Australia (201 & 123‡) at The Oval	1938
Inns & 360 runs	Australia (652-7 dec) v South Africa (159 & 133) at Johannesburg ..	2001-02
Inns & 336 runs	West Indies (614-5 dec) v India (124 & 154) at Calcutta...........	1958-59
Inns & 332 runs	Australia (645) v England (141 & 172) at Brisbane...............	1946-47
Inns & 324 runs	Pakistan (643) v New Zealand (73 & 246) at Lahore..............	2002
Inns & 322 runs	West Indies (660-5 dec) v New Zealand (216 & 122) at Wellington..	1994-95
Inns & 310 runs	West Indies (536) v Bangladesh (139 & 87) at Dhaka.............	2002-03
Inns & 294 runs	New Zealand (452-9 dec) v Zimbabwe (59 & 99) at Harare	2005-06
Inns & 285 runs	England (629) v India (302 & 42†) at Lord's...................	1974
Inns & 264 runs	Pakistan (546-3 dec) v Bangladesh (134 & 148) at Multan	2001-02
Inns & 261 runs	England (528-3 dec) v Bangladesh (108 & 159) at Lord's.........	2005
Inns & 259 runs	Australia (549-7 dec) v South Africa (158 & 132) at Port Elizabeth ..	1949-50
Inns & 254 runs	Sri Lanka (713-3 dec) v Zimbabwe (228 & 231) at Bulawayo	2003-04

‡ *Two men absent in both Australian innings.*   † *One man absent in India's second innings.*

Largest Victories by Runs Margin

675 runs	England (521 & 342-8 dec) v Australia (122 & 66†) at Brisbane...........	1928-29
562 runs	Australia (701 & 327) v England (321 & 145‡) at The Oval	1934
530 runs	Australia (328 & 578) v South Africa (205 & 171§) at Melbourne	1910-11
491 runs	Australia (381 & 361-5 dec) v Pakistan (179 & 72) at Perth..............	2004-05
465 runs	**Sri Lanka (384 and 447-6 dec) v Bangladesh (208 and 158) at Chittagong**	**2008-09**
425 runs	West Indies (211 & 411-5 dec) v England (71 & 126) at Manchester	1976
409 runs	Australia (350 & 460-7 dec) v England (215 & 186) at Lord's.............	1948
408 runs	West Indies (328 & 448) v Australia (203 & 165) at Adelaide.............	1979-80
384 runs	Australia (492 & 296-5 dec) v England (325 & 79) at Brisbane............	2002-03
382 runs	Australia (238 & 411) v England (124 & 143) at Adelaide................	1894-95
382 runs	Australia (619 & 394-8 dec) v West Indies (279 & 352) at Sydney	1968-69
379 runs	Australia (435 & 283-2 dec) v West Indies (210 & 129) at Brisbane	2005-06

† *One man absent in Australia's first innings; two men absent in their second.*
‡ *Two men absent in England's first innings; one man absent in their second.*
§ *One man absent in South Africa's second innings.*

Bold type denotes performances since January 1, 2009.

TIED TESTS

West Indies (453 & 284) v Australia (505 & 232) at Brisbane	1960-61
Australia (574-7 dec & 170-5 dec) v India (397 & 347) at Madras...................	1986-87

MOST CONSECUTIVE TEST VICTORIES

16	Australia...........	1999-00–2000-01	8	England	2004–2004-05
16	Australia...........	2005-06–2007-08	7	England	1884-85–1887-88
11	West Indies........	1983-84–1984-85	7	England	1928–1928-29
9	Sri Lanka	2001–2001-02	7	West Indies........	1984-85–1985-86
9	South Africa........	2001-02–2003	7	West Indies........	1988–1988-89
8	Australia...........	1920-21–1921	7	Australia...........	2002-03

MOST CONSECUTIVE TESTS WITHOUT VICTORY

44	New Zealand	1929-30–1955-56		23	New Zealand	1962-63–1967-68
34	Bangladesh	2000-01–2004-05		22	Pakistan	1958-59–1964-65
31	India	1981-82–1984-85		21	Sri Lanka	1985-86–1992-93
28	South Africa	1935–1949-50		20	West Indies	1968-69–1972-73
24	India	1932–1951-52		20	West Indies	2004-05–2007
24	**Bangladesh**	**2004-05–2008-09**				

Bold type denotes sequence which was still in progress after January 1, 2009.

WHITEWASHES

Teams winning every game in a series of four Tests or more:

Five-Test Series

Australia beat England	1920-21	West Indies beat England	1985-86
Australia beat South Africa	1931-32	South Africa beat West Indies	1998-99
England beat India	1959	Australia beat West Indies	2000-01
West Indies beat India	1961-62	Australia beat England	2006-07
West Indies beat England	1984		

Four-Test Series

Australia beat India	1967-68	England beat West Indies	2004
South Africa beat Australia	1969-70		

Note: The winning team in each instance was at home, except for West Indies in England, 1984.

PLAYERS

YOUNGEST TEST PLAYERS

Years	Days			
15	124	Mushtaq Mohammad	Pakistan v West Indies at Lahore	1958-59
15	128	Mohammad Sharif	Bangladesh v Zimbabwe at Bulawayo	2000-01
16	189	Aqib Javed	Pakistan v New Zealand at Wellington	1988-89
16	205	S. R. Tendulkar	India v Pakistan at Karachi	1989-90

The above table should be treated with caution. All birthdates for Bangladesh and Pakistan (after Partition) must be regarded as questionable because of deficiencies in record-keeping. Hasan Raza was claimed to be 14 years 227 days old when he played for Pakistan against Zimbabwe at Faisalabad in 1996-97; this age was rejected by the Pakistan Cricket Board, although no alternative has been offered. Suggestions that Enamul Haque jun. was 16 years 230 days old when he played for Bangladesh against England in Dhaka in 2003-04 have been discounted by well-informed local observers, who believe he was 18.

The youngest Test players for countries not mentioned above are:

17	122	J. E. D. Sealy	West Indies v England at Bridgetown	1929-30
17	189	C. D. U. S. Weerasinghe	Sri Lanka v India at Colombo (PSS)	1985-86
17	239	I. D. Craig	Australia v South Africa at Melbourne	1952-53
17	352	H. Masakadza	Zimbabwe v West Indies at Harare	2001
18	10	D. L. Vettori	New Zealand v England at Wellington	1996-97
18	149	D. B. Close	England v New Zealand at Manchester	1949
18	340	P. R. Adams	South Africa v England at Port Elizabeth	1995-96

OLDEST PLAYERS ON TEST DEBUT

Years	Days			
49	119	J. Southerton	England v Australia at Melbourne	1876-77
47	284	Miran Bux	Pakistan v India at Lahore	1954-55
46	253	D. D. Blackie	Australia v England at Sydney	1928-29
46	237	H. Ironmonger	Australia v England at Brisbane	1928-29
42	242	N. Betancourt	West Indies v England at Port-of-Spain	1929-30
41	337	E. R. Wilson	England v Australia at Sydney	1920-21
41	27	R. J. D. Jamshedji	India v England at Bombay	1933-34
40	345	C. A. Wiles	West Indies v England at Manchester	1933
40	295	O. Henry	South Africa v India at Durban	1992-93
40	216	S. P. Kinneir	England v Australia at Sydney	1911-12
40	110	H. W. Lee	England v South Africa at Johannesburg	1930-31
40	56	G. W. A. Chubb	South Africa v England at Nottingham	1951
40	37	C. Ramaswami	India v England at Manchester	1936

Note: The oldest Test player on debut for New Zealand was H. M. McGirr, 38 years 101 days, v England at Auckland, 1929-30; for Sri Lanka, D. S. de Silva, 39 years 251 days, v England at Colombo (PSS), 1981-82; for Zimbabwe, A. C. Waller, 37 years 84 days, v England at Bulawayo, 1996-97; for Bangladesh, Enamul Haque, sen. 35 years 58 days, v Zimbabwe at Harare, 2000-01. A. J. Traicos was 45 years 154 days old when he made his debut for Zimbabwe (v India at Harare, 1992-93) having played three Tests for South Africa in 1969-70.

OLDEST TEST PLAYERS

(Age on final day of their last Test match)

Years	Days			
52	165	W. Rhodes	England v West Indies at Kingston	1929-30
50	327	H. Ironmonger	Australia v England at Sydney	1932-33
50	320	W. G. Grace	England v Australia at Nottingham	1899
50	303	G. Gunn	England v West Indies at Kingston	1929-30
49	139	J. Southerton	England v Australia at Melbourne	1876-77
47	302	Miran Bux	Pakistan v India at Peshawar	1954-55
47	249	J. B. Hobbs	England v Australia at The Oval	1930
47	87	F. E. Woolley	England v Australia at The Oval	1934
46	309	D. D. Blackie	Australia v England at Adelaide	1928-29
46	206	A. W. Nourse	South Africa v England at The Oval	1924
46	202	H. Strudwick	England v Australia at The Oval	1926
46	41	E. H. Hendren	England v West Indies at Kingston	1934-35
45	304	A. J. Traicos	Zimbabwe v India at Delhi	1992-93
45	245	G. O. B. Allen	England v West Indies at Kingston	1947-48
45	215	P. Holmes	England v India at Lord's	1932
45	140	D. B. Close	England v West Indies at Manchester	1976

MOST TEST APPEARANCES

168	S. R. Waugh (Australia)	131	Kapil Dev (India)
164	**S. R. Tendulkar (India)**	131	B. C. Lara (West Indies/World)
156	A. R. Border (Australia)	**130**	**M. V. Boucher (South Africa/World)**
145	S. K. Warne (Australia)	128	M. E. Waugh (Australia)
142	**R. T. Ponting (Australia)**	125	S. M. Gavaskar (India)
139	**R. Dravid (India/World)**	124	Javed Miandad (Pakistan)
135	**J. H. Kallis (South Africa/World)**	124	G. D. McGrath (Australia)
133	A. J. Stewart (England)	**123**	**S. Chanderpaul (West Indies)**
132	A. Kumble (India)	121	I. V. A. Richards (West Indies)
132	**M. Muralitharan (Sri Lanka/World)**	120	Inzamam-ul-Haq (Pakistan/World)
132	C. A. Walsh (West Indies)		

Note: Excluding the Super Series Test, **J. H. Kallis** has made **134** appearances for South Africa and **M. Muralitharan 131** for Sri Lanka, both national records. The most appearances for New Zealand is 111 by S. P. Fleming; for Zimbabwe, 67 by G. W. Flower; and for Bangladesh **52** by **Mohammad Ashraful**.

Bold type denotes those who have played Test cricket since January 1, 2009.

MOST CONSECUTIVE TEST APPEARANCES FOR A COUNTRY

153	A. R. Border (Australia).	March 1979 to March 1994
107	M. E. Waugh (Australia)	June 1993 to October 2002
106	S. M. Gavaskar (India).	January 1975 to February 1987
96†	A. C. Gilchrist (Australia)	November 1999 to January 2008
93	R. Dravid (India)	June 1996 to December 2005
87	G. R. Viswanath (India).	March 1971 to February 1983
86	M. L. Hayden (Australia).	March 2000 to January 2008
85	G. S. Sobers (West Indies)	April 1955 to April 1972
84	S. R. Tendulkar (India)	November 1989 to June 2001
75	M. V. Boucher (South Africa)	February 1998 to August 2004
72	S. P. Fleming (New Zealand).	July 1999 to March 2008
72	D. L. Haynes (West Indies)	December 1979 to June 1988
71	I. M. Chappell (Australia)	January 1966 to February 1976
69	M. Azharuddin (India).	April 1989 to February 1999
66	Kapil Dev (India)	October 1978 to December 1984
65	I. T. Botham (England)	February 1978 to March 1984
65	Kapil Dev (India)	January 1985 to March 1994
65	A. P. E. Knott (England)	March 1971 to August 1977
65	**D. P. M. D. Jayawardene (Sri Lanka)**	**November 2002 to December 2009**

The most consecutive Test appearances for the countries not mentioned above are:

56	A. D. R. Campbell (Zimbabwe).	October 1992 to September 2001
53	Javed Miandad (Pakistan)	December 1977 to January 1984
37	**Mohammad Ashraful (Bangladesh)**	**February 2004 to January 2010**

† *Complete Test career.*

Bold type denotes sequence which was still in progress after January 1, 2009.

MOST TESTS AS CAPTAIN

	P	W	L	D		P	W	L	D
A. R. Border (A)	93	32	22	38*	B. C. Lara (WI)	47	10	26	11
S. P. Fleming (NZ)	80	28	27	25	N. Hussain (E)	45	17	15	13
C. H. Lloyd (WI)	74	36	12	26	P. B. H. May (E)	41	20	10	11
G. C. Smith (SA/World)	73	34	22†	17	Nawab of Pataudi jun. (I)	40	9	19	12
R. T. Ponting (A)	**67**	**44**	**11**	**12**	R. B. Simpson (A)	39	12	12	15
S. R. Waugh (A)	57	41	9	7	G. S. Sobers (WI)	39	9	10	20
A. Ranatunga (SL)	56	12	19	25	S. T. Jayasuriya (SL)	38	18	12	8
M. A. Atherton (E)	54	13	21	20	G. A. Gooch (E)	34	10	12	12
W. J. Cronje (SA)	53	27	11	15	Javed Miandad (P)	34	14	6	14
M. P. Vaughan (E)	51	26	11	14	Kapil Dev (I)	34	4	7	22*
I. V. A. Richards (WI)	50	27	8	15	J. R. Reid (NZ)	34	3	18	13
M. A. Taylor (A)	50	26	13	11	D. I. Gower (E)	32	5	18	9
S. C. Ganguly (I)	49	21	13	15	J. M. Brearley (E)	31	18	4	9
G. S. Chappell (A)	48	21	13	14	R. Illingworth (E)	31	12	5	14
Imran Khan (P)	48	14	8	26	Inzamam-ul-Haq (P)	31	11	11	9
M. Azharuddin (I)	47	14	14	19	I. M. Chappell (A)	30	15	5	10
S. M. Gavaskar (I)	47	9	8	30	E. R. Dexter (E)	30	9	7	14
					G. P. Howarth (NZ)	30	11	7	12

* *One match tied.*

† *Includes defeat as World XI captain in Super Series Test against Australia.*

Most Tests as captain of other countries:

	P	W	L	D
A. D. R. Campbell (Z)	21	2	12	7
Habibul Bashar (B)	18	1	13	4

Notes: A. R. Border captained Australia in 93 consecutive Tests.

W. W. Armstrong (Australia) captained his country in the most Tests without being defeated: ten matches with eight wins and two draws.

I. T. Botham (England) captained his country in 12 Tests without ever winning: eight draws and four defeats.

Bold type denotes those who have been captains since January 1, 2009.

UMPIRES

MOST TESTS

		First Test	Last Test
128	**S. A. Bucknor (West Indies)**	**1988-89**	**2008-09**
105	**R. E. Koertzen (South Africa)**	**1992-93**	**2009-10**
92	D. R. Shepherd (England)	1985	2004-05
88	**D. J. Harper (Australia)**	**1998-99**	**2009-10**
78	D. B. Hair (Australia)	1991-92	2008
73	S. Venkataraghavan (India)	1992-93	2003-04
66	H. D. Bird (England)	1973	1996
61	**S. J. A. Taufel (Australia)**	**2000-01**	**2009-10**
59	**Aleem Dar (Pakistan)**	**2003-04**	**2009-10**
59	**B. F. Bowden (New Zealand)**	**1999-2000**	**2009-10**
48	F. Chester (England)	1924	1955
44	D. L. Orchard (South Africa)	1995-96	2003-04
44	**R. B. Tiffin (Zimbabwe)**	**1995-96**	**2008-09**
43	**E. A. R. de Silva (Sri Lanka)**	**2000**	**2009-10**
42	C. S. Elliott (England)	1957	1974
39	R. S. Dunne (New Zealand)	1988-89	2001-02
36	D. J. Constant (England)	1971	1988
36	S. G. Randell (Australia)	1984-85	1997-98
34	Khizar Hayat (Pakistan)	1979-80	1996-97
33	J. S. Buller (England)	1956	1969
33	A. R. Crafter (Australia)	1978-79	1991-92
32	R. W. Crockett (Australia)	1901-02	1924-25
31	D. Sang Hue (West Indies)	1961-62	1980-81

Bold type indicates umpires who have stood since January 1, 2009.

SUMMARY OF TESTS

To January 27, 2010

	Opponents	Tests	E	A	SA	WI	NZ	I	P	SL	Z	B	Wld	Tied	Drawn
								Won by							
England	Australia	321	99	132	–	–	–	–	–	–	–	–	–	–	90
	South Africa	138	56	–	29	–	–	–	–	–	–	–	–	–	53
	West Indies	145	43	–	–	53	–	–	–	–	–	–	–	–	49
	New Zealand	94	45	–	–	–	8	–	–	–	–	–	–	–	41
	India	99	34	–	–	–	–	19	–	–	–	–	–	–	46
	Pakistan	67	19	–	–	–	–	–	12	–	–	–	–	–	36
	Sri Lanka	21	8	–	–	–	–	–	–	6	–	–	–	–	7
	Zimbabwe	6	3	–	–	–	–	–	–	–	0	–	–	–	3
	Bangladesh	4	4	–	–	–	–	–	–	–	–	0	–	–	0
Australia	South Africa	83	–	47	18	–	–	–	–	–	–	–	–	–	18
	West Indies	108	–	52	–	32	–	–	–	–	–	–	–	1	23
	New Zealand	48	–	24	–	–	7	–	–	–	–	–	–	–	17
	India	76	–	34	–	–	–	18	–	–	–	–	–	1	23
	Pakistan	55	–	27	–	–	–	–	11	–	–	–	–	–	17
	Sri Lanka	20	–	13	–	–	–	–	–	1	–	–	–	–	6
	Zimbabwe	3	–	3	–	–	–	–	–	–	0	–	–	–	0
	Bangladesh	4	–	4	–	–	–	–	–	–	–	0	–	–	0
	ICC World XI	1	–	1	–	–	–	–	–	–	–	–	0	–	0
South Africa	West Indies	22	–	–	14	3	–	–	–	–	–	–	–	–	5
	New Zealand	35	–	–	20	–	4	–	–	–	–	–	–	–	11
	India	22	–	–	10	–	–	5	–	–	–	–	–	–	7
	Pakistan	16	–	–	8	–	–	–	3	–	–	–	–	–	5
	Sri Lanka	17	–	–	8	–	–	–	–	4	–	–	–	–	5
	Zimbabwe	7	–	–	6	–	–	–	–	–	0	–	–	–	1
	Bangladesh	8	–	–	8	–	–	–	–	–	–	0	–	–	0
West Indies	New Zealand	37	–	–	–	10	9	–	–	–	–	–	–	–	18
	India	82	–	–	–	30	–	11	–	–	–	–	–	–	41
	Pakistan	44	–	–	–	14	–	–	15	–	–	–	–	–	15
	Sri Lanka	12	–	–	–	3	–	–	–	6	–	–	–	–	3
	Zimbabwe	6	–	–	–	4	–	–	–	–	0	–	–	–	2
	Bangladesh	6	–	–	–	3	–	–	–	–	–	2	–	–	1
New Zealand	India	47	–	–	–	–	9	15	–	–	–	–	–	–	23
	Pakistan	48	–	–	–	–	7	–	22	–	–	–	–	–	19
	Sri Lanka	26	–	–	–	–	9	–	–	7	–	–	–	–	10
	Zimbabwe	13	–	–	–	–	7	–	–	–	0	–	–	–	6
	Bangladesh	8	–	–	–	–	7	–	–	–	–	0	–	–	1
India	Pakistan	59	–	–	–	–	–	9	12	–	–	–	–	–	38
	Sri Lanka	32	–	–	–	–	–	13	–	5	–	–	–	–	14
	Zimbabwe	11	–	–	–	–	–	7	–	–	2	–	–	–	2
	Bangladesh	7	–	–	–	–	–	6	–	–	–	0	–	–	1
Pakistan	Sri Lanka	37	–	–	–	–	–	–	15	9	–	–	–	–	13
	Zimbabwe	14	–	–	–	–	–	–	8	–	2	–	–	–	4
	Bangladesh	6	–	–	–	–	–	–	6	–	–	0	–	–	0
Sri Lanka	Zimbabwe	15	–	–	–	–	–	–	–	10	0	–	–	–	5
	Bangladesh	12	–	–	–	–	–	–	–	12	–	0	–	–	0
Zimbabwe	Bangladesh	8	–	–	–	–	–	–	–	–	4	1	–	–	3
		1,950	311	337	121	152	67	103	104	60	8	3	0	2	682

	Tests	Won	Lost	Drawn	Tied	% Won	Toss Won
England	895	311	259	325	–	34.74	433
Australia	719†	337†	186	194	2	46.87	362
South Africa	348	121	122	105	–	34.77	166
West Indies	462	152	152	157	1	32.90	241
New Zealand	356	67	143	146	–	18.82	181
India	435	103	136	195	1	23.67	224
Pakistan	346	104	95	147	–	30.05	163
Sri Lanka	192	60	69	63	–	31.25	99
Zimbabwe	83	8	49	26	–	9.63	49
Bangladesh	63	3	54	6	–	4.76	32
ICC World XI	1	0	1	0	–	0.00	0

† *Includes Super Series Test between Australia and ICC World XI.*

ENGLAND v AUSTRALIA

Series notes: England have taken 20 wickets in only one of the last 15 Tests in Australia in which the Ashes were still at stake. They have won none and lost 12 of those matches. Only five of the last 34 Tests between the sides have been drawn and, excluding one-off Tests, there have been no drawn series since 1972. Australia have lost only two of their last 28 Tests against England at Lord's. Since 1990, Australia have a conversion-rate of fifties to hundreds of 39% (73 x 100, 114 x 50); England's is 18% (30 x 100; 140 x 50). D. G. Bradman is the only man to score 5,000 runs against one country; he made 5,028 at 89.78 against England. S. K. Warne's 195 English wickets are a record against one country; he is also the only man to take 100 wickets in another country, with 129 at 21.94 in England. I. T. Botham's 21 sixes are a record against Australia, shared with B. C. Lara.

		Captains					
Season	*England*		*Australia*	*T*	*E*	*A*	*D*
1876-77	James Lillywhite		D. W. Gregory	2	1	1	0
1878-79	Lord Harris		D. W. Gregory	1	0	1	0
1880	Lord Harris		W. L. Murdoch	1	1	0	0
1881-82	A. Shaw		W. L. Murdoch	4	0	2	2
1882	A. N. Hornby		W. L. Murdoch	1	0	1	0

THE ASHES

		Captains						
Season	*England*		*Australia*	*T*	*E*	*A*	*D*	*Held by*
1882-83	Hon. Ivo Bligh		W. L. Murdoch	4*	2	2	0	E
1884	Lord Harris[1]		W. L. Murdoch	3	1	0	2	E
1884-85	A. Shrewsbury		T. P. Horan[2]	5	3	2	0	E
1886	A. G. Steel		H. J. H. Scott	3	3	0	0	E
1886-87	A. Shrewsbury		P. S. McDonnell	2	2	0	0	E
1887-88	W. W. Read		P. S. McDonnell	1	1	0	0	E
1888	W. G. Grace[3]		P. S. McDonnell	3	2	1	0	E
1890†	W. G. Grace		W. L. Murdoch	2	2	0	0	E
1891-92	W. G. Grace		J. McC. Blackham	3	1	2	0	A
1893	W. G. Grace[4]		J. McC. Blackham	3	1	0	2	E
1894-95	A. E. Stoddart		G. Giffen[5]	5	3	2	0	E
1896	W. G. Grace		G. H. S. Trott	3	2	1	0	E
1897-98	A. E. Stoddart[6]		G. H. S. Trott	5	1	4	0	A
1899	A. C. MacLaren[7]		J. Darling	5	0	1	4	A
1901-02	A. C. MacLaren		J. Darling[8]	5	1	4	0	A
1902	A. C. MacLaren		J. Darling	5	1	2	2	A
1903-04	P. F. Warner		M. A. Noble	5	3	2	0	E
1905	Hon. F. S. Jackson		J. Darling	5	2	0	3	E
1907-08	A. O. Jones[9]		M. A. Noble	5	1	4	0	A
1909	A. C. MacLaren		M. A. Noble	5	1	2	2	A
1911-12	J. W. H. T. Douglas		C. Hill	5	4	1	0	E
1912	C. B. Fry		S. E. Gregory	3	1	0	2	E
1920-21	J. W. H. T. Douglas		W. W. Armstrong	5	0	5	0	A
1921	Hon. L. H. Tennyson[10]		W. W. Armstrong	5	0	3	2	A
1924-25	A. E. R. Gilligan		H. L. Collins	5	1	4	0	A
1926	A. W. Carr[11]		H. L. Collins[12]	5	1	0	4	E
1928-29	A. P. F. Chapman[13]		J. Ryder	5	4	1	0	E
1930	A. P. F. Chapman[14]		W. M. Woodfull	5	1	2	2	A
1932-33	D. R. Jardine		W. M. Woodfull	5	4	1	0	E
1934	R. E. S. Wyatt[15]		W. M. Woodfull	5	1	2	2	A
1936-37	G. O. B. Allen		D. G. Bradman	5	2	3	0	A
1938†	W. R. Hammond		D. G. Bradman	4	1	1	2	A
1946-47	W. R. Hammond[16]		D. G. Bradman	5	0	3	2	A
1948	N. W. D. Yardley		D. G. Bradman	5	0	4	1	A

Captains

Season	England	Australia	T	E	A	D	Held by
1950-51	F. R. Brown	A. L. Hassett	5	1	4	0	A
1953	L. Hutton	A. L. Hassett	5	1	0	4	E
1954-55	L. Hutton	I. W. Johnson[17]	5	3	1	1	E
1956	P. B. H. May	I. W. Johnson	5	2	1	2	E
1958-59	P. B. H. May	R. Benaud	5	0	4	1	A
1961	P. B. H. May[18]	R. Benaud[19]	5	1	2	2	A
1962-63	E. R. Dexter	R. Benaud	5	1	1	3	A
1964	E. R. Dexter	R. B. Simpson	5	0	1	4	A
1965-66	M. J. K. Smith	R. B. Simpson[20]	5	1	1	3	A
1968	M. C. Cowdrey[21]	W. M. Lawry[22]	5	1	1	3	A
1970-71†	R. Illingworth	W. M. Lawry[23]	6	2	0	4	E
1972	R. Illingworth	I. M. Chappell	5	2	2	1	E
1974-75	M. H. Denness[24]	I. M. Chappell	6	1	4	1	A
1975	A. W. Greig[25]	I. M. Chappell	4	0	1	3	A
1976-77‡	A. W. Greig	G. S. Chappell	1	0	1	0	—
1977	J. M. Brearley	G. S. Chappell	5	3	0	2	E
1978-79	J. M. Brearley	G. N. Yallop	6	5	1	0	E
1979-80‡	J. M. Brearley	G. S. Chappell	3	0	3	0	—
1980‡	I. T. Botham	G. S. Chappell	1	0	0	1	—
1981	J. M. Brearley[26]	K. J. Hughes	6	3	1	2	E
1982-83	R. G. D. Willis	G. S. Chappell	5	1	2	2	A
1985	D. I. Gower	A. R. Border	6	3	1	2	E
1986-87	M. W. Gatting	A. R. Border	5	2	1	2	E
1987-88‡	M. W. Gatting	A. R. Border	1	0	0	1	—
1989	D. I. Gower	A. R. Border	6	0	4	2	A
1990-91	G. A. Gooch[27]	A. R. Border	5	0	3	2	A
1993	G. A. Gooch[28]	A. R. Border	6	1	4	1	A
1994-95	M. A. Atherton	M. A. Taylor	5	1	3	1	A
1997	M. A. Atherton	M. A. Taylor	6	2	3	1	A
1998-99	A. J. Stewart	M. A. Taylor	5	1	3	1	A
2001	N. Hussain[29]	S. R. Waugh[30]	5	1	4	0	A
2002-03	N. Hussain	S. R. Waugh	5	1	4	0	A
2005	M. P. Vaughan	R. T. Ponting	5	2	1	2	A
2006-07	A. Flintoff	R. T. Ponting	5	0	5	0	A
2009	**A. J. Strauss**	**R. T. Ponting**	**5**	**2**	**1**	**2**	**E**
	In Australia		165	54	85	26	
	In England		**156**	**45**	**47**	**64**	
	Totals		**321**	**99**	**132**	**90**	

* The Ashes were awarded in 1882-83 after a series of three matches which England won 2–1. A fourth match was played and this was won by Australia.
† The matches at Manchester in 1890 and 1938 and at Melbourne (Third Test) in 1970-71 were abandoned without a ball being bowled and are excluded.
‡ The Ashes were not at stake in these series.

Notes: The following deputised for the official touring captain or were appointed by the home authority for only a minor proportion of the series:

[1]A. N. Hornby (First). [2]W. L. Murdoch (First), H. H. Massie (Third), J. McC. Blackham (Fourth). [3]A. G. Steel (First). [4]A. E. Stoddart (First). [5]J. McC. Blackham (First). [6]A. C. MacLaren (First, Second and Fifth). [7]W. G. Grace (First). [8]H. Trumble (Fourth and Fifth). [9]F. L. Fane (First, Second and Third). [10]J. W. H. T. Douglas (First and Second). [11]A. P. F. Chapman (Fifth). [12]W. Bardsley (Third and Fourth). [13]J. C. White (Fifth). [14]R. E. S. Wyatt (Fifth). [15]C. F. Walters (First). [16]N. W. D. Yardley (Fifth). [17]A. R. Morris (Second). [18]M. C. Cowdrey (First and Second). [19]R. N. Harvey (Second). [20]B. C. Booth (First and Third). [21]T. W. Graveney (Fourth). [22]B. N. Jarman (Fourth) [23]I. M. Chappell (Seventh). [24]J. H. Edrich (Fourth). [25]M. H. Denness (First). [26]I. T. Botham (First and Second). [27]A. J. Lamb (First). [28]M. A. Atherton (Fifth and Sixth). [29]M. A. Atherton (Second and Third). [30]A. C. Gilchrist (Fourth).

HIGHEST INNINGS TOTALS

For England in England: 903-7 dec at The Oval 1938
              in Australia: 636 at Sydney 1928-29

For Australia in England: 729-6 dec at Lord's 1930
              in Australia: 659-8 dec at Sydney 1946-47

LOWEST INNINGS TOTALS

For England in England: 52 at The Oval 1948
              in Australia: 45 at Sydney 1886-87

For Australia in England: 36 at Birmingham 1902
              in Australia: 42 at Sydney 1887-88

DOUBLE-HUNDREDS

For England (11)

364	L. Hutton at The Oval	1938		216*	E. Paynter at Nottingham	1938
287	R. E. Foster at Sydney	1903-04		215	D. I. Gower at Birmingham	1985
256	K. F. Barrington at Manchester	1964		207	N. Hussain at Birmingham	1997
251	W. R. Hammond at Sydney	1928-29		206	P. D. Collingwood at Adelaide	2006-07
240	W. R. Hammond at Lord's	1938		200	W. R. Hammond at Melbourne	1928-29
231*	W. R. Hammond at Sydney	1936-37				

For Australia (23)

334	D. G. Bradman at Leeds	1930		232	S. J. McCabe at Nottingham	1938
311	R. B. Simpson at Manchester	1964		225	R. B. Simpson at Adelaide	1965-66
307	R. M. Cowper at Melbourne	1965-66		219	M. A. Taylor at Nottingham	1989
304	D. G. Bradman at Leeds	1934		212	D. G. Bradman at Adelaide	1936-37
270	D. G. Bradman at Melbourne	1936-37		211	W. L. Murdoch at The Oval	1884
266	W. H. Ponsford at The Oval	1934		207	K. R. Stackpole at Brisbane	1970-71
254	D. G. Bradman at Lord's	1930		206*	W. A. Brown at Lord's	1938
250	J. L. Langer at Melbourne	2002-03		206	A. R. Morris at Adelaide	1950-51
244	D. G. Bradman at The Oval	1934		201*	J. Ryder at Adelaide	1924-25
234	S. G. Barnes at Sydney	1946-47		201	S. E. Gregory at Sydney	1894-95
234	D. G. Bradman at Sydney	1946-47		200*	A. R. Border at Leeds	1993
232	D. G. Bradman at The Oval	1930				

INDIVIDUAL HUNDREDS

For England (222)

12: J. B. Hobbs.

9: D. I. Gower, W. R. Hammond.

8: H. Sutcliffe.

7: G. Boycott, J. H. Edrich, M. Leyland.

5: K. F. Barrington, D. C. S. Compton, M. C. Cowdrey, L. Hutton, F. S. Jackson, A. C. MacLaren.

4: I. T. Botham, B. C. Broad, M. W. Gatting, G. A. Gooch, M. P. Vaughan.

3: M. A. Butcher, E. H. Hendren, P. B. H. May, D. W. Randall, A. C. Russell, A. Shrewsbury, **A. J. Strauss**, G. P. Thorpe, J. T. Tyldesley, R. A. Woolmer.

2: C. J. Barnett, L. C. Braund, E. R. Dexter, B. L. D'Oliveira, W. J. Edrich, W. G. Grace, G. Gunn, T. W. Hayward, N. Hussain, A. P. E. Knott, B. W. Luckhurst, **K. P. Pietersen**, K. S. Ranjitsinhji, R. T. Robinson, Rev. D. S. Sheppard, R. A. Smith, A. G. Steel, A. E. Stoddart, R. Subba Row, C. Washbrook, F. E. Woolley.

1: R. Abel, L. E. G. Ames, M. A. Atherton, R. W. Barber, W. Barnes, J. Briggs, J. T. Brown, A. P. F. Chapman, **P. D. Collingwood**, **A. N. Cook**, M. H. Denness, K. S. Duleepsinhji, K. W. R. Fletcher, **A. Flintoff**, R. E. Foster, C. B. Fry, T. W. Graveney, A. W. Greig, W. Gunn, J. Hardstaff, jun., J. W. Hearne, K. L. Hutchings, G. L. Jessop, A. J. Lamb, J. W. H. Makepeace, C. P. Mead, Nawab of Pataudi, sen., E. Paynter, M. R. Ramprakash, W. W. Read, W. Rhodes, C. J. Richards, P. E. Richardson, R. C. Russell, J. Sharp, R. T. Simpson, A. J. Stewart, **I. J. L. Trott**, G. Ulyett, A. Ward, W. Watson.

For Australia (284)

19: D. G. Bradman.

10: S. R. Waugh.

9: G. S. Chappell.

8: A. R. Border, A. R. Morris, **R. T. Ponting**.

7: D. C. Boon, W. M. Lawry, M. J. Slater.

6: R. N. Harvey, M. A. Taylor, V. T. Trumper, M. E. Waugh, W. M. Woodfull.

5: M. L. Hayden, J. L. Langer, C. G. Macartney, W. H. Ponsford.

4: W. W. Armstrong, P. J. Burge, I. M. Chappell, **M. J. Clarke**, S. E. Gregory, A. L. Hassett, C. Hill, S. J. McCabe, K. D. Walters.

3: W. Bardsley, G. S. Blewett, W. A. Brown, H. L. Collins, J. Darling, A. C. Gilchrist, K. J. Hughes, D. M. Jones, P. S. McDonnell, K. R. Miller, K. R. Stackpole, G. M. Wood, G. N. Yallop.

2: S. G. Barnes, B. C. Booth, R. A. Duff, R. Edwards, M. T. G. Elliott, J. H. Fingleton, H. Graham, I. A. Healy, **M. E. K. Hussey**, F. A. Iredale, R. B. McCosker, C. C. McDonald, G. R. Marsh, D. R. Martyn, W. L. Murdoch, **M. J. North**, N. C. O'Neill, C. E. Pellew, I. R. Redpath, J. Ryder, R. B. Simpson.

1: C. L. Badcock, C. Bannerman, G. J. Bonnor, J. W. Burke, R. M. Cowper, J. Dyson, G. Giffen, J. M. Gregory, **B. J. Haddin**, R. J. Hartigan, H. L. Hendry, A. M. J. Hilditch, T. P. Horan, A. A. Jackson, **S. M. Katich**, C. Kelleway, A. F. Kippax, R. R. Lindwall, J. J. Lyons, C. L. McCool, C. E. McLeod, R. W. Marsh, G. R. J. Matthews, M. A. Noble, V. S. Ransford, A. J. Richardson, V. Y. Richardson, A. M. Ritchie, H. J. H. Scott, A. Symonds, J. M. Taylor, G. H. S. Trott, D. M. Wellham, K. C. Wessels.

RECORD PARTNERSHIPS FOR EACH WICKET

For England

323 for 1st	J. B. Hobbs and W. Rhodes at Melbourne	1911-12
382 for 2nd†	L. Hutton and M. Leyland at The Oval	1938
262 for 3rd	W. R. Hammond and D. R. Jardine at Adelaide	1928-29
310 for 4th	P. D. Collingwood and K. P. Pietersen at Adelaide	2006-07
206 for 5th	E. Paynter and D. C. S. Compton at Nottingham	1938
215 for 6th	{ L. Hutton and J. Hardstaff jun. at The Oval	1938
	{ G. Boycott and A. P. E. Knott at Nottingham	1977
143 for 7th	F. E. Woolley and J. Vine at Sydney	1911-12
124 for 8th	E. H. Hendren and H. Larwood at Brisbane	1928-29
151 for 9th	W. H. Scotton and W. W. Read at The Oval	1884
130 for 10th†	R. E. Foster and W. Rhodes at Sydney	1903-04

For Australia

329 for 1st	G. R. Marsh and M. A. Taylor at Nottingham	1989
451 for 2nd†	W. H. Ponsford and D. G. Bradman at The Oval	1934
276 for 3rd	D. G. Bradman and A. L. Hassett at Brisbane	1946-47
388 for 4th†	W. H. Ponsford and D. G. Bradman at Leeds	1934
405 for 5th†	S. G. Barnes and D. G. Bradman at Sydney	1946-47
346 for 6th†	J. H. Fingleton and D. G. Bradman at Melbourne	1936-37
165 for 7th	C. Hill and H. Trumble at Melbourne	1897-98
243 for 8th†	R. J. Hartigan and C. Hill at Adelaide	1907-08
154 for 9th†	S. E. Gregory and J. McC. Blackham at Sydney	1894-95
127 for 10th†	J. M. Taylor and A. A. Mailey at Sydney	1924-25

† *Record partnership against all countries.*

MOST RUNS IN A SERIES

England in England	732 (average 81.33)	D. I. Gower	1985
England in Australia	905 (average 113.12)	W. R. Hammond	1928-29
Australia in England	974 (average 139.14)	D. G. Bradman	1930
Australia in Australia	810 (average 90.00)	D. G. Bradman	1936-37

TEN WICKETS OR MORE IN A MATCH

For England (38)

13-163 (6-42, 7-121)	S. F. Barnes, Melbourne	1901-02
14-102 (7-28, 7-74)	W. Bates, Melbourne	1882-83
10-105 (5-46, 5-59)	A. V. Bedser, Melbourne	1950-51
14-99 (7-55, 7-44)	A. V. Bedser, Nottingham	1953
11-102 (6-44, 5-58)	C. Blythe, Birmingham	1909
11-176 (6-78, 5-98)	I. T. Botham, Perth	1979-80
10-253 (6-125, 4-128)	I. T. Botham, The Oval	1981
11-74 (5-29, 6-45)	J. Briggs, Lord's	1886
12-136 (6-49, 6-87)	J. Briggs, Adelaide	1891-92
10-148 (5-34, 5-114)	J. Briggs, The Oval	1893
10-215 (3-121, 7-94)	A. R. Caddick, Sydney	2002-03
10-104 (6-77, 4-27)†	R. M. Ellison, Birmingham	1985
10-179 (5-102, 5-77)†	K. Farnes, Nottingham	1934
10-60 (6-41, 4-19)	J. T. Hearne, The Oval	1896
11-113 (5-58, 6-55)	J. C. Laker, Leeds	1956
19-90 (9-37, 10-53)	J. C. Laker, Manchester	1956
10-124 (5-96, 5-28)	H. Larwood, Sydney	1932-33
11-76 (6-48, 5-28)	W. H. Lockwood, Manchester	1902
12-104 (7-36, 5-68)	G. A. Lohmann, The Oval	1886
10-87 (8-35, 2-52)	G. A. Lohmann, Sydney	1886-87
10-142 (8-58, 2-84)	G. A. Lohmann, Sydney	1891-92
12-102 (6-50, 6-52)†	F. Martin, The Oval	1890
11-68 (7-31, 4-37)	R. Peel, Manchester	1888
15-124 (7-56, 8-68)	W. Rhodes, Melbourne	1903-04
10-156 (5-49, 5-107)†	T. Richardson, Manchester	1893
11-173 (6-39, 5-134)	T. Richardson, Lord's	1896
13-244 (7-168, 6-76)	T. Richardson, Manchester	1896
10-204 (8-94, 2-110)	T. Richardson, Sydney	1897-98
11-228 (6-130, 5-98)†	M. W. Tate, Sydney	1924-25
11-88 (5-58, 6-30)	F. S. Trueman, Leeds	1961
11-93 (7-66, 4-27)	P. C. R. Tufnell, The Oval	1997
10-130 (4-45, 6-85)	F. H. Tyson, Sydney	1954-55
10-82 (4-37, 6-45)	D. L. Underwood, Leeds	1972
11-215 (7-113, 4-102)	D. L. Underwood, Adelaide	1974-75
15-104 (7-61, 8-43)	H. Verity, Lord's	1934
10-57 (6-41, 4-16)	W. Voce, Brisbane	1936-37
13-256 (5-130, 8-126)	J. C. White, Adelaide	1928-29
10-49 (5-29, 5-20)	F. E. Woolley, The Oval	1912

For Australia (43)

10-151 (5-107, 5-44)	T. M. Alderman, Leeds	1989
10-239 (4-129, 6-110)	L. O'B. Fleetwood-Smith, Adelaide	1936-37
10-160 (4-88, 6-72)	G. Giffen, Sydney	1891-92
11-82 (5-45, 6-37)†	C. V. Grimmett, Sydney	1924-25
10-201 (5-107, 5-94)	C. V. Grimmett, Nottingham	1930
10-122 (5-65, 5-57)	R. M. Hogg, Perth	1978-79
10-66 (5-30, 5-36)	R. M. Hogg, Melbourne	1978-79
12-175 (5-85, 7-90)†	H. V. Hordern, Sydney	1911-12
10-161 (5-95, 5-66)	H. V. Hordern, Sydney	1911-12
10-164 (7-88, 3-76)	E. Jones, Lord's	1899
11-134 (6-47, 5-87)	G. F. Lawson, Brisbane	1982-83
10-181 (5-58, 5-123)	D. K. Lillee, The Oval	1972
11-165 (6-26, 5-139)	D. K. Lillee, Melbourne	1976-77
11-138 (6-60, 5-78)	D. K. Lillee, Melbourne	1979-80
11-159 (7-89, 4-70)	D. K. Lillee, The Oval	1981
11-85 (7-58, 4-27)	C. G. Macartney, Leeds	1909
11-157 (8-97, 3-60)	C. J. McDermott, Perth	1990-91

12-107 (5-57, 7-50)	S. C. G. MacGill, Sydney	1998-99
10-302 (5-160, 5-142)	A. A. Mailey, Adelaide	1920-21
13-236 (4-115, 9-121)	A. A. Mailey, Melbourne	1920-21
16-137 (8-84, 8-53)†	R. A. L. Massie, Lord's	1972
10-152 (5-72, 5-80)	K. R. Miller, Lord's	1956
13-77 (7-17, 6-60)	M. A. Noble, Melbourne	1901-02
11-103 (5-51, 6-52)	M. A. Noble, Sheffield	1902
10-129 (5-63, 5-66)	W. J. O'Reilly, Melbourne	1932-33
11-129 (4-75, 7-54)	W. J. O'Reilly, Nottingham	1934
10-122 (5-66, 5-56)	W. J. O'Reilly, Leeds	1938
11-165 (7-68, 4-97)	G. E. Palmer, Sydney	1881-82
10-126 (7-65, 3-61)	G. E. Palmer, Melbourne	1882-83
13-148 (6-97, 7-51)	B. A. Reid, Melbourne	1990-91
13-110 (6-48, 7-62)	F. R. Spofforth, Melbourne	1878-79
14-90 (7-46, 7-44)	F. R. Spofforth, The Oval	1882
11-117 (4-73, 7-44)	F. R. Spofforth, Sydney	1882-83
10-144 (4-54, 6-90)	F. R. Spofforth, Sydney	1884-85
12-89 (6-59, 6-30)	H. Trumble, The Oval	1896
10-128 (4-75, 6-53)	H. Trumble, Manchester	1902
12-173 (8-65, 4-108)	H. Trumble, The Oval	1902
12-87 (5-44, 7-43)	C. T. B. Turner, Sydney	1887-88
10-63 (5-27, 5-36)	C. T. B. Turner, Lord's	1888
11-110 (3-39, 8-71)	S. K. Warne, Brisbane	1994-95
11-229 (7-165, 4-64)	S. K. Warne, The Oval	2001
10-162 (4-116, 6-46)	S. K. Warne, Birmingham	2005
12-246 (6-122, 6-124)	S. K. Warne, The Oval	2005

† *On first appearance in England–Australia Tests.*

Note: A. V. Bedser, J. Briggs, J. C. Laker, T. Richardson in 1896, R. M. Hogg, A. A. Mailey, H. Trumble and C. T. B. Turner took ten wickets or more in successive Tests. J. Briggs was omitted, however, from the England team for the first Test match in 1893.

SEVEN WICKETS OR MORE IN AN INNINGS

In addition to those listed above, the following have taken seven wickets or more in an innings:

For England

7-40	R. G. Barlow, Sydney	1882-83	7-40	J. A. Snow, Sydney	1970-71
7-44	R. G. Barlow, Manchester	1886	7-57	J. B. Statham, Melbourne	1958-59
7-60	S. F. Barnes, Sydney	1907-08	7-79	F. J. Titmus, Melbourne	1962-63
8-107	B. J. T. Bosanquet, Nottingham	1905	7-27	F. H. Tyson, Melbourne	1954-55
8-81	L. C. Braund, Melbourne	1903-04	7-36	G. Ulyett, Lord's	1884
7-78	J. E. Emburey, Sydney	1986-87	7-50	D. L. Underwood, The Oval	1968
7-68	T. Emmett, Melbourne	1878-79	7-78	R. G. D. Willis, Lord's	1977
7-109	M. J. Hoggard, Adelaide	2006-07	8-43	R. G. D. Willis, Leeds	1981
7-71	W. H. Lockwood, The Oval	1899	7-105	D. V. P. Wright, Sydney	1946-47
7-17	W. Rhodes, Birmingham	1902			

For Australia

7-148	A. Cotter, The Oval	1905	7-63	R. R. Lindwall, Sydney	1946-47
7-117	G. Giffen, Sydney	1884-85	8-141	C. J. McDermott, Manchester	1985
7-128	G. Giffen, The Oval	1893	8-38	G. D. McGrath, Lord's	1997
7-37	J. N. Gillespie, Leeds	1997	7-76	G. D. McGrath, The Oval	1997
7-69	J. M. Gregory, Melbourne	1920-21	7-76	G. D. McGrath, Leeds	2001
7-105	N. J. N. Hawke, Sydney	1965-66	7-153	G. D. McKenzie, Manchester	1964
7-25	G. R. Hazlitt, The Oval	1912	7-60	K. R. Miller, Brisbane	1946-47
7-92	P. M. Hornibrook, The Oval	1930	7-100	M. A. Noble, Sydney	1903-04
7-36	M. S. Kasprowicz, The Oval	1997	7-189	W. J. O'Reilly, Manchester	1934
7-55	T. K. Kendall, Melbourne	1876-77	8-43	A. E. Trott, Adelaide	1894-95
7-64	F. J. Laver, Nottingham	1905	7-28	H. Trumble, Melbourne	1903-04
8-31	F. J. Laver, Manchester	1909	8-143	M. H. N. Walker, Melbourne	1974-75
7-81	G. F. Lawson, Lord's	1981			

MOST WICKETS IN A SERIES

England in England . . . . 46 (average 9.60)	J. C. Laker.	1956
England in Australia . . . . . 38 (average 23.18)	M. W. Tate	1924-25
Australia in England . . . . . 42 (average 21.26)	T. M. Alderman (6 Tests)	1981
Australia in Australia. . . . . 41 (average 12.85)	R. M. Hogg (6 Tests)	1978-79

WICKETKEEPING – MOST DISMISSALS

	M	Ct	St	Total
†R. W. Marsh (Australia)	42	141	7	148
I. A. Healy (Australia).	33	123	12	135
A. P. E. Knott (England)	34	97	8	105
A. C. Gilchrist (Australia)	20	89	7	96
†W. A. Oldfield (Australia)	38	59	31	90
A. A. Lilley (England).	32	65	19	84
A. J. Stewart (England)	26	76	2	78
A. T. W. Grout (Australia)	22	69	7	76
T. G. Evans (England).	31	64	12	76

† *The number of catches by R. W. Marsh (141) and stumpings by W. A. Oldfield (31) are respective records in England–Australia Tests.*

Note: Stewart held a further 6 catches in 7 matches when not keeping wicket.

SCORERS OF OVER 2,000 RUNS

	T	I	NO	R	HS	100s	Avge
D. G. Bradman.	37	63	7	5,028	334	19	89.78
J. B. Hobbs	41	71	4	3,636	187	12	54.26
A. R. Border	47	82	19	3,548	200*	8	56.31
D. I. Gower	42	77	4	3,269	215	9	44.78
S. R. Waugh.	46	73	18	3,200	177*	10	58.18
G. Boycott	38	71	9	2,945	191	7	47.50
W. R. Hammond	33	58	3	2,852	251	9	51.85
H. Sutcliffe.	27	46	5	2,741	194	8	66.85
C. Hill	41	76	1	2,660	188	4	35.46
J. H. Edrich	32	57	3	2,644	175	7	48.96
G. A. Gooch.	42	79	0	2,632	196	4	33.31
G. S. Chappell	35	65	8	2,619	144	9	45.94
M. A. Taylor	33	61	2	2,496	219	6	42.30
M. C. Cowdrey	43	75	4	2,433	113	5	34.26
L. Hutton	27	49	6	2,428	364	5	56.46
R. N. Harvey	37	68	5	2,416	167	6	38.34
R. T. Ponting	**31**	**50**	**1**	**2,363**	**196**	**8**	**48.22**
V. T. Trumper	40	74	5	2,263	185*	6	32.79
D. C. Boon.	31	57	8	2,237	184*	7	45.65
W. M. Lawry	29	51	5	2,233	166	7	48.54
M. E. Waugh	29	51	7	2,204	140	6	50.09
S. E. Gregory	52	92	7	2,193	201	4	25.80
W. W. Armstrong	42	71	9	2,172	158	4	35.03
I. M. Chappell	30	56	4	2,138	192	4	41.11
K. F. Barrington.	23	39	6	2,111	256	5	63.96
A. R. Morris.	24	43	2	2,080	206	8	50.73

BOWLERS WITH 100 WICKETS

	T	Balls	R	W	5W/i	10W/m	Avge
S. K. Warne	36	10,757	4,535	195	11	4	23.25
D. K. Lillee	29	8,516	3,507	167	11	4	21.00
G. D. McGrath	30	7,280	3,286	157	10	0	20.92
I. T. Botham	36	8,479	4,093	148	9	2	27.65
H. Trumble	31	7,895	2,945	141	9	3	20.88
R. G. D. Willis	35	7,294	3,346	128	7	0	26.14
M. A. Noble	39	6,895	2,860	115	9	2	24.86
R. R. Lindwall	29	6,728	2,559	114	6	0	22.44
W. Rhodes	41	5,790	2,616	109	6	1	24.00
S. F. Barnes	20	5,749	2,288	106	12	1	21.58
C. V. Grimmett	22	9,224	3,439	106	11	2	32.44
D. L. Underwood	29	8,000	2,770	105	4	2	26.38
A. V. Bedser	21	7,065	2,859	104	7	2	27.49
G. Giffen	31	6,391	2,791	103	7	1	27.09
W. J. O'Reilly	19	7,864	2,587	102	8	3	25.36
C. T. B. Turner	17	5,179	1,670	101	11	2	16.53
R. Peel	20	5,216	1,715	101	5	1	16.98
T. M. Alderman	17	4,717	2,117	100	11	1	21.17
J. R. Thomson	21	4,951	2,418	100	5	0	24.18

RESULTS ON EACH GROUND

In England

	Matches	England wins	Australia wins	Drawn
The Oval	35	16	6	13
Manchester	28	7	7	14†
Lord's	34	6‡	14	14
Nottingham	20	4	7	9
Leeds	24	7	9	8
Birmingham	13	5	3	5
Sheffield	1	0	1	0
Cardiff	1	0	0	1

† *Excludes two matches abandoned without a ball bowled.*
‡ *England have won only twice (1934 and 2009) since 1896.*

In Australia

	Matches	England wins	Australia wins	Drawn
Melbourne	53	19	27	7†
Sydney	53	21	25	7
Adelaide	29	8	16	5
Brisbane				
Exhibition Ground	1	1	0	0
Woolloongabba	18	4	10	4
Perth	11	1	7	3

† *Excludes one match abandoned without a ball bowled.*

Bold type denotes performances in the 2009 series or, in career figures, players who appeared in that series.

ENGLAND v SOUTH AFRICA

Series notes: South Africa have won only five of their last 24 Tests at home to England, and drawn 14. South Africa have failed to win in 13 attempts at The Oval. There has been no play on seven days of the 20 scheduled between the sides at Centurion. In their post-readmission Lord's Tests, South Africa have averaged 49.6 runs per wicket and England 27.4. A. Flintoff has struck 23 sixes, a record for any batsman against South Africa. S. F. Barnes took 83 wickets at 9.85 in seven Tests against South Africa. G. C. Smith has scored 523 runs at 174.33 in two Tests at Edgbaston.

		Captains				
Season	*England*	*South Africa*	*T*	*E*	*SA*	*D*
1888-89	C. A. Smith[1]	O. R. Dunell[2]	2	2	0	0
1891-92	W. W. Read	W. H. Milton	1	1	0	0
1895-96	Lord Hawke[3]	E. A. Halliwell[4]	3	3	0	0
1898-99	Lord Hawke	M. Bisset	2	2	0	0
1905-06	P. F. Warner	P. W. Sherwell	5	1	4	0
1907	R. E. Foster	P. W. Sherwell	3	1	0	2
1909-10	H. D. G. Leveson Gower[5]	S. J. Snooke	5	2	3	0
1912	C. B. Fry	F. Mitchell[6]	3	3	0	0
1913-14	J. W. H. T. Douglas	H. W. Taylor	5	4	0	1
1922-23	F. T. Mann	H. W. Taylor	5	2	1	2
1924	A. E. R. Gilligan[7]	H. W. Taylor	5	3	0	2
1927-28	R. T. Stanyforth[8]	H. G. Deane	5	2	2	1
1929	J. C. White[9]	H. G. Deane	5	2	0	3
1930-31	A. P. F. Chapman	H. G. Deane[10]	5	0	1	4
1935	R. E. S. Wyatt	H. F. Wade	5	0	1	4
1938-39	W. R. Hammond	A. Melville	5	1	0	4
1947	N. W. D. Yardley	A. Melville	5	3	0	2
1948-49	F. G. Mann	A. D. Nourse	5	2	0	3
1951	F. R. Brown	A. D. Nourse	5	3	1	1
1955	P. B. H. May	J. E. Cheetham[11]	5	3	2	0
1956-57	P. B. H. May	C. B. van Ryneveld[12]	5	2	2	1
1960	M. C. Cowdrey	D. J. McGlew	5	3	0	2
1964-65	M. J. K. Smith	T. L. Goddard	5	1	0	4
1965	M. J. K. Smith	P. L. van der Merwe	3	0	1	2
1994	M. A. Atherton	K. C. Wessels	3	1	1	1
1995-96	M. A. Atherton	W. J. Cronje	5	0	1	4
1998	A. J. Stewart	W. J. Cronje	5	2	1	2
1999-2000	N. Hussain	W. J. Cronje	5	1	2	2
2003	M. P. Vaughan[13]	G. C. Smith	5	2	2	1

THE BASIL D'OLIVEIRA TROPHY

		Captains					
Season	*England*	*South Africa*	*T*	*E*	*SA*	*D*	*Held by*
2004-05	M. P. Vaughan	G. C. Smith	5	2	1	2	E
2008	M. P. Vaughan[14]	G. C. Smith	4	1	2	1	SA
2009-10	**A. J. Strauss**	**G. C. Smith**	**4**	**1**	**1**	**2**	**SA**
	In South Africa		77	29	18	30	
	In England..........................		61	27	11	23	
	Totals		**138**	**56**	**29**	**53**	

Notes: The following deputised for the official touring captain or were appointed by the home authority for only a minor proportion of the series:

[1]M. P. Bowden (Second). [2]W. H. Milton (Second). [3]Sir T. C. O'Brien (First). [4]A. R. Richards (Third). [5]F. L. Fane (Fourth and Fifth). [6]L. J. Tancred (Second and Third). [7]J. W. H. T. Douglas (Fourth). [8]G. T. S. Stevens (Fifth). [9]A. W. Carr (Fourth and Fifth). [10]E. P. Nupen (First), H. B. Cameron (Fourth and Fifth). [11]D. J. McGlew (Third and Fourth). [12]D. J. McGlew (Second). [13]N. Hussain (First). [14]K. P. Pietersen (Fourth).

HIGHEST INNINGS TOTALS

For England in England: 604-9 dec at The Oval 2003
         in South Africa: 654-5 at Durban 1938-39

For South Africa in England: 682-6 dec at Lord's 2003
         in South Africa: 572-7 at Durban 1999-2000

LOWEST INNINGS TOTALS

For England in England: 76 at Leeds 1907
         in South Africa: 92 at Cape Town 1898-99

For South Africa in England: 30 at Birmingham 1924
         in South Africa: 30 at Port Elizabeth 1895-96

DOUBLE-HUNDREDS

For England (5)

243	E. Paynter at Durban	1938-39		211	J. B. Hobbs at Lord's	1924
219	W. J. Edrich at Durban	1938-39		208	D. C. S. Compton at Lord's	1947
219	M. E. Trescothick at The Oval	2003				

For South Africa (6)

277	G. C. Smith at Birmingham	2003		236	E. A. B. Rowan at Leeds	1951
275	G. Kirsten at Durban	1999-2000		210	G. Kirsten at Manchester	1998
259	G. C. Smith at Lord's	2003		208	A. D. Nourse at Nottingham	1951

INDIVIDUAL HUNDREDS

For England (114)

7: D. C. S. Compton.

6: W. R. Hammond, H. Sutcliffe.

4: L. Hutton.

3: M. A. Atherton, M. C. Cowdrey, W. J. Edrich, N. Hussain, P. B. H. May, C. P. Mead, E. Paynter, **A. J. Strauss**, M. E. Trescothick, F. E. Woolley.

2: L. E. G. Ames, K. F. Barrington, **I. R. Bell**, M. A. Butcher, P. A. Gibb, E. H. Hendren, G. A. Hick, J. B. Hobbs, M. Leyland, **K. P. Pietersen**, A. C. Russell, G. P. Thorpe, E. Tyldesley, R. E. S. Wyatt.

1: R. Abel, G. Boycott, L. C. Braund, **P. D. Collingwood**, **A. N. Cook**, D. Denton, E. R. Dexter, J. W. H. T. Douglas, F. L. Fane, A. Flintoff, C. B. Fry, T. W. Hayward, A. J. L. Hill, D. J. Insole, F. G. Mann, P. H. Parfitt, J. M. Parks, G. Pullar, W. Rhodes, P. E. Richardson, R. W. V. Robins, R. T. Simpson, M. J. K. Smith, R. H. Spooner, A. J. Stewart, M. W. Tate, J. T. Tyldesley, B. H. Valentine, M. P. Vaughan, P. F. Warner, C. Washbrook, A. J. Watkins, H. Wood.

For South Africa (96)

7: **J. H. Kallis**, B. Mitchell, A. D. Nourse, H. W. Taylor.

6: **G. C. Smith**.

5: G. Kirsten.

4: A. Melville.

3: R. H. Catterall, H. H. Gibbs, R. A. McLean.

2: **H. M. Amla**, K. C. Bland, D. J. Cullinan, E. L. Dalton, **A. B. de Villiers**, D. J. McGlew, R. G. Pollock, **A. G. Prince**, E. A. B. Rowan, G. C. White.

1: E. J. Barlow, **M. V. Boucher**, W. J. Cronje, H. H. Dippenaar, W. R. Endean, G. A. Faulkner, T. L. Goddard, C. M. H. Hathorn, P. N. Kirsten, L. Klusener, N. D. McKenzie, B. M. McMillan, H. G. Owen-Smith, A. J. Pithey, J. N. Rhodes, P. W. Sherwell, I. J. Siedle, J. H. Sinclair, P. G. van der Bijl, K. G. Viljoen, W. W. Wade, J. H. B. Waite, K. C. Wessels, P. L. Winslow.

MOST RUNS IN A SERIES

England in England	753 (average 94.12)	D. C. S. Compton	1947
England in South Africa	656 (average 72.88)	A. J. Strauss	2004-05
South Africa in England	714 (average 79.33)	G. C. Smith	2003
South Africa in South Africa	625 (average 69.44)	J. H. Kallis	2004-05

TEN WICKETS OR MORE IN A MATCH

For England (26)

11-110 (5-25, 6-85)†	S. F. Barnes, Lord's	1912
10-115 (6-52, 4-63)	S. F. Barnes, Leeds	1912
13-57 (5-28, 8-29)	S. F. Barnes, The Oval	1912
10-105 (5-57, 5-48)	S. F. Barnes, Durban	1913-14
17-159 (8-56, 9-103)	S. F. Barnes, Johannesburg	1913-14
14-144 (7-56, 7-88)	S. F. Barnes, Durban	1913-14
12-112 (7-58, 5-54)	A. V. Bedser, Manchester	1951
11-118 (6-68, 5-50)	C. Blythe, Cape Town	1905-06
15-99 (8-59, 7-40)	C. Blythe, Leeds	1907
10-104 (7-46, 3-58)	C. Blythe, Cape Town	1909-10
15-28 (7-17, 8-11)	J. Briggs, Cape Town	1888-89
13-91 (6-54, 7-37)†	J. J. Ferris, Cape Town	1891-92
10-122 (5-60, 5-62)	A. R. C. Fraser, Nottingham	1998
10-207 (7-115, 3-92)	A. P. Freeman, Leeds	1929
12-171 (7-71, 5-100)	A. P. Freeman, Manchester	1929
12-130 (7-70, 5-60)	G. Geary, Johannesburg	1927-28
11-90 (6-7, 5-83)	A. E. R. Gilligan, Birmingham	1924
12-205 (5-144, 7-61)	M. J. Hoggard, Johannesburg	2004-05
10-119 (4-64, 6-55)	J. C. Laker, The Oval	1951
15-45 (7-38, 8-7)†	G. A. Lohmann, Port Elizabeth	1895-96
12-71 (9-28, 3-43)	G. A. Lohmann, Johannesburg	1895-96
10-138 (1-81, 9-57)	D. E. Malcolm, The Oval	1994
11-97 (6-63, 5-34)	J. B. Statham, Lord's	1960
12-101 (7-52, 5-49)	R. Tattersall, Lord's	1951
12-89 (5-53, 7-36)	J. H. Wardle, Cape Town	1956-57
10-175 (5-95, 5-80)	D. V. P. Wright, Lord's	1947

For South Africa (8)

11-127 (6-53, 5-74)	A. A. Donald, Johannesburg	1999-2000
11-112 (4-49, 7-63)†	A. E. Hall, Cape Town	1922-23
10-220 (5-75, 5-145)	M. Ntini, Lord's	2003
11-150 (5-63, 6-87)	E. P. Nupen, Johannesburg	1930-31
10-87 (5-53, 5-34)	P. M. Pollock, Nottingham	1965
12-127 (4-57, 8-70)	S. J. Snooke, Johannesburg	1905-06
13-192 (4-79, 9-113)	H. J. Tayfield, Johannesburg	1956-57
12-181 (5-87, 7-94)	A. E. E. Vogler, Johannesburg	1909-10

† *On first appearance in England–South Africa Tests.*

Notes: S. F. Barnes took ten wickets or more in his first five Tests v South Africa and in six of his seven Tests v South Africa. A. P. Freeman and G. A. Lohmann took ten wickets or more in successive matches.

SEVEN WICKETS OR MORE IN AN INNINGS

In addition to those listed above, the following have taken seven wickets or more in an innings:

For England

7-46	A. R. Caddick, Durban	1999-2000	7-39　J. B. Statham, Lord's	1955
7-42	G. A. Lohmann, Cape Town	1895-96		

For South Africa

7-95	W. H. Ashley, Cape Town	1888-89	7-65	S. J. Pegler, Lord's	1912
7-29	G. F. Bissett, Durban	1927-28	8-69	H. J. Tayfield, Durban........	1956-57
7-84	G. A. Faulkner, The Oval	1912	7-128	A. E. E. Vogler, Lord's.......	1907

MOST WICKETS IN A SERIES

England in England	34 (average 8.29)	S. F. Barnes.............	1912
England in South Africa........	49 (average 10.93)	S. F. Barnes.............	1913-14
South Africa in England........	33 (average 19.78)	A. A. Donald.............	1998
South Africa in South Africa	37 (average 17.18)	H. J. Tayfield...........	1956-57

Bold type denotes performances in the 2009-10 series or, in career figures, players who appeared in that series.

ENGLAND v WEST INDIES

Series notes: England have won 15 and lost only one of the last 23 Tests between the sides. Only one of West Indies' 53 wins has come in a lost series, in 2000. West Indies' last three victories, going back to 1998, have been by an innings. England have batted first in 11 of the last 12 Tests. West Indies have bowled England out in only one of the last ten innings. West Indies have never lost in eight Tests at Nottingham; in seven Tests at St John's, they have averaged 62.3 runs per wicket and England 34.5. G. S. Sobers scored 3,214 runs against England, the most by any batsman against a single country outside Ashes Tests. I. V. A. Richards' 34 sixes are a record against one country.

		Captains				
Season	England	West Indies	T	E	WI	D
1928	A. P. F. Chapman	R. K. Nunes	3	3	0	0
1929-30	Hon. F. S. G. Calthorpe	E. L. G. Hoad[1]	4	1	1	2
1933	D. R. Jardine[2]	G. C. Grant	3	2	0	1
1934-35	R. E. S. Wyatt	G. C. Grant	4	1	2	1
1939	W. R. Hammond	R. S. Grant	3	1	0	2
1947-48	G. O. B. Allen[3]	J. D. C. Goddard[4]	4	0	2	2
1950	N. W. D. Yardley[5]	J. D. C. Goddard	4	1	3	0
1953-54	L. Hutton	J. B. Stollmeyer	5	2	2	1
1957	P. B. H. May	J. D. C. Goddard	5	3	0	2
1959-60	P. B. H. May[6]	F. C. M. Alexander	5	1	0	4

THE WISDEN TROPHY

		Captains					
Season	England	West Indies	T	E	WI	D	Held by
1963	E. R. Dexter	F. M. M. Worrell	5	1	3	1	WI
1966	M. C. Cowdrey[7]	G. S. Sobers	5	1	3	1	WI
1967-68	M. C. Cowdrey	G. S. Sobers	5	1	0	4	E
1969	R. Illingworth	G. S. Sobers	3	2	0	1	E
1973	R. Illingworth	R. B. Kanhai	3	0	2	1	WI
1973-74	M. H. Denness	R. B. Kanhai	5	1	1	3	WI
1976	A. W. Greig	C. H. Lloyd	5	0	3	2	WI
1980	I. T. Botham	C. H. Lloyd[8]	5	0	1	4	WI
1980-81†	I. T. Botham	C. H. Lloyd	4	0	2	2	WI
1984	D. I. Gower	C. H. Lloyd	5	0	5	0	WI
1985-86	D. I. Gower	I. V. A. Richards	5	0	5	0	WI
1988	J. E. Emburey[9]	I. V. A. Richards	5	0	4	1	WI
1989-90‡	G. A. Gooch[10]	I. V. A. Richards[11]	4	1	2	1	WI
1991	G. A. Gooch	I. V. A. Richards	5	2	2	1	WI
1993-94	M. A. Atherton	R. B. Richardson[12]	5	1	3	1	WI
1995	M. A. Atherton	R. B. Richardson	6	2	2	2	WI
1997-98§	M. A. Atherton	B. C. Lara	6	1	3	2	WI
2000	N. Hussain[13]	J. C. Adams	5	3	1	1	E

Captains

Season	England	West Indies	T	E	WI	D	Held by
2003-04	M. P. Vaughan	B. C. Lara	4	3	0	1	E
2004	M. P. Vaughan	B. C. Lara	4	4	0	0	E
2007	M. P. Vaughan[14]	R. R. Sarwan[15]	4	3	0	1	E
2008-09§	**A. J. Strauss**	**C. H. Gayle**	**5**	**0**	**1**	**4**	**WI**
2009	**A. J. Strauss**	**C. H. Gayle**	**2**	**2**	**0**	**0**	**E**
	In England............................		80	30	29	21	
	In West Indies......................		65	13	24	28	
	Totals................................		145	43	53	49	

† *The Second Test, at Georgetown, was cancelled owing to political pressure and is excluded.*
‡ *The Second Test, at Georgetown, was abandoned without a ball being bowled and is excluded.*
§ *The First Test at Kingston in 1997-98 and the Second Test at North Sound in 2008-09 were called off on their opening days because of unfit pitches and are shown as draws.*

Notes: The following deputised for the official touring captain or were appointed by the home authority for only a minor proportion of the series: [1]N. Betancourt (Second), M. P. Fernandes (Third); R. K. Nunes (Fourth). [2]R. E. S. Wyatt (Third). [3]K. Cranston (First). [4]G. A. Headley (First), G. E. Gomez (Second). [5]F. R. Brown (Fourth). [6]M. C. Cowdrey (Fourth and Fifth). [7]M. J. K. Smith (First), D. B. Close (Fifth). [8]I. V. A. Richards (Fifth). [9]M. W. Gatting (First), C. S. Cowdrey (Fourth), G. A. Gooch (Fifth). [10]A. J. Lamb (Fourth and Fifth). [11]D. L. Haynes (Third). [12]C. A. Walsh (Fifth). [13]A. J. Stewart (Second). [14]A. J. Strauss (First). [15]D. Ganga (Third and Fourth).

HIGHEST INNINGS TOTALS

For England in England: 619-6 dec at Nottingham 1957
    in West Indies: 849 at Kingston 1929-30

For West Indies in England: 692-8 dec at The Oval 1995
    in West Indies: 751-5 dec at St John's......................... 2003-04

LOWEST INNINGS TOTALS

For England in England: 71 at Manchester 1976
    in West Indies: 46 at Port-of-Spain.......................... 1993-94

For West Indies in England: 54 at Lord's 2000
    in West Indies: 47 at Kingston................................. 2003-04

DOUBLE-HUNDREDS

For England (10)

325	A. Sandham at Kingston.......	1929-30	221	R. W. T. Key at Lord's........	2004
285*	P. B. H. May at Birmingham ...	1957	205*	E. H. Hendren at Port-of-Spain .	1929-30
262*	D. L. Amiss at Kingston.......	1973-74	205	L. Hutton at Kingston..........	1953-54
258	T. W. Graveney at Nottingham .	1957	203	D. L. Amiss at The Oval.......	1976
226	K. P. Pietersen at Leeds	2007	202*	L. Hutton at The Oval.........	1950

For West Indies (16)

400*	B. C. Lara at St John's	2003-04	226	G. S. Sobers at Bridgetown.....	1959-60
375	B. C. Lara at St John's	1993-94	223	C. G. Greenidge at Manchester .	1984
302	L. G. Rowe at Bridgetown	1973-74	223	G. A. Headley at Kingston	1929-30
291	I. V. A. Richards at The Oval ...	1976	220	C. L. Walcott at Bridgetown....	1953-54
291	**R. R. Sarwan at Bridgetown** ..	**2008-09**	214*	C. G. Greenidge at Lord's......	1984
270*	G. A. Headley at Kingston	1934-35	209*	B. F. Butcher at Nottingham....	1966
261	F. M. M. Worrell at Nottingham	1950	209	C. A. Roach at Georgetown	1929-30
232	I. V. A. Richards at Nottingham.	1976	206	E. D. Weekes at Port-of-Spain ..	1953-54

INDIVIDUAL HUNDREDS

For England (132)

6: M. C. Cowdrey, A. J. Lamb.

5: G. Boycott, G. A. Gooch, T. W. Graveney, L. Hutton.

4: D. L. Amiss, M. A. Atherton, **P. D. Collingwood**, **A. N. Cook**, **A. J. Strauss**, M. P. Vaughan.

3: L. E. G. Ames, K. F. Barrington, **R. S. Bopara**, A. W. Greig, P. B. H. May, **K. P. Pietersen**, R. A. Smith, A. J. Stewart, G. P. Thorpe.

2: D. C. S. Compton, E. R. Dexter, **A. Flintoff**, E. H. Hendren, **M. J. Prior**, P. E. Richardson, A. Sandham, M. E. Trescothick, C. Washbrook, P. Willey.

1: A. H. Bakewell, **I. R. Bell**, J. H. Edrich, T. G. Evans, K. W. R. Fletcher, G. Fowler, D. I. Gower, S. C. Griffith, W. R. Hammond, J. H. Hampshire, F. C. Hayes, G. A. Hick, J. B. Hobbs, N. Hussain, R. Illingworth, D. R. Jardine, R. W. T. Key, A. P. E. Knott, C. Milburn, J. T. Murray, J. M. Parks, W. Place, M. R. Ramprakash, J. D. Robertson, M. J. K. Smith, D. S. Steele, R. Subba Row, E. Tyldesley, W. Watson.

For West Indies (128)

10: G. S. Sobers.

8: G. A. Headley, I. V. A. Richards.

7: C. G. Greenidge, B. C. Lara.

6: F. M. M. Worrell.

5: **S. Chanderpaul**, D. L. Haynes, R. B. Kanhai, C. H. Lloyd, **R. R. Sarwan**.

4: R. B. Richardson, C. L. Walcott.

3: R. C. Fredericks, **C. H. Gayle**, C. L. Hooper, C. C. Hunte, L. G. Rowe, E. D. Weekes.

2: B. F. Butcher, H. A. Gomes, A. I. Kallicharran, S. M. Nurse, A. F. Rae, C. A. Roach, O. G. Smith.

1: J. C. Adams, K. L. T. Arthurton, I. Barrow, C. A. Best, G. M. Carew, C. A. Davis, P. J. L. Dujon, A. G. Ganteaume, D. A. J. Holford, J. K. Holt, R. D. Jacobs, B. D. Julien, C. B. Lambert, **B. P. Nash**, **D. Ramdin**, **D. S. Smith**, K. H. Weekes.

TEN WICKETS OR MORE IN A MATCH

For England (13)

11-98 (7-44, 4-54)	T. E. Bailey, Lord's	1957
11-110 (8-53, 3-57)	A. R. C. Fraser, Port-of-Spain	1997-98
10-93 (5-54, 5-39)	A. P. Freeman, Manchester	1928
13-156 (8-86, 5-70)	A. W. Greig, Port-of-Spain	1973-74
11-48 (5-28, 6-20)	G. A. R. Lock, The Oval	1957
10-137 (4-60, 6-77)	D. E. Malcolm, Port-of-Spain	1989-90
11-96 (5-37, 6-59)†	C. S. Marriott, The Oval	1933
10-187 (4-50, 6-137)	M. S. Panesar, Manchester	2007
10-142 (4-82, 6-60)	J. A. Snow, Georgetown	1967-68
10-195 (5-105, 5-90)†	G. T. S. Stevens, Bridgetown	1929-30
11-152 (6-100, 5-52)	F. S. Trueman, Lord's	1963
12-119 (5-75, 7-44)	F. S. Trueman, Birmingham	1963
11-149 (4-79, 7-70)	W. Voce, Port-of-Spain	1929-30

For West Indies (15)

10-127 (2-82, 8-45)	C. E. L. Ambrose, Bridgetown	1989-90
11-84 (5-60, 6-24)	C. E. L. Ambrose, Port-of-Spain	1993-94
10-174 (5-105, 5-69)	K. C. G. Benjamin, Nottingham	1995
11-147 (5-70, 6-77)†	K. D. Boyce, The Oval	1973
11-229 (5-137, 6-92)	W. Ferguson, Port-of-Spain	1947-48
11-157 (5-59, 6-98)†	L. R. Gibbs, Manchester	1963
10-106 (5-37, 5-69)	L. R. Gibbs, Manchester	1966
14-149 (8-92, 6-57)	M. A. Holding, The Oval	1976
10-96 (5-41, 5-55)†	H. H. H. Johnson, Kingston	1947-48
10-92 (6-32, 4-60)	M. D. Marshall, Lord's	1988

11-152 (5-66, 6-86)	S. Ramadhin, Lord's	1950
10-123 (5-60, 5-63)	A. M. E. Roberts, Lord's	1976
11-204 (8-104, 3-100)†	A. L. Valentine, Manchester	1950
10-160 (4-121, 6-39)	A. L. Valentine, The Oval	1950
10-117 (4-43, 6-74)	C. A. Walsh, Lord's....................................	2000

† *On first appearance in England–West Indies Tests.*

Note: F. S. Trueman took ten wickets or more in successive matches.

SEVEN WICKETS OR MORE IN AN INNINGS

In addition to those listed above, the following have taken seven wickets or more in an innings:

For England

7-34	T. E. Bailey, Kingston	1953-54
8-103	I. T. Botham, Lord's	1984
7-43	D. G. Cork, Lord's	1995
8-75	A. R. C. Fraser, Bridgetown ...	1993-94
7-12	S. J. Harmison, Kingston	2003-04
7-50	W. E. Hollies, Georgetown....	1934-35
7-103	J. C. Laker, Bridgetown	1947-48
7-56	James Langridge, Manchester .	1933
7-49	J. A. Snow, Kingston	1967-68

For West Indies

7-69	W. W. Hall, Kingston	1959-60
7-53	M. D. Marshall, Leeds	1984
7-22	M. D. Marshall, Manchester....	1988
7-49	S. Ramadhin, Birmingham	1957
7-66	D. J. G. Sammy, Manchester ...	2007
7-70	F. M. M. Worrell, Leeds.......	1957

Bold type denotes performances in the 2008-09 or 2009 series or, in career figures, players who appeared in those series.

ENGLAND v NEW ZEALAND

Series notes: New Zealand's win at Lord's in 1999 was their only victory in 15 Tests there. England have a 100% record from four Tests at Birmingham. The teams' averages for runs per wicket are almost identical home and away: in 50 Tests at home, England average 37.1 to New Zealand's 25.9: in 44 Tests away, England average 36.1 to New Zealand's 25.8. W. R. Hammond's batting average of 112.77 is the highest for any batsman who has scored 1,000 Test runs against one country. G. P. Howarth is the only man to make twin hundreds in this fixture, at Auckland in 1977-78. R. J. Sidebottom has 41 wickets at 18.48 in six Tests against New Zealand.

		Captains				
Season	England	New Zealand	T	E	NZ	D
1929-30	A. H. H. Gilligan	T. C. Lowry	4	1	0	3
1931	D. R. Jardine	T. C. Lowry	3	1	0	2
1932-33	D. R. Jardine[1]	M. L. Page	2	0	0	2
1937	R. W. V. Robins	M. L. Page	3	1	0	2
1946-47	W. R. Hammond	W. A. Hadlee	1	0	0	1
1949	F. G. Mann[2]	W. A. Hadlee	4	0	0	4
1950-51	F. R. Brown	W. A. Hadlee	2	1	0	1
1954-55	L. Hutton	G. O. Rabone	2	2	0	0
1958	P. B. H. May	J. R. Reid	5	4	0	1
1958-59	P. B. H. May	J. R. Reid	2	1	0	1
1962-63	E. R. Dexter	J. R. Reid	3	3	0	0
1965	M. J. K. Smith	J. R. Reid	3	3	0	0
1965-66	M. J. K. Smith	B. W. Sinclair[3]	3	0	0	3
1969	R. Illingworth	G. T. Dowling	3	2	0	1
1970-71	R. Illingworth	G. T. Dowling	2	1	0	1
1973	R. Illingworth	B. E. Congdon	3	2	0	1
1974-75	M. H. Denness	B. E. Congdon	2	1	0	1
1977-78	G. Boycott	M. G. Burgess	3	1	1	1
1978	J. M. Brearley	M. G. Burgess	3	3	0	0
1983	R. G. D. Willis	G. P. Howarth	4	3	1	0
1983-84	R. G. D. Willis	G. P. Howarth	3	0	1	2

Captains

Season	England	New Zealand	T	E	NZ	D
1986	M. W. Gatting	J. V. Coney	3	0	1	2
1987-88	M. W. Gatting	J. J. Crowe[4]	3	0	0	3
1990	G. A. Gooch	J. G. Wright	3	1	0	2
1991-92	G. A. Gooch	M. D. Crowe	3	2	0	1
1994	M. A. Atherton	K. R. Rutherford	3	1	0	2
1996-97	M. A. Atherton	L. K. Germon[5]	3	2	0	1
1999	N. Hussain[6]	S. P. Fleming	4	1	2	1
2001-02	N. Hussain	S. P. Fleming	3	1	1	1
2004	M. P. Vaughan[7]	S. P. Fleming	3	3	0	0
2007-08	M. P. Vaughan	D. L. Vettori	3	2	1	0
2008	M. P. Vaughan	D. L. Vettori	3	2	0	1
	In New Zealand		44	18	4	22
	In England		50	27	4	19
	Totals		94	45	8	41

Notes: The following deputised for the official touring captain or were appointed by the home authority for only a minor proportion of the series:
[1]R. E. S. Wyatt (Second). [2]F. R. Brown (Third and Fourth). [3]M. E. Chapple (First). [4]J. G. Wright (Third). [5]S. P. Fleming (Third). [6]M. A. Butcher (Third). [7]M. E. Trescothick (First).

HIGHEST INNINGS TOTALS

For England in England: 567-8 dec at Nottingham 1994
in New Zealand: 593-6 dec at Auckland 1974-75

For New Zealand in England: 551-9 dec at Lord's 1973
in New Zealand: 537 at Wellington 1983-84

LOWEST INNINGS TOTALS

For England in England: 126 at Birmingham 1999
in New Zealand: 64 at Wellington 1977-78

For New Zealand in England: 47 at Lord's 1958
in New Zealand: 26 at Auckland 1954-55

DOUBLE-HUNDREDS

For England (7)

336* W. R. Hammond at Auckland. . . 1932-33 | 210 G. A. Gooch at Nottingham 1994
310* J. H. Edrich at Leeds . . . . 1965 | 206 L. Hutton at The Oval 1949
227 W. R. Hammond at Christchurch 1932-33 | 200* G. P. Thorpe at Christchurch . . . 2001-02
216 K. W. R. Fletcher at Auckland . . 1974-75 |

For New Zealand (2)

222 N. J. Astle at Christchurch . . . . . 2001-02 | 206 M. P. Donnelly at Lord's 1949

INDIVIDUAL HUNDREDS

For England (98)

4: M. A. Atherton, G. A. Gooch, D. I. Gower, W. R. Hammond, A. J. Stewart, G. P. Thorpe.

3: K. F. Barrington, I. T. Botham, J. H. Edrich, L. Hutton, A. J. Lamb, P. B. H. May, A. J. Strauss.

2: L. E. G. Ames, D. L. Amiss, G. Boycott, D. C. S. Compton, M. C. Cowdrey, K. S. Duleepsinhji, K. W. R. Fletcher, J. Hardstaff, jun., N. Hussain, K. P. Pietersen, D. W. Randall, H. Sutcliffe.

1: G. O. B. Allen, T. R. Ambrose, T. E. Bailey, I. R. Bell, E. H. Bowley, B. C. Broad, M. H. Denness, E. R. Dexter, B. L. D'Oliveira, W. J. Edrich, A. Flintoff, G. Fowler, M. W. Gatting, A. W. Greig, G. O. Jones, B. R. Knight, A. P. E. Knott, G. B. Legge, C. A. Milton, P. H. Parfitt, C. T. Radley, P. E. Richardson, J. D. Robertson, P. J. Sharpe, R. T. Simpson, C. J. Tavaré, M. E. Trescothick, M. P. Vaughan, C. Washbrook.

For New Zealand (50)

5: M. D. Crowe.

4: J. G. Wright.

3: N. J. Astle, B. E. Congdon, G. P. Howarth.

2: M. G. Burgess, C. S. Dempster, S. P. Fleming, V. Pollard, B. Sutcliffe, L. R. P. L. Taylor.

1: J. G. Bracewell, J. V. Coney, J. J. Crowe, M. P. Donnelly, T. J. Franklin, M. J. Greatbatch, W. A. Hadlee, M. J. Horne, A. H. Jones, C. D. McMillan, J. E. Mills, J. D. P. Oram, M. L. Page, J. M. Parker, J. R. Reid, M. H. Richardson, K. R. Rutherford, B. W. Sinclair, I. D. S. Smith, S. B. Styris.

TEN WICKETS OR MORE IN A MATCH

For England (9)

11-140 (6-101, 5-39)	I. T. Botham, Lord's	1978
10-149 (5-98, 5-51)	A. W. Greig, Auckland	1974-75
11-65 (4-14, 7-51)	G. A. R. Lock, Leeds	1958
11-84 (5-31, 6-53)	G. A. R. Lock, Christchurch	1958-59
10-139 (4-90, 6-49)†	R. J. Sidebottom, Hamilton	2007-08
11-147 (4-100, 7-47)†	P. C. R. Tufnell, Christchurch	1991-92
11-70 (4-38, 7-32)†	D. L. Underwood, Lord's	1969
12-101 (6-41, 6-60)	D. L. Underwood, The Oval	1969
12-97 (6-12, 6-85)	D. L. Underwood, Christchurch	1970-71

For New Zealand (5)

10-144 (7-74, 3-70)	B. L. Cairns, Leeds	1983
10-140 (4-73, 6-67)	J. Cowie, Manchester	1937
10-100 (4-74, 6-26)	R. J. Hadlee, Wellington	1977-78
10-140 (6-80, 4-60)	R. J. Hadlee, Nottingham	1986
11-169 (6-76, 5-93)	D. J. Nash, Lord's	1994

† *On first appearance in England–New Zealand Tests.*

Note: D. L. Underwood took 12 wickets in successive matches against New Zealand in 1969 and 1970-71.

SEVEN WICKETS OR MORE IN AN INNINGS

In addition to those listed above, the following have taken seven wickets or more in an innings:

For England

7-43	J. M. Anderson, Nottingham	2008	7-47 R. J. Sidebottom, Napier	2007-08
7-63	M. J. Hoggard, Christchurch	2001-02	7-75 F. S. Trueman, Christchurch	1962-63
7-35	G. A. R. Lock, Manchester	1958	7-76 F. E. Woolley, Wellington	1929-30

For New Zealand

7-143 B. L. Cairns, Wellington 1983-84

ENGLAND v INDIA

Series notes: England have won only four and lost ten of the last 27 Tests between the sides. The away side have won only three of the last 25 Tests. England have won only one Test in India since 1984-85, and have reached 400 only once in the last eight Tests between the sides. They are unbeaten in seven Tests at Delhi and in six at Kanpur – but have not played at either ground since 1984-85. India won their last two Tests at Leeds and have not lost there since 1967, but have failed to win in 13 Tests at Birmingham and Manchester. England lead 10–1 in 15 Tests at Lord's. S. R. Tendulkar has scored 2,150 runs against England at an average of 61.42. M. S. Panesar's 19 Test wickets against India have cost 53.57 runs apiece. I. R. Bell averages 24.66 from eight Tests against India. A. V. Bedser took 44 Indian wickets at a cost of 13.11 each; F. S. Trueman took 53 at 14.84.

		Captains				
Season	*England*	*India*	*T*	*E*	*I*	*D*
1932	D. R. Jardine	C. K. Nayudu	1	1	0	0
1933-34	D. R. Jardine	C. K. Nayudu	3	2	0	1
1936	G. O. B. Allen	Maharaj of Vizianagram	3	2	0	1
1946	W. R. Hammond	Nawab of Pataudi sen.	3	1	0	2
1951-52	N. D. Howard[1]	V. S. Hazare	5	1	1	3
1952	L. Hutton	V. S. Hazare	4	3	0	1
1959	P. B. H. May[2]	D. K. Gaekwad[3]	5	5	0	0
1961-62	E. R. Dexter	N. J. Contractor	5	0	2	3
1963-64	M. J. K. Smith	Nawab of Pataudi jun.	5	0	0	5
1967	D. B. Close	Nawab of Pataudi jun.	3	3	0	0
1971	R. Illingworth	A. L. Wadekar	3	0	1	2
1972-73	A. R. Lewis	A. L. Wadekar	5	1	2	2
1974	M. H. Denness	A. L. Wadekar	3	3	0	0
1976-77	A. W. Greig	B. S. Bedi	5	3	1	1
1979	J. M. Brearley	S. Venkataraghavan	4	1	0	3
1979-80	J. M. Brearley	G. R. Viswanath	1	1	0	0
1981-82	K. W. R. Fletcher	S. M. Gavaskar	6	0	1	5
1982	R. G. D. Willis	S. M. Gavaskar	3	1	0	2
1984-85	D. I. Gower	S. M. Gavaskar	5	2	1	2
1986	M. W. Gatting[4]	Kapil Dev	3	0	2	1
1990	G. A. Gooch	M. Azharuddin	3	1	0	2
1992-93	G. A. Gooch[5]	M. Azharuddin	3	0	3	0
1996	M. A. Atherton	M. Azharuddin	3	1	0	2
2001-02	N. Hussain	S. C. Ganguly	3	0	1	2
2002	N. Hussain	S. C. Ganguly	4	1	1	2
2005-06	A. Flintoff	R. Dravid	3	1	1	1

THE PATAUDI TROPHY

	Captains						
Season	*England*	*India*	*T*	*E*	*I*	*D*	*Held by*
2007	M. P. Vaughan	R. Dravid	3	0	1	2	I
2008-09	K. P. Pietersen	M. S. Dhoni	2	0	1	1	I
	In England.........................		48	23	5	20	
	In India		51	11	14	26	
	Totals		99	34	19	46	

Notes: The 1932 Indian touring team was captained by the Maharaj of Porbandar but he did not play in the Test match.

The following deputised for the official touring captain or were appointed by the home authority for only a minor proportion of the series:

[1]D. B. Carr (Fifth). [2]M. C. Cowdrey (Fourth and Fifth). [3]Pankaj Roy (Second). [4]D. I. Gower (First).
[5]A. J. Stewart (Second).

HIGHEST INNINGS TOTALS

For England in England: 653–4 dec at Lord's 1990
     in India: 652–7 dec at Madras 1984–85

For India in England: 664 at The Oval 2007
     in India: 591 at Bombay 1992-93

LOWEST INNINGS TOTALS

For England in England: 101 at The Oval....................................... 1971
     in India: 102 at Bombay 1981-82

For India in England: 42 at Lord's... 1974
     in India: 83 at Madras... 1976-77

DOUBLE-HUNDREDS

For England (9)

333	G. A. Gooch at Lord's	1990	207	M. W. Gatting at Madras	1984-85
246*	G. Boycott at Leeds	1967	205*	J. Hardstaff, jun. at Lord's	1946
217	W. R. Hammond at The Oval	1936	201	G. Fowler at Madras	1984-85
214*	D. Lloyd at Birmingham	1974	200*	D. I. Gower at Birmingham	1979
208	I. T. Botham at The Oval	1982			

For India (5)

224	V. G. Kambli at Bombay	1992-93	217	R. Dravid at The Oval	2002
222	G. R. Viswanath at Madras	1981-82	203*	Nawab of Pataudi, jun. at Delhi	1963-64
221	S. M. Gavaskar at The Oval	1979			

INDIVIDUAL HUNDREDS

For England (93)

5: I. T. Botham, G. A. Gooch.
4: G. Boycott, N. Hussain, M. P. Vaughan.
3: K. F. Barrington, M. C. Cowdrey, M. W. Gatting, A. W. Greig, A. J. Lamb, K. P. Pietersen, A. J. Strauss.
2: D. L. Amiss, M. A. Atherton, P. D. Collingwood, M. H. Denness, K. W. R. Fletcher, D. I. Gower, T. W. Graveney, W. R. Hammond, L. Hutton, G. Pullar, R. A. Smith.
1: A. N. Cook, J. P. Crawley, E. R. Dexter, B. L. D'Oliveira, J. H. Edrich, T. G. Evans, G. Fowler, J. Hardstaff, jun., G. A. Hick, R. Illingworth, B. R. Knight, A. R. Lewis, C. C. Lewis, D. Lloyd, B. W. Luckhurst, P. B. H. May, P. H. Parfitt, D. W. Randall, R. T. Robinson, R. C. Russell, Rev. D. S. Sheppard, M. J. K. Smith, C. J. Tavaré, B. H. Valentine, C. F. Walters, A. J. Watkins, C. White, T. S. Worthington.

For India (78)

7: S. R. Tendulkar.
6: M. Azharuddin.
5: D. B. Vengsarkar.
4: R. Dravid, S. M. Gavaskar, R. J. Shastri, G. R. Viswanath.
3: S. C. Ganguly, V. L. Manjrekar, V. M. Merchant, Nawab of Pataudi, jun., P. R. Umrigar.
2: V. S. Hazare, M. L. Jaisimha, Kapil Dev, B. K. Kunderan, Pankaj Roy.
1: A. B. Agarkar, L. Amarnath, A. A. Baig, D. Dasgupta, F. M. Engineer, G. Gambhir, Hanumant Singh, V. G. Kambli, S. M. H. Kirmani, A. Kumble, V. Mankad, Mushtaq Ali, R. G. Nadkarni, S. M. Patil, D. G. Phadkar, V. Sehwag, N. S. Sidhu, Wasim Jaffer, Yashpal Sharma.

Notes: G. A. Gooch's match aggregate of 456 (333 and 123) for England at Lord's in 1990 is the record in Test matches and the only instance of a batsman scoring a triple-hundred and a hundred in the same first-class match. His 333 is the highest innings in any match at Lord's.
  M. Azharuddin scored hundreds in each of his first three Tests.

TEN WICKETS OR MORE IN A MATCH

For England (7)

10-78 (5-35, 5-43)†	G. O. B. Allen, Lord's	1936
11-145 (7-49, 4-96)†	A. V. Bedser, Lord's	1946
11-93 (4-41, 7-52)	A. V. Bedser, Manchester	1946
13-106 (6-58, 7-48)	I. T. Botham, Bombay	1979-80
11-163 (6-104, 5-59)†	N. A. Foster, Madras	1984-85
10-70 (7-46, 3-24)†	J. K. Lever, Delhi....................................	1976-77
11-153 (7-49, 4-104)	H. Verity, Madras....................................	1933-34

For India (5)

10-177 (6-105, 4-72)	S. A. Durani, Madras	1961-62
10-233 (7-115, 3-118)	A. Kumble, Ahmedabad...............................	2001-02
12-108 (8-55, 4-53)	V. Mankad, Madras	1951-52
10-188 (4-130, 6-58)	Chetan Sharma, Birmingham...........................	1986
12-181 (6-64, 6-117)†	L. Sivaramakrishnan, Bombay..........................	1984-85

† *On first appearance in England–India Tests.*

Note: A. V. Bedser took 11 wickets in a match in each of the first two Tests of his career.

SEVEN WICKETS OR MORE IN AN INNINGS

In addition to those listed above, the following have taken seven wickets or more in an innings:

For England

7-80 G. O. B. Allen, The Oval ......   1936 | 8-31 F. S. Trueman, Manchester.....   1952

For India

7-86 L. Amar Singh, Madras .... 1933-34 | 8-79 B. S. Chandrasekhar, Delhi. 1972-73

ENGLAND v PAKISTAN

Series notes: Only one of the last 11 series has been drawn (2001). Exactly 75% of the matches in Pakistan have been drawn (18 out of 24), compared to 42% in England (18 out of 43). In 24 Tests in Pakistan, the team winning the toss – and the team batting first – have won only once: at Multan in 2005-06. In fact, there has been only one insertion: the draw at Lahore in 1983-84. England have never lost in six Tests where they have been put in – or in five more where they have put Pakistan in. Inzamam-ul-Haq is the top scorer with 1,584 runs, and is one of only two men to have made two hundreds in the same Test: Hanif Mohammad is the other. J. H. Wardle took 20 wickets at 8.80 against Pakistan.

		Captains				
Season	England	Pakistan	T	E	P	D
1954	L. Hutton[1]	A. H. Kardar	4	1	1	2
1961-62	E. R. Dexter	Imtiaz Ahmed	3	1	0	2
1962	E. R. Dexter[2]	Javed Burki	5	4	0	1
1967	D. B. Close	Hanif Mohammad	3	2	0	1
1968-69	M. C. Cowdrey	Saeed Ahmed	3	0	0	3
1971	R. Illingworth	Intikhab Alam	3	1	0	2
1972-73	A. R. Lewis	Majid Khan	3	0	0	3
1974	M. H. Denness	Intikhab Alam	3	0	0	3
1977-78	J. M. Brearley[3]	Wasim Bari	3	0	0	3
1978	J. M. Brearley	Wasim Bari	3	2	0	1
1982	R. G. D. Willis[4]	Imran Khan	3	2	1	0
1983-84	R. G. D. Willis[5]	Zaheer Abbas	3	0	1	2

                              Captains

Season	England	Pakistan	T	E	P	D
1987	M. W. Gatting	Imran Khan	5	0	1	4
1987-88	M. W. Gatting	Javed Miandad	3	0	1	2
1992	G. A. Gooch	Javed Miandad	5	1	2	2
1996	M. A. Atherton	Wasim Akram	3	0	2	1
2000-01	N. Hussain	Moin Khan	3	1	0	2
2001	N. Hussain[6]	Waqar Younis	2	1	1	0
2005-06	M. P. Vaughan[7]	Inzamam-ul-Haq	3	0	2	1
2006†	A. J. Strauss	Inzamam-ul-Haq	4	3	0	1
	In England		43	17	8	18
	In Pakistan		24	2	4	18
	Totals		67	19	12	36

† *In 2008, the ICC changed the result of the forfeited Oval Test of 2006 from an England win to a draw, in contravention of the Laws of Cricket, only to rescind their decision in January 2009.*

Notes: The following deputised for the official touring captain or were appointed by the home authority for only a minor proportion of the series:
[1]D. S. Sheppard (Second and Third). [2]M. C. Cowdrey (Third). [3]G. Boycott (Third). [4]D. I. Gower (Second). [5]D. I. Gower (Second and Third). [6]A. J. Stewart (Second). [7]M. E. Trescothick (First).

HIGHEST INNINGS TOTALS

For England in England: 558-6 dec at Nottingham	1954
in Pakistan: 546-8 dec at Faisalabad	1983-84
For Pakistan in England: 708 at The Oval	1987
in Pakistan: 636-8 dec at Lahore...................................	2005-06

LOWEST INNINGS TOTALS

For England in England: 130 at The Oval	1954
in Pakistan: 130 at Lahore......................................	1987-88
For Pakistan in England: 87 at Lord's	1954
in Pakistan: 158 at Karachi	2000-01

DOUBLE-HUNDREDS

For England (2)

278	D. C. S. Compton at Nottingham	1954	205	E. R. Dexter at Karachi........	1961-62

For Pakistan (7)

274	Zaheer Abbas at Birmingham...	1971	205	Aamir Sohail at Manchester	1992
260	Javed Miandad at The Oval	1987	200	Mohsin Khan at Lord's........	1982
240	Zaheer Abbas at The Oval	1974	202	Mohammad Yousuf at Lord's...	2006
223	Mohammad Yousuf at Lahore ..	2005-06				

INDIVIDUAL HUNDREDS

For England (64)

4: K. F. Barrington, I. R. Bell, P. H. Parfitt.

3: D. L. Amiss, G. Boycott, M. C. Cowdrey, T. W. Graveney.

2: I. T. Botham, A. N. Cook, E. R. Dexter, M. W. Gatting, D. I. Gower, K. P. Pietersen, A. J. Stewart, A. J. Strauss, G. P. Thorpe, M. E. Trescothick.

1: M. A. Atherton, C. W. J. Athey, B. C. Broad, P. D. Collingwood, D. C. S. Compton, J. P. Crawley, B. L. D'Oliveira, K. W. R. Fletcher, G. A. Gooch, N. V. Knight, A. P. E. Knott, B. W. Luckhurst, C. Milburn, G. Pullar, C. T. Radley, D. W. Randall, R. T. Robinson, R. T. Simpson, R. A. Smith, M. P. Vaughan.

For Pakistan (52)

6: Mohammad Yousuf.

5: Inzamam-ul-Haq.

4: Salim Malik.

3: Asif Iqbal, Hanif Mohammad, Javed Burki, Mudassar Nazar, Mushtaq Mohammad.

2: Haroon Rashid, Javed Miandad, Mohsin Khan, Zaheer Abbas.

1: Aamir Sohail, Abdul Razzaq, Alim-ud-Din, Ijaz Ahmed, sen., Imran Khan, Intikhab Alam, Kamran Akmal, Moin Khan, Nasim-ul-Ghani, Sadiq Mohammad, Saeed Anwar, Salman Butt, Wasim Raja, Younis Khan.

Note: Three batsmen – Majid Khan, Mushtaq Mohammad and D. L. Amiss – were dismissed for 99 at Karachi, 1972-73: the only instance in Test matches.

TEN WICKETS OR MORE IN A MATCH

For England (3)

11-83 (6-65, 5-18)†	N. G. B. Cook, Karachi	1983-84
11-76 (6-19, 5-57)	S. J. Harmison, Manchester	2006
13-71 (5-20, 8-51)	D. L. Underwood, Lord's	1974

For Pakistan (6)

10-194 (5-84, 5-110)	Abdul Qadir, Lahore......................................	1983-84
10-211 (7-96, 3-115)	Abdul Qadir, The Oval....................................	1987
13-101 (9-56, 4-45)	Abdul Qadir, Lahore......................................	1987-88
10-186 (5-88, 5-98)	Abdul Qadir, Karachi	1987-88
12-99 (6-53, 6-46)	Fazal Mahmood, The Oval..................................	1954
10-77 (3-37, 7-40)	Imran Khan, Leeds..	1987

† *On first appearance in England–Pakistan Tests.*

SEVEN WICKETS OR MORE IN AN INNINGS

In addition to those listed above, the following have taken seven wickets or more in an innings:

For England

8-34	I. T. Botham, Lord's	1978	7-50	C. M. Old, Birmingham	1978
7-66	P. H. Edmonds, Karachi	1977-78	7-56	J. H. Wardle, The Oval	1954
8-107	N. A. Foster, Leeds	1987			

For Pakistan

7-52	Imran Khan, Birmingham......	1982	8-164	Saqlain Mushtaq, Lahore 2000-01

ENGLAND v SRI LANKA

Series notes: All of England's three victories in Sri Lanka have come after losing the toss. The team batting first have won five and lost nine of the 21 matches. England have scored more than 500 in an innings in four of their last six Tests at home to Sri Lanka – but have never managed 400 in 22 innings overseas. They average 41.4 runs per wicket at home, but 27.3 away. M. Muralitharan has taken 112 England wickets, more than twice the next best on either side (W. P. U. J. C. Vaas, with 49); in the second innings, he has 47 wickets at 16.72. Muralitharan has also claimed all four ten-wicket hauls in this fixture. D. P. M. D. Jayawardene is the leading scorer with 1,581 runs, half as much again as the next best (K. C. Sangakkara, with 1,007).

		Captains				
Season	*England*	*Sri Lanka*	*T*	*E*	*SL*	*D*
1981-82	K. W. R. Fletcher	B. Warnapura	1	1	0	0
1984	D. I. Gower	L. R. D. Mendis	1	0	0	1
1988	G. A. Gooch	R. S. Madugalle	1	1	0	0
1991	G. A. Gooch	P. A. de Silva	1	1	0	0
1992-93	A. J. Stewart	A. Ranatunga	1	0	1	0
1998	A. J. Stewart	A. Ranatunga	1	0	1	0
2000-01	N. Hussain	S. T. Jayasuriya	3	2	1	0
2002	N. Hussain	S. T. Jayasuriya	3	2	0	1
2003-04	M. P. Vaughan	H. P. Tillekeratne	3	0	1	2
2006	A. Flintoff	D. P. M. D. Jayawardene	3	1	1	1
2007-08	M. P. Vaughan	D. P. M. D. Jayawardene	3	0	1	2
	In England		10	5	2	3
	In Sri Lanka		11	3	4	4
	Totals		21	8	6	7

HIGHEST INNINGS TOTALS

For England in England: 551-6 dec at Lord's 2006
in Sri Lanka: 387 at Kandy 2000-01

For Sri Lanka in England: 591 at The Oval.................................... 1998
in Sri Lanka: 628-8 dec at Colombo (SSC) 2003-04

LOWEST INNINGS TOTALS

For England in England: 181 at The Oval 1998
in Sri Lanka: 81 at Galle 2007-08

For Sri Lanka in England: 141 at Birmingham 2006
in Sri Lanka: 81 at Colombo (SSC) 2000-01

DOUBLE-HUNDREDS

For Sri Lanka (3)

213* D. P. M. D. Jayawardene at Galle 2007-08 | 201* M. S. Atapattu at Galle 2000-01
213 S. T. Jayasuriya at The Oval.... 1998 |

Highest score for England: 174 by G. A. Gooch at Lord's, 1991.

INDIVIDUAL HUNDREDS

For England (20)

3: M. E. Trescothick.
2: M. A. Butcher, A. J. Stewart, G. P. Thorpe, K. P. Pietersen, M. P. Vaughan.
1: A. N. Cook, J. P. Crawley, G. A. Gooch, G. A. Hick, N. Hussain, A. J. Lamb, R. A. Smith.

For Sri Lanka (20)

6: D. P. M. D. Jayawardene.
2: M. S. Atapattu, P. A. de Silva, M. G. Vandort.
1: R. P. Arnold, T. M. Dilshan, S. T. Jayasuriya, L. R. D. Mendis, T. T. Samaraweera, K. C. Sangakkara, S. A. R. Silva, S. Wettimuny.

TEN WICKETS OR MORE IN A MATCH

For Sri Lanka (4)

16-220 (7-155, 9-65)	M. Muralitharan, The Oval	1998
11-93 (7-46, 4-47)	M. Muralitharan, Galle	2003-04
10-115 (6-86, 4-29)	M. Muralitharan, Birmingham	2006
11-132 (3-62, 8-70)	M. Muralitharan, Nottingham	2006

Note: The best match figures for England are 8-95 (5-28, 3-67) by D. L. Underwood at Colombo (PSS), 1981-82.

SEVEN WICKETS OR MORE IN AN INNINGS

In addition to those listed above, the following has taken seven wickets or more in an innings:

For England

7-70   P. A. J. DeFreitas, Lord's   1991

ENGLAND v ZIMBABWE

Series notes: All three of England's victories have been by an innings. Since scoring 376 in their first innings against England, Zimbabwe have failed to reach 300 in ten attempts. In the two Tests at Lord's, England average 44.3 runs per wicket and Zimbabwe 14.6. Spin bowlers have taken only 1.75 wickets per Test when the sides have met in England (seven in four matches), and 12.5 per Test in Zimbabwe (25 in two).

Season	England	Captains Zimbabwe	T	E	Z	D
1996-97	M. A. Atherton	A. D. R. Campbell	2	0	0	2
2000	N. Hussain	A. Flower	2	1	0	1
2003	N. Hussain	H. H. Streak	2	2	0	0
	In England		4	3	0	1
	In Zimbabwe		2	0	0	2
	Totals		6	3	0	3

HIGHEST INNINGS TOTALS

For England in England: 472 at Lord's		2003
in Zimbabwe: 406 at Bulawayo		1996-97
For Zimbabwe in England: 285-4 dec at Nottingham		2000
in Zimbabwe: 376 at Bulawayo.		1996-97

LOWEST INNINGS TOTALS

For England in England: 147 at Nottingham..		2000
in Zimbabwe: 156 at Harare		1996-97
For Zimbabwe in England: 83 at Lord's		2000
in Zimbabwe: 215 at Harare		1996-97

HIGHEST INDIVIDUAL INNINGS

For England

137   M. A. Butcher at Lord's   2003

For Zimbabwe

148* M. W. Goodwin at Nottingham .   2000

INDIVIDUAL HUNDREDS

For England (7)

2: A. J. Stewart.
1: M. A. Atherton, M. A. Butcher, J. P. Crawley, G. A. Hick, N. Hussain.

For Zimbabwe (2)

1: A. Flower, M. W. Goodwin.

BEST MATCH BOWLING ANALYSES

For England

7-42 (5-15, 2-27)†   E. S. H. Giddins, Lord's............................   2000

For Zimbabwe

7-186 (5-123, 2-63)†   P. A. Strang, Bulawayo   1996-97

† *On first appearance in England–Zimbabwe Tests.*

ENGLAND v BANGLADESH

Series notes: Pending the series in 2009-10, England average 162.5 runs per wicket in home Tests; Bangladesh average 17.1. The away side have never won the toss. England's average opening partnership is 93.16; Bangladesh's is 18.50. The average fourth-wicket partnerships are 131.33 and 6.75 respectively. Bangladesh spinners have taken 44% of their team's wickets in this fixture (15 out of 34); England's spinners have managed only 5% (four of 79). I. R. Bell has scored 227 runs in two innings without being dismissed.

		Captains					
Season	*England*		*Bangladesh*	*T*	*E*	*B*	*D*
2003-04	M. P. Vaughan		Khaled Mahmud	2	2	0	0
2005	M. P. Vaughan		Habibul Bashar	2	2	0	0
	In England........................			2	2	0	0
	In Bangladesh....................			2	2	0	0
	Totals............................			4	4	0	0

HIGHEST INNINGS TOTALS

For England in England: 528-3 dec at Lord's 2005
            in Bangladesh: 326 at Chittagong 2003-04

For Bangladesh in England: 316 at Chester-le-Street 2005
              in Bangladesh: 255 at Dhaka 2003-04

LOWEST INNINGS TOTALS

For England in Bangladesh: 295 at Dhaka................................... 2003-04

For Bangladesh in England: 104 at Chester-le-Street 2005
              in Bangladesh: 138 at Chittagong 2003-04

HIGHEST INDIVIDUAL INNINGS

For England

194 M. E. Trescothick at Lord's 2005

For Bangladesh

82* Aftab Ahmed at Chester-le-Street 2005

INDIVIDUAL HUNDREDS

For England (5)

3: M. E. Trescothick.
1: I. R. Bell, M. P. Vaughan.

BEST MATCH BOWLING ANALYSES

For England

9-79 (5-35, 4-44)†   S. J. Harmison, Dhaka 2003-04

For Bangladesh

5-141 (3-84, 2-57)†   Mohammad Rafique, Dhaka 2003-04

† *On first appearance in England–Bangladesh Tests.*

AUSTRALIA v SOUTH AFRICA

Series notes: South Africa have not won a "live" Test at home to Australia since 1993-94. Australia have won nine of their 11 Tests at Cape Town. S. K. Warne has taken more South African wickets than any other bowler – he had 130 from 24 Tests at 24.16. R. T. Ponting is the top scorer in Tests between these teams, with 2,030 runs at an average of 56.38. M. J. Procter took 41 wickets at 15.02 in seven Tests against Australia.

		Captains				
Season	Australia	South Africa	T	A	SA	D
1902-03S	J. Darling	H. M. Taberer[1]	3	2	0	1
1910-11A	C. Hill	P. W. Sherwell	5	4	1	0
1912E	S. E. Gregory	F. Mitchell[2]	3	2	0	1
1921-22S	H. L. Collins	H. W. Taylor	3	1	0	2
1931-32A	W. M. Woodfull	H. B. Cameron	5	5	0	0
1935-36S	V. Y. Richardson	H. F. Wade	5	4	0	1
1949-50S	A. L. Hassett	A. D. Nourse	5	4	0	1
1952-53A	A. L. Hassett	J. E. Cheetham	5	2	2	1
1957-58S	I. D. Craig	C. B. van Ryneveld[3]	5	3	0	2

Captains

Season	Australia	South Africa	T	A	SA	D
1963-64*A*	R. B. Simpson[4]	T. L. Goddard	5	1	1	3
1966-67*S*	R. B. Simpson	P. L. van der Merwe	5	1	3	1
1969-70*S*	W. M. Lawry	A. Bacher	4	0	4	0
1993-94*A*	A. R. Border	K. C. Wessels[5]	3	1	1	1
1993-94*S*	A. R. Border	K. C. Wessels	3	1	1	1
1996-97*S*	M. A. Taylor	W. J. Cronje	3	2	1	0
1997-98*A*	M. A. Taylor	W. J. Cronje	3	1	0	2
2001-02*A*	S. R. Waugh	S. M. Pollock	3	3	0	0
2001-02*S*	S. R. Waugh	M. V. Boucher	3	2	1	0
2005-06*A*	R. T. Ponting	G. C. Smith	3	2	0	1
2005-06*S*	R. T. Ponting	G. C. Smith[6]	3	3	0	0
2008-09*A*	**R. T. Ponting**	**G. C. Smith**	**3**	**1**	**2**	**0**
2008-09*S*	**R. T. Ponting**	**G. C. Smith[7]**	**3**	**2**	**1**	**0**
	In South Africa		45	25	11	9
	In Australia		35	20	7	8
	In England		3	2	0	1
	Totals		**83**	**47**	**18**	**18**

S Played in South Africa.   A Played in Australia.   E Played in England.

Notes: The following deputised for the official touring captain or were appointed by the home authority for only a minor proportion of the series:
[1]J. H. Anderson (Second), E. A. Halliwell (Third). [2]L. J. Tancred (Third). [3]D. J. McGlew (First). [4]R. Benaud (First). [5]W. J. Cronje (Third). [6]J. H. Kallis (Third). [7]J. H. Kallis (Third).

HIGHEST INNINGS TOTALS

For Australia in Australia: 578 at Melbourne 1910-11
in South Africa: 652-7 dec at Johannesburg 2001-02

For South Africa in Australia: 595 at Adelaide 1963-64
in South Africa: 651 at Cape Town **2008-09**

LOWEST INNINGS TOTALS

For Australia in Australia: 111 at Sydney 1993-94
in South Africa: 75 at Durban 1949-50

For South Africa in Australia: 36† at Melbourne. 1931-32
in South Africa 85‡ at Johannesburg 1902-03
85‡ at Cape Town 1902-03

† *Scored 45 in the second innings, giving the smallest aggregate of 81 (12 extras) in Test cricket.*
‡ *In successive innings.*

DOUBLE-HUNDREDS

For Australia (8)

299*	D. G. Bradman at Adelaide.	1931-32		205	R. N. Harvey at Melbourne.	1952-53
226	D. G. Bradman at Brisbane.	1931-32		204*	A. C. Gilchrist at Johannesburg .	2001-02
214*	V. T. Trumper at Adelaide	1910-11		203*	B. J. Hodge at Perth	2005-06
214	G. S. Blewett at Johannesburg . .	1996-97		203	H. L. Collins at Johannesburg. . .	1921-22

For South Africa (5)

274	R. G. Pollock at Durban	1969-70		204	G. A. Faulkner at Melbourne . . .	1910-11
231	A. D. Nourse at Johannesburg . .	1935-36		201	E. J. Barlow at Adelaide	1963-64
209	R. G. Pollock at Cape Town. . . .	1966-67				

INDIVIDUAL HUNDREDS
For Australia (94)

8: R. N. Harvey, **R. T. Ponting**.

6: M. L. Hayden.

4: D. G. Bradman, D. R. Martyn, M. E. Waugh.

3: W. Bardsley, J. H. Fingleton, A. L. Hassett, C. Hill.

2: W. W. Armstrong, R. Benaud, B. C. Booth, A. C. Gilchrist, **P. J. Hughes**, C. Kelleway, J. L. Langer, C. G. Macartney, S. J. McCabe, J. Moroney, A. R. Morris, M. A. Taylor, V. T. Trumper, S. R. Waugh.

1: G. S. Blewett, W. A. Brown, J. W. Burke, A. G. Chipperfield, **M. J. Clarke**, H. L. Collins, J. M. Gregory, B. J. Hodge, **M. E. K. Hussey**, **M. G. Johnson**, **S. M. Katich**, W. M. Lawry, S. J. E. Loxton, C. C. McDonald, **M. J. North**, K. E. Rigg, J. Ryder, R. B. Simpson, K. R. Stackpole, W. M. Woodfull.

For South Africa (53)

5: E. J. Barlow, R. G. Pollock.

4: J. H. Kallis.

3: A. B. de Villiers, G. A. Faulkner, D. T. Lindsay.

2: G. Kirsten, D. J. McGlew, A. D. Nourse, **A. G. Prince**, B. A. Richards, J. H. Sinclair, J. H. B. Waite, J. W. Zulch.

1: K. C. Bland, W. J. Cronje, **J-P. Duminy**, W. R. Endean, C. N. Frank, H. H. Gibbs, A. C. Hudson, B. L. Irvine, A. W. Nourse, E. A. B. Rowan, J. A. Rudolph, **G. C. Smith**, S. J. Snooke, K. G. Viljoen.

TEN WICKETS OR MORE IN A MATCH
For Australia (8)

14-199 (7-116, 7-83)	C. V. Grimmett, Adelaide	1931-32
10-88 (5-32, 5-56)	C. V. Grimmett, Cape Town	1935-36
10-110 (3-70, 7-40)	C. V. Grimmett, Johannesburg	1935-36
13-173 (7-100, 6-73)	C. V. Grimmett, Durban	1935-36
11-24 (5-6, 6-18)	H. Ironmonger, Melbourne	1931-32
11-159 (8-61, 3-98)†	**M. G. Johnson, Perth**	**2008-09**
12-128 (7-56, 5-72)	S. K. Warne, Sydney	1993-94
11-109 (5-75, 6-34)	S. K. Warne, Sydney	1997-98

For South Africa (5)

10-123 (4-80, 6-43)	P. S. de Villiers, Sydney	1993-94
10-116 (5-43, 5-73)	C. B. Llewellyn, Johannesburg	1902-03
10-178 (6-100, 4-78)	M. Ntini, Johannesburg	2005-06
10-154 (5-87, 5-67)	**D. W. Steyn, Melbourne**	**2008-09**
13-165 (6-84, 7-81)	H. J. Tayfield, Melbourne	1952-53

† *On first appearance in Australia–South Africa Tests.*

Note: C. V. Grimmett took ten wickets or more in three consecutive matches in 1935-36, the last three of his career.

SEVEN WICKETS OR MORE IN AN INNINGS

In addition to those listed above, the following have taken seven wickets or more in an innings:

For Australia

7-34 J. V. Saunders, Johannesburg . . . 1902-03

For South Africa

7-91 J. T. Partridge, Sydney . . . . 1963-64 │ 7-23 H. J. Tayfield, Durban. 1949-50
7-87 S. M. Pollock, Adelaide . . . . 1997-98 │

Bold type denotes performances in the 2008-09 series in Australia and South Africa or, in career figures, players who appeared in those series.

AUSTRALIA v WEST INDIES

Series notes: There have been only two draws in the last 29 Tests. West Indies' last seven victories over Australia have come when they fielded first. They have lost 13 of the last 16 matches in Australia; before that, they had lost only four in 21. Australia have scored 400-plus in the first innings of 12 of their last 14 Tests against West Indies – the two times they failed, they did it in the second innings. Nobody has hit more sixes against Australia than B. C. Lara: he and I. T. Botham both struck 21. I. A. Healy's 78 dismissals are a record against West Indies, as are M. E. Waugh's 45 outfield catches.

| | | *Captains* | | | | | |
Season	Australia	West Indies	T	A	WI	T	D
1930-31A	W. M. Woodfull	G. C. Grant	5	4	1	0	0
1951-52A	A. L. Hassett[1]	J. D. C. Goddard[2]	5	4	1	0	0
1954-55W	I. W. Johnson	D. St E. Atkinson[3]	5	3	0	0	2

THE FRANK WORRELL TROPHY

| | | *Captains* | | | | | | |
Season	Australia	West Indies	T	A	WI	T	D	Held by
1960-61A	R. Benaud	F. M. M. Worrell	5	2	1	1	1	A
1964-65W	R. B. Simpson	G. S. Sobers	5	1	2	0	2	WI
1968-69A	W. M. Lawry	G. S. Sobers	5	3	1	0	1	A
1972-73W	I. M. Chappell	R. B. Kanhai	5	2	0	0	3	A
1975-76A	G. S. Chappell	C. H. Lloyd	6	5	1	0	0	A
1977-78W	R. B. Simpson	A. I. Kallicharran[4]	5	1	3	0	1	WI
1979-80A	G. S. Chappell	C. H. Lloyd[5]	3	0	2	0	1	WI
1981-82A	G. S. Chappell	C. H. Lloyd	3	1	1	0	1	WI
1983-84W	K. J. Hughes	C. H. Lloyd[6]	5	0	3	0	2	WI
1984-85A	A. R. Border[7]	C. H. Lloyd	5	1	3	0	1	WI
1988-89A	A. R. Border	I. V. A. Richards	5	1	3	0	1	WI
1990-91W	A. R. Border	I. V. A. Richards	5	1	2	0	2	WI
1992-93A	A. R. Border	R. B. Richardson	5	1	2	0	2	WI
1994-95W	M. A. Taylor	R. B. Richardson	4	2	1	0	1	A
1996-97A	M. A. Taylor	C. A. Walsh	5	3	2	0	0	A
1998-99W	S. R. Waugh	B. C. Lara	4	2	2	0	0	A
2000-01A	S. R. Waugh[8]	J. C. Adams	5	5	0	0	0	A
2002-03W	S. R. Waugh	B. C. Lara	4	3	1	0	0	A
2005-06A	R. T. Ponting	S. Chanderpaul	3	3	0	0	0	A
2007-08W	R. T. Ponting	R. R. Sarwan[9]	3	2	0	0	1	A
2009-10A	**R. T. Ponting**	**C. H. Gayle**	**3**	**2**	**0**	**0**	**1**	**A**
	In Australia		**63**	**35**	**18**	**1**	**9**	
	In West Indies		45	17	14	0	14	
	Totals		**108**	**52**	**32**	**1**	**23**	

A Played in Australia. W Played in West Indies.

Notes: The following deputised for the official touring captain or were appointed by the home authority for only a minor proportion of the series:

[1] A. R. Morris (Third). [2] J. B. Stollmeyer (Fifth). [3] J. B. Stollmeyer (Second and Third). [4] C. H. Lloyd (First and Second). [5] D. L. Murray (First). [6] I. V. A. Richards (Second). [7] K. J. Hughes (First and Second). [8] A. C. Gilchrist (Third). [9] C. H. Gayle (Third).

HIGHEST INNINGS TOTALS

For Australia in Australia: 619 at Sydney 1968-69
in West Indies: 758-8 dec at Kingston 1954-55

For West Indies in Australia: 616 at Adelaide 1968-69
in West Indies: 573 at Bridgetown 1964-65

LOWEST INNINGS TOTALS

For Australia in Australia: 76 at Perth 1984-85
in West Indies: 90 at Port-of-Spain 1977-78

For West Indies in Australia: 78 at Sydney 1951-52
in West Indies: 51 at Port-of-Spain 1998-99

DOUBLE-HUNDREDS

For Australia (9)

242	K. D. Walters at Sydney	1968-69	205	W. M. Lawry at Melbourne . . .	1968-69
223	D. G. Bradman at Brisbane	1930-31	204	R. N. Harvey at Kingston	1954-55
216	D. M. Jones at Adelaide	1988-89	201	R. B. Simpson at Bridgetown . . .	1964-65
210	W. M. Lawry at Bridgetown	1964-65	200	S. R. Waugh at Kingston	1994-95
206	R. T. Ponting at Port-of-Spain . .	2002-03			

For West Indies (7)

277	B. C. Lara at Sydney	1992-93	213	B. C. Lara at Kingston	1998-99
226	C. G. Greenidge at Bridgetown .	1990-91	208	I. V. A. Richards at Melbourne .	1984-85
226	B. C. Lara at Adelaide	2005-06	201	S. M. Nurse at Bridgetown	1964-65
219	D. St E. Atkinson at Bridgetown	1954-55			

INDIVIDUAL HUNDREDS

For Australia (107)

7: R. T. Ponting, S. R. Waugh.

6: K. D. Walters.

5: G. S. Chappell, I. M. Chappell, M. L. Hayden.

4: W. M. Lawry, K. R. Miller, I. R. Redpath, M. E. Waugh.

3: D. C. Boon, A. R. Border, R. N. Harvey, J. L. Langer.

2: D. G. Bradman, R. M. Cowper, A. L. Hassett, K. J. Hughes, **M. E. K. Hussey, S. M. Katich**, C. C. McDonald, W. H. Ponsford, G. M. Wood.

1: R. G. Archer, R. Benaud, B. C. Booth, **M. J. Clarke**, G. J. Cosier, J. Dyson, A. C. Gilchrist, I. A. Healy, A. M. J. Hilditch, P. A. Jaques, A. F. Kippax, D. S. Lehmann, R. R. Lindwall, R. B. McCosker, A. R. Morris, N. C. O'Neill, W. B. Phillips, C. S. Serjeant, R. B. Simpson, M. J. Slater, K. R. Stackpole, M. A. Taylor, P. M. Toohey, A. Turner, K. C. Wessels.

For West Indies (102)

9: B. C. Lara, R. B. Richardson.

6: H. A. Gomes, C. H. Lloyd.

5: D. L. Haynes, R. B. Kanhai, I. V. A. Richards, C. L. Walcott.

4: S. Chanderpaul, C. G. Greenidge, A. I. Kallicharran, G. S. Sobers.

3: B. F. Butcher.

2: D. J. Bravo, S. L. Campbell, P. J. L. Dujon, D. Ganga, **C. H. Gayle**, G. A. Headley, S. M. Nurse, **R. R. Sarwan**.

1: F. C. M. Alexander, K. L. T. Arthurton, D. St E. Atkinson, **A. B. Barath**, C. C. Depeiza, M. L. C. Foster, R. C. Fredericks, C. L. Hooper, C. C. Hunte, F. R. Martin, L. G. Rowe, P. V. Simmons, O. G. Smith, J. B. Stollmeyer, E. D. Weekes, A. B. Williams, F. M. M. Worrell.

Note: F. C. M. Alexander and C. C. Depeiza scored the only hundreds of their first-class careers in a Test match.

TEN WICKETS OR MORE IN A MATCH

For Australia (15)

10-113 (4-31, 6-82)	M. G. Bevan, Adelaide	1996-97
11-96 (7-46, 4-50)	A. R. Border, Sydney.	1988-89
11-222 (5-135, 6-87)†	A. K. Davidson, Brisbane	1960-61
11-183 (7-87, 4-96)†	C. V. Grimmett, Adelaide	1930-31
10-115 (6-72, 4-43)	N. J. N. Hawke, Georgetown	1964-65
10-144 (6-54, 4-90)	R. G. Holland, Sydney	1984-85
13-217 (5-130, 8-87)	M. G. Hughes, Perth	1988-89
11-79 (7-23, 4-56)	H. Ironmonger, Melbourne	1930-31
11-181 (8-112, 3-69)	G. F. Lawson, Adelaide	1984-85
10-127 (7-83, 3-44)	D. K. Lillee, Melbourne	1981-82
10-78 (5-50, 5-28)	G. D. McGrath, Port-of-Spain	1998-99
10-27 (6-17, 4-10)	G. D. McGrath, Brisbane	2000-01
10-159 (8-71, 2-88)	G. D. McKenzie, Melbourne	1968-69
10-113 (5-81, 5-32)	C. R. Miller, Adelaide	2000-01
10-185 (3-87, 7-98)	B. Yardley, Sydney	1981-82

For West Indies (4)

10-120 (6-74, 4-46)	C. E. L. Ambrose, Adelaide	1992-93
10-113 (7-55, 3-58)	G. E. Gomez, Sydney	1951-52
11-107 (5-45, 6-62)	M. A. Holding, Melbourne	1981-82
10-107 (5-45, 6-62)	M. D. Marshall, Adelaide	1984-85

† *On first appearance in Australia–West Indies Tests.*

SEVEN WICKETS OR MORE IN AN INNINGS

In addition to those listed above, the following have taken seven wickets or more in an innings:

For Australia

7-44	I. W. Johnson, Georgetown. . . .	1954-55	7-52	S. K. Warne, Melbourne	1992-93
7-104	S. C. G. MacGill, Sydney	2000-01	7-89	M. R. Whitney, Adelaide	1988-89

For West Indies

7-25	C. E. L. Ambrose, Perth	1992-93	7-54	A. M. E. Roberts, Perth.	1975-76
7-78	J. J. C. Lawson, St John's	2002-03			

Bold type denotes performances in the 2009-10 series or, in career figures, players who appeared in that series.

AUSTRALIA v NEW ZEALAND

Series notes: Pending the series in 2009-10, New Zealand have never beaten Australia in 20 Tests when they have batted first. The teams have never played more than a three-match series. Only one of the 31 victories has been in a losing series. In 26 Tests at home, Australia average 41.6 runs per wicket and New Zealand 27.2. In three Tests at Hobart, Australia average 63.0 and New Zealand 24.7 – but Australia have won only once. In the last 14 Tests in Australia, only 26 of a possible 56 innings have been completed. In the last seven series between the sides, Australia are unbeaten and have won 13 out of 19 Tests. In the same period, New Zealand have won 13 out of 19 tosses. New Zealand bowlers have taken eight of the top ten analyses in this fixture.

		Captains				
Season	*Australia*	*New Zealand*	*T*	*A*	*NZ*	*D*
1945-46*N*	W. A. Brown	W. A. Hadlee	1	1	0	0
1973-74*A*	I. M. Chappell	B. E. Congdon	3	2	0	1
1973-74*N*	I. M. Chappell	B. E. Congdon	3	1	1	1
1976-77*N*	G. S. Chappell	G. M. Turner	2	1	0	1
1980-81*A*	G. S. Chappell	G. P. Howarth[1]	3	2	0	1
1981-82*N*	G. S. Chappell	G. P. Howarth	3	1	1	1

TRANS-TASMAN TROPHY

Season	Australia	*Captains* New Zealand	T	A	NZ	D	Held by
1985-86A	A. R. Border	J. V. Coney	3	1	2	0	NZ
1985-86N	A. R. Border	J. V. Coney	3	0	1	2	NZ
1987-88A	A. R. Border	J. J. Crowe	3	1	0	2	A
1989-90A	A. R. Border	J. G. Wright	1	0	0	1	A
1989-90N	A. R. Border	J. G. Wright	1	0	1	0	NZ
1992-93N	A. R. Border	M. D. Crowe	3	1	1	1	NZ
1993-94A	A. R. Border	M. D. Crowe[2]	3	2	0	1	A
1997-98A	M. A. Taylor	S. P. Fleming	3	2	0	1	A
1999-2000N	S. R. Waugh	S. P. Fleming	3	3	0	0	A
2001-02A	S. R. Waugh	S. P. Fleming	3	0	0	3	A
2004-05A	R. T. Ponting	S. P. Fleming	2	2	0	0	A
2004-05N	R. T. Ponting	S. P. Fleming	3	2	0	1	A
2008-09A	R. T. Ponting	D. L. Vettori	2	2	0	0	A
	In Australia......................		26	14	2	10	
	In New Zealand		22	10	5	7	
	Totals		48	24	7	17	

A Played in Australia. N Played in New Zealand.

Notes: The following deputised for the official touring captain: [1]M. G. Burgess (Second). [2]K. R. Rutherford (Second and Third).

HIGHEST INNINGS TOTALS

For Australia in Australia: 607-6 dec at Brisbane 1993-94
in New Zealand: 570-8 dec at Wellington 2004-05

For New Zealand in Australia: 553-7 dec at Brisbane.......................... 1985-86
in New Zealand: 484 at Wellington 1973-74

LOWEST INNINGS TOTALS

For Australia in Australia: 162 at Sydney 1973-74
in New Zealand: 103 at Auckland 1985-86

For New Zealand in Australia: 76 at Brisbane......................... 2004-05
in New Zealand: 42 at Wellington 1945-46

DOUBLE-HUNDREDS

For Australia (5)

250	K. D. Walters at Christchurch...	1976-77	205	A. R. Border at Adelaide	1987-88
247*	G. S. Chappell at Wellington ...	1973-74	200	D. C. Boon at Perth...........	1989-90
215	J. L. Langer at Adelaide	2004-05			

Highest score for New Zealand: 188 by M. D. Crowe at Brisbane, 1985-86.

INDIVIDUAL HUNDREDS
For Australia (51)

5: A. R. Border.

4: A. C. Gilchrist, J. L. Langer.

3: D. C. Boon, G. S. Chappell, K. D. Walters.

2: I. M. Chappell, M. J. Clarke, S. M. Katich, G. R. J. Matthews, R. T. Ponting, M. J. Slater, M. A. Taylor, S. R. Waugh, G. M. Wood.

1: M. T. G. Elliott, G. J. Gilmour, B. J. Haddin, M. L. Hayden, I. A. Healy, G. R. Marsh, R. W. Marsh, D. R. Martyn, I. R. Redpath, K. R. Stackpole, M. E. Waugh.

For New Zealand (27)

3: M. D. Crowe.

2: B. E. Congdon, A. H. Jones, G. M. Turner, J. G. Wright.

1: N. J. Astle, C. L. Cairns, J. V. Coney, B. A. Edgar, S. P. Fleming, M. J. Greatbatch, B. F. Hastings, M. J. Horne, H. J. H. Marshall, J. F. M. Morrison, J. D. P. Oram, J. M. Parker, A. C. Parore, J. F. Reid, K. R. Rutherford, L. Vincent.

Note: G. S. and I. M. Chappell each hit two hundreds at Wellington in 1973-74, the only instance of two batsmen on the same side scoring twin hundreds in the same Test.

TEN WICKETS OR MORE IN A MATCH
For Australia (2)

10-174 (6-106, 4-68)	R. G. Holland, Sydney...................................	1985-86
11-123 (5-51, 6-72)	D. K. Lillee, Auckland.................................	1976-77

For New Zealand (5)

10-106 (4-74, 6-32)	J. G. Bracewell, Auckland............................	1985-86
15-123 (9-52, 6-71)	R. J. Hadlee, Brisbane	1985-86
11-155 (5-65, 6-90)	R. J. Hadlee, Perth....................................	1985-86
10-176 (5-109, 5-67)	R. J. Hadlee, Melbourne.............................	1987-88
12-149 (5-62, 7-87)	D. L. Vettori, Auckland..............................	1999-2000

SEVEN WICKETS OR MORE IN AN INNINGS

In addition to those listed above, the following have taken seven wickets or more in an innings:

For New Zealand

7-116 R. J. Hadlee, Christchurch .... 1985-86 | 7-89 D. K. Morrison, Wellington 1992-93

AUSTRALIA v INDIA

Series notes: India have never won a series in Australia, and have never won in ten Tests where they have put Australia in. The six highest individual scores between the sides have all been scored since the turn of the century. B. Lee is Australia's top wicket-taker against India, with 53 at 31.98, but six Indians have taken more wickets against Australia, led by A. Kumble with 111 at 30.32. S. R. Tendulkar is the top scorer with 2,748 runs at 56.08. R. T. Ponting averages 79.35 in 11 Tests at home to India but only 20.85 in 12 Tests away. Harbhajan Singh is the only man to take a hat-trick.

Captains

Season	Australia	India	T	A	I	T	D
1947-48*A*	D. G. Bradman	L. Amarnath	5	4	0	0	1
1956-57*I*	I. W. Johnson[1]	P. R. Umrigar	3	2	0	0	1
1959-60*I*	R. Benaud	G. S. Ramchand	5	2	1	0	2
1964-65*I*	R. B. Simpson	Nawab of Pataudi jun.	3	1	1	0	1
1967-68*A*	R. B. Simpson[2]	Nawab of Pataudi jun.[3]	4	4	0	0	0
1969-70*I*	W. M. Lawry	Nawab of Pataudi jun.	5	3	1	0	1
1977-78*A*	R. B. Simpson	B. S. Bedi	5	3	2	0	0
1979-80*I*	K. J. Hughes	S. M. Gavaskar	6	0	2	0	4
1980-81*A*	G. S. Chappell	S. M. Gavaskar	3	1	1	0	1
1985-86*A*	A. R. Border	Kapil Dev	3	0	0	0	3
1986-87*I*	A. R. Border	Kapil Dev	3	0	0	1	2
1991-92*A*	A. R. Border	M. Azharuddin	5	4	0	0	1

THE BORDER–GAVASKAR TROPHY

Captains

Season	Australia	India	T	A	I	T	D	Held by
1996-97*I*	M. A. Taylor	S. R. Tendulkar	1	0	1	0	0	I
1997-98*I*	M. A. Taylor	M. Azharuddin	3	1	2	0	0	I
1999-2000*A*	S. R. Waugh	S. R. Tendulkar	3	3	0	0	0	A
2000-01*I*	S. R. Waugh	S. C. Ganguly	3	1	2	0	0	I
2003-04*A*	S. R. Waugh	S. C. Ganguly	4	1	1	0	2	I
2004-05*I*	R. T. Ponting[4]	S. C. Ganguly[5]	4	2	1	0	1	A
2007-08*A*	R. T. Ponting	A. Kumble	4	2	1	0	1	A
2008-09*I*	R. T. Ponting	A. Kumble[6]	4	0	2	0	2	I

		T	A	I	T	D
In Australia.		36	22	5	0	9
In India.		40	12	13	1	14
Totals		76	34	18	1	23

A Played in Australia. I Played in India.

Notes: The following deputised for the official touring captain or were appointed by the home authority for only a minor proportion of the series:

[1]R. R. Lindwall (Second). [2]W. M. Lawry (Third and Fourth). [3]C. G. Borde (First). [4]A. C. Gilchrist (First, Second and Third). [5]R. Dravid (Third and Fourth). [6]M. S. Dhoni (Second and Fourth).

HIGHEST INNINGS TOTALS

For Australia in Australia: 674 at Adelaide 1947-48
           in India: 577 at Delhi 2008-09

For India in Australia: 705-7 dec at Sydney 2003-04
        in India: 657-7 dec at Kolkata 2000-01

LOWEST INNINGS TOTALS

For Australia in Australia: 83 at Melbourne 1980-81
           in India: 93 at Mumbai. 2004-05

For India in Australia: 58 at Brisbane 1947-48
        in India: 104 in Mumbai. 2004-05

DOUBLE-HUNDREDS

For Australia (8)

257	R. T. Ponting at Melbourne ...	2003-04	210	D. M. Jones at Madras	1986-87
242	R. T. Ponting at Adelaide	2003-04	204	G. S. Chappell at Sydney	1980-81
223	J. L. Langer at Sydney	1999-2000	203	M. L. Hayden at Chennai	2000-01
213	K. J. Hughes at Adelaide	1980-81	201	D. G. Bradman at Adelaide	1947-48

For India (4)

281	V. V. S. Laxman at Kolkata	2000-01	233	R. Dravid at Adelaide	2003-04
241*	S. R. Tendulkar at Sydney	2003-04	206	R. J. Shastri at Sydney	1991-92

INDIVIDUAL HUNDREDS

For Australia (82)

6: D. C. Boon, M. L. Hayden, R. T. Ponting.

4: A. R. Border, D. G. Bradman, R. N. Harvey, R. B. Simpson.

3: M. J. Clarke, J. L. Langer.

2: I. M. Chappell, R. M. Cowper, A. C. Gilchrist, K. J. Hughes, M. E. K. Hussey, D. M. Jones, S. M. Katich, D. R. Martyn, N. C. O'Neill, M. A. Taylor, S. R. Waugh, G. N. Yallop.

1: S. G. Barnes, J. W. Burke, G. S. Chappell, L. E. Favell, A. L. Hassett, W. M. Lawry, A. L. Mann, G. R. Marsh, G. R. J. Matthews, T. M. Moody, A. R. Morris, G. M. Ritchie, A. P. Sheahan, K. R. Stackpole, A. Symonds, K. D. Walters, M. E. Waugh, G. M. Wood.

For India (60)

10: S. R. Tendulkar.

8: S. M. Gavaskar.

6: V. V. S. Laxman.

4: G. R. Viswanath.

3: V. Sehwag.

2: M. Amarnath, M. Azharuddin, R. Dravid, G. Gambhir, S. C. Ganguly, V. S. Hazare, V. Mankad, R. J. Shastri, D. B. Vengsarkar.

N. J. Contractor, M. L. Jaisimha, Kapil Dev, S. M. H. Kirmani, N. R. Mongia, Nawab of Pataudi,

1: jun., S. M. Patil, D. G. Phadkar, G. S. Ramchand, K. Srikkanth, Yashpal Sharma.

TEN WICKETS OR MORE IN A MATCH

For Australia (13)

11-105 (6-52, 5-53)	R. Benaud, Calcutta	1956-57
12-124 (5-31, 7-93)	A. K. Davidson, Kanpur........................	1959-60
12-166 (5-99, 7-67)	G. Dymock, Kanpur............................	1979-80
12-358 (8-215, 4-143)†	J. J. Krejza, Nagpur	2008-09
10-168 (5-76, 5-92)	C. J. McDermott, Adelaide	1991-92
10-103 (5-48, 5-55)	G. D. McGrath, Sydney	1999-2000
10-91 (6-58, 4-33)†	G. D. McKenzie, Madras	1964-65
10-151 (7-66, 3-85)	G. D. McKenzie, Melbourne	1967-68
10-144 (5-91, 5-53)	A. A. Mallett, Madras	1969-70
10-249 (5-103, 5-146)	G. R. J. Matthews, Madras......................	1986-87
12-126 (6-66, 6-60)	B. A. Reid, Melbourne.........................	1991-92
11-31 (5-2, 6-29)†	E. R. H. Toshack, Brisbane	1947-48
11-95 (4-68, 7-27)	M. R. Whitney, Perth..........................	1991-92

For India (11)

10-194 (5-89, 5-105)	B. S. Bedi, Perth	1977-78
12-104 (6-52, 6-52)	B. S. Chandrasekhar, Melbourne	1977-78
10-130 (7-49, 3-81)	Ghulam Ahmed, Calcutta	1956-57
13-196 (7-123, 6-73)	Harbhajan Singh, Kolkata	2000-01
15-217 (7-133, 8-84)	Harbhajan Singh, Chennai	2000-01
11-224 (5-146, 6-78)	Harbhajan Singh, Bangalore	2004-05
12-279 (8-141, 4-138)	A. Kumble, Sydney	2003-04
13-181 (7-48, 6-133)	A. Kumble, Chennai	2004-05
11-122 (5-31, 6-91)	R. G. Nadkarni, Madras	1964-65
14-124 (9-69, 5-55)	J. M. Patel, Kanpur	1959-60
10-174 (4-100, 6-74)	E. A. S. Prasanna, Madras	1969-70

† *On first appearance in Australia–India Tests.*

SEVEN WICKETS OR MORE IN AN INNINGS

In addition to those listed above, the following have taken seven wickets or more in an innings:

For Australia

7-72	R. Benaud, Madras	1956-57	
7-143	J. D. Higgs, Madras	1979-80	
7-38	R. R. Lindwall, Adelaide	1947-48
7-43	R. R. Lindwall, Madras	1956-57

For India

7-98	B. S. Bedi, Calcutta	1969-70	
8-106	Kapil Dev, Adelaide	1985-86

AUSTRALIA v PAKISTAN

Series notes: Pakistan have lost their last 12 Tests against Australia, three by an innings, and one by 491 runs. Australia have won 66% of their matches at home, but only 15% in Pakistan. Australia have won all five Tests at Perth, and Pakistan none of their 16 Tests in Australia outside Sydney and Melbourne; but Pakistan have won five and lost none of the eight Tests at Karachi. In four Tests at Brisbane, Australia average 59.3 runs per wicket and Pakistan 24.1. In the second Test of a series, Australia lead 10–1 from 17 Tests. Only two of the 38 victories between these sides have come in a losing series – both of them for Pakistan in dead rubbers. D. W. Fleming took the only hat-trick, on his Test debut at Rawalpindi in 1994-95. R. T. Ponting averages 75.73 from 13 Tests against Pakistan despite making four ducks. R. W. Marsh's 68 dismissals are a record for any wicketkeeper against Pakistan.

		Captains					
Season	*Australia*		*Pakistan*	*T*	*A*	*P*	*D*
1956-57*P*	I. W. Johnson		A. H. Kardar	1	0	1	0
1959-60*P*	R. Benaud		Fazal Mahmood[1]	3	2	0	1
1964-65*P*	R. B. Simpson		Hanif Mohammad	1	0	0	1
1964-65*A*	R. B. Simpson		Hanif Mohammad	1	0	0	1
1972-73*A*	I. M. Chappell		Intikhab Alam	3	3	0	0
1976-77*A*	G. S. Chappell		Mushtaq Mohammad	3	1	1	1
1978-79*A*	G. N. Yallop[2]		Mushtaq Mohammad	2	1	1	0
1979-80*P*	G. S. Chappell		Javed Miandad	3	0	1	2
1981-82*A*	G. S. Chappell		Javed Miandad	3	2	1	0
1982-83*P*	K. J. Hughes		Imran Khan	3	0	3	0
1983-84*A*	K. J. Hughes		Imran Khan[3]	5	2	0	3
1988-89*P*	A. R. Border		Javed Miandad	3	0	1	2
1989-90*A*	A. R. Border		Imran Khan	3	1	0	2
1994-95*P*	M. A. Taylor		Salim Malik	3	0	1	2
1995-96*A*	M. A. Taylor		Wasim Akram	3	2	1	0
1998-99*P*	M. A. Taylor		Aamir Sohail	3	1	0	2
1999-2000*A*	S. R. Waugh		Wasim Akram	3	3	0	0
2002-03*S/U*	S. R. Waugh		Waqar Younis	3	3	0	0

	Captains					
Season	*Australia*	*Pakistan*	T	A	P	D
2004-05A	R. T. Ponting	Inzamam-ul-Haq[4]	3	3	0	0
2009-10A	**R. T. Ponting**	**Mohammad Yousuf**	**3**	**3**	**0**	**0**
	In Pakistan		20	3	7	10
	In Sri Lanka		1	1	0	0
	In United Arab Emirates		2	2	0	0
	In Australia		**32**	**21**	**4**	**7**
	Totals		**55**	**27**	**11**	**17**

A Played in Australia. P Played in Pakistan.
S/U First Test played in Sri Lanka, Second and Third Tests in United Arab Emirates.

Notes: The following deputised for the official touring captain or were appointed by the home authority for only a minor proportion of the series:
　[1]Imtiaz Ahmed (Second). [2]K. J. Hughes (Second). [3]Zaheer Abbas (First, Second and Third). [4]Yousuf Youhana *later known as Mohammad Yousuf* (Second and Third).

HIGHEST INNINGS TOTALS

For Australia in Australia: 585 at Adelaide	1972-73
in Pakistan: 617 at Faisalabad	1979-80
in Sri Lanka: 467 at Colombo (PSS)	2002-03
in United Arab Emirates: 444 at Sharjah	2002-03

For Pakistan in Australia: 624 at Adelaide	1983-84
in Pakistan: 580-9 dec at Peshawar	1998-99
in Sri Lanka: 279 at Colombo (PSS)	2002-03
in United Arab Emirates: 221 at Sharjah	2002-03

LOWEST INNINGS TOTALS

For Australia in Australia: 125 at Melbourne	1981-82
in Pakistan: 80 at Karachi	1956-57
in Sri Lanka: 127 at Colombo (PSS)	2002-03
in United Arab Emirates: 310 at Sharjah	2002-03

For Pakistan in Australia: 62 at Perth	1981-82
in Pakistan: 134 at Dacca	1959-60
in Sri Lanka: 274 at Colombo (PSS)	2002-03
in United Arab Emirates: 53 at Sharjah	2002-03

DOUBLE-HUNDREDS

For Australia (6)

334*	M. A. Taylor at Peshawar	1998-99	207	R. T. Ponting at Sydney	2004-05
268	G. N. Yallop at Melbourne	1983-84	**207**	**R. T. Ponting at Hobart**	**2009-10**
235	G. S. Chappell at Faisalabad	1979-80	201	G. S. Chappell at Brisbane	1981-82

For Pakistan (3)

237	Salim Malik at Rawalpindi	1994-95	210*	Taslim Arif at Faisalabad	1979-80
211	Javed Miandad at Karachi	1988-89			

INDIVIDUAL HUNDREDS

For Australia (67)

6: A. R. Border, G. S. Chappell.
5: R. T. Ponting.
4: J. L. Langer, M. A. Taylor.
3: M. J. Slater, M. E. Waugh, S. R. Waugh, G. N. Yallop.
2: A. C. Gilchrist, K. J. Hughes, D. M. Jones, D. R. Martyn, R. B. Simpson.
1: J. Benaud, D. C. Boon, I. M. Chappell, **M. J. Clarke**, G. J. Cosier, I. C. Davis, M. L. Hayden, **M. E. K. Hussey**, **S. M. Katich**, R. B. McCosker, R. W. Marsh, N. C. O'Neill, W. B. Phillips, I. R. Redpath, G. M. Ritchie, A. P. Sheahan, K. D. Walters, **S. R. Watson**, K. C. Wessels, G. M. Wood.

For Pakistan (47)

6: Ijaz Ahmed, sen., Javed Miandad.
3: Asif Iqbal, Majid Khan, Mohsin Khan, Saeed Anwar.
2: Aamir Sohail, Hanif Mohammad, Sadiq Mohammad, Salim Malik, **Salman Butt**, Zaheer Abbas.
1: Imran Khan, Inzamam-ul-Haq, Khalid Ibadulla, Mansoor Akhtar, **Mohammad Yousuf**, Moin Khan, Mushtaq Mohammad, Qasim Omar, Saeed Ahmed, Taslim Arif, Wasim Akram.

TEN WICKETS OR MORE IN A MATCH

For Australia (5)

10-111 (7-87, 3-24)†	R. J. Bright, Karachi.	1979-80
10-135 (6-82, 4-53)	D. K. Lillee, Melbourne.	1976-77
11-118 (5-32, 6-86)†	C. G. Rackemann, Perth.	1983-84
11-77 (7-23, 4-54)	S. K. Warne, Brisbane	1995-96
11-188 (7-94, 4-94)	S. K. Warne, Colombo (PSS).	2002-03

For Pakistan (6)

11-218 (4-76, 7-142)	Abdul Qadir, Faisalabad.	1982-83
13-114 (6-34, 7-80)†	Fazal Mahmood, Karachi.	1956-57
12-165 (6-102, 6-63)	Imran Khan, Sydney.	1976-77
11-118 (4-69, 7-49)	Iqbal Qasim, Karachi.	1979-80
11-125 (2-39, 9-86)	Sarfraz Nawaz, Melbourne.	1978-79
11-160 (6-62, 5-98)†	Wasim Akram, Melbourne.	1989-90

† *On first appearance in Australia–Pakistan Tests.*

SEVEN WICKETS OR MORE IN AN INNINGS

In addition to those listed above, the following have taken seven wickets or more in an innings:

For Australia

7-75	L. F. Kline, Lahore	1959-60	8-59 A. A. Mallett, Adelaide.	1972-73
8-24	G. D. McGrath, Perth	2004-05	7-187 B. Yardley, Melbourne.	1981-82

For Pakistan

7-188 Danish Kaneria, Sydney 2004-05

Bold type denotes performances in the 2009-10 series or, in career figures, players who appeared in that series.

AUSTRALIA v SRI LANKA

Series notes: Sri Lanka have never won in Australia. In ten Tests there, they average 27 runs per wicket and Australia 54. Australia have batted first in 18 of the 20 matches. Their last four victories in Sri Lanka have come after trailing on first innings. R. T. Ponting is the top scorer with 851 runs at 50.05. M. Muralitharan needs six wickets to overtake S. K. Warne (59) as the top wicket-taker. Of Muralitharan's 54 wickets at an average of 36.50, 47 have come in Sri Lanka, at 26.02, with his seven wickets in Australia costing 106.85 apiece. M. J. Clarke averages 216 in two Tests against Sri Lanka.

		Captains				
Season	*Australia*	*Sri Lanka*	*T*	*A*	*SL*	*D*
1982-83S	G. S. Chappell	L. R. D. Mendis	1	1	0	0
1987-88A	A. R. Border	R. S. Madugalle	1	1	0	0
1989-90A	A. R. Border	A. Ranatunga	2	1	0	1
1992-93S	A. R. Border	A. Ranatunga	3	1	0	2
1995-96A	M. A. Taylor	A. Ranatunga[1]	3	3	0	0
1999-2000S	S. R. Waugh	S. T. Jayasuriya	3	0	1	2
2003-04S	R. T. Ponting	H. P. Tillekeratne	3	3	0	0
2004A	R. T. Ponting[2]	M. S. Atapattu	2	1	0	1

THE WARNE–MURALITHARAN TROPHY

		Captains					
Season	*Australia*	*Sri Lanka*	*T*	*A*	*SL*	*D*	*Held by*
2007-08A	R. T. Ponting	D. P. M. D. Jayawardene	2	2	0	0	A
	In Australia.........................		10	8	0	2	
	In Sri Lanka		10	5	1	4	
	Totals		20	13	1	6	

A Played in Australia. S Played in Sri Lanka.

Note: The following deputised for the official touring captain:
[1]P. A. de Silva (Third). [2]A. C. Gilchrist (First).

HIGHEST INNINGS TOTALS

For Australia in Australia: 617-5 dec at Perth 1995-96
          in Sri Lanka: 514-4 dec at Kandy 1982-83

For Sri Lanka in Australia: 455 at Cairns 2004
          in Sri Lanka: 547-8 dec at Colombo (SSC) 1992-93

LOWEST INNINGS TOTALS

For Australia in Australia: 201 at Darwin 2004
          in Sri Lanka: 120 at Kandy 2003-04

For Sri Lanka in Australia: 97 at Darwin.. 2004
          in Sri Lanka: 154 at Galle 2003-04

DOUBLE-HUNDRED

For Australia (1)

219   M. J. Slater at Perth 1995-96

Highest score for Sri Lanka: 192 by K. C. Sangakkara at Hobart, 2007-08.

INDIVIDUAL HUNDREDS

For Australia (31)

3: M. L. Hayden, D. M. Jones, S. R. Waugh.

2: M. E. K. Hussey, P. A. Jaques, J. L. Langer, D. S. Lehmann, D. R. Martyn, M. A. Taylor.

1: D. C. Boon, A. R. Border, M. J. Clarke, A. C. Gilchrist, D. W. Hookes, T. M. Moody, R. T. Ponting, M. J. Slater, M. E. Waugh, K. C. Wessels.

For Sri Lanka (13)

2: M. S. Atapattu, A. P. Gurusinha, S. T. Jayasuriya.

1: P. A. de Silva, T. M. Dilshan, D. P. M. D. Jayawardene, R. S. Kaluwitharana, A. Ranatunga, K. C. Sangakkara, H. P. Tillekeratne.

TEN WICKETS OR MORE IN A MATCH

For Australia (2)

10-159 (5-116, 5-43)	S. K. Warne, Galle	2003-04
10-155 (5-65, 5-90)	S. K. Warne, Kandy	2003-04

For Sri Lanka (2)

11-212 (6-59, 5-153)	M. Muralitharan, Galle	2003-04
10-210 (5-109, 5-101)	U. D. U. Chandana, Cairns	2004

SEVEN WICKETS OR MORE IN AN INNINGS

For Australia

7-39 M. S. Kasprowicz, Darwin   2004

AUSTRALIA v ZIMBABWE

Series notes: Zimbabwe have won all three tosses – and lost all three Tests. Australia average 64.3 runs per wicket and Zimbabwe 26.0. Australia's lowest innings score (403) exceeds Zimbabwe's highest (321). Zimbabwe do lead 9–0 in one field, though: ducks.

		Captains				
Season	*Australia*	*Zimbabwe*	T	A	Z	D
1999-2000*Z*	S. R. Waugh	A. D. R. Campbell	1	1	0	0
2003-04*A*	S. R. Waugh	H. H. Streak	2	2	0	0
	In Australia		2	2	0	0
	In Zimbabwe		1	1	0	0
	Totals		3	3	0	0

A Played in Australia.   Z Played in Zimbabwe.

HIGHEST INNINGS TOTALS

For Australia in Australia: 735-6 dec at Perth		2003-04
in Zimbabwe: 422 at Harare		1999-2000
For Zimbabwe in Australia: 321 at Perth		2003-04
in Zimbabwe: 232 at Harare		1999-2000

LOWEST INNINGS TOTALS

For Australia in Australia: 403 at Sydney   2003-04
               in Zimbabwe: 422 at Harare   1999-2000

For Zimbabwe in Australia: 239 at Perth   2003-04
                in Zimbabwe: 194 at Harare   1999-2000

DOUBLE-HUNDRED
For Australia (1)

380   M. L. Hayden at Perth 2003-04

Highest score for Zimbabwe: 118 by S. V. Carlisle at Sydney, 2003-04.

INDIVIDUAL HUNDREDS
For Australia (5)

2: M. L. Hayden.
1: A. C. Gilchrist, R. T. Ponting, S. R. Waugh.

For Zimbabwe (1)

1: S. V. Carlisle.

BEST MATCH BOWLING ANALYSES
For Australia

6-90 (0-25, 6-65)   S. M. Katich, Sydney   2003-04

For Zimbabwe

6-184 (6-121, 0-63)   R. W. Price, Sydney   2003-04

AUSTRALIA v BANGLADESH

Series notes: The home side has won the toss in all four Tests. Australia have never batted first. M. L. Hayden's average against Bangladesh (33.60) is his lowest against any of the nine nations he has played. In four matches against Bangladesh, J. N. Gillespie averages 247.00 with the bat and 13.68 with the ball. All six five-wicket hauls have been taken by spinners, four of them by S. C. G. MacGill.

		Captains				
Season	*Australia*	*Bangladesh*	*T*	*A*	*B*	*D*
2003*A*	S. R. Waugh	Khaled Mahmud	2	2	0	0
2005-06*B*	R. T. Ponting	Habibul Bashar	2	2	0	0
	In Australia		2	2	0	0
	In Bangladesh		2	2	0	0
	Totals		4	4	0	0

A Played in Australia.   B Played in Bangladesh.

HIGHEST INNINGS TOTALS

For Australia in Australia: 556-4 dec at Cairns   2003
               in Bangladesh: 581-4 dec at Chittagong   2005-06

For Bangladesh in Australia: 295 at Cairns   2003
                 in Bangladesh: 427 at Fatullah   2005-06

LOWEST INNINGS TOTALS

For Australia in Bangladesh: 269 at Fatullah 2005-06

For Bangladesh in Australia: 97 at Darwin 2003
in Bangladesh: 148 at Fatullah 2005-06

DOUBLE-HUNDREDS
For Australia (1)
201* J. N. Gillespie at Chittagong 2005-06

Highest score for Bangladesh: 138 by Shahriar Nafees at Fatullah, 2005-06.

INDIVIDUAL HUNDREDS
For Australia (9)
2: D. S. Lehmann, S. R. Waugh.
1: A. C. Gilchrist, J. N. Gillespie, M. E. K. Hussey, M. L. Love, R. T. Ponting.

For Bangladesh (1)
1: Shahriar Nafees.

TEN WICKETS OR MORE IN A MATCH
For Australia (1)
10-133 (5-77, 5-56)   S. C. G. MacGill, Cairns 2003
Note: The best match figures for Bangladesh are 9-160 (5-62, 4-98) by Mohammad Rafique at Fatullah, 2005-06.

SEVEN WICKETS OR MORE IN AN INNINGS
For Australia
8-108 S. C. G. MacGill, Fatullah 2005-06

AUSTRALIA v ICC WORLD XI

Season	Australia	ICC World XI	T	A	ICC	D
2005-06*A*	R. T. Ponting	G. C. Smith	1	1	0	0

A Played in Australia.

HIGHEST INNINGS TOTALS

For Australia: 345 at Sydney 2005-06
For ICC World XI: 190 at Sydney 2005-06

LOWEST INNINGS TOTALS

For Australia: 199 at Sydney 2005-06
For ICC World XI: 144 at Sydney 2005-06

HIGHEST INDIVIDUAL INNINGS
For Australia

111   M. L. Hayden at Sydney 2005-06

For ICC World XI

76   V. Sehwag at Sydney 2005-06

BEST MATCH BOWLING ANALYSES
For Australia

9-82 (4-39, 5-43)   S. C. G. MacGill at Sydney 2005-06

For ICC World XI

7-107 (4-59, 3-48)   A. Flintoff at Sydney 2005-06

SOUTH AFRICA v WEST INDIES

Series notes: West Indies trail 7–0 from ten Tests in which they have fielded first. South Africa have scored over 500 in the first innings of seven of the last 11 Tests – before that, neither side had done so in 11 Tests. South Africa have been bowled out in the second innings in only five of the 22 matches; West Indies have been bowled out 17 times. In two Tests at Centurion, South Africa average 64.8 runs per wicket, more than double West Indies' 25.2. The top nine individual scores were all made in two series, in 2003-04 and 2004-05. J. H. Kallis is the leading run-scorer, with 2,073; he averages 74.03 against West Indies, while A. G. Prince averages 77.00 and G. C. Smith 71.88. Kallis needs three wickets to become the third person to score 2,000 runs and take 50 wickets against one Test team.

Season	South Africa	*Captains* West Indies	T	SA	WI	D
1991-92*W*	K. C. Wessels	R. B. Richardson	1	0	1	0
1998-99*S*	W. J. Cronje	B. C. Lara	5	5	0	0

SIR VIVIAN RICHARDS TROPHY

Season	South Africa	*Captains* West Indies	T	SA	WI	D	Held by
2000-01*W*	S. M. Pollock	C. L. Hooper	5	2	1	2	SA
2003-04*S*	G. C. Smith	B. C. Lara	4	3	0	1	SA
2004-05*W*	G. C. Smith	S. Chanderpaul	4	2	0	2	SA
2007-08 *S*	G. C. Smith	C. H. Gayle[1]	3	2	1	0	SA
	In South Africa		12	10	1	1	
	In West Indies		10	4	2	4	
	Totals		22	14	3	5	

S Played in South Africa.   W Played in West Indies.

Note: The following deputised for the official touring captain:
  [1]D. J. Bravo (Third).

HIGHEST INNINGS TOTALS

For South Africa in South Africa: 658-9 dec at Durban 2003-04
              in West Indies: 588-6 dec at St John's 2004-05

For West Indies in South Africa: 427 at Cape Town 2003-04
            in West Indies: 747 at St John's 2004-05

LOWEST INNINGS TOTALS

For South Africa in South Africa: 195 at Port Elizabeth 1998-99
              in West Indies: 141 at Kingston 2000-01

For West Indies in South Africa: 121 at Port Elizabeth 1998-99
            in West Indies: 140 at St John's 2000-01

DOUBLE-HUNDREDS

For West Indies (4)

317	C. H. Gayle at St John's	2004-05	203* S. Chanderpaul at Georgetown . .	2004-05
213	W. W. Hinds at Georgetown. . . .	2004-05	202 B. C. Lara at Johannesburg.	2003-04

Highest score for South Africa: 192 by H. H. Gibbs at Centurion, 2003-04.

INDIVIDUAL HUNDREDS

For South Africa (33)

7: J. H. Kallis.
6: G. C. Smith.
3: D. J. Cullinan, A. B. de Villiers, H. H. Gibbs, G. Kirsten.
2: M. V. Boucher, A. G. Prince.
1: A. C. Hudson, S. M. Pollock, J. N. Rhodes, J. A. Rudolph.

For West Indies (20)

4: S. Chanderpaul, B. C. Lara, R. R. Sarwan.
3: C. H. Gayle.
1: D. J. Bravo, W. W. Hinds, R. D. Jacobs, M. N. Samuels, D. R. Smith.

TEN WICKETS OR MORE IN A MATCH

For South Africa (2)

10-88 (4-56, 6-32)   A. Nel, Bridgetown 2004-05
13-132 (6-95, 7-37)   M. Ntini, Port-of-Spain 2004-05

Note: The best match figures for West Indies are 8-79 (2-28, 6-51) by C. E. L. Ambrose at Port Elizabeth, 1998-99.

SEVEN WICKETS OR MORE IN AN INNINGS

In addition to those listed above, the following has taken seven wickets or more in an innings.

For West Indies

7-84 F. A. Rose, Durban 1998-99

SOUTH AFRICA v NEW ZEALAND

Series notes: New Zealand have never won a series against South Africa and have beaten them only once in 14 home Tests. South Africa average 46.1 runs per wicket away, well ahead of New Zealand's 27.6 at home. All four New Zealand's wins have come after they won the toss. Eight of the last 12 victories between these sides have been by the team fielding first. J. H. Kallis is the top scorer for either country with 1,356 at an average of 67.80; only Javed Miandad (1,919), A. R. Border (1,500) and S. R. Tendulkar (1,406) have scored more Test runs against New Zealand. M. Ntini is the top wicket-taker with 46 at 25.21 in 11 Tests; D. W. Steyn has taken 36 at 16.66 in five Tests.

Season	South Africa	*Captains* New Zealand	T	SA	NZ	D
1931-32*N*	H. B. Cameron	M. L. Page	2	2	0	0
1952-53*N*	J. E. Cheetham	W. M. Wallace	2	1	0	1
1953-54*S*	J. E. Cheetham	G. O. Rabone[1]	5	4	0	1
1961-62*S*	D. J. McGlew	J. R. Reid	5	2	2	1
1963-64*N*	T. L. Goddard	J. R. Reid	3	0	0	3
1994-95*S*	W. J. Cronje	K. R. Rutherford	3	2	1	0
1994-95*N*	W. J. Cronje	K. R. Rutherford	1	1	0	0
1998-99*N*	W. J. Cronje	D. J. Nash	3	1	0	2
2000-01*S*	S. M. Pollock	S. P. Fleming	3	2	0	1
2003-04*N*	G. C. Smith	S. P. Fleming	3	1	1	1
2005-06*S*	G. C. Smith	S. P. Fleming	3	2	0	1
2007-08*S*	G. C. Smith	D. L. Vettori	2	2	0	0
	In New Zealand		14	6	1	7
	In South Africa.		21	14	3	4
	Totals		35	20	4	11

N Played in New Zealand.   S Played in South Africa.

Note: The following deputised for the official touring captain:
[1]B. Sutcliffe (Fourth and Fifth).

HIGHEST INNINGS TOTALS

For South Africa in South Africa: 512 at Cape Town 2005-06
                  in New Zealand: 621-5 dec at Auckland 1998-99

For New Zealand in South Africa: 593-8 dec at Cape Town. 2005-06
                  in New Zealand: 595 at Auckland. 2003-04

LOWEST INNINGS TOTALS

For South Africa in South Africa: 148 at Johannesburg 1953-54
                  in New Zealand: 223 at Dunedin 1963-64

For New Zealand in South Africa: 79 at Johannesburg. 1953-54
                  in New Zealand: 138 at Dunedin. 1963-64

DOUBLE-HUNDREDS

For South Africa (3)

275* D. J. Cullinan at Auckland . . . . . 1998-99 | 211* H. H. Gibbs at Christchurch 1998-99
255* D. J. McGlew at Wellington. . . . 1952-53 |

For New Zealand (1)

262   S. P. Fleming at Cape Town 2005-06

INDIVIDUAL HUNDREDS

For South Africa (33)

5: J. H. Kallis.
3: H. M. Amla, D. J. McGlew.
2: W. J. Cronje, D. J. Cullinan, H. H. Gibbs, G. Kirsten, R. A. McLean.
1: X. C. Balaskas, J. A. J. Christy, H. H. Dippenaar, W. R. Endean, N. D. McKenzie, B. Mitchell, A. R. A. Murray, A. G. Prince, D. J. Richardson, J. A. Rudolph, G. C. Smith, J. H. B. Waite.

For New Zealand (14)

2: J. D. P. Oram, J. R. Reid.
1: P. T. Barton, C. L. Cairns, S. P. Fleming, J. E. C. Franklin, P. G. Z. Harris, G. O. Rabone, B. W. Sinclair, M. S. Sinclair, S. B. Styris, H. G. Vivian.

TEN WICKETS OR MORE IN A MATCH

For South Africa (4)

11-196 (6-128, 5-68)†	S. F. Burke, Cape Town	1961-62
10-145 (5-94, 5-51)	M. Ntini, Centurion	2005-06
10-93 (5-34, 5-59)	D. W. Steyn, Johannesburg	2007-08
10-91 (4-42, 6-49)	D. W. Steyn, Centurion	2007-08

For New Zealand (1)

11-180 (6-76, 5-104)	C. S. Martin, Auckland	2003-04

† *On first appearance in South Africa–New Zealand Tests.*

SEVEN WICKETS OR MORE IN AN INNINGS

For South Africa

8-53 G. B. Lawrence, Johannesburg . . 1961-62

SOUTH AFRICA v INDIA

Series notes: India have lost all four series in South Africa. Pending the series in 2009-10, the side batting first have won two and lost seven of the last 13 matches; before that, the side batting first had won five in a row. S. R. Tendulkar and R. Dravid are the only men to score 1,000 runs, yet their averages (35.35 and 36.51 respectively) are their lowest against any Test team. G. Kirsta is the only man to make two centuries in a Test, at Kolkata in 1996-97.

		Captains				
Season	*South Africa*	*India*	*T*	*SA*	*I*	*D*
1992-93*S*	K. C. Wessels	M. Azharuddin	4	1	0	3
1996-97*I*	W. J. Cronje	S. R. Tendulkar	3	1	2	0
1996-97*S*	W. J. Cronje	S. R. Tendulkar	3	2	0	1
1999-2000*I*	W. J. Cronje	S. R. Tendulkar	2	2	0	0
2001-02*S*†	S. M. Pollock	S. C. Ganguly	2	1	0	1
2004-05*I*	G. C. Smith	S. C. Ganguly	2	0	1	1
2006-07*S*	G. C. Smith	R. Dravid	3	2	1	0
2007-08*I*	G. C. Smith	A. Kumble[1]	3	1	1	1
	In South Africa		12	6	1	5
	In India		10	4	4	2
	Totals		22	10	5	7

S Played in South Africa.   I Played in India.

† *The Third Test at Centurion was stripped of its official status by the ICC after a disciplinary dispute and is excluded.*

Note: The following was appointed by the home authority for only a minor proportion of the series:
[1]M. S. Dhoni (Third).

HIGHEST INNINGS TOTALS

For South Africa in South Africa: 563 at Bloemfontein 2001-02
              in India: 540 at Chennai 2007-08

For India in South Africa: 414 at Cape Town 2006-07
              in India: 627 at Chennai 2007-08

LOWEST INNINGS TOTALS

For South Africa in South Africa: 84 at Johannesburg 2006-07
              in India: 105 at Ahmedabad.................................... 1996-97

For India in South Africa: 66 at Durban 1996-97
              in India: 76 at Ahmedabad... 2007-08

DOUBLE-HUNDRED

For India (1)

319   V. Sehwag at Chennai 2007-08

Highest score for South Africa: 196 by H. H. Gibbs at Port Elizabeth, 2001-02.

INDIVIDUAL HUNDREDS

For South Africa (20)

3: G. Kirsten.
2: D. J. Cullinan, H. H. Gibbs, J. H. Kallis, L. Klusener.
1: H. M. Amla, W. J. Cronje, A. B. de Villiers, A. J. Hall, A. C. Hudson, N. D. McKenzie, B. M. McMillan, A. G. Prince, K. C. Wessels.

For India (15)

4: M. Azharuddin.
3: V. Sehwag, S. R. Tendulkar.
2: R. Dravid.
1: P. K. Amre, Kapil Dev, Wasim Jaffer.

TEN WICKETS OR MORE IN A MATCH

For South Africa (2)

| 12-139 (5-55, 7-84) | A. A. Donald, Port Elizabeth .... | 1992-93 |
| 10-147 (4-91, 6-56) | S. M. Pollock, Bloemfontein .... | 2001-02 |

For India (1)

| 10-153 (5-60, 5-93) | B. K. V. Prasad, Durban .... | 1996-97 |

SEVEN WICKETS OR MORE IN AN INNINGS

In addition to those listed above, the following have taken seven wickets or more in an innings:

For South Africa

8-64 L. Klusener, Calcutta 1996-97

For India

7-87 Harbhajan Singh, Kolkata...... 2004-05

SOUTH AFRICA v PAKISTAN

Series notes: South Africa have batted first in 12 of the 16 Tests between these sides. All three Pakistan victories came after losing the toss. South Africa average 35.1 runs per wicket on African soil, one and a half times Pakistan's 22.7. In Asia, however, South Africa average 35.5 and Pakistan 33.5. J. H. Kallis is the only man to score 1,000 runs, having amassed 1,149 at an average of 60.47. He is also the only man to make twin hundreds, at Karachi in 2007-08.

		Captains				
Season	*South Africa*	*Pakistan*	*T*	*SA*	*P*	*D*
1994-95*S*	W. J. Cronje	Salim Malik	1	1	0	0
1997-98*P*	W. J. Cronje	Saeed Anwar	3	1	0	2
1997-98*S*	W. J. Cronje[1]	Rashid Latif[2]	3	1	1	1
2002-03*S*	S. M. Pollock	Waqar Younis	2	2	0	0
2003-04*P*	G. C. Smith	Inzamam-ul-Haq[3]	2	0	1	1
2006-07*S*	G. C. Smith	Inzamam-ul-Haq	3	2	1	0
2007-08*P*	G. C. Smith	Shoaib Malik	2	1	0	1
	In South Africa....................		9	6	2	1
	In Pakistan		7	2	1	4
	Totals		16	8	3	5

S Played in South Africa.   P Played in Pakistan.

Notes: The following deputised for the official touring captain or were appointed by the home authority for only a minor proportion of the series:

[1]G. Kirsten (First). [2]Aamir Sohail (First and Second). [3]Yousuf Youhana *later known as Mohammad Yousuf* (First).

HIGHEST INNINGS TOTALS

For South Africa in South Africa: 620-7 dec at Cape Town 2002-03
            in Pakistan: 450 at Karachi 2007-08

For Pakistan in South Africa: 329 at Johannesburg............................... 1996-97
            in Pakistan: 456 at Rawalpindi 1997-98

LOWEST INNINGS TOTALS

For South Africa in South Africa: 124 at Port Elizabeth 2006-07
            in Pakistan: 214 at Faisalabad 1997-98

For Pakistan in South Africa: 106 at Port Elizabeth 1997-98
            in Pakistan: 92 at Faisalabad..................................... 1997-98

DOUBLE-HUNDRED

For South Africa (1)

228   H. H. Gibbs at Cape Town 2002-03

Highest score for Pakistan: 136 by Azhar Mahmood at Johannesburg, 1997-98.

INDIVIDUAL HUNDREDS

For South Africa (12)

4: J. H. Kallis.
2: G. Kirsten, G. C. Smith.
1: H. H. Gibbs, B. M. McMillan, A. G. Prince, P. L. Symcox.

For Pakistan (10)

3: Azhar Mahmood.
2: Taufeeq Umar, Younis Khan.
1: Ali Naqvi, Imran Farhat, Saeed Anwar.

TEN WICKETS OR MORE IN A MATCH

For South Africa (1)

10-108 (6-81, 4-27)   † P. S. de Villiers, Johannesburg   1994-95

For Pakistan (1)

10-133 (6-78, 4-55)   Waqar Younis, Port Elizabeth   1997-98
† *On first appearance in South Africa–Pakistan Tests.*

SEVEN WICKETS OR MORE IN AN INNINGS

For South Africa

7-128 P. R. Adams, Lahore 2003-04

SOUTH AFRICA v SRI LANKA

Series notes: Sri Lanka have never won a Test in South Africa. They average 37.5 runs per wicket at home but only 21.6 away. Half of the 12 victories have been by an innings. Six of South Africa's eight wins have come after they lost the toss. M. Muralitharan has taken 104 wickets, more than twice the next best (S. M. Pollock with 48). He has also taken 11 five-wicket hauls against South Africa – the rest of Sri Lanka have managed three between them.

		Captains					
Season	*South Africa*	*Sri Lanka*	*T*	*SA*	*SL*	*D*
1993-94*SL*	K. C. Wessels	A. Ranatunga	3	1	0	2
1997-98*SA*	W. J. Cronje	A. Ranatunga	2	2	0	0
2000*SL*	S. M. Pollock	S. T. Jayasuriya	3	1	1	1
2000-01*SA*	S. M. Pollock	S. T. Jayasuriya	3	2	0	1
2002-03*SA*	S. M. Pollock	S. T. Jayasuriya[1]	2	2	0	0
2004*SL*	G. C. Smith	M. S. Atapattu	2	0	1	1
2006*SL*	A. G. Prince	D. P. M. D. Jayawardene	2	0	2	0
	In South Africa.		7	6	0	1
	In Sri Lanka		10	2	4	4
	Totals		17	8	4	5

SA Played in South Africa.   SL Played in Sri Lanka.

Note: The following deputised for the official captain:
   [1]M. S. Atapattu (Second).

HIGHEST INNINGS TOTALS

For South Africa in South Africa: 504-7 dec at Cape Town   2000-01
                     in Sri Lanka: 495 at Colombo (SSC)   1993-94

For Sri Lanka in South Africa: 323 at Centurion   2002-03
                  in Sri Lanka: 756-5 dec at Colombo (SSC)   2006

LOWEST INNINGS TOTALS

For South Africa in South Africa: 200 at Centurion   1997-98
                     in Sri Lanka: 169 at Colombo (SSC)   2006

For Sri Lanka in South Africa: 95 at Cape Town   2000-01
                  in Sri Lanka: 119 at Colombo (SSC)   1993-94

DOUBLE-HUNDREDS

For Sri Lanka (4)

374	D. P. M. D. Jayawardene at Colombo (SSC).	2006	237 D. P. M. D. Jayawardene at Galle	2004
287	K. C. Sangakkara at Colombo (SSC)	2006	233 K. C. Sangakkara at Colombo (SSC)	2004

Highest score for South Africa: 180 by G. Kirsten at Durban, 2000-01.

INDIVIDUAL HUNDREDS

For South Africa (12)

5: D. J. Cullinan.
1: W. J. Cronje, G. Kirsten, L. Klusener, N. D. McKenzie, S. M. Pollock, J. N. Rhodes, J. A. Rudolph.

For Sri Lanka (11)

5: D. P. M. D. Jayawardene.
2: K. C. Sangakkara.
1: M. S. Atapattu, S. T. Jayasuriya, A. Ranatunga, H. P. Tillekeratne.

TEN WICKETS OR MORE IN A MATCH

For Sri Lanka (4)

13-171 (6-87, 7-84)	M. Muralitharan, Galle.	2000
11-161 (5-122, 6-39)	M. Muralitharan, Durban	2000-01
10-172 (4-41, 6-131)	M. Muralitharan, Colombo (SSC)	2006
12-225 (5-128, 7-97)	M. Muralitharan, Colombo (PSS).	2006

Note: The best match figures for South Africa are 9-106 (5-48, 4-58) by B. N. Schultz at Colombo (SSC), 1993-94.

SOUTH AFRICA v ZIMBABWE

Series notes: South Africa have won four of the seven Tests by an innings. They have a 100% record in three games at Harare, but drew their only match at Bulawayo. Zimbabwe have failed to bowl South Africa out in the last five Tests, and have managed it only twice in seven Tests overall. South Africa average 169.7 runs per wicket in the one Test when they batted first, against 53.4 in the six when they fielded. In Tests in Zimbabwe, South Africa's average is 62.1 and Zimbabwe's 26.2. A. Flower is the only man to make two centuries in the same Test: he scored 142 and 199 not out at Harare in 2001-02. In three Tests in Zimbabwe, J. H. Kallis averages 503.

	Captains					
Season	*South Africa*	*Zimbabwe*	*T*	*SA*	*Z*	*D*
1995-96Z	W. J. Cronje	A. Flower	1	1	0	0
1999-2000S	W. J. Cronje	A. D. R. Campbell	1	1	0	0
1999-2000Z	W. J. Cronje	A. Flower	1	1	0	0
2001-02Z	S. M. Pollock	H. H. Streak	2	1	0	1
2004-05S	G. C. Smith	T. Taibu	2	2	0	0
	In Zimbabwe		4	3	0	1
	In South Africa.		3	3	0	0
	Totals		7	6	0	1

S Played in South Africa. Z Played in Zimbabwe.

HIGHEST INNINGS TOTALS

For South Africa in South Africa: 480-7 dec at Centurion 2004-05
                    in Zimbabwe: 600-3 dec at Harare............................. 2001-02

For Zimbabwe in South Africa: 269 at Centurion 2004-05
                    in Zimbabwe: 419-9 dec at Bulawayo............................ 2001-02

LOWEST INNINGS TOTALS

For South Africa in South Africa: 417 in Bloemfontein 1999-2000
                    in Zimbabwe: 346 at Harare.................................   1995-96

For Zimbabwe in South Africa: 54 at Cape Town............................   2004-05
                    in Zimbabwe: 102 at Harare 1999-2000

DOUBLE-HUNDRED
For South Africa (1)
220   G. Kirsten at Harare 2001-02

Highest score for Zimbabwe: 199* by A. Flower at Harare, 2001-02.

INDIVIDUAL HUNDREDS
For South Africa (9)

3: J. H. Kallis.
1: M. V. Boucher, H. H. Gibbs, A. C. Hudson, G. Kirsten, A. G. Prince, G. C. Smith.

For Zimbabwe (2)

2: A. Flower.

TEN WICKETS OR MORE IN A MATCH
For South Africa (1)
11-113 (3-42, 8-71)†   A. A. Donald, Harare 1995-96

Note: The best match figures for Zimbabwe are 5-105 (3-68, 2-37) by A. C. I. Lock at Harare, 1995-96.

† *On first appearance in South Africa–Zimbabwe Tests.*

SOUTH AFRICA v BANGLADESH

Series notes: South Africa have won all eight Tests, seven by an innings. South Africa average 58.6 runs per wicket and Bangladesh 18.4. On average, Bangladesh have taken only 7.75 wickets per Test. G. C. Smith has scored 743 runs in Tests between these sides, more than twice the next best, J. H. Kallis with 317. J. A. Rudolph averages 293 against Bangladesh. M. Ntini is the top wicket-taker, with 35 at 16.37.

Season	South Africa	Captains Bangladesh	T	SA	B	D
2002-03*S*	S. M. Pollock[1]	Khaled Mashud	2	2	0	0
2003*B*	G. C. Smith	Khaled Mahmud	2	2	0	0
2007-08*B*	G. C. Smith	Mohammad Ashraful	2	2	0	0
2008-09*S*	G. C. Smith	Mohammad Ashraful	2	2	0	0
	In South Africa....................		4	4	0	0
	In Bangladesh.....................		4	4	0	0
	Totals...........................		8	8	0	0

S Played in South Africa.   B Played in Bangladesh.

Note: The following deputised for the official captain:
[1]M. V. Boucher (First).

HIGHEST INNINGS TOTALS

For South Africa in South Africa: 529-4 dec at East London 2002-03
in Bangladesh: 583-7 dec at Chittagong 2007-08

For Bangladesh in South Africa: 252 at East London 2002-03
in Bangladesh: 259 at Chittagong 2007-08

LOWEST INNINGS TOTALS

For South Africa in South Africa: 429 at Centurion 2008-09
in Bangladesh: 170 at Mirpur...................................... 2007-08

For Bangladesh in South Africa: 107 at Potchefstroom........................... 2002-03
in Bangladesh: 102 at Dhaka 2003

DOUBLE-HUNDREDS

For South Africa (4)

232	G. C. Smith at Chittagong...... 2007-08	222* J. A. Rudolph at Chittagong	2003
226	N. D. McKenzie at Chittagong .. 2007-08	200 G. C. Smith at East London	2002-03

Highest score for Bangladesh: 75 by Habibul Bashar at Chittagong, 2003.

INDIVIDUAL HUNDREDS

For South Africa (13)

3: G. C. Smith.
2: G. Kirsten.
1: H. M. Amla, M. V. Boucher, H. H. Dippenaar, H. H. Gibbs, J. H. Kallis, N. D. McKenzie, A. G. Prince, J. A. Rudolph.

TEN WICKETS OR MORE IN A MATCH

For South Africa (1)

10-106 (5-37, 5-69)   P. R. Adams, Chittagong.................................... 2003

Note: The best match figures for Bangladesh are 9-97 (6-27, 3-70) by Shahadat Hossain at Mirpur, 2007-08.

WEST INDIES v NEW ZEALAND

Series notes: New Zealand have won five and lost none of the last ten Tests between the sides, going back to 1995-96. All seven Tests in the Caribbean outside Bridgetown and Kingston have been drawn. In two Tests at Georgetown, New Zealand average 75.6 runs per wicket and West Indies 64.7. C. H. Gayle has scored 820 runs at 74.54 against New Zealand, and needs 63 runs to become the top scorer in Tests between these teams.

		Captains				
Season	*West Indies*	*New Zealand*	*T*	*WI*	*NZ*	*D*
1951-52N	J. D. C. Goddard	B. Sutcliffe	2	1	0	1
1955-56N	D. St E. Atkinson	J. R. Reid[1]	4	3	1	0
1968-69N	G. S. Sobers	G. T. Dowling	3	1	1	1
1971-72W	G. S. Sobers	G. T. Dowling[2]	5	0	0	5
1979-80N	C. H. Lloyd	G. P. Howarth	3	0	1	2
1984-85W	I. V. A. Richards	G. P. Howarth	4	2	0	2
1986-87N	I. V. A. Richards	J. V. Coney	3	1	1	1
1994-95N	C. A. Walsh	K. R. Rutherford	2	1	0	1
1995-96W	C. A. Walsh	L. K. Germon	2	1	0	1
1999-2000N	B. C. Lara	S. P. Fleming	2	0	2	0
2002W	C. L. Hooper	S. P. Fleming	2	0	1	1
2005-06N	S. Chanderpaul	S. P. Fleming	3	0	2	1
2008-09N	C. H. Gayle	D. L. Vettori	2	0	0	2
	In New Zealand.		24	7	8	9
	In West Indies.		13	3	1	9
	Totals		37	10	9	18

N Played in New Zealand.   W Played in West Indies.

Notes: The following deputised for the official touring captain or were appointed by the home authority for only a minor proportion of the series:
[1]H. B. Cave (First). [2]B. E. Congdon (Third, Fourth and Fifth).

HIGHEST INNINGS TOTALS

For West Indies in West Indies: 564-8 at Bridgetown.	1971-72
in New Zealand: 660-5 dec at Wellington.	1994-95
For New Zealand in West Indies: 543-3 dec at Georgetown.	1971-72
in New Zealand: 518-9 dec at Wellington.	1999-2000

LOWEST INNINGS TOTALS

For West Indies in West Indies: 107 at Bridgetown	2002
in New Zealand: 77 at Auckland.	1955-56
For New Zealand in West Indies: 94 at Bridgetown	1984-85
in New Zealand: 74 at Dunedin	1955-56

DOUBLE-HUNDREDS

For West Indies (6)

258	S. M. Nurse at Christchurch 1968-69	208* J. C. Adams at St John's. 1995-96
214	L. G. Rowe at Kingston 1971-72	208 S. L. Campbell at Bridgetown . . 1995-96
213	C. G. Greenidge at Auckland . . . 1986-87	204 C. H. Gayle at St George's 2002

For New Zealand (3)

259	G. M. Turner at Georgetown 1971-72	214 M. S. Sinclair at Wellington . . .1999-2000
223*	G. M. Turner at Kingston. 1971-72	

INDIVIDUAL HUNDREDS

For West Indies (37)

3: D. L. Haynes, L. G. Rowe, E. D. Weekes.

2: J. C. Adams, S. L. Campbell, C. H. Gayle, C. G. Greenidge, A. I. Kallicharran, S. M. Nurse.

1: M. C. Carew, S. Chanderpaul, C. A. Davis, R. C. Fredericks, A. F. G. Griffith, C. L. King, B. C. Lara, J. R. Murray, I. V. A. Richards, R. B. Richardson, R. G. Samuels, G. S. Sobers, J. B. Stollmeyer, J. E. Taylor, C. L. Walcott, F. M. M. Worrell.

For New Zealand (25)

3: M. D. Crowe.

2: N. J. Astle, B. E. Congdon, B. F. Hastings, S. B. Styris, G. M. Turner.

1: M. G. Burgess, J. J. Crowe, B. A. Edgar, S. P. Fleming, R. J. Hadlee, G. P. Howarth, T. W. Jarvis, T. G. McIntosh, A. C. Parore, M. S. Sinclair, B. R. Taylor, J. G. Wright.

Notes: E. D. Weekes in 1955-56 made three hundreds in consecutive innings.

L. G. Rowe and A. I. Kallicharran each scored hundreds in their first two innings in Test cricket. Rowe and Yasir Hameed (for Pakistan v Bangladesh) are the only two batsmen to do so in their first match.

TEN WICKETS OR MORE IN A MATCH

For West Indies (2)

11-120 (4-40, 7-80)	M. D. Marshall, Bridgetown	....	1984-85
13-55 (7-37, 6-18)	C. A. Walsh, Wellington	....	1994-95

For New Zealand (4)

10-100 (3-73, 7-27)†	C. L. Cairns, Hamilton	....	1999-2000
10-124 (4-51, 6-73)†	E. J. Chatfield, Port-of-Spain	....	1984-85
11-102 (5-34, 6-68)†	R. J. Hadlee, Dunedin	....	1979-80
10-166 (4-71, 6-95)	G. B. Troup, Auckland	....	1979-80

† *On first appearance in West Indies–New Zealand Tests.*

SEVEN WICKETS OR MORE IN AN INNINGS

In addition to those listed above, the following have taken seven wickets or more in an innings:

For West Indies

7-53 D. St E. Atkinson, Auckland ... 1955-56 | 7-87 F. H. Edwards, Napier 2008-09

For New Zealand

7-74 B. R. Taylor, Bridgetown 1971-72

WEST INDIES v INDIA

Series notes: These sides have drawn only two of their 18 Test series, but West Indies have not won a series in India since 1983-84. Of the last 20 Tests, the team batting second have won only two. West Indies have won seven out of eight Tests in Bridgetown, but all six in Georgetown have been drawn. Twenty-seven centuries have been scored in the last 12 Tests. Eight of the top ten analyses have been recorded by spinners. S. M. Gavaskar struck 13 centuries against West Indies; only D. G. Bradman, with 19 for Australia against England, has scored more against one Test side. I. V. A. Richards's 39 catches are a record against India for an outfielder.

	Captains					
Season	*West Indies*	*India*	*T*	*WI*	*I*	*D*
1948-49*I*	J. D. C. Goddard	L. Amarnath	5	1	0	4
1952-53*W*	J. B. Stollmeyer	V. S. Hazare	5	1	0	4
1958-59*I*	F. C. M. Alexander	Ghulam Ahmed[1]	5	3	0	2
1961-62*W*	F. M. M. Worrell	N. J. Contractor[2]	5	5	0	0

Captains

Season	West Indies	India	T	WI	I	D
1966-67*I*	G. S. Sobers	Nawab of Pataudi jun.	3	2	0	1
1970-71*W*	G. S. Sobers	A. L. Wadekar	5	0	1	4
1974-75*I*	C. H. Lloyd	Nawab of Pataudi jun.[3]	5	3	2	0
1975-76*W*	C. H. Lloyd	B. S. Bedi	4	2	1	1
1978-79*I*	A. I. Kallicharran	S. M. Gavaskar	6	0	1	5
1982-83*W*	C. H. Lloyd	Kapil Dev	5	2	0	3
1983-84*I*	C. H. Lloyd	Kapil Dev	6	3	0	3
1987-88*I*	I. V. A. Richards	D. B. Vengsarkar[4]	4	1	1	2
1988-89*W*	I. V. A. Richards	D. B. Vengsarkar	4	3	0	1
1994-95*I*	C. A. Walsh	M. Azharuddin	3	1	1	1
1996-97*W*	C. A. Walsh[5]	S. R. Tendulkar	5	1	0	4
2001-02*W*	C. L. Hooper	S. C. Ganguly	5	2	1	2
2002-03*I*	C. L. Hooper	S. C. Ganguly	3	0	2	1
2005-06*W*	B. C. Lara	R. Dravid	4	0	1	3
	In India............................		40	14	7	19
	In West Indies		42	16	4	22
	Totals		82	30	11	41

I Played in India.   W Played in West Indies.

Notes: The following deputised for the official touring captain or were appointed by the home authority for only a minor proportion of the series:
[1]P. R. Umrigar (First), V. Mankad (Fourth), H. R. Adhikari (Fifth). [2]Nawab of Pataudi jun. (Third, Fourth and Fifth). [3]S. Venkataraghavan (Second). [4]R. J. Shastri (Fourth). [5]B. C. Lara (Third).

HIGHEST INNINGS TOTALS

For West Indies in West Indies: 631-8 dec at Kingston............................ 1961-62
                in India: 644-8 dec at Delhi 1958-59

For India in West Indies: 588-8 dec at Gros Islet, St Lucia......................... 2005-06
               in India: 644-7 dec at Kanpur...................................... 1978-79

LOWEST INNINGS TOTALS

For West Indies in West Indies: 103 at Kingston................................. 2005-06
                in India: 127 at Delhi... 1987-88

For India in West Indies: 81 at Bridgetown.................................... 1996-97
               in India: 75 at Delhi 1987-88

DOUBLE-HUNDREDS

For West Indies (6)

256	R. B. Kanhai at Calcutta.......	1958-59	237	F. M. M. Worrell at Kingston...	1952-53
250	S. F. A. F. Bacchus at Kanpur ..	1978-79	233	C. L. Hooper at Georgetown....	2001-02
242*	C. H. Lloyd at Bombay........	1974-75	207	E. D. Weekes at Port-of-Spain ..	1952-53

For India (6)

236*	S. M. Gavaskar at Madras......	1983-84	212	Wasim Jaffer at St John's......	2005-06
220	S. M. Gavaskar at Port-of-Spain.	1970-71	205	S. M. Gavaskar at Bombay.....	1978-79
212	D. N. Sardesai at Kingston	1970-71	201	N. S. Sidhu at Port-of-Spain	1996-97

INDIVIDUAL HUNDREDS

For West Indies (96)

8: I. V. A. Richards, G. S. Sobers.

7: C. H. Lloyd, E. D. Weekes.

5: S. Chanderpaul, C. G. Greenidge, C. L. Hooper.

4: R. B. Kanhai, C. L. Walcott.

3: A. I. Kallicharran.

2: J. C. Adams, B. F. Butcher, C. A. Davis, R. C. Fredericks, D. L. Haynes, W. W. Hinds, B. C. Lara, A. L. Logie, A. F. Rae, R. B. Richardson, J. B. Stollmeyer.

1: S. F. A. F. Bacchus, R. J. Christiani, P. J. L. Dujon, D. Ganga, H. A. Gomes, G. E. Gomez, J. K. Holt, C. C. Hunte, R. D. Jacobs, E. D. A. McMorris, B. H. Pairaudeau, M. N. Samuels, R. R. Sarwan, O. G. Smith, J. S. Solomon, A. B. Williams, S. C. Williams, F. M. M. Worrell.

For India (72)

13: S. M. Gavaskar.

6: D. B. Vengsarkar.

4: G. R. Viswanath.

3: M. Amarnath, C. G. Borde, R. Dravid, Kapil Dev, V. V. S. Laxman, D. N. Sardesai, N. S. Sidhu, S. R. Tendulkar, P. R. Umrigar.

2: V. S. Hazare, V. Sehwag, R. J. Shastri.

1: H. R. Adhikari, M. L. Apte, S. A. Durani, F. M. Engineer, A. D. Gaekwad, M. Kaif, S. V. Manjrekar, V. L. Manjrekar, R. S. Modi, Mushtaq Ali, B. P. Patel, M. Prabhakar, A. Ratra, Pankaj Roy, E. D. Solkar, Wasim Jaffer.

TEN WICKETS OR MORE IN A MATCH

For West Indies (4)

11-126 (6-50, 5-76)	W. W. Hall, Kanpur	1958-59
11-89 (5-34, 6-55)	M. D. Marshall, Port-of-Spain	1988-89
12-12 (7-64, 5-57)	A. M. E. Roberts, Madras	1974-75
10-101 (6-62, 4-39)	C. A. Walsh, Kingston	1988-89

For India (4)

11-235 (7-157, 4-78)†	B. S. Chandrasekhar, Bombay	1966-67
10-223 (9-102, 1-121)	S. P. Gupte, Kanpur	1958-59
16-136 (8-61, 8-75)†	N. D. Hirwani, Madras	1987-88
10-135 (1-52, 9-83)	Kapil Dev, Ahmedabad	1983-84

† *On first appearance in West Indies–India Tests.*

SEVEN WICKETS OR MORE IN AN INNINGS

In addition to those listed above, the following have taken seven wickets or more in an innings:

For West Indies

8-38	L. R. Gibbs, Bridgetown	1961-62	9-95	J. M. Noreiga, Port-of-Spain	1970-71
7-98	L. R. Gibbs, Bombay	1974-75			

For India

7-162	S. P. Gupte, Port-of-Spain	1952-53	7-159	D. G. Phadkar, Madras	1948-49
7-48	Harbhajan Singh, Mumbai	2002-03			

WEST INDIES v PAKISTAN

Series notes: Pakistan have never won a series in the West Indies, though when they drew in 1987-88 they were the only team to avoid defeat between 1974 and 1994. West Indies have not won a series in Pakistan since 1980-81, and have won none of their seven Tests at Karachi. Pakistan have never won in eight Tests at Bridgetown and St John's. Pakistan lead 7–2 in the first Test of series between the sides, but West Indies lead 6– 4 in the second Test and 4–2 in the third. West Indies average 35.7 runs per wicket at home and 24.6 in Pakistan. Mohammad Yousuf is the top scorer with 1,214 runs at an average of 101.16.

		Captains				
Season	*West Indies*	*Pakistan*	*T*	*WI*	*P*	*D*
1957-58W	F. C. M. Alexander	A. H. Kardar	5	3	1	1
1958-59P	F. C. M. Alexander	Fazal Mahmood	3	1	2	0
1974-75P	C. H. Lloyd	Intikhab Alam	2	0	0	2
1976-77W	C. H. Lloyd	Mushtaq Mohammad	5	2	1	2
1980-81P	C. H. Lloyd	Javed Miandad	4	1	0	3
1986-87P	I. V. A. Richards	Imran Khan	3	1	1	1
1987-88W	I. V. A. Richards[1]	Imran Khan	3	1	1	1
1990-91P	D. L. Haynes	Imran Khan	3	1	1	1
1992-93W	R. B. Richardson	Wasim Akram	3	2	0	1
1997-98P	C. A. Walsh	Wasim Akram	3	0	3	0
1999-2000W	J. C. Adams	Moin Khan	3	1	0	2
2001-02U	C. L. Hooper	Waqar Younis	2	0	2	0
2004-05W	S. Chanderpaul	Inzamam-ul-Haq[2]	2	1	1	0
2006-07P	B. C. Lara	Inzamam-ul-Haq	3	0	2	1
	In West Indies		21	10	4	7
	In Pakistan		21	4	9	8
	In United Arab Emirates		2	0	2	0
	Totals		44	14	15	15

P Played in Pakistan.   W Played in West Indies.   U Played in United Arab Emirates.

Note: The following was appointed by the home authority for only a minor proportion of the series: [1]C. G. Greenidge (First). [2]Younis Khan (First).

HIGHEST INNINGS TOTALS

For West Indies in West Indies: 790-3 dec at Kingston............................	1957-58
in Pakistan: 591 at Multan.......................................	2006-07
in United Arab Emirates: 366 at Sharjah..........................	2001-02
For Pakistan in West Indies: 657-8 dec at Bridgetown	1957-58
in Pakistan: 485 at Lahore.......................................	2006-07
in United Arab Emirates: 493 at Sharjah	2001-02

LOWEST INNINGS TOTALS

For West Indies in West Indies: 127 at Port-of-Spain	1992-93
in Pakistan: 53 at Faisalabad	1986-87
in United Arab Emirates: 171 at Sharjah..........................	2001-02
For Pakistan in West Indies: 106 at Bridgetown	1957-58
in Pakistan: 77 at Lahore.......................................	1986-87
in United Arab Emirates: 472 at Sharjah	2001-02

DOUBLE-HUNDREDS

For West Indies (4)

365*	G. S. Sobers at Kingston	1957-58	217	R. B. Kanhai at Lahore	1958-59
260	C. C. Hunte at Kingston	1957-58	216	B. C. Lara at Multan	2006-07

For Pakistan (1)

337 Hanif Mohammad at Bridgetown. . 1957-58

INDIVIDUAL HUNDREDS

For West Indies (31)

4: B. C. Lara.
3: D. L. Haynes, C. L. Hooper, C. C. Hunte, G. S. Sobers.
2: I. V. A. Richards.
1: L. Baichan, S. Chanderpaul, P. J. L. Dujon, R. C. Fredericks, C. G. Greenidge, W. W. Hinds, B. D. Julien, A. I. Kallicharran, R. B. Kanhai, C. H. Lloyd, I. T. Shillingford, C. L. Walcott, E. D. Weekes.

For Pakistan (38)

7: Mohammad Yousuf.
4: Inzamam-ul-Haq.
2: Aamir Sohail, Hanif Mohammad, Javed Miandad, Majid Khan, Mushtaq Mohammad, Shahid Afridi, Wasim Raja, Wazir Mohammad, Younis Khan.
1: Asif Iqbal, Ijaz Ahmed, sen., Imran Khan, Imran Nazir, Imtiaz Ahmed, Mohammad Hafeez, Rashid Latif, Saeed Ahmed, Salim Malik.

TEN WICKETS OR MORE IN A MATCH

For Pakistan (4)

12-100 (6-34, 6-66)	Fazal Mahmood, Dacca	1958-59
11-121 (7-80, 4-41)	Imran Khan, Georgetown	1987-88
10-106 (5-35, 5-71)	Mushtaq Ahmed, Peshawar	1997-98
11-110 (6-61, 5-49)	Wasim Akram, St John's	1999-2000

For West Indies (1)

11-134 (7-78, 4-56)	C. D. Collymore at Kingston	2004-05

WEST INDIES v SRI LANKA

Series notes: West Indies have never won a Test in Sri Lanka. They have lost all three Tests where they won the toss and batted. Only ten of the 46 innings in this fixture have exceeded 300 (five for each side). M. Muralitharan has taken 82 wickets at an average of 19.62 in 12 Tests against West Indies; W. P. U. J. C. Vaas has taken 55 at 16.60 in nine Tests.

Season	West Indies	*Captains* Sri Lanka	T	WI	SL	D
1993-94*S*	R. B. Richardson	A. Ranatunga	1	0	0	1
1996-97*W*	C. A. Walsh	A. Ranatunga	2	1	0	1
2001-02*S*	C. L. Hooper	S. T. Jayasuriya	3	0	3	0
2003*W*	B. C. Lara	H. P. Tillekeratne	2	1	0	1
2005*S*	S. Chanderpaul	M. S. Atapattu	2	0	2	0
2007-08*W*	C. H. Gayle	D. P. M. D. Jayawardene	2	1	1	0
	In West Indies		6	3	1	2
	In Sri Lanka		6	0	5	1
	Totals		12	3	6	3

W Played in West Indies.   S Played in Sri Lanka.

HIGHEST INNINGS TOTALS

For West Indies in West Indies: 477-9 dec at Gros Islet, St Lucia.   2003
      in Sri Lanka: 448 at Galle   2001-02

For Sri Lanka in West Indies: 476-8 dec at Providence.   2007-08
      in Sri Lanka: 627-9 dec at Colombo (SSC)   2001-02

LOWEST INNINGS TOTALS

For West Indies in West Indies: 147 at St Vincent   1996-97
      in Sri Lanka: 113 at Colombo (SSC).   2005

For Sri Lanka in West Indies: 152 at St John's   1996-97
      in Sri Lanka: 150 at Kandy.   2005

DOUBLE-HUNDREDS

For West Indies (2)

221   B. C. Lara at Colombo (SSC). . . 2001-02 | 209   B. C. Lara at Gros Islet, St Lucia   2003

For Sri Lanka (1)

204*   H. P. Tillekeratne at Colombo (SSC).   2001-02

INDIVIDUAL HUNDREDS

For West Indies (7)

5: B. C. Lara.
1: W. W. Hinds, R. R. Sarwan.

For Sri Lanka (8)

2: K. C. Sangakkara, H. P. Tillekeratne.
1: M. S. Atapattu, D. P. M. D. Jayawardene, T. T. Samaraweera, B. S. M. Warnapura.

TEN WICKETS OR MORE IN A MATCH

For Sri Lanks (4)

11-170 (6-126, 5-44)	M. Muralitharan, Galle	2001-02
10-135 (4-54, 6-81)	M. Muralitharan, Kandy	2001-02
10-83 (2-37, 8-46)	M. Muralitharan at Kandy.	2005
14-191 (7-120, 7-71)	W. P. U. J. C. Vaas, Colombo (SSC)	2001-02

Note: The best match figures for West Indies are 9-85 (2-28, 7-57) by C. D. Collymore at Kingston, 2003.

WEST INDIES v ZIMBABWE

Series notes: West Indies have never lost a Test to Zimbabwe, and the two matches at Harare are the only ones in which Zimbabwe have not been beaten. Zimbabwe do outscore West Indies in centuries – six to four – though the three highest scores are all by West Indians.

Season	West Indies	Captains Zimbabwe	T	WI	Z	D
1999-2000W	J. C. Adams	A. Flower	2	2	0	0
2001Z	C. L. Hooper	H. H. Streak	2	1	0	1
2003-04Z	B. C. Lara	H. H. Streak	2	1	0	1
	In West Indies		2	2	0	0
	In Zimbabwe		4	2	0	2
	Totals		6	4	0	2

W Played in West Indies.   *Z Played in Zimbabwe.*

HIGHEST INNINGS TOTALS

For West Indies in West Indies: 339 at Kingston.............................. 1999-2000
                 in Zimbabwe: 559-6 dec at Bulawayo......................... 2001

For Zimbabwe in West Indies: 308 at Kingston 1999-2000
                in Zimbabwe: 563-9 dec at Harare 2001

LOWEST INNINGS TOTALS

For West Indies in West Indies: 147 at Port-of-Spain......................... 1999-2000
                 in Zimbabwe: 128 at Bulawayo............................... 2003-04

For Zimbabwe in West Indies: 63 at Port-of-Spain........................... 1999-2000
                in Zimbabwe: 104 at Bulawayo................................ 2003-04

HIGHEST INDIVIDUAL SCORES
For West Indies
191   B. C. Lara at Bulawayo........ 2003-04

For Zimbabwe
127*   H. H. Streak at Harare......... 2003-04

INDIVIDUAL HUNDREDS
For West Indies (4)
1: J. C. Adams, C. H. Gayle, C. L. Hooper, B. C. Lara.

For Zimbabwe (6)
1: A. D. R. Campbell, A. Flower, M. W. Goodwin, H. Masakadza, H. H. Streak, M. A. Vermeulen.

TEN WICKETS OR MORE IN A MATCH
For Zimbabwe
10-161 (6-73, 4-88)   R. W. Price, Harare...................................... 2003-04

Note: The best match figures for West Indies are 7-50 (4-42, 3-8) by C. E. L. Ambrose at Port-of-Spain, 1999-2000.

WEST INDIES v BANGLADESH

Series notes: West Indies are the only team to lose a Test and a series at home to Bangladesh. West Indies led on first innings in both their defeats. Bangladesh have batted first in five of the six Tests between the sides. They have recorded 19 ducks to West Indies' six. In two Tests at home to Bangladesh, R. R. Sarwan averages 301 with the bat and 13.12 with the ball.

		Captains				
Season	*West Indies*	*Bangladesh*	*T*	*WI*	*B*	*D*
2002-03*B*	R. D. Jacobs	Khaled Mashud	2	2	0	0
2003-04*W*	B. C. Lara	Habibul Bashar	2	1	0	1
2009*W*	**F. L. Reifer**	**Mashrafe bin Mortaza**[1]	**2**	**0**	**2**	**0**
	In West Indies....................		4	1	2	1
	In Bangladesh...................		2	2	0	0
	Totals...........................		**6**	**3**	**2**	**1**

B Played in Bangladesh.　W Played in West Indies.

Note: The following deputised for the official touring captain for a minor proportion of the series:
[1]Shakib Al Hasan (Second).

HIGHEST INNINGS TOTALS

For West Indies in West Indies: 559-4 dec at Kingston........................... 2003-04
　　　　　　　　　in Bangladesh: 536 at Dhaka.................................... 2002-03

For Bangladesh in West Indies: 416 at Gros Islet, St Lucia...................... 2003-04
　　　　　　　　　in Bangladesh: 212 at Chittagong 2002-03

LOWEST INNINGS TOTALS

For West Indies in West Indies: **181 at St Vincent**............................. **2009**
　　　　　　　　　in Bangladesh: 296 at Chittagong 2002-03

For Bangladesh in West Indies: 176 at Kingston................................. 2003-04
　　　　　　　　　in Bangladesh: 87 at Dhaka 2002-03

DOUBLE-HUNDRED

For West Indies (1)

261* R. R. Sarwan at Kingston 2003-04

Highest score for Bangladesh: **128 by Tamim Iqbal at St Vincent, 2009.**

INDIVIDUAL HUNDREDS

For West Indies (5)

2: R. R. Sarwan.
1: S. Chanderpaul, C. H. Gayle, B. C. Lara.

For Bangladesh (4)

1: Habibul Bashar, Khaled Mashud, Mohammad Rafique, **Tamim Iqbal**.

BEST BOWLING MATCH ANALYSES

For West Indies

9-117 (3-64, 6-53) P. T. Collins, Kingston 2003-04

For Bangladesh

6-117 (4-72, 2-45) Tapash Baisya, Chittagong 2002-03

Bold type denotes performances in the 2009 series or, in career figures, players who appeared in that series.

NEW ZEALAND v INDIA

Series notes: The team batting first have won none of the last 18 Tests between the sides. The away team have won just one of the last 20. Five of New Zealand's nine wins over India have come in the second Test of the series. New Zealand have lost only two of the last 14 Tests. R. Dravid is the only man to make twin centuries, at Hamilton in 1998-99.

		Captains				
Season	*New Zealand*	*India*	*T*	*NZ*	*I*	*D*
1955-56*I*	H. B. Cave	P. R. Umrigar[1]	5	0	2	3
1964-65*I*	J. R. Reid	Nawab of Pataudi jun.	4	0	1	3
1967-68*N*	G. T. Dowling[2]	Nawab of Pataudi jun.	4	1	3	0
1969-70*I*	G. T. Dowling	Nawab of Pataudi jun.	3	1	1	1
1975-76*N*	G. M. Turner	B. S. Bedi[3]	3	1	1	1
1976-77*I*	G. M. Turner	B. S. Bedi	3	0	2	1
1980-81*N*	G. P. Howarth	S. M. Gavaskar	3	1	0	2
1988-89*I*	J. G. Wright	D. B. Vengsarkar	3	1	2	0
1989-90*N*	J. G. Wright	M. Azharuddin	3	1	0	2
1993-94*N*	K. R. Rutherford	M. Azharuddin	1	0	0	1
1995-96*I*	L. K. Germon	M. Azharuddin	3	0	1	2
1998-99*N†*	S. P. Fleming	M. Azharuddin	2	1	0	1
1999-2000*I*	S. P. Fleming	S. R. Tendulkar	3	0	1	2
2002-03*N*	S. P. Fleming	S. C. Ganguly	2	2	0	0
2003-04*I*	S. P. Fleming	S. C. Ganguly[4]	2	0	0	2
2008-09*N*	**D. L. Vettori**	**M. S. Dhoni**[5]	**3**	**0**	**1**	**2**
	In India		26	2	10	14
	In New Zealand		**21**	**7**	**5**	**9**
	Totals		47	9	15	23

I Played in India.   N Played in New Zealand.

† *The First Test at Dunedin was abandoned without a ball being bowled and is excluded.*

Notes: The following deputised for the official touring captain or were appointed by the home authority for a minor proportion of the series:
[1]Ghulam Ahmed (First). [2]B. W. Sinclair (First). [3]S. M. Gavaskar (First). [4]R. Dravid (Second). [5]V. Sehwag (Second).

HIGHEST INNINGS TOTALS

For New Zealand in New Zealand: **619-9 dec at Napier** **2008-09**
                in India: 630-6 dec at Mohali 2003-04

For India in New Zealand: **520 at Hamilton** **2008-09**
                in India: 583-7 dec at Ahmedabad 1999-2000

LOWEST INNINGS TOTALS

For New Zealand in New Zealand: 94 at Hamilton   2002-03
                in India: 124 at Hyderabad   1988-89

For India in New Zealand: 81 at Wellington   1975-76
          in India: 83 at Mohali   1999-2000

DOUBLE-HUNDREDS

For New Zealand (3)

239	G. T. Dowling at Christchurch . . 1967-68	**201**	**J. D. Ryder at Napier** **2008-09**
230*	B. Sutcliffe at Delhi 1955-56		

For India (6)

231	V. Mankad at Madras 1955-56	222	R. Dravid at Ahmedabad 2003-04
223	V. Mankad at Bombay 1955-56	217	S. R. Tendulkar at Ahmedabad 1999-2000
223	P. R. Umrigar at Hyderabad 1955-56	200*	D. N. Sardesai at Bombay 1964-65

INDIVIDUAL HUNDREDS

For New Zealand (33)

3: G. T. Dowling, B. Sutcliffe, J. G. Wright.
2: J. R. Reid, **J. D. Ryder, L. R. P. L. Taylor**, G. M. Turner.
1: N. J. Astle, C. L. Cairns, M. D. Crowe, J. W. Guy, G. P. Howarth, A. H. Jones, **B. B. McCullum**, C. D. McMillan, J. M. Parker, J. F. Reid, M. H. Richardson, I. D. S. Smith, S. B. Styris, B. R. Taylor, **D. L. Vettori**, L. Vincent.

For India (40)

4: **R. Dravid, S. R. Tendulkar**.
3: S. C. Ganguly, V. L. Manjrekar.
2: M. Azharuddin, **G. Gambhir**, S. M. Gavaskar, **V. V. S. Laxman**, V. Mankad, Nawab of Pataudi, jun., Pankaj Roy, D. N. Sardesai.
1: S. Amarnath, C. G. Borde, A. G. Kripal Singh, G. S. Ramchand, S. Ramesh, **V. Sehwag**, N. S. Sidhu, P. R. Umrigar, G. R. Viswanath, A. L. Wadekar.

TEN WICKETS OR MORE IN A MATCH

For New Zealand (2)

11-58 (4-35, 7-23)	R. J. Hadlee, Wellington	1975-76
10-88 (6-49, 4-39)	R. J. Hadlee, Bombay	1988-89

For India (3)

10-134 (4-67, 6-67)	A. Kumble, Kanpur	1999-2000
11-140 (3-64, 8-76)	E. A. S. Prasanna, Auckland	1975-76
12-152 (8-72, 4-80)	S. Venkataraghavan, Delhi	1964-65

SEVEN WICKETS OR MORE IN AN INNINGS

In addition to those listed above, the following have taken seven wickets or more in an innings:

For New Zealand

7-65   S. B. Doull, Wellington 1998-99

For India

7-128 S. P. Gupte, Hyderabad........1955-56

Bold type denotes performances in the 2008-09 series or, in career figures, players who appeared in that series.

NEW ZEALAND v PAKISTAN

Series notes: New Zealand have won only two, and lost 12, of 22 Tests against Pakistan when they have batted first. Seven of the last 14 wins in this fixture, and ten of the last 21, have been achieved by sides trailing on first innings. New Zealand have failed to win in seven Tests at Wellington and six at Karachi. Pakistan lead 13-2 in Tests at home. Eight of the nine double-centuries have been made by Pakistanis. In two Tests against New Zealand, Shoaib Akhtar has taken 17 wickets at 5.23, with a wicket every 16.52 balls. Seven of his 17 were out for ducks, and nine were bowled. D. L. Vettori has taken 14 wickets in six Tests at 54.64.

		Captains				
Season	*New Zealand*	*Pakistan*	*T*	*NZ*	*P*	*D*
1955-56*P*	H. B. Cave	A. H. Kardar	3	0	2	1
1964-65*N*	J. R. Reid	Hanif Mohammad	3	0	0	3
1964-65*P*	J. R. Reid	Hanif Mohammad	3	0	2	1
1969-70*P*	G. T. Dowling	Intikhab Alam	3	1	0	2
1972-73*N*	B. E. Congdon	Intikhab Alam	3	0	1	2
1976-77*P*	G. M. Turner[1]	Mushtaq Mohammad	3	0	2	1
1978-79*N*	M. G. Burgess	Mushtaq Mohammad	3	0	1	2
1984-85*P*	J. V. Coney	Zaheer Abbas	3	0	2	1
1984-85*N*	G. P. Howarth	Javed Miandad	3	2	0	1
1988-89*N*†	J. G. Wright	Imran Khan	2	0	0	2
1990-91*P*	M. D. Crowe	Javed Miandad	3	0	3	0
1992-93*N*	K. R. Rutherford	Javed Miandad	1	0	1	0
1993-94*N*	K. R. Rutherford	Salim Malik	3	1	2	0
1995-96*N*	L. K. Germon	Wasim Akram	1	0	1	0
1996-97*P*	L. K. Germon	Saeed Anwar	2	1	1	0
2000-01*N*	S. P. Fleming	Moin Khan[2]	3	1	1	1
2002*P*‡	S. P. Fleming	Waqar Younis	1	0	1	0
2003-04*N*	S. P. Fleming	Inzamam-ul-Haq	2	0	1	1
2009-10*N*	**D. L. Vettori**	**Mohammad Yousuf**	**3**	**1**	**1**	**1**
	In Pakistan..................		21	2	13	6
	In New Zealand..............		**27**	**5**	**9**	**13**
	Totals..................		48	7	22	19

N Played in New Zealand.   P Played in Pakistan.

† *The First Test at Dunedin was abandoned without a ball being bowled and is excluded.*
‡ *The Second Test at Karachi was cancelled owing to civil disturbances.*

Note: The following were appointed by the home authority for only a minor proportion of the series or deputised for the official touring captain:
[1]J. M. Parker (Third). [2]Inzamam-ul-Haq (Third).

HIGHEST INNINGS TOTALS

For New Zealand in New Zealand: 563 at Hamilton............................... 2003-04
                in Pakistan: 482-6 dec at Lahore................................ 1964-65

For Pakistan in New Zealand: 616-5 dec at Auckland............................ 1988-89
                in Pakistan: 643 at Lahore... 2002

LOWEST INNINGS TOTALS

For New Zealand in New Zealand: 93 at Hamilton   1992-93
                in Pakistan: 70 at Dacca   1955-56

For Pakistan in New Zealand: 104 at Hamilton   2000-01
             in Pakistan: 102 at Faisalabad   1990-91

DOUBLE-HUNDREDS

For New Zealand (1)

204* M. S. Sinclair at Christchurch. . . 2000-01

For Pakistan (8)

329	Inzamam-ul-Haq at Lahore	2002	203*	Hanif Mohammad at Lahore	1964-65
271	Javed Miandad at Auckland	1988-89	203*	Shoaib Mohammad at Karachi . .	1990-91
209	Imtiaz Ahmed at Lahore	1955-56	203	Yousuf Youhana at Christchurch	2000-01
206	Javed Miandad at Karachi	1976-77	201	Mushtaq Mohammad at Dunedin	1972-73

INDIVIDUAL HUNDREDS

For New Zealand (27)

3: J. F. Reid.

2: M. G. Burgess, M. D. Crowe, **D. L. Vettori**.

1: M. D. Bell, J. V. Coney, B. A. Edgar, S. P. Fleming, M. J. Greatbatch, B. F. Hastings, G. P. Howarth, W. K. Lees, S. N. McGregor, R. E. Redmond, J. R. Reid, M. H. Richardson, B. W. Sinclair, M. S. Sinclair, S. A. Thomson, G. M. Turner, J. G. Wright, B. A. Young.

For Pakistan (50)

7: Javed Miandad.

5: Shoaib Mohammad.

3: Asif Iqbal, Hanif Mohammad, Inzamam-ul-Haq, Majid Khan, Mushtaq Mohammad.

2: Ijaz Ahmed, sen., Sadiq Mohammad, Saeed Anwar, Salim Malik.

1: Basit Ali, **Imran Farhat**, Imran Nazir, Imtiaz Ahmed, Mohammad Ilyas, Mohammad Wasim, **Mohammad Yousuf**, Moin Khan, Mudassar Nazar, Saeed Ahmed, Saqlain Mushtaq, **Umar Akmal**, Waqar Hassan, Younis Khan, Zaheer Abbas.

Note: Mushtaq and Sadiq Mohammad both hit hundreds at Hyderabad in 1976-77, the fourth time – after the Chappells (thrice) – that brothers had each scored hundreds in the same Test innings.

TEN WICKETS OR MORE IN A MATCH

For New Zealand (1)

11-152 (7-52, 4-100) C. Pringle, Faisalabad   1990-91

For Pakistan (11)

10-182 (5-91, 5-91)	Intikhab Alam, Dacca	1969-70
11-130 (7-52, 4-78)	Intikhab Alam, Dunedin	1972-73
11-130 (4-64, 7-66)†	Mohammad Zahid, Rawalpindi	1996-97
10-171 (3-115, 7-56)	Mushtaq Ahmed, Christchurch	1995-96
10-143 (4-59, 6-84)	Mushtaq Ahmed, Lahore	1996-97
11-78 (5-48, 6-30)	Shoaib Akhtar, Christchurch	2003-04
10-106 (3-20, 7-86)	Waqar Younis, Lahore	1990-91
12-130 (7-76, 5-54)	Waqar Younis, Faisalabad	1990-91
10-128 (5-56, 5-72)	Wasim Akram, Dunedin	1984-85
11-179 (4-60, 7-119)	Wasim Akram, Wellington	1993-94
11-79 (5-37, 6-42)†	Zulfiqar Ahmed, Karachi	1955-56

† *On first appearance in New Zealand–Pakistan Tests.*

Note: Waqar Younis's performances were in successive matches.

SEVEN WICKETS OR MORE IN AN INNINGS

In addition to those listed above, the following have taken seven wickets or more in an innings:

For New Zealand

7-87   S. L. Boock, Hyderabad 1984-85

For Pakistan

7-168 Danish Kaneria, Napier . . . . . **2009-10** | 7-74   Pervez Sajjad, Lahore 1969-70
7-99   Mohammad Nazir, Karachi . . . 1969-70 |

Bold type denotes performances in the 2009-10 series or, in career figures, players who appeared in that series.

NEW ZEALAND v SRI LANKA

Series notes: New Zealand have won only five of the last 21 Tests, having won four of the first five. Sri Lanka have won none of the five Tests in which they have chosen to field first. New Zealand's three highest individual scores have all come against Sri Lanka.

		Captains				
Season	*New Zealand*	*Sri Lanka*	*T*	*NZ*	*SL*	*D*
1982-83*N*	G. P. Howarth	D. S. de Silva	2	2	0	0
1983-84*S*	G. P. Howarth	L. R. D. Mendis	3	2	0	1
1986-87*S*†	J. J. Crowe	L. R. D. Mendis	1	0	0	1
1990-91*N*	M. D. Crowe[1]	A. Ranatunga	3	0	0	3
1992-93*S*	M. D. Crowe	A. Ranatunga	2	0	1	1
1994-95*N*	K. R. Rutherford	A. Ranatunga	2	0	1	1
1996-97*N*	S. P. Fleming	A. Ranatunga	2	2	0	0
1997-98*S*	S. P. Fleming	A. Ranatunga	3	1	2	0
2003*S*	S. P. Fleming	H. P. Tillekeratne	2	0	0	2
2004-05*N*	S. P. Fleming	M. S. Atapattu	2	1	0	1
2006-07*N*	S. P. Fleming	D. P. M. D. Jayawardene	2	1	1	0
2009*S*	**D. L. Vettori**	**K. C. Sangakkara**	**2**	**0**	**2**	**0**
	In New Zealand		13	6	2	5
	In Sri Lanka		**13**	**3**	**5**	**5**
	Totals		**26**	**9**	**7**	**10**

N Played in New Zealand.   S Played in Sri Lanka.

† *The Second and Third Tests were cancelled owing to civil disturbances.*

Note: The following was appointed by the home authority for only a minor proportion of the series:
   [1]I. D. S. Smith (Third).

HIGHEST INNINGS TOTALS

For New Zealand in New Zealand: 671-4 at Wellington 1990-91
   in Sri Lanka: 515-7 dec at Colombo (PSS) 2003

For Sri Lanka in New Zealand: 498 at Napier 2004-05
   in Sri Lanka: 483 at Colombo (PSS) 2003

LOWEST INNINGS TOTALS

For New Zealand in New Zealand: 109 at Napier 1994-95
                   in Sri Lanka: 102 at Colombo (SSC) 1992-93

For Sri Lanka in New Zealand: 93 at Wellington 1982-83
                in Sri Lanka: 97 at Kandy 1986-87

DOUBLE-HUNDREDS

For New Zealand (4)

299	M. D. Crowe at Wellington 1990-91	267* B. A. Young at Dunedin 1996-97
274*	S. P. Fleming at Colombo (PSS) 2003	224 L. Vincent at Wellington 2004-05

For Sri Lanka (2)

267   P. A. de Silva at Wellington .... 1990-91 | 201* D. S. B. P. Kuruppu at Colombo
                                                 | (CCC) 1986-87

INDIVIDUAL HUNDREDS

For New Zealand (18)

3: A. H. Jones.
2: M. D. Crowe, S. P. Fleming.
1: N. J. Astle, J. J. Crowe, R. J. Hadlee, C. D. McMillan, H. J. H. Marshall, J. F. Reid, K. R. Rutherford, **D. L. Vettori**, L. Vincent, J. G. Wright, B. A. Young.

For Sri Lanka (23)

3: A. P. Gurusinha, **D. P. M. D. Jayawardene, K. C. Sangakkara**.
2: P. A. de Silva, R. S. Mahanama, **T. T. Samaraweera**, H. P. Tillekeratne.
1: M. S. Atapattu, R. L. Dias, **T. M. Dilshan**, R. S. Kaluwitharana, D. S. B. P. Kuruppu, L. P. C. Silva.

Note: A. H. Jones and A. P. Gurusinha, on opposing sides, each hit two hundreds at Hamilton in 1990-91, the second time this had happened in Tests, after D. C. S. Compton and A. R. Morris, for England and Australia at Adelaide in 1946-47.

TEN WICKETS OR MORE IN A MATCH

For New Zealand (2)

10-102 (5-73, 5-29)   R. J. Hadlee, Colombo (CCC) 1983-84
10-183 (3-53, 7-130) D. L. Vettori, Wellington 2006-07

For Sri Lanka (2)

10-118 (4-31, 6-87)   M. Muralitharan, Wellington 2006-07
10-90 (5-47, 5-43)†   W. P. U. J. C. Vaas, Napier 1994-95

† *On first appearance in New Zealand–Sri Lanka Tests.*

Bold type denotes performances in the 2009 series or, in career figures, players who appeared in that series.

NEW ZEALAND v ZIMBABWE

Series notes: New Zealand have won six of the last seven Tests between the sides. The team winning the toss have batted first in ten of the 13 matches. In two Tests, S. E. Bond has taken 13 Zimbabwean wickets at an average of 9.23.

Season	*Captains* New Zealand	Zimbabwe	T	NZ	Z	D
1992-93Z	M. D. Crowe	D. L. Houghton	2	1	0	1
1995-96N	L. K. Germon	A. Flower	2	0	0	2
1997-98Z	S. P. Fleming	A. D. R. Campbell	2	0	0	2
1997-98N	S. P. Fleming	A. D. R. Campbell	2	2	0	0
2000-01Z	S. P. Fleming	H. H. Streak	2	2	0	0
2000-01N	S. P. Fleming	H. H. Streak	1	0	0	1
2005-06Z	S. P. Fleming	T. Taibu	2	2	0	0
	In New Zealand		5	2	0	3
	In Zimbabwe		8	5	0	3
	Totals		13	7	0	6

N Played in New Zealand. Z Played in Zimbabwe.

HIGHEST INNINGS TOTALS

For New Zealand in New Zealand: 487-7 dec at Wellington. 2000-01
in Zimbabwe: 484 at Bulawayo 2005-06

For Zimbabwe in New Zealand: 340-6 dec at Wellington 2000-01
in Zimbabwe: 461 at Bulawayo 1997-98

LOWEST INNINGS TOTALS

For New Zealand in New Zealand: 251 at Auckland 1995-96
in Zimbabwe: 207 at Harare 1997-98

For Zimbabwe in New Zealand: 170 at Auckland 1997-98
in Zimbabwe: 59 at Harare 2005-06

DOUBLE-HUNDRED

For Zimbabwe (1)

203* G. J. Whittall at Bulawayo 1997-98

Highest score for New Zealand: 157 by M. J. Horne at Auckland, 1997-98.

INDIVIDUAL HUNDREDS

For New Zealand (14)

3: N. J. Astle.
2: C. L. Cairns, M. J. Horne, C. D. McMillan.
1: M. D. Crowe, R. T. Latham, B. B. McCullum, C. M. Spearman, D. L. Vettori.

For Zimbabwe (6)

2: G. W. Flower, G. J. Whittall.
1: K. J. Arnott, D. L. Houghton.

TEN WICKETS OR MORE IN A MATCH

For New Zealand (1)

10-99 (6-51, 4-48)   S. E. Bond, Bulawayo.................................... 2005-06

For Zimbabwe (2)

11-255 (6-109, 5-146) A. G. Huckle, Bulawayo................................. 1997-98
10-158 (8-109, 2-49) P. A. Strang, Bulawayo................................. 2000-01

NEW ZEALAND v BANGLADESH

Series notes: Pending the one-off Test in 2009-10, New Zealand have been dismissed only four times in eight Tests; Bangladesh have been dismissed 14 times in their 15 innings and have never reached 300. D. L. Vettori has taken 46 wickets in Tests between the sides, more than three times the next best (C. S. Martin and I. E. O'Brien with 15). Vettori is also the second-highest run-scorer with 302, 95 behind S. P. Fleming. J. E. C. Franklin is the only man to take a hat-trick.

		Captains				
Season	*New Zealand*	*Bangladesh*	*T*	*NZ*	*B*	*D*
2001-02N	S. P. Fleming	Khaled Mashud	2	2	0	0
2004-05B	S. P. Fleming	Khaled Mashud	2	2	0	0
2007-08N	D. L. Vettori	Mohammad Ashraful	2	2	0	0
2008-09B	D. L. Vettori	Mohammad Ashraful	2	1	0	1
	In New Zealand		4	4	0	0
	In Bangladesh........................		4	3	0	1
	Totals		8	7	0	1

B Played in Bangladesh.   N Played in New Zealand.

HIGHEST INNINGS TOTALS

For New Zealand in New Zealand: 393 at Wellington 2007-08
               in Bangladesh: 545-6 at Chittagong 2004-05

For Bangladesh in New Zealand: 254 at Dunedin (Univ) 2007-08
               in Bangladesh: 262 at Chittagong 2004-05

LOWEST INNINGS TOTALS

For New Zealand in New Zealand: 357 at Dunedin (Univ)......................... 2007-08
               in Bangladesh: 171 at Chittagong 2008-09

For Bangladesh in New Zealand: 108 at Hamilton 2001-02
               in Bangladesh: 126 at Dhaka.................................... 2004-05

DOUBLE-HUNDRED

For New Zealand (1)

202   S. P. Fleming at Chittagong 2004-05

Highest score for Bangladesh: 84 by Tamim Iqbal at Dunedin (Univ), 2007-08.

INDIVIDUAL HUNDREDS

For New Zealand (6)

1: M. D. Bell, S. P. Fleming, B. B. McCullum, C. D. McMillan, J. D. P. Oram, M. H. Richardson.

TEN WICKETS OR MORE IN A MATCH

For New Zealand (1)

12-170 (6-70, 6-100) D. L. Vettori, Chittagong 2004-05

Note: The best match figures for Bangladesh are 9-115 (7-36, 2-79) by Shakib Al Hasan at Chittagong, 2008-09.

SEVEN WICKETS OR MORE IN AN INNINGS

For New Zealand

7-53 C. L. Cairns, Hamilton 2001-02

For Bangladesh

7-36 Shakib Al Hasan, Chittagong . . . 2008-09

INDIA v PAKISTAN

Series notes: India have scored 600 in five of the last 12 Tests against Pakistan. Their two victories in 2003-04 were their first in Pakistan after 20 without success. 64% of Tests between these sides have been drawn. There have been ten positive results in the last 15 Tests; this follows a run of 15 draws out of 16. Pakistan have never lost in six Tests when they have elected to field. They are unbeaten in five Tests at Bangalore, but have not won in five at Delhi. Younis Khan averages 88.06 from nine Tests against India, V. Sehwag 91.14 from nine against Pakistan. Younis Khan and Mohammed Yousuf average 171.50 from nine partnerships against India, a record for any partnership that has produced 1,000 runs against one country.

		Captains				
Season	*India*	*Pakistan*	*T*	*I*	*P*	*D*
1952-53*I*	L. Amarnath	A. H. Kardar	5	2	1	2
1954-55*P*	V. Mankad	A. H. Kardar	5	0	0	5
1960-61*I*	N. J. Contractor	Fazal Mahmood	5	0	0	5
1978-79*P*	B. S. Bedi	Mushtaq Mohammad	3	0	2	1
1979-80*I*	S. M. Gavaskar[1]	Asif Iqbal	6	2	0	4
1982-83*P*	S. M. Gavaskar	Imran Khan	6	0	3	3
1983-84*I*	Kapil Dev	Zaheer Abbas	3	0	0	3
1984-85*P*	S. M. Gavaskar	Zaheer Abbas	2	0	0	2
1986-87*I*	Kapil Dev	Imran Khan	5	0	1	4
1989-90*P*	K. Srikkanth	Imran Khan	4	0	0	4
1998-99*I*	M. Azharuddin	Wasim Akram	2	1	1	0
1998-99*I*†	M. Azharuddin	Wasim Akram	1	0	1	0
2003-04*P*	S. C. Ganguly[2]	Inzamam-ul-Haq	3	2	1	0
2004-05*I*	S. C. Ganguly	Inzamam-ul-Haq	3	1	1	1
2005-06*P*	R. Dravid	Inzamam-ul-Haq[3]	3	0	1	2
2007-08*I*	A. Kumble	Shoaib Malik[4]	3	1	0	2
	In India		33	7	5	21
	In Pakistan		26	2	7	17
	Totals		59	9	12	38

I Played in India. P Played in Pakistan.

† *This Test was part of the Asian Test Championship and was not counted as part of the preceding bilateral series.*

Note: The following were appointed by the home authority for only a minor proportion of the series or deputised for the official touring captain:
[1]G. R. Viswanath (Sixth). [2]R. Dravid (First and Second). [3]Younis Khan (Third). [4]Younis Khan (Second and Third).

HIGHEST INNINGS TOTALS

For India in India: 626 at Bangalore 2007-08
        in Pakistan: 675-5 dec at Multan 2003-04

For Pakistan in India: 570 at Bangalore. 2004-05
        in Pakistan: 699-5 at Lahore 1989-90

LOWEST INNINGS TOTALS

For India in India: 106 at Lucknow 1952-53
        in Pakistan: 145 at Karachi. 1954-55

For Pakistan in India: 116 at Bangalore. 1986-87
        in Pakistan: 158 at Dacca 1954-55

DOUBLE-HUNDREDS

For India (8)

309	V. Sehwag at Multan	2003-04	218	S. V. Manjrekar at Lahore	1989-90
270	R. Dravid at Rawalpindi	2003-04	202	Wasim Jaffer at Kolkata	2007-08
254	V. Sehwag at Lahore.	2005-06	201	A. D. Gaekwad at Jullundur	1983-84
239	S. C. Ganguly at Bangalore	2007-08	201	V. Sehwag at Bangalore	2004-05

For Pakistan (7)

280*	Javed Miandad at Hyderabad	1982-83	215	Zaheer Abbas at Lahore	1982-83
267	Younis Khan at Bangalore	2004-05	210	Qasim Omar at Faisalabad	1984-85
235*	Zaheer Abbas at Lahore	1978-79	203*	Shoaib Mohammad at Lahore	1989-90
231	Mudassar Nazar at Hyderabad	1982-83			

INDIVIDUAL HUNDREDS

For India (51)

5: R. Dravid, S. M. Gavaskar, P. R. Umrigar.
4: M. Amarnath, V. Sehwag.
3: M. Azharuddin, R. J. Shastri, Yuvraj Singh.
2: S. C. Ganguly, S. V. Manjrekar, S. R. Tendulkar, D. B. Vengsarkar.
1: C. G. Borde, M. S. Dhoni, A. D. Gaekwad, V. S. Hazare, V. V. S. Laxman, I. K. Pathan, S. M. Patil, R. H. Shodhan, K. Srikkanth, G. R. Viswanath, Wasim Jaffer.

For Pakistan (65)

6: Mudassar Nazar, Zaheer Abbas.
5: Javed Miandad, Younis Khan.
4: Kamran Akmal, Mohammad Yousuf.
3: Imran Khan, Inzamam-ul-Haq, Salim Malik, Shahid Afridi.
2: Aamer Malik, Hanif Mohammad, Misbah-ul-Haq, Saeed Ahmed, Shoaib Mohammad.
1: Alim-ud-Din, Asif Iqbal, Faisal Iqbal, Ijaz Faqih, Imran Farhat, Imtiaz Ahmed, Mohsin Khan, Mushtaq Mohammad, Nazar Mohammad, Qasim Omar, Ramiz Raja, Saeed Anwar, Wasim Raja.

TEN WICKETS OR MORE IN A MATCH

For India (6)

11-146 (4-90, 7-56)	Kapil Dev, Madras	1979-80
14-149 (4-75, 10-74)	A. Kumble, Delhi.	1998-99
10-161 (3-98, 7-63)	A. Kumble, Kolkata.	2004-05

10-126 (7-27, 3-99)	Maninder Singh, Bangalore	1986-87
13-131 (8-52, 5-79)†	V. Mankad, Delhi	1952-53
13-132 (5-46, 8-86)	J. Srinath, Calcutta	1998-99

For Pakistan (7)

12-94 (5-52, 7-42)	Fazal Mahmood, Lucknow	1952-53
11-79 (3-19, 8-60)	Imran Khan, Karachi	1982-83
11-180 (6-98, 5-82)	Imran Khan, Faisalabad	1982-83
10-175 (4-135, 6-40)	Iqbal Qasim, Bombay	1979-80
10-187 (5-94, 5-93)†	Saqlain Mushtaq, Chennai	1998-99
10-216 (5-94, 5-122)	Saqlain Mushtaq, Delhi	1998-99
11-190 (8-69, 3-121)	Sikander Bakht, Delhi	1979-80

† *On first appearance in India–Pakistan Tests.*

SEVEN WICKETS OR MORE IN AN INNINGS

In addition to those listed above, the following have taken seven wickets or more in an innings:

For India

7-220 Kapil Dev, Faisalabad .... 1982-83 | 8-85 Kapil Dev, Lahore 1982-83

INDIA v SRI LANKA

Series notes: Sri Lanka have never won a Test in India. In 17 Tests there, India average 49.8 runs per wicket and Sri Lanka 27.4. Of India's ten victories at home to Sri Lanka, eight have been by an innings. India have scored in excess of 400 in each of their last four innings, having failed to do so in their previous 18 attempts. S. R. Tendulkar is the top scorer with 1,605 runs. M. Muralitharan is the leading wicket-taker with 97, though they have come at an average of 33.34, his highest against any country except Australia. T. T. Samaraweera averages 115.33 from four Tests at home to India but just 24.12 from six Tests away. Nobody has hit more sixes against Sri Lanka than N. S. Sidhu's 18, or taken more than M. Azharuddin's 27 outfield catches.

Season	India	*Captains* Sri Lanka	T	I	SL	D
1982-83*I*	S. M. Gavaskar	B. Warnapura	1	0	0	1
1985-86*S*	Kapil Dev	L. R. D. Mendis	3	0	1	2
1986-87*I*	Kapil Dev	L. R. D. Mendis	3	2	0	1
1990-91*I*	M. Azharuddin	A. Ranatunga	1	1	0	0
1993-94*S*	M. Azharuddin	A. Ranatunga	3	1	0	2
1993-94*I*	M. Azharuddin	A. Ranatunga	3	3	0	0
1997-98*S*	S. R. Tendulkar	A. Ranatunga	2	0	0	2
1997-98*I*	S. R. Tendulkar	A. Ranatunga	3	0	0	3
1998-99*S*†	M. Azharuddin	A. Ranatunga	1	0	0	1
2001*S*	S. C. Ganguly	S. T. Jayasuriya	3	1	2	0
2005-06*I*	R. Dravid[1]	M. S. Atapattu	3	2	0	1
2008*S*	A. Kumble	D. P. M. D. Jayawardene	3	1	2	0
2009-10*I*	**M. S. Dhoni**	**K. C. Sangakkara**	**3**	**2**	**0**	**1**
	In India		17	10	0	7
	In Sri Lanka		15	3	5	7
	Totals		32	13	5	14

I Played in India.   S Played in Sri Lanka.

† *This Test was part of the Asian Test Championship.*

Note: The following was appointed by the home authority for only a minor proportion of the series:
  [1]V. Sehwag (Third).

HIGHEST INNINGS TOTALS

For India in India: **726-9 dec at Mumbai (BS)**.................................. **2009-10**
      in Sri Lanka: 537-8 dec at Colombo (RPS) 1997-98

For Sri Lanka in India: **760-7 dec at Ahmedabad** **2009-10**
      in Sri Lanka: 952-6 dec at Colombo (RPS) 1997-98

LOWEST INNINGS TOTALS

For India in India: 167 at Chennai... 2005-06
      in Sri Lanka: 138 at Colombo (SSC) 2008

For Sri Lanka in India: 82 at Chandigarh................................... 1990-91
      in Sri Lanka: 136 at Galle 2008

DOUBLE-HUNDREDS

For India (2)

293	V. Sehwag at Mumbai (BS) ... **2009-10**	201* V. Sehwag at Galle 2008

For Sri Lanka (4)

340	S. T. Jayasuriya at Colombo (RPS) 1997-98	242	D. P. M. D. Jayawardene at Colombo (SSC). 1998-99
275	**D. P. M. D. Jayawardene at Ahmedabad 2009-10**	225	R. S. Mahanama at Colombo (RPS) 1997-98

INDIVIDUAL HUNDREDS

For India (42)

8: **S. R. Tendulkar.**
5: M. Azharuddin.
4: N. S. Sidhu.
3: **R. Dravid**, S. C. Ganguly, **V. Sehwag**.
2: M. Amarnath, **M. S. Dhoni, G. Gambhir**, S. M. Gavaskar, V. G. Kambli, D. B. Vengsarkar.
1: Kapil Dev, **V. V. S. Laxman**, S. M. Patil, S. Ramesh.

For Sri Lanka (35)

5: P. A. de Silva, **D. P. M. D. Jayawardene**.
3: **T. M. Dilshan**, S. T. Jayasuriya, L. R. D. Mendis, **K. C. Sangakkara**.
2: M. S. Atapattu, R. S. Mahanama, **T. T. Samaraweera**.
1: R. L. Dias, **H. A. P. W. Jayawardene**, R. S. Madugalle, A. Ranatunga, S. A. R. Silva, H. P. Tillekeratne, B. S. M. Warnapura.

TEN WICKETS OR MORE IN A MATCH

For India (6)

10-141 (7-62, 3-79)	Harbhajan Singh, Ahmedabad.........................	2005-06
10-153 (6-102, 4-51)	Harbhajan Singh, Galle	2008
11-128 (4-69, 7-59)	A. Kumble, Lucknow	1993-94

10-157 (6-72, 4-85)	A. Kumble, Delhi	2005-06
10-107 (3-56, 7-51)	Maninder Singh, Nagpur	1986-87
11-125 (5-38, 6-87)	S. L. V. Raju, Ahmedabad	1993-94

For Sri Lanka (3)

10-209 (6-117, 4-92)	B. A. W. Mendis, Galle	2008
11-196 (8-87, 3-109)	M. Muralitharan, Colombo (SSC)	2001
11-110 (5-84, 6-26)	M. Muralitharan, Colombo (SSC)	2008

SEVEN WICKETS OR MORE IN AN INNINGS

In addition to those listed above, the following has taken seven wickets or more in an innings:

For Sri Lanka

7-100 M. Muralitharan, Delhi 2005-06

Bold type denotes performances in the 2009-10 series or, in career figures, players who appeared in that series.

INDIA v ZIMBABWE

Series notes: Both of Zimbabwe's victories over India have come at Harare, while India have won all three matches at Delhi. The team batting second have won each of the last six Tests. In two games at Nagpur, India average 90.6 runs per wicket and Zimbabwe 37.6. The seven highest individual scores were all made at Nagpur or Delhi. I. K. Pathan has taken 21 wickets at 11.28 against Zimbabwe. A. Flower is the only man with 1,000 runs in Tests between these sides; he scored 1,138 at 94.83 in nine matches, including 820 at 117.14 from five Tests in India.

| | | *Captains* | | | | |
Season	India	Zimbabwe	T	I	Z	D
1992-93Z	M. Azharuddin	D. L. Houghton	1	0	0	1
1992-93I	M. Azharuddin	D. L. Houghton	1	1	0	0
1998-99Z	M. Azharuddin	A. D. R. Campbell	1	0	1	0
2000-01I	S. C. Ganguly	H. H. Streak	2	1	0	1
2001Z	S. C. Ganguly	H. H. Streak	2	1	1	0
2001-02I	S. C. Ganguly	S. V. Carlisle	2	2	0	0
2005-06Z	S. C. Ganguly	T. Taibu	2	2	0	0
In India			5	4	0	1
In Zimbabwe			6	3	2	1
Totals			11	7	2	2

I Played in India.   Z Played in Zimbabwe.

HIGHEST INNINGS TOTALS

| For India in India: 609-6 dec at Nagpur | 2000-01 |
| in Zimbabwe: 554 at Bulawayo | 2005-06 |

| For Zimbabwe in India: 503-6 at Nagpur | 2000-01 |
| in Zimbabwe: 456 at Harare | 1992-93 |

LOWEST INNINGS TOTALS

| For India in India: 354 at Delhi | 2001-02 |
| in Zimbabwe: 173 at Harare | 1998-99 |

For Zimbabwe in India: 146 at Delhi... 2001-02
         in Zimbabwe: 161 at Harare 2005-06

DOUBLE-HUNDREDS

For India (3)

227   V. G. Kambli at Delhi......... 1992-93 | 200* R. Dravid at Delhi........... 2000-01
201* S. R. Tendulkar at Nagpur ..... 2000-01 |

For Zimbabwe (1)

232* A. Flower at Nagpur.......... 2000-01

INDIVIDUAL HUNDREDS

For India (14)

3: R. Dravid, S. R. Tendulkar.
2: S. S. Das, S. C. Ganguly.
1: S. B. Bangar, V. G. Kambli, V. V. S. Laxman, S. V. Manjrekar.

For Zimbabwe (6)

3: A. Flower.
1: A. D. R. Campbell, G. W. Flower, D. L. Houghton.

TEN WICKETS OR MORE IN A MATCH

For India (1)

12-126 (7-59, 5-67)   I. K. Pathan at Harare.................................. 2005-06

Note: The best match figures for Zimbabwe are 7-115 (3-69, 4-46) by H. H. Streak at Harare, 2001.

INDIA v BANGLADESH

Series notes: The sides have yet to meet in a Test in India. India average 52.1 runs per wicket against Bangladesh's 23.7. S. R. Tendulkar has played in all seven Tests, and scored 820 runs at 136.66. In two Tests, I. K. Pathan has taken 18 wickets at 11.88.

		Captains				
Season	*India*	*Bangladesh*	*T*	*I*	*B*	*D*
2000-01*B*	S. C. Ganguly	Naimur Rahman	1	1	0	0
2004-05*B*	S. C. Ganguly	Habibul Bashar	2	2	0	0
2007*B*	R. Dravid	Habibul Bashar	2	1	0	1
2009-10*B*	**M. S. Dhoni[1]**	**Shakib Al Hasan**	**2**	**2**	**0**	**0**
	In Bangladesh.....................		**7**	**6**	**0**	**1**

B Played in Bangladesh.

Note: The following deputised for the official touring captain for a minor proportion of the series:
  [1]V. Sehwag (First).

HIGHEST INNINGS TOTALS

For India: 610-3 dec at Mirpur 2007

For Bangladesh: 400 at Dhaka 2000-01

LOWEST INNINGS TOTALS

For India: **243 at Chittagong** **2009-10**

For Bangladesh: 91 at Dhaka 2000-01

DOUBLE-HUNDRED

For India (1)

248* S. R. Tendulkar at Dhaka 2004-05

Highest score for Bangladesh: 158* by Mohammad Ashraful at Chittagong, 2004-05.

INDIVIDUAL HUNDREDS

For India (13)

5: S. R. Tendulkar.
3: R. Dravid.
2: G. Gambhir.
1: S. C. Ganguly, **K. D. Karthik**, Wasim Jaffer.

For Bangladesh (4)

1: Aminul Islam, **Mohammad Ashraful, Mushfiqur Rahim, Tamim Iqbal**.

TEN WICKETS OR MORE IN A MATCH

For India (1)

11-96 (5-45, 6-51) I. K. Pathan, Dhaka 2004-05
10-149 (3-62, 7-87) Zaheer Khan, Mirpur **2009-10**

Note: The best match figures for Bangladesh are **7-174 (5-62, 2-112) by Shakib Al Hasan at Chittagong, 2009-10**.

Bold type denotes performances in the 2009-10 series or, in career figures, players who appeared in that series.

PAKISTAN v SRI LANKA

Series notes: Six of Sri Lanka's nine victories have come away from home. Six of Pakistan's 15 wins have been by an innings, while Sri Lanka have never beaten them by an innings. Sri Lanka have won only 13% of the Tests in which they have won the toss and batted (two of 15), but 50% when they have won the toss and fielded (three of six). In two Tests against Sri Lanka, Mohammad Asif has taken 17 wickets at 10.76, with a strike-rate of one every 26.1 balls.

Captains

Season	Pakistan	Sri Lanka	T	P	SL	D
1981-82*P*	Javed Miandad	B. Warnapura[1]	3	2	0	1
1985-86*P*	Javed Miandad	L. R. D. Mendis	3	2	0	1
1985-86*S*	Imran Khan	L. R. D. Mendis	3	1	1	1
1991-92*P*	Imran Khan	P. A. de Silva	3	1	0	2
1994-95*S*†	Salim Malik	A. Ranatunga	2	2	0	0
1995-96*P*	Ramiz Raja	A. Ranatunga	3	1	2	0
1996-97*S*	Ramiz Raja	A. Ranatunga	2	0	0	2
1998-99*P*‡	Wasim Akram	H. P. Tillekeratne	1	0	0	1
1998-99*B*‡	Wasim Akram	P. A. de Silva	1	1	0	0
1999-2000*P*	Saeed Anwar [2]	S. T. Jayasuriya	3	1	2	0
2000*S*	Moin Khan	S. T. Jayasuriya	3	2	0	1
2001-02*P*‡	Waqar Younis	S. T. Jayasuriya	1	0	1	0
2004-05*P*	Inzamam-ul-Haq	M. S. Atapattu	2	1	1	0
2005-06*S*	Inzamam-ul-Haq	D. P. M. D. Jayawardene	2	1	0	1
2008-09*P*§	**Younis Khan**	**D. P. M. D. Jayawardene**	**2**	**0**	**0**	**2**
2009*S*	**Younis Khan**	**K. C. Sangakkara**	**3**	**0**	**2**	**1**
	In Pakistan		21	8	6	7
	In Sri Lanka		15	6	3	6
	In Bangladesh........................		1	1	0	0
	Totals		**37**	**15**	**9**	**13**

P Played in Pakistan.   S Played in Sri Lanka.   B Played in Bangladesh.

† *One Test was cancelled owing to the threat of civil disturbances following a general election.*
‡ *These Tests were part of the Asian Test Championship.*
§ *The Second Test ended after a terrorist attack on the Sri Lankan team bus on the third day.*

Note: The following deputised for the official touring captain or were appointed by the home authority for only a minor proportion of the series:
[1]L. R. D. Mendis (Second). [2]Moin Khan (Third).

HIGHEST INNINGS TOTALS

For Pakistan in Pakistan: **765-6 dec at Karachi** **2008-09**
    in Sri Lanka: 600-8 dec at Galle 2000
    in Bangladesh: 594 at Dhaka................................. 1998-99

For Sri Lanka in Pakistan: **644-7 dec at Karachi** **2008-09**
    in Sri Lanka: 467-5 at Kandy 2000

LOWEST INNINGS TOTALS

For Pakistan in Pakistan: 182 at Rawalpindi 1999-2000
    in Sri Lanka: **90 at Colombo** **2009**

For Sri Lanka in Pakistan: 149 at Karachi 1981-82
    in Sri Lanka: 71 at Kandy 1994-95

DOUBLE-HUNDREDS

For Pakistan (5)

313	**Younis Khan at Karachi**......	**2008-09**	203*	Javed Miandad at Faisalabad	...	1985-86
211	Ijaz Ahmed, sen. at Dhaka	1998-99	200*	Inzamam-ul-Haq at Dhaka	.....	1998-99
206	Qasim Omar at Faisalabad	1985-86				

For Sri Lanka (6)

253	S. T. Jayasuriya at Faisalabad... 2004-05	230	K. C. Sangakkara at Lahore 2001-02
240	**D. P. M. D. Jayawardene at**	**214**	**T. T. Samaraweera at Lahore..... 2008-09**
	Karachi 2008-09	207*	M. S. Atapattu at Kandy 2000
231	**T. T. Samaraweera at Karachi 2008-09**		

INDIVIDUAL HUNDREDS

For Pakistan (31)

5: Inzamam-ul-Haq.
4: **Younis Khan**.
3: Salim Malik.
2: Ijaz Ahmed, sen., Saeed Anwar, **Shoaib Malik**, Wajahatullah Wasti.
1: **Fawad Alam**, Haroon Rashid, Javed Miandad, **Kamran Akmal**, **Mohammad Yousuf**, Mohsin Khan, Moin Khan, Qasim Omar, Ramiz Raja, Wasim Akram, Zaheer Abbas.

For Sri Lanka (31)

8: P. A. de Silva.
5: **K. C. Sangakkara**.
4: S. T. Jayasuriya.
3: **T. T. Samaraweera**.
2: H. P. Tillekeratne.
1: R. P. Arnold, M. S. Atapattu, R. L. Dias, **T. M. Dilshan**, A. P. Gurusinha, **D. P. M. D. Jayawardene**, R. S. Kaluwitharana, A. Ranatunga, S. Wettimuny.

TEN WICKETS OR MORE IN A MATCH

For Pakistan (4)

10-190 (3-72, 7-118)	Danish Kaneria, Karachi	2004-05
14-116 (8-58, 6-58)	Imran Khan, Lahore.....................................	1981-82
11-71 (6-44, 5-27)	Mohammad Asif, Kandy	2005-06
11-119 (6-34, 5-85)	Waqar Younis, Kandy	1994-95

For Sri Lanka (1)

10-148 (4-77, 6-71)	M. Muralitharan, Peshawar.............................	1999-2000

SEVEN WICKETS OR MORE IN AN INNINGS

In addition to those listed above, the following has taken seven wickets or more in an innings:

For Sri Lanka

8-83 J. R. Ratnayeke, Sialkot 1985-86

Bold type denotes performances in the 2008-09 or 2009 series or, in career figures, players who appeared in those series.

PAKISTAN v ZIMBABWE

Series notes: Zimbabwe have won the toss in 11 of the 14 Tests. Pakistan have a worse record at home to Zimbabwe (three wins and one defeat from seven matches) than away (five wins and one defeat from seven). Zimbabwe are the only team with an innings win. The team batting first have won only one of the last eight matches. Pakistan lead 3–1 in Tests at Harare, but Zimbabwe have a higher runs-per-wicket average there (31.3 to 28.0).

		Captains				
Season	*Pakistan*	*Zimbabwe*	*T*	*P*	*Z*	*D*
1993-94*P*	Wasim Akram[1]	A. Flower	3	2	0	1
1994-95*Z*	Salim Malik	A. Flower	3	2	1	0
1996-97*P*	Wasim Akram	A. D. R. Campbell	2	1	0	1
1997-98*Z*	Rashid Latif	A. D. R. Campbell	2	1	0	1
1998-99*P*†	Aamir Sohail[2]	A. D. R. Campbell	2	0	1	1
2002-03*Z*	Waqar Younis	A. D. R. Campbell	2	2	0	0
	In Pakistan		7	3	1	3
	In Zimbabwe		7	5	1	1
	Totals		14	8	2	4

P Played in Pakistan.   Z Played in Zimbabwe.

† *The Third Test at Faisalabad was abandoned without a ball being bowled and is excluded.*

Notes: The following were appointed by the home authority for only a minor proportion of the series:
  [1]Waqar Younis (First). [2]Moin Khan (Second).

HIGHEST INNINGS TOTALS

For Pakistan in Pakistan: 553 at Sheikhupura 1996-97
           in Zimbabwe: 403 at Bulawayo 2002-03

For Zimbabwe in Pakistan: 375 at Sheikhupura 1996-97
            in Zimbabwe: 544-4 dec at Harare 1994-95

LOWEST INNINGS TOTALS

For Pakistan in Pakistan: 103 at Peshawar...................................... 1998-99
           in Zimbabwe: 158 at Harare 1994-95

For Zimbabwe in Pakistan: 133 at Faisalabad 1996-97
            in Zimbabwe: 139 at Harare 1994-95

DOUBLE-HUNDREDS

For Pakistan (1)

257* Wasim Akram at Sheikhupura . . 1996-97

For Zimbabwe (1)

201* G. W. Flower at Harare........ 1994-95

INDIVIDUAL HUNDREDS

For Pakistan (7)

2: Inzamam-ul-Haq, Yousuf Youhana.
1: Mohammad Wasim, Taufeeq Umar, Wasim Akram.

For Zimbabwe (9)

3: G. W. Flower.
2: A. Flower.
1: M. W. Goodwin, N. C. Johnson, P. A. Strang, G. J. Whittall.

TEN WICKETS OR MORE IN A MATCH

For Pakistan (3)

10-155 (7-66, 3-89)   Saqlain Mushtaq, Bulawayo.   2002-03
13-135 (7-91, 6-44)† Waqar Younis, Karachi (DS).   1993-94
10-106 (6-48, 4-58)   Wasim Akram, Faisalabad   1996-97

Note: The best match figures for Zimbabwe are 9-105 (6-90, 3-15) by H. H. Streak at Harare, 1994-95.

† *On first appearance in Pakistan–Zimbabwe Tests.*

PAKISTAN v BANGLADESH

Series notes: Bangladesh have batted first in all six Tests between these sides. Pakistan have been bowled out only three times, while dismissing Bangladesh twice in each game. Inzamam-ul-Haq averaged 253 against Bangladesh in two Tests on his home ground at Multan. Mohammad Yousuf (formerly known as Yousuf Youhana) averages 251.50 against Bangladesh. Yasir Hameed is the only man to score twin hundreds in a Test, at Karachi in 2003, and Bangladesh leg-spinner Alok Kapali is the only man to take a hat-trick, at Peshawar in the same series.

Season	Pakistan	*Captains* Bangladesh	T	P	B	D
2001-02*P*†	Waqar Younis	Naimur Rahman	1	1	0	0
2001-02*B*	Waqar Younis	Khaled Mashud	2	2	0	0
2003*P*	Rashid Latif	Khaled Mahmud	3	3	0	0
	In Pakistan		4	4	0	0
	In Bangladesh.		2	2	0	0
	Totals		6	6	0	0

P Played in Pakistan. B Played in Bangladesh.

† *This Test was part of the Asian Test Championship.*

HIGHEST INNINGS TOTALS

For Pakistan in Pakistan: 546-3 dec at Multan.   2001-02
            in Bangladesh: 490-9 dec at Dhaka.   2001-02

For Bangladesh in Pakistan: 361 at Peshawar   2003
            in Bangladesh: 160 at Dhaka   2001-02

LOWEST INNINGS TOTALS

For Pakistan in Pakistan: 175 at Multan.   2003

For Bangladesh in Pakistan: 96 at Peshawar   2003
            in Bangladesh: 148 at Chittagong (in both innings)   2001-02

DOUBLE-HUNDRED

For Pakistan (1)

204* Yousuf Youhana at Chittagong . 2001-02

Highest score for Bangladesh: 119 by Javed Omar at Peshawar, 2003.

INDIVIDUAL HUNDREDS

For Pakistan (12)

2: Abdul Razzaq, Inzamam-ul-Haq, Yasir Hameed, Yousuf Youhana.
1: Mohammad Hafeez, Saeed Anwar, Taufeeq Umar, Younis Khan.

For Bangladesh (2)

1: Habibul Bashar, Javed Omar.

Note: Yasir Hameed and L. G. Rowe (for West Indies v New Zealand) are the only two batsmen to score two hundreds in their first Test.

TEN WICKETS OR MORE IN A MATCH

For Pakistan (2)

12-94 (6-42, 6-52)†	Danish Kaneria, Multan	2001-02
10-80 (6-50, 4-30)	Shoaib Akhtar, Peshawar	2003

Note: The best match figures for Bangladesh are 7-105 (4-37, 3-68) by Khaled Mahmud at Multan, 2003.

† *On first appearance in Pakistan–Bangladesh Tests.*

SEVEN WICKETS OR MORE IN AN INNINGS

For Pakistan

7-77 Danish Kaneria, Dhaka 2001-02

SRI LANKA v ZIMBABWE

Series notes: Zimbabwe have never beaten Sri Lanka, and have lost all seven Tests away from home. They passed 300 in their first three innings against Sri Lanka; since then, they have managed it only once in 24 innings. Sri Lanka have scored over 500 in the first innings of four of the last five Tests, having failed to do so in either innings of the first ten Tests. They have never been dismissed for under 200. M. Muralitharan has taken more wickets in Tests against Zimbabwe than any other bowler, and needs 13 more to reach 100.

		Captains					
Season	*Sri Lanka*	*Zimbabwe*	*T*	*SL*	*Z*	*D*	
1994-95Z	A. Ranatunga	A. Flower	3	0	0	3	
1996-97S	A. Ranatunga	A. D. R. Campbell	2	2	0	0	
1997-98S	A. Ranatunga	A. D. R. Campbell	2	2	0	0	
1999-2000Z	S. T. Jayasuriya	A. Flower	3	1	0	2	
2001-02S	S. T. Jayasuriya	S. V. Carlisle	3	3	0	0	
2003-04Z	M. S. Atapattu	T. Taibu	2	2	0	0	
	In Sri Lanka		7	7	0	0	
	In Zimbabwe		8	3	0	5	
	Totals		15	10	0	5	

S Played in Sri Lanka.   Z Played in Zimbabwe.

HIGHEST INNINGS TOTALS

For Sri Lanka in Sri Lanka: 586-6 dec at Colombo (SSC) 2001-02
    in Zimbabwe: 713-3 dec at Bulawayo 2003-04

For Zimbabwe in Sri Lanka: 338 at Kandy 1997-98
    in Zimbabwe: 462-9 dec at Bulawayo. 1994-95

LOWEST INNINGS TOTALS

For Sri Lanka in Sri Lanka: 225 at Colombo (SSC) 1997-98
    in Zimbabwe: 218 at Bulawayo   1994-95

For Zimbabwe in Sri Lanka: 79 at Galle 2001-02
    in Zimbabwe: 102 at Harare   2003-04

DOUBLE-HUNDREDS

For Sri Lanka (4)

270	K. C. Sangakkara at Bulawayo . .	2003-04	223 M. S. Atapattu at Kandy	1997-98
249	M. S. Atapattu at Bulawayo.	2003-04	216* M. S. Atapattu at Bulawayo . . .	1999-2000

For Zimbabwe (1)

266   D. L. Houghton at Bulawayo . . . 1994-95

INDIVIDUAL HUNDREDS

For Sri Lanka (19)

5: M. S. Atapattu.
2: S. T. Jayasuriya, S. Ranatunga, K. C. Sangakkara, H. P. Tillekeratne.
1: R. P. Arnold, P. A. de Silva, T. M. Dilshan, A. P. Gurusinha, D. P. M. D. Jayawardene, T. T. Samaraweera.

For Zimbabwe (4)

2: A. Flower, D. L. Houghton.

TEN WICKETS OR MORE IN A MATCH

For Sri Lanka (2)

12-117 (5-23, 7-94)   M. Muralitharan, Kandy. 1997-98
13-115 (9-51, 4-64)   M. Muralitharan, Kandy. 2001-02

Note: The best match figures for Zimbabwe are 6-112 (2-28, 4-84) by H. H. Streak at Colombo (SSC), 1997-98.

SEVEN WICKETS OR MORE IN AN INNINGS

In addition to those listed above, the following has taken seven wickets or more in an innings:

For Sri Lanka

7-116   K. R. Pushpakumara, Harare. . . . 1994-95

SRI LANKA v BANGLADESH

Series notes: Bangladesh have dismissed Sri Lanka only once in eight away Tests, but have done it in each of the four home games. M. Muralitharan has taken 11 of the 15 five-fors between these teams; in all, he has 89 wickets at an average of 13.37 against Bangladesh, more than three times the next best for either side (C. R. D. Fernando with 28).

		Captains				
Season	*Sri Lanka*	*Bangladesh*	*T*	*SL*	*B*	*D*
2001-02S†	S. T. Jayasuriya	Naimur Rahman	1	1	0	0
2002S	S. T. Jayasuriya	Khaled Mashud	2	2	0	0
2005-06S	M. S. Atapattu	Habibul Bashar	2	2	0	0
2005-06B	D. P. M. D. Jayawardene	Habibul Bashar	2	2	0	0
2007S	D. P. M. D. Jayawardene	Mohammad Ashraful	3	3	0	0
2008-09B	**D. P. M. D. Jayawardene**	**Mohammad Ashraful**	**2**	**2**	**0**	**0**
	In Sri Lanka................................		8	8	0	0
	In Bangladesh		**4**	**4**	**0**	**0**
	Totals		12	12	0	0

S Played in Sri Lanka.   B Played in Bangladesh.

† *This Test was part of the Asian Test Championship.*

HIGHEST INNINGS TOTALS

For Sri Lanka in Sri Lanka: 577-6 dec at Colombo (SSC) 2007
　　　　　　in Bangladesh: **447-6 dec at Chittagong** **2008-09**

For Bangladesh in Sri Lanka: 328 at Colombo (SSC)............................. 2001-02
　　　　　　　in Bangladesh: **413 at Mirpur**................................. **2008-09**

LOWEST INNINGS TOTALS

For Sri Lanka in Sri Lanka: 373 at Colombo (SSC) 2002
　　　　　　in Bangladesh: **293 at Mirpur** **2008-09**

For Bangladesh in Sri Lanka: 62 at Colombo (PSS) 2007
　　　　　　　in Bangladesh: **158 at Chittagong** **2008-09**

DOUBLE-HUNDREDS

For Sri Lanka (4)

222*	K. C. Sangakkara at Kandy.....	2007	201	M. S. Atapattu at Colombo (SSC) 2001-02
206	P. A. de Silva at Colombo (PSS)	2002	200*	K. C. Sangakkara at Colombo (PSS).................... 2007

Highest score for Bangladesh: 136 by Mohammad Ashraful at Chittagong, 2005-06.

INDIVIDUAL HUNDREDS

For Sri Lanka (18)

4: D. P. M. D. Jayawardene.

3: T. M. Dilshan.

2: K. C. Sangakkara, M. G. Vandort.

1: M. S. Atapattu, P. A. de Silva, S. T. Jayasuriya, **H. A. P.W. Jayawardene**, T. T. Samaraweera, W. U. Tharanga, W. P. U. J. C. Vaas.

For Bangladesh (4)

4: Mohammad Ashraful.

TEN WICKETS OR MORE IN A MATCH

For Sri Lanka (4)

10-111 (5-13, 5-98)	M. Muralitharan, Colombo (SSC)	2001-02
10-98 (5-39, 5-59)	M. Muralitharan, Colombo (PSS)	2002
12-82 (6-28, 6-54)	M. Muralitharan, Kandy	2007
10-190 (6-49, 4-141)	**M. Muralitharan, Mirpur**	**2008-09**

Note: The best match figures for Bangladesh are 5-114 (5-114) by Mohammad Rafique at Colombo (RPS), 2005-06.

Bold type denotes performances in the 2008-09 series or, in career figures, players who appeared in that series.

ZIMBABWE v BANGLADESH

Series notes: Zimbabwe are the only team to lose a Test or a series in Bangladesh, in 2004-05. Zimbabwe have won the toss in six out of eight Tests. The team batting first lost the first two Tests between the sides, but are unbeaten in the last six. Habibul Bashar is the leading scorer with 578; Zimbabwe's best is 447 by T. Taibu.

		Captains				
Season	Zimbabwe	Bangladesh	T	Z	B	D
2000-01Z	H. H. Streak	Naimur Rahman	2	2	0	0
2001-02B	B. A. Murphy[1]	Naimur Rahman	2	1	0	1
2003-04Z	H. H. Streak	Habibul Bashar	2	1	0	1
2004-05B	T. Taibu	Habibul Bashar	2	0	1	1
	In Zimbabwe		4	3	0	1
	In Bangladesh		4	1	1	2
	Totals		8	4	1	3

Z Played in Zimbabwe. B Played in Bangladesh.

Note: The following deputised for the official touring captain:

[1]S. V. Carlisle (Second).

HIGHEST INNINGS TOTALS

For Zimbabwe in Zimbabwe:	457 at Bulawayo	2000-01
in Bangladesh:	542-7 dec at Chittagong	2001-02
For Bangladesh in Zimbabwe:	331 at Harare	2003-04
in Bangladesh:	488 at Chittagong	2004-05

LOWEST INNINGS TOTALS

For Zimbabwe in Zimbabwe: 441 at Harare 2003-04
                   in Bangladesh: 154 at Chittagong 2004-05

For Bangladesh in Zimbabwe: 168 at Bulawayo................................. 2000-01
                        168 at Bulawayo................................. 2003-04
                   in Bangladesh: 107 at Dhaka. 2001-02

HIGHEST INDIVIDUAL INNINGS

For Zimbabwe

153   T. Taibu at Dhaka 2004-05

For Bangladesh

121   Nafis Iqbal at Dhaka 2004-05

INDIVIDUAL HUNDREDS

For Zimbabwe (6)

1: S. V. Carlisle, A. Flower, T. R. Gripper, T. Taibu, G. J. Whittall, C. B. Wishart.

For Bangladesh (2)

1: Habibul Bashar, Nafis Iqbal.

TEN WICKETS OR MORE IN A MATCH

For Bangladesh (1)

12-200 (7-95, 5-105)   Enamul Haque, jun., Dhaka 2004-05

Note: The best match figures for Zimbabwe are 8-104 (4-41, 4-63) by G. W. Flower at Chittagong, 2001-02.

TEST GROUNDS

in chronological order

City and Ground	First Test Match		Tests
1 **Melbourne, Melbourne Cricket Ground**	**March 15, 1877**	**A v E**	**102**
2 **London, Kennington Oval**	**September 6, 1880**	**E v A**	**92**
3 **Sydney, Sydney Cricket Ground (No. 1)**	**February 17, 1882**	**A v E**	**98**
4 Manchester, Old Trafford	July 11, 1884	E v A	73
5 **London, Lord's**	**July 21, 1884**	**E v A**	**118**
6 **Adelaide, Adelaide Oval**	**December 12, 1884**	**A v E**	**68**
7 Port Elizabeth, St George's Park	March 12, 1889	SA v E	23
8 **Cape Town, Newlands**	**March 25, 1889**	**SA v E**	**45**
9 Johannesburg, Old Wanderers	March 2, 1896	SA v E	22
Now the site of Johannesburg Railway Station.			
10 Nottingham, Trent Bridge	June 1, 1899	E v A	55
11 **Leeds, Headingley**	**June 29, 1899**	**E v A**	**69**
12 **Birmingham, Edgbaston**	**May 29, 1902**	**E v A**	**44**
13 Sheffield, Bramall Lane	July 3, 1902	E v A	1
Sheffield United Football Club have built a stand over the cricket pitch.			
14 Durban, Lord's	January 21, 1910	SA v E	4
Ground destroyed and built on.			
15 **Durban, Kingsmead**	**January 18, 1923**	**SA v E**	**37**
16 Brisbane, Exhibition Ground	November 30, 1928	A v E	2
No longer used for cricket.			

	City and Ground	First Test Match		Tests
17	Christchurch, Lancaster Park	January 10, 1930	NZ v E	40
	Ground also known under sponsors' names; currently Jade Stadium.			
18	**Bridgetown, Kensington Oval**	**January 11, 1930**	**WI v E**	**45**
19	**Wellington, Basin Reserve**	**January 24, 1930**	**NZ v E**	**50**
20	**Port-of-Spain, Queen's Park Oval**	**February 1, 1930**	**WI v E**	**56**
21	Auckland, Eden Park	February 17, 1930	NZ v E	47
22	Georgetown, Bourda	February 21, 1930	WI v E	30
23	**Kingston, Sabina Park**	**April 3, 1930**	**WI v E**	**44**
24	**Brisbane, Woolloongabba**	**November 27, 1931**	**A v SA**	**52**
25	Bombay, Gymkhana Ground	December 15, 1933	I v E	1
	No longer used for first-class cricket.			
26	Calcutta (*now Kolkata*), Eden Gardens	January 5, 1934	I v E	35
27	Madras (*now Chennai*), Chepauk (Chidambaram Stadium)	February 10, 1934	I v E	30
28	Delhi, Feroz Shah Kotla	November 10, 1948	I v WI	30
29	**Bombay (*now Mumbai*), Brabourne Stadium**	**December 9, 1948**	**I v WI**	**18**
	Rarely used for first-class cricket.			
30	Johannesburg, Ellis Park	December 27, 1948	SA v E	6
	Mainly a football and rugby stadium, no longer used for cricket.			
31	**Kanpur, Green Park (Modi Stadium)**	**January 12, 1952**	**I v E**	**21**
32	Lucknow, University Ground	October 25, 1952	I v P	1
	Ground destroyed, now partly under a river bed.			
33	Dacca (*now Dhaka*), Dacca (*now Bangabandhu*) Stadium	January 1, 1955	P v I	17
	Originally in East Pakistan, now Bangladesh, no longer used for cricket.			
34	Bahawalpur, Dring (*now Bahawal*) Stadium	January 15, 1955	P v I	1
	Still used for first-class cricket.			
35	Lahore, Lawrence Gardens (Bagh-e-Jinnah)	January 29, 1955	P v I	3
	Still used for club and occasional first-class matches.			
36	Peshawar, Services Ground	February 13, 1955	P v I	1
	Superseded by new stadium.			
37	**Karachi, National Stadium**	**February 26, 1955**	**P v I**	**41**
38	Dunedin, Carisbrook	March 11, 1955	NZ v E	10
39	Hyderabad, Fateh Maidan (Lal Bahadur Stadium)	November 19, 1955	I v NZ	3
40	Madras, Corporation Stadium	January 6, 1956	I v NZ	9
	Superseded by rebuilt Chepauk Stadium.			
41	**Johannesburg, Wanderers**	**December 24, 1956**	**SA v E**	**32**
42	**Lahore, Gaddafi Stadium**	**November 21, 1959**	**P v A**	**40**
43	Rawalpindi, Pindi Club Ground	March 27, 1965	P v NZ	1
	Superseded by new stadium.			
44	Nagpur, Vidarbha C.A. Ground	October 3, 1969	I v NZ	9
	Superseded by new stadium.			
45	**Perth, Western Australian C.A. Ground**	**December 11, 1970**	**A v E**	**37**
46	Hyderabad, Niaz Stadium	March 16, 1973	P v E	5
47	Bangalore, Karnataka State C.A. Ground (Chinnaswamy Stadium)	November 22, 1974	I v WI	18
48	Bombay (*now Mumbai*), Wankhede Stadium	January 23, 1975	I v WI	21
49	Faisalabad, Iqbal Stadium	October 16, 1978	P v I	24
50	**Napier, McLean Park**	**February 16, 1979**	**NZ v P**	**9**
51	Multan, Ibn-e-Qasim Bagh Stadium	December 30, 1980	P v WI	1
	Superseded by new stadium.			
52	**St John's (Antigua), Recreation Ground**	**March 27, 1981**	**WI v E**	**22**
53	**Colombo, P. Saravanamuttu (Sara) Stadium**	**February 17, 1982**	**SL v E**	**14**
54	Kandy, Asgiriya Stadium	April 22, 1983	SL v A	21
55	Jullundur, Burlton Park	September 24, 1983	I v P	1
56	**Ahmedabad, Sardar Patel (Gujarat) Stadium**	**November 12, 1983**	**I v WI**	**10**
57	**Colombo, Sinhalese Sports Club Ground**	**March 16, 1984**	**SL v NZ**	**33**
58	Colombo, Colombo Cricket Club Ground	March 24, 1984	SL v NZ	3
59	Sialkot, Jinnah Stadium	October 27, 1985	P v SL	4
60	Cuttack, Barabati Stadium	January 4, 1987	I v SL	2

	City and Ground	First Test Match		Tests
61	Jaipur, Sawai Mansingh Stadium	February 21, 1987	I v P	1
62	**Hobart, Bellerive Oval**	**December 16, 1989**	**A v SL**	**9**
63	Chandigarh, Sector 16 Stadium	November 23, 1990	I v SL	1
	Superseded by Mohali ground.			
64	**Hamilton, Seddon Park**	**February 22, 1991**	**NZ v SL**	**15**
	Ground also known under various sponsors' names.			
65	Gujranwala, Municipal Stadium	December 20, 1991	P v SL	1
66	Colombo, R. Premadasa (Khettarama) Stadium	August 28, 1992	SL v A	6
67	Moratuwa, Tyronne Fernando Stadium	September 8, 1992	SL v A	4
68	Harare, Harare Sports Club	October 18, 1992	Z v I	26
69	Bulawayo, Bulawayo Athletic Club	November 1, 1992	Z v NZ	1
	Superseded by Queens Sports Club ground.			
70	Karachi, Defence Stadium	December 1, 1993	P v Z	1
71	Rawalpindi, Rawalpindi Cricket Stadium	December 9, 1993	P v Z	8
72	Lucknow, K. D. "Babu" Singh Stadium	January 18, 1994	I v SL	1
73	Bulawayo, Queens Sports Club	October 20, 1994	Z v SL	17
74	Mohali, Punjab Cricket Association Stadium	December 10, 1994	I v WI	9
75	Peshawar, Arbab Niaz Stadium	September 8, 1995	P v SL	6
76	**Centurion (*formerly Verwoerdburg*), Centurion Park**	**November 16, 1995**	**SA v E**	**15**
77	Sheikhupura, Municipal Stadium	October 17, 1996	P v Z	2
78	**St Vincent, Arnos Vale**	**June 20, 1997**	**WI v SL**	**2**
79	**Galle, International Stadium**	**June 3, 1998**	**SL v NZ**	**15**
80	Bloemfontein, Springbok Park	October 29, 1999	SA v Z	4
	Ground also known under sponsor's name; currently OUTsurance Oval.			
81	Multan, Multan Cricket Stadium	August 29, 2001	P v B	5
82	Chittagong, Chittagong Stadium	November 15, 2001	B v Z	8
	Ground also known as M. A. Aziz Stadium.			
83	Sharjah, Sharjah Cricket Association Stadium	January 31, 2002	P v WI	4
84	**St George's, Grenada, Queen's Park New Stadium**	**June 28, 2002**	**WI v NZ**	**2**
85	East London, Buffalo Park	October 18, 2002	SA v B	1
86	Potchefstroom, North West Cricket Stadium	October 25, 2002	SA v B	1
	Ground now known under sponsor's name as Senwes Park.			
87	**Chester-le-Street, Riverside Ground**	**June 5, 2003**	**E v Z**	**4**
88	Gros Islet, St Lucia, Beausejour Stadium	June 20, 2003	WI v SL	3
89	Darwin, Marrara Cricket Ground	July 18, 2003	A v B	2
90	Cairns, Cazaly's Football Park	July 25, 2003	A v B	2
	Ground also known under sponsor's name as Bundaberg Rum Stadium.			
91	**Chittagong, Chittagong Divisional Stadium**	**February 28, 2006**	**B v SL**	**7**
	Ground also known as Bir Shrestha Shahid Ruhul Amin Stadium and Zohur Ahmed Chowdhury Stadium.			
92	Bogra, Shaheed Chandu Stadium	March 8, 2006	B v SL	1
93	Fatullah, Narayanganj Osmani Stadium	April 9, 2006	B v A	1
94	Basseterre (St Kitts), Warner Park	June 22, 2006	WI v I	1
95	**Mirpur (Dhaka), Shere Bangla National Stadium**	**May 25, 2007**	**B v I**	**5**
96	**Dunedin, University Oval**	**January 4, 2008**	**NZ v B**	**3**
97	Providence Stadium (Guyana)	March 22, 2008	WI v SL	1
98	**North Sound (Antigua), Sir Vivian Richards Stadium**	**May 30, 2008**	**WI v A**	**2**
99	Nagpur, Vidarbha C. A. Stadium, Jamtha	November 6, 2008	I v A	1
100	**Cardiff, Sophia Gardens**	**July 8, 2009**	**E v A**	**1**
	Ground now known under sponsor's name as Swalec Stadium.			

Bold type denotes grounds used for Test cricket since January 1, 2009.

ONE-DAY INTERNATIONAL RECORDS

Matches in this section do not have first-class status.

SUMMARY OF ONE-DAY INTERNATIONALS

1970-71 to December 31, 2009

	Opponents	Matches	Won by															Tied	NR
			E	A	SA	WI	NZ	I	P	SL	Z	B	Ass	Asia	Wld	Afr		
England	Australia	101	38	59	–	–	–	–	–	–	–	–	–	–	–	–	2	2
	South Africa	44	18	–	23	–	–	–	–	–	–	–	–	–	–	–	1	2
	West Indies	82	37	–	–	41	–	–	–	–	–	–	–	–	–	–	–	4
	New Zealand	70	29	–	–	–	35	–	–	–	–	–	–	–	–	–	2	4
	India	70	30	–	–	–	–	38	–	–	–	–	–	–	–	–	–	2
	Pakistan	63	35	–	–	–	–	–	26	–	–	–	–	–	–	–	–	2
	Sri Lanka	44	23	–	–	–	–	–	–	21	–	–	–	–	–	–	–	–
	Zimbabwe	30	21	–	–	–	–	–	–	–	8	–	–	–	–	–	–	1
	Bangladesh	8	8	–	–	–	–	–	–	–	–	0	–	–	–	–	–	–
	Associates	13	12	–	–	–	–	–	–	–	–	–	0	–	–	–	–	1
Australia	South Africa	77	–	39	35	–	–	–	–	–	–	–	–	–	–	–	3	–
	West Indies	120	–	59	–	57	–	–	–	–	–	–	–	–	–	–	2	2
	New Zealand	118	–	81	–	–	32	–	–	–	–	–	–	–	–	–	–	5
	India	103	–	61	–	–	–	34	–	–	–	–	–	–	–	–	–	8
	Pakistan	80	–	47	–	–	–	–	29	–	–	–	–	–	–	–	1	3
	Sri Lanka	68	–	46	–	–	–	–	–	20	–	–	–	–	–	–	–	2
	Zimbabwe	27	–	25	–	–	–	–	–	–	1	–	–	–	–	–	–	1
	Bangladesh	16	–	15	–	–	–	–	–	–	–	1	–	–	–	–	–	–
	Associates	13	–	13	–	–	–	–	–	–	–	–	0	–	–	–	–	–
	ICC World XI	3	–	3	–	–	–	–	–	–	–	–	–	–	0	–	–	–
South Africa	West Indies	45	–	–	32	12	–	–	–	–	–	–	–	–	–	–	–	1
	New Zealand	51	–	–	30	–	17	–	–	–	–	–	–	–	–	–	–	4
	India	57	–	–	35	–	–	20	–	–	–	–	–	–	–	–	–	2
	Pakistan	52	–	–	35	–	–	–	16	–	–	–	–	–	–	–	–	1
	Sri Lanka	46	–	–	22	–	–	–	–	22	–	–	–	–	–	–	1	1
	Zimbabwe	29	–	–	26	–	–	–	–	–	2	–	–	–	–	–	–	1
	Bangladesh	13	–	–	12	–	–	–	–	–	–	1	–	–	–	–	–	–
	Associates	17	–	–	17	–	–	–	–	–	–	–	0	–	–	–	–	–
West Indies	New Zealand	51	–	–	–	24	20	–	–	–	–	–	–	–	–	–	–	7
	India	95	–	–	–	54	–	38	–	–	–	–	–	–	–	–	1	2
	Pakistan	114	–	–	–	64	–	–	48	–	–	–	–	–	–	–	2	–
	Sri Lanka	46	–	–	–	26	–	–	–	18	–	–	–	–	–	–	–	2
	Zimbabwe	36	–	–	–	27	–	–	–	–	8	–	–	–	–	–	–	1
	Bangladesh	16	–	–	–	11	–	–	–	–	–	3	–	–	–	–	–	2
	Associates	15	–	–	–	13	–	–	–	–	–	–	1	–	–	–	–	1
New Zealand	India	81	–	–	–	–	36	40	–	–	–	–	–	–	–	–	–	5
	Pakistan	82	–	–	–	–	32	–	48	–	–	–	–	–	–	–	1	1
	Sri Lanka	70	–	–	–	–	35	–	–	31	–	–	–	–	–	–	1	3
	Zimbabwe	28	–	–	–	–	19	–	–	–	7	–	–	–	–	–	1	1
	Bangladesh	14	–	–	–	–	13	–	–	–	–	1	–	–	–	–	–	–
	Associates	11	–	–	–	–	11	–	–	–	–	–	0	–	–	–	–	–
India	Pakistan	118	–	–	–	–	–	45	69	–	–	–	–	–	–	–	–	4
	Sri Lanka	118	–	–	–	–	–	63	–	44	–	–	–	–	–	–	–	11
	Zimbabwe	49	–	–	–	–	–	39	–	–	8	–	–	–	–	–	2	–
	Bangladesh	19	–	–	–	–	–	17	–	–	–	2	–	–	–	–	–	–
	Associates	22	–	–	–	–	–	20	–	–	–	–	2	–	–	–	–	–
Pakistan	Sri Lanka	119	–	–	–	–	–	–	70	45	–	–	–	–	–	–	1	3
	Zimbabwe	40	–	–	–	–	–	–	36	–	2	–	–	–	–	–	1	1
	Bangladesh	25	–	–	–	–	–	–	24	–	–	1	–	–	–	–	–	–
	Associates	17	–	–	–	–	–	–	16	–	–	–	1	–	–	–	–	–
Sri Lanka	Zimbabwe	43	–	–	–	–	–	–	–	36	6	–	–	–	–	–	–	1
	Bangladesh	26	–	–	–	–	–	–	–	24	–	2	–	–	–	–	–	–
	Associates	13	–	–	–	–	–	–	–	12	–	–	1	–	–	–	–	–
Zimbabwe	Bangladesh	47	–	–	–	–	–	–	–	–	22	25	–	–	–	–	–	–
	Associates	38	–	–	–	–	–	–	–	–	30	–	5	–	–	–	1	2
Bangladesh	Associates	27	–	–	–	–	–	–	–	–	–	19	8	–	–	–	–	–
Associates	Associates	89	–	–	–	–	–	–	–	–	–	–	84	–	–	–	–	5
Asian CC XI	ICC World XI	1	–	–	–	–	–	–	–	–	–	–	–	0	1	–	–	–
	African XI	6	–	–	–	–	–	–	–	–	–	–	–	4	–	1	–	1
		2,936	251	448	267	329	250	354	382	273	94	55	102	4	1	1	23	102

Note: Associate Members of ICC who have played one-day internationals are Afghanistan, Bermuda, Canada, East Africa, Hong Kong, Ireland, Kenya, Namibia, Netherlands, Scotland, United Arab Emirates and USA. Sri Lanka, Zimbabwe and Bangladesh also played one-day internationals before being given Test status; these are not included among the Associates' results.

RESULTS SUMMARY OF ONE-DAY INTERNATIONALS

1970-71 to December 31, 2009 (2,936 matches)

	Matches	Won	Lost	Tied	No Result	% Won (excl. NR)
South Africa	431	267	147	5	12	64.31
Australia	726	448	247	8	23	64.29
West Indies	620	329	264	5	22	55.43
Pakistan	710	382	307	6	15	55.39
India	732	354	341	3	34	50.93
England	525	251	251	5	18	50.00
Sri Lanka.................	593	273	294	3	23	48.15
New Zealand..............	576	250	291	5	30	46.24
Zimbabwe.................	367	94	259	5	9	26.95
Bangladesh	211	55	154	–	2	26.31
Asian Cricket Council XI	7	4	2	–	1	66.66
Afghanistan...............	3	2	1	–	–	66.66
Ireland....................	41	17	20	1	3	46.05
Netherlands...............	45	18	25	–	2	41.86
Kenya	125	35	85	–	5	29.16
Scotland	40	10	27	–	3	27.02
Canada	49	12	36	–	1	25.00
ICC World XI	4	1	3	–	–	25.00
Bermuda..................	35	7	28	–	–	20.00
African XI................	6	1	4	–	1	20.00
United Arab Emirates	11	1	10	–	–	9.09
USA	2	–	2	–	–	0.00
East Africa	3	–	3	–	–	0.00
Hong Kong	4	–	4	–	–	0.00
Namibia..................	6	–	6	–	–	0.00

Note: Matches abandoned without a ball bowled are not included except (from 2004) where the toss took place, in accordance with an ICC ruling. Such matches, like those called off after play began, are now counted as official internationals in their own right, even when replayed on another day. In the percentages of matches won, ties are counted as half a win.

BATTING RECORDS

MOST RUNS

		M	I	NO	R	HS	100s	Avge
1	**S. R. Tendulkar (India)**	**440**	**429**	**40**	**17,394**	**186***	**45**	**44.71**
2	**S. T. Jayasuriya (Sri Lanka/Asia)**......	**444**	**432**	**18**	**13,428**	**189**	**28**	**32.43**
3	**R. T. Ponting (Australia/World)**.......	**330**	**321**	**36**	**12,311**	**164**	**28**	**43.19**
4	Inzamam-ul-Haq (Pakistan/Asia)........	378	350	53	11,739	137*	10	39.52
5	S. C. Ganguly (India/Asia)..............	311	300	23	11,363	183	22	41.02
6	**R. Dravid (India/World/Asia)**	**339**	**313**	**40**	**10,765**	**153**	**12**	**39.43**
7	**J. H. Kallis (S. Africa/World/Africa)** ...	**295**	**281**	**51**	**10,409**	**139**	**16**	**45.25**
8	B. C. Lara (West Indies/World).........	299	289	32	10,405	169	19	40.48
9	A. C. Gilchrist (Australia/World).......	287	279	11	9,619	172	16	35.89
10	**Mohammad Yousuf (Pakistan/Asia)**....	**278**	**263**	**40**	**9,543**	**141***	**15**	**42.79**
11	M. Azharuddin (India)................	334	308	54	9,378	153*	7	36.92
12	P. A. de Silva (Sri Lanka)	308	296	30	9,284	145	11	34.90
13	Saeed Anwar (Pakistan)...............	247	244	19	8,824	194	20	39.21
14	D. L. Haynes (West Indies)	238	237	28	8,648	152*	17	41.37

		M	I	NO	R	HS	100s	Avge
15	M. S. Atapattu (Sri Lanka).............	268	259	32	8,529	132*	11	37.57
16	**D. P. M. D. Jayawardene (SL/Asia)**	**314**	**295**	**29**	**8,518**	**128**	**11**	**32.02**
17	M. E. Waugh (Australia)..............	244	236	20	8,500	173	18	39.35
18	**S. Chanderpaul (West Indies)**.........	**252**	**236**	**38**	**8,250**	**150**	**10**	**41.66**
19	**H. H. Gibbs (South Africa)**	**245**	**238**	**16**	**8,060**	**175**	**21**	**36.30**
20	S. P. Fleming (New Zealand/World)	280	269	21	8,037	134*	8	32.40
21	**K. C. Sangakkara (SL/Asia/World)**	**262**	**245**	**26**	**7,878**	**138***	**10**	**35.97**
22	S. R. Waugh (Australia)...............	325	288	58	7,569	120*	3	32.90

Notes: The leading aggregates for players who have appeared for other Test countries are:

	M	I	NO	R	HS	100s	Avge
A. Flower (Zimbabwe)...................	213	208	16	6,786	145	4	35.34
A. J. Stewart (England)	170	162	14	4,677	116	4	31.60
Mohammad Ashraful (Bangladesh/Asia)	**152**	**145**	**13**	**3,140**	**109**	**3**	**23.78**

Excluding runs scored for combined teams, the record aggregate for Sri Lanka is **13,362** in 440 matches by **S. T. Jayasuriya**; for Australia, **12,196** in 329 matches by **R. T. Ponting**; for Pakistan, 11,701 in 375 matches by Inzamam-ul-Haq; for South Africa, **10,380** in 290 matches by **J. H. Kallis**; for West Indies, 10,348 in 295 matches by B. C. Lara; and for New Zealand, 8,007 in 279 matches by S. P. Fleming. Mohammad Ashraful scored no runs in his two matches for the Asian Cricket Council XI.

Bold type denotes those who played one-day internationals in the calendar year 2009.

BEST CAREER STRIKE-RATES BY BATSMEN

(Runs per 100 balls. Qualification: 700 runs)

SR		Position	M	I	R	Avge
110.85	**Shahid Afridi (P/World/Asia)** ...	**2/7**	**288**	**270**	**5,830**	**23.13**
105.80	**J. M. Davison (Canada)**	**1/2**	**27**	**27**	**766**	**29.46**
104.88	B. L. Cairns (NZ)	9/8	78	65	987	16.72
102.93	**V. Sehwag (I/World/Asia)**.......	**1/2**	**216**	**210**	**6,934**	**34.32**
101.54	D. R. Smith (WI)...............	6/7	71	56	791	14.92
99.43	I. D. S. Smith (NZ)	8	98	77	1,055	17.29
96.94	A. C. Gilchrist (A/World)........	1/2	287	279	9,619	35.89
96.66	R. L. Powell (WI)...............	6	109	100	2,085	24.82
95.07	Kapil Dev (I)...................	7/6	225	198	3,783	23.79
92.45	**A. Symonds (A)**	**5**	**198**	**161**	**5,088**	**39.75**
91.92	R. V. Uthappa (I)...............	1/7	38	34	786	27.10
91.22	**S. T. Jayasuriya (SL/Asia)**	**1/2**	**444**	**432**	**13,428**	**32.43**
90.20	I. V. A. Richards (WI)...........	4	187	167	6,721	47.00
90.09	**J. R. Hopes (A)**...............	**7**	**67**	**48**	**1,000**	**23.80**

Note: Position means a batsman's most usual position in the batting order.

Bold type denotes those who played one-day internationals in the calendar year 2009.

HIGHEST INDIVIDUAL INNINGS

194*	C. K. Coventry	Zimbabwe v Bangladesh at Bulawayo	2009
194	Saeed Anwar	Pakistan v India at Chennai	1996-97
189*	I. V. A. Richards	West Indies v England at Manchester	1984
189	S. T. Jayasuriya	Sri Lanka v India at Sharjah.....................	2000-01
188*	G. Kirsten	South Africa v UAE at Rawalpindi	1995-96
186*	S. R. Tendulkar	India v New Zealand at Hyderabad	1999-2000
183*	M. S. Dhoni	India v Sri Lanka at Jaipur	2005-06
183	S. C. Ganguly	India v Sri Lanka at Taunton	1999
181*	M. L. Hayden	Australia v New Zealand at Hamilton	2006-07
181	I. V. A. Richards	West Indies v Sri Lanka at Karachi	1987-88
178*	**H. Masakadza**	**Zimbabwe v Kenya at Harare**...................	**2009-10**
175*	Kapil Dev	India v Zimbabwe at Tunbridge Wells.............	1983

175	H. H. Gibbs	South Africa v Australia at Johannesburg	2005-06
175	**S. R. Tendulkar**	**India v Australia at Hyderabad**	**2009-10**
173	M. E. Waugh	Australia v West Indies at Melbourne	2000-01
172*	C. B. Wishart	Zimbabwe v Namibia at Harare	2002-03
172	A. C. Gilchrist	Australia v Zimbabwe at Hobart	2003-04
172	L. Vincent	New Zealand v Zimbabwe at Bulawayo............	2005-06
171*	G. M. Turner	New Zealand v East Africa at Birmingham	1975

Note: The highest individual scores for other Test countries are:

| 167* | R. A. Smith | England v Australia at Birmingham............... | 1993 |
| **154** | **Tamim Iqbal** | **Bangladesh v Zimbabwe at Bulawayo** .... | **2009** |

Bold type denotes performances in the calendar year 2009.

After the deadline for inclusion in this section S. R. Tendulkar set a new record with 200* for India v South Africa at Gwalior in February 2010.

MOST HUNDREDS

S. R. Tendulkar (I) **45**	J. H. Kallis (SA/Wld/Af).. 16	I. V. A. Richards (WI)... 11
S. T. Jayasuriya (SL/Asia) **28**	Mohammad Yousuf (P/As) 15	S. Chanderpaul (WI)... **10**
R. T. Ponting (A/World).. **28**	G. Kirsten (SA) 13	M. L. Hayden (A/World) 10
S. C. Ganguly (I/Asia)... 22	R. Dravid (I/World/Asia) **12**	Ijaz Ahmed, sen. (P) 10
H. H. Gibbs (SA) **21**	M. E. Trescothick (E) ... 12	Inzamam-ul-Haq (P/Asia) 10
Saeed Anwar (P) 20	V. Sehwag (I/World/As) . 12	K. C. Sangakkara (SL/W/
C. H. Gayle (WI/World).. **19**	Yuvraj Singh (I/Asia) .. **12**	Asia)................ **10**
B. C. Lara (WI/World) .. 19	M. S. Atapattu (SL)..... 11	*Most hundreds for other*
M. E. Waugh (A)....... 18	P. A. de Silva (SL)...... 11	*countries:*
D. L. Haynes (WI)...... 17	C. G. Greenidge (WI) ... 11	A. D. R. Campbell (Z)... 7
N. J. Astle (NZ)........ 16	D. P. M. D. Jayawardene	Shahriar Nafees (B)..... 4
A. C. Gilchrist (A/World).. 16	(SL/Asia) **11**	**Shakib Al Hasan (B) ... 4**

Note: Ponting's hundreds include one for the World XI; no other player reached three figures for a combined team.

Bold type denotes those who played one-day internationals in the calendar year 2009.

FASTEST ONE-DAY INTERNATIONAL FIFTIES

Balls

17	S. T. Jayasuriya	Sri Lanka v Pakistan at Singapore	1995-96
18	S. P. O'Donnell	Australia v Sri Lanka at Sharjah...................	1989-90
18	Shahid Afridi........	Pakistan v Sri Lanka at Nairobi	1996-97
18	Shahid Afridi........	Pakistan v Netherlands at Colombo (SSC)..........	2002
19	M. V. Boucher.......	South Africa v Kenya at Cape Town	2001-02
19	J. M. Kemp	South Africa v India at Durban	2004-05
19	B. B. McCullum	New Zealand v Bangladesh at Queenstown	2007-08
19	D. J. Hussey.........	Australia v West Indies at Basseterre	2008
20	Shahid Afridi........	Pakistan v India at Kanpur	2004-05
20	Shahid Afridi........	Pakistan v South Africa at Durban	2006-07
20	B. B. McCullum	New Zealand v Canada at Gros Islet	2006-07

FASTEST ONE-DAY INTERNATIONAL HUNDREDS

Balls

37	Shahid Afridi........	Pakistan v Sri Lanka at Nairobi	1996-97
44	M. V. Boucher.......	South Africa v Zimbabwe at Potchefstroom	2006-07
45	B. C. Lara	West Indies v Bangladesh at Dhaka................	1999-2000
45	Shahid Afridi........	Pakistan v India at Kanpur	2004-05
48	S. T. Jayasuriya	Sri Lanka v Pakistan at Singapore	1995-96

HIGHEST PARTNERSHIP FOR EACH WICKET

286	for 1st	W. U. Tharanga and S. T. Jayasuriya	SL v E	Leeds	2006
331	for 2nd	S. R. Tendulkar and R. Dravid	I v NZ	Hyderabad	1999-2000
237*	for 3rd	R. Dravid and S. R. Tendulkar	I v K	Bristol	1999
275*	for 4th	M. Azharuddin and A. Jadeja	I v Z	Cuttack.........	1997-98
223	for 5th	M. Azharuddin and A. Jadeja	I v SL	Colombo (RPS)..	1997-98
218	for 6th	D. P. M. D. Jayawardene and M. S. Dhoni	As v Af	Chennai	2007
130	for 7th	A. Flower and H. H. Streak	Z v E	Harare..........	2001-02
138*	for 8th	J. M. Kemp and A. J. Hall	SA v I	Cape Town......	2006-07
126*	for 9th	Kapil Dev and S. M. H. Kirmani	I v Z	Tunbridge Wells .	1983
106*	for 10th	I. V. A. Richards and M. A. Holding	WI v E	Manchester......	1984

BOWLING RECORDS

MOST WICKETS

		M	Balls	R	W	BB	4W/i	Avge
1	M. Muralitharan (SL/World/Asia) ...	334	18,001	11,742	512	7-30	24	22.93
2	Wasim Akram (Pakistan)	356	18,186	11,812	502	5-15	23	23.52
3	Waqar Younis (Pakistan)	262	12,698	9,919	416	7-36	27	23.84
4	W. P. U. J. C. Vaas (SL/Asia).......	322	15,775	11,014	400	8-19	13	27.53
5	S. M. Pollock (SA/World/Africa)......	303	15,712	9,631	393	6-35	17	24.50
6	G. D. McGrath (Australia/World)......	250	12,970	8,391	381	7-15	16	22.02
7	A. Kumble (India/Asia)	271	14,496	10,412	337	6-12	10	30.89
8	**B. Lee (Australia)**	186	9,478	7,456	324	5-22	20	23.01
9	**S. T. Jayasuriya (Sri Lanka/Asia)** ...	444	14,838	11,825	322	6-29	12	36.72
10	J. Srinath (India)	229	11,935	8,847	315	5-23	10	28.08
11	S. K. Warne (Australia/World)........	194	10,642	7,541	293	5-33	13	25.73
12	{ Saqlain Mushtaq (Pakistan)	169	8,770	6,275	288	5-20	17	21.78
	{ A. B. Agarkar (India)	191	9,484	8,021	288	6-42	12	27.85
14	A. A. Donald (South Africa).........	164	8,561	5,926	272	6-23	13	21.78
15	**Shahid Afridi (Pakistan/World/Asia)** ..	288	12,075	9,290	269	6-38	5	34.53
16	**M. Ntini (South Africa/World)**	173	8,687	6,559	266	6-22	12	24.65
17	**D. L. Vettori (New Zealand/World)** ...	248	11,709	8,120	256	5-7	9	31.71
18	Abdul Razzaq (Pakistan/Asia).......	237	10,103	7,905	254	6-35	11	31.12
19	Kapil Dev (India)	225	11,202	6,945	253	5-43	4	27.45
20	**J. H. Kallis (S. Africa/World/Asia)** ...	295	9,898	7,962	248	5-30	4	32.10
21	H. H. Streak (Zimbabwe)	189	9,468	7,129	239	5-32	8	29.82
22	D. Gough (England/World)	159	8,470	6,209	235	5-44	12	26.42
23	**Harbhajan Singh (India/Asia)**	206	10,757	7,696	233	5-31	5	33.03
24	**Zaheer Khan (India/Asia)**	167	8,367	6,846	232	5-42	8	29.50
25	C. A. Walsh (West Indies)	205	10,822	6,918	227	5-1	7	30.47
26	C. E. L. Ambrose (West Indies)	176	9,353	5,429	225	5-17	10	24.12

Notes: The leading aggregates for players who have appeared for other countries are:

Mashrafe bin Mortaza (Bangladesh/Asia)..	**103**	**5,280**	**4,025**	**135**	**6-26**	**6**	**29.81**

Excluding wickets taken for combined teams, the record aggregate for Sri Lanka is **501** in 327 matches by **M. Muralitharan**; for South Africa, 387 in 294 matches by S. M. Pollock; for Australia, 380 in 249 matches by G. D. McGrath; for India, 334 in 269 matches by A. Kumble; for New Zealand, **248** in 246 matches by **D. L. Vettori**; for Zimbabwe, 237 in 187 matches by H. H. Streak; for England, 234 in 158 matches by D. Gough; and for Bangladesh, **134** in 101 matches by **Mashrafe bin Mortaza**.

Bold type denotes those who played one-day internationals in the calendar year 2009.

BEST CAREER STRIKE-RATES BY BOWLERS

(Balls per wicket. Qualification: 1,500 balls)

SR		M	W
24.95	**B. A. W. Mendis (SL)**	**38**	**72**
29.24	**S. E. Bond (NZ)**...................	**77**	**138**
29.25	**B. Lee (A)**......................	**186**	**324**
29.38	G. I. Allott (NZ)	31	52
29.58	L. S. Pascoe (A)	29	53
30.34	**S. C. J. Broad (E)**	**57**	**94**
30.45	Saqlain Mushtaq (P)	169	288
30.48	**Shoaib Akhtar (P/World/Asia)**	**144**	**223**
30.52	Waqar Younis (P).................	262	416
30.61	**Naved-ul-Hasan (P)**.	**69**	**104**

Bold type denotes those who played one-day internationals in the calendar year 2009.

BEST CAREER ECONOMY-RATES

(Runs conceded per six balls. Qualification: 50 wickets)

ER		M	W
3.09	J. Garner (WI)....................	98	146
3.28	R. G. D. Willis (E)	64	80
3.30	R. J. Hadlee (NZ)	115	158
3.32	M. A. Holding (WI)	102	142
3.40	A. M. E. Roberts (WI)	56	87
3.48	C. E. L. Ambrose (WI)............	176	225

BEST BOWLING ANALYSES

8-19	W. P. U. J. C. Vaas	Sri Lanka v Zimbabwe at Colombo (SSC)	2001-02
7-15	G. D. McGrath	Australia v Namibia at Potchefstroom..........	2002-03
7-20	A. J. Bichel	Australia v England at Port Elizabeth	2002-03
7-30	M. Muralitharan	Sri Lanka v India at Sharjah	2000-01
7-36	Waqar Younis	Pakistan v England at Leeds	2001
7-37	Aqib Javed	Pakistan v India at Sharjah..................	1991-92
7-51	W. W. Davis	West Indies v Australia at Leeds	1983

Note: The best analyses for other countries are:

6-12	A. Kumble	India v West Indies at Calcutta	1993-94
6-19	S. E. Bond	New Zealand v India at Bulawayo.............	2005-06
6-19	H. K. Olonga	Zimbabwe v England at Cape Town	1999-2000
6-22	M. Ntini	South Africa v Australia at Cape Town	2005-06
6-26	Mashrafe bin Mortaza	Bangladesh v Kenya at Nairobi	2006
6-31	P. D. Collingwood	England v Bangladesh at Nottingham	2005

HAT-TRICKS

Jalal-ud-Din	Pakistan v Australia at Hyderabad	1982-83
B. A. Reid	Australia v New Zealand at Sydney	1985-86
Chetan Sharma	India v New Zealand at Nagpur	1987-88
Wasim Akram	Pakistan v West Indies at Sharjah.......................	1989-90
Wasim Akram	Pakistan v Australia at Sharjah..........................	1989-90
Kapil Dev	India v Sri Lanka at Calcutta	1990-91
Aqib Javed	Pakistan v India at Sharjah.............................	1991-92
D. K. Morrison	New Zealand v India at Napier..........................	1993-94
Waqar Younis	Pakistan v New Zealand at East London	1994-95
Saqlain Mushtaq‡	Pakistan v Zimbabwe at Peshawar.......................	1996-97

E. A. Brandes	Zimbabwe v England at Harare	1996-97
A. M. Stuart	Australia v Pakistan at Melbourne	1996-97
Saqlain Mushtaq	Pakistan v Zimbabwe at The Oval	1999
W. P. U. J. C. Vaas	Sri Lanka v Zimbabwe at Colombo (SSC)................	2001-02
Mohammad Sami	Pakistan v West Indies at Sharjah.......................	2001-02
W. P. U. J. C. Vaas§	Sri Lanka v Bangladesh at Pietermaritzburg	2002-03
B. Lee	Australia v Kenya at Durban	2002-03
J. M. Anderson	England v Pakistan at The Oval.........................	2003
S. J. Harmison	England v India at Nottingham..........................	2004
C. K. Langeveldt	South Africa v West Indies at Bridgetown................	2004-05
Shahadat Hossain	Bangladesh v Zimbabwe at Harare.......................	2006
J. E. Taylor	West Indies v Australia at Mumbai	2006-07
S. E. Bond	New Zealand v Australia at Hobart	2006-07
S. L. Malinga†	Sri Lanka v South Africa at Providence..................	2006-07
A. Flintoff	**England v West Indies at Gros Islet, St Lucia**	**2008-09**

† *Four wickets in four balls.*   ‡ *Four wickets in five balls.*   § *The first three balls of the match.*

Bold type denotes performances in the calendar year 2009.

WICKETKEEPING AND FIELDING RECORDS

MOST DISMISSALS IN AN INNINGS

6 (all ct)	A. C. Gilchrist	Australia v South Africa at Cape Town	1999-2000
6 (all ct)	A. J. Stewart	England v Zimbabwe at Manchester...........	2000
6 (5ct, 1st)	R. D. Jacobs	West Indies v Sri Lanka at Colombo (RPS)	2001-02
6 (5ct, 1st)	A. C. Gilchrist	Australia v England at Sydney	2002-03
6 (all ct)	A. C. Gilchrist	Australia v Namibia at Potchefstroom.........	2002-03
6 (all ct)	A. C. Gilchrist	Australia v Sri Lanka at Colombo (RPS)	2003-04
6 (all ct)	M. V. Boucher.......	South Africa v Pakistan at Cape Town	2006-07
6 (5ct, 1st)	M. S. Dhoni.........	India v England at Leeds....................	2007
6 (all ct)	A. C. Gilchrist	Australia v India at Vadodara	2007-08
6 (5ct, 1st)	A. C. Gilchrist	Australia v India at Sydney	2007-08
6 (all ct)	M. J. Prior	England v South Africa at Nottingham........	2008

MOST DISMISSALS

			M	*Ct*	*St*
1	472	A. C. Gilchrist (Australia/World)......................	282	417	55
2	**414**	**M. V. Boucher (South Africa/Africa)**	**288**	**393**	**21**
3	**294**	**K. C. Sangakkara (Sri Lanka/World/Asia)**	**218**	**229**	**65**
4	287	Moin Khan (Pakistan)	219	214	73
5	234	I. A. Healy (Australia)	168	195	39
6	220	Rashid Latif (Pakistan)..............................	166	182	38
7	206	R. S. Kaluwitharana (Sri Lanka)	186	131	75
8	204	P. J. L. Dujon (West Indies).........................	169	183	21
9	**202**	**M. S. Dhoni (India/Asia)**	**154**	**151**	**51**
10	189	R. D. Jacobs (West Indies)...........................	147	160	29
11	**187**	**B. B. McCullum (New Zealand)**	**147**	**174**	**13**
12	⎰ 165	D. J. Richardson (South Africa).......................	122	148	17
	⎱ 165	A. Flower (Zimbabwe)...............................	186	133	32
14	163	A. J. Stewart (England)	138	148	15
15	154	N. R. Mongia (India)	140	110	44
16	136	A. C. Parore (New Zealand)..........................	150	111	25
17	**132**	**Kamran Akmal (Pakistan)**.........................	**111**	**113**	**19**

			M	Ct	St
18	126	Khaled Mashud (Bangladesh)	126	91	35
19	124	R. W. Marsh (Australia).............................	92	120	4
20	**112**	**T. Taibu (Zimbabwe/Africa)**.......................	**108**	**97**	**15**
21	103	Salim Yousuf (Pakistan).............................	86	81	22

Notes: Excluding dismissals for combined teams, the most for Australia is 470 (416 ct, 54 st) in 281 matches by A. C. Gilchrist; for South Africa **405** (385 ct, 20 st) in 283 matches by **M. V. Boucher**; and for Sri Lanka, **285** (223 ct, 62 st) in 211 matches by **K. C. Sangakkara**.

  K. C. Sangakkara's record excludes 19 catches taken in 44 one-day internationals when not keeping wicket; R. S. Kaluwitharana's excludes 1 in 3; B. B. McCullum's 4 in 16; A. Flower's 8 in 27; A. J. Stewart's 11 in 32; A. C. Parore's 5 in 29; and T. Taibu's 2 in 4. A. C. Gilchrist played five one-day internationals without keeping wicket but made no catches. R. Dravid (India) has made 210 dismissals (196 ct, 14 st) in 339 one-day internationals but only 86 (72 ct, 14 st) in 74 as wicketkeeper (including one where he took over during the match).

Bold type denotes those who played one-day internationals in the calendar year 2009.

MOST CATCHES IN AN INNINGS

(Excluding wicket-keepers)

5   J. N. Rhodes .... South Africa v West Indies at Bombay 1993-94

Note: There have been 25 instances of four catches in an innings.

MOST CATCHES

Ct	M			Ct	M	
165	314	**D. P. M. D. Jayawardene (SL/Asia)**		108	244	M. E. Waugh (Australia)
156	334	M. Azharuddin (India)		108	303	S. M. Pollock (SA/World/Africa)
141	**330**	**R. T. Ponting (Australia/World)**		107	295	J. H. Kallis (SA/World/Africa)
134	**440**	**S. R. Tendulkar (India)**		106	245	H. H. Gibbs (South Africa)
133	280	S. P. Fleming (New Zealand/World)		105	245	J. N. Rhodes (South Africa)
128	**334**	**M. Muralitharan (SL/World/Asia)**		104	197	**Younis Khan (Pakistan)**
127	273	A. R. Border (Australia)		100	187	I. V. A. Richards (West Indies)
124	**266**	**R. Dravid (India/World/Asia)**		100	311	S. C. Ganguly (India/Asia)
123	444	S. T. Jayasuriya (Sri Lanka/Asia)				
120	227	C. L. Hooper (West Indies)				*Most catches for other countries:*
120	299	B. C. Lara (West Indies/World)		Ct	M	
113	378	Inzamam-ul-Haq (Pakistan/Asia)		**99**	**173**	**P. D. Collingwood (England)**
111	325	S. R. Waugh (Australia)		86	219	G. W. Flower (Zimbabwe)
109	213	R. S. Mahanama (Sri Lanka)		**33**	**103**	**Mashrafe bin Mortaza (Bang)**

Note: Excluding catches taken for combined teams, the record aggregate for Sri Lanka is **159** in 309 matches by **D. P. M. D. Jayawardene**; for Australia, **140** in 329 by **R. T. Ponting**; for New Zealand, 132 in 279 by S. P. Fleming; and for Pakistan, 113 in 375 by Inzamam-ul-Haq.

Bold type denotes those who played one-day internationals in the calendar year 2009.

TEAM RECORDS

HIGHEST INNINGS TOTALS

443-9	(50 overs)	Sri Lanka v Netherlands at Amstelveen	2006
438-9	(49.5 overs)	South Africa v Australia at Johannesburg............	2005-06
434-4	(50 overs)	Australia v South Africa at Johannesburg............	2005-06
418-5	(50 overs)	South Africa v Zimbabwe at Potchefstroom..........	2006-07
414-7	**(50 overs)**	**India v Sri Lanka at Rajkot**......................	**2009-10**
413-5	(50 overs)	India v Bermuda at Port-of-Spain...................	2006-07
411-8	**(50 overs)**	**Sri Lanka v India at Rajkot**......................	**2009-10**
402-2	(50 overs)	New Zealand v Ireland at Aberdeen	2008

398-5	(50 overs)	Sri Lanka v Kenya at Kandy.....................	1995-96
397-5	(44 overs)	New Zealand v Zimbabwe at Bulawayo.............	2005-06
392-4	**(50 overs)**	**India v New Zealand at Christchurch.**	**2008-09**
392-6	(50 overs)	South Africa v Pakistan at Centurion..............	2006-07
391-4	(50 overs)	England v Bangladesh at Nottingham...............	2005
387-5	(50 overs)	India v England at Rajkot.......................	2008-09
377-6	(50 overs)	Australia v South Africa at Basseterre	2006-07
376-2	(50 overs)	India v New Zealand at Hyderabad.................	1999-2000

Note: The highest totals by other countries are:

371-9	(50 overs)	Pakistan v Sri Lanka at Nairobi (Gymkhana)..........	1996-97
360-4	(50 overs)	West Indies v Sri Lanka at Karachi	1987-88
340-2	(50 overs)	Zimbabwe v Namibia at Harare	2002-03
301-7	(50 overs)	Bangladesh v Kenya at Bogra.....................	2005-06

Bold type denotes performances in the calendar year 2009.

HIGHEST TOTALS BATTING SECOND

438-9	(49.5 overs)	South Africa v Australia at Johannesburg	2005-06
		(Won by 1 wicket)	
411-8	**(50 overs)**	**Sri Lanka v India at Rajkot**	**2009-10**
		(Lost by 3 runs)	
350-9	(49.3 overs)	New Zealand v Australia at Hamilton	2006-07
		(Won by 1 wicket)	
347	**(49.4 overs)**	**India v Australia at Hyderabad**	**2009-10**
		(Lost by 3 runs)	
344-8	(50 overs)	Pakistan v India at Karachi	2003-04
		(Lost by 5 runs)	
340-5	(48.4 overs)	New Zealand v Australia at Auckland..................	2006-07
		(Won by 5 wickets)	
340-7	(50 overs)	New Zealand v England at Napier.....................	2007-08
		(Tied)	
335-5	(50 overs)	New Zealand v Australia at Perth	2006-07
		(Lost by 8 runs)	

Bold type denotes performances in the calendar year 2009.

HIGHEST MATCH AGGREGATES

872-13	(99.5 overs)	South Africa v Australia at Johannesburg	2005-06
825-15	**(100 overs)**	**India v Sri Lanka at Rajkot.**	**2009-10**
726-14	**(95.1 overs)**	**New Zealand v India at Christchurch**	**2008-09**
697-14	**(99.4 overs)**	**India v Australia at Hyderabad**	**2009-10**
696-14	(99.3 overs)	New Zealand v Australia at Hamilton	2006-07
693-15	(100 overs)	Pakistan v India at Karachi	2003-04
691-19	(98.3 overs)	Netherlands v Sri Lanka at Amstelveen................	2006
680-13	(100 overs)	New Zealand v England at Napier.....................	2007-08

Bold type denotes performances in the calendar year 2009.

LOWEST INNINGS TOTALS

35	(18 overs)	Zimbabwe v Sri Lanka at Harare......................	2003-04
36	(18.4 overs)	Canada v Sri Lanka at Paarl.........................	2002-03
38	(15.4 overs)	Zimbabwe v Sri Lanka at Colombo (SSC)...............	2001-02
43	(19.5 overs)	Pakistan v West Indies at Cape Town	1992-93
44	**(24.5 overs)**	**Zimbabwe v Bangladesh at Chittagong**	**2009-10**
45	(40.3 overs)	Canada v England at Manchester......................	1979
45	(14 overs)	Namibia v Australia at Potchefstroom	2002-03
54	(26.3 overs)	India v Sri Lanka at Sharjah........................	2000-01
54	(23.2 overs)	West Indies v South Africa at Cape Town..............	2003-04

55	(28.3 overs)	Sri Lanka v West Indies at Sharjah	1986-87
63	(25.5 overs)	India v Australia at Sydney	1980-81
64	(35.5 overs)	New Zealand v Pakistan at Sharjah	1985-86
65	(24 overs)	USA v Australia at Southampton	2004
65	(24.3 overs)	Zimbabwe v India at Harare	2005-06
67	(31 overs)	Zimbabwe v Sri Lanka at Harare	2008-09
68	(31.3 overs)	Scotland v West Indies at Leicester	1999
69	(28 overs)	South Africa v Australia at Sydney	1993-94
69	(22.5 overs)	Zimbabwe v Kenya at Harare	2005-06
70	(25.2 overs)	Australia v England at Birmingham	1977
70	(26.3 overs)	Australia v New Zealand at Adelaide	1985-86

The lowest totals by other Test-playing countries are:

| 74 | (27.4 overs) | Bangladesh v Australia at Darwin | 2008 |
| 86 | (32.4 overs) | England v Australia at Manchester | 2001 |

LARGEST VICTORIES

290 runs	New Zealand (402-2 in 50 overs) v Ireland (112 in 28.4 ov) at Aberdeen	2008
257 runs	India (413-5 in 50 overs) v Bermuda (156 in 43.1 overs) at Port-of-Spain	2006-07
256 runs	Australia (301-6 in 50 overs) v Namibia (45 in 14 overs) at Potchefstroom	2002-03
256 runs	India (374-4 in 50 overs) v Hong Kong (118 in 36.5 overs) at Karachi	2008
245 runs	Sri Lanka (299-5 in 50 overs) v India (54 in 26.3 overs) at Sharjah	2000-01
243 runs	Sri Lanka (321-6 in 50 overs) v Bermuda (78 in 24.4 overs) at P-of-Spain	2006-07
234 runs	**Sri Lanka (309-5 in 50 overs) v Pakistan (75 in 22.5 overs) at Lahore**	**2008-09**
233 runs	Pakistan (320-3 in 50 overs) v Bangladesh (87 in 34.2 overs) at Dhaka	1999-2000
232 runs	Australia (323-2 in 50 overs) v Sri Lanka (91 in 35.5 overs) at Adelaide	1984-85

There have been **38** instances of victory by ten wickets.

Bold type denotes performances in the calendar year 2009.

TIED MATCHES

There have been **23** tied one-day internationals. Australia have tied eight matches; Bangladesh are the only Test-playing country never to have tied. The most recent ties are:

South Africa (259-7 in 50 overs) v Australia (259-9 in 50 overs) at Potchefstroom	2001-02
Sri Lanka (268-9 in 50 overs) v South Africa (229-6 in 45 overs) at Durban (D/L method)	2002-03
England (270-5 in 50 overs) v South Africa (270-8 in 50 overs) at Bloemfontein	2004-05
Australia (196 in 48.5 overs) v England (196-9 in 50 overs) at Lord's	2005
Ireland (221-9 in 50 overs) v Zimbabwe (221 in 50 overs) at Kingston	2006-07
England (340-6 in 50 overs) v New Zealand (340-7 in 50 overs) at Napier	2007-08

OTHER RECORDS

MOST APPEARANCES

444	**S. T. Jayasuriya (SL/Asia)**	299	B. C. Lara (WI/World)
440	**S. R. Tendulkar (I)**	**295**	**J. H. Kallis (SA/World/Africa)**
378	Inzamam-ul-Haq (P/Asia)	**288**	**M. V. Boucher (SA/Africa)**
356	Wasim Akram (P)	**288**	**Shahid Afridi (P/World/Asia)**
339	**R. Dravid (I/World/Asia)**	287	A. C. Gilchrist (A/World)
334	M. Azharuddin (I)	283	Salim Malik (P)
334	**M. Muralitharan (SL/World/Asia)**	280	S. P. Fleming (NZ/World)
330	**R. T. Ponting (A/World)**	**278**	**Mohammad Yousuf (P/Asia)**
325	S. R. Waugh (A)	273	A. R. Border (A)
322	W. P. U. J. C. Vaas (SL/Asia)	271	A. Kumble (I/Asia)
314	**D. P. M. D. Jayawardene (SL/Asia)**	269	A. Ranatunga (SL)
311	S. C. Ganguly (I/Asia)	268	M. S. Atapattu (SL)
308	P. A. de Silva (SL)	**262**	**K. C. Sangakkara (SL/World/Asia)**
303	S. M. Pollock (SA/World/Africa)	262	Waqar Younis (P)

Notes: The most appearances for other countries are 219 by G. W. Flower (Z), **173** by **P. D. Collingwood** (E), and **152** by **Mohammad Ashraful** (B). Excluding appearances for combined teams, the record for Sri Lanka is **440** appearances by **S. T. Jayasuriya**; for Pakistan, 375 by Inzamam-ul-Haq; for West Indies, 295 by B. C. Lara; for South Africa, 294 by S. M. Pollock; and for New Zealand, 279 by S. P. Fleming.

Bold type denotes those who played one-day internationals in the calendar year 2009.

MOST MATCHES AS CAPTAIN

	P	W	L	T	NR		P	W	L	T	NR
S. P. Fleming (NZ)....	218	98	106	1	13	W. J. Cronje (SA).....	138	99	35	1	3
R. T. Ponting (A/World)	199	145	42	2	10	**G. C. Smith (SA/Af)** ..	127	74	46	1	6
A. Ranatunga (SL)....	193	89	95	1	8	B. C. Lara (WI)	125	59	59	0	7
A. R. Border (A)	178	107	67	1	3	S. T. Jayasuriya (SL) ..	118	66	47	2	3
M. Azharuddin (I)	174	90	76	2	6	Wasim Akram (P)	109	66	41	2	0
S. C. Ganguly (I/Asia)	147	76	66	0	5	S. R. Waugh (A)......	106	67	35	3	1
Imran Khan (P).......	139	75	59	1	4	I. V. A. Richards (WI) ..	105	67	36	0	2

Bold type denotes those who captained in one-day internationals in the calendar year 2009.

WORLD CUP RECORDS

WORLD CUP FINALS

1975	WEST INDIES (291-8) beat Australia (274) by 17 runs	Lord's
1979	WEST INDIES (286-9) beat England (194) by 92 runs	Lord's
1983	INDIA (183) beat West Indies (140) by 43 runs	Lord's
1987	AUSTRALIA (253-5) beat England (246-8) by seven runs	Calcutta
1992	PAKISTAN (249-6) beat England (227) by 22 runs....................	Melbourne
1996	SRI LANKA (245-3) beat Australia (241-7) by seven wickets	Lahore
1999	AUSTRALIA (133-2) beat Pakistan (132) by eight wickets.............	Lord's
2003	AUSTRALIA (359-2) beat India (234) by 125 runs...................	Johannesburg
2007	AUSTRALIA (281-4) beat Sri Lanka (215-8) by 53 runs (D/L method)	Bridgetown

TEAM RESULTS

	Rounds reached				Matches			
	W	F	SF	P	W	L	T	NR
Australia (9)................	4	6	6	69	51	17	1	0
England (9)	0	3	5	59	36	22	0	1
West Indies (9).............	2	3	4	57	35	21	0	1
New Zealand (9)	0	0	5	62	35	26	0	1
India (9)....................	1	2	4	58	32	25	0	1
Pakistan (9)	1	2	5	56	30	24	0	2
South Africa (5)............	0	0	3	40	25	13	2	0
Sri Lanka (9)	1	2	3	57	25	30	1	1
Zimbabwe (7)	0	0	0	45	8	33	1	3
Kenya (4)..................	0	0	1	23	6	16	0	1
Bangladesh (3)..............	0	0	0	20	5	14	0	1
Ireland (1)	0	0	0	9	2	6	1	0
Netherlands (3)	0	0	0	14	2	12	0	0
United Arab Emirates (1).....	0	0	0	5	1	4	0	0
Canada (3)	0	0	0	12	1	11	0	0
Bermuda (1)................	0	0	0	3	0	3	0	0
East Africa (1)	0	0	0	3	0	3	0	0
Namibia (1)	0	0	0	6	0	6	0	0
Scotland (2)	0	0	0	8	0	8	0	0

The number of tournaments each team has played in is shown in brackets.

BATTING RECORDS

Most Runs

	M	I	NO	R	HS	100s	Avge
S. R. Tendulkar (India)........	36	35	4	1,796	152	4	57.93
R. T. Ponting (Australia)	39	36	4	1,537	140*	4	48.03
B. C. Lara (West Indies)	34	33	4	1,225	116	2	42.24
S. T. Jayasuriya (Sri Lanka).....	38	37	3	1,165	120	3	34.26
A. C. Gilchrist (Australia)	31	31	1	1,085	149	1	36.16
Javed Miandad (P)............	33	30	5	1,083	103*	1	43.32
S. P. Fleming (New Zealand)....	33	33	3	1,075	134*	2	35.83
H. H. Gibbs (South Africa)	25	23	4	1,067	143	2	56.15
P. A. de Silva (SL)...........	35	32	3	1,064	145	2	36.68
I. V. A. Richards (WI)	23	21	5	1,013	181	3	63.31
S. C. Ganguly (India)..........	21	21	3	1,006	183	4	55.88
M. E. Waugh (A)..............	22	22	3	1,004	130	4	52.84

Highest Scores

188*	G. Kirsten	South Africa v United Arab Emirates at Rawalpindi ...	1995-96
183	S. C. Ganguly	India v Sri Lanka at Taunton.......................	1999
181	I. V. A. Richards	West Indies v Sri Lanka at Karachi.................	1987-88
175*	Kapil Dev	India v Zimbabwe at Tunbridge Wells	1983
172*	C. B. Wishart	Zimbabwe v Namibia at Harare	2002-03
171*	G. M. Turner†	New Zealand v East Africa at Birmingham	1975
161	A. C. Hudson	South Africa v Netherlands at Rawalpindi	1995-96
160	Imran Nazir	Pakistan v Zimbabwe at Kingston..................	2006-07
158	M. L. Hayden	Australia v West Indies at North Sound	2006-07
152	S. R. Tendulkar	India v Namibia at Pietermaritzburg	2002-03

Highest scores for other Test-playing countries:

145	P. A. de Silva	Sri Lanka v Kenya at Kandy.......................	1995-96
137	D. L. Amiss†	England v India at Lord's	1975
87	Mohammad Ashraful	Bangladesh v South Africa at Providence............	2006-07

† *Amiss scored 137 and Turner 171* on the opening day of the inaugural World Cup in 1975; both remain national World Cup records.*

Most Hundreds

4, S. C. Ganguly (I), R. T. Ponting (A), S. R. Tendulkar (I) and M. E. Waugh (A); 3, M. L. Hayden (A), S. T. Jayasuriya (SL), Ramiz Raja (P), I. V. A. Richards (WI) and Saeed Anwar (P).

Most Runs in a Tournament

673, S. R. Tendulkar (I) 2002-03; 659, M. L. Hayden (A) 2006-07; 548, D. P. M. D. Jayawardene (SL) 2006-07; 539, R. T. Ponting (A) 2006-07; 523, S. R. Tendulkar (I) 1995-96; 499, S. B. Styris (NZ) 2006-07; 485, J. H. Kallis (SA) 2006-07; 484, M. E. Waugh (A) 1995-96.

Highest Partnership for Each Wicket

194	for 1st	Saeed Anwar and Wajahatullah Wasti	P v NZ	Manchester	1999
318	for 2nd	S. C. Ganguly and R. Dravid	I v SL	Taunton	1999
237*	for 3rd	R. Dravid and S. R. Tendulkar	I v K	Bristol	1999
204	for 4th	M. J. Clarke and B. J. Hodge	A v Neth	Basseterre	2006-07
148	for 5th	R. G. Twose and C. L. Cairns	NZ v A	Cardiff	1999
161	for 6th	M. O. Odumbe and A. V. Vadher	K v SL	Southampton	1999
98	for 7th	R. R. Sarwan and R. D. Jacobs	WI v NZ	Port Elizabeth	2002-03
117	for 8th	D. L. Houghton and I. P. Butchart	Z v NZ	Hyderabad (India)	1987-88
126*	for 9th	Kapil Dev and S. M. H. Kirmani	I v Z	Tunbridge Wells	1983
71	for 10th	A. M. E. Roberts and J. Garner	WI v I	Manchester	1983

BOWLING RECORDS

Most Wickets

	O	R	W	BB	4W/i	Avge
G. D. McGrath (A)	325.5	1,292	71	7-15	2	18.19
Wasim Akram (P).	324.3	1,311	55	5-28	3	23.83
M. Muralitharan (SL)	272.3	1,044	53	4-19	3	19.69
W. P. U. J. C. Vaas (SL).	261.4	1,040	49	6-25	2	21.22
J. Srinath (I)	283.2	1,224	44	4-30	2	27.81
A. A. Donald (SA)	218.5	913	38	4-17	2	24.02
G. B. Hogg (A).	158.3	654	34	4-27	2	19.23
Imran Khan (P).	169.3	655	34	4-37	2	19.26
S. K. Warne (A)	162.5	624	32	4-29	4	19.50
C. Z. Harris (NZ)	194.2	861	32	4-70	1	26.90
A. Kumble (I)	173.1	708	31	4-32	1	22.83
S. M. Pollock (SA)	269.0	970	31	5-36	1	31.29

Best Bowling

7-15	G. D. McGrath	Australia v Namibia at Potchefstroom	2002-03
7-20	A. J. Bichel	Australia v England at Port Elizabeth	2002-03
7-51	W. W. Davis	West Indies v Australia at Leeds	1983
6-14	G. J. Gilmour	Australia v England at Leeds	1975
6-23	A. Nehra	India v England at Durban	2002-03
6-23	S. E. Bond	New Zealand v Australia at Port Elizabeth	2002-03
6-25	W. P. U. J. C. Vaas	Sri Lanka v Bangladesh at Pietermaritzburg	2002-03
6-39	K. H. MacLeay	Australia v India at Nottingham	1983

Best analyses for other Test-playing countries:

5-18	A. J. Hall	South Africa v England at Bridgetown	2006-07
5-21	P. A. Strang	Zimbabwe v Kenya at Patna.	1995-96
5-28	Wasim Akram	Pakistan v Namibia at Kimberley	2002-03
5-39	V. J. Marks	England v Sri Lanka at Taunton.	1983
4-38	Mashrafe bin Mortaza	Bangladesh v India at Port-of-Spain.	2006-07

Other Bowling Records

Hat-tricks: Chetan Sharma, India v New Zealand at Nagpur, 1987-88; Saqlain Mushtaq, Pakistan v Zimbabwe at The Oval, 1999; W. P. U. J. C. Vaas, Sri Lanka v Bangladesh at Pietermaritzburg, 2002-03 (the first three balls of the match); B. Lee, Australia v Kenya at Durban, 2002-03; S. L. Malinga, Sri Lanka v South Africa at Providence, 2006-07 (four wickets in four balls).

Most economical bowling (minimum 10 overs): 12–8–6–1, B. S. Bedi, India v East Africa at Leeds, 1975.

Most expensive bowling (minimum 10 overs): 12–1–105–2, M. C. Snedden, New Zealand v England at The Oval, 1983; 10–0–97–1, A. L. F. de Mel, Sri Lanka v West Indies at Karachi, 1987-88.

Most Wickets in a Tournament

26, G. D. McGrath (A) 2006-07; 23, M. Muralitharan (SL) 2006-07, S. W. Tait (A) 2006-07 and W. P. U. J. C. Vaas (SL) 2002-03; 22, B. Lee (A) 2002-03; 21, G. B. Hogg (A) 2006-07 and G. D. McGrath (A) 2002-03; 20, G. I. Allott (NZ) 1999 and S. K. Warne (A) 1999.

WICKETKEEPING RECORDS

Most Dismissals

A. C. Gilchrist (A)	52 (45ct, 7st)	A. J. Stewart (E)	23 (21ct, 2st)
K. C. Sangakkara (SL)	32 (26ct, 6st)	R. D. Jacobs (WI)	22 (21ct, 1st)
M. V. Boucher (SA)	31 (all ct)	Wasim Bari (P)	22 (18ct, 4st)
Moin Khan (P)	30 (23ct, 7st)	I. A. Healy (A)	21 (18ct, 3st)
B. B. McCullum (NZ)	23 (22ct, 1st)	P. J. L. Dujon (WI)	20 (19ct, 1st)

Most Dismissals in an Innings

6 (6ct)	A. C. Gilchrist	Australia v Namibia at Potchefstroom	2002-03
5 (5ct)	S. M. H. Kirmani	India v Zimbabwe at Leicester	1983
5 (4ct, 1st)	J. C. Adams	West Indies v Kenya at Pune	1995-96
5 (4ct, 1st)	Rashid Latif	Pakistan v New Zealand at Lahore	1995-96
5 (5ct)	R. D. Jacobs	West Indies v New Zealand at Southampton	1999
5 (4ct, 1st)	N. R. Mongia	India v Zimbabwe at Leicester	1999

Most Dismissals in a Tournament

21, A. C. Gilchrist (A) 2002-03; 17, A. C. Gilchrist (A) 2006-07 and K. C. Sangakkara (SL) 2002-03; 16, R. Dravid (I) 2002-03, P. J. L. Dujon (WI) 1983 and Moin Khan (P) 1999; 15, D. J. Richardson (SA) 1991-92 and K. C. Sangakkara (SL) 2006-07.

FIELDING RECORDS

Most Catches

25, R. T. Ponting (A); 18, S. T. Jayasuriya (SL); 16, C. L. Cairns (NZ), Inzamam-ul-Haq (P) and B. C. Lara (WI); 14, P. A. de Silva (SL), A. Kumble (I) and S. R. Waugh (A).

MOST APPEARANCES

39, G. D. McGrath (A) and R. T. Ponting (A); 38, S. T. Jayasuriya (SL) and Wasim Akram (P); 36, S. R. Tendulkar (I); 35, P. A. de Silva (SL) and Inzamam-ul-Haq (P); 34, B. C. Lara (WI) and J. Srinath (I); 33, S. P. Fleming (NZ), Javed Miandad (P) and S. R. Waugh (A).

TEAM RECORDS

Highest Totals

413-5	(50 overs)	India v Bermuda at Port-of-Spain	2006-07
398-5	(50 overs)	Sri Lanka v Kenya at Kandy	1995-96
377-6	(50 overs)	Australia v South Africa at Basseterre.	2006-07
373-6	(50 overs)	India v Sri Lanka at Taunton.	1999
363-5	(50 overs)	New Zealand v Canada at Gros Islet, St Lucia	2006-07
360-4	(50 overs)	West Indies v Sri Lanka at Karachi.	1987-88
359-2	(50 overs)	Australia v India at Johannesburg	2002-03
358-5	(50 overs)	Australia v Netherlands at Basseterre	2006-07
356-4	(50 overs)	South Africa v West Indies at St George's	2006-07
353-3	(40 overs)	South Africa v Netherlands at Basseterre	2006-07

Highest totals for other Test-playing countries:

349	(49.5 overs)	Pakistan v Zimbabwe at Kingston.	2006-07
340-2	(50 overs)	Zimbabwe v Namibia at Harare.	2002-03
334-4	(60 overs)	England v India at Lord's	1975
251-8	(50 overs)	Bangladesh v South Africa at Providence	2006-07

Highest total batting second:

313-7	(49.2 overs)	Sri Lanka v Zimbabwe at New Plymouth	1991-92

Lowest Totals

36	(18.4 overs)	Canada v Sri Lanka at Paarl	2002-03
45	(40.3 overs)	Canada v England at Manchester	1979
45	(14 overs)	Namibia v Australia at Potchefstroom	2002-03
68	(31.3 overs)	Scotland v West Indies at Leicester	1999
74	(40.2 overs)	Pakistan v England at Adelaide	1991-92
77	(27.4 overs)	Ireland v Sri Lanka at St George's	2006-07
78	(24.4 overs)	Bermuda v Sri Lanka at Port-of-Spain	2006-07
84	(17.4 overs)	Namibia v Pakistan at Kimberley	2002-03
86	(37.2 overs)	Sri Lanka v West Indies at Manchester	1975

Highest Aggregate

671-16	(98 overs)	Australia v South Africa at Basseterre	2006-07

RESULTS

Largest Victories

10 wkts	India beat East Africa at Leeds	1975
10 wkts	West Indies beat Zimbabwe at Birmingham	1983
10 wkts	West Indies beat Pakistan at Melbourne	1991-92
10 wkts	South Africa beat Kenya at Potchefstroom	2002-03
10 wkts	Sri Lanka beat Bangladesh at Pietermaritzburg	2002-03
10 wkts	South Africa beat Bangladesh at Bloemfontein	2002-03
10 wkts	Australia beat Bangladesh at North Sound	2006-07
257 runs	India beat Bermuda at Port-of-Spain	2006-07
256 runs	Australia beat Namibia at Potchefstroom	2002-03
243 runs	Sri Lanka beat Bermuda at Port-of-Spain	2006-07

Narrowest Victories

1 wkt	West Indies beat Pakistan at Birmingham	1975
1 wkt	Pakistan beat West Indies at Lahore	1987-88
1 wkt	South Africa beat Sri Lanka at Providence	2006-07
1 wkt	England beat West Indies at Bridgetown	2006-07
1 run	Australia beat India at Madras	1987-88
1 run	Australia beat India at Brisbane	1991-92
2 runs	Sri Lanka beat England at North Sound	2006-07

Ties

Australia v South Africa at Birmingham	1999
South Africa v Sri Lanka (D/L method) at Durban	2002-03
Ireland v Zimbabwe at Kingston	2006-07

TWENTY20 INTERNATIONAL RECORDS

Matches in this section do not have first-class status.

RESULTS SUMMARY OF TWENTY20 INTERNATIONALS

2004-05 to December 31, 2009 (127 matches)

	Matches	Won	Lost	No Result	% Won (excl. NR)
Pakistan...................	27	21	6	0	77.77
South Africa................	26	17	9	0	65.38
Sri Lanka	25	15	10	0	60.00
India......................	20	11	8	1	57.89
West Indies................	18	9	9	0	50.00
Australia...................	24	11	12	1	47.82
New Zealand................	30	13	17	0	43.33
Zimbabwe..................	7	3	4	0	42.85
England...................	23	9	13	1	40.90
Bangladesh	13	3	10	0	23.07
Netherlands................	6	3	2	1	60.00
Ireland....................	9	4	4	1	50.00
Canada	7	2	5	0	28.57
Scotland	8	2	5	1	28.57
Kenya.....................	8	1	7	0	12.50
Bermuda	3	0	3	0	0.00

* New Zealand, India and Zimbabwe won tied matches with West Indies, Pakistan and Canada respectively in bowling contests. West Indies won a tied match with New Zealand in a one-over eliminator.

BATTING RECORDS

HIGHEST INDIVIDUAL INNINGS

117	C. H. Gayle	West Indies v South Africa at Johannesburg.........	2007-08
98*	R. T. Ponting	Australia v New Zealand at Auckland	2004-05
96*	**T. M. Dilshan**	**Sri Lanka v West Indies at The Oval**	**2009**
96	D. R. Martyn	Australia v South Africa at Brisbane................	2005-06
94	**L. L. Bosman**	**South Africa v England at Centurion**	**2009-10**
90*	H. H. Gibbs	South Africa v West Indies at Johannesburg..........	2007-08

MOST RUNS

		M	I	NO	R	HS	100s	Avge
1	**B. B. McCullum (NZ)** ...	30	30	4	813	69*	0	31.26
2	**G. C. Smith (SA)**	20	20	2	642	89*	0	35.66
3	**T. M. Dilshan (SL)**......	23	22	3	607	96*	0	31.94
4	**S. T. Jayasuriya (SL)**....	23	23	1	606	88	0	27.54
5	**K. C. Sangakkara (SL)** ..	20	19	2	572	78	0	33.64
6	**K. P. Pietersen (E)**......	20	20	1	558	79	0	29.36
7	**Shoaib Malik (P)**	27	26	6	554	57	0	27.70
8	**G. Gambhir (I)**.........	19	18	0	552	75	0	30.66
9	**Misbah-ul-Haq (P)**......	23	19	8	509	87*	0	46.27

HIGHEST PARTNERSHIP FOR EACH WICKET

170	**for 1st**	G. C. Smith and L. L. Bosman	SA v E	Centurion	**2009-10**
111	for 2nd	G. C. Smith and H. H. Gibbs	SA v A	Johannesburg	2005-06
120*	for 3rd	H. H. Gibbs and J. M. Kemp	SA v WI	Johannesburg	2005-06
101	for 4th	Younis Khan and Shoaib Malik	P v SL	Johannesburg	2007-08
119*	for 5th	Shoaib Malik and Misbah-ul-Haq	P v A	Johannesburg	2007-08
77*	for 6th	R. T. Ponting and M. E. K. Hussey	A v NZ	Auckland	2004-05
91	for 7th	P. D. Collingwood and M. H. Yardy	E v WI	The Oval	2007
61	**for 8th**	**S. K. Raina and Harbhajan Singh**	**I v NZ**	**Christchurch**	**2008-09**
44	for 9th	S. L. Malinga and C. R. D. Fernando	SL v NZ	Auckland	2006-07
28	for 10th	J. D. P. Oram and J. S. Patel	NZ v A	Perth	2007-08

BOWLING RECORDS

BEST BOWLING ANALYSES

5-6	Umar Gul	Pakistan v New Zealand at The Oval	**2009**
4-7	M. R. Gillespie	New Zealand v Kenya at Durban	2007-08
4-8	**Umar Gul**	**Pakistan v Australia at Dubai**	**2008-09**
4-9	D. W. Steyn	South Africa v West Indies at Port Elizabeth	2007-08
4-11	**Shahid Afridi**	**Pakistan v Netherlands at The Oval**	**2009**

HAT-TRICKS

B. Lee	Australia v Bangladesh at Cape Town	2007-08
J. D. P. Oram	**New Zealand v Sri Lanka at Colombo**	**2009**

MOST WICKETS

		M	*B*	*R*	*W*	*BB*	*4W/i*	*Avge*
1	Umar Gul (P).	23	493	452	39	5-6	4	11.58
2	Shahid Afridi (P).	16	600	577	37	4-11	2	15.59
3	D. L. Vettori (NZ)	18	426	390	27	4-20	1	14.44
4	B. A. W. Mendis (SL) . . .	12	276	244	25	4-15	2	9.76
5	S. L. Malinga (SL).	20	400	500	24	3-17	0	20.83
6	D. W. Steyn (SA).	14	306	359	23	4-9	1	15.60
7	S. C. J. Broad (E)	18	390	518	22	3-17	0	23.54

WICKETKEEPING RECORDS

MOST DISMISSALS IN AN INNINGS

4 (all ct)	A. C. Gilchrist	Australia v Zimbabwe at Cape Town	2007-08
4 (all ct)	M. J. Prior	England v South Africa at Cape Town	2007-08
4 (all ct)	A. C. Gilchrist	Australia v New Zealand at Perth.	2007-08
4 (all st)	**Kamran Akmal**	**Pakistan v Netherlands at Lord's**	**2009**
4 (3ct, 1st)	N. J. O'Brien	Ireland v Sri Lanka at Lord's	2009

MOST DISMISSALS

			M	*Ct*	*St*
1	30	Kamran Akmal (P).	27	12	18
2	25	A. B. de Villiers (SA)	23	23	2
3	22	B. B. McCullum (NZ).	30	19	3

Note: A. B. de Villiers's record includes 17 catches taken in 18 Twenty20 internationals when not keeping wicket; B. B. McCullum's includes 6 in 10. Kamran Akmal played one Twenty20 international in which he did not keep wicket but he did not take a catch in that game.

TEAM RECORDS

HIGHEST INNINGS TOTALS

260-6	(20 overs)	Sri Lanka v Kenya at Johannesburg	2007-08
241-6	**(20 overs)**	**South Africa v England at Centurion**	**2009-10**
221-5	(20 overs)	Australia v England at Sydney	2006-07
218-4	(20 overs)	India v England at Durban	2007-08
215-5	**(20 overs)**	**Sri Lanka v India at Nagpur**	**2009-10**
214-5	(20 overs)	Australia v New Zealand at Auckland	2004-05

LOWEST INNINGS TOTALS

67	(17.2 overs)	Kenya v Ireland at Belfast	2008
70	(20 overs)	Bermuda v Canada at Belfast............................	2008
73	(16.5 overs)	Kenya v New Zealand at Durban........................	2007-08
74	(17.3 overs)	India v Australia at Melbourne.........................	2007-08
75	(19.2 overs)	Canada v Zimbabwe at King City	2007-08

OTHER RECORDS

MOST APPEARANCES

30	**B. B. McCullum (NZ)**	27	**Shoaib Malik (P)**
27	**Kamran Akmal (P)**	26	**Shahid Afridi (P)**

Bold type denotes performances in the calendar year 2009 or, in career figures, players who appeared in Twenty20 internationals in that year.

MISCELLANEOUS RECORDS

LARGE ATTENDANCES

Test Series

943,000	Australia v England (5 Tests)	1936-37

In England

549,650	England v Australia (5 Tests)	1953

Test Matches

†‡465,000	India v Pakistan, Calcutta	1998-99
350,534	Australia v England, Melbourne (Third Test)	1936-37

Note: Attendance at India v England at Calcutta in 1981-82 may have exceeded 350,000.

In England

158,000+	England v Australia, Leeds	1948
137,915	England v Australia, Lord's..............................	1953

Test Match Day

‡100,000	India v Pakistan, Calcutta (first four days)....................	1998-99
90,800	Australia v West Indies, Melbourne (Fifth Test, second day)	1960-61
89,155	Australia v England, Melbourne (Fourth Test, first day)..........	2006-07

Other First-Class Matches in England

93,000	England v Australia, Lord's (Fourth Victory Match, 3 days)	1945
80,000+	Surrey v Yorkshire, The Oval (3 days)	1906
78,792	Yorkshire v Lancashire, Leeds (3 days).....................	1904
76,617	Lancashire v Yorkshire, Manchester (3 days)	1926

One-Day Internationals

‡100,000	India v South Africa, Calcutta.............................	1993-94
‡100,000	India v West Indies, Calcutta..............................	1993-94
‡100,000	India v West Indies, Calcutta..............................	1994-95
‡100,000	India v Sri Lanka, Calcutta (World Cup semi-final)	1995-96
‡100,000	India v Australia, Kolkata	2003-04
‡90,000	India v Pakistan, Calcutta	1986-87
‡90,000	India v South Africa, Calcutta.............................	1991-92
87,182	England v Pakistan, Melbourne (World Cup final)	1991-92
86,133	Australia v West Indies, Melbourne	1983-84

Twenty20 International

84,041	Australia v India, Melbourne................................	2007-08

† *Estimated.*
‡ *No official attendance figures were issued for these games, but capacity at Calcutta (now Kolkata) is believed to have reached 100,000 following rebuilding in 1993.*

LORD'S CRICKET GROUND

Lord's and the Marylebone Cricket Club were founded in London in 1787. The Club has enjoyed an uninterrupted career since that date, but there have been three grounds known as Lord's. The first (1787–1810) was situated where Dorset Square now is; the second (1809–13), at North Bank, had to be abandoned owing to the cutting of the Regent's Canal; and the third, opened in 1814, is the present one at St John's Wood. It was not until 1866 that the freehold of Lord's was secured by MCC. The present pavilion was erected in 1890 at a cost of £21,000.

HIGHEST INDIVIDUAL SCORES MADE AT LORD'S

333	G. A. Gooch	England v India	1990
316*	J. B. Hobbs	Surrey v Middlesex	1926
315*	P. Holmes	Yorkshire v Middlesex	1925
315	M. A. Wagh......	Warwickshire v Middlesex	2001
303*	N. V. Knight	Warwickshire v Middlesex	2004

Note: The longest innings in a first-class match at Lord's was N. V. Knight's, which lasted 644 minutes.

HIGHEST TOTALS AT LORD'S

First-Class Matches

729-6 dec	Australia v England..	1930
682-6 dec	South Africa v England...	2003
665	West Indians v Middlesex.......................................	1939
653-4 dec	England v India...	1990
652-8 dec	West Indies v England	1973

Minor Matches

735-9 dec	MCC and Ground v Wiltshire....................................	1888

BIGGEST HIT AT LORD'S

The only known instance of a batsman hitting a ball over the present pavilion at Lord's occurred when A. E. Trott, appearing for MCC against Australians on July 31, August 1, 2, 1899, drove M. A. Noble so far and high that the ball struck a chimney pot and fell behind the building.

MINOR CRICKET

HIGHEST INDIVIDUAL SCORES

628*	A. E. J. Collins, Clark's House v North Town at Clifton College.	
	A junior house match. His innings of 6 hours 50 minutes was spread over four	
	afternoons	1899
566	C. J. Eady, Break-o'-Day v Wellington at Hobart	1901-02
515	D. R. Havewalla, B. B. and C. I. Railways v St Xavier's at Bombay	1933-34
506*	J. C. Sharp, Melbourne GS v Geelong College at Melbourne	1914-15
502*	Chaman Lal, Mehandra Coll., Patiala v Government Coll., Rupar at Patiala	1956-57
485	A. E. Stoddart, Hampstead v Stoics at Hampstead.	1886
475*	Mohammad Iqbal, Muslim Model HS v Islamia HS, Sialkot at Lahore.	1958-59
466*	G. T. S. Stevens, Beta v Lambda (University College School house match) at	
	Neasden. *Stevens scored his 466 and took 14 wickets on one day*	1919
459	J. A. Prout, Wesley College v Geelong College at Geelong	1908-09

Note: The highest score in a Minor County match is 323* by F. E. Lacey for Hampshire v Norfolk at Southampton in 1887; the highest in the Minor Counties Championship is 282 by E. Garnett for Berkshire v Wiltshire at Reading in 1908.

HIGHEST PARTNERSHIPS

721* for 1st	B. Manoj Kumar and M. S. Tumbi, St Peter's High School v St Philip's	
	High School at Secunderabad	2006-07
664* for 3rd	V. G. Kambli and S. R. Tendulkar, Sharadashram Vidyamandir School v	
	St Xavier's High School at Bombay	1987-88

Notes: Manoj Kumar and Tumbi scored 721 in 40 overs in an Under-13 inter-school match; they hit 103 fours between them, but no sixes. Their opponents were all out for 21 in seven overs.

Kambli was 16 years old, Tendulkar 14. Tendulkar made his Test debut 21 months later.

MOST WICKETS WITH CONSECUTIVE BALLS

There are **two** recorded instances of a bowler taking nine wickets with consecutive balls. Both came in school games: Paul Hugo, for Smithfield School v Aliwal North at Smithfield, South Africa, in 1930-31, and Stephen Fleming (not the future Test captain), for Marlborough College A v Bohally School at Blenheim, New Zealand, in 1967-68. There are five further verified instances of eight wickets in eight balls, the most recent by Mike Walters for the Royal Army Educational Corps v Joint Air Transport Establishment at Beaconsfield in 1979.

TEN WICKETS FOR NO RUNS

There are **24** recorded instances of a bowler taking all ten wickets in an innings for no runs, the most recent by David Morton, for Bayside Muddies v Ranatungas in Brisbane in 1998-99. The previous instance was also in Australia, by the schoolgirl Emma Liddell, for Metropolitan East v West at Penrith (Sydney) in 1995-96. When Jennings Tune did it, for the Yorkshire club Cliffe v Eastrington at Cliffe in 1923, all ten of his victims were bowled.

NOUGHT ALL OUT

In minor matches, this is more common than might be imagined. The historian Peter Wynne-Thomas says the first recorded example was in Norfolk, where an Eleven of Fakenham, Walsingham and Hempton were dismissed for nought by an Eleven of Licham, Dunham and Brisley in July 1815.

MOST DISMISSALS IN AN INNINGS

The only recorded instance of a wicketkeeper being involved in all ten dismissals in an innings was by Welihinda Badalge Bennett, for Mahinda College against Richmond College in Ceylon (now Sri Lanka) in 1952-53. His feat comprised six catches and four stumpings. There are three other known instances of nine dismissals in the same innings, one of which – by H. W. P. Middleton for Priory v Mitre in a Repton School house match in 1930 – included eight stumpings. Young Rangers' innings against Bohran Gymkhana in Karachi in 1969-70 included nine run-outs.

The widespread nature – and differing levels of supervision – of minor cricket matches mean that record claims have to be treated with caution. Additions and corrections to the above records for minor cricket will only be considered for inclusion in Wisden *if they are corroborated by independent evidence of the achievement.*

Research: Steven Lynch

RECORD HIT

The Rev. W. Fellows, while at practice on the Christ Church ground at Oxford in 1856, drove a ball bowled by Charles Rogers 175 yards from hit to pitch.

THROWING THE CRICKET BALL

140 yards 2 feet, Robert Percival, on the Durham Sands racecourse, Co. Durham.	c1882
140 yards 9 inches, Ross Mackenzie, at Toronto	1872
140 yards, "King Billy" the Aborigine, at Clermont, Queensland	1872

Note: Extensive research by David Rayvern Allen has shown that these traditional records are probably authentic, if not necessarily wholly accurate. Modern competitions have failed to produce similar distances although Ian Pont, the Essex all-rounder who also played baseball, was reported to have thrown 138 yards in Cape Town in 1981. There have been speculative reports attributing throws of 150 yards or more to figures as diverse as the South African Test player Colin Bland, the Latvian javelin thrower Janis Lusis, who won a gold medal for the Soviet Union in the 1968 Olympics, and the British sprinter Charley Ransome. The definitive record is still awaited.

COUNTY CHAMPIONSHIP

MOST APPEARANCES

762	W. Rhodes	Yorkshire	1898–1930
707	F. E. Woolley	Kent	1906–1938
668	C. P. Mead	Hampshire	1906–1936
617	N. Gifford	Worcestershire (484), Warwickshire (133)	1960–1988
611	W. G. Quaife	Warwickshire	1895–1928
601	G. H. Hirst	Yorkshire	1891–1921

MOST CONSECUTIVE APPEARANCES

423	K. G. Suttle	Sussex	1954–1969
412	J. G. Binks	Yorkshire	1955–1969

Notes: J. Vine made 417 consecutive appearances for Sussex in all first-class matches (399 of them in the Championship) between July 1900 and September 1914.

J. G. Binks did not miss a Championship match for Yorkshire between making his debut in June 1955 and retiring at the end of the 1969 season.

UMPIRES

MOST COUNTY CHAMPIONSHIP APPEARANCES

570	T. W. Spencer	1950–1980	517	H. G. Baldwin	1932–1962
531	F. Chester	1922–1955	511	A. G. T. Whitehead	1970–2005
523	D. J. Constant	1969–2006			

MOST SEASONS ON ENGLISH FIRST-CLASS LIST

38	D. J. Constant	1969–2006	27	**J. W. Holder**	**1983–2009**
36	A. G. T. Whitehead	1970–2005	27	J. Moss	1899–1929
31	K. E. Palmer	1972–2002	26	**B. Dudleston**	**1984–2009**
31	T. W. Spencer	1950–1980	26	W. A. J. West	1896–1925
30	R. Julian	1972–2001	25	H. G. Baldwin	1932–1962
30	P. B. Wight	1966–1995	25	A. Jepson	1960–1984
29	H. D. Bird	1970–1998	25	J. G. Langridge	1956–1980
28	F. Chester	1922–1955	25	B. J. Meyer	1973–1997
28	B. Leadbeater	1981–2008	25	D. R. Shepherd	1981–2005
28	R. Palmer	1980–2007			

Bold type denotes umpires who stood in the 2009 season.

WOMEN'S TEST RECORDS

Amended to December 31, 2009

BATTING RECORDS

HIGHEST INDIVIDUAL INNINGS

242	Kiran Baluch	Pakistan v West Indies at Karachi	2003-04
214	M. Raj	India v England at Taunton	2002
209*	K. L. Rolton	Australia v England at Leeds	2001
204	K. E. Flavell	New Zealand v England at Scarborough	1996
204	M. A. J. Goszko	Australia v England at Shenley Park	2001
200	J. Broadbent	Australia v England at Guildford	1998
193	D. A. Annetts	Australia v England at Collingham	1987
190	S. Agarwal	India v England at Worcester	1986
189	E. A. Snowball	England v New Zealand at Christchurch	1934-35
179	R. Heyhoe-Flint	England v Australia at The Oval	1976
177	S. C. Taylor	England v South Africa at Shenley Park	2003
176*	K. L. Rolton	Australia v England at Worcester	1998

1,000 RUNS IN A CAREER

R	T		R	T	
1,935	27	J. A. Brittin (England)	1,110	13	S. Agarwal (India)
1,594	22	R. Heyhoe-Flint (England)	1,078	12	E. Bakewell (England)
1,380	**18**	**C. M. Edwards (England)**	**1,030**	**15**	**S. C. Taylor (England)**
1,301	19	D. A. Hockley (New Zealand)	1,007	14	M. E. Maclagan (England)
1,164	18	C. A. Hodges (England)	**1,002**	**14**	**K. L. Rolton (Australia)**

BOWLING RECORDS

BEST BOWLING ANALYSES

8-53	N. David	India v England at Jamshedpur	1995-96
7-6	M. B. Duggan	England v Australia at Melbourne	1957-58
7-7	E. R. Wilson	Australia v England at Melbourne	1957-58
7-10	M. E. Maclagan	England v Australia at Brisbane	1934-35
7-18	A. Palmer.	Australia v England at Brisbane	1934-35
7-24	L. Johnston	Australia v New Zealand at Melbourne	1971-72
7-34	G. E. McConway	England v India at Worcester.	1986
7-41	J. A. Burley	New Zealand v England at The Oval	1966
7-51	L. C. Pearson	England v Australia at Sydney	2002-03
7-59	Shaiza Khan.	Pakistan v West Indies at Karachi	2003-04
7-61	E. Bakewell	England v West Indies at Birmingham	1979

MOST WICKETS IN A MATCH

13-226	Shaiza Khan.	Pakistan v West Indies at Karachi	2003-04

50 WICKETS IN A CAREER

W	T		W	T	
77	17	M. B. Duggan (England)	60	19	S. Kulkarni (India)
68	11	E. R. Wilson (Australia)	57	16	R. H. Thompson (Australia)
63	20	D. F. Edulji (India)	55	15	J. Lord (New Zealand)
60	13	C. L. Fitzpatrick (Australia)	50	12	E. Bakewell (England)
60	14	M. E. Maclagan (England)			

WICKETKEEPING RECORDS

SIX DISMISSALS IN AN INNINGS

8 (6ct, 2st)	L. Nye.	England v New Zealand at New Plymouth	1991-92
6 (2ct, 4st)	B. A. Brentnall	New Zealand v South Africa at Johannesburg	1971-72

25 DISMISSALS IN A CAREER

		T	Ct	St
58	C. Matthews (Australia)	20	46	12
43	J. Smit (England).	21	39	4
36	S. A. Hodges (England).	11	19	17
28	B. A. Brentnall (New Zealand)	10	16	12

TEAM RECORDS

HIGHEST INNINGS TOTALS

569-6 dec	Australia v England at Guildford	1998
525	Australia v India at Ahmedabad	1983-84
517-8	New Zealand v England at Scarborough	1996
503-5 dec	England v New Zealand at Christchurch	1934-35

LOWEST INNINGS TOTALS

35	England v Australia at Melbourne	1957-58
38	Australia v England at Melbourne	1957-58
44	New Zealand v England at Christchurch	1934-35
47	Australia v England at Brisbane	1934-35
50	Netherlands v South Africa at Rotterdam..................................	2007

Bold type denotes performances in the calendar year 2009 or, in career figures, players who appeared in Tests in that year.

WOMEN'S ONE-DAY INTERNATIONAL RECORDS

Amended to December 31, 2009

BATTING RECORDS

HIGHEST INDIVIDUAL INNINGS

229*	B. J. Clark	Australia v Denmark at Mumbai..................	1997-98
173*	C. M. Edwards.......	England v Ireland at Pune	1997-98
168	**S. W. Bates**	**New Zealand v Pakistan at Sydney**	**2008-09**
156*	L. M. Keightley......	Australia v Pakistan at Melbourne..................	1996-97
156*	S. C. Taylor	England v India at Lord's	2006
154*	K. L. Rolton.........	Australia v Sri Lanka at Christchurch	2000-01
153*	J. Logtenberg........	South Africa v Netherlands at Deventer	2007
151	K. L. Rolton.........	Australia v Ireland at Dublin	2005

MOST RUNS IN A CAREER

R	M		R	M	
4,844	118	B. J. Clark (Australia)	3,829	130	C. M. Edwards (England)
4,814	**141**	**K. L. Rolton (Australia)**	3,690	114	S. C. Taylor (England)
4,064	118	D. A. Hockley (New Zealand)	3,549	115	M. Raj (India)

BOWLING RECORDS

BEST BOWLING ANALYSES

7-4	Sajjida Shah...........	Pakistan v Japan at Amsterdam.................	2003
7-8	J. M. Chamberlain.......	England v Denmark at Haarlem	1991
7-24	S. Nitschke.............	Australia v England at Kidderminster............	2005
6-10	J. Lord	New Zealand v India at Auckland..............	1981-82
6-10	M. Maben	India v Sri Lanka at Kandy	2003-04
6-20	G. L. Page	New Zealand v Trinidad & Tobago at St Albans ...	1973
6-32	B. H. McNeill	New Zealand v England at Lincoln..............	2007-08

MOST WICKETS IN A CAREER

W	M		W	M	
180	109	C. L. Fitzpatrick (Australia)	102	105	C. E. Taylor (England)
141	97	N. David (India)	**100**	**93**	**L. C. Sthalekar (Australia)**
109	**100**	**J. Goswami (India)**			

WICKETKEEPING RECORDS

MOST DISMISSALS IN AN INNINGS

6 (4ct, 2st)	S. L. Illingworth	New Zealand v Australia at Beckenham.........	1993
6 (1ct, 5st)	V. Kalpana..........	India v Denmark at Slough	1993
6 (2ct, 4st)	Batool Fatima	Pakistan v West Indies at Karachi.............	2003-04

MOST DISMISSALS IN A CAREER

		M	*Ct*	*St*
133	R. J. Rolls (New Zealand)	104	89	44
114	J. Smit (England)	109	69	45
100	J. C. Price (Australia)..............	84	70	30

TEAM RECORDS

HIGHEST INNINGS TOTALS

455-5	New Zealand v Pakistan at Christchurch	1996-97
412-3	Australia v Denmark at Mumbai	1997-98
397-4	Australia v Pakistan at Melbourne	1996-97
376-2	England v Pakistan at Vijayawada	1997-98
375-5	Netherlands v Japan at Schiedam...................................	2003
373-7	**New Zealand v Pakistan at Sydney**...............................	**2008-09**

LOWEST INNINGS TOTALS

22	Netherlands v West Indies at Deventer.................................	2008
23	Pakistan v Australia at Melbourne....................................	1996-97
24	Scotland v England at Reading.......................................	2001
26	India v New Zealand as St Saviour	2002
27	Pakistan v Australia at Hyderabad (India).............................	1997-98
28	Japan v Pakistan at Amsterdam......................................	2003
29	Netherlands v Australia at Perth	1988-89

Bold type denotes performances in the calendar year 2009 or, in career figures, players who appeared in one-day internationals in that year.

WOMEN'S WORLD CUP WINNERS

1973	England	1988-89	Australia	2000-01	New Zealand
1977-78	Australia	1993	England	2004-05	Australia
1981-82	Australia	1997-98	Australia	**2008-09**	**England**

BIRTHS AND DEATHS

TEST CRICKETERS

Full list from 1876-77 to January 27, 2010

In the Test career column, dates in italics indicate seasons embracing two different years (i.e. non-English seasons). In these cases, only the first year is given, e.g. *1876* for 1876-77. Some non-English series taking place outside the host country's normal season are dated by a single year.

The Test career figures are complete up to January 27, 2010; the one-day international and Twenty20 international totals are complete up to December 31, 2009. Career figures are for one national team only; those players who have appeared for more than one Test team are listed on page 395 and for more than one one-day and international team on page 397.

The forename by which a player is known is underlined if it is not his first name.

Family relationships are indicated by superscript numbers; where the relationship is not immediately apparent from a shared name, see the notes at the end of this section. The 5/10 column indicates instances of a player taking five wickets in a Test innings and ten wickets in a match. O/T signifies number of one-day and Twenty20 internationals played.

¹ *Father and son(s).*   ² *Brothers.*   ³ *Grandfather, father and son.*   ⁴ *Grandfather and grandson.*   ⁵ *Great-grandfather and great-grandson.*
† *Excludes matches for another Test team.*   ‡ *Excludes matches for another ODI team.*

ENGLAND (645 players)

	Born	Died	Tests	Test Career	Runs	HS	100s	Avge	Wkts	BB	5/10	Avge	Ct/St	O/T
Abel Robert.....	30.11.1857	10.12.1936	13	1888-1902	744	132*	2	37.20	1	–	–/–	–	13	
Absolom Charles Alfred	7.6.1846	30.7.1889	1	*1878*	58	52	0	29.00	1	–	–/–	–	0	
Adams Christopher John	6.5.1970		5	1999	104	31	0	13.00	1	1-42	0/0	59.00	6	5
Afzaal Usman.....	9.6.1977		3	2001	83	54	0	16.60	1	1-49	0/0	49.00	0	
Agnew Jonathan Philip	4.4.1960		3	1984-1985	10	5	0	10.00	4	2-51	0/0	93.25	0	3
Ali Kabir	24.11.1980		1	2003	10	9	0	5.00	5	3-80	0/0	27.20	0	14
Allen David Arthur	29.10.1935		39	1959-1966	918	88	0	25.50	122	5-30	4/0	30.97	10	
Allen Sir George Oswald Browning ("Gubby")	31.7.1902	29.11.1989	25	1930-1947	750	122	1	24.19	81	7-80	5/1	29.37	20	
Allom Maurice James Carrick	23.3.1906	8.4.1995	5	1929-1930	14	8*	0	14.00	14	5-38	1/0	18.92	2	
Allott Paul John Walter	14.9.1956		13	1981-1985	213	52*	0	14.20	26	6-61	1/0	41.69	4	13
Ambrose Timothy Raymond	1.12.1982		11	2007-2008	447	102	1	29.80	–	–	–/–	–	31	5/1
Ames Leslie Ethelbert George CBE	3.12.1905	27.2.1990	47	1929-1938	2,434	149	8	40.56	–	–	–/–	–	74/23	
Amiss Dennis Leslie MBE...	7.4.1943		50	1966-1977	3,612	262*	11	46.30	–	–	–/–	–	24	18

Name	Born	Died	Tests	Test Career	Runs	HS	100s	Avge	Wkts	BB	5/10	Avge	Ct/St	O/T
Anderson James Michael	30.7.1982		46	2003–2009	468	34	0	14.18	156	7-43	8/0	34.81	18	120/19
Andrew Keith Vincent	15.12.1929		2	1954–1963	29	15	0	9.66	–	–	–/–	–	1	
Appleyard Robert MBE	27.6.1924		9	1954–1956	51	19*	0	17.00	31	5-51	1/0	17.87	4	
Archer Alfred German	6.12.1871	15.7.1935	1	1898	31	24*	0	31.00	–	–	–/–	–	0	
Armitage Thomas	25.4.1848	21.9.1922	2	1876	33	21	0	11.00	0	0-15	0/0	–	0	
Arnold Edward George	7.11.1876	25.10.1942	10	1903–1907	160	40	0	13.33	31	5-37	1/0	25.41	8	14
Arnold Geoffrey Graham	3.9.1944		34	1967–1975	421	59	0	12.02	115	6-45	6/0	28.29	9	
Arnold John	30.11.1907	4.4.1984	1	1931	34	34	0	17.00	–	–	–/–	–	0	
Astill William Ewart	1.3.1888	10.2.1948	9	1927–1929	190	40	0	12.66	25	4-58	0/0	34.24	7	
Atherton Michael Andrew OBE.	23.3.1968		115	1989–2001	7,728	185*	16	37.69	2	1-20	0/0	151.00	83	54
Athey Charles William Jeffrey	27.9.1957		23	1980–1988	919	123	1	22.97	–	–	–/–	–	13	31
Attewell William	12.6.1861	11.6.1927	10	1884–1891	150	43*	0	16.66	28	4-42	0/0	22.35	9	
Bailey Robert John	28.10.1963		4	1988–1989	119	43	0	14.87	1	1-80	0/0	80.00	0	4
Bailey Trevor Edward CBE.	3.12.1923		61	1949–1958	2,290	134*	1	29.74	132	7-34	5/1	29.21	32	
Bairstow David Leslie.	1.9.1951	5.1.1998	4	1979–1980	125	59	0	20.83	–	–	–/–	–	12/1	21
Bakewell Alfred Harry	2.11.1908	23.1.1983	6	1931–1935	409	107	1	45.44	0	0-8	0/0	–	3	
Balderstone John Christopher	16.11.1940	6.3.2000	2	1976	39	35	0	9.75	1	1-80	0/0	80.00	–	
Barber Robert William	26.9.1935		28	1960–1968	1,495	185	1	35.59	42	4-132	0/0	43.00	21	
Barber Wilfred.	18.4.1901	10.9.1968	2	1935	83	44	0	20.75	1	1-0	0/0	0.00	0	
Barlow Graham Derek.	26.3.1950		3	1976–1977	17	7*	0	4.25	–	–	–/–	–	1	6
Barlow Richard Gorton.	28.5.1851	31.7.1919	17	1881–1886	591	62	0	22.73	34	7-40	3/0	22.55	14	
Barnes Sydney Francis	19.4.1873	26.12.1967	27	1901–1913	242	38*	0	8.06	189	9-103	24/7	16.43	12	
Barnes William	27.5.1852	24.3.1899	21	1880–1890	725	134	1	23.38	51	6-28	3/0	15.54	19	
Barnett Charles John.	3.7.1910	28.5.1993	20	1933–1948	1,098	129	2	35.41	0	0-1	0/0	–	14	
Barnett Kim John.	17.7.1960		4	1988–1989	207	80	0	29.57	0	0-32	0/0	–	–	1
Barratt Fred.	12.4.1894	29.1.1947	5	1929–1929	28	17	0	9.33	5	1-8	0/0	47.00	2	
Barrington Kenneth Frank.	24.11.1930	14.3.1981	82	1955–1968	6,806	256	20	58.67	29	3-4	0/0	44.82	58	
Barton Victor Alexander	6.10.1867	23.3.1906	1	1891	23	23	0	23.00	–	–	–/–	–	0	
Bates Willie	19.11.1855	8.1.1900	15	1881–1886	656	64	0	27.33	50	7-28	4/1	16.42	9	
Batty Gareth Jon	13.10.1977		7	2003–2005	144	38	0	20.57	11	3-55	0/0	66.63	3	10/1
Bean George	7.3.1864	16.3.1923	3	1891	92	50	0	18.40	–	–	–/–	–	4	
Bedser Sir Alec Victor	4.7.1918		51	1946–1955	714	79	0	12.75	236	7-44	15/5	24.89	26	79/5
Bell Ian Ronald MBE.	11.4.1982		53	2004–2009	3,457	199	9	40.19	1	1-33	0/0	76.00	48	2
Benjamin Joseph Emmanuel	2.2.1961		1	1994	0	0	0	0.00	4	4-42	0/0	20.00	0	1
Benson Mark Richard	6.7.1958		1	1986	51	30	0	25.50	–	–	–/–	–	0	

	Born	Died	Tests	Test Career	Runs	HS	100s	Avge	Wkts	BB	5/10	Avge	Ct/St	O/T
Berry Robert	29.1.1926	2.12.2006	2	1950	6	4*	0	3.00	9	5-63	1/0	25.33	2	7
Bicknell Martin Paul	14.11.1969		4	1993–2003	45	15	0	6.42	14	4-84	0/0	38.78	2	
Binks James Graham	5.10.1935		2	1963	91	55	0	22.75					8	
Bird Morice Carlos	25.3.1888	9.12.1933	10	1909–1913	280	61	0	18.66	8	3-11	-/-	15.00	5	
Birkenshaw Jack	13.11.1940		5	1972–1973	148	64	0	21.14	13	5-57	1/0	36.07	3	
Blackwell Ian David	10.6.1978		1	2005	4	4	0	4.00	0	0-28	0/0	–	–	34
Blakey Richard John	15.1.1967		2	1992	7	6	0	1.75					2	3
Bligh *Hon.* Ivo Francis Walter	13.3.1859	10.4.1927	4	1882	62	19	0	10.33					7	
Blythe Colin	30.5.1879	8.11.1917	19	1901–1909	183	27	0	9.63	100	8-59	9/4	18.63	6	
Board John Henry	23.2.1867	15.4.1924	6	1898–1905	108	29	0	10.80					8/3	
Bolus John Brian	31.1.1934		7	1963–1963	496	88	0	41.33	0	0-16	0/0	–	2	
Booth Major William	10.12.1886	1.7.1916	2	1913	46	32	0	23.00	7	4-49	0/0	18.57	0	
Bopara Ravinder Singh	4.5.1985		10	2007–2009	502	143	3	33.46	1	1-39	0/0	199.00	5	50/8
Bosanquet Bernard James Tindal	13.10.1877	12.10.1936	7	1903–1905	147	27	0	13.36	25	8-107	2/0	24.16	9	
Botham Sir Ian Terence OBE	24.11.1955		102	1977–1992	5,200	208	14	33.54	383	8-34	27/4	28.40	120	116
Bowden Montague Parker	1.11.1865	19.2.1892	2	1888	25	25	0	12.50					1	
Bowes William Eric	25.7.1908	4.9.1987	15	1932–1946	28	10*	0	4.66	68	6-33	6/0	22.33	2	
Bowley Edward Henry	6.6.1890	9.7.1974	5	1929–1929	252	109	1	36.00	0	0-7	0/0	–	2	
Boycott Geoffrey OBE	21.10.1940		108	1964–1981	8,114	246*	22	47.72	7	3-47	0/0	54.57	33	
Bradley Walter Morris	2.1.1875	19.6.1944	2	1899	23	23*	0	23.00	6	5-67	1/0	38.83	0	
Braund Leonard Charles	18.10.1875	23.12.1955	23	1901–1907	987	104	3	25.97	47	8-81	3/0	38.51	39	36
Brearley John Michael OBE	28.4.1942		39	1976–1981	1,442	91	0	22.88					52	25
Brearley Walter	11.3.1876	30.1.1937	4	1905–1912	21	11*	0	7.00	17	5-110	1/0	21.11	0	
Brennan Donald Vincent	10.2.1920	9.1.1985	2	1951	16	16	0	8.00					0/1	
Bresnan Timothy Thomas	28.2.1985		3	2009	9	9	0	9.00	3	3-45	0/0	32.33	2	18/3
Briggs John	3.10.1862	11.1.1902	33	1884–1899	815	121	0	18.11	118	8-11	9/4	17.75	12	34
Broad Brian Christopher	29.9.1957		25	1984–1989	1,661	162	6	39.54	0	0-4	0/0	–	10	34
Broad Stuart Christopher John	24.6.1986		26	2007–2009	843	76	0	26.34	77	6-91	3/0	35.38	7	57/18
Brockwell William	21.1.1865	30.6.1935	7	1893–1899	202	49	0	16.83	5	3-33	0/0	61.80	6	
Bromley-Davenport Hugh Richard	18.8.1870	23.5.1954	4	1895–1898	128	84	0	21.33	4	2-46	0/0	24.50	1	
Brookes Dennis	29.10.1915	9.3.2006	1	1947	17	10	0	8.50					–	
Brown Alan	17.10.1935		2	1961	3	3*	0	–	3	3-27	0/0	50.00	1	
Brown David John	30.1.1942		26	1965–1969	342	44*	0	11.79	79	5-42	2/0	28.31	7	
Brown Frederick Richard MBE	16.12.1910	24.7.1991	22	1931–1953	734	79	0	25.31	45	5-49	1/0	31.06	22	
Brown George	6.10.1887	3.12.1964	7	1921–1922	299	84	0	29.90					9/3	

	Born	Died	Tests	Test Career	Runs	HS	100s	Avge	Wkts	BB	5/10	Avge	Ct/St	O/T
Brown John Thomas	20.8.1869	4.11.1904	8	1894–1899	470	140	1	36.15	0	0-22	00	–	7	
Brown Simon John Emmerson	29.6.1969		1	1996	11	10*	0	11.00	2	1-60	00	69.00	1	
Buckenham Claude Percival	16.1.1876	23.2.1937	4	1909	43	17	0	6.14	21	5-115	10	28.23	2	
Butcher Alan Raymond	7.1.1954		1	1979	34	20	0	17.00	0	0-9	00	–	1	1
Butcher Mark Alan	23.8.1972		71	1997–2004	4,288	173*	8	34.58	15	4-42	–/–	36.06	61	
Butcher Roland Orlando	14.10.1953		3	1980	71	32	0	14.20					3	3
Butler Harold James	12.3.1913	17.7.1991	2	1947–1947	15	15*	0	15.00	12	4-34	00	17.91	1	
Butt Henry Rigden	27.12.1865	21.12.1928	3	1895	22	13	0	7.33					1/1	
Caddick Andrew Richard	21.11.1968		62	1993–2002	861	49*	0	10.37	234	7-46	13/1	29.91	21	54
Calthorpe Hon. Frederick Somerset Gough	27.5.1892	19.11.1935	4	1929	129	49	0	18.42	1	1-38	00	91.00	3	
Capel David John	6.2.1963		15	1987–1989	374	98	0	15.58	21	3-88	00	50.66	6	23
Carr Arthur William	21.5.1893	7.2.1963	11	1922–1929	237	63	0	19.75				–	3	
Carr Donald Bryce OBE	28.12.1926		2	1951	135	76	0	33.75	2	2-84	00	70.00	0	
Carr Douglas Ward	17.3.1872	23.3.1950	1	1909	0	0	0	0.00	7	5-146	10	40.28	0	
Cartwright Thomas William MBE	22.7.1935	30.4.2007	5	1964–1965	26	9	0	5.20	15	6-94	10	36.26	2	
Chapman Arthur Percy Frank	3.9.1900	16.9.1961	26	1924–1930	925	121	1	28.90	0	0-10	00	–	32	
Charlwood Henry Rupert James	19.12.1846	6.6.1888	2	1876	63	36	0	15.75				–	0	
Chatterton William	27.12.1861	19.3.1913	1	1891	48	48	0	48.00				–	1	
Childs John Henry	15.8.1951		2	1988	2	2*	0	–	3	1-13	00	61.00	1	
Christopherson Stanley	11.11.1861	6.4.1949	1	1884	17	17	0	17.00	1	1-52	00	69.00	0	
Clark Edward Winchester	9.8.1902	28.4.1982	8	1929–1934	36	10	0	9.00	32	5-98	10	28.09	0	
Clarke Rikki	29.9.1981		2	2003	96	55	0	32.00	4	2-7	00	15.00	1	20
Clay John Charles	18.3.1898	11.8.1973	1	1935	–	–	–	–	0	0-30	00	–	1	
Close Dennis Brian CBE	24.2.1931		22	1949–1976	887	70	0	25.34	18	4-35	00	29.55	24	3
Coldwell Leonard John	10.1.1933	6.8.1996	7	1962–1964	9	6*	0	4.50	22	6-85	10	27.72	1	
Collingwood Paul David MBE	26.5.1976		57	2003–2009	3,909	206	9	43.43	15	3-23	00	60.80	75	173/22
Compton Denis Charles Scott CBE	23.5.1918	23.4.1997	78	1937–1956	5,807	278	17	50.06	25	5-70	10	56.40	49	23/4
Cook Alastair Nathan	25.12.1984		52	2005–2009	3,796	160	10	42.65	0	0-1	00	–	48	
Cook Cecil ("Sam")	23.8.1921	5.9.1996	1	1947	4	4	0	2.00	0	0-40	00	–	0	
Cook Geoffrey	9.10.1951		7	1981–1982	203	66	0	15.61	0	0-4	00	–	9	6
Cook Nicholas Grant Billson	17.6.1956		15	1983–1989	179	31	0	8.52	52	6-65	4/1	32.48	5	3
Cope Geoffrey Alan	23.2.1947		3	1977	40	22	0	13.33	8	3-102	10	34.62	2	2
Copson William Henry	27.4.1908	13.9.1971	3	1939–1947	6	6	0	6.00	15	5-85	10	19.80	1	
Cork Dominic Gerald	7.8.1971		37	1995–2002	864	59	0	18.00	131	7-43	50	29.81	18	32
Cornford Walter Latter	25.12.1900	6.2.1964	4	1929	36	18	0	9.00		–	–/–	–	5/3	

	Born	Died	Tests	Test Career	Runs	HS	100s	Avge	Wkts	BB	5/10	Avge	Ct/St	O/T
Cottam Robert Michael Henry	16.10.1944		4	1968–1972	27	13	0	6.75	14	4-50	0/0	23.35	2	
Coventry *Hon.* Charles John	26.2.1867	2.6.1929	2	1888	13	12	0	13.00				–	0	
Cowans Norman George	17.4.1961		19	1982–1985	175	36	0	7.95	51	6-77	2/0	39.27	9	23
Cowdrey Christopher Stuart	20.10.1957		6	1984–1988	101	38	0	14.42	4	2-65	0/0	77.25	5	3
Cowdrey *Lord* [Michael Colin] CBE	24.12.1932	4.12.2000	114	1954–1974	7,624	182	22	44.06	–	0-1		–	120	1
Coxon Alexander	18.1.1916	22.1.2006	1	1948	19	19	0	9.50	3	2-90	0/0	57.33	1	
Cranston James	9.1.1859	10.12.1904	1	1890	31	16	0	15.50				–	0	
Cranston Kenneth	20.10.1917	8.1.2007	8	1947–1948	209	45	0	14.92	18	4-12	0/0	25.61	3	
Crapp John Frederick	14.10.1912	13.2.1981	7	1948–1949	319	56	0	29.00				–	7	
Crawford John Neville	1.12.1886	2.5.1963	12	1905–1907	469	74	0	22.33	39	5-48	3/0	29.48	13	
Crawley John Paul	21.9.1971		37	1994–2002	1,800	156*	4	34.61				–	29	13
Croft Robert Damien Bale	25.5.1970		21	1996–2001	421	37*	0	16.19	49	5-95	1/0	37.24	10	50
Curtis Timothy Stephen	15.1.1960		5	1988–1989	140	41	0	15.55				–	3	
Cuttell Willis Robert	13.9.1863	9.12.1929	2	1898	65	21	0	16.25	6	3-17	0/0	12.16	3	
Dawson Edward William	13.2.1904	4.6.1979	5	1927–1929	175	55	0	19.44				–	2	
Dawson Richard Kevin James	4.8.1980		7	2001–2002	114	19*	0	11.40	11	4-134	0/0	61.54	3	
Dean Harry	13.8.1884	12.3.1957	3	1912	10	8	0	5.00	11	4-19	0/0	13.90	2	
DeFreitas Phillip Anthony Jason	18.2.1966		44	1986–1995	934	88	0	14.82	140	7-70	4/0	33.57	14	103
Denness Michael Henry	1.12.1940		28	1969–1975	1,667	188	4	39.69	–			–	28	12
Denton David	4.7.1874	16.2.1950	11	1905–1909	424	104	1	20.19				–	8	
Dewes John Gordon	11.10.1926		5	1948–1950	121	67	0	12.10				–	0	
Dexter Edward Ralph CBE	15.5.1935		62	1958–1968	4,502	205	9	47.89	66	4-10	0/0	34.93	29	
Dilley Graham Roy	18.5.1959		41	1979–1989	521	56	0	13.35	138	6-38	6/0	29.76	10	36
Dipper Alfred Ernest	9.11.1885	7.11.1945	1	1921	51	40	0	25.50				–	0	
Doggart George Hubert Graham OBE	18.7.1925		2	1950	76	29	0	19.00				–	3	
D'Oliveira Basil Lewis CBE	4.10.1931		44	1966–1972	2,484	158	5	40.06	47	3-46	0/0	39.55	29	4
Dollery Horace Edgar ("Tom")	14.10.1914	20.1.1987	4	1947–1950	72	37	0	10.28				–	1	
Dolphin Arthur	24.12.1885	23.10.1942	1	1920	1	1	0	0.50				–	1	
Douglas John William Henry Tyler	3.9.1882	19.12.1930	23	1911–1924	962	119	1	29.15	45	5-46	1/0	33.02	9	
Downton Paul Rupert	4.4.1957		30	1980–1988	785	74	0	19.62				–	70/5	28
Druce Norman Frank	1.1.1875	27.10.1954	5	1897	252	64	0	28.00				–	5	
Ducat Andrew	16.2.1886	23.7.1942	1	1921	5	3	0	2.50				–	1	
Duckworth George	9.5.1901	5.1.1966	24	1924–1936	234	39*	0	14.62				–	45/15	
Duleepsinhji Kumar Shri	13.6.1905	5.12.1959	12	1929–1931	995	173	3	58.52	0	0-7		–	10	
Durston Frederick John	11.7.1893	8.4.1965	1	1921	8	6*	0	8.00	5	4-102	0/0	27.20	0	

	Born	Died	Tests	Test Career	Runs	HS	100s	Avge	Wkts	BB	5/O	Avge	Ct/St	O/T
Ealham Mark Alan	27.8.1969		8	1996–1999	210	53*	0	21.00	17	4-21	0/0	28.70	4	64
Edmonds Philippe-Henri	8.3.1951		51	1975–1987	875	64	0	17.50	125	7-66	2/0	34.18	42	29
Edrich John Hugh MBE	21.6.1937		77	1963–1976	5,138	310*	12	43.54	0	0-6	0/0	–	43	7
Edrich William John	26.3.1916	24.4.1986	39	1938–1954	2,440	219	6	40.00	41	4-68	0/0	41.29	39	
Elliott Harry	2.11.1891	2.2.1976	4	1927–1933	61	37*	0	15.25	–	–	–/–	–	8/3	
Ellison Richard Mark	21.9.1959		11	1984–1986	202	41	0	13.46	35	6-77	3/1	29.94	2	14
Embury John Ernest	20.8.1952		64	1978–1995	1,713	75	0	22.53	147	7-78	6/0	38.40	34	61
Emmett George Malcolm	2.12.1912	18.12.1976	1	1948	10	10	0	5.00	–		–/–	–	0	
Emmett Thomas	3.9.1841	30.6.1904	7	1876–1881	160	48	0	13.33	9	7-68	1/0	31.55	9	
Evans Alfred John	1.5.1889	18.9.1960	1	1921	18	14	0	9.00	–		–/–	–	0	
Evans Thomas Godfrey CBE	18.8.1920	3.5.1999	91	1946–1959	2,439	104	2	20.49	–		–/–	–	173/46	
Fagg Arthur Edward	18.6.1915	13.9.1977	5	1936–1939	150	39	0	18.75	–		–/–	–	5	
Fairbrother Neil Harvey	9.9.1963		10	1987–1992	219	83	0	15.64	0	0-9	0/0	–	4	75
Fane Frederick Luther	27.4.1875	27.11.1960	14	1905–1909	682	143	1	26.23	–		–/–	–	6	
Farnes Kenneth	8.7.1911	20.10.1941	15	1934–1938	58	20	0	4.83	60	6-96	3/1	28.65	1	
Farrimond William	23.5.1903	15.11.1979	4	1930–1935	116	35	0	16.57	–		–/–	–	5/2	
Fender Percy George Herbert	22.8.1892	15.6.1985	13	1920–1929	380	60	0	19.00	29	5-90	2/0	40.86	14	24
Ferris John James	21.5.1867	17.11.1900	1†	1891	16	16	0	16.00	13	7-37	2/1	7.00	0	
Fielder Arthur	19.7.1877	30.8.1949	6	1903–1907	78	20	0	11.14	26	6-82	1/0	27.34	4	
Fishlock Laurence Barnard	2.1.1907	25.6.1986	4	1936–1946	47	19*	0	11.75	–		–/–	–	1	
Flavell John Alfred	15.5.1929	25.2.2004	4	1961–1964	31	14	0	7.75	7	2-65	0/0	52.42	0	
Fletcher Keith William Robert OBE	20.5.1944		59	1968–1981	3,272	216	7	39.90	2	1-6	0/0	96.50	54	24
Flintoff Andrew MBE	6.12.1977		78§	1998–2009	3,795	167	5	31.89	219	5-58	3/0	33.34	52	138‡/7
Flowers Wilfred	7.12.1856	1.11.1926	8	1884–1893	254	56	0	18.14	14	5-46	1/0	21.14	2	
Ford Francis Gilbertson Justice	14.12.1866	7.2.1940	5	1894	168	48	0	18.66	1	1-47	0/0	129.00	5	
Foster Frank Rowbotham	31.1.1889	3.5.1958	11	1911–1912	330	71	0	23.57	45	6-91	4/0	20.57	11	
Foster James Savin	15.4.1980		7	2001–2002	226	48	0	25.11	–		–/–	–	17/1	11/5
Foster Neil Alan	6.5.1962		29	1983–1993	446	39	0	11.73	88	8-107	5/1	32.85	7	48
Foster Reginald Erskine ("Tip")	16.4.1878	13.5.1914	8	1903–1907	602	287	1	46.30	–		–/–	–	13	
Fothergill Arnold James	26.8.1854	1.8.1932	2	1888	33	32	0	16.50	8	4-19	0/0	11.25	0	
Fowler Graeme	20.4.1957		21	1982–1984	1,307	201	3	35.32	0	0-0	0/0	–	10	26
Fraser Angus Robert Charles MBE	8.8.1965		46	1989–1998	388	32	0	7.46	177	8-53	13/2	27.32	9	42
Freeman Alfred Percy ("Tich")	17.5.1888	28.1.1965	12	1924–1929	154	50*	0	14.00	66	7-71	5/3	25.86	4	
French Bruce Nicholas	13.8.1959		16	1986–1987	308	59	0	18.11	–		–/–	–	38/1	13

§ *Flintoff's figures exclude 50 runs and seven wickets for the ICC World XI v Australia in the Super Series Test in 2005-06.*

	Born	Died	Tests	Test Career	Runs	HS	100s	Avge	Wkts	BB	5/10	Avge	Ct/St	O/T
Fry Charles Burgess	25.4.1872	7.9.1956	26	1895–1912	1,223	144	2	32.18	0	0-3	0/0	–	17	–
Gallian Jason Edward Riche	25.6.1971		3	1995–1995	74	28	0	12.33	0	0-6	0/0	–	1	–
Gatting Michael William OBE	6.6.1957		79	1977–1994	4,409	207	10	35.55	4	1-14	0/0	79.25	59	92
Gay Leslie Hewitt	24.3.1871	1.11.1949	1	1894	37	33	0	18.50		–	–/–	–	3/1	
Geary George	9.7.1893	6.3.1981	14	1924–1934	249	66	0	15.56	46	7-70	4/1	29.41	13	
Gibb Paul Antony	11.7.1913	7.12.1977	8	1938–1946	581	120	2	44.69		–	–/–	–	3/1	
Giddins Edward Simon Hunter	20.7.1971		4	1999–2000	10	7	0	2.50	12	5-15	1/0	20.00	0	
Gifford Norman MBE	30.3.1940		15	1964–1973	179	25*	0	16.27	33	5-55	1/0	31.09	8	2
Giles Ashley Fraser MBE	19.3.1973		54	1998–2006	1,421	59	0	20.89	143	5-57	5/0	40.60	33	62
Gilligan Alfred Herbert Harold	29.6.1896	5.5.1978	4	1929	71	32	0	17.75		–	–/–	–	0	
Gilligan Arthur Edward Robert	23.12.1894	5.9.1976	11	1922–1924	209	39*	0	16.07	36	6-7	2/1	29.05	3	
Gimblett Harold	19.10.1914	30.3.1978	3	1936–1939	129	67*	0	32.25		–	–/–	–	1	
Gladwin Clifford	3.4.1916	9.4.1988	8	1947–1949	170	51*	0	28.33	15	3-21	0/0	38.06	1	
Goddard Thomas William John	1.10.1900	22.5.1966	8	1930–1939	13	8	0	6.50	22	6-29	1/0	26.72	3	
Gooch Graham Alan OBE	23.7.1953		118	1975–1994	8,900	333	20	42.58	23	3-39	0/0	46.47	103	125
Gough Darren	18.9.1970		58	1994–2003	855	65	0	12.57	229	6-42	9/0	28.39	13	158†/2
Gover Alfred Richard MBE	29.2.1908	7.10.2001	4	1936–1946	2	2*	0	–	8	3-85	0/0	44.87	1	
Gower David Ivon OBE	1.4.1957		117	1978–1992	8,231	215	18	44.25	1	1-1	0/0	20.00	74	114
Grace Edward Mills	28.11.1841	20.5.1911	1	1880	36	36	0	18.00		–	–/–	–	1	
Grace George Frederick	13.12.1850	22.9.1880	1	1880	0	0	0	0.00		–	–/–	–	2	
Grace William Gilbert (W.G.)	18.7.1848	23.10.1915	22	1880–1899	1,098	170	2	32.29	9	2-12	0/0	26.22	39	
Graveney Thomas William OBE	16.6.1927		79	1951–1969	4,882	258	11	44.38	1	1-34	0/0	167.00	80	
Greenough Thomas	9.11.1931		4	1959–1960	4	2	0	1.33	16	5-35	1/0	22.31	1	
Greenwood Andrew	20.8.1847	12.2.1889	2	1876	77	49	0	19.25		–	–/–	–	2	
Greig Anthony William	6.10.1946		58	1972–1977	3,599	148	8	40.43	141	8-86	6/2	32.20	87	22
Greig Ian Alexander	8.12.1955		2	1982	26	14	0	6.50	4	4-53	0/0	28.50	0	
Grieve Basil Arthur Firebrace	28.5.1864	19.11.1917	2	1888	40	14*	0	40.00		–	–/–	–	0	
Griffith Stewart Cathie CBE ("Billy")	16.6.1914	7.4.1993	3	1947–1948	157	140	1	31.40		–	–/–	–	5	
Gunn George	13.6.1879	29.6.1958	15	1907–1929	1,120	122*	2	40.00	1	0-8	0/0	–	15	
Gunn John Richmond	19.7.1876	21.8.1963	6	1901–1905	85	24	0	10.62	18	5-76	0/0	21.50	3	
Gunn William	4.12.1858	29.1.1921	11	1886–1899	392	102*	1	21.77		–	–/–	–	5	
Habib Aftab	7.2.1972		2	1999	26	19	0	8.66		–	–/–	–	1	
Haig Nigel Esmé	12.12.1887	27.10.1966	5	1921–1929	126	47	0	14.00	13	3-73	0/0	34.46	4	
Haigh Schofield	19.3.1871	27.2.1921	11	1898–1912	113	25	0	7.53	24	6-11	1/0	25.91	8	
Hallows Charles	4.4.1895	10.11.1972	2	1921–1928	42	26	0	42.00		–	–/–	–	0	

	Born	Died	Tests	Test Career	Runs	HS	100s	Avge	Wkts	BB	5/10	Avge	Ct/St	O/T 0‡
Hamilton Gavin Mark	16.9.1974		1	1999	0	0	0	–	0	–	–	–	0	
Hammond Walter Reginald	19.6.1903	1.7.1965	85	1927–1946	7,249	336*	22	58.45	83	5-36	2/0	37.80	110	3
Hampshire John Harry	10.2.1941		8	1969–1975	403	107	1	26.86	–	–	–	–	9	
Harding Harold Thomas William ("Wally")	25.2.1886	8.5.1965	1	1921	30	25	0	15.00	–	–	–/–	–	0	
‡Hardstaff Joseph, sen	9.11.1882	2.4.1947	5	1907	311	72	0	31.10	–	–	–/–	–	1	
‡Hardstaff Joseph, jun	3.7.1911	1.1.1990	23	1935–1948	1,636	205*	4	46.74	–	–	–/–	–	9	
Harmison Stephen James MBE	23.10.1978		62§	2002–2009	742	49*	0	12.16	222	7-12	8/1	31.94	7	58/2
Harris *Lord* [George Robert Canning]	3.2.1851	24.3.1932	4	1878–1884	145	52	0	29.00	0	0-14	0/0	–	2	
Hartley John Cabourn	15.11.1874	8.3.1963	2	1905	15	9	0	3.75	1	1-62	0/0	115.00	2	
Hawke *Lord* [Martin Bladen]	16.8.1860	10.10.1938	5	1895–1898	55	30	0	7.85	–	–	–/–	–	3	
Hayes Ernest George	6.11.1876	2.12.1953	5	1905–1912	86	35	0	10.75	1	1-28	0/0	52.00	2	
Hayes Frank Charles	6.12.1946		9	1973–1976	244	106*	1	15.25	–	–	–	–	7	
Hayward Thomas Walter	29.3.1871	19.7.1939	35	1895–1909	1,999	137	3	34.46	14	4-22	0/0	36.71	19	6
³Headley Dean Warren	27.1.1970		15	1997–1999	186	31	0	8.45	60	6-60	1/0	27.85	7	13
²Hearne Alec	22.7.1863	16.5.1952	1	1895–1898	9	9	0	9.00	–	–	–/–	–	1	
¹,²Hearne Frank	23.11.1858	14.7.1949	2‡	1888	47	27	0	23.50	–	–	–/–	–	0	
²Hearne George Gibbons	7.7.1856	13.2.1932	1	1891	0	0	0	0.00	–	–	–	–	0	
²Hearne John Thomas	3.5.1867	17.4.1944	12	1891–1899	126	40	0	9.00	49	6-41	4/1	22.08	4	
¹,²Hearne John William	11.2.1891	14.9.1965	24	1911–1926	806	114	1	26.00	30	5-49	1/0	48.73	13	
Hegg Warren Kevin	23.2.1968		2	1998	30	15	0	7.50	–	–	–	–	8	
Hemmings Edward Ernest	20.2.1949		16	1982–1990	383	95	0	22.52	43	6-58	1/0	42.44	5	33
Hendren Elias Henry ("Patsy")	5.2.1889	4.10.1962	51	1920–1934	3,525	205*	7	47.63	1	1-27	0/0	31.00	33	
Hendrick Michael	22.10.1948		30	1974–1981	128	15	0	6.40	87	4-28	0/0	25.83	25	22
Heseltine Christopher	26.11.1869	13.6.1944	2	1895	18	18	0	9.00	5	5-38	1/0	16.80	3	
Hick Graeme Ashley MBE	23.5.1966		65	1991–2000	3,383	178	6	31.32	23	4-126	0/0	56.78	90	120
Higgs Kenneth	14.1.1937		15	1965–1968	185	63	0	11.56	71	6-91	2/0	20.74	4	
Hill Allen	14.11.1843	28.8.1910	2	1876	101	49	0	50.50	7	4-27	0/0	18.57	1	
Hill Arthur James Ledger	26.7.1871	6.9.1950	3	1895	251	124	1	62.75	4	4-8	0/0	2.00	1	
Hilton Malcolm Jameson	2.8.1928	8.7.1990	4	1950–1951	37	15	0	7.40	14	5-61	1/0	34.07	1	
Hirst George Herbert	7.9.1871	10.5.1954	24	1897–1909	790	85	0	22.57	59	5-48	3/0	30.00	18	
Hitch John William	7.5.1886	7.7.1965	7	1911–1921	103	51*	0	14.71	7	2-31	0/0	46.42	4	
Hobbs Sir John Berry	16.12.1882	21.12.1963	61	1907–1930	5,410	211	15	56.94	1	1-19	0/0	165.00	17	
Hobbs Robin Nicholas Stuart	8.5.1942		7	1967–1971	34	15*	0	6.80	12	3-25	0/0	40.08	8	
Hoggard Matthew James MBE	31.12.1976		67	2000–2007	473	38	0	7.27	248	7-61	7/1	30.50	24	26

§ *Harmison's figures exclude one run and four wickets for the ICC World XI v Australia in the Super Series Test in 2005-06.*

	Born	Died	Tests	Test Career	Runs	HS	100s	Avge	Wkts	BB	5/10	Avge	Ct/St	O/T
Hollies William Eric	5.6.1912	16.4.1981	13	1934–1950	37	18*	0	5.28	44	7-50	5/0	30.27	2	35
[2] Hollioake Adam John	5.9.1971		4	1997–1997	65	45	0	10.83	2	2-31	0/0	33.50	4	20
Hollioake Benjamin Caine	11.11.1977	23.3.2002	2	1997–1998	44	28	0	11.00	4	2-105	0/0	49.75	2	
Holmes Errol Reginald Thorold	21.8.1905	16.8.1960	5	1934–1935	114	85*	0	16.28	2	1-10	0/0	38.00	4	
Holmes Percy	25.11.1886	3.9.1971	7	1921–1932	357	88	0	27.46				–	3	
Hone Leland	30.1.1853	31.12.1896	1	1878	13	7	0	6.50				–	2/1	
Hopwood John Leonard	30.10.1903	15.6.1985	2	1934	12	8	0	6.00	0	0-16	0/0	–	0	
Hornby Albert Neilson ("Monkey")	10.2.1847	17.12.1925	3	1878–1884	21	9	0	3.50	1	1-0	0/0	0.00	0	
Horton Martin John	21.4.1934		2	1959	60	58	0	30.00	2	2-24	0/0	29.50	2	
Howard Nigel David	18.5.1925	31.5.1979	4	1951	86	23	0	17.20				–	4	
Howell Henry	29.11.1890	9.7.1932	5	1920–1924	15	5	0	7.50	7	4-115	0/0	79.85	2	
Howorth Richard	26.4.1909	2.4.1980	5	1947–1947	145	45*	0	18.12	19	6-124	1/0	33.42	2	
Humphries Joseph	19.5.1876	7.5.1946	3	1907	44	16	0	8.80				–	7	
Hunter Joseph	3.8.1855	4.1.1891	5	1884	93	39*	0	18.60				–	8/3	
Hussain Nasser OBE	28.3.1968		96	1989–2004	5,764	207	14	37.18	0	0-15	0/0	–	67	88
Hutchings Kenneth Lotherington	7.12.1882	3.9.1916	7	1907–1909	341	126	1	28.41	1	1-5	0/0	81.00	9	
[1] Hutton *Sir* Leonard	23.6.1916	6.9.1990	79	1937–1954	6,971	364	19	56.67	3	1-2	0/0	77.33	57	
Hutton Richard Anthony	6.9.1942		5	1971	219	81	0	36.50	9	3-72	0/0	28.55	9	
Iddon John	8.1.1902	17.4.1946	5	1934–1935	170	73	0	28.33	0	0-3	0/0	–	0	
Igglesden Alan Paul	8.10.1964		3	1989–1993	6	3*	0	3.00	6	2-91	0/0	54.83	1	4
Ikin John Thomas	7.3.1918	15.9.1984	18	1946–1955	606	60	0	20.89	3	1-38	0/0	118.00	31	
Illingworth Raymond CBE	8.6.1932		61	1958–1973	1,836	113	2	23.24	122	6-29	3/0	31.20	45	31
Illingworth Richard Keith	23.8.1963		9	1991–1995	128	28	0	18.28	19	4-96	0/0	32.36	5	25
Ilott Mark Christopher	27.8.1970		5	1993–1995	28	15	0	7.00	12	3-48	0/0	45.16	0	
Insole Douglas John CBE	18.4.1926		9	1950–1957	408	110*	1	27.20				–	8	
Irani Ronald Charles	26.10.1971		3	1996–1999	86	41	0	17.20	3	1-22	0/0	37.33	2	31
Jackman Robin David	13.8.1945		4	1980–1982	42	17	0	7.00	14	4-110	0/0	31.78	0	15
Jackson *Sir* Francis Stanley	21.11.1870	9.3.1947	20	1893–1905	1,415	144*	5	48.79	24	5-52	1/0	33.29	10	
Jackson Herbert Leslie	5.4.1921	25.4.2007	2	1949–1961	15	8	0	15.00	7	2-26	0/0	22.14	1	
James Stephen Peter	7.9.1967		2	1998	71	36	0	17.75				–	0	
Jameson John Alexander	30.6.1941		4	1971–1973	214	82	0	26.75	1	1-17	0/0	17.00	2	3
Jardine Douglas Robert	23.10.1900	18.6.1958	22	1928–1933	1,296	127	1	48.00	0	0-10	0/0	–	26	
Jarvis Paul William	29.6.1965		9	1987–1992	132	29*	0	10.15	21	4-107	0/0	45.95	2	16
Jenkins Roland Oliver	24.11.1918	22.7.1995	9	1948–1952	198	39	0	18.00	32	5-116	1/0	34.31	4	
Jessop Gilbert Laird	19.5.1874	11.5.1955	18	1899–1912	569	104	1	21.88	10	4-68	0/0	35.40	11	

	Born	Died	Tests	Test Career	Runs	HS	100s	Avge	Wks	BB	5/10	Avge	Ct/St	O/T
Johnson Richard Leonard	29.12.1974		3	2003–2003	59	26	0	14.75	16	6-33	2/0	17.18	0	10
Jones Arthur Owen	16.8.1872	21.12.1914	12	1899–1909	291	34	0	13.85	3	3-73	0/0	44.33	15	
Jones Geraint Owen MBE.	14.7.1976		34	2003–2006	1,172	100	1	23.91					128/5	49/2
Jones Ivor Jeffrey	10.12.1941		15	1963–1967	38	16	0	4.75	44	6-118	1/0	40.20	4	
Jones Simon Philip MBE.	25.12.1978		18	2002–2005	205	44	0	15.76	59	6-53	3/0	28.23	4	8
Jupp Henry	19.11.1841	8.4.1889	2	1876	68	63	0	17.00					2	
Jupp Vallance William Crisp	27.3.1891	9.7.1960	8	1921–1928	208	38	0	17.33	28	4-37	–/–	22.00	5	
Keeton William Walter	30.4.1905	10.10.1980	2	1934–1939	57	25	0	14.25					0	
Kennedy Alexander Stuart	24.1.1891	15.11.1959	5	1922	93	41*	0	15.50	31	5-76	2/0	19.32	5	
Kenyon Donald	15.5.1924	12.11.1996	8	1951–1955	192	87	0	12.80					5	
Key Robert William Trevor	12.5.1979		15	2002–2004	775	221	1	31.00					11	5/1
Khan Amjad	14.10.1980		1	2008	–	–	–	–	1	1-111	0/0	122.00	0	0/1
Killick *Rev.* **Edgar Thomas**	9.5.1907	18.5.1953	2	1929	81	31	0	20.25					2	
Kilner Roy	17.10.1890	5.4.1928	9	1924–1926	233	74	0	33.28	24	4-51	0/0	30.58	6	
King John Herbert	16.4.1871	18.11.1946	1	1909	64	60	0	32.00	1	1-99	0/0	99.00	0	
Kinneir Septimus Paul	13.5.1871	16.10.1928	1	1911	52	30	0	26.00					0	
Kirtley Robert James	10.1.1975		4	2003–2003	32	12	0	5.33	19	6-34	1/0	29.52	3	11/1
Knight Albert Ernest	8.10.1872	25.4.1946	3	1903	81	70*	0	16.20					0	
Knight Barry Rolfe	18.2.1938		29	1961–1969	812	127	2	26.19	70	4-38	0/0	31.75	14	
Knight Donald John	12.5.1894	5.1.1960	2	1921	54	38	0	13.50					1	
Knight Nicholas Verity	28.11.1969		17	1995–2001	719	113	1	23.96					26	100
Knott Alan Philip Eric	9.4.1946		95	1967–1981	4,389	135	5	32.75					250/19	20
Knox Neville Alexander	10.10.1884	3.3.1935	2	1907	24	8*	0	8.00	3	2-39	0/0	35.00	0	
Laker James Charles	9.2.1922	23.4.1986	46	1947–1958	676	63	0	14.08	193	10-53	9/3	21.24	12	122
Lamb Allan Joseph	20.6.1954		79	1982–1992	4,656	142	14	36.09	1	1-6	0/0	23.00	75	
Langridge James	10.7.1906	10.9.1966	8	1933–1946	242	70	0	26.88	19	7-56	2/0	21.73	6	
Larkins Wayne	22.11.1953		13	1979–1990	493	64	0	20.54					8	25
Larter John David Frederick	24.4.1940		10	1962–1965	16	10	0	3.20	37	5-57	2/0	25.43	5	
Larwood Harold MBE.	14.11.1904	22.7.1995	21	1926–1932	485	98	0	19.40	78	6-32	4/1	28.35	15	
Lathwell Mark Nicholas	26.12.1971		2	1993	78	33	0	19.50					0	
Lawrence David Valentine ("Syd").	28.1.1964		5	1988–1991	60	34	0	10.00	18	5-106	1/0	37.55	0	1
Leadbeater Edric	15.8.1927		2	1951	40	38	0	20.00	2	1-38	0/0	109.00	3	
Lee Henry William	26.10.1890	21.4.1981	1	1930	19	18	0	9.50					0	
Lees Walter Scott	25.12.1875	10.9.1924	5	1905	66	25*	0	11.00	26	6-78	2/0	17.96	2	
Legge Geoffrey Bevington	26.1.1903	21.11.1940	5	1927–1929	299	196	1	49.83					1	

Name	Born	Died	Tests	Test Career	Runs	HS	100s	Avge	Wkts	BB	5/10	Avge	Ct/St	O/T
Leslie Charles Frederick Henry	8.12.1861	12.2.1921	4	1882	106	54	0	15.14		3-31	–/–	11.00	1	22
Lever John Kenneth MBE	24.2.1949		21	1976-1986	306	53	0	11.76	73	7-46	3/1	26.72	11	10
Lever Peter	17.9.1940		17	1970-1975	350	88*	0	21.87	41	6-38	2/0	36.80	11	
Leveson Gower Sir Henry Dudley Gresham	8.5.1873	1.2.1954	3	1909	95	31	0	23.75	–	–	–/–	–		
Levett William Howard Vincent ("Hopper")	25.1.1908	1.12.1995	1	1933	7	5	0	7.00	–	–	–/–	–	3	
Lewis Anthony Robert CBE	6.7.1938		9	1972-1973	457	125	1	32.64	–	–	–/–	–	0	53
Lewis Clairmonte Christopher	14.2.1968		32	1990-1996	1,105	117	1	23.02	93	6-111	3/0	37.52	0	13/2
Lewis Jonathan	26.8.1975		1	2006	27	20	0	13.50	3	3-68	0/0	40.66		
Leyland Maurice	20.7.1900	1.1.1967	41	1928-1938	2,764	187	9	46.06	6	3-91	0/0	97.50	13	8
Lilley Arthur Frederick Augustus ("Dick")	28.11.1866	17.11.1929	35	1896-1909	903	84	0	20.52	1	1-23	0/0	23.00	70/22	3
Lillywhite James	23.2.1842	25.10.1929	2	1876	16	10	0	8.00	8	4-70	0/0	15.75		
Lloyd David	18.3.1947		9	1974-1974	552	214*	1	42.46	0	0-4	0/0	–	11	
Lloyd Timothy Andrew	5.11.1956		1	1984	10	10*	0	–	–	–	–/–	–	0	
Loader Peter James	25.10.1929		13	1954-1958	76	17	0	5.84	39	6-36	1/0	22.51	2	
Lock Graham Anthony Richard	5.7.1929	30.3.1995	49	1952-1967	742	89	0	13.74	174	7-35	9/3	25.58	59	
Lockwood William Henry	25.3.1868	26.4.1932	12	1893-1902	231	52*	0	17.76	43	7-71	5/1	20.53	4	
Lohmann George Alfred	2.6.1865	1.12.1901	18	1886-1896	213	62*	0	8.87	112	9-28	9/5	10.75	28	
Lowson Frank Anderson	1.7.1925	8.9.1984	7	1951-1955	245	68	0	18.84	–	–			5	
Lucas Alfred Perry	20.2.1857	12.10.1923	5	1878-1884	157	55	0	19.62	0	0-23	0/0	–	1	
Luckhurst Brian William	5.2.1939	1.3.2005	21	1970-1974	1,298	131	4	36.05	1	1-9	0/0	32.00	14	
Lyttelton Hon. Alfred	7.2.1857	5.7.1913	4	1880-1884	94	31	0	15.66	4	4-19	1/0	4.75	2	3
Macaulay George Gibson	7.12.1897	13.12.1940	8	1922-1933	112	76	0	18.66	24	5-64	1/0	27.58	5	
MacBryan John Crawford William	22.7.1892	14.7.1983	1	1924	21	11	0	–	–	–	–/–	–	1	
McCague Martin John	24.5.1969		3	1993-1994	21	11	0	4.20	6	4-121	0/0	65.00		
McConnon James Edward	21.6.1922	26.1.2003	2	1954	18	11	0	9.00	4	3-19	0/0	18.50	4	
McGahey Charles Percy	12.2.1871	10.1.1935	2	1901	38	18	0	9.50	–	–	–/–	–		
McGrath Anthony	6.10.1975		4	2003	201	81	0	40.20	4	3-16	0/0	14.00	3	14
MacGregor Gregor	31.8.1869	20.8.1919	8	1890-1893	96	31	0	12.00	–	–	–/–	–	14/3	
McIntyre Arthur John William	14.5.1918	26.12.2009	3	1950-1955	19	7	0	3.16	–	–	–/–	–	8	
MacKinnon Francis Alexander	9.4.1848	27.2.1947	1	1878	5	5	0	2.50	–	–	–/–	–	0	
MacLaren Archibald Campbell	1.12.1871	17.11.1944	35	1894-1909	1,931	140	5	33.87	0	–	–/–	–	29	
McMaster Joseph Emile Patrick	16.3.1861	7.6.1929	1	1888	0	0	0	0.00	–	–	–/–	–		
Maddy Darren Lee	23.5.1974		3	1999-1999	46	24	0	11.50	0	0-40	0/0	–	4	8/4
Mahmood Sajid Iqbal	21.12.1981		8	2006-2006	81	34	0	8.10	20	4-22	0/0	38.10	0	26/4
Makepeace Joseph William Henry	22.8.1881	19.12.1952	4	1920	279	117	1	34.87	–	–	–/–	–		

	Born	Died	Tests	Test Career	Runs	HS	100s	Avge	Wkts	BB	5/10	Avge	Ct/St	O/T
Malcolm Devon Eugene	22.2.1963		40	1989–1997	236	29	0	6.05	128	9-57	5/2	37.09	7	10
Mallender Neil Alan	13.8.1961		2	1992	8	4	0	2.66	10	5-50	1/0	21.50	0	
Mann Francis George CBE	6.9.1917	8.8.2001	7	1948–1949	376	136*	1	37.60	–	–	–/–	–	3	
Mann Francis Thomas	3.3.1888	6.10.1964	5	1922	281	84	0	35.12	–	–	–/–	–	4	
Marks Victor James	25.6.1955		6	1982–1983	249	83	0	27.66	11	3-78	–/–	44.00	0	34
Marriott Charles Stowell ("Father")	14.9.1895	13.10.1966	1	1933	0	0	0	0.00	11	6-59	2/1	8.72	0	
Martin Frederick	12.10.1861	13.12.1921	2	1890–1891	14	13	0	7.00	14	6-50	2/1	10.07	2	
Martin John William	16.2.1917	4.1.1987	1	1947	26	26	0	13.00	1	1-111	0/0	129.00	2	
Martin Peter James	15.11.1968		8	1995–1997	115	29	0	8.84	17	4-60	0/0	34.11	6	20
Mason John Richard	26.3.1874	15.10.1958	5	1897	129	32	0	12.90	2	1-8	0/0	74.50	3	
Matthews Austin David George	3.5.1904	29.7.1977	1	1937	2	2*	0	–	2	1-13	0/0	32.50	1	
May Peter Barker Howard CBE	31.12.1929	27.12.1994	66	1951–1961	4,537	285*	13	46.77	–	–	–/–	–	42	
Maynard Matthew Peter	21.3.1966		4	1988–1993	87	35	0	10.87	–	–	–/–	–	3	14
Mead Charles Philip	9.3.1887	26.3.1958	17	1911–1928	1,185	182*	4	49.37	–	–	–/–	–	4	
Mead Walter	1.4.1868	18.3.1954	1	1899	7	7	0	3.50	1	1-91	0/0	91.00	1	
Midwinter William Evans	19.6.1851	3.12.1890	4†	1887	95	36	0	13.57	10	4-81	–/–	27.20	5	
Milburn Colin	23.10.1941	28.2.1990	9	1966–1968	654	139	2	46.71	–	–	–/–	–	7	
Miller Audley Montague	19.10.1869	26.6.1959	1	1895	24	20*	0	–	–	–	–/–	–	0	
Milligan Frank William	19.3.1870	31.3.1900	2	1898	58	38	0	14.50	6	5-44	1/0	25.80	1	25
Millman Geoffrey	2.10.1934	6.4.2005	6	1961–1962	60	32*	0	12.00	0	0-12	0/0	–	13/2	
Milton Clement Arthur	10.3.1928	25.4.2007	6	1958–1959	204	104*	1	25.50	0	0-4	0/0	–	5	
Mitchell Arthur	13.9.1902	25.12.1976	6	1933–1936	298	72	0	29.80	0	–	–/–	–	9	
Mitchell Frank	13.8.1872	11.10.1935	2†	1898	88	41	0	22.00	0	–	–/–	–	2	
Mitchell Thomas Bignall	4.9.1902	27.1.1996	5	1932–1935	20	9	0	5.00	8	2-49	0/0	62.25	1	
Mitchell-Innes Norman Stewart ("Mandy")	7.9.1914	28.12.2006	1	1935	5	5	0	5.00	–	–	–/–	–	0	
Mold Arthur Webb	27.5.1863	29.4.1921	3	1893	0	0*	0	0.00	7	3-44	0/0	33.42	1	
Moon Leonard James	9.2.1878	23.11.1916	1	1905	182	36	0	22.75	–	–	–/–	–	4	
Morley Frederick	16.12.1850	28.9.1884	4	1880–1882	6	2*	0	1.50	16	5-56	1/0	18.50	4	
Morris Hugh	5.10.1963		3	1991	115	44	0	19.16	–	–	–/–	–	3	
Morris John Edward	1.4.1964		3	1990	71	32	0	23.66	–	–	–/–	–	3	8
Mortimore John Brian	14.5.1933		9	1958–1964	243	73*	0	24.30	13	3-36	0/0	56.38	3	
Moss Alan Edward	14.11.1930		9	1953–1960	61	26	0	10.16	21	4-35	0/0	29.80	1	
Moxon Martyn Douglas	4.5.1960		10	1986–1989	455	99	0	28.43	0	0-3	0/0	–	10	8
Mullally Alan David	12.7.1969		19	1996–2001	127	24	0	5.52	58	5-105	1/0	31.24	6	50

	Born	Died	Tests	Test Career	Runs	HS	100s	Avge	Wkts	BB	5/10	Avge	Ct/St	O/T
Munton Timothy Alan	30.7.1965		2	1992	25	25*	0	50.00	4	2-22	0/0	25.00	0	
Murdoch William Lloyd	18.10.1854	18.2.1911	1†	1891	12	12	0	12.00	–	–	–/–	–	0/1	
Murray John Thomas MBE	1.4.1935		21	1961–1967	506	112	0	22.00	–	–	–/–	–	52/3	
Newham William	12.12.1860	26.6.1944	1	1887	26	17	0	13.00	–	–	–/–	–	0	
Newport Philip John	11.10.1962		3	1988–1990	110	40*	0	27.50	10	4-87	0/0	41.70	1	
Nichols Morris Stanley	6.10.1900	26.1.1961	14	1929–1939	355	78*	0	29.58	41	6-35	2/0	28.09	11	
Oakman Alan Stanley Myles	20.4.1930		2	1956	14	10	0	7.00	0	0-21	0/0	–	7	
O'Brien *Sir* Timothy Carew	5.11.1861	9.12.1948	5	1884–1895	59	20	0	7.37	–	–	–/–	–	4	
O'Connor Jack	6.11.1897	22.2.1977	4	1929–1929	153	51	0	21.85	1	1-31	0/0	72.00	4	
Old Christopher Middleton	22.12.1948		46	1972–1981	845	65	0	14.82	143	7-50	4/0	28.11	22	32
Oldfield Norman	5.5.1911	19.4.1996	1	1939	99	80	0	49.50	–	–	–/–	–	0	
Onions Graham	9.9.1982		8	2009–2009	30	17*	0	10.00	28	5-38	1/0	31.03	0	
Ormond James	20.8.1977		2	2001–2001	38	18	0	10.00	28	1-70	0/0	92.50	0	4
Padgett Douglas Ernest Vernon	20.7.1934		2	1960	51	31	0	12.75	0	0-8	0/0	–	0	
Paine George Alfred Edward	11.6.1908	30.3.1978	4	1934	97	49	0	16.16	17	5-168	1/0	27.47	5	
Palairet Lionel Charles Hamilton	27.5.1870	27.3.1933	2	1902	49	20	0	12.25	–	–	–/–	–	2	
Palmer Charles Henry CBE	15.5.1919	31.3.2005	1	1953	22	22	0	11.00	0	0-15	0/0	–	0	
Palmer Kenneth Ernest MBE	22.4.1937		1	1964	10	10	0	10.00	1	1-113	0/0	189.00	0	
Panesar Mudhsuden Singh ("Monty")	25.4.1982		39	2005–2009	187	26	0	5.50	126	6-37	8/1	34.37	9	26/1
Parfitt Peter Howard	8.12.1936		37	1961–1972	1,882	131*	7	40.91	12	2-5	0/0	47.83	42	
Parker Charles Warrington Leonard	14.10.1882	11.7.1959	1	1921	3	3*	0	6.50	2	2-32	0/0	16.00	0	
Parker Paul William Giles	15.1.1956		1	1981	13	13	0	6.50	–	–	–/–	–	0	
Parkhouse William Gilbert Anthony	12.10.1925	10.8.2000	7	1950–1959	373	78	0	28.69	–	–	–/–	–	3	
Parkin Cecil Harry	18.2.1886	15.6.1943	10	1920–1924	160	36	0	12.30	32	5-38	2/0	35.25	3	
Parks James Horace	12.5.1903	21.11.1980	1	1937	29	22	0	14.50	3	2-26	0/0	12.00	3	
Parks James Michael	21.10.1931		46	1954–1967	1,962	108*	2	32.16	1	1-43	0/0	51.00	103/11	
Pataudi Iftikhar Ali Khan, Nawab of	16.3.1910	5.1.1952	3†	1932–1934	144	102	1	28.80	–	–	–/–	–	0	
Patel Minal Mahesh	7.7.1970		2	1996	45	27	0	22.50	1	1-101	0/0	180.00	2	
Pattinson Darren John	2.8.1979		1	2008	21	13	0	10.50	2	2-95	0/0	48.00	0	
Paynter Edward	5.11.1901	5.2.1979	20	1931–1939	1,540	243	4	59.23	–	–	–/–	–	7	
Peate Edmund	2.3.1855	11.3.1900	9	1881–1886	70	13	0	11.66	31	6-85	2/0	22.03	2	
Peebles Ian Alexander Ross	20.1.1908	27.2.1980	13	1927–1931	98	26	0	10.88	45	6-63	3/0	30.91	5	
Peel Robert	12.2.1857	12.8.1941	20	1884–1896	427	83	0	14.72	101	7-31	5/1	16.98	17	
Penn Frank	7.3.1851	26.12.1916	1	1880	50	27*	0	50.00	0	0-2	0/0	–	1	
Perks Reginald Thomas David	4.10.1911	22.11.1977	2	1938–1939	3	2*	0	–	11	5-100	2/0	32.27	0	

Name	Born	Died	Tests	Test Career	Runs	HS	100s	Avge	Wkts	BB	5/10	Avge	Ct/St	O/T
Philipson Hylton	8.6.1866	4.12.1935	5	1891–1894	63	30	0	9.00					8/3	
Pietersen Kevin Peter MBE	27.6.1980		58	2005–2009	4,824	226	16	48.24	4	1-0	0/0	137.00	32	93t/20
Pigott Anthony Charles Shackleton	4.6.1958		1	1983	12	8*	0	12.00	2	2-75	0/0	37.50	0	
Pilling Richard	11.8.1855	28.3.1891	8	1881–1888	91	23	0	7.58					10/4	
Place Winston	7.12.1914	25.1.2002	3	1947	144	107	1	28.80					0	
Plunkett Liam Edward	6.4.1985		9	2005–2007	126	44*	0	11.45	23	3-17	0/0	39.82	3	27/1
Pocock Patrick Ian	24.9.1946		25	1967–1984	206	33	0	6.24	67	6-79	3/0	44.41	15	1
Pollard Richard	19.6.1912	16.12.1985	4	1946–1948	13	10*	0	13.00	15	5-24	1/0	25.20	3	
Poole Cyril John	13.3.1921	11.2.1996	3	1951	161	69*	0	40.25		0-9			1	
Pope George Henry	27.1.1911	29.10.1993	1	1947	8	8*	0	–	1	1-49	0/0	85.00	0	
Pougher Arthur Dick	19.4.1865	20.5.1926	1	1891	17	17	0	17.00	3	3-26	1/0	8.66	2	
Price John Sidney Ernest	22.7.1937		15	1963–1972	66	32	0	7.33	40	5-73	1/0	35.02	7	
Price Wilfred Frederick Frank	25.4.1902	13.1.1969	1	1938	6	6	0	3.00					2	
Prideaux Roger Malcolm	31.7.1939		3	1968	102	64	0	20.40					0	
Pringle Derek Raymond	18.9.1958		30	1982–1992	695	63	0	15.10	70	5-95	3/0	35.97	10	44
Prior Matthew James	26.2.1982		27	2007–2009	1,484	131*	2	40.10					63/2	52/8
Pullar Geoffrey	1.8.1935		28	1959–1962	1,974	175	4	43.86	1	1-1	0/0	37.00	2	
Quaife William George	17.3.1872	13.10.1951	7	1899–1901	228	68	0	19.00		0-6			4	
Radford Neal Victor	7.6.1957		3	1986–1987	21	12*	0	7.00	4	2-131	0/0	87.75	0	6
Radley Clive Thornton MBE	13.5.1944		8	1977–1978	481	158	2	48.10					4	4
Ramprakash Mark Ravin	5.9.1969		52	1991–2001	2,350	154	2	27.32	4	1-2	0/0	119.25	39	18
Randall Derek William	24.2.1951		47	1976–1984	2,470	174	7	33.37		0-1			31	49
Ranjitsinhji Kumar Shri	10.9.1872	2.4.1933	15	1896–1902	989	175	2	44.95	1	1-23	0/0	39.00	13	
Read Christopher Mark Wells	10.8.1978		15	1999–2006	360	55	0	18.94					48/6	36/1
Read Holcombe Douglas ("Hopper")	28.11.1910	5.1.2000	1	1935	–	–	–	–	6	4-136	0/0	33.33	0	
Read John Maurice	9.2.1859	17.2.1929	17	1882–1893	461	57	0	17.07		0-0			8	
Read Walter William	23.11.1855	6.1.1907	18	1882–1893	720	117	1	27.69		0-27			16	
Reeve Dermot Alexander OBE	2.4.1963		3	1991	124	59	0	24.80	2	1-4	0/0	30.00	1	29
Relf Albert Edward	26.6.1874	26.3.1937	13	1903–1913	416	63	0	23.11	25	5-85	1/0	24.96	14	
Rhodes Harold James	22.7.1936		2	1959	–	0*	0	–	9	4-50	0/0	27.11	0	
Rhodes Steven John	17.6.1964		11	1994–1994	294	65*	0	24.50					46/3	9
Rhodes Wilfred	29.10.1877	8.7.1973	58	1899–1929	2,325	179	1	30.19	127	8-68	6/1	26.96	60	
Richards Clifton James ("Jack")	10.8.1958		8	1986–1988	285	133	1	21.92					20/1	22
[2] Richardson Derek Walter ("Dick")	3.11.1934		1	1957	33	33	0	33.00					0	
[2] Richardson Peter Edward	4.7.1931		34	1956–1963	2,061	126	5	37.47	3	2-10	0/0	16.00	6	

Name	Born	Died	Tests	Test Career	Runs	HS	100s	Avge	Wkts	BB	5/10	Avge	Ct/St	O/T
Richardson Thomas	11.8.1870	2.7.1912	14	1893–1897	177	25*		11.06	88	8-94	11/4	25.22	5	
Richmond Thomas Leonard	23.6.1890	29.12.1957	1	1921	6	4		3.00	2	2-69	00	43.00		
Ridgway Frederick	10.8.1923		5	1951	49	24		8.16	7	4-83	00	54.14	3	
Robertson John David Benbow	22.2.1917	12.10.1996	11	1947–1951	881	133	2	46.36	2	2-17	00	29.00	6	
Robins Robert Walter Vivian	3.6.1906	12.12.1968	19	1929–1937	612	108	1	26.60	64	6-32	1/0	27.46	12	
Robinson Robert Timothy	21.11.1958		29	1984–1989	1,601	175	4	36.38	0	0-0	00	–	8	26
Roope Graham Richard James	12.7.1946	26.11.2006	21	1972–1978	860	77	0	30.71	0	0-2	00	–	35	8
Root Charles Frederick	16.4.1890	20.1.1954	3	1926	–	–		–	8	4-84	00	24.25	1	
Rose Brian Charles	4.6.1950		9	1977–1980	358	70	0	25.57			–/–	–	4	2
Royle Vernon Peter Fanshawe Archer	29.1.1854	21.5.1929	1	1878	21	18	0	10.50	0	0-6	00	–	2	
Rumsey Frederick Edward	4.12.1935		5	1964–1965	30	21*	0	15.00	17	4-25	00	27.11	0	
Russell Albert Charles ("Jack")	7.10.1887	23.3.1961	10	1920–1922	910	140	5	56.87			–/–	–	8	
Russell Robert Charles ("Jack")	15.8.1963		54	1988–1997	1,897	128*	2	27.10			–/–	–	153/12	40
Russell William Eric	3.7.1936		10	1961–1967	362	70	0	21.29	1	0-19	00	–	4	
Saggers Martin John	23.5.1972		3	2003–2004	1	1	0	0.33	7	2-29	00	35.28		
Salisbury Ian David Kenneth	21.11.1970		15	1992–2000	368	50	0	16.72	20	4-163	00	76.95	5	4
Sandham Andrew	6.7.1890	20.4.1982	14	1921–1929	879	325	2	38.21	0		–/–	–	4	
Schofield Christopher Paul	6.10.1978		2	2000	67	57	0	22.33	0	0-73	00	–	0	0/4
Schultz Sandford Spence	29.8.1857	18.12.1937	1	1878	20	20	0	20.00	1	1-16	00	26.00	0	
Scotton William Henry	15.1.1856	9.7.1893	15	1881–1886	510	90	0	22.17	0	0-20	00	–	4	
Selby John	1.7.1849	11.3.1894	6	1876–1881	256	70	0	23.27			–/–	–	5/2	
Selvey Michael Walter William	25.4.1948		3	1976–1976	15	5*	0	7.50	6	4-41	00	57.16	1	
Shackleton Derek	12.8.1924	28.9.2007	7	1950–1963	113	42	0	18.83	18	4-72	00	42.66	1	
Shah Owais Alam	22.10.1978		6	2005–2008	269	88	0	26.90	0	0-12	00	–	2	
Sharp John	15.2.1878	28.1.1938	3	1909	188	105	1	47.00	3	3-67	00	37.00	2	
Sharpe John William	9.12.1866	19.6.1936	3	1890–1891	44	26	0	22.00	11	6-84	1/0	27.72	2	
Sharpe Philip John	27.12.1936		12	1963–1969	786	111	1	46.23	0		–/–	–	17	
Shaw Alfred	29.8.1842	16.1.1907	7	1876–1881	111	40	0	10.09	12	5-38	1/0	23.75	4	
Sheppard Rt. Rev. Lord [David Stuart]	6.3.1929	5.3.2005	22	1950–1962	1,172	119	3	37.80			–/–	–	12	71/17
Sherwin Mordecai	26.2.1851	3.7.1910	3	1886–1888	30	21*	0	15.00			–/–	–	5/2	
Shrewsbury Arthur	11.4.1856	19.5.1903	23	1887–1893	1,277	164	3	35.47	0		–/–	–	29	
Shuter John	9.2.1855	5.7.1920	1	1888	28	28	0	28.00			–/–	–	0	
Shuttleworth Kenneth	13.11.1944		5	1970–1971	46	21	0	7.66	12	5-47	1/0	35.58	1	
Sidebottom Arnold	1.4.1954		1	1985	2	2	0	2.00	1	1-65	00	65.00	0	
Sidebottom Ryan Jay	15.1.1978		22	2001–2009	313	31	0	15.65	79	7-47	5/1	28.24	5	24/8

Name	Born	Died	Tests	Test Career	Runs	HS	100s	Avge	Wkts	BB	5/10	Avge	Ct/St	O/T
Silverwood Christopher Eric Wilfred	5.3.1975	—	6	1996–2002	29	10	0	7.25	11	5-91	1/0	40.36	2	7
Simpson Reginald Thomas	27.2.1920	—	27	1948–1954	1,401	156*	4	33.35	2	2-4	0/0	11.00	5	—
Simpson-Hayward George Hayward Thomas	7.6.1875	2.10.1936	1	1909	105	29*	0	15.00	23	6-43	2/0	18.26	1	—
Sims James Morton	13.5.1903	27.4.1973	4	1935–1936	16	12	0	4.00	11	5-73	2/0	43.63	6	—
Sinfield Reginald Albert	24.12.1900	17.3.1988	1	1938	6	6	0	6.00	2	1-51	0/0	61.50	3	—
Slack Wilfred Norris	12.12.1954	15.11.1989	3	1985–1986	81	52	0	13.50	—	—	—	—	0	2
Smailes Thomas Francis	27.3.1910	1.12.1970	1	1946	25	25	0	25.00	3	3-44	0/0	20.66	—	—
Small Gladstone Cleophas	18.10.1961	—	17	1986–1990	263	59	0	15.47	55	5-48	2/0	34.01	9	53
Smith Alan Christopher CBE	25.10.1936	—	6	1962	118	69*	0	29.50	—	—	—	—	20	—
Smith Andrew Michael	1.10.1967	—	1	1997	4	4*	0	4.00	0	0-89	0/0	—	0	—
Smith Cedric Ivan James	25.8.1906	8.2.1979	5	1934–1937	102	27	0	10.20	15	5-16	1/0	26.20	1	—
Smith Sir Charles Aubrey	21.7.1863	20.12.1948	1	1888	3	3	0	3.00	7	5-19	1/0	8.71	0	—
[2]Smith Christopher Lyall	15.10.1958	—	8	1983–1986	392	91	0	30.15	3	2-31	0/0	13.00	5	4
Smith David Mark	9.1.1956	—	2	1985	80	47	0	20.00	—	—	—	—	0	2
Smith David Robert	5.10.1934	17.12.2003	5	1961	38	34	0	9.50	6	2-60	0/0	59.83	2	—
Smith Denis	24.1.1907	12.9.1979	3	1935	128	57	0	32.00	—	—	—	—	—	—
Smith Donald Victor	14.6.1923	—	2	1957	25	16*	0	8.33	1	1-12	0/0	97.00	0	—
Smith Edward Thomas	19.7.1977	—	3	2003	87	64	0	17.40	—	—	—	—	5	—
Smith Ernest James ("Tiger")	6.2.1886	31.8.1979	11	1911–1913	113	22	0	8.69	1	—	—	—	17/3	—
Smith Harry	21.5.1891	12.11.1937	2	1928	7	7	0	7.00	—	—	—	—	—	—
[2]Smith Michael John Knight OBE	30.6.1933	—	50	1958–1972	2,278	121	3	31.63	1	1-10	0/0	128.00	53	71
Smith Robin Arnold	13.9.1963	—	62	1988–1995	4,236	175	9	43.67	0	0-6	0/0	—	39	—
Smith Thomas Peter Bromley	30.10.1908	4.8.1967	4	1946–1946	33	24	0	6.60	3	2-172	0/0	106.33	1	—
Smithson Gerald Arthur	1.11.1926	6.9.1970	2	1947	70	35	0	23.33	—	—	—	—	0	—
Snow John Augustine	13.10.1941	—	49	1965–1976	772	73	0	13.54	202	7-40	8/1	26.66	16	9
Southerton James	16.11.1827	16.6.1880	2	1876	7	6	0	3.50	7	4-46	0/0	15.28	2	—
Spooner Reginald Herbert	21.10.1880	2.10.1961	10	1905–1912	481	119	1	32.06	—	—	—	—	4	—
Spooner Richard Thompson	30.12.1919	20.12.1997	7	1951–1955	354	92	0	27.23	—	—	—	—	10/2	—
Stanyforth Ronald Thomas	30.5.1892	20.2.1964	4	1927	13	6*	0	2.60	—	—	—	—	7/2	—
Staples Samuel James	18.9.1892	4.6.1950	3	1927	65	39	0	13.00	15	3-50	0/0	29.00	0	—
Statham John Brian CBE	17.6.1930	10.6.2000	70	1950–1965	675	38	0	11.44	252	7-39	9/1	24.84	28	—
Steel Allan Gibson	24.9.1858	15.6.1914	13	1880–1888	600	148	2	35.29	29	3-27	0/0	20.86	5	—
Steele David Stanley OBE	29.9.1941	—	8	1975–1976	673	106	1	42.06	2	1-1	0/0	19.50	7	—
Stephenson John Patrick	14.3.1965	—	1	1989	36	25	0	18.00	—	—	—	—	0	—
Stevens Greville Thomas Scott	7.1.1901	19.9.1970	10	1922–1929	263	69	0	15.47	20	5-90	2/1	32.40	9	1

	Born	Died	Tests	Test Career	Runs	HS	100s	Avge	Wkts	BB	5/10	Avge	Ct/St	O/T
Stevenson Graham Barry	16.12.1955		2	1979–1980	28	27*	0	28.00	5	3-111	0/0	36.60	0	4
Stewart Alec James OBE	8.4.1963		133	1989–2003	8,463	190	15	39.54	0	0-5	0/0	–	263/14	170
¹Stewart Michael James OBE	16.9.1932		8	1962–1963	385	87	0	35.00	–	–	–/–	–	6	
Stoddart Andrew Ernest	11.3.1863	3.4.1915	16	1887–1897	996	173	2	35.57	2	1-10	0/0	47.00	6	
Storer William	25.1.1867	28.2.1912	6	1897–1899	215	51	0	19.54	2	1-24	0/0	54.00	11	
Strauss Andrew John MBE	2.3.1977		71	2004–2009	5,436	177	18	43.48	–	–	–/–	–	77	99/4
Street George Benjamin	6.12.1889	24.4.1924	1	1922	11	7*	0	11.00	–	–	–/–	–	0/1	
Strudwick Herbert	28.1.1880	14.2.1970	28	1909–1926	230	24	0	7.93	–	–	–/–	–	61/12	
²Studd Charles Thomas	2.12.1860	16.7.1931	5	1882–1882	160	48	0	20.00	3	2-35	0/0	32.66	5	
²Studd George Brown	20.10.1859	13.2.1945	4	1882	31	9	0	4.42	–	–	–/–	–	8	
Subba Row Raman CBE	29.1.1932		13	1958–1961	984	137	3	46.85	0	0-2	0/0	–	5	
Such Peter Mark	12.6.1964		11	1993–1999	67	14*	0	6.09	37	6-67	2/0	33.56	4	
Sugg Frank Howe	11.1.1862	29.5.1933	2	1888	55	31	0	27.50	–	–	–/–	–	0	
Sutcliffe Herbert	24.11.1894	22.1.1978	54	1924–1935	4,555	194	16	60.73	–	–	–/–	–	23	
Swann Graeme Peter	24.3.1979		16	2008–2009	525	85	0	32.81	69	5-54	4/0	30.69	10	29/9
Swetman Roy	25.10.1933		11	1958–1959	254	65	0	16.93	–	–	–/–	–	24/2	
¹Tate Frederick William	24.7.1867	24.2.1943	1	1902	9	5*	0	9.00	2	2-7	0/0	25.50	2	
¹Tate Maurice William	30.5.1895	18.5.1956	39	1924–1935	1,198	100*	1	25.48	155	6-42	7/1	26.16	11	
Tattersall Roy	17.8.1922		16	1950–1954	50	10*	0	5.00	58	7-52	4/1	26.08	8	
Tavaré Christopher James	27.10.1954		31	1980–1989	1,755	149	2	32.50	0	0-0	0/0	–	20	29
Taylor Jonathan Paul	8.8.1964		2	1992–1994	34	17*	0	17.00	3	1-18	0/0	52.00	–	1
Taylor Kenneth	21.8.1935		3	1959–1964	57	24	0	11.40	0	0-6	0/0	–	1	
Taylor Leslie Brian	25.10.1953		2	1985	1	1*	0	–	4	2-34	0/0	44.50	–	2
Taylor Robert William MBE	17.7.1941		57	1970–1983	1,156	97	0	16.28	0	0-6	0/0	–	167/7	27
Tennyson *Lord* Lionel Hallam	7.11.1889	6.6.1951	9	1913–1921	345	74*	0	31.36	0	0-1	0/0	–	6	
Terry Vivian Paul	14.1.1959		2	1984	16	8	0	5.33	–	–	–/–	–	2	
Thomas John Gregory	12.8.1960		5	1985–1986	83	31*	0	13.83	10	4-70	0/0	50.40	2	
Thompson George Joseph	27.10.1877	3.3.1943	6	1909–1909	273	63	0	30.33	23	4-50	0/0	27.73	5	3
Thomson Norman Ian	23.1.1929		5	1964	69	39	0	23.00	9	2-55	0/0	63.11	3	
Thorpe Graham Paul MBE	1.8.1969		100	1993–2005	6,744	200*	16	44.66	0	0-0	0/0	–	105	82
Titmus Frederick John MBE	24.11.1932		53	1955–1974	1,449	84*	0	22.29	153	7-79	7/0	32.22	35	2
Tolchard Roger William	15.6.1946		4	1976	129	67	0	25.80	–	–	–/–	–	5	1
¹Townsend Charles Lucas	7.11.1876	17.10.1958	2	1899	51	38	0	17.00	3	3-50	0/0	25.00	0	
¹Townsend David Charles Humphrey	20.4.1912	27.1.1997	3	1934	77	36	0	12.83	0	0-9	0/0	–	1	
Townsend Leslie Fletcher	8.6.1903	17.2.1993	4	1929–1933	97	40	0	16.16	6	2-22	0/0	34.16	2	

	Born	Died	Tests	Test Career	Runs	HS	100s	Avge	Wkts	BB	5/10	Avge	Ct/St	O/T
¹Tremlett Christopher Timothy	2.9.1981		3	2007	50	25*	0	12.50	13	3-12	0/0	29.69	1	9/1
¹Tremlett Maurice Fletcher	5.7.1923	30.7.1984	3	1947	20	18*	0	6.66	4	2-98	0/0	56.50	1	
Trescothick Marcus Edward MBE	25.12.1975		76	2000–2006	5,825	219	14	43.79	1	1-34	0/0	155.00	95	123/3
²Trott Albert Edwin	6.2.1873	30.7.1914	2‡	1898	23	16	0	5.75	17	5-49	1/0	11.64	4	
Trott Ian Jonathan Leonard	22.4.1981		5	2009–2009	350	119	1	38.88	0	0-9	0/0	–	3	4/5
Trueman Frederick Sewards OBE	6.2.1931	1.7.2006	67	1952–1965	981	39*	0	13.81	307	8-31	17/3	21.57	64	
Tudor Alex Jeremy	23.10.1977		10	1998–2002	229	99*	0	19.08	28	5-44	1/0	34.39	3	3
Tufnell Neville Charsley	13.6.1887	3.8.1951	1	1909	14	14	0	14.00	–	–	–/–	–	0/1	
Tufnell Philip Clive Roderick	29.4.1966		42	1990–2001	153	22*	0	5.10	121	7-47	5/2	37.68	12	20
Turnbull Maurice Joseph Lawson	16.3.1906	5.8.1944	9	1929–1936	224	61	0	20.36	–	–	–/–	–	1	
²Tyldesley [George] Ernest	5.2.1889	5.5.1962	14	1921–1928	990	122	3	55.00	0	0-2	0/0	–	2	
²Tyldesley John Thomas	22.11.1873	27.11.1930	31	1898–1909	1,661	138	4	30.75	–	–	–/–	–	16	
Tyldesley Richard Knowles	11.3.1897	17.9.1943	7	1924–1930	47	29	0	7.83	19	3-50	0/0	32.57	1	
Tylecote Edward Ferdinando Sutton	23.6.1849	15.3.1938	6	1882–1886	152	66	0	19.00	–	–	–/–	–	5/5	26
Tyler Edwin James	13.10.1864	25.1.1917	1	1895	0	0	0	0.00	4	3-49	0/0	16.25	0	
Tyson Frank Holmes	6.6.1930		17	1954–1958	230	37*	0	10.95	76	7-27	4/1	18.56	4	
Udal Shaun David	18.3.1969		4	2005	109	33*	0	18.16	8	4-14	0/0	43.00	1	11
Ulyett George	21.10.1851	18.6.1898	25	1876–1890	949	149	1	24.33	50	7-36	1/0	20.40	19	
Underwood Derek Leslie MBE	8.6.1945		86	1966–1981	937	45*	0	11.56	297	8-51	17/6	25.83	44	26
Valentine Bryan Herbert	17.1.1908	2.2.1983	7	1933–1938	454	136	2	64.85	–	–	–/–	–	2	
Vaughan Michael Paul OBE	29.10.1974		82	1999–2008	5,719	197	18	41.44	6	2-71	0/0	93.50	44	86/2
Verity Hedley	18.5.1905	31.7.1943	40	1931–1939	669	66*	0	20.90	144	8-43	5/2	24.37	30	
Vernon George Frederick	20.6.1856	10.8.1902	1	1882	14	11*	0	14.00	–	–	–/–	–	0	
Vine Joseph	15.5.1875	25.4.1946	2	1911	46	36	0	46.00	–	–	–/–	–	0	
Voce William	8.8.1909	6.6.1984	27	1929–1946	308	66	0	13.39	98	7-70	3/2	27.88	15	
Waddington Abraham	4.2.1893	28.10.1959	2	1920	16	7	0	4.00	1	1-35	0/0	119.00	1	
Wainwright Edward	8.4.1865	28.10.1919	5	1893–1897	132	49	0	14.66	0	0-11	0/0	–	2	
Walker Peter Michael	17.2.1936		3	1960	128	52	0	32.00	0	0-8	0/0	–	5	
Walters Cyril Frederick	28.8.1905	23.12.1992	11	1933–1934	784	102	1	52.26	–	–	–/–	–	6	
Ward Alan	10.8.1947		5	1969–1976	40	21	0	8.00	14	4-61	0/0	32.35	3	
Ward Albert	21.11.1865	6.1.1939	7	1893–1894	487	117	1	37.46	–	–	–/–	–	1	
Ward Ian James	30.9.1972		5	2001	129	39	0	16.12	–	–	–/–	–	1	
Wardle John Henry	8.1.1923	23.7.1985	28	1947–1957	653	66	0	19.78	102	7-36	5/1	20.39	12	
Warner Sir Pelham Francis	2.10.1873	30.1.1963	15	1898–1912	622	132*	1	23.92	–	–	–/–	–	3	
Warr John James	16.7.1927		2	1950	4	4	0	1.00	1	1-76	0/0	281.00	0	

Name	Born	Died	Tests	Test Career	Runs	HS	100s	Avge	Wkts	BB	5/10	Avge	Ct/St	O/T
Warren Arnold	2.4.1875	3.9.1951	1	1905	7	7	0	7.00	6	5-57	1/0	18.83	1	
Washbrook Cyril CBE	6.12.1914	27.4.1999	37	1937–1956	2,569	195	6	42.81	–	–	–	–	12	
Watkin Steven Llewellyn	15.9.1964		3	1991–1993	25	13	0	5.00	11	1-25	0/0	33.00	1	4
Watkins Albert John ("Allan")	21.4.1922		15	1948–1952	810	137*	2	40.50	11	3-20	0/0	27.72	17	
Watkinson Michael	1.8.1961		4	1995–1995	167	82*	0	33.40	10	3-64	0/0	50.36	1	1
Watson Willie	7.3.1920	23.4.2004	23	1951–1958	879	116	2	25.85	–	–	–/–	–	8	
Webbe Alexander Josiah	16.1.1855	19.2.1941	1	1878	4	4	0	2.00	–	–	–	–	2	
Wellard Arthur William	8.4.1902	31.12.1980	2	1937–1938	47	38	0	11.75	7	4-81	0/0	33.85	2	
Wells Alan Peter	2.10.1961		1	1995	3	3*	0	3.00	–	–	–	–	0	
Wharton Alan	30.4.1923	26.8.1993	1	1949	20	13	0	10.00	–	–	–	–	0	1
Whitaker John James	5.5.1962		1	1986	11	11	0	11.00	–	–	–	–	0	2
White Craig	16.12.1969		30	1994–2002	1,052	121	2	24.46	59	5-32	3/0	37.62	14	51
White David William ("Butch")	14.12.1935	1.8.2008	2	1961	0	0	0	0.00	4	3-65	0/0	29.75	0	
White John Cornish	19.2.1891	2.5.1961	15	1921–1930	239	29	0	18.38	49	8-126	3/1	32.26	6	
Whysall William Wilfrid	31.10.1887	11.11.1930	4	1924–1930	209	76	0	29.85	0	0-9	0/0	–	7	
Wilkinson Leonard Litton	5.11.1916	3.9.2002	3	1938	3	3	0	3.00	7	2-12	0/0	38.71	0	
Willey Peter	6.12.1949		26	1976–1986	1,184	102*	2	26.90	7	2-73	0/0	65.14	3	26
Williams Neil FitzGerald	2.7.1962	27.3.2006	1	1990	38	38	0	38.00	2	2-148	0/0	74.00	0	
Willis Robert George Dylan MBE	30.5.1949		90	1970–1984	840	28*	0	11.50	325	8-43	16/0	25.20	39	64
[2]Wilson Clement Eustace Macro	15.5.1875	8.2.1944	2	1898	42	18	0	14.00	–	–	–/–	–	0	
Wilson Donald	7.8.1937		6	1963–1970	75	42	0	12.50	11	2-17	0/0	42.36	1	
[2]Wilson Evelyn Rockley	25.3.1879	21.7.1957	1	1920	10	5	0	5.00	3	2-28	–/–	12.00	0	
Wood Arthur	25.8.1898	1.4.1973	4	1938–1939	80	53	0	20.00	–	–	–	–	10/1	
Wood Barry	26.12.1942		12	1972–1978	454	90	0	21.61	0	0-2	0/0	–	6	13
Wood George Edward Charles	22.8.1893	18.3.1971	3	1924	7	6	0	3.50	–	–	–	–	5/1	
Wood Henry	14.12.1853	30.4.1919	4	1888–1891	204	134*	1	68.00	–	–	–/–	–	2/1	
Wood Reginald	7.3.1860	6.1.1915	1	1886	6	6	0	3.00	–	–	–	–	0	
Woods Samuel Moses James	13.4.1867	30.4.1931	3†	1895	122	53	0	30.50	5	3-28	0/0	25.80	4	
Woolley Frank Edward	27.5.1887	18.10.1978	64	1909–1934	3,283	154	5	36.07	83	7-76	4/1	33.91	64	
Woolmer Robert Andrew	14.5.1948	18.3.2007	19	1975–1981	1,059	149	3	33.09	4	1-8	0/0	74.75	10	6
Worthington Thomas Stanley	21.8.1905	31.8.1973	9	1929–1936	321	128	1	29.18	8	2-19	0/0	39.50	8	
Wright Charles William	27.5.1863	10.1.1936	3	1895	125	71	0	31.25	–	–	–	–	0	
Wright Douglas Vivian Parson	21.8.1914	13.11.1998	34	1938–1950	289	45	0	11.11	108	7-105	6/1	39.11	10	
Wyatt Robert Elliott Storey	2.5.1901	20.4.1995	40	1927–1936	1,839	149	2	31.70	18	3-4	0/0	35.66	16	
Wynyard Edward George	1.4.1861	30.10.1936	3	1896–1905	72	30	0	12.00	0	0-2	0/0	–	0	

	Born	Died	Tests	Test Career	Runs	HS	100s	Avge	Wkts	BB	5/10	Avge	Ct/St	O/T
Yardley Norman Walter Dransfield	19.3.1915	3.10.1989	20	1938–1950	812	99	0	25.37	21	3-67	0/0	33.66	14	
Young Harding Isaac ("Sailor")	5.2.1876	12.12.1964	2	1899	43	43	0	21.50	12	4-30	0/0	21.83	1	65
Young John Albert	14.10.1912	5.2.1993	8	1947–1949	28	10*	0	5.60	17	3-65	0/0	44.52	5	
Young Richard Alfred	16.9.1885	1.7.1968	2	1907	27	13	0	6.75	–	–	–/–	–	6	

AUSTRALIA (412 players)

	Born	Died	Tests	Test Career	Runs	HS	100s	Avge	Wkts	BB	5/10	Avge	Ct/St	O/T
a'Beckett Edward Lambert	11.8.1907	2.6.1989	4	1928–1931	143	41	0	20.42	3	1-41	0/0	105.66	4	
Alderman Terence Michael	12.6.1956		41	1981–1990	203	26*	0	6.54	170	6-47	14/1	27.15	27	
Alexander George	22.4.1851	6.11.1930	2	1880–1884	52	33	0	13.00	2	2-69	0/0	46.50	2	
Alexander Harry Houston	9.6.1905	15.4.1993	1	1932	17	17*	0	17.00	1	1-129	0/0	154.00	0	
Allan Francis Erskine	2.12.1849	9.2.1917	1	1878	5	5	0	5.00	4	2-30	0/0	20.00	0	
Allan Peter John	31.12.1935		1	1965	–	–	–	–	2	2-58	0/0	–	0	
Allen Reginald Charles	2.7.1858	2.5.1952	1	1886	44	30	0	22.00	–	–	–/–	–	2	
Andrews Thomas James Edwin	26.8.1890	28.1.1970	16	1921–1926	592	94	0	26.90	1	1-23	0/0	116.00	12	
Angel Jo	22.4.1968		4	1992–1994	35	11	0	5.83	10	3-54	0/0	46.30	1	3
Archer Kenneth Alan	17.1.1928		5	1950–1951	234	48	0	26.00	–	–	–/–	–	0	
Archer Ronald Graham	25.10.1933	27.5.2007	19	1952–1956	713	128	1	24.58	48	5-53	0/0	27.45	20	
Armstrong Warwick Windridge	22.5.1879	13.7.1947	50	1901–1921	2,863	159*	6	38.68	87	6-35	3/0	33.59	44	
Badcock Clayvel Lindsay ("Jack")	10.4.1914	13.12.1982	7	1936–1938	160	118	0	14.54	–	–	–/–	–	3	
Bannerman Alexander Chalmers	21.3.1854	19.9.1924	28	1878–1893	1,108	94	0	23.08	4	3-111	0/0	40.75	21	
Bannerman Charles	23.7.1851	20.8.1930	3	1876–1878	239	165*	1	59.75	–	–	–/–	–	0	
Bardsley Warren	6.12.1882	20.1.1954	41	1909–1926	2,469	193*	6	40.47	–	–	–/–	–	12	
Barnes Sidney George	5.6.1916	16.12.1973	13	1938–1948	1,072	234	3	63.05	4	2-25	0/0	54.50	14	
Barnett Benjamin Arthur	23.3.1908	29.6.1979	4	1938	195	57	0	27.85	–	–	–/–	–	3/2	
Barrett John Edward	15.10.1866	6.2.1916	2	1890	80	67*	0	26.66	–	–	–/–	–	1	
Beard Graeme Robert	19.8.1950		3	1979	114	49	0	22.80	1	1-26	0/0	109.00	0	2
Benaud John	11.5.1944		3	1972	223	142	1	44.60	2	2-12	0/0	6.00	0	
Benaud Richard OBE	6.10.1930		63	1951–1963	2,201	122	3	24.45	248	7-72	16/1	27.03	65	
Bennett Murray John	6.10.1956		3	1984–1985	71	23	0	23.66	6	3-79	0/0	54.16	5	
Bevan Michael Gwyl	8.5.1970		18	1994–1997	785	91	0	29.07	29	6-82	1/1	24.24	8	8
Bichel Andrew John	27.8.1970		19	1996–2003	355	71	0	16.90	58	5-60	1/0	32.24	16	232
Blackham John McCarthy	11.5.1854	28.12.1932	35	1876–1894	800	74	0	15.68	–	–	–/–	–	37/24	67

	Born	Died	Tests	Test Career	Runs	HS	100s	Avge	Wkts	BB	5/10	Avge	Ct/St	O/T
Blackie Donald Dearness	5.4.1882	18.4.1955	3	1928	24	11*		8.00	14	6-94	1/0	31.71	2	
Blewett Gregory Scott	28.10.1971		46	1994–1999	2,552	214	4	34.02	14	2-9	0/0	51.42	45	32
Bollinger Douglas Erwin	24.7.1981		6	2008–2009	11	9		3.66	27	5-70	1/0	24.11	2	7
Bonnor George John	25.2.1855	27.6.1912	17	1880–1888	512	128	1	17.06	2	1-5	0/0	42.00	16	
Boon David Clarence	29.12.1960		107	1984–1995	7,422	200	21	43.65	0	0-0	0/0	–	99	181
Booth Brian Charles MBE	19.10.1933		29	1961–1965	1,773	169	5	42.21	3	2-33	0/0	48.66	17	
Border Allan Robert	27.7.1955		156	1978–1993	11,174	205	27	50.56	39	7-46	2/1	39.10	156	273
Boyle Henry Frederick	10.12.1847	21.11.1907	12	1878–1884	153	36*	0	12.75	32	6-42	1/0	20.03	10	
Bracken Nathan Wade	12.9.1977		5	2003–2005	70	37	0	17.50	12	4-48	0/0	42.08	2	116/19
Bradman Sir Donald George AC	27.8.1908	25.2.2001	52	1928–1948	6,996	334	29	99.94	2	1-8	0/0	36.00	32	
Bright Raymond James	13.7.1954		25	1977–1986	445	33	0	14.35	53	7-87	4/1	41.13	13	11
Bromley Ernest Harvey	2.9.1912	1.2.1967	2	1932–1934	38	26	0	9.50	0	0-19	0/0	–	2	
Brown William Alfred	31.7.1912	16.3.2008	22	1934–1948	1,592	206*	4	46.82	–	–	–/–	–	14	
Bruce William	22.5.1864	3.8.1925	14	1884–1894	702	80	0	29.25	12	3-88	0/0	36.66	12	
Burge Peter John [Parnell]	17.5.1932	5.10.2001	42	1954–1965	2,290	181	4	38.16	–	–	–/–	–	23	
Burke James Wallace	12.6.1930	2.2.1979	24	1950–1958	1,280	189	3	34.59	8	4-37	0/0	28.75	18	
Burn Edwin James Kenneth (K. E.)	17.9.1862	20.7.1956	2	1890	41	19	0	10.25	–	–	–/–	–	0	
Burton Frederick John	2.11.1865	25.8.1929	2	1886–1887	4	2*	0	2.00	–	–	–/–	–	1/1	
Callaway Sydney Thomas	6.2.1868	25.11.1923	3	1891–1894	87	41	0	17.40	6	5-37	1/0	23.66	2	
Callen Ian Wayne	2.5.1955		1	1977	26	22*	0		6	3-83	0/0	31.83	1	5
Campbell Gregory Dale	10.3.1964		4	1989–1989	10	6	0	2.50	13	3-79	0/0	38.69	1	12
Carkeek William ("Barlow")	17.10.1878	20.2.1937	6	1912	16	6*	0	5.33	–	–	–/–	–	6	
Carlson Phillip Henry	8.8.1951		2	1978	23	21	0	5.75	2	2-41	0/0	49.50	2	4
Carter Hanson	15.3.1878	8.6.1948	28	1907–1921	873	72	0	22.97	–	–	–/–	–	44/21	
Casson Beau	7.12.1982		1	2007	10	10	0	10.00	3	3-86	0/0	43.00	2	
[2,4] **Chappell** Gregory Stephen MBE	7.8.1948		87	1970–1983	7,110	247*	24	53.86	47	5-61	1/0	40.70	122	74
[2,4] **Chappell** Ian Michael	26.9.1943		75	1964–1979	5,345	196	14	42.42	20	2-21	0/0	65.80	105	16
[2,4] **Chappell** Trevor Martin	21.10.1952		3	1981	79	27	0	15.80	–	–	–/–	–	2	20
Charlton Percie Chater	9.4.1867	30.9.1954	2	1890	29	11	0	7.25	3	3-18	0/0	8.00	2	
Chipperfield Arthur Gordon	17.11.1905	29.7.1987	14	1934–1938	552	109	0	32.47	5	3-91	0/0	87.40	15	
Clark Stuart Rupert	28.9.1975		24	2005–2009	248	39	0	13.05	94	5-32	2/0	23.86	4	39/9
Clark Wayne Maxwell	19.9.1953		10	1977–1978	98	33	0	5.76	44	4-46	0/0	28.75	6	2
§ **Clarke** Michael John	2.4.1981		58	2004–2009	4,116	166	13	50.19	19	6-9	1/0	39.73	56	163/19
Colley David John	15.3.1947		3	1972	84	54	0	21.00	6	3-83	0/0	52.00	1	1

§ *Clarke's figures include 44 runs and one catch for Australia v the ICC World XI in the Super Series Test in 2005-06.*

	Born	Died	Tests	Test Career	Runs	HS	100s	Avge	Wkts	BB	5/10	Avge	Ct/St	O/T
Collins Herbert Leslie	21.1.1888	28.5.1959	19	1920–1926	1,352	203	4	45.06	4	2-47	000	63.00	13	1
Coningham Arthur	14.7.1863	13.6.1939	1	1894	13	10	0	6.50	2	2-17	000	38.00	0	
Connolly Alan Norman	29.6.1939		29	1963–1970	260	37	0	10.40	102	6-47	400	29.22	17	
Cook Simon Hewitt	29.1.1972		2	1997	3	3*	0	-	7	5-39	100	20.28	0	
Cooper Bransby Beauchamp	15.3.1844	7.8.1914	1	1876	18	15	0	9.00	-	-	-/-	-	2	
5 Cooper William Henry	11.9.1849	5.4.1939	2	1881–1884	13	7	0	6.50	9	6-120	1/0	25.11	1	
Corling Grahame Edward	13.7.1941		5	1964	5	3	0	1.66	12	4-60	000	37.25	0	
Cosier Gary John	25.4.1953		18	1975–1978	897	168	2	28.93	5	2-26	000	68.20	14	9
Cottam John Thomas	5.9.1867	30.1.1897	1	1886	4	3	0	2.00	-	-	-/-	-	1	
Cotter Albert ("Tibby")	3.12.1883	31.10.1917	21	1903–1911	457	45	0	13.05	89	7-148	7/0	28.64	8	
Coulthard George	1.8.1856	22.10.1883	1	1881	6	6*	0	-	-	-	-	-	0	
Cowper Robert Maskew	5.10.1940		27	1964–1968	2,061	307	5	46.84	36	4-48	000	31.63	21	
Craig Ian David	12.6.1935		11	1952–1957	358	53	0	19.88	-	-	-/-	-	2	
Crawford William Patrick Anthony	3.8.1933	21.11.2009	4	1956–1956	53	34	0	17.66	7	3-28	000	15.28	1	
Cullen Daniel James	10.4.1984		1	2005	-	-	0	-	1	1-25	000	54.00	0	5
Dale Adam Craig	30.12.1968		2	1997–1998	6	5	0	2.00	6	3-71	000	31.16	0	30
Darling Joseph	21.11.1870	2.1.1946	34	1894–1905	1,657	178	3	28.56	-	-	-/-	-	27	
Darling Leonard Stuart	14.8.1909	24.6.1992	12	1932–1936	474	85	0	27.88	0	0-3	000	-	8	
Darling Warrick Maxwell	1.5.1957		14	1977–1979	697	91	0	26.80	-	-	-/-	-	5	
Davidson Alan Keith MBE	14.6.1929		44	1953–1962	1,328	80	0	24.59	186	7-93	14/2	20.53	42	18
Davis Ian Charles	25.6.1953		15	1973–1977	692	105	0	26.61	-	-	-/-	-	9	
Davis Simon Peter	8.11.1959		1	1985	0	0	0	0.00	0	0-70	000	-	0	3
De Courcy James Harry	18.4.1927	20.6.2000	3	1953	81	41	0	16.20	-	-	-/-	-	3	39
Dell Anthony Ross	6.8.1947		2	1970–1973	6	3*	0	-	6	3-65	000	26.66	3	
Dodemaide Anthony Ian Christopher	5.10.1963		10	1987–1992	202	50	0	22.44	34	6-58	1/0	28.02	6	24
Donnan Henry	12.11.1864	13.8.1956	5	1891–1896	75	15	0	8.33	0	0-22	000	-	2	
Dooland Bruce	1.11.1923	8.9.1980	3	1946–1947	76	29	0	19.00	9	4-69	000	46.55	3	
Duff Reginald Alexander	17.8.1878	13.12.1911	22	1901–1905	1,317	146	2	35.59	4	2-43	000	21.25	14	
Duncan John Ross Frederick	25.3.1944		1	1970	3	3	0	3.00	0	0-30	000	-	0	
Dyer Gregory Charles	16.3.1959		6	1986–1987	131	60	0	21.83	-	-	-/-	-	22/2	23
Dymock Geoffrey	21.7.1945		21	1973–1979	236	31*	0	9.44	78	7-67	5/1	27.12	9	
Dyson John	11.6.1954		30	1977–1984	1,359	127*	2	26.64	-	-	-/-	-	10	15
Eady Charles John	29.10.1870	20.12.1945	2	1896–1901	20	10*	0	6.66	7	3-30	000	16.00	2	29
Eastwood Kenneth Humphrey	23.11.1935		1	1970	5	5	0	2.50	1	1-21	000	21.00	0	
Ebeling Hans Irvine	1.1.1905	12.1.1980	1	1934	43	41	0	21.50	3	3-74	000	29.66	0	

	Born	Died	Tests	Test Career	Runs	HS	100s	Avge	Wkts	BB	5/10	Avge	Ct/St	O/T
Edwards John Dunlop	12.6.1860	31.7.1911	3	1888	48	26	–	9.60	0	–	–/–	–	1	–
Edwards Ross	1.12.1942		20	1972–1975	1,171	170*	2	40.37	0	0-20	0/0	–	7	9
Edwards Walter John	23.12.1949		3	1974	68	30	–	11.33	–	–		–	0	1
Elliott Matthew Thomas Gray	28.9.1971		21	1996–2004	1,172	199	3	33.48	–	–		–	14	1
Emery Philip Allen	25.6.1964		1	1994	8	8*	0	–	–	–	–/–	–	5/1	1
Emery Sidney Hand	15.10.1885	7.1.1967	4	1912	6	5	0	3.00	5	2-46	0/0	49.80	2	
Evans Edwin	26.3.1849	2.7.1921	6	1881–1886	82	33	0	10.25	7	3-64	0/0	47.42	5	
Fairfax Alan George	16.6.1906	17.5.1955	10	1928–1930	410	65	0	51.25	21	4-31	0/0	30.71	15	
Favell Leslie Ernest MBE	6.10.1929	14.6.1987	19	1954–1960	757	101	1	27.03	–	–		–	9	
Ferris John James	21.5.1867	17.11.1900	8†	1886–1890	98	20*	0	8.16	48	5-26	4/0	14.25	4	
Fingleton John Henry Webb OBE	28.4.1908	22.11.1981	18	1931–1938	1,189	136	5	42.46	–	–		–	13	
Fleetwood-Smith Leslie O'Brien ("Chuck")	30.3.1908	16.3.1971	10	1935–1938	54	16*	0	9.00	42	6-110	2/1	37.38	0	
Fleming Damien William	24.4.1970		20	1994–2000	305	71*	0	19.06	75	5-30	3/0	25.89	9	88
Francis Bruce Colin	18.2.1948		3	1972	52	27	0	10.40	–	–		–	0	
Freeman Eric Walter	13.7.1944		11	1967–1969	345	76	0	19.16	34	4-52	–/–	33.17	5	
Freer Frederick Alfred William	4.12.1915	2.11.1998	1	1946	28	28*	0	–	3	2-49	0/0	24.66	0	
Gannon John Bryant ("Sam")	8.2.1947		3	1977	3	3*	0	3.00	11	4-77	0/0	32.81	3	
Garrett Thomas William	26.7.1858	6.8.1943	19	1876–1887	339	51*	0	12.55	36	6-78	2/0	26.94	7	
Gaunt Ronald Arthur	26.2.1934		3	1957–1963	6	3	0	3.00	7	3-53	0/0	44.28	3	
Gehrs Donald Raebum Algernon	29.11.1880	25.6.1953	6	1903–1910	221	67	0	20.09	0	0-4	0/0	–	6	
Giffen George	27.3.1859	29.11.1927	31	1881–1896	1,238	161	1	23.35	103	7-117	7/1	27.09	24	
Giffen Walter Frank	20.9.1861	28.6.1949	3	1886–1891	11	3	0	1.83	–	–		–	1	
Gilbert David Robert	29.12.1960		9	1985–1986	57	15	0	7.12	16	3-48	–/–	52.68	1	
Gilchrist Adam Craig	14.11.1971		96§	1999–2007	5,570	204*	17	47.60	0	–		–	379/37	286§/13
Gillespie Jason Neil	19.4.1975		71	1996–2005	1,218	201*	0	18.73	259	7-37	8/0	26.13	27	97/1
Gilmour Gary John	26.6.1951		15	1973–1976	483	101	1	23.00	54	6-85	3/0	26.03	8	5
Gleeson John William	14.3.1938		29	1967–1972	395	45	0	10.39	93	5-61	3/0	36.20	17	
Graham Henry	22.11.1870	7.2.1911	6	1893–1896	301	107	2	30.10	–	–		–	3	
Gregory David William	15.4.1845	4.8.1919	3	1876–1878	60	43	0	20.00	0	0-9	–/–	–	0	
Gregory Edward James	29.5.1839	22.4.1899	1	1876	11	11	0	5.50	–	–		–	1	
Gregory Jack Morrison	14.8.1895	7.8.1973	24	1920–1928	1,146	119	2	36.96	85	7-69	4/0	31.15	37	
Gregory Ross Gerald	28.2.1916	10.6.1942	2	1936	153	80	0	51.00	0	0-14	0/0	–	1	
Gregory Sydney Edward	14.4.1870	1.8.1929	58	1890–1912	2,282	201	4	24.53	0	0-4	0/0	–	25	
Grimmett Clarence Victor	25.12.1891	2.5.1980	37	1924–1935	557	50	0	13.92	216	7-40	21/7	24.21	17	

§ Gilchrist's figures include 95 runs, five catches and two stumpings for Australia v the ICC World XI in the Super Series Test in 2005-06.

	Born	Died	Tests	Test Career	Runs	HS	100s	Avge	Wkts	BB	5/10	Avge	Ct/St	O/T
Groube Thomas Underwood	2.9.1857	5.8.1927	1	1880	11	11	0	5.50	–	–	–/–	–	0	–
Grout Arthur Theodore Wallace	30.3.1927	9.11.1968	51	1957–1965	890	74	0	15.08	0	–	–/–	–	163/24	–
Guest Colin Ernest John	7.10.1937		1	1962	11	11	0	11.00	0	0-8	0/0	–	1	–
Haddin Bradley James	23.10.1977		25	2007–2009	1,474	169	2	38.78	–	–	–/–	–	101/2	53/10
Hamence Ronald Arthur	25.11.1915		3	1946–1947	81	30*	0	27.00	–	–	–/–	–	1	–
Hammond Jeffrey Roy	19.4.1950		5	1972	28	19	0	9.33	15	4-38	1/0	32.53	2	1
Harry John	1.8.1857	27.10.1919	1	1894	8	6	0	4.00	0	–	–/–	–	2	–
Hartigan Roger Joseph	12.12.1879	7.6.1958	2	1907	170	116	1	42.50	0	0-7	0/0	–	1	–
Hartkopf Albert Ernst Victor	28.12.1889	20.5.1968	1	1924	80	80	0	40.00	1	1-120	0/0	134.00	0	–
Harvey Mervyn Roye	29.4.1918	18.3.1995	1	1946	43	31	0	21.50	–	–	–/–	–	0	–
²Harvey Robert Neil MBE	8.10.1928		79	1947–1962	6,149	205	21	48.41	3	1-8	0/0	40.00	64	–
Hassett Arthur Lindsay MBE	28.8.1913	16.6.1993	43	1938–1953	3,073	198*	10	46.56	0	0-1	0/0	–	30	–
Hauritz Nathan Michael	18.10.1981		13	2004–2009	317	75	0	22.64	53	5-53	2/0	29.26	9	38/3
Hawke Neil James Napier	27.6.1939	25.12.2000	27	1962–1968	365	45*	0	16.59	91	7-105	6/1	29.41	9	–
Hayden Matthew Lawrence	29.10.1971		103§	1993–2008	8,625	380	30	50.73	0	0-7	0/0	–	128	160§/9
Hazlitt Gervys Rignold	4.9.1888	30.10.1915	9	1907–1912	89	34*	0	11.12	23	7-25	1/0	27.08	4	–
Healy Ian Andrew	30.4.1964		119	1988–1999	4,356	161*	4	27.39	0	–	–/–	–	366/29	168
Hendry Hunter Scott Thomas Laurie ("Stork")	24.5.1895	16.12.1988	11	1921–1928	335	112	1	20.93	16	3-36	0/0	40.00	10	–
Hibbert Paul Anthony	23.7.1952	27.11.2008	1	1977	15	13	0	7.50	–	–	–/–	–	1	–
Higgs James Donald	11.7.1950		22	1977–1980	111	16	0	5.55	66	7-143	2/0	31.16	3	–
Hilditch Andrew Mark Jefferson	20.5.1956		18	1978–1985	1,073	119	2	31.55	–	–	–/–	–	13	8
Hilfenhaus Benjamin William	15.3.1983		9	2008–2009	68	20	0	11.33	34	4-60	0/0	30.58	3	15/6
Hill Clement	18.3.1877	5.9.1945	49	1896–1911	3,412	191	7	39.21	–	–	–/–	–	33	–
Hill John Charles	25.6.1923	11.8.1974	3	1953–1954	21	8*	0	7.00	8	3-35	0/0	34.12	2	–
Hoare Desmond Edward	19.10.1934		1	1960	35	35	0	17.50	2	2-68	0/0	78.00	2	–
Hodge Bradley John	29.12.1974		6	2005–2007	503	203*	1	55.88	0	0-8	0/0	–	9	25/8
Hodges John Robart	11.8.1855	d unknown	2	1876	10	8	0	3.33	6	2-7	0/0	14.00	0	–
Hogan Tom George	23.9.1956		7	1982–1983	205	42*	0	18.63	15	5-66	1/0	47.06	2	16
Hogg George Bradley	6.2.1971		7	1996–2007	186	79	0	26.57	17	2-40	0/0	54.88	1	123/2
Hogg Rodney Malcolm	5.3.1951		38	1978–1984	439	52	0	9.75	123	6-74	6/2	28.47	7	71
Hohns Trevor Victor	23.1.1954		7	1988–1989	136	40	0	22.66	17	3-59	0/0	34.11	3	–
Hole Graeme Blake	6.1.1931	14.2.1990	18	1950–1954	789	66	0	25.45	3	1-9	0/0	42.00	21	–
Holland Robert George	19.10.1946		11	1984–1985	35	10	0	3.18	34	6-54	3/2	39.76	5	2
Hookes David William	3.5.1955	19.1.2004	23	1976–1985	1,306	143*	1	34.36	1	1-4	0/0	41.00	12	39

§ Hayden's figures include 188 runs and three catches for Australia v the ICC World XI in the Super Series Test in 2005-06.

	Born	Died	Tests	Test Career	Runs	HS	100s	Avge	Wkts	BB	Avge	5/10	Ct/St	O/T
Hopkins Albert John Young	3.5.1874	25.4.1931	20	1901–1909	509	43	0	16.41	26	4-81	26.76	0/0	11	
Horan Thomas Patrick	8.3.1854	16.4.1916	15	1876–1884	471	124	1	18.84	11	6-40	13.00	1/0	6	
Hordern Herbert Vivian MBE	10.2.1883	17.6.1938	7	1910–1911	254	50	0	23.09	46	7-90	23.36	5/2	6	
Hornbrook Percival Mitchell	27.7.1899	25.8.1976	6	1928–1930	60	26	0	10.00	17	7-92	39.05	1/0	7	
Howell William Peter	29.12.1869	14.7.1940	18	1897–1903	158	35	0	7.52	49	5-81	28.71	1/0	12	
Hughes Kimberley John	26.1.1954		70	1977–1984	4,415	213	9	37.41	0	0-0	–	0/0	50	97
Hughes Mervyn Gregory	23.11.1961		53	1985–1993	1,032	72*	0	16.64	212	8-87	28.38	7/1	23	33
Hughes Phillip Joel	30.11.1988		6	2008–2009	509	160	2	46.27					3	
Hunt William Alfred	26.8.1908	30.12.1983	1	1931	0	0	0	0.00	0	0-14	–		1	
Hurst Alan George	15.7.1950		12	1973–1979	102	26	0	6.00	43	5-28	27.90	2/0	3	8
Hurwood Alexander	17.6.1902	26.9.1982	2	1930	5	5	0	2.50	11	4-22	15.45	0/0	2	
Hussey Michael Edward Killeen	27.5.1975		48	2005–2009	3,819	182	11	53.04	2	1-3	51.50	0/0	45	126/18
Inverarity Robert John	31.1.1944		6	1968–1972	174	56	0	17.40	4	3-26	23.25	0/0	4	
Iredale Francis Adams	19.6.1867	15.4.1926	14	1894–1899	807	140	2	36.68	0	0-3	–		16	
Ironmonger Herbert	7.4.1882	31.5.1971	14	1928–1932	42	12	0	2.62	74	7-23	17.97	4/2	3	
Iverson John Brian	27.7.1915	24.10.1973	5	1950	3	1*	0	0.75	21	6-27	15.23	1/0	2	
Jackson Archibald Alexander	5.9.1909	16.2.1933	8	1928–1930	474	164	1	47.40	0		–		7	
Jaques Philip Anthony	3.5.1979		11	2005–2007	902	150	3	47.47					7	6
Jarman Barrington Noel	17.2.1936		19	1959–1968	400	78	0	14.81					50/4	
Jarvis Arthur Harwood	19.10.1860	15.11.1933	11	1884–1894	303	82	0	16.83					9/9	
Jenner Terrence James	8.9.1944		9	1970–1975	208	74	0	23.11	24	5-90	31.20	1/0	5	1
Jennings Claude Burrows	5.6.1884	20.6.1950	6	1912	107	32	0	17.83					5	
Johnson Ian William Geddes CBE	8.12.1917	9.10.1998	45	1945–1956	1,000	77	0	18.51	109	7-44	29.19	3/0	30	
Johnson Leonard Joseph	18.3.1919	20.4.1977	1	1947	25	25*	0	–	6	3-8	12.33	0/0	2	
Johnson Mitchell Guy	2.11.1981		32	2007–2009	924	123*	1	26.40	143	8-61	28.45	4/1	8	72/12
Johnston William Arras	26.2.1922	25.5.2007	40	1947–1954	273	29	0	11.37	160	6-44	23.91	7/0	16	
Jones Dean Mervyn	24.3.1961		52	1983–1992	3,631	216	11	46.55	1	1-5	64.00	0/0	34	164
Jones Ernest	30.9.1869	23.11.1943	19	1894–1902	126	20	0	5.04	64	7-88	29.01	3/1	21	
Jones Samuel Percy	1.8.1861	14.7.1951	12	1881–1887	428	87	0	21.40	6	4-47	18.66	0/0	12	
Joslin Leslie Ronald	13.12.1947		1	1967	9	7	0	4.50					0	
Julian Brendon Paul	10.8.1970		7	1993–1995	128	56*	0	16.00	15	4-36	39.93	0/0	4	25
Kasprowicz Michael Scott	10.2.1972		38	1996–2005	445	25	0	10.59	113	7-36	32.88	4/0	16	43/2
Katich Simon Mathew §	21.8.1975		45	2001–2009	3,503	157	9	44.91	21	6-65	29.38	1/0	36	45/3
Kelleway Charles	25.4.1886	16.11.1944	26	1910–1928	1,422	147	3	37.42	52	5-33	32.36	1/0	24	

§ Katich's figures include two runs and one catch for Australia v the ICC World XI in the Super Series Test in 2005-06.

	Born	Died	Tests	Test Career	Runs	HS	100s	Avge	Wkts	BB	5/10	Avge	Ct/St	O/T
Kelly James Joseph	10.5.1867	14.8.1938	36	1896–1905	664	46*	0	17.02	–	–	–/–	–	43/20	
Kelly Thomas Joseph Dart	3.5.1844	20.7.1893	2	1876–1878	64	35	0	21.33	–	–	–/–	–	1	
Kendall Thomas Kingston	24.8.1851	17.8.1924	2	1876	39	17*	0	13.00	14	7-55	1/0	15.35	2	5
Kent Martin Francis	23.11.1953		3	1981	171	54	0	28.50	–	–	–/–	–	6	4
Kerr Robert Byers	16.6.1961		2	1985	31	17	0	7.75	–	–	–/–	–	1	
Kippax Alan Falconer	25.5.1897	5.9.1972	22	1924–1934	1,192	146	2	36.12	0	0-2	0/0	–	13	
Kline Lindsay Francis	29.9.1934		13	1957–1960	58	15*	0	8.28	34	7-75	1/0	22.82	9	
Krejza Jason John	14.11.1983		2	2008	71	32	0	23.66	13	8-215	1/1	43.23	4	
Laird Bruce Malcolm	21.11.1950		21	1979–1982	1,341	92	0	35.28	0	0-3	0/0	–	16	23
Langer Justin Lee	21.11.1970		105§	1992–2006	7,696	250	23	45.27	0	0-3	0/0	–	73	8
Langley Gilbert Roche Andrews	14.9.1919	14.5.2001	26	1951–1956	374	53	0	14.96	–	–	–/–	–	83/15	
Laughlin Trevor John	30.1.1951		3	1977–1978	87	35	0	17.40	6	5-101	1/0	43.66	3	6
Laver Frank Jonas	7.12.1869	24.9.1919	15	1899–1909	196	45	0	11.52	37	8-31	2/0	26.05	8	
Law Stuart Grant	18.10.1968		1	1995	54	54*	0	–	0	0-9	0/0	–	1	54
Lawry William Morris	11.2.1937		67	1961–1970	5,234	210	13	47.15	–	–	–/–	–	30	1
Lawson Geoffrey Francis	7.12.1957		46	1980–1989	894	74	0	15.96	180	8-112	11/2	30.56	10	79
Lee Brett	8.11.1976		76§	1999–2008	1,451	64	0	20.15	310	5-30	10/0	30.81	23	186/17
Lee Philip Keith	15.9.1904	9.8.1980	2	1931–1932	57	42	0	19.00	5	4-111	0/0	42.40	1	
Lehmann Darren Scott	5.2.1970		27	1997–2004	1,798	177	5	44.95	15	3-42	0/0	27.46	11	117
Lillee Dennis Keith MBE.	18.7.1949		70	1970–1983	905	73*	0	13.71	355	7-83	23/7	23.92	23	63
Lindwall Raymond Russell MBE.	3.10.1921	23.6.1996	61	1945–1959	1,502	118	2	21.15	228	7-38	12/0	23.03	26	
Love Hampden Stanley Bray	10.8.1895	22.7.1969	1	1932	8	5	0	4.00	–	–	–/–	–	3	
Love Martin Lloyd	30.3.1974		5	2002–2003	233	100*	1	46.60	–	–	–/–	–	7	
Loxton Samuel John Everett	29.3.1921		12	1947–1950	554	101	1	36.93	8	3-55	0/0	43.62	7	
Lyons John James	21.5.1863	21.7.1927	14	1886–1897	731	134	1	27.07	6	5-30	1/0	24.83	3	
McAlister Peter Alexander	11.7.1869	10.5.1938	8	1903–1909	252	41	0	16.80	–	–	–/–	–	10	
Macartney Charles George	27.6.1886	9.9.1958	35	1907–1926	2,131	170	7	41.78	45	7-58	2/1	27.55	17	
McCabe Stanley Joseph	16.7.1910	25.8.1968	39	1930–1938	2,748	232	6	48.21	36	4-13	0/0	42.86	41	
McCool Colin Leslie	9.12.1916	5.4.1986	14	1945–1949	459	104*	1	35.30	36	5-41	3/0	26.61	14	
McCormick Ernest Leslie	16.5.1906	28.6.1991	12	1935–1938	54	17*	0	6.00	36	4-101	0/0	29.97	8	
McCosker Richard Bede	11.12.1946		25	1974–1979	1,622	127	4	39.56	–	–	–/–	–	21	14
McDermott Craig John	14.4.1965		71	1984–1995	940	42*	0	12.20	291	8-97	14/2	28.63	19	138
McDonald Andrew Barry	15.6.1981		4	2008	107	68	0	21.40	9	3-25	0/0	33.33	2	
McDonald Colin Campbell	17.11.1928		47	1951–1961	3,107	170	5	39.32	0	0-3	0/0	–	14	

§ Langer's figures include 22 runs and one catch and Lee's four runs, two wickets and one catch for Australia v the ICC World XI in the Super Series Test in 2005-06.

	Born	Died	Tests	Test Career	Runs	HS	100s	Avge	Wkts	BB	5/10	Avge	Ct/St	O/T
McDonald Edgar Arthur	6.1.1891	22.7.1937	11	1920–1921	116	36	0	16.57	43	5-32	2/0	33.27	3	
McDonnell Percy Stanislaus	13.11.1858	24.9.1896	19	1880–1888	955	147	3	28.93	0	0-11	0/0	–	6	
McGain Bryce Edward	25.3.1972		1	2008	2	2	0	1.00	0	0-149	0/0	–	0	
MacGill Stuart Charles Glydwr	25.2.1971		44§	1997–2007	349	43	0	9.69	208	8-108	12/2	29.02	16	3
McGrath Glenn Donald	9.2.1970		124§	1993–2006	641	61	0	7.36	563	8-24	29/3	21.64	38	249+½
McIlwraith John	7.9.1857	5.7.1938	1	1886	9	7	0	4.50					3	
McIntyre Peter Edward	27.4.1966		2	1994–1996	22	16	0	7.33	5	3-103	0/0	38.80	0	
McKay Clinton James	22.2.1983		1	2009	10	10	0	10.00	1	1-56	0/0	101.00	1	2
Mackay Kenneth Donald MBE	24.10.1925	13.6.1982	37	1956–1962	1,507	89	0	33.48	50	6-42	2/0	34.42	16	
McKenzie Graham Douglas	24.6.1941		60	1961–1970	945	76	0	12.27	246	8-71	16/3	29.78	34	1
McKibbin Thomas Robert	10.12.1870	15.12.1939	5	1894–1897	88	28*	0	14.66	17	3-35	0/0	29.17	4	
McLaren John William	22.12.1886	17.11.1921	1	1911	0	0*	0	–	1	1-23	0/0	70.00	0	
Maclean John Alexander	27.4.1946		4	1978	79	33*	0	11.28					18	2
²McLeod Charles Edward	24.10.1869	26.11.1918	17	1894–1905	573	112	1	23.87	33	5-65	2/0	40.15	9	
²McLeod Robert William	19.1.1868	14.6.1907	6	1891–1893	146	31	0	13.27	12	5-53	1/0	31.83	3	
McShane Patrick George	18.4.1858	11.12.1903	3	1884–1887	26	12*	0	5.20	1	1-39	0/0	48.00	2	
Maddocks Leonard Victor	24.5.1926		7	1954–1956	177	69	0	17.70					19/1	
Maguire John Norman	15.9.1956		3	1983	28	15*	0	7.00	10	4-57	0/0	32.30	2	23
Mailey Arthur Alfred	3.1.1886	31.12.1967	21	1920–1926	222	46*	0	11.10	99	9-121	6/2	33.91	14	
Mallett Ashley Alexander	13.7.1945		38	1968–1980	430	43*	0	11.62	132	8-59	6/1	29.84	30	9
Malone Michael Francis	9.10.1950		1	1977	46	46	0	46.00	6	5-63	0/0	12.83	0	10
Mann Anthony Longford	8.11.1945		4	1977	189	105	1	23.62	4	3-12	0/0	79.00	2	
Manou Graham Allan	23.4.1979		1	2009	21	13*	0	21.00					3	4
Marr Alfred Percy	28.3.1862	15.3.1940	1	1884	5	5	0	2.50	0	0-3	0/0	–	0	
Marsh Geoffrey Robert	31.12.1958		50	1985–1991	2,854	138	4	33.18	0	–	–/–	–	38	117
Marsh Rodney William MBE	4.11.1947		96	1970–1983	3,633	132	3	26.51	0	0-3	0/0	–	343/12	92
Martin John Wesley	28.7.1931	16.7.1992	8	1960–1966	214	55	0	17.83	17	3-56	0/0	48.94	5	
Martyn Damien Richard	21.10.1971		67	1992–2006	4,406	165	13	46.37	2	1-0	0/0	84.00	36	208/4
Massie Hugh Hamon	11.4.1854	12.10.1938	9	1881–1884	249	55	0	15.56					5	
Massie Robert Arnold Lockyer	14.4.1947		6	1972–1972	78	42	0	11.14	31	8-53	2/1	20.87	1	3
Matthews Christopher Darrell	22.9.1962		3	1986–1988	54	32	0	10.80	6	3-95	0/0	52.16	1	
Matthews Gregory Richard John	15.12.1959		33	1983–1992	1,849	130	4	41.08	61	5-103	2/1	48.22	17	59
Matthews Thomas James	3.4.1884	14.10.1943	8	1911–1912	153	53	0	17.00	16	4-29	0/0	26.18	7	
May Timothy Brian Alexander	26.1.1962		24	1987–1994	225	42*	0	14.06	75	5-9	3/0	34.74	6	47

§ MacGill's figures include no runs and nine wickets and McGrath's two runs and three wickets for Australia v the ICC World XI in the Super Series Test in 2005-06.

Name	Born	Died	Tests	Test Career	Runs	HS	100s	Avge	Wkts	BB	5/10	Avge	Ct/St	O/T
Mayne Edgar Richard	2.7.1882	26.10.1961	4	1912–1921	64	25*	0	21.33	0	0-1	00	–	2	
Mayne Lawrence Charles	23.1.1942		6	1964–1969	76	13	0	9.50	19	4-43	00	33.05	3	
Meckiff Ian	6.1.1935		18	1957–1963	154	45*	0	11.84	45	6-38	2/0	31.62	9	
Meuleman Kenneth Douglas	5.9.1923		1	1945	0	0	0	0.00	–	–	–/–	–	1	
Midwinter William Evans	19.6.1851	3.12.1890	8†	1876–1886	174	37	0	13.38	14	5-78	1/0	23.78	5	
Miller Colin Reid	6.2.1964		18	1998–2000	174	43	0	8.28	69	5-32	3/1	26.15	6	
Miller Keith Ross MBE	28.11.1919	11.10.2004	55	1945–1956	2,958	147	7	36.97	170	7-60	7/1	22.97	38	
Minnett Roy Baldwin	13.6.1888	21.10.1955	9	1911–1912	391	90	0	26.06	11	4-34	00	26.36	0	
Misson Francis Michael	19.11.1938		5	1960–1961	38	25*	0	19.00	16	4-58	00	38.50	6	
Moody Thomas Masson	2.10.1965		8	1989–1992	456	106	0	32.57	2	1-17	00	73.50	9	76
Moroney John	24.7.1917	1.7.1999	7	1949–1951	383	118	2	34.81	–	–	–/–	–	0	
Morris Arthur Robert MBE	19.1.1922		46	1946–1954	3,533	206	12	46.48	2	1-5	00	25.00	15	
Morris Samuel	22.6.1855	20.9.1931	1	1884	14	10*	0	14.00	2	2-73	00	36.50	0	
Moses Henry	13.2.1858	7.12.1938	6	1886–1894	198	33	0	19.80	–	–	–/–	–	0	
Moss Jeffrey Kenneth	29.6.1947		1	1978	60	38*	0	60.00	–	–	–/–	–	0	1
Moule William Henry	31.1.1858	24.8.1939	1	1880	40	34*	0	20.00	3	3-23	00	7.66	1	
Muller Scott Andrew	11.7.1971		2	1999	6	6*	0	–	7	3-68	00	36.85	2	
Murdoch William Lloyd	18.10.1854	18.2.1911	18†	1876–1890	896	211	2	32.00	–	–	–/–	–	14	
Musgrove Henry Alfred	27.11.1858	2.11.1931	1	1884	13	9	0	6.50	–	–	–/–	–	0	
Nagel Lisle Ernest	6.3.1905	23.11.1971	1	1932	21	21*	0	21.00	2	2-110	00	55.00	0	
Nash Laurence John	2.5.1910	24.7.1986	2	1931–1936	30	17	0	15.00	10	4-18	00	12.60	6	
Nicholson Matthew James	2.10.1974		1	1998	14	9	0	7.00	4	3-56	00	28.75	0	
Nitschke Holmesdale Carl ("Jack")	14.4.1905	29.9.1982	2	1931	53	47	0	26.50	–	–	–/–	–	3	
Noble Montague Alfred	28.1.1873	22.6.1940	42	1897–1909	1,997	133	1	30.25	121	7-17	9/2	25.00	26	
Noblet Geffery	14.9.1916	16.8.2006	3	1949–1952	22	13*	0	7.33	7	3-21	00	26.14	1	
North Marcus James	28.7.1979		13	2008–2009	734	125*	5	36.70	6	4-98	00	60.66	8	2/1
Nothling Otto Ernest	1.8.1900	26.9.1965	1	1928	52	44	0	26.00	0	0-12	00	–	1	
O'Brien Leo Patrick Joseph	2.7.1907	13.3.1997	5	1932–1936	211	61	0	26.37	–	–	–/–	–	3	
O'Connor John Denis Alphonsus	9.9.1875	23.8.1941	4	1907–1909	86	20	0	12.28	13	5-40	1/0	26.15	3	
O'Donnell Simon Patrick	26.1.1963		6	1985–1985	206	48	0	29.42	6	3-37	00	84.00	4	87
Ogilvie Alan David	3.6.1951		5	1977	178	47	0	17.80	–	–	–/–	–	5	
O'Keeffe Kerry James	25.11.1949		24	1970–1977	644	85	0	25.76	53	5-101	1/0	38.07	15	2
Oldfield William Albert [Stanley] MBE	9.9.1894	10.8.1976	54	1920–1936	1,427	65*	0	22.65	–	–	–/–	–	78/52	
O'Neill Norman Clifford	19.2.1937	3.3.2008	42	1958–1964	2,779	181	6	45.55	17	4-41	00	39.23	21	
O'Reilly William Joseph OBE	20.12.1905	6.10.1992	27	1931–1945	410	56*	0	12.81	144	7-54	11/3	22.59	7	

	Born	Died	Tests	Test Career	Runs	HS	100s	Avge	Wkts	BB	5/10	Avge	Ct/St	O/T
Oxenham Ronald Keven	28.7.1891	16.8.1910	7	1928–1931	151	48	0	15.10	14	4-39	0-0	37.28	4	
Palmer George Eugene	22.2.1859	22.8.1910	17	1880–1886	296	48	0	14.09	78	7-65	6-2	21.51	13	
Park Roy Lindsay	30.7.1892	23.1.1947	1	1920	0	0	0	0.00	0	0-9	0-0	–	0	
Pascoe Leonard Stephen	13.2.1950		14	1977–1981	106	30*	0	10.60	64	5-59	1-0	26.06	2	29
Pellew Clarence Everard ("Nip")	21.9.1893	9.5.1981	10	1920–1921	484	116	2	37.23	0	0-3	0-0	–	4	
Phillips Wayne Bentley	1.3.1958		27	1983–1985	1,485	159	2	32.28	–	–	–/–	–	52	48
Phillips Wayne Norman	7.11.1962		1	1991	22	14	0	11.00	–	–	–/–	–	0	
Philpott Peter Ian	21.11.1934		8	1964–1965	93	22	0	10.33	26	5-90	1-0	38.46	5	
Ponsford William Harold MBE	19.10.1900	6.4.1991	29	1924–1934	2,122	266	7	48.22	–	–	–/–	–	21	
Ponting Ricky Thomas	19.12.1974		142§	1995–2009	11,859	257	39	55.67	5	1-0	0-0	48.40	164	329†/17
Pope Roland James	18.2.1864	27.7.1952	1	1884	3	3	0	1.50	–	–	–/–	–	0	
Rackemann Carl Gray	3.6.1960		12	1982–1990	53	15*	0	5.30	39	6-86	3-1	29.15	2	52
Ransford Vernon Seymour	20.3.1885	19.3.1958	20	1907–1911	1,211	143*	1	37.84	1	1-9	0-0	28.00	10	
Redpath Ian Ritchie MBE	11.5.1941		66	1963–1975	4,737	171	8	43.45	0	0-0	0-0	–	83	5
Reedman John Cole	9.10.1865	25.3.1924	1	1894	21	17	0	10.50	1	1-12	0-0	24.00	1	
Reid Bruce Anthony	14.3.1963		27	1985–1992	93	13	0	4.65	113	7-51	5-2	24.63	5	61
Reiffel Paul Ronald	19.4.1966		35	1991–1997	955	79*	0	26.52	104	6-71	5-0	26.96	15	92
Renneberg David Alexander	23.9.1942		8	1966–1967	22	9	0	3.66	23	5-39	2-0	36.08	2	
Richardson Arthur John	24.7.1888	23.12.1973	9	1924–1926	403	100	1	31.00	12	2-20	0-0	43.41	1	
[4] Richardson Victor York	7.9.1894	30.10.1969	19	1924–1935	706	138	1	23.53	–	–	–/–	–	24	
Rigg Keith Edward	21.5.1906	28.2.1995	8	1930–1936	401	127	1	33.41	–	–	–/–	–	5	
Ring Douglas Thomas	14.10.1918	23.6.2003	13	1947–1953	426	67	0	22.42	35	6-72	2-0	37.28	5	
Ritchie Gregory Michael	23.1.1960		30	1982–1986	1,690	146	3	35.20	1	0-10	0-0	–	14	44
Rixon Stephen John	25.2.1954		13	1977–1984	394	54	0	18.76	–	–	–/–	–	42/5	6
Robertson Gavin Ron	28.5.1966		4	1997–1998	140	57	0	20.00	13	4-72	0-0	39.61	1	13
Robertson William Roderick	6.10.1861	24.6.1938	1	1884	2	2	0	1.00	0	0-24	0-0	–	0	
Robinson Richard Daryl	8.6.1946		3	1977	100	34	0	16.66	–	–	–/–	–	4	
Robinson Rayford Harold	26.3.1914	10.8.1965	1	1936	5	3	0	2.50	–	–	–/–	–	1	
Rogers Christopher John Llewellyn	31.8.1977		1	2007	19	15	0	9.50	–	–	–/–	–	1	
Rorke Gordon Frederick	27.6.1938		4	1958–1959	9	7	0	4.50	10	3-23	0-0	20.30	1	
Rutherford John Walter	25.9.1929		1	1956	30	30	0	30.00	1	1-11	0-0	15.00	0	
Ryder John	8.8.1889	3.4.1977	20	1920–1928	1,394	201*	3	51.62	17	2-20	0-0	43.70	17	2
Saggers Ronald Arthur	15.5.1917	17.3.1987	6	1948–1949	30	14	0	10.00	–	–	–/–	–	16/8	
Saunders John Victor	21.3.1876	21.12.1927	14	1901–1907	39	11*	0	2.29	79	7-34	6-0	22.73	5	

§ Ponting's figures include 100 runs and one catch for Australia v the ICC World XI in the Super Series Test in 2005-06.

	Born	Died	Tests	Test Career	Runs	HS	100s	Avge	Wkts	BB	5/10	Avge	Ct/St	O/T
Scott Henry James Herbert	26.12.1858	23.9.1910	8	1884–1886	359	102	1	27.61	0	0-9	0/0	–	8	–
Sellers Reginald Hugh Durning	20.8.1940		1	1964	0	0		0.00	0	0-17	0/0	–	–	–
Serjeant Craig Stanton	1.11.1951		12	1977–1977	522	124	1	23.72	–	–	–/–	–	13	3
Sheahan Andrew Paul	30.9.1946		31	1967–1973	1,594	127	2	33.91	–	0-3	–/–	–	17	3
Shepherd Barry Kenneth	23.4.1937	17.9.2001	9	1962–1964	502	96		41.83	0	0-3	0/0	–	2	–
Siddle Peter Matthew	25.11.1984		17	2008–2009	256	38		16.00	60	5-21	2/0	31.53	10	12/1
Sievers Morris William	13.4.1912	10.5.1968	3	1936	67	25*		13.40	9	5-21	1/0	17.88	4	–
Simpson Robert Baddeley	3.2.1936		62	1957–1977	4,869	311	10	46.81	71	5-57	2/0	42.26	110	2
Simcock David John	1.2.1942		3	1964–1965	80	29		26.66	8	3-67	0/0	51.25	2	–
Slater Keith Nichol	12.3.1936		1	1958		1*		–	2	2-40	0/0	50.50	2	–
Slater Michael Jonathon	21.2.1970		74	1993–2001	5,312	219	14	42.83	1	1-4	0/0	10.00	33	42
Sleep Peter Raymond	4.5.1957		14	1978–1989	483	90		24.15	31	5-72	1/0	45.06	4	–
Slight James	20.10.1855	9.12.1930	1	1880	11	11		5.50	–	–	–/–	–	0	–
Smith David Bertram Miller	14.9.1884	29.7.1963	2	1912	30	24*		15.00	–	–	–/–	–	0	–
Smith Steven Barry	18.10.1961		3	1983	41	12		8.20	–	–	–/–	–	1	28
Spofforth Frederick Robert	9.9.1853	4.6.1926	18	1876–1886	217	50		9.43	94	7-44	7/4	18.41	11	–
Stackpole Keith Raymond MBE.	10.7.1940		43	1965–1977	2,807	207	7	37.42	15	2-33	0/0	66.73	47	6
Stevens Gavin Byron	29.2.1932		4	1959	112	28		16.00	–	–	–/–	–	2	–
Symonds Andrew	9.6.1975		26	2003–2008	1,462	162*	2	40.61	24	3-50	0/0	37.33	22	198/14
Taber Hedley Brian	29.4.1940		16	1966–1969	353	48		16.04	–	–	–/–	–	56/4	–
Tait Shaun William	22.2.1983		3	2005–2007	20	8		6.66	5	3-97	0/0	60.40	1	22/3
Tallon Donald	17.2.1916	7.9.1984	21	1945–1953	394	92		17.13	–	–	–/–	–	50/8	–
Taylor John Morris	10.10.1895	12.5.1971	20	1920–1926	997	108	1	35.60	1	1-25	0/0	45.00	11	–
Taylor Mark Anthony	27.10.1964		104	1988–1999	7,525	334*	19	43.49	1	1-11	0/0	26.00	157	113
Taylor Peter Laurence	22.8.1956		13	1986–1991	431	87		26.93	27	6-78	1/0	39.55	10	83
Thomas Grahame	21.3.1938		8	1964–1965	325	61		29.54	–	–	–/–	–	3	–
Thoms George Ronald	22.3.1927	29.8.2003	1	1951	44	28		22.00	–	–	–/–	–	0	–
Thomson Alan Lloyd ("Froggy")	2.12.1945		4	1970	22	12*		22.00	12	3-79	0/0	54.50	0	1
Thomson Jeffrey Robert	16.8.1950		51	1972–1985	679	49		12.81	200	6-46	8/0	28.00	20	50
Thomson Nathaniel Frampton Davis	29.5.1839	2.9.1896	2	1876	67	41		16.75	1	1-14	0/0	31.00	3	–
Thurlow Hugh Motley ("Pud")	10.11.1903	3.12.1975	1	1931	0	0		0.00	0	0-33	0/0	–	0	–
Toohey Peter Michael	20.4.1954		15	1977–1979	893	122	1	31.89	0	0-4	0/0	–	9	5
Toshack Ernest Raymond Herbert	8.12.1914	11.5.2003	12	1945–1948	73	20*		14.60	47	6-29	4/1	21.04	4	–
Travers Joseph Patrick Francis	10.1.1871	15.9.1942	1	1901	10	9		5.00	1	1-14	0/0	14.00	1	–
Tribe George Edward	4.10.1920	5.4.2009	3	1946	35	25*		17.50	2	2-48	0/0	165.00	0	–

	Born	Died	Tests	Test Career	Runs	HS	100s	Avge	Wkts	BB	Avge	5/10	Ct/St	O/T
[2]Trott Albert Edwin	6.2.1873	30.7.1914	3†	1894	205	85*	0	102.50	9	8-43	21.33	1/0	4	
[2]Trott George Henry Stevens	5.8.1866	10.11.1917	24	1888–1897	921	143	1	21.92	29	4-71	35.13	0/0	21	
[2]Trumble Hugh	12.5.1867	14.8.1938	32	1890–1903	851	70	0	19.79	141	8-65	21.78	9/3	45	
[2]Trumble John William	16.9.1863	17.8.1944	7	1884–1886	243	59	0	20.25	10	3-29	22.20	0/0	3	
Trumper Victor Thomas	2.11.1877	28.6.1915	48	1899–1911	3,163	214*	8	39.04	8	3-60	39.62	0/0	31	
Turner Alan	23.7.1950		14	1975–1976	768	136	1	29.53	–		–	–/–	15	6
Turner Charles Thomas Biass	16.11.1862	1.1.1944	17	1886–1894	323	29	0	11.53	101	7-43	16.53	11/2	8	
Veivers Thomas Robert	6.4.1937		21	1963–1966	813	88	0	31.26	33	4-68	41.66	0/0	7	
Veletta Michael Robert John	30.10.1963		8	1987–1989	207	39	0	18.81	–		–	–/–	12	20
Waite Mervyn George	7.1.1911	16.12.1985	2	1938	11	8	0	3.66	1	1-150	190.00	0/0	1	
Walker Maxwell Henry Norman	12.9.1948		34	1972–1977	586	78*	0	19.53	138	8-143	27.47	6/0	12	17
Wall Thomas Welbourn ("Tim")	13.5.1904	26.3.1981	18	1928–1934	121	20	0	6.36	56	5-14	35.89	3/0	11	
Walters Francis Henry	9.2.1860	1.6.1922	1	1884	12	7	0	6.00	–		–	–/–	2	
Walters Kevin Douglas MBE	21.12.1945		74	1965–1980	5,357	250	15	48.26	49	5-66	29.08	1/0	43	28
Ward Francis Anthony	23.12.1906	25.3.1974	4	1936–1938	36	18	0	6.00	11	6-102	52.18	1/0	1	
Warne Shane Keith	13.9.1969		145§	1991–2006	3,154	99	0	17.32	708	8-71	25.41	37/10	125	193‡
Watkins John Russell	16.4.1943		1	1972	39	36	0	39.00	6	0-21	–	0/0	1	
Watson Graeme Donald	8.3.1945		5	1966–1972	97	50	0	10.77	6	2-67	42.33	0/0	5	2
Watson Shane Robert	17.6.1981		17§	2004–2009	1,106	120*	1	39.50	27	4-42	32.70	0/0	13	96/7
Watson William James	31.3.1931		4	1954	106	30	0	17.66	0	0-5	–	0/0	2	
[2]Waugh Mark Edward	2.6.1965		128	1990–2002	8,029	153*	20	41.81	59	5-40	41.16	1/0	181	244
[2]Waugh Stephen Rodger	2.6.1965		168	1985–2003	10,927	200	32	51.06	92	5-28	37.44	3/0	112	325
Wellham Dirk Macdonald	13.3.1959		6	1981–1986	257	103	1	23.36	0		–	0/0	5	17
Wessels Kepler Christoffel	14.9.1957		24†	1982–1985	1,761	179	4	42.95	0	0-2	–	0/0	18	54‡
Whatmore Davenell Frederick	16.3.1954		7	1978–1979	293	77	0	22.53	0	0-11	–	0/0	13	
White Cameron Leon	18.8.1983		4	2008	146	46	0	29.20	5	2-71	68.40	0/0	2	47/8
Whitney Michael Roy	24.2.1959		12	1981–1992	68	13	0	6.18	39	7-27	33.97	2/1	2	38
Whitty William James	15.8.1886	30.1.1974	14	1909–1912	161	39*	0	13.41	65	6-17	21.12	3/0	4	
Wiener Julien Mark	1.5.1955		6	1979	281	93	0	25.54	0	0-19	–	0/0	4	7
Williams Brad Andrew	20.11.1974		4	2003	23	10*	0	7.66	9	4-53	45.11	0/0	4	25
Wilson John William	20.8.1921	13.10.1985	1	1956	0	0*	–	–	1	1-25	64.00	0/0	0	
Wilson Paul	12.1.1972		1	1997	0	0*	0	–	0	0-50	–	0/0	0	11
Wood Graeme Malcolm	6.11.1956		59	1977–1988	3,374	172	9	31.83	–		–	–/–	41	83
Woodcock Ashley James	27.2.1947		1	1973	27	27	0	27.00	–		–	–/–	1	1

§ Warne's figures include 12 runs and six wickets and Watson's 34 runs and no wicket for Australia v the ICC World XI in the Super Series Test in 2005-06.

	Born	Died	Tests	Test Career	Runs	HS	100s	Avge	Wkts	BB	5/10	Avge	Ct/St	O/T
Woodfull William Maldon OBE	22.8.1897	11.8.1965	35	1926–1934	2,300	161	7	46.00	–	–	–/–	–	7	–
Woods Samuel Moses James	13.4.1867	30.4.1931	3†	1888	32	18	0	5.33	5	2-35	0/0	24.20	1	–
Woolley Roger Douglas	16.9.1954		2	1982–1983	21	13	0	10.50	–	–	0/0	–	7	4
Worrall John	20.6.1860	17.11.1937	11	1884–1899	478	76	0	25.15	1	1-97	0/0	127.00	13	–
Wright Kevin John	27.12.1953		10	1978–1979	219	55*	0	16.84	–	–	–/–	–	31/4	5
Yallop Graham Neil	7.10.1952		39	1975–1984	2,756	268	8	41.13	1	1-21	0/0	116.00	23	30
Yardley Bruce	5.9.1947		33	1977–1982	978	74	0	19.56	126	7-98	6/1	31.63	31	7
Young Shaun	13.6.1970		1	1997	4	4*	0	4.00	0	0-5	0/0	–	–	–
Zoehrer Timothy Joseph	25.9.1961		10	1985–1986	246	52*	0	20.50	–	–	–/–	–	18/1	22

SOUTH AFRICA (307 players)

	Born	Died	Tests	Test Career	Runs	HS	100s	Avge	Wkts	BB	5/10	Avge	Ct/St	O/T
Ackerman Hylton Deon	14.2.1973		4	1997	161	57	0	20.12	–	–	–/–	–	1	24
Adams Paul Regan	20.1.1977		45	1995–2003	360	35	0	9.00	134	7-128	4/1	32.87	29	24
Adcock Neil Amwin Treharne	8.3.1931		26	1953–1961	146	24	0	5.40	104	6-43	5/0	21.10	4	–
Amla Hashim Mahomed	31.3.1983		41	2004–2009	2,771	176*	7	40.75	0	0-4	0/0	–	36	22/2
Anderson James Henry	26.4.1874	11.3.1926	1	1902	43	32	0	21.50	–	–	–/–	–	1	–
Ashley William Hare	10.2.1862	14.7.1930	1	1888	1	1	0	0.50	7	7-95	1/0	13.57	0	–
Bacher Adam Marc	29.10.1973		19	1996–1999	833	96	0	26.03	0	0-4	0/0	–	11	13
Bacher Aron ("Ali")	24.5.1942		12	1965–1969	679	73	0	32.33	–	–	–/–	–	10	–
Balaskas Xenophon Constantine	15.10.1910	12.5.1994	9	1930–1938	174	122*	1	14.50	22	5-49	1/0	36.63	5	–
Barlow Edgar John	12.8.1940	30.12.2005	30	1961–1969	2,516	201	6	45.74	40	5-85	1/0	34.05	35	–
Baumgartner Harold Vane	17.11.1883	8.4.1938	1	1913	19	16	0	9.50	2	2-99	0/0	49.50	1	–
Beaumont Rolland	4.2.1884	25.5.1958	5	1912–1913	70	31	0	7.77	0	0-0	0/0	–	2	–
Begbie Denis Warburton	12.12.1914	10.3.2009	5	1948–1949	138	48	0	19.71	1	1-38	0/0	130.00	2	–
Bell Alexander John	15.4.1906	1.8.1985	16	1929–1935	69	26*	0	6.27	48	6-99	4/0	32.64	6	–
Bisset Sir Murray	14.4.1876	24.10.1931	3	1898–1909	103	35	0	25.75	–	–	–/–	–	2/1	–
Bisset George Finlay	5.11.1905	14.11.1965	4	1927	38	23	0	19.00	25	7-29	2/0	18.76	0	–
Blanckenberg James Manuel	31.12.1892	d unknown	18	1913–1924	455	59	0	19.78	60	6-76	4/0	30.28	9	–
Bland Kenneth Colin	5.4.1938		21	1961–1966	1,669	144*	3	49.08	2	2-16	0/0	62.50	10	–
Bock Ernest George	17.9.1908	5.9.1961	1	1935	11	9*	0	–	0	0-42	0/0	–	0	–
Boje Nico	20.3.1973		43	1999–2006	1,312	85	0	25.23	100	5-62	3/0	42.65	18	113½/1
Bond Gerald Edward	5.4.1909	27.8.1965	1	1938	0	0	0	0.00	0	0-16	0/0	–	0	–

Name	Born	Died	Tests	Test Career	Runs	HS	100s	Avge	Wkts	BB	5/10	Avge	Ct/St	O/T
Bosch Tertius	14.3.1966	14.2.2000	1	1991	5	5*	0	–	3	2-61	0/0	34.66	0	2
Botha Johan	2.5.1982		3	2005-2007	45	25	0	45.00	4	2-57	0/0	44.50	1	48/16
Botten James Thomas ("Jackie")	21.6.1938	14.5.2006	3	1965	65	33	0	10.83	8	2-56	0/0	42.12	1	
Boucher Mark Verdon	3.12.1976		128	1997-2009	5,012	125	5	31.13	1	1-6	0/0	6.00	467/22	283†/20
Brann William Henry	4.4.1899	22.9.1953	3	1922	71	50	0	14.20			–/–		2	
Briscoe Arthur Wellesley ("Dooley")	6.2.1911	22.4.1941	2	1935-1938	33	16	0	11.00			–/–		1	
Bromfield Harry Dudley	26.6.1932		9	1961-1965	59	21	0	11.80	17	5-88	1/0	35.23	13	
Brown Lennox Sidney	24.11.1910	1.9.1983	2	1931	17	8	0	5.66	3	1-30	0/0	63.00	1	
Burger Christopher George de Villiers	12.7.1935		2	1957	62	37*	0	20.66			–		0	
Burke Sydney Frank	11.3.1934		2	1961-1964	42	20	0	14.00	11	6-128	2/1	23.36	1	
Buys Isaac Daniel	4.2.1895	d unknown	1	1922	4	4*	0	4.00	0	0-20	0/0	–	0	
Cameron Horace Brakenridge ("Jock")	5.7.1905	2.11.1935	26	1927-1935	1,239	90	0	30.21			–/–		39/12	
Campbell Thomas	9.2.1882	5.10.1924	5	1909-1912	90	48	0	15.00			–		7/1	
Carlstein Peter Rudolph	28.10.1938		8	1957-1963	190	42	0	14.61			–		3	
Carter Claude Pagdet	23.4.1881	8.11.1952	10	1912-1924	181	45	0	18.10	28	6-50	2/0	24.78	2	
Catterall Robert Hector	10.7.1900	3.1.1961	24	1922-1930	1,555	120	3	37.92	7	3-15	0/0	23.14	12	
Chapman Horace William	30.6.1890	1.12.1941	2	1913-1921	39	17	0	13.00	1	1-51	0/0	104.00	1	
Cheetham John Erskine	26.5.1920	21.8.1980	24	1948-1955	883	89	0	23.86	0	0-2	0/0	–	13	
Chevallier Grahame Anton	9.3.1937		1	1969	0	0*	0	0.00	5	3-68	0/0	20.00	0	
Christy James Alexander Joseph	12.12.1904	1.2.1971	10	1929-1931	618	103	1	34.33	2	1-15	0/0	46.00	3	
Chubb Geoffrey Walter Ashton	12.4.1911	28.8.1982	5	1951	63	15*	0	10.50	21	6-51	2/0	27.47	1	
Cochran John Alexander Kennedy	15.7.1909	15.6.1987	1	1930	4	4	0	4.00	0	0-47	0/0	–	0	
Coen Stanley Keppel ("Shunter")	14.10.1902	29.1.1967	2	1927	101	41*	0	50.50	0	0-7	0/0	–	0	
Commaille John McIllwaine Moore ("Mick")	21.2.1883	28.7.1956	12	1909-1927	355	47	0	16.90			–		1	
Commins John Brian	19.2.1965		3	1994	125	45	0	25.00			–		2	
Conyngham Dalton Parry	10.5.1897	7.7.1979	1	1922	6	5*	0	–	2	1-40	0/0	51.50	0	
Cook Frederick James	1870	30.11.1915	1	1895	7	7	0	3.50			–		0	
Cook Stephen James	31.7.1953		3	1992-1993	107	43	0	17.83			–		1	4
Cooper Alfred Henry Cecil	2.9.1893	18.7.1963	1	1913	6	6	0	3.00			–		0	
Cox Joseph Lovell	28.6.1886	4.7.1971	3	1913	17	12*	0	3.40	4	2-74	0/0	61.25	1	
Cripps Godfrey	19.10.1865	27.7.1943	1	1891	21	18	0	10.50	0	0-23	0/0	–	0	
Crisp Robert James	28.5.1911	2.3.1994	9	1935-1935	123	35	0	10.25	20	5-99	1/0	37.35	3	
Cronje Wessel Johannes ("Hansie")	25.9.1969	1.6.2002	68	1991-1999	3,714	135	6	36.41	43	3-14	0/0	29.95	33	188
Cullinan Daryll John	4.3.1967		70	1992-2000	4,554	275*	14	44.21	2	1-10	0/0	35.50	67	138

§ Boucher's figures exclude 17 runs and two catches for the ICC World XI v Australia in the Super Series Test in 2005-06.

Name	Born	Died	Tests	Test Career	Runs	HS	100s	Avge	Wkts	BB	5/10	Avge	Ct/St	O/T
Curnow Sydney Harry	16.12.1907	28.7.1986	7	1930–1931	168	47	0	12.00	–	–	–	–	5	
Dalton Eric Londesbrough	2.12.1906	3.6.1981	15	1929–1938	698	117	2	31.72	12	4-59	0/0	40.83	5	
Davies Eric Quail	26.8.1909	11.11.1976	2	1935–1938	9	3	0	1.80	7	4-75	0/0	68.71	0	
Dawson Alan Charles	27.11.1969		2	2003	10	10	0	10.00	5	2-20	0/0	23.40	0	19
Dawson Oswald Charles	1.9.1919	22.12.2008	9	1947–1948	293	55	0	20.92	2	2-57	0/0	57.80	10	
Deane Hubert Gouvaine ("Nummy")	21.7.1895	21.10.1939	17	1924–1930	628	93	2	25.12	3	2-32	0/0	30.66	8	
de Bruyn Zander	5.7.1975		3	2004	155	83	0	38.75	–	–	–	–	3	
de Villiers Abraham Benjamin	17.2.1984		56	2004–2009	3,834	217*	9	43.56	2	2-49	0/0	49.50	60/1	88/23
de Villiers Petrus Stephanus ("Fanie")	13.10.1964		18	1993–1997	359	67*	0	18.89	85	6-23	5/2	24.27	11	83
de Wet Friedel	26.6.1980		2	2009	20	20	0	10.00	6	4-55	0/0	31.00	1	
Dippenaar Hendrik Human ("Boeta")	14.6.1977		38	1999–2006	1,718	177*	3	30.14	–	0-1	–	–	27	101/1
Dixon Cecil Donovan	12.2.1891	9.9.1969	1	1913	0	0	0	0.00	3	2-62	0/0	39.33	1	
Donald Allan Anthony	20.10.1966		72	1991–2001	652	37	0	10.68	330	8-71	20/3	22.25	18	164
Dower Robert Reid	4.6.1876	15.9.1964	1	1898	9	9	0	4.50	1	–	0/0	37.33	2	
Draper Ronald George	24.12.1926		2	1949	25	15	0	8.33	–	–	–	–	0	
Duckworth Christopher Anthony Russell	22.3.1933		2	1956	28	13	0	7.00	–	–	–	–	3	
Dumbrill Richard	19.11.1938	31.1.1980	5	1965–1966	153	36	0	15.30	9	4-30	0/0	39.00	3	
Duminy Jacobus Petrus	16.12.1897		3	1927–1929	30	12	0	5.00	3	1-17	0/0		3	
Duminy Jean-Paul	14.4.1984		10	2008–2009	503	166	1	33.53	10	3-89	0/0	29.40	11	54/18
Dunell Owen Robert	15.7.1856	21.10.1929	2	1888	42	26*	0	14.00	–	–	–	–	1	
Du Preez John Harcourt	14.11.1942		2	1966	0	0	0	–	3	2-22	0/0	17.00	2	
Du Toit Jacobus Francois	2.4.1869	10.7.1909	1	1891	2	2*	0	0.00	1	1-47	0/0	47.00	0	
Dyer Dennis Victor	2.5.1914	16.6.1990	3	1947	96	62	0	16.00	–	–	–	–	2	
Eksteen Clive Edward	2.12.1966		7	1993–1999	91	22	0	10.11	8	3-12	0/0	61.75	0	6
Elgie Michael Kelsey ("Kim")	6.3.1933		3	1961	75	56	0	12.50	0	0-18	0/0	–	5	
Elworthy Steven	23.2.1965		4	1998–2002	72	48	0	18.00	13	4-66	0/0	34.15	4	39
Endean William Russell	31.5.1924	28.6.2003	28	1951–1957	1,630	162*	3	33.95	–	–	–	–	41	
Farrer William Stephen ("Buster")	8.12.1936		6	1961–1963	221	40	0	27.62	–	–	–	–	2	
Faulkner George Aubrey	17.12.1881	10.9.1930	25	1905–1924	1,754	204	4	40.79	82	7-84	4/0	26.58	20	
Fellows-Smith Jonathan Payn	3.2.1932		4	1960	166	35	0	27.66	0	0-13	0/0	–	2	
Fichardt Charles Gustav	20.3.1870	30.5.1923	2	1891–1895	15	10	0	3.75	0	0-7	0/0	–	2	
Finlason Charles Edward	19.2.1860	31.7.1917	1	1888	6	6	0	3.00	0	0-24	0/0	–	0	
Floquet Claude Eugene	3.11.1884	22.11.1963	1	1909	12	11*	0	12.00	0	–	0/0	–	0	
Francis Howard Henry	26.5.1868	7.1.1936	2	1898	39	29	0	9.75	0	–	–	–	1	
Francois Cyril Matthew	20.6.1897	26.5.1944	5	1922	252	72	0	31.50	6	3-23	0/0	37.50	5	

Name	Born	Died	Tests	Test Career	Runs	HS	100s	Avge	Wkts	BB	5/10	Avge	Ct/St	O/T
Frank Charles Newton	27.1.1891	25.12.1961	3	1921	236	152	1	39.33	–	–	–/–	–	0	
Frank William Hughes Bowker	23.11.1872	16.2.1945	1	1895	7	5	0	3.50	–	–	–/–	–	0	
Fuller Edward Russell Henry	2.8.1931	19.7.2008	7	1952–1957	64	17	0	8.00	22	5-66	1/0	30.36	3	
Fullerton George Murray	8.12.1922	19.11.2002	7	1947–1951	325	88	0	25.00	1	1-52	0/0	52.00	10/2	
Funston Kenneth James	3.12.1925	15.4.2005	18	1952–1957	824	92	0	25.75	–	–	–/–	–	7	
Gamsy Dennis	17.2.1940		2	1969	39	30*	0	19.50	–	–	–/–	–	5	245/20
Gibbs Herschelle Herman	23.2.1974		90	1996–2007	6,167	228	14	41.95	0	0-4	0/0	–	94	
Gleeson Robert Anthony	6.12.1873	27.9.1919	1	1895	4	3	0	4.00	–	–	–/–	–	2	
Glover George Keyworth	13.5.1870	15.11.1938	1	1895	21	18*	0	21.00	1	1-28	0/0	28.00	0	
Goddard Trevor Leslie	1.8.1931		41	1955–1969	2,516	112	1	34.46	123	6-53	5/0	26.22	48	
Gordon Norman	6.8.1911		5	1938	8	7*	0	2.00	20	5-103	2/0	40.35	1	
Graham Robert	16.9.1877	21.4.1946	2	1898	6	4	0	1.50	3	2-22	0/0	42.33	2	
Grieveson Ronald Eustace	24.8.1909	24.7.1998	2	1938	114	75	0	57.00	–	–	–/–	–	7/3	
Griffin Geoffrey Merton	12.6.1939	16.11.2006	2	1960	25	14	0	6.25	8	4-87	0/0	24.00	0	
Hall Alfred Ewart	23.1.1896	1.1.1964	7	1922–1930	11	5	0	1.83	40	7-63	3/1	22.15	4	
Hall Andrew James	31.7.1975		21	2001–2006	760	163	1	26.20	45	3-1	0/0	35.93	16	88/2
Hall Glen Gordon	24.5.1938	26.6.1987	1	1964	0	0	0	0.00	1	1-94	0/0	94.00	0	
Halliwell Ernest Austin	7.9.1864	2.10.1919	8	1891–1902	188	57	0	12.53	–	–	–/–	–	10/2	
Halse Clive Gray	28.2.1935	28.5.2002	3	1963	30	19*	0	–	6	3-50	0/0	43.33	0	
² Hands Philip Albert Myburgh	18.3.1890	27.4.1951	7	1913–1924	300	83	0	25.00	0	0-1	0/0	–	3	
² Hands Reginald Harry Myburgh	26.7.1888	20.4.1918	1	1913	7	7	0	3.50	–	–	–/–	–	0	
Hanley Martin Andrew	10.11.1918	2.6.2000	1	1948	0	0	0	0.00	–	–	–/–	–	0	
Harris Paul Lee	2.11.1978		27	2006–2009	401	46	0	12.15	82	6-127	3/0	33.64	12	3
Harris Terence Anthony	27.8.1916	7.3.1993	3	1947–1948	100	60	0	25.00	–	–	–/–	–	1	
Hartigan Gerald Patrick Desmond	30.12.1884	7.1.1955	5	1912–1913	114	51	0	11.40	1	1-72	0/0	141.00	0	
Harvey Robert Lyon	14.9.1911	20.7.2000	2	1935	51	28	0	12.75	–	–	–/–	–	0	
Hathorn Christopher Maitland Howard	7.4.1878	17.5.1920	12	1902–1910	325	102	1	17.10	–	–	–/–	–	5	
Hayward Mornantau ("Nantie")	6.3.1977		16	1999–2004	66	14	0	7.33	54	5-56	1/0	29.79	4	21
¹,² Hearne Frank	23.11.1858	14.7.1949	4†	1891–1895	121	30	0	15.12	2	2-40	0/0	20.00	2	
Hearne George Alfred Lawrence	27.3.1888	13.11.1978	3	1922–1924	59	28	0	11.80	–	–	–/–	–	3	
Heine Peter Samuel	28.6.1928	4.2.2005	14	1955–1961	209	31	0	9.95	58	6-58	4/0	25.08	8	
Henderson Claude William	14.6.1972		7	2001–2002	65	30	0	9.28	22	4-116	0/0	42.18	2	4
Henry Omar	23.1.1952		3	1992	53	34	0	17.66	3	2-56	0/0	63.00	2	3
Hime Charles Frederick William	24.10.1869	6.12.1940	1	1895	8	8	0	4.00	1	1-20	0/0	31.00	0	
Hudson Andrew Charles	17.3.1965		35	1991–1997	2,007	163	4	33.45	–	–	–/–	–	36	89

	Born	Died	Tests	Test Career	Runs	HS	100s	Avge	Wkts	BB	5/10	Avge	Ct/St	O/T
Hutchinson Philip	25.1.1862	30.9.1925	2	1888	14	11	0	3.50	–	–	–/–	–	3	
Ironside David Ernest James	2.5.1925	21.8.2005	3	1953	37	13	0	18.50	15	5-51	1/0	18.33	1	
Irvine Brian Lee	9.3.1944		4	1969	353	102	1	50.42	–	–	–/–	–	2	
Jack Steven Douglas	4.8.1970		2	1994	7	7	0	3.50	8	4-69	0/0	24.50	–	2
Johnson Clement Lecky	31.3.1871	31.5.1908	1	1895	10	7	0	5.00	0	0-57	0/0	–	1	
[2] Kallis Jacques Henry	16.10.1975		134§	1995–2009	10,557	189*	33	54.41	259	6-54	5/0	31.37	148	290§/10
Keith Headley James	25.10.1927	17.11.1997	8	1952–1956	318	73	0	21.20	9	0-19	0/0	–	9	
Kemp Justin Miles	2.10.1977		4	2000–2005	80	55	0	13.33	9	3-33	0/0	24.66	3	79§/8
Kempis Gustav Adolph	4.8.1865	19.5.1890	1	1888	0	0*	0	0.00	4	3-53	0/0	19.00	0	
Khan Imran	27.4.1984		1	2008	20	20	0	20.00	–	–	–/–	–	0	
[2] Kirsten Gary	23.11.1967		101	1993–2003	7,289	275	21	45.27	2	1-0	0/0	71.00	83	185
[2] Kirsten Peter Noel	14.5.1955		12	1991–1994	626	104	1	31.30	0	0-5	0/0	–	8	40
[2] Klusener Lance	4.9.1971		49	1996–2004	1,906	174	4	32.86	80	8-64	1/0	37.91	34	171
Kotze Johannes Jacobus ("Kodgee")	7.8.1879	7.7.1931	3	1902–1907	2	2	0	0.40	6	3-64	0/0	40.50	3	
Kuiper Adrian Paul	24.8.1959		1	1991	34	34	0	17.00	–	–	–/–	–	1	25
Kuys Frederick	21.3.1870	12.9.1953	1	1898	26	26	0	13.00	2	2-31	0/0	15.50	0	
Lance Herbert Roy ("Tiger")	6.6.1940		13	1961–1969	591	70	0	28.14	12	3-30	0/0	39.91	7	
Langeveldt Charl Kenneth	17.12.1974		6	2004–2005	16	10	0	8.00	16	5-46	1/0	37.06	2	63/4
Langton Arthur Chudleigh Beaumont	2.3.1912	27.11.1942	15	1935–1938	298	73*	0	15.68	40	5-58	1/0	45.67	8	
Lawrence Godfrey Bernard	31.3.1932		5	1961	141	43	0	17.62	28	8-53	2/0	18.28	2	
le Roux Frederick Louis	5.2.1882	22.9.1963	1	1913	1	1	0	0.50	0	0-5	0/0	–	0	
Lewis Percy Tyson	2.10.1884	30.1.1976	1	1913	0	0	0	0.00	–	–	–/–	–	0	
Liebenberg Gerhardus Frederick Johannes	7.4.1972		5	1997–1998	104	45	0	13.00	–	–	–/–	–	0	4
[1] Lindsay Denis Thomson	4.9.1939	30.11.2005	19	1963–1969	1,130	182	3	37.66	–	–	–/–	–	57/2	
[1] Lindsay John Dixon	8.9.1908	31.8.1990	3	1947	21	9*	0	7.00	–	–	–/–	–	4/1	
Lindsay Nevil Vernon	30.7.1886	2.2.1976	1	1921	35	29	0	17.50	0	0-20	0/0	–	1	
Ling William Victor Stone	26.9.1891	26.9.1960	6	1921–1922	168	38	0	16.80	0	0-92	0/0	–	7	
Llewellyn Charles Bennett	26.9.1876	7.6.1964	15	1895–1912	544	90	0	20.14	48	6-92	4/1	29.60	7	
Lundie Eric Balfour	15.3.1888	12.9.1917	1	1913	1	1	0	1.00	4	4-101	0/0	26.75	0	
Macaulay Michael John	19.4.1939		1	1964	33	21	0	16.50	2	1-10	0/0	36.50	0	
McCarthy Cuan Neil	24.3.1929	14.8.2000	15	1948–1951	28	5	0	3.11	36	6-43	2/0	41.94	6	
McGlew Derrick John ("Jackie")	11.3.1929	9.6.1998	34	1951–1961	2,440	255*	7	42.06	0	0-7	0/0	–	18	
McKenzie Neil Douglas	24.11.1975		58	2000–2008	3,253	226	5	37.39	0	0-1	0/0	–	54	64/2
McKinnon Atholl Henry	20.8.1932	2.12.1983	8	1960–1966	107	27	0	17.83	26	4-128	0/0	35.57	1	

§ Kallis's figures exclude 83 runs, one wicket and four catches for the ICC World XI v Australia in the Super Series Test in 2005-06.

	Born	Died	Tests	Test Career	Runs	HS	100s	Avge	Wkts	BB	5/10	Avge	Ct/St	O/T
McLaren Ryan	9.2.1983		1	2009	33	33*		–	1	1-30	0/0	43.00		5/2
McLean Roy Alastair	9.7.1930	26.8.2007	40	1951–1964	2,120	142	5	30.28					23	
McMillan Brian Mervin	22.12.1963		38	1992–1998	1,968	113	3	39.36	75	4-65	0/0	33.82	49	78
McMillan Quintin	23.6.1904	3.7.1948	13	1929–1931	306	50*	0	18.00	36	5-66	2/0	34.52	8	
Mann Norman Bertram Fleetwood ("Tufty")	28.12.1920	31.7.1952	19	1947–1951	400	52	0	13.33	28	6-59	1/0	33.10	3	
Mansell Percy Neville Frank MBE	16.3.1920	9.5.1995	13	1951–1955	355	90	0	17.75	11	3-58	0/0	66.90	15	
Markham Lawrence Anderson	12.9.1924	5.8.2000	1	1948	20	20	0	20.00	1	1-34	0/0	72.00	0	
Marx Waldemar Frederick Eric	4.7.1895	2.6.1974	3	1921	125	36	0	20.83	4	3-85	0/0	36.00	0	
Matthews Craig Russell	15.2.1965		18	1992–1995	348	62*	0	18.31	52	5-42	2/0	28.88	4	56
Meintjes Douglas James	9.6.1890	17.7.1979	2	1922	43	21	0	14.33	6	3-38	0/0	19.16	3	
Melle Michael George	3.6.1930	28.12.2003	7	1949–1952	68	17	0	8.50	26	6-71	2/0	32.73	4	
Melville Alan	19.5.1910	18.4.1983	11	1938–1948	894	189	4	52.58			–/–		8	
Middleton James	30.9.1865	23.12.1913	6	1895–1902	52	22	0	7.42	24	5-51	2/0	18.41	1	
Mills Charles Henry	26.11.1867	26.7.1948	1	1891	25	21	0	12.50	2	2-83	0/0	41.50	1	
Milton Sir William Henry	3.12.1854	6.3.1930	3	1888–1891	68	21	0	11.33	2	1-5	0/0	24.00	2	
Mitchell Bruce	8.1.1909	1.7.1995	42	1929–1948	3,471	189*	8	48.88	27	5-87	1/0	51.11	56	
Mitchell Frank	13.8.1872	11.10.1935	3†	1912	28	12	0	4.66			–/–		0	
Morkel Denijs Paul Beck	25.1.1906	6.10.1980	16	1927–1931	663	88	0	24.55	18	4-93	0/0	45.61	13	
Morkel Johannes Albertus	10.6.1981		1	2008	58	58	0	58.00	1	1-44	0/0	132.00	0	44±/24
Morkel Morne	6.10.1984		21	2006–2009	336	40	0	13.44	74	5-50	2/0	31.45	6	20±/9
Murray Anton Ronald Andrew	30.4.1922	17.4.1995	10	1952–1953	289	109	1	22.23	18	4-169	0/0	39.44	3	
Nel Andre	15.7.1977		36	2001–2008	337	34	0	9.91	123	6-32	3/1	31.86	16	79/2
Nel John Desmond	10.7.1928		6	1949–1957	150	38	0	13.63			–/–		1	
Newberry Claude	1889	1.8.1916	4	1913	62	16	0	7.75	11	4-72	0/0	24.36	3	
Newson Edward Serrurier OBE	2.12.1910	24.4.1988	3	1930–1938	30	16	0	7.50	4	2-58	0/0	66.25	3	
Ngam Mfuneko	29.1.1979		3	2000	0	0*	0	–	11	3-26	0/0	17.18	1	
Nicholson Frank	17.9.1909	30.7.1982	4	1935	76	29	0	10.85			–/–		3	
Nicolson John Fairless William	19.7.1899	13.12.1935	3	1927	179	78	0	35.80			–/–		3	
Norton Norman Ogilvie	11.5.1881	27.6.1968	1	1909	9	7	0	4.50	4	0-5	0/0	4.47	0	
Nourse Arthur Dudley	12.11.1910	14.8.1981	34	1935–1951	2,960	231	9	53.81			–/–		12	
Nourse Arthur William ("Dave")	25.1.1879	8.7.1948	45	1902–1924	2,234	111	1	29.78	41	4-25	0/0	37.87	43	
Ntini Makhaya	6.7.1977		101	1998–2009	699	32*	0	9.84	390	7-37	18/4	28.82	25	172±/9
Nupen Eiulf Peter ("Buster")	1.1.1902	29.1.1977	17	1921–1935	348	69	0	14.50	50	6-46	5/1	35.76	9	
Oehse Arthur Edward	13.3.1870	11.4.1918	2	1888	16	8	0	4.00			–/–		0	
Oehse Arthur Lemox	11.10.1899	5.5.1949	3	1927–1929	11	4*	0	3.66	10	4-79	0/0	36.20	1	

Name	Born	Died	Tests	Test Career	Runs	HS	100s	Avge	Wkts	BB	5/10	Avge	Ct/St	O/T
O'Linn Sidney	5.5.1927		7	1960–1961	297	98	0	27.00	–	–	–/–	–	4	25‡/3
Ontong Justin Lee	4.1.1980		2	2001–2004	57	32	0	19.00	1	1–79	0/0	133.00	1	–
Owen-Smith Harold Geoffrey ("Tuppy")	18.2.1909	28.2.1990	5	1929	252	129	1	42.00	0	0–3	0/0	–	4	–
Palm Archibald William	8.6.1901	17.8.1966	1	1927	15	13	0	7.50	–	–	–/–	–	1	–
Parker George Macdonald	27.5.1899	1.5.1969	2	1924	3	2*	0	1.50	8	6–152	1/0	34.12	0	–
Parkin Durant Clifford	20.2.1873	20.3.1936	1	1891	–	–	–	–	3	3–82	0/0	27.33	1	–
Parnell Wayne Dillon	30.7.1989		1	2009	–	–	–	–	2	2–17	0/0	17.50	–	9/8
Partridge Joseph Titus	9.12.1932	6.6.1988	11	1963–1964	73	13*	0	10.42	44	7–91	3/0	31.20	6	–
Pearse Charles Ormerod Cato	10.10.1884	7.5.1953	3	1910	55	31	0	9.16	3	3–56	0/0	35.33	3	–
Pegler Sidney James	28.7.1888	10.9.1972	16	1909–1924	356	35*	0	15.47	47	7–65	2/0	33.44	5	–
Peterson Robin John	4.8.1979		6	2003–2007	163	61	0	27.16	14	5–33	1/0	35.50	5	35/5
[2]Pithey Anthony John	17.7.1933	17.11.2006	17	1956–1964	819	154	1	31.50	0	0–5	0/0	–	3	–
Pithey David Bartlett	4.10.1936		8	1963–1966	138	55	0	12.54	12	6–58	1/0	48.08	6	–
Plimsoll Jack Bruce	27.10.1917	11.11.1999	1	1947	16	8*	0	16.00	3	3–128	0/0	47.66	0	–
[1,2]Pollock Peter Maclean	30.6.1941		28	1961–1969	607	75*	0	21.67	116	6–38	9/1	24.18	9	–
[2]Pollock Robert Graeme	27.2.1944		23	1963–1969	2,256	274	7	60.97	4	2–50	0/0	51.00	17	–
[1]Pollock Shaun Maclean	16.7.1973		108	1995–2007	3,781	111	2	32.31	421	7–87	16/1	23.11	72	294‡/12
Poore Robert Montagu	20.3.1866	14.7.1938	3	1895	76	20	0	12.66	4	1–4	0/0	4.00	3	–
Potheacary James Edward	6.12.1933		3	1960	26	12	0	6.50	9	4–58	0/0	39.33	2	–
Powell Albert William	18.7.1873	11.9.1948	3	1898	16	11	0	8.00	1	1–10	0/0	10.00	2	–
Pretorius Dewald	6.12.1977		4	2001–2003	22	9	0	7.33	6	4–115	0/0	71.66	0	–
Prince Ashwell Gavin	28.5.1977		52	2001–2009	3,171	162*	11	44.04	1	1–2	0/0	47.00	32	49‡/1
Prince Charles Frederick Henry	11.9.1874	2.2.1949	1	1898	6	5	0	3.00	–	–	–/–	–	0	–
Pringle Meyrick Wayne	22.6.1966		4	1991–1995	67	33	0	16.75	5	2–62	0/0	54.00	0	–
Procter Michael John	15.9.1946		7	1966–1969	226	48	0	25.11	41	6–73	1/0	15.02	4	17
Promnitz Henry Louis Ernest	23.2.1904	7.9.1983	2	1927	14	5	0	3.50	8	5–58	1/0	20.12	2	–
Quinn Neville Anthony	21.2.1908	5.8.1934	12	1929–1931	90	11	0	6.00	35	6–92	1/0	32.71	1	–
Reid Norman	26.12.1890	6.6.1947	1	1921	17	11	0	8.50	2	2–63	0/0	31.50	0	–
Rhodes Jonathan Neil	27.7.1969		52	1992–2000	2,532	117	3	35.66	0	0–0	0/0	–	34	245
Richards Alfred Renfrew	14.12.1867	9.11.1904	1	1895	6	6	0	3.00	–	–	–/–	–	0	–
Richards Barry Anderson	21.7.1945		4	1969	508	140	2	72.57	1	1–12	0/0	26.00	3	–
[2]Richards William Henry Matthews	26.3.1862	4.1.1903	1	1888	4	4	0	2.00	–	–	–/–	–	0	–
Richardson David John	16.9.1959		42	1991–1997	1,359	109	1	24.26	–	–	–/–	–	150/2	122
Robertson John Benjamin	5.6.1906	5.7.1985	3	1935	51	17	0	10.20	6	3–143	0/0	53.50	2	–
Rose-Innes Albert	16.2.1868	22.11.1946	2	1888	14	13	0	3.50	5	5–43	1/0	17.80	2	–

	Born	Died	Tests	Test Career	Runs	HS	100s	Avge	Wkts	BB	5/10	Avge	Ct/St	O/T
Routledge Thomas William	18.4.1867	9.5.1927	4	1891–1895	72	24	0	9.00			–/–	–	2	
[2] Rowan Athol Matthew Burchell	7.2.1921	22.2.1998	15	1947–1951	290	41	0	17.05	54	5-68	4/0	38.59	7	4
[2] Rowan Eric Alfred Burchell	20.7.1909	30.4.1993	26	1935–1951	1,965	236	3	43.66	0	0-0	0/0	–	14	
Rowe George Alexander	15.6.1874	8.1.1950	5	1895–1902	26	13*	0	4.33	15	5-115	1/0	30.40	4	
Rudolph Jacobus Andries	4.5.1981		35	2003–2006	2,028	222*	5	36.21	4	1-1	0/0	108.00	22	43±/1
Rushmere Mark Weir	7.1.1965		1	1991	6	3	0	3.00			–/–	–	0	4
Samuelson Sivert Vause	21.11.1883	18.11.1958	1	1909	22	15	0	11.00	0	0-64	0/0	–	0	
Schultz Brett Nolan	26.8.1970		9	1992–1997	9	6	0	1.50	37	5-48	2/0	20.24	2	1
Schwarz Reginald Oscar	4.5.1875	18.11.1918	20	1905–1912	374	61	0	13.85	55	6-47	2/0	25.76	18	
Seccull Arthur William	14.9.1868	20.7.1945	1	1895	23	17*	0	23.00	2	2-37	0/0	18.50	1	
Seymour Michael Arthur ("Kelly")	5.6.1936		7	1963–1969	84	36	0	12.00	9	3-80	0/0	65.33	2	
Shalders William Alfred	12.2.1880	18.3.1917	12	1898–1907	355	42	0	16.13	1	1-6	0/0	6.00	3	
Shepstone George Harold	9.4.1876	3.7.1940	2	1895–1898	38	21	0	9.50	1	0-8	0/0	–	2	
Sherwell Percy William	17.8.1880	17.4.1948	13	1905–1910	427	115	1	23.72			–/–	–	20/16	
Siedle Ivan Julian ("Jack")	11.1.1903	24.8.1982	18	1927–1935	977	141	1	28.73	1	1-7	–/–	7.00	7	
Sinclair James Hugh	16.10.1876	23.2.1913	25	1895–1910	1,069	106	3	23.23	63	6-26	1/0	31.68	9	
Smith Charles James Edward	25.12.1872	27.3.1947	3	1902	106	45	0	21.20			–/–	–	2	
Smith Frederick William	31.3.1861	17.4.1914	3	1888–1895	45	12	0	9.00			–/–	–	2	
Smith Graeme Craig	1.2.1981		808	2001–2009	6,757	277	20	51.58	8	2-145	0/0	100.12	108	148±/20
Smith Vivian Ian	23.2.1925		9	1947–1957	39	11*	0	3.90	12	4-143	0/0	64.08	3	
Snell Richard Peter	12.9.1968		5	1991–1994	95	48	0	13.57	19	4-74	0/0	28.31	1	42
[2] Snooke Sibley John ("Tip")	1.2.1881	14.8.1966	26	1905–1922	1,008	103	1	22.40	35	8-70	1/1	20.05	24	
[2] Snooke Stanley de la Courtte	11.11.1878	6.4.1959	1	1907	0	0	0	0.00			–/–	–	2	
Solomon William Rodger Thomson	23.4.1872	13.7.1964	1	1898	4	2	0	2.00			–/–	–	1	
Stewart Robert Burnard	3.9.1856	12.9.1913	1	1888	13	9	0	6.50			–/–	–	2	
Steyn Dale Willem	27.6.1983		36	2004–2009	471	76	0	13.08	185	6-49	12/3	23.70	10	33±/14
Steyn Philippus Jeremia Rudolf	30.6.1967		3	1994	127	46	0	21.16			–/–	–	1	1
Stricker Louis Anthony	26.5.1884	5.2.1960	13	1909–1912	344	48	0	14.33	1	1-36	0/0	105.00	3	
Strydom Pieter Coenraad	8.6.1969		2	1999	35	30	0	11.66	0	0-27	0/0	–	3	10
Susskind Manfred John	8.6.1891	9.7.1957	5	1924	268	65	0	33.50			–/–	–	1	
Symcox Patrick Leonard	14.4.1960		20	1993–1998	741	108	1	28.50	37	4-69	0/0	43.32	5	80
Taberer Henry Melville	7.10.1870	5.6.1932	1	1902	2	2	0	2.00	1	1-25	0/0	48.00	0	
[2] Tancred Augustus Bernard	20.8.1865	23.11.1911	2	1888	87	29	0	29.00			–/–	–	2	
[2] Tancred Louis Joseph	7.10.1876	28.7.1934	14	1902–1913	530	97	0	21.20			–/–	–	3	

§ G. C. Smith's figures exclude 12 runs and three catches for the ICC World XI v Australia in the Super Series Test in 2005-06.

	Born	Died	Tests	Test Career	Runs	HS	100s	Avge	Wkts	BB	5/10	Avge	Ct/St	O/T
2Tancred Vincent Maximilian.	7.7.1875	3.6.1904	1	1898	25	18	0	12.50	–	–	–/–	–	0	
2Tapscott George Lancelot ("Dusty").	7.11.1889	13.12.1940	1	1913	5	4	0	2.50	–	–	–/–	–	1	
2Tapscott Lionel Eric ("Doodles").	18.3.1894	7.7.1934	2	1922	58	50*	0	29.00	0	0-2	0/0	–	0	
Tayfield Hugh Joseph.	30.1.1929	24.2.1994	37	1949–1960	862	75	0	16.90	170	9-113	14/2	25.91	26	4
Taylor Alistair Innes ("Scotch").	25.7.1925	7.2.2004	1	1956	18	12	0	9.00	–	–	–	–	0	
2Taylor Daniel.	9.1.1887	24.1.1957	2	1913	85	36	0	21.25	–	–	–/–	–	0	
2Taylor Herbert Wilfred.	5.5.1889	8.2.1973	42	1912–1931	2,936	176	7	40.77	5	3-15	0/0	31.20	19	
Terbrugge David John.	31.1.1977		7	1998–2003	16	4*	0	5.33	20	5-46	1/0	25.85	4	
Theunissen Nicolaas Hendrik Christiaan de Jong.	4.5.1867	9.11.1929	1	1888	2	2*	0	2.00	0	0-51	0/0	–	0	
Thornton George.	24.12.1867	31.1.1939	1	1902	1	1*	0	–	1	1-20	0/0	20.00	1	
Tomlinson Denis Stanley.	4.9.1910	11.7.1993	1	1935	9	9	0	9.00	0	0-38	0/0	–	0	0‡
Traicos Athanasios John.	17.5.1947		3†	1969	8	5*	0	4.00	4	2-70	0/0	51.75	4	
Trimborn Patrick Henry Joseph.	18.5.1940		4	1966–1969	13	11*	0	6.50	11	3-12	0/0	23.36	7	
Tsolekile Thami Lungisa.	9.10.1980		3	2004	47	22	0	9.40	–	–	–/–	–	6	
1Tuckett Lindsay.	6.2.1919		9	1947–1948	131	40*	0	11.90	19	5-68	2/0	51.57	9	
1Tuckett Lindsay Richard ("Len").	19.4.1885	8.4.1963	1	1913	0	0*	0	0.00	0	0-24	0/0	–	2	
Twentyman-Jones Percy Sydney.	13.9.1876	8.3.1954	1	1902	0	0	0	0.00	–	–	–	–	0	
van der Bijl Pieter Gerhard Vintcent.	21.10.1907	16.2.1973	5	1938	460	125	1	51.11	–	–	–/–	–	1	
van der Merwe Edward Alexander.	9.11.1903	26.2.1971	2	1929–1935	27	19	0	9.00	0	–	–	–	3	
van der Merwe Peter Laurence.	14.3.1937		15	1963–1966	533	76	0	25.38	1	1-6	0/0	22.00	11	
van Jaarsveld Martin.	18.6.1974		9	2002–2004	397	73	0	30.53	0	0-28	0/0	–	11	
van Ryneveld Clive Berrange.	19.3.1928		19	1951–1957	724	83	0	26.81	17	4-67	0/0	39.47	14	
Varnals George Derek.	24.7.1935		3	1964	97	23	0	16.16	0	0-2	0/0	–	0	
Viljoen Kenneth George.	14.5.1910	21.1.1974	27	1930–1948	1,365	124	2	28.43	2	0-10	0/0	–	5	
Vincent Cyril Leverton.	16.2.1902	24.8.1968	25	1927–1935	526	60	0	20.23	84	6-51	3/0	31.32	27	
Vintcent Charles Henry.	2.9.1866	28.9.1943	3	1888–1891	26	9	0	4.33	4	3-88	0/0	48.25	1	
Vogler Albert Edward Ernest.	28.11.1876	9.8.1946	15	1905–1910	340	65	0	17.00	64	7-94	5/1	22.73	20	
2Wade Herbert Frederick.	14.9.1905	23.11.1980	10	1935–1935	327	40*	0	20.43	–	–	–/–	–	4	
2Wade Walter Wareham ("Billy").	18.6.1914	31.5.2003	11	1938–1949	511	125	2	28.38	–	–	–/–	–	15/2	
Waite John Henry Bickford.	19.1.1930		50	1951–1964	2,405	134	4	30.44	–	–	–/–	–	124/17	
Walter Kenneth Alexander.	5.11.1939	13.9.2003	2	1961	11	10	0	3.66	6	4-63	0/0	32.83	3	
Ward Thomas Alfred.	2.8.1887	16.2.1936	23	1912–1924	459	64	0	13.90	0	–	–	–	19/13	
Watkins John Cecil.	10.4.1923		15	1949–1956	612	92	0	23.53	29	4-22	0/0	28.13	12	
Wesley Colin.	5.9.1937		3	1960	49	35	0	9.80	–	–	–/–	–	1	
Wessels Kepler Christoffel.	14.9.1957		16†	1991–1994	1,027	118	2	38.03	–	–	–/–	–	12	55‡

	Born	Died	Tests	Test Career	Runs	HS	100s	Avge	Wkts	BB	5/10	Avge	Ct/St	O/T
Westcott Richard John	19.9.1927		5	1953–1957	166	62	0	18.44	–	0-22	0/0	–	0	
White Gordon Charles	5.2.1882	17.10.1918	17	1905–1912	872	147	2	30.06	9	4-47	0/0	33.44	10	
Willoughby Charl Myles	3.12.1974		2	2003	–	–	–	–	1	1-47	0/0	125.00	0	3
Willoughby Joseph Thomas	7.11.1874	11.3.1952	2	1895	8	5	0	2.00	6	2-37	0/0	26.50	0	
Wimble Clarence Skelton	22.4.1861	28.1.1930	1	1891	0	0	0	0.00	–	–	–/–	–	0	
Winslow Paul Lyndhurst	21.5.1929		5	1949–1955	186	108	1	20.66	–	–	–/–	–	1	
Wynne Owen Edgar	1.6.1919	13.7.1975	6	1948–1949	219	50	0	18.25	–	–	–/–	–	3	
Zondeki Monde	25.7.1982		6	2003–2008	82	59	0	16.40	19	6-39	1/0	25.26	1	11½/1
Zulch Johan Wilhelm	2.1.1886	19.5.1924	16	1909–1921	983	150	2	32.76	0	0-2	0/0	–	4	

WEST INDIES (283 players)

	Born	Died	Tests	Test Career	Runs	HS	100s	Avge	Wkts	BB	5/10	Avge	Ct/St	O/T
Achong Ellis Edgar	16.2.1904	30.8.1986	6	1929–1934	81	22	0	8.10	8	2-64	0/0	47.25	6	
Adams James Clive	9.1.1968		54	1991–2000	3,012	208*	6	41.26	27	5-17	1/0	49.48	48	127
Alexander Franz Copeland Murray ("Gerry")	2.11.1928		25	1957–1960	961	108	0	30.03	–	–	–/–	–	85/5	
Ali Imtiaz	28.7.1954		1	1975	–	1*	0	–	–	–	–/–	–	0	
Ali Inshan	25.9.1949	24.6.1995	12	1970–1976	172	25	0	10.75	34	5-59	1/0	47.67	7	
Allan David Walter	5.11.1937		5	1961–1966	75	40*	0	12.50	–	–	–/–	–	15/3	
Allen Ian Basil Alston	6.10.1965		2	1991	5	4*	0	–	5	2-69	0/0	36.00	1	
Ambrose Curtly Elconn Lynwall	21.9.1963		98	1987–2000	1,439	53	0	12.40	405	8-45	22/3	20.99	18	176
Arthurton Keith Lloyd Thomas	21.2.1965		33	1988–1995	1,382	157*	2	30.71	1	1-17	0/0	183.00	22	105
Asgarali Nyron Sultan	28.12.1920	5.11.2006	2	1957	62	29	0	15.50	–	–	–/–	–	0	
[2] Atkinson Denis St Eval	9.8.1926	9.11.2001	22	1948–1957	922	219	1	31.79	47	7-53	3/0	35.04	11	
[2] Atkinson Eric St Eval	6.11.1927	29.5.1998	8	1957–1958	126	37	0	15.75	25	5-42	1/0	23.56	2	
Austin Richard Arkwright	5.9.1954		2	1977	22	20	0	11.00	2	0-5	0/0	–	2	1
Austin Ryan Anthony	15.11.1981		2	2009	39	19	0	9.75	3	1-29	0/0	51.66	3	
Bacchus Sheik Faoud Ahamul Fasiel	31.1.1954		19	1977–1981	782	250	1	26.06	–	0-3	0/0	–	17	29
Baichan Leonard	12.5.1946		3	1974–1975	184	105*	1	46.00	–	–	–/–	–	2	
Baker Lionel Sionne	6.9.1984		4	2008–2009	23	17	0	11.50	5	2-39	0/0	79.00	1	10/3
Banks Omari Ahmed Clemente	17.7.1982		10	2002–2003	318	50*	0	26.50	28	4-87	0/0	48.82	6	5
Baptiste Eldine Ashworth Elderfield	12.3.1960		10	1983–1989	233	87*	0	23.30	16	3-31	0/0	35.18	2	43
Barath Adrian Boris	14.4.1990		2	2009	139	104	1	34.75	–	0-4	0/0	–	2	
Barrett Arthur George	4.4.1944		6	1970–1974	40	19	0	6.66	13	3-43	0/0	46.38	0	

	Born	Died	Tests	Test Career	Runs	HS	100s	Avge	Wkts	BB	5/10	Avge	Ct/St	O/T
Barrow Ivanhoe Mordecai	16.1.1911	2.4.1979	11	1929-1939	276	105	1	16.23	-	-	-/-	-	17/5	
Bartlett Edward Lawson	10.3.1906	21.12.1976	5	1928-1930	131	84	0	18.71	-	-	-/-	-	2	
Baugh Carlton Seymour	23.6.1982		5	2002-2004	196	68	0	19.60	-	-	-/-	-	4/1	30/1
Benjamin Kenneth Charlie Griffith	8.4.1967		26	1991-1997	222	43*	0	7.92	92	6-66	4/1	30.27	2	26
Benjamin Winston Keithroy Matthew	31.12.1964		21	1987-1994	470	85	0	18.80	61	4-46	0/0	27.01	12	85
Benn Sulieman Jamaal	22.7.1981		12	2007-2009	251	35	0	13.94	35	5-155	1/0	45.31	6	11/10
Bernard David Eddison	19.7.1981		3	2002-2009	202	69	0	40.40	4	2-30	0/0	46.25	8	14/1
Best Carlisle Alonza	14.5.1959		8	1985-1990	342	164	1	28.50	0	0-2	0/0	-	1	24
Best Tino la Bertram	26.8.1981		14	2002-2009	196	27	0	9.80	28	4-46	0/0	48.67	0	12
Betancourt Nelson	4.6.1887	12.10.1947	1	1929	52	39	0	26.00	-	-	-/-	-		
Binns Alfred Phillip	24.7.1929		5	1952-1955	64	27	0	9.14	-	-	-/-	-	14/3	
Birkett Lionel Sydney	14.4.1905	16.1.1998	4	1930	136	64	0	17.00	1	1-16	0/0	71.00	8	
Bishop Ian Raphael	24.10.1967		43	1988-1997	632	48	0	12.15	161	6-40	6/0	24.27	8	84
Black Marlon Ian	7.6.1975		6	2000-2001	21	6	0	2.62	12	4-83	0/0	49.75	3	5
Boyce Keith David	11.10.1943	11.10.1996	21	1970-1975	657	95*	0	24.33	60	6-77	2/1	30.01		8
Bradshaw Ian David Russell	9.7.1974		5	2005	96	33	0	13.71	9	3-73	0/0	60.00		62/1
Bravo Dwayne John	7.10.1983		34	2004-2009	2,009	113	3	32.40	81	6-55	2/0	38.14	35	99/15
Breese Gareth Rohan	9.1.1976		1	2002	5	5	0	2.50	2	2-108	0/0	67.50	1	
Browne Courtney Oswald	7.12.1970		20	1994-2004	387	68	0	16.12	6	2-72	0/0	48.00	79/2	46
Browne Cyril Rutherford	8.10.1890	12.11.1964	4	1928-1929	176	70*	0	25.14	-	-	-/-	-	1	
Butcher Basil Fitzherbert	3.9.1933		44	1958-1969	3,104	209*	7	43.11	5	5-34	1/0	18.00	15	
Butler Lennox Stephen	9.2.1929		1	1954	16	16	0	16.00	5	2-151	0/0	75.50	0	
Butts Clyde Godfrey	8.7.1957		7	1984-1987	108	38	0	15.42	10	4-73	0/0	59.50	2	
Bynoe Michael Robin	23.2.1941		4	1958-1966	111	48	0	18.50	1	1-5	0/0	5.00	4	
Camacho George Stephen	15.10.1945		11	1967-1970	640	87	0	29.09	0	0-12	0/0	-	4	
[2]Cameron Francis James	22.6.1923	10.6.1994	5	1948	151	75*	0	25.16	3	2-74	0/0	92.66		
[2]Cameron John Hemsley	8.4.1914	13.2.2000	2	1939	6	6	0	2.00	3	3-66	0/0	29.33		
Campbell Sherwin Legay	1.11.1970		52	1994-2001	2,882	208	4	32.38	-	-	-/-	-	47	90
Carew George McDonald	4.6.1910	9.12.1974	4	1934-1948	170	107	0	28.33	0	0-2	0/0	-	1	
Carew Michael Conrad ("Joey")	15.9.1937		19	1963-1971	1,127	109	1	34.15	8	1-11	0/0	54.62	13	
Challenor George	28.6.1888	30.7.1947	3	1928	101	46	0	16.83	-	-	-/-	-		
Chanderpaul Shivnarine	16.8.1974		123	1993-2009	8,669	203*	21	48.70	8	1-2	0/0	105.62	50	252/15
Chang Herbert Samuel	27.1.1952		1	1978	8	6	0	4.00	-	-	-/-	-	0	
Chattergoon Sewnarine	3.4.1981		4	2007-2008	127	46	0	18.14	-	-	-/-	-	4	18
[2]Christiani Cyril Marcel	28.10.1913	4.4.1938	4	1934	98	32*	0	19.60	-	-	-/-	-	6/1	

	Born	Died	Tests	Test Career	Runs	HS	100s	Avge	Wkts	BB	Avge	5/10	Ct/St	O/T
[2] Christiani Robert Julian	19.7.1920	4.1.2005	22	1947–1953	896	107	1	26.35	3	3-52	36.00	0/0	19/2	
Clarke Carlos Bertram OBE	7.4.1918	14.10.1993	3	1939	3	2	0	1.00	6	3-59	43.50	0/0	0	10
[2] Clarke Sylvester Theophilus	11.12.1954		11	1977–1981	172	35*	0	15.63	42	5-126	27.85	1/0	2	30
[2] Collins Pedro Tyrone	12.8.1976		32	1998–2005	235	24	0	5.87	106	6-53	34.63	3/0	7	84
Collymore Corey Dalanelo	21.12.1977		30	1998–2007	197	16*	0	7.88	93	7-57	32.30	4/1	6	
Constantine *Lord* [Learie Nicholas]	21.9.1901	1.7.1971	18	1928–1939	635	90	0	19.24	58	5-75	30.10	2/0	28	
Croft Colin Everton Hunte	15.3.1953		27	1976–1981	158	33	0	10.53	125	8-29	23.30	3/0	8	19
Cuffy Cameron Eustace	8.2.1970		15	1994–2002	58	15	0	4.14	43	4-82	33.83	0/0	5	41
Cummins Anderson Cleophas	7.5.1966		5	1992–1994	98	50	0	19.60	8	4-54	42.75	0/0	1	63
Da Costa Oscar Constantine	11.9.1907	1.10.1936	5	1929–1934	153	39	0	19.12	3	1-14	58.33	0/0	5	
Daniel Wayne Wendell	16.1.1956		10	1975–1983	46	11	0	6.57	36	5-39	25.27	1/0	4	18
[2] Davis Bryan Allan	2.5.1940		4	1964	245	68	0	30.62	–	–	–	–/–	1	
[2] Davis Charles Allan	1.1.1944		15	1968–1972	1,301	183	4	54.20	2	1-27	165.00	0/0	4	
Davis Winston Walter	18.9.1958		15	1982–1987	202	77	0	15.53	45	4-19	32.71	0/0	10	35
De Caires Francis Ignatius	12.5.1909	2.2.1959	3	1929	232	80	0	38.66	0	0-9	–	0/0	1	
Deomarine Narsingh	16.8.1983		5	2004–2009	207	82	0	29.57	4	2-74	56.50	0/0	4	5
Depeiza Cyril Clairmonte	10.10.1928	10.11.1995	5	1954–1955	187	122	1	31.16	0	0-3	–	0/0	7/4	
Dewdney David Thomas	23.10.1933		9	1954–1957	17	5*	0	2.42	21	5-21	38.42	1/0	0	
Dhanraj Rajindra	6.2.1969		4	1994–1995	17	9	0	4.25	8	2-49	74.37	0/0	1	6
Dillon Mervyn	5.6.1974		38	1996–2003	549	43	0	8.44	131	5-71	33.57	2/0	16	108
Dowe Uton George	29.3.1949		4	1970–1972	8	5*	0	8.00	12	4-69	44.50	0/0	3	
Dowlin Travis Montague	24.2.1977		12	2009–2009	328	95	0	41.00	–	–	–	–/–	4	6/1
Drakes Vasbert Conniel	5.8.1969		12	2002–2003	386	67	0	21.44	33	5-93	41.27	1/0	2	34
Dujon Peter Jeffrey Leroy	28.5.1956		81	1981–1991	3,322	139	5	31.94	–	–	–	–/–	267/5	169
[2] Edwards Fidel Henderson	6.2.1982		43	2003–2009	248	21	0	5.16	122	7-87	39.43	8/0	7	50/12
Edwards Richard Martin	3.6.1940		5	1968	65	22	0	9.28	18	5-84	34.77	1/0	0	
Ferguson Wilfred	14.12.1917	23.2.1961	8	1947–1953	200	75	0	28.57	34	6-92	34.26	3/1	11	
Fernandes Maurius Pacheco	12.8.1897	8.5.1981	2	1928–1929	49	22	0	12.25	–	–	–	–/–	0	
Findlay Thaddeus Michael MBE	19.10.1943		10	1969–1972	212	44*	0	16.30	–	–	–	–/–	19/2	
Foster Maurice Linton Churchill	9.5.1943		14	1969–1977	580	125	1	30.52	9	2-41	66.66	0/0	3	2
Francis George Nathaniel	11.12.1897	12.1.1942	10	1928–1933	81	19*	0	5.78	23	4-40	33.17	0/0	7	
Frederick Michael Campbell	6.5.1927		1	1953	30	30	0	15.00	–	–	–	–/–	0	
Fredericks Roy Clifton	11.11.1942	5.9.2000	59	1968–1976	4,334	169	8	42.49	7	1-12	78.28	0/0	62	12
Fuller Richard Livingston	30.1.1913	3.5.1987	1	1934	1	1	0	1.00	0	0-2	–	0/0	0	
Furlonge Hammond Allan	19.6.1934		3	1954–1955	99	64	0	19.80	–	–	–	–/–	0	

Name	Born	Died	Tests	Test Career	Runs	HS	100s	Avge	Wkts	BB	5/10	Avge	Ct/St	O/T
Ganga Daren	14.1.1979		48	1998–2007	2,160	135	3	25.71	1	1-20	0/0	106.00	30	35/1
Ganteaume Andrew Gordon	22.1.1921		1	1947	112	112	0	112.00	–	–	–/–	–	0	
Garner Joel MBE	16.12.1952		58	1976–1986	672	60	0	12.44	259	6-56	7/0	20.97	42	98
Garrick Leon Vivian	11.11.1976		2	2000	27	27	0	13.50	–	–	–/–	–	2	3
Gaskin Berkeley Bertram McGarrell	21.3.1908	2.5.1979	2	1947	17	10	0	5.66	2	1-15	0/0	79.00	1	
Gayle Christopher Henry	21.9.1979		85	1999–2009	5,848	317	12	40.61	71	5-34	2/0	42.08	82	202/12
Gibbs Glendon Lionel	27.12.1925	21.2.1979	1	1954	12	12	0	6.00	0	0-2	0/0	–	1	
Gibbs Lancelot Richard	29.9.1934		79	1957–1975	488	25	0	6.97	309	8-38	18/2	29.09	52	3
Gibson Ottis Delroy	16.3.1969		2	1995–1998	93	37	0	23.25	3	2-81	0/0	91.66	0	15
Gilchrist Roy	28.6.1934	18.7.2001	13	1957–1958	60	12	0	5.45	57	6-55	1/0	26.68	4	
Gladstone Morais George	14.1.1901	19.5.1978	1	1929	12	12*	0	–	1	1-139	0/0	189.00	0	
Goddard John Douglas Claude OBE	21.4.1919	26.8.1987	27	1947–1957	859	83*	0	30.67	33	5-31	1/0	31.81	22	83
Gomes Hilary Angelo ("Larry")	13.7.1953		60	1976–1987	3,171	143	9	39.63	15	2-20	0/0	62.00	18	
Gomez Gerald Ethridge	10.10.1919	6.8.1996	29	1939–1953	1,243	101	1	30.31	58	7-55	1/1	27.41	18	
[2]Grant George Copeland ("Jackie")	9.5.1907	26.10.1978	12	1930–1934	413	71*	0	25.81	0	0-1	0/0	–	10	
[2]Grant Rolph Stewart	15.12.1909	18.10.1977	7	1934–1939	220	77	0	22.00	11	3-68	0/0	32.09	13	
Gray Anthony Hollis	23.5.1963		5	1986	48	12*	0	8.00	22	4-39	0/0	17.13	6	25
Greenidge Alvin Ethelbert	20.8.1956		6	1977–1978	222	69	0	22.20	–	–	–/–	–	5	1
Greenidge Cuthbert Gordon MBE	1.5.1951		108	1974–1990	7,558	226	19	44.72	0	0-0	0/0	–	96	128
Greenidge Geoffrey Alan	26.5.1948		5	1971–1972	209	50	0	29.85	0	0-2	0/0	–	3	
Grell Mervyn George	18.12.1899	11.1.1976	1	1929	34	21	0	17.00	0	0-7	0/0	–	–	
Griffith Adrian Frank Gordon	19.11.1971		14	1996–2000	638	114	1	24.53	–	–	–/–	–	5	9
Griffith Charles Christopher	14.12.1938		28	1959–1968	530	54	0	16.56	94	6-36	5/0	28.54	16	
Griffith Herman Clarence	1.12.1893	18.3.1980	13	1928–1933	91	18	0	5.05	44	6-103	2/0	28.25	4	
Guillen Simpson Clairmonte ("Sammy")	24.9.1924		5†	1951	104	54	0	26.00	–	–	–/–	–	9/2	
Hall Wesley Winfield	12.9.1937		48	1958–1968	818	50*	0	15.73	192	7-69	9/1	26.38	11	
Harper Roger Andrew	17.3.1963		25	1983–1993	535	74	0	18.44	46	6-57	1/0	28.06	36	105
Haynes Desmond Leo	15.2.1956		116	1977–1993	7,487	184	18	42.29	1	1-2	0/0	8.00	65	238
[3]Headley George Alphonso MBE	30.5.1909	30.11.1983	22	1929–1953	2,190	270*	10	60.83	–	–	–/–	–	14	
[3]Headley Ronald George Alphonso	29.6.1939		2	1973	62	42	0	15.50	0	0-0	0/0	–	2	1
Hendriks John Leslie	21.12.1933		20	1961–1969	447	64	0	18.62	–	–	–/–	–	42/5	
Hinds Ryan O'Neal	17.2.1981		15	2001–2009	505	84	0	21.04	13	2-45	0/0	66.92	7	14
Hinds Wavell Wayne	7.9.1976		45	1995–2005	2,608	213	5	33.01	16	3-79	0/0	36.87	32	114/1
Hoad Edward Lisle Goldsworthy	29.1.1896	5.3.1986	4	1928–1933	98	36	0	12.25	–	–	–/–	–	1	
Holder Roland Irwin Christopher	22.12.1967		11	1996–1998	380	91	0	25.33	–	–	–/–	–	9	37

	Born	Died	Tests	Test Career	Runs	HS	100s	Avge	Wkts	BB	Avge	5/10	Ct/St	O/T
Holder Vanburn Alonzo	10.10.1945		40	1969–1978	682	42	0	14.20	109	6-28	33.27	3/0	16	12
Holding Michael Anthony	16.2.1954		60	1975–1986	910	73	0	13.78	249	8-92	23.68	13/2	22	102
Holford David Anthony Jerome	16.4.1940	3.6.1997	24	1966–1976	768	105*	1	22.58	51	5-23	39.39	1/0	18	
Holt John Kenneth Constantine	12.8.1923		17	1953–1958	1,066	166	2	36.75	1	1-20	20.00	0/0	8	
Hooper Carl Llewellyn	15.12.1966		102	1987–2002	5,762	233	13	36.46	114	5-26	49.42	4/0	115	227
Howard Anthony Bourne	27.8.1946		1	1971					2	2-140	70.00	0/0	0	
Hunte *Sir* Conrad Cleophas	9.5.1932	3.12.1999	44	1957–1966	3,245	260	8	45.06	2	1-17	55.00	0/0	16	
Hunte Errol Ashton Clairmonte	3.10.1905	26.6.1967	3	1929	166	58	0	33.20				-/-	5	
Hylton Leslie George	29.3.1905	17.5.1955	6	1934–1939	70	19	0	11.66	16	4-27	26.12	0/0	1	
Jacobs Ridley Detamore	26.11.1967		65	1998–2004	2,577	118	3	28.31				-/-	207/12	147
Jaggernauth Amit Sheldon	16.11.1983			2007	0	0*	0	0.00	1	1-74	96.00	0/0	0	
Johnson Hophnie Hobah Hines	13.7.1910	24.6.1987	3	1947–1950	38	22	0	9.50	13	5-41	18.30	2/1	0	
Johnson Tyrell Fabian	10.1.1917	5.4.1985	1	1939	9	9*	0	–	3	2-53	43.00	0/0	1	
Jones Charles Ernest Llewellyn	3.11.1902	10.12.1959	4	1929–1934	63	19	0	9.00	0	0-2	–	0/0	3	
Jones Prior Erskine Waverley	6.6.1917	21.11.1991	9	1947–1951	47	10*	0	5.22	25	5-85	30.04	1/0	4	
Joseph David Rolston Emmanuel	15.11.1969		4	1998	141	50	0	20.14	0	0-1	–	0/0	10	
Joseph Sylvester Cleofoster	5.9.1978		5	2004–2007	147	45	0	14.70	0	0-8	–	0/0	3	
Julien Bernard Denis	13.3.1950		24	1973–1976	866	121	2	30.92	50	5-57	37.36	1/0	14	13
Jumadeen Raphick Rasif	12.4.1948		12	1971–1978	84	56	0	21.00	29	4-72	39.34	0/0	4	12
Kallicharran Alvin Isaac	21.3.1949		66	1971–1980	4,399	187	12	44.43	4	2-16	39.50	0/0	51	31
Kanhai Rohan Bholalall	26.12.1935		79	1957–1973	6,227	256	15	47.53	0	0-1	–	0/0	50	7
Kentish Esmond Seymour Maurice	21.11.1916	23.12.1990	2	1947–1953	1	1*	0	1.00	8	5-49	22.25	1/0	1	
King Collis Llewellyn	11.6.1951		9	1976–1980	418	100*	1	32.15	3	1-30	94.00	0/0	5	18
King Frank McDonald	14.12.1926	9.7.1990	14	1952–1955	116	21	0	8.28	29	5-74	39.96	1/0	5	
King Lester Anthony	27.2.1939		2	1961–1967	41	20	0	10.25	9	5-46	17.11	1/0	2	
King Reon Dane	6.10.1975		19	1998–2004	66	12*	0	3.47	53	5-51	32.69	1/0	2	50
Lambert Clayton Benjamin	10.2.1962		5	1991–1998	284	104	1	31.55	1	1-4	5.00	0/0	8	11
Lara Brian Charles	2.5.1969		131	1990–2006	11,912 §	400*	34	53.17	0	0-0	–	0/0	164	295‡
Lashley Patrick Douglas ("Peter")	11.2.1937		4	1960–1966	159	49	0	22.71	1	1-1	1.00	0/0	4	
Lawson Jermaine Jay Charles	13.1.1982		13	2002–2005	52	14	0	3.46	51	7-78	29.64	2/0	3	13
Legall Ralph Archibald	1.12.1925	2003	4	1952	50	23	0	10.00				-/-	8/1	
Lewis Desmond Michael	21.2.1946		3	1970	259	88	0	86.33				-/-	8	
Lewis Rawl Nicholas	5.9.1974		5	1997–2007	89	40	0	8.90	4	2-42	114.00	0/0	0	28/1
Lloyd Clive Hubert CBE	31.8.1944		110	1966–1984	7,515	242*	19	46.67	10	2-13	62.20	0/0	90	87

§ Lara's figures exclude 41 runs for the ICC World XI v Australia in the Super Series Test in 2005-06.

	Born	Died	Tests	Test Career	Runs	HS	100s	Avge	Wkts	BB	5/10	Avge	Ct/St	O/1T
Logie Augustine Lawrence	28.9.1960		52	1982–1991	2,470	130	4	35.79	0	0-0	0/0	–	57	158
McGarrell Neil Christopher	12.7.1972		4	2000–2001	61	33	0	15.25	17	4-23	0/0	26.64	2	17
McLean Nixon Alexei McNamara	20.7.1973		19	1997–2000	368	46	0	12.26	44	3-53	0/0	42.56	5	45
McMorris Easton Dudley Ashton St John	4.4.1935		13	1957–1966	564	125	1	26.85	1	1-16	–/–	–	5	–
McWatt Clifford Aubrey	1.2.1922	20.7.1997	6	1953–1954	202	54	0	28.85	–	–	–/–	16.00	9/1	–
Madray Ivan Samuel	2.7.1934	23.4.2009	2	1957	3	2	0	1.00	0	0-12	0/0	–	2	–
Marshall Malcolm Denzil	18.4.1958	4.11.1999	81	1978–1991	1,810	92	0	18.85	376	7-22	22/4	20.94	25	136
Marshall Norman Edgar	27.2.1924	11.8.2007	1	1954	8	8	0	4.00	2	1-22	0/0	31.00	–	–
Marshall Roy Edwin	25.4.1930	27.10.1992	4	1951	143	30	0	20.42	0	0-3	0/0	–	1	–
Marshall Xavier Melbourne	27.3.1986		7	2005–2008	243	85	0	20.25	0	0-0	0/0	–	7	24/6
Martin Frank Reginald	12.10.1893	23.11.1967	9	1928–1930	486	123*	1	28.58	8	3-91	0/0	77.37	2	–
Martindale Emmanuel Alfred	25.11.1909	17.3.1972	10	1933–1939	58	22	0	5.27	37	5-22	3/0	21.72	5	–
Mattis Everton Hugh	11.4.1957		4	1980	145	71	0	29.00	0	0-4	0/0	–	3	2
Mendonca Ivor Leon	13.7.1934		2	1961	81	78	0	40.50	–	–	–/–	–	8/2	–
Merry Cyril Arthur	20.1.1911	19.4.1964	2	1933	34	13	0	8.50	–	–	–/–	–	1	–
Miller Nikita O'Neil	16.5.1982		1	2009	5	5	0	2.50	0	0-27	0/0	–	0	20/1
Miller Roy	24.12.1924		1	1952	23	23	0	23.00	0	0-28	0/0	–	0	–
Mohammed Dave	8.10.1979		5	2003–2006	225	52	0	32.14	13	3-98	0/0	51.38	1	7
Moodie George Horatio	26.11.1915	8.6.2002	1	1934	5	5	0	5.00	3	2-23	0/0	13.33	0	–
Morton Runako Shakur	22.7.1978		15	2005–2007	573	70*	0	22.03	0	0-4	0/0	–	20	54/5
Moseley Ezra Alphonsa	5.1.1958		2	1989	35	26	0	8.75	6	2-70	0/0	43.50	0	9
Murray David Anthony	29.5.1950		19	1977–1981	601	84	0	21.46	–	–	–/–	–	57/5	10
Murray Deryck Lance	20.5.1943		62	1963–1980	1,993	91	0	22.90	–	–	–/–	–	181/8	26
Murray Junior Randalph	20.1.1968		33	1992–2001	918	101*	1	22.39	–	–	–/–	–	99/3	55
Nagamootoo Mahendra Veeren	9.10.1975		5	2000–2002	185	68	0	26.42	12	3-119	0/0	53.08	2	24
Nanan Rangy	29.5.1953		1	1980	16	8	0	8.00	4	2-37	0/0	22.75	2	–
Nash Brendan Paul	14.12.1977		12	2008–2009	747	109	1	39.31	1	1-34	0/0	178.00	4	9
Neblett James Montague	13.11.1901	28.3.1959	1	1934	16	11*	0	16.00	1	1-44	0/0	75.00	0	–
Noreiga Jack Mollinson	15.4.1936	8.8.2003	4	1970	11	9	0	3.66	17	9-95	2/0	29.00	2	–
Nunes Robert Karl	7.6.1894	23.7.1958	4	1928–1929	245	92	0	30.62	–	–	–/–	–	2	–
Nurse Seymour MacDonald	10.11.1933		29	1959–1968	2,523	258	6	47.60	0	0-0	0/0	–	21	–
Padmore Albert Leroy	17.12.1946		2	1975–1976	8	8*	0	8.00	1	1-36	0/0	135.00	0	9
Pagon Donovan Jomo	13.9.1982		2	2004	37	35	0	12.33	–	–	–/–	–	0	–
Pairaudeau Bruce Hamilton	14.4.1931		13	1952–1957	454	115	1	21.61	0	0-3	0/0	–	6	–
Parchment Brenton Anthony	24.6.1982		2	2007	55	20	0	13.75	–	–	–/–	–	–	7/1

	Born	Died	Tests	Test Career	Runs	HS	100s	Avge	Wkts	BB	5/10	Avge	Ct/St	O/T
Parry Derick Recaldo	22.12.1954		12	1977–1979	381	65	0	22.41	23	5-15	1/0	40.69	4	6
Passailaigue Charles Clarence	4.8.1901	7.1.1972	1	1929	46	44	0	46.00	0			–	3	
Patterson Balfour Patrick	15.9.1961		28	1985–1992	145	21*	0	6.59	93	5-24	5/0	30.90	5	59
Payne Thelston Rodney O'Neale	13.2.1957		1	1985	5	5	0	5.00	0		–/–	–	5/1	7
Perry Nehemiah Odolphus	16.6.1968		4	1998–1999	74	26	0	12.33	10	5-70	1/0	44.60	1	21
Phillip Norbert	12.6.1948		9	1977–1978	297	47	0	29.70	28	4-48	–/–	37.17	5	1
Phillips Omar Jamel	12.10.1986		2	2009	160	94	0	40.00	0		–/–	–	2	
Pierre Lancelot Richard	5.6.1921	14.4.1989	1	1947	–	–	–	–	0	0-9	0/0	–	0	
Powell Daren Brentlyle	15.4.1978		37	2002–2008	407	36*	0	7.82	85	5-25	1/0	47.85	8	55/5
Powell Ricardo Lloyd	16.12.1978		2	1999–2003	53	30	0	17.66	0	0-13	0/0	–	1	109
Rae Allan Fitzroy	30.9.1922	27.2.2005	15	1948–1952	1,016	109	4	46.18	–			–	10	
Ragoonath Suruj	22.3.1968		2	1998	13	9	0	4.33	–			–	0	
Ramadhin Sonny	1.5.1929		43	1950–1960	361	44	0	8.20	158	7-49	10/1	28.98	9	1
Ramdass Ryan Rakesh	3.7.1983		1	2005	26	23	0	13.00	–			–	2	
Ramdin Denesh	13.3.1985		39	2005–2009	1,419	166	1	23.26	–			–	116/2	67/16
Rammarine Dinanath	4.6.1975		12	1997–2001	106	35*	0	6.23	45	5-78	1/0	30.73	8	4
Rampaul Ravindranath	15.10.1984		3	2009	65	40*	0	16.25	4	1-21	0/0	72.50	0	36/5
Reifer Floyd Lamonte	23.7.1972		6	1996–2009	111	29	0	9.25	–			–	6	8/1
Richards Dale Maurice	16.7.1976		2	2009	108	69	0	27.00	–			–	3	4/1
Richards Sir Isaac Vivian Alexander	7.3.1952		121	1974–1991	8,540	291	24	50.23	32	2-17	0/0	61.37	122	187
Richardson Richard Benjamin	12.1.1962		86	1983–1995	5,949	194	16	44.39	0	0-0	0/0	–	90	224
Rickards Kenneth Roy	22.8.1923	21.8.1995	2	1947–1951	104	67	0	34.66	–			–	0	
Roach Clifford Archibald	13.3.1904	16.4.1988	16	1928–1934	952	209	2	30.70	2	1-18	0/0	51.50	5	
Roach Kemar Andre Jamal	30.6.1988		2	2009–2009	46	17	0	6.57	20	6-48	1/0	29.30	3	7/2
Roberts Alphonso Theodore	18.9.1937	24.7.1996	1	1955	28	28	0	14.00	–			–	0	
Roberts Anderson Montgomery Everton CBE	29.1.1951		47	1973–1983	762	68	0	14.94	202	7-54	11/2	25.61	9	56
Roberts Lincoln Abraham	4.9.1974		1	1998	0	0	0	0.00	–		–/–	–	0	
Rodriguez William Vicente	25.6.1934		5	1961–1967	96	50	0	13.71	7	3-51	0/0	53.42	3	
Rose Franklyn Albert	1.2.1972		19	1996–2000	344	69	0	13.23	53	7-84	2/0	30.88	4	27
Rowe Lawrence George	8.1.1949		30	1971–1979	2,047	302	7	43.55	0	0-1	0/0	–	17	11
[2] St Hill Edwin Lloyd	9.3.1904	21.5.1957	2	1929	18	12	0	4.50	3	2-110	0/0	73.66	0	
[2] St Hill Wilton H.	6.7.1893	d unknown	3	1928–1929	117	38	0	19.50	0	0-9	0/0	–	0	
Sammy Darren Julius Garvey	20.12.1983		8	2007–2009	291	48	0	19.40	27	7-66	3/0	27.74	1	29/9
[2] Samuels Marlon Nathaniel	5.1.1981		29	2000–2007	1,408	105	2	28.73	7	2-49	0/0	127.00	8	107/6
[2] Samuels Robert George	13.3.1971		6	1995–1996	372	125	1	37.20	–		–/–	–	8	8

	Born	Died	Tests	Test Career	Runs	HS	100s	Avge	Wkts	BB	5/10	Avge	Ct/St	O/T
Sanford Adam	12.7.1975		11	2001–2003	72	18*	0	4.80	1	4-132	0/0	43.86	4	—
Sarwan Ramnaresh Ronnie	23.6.1980		83	1999–2009	5,759	291	15	41.73	23	4-37	0/0	50.56	50	152/11
Scarlett Reginald Osmond	15.8.1934		3	1959	54	29*	0	18.00	2	1-46	0/0	104.50	2	—
Scott Alfred Homer Patrick	29.7.1934		1	1952	5	5	0	5.00	0	0-52	0/0	—	1	—
Scott Oscar Charles ("Tommy")	14.8.1892	15.6.1961	8	1928–1930	171	35	0	17.10	22	5-266	1/0	42.04	0	—
Sealey Benjamin James	12.8.1899	12.9.1963	1	1933	41	29	0	20.50	1	1-10	0/0	10.00	0	—
Sealy James Edward Derrick	11.9.1912	3.1.1982	11	1929–1939	478	92	0	28.11	3	2-7	0/0	31.33	6/1	—
Shepherd John Neil	9.11.1943		5	1969–1970	77	32	0	9.62	19	5-104	1/0	25.21	4	—
Shillingford Grayson Cleophas	25.9.1944	23.12.2009	7	1969–1971	57	25	0	8.14	15	3-63	0/0	35.80	2	—
Shillingford Irvine Theodore	18.4.1944		4	1976–1977	218	120	1	31.14	—	—	–/–	—	1	2
Shivnarine Sewdatt	13.5.1952		8	1977–1978	379	63	0	29.15	1	1-13	0/0	167.00	6	1
Simmons Lendl Mark Platter	25.1.1985		3	2008–2009	87	24	0	14.50	1	1-60	0/0	139.00	3	147
Simmons Philip Verant	18.4.1963		26	1987–1997	1,002	110	1	22.26	4	2-34	0/0	64.25	26	143
Singh Charran Kamkaran	27.11.1935		2	1959	11	11	0	3.66	5	2-28	0/0	33.20	2	—
Small Joseph A.	3.11.1892	26.4.1958	3	1928–1929	79	52	0	13.16	3	2-67	0/0	61.33	3	—
Small Milton Aster	12.2.1964		2	1983–1984	3	3*	0	—	4	3-40	0/0	38.25	0	2
Smith Cameron Wilberforce	29.7.1933	9.9.1959	5	1960–1961	222	55	0	24.66	—	—	–/–	—	4/1	—
Smith Devon Sheldon	21.10.1981		31	2002–2009	1,315	108	1	24.81	—	—	–/–	—	27	32/6
Smith Dwayne Romel	12.4.1983		10	2003–2005	320	105*	1	24.61	7	3-71	0/0	49.14	9	71/5
Smith O'Neil Gordon ("Collie")	5.5.1933	9.9.1959	26	1954–1958	1,331	168	4	31.69	48	5-90	1/0	33.85	9	—
Sobers Sir Garfield St Aubrun	28.7.1936		93	1953–1973	8,032	365*	26	57.78	235	6-73	6/0	34.03	109	1
Solomon Joseph Stanislaus	26.8.1930		27	1958–1964	1,326	100*	1	34.00	4	1-20	0/0	67.00	13	—
Stayers Sven Conrad ("Charlie")	9.6.1937	6.1.2005	4	1961	58	35*	0	19.33	9	3-65	0/0	40.44	0	—
Stollmeyer Jeffrey Baxter	11.3.1921	10.9.1989	32	1939–1954	2,159	160	4	42.33	13	3-32	0/0	39.00	20	—
Stollmeyer Victor Humphrey	24.1.1916	21.9.1999	1	1939	96	96	0	96.00	—	—	–/–	—	0	—
Stuart Colin Ellsworth Laurie	28.9.1973		6	2000–2001	24	12*	0	3.42	20	3-33	0/0	31.40	2	5
Taylor Jaswick Ossie	3.1.1932	13.11.1999	3	1957–1958	4	4*	0	2.00	10	5-109	1/0	27.30	3	—
Taylor Jerome Everton	22.6.1984		29	2003–2009	629	106	1	15.72	82	5-11	3/0	35.64	5	62/12
Thompson Patterson Ian Chesterfield	26.9.1971		2	1995–1996	17	10*	0	8.50	5	2-58	0/0	43.00	0	2
Tonge Gavin Courtney	13.2.1983		1	2009	25	23*	0	25.00	1	1-28	0/0	113.00	0	5/1
Trim John	25.1.1915	12.11.1960	4	1947–1951	21	12	0	5.25	18	5-34	1/0	16.16	2	—
Valentine Alfred Louis	28.4.1930	11.5.2004	36	1950–1961	141	14	0	4.70	139	8-104	8/2	30.32	13	—
Valentine Vincent Adolphus	4.4.1908	6.7.1972	2	1933	35	19*	0	11.66	1	1-55	0/0	104.00	0	—
Walcott Sir Clyde Leopold	17.1.1926	26.8.2006	44	1947–1959	3,798	220	15	56.68	11	3-50	0/0	37.09	53/11	—
Walcott Leslie Arthur	18.1.1894	27.2.1984	1	1929	40	24	0	40.00	1	1-17	0/0	32.00	0	—

	Born	Died	Tests	Test Career	Runs	HS	100s	Avge	Wkts	BB	5/10	Avge	Ct/St	O/T
Wallace Philo Alphonso	2.8.1970		7	1997–1998	279	92	0	21.46	–	–	–/–	–	9	33
Walsh Courtney Andrew	30.10.1962		132	1984–2000	936	30*	0	7.54	519	7-37	22/3	24.44	29	205
Walton Chadwick Antonio Kirkpatrick	3.7.1985		1	2009	13	10	0	3.25					10	2
Washington Dwight Marlon	5.3.1983		1	2004	7	7*	0	–	0	0-20	0/0	–	3	
Watson Chester Donald	1.7.1938		7	1959–1961	12	5	0	2.40	19	4-62	0/0	38.10	1	
Weekes *Sir* Everton de Courcy	26.2.1925		48	1947–1957	4,455	207	15	58.61	1	1-8	0/0	77.00	49	
Weekes Kenneth Hunnell	24.1.1912	9.2.1998	2	1939	173	137	1	57.66			–/–		0	
White Anthony Wilbur	20.11.1938		2	1964	71	57*	0	23.66	3	2-34	0/0	50.66	1	
Wight Claude Vibart	28.7.1902	4.10.1969	2	1928–1929	67	23	0	22.33	0	0-6	0/0	–	0	
Wight George Leslie	28.5.1929	4.1.2004	1	1952	21	21	0	21.00	–		–/–		0	
Wiles Charles Archibald	11.8.1892	4.11.1957	1	1933	2	2	0	1.00			–/–		0	
Willett Elquemedo Tonito	1.5.1953		5	1972–1974	74	26	0	14.80	11	3-33	0/0	43.81	0	
Williams Alvadon Basil	21.11.1949		7	1977–1978	469	111	2	39.08			–/–		5	
Williams David	4.11.1963		11	1991–1997	242	65	0	13.44	–		–/–		40/2	36
Williams Ernest Albert Vivian ("Foffie")	10.4.1914	13.4.1997	4	1939–1947	113	72	0	18.83	9	3-51	0/0	26.77	2	
Williams Stuart Clayton	12.8.1969		31	1993–2001	1,183	128	1	24.14	0	0-19	0/0	–	27	57
Wishart Kenneth Leslie	28.11.1908	18.10.1972	1	1934	52	52	0	26.00			–/–		0	
Worrell *Sir* Frank Mortimer Maglinne	1.8.1924	13.3.1967	51	1947–1963	3,860	261	9	49.48	69	7-70	2/0	38.72	43	

NEW ZEALAND (244 players)

	Born	Died	Tests	Test Career	Runs	HS	100s	Avge	Wkts	BB	5/10	Avge	Ct/St	O/T
Adams Andre Ryan	17.1.1975		1	2001	18	11	0	9.00	6	3-44	0/0	17.50	1	42/4
Alabaster John Chaloner	11.7.1930		21	1955–1971	272	34	0	9.71	49	4-46	0/0	38.02	7	
Allcott Cyril Francis Walter	7.10.1896	19.11.1973	6	1929–1931	113	33	0	22.60	6	2-102	0/0	90.16	3	
Allott Geoffrey Ian	24.12.1971		10	1995–1999	27	8*	0	3.37	19	4-74	0/0	58.47	2	31
Anderson Robert Wickham	2.10.1948		9	1976–1978	423	92	0	23.50			–/–		1	2
Anderson William McDougall	8.10.1919	21.12.1979	1	1945	5	4	0	2.50					0	
Andrews Bryan	4.4.1945		2	1973	22	17	0	22.00	2	2-40	0/0	77.00	0	
Astle Nathan John	15.9.1971		81	1995–2006	4,702	222	11	37.02	51	3-27	0/0	42.01	70	223/4
Badcock Frederick Theodore ("Ted")	9.8.1897	19.9.1982	7	1929–1932	137	64	0	19.57	16	4-80	0/0	38.12	1	
Barber Richard Trevor	3.6.1925		1	1955	17	12	0	8.50					1	
Bartlett Gary Alex	3.2.1941		10	1961–1967	263	40	0	15.47	24	6-38	1/0	33.00	8	
Barton Paul Thomas	9.10.1935		7	1961–1962	285	109	1	20.35	–		–/–		4	

Name	Born	Died	Tests	Test Career	Runs	HS	100s	Avge	Wkts	BB	5/10	Avge	Ct/St	O/T
Beard Donald Derek	14.1.1920	15.7.1982	4	1951–1955	101	31	0	20.20	9	3-22	0/0	33.55	2	—
Beck John Edward Francis	1.8.1934	23.4.2000	8	1953–1955	394	99	0	26.26	–	–	–/–	–	0	7
Bell Matthew David	25.2.1977		18	1998–2007	729	107	2	24.30	–	–	–/–	–	19	
Bell William	5.9.1931	23.7.2002	2	1953	21	21*	0	–	2	1-54	0/0	117.50	1	
Bilby Grahame Paul	7.5.1941		2	1965	55	28	0	13.75	–	–	–/–	–	3	
Blain Tony Elston	17.2.1962		11	1986–1993	456	78	0	26.82	–	–	–/–	–	192	38
Blair Robert William	23.6.1932		19	1952–1963	189	64*	0	6.75	43	4-85	0/0	35.23	5	
Blunt Roger Charles	3.11.1900	22.6.1966	9	1929–1931	330	96	0	27.50	12	3-17	0/0	39.33	5	
Bolton Bruce Alfred	31.5.1935		2	1958	59	33	0	19.66	–	–	–/–	–	1	
Bond Shane Edward	7.6.1975		18	2001–2009	168	41*	0	12.92	87	6-51	5/1	22.09	8	77/13
Boock Stephen Lewis	20.9.1951		30	1977–1988	207	37	0	6.27	74	7-87	4/0	34.64	14	14
2 Bracewell Brendon Paul	14.9.1959		6	1978–1984	24	8	0	2.40	14	3-110	0/0	41.78	1	1
2 Bracewell John Garry	15.4.1958		41	1980–1990	1,001	110	1	20.42	102	6-32	4/1	35.81	31	53
1 Bradburn Grant Eric	26.5.1966		7	1990–2000	105	30*	0	13.12	6	3-134	0/0	76.66	6	11
1 Bradburn Wynne Pennell	24.11.1938	25.9.2008	4	1963	62	32	0	15.50	–	–	–/–	–	2	
Brown Vaughan Raymond	3.11.1959		2	1985	51	36*	0	25.50	1	1-17	0/0	176.00	3	3
Burgess Mark Gordon	17.7.1944		50	1967–1980	2,684	119*	5	31.20	6	3-23	0/0	35.33	34	26
Burke Cecil	27.3.1914	4.8.1997	1	1945	4	3	0	2.00	2	2-30	0/0	15.00	0	
Burtt Thomas Browning	22.1.1915	24.5.1988	10	1946–1952	252	42	0	21.00	33	6-162	3/0	35.45	2	
1 Butler Ian Gareth	24.11.1981		8	2001–2004	76	26	0	9.50	24	6-46	1/0	36.83	4	24/12
Butterfield Leonard Arthur	29.8.1913	5.7.1999	1	1945	0	0	0	0.00	0	0-24	0/0	–	0	
1 Cairns Bernard Lance	10.10.1949		43	1973–1985	928	64	0	16.28	130	7-74	6/1	32.91	30	78
1 Cairns Christopher Lance	13.6.1970		62	1989–2004	3,320	158	5	33.53	218	7-27	13/1	29.40	14	214‡2
Cameron Francis James MBE	1.6.1932		19	1961–1965	116	27*	0	11.60	62	5-34	3/0	29.82	1	
Cave Henry Butler	10.10.1922	15.9.1989	19	1949–1958	229	22*	0	8.80	34	4-21	0/0	43.14	8	
Chapple Murray Ernest	25.7.1930	31.7.1985	14	1952–1965	497	76	0	19.11	1	1-24	0/0	84.00	10	
Chatfield Ewen John MBE	3.7.1950		43	1974–1988	180	21*	0	8.57	123	6-73	3/1	32.17	7	114
Cleverley Donald Charles	23.12.1909	16.2.2004	2	1931–1945	19	10*	0	19.00	0	0-51	0/0	–	0	
Collinge Richard Owen	2.4.1946		35	1964–1978	533	68*	0	14.40	116	6-63	3/0	29.25	10	15
Colquhoun Ian Alexander	8.6.1924	26.2.2005	2	1954	1	1*	0	0.50	–	–	–/–	–	4	
Coney Jeremy Vernon MBE	21.6.1952		52	1973–1986	2,668	174*	3	37.57	27	3-28	0/0	35.77	64	88
Congdon Bevan Ernest OBE	11.2.1938		61	1964–1978	3,448	176	7	32.22	59	5-65	1/0	36.50	44	11
Cowie John OBE	30.3.1912	3.6.1994	9	1937–1949	90	45	0	10.00	45	6-40	4/1	21.53	3	
Cresswell George Fenwick	22.3.1915	10.1.1966	3	1949–1950	14	12*	0	7.00	13	6-168	1/0	22.46	0	
Cromb Ian Burns	25.6.1905	6.3.1984	5	1931–1937	123	51*	0	20.50	8	3-113	0/0	55.25	1	

	Born	Died	Tests	Test Career	Runs	HS	100s	Avge	Wkts	BB	5/10	Avge	Ct/St	O/T
²Crowe Jeffrey John.	14.9.1958		39	1982–1989	1,601	128	3	26.24	–	0-0	0/0	–	41	75
²Crowe Martin David MBE.	22.9.1962		77	1981–1995	5,444	299	17	45.36	14	2-25	0/0	48.28	71	143
Cumming Craig Derek	31.8.1975		11	2004–2007	441	74	0	25.94	–	–	–/–	–	3	13
Cunis Robert Smith.	5.1.1941	9.8.2008	20	1963–1971	295	33	0	12.82	51	6-76	1/0	37.00	1	
D'Arcy John William	23.4.1936		5	1958	136	33	0	13.60	–	–	–/–	–	0	
Davis Heath Te-Ihi-O-Te-Rangi	30.11.1971		5	1994–1997	20	8*	0	6.66	17	5-63	1/0	29.35	4	11
de Groen Richard Paul	5.8.1962		5	1993–1994	45	26	0	7.50	11	3-40	0/0	45.90	0	12
Dempster Charles Stewart	15.11.1903	14.2.1974	10	1929–1932	723	136	2	65.72	0	0-10	0/0	–	2	
Dempster Eric William	25.1.1925		5	1952–1953	106	47	0	17.66	2	1-24	0/0	109.50	1	
Dick Arthur Edward	10.10.1936		17	1961–1965	370	50*	0	14.23	–	–	–/–	–	47/4	
Dickinson George Ritchie	11.3.1903	17.3.1978	3	1929–1931	31	11	0	6.20	8	3-66	0/0	30.62	3	
Donnelly Martin Paterson.	17.10.1917	22.10.1999	7	1937–1949	582	206	1	52.90	0	0-20	0/0	–	7	
Doull Simon Blair	6.8.1969		32	1992–1999	570	46	0	14.61	98	7-65	6/0	29.30	16	42
Dowling Graham Thorne OBE.	4.3.1937		39	1961–1971	2,306	239	3	31.16	1	1-19	0/0	19.00	23	
Drum Christopher James	10.7.1974		5	2000–2001	10	4	0	3.33	16	3-36	0/0	30.12	4	5
Dunning John Angus.	6.2.1903	24.6.1971	4	1932–1937	38	19	0	7.60	5	2-35	0/0	98.60	2	
Edgar Bruce Adrian	23.11.1956		39	1978–1986	1,958	161	3	30.59	0	0-3	0/0	–	14	64
Edwards Graham Neil ("Jock")	27.5.1955		8	1976–1980	377	55	0	25.13	–	–	–/–	–	4	6
Elliott Grant David	21.3.1979		5	2007–2009	86	25	0	10.75	4	2-8	0/0	35.00	7	28/1
Emery Raymond William George	28.3.1915	18.12.1982	2	1951	46	28	0	11.50	2	2-52	0/0	26.00	0	
Fisher Frederick Eric.	28.7.1924	19.6.1996	1	1952	23	14	0	11.50	1	1-78	0/0	78.00	0	
Fleming Stephen Paul	1.4.1973		111	1993–2007	7,172	274*	9	40.06	–	–	–/–	–	171	279/5
Flynn Daniel Raymond	16.4.1985		16	2008–2009	689	95	0	28.70	–	–	–/–	–	7	16/4
Foley Henry	28.11.1906	16.10.1948	1	1929	4	2	0	2.00	–	–	–/–	–	0	
Franklin James Edward Charles.	7.11.1980		26	2000–2008	644	122*	1	21.46	80	6-119	3/0	32.65	11	69/10
Franklin Trevor John	15.3.1962		21	1983–1990	828	101	1	23.00	–	–	–/–	–	8	3
Freeman Douglas Linford	8.9.1914	31.5.1994	2	1932	2	1	0	1.00	1	1-91	0/0	169.00	0	
Fulton Peter Gordon	1.2.1979		10	2005–2009	314	75	0	20.93	–	–	–/–	–	12	49/11
Gallichan Norman	3.6.1906	25.3.1969	1	1937	32	30	0	16.00	3	3-99	0/0	37.66	0	
Gedye Sidney Graham	2.5.1929		4	1963–1964	193	55	0	24.12	–	–	–/–	–	1	
Germon Lee Kenneth	4.11.1968		12	1995–1996	382	55	0	21.22	–	–	–/–	–	27/2	37
Gillespie Mark Raymond	17.10.1979		3	2007–2008	25	16*	0	6.25	11	5-136	1/0	34.54	1	32/11
Gillespie Stuart Ross	2.3.1957		1	1985	28	28	0	28.00	1	1-79	0/0	79.00	0	19
Gray Evan John	18.11.1954		10	1983–1988	248	50	0	15.50	17	3-73	0/0	52.11	6	10
Greatbatch Mark John	11.12.1963		41	1987–1996	2,021	146*	3	30.62	0	0-0	0/0	–	27	84

Name	Born	Died	Tests	Test Career	Runs	HS	100s	Avge	Wkts	BB	5/10	Avge	Ct/St	O/T
Guillen Simpson Clairmonte ("Sammy")	24.9.1924		3†	1955	98	41	0	16.33	–	–	–/–	–	4/1	
Guptill Martin James	30.9.1986		8	2008–2009	329	60	0	23.50	3	3-37	0/0	12.33	7	22/12
Guy John William	29.8.1934		12	1955–1961	440	102	1	20.95	–	–	–/–	–	2	
[1,2] Hadlee Dayle Robert	6.1.1948		26	1969–1977	530	56	0	14.32	71	4-30	0/0	33.64	8	11
[1,2] Hadlee Sir Richard John	3.7.1951		86	1972–1990	3,124	151*	2	27.16	431	9-52	36/9	22.29	39	115
[1] Hadlee Walter Arnold CBE	4.6.1915	29.9.2006	11	1937–1950	543	116	0	30.16	–	–	–/–	–	6	
Harford Noel Sherwin	30.8.1930	30.3.1981	8	1955–1958	229	93	0	15.26	–	–	–/–	–	0	
Harford Roy Ivan	30.5.1936		3	1967	7	6	0	2.33	–	–	–/–	–	11	
[1] Harris Chris Zinzan	20.11.1969		23	1992–2002	777	71	0	20.44	16	2-16	0/0	73.12	14	250
[1] Harris Parke Gerald Zinzan	18.7.1927	1.12.1991	9	1955–1964	378	101	0	22.23	0	0-14	0/0	–	6	
Harris Roger Meredith	27.7.1933		2	1958	31	13	0	10.33	–	–	–/–	–	0	
[2] Hart Matthew Norman	16.5.1972		14	1993–1995	353	45	0	17.65	29	5-77	1/0	49.58	9	13
[2] Hart Robert Garry	2.12.1974		11	2002–2003	260	57*	0	16.25	–	–	–/–	–	29/1	2
Hartland Blair Robert	22.10.1966		9	1991–1994	303	52	0	16.83	–	–	–/–	–	5	16
Haslam Mark James	26.9.1972		4	1992–1995	4	3	0	4.00	2	0-3	0/0	122.50	2	1
Hastings Brian Frederick	23.3.1940		31	1968–1975	1,510	117*	4	30.20	30	4-36	0/0	40.56	23	11
Hayes Chris Arthur	11.11.1927	25.12.2007	15	1950–1958	73	19	0	4.86	2	2-38	0/0	32.00	3	
Henderson Matthew	2.8.1895	17.6.1970	1	1929	8	6	0	8.00	0	0-4	0/0	–	1	
Hopkins Gareth James	24.11.1976		1	2008	27	15	0	13.50	–	–	–/–	–	3	14/1
[2] Horne Matthew Jeffery	5.12.1970		35	1996–2003	1,788	157	4	28.38	–	–	–/–	–	17	50
[2] Horne Philip Andrew	21.1.1960		4	1986–1990	71	27	0	10.14	–	–	–/–	–	3	4
Hough Kenneth William	24.10.1928	20.9.2009	2	1958	62	31*	0	62.00	6	3-79	0/0	29.16		31/5
How Jamie Michael	19.5.1981		19	2005–2008	772	92	1	22.70	0	0-0	0/0	–	18	
[1] Howarth Geoffrey Philip OBE	29.3.1951		47	1974–1984	2,531	147	0	32.44	3	1-13	0/0	90.33	29	70
[2] Howarth Hedley John	25.12.1942	7.11.2008	30	1972–1976	291	61	0	12.12	86	5-34	2/0	36.95	33	9
James Kenneth Cecil	12.3.1904	21.8.1976	11	1929–1932	52	14	0	4.72	–	–	–/–	–	11/5	
Jarvis Terrence Wayne	29.7.1944		13	1964–1972	625	182	1	29.76	0	0-0	0/0	–	3	
Jones Andrew Howard	9.5.1959		39	1986–1994	2,922	186	2	44.27	1	1-40	0/0	194.00	25	87
Jones Richard Andrew	22.10.1973		1	2003	23	16	0	11.50	–	–	–/–	–	0	5
Kennedy Robert John	3.6.1972		4	1995	28	22	0	7.00	6	3-28	0/0	63.33	4	7
Kerr John Lambert	28.12.1910	27.5.2007	7	1931–1937	212	59	0	19.27	–	–	–/–	–	1	
Kuggeleijn Christopher Mary	10.5.1956		2	1988	7	7	0	1.75	1	1-50	0/0	67.00	5	16
Larsen Gavin Rolf	27.9.1962		8	1994–1995	127	26*	0	14.11	24	3-57	0/0	28.70	5	121
Latham Rodney Terry	12.6.1961		4	1991–1992	219	119	1	31.28	0	0-6	0/0	–		33
Lees Warren Kenneth MBE	19.3.1952		21	1976–1983	778	152	1	23.57	0	0-4	0/0	–	52/7	31

	Born	Died	Tests	Test Career	Runs	HS	100s	Avge	Wkts	BB	5/10	Avge	Ct/St	O/T
Leggat Ian Bruce	7.6.1930	9.3.1973	1	1953	0	0	0	0.00	–	0-6	0/0	–	2	–
Leggat John Gordon	27.5.1926	24.1.1973	9	1951–1955	351	61	0	21.93	–	–	–/–	–	2	
Lissette Allen Fisher	6.11.1919		2	1955	2	1*	0	1.00	3	2-73	0/0	41.33	0	
Loveridge Greg Riaka	15.1.1975		1	1995	4	4*	0	–	–	–	–/–	–	1	
Lowry Thomas Coleman	17.2.1898	20.7.1976	7	1929–1931	223	80	0	27.87	0	0-0	0/0	–	8	
McCullum Brendon Barrie	27.9.1981		49	2003–2009	2,474	143	3	32.12	–	–	–/–	–	154/10	163/30
McEwan Paul Ernest	19.12.1953		4	1979–1984	96	40*	0	16.00	0	0-6	0/0	–	4	17
MacGibbon Anthony Roy	28.8.1924		26	1950–1958	814	66	0	19.85	70	5-64	1/0	30.85	13	
McGirr Herbert Mendelson	5.11.1891	14.4.1964	2	1929	51	51	0	51.00	1	1-65	0/0	115.00	0	
McGregor Spencer Noel	18.12.1931	21.11.2007	25	1954–1964	892	111	0	19.82	–	–	–/–	–	9	
McIntosh Timothy Gavin	4.12.1979		10	2008–2009	472	136	1	27.76	–	–	–/–	–	6	
McLeod Edwin George	14.10.1900	14.9.1989	1	1929	18	16	0	18.00	0	0-5	0/0	–	0	
McMahon Trevor George	8.11.1929		5	1955	7	4*	0	2.33	–	–	–/–	–	7/1	
McMillan Craig Douglas	13.9.1976		55	1997–2004	3,116	142	6	38.46	28	3-48	0/0	44.89	22	197/8
McRae Donald Alexander Noel	25.12.1912	10.8.1986	1	1945	8	8	0	4.00	0	0-44	0/0	–	0	
[2] Marshall Hamish John Hamilton	15.2.1979		13	2000–2005	652	160	2	38.35	0	0-4	0/0	–	1	66/3
[2] Marshall James Andrew Hamilton	15.2.1979		7	2004–2008	218	52	0	19.81	–	–	–/–	–	5	10/3
Martin Christopher Stewart	10.12.1974		53	2000–2009	83	12*	0	2.24	176	6-54	8/1	33.61	12	20/6
Mason Michael James	27.8.1974		1	2003	3	3	0	1.50	0	0-32	0/0	–	0	25/3
Matheson Alexander Malcolm	27.2.1906	31.12.1985	2	1929–1931	7	7	0	7.00	2	2-7	0/0	68.00	2	
Meale Trevor	11.11.1928		2	1958	21	10	0	5.25	–	–	–/–	–	0	
Merritt William Edward	18.8.1908	9.6.1977	6	1929–1931	73	19	0	10.42	12	4-104	0/0	51.41	2	
Meuli Edgar Milton	20.2.1926	15.4.2007	1	1952	38	23	0	19.00	–	–	–/–	–	2	
Milburn Barry Douglas	24.11.1943		3	1968	8	4*	0	8.00	–	–	–/–	–	6/2	
Miller Lawrence Somerville Martin	31.3.1923	17.12.1996	13	1952–1958	346	47	0	13.84	1	0-1	0/0	–	1	
Mills John Ernest	3.9.1905	11.12.1972	7	1929–1932	241	117	1	26.77	–	–	–/–	–	1	110/15
Mills Kyle David	15.3.1979		19	2004–2008	289	57	0	11.56	44	4-16	0/0	33.02	4	
Moir Alexander McKenzie	17.7.1919	17.6.2000	17	1950–1958	327	41*	0	14.86	28	6-155	2/0	50.64	2	
Moloney Denis Andrew Robert ("Sonny")	11.8.1910	15.7.1942	3	1937	156	64	0	26.00	0	0-9	0/0	–	3	
Mooney Francis Leonard Hugh	26.5.1921	8.3.2004	14	1949–1953	343	46	0	17.15	0	0-0	0/0	–	22/8	
Morgan Ross Winston	12.2.1941		20	1964–1971	734	97	0	22.24	5	1-16	0/0	121.80	12	
Morrison Bruce Donald	17.12.1933		1	1962	10	10	0	5.00	2	2-129	0/0	64.50	1	
Morrison Daniel Kyle	3.2.1966		48	1987–1996	379	42	0	8.42	160	7-89	1/0	34.68	14	96
Morrison John Francis MacLean	27.8.1947		17	1973–1981	656	117	1	22.62	2	2-52	0/0	35.50	9	18
Motz Richard Charles	12.1.1940	29.4.2007	32	1961–1969	612	60	0	11.54	100	6-63	5/0	31.48	9	

	Born	Died	Tests	Test Career	Runs	HS	100s	Avge	Wkts	BB	5/10	Avge	Ct/St	O/T
Murray Bruce Alexander Grenfell	18.9.1940		13	1967–1970	598	90	0	23.92	1	1-0	0/0	0.00	21	1
Murray Darrin James	4.9.1967		8	1994	303	52	0	20.20				–	6	
Nash Dion Joseph	20.11.1971		32	1992–2001	729	89*	0	23.51	93	6-27	3/1	28.48	13	81
Newman Sir Jack	3.7.1902	23.9.1996	3	1931–1932	33	19	0	8.25	2	2-76	0/0	127.00	0	
O'Brien Iain Edward	10.7.1976		22	2004–2009	219	31	0	7.55	73	6-75	0/0	33.27	7	10/4
O'Connor Shayne Barry	15.11.1973		19	1997–2001	103	20	0	5.72	53	5-51	1/0	32.52	6	38
Oram Jacob David Philip	28.7.1978		33	2002–2009	1,780	133	5	36.32	60	4-41	0/0	33.05	15	135/20
O'Sullivan David Robert	16.11.1944		11	1972–1976	158	23*	0	9.29	18	5-148	1/0	67.83	2	3
Overton Guy William Fitzroy	8.6.1919	7.9.1993	3	1953	8	3*	0	1.60	9	3-65	0/0	28.66	1	
Owens Michael Barry	11.11.1969		8	1992–1994	16	8*	0	2.66	17	4-99	0/0	34.41	3	1
Page Milford Laurenson ("Curly")	8.5.1902	13.2.1987	14	1929–1937	492	104	1	24.60	5	2-21	0/0	46.20	6	
Papps Michael Hugh William	2.7.1979		8	2003–2007	246	86	0	16.40				–	11	6
[2]Parker John Morton	21.2.1951		36	1972–1980	1,498	121	3	24.55	1	1-24	0/0	24.00	30	24
[2]Parker Norman Murray	28.8.1948		3	1976	89	40	0	14.83				–	2	1
Parore Adam Craig	23.1.1971		78	1990–2001	2,865	110	2	26.28				–	197/7	179
Patel Dipak Narshibhai	25.10.1958		37	1986–1996	1,200	99	0	20.68	75	6-50	3/0	42.05	15	75
Patel Jeetan Shashi	7.5.1980		9	2005–2009	131	27*	0	13.10	33	5-110	1/0	39.06	5	39/11
Petherick Peter James	25.9.1942		6	1976	34	13	0	4.85	16	3-90	0/0	42.81	4	
Petrie Eric Charlton	22.5.1927	14.8.2004	14	1955–1965	258	55	0	12.90				–	25	
Playle William Rodger	1.12.1938		8	1958–1962	151	65	0	10.06				–	4	
Pocock Blair Andrew	18.6.1971		15	1993–1997	665	85	2	22.93	0	0-10	0/0	–	5	3
Pollard Victor	7.9.1945		32	1964–1973	1,266	116	5	24.34	40	3-3	0/0	46.32	19	
Poore Matt Beresford	1.6.1930		14	1952–1955	355	45	0	15.43	9	2-28	0/0	40.77	1	18
Priest Mark Wellings	12.8.1961		3	1990–1997	56	26	0	14.00	3	2-42	0/0	52.66	0	
Pringle Christopher	26.1.1968		14	1990–1994	175	30	0	10.29	30	7-52	1/1	46.30	3	64
Puna Narotam	28.10.1929	7.6.1996	3	1965	31	18*	0	15.50	4	2-40	0/0	60.00	5	
Rabone Geoffrey Osborne	6.11.1921	19.1.2006	12	1949–1954	562	107	5	31.22	16	6-68	1/0	39.68	5	3
[1]Redmond Aaron James	23.9.1979		7	2008–2009	299	83	0	23.00	3	2-47	0/0	20.66	5	
Redmond Rodney Ernest	29.12.1944		1	1972	163	107	1	81.50				–	0	
Reid John Fulton	3.3.1956		19	1978–1985	1,296	180	6	46.28	0	0-0	0/0	–	9	25
Reid John Richard OBE	3.6.1928		58	1949–1965	3,428	142	6	33.28	85	6-60	1/0	33.35	43/1	4
Richardson Mark Hunter	11.6.1971		38	2000–2004	2,776	145	4	44.77	1	1-16	0/0	21.00	26	
Roberts Albert William	20.8.1909	13.5.1978	5	1929–1937	248	66*	0	27.55	7	4-101	0/0	29.85	5	1
Roberts Andrew Duncan Glenn	6.5.1947	26.10.1989	7	1975–1976	254	84*	0	23.09	4	1-12	0/0	45.50	4	10
Robertson Gary Keith	15.7.1960		1	1985	12	12	0	12.00	1	1-91	0/0	91.00	0	

	Born	Died	Tests	Test Career	Runs	HS	100s	Avge	Wkts	BB	5/10	Avge	Ct/St	O/T
Rowe Charles Gordon	30.6.1915	9.6.1995	1	1945	0	0	0	0.00	-	-	-/-	-	1	
Rutherford Kenneth Robert	26.10.1965		56	1984–1994	2,465	107*	3	27.08	1	1-38	0/0	161.00	32	121
Ryder Jesse Daniel	6.8.1984		11	2008–2009	898	201	3	49.88	4	2-7	0/0	53.00	8	21/9
Scott Roy Hamilton	6.3.1917	5.8.2005	1	1946	18	18	0	18.00	1	1-74	0/0	74.00		
Scott Verdun John	31.7.1916	2.8.1980	10	1945–1951	458	84	0	28.62	0	0-9	0/0	-	7	
Sewell David Graham	20.10.1977		1	1997	1	1*	0	-	0	0-5	0/0	-		
Shrimpton Michael John Froud	23.6.1940		10	1962–1973	265	46	0	13.94	5	3-35	0/0	31.60	2	
Sinclair Barry Whitley	23.10.1936		21	1962–1967	1,148	138	3	29.43	5	2-32	0/0	16.00	8	
Sinclair Ian McKay	1.6.1933		2	1955	25	18*	0	8.33	1	1-79	0/0	120.00		
Sinclair Mathew Stuart	9.11.1975		32	1999–2007	1,595	214	3	32.55	0	0-13	0/0	-	31	54/2
Smith Frank Brunton	13.3.1922	6.7.1997	4	1946–1951	237	96	0	47.40	1	1-113	0/0	113.00	0	
Smith Horace Dennis	8.1.1913	25.1.1986	1	1932	4	4	0	4.00	0	0-5	0/0	-	0	
Smith Ian David Stockley MBE	28.2.1957		63	1980–1991	1,815	173	2	25.56	-	-	-/-	-	168/8	98
Snedden Colin Alexander	7.1.1918		1	1946	-	-	-	-	0	0-46	0/0	-		
Snedden Martin Colin	23.11.1958		25	1980–1990	327	33*	0	14.86	58	5-68	1/0	37.91	7	93
Southee Timothy Grant	11.12.1988		6	2007–2009	127	77*	0	15.87	15	5-55	1/0	46.73	4	24/9
Sparling John Trevor	24.7.1938		11	1958–1963	229	50	0	12.72	5	1-9	0/0	65.40		
Spearman Craig Murray	4.7.1972		19	1995–2000	922	112	1	26.34	-	-	-/-	-	21	51
Stead Gary Raymond	9.1.1972		5	1998–1999	278	78	0	34.75	0	0-1	0/0	-	2	
Stirling Derek Alexander	5.10.1961		6	1984–1986	108	26	0	15.42	13	4-88	0/0	46.23	1	6
Styris Scott Bernard	10.7.1975		29	2002–2007	1,586	170	5	36.04	20	3-28	0/0	50.75	23	160/22
Su'a Murphy Logo	7.11.1966		13	1991–1994	165	44	0	12.69	36	5-73	2/0	38.25	8	12
Sutcliffe Bert MBE	17.11.1923	20.4.2001	42	1946–1965	2,727	230*	5	40.10	4	2-38	0/0	86.00	20	
Taylor Bruce Richard	12.7.1943		30	1964–1973	898	124	2	20.40	111	7-74	4/0	26.60	10	2
Taylor Donald Dougald	2.3.1923	5.12.1980	3	1946–1955	159	77	0	31.80	-	-	-/-	-	2	
Taylor Lutero Ross Poutoa Lote	8.3.1984		22	2007–2009	1,644	154*	4	42.15	0	0-4	0/0	-	41	73/24
Thomson Keith	26.2.1941		2	1967	94	69	0	31.33	1	1-9	0/0	9.00		
Thomson Shane Alexander	27.11.1969		19	1989–1995	958	120*	1	30.90	19	3-63	0/0	50.15	7	56
Tindill Eric William Thomas	18.12.1910		5	1937–1946	73	37*	0	9.12	-	-	-/-	-	6/1	
Troup Gary Bertram	3.10.1952		15	1976–1985	55	13*	0	4.58	39	6-95	1/0	37.28	2	22
Truscott Peter Bennetts	14.8.1941		1	1964	29	26	0	14.50	-	-	-/-	-		
Tuffey Daryl Raymond	11.6.1978		24	1999–2009	349	80*	0	13.96	74	6-54	2/0	30.79	13	83/1
Turner Glenn Maitland	26.5.1947		41	1968–1982	2,991	259	7	44.64	0	0-5	0/0	-	42	41
Twose Roger Graham	17.4.1968		16	1995–1999	628	94	0	25.12	3	2-36	0/0	43.33	5	87
Vance Robert Howard	31.3.1955		4	1987–1989	207	68	0	29.57	-	-	-/-	-	0	8

	Born	Died	Tests	Test Career	Runs	HS	100s	Avge	Wkts	BB	5/10	Avge	Ct/St	O/T
Vaughan Justin Thomas Caldwell	30.8.1967		6	1992–1996	201	44	0	18.27	11	4-27	0/0	40.90	4	18
Vettori Daniel Luca	27.1.1979		96	1996–2009	3,771	140	5	30.90	312	7-87	18/3	33.36	55	2444/18
Vincent Lou	11.11.1978		23	2001–2007	1,332	224	3	34.15	–	–	–	–	19	102/9
1 **Vivian Graham Ellery**	28.2.1946		5	1964–1971	110	43	0	18.33	1	1-14	0/0	107.00	3	
1 **Vivian Henry**	4.11.1912	12.8.1983	7	1931–1937	421	100	1	42.10	17	4-58	0/0	38.23	4	
Wadsworth Kenneth John	30.11.1946	19.8.1976	33	1969–1975	1,010	80	0	21.48	–	–	–	–	92/4	13
Walker Brooke Graeme Keith	25.3.1977		5	2000–2002	118	27*	0	19.66	5	2-92	0/0	79.80	0	11
Wallace Walter Mervyn	19.12.1916	21.3.2008	13	1937–1952	439	66	0	20.90	–	–	–	–	5	
Walmsley Kerry Peter	23.8.1973		3	1994–2000	13	5	0	2.60	9	3-70	0/0	43.44	0	2
Ward John Thomas	11.3.1937		8	1963–1967	75	35*	0	12.50	–	–	–	–	16/1	
Watling Bradley-John	9.7.1985		1	2009	78	60*	0	78.00	–	–	–	–	0	0/2
Watson William	31.8.1965	15.11.1996	15	1986–1993	60	11	0	5.00	40	6-78	1/0	34.67	4	61
Watt Leslie	17.9.1924		1	1954	2	2	0	1.00	–	–	–	–	0	
Webb Murray George	22.6.1947		3	1970–1973	12	2	0	6.00	4	2-114	0/0	117.75	0	
Webb Peter Neil	14.7.1957		2	1979	11	5	0	3.66	–	–	–	–	2	5
Weir Gordon Lindsay	2.6.1908	31.10.2003	11	1929–1937	416	74*	0	29.71	7	3-38	0/0	29.85	3	
White David John	26.6.1961		2	1990	31	18	0	7.75	–	–	–	–	0	3
Whitelaw Paul Erskine	10.2.1910	28.8.1988	2	1932	64	30	0	32.00	–	–	–	–	0	
Wiseman Paul John	4.5.1970		25	1997–2004	366	30	0	14.07	61	5-82	0/0	47.59	11	15
Wright John Geoffrey MBE	5.7.1954		82	1977–1992	5,334	185	12	37.82	0	0-1	0/0	–	38	149
Young Bryan Andrew	3.11.1964		35	1993–1998	2,034	267*	2	31.78	–	–	–	–	54	74
Yuile Bryan William	29.10.1941		17	1962–1969	481	64	0	17.81	34	4-43	0/0	35.67	12	

§ *Vettori's figures exclude eight runs and one wicket for the ICC World XI v Australia in the Super Series Test in 2005-06.*

INDIA (261 players)

	Born	Died	Tests	Test Career	Runs	HS	100s	Avge	Wkts	BB	5/10	Avge	Ct/St	O/T
Abid Ali Syed	9.9.1941		29	1967–1974	1,018	81	0	20.36	47	6-55	1/0	42.12	32	5
Adhikari Hemchandra Ramachandra	31.7.1919	25.10.2003	21	1947–1958	872	114*	1	31.14	3	3-68	0/0	27.33	8	
Agarkar Ajit Bhalchandra	4.12.1977		26	1998–2005	571	109*	1	16.79	58	6-41	1/0	47.32	6	191/4
2 **Amar Singh Ladha**	4.12.1910	21.5.1940	7	1932–1936	292	51	0	22.46	28	7-86	2/0	30.64	3	
1,2 **Amarnath Mohinder**	24.9.1950		69	1969–1987	4,378	138	11	42.50	32	4-63	0/0	55.68	47	85
1 **Amarnath Nanik ("Lala")**	11.9.1911	5.8.2000	24	1933–1952	878	118	1	24.38	45	5-96	2/0	32.91	13	
1,2 **Amarnath Surinder**	30.12.1948		10	1975–1978	550	124	1	30.55	1	1-5	0/0	5.00	4	3

	Born	Died	Tests	Test Career	Runs	HS	100s	Avge	Wkts	BB	5/10	Avge	Ct/St	O/T
Amir Elahi	1.9.1908	28.12.1980	1†	1947	17	13	0	8.50	–	–	–/–	–	0	37
Amre Pravin Kalyan	14.8.1968		11	1992–1993	425	103	1	42.50	–	–	–/–	–	9	20
Ankola Salil Ashok	1.3.1968		1	1989	6	6	0	6.00	2	1-35	–/–	64.00	0	
² Apte Arvindrao Laxmanrao	24.10.1934		1	1959	15	8	0	7.50	–	–	–/–	–	0	
² Apte Madhavrao Laxmanrao	5.10.1932		7	1952	542	163*	1	49.27	0	0-3	0/0	–	2	
Arshad Ayub	2.8.1958		13	1987–1989	257	57	0	17.13	41	5-50	3/0	35.07	2	32
Arun Bharathi	14.12.1962		2	1986	4	2*	0	4.00	4	3-76	0/0	29.00	2	4
Arun Lal	1.8.1955		16	1982–1988	729	93	0	26.03	0	0-0	0/0	–	13	13
Azad Kirtivardhan	2.1.1959		7	1980–1983	135	24	0	11.25	3	2-84	0/0	124.33	3	25
Azharuddin Mohammad	8.2.1963		99	1984–1999	6,215	199	22	45.03	0	0-4	0/0	–	105	334
Badani Hemang Kamal	14.11.1976		4	2001	94	38	0	15.66	0	0-17	0/0	–	6	40
Bahutule Sairaj Vasant	6.1.1973		2	2000–2001	39	21*	0	13.00	3	1-32	0/0	67.66	1	8
Baig Abbas Ali	19.3.1939		10	1959–1966	428	112	1	23.77	0	0-2	0/0	–	6	
Balaji Lakshmipathy	27.9.1981		8	2003–2004	51	31	0	5.66	27	5-76	1/0	37.18	1	30
Banerjee Sarobindu Nath ("Shute")	3.10.1911	14.10.1980	1	1948	13	8	0	6.50	5	4-54	0/0	25.40	0	
Banerjee Subroto Tara	13.2.1969		1	1991	3	3	0	3.00	3	3-47	0/0	15.66	0	6
Banerjee Sudangsu Abinash	1.11.1917	14.9.1992	1	1948	0	0	0	0.00	5	4-120	0/0	36.20	3	
Bangar Sanjay Bapusaheb	11.10.1972		12	2001–2002	470	100*	1	29.37	7	2-23	0/0	49.00	4	15
Baqa Jilani Mohammad	20.7.1911	2.7.1941	1	1936	16	12	0	16.00	0	0-55	0/0	–	0	
Bedi Bishan Singh	25.9.1946		67	1966–1979	656	50*	0	8.98	266	7-98	14/1	28.71	26	10
Bhandari Prakash	27.11.1935		3	1954–1956	77	39	0	19.25	0	0-12	0/0	–	1	
Bharadwaj Raghvendrarao Vijay	15.8.1975		3	1999	28	22	0	9.33	4	1-26	0/0	107.00	3	10
Bhat Adwai Raghuram	16.4.1958		2	1983	6	6	0	3.00	4	2-65	0/0	37.75	0	
Binny Roger Michael Humphrey	19.7.1955		27	1979–1986	830	83*	0	23.05	47	6-56	2/0	32.63	11	72
Borde Chandrakant Gulabrao	21.7.1934		55	1958–1969	3,061	177*	5	35.59	52	5-88	1/0	46.48	37	
Chandrasekhar Bhagwat Subramanya	17.5.1945		58	1963–1979	167	22	0	4.07	242	8-79	16/2	29.74	25	
Chauhan Chetandra Pratap Singh	21.7.1947		40	1969–1980	2,084	97	0	31.57	2	1-4	0/0	53.00	38	1
Chauhan Rajesh Kumar	19.12.1966		21	1992–1997	98	23	0	7.00	47	4-48	0/0	39.51	12	7
Chawla Piyush Pramod	24.12.1988		2	2005–2007	5	4	0	2.50	3	2-66	0/0	45.66	0	35
Chopra Aakash	19.9.1977		10	2003–2004	437	60	0	23.00	–	–	–/–	–	15	21
Chopra Nikhil	26.12.1973		1	1999	7	4	0	3.50	0	0-78	0/0	–	0	39
Chowdhury Nirode Ranjan	23.5.1923	14.12.1979	2	1948–1951	3	3*	0	3.00	1	1-130	0/0	205.00	0	
Colah Sorabji Hormasji Munchersha	22.9.1902	11.9.1950	2	1932–1933	69	31	0	17.25	–	–	–/–	–	2	
Contractor Nariman Jamshedji	7.3.1934		31	1955–1961	1,611	108	1	31.58	1	1-9	0/0	80.00	18	
Dahiya Vijay	10.5.1973		2	2000	2	2*	0	–	–	–	–/–	–	6	19

	Born	Died	Tests	Test Career	Runs	HS	100s	Avge	Wkts	BB	5/10	Avge	Ct/St	O/T
Dani Hemchandra Tukaram	24.5.1933	19.12.1999	1	1952	–	–	–	–	0	1-9	0/0	19.00	1	4
Das Shiv Sunder	5.11.1977		23	2000–2001	1,326	110	1	34.89	0	0-7	0/0	–	34	5
Dasgupta Deep	7.6.1977		8	2001	344	100	2	28.66	–				13	
Desai Ramakant Bhikaji	20.6.1939	27.4.1998	28	1958–1967	418	85	–	13.48	74	6-56	2/0	37.31	9	
Dhoni Mahendra Singh	7.7.1981		41	2005–2009	2,265	148	3	41.18	–	0-1	–/–	–	108/20	151‡/20
Dighe Sameer Sudhakar	8.10.1968	–	6	2000–2001	141	47	–	15.66	–				12/2	23
Dilawar Hussain	19.3.1907	26.8.1967	3	1933–1936	254	59	–	42.33	11	3-102	–/–	32.81	6/1	
Divecha Ramesh Vithaldas	18.10.1927	11.2.2003	5	1951–1952	60	26	–	12.00	114	6-102	6/0	30.71	5	
Doshi Dilip Rasiklal	22.12.1947		33	1979–1983	129	20	–	4.60	1	1-18	0/0	39.00	10	15
Dravid Rahul	11.1.1973		388	1996–2009	11,372	270	29	54.15	1				192	335‡
Durani Salim Aziz	11.12.1934		29	1959–1972	1,202	104	1	25.04	75	6-73	3/1	35.42	14	
Engineer Farokh Maneksha	25.2.1938		46	1961–1974	2,611	121	2	31.08	–				66/16	5
Gadkari Chandrasekhar Vaman	3.2.1928	11.11.1998	6	1952–1954	129	50*	–	21.50	0	0-8	–/–	–	6	
Gaekwad Anshuman Dattajirao	23.9.1952		40	1974–1984	1,985	201	2	30.07	2	1-4	0/0	93.50	15	15
Gaekwad Dattajirao Krishnarao	27.10.1928		11	1952–1960	350	52	–	18.42	0	0-4	0/0	–	5	
Gaekwad Hiralal Ghasilal	29.8.1923	2.1.2003	1	1952	22	14	–	11.00	–				0	
Gambhir Gautam	14.10.1981		29	2004–2009	2,760	206	9	57.50	–				25	91/19
Gandhi Devang Jayant	6.9.1971		4	1999	204	88	–	34.00	0				3	3
Gandotra Ashok	24.11.1948		2	1969	54	18	–	13.50	0	0-5	–/–	–	1	
Ganesh Doddanarasiah	30.6.1973		4	1996	25	8	–	6.25	5	2-28	0/0	57.40	0	1
Ganguly Sourav Chandidas	8.7.1972		113	1996–2008	7,212	239	16	42.17	32	3-28	0/0	52.53	71	308‡
Gavaskar Sunil Manohar	10.7.1949		125	1970–1986	10,122	236*	34	51.12	1	1-34	0/0	206.00	108	108
Ghavri Karsan Devjibhai	28.2.1951		39	1974–1980	913	86	–	21.23	109	5-33	4/0	33.54	16	19
Ghorpade Jayasinghrao Mansinghrao	2.10.1930	29.3.1978	8	1952–1959	229	41	–	15.26	–	0-17	0/0	–	4	
Ghulam Ahmed	4.7.1922	28.10.1998	22	1948–1958	192	50	–	8.72	68	7-49	4/1	30.17	11	
Gopalan Morappakam Joysam	6.6.1909	21.12.2003	1	1933	18	11*	–	18.00	1	1-39	0/0	39.00	3	
Gopinath Coimbatarao Doraikannu	1.3.1930		8	1951–1959	242	50*	–	22.00	–	1-11	0/0	11.00	2	
Guard Ghulam Mustafa	12.12.1925	13.3.1978	2	1958–1959	11	7	–	5.50	3	2-69	0/0	60.66	2	
Guha Subrata	31.1.1946	5.11.2003	4	1967–1969	17	6	–	3.40	3	2-55	0/0	103.66	2	
Gul Mahomed	15.10.1921	8.5.1992	8†	1946–1952	166	34	–	11.06	2	2-21	0/0	12.00	3	
² Gupte Balkrishna Pandharinath	30.8.1934	5.7.2005	3	1960–1964	28	17*	–	28.00	3	1-54	0/0	116.33		
² Gupte Subhashchandra Pandharinath	11.12.1929	31.5.2002	36	1951–1961	183	21	–	6.31	149	9-102	12/1	29.55	14	
Gursharan Singh	8.3.1963		1	1989	18	18	–	18.00	–		–/–		2	1
Hafeez Abdul (see Kardar)														

§ *Dravid's figures exclude 23 runs and one catch for the ICC World XI v Australia in the Super Series Test in 2005-06.*

	Born	Died	Tests	Test Career	Runs	HS	100s	Avge	Wkts	BB	5/10	Avge	Ct/St	O/T
Hanumant Singh	29.3.1939	29.11.2006	14	1963–1969	686	105	1	31.18	—	—	—	—	11	204¼/17
Harbhajan Singh	3.7.1980	—	81	1998–2009	1,537	66	0	16.70	345	8-84	23/5	31.00	39	—
Hardikar Manohar Shankar	8.2.1936	4.2.1995	2	1958	56	32*	0	18.66	4	1-9	0/0	55.00	3	—
Harvinder Singh	23.12.1977	—	3	1997–2001	6	6	0	2.00	4	2-62	0/0	46.25	0	16
Hazare Vijay Samuel	11.3.1915	18.12.2004	30	1946–1952	2,192	164*	7	47.65	20	4-29	0/0	61.00	11	—
Hindlekar Dattaram Dharmaji	1.1.1909	30.3.1949	4	1936–1946	71	26	0	14.20	—	—	—	—	3	—
Hirwani Narendra Deepchand	18.10.1968	—	17	1987–1996	54	17	0	5.40	66	8-61	4/1	30.10	5	18
Ibrahim Khanmohammad Cassumbhoy	26.1.1919	12.11.2007	4	1948	169	85	0	21.12	—	—	—	—	5	—
Indrajitsinhji Kumar Shri	15.6.1937	—	4	1964–1969	51	23	0	8.50	—	—	—	—	6/3	—
Irani Jamshed Khudadad	18.8.1923	25.2.1982	2	1947	19	2*	0	3.00	—	—	—	—	2/1	—
Jadeja Ajaysinhji	1.2.1971	—	15	1992–1999	576	96	0	26.18	—	—	—	—	5	196
[3]Jahangir Khan Mohammad	1.2.1910	23.7.1988	4	1932–1936	39	13	0	5.57	4	4-60	0/0	63.75	4	—
Jai Laxmidas Purshottamdas	1.4.1902	29.1.1968	1	1933	19	19	0	9.50	—	—	—	—	-	—
Jaisimha Motganhalli Laxmanarsu	3.3.1939	6.7.1999	39	1959–1970	2,056	129	3	30.68	9	2-54	0/0	92.11	17	—
Jamshedji Rustomji Jamshedji Dorabji	18.11.1892	5.4.1976	1	1933	5	4*	0	—	3	3-137	0/0	45.66	2	—
Jayantilal Kenia	13.1.1948	—	1	1970	5	5	0	5.00	—	—	—	—	-	—
Johnson David Jude	16.10.1971	—	2	1996	8	5	0	4.00	3	2-52	0/0	47.66	7	—
Joshi Padmanabh Govind	27.10.1926	8.1.1987	12	1951–1960	207	52*	0	10.89	—	—	—	—	18/9	—
Joshi Sunil Bandacharya	6.6.1969	—	15	1996–2000	352	92	0	20.70	41	5-142	1/0	35.85	7	69
Kaif Mohammad	1.12.1980	—	13	1999–2005	624	148*	1	32.84	0	0-4	—	—	14	125
Kambli Vinod Ganpat	18.1.1972	—	17	1992–1995	1,084	227	4	54.20	0	0-4	0/0	—	7	104
[1]Kanitkar Hrishikesh Hemant	14.11.1974	—	2	1999	74	45	0	18.50	0	0-2	0/0	—	0	34
[1]Kanitkar Hemant Shamsunder	8.12.1942	—	2	1974	111	65	0	27.75	—	—	—	—	0	—
Kapil Dev	6.1.1959	—	131	1978–1993	5,248	163	8	31.05	434	9-83	23/2	29.64	64	225
Kapoor Aashish Rakesh	25.3.1971	—	4	1994–1996	97	42	0	19.40	6	2-19	0/0	42.50	1	17
Kardar Abdul Hafeez	17.1.1925	21.4.1996	3†	1946	80	43	0	16.00	—	—	—	—	1	—
Karim Syed Saba	14.11.1967	—	1	2000	15	15	0	15.00	—	—	—	—	2	34
Kartik Krishankumar Dinesh	1.6.1985	—	23	2004–2009	1,000	129	2	27.77	—	—	—	—	51/5	36/7
Kartik Murali	11.9.1976	—	8	1999–2004	88	43	0	9.77	24	4-44	0/0	34.16	2	37/1
Kenny Ramnath Baburao	29.9.1930	21.11.1985	4	1958–1959	245	62	0	27.22	—	—	—	—	—	—
Kirmani Syed Mujtaba Hussein	29.12.1949	—	88	1975–1985	2,759	102	2	27.04	—	—	—	—	160/38	49
Kishenchand Gogumal	14.4.1925	16.4.1997	5	1947–1952	89	44	0	8.90	1	1-9	0/0	13.00	1	—
[1]Kripal Singh Amritsar Govindsingh	6.8.1933	22.7.1987	14	1955–1964	422	100*	0	28.13	10	3-43	0/0	58.40	4	—
Krishnamurthy Pochiah	12.7.1947	28.11.1999	5	1970	33	20	0	5.50	—	—	—	—	7/1	1
Kulkarni Nilesh Moreshwar	3.4.1973	—	3	1997–2000	5	4	0	5.00	2	1-70	0/0	166.00	1	10

	Born	Died	Tests	Test Career	Runs	HS	100s	Avge	Wkts	BB	5/10	Avge	Ct/St	O/T
Kulkarni Rajiv Ramesh	25.9.1962		3	1986	2	2	0	1.00	5	3-85	0/0	45.40	1	10
Kulkarni Umesh Narayan	7.3.1942		4	1967	13	2	0	4.33	5	2-37	0/0	47.60	1	
Kumar Vaman Viswanath	22.6.1935		2	1960–1961	6	6	0	3.00	7	5-64	1/0	28.85	2	
Kumble Anil	17.10.1970		132	1990–2008	2,506	110*	1	17.77	619	10-74	35/8	29.65	60	269‡
Kunderan Budhisagar Krishnappa	2.10.1939	23.6.2006	18	1959–1967	981	192	2	32.70		0-13		–	23/7	
Kuruvilla Abey	8.8.1968		10	1996–1997	66	35*	0	6.60	25	5-68	1/0	35.68	1	25
Lall Singh	16.12.1909	19.11.1985	1	1932	44	29	0	22.00	–	–	–/–	–	1	
Lamba Raman	2.1.1960	22.2.1998	4	1986–1987	102	53	0	20.40	–	–		–	1	32
Laxman Vangipurappu Venkata Sai	1.11.1974		109	1996–2009	6,993	281	14	45.70	2	1-2	0/0	63.00	114	86
Madan Lal	20.3.1951		39	1974–1986	1,042	74	0	22.65	71	5-23	4/0	40.08	15	67
Maka Ebrahim Suleman	5.3.1922	d unknown	2	1952	2	2*	0	–	0	–	–/–	–	2/1	
Malhotra Ashok Omprakash	26.1.1957		7	1981–1984	226	72*	0	25.11	0	0-0	0/0	–	2	20
Maninder Singh	13.6.1965		35	1982–1992	99	15	0	3.80	88	7-27	3/2	37.36	9	59
Manjrekar Sanjay Vijay	12.7.1965		37	1987–1996	2,043	218	4	37.14	0	0-4	0/0	–	25/1	74
Manjrekar Vijay Laxman	26.9.1931	18.10.1983	55	1951–1964	3,208	189*	7	39.12	1	1-16	0/0	44.00	19/2	
Mankad Ashok Vinoo	12.10.1946	1.8.2008	22	1969–1977	991	97	0	25.41	0	0-0	0/0	–	12	1
Mankad Mulvantrai Himmatlal ("Vinoo")	12.4.1917	21.8.1978	44	1946–1958	2,109	231	5	31.47	162	8-52	8/2	32.32	33	
Mantri Madhav Krishnaji	1.9.1921	10.2.1982	4	1951–1954	67	39	0	9.57	–	–		–	8/1	
Meherhomji Khershedji Rustomji	9.8.1911		1	1936	0	0*	0	–	–	–		–	1	
Mehra Vijay Laxman	12.3.1938	25.8.2006	8	1955–1963	329	62	0	25.30	0	0-1	0/0	–	1	
Merchant Vijay Madhavji	12.10.1911	27.10.1987	10	1933–1951	859	154	3	47.72	0	0-17	0/0	–	7	
Mhambrey Paras Laxmikant	20.6.1972		2	1996	58	28	0	29.00	2	1-43	0/0	74.00	1	3
Milkha Singh Amritsar Govindsingh	31.12.1941		4	1959–1961	92	35	0	15.33	0	0-2	0/0	–	2	
Mishra Amit	24.11.1982		7	2008–2009	137	50	0	19.57	28	5-71	1/0	34.07	4	5
Modi Rustomji Sheryar	11.11.1924	17.5.1996	10	1946–1952	736	112	1	46.00	0	0-14	0/0	–	3	
Mohanty Debasis Sarbeswar	20.7.1976		2	1997	0	0*	0	–	4	4-78	0/0	59.75	0	45
Mongia Nayan Ramlal	19.12.1969		44	1993–2000	1,442	152	1	24.03	0	0-0	–/–	–	99/8	140
More Kiran Shankar	4.9.1962		49	1986–1993	1,285	73	0	25.70	0	0-12	0/0	–	110/20	94
Muddiah Venatappa Musandra	8.6.1929	1.10.2009	2	1959–1960	11	11	0	5.50	3	2-40	0/0	44.66	1	
Mushtaq Ali Syed	17.12.1914	18.6.2005	11	1933–1951	612	112	2	32.21	3	1-45	0/0	67.33	7	
Nadkarni Rameshchandra Gangaram ("Bapu")	4.4.1933		41	1955–1967	1,414	122*	1	25.70	88	6-43	4/1	29.07	22	
Naik Sudhir Sakharam	21.2.1945		3	1974–1974	141	77	0	23.50	0	–	–/–	–	0	
Naoomal Jeoomal	17.4.1904	28.7.1980	3	1932–1933	108	43	0	27.00	2	1-4	0/0	34.00	0	2
Narasimha Rao Modireddy Venkateshwar	11.8.1954		4	1978–1979	46	20*	0	9.20	3	2-46	0/0	75.66	8	
Navle Janardan Gyanoba	7.12.1902	7.9.1979	2	1932–1933	42	13	0	10.50	–	–	–/–	–	1	

Name	Born	Died	Tests	Test Career	Runs	HS	100s	Avge	Wkts	BB	5/10	Avge	Ct/St	O/T
Nayak Surendra Vithal	20.10.1954		2	1982	19	11	0	9.50	9	1-16	0/0	132.00	1	4
[2] Nayudu Cottari Kanakaiya	31.10.1895	14.11.1967	7	1932–1936	350	81	0	25.00	9	3-40	0/0	42.88	4	
[2] Nayudu Cottari Subbanna	18.4.1914	22.11.2002	11	1933–1951	147	36	0	9.18	2	1-19	0/0	179.50	3	
[2] Nazir Ali Syed	8.6.1906	18.2.1975	2	1932–1933	30	13	0	7.50	4	4-83	0/0	20.75	0	90½/2
Nehra Ashish	29.4.1979		17	1998–2003	77	19	0	5.50	44	4-72	0/0	42.40	5	
Nissar Mohammad	1.8.1910	11.3.1963	6	1932–1936	55	14	0	6.87	25	5-90	3/0	28.28	2	
Nyalchand Shah	14.9.1919	4.1.1997	1	1952	7	6*	0	7.00	3	3-97	0/0	32.33	0	
Ojha Pragyan Prayish	5.9.1986		3	2009	7	5*	0	–	13	3-101	0/0	29.53	3	9/4
Pai Ajit Manohar	28.4.1945		1	1969	10	9	0	5.00	2	2-29	0/0	15.50	0	
Palia Phiroze Edulji	5.9.1910	9.9.1981	2	1932–1936	29	16	0	9.66	0	0-2	–/–	–	0	
Pandit Chandrakant Sitaram	30.9.1961		5	1986–1991	171	39	0	24.42	–	–	–/–	–	14/2	36
Parkar Ghulam Ahmed	25.10.1955		1	1982	7	6	0	3.50	–	–	–/–	–	0	10
Parkar Ramnath Dhondu	31.10.1946	11.8.1999	2	1972	80	35	0	20.00	–	–	–/–	–	1	
Parsana Dhiraj Devshibhai	2.12.1947		2	1978	1	1	0	0.50	1	1-32	0/0	50.00	0	
Patankar Chandrakant Trimbak	24.11.1930		1	1955	14	13	0	14.00	–	–	–/–	–	3/1	
[1] Pataudi Iftikhar Ali Khan, Nawab of	16.3.1910	5.1.1952	3†	1946	55	22	0	11.00	–	–	–/–	–	0	
[1] Pataudi Mansur Ali Khan, Nawab of	5.1.1941		46	1961–1974	2,793	203*	6	34.91	1	1-10	0/0	88.00	27	
Patel Brijesh Pursuram	24.11.1952		21	1974–1977	972	115*	1	29.45	–	–	–/–	–	17	
Patel Jasubhai Motibhai	26.11.1924	12.12.1992	7	1954–1959	25	12	0	2.77	29	9-69	2/1	21.96	2	10
Patel Munaf Musa	12.7.1983		12	2005–2008	56	15*	0	7.00	34	4-25	0/0	36.17	6	43
Patel Parthiv Ajay	9.3.1985		20	2002–2008	683	69	0	29.69	0	0-14	–/–	–	41/8	14
Patel Rashid	1.6.1964		1	1988	0	0	0	0.00	0	0-59	0/0	–	0	1
Pathan Irfan Khan	27.10.1984		29	2003–2007	1,105	102	1	31.57	100	7-59	7/2	32.26	8	107/16
Patiala Maharaja of (Yadavendra Singh)	17.1.1913	17.6.1974	1	1933	84	60	0	42.00	–	–	–/–	–	2	
Patil Sadashiv Raoji	10.10.1933		1	1955	14	14*	0	–	2	1-15	0/0	25.50	1	
Patil Sandeep Madhusudan	18.8.1956		29	1979–1984	1,588	174	4	36.93	9	2-28	0/0	26.66	12	45
Phadkar Dattatraya Gajanan	12.12.1925	17.3.1985	31	1947–1958	1,229	123	2	32.34	62	7-159	3/0	36.85	21	
Powar Ramesh Rajaram	20.5.1978		2	2007	13	10	0	6.50	6	3-33	0/0	19.66	0	31
Prabhakar Manoj	15.4.1963		39	1984–1995	1,600	120	1	32.65	96	6-132	3/0	37.30	20	130
Prasad Bapu Krishnarao Venkatesh	5.8.1969		33	1996–2001	203	30*	0	7.51	96	6-33	7/1	35.00	6	161
Prasad Mannava Sri Kanth	24.4.1975		6	1999	106	19	0	11.77	–	–	–/–	–	15	17
Prasanna Erapalli Anatharao Srinivas	22.5.1940		49	1961–1978	735	37	0	11.48	189	8-76	10/2	30.38	18	
Punjabi Pananmal Hotchand	20.9.1921		5	1954	164	33	0	16.40	–	–	–/–	–	5	
Rai Singh Kanwar	24.2.1922		1	1947	26	24	0	13.00	–	–	–/–	–	0	
Rajinder Pal	18.11.1937		1	1963	6	3*	0	6.00	0	0-3	0/0	–	–	

	Born	Died	Tests	Test Career	Runs	HS	100s	Avge	Wkts	BB	5/10	Avge	Ct/St	O/T
Rajindernath Vijay	7.1.1928	22.11.1989	1	1952	–	–	0	–	–	–	–/–	–	0/4	
Rajput Lalchand Sitaram	18.12.1961		2	1985	105	61	0	26.25	–	–	–/–	–	1	4
Raju Sagi Lakshmi Venkatapathy	9.7.1969		28	1989-2000	240	31	0	10.00	93	6-12	5/1	30.72	6	53
Raman Woorkeri Venkat	23.5.1965		11	1987-1996	448	96	0	24.88	2	1-7	0/0	64.50	6	27
Ramaswami Cotar	16.6.1896	1.1990	2	1936	170	60	0	56.66	–	–	–/–	–	0	
Ramchand Gulabrai Sipahimalani	26.7.1927	8.9.2003	33	1952-1959	1,180	109	2	24.58	41	6-49	1/0	46.31	20	
Ramesh Sadagoppan	16.10.1975		19	1998-2001	1,367	143	2	37.97	0	0-5	0/0	–	18	24
²Ramji Ladha	10.2.1900	20.12.1948	1	1933	1	1	0	0.50	0	0-64	0/0	–	1	
Rangachari Commandur Rajagopalachari	14.4.1916	9.10.1993	4	1947-1948	8	8*	0	2.66	9	5-107	1/0	54.77	0	
Rangnekar Khanderao Moreshwar	27.6.1917	11.10.1984	3	1947	33	18	0	5.50	–	–	–/–	–		
Ranjane Vasant Baburao	22.7.1937		7	1958-1964	40	16	0	6.66	19	4-72	0/0	34.15	0	
Rathore Vikram	26.3.1969		6	1996-1996	131	44	0	13.10	–	–	–/–	–	12	7
Ratra Ajay	13.12.1981		6	2001-2002	163	115*	0	18.11	0	0-1	0/0	–	11/2	12
Razdan Vivek	25.8.1969		2	1989	6	6*	0	6.00	5	5-79	1/0	28.20	0	3
Reddy Bharath	12.11.1954		4	1979	38	21	0	9.50	–	–	–/–	–	9/2	3
Rege Madhusudan Ramachandra	18.3.1924		1	1948	15	15	0	7.50	–	–	–/–	–	0	
Roy Ambar	5.6.1945	19.9.1997	4	1969	91	48	0	13.00	1	1-6	0/0	66.00	0	
¹Roy Pankaj	31.5.1928	4.2.2001	43	1951-1960	2,442	173	5	32.56	–	–	–/–	–	16	
Roy Pranab	10.2.1957		2	1981	71	60*	0	35.50	–	–	–/–	–	1	
Sandhu Balwinder Singh	3.8.1956		8	1982-1983	214	71	0	30.57	10	3-87	0/0	55.70	4	22
Sanghvi Rahul Laxman	3.9.1974		1	2000	2	2	0	1.00	2	2-67	0/0	39.00	0	10
Sarandeep Singh	21.10.1979		3	2000-2001	43	39*	0	43.00	10	4-136	0/0	34.00	1	5
Sardesai Dilip Narayan	8.8.1940	2.7.2007	30	1961-1972	2,001	212	5	39.23	0	0-3	0/0	–	4	
Sarwate Chandrasekhar Trimbak	22.7.1920	23.12.2003	9	1946-1951	208	37	0	13.00	3	1-16	0/0	124.66		
Saxena Ramesh Chandra	20.9.1944		1	1967	25	16	0	12.50	0	0-11	0/0	–	1	
Sehwag Virender§	20.10.1978		73	2001-2009	6,318	319	17	52.65	31	5-104	1/0	42.90	59	206/14
Sekhar Thirumalai Ananthanpillai	28.3.1956		2	1982	–	0*	0	–	0	0-43	0/0	–	0	4
Sen Probir Kumar ("Khokhan")	31.5.1926	27.1.1970	14	1947-1952	165	25	0	11.78	–	–	–/–	–	20/11	
Sen Gupta Apoorva Kumar	3.8.1939		1	1958	9	8	0	4.50	–	–	–/–	–		
Sharma Ajay Kumar	3.4.1964		1	1987	53	30	0	26.50	0	0-9	0/0	–	1	31
Sharma Chetan	3.1.1966		23	1984-1988	396	54	0	22.00	61	6-58	4/1	35.45	2	65
Sharma Gopal	3.8.1960		5	1984-1990	11	10*	0	3.66	10	4-88	0/0	41.80	6	11
Sharma Ishant	2.9.1988		21	2007-2009	163	23	0	10.86	63	5-118	1/0	32.85	1	41/11
Sharma Parthasarathy Harishchandra	5.1.1948		5	1974-1976	187	54	0	18.70	0	0-2	0/0	–	1	2

§ *Sehwag's figures exclude 83 runs and one catch for the ICC World XI v Australia in the Super Series Test in 2005-06.*

	Born	Died	Tests	Test Career	Runs	HS	100s	Avge	Wks	BB	5/10	Avge	Ct/St	O/T
Sharma Sanjeev Kumar	25.8.1965		2	1988–1990	56	38	0	28.00	6	3-37	0/0	41.16	0	23
Shastri Ravishankar Jayadritha	27.5.1962		80	1980–1992	3,830	206	11	35.79	151	5-75	2/0	40.96	36	150
Shinde Sadashiv Ganpatrao	18.8.1923	22.6.1955	7	1946–1952	85	14	0	14.16	12	6-91	1/0	59.75	1	
Shodhan Roshan Harshadlal ("Deepak")	18.10.1928		3	1952	181	110	1	60.33	0	0-1	0/0	–	0	
Shukla Rakesh Chandra	4.2.1948		1	1982	–	–	–	–	2	2-82	0/0	76.00	0	
Siddiqui Iqbal Rashid	26.12.1974		1	2001	29	24	0	29.00	1	1-32	0/0	48.00	0	
Sidhu Navjot Singh	20.10.1963		51	1983–1998	3,202	201	9	42.13	0	0-9	0/0	–	9	136
Singh Rabindra Ramanarayan ("Robin")	14.9.1963		1	1998	27	15	0	13.50	0	0-16	0/0	–	5	136
Singh Robin	1.1.1970		1	1998	0	0	0	0.00	3	2-74	0/0	58.66	1	
Singh Rudra Pratap	6.12.1985		13	2005–2007	91	30	0	6.50	40	5-59	1/0	39.10	6	55/10
Singh Vikram Rajvir	17.9.1984		5	2005–2007	47	29	0	11.75	8	3-48	0/0	53.37	9	2
Sivaramakrishnan Laxman	31.12.1965		9	1982–1985	130	25	0	16.25	26	6-64	3/1	44.03	9	16
Sohoni Sriranga Wasudev	5.3.1918	19.5.1993	4	1946–1951	83	29*	0	16.60	2	1-16	0/0	101.00	2	
Solkar Eknath Dhondu	18.3.1948	26.6.2005	27	1969–1976	1,068	102	0	25.42	18	3-28	0/0	59.44	53	7
Sood Man Mohan	6.7.1939		1	1959	3	3	0	1.50	–	–	–	–	0	
Sreesanth Shanthakumaran	6.2.1983		17	2005–2009	226	35	0	13.29	60	5-40	2/0	32.01	2	41/10
Srikkanth Krishnamachari	21.12.1959		43	1981–1991	2,062	123	2	29.88	0	0-1	0/0	–	40	146
Srinath Javagal	31.8.1969		67	1991–2002	1,009	76	0	14.21	236	8-86	10/1	30.49	22	229
Srinivasan Thirumalai Echambadi	26.10.1950		1	1980	48	29	0	24.00	0	0-3	0/0	–	0	2
Subramanya Venkataraman	16.7.1936		9	1964–1967	263	75	0	18.78	3	2-32	0/0	67.00	9	
Sunderam Gundibail Rama	29.3.1930		2	1955	3	3*	0	–	26	2-46	2/0	55.33	0	
Surendranath	4.1.1937		11	1958–1960	136	27	0	10.46	26	5-75	2/0	40.50	4	
Surti Rusi Framroze	25.5.1936	1.5.1983	26	1960–1969	1,263	99	0	28.70	42	5-74	1/0	46.71	26	
Swamy Venkatraman Narayan	23.5.1924	19.3.2002	1	1955	–	–	–	–	0	0-15	0/0	–	0	
Tamhane Narendra Shankar	4.8.1931		21	1954–1960	225	54*	0	10.22	–	–	–	–	35/16	
Tarapore Keki Khurshedji	17.12.1910	15.6.1986	1	1948	2	2	0	2.00	0	0-72	0/0	–	0	
Tendulkar Sachin Ramesh	24.4.1973		164	1989–2009	13,234	248*	45	55.37	44	3-10	0/0	52.22	104	440/1
Umrigar Pahlanji Ratanji ("Polly")	28.3.1926	7.11.2006	59	1948–1961	3,631	223	12	42.22	35	6-74	2/0	42.08	33	
Vengsarkar Dilip Balwant	6.4.1956		116	1975–1991	6,868	166	17	42.13	1	0-3	0/0	–	78	129
Venkataraghavan Srinivasaraghavan	21.4.1945		57	1964–1983	748	64	0	11.68	156	8-72	3/1	36.11	44	15
Venkataramana Margashayam	24.4.1966		1	1988	0	0*	0	–	1	1-10	0/0	58.00	1	
Vijay Murali	1.4.1984		3	2008–2009	191	87	0	47.75	–	–	–	–	4	
Viswanath Gundappa Rangnath	12.2.1949		91	1969–1982	6,080	222	14	41.93	1	1-11	0/0	46.00	63	25
Viswanath Sadanand	29.11.1962		3	1985	31	20	0	6.20	–	–	–	–	11	22

	Born	Died	Test Career	Tests	Runs	HS	100s	Avge	Wkts	BB	5/10	Avge	Ct/St	O/T
Vizianagram Maharaja Kumar of (*Sir Vijaya Anand*)...	28.12.1905	2.12.1965	1936	3	33	19*	0	8.25	0	–	–/–	–	1	
Wadekar Ajit Laxman...	1.4.1941		1966–1974	37	2,113	143	1	31.07	0	0-0	0/0	–	46	2
Wasim Jaffer...	16.2.1978		1999–2007	31	1,944	212	5	34.10	2	2-18	0/0	9.00	27	2
Wassan Atul Satish...	23.3.1968		1989–1990	4	94	53	0	23.50	10	4-108	0/0	50.40	1	9
[1,2] Wazir Ali Syed...	15.9.1903	17.6.1950	1932–1936	7	237	42	0	16.92	0	0-0	0/0	–	1	
Yadav Nandlal Shivlal...	26.1.1957		1979–1986	35	403	43	0	14.39	102	5-76	3/0	35.09	10	7
Yadav Vijay...	14.3.1967		1992	1	30	30	0	30.00	0	–	–/–	–	1/2	19
Yajurvindra Singh...	1.8.1952		1976–1979	4	109	43*	0	18.16	1	0-2	0/0	–	11	
Yashpal Sharma...	11.8.1954		1979–1983	37	1,606	140	2	33.45	1	1-6	0/0	17.00	16	42
[1] Yograj Singh...	25.3.1958		1980	1	10	6	0	5.00	1	1-63	0/0	63.00	0	6
Yohannan Tinu...	18.2.1979		2001–2002	3	13	8*	0	–	5	2-56	0/0	51.20	1	3
[1] Yuvraj Singh...	12.12.1981		2003–2009	33	1,582	169	3	35.95	8	2-9	0/0	53.87	30	242±17
Zaheer Khan...	7.10.1978		2000–2009	70	935	75	0	13.35	235	7-87	9/1	33.04	18	161±9

PAKISTAN (199 players)

	Born	Died	Test Career	Tests	Runs	HS	100s	Avge	Wkts	BB	5/10	Avge	Ct/St	O/T
Aamer Malik...	3.1.1963		1987–1994	14	565	117	2	35.31	1	1-0	0/0	89.00	15/1	24
Aamir Nazir...	2.1.1971		1992–1995	6	31	11	0	6.20	20	5-46	1/0	29.85	1	9
Aamir Sohail...	14.9.1966		1992–1999	47	2,823	205	5	35.28	25	4-54	0/0	41.96	36	156
Abdul Kadir...	10.5.1944	12.3.2002	1964	4	272	95	0	34.00	0	–	–/–	–	0/1	
Abdul Qadir...	15.9.1955		1977–1990	67	1,029	61	0	15.59	236	9-56	15/5	32.80	15	104
Abdul Razzaq...	2.12.1979		1999–2006	46	1,946	134	3	28.61	100	5-35	1/0	36.94	15	233±9
Abdur Rauf...	9.12.1980		2009–2009	3	52	31	0	8.66	6	2-59	0/0	46.33	0	4/1
Abdur Rehman...	1.3.1980		2007	2	34	25*	0	17.00	11	4-105	0/0	32.00	1	11/2
Afaq Hussain...	31.12.1939		1961–1964	2	66	35*	0	–	1	1-40	0/0	106.00	2	
Aftab Baloch...	1.4.1953		1969–1974	2	97	60*	0	48.50	0	0-2	0/0	–	0	
Aftab Gul...	31.3.1946		1968–1971	6	182	33	0	22.75	0	0-4	0/0	–	3	
Agha Saadat Ali...	21.6.1929	25.10.1995	1955	1	8	8*	0	–	0	–	–/–	–	3	
Agha Zahid...	7.1.1953		1974	1	15	14	0	7.50	0	–	–/–	–	0	
Akram Raza...	22.11.1964		1989–1994	9	153	32	0	15.30	13	3-46	0/0	56.30	8	49
Ali Hussain Rizvi...	6.1.1974		1997	1	–	–	–	–	2	2-72	0/0	36.00	0	
Ali Naqvi...	19.3.1977		1997	5	242	115	1	30.25	0	0-11	0/0	–	1	

	Born	Died	Tests	Test Career	Runs	HS	100s	Avge	Wkts	BB	5/10	Avge	Ct/St	O/T
Alim-ud-Din	15.12.1930		25	1954–1962	1,091	109	2	25.37		1-17	0/0	75.00	8	
Amir Elahi	1.9.1908	28.12.1980	5†	1952	65	47	0	10.83	7	4-134	0/0	35.42	0	15
Anil Dalpat	20.9.1963		9	1983–1984	167	52	0	15.18				–	22/3	
Anwar Hussain	16.7.1920	9.10.2002	4	1952	42	17	0	7.00	1	1-25	0/0	29.00	0	
Anwar Khan	24.12.1955		1	1978	15	12	0	15.00	0	0-12		–	0	
Aqib Javed	5.8.1972		22	1988–1998	101	28*	0	5.05	54	5-84	1/0	34.70	2	163
Arif Butt	17.5.1944		3	1964	59	20	0	11.80	14	6-89	1/0	20.57	3	
Arshad Khan	22.3.1971		9	1997–2004	31	9*	0	5.16	32	5-38	1/0	30.00	0	58
Ashfaq Ahmed	6.6.1973		1	1993	1	1*	0	1.00	2	2-31	0/0	26.50	0	3
Ashraf Ali	22.4.1958		8	1981–1987	229	65	0	45.80				–	17/5	16
Asif Iqbal	6.6.1943		58	1964–1979	3,575	175	11	38.85	53	5-48	2/0	28.33	36	10
Asif Masood	23.1.1946		16	1968–1976	93	30*	0	10.33	38	5-111	1/0	41.26	5	7
Asif Mujtaba	4.11.1967		25	1986–1996	928	65*	0	24.42	4	1-0	0/0	75.75	19	66
Asim Kamal	31.5.1976		12	2003–2005	717	99	0	37.73				–	10	
Ata-ur-Rehman	28.3.1975		13	1992–1996	76	19	0	8.44	31	4-50	0/0	34.54	2	30
Atif Rauf	3.3.1964		1	1993	25	16	0	12.50		–		–	0	
Atiq-uz-Zaman	20.7.1975		1	1999	26	25	0	13.00		–		–	5	3
Azam Khan	1.3.1969		1	1996	14	14	0	14.00		–		–	0	6
Azeem Hafeez	29.7.1963		18	1983–1984	134	24	0	8.37	63	6-46	4/0	34.98	1	15
Azhar Khan	7.9.1955		1	1979	14	14	0	14.00	1	1-1	0/0	2.00	0	
[2] Azhar Mahmood	28.2.1975		21	1997–2001	900	136	3	30.00	39	4-50	0/0	35.94	14	143
[2] Azmat Rana	3.11.1951		1	1979	49	49	0	49.00		–		–	0	2
Basit Ali	13.12.1970		19	1992–1995	858	103	1	26.81	0	0-6	0/0	–	6	50
[3] Bazid Khan	25.3.1981		1	2004	32	23	0	16.00				–	2	5
Danish Kaneria	16.12.1980		58	2000–2009	306	29	0	6.51	254	7-77	15/2	34.27	18	18
D'Souza Antao	17.1.1939		6	1958–1962	76	23*	0	38.00	17	5-112	1/0	43.82	3	
Ehtesham-ud-Din	4.9.1950		5	1979–1982	2	2	0	1.00	16	5-47	1/0	23.43	2	
Faisal Iqbal	30.12.1981		26	2000–2009	1,124	139	1	26.76	0	0-7	0/0	–	22	18
Farhan Adil	25.9.1977		1	2003	33	25	0	16.50		–		–	0	
Farooq Hamid	3.3.1945		1	1964	3	3	0	1.50	1	1-82	0/0	107.00	0	
Farrukh Zaman	2.4.1956		1	1976	–		–	–	0	0-7	0/0	–	0	
Fawad Alam	8.10.1985		3	2009–2009	250	168	1	41.66		–		–	3	14/15
Fazal Mahmood	18.2.1927	30.5.2005	34	1952–1962	620	60	0	14.09	139	7-42	13/4	24.70	11	
Fazl-e-Akbar	20.10.1980		5	1997–2003	52	25	0	13.00	11	3-85	0/0	46.45	2	2
[3] Ghazali Mohammad Ebrahim Zainuddin	15.6.1924	26.4.2003	2	1954	32	18	0	8.00	0	0-18	0/0	–	0	

	Born	Died	Tests	Test Career	Runs	HS	100s	Avge	Wkts	BB	5/10	Avge	Ct/St	O/T
Ghulam Abbas	1.5.1947		1	1967	12	12	0	6.00	–	–	–/–	–	0	
Gul Mahomed	15.10.1921	8.5.1992	1†	1956	39	27*	0	39.00	1	–	–/–	–	0	
1,2 Hanif Mohammad	21.12.1934		55	1952–1969	3,915	337	12	43.98	1	1-1	0/0	95.00	40	12
Haroon Rashid	25.3.1953		23	1976–1982	1,217	153	3	34.77	0	0-3	0/0	–	16	16
Hasan Raza	11.3.1982		7	1996–2005	235	68	0	26.11	0	0-1	0/0	–	5	
Haseeb Ahsan	15.7.1939		12	1957–1961	61	14	0	6.77	27	6-202	2/0	49.25	1	
2 Humayun Farhat	24.1.1981		1	2000	54	28	0	27.00	–	–	–/–	–	1	5
Ibadulla Khalid ("Billy")	20.12.1935		4	1964–1967	253	166	1	31.62	1	1-42	0/0	99.00	3	
Iftikhar Anjum	1.12.1980			2005	9	9*	0	–	0	0-8	0/0	–	0	60/2
Ijaz Ahmed sen	20.9.1968		60	1986–2000	3,315	211	12	37.67	2	1-9	0/0	38.50	45	250
Ijaz Ahmed jun	2.2.1969		2	1995	29	16	0	9.66	–	0-1	0/0	–	3	2
Ijaz Butt	10.3.1938		8	1958–1962	279	58	0	19.92	–	–	–/–	–	5	
Ijaz Faqih	24.3.1956		5	1980–1987	183	105	1	26.14	4	1-38	0/0	74.75	5	27
2 Imran Farhat	20.5.1982		33	2000–2009	2,071	128	3	33.95	3	2-69	0/0	81.33	35	33
Imran Khan	25.11.1952		88	1971–1991	3,807	136	6	37.69	362	8-58	23/6	22.81	28	175
Imran Nazir	16.12.1981		8	1998–2002	427	131	2	32.84	–	–	–/–	–	4	79/13
Imtiaz Ahmed	5.1.1928		41	1952–1962	2,079	209	3	29.28	0	0-0	0/0	–	77/16	
Intikhab Alam	28.12.1941		47	1959–1976	1,493	138	1	22.28	125	7-52	5/2	35.95	20	4
Inzamam-ul-Haq	3.3.1970		119§	1992–2007	8,829	329	25	50.16	0	0-8	0/0	–	81	375/1
Iqbal Qasim	6.8.1953		50	1976–1988	549	56	0	13.07	171	7-49	8/2	28.11	42	15
Irfan Fazil	2.11.1981		1	1999	4	3	0	4.00	2	1-30	0/0	32.50	2	1
Israr Ali	1.5.1927		4	1952–1959	33	10	0	4.71	6	2-29	0/0	27.50	1	
Jalal-ud-Din	12.6.1959		6	1982–1985	3	2	0	3.00	11	3-77	0/0	48.81	0	8
Javed Akhtar	21.11.1940		1	1962	4	2*	0	4.00	0	0-52	0/0	–	0	
Javed Burki	8.5.1938		25	1960–1969	1,341	140	3	30.47	0	0-2	0/0	–	7	
Javed Miandad	12.6.1957		124	1976–1993	8,832	280*	23	52.57	17	3-74	0/0	40.11	93/1	233
Kabir Khan	12.4.1974		4	1994	24	10	0	8.00	9	3-26	0/0	41.11	1	10
2 Kamran Akmal	13.11.1982		48	2002–2009	2,550	158*	6	33.55	–	–	–/–	–	159/22	111/27
Kardar Abdul Hafeez	17.1.1925	21.4.1996	23†	1952–1957	847	93	0	24.91	21	3-35	0/0	45.42	15	
Khalid Hassan	14.7.1937		1	1954	17	10	0	17.00	2	2-116	0/0	58.00	0	
1 Khalid Wazir	27.4.1936		2	1954	14	9*	0	7.00	–	–	–/–	–	0	
Khan Mohammad	1.1.1928	4.7.2009	13	1952–1957	100	26*	0	10.00	54	6-21	4/0	23.92	4	3
Khurram Manzoor	10.6.1986		7	2008–2009	326	93	0	29.63	–	–	–/–	–	4	
Liaqat Ali Khan	21.5.1955		5	1974–1978	28	12	0	7.00	6	3-80	0/0	59.83	1	3

§ Inzamam-ul-Haq's figures exclude one run for the ICC World XI v Australia in the Super Series Test in 2005-06.

Name	Born	Died	Tests	Test Career	Runs	HS	100s	Avge	Wkts	BB	Avge	5/10	Ct/St	O/T
Mahmood Hussain	2.4.1932	25.12.1991	27	1952-1962	336	35	0	10.18	68	6-67	38.64	2/0	5	23
[3] Majid [Jahangir] Khan	28.9.1946		63	1964-1982	3,931	167	8	38.92	27	4-45	53.92	0/0	70	5
Mansoor Akhtar	25.12.1957		19	1980-1989	655	111	1	25.19	—	—	—	—	9	41
[2] Manzoor Elahi	15.4.1963		6	1984-1994	123	52	0	15.37	7	2-38	27.71	0/0	7	54
Maqsood Ahmed	26.3.1925	4.1.1999	16	1952-1955	507	99	0	19.50	3	2-12	63.66	0/0	13	
Masood Anwar	12.12.1967		1	1990	39	37	0	19.50	2	2-59	34.00	0/0	0	
Mathias Wallis	4.2.1935	1.9.1994	21	1955-1962	783	77	0	23.72	0	0-20	—	0/0	22	
Miran Bux	20.4.1907	8.2.1991	2	1954	1	1*	0	1.00	2	2-82	57.50	0/0	0	
Misbah-ul-Haq	28.5.1974		19	2000-2009	1,008	161*	1	33.60	—	—	—	—	24	56/23
Mohammad Aamer	13.4.1992		8	2009-2009	187	30*	0	15.58	21	5-79	42.38	1/0	0	11/10
Mohammad Akram	10.9.1974		9	1995-2000	24	10*	0	2.66	21	5-138	50.52	1/0	4	23
Mohammad Asif	20.12.1982		17	2004-2009	104	29	0	5.77	83	6-41	23.20	6/1	2	29†/9
Mohammad Aslam	5.1.1920		1	1954	34	18	0	17.00	—	—	—	—	0	
Mohammad Farooq	8.4.1938		7	1960-1964	85	47	0	17.00	21	4-70	32.47	1/0	1	
Mohammad Hafeez	17.10.1980		11	2003-2007	677	104	2	33.85	4	1-11	79.75	0/0	4	48/9
Mohammad Hussain	8.10.1976		2	1996-1998	18	17	0	6.00	3	2-66	29.00	0/0	1	14
Mohammad Ilyas	19.3.1946		10	1964-1968	441	126	1	23.21	1	0-1	—	0/0	6	
Mohammad Khalil	11.11.1982		1	2004	9	5	0	3.00	0	0-38	—	0/0	0	3
Mohammad Munaf	2.11.1935		4	1959-1961	63	19	0	12.60	11	4-42	31.00	0/0	0	
Mohammad Nazir	8.3.1946		14	1969-1983	144	29*	0	18.00	34	7-99	33.05	3/0	4	4
Mohammad Ramzan	25.12.1970		1	1997	36	29	0	18.00	0	—	—	—	0	
Mohammad Sami	24.2.1981		34	2000-2009	473	49	0	11.82	84	5-36	50.73	2/0	7	83
Mohammad Talha	15.10.1988		1	2008	—	—	—	—	1	1-88	88.00	0/0	0	
Mohammad Wasim	8.8.1977		18	1996-2000	783	192	2	30.11	—	—	—	—	22/2	25
Mohammad Yousuf (formerly Yousuf Youhana)	27.8.1974		88	1997-2009	7,431	223	24	53.07	0	0-3	—	0/0	65	271†/1
Mohammad Zahid	2.8.1976		5	1996-2002	7	6*	0	1.40	15	7-66	33.46	1/1	4	11
Mohsin Kamal	16.6.1963		9	1983-1994	37	13*	0	9.25	24	4-116	34.25	0/0	4	19
Mohsin Khan	15.3.1955		48	1977-1986	2,709	200	7	37.10	0	0-0	—	—	34	75
[2] Moin Khan	23.9.1971		69	1990-2004	2,741	137	4	28.55	—	—	—	—	128/20	219
[1] Mudassar Nazar	6.4.1956		76	1976-1988	4,114	231	10	38.09	66	6-32	38.36	1/0	48	122
Mufasir-ul-Haq	16.8.1944	27.7.1983	1	1964	8	8*	0	—	3	2-50	28.00	0/0	1	
Munir Malik	10.7.1934		3	1959-1962	7	4	0	2.33	9	5-128	39.77	1/0	1	
Mushtaq Ahmed	28.6.1970		52	1989-2003	656	59	0	11.71	185	7-56	32.97	10/3	23	144
[2] Mushtaq Mohammad	22.11.1943		57	1958-1978	3,643	201	10	39.17	79	5-28	29.22	3/0	42	10

	Born	Died	Tests	Test Career	Runs	HS	100s	Avge	Wkts	BB	5/10	Avge	Ct/St	O/T
Nadeem Abbasi	15.4.1964		3	1989	46	36	0	23.00	0	–	–/–	–	6	6
Nadeem Ghauri	12.10.1962		1	1989	0	0	0	0.00	0	0-20	0/0	–	0	2
[2]Nadeem Khan	10.12.1969		2	1992-1998	34	25	0	17.00	2	2-147	0/0	115.00	0	1
Nasim-ul-Ghani	14.5.1941		29	1957-1972	747	101	1	16.60	52	6-67	2/0	37.67	11	
Naushad Ali	1.10.1943		6	1964	156	39	0	14.18	–	–	–/–	–	9	
Naved Anjum	27.7.1963		2	1989-1990	44	22	0	14.66	4	2-57	0/0	40.50	0	13
Naved Ashraf	4.9.1974		2	1998-1999	64	32	0	21.33	–	–	–/–	–	0	
Naved Latif	21.2.1976		1	2001	20	20	0	10.00	–	–	–/–	–	0	11
Naved-ul-Hasan	28.2.1978		9	2004-2006	239	42*	0	19.91	18	3-30	0/0	58.00	3	69/3
[1]Nazar Mohammad	5.3.1921	12.7.1996	5	1952	277	124*	1	39.57	0	0-4	0/0	–	7	
Niaz Ahmed	11.11.1945		2	1967-1968	17	16*	0	–	3	2-72	0/0	31.33	1	
[2]Pervez Sajjad	30.8.1942	12.4.2000	19	1964-1972	123	24	0	13.66	59	7-74	3/0	23.89	9	
Qaiser Abbas	7.5.1982		1	2000	2	2	0	2.00	0	0-35	0/0	–	0	
Qasim Omar	9.2.1957		26	1983-1986	1,502	210	3	36.63	0	0-0	0/0	–	15	31
[2]Ramiz Raja	14.8.1962		57	1983-1996	2,833	122	2	31.83	–	–	–/–	–	34	198
Rashid Khan	15.12.1959		4	1981-1984	155	59	0	51.66	8	3-129	0/0	45.00	2	29
Rashid Latif	14.10.1968		37	1992-2003	1,381	150	1	28.77	0	0-10	0/0	–	119/11	166
Rehman Sheikh Fazalur	11.6.1935		1	1957	10	8	0	5.00	1	1-43	0/0	99.00	1	
[2]Riaz Afridi	21.11.1985		1	2004	9	9	0	9.00	2	2-42	0/0	43.50	0	
Rizwan-uz-Zaman	4.9.1961		11	1981-1988	345	60	0	19.16	4	3-26	0/0	11.50	4	3
[2]Sadiq Mohammad	3.5.1945		41	1969-1980	2,579	166	5	35.81	0	0-0	0/0	–	28	19
Saeed Ahmed	1.10.1937		41	1957-1972	2,991	172	5	40.41	22	4-64	0/0	36.45	13	
Saeed Ajmal	14.10.1977		5	2009-2009	29	10	0	5.80	18	4-87	0/0	42.27	0	22/11
Saeed Anwar	6.9.1968		55	1990-2001	4,052	188*	11	45.52	0	0-0	0/0	–	18	247
Salah-ud-Din	14.2.1947		5	1964-1969	117	34*	0	19.50	7	2-36	0/0	26.71	3	
Saleem Jaffer	19.11.1962		14	1986-1991	42	10*	0	5.25	36	5-40	1/0	31.63	2	39
Salim Altaf	19.4.1944		21	1967-1978	276	53*	0	14.52	46	4-11	0/0	37.17	3	6
[2]Salim Elahi	21.11.1976		13	1995-2002	436	72	0	18.95	0	–	–/–	–	10/1	48
Salim Malik	16.4.1963		103	1981-1998	5,768	237	15	43.69	5	1-3	0/0	82.80	65	283
Salim Yousuf	7.12.1959		32	1981-1990	1,055	91*	0	27.05	–	–	–/–	–	91/13	86
Salman Butt	7.10.1984		27	2003-2009	1,548	122	3	30.96	1	1-36	0/0	106.00	12	71/16
Saqlain Mushtaq	29.12.1976		49	1995-2003	927	101*	1	14.48	208	8-164	13/3	29.83	15	169
Sarfraz Ahmed	22.5.1987		1	2009	6	5	0	3.00	0	–	–/–	–	4	8
Sarfraz Nawaz Malik	1.12.1948		55	1968-1983	1,045	90	0	17.71	177	9-86	4/1	32.75	26	45
Shabbir Ahmed	21.4.1976		10	2003-2005	88	24*	0	8.80	51	5-48	2/0	23.03	3	32/1

	Born	Died	Tests	Test Career	Runs	HS	100s	Avge	Wks	BB	5/10	Avge	Ct/St	O/T
Shadab Kabir	12.11.1977		5	1996–2001	148	55	0	21.14	0	0-9	0/0	–	11	3
Shafiq Ahmed	28.3.1949		6	1974–1980	99	27*	0	11.00	0	0-1	0/0	–	1	3
²Shafqat Rana	10.8.1943		5	1964–1969	221	95	0	31.57	1	1-2	0/0	9.00	5	
Shahid Afridi	1.3.1980		26	1998–2006	1,683	156	5	37.40	47	5-52	1/0	34.89	10	283‡/26
Shahid Israr	1.3.1950		1	1976	7	7*	0	–			–/–	–	2	
Shahid Mahboob	25.8.1962		1	1989	–	–	–	–	2	2-131	0/0	65.50	0	10
Shahid Mahmood	17.3.1939		1	1962	25	16	0	12.50	0	0-23	0/0	–	0	
Shahid Nazir	4.12.1977		15	1996–2006	194	40	0	12.12	36	5-53	1/0	35.33	5	17
Shahid Saeed	6.1.1966		1	1989	12	12	0	12.00	0	0-7	0/0	–	0	10
Shakeel Ahmed, sen.	12.2.1966		1	1998	1	1	0	1.00	4	4-91	0/0	34.75	1	
Shakeel Ahmed, jun.	12.11.1971		3	1992–1994	74	33	0	14.80			–/–	–	4	2
Sharpe Duncan Albert.	3.8.1937		3	1959	134	56	0	22.33			–/–	–	2	
Shoaib Akhtar	13.8.1975		46	1997–2007	544	47	0	10.07	178	6-11	12/2	25.69	12	139‡/7
Shoaib Malik	1.2.1982		29	2001–2009	1,517	148*	2	36.11	19	4-42	0/0	63.21	16	187/27
Shoaib Mohammad	8.1.1961		45	1983–1995	2,705	203*	7	44.34	5	2-8	0/0	34.00	22	63
Shuja-ud-Din Butt	10.4.1930	7.2.2006	19	1954–1961	395	47	0	15.19	20	3-18	0/0	40.05	8	
Sikander Bakht	25.8.1957		26	1976–1982	146	22*	0	6.34	67	8-69	3/1	36.00	7	27
Sohail Khan	6.3.1984		1	2008			–	–	0	0-33	0/0	–	0	4/1
Sohail Tanvir	12.12.1984		2	2007	17	13	0	5.66	5	3-83	0/0	63.20	0	31/15
Tahir Naqqash	6.6.1959		15	1981–1984	300	57	0	21.42	34	5-40	2/0	41.11	3	40
Talat Ali Malik	29.5.1950		10	1972–1978	370	61	0	23.12	0	0-1	0/0	–	4	
Taslim Arif	1.5.1954	13.3.2008	6	1979–1980	501	210*	1	62.62	1	1-28	0/0	28.00	63	67/23
Taufeeq Umar	20.6.1981		25	2001–2006	1,729	135	4	39.29	0	0-10	0/0	–	33	15
Tauseef Ahmed	10.5.1958		34	1979–1993	318	35*	0	17.66	93	6-45	3/0	31.72	9	19
²Umar Akmal	26.5.1990		6	2009	578	129	1	48.16			–/–	–	3	70
Umar Gul	14.4.1984		26	2003–2009	325	46	0	9.84	96	6-135	4/0	34.62	7	10/3
Wajahatullah Wasti	11.11.1974		6	1998–1999	329	133	1	36.55	0	0-0	0/0	–	7	
²Waqar Hassan	12.9.1932		21	1952–1959	1,071	189	1	31.50	0	0-10	0/0	–	10	
Waqar Younis	16.11.1971		87	1989–2002	1,010	45	0	10.20	373	7-76	22/5	23.56	18	262
Wasim Akram	3.6.1966		104	1984–2001	2,898	257*	3	22.64	414	7-119	25/5	23.62	44	356
Wasim Bari	23.3.1948		81	1967–1983	1,366	85	0	15.88	0	0-2	0/0	–	201/27	51
²Wasim Raja	3.7.1952	23.8.2006	57	1972–1984	2,821	125	4	36.16	51	4-50	0/0	35.80	20	54
²Wazir Mohammad	22.12.1929		20	1952–1959	801	189	2	27.62	0	0-2	0/0	–	5	
Yasir Ali	15.10.1985		1	2003	1	1*	0	–	2	1-12	0/0	27.50	0	
Yasir Arafat	12.3.1982		3	2007–2008	94	50*	0	47.00	9	5-161	1/0	48.66	0	11/5

	Born	Died	Tests	Test Career	Runs	HS	100s	Avge	Wkts	BB	5/10	Avge	Ct/St	O/T
Yasir Hameed	28.2.1978		23	2003–2007	1,450	170	2	34.52	0	0-5	0/0	–	16	56
2 **Younis Ahmed**	20.10.1947		4	1969–1986	177	62	0	29.50	0	0-6	0/0	–	0	2
Younis Khan	29.11.1977		63	1999–2009	5,260	313	16	50.09	7	2-23	0/0	48.71	67	197/22
Yousuf Youhana (*see Mohammad Yousuf*)														
Zaheer Abbas	24.7.1947		78	1969–1985	5,062	274	12	44.79	3	2-21	0/0	44.00	34	62
Zahid Fazal	10.11.1973		9	1990–1995	288	78	0	18.00	–		–/–	–	5	19
2 **Zahoor Elahi**	1.3.1971		2	1996	30	22	0	10.00	–		–/–	–	1	14
Zakir Khan	3.4.1963		2	1985–1989	9	9*			5	3-80	0/0	51.80	1	17
Zulfiqar Ahmed	22.11.1926	3.10.2008	9	1952–1956	200	63*	0	33.33	20	6-42	2/1	18.30	5	
Zulqarnain	25.5.1962		3	1985	24	13	0	6.00	–		–/–	–	8/2	16

SRI LANKA (112 players)

	Born	Died	Tests	Test Career	Runs	HS	100s	Avge	Wkts	BB	5/10	Avge	Ct/St	O/T
Ahangama Franklyn Saliya	14.9.1959		3	1985	11	11	0	5.50	18	5-52	1/0	19.33	1	1
Amalean Kaushik Naginda	7.4.1965		2	1985–1987	9	7*	0	9.00	7	4-97	0/0	22.28	1	8
Amerasinghe Amerasinghe Mudalige Jayantha Gamini	2.2.1954		2	1983	54	34	0	18.00	3	2-73	0/0	50.00	3	
Amerasinghe Merenna Koralage Don Ishara	5.3.1978		1	2007	0	0*	0	–	1	1-62	0/0	105.00	–	8
Anurasiri Sangarange Don	25.2.1966		18	1985–1997	91	24	0	5.35	41	4-71	0/0	37.75	4	45
Arnold Russel Premakumaran	25.10.1973		44	1996–2004	1,821	123	3	28.01	11	3-76	0/0	54.36	51	180/1
Atapattu Marvan Samson	22.11.1970		90	1990–2007	5,502	249	16	39.02	1	1-9	0/0	24.00	58	268/2
Bandara Charitha Malinga	31.12.1979		8	1997–2005	124	43	0	15.50	16	3-84	0/0	39.56	4	30/4
Bandaratilleke Mapa Rallage Chandima Niroshan	16.5.1975		7	1997–2001	93	25	0	11.62	23	5-36	1/0	30.34	0	3
Chandana Umagiliya Durage Upul	7.5.1972		16	1998–2004	616	92	0	26.78	37	6-179	3/1	41.48	7	147
Dassanayake Pubudu Bathiya	11.7.1970		11	1993–1994	196	36	0	13.06	–		–/–	–	19/5	16
de Alwis Ronald Guy	15.2.1959		11	1982–1987	152	28	0	8.00	–		–/–	–	21/2	31
de Mel Ashantha Lakdasa Francis	9.5.1959		17	1981–1986	326	34	0	14.17	59	6-109	3/0	36.94	9	57
de Saram Samantha Indika	2.9.1973		4	1999	117	39	0	23.40	–		–/–	–	2	15/1
de Silva Ashley Mathew	3.12.1963		3	1992–1993	10	9	0	3.33	–		–/–	–	4/1	4
de Silva Dandeniyage Somachandra	11.6.1942		12	1981–1984	406	61	0	21.36	37	5-59	1/0	36.40	5	41
de Silva Ellawalakankanamge Asoka Ranjit	28.3.1956		10	1985–1990	185	50	0	15.41	8	2-67	0/0	129.00	4	28
de Silva Ginigalpodage Ramba Ajit	12.12.1952		4	1981–1982	41	14	0	8.20	7	2-38	0/0	55.00	0	6
de Silva Karunakalage Sajeewa Chanaka	11.1.1971		8	1996–1998	65	27	0	9.28	16	5-85	1/0	55.56	5	38

	Born	Died	Test Career	Tests	Runs	HS	100s	Avge	Wkts	BB	5/10	Avge	Ct/St	O/T
de Silva Pinnaduwage Aravinda	17.10.1965		1984–2002	93	6,361	267	20	42.97	29	3-30	0/0	41.65	43	308
de Silva Sanjeewa Kumara Lanka	29.7.1975		1997	3	36	20*	0	18.00	–	–	–/–	–	1	11
de Silva Weddikkara Ruwan Sujeewa	7.10.1979		2002–2007	3	10	5*	0	10.00	11	4-35	0/0	19.00	1	–
Dharmasena Handunnettige Deepthi Priyantha Kumar	24.4.1971		1993–2003	31	868	62*	0	19.72	69	6-72	3/0	42.31	14	141
Dias Roy Luke	18.10.1952		1981–1986	20	1,285	109	3	36.71	–	0-17	0/0	–	6	58
Dilshan Tillekeratne Mudiyanselage	14.10.1976		1999–2009	60	3,691	168	11	43.42	13	4-10	0/0	36.23	70	171/23
Dunusinghe Chamara Iroshan	19.10.1970		1994–1995	5	160	91	0	16.00	–	–	–/–	–	13/2	1
Fernando Congenige Randhi Dilhara	19.7.1979		2000–2008	33	198	36*	0	7.33	88	5-42	3/0	34.90	10	133½/15
Fernando Ellekutige Rufus Nemesion Susil	19.12.1955		1982–1983	5	112	46	0	11.20	–	–	–/–	–	0	7
Fernando Kandage Hasantha Ruwan Kumara	14.10.1979		2002	2	38	24	0	9.50	4	3-63	0/0	27.00	1	7
Fernando Kandana Arachchige Dinusha Manoj	10.8.1979		2003	2	56	51*	0	28.00	1	1-29	0/0	107.00	0	–
Fernando Thudellage Charitha Buddhika	22.8.1980		2001–2002	9	132	45	0	26.40	18	4-27	0/0	44.00	4	17
Gallage Indika Sanjeewa	22.11.1975		1999	1	3	3	0	3.00	–	0-24	0/0	–	0	3
Goonatillake Hettiarachige Mahes	16.8.1952		1981–1982	5	177	56	0	22.12	–	–	–/–	–	10/3	6
Gunasekera Yohan	8.11.1957		1982	2	48	23	0	12.00	–	–	–/–	–	6	3
Gunawardene Dihan Avishka	26.5.1977		1998–2005	6	181	43	0	16.45	–	–	–/–	–	2	61
Guneratne Roshan Punyajith Wijesinghe	26.1.1962	21.7.2005	1982	1	0	0*	0	–	–	0-84	0/0	–	0	–
Gurusinha Asanka Pradeep	16.9.1966		1985–1996	41	2,452	143	7	38.92	20	2-7	0/0	34.05	33	147
Hathurusinghe Upul Chandika	13.9.1968		1990–1998	26	1,274	83	0	29.62	17	4-66	0/0	46.41	7	35
Herath Herath Mudiyanselage Rangana Keerthi Bandara	19.3.1978		1999–2009	21	207	33*	0	9.00	70	5-99	4/0	36.68	4	6
Hettiarachchi Dinuka	15.7.1976		2000	1	0	0*	0	0.00	2	2-36	0/0	20.50	0	–
Jayasekera Rohan Stanley Amarasiriwardene	7.12.1957		1981	1	2	2	0	1.00	–	–	–/–	–	0	2
Jayasuriya Sanath Teran	30.6.1969		1990–2007	110	6,973	340	14	40.07	98	5-34	2/0	34.34	78	440½/23
Jayawardene Denagamage Proboth Mahela de Silva	27.5.1977		1997–2009	110	9,120	374	27	53.96	6	2-32	0/0	48.66	152	309½/23
Jayawardene Hewasandatchige Asiri Prasanna Wishvanath	9.10.1979		2000–2009	30	1,044	154*	2	30.70	–	–	–/–	–	61/20	6
Jeganathan Sridharan	11.7.1951	14.5.1996	1982	2	19	8	0	4.75	–	0-12	0/0	–	0	6
John Vinothen Bede	27.5.1960		1982–1984	6	53	27*	0	10.60	28	5-60	2/0	21.92	2	5
Jurangpathy Baba Roshan	25.6.1967		1985–1986	2	1	1	0	0.25	1	1-69	0/0	93.00	2	45
Kalaviltgoda Shantha	23.12.1977		2004	1	8	7	0	4.00	–	–	–/–	–	2	–
Kalpage Ruwan Senani	19.2.1970		1993–1998	11	294	63	0	18.37	12	2-27	0/0	64.50	10	86
² Kaluperuma Lalith Wasantha Silva	25.6.1949		1981	2	12	11*	0	4.00	0	0-24	0/0	–	2	4

	Born	Died	Tests	Test Career	Runs	HS	100s	Avge	Wkts	BB	5/10	Avge	Ct/St	O/T
[2] Kaluperuma Sanath Mohan Silva	22.10.1961		4	1983–1987	88	23	0	11.00	2	2-17	00	62.00	6	2
Kaluwitharana Romesh Shantha	24.11.1969		49	1992–2004	1,933	132*	3	26.12		–	–/–	–	93/26	189
Kapugedera Chamara Kantha	24.2.1987		8	2006–2009	418	96	0	34.83	0	0-9	00	–	6	68/11
Kulasekara Kulasekara Mudiyanselage Dinesh Nuwan	22.7.1982		11	2004–2009	245	64	0	16.33	25	4-21	00	34.48	4	64/9
Kuruppu Don Sardha Brendon Priyantha	5.11.1962		4	1986–1991	320	201*	1	53.33		–	–/–	–	1	54
Kuruppuarachchi Ajith Kosala	1.11.1964		2	1985–1986	0	0*	0	–	8	5-44	1/0	18.62	0	
Labrooy Graeme Fredrick	7.6.1964		9	1986–1990	158	70*	0	14.36	27	5-133	1/0	44.22	3	44
Lakshitha Materba Kanatha Gamage Chamila Premanath	4.1.1979		2	2002–2002	42	40	0	14.00	5	2-33	00	31.60	1	7
Liyanage Dulip Kapila	6.6.1972		9	1992–2001	69	23	0	7.66	17	4-56	00	39.17	1	16
Lokuarachchi Kaushal Samaraweera	20.5.1982		4	2003–2003	94	28*	0	23.50	5	2-47	00	59.00	0	21
Madugalle Ranjan Senerath	22.4.1959		21	1981–1988	1,029	103	1	29.40	0	0-0	00	–	9	63
Madurasinghe Madurasinghe Arachchige Wijayasiri Ranjith	30.1.1961		3	1988–1992	24	11	0	4.80	3	3-60	00	57.33	0	12
Mahanama Roshan Siriwardene	31.5.1966		52	1985–1997	2,576	225	4	29.27	0	0-3	00	–	56	213
Maharoof Mohamed Farveez	7.9.1984		20	2003–2007	538	72	0	19.92	24	4-52	00	60.75	6	91/7
Malinga Separamadu Lasith	28.8.1983		28	2004–2007	192	42*	0	9.14	91	5-68	2/0	33.80	7	64/20
Mathews Angelo Davis	2.6.1987		7	2009–2009	379	99	0	37.90	5	1-13	00	60.40	2	18/12
Mendis Balapuwaduge Ajantha Winslo	11.3.1985		10	2008–2009	64	27	0	9.14	44	6-117	2/1	29.50	2	38/12
Mendis Louis Rohan Duleep	25.8.1952		24	1981–1988	1,329	124	4	31.64		–	–/–	–	9	79
Mirando Magina Thilan Thushara	1.3.1981		9	2003–2009	90	15*	0	8.18	28	5-83	1/0	34.32	3	32/5
Mubarak Jehan	10.1.1981		10	2002–2007	254	48	0	15.87	0	0-1	00	–	13	38/16
Muralitharan Muttiah	17.4.1972		131§	1992–2009	1,254	67	0	11.83	787	9-51	66/22	22.65	70	327+9
Nawaz Mohamed Naveed	20.9.1973		1	2002	99	78*	0	99.00	0	–	–/–	–	3	3
Nissanka Ratnayake Arachchige Prabath	25.10.1980		4	2003	18	12*	0	6.00	10	5-64	00	36.60		23
Paranavitana Nishad Tharanga	15.4.1982		10	2008–2009	530	73	0	29.44	1	1-26	00	76.00	4	
Perera Anhettige Suresh Asanka	16.2.1978		3	1998–2001	77	43*	0	25.66	1	1-104	00	180.00	1	20
Perera Panagodage Don Ruchira Laksiri	6.4.1977		8	1998–2002	33	11*	0	11.00	17	3-40	00	38.88	2	192
Prasad Kariyawasam Tirana Gamage Dammika	30.5.1983		8	2008–2009	66	36	0	16.50	13	3-82	00	43.61	10	5
Pushpakumara Karuppiahyage Ravindra	21.7.1975		23	1994–2001	166	44	0	8.73	58	7-116	4/0	38.65	6	31
Ramanayake Champaka Priyadarshana Hewage	8.1.1965		18	1987–1993	143	34*	0	9.53	44	5-82	1/0	42.72		62
Ramyakumara Wijekoon Mudiyanselage Gayan	21.12.1976		2	2005	38	14	0	12.66	2	2-49	00	33.00	0	0/3

§ Muralitharan's figures exclude two runs, five wickets and two catches for the ICC World XI v Australia in the Super Series Test in 2005-06.

Name	Born	Died	Tests	Test Career	Runs	HS	100s	Avge	Wkts	BB	5/10	Avge	Ct/St	O/T
Ranasinghe Anura Nandana	13.10.1956	9.11.1998	2	1981–1982	88	77	0	22.00	1	1-23	0/0	69.00	0	9
[2]Ranatunga Arjuna	1.12.1963		93	1981–2000	5,105	135*	4	35.69	16	2-17	0/0	65.00	47	269
[2]Ranatunga Dammika	12.10.1962		2	1989	87	45	0	29.00	-	-	-	-	0	4
[2]Ranatunga Sanjeeva	25.4.1969		4	1994–1996	531	118	0	33.18	-	-	-	-	2	13
Ratnayake Rumesh Joseph	2.1.1964		23	1982–1991	433	56	0	14.43	73	6-66	-/-	35.10	9	70
Ratnayake Joseph Ravindran	2.5.1960		22	1981–1989	807	93	0	25.21	56	8-83	4/0	35.21	7	78
Samarasekera Maitipage Athula Rohitha	5.8.1961		4	1988–1991	118	57	0	16.85	3	2-38	0/0	34.66	3	39
[2]Samaraweera Dulip Prasanna	12.2.1972		7	1993–1994	211	42	0	15.07	-	-	-	-	5	5
[2]Samaraweera Thilan Thusara	22.9.1976		57	2001–2009	3,938	231	11	51.14	14	4-49	0/0	48.50	36	28
Sangakkara Kumar Chokshanada	27.10.1977		88	2000–2009	7,549	287	21	55.10	-	0-4	-/-	-	157/20	255±20
Senamayake Charith Pandika	19.12.1962		3	1990	97	64	0	19.40	-	-	-	-	7	2
Silva Kelaniyage Jayantha	2.6.1973		7	1995–1997	6	6*	0	2.00	20	4-16	0/0	32.35	2	1
[2]Silva Lindamullage Prageeth Chamara	14.12.1979		11	2006–2007	537	152*	1	33.56	1	1-57	0/0	65.00	7	55/15
Silva Sampathawaduge Amal Rohitha	12.12.1960		9	1982–1988	353	111	1	25.21	-	-	-	-	33/1	20
Tharanga Warushavithana Upul	2.2.1985		15	2005–2007	713	165	1	28.52	-	-	-	-	11	86±8
Tillekeratne Hashan Prasanna	14.7.1967		83	1989–2009	4,545	204*	11	42.87	0	0-0	0/0	-	122/2	200
Upashantha Kalutarage Eric Amila	10.6.1972		2	1998–2002	10	6	0	3.33	4	2-41	0/0	50.00	0	12
Vaas Warnakulasuriya Patabendige Ushantha Joseph Chaminda	27.1.1974		111	1994–2009	3,089	100*	1	24.32	355	7-71	12/2	29.58	31	321±6
Vandort Michael Graydon	19.11.1980		20	2001–2008	1,144	140	4	36.90	0	0-1	-/-	-	6	1
Warnapura Bandula	1.3.1953		4	1981–1982	96	38	0	12.00	0	0-1	-/-	-	2	12
Warnapura Basnayake Shalith Malinda	26.5.1979		14	2007–2009	821	120	2	35.69	0	0-40	0/0	-	14	3
Warnaweera Kahakatchchi Patabandige Jayananda	23.11.1960		10	1985–1994	39	20	0	4.33	32	4-25	0/0	31.90	0	6
Weerasinghe Colombage Don Udesh Sanjeewa	1.3.1968		1	1985	3	3	0	3.00	0	0-8	0/0	-	0	-
Wedagedara Uda Walawwe Mahim Bandaralage Chanaka Asanka	20.3.1981		4	2007–2009	19	8	0	6.33	10	4-87	0/0	47.30	1	4
[2]Wettimuny Mithra de Silva	11.6.1951		2	1982	28	17	0	7.00	-	-	-	-	2	1
[2]Wettimuny Sidath	12.8.1956		23	1981–1986	1,221	190	2	29.07	0	0-16	-/-	-	10	35
Wickremasinghe Angurupulge Gamini Dayantha	27.12.1965		3	1989–1992	17	13*	0	8.50	-	-	-	-	9/1	4
Wickremasinghe Gallage Pramodya	14.8.1971		40	1991–2000	555	51	0	9.40	85	6-60	3/0	41.87	18	134
Wijegunawardene Kapila Indaka Weerakkody	23.11.1964		2	1991–1991	14	6*	0	4.66	7	4-51	0/0	21.00	0	26
Wijesuriya Roger Gerard Christopher Ediriweera	18.2.1960		4	1981–1985	22	8	0	4.40	1	1-68	0/0	294.00	1	8

	Born	Died	Tests	Test Career	Runs	HS	100s	Avge	Wkts	BB	5/10	Avge	Ct/St	O/T
Wijetunge Piyal Kashyapa	6.8.1971		1	1993	10	10	0	5.00	2	1-58	0/0	59.00	0	
Zoysa Demuni Nuwan Tharanga	13.5.1978		30	1996–2004	288	28*	0	8.47	64	5-20	1/0	33.70	4	9

ZIMBABWE (74 players)

	Born	Died	Tests	Test Career	Runs	HS	100s	Avge	Wkts	BB	5/10	Avge	Ct/St	O/T
Arnott Kevin John	8.3.1961		4	1992	302	101*	1	43.14	–	–	–/–	–	4	13
Blignaut Arnoldus Mauritius ("Andy")	1.8.1978		19	2000–2005	886	92	0	26.84	53	5-73	3/0	37.05	13	51
Brain David Hayden	4.10.1964		9	1992–1994	115	28	0	10.45	30	5-42	1/0	30.50	4	23
Brandes Eddo André	5.3.1963		10	1992–1999	121	39	0	10.08	26	3-45	0/0	36.57	4	59
Brent Gary Bazil	13.1.1976		4	1999–2001	35	25	0	5.83	7	3-21	0/0	44.85	–	70/3
Briant Gavin Aubrey	11.4.1969		1	1992	17	16	0	8.50					0	5
Bruk-Jackson Glen Keith	25.4.1969		2	1993	39	31	0	9.75					–	1
Burmester Mark Greville	24.1.1968		3	1992	54	30*	0	27.00	3	3-78	0/0	75.66	1	8
Butchart Iain Peter	9.5.1960		1	1994	23	15	0	11.50	1	0-11	0/0	–	–	20
Campbell Alistair Douglas Ross	23.9.1972		60	1992–2002	2,858	103	2	27.21	0	0-1	0/0	–	60	188
Carlisle Stuart Vance	10.5.1972		37	1994–2005	1,615	118	2	26.91	–	–	–/–	–	34	111
Chigumbura Elton	14.3.1986		6	2003–2004	187	71	0	15.58	9	5-54	1/0	55.33	2	100†/7
Coventry Charles Kevin	8.3.1983		2	2005	88	37	0	22.00					3	26
Cremer Alexander Graeme	19.9.1986		2	2004–2005	29	12	0	2.63	13	3-86	0/0	45.76	3	19/1
Crocker Gary John	16.5.1962		6	1992	69	23	0	23.00	3	2-65	0/0	72.33	0	6
Dabengwa Keith Mbusi	17.8.1980		3	2005	90	35	0	15.00	5	3-127	0/0	49.80	1	32/6
Dekker Mark Hamilton	5.12.1969		14	1993–1996	333	68*	0	15.85	0	0-5	0/0	–	12	23
Duffin Terrence	20.3.1982		2	2005	80	56	0	20.00					2	23
Ebrahim Dion Digby	7.8.1980		29	2000–2005	1,226	94	0	22.70					16	82
Ervine Sean Michael	6.12.1982		5	2003–2003	261	86	0	32.62	9	4-146	0/0	43.11	7	42
Evans Craig Neil	29.11.1969		3	1996–2003	52	22	0	8.66	0	0-8	0/0	–	1	53
Ewing Gavin Mackie	21.11.1981		1	2003–2005	108	71	0	18.00	2	1-27	0/0	130.00	1	7
Ferreira Neil Robert	3.6.1979		1	2005	21	16	0	10.50					0	–
Flower Andrew	28.4.1968		63	1992–2002	4,794	232*	12	51.54	0	0-0	0/0	–	151/9	213
[2]Flower Grant William	20.12.1970		67	1992–2003	3,457	201*	6	29.54	25	4-41	0/0	61.48	43	219
Friend Travis John	7.1.1981		13	2001–2003	447	81	0	29.80	25	5-31	1/0	43.60	2	51
Goodwin Murray William	11.12.1972		19	1997–2000	1,414	166*	3	42.84	0	0-3	0/0	–	10	71

	Born	Died	Tests	Test Career	Runs	HS	100s	Avge	Wkts	BB	5/10	Avge	Ct/St	O/T
Gripper Trevor Raymond	28.12.1975		20	1999-2003	809	112	1	21.86	6	2-91	0/0	84.83	14	8
Hondo Douglas Tafadzwa	7.7.1979		9	2001-2004	83	19	0	9.22	21	6-59	1/0	36.85	5	56
Houghton David Laud	23.6.1957		22	1992-1997	1,464	266	4	43.05	0	0-0	0/0	–	17	63
Huckle Adam George	21.9.1971		8	1997-1998	74	28*	0	6.72	25	6-109	2/1	34.88	3	19
James Wayne Robert	27.8.1965		4	1993-1994	61	33	0	15.25	–	–	–/–	–	16	11
Jarvis Malcolm Peter	6.12.1955		5	1992-1994	5	2*	0	2.00	11	3-30	0/0	35.72	2	12
Johnson Neil Clarkson	24.11.1970		13	1998-2000	532	107	1	24.18	15	4-77	0/0	39.60	12	48
Lock Alan Charles Ingram	10.9.1962		1	1995	17	8*	0	8.00	5	3-68	0/0	21.00	–	8
Madondo Trevor Nyasha	22.11.1976	11.6.2001	3	1997-2000	90	74*	0	30.00	–	–	–/–	–	1	13
Mahwire Ngonidzashe Blessing	31.7.1982		10	2002-2005	147	50*	0	13.36	18	4-92	0/0	50.83	1	23
Maregwede Alester	5.8.1981		2	2003	74	28	0	18.50	–	–	–/–	–	2	11
Marillier Douglas Anthony	24.4.1978		5	2000-2001	185	73	0	30.83	11	4-57	0/0	29.27	2	48
Masakadza Hamilton	9.8.1983		15	2001-2005	785	119	1	27.06	2	1-9	0/0	19.50	8	85/7
Matambanadzo Everton Zvikomborero	13.4.1976		3	1996-1999	17	7	0	4.25	4	2-62	0/0	62.50	0	7
Matsikenyeri Stuart	3.5.1983		8	2003-2004	351	57	0	23.40	2	1-58	0/0	172.50	7	105/7
Mbangwa Mpumelelo ("Pommie")	26.6.1976		15	1996-2000	34	8	0	2.00	32	3-23	0/0	31.43	2	29
Mpofu Christopher Bobby	27.11.1985		6	2004-2005	17	7	0	2.83	8	4-109	0/0	69.50	0	37/3
Mupariwa Tawanda	16.4.1985		1	2003	15	14	0	15.00	0	0-136	0/0	–	0	35/4
Murphy Brian Andrew	1.12.1976		11	1999-2001	123	30	0	10.25	18	3-32	0/0	61.83	11	31
Mutendera David Travolta	25.1.1979		1	2000	10	10	0	5.00	0	0-29	0/0	–	0	9
Mwayenga Waddington	20.6.1984		1	2005	15	14*	0	15.00	1	1-79	0/0	79.00	0	3
Nkala Mluleki Luke	1.4.1981		10	2000-2004	187	47	0	14.38	11	3-82	0/0	66.09	4	50/1
Olonga Henry Khaaba	3.7.1976		30	1994-2002	184	24	0	5.41	68	5-70	2/0	38.52	10	50
Panyangara Tinashe	21.10.1985		3	2003-2004	128	40*	0	32.00	8	3-28	0/0	35.75	0	23
Peall Stephen Guy	2.9.1969		4	1993-1994	60	30	0	15.00	4	2-89	0/0	75.75	1	21
Price Raymond William	12.6.1976		18	1999-2003	224	36	0	9.73	69	6-73	5/1	35.86	3	69/4
Pycroft Andrew John	6.6.1956		3	1992	152	60	0	30.40	–	–	–/–	–	2	20
Ranchod Ujesh	17.5.1969		1	1992	8	7	0	4.00	1	1-45	0/0	45.00	0	3
[2] Rennie Gavin James	12.1.1976		23	1997-2001	1,023	93	0	22.73	1	1-40	0/0	84.00	13	40
[2] Rennie John Alexander	29.7.1970		4	1993-1997	62	22	0	12.40	3	2-22	0/0	97.66	1	44
Rogers Barney Guy	20.8.1982		4	2004	90	29	0	11.25	0	0-17	0/0	–	0	15
Shah Ali Hassimshah	7.8.1959		3	1992-1996	122	62	0	24.40	1	1-46	0/0	125.00	0	28
Sibanda Vusimuzi	10.10.1983		3	2003-2004	48	18	0	8.00	–	–	–/–	–	4	20
[2] Strang Bryan Colin	9.6.1972		26	1994-2001	465	53	0	12.91	56	5-101	1/0	39.33	11	77½/2
[2] Strang Paul Andrew	28.7.1970		24	1994-2001	839	106*	1	27.06	70	8-109	4/1	36.02	15	95

	Born	Died	Tests	Test Career	Runs	HS	100s	Avge	Wkts	BB	5/10	Avge	Ct/St	O/T
Streak Heath Hilton	16.3.1974		65	1993–2005	1,990	127*	1	22.35	216	6-73	7/0	28.14	17	187‡
Taibu Tatenda	14.5.1983		24	2001–2005	1,273	153	1	29.60	1	1-27	0/0	27.00	48/4	111‡/6
Taylor Brendan Ross Murray	6.2.1986		10	2003–2005	422	78	0	21.10	0	0-6	0/0	–	7	92/3
Traicos Athanasios John	17.5.1947		4†	1992	11	5	0	2.75	14	5-86	1/0	40.14	4	27
Useya Prosper	26.3.1985		1	2003	45	45	0	22.50	0	0-55	0/0	–	2	101/7
Vermeulen Mark Andrew	2.3.1979		8	2002–2003	414	118	1	25.87	–	–	–	–	6	43
Viljoen Dirk Peter	11.3.1977		2	1997–2000	57	38	0	14.25	1	1-14	0/0	65.00	1	53
Waller Andrew Christopher	25.9.1959		2	1996	69	50	0	23.00	–	–	–	–	1	39
Watambwa Brighton Tonderai	9.6.1977		6	2000–2001	11	4*	0	3.66	14	4-64	0/0	35.00	0	
Whittall Andrew Richard	28.3.1973		10	1996–1999	114	17	0	7.60	7	3-73	0/0	105.14	8	63
Whittall Guy James	5.9.1972		46	1993–2002	2,207	203*	4	29.42	51	4-18	0/0	40.94	19	147
Wishart Craig Brian	9.1.1974		27	1995–2005	1,098	114	1	22.40	–	–	–/–	–	15	90

BANGLADESH (57 players)

	Born	Died	Tests	Test Career	Runs	HS	100s	Avge	Wkts	BB	5/10	Avge	Ct/St	O/T
Abdur Razzak	15.6.1982		5	2005–2008	129	33	0	21.50	7	3-93	0/0	80.71	2	89/11
Aftab Ahmed	10.11.1985		14	2004–2007	514	82*	0	21.41	5	2-31	0/0	45.00	6	80/9
Akram Khan	1.11.1968		8	2000–2003	259	44	0	16.18	–	–	–/–	–	6	44
Al Sahariar	23.4.1978		15	2000–2003	683	71	0	22.76	–	–	–/–	–	10	29
Alamgir Kabir	10.1.1981		3	2002–2003	8	4	0	2.00	0	0-39	0/0	–	0	
Alok Kapali	1.1.1984		17	2002–2005	584	85	0	17.69	6	3-3	0/0	118.16	5	65/5
Aminul Islam	2.2.1968		13	2000–2002	530	145	1	21.20	1	1-66	0/0	149.00	5	39
Anwar Hossain Monir	31.12.1981		3	2003–2005	22	13	0	7.33	0	0-95	0/0	–	0	1
Anwar Hossain Piju	10.12.1983		2	2002	14	12	0	7.00	–	–	–/–	–	0	1
Bikash Ranjan Das	14.7.1982		1	2000	2	2	0	1.00	1	1-64	0/0	72.00	1	
Ehsanul Haque	1.12.1979		7	2002	5	5	0	3.50	0	0-18	0/0	–	1	6
Enamul Haque, sen.	27.2.1966		10	2000–2003	180	24*	0	12.00	18	4-136	0/0	57.05	1	29
Enamul Haque, jun.	5.12.1986		14	2003–2009	53	13	0	5.88	41	7-95	3/1	39.24	3	10
Fahim Muntasir	1.11.1980		3	2001–2002	52	33	0	8.66	5	3-131	0/0	68.40	1	3
Faisal Hossain	26.10.1978		1	2003	5	5	0	3.50	–	–	–/–	–	0	4
Habibul Bashar	17.8.1972		50	2000–2007	3,026	113	3	30.87	0	0-1	0/0	–	22	111
Hannan Sarkar	1.12.1982		17	2002–2004	662	76	0	20.06	–	–	–/–	–	7	20

	Born	Died	Tests	Test Career	Runs	HS	100s	Avge	Wkts	BB	5/10	Avge	Ct/St	O/T
Hasibul Hossain	3.6.1977		5	2000–2001	97	31	0	10.77	6	2-125	–/–	95.16	1	32
Imrul Kayes	2.2.1987		8	2008–2009	190	33	0	11.87	–	0-7	0/0	–	1	3
Javed Omar Belim	25.11.1976		40	2000–2007	1,720	119	1	22.05	0	0-12	0/0	–	6	59
Junaid Siddique	30.10.1987		13	2007–2009	588	78	0	23.52	0	0-2	0/0	–	10	29/5
Khaled Mahmud	26.7.1971		12	2001–2003	266	45	0	12.09	13	4-37	0/0	64.00	2	77
Khaled Mashud	8.2.1976		44	2000–2007	1,409	103*	1	19.04	–	–	–/–	–	78/9	126
Mahbubul Alam	1.12.1983		4	2008	5	2	0	1.25	5	2-62	0/0	62.80	0	5
Mahmudullah	4.2.1986		4	2009–2009	230	96*	0	38.33	14	5-51	1/0	24.14	5	37/8
Manjural Islam	7.11.1979		17	2000–2003	81	21	0	3.68	28	6-81	1/0	57.32	4	34
Manjural Islam Rana	4.5.1984	16.3.2007	6	2003–2004	257	69	0	25.70	5	3-84	0/0	80.20	3	25
Mashrafe bin Mortaza	5.10.1983		36	2001–2009	797	79	0	12.85	78	4-60	0/0	41.52	9	101‡/11
Mehrab Hossain, sen.	22.9.1978		9	2000–2003	241	71	0	13.38	0	0-5	0/0	–	6	18
Mehrab Hossain, jun.	8.7.1987		7	2007–2008	243	83	0	20.25	4	2-29	0/0	70.25	2	18/2
Mohammad Ashraful	9.9.1984		52	2001–2009	2,242	158*	5	23.11	20	2-42	0/0	58.30	23	150‡/12
Mohammad Rafique	5.9.1970		33	2000–2007	1,059	111	1	18.57	100	6-77	7/0	40.76	7	123‡/1
Mohammad Salim	15.10.1981		2	2003	49	26	0	16.33	–	–	–/–	–	3/1	1
Mohammad Sharif	12.12.1985		10	2000–2007	122	24*	0	7.17	14	4-98	0/0	79.00	5	9
Mushfiqur Rahim	1.9.1988		18	2005–2009	864	101	1	27.00	–	–	–/–	–	27/4	59/12
Mushfiqur Rahman	1.1.1980		10	2000–2004	232	46*	0	13.64	13	4-65	0/0	63.30	6	28
Naeem Islam	31.12.1986		2	2008	44	19	0	11.00	1	1-11	0/0	46.00		244
²Nafis Iqbal	31.1.1985		11	2004–2005	518	121	1	23.54	–	–	–/–	–	2	16
Naimur Rahman	19.9.1974		8	2000–2002	210	48	0	15.00	12	6-132	1/0	59.83	4	29
Nazmul Hossain	5.10.1987		1	2004	8	8*	0	8.00	2	2-114	0/0	57.00	0	31/1
Rafiqul Islam	7.11.1977		1	2002	7	6	0	3.50	–	–	–/–	–	1	3
Rajin Saleh	20.11.1983		24	2003–2008	1,141	89	0	23.93	2	1-9	0/0	134.00	15	43
Raqibul Hasan	8.10.1987		7	2008–2009	268	65	0	19.14	1	1-0	0/0	5.00	7	36/4
Rubel Hossain	1.1.1990		4	2009–2009	13	4*	0	4.33	4	3-76	0/0	107.75	2	8/3
Sajidul Islam	18.11.1988		2	2007	14	6	0	3.50	3	2-71	0/0	58.33	0	
Sanwar Hossain	5.8.1973		9	2001–2003	345	49	0	19.16	5	2-128	0/0	62.00	1	27
Shafiul Islam	6.10.1989		2	2009	23	9	0	5.75	4	3-86	0/0	53.50	0	
Shahadat Hossain	7.8.1986		25	2005–2009	314	40	0	9.23	60	6-27	3/0	42.18	5	43/4
Shahriar Hossain	1.6.1976		3	2000–2003	99	48	0	19.80	–	–	–/–	–	0/1	20
Shahriar Nafees	25.1.1986		16	2005–2009	835	138	1	26.09	–	–	–/–	–	12	60/1
Shakib Al Hasan	24.3.1987		16	2007–2009	790	96*	0	28.21	57	7-36	6/0	28.92	8	75/11
Syed Rasel	3.7.1984		6	2005–2007	37	19	0	4.62	12	4-129	0/0	47.75	0	46/8

	Born	Died	Tests	Test Career	Runs	HS	100s	Avge	Wkts	BB	5/10	Avge	Ct/St	O/T
Talha Jubair	10.12.1985		7	2002–2004	52	31	0	6.50	14	3-135	0/0	55.07	1	6
²Tamim Iqbal	20.3.1989		14	2007–2009	842	151	2	32.38	0	0-1	0/0	–	7	66/12
Tapash Baisya	25.12.1982		21	2002–2005	384	66	0	11.29	36	4-72	0/0	59.36	6	56
Tareq Aziz	4.9.1983		3	2003–2004	22	10*	0	11.00	1	1-76	0/0	261.00	–	10
Tushar Imran	10.12.1983		5	2002–2007	89	28	0	8.90	0	0-48	0/0	–	1	41

Notes

In one Test, A. and G. G. Hearne played for England; their brother, F. Hearne, for South Africa.

The Waughs and New Zealand's Marshalls are the only instance of Test-playing twins.

P. N. and G. Kirsten: half-brothers.

Amarsingh, L.: brother of L. Ramji.

Azmat Rana: brother of Shafqat Rana.

Bazid Khan: son of Majid Khan and grandson of M. Jahangir Khan.

Chappell, G. S., I. M. and T. M.: grandsons of V. Y. Richardson.

Collins, P. T.: half-brother of F. H. Edwards.

Cooper, W. H.: great-grandfather of A. P. Sheahan.

Edwards, F. H.: half-brother of P. T. Collins.

Hanif Mohammad: brother of Mushtaq, Sadiq and Wazir Mohammad, and father of Shoaib Mohammad.

Hearne, F.: father of G. A. L. Hearne (South Africa).

Jahangir Khan, M.: father of Majid Khan and grandfather of Bazid Khan.

Kamran Akmal: brother of Umar Akmal.

Khalid Wazir: son of S. Wazir Ali.

Majid Khan: son of M. Jahangir Khan and father of Bazid Khan.

Manzoor Elahi: brother of Salim and Zahoor Elahi.

Moin Khan: brother of Nadeem Khan.

Mudassar Nazar: son of Nazar Mohammad.

Mushtaq Mohammad: brother of Hanif, Sadiq and Wazir Mohammad.

Nadeem Khan: brother of Moin Khan.

Nafis Iqbal: brother of Tamim Iqbal.

Nazar Mohammad: father of Mudassar Nazar.

Nazir Ali, S.: brother of S. Wazir Ali.

Pervez Sajjad: brother of Waqar Hassan.

Ramiz Raja: brother of Wasim Raja.

Ramji, L.: brother of L. Amarsingh.

Richardson, V. Y.: grandfather of G. S., I. M. and T. M. Chappell.

Sadiq Mohammad: brother of Hanif, Mushtaq and Wazir Mohammad.

Saeed Ahmed: brother of Younis Ahmed.

Salim Elahi: brother of Manzoor and Zahoor Elahi.

Shafqat Rana: brother of Azmat Rana.

Sheahan, A. P.: great-grandson of W. H. Cooper.

Shoaib Mohammad: son of Hanif Mohammad.

Tamim Iqbal: brother of Nafis Iqbal.

Umar Akmal: brother of Kamran Akmal.

Waqar Hassan: brother of Pervez Sajjad.

Wasim Raja: brother of Ramiz Raja.

Wazir Ali, S.: brother of S. Nazir Ali and father of Khalid Wazir.

Wazir Mohammad: brother of Hanif, Mushtaq and Sadiq Mohammad.

Yograj Singh: father of Yuvraj Singh.

Younis Ahmed: brother of Saeed Ahmed.

Yuvraj Singh: son of Yograj Singh.

Zahoor Elahi: brother of Manzoor and Salim Elahi.

PLAYERS APPEARING FOR MORE THAN ONE TEST TEAM

Fourteen cricketers have appeared for two countries in Test matches, namely:

Amir Elahi (India 1, Pakistan 5)
J. J. Ferris (Australia 8, England 1)
S. C. Guillen (West Indies 5, New Zealand 3)
Gul Mahomed (India 8, Pakistan 1)
F. Hearne (England 2, South Africa 4)
A. H. Kardar (India 3, Pakistan 23)
W. E. Midwinter (England 4, Australia 8)

F. Mitchell (England 2, South Africa 3)
W. L. Murdoch (Australia 18, England 1)
Nawab of Pataudi, sen. (England 3, India 3)
A. J. Traicos (South Africa 3, Zimbabwe 4)
A. E. Trott (Australia 3, England 2)
K. C. Wessels (Australia 24, South Africa 16)
S. M. J. Woods (Australia 3, England 3)

Wessels also played 54 one-day internationals for Australia and 55 for South Africa.

The following players appeared for the ICC World XI against Australia in the Super Series Test in 2005–06: M. V. Boucher, R. Dravid, A. Flintoff, S. J. Harmison, Inzamam-ul-Haq, J. H. Kallis, B. C. Lara, M. Muralitharan, V. Sehwag, G. C. Smith, D. L. Vettori.

Note In 1970, England played five first-class matches against the Rest of the World after the cancellation of South Africa's tour. Players were awarded England caps, but the matches are no longer considered to have Test status. Alan Jones (born 4.11.1938) made his only appearance for England in this series, scoring 5 and 0; he did not bowl and took no catches.

ONE-DAY INTERNATIONAL CRICKETERS

The following players have appeared for Test-playing countries in one-day internationals but had not represented their countries in Test matches by December 31, 2009. (Numbers in brackets signify number of one-day internationals for each player: where a second number appears, e.g. (5/1), it signifies the number of Twenty20 internationals for that player.)

England

M. W. Alleyne (10), I. D. Austin (9), A. D. Brown (16), D. R. Brown (9), G. Chapple (1), J. W. M. Dalrymple (27/3), S. M. Davies (1/1), J. L. Denly (9/3), M. V. Fleming (11), P. J. Franks (1), I. J. Gould (18), A. P. Grayson (2), G. W. Humpage (3), T. E. Jesty (10), E. C. Joyce (17/2), G. D. Lloyd (6), A. G. R. Loudon (1), J. D. Love (3), M. B. Loye (7), M. A. Lynch (3), A. D. Mascarenhas (20/14), E. J. G. Morgan (15/3), P. Mustard (10/2), P. A. Nixon (19/1), S. R. Patel (11), A. U. Rashid (5/5), M. J. Smith (5), N. M. K. Smith (7), J. N. Snape (10/1), V. S. Solanki (51/3), J. O. Troughton (6), C. M. Wells (2), V. J. Wells (9), A. G. Wharf (13), L. J. Wright (28/16), M. H. Yardy (6/3).
Note: D. R. Brown also played 16 one-day internationals for Scotland and E. J. G. Morgan 23 for Ireland.

Australia

G. A. Bishop (2), R. J. Campbell (2), M. J. Cosgrove (3), M. J. Di Venuto (9), B. R. Dorey (4), C. J. Ferguson (25/3), B. Geeves (2/1), S. F. Graf (11), R. J. Harris (1), S. M. Harwood (1/3), I. J. Harvey (73), M. C. Henriques (2/1), J. R. Hopes (67/11), D. J. Hussey (23/11), B. Laughlin (5/1), S. Lee (45), M. L. Lewis (7/2), R. J. McCurdy (11), K. H. MacLeay (16), J. P. Maher (26), S. E. Marsh (19/3), D. P. Nannes (1/1), A. A. Noffke (1/2), T. D. Paine (15/1), G. D. Porter (2), L. Ronchi (4/3), J. D. Siddons (1), A. M. Stuart (3), G. S. Trimble (2), A. C. Voges (7/4), D. A. Warner (7/8), B. E. Young (6), A. K. Zesers (2).
Notes: A. Symonds appeared for Australia in 94 one-day internationals before making his Test debut. D. P. Nannes also played two Twenty20 internationals for the Netherlands.

South Africa

S. Abrahams (1), D. M. Benkenstein (23), G. H. Bodi (2/1), L. L. Bosman (11/6), R. E. Bryson (7), D. J. Callaghan (29), D. N. Crookes (32), J. C. Kent (2), L. J. Koen (5), G. J-P. Kruger (3/1), J. Louw (3/2), P. V. Mpitsang (1), S. J. Palframan (7), A. N. Petersen (10), V. D. Philander (7/7), N. Pothas (3), A. G. Puttick (1), C. E. B. Rice (3), M. J. R. Rindel (22), D. B. Rundle (2), T. G. Shaw (9), E. O. Simons (23), E. L. R. Stewart (6), R. Telemachus (37/3), T. Tshabalala (4), L. L. Tsotsobe (3/1), R. E. van der Merwe (10/9), J. J. van der Wath (10/8), V. B. van Jaarsveld (2/3), M. N. van Wyk (6/2), C. J. P. G. van Zyl (2), H. S. Williams (7), M. Yachad (1).

West Indies
H. A. G. Anthony (3), D. M. Bravo (4), D. Brown (3), B. St A. Browne (4), P. A. Browne (5), H. R. Bryan (15), D. C. Butler (5/1), R. T. Crandon (1), R. R. Emrit (2), S. E. Findlay (9/2), A. D. S. Fletcher (10/8), R. S. Gabriel (11), R. C. Haynes (8), R. O. Hurley (9), K. C. B. Jeremy (6), L. R. Johnson (3), N. T. Pascal (1), K. A. Pollard (15/10), K. O. A. Powell (2), M. R. Pydanna (3), A. C. L. Richards (1/1), K. F. Semple (7), D. C. Thomas (2/1), C. M. Tuckett (1), L. R. Williams (15).

New Zealand
M. D. Bailey (1), B. R. Blair (14), N. T. Broom (16/9), C. E. Bulfin (4), T. K. Canning (4), P. G. Coman (3), B. J. Diamanti (1/1), M. W. Douglas (6), B. G. Hadlee (2), L. J. Hamilton (2), R. T. Hart (1), R. L. Hayes (1), P. A. Hitchcock (14/1), L. G. Howell (12), N. L. McCullum (2/12), P. D. McGlashan (4/8), B. J. McKechnie (14), E. B. McSweeney (16), J. P. Millmow (5), C. J. Nevin (37), A. J. Penn (5), R. G. Petrie (12), R. B. Reid (9), S. J. Roberts (2), L. W. Stott (1), G. P. Sulzberger (3), A. R. Tait (5), E. P. Thompson (1/1), M. D. J. Walker (3), R. J. Webb (3), J. W. Wilson (6), W. A. Wisneski (3).

India
S. Badrinath (3), A. C. Bedade (13), A. Bhandari (2), Bhupinder Singh, sen. (2), G. Bose (1), V. B. Chandrasekhar (7), U. Chatterjee (3), N. A. David (4), P. Dharmani (1), R. S. Gavaskar (11), R. S. Ghai (6), M. S. Gony (2), R. A. Jadeja (14/5), Joginder Sharma (4/4), A. V. Kale (1), S. C. Khanna (10), G. K. Khoda (8), A. R. Khurasiya (12), V. Kohli (15), P. Kumar (34/1), T. Kumaran (8), J. J. Martin (10), D. Mongia (57/1), S. P. Mukherjee (8), A. M. Nayar (3), G. K. Pandey (2), J. V. Paranjpe (4), A. K. Patel (8), Y. K. Pathan (30/11), S. K. Raina (82/11), Randhir Singh (2), S. S. Raul (2), A. M. Salvi (4), R. G. Sharma (41/14), L. R. Shukla (3), R. P. Singh (2), R. S. Sodhi (18), S. Somasunder (2), S. Sriram (8), Sudhakar Rao (1), M. K. Tiwary (1), S. Tyagi (1/1), R. V. Uthappa (38/9), P. S. Vaidya (4), Y. Venugopal Rao (16), Jai P. Yadav (12).

Pakistan
Aamer Hameed (2), Aamer Hanif (5), Ahmed Shehzad (4/2), Akhtar Sarfraz (4), Arshad Pervez (2), Asif Mahmood (2), Faisal Athar (1), Ghulam Ali (3), Haafiz Shahid (3), Hasan Jamil (6), Imran Abbas (2), Iqbal Sikandar (4), Irfan Bhatti (1), Javed Qadir (1), Junaid Zia (4), Kamran Hussain (2), Kashif Raza (1), Khalid Latif (4/1), Mahmood Hamid (1), Mansoor Amjad (1/1), Mansoor Rana (2), Manzoor Akhtar (7), Maqsood Rana (1), Masood Iqbal (1), Moin-ul-Atiq (5), Mujahid Jamshed (4), Naeem Ahmed (1), Naeem Ashraf (2), Najaf Shah (1), Naseer Malik (3), Nasir Jamshed (12), Naumanullah (1), Parvez Mir (3), Rizwan Ahmed (1), Saadat Ali (8), Saeed Azad (1), Sajid Ali (13), Sajjad Akbar (2), Salim Pervez (1), Samiullah Khan (2), Shahid Anwar (1), Shakil Khan (1), Sohail Fazal (1), Tanvir Mehdi (1), Wahab Riaz (5/1), Wasim Haider (3), Zafar Iqbal (8), Zahid Ahmed (2).

Sri Lanka
J. W. H. D. Boteju (2), D. L. S. de Silva (2), G. N. de Silva (4), L. H. D. Dilhara (8/2), E. R. Fernando (3), T. L. Fernando (1), U. N. K. Fernando (2), J. C. Gamage (4), W. C. A. Ganegama (4), F. R. M. Goonatilleke (1), P. W. Gunaratne (23), A. A. W. Gunawardene (1), P. D. Heyn (2), W. S. Jayantha (17), P. S. Jayaprakashdaran (1), S. A. Jayasinghe (2), S. H. T. Kandamby (26/4), S. H. U. Karnain (19), R. A. S. Lakmal (3), C. Mendis (1), A. M. N. Munasinghe (5), H. G. D. Nayanakantha (3), A. R. M. Opatha (5), S. P. Pasqual (2), K. G. Perera (1), M. D. K. Perera (4), N. L. T. C. Perera (2), H. S. M. Pieris (3), M. Pushpakumara (1/1), S. K. Ranasinghe (4), N. Ranatunga (2), S. Randiv (4), N. L. K. Ratnayake (2), A. P. B. Tennekoon (4), M. H. Tissera (3), M. L. Udawatte (9/5), D. M. Vonhagt (1), A. P. Weerakkody (1), K. Weeraratne (15/5), S. R. de S. Wettimuny (3), R. P. A. H. Wickremaratne (3).

Zimbabwe
R. D. Brown (7), R. W. Chakabva (1/1), C. J. Chibhabha (49/7), K. M. Curran (11), S. G. Davies (4), K. G. Duers (6), E. A. Essop-Adam (1), D. A. G. Fletcher (6), T. N. Garwe (1), J. G. Heron (6), R. S. Higgins (1), V. R. Hogg (2), A. J. Ireland (26/1), K. M. Jarvis (9), T. Kamungozi (4), F. Kasteni (3), A. J. Mackay (3), G. C. Martin (5), T. Maruma (5/3), T. M. K. Mawoyo (2), M. A. Meman (1), K. O. Meth (5), T. V. Mufambisi (6), F. Mutizwa (9), G. A. Paterson (10), G. E. Peckover (1), E. C. Rainsford (36), P. W. E. Rawson (10), H. P. Rinke (18), R. W. Sims (3), G. M. Strydom (12), M. N. Waller (14), S. C. Williams (41/1), C. Zhuwawo (1/3).

Bangladesh
Ahmed Kamal (1), Alam Talukdar (2), Aminul Islam, jun. (1), Anisur Rahman (2), Ather Ali Khan (19), Azhar Hussain (7), Dhiman Ghosh (14/1), Dolar Mahmud (7), Farhad Reza (32/7), Faruq Ahmed (7), Gazi Ashraf (7), Ghulam Faruq (5), Ghulam Nausher (9), Hafizur Rahman (7), Harunur Rashid (2), Jahangir Alam (3), Jahangir Badshah (5), Jamaluddin Ahmed (1), Mafizur Rahman (4), Mahbubur Rahman (1), Mazharul Haque (1), Minhazul Abedin (27), Moniruzzaman (2), Morshed Ali Khan (3), Mosharraf Hossain (3), Nasir Ahmed (7), Nazimuddin (7/7), Neeyamur Rashid (2), Nurul Abedin (4), Rafiqul Alam (2), Raqibul Hasan, sen. (2), Saiful Islam (7), Sajjad Ahmed (2), Samiur Rahman (2), Shafiuddin Ahmed (11), Shahidur Rahman (2), Shariful Haq (1), Sheikh Salahuddin (6), Wahidul Gani (1), Zahid Razzak (3), Zakir Hassan (2).

PLAYERS APPEARING FOR MORE THAN ONE ONE-DAY INTERNATIONAL TEAM

The following players have played one-day internationals for the **African XI** in addition to their national side:

N. Boje (2), L. L. Bosman (1), J. Botha (2), M. V. Boucher (5), E. Chigumbura (3), A. B. de Villiers (5), H. H. Dippenaar (6), J. H. Kallis (2), J. M. Kemp (6), J. A. Morkel (2), M. Morkel (3), T. M. Odoyo (5), P. J. Ongondo (1), J. L. Ontong (1), S. M. Pollock (6), A. G. Prince (3), J. A. Rudolph (2), V. Sibanda (2), G. C. Smith (10), D. W. Steyn (2), H. H. Streak (3), T. Taibu (10), S. O. Tikolo (4), M. Zondeki (2). (Odoyo, Ongondo and Tikolo play for Kenya, which does not have Test status.)

The following players have played one-day internationals for the **Asian Cricket Council XI** in addition to their national side:

Abdul Razzaq (4), M. S. Dhoni (3), R. Dravid (1), C. R. D. Fernando (1), S. C. Ganguly (3), Harbhajan Singh (2), Inzamam-ul-Haq (3), S. T. Jayasuriya (4), D. P. M. D. Jayawardene (5), A. Kumble (2), Mashrafe bin Mortaza (2), Mohammad Ashraful (2), Mohammad Asif (3), Mohammad Rafique (2), Mohammad Yousuf (7), M. Muralitharan (4), A. Nehra (3), K. C. Sangakkara (4), V. Sehwag (7), Shahid Afridi (3), Shoaib Akhtar (3), W. U. Tharanga (1), W. P. U. J. C. Vaas (1), Yuvraj Singh (3), Zaheer Khan (6).

The following players have played one-day internationals for the **ICC World XI** in addition to their national side:

C. L. Cairns (1), R. Dravid (3), S. P. Fleming (1), A. Flintoff (3), C. H. Gayle (3), A. C. Gilchrist (1), D. Gough (1), M. L. Hayden (3), J. H. Kallis (3), B. C. Lara (4), G. D. McGrath (1), M. Muralitharan (3), M. Ntini (1), K. P. Pietersen (2), S. M. Pollock (3), R. T. Ponting (3), K. C. Sangakkara (3), V. Sehwag (3), Shahid Afridi (3), Shoaib Akhtar (2), D. L. Vettori (4), S. K. Warne (1).

K. C. Wessels has appeared for both Australia and South Africa. D. R. Brown has appeared for both England and Scotland. E. J. G. Morgan has appeared for both Ireland and England.

  G. M. Hamilton has played Test cricket for England and one-day internationals for Scotland. D. P. Nannes has played one-day and Twenty20 internationals for Australia and Twenty20 internationals for the Netherlands.

TWENTY20 INTERNATIONAL CRICKETERS

The following players have appeared for Test-playing countries in Twenty20 internationals but had not represented their countries in Test matches or one-day internationals by December 31, 2009:

Australia L. A. Pomersbach (1); **South Africa** Y. A. Abdulla (2), T. Henderson (1), R. K. Kleinveldt (1), H. G. Kuhn (1), A. C. Thomas (1); **West Indies** W. K. D. Perkins (1); **India** A. B. Dinda (1); **Pakistan** Anwar Ali (1), Shahzaib Hasan (1), Shoaib Khan (1), Zulqarnain Haider (1); **Sri Lanka** C. U. Jayasinghe (2), H. G. J. M. Kulatunga (2), R. J. M. G. M. Rupasinghe (2), I. Udana (5); **Bangladesh** Nadif Chowdhury (3), Nazmus Sadat (1).

ELITE TEST UMPIRES

The following umpires were on the ICC's elite panel in January 2010. The figures for Tests, one-day internationals and Twenty20 internationals and the Test Career dates refer to matches in which they have officiated as umpires (excluding abandoned games). The totals of Tests are complete up to January 27, 2010, the totals of one-day internationals up to December 31, 2009, and the Twenty20 internationals up to December 31, 2009.

	Country	Born	Tests	Test Career	ODIs	T20Is
Aleem Dar.......................	P	6.6.1968	59	*2003–2009*	126	6
Asad Rauf.......................	P	12.5.1956	28	*2004–2009*	69	11
Benson Mark Richard	E	6.7.1958	28	*2004–2009*	72	19
Bowden Brent Fraser ("Billy")	NZ	11.4.1963	59	*1999–2009*	136	11
Davis Stephen James...............	A	9.4.1952	21	*1997–2009*	94	8
de Silva Ellawalakankanamge <u>Asoka</u> Ranjit	SL	28.3.1956	43	*2000–2009*	95	5
Doctrove Billy Raymond	WI	3.7.1955	29	*1999–2009*	89	10
Gould Ian James	E	19.8.1957	9	*2008–2009*	38	7
Harper Daryl John	A	23.10.1951	88	*1998–2009*	161	10
Hill Anthony Lloyd.................	NZ	26.6.1951	15	*2001–2009*	74	13
Koertzen Rudolf Eric	SA	26.3.1949	105	*1992–2009*	202	8
Taufel Simon James Arthur	A	21.1.1971	61	*2000–2009*	143	16

Note: S. A. Bucknor left the panel in 2009; his final figures were as follows:

	Country	Born	Tests	Test Career	ODIs	T20Is
Bucknor Stephen Anthony	WI	31.5.1946	128	*1988–2008*	181	–

BIRTHS AND DEATHS

OTHER CRICKETING NOTABLES

The following list shows the births and deaths of cricketers, and people associated with cricket, who have *not* played in Test matches.

Criteria for inclusion The following are included: all non-Test players who have either (1) scored 20,000 runs in first-class cricket, or (2) taken 1,500 first-class wickets, or (3) achieved 750 dismissals, or (4) reached *both* 15,000 runs *and* 750 wickets. It also includes (5) the leading players who flourished before the start of Test cricket and (6) all others deemed of sufficient merit or interest for inclusion, either because of their playing skill, their present position, their contribution to the game in whatever capacity or their fame in other walks of life.

Names Where players were normally known by a name other than their first, this is underlined.

Teams Where only one team is listed, this is normally the one for which the player made most first-class appearances. Additional teams are listed only if the player appeared for them in more than 20 first-class matches or if they are especially relevant to their career. School and university teams are not given unless especially relevant (e.g. for the schoolboys chosen as wartime Cricketers of the Year in the 1918 and 1919 *Wisdens*).

	Teams	*Born*	*Died*
Aird Ronald MC	Hampshire	4.5.1902	16.8.1986
Secretary of MCC 1953–62; president of MCC 1968–69.			
Aislabie Benjamin	Surrey, Secretary of MCC 1822– 42	14.1.1774	2.6.1842
Alcock Charles William	Secretary of Surrey 1872–1907	2.12.1842	26.2.1907
Editor, Cricket magazine, 1882–1907. Captain of Wanderers and England football teams.			
Alley William Edward	NSW, Somerset; Test umpire	3.2.1919	26.11.2004
Altham Harry Surtees CBE	Surrey, Hampshire; historian	30.11.1888	11.3.1965
Coach at Winchester for 30 years; president of MCC 1959–60.			
Arlott Leslie Thomas <u>John</u> OBE	Broadcaster and writer	25.2.1914	14.12.1991
Arthur <u>John</u> Michael	Griq. W., OFS, South Africa Coach 2005–2010	17.5.1968	
Ashdown William Henry	Kent	27.12.1898	15.9.1979
The only cricketer to appear in English first-class cricket before and after the two wars.			
Ashley-Cooper Frederick Samuel	Historian	22.3.1877	31.1.1932
Austin *Sir* Harold Bruce Gardiner	Barbados	15.7.1877	27.7.1943
Bailey Jack Arthur		22.6.1930	
Bannister John David	Warwickshire; writer and broadcaster	23.8.1930	
Barker Gordon	Essex	6.7.1931	10.2.2006
Bayliss Trevor Harley	NSW, Sri Lanka coach 2007–	21.12.1962	
Beauclerk *Rev. Lord* Frederick	Middlesex, Surrey, MCC	8.5.1773	22.4.1850
Beldam George William	Middlesex; photographer	1.5.1868	23.11.1937
Beldham William ("Silver Billy")	Hambledon, Surrey	5.2.1766	26.2.1862
Berry Leslie George	Leicestershire	28.4.1906	5.2.1985
Bird Harold Dennis MBE	Yorkshire, Leicestershire; Test umpire	19.4.1933	
Blofeld Henry Calthorpe OBE	Cambridge Univ; broadcaster	23.9.1939	
Booth Roy	Yorkshire, Worcestershire	1.10.1926	
Bowley Frederick Lloyd	Worcestershire	9.11.1873	31.5.1943
Bradshaw Keith	Tasmania, Secretary/chief executive MCC 2006–	2.10.1963	
Buchanan John Marshall	Queensland; Aust. coach 1999–2007	5.4.1953	
Bucknor Stephen Anthony	ICC umpire	31.5.1946	
Umpire of 128 Tests, a record.			
Buller John Sydney MBE	Worcestershire; Test umpire	23.8.1909	7.8.1970
Cardus *Sir* Neville	Writer	3.4.1888	27.2.1975
Chester Frank	Worcestershire; Test umpire	20.1.1895	8.4.1957
Stood in 48 Tests between 1924 and 1955, a record that lasted until 1992.			
Clark David Graham	Kent; president of MCC 1977–78	27.1.1919	
Clarke Charles <u>Giles</u>	Chairman of ECB, 2007–	9.5.1953	
Clarke William	Nottinghamshire	24.12.1798	25.8.1856
Founded the All-England XI, Trent Bridge ground.			

	Teams	Born	Died
Collier David Gordon	Chief executive of ECB, 2005–	22.4.1955	
Collins Arthur Edward Jeune	Clifton College	18.8.1885	11.11.1914
Made the highest score in any cricket, 628* in a house match in 1899.			
Conan Doyle *Dr Sir* Arthur Ignatius	MCC	22.5.1859	7.7.1930
Creator of Sherlock Holmes; his only victim in first-class cricket was W. G. Grace.			
Cook Thomas Edwin Reed	Sussex	5.1.1901	15.1.1950
Cox George, jun.	Sussex	23.8.1911	30.3.1985
Cox George, sen.	Sussex	29.11.1873	24.3.1949
Cozier Tony	Broadcaster and writer	10.7.1940	
Dalmiya Jagmohan	President of ICC 1997–2000	30.5.1940	
Davies Emrys	Glamorgan; Test umpire	27.6.1904	10.11.1975
Davison Brian Fettes	Rhodesia, Leics, Tasmania, Gloucestershire	21.12.1946	
Dawkes George Owen	Leicestershire, Derbyshire	19.7.1920	10.8.2006
de Lisle Timothy John March Phillipps	Editor of *Wisden* 2003	25.6.1962	
Dennett George	Gloucestershire	27.4.1880	14.9.1937
Di Venuto Michael James	Tasmania, Derbys, Durham	12.12.1973	
Eagar Edward *Patrick*	Photographer	9.3.1944	
Edwards Charlotte Marie MBE	England Women	17.12.1979	
Ehsan Mani	President of ICC 2003–06	23.3.1945	
Engel Matthew Lewis	Editor of *Wisden* 1993–2000, 2004–07	11.6.1951	
"Felix" (Nicholas Wanostrocht)	Kent, Surrey, All-England	4.10.1804	3.9.1876
Batsman, artist, author (Felix on the Bat) and inventor of the Catapulta bowling machine.			
Ferguson William Henry BEM	Scorer	6.6.1880	22.9.1957
Scorer and baggage-master for five Test nations on 43 tours over 52 years: "never lost a bag".			
Fletcher Duncan Andrew Gwynne	Zimbabwe, England coach 1999–2007	27.9.1948	
Frindall William Howard MBE	Statistician	3.3.1939	30.1.2009
Gibbons Harold Harry Haywood	Worcestershire	8.10.1904	16.2.1973
Grace *Mrs* Martha	Mother and cricketing mentor of W.G.	18.7.1812	25.7.1884
Grace William Gilbert	Gloucestershire; son of W.G.	6.7.1874	2.3.1905
Graveney David Anthony	Gloucestershire, Somerset, Durham	2.1.1953	
Chairman of England selectors 1997–2008			
Gray James Roy	Hampshire	19.5.1926	
Gray Malcolm Alexander	President of ICC 2000–03	30.5.1940	
Grieves Kenneth James	New South Wales, Lancashire	27.8.1925	3.1.1992
Hair Darrell Bruce	ICC umpire	30.9.1952	
Hallam Maurice Raymond	Leicestershire	10.9.1931	1.1.2000
Heyhoe-Flint Rachael	England Women	11.6.1939	
Horton Henry	Hampshire	18.4.1923	2.11.1998
Howard Cecil *Geoffrey*	Middlesex; administrator	14.2.1909	8.11.2002
Huish Frederick Henry	Kent	15.11.1869	16.3.1957
Hunter David	Yorkshire	23.2.1860	11.1.1927
Hutchinson James Metcalf	Derbyshire	29.11.1896	7.11.2000
Believed to be the longest-lived first-class cricketer at 103 years 344 days.			
Ingleby-Mackenzie Alexander Colin David OBE	Hampshire	15.9.1933	9.3.2006
President of MCC 1996–98.			
Jackson Victor Edward	NSW, Leicestershire	25.10.1916	30.1.1965
James Cyril Lionel Robert	Writer	4.1.1901	31.5.1989
Jesty Trevor Edward	Hants, Griqualand W, Surrey, Lancs; umpire	2.6.1948	
Johnson Paul	Nottinghamshire	24.4.1965	
Johnston Brian Alexander CBE, MC	Broadcaster	24.6.1912	5.1.1994
Jones Alan MBE	Glamorgan	4.11.1938	
Played once for England v Rest of the World, 1970, regarded at the time as a Test match.			
King John Barton	Philadelphia	19.10.1873	17.10.1965
"Beyond question the greatest all-round cricketer produced by America." – Wisden.			
Knight Roger David Verdon CBE	Surrey, Gloucestershire, Sussex	6.9.1946	
Secretary of MCC 1994–2005			
Lacey *Sir* Francis Eden	Hants; Secretary of MCC 1898–1926	19.10.1859	26.5.1946
Lamb Timothy Michael	Middlesex, Northants	24.3.1953	
Chief Executive of ECB, 1997–2004.			
Langridge John George MBE	Sussex; Test umpire	10.2.1910	27.6.1999

	Teams	Born	Died
Lillywhite Frederick William	Sussex	13.6.1792	21.8.1854
Long Arnold	Surrey, Sussex	18.12.1940	
Lord Thomas	Middlesex; founder of Lord's Cricket Ground	23.11.1755	13.1.1832
Lorgat Haroon	Chief executive of ICC, 2008–	26.5.1960	
McEwan Kenneth Scott	E. Province, Essex	16.7.1952	
McGilvray Alan David MBE	NSW; broadcaster	6.12.1909	17.7.1996
MacLaurin of Knebworth, Lord	Chairman of ECB 1997–2002	30.3.1937	
Majola Mongezi <u>Gerald</u>	Chief executive, Cricket South Africa	20.11.1959	
Marlar Robin Geoffrey	Sussex; writer	2.1.1931	
Martin-Jenkins Christopher Dennis Alexander MBE	Writer; broadcaster	20.1.1945	
Mendis Gehan Dixon	Sussex, Lancashire	20.4.1955	
Mercer John	Sussex, Glamorgan; coach and scorer	22.4.1893	31.8.1987
Meyer Rollo John Oliver OBE	Somerset	15.3.1905	9.3.1991
Modi Lalit Kumar	Chairman, Indian Premier League	29.11.1963	
Moles Andrew James	Warwickshire, NZ coach 2008–09	12.2.1961	
Moores Peter	Sussex; England coach 2007–09	18.12.1962	
Morgan Derek Clifton	Derbyshire	26.2.1929	
Morgan Frederick <u>David</u>	Chairman of ECB 2003–07, President of ICC 2008–10	6.10.1937	
Mynn Alfred	Kent, All-England	19.1.1807	1.11.1861
Neale Phillip Anthony	Worcestershire; England manager	5.6.1954	
Newman John Alfred	Hampshire	12.11.1884	21.12.1973
Nicholas Mark Charles Jefford	Hampshire; broadcaster	29.9.1957	
Nicholls Ronald Bernard	Gloucestershire	4.12.1933	21.7.1994
Nielsen Timothy John	South Australia, Australia coach, 2007–	5.5.1968	
Nyren John	Hampshire	15.12.1764	28.6.1837
Author of The Young Cricketer's Tutor, *1833.*			
Nyren Richard	Hampshire	1734	25.4.1797
Proprietor Bat & Ball Inn, Broadhalfpenny Down.			
Ontong Rodney Craig	Border, Glamorgan, N. Transvaal	9.9.1955	
Ormrod Joseph <u>Alan</u>	Worcestershire, Lancashire	22.12.1942	
Pardon Sydney Herbert	Editor of *Wisden* 1891–1925	23.9.1855	20.11.1925
Parks Henry William	Sussex	18.7.1906	7.5.1984
Parr George	Nottinghamshire, All-England	22.5.1826	23.6.1891
Captain and manager of the All-England XI.			
Pawar Sharadchandra Govindrao	President of BCCI 2005–08, President-elect of ICC	12.12.1940	
Payton Wilfred Richard Daniel	Nottinghamshire	13.2.1882	2.5.1943
Pearce Thomas Neill	Essex; administrator	3.11.1905	10.4.1994
Pearson Frederick	Worcestershire	23.9.1880	10.11.1963
Perrin Percival Albert	Essex	26.5.1876	20.11.1945
Pilch Fuller	Norfolk, Kent	17.3.1804	1.5.1870
"The best batsman that has ever yet appeared" – Arthur Haygarth, 1862.			
Preston Norman MBE	Editor of *Wisden* 1952–80	18.3.1903	6.3.1980
Rait-Kerr *Colonel* Rowan Scrope	Europeans; sec. MCC 1936–52	13.4.1891	2.4.1961
Reeves William	Essex; Test umpire	22.1.1875	22.3.1944
Rice Clive Edward Butler	Transvaal, Nottinghamshire	23.7.1949	
Robertson-Glasgow Raymond Charles	Somerset; writer	15.7.1901	4.3.1965
Robins Derrick Harold	Warwickshire; tour promoter	27.6.1914	3.5.2004
Robinson Mark Andrew	Northants, Yorkshire, Sussex, coach	23.11.1966	
Roebuck Peter Michael	Somerset; writer	6.3.1956	
Sainsbury Peter James	Hampshire	13.6.1934	
Sellers Arthur Brian MBE	Yorkshire	5.3.1907	20.2.1981
Seymour James	Kent	25.10.1879	30.9.1930
Shepherd David Robert MBE	Gloucestershire; ICC umpire	27.12.1940	27.10.2009
Shepherd Donald John	Glamorgan	12.8.1927	
Siddons James Darren	Victoria, S. Australia, Bangladesh coach	25.4.1964	
Silk Dennis Raoul Whitehall CBE	Somerset	8.10.1931	
President of MCC 1992–94; chairman of TCCB 1994–96.			
Simmons Jack MBE	Lancashire, Tasmania	28.3.1941	

	Teams	Born	Died
Skelding Alexander	Leicestershire; umpire	5.9.1886	17.4.1960
First-class umpire 1931–1958, when he was 72.			
Smith William Charles	Surrey	4.10.1877	15.7.1946
Speed Malcolm Walter	Chief Executive of ICC 2001–08	14.9.1948	
Spencer Thomas William OBE	Kent; Test umpire	22.3.1914	1.11.1995
Stephenson Harold William	Somerset	18.7.1920	23.4.2008
Stephenson Heathfield Harman	Surrey, All-England	3.5.1832	17.12.1896
Captained first English team to Australia, 1861-62; umpired first Test in England, 1880.			
Stephenson *Lt.-Col.* John Robin CBE	Sec. MCC 1987–93	25.2.1931	2.6.2003
Studd *Sir* John Edward Kynaston	Middlesex	26.7.1858	14.1.1944
Lord Mayor of London 1928–29; President of MCC 1930.			
Surridge Walter Stuart	Surrey	3.9.1917	13.4.1992
Sutherland James Alexander	Vic.; CEO Cricket Australia 2001–	14.7.1965	
Suttle Kenneth George	Sussex	25.8.1928	25.3.2005
Swanton Ernest William CBE	Middlesex; writer	11.2.1907	22.1.2000
Tarrant Francis Alfred	Victoria, Middlesex	11.12.1880	29.1.1951
Taylor Brian	Essex	19.6.1932	
Taylor Samantha Claire MBE	England Women	25.9.1975	
Thornton Charles Inglis	Middlesex	20.3.1850	10.12.1929
Timms John Edward	Northamptonshire	3.11.1906	18.5.1980
Todd Leslie John	Kent	19.6.1907	20.8.1967
Tunnicliffe John	Yorkshire	26.8.1866	11.7.1948
Turner Francis Michael MBE	Leicestershire; administrator	8.8.1934	
Turner Robert Julian	Somerset	25.11.1967	
Ufton Derek Gilbert	Kent	31.5.1928	
van der Bijl Vintcent Adriaan Pieter	Natal, Middx, Transvaal	19.3.1948	
Virgin Roy Thomas	Somerset, Northamptonshire	26.8.1939	
Ward William	Hampshire	24.7.1787	30.6.1849
Scorer of the first double-century: 278 for MCC v Norfolk, 1820.			
Wass Thomas George	Nottinghamshire	26.12.1873	27.10.1953
Watson Frank	Lancashire	17.9.1898	1.2.1976
Webber Roy	Statistician	23.7.1914	14.11.1962
Weigall Gerald John Villiers	Kent; coach	19.10.1870	17.5.1944
Wheatley Oswald Stephen CBE	Warwickshire, Glamorgan	28.5.1935	
Wight Peter Bernard	Somerset; umpire	25.6.1930	
Wilson John Victor	Yorkshire	17.1.1921	5.6.2008
Wisden John	Sussex	5.9.1826	5.4.1884
"The Little Wonder"; founder of Wisden Cricketers' Almanack, 1864.			
Wood Cecil John Burditt	Leicestershire	21.11.1875	5.6.1960
Woodcock John Charles OBE	Writer; editor of *Wisden* 1981–86	7.8.1926	
Wooller Wilfred	Glamorgan	20.11.1912	10.3.1997
Wright Graeme Alexander	Editor of *Wisden* 1987–92, 2001–02	23.4.1943	
Young Douglas Martin	Worcestershire, Gloucestershire	15.4.1924	18.6.1993

REGISTER OF CURRENT PLAYERS

The qualifications for inclusion are as follows:
1. All players who appeared in Tests, one-day internationals or Twenty20 internationals for a Test-playing country in the calendar year 2009.
2. All players who appeared in the County Championship, the Sheffield Shield, the SuperSport Series, the West Indian four-day regional competition for the WICB President's Trophy, or the Duleep Trophy in the calendar year 2009.
3. All players who appeared in a first-class match in a Test-playing country in the calendar year 2009 who have previously played Tests, one-day international cricket or Twenty20 international cricket for a Test-playing country.
4. All players who appeared in a first-class match for a Test-playing country on tour or the A-team of a Test-playing country in the calendar year 2009.

Notes: The forename by which the player is known is underlined if it is not his first name.

Teams are those played for in the calendar year 2009, or the last domestic team for which that player appeared.

Countries are those for which players are qualified.

The country of birth is given if it is not the one for which a player is qualified. It is also given to differentiate between West Indian nations, and where it is essential for clarity.

* *Denotes Test player.*

	Team	Country	Born	Birthplace
Abbott Kyle John	Dolphins/KwaZulu-Natal	SA	18.6.1987	*Empangeni*
Abdulla Yusuf Adam	Dolphins	SA	17.1.1983	*Johannesburg*
***Abdul Razzaq**	ZTBL	P	2.12.1979	*Lahore*
***Abdur Rauf**	Multan	P	9.12.1978	*Renala Khurd*
***Abdur Razzak**	Khulna	B	15.6.1982	*Khulna*
***Abdur Rehman**	Habib Bank	P	1.3.1980	*Sialkot*
***Ackerman** Hylton Deon	Dolphins/Leicestershire	SA	14.2.1973	*Cape Town*
***Adams** Andre Ryan	Nottinghamshire	NZ	17.7.1975	*Auckland*
Adams James Henry Kenneth	Hampshire	E	23.9.1980	*Winchester*
Adshead Stephen John	Gloucestershire	E	29.1.1980	*Redditch*
***Afzaal** Usman	Surrey	E	9.6.1977	*Rawalpindi, Pakistan*
Aga Ragheb Gul	Sussex/Kenya	K	10.7.1984	*Nairobi*
***Agarkar** Ajit Bhalchandra	Mumbai	I	4.12.1977	*Bombay*
Agathagelou Andrea Peter	Lions/North West	SA	16.11.1989	*Rustenberg*
Ahmed Mehraj	Worcestershire	E	5.1.1989	*Birmingham*
Ahmed Shehzad	Habib Bank	P	23.11.1991	*Lahore*
Akoojee Muhammad	Lions/North West	SA	21.11.1984	*Klerksdorp*
Alexander Camilus Christopher	Windward Islands	WI	20.10.1981	*Mount Horne, Grenada*
Alexander Craig John	Lions/North West	SA	5.1.1987	*Cape Town*
***Ali** Kabir	Worcestershire	E	24.11.1980	*Moseley*
Ali Kadeer	Gloucestershire	E	7.3.1983	*Moseley*
Ali Moeen Munir	Worcestershire	E	18.6.1987	*Birmingham*
***Ali Naqvi**	KRL	P	19.3.1977	*Lahore*
Allenby James	Glamorgan/Leicestershire	E	12.9.1982	*Perth, Australia*
Allert Atiba Kerry	Trinidad & Tobago	WI	27.6.1981	*McBean, Trinidad*
***Ambrose** Timothy Raymond	Warwickshire	E	1.12.1982	*Newcastle, Australia*
***Amerasinghe** Merenna Koralage Don Ishara	Colts/Wayamba	SL	5.3.1978	*Colombo*
Amla Ahmed Mahomed	Dolphins	SA	15.9.1979	*Durban*
***Amla** Hashim Mahomed	Dolphins/Essex	SA	31.3.1983	*Durban*
***Anderson** James Michael	Lancashire	E	30.7.1982	*Burnley*
Andrew Gareth Mark	Worcestershire	E	27.12.1983	*Yeovil*
Anwar Ali	PIA	P	25.11.1987	*Karachi*
Anyon James Edward	Surrey/Warwickshire	E	5.5.1983	*Lancaster*
Arjune Krishna	Guyana	WI	3.9.1980	*Unity Village, Guyana*
Arnel Brent John	Northern Districts	NZ	3.1.1979	*Te Awamutu*

	Team	Country	Born	Birthplace
*Arshad Khan	Quetta	P	22.3.1971	Peshawar
Ashling Christopher Paul	Glamorgan	E	26.11.1988	Manchester
Ashwin Ravichandran	Tamil Nadu	I	17.9.1986	Madras
Asif Mahmood	KRL	P	18.12.1975	Rawalpindi
*Asim Kamal	Karachi	P	31.5.1976	Karachi
Athanaze Justin Jason	Leeward Islands	WI	29.1.1988	Antigua
*Austin Ryan Anthony	Com. Campuses & Colls.	WI	15.11.1981	Arima, Trinidad
Awana Parvinder	Delhi	I	19.7.1986	Noida
Azeem Rafiq	Yorkshire	E	27.2.1991	Karachi, Pakistan
Azhar Ali	KRL	P	19.2.1985	Lahore
*Azhar Mahmood	Kent	P	28.2.1975	Rawalpindi
Badree Samuel	Trinidad & Tobago	WI	8.3.1981	Barrackpore, Trinidad
Badrinath Subramaniam	Tamil Nadu	I	30.8.1980	Madras
*Bahutule Sairaj Vasant	Mumbai/Assam	I	6.1.1973	Bombay
Bailey Cullen Benjamin	South Australia	A	26.2.1985	Bedford Park
Bailey George John	Tasmania	A	7.9.1982	Launceston
Bailey Ryan Tyrone	Eagles	SA	8.9.1982	Cape Town
Bairstow Jonathan Marc	Yorkshire	E	26.9.1989	Bradford
*Baker Lionel Sionne	Leeward Islands	WI	6.9.1984	Montserrat
*Balaji Lakshmipathy	Tamil Nadu/Wellington	I	27.9.1981	Madras
Balcombe David John	Hampshire	E	24.12.1984	London
*Bandara Charitha Malinga	Ragama/Basnahira South	SL	31.12.1979	Kalutara
*Bandaratilleke Mapa Rallalage				
Chandima Niroshan	Badureliya/Basnahira N.	SL	16.5.1975	Colombo
Bandekar Saurab Sushant	Goa	I	16.10.1987	Bombay
Bandy David Charles	Western Australia	A	19.7.1978	Subiaco
Banerjee Vikram	Gloucestershire	E	20.3.1984	Bradford
*Bangar Sanjay Bapusaheb	Railways	I	11.10.1972	Bid
*Banks Omari Ahmed Clemente	Leeward Islands/Somerset	WI	17.7.1982	Road Bay, Antigua
*Barath Adrian Boris	Trinidad & Tobago	WI	14.4.1990	Chaguanas, Trinidad
Barker Keith Hubert Douglas	Warwickshire	E	21.10.1986	Manchester
Barnes Bradley Graeme	Dolphins/KwaZulu-Natal	SA	20.10.1988	Johannesburg
Barnwell Christopher Dion	Guyana	WI	6.1.1987	McKenzie, Guyana
Barrington Shemroy	Guyana	WI	20.1.1988	McKenzie, Guyana
Bascombe Miles Cameron	Windward Islands	WI	12.1.1986	St Vincent
Batticciotto Glen Charles	Queensland	A	18.8.1981	Redcliffe
*Batty Gareth Jon	Worcestershire	E	13.10.1977	Bradford
Batty Jonathan Neil	Surrey	E	18.4.1974	Chesterfield
*Baugh Carlton Seymour	Jamaica	WI	23.6.1982	Kingston, Jamaica
*Bazid Khan	KRL	P	25.3.1981	Lahore
Behardien Farhaan	Titans/Northerns	SA	9.10.1983	Johannesburg
Bekker Martin	Dolphins/KwaZulu-Natal	SA	15.5.1985	Durban
*Bell Ian Ronald	Warwickshire	E	11.4.1982	Walsgrave
*Bell Matthew David	Wellington	NZ	25.2.1977	Dunedin
Benham Christopher Charles	Hampshire	E	24.3.1983	Frimley
Benkenstein Dale Martin	Durham	SA	9.6.1974	Salisbury, Zimbabwe
*Benn Sulieman Jamaal	Barbados	WI	22.7.1981	Haynesville, Barbados
Benning James Graham Edward	Leicestershire/Surrey	E	4.5.1983	Mill Hill
Berg Gareth Kyle	Middlesex	SA	18.1.1981	Cape Town
*Bernard David Eddison	Jamaica	WI	19.7.1981	Kingston, Jamaica
Bess Brandon Jeremy	Guyana	WI	13.12.1987	Rosignol, Guyana
*Best Tino la Bertram	Barbados	WI	26.8.1981	3rd Avenue, Barbados
Bhatia Rajat	Delhi	I	22.10.1979	Delhi
Bhuvneshwar Singh	Uttar Pradesh	I	5.2.1990	Meerut
Birch Andrew Charles Ross	Warriors/Eastern Province	SA	7.6.1985	East London
Bird Aaron Christopher	New South Wales	A	28.9.1983	Taree
Birt Travis Rodney	Tasmania	A	9.12.1981	Sale
Bishoo Devendra	Guyana	WI	6.11.1985	New Amsterdam, Guy.
*Blackwell Ian David	Durham	E	10.6.1978	Chesterfield

	Team	Country	Born	Birthplace
Blake Alexander James	Kent	E	25.1.1989	Farnborough
Bobb Alston Brenton Winston	Windward Islands	WI	17.1.1984	St Vincent
Bodi Goolam Hussain	Titans/Easterns	SA	4.1.1979	Hathuran, India
Bodibe Tumelo Mphunzi	Titans/Easterns	SA	22.6.1987	Vosloorus
*****Boje** Nico	Northamptonshire	SA	20.3.1973	Bloemfontein
*****Bollinger** Douglas Erwin	New South Wales	A	24.7.1981	Baulkham Hills
*****Bond** Shane Edward	Canterbury	NZ	7.6.1975	Christchurch
*****Bopara** Ravinder Singh	Essex/Auckland	E	4.5.1985	Forest Gate
Borgas Cameron James	South Australia	A	1.9.1983	Melrose Park
Borthwick Scott George	Durham	E	19.4.1990	Sunderland
Bose Ranadeb Ranjit	Bengal	I	27.2.1979	Calcutta
Bosman Lungile Loots	Dolphins/KwaZulu-Natal	SA	14.4.1977	Kimberley
Boteju Jayawardene Welathanthrige				
Hemantha Devapriya	Sebastianites/Lankan	SL	3.11.1977	Colombo
Botha Anthony Greyvensteyn	Warwickshire	SA	17.11.1976	Pretoria
*****Botha** Johan	Warriors	SA	2.5.1982	Johannesburg
Bothma Johannes Paulus	Cape Cobras/Boland	SA	28.3.1988	Bellville
*****Boucher** Mark Verdon	Warriors	SA	3.12.1976	East London
Boucher Rashidi Hasani	Barbados	WI	17.7.1990	St Michael, Barbados
Boult Trent Alexander	Northern Districts	NZ	22.7.1989	Rotorua
Boyce Matthew Andrew Golding	Leicestershire	E	13.8.1985	Cheltenham
*****Bracken** Nathan Wade	New South Wales	A	12.9.1977	Penrith
Bragg William David	Glamorgan	E	24.10.1986	Newport
Brathwaite Kraigg Clairmonte	Barbados	WI	1.12.1992	Belfield, Barbados
*****Bravo** Dwayne John	Trinidad & Tobago	WI	7.10.1983	Santa Cruz, Trinidad
Bravo Darren Michael	Trinidad & Tobago	WI	6.2.1989	Santa Cruz, Trinidad
*****Breese** Gareth Rohan	Durham	WI	9.1.1976	Montego Bay, Jamaica
*****Bresnan** Timothy Thomas	Yorkshire	E	28.2.1985	Pontefract
Briggs Danny Richard	Hampshire	E	30.4.1991	Newport
Broad Ryan Andrew	Queensland	A	9.3.1982	Herston
*****Broad** Stuart Christopher John	Nottinghamshire	E	24.6.1986	Nottingham
Brooks Jack Alexander	Northamptonshire	E	4.6.1984	Oxford
Brooks Sharmarh Shaqad Joshua	Barbados	WI	1.10.1988	St John's Land, Barb.
Broom Neil Trevor	Otago	NZ	20.11.1983	Christchurch
Brophy Gerard Louis	Yorkshire	E	26.11.1975	Welkom
Brown Alistair Duncan	Nottinghamshire	E	11.2.1970	Beckenham
Brown Bevon Mark	Jamaica	WI	2.9.1979	Kingston, Jamaica
Brown Darryl Lewis	Warriors/Border	SA	25.3.1983	East London
Brown Karl Robert	Lancashire	E	17.5.1988	Bolton
Brown Michael James	Surrey	E	9.2.1980	Burnley
Brown Odean Vernon	Jamaica	WI	8.2.1982	Westmoreland, Jam.
Browne Patrick Anderson	Barbados	WI	26.1.1982	Bayfield, Barbados
Browne Salvan Royston	Windward Islands	WI	19.3.1982	St Vincent
Buck Nathan Liam	Leicestershire	E	26.4.1991	Leicester
Burrows Thomas George	Hampshire	E	5.5.1985	Wokingham
Burton David Alexander	Middlesex	E	23.8.1985	Dulwich
*****Butcher** Mark Alan	Surrey	E	23.8.1972	Croydon
Butler Deighton Kelvin	Windward Islands	WI	17.7.1974	South Rivers, St Vinc.
*****Butler** Ian Gareth	Otago	NZ	24.11.1981	Middlemore
Butterworth Luke Rex	Tasmania	A	28.10.1983	Hobart
Buttler Joseph Charles	Somerset	E	8.9.1990	Taunton
*****Caddick** Andrew Richard	Somerset	E	21.11.1968	Christchurch, NZ
Cameron Mark Alan	New South Wales	A	31.1.1981	Waratah
Canning Ryan Clement Cavanagh	Cape Cobras/W. Province	SA	22.2.1984	Cape Town
Carberry Michael Alexander	Hampshire	E	29.9.1980	Croydon
Carolus Deon Dean	Eagles/Griqualand West	SA	10.7.1978	Port Elizabeth
Carseldine Lee Andrew	Queensland	A	17.11.1975	Nambour
Carter Andrew	Nottinghamshire	E	27.8.1988	Lincoln
Carter Jonathan Lyndon	Barbados	WI	16.11.1987	Belleplaine, Barbados

	Team	Country	Born	Birthplace
Carter Neil Miller	Warwickshire	SA	29.1.1975	*Cape Town*
Casimir Raymond	Windward Islands	WI	28.10.1976	*Dominica*
*****Casson** Beau	New South Wales	A	7.12.1982	*Subiaco*
Catlin Khismar	Com. Campuses & Colls.	WI	15.10.1985	*Shop Hill, Barbados*
Chakabva Regis Wiriranai	Northerns/Mash. Eagles	Z	20.9.1987	*Harare*
Chakrabarty Dibyendu Pratul	Bengal	I	15.11.1982	*Howrah*
Chambers Maurice Anthony	Essex	E	14.9.1987	*Port Antonio, Jamaica*
*****Chandana** Umagiliya Durage Upul	Nondescripts	SL	7.5.1972	*Galle*
*****Chanderpaul** Shivnarine	Durham	WI	16.8.1974	*Unity Village, Guyana*
Chapple Glen	Lancashire	E	23.1.1974	*Skipton*
Charles Johnson	Windward Islands	WI	14.1.1989	*St Lucia*
Charles Nikolai Gabriel Ramon	Barbados	WI	1.10.1986	*Wildey, Barbados*
*****Chattergoon** Sewnarine	Guyana	WI	3.4.1981	*Fyrish, Guyana*
Chawla Piyush Pramod	Uttar Pradesh/Sussex	I	24.12.1988	*Aligarh*
Chibhabha Chamunorwa Justice	Centrals/Southern Rocks	Z	6.9.1986	*Masvingo*
*****Chigumbura** Elton	Northerns/Mash. Eagles	Z	14.3.1986	*Kwekwe*
Chilton Mark James	Lancashire	E	2.10.1976	*Sheffield*
Chisoro Tendai Sam	Centrals/Southern Rocks	Z	12.2.1988	*Masvingo*
*****Chopra** Aakash	Delhi	I	19.9.1977	*Agra*
Chopra Varun	Essex	E	21.6.1987	*Barking*
Christian Derwin O'Neil	Guyana	WI	9.5.1983	*Kilen, Guyana*
Christian Daniel Trevor	South Australia	A	4.5.1983	*Camperdown*
Clare Jonathan Luke	Derbyshire	E	14.6.1986	*Burnley*
*****Clark** Stuart Rupert	New South Wales	A	28.9.1975	*Sutherland*
*****Clarke** Michael John	New South Wales	A	2.4.1981	*Liverpool*
*****Clarke** Rikki	Warwickshire	E	29.9.1981	*Orsett*
Claydon Mitchell Eric	Durham	E	25.11.1982	*Fairfield, Australia*
Cleary Mark Francis	South Australia	A	19.7.1980	*Moorabbin*
Cliff Samuel James	Leicestershire	E	3.10.1987	*Nottingham*
Cobb Joshua James	Leicestershire	E	17.8.1990	*Leicester*
Cockley Burt Tom	New South Wales	A	3.4.1986	*Waratah*
Coetsee Werner Loubser	Lions/North West	SA	16.3.1983	*Bethlehem*
Coetzee Justin Petrus	Western Australia	A	12.6.1984	*Durban, SA*
Coetzer Kyle James	Durham	Scotland	14.4.1984	*Aberdeen*
Coles Matthew Thomas	Kent	E	26.5.1990	*Maidstone*
*****Collingwood** Paul David	Durham	E	26.5.1976	*Shotley Bridge*
*****Collins** Pedro Tyrone	Barbados/Surrey	WI	12.8.1976	*Boscobelle, Barbados*
*****Collymore** Corey Dalanelo	Barbados/Sussex	WI	21.12.1977	*Boscobelle, Barbados*
Compton Nicholas Richard Denis	Middlesex	E	26.6.1983	*Durban, SA*
*****Cook** Alastair Nathan	Essex	E	25.12.1984	*Gloucester*
Cook Stephen Craig	Lions/Gauteng	SA	29.11.1982	*Johannesburg*
Cook Simon James	Kent	E	15.1.1977	*Oxford*
Cooper Tom Lexley William	South Australia	A	26.11.1986	*Wollongong*
Corbin Kyle Anthony McDonald	Com. Campuses & Colls.	WI	15.5.1990	*Newbury, Barbados*
*****Cork** Dominic Gerald	Hampshire	E	7.8.1971	*Newcastle-under-Lyme*
Cornwall Wilden Winston	Leeward Islands	WI	29.4.1973	*Liberta, Antigua*
Cosgrove Mark James	S. Australia/Glamorgan	A	14.6.1984	*Elizabeth*
Cosker Dean Andrew	Glamorgan	E	7.1.1978	*Weymouth*
*****Coventry** Charles Kevin	Westerns/Mata. Tuskers	Z	8.3.1983	*Kwekwe*
Cowan Edward James McKenzie	NSW/Tasmania	A	16.6.1982	*Paddington*
Cox Oliver Benjamin	Worcestershire	E	2.2.1992	*Wordsley*
Crandon Esuan Asqui	Guyana	WI	17.12.1981	*Rose Hall, Guyana*
Crandon Royston Tycho	Guyana	WI	31.5.1983	*Courtland, Guyana*
*****Crawley** John Paul	Hampshire	E	21.9.1971	*Maldon*
Creary Andre St Aubin	West Indies A	WI	17.11.1990	*Jamaica*
*****Cremer** Alexander Graeme	Northerns/ MW Rhinos	Z	19.9.1986	*Harare*
*****Croft** Robert Damien Bale	Glamorgan	E	25.5.1970	*Morriston*
Croft Steven John	Lancashire/Auckland	E	11.10.1984	*Blackpool*
Crook Steven Paul	Northamptonshire	E	28.5.1983	*Modbury, Australia*
Crosthwaite Adam John	Victoria	A	22.9.1984	*Melbourne*

	Team	Country	Born	Birthplace
Crowe Carl Daniel	Leicestershire	E	25.11.1975	*Leicester*
Cruickshank Daron Alfred	Trinidad & Tobago	WI	17.6.1988	*Port-of-Spain, Trinidad*
*****Cullen** Daniel James	South Australia	A	10.4.1984	*Woodville*
*****Cumming** Craig Derek	Otago	NZ	31.8.1975	*Timaru*
Currency Romel Kwesi	Com. Campuses & Colls.	WI	7.5.1982	*Mesopotamia, St Vinc.*
Cutting Benjamin Colin James	Queensland	A	30.1.1987	*Sunnybank*
*****Dabengwa** Keith Mbusi	Westerns/Mata. Tuskers	Z	17.8.1980	*Bulawayo*
Daggett Lee Martin	Northamptonshire	E	1.10.1982	*Bury*
Dalrymple James William Murray	Glamorgan	E	21.1.1981	*Nairobi, Kenya*
*****Danish Kaneria**	Habib Bank/Essex	P	16.12.1980	*Karachi*
Darshanpriya Thawalampolage Dinesh Daminda	Ragama/Basnahira North	SL	23.10.1983	*Ragama*
Das Halhadar Michu	Orissa	I	10.12.1986	*Dhenkamal*
Das Shiv Sunder	Orissa	I	5.11.1977	*Bhubaneswar*
*****Dasgupta** Deep	Bengal	I	7.6.1977	*Calcutta*
Davids Henry	Cape Cobras/Boland	SA	19.1.1980	*Stellenbosch*
Davies Mark	Durham	E	4.10.1980	*Stockton-on-Tees*
Davies Steven Michael	Worcestershire	E	17.6.1986	*Bromsgrove*
Davis Liam Murray	Western Australia	A	2.8.1984	*Perth*
Dawes Jason O'Brian	Jamaica	WI	27.12.1988	*Westmoreland, Jam.*
Dawson David Graham	Tasmania	A	7.3.1982	*Weekangeria*
Dawson Liam Andrew	Hampshire	E	1.3.1990	*Swindon*
*****Dawson** Richard Kevin James	Gloucestershire	E	4.8.1980	*Doncaster*
Deacon Wycliffe Andrew	Lions/North West	SA	23.6.1980	*Kroonstad*
de Bruyn Pierre	Dolphins/KwaZulu-Natal	SA	31.3.1977	*Pretoria*
*****de Bruyn** Zander	Warriors/Lions/Somerset	SA	5.7.1975	*Johannesburg*
DeFreitas Bront Arson	Leeward Islands	WI	12.11.1978	*St Vincent*
de Lange Con de Wet	Eagles	SA	11.2.1981	*Bellville*
Delport Cameron	Dolphins/KwaZulu-Natal	SA	12.5.1989	*Durban*
Denly Joseph Liam	Kent	E	16.3.1986	*Canterbury*
Denton Gerard John	Tasmania	A	7.8.1975	*Mount Isa*
*****Deonarine** Narsingh	Guyana	WI	16.8.1983	*Chesney Estate, Guy.*
Dernbach Jade Winston	Surrey	E	3.3.1986	*Johannesburg, SA*
*****de Saram** Samantha Indika	Ragama/Ruhuna	SL	2.9.1973	*Matara*
*****de Silva** Sanjeewa Kumara Lanka	Tamil Union/Wayamba	SL	29.7.1975	*Kurunegala*
*****de Silva** Weddikkara Ruwan Sujeewa	Colombo/Ruhuna	SL	7.10.1979	*Beruwala*
*****de Villiers** Abraham Benjamin	Titans	SA	17.2.1984	*Pretoria*
de Villiers Cornelius Johannes du Preez	Eagles/Free State	SA	16.3.1986	*Kroonstad*
Dewan Rahul	Haryana	I	15.7.1986	*Delhi*
*****de Wet** Friedel	Lions	SA	26.6.1980	*Durban*
Dexter Neil John	Middlesex	E	21.8.1984	*Johannesburg, SA*
Dharmani Pankaj	Punjab	I	27.9.1974	*Delhi*
Dhawan Shikhar	Delhi	I	5.12.1985	*Delhi*
*****Dhoni** Mahendra Singh	Jharkhand	I	7.7.1981	*Ranchi*
Diamanti Brendon John	Central Districts	NZ	30.4.1981	*Blenheim*
Dilhara Loku Hettige Danushka	Moors/Ruhuna	SL	3.7.1980	*Colombo*
Also known as Dilhara Lokuhettige				
*****Dilshan** Tillekeratne Mudiyanselage	Bloomfield	SL	14.10.1976	*Kalutara*
Dinda Ashok Bhimchandra	Bengal	I	25.3.1984	*Medinipur*
*****Dippenaar** Hendrik Human (Boeta)	Eagles/Leicestershire	SA	14.6.1977	*Kimberley*
Di Venuto Michael James	Durham	A	12.12.1973	*Hobart*
Dolar Mahmud	Khulna	B	30.12.1988	*Narail*
Dolley Corbyn Richard	Warriors/Eastern Province	SA	26.11.1987	*Port Elizabeth*
Doolan Alexander James	Tasmania	A	29.11.1985	*Launceston*
Doran Daniel John	Queensland	A	18.6.1981	*Hobart*
Dorey Brett Raymond	Western Australia	A	3.10.1977	*East Fremantle*
Doropoulos Theo Paul	Western Australia	A	25.4.1985	*Subiaco*

	Team	Country	Born	Birthplace
***Dowlin** Travis Montague	Guyana	WI	24.2.1977	*Guyhock Gardens, Guy.*
***Dravid** Rahul	Karnataka/Canterbury	I	11.1.1973	*Indore*
Drew Brendan Gerard	Tasmania	A	16.12.1983	*Lismore*
***Duffin** Terrence	Matabeleland Tuskers	Z	20.3.1982	*Kwekwe*
***Duminy** Jean-Paul	Cape Cobras	SA	14.4.1984	*Strandfontein*
du Plessis Francois	Titans/Lancashire	SA	13.7.1984	*Pretoria*
du Preez Dillon	Eagles	SA	8.11.1981	*Queenstown*
Durston Wesley John	Somerset	E	6.10.1980	*Taunton*
du Toit Jacques	Leicestershire	SA	2.1.1980	*Port Elizabeth*
Duval Chris John	Tasmania/S. Australia	A	3.8.1983	*Elizabethvale*
Dyili Athenkosi Ziphozihle Madoda	Warriors/Eastern Province	SA	17.7.1984	*King William's Town*
***Ealham** Mark Alan	Nottinghamshire	E	27.8.1969	*Willesborough*
***Ebrahim** Dion Digby	Matabeleland Tuskers	Z	7.8.1980	*Bulawayo*
Edmondson Ben Matthew	Western Australia	A	28.9.1978	*Southport*
***Edwards** Fidel Henderson	Barbados	WI	6.2.1982	*Gays, Barbados*
Edwards Kirk Anton	Barbados	WI	3.11.1984	*Mile & a Quarter, Barbados*
Edwards Philip Duncan	Kent	E	16.4.1984	*Minster*
Elgar Dean	Eagles	SA	11.6.1987	*Welkom*
***Elliott** Grant David	Wellington/Surrey	NZ	21.3.1979	*Johannesburg, SA*
Emmanuel Craig Walt	Com. Campuses & Colls.	WI	5.5.1986	*Mon Repos, St Lucia*
Emrit Rayad Ryan	Trinidad & Tobago	WI	8.3.1981	*Mount Hope, Trinidad*
***Enamul Haque, jun.**	Sylhet	B	5.12.1986	*Sylhet*
Engelbrecht Sybrand Abraham	Cape Cobras/W. Province	SA	15.9.1988	*Johannesburg*
***Ervine** Sean Michael	Hampshire	Z	6.12.1982	*Harare*
Evans Daniel	Middlesex	E	24.7.1987	*Hartlepool*
Evans Laurie John	Surrey	E	12.10.1987	*Lambeth*
***Ewing** Gavin Mackie	Matabeleland Tuskers	Z	21.1.1981	*Harare*
Fahad Iqbal	PIA	P	25.2.1986	*Karachi*
Fahad Masood	Habib Bank	P	14.8.1981	*Gaggu Mandi*
Faisal Athar	Hyderabad	P	15.10.1975	*Hyderabad*
***Faisal Iqbal**	PIA	P	30.12.1981	*Karachi*
Fallah Samad Mohammed	Maharashtra	I	2.5.1985	*Hyderabad*
Faulkner James Peter	Tasmania	A	29.4.1990	*Launceston*
***Fawad Alam**	National Bank	P	8.10.1985	*Karachi*
***Fazl-e-Akbar**	PIA	P	20.10.1980	*Peshawar*
Feldman Luke William	Queensland	A	1.8.1984	*Sunnybank*
Ferguson Callum James	South Australia	A	21.11.1984	*North Adelaide*
Ferley Robert Steven	Kent	E	4.2.1982	*Norwich*
***Fernando** Congenige Randhi Dilhara	Sinhalese	SL	19.7.1979	*Colombo*
***Fernando** Kandana Arachchige Dinusha Manoj	Panadura/Nondescripts	SL	10.8.1979	*Panadura*
***Fernando** Kandage <u>Hasantha</u> Ruwan Kumara	Moors/Basnahira South	SL	14.10.1979	*Panadura*
***Fernando** Thudellage <u>Charitha</u> <u>Buddhika</u> *Also known as Charitha Buddhika*	Bloomfield	SL	22.8.1980	Panadura
Findlay Shawn Eli	Jamaica	WI	3.3.1984	*Mandeville, Jamaica*
Finn Steven Thomas	Middlesex	E	4.4.1989	*Watford*
Fletcher Andre David Stephon	Windward Islands	WI	28.11.1987	*La Tante, Grenada*
Fletcher Luke Jack	Nottinghamshire	E	18.9.1988	*Nottingham*
***Flintoff** Andrew	Lancashire	E	6.12.1977	*Preston*
***Flower** Grant William	Essex	Z	20.12.1970	*Salisbury*
***Flynn** Daniel Raymond	Northern Districts	NZ	16.4.1985	*Rotorua*
Forrest Peter James	New South Wales	A	15.11.1985	*Windsor, Australia*
***Foster** James Savin	Essex	E	15.4.1980	*Whipps Cross*
***Franklin** James Edward Charles	Wellington/Glos	NZ	7.11.1980	*Wellington*

	Team	Country	Born	Birthplace
Franks Paul John	Nottinghamshire	E	3.2.1979	*Mansfield*
Friend Quinton	Dolphins/KwaZulu-Natal	SA	16.2.1982	*Bellville*
Frost Tony	Warwickshire	E	17.11.1975	*Stoke-on-Trent*
Frylinck Robert	Lions/Gauteng	SA	27.9.1984	*Durban*
Fudadin Assad Badyr	Guyana	WI	1.8.1985	*Rose Hall, Guyana*
*****Fulton** Peter Gordon	Canterbury	NZ	1.2.1979	*Christchurch*
Gale Andrew William	Yorkshire	E	28.11.1983	*Dewsbury*
*****Gallian** Jason Edward Riche	Essex	E	25.6.1971	*Manly, Australia*
*****Gambhir** Gautam	Delhi	I	14.10.1981	*Delhi*
Ganegama Withanaarchchige Chamara <u>Akalanka</u>	Nondescripts/Kandurata	SL	29.3.1981	*Colombo*
*****Ganga** Daren	Trinidad & Tobago	WI	14.1.1979	*Barrackpore, Trinidad*
Ganga Sherwin	Trinidad & Tobago	WI	13.2.1982	*Barrackpore, Trinidad*
*****Ganguly** Sourav Chandidas	Bengal	I	8.7.1972	*Calcutta*
Garraway Trevon Cabello	Guyana	WI	11.1.1984	*Suddie, Guyana*
Garwe Trevor Nyasha	Northerns/Mash. Eagles	Z	7.1.1982	*Harare*
Gatting Joe Stephen	Sussex	E	25.11.1987	*Brighton*
Gavaskar Rohan Sunil	Bengal	I	20.2.1976	*Kanpur*
*****Gayle** Christopher Henry	Jamaica	WI	21.9.1979	*Kingston, Jamaica*
*****Geeves** Brett	Tasmania	A	13.6.1982	*Claremont*
George Dennis Martin	Windward Islands	WI	3.12.1981	*St Patricks, Grenada*
George Peter Robert	South Australia	A	16.10.1986	*Woodville*
Gerber Etienne	Lions/North West	SA	6.7.1988	*Kempton Park*
*****Gibbs** Herschelle Herman	Cape Cobras/Glamorgan	SA	23.2.1974	*Green Point*
Gidman Alexander Peter Richard	Gloucestershire	E	22.6.1981	*High Wycombe*
*****Gillespie** Mark Raymond	Wellington	NZ	17.10.1979	*Wanganui*
Gilmour Steven Thomas	Victoria	A	16.10.1986	*Numurkah*
Gobind Viyash	Dolphins/KwaZulu-Natal	SA	22.12.1984	*Durban*
Godleman Billy Ashley	Middlesex	E	11.2.1989	*Camden*
Gony Manpreet Singh	Punjab	I	4.1.1984	*Roopnagar*
*****Goodwin** Murray William	Sussex	Z	11.12.1972	*Salisbury*
Goud Yere Karekal Thippana	Railways	I	27.11.1971	*Raichur*
Govender Ugasen	Dolphins/KZN/Lions/Gau.	SA	17.12.1983	*Tongaat*
Gray Alistair John Alec	Cape Cobras/W. Province	SA	8.7.1982	*Johannesburg*
Griffiths David Andrew	Hampshire	E	10.9.1985	*Newport, Isle of Wight*
Groenewald Timothy Duncan	Derbyshire	SA	10.11.1984	*Pietermaritzburg*
Guillen Justin Christopher	Trinidad & Tobago	WI	2.1.1986	*Port-of-Spain, Trinidad*
*****Gunawardene** Dihan <u>Avishka</u>	Sinhalese	SL	26.5.1977	*Colombo*
*****Guptill** Martin James	Auckland	NZ	30.9.1986	*Auckland*
Gurney Harry Frederick	Leicestershire	E	25.10.1986	*Nottingham*
Haberfield Jake Andy	South Australia	A	18.6.1986	*Townsville*
*****Haddin** Bradley James	New South Wales	A	23.10.1977	*Cowra*
Hales Alexander Daniel	Nottinghamshire	E	3.1.1989	*Hillingdon*
Hall Andrew James	Dolphins/Northants	SA	31.7.1975	*Johannesburg*
Hamilton Jahmar Neville	Leeward Islands	WI	22.9.1990	*St Thomas, Anguilla*
Hamilton-Brown Rory James	Sussex	E	3.9.1987	*St John's Wood*
*****Harbhajan Singh**	Punjab	I	3.7.1980	*Jullundur*
Harinath Arun	Surrey	E	26.3.1987	*Sutton*
*****Harmison** Stephen James	Durham	E	23.10.1978	*Ashington*
Harris Andrew James	Leicestershire	E	26.6.1973	*Ashton-under-Lyne*
*****Harris** Chris Zinzan	Canterbury	NZ	20.11.1969	*Christchurch*
Harris Daniel Joseph	South Australia	A	31.12.1979	*North Adelaide*
Harris James Alexander Russell	Glamorgan	E	16.5.1990	*Morriston*
*****Harris** Paul Lee	Titans	SA	2.11.1978	*Salisbury, Zimbabwe*
Harris Ryan James	Queensland/Surrey	A	11.10.1979	*Nowra*
Harrison David Stuart	Glamorgan	E	30.7.1981	*Newport*
Harrison Paul William	Northamptonshire	E	22.5.1984	*Cuckfield*
Hartley Christopher Desmond	Queensland	A	24.5.1982	*Nambour*

	Team	Country	Born	Birthplace
Harwood Shane Michael	Victoria	A	1.3.1974	*Ballarat*
*****Hasan Raza**	Habib Bank	P	11.3.1982	*Karachi*
Hastings John Wayne	Victoria	A	4.11.1985	*Nepean*
*****Hauritz** Nathan Michael	New South Wales	A	18.10.1981	*Wondai*
*****Hayden** Matthew Lawrence	Queensland	A	29.10.1971	*Kingaroy*
Haynes Jason Adrian McCarthy	Barbados	WI	3.7.1981	*Jackman Main Rd, Barbados*
*****Hayward** Mornantau (Nantie)	Derbyshire	SA	6.3.1977	*Uitenhage*
Hazlewood Josh Reginald	New South Wales	A	8.1.1991	*Tamworth*
Heal Aaron Keith	Western Australia	A	13.3.1983	*Armadale*
Hector Donwell Banister	Windward Islands	WI	31.10.1988	*St Vincent*
*****Henderson** Claude William	Cape Cobras/Leics	SA	14.6.1972	*Worcester*
Hendricks Reeza Raphael	Eagles/Griqualand West	SA	14.8.1989	*Kimberley*
Henriques Moises Consantino	New South Wales	A	1.2.1987	*Funchal, Portugal*
Herath Herath Mudiyanselage Rangana Keerthi Bandara	Moors/Wayamba/Surrey	SL	19.3.1978	*Kurunegala*
*****Hettiarachchi** Dinuka	Chilaw M./Basnahira S.	SL	15.7.1976	*Colombo*
Hewer Nicolas David	Dolphins/KwaZulu-Natal	SA	6.7.1984	*Durban*
Hibbert Keith Hugh	Jamaica	WI	14.6.1980	*St Catherine, Jamaica*
Hicks Delbert	Guyana	WI	11.11.1983	*New Amsterdam, Guy.*
Hildreth James Charles	Somerset	E	9.9.1984	*Milton Keynes*
*****Hilfenhaus** Benjamin William	Tasmania	A	15.3.1983	*Ulverstone*
*****Hinds** Ryan O'Neal	Barbados	WI	17.2.1981	*Holders Hill, Barb.*
*****Hinds** Wavell Wayne	Jamaica/Derbyshire	WI	7.9.1976	*Kingston, Jamaica*
Hockley James Bernard	Kent	E	16.4.1979	*Beckenham*
Hodd Andrew John	Sussex	E	12.1.1984	*Chichester*
*****Hodge** Bradley John	Victoria	A	29.12.1974	*Sandringham*
Hodge Montcin Verniel	Leeward Islands	WI	29.9.1987	*Anguilla*
Hodnett Grant Phillip	Gloucestershire	E	17.8.1982	*Johannesburg, SA*
Hogan Michael Garry	Western Australia	A	31.5.1981	*Newcastle*
Hogg Kyle William	Lancashire	E	2.7.1983	*Birmingham*
*****Hoggard** Matthew James	Yorkshire	E	31.12.1976	*Leeds*
Holder Jason Omar	Barbados	WI	5.11.1991	*Rouens Village, Barb.*
Holland Jonathan Mark	Victoria	A	29.5.1987	*Sandringham*
Hondo Douglas Tafadzwa	Easterns/Mash. Eagles	Z	7.7.1979	*Bulawayo*
Hopes James Redfern	Queensland	A	24.10.1978	*Townsville*
*****Hopkins** Gareth James	Auckland	NZ	24.11.1976	*Lower Hutt*
Hopkinson Carl Daniel	Sussex	E	14.9.1981	*Brighton*
Horton Paul James	Lancashire	E	20.9.1982	*Sydney, Australia*
Housego Daniel Mark	Middlesex	E	12.10.1988	*Windsor*
*****How** Jamie Michael	Central Districts	NZ	19.5.1981	*New Plymouth*
Howgego Benjamin Harry Nicholas	Northamptonshire	E	3.3.1988	*Kings Lynn*
*****Hughes** Phillip Joel	New South Wales/Middx	A	30.11.1988	*Macksville*
*****Humayun Farhat**	Habib Bank	P	24.1.1981	*Lahore*
Hunter Ian David	Derbyshire	E	11.9.1979	*Durham*
Hussain Gemaal Maqsood	Gloucestershire	E	10.10.1983	*Waltham Forest*
Hussey David John	Victoria/Nottinghamshire	A	15.7.1977	*Morley*
*****Hussey** Michael Edward Killeen	Western Australia	A	27.5.1975	*Morley*
Hutchinson Boris	Com. Campuses & Colls.	WI	4.11.1985	*Jamaica*
Hyatt Danza Pacino	Jamaica	WI	17.3.1983	*St Catherine, Jamaica*
*****Iftikhar Anjum**	ZTBL	P	1.12.1980	*Khanewal*
*****Ijaz Ahmed, jun.**	Faisalabad	P	2.2.1969	*Lyallpur*
Imran Abbas	Sui Southern	P	25.3.1978	*Gujranwala*
Imran Arif	Worcestershire	P	15.1.1984	*Kotli*
*****Imran Farhat**	Habib Bank	P	20.5.1982	*Lahore*
*****Imran Nazir**	ZTBL	P	16.12.1981	*Gujranwala*
Imran Tahir	Titans/Easterns/Hants	P	27.3.1979	*Lahore*
*****Imrul Kayes**	Khulna	B	2.2.1987	*Meherpur*
Ingram Colin Alexander	Warriors/E. Province	SA	3.7.1985	*Port Elizabeth*

	Team	Country	Born	Birthplace
Ingram Peter John	Central Districts	NZ	25.10.1978	*Hawera*
Ireland Anthony John	Gloucestershire	Z	30.8.1984	*Masvingo*
*__Irfan Fazil__	Habib Bank	P	2.11.1981	*Lahore*
Jackson Simon	Com. Campuses & Colls.	WI	18.5.1985	*Jamaica*
Jacobs Arno	Warriors	SA	13.3.1977	*Potchefstroom*
Jacobs David Johan	Warriors	SA	4.11.1982	*Klerksdorp*
Jacobs Steven Anthony	Guyana	WI	13.9.1988	*Georgetown, Guyana*
Jadeja Ravindrasinh Anirudhsinh	Saurashtra	I	6.12.1988	*Navagam-Khed*
Jadhav Kedar Mahadev	Maharashtra	I	26.3.1985	*Pune*
*__Jaggernauth__ Amit Shelden	Trinidad & Tobago	WI	16.11.1983	*Lennard St, Trinidad*
Jakati Shadab Bashir	Goa	I	27.11.1980	*Vasco da Gama*
James Kevin Arthur	Windward Islands	WI	9.12.1987	*Goodwill, Dominica*
James Lindon Omrick Dinsley	Windward Islands	WI	30.12.1984	*South Rivers, St Vinc.*
*__Jaques__ Philip Anthony	New South Wales	A	3.5.1979	*Wollongong*
Jarvis Kyle Malcolm	Mashonaland Eagles	Z	16.2.1989	*Harare*
Javid Ateeq	Warwickshire	E	15.10.1991	*Birmingham*
Jayantha Warushavithana Saman	Bloomfield	SL	26.1.1974	*Ambalangoda*
Jayaprakashdaran Pradeep Sri	Badureliya/Tamil Union	SL	13.1.1984	*Colombo*
Jayasinghe Chinthaka Umesh	Bloomfield/Kandurata	SL	19.5.1978	*Kalutara*
*__Jayasuriya__ Sanath Teran	Bloomfield	SL	30.6.1969	*Matara*
*__Jayawardene__ Denagamage Proboth Mahela de Silva	Sinhalese	SL	27.5.1977	*Colombo*
*__Jayawardene__ Hewasandatchige Asiri Prasanna Wishvanath	Bloomfield	SL	9.10.1979	*Colombo*
Jeffers Shane Melvon	Leeward Islands	WI	12.9.1981	*Sandy Point, St Kitts*
Jefferson William Ingleby	Nottinghamshire	E	25.10.1979	*Derby*
Jeggels Riaan Ruche	Warriors/E. Province	SA	10.9.1981	*Port Elizabeth*
Jewell Nicholas	Victoria	A	27.8.1977	*Melbourne*
Johnson Leon Rayon	Guyana	WI	8.8.1987	*Georgetown, Guyana*
Johnson Michael Anthony	Western Australia	A	11.8.1988	*Perth*
*__Johnson__ Mitchell Guy	Queensland	A	2.11.1981	*Townsville*
Jones Brady	Tasmania	A	16.9.1988	*Franklin*
*__Jones__ Geraint Owen	Kent	E	14.7.1976	*Kundiawa, Papua N. G.*
Jones Philip Steffan	Derbyshire/Kent	E	9.2.1974	*Llanelli*
Jones Richard Alan	Worcestershire	E	6.11.1986	*Stourbridge*
*__Jones__ Richard Andrew	Auckland	NZ	22.10.1973	*Auckland*
Jordan Christopher James	Surrey	E	4.10.1988	*Lowlands, Barbados*
Joseph Robert Hartman	Kent/Leeward Islands	E	20.1.1982	*St John's, Antigua*
Joshi Sunil Bandacharya	Karnataka	I	6.6.1969	*Gadag*
Joubert Pierre	Titans	SA	2.5.1978	*Pretoria*
Joyce Edmund Christopher	Sussex	E	22.9.1978	*Dublin, Ireland*
*__Junaid Siddique__	Rajshahi	B	30.10.1987	*Rajshahi*
Junaid Zia	Lahore	P	11.12.1983	*Lahore*
*__Kaif__ Mohammad	Uttar Pradesh	I	1.12.1980	*Allahabad*
*__Kalavitigoda__ Shantha	Bloomfield/Moors	SL	23.12.1977	*Colombo*
*__Kallis__ Jacques Henry	Warriors	SA	16.10.1975	*Pinelands*
*__Kamran Akmal__	National Bank	P	13.1.1982	*Lahore*
Kamran Hussain	Habib Bank	P	9.5.1977	*Bahawalpur*
Kamungozi Tafadzwa	Centrals/S. Rocks	Z	8.6.1987	*Harare*
Kandamby Sahan Hewa Thilina	Sinhalese/Basnahira N.	SL	4.6.1982	*Colombo*
*__Kanitkar__ Hrishikesh Hemant	Madhya Pradesh	I	14.11.1974	*Pune*
Kantasingh Kavesh	Com. Campuses & Colls.	WI	30.9.1986	*Trinidad*
Kapugedera Chamara Kantha	Colombo	SL	24.2.1987	*Kandy*
Karthik Krishankumar Dinesh	Tamil Nadu	I	1.6.1985	*Madras*
*__Kartik__ Murali	Railways/Middlesex	I	11.9.1976	*Madras*
Kashif Raza	WAPDA	P	29.12.1979	*Sheikhupura*
Kasteni Friday	Centrals/MW Rhinos	Z	25.3.1988	*Kadoma*
*__Katich__ Simon Mathew	New South Wales	A	21.8.1975	*Middle Swan*

	Team	Country	Born	Birthplace
Katti Anand	Assam	I	11.7.1972	*Belgaum*
Kaul Uday	Punjab	I	2.12.1987	*Kangra*
Keedy Gary	Lancashire	E	27.11.1974	*Sandal*
Kelly Richard Alexander	Trinidad & Tobago	WI	19.2.1984	*Trinidad*
*****Kemp** Justin Miles	Cape Cobras/Kent	SA	2.10.1977	*Queenstown*
Kent Jon Carter	Dolphins/KwaZulu-Natal	SA	7.5.1979	*Cape Town*
Kervezee Alexei Nicolaas	Worcestershire	NL	11.9.1989	*Walvis Bay, Namibia*
*****Key** Robert William Trevor	Kent	E	12.5.1979	*East Dulwich*
Khalid Latif	Karachi	P	4.11.1985	*Karachi*
*****Khan** Amjad	Kent	E	14.10.1980	*Copenhagen, Denmark*
*****Khan** Imraan	Dolphins	SA	27.4.1984	*Durban*
Khan Imran	Trinidad & Tobago	WI	6.12.1984	*Port-of-Spain, Trinidad*
Khawaja Usman Tariq	New South Wales	A	18.12.1986	*Islamabad, Pakistan*
Khoda Gagan Kishanlal	Rajasthan	I	24.10.1974	*Barmer*
*****Khurram Manzoor**	PIA	P	10.6.1986	*Karachi*
Kieswetter Craig	Somerset	SA	28.11.1987	*Johannesburg*
King Simon James	Surrey	E	4.9.1987	*Warlingham*
Kirby Steven Paul	Gloucestershire	E	4.10.1977	*Ainsworth*
*****Kirtley** Robert James	Sussex	E	10.1.1975	*Eastbourne*
Kleinveldt Rory Keith	Cape Cobras	SA	15.3.1983	*Cape Town*
Klinger Michael	South Australia	A	4.7.1980	*Kew*
Klokker Frederik Andreas	Derbyshire	Denmark	13.3.1983	*Odense*
Knappett Joshua Philip Thomas	Worcestershire	E	15.4.1985	*Westminster*
Knowles Bradley Aaron	Western Australia	A	29.10.1981	*Moe*
Kohli Virat	Delhi	I	5.11.1988	*Delhi*
*****Krejza** Jason John	Tasmania	A	14.1.1983	*Newtown*
Kreusch Justin Peter	Warriors	SA	27.9.1979	*East London*
Kruger Garnett John-Peter	Lions/Warriors/Glam	SA	5.1.1977	*Port Elizabeth*
Kruger Nicholas James	Queensland	A	14.8.1983	*Paddington, Australia*
Kruis Gideon Jacobus (Deon)	Yorkshire	SA	9.5.1974	*Pretoria*
Kuhn Heino Gunther	Titans/Northerns	SA	1.4.1984	*Piet Retief*
*****Kulasekara** Kulasekara Mudiyanselage Dinesh Nuwan	Colts/Basnahira North	SL	22.7.1982	*Nittambuwa*
Kulatunga Hettiarachchi Gamage Jeevantha Mahesh	Colts/Wayamba	SL	2.11.1973	*Kurunegala*
Kulkarni Dhawal Sunil	Mumbai/Wellington	I	10.12.1988	*Bombay*
Kumar Praveenkumar	Uttar Pradesh	I	2.10.1986	*Meerut*
Lakmal Ranasinghe Arachchige Suranga	Tamil Union	SL	10.3.1987	*Matara*
*****Lakshitha** Materba Kanatha Gamage Chamila Premanath	Air Force	SL	4.1.1979	*Unawatuna*
Also known as Chamila Gamage				
Lambert Grant Michael	New South Wales	A	5.8.1977	*Parramatta*
Lambert Tamar Lansford	Jamaica	WI	15.7.1981	*St Catherine, Jamaica*
*****Langer** Justin Lee	Somerset	A	21.11.1970	*Perth*
*****Langeveldt** Charl Kenneth	Cape Cobras	SA	17.12.1974	*Stellenbosch*
Laughlin Ben	Queensland	A	3.10.1982	*Box Hill*
*****Law** Stuart Grant	Derbyshire	A	18.10.1968	*Herston*
Lawson Mark Anthony Kenneth	Derbyshire	E	24.10.1985	*Leeds*
*****Laxman** Vangipurappu Venkata Sai	Hyderabad/Otago/Lancs	I	1.11.1974	*Hyderabad*
*****Lee** Brett	New South Wales	A	8.11.1976	*Wollongong*
Lee James Edward	Yorkshire	E	23.12.1988	*Sheffield*
Lesporis Keddy	Windward Islands	WI	27.12.1988	*St Lucia*
Levi Richard Ernst	Cape Cobras	SA	14.1.1988	*Johannesburg*
*****Lewis** Jonathan	Gloucestershire	E	26.8.1975	*Aylesbury*
*****Lewis** Rawl Nicholas	Windward Islands	WI	5.9.1974	*Union Village, Grenada*
Lewry Jason David	Sussex	E	2.4.1971	*Worthing*
Liburd Steve Stuart Wayne	Leeward Islands	WI	26.2.1985	*Basseterre, St Kitts*

	Team	Country	Born	Birthplace
Linley Timothy Edward	Surrey	E	23.3.1982	*Leeds*
Lockyear Rhett John Gaven	Tasmania	A	28.2.1983	*Mudgee*
Logan Richard James	Surrey	E	28.1.1980	*Stone*
***Lokuarachchi** Kaushal Samaraweera	Sinhalese/Wayamba	SL	20.5.1982	*Colombo*
London Adam Brian	Middlesex	E	12.10.1988	*Ashford*
Lotter Richard Bryan	Cape Cobras/W. Province	SA	22.4.1986	*Cape Town*
Louw Johann	Dolphins	SA	12.4.1979	*Cape Town*
***Love** Martin Lloyd	Queensland	A	30.3.1974	*Mundubbera*
Loye Malachy Bernard	Lancashire	E	27.9.1972	*Northampton*
Lucas David Scott	Northamptonshire	E	19.8.1978	*Nottingham*
Ludeman Timothy Paul	South Australia	A	23.6.1987	*Warrnambool*
Lumb Michael John	Hampshire	E	12.2.1980	*Johannesburg, SA*
Lungley Tom	Derbyshire/Lancashire	E	25.7.1979	*Derby*
Lyth Adam	Yorkshire	E	25.9.1987	*Whitby*
McClean Kevin Ramon	Com. Campuses & Colls.	WI	24.1.1988	*Castle, Barbados*
McClenaghan Mitchell John	Central Districts	NZ	11.6.1986	*Hastings*
***McCullum** Brendon Barrie	Otago	NZ	27.9.1981	*Dunedin*
McCullum Nathan Leslie	Otago	NZ	1.9.1980	*Dunedin*
***McDonald** Andrew Barry	Victoria	A	15.6.1981	*Wodonga*
Macdonald Timothy Peter	Tasmania	A	7.9.1980	*Subiaco*
***McGain** Bryce Edward	Victoria	A	25.3.1972	*Mornington*
McGlashan Peter Donald	Northern Districts	NZ	22.6.1979	*Napier*
***McGrath** Anthony	Yorkshire	E	6.10.1975	*Bradford*
***McIntosh** Timothy Gavin	Auckland	NZ	4.12.1979	*Auckland*
***McKay** Clinton James	Victoria	A	22.2.1983	*Melbourne*
***McKenzie** Neil Douglas	Lions	SA	24.11.1975	*Johannesburg*
McLaren Adrian Peter	Eagles/Griqualand West	SA	21.4.1980	*Kimberley*
***McLaren** Ryan	Eagles/Kent	SA	9.2.1983	*Kimberley*
***Maddy** Darren Lee	Warwickshire	E	23.5.1974	*Leicester*
Madsen Wayne Lee	Derbyshire	SA	2.1.1984	*Durban*
Magoffin Steven James	Western Australia	A	17.12.1979	*Corinda*
***Maharoof** Mohamed Farveez	Nondescripts	SL	7.9.1984	*Colombo*
***Mahbubul Alam**	Dhaka	B	1.12.1983	*Faridpur*
***Mahmood** Sajid Iqbal	Lancashire	E	21.12.1981	*Bolton*
***Mahmudullah**	Dhaka	B	4.2.1986	*Mymensingh*
***Mahwire** Ngonidzashe Blessing	Centrals/S. Rocks	Z	31.7.1982	*Bikita*
Mail Gregory John	New South Wales	A	29.4.1978	*Penrith*
Malan Dawid Johannes	Middlesex	E	3.9.1987	*Roehampton*
Malan Pieter Jacobus	Titans/Northerns	SA	13.8.1989	*Nelspruit*
Malik Vikramjeet	Himachal Pradesh	I	9.5.1983	*Solan*
***Malinga** Separamadu Lasith	Nondescripts	SL	4.9.1983	*Galle*
Mangan Joshua Patrick	Western Australia	A	15.1.1986	*Rutherglen*
***Manou** Graham Allan	South Australia	A	23.4.1979	*Modbury*
Mansoor Amjad	National Bank	P	25.12.1986	*Sialkot*
Manyumwa Admire Marvellous	Northerns/Mash. Eagles	Z	28.12.1987	*Chitungwiza*
***Maregwede** Alester	Southern Rocks	Z	5.8.1981	*Harare*
Marsh Daniel James	Tasmania	A	14.6.1973	*Subiaco*
Marsh Mitchell Ross	Western Australia	A	20.10.1991	*Armadale*
Marsh Shaun Edward	Western Australia	A	9.7.1983	*Narrogin*
***Marshall** Hamish John Hamilton	Northern Districts/Glos	NZ	15.2.1979	*Warkworth*
***Marshall** James Andrew Hamilton	Northern Districts	NZ	15.2.1979	*Warkworth*
***Marshall** Xavier Melbourne	Jamaica	WI	27.3.1986	*St Ann, Jamaica*
Martin Anthony	Leeward Islands	WI	18.11.1982	*Bethesda, Antigua*
Martin Bruce Philip	Northern Districts	NZ	25.4.1980	*Whangarei*
***Martin** Christopher Stewart	Auckland/Canterbury	NZ	10.12.1974	*Christchurch*
Martin Jacob Joseph	Baroda	I	11.5.1972	*Baroda*
Martin-Jenkins Robin Simon Christopher	Sussex	E	28.10.1975	*Guildford*

	Team	Country	Born	Birthplace
Maruma Timycen	Easterns/Mountaineers	Z	19.4.1988	*Harare*
*****Masakadza** Hamilton	Easterns/Mountaineers	Z	9.8.1983	*Harare*
Masakadza Shingirai Winston	Easterns/Mountaineers	Z	4.9.1986	*Harare*
Mascarenhas Adrian Dimitri	Hampshire	E	30.10.1977	*Chiswick*
Masekela Lerutla Matheko Gershon	Titans/Northerns	SA	21.7.1987	*Pietersburg*
Mash Lloyd Ryan	Victoria	A	1.12.1981	*Melbourne*
*****Mashrafe bin Mortaza**	Khulna	B	5.10.1983	*Narail*
*****Mason** Michael James	Central Districts	NZ	27.8.1974	*Carterton*
Mason Matthew Sean	Worcestershire	A	20.3.1974	*Claremont*
Masters David Daniel	Essex	E	22.4.1978	*Chatham*
Mathews Angelo Davis	Colts/Basnahira North	SL	2.6.1987	*Colombo*
Matshikwe Pumelela	Lions/Gauteng	SA	19.6.1984	*Johannesburg*
*****Matsikenyeri** Stuart	Easterns/Mountaineers	Z	3.5.1983	*Harare*
Matthew Mervin	Windward Islands	WI	23.9.1985	*Soufriere, Dominica*
Maunders John Kenneth	Essex	E	4.4.1981	*Ashford*
Mawoyo Tinotenda Mbiri Kanayi	Easterns/Mountaineers	Z	8.1.1986	*Umtali*
Maynard Thomas Lloyd	Glamorgan	E	25.3.1989	*Cardiff*
Mbhalati Nkateko Ethy	Titans	SA	18.11.1981	*Tzaneen*
Meaker Stuart Christopher	Surrey	E	21.1.1989	*Durban, SA*
*****Mehrab Hossain, jun.**	Dhaka	B	8.7.1987	*Rajshahi*
*****Mendis** Balapuwaduge Ajantha Winslo	Army	SL	11.3.1985	*Moratuwa*
Meth Keagan Orry	Matabeleland Tuskers	Z	8.2.1988	*Bulawayo*
Meyer Lyall	Warriors/Eastern Province	SA	23.3.1982	*Port Elizabeth*
Mickleburgh Jaik Charles	Essex	E	30.3.1990	*Norwich*
Middlebrook James Daniel	Essex	E	13.5.1977	*Leeds*
Miller Andrew Stephen	Warwickshire	E	27.9.1987	*Preston*
Miller David Andrew	Dolphins/KwaZulu-Natal	SA	10.6.1989	*Pietermaritzburg*
*****Miller** Nikita O'Neil	Jamaica	WI	16.5.1982	*St Elizabeth, Jamaica*
*****Mills** Kyle David	Auckland	NZ	15.3.1979	*Auckland*
*****Mirando** Magina Thilan Thushara				
Also known as Thilan Thushara	Sinhalese	SL	3.1.1981	*Balapitiya*
*****Misbah-ul-Haq**	Sui Northern	P	28.5.1974	*Mianwali*
*****Mishra** Amit	Haryana/C. Districts	I	24.11.1982	*Delhi*
Mitchell Daryl Keith Henry	Worcestershire	E	25.11.1983	*Badsey*
Mlongo Saidi	Dolphins/KwaZulu-Natal	SA	21.9.1983	*Stanger*
Mohamed Zaheer	Guyana	WI	10.10.1985	*Georgetown, Guyana*
*****Mohammad Aamer**	National Bank	P	13.4.1992	*Gujjar Khan*
*****Mohammad Ashraful**	Dhaka	B	9.9.1984	*Dhaka*
*****Mohammad Asif**	National Bank	P	20.12.1982	*Sheikhupura*
*****Mohammad Hafeez**	Sui Northern	P	17.10.1980	*Sargodha*
*****Mohammad Hussain**	Customs	P	8.10.1976	*Lahore*
*****Mohammad Khalil**	ZTBL	P	11.11.1982	*Lahore*
*****Mohammad Sami**	Karachi	P	24.2.1981	*Karachi*
*****Mohammad Talha**	National Bank	P	15.10.1988	*Faisalabad*
*****Mohammad Wasim**	KRL	P	8.8.1977	*Rawalpindi*
*****Mohammad Yousuf**	WAPDA	P	27.8.1974	*Lahore*
Formerly known as Yousuf Youhana				
*****Mohammad Zahid**	Customs	P	2.8.1976	*Gaggu Mandi*
*****Mohammed** Dave	Trinidad & Tobago	WI	8.10.1979	*Knolly Street, Trinidad*
Mohammed Gibran	Trinidad & Tobago	WI	31.7.1983	*Barrackpore, Trinidad*
Mohammed Jason Nazimuddin	Trinidad & Tobago	WI	23.9.1986	*Barrackpore, Trinidad*
Mohanty Basantkumar Chintamani	Orissa	I	24.11.1986	*Bhubaneswar*
*****Mohanty** Debasis Sarbeswar	Orissa	I	20.7.1976	*Bhubaneswar*
Mokoena Thabang Grant	Lions/Gauteng	SA	15.8.1987	*Johannesburg*
Moller Gregory David	Queensland	A	29.11.1983	*Boonah*
Moore Gilford	Com. Campuses & Colls.	WI	26.2.1982	*Henrietta, Guyana*
Moore Stephen Colin	Worcestershire	E	4.11.1980	*Johannesburg, SA*
Morgan Eoin Joseph Gerard	Middlesex	Ireland/E	10.9.1986	*Dublin*
*****Morkel** Johannes Albertus	Titans	SA	10.6.1981	*Vereeniging*

	Team	Country	Born	Birthplace
***Morkel** Morne	Titans	SA	6.10.1984	Vereeniging
Morris Carlo Antonio	Barbados	WI	13.1.1980	Westmorland, Barbados
***Morton** Runako Shakur	Leeward Islands	WI	22.7.1978	Rawlins, Nevis
Mosehle Mangaliso	Titans/Easterns	SA	24.4.1990	Duduza
Mpitsang Phenyo Victor	Eagles/Free State	SA	28.3.1980	Kimberley
***Mpofu** Christopher Bobby	Westerns/Mata. Tuskers	Z	27.11.1985	Plumtree
Mubarak Jehan	Colombo/Wayamba	SL	10.1.1981	Washington, USA
Muchall Gordon James	Durham	E	2.11.1982	Newcastle-upon-Tyne
Mufambisi Tafadzwa Vintlane	Northerns/Mash. Eagles	Z	17.12.1986	Glen View
Mukund Abhinav	Tamil Nadu	I	6.1.1990	Madras
Munday Michael Kenneth	Somerset	E	22.10.1984	Nottingham
Mupariwa Tawanda	Westerns/Mata. Tuskers	Z	16.4.1985	Bulawayo
***Muralitharan** Muttiah	Tamil Union	SL	17.4.1972	Kandy
Murphy David	Northamptonshire	E	24.7.1989	Welwyn Garden City
Murtagh Christopher Paul	Surrey	E	14.10.1984	Lambeth
Murtagh Timothy James	Middlesex	E	2.8.1981	Lambeth
Murtaza Hussain	Customs/Surrey	P	20.12.1974	Bahawalpur
***Mushfiqur Rahim**	Sylhet	B	1.9.1988	Bogra
Mustard Philip	Durham	E	8.10.1982	Sunderland
Mutizwa Forster	Easterns/Mash. Eagles	Z	24.8.1985	Harare
***Naeem Islam**	Rajshahi	B	31.12.1986	Gaibandha
Naik Jigar Kumar Hakumatrai	Leicestershire	E	10.8.1984	Leicester
Najaf Shah	PIA	P	17.12.1984	Gujarkhan
Nanan Magnum	Trinidad & Tobago	WI		
Nannes Dirk Peter	Victoria	NL/A	16.5.1976	Mount Waverly
Napier Graham Richard	Essex	E	6.1.1980	Colchester
***Narine** Sunil Philip	Trinidad & Tobago	WI	26.5.1988	Trinidad
***Nash** Brendan Paul	Jamaica	WI	14.12.1977	Attadale, Australia
Nash Christopher David	Sussex	E	19.5.1983	Cuckfield
Nash David Charles	Middlesex	E	19.1.1978	Chertsey
Nasir Jamshed	National Bank	P	6.12.1989	Lahore
Naumanullah	National Bank	P	20.5.1975	Karachi
Naved Arif	Sialkot	P	2.11.1981	Mandi Bahauddin
***Naved Ashraf**	Rawalpindi	P	4.9.1974	Rawalpindi
***Naved Latif**	Faisalabad	P	21.2.1976	Sargodha
***Naved-ul-Hasan**	WAPDA/Yorkshire	P	28.2.1978	Sheikhupura
Also known as Rana Naved				
Nayanakantha Hewawasam Gamage Dharshana	Ragama/Kandurata	SL	2.3.1979	Colombo
Also known as Dharshana Gamage				
Nayar Abhishek Mohan	Mumbai	I	26.10.1983	Secunderabad
***Nazmul Hossain**	Sylhet	B	5.10.1987	Hobigonj
Needham Jake	Derbyshire	E	30.9.1986	Portsmouth
***Nehra** Ashish	Delhi	I	29.4.1979	Delhi
***Nel** Andre	Lions/Gauteng/Surrey	SA	15.7.1977	Germiston
Nelson Mark Anthony George	Northamptonshire	E	24.9.1986	Milton Keynes
Nevill Peter Michael	New South Wales	A	13.10.1985	Hawthorne
Nevin Christopher John	Wellington	NZ	3.8.1975	Dunedin
New Thomas James	Leicestershire	E	18.1.1985	Sutton-in-Ashfield
Newby Oliver James	Lancashire	E	26.8.1984	Blackburn
Newman Scott Alexander	Nottinghamshire/Surrey	E	3.11.1979	Epsom
Newport Nathan Alexander	Warwickshire	E	10.5.1989	Worcester
Nixon Paul Andrew	Leicestershire	E	21.10.1970	Carlisle
Nkwe Enoch Thabiso	Lions/Gauteng	SA	8.2.1983	Soweto
Noel Jamal	Com. Campuses & Colls.	WI	21.4.1984	Foster Hall, Barbados
Noffke Ashley Allan	Qld/W. Australia/Worcs	A	30.4.1977	Nambour
***North** Marcus James	Western Australia/Hants	A	28.7.1979	Pakenham
Northeast Sam Alexander	Kent	E	16.10.1989	Ashford

	Team	Country	Born	Birthplace
Nowak Sean Andrew	Titans/Northerns	SA	6.1.1987	*Pretoria*
***Ntini** Makhaya	Warriors	SA	6.7.1977	*Mdingi*
Nurse Rohan Renee	Barbados	WI	21.8.1983	*Forde Rd Village, Barb.*
Nyumbu John	Westerns/Mata. Tuskers	Z	1.3.1983	*Harare*
O'Brien Aaron Warren	South Australia	A	2.10.1981	*St Leonards*
***O'Brien** Iain Edward	Wellington/Leics	NZ	10.7.1976	*Lower Hutt*
O'Brien Niall John	Northamptonshire	Ireland	8.11.1981	*Dublin*
Ojha Naman Vijaykumar	Madhya Pradesh	I	20.7.1983	*Ujjain*
***Ojha** Pragyan Prayish	Hyderabad	I	5.9.1986	*Khurda*
O'Keefe Stephen Norman John	New South Wales	A	9.12.1984	*Malaysia*
Olivier Mario Wicus	War./Bor./C. Cob/W. Prov	SA	3.11.1982	*Pretoria*
***Onions** Graham	Durham	E	9.9.1982	*Gateshead*
***Ontong** Justin Lee	Cape Cobras	SA	4.1.1980	*Paarl*
***Oram** Jacob David Philip	Central Districts	NZ	28.7.1978	*Palmerston North*
O'Shea Michael Peter	Glamorgan	E	4.9.1987	*Cardiff*
***Pagon** Donovan Jomo	Jamaica	WI	13.9.1982	*Kingston, Jamaica*
Paine Timothy David	Tasmania	A	8.12.1984	*Hobart*
Palladino Antonio Paul	Essex/Namibia	E	29.6.1983	*Tower Hamlets*
***Panesar** Mudhsuden Singh (Monty)	Northamptonshire/Lions	E	25.4.1982	*Luton*
Pankaj Singh	Rajasthan	I	6.5.1985	*Sultanpur*
***Papps** Michael Hugh William	Canterbury	NZ	2.7.1979	*Christchurch*
***Paranavitana** Nishad Tharanga	Sinhalese	SL	15.4.1982	*Kegalle*
***Parchment** Brenton Anthony	Jamaica	WI	24.6.1982	*St Elizabeth, Jamaica*
Parida Rashmi Ranjan	Orissa	I	7.9.1974	*Bhubaneswar*
Park Garry Terence	Derbyshire	E	19.4.1983	*Empangeni, SA*
***Parnell** Wayne Dillon	Warriors/Kent	SA	30.7.1989	*Port Elizabeth*
Parris Jason Andre	Barbados	WI	5.6.1982	*Ashdean, Barbados*
Parris Nekoli	Com. Campuses & Colls.	WI	6.6.1987	*Lowland Park, Barb.*
Parry Stephen David	Lancashire	E	12.1.1986	*Manchester*
Parvinder Singh	Uttar Pradesh	I	8.12.1981	*Meerut*
Pascal Nelon Troy	Windward Islands	WI	25.4.1987	*St David's, Grenada*
Patel Akhil	Nottinghamshire	E	18.6.1990	*Nottingham*
***Patel** Jeetan Shashi	Wellington/Warwickshire	NZ	7.5.1980	*Wellington*
***Patel** Munaf Musa	Baroda	I	12.7.1983	*Ikhar*
***Patel** Parthiv Ajay	Gujarat	I	9.3.1985	*Ahmedabad*
Patel Samit Rohit	Nottinghamshire	E	30.11.1984	*Leicester*
***Pathan** Irfan Khan	Baroda	I	27.10.1984	*Baroda*
Pathan Yusuf Khan	Baroda	I	27.11.1984	*Baroda*
Patterson Steven Andrew	Yorkshire	E	3.10.1983	*Hull*
***Pattinson** Darren John	Nottinghamshire/Victoria	E	2.8.1979	*Grimsby*
Pattinson James Lee	Victoria	A	3.5.1990	*Melbourne*
Pawar Rajesh Vithal	Baroda	I	6.9.1979	*Bombay*
Penco Shervon	Com. Campuses & Colls.	WI	24.9.1983	*Tunapuna, Trinidad*
***Perera** Anhettige Suresh Asanka	Moors	SL	16.2.1978	*Colombo*
Perera Mahawaduge Dilruwan Kamalaneth	Colts/Basnahira South	SL	22.7.1982	*Panadura*
Perera Narangoda Liyanaarachchilage Tissara Chirantha	Colts/Wayamba	SL	3.4.1989	*Colombo*
***Perera** Panagodage Don Ruchira Laksiri	Colts/Basnahira South	SL	6.4.1977	*Colombo*
Permaul Veerasammy	Guyana	WI	11.8.1989	*Belvedere, Guyana*
Peters Keon Kenroy	Windward Islands	WI	24.2.1982	*Mesopotamia, St Vincent*
Peters Orlando	Leeward Islands	WI	10.5.1988	*Antigua*
Peters Stephen David	Northamptonshire	E	10.12.1978	*Harold Wood*
Petersen Alviro Nathan	Lions/North West	SA	25.11.1980	*Port Elizabeth*
***Peterson** Robin John	Warriors/Cape Cobras	SA	4.8.1979	*Port Elizabeth*

	Team	Country	Born	Birthplace
Pettini Mark Lewis	Essex	E	7.8.1983	*Brighton*
Phangiso Aaron Mpho	Lions/Gauteng	SA	21.1.1984	*Garunkuwa*
Philander Vernon Darryl	Cape Cobras/W. Province	SA	24.6.1985	*Bellville*
Philipson Craig Andrew	Queensland	A	18.11.1982	*Herston*
Phillips Ben James	Somerset	E	30.9.1974	*Lewisham*
*Phillips Omar Jamel	Com. Campuses & Colls.	WI	12.10.1986	*Boscobel, Barbados*
Phillips Timothy James	Essex	E	13.3.1981	*Cambridge*
Pienaar Abraham Jacobus (Obus)	Eagles/Free State	SA	12.12.1989	*Bloemfontein*
Pietersen Charl	Eagles/Griqualand West	SA	6.1.1983	*Kimberley*
*Pietersen Kevin Peter	Hampshire	E	27.6.1980	*Pietermaritzburg, SA*
Pipe David James	Derbyshire	E	16.12.1977	*Bradford*
Plaatjies Francois Chessley	Cape Cobras/W. Province	SA	26.8.1986	*Oudtshoorn*
Plunkett Liam Edward	Durham	E	6.4.1985	*Middlesbrough*
Pollard Kieron Adrian	Trinidad & Tobago	WI	12.5.1987	*Cacariqua, Trinidad*
Pomersbach Luke Anthony	Western Australia	A	28.9.1984	*Bentley*
*Ponting Ricky Thomas	Tasmania	A	19.12.1974	*Launceston*
Pooran Homchand	Guyana	WI	14.2.1979	*Port Mourant, Guyana*
Porter Drew Nathan	Western Australia	A	7.9.1985	*Attadale*
Porterfield William Thomas Stuart	Gloucestershire	Ireland	6.9.1984	*Londonderry*
Pothas Nic	Hampshire	SA	18.11.1973	*Johannesburg*
*Powar Ramesh Rajaram	Mumbai	I	20.5.1978	*Bombay*
*Powell Daren Brentlyle	Jamaica	WI	15.4.1978	*Malvenn, Jamaica*
Powell Kieran Omar Akeem	Leeward Islands	WI	6.3.1990	*Government Road, Nevis*
Powell Michael John	Glamorgan	E	3.2.1977	*Abergavenny*
*Prasad Kariyawasam Tirana Gamage Dammika	Sinhalese/Basnahira N.	SL	30.5.1983	*Ragama*
*Price Raymond William	Northerns/Mash. Eagles	Z	12.6.1976	*Salisbury*
*Prince Ashwell Gavin	Warriors/Lancashire	SA	28.5.1977	*Port Elizabeth*
Prince Tarrick	Leeward Islands	WI		*Antigua*
*Prior Matthew James	Sussex	E	26.2.1982	*Johannesburg, SA*
Pujara Cheteshwar Arvind	Saurashtra	I	25.1.1988	*Rajkot*
Pushpakumara Muthumudalige	Tamil Union/Basnahira N.	SL	26.9.1981	*Colombo*
Puttick Andrew George	Cape Cobras	SA	11.12.1980	*Cape Town*
Pyrah Richard Michael	Yorkshire	E	1.11.1982	*Dewsbury*
*Qaiser Abbas	National Bank	P	7.5.1982	*Muridke*
Quiney Robert John	Victoria	A	20.8.1982	*Brighton, Australia*
Rabie Gurshwin Renier	Cape Cobras/W. Province	SA	26.6.1983	*Oudtshoorn*
Rahane Ajinkya Madhukar	Mumbai	I	6.6.1988	*Ashwi Khurd*
Raina Suresh Kumar	Uttar Pradesh	I	27.11.1986	*Ghaziabad*
Rainsford Edward Charles	Centrals/MW Rhinos	Z	14.12.1984	*Kadoma*
*Ramdin Denesh	Trinidad & Tobago	WI	13.3.1985	*Mission Road, Trinidad*
Ramela Omphile Abel	Cape Cobras/Boland	SA	14.3.1988	*Soweto*
*Rampaul Ravindranath	Trinidad & Tobago	WI	15.10.1984	*Preysal, Trinidad*
*Ramprakash Mark Ravin	Surrey	E	5.9.1969	*Bushey*
Ramsay Shane Gerry	Barbados	WI	3.12.1985	*Farm Road, Barbados*
*Ramyakumara Wijekoon Mudiyanselage Gayan	Chilaw M./Basnahira N.	SL	21.12.1976	*Gampaha*
Also known as Gayan Wijekoon				
Randiv Suraj	Bloomfield/Kandurata	SL	30.1.1985	*Matara*
Also known as Hewa Kaluhalamullage Suraj Randiv Kaluhalamulla; formerly known as Mohamed Marshuk Mohamed Suraj				
Rankin William Boyd	Warwickshire	Ireland	5.7.1984	*Londonderry*
*Raqibul Hasan	Barisal	B	8.10.1987	*Jamalpur*
Rashid Adil Usman	Yorkshire	E	17.2.1988	*Bradford*

	Team	Country	Born	Birthplace
***Ratra** Ajay	Goa	I	13.12.1981	Faridabad
Rayner Oliver Philip	Sussex	E	1.11.1985	Fallingbostel, Germany
***Read** Christopher Mark Wells	Nottinghamshire	E	10.8.1978	Paignton
Reardon Nathan Jon	Queensland	A	8.11.1984	Chinchilla
Redfern Daniel James	Derbyshire	E	18.4.1990	Shrewsbury
***Redmond** Aaron James	Otago	NZ	23.9.1979	Auckland
Rees Gareth Peter	Glamorgan	E	8.4.1985	Swansea
***Reifer** Floyd Lamonte	Com. Campuses & Colls.	WI	23.7.1972	Parish Land, Barbados
***Riaz Afridi**	Peshawar	P	21.1.1985	Peshawar
Richards Austin Conroy Lenroy	Leeward Islands	WI	14.11.1983	Freetown, Antigua
***Richards** Dale Maurice	Barbados	WI	16.7.1976	Isolation Rd, Barbados
Richardson Alan	Middlesex	E	6.5.1975	Newcastle-under-Lyme
Richardson Andrew Peter	Jamaica	WI	6.9.1981	Kingston, Jamaica
Rimmington Nathan John	Queensland	A	11.11.1982	Redcliffe
Rizwan Ahmed	KRL/Sui Southern	P	1.10.1978	Hyderabad
***Roach** Kemar Andre Jamal	Barbados	WI	30.6.1988	Checker Hall, Barb.
Roberts Garvin Raphael	Windward Islands	WI	10.12.1982	St Paul's, Grenada
Robertson Iain Anthony	Canterbury	NZ	9.11.1982	Christchurch
Robinson Wesley Michael	Western Australia	A	26.12.1980	Duncraig
Robson Samuel David	Middlesex	A	1.7.1989	Paddington, Australia
***Rogers** Christopher John Llewellyn	Victoria/Derbyshire	A	31.8.1977	St George
Rogers Codville Leon	Leeward Islands	WI	4.7.1976	Sinletts, Nevis
Rohrer Ben James	New South Wales	A	26.3.1981	Bankstown
Ronchi Luke	Western Australia	A	23.4.1981	Dannevirke, NZ
Rossouw Riley Roscoe	Eagles/Free State	SA	9.10.1989	Bloemfontein
***Rubel Hossain**	Chittagong	B	1.1.1990	Bagerhat
***Rudolph** Jacobus Andries	Titans/Yorkshire	SA	4.5.1981	Springs
Rupasinghe Rupasinghe Jayawardene Mudiyanselage Gihan Madushanka	Tamil Union/Basnahira S.	SL	5.3.1986	Watupitiwala
Russell Andre Dwayne	Jamaica	WI	29.4.1988	Jamaica
***Ryder** Jesse Daniel	Wellington	NZ	6.8.1984	Masterton
Sadler John Leonard	Derbyshire	E	19.11.1981	Dewsbury
***Saeed Ajmal**	KRL/ZTBL	P	14.10.1977	Faisalabad
***Saggers** Martin John	Kent	E	23.5.1972	King's Lynn
Saha Wriddhaman Prasanta	Bengal	I	24.10.1984	Siliguri
***Sajidul Islam**	Barisal	B	18.1.1988	Rangpur
***Salim Elahi**	Habib Bank	P	21.11.1976	Sahiwal
***Salman Butt**	National Bank	P	7.10.1984	Lahore
Salvi Aavishkar Madhav	Mumbai	I	20.10.1981	Bombay
***Samaraweera** Thilan Thusara	Sinhalese	SL	22.9.1976	Colombo
Samiullah Khan	Sui Northern	P	4.8.1982	Mianwali
***Sammy** Darren Julius Garvey	Windward Islands	WI	20.12.1983	Micoud, St Lucia
Sandri Pepler Sacto Emiliano	C. Cobras/Boland/Sussex	SA	14.1.1983	Cape Town
***Sangakkara** Kumar Chokshanada	Nondescripts	SL	27.10.1977	Matale
***Sarandeep Singh**	Himachal Pradesh	I	21.10.1979	Amritsar
***Sarfraz Ahmed**	PIA	P	22.5.1987	Karachi
***Sarwan** Ramnaresh Ronnie	Guyana	WI	23.6.1980	Wakenaam Island, Guy.
Saxelby Ian David	Gloucestershire	E	22.5.1989	Nottingham
Sayers Joseph John	Yorkshire	E	5.11.1983	Leeds
Scantlebury-Searles Javon Philip Ramon	Barbados	WI	21.12.1986	Durants Village, Barb.
***Schofield** Christopher Paul	Surrey	E	6.10.1978	Wardle
Scott Ben James Matthew	Middlesex	E	4.8.1981	Isleworth
Sealy Anderson Wendle Leandro	Com. Campuses & Colls.	WI	10.7.1982	Government Hill, Barb.
Sebastien Liam Andrew Shannon	Windward Islands	WI	9.9.1984	Roseau, Dominica
***Sehwag** Virender	Delhi	I	20.10.1978	Delhi
***Shabbir Ahmed**	WAPDA	P	21.4.1976	Khanewal
***Shadab Kabir**	Karachi	P	12.11.1977	Karachi

	Team	Country	Born	Birthplace
Shafayat Bilal Mustapha	Nottinghamshire/Customs	E	10.7.1984	Nottingham
*****Shah** Owais Alam	Middlesex	E	22.10.1978	Karachi, Pakistan
*****Shahadat Hossain**	Dhaka	B	7.8.1986	Narayanganj
*****Shahid Afridi**	Habib Bank	P	1.3.1980	Khyber Agency
*****Shahid Nazir**	Habib Bank	P	4.12.1977	Faisalabad
Shahzad Ajmal	Yorkshire	E	27.7.1985	Huddersfield
Shahzaib Hasan	Karachi	P	25.12.1989	Karachi
*****Shakib Al Hasan**	Khulna	B	24.3.1987	Magura
Shantry Adam John	Glamorgan	E	13.11.1982	Bristol
Shantry Jack David	Worcestershire	E	29.1.1988	Shrewsbury
*****Sharma** Ishant	Delhi	I	2.9.1988	Delhi
Sharma Joginder	Haryana	I	23.10.1983	Rohtak
Sharma Rohit Gurunath	Mumbai	I	30.4.1987	Bansod
Sheharyar Ghani	Karachi	P	9.9.1985	Karachi
Sheridan William David	Victoria	A	5.7.1987	Chertsey, England
Shezi Mthokozisi	Dolphins/KwaZulu-Natal	SA	9.9.1987	Imbali
Shillingford Shane	Windward Islands	WI	22.2.1983	Dominica
*****Shoaib Akhtar**	KRL	P	13.8.1975	Rawalpindi
Shoaib Khan	Quetta	P	13.4.1985	Bostan
*****Shoaib Malik**	PIA	P	1.2.1982	Sialkot
Shreck Charles Edward	Nottinghamshire	E	6.1.1978	Truro
Shukla Laxmi Ratan	Bengal	I	6.5.1981	Howrah
Shukla Shivakant S.	Uttar Pradesh	I	26.1.1986	Allahabad
*****Sibanda** Vusimuzi	Mid West Rhinos	Z	10.10.1983	Highfields
*****Siddle** Peter Matthew	Victoria	A	25.11.1984	Traralgon
*****Sidebottom** Ryan Jay	Nottinghamshire	E	15.1.1978	Huddersfield
Silva Jayan Kaushal	Sinhalese/Basnahira North	SL	27.5.1986	Colombo
Silva Lindamlilage Prageeth Chamara	Bloomfield/Basnahira S.	SL	14.12.1979	Panadura
*****Silverwood** Christopher Eric Wilfred	Middlesex/Mash. Eagles	E	5.3.1975	Pontefract
Simmons Craig Joseph	Western Australia	A	1.12.1982	Paddington
*****Simmons** Lendl Mark Platter	Trinidad & Tobago	WI	25.1.1985	Port-of-Spain, Trinidad
Simpson Christopher Patrick	Queensland	A	9.1.1982	Brisbane
Simpson John Andrew	Middlesex	E	13.7.1988	Bury
*****Sinclair** Mathew Stuart	Central Districts	NZ	9.11.1975	Katherine, Australia
Singh Gajanand	Guyana	WI	3.10.1987	Cumberland, Guyana
*****Singh** Rudra Pratap	Uttar Pradesh	I	6.12.1985	Rae Bareli
Singh Vishan Anthony	Guyana	WI	12.1.1989	Georgetown, Guyana
Smit Darren	Dolphins	SA	28.1.1984	Durban
Smith Benjamin Francis	Worcestershire	E	3.4.1972	Corby
Smith Daniel Lindsay Richard	New South Wales	A	17.3.1982	Westmead
*****Smith** Dwayne Romel	Barbados/Sussex	WI	12.4.1983	Storey Gap, Barbados
*****Smith** Devon Sheldon	Windward Islands	WI	21.10.1981	Hermitage, Grenada
*****Smith** Graeme Craig	Cape Cobras	SA	1.2.1981	Johannesburg
Smith Gregory Marc	Derbyshire	SA	20.4.1983	Johannesburg
Smith Greg Phillip	Leicestershire	E	16.11.1988	Leicester
Smith Jamal	Com. Campuses & Colls.	WI	16.10.1984	Deacon Road, Barbados
Smith James David	South Australia	A	11.10.1988	Murray Bridge
Smith Jeremy Stewart	Tasmania	A	23.10.1988	Launceston
Smith Michael Bruce Argo	Warriors/E. Province	SA	5.5.1980	King William's Town
Smith Steven Peter Devereux	New South Wales	A	2.6.1989	Sydney
Smith Thomas Christopher	Lancashire	E	26.12.1985	Liverpool
Smith Thomas Michael John	Sussex	E	22.8.1987	Eastbourne
Smith William Rew	Durham	E	28.9.1982	Luton
Smuts Jon-Jon Trevor	Warriors/E. Province	SA	21.8.1988	Grahamstown
Snell Stephen David	Gloucestershire	E	27.2.1983	Winchester
Snijman Blake Douglas	Titans/Northerns	SA	28.10.1985	Krugersdorp
*****Sohail Khan**	Sui Southern	P	6.3.1984	Malakand

Name	Team	Country	Born	Birthplace
*Sohail Tanvir	KRL/ZTBL	P	12.12.1984	Rawalpindi
Sohal Sunny	Punjab	I	10.11.1987	Mohali
Solanki Vikram Singh	Worcestershire	E	1.4.1976	Udaipur, India
*Southee Timothy Grant	Northern Districts	NZ	11.12.1988	Whangarei
*Spearman Craig Murray	Gloucestershire	NZ	4.7.1972	Auckland
Spriegel Matthew Neil William	Surrey	E	4.3.1987	Epsom
*Sreesanth Shanthakumaran	Kerala/Warwickshire	I	6.2.1983	Kothamangalam
Sriram Sridharan	Goa	I	21.2.1976	Madras
Srivastava Tanmay Manoj	Uttar Pradesh	I	7.11.1989	Lucknow
Starc Mitchell Aaron	New South Wales	A	13.1.1990	Baulkham Hills
Stayt Thomas Patrick	Gloucestershire	E	20.1.1986	Salisbury
Stevens Darren Ian	Kent	E	30.4.1976	Leicester
Stewart Navin Derrick	Trinidad & Tobago	WI	13.6.1983	Roxborough, Tobago
*Steyn Dale Willem	Titans	SA	27.6.1983	Phalaborwa
Stiff David Alexander	Somerset	E	20.10.1984	Dewsbury
Stoinis Marcus Peter	Western Australia	A	16.8.1989	Perth
Stoneman Mark Daniel	Durham	E	26.6.1987	Newcastle-upon-Tyne
Stoute Kevin Andre	Barbados	WI	12.11.1985	Black Rock, Barbados
*Strauss Andrew John	Middlesex	E	2.3.1977	Johannesburg, SA
Strydom Gregory Mark	Matabeleland Tuskers	Z	26.3.1984	Pretoria, SA
Stubbings Stephen David	Derbyshire	E	31.3.1978	Huddersfield
*Styris Scott Bernard	Auckland	NZ	10.7.1975	Brisbane, Australia
Sullivan Grant James	Queensland	A	7.3.1984	Mackay
Suppiah Arul Vivasvan	Somerset	E	30.8.1983	Kuala Lumpur, Malay.
Suresh Manipuri	Railways	I	21.12.1983	Cuddapah
Sutton Luke David	Lancashire	E	4.10.1976	Keynsham
Swan Christopher Richard	Queensland	A	10.8.1978	Southport
*Swann Graeme Peter	Nottinghamshire	E	24.3.1979	Northampton
*Syed Rasel	Khulna	B	3.7.1984	Jessore
Symes Jean	Lions/Gauteng	SA	13.11.1986	Johannesburg
*Symonds Andrew	Queensland	A	9.6.1975	Birmingham, England
Tahir Naqaash Sarosh	Warwickshire	E	14.11.1983	Birmingham
*Taibu Tatenda	Northerns/Mountaineers	Z	14.5.1983	Harare
*Tait Shaun William	South Australia	A	22.2.1983	Bedford Park
*Tamim Iqbal	Chittagong	B	20.3.1989	Chittagong
*Taufeeq Umar	Habib Bank	P	20.6.1981	Lahore
*Taylor Brendan Ross Murray	Northerns/MW Rhinos	Z	6.2.1986	Harare
Taylor Billy Victor	Hampshire	E	11.1.1977	Southampton
Taylor Christopher Glyn	Gloucestershire	E	27.9.1976	Bristol
*Taylor Jerome Everton	Jamaica	WI	22.6.1984	St Elizabeth, Jamaica
Taylor James William Arthur	Leicestershire	E	6.1.1990	Nottingham
*Taylor Luteru Ross Poutoa Lote	Central Districts	NZ	8.3.1984	Lower Hutt
ten Doeschate Ryan Neil	Essex	NL	30.6.1980	Port Elizabeth, SA
*Tendulkar Sachin Ramesh	Mumbai	I	24.4.1973	Bombay
Thaker Bhavik Dinbandhubhai	Gujarat	I	23.10.1982	Ahmedabad
*Tharanga Warushavithana Upul	Nondescripts/Ruhuna	SL	2.2.1985	Balapitiya
Theron Juan	Warriors	SA	24.7.1985	Vereeniging
Thirimanne Hettige Don Rumesh Lahiru	Ragama/Basnahira South	SL	8.9.1989	Moratuwa
Thomas Alfonso Clive	Somerset	SA	9.2.1977	Cape Town
Thomas Devon Cuthbert	Leeward Islands	WI	12.11.1989	Bethesda, Antigua
Thompson Christopher Everton Junior	Leicestershire	E	26.6.1987	Waterloo
Thompson Ewen Paul	Central Districts	NZ	17.12.1979	Warkworth
Thornely Dominic John	New South Wales	A	1.10.1978	Albury
Thornely Michael Alistair	Sussex	E	19.10.1987	Camden
Thorp Callum David	Durham	A	11.2.1975	Mount Lawley
Thyssen Craig Andre	Warriors/Border	SA	25.3.1984	Port Elizabeth
Tiwary Manoj Kumar	Bengal	I	14.11.1985	Howrah

	Team	Country	Born	Birthplace
Tiwary Saurabh Sunil	Jharkhand	I	30.12.1989	Jamshedpur
Tomlinson James Andrew	Hampshire	E	12.6.1982	Winchester
***Tonge** Gavin Courtney	Leeward Islands	WI	13.2.1983	St John's, Antigua
Towers Luke James Charles	Western Australia	A	18.6.1988	Subiaco
Townsend Wade James	Queensland	A	29.1.1986	Herston
Tredwell James Cullum	Kent	E	27.2.1982	Ashford
Trego Peter David	Somerset	E	12.6.1981	Weston-super-Mare
***Tremlett** Christopher Timothy	Hampshire	E	2.9.1981	Southampton
***Trescothick** Marcus Edward	Somerset	E	25.12.1975	Keynsham
Trivedi Siddharth Kishorkumar	Gujarat	I	4.9.1982	Ahmedabad
***Trott** Ian Jonathan Leonard	Warwickshire	E	22.4.1981	Cape Town, SA
Troughton Jamie Oliver	Warwickshire	E	2.3.1979	Camden
Tshabalala Thandi	Eagles/Free State	SA	19.11.1984	Welkom
***Tsolekile** Thami Lungisa	Lions/Western Province	SA	9.10.1980	Cape Town
Tsotsobe Lonwabo Lennox	Warriors	SA	7.3.1984	Port Elizabeth
***Tudor** Alex Jeremy	Surrey	E	23.10.1977	West Brompton
***Tuffey** Daryl Raymond	Auckland	NZ	11.6.1978	Milton
Turner Mark Leif	Somerset	E	23.10.1984	Sunderland
Tyagi Sudeep	Uttar Pradesh	I	19.9.1987	Ghaziabad
***Udal** Shaun David	Middlesex	E	18.3.1969	Cove
Udana Isuru	Tamil Union/Wayamba	SL	17.2.1988	Balangoda
Udawatte Mahela Lakmal	Chilaw M./Wayamba	SL	19.7.1986	Colombo
***Umar Akmal**	Sui Northern	P	26.5.1990	Lahore
Umar Amin	National Bank	P	16.10.1989	Rawalpindi
***Umar Gul**	Habib Bank	P	14.4.1984	Peshawar
Uthappa Robin Venu	Karnataka	I	11.11.1985	Coorg
***Utseya** Prosper	Easterns/Mountaineers	Z	26.3.1985	Harare
***Vaas** Warnakulasuriya Patabendige Ushantha Joseph Chaminda	Colts	SL	27.1.1974	Mattumagala
van der Merwe Roelof Erasmus	Titans/Northerns	SA	31.12.1984	Johannesburg
van der Wath Johannes Jacobus	Eagles/Northants	SA	10.1.1978	Newcastle
Vandiar Jonathan David	Lions	SA	25.4.1990	Paarl
***Vandort** Michael Graydon	Colombo/Wayamba	SL	19.1.1980	Colombo
***van Jaarsveld** Martin	Kent	SA	18.6.1974	Klerksdorp
van Jaarsveld Vaughn Bernard	Lions/Gauteng	SA	2.2.1985	Johannesburg
van Schalkwyk Shadley Claude	Eagles/Free State	SA	5.8.1988	Cape Town
van Wyk Divan Jaco	Eagles/Free State	SA	25.2.1985	Bloemfontein
van Wyk Morne Nico	Eagles	SA	20.3.1979	Bloemfontein
van Zyl Stiaan	Cape Cobras	SA	19.9.1987	Cape Town
***Vaughan** Michael Paul	Yorkshire	E	29.10.1974	Manchester
Venugopal Rao Yalaka	Andhra	I	26.2.1982	Visakhapatnam
***Vermeulen** Mark Andrew	Westerns/Mata. Tuskers	Z	2.3.1979	Salisbury
***Vettori** Daniel Luca	Northern Districts	NZ	27.1.1979	Auckland
Vidanapathirana Chaminda Wijayakumara	Colombo/Kandurata	SL	25.1.1983	Morawake
***Vijay** Murali	Tamil Nadu/C. Districts	I	1.4.1984	Madras
Vilas Dane James	Lions/Gauteng	SA	10.6.1985	Johannesburg
Vinay Kumar Ranganath	Karnataka	I	12.2.1984	Davanagere
Vince James Michael	Hampshire	E	14.3.1991	Cuckfield
Voges Adam Charles	Western Australia/Notts	A	4.10.1979	Perth
von Berg Shaun	Titans/Northerns	SA	16.9.1986	Pretoria
Vries Gino Angelo	Eagles/Free State	SA	14.11.1987	Bloemfontein
Wade Matthew Scott	Victoria	A	26.12.1987	Hobart
Wagg Graham Grant	Derbyshire	E	28.4.1983	Rugby
Wagh Mark Anant	Nottinghamshire	E	20.10.1976	Birmingham
Wahab Riaz	National Bank	P	28.6.1985	Lahore
Wainwright David John	Yorkshire	E	21.3.1985	Pontefract

	Team	Country	Born	Birthplace
*Wajahatullah Wasti	ZTBL	P	11.11.1974	Peshawar
Wakely Alexander George	Northamptonshire	E	3.11.1988	Hammersmith
Walker George William	Leicestershire	E	12.5.1984	Norwich
Walker Matthew Jonathan	Essex	E	2.1.1974	Gravesend
Wallace Gavin	Jamaica	WI	22.12.1984	Jamaica
Wallace Mark Alexander	Glamorgan	E	19.11.1981	Abergavenny
Waller Malcolm Noel	Centrals/MW Rhinos	Z	28.9.1984	Harare
Waller Max Thomas Charles	Somerset	E	3.3.1988	Salisbury
Walter Scott Hugh	Queensland	A	2.5.1989	South Brisbane
Walters Basheeru-Deen	Titans/Easterns	SA	16.9.1986	Port Elizabeth
Walters Martin Dennis	Cape Cobras/W. Province	SA	12.3.1985	East London
Walters Stewart Jonathan	Surrey	E	25.6.1983	Mornington, Australia
*Walton Chadwick Antonio Kirkpatrick	Com. Campuses & Colls.	WI	3.7.1985	Jamaica
*Warnapura Basnayake Shalith Malinda	Colts	SL	26.5.1979	Colombo
Warner David Andrew	New South Wales	A	27.10.1986	Paddington
*Wasim Jaffer	Mumbai	I	16.2.1978	Bombay
*Watling Bradley-John	Northern Districts	NZ	9.7.1985	Durban, SA
*Watson Shane Robert	Queensland	A	17.6.1981	Ipswich
Weeks Matthew Craig	South Australia	A	4.10.1982	Adelaide
Weerakoon Sajeewa	Colts/Ruhuna	SL	17.2.1978	Galle
Weeraratne Kaushalya	Ragama/Kandurata	SL	29.1.1981	Gampola
*Welagedara Uda Walawwe Mahim Bandaralage Chanaka Asanka	Moors/Wayamba	SL	20.3.1981	Matale
Wells Jonathan Wayne	Tasmania	A	13.8.1988	Hobart
Wessels Mattheus Hendrik (Riki)	Northants/MW Rhinos	E	12.11.1985	Marogudoore, Aust.
Westley Thomas	Essex	E	13.3.1989	Cambridge
Westwood Ian James	Warwickshire	E	13.7.1982	Birmingham
Wheater Adam Jack	Essex	E	13.2.1990	Whipps Cross
Wheeldon David Antony	Worcestershire	E	12.4.1989	Staffordshire
Whelan Christopher David	Worcestershire	E	8.5.1986	Liverpool
*White Cameron Leon	Victoria	A	18.8.1983	Bairnsdale
White Graeme Geoffrey	Northamptonshire	E	18.4.1987	Milton Keynes
White Robert Allan	Northamptonshire	E	15.10.1979	Chelmsford
White Wayne Andrew	Leicestershire	E	22.4.1985	Derby
Wickremaratne Ranasinghe Pattikirikoralalage Aruna Hemantha	Ragama/Badureliya	SL	21.2.1971	Colombo
Wigley David Harry	Northamptonshire	E	26.10.1981	Bradford
Wilkinson Kurt Jason	Com. Campuses & Colls.	WI	14.8.1981	Applethwaites, Barb.
Willett Akito Elquemedo	Leeward Islands	WI	22.6.1988	Hamilton Estate, Nevis
Willett Tonito Akanni	Leeward Islands	WI	6.2.1983	Government Rd, Nevis
Willey David Jonathan	Northamptonshire	E	28.2.1990	Northampton
Williams Sean Colin	Westerns/Mata. Tuskers	Z	26.9.1986	Bulawayo
Williamson Kane Stuart	Northern Districts	NZ	8.8.1990	Tauranga
*Willoughby Charl Myles	Somerset	SA	3.12.1974	Cape Town
Woakes Christopher Roger	Warwickshire	E	2.3.1989	Birmingham
Wood Matthew James	Nottinghamshire	E	30.9.1980	Exeter
Woodcock Luke James	Wellington	NZ	19.3.1982	Wellington
Woodman Robert James	Gloucestershire	E	12.10.1986	Taunton
Wright Ben James	Glamorgan	E	5.12.1987	Preston
Wright Christopher Julian Clement	Essex	E	14.7.1985	Chipping Norton
Wright Damien Geoffrey	Victoria/Sussex	A	25.7.1975	Casino
Wright Luke James	Sussex	E	7.3.1985	Grantham
Wyatt Alexander Charles Frederick	Leicestershire	E	23.7.1990	Roehampton
Yadav Arjun Shivlal	Hyderabad	I	23.12.1981	Palghat
Yadav Umeshkumar Tilak	Vidarbha	I	25.10.1987	Nagpur
Yardy Michael Howard	Sussex	E	27.11.1980	Pembury

	Team	Country	Born	Birthplace
*Yasir Ali	KRL	P	15.10.1985	Hazro
*Yasir Arafat	KRL/Sussex	P	12.3.1982	Rawalpindi
*Yasir Hameed	PIA	P	28.2.1978	Peshawar
Yearwood Barrington Bjorn Beckenbauer	Barbados	WI	18.8.1986	St Peter, Barbados
*Yohannan Tinu	Kerala	I	18.2.1979	Quilon
Young Reece Alan	Auckland	NZ	15.9.1979	Auckland
*Younis Khan	Habib Bank	P	29.11.1977	Mardan
*Yuvraj Singh	Punjab	I	12.12.1981	Chandigarh
*Zaheer Khan	Mumbai	I	7.10.1978	Shrirampur
*Zahoor Elahi	Customs/KRL	P	1.3.1971	Sahiwal
Zhuwawo Cephas	Northerns/Mash. Eagles	Z	15.12.1984	Harare
*Zondeki Monde	Cape Cobras	SA	25.7.1982	King William's Town
Zondo Khayelihle	Dolphins/KwaZulu-Natal	SA	7.3.1990	Durban
*Zoysa Demuni Nuwan Tharanga	Sinhalese/Basnahira S.	SL	13.5.1978	Colombo
Zulqarnain Haider	Lahore/ZTBL	P	3.4.1986	Lahore

REGISTER OF WOMEN PLAYERS

The qualifications for inclusion are as follows:

All players who appeared in an international match, or in the County Championship in England, the Women's National Cricket League in Australia, or the State League in New Zealand, in the calendar year 2009

AND have scored 1,000 runs/taken 50 wickets in one-day internationals, or scored a hundred/taken five in an innings in a Test or one-day international since 2007.

Denotes Test player.

	Team	Country	Born	Birthplace
*Al Khader Nooshin	Railways	I	13.2.1981	Tehran, Iran
*Atkins Caroline Mary Ghislaine	Sussex	E	13.1.1981	Brighton
Bates Suzannah Wilson	Otago	NZ	16.9.1987	Dunedin
*Blackwell Alexandra Joy	New South Wales	A	31.8.1983	Wagga Wagga
*Brindle Arran	Lancashire	E	23.11.1981	Steeton
*Brits Cri-Zelda	Gauteng	SA	20.11.1983	Rustenburg
*Browne Nicola Jane	Northern Districts	NZ	14.9.1983	Matamata
*Brunt Katherine Helen	Yorkshire	E	2.7.1985	Barnsley
*Chopra Anjum	Delhi	I	20.5.1977	Delhi
*Colvin Holly Louise	Sussex	E	7.9.1989	Chichester
*Drumm Emily Cecilia	Kent	NZ	15.9.1974	Avondale
*Edwards Charlotte Marie	Kent	E	17.12.1979	Huntingdon
*Fahey Maria Frances	Canterbury	NZ	5.3.1984	Timaru
*Fields Jodie Maree (née Purves)	Queensland	A	19.6.1984	Toowoomba
*Goswami Jhulan	Bengal	I	25.11.1982	Kalyani
*Guha Isa Tara	Berkshire	E	21.5.1985	High Wycombe
*Gunn Jennifer Louise	Notts/W. Australia	E	9.5.1986	Nottingham
*Jones Melanie	Victoria/Tasmania	A	11.8.1972	Barnstaple, England
*Kala Hemlata	Railways	I	15.8.1975	Agra
*Keightley Lisa Maree	Warwickshire	A	26.8.1971	Mudgee
*Loubser Sunette	Boland	SA	26.9.1982	Paarl
*McGlashan Sara Jade	Central Districts	NZ	28.3.1982	Napier
McNeill Beth Hannah	Canterbury	NZ	10.11.1982	Wellington
*Marsh Laura Alexandra	Sussex	E	5.12.1986	Pembury
*Metcalfe Ciara Johanna	Pembroke	Ireland	29.9.1979	Dublin
*Milliken Louise Elizabeth	Northern Districts	NZ	19.9.1983	Morrinsville
*Newton Laura Kelly	Cheshire	E	27.11.1977	Congleton
*Nitschke Shelley	South Australia	A	3.12.1976	Adelaide
*Raj Mithali	Railways	I	3.12.1982	Jodhpur
Richardson Eimear Ann Jermyn	Leinster	Ireland	14.9.1986	Dublin
*Rolton Karen Louise	South Australia	A	21.11.1974	Adelaide
*Sajjida Shah	Hyderabad	P	3.2.1988	Hyderabad
*Sampson Emma Margaret	S. Australia/Surrey	A	29.7.1985	Adelaide
*Sharma Amita	Railways	I	12.9.1982	Delhi
*Smit Jane	Nottinghamshire	E	24.12.1972	Ilkeston
*Smith Alicia Esther	Boland	SA	13.3.1984	Cape Town
*Sthalekar Lisa Caprini	New South Wales	A	13.8.1979	Poona, India
*Tanke Annemarie Suzanne	Rood en Wit	NL	27.2.1978	Velsen
*Taylor Clare Elizabeth	Otago	E	22.5.1965	Huddersfield
*Taylor Samantha Claire	Berkshire	E	25.9.1975	Amersham
*Taylor Sarah Jane	Sussex	E	20.5.1989	Whitechapel
Taylor Stafanie Roxann	Jamaica	WI	11.6.1991	Jamaica
*Tiffen Haidee Maree	Canterbury	NZ	4.9.1979	Timaru
*Urooj Mumtaz	Karachi	P	1.10.1985	Karachi
*Watkins Aimee Louise (née Mason)	Central Districts	NZ	11.10.1982	New Plymouth
Watson Helen Maree	Canterbury	NZ	17.2.1972	Ashburton

CRICKETERS OF THE YEAR, 1889–2010

1889   *Six Great Bowlers of the Year:* J. Briggs, J. J. Ferris, G. A. Lohmann, R. Peel, C. T. B. Turner, S. M. J. Woods.

1890   *Nine Great Batsmen of the Year:* R. Abel, W. Barnes, W. Gunn, L. Hall, R. Henderson, J. M. Read, A. Shrewsbury, F. H. Sugg, A. Ward.

1891   *Five Great Wicketkeepers:* J. McC. Blackham, G. MacGregor, R. Pilling, M. Sherwin, H. Wood.

1892   *Five Great Bowlers:* W. Attewell, J. T. Hearne, F. Martin, A. W. Mold, J. W. Sharpe.

1893   *Five Batsmen of the Year:* H. T. Hewett, L. C. H. Palairet, W. W. Read, S. W. Scott, A. E. Stoddart.

1894   *Five All-Round Cricketers:* G. Giffen, A. Hearne, F. S. Jackson, G. H. S. Trott, E. Wainwright.

1895   *Five Young Batsmen of the Season:* W. Brockwell, J. T. Brown, C. B. Fry, T. W. Hayward, A. C. MacLaren.

1896   W. G. Grace.

1897   *Five Cricketers of the Season:* S. E. Gregory, A. A. Lilley, K. S. Ranjitsinhji, T. Richardson, H. Trumble.

1898   *Five Cricketers of the Year:* F. G. Bull, W. R. Cuttell, N. F. Druce, G. L. Jessop, J. R. Mason.

1899   *Five Great Players of the Season:* W. H. Lockwood, W. Rhodes, W. Storer, C. L. Townsend, A. E. Trott.

1900   *Five Cricketers of the Season:* J. Darling, C. Hill, A. O. Jones, M. A. Noble, Major R. M. Poore.

1901   *Mr R. E. Foster and Four Yorkshiremen:* R. E. Foster, S. Haigh, G. H. Hirst, T. L. Taylor, J. Tunnicliffe.

1902   L. C. Braund, C. P. McGahey, F. Mitchell, W. G. Quaife, J. T. Tyldesley.

1903   W. W. Armstrong, C. J. Burnup, J. Iremonger, J. J. Kelly, V. T. Trumper.

1904   C. Blythe, J. Gunn, A. E. Knight, W. Mead, P. F. Warner.

1905   B. J. T. Bosanquet, E. A. Halliwell, J. Hallows, P. A. Perrin, R. H. Spooner.

1906   D. Denton, W. S. Lees, G. J. Thompson, J. Vine, L. G. Wright.

1907   J. N. Crawford, A. Fielder, E. G. Hayes, K. L. Hutchings, N. A. Knox.

1908   A. W. Hallam, R. O. Schwarz, F. A. Tarrant, A. E. E. Vogler, T. G. Wass.

1909   *Lord Hawke and Four Cricketers of the Year:* W. Brearley, Lord Hawke, J. B. Hobbs, A. Marshal, J. T. Newstead.

1910   W. Bardsley, S. F. Barnes, D. W. Carr, A. P. Day, V. S. Ransford.

1911   H. K. Foster, A. Hartley, C. B. Llewellyn, W. C. Smith, F. E. Woolley.

1912   *Five Members of the MCC's Team in Australia:* F. R. Foster, J. W. Hearne, S. P. Kinneir, C. P. Mead, H. Strudwick.

1913   John Wisden: Personal Recollections.

1914   M. W. Booth, G. Gunn, J. W. Hitch, A. E. Relf, Hon. L. H. Tennyson.

1915   J. W. H. T. Douglas, P. G. H. Fender, H. T. W. Hardinge, D. J. Knight, S. G. Smith.

1916–17   No portraits appeared.

1918   *School Bowlers of the Year:* H. L. Calder, J. E. D'E. Firth, C. H. Gibson, G. A. Rotherham, G. T. S. Stevens.

1919   *Five Public School Cricketers of the Year:* P. W. Adams, A. P. F. Chapman, A. C. Gore, L. P. Hedges, N. E. Partridge.

1920   *Five Batsmen of the Year:* A. Ducat, E. H. Hendren, P. Holmes, H. Sutcliffe, E. Tyldesley.

1921   P. F. Warner.

1922   H. Ashton, J. L. Bryan, J. M. Gregory, C. G. Macartney, E. A. McDonald.

1923   A. W. Carr, A. P. Freeman, C. W. L. Parker, A. C. Russell, A. Sandham.

1924   *Five Bowlers of the Year:* A. E. R. Gilligan, R. Kilner, G. G. Macaulay, C. H. Parkin, M. W. Tate.

1925   R. H. Catterall, J. C. W. MacBryan, H. W. Taylor, R. K. Tyldesley, W. W. Whysall.

1926   J. B. Hobbs.

1927   G. Geary, H. Larwood, J. Mercer, W. A. Oldfield, W. M. Woodfull.

1928   R. C. Blunt, C. Hallows, W. R. Hammond, D. R. Jardine, V. W. C. Jupp.

1929   L. E. G. Ames, G. Duckworth, M. Leyland, S. J. Staples, J. C. White.

1930   E. H. Bowley, K. S. Duleepsinhji, H. G. Owen-Smith, R. W. V. Robins, R. E. S. Wyatt.

1931   D. G. Bradman, C. V. Grimmett, B. H. Lyon, I. A. R. Peebles, M. J. Turnbull.

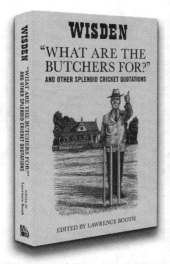

1932	W. E. Bowes, C. S. Dempster, James Langridge, Nawab of Pataudi sen., H. Verity.
1933	W. E. Astill, F. R. Brown, A. S. Kennedy, C. K. Nayudu, W. Voce.
1934	A. H. Bakewell, G. A. Headley, M. S. Nichols, L. F. Townsend, C. F. Walters.
1935	S. J. McCabe, W. J. O'Reilly, G. A. E. Paine, W. H. Ponsford, C. I. J. Smith.
1936	H. B. Cameron, E. R. T. Holmes, B. Mitchell, D. Smith, A. W. Wellard.
1937	C. J. Barnett, W. H. Copson, A. R. Gover, V. M. Merchant, T. S. Worthington.
1938	T. W. J. Goddard, J. Hardstaff jun., L. Hutton, J. H. Parks, E. Paynter.
1939	H. T. Bartlett, W. A. Brown, D. C. S. Compton, K. Farnes, A. Wood.
1940	L. N. Constantine, W. J. Edrich, W. W. Keeton, A. B. Sellers, D. V. P. Wright.
1941– 46	No portraits appeared.
1947	A. V. Bedser, L. B. Fishlock, V. (M. H.) Mankad, T. P. B. Smith, C. Washbrook.
1948	M. P. Donnelly, A. Melville, A. D. Nourse, J. D. Robertson, N. W. D. Yardley.
1949	A. L. Hassett, W. A. Johnston, R. R. Lindwall, A. R. Morris, D. Tallon.
1950	T. E. Bailey, R. O. Jenkins, John Langridge, R. T. Simpson, B. Sutcliffe.
1951	T. G. Evans, S. Ramadhin, A. L. Valentine, E. D. Weekes, F. M. M. Worrell.
1952	R. Appleyard, H. E. Dollery, J. C. Laker, P. B. H. May, E. A. B. Rowan.
1953	H. Gimblett, T. W. Graveney, D. S. Sheppard, W. S. Surridge, F. S. Trueman.
1954	R. N. Harvey, G. A. R. Lock, K. R. Miller, J. H. Wardle, W. Watson.
1955	B. Dooland, Fazal Mahmood, W. E. Hollies, J. B. Statham, G. E. Tribe.
1956	M. C. Cowdrey, D. J. Insole, D. J. McGlew, H. J. Tayfield, F. H. Tyson.
1957	D. Brookes, J. W. Burke, M. J. Hilton, G. R. A. Langley, P. E. Richardson.
1958	P. J. Loader, A. J. McIntyre, O. G. Smith, M. J. Stewart, C. L. Walcott.
1959	H. L. Jackson, R. E. Marshall, C. A. Milton, J. R. Reid, D. Shackleton.
1960	K. F. Barrington, D. B. Carr, R. Illingworth, G. Pullar, M. J. K. Smith.
1961	N. A. T. Adcock, E. R. Dexter, R. A. McLean, R. Subba Row, J. V. Wilson.
1962	W. E. Alley, R. Benaud, A. K. Davidson, W. M. Lawry, N. C. O'Neill.
1963	D. Kenyon, Mushtaq Mohammad, P. H. Parfitt, P. J. Sharpe, F. J. Titmus.
1964	D. B. Close, C. C. Griffith, C. C. Hunte, R. B. Kanhai, G. S. Sobers.
1965	G. Boycott, P. J. Burge, J. A. Flavell, G. D. McKenzie, R. B. Simpson.
1966	K. C. Bland, J. H. Edrich, R. C. Motz, P. M. Pollock, R. G. Pollock.
1967	R. W. Barber, B. L. D'Oliveira, C. Milburn, J. T. Murray, S. M. Nurse.
1968	Asif Iqbal, Hanif Mohammad, K. Higgs, J. M. Parks, Nawab of Pataudi jun.
1969	J. G. Binks, D. M. Green, B. A. Richards, D. L. Underwood, O. S. Wheatley.
1970	B. F. Butcher, A. P. E. Knott, Majid Khan, M. J. Procter, D. J. Shepherd.
1971	J. D. Bond, C. H. Lloyd, B. W. Luckhurst, G. M. Turner, R. T. Virgin.
1972	G. G. Arnold, B. S. Chandrasekhar, L. R. Gibbs, B. Taylor, Zaheer Abbas.
1973	G. S. Chappell, D. K. Lillee, R. A. L. Massie, J. A. Snow, K. R. Stackpole.
1974	K. D. Boyce, B. E. Congdon, K. W. R. Fletcher, R. C. Fredericks, P. J. Sainsbury.
1975	D. L. Amiss, M. H. Denness, N. Gifford, A. W. Greig, A. M. E. Roberts.
1976	I. M. Chappell, P. G. Lee, R. B. McCosker, D. S. Steele, R. A. Woolmer.
1977	J. M. Brearley, C. G. Greenidge, M. A. Holding, I. V. A. Richards, R. W. Taylor.
1978	I. T. Botham, M. Hendrick, A. Jones, K. S. McEwan, R. G. D. Willis.
1979	D. I. Gower, A. J. K. Lever, C. M. Old, C. T. Radley, J. N. Shepherd.
1980	J. Garner, S. M. Gavaskar, G. A. Gooch, D. W. Randall, B. C. Rose.
1981	K. J. Hughes, R. D. Jackman, A. J. Lamb, C. E. B. Rice, V. A. P. van der Bijl.
1982	T. M. Alderman, A. R. Border, R. J. Hadlee, Javed Miandad, R. W. Marsh.
1983	Imran Khan, T. E. Jesty, A. I. Kallicharran, Kapil Dev, M. D. Marshall.
1984	M. Amarnath, J. V. Coney, J. E. Emburey, M. W. Gatting, C. L. Smith.
1985	M. D. Crowe, H. A. Gomes, G. W. Humpage, J. Simmons, S. Wettimuny.
1986	P. Bainbridge, R. M. Ellison, C. J. McDermott, N. V. Radford, R. T. Robinson.
1987	J. H. Childs, G. A. Hick, D. B. Vengsarkar, C. A. Walsh, J. J. Whitaker.
1988	J. P. Agnew, N. A. Foster, D. P. Hughes, P. M. Roebuck, Salim Malik.
1989	K. J. Barnett, P. J. L. Dujon, P. A. Neale, F. D. Stephenson, S. R. Waugh.
1990	S. J. Cook, D. M. Jones, R. C. Russell, R. A. Smith, M. A. Taylor.
1991	M. A. Atherton, M. Azharuddin, A. R. Butcher, D. L. Haynes, M. E. Waugh.
1992	C. E. L. Ambrose, P. A. J. DeFreitas, A. A. Donald, R. B. Richardson, Waqar Younis.
1993	N. E. Briers, M. D. Moxon, I. D. K. Salisbury, A. J. Stewart, Wasim Akram.
1994	D. C. Boon, I. A. Healy, M. G. Hughes, S. K. Warne, S. L. Watkin.
1995	B. C. Lara, D. E. Malcolm, T. A. Munton, S. J. Rhodes, K. C. Wessels.
1996	D. G. Cork, P. A. de Silva, A. R. C. Fraser, A. Kumble, D. A. Reeve.
1997	S. T. Jayasuriya, Mushtaq Ahmed, Saeed Anwar, P. V. Simmons, S. R. Tendulkar.

1998	M. T. G. Elliott, S. G. Law, G. D. McGrath, M. P. Maynard, G. P. Thorpe.
1999	I. D. Austin, D. Gough, M. Muralitharan, A. Ranatunga, J. N. Rhodes.
2000	C. L. Cairns, R. Dravid, L. Klusener, T. M. Moody, Saqlain Mushtaq.

Cricketers of the Century D. G. Bradman, G. S. Sobers, J. B. Hobbs, S. K. Warne, I. V. A. Richards.

2001	M. W. Alleyne, M. P. Bicknell, A. R. Caddick, J. L. Langer, D. S. Lehmann.
2002	A. Flower, A. C. Gilchrist, J. N. Gillespie, V. V. S. Laxman, D. R. Martyn.
2003	M. L. Hayden, A. J. Hollioake, N. Hussain, S. M. Pollock, M. P. Vaughan.
2004	C. J. Adams, A. Flintoff, I. J. Harvey, G. Kirsten, G. C. Smith.
2005	A. F. Giles, S. J. Harmison, R. W. T. Key, A. J. Strauss, M. E. Trescothick.
2006	M. J. Hoggard, S. P. Jones, B. Lee, K. P. Pietersen, R. T. Ponting.
2007	P. D. Collingwood, D. P. M. D. Jayawardene, Mohammad Yousuf, M. S. Panesar, M. R. Ramprakash.
2008	I. R. Bell, S. Chanderpaul, O. D. Gibson, R. J. Sidebottom, Zaheer Khan.
2009	J. M. Anderson, D. M. Benkenstein, M. V. Boucher, N. D. McKenzie, S. C. Taylor.
2010	S. C. J. Broad, M. J. Clarke, G. Onions, M. J. Prior, G. P. Swann.

Note: From 2000 to 2003 the award was made on the basis of all cricket round the world, not just the English season. This ended in 2004 with the start of *Wisden's* Leading Cricketer in the World award. Jayasuriya in 1997 was chosen for his "influence" on the English season, stemming from the 1996 World Cup.

CRICKETERS OF THE YEAR: AN ANALYSIS

The five players selected to be Cricketers of the Year for 2010 bring the number chosen since selection began in 1889 to 557. They have been chosen from 39 different teams as follows:

Derbyshire	13	Northants	14	Australians	71	Cranleigh School	1
Durham	5	Nottinghamshire	28	South Africans	26	Eton College	2
Essex	23	Somerset	18	West Indians	24	Malvern College	1
Glamorgan	11	Surrey	49	New Zealanders	8	Rugby School	1
Gloucestershire	17	Sussex	22	Indians	14	Tonbridge School	1
Hampshire	15	Warwickshire	21	Pakistanis	12	Univ. Coll. School	1
Kent	26	Worcestershire	15	Sri Lankans	5	Uppingham School	1
Lancashire	33	Yorkshire	42	Zimbabweans	1	Winchester College	1
Leicestershire	8	Oxford Univ.	6	Staffordshire	1	England Women	1
Middlesex	27	Cambridge Univ.	10	Cheltenham College	1		

Notes: Schoolboys were chosen in 1918 and 1919 when first-class cricket was suspended due to war. The total of sides comes to 576 because 19 players played regularly for two teams (England excluded) in the year for which they were chosen. John Wisden, listed as a Sussex player, retired 50 years before his posthumous selection.

Types of Players

Of the 557 Cricketers of the Year, 281 are best classified as batsmen, 161 as bowlers, 79 as all-rounders and 36 as wicketkeepers or wicketkeeper-batsmen.

Research: Robert Brooke

PART THREE

English and
European Cricket

THE ENGLAND TEAM IN 2009

From shambles to Shangri-La

VIC MARKS

From shambles to Shangri-La, all in the space of 12 months. Some luck, some judgment and the union of two extremely impressive and compatible men at the helm of English cricket meant that the national side ended 2009 heading steadily in the right direction. The two Andrews – Strauss and Flower – are both very sensible human beings, which can sound too much like faint praise. So, just to clarify: they are also honest, strong, clear-thinking and devoid of ego. With these qualities combined it was not so surprising that England were a credible Test and 50-over team by year's end.

Order had been restored. The Ashes were in the bag – not such a difficult undertaking as in 2005, but a compelling series, nonetheless – and in the Boxing Day Test, staged in Durban, mighty South Africa – only just below the new top team, India, in the world rankings – were defeated by an innings and 98 runs.

Twelve months previously England had just returned from a traumatic tour of India, which had been torn asunder by terrorism in Mumbai and, to general consternation, they were about to lose both captain and coach simultaneously, prompting Wildean thoughts of carelessness rather than misfortune at the ECB.

ENGLAND IN 2009

	Played	Won	Lost	Drawn/No result
Tests	14	5	2	7
One-day internationals	22	11	11	–
Twenty20 internationals	9	3	5	1

JANUARY		
FEBRUARY		
MARCH	5 Tests, 5 ODIs and 1 T20I (a) v West Indies	(page 1386)
APRIL		
MAY	2 Tests and 3 ODIs (h) v West Indies	(page 463)
JUNE	World Twenty20 (in England)	(page 527)
JULY		
AUGUST	5 Tests, 7 ODIs and 2 T20Is (h) v Australia; 1 ODI (a) v Ireland	(page 479)
SEPTEMBER		
OCTOBER	Champions Trophy (in South Africa)	(page 1015)
NOVEMBER		
DECEMBER	4 Tests, 5 ODIs and 2 T20Is (a) v South Africa	(page 1269)
JANUARY		

That was the first crisis of a year in which England seemed to make a virtue out of adversity. In January 2009 the ECB had the chance to extricate themselves from two very poor appointments. And they grabbed it. Curiously neither Peter Moores nor Kevin Pietersen did much wrong while they were coach and captain of England, but they found themselves in the wrong place at the wrong time.

Moores, landed with the tricky task of succeeding Duncan Fletcher, was surprisingly slow to recognise that there is a huge difference between coaching at international level and on the county circuit or at the Academy. At the top, players have to be challenged more subtly, and sometimes the art is to reduce rather than increase the pressure upon them.

It was not Moores's inability to gel with Pietersen that was so striking, for Pietersen will always be abrasive and provocative. It was the fact that Moores was unable to work effectively with Michael Vaughan, a vastly experienced captain, which dented his credibility as an international coach.

As for Pietersen, in his blunderbuss way he was simply and honestly following his gut instincts as captain when he tried to oust Moores. He thought England would be a better side with a different coach, and reckoned on the unblinking support of the decision-makers at Lord's. But the men at the ECB were taken aback by the abrupt, gung-ho manner in which Pietersen wished to jettison Moores. They should not have been so surprised. Nor should they have ever appointed Pietersen just because he was about the only man in the squad who could be guaranteed a place in all three forms of international cricket.

However, Machiavelli would have been proud of how the ECB exploited the situation in January, even though Hugh Morris, the England team's managing director, has always seemed the least Machiavellian of men (maybe that's his secret). Thus the ECB seized their chance to sack both Moores and Pietersen; to appoint Strauss, who should have been given the job in the first place (for Tests and 50-over cricket); and, out of necessity, to ask Flower to be in temporary charge of the coaching team for the West Indies tour.

The next moment of adversity cropped up on that tour in Jamaica on February 7. England were bowled out for 51 at Kingston to lose the First Test by an innings. It was a defeat that required some serious soul-searching within the England camp, and it was around then that Flower came to realise that he was stimulated by his temporary role and that he would consider putting his name forward for the permanent post. Handling that crisis clearly energised him. Now Flower and Strauss began to put their own imprint on the team.

The defeat in Jamaica was humiliating, and the two Andrews took decisive and difficult action. For the next game, Ian Bell and Steve Harmison were dropped (though Harmison would return for the match at the Recreation Ground after the ten-ball Test at the Viv Richards Stadium in Antigua). The captain and coach demonstrated that the new regime was not tolerating any more cosiness within the English camp. They were prepared to take the tough decisions.

England were unable to square the series in the Caribbean. On the face of it this was a very poor result, the type of which is bound to prompt the routine sacking of any football manager. Fortunately the ECB exercised some common

Dejected: England faces reflect the surrender of the Wisden Trophy to West Indies at Port-of-Spain, March 2009.

sense by recognising that Flower, despite the results, was doing a fine job and that his relationship with Strauss was strong and constructive. Moreover there was an absence of other candidates. So, in April, Flower got the job on a permanent basis.

The next crisis arrived on August 9. At Headingley, Australia beat England by an innings and 80 runs. It was a crushing defeat; the Ashes series was levelled and the mood in the country was one of despair. It was widely assumed that the quest for the Ashes was over; some sages called for desperate measures for the last Test at The Oval after England's abject performance at Leeds. Marcus Trescothick should be persuaded out of retirement. Recall Mark Ramprakash was the siren cry; Rob Key, too.

Flower and Strauss – and the selectors (better include them since they are usually pilloried when it all goes wrong) – refused to panic. All they did was to bring back Andrew Flintoff, who was now something approaching fit enough to play a game of cricket, and to drop Ravi Bopara, who had been shell-shocked by the Ashes experience. To replace Bopara they stuck with the established pecking order and chose Jonathan Trott to make his Test debut, a decision which filled very few onlookers with glee before the match.

However, the greatest achievement after Headingley, which mirrored what Vaughan and Fletcher had managed after the 2005 Lord's Test, was to convince a group of players who had just been thrashed by Ricky Ponting's Australians that they could still win. They did this by remaining calm in the storm, quietly expressing confidence in those who had played the majority of the series, and by some more open and honest talking. They were given a hand by a sympathetic Oval groundsman and by an intransigent Australian management team, who opted not to believe the evidence of their own eyes when they inspected the playing surface and left out their specialist spinner.

Delighted: England faces reflect the innings victory over South Africa at Durban, December 2009.

By now it was obvious that the problems of December 2008 had been resolved. Strauss clearly relished the responsibility of leading the team, while Flower acknowledged that his role was "as satisfying as I thought it would be and as satisfying as any playing experience".

By the end of the year the ledger was encouraging, with England winning five and losing two of their 14 Tests. The most rare of those victories was at Lord's, because it was against Australia, the most exciting at The Oval (ditto), the most complete was at Durban at the end of December, when England were exceptional throughout. The victories over West Indies at Lord's and Chester-le-Street in May were devalued because the opposition was generally freezing and uninterested – as were some of the spectators.

Strauss was outstanding as a batsman (as well as a captain in 2009), as was Paul Collingwood, now the acknowledged master of the rearguard action. In South Africa Alastair Cook and Ian Bell restored waning reputations, Trott soon established a rather healthy one after his Oval heroics, but Pietersen, who missed three Ashes Tests because of an Achilles problem, had a very mortal year. Nobody was sure whether this was because of his injury or because of his sudden removal from the captaincy back in January, but just about everyone agreed that he would come again.

James Anderson became the first-choice pace bowler. While he never guaranteed consistency, he was capable of mesmerising spells when the ball was swinging. Arguably he was also England's most improved batsman. Stuart Broad was always selected; his bowling was sometimes bland and his batting is taking time to develop – since he is ever-present there is hardly any space for him to work quietly at this aspect of his game. But his obvious combativeness was highly valued, and his spells at The Oval and Durban were critical to famous victories.

Graeme Swann, despite the encumbrance of being an orthodox finger-spinner and being incapable of resisting a one-liner, was outstanding throughout, snatching lbws at a rate that left the likes of Ray Illingworth and Fred Titmus exasperatedly adding a notional 500 wickets to their career aggregates. His carefree batting was also invaluable down the order.

Meanwhile Ryan Sidebottom, Monty Panesar, Steve Harmison, Bopara (despite three consecutive Test centuries against West Indies) and – with justifiable fanfare – Flintoff faded from the scene in 2009. Some may return, but almost certainly not Flintoff, who announced his retirement from Test cricket just before the Lord's Test against Australia, and bade farewell with his brilliant run-out of Ponting at The Oval.

Flintoff's permanent absence focused attention on the perennial problem of balancing the team, a subject which aroused surprising passions throughout the second half of 2009. Nobody wanted to have just four bowlers; nobody wanted Broad to bat at No. 7 either. A few wanted an all-rounder in the team just for the sake of it. Those in charge avoided being dogmatic on the issue – that was left to the armchair critics. Instead, pragmatism demanded that they fit the system to the best players available, which led to the campaign in South Africa being conducted with six batsmen.

As ever, the progress in one-day cricket was not so pronounced. England managed to win the series 3–2 in the Caribbean; there was a rousing victory over South Africa in the Champions Trophy, and in November they beat the South Africans 2–1 in a rain-drenched one-day series. But these successes were countered by another moribund performance in an ICC competition, the World Twenty20 tournament held in England (the lowlight of which was the opening-night defeat by the Netherlands at Lord's), and a chastening 6–1 drubbing from Australia after the Ashes triumph.

Once again Strauss and Flower were prepared to take decisive action. Bopara was ditched. So too, more strikingly, was Owais Shah. He had been a regular in England's one-day side throughout 2009 and before, and he had scored his quota of runs – although no more – with wristy, unorthodox strokeplay. But it was all a question of running. Shah was unreliable between the wickets and slow in the outfield. Therefore, they decided, he had to go.

The goal now was for a more dynamic side: aggressive at the start of the innings, quicksilver between the wickets and in the field. So the one-day team began to evolve in South Africa, with Eoin Morgan establishing himself down the order in a similar role to Neil Fairbrother a decade or two previously. Meanwhile Tim Bresnan and Luke Wright, two plucky all-rounders, joined with the established Test players to suggest that the one-day team might also be moving in the right direction, though much more evidence was required before anyone could seriously contemplate England winning an international tournament.

So progress could be spied on all fronts, and while it might be possible in the 21st century to consult the ever-increasing number of analysts, who detail every contribution of every player, the simple explanation for England's improvement in 2009 was surely this: at the top they had the right men in the right jobs.

ENGLAND PLAYERS IN 2009

LAWRENCE BOOTH

The following 30 players (compared to 25 in 2008, and 36 in 2007) appeared for England in the calendar year 2009, when England played 14 Tests (though one lasted only ten balls), 22 one-day internationals and nine Twenty20 internationals. All statistics refer to the full year, not the 2009 season.

TIM AMBROSE   **Warwickshire**

The absence of Prior, who had flown home for the birth of his first child, allowed Ambrose a no-pressure, one-off return to international cricket, and he duly responded with a carefree undefeated 76 from 95 balls as England racked up 600 in Barbados. His keeping was tidy, too, as West Indies replied with 749 for nine, but stop-gaps do not come any more temporary, and the whole exercise had an academic feel. As if to prove the point, Ambrose – never quite strong enough to bat at No. 6 – would not have been considered had Prior not recovered from his back spasm moments before the start of the Headingley Test, and he was subsequently overtaken by Davies.

2009   1 Test: 76 runs without being dismissed; 1 catch.

JAMES ANDERSON   **Lancashire**

As so often, Anderson's year had the feel of two steps forward, one step back. At times, he could be brilliant: at Chester-le-Street, where he swung the ball both ways to take nine wickets against West Indies; on the second morning at both Lord's and, in particular, Edgbaston, where Australia's middle order could barely lay a bat on him; and in one-day internationals against Sri Lanka at Johannesburg and South Africa at Port Elizabeth. But his oft-stated desire to be regarded as England's undisputed attack leader was occasionally undermined too: he went missing at Headingley, possibly because of a hamstring twinge, and the more he bowled to left-handers, especially during the Ashes, the less he seemed capable of sending down outswingers to right-handers. Even so, Anderson remained England's go-to man on cloudy days, was regularly consulted in the field by Strauss, and worked hard to overcome his natural diffidence, even insisting he would one day like a crack at the captaincy. His batting continued to improve, with one or two strokes now complementing his lower-order grit, and five night-watchman innings each resumed the following morning. A duck at The Oval was his first in 54 Test innings – placing him fourth in the all-time list – but this was more than a statto's delight. It was evidence of England's improved professionalism, and without Anderson's resistance at Cardiff, the Ashes would probably not have been won.

2009   13 Tests: 178 runs @ 14.83; 40 wickets @ 33.87.
             19 ODI: 21 runs @ 7.00; 34 wickets @ 23.61.
              9 T20I: 0 runs @ 0.00; 7 wickets @ 32.85.

GARETH BATTY
Worcestershire/Surrey

Injury to Swann gave Batty an unlikely route back into international cricket nearly three years after his last game. But his latest stint lasted only 12 days and four limited-overs matches, the highlight of which was a ninth-wicket stand of 51 with Mascarenhas at Bridgetown after England had slumped to 68 for eight. Batty remained what he had always been: a committed yet limited off-spinning all-rounder who failed to get as much work on the ball as Swann, and after three matches of the five-game ODI series England concluded they could live without him.

2009   3 ODI: 24 runs @ 12.00; 1 wicket @ 72.00.
            1 T20I: 4 runs @ 4.00; no wicket for 17.

IAN BELL
Warwickshire

It was the usual mixture of the good, the bad and the beautiful: as such, Bell's ten Test innings in the calendar year provided a neat summary of his career. Five single-figure scores provoked the usual hand-wringing, while the first of them – courtesy of a tame cut on the stroke of lunch to kick-start the collapse in Jamaica – cost him his place for almost six months. But even his critics had to concede there were displays of character too. If his first-innings 53 at Edgbaston owed as much to luck as skill, then his gutsy 72 at The Oval after being promoted to No. 3 may have been the most important innings of his career, however overshadowed it was by the feats of Broad and Trott. Brownie points were sacrificed once more when – now batting at No. 6 – he ushered a straight one on to his stumps at Centurion, but there was no doubting the class of his 140 in the next game at Durban. And when he held South Africa at bay for most of the final day at Cape Town early in 2010, there was hope Bell had finally found his inner mongrel, even though he had lost his one-day place.

2009   6 Tests: 319 runs @ 31.90.

RAVI BOPARA
Essex

It was truly a year of two halves. Recalled to the Test team after a 14-month hiatus caused by three straight ducks in Sri Lanka, Bopara responded with three straight hundreds against West Indies, first from No. 6 in Bridgetown, then three places higher at Lord's and Chester-le-Street. There were moments of luck, but England's eagerness to identify their No. 3 against Australia overrode all else. Then, thrown in at the deepest end, Bopara found the tide turning. Seven Ashes innings, each more harrowing than the last, produced 105 runs. Ben Hilfen-haus exposed a lack of judgment outside off to remove him five times and, after Bopara made one and nought at Headingley, the selectors put him out of his misery. There was little joy elsewhere: he failed to score a single one-day half-century, was dropped first down the order, then out of the team altogether, and ended the year trying to rebuild his game and his confidence in domestic cricket in New Zealand.

2009   7 Tests: 460 runs @ 46.00; no wicket for 118.
             17 ODI: 436 runs @ 25.64; 1 wicket @ 53.00.
              7 T20I: 159 runs @ 22.71.

TIM BRESNAN   **Yorkshire**

In a mixed year, Bresnan oscillated between the virtually anonymous, the briefly notorious and the momentarily glorious, but the overall impression was of a gutsy seamer whose best may not quite have been good enough. For much of his debut Test series he resembled the Invisible Man, sending down only 17 of the 189.2 overs West Indies faced in their first three innings, and it needed a final-morning burst at Chester-le-Street to justify his presence before the inevitable return of Flintoff – the man he had supposedly replaced – for the Ashes. His most telling moment in the one-day side came immediately after he had been chastised for aiming earthy language at a member of the public on the twitter website: a 76-ball 80 against Australia in the Champions Trophy, the highest one-day score by an England No. 8, was a much better retort. But that innings was part of the problem. Bresnan was in the side primarily for his wickets, and there were never more than two of those in an innings.

2009   2 Tests: 9 runs @ 9.00; 3 wickets @ 32.33.
             13 ODI: 202 runs @ 40.40; 13 wickets @ 39.38.
              2 T20I: 3 runs @ 3.00; no wicket for 73.

STUART BROAD   **Nottinghamshire**

No England cricketer earned more bouquets than Broad, whose Ashes-settling spell at The Oval seared him on to the national consciousness and even earned him an appearance on the BBC's *Friday Night with Jonathan Ross*. The "new Flintoff" tag was as misleading as it was inevitable, for here – when he wasn't being misused as a battering ram – was a more thoughtful bowler than the Lancastrian, and a more refined, if less potentially destructive, batsman. A tally of 88 international wickets in all forms of the game – 40 more than in 2008 – was seven more than his next-best team-mate, Anderson, and 47 Test wickets placed him third in the world. All the while, he wrestled with the seam bowler's equivalent of an identity crisis: bang it in or pitch it up? Often his role depended on the make-up of England's attack, and his fondness for experimentation at times clouded the issue, yet it was clear – both at The Oval and Durban – that Broad threatened most when he aimed for the top of off, with a hint of swing either way. His batting failed to make a strong enough case for the No. 7 role, and for the time being counter-attacking innings from one place below were his forte. But Broad was one of England's most exciting long-term projects, and all he needed to do now was stay on the right side of the match referees, his own father among them. Temper tantrums occasionally trod the fine line between adrenalin rush and petulance, and he pushed his luck when he fielded the ball off his own bowling at Cape Town early in 2010 with the studded sole of his boot. England, though, were in no mind to extinguish the fire within.

2009   14 Tests: 431 runs @ 25.35; 47 wickets @ 28.36.
            15 ODI: 54 runs @ 6.00; 32 wickets @ 22.84.
             7 T20I: 24 runs @ 12.00; 9 wickets @ 18.11.

PAUL COLLINGWOOD   Durham

Attempts to force Collingwood into a pigeon-hole were once more thwarted by his adaptability. At the more familiar end of the spectrum were the defensive nail-biters at Cardiff, Centurion and Cape Town, the first of which seemed to drain him of most of his Ashes energy. But his perennially underrated class shone in 50-over cricket too, most notably after an enforced rest during the one-day debacle against Australia. As a result of his recharged batteries, no England player came close to Collingwood's 16 sixes, and a trio of innings in South Africa – 82 and 105 not out at Centurion, 86 at Cape Town – were the product of a man on top of his game, form he carried into the Test series. In all cricket, no colleague passed fifty more times than Collingwood's 15 – and one of them, a 32-ball 57 in the narrow Twenty20 win at Johannesburg, suggested he had finally adapted to the captaincy in that format. Seventeen one-day wickets, bettered only by Broad and Anderson, were a pleasant bonus, and his all-round fielding was peerless once more. If the over-reliance on the bottom hand lingered – and with it an occasional tendency to play round straight balls – then Collingwood's man-for-all-seasons persona remained one of England's bankers.

2009   14 Tests: 915 runs @ 48.15; 1 wicket @ 194.00.
            19 ODI: 705 runs @ 50.35; 17 wickets @ 32.47.
             8 T20I: 134 runs @ 19.14; 3 wickets @ 15.00.

ALASTAIR COOK   Essex

The statistics masked something of an odyssey. Cook began the year by ridding himself of an albatross: his second-innings hundred at Bridgetown was his first in 28 Test innings. But easy pickings against West Indies were merely ill preparation for another grilling by Australia's seamers. An old tendency to play round his front pad resurfaced, followed by some iffy driving outside off. Only 95 at Lord's, an innings aided and abetted by dismal bowling, stopped the Ashes being a personal disaster. But there followed a period of technical rehab at the hands of his Essex mentor Graham Gooch, who encouraged him to stand straighter, pare down his backlift, and get more side-on. After two failures at Centurion, the work paid off during a 401-minute 118 at Durban in which Cook turned his nose up at the South African seamers' pitched-up offerings outside off stump, and a pair of fifties at Cape Town – three innings which persuaded the selectors he was in the right frame of mind to lead England in Bangladesh in 2010 after all. Critics had previously questioned his elevation to the vice-captaincy, a doubt that was hardly quelled by a faltering performance in the field during the Twenty20 drubbing at Centurion. Even so, ten Test centuries at the age of 25 were not to be sniffed at, and the abiding sense was there were plenty more to come.

2009   14 Tests: 960 runs @ 45.71.
         2 T20I: 37 runs @ 18.50.

STEVEN DAVIES   Worcestershire/Surrey

Two appearances as wicketkeeper separated by more than six months were little more than unexpected bonuses, but Davies's 21-ball 27 in a Twenty20 game at Port-of-Spain confirmed a neat cover-drive and a punchy pull – as well as great hands, if minimal footwork – and turned out to be England's top score. When Prior fell ill at the Champions Trophy, his presence at No. 6 in the semi-final against Australia seemed less reassuring, and by that time he had already lost out on World Twenty20 selection to Foster. But these were early days, and a close-season move to Surrey suggested a young cricketer who wanted to go places.

2009   1 ODI: 5 runs @ 5.00; 1 catch.
         1 T20I: 27 runs @ 27.00.

JOE DENLY   Kent

There were moments when Denly looked the part as England sought a one-day natural at the top of the order: his intent was generally aggressive, the straight-

drive oozed class, and he could hit over the top off both front and back foot. But vertigo kept striking. In six innings of nine he passed 20; not once did he go beyond the 67 he made while top-scoring on debut in Ireland. An injury sustained when Shah fouled him in a football match did not help his progress; neither did two first-ballers in his first two Twenty20 knocks. But even though Trott replaced him for the 50-over matches in South Africa, there was enough here to merit another look.

2009   9 ODI: 268 runs @ 29.77.
         3 T20I: 14 runs @ 4.66; 1 wicket @ 9.00.

Philip Brown

ANDREW FLINTOFF   Lancashire

The mind was willing, but the body struggled to keep up. As ever, Flintoff's deeds demanded – and received – special attention: a rare but tub-thumping five-for at Lord's, where he finally located a fuller length; a cobwebs-dispersing 74 at Edgbaston; and the raucous run-out of Ponting at The Oval. Hyperbole was rarely in short supply – although a series-clinching hat-trick in the final one-day international in St Lucia earned its accolades – and there were moments when the talisman felt more like a distraction. Inevitable speculation surrounded his role in the demise of Moores and Pietersen, and the never-ending saga of his right knee, injured while on IPL duty, was the summer's major subplot. Critics felt he should not have announced his retirement from Tests on the eve of the Lord's game and, when England left him out at Headingley, his agent immediately hit back by claiming Flintoff, plainly peeved, had been fit to play. After rejecting the ECB's offer of an incremental contract to concentrate on life as a globe-trotting freelancer, Flintoff's close-season, post-operative move to the warmth of Dubai removed him from the limelight for a while. But no one – not least the man himself – could say with any certainty what the future held. And England had long been planning for life without him.

2009   7 Tests: 267 runs @ 26.70; 13 wickets @ 43.69.
           3 ODI: 3 runs @ 1.50; 6 wickets @ 16.00.

JAMES FOSTER   Essex

More than seven years after England had tried to turn him into Alec Stewart's long-term replacement, Foster re-emerged for the World Twenty20, where he duly conformed to stereotype. His glovework was at times electric, and purists purred over the stumpings of Yuvraj Singh and Dwayne Bravo. But his batting remained lightweight: 32 balls yielded a single six and no fours, and in two games he was a place too high at No. 6. It was never going to be enough to displace Prior in the longer forms of the game, and Foster soon lost his Twenty20 place too.

2009   5 T20I: 37 runs @ 12.33; 3 catches, 3 stumpings.

STEVE HARMISON   Durham

When Harmison found himself on an Ashes hat-trick on the final day of the Test summer, it was tempting to imagine that England's only bowler with the ability to intimidate really had rediscovered his snarl. But the moment was as fleeting as it was illusory and, for the fifth time in a little over a year and a half, Harmison – his protests ringing increasingly hollow – was dropped, possibly for good. Goodwill had already been sacrificed by another insipid winter tour, this time in the Caribbean where he failed to take advantage of the extra bounce at St John's. A familiar template ensued: Harmison spent much of the summer helping Durham win the County Championship, and was then called up for the Headingley Test, where a rib-tickler to Katich set the tone for England's mindlessly short-pitched approach. The Oval, as ever, suited him better, but – with a rumour circulating that Harmison had expressed his reluctance to tour Australia in 2010-11 – England decided to go to South Africa without him. Previous omissions felt like temporary measures; this seemed more like a fresh start.

2009   4 Tests: 45 runs @ 15.00; 9 wickets @ 34.88.
           4 ODI: 18 runs without being dismissed; no wicket for 139.

ROBERT KEY   Kent

It said much for England's confusion over their best Twenty20 side that Key –
absent from the international scene since the South Africa tour of 2004-05
– was touted both as captain and opener. In the event, he was neither, coming
in at No. 6 in his only appearance – in the embarrassment against the
Netherlands at Lord's – and later having to deny rumours he had fallen out
with the management.

2009   1 T20I: 10 runs without being dismissed.

AMJAD KHAN   Kent

Drafted in for an unlikely Test debut in Trinidad as England desperately sought
a cutting-edge, particularly with the old ball, the Copenhagen-born Khan
inflicted Sarwan's first failure of a prolific series, but spoiled the effect with a
plague of no-balls. Pace vied with profligacy as the dominant feature, although
a smattering of reverse-swing was encouraging. But when Strauss needed
wickets on the final day of the series, Khan was given only four overs. One
Twenty20 appearance later, he was dropped.

2009   1 Test: 1 wicket @ 122.00.
            1 T20I: 2 runs @ 2.00; 2 wickets @ 17.00.

SAJID MAHMOOD   Lancashire

Concerns that Mahmood's return to the England set-up owed more to hope
than conviction were borne out when his two Twenty20 outings in South
Africa produced figures of 7–0–92–2. A single 50-over appearance proved
little better, leaving Mahmood's claim that he had ironed out inconsistencies
in line and length splattered all over the high veld. Realising as much, England
released him to join up with their performance squad instead.

2009   1 ODI: 1 wicket @ 41.00.
            2 T20I: 1 run without being dismissed; 2 wickets @ 46.00

DIMITRI MASCARENHAS   Hampshire

The emergence of the more dynamic Wright left Mascarenhas in limbo. In
some respects this was harsh. England's most economical Twenty20 bowler,
he was also their most miserly seamer in the 50-over game. But wickets and
runs proved hard to come by, and any sense of belonging evaporated in a fug
of selectorial inconsistency: only once did he bat in the same position in
successive one-day internationals. The upshot, perhaps, was that Mascarenhas
managed only one six all year – and without his trademark explosiveness, he
found it hard to justify a regular place.

2009   9 ODI: 95 runs @ 15.83; 7 wickets @ 45.28.
            4 T20I: 42 runs @ 21.00; 2 wickets @ 31.00.

EOIN MORGAN   Middlesex

Ireland's loss was England's gain, for few freer innings were played all year
than Morgan's unbeaten 85 off 45 balls in the Johannesburg Twenty20
international – a performance at altitude to match the dizzying heights he

was now reaching. Natural hand–eye co-ordination, impish wit and deceptive power – only Collingwood hit more than his 15 sixes in one-day and Twenty20 internationals – helped turn Morgan into the team's innovator par excellence,

Philip Brown

and his ability to hit both in the air and along the ground all round the wicket felt unprecedented in English cricket. Reverse-sweeps, even reverse-reverse-sweeps, were his special delight, but this was more than gimmickry, and his 41-ball 58 in the defeat by Australia at Trent Bridge was the catalyst for England to chance their arm. A sparkling knock of 67 from 34 balls at Centurion lit up the Champions Trophy, while his fielding, both close in and deep, was spectacular. Only a queue he now had hopes of jumping prevented a Test debut.

2009   15 ODI: 363 runs @ 36.30.
        3 T20I: 101 runs @ 50.50.

GRAHAM ONIONS   Durham

In helping to see out the last 19 balls of the Centurion Test, then the final 17 at Cape Town, Onions – called a "legend" by his captain – personified England's new-found backbone. But he was far more than a backs-to-the-wall specialist, and by the end of the year he had graduated from third-change to the new ball, a reflection of his wicket-to-wicket style that lost some of its effectiveness only when he dropped short. Four wickets in seven balls on Test debut against West Indies at Lord's could have been a fluke, but useful contributions against Australia, first at Lord's, then at Edgbaston – where the wickets of Watson and Hussey with the first two balls of the second day were an Ashes champagne moment – scotched that notion. In South Africa he bowled better than his figures suggested, especially against Smith, and made the batsmen play more often than any of his colleagues. If he wasn't quite Mr Dependable just yet, he had made a good start – and his omission from the Johannesburg Test in January 2010 felt harsh.

2009   7 Tests: 26 runs @ 8.66; 25 wickets @ 28.52.
        4 ODI: 1 run @ 1.00; 4 wickets @ 46.25.

MONTY PANESAR   Northamptonshire/Sussex

Panesar's heart-warming role in saving the Cardiff Test with the bat quickly gave way to a colder reality: his bowling had not simply stalled, it had gone backwards. Four Tests, of which Cardiff was the last, yielded six wickets in almost 145 overs and a painful sense that Panesar had badly mislaid his A-game. In an attempt to counter mounting criticism, he tried to add variety, but it felt like an uncle hitting the disco dance-floor: well-intentioned but incongruous. Already behind Swann in England's spin-bowling hierarchy at the start of the year, Panesar dropped behind Rashid towards the end, and was left to reassert his belief in his old methods during a spell with Highveld Lions and to switch counties in search of a change of fortune. The selectors' preference for Tredwell as a second spinner in Bangladesh underlined how far he had fallen.

2009   4 Tests: 11 runs @ 5.50; 6 wickets @ 64.16.

KEVIN PIETERSEN   Hampshire

It was to Pietersen's credit that a subdued, injury-hit year still produced a Test average worthy of the name. But, maybe for the first time in his career, the spark was missing. In Tests he hit only four sixes (out of a career tally of 49) and in 50-over cricket only three (out of 59). If his performances in the World Twenty20 were better – there were match-winning innings against Pakistan and India – then the overall effect felt like a post-captaincy comedown after he was sacked at the start of the year. An Achilles problem that was aggravated during an ill-fated stint as captain of Bangalore in the IPL and ensured only a bit-part in the Ashes did not help. Neither did a tendency towards aberration: most notably, a hubristic slog-sweep on 97 in Jamaica; an ugly-looking sweep at Cardiff, even if it attracted more attention than it deserved; and a hare-brained run-out after doing the hard work at Centurion. Yet for all that – and despite the excellence of Strauss – Pietersen's remained the wicket the opposition cherished most, and only four single-figure scores in 18 Test innings was a consistency of sorts, even if his double failures at Cape Town and Johannesburg in the new year prompted a renewed bout of concern about his tendency to fall away to the off side and hit straight balls through midwicket.

2009   11 Tests: 760 runs @ 47.50; no wicket for 94.
           8 ODI: 132 runs @ 18.85; no wicket for 0.
           6 T20I: 195 runs @ 32.50; 1 wicket @ 36.00.

MATT PRIOR   Sussex

For the first time in years England were able to operate without the wicketkeeping debate rumbling on in the background. If Prior briefly lost his Twenty20 place to Foster, then he was the first choice in all three formats by the year's end. The blunders all but vanished, thanks in part to some diligent work with Bruce French and the decision to place nimbleness ahead of bulk, and in Tests Prior was equally at home at No. 6, when Flintoff was available, and No. 7, when he wasn't. He may not quite have been Gilchristian, but Prior did inject urgency often enough, his speciality the busy 60 – never bettered than when he ran Australia ragged on the third evening at Lord's. Defensive rearguards and slower pitches suited his off-side game less well, and he had yet to nail down a match-winning innings in the one-day side. But the doomsday scenario of an England keeper dropping the opposition captain two runs into an innings of 150 gradually faded from the mind.

2009   13 Tests: 740 runs @ 43.52; 25 catches, 2 stumpings.
           19 ODI: 357 runs @ 27.46; 18 catches, 1 stumping.
            3 T20I: 10 runs @ 10.00; 1 stumping.

ADIL RASHID   Yorkshire

Rashid may have paid the price as much for his art as his age. England seemed unsure how to use a 21-year-old leg-spinner, although there were moments of real promise: two six-an-over World Twenty20 returns against South Africa and Pakistan, followed by 10–0–37–0 against Australia at The Oval, where an undefeated 31 from 23 balls also hinted at wristy potential with the bat. But England, possibly encouraging him to push the ball through more quickly than he was used to with Yorkshire, omitted him from the next game, and his confidence took a further hit when South Africa – publicly encouraged by their coach, Mickey Arthur – targeted Rashid at the start of England's tour. One over for 25 in the Twenty20 mauling at

Philip Brown

Centurion lent credence to their tactics, and Rashid, struggling to find bounce, was handed over to the Performance squad, knowing at least that time was on his side.

2009   5 ODI: 60 runs @ 20.00; 3 wickets @ 63.66.
       5 T20I: 10 runs @ 10.00; 3 wickets @ 40.00.

OWAIS SHAH   Middlesex

Not since the days of Geoff Boycott had an England batsman's uncertainty between the wickets attracted so much attention. If Shah's talent was never in doubt, neither was his ability to unnerve his partner, and two run-outs in six innings on the Caribbean's featherbeds – and a solitary half-century – cost him any hope of an Ashes place. They were followed by two more in the NatWest Series (plus an equally hapless hit wicket), taking his career tally of run-outs in all internationals to ten. And while his 89-ball 98 against South Africa in the Champions Trophy thrillingly embodied England's brave new one-day tactics, it was also one of only two half-centuries in 17 one-day innings, and subsequent failures against New Zealand and Australia reinforced the suspicion that his shot selection was flawed. For the selectors – equally unimpressed by his fielding – enough was enough, and Shah was not taken to South Africa. An outburst several weeks later questioning that decision hardly helped his cause.

2009   4 Tests: 133 runs @ 22.16; no wicket for 31.
       19 ODI: 546 runs @ 30.33; 4 wickets @ 14.50.
       7 T20I: 112 runs @ 18.66.

RYAN SIDEBOTTOM   Nottinghamshire

After a couple of unpenetrative performances in the Caribbean and a place in the starting line-up for the Antigua Test that never was, Sidebottom – England's leading Test wicket-taker the previous year – was reduced to a bit-part in the limited-overs sides. The Ashes passed him by as concerns over his stamina persuaded the selectors to look elsewhere, and a cheap five-for in a warm-up game at East London did not earn him a Test spot in South Africa until the final game at Johannesburg, where he bowled adequately. In the build-up to that trip he had never worked harder on his fitness, but the concern at the end of 2008 – that England had seen the best of Sidebottom – was in danger of becoming reality.

2009   3 Tests: 32 runs @ 32.00; 1 wicket @ 181.00.
           8 ODI: 82 runs @ 16.40; 4 wickets @ 83.00.
           4 T20I: did not bat; 3 wickets @ 33.33.

ANDREW STRAUSS   Middlesex

Strauss's calm decency and quiet authority proved to be just what England needed after Pietersen's chaotic interregnum, although depths were plumbed before the Ashes high. His first Test back in charge after almost two and a half years in and out of the ranks was the debacle in Jamaica, but defeat by West Indies with a team Strauss had no part in choosing was tempered by his obvious relish for the job – he made big first-innings hundreds in each of the remaining three Caribbean Tests – and a blossoming partnership with Andy Flower. Against Australia he was simply momentous, scoring a decisive 161 at Lord's and equally game-shaping half-centuries at The Oval, and also lucky, winning four tosses out of five. His all-round influence was reflected in both a successful return as a one-day opener – it was no coincidence that the Twenty20 team, the only format he did not play, struggled – and England's overt improvement in 50-over cricket after losing the ill-timed one-day series 6–1 to Australia. Meanwhile, his calculated assault on Ntini at Durban paved the way for a famous win, even if his form fell away at Cape Town and Johannesburg. By the end of the year, only Sri Lanka's Samaraweera and Jayawardene had scored more Test runs, and Strauss – initially erring on the side of caution when declaring in the Caribbean – had developed into a captain capable of seizing the moment. England had ignored his leadership claims ahead of the 2006-07 Ashes in favour of Flintoff, but the unwitting upshot – stability, at last – almost justified the means, which is partly why his decision to skip the tour of Bangladesh in the spring of 2010 attracted such criticism.

2009   14 Tests: 1,172 runs @ 53.27.
           21 ODI: 647 runs @ 32.35.
            1 T20I: 22 runs @ 22.00.

GRAEME SWANN   Nottinghamshire

Swann had always played up to his court-jester persona, but now his performances on the field proved as entertaining as those off it. His haul of 54 Test wickets was second only to Mitchell Johnson, while his perky presence in the lower order – he combined a top-order average with a game-changing strike-rate of nearly 86 – meant England wagged as enthusiastically as anyone. Against left-handers, Swann could be unplayable: 35 of them were Test victims, of which 17 were trapped leg-before. The modern umpires' impatience with pad play certainly helped his cause, as did the new review system, which favoured bowlers capable of straightening the ball on the line of the stumps.

But if Swann was plying his trade in a fortuitous mini-era for off-spinners, then at least he had the self-belief and sunny optimism to exploit the fact, and a first-innings bowling average of 29 went beyond the call of duty. He picked up four wickets or more in a Test innings on eight occasions, and – typically – claimed the winning scalp in both England's Ashes wins, before taking 21 wickets, more than any player on either side, in the drawn series in South Africa. The over in which he dismissed Ponting at Edgbaston was one of the most memorable of the year. His one-day stats relied heavily on a canny five-for in the deadest of rubbers at Chester-le-Street, but no one – except possibly the almost-forgotten Panesar – was complaining. While Swann had the ball, finger-spin felt anything but a dying art.

2009   12 Tests: 452 runs @ 45.20; 54 wickets @ 27.92.
           14 ODI: 81 runs @ 11.57; 13 wickets @ 30.92.
            6 T20I: 15 runs @ 7.50; 6 wickets @ 25.16.

JONATHAN TROTT   Warwickshire

Two years after flirting with England's Twenty20 side, Trott returned for something more substantial. His second-innings hundred at The Oval was a Test debut for the ages and instant Ashes folklore (not to mention a pat on the back by proxy for the selectors), and although his next outing was a back-to-earth one-day duck in Belfast, England rewarded him with the No. 3 slot in his native South Africa. A patient last-day 69 to help save the Centurion Test revealed other, adhesive, qualities. But that game also suggested he needed to expand his tactics against spin, and as the runs dried up towards the end of the series, there were concerns too about his intensity and position in the order. Even so, England had already trusted him enough to make him their latest one-day opener, and he rarely exuded less than solidity. This was not always straightforward: he was accused by Michael Vaughan of celebrating with the South Africans at Edgbaston in 2008, a charge he denied, and annoyed his former compatriots with his time-gobbling fussiness at the crease. If anything, the barbs forced him deeper into his shell.

2009   3 Tests: 275 runs @ 55.00; no wicket for 28.
          4 ODI: 148 runs @ 49.33; no wicket for 29.
          3 T20I: 84 runs @ 42.00.

LUKE WRIGHT   Sussex

Wright's continued selection in the two limited-overs teams appeared to be based on the promise of things to come. Sixteen one-day international and Twenty20 innings produced a single half-century – in the defeat by the Netherlands – and one or two moments of substance, most notably when he shared a century stand with Bresnan against Australia in the Champions Trophy. But his supposed high-impact presence never quite lived up to its billing, and a stint as Twenty20 opener came to an end after 22 runs in five innings. Neither did ten expensive wickets do much for the claim that he was a Test-match all-rounder in the making and, when he failed to earn a place at No. 7 in the post-Flintoff series in South Africa, it seemed the selectors agreed.

2009   12 ODI: 199 runs @ 22.11; 7 wickets @ 44.42.
          8 T20I: 127 runs @ 18.14; 3 wickets @ 40.33.

ENGLAND TEST AVERAGES IN CALENDAR YEAR 2009

The averages in this section refer to the calendar year 2009.

BATTING AND FIELDING

	T	I	NO	R	HS	100s	Avge	SR	Ct/St
I. J. L. Trott	3	5	0	275	119	1	55.00	43.37	1
†A. J. Strauss	14	24	2	1,172	169	4	53.27	54.13	9
P. D. Collingwood	14	21	2	915	161	2	48.15	48.10	19
K. P. Pietersen	11	17	1	760	102	1	47.50	58.28	2
R. S. Bopara	7	10	0	460	143	3	46.00	53.30	4
†A. N. Cook	14	24	3	960	160	3	45.71	48.38	13
G. P. Swann	12	14	4	452	85	0	45.20	85.93	6
M. J. Prior	13	20	3	740	131*	1	43.52	72.69	25/2
†R. J. Sidebottom	3	2	1	32	26*	0	32.00	27.82	0
I. R. Bell	6	10	0	319	140	1	31.90	49.61	3
A. Flintoff	7	11	1	267	74	0	26.70	55.74	3
†S. C. J. Broad	14	21	4	431	61	0	25.35	66.61	2
O. A. Shah	4	6	0	133	57	0	22.16	39.34	1
S. J. Harmison	4	6	3	45	19*	0	15.00	43.26	0
†J. M. Anderson	13	15	3	178	29	0	14.83	43.30	4
T. T. Bresnan	2	1	0	9	9	0	9.00	56.25	2
G. Onions	7	8	5	26	17*	0	8.66	33.76	0
†M. S. Panesar	4	4	2	11	7*	0	5.50	18.96	0
T. R. Ambrose	1	1	1	76	76*	0	–	80.00	1
A. Khan	1	–	–	–	–	–	–	–	0

† *Left-handed batsman.*

BOWLING

	Style	O	M	R	W	BB	5W/i	Avge	SR
G. P. Swann	OB	518	111	1,508	54	5-54	4	27.92	57.55
S. C. J. Broad	RFM	421.3	84	1,333	47	6-91	3	28.36	53.80
G. Onions	RFM	196.1	35	713	25	5-38	1	28.52	47.08
T. T. Bresnan	RFM	31	7	97	3	3-45	0	32.33	62.00
J. M. Anderson	RFM	440.5	100	1,355	40	5-80	2	33.87	66.12
S. J. Harmison	RF	97.4	20	314	9	3-54	0	34.88	65.11
A. Flintoff	RF	191.1	37	568	13	5-92	1	43.69	88.23
M. S. Panesar	SLA	144.5	33	385	6	2-34	0	64.16	144.83
A. Khan	RF	29	1	122	1	1-111	0	122.00	174.00
R. J. Sidebottom	LFM	59	9	181	1	1-146	0	181.00	354.00
P. D. Collingwood	RM	52	4	194	1	1-38	0	194.00	312.00
I. J. L. Trott	RM	6	0	28	0	–	–	–	–
O. A. Shah	OB	5	0	31	0	–	–	–	–
K. P. Pietersen	OB	23	2	94	0	–	–	–	–
R. S. Bopara	RM	23.2	1	118	0	–	–	–	–

> **❝** The New Zealanders ate a tasteless lunch at 61 for six.❞
> New Zealand v India, First Test, page 1171

ENGLAND ONE-DAY INTERNATIONAL AVERAGES IN CALENDAR YEAR 2009

BATTING AND FIELDING

	M	I	NO	R	HS	100s	Avge	SR	Ct/St
P. D. Collingwood	19	18	4	705	105*	1	50.35	83.92	11
I. J. L. Trott	4	4	1	148	87	0	49.33	68.83	2
T. T. Bresnan	13	10	5	202	80	0	40.40	92.23	2
†E. J. G. Morgan	15	15	5	363	67	0	36.30	82.68	7
†A. J. Strauss	21	21	1	647	105	1	32.35	78.14	10
O. A. Shah	19	18	0	546	98	0	30.33	75.93	6
J. L. Denly	9	9	0	268	67	0	29.77	65.52	5
M. J. Prior.	19	17	4	357	87	0	27.46	76.28	18/1
R. S. Bopara	17	17	0	436	49	0	25.64	69.31	6
L. J. Wright	12	9	0	199	48	0	22.11	100.50	4
A. U. Rashid.	5	4	1	60	31*	0	20.00	111.11	1
K. P. Pietersen	8	7	0	132	48	0	18.85	79.04	1
†R. J. Sidebottom	8	8	3	82	24	0	16.40	74.54	3
A. D. Mascarenhas	9	6	0	95	36	0	15.83	64.18	1
G. J. Batty.	3	3	1	24	17	0	12.00	44.44	0
G. P. Swann	14	9	2	81	18	0	11.57	79.41	6
†J. M. Anderson	19	8	5	21	8	0	7.00	38.88	2
†S. C. J. Broad	15	10	1	54	22	0	6.00	90.00	1
†S. M. Davies.	1	1	0	5	5	0	5.00	125.00	1
A. Flintoff.	3	2	0	3	3	0	1.50	25.00	4
G. Onions	4	1	0	1	1	0	1.00	50.00	1
S. J. Harmison	4	1	1	18	18*	0	–	100.00	2
S. I. Mahmood	1	–	–	–	–	–	–	–	0

† Left-handed batsman.

BOWLING

	Style	O	M	R	W	BB	4W/i	Avge	SR	ER
O. A. Shah	OB	13.1	1	58	4	3-15	0	14.50	19.75	4.40
A. Flintoff	RF	19	0	96	6	5-19	1	16.00	19.00	5.05
S. C. J. Broad	RFM	129.3	6	731	32	4-39	3	22.84	24.28	5.64
J. M. Anderson	RFM	161.3	9	803	34	5-23	2	23.61	28.50	4.97
G. P. Swann	OB	86	2	402	13	5-28	1	30.92	39.69	4.67
P. D. Collingwood . . .	RM	108	0	552	17	3-16	0	32.47	38.11	5.11
T. T. Bresnan	RFM	102.5	4	512	13	2-10	0	39.38	47.46	4.97
S. I. Mahmood	RFM	7	0	41	1	1-41	0	41.00	42.00	5.85
L. J. Wright	RFM	58	1	311	7	2-52	0	44.42	49.71	5.36
A. D. Mascarenhas . . .	RM	66	1	317	7	3-26	0	45.28	56.57	4.80
G. Onions	RFM	34	1	185	4	2-58	0	46.25	51.00	5.44
R. S. Bopara	RM	10	0	53	1	1-12	0	53.00	60.00	5.30
A. U. Rashid.	LBG	34	0	191	3	1-16	0	63.66	68.00	5.61
G. J. Batty	OB	13	0	72	1	1-34	0	72.00	78.00	5.53
R. J. Sidebottom.	LFM	61	1	332	4	1-32	0	83.00	91.50	5.44
K. P. Pietersen	OB	0.5	0	0	0	–	–	–	–	0.00
I. J. L. Trott	RM	8	0	29	0	–	–	–	–	3.62
S. J. Harmison	RF	25	0	139	0	–	–	–	–	5.56

ENGLAND TWENTY20 INTERNATIONAL AVERAGES IN CALENDAR YEAR 2009

BATTING AND FIELDING

	M	I	NO	R	HS	50s	Avge	SR	4	6	Ct/St
†E. J. G. Morgan	3	3	1	101	85*	1	50.50	168.33	9	5	1
I. J. L. Trott	3	3	1	84	51	1	42.00	121.73	6	3	0
K. P. Pietersen	6	6	0	195	58	1	32.50	143.38	20	6	1
†S. M. Davies	1	1	0	27	27	0	27.00	128.57	5	0	0
R. S. Bopara	7	7	0	159	55	1	22.71	111.18	16	1	2
†A. J. Strauss	1	1	0	22	22	0	22.00	88.00	2	0	0
A. D. Mascarenhas	4	4	2	42	25*	0	21.00	93.33	3	0	1
P. D. Collingwood	8	7	0	134	57	1	19.14	136.73	11	4	5
O. A. Shah	7	6	0	112	38	0	18.66	101.81	8	4	2
†A. N. Cook	2	2	0	37	26	0	18.50	127.58	6	0	0
L. J. Wright	8	7	0	127	71	1	18.14	135.10	16	2	5
J. S. Foster	5	5	2	37	14*	0	12.33	115.62	0	1	3/3
†S. C. J. Broad	7	4	2	24	10*	0	12.00	150.00	2	1	3
M. J. Prior	3	2	1	10	10*	0	10.00	111.11	1	0	0/1
A. U. Rashid	5	2	1	10	9*	0	10.00	52.63	0	0	0
G. P. Swann	6	3	1	15	10*	0	7.50	93.75	0	0	0
J. L. Denly	3	3	0	14	14	0	4.66	87.50	2	0	0
G. J. Batty	1	1	0	4	4	0	4.00	57.14	0	0	0
T. T. Bresnan	2	2	1	3	3*	0	3.00	50.00	0	0	1
A. Khan	1	1	0	2	2	0	2.00	50.00	0	0	0
†J. M. Anderson	9	2	1	0	0*	0	0.00	0.00	0	0	1
R. W. T. Key	1	1	1	10	10*	0	–	125.00	0	0	1
S. I. Mahmood	2	1	1	1	1*	0	–	100.00	0	0	1
†R. J. Sidebottom	4	–	–	–	–	–	–	–	–	–	1

† Left-handed batsman.

BOWLING

	Style	O	M	R	W	BB	4W/i	Avge	SR	ER
J. L. Denly	LB	1	0	9	1	1-9	0	9.00	6.00	9.00
P. D. Collingwood	RM	7	0	45	3	2-20	0	15.00	14.00	6.42
A. Khan	RF	4	0	34	2	2-34	0	17.00	12.00	8.50
S. C. J. Broad	RFM	23	0	163	9	3-17	0	18.11	15.33	7.08
G. P. Swann	OB	20	0	151	6	2-28	0	25.16	20.00	7.55
A. D. Mascarenhas	RM	11	0	62	2	1-9	0	31.00	33.00	5.63
J. M. Anderson	RFM	31.2	0	230	7	3-23	0	32.85	26.85	7.34
R. J. Sidebottom	LFM	13.2	0	100	3	2-31	0	33.33	26.66	7.50
K. P. Pietersen	OB	3	0	36	1	1-27	0	36.00	18.00	12.00
A. U. Rashid	LBG	14	0	120	3	1-11	0	40.00	28.00	8.57
L. J. Wright	RFM	14	0	121	3	1-17	0	40.33	28.00	8.64
S. I. Mahmood	RFM	7	0	92	2	1-31	0	46.00	21.00	13.14
G. J. Batty	OB	3	0	17	0	–	–	–	–	5.66
T. T. Bresnan	RFM	6	0	73	0	–	–	–	–	12.16

FIRST-CLASS AVERAGES, 2009

BATTING AND FIELDING

(Qualification: 10 innings)

† Left-handed batsman.

		M	I	NO	R	HS	100s	50s	Avge	Ct/St
1	M. R. Ramprakash (*Surrey*).........	11	17	2	1,350	274	5	4	90.00	5
2	†S. Chanderpaul (*West Indians & Durham*)	9	13	5	683	201*	3	2	85.37	3
3	†M. J. Di Venuto (*Durham*)..........	17	27	6	1,654	254*	6	6	78.76	23
4	A. C. Voges (*Notts*)...............	8	10	1	697	139	1	6	77.44	8
5	†M. E. Trescothick (*Somerset*)........	16	26	2	1,817	146	8	9	75.70	21
6	C. M. W. Read (*Notts*).............	16	22	6	1,203	125	4	6	75.18	46/4
7	N. Pothas (*Hants*)................	11	15	4	816	122*	1	6	74.18	24
8	I. J. L. Trott (*Warwicks, England Lions & England*)	17	25	6	1,400	184*	5	5	73.68	13
9	†C. J. L. Rogers (*Derbys*)	13	21	1	1,461	222	6	4	73.05	21
10	†M. A. Carberry (*Hants*)	12	21	3	1,251	204	4	8	69.50	6
11	M. van Jaarsveld (*Kent*)............	16	25	3	1,509	182	7	7	68.59	30
12	A. U. Rashid (*MCC, Yorks & Eng. Lions*)	10	12	4	545	157*	2	3	68.12	6
13	V. V. S. Laxman (*Lancs*)...........	11	16	3	857	135	4	4	65.92	15
14	†P. J. Hughes (*Middx & Australians*) ...	7	12	1	724	195	3	3	65.81	6
15	†M. J. North (*Hants & Australians*).....	8	12	2	613	191*	3	1	61.30	4
16	†M. J. Cosgrove (*Glam*).............	10	15	2	780	175	3	5	60.00	4
17	R. S. Bopara (*England & Essex*)	9	15	2	772	201	4	1	59.38	7
18	C. Kieswetter (*Somerset*)...........	16	24	3	1,242	153	4	7	59.14	48
19	M. J. Clarke (*Australians*)	6	10	1	532	136	2	3	59.11	9
20	W. L. Madsen (*Derbys*)	9	16	2	809	170*	3	3	57.78	8
21	†U. Afzaal (*Surrey*)	16	28	6	1,269	204*	3	7	57.68	3
22	J. W. A. Taylor (*Leics*).............	17	28	7	1,207	207*	3	6	57.47	9
23	C. D. Nash (*Sussex*)...............	15	26	3	1,321	157	4	6	57.43	3
24	†M. E. K. Hussey (*Australians*)........	7	12	2	572	150	2	4	57.20	7
25	M. B. Loye (*Lancs*)	14	22	4	996	151*	2	6	55.33	4
26	†A. G. Prince (*Lancs*)	6	12	2	526	135*	1	3	52.60	9
27	M. J. Chilton (*Lancs*)..............	16	23	6	891	114	2	6	52.41	15
28	†J. H. K. Adams (*Hants*)	17	30	4	1,350	147	3	10	51.92	17
29	G. O. Jones (*Kent*)	17	26	0	1,345	156	5	6	51.73	41/3
30	†A. J. Strauss (*Middx & England*)......	11	19	1	917	161	2	5	50.94	12
31	A. J. Hall (*Northants*).............	16	25	2	1,161	159	2	6	50.47	16
32	J. W. M. Dalrymple (*Glam*).........	17	23	3	1,009	128	3	5	50.45	17
33	R. W. T. Key (*MCC, Kent & Eng. Lions*)	17	28	4	1,209	270*	4	7	50.37	15
34	†J. E. C. Franklin (*Glos*)	14	22	4	904	109	3	4	50.22	6
35	D. I. Stevens (*Kent*)	17	24	3	1,050	208	4	2	50.00	11
36	L. J. Wright (*Sussex & England Lions*).	10	15	2	637	118*	3	3	49.00	1
37	†J. A. Rudolph (*Yorks*)..............	17	29	1	1,366	198	4	6	48.78	14
38	D. M. Benkenstein (*Durham*)........	18	24	0	1,168	181	5	4	48.66	10
39	A. V. Suppiah (*Somerset*)	16	26	1	1,201	151	3	6	48.04	18
40	†G. P. Rees (*Glam*)	17	25	2	1,061	154	3	4	46.13	15
41	R. N. ten Doeschate (*Essex*).........	14	22	4	823	159*	2	2	45.72	5
42	J. M. Bairstow (*Yorks*).............	12	19	6	592	84*	0	6	45.53	21
43	†S. M. Katich (*Australians*)..........	7	11	0	498	122	1	2	45.27	10
44	†I. D. Blackwell (*Durham*)..........	18	24	3	949	158	2	6	45.19	4
45	A. P. R. Gidman (*Glos*)	15	23	0	1,028	176	4	4	44.69	9
46	J. C. Hildreth (*Somerset*)	15	23	2	934	303*	2	4	44.47	10
47	G. L. Brophy (*Yorks*)	14	22	5	748	99	0	6	44.00	37/2
48	I. R. Bell (*MCC, Warwicks, England Lions & England*)..............	19	30	3	1,185	172	4	6	43.88	15
49	S. D. Peters (*Northants*)............	14	25	1	1,050	175	3	5	43.75	12

		M	I	NO	R	HS	100s	50s	Avge	Ct/St
50	†M. J. Lumb (*Hants*)	16	24	1	1,006	219	2	5	43.73	10
51	†J. L. Langer (*Somerset*)	15	21	2	831	122*	2	4	43.73	17
52	J. M. Kemp (*Kent*)	14	21	3	780	183	2	3	43.33	30
53	†A. N. Cook (*Essex & England*)	17	30	3	1,168	160	2	6	43.25	20
54	H. H. Dippenaar (*Leics*)	17	31	5	1,121	143	2	8	43.11	6
55	†J. J. Sayers (*Yorks*)	17	29	2	1,150	173	2	2	42.59	16
56	†J. L. Denly (*Kent & England Lions*)	11	17	1	680	123	3	2	42.50	7
57	G. M. Smith (*Derbys*)	16	27	4	977	126	1	6	42.47	5
58	G. T. Park (*Derbys*)	16	27	2	1,059	178*	2	8	42.36	14
59	O. A. Shah (*Middx*)	8	16	2	591	159	2	2	42.21	5
60	†M. H. Yardy (*Sussex*)	17	29	3	1,096	152	2	6	42.15	13
61	†D. J. Wainwright (*Yorks*)	10	13	4	378	102*	1	1	42.00	0
62	†P. Mustard (*Durham*)	18	22	7	627	94*	0	5	41.80	69/1
63	N. J. Dexter (*Middx*)	10	19	2	709	146	2	2	41.70	15
64	†S. M. Ervine (*Hants*)	15	22	2	832	114	3	3	41.60	6
65	M. J. Prior (*Sussex & England*)	13	21	2	788	140	1	6	41.47	30/1
66	J. Allenby (*Leics & Glam*)	12	18	2	662	137	1	6	41.37	10
67	H. D. Ackerman (*Leics*)	12	21	1	827	180	1	5	41.35	5
68	†E. C. Joyce (*Sussex*)	15	24	1	945	183	3	3	41.08	12
69	†S. M. Davies (*Worcs & England Lions*)	15	28	3	1,023	126	2	5	40.92	40/2
70	S. J. Adshead (*Glos.*)	7	10	1	367	156*	2	0	40.77	22/1
71	A. D. Hales (*Notts*)	7	12	1	447	78	0	4	40.63	3
72	M. J. Powell (*Glam*)	17	25	2	934	108	2	7	40.60	8
73	A. D. Brown (*Notts*)	16	24	3	849	148	1	6	40.42	10
74	R. T. Ponting (*Australians*)	6	10	0	401	150	1	2	40.10	12
75	†N. Boje (*Northants*)	15	25	5	801	98	0	8	40.05	7
76	M. L. Pettini (*Essex*)	15	28	6	870	101*	1	4	39.54	10
77	S. A. Northeast (*Kent*)	11	19	2	667	128*	1	3	39.23	10
78	J. S. Foster (*MCC & Essex*)	17	27	2	980	103*	1	6	39.20	61/4
79	T. Westley (*MCC, Durham UCCE & Essex*)	10	17	3	547	132	1	2	39.07	6
80	D. K. H. Mitchell (*Worcs*)	17	31	1	1,162	298	2	5	38.73	18
81	L. E. Plunkett (*Durham & Eng. Lions*)	15	14	3	425	94*	0	3	38.63	13
82	†S. C. J. Broad (*Notts & England*)	9	13	3	382	61	0	3	38.20	3
83	D. J. Pipe (*Derbys*)	14	18	5	493	64*	0	3	37.92	36/2
	M. A. Ealham (*Notts*)	14	20	7	493	70	0	2	37.92	6
85	W. R. Smith (*Durham*)	17	25	3	834	150	2	5	37.90	6
86	A. Shahzad (*Notts*)	14	18	6	451	88	0	2	37.58	4
87	P. D. Collingwood (*England*)	8	13	2	413	79*	0	5	37.54	7
88	†D. J. Malan (*Middx*)	15	28	3	930	88	0	8	37.20	19
89	R. Clarke (*Warwicks*)	14	18	1	631	112	1	5	37.11	25
90	T. R. Ambrose (*Warwicks & Eng. Lions*)	18	24	2	814	153	3	3	37.00	43/2
	M. A. Wagh (*Notts*)	15	24	2	814	147	3	2	37.00	4
92	C. D. Hopkinson (*Sussex*)	9	13	1	443	139	2	0	36.91	2
93	†A. W. Gale (*Yorks*)	17	26	1	921	121	2	5	36.84	6
94	M. J. Brown (*Surrey*)	16	28	1	992	120	2	4	36.74	7
	R. A. White (*Northants*)	17	31	4	992	193	1	7	36.74	11
96	J. N. Batty (*Surrey*)	16	26	0	937	120	2	1	36.03	46/4
97	†J. O. Troughton (*Warwicks*)	17	23	0	828	223	2	3	36.00	10
98	†M. J. Walker (*Essex*)	17	31	3	1,004	150	2	3	35.85	13
99	†C. P. Schofield (*Surrey*)	14	21	3	644	144	1	3	35.77	7
100	†G. M. Andrew (*Worcs*)	10	16	5	391	92*	0	3	35.54	0
101	M. H. Wessels (*Northants*)	15	25	0	887	109	1	7	35.48	27/1
102	†P. A. Nixon (*Leics*)	9	17	2	531	173*	1	3	35.40	10
103	G. P. Swann (*Notts & England*)	10	12	2	352	63*	0	3	35.20	1
104	H. J. H. Marshall (*Glos*)	16	26	2	844	158	1	5	35.16	13
105	†W. W. Hinds (*Derbys*)	16	26	2	841	148	2	2	35.04	7
106	G. R. Napier (*Essex*)	10	16	6	348	64*	0	2	34.80	3
107	Kadeer Ali (*Glos*)	16	28	4	834	90	0	4	34.75	10
108	†J. K. Maunders (*Essex*).	11	18	0	621	150	1	3	34.50	12
109	S. D. Robson (*Middx*)	7	13	0	441	110	1	2	33.92	12

		M	I	NO	R	HS	100s	50s	Avge	Ct/St
110	P. D. Trego (*Somerset*)	16	23	5	610	103*	1	5	33.88	5
111	V. S. Solanki (*Worcs & England Lions*)	17	31	1	1,016	206*	1	4	33.86	14
112	R. D. B. Croft (*Glam*)	17	21	4	574	121	1	1	33.76	4
113	C. G. Taylor (*Glos*)	15	22	1	705	111	1	5	33.57	11
114	A. McGrath (*Yorks*)	17	27	1	871	211	2	2	33.50	11
115	M. W. Goodwin (*Sussex*)	16	27	3	800	344*	1	2	33.33	6
116	N. R. D. Compton (*Middx*)	14	28	2	860	178	2	3	33.07	8
117	C. R. Woakes (*MCC, Warwicks & England Lions*)	19	23	8	495	131*	1	1	33.00	5
118 {	G. Chapple (*Lancs*)	11	14	2	390	89	0	3	32.50	3
	†T. C. Smith (*Lancs*)	9	15	3	390	104*	1	2	32.50	7
120	S. J. Walters (*Surrey*)	11	18	0	573	188	2	1	31.83	15
121	G. K. Berg (*Middx*)	13	23	2	668	98	0	7	31.80	9
122	S. R. Patel (*Notts & England Lions*)	17	26	0	821	95	0	4	31.57	11
123	P. J. Horton (*Lancs*)	17	30	2	881	173	2	4	31.46	16
124	†T. J. New (*Leics*)	18	30	4	813	85*	0	6	31.26	29/1
125	F. du Plessis (*Lancs*)	13	20	3	531	86*	0	5	31.23	8
126	Z. de Bruyn (*Somerset*)	16	25	3	686	106	1	6	31.18	3
127	S.C. Moore (*MCC, Worcs & Eng. Lions*)	17	32	1	952	120	2	5	30.70	6
128	†W. D. Bragg (*Glam*)	9	12	0	367	92	0	2	30.58	4
129	C. J. Jordan (*Surrey*)	8	10	3	213	42	0	0	30.42	4
130	†D. J. Redfern (*Derbys*)	14	23	1	668	95	0	5	30.36	8
131	G. J. Muchall (*Durham*)	13	19	2	515	106*	1	2	30.29	14
132	†J. C. Tredwell (*Kent*)	17	21	5	484	86*	0	4	30.25	12
133	L. A. Dawson (*Hants*)	15	23	4	571	69	0	4	30.05	13
134	S. J. Croft (*Lancs*)	9	14	2	360	79	0	2	30.00	6
135	†S. D. Stubbings (*Derbys*)	7	11	1	296	83	0	1	29.60	4
136	P. P. Chawla (*Sussex*)	6	10	3	206	102*	1	0	29.42	2
137	†M. A. Wallace (*Glam*)	17	22	0	645	139	2	0	29.31	31/6
138	†M M. Ali (*Worcs*)	17	30	2	803	153	2	3	28.67	4
139	J. K. H. Naik (*Leics*)	6	10	3	200	109*	1	0	28.57	1
140	A. D. Mascarenhas (*Hants*)	10	11	2	254	108	1	0	28.22	4
141	J. G. E. Benning (*Surrey & Leics*)	7	12	2	282	72	0	1	28.20	2
142	A. C. Thomas (*Somerset*)	14	15	3	338	70	0	3	28.16	2
143	J. P. Crawley (*Hants*)	8	14	3	308	81*	0	2	28.00	8
144	†I. J. Westwood (*Warwicks*)	15	25	3	612	133	1	4	27.81	10
145	L. D. Sutton (*Lancs*)	17	23	7	438	53*	0	1	27.37	56/3
146	†M. A. G. Boyce (*Leics*)	15	29	2	738	98	0	5	27.33	5
147	A. N. Kervezee (*Worcs*)	8	14	0	381	66	0	2	27.21	2
148	T. Frost (*Warwicks*)	15	23	1	598	105	1	2	27.18	8
149	†N. J. O'Brien (*Northants*)	9	16	0	434	128	1	1	27.12	34/1
150	M. J. Wood (*Notts*)	7	11	1	270	86	0	1	27.00	0
151	B. M. Shafayat (*Notts*)	14	23	1	590	90*	0	3	26.81	13
152	†M. N. W. Spriegel (*Surrey*)	6	11	0	294	100	1	2	26.72	7
153	A. Flintoff (*Lancs & England*)	7	12	1	288	74	0	2	26.18	5
154	†A. G. Botha (*Warwicks*)	14	19	2	444	64	0	2	26.11	5
155	B. F. Smith (*Worcs*)	14	27	3	626	80*	0	4	26.08	9
156	T. T. Bresnan (*MCC, Yorks, England & England Lions*)	14	17	2	386	97	0	1	25.73	7
157	K. W. Hogg (*Lancs*)	14	15	2	333	69	0	2	25.61	2
158	V. Chopra (*Essex*)	12	21	0	537	88	0	5	25.57	6
159	R. K. J. Dawson (*Glos*)	7	10	0	254	50	0	1	25.40	12
160	J. J. van der Wath (*Northants*)	13	19	1	452	85	0	3	25.11	4
161	J. M. Vince (*Hants*)	9	13	1	301	75	0	1	25.08	3
162	A. R. Adams (*Notts*)	11	13	1	300	84	0	1	25.00	13
163	A. J. Hodd (*Sussex*)	16	23	3	499	101	1	2	24.95	25/3
164	†E. J. G. Morgan (*Middx & Eng. Lions*)	11	20	2	445	114*	1	1	24.72	13
165	†S. A. Newman (*Surrey & Notts*)	12	19	0	466	124	1	2	24.52	5
166	J. D. Middlebrook (*Essex*)	8	11	3	196	46	0	0	24.50	2
167	†N. M. Carter (*Warwicks*)	9	13	0	318	67	0	2	24.46	0

		M	I	NO	R	HS	100s	50s	Avge	Ct/St
168	S. J. Cook (*Kent*)	13	13	4	220	60*	0	1	24.44	0
169	A. G. Wakely (*Northants*)	12	20	1	457	113*	1	2	24.05	10
170	†M. Kartik (*Middx*)	10	19	5	336	62*	0	2	24.00	11
171	J. C. Mickleburgh (*Essex*)	6	12	0	285	62	0	2	23.75	3
172	†M. D. Stoneman (*Durham*)	13	21	1	466	64	0	1	23.30	14
173	R. A. Jones (*Worcs*)	7	11	2	209	53*	0	1	23.22	3
174	†W. T. S. Porterfield (*Glos*)	9	16	1	341	81	0	2	22.73	17
	D. D. Masters (*Essex*)	15	16	1	341	67	0	2	22.73	7
176	P. S. Jones (*Kent & Derbys*)	12	13	3	225	54*	0	2	22.50	5
177	†A. J. Shantry (*Glam*)	13	17	3	314	100	1	0	22.42	0
178	J. Lewis (*Glos*)	15	22	6	358	61*	0	2	22.37	5
179	D. G. Cork (*Hants*)	12	15	2	290	52	0	1	22.30	18
180	C. W. Henderson (*Leics*)	10	13	2	241	79*	0	1	21.90	1
181	†B. H. N. Howgego (*Northants*)	6	11	1	219	47	0	0	21.90	3
182	D. A. Stiff (*Somerset*)	10	14	5	193	49	0	0	21.44	0
183	G. G. Wagg (*Derbys*)	14	14	1	273	71	0	1	21.00	4
184	†D. J. Willey (*Northants*)	10	17	1	331	60	0	1	20.68	3
185	J. E. R. Gallian (*Essex*)	7	13	1	245	125	1	0	20.41	5
186	W. A. White (*Leics*)	12	19	2	340	68	0	1	20.00	5
187	R. S. C. Martin-Jenkins (*Sussex*)	13	17	2	299	67	0	1	19.93	5
188	B. J. Wright (*Glam*)	9	14	0	279	81	0	1	19.92	3
189	S. D. Udal (*Middx*)	14	24	4	398	55	0	1	19.90	4
190	J. A. R. Harris (*Glam*)	14	16	3	256	76*	0	1	19.69	1
191	J. J. Cobb (*Leics*)	14	26	0	510	95	0	4	19.61	4
192	T. D. Groenewald (*Derbys*)	9	11	1	194	50	0	1	19.40	2
193	Imran Tahir (*Hants*)	12	15	4	206	77*	0	1	18.72	4
194	D. R. Smith (*Sussex*)	9	14	0	261	80	0	2	18.64	1
195	D. S. Lucas (*Northants*)	16	24	7	312	55*	0	1	18.35	5
196	†T. J. Murtagh (*Middx*)	13	20	6	249	51*	0	1	17.78	2
197	G. P. Smith (*Durham UCCE & Leics*)	7	14	1	231	51	0	1	17.76	3
198	O. P. Rayner (*Sussex*)	11	11	1	173	60	0	1	17.30	15
199	C. D. Thorp (*Durham*)	13	12	0	207	42	0	0	17.25	15
200	A. Khan (*Kent*)	11	12	3	153	62*	0	1	17.00	2
201	I. D. Saxelby (*Glos*)	9	13	3	168	60*	0	1	16.80	5
202	S. D. Snell (*Glos*)	9	14	1	215	85	0	1	16.53	28/2
203	†R. J. Woodman (*Glos*)	6	10	1	144	32	0	0	16.00	3
204	†J. M. Anderson (*Lancs & England*)	9	11	3	123	29	0	0	15.37	4
205	N. S. Tahir (*Warwicks*)	12	14	4	152	24	0	0	15.20	2
206	G. J-P. Kruger (*Glam*)	13	13	7	91	28*	0	0	15.16	2
207	M. J. Hoggard (*Yorks*)	16	17	4	195	56*	0	1	15.00	5
208	C. D. Whelan (*Worcs*)	12	17	3	205	47	0	0	14.64	2
209	A. Nel (*Surrey*)	9	10	2	117	32	0	0	14.62	3
210	C. J. C. Wright (*Essex*)	14	16	7	130	24*	0	0	14.44	2
211	Imran Arif (*Worcs*)	9	13	7	81	35	0	0	13.50	4
212	D. A. Cosker (*Glam*)	8	11	3	107	46*	0	0	13.37	5
213	†J. A. Tomlinson (*Hants*)	12	14	7	92	23	0	0	13.14	3
214	B. J. M. Scott (*Middx*)	8	14	1	167	44	0	0	12.84	18/2
215	M. S. Mason (*Worcs*)	14	23	6	207	28	0	0	12.17	6
216	Danish Kaneria (*Essex*)	11	15	2	158	37	0	0	12.15	5
217	†M. S. Panesar (*Northants & England*)	15	22	6	193	38	0	0	12.06	0
218	S. P. Kirby (*Glos*)	16	22	8	157	27	0	0	11.21	2
219	G. J. Batty (*Worcs*)	11	16	0	175	46	0	0	10.93	9
220	H. F. Gurney (*Leics*)	10	11	6	54	24*	0	0	10.80	2
221	J. W. Dernbach (*Surrey*)	14	19	6	138	19	0	0	10.61	1
222	D. H. Wigley (*Northants*)	12	15	8	74	16	0	0	10.57	5
223	M. E. Claydon (*Durham*)	12	12	1	110	38	0	0	10.00	3
224	A. J. Harris (*Leics*)	16	19	3	143	22*	0	0	8.93	0
225	†J. D. Lewry (*Sussex*)	6	10	4	51	25	0	0	8.50	0
226	S. J. Harmison (*Durham, England Lions & England*)	17	15	5	79	25*	0	0	7.90	2

		M	I	NO	R	HS	100s	50s	Avge	Ct/St
227	†V. Banerjee (*Glos*)	7	12	3	71	16	0	0	7.88	2
228	S. I. Mahmood (*MCC, Lancs & England Lions*)	14	14	1	100	30*	0	0	7.69	6
229	C. D. Collymore (*Sussex*)	14	17	5	89	23	0	0	7.41	2
230	†G. Keedy (*Lancs*)	17	16	7	63	18	0	0	7.00	0
231	G. Onions (*Durham, England & England Lions*)	14	14	6	52	17*	0	0	6.50	5
232	O. J. Newby (*Lancs*)	13	11	1	64	15	0	0	6.40	2
233	S. T. Finn (*Middx*)	14	22	4	107	24*	0	0	5.94	4
234	C. E. Shreck (*Notts*)	11	12	7	28	12*	0	0	5.60	1
235	†D. A. Griffiths (*Hants*)	10	13	4	45	20*	0	0	5.00	0
236	†C. M. Willoughby (*Somerset*)	16	13	4	40	23	0	0	4.44	4
237	†W. B. Rankin (*Warwicks*)	13	13	4	19	7	0	0	2.11	2

BOWLING

(Qualification: 10 wickets in 5 innings)

		Style	O	M	R	W	BB	5Wi/i	Avge
1	Azhar Mahmood (*Kent*)	RFM	130.3	38	382	21	5-39	1	18.19
2	G. Onions (*Durham, England & England Lions*)	RFM	428.4	88	1,377	69	7-38	5	19.95
3	J. Lewis (*Glos*)	RFM	426.3	110	1,146	57	5-73	1	20.10
4	D. S. Lucas (*Northants*)	LFM	414.3	86	1,299	60	7-24	3	21.65
5	N. S. Tahir (*Warwicks*)	RFM	274.2	62	843	38	5-67	1	22.18
6	S. P. Kirby (*Glos*)	RFM	472.4	107	1,420	64	5-44	1	22.18
7	H. J. H. Marshall (*Glos*)	RM	104	24	360	16	4-24	0	22.50
8	I. D. Blackwell (*Durham*)	SLA	456.5	135	1,064	47	7-85	3	22.63
9	J. M. Anderson (*Lancs & England*)	RFM	290.3	72	886	39	6-56	5	22.71
10	A. J. Hall (*Northants*)	RFM	310.2	76	911	40	5-29	1	22.77
11	M. Kartik (*Middx*)	SLA	317.1	103	755	33	5-65	1	22.87
12	L. E. Plunkett (*Durham & Eng. Lions*)	RFM	409.3	75	1,401	60	6-63	3	23.35
13	Danish Kaneria (*Essex*)	LBG	597.5	124	1,777	75	8-116	6	23.69
14	S. J. Harmison (*Durham, England Lions & England*)	RF	513.2	131	1,503	63	6-20	4	23.85
15	R. J. Sidebottom (*Notts*)	LFM	260.2	70	760	31	5-59	2	24.51
16	J. J. van der Wath (*Northants*)	RFM	364.3	75	1,237	50	5-71	1	24.74
17	C. D. Thorp (*Durham*)	RFM	320.5	94	846	34	5-49	2	24.88
18	G. Chapple (*Lancs*)	RFM	335.4	87	884	35	6-19	2	25.25
19	T. J. Murtagh (*Middx*)	RFM	443	81	1,521	60	7-82	3	25.35
20	I. E. O'Brien (*Leics*)	RFM	181.2	38	547	21	6-39	2	26.04
21	S. C. J. Broad (*Notts & England*)	RFM	268.3	47	887	34	6-91	3	26.08
22	M. J. Saggers (*Kent*)	RFM	108.5	34	264	10	3-45	0	26.40
23	J. C. Tredwell (*Kent*)	OB	681.5	178	1,838	69	8-66	4	26.63
24	D. D. Masters (*Essex*)	RFM	557.2	184	1,212	45	5-65	1	26.93
25	T. D. Groenewald (*Derbys*)	RFM	273.2	49	921	34	6-50	2	27.08
26	S. D. Udal (*Middx*)	OB	368.5	67	1,007	37	6-36	2	27.21
27	P. P. Chawla (*Sussex*)	LBG	341.5	72	981	36	6-52	4	27.25
28	B. W. Hilfenhaus (*Australians*)	RFM	180.5	40	604	22	4-60	0	27.45
29	M. S. Mason (*Worcs*)	RFM	418.4	125	1,186	43	7-39	2	27.58
30	L. J. Fletcher (*Notts*)	RFM	245.3	62	800	29	4-38	0	27.58
31	J. Allenby (*Leics & Glam*)	RM	190.4	52	471	17	3-70	0	27.70
32	A. Nel (*Surrey*)	RFM	260.4	69	754	27	6-36	1	27.92
33	I. D. Hunter (*Derbys*)	RFM	181.4	33	593	21	5-46	2	28.23
34	D. G. Cork (*Hants*)	RFM	287	69	767	27	5-14	1	28.40
35	A. R. Adams (*Notts*)	RFM	409	103	1,224	43	4-39	0	28.46
36	J. E. C. Franklin (*Glos*)	LFM	292.4	62	904	31	5-30	1	29.16
37	K. W. Hogg (*Lancs*)	RFM	338.2	91	1,000	34	4-22	0	29.41
38	P. M. Siddle (*Australians*)	RFM	175.1	25	680	23	5-21	1	29.56
39	D. A. Cosker (*Glam*)	SLA	312.1	83	769	26	6-91	2	29.57

		Style	O	M	R	W	BB	5W/i	Avge
40	M. Davies (*Durham*)	RFM	217.1	60	562	19	4-87	0	29.57
41	N. Boje (*Northants*)	SLA	311	81	891	30	4-59	0	29.70
42	R. D. B. Croft (*Glam*)	OB	737	154	1,727	58	5-65	1	29.77
43	C. M. Willoughby (*Somerset*)	LFM	555.4	161	1,621	54	5-56	3	30.01
44	S. R. Clark (*Australians*)	RFM	94	19	301	10	3-18	0	30.10
45	G. P. Swann (*Notts & England*)	OB	269.2	55	824	27	4-38	0	30.51
46	S. T. Finn (*Middx*)	RFM	418.3	64	1,624	53	5-57	1	30.64
47	S. J. Cook (*Kent*)	RFM	374.1	88	1,047	34	5-22	3	30.79
48	A. Flintoff (*Lancs & England*)	RF	193.2	39	586	19	5-92	1	30.84
49	A. J. Shantry (*Glam*)	LFM	278	47	898	29	5-62	1	30.96
50	I. D. Saxelby (*Glos*)	RFM	185.2	30	620	20	3-31	0	31.00
51	M. E. Claydon (*Durham*)	RFM	234	51	777	25	4-90	0	31.08
52	R. H. Joseph (*Kent*)	RF	97.2	9	373	12	6-55	1	31.08
53	W. D. Parnell (*Kent*)	LFM	166.3	35	529	17	4-78	0	31.11
54	P. T. Collins (*Surrey*)	LFM	137.2	25	504	16	5-75	1	31.50
55	A. J. Ireland (*Glos*)	RFM	167	34	664	21	6-31	1	31.61
56	D. J. Wainwright (*Yorks*)	SLA	250.2	50	824	26	5-134	1	31.69
57	V. Banerjee (*Glos*)	SLA	200.3	38	667	21	4-58	0	31.76
58	A. Khan (*Kent*)	RF	339.1	65	1,146	36	5-113	1	31.83
59	R. McLaren (*Kent*)	RFM	164.5	37	608	19	4-51	0	32.00
60	J. D. Middlebrook (*Essex*)	OB	138	29	449	14	3-80	0	32.07
61	S. Sreesanth (*Warwicks*)	RFM	109.3	21	418	13	5-93	1	32.15
62	M. J. Hoggard (*Yorks*)	RFM	479.1	107	1,486	46	5-56	2	32.30
63	D. A. Griffiths (*Hants*)	RFM	283.2	52	1,039	32	4-48	0	32.46
64	D. R. Smith (*Sussex*)	RM	301	84	814	25	4-58	0	32.56
65	Imran Tahir (*Hants*)	LBG	487.4	81	1,711	52	7-140	4	32.90
66	R. M. R. Brathwaite (*Cambridge UCCE/Univ.*)	RFM	142.4	31	428	13	5-54	1	32.92
67	J. W. M. Dalrymple (*Glam*)	OB	231.5	29	726	22	3-11	0	33.00
68	C. D. Collymore (*Sussex*)	RFM	396	102	1,104	33	4-66	0	33.45
69	C. R. Woakes (*MCC, Warwicks & England Lions*)	RFM	489.5	105	1,576	47	6-43	2	33.53
70	R. A. Jones (*Worcs*)	RFM	174	25	745	22	6-100	1	33.86
71	S. I. Mahmood (*MCC, Lancs & England Lions*)	RFM	379.3	67	1,394	41	6-30	2	34.00
72	G. Keedy (*Lancs*)	SLA	543.5	107	1,540	45	6-50	3	34.22
73	A. Shahzad (*Yorks*)	RFM	422.5	86	1,405	41	4-72	0	34.26
74	G. M. Smith (*Derbys*)	RM/OB	330.2	64	1,098	32	5-65	1	34.31
75	R. S. C. Martin-Jenkins (*Sussex*)	RFM	277.4	74	793	23	5-43	1	34.47
76	W. B. Rankin (*Warwicks*)	RFM	340.1	54	1,279	37	5-85	1	34.56
77	G. R. Napier (*Essex*)	RFM	271.3	55	1,005	29	4-32	0	34.65
78	L. J. Wright (*Sussex & Eng. Lions*)	RFM	224.1	38	764	22	5-66	2	34.72
79	J. A. R. Harris (*Glam*)	RFM	439.2	86	1,498	43	4-69	0	34.83
80	M. A. Chambers (*Essex*)	RFM	141.4	19	526	15	4-62	0	35.06
81	M. A. Ealham (*Notts*)	RM	387	117	983	28	5-31	1	35.10
82	S. J. Benn (*West Indians*)	SLA	120	23	353	10	4-31	0	35.30
83	P. S. Jones (*Kent & Derbys*)	RFM	398	84	1,210	34	5-35	1	35.58
84	O. J. Newby (*Lancs*)	RFM	297.1	43	1,107	31	4-21	0	35.70
85	A. U. Rashid (*MCC, Yorks & England Lions*)	LBG	306.4	41	1,118	31	5-41	2	36.06
86	D. A. Stiff (*Somerset*)	RFM	268.2	33	1,120	31	5-91	1	36.12
87	T. T. Bresnan (*MCC, Yorks, England & England Lions*)	RFM	443.4	111	1,168	32	4-116	0	36.50
88	G. J. Kruis (*Yorks*)	RFM	252.1	56	816	22	3-51	0	37.09
89	A. C. Thomas (*Somerset*)	RFM	401.1	77	1,317	35	5-53	1	37.62
90	G. G. Wagg (*Derbys*)	LFM/SLA	521.3	85	1,773	47	6-35	3	37.72
91	B. J. Phillips (*Somerset*)	RFM	158.1	37	456	12	4-46	0	38.00
92	D. H. Wigley (*Northants*)	RFM	314.1	60	1,230	32	6-72	2	38.43
93	C. J. C. Wright (*Essex*)	RFM	437.1	67	1,538	40	4-43	0	38.45

	Style	O	M	R	W	BB	5W/i	Avge
94 {M. G. Johnson (*Australians*)	LF	215.2	19	924	24	5-69	1	38.50
{D. S. Harrison (*Glam*)	RFM	207.1	32	770	20	4-60	0	38.50
96 G. K. Berg (*Middx*)	RFM	249.1	46	886	23	5-55	2	38.52
97 J. W. Dernbach (*Surrey*).........	RFM	395.2	67	1,436	37	6-47	2	38.81
98 G. J-P. Kruger (*Glam*)	RFM	353.4	59	1,283	33	6-93	1	38.87
99 P. J. Franks (*Notts*).............	RFM	141	37	428	11	3-52	0	38.90
100 J. A. Tomlinson (*Hants*)........	LFM	318.1	57	1,193	30	3-53	0	39.76
101 C. T. Tremlett (*Hants*)	RFM	173	34	564	14	4-49	0	40.28
102 J. L. Clare (*Derbys*)	RFM	119	27	407	10	3-64	0	40.70
103 T. Lungley (*Derbys & Lancs*)	RFM	132.5	16	531	13	3-56	0	40.84
104 A. G. Botha (*Warwicks*).........	SLA	316.3	61	941	23	5-51	1	40.91
105 N. M. Hauritz (*Australians*)	OB	154.4	26	492	12	3-63	0	41.00
106 A. J. Harris (*Leics*)	RFM	395.1	79	1,439	35	5-26	1	41.11
107 Naved-ul-Hasan (*Yorks*)........	RFM	124	23	412	10	3-102	0	41.20
108 T. C. Smith (*Lancs*)	RFM	199.4	45	623	15	6-46	1	41.53
109 L. A. Dawson (*Hants*)	SLA	97	11	421	10	2-3	0	42.10
110 M. Hayward (*Derbys*)	RFM	123.2	19	472	11	4-99	0	42.90
111 G. M. Andrew (*Worcs*).........	RFM	257.3	38	991	23	5-117	1	43.08
112 Murtaza Hussain (*Surrey*)	OB	271	47	825	19	4-70	0	43.42
113 O. P. Rayner (*Sussex*)...........	OB	294.3	48	870	20	4-186	0	43.50
114 N. M. Carter (*Warwicks*)	LFM	190	30	704	16	5-37	1	44.00
115 {R. N. ten Doeschate (*Essex*).....	RM	246	32	970	22	5-62	1	44.09
{Kabir Ali (*MCC & Worcs*).......	RFM	117	12	485	11	6-68	1	44.09
117 W. A. White (*Leics*)...........	RM	197.3	23	852	19	3-91	0	44.84
118 A. A. Noffke (*Worcs*)..........	RFM	158	38	452	10	4-92	0	45.20
119 C. W. Henderson (*Leics*)	SLA	394.5	70	1,044	23	6-152	1	45.39
120 A. V. Suppiah (*Somerset*)........	SLA	212.5	47	682	15	3-58	0	45.46
121 P. D. Trego (*Somerset*).........	RFM	256.5	57	889	19	3-53	0	46.78
122 S. R. Patel (*Notts & England Lions*)	SLA	484.2	86	1,558	33	6-84	2	47.21
123 A. D. Mascarenhas (*Hants*)	RM	241	70	618	13	2-46	0	47.53
124 C. D. Whelan (*Worcs*)	RFM	232	24	1,067	22	5-95	1	48.50
125 Azeem Rafiq (*Yorks*)	OB	124.3	9	487	10	3-34	0	48.70
126 S. C. Meaker (*Surrey*)	RFM	110.4	11	498	10	3-114	0	49.80
127 R. K. J. Dawson (*Glos*)	OB	158.4	13	610	12	4-76	0	50.83
128 Yasir Arafat (*Sussex*)	RFM	151	24	621	12	3-83	0	51.75
129 H. F. Gurney (*Leics*)...........	LFM	228.5	42	829	16	5-82	1	51.81
130 A. R. Caddick (*Somerset*)	RFM	131.1	24	525	10	3-53	0	52.50
131 Imran Arif (*Worcs*)............	RFM	184.5	21	899	17	5-93	1	52.88
132 J. D. Lewry (*Sussex*)..........	RFM	159.1	39	535	10	2-53	0	53.50
133 M. S. Panesar (*Northants & Eng.*).	SLA	454.5	97	1,195	22	3-10	0	54.31
134 A. Richardson (*Middx*)..........	RFM	222.2	53	618	11	3-52	0	56.18
135 R. Clarke (*Warwicks*)..........	RFM	164.1	23	640	11	2-15	0	58.18
136 C. J. Jordan (*Surrey*)	RFM	208.2	36	764	13	4-84	0	58.76
137 {C. E. Shreck (*Notts*)	RFM	363.2	77	1,281	21	4-63	0	61.00
{S. M. Ervine (*Hants*)	RFM	233.3	55	793	13	3-22	0	61.00
139 C. P. Schofield (*Surrey*)	LBG	363.5	35	1,357	22	5-40	1	61.68
140 G. J. Batty (*Worcs*)..............	OB	227.1	37	724	10	2-71	0	72.40
141 D. J. Pattinson (*Notts*)	RFM	219.5	40	872	10	4-53	0	87.20

The following bowler took ten wickets in a single match:

S. A. Piolet (*Warwicks*)	RM	27	13	43	10	6-17	1	4.30

BOWLING STYLES

LBG	Leg-breaks and googlies (5)	**RF**	Right-arm fast (4)
LF	Left-arm fast (1)	**RFM**	Right-arm fast medium (85)
LFM	Left-arm fast medium (12)	**RM**	Right-arm medium (9)
OB	Off-breaks (13)	**SLA**	Slow left-arm (15)

Note: The total comes to 144 because G. G. Wagg and G. M. Smith have two styles of bowling.

INDIVIDUAL SCORES OF 100 AND OVER

There were **292** three-figure innings in 171 first-class matches in 2009, 54 more than in 2008 when 172 first-class matches were played. Of these, 19 were double-hundreds, compared with ten in 2008. The list includes 253 hundreds hit in the County Championship, compared with 189 in 2008.

M. E. Trescothick (8)

105	Somerset v Durham, Taunton
109	Somerset v Sussex, Hove
146	Somerset v Yorks, Taunton
142	Somerset v Worcs, Worcester
108 107* }	Somerset v Warwicks, Birmingham
118	Somerset v Hants, Southampton
102	Somerset v Lancs, Taunton

M. van Jaarsveld (7)

107	Kent v Northants, Canterbury
102	Kent v Essex, Chelmsford
182	Kent v Glam, Canterbury
110	Kent v Surrey, The Oval
100*	Kent v Northants, Northampton
101*	Kent v Derbys, Derby
146	Kent v Leics, Canterbury

M. J. Di Venuto (6)

143	Durham v Yorks, Chester-le-Street
103	Durham v Sussex, Hove
100*	Durham v Worcs, Chester-le-Street
254*	Durham v Sussex, Chester-le-Street
219	Durham v Notts, Chester-le-Street
113	Durham v Worcs, Worcester

C. J. L. Rogers (6)

104	Derbys v Glos, Chesterfield
107	Derbys v Kent, Canterbury
163	Derbys v Leics, Leicester
208	Derbys v Kent, Derby
112*	Derbys v Middx, Uxbridge
222	Derbys v Essex, Derby

D. M. Benkenstein (5)

181	Durham v Somerset, Taunton
136	Durham v Sussex, Hove
105	Durham v Notts, Nottingham
105	Durham v Notts, Chester-le-Street
109	Durham v Worcs, Worcester

G. O. Jones (5)

103	Kent v Northants, Canterbury
133	Kent v Glam, Canterbury
100	Kent v Derbys, Canterbury
156	Kent v Surrey, Canterbury
108	Kent v Derbys, Derby

M. R. Ramprakash (5)

133	Surrey v Middx, The Oval
138	Surrey v Glam, Cardiff
136	Surrey v Middx, Lord's
274	Surrey v Leics, The Oval
134*	Surrey v Derbys, Whitgift School

I. J. L. Trott (5)

161*	Warwicks v Yorks, Birmingham
166	Warwicks v Sussex, Birmingham
184*	Warwicks v Hants, Southampton
121	Warwicks v Notts, Nottingham
119	England v Australia, The Oval

I. R. Bell (4)

172	Warwicks v Somerset, Taunton
106	Warwicks v Lancs, Birmingham
126	Warwicks v Notts, Nottingham
104	Warwicks v Sussex, Hove

R. S. Bopara (4)

143	England v West Indies, Lord's
108	England v West Indies, Chester-le-Street
104	England XI v Warwicks, Birmingham
201	Essex v Surrey, Colchester

M. A. Carberry (4)

123	Hants v Somerset, Taunton
112	Hants v Sussex, Arundel
204	Hants v Warwicks, Southampton
136*	Hants v Lancs, Southampton

A. P. R. Gidman (4)

159	Glos v Leics, Bristol
135	Glos v Derbys, Chesterfield
128	Glos v Glam, Bristol
176	Glos v Surrey, Bristol

R. W. T. Key (4)

123	Kent v Surrey, The Oval
270*	Kent v Glam, Cardiff
110	Kent v Derbys, Canterbury
141*	Kent v Derbys, Derby

C. Kieswetter (4)

150*	Somerset v Warwicks, Taunton
106	Somerset v Durham, Taunton
135*	Somerset v Sussex, Taunton
153	Somerset v Lancs, Taunton

V. V. S. Laxman (4)
109	Lancs v Yorks, Manchester
135	Lancs v Hants, Southampton
113*	Lancs v Somerset, Taunton
113	Lancs v Warwicks, Manchester

C. D. Nash (4)
134	Sussex v Somerset, Hove
100*	Sussex v Worcs, Hove
157	Sussex v Somerset, Taunton
135	Sussex v Notts, Nottingham

C. M. W. Read (4)
125	Notts v Worcs, Nottingham
116*	Notts v Hants, Southampton
110	Notts v Warwicks, Nottingham
119*	Notts v Hants, Nottingham

J. A. Rudolph (4)
198	Yorks v Worcs, Leeds
191	Yorks v Somerset, Taunton
127	Yorks v Lancs, Manchester
149	Yorks v Notts, Nottingham

D. I. Stevens (4)
193*	Kent v Loughborough UCCE, Canterbury
136*	Kent v Essex, Chelmsford
112	Kent v Surrey, Canterbury
208	Kent v Middx, Uxbridge

J. H. K. Adams (3)
112	Hants v Notts, Southampton
107	Hants v Lancs, Southampton
147	Hants v Somerset, Southampton

U. Afzaal (3)
204*	Surrey v Northants, Northampton
116	Surrey v Essex, Guildford
170	Surrey v Glam, The Oval

T. R. Ambrose (3)
153	Warwicks v Hants, Birmingham
117	England Lions v West Indians, Derby
113	Warwicks v Yorks, Scarborough

S. Chanderpaul (3)
117*	Durham v Somerset, Chester-le-Street
109*	Durham v Notts, Chester-le-Street
201*	Durham v Worcs, Worcester

M. J. Cosgrove (3)
120	Glam v Middx, Lord's
102*	Glam v Northants, Cardiff
175	Glam v Surrey, The Oval

J. W. M. Dalrymple (3)
112*	Glam v Middx, Lord's
102	Glam v Derbys, Cardiff
128	Glam v Derbys, Derby

J. L. Denly (3)
116*	Kent v Leics, Leicester
123	Kent v Essex, Tunbridge Wells
123	Kent v Surrey, The Oval

S. M. Ervine (3)
109	Hants v Sussex, Southampton
114	Hants v Lancs, Southampton
104	Hants v Notts, Nottingham

J. E. C. Franklin (3)
109	Glos v Derbys, Cheltenham
100	Glos v Essex, Southend
104*	Glos v Kent, Bristol

P. J. Hughes (3)
118	Middx v Glam, Lord's
139	Middx v Leics, Southgate
195	Middx v Surrey, The Oval

E. C. Joyce (3)
100*	Sussex v Yorks, Leeds
183	Sussex v Notts, Horsham
107	Sussex v Warwicks, Hove

W. L. Madsen (3)
170*	Derbys v Glos, Cheltenham
108*	Derbys v Surrey, Whitgift School
167	Derbys v Middx, Uxbridge

M. J. North (3)
191*	Australians v England Lions, Worcester
125*	Australia v England, Cardiff
110	Australia v England, Leeds

S. D. Peters (3)
107	Northants v Kent, Canterbury
175	Northants v Derbys, Northampton
163	Northants v Glam, Northampton

G. P. Rees (3)
116*	Glam v Northants, Cardiff
122	Glam v Essex, Cardiff
154	Glam v Surrey, The Oval

A. V. Suppiah (3)
131	Somerset v Yorks, Taunton
151	Somerset v Notts, Taunton
133	Somerset v Sussex, Taunton

J. W. A. Taylor (3)
122*	Leics v Middx, Southgate
207*	Leics v Surrey, The Oval
112*	Leics v Essex, Chelmsford

M. A. Wagh (3)
147	Notts v Warwicks, Birmingham
131	Notts v Lancs, Nottingham
136*	Notts v Hants, Nottingham

L. J. Wright (3)

106	Sussex v Cambridge UCCE, Cambridge
104	Sussex v Hants, Arundel
118*	Sussex v Durham, Chester-le-Street

S. J. Adshead (2)

156*	Glos v Essex, Southend
114	Glos v Kent, Bristol

M. M. Ali (2)

153	Worcs v Yorks, Leeds
124	Worcs v Sussex, Worcester

H. M. Amla (2)

181	Essex v Glam, Chelmsford
118	Essex v Leics, Leicester

J. N. Batty (2)

110	Surrey v Northants, The Oval
120	Surrey v Glam, The Oval

C. C. Benham (2)

111	Hants v Loughborough UCCE, Southampton
100	Hants v Durham, Southampton

I. D. Blackwell (2)

102*	Durham v MCC, Lord's
158	Durham v Warwicks, Birmingham

M. J. Brown (2)

101	Surrey v Leics, Leicester
120	Surrey v Derbys, Whitgift School

M. J. Chilton (2)

114	Lancs v Durham UCCE, Durham
111*	Lancs v Yorks, Leeds

M. J. Clarke (2)

136	Australia v England, Lord's
103*	Australia v England, Birmingham

N. R. D. Compton (2)

100*	Middx v Surrey, Lord's
178	Middx v Derbys, Uxbridge

A. N. Cook (2)

160	England v West Indies, Chester-le-Street
124	England XI v Warwicks, Birmingham

S. M. Davies (2)

126	Worcs v Notts, Nottingham
112	Worcs v Yorks, Worcester

N. J. Dexter (2)

146 }	Middx v Kent, Uxbridge
118 }	

H. H. Dippenaar (2)

143	Leics v Surrey, Leicester
115*	Leics v Essex, Chelmsford

A. W. Gale (2)

101	Yorks v Worcs, Worcester
121	Yorks v Lancs, Manchester

A. J. Hall (2)

124*	Northants v Leics, Leicester
159	Northants v Leics, Northampton

R. J. Hamilton-Brown (2)

106*	Sussex v Cambridge UCCE, Cambridge
171*	Sussex v Yorks, Hove

J. C. Hildreth (2)

303*	Somerset v Warwicks, Taunton
155	Somerset v Hants, Taunton

W. W. Hinds (2)

119*	Derbys v Glam, Derby
148	Derbys v Northants, Northampton

C. D. Hopkinson (2)

119	Sussex v Warwicks, Birmingham
139	Sussex v Somerset, Taunton

P. J. Horton (2)

105	Lancs v Durham UCCE, Durham
173	Lancs v Somerset, Taunton

D. J. Hussey (2)

126	Notts v Lancs, Nottingham
189	Notts v Yorks, Scarborough

M. E. K. Hussey (2)

150	Australians v England Lions, Worcester
121	Australia v England, The Oval

J. M. Kemp (2)

183	Kent v Surrey, The Oval
138*	Kent v Middx, Uxbridge

J. L. Langer (2)

122*	Somerset v Durham, Taunton
107	Somerset v Worcs, Worcester

M. B. Loye (2)

146	Lancs v Yorks, Manchester
151*	Lancs v Somerset, Taunton

M. J. Lumb (2)

172	Hants v Loughborough UCCE, Southampton
219	Hants v Notts, Nottingham

A. McGrath (2)

120	Yorks v Worcs, Leeds
211	Yorks v Warwicks, Birmingham

D. K. H. Mitchell (2)
140*   Worcs v Oxford UCCE, Oxford
298   Worcs v Somerset, Taunton

S. C. Moore (2)
120   England Lions v Australians, Worcester
107   Worcs v Lancs, Manchester

G. T. Park (2)
178*   Derbys v Kent, Derby
103*   Derbys v Essex, Derby

M. J. Powell (2)
108   Glam v Derbys, Cardiff
102   Glam v Essex, Chelmsford

A. U. Rashid (2)
117*   Yorks v Hants, Basingstoke
157*   Yorks v Lancs, Leeds

J. J. Sayers (2)
173   Yorks v Warwicks, Birmingham
152   Yorks v Somerset, Taunton

O. A. Shah (2)
159   Middx v Surrey, Lord's
129*   Middx v Derbys, Derby

W. R. Smith (2)
101   Durham v Sussex, Chester-le-Street
150   Durham v Hants, Southampton

A. J. Strauss (2)
150   Middx v Leics, Southgate
161   England v Australia, Lord's

R. N. ten Doeschate (2)
159*   Essex v Surrey, Guildford
108*   Essex v Derbys, Derby

J. O. Troughton (2)
223   Warwicks v Hants, Birmingham
111   Warwicks v Durham, Chester-le-Street

M. J. Walker (2)
116*   Essex v Leics, Leicester
150   Essex v Middx, Lord's

M. A. Wallace (2)
128   Glam v Middx, Lord's
139   Glam v Surrey, The Oval

S. J. Walters (2)
142   Surrey v Essex, Guildford
188   Surrey v Leics, The Oval

M. H. Yardy (2)
110   Sussex v Yorks, Leeds
152   Sussex v Worcs, Worcester

The following each played one three-figure innings:

H. D. Ackerman, 180, Leics v Surrey, Leicester; J. Allenby, 137, Glam v Surrey, The Oval; A. S. Ansari, 132, Cambridge U. v Oxford U., Cambridge; A. Ashok, 112, Cambridge U. v Oxford U., Cambridge; Azeem Rafiq, 100, Yorks v Worcs, Worcester.

P. M. Borrington, 105, Loughborough UCCE v Hants, Southampton; A. D. Brown, 148, Notts v Hants, Southampton.

P. P. Chawla, 102*, Sussex v Worcs, Worcester; R. Clarke, 112, Warwicks v Hants, Birmingham; K. J. Coetzer, 107, Durham v Notts, Chester-le-Street; R. D. B. Croft, 121, Glam v Leics, Colwyn Bay.

Z. de Bruyn, 106, Somerset v Worcs, Taunton; P. G. Dixey, 103, Durham UCCE v Lancs, Durham; J. du Toit, 100*, Leics v Surrey, The Oval.

J. S. Foster, 103*, Essex v Leics, Chelmsford; T. Frost, 105, Warwicks v Durham UCCE, Durham.

J. E. R. Gallian, 125, Essex v Cambridge UCCE, Cambridge; J. S. Gatting, 152, Sussex v Cambridge UCCE, Cambridge; M. W. Goodwin, 344*, Sussex v Somerset, Taunton.

B. J. Haddin, 121, Australia v England, Cardiff; A. J. Hodd, 101, Sussex v Durham, Hove.

W. I. Jefferson, 133, Notts v Oxford UCCE, Oxford.

S. M. Katich, 122, Australia v England, Cardiff.

H. J. H. Marshall, 158, Glos v Derbys, Chesterfield; A. D. Mascarenhas, 108, Hants v Lancs, Liverpool; J. K. Maunders, 150, Essex v Leics, Chelmsford; E. J. G. Morgan, 114*, Middx v Leics, Southgate; G. J. Muchall, 106*, Durham v Sussex, Hove.

J. H. K. Naik, 109*, Leics v Derbys, Leicester; S. A. Newman, 124, Surrey v Derbys, Derby; P. A. Nixon, 173*, Leics v Kent, Canterbury; S. A. Northeast, 128*, Kent v Glos, Bristol.

N. J. O'Brien, 128, Northants v Surrey, The Oval.

J. S. Patel, 120, Warwicks v Yorks, Birmingham; M. L. Pettini, 101*, Essex v Kent, Tunbridge Wells; R. T. Ponting, 150, Australia v England, Cardiff; N. Pothas, 122*, Hants v Warwicks, Birmingham; A. G. Prince, 135*, Lancs v Notts, Manchester; M. J. Prior, 140, Sussex v Hants, Southampton.

S. D. Robson, 110, Middx v Essex, Lord's.

R. R. Sarwan, 100, West Indies v England, Chester-le-Street; C. P. Schofield, 144, Surrey v Essex, Colchester; A. J. Shantry, 100, Glam v Leics, Colwyn Bay; L. M. P. Simmons, 102*, West Indians v Leics, Leicester; G. M. Smith, 126, Derbys v Glos, Cheltenham; T. C. Smith, 104*, Lancs v Durham UCCE, Durham; V. S. Solanki, 206*, Worcs v Yorks, Leeds; M. N. W. Spriegel, 100, Surrey v Glam, The Oval.

C. G. Taylor, 111, Glos v Surrey, Bristol; P. D. Trego, 103*, Somerset v Yorks, Taunton.

A. C. Voges, 139, Notts v Sussex, Horsham.

D. J. Wainwright, 102*, Yorks v Warwicks, Scarborough; A. G. Wakely, 113*, Northants v Glam, Cardiff; M. H. Wessels, 109, Northants v Surrey, The Oval; T. Westley, 132, Essex v Derbys, Derby; I. J. Westwood, 133, Warwicks v Worcs, Birmingham; R. A. White, 193, Northants v Leics, Northampton; C. R. Woakes, 131*, Warwicks v Hants, Southampton.

FASTEST HUNDREDS BY BALLS...

Balls	Mins		
54	65	P. D. Trego	Somerset v Yorkshire, Taunton.
57	68	R. N. ten Doeschate............	Essex v Derbys, Derby.
78	104	R. Clarke	Warwicks v Hants, Birmingham.
82	93	P. P. Chawla	Sussex v Worcs, Worcester.
84	107	G. O. Jones	Kent v Surrey, Canterbury.
85	106	L. J. Wright	Sussex v Cambridge UCCE, Cambridge.
92	105	Azeem Rafiq	Yorks v Worcs, Worcester.
94	101	M. H. Wessels	Northants v Surrey, The Oval.
97	121	C. G. Taylor.................	Glos v Surrey, Bristol.
99	146	C. D. Nash...................	Sussex v Worcs, Hove.
100	123	M. E. Trescothick	Somerset v Warwicks, Birmingham.

The fastest hundreds in terms of minutes not in the above list were by R. J. Hamilton-Brown (121 minutes, 126 balls) for Sussex v Cambridge UCCE, Cambridge; M. A. Wallace (122 minutes, 105 balls) for Glam v Surrey, The Oval; and C. M. W. Read (126 minutes, 125 balls) for Notts v Hants, Southampton.

...AND THE SLOWEST

Balls	Mins		
291	294	W. R. Smith...................	Durham v Sussex, Chester-le-Street.
288	348	M. J. Brown...................	Surrey v Leics, Leicester.
271	314	J. N. Batty	Surrey v Northants, The Oval.
270	267	W. W. Hinds	Derbys v Glam, Derby.

TEN WICKETS IN A MATCH

There were **12** instances of bowlers taking ten or more wickets in a first-class match in 2009, two more than in 2008. All but one were in the County Championship.

J. M. Tredwell (2)
11-120, Kent v Glam, Canterbury; 10-100, Kent v Northants, Northampton.

Danish Kaneria (2)
12-203, Essex v Leics, Chelmsford; 10-219, Essex v Glam, Cardiff.

The following each took ten wickets in a match on one occasion:

J. M. Anderson, 11-109, Lancs v Sussex, Hove.
P. P. Chawla, 11-170, Sussex v Somerset, Hove; D. A. Cosker, 11-126, Glam v Essex, Cardiff.
D. S. Lucas, 12-73, Northants v Glos, Cheltenham.
S. I. Mahmood, 10-140, Lancs v Worcs, Worcester.
S. A. Piolet, 10-43, Warwicks v Durham UCCE, Durham; L. E. Plunkett, 11-119, Durham v Worcs, Chester-le-Street.
S. D. Udal, 10-95, Middx v Glam, Swansea.

ENGLAND v WEST INDIES, 2009

REVIEW BY TONY COZIER

Test matches (2): England 2, West Indies 0
One-day internationals (3): England 2, West Indies 0

West Indies had suffered such indignities in England since the turn of the century – a 4–0 whitewash in 2004, all-out totals of 54 and 61 in 2000, ten defeats in 13 Tests including a two-day thrashing – that it required the most compelling of incentives, money, to lure them back, out of turn, at the start of a season in which only the Ashes mattered.

While the impoverished West Indies Cricket Board grabbed the unexpected chance to make a quick buck (over $US2m to be precise) as a belated replacement for Zimbabwe, there was a host of cricketing reasons why the tour was ill-conceived.

It was not surprising that the outcome was yet another debacle. England won the First Test at Lord's by ten wickets in three days, the Second at Chester-le-Street by an innings and 83 runs, effectively in four days because of a washout. They were equally dominant in the two completed one-day internationals. Even before meeting the senior England side, the tourists suffered the humiliation of losing to the England Lions by ten wickets with a day to spare.

There were extenuating circumstances for which the West Indians were simply not prepared. Apart from a single day of Caribbean sunshine for the one-day international in Bristol, the weather was bitingly cold, especially at Riverside, Test cricket's northern-most venue. The management purchased 200 hand-warmers for the players, whose body language spoke loudly of a reluctance to be in such an unwelcoming environment. Meanwhile, after their struggles in the heat of India and the Caribbean, England relished the return to conditions in which they had been nurtured and now prospered. They found none of the fierce resistance that had clinched a 1–0 triumph and regained the Wisden Trophy for West Indies a couple of months earlier. It seemed a travesty that West Indies had to hand the Trophy back on the basis of just two hastily arranged Tests; their board president Julian Hunte seemed surprised that it was at stake, but the ECB insisted this had been agreed by WICB chief executive Donald Peters, who had since resigned.

West Indies were, in fact, the ECB's third choice to fill out the number of international matches required by its television contract. Once Zimbabwe, originally scheduled to tour on the ICC programme, were eliminated by the realities of international politics, Sri Lanka were invited but eventually declined when their main players were adamant they would not miss out on lucrative, pre-existing contracts in the simultaneous Indian Premier League.

Eager to accept the offer, the WICB failed to consult the West Indies Players' Association. Predictably aggrieved, it presented its misgivings and demands – principally, as with the Sri Lankans, concern for its IPL-contracted

Philip Brown

Losing their grip: a farrago of fumbles in the field cost West Indies dear during the Lord's Test. The culprits this time are Chris Gayle and Devon Smith.

members. The scheduling of the series in England "at a time of year when no other team has ever played in the history of over 100 years of international cricket" was another WIPA objection. England had staged Tests in mid-May for a decade, and West Indies themselves had played two in 2007, but no Test had ever started as early as May 6 – a date dictated by the need to fit the tour in before the World Twenty20 tournament in June. The IPL, on the other hand, was starting a week later than planned because security concerns had forced it to move to South Africa.

There was even the threat of another players' boycott before the board agreed the squad should share $US1.5m, a five-fold increase on their usual fee, and compensated IPL players (eventually only captain Chris Gayle and Fidel Edwards) for their loss of earnings.

Gayle typified the general attitude of his team. In a compromise with the WICB, he was allowed to stay in South Africa with the Kolkata Knight Riders until May 1, five days before the First Test. Then he wrung a further concession from the board and remained for one more match before flying to London on May 3, giving himself two days to prepare.

Any lingering doubt over where his priorities lay was erased a week later when he said in an interview with *The Guardian* – ironically, arranged to promote Sky Sports' coverage of the series – that he preferred Twenty20 to the traditional game, that he "wouldn't be so sad" if Test cricket died, and that he was so drained by the captaincy he would be "giving it up shortly". Although he later claimed he was misinterpreted and misquoted, his widely reported, and criticised, words had the understandable effect of further alienating the public. Lord's had been seldom more than half full for the First Test and, with the Saturday and Sunday lost because of the premature finish, the ECB estimated a shortfall of £300,000 in gate receipts. Durham, which had bid £500,000 to stage the Second Test, were similarly hard hit; no more than 3,000 turned up on the first and fourth days.

The all-round talent and ebullience of Dwayne Bravo might have infused the team with necessary fervour. An operation on his left ankle had kept him out of action since August 2008, but he returned in March for the limited-overs matches against England in the Caribbean, seemingly with no ill effects. Mysteriously, the WICB's medical staff ruled him still unready for the rigours of five-day Test cricket, so he joined the team in England only for the one-day series – but in the interim he played 11 games for the Mumbai Indians in the IPL. It was one more odd piece in the puzzle.

Yet West Indies began promisingly. When Fidel Edwards, fast and always threatening with late swing, claimed Matt Prior as his fourth victim just after tea on the opening day at Lord's, England were 193 for five with only the five bowlers remaining to partner Ravi Bopara, the new No. 3.

What followed in the final session effectively settled the match and the series. Six catches were dropped, three off Edwards. Bopara's life, on 76, was the costliest. West Indian heads drooped lower and cold hands were pressed deeper into pockets and hand-warmers with every error. Bopara followed his century in Barbados ten weeks earlier with another (he completed a hat-trick of hundreds at Chester-le-Street the following week), temporarily settling the one-down spot as his own. Stuart Broad and Graeme Swann joined the fun, and West Indies were a dispirited and beaten team once England reached as many as 377.

In response, the tourists were rolled over for 152, the last eight wickets managing just 53, and made to follow on. Gayle and Ramnaresh Sarwan, the run-pirate of the Caribbean, were out twice on the second day; Shivnarine Chanderpaul, who could not be dislodged in either innings as he compiled 128 and 97 in the Lord's Test five years earlier, managed just six balls and four runs in all, undone each time by close catches off Swann's off-spin. Only an enterprising second-innings partnership of 143 for the sixth wicket between left-hander Brendan Nash and wicketkeeper Denesh Ramdin avoided the total embarrassment of an innings defeat, if not the three-day loss.

Three of England's wicket-takers, Broad, Swann and James Anderson, were familiar; the other was not. "I never even taste Onions," Gayle quipped at the pre-match media conference. He pre-empted eager sub-editors who indulged themselves in predictable puns two days later when Graham Onions's swing earned him five wickets in the first innings, and seven in the match, on Test debut.

The West Indian mood became distinctly bleaker the following week in the gloomy, arctic weather of the North-East. Alastair Cook joined Bopara, his Essex colleague in the run-feast, helping himself to 160, the highest of his nine Test hundreds, as their stand of 213 set up a total of 569 for six declared. England had amassed similarly imposing positions in three successive Tests in the Caribbean but, on lifeless pitches, their bowlers could not capitalise. This was different.

The sky was filled with low, grey clouds, the temperature hovered in the low teens, and Anderson especially made the ball talk in a dialect alien to West

Three of a kind: at Riverside, Ravi Bopara, after a run of three successive ducks, all against Sri Lanka, heads for a third successive hundred, all against West Indies.

Indian batsmen. As the Test hurried towards its end on the fifth day (the second had been washed out), they could hardly make contact against Anderson or the supporting swing of Onions and Tim Bresnan. Amid the first-innings ruins, Sarwan compiled an even hundred with the class that had characterised his batting in the Caribbean; it took a clinical bouncer barrage from Broad, of the type once the preserve of West Indian attacks, to disconcert and dismiss him. There was another spirited half-century from Ramdin, and the distracted Gayle finally managed one himself, but there was no fight left, if there ever had been.

In 2007, success in the one-day internationals, Gayle's first as captain, provided a welcome lift after a 3–0 drubbing in the Tests. There was never going to be a repeat this time. Whatever West Indies' woes, a clean sweep for England made pleasant if undemanding preparation for the more serious business of the Ashes. Most of the pieces fell neatly into place following the disarray and the disappointments of their winter, with the controversial change of captain and coach, and the blank sheet from Tests in India and the Caribbean.

In contrast, West Indies took a few unmistakable steps back towards mediocrity after a couple of years' encouraging progress. Gayle's tenure, both as captain and the one constant opener, was in doubt, but there was no obvious replacement in either position. With the notable exception of Edwards, the bowling lacked penetration; the batting still rested heavily on Gayle, Sarwan and Chanderpaul; and there was no perceptible advance on tour by the newer players such as Lendl Simmons, Lionel Baker, Nelon Pascal and Andrew Richardson. With the prospect of dividing Test cricket into two divisions gaining support within the ICC, it was an inopportune setback for West Indies, for so long the game's strongest and most revered entity.

WEST INDIAN TOURING PARTY

C. H. Gayle (*captain*), D. Ramdin (*vice-captain*), L. S. Baker, S. J. Benn, D. E. Bernard, S. Chanderpaul, N. Deonarine, F. H. Edwards, B. P. Nash, N. T. Pascal, D. M. Richards, A. P. Richardson, D. J. G. Sammy, R. R. Sarwan, L. M. P. Simmons, D. S. Smith, J. E. Taylor.

Gayle and Edwards were playing in the IPL and joined the party shortly before the First Test. Richards flew home during the Test series because of a shoulder injury; he was replaced by R. S. Morton for the one-day series, while D. J. Bravo, K. A. Pollard and R. Rampaul replaced Bernard, Deonarine, Nash, Pascal, Richardson and Smith.

Coach: J. Dyson. *Team manager:* O. Khan. *Assistant coach:* D. Williams. *Team analyst:* R. Berridge. *Physiotherapist:* C. J. Clark. *Strength and conditioning coach:* S. Folkes. *Massage therapist:* V. A. Browne. *Media officer:* P. Spooner.

Note: Matches in this section which were not first-class are signified by a dagger.

LEICESTERSHIRE v WEST INDIANS

At Leicester, April 20, 21, 22. Drawn. Toss: Leicestershire.

After 14 wickets on the first day, the match settled down into a gentle introduction to English conditions for the West Indians. Lendl Simmons – whose uncle Phil had helped Leicestershire win two Championships in 1996 and 1998 – and Nash added 163 for the next wicket, and were separated only when Simmons retired after reaching his second century at Grace Road (he scored one for West Indies A in 2006). He cited cramp in his right arm; Nash soon went off too, complaining of stiff legs. The tourists eventually built a lead of 138, but the young Leicestershire side, troubled by Richardson's pace and Benn's spin in their first innings, had much less bother securing the draw. West Indies coach John Dyson had criticised the pitch after the first day, which rebounded on him when he asked if they could practise on it the day after the match: "I don't think it's appropriate after his comments," said David Smith, Leicestershire's chief executive. "They can practise in the nets and they're very welcome." Dyson was unperturbed: "There's a nice big field here. We'll find something to do."

Close of play: First day, West Indians 80-4 (Simmons 21); Second day, Leicestershire 51-1 (Boyce 19, Cobb 17).

Leicestershire

M. A. G. Boyce c Simmons b Benn	45	– c Richards b Simmons	55
†T. J. New lbw b Baker	4	– c Sammy b Richardson	0
J. J. Cobb b Benn	11	– c Ramdin b Benn	53
J. Allenby c Smith b Benn	28		
J. W. A. Taylor lbw b Sammy	4	– (4) c Simmons b Benn	5
*H. H. Dippenaar c Smith b Benn	4	– (5) not out	40
W. A. White not out	37	– (6) c Ramdin b Baker	18
C. D. Crowe b Richardson	21	– (7) b Sammy	16
J. K. H. Naik c Sammy b Richardson	0	– (8) not out	16
H. F. Gurney b Richardson	0		
A. C. F. Wyatt run out	3		
B 20, l-b 2, w 3	25	B 18, l-b 13, w 1, n-b 3	35

1/30 (2) 2/77 (3) 3/90 (1) 4/95 (5) (62.3 overs) 182
5/108 (6) 6/129 (4) 7/166 (8)
8/166 (9) 9/174 (10) 10/182 (11)

1/13 (2) (6 wkts, 91 overs) 238
2/117 (1) 3/129 (3)
4/134 (4) 5/185 (6) 6/214 (7)

Baker 9–2–11–1; Richardson 14.3–5–46–3; Nash 5–3–7–0; Sammy 14–2–51–1; Benn 15–5–31–4; Deonarine 5–2–14–0. *Second Innings*—Baker 21–7–62–1; Richardson 19–8–32–1; Sammy 17–7–36–1; Deonarine 1–0–2–0; Benn 25–5–53–2; Simmons 8–2–22–1.

West Indians

D. S. Smith lbw b Naik	24	D. J. G. Sammy c Dippenaar b Wyatt	3
D. M. Richards c Taylor b Wyatt	15	S. J. Benn not out	23
R. R. Sarwan c Allenby b Wyatt	4	B 8, l-b 6, n-b 1, p 5	20
L. M. P. Simmons retired hurt	102		
N. Deonarine lbw b Gurney	15	1/16 (2) (6 wkts dec, 99.5 overs)	320
B. P. Nash retired hurt	78	2/34 (3) 3/56 (1)	
*†D. Ramdin c Boyce b Dippenaar	36	4/80 (5) 5/266 (8) 6/320 (7)	

L. S. Baker and A. P. Richardson did not bat.

Simmons retired hurt at 243; Nash retired hurt at 258.

Gurney 22–6–58–1; Wyatt 21–7–42–3; Allenby 4.1–2–13–0; Naik 16.5–6–33–1; Crowe 17–3–48–0; White 14–1–82–0; Cobb 4–0–19–0; Dippenaar 0.5–0–6–1.

Umpires: M. J. D. Bodenham and A. Hicks.

ESSEX v WEST INDIANS

At Chelmsford, April 25, 26, 27. Drawn. Toss: Essex.

Rain wiped out the final day, depriving Essex, who led by 292, of the chance to push for victory and Cook of a morale-boosting pre-Test century. It was his first match of the summer after he broke his left index finger, and lingering discomfort forced him to field much of each innings. He timed the ball well, although he was dropped by wicketkeeper Simmons off Pascal before scoring. Gallian bagged a duck, dismissed by the third delivery of each innings. In between, the tourists collapsed inside 45 overs against Essex's inexperienced swing bowlers, with Chambers and Westfield, both of West Indian origin, the pick. Three wickets fell in six deliveries at the start of the second day, catching Nash by surprise; he was still dressing for action on his way from the crease, and dropped his box attempting to pull on his sweater. Only the class of Chanderpaul shone through. He faced 107 balls in 165 minutes for an unbeaten 66, when the next highest contribution was 15 from Extras.

Close of play: First day, West Indians 24-1 (Richards 8); Second day, Essex 175-3 (Cook 74, Foster 48).

Essex

J. E. R. Gallian c Sammy b Baker	0	– lbw b Baker	0
A. N. Cook c Smith b Sammy	46	– not out	74
V. Chopra c Deonarine b Richardson	50	– c Simmons b Pascal	14
J. C. Mickleburgh lbw b Richardson	58	– lbw b Baker	23
*†J. S. Foster b Baker	23	– not out	48
T. Westley c Simmons b Deonarine	4		
G. W. Flower run out	9		
J. D. Middlebrook lbw b Bernard	46		
M. S. Westfield b Deonarine	1		
J. S. Ahmed c Smith b Deonarine	5		
M. A. Chambers not out	0		
B 9, l-b 5, w 3, n-b 4	21	B 8, l-b 3, w 2, n-b 3	16

1/0 (1) 2/87 (3) 3/102 (2)	(80.2 overs)	263
4/168 (5) 5/189 (6) 6/195 (4)		
7/210 (7) 8/235 (9) 9/263 (8) 10/263 (10)		

1/0 (1) 2/31 (3)	(3 wkts, 47 overs)	175
3/98 (4)		

Baker 13–2–39–2; Pascal 14–0–76–0; Bernard 14–7–19–1; Richardson 13–3–51–2; Sammy 14–5–32–1; Deonarine 12.2–1–32–3. *Second Innings*—Baker 9–1–31–2; Pascal 8–1–23–1; Richardson 7–1–31–0; Sammy 6–1–23–0; Bernard 11–1–29–0; Deonarine 6–0–27–0.

West Indians

D. S. Smith c Mickleburgh b Middlebrook	13	L. S. Baker lbw b Chambers		9
D. M. Richards c Foster b Chambers	8	A. P. Richardson c Middlebrook b Westfield		4
†L. M. P. Simmons c Foster b Ahmed	4	N. T. Pascal c Chambers b Westfield		0
N. Deonarine b Chambers	0	L-b 1, w 4, n-b 10		15
S. Chanderpaul not out	66			—
B. P. Nash b Chambers	14	1/24 (1) 2/24 (2) 3/24 (4) (44.1 overs)		146
D. E. Bernard c Foster b Ahmed	12	4/29 (3) 5/64 (6) 6/79 (7)		
*D. J. G. Sammy lbw b Westfield	1	7/80 (8) 8/117 (9) 9/141 (10) 10/146 (11)		

Chambers 14–3–62–4; Ahmed 11–1–55–2; Middlebrook 4–3–2–1; Westfield 13.1–5–25–3; Chopra 2–1–1–0.

Umpires: D. J. Millns and S. J. O'Shaughnessy.

ENGLAND LIONS v WEST INDIANS

At Derby, April 30, May 1, 2. England Lions won by ten wickets. Toss: England Lions.

England's second string gave their seniors a psychological boost, inflicting a heavy defeat on the tourists, who were still waiting for their captain, Gayle, and strike bowler, Edwards, to return from the IPL. Their batsmen had little answer to Chris Woakes, a tall, brisk 20-year-old from Warwickshire, who took the first six wickets on his way to career-best figures. "It swung, I got a bit of nip and thankfully I got the edges," he said. Taylor, another late arrival (he had been recovering from a hip injury after a car accident), grabbed the Lions' first three wickets in an 11-ball spell, but Ambrose's punchy century – he hit 20 fours and a six, and put on 152 with Rashid – set up a lead of 108. The West Indians then produced another sorry batting display. Rashid's leg-spin accounted for top scorers Simmons and Chanderpaul, who misread a googly, before Plunkett claimed four late scalps as six clattered for 25 in eight overs. Moore and Key galloped past a target of 72 inside ten overs. Even though only 28 overs were possible on the first day, the Lions won with a day to spare.

Close of play: First day, West Indians 76-4 (Chanderpaul 15, Nash 11); Second day, England Lions 143-6 (Ambrose 49, Rashid 13).

West Indians

D. S. Smith c Ambrose b Woakes	8	– b Mahmood	1
L. M. P. Simmons c Ambrose b Woakes	4	– lbw b Rashid	63
R. R. Sarwan c Patel b Woakes	31	– c Ambrose b Woakes	13
*†D. Ramdin c Bell b Woakes	4	– c Bell b Woakes	4
S. Chanderpaul c Ambrose b Woakes	21	– lbw b Rashid	50
B. P. Nash c Patel b Woakes	20	– c Bell b Rashid	19
D. E. Bernard lbw b Rashid	58	– not out	10
D. J. G. Sammy lbw b Wright	22	– c Woakes b Plunkett	4
J. E. Taylor b Mahmood	0	– b Plunkett	5
S. J. Benn c Ambrose b Plunkett	26	– c Trott b Plunkett	0
N. T. Pascal not out	1	– b Plunkett	1
L-b 4, n-b 4	8	B 4, l-b 2, n-b 3	9

1/8 (2) 2/20 (1) 3/34 (4) 4/55 (3) (64 overs) 203
5/90 (5) 6/91 (6) 7/127 (8) 8/131 (9)
9/201 (10) 10/203 (7)

1/2 (1) 2/21 (3) (45.1 overs) 179
3/29 (4) 4/116 (2)
5/154 (5) 6/157 (6) 7/170 (8) 8/176 (9)
9/177 (10) 10/179 (11)

Mahmood 12–1–46–1; Woakes 18–6–43–6; Plunkett 18–2–53–1; Trott 4–1–9–0; Wright 5–1–23–1; Rashid 7–0–25–1. *Second Innings*—Mahmood 8–0–32–1; Woakes 6–1–21–2; Wright 6–2–24–0; Rashid 15–1–66–3; Plunkett 10.1–0–30–4.

England Lions

S. C. Moore c Smith b Taylor	3	– not out	30
*R. W. T. Key lbw b Taylor	0	– not out	33
I. R. Bell lbw b Bernard	27		
I. J. L. Trott c Ramdin b Taylor	0		
S. R. Patel c Simmons b Pascal	27		
†T. R. Ambrose c Sammy b Simmons	117		
L. J. Wright b Bernard	4		
A. U. Rashid c Bernard b Pascal	72		
L. E. Plunkett c Sarwan b Pascal	17		
C. R. Woakes not out	2		
S. I. Mahmood lbw b Pascal	0		
B 17, l-b 11, w 1, n-b 13	42	B 8, w 1	9

1/1 (2) 2/9 (1) 3/13 (4) 4/57 (3)   (72.5 overs) 311
5/78 (5) 6/117 (7) 7/269 (6)   (no wkt, 9.5 overs) 72
8/305 (8) 9/311 (9) 10/311 (11)

Taylor 17–2–54–3; Pascal 15.5–1–68–4; Bernard 21–1–86–2; Sammy 7–1–26–0; Benn 10–1–39–0; Simmons 2–0–10–1. *Second Innings*—Taylor 3–0–14–0; Pascal 3–0–17–0; Simmons 2–0–18–0; Sammy 1.5–0–15–0.

Umpires: N. A. Mallender and P. Willey.

ENGLAND v WEST INDIES

First npower Test

SCYLD BERRY

At Lord's, May 6, 7, 8. England won by ten wickets. Toss: West Indies. Test debuts: T. T. Bresnan, G. Onions.

It was an unsatisfactory game except for England's players and their most committed supporters. The first Lord's Test to start on a Wednesday (excluding England v Rest of the World in 1970, no longer regarded as a genuine Test) was finished before the weekend. The weather was cool at best, mostly windy and cold, and the ground was little more than half full on any of the three days. But, after six consecutive draws at Lord's, England were delighted to find that the ball swung about throughout, and they won a "live" Test against a country other than New Zealand for the first time since an equally unprepared West Indian side visited two years earlier.

As West Indies lost seven for 29 on the second afternoon, Benn was so unready that, like Nash in one of the warm-ups, he came out to bat before he had finished putting on his gear, to avoid being timed out. It made little difference: he became Graham Onions's third victim in one over. The moment captured the tourists' state of mind. They had boarded their plane to London less than a fortnight after hosting England's visit – far too soon for a return series. They did play three first-class practice games (the 2007 West Indians had less than a day of outdoor play before the First Test), but had hardly "warmed up". After competing for the first two sessions, West Indies fell apart when they missed six chances – none very difficult – in the evening. One was dropped by Gayle, their captain, who had arrived from the IPL in South Africa only two days before, although the tour management had expected him to come three days earlier. Following the example of their fielding, their bowling fell apart on the second morning, their batting on the second afternoon.

As the six most experienced batsmen – three on each side – scored 84 runs between them, this match was decided by junior players: in England's case, by Bopara, Swann and, on his debut, Onions. After failing to win the opening Test for the last 14 series, since beating Bangladesh at Lord's in 2005, England's new regime of Andrew Strauss and Andy

Philip Brown

Middle, please: Graham Onions, on Test debut, makes short work of Devon Smith.

Flower were determined to hit the ground running, and introduced the form bowler of the county season to date: Onions had already taken five-fors against Yorkshire and Somerset. The first selection in which the pair had a free hand was a fresh, youthful and almost exuberant team, with the caveat that two months before the Ashes was late in the day for experiments. Bopara's selection in the first place, plus his promotion to No. 3, was one defining decision of the new regime – Flower had watched Bopara grow up at Essex since he was 17.

England's IPL players had been told to return home by lunchtime on May 1 (as opposed to Gayle on the night of May 3), but even that was not long enough. After England were put in, Collingwood, who had not played a game in South Africa, and Pietersen were blown away in a fine spell by Edwards, who had just flown in himself and bowled fiercely from the Nursery End; and Bopara was all at sea with his footwork early on. He had been the only England player to make a significant score in the IPL, and initially he continued to back away to give himself room to hit through the off side, before readjusting his footwork. Once settled, Bopara filled the No. 3 role after Vaughan, Bell and Shah had scored only one fifty between them in that position since Vaughan's hundred at Lord's a year before.

Edwards enjoyed the swinging conditions as much as England's pace bowlers, but was let down and demoralised by his fielders, whereas England missed little (one of the few drops was a return chance to Onions). After Cook had inside-edged, Pietersen lunged at an outswinger shaping towards the top of his off stump for a spectacular first-baller, caught by the keeper Ramdin to his right after he had headed to leg side. But after a consolidating stand between Bopara and Prior, who had been promoted to No. 6 in the Trinidad Test, Edwards's fieriness waned as he had three catches put down, the first a regulation chance to Nash at square leg when Bopara was 76. Broad was dropped four times in all, twice off Edwards, while Benn missed two catches.

Perhaps the finest strokes in Bopara's second Test hundred – he had been left out after the first in Barbados – were his drives to the on side of straight, in the manner of his hero

Sachin Tendulkar, and the cover-drives off Benn with a whip of the wrists. Approaching a century in his first home Test, he was content to reach it in singles then signal to the dressing-room for his name to be written on the honours board. Bopara could have been given lbw to Benn by Steve Davis when 40, and Smith at second slip dropped him on 100. But batsmen needed some luck when the ball was not only swinging but occasionally seaming off a pitch that started damp and was grassier than previous ones at Lord's.

At the start of the second morning West Indies were still in the game, but not mentally. Taylor and Edwards bowled swinging half-volleys to Swann, who hammered them, and by the time they pitched a few short a player not renowned for liking bouncers was well on his way to his highest Test score. Swann went on to take the new ball for two overs, which divided opinion. The off-spinner had dismissed left-hander Devon Smith for a pastime in the Caribbean; and Strauss had noted that the 2009 Dukes ball did not swing until after roughly ten overs, so it made sense to keep Anderson back until then. But if ever conditions favoured swing bowling it was here and now; and it may have alerted the Australians to the possibility that Swann might open against their own left-handed openers in the Ashes series.

The West Indian collapse – eight wickets falling for 53 was some revenge for England's 51 in Jamaica – was the work of Swann, when he returned for his second spell, and Onions, bowling from the Nursery End like Edwards. In his first over back, Swann bowled Smith through his rather large gate (by the end of the game Smith had scored one fifty in 28 Test innings since November 2005) and had Chanderpaul edging to Collingwood at slip. Collingwood then took an exceptional catch when Nash edged a drive well to his left. Onions's best delivery was a lifter that gave him his maiden Test wicket – Simmons edging high to first slip – then he mopped up the tail at good pace.

Anderson and Broad, as well as Onions and Swann, were all over the tourists when they followed on. Swann dismissed Chanderpaul again, this time bat-pad, and removed him from No. 1 in the ICC rankings. It was only when the sun came out on the third afternoon that England were halted. Nash and Ramdin, adding 143, showed up areas which the home side still had to work on. Swann, having taken two catches at third slip to his left, missed Nash on nought when he went for a chance to his right with only one hand. The ball stopped swinging conventionally, and the square was too immaculately grassed to allow reverse swing; Strauss said the bowling hereabouts could have been "more disciplined"; and Prior's wicketkeeping, while functional, still lacked the polish to lift his side. But England, overall, started their home season and their new regime in fine style.

Man of the Match: G. P. Swann. *Attendance:* 57,417.

Close of play: First day, England 289-7 (Bopara 118, Swann 7); Second day, West Indies 39-2 (Smith 26, Simmons 7).

England

*A. J. Strauss c Ramdin b Taylor	16	– not out	14
A. N. Cook b Edwards	35	– not out	14
R. S. Bopara c Nash b Taylor	143		
K. P. Pietersen c Ramdin b Edwards	0		
P. D. Collingwood c Smith b Edwards	8		
†M. J. Prior c Simmons b Edwards	42		
S. C. J. Broad c Taylor b Benn	38		
T. T. Bresnan lbw b Benn	9		
G. P. Swann not out	63		
J. M. Anderson c Ramdin b Edwards	1		
G. Onions b Edwards	0		
B 1, l-b 5, w 7, n-b 9	22	N-b 4	4

1/28 (1) 2/92 (2) 3/92 (4) (111.3 overs) 377 (no wkt, 6.1 overs) 32
4/109 (5) 5/193 (6) 6/262 (7)
7/275 (8) 8/368 (3) 9/377 (10) 10/377 (11)

Taylor 24–2–83–2; Edwards 26.3–4–92–6; Baker 24–5–75–0; Benn 27–4–84–2; Nash 2–1–2–0;
Simmons 5–1–24–0; Gayle 3–0–11–0. *Second Innings*—Edwards 3.1–0–12–0; Taylor 3–0–20–0.

West Indies

*C. H. Gayle b Broad		28	– c Swann b Anderson	0
D. S. Smith b Swann		46	– b Onions	41
R. R. Sarwan c Prior b Broad		13	– b Anderson	1
L. M. P. Simmons c Strauss b Onions		16	– c Cook b Onions	21
S. Chanderpaul c Collingwood b Swann		0	– c Bopara b Swann	4
B. P. Nash c Collingwood b Swann		4	– c Cook b Broad	81
†D. Ramdin lbw b Onions		5	– b Broad	61
J. E. Taylor c Prior b Onions		0	– lbw b Swann	15
S. J. Benn c Swann b Onions		2	– b Swann	0
F. H. Edwards not out		10	– c Bresnan b Broad	2
L. S. Baker lbw b Onions		17	– not out	2
L-b 10, w 1		11	B 8, l-b 18, w 2	28

1/46 (1) 2/70 (3) 3/99 (2) 4/99 (5)   (32.3 overs) 152   1/14 (1) 2/22 (3)   (72.2 overs) 256
5/117 (6) 6/117 (4) 7/117 (8)   3/70 (4) 4/75 (5)
8/119 (9) 9/128 (7) 10/152 (11)   5/79 (2) 6/222 (7) 7/243 (8)
    8/246 (9) 9/249 (10) 10/256 (6)

Broad 11–0–56–2; Swann 5–2–16–3; Anderson 7–0–32–0; Onions 9.3–1–38–5. *Second Innings*—
Anderson 15–6–38–2; Broad 19.2–2–64–3; Bresnan 7–3–17–0; Swann 17–4–39–3; Onions
12–2–64–2; Bopara 2–0–8–0.

Umpires: S. J. Davis and E. A. R. de Silva.
Third umpire: I. J. Gould.   Referee: A. J. Pycroft.

ENGLAND v WEST INDIES

Second npower Test

STEPHEN BRENKLEY

At Chester-le-Street, May 14, 15, 16, 17, 18. England won by an innings and 83 runs.
Toss: England.

There were times before, during and immediately after this match when it felt as if Test
cricket in England had reached its nadir. Although the hosts were occasionally as inspired
as the tourists were lacklustre, the suspicion was never shaken off that this was a game
few wanted to play or to watch. The surrender of the Wisden Trophy by West Indies, who
had held it for a mere 69 days – following a gap of nine years – seemed as inevitable as
had, once upon a time, their continued possession of it.

The match was conducted throughout in cold temperatures: early in the piece, when the
ground was barely a quarter full, spectators looked as if they were venturing forth on a
polar expedition rather than spending a day at the cricket. Tickets had been difficult to sell,
partly because the tour was confirmed so late, partly because West Indies had played a
Test at Chester-le-Street only two years earlier, partly because there was a genuine sense
of grievance in the North-East that they had been overlooked for an Ashes Test.

All this was compounded in spectacular fashion by an interview with Chris Gayle
published on the eve of the match, in which he promoted the virtues of Twenty20, said he
would not be sad if Test cricket died, and made it clear that he intended to resign as West
Indian captain sooner rather than later. It was impossible, as the game unfolded, to

dissociate those comments from the manner in which Gayle's side played, which aggravated a plethora of concerns. The future for West Indies as a Test team – certainly away from deliberately benign surfaces at home – looked as bleak as at any moment in the previous five years, during which one low point had followed another.

The idea that Test cricket, or international cricket of any kind, could be played so early in England was made to look ridiculous. Durham, whose organisation of the match was close to faultless, seemed and felt badly treated by the authorities. They were not about to decline the opportunity of staging a Test – not least for fear of what it might do to their future international chances – but they would have preferred a different opposition at a different time, and felt resoundingly that they had done enough to deserve that.

When rain prevented play on the second day and exacerbated the general gloom, the chief executive of the England and Wales Cricket Board, David Collier, felt impelled to mount a staunch defence of the series. He insisted it had been important for cricketing reasons: England needed two home Tests to prepare for the Ashes, he said, playing down the commercial imperative of staging seven Tests to fulfil the ECB's TV contract with Sky Sports.

England, for their part, ignored the apathy all round them and hardly put a foot wrong on any of the four days when cricket took place. Bopara became only the fifth England batsman to score hundreds in three consecutive Test innings, and the first to do it following three consecutive ducks; Cook became the only England batsman to have scored nine Test hundreds before his 25th birthday. Add the control of Anderson, not to mention his late swing, especially in the second innings, and England had almost enough to keep them warm without two sweaters.

THREE CONSECUTIVE TEST HUNDREDS FOR ENGLAND

H. Sutcliffe . . . . 115, 176 and 127 v Australia, 1924-25
D. C. S. Compton . . . . 163, 208 and 115 v South Africa, 1947
G. Boycott . . . . 119* v Australia, 1970-71; 121* and 112 v Pakistan, 1971
G. A. Gooch . . . . 333, 123 and 116 v India, 1990
R. S. Bopara . . . . **104 v West Indies, 2008-09; 143 and 108 v West Indies, 2009**

Sutcliffe and Gooch achieved the feat in two Tests; Compton, Boycott and Bopara over three.

The overall record is five consecutive innings, by E. D. Weekes (West Indies) v England in 1947-48 and India in 1948-49; J. H. W. Fingleton (Australia), A. Melville (South Africa) and R. Dravid (India) have done it in four.

Neither side made any changes from the teams at Lord's, though England had called both Sidebottom and Bell into their squad, perhaps as a sign of future intentions. Strauss decided to bat, and once Essex team-mates Bopara and Cook came together before lunch they were not parted until just before the close, by which time they had added 213 in a little over four hours. Bopara's class and temperament were illustrated by the way he raced from 84 to 98 in three balls, straight-driving Benn for four, six and four – the last boundary flying through the bowler's hands.

Cook, who had not scored a century at home since West Indies's previous visit two years earlier, was much stealthier in approach, and betrayed his anxiety when he was on 99 by almost running out his partner. He went on to his highest Test score after the washout on the second day. England declared at tea on the third and, if they might have done so earlier, it was plain that they had no intention of batting again. Their total of 569 for six was then the highest in all first-class cricket at Riverside.

There was a period of comic relief on the third morning when Anderson, who for no valid reason had been sent in as night-watchman when England were well in control, was peppered with fast and vicious bouncers by Edwards. It was thrilling stuff, but Edwards's effort, apparent against none of the other, more proficient batsmen, seemed wasted, while Anderson responded by knocking the top off the tourists' reply.

Pretty well wrapped up: spectators huddle against the cold (*above*), while the England team huddle in celebration of stand-in wicketkeeper Paul Collingwood's catch to remove Shivnarine Chanderpaul, leaving West Indies one wicket from defeat.

Although Sarwan and Chanderpaul (who batted 138 minutes for his 23) offered some world-weary resistance, it never convinced. Both were undone by skilful bowling from Broad, coming round the wicket to Chanderpaul and then bouncing out Sarwan immediately after he had made his fourth hundred in his last nine Test innings, all against England.

By the time stumps were drawn on the fourth day, West Indies, following on for the second match running, had already lost their top three, including Gayle and Sarwan. On the final morning their resistance, as it had been since their arrival in England, was minimal. Against bowling of the standard that Anderson produced, they needed far better method and temperament. Collingwood kept wicket in front of his home crowd in place of Prior, who had bruised his right ring finger, and to his obvious delight held a catch off an edge from Chanderpaul on the final day. There were catches, too, for both the substitute fielders provided by the Durham club.

So dominant were England that they could spend much of the last morning – when Anderson was not swinging his way through the West Indian batting – trying to ensure that Bresnan secured his first Test wicket. It seemed as though he would be denied until Nash obliged by clipping him to square leg. Wickets for Bresnan then came along like buses, and it was he who finished matters off three overs after lunch.

If England could feel pleased with themselves, after having been denied so frequently in the Caribbean a few months earlier, almost everybody else was relieved that a one-sided, undistinguished series was done. Rarely can a Test series win for England in England have been perceived as quite so unsatisfactory, not so much because of the poor opposition but because of the circumstances. There was an overwhelming feeling that it should not be permitted to happen again.

Man of the Match: J. M. Anderson. *Attendance:* 28,841.

Men of the Series: England – R. S. Bopara; West Indies – F. H. Edwards.

Close of play: First day, England 302-2 (Cook 126, Anderson 4); Second day, No play; Third day, West Indies 94-3 (Sarwan 41, Chanderpaul 3); Fourth day, West Indies 115-3 (Simmons 3, Chanderpaul 18).

England

*A. J. Strauss c Ramdin b Gayle	26
A. N. Cook c Gayle b Benn	160
R. S. Bopara b Baker	108
J. M. Anderson b Edwards	14
K. P. Pietersen c Simmons b Benn	49
P. D. Collingwood not out	60
†M. J. Prior c Benn b Simmons	63

S. C. J. Broad not out	28
B 20, l-b 5, w 8, n-b 28	61
	—
1/69 (1) 2/282 (3) (6 wkts dec, 147 overs)	569
3/326 (4) 4/410 (2)	
5/419 (5) 6/513 (7)	

T. T. Bresnan, G. P. Swann and G. Onions did not bat.

Taylor 20–2–68–0; Edwards 25–1–113–1; Baker 30–3–119–1; Gayle 14–2–31–1; Benn 43–8–146–2; Simmons 14–0–60–1; Sarwan 1–0–7–0.

West Indies

D. S. Smith b Anderson	7	– lbw b Swann	11
*C. H. Gayle lbw b Anderson	19	– c Strauss b Onions	54
R. R. Sarwan c Bresnan b Broad	100	– lbw b Onions	22
L. M. P. Simmons c Strauss b Anderson	8	– c sub (S. G. Borthwick) b Anderson	10
S. Chanderpaul c Prior b Broad	23	– c Collingwood b Anderson	47
B. P. Nash b Anderson	10	– c sub (S. G. Borthwick) b Bresnan	1
†D. Ramdin c Swann b Anderson	55	– c Anderson b Bresnan	0
J. E. Taylor lbw b Onions	10	– b Anderson	5
S. J. Benn run out	35	– b Anderson	0
F. H. Edwards c Strauss b Broad	11	– c sub (K. Turner) b Bresnan	4
L. S. Baker not out	0	– not out	4
B 2, l-b 21, w 2, n-b 7	32	B 8, l-b 5, w 5	18

1/18 (1) 2/38 (2) 3/68 (4) 4/167 (5) (84.3 overs) 310	1/53 (1) 2/88 (3) (44 overs) 176
5/188 (3) 6/205 (6) 7/216 (8)	3/89 (2) 4/141 (4)
8/286 (9) 9/310 (10) 10/310 (7)	5/142 (6) 6/146 (7) 7/163 (8)
	8/167 (9) 9/168 (5) 10/176 (10)

Anderson 26.3–5–87–5; Broad 16–2–62–3; Onions 18–6–52–1; Bresnan 10–2–35–0; Swann 14–4–51–0. *Second Innings*—Anderson 16–5–38–4; Broad 5–1–21–0; Swann 3–0–13–1; Onions 6–0–46–2; Bresnan 14–2–45–3.

Umpires: S. J. Davis and E. A. R. de Silva.
Third umpire: P. J. Hartley. Referee: A. J. Pycroft.

ONE-DAY INTERNATIONAL REPORTS BY TONY COZIER

†ENGLAND v WEST INDIES

First One-Day International

At Leeds, May 21. Abandoned.

Yorkshire chief executive Stewart Regan defended Headingley's new drainage system, installed during the winter with a £600,000 ECB grant, when the match was abandoned shortly after 3 p.m. Torrential downpours overnight and in the early morning left the relaid outfield swamped; the sun eventually streamed down, but parts remained boggy, and umpires Steve Davis and Nigel Llong called off the match after several inspections. Although their money was refunded, just over 11,000 spectators were not pleased, and there were questions over the Ashes Test, scheduled for early August. Regan pleaded unusual circumstances, explained that the new outfield would take time to "bed in", and was confident the drainage would get better in time.

†ENGLAND v WEST INDIES

Second One-Day International

At Bristol, May 24. England won by six wickets. Toss: England.

The big freeze of the North-East gave way to a day of clear, cloudless sunshine – a few degrees warmer and it could have been Barbados. What didn't change was the standard of West Indies' cricket. To be bowled out with 11.3 overs unused, in favourable conditions on a county ground with close boundaries, short-changed spectators who had filled the temporary stands to capacity. A few hundred came from local Afro-Caribbean communities, carrying flags, wearing maroon shirts and shouting encouragement in the hope of inspiring West Indies. Instead, their team fell flat again. Sent in, the middle order succumbed to Collingwood's uncomplicated, wicket-to-wicket medium-pace, while Broad took care of the top and bottom. Gayle looked in the mood, with 31 off 28 balls, but, after greeting Swann's first delivery with a straight hit for his second six, he was bowled by the next attempting a repeat. In his first match since arriving from the IPL, Bravo top-scored with 50 from 58 balls before he became Collingwood's first victim. England faltered briefly at 81 for three, but Shah and Collingwood shared a 76-run stand that carried them to within four of their goal.

Man of the Match: P. D. Collingwood.   *Attendance:* 13,955.

West Indies

*C. H. Gayle b Swann	31		S. J. Benn c Bopara b Broad		1
L. M. P. Simmons lbw b Broad	0		R. Rampaul c Swann b Broad		7
R. R. Sarwan c Prior b Broad	0				
S. Chanderpaul c Strauss b Bresnan	27		B 2, l-b 2, w 5		14
D. J. Bravo b Collingwood	50				
†D. Ramdin lbw b Collingwood	8		1/2 (2) 2/7 (3) 3/44 (1) (38.3 overs)		160
K. A. Pollard b Collingwood	8		4/107 (4) 5/128 (5) 6/131 (6)		
J. E. Taylor run out	1		7/134 (8) 8/150 (7) 9/153 (10)		
D. J. G. Sammy not out	13		10/160 (11)	10 overs: 46-3	

Anderson 6–1–19–0; Broad 8.3–1–46–4; Swann 8–1–26–1; Mascarenhas 6–0–24–0; Bresnan 4–0–20–1; Collingwood 6–0–16–3.

England

*A. J. Strauss c Sammy b Taylor	4		E. J. G. Morgan not out		2
R. S. Bopara lbw b Bravo	43		L-b 9, w 6, n-b 1		16
†M. J. Prior c Gayle b Sammy	11				
O. A. Shah run out	38		1/31 (1) 2/61 (3) (4 wkts, 36 overs)		161
P. D. Collingwood not out	47		3/81 (2) 4/157 (4)	10 overs: 48-1	

A. D. Mascarenhas, S. C. J. Broad, G. P. Swann, T. T. Bresnan and J. M. Anderson did not bat.

Taylor 7–2–29–1; Rampaul 6–0–23–0; Sammy 5–0–15–1; Bravo 6–0–30–1; Benn 9–0–38–0; Pollard 3–0–17–0.

Umpires: E. A. R. de Silva and P. J. Hartley.
Third umpire: I. J. Gould.   Referee: A. J. Pycroft.

†ENGLAND v WEST INDIES

Third One-Day International

At Birmingham, May 26. England won by 58 runs. Toss: West Indies.

Another massive defeat brought a distressing tour to a predictable end. Realistically, the margin of England's sixth consecutive victory over West Indies in all cricket was far wider than 58 runs. Against indisciplined bowling and shoddy fielding, the tourists' hallmark throughout, England efficiently compiled 328, the highest total for either side in their 82 one-day games against each other, and the highest in any one-day international at Edgbaston. West Indies were effectively beaten once Gayle and Sarwan were out within the first four overs; only Chanderpaul's tedious 68 off 108 balls and a few meaningless blows from Ramdin and the tail stretched the contest into the final over. On another chilly though sunny day, the foundation for England's daunting total was set by Strauss and Bopara in an opening stand of 81 in 15 overs. Prior and Shah built on it, adding 149 from 20: Prior helped himself to 87 off 86 balls, Shah to 75 off 65. They were never under any pressure, the batting powerplay yielding 55 off five overs, the last ten overs bringing 90. Long before then, West Indies' spirits were broken. The drudgery of Chanderpaul – the shining light of their batting for the previous two years – and three schoolboyish run-outs simply typified their mood.

Man of the Match: M. J. Prior.   *Attendance:* 16,095.
Man of the Series: S. C. J. Broad.

England

*A. J. Strauss st Ramdin b Benn	52	T. T. Bresnan c Rampaul b Pollard		9
R. S. Bopara b Bravo	49	S. C. J. Broad not out		6
†M. J. Prior b Taylor	87	B 2, l-b 7, w 10, n-b 2		21
O. A. Shah c Morton b Taylor	75			—
A. D. Mascarenhas c and b Pollard	0	1/81 (2) 2/129 (1)	(7 wkts, 50 overs)	328
P. D. Collingwood b Taylor	23	3/278 (4) 4/279 (5)		
E. J. G. Morgan not out	6	5/289 (3) 6/308 (6) 7/317 (8)	10 overs: 50-0	

G. P. Swann and J. M. Anderson did not bat.

Taylor 10–1–59–3; Rampaul 4–0–29–0; Edwards 6–0–43–0; Bravo 6–0–43–1; Benn 10–1–51–1; Gayle 5–0–31–0; Pollard 9–0–63–2.

West Indies

*C. H. Gayle c Bopara b Broad	11	R. Rampaul b Swann		16
R. S. Morton run out	21	F. H. Edwards not out		4
R. R. Sarwan c Strauss b Anderson	9			
S. Chanderpaul c Bopara b Broad	68	B 2, l-b 2, w 5		9
D. J. Bravo lbw b Bresnan	26			—
†D. Ramdin c Prior b Anderson	45	1/13 (1) 2/22 (3) 3/66 (2)	(49.4 overs)	270
K. A. Pollard run out	12	4/99 (5) 5/181 (4) 6/189 (6)		
J. E. Taylor run out	18	7/212 (7) 8/223 (8) 9/254 (10)		
S. J. Benn b Anderson	31	10/270 (9)	10 overs: 53-2	

Broad 10–0–63–2; Anderson 9.4–0–58–3; Mascarenhas 7–0–43–0; Bresnan 10–0–36–1; Swann 8–0–38–1; Collingwood 5–0–28–0.

Umpires: S. J. Davis and I. J. Gould.
Third umpire: N. J. Llong.   Referee: A. J. Pycroft.

Details of West Indies' matches in the World Twenty20 tournament in June can be found in that section (see page 527).

ENGLAND v AUSTRALIA, 2009

Review by Christopher Martin-Jenkins

Test matches (5): England 2, Australia 1
One-day internationals (7): England 1, Australia 6
Twenty20 internationals (2): England 0, Australia 0

One hot and airless day in Hamilton, in the southern summer of 2007-08, a lonely, perspiring figure ran with steady, determined tread along the banks of the broad Waikato river. The cicadas were in full voice, a burning sun was at its zenith: only mad dogs and Andrew Strauss could have been pounding the road at such an hour. England had just lost a Test against New Zealand that they had been expected to win, and Strauss, dropped for the previous series in Sri Lanka, had been part of the general failure. By the time the Third and deciding Test arrived, in Napier, he had no immediate future as an international cricketer unless he scored a century.

It was the ultimate time of trial but, like W. E. Henley's "unconquerable soul", Strauss prevailed. By character as much as resolute batting, he scored 177 to lay the base for victory in that game. Less than 18 months later, having assumed the captaincy in his own right, expanded his batting repertoire and made seven more Test hundreds to lift his tally to 18, he led England to a 2–1 victory against Australia.

The final result remained in doubt until Stuart Broad ran suddenly through Australia's main batting on the dramatic second afternoon of the final Test at The Oval. It went against the general run of play and owed much to Strauss's thoughtful leadership, bottomless determination and quite outstanding batting. Rightly he won the Compton–Miller medal, awarded to Andrew Flintoff and Ricky Ponting in the two previous series.

Ponting became the first Australian captain since Billy Murdoch in 1890 to lose two Ashes series in England, but emerged with immense credit and renewed respect from knowledgeable cricket followers, despite regular boorish booing from a minority who apparently believed he might be goaded into indiscretions. On the contrary, he handled the media with patience and a sense of humour, and batted with customary dash and authority, playing leading roles both in the match that Australia won, and the one they ought to have won. Only a poor shot against Graeme Swann at Edgbaston – shades of past problems against Harbhajan Singh – and some ill luck at Lord's prevented him averaging well over 50. As a captain, he used his inexperienced attack wisely for the greater part of Australia's time in the field, allowing the initiative to slip only in the vital final stage of the First Test and at the start of the Second, when his bowlers let him down.

Even after England had fought their way to a first-innings lead of 172 on a dry, pitted but slow Oval pitch, a partnership of 127 between Ponting and Michael Hussey raised the possibility of a miraculous Australian escape from a hopeless position. England had achieved a minor miracle in the First Test six

The clincher: Andrew Strauss and Graeme Swann, on his knees in ecstasy after taking the last Australian wicket at The Oval, embrace in celebration.

weeks previously, but a last act in Test cricket from the injury-ravaged titan, Flintoff, effectively settled the destiny of the urn. His direct hit from mid-on to throw out an unwary Ponting, followed next over by the freakish run-out of vice-captain Michael Clarke, the most fluent batsman in the series on either side, resolved the issue.

Swann, the only specialist spinner in conditions perfect for his craft, took eight wickets in the deciding game. He finally underlined a difference between the teams that had been foreseen when the series started: England's apparent advantage in slow bowling. In the event, Swann had been outbowled on a placid pitch in the First Test at Cardiff by Australia's only specialist, Nathan Hauritz, whose foolish omission from the last Test arguably cost them the Ashes.

Throughout its topsy-turvy course the series had been mercurial and unpredictable, one side plumbing the depths as the other found temporary inspiration. The cricket was exciting but consistently fallible. Eleven of the players in the First Test (seven of them Australian) had never played Ashes cricket before, with four more to join them by August.

Great vintages seldom follow one another, so it was remarkable that the 2009 series came even close to equalling 2005. Because of the nature of that classic battle between two teams of exalted quality, the build-up to this one was long and exaggerated. So grossly does the contemporary British press indulge the Big Event, at the expense of offering the solid core of genuine cricket (and sports) followers a rounded service, that the next home series could easily have been an anticlimax, swiftly leaving the front pages. Remarkably, that did not happen.

The 2005 Ashes, with its high-octane cricket, sustained tension and vivid, unpredictable action, had been truly an unforgettable epic; four years later it was followed by an intriguing whodunnit, with as many twists and misleading clues as an Agatha Christie. The final oddity was that the losing team was the one with the stronger and more effective batting, especially once Kevin Pietersen had limped out after two Tests to have an operation on a damaged Achilles tendon. For the first time in more than 130 years of Test cricket, a side scoring six more individual hundreds than its opponents managed to lose the series. How do you explain that, Miss Marple?

When it was all over, the two captains attempted to offer their own solutions by resorting to one of the great mantras of contemporary sport. What matters, say the professionals, is recognising the big moments, the potential turning points of a match, and winning them. "If we've had a bad session we've had a really bad session," said Ponting. "When we were bad we were very bad, but when we were good we were just good enough," said Strauss.

That it was so was the cause, once again, of national rejoicing and, yes, front-page coverage in the newspapers. Even BBC television, long estranged from covering Test cricket to the serious detriment of the game in Britain, led its 10 p.m. news with five minutes of reflection on what it deemed to be the biggest event in the world on the Sunday evening of August 23. They even took a live report from a journalist posted outside the hotel to which the triumphant team, still savouring victory with their families in the pavilion, would not return for some time.

It was gratifying for officials of the England and Wales Cricket Board, both in the public relations department and the populous one that looks after all aspects of England teams under the command of Hugh Morris. They had planned long and thoroughly for what they hoped would be a repeat of the heightened interest in cricket throughout the land engendered by an Ashes success. This time they celebrated the narrow triumph – two matches to one, as it had been four years earlier, after the eight-series domination by Australia – with greater dignity and less excess.

Yet in 2005 England's triumph had been the culmination of a period of sustained success by a mature, talented and settled side. Eight months before the Oval Test of 2009, Morris had presided with profound embarrassment over a press conference at the same ground, in which he had announced to the world that the England captain, Kevin Pietersen, and the England director of cricket, Peter Moores, had both been sacked. Pietersen was supposed to have resigned, but in fact he had been told to do so. Moores was removed because he had lost the confidence of Pietersen and did not appear to have sufficient support from other senior players for his inflexible belief in remorseless hard work.

HOW THEY MEASURED UP

England		Australia
4	Tosses won	1
2,869	Runs scored	2,886
84	Wickets lost	71
759.3	Overs faced	793.2
34.15	Runs per wicket	40.64
3.77	Runs per over	3.63
2	100s	8
61 / 32	10–99s / 0–9s	42 / 30

Partnership averages

England		Australia
44.55	1st	48.25
29.00	2nd	55.37
37.22	3rd	48.25
40.66	4th	16.87
25.66	5th	68.62
40.66	6th	80.42
29.37	7th	20.66
47.00	8th	8.16
21.37	9th	25.50
21.16	10th	16.33
55.55 / 44.44	% runs by wkts 1–5 / 6–10	65.80 / 34.19

Average by batting position

England		Australia
52.66	No. 1	37.12
24.66	No. 2	42.62
20.11	No. 3	48.12
26.88	No. 4	34.50
42.77	No. 5	64.00
30.37	No. 6	52.42
28.12	No. 7	42.71
29.75	No. 8	17.50
27.62	No. 9	20.25
33.75	No. 10	15.50
14.00	No. 11	20.00

England		Australia
54 @ 38.75 / 15 @ 45.46	Wickets taken by seam / spin	66 @ 31.75 / 15 @ 41.80
14.19	Over-rate per hour	13.99
4	Five-wicket hauls	2
67.04	Bowling strike-rate	54.25
44 / 67 / 12 / 31 / 154	B / l-b / w / n-b / total extras	78 / 68 / 29 / 86 / 261
9.09	% total runs scored in extras	5.33
53.91	% runs off bat in boundaries	54.90
347 / 3	Fours / sixes	360 / 10

How wickets fell

England		Australia
10	Bowled	17
18 / 41	Caught behind / elsewhere	11 / 26
12	lbw	14
3	Run out	2
0	Stumped	1
11	Dropped catches	11

Research: Benedict Bermange

Moores went to coach Lancashire, Pietersen returned to the ranks, badly stung but big enough to appreciate that it was Test cricket that had made his reputation and could still sustain it, especially if he played a leading role in regaining the Ashes. Under Strauss and Andy Flower, the widely respected former captain of Zimbabwe and newly appointed director of cricket, with whom Strauss was instinctively comfortable, the urgent mending of fences started in the West Indies in late January.

Australia, meanwhile, were on their own rebuilding mission, having lost three great players – Shane Warne, Glenn McGrath and Adam Gilchrist – another of huge achievement in Matthew Hayden, and one of the feistiest and most effective of all their opening batsmen, Justin Langer, since humiliating England 5–0 at home in 2006-07. At the end of 2008 they had lost successive series to the two other strongest Test teams in the world, India and South Africa, only to come back under Ponting's tenacious lead to beard the South African lion in his den in March.

ENGLAND'S GOOD HOUSEKEEPING

No-balls and wides bowled during the 2009 Ashes series:

England	Legitimate balls	No-balls	Wides	Illegitimate balls %	Australia	Legitimate balls	No-balls	Wides	Illegitimate balls %
Flintoff....	773	19	2	2.71	Hilfenhaus .	1,085	39	1	3.68
Harmison ..	258	5	1	2.32	Johnson ...	973	20	12	3.28
Onions	466	2	3	1.07	Siddle.....	970	17	5	2.26
Broad	925	1	4	0.54	Hauritz....	620	6	–	0.96
Anderson ..	948	2	2	0.42	North	405	1	1	0.49
Swann	1,022	–	–	–	Clark	282	–	1	0.35
Others.....	368	2	–	0.54	Others.....	222	–	–	–

The percentage represents illegitimate balls (no-balls and wides) divided by total legitimate balls.

Other bowlers: R. S. Bopara (2 no-balls), P. D. Collingwood, M. S. Panesar; M. J. Clarke, S. M. Katich, S. R. Watson.

So recent a demonstration of resilience made them most people's favourites to retain the Ashes, despite the fact that only Brett Lee of their main bowlers had ever played a Test in England before. Lee, who had missed the trip to South Africa because of a broken foot, was ready to return to the Test side after a devastating spell of reverse-swing bowling at Worcester in the game before the First Test, but sustained an intercostal injury in extending himself there and did not bowl in another match until mid-August.

Australia's strong performance in South Africa had centred instead on outstanding fast bowling by the sturdy, athletic Queenslander Mitchell Johnson, the latest in a line of left-arm, over-the-wicket pace bowlers who had excelled for Australia since the Second World War, notably Bill Johnston, Alan Davidson and Bruce Reid. But in England Johnson, despite averaging four wickets a Test, did not live up to expectations. His relative failure owed something to nervousness caused by finding himself thrust into his first Ashes series as a leader, and possibly something to domestic problems; but the biggest reason was a simple loss of rhythm in a bowling action lacking classical

Body language: Mitchell Johnson struggles to live up to the pre-tour hype.

simplicity. He was also unable to bowl more than an occasional inswinger to right-handers. A shortage of pace in all the pitches except Lord's, where he was at his most wayward, also reduced his potency, although 20 wickets at 32 was no disgrace. Vengeance may well be his on livelier pitches in 2010-11.

Johnson soon had to concede the new ball to less established bowlers, but his inability to lead the attack was cancelled out by a similar underperformance from England's "hot" bowler at the start of the series, James Anderson, with whom Johnson seems to share a natural distaste for the spotlight. Anderson's shortcomings were overcome by good performances at different times from Broad, Graham Onions and Flintoff, whose latest injury, to his right knee, obliged him to announce before Lord's that he would retire from Test cricket at the end of the series. For Australia two fast bowlers with scant international experience, Peter Siddle and Ben Hilfenhaus, moved seamlessly into the vacuum.

Siddle, tall and bullishly round-shouldered, bowled with persistent pace and hostility, if not always with sufficient control, but he was often too hot for tailenders. Hilfenhaus in particular excelled as an old-fashioned outswing bowler with a superb, economical action, who got on with the job without any need for gamesmanship or showmanship. Biblical-faced, strong, willing and consistent, with a hint of F. S. Trueman or Graham McKenzie about his pigeon-toed approach and long final stride (which often resulted in no-balls), he pitched the ball up at a brisk pace, seldom bothering with bouncers, and finished as the leading wicket-taker on either side. Ten of his wickets – five in each – came in the two games dominated by Australia, at Cardiff and Headingley.

Another cricketer whose reputation was greatly enhanced excelled in the same two matches. Marcus North added steady, virtually error-free Test centuries in Cardiff and Leeds to the one that he had scored on his debut at the Wanderers in his only previous series. His 96 at Edgbaston was no less influential in saving the Third Test. His attitude was refreshing, too. Both when falling four short of a hundred in that game and, more vitally, being given out lbw at The Oval despite getting a palpable inside edge on to his pad, he merely smiled in resignation.

An experienced, technically accomplished left-hander, North was a reminder that not all successful Australian Test players are youthful prodigies. Celebrating his 30th birthday in the middle of the series, he proved that there is value also in making your early mistakes at a little below the top level, and in learning your trade in different conditions. North had appeared for no fewer than five English counties, which at once demonstrated his competence and the shameless opportunism of employers who prefer the quick fix to patient nurturing of their own young players.

The faults and lingering virtues of the contrasting English "system" were highlighted by the experiences of two other batsmen making their first appearances in an Ashes series. Ravi Bopara (an exact contemporary of Alastair Cook in the Essex side) had appeared ready for Test cricket at the start of England's tour of Sri Lanka late in 2007, a misjudgment by the selectors that deprived the much riper Owais Shah of his best chance of establishing himself. Bopara managed 42 runs in five Test innings but, given another chance, under Strauss and Flower in the Caribbean, he responded with an elegant, chancy hundred in Barbados on one of the truest batting pitches ever prepared. Two more followed against the same West Indies attack in the early summer of 2009.

Geoff Miller, whose record as the national selector has been mixed, decided in conjunction with his two colleagues, James Whitaker and Ashley Giles, and with the approval of Strauss and Flower, to entrust Bopara with the No. 3 position against Australia. Experienced judges, among them Warne and Geoff Boycott, warned that he was too loose. They were right. Bopara had enjoyed a lot of luck against the weak West Indies, especially when hooking and chasing balls speculatively outside his off stump. The Australians exploited the second failing, the batsman's confidence deserted him and, after a final dismissal at Headingley attributable to one of the summer's many umpiring errors – the referral system was not in use for this series – Bopara was dropped.

Despite calls to reinstate Mark Ramprakash purely for the purposes of the final Test at a ground on which he averaged 73 in first-class cricket and had already made a Test hundred against Australia, the selectors instead promoted the 28-year-old South African-bred batsman from Warwickshire, Jonathan Trott. After only a few balls of his first innings, in particular two that reared towards his ribs but were calmly prodded into the ground, with hands on top and body behind the ball, it was clear that Trott had both the temperament and technique for Test cricket.

It is debatable whether this was because he had, as he said, "done the hard yards" in first division County Championship cricket – certainly more

Graham Morris

Picking himself up: like England, Stuart Broad fell at Leeds before rising to the occasion at The Oval.

demanding now than the second division – or because his upbringing had been in Cape Town, as the son of an English cricket coach and a Rhodesian mother. What was undeniable was that four of England's top six batsmen in the final Test had disproved the idea of a yawning gap between county and Test cricket by scoring hundreds in their maiden Tests.

One of them, Cook, seemed hardly to have improved in the three international-packed years since his auspicious debut at Nagpur. Both calmer and intellectually sharper than his young Essex contemporary, he was nevertheless unable to overcome Australia's diligently executed bowling plans, and looked to be in need of a winter's technical remedial work by the end of a series in which he could average only 24 from his nine innings. The fast bowlers pitched the ball up to him and waited until he either played round a firmly planted long right leg or, more frequently, followed the path of balls angled across him, sometimes as if giving catching practice to the slips and gullies.

Much the same policy worked for Paul Collingwood, whose heroic defiance in the second innings at Cardiff gave way to a series of dismissals outside his off stump. Starved of his bread-and-butter runs to midwicket off straight balls, he was surprisingly prone to temptation on quicker pitches. When he also seemed suddenly incapable of getting out of the way of short-pitched balls aimed at his body at The Oval, his future as a Test batsman appeared to be in serious doubt.

Cook looked capable of making the same improvement as Simon Katich, whose brilliant fielding, especially at short leg, added to his value as a solid and well-organised opener. A disappointing, albeit sometimes unlucky batsman four years earlier, he continued to look like an ideal replacement for Langer. Keeping the ball under his nose and clipping it wristily away when the length and line were right, Katich was forming a promising first-wicket partnership with the gifted Shane Watson by the end of the series.

The duel between the two sets of selectors, like that between the two captains and the teams, was close. England's got Bopara wrong and Trott right, but their key decision was probably to resist any temptation to drop Broad, the burgeoning all-rounder, after he had taken only one for 129 in Cardiff as one of three pace bowlers. Stephen Harmison was replete with wickets for Durham at the time and had already performed a valuable service by twice unsettling and dismissing the young prodigy, Phillip Hughes, when bowling for the England Lions immediately before the First Test. In the event, the selectors kept Harmison as a shadow for Flintoff until the last two Tests, telling him privately before the Headingley match that he would play those games, come what may.

Australia's choices were less sound. They risked Hughes at the start of the series, despite evidence that his weakness against balls bouncing towards his right shoulder would undo him until he found a method for getting out of the way. They backed Watson as his replacement and were duly vindicated, but the omission of Hauritz for the last match proved fatal.

Hauritz, chosen for the tour ahead of other spinners of modest attainment despite never having taken a five-wicket haul in a first-class match, had been successfully targeted by Sussex and the Lions in the two warm-up games, but bowled with good control and nice variations of pace to take three wickets in each innings of the First Test.

Sophia Gardens, unfurled in all its modern splendour as the Swalec Stadium (though broadcasters dared not mention its name since Swalec was a competitor of the main series sponsor, npower), was a controversial choice to stage the opening Test in the second week of July. Unashamed that they had bought the rights by outbidding everyone else with the help of Welsh government money, Glamorgan, driven by their chairman Paul Russell, ran the match perfectly. Smiling faces greeted all visitors, were they English, Australian or even from Swansea. On the blandest of pitches, Strauss won a theoretically important toss, the first of four wrong calls by Ponting of which only the last proved really significant. At 90 for three just before lunch England were faltering, but Pietersen and Collingwood had established supremacy when Hilfenhaus produced a fine ball to have Collingwood caught behind, whereupon Pietersen gave his wicket away with a premeditated shot that great players ought not to need.

Dashing batting by Flintoff and Matt Prior (for fluency England's nearest equivalent to Clarke) restored equality, and England were quite pleased with an eventual total of 435. They were soon disabused. Although Hughes fell during Flintoff's first fiery and well-directed spell, Australia had reached 281 for one by the time the second new ball was taken, 20 minutes after the start of the third day. Katich, balanced and wristy, and the inevitable Ponting, making a familiar stamp on the series at the first opportunity, eventually added 239.

Patrick Eagar

Cardiff quartet: Brad Haddin (*left*) joins Marcus North (*right*), Simon Katich and Ricky Ponting in becoming the first four Australians to score hundreds in a single Ashes innings.

Ponting went on to a brilliant 150 before becoming Monty Panesar's only victim in the series.

The die was cast. Clarke, with elegant strokes and dazzlingly quick footwork, kept the pressure on a deflated England attack, before North and Brad Haddin added the third and fourth individual centuries of a triumphant total of 674 for six declared. By the close of the fourth day England, facing a deficit of 239, had lost Cook and Bopara for 17 runs. Already there were gloomy clutchings at straws marked "Headingley 1981".

The impossible escape came in the unlikeliest circumstances imaginable. By lunch on the last day, Pietersen and Strauss had gone and the score was 102 for five. The ball was turning for Hauritz and, despite a flinty and utterly single-minded innings of resistance by Collingwood, England lost two more wickets, those of Flintoff and Broad, in the 34 overs before tea. They were still six runs behind when Collingwood was ninth out after holding up an end for 344 minutes. The improved but strictly limited Anderson faced what turned out to be 11.3 overs in the company of everyone's favourite No. 11, Panesar. Incredibly, neither succumbed.

It was fairer to praise batting of profound spirit, and the advances that both the left-handers had made by diligent net practice since starting their Test careers as utterly hopeless batsmen, than it was to berate Ponting and his bowlers for failing to finish the job. Almost certainly, however, Ponting erred towards the end in not bringing back a fast bowler, and there was no denying the significance of England's astounding reprieve.

It was cruelly emphasised when they beat Australia at Lord's for the first time since Hedley Verity's 15 wickets had bowled them to victory in 1934. The game saw Strauss and his team at their resilient best from the outset. Batting with the same authority that he had shown against West Indies, Strauss put on 196 for the first wicket with Cook, and ended the opening day with an unbeaten 161 out of 364 for six.

He was bowled by the second ball of the second day, playing no shot at Hilfenhaus, but Anderson, swinging the new ball at pace both ways and finding useful support from Flintoff and the wiry and vibrant Onions, bowled Australia out for 215. The tourists had no luck, especially when Rudi Koertzen gave Ponting out caught, mistaking a clash of bat on boot for an inside edge. Hawk-Eye suggested he might have been lbw instead. But England continued to have more of the luck with borderline decisions, as winning sides, who create more chances, invariably do.

RUN-RATES OVER PAST FIVE ASHES SERIES

Ashes series	Runs per over		Runs per wicket		Series result
	England	Australia	England	Australia	
2001	3.50	4.26	26.44	49.11	Australia 4–1
2002-03	3.02	4.09	29.30	46.81	Australia 4–1
2005	3.87	3.72	31.84	31.57	England 2–1
2006-07	2.84	3.90	26.35	52.77	Australia 5–0
2009	**3.77**	**3.63**	**34.15**	**40.64**	**England 2–1**

Research: Benedict Bermange

Strauss chose not to enforce the follow-on, aware that Flintoff's knee injury had to be managed. When the crunch came at Lord's, Flintoff produced a magnificently fast, straight and hostile first spell of two for nine in seven overs from the Pavilion End, then on the fifth morning he broke a brilliant partnership between Clarke and Haddin that had given Australia a distant glimpse of making a record 522 to win. If anything even more irresistible now, Flintoff completed his last match-winning feat in Test cricket to finish with five for 92, only his third five-wicket analysis in a Test innings. His potentially great career had been ruined by injuries, but he played in two of the three remaining games and missed only England's humiliation at Headingley.

The Third Test at Edgbaston was spoiled by bad weather after an unlucky prologue for Australia. Haddin, who had already done a remarkably effective job in filling the chasm left by Gilchrist, broke a finger in a last-minute practice after the teams had been announced and the coin had been spun. Strauss properly allowed his opponents to change wicketkeepers, thus proving that cricket's true spirit depends on sound instinct and education in the game's traditions. Any right-thinking captain of any nationality would have done the same, despite the law. Graham Manou was thus given the chance to show that, when it comes to wicketkeepers, Australia are at least as well stocked with capable reserves as England.

Australia made the most at first of a bland pitch after Ponting had won his only toss of the series, but on the second day Onions and Anderson made outstanding use of good swing-bowling conditions, and from 126 for one they subsided to 263 all out. Staunch innings by Strauss and Ian Bell, returning to the England team in Pietersen's place, paved the way for breezier contributions from Prior (41 from 59 balls) and Flintoff, whose 74 included ten fours and a

Crowd-pleaser: the England team at Lord's applaud as umpire Koertzen confirms the dismissal of Ricky Ponting.

six to delight the usual patriotic Birmingham crowd. Another solid fifty by Watson, determined ones by the left-handed Hussey and North, and an unbeaten hundred from Clarke ensured a draw.

For England, the two-and-a-half-day Test in Leeds was a nightmare; for Australia, a sweet dream. Flintoff had been left out against his will by Flower and Strauss, but Stuart Clark returned for Australia in just the right conditions, with the ball seaming and swinging, to help whistle out England for 102. There was just as much movement for the home fast bowlers, but they bowled horrendously short and wide instead of putting the ball on a length around the off stump. Ponting ruthlessly punished them, striking 12 fours and a six from his 101 balls, and both Clarke and North maintained the impetus in more comfortable batting conditions on the second day.

Broad's all-round form was England's only consolation for a wretched innings defeat, but Flower and Strauss insisted on a team meeting before the players dispersed for ten days of sober reflection and, in most cases, some county cricket. The resilience that followed might have surprised some.

Flintoff was back in the fold for the deciding Test but it was Broad, bowling straight and pitching the ball up, and Swann, on the sort of dry, turning pitch on which Australian sides had often buckled against tidy finger-spin in the past, who delivered the crucial first-innings wickets and a lead of 172. Trott's calm, accomplished century in the second innings underlined England's good fortune in winning the toss. Had the two teams met again ten days later, it would have been no surprise if Australia had won. There was really nothing between them but luck, destiny and Strauss.

John Etheridge's review of the limited-overs series appears on page 518.

AUSTRALIAN TOURING PARTY

R. T. Ponting (*captain*), M. J. Clarke (*vice-captain*), S. R. Clark, B. J. Haddin, N. M. Hauritz, B. W. Hilfenhaus, P. J. Hughes, M. E. K. Hussey, M. G. Johnson, S. M. Katich, B. Lee, A. B. McDonald, G. A. Manou, M. J. North, T. D. Paine, P. M. Siddle, S. R. Watson.

Coach: T. J. Nielsen. *Manager:* S. R. Bernard. *Bowling coach:* T. J. Cooley. *Assistant coaches:* S. G. Helmot and T. J. Barsby. *Analyst:* M. P. Marshall. *Physiotherapist:* A. Kountouris. *Strength and conditioning coach:* S. J. Karppinen. *Massage therapist:* C. F. Binder. *Psychologist:* R. A. Chapman. *Security manager:* F. A. Dimasi. *Media managers:* P. N. D. Pope and A. L. Patterson.

C. D. Hartley was drafted in to cover for Haddin for one two-day game. For the limited-overs internationals which followed the Tests N. W. Bracken, C. J. Ferguson, J. R. Hopes, D. J. Hussey, D. P. Nannes, A. C. Voges, D. A. Warner and C. L. White replaced Clark, Hughes, Katich, McDonald, North and Siddle. Ponting went home until halfway through the one-day series, and Clarke assumed the captaincy in his absence; Haddin withdrew for the limited-overs games because of injury.

The squad for the World Twenty20 tournament which preceded the tour may be found on page 534.

TEST MATCH AVERAGES

ENGLAND – BATTING AND FIELDING

	T	I	NO	R	HS	100s	50s	Avge	Ct/St
†A. J. Strauss	5	9	0	474	161	1	3	52.66	4
K. P. Pietersen	2	4	0	153	69	0	1	38.25	1
G. P. Swann	5	8	1	249	63	0	2	35.57	1
A. Flintoff	4	7	1	200	74	0	1	33.33	1
M. J. Prior	5	9	1	261	61	0	2	32.62	11/1
S. J. Harmison	2	3	2	31	19*	0	0	31.00	0
†S. C. J. Broad	5	9	1	234	61	0	2	29.25	1
I. R. Bell	3	5	0	140	72	0	2	28.00	1
P. D. Collingwood	5	9	0	250	74	0	3	27.77	4
†A. N. Cook	5	9	0	222	95	0	1	24.66	7
†J. M. Anderson	5	8	2	99	29	0	0	16.50	2
R. S. Bopara	4	7	0	105	35	0	0	15.00	3
G. Onions	3	4	2	19	17*	0	0	9.50	0

Played in one Test: †M. S. Panesar 4, 7*; I. J. L. Trott 41, 119 (1 ct).

† *Left-handed batsman.*

BOWLING

	Style	O	M	R	W	BB	5W/i	Avge
S. C. J. Broad	RFM	154.1	25	544	18	6-91	2	30.22
G. Onions	RFM	77.4	11	303	10	4-58	0	30.30
S. J. Harmison	RF	43	10	167	5	3-54	0	33.40
G. P. Swann	OB	170.2	30	567	14	4-38	0	40.50
J. M. Anderson	RFM	158	38	542	12	5-80	1	45.16
A. Flintoff	RF	128.5	18	417	8	5-92	1	52.12

Also bowled: R. S. Bopara (RM) 8.2–1–44–0; P. D. Collingwood (RM) 18–1–76–1; M. S. Panesar (SLA) 35–4–115–1.

AUSTRALIA – BATTING AND FIELDING

	T	I	NO	R	HS	100s	50s	Avge	Ct
M. J. Clarke............	5	8	1	448	136	2	2	64.00	8
†M. J. North.............	5	8	1	367	125*	2	1	52.42	3
R. T. Ponting...........	5	8	0	385	150	1	2	48.12	11
S. R. Watson...........	3	5	0	240	62	0	3	48.00	2
B. J. Haddin...........	4	6	0	278	121	1	1	46.33	15
†S. M. Katich............	5	8	0	341	122	1	1	42.62	6
†M. E. K. Hussey.......	5	8	0	276	121	1	2	34.50	6
N. M. Hauritz	3	3	1	45	24	0	0	22.50	0
B. W. Hilfenhaus........	5	6	4	40	20	0	0	20.00	0
†P. J. Hughes...........	2	3	0	57	36	0	0	19.00	1
P. M. Siddle............	5	6	1	91	35	0	0	18.20	3
†M. G. Johnson..........	5	6	0	105	63	0	1	17.50	0
S. R. Clark.............	2	3	0	38	32	0	0	12.66	0

Played in one Test: G. A. Manou 8, 13* (3 ct).

† *Left-handed batsman.*

BOWLING

	Style	O	M	R	W	BB	5W/i	Avge
B. W. Hilfenhaus....	RFM	180.5	40	604	22	4-60	0	27.45
P. M. Siddle........	RFM	161.4	24	616	20	5-21	1	30.80
N. M. Hauritz	OB	103.2	17	321	10	3-63	0	32.10
M. G. Johnson	LF	162.1	15	651	20	5-69	1	32.55
S. R. Clark	RFM	47	12	176	4	3-18	0	44.00
M. J. North........	OB	67.3	13	204	4	4-98	0	51.00

Also bowled: M. J. Clarke (SLA) 19–1–75–1; S. M. Katich (SLC) 10–2–27–0; S. R. Watson (RFM) 8–0–49–0.

Note: Matches in this section which were not first-class are signified by a dagger.

Details of Australia's matches in the World Twenty20 tournament in June can be found in that section (pages 527–559).

†At Hove, June 24, 25, 26, 27. **Drawn.** Toss: Australians. **Australians 349-7 dec** (S. M. Katich 49, M. E. K. Hussey 32, M. J. Clarke 45, B. J. Haddin 69, B. Lee 47*, N. M. Hauritz 65*; P. S. E. Sandri 3-73) **and 379-7 dec** (P. J. Hughes 78, S. M. Katich 40, R. T. Ponting 71, M. E. K. Hussey 40, M. J. Clarke 75*, B. Lee 33); **Sussex 311** (C. D. Nash 45, R. J. Hamilton-Brown 37, A. J. Hodd 40, R. S. C. Martin-Jenkins 35, Extras 40; B. Lee 3-53, S. R. Clark 3-46) **and 373-7** (M. H. Yardy 67, E. C. Joyce 34, C. D. Hopkinson 115, L. J. Wright 35, A. J. Hodd 37*, Extras 36). *County debut:* P. S. E. Sandri.

The match lost first-class status after the Australians – most of whom had played only one-day cricket for three months – requested a 12-a-side game. It attracted more than 25,000 spectators over four days. In a cracking finish Hopkinson, badly dropped on 69 by Ponting, almost led Sussex to a target of 418; he added 81 in 13 overs with Wright, and they needed 75 off ten, but lost momentum when Hopkinson fell for 115. On a slow, low pitch, the tourists got a wake-up call from Pepler Sandri, a South African of Italian parentage who might not have played had it been 11-a-side. He ripped out both openers with raw pace, and left the Australians on 114-5 before Clarke and Haddin doubled that, while Lee and Hauritz shared an unbroken eighth-wicket stand of 117. Siddle apart, the Australian seamers struggled for consistency, and off-spinner Hauritz's 18 first-innings overs went for 98. Clark struck Hodd's throat with a lifter, but he recovered and brought Sussex close to parity. Hughes and Ponting prospered on the third day, though North took 22 deliveries to get off the mark and struck just one four in 50 balls. A century partnership from Clarke and Lee injected some impetus.

ENGLAND LIONS v AUSTRALIANS

At Worcester, July 1, 2, 3, 4. Drawn. Toss: Australians.

The Australians' uncertain preparations continued, with one of their biggest pluses from this match swiftly negated. Brett Lee, having demonstrated his recovery from ankle surgery in a spell of fast reverse swing that claimed five wickets in 40 balls, was then forced out of contention by a torn abdominal muscle. Their batsmen's form was uneven against the northern seamers; Hussey had to rebuild the Australian innings twice on the opening day, first with Katich and again with Johnson. They looked more convincing over the last two days, though for the second time Hughes, recently prolific for Middlesex, fell cheaply fending a short-pitched ball from Harmison into the slips. North, who had scraped 13 from his last three innings, emulated Hussey by batting more than six hours, missing a double-century when Ponting declared at lunch. In between, Denly and Moore had opened with 172 for the Lions before Lee seized the first five wickets, including home captain Bell first ball, to earn his best figures on English soil. The match ended early when umpire Jeff Evans became dizzy and collapsed; Australian physio Alex Kountouris helped to treat him, and Evans walked off with the players.

Close of play: First day, Australians 337-8 (Hussey 143, Hauritz 7); Second day, England Lions 302-6 (Rashid 36, Bresnan 0); Third day, Australians 276-4 (North 106, Hussey 11).

Australians

P. J. Hughes c Denly b Harmison	7	– c Morgan b Harmison 8
S. M. Katich c Onions b Harmison	95	– c Moore b Rashid 37
*R. T. Ponting c Solanki b Onions	1	– c Rashid b Harmison 15
M. E. K. Hussey b Harmison	150	– (6) retired hurt 62
M. J. Clarke c Rashid b Bresnan	4	– c Onions b Solanki 80
M. J. North b Onions	1	– (4) not out. 191
†B. J. Haddin lbw b Bresnan	7	– not out 25
M. G. Johnson c Davies b Bresnan	47	
B. Lee b Harmison	6	
N. M. Hauritz c Denly b Onions	11	
S. R. Clark not out	10	
B 6, l-b 10, n-b 3	19	B 11, l-b 8, n-b 1 20

1/19 (1) 2/24 (3) 3/165 (2)   (96.4 overs) 358   1/17 (1)   (4 wkts dec, 103 overs) 438
4/185 (5) 5/186 (6) 6/197 (7)   2/41 (3) 3/90 (2)
7/306 (8) 8/315 (9) 9/348 (4) 10/358 (10)   4/260 (5)

In the second innings Hussey retired hurt at 365.

Onions 23.4–3–70–3; Harmison 25–3–80–4; Bresnan 17–1–46–3; Mahmood 17–2–74–0; Rashid 14–1–72–0. *Second Innings*—Onions 19–2–74–0; Harmison 17–3–55–2; Mahmood 18–2–56–0; Bresnan 18–6–60–0; Rashid 22–2–109–1; Solanki 5–0–32–1; Denly 4–0–33–0.

England Lions

J. L. Denly b Lee	66	– c Haddin b Johnson 36
S. C. Moore c Haddin b Lee.	120	– c Ponting b Johnson 16
*I. R. Bell lbw b Lee	0	– c Katich b Hauritz 20
V. S. Solanki b Lee	8	– b Lee. 28
E. J. G. Morgan lbw b Lee	4	– not out 28
†S. M. Davies c Clarke b North	53	– not out 18
A. U. Rashid c Hussey b Clark	66	
T. T. Bresnan b Johnson.	5	
S. I. Mahmood b Lee	0	
S. J. Harmison not out	7	
G. Onions c Hughes b Clark	8	
B 5, l-b 2, n-b 8	15	B 4, l-b 11, n-b 1 16

1/172 (1) 2/172 (3) 3/198 (4)   (96 overs) 352   1/29 (2)   (4 wkts, 47.2 overs) 162
4/209 (2) 5/209 (5) 6/295 (6) 7/315 (8)   2/62 (1) 3/105 (3)
8/316 (9) 9/344 (7) 10/352 (11)   4/115 (4)

Johnson 26–1–118–1; Lee 27–6–76–6; Clark 16–2–40–2; Hauritz 18–1–80–0; Clarke 4–0–15–0; North 5–1–16–1. *Second Innings*—Johnson 9–2–48–2; Lee 8–1–38–1; Clark 8–2–11–0; North 5–0–17–0; Hauritz 12.2–4–22–1; Katich 5–0–11–0.

Umpires: J. H. Evans and J. W. Lloyds.

ENGLAND v AUSTRALIA

First npower Test

STEVE JAMES

At Cardiff, July 8, 9, 10, 11, 12. Drawn. Toss: England.

Wales's first Test match was a triumph in every respect bar the provision of an England victory. But a thrilling draw, with England's last pair surviving 11.3 nerve-shredding overs, was more than ample consolation, another mini-epic to add to a lengthy list in Ashes history. The throbbing atmosphere lost little in comparison with even the greatest of rugby days at the nearby Millennium Stadium. But never before had English defiance been so fanatically cheered by the Welsh.

Test cricket's 100th venue could have done little more. Controversially awarded this Test, courtesy of a reported £3.2m bid, Glamorgan set new standards in hospitality and warmth of welcome. The setting, small at a capacity of 16,000 but intimate and sylvan, was well received, not least by those taking afternoon strolls along the bank of the River Taff who could catch a sneak view of the action. Doubters and critics were silenced. Not a word of complaint was heard.

Except from Australians disappointed at the result. Because, in truth, England were extremely lucky to escape. They were thoroughly outplayed throughout, requiring some timely, if delayed, rain on the fourth afternoon and a typically gritty, over-my-dead-body innings of 74 from Collingwood on the last day to salvage a most unexpected draw.

FEWEST MATCHES TO SCORE 1,000 RUNS IN ASHES TESTS

Tests	Inns		Years	Days
7	13	D. G. Bradman (A)	1	224
8	14	W. R. Hammond (E)	1	225
9	16	A. R. Morris (A)	1	242
9	17	M. A. Taylor (A)	1	214
10	15	H. Sutcliffe (E)	1	239
10	17	L. Hutton (E)	10	19
11	19	M. E. Waugh (A)	3	346
11	20	M. J. Slater (A)	1	248
11	21	K. F. Barrington (E)	3	2
11	**21**	**K. P. Pietersen (E)**	**3**	**353**
11	21	J. B. Hobbs (E)	4	41

Australia's D. M. Jones and J. L. Langer took 20 innings but 12 Tests; England's J. H. Edrich took 20 innings and 13 Tests.

England won the toss on a turgid surface and, for the first time in a home Test since Old Trafford in 1999, fielded two spinners, as they had desired ever since a strip nearby had been censured earlier in the season for "excessive turn", but thereafter did little right. Lacking the later patience of Australia's batsmen, England endured a nervy first session. Strauss and Cook's 55th opening partnership – a national record, beating 54 by Marcus Trescothick and Michael Vaughan – lasted only eight overs as England lost three wickets for 90, two to Johnson, a bouncer gloving Strauss and a slower cutter deceiving Bopara. Even though they probably encountered the most pronounced of the pitch's "tennis-ball" bounce, 435 was an inadequate opening salvo with, disappointingly, none of three players who passed fifty converting into a century. Most heavily criticised was Pietersen, who attempted an unlikely sweep shot at a ball from off-spinner Hauritz that was seemingly nearer the Caerphilly Mountain lurking way beyond the pavilion than his off stump. The ball went tamely, via a deflection from his helmet, to short leg. The media reaction was hysterical, and in his second innings, as if turned ultra-defensive by accusations of profligacy, he left a ball from Hilfenhaus and was bowled.

With Brett Lee ruled out by a side injury, Hilfenhaus was a surprise selection ahead of Stuart Clark. But he was a good one. He swung the new ball consistently and proved the best seamer on show in the match. Siddle, always oozing aggression, ran him close, most especially in a hostile spell before tea on the final day which put Swann through the wringer: he was hit several times by bouncers. The left-armer Johnson was, though, a disappointment. His wild, insipid spell with the new ball in the game's last session may well have cost Australia victory.

England's bowlers were awful, full stop. The smallest of beacons was Flintoff's first spell to Hughes, bowling short and fast from the River Taff End with a ferocity that was too much for the quirky left-hander. Memories of 2005 were briefly rekindled; they did not last. Flintoff blended into the mediocrity as Broad bowled too short, Anderson mislaid the key to his swing, an overawed Swann initially bowled too quickly and Panesar merely continued his poor season's form. That Collingwood's off-cutters found most response from the characteristically Welsh pitch – as the great uncapped Welshman Don Shepherd had once done so effectively in these parts – summed up the plight neatly.

For the first time in an Ashes Test innings, four Australians recorded centuries (while five Englishmen conceded them). The best and most predictable came from Ponting, his gimlet-eyed determination evident from his first ball and through every milestone; his celebrations were cursory. On 40, he became only the fourth batsman behind Sachin Tendulkar, Brian Lara and Allan Border to reach 11,000 Test runs; he advanced to his eighth hundred against England, and his 13th Test score of 150 or more.

AUSTRALIA'S HIGHEST TEST TOTALS AGAINST ENGLAND

729-6 dec	Lord's	1930	656-8 dec	Manchester	1964
701	The Oval	1934	653-4 dec	Leeds	1993
695	The Oval	1930	645	Brisbane.	1946-47
674-6 dec	**Cardiff**	**2009**	641-4 dec	The Oval	2001
659-8 dec	Sydney.	1946-47	632-4 dec	Lord's	1993

Katich had never scored a century against England, and this was revenge for a moderate 2005 Ashes series. But Katich was a No. 6 then, and a limited player, strong only behind square on the off side. Now he revealed himself as an adhesive opener. He still had a crabby pre-delivery movement across the crease, but had added an ability to hit down the ground. There were centuries on Ashes debut for the tall left-hander North and wicketkeeper Haddin. Achieved from a considerable position of strength they might have been, but both surprised observers; North with his ability to drive straight and crisply, and Haddin with a fierce square cut and a natural preference for the leg side.

Rain was forecast for the whole of the fourth day – and England fielded and bowled as if waiting for it. Australia's eventual declaration, 239 ahead, left them half an hour's batting before tea. History had been created the previous day when, as agreed before the series, floodlights were used in a Test for the first time in England and Wales. Now they came on again and the home side lost two quick wickets before the last session was wiped out.

So England began the final day still 219 behind Australia's first innings. Three more wickets fell and they lunched at 102 for five, with all seeming lost. But Collingwood

Philip Brown

No surrender: James Anderson and Monty Panesar leave the field after defying the Australians for the last 69 balls.

simply refused to concede defeat. His short backlift and soft hands blunted the attack, especially the spin of Hauritz, whose performance had mocked pre-match predictions of ineffectiveness. He was not Jim Laker, but Hauritz looked here to be a decent off-spinner. He barely bowled a bad ball, and easily outshone Swann and Panesar.

Collingwood eventually fell, ninth out at 233, caught off a jab to gully after 245 balls and five and three-quarter hours of grim resistance. He was a broken man, unable at first to drag himself from the crease, thinking the game had gone. But last man Panesar had other ideas. On such a slow pitch, his defensive technique was as sound as Ponting's use of North's part-time off-spin was mystifying. Panesar lasted 35 balls, his partner Anderson 53: two southpaw heroes whose stumps were seldom threatened by the Australian bowlers. The 69 deliveries they survived together represented the longest stand recorded in terms of balls by a No. 10 and 11 pair holding out for a draw (beating 64 by New Zealanders Simon Doull and Shayne O'Connor at Hobart in 1997-98, and 60 by Daren Powell and Fidel Edwards against England at St John's in February 2009).

There was controversy, too. Twice in the closing stages England sent twelfth man Bilal Shafayat on to the field. On the second occasion he was accompanied by the stand-in physiotherapist Steve McCaig, an Australian. Even Anderson, obviously unhurt, looked embarrassed. The visitors accused England of time-wasting to prevent Australia bowling more than the minimum 15 overs in the final hour. In the second instance they may well have been correct. Probably not in the first, though: a message was required because there was much confusion all round as to how long England had to survive. They even inched 13 runs ahead of Australia to add to the flurry of calculations. But survive they did.

Man of the Match: R. T. Ponting.   *Attendance:* 75,510.

TIMELINE FOR THE FINAL SESSION AT CARDIFF

England resumed on 169-7 (70 behind) from 71 overs, Collingwood on 55 and Swann 4, and a minimum of 34 overs to be bowled. Siddle and Hauritz continued their spells from before tea.

Time	Over			Score
4.30	72nd	. 1	Collingwood takes a single off Siddle's second ball	170-7
4.35	73rd	. . 1 1 1 .	Collingwood and Swann take three singles off Hauritz	173-7
4.38	74th	1 . 4 . 2lb .	A four for Swann, and two leg-byes bounced off his helmet	180-7
4.43	75th	. 1	Collingwood hits a single to deep point	181-7
4.46	76th	. . 1 . . 1	Katich replaces Siddle for his first bowl of the innings	183-7
4.50	77th	. 1 . . 2 .	Collingwood cover-drives two	186-7
4.53	78th	2 . . . 1 .	Swann runs two off a thick outside edge…	189-7
4.56	79th	. 2 . 3 . .	…and picks up five more, both shots off the back foot	194-7
4.59	80th	. . 4b . . 2	Katich beats Swann and the keeper for four byes.	200-7
5.02	81st	 1	Hilfenhaus replaces Hauritz, and takes the new ball after four deliveries	201-7
5.08	82nd	. w	Johnson replaces Katich, and bowls a wide	202-7
5.13	83rd	. . 4 . 2 .	Swann survives lbw appeal, then edges four through the slips	208-7
5.17	84th	w 2	Another wide from Johnson brings up the fifty partnership for Collingwood and Swann	211-7
5.21	85th	. 4	Swann cover-drives for four	215-7
5.25	86th	. . 4 . 2	Collingwood gloves four off his pads to fine leg	217-7
5.29	87th	W	**5.30 – Hilfenhaus traps Swann lbw: 221-8. Enter Anderson**	221-8
5.35	88th	. . 2 . . .	Collingwood drives for two	223-8
5.40	89th	1	Hauritz replaces Hilfenhaus. Collingwood survives Ponting's bat-pad appeal. Drinks taken	224-8
5.45	90th	. . . . 1 .	Collingwood nearly run out off first ball as Anderson sends him back	225-8
5.50	91st	3	**Umpires signal last hour;** play may continue until 6.50 or until a minimum of 15 overs has been bowled, whichever is later.	228-8
			Anderson runs three; Collingwood survives lbw appeal	
5.53	92nd	. 4	Anderson hits four, and edges last ball short of slips	232-8
5.57	93rd	. . . . . .	Collingwood edges the second ball short of Ponting at silly point.	232-8
6.00	94th	1 . W . 1 1	Siddle replaces Johnson. **6.02 – Collingwood edges catch to gully: 233-9. Enter Panesar, with a minimum of 11.3 overs left**	235-9
6.06	95th	. . . . . .	Anderson survives appeal for catch by Haddin, and for lbw next ball	235-9
6.09	96th	 1	Panesar defends five balls from Siddle, then takes a single…	236-9
6.13	97th	. . . . . .	…and survives another six balls from Hauritz	236-9
6.15	98th	. . . 4 4 .	Anderson hits two fours off Siddle; **the first, through the slips, puts England ahead**, meaning that Australia must bat again to win. Two overs/ten minutes will be deducted for the innings change, so England can survive by batting until 6.40	244-9
6.19	99th	1	Anderson edges Hauritz, but safely	245-9
6.22	100th	. . . . . .	Panesar survives lbw appeal off Siddle's first ball	245-9
6.26	101st	. . 1 . . .	Anderson takes a single to third man	246-9
6.29	102nd	1 4	North replaces Siddle. England twelfth man runs on with a message for the batsmen. Panesar hits North for four to bring up 250	251-9
6.34	103rd	. . . . . .	Twelfth man brings out gloves, accompanied by physiotherapist	251-9
6.36	104th	. . . . . .	Panesar keeps out another six balls from North	251-9
6.39	105th	. . . . . 1b	Anderson runs a bye off the final ball of the match, from Hauritz	252-9
6.42			Players shake hands as the Test is drawn	

Close of play: First day, England 336-7 (Anderson 2, Broad 4); Second day, Australia 249-1 (Katich 104, Ponting 100); Third day, Australia 479-5 (North 54, Haddin 4); Fourth day, England 20-2 (Strauss 6, Pietersen 3).

England

*A. J. Strauss c Clarke b Johnson	30	– c Haddin b Hauritz	17
A. N. Cook c Hussey b Hilfenhaus	10	– lbw b Johnson	6
R. S. Bopara c Hughes b Johnson	35	– lbw b Hilfenhaus	1
K. P. Pietersen c Katich b Hauritz	69	– b Hilfenhaus	8
P. D. Collingwood c Haddin b Hilfenhaus	64	– c Hussey b Siddle	74
†M. J. Prior b Siddle	56	– c Clarke b Hauritz	14
A. Flintoff b Siddle	37	– c Ponting b Johnson	26
J. M. Anderson c Hussey b Hauritz	26	– (10) not out	21
S. C. J. Broad b Johnson	19	– (8) lbw b Hauritz	14
G. P. Swann not out	47	– (9) lbw b Hilfenhaus	31
M. S. Panesar c Ponting b Hauritz	4	– not out	7
B 13, l-b 11, w 2, n-b 12	38	B 9, l-b 9, w 4, n-b 11	33

1/21 (2) 2/67 (1) 3/90 (3)   (106.5 overs) **435**   1/13 (2)   (9 wkts, 105 overs) **252**
4/228 (5) 5/241 (4) 6/327 (7)   2/17 (3) 3/31 (4)
7/329 (6) 8/355 (9) 9/423 (8) 10/435 (11)   4/46 (1) 5/70 (6) 6/127 (7)
                                            7/159 (8) 8/221 (9) 9/233 (5)

Johnson 22–2–87–3; Hilfenhaus 27–5–77–2; Siddle 27–3–121–2; Hauritz 23.5–1–95–3; Clarke 5–0–20–0; Katich 2–0–11–0. *Second Innings*—Johnson 22.4–44–2; Hilfenhaus 15.3–3–47–3; Siddle 18–2–51–1; Hauritz 37–12–63–3; Clarke 3–0–8–0; North 7–4–14–0; Katich 3–0–7–0.

Australia

P. J. Hughes c Prior b Flintoff	36	†B. J. Haddin c Bopara b Collingwood	121
S. M. Katich lbw b Anderson	122	B 9, l-b 14, w 4, n-b 7	34
*R. T. Ponting b Panesar	150		
M. E. K. Hussey c Prior b Anderson	3	1/60 (1) (6 wkts dec, 181 overs)	**674**
M. J. Clarke c Prior b Broad	83	2/299 (2) 3/325 (4)	
M. J. North not out	125	4/331 (3) 5/474 (5) 6/674 (7)	

M. G. Johnson, N. M. Hauritz, P. M. Siddle and B. W. Hilfenhaus did not bat.

Anderson 32–6–110–2; Broad 32–6–129–1; Swann 38–8–131–0; Flintoff 35–3–128–1; Panesar 35–4–115–1; Collingwood 9–0–38–1.

Umpires: Aleem Dar and B. R. Doctrove.
Third umpire: R. A. Kettleborough.   Referee: J. J. Crowe.

ENGLAND v AUSTRALIA

Second npower Test

HUGH CHEVALLIER

At Lord's, July 16, 17, 18, 19, 20. England won by 115 runs. Toss: England.

Shortly before lunch on the last day Swann, who had been giving his off-breaks a tempting flight, saw Johnson advancing and darted an arm-ball in faster. It beat the bat, crashed into middle, and, as Lord's went up in ecstasy, the Australian fortress came down in ruins. For the first time since June 1934, when Hedley Verity crafted 15 wickets with his left-arm spin on a wet pitch, Australia had lost an Ashes Test at HQ – an event as rare as a sighting of Halley's Comet, which also comes once every 75 years.

It was just one match, one victory, with three Tests left, but it felt dangerously as though the Ashes were reclaimed already. Even in the heady days of 2005, England came a cropper here. Now they had won, and won handsomely. England's cricketers, none more prominently than Flintoff, appeared on almost every front page.

Beforehand, Flintoff was also the talk of the back pages. On the eve of the match, he announced that his creaking body (especially the right knee he had injured during the IPL in April) had told him the Ashes would be his Test swansong. Ponting, ever on the watch for a psychological stick with which to beat his opponents, said a four-Test farewell could only distract England. From the available evidence, he could not have been more wrong. A galvanised Flintoff, driven by his last chance of glory at Lord's, produced one of the most relentlessly hostile spells by an England bowler for a generation. For someone with just one serviceable knee, it was astonishing.

Flintoff, who pitched too short in the first innings, was deadliest on the last morning. Thanks to an iron-willed fightback by Clarke and Haddin, Australia had recovered from 128 for five to begin the day at 313, still five down. The sun was shining, the pitch true, and conditions for batting the best Australia enjoyed all match. Their target was the small matter of 522 (nine more than the highest winning fourth-innings total in all first-class cricket), but the unbeaten stand of 185 had instilled doubts – Strauss admitted to a poor night's sleep. Flintoff, sporting aggression made flesh, thundered in; not once in his first over of the day did he fall below 90mph. Unsure whether the ball would move down the slope, Haddin edged low to Collingwood at second slip. Flintoff then told his captain he was staying on until the last wicket fell. "It seemed a good plan to me," said Strauss.

CENTURY AND FIVE WICKETS IN AN INNINGS AT LORD'S

I. T. Botham (England)	108 v Pakistan, 1978	8-34 v Pakistan, 1978
		6-101 and 5-39 v New Zealand, 1978
		5-35 v India, 1979
		5-46 v India, 1982
		8-103 v West Indies, 1984
		6-90 v Sri Lanka, 1984
		5-109 v Australia, 1985
G. O. B. Allen (England) . . .	122 v New Zealand, 1931	5-35 and 5-43 v India, 1936
K. R. Miller (Australia).	109 v England, 1953	5-72 and 5-80 v England, 1956
V. Mankad (India)	184 v England, 1952	5-196 v England, 1952
R. Illingworth (England). . . .	113 v West Indies, 1969	6-29 v India, 1967
A. Flintoff (England).	142 v South Africa, 2003	**5-92 v Australia, 2009**

Only Botham and Mankad have scored a hundred and taken five in an innings in the same Lord's Test.

G. S. Sobers (West Indies) scored 163* at Lord's in 1966 and 150* in 1973, and also took 6-21 for Rest of the World v England there in 1970.

Haddin's obduracy had held for 49 overs, and his wicket was the break England craved. Johnson helped add 43 before Clarke fell for an outstanding, chanceless 136. His concentration was exceptional, his cover-drives of such beauty that spectators cooed with delight. His deft footwork to spin had been faultless, yet in his strength lay his downfall: a dipping, curving ball from Swann beat his advancing bat and spun in to hit off. Their overnight heroes gone, Australia had no route back from 356 for seven. The session belonged to Flintoff, who bowled all ten overs from the Pavilion End at a ferocious pace, honouring his word to his captain but horrifying the medical staff. Twice he demolished the stumps with unplayable balls that swung in and jagged down the slope. Siddle's wicket gave Flintoff a coveted Lord's five-for, only his third in any Test.

England had replaced Panesar's spin with Onions's swing and seam, while Australia were unchanged. Strauss won an important toss to gain first use of a belter, and was helped by Johnson, who pitched far too short – his bowling arm as low as his confidence after a shoddy performance in Wales. By lunch on the first day, his eight overs had yielded 11 fours. Although he later removed Cook (his 100th Test wicket) for a sprightly 95 containing 18 boundaries, the openers had put on 196, and Australia were doomed to play catch-up.

That first-wicket stand was a firm rejoinder to the accusation that England's batsmen had not imposed themselves at Cardiff – and yet the accusation still applied. Bopara fell just as he seemed to settle, when Hilfenhaus varied his stock outswinger; Pietersen, hampered by an Achilles injury that required surgery the following week, showed flashes of brilliance before flashing at Siddle; Collingwood chipped horribly to mid-on; Prior was bowled when Johnson swung the old ball between bat and pad; and Flintoff was beaten by one that came down the slope. The glorious exception was Strauss, who cut, pulled and swept with power and judgment to maintain the morning's tempo. He gave a couple of half-chances, including a return catch that dislocated a finger on Hauritz's right hand, but his fourth hundred in 12 Tests at Lord's was his highest and arguably his best. At the close he was on 161, precisely 5,000 Test runs to his name, and England were 364 for six, not quite the promised land they had glimpsed from the heights of 196 for none.

Next morning, the admirable Hilfenhaus removed Strauss, who unwisely ignored the second ball of the day. Two more wickets had England 378 for nine before an ebullient partnership put the wind back in their sails. Anderson's batting was a known and useful commodity, Onions's a pleasant surprise; between them they added 47, bettered only by the opening stand (both were Ashes records for England at Lord's). It was the first time England had reached 400 against Australia here since 1975.

Under slate-grey clouds that saw the new floodlights on soon after lunch, the ball moved far more than on the first day. Batting was a trickier proposition – and so were England's bowlers. Anderson shared the new ball not with the off-colour Broad, but with Flintoff, in theory available only for short bursts. Their swing and accuracy complemented each other well, and the pity was their pairing could not outlive the series. Hughes gloved an attempted pull before Lord's erupted at the fall of Ponting, caught at slip after apparently edging an inswinger from Anderson into his pads. The umpires asked for confirmation that the catch was good; it was, but the noise Koertzen heard was bat on boot, not ball on bat. Ponting was livid, but there was some justice: Hawk-Eye revealed he was probably lbw.

Katich oversaw a recovery from ten for two before being spectacularly caught at long leg – one of five Australians to fall pulling – to trigger a collapse of six for 49. The tail rallied under sunnier skies next morning, but the deficit was 210, providing only the second opportunity for an England captain to enforce the follow-on against Australia since 1987-88. With the game little more than two days old, and mindful of the injuries sustained by the pace attack when England had asked South Africa to follow on here a year earlier, Strauss chose to bat. He and Cook rattled along before both succumbed to the underrated and persevering Hauritz. Then came a curious contest within a contest, in which Bopara, Pietersen and Johnson – all badly out-of-sorts – struggled to regain form. Bopara was even gifted two lives: Ponting, his fingers pointing up though the ball was low, shelled a straightforward chance at slip, and Hauritz seemed to hold one at mid-on. He was convinced the catch was clean, but Bopara stood his ground; the umpires called for a replay which, as so often, only muddied the waters. Pietersen had rarely been less fluent.

After such introspection, the extroverts at Nos 5, 6 and 7 were a breath of fresh air. In the 31 overs possible after tea, they piled on 181 runs, Collingwood beginning the acceleration and Prior batting at Gilchristian tempo. Indeed in Ashes cricket only Gilchrist had hit an innings of 50-plus at a faster strike-rate than Prior's 145 per hundred balls. Some urged Strauss to continue batting on the Sunday morning, but he ignored them: the forecast for later was mixed and, after a 15-minute delay, the conditions were ideal for bowling. His declaration set a gargantuan target of 522.

England's brisk scoring had given them two days to dismiss Australia, though it briefly looked as if one would be enough. First blood came when Katich edged to gully, though replays showed Flintoff, unnoticed by Koertzen, overstepping. The umpire, who became the second after Steve Bucknor to stand in 100 Tests, was in the thick of it again when Strauss claimed a low slip catch, but Ponting, the non-striker, urged Hughes not to walk.

Cut and thrust: Andrew Strauss bats England into a strong position on the first day at Lord's; a ferocious last-morning spell from Andrew Flintoff converts advantage into victory.

Koertzen was unsure about the carry, but not Doctrove – and Hughes was on his way without recourse to the third umpire. The contrast with Bopara's reprieve was stark, though the playing conditions unambiguously stated that a catch could be referred only if *both* on-field umpires were unable to make a decision. Television also raised questions about the catch, but answered none.

Australia, now 34 for two, desperately needed Ponting to redress his Lord's record: 71 runs in five Test innings. He had shown a few promising signs when he cut a full ball into his stumps – Broad's 50th Test wicket. Next was Hussey, neatly caught edging Swann to slip. No one queried Doctrove's verdict except the batsman, who looked nonplussed. But once the technological panoply of "snicko", "hot-spot" and endless replays was unleashed, it emerged that the ball had turned sharply out of the rough and that the sound was that of the bat striking the pitch. It was a perfect illustration of the plight of the 21st-century umpire, dependent on ageing eyes and ears when the rest of the world has recourse to heat-sensing cameras, long lenses and hypersensitive microphones. Australia, who might in other circumstances have been one down (Ponting could have no argument with his dismissal) were 120 for four. Swann soon bowled North between bat and pad to leave them 128 for five in the 39th over of the day.

YOUNGEST PLAYERS WITH 50 WICKETS FOR ENGLAND

Years	Days		Tests for 50 wickets
22	261	I. T. Botham	10
23	**25**	**S. C. J. Broad**	**19**
23	120	W. Voce	12
24	50	D. L. Underwood	14
24	57	N. G. Cowans	19
24	198	J. B. Statham	20
24	304	G. R. Dilley	18
24	306	D. G. Cork	11
24	356	J. M. Anderson	17
25	7	F. H. Tyson	9

When Strauss took the new ball beneath skies inky enough for the floodlights to be on again, Clarke and Haddin's resistance had already spanned 41 overs. Tired limbs could make no impression, but in this game luck was an England supporter, and losing 12 overs at the end of the fourth day was a blessing: it allowed a fiery Flintoff another and more ferocious blast with the hard ball on the fifth. His subsequent apotheosis by the media might have been overdone (Strauss's century set up the victory), but it was impossible to overstate his worth to the England attack.

Man of the Match: A. Flintoff. *Attendance:* 142,945.

Close of play: First day, England 364-6 (Strauss 161, Broad 7); Second day, Australia 156-8 (Hauritz 3, Siddle 3); Third day, England 311-6 (Flintoff 30, Broad 0); Fourth day, Australia 313-5 (Clarke 125, Haddin 80).

England

*A. J. Strauss b Hilfenhaus	161	– c Clarke b Hauritz	32
A. N. Cook lbw b Johnson	95	– lbw b Hauritz	32
R. S. Bopara lbw b Hilfenhaus	18	– c Katich b Hauritz	27
K. P. Pietersen c Haddin b Siddle	32	– c Haddin b Siddle	44
P. D. Collingwood c Siddle b Clarke	16	– c Haddin b Siddle	54
†M. J. Prior b Johnson	8	– run out	61
A. Flintoff c Ponting b Hilfenhaus	4	– not out	30
S. C. J. Broad b Hilfenhaus	16	– not out	0
G. P. Swann c Ponting b Siddle	4		
J. M. Anderson c Hussey b Johnson	29		
G. Onions not out	17		
B 15, l-b 2, n-b 8	25	B 16, l-b 9, w 1, n-b 5	31

1/196 (2) 2/222 (3) 3/267 (4)   (101.4 overs) 425   1/61 (2)   (6 wkts dec, 71.2 overs) 311
4/302 (5) 5/317 (6) 6/333 (7)   2/74 (1) 3/147 (3)
7/364 (1) 8/370 (9) 9/378 (8) 10/425 (10)   4/174 (4) 5/260 (6) 6/311 (5)

Hilfenhaus 31–12–103–4; Johnson 21.4–2–132–3; Siddle 20–1–76–2; Hauritz 8.3–1–26–0; North 16.3–2–59–0; Clarke 4–1–12–1. *Second Innings*—Hilfenhaus 19–5–59–0; Johnson 17–2–68–0; Siddle 15.2–4–64–2; Hauritz 16–1–80–3; Clarke 4–0–15–0.

Australia

P. J. Hughes c Prior b Anderson	4	– c Strauss b Flintoff	17
S. M. Katich c Broad b Onions	48	– c Pietersen b Flintoff	6
*R. T. Ponting c Strauss b Anderson	2	– b Broad	38
M. E. K. Hussey b Flintoff	51	– c Collingwood b Swann	27
M. J. Clarke c Cook b Anderson	1	– b Swann	136
M. J. North b Anderson	0	– b Swann	6
†B. J. Haddin c Cook b Broad	28	– c Collingwood b Flintoff	80
M. G. Johnson c Cook b Broad	4	– b Swann	63
N. M. Hauritz c Collingwood b Onions	24	– b Flintoff	1
P. M. Siddle c Strauss b Onions	35	– b Flintoff	7
B. W. Hilfenhaus not out	6	– not out	4
B 4, l-b 6, n-b 2	12	B 5, l-b 8, n-b 8	21

1/4 (1) 2/10 (3) 3/103 (2) 4/111 (4) (63 overs) 215
5/111 (5) 6/139 (6) 7/148 (8) 8/152 (7)
9/196 (9) 10/215 (10)

1/17 (2) 2/34 (1) (107 overs) 406
3/78 (3) 4/120 (4)
5/128 (6) 6/313 (7) 7/356 (5)
8/363 (9) 9/388 (10) 10/406 (8)

Anderson 21–5–55–4; Flintoff 12–4–27–1; Broad 18–1–78–2; Onions 11–1–41–3; Swann 1–0–4–0. *Second Innings*—Anderson 21–4–86–0; Flintoff 27–4–92–5; Onions 9–0–50–0; Broad 16–3–49–1; Swann 28–3–87–4; Collingwood 6–1–29–0.

Umpires: B. R. Doctrove and R. E. Koertzen.
Third umpire: N. J. Llong.   Referee: J. J. Crowe.

NORTHAMPTONSHIRE v AUSTRALIANS

At Northampton, July 24, 25, 26. Australians won by 135 runs. Toss: Australians. First-class debut: J. A. Brooks.

Needing to regroup after their defeat at Lord's, the tourists claimed a morale-boosting victory in a game from which – according to coach Tim Nielsen – they derived "nothing but positives". Yet questions persisted about the form of some players. Johnson continued to struggle, failing to take a wicket until the final ball of the match, while conceding nearly six an over against a young line-up. Hughes fell to a short-pitched ball again, this time from Wigley on the rain-shortened opening day, though he made amends second time round, reaching an enterprising fifty with a six. Watson, however, struck the ball handsomely and played his way into the Test side, while Clark bowled accurately to make his own strong case. For Northamptonshire, Jack Brooks – a 25-year-old seamer from Oxfordshire – dismissed two late-order batsmen on first-class debut. Wakely, Wessels and Howgego gained useful batting experience against high-quality opposition, until a collapse of eight for 66 on the final afternoon disappointed the home crowd.

Close of play: First day, Australians 231-3 (Hussey 75, North 32); Second day, Australians 139-0 (Hughes 69, McDonald 69).

Australians

P. J. Hughes c Wakely b Wigley	10	– b Wigley	68
S. M. Katich c O'Brien b Willey	25		
S. R. Watson c O'Brien b G. G. White	84	– c Wessels b G. G. White	50
*M. E. K. Hussey retired out	75	– (5) not out	9
M. J. North c Willey b Lucas	39		
A. B. McDonald b Brooks	32	– (2) c Nelson b Willey	75
†G. A. Manou lbw b Lucas	0	– (4) not out	59
M. G. Johnson c Wessels b Brooks	14		
N. M. Hauritz not out	12		
P. M. Siddle not out	11		
L-b 6	6	L-b 9	9

1/18 (1) 2/48 (2) (8 wkts dec, 79 overs) 308
3/147 (3) 4/231 (4)
5/245 (5) 6/245 (7) 7/285 (6) 8/286 (8)

1/146 (2) (3 wkts dec, 53 overs) 270
2/150 (1) 3/224 (3)

S. R. Clark did not bat.

Wigley 16–3–63–1; Lucas 15–3–44–2; Brooks 20–3–89–2; Willey 15–1–58–1; G. G. White 13–1–48–1. *Second Innings*—Wigley 14–3–77–1; Lucas 6–0–31–0; Brooks 11–1–52–0; G. G. White 11–1–49–1; Willey 11–0–52–1.

Northamptonshire

B. H. N. Howgego c Manou b Clark	9	– c Hauritz b McDonald	46
N. J. O'Brien b Siddle	30	– c Siddle b Watson	58
*R. A. White b Clark	5	– c Manou b Clark	1
A. G. Wakely c Katich b Watson	62	– c Manou b Clark	1
†M. H. Wessels c Johnson b Watson	50	– c Manou b McDonald	33
M. A. G. Nelson c Katich b Siddle	34	– run out	9
D. J. Willey b North b Siddle	19	– c Katich b McDonald	2
G. G. White not out	3	– b McDonald	0
D. S. Lucas (did not bat)		– c Manou b Hauritz	22
D. H. Wigley (did not bat)		– c Siddle b Johnson	16
J. A. Brooks (did not bat)		– not out	10
B 5, l-b 5, w 1, n-b 3	14	B 12, l-b 3, w 1, n-b 3	19

1/16 (1) 2/41 (3)   (7 wkts dec, 49.3 overs) 226   1/99 (2) 2/104 (3)   (64.1 overs) 217
3/57 (2) 4/149 (4)   3/118 (4) 4/140 (1)
5/175 (5) 6/212 (7) 7/226 (6)   5/153 (6) 6/162 (7) 7/164 (8)
                                         8/165 (5) 9/203 (9) 10/217 (10)

Siddle 9.3–0–53–3; Clark 14–2–45–2; Johnson 7–0–42–0; McDonald 5–0–23–0; Hauritz 9–2–33–0; Watson 5–0–20–2. *Second Innings*—Siddle 4–1–11–0; Clark 9–1–29–2; Johnson 11.1–1–65–1; Watson 10–3–34–1; Hauritz 12–2–36–1; McDonald 11–5–15–4; North 7–1–12–0.

Umpires: M. J. D. Bodenham and M. A. Eggleston.

ENGLAND v AUSTRALIA

Third npower Test

S T E V E N   L Y N C H

At Birmingham, July 30, 31, August 1, 2, 3. Drawn. Toss: Australia. Test debut: G. A. Manou.

Two superb sessions gave England the upper hand in this match, but they could not conjure up a third when they needed one on the final day. In the end Australia survived comfortably enough, helped by the loss of the entire third day and most of the first to rain, and when a soggy match dribbled to its conclusion they were arguably in the stronger position, leading by 262 with five wickets standing.

The first of England's purple passages came on the second day, after a lacklustre bowling performance in the two hours possible on the first had let Australia – for whom Ponting had won the toss and decided to bat despite the overcast conditions and sodden outfield – sprint out of the blocks. The overnight 126 for one was transformed when Onions pinned Watson in front with the first ball of the day, then Hussey let the second one go, only for it to clip his off stump. Hussey, who had bustled bristlingly out to the centre, marched off equally quickly. It was thought to be only the second time that wickets had fallen to the first two balls of any day's play in a Test, after 1936-37, when 12,000 spectators at Melbourne saw "Chuck" Fleetwood-Smith seal Australia's 3–2 series triumph by taking England's last two wickets on the fifth morning.

As at Lord's, and later at The Oval, quick strikes gave England an irresistible momentum for a while, and Australia lost seven wickets for 77 in the session, dipping to 203 for eight by lunch. Onions also removed Ponting, who thin-edged an attempted pull not long after passing Allan Border's 11,174 to become Australia's leading Test run-scorer – having reached 20,000 first-class runs earlier on. Then Anderson took over. Swinging the ball as if attached to a piece of (English-made) elastic, he trapped Clarke with a big inswinger that Hawk-Eye suggested might have slipped down leg (umpire Koertzen also ignored Clarke's big stride forward). North was well caught by Prior, diving in front of first slip, then Johnson padded up to his first delivery, which swung in late. Finally Manou was beaten by a superb ball, angled in from wide of the crease but straightening, which extracted his off stump: Anderson had taken four wickets in 14 balls, and Australia were on the ropes.

Some tail-end resistance pushed the total to 263 before Anderson completed a deserved five-for – his first against Australia – but England made a poor start when Cook stretched to nick a widish delivery in Siddle's first over. Bopara started with a pleasing clip for four off his pads, but although he survived until tea he departed immediately afterwards, inside-edging Hilfenhaus into his stumps. This brought in Bell, given the onerous task of replacing the injured Kevin Pietersen, and he settled in alongside the impressive Strauss, passing 10,000 first-class runs early in his innings and later skipping down the pitch to loft Hauritz for six, although Bell was lucky to escape – courtesy of Koertzen, who had another undistinguished game – what looked a plumb lbw shout by Johnson on 18.

England were 147 behind when bad light brought an early end to the second day, then the rain returned in earnest to wash out the third: even though groundsman Steve Rouse and his staff carried on the tireless efforts that had allowed the game to begin in the first place, play never looked likely, and the umpires gave up at 2.40. Matters were not helped by Edgbaston's antiquated drainage system which, like the pavilion, was due for replacement in 2010. The restart was delayed a further hour on the fourth morning, after which Strauss and Collingwood soon fell, but then came England's second superb session. After lunch Bell made a neat half-century

Good weather for ducks: rain washes out the third day's play.

Philip Brown

before he was trapped in front by Johnson, who was finally showing signs of the form he had mislaid after a successful South African tour, pitching it up more and preferring the older ball. But Prior and Flintoff tucked in, with Flintoff taking a particular liking to the military-mediums of Watson, who obligingly pitched too full at him during three oddly timed overs.

Prior, looking more and more like his mentor Alec Stewart at the crease, attacked well. He had 41 from 59 balls when, perhaps over-confident, he skied a pull straight to mid-on. But in the next over Flintoff mowed Hauritz for six to level the scores, then swept a four to complete his fifty and put England in front. He and Broad took 15 from six balls from Siddle as they piled on 52 in nine overs; Flintoff prolonged the underused Johnson's agony with two fours in an otherwise hostile over. He sprinted to 74, taking his Test batting average at Edgbaston to exactly 50 (by his retirement, Flintoff's highest at any ground on which he played more than one match), before failing to remove his gloves from the path of his 79th ball, an off-break from Hauritz that spat up out of the rough. However, Swann leaned back to hammer Hauritz through the covers to give England 157 runs from 32.1 overs in another sparkling session.

Again the momentum could not quite be maintained. The final three wickets soon fell to the new ball for a lead of 113, though Anderson beat Geraint Jones's England record by achieving his 52nd Test innings without a duck, and Broad was the last to go after a stroke-filled fifty. Australia's openers negotiated the first 13 overs with few alarms, but England briefly sniffed victory when Katich nicked Onions, and then Ponting – trying to push against the spin into the covers – was gated by a big-turning off-break from Swann. Next came what, in hindsight, might have been England's last chance to force victory: Hussey, on a king pair, inside-edged his first ball on to his body, from where it looped back up the

pitch. Despite a despairing dive, the bowler Onions just failed to reach it, but short leg might well have done... had one been posted by Strauss, never the most attacking of captains. The next wicket did not fall until after the drinks interval on the final morning, by which time Australia were back in front.

Watson, playing his second resolute innings of the match, and Hussey both passed 50, then Clarke and North batted throughout what was for England's bowlers a rather flat afternoon to make the match safe. It might have been different if Strauss had caught a pull by Clarke, then 38, at short midwicket from Bopara's second ball of the series: Australia would effectively have been 106 for five. North, after some peachy cover-drives and three fine fours in a Bopara over, fell to a sharp gully catch when 96. When Clarke reached his 12th hundred, in his 50th Test, the match concluded.

It was arguably the first dull draw in a live Ashes Test since Lord's in 1997. Indeed, much of the drama outside England's spasmodic brilliance occurred before the start. Pietersen had undergone surgery on the Achilles problem that clearly hindered him at Lord's, so Bell returned for England on his home ground. For Australia, Phillip Hughes was jettisoned after three unconvincing innings and replaced by

Stroke of luck: Michael Clarke nibbles to slip on 96, but umpire Koertzen signals a no-ball.

Watson, who had opened in one-day internationals but only six times in first-class cricket, where he averaged 4.66. In a first for international cricket, Hughes let slip news of his axing via the Twitter website before the official announcement ("Disappointed not to be on the field with the lads today, will be supporting the guys, it's a BIG test match 4 us. Thanks 4 all the support!"). The choice of Watson to open was described by one Australian journalist as "not from left field but out of the car park", but he applied himself well for his two fifties, although his liking for the clipped on-drive suggested he was a possible lbw candidate. He was the first right-hander to open in a Test for Australia since Michael Slater at Headingley in 2001.

An unscheduled change came shortly before the start, when Brad Haddin broke the ring finger on his left hand in practice. The toss had just taken place, so the teams were

(Graham Morris)

theoretically finalised, but England agreed that the reserve wicketkeeper, South Australia's Graham Manou, could play instead. It was believed to be the first time a Test side had been changed after the toss had been made. Manou was the 411th man to wear the baggy green, although the last-minute rush meant he was not officially presented with his cap until the second morning. Edgbaston was an unlucky ground for Haddin: in 2005 he had been playing touch rugby with Glenn McGrath when McGrath stepped on a ball and injured his ankle, forcing him out of that epic encounter which England won by two runs.

Man of the Match: M. J. Clarke.   *Attendance:* 101,538.

Close of play: First day, Australia 126-1 (Watson 62, Ponting 17); Second day, England 116-2 (Strauss 64, Bell 26); Third day, No play; Fourth day, Australia 88-2 (Watson 34, Hussey 18).

Australia

S. R. Watson lbw b Onions	62	– c Prior b Anderson	53
S. M. Katich lbw b Swann	46	– c Prior b Onions	26
*R. T. Ponting c Prior b Onions	38	– b Swann	5
M. E. K. Hussey b Onions	0	– c Prior b Broad	64
M. J. Clarke lbw b Anderson	29	– not out	103
M. J. North c Prior b Anderson	12	– c Anderson b Broad	96
*G. A. Manou b Anderson	8	– not out	13
N. M. Hauritz not out	20		
M. G. Johnson lbw b Anderson	0		
P. M. Siddle c Prior b Anderson	13		
B. W. Hilfenhaus c Swann b Onions	20		
B 5, l-b 7, w 2, n-b 1	15	B 4, l-b 6, w 2, n-b 3	15

1/85 (2) 2/126 (1) 3/126 (4)   (70.4 overs) 263   1/47 (1)   (5 wkts, 112.2 overs) 375
4/163 (3) 5/193 (5) 6/202 (6)   2/52 (3) 3/137 (1)
7/202 (8) 8/203 (7) 9/229 (10) 10/263 (11)   4/161 (4) 5/346 (6)

Anderson 24–7–80–5; Flintoff 15–2–58–0; Onions 16.4–2–59–4; Broad 13–2–51–0; Swann 2–0–4–1. *Second Innings*—Anderson 21–8–47–1; Flintoff 15–0–35–0; Onions 19–3–74–1; Swann 31–4–119–1; Broad 16–2–38–2; Bopara 8.2–1–44–0; Collingwood 2–0–8–0.

England

*A. J. Strauss c Manou b Hilfenhaus	69	G. P. Swann c North b Johnson	24
A. N. Cook c Manou b Siddle	0	J. M. Anderson c Manou b Hilfenhaus	1
R. S. Bopara b Hilfenhaus	23	G. Onions not out	2
I. R. Bell lbw b Johnson	53	B 2, l-b 4, w 6, n-b 9	21
P. D. Collingwood c Ponting b Hilfenhaus	13		
*M. J. Prior c sub (P. J. Hughes) b Siddle	41	1/2 (2) 2/60 (3) 3/141 (1) (93.3 overs) 376
A. Flintoff c Clarke b Hauritz	74	4/159 (5) 5/168 (4) 6/257 (6)
S. C. J. Broad c and b Siddle	55	7/309 (7) 8/348 (9) 9/355 (10) 10/376 (8)

Hilfenhaus 30–7–109–4; Siddle 21.3–3–89–3; Hauritz 18–2–57–1; Johnson 21–1–92–2; Watson 3–0–23–0.

Umpires: Aleem Dar and R. E. Koertzen.
Third umpire: R. A. Kettleborough.   Referee: J. J. Crowe.

ENGLAND v AUSTRALIA

Fourth npower Test

SCYLD BERRY

At Leeds, August 7, 8, 9. Australia won by an innings and 80 runs. Toss: England.

This was a shattering let-down for England's players, who went to Leeds knowing that one good game would regain the Ashes. They were beaten by an innings in less than two

North star: Marcus North takes a blinder to remove Andrew Strauss for three, and the tone is set.

and a half days, and forced to the verge of mental disintegration, as in so many Ashes series of the last two decades, before a significant last-minute rally. Strauss admitted that England "didn't really turn up".

The very knowledge that the Ashes were within reach seemed to cause England to freeze. They had several distractions before the start, but the fundamental reason was that they succumbed to the pressure in what everybody prophesied would be the decisive match of the series following the rain-affected draw at Edgbaston. If they were nervous at Cardiff, here England could not perform at all until, with nothing left to play for except some self-respect, Broad and Swann finally gave the crowd something to cheer.

While England saved their worst for Headingley, as they had done against South Africa the previous year and India in 2002, Australia turned on their best cricket. In place of Hauritz, they finally selected Clark, who proceeded to give a masterclass on how to use the conditions on the first morning and set England too far back to recover. As a unit, Australia's pace bowlers were as disciplined as South Africa's had been, while the home batsmen and bowlers were ill-disciplined in typically English conditions, when everything hinged on putting the ball in the right place to maximise the seam and swing movement.

The distractions for England included a fire alarm in their hotel at 5 a.m. on the first morning of the match, which had them standing in the street for half an hour. Then there was Andrew Flintoff, who wanted to play but was not selected after labouring through a bowling fitness test on the eve of the game. Strauss and coach Andy Flower wanted him to be able to bowl more than one or two spells per day and, with the advice of the medical staff, decided his right knee was not up to the task. The omission of Flintoff, while medically correct, had the same deflating effect on the chemistry as Darren Pattinson's inclusion at Headingley the year before. The team and spectators had nobody to inspire the same bullish confidence. The crowd, which had been told by the ECB chairman Giles Clarke to have more respect for Ponting after he had been booed loudly at Edgbaston, was mute while England collapsed on the opening day.

As if these were not distractions enough, Prior suffered a back spasm (the second of his life) an hour before the game. Chaos ensued as the medical staff gave him an injection and a fitness test, while Collingwood practised his rusty wicketkeeping (he had done a bit in the Chester-le-Street Test three months before). England asked for the toss to be delayed by ten minutes, which Australia granted for the favour which Strauss had done them by allowing Haddin to be replaced after the toss in the previous Test. Prior said afterwards that he would not have been able to declare himself ready by 10.30.

After deciding to bat at 10.40, and then conducting three media interviews, Strauss had too little time to prepare himself mentally for batting; but if he had chosen to bowl first on a remarkably dry pitch and Australia had survived the opening exchanges, he would have been more than pilloried. Strauss played all round his first ball, an inswinger from Hilfenhaus. An indifferent match for the umpires – except for their cutting down on England players leaving the field for unacceptable reasons – began with Bowden turning down the appeal. Not long afterwards Strauss drove at a ball angled across him and North at third slip began his man-of-the-match campaign by holding on with his right hand to a screamer. The pattern of the series whereby England made a good score if their captain did, and not if he didn't, was maintained.

Bopara and Bell were found wanting as Bopara hung out his bat and was caught at gully, and Bell, after a couple of loose shots, fended a bouncer. The techniques of Collingwood and Cook were exposed as the Australians' full length drew them into front-foot off-drives. A bustling innings of 37 not out from 43 balls by Prior was all that remained. Siddle recorded the best figures of his Test career by mixing in some short balls at England's tailenders along with the requisite length. The fact that all ten wickets went to catches emphasised the standard of shot selection.

England began to make some amends for their batting by quickly dismissing Katich, a snorter from Harmison who had taken the new ball on his recall. Unfortunately, they seemed to be encouraged by this dismissal to think that short balls were a good tactic on this pitch, rather than Clark-like line and length. Ponting, on the back foot, feasted on this fare and shut England out of the game. Watson had put away to the third-man boundary the first two balls of the innings from Anderson, which were short and wide. England's leading bowler to that point, Anderson had tweaked a hamstring in his left leg when going for a quick single to get off the mark and was thereafter a disconsolate figure.

MOST CENTURIES BY AN AUSTRALIAN IN HIS FIRST SIX TESTS

4	D. G. Bradman		3	A. R. Morris		3	M. E. K. Hussey
3	W. Bardsley		3	R. N. Harvey		**3**	**M. J. North**

In addition to Bradman, G. A. Headley (West Indies) and S. M. Gavaskar (India) scored four centuries in their first six Tests. Nine other players have scored three.

Before the close of the first day England took three more wickets, by pitching the ball up, although they were 94 behind already. But the lesson was lost again on the second morning when they kept banging it in. Hitting Clarke on the helmet on the first evening seemed to be further inducement, but Australia's form batsman, even though restricted by a stomach strain, pulled the short stuff as well as stroking it through the off side. He and North, determined to build the big first innings which had been missing in the two previous Tests, carried on from where they had left off at Edgbaston with another stand of 150-plus. North thought the Australians had brought the momentum with them from there, and believing it helped to make it so. The left-hander, raised in Perth, was given plenty to pull, and he cover-drove with a growing flourish on the rare occasions the ball was full, before reaching his third hundred in six Tests with a slog-sweep for six off Swann.

During the match, a Sunday newspaper published a dossier which Justin Langer had drawn up for the Australian players, saying that English cricketers went soft when the going got tough. And as the latter became ever more downcast, Langer could claim to have had a point. Broad got stuck in, after bowling wide of off stump until Australia's lead was approaching 300. With the second new ball he mopped up the tail for his best Test figures, but only after Clark had pulled him for two consecutive sixes.

Even after a start of 58, England's second innings disintegrated to 82 for five by the end of the second day – and if Prior had not been dropped by North at third slip off its final ball, from Johnson, Australia would have claimed the extra half-hour and probably wrapped up the game by an innings and more than 200 runs. Strauss had been beaten by a delivery which took something out of the dry surface and cut back. This was the cue for Bopara to go first ball when he got the faintest of inside edges to Hilfenhaus's inswinging variation, and for Cook and Bell to repeat their first-innings dismissals. When Collingwood was beaten by Johnson's fast, late inswing, England's Nos 3, 4 and 5 had been dismissed for 16 runs in the match (it was only the second time in England's history that all three had been out for single figures in both innings, and the first since 1888). Johnson, relieved of the new ball, came back to his best by bowling a length, making the odd ball swing in and forcing the batsmen back with a few ferocious bouncers.

A significant team talk occurred on the third and final morning. England's coach Andy Flower told his players that, although the Fourth Test was probably lost, preparations for the Fifth Test started now. England rallied: there was a little more fluency from Prior, then Broad and Swann hit 108 off only 12.3 overs of swashbuckling strokeplay; the hundred stand was raised from just 76 balls. A morning session of 163 runs in only 24 overs brought the crowd, ready to be disgruntled at very little play, back on their side. The Australians became a little ragged as two boundary catches were missed, Clark was taken apart – Broad and Swann each hit him for 16 in an over – and some gloss was taken from what had hitherto been a complete walkover. After the match England had a two-hour meeting in their hotel to effect "closure" on their defeat. A merciful ten-day gap before the final Test then allowed them to regroup, which would have been far more difficult if the last two Tests had been back to back.

Man of the Match: M. J. North.   *Attendance:* 49,042.

Close of play: First day, Australia 196-4 (Clarke 34, North 7); Second day, England 82-5 (Anderson 0, Prior 4).

England

*A. J. Strauss c North b Siddle	3	– lbw b Hilfenhaus	32
A. N. Cook c Clarke b Clark	30	– c Haddin b Johnson	30
R. S. Bopara c Hussey b Hilfenhaus	1	– lbw b Hilfenhaus	0
I. R. Bell c Haddin b Johnson	8	– c Ponting b Johnson	3
P. D. Collingwood c Ponting b Clark	0	– lbw b Johnson	4
†M. J. Prior not out	37	– (7) c Haddin b Hilfenhaus	22
S. C. J. Broad c Katich b Clark	3	– (8) c Watson b Siddle	61
G. P. Swann c Clarke b Siddle	0	– (9) c Haddin b Johnson	62
S. J. Harmison c Haddin b Siddle	0	– (10) not out	19
J. M. Anderson c Haddin b Siddle	3	– (6) c Ponting b Hilfenhaus	4
G. Onions c Katich b Siddle	0	– b Johnson	0
B 5, l-b 8, w 1, n-b 3	17	B 5, l-b 5, w 5, n-b 11	26

1/11 (1) 2/16 (3) 3/39 (4) 4/42 (5)   (33.5 overs) 102   1/58 (1) 2/58 (3)   (61.3 overs) 263
5/63 (2) 6/72 (7) 7/92 (8) 8/98 (9)   3/67 (4) 4/74 (5)
9/102 (10) 10/102 (11)   5/78 (2) 6/86 (6) 7/120 (7)
8/228 (8) 9/259 (9) 10/263 (11)

Hilfenhaus 7–0–20–1; Siddle 9.5–0–21–5; Johnson 7–0–30–1; Clark 10–4–18–3. *Second Innings—* Hilfenhaus 19–2–60–4; Siddle 12–2–50–1; Clark 11–1–74–0; Johnson 19.3–3–69–5.

Australia

S. R. Watson lbw b Onions	51	S. R. Clark b Broad	32
S. M. Katich c Bopara b Harmison	0	B. W. Hilfenhaus not out	0
*R. T. Ponting lbw b Broad	78		
M. E. K. Hussey lbw b Broad	10	B 9, l-b 14, w 4, n-b 3	30
M. J. Clarke lbw b Onions	93		
M. J. North c Anderson b Broad	110	1/14 (2) 2/133 (1) (104.1 overs) 445
†B. J. Haddin c Bell b Harmison	14	3/140 (3) 4/151 (4)
M. G. Johnson c Bopara b Broad	27	5/303 (5) 6/323 (7) 7/393 (8)
P. M. Siddle b Broad	0	8/394 (9) 9/440 (10) 10/445 (6)

Anderson 18–3–89–0; Harmison 23–4–98–2; Onions 22–5–80–2; Broad 25.1–6–91–6; Swann 16–4–64–0.

Umpires: Asad Rauf and B. F. Bowden.
Third umpire: I. J. Gould.   Referee: R. S. Madugalle.

†At Canterbury, August 15, 16. **Australians won by 103 runs.** Toss: England Lions. **Australians 340-9 dec** (S. R. Watson 95, R. T. Ponting 45, M. E. K. Hussey 65, N. M. Hauritz 34*; G. Keedy 3-70); **England Lions 237** (S. C. Moore 30, A. W. Gale 31, J. W. M. Dalrymple 58, C. R. Woakes 36, L. E. Plunkett 34, Extras 30; B. Lee 3-37).

The Australians maintained their winning form in this two-day single-innings match. Queensland keeper Chris Hartley was drafted in from the Northern League as Brad Haddin and Graham Manou both had finger injuries. All the Australian specialist bowlers played except Ben Hilfenhaus. Watson hit 92 off 80 balls before lunch, with 15 fours and a six off 85 balls in all. In his first game for six weeks – since the previous encounter with the Lions, at Worcester – Lee dismissed both openers and bowled Liam Plunkett, whereupon a seagull swooped down and stole one of the bails. Lee pursued the bird across the outfield but failed to recover the bail, which had to be replaced for the remaining nine balls.*

ENGLAND v AUSTRALIA

Fifth npower Test

MATTHEW ENGEL

At The Oval, August 20, 21, 22, 23. England won by 197 runs. Toss: England. Test debut: I. J. L. Trott.

At 5.49 p.m. on a warm and mellow summer's evening, Alastair Cook snapped up a bat-pad catch off Graeme Swann, and England recaptured the urn that had been confiscated from them in disgrace at Perth seven Tests, two years and 248 days earlier. In all Ashes history this was one of the shortest Australian reigns, which have a habit of lasting nearer to infinity.

The victory also came about 50 hours after all cricketing logic suggested it was inevitable. Once Australia had collapsed on the second day, it was extremely difficult for England to avoid victory, given that rain had finally vanished from the Met Office's radar screen. But this was not a logical Test match, nor a logical series. And English cricket has never embraced the word "doddle".

Australia were set 546 to win on a pitch variously condemned by commentators – not all of them Australian – as "dodgy", "an abuse", "overbaked" and "crumbling". This figure was 128 beyond the existing Test record for a winning total in the fourth innings, and even 33 beyond the record in all first-class cricket. Yet even so, the stands and press box (and perhaps, for all we know, the dressing-room) were full of English defeatists, convinced that it was not the ball that was liable to kick spitefully and unpredictably, but fate.

Indeed, at 217 for two and 327 for five, even the stoutest English heart began to quiver a little. But when the end came, it came quickly, with a day to spare: a spectacular reversal of the events of Headingley. This was not so much cricket as judo, in which the seemingly prostrate contestant is the one just about to flip his opponent and emerge in triumph.

It was a series of many mysteries, but the Oval pitch was perhaps the greatest mystery of all. Solving it was made no easier by the groundsman, Bill Gordon, who evaded the media and refused to discuss in public what on earth he had been playing at. He was then vilified all round Australia – a situation the battalion of ECB and Surrey PR people should have averted.

The surface was certainly unusually dry, with the ball going through the top on the first day and clouds of dust appearing from the first minute. It offered bounce, as The Oval usually does, but not predictably so. This bounce got slower as the game progressed, giving the batsmen time to adjust. It was one of those pitches that was not, theoretically, ideal but actually produces heroic cricket. What irked the Aussies was the persistent rumour that it had been prepared to the precise specifications of the ECB.

Well, one hopes someone did say something to Gordon (if they managed to find him). In 1995, a tense and brilliant England–West Indies series reached The Oval 2–2 and was killed stone dead by a pitch flat enough to last a fortnight. This situation demanded a result wicket. What was completely barmy was the idea that the pitch could somehow have been tailored to create an England victory. The evidence of Leeds was that Australia could beat them if they played on the Goodwin Sands or Andrew Strauss's living-room carpet.

The ECB did not tell Ponting to guess wrong at the toss (for the fourth time out of five). Nor did they tell the Australian selectors to stick with their Headingley team and omit their sole specialist spinner, Nathan Hauritz. It was the Oval Test precisely a hundred years earlier that moved *Wisden's* editor Sydney Pardon (in his 1910 Notes) to his most famous phrase – that the England selectors had "touched the confines of lunacy". Now the press, seated in the Sydney Pardon gallery, saw Australia's selectors not merely touch those confines but burst though them. Even if you presumed the pitch to be more Ovalish, you could not possibly justify playing without a front-line spinner.

All the pre-match worry had been England's. The team was engulfed by speculation about whether Flintoff would be fit for his farewell (he was deemed to be) and who might replace the fading Bopara. There were improbable campaigns to recall Mark Ramprakash or Marcus Trescothick, and a more plausible argument for Robert Key – all of them a waste of breath. National selector Geoff Miller had indicated at the start of the debate that Jonathan Trott, from South Africa (England's chief breeding-ground) via Warwickshire, was next in line, having been put on standby for Leeds. And it came to pass: Trott became the first man to make his Test debut for England in an Ashes decider since E. G. Wynyard in 1896. Onions made way to accommodate Flintoff's return.

DEBUT IN FINAL TEST WITH ASHES UNDECIDED

	Performance	Debut Test	Season	State of series	Result of decider
F. H. Walters (A)	7, 5	5th Test at Melbourne	1884-85	2–2	England won
P. G. McShane (A)	9, 12*; 0-3	5th Test at Melbourne	1884-85	2–2	England won
A. E. Stoddart (E)	16, 17	Only Test at Sydney	1887-88	0–0	England won
W. Newham (E)	9, 17	Only Test at Sydney	1887-88	0–0	England won
T. Richardson (E)	16; 5-49, 5-107	3rd Test at Manchester	1893	1–0 to E	Drawn
T. R. McKibbin (A)	23, 13; 1-73, 1-47	5th Test at Melbourne	1894-95	2–2	England won
E. G. Wynyard (E)	10, 3	3rd Test at The Oval	1896	1–1	England won
H. I. Ebeling (A)	2, 41; 3-74, 0-15	5th Test at The Oval	1934	1–1	Australia won
N. J. N. Hawke (A)	14; 2-51, 0-38	5th Test at Sydney	1962-63	1–1	Drawn†
K. H. Eastwood (A)	5, 0; 1-21	7th Test at Sydney	1970-71	1–0 to E	England won
A. R. Dell (A)	3*, 3*; 2-32, 3-65	7th Test at Sydney	1970-71	1–0 to E	England won
D. R. Gilbert (A)	1, 0*; 1-96	6th Test at The Oval	1985	2–1 to E	England won
I. J. L. Trott (E)	**41, 119**	**5th Test at The Oval**	**2009**	**1–1**	**England won**

† *Australia retained the Ashes.*   *Research: Philip Bailey*

In the instances where England were leading, Australia would have retained the Ashes by drawing the series.

Strauss had no doubt about batting first (it was an insertion-free series) and once again batted serenely himself before playing a rare false stroke (to what should have been called a no-ball) on 55. Even with this lapse, England still reached 176 for two, although the evidence was piling up that this was not a straightforward pitch. Bell received a physical pummelling from Johnson but came through, so that shortly before tea Ponting was forced to confront the reality of Australia's selection error by bringing on North's clubby off-breaks, which would be better reserved for charity matches.

Curiously, that heralded the collapse, though North did not take a wicket. Perhaps the batsmen got overexcited by the sight of him, so that one after another they got out in silly ways. Trott, who had progressed to a fidgety but competent 41, was unfortunate: he was run out – stumped, almost – by a reflex throw from Katich at short leg. Most of the others were culpable. All out for 332 early on the second morning (Anderson's nought ending his England-record 54 duckless Test innings), they seemed – as at Cardiff – to have wasted a chance to seize control. As Watson and Katich put on 73 for the first wicket, English gloom was intense, even though Swann was already getting turn and bounce.

Just before lunch, it started to rain, and nearly an hour was lost. On the restart, Strauss rejected Swann and turned (inspiration? desperation?) to his fifth-choice bowler, Broad. And suddenly, the 2009 Ashes turned head-over-heels again – for one final time. Bowling from the Vauxhall End, Broad took four wickets in his first five overs: Watson and Hussey were plumb lbw; Ponting played on; and the burst culminated in Australia's most dangerous batsman of the summer, Clarke, being brilliantly snaffled by Trott at short extra cover. He later bowled Haddin with an away-swinging yorker and completed his single 12-over spell just before tea with five for 37. The crowd forgot Flintoff and hailed Broad as their new hero.

Old bowlers often maintain that their most famous spells were not necessarily their best. It was not wholly clear what Broad, who had looked so innocuous early in the series, was doing differently. But his natural length – a shade short on more trustworthy pitches – was now just right and, when the ball swung, it was unerringly on target. Success made him strong and reduced the Australians to gibberers. Lunch: 61 for nought. Tea: 133 for eight.

Australia had just avoided the follow-on (not that Strauss would have dreamed of enforcing it) and the eventual lead was 172. England themselves lost three wickets before the close to make it a 15-wicket day. The Australian press vented their fury on the pitch and Gordon, although Katich, speaking on behalf of the team, credited good bowling and bad batting, which undermined the whole theory – as did Saturday morning's play, when Strauss and Trott remained together until the over before lunch.

The two teams' selection decisions now came home to roost. The Australian attack was in such a pickle that North – to general embarrassment – became the mainstay of their attack. In Trott, however, England had found a player of sound technique, considerable self-confidence and a big-match temperament. It was Strauss who went, to North for 75 (having reached the slowest Test fifty of his career in 154 balls), and Trott who went on to a remarkable century. Swann kept him cheery company, making 63 inside an hour.

Strauss felt confident enough to declare with 21 overs plus two days remaining. Again, there was a strong first-wicket stand, and Australia were 80 for nought at the close before both openers went early next morning. Hussey, on a pair and with his Test career in jeopardy, had five men round the bat as his old Northamptonshire team-mate Swann tormented him.

This time, there was no collapse. The crowd grew anxious. But then The Man intervened. Flintoff had hardly been at the races at all: word had leaked before the game about his impending knee operation and he was obviously not match-fit – he had been bowled sparingly, taken a solitary wicket (Hilfenhaus), twice been clapped to the crease and quickly clapped back in again. Now his moment came.

Hussey played the ball to mid-on; Flintoff threw to the far end, and hit, with Ponting short of his ground. Flintoff marked the occasion with another of his Christ-like poses destined to adorn countless adverts. Five balls later, Clarke was even more narrowly run out by Strauss from backward short leg, after the ball was deflected by forward short leg's boot. Then Prior, neatly, made North the only stumping victim of the series.

Order was restored, slowly: a couple of catches went down; Hussey and Haddin regrouped; the crowd, abuzz after the dramas, became nervy again. But when the dam burst, Australia were swamped. Harmison, having done little all match, had unsettled them

Sizing it all up Down Under

Paul Coupar

As Australia's Ashes hopes vanished in a puff of South London dust, one Aussie writer found a hint of a glimmer of a consolation: at least they lost to the best team in the world… South Africa.

"Is it England or South Africa tormenting Australia in this Ashes series?" wondered Ben Dorries as he totted up England's African-born players in Sydney's *Daily Telegraph*. "After England's latest South African-born hero Jonathan Trott made 119 on debut in the Fifth Test, it seems the Rainbow Nation is more of a factor than the Mother Country."

Pausing only to quote Trott ("speaking in a strong South African accent"), the piece reflected that Andrew Strauss (born Johannesburg), Matt Prior (ditto), Kevin Pietersen (Pietermaritzburg) and Trott had scored 1,048 runs in the series – "over 40% of England's total".

For most, though, there was no consolation. The post-Oval headlines told the tale: "A defeat that's too bitter to swallow" (*Sydney Morning Herald*); "Ricky's Homecoming: Voyage of the damned" (*Illawarra Mercury*); "The Picture We Never Wanted To See Again" (*Herald Sun*), a smiling England team cavorting amid spumes of champagne.

Indeed Melbourne's *Age* couldn't bring itself to print the photo at all. The paper's sports supplement led with a blank page and a message reading: "WARNING: Some of you will find the following pages extremely disturbing. The rest of you will be interested to read about England winning the Ashes."

Inside, Peter Roebuck was magnanimous: "England deserved to win… That Australia provided five of the six highest scorers and the three leading wicket-takers and still lost is merely a mathematical quirk. Cricket is not to be put in a statistical box. It is a hot-blooded game. Plain and simple, England produced the three most incisive spells of bowling in the series: Andrew Flintoff's thunder at Lord's, Jimmy Anderson's waspish swingers in Birmingham, and Stuart Broad's irresistible intervention at The Oval."

On the opposite page, Richard Hinds offered an alternative analysis. "Well played [England]. An especially heroic victory having lost one of your most influential performers for the decider. Kevin Pietersen? No, I meant Rudi Koertzen."

Other explanations for defeat ranged from selector Merv Hughes's intrusive TV work, to magic in the stands, in the form of Daniel Radcliffe, aka Harry Potter ("Expelliarmus! Incendio! LBW-o!"). But two main culprits emerged: the Oval pitch and, especially, the selection panel who misread it. As Australia crumbled as fast as an "overbaked" SE11 wicket (Shane Warne), the hunt began for the elusive groundsman, Bill Gordon – described by News Ltd's journalists as an "eccentric recluse", apparently, as Gideon Haigh pointed out, "because he won't speak to them, even if it's not quite clear what he might gain from doing so". When finally cornered, Gordon reportedly pretended his name was "John" and offered to pass on a message.

In Gordon's absence, *The Australian's* Malcolm Conn reserved his ire for his "dusty… dodgy… manufactured" pitch, on which even England's "inconsistent" off-spinner Graeme Swann found success. "Heck, Bill Gordon might even receive an MBE." (Conn, though, did concede the pitch was "not likely to have made any decisive difference, given another poor Australian first-innings batting performance".) Another journalist said it was the "first time I've ever seen a drought 22 yards long and three yards wide".

Given all that, why was no spinner selected at The Oval? *The Telegraph* savaged the selection panel: "Australian cricket chief James Sutherland lifted his head out of the sand just long enough to assure Test skipper Ricky Ponting his job was safe and to decree chairman of selectors Andrew Hilditch was not to blame." Ian Chappell was quoted as saying the panel "handcuffed" Ponting at The Oval, "a crime punishable by demotion". The *SMH* said that "Any way you spin it, selectors [are] in the gun."

Not that dodgy judgments were the sole preserve of the selectors: "Australia, breathe a sigh of relief," the *Herald* had announced after the Fourth Test, "for the Ashes will remain ours for at least two more years." Despite the series being tied 1–1 with one to go, the "horror", "massacre" and "devastation" of the Headingley Test persuaded the *SMH's* man that England were done for.

"Sure, England may conjure a remarkable victory at The Oval… but those who seriously believe that underestimate their lack of resolve, as outlined by the former opener Justin Langer in a humiliating dossier…" Cue several paragraphs quoting Langer's "pussy-gate" revelations at length.

After the series was lost, the *SMH* diagnosed a deeper malaise. "Whereas English cricket… is peopled by players from a wide spectrum of cultural backgrounds – British, Indian, Pakistani, South African – Australian cricket, at the top level, is almost exclusively monocultural… Thousands of young migrants from India, Sri Lanka and Pakistan play cricket in Australia… Yet they do not continue in the sport. Are all Australians getting a fair go?"

So, for the *Herald*, the key was to start looking beyond the white, Anglo-Saxon core for talent. Heck, they might even start picking South Africans.

Caught short: a direct hit from the unseen Andrew Flintoff finds Ricky Ponting out by millimetres.

before the run-outs; now he gained some reward with three quick wickets, and the last five went down for 21.

I swear I saw complete strangers embrace at the Vauxhall End. The England players did all the regulation cavorting. The vanquished Australians were appropriately gracious. But this was not 2005 or even 1953. There was a sense of restraint in the crowd, partly because a four-year gap is not the same as a 20-year gap and partly because – for the first time all series – this was a real crickety kind of crowd. After the novelty-seekers at Cardiff, the social set at Lord's, the amiable drunks at Edgbaston, and the nasty drunks at Headingley, these were spectators who knew the game, and remembered what had happened four years earlier, of how the joy turned so quickly to, well, ashes.

The ECB and the players remembered, too, so the late-night celebrations were discreet and open-top buses forgotten. Four days later, England faced a one-day international in Belfast: even cricket's greatest prize has to bow to the banality of the modern fixture list.

Man of the Match: S. C. J. Broad.   *Attendance:* 89,304.

Men of the Series: England – A. J. Strauss; Australia – M. J. Clarke.

Compton–Miller Medal: A. J. Strauss.

Close of play: First day, England 307-8 (Broad 26); Second day, England 58-3 (Strauss 32, Trott 8); Third day, Australia 80-0 (Watson 31, Katich 42).

England

*A. J. Strauss c Haddin b Hilfenhaus	55	– c Clarke b North	75
A. N. Cook c Ponting b Siddle	10	– c Clarke b North	9
I. R. Bell b Siddle	72	– c Katich b Johnson	4
P. D. Collingwood c Hussey b Siddle	24	– c Katich b Johnson	1
I. J. L. Trott run out	41	– c North b Clark	119
†M. J. Prior c Watson b Johnson	18	– run out	4
A. Flintoff c Haddin b Johnson	7	– c Siddle b North	22
S. C. J. Broad c Ponting b Hilfenhaus	37	– c Ponting b North	29
G. P. Swann c Haddin b Siddle	18	– c Haddin b Hilfenhaus	63
J. M. Anderson lbw b Hilfenhaus	0	– not out	15
S. J. Harmison not out	12		
B 12, l-b 5, w 3, n-b 18	38	B 1, l-b 15, w 7, n-b 9	32

1/12 (2) 2/114 (1) 3/176 (4)   (90.5 overs) 332
4/181 (3) 5/229 (6) 6/247 (7)
7/268 (5) 8/307 (9) 9/308 (10) 10/332 (8)

1/27 (2)   (9 wkts dec, 95 overs) 373
2/34 (3) 3/39 (4)
4/157 (1) 5/168 (6) 6/200 (7)
7/243 (8) 8/333 (9) 9/373 (5)

Hilfenhaus 21.5–5–71–3; Siddle 21–6–75–4; Clark 14–5–41–0; Johnson 15–0–69–2; North 14–3–33–0; Watson 5–0–26–0. *Second Innings*—Hilfenhaus 11–1–58–1; Siddle 17–3–69–0; North 30–4–98–4; Johnson 17–1–60–2; Katich 5–2–9–0; Clark 12–2–43–1; Clarke 3–0–20–0.

Australia

S. R. Watson lbw b Broad	34	– lbw b Broad	40
S. M. Katich c Cook b Swann	50	– lbw b Swann	43
*R. T. Ponting b Broad	8	– run out	66
M. E. K. Hussey lbw b Broad	0	– c Cook b Swann	121
M. J. Clarke b Trott b Broad	3	– run out	0
M. J. North lbw b Swann	8	– st Prior b Swann	10
†B. J. Haddin b Broad	1	– c Strauss b Swann	34
M. G. Johnson c Prior b Swann	11	– c Collingwood b Harmison	0
P. M. Siddle not out	26	– c Flintoff b Harmison	10
S. R. Clark c Cook b Swann	6	– c Cook b Harmison	0
B. W. Hilfenhaus b Flintoff	6	– not out	4
B 1, l-b 5, n-b 1	7	B 7, l-b 7, n-b 6	20

1/73 (1) 2/85 (3) 3/89 (4) 4/93 (5)   (52.5 overs) 160
5/108 (6) 6/109 (2) 7/111 (7)
8/131 (8) 9/143 (10) 10/160 (11)

1/86 (2) 2/90 (1)   (102.2 overs) 348
3/217 (3) 4/220 (5)
5/236 (6) 6/327 (7) 7/327 (8)
8/343 (9) 9/343 (10) 10/348 (4)

Anderson 9–3–29–0; Flintoff 13.5–4–35–1; Swann 14–3–38–4; Harmison 4–1–15–0; Broad 12–1–37–5. *Second Innings*—Anderson 12–2–46–0; Flintoff 11–1–42–0; Harmison 16–5–54–3; Swann 40.2–8–120–4; Broad 22–4–71–1; Collingwood 1–0–1–0.

Umpires: Asad Rauf and B. F. Bowden.
Third umpire: P. J. Hartley.   Referee: R. S. Madugalle.

Details of England's one-day international against Ireland (August 27) can be found in Irish Cricket (page 979); details of Australia's one-day international against Scotland (August 28) can be found in Scottish Cricket (page 983).

TWENTY20 AND ONE-DAY INTERNATIONALS

REVIEW AND REPORTS BY JOHN ETHERIDGE

A total of ten limited-overs matches (including one in Belfast) was squeezed into the four weeks following England's Ashes triumph. What potential for anticlimax. And so it proved – for England, at least. They won two games (narrowly against Ireland, and in the dead-rubber seventh one-day match against Australia) and escaped with two washouts in the Twenty20 internationals. In the remaining six games they were beaten, often convincingly.

England's main problem was batting. They collapsed meekly and frequently, whether setting targets or chasing them. Batsmen usually got in but then surrendered to tame shots, such as clips to mid-off, or appalling running between the wickets. Owais Shah and Ravi Bopara were normally at the centre of the mix-up madness, and this area of unprofessionalism in their game was a factor in their dropping from the one-day squad for the tour of South Africa.

While Andrew Strauss was the leading scorer on either side in the one-dayers, having had a week's rest after The Oval, the next five on the list all came from Australia. There was another telling statistic – Australia scored three hundreds and nine fifties, England just five half-centuries. The top three wicket-takers were all Australian, too.

England's players were unhappy at playing in Belfast so soon after their Ashes win. They scarcely had time to catch their breath, let alone revel in the national euphoria. The seven-match NatWest Series was at least two games too long. Instead of doubling up at Lord's and Trent Bridge, surely a single match could have been scheduled for each venue. Rather than playing their best eleven, which they had to do if they were going to compete, England had to rest James Anderson, Stuart Broad and Paul Collingwood at various stages – arguably, their three best one-day players, given the absence through injury of Kevin Pietersen and Andrew Flintoff. Even a week off seemed to revitalise Anderson and Collingwood for the end of this series and for the Champions Trophy in South Africa.

Although fatigue and burnout might have been a factor in England's demise, the plain truth was that Australia, desperate to salvage something from their four-month tour, were vastly superior in every department. England showed no sign of overcoming the failings in one-day cricket that have damaged them for many years – the failure of individuals to build big scores, poor running by the batsmen, an inability to take wickets in the middle overs and a general lack of dynamism.

Ricky Ponting flew home for a rest and missed the Twenty20s and first three 50-over matches. The break did him good: he batted superbly and continued his form into the Champions Trophy. His century at Trent Bridge was the perfect way to orchestrate a run-chase. Ponting's absence allowed Cameron White a place up the order in the early part of the series and his judicious strokeplay – as opposed to the slogging-by-numbers he has sometimes produced – could transform his career. Similarly, Brad Haddin's absence with a broken finger was overcome by Tim Paine's elevation to opener: Paine scored a maiden century for Australia at Trent Bridge. Brett Lee was brilliant once the ball began to reverse-swing, and Mitchell Johnson did not compromise on hostility in an attempt to stop runs.

†ENGLAND v AUSTRALIA

First Twenty20 International

At Manchester, August 30. No result. Toss: England. Twenty20 international debuts: J. L. Denly; T. D. Paine.

England were already struggling when rain halted play seven deliveries into their reply to Australia's 145 for four, which was built around White's powerful 55 from 36 balls. Lee gave Joe Denly a merciless introduction into top-level international cricket with a first-ball bouncer directed towards his head – and Denly's attempted hook shot lobbed to square leg. Then Bopara was held at slip from Johnson's only legitimate delivery. Bopara and Denly were England's 13th opening pair in their 21st Twenty20 international.

Attendance: 19,132.

Australia

		B	4	6
S. R. Watson *c 1 b 8*	10	14	0	0
D. A. Warner *lbw b 5*	33	26	3	0
*M. J. Clarke *not out*	27	34	1	0
D. J. Hussey *st 4 b 5*	0	2	0	0
C. L. White *c 5 b 8*	55	36	1	3
A. C. Voges *not out*	11	8	1	0
L-b 3, w 6	9			

6 overs: 43-1   (20 overs) 145-4

1/35 2/54 3/54 4/132

†T. D. Paine, M. G. Johnson, B. Lee, N. M. Hauritz and D. P. Nannes did not bat.

Anderson 4–0–28–0; Sidebottom 4–0–31–0; Broad 4–0–33–2; Collingwood 4–0–20–2; Wright 1–0–6–0; Swann 3–0–24–0.

England

		B	4	6
R. S. Bopara *c 1 b 8*	1	3	0	0
J. L. Denly *c 10 b 9*	0	1	0	0
I. J. L. Trott *not out*	0	4	0	0
W 2, n-b 1	3			

(1.1 overs)   4-2

1/1 2/4

†M. J. Prior, *P. D. Collingwood, O. A. Shah, L. J. Wright, S. C. J. Broad, G. P. Swann, R. J. Sidebottom and J. M. Anderson did not bat.

Lee 1–0–3–1; Johnson 0.1–0–1–1.

Umpires: I. J. Gould and R. A. Kettleborough.   Third umpire: P. J. Hartley.   Referee: R. S. Madugalle.

†ENGLAND v AUSTRALIA

Second Twenty20 International

At Manchester, September 1 (floodlit). Abandoned.

A soggy patch, two metres square and around three metres from the stumps at the Brian Statham End, was the main reason why no play was possible. The drainage under the outfield had been relaid the previous winter, but this area, on the bowler's run-up, had not been included as it was to become part of the new square when the Old Trafford pitches were reoriented from east–west to north–south in 2010-11. The decision by umpires Nigel Llong and Peter Hartley to abandon the game – endorsed by the captains – opened a debate about whether Twenty20 should be regarded in the same light as other international cricket, or as a different sort of entertainment, with more flexibility in getting play under way. The officials clearly thought the former: no serious consideration was given to mowing another strip, or removing the game's international status and bowling from one end to entertain a crowd of almost 20,000. Ten days later, an ECB enquiry cleared Lancashire of any blame for inadequate covering.

†ENGLAND v AUSTRALIA

First One-Day International

At The Oval, September 4 (day/night). Australia won by four runs. Toss: England.

The day before the match – and less than 48 hours after the ground at Old Trafford was deemed too dangerous for cricket – Shah tackled Joe Denly in a warm-up football game and sent him to hospital with a damaged left knee. The England management were particularly angry because their kickabout was a "no tackle" rule. Shah put his foot in the wrong place in the main game, too, because he trod on his stumps for 40, and after that England were behind the rate in their struggle to reach 261. Most of their batsmen succumbed softly at the scene of their Ashes victory less than two weeks earlier. Rashid followed a ten-over spell of 37 runs by scoring 31 from 23 deliveries, and was promptly dropped for the next two matches. For England to win, Sidebottom needed to hit the final ball for six – something he had never done in international cricket. Earlier, acting-captain Clarke laboured for 45 runs from 72 balls, but a late flurry led by Ferguson, who hit 71 in 75, took Australia to a competitive total.

Man of the Match: C. J. Ferguson. *Attendance:* 20,480.

Australia

S. R. Watson c and b Collingwood	46	J. R. Hopes not out		18
†T. D. Paine run out	0	L-b 3, w 4		7
C. L. White run out	53			
*M. J. Clarke c Shah b Collingwood	45	1/11 (2) 2/93 (1)	(5 wkts, 50 overs)	260
C. J. Ferguson not out	71	3/111 (3) 4/190 (4)		
M. E. K. Hussey b Sidebottom	20	5/237 (6)	10 overs: 41-1	

M. G. Johnson, B. Lee, N. M. Hauritz and N. W. Bracken did not bat.

Anderson 7–0–35–0; Broad 9–1–52–0; Sidebottom 7–0–48–1; Wright 1–0–9–0; Rashid 10–0–37–0; Collingwood 9–0–47–2; Swann 7–0–29–0.

England

*A. J. Strauss c White b Lee	12	G. P. Swann c Paine b Watson		4
R. S. Bopara st Paine b Hauritz	49	R. J. Sidebottom not out		13
†M. J. Prior c Johnson b Hauritz	28	B 3, w 10, n-b 3		16
O. A. Shah hit wkt b Johnson	40			
P. D. Collingwood c Watson b Johnson	23	1/22 (1) 2/83 (3)	(8 wkts, 50 overs)	256
L. J. Wright run out	38	3/124 (2) 4/161 (4)		
S. C. J. Broad c Clarke b Johnson	2	5/168 (5) 6/178 (7)		
A. U. Rashid not out	31	7/224 (6) 8/229 (9)	10 overs: 45-1	

J. M. Anderson did not bat.

Lee 9–0–65–1; Bracken 10–0–48–0; Johnson 7–0–24–3; Hopes 5–1–14–0; Hauritz 9–0–44–2; Clarke 4–0–18–0; Watson 6–0–40–1.

Umpires: A. L. Hill and N. J. Llong.
Third umpire: P. J. Hartley. Referee: R. S. Mahanama.

†ENGLAND v AUSTRALIA

Second One-Day International

At Lord's, September 6. Australia won by 39 runs. Toss: England.

England produced an even worse run-chase than two days before. Openers Strauss and Bopara reached 74 in the 14th over, but so feeble was the subsequent capitulation that they succumbed by 39 runs. Strauss was out two balls after a fly-past by a Lancaster bomber commemorating Lord's role as an RAF receiving base during the Second World War. Shah extended his accident-prone series by being run out and, by the time England called their batting powerplay, last man Anderson had joined Collingwood at the wicket. Strauss accused his players of tossing away victory. "We were the architects of our own downfall," he said. "We keep talking about batsmen getting big scores and taking responsibility, but they haven't done that in the last two games." Australia had been reduced to 179 for six in the 43rd over, but Johnson whacked 43 not out from 23 balls.

Man of the Match: M. G. Johnson.   *Attendance:* 27,407.

Australia

S. R. Watson c Wright b Bresnan	34	B. Lee c Shah b Sidebottom		0
†T. D. Paine c Morgan b Wright	26	N. M. Hauritz not out		10
C. L. White c Prior b Bopara	42	L-b 8, w 8		16
*M. J. Clarke c Prior b Wright	4			
C. J. Ferguson b Anderson	55	1/62 (1) 2/64 (2)	(8 wkts, 50 overs)	249
M. E. K. Hussey b Swann	8	3/73 (4) 4/142 (3)		
J. R. Hopes lbw b Swann	11	5/155 (6) 6/179 (7)		
M. G. Johnson not out	43	7/201 (5) 8/208 (9)	10 overs: 43-0	

N. W. Bracken did not bat.

Anderson 9–0–57–1; Sidebottom 9–0–45–1; Bresnan 7–0–25–1; Wright 10–0–52–2; Collingwood 4–0–19–0; Swann 8–0–31–2; Bopara 3–0–12–1.

England

*A. J. Strauss c and b Hauritz	47	R. J. Sidebottom b Bracken		0
R. S. Bopara lbw b Watson	27	J. M. Anderson not out		0
†M. J. Prior c Paine b Watson	1			
O. A. Shah run out	12	B 5, l-b 2, w 6, n-b 1		14
P. D. Collingwood b Lee	56			
E. J. G. Morgan lbw b Johnson	14	1/74 (2) 2/76 (3) 3/85 (1)	(46.1 overs)	210
L. J. Wright c Paine b Lee	20	4/97 (4) 5/129 (6) 6/157 (7)		
T. T. Bresnan c Paine b Johnson	5	7/168 (8) 8/204 (9)		
G. P. Swann b Bracken	14	9/204 (10) 10/210 (5)	10 overs: 42-0	

Lee 8.1–0–22–2; Bracken 10–1–37–2; Johnson 9–1–50–2; Hopes 3–0–22–0; Hauritz 9–0–46–1; Watson 7–1–26–2.

Umpires: I. J. Gould and A. L. Hill.
Third umpire: N. J. Llong.   Referee: R. S. Mahanama.

†ENGLAND v AUSTRALIA

Third One-Day International

At Southampton, September 9 (day/night). Australia won by six wickets. Toss: England.

England were crushed again – Strauss called it "groundhog day" – although this time they succumbed batting first. There was hardly a moment when Australia did not look like winning. England raised an inadequate 228 for nine, and White's first international century (he had made his maiden Twenty20 and one-day international fifties in the previous ten days) steered Australia to victory with nine balls to spare. Strauss struck Lee for three consecutive fours, but after that England's batsmen looked timid and bereft of confidence. Their shot selection was woeful, too, with six of the top seven caught in the single-saving ring. White, enjoying his promotion to No. 3 while Ponting was resting for the first three matches, would have been run out on 46 if Anderson, throwing with his

White heat: Cameron White sparkles under the Southampton lights.

weaker left hand, had not missed the stumps from five yards, and he narrowly got home on 70 with Anderson involved again. He was also badly dropped by Bresnan at long-on when 92. White and Clarke put on 143 in 30 overs for the third wicket.

Man of the Match: C. L. White.   *Attendance:* 20,569.

England

*A. J. Strauss c Clarke b Hauritz	63	G. P. Swann lbw b Watson	3
R. S. Bopara c Hopes b Bracken	10	R. J. Sidebottom c White b Watson	24
†M. J. Prior c Hopes b Johnson	0	L-b 1, w 4, n-b 4	9
O. A. Shah lbw b Johnson	8		
P. D. Collingwood c Bracken b Watson	28	1/41 (2) 2/41 (3) (9 wkts, 50 overs) 228	
E. J. G. Morgan c Johnson b Lee	43	3/62 (4) 4/98 (1)	
L. J. Wright c sub (A. C. Voges) b Hopes	9	5/132 (5) 6/147 (7) 7/183 (6)	
T. T. Bresnan not out	31	8/188 (9) 9/228 (10) 10 overs: 43-2	

J. M. Anderson did not bat.

Lee 9–1–58–1; Bracken 10–0–36–1; Johnson 10–1–39–2; Hopes 7–0–34–1; Hauritz 6–0–24–1; Watson 8–0–36–3.

Australia

S. R. Watson lbw b Anderson	7	M. E. K. Hussey not out	8
†T. D. Paine lbw b Collingwood	29	B 1, l-b 2, w 6	9
C. L. White c Sidebottom b Wright	105		
*M. J. Clarke b Swann	52	1/16 (1) 2/52 (2) (4 wkts, 48.3 overs) 230	
C. J. Ferguson not out	20	3/195 (4) 4/220 (3) 10 overs: 29-1	

J. R. Hopes, M. G. Johnson, B. Lee, N. M. Hauritz and N. W. Bracken did not bat.

Anderson 9.3–1–52–1; Sidebottom 10–1–39–0; Bresnan 10–1–46–0; Collingwood 7–0–39–1; Wright 7–1–16–1; Swann 5–0–35–1.

Umpires: P. J. Hartley and A. L. Hill.
Third umpire: R. A. Kettleborough.   Referee: R. S. Mahanama.

†ENGLAND v AUSTRALIA

Fourth One-Day International

At Lord's, September 12. Australia won by seven wickets. Toss: England.

Brett Lee wrecked England with a magnificent demonstration of high-velocity, reverse-swing bowling. What is a batsman meant to do with a 95mph ball swerving in towards his toes? Miss it, that's what, and have his stumps rearranged. After the returning Denly was caught at slip in his opening spell, Lee bowled his next four victims for his ninth five-wicket return in one-day internationals: England in their history had taken only 21 five-fors. England again failed to last their 50 overs despite being 96 for one in the 19th over. Strauss was dismissed for 63 by Hauritz for the second game running, and the rest of the home batsmen were suffocated by Hauritz and obliterated by Lee. A target of 221 on a decent pitch was never going to challenge Australia, now reinforced by Ponting. Paine set them on their way with a maiden international fifty and they won with 6.2 overs in hand to secure the series. The remaining three matches offered the macabre fascination of whether England could avoid a whitewash.

Man of the Match: B. Lee.   *Attendance:* 26,805.

England

*A. J. Strauss c Bracken b Hauritz	63		T. T. Bresnan not out	11
J. L. Denly c White b Lee	11		R. J. Sidebottom b Johnson	2
R. S. Bopara lbw b Hauritz	26			
†M. J. Prior b Lee	29		B 1, l-b 1, w 2, n-b 4	8
O. A. Shah c Ferguson b Watson	39			
E. J. G. Morgan st Paine b Bracken	13		1/29 (2) 2/96 (3) 3/111 (1) (46.3 overs)	220
L. J. Wright b Lee	12		4/146 (4) 5/174 (6) 6/200 (7)	
S. C. J. Broad b Lee	2		7/202 (8) 8/206 (5)	
A. U. Rashid b Lee	4		9/212 (9) 10/220 (11) 10 overs: 59-1	

Lee 9–1–49–5; Bracken 8–0–40–1; Johnson 8.3–0–42–1; Watson 8–0–46–1; Hauritz 10–0–23–2; Clarke 3–0–18–0.

Australia

S. R. Watson lbw b Bresnan	26
†T. D. Paine c Prior b Rashid	51
*R. T. Ponting c Bopara b Bresnan	48
M. J. Clarke not out	62
C. J. Ferguson not out	23
B 1, l-b 1, w 7, n-b 2	11

1/51 (1) 2/108 (2)   (3 wkts, 43.4 overs) 221
3/168 (3)   10 overs: 51-1

M. E. K. Hussey, C. L. White, M. G. Johnson, B. Lee, N. M. Hauritz and N. W. Bracken did not bat.

Broad 9–0–43–0; Sidebottom 7.4–0–41–0; Bresnan 8–1–41–2; Rashid 10–0–56–1; Shah 3–0–12–0; Wright 6–0–26–0.

Umpires: Asad Rauf and N. J. Llong.
Third umpire: I. J. Gould.   Referee: R. S. Mahanama.

†ENGLAND v AUSTRALIA

Fifth One-Day International

At Nottingham, September 15 (day/night). Australia won by four wickets. Toss: England.

In his second match since returning from a break in Australia, Ricky Ponting scored his 27th one-day international century. A dazzling 126 from 109 balls was the foundation for another comprehensive Australian victory, although this time England at least performed well with the bat. Ponting was breathtakingly good. The first of his three sixes – an apparently effortless straight blow off Sidebottom that landed next to the TV commentary box – was described on air by Mike Atherton as the greatest shot in the history of cricket; his tongue was only partly in his cheek. Ponting and Clarke added 133 in 22 overs, and Australia won with ten balls to spare. Again, no England batsman made a big score, but enough contributed for them to reach 299, their best total of the series. Morgan, with his mixture of hurling-inspired reverse sweeps and dabs, stood out with 58 from 41 balls – his first fifty for England following six for Ireland – although he was reprieved on 38 when Hussey, juggling at deep square leg, eventually dropped the ball at the fourth attempt. Luke Wright missed the match after being hit on the toe by a bowling machine.

Man of the Match: R. T. Ponting.   *Attendance:* 16,959.

England

*A. J. Strauss lbw b Hauritz	35	T. T. Bresnan c Bracken b Siddle		4
J. L. Denly c Hussey b Johnson	45	R. J. Sidebottom not out		3
R. S. Bopara c Hauritz b Watson	18			
†M. J. Prior b Hauritz	37	L-b 1, w 6, n-b 2		9
O. A. Shah c Paine b Johnson	31			
E. J. G. Morgan c Siddle b Bracken	58	1/61 (1) 2/95 (3) 3/105 (2) (50 overs)		299
A. D. Mascarenhas c Johnson b Watson	19	4/165 (4) 5/192 (5) 6/230 (7)		
S. C. J. Broad run out	22	7/267 (8) 8/272 (6)		
A. U. Rashid run out	18	9/278 (10) 10/299 (9) 10 overs: 47-0		

Siddle 10–1–50–1; Bracken 8–1–43–1; Johnson 10–0–80–2; Watson 10–0–60–2; Hauritz 10–0–54–2; Clarke 2–0–11–0.

Australia

S. R. Watson c Mascarenhas b Bresnan	36	C. L. White not out		24
†T. D. Paine c Rashid b Bresnan	16	M. G. Johnson not out		18
*R. T. Ponting c Shah b Broad	126	B 1, w 6		7
M. J. Clarke c Shah b Rashid	52			
M. E. K. Hussey c Sidebottom b Mascarenhas	6	1/45 (2) 2/76 (1) (6 wkts, 48.2 overs)		302
		3/209 (4) 4/226 (5)		
C. J. Ferguson lbw b Broad	17	5/255 (6) 6/261 (3) 10 overs: 50-1		

N. M. Hauritz, P. M. Siddle and N. W. Bracken did not bat.

Broad 9–0–57–2; Sidebottom 9.2–0–43–0; Bresnan 10–0–76–2; Mascarenhas 10–0–49–1; Rashid 7–0–55–1; Bopara 3–0–21–0.

Umpires: Asad Rauf and R. A. Kettleborough.
Third umpire: N. J. Llong.   Referee: R. S. Mahanama.

†ENGLAND v AUSTRALIA

Sixth One-Day International

At Nottingham, September 17 (day/night). Australia won by 111 runs. Toss: Australia.
    Nothing demonstrated the gulf between the teams more vividly than two brilliant run-outs by Ponting to dismiss Prior and Bopara. Australia's captain was razor-sharp and alert to every possibility, while England's batsmen were hesitant and totally lacking confidence in each other's judgment. Ponting swooped, swivelled and threw out Prior at the non-striker's end and then, in the next over, another direct hit left Bopara yards short of his ground. He missed the stumps with two further run-out chances. There was irony in Ponting punishing England with run-outs at Trent Bridge: one of the enduring memories of the 2005 Ashes was Ponting himself being run out here by twelfth man Gary Pratt and angrily complaining to Duncan Fletcher on the balcony about the use of substitute fielders. Wicketkeeper Paine made his first century for Australia, three weeks after his debut, during a 163-run stand with Hussey, and White and Hopes produced a late flurry. For England, Bresnan top-scored with 31 from No. 8, but could not prevent their third-heaviest home defeat. By the time they took the batting powerplay in the 38th over they were already eight down. Australia became the first team to take a 6–0 lead in a bilateral one-day series.

Man of the Match: T. D. Paine.   *Attendance:* 16,959.

A ROUND HALF-DOZEN

There have been five instances of a team winning six games in a one-day bilateral international series (all series were of seven games).

6–1	West Indies beat India* (WWLWWWW)	1987-88
6–1	South Africa* beat England (WLWWWWW)	1995-96
6–1	South Africa* beat West Indies (WLWWWWW)	1998-99
6–1	India* beat Sri Lanka (WWWWLWW)	2005-06
6–1	**Australia beat England* (WWWWWWL)**	**2009**

* Home team.

Australia beat England 6–0 in a triangular series also involving Sri Lanka in 2002-03, four times in the group games and twice in the best-of-three finals.

Australia

S. R. Watson b Anderson	4	N. M. Hauritz not out	1
†T. D. Paine c Prior b Mascarenhas	111	P. M. Siddle not out	8
*R. T. Ponting c Sidebottom b Anderson	6	B 1, l-b 7, w 14	22
M. E. K. Hussey c Denly b Swann	65		
C. J. Ferguson b Anderson	6	1/19 (1) 2/40 (3) (8 wkts, 50 overs)	296
C. L. White c Denly b Anderson	35	3/203 (4) 4/206 (2)	
J. R. Hopes c Strauss b Sidebottom	38	5/220 (5) 6/273 (6)	
B. Lee run out	0	7/281 (8) 8/288 (7) 10 overs: 41-2	

N. W. Bracken did not bat.

Anderson 10–0–55–4; Sidebottom 9–0–65–1; Mascarenhas 10–0–49–1; Bresnan 9–0–60–0; Swann 10–0–48–1; Bopara 2–0–11–0.

England

*A. J. Strauss c Paine b Lee	0	R. J. Sidebottom b Siddle	15
J. L. Denly c Lee b Hopes	25	J. M. Anderson b Lee	1
R. S. Bopara run out	24		
†M. J. Prior run out	6	L-b 3, w 8, n-b 3	14
O. A. Shah c Watson b Hopes	23		
E. J. G. Morgan c Hussey b Bracken	23	1/0 (1) 2/45 (2) 3/59 (4) (41 overs)	185
A. D. Mascarenhas b Hopes	11	4/60 (3) 5/100 (6) 6/114 (5)	
T. T. Bresnan not out	31	7/125 (7) 8/159 (9)	
G. P. Swann b Bracken	12	9/182 (10) 10/185 (11) 10 overs: 42-1	

Lee 8–0–48–2; Bracken 10–0–42–2; Siddle 8–1–22–1; Hopes 9–0–32–3; Hauritz 6–0–38–0.

Umpires: Asad Rauf and N. J. Llong.
Third umpire: R. A. Kettleborough. Referee: R. S. Mahanama.

†ENGLAND v AUSTRALIA

Seventh One-Day International

At Chester-le-Street, September 20. England won by four wickets. Toss: England. One-day international debut: G. Onions.

England avoided an unprecedented 7–0 whitewash thanks mainly to Swann, whose off-spin extracted turn and bounce to remove Australia's middle order. Some of his balls fizzed, which was not what most people expected in the North-East in late September. Swann took five for 28, his best figures in all international cricket, and, for a game at least, the series was turned upside down. England captured a couple of early wickets and, although Ponting was again in imperious form, Australia never fully recovered. Their total of 176 was the lowest by either side in this series, and

Clarke's 38 runs spanned 81 deliveries. Strauss and Denly compiled a century partnership but, once Strauss was dismissed by Hauritz – for the fifth time in six games and second time running to a reverse sweep – England wobbled. They subsided from 106 for nought to 162 for six before Collingwood, back after being rested for three matches, and Bresnan pushed them across the line. Strauss said: "It was a relief to win and avoid the whitewash, but I'm not jumping for joy – we still lost the series 6–1."

Man of the Match: G. P. Swann.   *Attendance:* 17,018.

Man of the Series: C. L. White.

Australia

S. R. Watson c Swann b Anderson	0	N. M. Hauritz c and b Shah	3
†T. D. Paine c Prior b Onions	4	B. W. Hilfenhaus not out	2
*R. T. Ponting c Collingwood b Swann	53		
M. J. Clarke run out	38	L-b 1, w 4	5
M. E. K. Hussey c Denly b Bresnan	49		
C. L. White b Swann	1	1/0 (1) 2/17 (2) 3/96 (3) (45.5 overs) 176
J. R. Hopes c and b Swann	11	4/110 (4) 5/112 (6) 6/138 (7)
M. G. Johnson c Anderson b Swann	10	7/158 (8) 8/158 (9)
B. Lee b Swann	0	9/163 (10) 10/176 (5) 10 overs: 32-2

Anderson 7–0–36–1; Onions 9–1–28–1; Bresnan 6.5–0–25–1; Collingwood 7–0–37–0; Swann 10–1–28–5; Bopara 1–0–7–0; Shah 5–1–14–1.

England

*A. J. Strauss c Hilfenhaus b Hauritz	47	T. T. Bresnan not out	10
J. L. Denly run out	53		
R. S. Bopara lbw b Watson	13	B 4, l-b 2, w 6, n-b 9	21
O. A. Shah c Paine b Hopes	7		
P. D. Collingwood not out	13	1/106 (1) 2/129 (2) (6 wkts, 40 overs) 177
E. J. G. Morgan c Paine b Lee	2	3/133 (3) 4/137 (4)
†M. J. Prior c Ponting b Hilfenhaus	11	5/141 (6) 6/162 (7) 10 overs: 47-0

G. P. Swann, J. M. Anderson and G. Onions did not bat.

Lee 10–3–33–1; Hilfenhaus 6–1–38–1; Johnson 5–0–29–0; Hauritz 8–0–30–1; Hopes 6–1–29–1; Watson 5–0–12–1.

Umpires: Asad Rauf and N. J. Llong.
Third umpire: P. J. Hartley.   Referee: R. S. Mahanama.

ICC WORLD TWENTY20, 2009

Hugh Chevallier

1. Pakistan   2. Sri Lanka   3= South Africa and West Indies

After March's terrorist outrage in Lahore brought international cricket in Pakistan to an abrupt halt, some questioned whether the national team, seemingly destined to wander the globe as a latter-day *Flying Dutchman*, could remain a force in world cricket. At Lord's, on the longest day, Pakistan gave an eloquent riposte to the doubters by outplaying Sri Lanka and winning the second ICC World Twenty20. No other nation needed this triumph as much as Pakistan and, after they put a ropy start behind them, no other nation deserved this triumph as much as Pakistan. The fortnight made a compelling story (complete with its own flying Dutchmen), touchingly concluded by Younis Khan dedicating victory to the memory of Bob Woolmer, the Pakistan coach who died during the 2007 World Cup.

   Younis also implored touring teams to return to Pakistan. That seemed unlikely, but the stock of Pakistani cricket had risen, and as well as giving a huge boost to millions at home it would have served to endorse the ECB's decision, announced less than a week after the tournament, to host a Pakistan v Australia Test series in July 2010. This was not entirely an act of altruism by the ECB, who can often spot a commercial opportunity when they see one (sometimes to the detriment of the cricket). In the UK, only England and India, though not necessarily in that order, enjoy a bigger following than Pakistan. Indeed the cosmopolitan nature of the consistently large crowds was a distinctive characteristic of the World Twenty20: all 12 teams attracted decent support. The ICC claimed roughly 96% of seats were sold, suggesting that ticket prices were pitched about right. For adults, the range was from £15–£90; for children, it was an enlightened £8–£15.

   For pretty much everyone, that represented excellent value for money: most tickets were for double-headers, and if one match was one-sided, chances were the other was a minor gem. It all got off to a cracking start, too, provided you weren't at Lord's hoping to see England move smoothly towards the next phase with a morale-boosting win over supposed Dutch makeweights, or Alesha Dixon sing for her supper. Late May and the beginning of June had seen England basking in early summer sun, but the weather broke at the wrong time, scuppering the opening ceremony and delaying the England–Netherlands game.

   It was worth the wait. The match was a classic: a final over of delicious tension ended in a memorable upset, a pitch invasion by sprinting Dutchmen and headlines the world over. "CLOGS 1, CLOTS 0" was the *Sun's* take on England's humbling, while the *News of the World* chose "EDAMMED". Others preferred fruitier options, insisting that England had been reduced to lemons by slipping on an Orange banana skin. It was nothing less than either side deserved, one harrying and fighting for all they were worth, the other

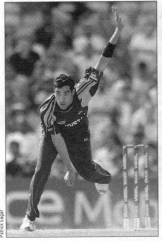

Master craftsmen: Umar Gul, of Pakistan, used reverse swing to deadly effect, while few could read the spin variations of Sri Lanka's Ajantha Mendis.

treating the game as glorified practice. Defeat raised the spectre of England's ignominious World Cup campaign of 1999 when they crashed out of their own tournament at the first hurdle. Their minds focused, England made light of a rusty Pakistan to qualify for the Super Eights; the Dutch would join them if they avoided a heavy defeat by Pakistan. That proved a step too far, but they returned to the Netherlands buoyed by the biggest night in their cricketing history.

The seeding system dictated that West Indies, because of their failure at the first World Twenty20, joined Australia and Sri Lanka in the toughest group. Just as he had in the opening game in 2007, Chris Gayle lit up the tournament with an innings of sheer brilliance, only this time it brought victory, against the shell-shocked Australians. Two days later, Australia lost to Sri Lanka, and were gone; Ricky Ponting's Ashes-bound team were left kicking their heels for a fortnight. The only Test side ousted before them were Bangladesh, well beaten by both India and Ireland. In the last group, Scotland fought spiritedly in a rain-reduced contest with New Zealand, but collapsed in a heap against a well-drilled South Africa.

Because time prevented a single Super Eight group in which all played all, no points were carried from the group stages. And because the organisers were keen to allow spectators to book ahead to follow their team, fixtures and venues were preordained, provided the seeded team progressed. (In reality, Australia's place was taken by West Indies, and Bangladesh's by Ireland.) The result was the fortnight's one structural weakness: with no incentive for a team to finish top of the table, the last three group matches were meaningless.

Meaning kicked in again for the Super Eights. In Group E, South Africa brushed England aside with disdainful ease and followed up with a convincing win over West Indies, all but guaranteeing a place in the semis. West Indies, thanks to the all-round excellence of Dwayne Bravo, defeated India, who never found the zest and confidence that brought them the first World Twenty20. Their captain, Mahendra Singh Dhoni, repeatedly denied that his players were exhausted by the recently concluded IPL; and they had to cope without Virender Sehwag, who had a shoulder injury, and whose absence left India's top order vulnerable to the short ball. Once they lost to England in a frenzied atmosphere at Lord's, the holders were out. That set up a virtual quarter-final between England and West Indies. But the game was sabotaged by the weather briefly forgetting its manners – and the Duckworth/Lewis method its even-handedness. Or so it seemed: a revised target of 80 from nine overs surely provided a lesser obstacle than 162 from 20, and West Indies, not England, progressed.

Sri Lanka sailed through Group F unbeaten and Ireland bumped winless along the bottom, only that doesn't quite tell the story. Ireland were never humbled, and even threatened an upset against Sri Lanka, who had to fight hard to defend 144 after a rare failure from Tillekeratne Dilshan. Pakistan lost to Sri Lanka before despatching New Zealand thanks to the bowling performance of the fortnight: Umar Gul's late-swinging yorkers left the batting in tatters. In fact, New Zealand had been in tatters since arriving in England. Fancied by some as possible winners, they were hamstrung by injuries. Daniel Vettori, the captain and canniest of slow bowlers, was never fully fit, while an infection meant Jesse Ryder, possibly Gayle's rival as the hardest hitter, withdrew after one match; Ross Taylor also struggled for fitness.

The semis pitted South Africa and Sri Lanka, both still unbeaten, against the volatile forces of Pakistan and West Indies. In the first, the hit-or-miss phenomenon that is Shahid Afridi proved a very palpable hit and condemned South Africa to the familiar fate of promising much and delivering little. In the second, the West Indies batting inexplicably committed collective hara-kiri and, genius though he is, Gayle could not overhaul Sri Lanka single-handed. Spectators were given a variation on the double-header when the semi-finals and final of the men's and women's events coincided. This laudable move brought women's cricket to a wider audience (and, in England's magnificently cool-headed pursuit of a stiff Australian target in the second semi-final, one of the matches of the fortnight – see page 563). Neither of the 2009 finals was one to savour. The side bowling first – the English women and the Pakistani men – were in dominant positions before the halfway mark, and won with few scares.

Structurally, the second tournament was a clone of the first. That's no criticism: the South African was an out-and-out winner, and the ICC wisely, if uncharacteristically, decided that if it ain't broke, don't fix it. So Steve Elworthy, tournament director in 2007, reprised his role to oversee another hugely successful contest. Some fringe elements, such as the dancers and resident DJ, lacked the freshness and vitality they had before, while it is kindest not to dwell on one addition, an utterly pointless episode before each match in which a member of the crowd was driven round the outfield in a golf buggy and lobbed a single delivery at a retired international player.

But they were minor cavils and, in at least one important respect, the second coming was an improvement on the first. This time there was a greater balance between bat and ball. Although the average first-innings score fell only slightly from 160 to 156, the drop was significant, especially in the Super Eight and knockout stages, when it fell from 159 to 150. The lower altitude of the English grounds was partly the cause, with the number of sixes tumbling from 265 to 166. But so were the slow pitches at Trent Bridge and, later in the tournament, at Lord's, and the spinners' ability to exploit them.

Research published on Cricinfo showed that between the seventh and 14th overs of the 2009 tournament, typically bowled by the spinners after the end of the powerplay, the run-rate dwindled from 7.75 to 6.77. (Two years before, the rate had risen slightly, from 7.45 to 7.70.) With batsmen under constant pressure to attack, it is axiomatic that stifling bowling can also be penetrative. Four bowlers – Shahid Afridi, Ajantha Mendis, Roelof van der Merwe and Saeed Ajmal – combined an economy-rate of under six with ten or more wickets, and all were spinners. It was no accident that the teams with the most inventive slow-bowling attacks, Pakistan and Sri Lanka, contested the final.

Not that slow bowling necessarily meant bowling slowly. For Afridi and Mendis, in particular, the full ball shooting through as fast as a medium-pacer, with or without spin, proved a deadly weapon; Afridi hit the stumps seven times. Come to that, off-spinner Ajmal didn't send down many off-breaks, relying more and more on the *doosra*; Kamran Akmal made five stumpings off his bowling. The message was clear: innovate and prosper.

If a successful team needed at least one inventive slow bowler – South Africa looked a far slicker outfit with the confident slow left-armer van der Merwe in the side – then the ideal foil was a bowler of genuine speed who could spear in yorker after yorker. The acknowledged master of the art was Umar Gul. Not usually brought on until around the 12th over to maximise the chance of finding reverse swing, he was utterly unplayable in the Super Eights match against New Zealand at The Oval, when he claimed the first five-for in Twenty20 internationals. Some in the New Zealand camp hinted that Gul's performance might have relied on the black art of ball-tampering, an accusation never voiced publicly. The umpires, however, were adamant nothing was amiss, and the lasting odour was of sour New Zealand grapes.

The lasting odour was of sour New Zealand grapes

Just as in 2007, Gul was the leading wicket-taker – as before he claimed 13 at around 12 each – though the most potent new-ball pairing was South Africa's Dale Steyn and Wayne Parnell. Steyn's speed and aggression was expected, but Parnell's mastery of length at pace was phenomenal, especially for a 19-year-old. As a left-armer, he also offered variety, even if his stock delivery was in the blockhole. Sri Lanka also had a ready-made yorker-machine in Lasith Malinga, though the 2009 model had added a slow bouncer and a deliberate slow full toss.

Overhead projector: Tillekeratne Dilshan's "starfish" shot sent the ball hurtling over his helmet towards the boundary.

Meanwhile, England's Stuart Broad experimented in the death overs with bowling round the wicket from very wide of the crease; the combination of unfamiliar angle and full length (again) made it awkward for batsmen to free their arms for a big hit. However, the ICC ruled out another Broad ruse when he tried to distract the batsman by pointing his left arm towards mid-off as he neared his delivery stride. Slow bowlers were already doing something similar when they came to a standstill in their delivery stride, deliberately delaying the release of the ball *à la* Robert Croft. Scotland's Majid Haq used the ploy against South Africa. Harbhajan Singh took it further in the England v India game. Seeing Kevin Pietersen changing his grip from right- to left-hander, Harbhajan simply did not let go of the ball.

The stroke of the tournament was the "starfish", which pinged several times from Dilshan's bat. It wasn't actually new, but the brio with which he played it – and its satisfying ability to render the wicketkeeper a hapless bystander as the ball flew over his head – made it an instant hit. Essentially it was a ramp played with the bat pointing down the wicket, a shot risky enough, according to the Sri Lankans, to be the sole preserve of those with no brain, which explains the (apparently brainless) starfish. Whatever the name, it threatened to restore long-stop to the international game after more than a century's absence.

Dilshan's batting comprised more than one shot, though he was heavily dependent on runs behind the wicket. He failed to pass 45 only twice in seven games, with ducks against Ireland and, crucially, in the final. Gayle, who preferred to slam the ball in front of square, also left an indelible mark on the competition, and his innings against Australia was the perfect balance of power and precision. As a rueful Ricky Ponting said afterwards, no team could have contained Gayle in that mood. Jacques Kallis underlined his adaptability, too. Controversially omitted from the first World Twenty20, he showed what might have been, hitting 238 runs at a strike-rate of 126.

The standard of fielding had dipped fractionally since 2007; perhaps the chill of the early English summer was to blame for the fallibility, especially notable in Indian and West Indian hands. There was no better fielding side than South Africa – and no better fieldsman than A. B. de Villiers, often to be seen diving, leaping or catching at backward point. The catch of the tournament came when Kyle Coetzer of Scotland leapt unfeasibly high to pluck a certain six from the air at long-on to remove Mark Boucher. But the real talking point was an astonishing piece of agility and quick thinking by Sri Lanka's Angelo Mathews that showed innovation was as applicable to fielding as other disciplines. Unable to stay within the boundary when trying to take a catch against West Indies, he threw the ball in the air before his momentum carried him over the rope; he then jumped up and, mid-air, parried the ball back into the field of play, saving three runs. The incident was emblematic of all that was best about Twenty20: athletic, inventive, entertaining and fast.

Even so, scheduling the next tournament to start in April 2010 was misguided. The ICC should beware: despite what Mae West said, too much of a good thing is not always wonderful.

ICC WORLD TWENTY20 STATISTICS

Leading run-scorers

	M	I	NO	R	HS	50s	Avge	SR	4	6
T. M. Dilshan (SL)	7	7	1	317	96*	3	52.83	144.74	46	3
J. H. Kallis (SA)	5	5	1	238	64	2	59.50	126.59	28	4
C. H. Gayle (WI)	5	5	1	193	88	2	48.25	134.02	21	8
Kamran Akmal (P)	7	7	0	188	57	1	26.85	125.33	15	7
A. B. de Villiers (SA)	6	6	1	186	79*	2	37.20	155.00	16	6
S. T. Jayasuriya (SL)	7	7	0	177	81	1	25.28	115.68	22	5
K. C. Sangakkara (SL)	7	7	2	177	64*	2	35.40	108.58	15	2
Shahid Afridi (P)	7	7	2	176	54*	2	35.20	140.80	16	3
Younis Khan (P)	7	6	3	172	50	1	57.33	139.83	11	3
K. P. Pietersen (E)	4	4	0	154	58	1	38.50	152.47	19	4
D. J. Bravo (WI)	6	5	1	154	66*	2	38.50	145.28	12	6
D. P. M. D. Jayawardene (SL) . . .	7	7	1	154	78	1	25.66	122.22	17	2
Yuvraj Singh (I)	5	5	1	153	67	1	38.25	154.54	10	9
L. M. P. Simmons (WI)	5	5	0	150	77	1	30.00	137.61	22	1

Best strike-rates – most runs scored per 100 balls

	SR	Runs		SR	Runs
A. J. Redmond (NZ)	177.19	101	K. P. Pietersen (E)	152.47	154
K. J. Coetzer (Scot)	159.57	75	D. J. Bravo (WI)	145.28	154
A. B. de Villiers (SA)	155.00	186	T. M. Dilshan (SL)	144.74	317
Yuvraj Singh (I)	154.54	153	Shahid Afridi (P)	140.80	176
A. D. Mathews (SL)	153.06	75			

Minimum 75 runs.

Leading wicket-takers

	Style	O	M	R	W	BB	4W/i	Avge	SR	ER
Umar Gul (P)	RFM	24.3	0	158	13	5-6	1	12.15	11.30	6.44
B. A. W. Mendis (SL) . . .	OB/LBG	26	0	143	12	3-9	0	11.91	13.00	5.50
Saeed Ajmal (P)	OB	28	0	163	12	4-19	1	13.58	14.00	5.82
S. L. Malinga (SL)	RF	25.2	0	181	12	3-17	0	15.08	12.66	7.14
Shahid Afridi (P)	LBG	28	0	149	11	4-11	1	13.54	15.27	5.32
R. E. van der Merwe (SA)	SLA	24	0	135	10	2-14	0	13.50	14.40	5.62
D. J. Bravo (WI)	RFM	21	0	184	10	4-38	1	18.40	12.60	8.76
W. D. Parnell (SA)	LFM	20.5	0	119	9	4-13	1	13.22	13.88	5.71
D. W. Steyn (SA)	RF	22	0	145	9	2-21	0	16.11	14.66	6.59
M. Muralitharan (SL)	OB	27	0	158	9	3-29	0	17.55	18.00	5.85

Most economical bowlers – runs per over

Shahid Afridi (P)	5.32	Saeed Ajmal (P)	5.82
N. L. McCullum (NZ)	5.42	M. Muralitharan (SL)	5.85
B. A. W. Mendis (SL)	5.50	Abdul Razzaq (P)	5.92
R. E. van der Merwe (SA)	5.62	P. P. Ojha (I)	6.18
W. D. Parnell (SA)	5.71	J. Botha (SA)	6.21

Minimum 10 overs. There were five maidens bowled: one each by Abdul Razzaq (P), Harbhajan Singh (I), D. T. Johnston (Ire), Mohammad Aamer (P) and J. A. Morkel (SA).

Leading wicketkeepers

K. C. Sangakkara (SL)	9 (5 ct, 4 st)	N. J. O'Brien (Ire)	6 (4 ct, 2 st)
Kamran Akmal (P)	8 (1 ct, 7 st)	D. Ramdin (WI)	6 (all ct)
J. S. Foster (E)	6 (3 ct, 3 st)		

Leading fielders – most catches

A. D. S. Fletcher (WI)	6	A. B. de Villiers (SA)	5

NATIONAL SQUADS

* Captain. ‡ Did not play in ICC World Twenty20.

Australia *R. T. Ponting, N. W. Bracken, M. J. Clarke, B. J. Haddin, N. M. Hauritz, ‡B. W. Hilfenhaus, J. R. Hopes, D. J. Hussey, M. E. K. Hussey, M. G. Johnson, B. Lee, ‡P. M. Siddle, D. A. Warner, S. R. Watson, ‡C. L. White. *Coach:* T. J. Nielsen.
White replaced A. Symonds, who was sent home on disciplinary grounds before the tournament started.

Bangladesh *Mohammad Ashraful, ‡Abdur Razzak, Junaid Siddique, Mahmudullah, Mashrafe bin Mortaza, ‡Mithun Ali, Mushfiqur Rahim, Naeem Islam, Raqibul Hasan, Rubel Hossain, Shahadat Hossain, Shakib Al Hasan, ‡Shamsur Rahman, ‡Syed Rasel, Tamim Iqbal. *Coach:* J. D. Siddons.

England *P. D. Collingwood, J. M. Anderson, R. S. Bopara, S. C. J. Broad, J. S. Foster, R. W. T. Key, A. D. Mascarenhas, E. J. G. Morgan, ‡G. R. Napier, K. P. Pietersen, A. U. Rashid, O. A. Shah, R. J. Sidebottom, G. P. Swann, L. J. Wright. *Coach:* A. Flower.
Rashid replaced A. Flintoff, who had not fully recovered from knee surgery.

India *M. S. Dhoni, G. Gambhir, Harbhajan Singh, R. A. Jadeja, ‡K. D. Karthik, ‡P. Kumar, P. P. Ojha, I. K. Pathan, Y. K. Pathan, S. K. Raina, I. Sharma, R. G. Sharma, R. P. Singh, Yuvraj Singh, Zaheer Khan. *Coach:* G. Kirsten.
Karthik replaced V. Sehwag, who withdrew with a shoulder injury soon after the tournament started.

Ireland *W. T. S. Porterfield, A. C. Botha, J. P. Bray, P. Connell, A. R. Cusack, D. T. Johnston, W. K. McCallan, J. F. Mooney, K. J. O'Brien, N. J. O'Brien, W. B. Rankin, P. R. Stirling, R. M. West, A. R. White, G. C. Wilson. *Coach:* P. V. Simmons.

Netherlands *J. Smits, P. W. Borren, ‡M. Bukhari, T. N. de Grooth, ‡T. J. G. Gruijters, ‡M. M. A. Jonkman, A. N. Kervezee, D. P. Nannes, D. J. Reekers, E. Schiferli, P. M. Seelaar, ‡E. S. Szwarczynski, R. N. ten Doeschate, D. L. S. van Bunge, B. Zuiderent. *Coach:* P. J. Drinnen.

New Zealand *D. L. Vettori, N. T. Broom, I. G. Butler, B. J. Diamanti, J. E. C. Franklin, M. J. Guptill, B. B. McCullum, N. L. McCullum, P. D. McGlashan, K. D. Mills, I. E. O'Brien, J. D. P. Oram, J. D. Ryder, S. B. Styris, L. R. P. L. Taylor. *Coach:* A. J. Moles.
Ryder suffered a groin infection after New Zealand's first game; his place was taken by A. J. Redmond.

Pakistan *Younis Khan, Abdul Razzaq, Ahmed Shehzad, Fawad Alam, ‡Iftikhar Anjum, Kamran Akmal, Misbah-ul-Haq, Mohammad Aamer, Saeed Ajmal, Salman Butt, Shahid Afridi, Shahzaib Hasan, Shoaib Malik, Sohail Tanvir, Umar Gul, Yasir Arafat. *Coach:* Intikhab Alam.
Shoaib Akhtar was named in the original squad but withdrew with genital warts, and was replaced by Iftikhar Anjum. Abdul Razzaq joined the squad after Yasir Arafat tore his hamstring v England.

Scotland *G. M. Hamilton, ‡R. D. Berrington, K. J. Coetzer, G. D. Drummond, R. M. Haq, N. F. I. McCallum, C. S. MacLeod, ‡J. D. Nel, N. S. Poonia, G. A. Rogers, C. J. O. Smith, J. H. Stander, R. R. Watson, D. F. Watts, C. M. Wright. *Coach:* P. D. Steindl.
J. A. R. Blain, originally selected for the squad, withdrew after a disagreement with his captain, and was replaced by MacLeod. Nel broke a finger before the tournament began, but was not replaced.

South Africa *G. C. Smith, ‡Y. A. Abdulla, J. Botha, M. V. Boucher, A. B. de Villiers, J-P. Duminy, H. H. Gibbs, J. H. Kallis, J. A. Morkel, M. Morkel, ‡J. L. Ontong, W. D. Parnell, ‡R. J. Peterson, D. W. Steyn, R. E. van der Merwe. *Coach:* J. M. Arthur.

Sri Lanka *K. C. Sangakkara, ‡S. I. de Saram, T. M. Dilshan, S. T. Jayasuriya, D. P. M. D. Jayawardene, K. M. D. N. Kulasekara, ‡M. F. Maharoof, S. L. Malinga, A. D. Mathews, B. A. W. Mendis, ‡M. T. T. Mirando, J. Mubarak, M. Muralitharan, L. P. C. Silva, I. Udana. *Coach:* T. H. Bayliss.

West Indies *C. H. Gayle, ‡L. S. Baker, S. J. Benn, ‡D. E. Bernard, D. J. Bravo, S. Chanderpaul, F. H. Edwards, A. D. S. Fletcher, X. M. Marshall, K. A. Pollard, D. Ramdin, D. J. G. Sammy, R. R. Sarwan, L. M. P. Simmons, J. E. Taylor. *Coach:* J. Dyson.

Note: Where a venue hosted two matches on one day, the same attendance figure is given for both matches.

MATCH REPORTS BY SCYLD BERRY, HUGH CHEVALLIER AND STEVEN LYNCH

GROUP A

BANGLADESH v INDIA

At Nottingham, June 6 (floodlit). India won by 25 runs. India 2 pts. Toss: India. Twenty20 international debuts: Rubel Hossain; P. P. Ojha.

A late flourish from Yuvraj Singh, who collected three sixes in four balls from off-spinner Naeem Islam, then next over (the 18th) clouted medium-pacer Rubel Hossain for six, four and four in an arc on the leg side, propelled India to an imposing total. Junaid Siddique briefly replied in kind, hoisting his first ball, from Irfan Pathan, into the crowd at midwicket and later adding two more sixes, but the introduction of Ojha changed the complexion of the match. Flighting his left-arm spin at less than 50mph, Ojha induced Shakib Al Hasan to top-edge a pull with his first delivery in Twenty20 internationals, and removed Junaid with his fifth. He finished with four wickets as Bangladesh fell short, despite Naeem's late burst, which included two impressive straight sixes off successive balls from Ishant Sharma.

Man of the Match: P. P. Ojha.   *Attendance:* 15,876.

India

		B	4	6
G. Gambhir c 4 b 9	50	46	4	0
R. G. Sharma b 4	36	23	3	2
*†M. S. Dhoni b 9	26	21	0	1
Yuvraj Singh c 1 b 10	41	18	3	4
S. K. Raina b 11	10	8	1	0
Y. K. Pathan not out	1	1	0	0
I. K. Pathan not out	11	3	1	1
W 5	5			

6 overs: 54-0   (20 overs)   180-5

1/59 2/112 3/140 4/157 5/169

Harbhajan Singh, Zaheer Khan, P. P. Ojha and I. Sharma did not bat.

Mashrafe bin Mortaza 4–0–29–0; Rubel Hossain 4–0–49–1; Shahadat Hossain 3–0–31–1; Mahmudullah 2–0–15–0; Shakib Al Hasan 4–0–24–1; Naeem Islam 3–0–32–2.

Bangladesh

		B	4	6
Tamim Iqbal st 3 b 6	15	10	3	0
Junaid Siddique c 8 b 10	41	22	2	3
*Mohammad Ashraful c 1 b 11 ..	11	9	1	0
Shakib Al Hasan c 3 b 10	8	10	0	0
Mahmudullah c 4 b 10	8	13	0	0
Raqibul Hasan c 10 b 9	16	20	1	0
Mashrafe bin Mortaza b 10	11	8	0	1
†Mushfiqur Rahim not out	11	11	1	0
Naeem Islam c 4 b 11	28	17	0	3
Shahadat Hossain not out	0	0	0	0
L-b 3, w 3	6			

6 overs: 55-2   (20 overs)   155-8

1/24 2/55 3/74 4/77 5/95 6/111 7/121 8/154

Rubel Hossain did not bat.

Zaheer Khan 3–0–26–1; I. K. Pathan 2–0–20–0; Y. K. Pathan 3–0–26–1; I. Sharma 4–0–34–2; Harbhajan Singh 4–0–25–0; Ojha 4–0–21–4.

Umpires: B. F. Bowden and S. J. A. Taufel.   Third umpire: N. J. Llong.   Referee: B. C. Broad.

BANGLADESH v IRELAND

At Nottingham, June 8. Ireland won by six wickets. Ireland 2 pts. Toss: Ireland. Twenty20 international debuts: J. P. Bray, J. F. Mooney, W. B. Rankin, R. M. West.

Ireland repeated their victory over Bangladesh in the 2007 World Cup, ensuring they would reach the Super Eight stage at their expense. They were helped enormously by some brainless shot selection by the Bangladeshis, which left their coach Jamie Siddons fuming: "There's nothing we can do if they're going to keep making mental errors like that, the same mistakes over and over... if the boys keep disobeying the plan you end up with a shitty little score like 130." The worst offenders were the captain, Mohammad Ashraful, who guided a simple chance to slip two overs after being dropped there from a similar shot, and Shakib Al Hasan, who perished mis-pulling for what Siddons reckoned was "the fifth time this tour". Johnston took advantage, collecting three wickets as he bowled his four overs off the reel. The final over, from Cusack, cost 20, including two sixes by Mashrafe bin Mortaza. But Niall O'Brien repaid him in kind, collecting three soaring leg-side sixes in an over on his way to 40 from 25 balls to launch Ireland's run-chase. His brother Kevin finished the job, pulling two sixes of his own. Bangladesh could console themselves with some home cooking after they paid to have it helicoptered in from the Bollywood Spice restaurant in Warmley, near Bristol. "If we eat too much before a match it will be bad for us," said Shakib, "so we are having it brought here after we play Ireland."

Man of the Match: N. J. O'Brien.   *Attendance:* 13,012.

Bangladesh

		B	4	6
Tamim Iqbal *run out*	22	28	2	0
Junaid Siddique *c 1 b 7*	13	5	3	0
*Mohammad Ashraful *c 6 b 7*	14	10	1	1
Shakib Al Hasan *c 4 b 7*	7	7	1	0
Mahmudullah *st 3 b 8*	7	10	0	0
Raqibul Hasan *b 9*	13	20	0	0
†Mushfiqur Rahim *c 5 b 10*	14	15	0	0
Mashrafe bin Mortaza *not out*	33	16	1	2
Naeem Islam *b 11*	7	9	0	0
Abdur Razzak *not out*	0	0	0	0
L-b 1, w 6	7			

6 overs: 42-2   (20 overs) 137-8

1/15 2/40 3/50 4/61 5/66 6/90 7/94 8/117

Rubel Hossain did not bat.

Rankin 4–0–36–1; Johnston 4–0–20–3; West 4–0–25–1; McCallan 4–0–17–1; Cusack 4–0–38–1.

Ireland

		B	4	6
J. P. Bray *c 6 b 8*	2	10	0	0
*W. T. S. Porterfield *c and b 10*	23	29	3	0
†N. J. O'Brien *c 11 b 4*	40	25	3	3
G. C. Wilson *c 3 b 8*	10	15	0	0
J. F. Mooney *not out*	17	14	2	0
K. J. O'Brien *not out*	39	17	4	2
L-b 4, w 3	7			

6 overs: 47-1   (18.2 overs) 138-4

1/6 2/61 3/71 4/89

D. T. Johnston, A. R. Cusack, W. K. McCallan, R. M. West and W. B. Rankin did not bat.

Mashrafe bin Mortaza 4–0–30–2; Rubel Hossain 3.2–0–31–0; Mahmudullah 3–0–23–0; Naeem Islam 2–0–9–0; Shakib Al Hasan 3–0–23–1; Abdur Razzak 3–0–18–1.

Umpires: N. J. Llong and S. J. A. Taufel.   Third umpire: I. J. Gould.   Referee: B. C. Broad.

INDIA v IRELAND

At Nottingham, June 10. India won by eight wickets. India 2 pts. Toss: India.

Ireland's undefeated record in Twenty20 internationals came to a sticky end in a match reduced by drizzle to 18 overs a side; before this they had four wins and a no-result against Associates and Bangladesh. As they had already qualified, Ireland rested Johnston (shoulder niggle) and Niall O'Brien (ankle), but were soon in trouble against the swing of Zaheer Khan, who had three for ten after his first two overs. A plucky display from White helped Ireland set a three-figure target, but Gambhir and Rohit Sharma took few risks in putting on 77 before Gambhir sliced the burly New Zealand-born slow left-armer West – who had earlier been run out after failing to ground his bat – to point.

Man of the Match: Zaheer Khan.   *Attendance:* 15,645.

Ireland

		B	4	6
*W. T. S. Porterfield *c 6 b 9*	5	8	0	0
J. P. Bray *b 9*	0	7	0	0
†G. C. Wilson *b 8*	19	23	1	0
A. C. Botha *c 6 b 9*	8	5	1	0
K. J. O'Brien *b 10*	2	4	0	0
J. F. Mooney *c 4 b 10*	19	22	1	0
A. R. White *c 3 b 9*	29	25	3	1
R. M. West *run out*	1	4	0	0
A. R. Cusack *not out*	12	6	2	0
W. K. McCallan *not out*	9	7	1	0
L-b 6, w 2	8			

5 overs: 24-3   (18 overs) 112-8

1/4 2/9 3/17 4/28 5/48 6/72 7/73 8/92

W. B. Rankin did not bat.

I. K. Pathan 3–0–22–0; Zaheer Khan 3–0–19–4; I. Sharma 3–0–18–0; Yuvraj Singh 1–0–4–0; Ojha 4–0–18–2; Harbhajan Singh 4–0–25–1.

India

		B	4	6
G. Gambhir *c 11 b 8*	37	31	3	1
R. G. Sharma *not out*	52	45	4	1
*†M. S. Dhoni *c 2 b 10*	14	13	1	0
Yuvraj Singh *not out*	3	4	0	0
L-b 4, w 3	7			

5 overs: 38-0   (15.3 overs) 113-2

1/77 2/100

S. K. Raina, Y. K. Pathan, I. K. Pathan, Harbhajan Singh, Zaheer Khan, P. P. Ojha and I. Sharma did not bat.

Rankin 4–0–28–0; O'Brien 2–0–17–0; Cusack 2–0–13–0; West 4–0–23–1; McCallan 3.3–0–28–1.

Umpires: I. J. Gould and N. J. Llong.   Third umpire: B. F. Bowden.   Referee: B. C. Broad.

GROUP B

ENGLAND v NETHERLANDS

At Lord's, June 5 (floodlit). Netherlands won by four wickets. Netherlands 2 pts. Toss: Netherlands. Twenty20 debut: A. N. Kervezee. Twenty20 international debuts: J. S. Foster, R. W. T. Key, E. J. G. Morgan, A. U. Rashid; D. P. Nannes, B. Zuiderent.

A stunning victory for the Netherlands on their first senior visit to Lord's marked a wretched nadir in the painful saga of England's one-day humiliations. The tension built throughout the Dutch reply, culminating in a final over of impossible drama that included three missed run-outs and a dropped catch. Bowling round the wicket from wide of the crease, Broad stifled the scoring by maintaining a full length, but since he committed all four fluffs, here was England's villain. The Dutch needed seven from that last over. From the first ball Broad somehow missed the non-striker's stumps from close range; from the second he tried a Jonty Rhodes dive, but broke the wicket with his hand, not the ball. From the third he put down a sharp return catch from ten Doeschate. Three balls, three missed chances, three singles. A scrambled bye – Foster's offers to stand up were ignored – and a run to mid-on left Schiferli needing two from the final ball. Lord's held its breath. Schiferli mistimed his shot; he knew there wasn't a single, let alone two, but he had no option, and charged for the other end as the bowler fielded in his follow-through. Hard-wired to attack, Broad turned, shied at the stumps and, to his utter horror, missed, as England had all night. The courageous Dutch filched an overthrow – and thousands of orange supporters were tickled pink. Had Broad allowed the tie, England would have had a tilt at victory in a "super over". But this was the right result; they had been punished for disdainfully underestimating their opponents, rashly giving a debut to Rashid rather than playing the

Dutch courage: Edgar Schiferli holds his nerve to steal two from the final ball; Stuart Broad holds his head in disbelief.

Philip Brown

reliable Swann. A tense finish looked improbable after Bopara and Wright had put on 102 to equal England's best stand in Twenty20 internationals. But Pietersen was absent with an injured Achilles heel, and England had an Achilles heel of their own. Key, a strange selection for the squad as he had been out of form, was played in the unfamiliar position of No. 6, instead of Graham Napier. After their opening stand, England scored 60 from 8.4 overs, and their other five batsmen hit one boundary from 37 balls. Having clawed back the initiative, the Dutch batsmen started out with belief. The stocky Reekers pummelled two leg-side sixes before de Grooth combined powerful strokes, some learned on the hockey field, with deft placement. They scored predominantly on the on side, while the English batsmen, against a more disciplined line, had favoured the off. Borren weighed in to ensure that, as rain fell, the Dutch were always ahead of the Duckworth/Lewis par score. Then came the riveting denouement…

Man of the Match: T. N. de Groth.   *Attendance:* 23,665.

England

		B	*4*	*6*
R. S. Bopara *c 11 b 6*	46	34	5	0
L. J. Wright *c 5 b 6*	71	49	8	0
O. A. Shah *c 1 b 8*	5	8	0	0
E. J. G. Morgan *c 3 b 5*	6	8	0	0
*P. D. Collingwood *c 8 b 11*	11	10	1	0
R. W. T. Key *not out*	10	8	0	0
†J. S. Foster *not out*	3	3	0	0
W 10	10			

6 overs: 51-0   (20 overs)   162-5

1/102 2/113 3/127 4/144 5/153

A. U. Rashid, S. C. J. Broad, R. J. Sidebottom and J. M. Anderson did not bat.

Nannes 4–0–30–0; Schiferli 4–0–33–1; ten Doeschate 4–0–35–2; Seelaar 4–0–33–1; Borren 4–0–31–1.

Netherlands

		B	*4*	*6*
A. N. Kervezee *c 9 b 11*	1	4	0	0
D. J. Reekers *c 3 b 9*	20	13	1	2
B. Zuiderent *st 7 b 8*	12	16	1	0
T. N. de Groth *c 6 b 5*	49	30	6	1
P. W. Borren *c 3 b 11*	30	25	1	1
R. N. ten Doeschate *not out*	22	17	2	0
D. L. S. van Bunge *c 2 b 11*	8	8	1	0
E. Schiferli *not out*	5	7	0	0
B 1, l-b 13, w 2	16			

6 overs: 52-2   (20 overs)   163-6

1/2 2/23 3/66 4/116 5/133 6/146

*†J. Smits, D. P. Nannes and P. M. Seelaar did not bat.

Anderson 4–0–23–3; Sidebottom 4–0–23–0; Broad 4–0–32–1; Rashid 4–0–36–1; Wright 2–0–18–0; Collingwood 2–0–17–1.

Umpires: S. J. Davis and E. A. R. de Silva.   Third umpire: A. L. Hill.   Referee: A. G. Hurst.

ENGLAND v PAKISTAN

At The Oval, June 7. England won by 48 runs. England 2 pts. Toss: Pakistan. Twenty20 international debut: Mohammad Aamer.

After the Dutch disaster, England shuffled their pack to play two specialist spinners. More importantly, Pietersen was back after injury – and the team found the passion and fight they lacked 48 hours before to breeze into the Super Eights. Bopara fell early to a stupendous diving catch by Shoaib Malik at backward point, but generally Pakistan's fielding was more 1920 village green than Twenty20 international. ("I have no idea why our fielders are unable to field properly," Younis Khan later lamented.) Wright crashed England's first six of the tournament as they made good use of the powerplay overs, and when he fell to an Umar Gul yorker – others would suffer the same fate over the next fortnight – the score was 62 for two in the sixth over. Saeed Ajmal's *doosras* reined in the scoring, but England still powered past 180, with Pietersen hitting three sixes – one an audacious strike over extra cover. England's aggressive short-of-a-length bowling and nimbler fielding never allowed their opponents to settle, and the final margin left Pakistan needing a substantial win against the Netherlands to progress.

Man of the Match: L. J. Wright.   *Attendance:* 20,332.

England

		B	4	6
R. S. Bopara *c 4 b 10*	5	6	1	0
L. J. Wright *b 9*	34	16	6	1
K. P. Pietersen *c 9 b 11*	58	38	5	3
O. A. Shah *b 9*	33	32	3	1
*P. D. Collingwood *c 6 b 11*	15	11	2	0
A. D. Mascarenhas *not out*	16	12	1	0
†J. S. Foster *not out*	14	8	0	1
L-b 3, w 4, n-b 3	10			

6 overs: 63-2   (20 overs) 185-5

1/9 2/62 3/128 4/152 5/156

A. U. Rashid, G. P. Swann, S. C. J. Broad and J. M. Anderson did not bat.

Yasir Arafat 4–0–42–0; Mohammad Aamer 3–0–31–1; Umar Gul 4–0–37–2; Shoaib Malik 1–0–13–0; Shahid Afridi 4–0–36–0; Saeed Ajmal 4–0–23–2.

12th man E. J. G. Morgan.

Pakistan

		B	4	6
Ahmed Shehzad *c 5 b 6*	4	7	0	0
Salman Butt *c 1 b 10*	28	23	5	0
†Kamran Akmal *c 2 b 10*	6	6	0	0
Shoaib Malik *c 7 b 2*	20	21	1	0
*Younis Khan *not out*	46	31	5	0
Shahid Afridi *c 12 b 9*	5	12	0	0
Misbah-ul-Haq *c 12 b 11*	10	8	0	1
Yasir Arafat *c 2 b 10*	4	6	0	0
Umar Gul *not out*	8	6	1	0
L-b 1, w 5	6			

6 overs: 41-3   (20 overs) 137-7

1/13 2/41 3/41 4/87 5/102 6/117 7/129

Mohammad Aamer and Saeed Ajmal did not bat.

Mascarenhas 2–0–14–1; Anderson 4–0–30–1; Broad 3–0–17–3; Rashid 4–0–24–0; Swann 4–0–27–1; Wright 3–0–24–1.

Umpires: B. R. Doctrove and D. J. Harper.   Third umpire: A. M. Saheba.   Referee: R. S. Madugalle.

NETHERLANDS v PAKISTAN

At Lord's, June 9. Pakistan won by 82 runs. Pakistan 2 pts. Toss: Pakistan.

Pakistan's phalanx of slow bowlers together claimed eight for 49 to bring the great Dutch adventure to an abrupt and decisive end. The batsmen found Shahid Afridi's variations especially tricky to decipher: he yorked Zuiderent with his first ball, castled de Grooth as he stepped back to cut, beat the advancing van Bunge to have him stumped, and finally deceived Schiferli in the flight. Saeed Ajmal's *doosra* claimed three victims, including two stumpings, while Shoaib Malik also had Kamran Akmal's slick glovery work to thank for dismissing the dangerous ten Doeschate. Akmal became the first wicketkeeper to make four stumpings in any form of limited-overs international. Earlier, the Pakistani batsmen had shown far more spine than against England. Akmal, particularly strong driving square of the wicket, gained combative support from the middle order as Pakistan reached a demanding total. The real target faced by the Netherlands, though, was slightly less: defeat by 24 runs or fewer would have seen them through on net run-rate.

Man of the Match: Kamran Akmal.   *Attendance:* 21,809.

Pakistan

		B	4	6
†Kamran Akmal *c 8 b 11*	41	30	3	2
Salman Butt *c 4 b 5*	18	13	2	1
Shoaib Malik *c 11 b 4*	30	28	2	0
*Younis Khan *c 6 b 11*	36	20	0	3
Misbah-ul-Haq *not out*	31	20	3	0
Shahid Afridi *b 10*	13	7	0	1
Fawad Alam *not out*	3	2	0	0
L-b 1, w 2	3			

6 overs: 50-1   (20 overs) 175-5

1/38 2/81 3/99 4/152 5/171

Sohail Tanvir, Umar Gul, Mohammad Aamer and Saeed Ajmal did not bat.

Netherlands

		B	4	6
D. J. Reekers *c 8 b 10*	13	6	3	0
A. N. Kervezee *st 1 b 11*	21	29	1	0
B. Zuiderent *b 6*	13	15	2	0
P. W. Borren *c 2 b 11*	2	4	0	0
R. N. ten Doeschate *st 1 b 3*	14	10	0	1
T. N. de Grooth *b 6*	4	7	0	0
D. L. S. van Bunge *st 1 b 6*	0	2	0	0
E. Schiferli *c 11 b 6*	2	6	0	0
*†J. Smits *not out*	11	17	0	0
D. P. Nannes *st 1 b 11*	6	7	0	0
P. M. Seelaar *b 9*	1	2	0	0
L-b 1, w 5	6			

6 overs: 37-1   (17.3 overs) 93

1/13 2/42 3/47 4/49 5/61 6/61 7/71 8/74 9/90

Nannes 4–0–26–1; Schiferli 4–0–36–0; ten Doeschate 4–0–42–1; Seelaar 4–0–36–2; Borren 4–0–34–1.

Sohail Tanvir 3–0–13–0; Mohammad Aamer 2–0–16–1; Umar Gul 2.3–0–14–1; Saeed Ajmal 4–0–20–3; Shahid Afridi 4–0–11–4; Shoaib Malik 2–0–18–1.

Umpires: B. R. Doctrove and A. M. Saheba.　Third umpire: D. J. Harper.　Referee: A. G. Hurst.

GROUP C

AUSTRALIA v WEST INDIES

At The Oval, June 6. West Indies won by seven wickets. West Indies 2 pts. Toss: Australia.

This match was decided by Chris Gayle's batting. Others pitched in, but it was Gayle's power that left the lasting impression – almost literally in the case of the road outside Archbishop Tenison's School and the roof of the Bedser Stand. He slammed his first and third balls for four, but really got going in Lee's third over. A six over midwicket to Tenison's was followed by a dot ball and a six on to the Bedser beyond long-on; then came another dot before the fifth delivery, a no-ball, was thumped to cover for four, and the free hit to long-off for four more; the last was a six to midwicket. Twenty-seven came off the over as West Indies reached a blistering 83 for none by the end of the powerplay, while Lee nursed figures of 3–0–51–0. It wasn't much quieter at the other end, with Fletcher, who initially outscored his captain, pummelling a 31-ball fifty; Gayle needed 23 for his. The pair had put on 133, the third-highest partnership in Twenty20 internationals, when Fletcher departed in the 12th over, by when the result was clear. Earlier, Australia had begun dreadfully, with Watson and Ponting, who got in a muddle and missed a straight

After the storm: Brett Lee smiles after dismissing Chris Gayle for a whirlwind 88, but the damage is done.

ball, gone in the first over, from Taylor. Despite being troubled by Edwards's pace, Warner played an aggressive hand to build the recovery from 15 for three. Setting a target of 170 was an achievement, but against Gayle on song, it was nothing like enough.

Man of the Match: C. H. Gayle.   *Attendance:* 18,731.

Australia

		B	4	6
S. R. Watson *c 5 b 9*	0	3	0	0
D. A. Warner *c 11 b 6*	63	53	6	1
*R. T. Ponting *lbw b 9*	0	1	0	0
M. J. Clarke *c 11 b 10*	2	7	0	0
†B. J. Haddin *c 11 b 7*	24	19	2	1
D. J. Hussey *c 2 b 6*	27	16	0	3
M. E. K. Hussey *not out*	28	15	3	1
M. G. Johnson *c 6 b 10*	9	7	1	0
B. Lee *not out*	1	1	0	0
B 1, l-b 5, w 7, n-b 2	15			

6 overs: 35-3   (20 overs) 169-7

1/1 2/3 3/15 4/81 5/113 6/143 7/153

J. R. Hopes and N. W. Bracken did not bat.

Taylor 4–0–33–2; Edwards 4–0–34–2; Bravo 4–0–31–2; Benn 4–0–35–0; Gayle 2–0–13–0; Pollard 2–0–17–1.

West Indies

		B	4	6
*C. H. Gayle *c 1 b 9*	88	50	6	6
A. D. S. Fletcher *c 6 b 8*	53	32	7	1
X. M. Marshall *c 10 b 8*	8	12	0	0
S. Chanderpaul *not out*	0	1	0	0
R. R. Sarwan *not out*	8	2	2	0
L-b 5, w 8, n-b 2	15			

6 overs: 83-0   (15.5 overs) 172-3

1/133 2/157 3/162

D. J. Bravo, K. A. Pollard, †D. Ramdin, J. E. Taylor, F. H. Edwards and S. J. Benn did not bat.

Lee 4–0–56–1; Johnson 3.5–0–36–2; Bracken 2–0–21–0; Hopes 2–0–13–0; D. J. Hussey 1–0–16–0; Watson 2–0–13–0; Clarke 1–0–12–0.

Umpires: Aleem Dar and Asad Rauf.   Third umpire: M. R. Benson.   Referee: R. S. Madugalle.

AUSTRALIA v SRI LANKA

At Nottingham, June 8. Sri Lanka won by six wickets. Sri Lanka 2 pts. Toss: Sri Lanka. Twenty20 international debuts: A. D. Mathews, I. Udana.

In a match of twists and turns – almost a mini-Test – Sri Lanka eventually triumphed, sentencing Australia to an early exit after two defeats: not the Ashes build-up they had envisaged. Sangakkara took the match award for a well-paced 55, but the main destroyer was Mendis, whose spin variations the Australians were encountering for the first time. In his opening over he bowled a nervous-looking Ponting, who had been orchestrating a recovery after the first-over dismissal of Warner. Next over Mendis trapped Watson, who missed a sweep; he returned to deceive Michael Hussey just after his brother David, back at his old home ground, had tonked him for six. From 94 for six off 14.5 overs, the Australians batted resiliently to hit 65 from 31 balls. Johnson spoiled Muralitharan's figures – 21 came from his last over, including two slog-swept sixes. After Jayasuriya's quick departure to Warner's backward-leaping catch, Dilshan improvised well, reaching 50 in 26 balls by flicking the ball over his shoulder for four, as if tossing a pancake: it soon became his signature shot. A late wobble was overcome by Sangakkara, who hit two sixes in Hauritz's final over, and finally by Mubarak, who tucked into an obliging length and wafted Lee for two huge sixes. The end came when the first ball of the last over, bowled by Johnson, was a leg-side wide.

Man of the Match: K. C. Sangakkara.   *Attendance:* 13,012.

Australia

		B	4	6
S. R. Watson *lbw b 11*	22	21	2	1
D. A. Warner *c 1 b 7*	0	3	0	0
*R. T. Ponting *b 11*	25	15	5	0
†B. J. Haddin *b 10*	16	17	0	1
M. J. Clarke *c and b 8*	11	15	0	0
D. J. Hussey *c 2 b 8*	28	22	1	2
M. E. K. Hussey *lbw b 11*	1	5	0	0
M. G. Johnson *not out*	28	13	2	2
B. Lee *b 10*	15	5	2	1
N. M. Hauritz *c 3 b 10*	4	3	1	0
N. W. Bracken *not out*	4	1	1	0
W 5	5			

6 overs: 48-2   (20 overs)   159-9

1/1 2/48 3/59 4/74 5/79 6/94 7/135 8/151 9/155

Mathews 2–0–10–1; Jayasuriya 2–0–17–0;
Udana 4–0–47–2; Malinga 4–0–36–3; Mendis
4–0–20–3; Muralitharan 4–0–29–0.

Sri Lanka

		B	4	6
T. M. Dilshan *b 5*	53	32	10	0
S. T. Jayasuriya *c 2 b 9*	2	7	0	0
*†K. C. Sangakkara *not out*	55	42	4	2
D. P. M. D. Jayawardene *c 11 b 10*	9	12	0	0
L. P. C. Silva *c 3 b 9*	11	11	1	0
J. Mubarak *not out*	21	12	1	2
L-b 1, w 6, n-b 2	9			

6 overs: 62-1   (19 overs)   160-4

1/19 2/81 3/98 4/127

A. D. Mathews, I. Udana, M. Muralitharan,
S. L. Malinga and B. A. W. Mendis did not bat.

Lee 4–0–39–2; Johnson 2–0–17–0; Bracken
4–0–33–0; Watson 2–0–24–0; Hauritz
4–0–27–1; Clarke 3–0–19–1.

Umpires: B. F. Bowden and I. J. Gould.   Third umpire: N. J. Llong.   Referee: B. C. Broad.

SRI LANKA v WEST INDIES

At Nottingham, June 10. Sri Lanka won by 15 runs. Sri Lanka 2 pts. Toss: West Indies.
  This match – thought to be of academic interest only as both teams had already qualified
by beating Australia but, as it turned out, a dry run for the semi-final – was virtually settled
by an opening partnership of 124 (the second-highest stand of the tournament) in 12.3
overs. It was dominated by Jayasuriya, rising 40, who used his powerful forearms to pull
Edwards for six and smack fours through mid-off and over point in an over costing 17.
Dilshan was no slouch, reaching his own fifty in 35 balls, but he received less of the strike
during Jayasuriya's virtuoso performance. When Pollard came on, Dilshan greeted him
with his "starfish" shot, then whirled him over backward point for six and slashed a back-
foot four; Jayasuriya completed the torture, in an over costing 19, by finding the long-off
boundary. West Indies did well to limit the damage after that – only 52 came from the last
six overs – but, with Gayle resting a knee injury, the target looked a tall order. They also
made a decent start, but Muralitharan and Mendis took three wickets in nine deliveries
between them, after which the only resistance came from Bravo, whose shots included a
lunging cover-driven four, off his feet after initially giving himself room, against the pacy
Malinga.
  Man of the Match: S. T. Jayasuriya.   *Attendance:* 15,645.

Sri Lanka

		B	4	6
T. M. Dilshan *c 10 b 1*	74	47	11	1
S. T. Jayasuriya *lbw b 1*	81	47	10	3
*†K. C. Sangakkara *c 2 b 1*	5	6	0	0
D. P. M. D. Jayawardene *c 8 b 1*	4	7	0	0
J. Mubarak *not out*	8	5	1	0
L. P. C. Silva *c 8 b 9*	7	7	1	0
A. D. Mathews *not out*	3	2	0	0
L-b 5, w 4, n-b 1	10			

6 overs: 66-0   (20 overs)   192-5

1/124 2/147 3/168 4/172 5/189

I. Udana, M. Muralitharan, S. L. Malinga and
B. A. W. Mendis did not bat.

West Indies

		B	4	6
L. M. P. Simmons *c 4 b 9*	29	19	5	0
A. D. S. Fletcher *b 10*	13	11	1	0
X. M. Marshall *c 6 b 11*	14	11	1	0
S. Chanderpaul *b 11*	1	5	0	0
R. R. Sarwan *not out*	28	26	0	0
D. J. Bravo *c 5 b 10*	51	38	5	2
K. A. Pollard *not out*	19	11	3	0
L-b 4, w 17, n-b 1	22			

6 overs: 65-1   (20 overs)   177-5

1/38 2/70 3/71 4/73 5/150

*†D. Ramdin, J. E. Taylor, S. J. Benn and F. H.
Edwards did not bat.

Taylor 4–0–32–1; Edwards 2–0–37–0; Bravo 4–0–29–0; Benn 4–0–25–0; Pollard 3–0–45–0; Simmons 3–0–19–4.

Jayasuriya 3–0–34–0; Malinga 4–0–45–2; Udana 4–0–36–0; Mendis 4–0–25–2; Muralitharan 4–0–21–1; Mathews 1–0–12–0.

Umpires: B. F. Bowden and S. J. A. Taufel. Third umpire: I. J. Gould. Referee: B. C. Broad.

GROUP D

NEW ZEALAND v SCOTLAND

At The Oval, June 6. New Zealand won by seven wickets. New Zealand 2 pts. Toss: New Zealand. Twenty20 international debuts: C. S. MacLeod, J. H. Stander.

After England's humbling the night before, it briefly looked as if New Zealand might be ambushed by a Scotland team missing three of their fastest bowlers. Rain delayed the 10 a.m. start by over two hours, allowing only a seven-over slog on what remained a true pitch. Watson greeted the first ball with an edged four over the keeper, and finished the over with three more boundaries. When the shortened powerplay ended, six balls later, Scotland were flying at 30 without loss. Butler's off-cutter deceived Watson, but Coetzer maintained the tempo against Ryder's inviting medium-pace. Scotland, however, lost three wickets from the last three balls – two for Butler sandwiching a run-out – as the momentum shifted. Ryder reverted to his stronger suit, hammering the ball so hard the Scots risked life and limb in the field; New Zealand passed 50 from the fourth ball of the third over. That base was enough to bring victory, despite slapstick running that saw Brendon McCullum run out off a free hit, and a stand-out over by Watson, whose off-spin was Scotland's only variation on military-medium. He conceded just one scoring shot – and that a dropped catch. What havoc might Vettori, absent with a sore shoulder, have wreaked?

Man of the Match: I. G. Butler. *Attendance:* 18,731.

Scotland

	B	4	6
R. R. Watson *c 3 b 10*	27	10	6	0
N. S. Poonia *run out*	27	15	2	1
K. J. Coetzer *c 7 b 10*	33	15	3	2
J. H. Stander *not out*	0	1	0	0
†C. J. O. Smith *b 10*	0	1	0	0
L-b 2	2			

2 overs: 30-0   (7 overs)   89-4

1/30 2/89 3/89 4/89

*G. M. Hamilton, D. F. Watts, N. F. I. McCullum, C. M. Wright, G. D. Drummond and C. S. MacLeod did not bat.

O'Brien 1–0–16–0; Franklin 1–0–12–0; Butler 2–0–19–3; Oram 2–0–21–0; Ryder 1–0–19–0.

New Zealand

	B	4	6
*B. B. McCullum *run out*	18	7	4	0
J. D. Ryder *c 11 b 9*	31	12	3	2
L. R. P. L. Taylor *not out*	21	10	1	2
J. D. P. Oram *c 4 b 1*	8	6	1	0
S. B. Styris *not out*	8	4	0	1
W 1, n-b 3	4			

2 overs: 31-0   (6 overs)   90-3

1/51 2/59 3/68

M. J. Guptill, †P. D. McGlashan, J. E. C. Franklin, N. L. McCullum, I. G. Butler and I. E. O'Brien did not bat.

MacLeod 1–0–19–0; Drummond 2–0–25–0; Wright 1–0–20–1; Watson 1–0–4–1; Stander 1–0–22–0.

Umpires: B. R. Doctrove and D. J. Harper. Third umpire: R. E. Koertzen. Referee: R. S. Madugalle.

SCOTLAND v SOUTH AFRICA

At The Oval, June 7. South Africa won by 130 runs. South Africa 2 pts. Toss: Scotland.

South Africa gave a sublime display of how to dismiss associate opposition. After reconnoitring for a couple of overs, Smith and Kallis began the assault on Scotland's dobbers. De Villiers was the star, mixing twinkling footwork against spin with power and placement against seam, while Morkel produced a beguiling cameo. His hitting down the ground brought two vast sixes, and the pair added 51 in 19 balls. De Villiers then sped South Africa on to their highest total in Twenty20 internationals before Scotland disintegrated against threatening pace and throttling spin. Amid the slaughter, there were significant performances from two players who, despite their names, were Scottish born and bred: off-spinner Majid Haq intelligently varied his pace and removed the openers; Kyle Coetzer, meanwhile, produced a breathtakingly athletic leap to catch Boucher, somehow holding on as he crashed to the ground inches from the long-on boundary; he also held the Scotland innings together while wickets fell pell-mell at the other end. South African born Jan Stander enjoyed his tournament rather less: all told, 43 runs flooded from his 12 balls.

Man of the Match: A. B. de Villiers.   *Attendance:* 20,332.

South Africa

		B	4	6
*G. C. Smith *c 5 b 8*	38	29	6	1
J. H. Kallis *b 8*	48	31	8	0
H. H. Gibbs *st 5 b 2*	16	14	0	0
A. B. de Villiers *not out*	79	34	5	6
J. A. Morkel *c 4 b 9*	24	11	1	2
†M. V. Boucher *c 4 b 9*	2	3	0	0
J-P. Duminy *not out*	0	0	0	0
W 1, n-b 3	4			

6 overs: 55-0   (20 overs) 211-5

1/87 2/88 3/125 4/176 5/195

R. E. van der Merwe, J. Botha, W. D. Parnell and D. W. Steyn did not bat.

MacLeod 4–0–37–0; Drummond 4–0–40–2; Stander 1–0–21–0; Rogers 4–0–52–0; Haq 4–0–25–2; Watson 3–0–36–1.

Scotland

		B	4	6
*G. M. Hamilton *c 7 b 10*	5	6	1	0
R. R. Watson *b 11*	4	4	1	0
N. S. Poonia *run out*	0	1	0	0
K. J. Coetzer *c and b 8*	42	32	1	3
†C. J. O. Smith *b 11*	0	1	0	0
N. F. I. McCullum *b 9*	8	16	1	0
J. H. Stander *lbw b 9*	2	6	0	0
R. M. Haq *b 8*	15	20	1	0
G. D. Drummond *b 5*	1	2	0	0
G. A. Rogers *not out*	1	3	0	0
C. S. MacLeod *b 5*	0	3	0	0
L-b 1, w 2	3			

6 overs: 32-4   (15.4 overs) 81

1/6 2/10 3/13 4/13 5/35 6/41 7/79 8/79 9/81

Steyn 3–0–21–2; Parnell 2–0–6–1; Kallis 1–0–4–0; Botha 4–0–17–2; van der Merwe 4–0–17–2; Morkel 1.4–0–15–2.

Umpires: Asad Rauf and A. M. Saheba.   Third umpire: D. J. Harper.   Referee: R. S. Madugalle.

NEW ZEALAND v SOUTH AFRICA

At Lord's, June 9 (floodlit). South Africa won by one run. South Africa 2 pts. Toss: New Zealand. Twenty20 international debut: B. J. Diamanti.

Both teams had qualified for the next phase, and New Zealand, struggling with injuries, omitted three first-choice players. Yet this match fizzed into life to spark a memorable if meaningless conclusion. South Africa set off at a daunting pace, but the advent of spin, as so often, transformed the innings. Nathan McCullum's first over of off-breaks cost just two, and South Africa lost all impetus. Sharp fielding, typified by stand-in captain Brendon McCullum's lightning pick-up-and-throw to remove Kallis, was almost as restrictive as the slow bowling. South Africa limped to 128. Brendon McCullum seemed determined to claim bragging rights with a swift and comprehensive win, but South Africa had two spinners to New Zealand's one and, ultimately, Daniel Vettori's absence proved vital. Van der Merwe's accuracy was exceptional; Botha's not far behind. New Zealand, flattered by the final margin, simply lost control of the run-chase. Worse still, Taylor suffered an injured hamstring as South Africa set a record for the lowest winning total in full-length Twenty20 internationals.

Man of the Match: R. E. van der Merwe.   *Attendance:* 21,809.

South Africa

		B	4	6
J. H. Kallis *run out*	24	23	2	1
*G. C. Smith *b 11*	33	35	4	0
H. H. Gibbs *c and b 6*	3	7	0	0
R. E. van der Merwe *b 8*	0	6	0	0
J-P. Duminy *c 3 b 9*	29	23	1	2
A. B. de Villiers *run out*	15	8	2	0
†M. V. Boucher *c 1 b 11*	6	6	0	0
J. A. Morkel *not out*	10	10	0	0
J. Botha *not out*	2	2	0	0
L-b 4, w 2	6			

6 overs: 47-0   (20 overs) 128-7

1/49 2/63 3/63 4/65 5/85 6/107 7/121

D. W. Steyn and W. D. Parnell did not bat.

Mills 4–0–34–1; Oram 4–0–30–0; Butler 4–0–13–2; Diamanti 2–0–19–0; N. L. McCullum 4–0–18–1; Styris 2–0–10–1.

New Zealand

		B	4	6
*B. B. McCullum *st 7 b 4*	57	54	6	0
M. J. Guptill *c 4 b 10*	6	5	1	0
N. T. Broom *c and b 1*	1	5	0	0
L. R. P. L. Taylor *b 4*	22	31	2	0
J. D. P. Oram *run out*	24	18	2	0
S. B. Styris *not out*	7	7	0	0
B 4, l-b 1, w 5	10			

6 overs: 35-2   (20 overs) 127-5

1/19 2/26 3/82 4/93 5/127

†P. D. McGlashan, N. L. McCullum, K. D. Mills, B. J. Diamanti and I. G. Butler did not bat.

Steyn 4–0–22–1; Parnell 4–0–38–1; Kallis 3–0–17–1; Botha 3–0–17–0; Morkel 2–0–14–0; van der Merwe 4–0–14–2.

Umpires: Asad Rauf and D. J. Harper.   Third umpire: A. M. Saheba.   Referee: A. G. Hurst.

FINAL GROUP TABLES

Group A

	Played	Won	Lost	Points	Net run-rate
INDIA	2	2	0	4	1.22
IRELAND	2	1	1	2	–0.16
Bangladesh	2	0	2	0	–0.99

Group B

	Played	Won	Lost	Points	Net run-rate
ENGLAND	2	1	1	2	1.17
PAKISTAN	2	1	1	2	0.85
Netherlands	2	1	1	2	–2.02

Group C

	Played	Won	Lost	Points	Net run-rate
SRI LANKA	2	2	0	4	0.62
WEST INDIES	2	1	1	2	0.71
Australia	2	0	2	0	–1.33

Group D

	Played	Won	Lost	Points	Net run-rate
SOUTH AFRICA	2	2	0	4	3.27
NEW ZEALAND	2	1	1	2	0.30
Scotland	2	0	2	0	–5.28

SUPER EIGHT MATCHES – GROUP E

ENGLAND v SOUTH AFRICA

At Nottingham, June 11 (floodlit). South Africa won by seven wickets. South Africa 2 pts. Toss: England.

England continued their up-and-down time by being thoroughly outplayed by South Africa, who lived up to their billing as tournament favourites in a clinical display. England's bright new opening pair were swept away in the first 11 balls, then in the sixth over Morkel made a crucial breakthrough when Pietersen cracked a full toss uppishly to mid-on, where van der Merwe caught it with a salmon leap. Morkel came off after that solitary over, the first maiden of the tournament, but had done his job. Only Shah stayed for long, and he was also the only batsman to clear the ropes: England's last six managed

25 runs (and one four) between them. South Africa made leisurely progress towards their undemanding target, only Kallis scoring at better than a run a ball, but the result was never in doubt. Just about the only bright spot for England came when Rashid made one turn and bounce on de Villiers, resulting in a slick slip catch for Collingwood.

Man of the Match: J. H. Kallis.   *Attendance:* 14,997.

England

		B	4	6
R. S. Bopara b 10	2	5	0	0
L. J. Wright c 7 b 11	1	6	0	0
K. P. Pietersen c 8 b 6	19	17	4	0
O. A. Shah c 7 b 2	38	33	3	2
*P. D. Collingwood b 2	19	19	2	0
†J. S. Foster c 6 b 8	1	4	0	0
A. D. Mascarenhas b 8	1	3	0	0
G. P. Swann c 6 b 9	5	6	0	0
S. C. J. Broad b 11	9	8	1	0
A. U. Rashid not out	9	17	0	0
J. M. Anderson b 11	0	1	0	0
L-b 1, w 6	7			

6 overs: 25-3   (19.5 overs) 111

1/4 2/4 3/25 4/78 5/79 6/82 7/88 8/92 9/111

Steyn 4–0–19–1; Parnell 3.5–0–14–3; Kallis 3–0–20–2; Morkel 1–1–0–1; Botha 4–0–25–1; van der Merwe 4–0–32–2.

South Africa

		B	4	6
*G. C. Smith c 6 b 9	11	15	2	0
J. H. Kallis not out	57	49	5	1
H. H. Gibbs b 8	30	30	2	1
A. B. de Villiers c 5 b 10	11	12	0	0
J-P. Duminy not out	2	4	0	0
L-b 1, w 2	3			

6 overs: 28-1   (18.2 overs) 114-3

1/17 2/91 3/108

J. A. Morkel, †M. V. Boucher, R. E. van der Merwe, J. Botha, D. W. Steyn and W. D. Parnell did not bat.

Mascarenhas 4–0–22–0; Anderson 3.2–0–27–0; Broad 3–0–14–1; Swann 4–0–26–1; Rashid 4–0–24–1.

Umpires: S. J. Davis and A. L. Hill.   Third umpire: E. A. R. de Silva.   Referee: A. G. Hurst.

INDIA v WEST INDIES

At Lord's, June 12 (floodlit). West Indies won by seven wickets. West Indies 2 pts. Toss: India.

This compelling game proved West Indies could down quality opponents even when Gayle was not firing on all 12 cylinders. The all-action hero was Bravo, although the early damage was done by the pace of Edwards, clocked at 93.9mph. Both adopted a relentlessly short length that flustered the Indian batsmen, Bravo picking up his first wicket courtesy of an extraordinary sprinting – running would do it no justice – catch by Simmons at square leg. Dhoni laboured on a relatively grudging pitch, and it needed the genius of Yuvraj Singh to dig India out of a hole, though he was dropped by Fletcher on 32, the main blemish in an improved West Indies fielding display. Lord's erupted when Gayle, after playing out a maiden from Harbhajan Singh, buckled beneath the pressure and top-edged a steepling catch to short fine leg. That, however, brought in Bravo; singles became twos as he and Simmons ran hard, and fielders found themselves fetching the ball from the extra cover boundary after Bravo hit inside-out over the infield. West Indies timed the chase perfectly, Bravo bringing victory with an elegant six.

Man of the Match: D. J. Bravo.   *Attendance:* 27,625.

India

		B	4	6
G. Gambhir *c 3 b 4*	14	13	2	0
R. G. Sharma *c 3 b 11*	5	3	1	0
S. K. Raina *c 8 b 11*	5	8	0	0
Yuvraj Singh *c and b 11*	67	43	6	2
*†M. S. Dhoni *c 2 b 4*	11	23	0	0
Y. K. Pathan *b 4*	31	23	3	1
I. K. Pathan *c 3 b 4*	2	3	0	0
Harbhajan Singh *not out*	13	4	3	0
Zaheer Khan *not out*	0	0	0	0
L-b 1, w 4	5			

6 overs: 40-3   (20 overs) 153-7

1/12 2/27 3/29 4/66 5/130 6/140 7/141

I. Sharma and P. P. Ojha did not bat.

Taylor 4–0–44–0; Edwards 4–0–24–3; Bravo 4–0–38–4; Gayle 3–0–13–0; Pollard 2–0–7–0; Benn 3–0–26–0.

West Indies

		B	4	6
*C. H. Gayle *c 9 b 6*	22	28	4	0
A. D. S. Fletcher *c 4 b 7*	0	2	0	0
L. M. P. Simmons *c 7 b 11*	44	37	5	0
D. J. Bravo *not out*	66	36	4	3
S. Chanderpaul *not out*	18	9	3	0
L-b 3, w 3	6			

6 overs: 32-1   (18.4 overs) 156-3

1/9 2/42 3/100

R. R. Sarwan, K. A. Pollard, †D. Ramdin, J. E. Taylor, S. J. Benn and F. H. Edwards did not bat.

Zaheer Khan 2.4–0–26–0; I. K. Pathan 2–0–9–1; Y. K. Pathan 4–0–27–1; Harbhajan Singh 4–1–31–0; I. Sharma 3–0–31–0; Ojha 3–0–29–1.

Umpires: Aleem Dar and R. E. Koertzen.   Third umpire: M. R. Benson.   Referee: B. C. Broad.

SOUTH AFRICA v WEST INDIES

At The Oval, June 13. South Africa won by 20 runs. South Africa 2 pts. Toss: West Indies.
Admirable full-length fast left-arm bowling by Wayne Parnell was the main difference between the sides, plus the fact that West Indies had played the evening before and Dwayne Bravo was drained by the effort of beating India. Gayle, having questionably decided to chase, clipped Parnell to midwicket after Fletcher had missed a wild swing, and

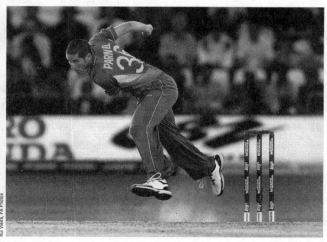

Rui Vieira, PA Photos

In the swing: Wayne Parnell removed both openers and ended with four for 13.

only Simmons – kicking on from the previous evening with 77 from 50 balls – kept West Indies in the game. Conventional swing having been missing from the tournament, Parnell swung it enough on a warm afternoon and a belter of a pitch with a glassy outfield. Earlier, South Africa's opening pair began with powerful driving, even though they hit in orthodox areas, and Gibbs struck 55 from 35 balls. A two-wicket over from Taylor stopped South Africa reaching much more than par on the highest scoring of the three grounds. But West Indies lacked a full-length opening and death bowler like Parnell.

Man of the Match: W. D. Parnell.   *Attendance*: 20,226.

South Africa

		B	4	6
J. H. Kallis *c 7 b 3*	45	31	6	1
*G. C. Smith *c 2 b 10*	31	18	6	0
H. H. Gibbs *c 9 b 7*	55	35	8	1
A. B. de Villiers *c 1 b 9*	17	10	2	0
J. A. Morkel *b 9*	10	8	2	0
†M. V. Boucher *not out*	17	12	0	1
J-P. Duminy *c 6 b 11*	0	1	0	0
R. E. van der Merwe *c 8 b 9*	1	3	0	0
J. Botha *not out*	4	2	0	0
L-b 1, w 2	3			

6 overs: 54-1   (20 overs) 183-7

1/54 2/105 3/136 4/155 5/159 6/163 7/166

D. W. Steyn and W. D. Parnell did not bat.

Taylor 4–0–30–3; Edwards 4–0–34–1; Bravo 2–0–24–0; Benn 4–0–36–1; Pollard 3–0–29–1; Gayle 1–0–7–0; Simmons 2–0–22–1.

West Indies

		B	4	6
*C. H. Gayle *c 9 b 11*	5	8	0	0
A. D. S. Fletcher *b 11*	0	5	0	0
L. M. P. Simmons *c 4 b 8*	77	50	12	1
D. J. Bravo *c 10 b 8*	19	17	2	0
S. Chanderpaul *c and b 7*	8	7	1	0
R. R. Sarwan *c 9 b 10*	8	11	0	0
K. A. Pollard *c 2 b 11*	6	4	1	0
†D. Ramdin *b 10*	8	7	1	0
J. E. Taylor *b 11*	0	1	0	0
S. J. Benn *not out*	13	9	2	0
F. H. Edwards *not out*	2	2	0	0
B 1, l-b 9, w 6, n-b 1	17			

6 overs: 45-2   (20 overs) 163-9

1/4 2/13 3/70 4/91 5/133 6/133 7/142 8/143 9/159

Steyn 4–0–30–2; Parnell 4–0–13–4; Kallis 2–0–23–0; Morkel 2–0–21–0; Botha 2–0–20–0; van der Merwe 4–0–30–2; Duminy 2–0–16–1.

Umpires: Aleem Dar and M. R. Benson.   Third umpire: R. J. Tucker.   Referee: R. S. Madugalle.

ENGLAND v INDIA

At Lords, June 14 (floodlit). England won by three runs. England 2 pts. Toss: India.

Indias astonishing decision to promote to No. 4 Ravindra Jadeja, a 20-year-old left-arm spinning all-rounder, ahead of three of the finest strikers in contemporary cricket cost them this match and their title as World Twenty20 champions. When Jadeja was dismissed by the third ball of the 14th over, Yuvraj Singh, Dhoni and Yusuf Pathan had to score 69 from 39 balls, and the fact that they hit 11 off the last three balls made the finish look closer than it was. Earlier, Pietersen underlined his value by making a brisk 46, but England looked like adding another defeat to those by the Netherlands and South Africa until Harbhajan Singh fired five wides down the leg side past Dhoni from what should have been the last balls of both the 18th and 20th overs, and gave them something to bowl at. England then borrowed the West Indian plan of pitching short against India's inexperienced top order, and made the elevation of Jadeja – 24 runs off 23 balls in his two previous Twenty20 internationals – all the more curious. India, the holders and pre-tournament favourites, were out. If England could beat West Indies, they would reach the semis. Collingwood later said being booed by Indian supporters had done his motivational speech for him.

Man of the Match: R. J. Sidebottom.   *Attendance:* 27,641.

England

	B	4	6
R. S. Bopara b 4 37	37	3	1
L. J. Wright c 7 b 11 1	7	0	0
K. P. Pietersen lbw b 4 46	27	5	1
A. D. Mascarenhas not out .. 25	27	2	0
O. A. Shah c 4 b 8 12	10	1	0
*P. D. Collingwood lbw b 9 7	5	1	0
†J. S. Foster c and b 8 6	5	0	0
G. P. Swann b 8 0	1	0	0
S. C. J. Broad not out 3	1	0	0
L-b 2, w 14 16			

6 overs: 40-1   (20 overs) 153-7

1/3 2/74 3/92 4/122 5/138 6/145 7/145

R. J. Sidebottom and J. M. Anderson did not bat.

Zaheer Khan 3–0–26–1; R. P. Singh 3–0–13–1; I. Sharma 4–0–36–0; Yuvraj Singh 2–0–20–0; Harbhajan Singh 4–0–30–3; Jadeja 4–0–26–2.

India

	B	4	6
G. Gambhir c 9 b 4 26	26	4	0
R. G. Sharma b 10........... 9	8	1	0
S. K. Raina c 2 b 10 2	5	0	0
R. A. Jadeja c 9 b 8......... 25	35	1	0
Yuvraj Singh st 7 b 8 17	9	0	2
**†M. S. Dhoni not out 30	20	3	0
Y. K. Pathan not out 33	17	1	2
L-b 4, w 4 8			

6 overs: 36-2   (20 overs) 150-5

1/12 2/24 3/62 4/85 5/87

Harbhajan Singh, Zaheer Khan, I. Sharma and R. P. Singh did not bat.

Anderson 4–0–32–0; Sidebottom 4–0–31–0; Broad 4–0–21–0; Pietersen 1–0–9–0; Wright 2–0–16–0; Swann 4–0–28–2; Mascarenhas 1–0–9–1.

Umpires: S. J. Davis and E. A. R. de Silva.   Third umpire: M. Erasmus.   Referee: A. G. Hurst.

ENGLAND v WEST INDIES

At The Oval, June 15 (floodlit). West Indies won by five wickets (D/L method). West Indies 2 pts. Toss: England.

England's stop-start progress in the tournament came to a permanent halt after the Duckworth/Lewis method seemed to weight the game in West Indies' favour. Rain in the interval caused the reduction of their task from 162 in 20 overs to just 80 in nine. West Indies slipped to 45 for five against feisty bowling, but then Sarwan teamed up with Chanderpaul, and the task of taking 35 from 22 balls proved simple for the tournament's most experienced sixth-wicket pair. England's own sixth-wicket pair also played beautifully, though not as batsmen: Foster and Swann combined to dismiss the dangerous Bravo with a quicksilver stumping, but their earlier run-making was less successful. After Wright again departed quickly to a mistimed heave, Bopara and Pietersen laid the foundations for what should have become a decent total. However, England's high-risk strategy of replacing Mascarenhas with Rashid – it meant Foster was two places too high at No. 6 – failed along with the middle order. Had Broad not smitten ten from the last two balls, the total would have been feeble. West Indies won without Fidel Edwards, their leading strike bowler, who injured his back moments before the toss. On National Wind Day, play was held up when a gust sent umpire Koertzen's floppy hat scurrying across the ground. Those who felt the new target did not offer a fair distillation of the original gained some support in September, when, after a scheduled four-year review, Duckworth and Lewis issued new tables reflecting increased scoring-rates. West Indies' revised target would have become 84; chances are they still would have made it.

Man of the Match: R. R. Sarwan.   *Attendance*: 20,465.

England

		B	4	6
R. S. Bopara lbw b 1	55	47	5	0
L. J. Wright c 8 b 5	6	6	1	0
K. P. Pietersen c 2 b 3	31	19	5	0
O. A. Shah c 2 b 4	18	15	1	1
*P. D. Collingwood lbw b 4	11	10	0	0
†J. S. Foster c 5 b 11	13	12	0	0
G. P. Swann not out	10	9	0	0
S. C. J. Broad not out	10	2	1	1
L-b 4, w 3	7			

6 overs: 49-1   (20 overs)   161-6

1/8 2/64 3/98 4/121 5/132 6/150

A. U. Rashid, R. J. Sidebottom and J. M. Anderson did not bat.

Sammy 4–0–24–0; Pollard 1–0–10–1; Benn 4–0–30–1; Taylor 2–0–24–0; Gayle 4–0–25–1; Simmons 1–0–14–1; Bravo 4–0–30–2.

West Indies

		B	4	6
*C. H. Gayle b 10	15	8	3	0
A. D. S. Fletcher c 6 b 11	0	3	0	0
L. M. P. Simmons c 10 b 8	0	1	0	0
D. J. Bravo st 6 b 7	18	13	1	1
K. A. Pollard b 9	9	6	0	1
S. Chanderpaul not out	17	10	1	0
R. R. Sarwan not out	19	9	3	0
L-b 1, w 3	4			

3 overs: 23-3   (8.2 overs)   82-5

1/6 2/16 3/16 4/41 5/45

†D. Ramdin, J. E. Taylor, D. J. G. Sammy and S. J. Benn did not bat.

Anderson 2–0–19–1; Sidebottom 1.2–0–15–1; Broad 2–0–20–1; Swann 2–0–16–1; Rashid 1–0–11–1.

Umpires: Aleem Dar and R. E. Koertzen.   Third umpire: R. J. Tucker.   Referee: R. S. Madugalle.

INDIA v SOUTH AFRICA

At Nottingham, June 16 (floodlit). South Africa won by 12 runs. South Africa 2 pts. Toss: South Africa.

The only interest for the neutral in this otherwise dead rubber was in whether India could win heavily enough to knock South Africa off the top of their group, and when they started their run-chase brightly, reaching 47 without loss in six overs, that looked possible. But on a slow pitch occasionally allowing extravagant turn, India's batsmen – normally so masterful against spin bowling – lost five wickets and scored only 32 runs in nine overs of spin. When Yuvraj Singh was eventually adjudged caught low down after scuffing Steyn to Boucher, the match was decided. South Africa, after making 47 in the powerplay, managed only 83 more off the last 14 overs. Despite leaving out Ojha, India still used five spinners of varying types, and between them they took three for 75 in 14 overs, the first eight of which featured no boundaries. India, the 2007 champions, departed this competition having been beaten only by Bangladesh and Ireland.

Man of the Match: A. B. de Villiers.   *Attendance:* 15,880.

South Africa

		B	4	6
*G. C. Smith c 8 b 7	26	26	2	0
H. H. Gibbs b 10	5	3	1	0
A. B. de Villiers c and b 8	63	51	7	0
J-P. Duminy st 5 b 3	10	15	0	0
†M. V. Boucher c 10 b 9	11	15	1	0
J. A. Morkel not out	8	8	1	0
J. Botha not out	4	2	1	0
L-b 2, w 1	3			

6 overs: 47-1   (20 overs)   130-5

1/13 2/59 3/98 4/110 5/120

R. E. van der Merwe, D. W. Steyn, M. Morkel and W. D. Parnell did not bat.

India

		B	4	6
G. Gambhir c 4 b 7	21	19	3	0
R. G. Sharma c 9 b 4	29	28	3	0
S. K. Raina c 10 b 7	3	8	0	0
Yuvraj Singh c 5 b 9	25	25	1	1
*†M. S. Dhoni run out	5	12	0	0
Y. K. Pathan c 3 b 8	0	2	0	0
Harbhajan Singh c 3 b 7	14	15	1	1
R. A. Jadeja not out	7	6	0	0
Zaheer Khan c 3 b 9	4	3	0	0
R. P. Singh not out	2	2	0	0
L-b 4, w 4	8			

6 overs: 47-0   (20 overs)   118-8

1/48 2/55 3/56 4/67 5/69 6/100 7/106 8/110

I. Sharma did not bat.

Zaheer Khan 3–0–26–1; R. P. Singh 2–0–21–1; I. Sharma 1–0–6–0; Jadeja 3–0–9–1; R. G. Sharma 2–0–15–0; Yuvraj Singh 4–0–25–0; Harbhajan Singh 4–0–20–1; Raina 1–0–6–1.

Steyn 3–0–25–2; Parnell 3–0–22–0; M. Morkel 4–0–23–0; J. A. Morkel 1–0–12–0; Botha 4–0–16–3; van der Merwe 4–0–13–1; Duminy 1–0–3–1.

Umpires: B. F. Bowden and I. J. Gould.   Third umpire: S. J. A. Taufel.   Referee: B. C. Broad.

SUPER EIGHT MATCHES – GROUP F

IRELAND v NEW ZEALAND

At Nottingham, June 11. New Zealand won by 83 runs. New Zealand 2 pts. Toss: Ireland. Twenty20 international debut: A. J. Redmond.

Ireland slumped to their second heavy defeat inside 24 hours, in the face of fine batting – and inspired fielding. An imposing total was set up by Aaron Redmond, who was only added to New Zealand's squad on the day of the match as a replacement for the unwell Jesse Ryder. Redmond, who had been playing club cricket in the Bolton League, sprinted off the blocks with seven fours from his first ten balls, and achieved the not-inconsiderable feat of outshining Brendon McCullum (one of whose shirts he had been forced to borrow, with the name taped over). Guptill, whose four boundaries were all sixes, and Styris kept up the momentum. Ireland needed a good start if they were to compete, but Porterfield was unluckily run out in the first over when the bowler Mills touched a straight-drive into the stumps. That was the first of four run-outs, two down to quicksilver direct hits from Brendon McCullum (in the outfield, and captaining because of New Zealand's continuing injury problems), who also made a sharp catch at midwicket off his brother's bowling look easy.

Man of the Match: A. J. Redmond.   *Attendance:* 14,997.

New Zealand

		B	4	6
*B. B. McCullum *c 10 b 9*	10	14	0	1
A. J. Redmond *lbw b 7*	63	30	13	0
M. J. Guptill *not out*	45	32	0	4
S. B. Styris *c 5 b 9*	42	25	1	3
J. D. P. Oram *c 4 b 7*	15	7	1	1
†P. D. McGlashan *b 8*	5	5	0	0
J. E. C. Franklin *not out*	7	7	0	0
B 3, l-b 4, w 4	11			

6 overs: 52-1   (20 overs)   198-5

1/51 2/91 3/152 4/168 5/176

N. T. Broom, N. L. McCullum, I. G. Butler and K. D. Mills did not bat.

Connell 1–0–14–0; Johnston 4–0–43–1; K. J. O'Brien 4–0–31–0; McCallan 4–0–33–2; Cusack 4–0–42–2; West 3–0–27–0.

Ireland

		B	4	6
*W. T. S. Porterfield *run out*	1	1	0	0
G. C. Wilson *c 7 b 4*	23	28	2	0
†N. J. O'Brien *c 5 b 11*	3	4	0	0
A. C. Botha *run out*	28	17	5	0
K. J. O'Brien *c 7 b 9*	2	3	0	0
J. F. Mooney *run out*	12	14	1	0
A. R. Cusack *c 1 b 9*	20	12	1	1
D. T. Johnston *run out*	14	9	0	1
W. K. McCallan *lbw b 9*	0	2	0	0
R. M. West *b 11*	8	8	1	0
P. Connell *not out*	1	2	0	0
L-b 2, w 1	3			

6 overs: 42-2   (16.4 overs)   115

1/1 2/15 3/57 4/58 5/67 6/86 7/104 8/104 9/112

Mills 2.4–0–12–2; Franklin 3–0–17–0; Butler 2–0–15–0; Oram 3–0–25–0; Styris 3–0–29–1; N. L. McCullum 3–0–15–3.

Umpires: E. A. R. de Silva and M. Erasmus.   Third umpire: S. J. Davis.   Referee: A. G. Hurst.

PAKISTAN v SRI LANKA

At Lord's, June 12. Sri Lanka won by 19 runs. Sri Lanka 2 pts. Toss: Sri Lanka.

This was the first time the teams had met since the Lahore attack in March; the players lined up together for the anthems rather than in separate groups, and wore black armbands. Boosted by two Sohail Tanvir overs that contained five wides, three no-balls and a total of 20 deliveries, Sri Lanka were 65 for none by the end of the powerplay. However, Pakistan's slower bowlers gained control, conceding just 11 from one four-over sequence – and only 54 from their combined ten overs. Shahid Afridi, disguising his change of pace so expertly that his meagre spin barely mattered, removed the openers, Dilshan for a typically inventive 46 that included his characteristic flick over his head and the keeper's, and the impish Jayasuriya. The middle order stalled, and Sri Lanka limped to 150, about par on a sluggish pitch. Pakistan's reply picked up the sedate tempo, leaving their own middle order much to do against another set of accomplished spinners. They had a chance while the fluent Younis Khan and more hesitant Misbah-ul-Haq were together, but once Murali grabbed two wickets in two balls – Afridi slogging first ball to deep midwicket – the game was up.

Man of the Match: T. M. Dilshan.   *Attendance*: 27,625.

Sri Lanka

		B	4	6
T. M. Dilshan *b 6*	46	39	8	0
S. T. Jayasuriya *c 4 b 6*	26	24	2	1
*†K. C. Sangakkara *st 2 b 11*	15	16	1	0
D. P. M. D. Jayawardene *c 6 b 11*	19	18	2	0
L. P. C. Silva *c 2 b 9*	8	6	1	0
J. Mubarak *run out*	5	10	0	0
A. D. Mathews *not out*	9	8	1	0
K. M. D. N. Kulasekara *lbw b 9*	0	1	0	0
S. L. Malinga *not out*	2	1	0	0
L-b 7, w 10, n-b 3	20			

6 overs: 65-0   (20 overs) 150-7

1/81 2/89 3/110 4/128 5/132 6/148 7/148

M. Muralitharan and B. A. W. Mendis did not bat.

Sohail Tanvir 2–0–29–0; Mohammad Aamer 4–0–26–0; Umar Gul 4–0–34–2; Shahid Afridi 4–0–23–2; Saeed Ajmal 4–0–26–2; Shoaib Malik 2–0–5–0.

Pakistan

		B	4	6
Salman Butt *b 7*	0	3	0	0
†Kamran Akmal *run out*	5	9	0	0
Shoaib Malik *c 8 b 9*	28	20	5	0
*Younis Khan *c 3 b 9*	50	37	4	0
Misbah-ul-Haq *c 5 b 10*	21	28	0	0
Shahid Afridi *c 1 b 10*	0	1	0	0
Fawad Alam *c 3 b 8*	12	11	1	0
Sohail Tanvir *c and b 9*	3	7	0	0
Umar Gul *not out*	9	4	0	1
Mohammad Aamer *run out*	0	0	0	0
Saeed Ajmal *not out*	0	0	0	0
B 1, w 2	3			

6 overs: 36-3   (20 overs) 131-9

1/0 2/34 3/35 4/101 5/101 6/108 7/121 8/123 9/124

Mathews 4–0–23–1; Kulasekara 4–0–30–1; Malinga 4–0–17–3; Muralitharan 4–0–28–2; Mendis 3–0–24–0; Jayasuriya 1–0–8–0.

Umpires: M. R. Benson and R. E. Koertzen.   Third umpire: R. J. Tucker.   Referee: B. C. Broad.

NEW ZEALAND v PAKISTAN

At The Oval, June 13 (floodlit). Pakistan won by six wickets. Pakistan 2 pts. Toss: New Zealand. Twenty20 international debut: Shahzaib Hasan.

Allegations of ball-tampering that were made by New Zealand, and rejected by the umpires, seemed an attempt to cover up the lack of class in their batting in the absence of Ross Taylor and Jesse Ryder. Before reverse swing was conceivable, New Zealand faltered to 37 for three, thanks to a fine start by Abdul Razzaq – the first ICL player to return to the official international game – and their final collapse was sparked by Shahid Afridi running back from mid-on to catch Styris within feet of the long-on rope. Umar Gul then switched to the Pavilion End and, simply by bowling quick, full and straight, mopped up a feeble tail for the first five-for in Twenty20 internationals. Pakistan did not bat well, but they knocked off the runs quickly to improve their net run-rate.

Man of the Match: Umar Gul.   *Attendance*: 20,226.

Kiwi in flight: Nathan McCullum fields off his own bowling.

Philip Brown

New Zealand

		B	4	6
B. B. McCullum *c 8 b 3*	12	6	2	0
A. J. Redmond *c 9 b 10*	15	14	2	0
M. J. Guptill *lbw b 3*	8	8	1	0
S. B. Styris *c 5 b 9*	22	29	0	1
J. D. P. Oram *c 7 b 5*	5	11	0	0
†P. D. McGlashan *lbw b 9*	8	8	1	0
N. L. McCullum *b 9*	7	11	1	0
J. E. C. Franklin *b 9*	7	13	0	0
*D. L. Vettori *run out*	8	9	1	0
K. D. Mills *c 2 b 9*	0	1	0	0
I. G. Butler *not out*	1	1	0	0
L-b 4, w 2	6			

6 overs: 37-3   (18.3 overs)   99

1/17 2/33 3/37 4/55 5/73 6/73 7/88 8/93 9/93

Mohammad Aamer 3–0–23–1; Abdul Razzaq 3.3–1–17–2; Saeed Ajmal 4–0–24–0; Shahid Afridi 4–0–17–1; Shoaib Malik 1–0–8–0; Umar Gul 3–0–6–5.

Pakistan

		B	4	6
†Kamran Akmal *c 3 b 10*	19	14	1	1
Shahzaib Hasan *run out*	35	28	4	2
Abdul Razzaq *c 6 b 9*	5	8	0	0
Shoaib Malik *c 1 b 9*	4	3	1	0
Shahid Afridi *not out*	29	18	3	0
*Younis Khan *not out*	6	9	0	0
W 1, n-b 1	2			

6 overs: 54-1   (13.1 overs)   100-4

1/36 2/61 3/61 4/71

Misbah-ul-Haq, Fawad Alam, Umar Gul, Mohammad Aamer and Saeed Ajmal did not bat.

Mills 4–0–28–1; Franklin 2–0–19–0; Vettori 4–0–20–2; Butler 2–0–22–0; N. L. McCullum 1.1–0–11–0.

Umpires: M. R. Benson and R. J. Tucker.   Third umpire: R. E. Koertzen.   Referee: R. S. Madugalle.

IRELAND v SRI LANKA

At Lord's, June 14. Sri Lanka won by nine runs. Sri Lanka 2 pts. Toss: Sri Lanka.

Sri Lanka clung on to their unbeaten record, but only after a jolt from the Irish, who began both innings the stronger. Indeed without a steadying Twenty20-best from Jayawardene, Sri Lanka might have been seriously embarrassed. They quickly lost Dilshan and Sangakkara as the Irish seamers kept them to just 28 from the powerplay. Jayasuriya briefly feasted on the slow bowling before missing a sweep. Ireland embarked jauntily on their ascent of 145, and Porterfield's freedom of strokeplay persuaded Sangakkara to turn to spin in the fifth over. However, the turning point came when Niall O'Brien aggravated an ankle injury diving to make his ground. Not entitled to a runner, he struggled on: incapacitated and facing the accuracy of Mendis and Muralitharan, he failed to unleash the big shots. Even so, at 87 for one in the 14th over, Ireland retained a chance. Then White launched himself once too often at Kulasekara, Mendis followed up with two quick wickets and Malinga quelled Irish ambitions. Despite the excellent entertainment, this game was essentially an optional hors d'oeuvre for the England v India main course that followed: many preferred to watch the Indian galacticos practising on the Nursery ground.

Man of the Match: D. P. M. D. Jayawardene.   *Attendance:* 27,641.

Sri Lanka

		B	4	6
T. M. Dilshan c 2 b 11	0	2	0	0
S. T. Jayasuriya lbw b 10	27	27	5	0
*†K. C. Sangakkara c 2 b 6	3	10	0	0
D. P. M. D. Jayawardene b 8	78	53	9	1
L. P. C. Silva c 11 b 10	4	6	0	0
J. Mubarak c 2 b 8	7	9	0	0
A. D. Mathews b 8	10	7	1	0
K. M. D. N. Kulasekara c 5 b 11	1	2	0	0
M. Muralitharan st 2 b 8	0	1	0	0
S. L. Malinga not out	1	2	0	0
B. A. W. Mendis not out	4	1	1	0
L-b 5, w 4	9			

6 overs: 28-2   (20 overs) 144-9

1/0 2/14 3/81 4/97 5/126 6/128 7/132 8/139 9/140

Rankin 4–0–27–2; Johnston 4–1–18–1; West 4–0–34–0; McCallan 4–0–33–2; Cusack 3–0–18–4; K. J. O'Brien 1–0–9–0.

Ireland

		B	4	6
*W. T. S. Porterfield c 3 b 9	31	29	5	0
†N. J. O'Brien st 3 b 11	31	37	4	0
A. R. White c 3 b 8	22	21	1	1
K. J. O'Brien c 1 b 11	0	2	0	0
J. F. Mooney not out	31	21	4	0
D. T. Johnston b 10	9	6	0	1
A. C. Botha b 10	0	1	0	0
A. R. Cusack run out	2	3	0	0
R. M. West not out	1	1	0	0
B 1, l-b 3, w 3, n-b 1	8			

6 overs: 37-0   (20 overs) 135-7

1/59 2/87 3/89 4/91 5/106 6/106 7/129

W. K. McCallan and W. B. Rankin did not bat.

Mathews 3–0–23–0; Kulasekara 4–0–47–1; Mendis 4–0–22–2; Malinga 4–0–19–2; Muralitharan 4–0–13–1; Jayasuriya 1–0–7–0.

Umpires: M. Erasmus and A. L. Hill.   Third umpire: S. J. Davis.   Referee: A. G. Hurst.

IRELAND v PAKISTAN

At The Oval, June 15. Pakistan won by 39 runs. Pakistan 2 pts. Toss: Pakistan. Twenty20 international debut: P. R. Stirling.

When these teams last met, in the 2007 World Cup, Ireland pulled off one of the game's greatest upsets, only for the result to be lost next morning in the turmoil surrounding the death of Pakistan coach Bob Woolmer. This game proved less eventful, with Younis Khan's team confirming a place in the semi-finals with what eventually became a straightforward win. Although a third defeat in the Super Eights spelled elimination, Ireland remained competitive, especially in the field, scampering and chasing as athletically as any side they played. With the ball, too, they gave nothing away. In a masterclass of short-of-a-length bowling Rankin yielded just 11 runs; only Ajantha Mendis, who conceded nine in the semi-final against West Indies, managed a more miserly four overs. Rankin helped restrict the total to 159, but Ireland's modest batting and Pakistan's strong attack – this time it was Saeed Ajmal who led the way – ensured that was plenty. Kamran Akmal cemented his place as an opener with a steady fifty, and made two more stumpings, taking his total in the tournament to seven.

Man of the Match: Kamran Akmal.   *Attendance:* 20,465.

Pakistan

		B	4	6
†Kamran Akmal *b 6*	57	51	5	1
Shahzaib Hasan *c 9 b 8*	23	19	3	1
Shahid Afridi *c 5 b 9*	24	13	3	0
*Younis Khan *b 10*	10	8	1	0
Misbah-ul-Haq *c 2 b 9*	20	14	1	1
Abdul Razzaq *not out*	15	9	0	1
Shoaib Malik *not out*	4	7	0	0
L-b 3, w 2, n-b 1	6			

6 overs: 38-1   (20 overs) 159-5

1/38 2/78 3/102 4/133 5/141

Fawad Alam, Umar Gul, Mohammad Aamer and Saeed Ajmal did not bat.

Rankin 4–0–11–0; Johnston 4–0–45–1; Cusack 4–0–41–1; West 4–0–33–1; McCallan 4–0–26–2.

Ireland

		B	4	6
*W. T. S. Porterfield *c 4 b 11*	40	36	2	0
†N. J. O'Brien *c and b 10*	7	10	1	0
P. R. Stirling *b 3*	17	16	2	0
K. J. O'Brien *st 1 b 11*	26	30	1	0
J. F. Mooney *c 6 b 11*	2	8	0	0
D. T. Johnston *b 9*	0	1	0	0
A. R. White *b 9*	5	5	0	0
A. R. Cusack *st 1 b 11*	2	2	0	0
W. K. McCallan *not out*	2	6	0	0
R. M. West *run out*	1	1	0	0
W. B. Rankin *not out*	5	5	0	0
B 1, l-b 7, w 3, n-b 2	13			

6 overs: 37-1   (20 overs) 120-9

1/13 2/42 3/87 4/93 5/99 6/108 7/110 8/110 9/111

Mohammad Aamer 4–0–19–1; Abdul Razzaq 3–0–18–0; Shahid Afridi 4–0–26–1; Saeed Ajmal 4–0–19–4; Shoaib Malik 1–0–11–0; Umar Gul 4–0–19–2.

Umpires: R. E. Koertzen and R. J. Tucker.   Third umpire: M. R. Benson.   Referee: R. S. Madugalle.

NEW ZEALAND v SRI LANKA

At Nottingham, June 16. Sri Lanka won by 48 runs. Sri Lanka 2 pts. Toss: Sri Lanka.

A virtual quarter-final – the winner progressed to the semis, the loser went out – was again decided by Sri Lanka's spinners, who derailed a promising run-chase. Mendis deceived Taylor and Styris (two of several New Zealanders carrying niggling injuries) in his second over to start a collapse in which eight wickets tumbled for 46. New Zealand had started well enough, Redmond spanking most of the 20 which came from the second over, bowled by Jayasuriya (who was earlier out first ball), but he spooned Malinga's slower ball to midwicket in the fifth over. After that, only the lanky Guptill survived for long. Sri Lanka had also struggled a little on the slow pitch, only just exceeding the average Trent Bridge tournament total of 155, despite another sparkling display from Dilshan, who brought up the fifty with three fine fours in a Mills over, and a patient run-a-ball knock from Sangakkara. Vettori, feeling his shoulder injury, overstepped in his third over: Jayawardene stroked the resultant free hit back for a huge straight six, and in the final over he reverse-swept Oram for four using the back of the bat.

Man of the Match: B. A. W. Mendis.   *Attendance:* 15,880.

Sri Lanka

		B	4	6
T. M. Dilshan *c 1 b 9*	48	37	5	0
S. T. Jayasuriya *c 4 b 8*.......	0	1	0	0
L. P. C. Silva *c 6 b 10*........	13	10	2	0
*†K. C. Sangakkara *c 5 b 9*	35	35	3	0
D. P. M. D. Jayawardene *not out*	41	29	6	1
J. Mubarak *lbw b 11*	8	5	1	0
A. D. Mathews *not out*	6	4	0	0
B 1, l-b 1, w 4, n-b 1........	7			

6 overs: 51-2   (20 overs) 158-5

1/3 2/25 3/87 4/137 5/147

I. Udana, S. L. Malinga, M. Muralitharan and B. A. W. Mendis did not bat.

N. L. McCullum 4–0–22–1; Mills 4–0–41–1; Oram 4–0–23–0; Butler 3–0–29–1; Vettori 4–0–32–2; Styris 1–0–9–0.

New Zealand

		B	4	6
B. B. McCullum *c 6 b 8*	10	12	2	0
A. J. Redmond *c 3 b 9*	23	13	3	1
M. J. Guptill *c 7 b 2*	43	34	4	1
L. R. P. L. Taylor *st 4 b 11*.....	8	8	1	0
S. B. Styris *b 11*	2	3	0	0
J. D. P. Oram *b 8*.............	7	12	0	0
†P. D. McGlashan *c 6 b 11*......	2	3	0	0
N. L. McCullum *run out*.......	2	4	0	0
*D. L. Vettori *c 9 b 10*.........	3	5	0	0
K. D. Mills *run out*	4	6	1	0
I. G. Butler *not out*	2	2	0	0
L-b 1, w 3...............	4			

6 overs: 46-2   (17 overs) 110

1/30 2/39 3/64 4/66 5/93 6/95 7/98 8/100 9/102

Udana 3–0–17–2; Jayasuriya 3–0–28–1; Muralitharan 4–0–18–1; Malinga 3–0–26–1; Mendis 3–0–9–3; Dilshan 1–0–11–0.

Umpires: S. J. Davis and S. J. A. Taufel.   Third umpire: N. J. Llong.   Referee: B. C. Broad.

FINAL SUPER EIGHT TABLES

Group E	Played	Won	Lost	Points	Net run-rate
SOUTH AFRICA	3	3	0	6	0.78
WEST INDIES	3	2	1	4	0.06
England	3	1	2	2	−0.41
India........................	3	0	3	0	−0.46

Group F	Played	Won	Lost	Points	Net run-rate
SRI LANKA	3	3	0	6	1.26
PAKISTAN	3	2	1	4	1.18
New Zealand	3	1	2	2	−0.23
Ireland	3	0	3	0	−2.18

SEMI-FINALS

PAKISTAN v SOUTH AFRICA

At Nottingham, June 18 (floodlit). Pakistan won by seven runs. Toss: Pakistan.

Shahid Afridi had been all but written off as a batting power before this match after some scratchy efforts, but when it counted he came in at No. 3 – surely the ideal place for him in a 20-over contest, rather than being kept back for the final overs – and bossed the innings. Not that he exactly played himself in: after watching a high bouncer (called a wide) from Parnell sail past, he smacked the next ball over mid-on for four. Once he really got his eye in he pulled Kallis for two fours in an over, then blasted Botha out of the attack with four successive fours – three lofted inside-out over the covers followed by a delicate late cut. Afridi, who put on 67 with Shoaib Malik, was suckered by Duminy's first ball after galloping to 51 from 33 balls, but he had done enough to ensure a par score. Then he took the ball. Afridi whistled one through Gibbs, and next over repeated the dose to castle de Villiers, the ball after he was put down by the wicketkeeper. From then on Pakistan held a firm grip, loosened only slightly when Younis Khan perplexingly gave Fawad Alam his first bowl of the tournament in the 15th over and his loopy left-armers went for 15. The slow start by South Africa against pace, including the 17-year-old Mohammad Aamer, had left them with too much to do against Pakistan's spinners. Again South Africa had found the penultimate step on the staircase too tricky.

Man of the Match: Shahid Afridi.   *Attendance:* 15,902.

Pakistan

		B	4	6
†Kamran Akmal *c 6 b 11*	23	12	4	1
Shahzaib Hasan *c 8 b 10*	0	2	0	0
Shahid Afridi *c 4 b 5*	51	34	8	0
Shoaib Malik *c 9 b 8*	34	39	2	0
*Younis Khan *not out*	24	18	1	0
Abdul Razzaq *not out*	12	15	0	0
L-b 2, w 3	5			

6 overs: 47-2   (20 overs) 149-4

1/8 2/28 3/95 4/124

Misbah-ul-Haq, Fawad Alam, Umar Gul, Mohammad Aamer and Saeed Ajmal did not bat.

Steyn 4–0–28–1; Parnell 4–0–26–1; Kallis 2–0–13–0; Morkel 2–0–13–0; van der Merwe 4–0–29–1; Botha 2–0–23–0; Duminy 2–0–14–1.

South Africa

		B	4	6
J. H. Kallis *c 4 b 11*	64	54	7	1
*G. C. Smith *c and b 10*	10	14	1	0
H. H. Gibbs *b 3*	5	4	1	0
A. B. de Villiers *b 3*	1	5	0	0
J-P. Duminy *not out*	44	39	3	1
J. A. Morkel *run out*	2	4	0	0
†M. V. Boucher *not out*	0	0	0	0
B 4, l-b 11, w 1	16			

6 overs: 40-1   (20 overs) 142-5

1/40 2/46 3/50 4/111 5/134

R. E. van der Merwe, J. Botha, W. D. Parnell and D. W. Steyn did not bat.

Abdul Razzaq 3–0–19–0; Mohammad Aamer 4–0–30–1; Shahid Afridi 4–0–16–2; Saeed Ajmal 4–0–23–1; Shoaib Malik 1–0–5–0; Umar Gul 3–0–19–0; Fawad Alam 1–0–15–0.

Umpires: B. F. Bowden and S. J. Davis.   Third umpire: S. J. A. Taufel.   Referee: B. C. Broad.

SRI LANKA v WEST INDIES

At The Oval, June 19 (floodlit). Sri Lanka won by 57 runs. Toss: West Indies.

The received wisdom was that, if Gayle were at the crease come the final ball, he would have guided his side to victory. Gayle was there at the end all right, but was surrounded by the mangled wreckage of the West Indian innings as he became the first to carry his bat in Twenty20 internationals. Needing a gettable if tricky 159, West Indies began catastrophically, thanks to an astounding opening over by Mathews, who hit the stumps with his second, fourth and sixth deliveries. All three victims played on, though Simmons was unlucky that the ball ricocheted down from the bottom of his thigh pad into leg stump. Gayle hit with awesome power, but those early blows knocked the sense out of his side. Batsman after batsman fell to reckless swings, swipes and swishes when the primary aim should have been to give Gayle the strike. Sri Lanka had also relied on the brilliance of an opener: Dilshan came within a shot of becoming only the second player, after Gayle, to hit a hundred in Twenty20 internationals. He took advantage of a diet of full tosses as the bowlers struggled to find a yorker length. He allowed only 15 dot balls, and scored 20 singles and eight twos to go with his 14 boundaries.

Man of the Match: T. M. Dilshan.   *Attendance*: 19,909.

Sri Lanka

		B	4	6
T. M. Dilshan *not out*	96	57	12	2
S. T. Jayasuriya *c 9 b 4*	24	37	3	0
*K. C. Sangakkara *c 7 b 4*	0	2	0	0
D. P. M. D. Jayawardene *c 5 b 7*	2	3	0	0
L. P. C. Silva *c 8 b 11*	11	12	2	0
J. Mubarak *c 10 b 9*	7	5	1	0
A. D. Mathews *not out*	12	4	1	1
L-b 3, w 3	6			

6 overs: 44-0   (20 overs) 158-5

1/73 2/73 3/77 4/127 5/134

I. Udana, S. L. Malinga, M. Muralitharan and B. A. W. Mendis did not bat.

West Indies

		B	4	6
*C. H. Gayle *not out*	63	50	8	2
X. M. Marshall *b 7*	0	1	0	0
L. M. P. Simmons *b 7*	0	2	0	0
D. J. Bravo *b 7*	0	2	0	0
S. Chanderpaul *lbw b 11*	7	15	0	0
R. R. Sarwan *c 7 b 10*	5	12	0	0
K. A. Pollard *st 3 b 10*	3	10	0	0
†D. Ramdin *c 4 b 8*	9	5	2	0
J. E. Taylor *c 12 b 10*	2	2	0	0
D. J. G. Sammy *c 6 b 11*	1	4	0	0
S. J. Benn *b 9*	0	4	0	0
B 1, l-b 2, w 7, n-b 1	11			

6 overs: 29-3   (17.4 overs) 101

1/1 2/1 3/1 4/43 5/64 6/75 7/86 8/95 9/97

Sammy 4–0–19–0; Taylor 4–0–31–1; Bravo 3–0–32–2; Benn 4–0–24–1; Gayle 3–0–35–0; Pollard 2–0–14–1.

Mathews 4–0–16–3; Udana 3–0–20–1; Malinga 2.4–0–24–1; Mendis 4–0–9–2; Muralitharan 4–0–29–3.

12th man K. M. D. N. Kulasekara.

Umpires: Aleem Dar and R. E. Koertzen.   Third umpire: D. J. Harper.   Referee: A. G. Hurst.

FINAL

PAKISTAN v SRI LANKA

At Lord's, June 21. Pakistan won by eight wickets. Toss: Sri Lanka.

In front of a boisterous full house at Lord's, this hugely successful tournament came to a satisfying, if not gripping, climax as Pakistan ultimately ran out comfortable winners under a warm midsummer sun. Younis Khan dedicated the triumph to Bob Woolmer, his mentor and former coach who died in the dark hours following defeat by Ireland in the 2007 World Cup, a terrible low in the history of Pakistan cricket. Now, however, came a high every bit as uplifting as winning the 1992 World Cup – perhaps more so given the world's unwillingness to travel to Pakistan in the wake of the Lahore terrorist atrocity in March, an attack which injured seven Sri Lankan cricketers (including three, Sangakkara, Jayawardene and Mendis playing here). Younis also made an impassioned plea for international cricket to return to Pakistan, as well as announcing his immediate retirement from Twenty20 internationals.

As in the semi-final victory over South Africa, Shahid Afridi claimed the match award for an all-round performance of sheer brilliance. Once again he abandoned his trademark fire-and-brimstone approach, giving a display of maturity that had long seemed beyond him, especially with a bat in his hand. A target of 139 was not daunting yet, in a Lord's final against a team so adept at defending a total, it was far from straightforward. The aggressive Kamran Akmal gave Pakistan the perfect start with 37 from 28 balls. The old

Six of clubs: Shahid Afridi hammers Muttiah Muralitharan for a maximum to midwicket.

Glyn Kirk, AFP/Getty Images

Afridi, spurred on by the adoring crowd chanting his name, might have been tempted to outdo Akmal from the word go. Instead he was content to accumulate, moving to a boundaryless 17 from 19 balls before opening out to pull Murali from outside off for a six over midwicket, followed next ball by a four over extra cover. Coming as the Sri Lankan spinners were threatening to take the asking-rate above eight, it kept Pakistan in front. Afridi repeated the trick in the 18th over when, with 26 needed from 18 balls, Sangakkara gambled by bringing back the inexperienced Udana rather than the cannier Jayasuriya. Another leg-side six followed by a four; 19 from the over put the result beyond doubt.

The match had begun with the tournament's dominant batsman facing its youngest bowler. Yet it was Dilshan who betrayed nerves to Mohammad Aamer, a 17-year-old left-armer, continually pitched short. The plan worked: Dilshan mistimed a scoop to short fine leg for a fifth-ball duck. Mubarak came and went with a flash and, when Jayasuriya ended his feisty ten-ball innings by playing on, Sri Lanka were in tatters at 26 for three.

The middle order, their major weakness on an unbeaten journey to the final, had one last chance to prove itself. Silva hung around briefly with Sangakkara, but Udana, oddly promoted to No. 7, did not, instead becoming the seventh batsman bowled by Afridi in the competition – most trying to cut – and his 11th victim in all. Then came the only passage of play to go Sri Lanka's way. From the depths of 70 for six in the 13th over, Sangakkara, playing with increasing aggression, and Mathews, hitting the ball sweetly, added 68 in a stand as remarkable for its intelligence as its acceleration. Despite facing Umar Gul, the master of the reverse-swinging yorker, for two of the last four overs, they cracked 50 from 24 balls, keeping Sri Lanka in the game. But the Pakistani batsmen played the three Ms – Malinga, Mendis and Muralitharan – as well as anyone, certainly with less fear, and Afridi was there to soak up the adulation when the winning run came.

Man of the Match: Shahid Afridi.   *Attendance:* 28,048.

Man of the Tournament: T. M. Dilshan.

Sri Lanka

		B	4	6
T. M. Dilshan *c 2 b 10*	....	0	5	0	0
S. T. Jayasuriya *b 6*	....	17	10	2	1
J. Mubarak *c 2 b 6*	....	0	2	0	0
*†K. C. Sangakkara *not out*	......	64	52	7	0
D. P. M. D. Jayawardene *c 7 b 6*		1	4	0	0
L. P. C. Silva *c 11 b 9*	....	14	19	2	0
I. Udana *b 3*	....	1	5	0	0
A. D. Mathews *not out*	....	35	24	3	1
L-b 3, w 2, n-b 1	....	6			

6 overs: 34-4   (20 overs)   138-6

1/0 2/2 3/26 4/32 5/67 6/70

S. L. Malinga, M. Muralitharan and B. A. W. Mendis did not bat.

Mohammad Aamer 4–1–30–1; Abdul Razzaq 3–0–20–3; Shahid Afridi 4–0–20–1; Saeed Ajmal 4–0–28–0; Shoaib Malik 1–0–8–0; Umar Gul 4–0–29–1.

Pakistan

		B	4	6
†Kamran Akmal *st 4 b 2*	....	37	28	2	2
Shahzaib Hasan *c 2 b 10*	......	19	23	3	0
Shahid Afridi *not out*	....	54	40	2	2
Shoaib Malik *not out*	....	24	22	1	0
L-b 2, w 2, n-b 1	....	5			

6 overs: 39-0   (18.4 overs)   139-2

1/48 2/63

*Younis Khan, Abdul Razzaq, Misbah-ul-Haq, Fawad Alam, Umar Gul, Mohammad Aamer and Saeed Ajmal did not bat.

Mathews 2–0–17–0; Udana 4–0–44–0; Malinga 3.4–0–14–0; Muralitharan 3–0–20–1; Mendis 4–0–34–0; Jayasuriya 2–0–8–1.

Umpires: D. J. Harper and S. J. A. Taufel.   Third umpire: S. J. Davis.   Referee: B. C. Broad.

ICC WORLD TWENTY20 WINNERS

2007-08   India   2009   Pakistan

ICC WOMEN'S WORLD TWENTY20, 2009

Sarah Potter

1. England   2. New Zealand   3= Australia and India

When Claire Taylor was revealed as one of *Wisden's* Five Cricketers of the
Year in 2009, most cricket writers felt the award was a momentous personal
achievement without wider significance for the women's game. It would not,
they agreed, alter perceptions or inspire schoolgirls to pick up a bat or ball.
Taylor and the World Twenty20, though, was a pairing which changed all that
– and a lot of correspondents' copy.

Mike Selvey of *The Guardian*, previously ambivalent towards women's
cricket, gushed enlightenment after Taylor's perfectly paced run-chase with
Beth Morgan as England beat Australia in the second semi-final at The Oval.
He urged his readers to go and watch future matches, judge the play on merit
(meaning don't compare women against men any more than you would in
tennis, golf or cycling) and be prepared for conversion. Similar endorsements
came from Mike Atherton in *The Times* and Nick Hoult in the *Daily Telegraph*.
Heady stuff!

Except that was only half the story. The initial moment of genius had come
from the ICC, not simply for going ahead with the inaugural women's event,
but for running it alongside the men's version, with the semis and final played
– and televised live – immediately before the men's equivalents.

With such varying standards in international women's cricket it was a risk,
but not a shot in the dark; the best of the distaff side had successfully shared
the men's stage at domestic and international level several times over the last
few years. It was clever, too – and another reason for the initiative's success –
to hold all the group matches in Taunton, where the less skilled sides were far
away from the forensic attention devoted to the men's tournament.

Over six well-organised days, there was barely time to blink before the
predictable elimination of West Indies, South Africa, Sri Lanka and Pakistan,
leaving the Big Four of women's cricket – New Zealand, India, Australia and
England – to head off to the semi-finals in Nottingham and London. Those
games produced the same finalists, New Zealand and England, as the World
Cup in Sydney three months earlier, and ultimately the same champions,
England.

The cheering in the first week was more high-pitched than most cricket
punters are used to, as the crowds were largely made up of enthusiastic
schoolchildren. On the field, thanks partly to the excellent batting tracks at
Somerset's ground (and, perhaps, the fielding-drill accident which gave
England's spearhead bowler, Katherine Brunt, a black eye and forced her to
miss the matches against Sri Lanka and Pakistan), there were no outrageous
embarrassments; Pakistan were dismissed by England for 60 in 16.5 overs, Sri
Lanka made 69 against the same attack, but at least saw out their allotted overs.

While none of the minnows came close to causing an upset, there were
unexpected flashes of flair; West Indies opener Deandra Dottin briefly rattled

Australia with a 22-ball fifty, the fastest in women's Twenty20 internationals. The other unexpected high was the number of sixes: 22 in the 12 group games, five in the two semis, although there were none for the Lord's crowd to celebrate in the final.

The first semi-final between New Zealand and India at Trent Bridge was too one-sided to deliver the oscillating tension that can make the shortest format of the game so compelling, but Aimee Watkins's unbeaten 89 from 58 balls was a silky masterclass showcasing some of the best of women's cricket. Likewise, the lopsided final was counter-balanced by Brunt's match-winning brilliance – three for six off four overs – and, of course, a home win at HQ.

Truth is, all the necessary convincing and converting had been done at The Oval by Morgan and, most of all, by Taylor (unsurprisingly named the ICC Women's Cricketer of the Year in October). It not only showed the watching world why *Wisden* had picked her as one of its Five Cricketers of the Year, but made the Women's World Twenty20 an unqualified success, justifying the decision to run the tournaments in parallel again in the Caribbean in May 2010. The players had been given a chance to prove their worth, and they grasped their chance with eager hands. And they even managed to romance a few gnarled old commentators along the way.

Note: Matches in this section were not first-class.

Group A

At Taunton, June 11. **West Indies won by three runs.** Toss: West Indies. **West Indies 123-7** (20 overs) (S. R. Taylor 50); **South Africa 120** (19.4 overs) (M. du Preez 38). *West Indies 2 pts. Twenty20 international debuts:* D. van Niekerk (South Africa); M. R. Aguilleira, P. Y. Lavine (West Indies). *Player of the Match:* S. R. Taylor.

South Africa's 16-year-old leg-spinner Dane van Niekerk lined up against 40-year-old Bajan opener Pamela Lavine. Lavine's opening partner Stafanie Taylor set up West Indies' win with a run-a-ball fifty on her 18th birthday.

At Taunton, June 12. **New Zealand won by nine wickets.** Toss: Australia. **Australia 123-8** (20 overs) (L. C. Sthalekar 46; S. E. A. Ruck 3-12); **New Zealand 127-1** (16.2 overs) (S. W. Bates 41*, A. L. Watkins 73*). *New Zealand 2 pts. Player of the Match:* S. E. A. Ruck.

New Zealand reduced Australia to 51-6 in the 12th over, with left-armer Sian Ruck removing the top three; later, Suzie Bates and Aimee Watkins, who hit 73 in 51 balls, added 118, a second-wicket record in women's Twenty20 internationals, to complete a crushing victory.*

At Taunton, June 13. **New Zealand won by 52 runs.** Toss: New Zealand. **New Zealand 158-6** (20 overs) (S. W. Bates 60, L. R. Doolan 41); **West Indies 106-7** (20 overs) (S. R. Taylor 58*; L. R. Doolan 3-16). *New Zealand 2 pts. Twenty20 international debut:* S. F. Daley (West Indies). *Player of the Match:* S. W. Bates.

Suzie Bates (11 fours in 39 balls) and Lucy Doolan opened New Zealand's innings with 94 in two overs; Doolan followed up her highest score at this level with her best bowling return. Stafanie Taylor batted throughout West Indies' innings for another run-a-ball fifty.

At Taunton, June 14. **Australia won by eight wickets.** Toss: West Indies. **West Indies 135-8** (20 overs) (D. J. S. Dottin 53); **Australia 136-2** (17.2 overs) (S. Nitschke 56, L. C. Sthalekar 34*, R. M. Farrell 31*). *Australia 2 pts. Twenty20 international debut:* C. P. Jack (West Indies). *Player of the Match:* S. Nitschke.

Deandra Dottin reached the fastest fifty in women's Twenty20 internationals in 22 balls; in all she hit nine fours and a six in 25 balls. Later, West Indies used eight bowlers in an attempt to curb Australia's charge to victory, led by Shelley Nitschke's 38-ball 56.

At Taunton, June 15. **New Zealand won by six wickets.** Toss: New Zealand. **South Africa 124-4** (20 overs) (C-Z. Brits 57*, S. M. Benade 44); **New Zealand 127-4** (18.1 overs) (A. L. Watkins 35). *New Zealand 2 pts. Player of the Match:* C-Z. Brits.

Cri-Zelda Brits and Susan Benade added 91 for South Africa's fourth wicket, but could not prevent New Zealand's third straight win.

At Taunton, June 16. **Australia won by 24 runs.** Toss: Australia. **Australia 164-6** (20 overs) (K. L. Rolton 43, A. J. Blackwell 40*; S. Ismail 3-27); **South Africa 140-7** (20 overs) (S. A. Fritz 39, T. Chetty 36; S. Nitschke 4-21). *Australia 2 pts. Twenty20 international debut:* M. Kapp (South Africa). *Player of the Match:* S. Nitschke.

Karen Rolton and Alex Blackwell fought back from 79-5, adding 68, before Shelley Nitschke took a career-best 4-21 with her left-arm spin. South Africa went down to their sixth consecutive Twenty20 defeat, all on English soil.

Group B

At Taunton, June 11. **England won by ten wickets.** Toss: India. **India 112-8** (20 overs) (H. L. Colvin 3-20); **England 113-0** (15.4 overs) (S. J. Taylor 50*, C. M. Edwards 61*). *England 2 pts. Twenty20 international debuts:* H. Kaur, L. Kumari, P. Roy (India). *Player of the Match:* C. M. Edwards.

Sarah Taylor and Charlotte Edwards shared the first century opening partnership in women's Twenty20 internationals to complete the first ten-wicket victory at this level.

At Taunton, June 12. **Sri Lanka won by four wickets.** Toss: Pakistan. **Pakistan 104-7** (20 overs) (Bismah Maroof 50*; L. E. Kaushalya 3-16); **Sri Lanka 105-6** (18.2 overs) (S. I. Galagedara 37). *Sri Lanka 2 pts. Twenty20 international debuts:* Sri Lanka (all). *Player of the Match:* L. E. Kaushalya.

Sri Lanka won their first Twenty20 international.

At Taunton, June 13. **India won by five wickets.** Toss: Pakistan. **Pakistan 75** (19.5 overs) (R. Dhar 3-13, P. Roy 5-16); **India 78-5** (17.4 overs) (A. Chopra 37*). *India 2 pts. Twenty20 international debut:* P. G. Raut (India). *Player of the Match:* P. Roy.

Leg-spinner Priyanka Roy collected the only five-wicket return of this tournament as Pakistan succumbed for 75; India stumbled to 36-4 in the eighth over, but Anjum Chopra steered them home.

At Taunton, June 14. **England won by 71 runs.** Toss: England. **England 140-7** (20 overs) (S. C. Taylor 75*; L. E. Kaushalya 4-18); **Sri Lanka 69-8** (20 overs). *England 2 pts. Player of the Match:* S. C. Taylor.

Claire Taylor hit 75 in 54 balls, with 11 fours, in a match where no one else passed 24; Isa Guha's figures of 4–2–4–2 for England were the most economical in women's Twenty20 internationals.

At Taunton, June 15. **India won by five wickets.** Reduced to 18 overs a side. Toss: Sri Lanka. **Sri Lanka 94-6** (18 overs); **India 95-5** (16.5 overs) (P. G. Raut 30, M. Raj 32*). *India 2 pts. Twenty20 international debuts:* A. C. Jayangani, A. P. S. Lakshika (Sri Lanka). *Player of the Match:* M. Raj.

India's Rumeli Dhar matched Isa Guha's record for economical figures the previous day, against the same opponents.

At Taunton, June 16. **England won by 63 runs.** Toss: Pakistan. **England 123** (20 overs) (C. M. Edwards 43); **Pakistan 60** (16.5 overs) (H. L. Colvin 3-18). *England 2 pts. Player of the Match:* C. M. Edwards.

Five of England's last six wickets fell to run-outs, and they were all out for the only time in this tournament. But Pakistan were bowled out in double figures for the second time in four days – their 60 was the lowest total in women's Twenty20 internationals.

GROUP TABLES

Group A	Played	Won	Lost	Points	Net run-rate
NEW ZEALAND	3	3	0	6	1.67
AUSTRALIA............	3	2	1	4	0.24
West Indies	3	1	2	2	−1.15
South Africa.............	3	0	3	0	−0.71

Group B

	Played	Won	Lost	Points	Net run-rate
ENGLAND	3	3	0	6	2.73
INDIA	3	2	1	4	−0.02
Sri Lanka	3	1	2	2	−1.20
Pakistan	3	0	3	0	−1.48

SEMI-FINALS AND FINAL REPORTS BY JENNY ROESLER

SEMI-FINALS

INDIA v NEW ZEALAND

At Nottingham, June 18. New Zealand won by 52 runs. Toss: New Zealand.

The first semi-final proved something of a false dawn, with crowds and press attention modest, and New Zealand's fourth straight victory too easy. Their captain, Aimee Watkins, struck a commanding 89 not out from 58 balls, with ten fours and two sixes – the first when she swung Gouhar Sultana's off-spin over square leg into the stand, the second over extra cover off the final ball of the innings, from Rumeli Dhar. It was the highest innings in the women's or men's tournaments until the following day, when Tillekeratne Dilshan scored 96 not out against West Indies in the men's semi-final. Needing 7.3 an over, India were hemmed in by disciplined seam bowling and, though they survived their 20 overs, mustered only 93 runs.

Player of the Match: A. L. Watkins.

New Zealand

		B	4	6
L. R. Doolan *c 2 b 8*	3	6	0	0
S. W. Bates *c 4 b 6*	10	15	1	0
*A. L. Watkins *not out*	89	58	10	2
A. E. Satterthwaite *run out* ..	10	16	1	0
N. J. Browne *st 7 b 9*.........	5	9	0	0
S. J. McGlashan *b 6*	4	8	0	0
S. F. M. Devine *not out*.......	14	8	0	1
L-b 2, w 8	10			

6 overs: 32-1   (20 overs)   145-5

1/5 2/45 3/69 4/96 5/120

†R. H. Priest, S. J. Tsukigawa, K. L. Pulford and S. E. A. Ruck did not bat.

Goswami 4–0–22–0; Dhar 4–1–35–1; Sharma 4–0–21–2; Kaur 1–0–14–0; Raut 3–0–17–0; Sultana 3–0–28–0; Roy 1–0–6–1.

India

		B	4	6
P. G. Raut *c 7 b 11*	5	6	1	0
A. Chopra *c 2 b 10*	15	24	1	0
M. Raj *c 6 b 4*	20	22	2	0
H. Kaur *b 11*	0	1	0	0
R. Malhotra *run out*	4	10	0	0
A. Sharma *c 3 b 4*	24	27	2	1
†S. Naik *c 6 b 2*.............	2	3	0	0
R. Dhar *c 2 b 7*	4	5	0	0
P. Roy *run out*..............	5	7	0	0
*J. Goswami *not out*..........	9	14	0	0
G. Sultana *not out*	2	2	0	0
L-b 1, w 1, n-b 1	3			

6 overs: 25-1   (20 overs)   93-9

1/7 2/30 3/30 4/42 5/49 6/58 7/76 8/77 9/87

Devine 4–0–17–1; Ruck 4–0–18–2; Pulford 4–0–17–1; Satterthwaite 4–0–20–2; Bates 4–0–20–1.

Umpires: Asad Rauf and M. R. Benson.   Third umpire: I. J. Gould.   Referee: B. C. Broad.

ENGLAND v AUSTRALIA

At The Oval, June 19. England won by eight wickets. Toss: England.

England's ambitions to own both world titles and the Ashes nearly came unstuck when they faced Australia in the finest women's Twenty20 match to date. It justified the growing reputation of a game which had been improving for years, but largely behind a curtain: when the women emerged on to the Oval stage, they bestrode it with immeasurable confidence. Australia happily played their shots after being sent in, with Karen Rolton's pulled six over midwicket one of many highlights. Their total was one short of the tournament's highest to date, their own 164 for six against South Africa. When England captain Charlotte Edwards fell in the seventh over, the asking-rate was 9.3. Then, with the 10,000-strong crowd enthralled, Claire Taylor and Beth Morgan silenced some senseless sledging with an exquisitely paced, unbeaten partnership of 122 (the second-highest for any wicket in women's Twenty20 internationals) which pushed England to their towering target with three balls remaining. Taylor masterminded the best run-chase of the fortnight – by men or women – with a 53-ball 76, winning it with her eighth four, while Morgan thumbed her nose at critics of the middle order. With Rolton about to hand over the captaincy, how Australia would have loved to contest the final, to make up for their World Cup failure on home soil in March! Playing their part in boosting the game's profile was little consolation; yet the world had woken up to women's cricket at last.

Player of the Match: S. C. Taylor.

Australia

		B	4	6
S. Nitschke *c 1 b 10*	37	25	6	0
L. J. Poulton *b 11*	39	31	6	0
L. C. Sthalekar *b 9*	28	21	3	0
*L. K. Rolton *c 9 b 8*	38	32	4	1
A. J. Blackwell *b 6*	5	7	0	0
L. K. Ebsary *not out*	8	4	1	0
R. M. Farrell *not out*	1	1	0	0
L-b 2, w 4, n-b 1	7			

6 overs: 49-0   (20 overs)   163-5

1/78 2/78 3/138 4/151 5/154

†J. M. Fields, E. A. Perry, K. E. Pike and S. J. Andrews did not bat.

Marsh 4–1–12–1; Brunt 4–0–39–1; Shaw 4–0–31–1; Colvin 4–0–37–1; Edwards 1–0–13–0; Gunn 3–0–29–1.

England

		B	4	6
†S. J. Taylor *c 3 b 7*	6	7	1	0
*C. M. Edwards *c 8 b 9*	25	23	4	0
S. C. Taylor *not out*	76	53	8	0
B. L. Morgan *not out*	46	34	5	0
L-b 4, w 8	12			

6 overs: 37-1   (19.3 overs)   165-2

1/23 2/43

L. S. Greenway, J. L. Gunn, C. M. G. Atkins, N. J. Shaw, K. H. Brunt, H. L. Colvin and L. A. Marsh did not bat.

Farrell 4–0–32–1; Andrews 2.3–0–24–0; Perry 4–0–32–1; Nitschke 4–0–22–0; Sthalekar 2–0–23–0; Pike 3–0–28–0.

Umpires: B. R. Doctrove and A. L. Hill.   Third umpire: E. A. R. de Silva.   Referee: A. G. Hurst.

FINAL

ENGLAND v NEW ZEALAND

At Lord's, June 21. England won by six wickets. Toss: England.

Three months after they contested the World Cup final in North Sydney, England and New Zealand met for a rematch at Lord's – and it followed a similar script, with New Zealand's batsmen failing again. "Everything we tried turned to custard," said their captain, Aimee Watkins. Custard and crumble – New Zealand folded for 85 after Katherine Brunt, the fiery Yorkshirewoman sporting a menacing black eye, punched through the top order with a career-best three for six. She removed Watkins, the tournament's leading scorer, for two, bowling her with an inswinger. England took their time over the target, but never looked in danger; New Zealand squandered their best chance when the keeper dropped Claire Taylor on nought. Taylor took England home, hitting the winning boundary and finishing the World Twenty20 with 199 runs (one behind Watkins) for once out, to earn a second successive Player of the Tournament trophy. Curiously, England captain Charlotte Edwards said she had wanted to prove the World Cup win "was no fluke"; nobody had thought it was, but if that was the motivation it worked to stunningly professional effect. In Sydney, England had been ecstatic; in London, they accepted the inaugural World Twenty20 trophy with controlled satisfaction. They appeared on the front and back pages of newspapers, and accepted an invitation to Downing Street. The ICC's gamble in staging the women's event alongside the men's had paid off, beautifully. And England remained on top of the world.

Player of the Match: K. H. Brunt.   *Player of the Tournament:* S. C. Taylor.

New Zealand

		B	4	6
S. W. Bates *st 1 b 11*	1	4	0	0
L. R. Doolan *c 1 b 9*	14	19	2	0
*A. L. Watkins *b 9*	2	6	0	0
A. E. Satterthwaite *c 3 b 8*	19	42	0	0
†R. H. Priest *c and b 9*	0	3	0	0
N. J. Browne *b 8*	1	9	0	0
S. J. McGlashan *c 5 b 6*	9	13	0	0
S. J. Tsukigawa *c 1 b 6*	5	9	0	0
S. F. M. Devine *run out*	10	6	1	0
K. L. Pulford *c 3 b 2*	14	10	2	0
S. E. A. Ruck *not out*	0	0	0	0
B 1, l-b 4, w 4, n-b 1	10			

6 overs: 18-2   (20 overs)   85

1/2 2/10 3/23 4/23 5/31 6/48 7/58 8/62 9/84
10/85

Marsh 4–0–16–1; Brunt 4–2–6–3; Shaw
4–0–17–2;   Colvin   4–0–16–0;   Gunn
3–0–19–2; Edwards 1–0–6–1.

England

		B	4	6
†S. J. Taylor *c 5 b 10*	23	33	3	0
*C. M. Edwards *b 11*	9	10	2	0
S. C. Taylor *not out*	39	32	4	0
B. L. Morgan *c 7 b 6*	6	17	0	0
L. S. Greenway *b 7*	3	7	0	0
J. L. Gunn *not out*	2	3	0	0
L-b 1, w 3	4			

6 overs: 23-1   (17 overs)   86-4

1/19 2/39 3/70 4/74

C. M. G. Atkins, N. J. Shaw, K. H. Brunt, H. L.
Colvin and L. A. Marsh did not bat.

Devine 3–0–12–1; Ruck 4–0–17–1; Pulford
4–0–20–1;   Bates   2–0–8–0;   Browne
3–0–18–1; Doolan 1–0–10–0.

Umpires: Aleem Dar and R. E. Koertzen.   Third umpire: Asad Rauf.   Referee: A. G. Hurst.

LV= COUNTY CHAMPIONSHIP, 2009

NEVILLE SCOTT

After three summers of fiercely tight cricket, with the title decided only in the final hours, 2009 brought the least compelling campaign in a decade of two-division play. It was like following a weekend at Silvio Berlusconi's villa with a tea dance at E. W. Swanton's. To adapt Gabriel García Márquez, we had feared "cricket in the time of swine flu"; what we received was a summer of sterility and stalemate.

Only 44% of matches produced a winner, the lowest proportion in 17 years of purely four-day play. The first division percentage (40.27) was barely better than in 1985, the least productive of all summers at 37.62. On September 11, when Worcestershire were relegated, 16 of 24 results in the top tier up to that point had involved either Durham wins or Worcestershire defeats: in a ritual of mutual negation, the other seven sides had managed 28 draws from 36 games between them. Sussex then blinked first. Beset by a loss of batting nerve, they surrendered each of their last three matches, two at Hove to key rivals, and became the second side demoted as the log-jam at last broke. The day after Worcestershire's demise, Durham retained the Championship with a fortnight to spare. Both outcomes, plus Kent's promotion 24 hours later, had looked likely in April, certain by mid-season.

COUNTY CHAMPIONSHIP TABLE

Division One	Matches	Won	Lost	Drawn	Bonus points Batting	Bonus points Bowling	Penalty	Points
1 – Durham (1)............	16	8	0	8	49	48	1	240
2 – Nottinghamshire (2)...	16	4	2	10	56	41	0	193
3 – Somerset (4)...........	16	3	1	12	50	43	1	182
4 – Lancashire (5)	16	4	2	10	35	44	0	175
5 – Warwickshire (1)	16	3	3	10	54	38	0	174
6 – Hampshire (3)	16	3	3	10	50	40	3	169
7 – Yorkshire (7)	16	2	2	12	46	44	0	166
8 – Sussex (6)............	16	2	6	8	45	39	1	143
9 – Worcestershire (2)	16	0	10	6	30	40	0	94

Division Two	Matches	Won	Lost	Drawn	Bonus points Batting	Bonus points Bowling	Penalty	Points
1 – Kent (8)	16	8	3	5	43	44	0	219
2 – Essex (5).............	16	6	3	7	40	43	1	194
3 – Northamptonshire (4)..	16	6	4	6	40	45	0	193
4 – Gloucestershire (9)....	16	6	6	4	39	46	0	185
5 – Glamorgan (8)	16	2	2	12	56	43	0	175
6 – Derbyshire (6)	16	2	3	11	55	45	0	172
7 – Surrey (9)............	16	1	4	11	54	36	0	148
8 – Middlesex (3).........	16	2	7	7	43	41	0	140
9 – Leicestershire (7)	16	2	3	11	31	35	0	138

2008 positions are shown in brackets: Division One in bold, Division Two in italic.

* Includes one match abandoned.

Win = 14 pts; draw = 4 pts. Penalties were deducted for slow over-rates.

Double success: Will Smith and Geoff Cook celebrate retaining the County Championship.

You could hardly blame **Durham** for proving so dominant. And the assessment of their head coach, Geoff Cook, was surely valid: "Other teams were less strong, perhaps, but Durham would have been a force in any year.

"Our team effort was total – best reflected in the fact that four men took between 43 and 51 wickets. There were big differentials between our first-innings scores and other sides'. The tremendous personal drive and focus of our imports, Di Venuto and Benkenstein, was backed up by Blackwell at six and Mustard, with a lot more cleverness and maturity, at seven. It was a formidable middle order."

Happily for England, who would founder without it, the hard labour of fast bowling is still embraced by club cricketers in the north. Pace offers Durham the prospect, next season, of becoming the first team for 42 years to secure three successive titles. Stuart Broad apart, no England pace bowler with even five caps since August 2005 has been born south of Bolton. This time Durham's England-nurtured, wicket-sharing quartet even included a spinner after the

PERCENTAGE OF WINS IN A CHAMPIONSHIP SEASON

	Both Divisions	Division One	Division Two		Both Divisions	Division One	Division Two
2000	53.47	55.55	51.38	2005	62.50	68.05	56.94
2001	54.16	51.38	56.94	2006	61.11	59.72	62.50
2002	65.97	59.72	72.22	2007	57.85	56.52	59.15
2003	61.11	56.94	65.27	2008	46.09	45.71	46.47
2004	51.38	47.22	55.55	**2009**	**44.44**	**40.27**	**48.61**

Statistics cover all seasons since the introduction of two divisions into the Championship. The percentage is that of victories in all matches played, excluding those abandoned without a ball bowled.

---

one-Test cap Ian Blackwell was signed from Somerset, where his fitness and rigour were doubted. The tutelage of the quicker men was left to Alan Walker, largely unheralded but, like Cook, one of the most decent and committed mentors in the game. He is the last in that noble line of fast bowlers whose first job was down a mine.

Of the pace nursery, Cook says: "There are still one or two lads in the pipeline. We make a special effort to spot bowlers with the right physique. After remedial work, we have much better pitches at Riverside, where the ball even spun a bit, and there is plenty of carry and bounce. Teams try to nullify our attack by playing on used wickets – a lot created turn but Blackwell answered there. In the past, Riverside moved more off the seam and that's a factor in the slow development of batsmen. But we expect them to come through in the next few years. The experience gained will stand them in good stead: we have batsmen who score heavily in the academy."

Bounce and carry are decidedly not the hallmark of many pitches elsewhere. With the exception of Old Trafford, that home to good contests between bat and ball, the norm is accumulation. Taunton's version of "quantitative easing" gave batsmen a licence to print runs. Somerset, at least, would dearly love to rectify this problem: moribund squares at Edgbaston, Headingley, the Rose Bowl, Derby, Cardiff, Leicester and The Oval owe rather more to design. It defeats the object of cricket when, at so many county headquarters, the draw can be forecast by tea on day one.

Before the season, only Nottinghamshire and Lancashire appeared to possess attacks with the bite to challenge Durham's. **Somerset** had the will and the imported pace – but also faced that Taunton pitch. In the early wet, **Nottinghamshire** did indeed win three of their first five games, powered by Chris Read, who averaged more (75.18) than any county keeper except Tony Frost in 2008. With Charlie Shreck and Darren Pattinson enduring abysmal summers, however, their one further success came in the final game, where lack of full batting points condemned Sussex by the second day. **Lancashire**, the single county to field exclusively English fast bowlers, had won three times at the halfway stage but Glen Chapple, their venerable leader, then succumbed to injury and missed five games.

Nottinghamshire finished runners-up and Lancashire, despite an identical playing record of four wins and two defeats, ended fourth behind Somerset.

Their lack of batting points, a perennial Lancashire problem explained partly by the very vigour of their pitches, left them barely clear of the trio behind, each of whom, amid the draws, lost as often as they won. But Lancashire were never really in danger.

By August 23, four genuinely threatened teams were separated by four points, all with four games to come. One of this clique was doomed to fall with **Worcestershire**. But both **Warwickshire** and **Hampshire**, who finished fifth and sixth, still had Worcestershire to meet – and trounce. Warwickshire then won the first of those two decisive games at Hove, where, a week later, Yorkshire delivered the *coup de grâce* to **Sussex** with a rare, last-afternoon bowling triumph. **Yorkshire**, coming seventh, achieved an average 39 runs per wicket through the season – not quite the feat it seemed: scoring at 3.17 runs per over, only twice did they create sufficient space to win.

A points regime placing heavy emphasis on runs and draws had clearly outlived its purpose. In games now scheduled to last only 384 overs, pursuing maximum batting points allowed little time for a result. Points for the draw were introduced in 1996 as a legitimate counter to teams throwing in the towel as soon as they could not win, a widespread problem that informed England's spineless batting in Tests. But, in two-division play, the need to thwart rivals should be clear. In December the ECB, acknowledging some of these problems, increased the reward for a win by two points to 16 and reduced that for a draw by one point to three. They also lowered the threshold for scoring bonus points from 120 overs (already down from 130 in 2008) to 110, encouraging a faster scoring-rate.

The myth is sides must bat first

The points debate is not straightforward, however. What the ECB are desperate to avoid is a return to the "result pitch" lottery of the 1980s, when banal seamers could thrive in the Championship yet rarely succeeded in Tests. In the second division last year, all five victories at Bristol went to sides winning the toss and inserting – and **Gloucestershire** called correctly four times. This strategy underlay their rise from bottom to fourth. To be fair, they played to their clear strength in good seam bowling, and batting second has often been the answer on modern squares. But any wider return to "win the toss and win the game" would arguably be worse than draws. A novel, if radical, possible solution might be to rescind any bowling points gained in a home defeat.

Of 32 wins by the end of July (exactly half the season's total), no fewer than 21 had fallen to teams batting second. The myth persists that sides must always bat first: this has been unfounded in the Championship for years. Such life as pitches retain habitually disappears in two sessions. Even when spin intervened in August and September, more wins still went to teams batting second, just.

Spin proved the key in the promotion race. James Tredwell's off-breaks led **Kent's** progress to the title, though, ironically, he faded markedly in the final five games. But Danish Kaneria came into his own. As **Essex** won four of their last six matches to rise from the dead (or seventh place), the Pakistan leg-spinner returned 52 wickets.

Even this was not the full story. Two of Essex's late wins came after they were challenged to run-chases, the first after the oddest declaration since Margaret Thatcher announced "we are a grandmother": **Middlesex**, fearing the wooden spoon, left themselves only 45 overs to take ten wickets and predictably failed to defend a target of 241. After seven defeats, they ended eighth.

Essex's more severe task, to make 359 at 5.5 per over, came on the season's last day. Five sides entered the final round with hopes of promotion but Northamptonshire had won in three days, removing Gloucestershire, Glamorgan and Derbyshire from contention. In a case of the biter bit, Derbyshire, who almost invariably played foreign-raised batsmen in five of their first six places, set the challenge but fell foul of Ryan ten Doeschate, Essex's South African Dutchman. His remarkable, promotion-seizing 108 not out required only 59 balls.

Crucially Essex had beaten Northamptonshire off the penultimate ball in their previous game, perhaps the best single match of the summer. **Northamptonshire** relied on a switch to result pitches for their seamers at Wantage Road but were unlucky to win only two tosses all year, neither of them at home. **Glamorgan**, backing spin, finished fifth but critically failed to finish off Gloucestershire or Essex, both with nine wickets down, in their last two games at home. **Derbyshire** scored quick runs, but their caution was reflected in the flatness of Derby pitches, so influential on that final day.

With almost nothing between them, except the trick of winning, any of these five sides might have gone up. But, sadly, the first division will see little of Kaneria in 2010 if he is chosen to tour with Pakistan. Blackwell apart, spin was less prominent throughout the upper echelon. England calls meant that Nottinghamshire lacked Graeme Swann for all but two games and Yorkshire lost Adil Rashid for more than half the season. Imran Tahir failed to repeat his Hampshire success of 2008.

The Tiflex ball was trialled in the second division to ensure that Dukes did not enjoy a monopoly. Dukes balls apparently swung more and the early Tiflex batches tended to go soft. But the final ECB verdict was positive: "Latterly, they were excellent; we were very satisfied." Tiflex balls certainly did little for **Surrey**. Conceding an average 46 runs per wicket, they were marginally more profligate than Leicestershire, who went for 44. The decline of Surrey, who finished seventh and used an unheard-of 27 players, can be identified with precision to July 12, 2003. They were then 26 points clear at the head of the table and apparently assured of a fourth title in five years. Since then, they have plummeted, completely failing to renew an attack that had made them the Durham of their day.

At least Surrey have the cash to address the problem; **Leicestershire**, alas, do not. Veering suddenly away from Kolpaks, they came last but beat Gloucestershire in mid-August with a side containing nine Englishmen, seven aged 27 or under. How many will be poached remains to be seen. Much more needs to be done to feed ECB money to clubs like Leicestershire, but extra payments in 2010 for those who foster home youth at least makes a start. With Kolpaks arriving in force since 2004, the average age of county sides has risen from 28 years 11 months to 29 years three months in 2009.

Typically, second-rank South Africans in their thirties have set back young English players by two or three seasons. Other South Africans have come from Under-19 cricket, opting early for better pay. Even with delays over work permits, 31.85% of Championship appearances last year were made by those who learned their cricket abroad. With the Home Office, the ECB have at last agreed more stringent criteria for Kolpak visas, limiting those without international caps. But, since players with four consecutive seasons in Britain are exempt, and five Tests in the previous five years remains a qualification, it may be the best part of a decade before real change comes.

Pre-season betting (best available prices): *Division One* – 7-2 DURHAM; 5-1 Nottinghamshire; 15-2 Hampshire and Somerset; 9-1 Sussex; 10-1 Lancashire; 11-1 Yorkshire; 14-1 Worcestershire; 16-1 Warwickshire. *Division Two* – 9-4 KENT; 5-1 Essex and Middlesex; 6-1 Surrey; 14-1 Northamptonshire; 25-1 Derbyshire; 28-1 Glamorgan; 33-1 Leicestershire and Gloucestershire.

Prize money

Division One
£500,000 for winners: DURHAM.
£225,000 for runners-up: NOTTINGHAMSHIRE.
£115,000 for third: SOMERSET.
£35,000 for fourth: LANCASHIRE.

Division Two
£115,000 for winners: KENT.
£70,000 for runners-up: ESSEX.

(These prizes are divided between players' prize money and a county performance payment. For the winners, players receive £350,000 and the county £150,000; for runners-up, the split is £175,000/£50,000; for third, £100,000/£15,000; for fourth, £30,000/£5,000. In the second division, the split for the winners is £90,000/£25,000, and for the runners-up £60,000/£10,000.)

Winners of each match (both divisions): £1,350.

Leaders: *Division One* – from April 17 Hampshire; May 9 Nottinghamshire; June 19 Durham. Durham became champions on September 12.
Division Two – from April 18 Northamptonshire; April 25 Derbyshire; May 9 Gloucestershire; July 15 Derbyshire; July 18 Kent. Kent became champions on September 17.

Bottom place: *Division One* – from April 24 Sussex; May 9 Somerset and Worcestershire; June 9 Worcestershire.
Division Two – from April 25 Leicestershire; May 2 Surrey; May 9 Leicestershire; July 12 Middlesex; August 8 Leicestershire; August 22 Middlesex; August 30 Leicestershire; September 5 Middlesex; September 12 Leicestershire.

Scoring of Points

(*a*) For a win, 14 points plus any points scored in the first innings. (*From 2010, 16 points.*)

(*b*) In a tie, each side scores seven points (*from 2010, eight points*), plus any points scored in the first innings.

(*c*) In a drawn match, each side scores four points (*from 2010, three points*), plus any points scored in the first innings.

(*d*) If the scores are equal in a drawn match, the side batting in the fourth innings scores seven points, plus any points scored in the first innings, and the opposing side scores four points plus any points scored in the first innings. (*From 2010, eight points and three points respectively.*)

(*e*) First-innings points (awarded only for performances in the first 120 overs of each first innings and retained whatever the result of the match). (*From 2010, 110 overs.*)

   (i) A maximum of five batting points to be available: 200 to 249 runs – 1 point; 250 to 299 runs – 2 points; 300 to 349 runs – 3 points; 350 to 399 runs – 4 points; 400 runs or over –

5 points. Penalty runs awarded within the first 120 (*from 2010, 110*) overs of each first innings count towards the award of bonus points.

(ii) A maximum of three bowling points to be available: 3 to 5 wickets taken – 1 point; 6 to 8 wickets taken – 2 points; 9 to 10 wickets taken – 3 points.

(*f*) If a match is abandoned without a ball being bowled, each side scores four points. (*From 2010, three points.*)

(*g*) The side which has the highest aggregate of points shall be the Champion County of their respective division. Should any sides in the Championship table be equal on points, the following tie-breakers will be applied in the order stated: most wins, fewest losses, team achieving most points in head-to-head contests between teams level on points, most wickets taken, most runs scored. At the end of the season, the top two teams from the second division will be promoted and the bottom two teams from the first division will be relegated.

(*h*) The minimum over-rate to be achieved by counties will be 16 overs per hour. Overs will be calculated at the end of the match and penalties applied on a match-by-match basis. For each over (ignoring fractions) that a side has bowled short of the target number, one point will be deducted from their Championship total.

(*i*) A county which is adjudged to have prepared a pitch unfit for four-day first-class cricket will have 22 points deducted. (*From 2010, 24 points*) A county adjudged to have prepared a poor pitch will have eight points deducted. This penalty will rise to 12 points if the county has prepared a poor pitch or unfit pitch within the previous 12 months. A county adjudged to have provided a playing area in a condition substantially reducing the possibility of play (subsequent to actions within that county's control) will have eight points deducted.

Under ECB playing conditions, two extras were scored for every no-ball bowled whether scored off or not, and one for every wide. Any runs scored off the bat were credited to the batsman, while byes and leg-byes were counted as no-balls or wides, as appropriate, in accordance with Law 24.13, in addition to the initial penalty.

CONSTITUTION OF COUNTY CHAMPIONSHIP

At least four possible dates have been given for the start of county cricket in England. The first, patchy, references began in 1825. The earliest mention in any cricket publication is in 1864 and eight counties have come to be regarded as first-class from that date, including Cambridgeshire, who dropped out after 1871. For many years, the County Championship was considered to have started in 1873, when regulations governing qualification first applied; indeed, a special commemorative stamp was issued by the Post Office in 1973. However, the Championship was not formally organised until 1890 and before then champions were proclaimed by the press; sometimes publications differed in their views and no definitive list of champions can start before that date. Eight teams contested the 1890 competition – Gloucestershire, Kent, Lancashire, Middlesex, Nottinghamshire, Surrey, Sussex and Yorkshire. Somerset joined in the following year, and in 1895 the Championship began to acquire something of its modern shape when Derbyshire, Essex, Hampshire, Leicestershire and Warwickshire were added. At that point MCC officially recognised the competition's existence. Worcestershire, Northamptonshire and Glamorgan were admitted to the Championship in 1899, 1905 and 1921 respectively and are regarded as first-class from these dates. An invitation in 1921 to Buckinghamshire to enter the Championship was declined, owing to the lack of necessary playing facilities, and an application by Devon in 1948 was unsuccessful. Durham were admitted to the Championship in 1992 and were granted first-class status prior to their pre-season tour of Zimbabwe. In 2000, the Championship was split for the first time into two divisions, on the basis of counties' standings in the 1999 competition. From 2000 onwards, the bottom three teams in Division One were relegated at the end of the season, and the top three teams in Division Two promoted. From 2006, this was changed to two teams relegated and two promoted.

COUNTY CHAMPIONS

The title of champion county is unreliable before 1890. In 1963, *Wisden* formally accepted the list of champions "most generally selected" by contemporaries, as researched by the late Rowland Bowen (see *Wisden 1959*, pp 91–98). This appears to be the most accurate available list but has no official status. The county champions from 1864 to 1889 were, according to Bowen: 1864 Surrey; 1865

Nottinghamshire; 1866 Middlesex; 1867 Yorkshire; 1868 Nottinghamshire; 1869 Nottinghamshire and Yorkshire; 1870 Yorkshire; 1871 Nottinghamshire; 1872 Nottinghamshire; 1873 Gloucestershire and Nottinghamshire; 1874 Gloucestershire; 1875 Nottinghamshire; 1876 Gloucestershire; 1877 Gloucestershire; 1878 undecided; 1879 Lancashire and Nottinghamshire; 1880 Nottinghamshire; 1881 Lancashire; 1882 Lancashire and Nottinghamshire; 1883 Nottinghamshire; 1884 Nottinghamshire; 1885 Nottinghamshire; 1886 Nottinghamshire; 1887 Surrey; 1888 Surrey; 1889 Lancashire, Nottinghamshire and Surrey.

Official champions		*Official champions*		*Official champions*	
1890	Surrey	1931	Yorkshire	1973	Hampshire
1891	Surrey	1932	Yorkshire	1974	Worcestershire
1892	Surrey	1933	Yorkshire	1975	Leicestershire
1893	Yorkshire	1934	Lancashire	1976	Middlesex
1894	Surrey	1935	Yorkshire	1977	Middlesex
1895	Surrey	1936	Derbyshire	1977	Kent
1896	Yorkshire	1937	Yorkshire	1978	Kent
1897	Lancashire	1938	Yorkshire	1979	Essex
1898	Yorkshire	1939	Yorkshire	1980	Middlesex
1899	Surrey	1946	Yorkshire	1981	Nottinghamshire
1900	Yorkshire	1947	Middlesex	1982	Middlesex
1901	Yorkshire	1948	Glamorgan	1983	Essex
1902	Yorkshire	1949	Middlesex	1984	Essex
1903	Middlesex	1949	Yorkshire	1985	Middlesex
1904	Lancashire	1950	Lancashire	1986	Essex
1905	Yorkshire	1950	Surrey	1987	Nottinghamshire
1906	Kent	1951	Warwickshire	1988	Worcestershire
1907	Nottinghamshire	1952	Surrey	1989	Worcestershire
1908	Yorkshire	1953	Surrey	1990	Middlesex
1909	Kent	1954	Surrey	1991	Essex
1910	Kent	1955	Surrey	1992	Essex
1911	Warwickshire	1956	Surrey	1993	Middlesex
1912	Yorkshire	1957	Surrey	1994	Warwickshire
1913	Kent	1958	Surrey	1995	Warwickshire
1914	Surrey	1959	Yorkshire	1996	Leicestershire
1919	Yorkshire	1960	Yorkshire	1997	Glamorgan
1920	Middlesex	1961	Hampshire	1998	Leicestershire
1921	Middlesex	1962	Yorkshire	1999	Surrey
1922	Yorkshire	1963	Yorkshire	2000	Surrey
1923	Yorkshire	1964	Worcestershire	2001	Yorkshire
1924	Yorkshire	1965	Worcestershire	2002	Surrey
1925	Yorkshire	1966	Yorkshire	2003	Sussex
1926	Lancashire	1967	Yorkshire	2004	Warwickshire
1927	Lancashire	1968	Yorkshire	2005	Nottinghamshire
1928	Lancashire	1969	Glamorgan	2006	Sussex
1929	Nottinghamshire	1970	Kent	2007	Sussex
1930	Lancashire	1971	Surrey	2008	Durham
		1972	Warwickshire	2009	Durham

Notes: Since the Championship was constituted in 1890 it has been won outright as follows: Yorkshire 30 times, Surrey 18, Middlesex 10, Lancashire 7, Essex, Kent and Warwickshire 6, Nottinghamshire and Worcestershire 5, Glamorgan, Leicestershire and Sussex 3, Durham and Hampshire 2, Derbyshire 1. Gloucestershire, Northamptonshire and Somerset have never won.

The title has been shared three times since 1890, involving Middlesex twice, Kent, Lancashire, Surrey and Yorkshire.

Wooden Spoons Since the major expansion of the Championship from nine teams to 14 in 1895, the counties have finished outright bottom as follows: Derbyshire 14; Somerset 12; Northamptonshire 11; Glamorgan 10; Gloucestershire, Leicestershire, Nottinghamshire and Sussex 8; Worcestershire 6; Durham and Hampshire 5; Warwickshire 3; Essex and Kent 2; Yorkshire 1. Lancashire, Middlesex and Surrey have never finished bottom. Leicestershire have also shared bottom place twice, once with Hampshire and once with Somerset.

From 1977 to 1983 the Championship was sponsored by Schweppes, from 1984 to 1998 by Britannic Assurance, from 1999 to 2000 by PPP healthcare, in 2001 by Cricinfo, from 2002 to 2005 by Frizzell and from 2006 by Liverpool Victoria (LV).

COUNTY CHAMPIONSHIP – FINAL POSITIONS, 1890–2009

	Derbyshire	Durham	Essex	Glamorgan	Gloucestershire	Hampshire	Kent	Lancashire	Leicestershire	Middlesex	Northamptonshire	Nottinghamshire	Somerset	Surrey	Sussex	Warwickshire	Worcestershire	Yorkshire
1890	–	–	–	–	6	–	3	2	–	7	–	5	–	1	8	–	–	3
1891	–	–	–	–	9	–	5	2	–	3	–	4	5	1	7	–	–	8
1892	–	–	–	–	7	–	7	4	–	5	–	2	3	1	9	–	–	6
1893	–	–	–	–	9	–	4	2	–	3	–	6	8	5	7	–	–	1
1894	–	–	–	–	9	–	4	4	–	3	–	7	6	1	8	–	–	2
1895	5	–	9	–	4	10	14	2	12	6	–	12	8	1	11	6	–	3
1896	7	–	5	–	10	8	9	2	13	3	–	6	11	4	14	12	–	1
1897	14	–	3	–	5	9	12	1	13	8	–	10	11	2	6	7	–	4
1898	9	–	5	–	3	12	7	6	13	2	–	8	13	4	9	9	–	1
1899	15	–	6	–	9	10	8	4	13	2	–	10	13	1	5	7	12	3
1900	13	–	10	–	7	15	3	2	14	7	–	5	11	7	3	6	12	1
1901	15	–	10	–	14	7	7	3	12	2	–	9	12	6	4	5	11	1
1902	10	–	13	–	14	15	7	5	11	12	–	3	7	4	2	6	9	1
1903	12	–	8	–	13	14	8	4	14	1	–	5	10	11	2	7	6	3
1904	10	–	14	–	9	15	3	1	7	4	–	5	12	11	6	7	13	2
1905	14	–	12	–	8	16	6	2	5	11	13	10	15	4	3	7	8	1
1906	16	–	7	–	9	8	1	4	15	11	11	5	11	3	10	6	14	2
1907	16	–	7	–	10	12	8	6	11	5	15	1	14	4	13	9	2	2
1908	14	–	11	–	10	9	2	7	13	4	15	8	16	3	5	12	6	1
1909	15	–	14	–	16	8	1	2	13	6	7	10	11	5	4	12	8	3
1910	15	–	11	–	12	6	1	4	10	3	9	5	16	2	7	14	13	8
1911	14	–	6	–	12	11	2	4	15	3	10	8	16	5	13	1	9	7
1912	12	–	15	–	11	6	3	4	13	5	2	8	14	7	10	9	16	1
1913	13	–	15	–	9	10	1	8	14	6	4	5	16	3	7	11	12	2
1914	12	–	8	–	16	5	3	11	13	2	9	10	15	1	6	7	14	4
1919	9	–	14	–	8	7	2	5	9	13	12	3	5	4	11	15	–	1
1920	16	–	9	–	8	11	5	2	13	1	14	7	10	3	6	12	15	4
1921	12	–	15	17	7	6	4	5	11	1	13	8	10	2	9	16	14	3
1922	11	–	8	16	13	6	4	5	14	7	15	2	10	3	9	12	17	1
1923	10	–	13	16	11	7	5	3	14	8	17	2	9	4	6	12	15	1
1924	17	–	15	13	6	12	5	4	11	2	16	6	8	3	10	9	14	1
1925	14	–	7	17	10	9	5	3	12	6	11	4	15	2	13	8	16	1
1926	11	–	9	8	15	7	3	1	13	6	16	4	14	5	10	12	17	2
1927	5	–	8	15	12	13	4	1	7	9	16	2	14	6	10	11	17	3
1928	10	–	16	15	5	12	2	1	9	8	13	3	14	6	7	11	17	4
1929	7	–	12	17	4	11	8	2	9	6	13	1	15	10	4	14	16	2
1930	9	–	6	11	2	13	5	1	12	16	17	4	13	8	7	15	10	3
1931	7	–	10	15	2	12	3	6	16	11	17	5	13	8	4	9	14	1
1932	10	–	14	15	13	8	3	6	12	10	16	4	7	5	2	9	17	1
1933	6	–	4	16	10	14	3	5	17	12	13	8	11	9	2	7	15	1
1934	3	–	8	13	7	14	5	1	12	10	17	9	15	11	2	4	16	5
1935	2	–	9	13	15	16	10	4	6	3	17	5	14	11	7	8	12	1
1936	1	–	9	16	4	10	8	11	15	2	17	5	7	6	14	13	12	3
1937	3	–	6	7	4	14	12	9	16	2	17	10	13	8	5	11	15	1
1938	5	–	6	16	10	14	9	4	15	2	17	12	7	3	8	13	11	1
1939	9	–	4	13	3	15	5	6	17	2	16	12	14	8	10	11	7	1
1946	15	–	8	6	5	10	6	3	11	2	16	13	4	11	17	14	8	1
1947	5	–	11	9	2	16	4	3	14	1	17	11	11	6	9	15	7	7

	Derbyshire	Durham	Essex	Glamorgan	Gloucestershire	Hampshire	Kent	Lancashire	Leicestershire	Middlesex	Northamptonshire	Nottinghamshire	Somerset	Surrey	Sussex	Warwickshire	Worcestershire	Yorkshire
1948	6	–	13	1	8	9	15	5	11	3	17	14	12	2	16	7	10	4
1949	15	–	9	8	7	16	13	11	17	1	6	11	9	5	13	4	3	1
1950	5	–	17	11	7	12	9	1	16	14	10	15	7	1	13	4	6	3
1951	11	–	8	5	12	9	16	3	15	7	13	17	14	6	10	1	4	2
1952	4	–	10	7	9	12	15	3	6	5	8	16	17	1	13	10	14	2
1953	6	–	12	10	6	14	16	3	3	5	11	8	17	1	2	9	15	12
1954	3	–	15	4	13	14	11	10	16	7	7	5	17	1	9	6	11	2
1955	8	–	14	16	12	3	13	9	6	5	7	11	17	1	4	9	15	2
1956	12	–	11	13	3	6	16	2	17	5	4	8	15	1	9	14	9	7
1957	4	–	5	9	12	13	14	6	17	7	2	15	8	1	9	11	16	3
1958	5	–	6	15	14	2	8	7	12	10	4	17	3	1	13	16	9	11
1959	7	–	9	6	2	8	13	5	16	10	11	17	12	3	15	4	14	1
1960	5	–	6	11	8	12	10	2	17	3	9	16	14	7	4	15	13	1
1961	7	–	6	14	5	1	11	13	9	3	16	17	10	15	8	12	4	2
1962	7	–	9	14	4	10	11	16	17	13	8	15	6	5	12	3	2	1
1963	17	–	12	2	8	10	13	15	16	6	7	9	3	11	4	4	14	1
1964	12	–	10	11	17	12	7	14	16	6	3	15	8	4	9	2	1	5
1965	9	–	15	3	10	12	5	13	14	6	2	17	7	8	16	11	1	4
1966	9	–	16	14	15	11	4	12	8	12	5	17	3	7	10	6	2	1
1967	6	–	15	14	17	12	2	11	2	7	9	15	8	4	13	10	5	1
1968	8	–	14	3	16	5	2	6	9	10	13	4	12	15	17	11	7	1
1969	16	–	6	1	2	5	10	15	14	11	9	8	17	3	7	4	12	13
1970	7	–	12	2	17	10	1	3	15	16	14	11	13	5	9	7	6	4
1971	17	–	10	16	8	9	4	3	5	6	14	12	7	1	11	2	15	13
1972	17	–	5	13	3	9	2	15	6	8	4	14	11	12	16	1	7	10
1973	16	–	8	11	5	1	4	12	9	13	3	17	10	2	15	7	6	14
1974	17	–	12	16	14	2	10	8	4	6	3	15	5	7	13	9	1	11
1975	15	–	7	9	16	3	5	4	1	11	8	13	12	6	17	14	10	2
1976	15	–	6	17	3	12	14	16	4	1	2	13	7	9	10	5	11	8
1977	7	–	6	14	3	11	1	16	5	1	9	17	4	14	8	10	13	12
1978	14	–	2	13	10	8	1	12	6	3	17	7	5	16	9	11	15	4
1979	16	–	1	17	10	12	5	13	6	14	11	9	8	3	4	15	2	7
1980	9	–	8	13	7	17	16	15	10	1	12	3	5	2	4	14	11	6
1981	12	–	5	14	13	7	9	16	8	4	15	1	3	6	2	17	11	10
1982	11	–	7	16	15	3	13	12	2	1	9	4	6	5	8	17	14	10
1983	9	–	1	15	12	3	7	12	4	2	6	14	10	8	11	5	16	17
1984	12	–	1	13	17	15	5	16	4	3	11	2	7	8	6	9	10	14
1985	13	–	4	12	3	2	9	14	16	1	10	8	17	6	7	15	5	11
1986	11	–	1	17	2	6	8	15	7	12	9	4	16	3	14	12	5	10
1987	6	–	12	13	10	5	14	2	3	16	7	1	11	4	17	15	9	8
1988	14	–	3	17	10	15	2	9	8	7	12	5	11	4	16	6	1	13
1989	6	–	2	17	9	6	13	4	13	3	5	11	14	10	8	1	16	
1990	12	–	2	8	13	3	16	6	7	1	11	13	15	9	17	5	4	10
1991	3	–	1	12	13	9	6	8	16	15	10	4	17	5	11	2	6	14
1992	5	18	1	14	10	15	2	12	8	11	3	4	9	13	7	6	17	16
1993	15	18	11	3	17	13	8	13	9	1	4	7	5	6	10	16	2	12
1994	17	16	6	18	12	13	9	10	2	4	5	3	11	7	8	1	15	13
1995	14	17	5	16	6	13	18	4	7	2	3	11	9	12	15	1	10	8
1996	2	18	5	10	13	14	4	15	1	9	16	17	11	3	12	8	7	6
1997	16	17	8	1	7	14	2	11	10	4	15	13	12	8	18	4	3	6
1998	10	14	18	12	4	6	11	2	1	17	15	16	9	5	7	8	13	3
1999	9	8	12	14	18	7	5	2	3	16	13	17	4	11	10	15	6	
2000	*9*	*8*	*2*	*3*	*4*	*7*	*6*	*2*	*4*	*8*	*1*	*7*	*5*	*1*	*9*	*6*	*5*	*3*
2001	**9**	**8**	**9**	**8**	**4**	**2**	**3**	**6**	**5**	**5**	**7**	**7**	**2**	**4**	**1**	**3**	**6**	**1**

	Derbyshire	Durham	Essex	Glamorgan	Gloucestershire	Hampshire	Kent	Lancashire	Leicestershire	Middlesex	Northamptonshire	Nottinghamshire	Somerset	Surrey	Sussex	Warwickshire	Worcestershire	Yorkshire
2002	6	9	*1*	*5*	*8*	7	3	4	5	2	*7*	*3*	8	1	6	2	*4*	9
2003	*9*	6	7	*5*	*3*	8	4	2	*9*	6	2	8	*7*	3	1	5	*1*	4
2004	8	*9*	5	3	*6*	2	2	8	6	4	*9*	*1*	4	3	5	1	7	7
2005	*9*	2	5	*9*	8	2	5	*1*	7	6	4	1	8	*7*	3	4	*6*	3
2006	5	*7*	3	8	7	3	5	2	4	9	6	8	*9*	*1*	1	4	2	6
2007	6	2	4	*9*	7	5	7	3	*8*	3	5	2	*1*	4	1	8	9	6
2008	6	1	5	*8*	*9*	3	8	5	7	3	4	2	*4*	9	6	*1*	2	7
2009	6	1	2	5	4	6	*1*	4	9	8	3	2	3	7	8	5	9	7

Note: For the 2000–2009 Championships, Division One placings are shown in bold, Division Two in italic.

MATCH RESULTS, 1864–2009

County	Years of Play	Played	Won	Lost	Drawn	Tied	% Won
Derbyshire	1871–87; 1895–2009	2,435	596	895	943	1	24.47
Durham	1992–2009	299	67	138	94	0	22.40
Essex	1895–2009	2,397	698	700	993	6	29.11
Glamorgan	1921–2009	1,929	424	661	844	0	21.98
Gloucestershire	1870–2009	2,671	779	985	905	2	29.16
Hampshire	1864–85; 1895–2009	2,506	662	847	993	4	26.41
Kent	1864–2009	2,794	1,006	833	950	5	36.00
Lancashire	1865–2009	2,868	1,061	593	1,211	3	36.99
Leicestershire.......	1895–2009	2,363	536	851	975	1	22.68
Middlesex..........	1864–2009	2,574	937	657	975	5	36.40
Northamptonshire ...	1905–2009	2,132	531	730	868	3	24.90
Nottinghamshire.....	1864–2009	2,703	820	730	1,152	1	30.33
Somerset	1882–85; 1891–2009	2,405	574	945	883	3	23.86
Surrey.............	1864–2009	2,949	1,161	651	1,133	4	39.36
Sussex	1864–2009	2,843	803	970	1,064	6	28.24
Warwickshire.......	1895–2009	2,377	654	676	1,045	2	27.51
Worcestershire	1899–2009	2,316	590	799	925	2	25.47
Yorkshire	1864–2009	2,972	1,290	528	1,152	2	43.40
Cambridgeshire	1864–69; 1871	19	8	8	3	0	42.10
		21,776	13,197	13,197	8,554	25	

Notes: Matches abandoned without a ball bowled are wholly excluded.

Counties participated in the years shown, except that there were no matches in the years 1915–1918 and 1940–1945; Hampshire did not play inter-county matches in 1868–1869, 1871–1874 and 1879; Worcestershire did not take part in the Championship in 1919.

COUNTY CHAMPIONSHIP STATISTICS FOR 2009

	For			Runs scored	Against		
County	Runs	Wickets	Avge	per 100 balls	Runs	Wickets	Avge
Derbyshire (6)	8,384	210	39.92	59.58	8,360	224	37.32
Durham (1)	7,893	189	41.76	56.13	6,804	272	25.01
Essex (2)	8,139	232	35.08	54.41	8,460	250	33.84
Glamorgan (5)	7,730	212	36.46	56.19	8,394	245	34.26
Gloucestershire (4)...........	7,206	233	30.92	54.84	7,311	262	27.90
Hampshire (6)	7,819	207	37.77	54.50	8,000	204	39.21
Kent (1)	8,824	212	41.62	63.13	8,627	260	33.18
Lancashire (4)	6,889	199	34.61	51.47	7,283	225	32.36

County	Runs	For Wickets	Avge	Runs scored per 100 balls	Runs	Against Wickets	Avge
Leicestershire (9)	8,032	243	33.05	52.47	6,878	154	44.66
Middlesex (8)	8,125	269	30.20	57.12	8,242	247	33.36
Northamptonshire (3)	7,811	242	32.27	56.53	7,673	252	30.44
Nottinghamshire (2)	7,958	210	37.89	61.10	8,782	228	38.51
Somerset (3)	8,911	201	44.33	63.23	8,474	202	41.95
Surrey (7)	8,596	234	36.73	52.03	8,902	193	46.12
Sussex (8)	8,114	233	34.82	58.55	8,248	212	38.90
Warwickshire (5)	7,624	206	37.00	57.04	7,470	189	39.52
Worcestershire (9)	7,792	273	28.54	54.69	7,852	182	43.14
Yorkshire (7)	8,556	217	39.42	52.84	8,643	221	39.10
	144,399	4,024	35.88	56.31	144,399	4,024	35.88

2009 Championship positions are shown in brackets; Division One in bold, Division Two in italic.

ECB PITCHES TABLE OF MERIT, 2009

	First-class	One-day		First-class	One-day
Derbyshire	5.09	5.46	Surrey	5.10	5.43
Durham	4.89	5.08	Sussex	4.72	4.65
Essex	4.89	5.07	Warwickshire	5.00	5.13
Glamorgan	4.44	4.00	Worcestershire	4.50	4.42
Gloucestershire	4.63	5.60	Yorkshire	5.00	5.15
Hampshire	4.78	5.33	Ireland		3.50
Kent	4.90	5.07	Scotland		4.25
Lancashire	5.38	4.50	Cambridge UCCE	5.17	
Leicestershire	4.10	4.67	Cardiff UCCE	5.00	
Middlesex	4.83	5.16	Durham UCCE	4.17	
Northamptonshire	5.00	5.36	Leeds/Bradford UCCE	3.67	
Nottinghamshire	4.75	4.87	Loughborough UCCE . .	4.00	4.40
Somerset	5.11	5.46	Oxford UCCE	5.00	

Each umpire in a match marks the pitch on the following scale: 6 – Very good; 5 – Good; 4 – above average; 3 – Below average; 2 – Poor; 1 – Unfit.

The tables, provided by the ECB, cover major matches, including Tests, Under-19 internationals, women's internationals and UCCE games, played on grounds under the county or UCCE's jurisdiction. Middlesex pitches at Lord's are the responsibility of MCC. The "First-class" column includes Under-19 and women's Tests, and inter-UCCE games.

Lancashire had the highest marks for first-class cricket and Gloucestershire for one-day cricket, though the ECB points out that the tables of merit are not a direct assessment of the groundsmen's ability. Marks may be affected by many factors including weather, soil conditions and the resources available.

COUNTY BENEFITS AWARDED FOR 2010

Glamorgan	D. A. Cosker.	Nottinghamshire	R. J. Sidebottom.
Hampshire	B. V. Taylor (Testimonial).	Sussex	Mushtaq Ahmed (Testimonial).

The ECB had not supplied details of performance-related fee payments at the time of going to press.

DERBYSHIRE

Sixth sensed again

GERALD MORTIMER

Throughout the season, Derbyshire were authentic challengers for promotion from the second division. There was still a faint hope as they entered the last round of matches but, by then, they were relying on results elsewhere, and hopes died as Leicestershire were beaten in three days at Northampton. Derby then became the focal point as Essex cruised to a steep target to go up with Kent. Derbyshire ended up sixth for the third successive season and, while that position confirmed their shortcomings, it also masked some significant progress. The problem was an inability to finish the job. They achieved winning positions but could not turn them into victories – most notably at Grace Road where, with two sessions in which to take three wickets, they were thwarted by James Taylor and Jigar Naik, who added 195 for the eighth wicket.

At times like that, Derbyshire yearned for Charl Langeveldt in his 2008 form. He was offered a place in the Indian Premier League, which was played in his native South Africa, and Derbyshire felt they could not deny a 34-year-old such a handsome payday. Infuriatingly, he was injured in the final game – his only appearance for Kolkata Knight Riders – and required a shoulder operation. That ruled him out of Derbyshire's calculations and his replacement, Nantie Hayward, was short of cricket and wildly expensive at times.

Langeveldt was not the only false start. The captain, Chris Rogers, was held up in Australia as he tried to unravel new visa regulations, and did not arrive until May, although the Jamaican authorities did allow Wavell Hinds to be on parade for the opening day of the season. While Rogers was fretting at home, Derbyshire beat Surrey, helped by career-best bowling from Graham Wagg and a stabilising innings by Steve Stubbings. It was one of only two Championship victories: Derbyshire might have been hard to beat, but they found it even harder to win.

The absence of Rogers brought a brief return to Championship action for 40-year-old Stuart Law, who had been signed solely with one-day games in mind. Wicketkeeper Jamie Pipe led the side in the early matches with customary verve, but startled even close colleagues by announcing his retirement at the end of the season. He did not go far: he is now the club's physiotherapist, a career change for which he prepared, even if he did not expect this particular opportunity to arise so soon. Derbyshire quickly re-signed Lee Goddard, who had played for them before joining Durham.

Once Rogers was allowed to travel, he again dominated the batting. He is not a complicated player: when settled, he stood still and hit the ball through the gaps. His captaincy was similarly level-headed, and he is again in charge for 2010. He ended the 2009 season in imposing form, with four centuries – two of them doubles – in the last five matches.

The two main winter recruits were successful. Garry Park turned down a contract with Durham in the hope of more regular cricket. He established himself at No. 3 once Rogers was available, demonstrating quick feet and an array of strokes, as well as being a fine outfielder. Reaching 50 seven times without going on to three figures began to make him edgy, but he cracked the barrier with a fine 178 against Kent and, along with Rogers, completed 1,000 runs. Tim Groenewald headed the bowling averages after leaving Warwickshire, although Wagg, who switched effortlessly between seam

Tim Groenewald

and spin, took most wickets. Ian Hunter had some good days, and Steffen Jones boosted the attack while on loan from Somerset, a move now made permanent, but it was a disappointing summer for Jon Clare, whose impact in 2008 earned him a winter of intensive coaching.

In July, Derbyshire brought in Wayne Madsen, who began with 170 not out at Cheltenham, the highest debut score for the county. Madsen, who has an Italian passport, had played for KwaZulu-Natal and Dolphins in South Africa, but when he arrived had figured in more hockey internationals than first-class cricket matches. His inclination to occupy the crease as an opener, while making good use of his hockey-player's wrists, spelled the end for Stubbings, who served Derbyshire well for 13 seasons, scoring just over 7,500 first-class runs. Hinds, meanwhile, was capped and released in the same season. He did not score runs regularly enough, but the decision also took heed of the impending changes in regulations about Kolpak players. Greg Smith stepped up to become an integral part of the side and, like Wagg, offered both seam and spin. Their efforts were praiseworthy, but in 2010 South African slow left-armer Robin Peterson might influence some of the tight finishes in Derbyshire's favour. Dan Redfern, 19, showed up as the best of the home-grown players and, at Northampton, was a tantalising five runs short of being the youngest player to score a century for Derbyshire.

In the one-day competitions, Derbyshire were not good enough to be consistent. It was an area in which work was needed to remind them that they won trophies in the not-too-distant past. There was, however, a sense of stability about the club. They were running at a profit, and John Morris accepted a lengthened contract as head of cricket. Don Amott, the chairman, saluted Keith Loring as the best county chief executive "by a million miles". Development was planned at the ground, while work on the square has gone so well that Derbyshire felt able to play on a north–south axis in 2010, a year earlier than expected. Sun will stop play no more.

DERBYSHIRE RESULTS

All first-class matches – Played 16: Won 2, Lost 3, Drawn 11.
County Championship matches – Played 16: Won 2, Lost 3, Drawn 11.

LV County Championship, 6th in Division 2; Friends Provident Trophy, 3rd in Group D;
Pro40 League, 7th in Division 2; Twenty20 Cup, 6th in North Division.

COUNTY CHAMPIONSHIP AVERAGES, BATTING AND FIELDING

Cap		M	I	NO	R	HS	100s	50s	Avge	Ct/St
2008	C. J. L. Rogers§	13	21	1	1,461	222	6	4	73.05	21
	J. L. Sadler	3	4	3	71	27*	0	0	71.00	3
	W. L. Madsen¶	9	16	2	809	170*	1	3	57.78	8
2009	G. M. Smith¶	16	27	4	977	126	1	6	42.47	5
	G. T. Park	16	27	2	1,059	178*	2	8	42.36	14
2007	D. J. Pipe	14	18	5	493	64*	0	3	37.92	36/2
2009	W. W. Hinds¶	16	26	2	841	148	2	2	35.04	7
	P. S. Jones	9	9	3	199	54*	0	2	33.16	4
	I. D. Hunter	7	7	3	129	47	0	0	32.25	2
	D. J. Redfern	14	23	1	668	95	0	5	30.36	8
2001	S. D. Stubbings	7	11	1	296	83	0	1	29.60	4
	M. A. K. Lawson	6	5	2	75	24*	0	0	25.00	3
2007	G. G. Wagg	14	14	1	273	71	0	1	21.00	4
2007	T. Lungley†	4	4	1	62	33	0	0	20.66	2
	T. D. Groenewald¶...	9	11	1	194	50	0	1	19.40	2
	F. A. Klokker¶	2	4	1	53	32*	0	0	17.66	3
	J. Needham...........	5	7	3	55	20	0	0	13.75	3
	S. G. Law	2	4	0	39	29	0	0	9.75	2
	M. Hayward¶........	5	5	2	14	6	0	0	4.66	1
	J. L. Clare............	5	5	0	13	6	0	0	2.60	1

† *Born in Derbyshire.* § *Official overseas player.* ¶ *Other non-England-qualified player.*

BOWLING

	O	M	R	W	BB	5W/i	Avge
T. D. Groenewald	273.2	49	921	34	6-50	2	27.08
I. D. Hunter	181.4	33	593	21	5-46	2	28.23
P. S. Jones	318	65	970	30	5-35	1	32.33
G. M. Smith................	330.2	64	1,098	32	5-65	1	34.31
G. G. Wagg	521.3	85	1,773	47	6-35	3	37.72
J. L. Clare	119	27	407	10	3-64	0	40.70
M. Hayward................	123.2	19	472	11	4-99	0	42.90

Also bowled: W. W. Hinds 60–6–181–4; M. A. K. Lawson 105–15–333–4; T. Lungley 92.5–8–392–8; W. L. Madsen 18–2–67–0; J. Needham 101.4–11–353–7; G. T. Park 90.3–8–311–7; D. J. Pipe 1–0–5–0; D. J. Redfern 32–3–117–2.

COUNTY RECORDS

Highest score for:	274	G. Davidson v Lancashire at Manchester	1896
Highest score against:	343*	P. A. Perrin (Essex) at Chesterfield	1904
Leading run-scorer:	23,854	K. J. Barnett (avge 41.12)	1979–1998
Best bowling for:	10-40	W. Bestwick v Glamorgan at Cardiff	1921
Best bowling against:	10-45	R. L. Johnson (Middlesex) at Derby	1994
Leading wicket-taker:	1,670	H. L. Jackson (avge 17.11)	1947–1963
Highest total for:	801-8 dec	v Somerset at Taunton....................	2007
Highest total against:	662	by Yorkshire at Chesterfield	1898
Lowest total for:	16	v Nottinghamshire at Nottingham...........	1879
Lowest total against:	23	by Hampshire at Burton upon Trent	1958

ADDRESS

County Ground, Nottingham Road, Derby DE21 6DA (01332 388101; **email** info@
derbyshireccc.com). **Website** www.derbyshireccc.com.

OFFICIALS

Captain C. J. L. Rogers
Head of cricket J. E. Morris
Director of academy K. M. Krikken
President R. W. Taylor

Chairman D. K. Amott
Chief executive K. A. Loring
Head groundsman N. Godrich
Scorer J. M. Brown

HIGHEST SCORES ON FIRST-CLASS DEBUT FOR DERBYSHIRE

170*	**W. L. Madsen† v Gloucestershire at Cheltenham**	**2009**
155*	P. D. Bowler v Cambridge University at Cambridge	1988
136	I. J. Harvey v Essex at Chelmsford	2007
134	D. J. Cullinan v Sussex at Derby	1995
132	M. J. North v Somerset at Taunton	2006
130	D. J. Birch‡ v Cambridge UCCE at Cambridge	2007
	before lunch on first day	
119*	W. A. Dessau v Oxford University at Oxford	1995
118	R. J. Bailey v Leicestershire at Derby	2000
110*	A. J. Harvey-Walker†‡ v Oxford University at Burton upon Trent	1971
102*	D. R. Hewson† v Glamorgan at Cardiff	2002
102	C. R. Taylor v Oxford UCCE at Oxford	2006
100*	F. A. Klokker v Cambridge UCCE at Cambridge	2007

† In the second innings.

‡ On first-class debut in all cricket.

Bowler also hit 100 on his first-class debut for Leicestershire (v Hampshire at Leicester in 1986); Cullinan made 131 in his next innings, v Nottinghamshire at Nottingham; Harvey made 153 in his next match, v Somerset at Taunton. In his second match for Derbyshire, M. Azharuddin made 116* v Cambridge University at Cambridge in 1991, not having batted in the first.*

Research: David Baggett

At Chelmsford, April 15, 16, 17, 18. DERBYSHIRE drew with ESSEX.

DERBYSHIRE v SURREY

At Derby, April 22, 23, 24, 25. Derbyshire won by five wickets. Derbyshire 19 pts, Surrey 3 pts.
Toss: Surrey.

The Tiflex ball, with a propensity to swing that caused wicketkeepers to dive around, had much to do with the fall of 17 wickets on the first day; Jack Birkenshaw, the pitch liaison officer summoned, had no complaints about the pitch. Wagg took five wickets before lunch on his way to career-best figures, then batted well enough with Smith to give Derbyshire the lead before the close, after a burst of three for eight in 12 balls from Collins. The eighth-wicket pair carried their stand to 102, then shrewd hitting by last man Hunter stretched Derbyshire's lead to 143 before a composed century by Newman put Surrey back in the game. Park took three wickets and then helped Stubbings to move towards the target in an opening stand of 89 before Pipe – captain in the absence of Rogers – struck the winning runs. Surrey were also missing their captain, the injured Mark Butcher, while Mark Ramprakash was completing a suspension, and was seen only in the nets.

Close of play: First day, Derbyshire 152-7 (Smith 35, Wagg 22); Second day, Surrey 213-3 (Afzaal 28, Dernbach 5); Third day, Derbyshire 145-2 (Stubbings 66, Redfern 11).

Surrey

S. A. Newman c Lawson b Wagg	12	– c Pipe b Park	124
*M. J. Brown c Stubbings b Wagg	1	– c Law b Hunter	28
L. J. Evans c Law b Wagg	6	– b Clare	7
U. Afzaal b Wagg	3	– c and b Clare	59
†J. N. Batty lbw b Wagg	36	– (6) c Pipe b Hunter	9
J. G. E. Benning c Park b Smith	5	– (7) c Hunter b Smith	36
C. J. Jordan lbw b Wagg	6	– (8) b Wagg	3
C. P. Schofield lbw b Clare	10	– (9) not out	31
A. Nel b Smith	12	– (10) b Park	15
J. W. Dernbach not out	4	– (5) c Smith b Hunter	6
P. T. Collins c Pipe b Smith	1	– b Park	8
B 13, l-b 7, w 1, n-b 14	35	B 10, l-b 16, w 2, n-b 6	34

1/5 (2) 2/19 (3) 3/31 (4) 4/32 (1)   (53 overs) 131
5/43 (6) 6/58 (7) 7/124 (5) 8/125 (9)
9/126 (8) 10/131 (11)

1/83 (2) 2/129 (3)   (107.3 overs) 360
3/204 (4) 4/217 (5)
5/255 (4) 6/259 (6) 7/276 (8)
8/314 (9) 9/342 (10) 10/360 (11)

In the first innings Schofield, when 10, retired hurt at 99 and resumed at 125.

Wagg 15.4–5–35–6; Hunter 12–3–27–0; Clare 14–5–31–1; Smith 11.2–7–18–3. *Second Innings—* Wagg 29–6–94–1; Hunter 26–2–88–3; Smith 14–5–35–1; Clare 17–3–53–2; Lawson 12–1–39–0; Park 9.3–1–25–3.

Derbyshire

S. D. Stubbings c Batty b Collins	7	– b Schofield	83
G. T. Park c Jordan b Dernbach	4	– lbw b Collins	50
S. G. Law c Batty b Nel	0	– c Schofield b Nel	7
D. J. Redfern c Batty b Collins	28	– c Nel b Jordan	17
W. W. Hinds lbw b Jordan	26	– c Batty b Schofield	9
G. M. Smith not out	94	– not out	27
*†D. J. Pipe lbw b Collins	6	– not out	8
J. L. Clare b Collins	0		
G. G. Wagg lbw b Schofield	35		
M. A. K. Lawson c Batty b Jordan	0		
I. D. Hunter b Collins	47		
B 5, l-b 6, n-b 16	27	L-b 4, w 7, n-b 8	19

1/6 (2) 2/7 (3) 3/21 (1) 4/68 (5)   (71.4 overs) 274
5/76 (4) 6/88 (7) 7/88 (8) 8/190 (9)
9/191 (10) 10/274 (11)

1/89 (2)   (5 wkts, 75.5 overs) 220
2/116 (3) 3/166 (4)
4/183 (5) 5/192 (1)

Nel 7.4–1–26–1; Dernbach 18.2–4–64–1; Collins 19.4–5–75–5; Benning 3–0–5–0; Jordan 14–0–59–2; Afzaal 2–1–1–0; Schofield 7–1–33–1. *Second Innings*—Dernbach 16–6–38–0; Collins 15–3–47–1; Nel 14–6–23–1; Schofield 13.5–4–42–2; Jordan 11–2–44–1; Benning 5–1–22–0; Afzaal 1–1–0–0.

Umpires: T. E. Jesty and J. F. Steele.

At Cardiff, April 28, 29, 30, May 1. DERBYSHIRE drew with GLAMORGAN.

At Derby, May 6, 7, 8 (not first-class). **Drawn.** Toss: Leeds/Bradford UCCE. **Derbyshire 424-9 dec.** (S. D. Stubbings 125, W. W. Hinds 126, J. L. Clare 41, R. A. Whiteley 45*; T. S. Roland-Jones 5–81) **and 283-2 dec.** (R. A. Whiteley 103, J. L. Sadler 100*, F. D. Telo 53*); **Leeds/Bradford UCCE 219** (A. J. Blake 44, J. R. Moorhouse 34, J. A. Hawley 42; J. L. Clare 3-34, M. A. K. Lawson 3-58) **and 44-2.** County debut: A. Sheikh.

As Derbyshire tried to play batsmen into form, Steve Stubbings and Wavell Hinds put on 210 before Toby Roland-Jones took four wickets for eight runs in 19 balls. In the second innings Ross Whiteley, in his only match of the season for Derbyshire's first team until three Pro40 appearances in September, retired out after making 103 in 224 minutes as practice took precedence over a contest.

DERBYSHIRE v GLOUCESTERSHIRE

At Chesterfield, June 6, 7, 8, 9. Drawn. Derbyshire 10 pts, Gloucestershire 11 pts. Toss: Gloucestershire.

The only surprise was that 99 balls were sent down on the second day at a time when the rest of the county was experiencing heavy rain. Bowlers toiled when play began in earnest. The pitch was placid and, despite the earlier rain, the outfield remained slick. Marshall, in prime form from the start, hit 21 fours and put on 233 for the third wicket with Gidman, whose second century of the season put a dismal 2008 further behind him, although he was content to stay in his partner's shadow. After being delayed in Australia by visa problems, Rogers responded with a century in his first Championship innings of the summer, receiving significant help from Redfern (who made his highest score) and Park, before sensible hitting by Lungley and Hunter ensured maximum batting points.

Close of play: First day, No play; Second day, Gloucestershire 58-1 (Hodnett 28, Marshall 30); Third day, Derbyshire 19-0 (Stubbings 2, Rogers 17).

Gloucestershire

Kadeer Ali c Lawson b Hunter	0	†S. D. Snell not out	4
G. P. Hodnett c Park b Wagg	31	B 3, l-b 8, w 10	21
H. J. H. Marshall c Pipe b Hunter	158		
*A. P. R. Gidman b Hinds	135	1/1 (1) (5 wkts dec, 107.5 overs)	403
C. G. Taylor not out	38	2/73 (2) 3/306 (3)	
C. M. Spearman b Lungley	16	4/361 (4) 5/390 (6)	

J. Lewis, A. J. Ireland, S. P. Kirby and R. K. J. Dawson did not bat.

Wagg 24–5–71–1; Hunter 15–3–65–2; Lungley 20.5–0–88–1; Smith 17–2–64–0; Lawson 10–0–46–0; Hinds 11–1–28–1; Park 10–0–30–0.

Derbyshire

S. D. Stubbings b Ireland	6	T. Lungley not out	29
*C. J. L. Rogers lbw b Lewis	104	I. D. Hunter not out	29
G. T. Park c Snell b Hodnett	62		
D. J. Redfern st Snell b Taylor	74	L-b 10, w 6	16
W. W. Hinds c Snell b Ireland	30		
G. M. Smith c Taylor b Kirby	24	1/31 (1) 2/177 (2) (8 wkts dec, 95 overs) 402
†D. J. Pipe c and b Dawson	0	3/201 (3) 4/262 (5)
G. G. Wagg c Spearman b Lewis	28	5/293 (4) 6/298 (7) 7/334 (8) 8/345 (6)

M. A. K. Lawson did not bat.

Kirby 22–8–51–1; Ireland 14–2–77–2; Lewis 17–3–71–2; Dawson 25–3–118–1; Gidman 5–1–23–0; Marshall 1–0–4–0; Hodnett 6–0–41–1; Taylor 5–3–7–1.

Umpires: S. A. Garratt and M. A. Gough.

DERBYSHIRE v GLAMORGAN

At Derby, June 11, 12, 13, 14. Drawn. Derbyshire 10 pts, Glamorgan 10 pts. Toss: Derbyshire.

Both teams had chances to take a grip but were unable to accept them, and Glamorgan were ultimately frustrated by Hinds's first Championship century. After a good start to their first innings, Derbyshire wavered, despite Powell missing three chances at slip, and not for the first time were grateful for Hunter's batting during a last-wicket stand of 62 with Groenewald, who was playing his first first-class match for Derbyshire after 13 one-day appearances for them. Dalrymple was again the obstacle: his immaculate century took his total against Derbyshire to 383 in four innings in Championship and one-day cricket in 2009. With no specialist spinner picked, Wagg had to employ his variations, but Derbyshire were on the ropes at the end of the third day, only 132 ahead with six wickets down. Croft dismissed Wagg to take his 100th Championship wicket against Derbyshire, but nobody could shift Hinds, who batted with restraint for almost five hours in his first first-class century since January 2007 (for Jamaica). With excellent support from Lungley and Groenewald, Derbyshire were able to set a steep target and escape.

Close of play: First day, Derbyshire 261-9 (Groenewald 10, Hunter 8); Second day, Glamorgan 225-6 (Dalrymple 105, Croft 24); Third day, Derbyshire 142-6 (Hinds 42, Wagg 0).

Derbyshire

*C. J. L. Rogers c Wallace b Cosgrove	27	– (2) c Cosker b Shantry	21
S. D. Stubbings lbw b Croft	43	– (1) lbw b Croft	49
G. T. Park c Kruger b Cosker	76	– b Dalrymple	10
D. J. Redfern c Powell b Shantry	11	– c Powell b Dalrymple	1
W. W. Hinds lbw b Cosgrove	30	– not out	119
G. M. Smith b Cosgrove	12	– run out	0
†D. J. Pipe b Kruger	22	– c Rees b Croft	10
G. G. Wagg st Wallace b Croft	0	– c Dalrymple b Croft	4
T. Lungley lbw b Croft	0	– lbw b Croft	33
T. D. Groenewald c Powell b Croft	24	– not out	27
I. D. Hunter not out	33		
B 9, l-b 16, n-b 4	29	B 6, l-b 7, w 1, n-b 6	20

1/56 (1) 2/129 (2) 3/150 (4) (120.4 overs) 307	1/44 (2) (8 wkts dec, 107 overs) 294
4/191 (3) 5/215 (5) 6/222 (6)	2/55 (3)
7/227 (8) 8/227 (9) 9/245 (7)	3/59 (4) 4/118 (1) 5/118 (6)
10/307 (10)	6/139 (7) 7/149 (8) 8/213 (9)
120 overs: 307-9	

Harris 20–4–59–0; Kruger 20–4–46–1; Shantry 18–2–44–1; Cosgrove 8–1–30–3; Cosker 17–5–29–1; Croft 37.4–14–74–4. *Second Innings*—Kruger 6–0–56–0; Harris 5–0–16–0; Shantry 4–1–15–1; Dalrymple 23–4–73–2; Croft 42–13–62–4; Cosker 27–5–59–0.

Glamorgan

G. P. Rees lbw b Smith	42	– c Redfern b Wagg	0
M. J. Cosgrove lbw b Wagg	0	– not out	74
B. J. Wright lbw b Lungley	14	– b Wagg	4
M. J. Powell c Park b Lungley	0	– not out	42
*J. W. M. Dalrymple c Park b Hunter	128		
†M. A. Wallace c Pipe b Wagg	0		
J. A. R. Harris c Pipe b Smith	20		
R. D. B. Croft c and b Groenewald	28		
D. A. Cosker not out	46		
A. J. Shantry lbw b Smith	13		
G. J-P. Kruger c Lungley b Wagg	0		
B 7, l-b 9, w 4, n-b 6	26	B 8, l-b 2, n-b 2	16

1/1 (2) 2/31 (3) 3/35 (4) 4/117 (1) (111 overs) 317   1/2 (1) 2/10 (3) (2 wkts, 38 overs) 136
5/118 (6) 6/166 (7) 7/236 (8)
8/273 (5) 9/316 (10) 10/317 (11)

Wagg 35–6–87–3; Hunter 12–0–39–1; Lungley 18–2–67–2; Groenewald 18–3–45–1; Hinds 4–0–10–0; Smith 21–7–41–3; Park 3–0–12–0. *Second Innings*—Wagg 13–1–46–2; Smith 5–1–13–0; Lungley 3–1–4–0; Hunter 7–2–17–0; Redfern 5–0–23–0; Groenewald 4–1–18–0; Park 1–0–5–0.

Umpires: T. E. Jesty and D. J. Millns.

DERBYSHIRE v LEICESTERSHIRE

At Derby, June 30, July 1, 2, 3. Drawn. Derbyshire 11 pts, Leicestershire 12 pts. Toss: Derbyshire.

Tom New, who had endured a difficult time on loan to Derbyshire in 2008, now showed his pedigree against them with a fine all-round performance – six catches behind the stumps and two half-centuries in front of them. He was in a position to shape an interesting finish had rain not washed out the final day. At the start, Derbyshire failed to control the swing in humid conditions, and Ackerman's first eight scoring strokes were boundaries. Allenby, who just missed his first Championship century since September 2006, built a sound position in a partnership of 177 with Taylor. Hunter took five wickets, although he admitted his bowling was a mixed bag. Derbyshire dug in, with avoiding the follow-on their main objective, but the third day was more eventful: 15 wickets went down. O'Brien belatedly found that a fuller length brought greater rewards, and took the last six wickets of Derbyshire's innings. By the close, Leicestershire were 256 ahead with three wickets standing, and all outcomes were possible until rain intervened.

Close of play: First day, Leicestershire 341-5 (Taylor 86, New 24); Second day, Derbyshire 188-2 (Park 70, Redfern 36); Third day, Leicestershire 209-7 (New 63, O'Brien 0).

Leicestershire

M. A. G. Boyce b Hunter	9	– c Hunter b Hayward	7
J. J. Cobb lbw b Wagg	8	– c Pipe b Wagg	4
*H. H. Dippenaar b Hunter	38	– run out	1
H. D. Ackerman c Pipe b Hunter	49	– c Wagg b Needham	31
J. Allenby run out	96	– c Pipe b Hunter	52
J. W. A. Taylor lbw b Hunter	89	– lbw b Wagg	4
†T. J. New c Stubbings b Smith	66	– not out	63
G. W. Walker lbw b Hunter	3	– c sub (B. Slater) b Wagg	13
I. E. O'Brien c Pipe b Hayward	5	– not out	0
A. J. Harris b Wagg	4		
H. F. Gurney not out	1		
B 16, l-b 17, w 7, n-b 4	44	B 6, l-b 10, w 2, n-b 16	34

1/21 (2) 2/25 (1) 3/115 (4) (118.1 overs) 412   1/7 (2) 2/19 (3) (7 wkts, 51 overs) 209
4/116 (3) 5/293 (5) 6/349 (6)   3/47 (1) 4/73 (4)
7/375 (8) 8/386 (9) 9/401 (10) 10/401 (7)   5/92 (6) 6/143 (5) 7/208 (8)

Wagg 22.1–6–72–2; Hayward 25–6–68–1; Hunter 26–6–82–5; Smith 19–5–64–1; Needham 12–0–51–0; Hinds 7–1–24–0; Park 7–0–18–0. *Second Innings*—Wagg 15–3–70–3; Hunter 7–2–34–1; Hinds 5–0–15–0; Hayward 10–0–36–1; Needham 11–3–29–1; Smith 3–0–9–0.

Derbyshire

*C. J. L. Rogers c New b Gurney	47	I. D. Hunter not out	3
S. D. Stubbings lbw b Gurney	19	M. Hayward c New b O'Brien	0
G. T. Park c Dippenaar b Walker	72		
D. J. Redfern c New b Allenby	50	B 8, l-b 5, n-b 10	23
W. W. Hinds c New b O'Brien	40		
G. M. Smith c Allenby b O'Brien	40	1/60 (1) 2/103 (2)	(113.3 overs) 365
†D. J. Pipe c New b O'Brien	49	3/207 (3) 4/213 (4)	
G. G. Wagg c Ackerman b O'Brien	16	5/279 (5) 6/336 (6) 7/345 (7)	
J. Needham c New b O'Brien	6	8/356 (8) 9/365 (9) 10/365 (11)	

O'Brien 29.3–3–87–6; Harris 20–4–92–0; Allenby 18–4–30–1; Gurney 20–4–68–2; Walker 26–7–75–1.

Umpires: N. G. Cowley and V. A. Holder.

At Northampton, July 7, 8, 9, 10. DERBYSHIRE drew with NORTHAMPTONSHIRE.

At Cheltenham, July 12, 13, 14, 15. DERBYSHIRE beat GLOUCESTERSHIRE by 185 runs.

DERBYSHIRE v MIDDLESEX

At Derby, July 21, 22, 23, 24. Drawn. Derbyshire 8 pts, Middlesex 8 pts. Toss: Middlesex.

Kevin Pietersen's Achilles injury (he had an operation on it during this match) was an invitation to English batsmen to show their credentials, and Shah did so with a masterly century. Sadly for him, it provoked no response from the selectors. After the first day was washed out, batting was tricky, but Middlesex did not make full use of the conditions in the morning. Later, they did have Derbyshire in trouble at 139 for seven, with Murtagh on the way to career-best figures. But, as on several occasions through the season, Derbyshire's tailenders built a competitive score, with Groenewald and Jones adding 91. Then Shah appeared to be playing in a different game from the rest of the Middlesex batsmen, none of whom reached 20. He was in control while the others came and went, with Wagg, again mixing seam and spin, taking five wickets. Pipe, who had turned an ankle while batting, was replaced as wicketkeeper by Tom Poynton. A surprise declaration by Udal opened the game up. Rogers immediately went on the attack – his 76 came from 82 balls – and ultimately offered a target of 280 in 68 overs. A shower cut out 18 overs but, after a good start from Robson and Compton, Shah scented victory, hitting 23 from 13 balls... before the rain returned. Hinds was awarded his county cap at lunch on the third day.

Close of play: First day, No play; Second day, Middlesex 16-1 (Compton 0, Shah 13); Third day, Derbyshire 138-2 (Madsen 34, Redfern 2).

Derbyshire

*C. J. L. Rogers lbw b Murtagh	0	– c Robson b Malan	76
W. L. Madsen c Morgan b Finn	43	– c Shah b Udal	71
G. T. Park c Richardson b Finn	32	– c Finn b Udal	16
D. J. Redfern lbw b Murtagh	13	– c Malan b Udal	43
W. W. Hinds lbw b Murtagh	7	– not out	25
G. M. Smith c Nash b Murtagh	6	– (7) c Robson b Finn	4
†D. J. Pipe c Nash b Murtagh	7		
G. G. Wagg c Nash b Murtagh	14	– (6) c Malan b Finn	5
T. D. Groenewald c Morgan b Murtagh	48	– (8) c Nash b Finn	7
P. S. Jones not out	54		
M. Hayward b Finn	6		
B 4, l-b 5, n-b 8	17	L-b 3, w 2, n-b 6	11

1/6 (1) 2/83 (2) 3/92 (3) 4/106 (5)   (75.4 overs) 247   1/97 (1)   (7 wkts dec, 61.1 overs) 258
5/109 (4) 6/120 (6) 7/139 (8)   2/130 (3)
8/230 (9) 9/230 (7) 10/247 (11)   3/199 (4) 4/220 (2) 5/231 (6)
                                                                                            6/241 (7) 7/258 (8)

In the first innings Pipe, when 7, retired hurt at 120-5 and resumed at 230-8.

Murtagh 22–5–82–7; Finn 18.4–0–59–3; Richardson 15–6–32–0; Berg 15–5–45–0; Udal 5–1–20–0. *Second Innings*—Murtagh 11–1–52–0; Finn 10.1–0–49–3; Richardson 12–0–53–0; Berg 4–0–19–0; Udal 16–3–53–3; Malan 8–1–29–1.

Middlesex

S. D. Robson c Rogers b Wagg	1	– run out	29
N. R. D. Compton b Hayward	6	– not out	62
O. A. Shah not out	129	– not out	23
E. J. G. Morgan c sub (T. Poynton) b Wagg	7		
D. J. Malan lbw b Jones	11		
†D. C. Nash c Redfern b Wagg	9		
G. K. Berg b Wagg	12		
*S. D. Udal b Groenewald	0		
T. J. Murtagh c sub (T. Poynton) b Groenewald	5		
S. T. Finn b Wagg	8		
A. Richardson not out	18		
B 7, w 1, n-b 12	20	B 1, l-b 3, w 3	7

1/1 (1) 2/39 (2)   (9 wkts dec, 68.4 overs) 226   1/86 (1)   (1 wkt, 24 overs) 121
3/62 (4) 4/107 (5) 5/141 (6)
6/157 (7) 7/158 (8) 8/168 (9) 9/195 (10)

Jones 12.4–3–30–1; Wagg 30–4–88–5; Hayward 11–3–43–1; Groenewald 13–2–41–2; Smith 2–0–17–0. *Second Innings*—Hayward 4–1–13–0; Wagg 12–0–56–0; Jones 3–1–12–0; Smith 3–0–19–0; Groenewald 2–0–17–0.

Umpires: N. G. B. Cook and J. H. Evans.

At Canterbury, July 31, August 1, 2, 3. DERBYSHIRE lost to KENT by three wickets.

At Whitgift School, Croydon, August 6, 7, 8, 9. DERBYSHIRE drew with SURREY.

At Leicester, August 11, 12, 13, 14. DERBYSHIRE drew with LEICESTERSHIRE. *Derbyshire are denied victory by an eighth-wicket stand of 195 between James Taylor and Jigar Naik.*

DERBYSHIRE v NORTHAMPTONSHIRE

At Chesterfield, August 19, 20, 21. Northamptonshire won by two wickets. Northamptonshire 18 pts, Derbyshire 5 pts. Toss: Derbyshire. Championship debut: J. A. Brooks.

As in their previous match at Leicester (and, later, at Uxbridge), Derbyshire achieved a winning position but were unable to see it through. Northamptonshire's narrow victory improved their chances of promotion – especially as, at the time, they had played two fewer games than Derbyshire. There was pace and life in the Queen's Park pitch to encourage the seam bowlers. Pipe, going for the bold approach and hitting 58 from 34 balls, with 12 fours, made most impact as Derbyshire were bowled out by tea on the first day. Rob White adopted a similar approach as Northamptonshire ended only nine behind, Groenewald's disciplined bowling earning him six wickets. He followed this with a valuable half-century to set a testing target in the conditions. When Northamptonshire were 168 for seven, the odds were on Derbyshire, for whom Jones took four wickets. Some sharp chances were missed, and Lucas and Graeme White, admirably determined, held out for victory.

Close of play: First day, Northamptonshire 137-3 (Lucas 1, Wakely 1); Second day, Derbyshire 212-8 (Groenewald 45, Lawson 7).

Derbyshire

*C. J. L. Rogers lbw b Brooks	27	– b Lucas 14
W. L. Madsen c R. A. White b van der Wath	19	– c R. A. White b van der Wath 2
G. T. Park c Peters b Brooks	55	– c O'Brien b van der Wath 3
G. M. Smith c Wessels b Hall	25	– c O'Brien b Lucas 19
W. W. Hinds b van der Wath	10	– c Brooks b Hall 36
D. J. Redfern c O'Brien b van der Wath	4	– c Hall b Willey 28
†D. J. Pipe b Lucas	58	– c and b van der Wath 10
T. D. Groenewald c O'Brien b Brooks	1	– b van der Wath 50
P. S. Jones b Brooks	22	– c Hall b Brooks 27
M. A. K. Lawson c van der Wath b Lucas	16	– b Lucas 21
M. Hayward not out	4	– not out 2
B 1, l-b 2, w 1, n-b 10	14	B 4, l-b 3, w 2, n-b 12 21

1/47 (2) 2/57 (1) 3/108 (4)   (58.3 overs) 255
4/129 (5) 5/133 (6) 6/179 (3)
7/193 (8) 8/229 (7) 9/233 (9) 10/255 (10)

1/6 (2) 2/14 (3)   (62.4 overs) 233
3/36 (1) 4/53 (4)
5/84 (5) 6/102 (7) 7/140 (6) 8/203 (9)
9/227 (10) 10/233 (8)

Van der Wath 19–3–92–3; Lucas 13.3–3–56–2; Brooks 16–1–76–4; Willey 2–0–17–0; Hall 8–2–11–1. *Second Innings*—van der Wath 16.4–2–55–4; Lucas 17–3–65–3; Brooks 10–0–38–1; Hall 11–3–34–1; Willey 4–0–21–1; G. G. White 4–0–13–0.

Northamptonshire

S. D. Peters lbw b Groenewald	39	– c Pipe b Hinds 13
N. J. O'Brien c Pipe b Groenewald	15	– c Pipe b Jones 13
R. A. White lbw b Hinds	62	– c Pipe b Groenewald 37
D. S. Lucas c Pipe b Smith	14	– (10) not out. 19
A. G. Wakely c Pipe b Hinds	26	– (4) b Jones 33
†M. H. Wessels c Rogers b Smith	3	– (5) c Park b Jones 31
*A. J. Hall c Rogers b Groenewald	36	– (6) c Rogers b Hayward 20
D. J. Willey c Hinds b Groenewald	12	– (7) c Rogers b Jones 42
J. J. van der Wath c Redfern b Groenewald	2	– (8) c Rogers b Hayward 0
G. G. White b Groenewald	0	– (9) not out. 29
J. A. Brooks not out	0	
B 9, l-b 12, n-b 16	37	L-b 5, w 1, n-b 2. 8

1/42 (2) 2/131 (3) 3/135 (1)   (67.1 overs) 246
4/164 (4) 5/170 (6) 6/224 (7)
7/232 (5) 8/245 (9) 9/245 (10) 10/246 (8)

1/21 (2)   (8 wkts, 61.2 overs) 245
2/61 (1) 3/83 (3)
4/130 (4) 5/137 (5) 6/168 (6)
7/168 (8) 8/208 (7)

Jones 15–4–51–0; Hayward 15–2–52–0; Groenewald 19.1–6–61–6; Smith 9–1–42–2; Hinds 9–2–19–2. *Second Innings*—Jones 22–2–79–4; Hayward 9.2–0–66–2; Hinds 12–1–38–1; Groenewald 14–1–46–1; Smith 4–2–11–0.

Umpires: N. G. B. Cook and N. A. Mallender.

DERBYSHIRE v KENT

At Derby, September 2, 3, 4, 5. Drawn. Derbyshire 12 pts, Kent 7 pts. Toss: Derbyshire.

Geraint Jones made the point that more than one English wicketkeeper can bat, with his fifth century of the season on a curtailed first day. His composure stood out in an unusually erratic Kent batting display, provoked by fine bowling from Steffan Jones and useful interventions by Lungley, back from a loan spell with Lancashire. The rapid fall of Kent's last five wickets, while only 47 runs were added, opened the way for some dominant batting. Rogers, ending the season in majestic form, and Madsen started with an opening stand of 216. Rogers went on to a double-century, facing 277 balls in 339 minutes and hitting 27 fours and a six in all, and there was widespread pleasure when Park completed his first century for Derbyshire. He had reached 50 seven times and was beginning to wonder but, once the hundred was in the bag, he showed an impressive range of strokes and hit 22 fours, all told. For the first time, a Derbyshire innings contained four century partnerships. Rogers declared with a lead of 302 but, on an immaculate batting surface, a Kent capitulation was unlikely. Sure enough, they gave Derbyshire an unrewarding last day, Key and van Jaarsveld scoring centuries in an unbroken partnership of 194.

Close of play: First day, Kent 232-5 (Jones 107, Blake 30); Second day, Derbyshire 186-0 (Rogers 116, Madsen 65); Third day, Kent 44-1 (Key 17, Jones 15).

Kent

S. A. Northeast c Hinds b Lungley	7	– c Smith b Lungley 6
*R. W. T. Key lbw b Jones	30	– not out 141
†G. O. Jones c Madsen b Lungley	108	– c Madsen b Smith 60
M. van Jaarsveld c Hinds b Jones	4	– not out 101
D. I. Stevens c Sadler b Lungley	16	
J. M. Kemp c Pipe b Jones	19	
A. J. Blake c Park b Jones	44	
J. C. Tredwell not out	22	
S. J. Cook c and b Wagg	2	
A. Khan lbw b Groenewald	0	
P. D. Edwards c Pipe b Jones	5	
L-b 15, w 1, n-b 8	24	B 9, l-b 2, n-b 14 25

1/34 (1) 2/46 (2) 3/68 (4) 4/121 (5) (83.5 overs) 281 1/6 (1) 2/139 (3) (2 wkts, 88 overs) 333
5/158 (6) 6/234 (3) 7/258 (7)
8/263 (9) 9/264 (10) 10/281 (11)

Lungley 17–1–56–3; Wagg 21–3–86–1; Jones 20.5–6–35–5; Groenewald 16–2–52–1; Smith 6–0–27–0; Park 3–0–10–0. *Second Innings*—Lungley 11–1–55–1; Wagg 20–2–80–0; Jones 10–3–21–0; Groenewald 14–1–57–0; Smith 20–2–55–1; Park 6–0–27–0; Madsen 6–0–22–0; Pipe 1–0–5–0.

Derbyshire

*C. J. L. Rogers lbw b Khan	208
W. L. Madsen c Jones b Khan	75
G. T. Park not out	178
G. M. Smith c Stevens b Khan	59
W. W. Hinds c Kemp b Khan	18
J. L. Sadler not out	24
B 7, l-b 11, w 1, n-b 2	21

1/216 (2) (4 wkts dec, 132 overs) 583
2/341 (1) 3/459 (4)
4/483 (5) 120 overs: 472-3

†D. J. Pipe, G. G. Wagg, T. D. Groenewald, T. Lungley and P. S. Jones did not bat.

Khan 26–3–110–4; Cook 28–4–94–0; Edwards 16–4–84–0; Kemp 25–5–79–0; Tredwell 31–3–137–0; Stevens 4–0–35–0; van Jaarsveld 2–0–26–0.

Umpires: V. A. Holder and T. E. Jesty.

At Uxbridge, September 15, 16, 17, 18. DERBYSHIRE drew with MIDDLESEX. *Middlesex's last pair survive the final 16 balls.*

DERBYSHIRE v ESSEX

At Derby, September 23, 24, 25, 26. Essex won by five wickets. Essex 20 pts, Derbyshire 8 pts. Toss: Essex.

The situation was clear. Essex, three points ahead of Northamptonshire, would be promoted if they scored 20 points in beating Derbyshire. For their part, Derbyshire had a chance if they won and other results went their way. Home hopes died on the third day, when Northamptonshire completed their rout of Leicestershire. Groenewald was ruled out by swine flu (his problems were revealed on a flippant poster in the dressing-room window) and others felt seedy – but Rogers provided the perfect tonic with his second double-century in successive home games. This time he batted for 410 minutes, faced 329 balls, and stroked 31 fours and a six. Danish Kaneria polished off the innings with the first hat-trick of his career; a maiden century by Westley, well supported by Walker, kept Essex in touch before their declaration. It was then a question of what target Derbyshire, still keen to end with a win, would set. It turned out to be 359 from 65 overs, a long chase at 5.5 an over. As Essex won by five wickets with five overs to spare, it was made to look easy, but it became reality only thanks to a remarkable innings from ten Doeschate. He pummelled an unbeaten 108 from 59 balls, hitting eight sixes and nine fours, and drove Essex to promotion by a single point. Until his crucial partnership of 156 in 17.3 overs with Pettini, Derbyshire were favourites – but in the end it was joy for Essex, and dark looks from Northampton.

Close of play: First day, Derbyshire 368-3 (Rogers 204, Hinds 19); Second day, Essex 166-2 (Westley 90, Walker 50); Third day, Derbyshire 103-3 (Park 25, Hinds 11).

Derbyshire

*C. J. L. Rogers c Masters b Napier	222	– c Cook b Danish Kaneria	42
W. L. Madsen lbw b Wright	16	– c Walker b Wright	0
G. T. Park c Walker b Wright	57	– not out	103
D. J. Redfern c Maunders b Wright	48		
W. W. Hinds b Masters	37	– b Danish Kaneria	36
J. L. Sadler c Walker b Masters	8	– not out	27
G. M. Smith b Danish Kaneria	6	– (4) c and b Danish Kaneria	16
†D. J. Pipe c Walker b Wright	21		
G. G. Wagg lbw b Danish Kaneria	0		
J. L. Clare lbw b Danish Kaneria	0		
P. S. Jones not out	19		
B 5, l-b 24, w 1, n-b 10	40	L-b 8, n-b 8	16

1/61 (2) 2/182 (3) 3/312 (4) (128.4 overs) 474
4/400 (1) 5/420 (6) 6/429 (5)
7/439 (7) 8/439 (9) 9/439 (10)
10/474 (8) 120 overs: 429-6

1/20 (2) (4 wkts dec, 64 overs) 240
2/63 (1) 3/85 (4)
4/143 (5)

Masters 33–10–72–2; Wright 27.4–5–97–4; Napier 34–6–111–1; Danish Kaneria 22–1–114–3; ten Doeschate 7–1–34–0; Westley 5–1–17–0. *Second Innings*—Napier 10–2–30–0; Wright 16–2–59–1; ten Doeschate 5–0–26–0; Danish Kaneria 17–1–36–3; Westley 3–0–3–0; Cook 7–0–40–0; Pettini 6–0–38–0.

Essex

J. K. Maunders c Rogers b Wagg	5	– c Wagg b Smith	55
A. N. Cook c Pipe b Wagg	8	– c Sadler b Clare	25
T. Westley c Pipe b Jones	132	– c Jones b Wagg	40
M. J. Walker c Hinds b Clare	75	– c Sadler b Smith	18
*M. L. Pettini c Madsen b Jones	14	– not out	85
†J. S. Foster c Redfern b Clare	15	– c Park b Smith	13
R. N. ten Doeschate run out	41	– not out	108
G. R. Napier c Pipe b Clare	0		
C. J. C. Wright not out	24		
Danish Kaneria c Madsen b Wagg	10		
B 11, l-b 6, w 1, n-b 14	32	B 5, l-b 4, w 2, n-b 4	15

1/9 (1) 2/14 (2)   (9 wkts dec, 107.5 overs) 356   1/45 (2)   (5 wkts, 60 overs) 359
3/238 (4) 4/244 (3) 5/271 (5)   2/114 (3) 3/139 (1)
6/299 (6) 7/299 (8) 8/346 (7) 9/356 (10)   4/160 (4) 5/203 (6)

D. D. Masters did not bat.

Jones 28–3–87–2; Wagg 31.5–10–79–3; Smith 10–0–41–0; Clare 23–4–64–3; Park 9–0–43–0; Hinds 6–0–25–0. *Second Innings*—Jones 11–0–68–0; Wagg 19–0–102–1; Clare 6–0–35–1; Smith 18–0–96–3; Park 1–0–12–0; Madsen 4–0–29–0; Redfern 1–0–8–0.

Umpires: S. A. Garratt and R. A. Kettleborough. Third umpire: R. J. Bailey.

DURHAM

A class of their own

TIM WELLOCK

Durham have gone from doormats to dominant force, whipping boys to whippers. When they won the Championship for the first time in 2008, it was considered something of a fairytale; suddenly, in 2009, they were in a class of their own.

Their winning margin of 47 points was a record since the advent of two divisions in 2000, even though their last two games were drawn with the title already secured. Durham were unbeaten, won twice as many matches as any other first division side, and conceded a first-innings deficit only once, at Headingley. The £500,000 prize money for retaining the title was a five-fold increase, designed to counter the possibility of counties concentrating on chasing Twenty20 riches. It didn't work: while Durham strengthened, largely through the acquisition of Ian Blackwell, the rest went backwards.

Durham were under pressure in four-day cricket only when Worcestershire's Kabir Ali – during the brief period in mid-season when he was fit – had them rocking on 59 for six at Riverside, and when they trailed by 135 against Yorkshire. They recovered to beat Worcestershire by five wickets, and at Headingley comfortably turned the tables by scoring 421 for nine declared in their second innings. That was one of several cases where they played on a used pitch that became increasingly dead; coach Geoff Cook thought too many chemicals were being used. While draws abounded elsewhere, six of Durham's eight wins came at Riverside, but Cook disagreed with the perception that they played on "result" wickets: "Our pitches are getting better and better. If you bat well you can score runs, and they are also now taking spin." That point was highlighted by Blackwell taking five for seven against his former Somerset colleagues. He finished with 43 Championship wickets, ten more than his fellow slow left-armer David Graveney's record haul for a Durham spinner in 1993.

No other side came close to matching Durham's bowling. After six Championship matches – one of which he missed to make his Test debut – Graham Onions had 40 wickets. His nearest rival in the country was team-mate Steve Harmison, on 30. Onions played only two more Championship games because of international duties, but that allowed Liam Plunkett to come to the fore. The phrase "world-beater one day, panel-beater the next" could have been coined for Plunkett, but his consistency steadily improved, and he averaged 44 with the bat; by September he looked worthy of his return to the England squad. Harmison finished as the leading wicket-taker, with 51, while Mark Davies, Callum Thorp and Mitch Claydon played their parts.

After having the better of three draws at the start of the season, Durham won four in succession to go 18 points clear. They then won three of the next five, to look unassailable. They twice beat runners-up Nottinghamshire by an innings, clinching the title in the home encounter, which was packed with landmarks. Durham's 648 for five was their highest total, beating 645 for six at Lord's in 2002; there were four century-makers in a Durham innings for the first time, in Michael Di Venuto, Kyle Coetzer, Shivnarine Chanderpaul and Dale Benkenstein; Benkenstein's hundred was his 15th for Durham, taking him to the top of their list ahead of John Morris and Paul Collingwood; and victory gave Durham eight Championship wins, beating the seven they achieved when finishing second to Sussex two years earlier.

Ian Blackwell

Matthew Lewis, Getty Images

In his first season after leaving Somerset, Blackwell scored an unbeaten century on county debut against MCC, followed up with 801 Championship runs and 43 wickets, and was voted player of the year by the members. It was also a memorable summer for Di Venuto, whose 254 not out at Hove to Sussex was a personal best. He went on to equal Collingwood's club record of six Championship centuries in a season, and raised the record run-aggregate to 1,601. It was hardly surprising that, by throwing his heart and soul into the captaincy, Will Smith sacrificed some of his 2008 batting form. But it scarcely mattered. With Phil Mustard showing greater consistency in all forms of the game, and Plunkett at No. 8, the batting had plenty of depth.

Chanderpaul, initially expected in early July, was delayed until mid-August; though he averaged 236 in six innings, his contribution was effectively irrelevant. The title would have been won without him, but the fact that he, Di Venuto and Benkenstein sat on top of the averages underlined the one disappointment: the lack of progress by home-grown batsmen to follow Collingwood.

Of two Newcastle boys, Gordon Muchall, who played no Championship cricket in 2008, was given the chance to re-establish himself but could not build on an early century. Mark Stoneman opened for most of the season, making only one fifty, though he remained highly rated, and was still only 22.

Leg-spinning all-rounder Scott Borthwick made an impressive first-class debut in the penultimate match, at the Rose Bowl, and became a regular member of the one-day side, as did Ben Harmison, who did not appear in the Championship. The one-day emphasis switched towards youth after a disappointing start in the FPT. Momentum picked up in the Twenty20 once Australian 20-over specialist David Warner arrived. But after scraping into the quarter-finals, Durham lost heavily at Canterbury, where they had clinched the four-day title so memorably the previous year.

Given the choice of Championship glory or Twenty20 riches, no one at Durham was in any doubt about which they preferred.

DURHAM RESULTS

All first-class matches – Played 18: Won 9, Lost 0, Drawn 9.
County Championship matches – Played 16: Won 8, Lost 0, Drawn 8.

LV County Championship, winners in Division 1; Friends Provident Trophy, 4th in Group C;
Pro40 League, 6th in Division 1; Twenty20 Cup, q-f.

COUNTY CHAMPIONSHIP AVERAGES, BATTING AND FIELDING

Cap		M	I	NO	R	HS	100s	50s	Avge	Ct/St
	S. Chanderpaul§	5	6	4	472	201*	3	0	236.00	3
	M. J. Di Venuto¶	16	26	6	1,601	254*	6	5	80.05	23
2005	D. M. Benkenstein¶	16	22	0	1,155	181	5	4	52.50	10
	L. E. Plunkett	12	13	3	400	94*	0	3	44.44	12
	P. Mustard†	16	20	6	592	94*	0	5	42.28	61/1
	I. D. Blackwell	16	22	2	801	158	1	6	40.05	4
	K. J. Coetzer	6	9	1	284	107	1	0	35.50	7
	W. R. Smith	15	23	2	700	150	2	3	33.33	6
2005	G. J. Muchall	11	17	2	497	106*	1	2	33.13	13
	M. D. Stoneman	11	18	0	376	64	0	1	20.88	10
	C. D. Thorp¶	12	12	0	207	42	0	0	17.25	15
	M. E. Claydon	10	11	1	110	38	0	0	11.00	3
2005	M. Davies†	9	8	4	37	16*	0	0	9.25	2
	G. Onions†‡	7	8	4	25	12*	0	0	6.25	3
1999	S. J. Harmison‡	13	10	1	16	10*	0	0	1.77	2

Also batted: G. R. Breese¶ (cap 2005) (1 match) 48 (2 ct); S. G. Borthwick† (1 match) 26*.

† *Born in Durham.* ‡ *ECB contract.* § *Official overseas player.* ¶ *Other non-England-qualified player. Durham ceased to award caps after 2005.*

BOWLING

	O	M	R	W	BB	5W/i	Avge
G. Onions	248.5	61	688	45	7-38	4	15.28
S. J. Harmison	412.2	109	1,154	51	6-20	4	22.62
I. D. Blackwell	430.1	121	1,012	43	7-85	3	23.53
L. E. Plunkett	346.2	65	1,217	49	6-63	3	24.83
C. D. Thorp	307.5	89	831	30	5-49	2	27.70
M. Davies	217.1	60	562	19	4-87	0	29.57
M. E. Claydon	210	40	734	22	4-90	0	33.36

Also bowled: D. M. Benkenstein 42–10–150–8; S. G. Borthwick 27–2–95–3; G. R. Breese 17–6–50–0; W. R. Smith 10–2–31–0.

COUNTY RECORDS

Highest score for:	273	M. L. Love v Hampshire at Chester-le-Street . . .	2003
Highest score against:	501*	B. C. Lara (Warwickshire) at Birmingham	1994
Leading run-scorer:	7,854	J. J. B. Lewis (avge 31.41)	1997–2006
Best bowling for:	10-47	O. D. Gibson v Hampshire at Chester-le-Street .	2007
Best bowling against:	9-36	M. S. Kasprowicz (Glamorgan) at Cardiff	2003
Leading wicket-taker:	518	S. J. E. Brown (avge 28.30)	1992–2002
Highest total for:	**648-5 dec**	**v Nottinghamshire at Chester-le-Street**	**2009**
Highest total against:	810-4 dec	by Warwickshire at Birmingham	1994
Lowest total for:	67	v Middlesex at Lord's	1996
Lowest total against:	56	by Somerset at Chester-le-Street	2003

ADDRESS

County Ground, Riverside, Chester-le-Street, County Durham DH3 3QR (0191 387 1717; **email** reception@durhamccc.co.uk). **Website** www.durhamccc.co.uk

OFFICIALS

Captain W. R. Smith
Head coach G. Cook
President I. D. Mills
Chairman C. W. Leach

Chief executive D. Harker
Head groundsman D. Measor
Scorer B. Hunt

Italy's finest slip fielder

Along with developing local talent, Durham have imported shrewdly in the last few years, and the Tasmanian Michael Di Venuto has become one of the experienced pillars around which their success has been built. Since he joined in 2007 – ten years after the last of his nine one-day internationals for Australia – his runs have reduced Durham's reliance on their bowlers, while his slip catching has played a central role in the dominance of their seam attack.

His statistics with the bat in 2009 speak for themselves: 1,601 runs at 80.05 was the second-highest in the County Championship after Marcus Trescothick's 1,817 and was, arguably, a more significant achievement, given that half his matches were played at Riverside, rather than at Taunton. He made six hundreds, including doubles against Sussex and Nottinghamshire.

Di Venuto's success at second slip perhaps requires greater explanation, for he took 23 catches, the most by a fielder in the first division, snapping up the plentiful offerings from an attack led by Steve Harmison. "You're always in the game as a catcher at the Riverside," said Harmison. "Divver practises hard and catches a lot of balls. Along with Marcus Trescothick, he's the best slip catcher I've ever played with. The two of them catch the low ones, below the knees, better than anybody else I've seen."

The reason that Di Venuto takes so many low slip catches is that his positioning creates more chances. While there is plenty of lateral movement at Riverside, there is a lack of pace and bounce, so Durham's slips stand a lot closer at home than at other grounds, with Di Venuto, at second slip, the furthest forward. "It means that a lot of the lower edges carry to him when they wouldn't carry to others," said Jon Lewis, the assistant coach. "But it also means that the chances come more quickly, especially off the likes of Steve Harmison. You've got to be good to do that. And Divver is as good as they come."

Di Venuto, a non-overseas player since 2008 thanks to his Italian passport, is now 36, but there is little sign of his reflexes slowing down. If the chances keep coming, he will keep taking them.   JOHN WESTERBY

At Lord's, April 9, 10, 11, 12. DURHAM drew with MCC (see MCC in 2009).

At Durham, April 15, 16, 17. DURHAM beat DURHAM UCCE by ten wickets.

DURHAM v YORKSHIRE

At Chester-le-Street, April 22, 23, 24, 25. Drawn. Durham 11 pts, Yorkshire 9 pts. Toss: Durham.

A match billed as Vaughan v Harmison battling for an England recall ended with selector James Whitaker being impressed by Onions, who took five for 56 in 28 overs of unrelenting accuracy and effort. Despite his endeavours, Yorkshire hung on throughout the final day, helped by a placid pitch and a 35-minute shower, to finish on 193 for seven, still 200 behind. In the first innings, Vaughan hit five fours in his 24 and was dismayed to be given out caught behind when a ball from Harmison appeared to umpire Cook to brush his glove; on the last day, he suppressed his attacking instincts for nearly two hours in the team's interests. In a good game for wicketkeepers, Mustard's unbeaten 94 was his highest Riverside score, and Brophy made six catches in the same innings. As a batsman, Brophy looked like achieving parity for Yorkshire until he charged Blackwell on 75 and Mustard pulled off a leg-side stumping. It proved a turning point: they slumped from 247 for four to 272. Di Venuto's fluent century allowed Durham to declare in time to bowl four overs on the third evening.

Close of play: First day, Durham 303-7 (Mustard 62, Thorp 24); Second day, Yorkshire 264-6 (Rashid 8, Sayers 4); Third day, Yorkshire 3-0 (Rudolph 2, Sayers 1).

Durham

M. J. Di Venuto c Hoggard b Bresnan	36	– (2) c Bresnan b Rashid	143
M. D. Stoneman c Brophy b Bresnan	2	– (1) lbw b Hoggard	0
*W. R. Smith c Brophy b Hoggard	21	– c and b Rashid	67
G. J. Muchall c Brophy b Patterson	13	– not out	51
D. M. Benkenstein c Brophy b Kruis	17	– (6) c Rashid b Hoggard	22
I. D. Blackwell c Brophy b Hoggard	95	– (5) c Rudolph b Rashid	6
†P. Mustard not out	94	– not out	1
L. E. Plunkett c sub (J. M. Finch) b Bresnan	10		
C. D. Thorp c and b Hoggard	42		
G. Onions c Brophy b Hoggard	4		
S. J. Harmison lbw b Rashid	3		
B 10, l-b 10, w 5	25	B 4, l-b 6, w 3	13

1/20 (2) 2/41 (1) 3/69 (4)	(112.3 overs)	362	1/0 (1)	(5 wkts dec, 79 overs) 303
4/82 (3) 5/129 (5) 6/236 (6)			2/204 (3) 3/233 (2)	
7/257 (8) 8/343 (9) 9/353 (10) 10/362 (11)			4/239 (5) 5/295 (6)	

Hoggard 24–5–82–4; Bresnan 27–8–63–3; Kruis 22–2–80–1; Patterson 22–6–61–1; McGrath 9–5–19–0; Rashid 8.3–0–37–1. *Second Innings*—Hoggard 15–1–57–2; Bresnan 9–2–40–0; Kruis 9–1–31–0; Patterson 17–2–62–0; Rashid 26–1–88–3; McGrath 3–0–15–0.

Yorkshire

A. W. Gale b Onions	11	– (5) c Muchall b Plunkett	27
J. A. Rudolph c Mustard b Harmison	51	– (1) b Onions	16
M. P. Vaughan c Mustard b Harmison	24	– c Mustard b Onions	20
*A. McGrath c Stoneman b Thorp	27	– c Di Venuto b Onions	26
†G. L. Brophy st Mustard b Blackwell	75	– (6) c Onions b Harmison	27
T. T. Bresnan b Plunkett	40	– (7) c Mustard b Onions	20
A. U. Rashid c Benkenstein b Harmison	11	– (8) not out	6
J. J. Sayers c Plunkett b Harmison	5	– (2) c Mustard b Onions	30
S. A. Patterson c Mustard b Onions	3	– not out	4
M. J. Hoggard lbw b Onions	1		
G. J. Kruis not out	0		
B 10, l-b 8, n-b 6	24	B 4, l-b 7, w 2, n-b 4	17

1/40 (1) 2/83 (3) 3/96 (2)	(85.1 overs)	272	1/29 (1)	(7 wkts, 90.4 overs) 193
4/142 (4) 5/247 (5) 6/247 (6)			2/71 (2) 3/72 (3)	
7/267 (8) 8/270 (9) 9/272 (10) 10/272 (7)			4/116 (5) 5/150 (4) 6/174 (6) 7/186 (7)	

Harmison 23.1–3–76–4; Thorp 18–2–57–1; Onions 19–4–49–3; Plunkett 13–3–38–1; Benkenstein 2–0–15–0; Blackwell 10–5–19–1. *Second Innings*—Harmison 23–8–32–1; Onions 28–9–56–5; Thorp 11.4–5–18–0; Blackwell 11–2–21–0; Plunkett 17–3–55–1.

Umpires: N. G. B. Cook and P. Willey.

At Taunton, April 28, 29, 30, May 1. DURHAM drew with SOMERSET.

At Hove, May 6, 7, 8, 9. DURHAM drew with SUSSEX.

DURHAM v HAMPSHIRE

At Chester-le-Street, June 6, 7, 8. Durham won by an innings and 110 runs. Durham 20 pts, Hampshire 3 pts. Toss: Durham.

This match started 75 minutes late, following rain, but Durham still gained their first Championship victory of the season 52 minutes into the third day, when Hampshire surrendered five of their six remaining wickets to Onions. Throughout the game he displayed the form that had won him a Test debut in May, taking three of the wickets that reduced Hampshire to 26 for four in the first 21 overs, and finishing with match figures of nine for 80. On all three days, he struck in his opening over. There were also six wickets for Harmison, who improved steadily after a wayward start. Much the same could be said of Imran Tahir, who took Durham's last three wickets in one over to complete an unlikely five-wicket haul. In tricky conditions on the second morning Will Smith, the Durham captain, studiously survived a testing spell from Tomlinson before profiting from some Tahir long-hops. By the time he had made 80 off 237 balls, the game was beyond a Hampshire side showing little fight. Blackwell enjoyed the opportunity, hitting a 60-ball fifty.

Close of play: First day, Durham 84-2 (Smith 21, Muchall 6); Second day, Hampshire 52-4 (Adams 11, Griffiths 1).

Hampshire

M. A. Carberry c Muchall b Onions	0	– lbw b Onions		0
J. H. K. Adams c Harmison b Thorp	8	– b Onions		11
J. P. Crawley c Di Venuto b Onions	10	– c Smith b Harmison		5
M. J. Lumb lbw b Claydon	20	– c Mustard b Harmison		32
S. M. Ervine c Mustard b Onions	2	– (7) c Claydon b Thorp		22
*†N. Pothas c Muchall b Harmison	35	– (8) lbw b Onions		8
L. A. Dawson b Claydon	0	– (9) not out		6
D. G. Cork c Di Venuto b Harmison	13	– (10) c Di Venuto b Onions		6
Imran Tahir b Harmison	0	– (11) c Mustard b Onions		0
D. A. Griffiths c Thorp b Harmison	0	– (6) b Onions		2
J. A. Tomlinson not out	6	– (5) b Thorp		1
L-b 4, w 1, n-b 6	11	L-b 2, w 1		3

1/0 (1) 2/20 (2) 3/20 (3) 4/26 (5) (50.4 overs) 105   1/0 (1) 2/13 (3) (34.2 overs) 96
5/59 (4) 6/59 (7) 7/88 (8) 8/88 (9)   3/49 (4) 4/50 (5)
9/92 (10) 10/105 (6)   5/53 (6) 6/66 (2) 7/76 (8)
   8/86 (7) 9/96 (10) 10/96 (11)

Onions 19–7–22–3; Harmison 17.4–5–43–4; Thorp 9–4–16–1; Claydon 5–0–20–2. *Second Innings*—Onions 14.2–2–58–6; Harmison 8–4–15–2; Thorp 12–4–21–2.

Durham

M. J. Di Venuto c Crawley b Tomlinson...	7	M. E. Claydon b Imran Tahir	10
M. D. Stoneman c Cork b Imran Tahir	44	G. Onions not out	1
*W. R. Smith lbw b Griffiths	80	S. J. Harmison b Imran Tahir	0
G. J. Muchall c Dawson b Cork	28	B 4, l-b 3, w 2, n-b 10	19
D. M. Benkenstein c Dawson b Imran Tahir	22		
I. D. Blackwell c Pothas b Imran Tahir....	68	1/7 (1) 2/75 (2) 3/140 (4) (103 overs) 311	
†P. Mustard b Ervine	32	4/191 (5) 5/208 (3) 6/280 (7)	
C. D. Thorp b Tomlinson	0	7/281 (8) 8/308 (6) 9/311 (9) 10/311 (11)	

Cork 20–5–45–1; Tomlinson 23–7–72–2; Griffiths 20–6–73–1; Imran Tahir 27–7–85–5; Ervine 13–5–29–1.

Umpires: N. G. B. Cook and R. K. Illingworth.

DURHAM v LANCASHIRE

At Chester-le-Street, June 11, 12, 13. Durham won by 138 runs. Durham 18 pts, Lancashire 3 pts. Toss: Lancashire.

Although not named in Lancashire's squad, Flintoff made his comeback six weeks after knee surgery when Tom Smith pulled out, and had Di Venuto caught behind off his second ball on his way to four for 47. He scored three and nought, but added two more wickets in the second innings, which he opened with a six-over spell costing one run as Durham slumped to ten for four. Sixteen wickets fell in the first 65 overs of the second day. Lancashire's 116 was their lowest total against Durham, and Blackwell, dropped on 18, scored 74 to set up another three-day win. Batting was never easy. There was some excellent swing bowling by Chapple on the first day, but the umpires had no complaints about the pitch other than that it was two-paced. Umpire Mallender might, however, have taken exception to the way Prince, in his final game for Lancashire, stood his ground in both innings after being given out lbw. The height of Mahmood and Harmison helped them achieve good bounce, with Mahmood recording a career-best six for 30. Harmison's steady improvement continued: he produced some unplayable balls in taking the first four second-innings wickets.

Close of play: First day, Durham 212-8 (Mustard 31, Onions 2); Second day, Durham 122-6 (Blackwell 65, Thorp 19).

Durham

M. J. Di Venuto c Sutton b Flintoff	16	– (2) c Newby b Mahmood	0
M. D. Stoneman c Flintoff b Mahmood	45	– (1) c Flintoff b Mahmood	2
*W. R. Smith c Sutton b Newby	11	– c Sutton b Mahmood	1
G. J. Muchall c du Plessis b Mahmood	18	– lbw b Newby	18
D. M. Benkenstein c Flintoff b Chapple	26	– c Prince b Chapple	1
I. D. Blackwell b Chapple	20	– c and b Mahmood	74
†P. Mustard c du Plessis b Flintoff	51	– c Sutton b Flintoff	7
C. D. Thorp c Horton b Chapple	4	– c Horton b Mahmood	24
M. E. Claydon c Sutton b Flintoff	6	– c Prince b Mahmood	0
G. Onions not out	12	– not out	7
S. J. Harmison c Loye b Flintoff	0	– c du Plessis b Flintoff	0
B 2, l-b 10, w 9, n-b 14	35	L-b 6, w 1, n-b 4	11

1/42 (1) 2/84 (3) 3/84 (2)   (69.5 overs) 244   1/0 (2) 2/2 (1)   (50.4 overs) 145
4/117 (4) 5/143 (6) 6/166 (5)   3/3 (3) 4/10 (5) 5/40 (4)
7/172 (8) 8/203 (9) 9/244 (7) 10/244 (11)   6/57 (7) 7/138 (6) 8/138 (9)
                                                      9/138 (8) 10/145 (11)

Chapple 25–5–58–3; Mahmood 14–4–62–2; Flintoff 15.5–3–47–4; Newby 15–2–65–1. *Second Innings*—Flintoff 15.4–9–30–2; Mahmood 14–7–30–6; Chapple 9–2–33–1; Newby 6–0–26–1; Keedy 5–0–19–0; du Plessis 1–0–1–0.

Lancashire

P. J. Horton c Mustard b Onions	0	– (2) c Mustard b Harmison	11
M. B. Loye lbw b Onions	14	– (1) c Muchall b Harmison	30
A. G. Prince lbw b Onions	17	– lbw b Harmison	3
F. du Plessis c Mustard b Harmison	41	– c Mustard b Harmison	5
M. J. Chilton c Stoneman b Harmison	2	– c Mustard b Claydon	22
A. Flintoff b Harmison	3	– c Claydon b Onions	0
†L. D. Sutton c Thorp b Claydon	21	– not out	19
*G. Chapple c Mustard b Claydon	0	– c Di Venuto b Harmison	21
S. I. Mahmood c Mustard b Harmison	7	– c Mustard b Onions	16
O. J. Newby c Blackwell b Onions	1	– b Blackwell	0
G. Keedy not out	0	– b Onions	0
B 4, l-b 4, n-b 2	10	B 1, l-b 2, w 1, n-b 4	8

1/4 (1) 2/34 (3) 3/37 (2) 4/48 (5)   (43.2 overs) 116
5/56 (6) 6/83 (7) 7/83 (8) 8/115 (4)
9/116 (10) 10/116 (9)

1/18 (2) 2/36 (3)   (52 overs) 135
3/50 (4) 4/63 (1) 5/64 (6)
6/78 (5) 7/113 (8) 8/133 (9)
9/134 (10) 10/135 (11)

Onions 13–4–40–4; Harmison 14.2–4–28–4; Claydon 9–4–19–2; Thorp 7–2–21–0. *Second Innings*—Onions 14–4–28–3; Harmison 17–7–46–5; Claydon 9–1–29–1; Thorp 10–4–19–0; Blackwell 2–0–10–1.

Umpires: N. A. Mallender and R. T. Robinson.

At Birmingham, June 16, 17, 18, 19. DURHAM beat WARWICKSHIRE by ten wickets.

DURHAM v WORCESTERSHIRE

At Chester-le-Street, June 30, July 1, 2, 3. Durham won by five wickets. Durham 17 pts, Worcestershire 3 pts. Toss: Durham.

Top met bottom with five men absent, playing for England Lions against the Australians. But Worcestershire suffered more from losing three batsmen – Solanki, Moore and Davies. Durham, without Harmison and Onions, called up Plunkett after five weeks out with a groin injury, while Davies made his first appearance of the season. Plunkett proved the match-winner after an erratic start, taking six in an innings for the second time, then five more for his first ten-wicket haul: a reward for pace, aggression and stamina, as well as improved accuracy. In humid conditions the ball swung on the first two days, helping Kabir Ali to take six too, but Mustard underlined his growing maturity as he dragged Durham from 59 for six to 194, a lead of one. Kervezee was the only visiting batsman to benefit from improved conditions on the third day, scoring his maiden Championship half-century while several colleagues brought about their own downfall. On the final morning Durham needed a further 115, with rain forecast at lunch. They reached their target at 12.14; Di Venuto completed his 50th first-class century with the single that levelled the scores, before Mustard secured Durham's fourth consecutive victory.

Close of play: First day, Durham 40-3 (Coetzer 20, Benkenstein 17); Second day, Worcestershire 0-0 (Mitchell 0, Kervezee 0); Third day, Durham 64-1 (Di Venuto 43, Smith 3).

Worcestershire

D. K. H. Mitchell c Mustard b Plunkett	13	– c Di Venuto b Davies	15
A. N. Kervezee c Di Venuto b Davies	6	– c Mustard b Plunkett	66
M. M. Ali c Plunkett b Benkenstein	9	– c Coetzer b Plunkett	10
B. F. Smith b Claydon	33	– c Coetzer b Thorp	3
D. A. Wheeldon c Di Venuto b Thorp	7	– c Di Venuto b Claydon	0
A. A. Noffke c Mustard b Plunkett	50	– lbw b Blackwell	11
*G. J. Batty b Plunkett	19	– b Plunkett	4
Kabir Ali c Thorp b Plunkett	28	– not out	30
†J. P. T. Knappett not out	4	– c Mustard b Blackwell	1
C. D. Whelan b Plunkett	0	– b Plunkett	21
M. S. Mason c Thorp b Plunkett	2	– c Thorp b Plunkett	5
B 9, l-b 5, w 2, n-b 6	22	L-b 5, n-b 8	13

1/18 (2) 2/26 (1) 3/56 (3) 4/80 (4)   (79.1 overs) 193   1/36 (1) 2/57 (3)   (74 overs) 179
5/80 (5) 6/137 (7) 7/187 (6)   3/66 (4) 4/71 (5)
8/187 (8) 9/191 (10) 10/193 (11)   5/108 (6) 6/116 (2) 7/117 (7) 8/124 (9)
                                                          9/169 (10) 10/179 (11)

Thorp 16–8–34–1; Claydon 17–4–32–1; Davies 13–5–29–1; Plunkett 23.1–3–63–6; Benkenstein 2–1–11–1; Blackwell 8–5–10–0. *Second Innings*—Claydon 11–0–50–1; Thorp 13–6–27–1; Davies 10–2–19–1; Plunkett 24–6–56–5; Blackwell 16–7–22–2.

Durham

M. J. Di Venuto c Kabir Ali	0	– not out	100
K. J. Coetzer b Kabir Ali	30	– c Knappett b Noffke	15
*W. R. Smith b Kabir Ali	0	– c Smith b Whelan	16
G. J. Muchall c Knappett b Mason	0	– c Mitchell b Mason	14
D. M. Benkenstein c Knappett b Kabir Ali	25	– c Knappett b Mason	17
I. D. Blackwell b Mason	1	– c Wheeldon b Mason	3
†P. Mustard not out	63	– not out	2
L. E. Plunkett c Batty b Mason	29		
C. D. Thorp lbw b Kabir Ali	17		
M. E. Claydon c Knappett b Kabir Ali	6		
M. Davies b Whelan	6		
B 4, l-b 5, w 2, n-b 6	17	B 2, l-b 6, n-b 4	12

1/0 (1) 2/0 (3) 3/1 (4) 4/56 (5)   (55.5 overs) 194   1/47 (2) 2/90 (3) (5 wkts, 41 overs) 179
5/59 (6) 6/59 (2) 7/105 (8) 8/140 (9)   3/115 (4)
9/171 (10) 10/194 (11)   4/137 (5) 5/155 (6)

Kabir Ali 18–4–68–6; Mason 21–8–55–3; Noffke 10–4–28–0; Whelan 6.5–1–34–1. *Second Innings*—Kabir Ali 6–0–23–0; Mason 11–2–35–3; Noffke 7–2–11–1; Batty 10–1–48–0; Whelan 5–0–37–1; M. M. Ali 2–0–17–0.

Umpires: R. J. Bailey and N. G. B. Cook.

At Leeds, July 10, 11, 12, 13. DURHAM drew with YORKSHIRE.

At Nottingham, July 15, 16, 17, 18. DURHAM beat NOTTINGHAMSHIRE by an innings and 102 runs.

DURHAM v SUSSEX

At Chester-le-Street, July 31, August 1, 2, 3. Durham won by nine wickets. Durham 20 pts (after 1 pt penalty), Sussex 2 pts. Toss: Durham.

After 592 runs and only five wickets on the first two days, Sussex lost 14 wickets on the third, mainly through swing. Di Venuto observed after his career-best 254: "There's plenty in the pitch, but when the ball seams, it seams big and beats the bat." He was happy for Will Smith to hog the strike during their stand of 231, the captain batting stoically to reach his first century of the season, from 291 balls. Di Venuto's fourth took 150, and he faced 368 in all, hitting 35 fours and one six, and offering one chance, at 180. Only Martin Love, with 273 against Hampshire in 2003, has scored more for Durham. Sussex subsided rapidly as Thorp ended a lean spell with five wickets; Yardy's attempts to hold them together ended with his run-out for 97. Following on, they slipped to 115 for five, but Wright and Hodd survived and took their stand to 112 on the final morning before Harmison, who had been struggling with blistered feet, claimed the last three wickets. Wright batted fearlessly, following a maiden Championship century in Sussex's previous game with another, reached by hooking successive sixes off Harmison. Di Venuto's unbeaten 39 took his match total to 293 without dismissal, and his season's aggregate past 1,000.

Close of play: First day, Durham 264-2 (Di Venuto 141, Muchall 1); Second day, Sussex 119-1 (Yardy 54, Goodwin 2); Third day, Sussex 208-5 (Wright 64, Hodd 22).

Durham

M. J. Di Venuto not out 254	– (2) not out	39
M. D. Stoneman c Yardy b Yasir Arafat 5	– (1) c Yardy b Rayner	18
*W. R. Smith b Collymore 101	– not out	21
G. J. Muchall c Hodd b Yasir Arafat 14		
D. M. Benkenstein c Joyce b Nash 69		
I. D. Blackwell not out 2		
B 2, l-b 11, w 1, n-b 14 28	N-b 2	2

1/16 (2) 2/247 (3) (4 wkts dec, 137 overs) 473   1/49 (1) (1 wkt, 18.4 overs) 80
3/280 (4) 4/453 (5) 120 overs: 380-3

†P. Mustard, L. E. Plunkett, C. D. Thorp, S. J. Harmison and M. Davies did not bat.

Lewry 21–8–56–0; Yasir Arafat 30–6–96–2; Wright 19–1–75–0; Collymore 24–6–61–1; Rayner 29–2–107–0; Yardy 10–1–56–0; Nash 4–1–9–1. *Second Innings*—Yasir Arafat 4–0–32–0; Collymore 1–0–5–0; Rayner 8–3–16–1; Nash 5.4–1–27–0.

Sussex

*M. H. Yardy run out 97	– c Muchall b Davies	20
C. D. Nash lbw b Thorp 19	– c Mustard b Thorp	55
E. C. Joyce c Mustard b Davies 36	– b Blackwell	14
M. W. Goodwin b Thorp 6	– c Mustard b Thorp	13
C. D. Hopkinson b Thorp 14	– lbw b Davies	7
L. J. Wright c Stoneman b Thorp 0	– not out 118
†A. J. Hodd c Smith b Plunkett 4	– c Plunkett b Davies	33
Yasir Arafat c Di Venuto b Plunkett 10	– c Di Venuto b Blackwell	18
O. P. Rayner c Muchall b Harmison 24	– lbw b Harmison	1
C. D. Collymore c Muchall b Thorp 11	– b Harmison	10
J. D. Lewry not out 4	– b Harmison	0
L-b 11, w 1, n-b 8 20	B 4, l-b 7, n-b 4	15

1/38 (2) 2/131 (4) 3/155 (5) (76.2 overs) 245   1/34 (1) 2/71 (3) (79.3 overs) 304
4/166 (3) 5/167 (6) 6/181 (7) 3/97 (2) 4/104 (4)
7/205 (8) 8/205 (1) 9/241 (10) 10/245 (9) 5/115 (5) 6/227 (7) 7/257 (8)
8/258 (9) 9/304 (10) 10/304 (11)

In the first innings Joyce, when 32, retired hurt at 101 and resumed at 155.

Harmison 20.2–5–58–1; Davies 16–4–41–1; Thorp 25–5–86–5; Plunkett 11–2–34–2; Blackwell 4–0–15–0. *Second Innings*—Davies 18–5–44–3; Harmison 12.3–1–68–3; Plunkett 8–2–50–0; Thorp 16–0–79–2; Blackwell 25–10–52–2.

Umpires: T. E. Jesty and P. Willey.

At Manchester, August 11, 12, 13, 14. DURHAM drew with LANCASHIRE.

DURHAM v WARWICKSHIRE

At Chester-le-Street, August 19, 20, 21. Durham won by eight wickets. Durham 19 pts, Warwickshire 3 pts. Toss: Warwickshire. Championship debut: A. Javid.

Durham cruised to their fifth successive home win, again demonstrating the depth of their attack without Harmison and Onions, while Warwickshire badly missed Bell and Trott – all four down at the Oval Test. Even when Davies retired with a back spasm after bowling two overs on the first morning, Durham could turn to Benkenstein's gentle medium-pace: he harnessed the swing almost as successfully as Thorp, reducing Warwickshire from 70 for two to 71 for five, and Thorp took five for the second time in two home games. Benkenstein had steered Durham into the lead by the close, with Rankin conceding almost a run a ball in eight overs, though he had Chanderpaul, in his first county game of the season, caught at backward square leg for a duck. With good bounce available, Rankin claimed his maiden Championship five-for next day. But at 34 for three, still 104 behind, Warwickshire were in danger of a two-day innings defeat. Then Troughton and Ambrose chanced their arms, before Troughton settled down with a well-constructed century. Chanderpaul hurried Durham past a target of 101, ending the match with a six over long-on.

Close of play: First day, Durham 173-4 (Benkenstein 59, Blackwell 48); Second day, Warwickshire 127-4 (Troughton 55, Clarke 7).

Warwickshire

*I. J. Westwood lbw b Thorp	5	– c Plunkett b Claydon	2
A. G. Botha c Stoneman b Benkenstein	23	– c Mustard b Thorp	14
J. O. Troughton lbw b Thorp	14	– c Di Venuto b Blackwell	111
T. Frost c Mustard b Benkenstein	19	– c Thorp b Claydon	4
†T. R. Ambrose c Mustard b Benkenstein	0	– c Di Venuto b Blackwell	39
R. Clarke lbw b Thorp	32	– c Thorp b Blackwell	13
A. Javid lbw b Thorp	8	– c Mustard b Davies	21
C. R. Woakes c Mustard b Claydon	0	– lbw b Davies	13
N. S. Tahir c Thorp b Plunkett	10	– c Blackwell b Davies	1
S. Sreesanth c Blackwell b Thorp	5	– c Chanderpaul b Claydon	4
W. B. Rankin not out	2	– not out	0
B 1, l-b 5, w 1, n-b 10	17	L-b 2, w 4, n-b 10	16

1/11 (1) 2/41 (3) 3/70 (2) 4/70 (5)   (55.1 overs) 135
5/71 (4) 6/101 (7) 7/103 (8)
8/123 (6) 9/127 (9) 10/135 (10)

1/4 (1) 2/29 (2)   (93.4 overs) 238
3/34 (4) 4/116 (5)
5/150 (6) 6/201 (3) 7/228 (7)
8/231 (8) 9/238 (10) 10/238 (9)

Claydon 15–8–25–1; Davies 2–1–1–0; Thorp 20.1–5–49–5; Plunkett 10–3–34–1; Benkenstein 8–2–20–3. *Second Innings*—Claydon 21–4–75–3; Davies 14.4–6–19–3; Thorp 20–11–31–1; Plunkett 15–4–67–0; Blackwell 23–9–44–3.

Durham

M. J. Di Venuto c Ambrose b Tahir	40	– (2) not out	41
M. D. Stoneman c Ambrose b Woakes	3	– (1) c Ambrose b Tahir	5
*W. R. Smith c Westwood b Rankin	16	– c sub (C. S. MacLeod) b Woakes	11
D. M. Benkenstein c Clarke b Rankin	73		
S. Chanderpaul c Javid b Rankin	0	– (4) not out	41
I. D. Blackwell c Ambrose b Tahir	53		
†P. Mustard c Troughton b Rankin	25		
L. E. Plunkett not out	31		
C. D. Thorp b Rankin	0		
M. E. Claydon c Sreesanth b Woakes	10		
M. Davies c Ambrose b Sreesanth	8		
B 6, l-b 2, n-b 6	14	N-b 8	8

1/43 (2) 2/43 (1) 3/87 (3) 4/97 (5)   (72.1 overs) 273
5/182 (6) 6/202 (4) 7/233 (7)
8/233 (9) 9/254 (10) 10/273 (11)

1/18 (1)   (2 wkts, 20.3 overs) 106
2/38 (3)

Rankin 21–1–85–5; Tahir 21–5–57–2; Woakes 17–3–72–2; Sreesanth 10.1–1–35–1; Clarke 3–0–16–0. *Second Innings*—Tahir 4–0–16–1; Sreesanth 6–0–27–0; Woakes 6–1–30–1; Clarke 2–0–21–0; Botha 2.3–0–12–0.

Umpires: D. J. Millns and J. F. Steele.

DURHAM v SOMERSET

At Chester-le-Street, September 1, 2, 3, 4. Drawn. Durham 9 pts, Somerset 6 pts (after 1 pt penalty). Toss: Somerset.

Rain wiped out the last two days, but Durham inched a little further out of third-placed Somerset's reach. On the first day, the visitors subsided from 89 without loss to 174 all out. Returning from England duty, Onions started the collapse by removing Trescothick and Langer, to whom he gave a torrid time, twice striking him in the midriff before swinging one in to hit leg and middle. A sudden return to form for Plunkett, on a pitch offering some help, would have been rewarded with five wickets but for dropped slip catches; instead, Blackwell stole the headlines, though he got the ball only when Harmison briefly left the field for treatment on a blistered toe. Probably surprised that he found some turn, Somerset were mesmerised by their former colleague, who took five for seven in 8.1 overs. Willoughby and Phillips troubled most of the Durham batsmen, but Chanderpaul provided a masterclass in survival, remaining unbeaten on 117 from 220 balls.

Close of play: First day, Durham 110-3 (Chanderpaul 49, Benkenstein 1); Second day, Somerset 41-0 (Trescothick 18, Suppiah 21); Third day, No play.

Somerset

M. E. Trescothick c Smith b Onions	31	– not out ... 18
A. V. Suppiah c Mustard b Plunkett	53	– not out ... 21
*J. L. Langer b Onions	12	
J. C. Hildreth c Thorp b Blackwell	27	
Z. de Bruyn lbw b Blackwell	16	
†C. Kieswetter c Di Venuto b Plunkett	0	
P. D. Trego c Di Venuto b Plunkett	4	
O. A. C. Banks not out	16	
B. J. Phillips lbw b Blackwell	0	
A. C. Thomas c Di Venuto b Blackwell	0	
C. M. Willoughby b Blackwell	0	
L-b 8, w 3, n-b 4	15	B 1, l-b 1 ... 2

1/89 (1) 2/89 (2) 3/127 (3)   (59.1 overs) 174
4/147 (4) 5/148 (6) 6/152 (7)
7/162 (5) 8/162 (9) 9/166 (10) 10/174 (11)

(no wkt, 12.5 overs) 41

Onions 17–2–49–2; Harmison 8–3–24–0; Thorp 5–0–21–0; Plunkett 21–6–65–3; Blackwell 8.1–5–7–5. *Second Innings*—Onions 6–0–25–0; Harmison 6–2–14–0; Plunkett 0.5–0–0–0.

Durham

M. J. Di Venuto c Trescothick b Willoughby	22	C. D. Thorp c Hildreth b Willoughby ... 15
K. J. Coetzer b Phillips	30	G. Onions c Kieswetter b Willoughby ... 0
*W. R. Smith c Kieswetter b Willoughby	0	S. J. Harmison c Kieswetter b Trego ... 1
S. Chanderpaul not out	117	B 9, l-b 12, w 2 ... 23
D. M. Benkenstein c Suppiah b de Bruyn	30	
I. D. Blackwell c Kieswetter b Phillips	0	1/24 (1) 2/24 (3) 3/104 (2) (89.5 overs) 272
†P. Mustard c Langer b Phillips	2	4/161 (5) 5/162 (6) 6/166 (7)
L. E. Plunkett b Willoughby	32	7/235 (8) 8/267 (9) 9/271 (10) 10/272 (11)

Willoughby 22–7–56–5; Thomas 20–4–54–0; Phillips 20.2–2–46–3; Trego 11.5–4–42–1; Banks 2–0–15–0; de Bruyn 11–3–31–1; Suppiah 3–1–7–0.

Umpires: R. J. Bailey and J. H. Evans.

DURHAM v NOTTINGHAMSHIRE

At Chester-le-Street, September 9, 10, 11, 12. Durham won by an innings and 52 runs. Durham 22 pts, Nottinghamshire 5 pts. Toss: Durham.

Durham were keen to make sure of retaining the Championship in their final home game, so that this time they could celebrate in front of their own fans: free admission on the last two days brought crowds of 4,000. And they effectively sealed the title on the third afternoon, when Davies had Brown caught behind to gain a second bowling point. They started the match needing 11 points; that gave them seven and, although Durham had to wait until the finish to be officially declared champions, Nottinghamshire had no chance of denying them four for the draw. The visitors had lost Read, their captain and wicketkeeper, with a dislocated thumb on the first morning (though he managed to bat), then in the afternoon Shreck limped off with a knee injury, and Ealham was unfit to bowl after damaging ribs as he completed a run-out. His victim was Coetzer, who had contributed 107 to an

HIGHEST TOTALS FOR DURHAM

648-5 dec	**v Nottinghamshire at Chester-le-Street**	**2009**
645-6 dec	v Middlesex at Lord's	2002
634-8 dec	**v Worcestershire at Worcester**	**2009**
625-6 dec	v Derbyshire at Chesterfield	1994
575	v Kent at Canterbury	2006
556-8 dec	v Warwickshire at Birmingham	1994
552	v Gloucestershire at Cheltenham	1999
545-8 dec	v Northamptonshire at Hartlepool	1994
543	**v Somerset at Taunton**	**2009**

HIGHEST TOTALS AT CHESTER-LE-STREET

648-5 dec	**Durham v Nottinghamshire**	**2009**
569-6 dec	**England v West Indies**	**2009**
530	Lancashire v Durham	2005
523	Nottinghamshire v Durham	2004
516-6 dec	Leicestershire v Durham	1996
515	Durham v Hampshire	2003
508	Leicestershire v Durham	2004
505	Durham v Essex	2005

opening stand of 314 – one short of Durham's all-wicket Championship record. Patel was left to carry the attack, and did not take a wicket until his 59th over. Di Venuto, who scored 105 between lunch and tea, batted through the day for 219 before edging the first ball of the second day, from Fletcher, to stand-in keeper Shafayat. Chanderpaul advanced to his 50th first-class hundred, while Benkenstein's 15th for Durham made him their leading century-maker, overtaking John Morris and Paul Collingwood. It was the first time Durham had had four hundreds in one innings. They declared after passing their previous highest total, 645 for six at Lord's in 2002, and showed their determination to push for the win, rather than settling for the draw which would still have made them champions, by making Nottinghamshire follow on. Plunkett bowled with good pace and direction, generally shaping the ball away, to take nine wickets in the match. Harmison, who lost his England contract to team-mate Onions on the third day, had three catches dropped in taking none for 108, but picked up three in the second innings, including the final one – just as he had to clinch their first Championship title at Canterbury a year earlier. Durham's second innings victory over Nottinghamshire left them 43 points clear.

Close of play: First day, Durham 377-1 (Di Venuto 219, Smith 22); Second day, Nottinghamshire 65-2 (Hales 23, Patel 15); Third day, Nottinghamshire 52-2 (Hales 33, Pattinson 4).

Durham

M. J. Di Venuto c Shafayat b Fletcher	219	†P. Mustard not out	6
K. J. Coetzer run out	107	B 13, l-b 20, w 1, n-b 12	46
*W. R. Smith c Shafayat b Fletcher	27		
S. Chanderpaul not out	109	1/314 (2) (5 wkts dec, 171 overs)	648
D. M. Benkenstein c Shafayat b Hales	105	2/377 (1) 3/382 (3)	
I. D. Blackwell c Hales b Patel	29	4/585 (5) 5/632 (6) 120 overs: 440-3	

L. E. Plunkett, M. E. Claydon, S. J. Harmison and M. Davies did not bat.

Shreck 7–3–26–0; Pattinson 28–7–106–0; Fletcher 34–6–125–2; Ealham 16–0–49–0; Patel 60–7–206–1; Hales 19–2–74–1; Brown 7–0–29–0.

Nottinghamshire

S. A. Newman lbw b Davies	16	– c Plunkett b Claydon	9
A. D. Hales b Plunkett	62	– c Coetzer b Blackwell	78
M. A. Wagh c Plunkett b Davies	3	– c Mustard b Davies	6
S. R. Patel c Coetzer b Plunkett	44	– (5) c Davies b Harmison	4
B. M. Shafayat lbw b Plunkett	4	– (6) run out	32
A. D. Brown c Mustard b Davies	59	– (7) b Plunkett	28
*†C. M. W. Read c Benkenstein b Plunkett	65	– (8) lbw b Plunkett	24
M. A. Ealham c Benkenstein b Plunkett	49	– (9) b Harmison	18
L. J. Fletcher b Davies	1	– (10) c Coetzer b Harmison	1
D. J. Pattinson c Mustard b Plunkett	59	– (4) b Plunkett	4
C. E. Shreck not out	0	– not out	0
B 6, l-b 16	22	L-b 8	8

1/23 (1) 2/33 (3) 3/129 (4) (102 overs)	384	1/21 (1) 2/48 (3) (85.2 overs) 212
4/133 (5) 5/152 (6) 6/247 (6)		3/52 (4) 4/61 (5)
7/269 (7) 8/270 (9) 9/383 (8) 10/384 (10)		5/119 (6) 6/163 (2) 7/187 (7)
		8/204 (8) 9/205 (10) 10/212 (9)

Harmison 28–1–108–0; Davies 25–5–87–4; Blackwell 17–3–46–0; Claydon 11–1–36–0; Plunkett 21–4–85–6. *Second Innings*—Plunkett 21–6–64–3; Claydon 11–3–31–1; Davies 14–4–29–1; Blackwell 19–11–27–1; Harmison 18.2–6–38–3; Benkenstein 2–0–15–0.

Umpires: R. K. Illingworth and J. W. Lloyds.

At Southampton, September 15, 16, 17, 18. DURHAM drew with HAMPSHIRE.

At Worcester, September 23, 24, 25, 26. DURHAM drew with WORCESTERSHIRE. *Durham end the season unbeaten in the Championship, 47 points ahead of runners-up Nottinghamshire.*

ESSEX

Back where they belong?

PAUL HISCOCK

A stunning last-gasp victory at Derby in the final session of the 2009 Championship ensured a return to the top tier for Essex after a six-year spell in the wilderness. It was due reward for their enterprise as they played with a refreshing self-belief to win four of their last six matches. The contribution from leg-spinner Danish Kaneria was immense. He took 75 Championship wickets, six more than anyone else in county cricket, and in those last half-dozen matches – just after returning from Pakistan's tour of Sri Lanka – he captured 52 to spearhead the thrust into Division One.

Captain Mark Pettini and coach Paul Grayson have now justified the county committee's faith since being appointed in July 2007. First, they restored the club's one-day reputation by lifting both the Friends Provident Trophy and the Pro40 Division Two title in 2008, before turning their attention to Championship matters. "Winning promotion is an achievement that we are all hugely proud of," Pettini purred. "It's a different feeling from winning a one-day trophy because the Championship campaign goes on for a long time. It's ridiculous that our whole season came down to that last session."

Remarkably, it was not until mid-June that Pettini became the first Essex batsman to hit a Championship century, but then the floodgates opened: seven of his colleagues reached hundreds, including two for Kaneria's short-term replacement, South African Test batsman Hashim Amla, and a couple for Ryan ten Doeschate; his unbeaten 59-ball 108 – including eight sixes – in the final match proved crucial as Essex powered to their target of 359 at six an over.

Amla, whose 181 was the highest on Essex debut, boasted quality and class, yet, despite hitting another century in one of his two Pro40 matches, he never finished on the winning side in his five-match stay. Essex had to wait nine games before eventually gaining full batting points, but thereafter the batsmen displayed greater substance. Matt Walker, alone in reaching 1,000 first-class runs, proved a sound signing from Kent, while James Foster's consistency saw him fall just 20 short; he also kept sublimely. Foster forced his way into the England team for the World Twenty20, though his subsequent omission from all international squads had Essex supporters – and some neutrals – puzzled.

The presence of Alastair Cook for eight matches was an unexpected bonus, but his England colleague Ravi Bopara made just two Championship appearances, both in the latter stages of the season after he had been axed for the last Ashes Test. Bopara's response was an unbeaten fifty in the successful run-chase against Middlesex and a double-century that underpinned the victory over Surrey at Colchester, before he was recalled for the one-day internationals against Australia.

Kaneria was in a class of his own in the bowling department. On six occasions he returned five or more wickets in an innings, including his county-best figures of eight for 116 against Leicestershire. David Masters, an economical workhorse with the new ball, offered valuable support with 45 Championship wickets, and former Middlesex player Chris Wright continued to progress with 40. Because of commitments with the IPL and the World Twenty20 (although he played only once for Mumbai Indians and not at all for England), Graham Napier missed several matches, but made valuable all-round contributions. Ten Doeschate, meanwhile, was a useful partnership-breaker, even if the value of his batting outweighed his bowling.

Danish Kaneria

Hannah Johnston, Getty Images

The one-day competitions proved a disappointment. Essex, the title-holders, were eliminated in the quarter-final stages of the Friends Provident by Lancashire, whom they had beaten three days earlier in a group match. Defeat by Hampshire in the last Twenty20 group match also saw Essex eliminated, while three reversals in the first four Pro40 games put paid to any hopes.

Tight purse strings reduced the likelihood of big-money signings before the new season. The availability of Kaneria was crucial to their planning but, with Pakistan's heavy schedule in England in 2010, his involvement with Essex could be severely restricted – if he is available at all. While Amla was again mentioned as a possible replacement, a match-winning bowler should be the priority in Kaneria's absence.

The county have been patient with their two young fast-bowling prospects, Maurice Chambers and Mervyn Westfield, but one – ideally both – needed to step forward and become a regular member of the first team. James Middlebrook, omitted in the second half of the season, left for Northamptonshire, leaving left-armer Tim Phillips to fulfil the spin duties in Kaneria's absence. Tom Westley, who scored his maiden first-class century in the memorable win at Derby, will also be encouraged to bowl his off-breaks when his Durham University studies permit. Jason Gallian retired at the end of the season, and Varun Chopra opted to join Warwickshire, but young batsmen Jaik Mickleburgh and former England Under-19 batsman Billy Godleman, newly arrived from Middlesex, will ensure there is competition for batting places.

Grayson reckoned his side would become established in the Championship's first division, though he was realistic. "I believe that with our squad, we do have a chance of competing this year," he said. "It's been too long since Essex were in Division One, going to Old Trafford and Headingley and places like that, and I'm absolutely delighted for the lads. We have some good young cricketers coming through, and hopefully we'll have Danish Kaneria for part of the season. I'm confident we can continue our progress."

ESSEX RESULTS

All first-class matches – Played 18: Won 6, Lost 3, Drawn 9.
County Championship matches – Played 16: Won 6, Lost 3, Drawn 7.

LV County Championship, 2nd in Division 2; Friends Provident Trophy, q-f;
Pro40 League, 4th in Division 1; Twenty20 Cup, 4th in South Division.

COUNTY CHAMPIONSHIP AVERAGES, BATTING AND FIELDING

Cap		M	I	NO	R	HS	100s	50s	Avge	Ct/St
2005	R. S. Bopara‡	2	4	2	269	201	1	1	134.50	2
	H. M. Amla§	3	5	1	410	181	2	1	102.50	2
2006	R. N. ten Doeschate¶ . . .	14	22	4	823	159*	2	2	45.72	5
	T. Westley	6	11	2	383	132	1	1	42.55	3
2006	M. L. Pettini	15	28	6	870	101*	1	4	39.54	10
2001	J. S. Foster†	15	24	1	905	103*	1	6	39.34	57/4
2005	A. N. Cook‡	8	15	1	493	87	0	4	35.21	11
2003	G. R. Napier†	10	16	6	348	64*	0	2	34.80	3
	M. J. Walker.	16	29	2	933	150	2	2	34.55	12
	J. K. Maunders	10	17	0	560	150	1	2	32.94	12
2006	T. J. Phillips	3	4	0	111	69	0	1	27.75	2
2008	D. D. Masters	15	16	1	341	67	0	2	22.73	7
	V. Chopra†	10	18	0	385	85	0	3	21.38	6
	M. A. Chambers	5	7	6	19	8*	0	0	19.00	0
	J. C. Mickleburgh.	4	8	0	138	62	0	1	17.25	2
2003	J. D. Middlebrook	6	8	2	96	19	0	0	16.00	1
	C. J. C. Wright	14	16	7	130	24*	0	0	14.44	2
2008	J. E. R. Gallian	5	10	1	120	44*	0	0	13.33	2
2004	Danish Kania§.	11	15	2	158	37	0	0	12.15	5

Also batted: A. P. Palladino (3 matches) 5, 0; A. J. Wheater† (1 match) 0 (4 ct).

† *Born in Essex.*   ‡ *ECB contract.*   § *Official overseas player.*   ¶ *Other non-England-qualified player.*

BOWLING

	O	M	R	W	BB	5W/i	Avge
Danish Kaneria	597.5	124	1,777	75	8-116	6	23.69
D. D. Masters.	557.2	184	1,212	45	5-65	1	26.93
G. R. Napier	271.3	55	1,005	29	4-32	0	34.65
C. J. C. Wright.	437.1	67	1,538	40	4-43	0	38.45
M. A. Chambers	117.4	13	438	10	3-30	0	43.80
R. N. ten Doeschate.	246	32	970	22	5-62	1	44.09

Also bowled: R. S. Bopara 8–3–30–0; V. Chopra 8.1–1–27–0; A. N. Cook 10–0–51–2; J. C. Mickleburgh 7.5–1–28–0; J. D. Middlebrook 99–16–345–9; A. P. Palladino 82–19–258–7; M. L. Pettini 6.5–0–62–0; T. J. Phillips 105–23–279–6; M. J. Walker 3.2–0–22–0; T. Westley 29–2–104–2.

COUNTY RECORDS

Highest score for:	343*	P. A. Perrin v Derbyshire at Chesterfield	1904
Highest score against:	332	W. H. Ashdown (Kent) at Brentwood	1934
Leading run-scorer:	30,701	G. A. Gooch (avge 51.77)	1973–1997
Best bowling for:	10-32	H. Pickett v Leicestershire at Leyton	1895
Best bowling against:	10-40	E. G. Dennett (Gloucestershire) at Bristol . . .	1906
Leading wicket-taker:	1,610	T. P. B. Smith (avge 26.68)	1929–1951
Highest total for:	761-6 dec	v Leicestershire at Chelmsford	1990
Highest total against:	803-4 dec	by Kent at Brentwood.	1934
Lowest total for:	30	v Yorkshire at Leyton	1901
Lowest total against:	14	by Surrey at Chelmsford.	1983

ADDRESS

County Ground, New Writtle Street, Chelmsford CM2 0PG (01245 252420; **email** administration.essex@ecb.co.uk). **Website** www.essexcricket.org.uk

OFFICIALS

Captain M. L. Pettini
First team coach A. P. Grayson
Batting coach G. A. Gooch
Bowling coach C. E. W. Silverwood
President D. J. Insole

Chairman N. R. A. Hilliard
Chief executive D. E. East
Chairman, cricket committee G. J. Saville
Head groundsman S. Kerrison
Scorer A. E. Choat

Kieran Galvin

This way up: Ryan ten Doeschate powers Essex to promotion at Derby on the last day of the Championship season, reaching a brutal hundred from 57 balls.

ESSEX v DERBYSHIRE

At Chelmsford, April 15, 16, 17, 18. Drawn. Essex 7 pts, Derbyshire 10 pts. Toss: Essex. County debuts: M. J. Walker; S. G. Law, G. T. Park.

Derbyshire had not won at Chelmsford since 1937, and the loss of more than 100 overs proved a major factor in extending that run after the visitors had controlled the match on a well-grassed pitch offering seam assistance. Derbyshire were grateful for 51 extras after each of their top eight reached 24 without passing 50. Essex were in danger of following on when four wickets fell for 11 runs, only for a ninth-wicket stand of 37 between Foster, dropped by Stubbings at first slip, and Masters to avert the danger; Hunter's career-best figures ultimately proved in vain. Despite a lead of 132, Derbyshire opted for a safety-first approach, as Foster took his haul of catches to eight, before they eventually declared 311 ahead on the final afternoon. With Chopra and Gallian posting their second half-century partnership, the match limped to a draw. Neither county was able to include an overseas player: both Danish Kaneria and Chris Rogers were still awaiting visas.

Close of play: First day, Derbyshire 306-7 (Wagg 17, Clare 2); Second day, Essex 29-0 (Chopra 16, Gallian 7); Third day, Derbyshire 4-1 (Park 2, Law 1).

Derbyshire

S. D. Stubbings c Foster b ten Doeschate	28	– c Gallian b Masters	0
G. T. Park b Wright	41	– c Foster b Chambers	7
S. G. Law c Foster b Wright	29	– c Foster b Wright	3
D. J. Redfern c Foster b Masters	50	– c Foster b ten Doeschate	26
W. W. Hinds c Masters b ten Doeschate	24	– (7) c Foster b Middlebrook	8
G. M. Smith lbw b Middlebrook	36	– (5) c ten Doeschate b Middlebrook	59
*†D. J. Pipe c Mickleburgh b Chambers	39	– (6) not out	64
G. G. Wagg not out	24		
J. L. Clare c Foster b Masters	2		
T. Lungley b Wright	0		
I. D. Hunter b Wright	2		
B 1, l-b 18, w 2, n-b 30	51	L-b 3, w 1, n-b 8	12

1/75 (1) 2/101 (2) 3/132 (3)   (105.4 overs) 326   1/0 (1)   (6 wkts dec, 55 overs) 179
4/166 (5) 5/235 (6) 6/260 (4)   2/9 (3) 3/19 (2)
7/295 (7) 8/307 (9) 9/318 (10) 10/326 (11)   4/64 (4) 5/153 (5) 6/179 (7)

Masters 28–11–40–2; Wright 29.4–7–86–4; Chambers 17–3–63–1; ten Doeschate 19–1–95–2; Middlebrook 12–5–23–1. *Second Innings*—Masters 9–5–6–1; Wright 10–2–17–1; Chambers 10–0–53–1; ten Doeschate 11–1–57–1; Middlebrook 15–3–43–2.

Essex

V. Chopra c Pipe b Lungley	39	– c Park b Hunter	56
J. E. R. Gallian c Stubbings b Hunter	11	– not out	44
J. C. Mickleburgh c Pipe b Hunter	5	– lbw b Hunter	1
M. J. Walker c Park b Smith	17	– c Pipe b Clare	7
*M. L. Pettini c Pipe b Hunter	28	– not out	1
†J. S. Foster c Lungley b Hunter	40		
R. N. ten Doeschate c Pipe b Clare	1		
J. D. Middlebrook lbw b Hunter	0		
C. J. C. Wright c sub (J. Needham) b Clare	8		
D. D. Masters c Redfern b Smith	20		
M. A. Chambers not out	2		
B 2, l-b 6, w 7, n-b 8	23	L-b 1, w 6, n-b 4	11

1/50 (2) 2/56 (3) 3/87 (4) 4/93 (1)   (69 overs) 194   1/88 (1)   (3 wkts, 29 overs) 120
5/140 (5) 6/141 (7) 7/142 (8) 8/151 (9)   2/100 (3) 3/114 (4)
9/188 (6) 10/194 (10)

Lungley 12–2–60–1; Hunter 23–4–46–5; Clare 18–7–44–2; Park 5–0–12–0; Smith 11–4–24–2. *Second Innings*—Lungley 11–1–62–0; Hunter 10–2–42–2; Smith 2–0–7–0; Park 1–1–0–0; Clare 3–2–1–1; Redfern 2–0–7–0.

Umpires: V. A. Holder and G. Sharp.

At Bristol, April 21, 22, 23. ESSEX beat GLOUCESTERSHIRE by seven wickets.

At Chelmsford, April 25, 26, 27. ESSEX drew with WEST INDIANS (see West Indian tour section).

ESSEX v KENT

At Chelmsford, April 29, 30, May 1, 2. Kent won by 192 runs. Kent 18 pts, Essex 7 pts. Toss: Kent. County debut: W. D. Parnell.

Kent completed their first victory after following on since 1992 thanks to a momentous second-innings rearguard and some blistering new-ball bowling from Parnell and Joseph. Asked to bat again after falling 165 behind first time round, Kent rode on a combination of luck and skill to turn the match on its head. Tredwell was dropped twice while making 79 in 13 minutes short of five hours, eventually adding 124 for the third wicket with van Jaarsveld, before Stevens and Hockley took up the baton with a sixth-wicket alliance of 166. The declaration set Essex 348 in 61 overs on a pitch still good for batting, but Parnell removed both openers, before Joseph ripped through the middle order to reduce the home side to 79 for seven. Masters and ten Doeschate resisted for 82 minutes, but the last three wickets fell in a hurry to round off an astonishing victory – the largest by a team asked to follow on – with 22 balls to spare (see *Wisden 2009*, page 1287). Earlier, Walker, missed before he had scored by van Jaarsveld at second slip against his former county, and Foster came agonisingly close to hundreds. After Kent had slipped to 96 for six in reply, Parnell, dropped on three, belted his maiden fifty to hint at the defiance still to come. Quite how much defiance, no one could have predicted.

Close of play: First day, Essex 330-7 (Foster 95, Wright 0); Second day, Kent 54-1 (Tredwell 15, G. O. Jones 14); Third day, Kent 391-5 (Stevens 74, Hockley 33).

Essex

V. Chopra b Parnell	12	– c G. O. Jones b Parnell	10
A. N. Cook c Hockley b Saggers	41	– c Tredwell b Parnell	4
J. C. Mickleburgh c van Jaarsveld b Parnell	7	– lbw b Joseph	15
M. J. Walker lbw b Joseph	98	– b Joseph	16
*M. L. Pettini b Saggers	27	– lbw b Joseph	0
†J. S. Foster c G. O. Jones b Saggers	99	– c Kemp b Joseph	13
D. D. Masters c van Jaarsveld b Joseph	0	– (9) c Denly b Tredwell	20
R. N. ten Doeschate c G. O. Jones b P. S. Jones	3	– (7) c van Jaarsveld b Parnell	36
C. J. C. Wright c Kemp b Parnell	6	– (8) b Joseph	0
Danish Kaneria c Denly b Parnell	23	– c Stevens b Joseph	4
M. A. Chambers not out	4	– not out	0
B 6, l-b 13, w 1, n-b 30	50	B 4, l-b 5, n-b 28	37

1/31 (1) 2/69 (2) 3/72 (3) (104.5 overs) 370
4/115 (5) 5/309 (4) 6/313 (7)
7/320 (8) 8/338 (9) 9/366 (6) 10/370 (10)

1/11 (2) 2/22 (1) (57.2 overs) 155
3/34 (3) 4/34 (5)
5/74 (6) 6/79 (4) 7/79 (8) 8/151 (9)
9/153 (7) 10/155 (10)

Joseph 20–2–104–2; Parnell 27.5–7–78–4; Saggers 22–8–45–3; P. S. Jones 17–3–61–1; Stevens 7–1–15–0; Kemp 9–2–35–0; Tredwell 2–0–13–0. *Second Innings*—Parnell 19–3–56–3; Saggers 8–3–17–0; Joseph 13.2–0–55–6; P. S. Jones 9–5–9–0; Tredwell 8–5–9–1.

Kent

J. L. Denly c Foster b Masters	0	– c sub (T. J. Phillips) b Wright	19
J. C. Tredwell c Foster b ten Doeschate	10	– c Cook b Danish Kaneria	79
†G. O. Jones c Foster b Wright	1	– b Chambers	45
*M. van Jaarsveld run out	35	– c Foster b Masters	102
D. I. Stevens lbw b Chambers	15	– not out	136
J. M. Kemp c Foster b Masters	3	– c Cook b Danish Kaneria	22
J. B. Hockley b Danish Kaneria	46	– c Pettini b Wright	72
W. D. Parnell c Masters b Wright	69	– c Chopra b Danish Kaneria	3
P. S. Jones lbw b Danish Kaneria	0	– c Cook b Chambers	16
R. H. Joseph c sub (T. J. Phillips) b Chambers	1	– lbw b Danish Kaneria	0
M. J. Saggers not out	5	– not out	0
B 4, l-b 1, w 1, n-b 14	20	L-b 6, w 2, n-b 10	18

1/4 (1) 2/13 (3) 3/19 (2) 4/54 (5) (62 overs) 205
5/57 (6) 6/96 (4) 7/134 (7) 8/134 (9)
9/159 (10) 10/205 (8)

1/35 (1) (9 wkts dec, 149.4 overs) 512
2/113 (3)
3/237 (2) 4/272 (4) 5/312 (6) 6/478 (7)
7/481 (8) 8/509 (9) 9/510 (10)

Masters 14–6–18–2; Wright 13–2–49–2; ten Doeschate 11–2–40–1; Chambers 11–1–45–2; Danish Kaneria 13–2–48–2. *Second Innings*—Masters 31–9–82–1; Wright 32–5–98–2; Danish Kaneria 46–7–172–4; ten Doeschate 16–3–51–0; Chambers 12.4–1–58–2; Chopra 4.1–1–17–0; Mickleburgh 7.5–1–28–0.

Umpires: N. L. Bainton and M. J. D. Bodenham.

At Northampton, May 6, 7, 8, 9. ESSEX lost to NORTHAMPTONSHIRE by eight wickets.

ESSEX v MIDDLESEX

At Chelmsford, June 6, 7, 8, 9. Drawn. Essex 7 pts, Middlesex 9 pts. Toss: Essex. First-class debut: S. D. Robson.

Essex failed to drive home their early advantage after Middlesex subsided from 117 for two to 139 for seven on the first afternoon. Then Berg, with a maiden first-class half-century, and Kartik added 99 for the eighth wicket, and the fightback continued as the lively Finn, finding bounce to complete his first five-wicket haul, and Berg – with another career-best – helped skittle Essex for 157, a total that would have been worse without Danish Kaneria's unorthodox 30-ball 37. Strauss rammed home Middlesex's advantage with a classy 97 that ended when he lost his off stump to Chambers playing down the wrong line, and the teatime declaration on the third day set Essex 415. Two scalps were claimed by the close, but Cook – who might have been run out on 24 after Walker scampered a quick single to get off the mark – survived, and when the weather delayed the start on the final day until three o'clock, a draw seemed inevitable.

Close of play: First day, Essex 54-4 (Masters 5, Pettini 0); Second day, Middlesex 60-0 (Strauss 35, Compton 24); Third day, Essex 79-2 (Cook 43, Walker 16).

Middlesex

A. J. Strauss c Wheater b Wright	16	– b Chambers	97
N. R. D. Compton b Wright	24	– lbw b Masters	44
S. D. Robson c Wheater b Masters	43	– lbw b Danish Kaneria	23
N. J. Dexter c Wheater b Masters	29	– lbw b Danish Kaneria	42
D. J. Malan b Wright	1	– c Cook b Danish Kaneria	3
†D. C. Nash c and b Wright	3	– c Wheater b Masters	26
G. K. Berg b Masters	56	– c and b Danish Kaneria	9
*S. D. Udal lbw b Danish Kaneria	7	– not out	36
M. Kartik not out	62		
C. E. W. Silverwood c Cook b Masters	9		
S. T. Finn c Cook b Masters	12		
L-b 8, n-b 4	12	B 11, l-b 4, n-b 2	17

1/23 (1) 2/60 (2) 3/117 (4)   (72.4 overs) 274
4/120 (5) 5/124 (3) 6/124 (6)
7/139 (8) 8/238 (7) 9/248 (10) 10/274 (11)

1/146 (2)   (7 wkts dec, 88.1 overs) 297
2/152 (1) 3/201 (3)
4/213 (5) 5/232 (4)
6/242 (7) 7/297 (6)

Masters 20.4–4–65–5; Wright 21–5–71–4; Chambers 14–0–50–0; Danish Kaneria 12–0–52–1; Middlebrook 4–0–21–0; Walker 1–0–7–0. *Second Innings*—Masters 20.1–3–39–2; Wright 16–1–60–0; Chambers 11–1–35–1; Danish Kaneria 28–6–85–4; Middlebrook 13–1–63–0.

Essex

A. N. Cook c Strauss b Kartik	31	– not out	84
J. E. R. Gallian c Kartik b Finn	10	– b Finn	12
V. Chopra c Dexter b Finn	0	– b Finn	0
M. J. Walker c Nash b Finn	5	– c Nash b Finn	19
D. D. Masters lbw b Berg	22		
*M. L. Pettini b Berg	10	– (5) lbw b Kartik	21
J. D. Middlebrook c Nash b Berg	2	– (6) not out	9
†A. G. Wheater c Kartik b Berg	0		
C. J. C. Wright c Nash b Finn	19		
Danish Kaneria c Dexter b Finn	37		
M. A. Chambers not out	8		
B 4, l-b 8, w 1	13	B 8, l-b 2, n-b 4	14

1/34 (2) 2/34 (1) 3/48 (4) 4/48 (4)   (55.3 overs) 157
5/86 (6) 6/87 (5) 7/87 (8) 8/98 (7)
9/120 (9) 10/157 (10)

1/34 (1)   (4 wkts, 62.1 overs) 159
2/40 (3) 3/90 (4)
4/145 (5)

Silverwood 15–5–40–0; Finn 21.3–8–57–5; Kartik 2–1–1–1; Berg 13.2–2–35–4; Dexter 4–2–12–0. *Second Innings*—Silverwood 12–2–34–0; Finn 17–1–67–3; Berg 8–3–14–0; Kartik 15.1–7–19–1; Udal 10–3–15–0.

Umpires: V. A. Holder and D. J. Millns.

At Cambridge, June 11, 12, 13. ESSEX drew with CAMBRIDGE UCCE.

At Tunbridge Wells, June 16, 17, 18, 19. ESSEX beat KENT by 122 runs.

ESSEX v GLAMORGAN

At Chelmsford, July 7, 8, 9, 10. Drawn. Essex 7 pts, Glamorgan 12 pts. Toss: Glamorgan. County debut: H. M. Amla. Championship debut: H. H. Gibbs.

    Glamorgan were in control from the moment Rees and Gibbs put on 115 for the first wicket on an easy-paced pitch. Powell compiled his fourth hundred against Essex and 25th in all, while Shantry's 38 as night-watchman – equalling his career-best – exposed the toothlessness of an Essex attack missing Danish Kaneria, who was playing for Pakistan in Sri Lanka. Shantry then made inroads with the ball, taking three for six in 15 deliveries in a 13-over spell that brought him five for 50. Essex's tame capitulation left them 315 adrift on first innings and, after the follow-on was enforced, they were in trouble again at 17 for two and 85 for four. But Amla, their interim signing from South Africa, stopped the rot, batting for nine minutes short of seven hours to make a magnificent 181. Amla, who was dropped off Croft at short leg on 78, added 142 with Foster and 153 with ten Doeschate, and within an hour of his dismissal the captains had settled for the draw.

Close of play: First day, Glamorgan 155-3 (Powell 20, Shantry 7); Second day, Essex 34-0 (Chopra 24, Maunders 8); Third day, Essex 133-4 (Amla 44, Foster 26).

Glamorgan

G. P. Rees c Foster b Masters	59	D. S. Harrison c Amla b Middlebrook	13
H. H. Gibbs b ten Doeschate	53	G. J-P. Kruger not out	28
B. J. Wright lbw b Napier	1		
M. J. Powell c Maunders b Napier	102	B 1, l-b 7, n-b 20	28
A. J. Shantry b Middlebrook	38		
*J. W. M. Dalrymple c Maunders b Wright	50	1/115 (2) (9 wkts dec, 132 overs)	515
†M. A. Wallace c Amla b Napier	37	2/118 (3) 3/138 (1)	
J. A. R. Harris not out	76	4/210 (5) 5/299 (6) 6/350 (4) 7/365 (7)	
R. D. B. Croft c Maunders b Middlebrook	30	8/410 (9) 9/452 (10) 120 overs: 424-8	

Masters 34–7–79–1; Wright 26–2–119–1; Napier 27–5–112–3; ten Doeschate 24–0–110–1; Middlebrook 21–3–87–3.

Essex

V. Chopra b Shantry	31	– lbw b Harrison	8
J. K. Maunders lbw b Harris	35	– c Gibbs b Harrison	8
H. M. Amla b Harris	4	– lbw b Croft	181
M. J. Walker c Wallace b Shantry	4	– c Wallace b Harris	15
*M. L. Pettini c Wallace b Shantry	10	– c Dalrymple b Croft	21
†J. S. Foster c Dalrymple b Shantry	0	– b Dalrymple	64
R. N. ten Doeschate c Wallace b Harris	26	– not out	88
G. R. Napier c Gibbs b Shantry	13	– not out	10
J. D. Middlebrook not out	15		
D. D. Masters c Dalrymple b Kruger	33		
C. J. C. Wright c Rees b Croft	1		
B 12, l-b 11, w 1, n-b 4	28	B 4, l-b 6, n-b 6	16

1/53 (1) 2/76 (3) 3/83 (4) 4/93 (5)	(57.5 overs) 200	1/16 (2) (6 wkts, 127 overs)	411
5/93 (6) 6/93 (2) 7/118 (8) 8/145 (7)		2/17 (1) 3/56 (4)	
9/199 (10) 10/200 (11)		4/85 (5) 5/227 (6) 6/380 (3)	

Harrison 12–2–39–0; Harris 15–3–37–3; Kruger 13–4–34–1; Shantry 15–0–62–5; Croft 2.5–0–5–1. *Second Innings*—Harris 23–8–58–1; Harrison 19–2–64–2; Shantry 17–6–56–0; Croft 41–4–107–2; Kruger 14–2–64–0; Dalrymple 13–0–52–1.

Umpires: J. H. Evans and D. J. Millns.

At Guildford, July 15, 16, 17, 18. ESSEX drew with SURREY.

At Leicester, July 21, 22, 23, 24. ESSEX drew with LEICESTERSHIRE.

ESSEX v GLOUCESTERSHIRE

At Southend, August 5, 6, 7, 8. Gloucestershire won by ten wickets. Gloucestershire 21 pts, Essex 5 pts. Toss: Essex.

Gloucestershire completed their second successive win at Garon Park, having previously won there in 2007, by comprehensively outplaying Essex in all facets of the game. Essex initially did well to reach 300 after slipping to 47 for five, as Pettini marshalled the lower order and Masters hit a maiden half-century for them. And when Gloucestershire subsided to 170 for six in reply, the Essex recovery seemed to be gathering momentum. But Franklin and Adshead responded with admirable hundreds in a game-changing stand of 169 for the seventh wicket, with Adshead going on to a career-best unbeaten 156 spanning more than six hours. A first-innings deficit of 198 proved too much for Essex, who lost seven wickets wiping off the arrears against some disciplined medium-pace bowling from Gloucestershire before inevitably going down to their third straight defeat at a venue unloved by their members.

Close of play: First day, Gloucestershire 13-1 (Kadeer Ali 9, Kirby 0); Second day, Gloucestershire 319-6 (Franklin 92, Adshead 56); Third day, Essex 75-3 (Westley 25, Pettini 21).

Essex

J. K. Maunders lbw b Saxelby	28	– c Dawson b Lewis	8
J. E. R. Gallian c Taylor b Franklin	3	– c Adshead b Lewis	6
T. Westley c Dawson b Kirby	7	– c Gidman b Dawson	32
M. J. Walker c Kadeer Ali b Kirby	0	– c Dawson b Kirby	7
*M. L. Pettini c Taylor b Lewis	91	– lbw b Franklin	36
†J. S. Foster c Adshead b Franklin	4	– c Marshall b Saxelby	20
R. N. ten Doeschate c Woodman b Dawson	43	– lbw b Saxelby	33
G. R. Napier c Adshead b Kirby	50	– c Kadeer Ali b Saxelby	39
D. D. Masters c Woodman b Franklin	55	– c Dawson b Franklin	19
Danish Kaneria c Taylor b Lewis	0	– c Saxelby b Franklin	1
C. J. C. Wright not out	0	– not out	15
B 2, l-b 11, n-b 6	19	B 8, l-b 8, w 2, n-b 2	20

1/16 (2) 2/26 (3) 3/26 (4) 4/42 (1) (86.1 overs) 300
5/47 (6) 6/138 (7) 7/208 (8)
8/296 (9) 9/297 (10) 10/300 (5)

1/10 (2) 2/17 (1) (93.5 overs) 236
3/31 (4) 4/87 (3)
5/113 (5) 6/148 (6) 7/183 (7) 8/215 (9)
9/217 (10) 10/236 (8)

Lewis 18.1–7–31–2; Franklin 16–1–61–3; Kirby 16–5–51–3; Saxelby 17–1–63–1; Dawson 12–0–61–1; Marshall 7–1–20–0. *Second Innings*—Kirby 18–4–36–1; Lewis 18–5–42–2; Franklin 16–5–23–3; Saxelby 16.5–4–31–3; Marshall 1–0–2–0; Dawson 24–2–86–1.

Gloucestershire

Kadeer Ali c Foster b Napier	76	– (2) not out	13
R. J. Woodman c Maunders b Masters	1	– (1) not out	23
S. P. Kirby c Pettini b Napier	19		
H. J. H. Marshall c Napier b ten Doeschate	20		
*A. P. R. Gidman c Foster b Danish Kaneria	14		
C. G. Taylor b Wright	21		
J. E. C. Franklin lbw b Danish Kaneria	100		
†S. J. Adshead not out	156		
R. K. J. Dawson b Wright	8		
I. D. Saxelby lbw b Danish Kaneria	20		
J. Lewis c Foster b Napier	32		
B 3, l-b 12, w 4, n-b 12	31	L-b 1, n-b 2	3

1/11 (2) 2/61 (3) 3/94 (4) (152.2 overs) 498
4/119 (5) 5/163 (1) 6/170 (6)
7/339 (7) 8/354 (9) 9/428 (10)
10/498 (11) 120 overs: 353-7

(no wkt, 10.2 overs) 39

Masters 35–12–68–1; Wright 27–2–96–2; Danish Kaneria 44–9–158–3; Napier 28.2–5–99–3; ten Doeschate 16–2–48–1; Westley 2–0–14–0. *Second Innings*—Wright 5.2–0–19–0; Danish Kaneria 5–1–19–0.

Umpires: R. A. Kettleborough and J. W. Lloyds.

At Lord's, August 11, 12, 13, 14. ESSEX beat MIDDLESEX by five wickets.

ESSEX v SURREY

At Colchester, August 19, 20, 21, 22. Essex won by nine wickets. Essex 21 pts, Surrey 6 pts. Toss: Surrey.

Career-best performances with the bat from Schofield – who hit a maiden first-class hundred with 22 fours – Spriegel and Meaker earned Surrey an unlikely fifth batting point with a ball to spare after they had collapsed to 136 for five. But those efforts were overshadowed by a superb double-century from Bopara, who responded to being dropped by England with some trademark drives on both sides of the wicket to take Essex to their highest total of the summer – despite injuries to Pettini, who had a disc problem in his back, and ten Doeschate, who was hit on the hand by Dernbach. Danish Kaneria then got stuck in with the ball, taking six for 50 – his 21st haul of five wickets or more for Essex – to move to 250 Championship victims. One of them was Ramprakash, who questioned a catch by Foster and departed for the pavilion reluctantly after exchanging words with the fielders. Essex galloped to their target at nearly six an over.

Close of play: First day, Surrey 304-6 (Schofield 87, Meaker 22); Second day, Essex 221-3 (Bopara 83, Pettini 33); Third day, Surrey 6-2 (Brown 6).

Surrey

†J. N. Batty c Pettini b Danish Kaneria	23	–	lbw b Danish Kaneria	0
M. J. Brown c Foster b Wright	0	–	c Westley b Wright	37
M. R. Ramprakash c Foster b Masters	33	– (4)	c Foster b Danish Kaneria	62
*S. J. Walters c Foster b Wright	41	– (5)	c Danish Kaneria b Phillips	9
U. Afzaal c Pettini b Danish Kaneria	17	– (6)	c ten Doeschate b Phillips	6
M. N. W. Spriegel c Westley b Phillips	61	– (7)	c Walker b Danish Kaneria	6
C. P. Schofield c Foster b ten Doeschate	144	– (8)	lbw b Danish Kaneria	24
S. C. Meaker c Pettini b Danish Kaneria	72	– (9)	c Maunders b Danish Kaneria	23
J. W. Dernbach c Pettini b ten Doeschate	10	– (10)	c Bopara b Phillips	2
T. E. Linley run out	4	– (3)	c Maunders b Danish Kaneria	0
P. T. Collins not out	0	–	not out	0
B 4, l-b 11, n-b 8	23		B 8, l-b 1, n-b 12	21

1/2 (2) 2/39 (1) 3/100 (3) 4/124 (4)   (128 overs) 428
5/136 (5) 6/263 (6) 7/388 (7)
8/404 (9) 9/428 (10) 10/428 (8)   120 overs: 402-7

1/0 (1) 2/6 (3) 3/88 (2)   (69 overs) 190
4/101 (5) 5/115 (6)
6/134 (7) 7/135 (4)
8/187 (8) 9/190 (10) 10/190 (9)

Masters 27–10–61–1; Wright 28–6–91–2; Danish Kaneria 38–7–120–3; ten Doeschate 18–4–71–2; Phillips 12–1–63–1; Bopara 2–1–2–0; Westley 3–0–5–0. *Second Innings*—Danish Kaneria 27–13–50–6; Masters 7–3–16–0; Phillips 24–4–61–3; Wright 11–0–54–1.

Essex

J. K. Maunders lbw b Schofield	39	–	c Walters b Dernbach	10
T. Westley c Batty b Collins	35	–	not out	45
R. S. Bopara c Spriegel b Collins	201	–	not out	15
M. J. Walker c Batty b Meaker	22			
*M. L. Pettini retired hurt	42			
†J. S. Foster c Batty b Meaker	11			
R. N. ten Doeschate not out	7			
T. J. Phillips c Linley b Schofield	69			
D. D. Masters c Brown b Dernbach	43			
C. J. C. Wright b Collins	16			
Danish Kaneria c Schofield b Collins	31			
B 8, l-b 7, w 8, n-b 6	29		L-b 1, w 1, n-b 2	4

1/77 (2) 2/79 (1) 3/137 (4)   (152.4 overs) 545
4/269 (6) 5/412 (3) 6/472 (8)
7/487 (9) 8/535 (11) 9/545 (10)   120 overs: 412-5

1/20 (1)   (1 wkt, 12.4 overs) 74

In the first innings Pettini retired hurt at 254; ten Doeschate, when 4, retired hurt at 282 and resumed at 535.

Dernbach 32–6–99–1; Collins 25.4–3–96–4; Linley 22–5–55–0; Schofield 27–1–117–2; Meaker 27–6–91–2; Spriegel 11–0–46–0; Afzaal 8–0–26–0. *Second Innings*—Dernbach 6–0–31–1; Schofield 5–0–22–0; Afzaal 1–0–9–0; Spriegel 0.4–0–11–0.

Umpires: M. J. D. Bodenham and M. A. Gough.

ESSEX v LEICESTERSHIRE

At Chelmsford, August 26, 27, 28, 29. Drawn. Essex 11 pts, Leicestershire 9 pts. Toss: Essex.

Backs-to-the-wall batting from Dippenaar and Taylor denied Essex a third straight victory after Leicestershire, following on 173 adrift, had slumped to 89 for four second time round. The defiant Dippenaar, dropped on 39 by Cook, held out for six hours, while Taylor kept him company in a fifth-wicket stand of 129, in the process passing 1,000 Championship runs for the season. The result, on a pitch offering slow turn throughout, was hard on Danish Kaneria, who sent down 86.3 overs for a match haul of 12 for 203 – including a county-best eight for 116 in the first innings. Earlier, Essex passed 500 for the second game in succession as Maunders struck his highest score for the club (against his former county) and Foster, the acting-captain in Pettini's absence, reached three figures for the first time all summer after putting on 104 for the ninth wicket with Masters, who also made his highest score for Essex. Taylor then kept Leicestershire afloat with a hundred of his own, but his attempts to avoid the follow-on were not helped when Benning was taken to hospital after being hit on the cheekbone by Masters. Naik twice found himself in the night-watchman role on the third day, while umpire Holder had to retire hurt briefly on the final day after being hit on the back by a throw from Masters.

Close of play: First day, Essex 310-3 (Maunders 142, Westley 71); Second day, Leicestershire 93-2 (Boyce 47, Naik 0); Third day, Leicestershire 42-2 (Dippenaar 17, Naik 0).

Essex

J. K. Maunders c Nixon b Harris	150	D. D. Masters run out		67
A. N. Cook b White	31	C. J. C. Wright not out		1
V. Chopra c New b White	13	B 8, l-b 14, w 1, n-b 4		27
M. J. Walker lbw b Naik	31			
T. Westley lbw b Harris	71	1/52 (2)	(9 wkts dec, 151.1 overs)	517
*†J. S. Foster not out	103	2/80 (3) 3/151 (4)		
T. J. Phillips st New b Henderson	22	4/310 (5) 5/321 (1) 6/392 (7)		
Danish Kaneria c Benning b Henderson	0	7/392 (8) 8/399 (9) 9/503 (10)		
R. N. ten Doeschate c and b Naik	1		120 overs: 392-7	

Harris 29–6–109–2; Benning 36–6–111–0; White 21–0–101–2; Naik 25–3–73–2; Henderson 40.1–6–101–2.

Leicestershire

P. A. Nixon c Foster b Danish Kaneria	40	– c Foster b Wright		4
M. A. G. Boyce b Danish Kaneria	70	– c Walker b Danish Kaneria		14
*H. H. Dippenaar c Phillips b Danish Kaneria	0	– not out		115
J. K. H. Naik c Phillips b Danish Kaneria	10	– c Danish Kaneria b Phillips		20
J. J. Cobb c and b Danish Kaneria	4	– b Danish Kaneria		1
J. W. A. Taylor not out	112	– lbw b Danish Kaneria		62
†T. J. New c Maunders b Danish Kaneria	14	– lbw b Danish Kaneria		10
J. G. E. Benning retired hurt	36	– not out		21
W. A. White c Foster b ten Doeschate	11			
C. W. Henderson lbw b Danish Kaneria	14			
A. J. Harris lbw b Danish Kaneria	7			
B 9, l-b 10, w 1, n-b 6	26	B 6, l-b 1, n-b 4		11

1/83 (1) 2/87 (3) 3/111 (4)	(118.4 overs) 344	1/9 (1)	(6 wkts, 101.5 overs) 258
4/115 (5) 5/152 (2) 6/178 (7)		2/34 (2) 3/88 (4)	
7/277 (9) 8/322 (10) 9/344 (11)		4/89 (5) 5/218 (6) 6/230 (7)	

In the first innings Benning retired hurt at 247.

Masters 21–9–61–0; Wright 16–3–59–0; Danish Kaneria 49.4–16–116–8; ten Doeschate 14–2–55–1; Phillips 18–7–34–0. *Second Innings*—Masters 14–4–27–0; Wright 15–0–48–1; Phillips 25–9–44–1; Danish Kaneria 36.5–12–87–4; ten Doeschate 4–1–18–0; Westley 4–0–18–0; Cook 1–0–3–0; Chopra 2–0–6–0.

Umpires: V. A. Holder and J. F. Steele. P. Adams deputised for Holder on the fourth day.

At Cardiff, September 10, 11, 12, 13. ESSEX drew with GLAMORGAN.

ESSEX v NORTHAMPTONSHIRE

At Chelmsford, September 15, 16, 17, 18. Essex won by four wickets. Essex 19 pts, Northamptonshire 4 pts. Toss: Essex. Championship debut: P. W. Harrison.

Twelve points behind second-placed Northamptonshire at the start of play, Essex won a thriller off the penultimate ball to keep alive their promotion hopes after the whole of the first day had been lost to rain. Set 242 in 52 overs, they were boosted by an opening stand of 130 inside 32 between Cook and Maunders, only for van der Wath to halt their momentum by taking five of the next six wickets, which fell for 75 runs in 16 overs. But, with Essex needing 28 off the final three, van der Wath conceded 16 in an over and Westley and Napier scrambled the winning bye with a ball to spare. Victory had been set up by Danish Kaneria, who claimed his 24th five-wicket haul in his 50th first-class game for Essex. Ten Doeschate and Foster engineered a revival after they had slipped to 128 for five. Northamptonshire then collapsed to 90 for seven, only for Lucas – dropped on 18 by Pettini, who was standing in behind the stumps after Foster broke a cheek bone in the warm-up – to compile a maiden half-century and set up the nail-biting finale.

Close of play: First day, No play; Second day, Essex 3-0 (Maunders 3, Cook 0); Third day, Northamptonshire 41-2 (O'Brien 28, Wessels 5).

Northamptonshire

S. D. Peters lbw b Danish Kaneria	37	– lbw b Masters	2
†N. J. O'Brien c Napier b Wright	14	– c Pettini b Napier	38
P. W. Harrison c Cook b Masters	32	– lbw b Masters	3
M. H. Wessels st Foster b Danish Kaneria	10	– c Pettini b Wright	8
R. A. White c Maunders b Danish Kaneria	30	– b Wright	8
*N. Boje lbw b Danish Kaneria	8	– c ten Doeschate b Wright	8
A. J. Hall c Foster b Masters	85	– b Danish Kaneria	29
J. J. van der Wath c Foster b Napier	10	– b Napier	0
D. S. Lucas c Foster b Danish Kaneria	20	– not out	55
M. S. Panesar not out	32	– c Walker b Wright	19
L. M. Daggett b Masters	0	– c Walker b Napier	2
B 6, l-b 3, n-b 12	21	B 1, l-b 6, w 2, n-b 14	23

1/40 (2) 2/67 (1) 3/79 (4) 4/143 (5) (90.3 overs) 299
5/143 (3) 6/153 (6) 7/180 (8)
8/251 (9) 9/297 (7) 10/299 (11)

1/8 (1) 2/28 (3) (59.3 overs) 195
3/55 (4) 4/71 (5)
5/85 (6) 6/85 (2) 7/90 (8)
8/150 (7) 9/183 (10) 10/195 (11)

Masters 19.3–7–57–3; Wright 15–1–61–1; Napier 18–4–74–1; Danish Kaneria 36–12–86–5; Westley 2–0–12–0. *Second Innings*—Masters 19–5–35–2; Danish Kaneria 21–3–64–1; Napier 7.3–1–46–3; Wright 12–3–43–4.

Essex

J. K. Maunders c White b van der Wath	10	– c O'Brien b van der Wath	46
A. N. Cook c Peters b Lucas	0	– c O'Brien b van der Wath	87
T. Westley b Lucas	3	– (8) not out	15
M. J. Walker c Hall b Panesar	40	– (3) c O'Brien b van der Wath	39
*M. L. Pettini c Hall b Boje	47	– b Hall	5
†J. S. Foster c Peters b Hall	28	– b van der Wath	5
R. N. ten Doeschate c Daggett b Hall	75	– (4) c O'Brien b van der Wath	7
G. R. Napier not out	7	– (7) not out	22
D. D. Masters c Hall b Panesar	5		
Danish Kaneria not out	15		
B 4, l-b 11, n-b 8	23	B 4, l-b 11, w 1	16

1/14 (1) 2/14 (2)   (8 wkts dec, 78.4 overs) 253   1/130 (1)   (6 wkts, 51.5 overs) 242
3/21 (3) 4/102 (4)   2/159 (2) 3/175 (4)
5/128 (5) 6/217 (6) 7/226 (7) 8/231 (9)   4/192 (5) 5/204 (3) 6/205 (6)

C. J. C. Wright did not bat.

Van der Wath 14–4–37–1; Lucas 11–4–16–2; Daggett 8–4–23–0; Hall 12.4–3–38–2; Panesar 25–6–71–2; Boje 8–0–53–1. *Second Innings*—van der Wath 17.5–3–71–5; Lucas 5–1–30–0; Hall 14–0–51–1; Boje 5–0–29–0; Panesar 8–0–29–0; Daggett 2–0–17–0.

Umpires: N. G. Cowley and B. Dudleston.

At Derby, September 23, 24, 25, 26. ESSEX beat DERBYSHIRE by five wickets. *Essex secure promotion by a single point.*

GLAMORGAN

More records, fewer wins

EDWARD BEVAN

With three weeks of the season to go, Glamorgan were in real contention for promotion, but they failed to take the tenth wicket against both Essex and Gloucestershire, and drew the last game, against Surrey, as well. If two Championship victories seemed inadequate recompense for the county's record-breaking batting achievements, they starkly highlighted the imperative of bowling sides out twice. Chairman Paul Russell and director of cricket Matthew Maynard were completely at odds with their verdicts on the season. While Maynard maintained Glamorgan had made positive strides during the season, the chairman disagreed. "It has been a very poor season," Russell said. "You cannot be enamoured with eight wins from 42 games – four fewer than last year." Maynard's future had appeared uncertain until his appraisal in the autumn, and a new two-year contract.

Unlike in 2008, the batsmen prospered. They struck 16 centuries and collected 56 batting points – no team in either division managed more – compared with a meagre 26 in 2008. In the final game at The Oval they racked up 702 for eight, just 16 short of their highest-ever total. Four of their batsmen scored centuries in that game, with openers Gareth Rees and Mark Cosgrove hitting 315, an all-wicket record for Glamorgan against Surrey.

However, Glamorgan's one-day results were dismal. They ended next to bottom in their Friends Provident group, and were deducted two points for producing a "poor" pitch at Cardiff against Essex. (The penalty will be implemented in the 40-over League since the 50-over competition was scrapped at the end of the 2009 season.) They also made little impression in the Twenty20 Cup, winning only twice, while their 40-over performances improved only during the last two games.

After a poor start, Rees once more passed 1,000 runs and hit three centuries. He made a formidable left-handed opening combination with Cosgrove, whose return to the club was a great success. Maynard had never seen the South Australian bat, but signed him on the recommendation of those who had played with Cosgrove in 2006. He reached 50 in eight of his 14 innings and averaged 63.08; he was due to return as the overseas signing in 2010. Herschelle Gibbs, the club's alternative overseas player in mid-season, appeared in five Championship matches and only two one-day games. He made little impression and also suffered an injury. Many supporters were disappointed with his performances; some questioned his commitment.

Jamie Dalrymple, in his first year as captain, led by example, scoring centuries in three of the first five games and passing 1,000 runs for the first time in his career. Michael Powell ended 66 short of the landmark and might feel he should have done better; he was ultimately left out of the one-day team after he often failed to capitalise on a start. Mark Wallace kept beautifully throughout the season and hit centuries in the first and last games, yet he was seldom effective in the shorter game – his forte in previous seasons. Adam Shantry, the left-arm swing bowler, struck a remarkable maiden century, against Leicestershire at Colwyn Bay: batting at No. 10, he helped Robert Croft add 197 for the ninth wicket, only six short of the county record, which has stood since 1929.

Jamie Dalrymple

The club signed all-rounder Jim Allenby on loan from Leicestershire in early August; he agreed to a three-year contract from the end of the season and celebrated by sharing a stand of 240 with Wallace in the final game, against Surrey. Their partnership eclipsed Glamorgan's previous sixth-wicket record, set by Willie Jones and Len Muncer at Worcester in 1953.

Despite Glamorgan's indifferent form in the one-day competitions, 20-year-old Tom Maynard played a number of thrilling innings. He struck a century from just 57 deliveries against Northamptonshire at Colwyn Bay to beat his father's one-day record by one ball; he reached three figures in style with an on-drive for six into an adjoining garden.

Yet again, Croft was Glamorgan's leading wicket-taker with 56 Championship victims. At 39, he thrived on hard work; he bowled more overs than anyone else in the country and also struck 574 runs, including a century in the game against Leicestershire. The pace attack depended too much on the youthful shoulders of James Harris, 19, who took 41 wickets; he received only fitful support from Garnett Kruger and David Harrison. Kruger, the county's first Kolpak signing, bowled fast at times, but was often ineffective. Harrison again experienced a disappointing year, while Alex Wharf announced his retirement after an injury-prone season, and planned to become a first-class umpire. Dean Cosker, awarded a benefit for 2010, topped the bowling averages, thanks largely to a match haul of 11 for 126 against Essex.

Paul Russell received 157 letters, 102 text messages and more than 50 emails following the successful staging of the First Ashes Test at Cardiff. There had been plenty of detractors when the ground was granted Test status, but there was praise from all quarters afterwards. The club was rewarded with an England v Australia one-day international for 2010, followed by two Twenty20 games between England and Pakistan. At the end of the season, Alan Hamer, previously the finance and commercial director, and a prominent figure before and during the staging of the Test match, was promoted to chief executive.

GLAMORGAN RESULTS

All first-class matches – Played 17: Won 2, Lost 2, Drawn 13.
County Championship matches – Played 16: Won 2, Lost 2, Drawn 12.

LV County Championship, 5th in Division 2; Friends Provident Trophy, 4th in Group D;
Pro40 League, 6th in Division 2; Twenty20 Cup, 5th in Midlands/Wales/West Division.

COUNTY CHAMPIONSHIP AVERAGES, BATTING AND FIELDING

Cap		M	I	NO	R	HS	100s	50s	Avge	Ct/St
	M. J. Cosgrove§	9	14	2	757	175	3	5	63.08	4
	J. W. M. Dalrymple	16	23	3	1,009	128	3	5	50.45	17
2009	G. P. Rees†	16	24	1	1,028	154	3	4	44.69	13
2000	M. J. Powell†	16	24	1	934	108	2	7	40.60	7
	J. Allenby	5	8	0	299	137	1	2	37.37	6
	H. H. Gibbs§	5	7	0	259	96	0	2	37.00	7
1992	R. D. B. Croft†	16	21	4	574	121	1	1	33.76	4
	W. D. Bragg†	9	12	0	367	92	0	2	30.58	4
2003	M. A. Wallace†	16	22	0	645	139	2	0	29.31	30/6
	A. J. Shantry	12	17	3	314	100	1	0	22.42	0
	B. J. Wright	8	13	0	271	81	0	1	20.84	3
	J. A. R. Harris†	13	16	3	256	76*	0	1	19.69	1
2006	D. S. Harrison†	7	7	2	98	51	0	1	19.60	2
	T. L. Maynard†	5	7	1	115	51*	0	1	19.16	5
	G. J-P. Kruger¶	13	13	7	91	28*	0	0	15.16	2
2000	D. A. Cosker	8	11	3	107	46*	0	0	13.37	5

Also batted: C. P. Ashling (1 match) 12; M. P. O'Shea† (1 match) 50, 25.

† *Born in Wales.*   § *Official overseas player.*   ¶ *Other non-England-qualified player.*

BOWLING

	O	M	R	W	BB	5W/i	Avge
D. A. Cosker	312.1	83	769	26	6-91	2	29.57
R. D. B. Croft	720	152	1,681	56	5-65	1	30.01
A. J. Shantry	266	46	867	27	5-62	1	32.11
J. A. R. Harris	425.2	83	1,441	41	4-69	0	35.14
J. W. M. Dalrymple	224.2	27	709	20	3-11	0	35.45
D. S. Harrison	194.1	29	732	19	4-60	0	38.52
G. J-P. Kruger	353.4	59	1,283	33	6-93	1	38.87

Also bowled: J. Allenby 78–19–209–6; C. P. Ashling 28–3–116–3; W. D. Bragg 5–0–23–0; M. J. Cosgrove 51–7–188–5; B. J. Wright 8–0–41–0.

COUNTY RECORDS

Highest score for:	309*	S. P. James v Sussex at Colwyn Bay	2000
Highest score against:	322*	M. B. Loye (Northamptonshire) at Northampton .	1998
Leading run-scorer:	34,056	A. Jones (avge 33.03)	1957–1983
Best bowling for:	10-51	J. Mercer v Worcestershire at Worcester	1936
Best bowling against:	10-18	G. Geary (Leicestershire) at Pontypridd	1929
Leading wicket-taker:	2,174	D. J. Shepherd (avge 20.95).	1950–1972
Highest total for:	718-3 dec	v Sussex at Colwyn Bay	2000
Highest total against:	712	by Northamptonshire at Northampton	1998
Lowest total for:	22	v Lancashire at Liverpool	1924
Lowest total against:	33	by Leicestershire at Ebbw Vale	1965

ADDRESS

Swalec Stadium, Sophia Gardens, Cardiff CF11 9XR (029 2040 9380; **email** info@glamorgancricket.co.uk). **Website** www.glamorgancricket.com

OFFICIALS

Captain J. W. M. Dalrymple
Director of cricket M. P. Maynard
President P. M. Walker
Chairman R. P. Russell

Chief executive A. Hamer
Head groundsman K. Exton
Scorer/archivist Dr A. K. Hignell

Cardiff's Ashes bonanza

Cardiff's future as an international venue was definitely looking rosy after the First Ashes Test at the Swalec Stadium in July 2009. England will play Australia there in a one-day game on June 24 this summer, followed by two Twenty20 games against Pakistan in September. And there will be further internationals: England–Sri Lanka Tests in 2011 and 2014, and one-day games in each of the next six seasons, for a start.

The Ashes Test was a huge success, and many who had criticised the decision to take the game to Wales beforehand were apologetic and complimentary afterwards. The game generated £6m for Glamorgan, which equated to around two years' worth of revenue in recent years. The club had sold every ticket for the exciting final day, taking advantage of it falling on a Sunday. They also insured that day's ticket sales, so customers would get a full refund in the event of the game finishing earlier. With 1,700 temporary catering staff serving 152,000 pints of beer and supplying 12,500 bacon rolls from mostly Welsh suppliers, conservative estimates indicated that the Welsh economy was boosted by £20m as a direct result of the game.

Glamorgan's new chief executive Alan Hamer recognised, however, that more counties are developing their own grounds, so bidding will become more competitive. "Everyone knows how well we organised and handled the Test," he said, "and we hope that will be taken into account when we bid for future games. There are so many internationals – in all categories – due to be played in the next five years, and we are determined to establish the Swalec Stadium as a regular Test match venue."

Glamorgan's members, meanwhile, are seeking improvement on the field after five lean county seasons, and are desperate to have a team worthy of the stadium. The county has one of the smallest playing budgets in the country, and relies on home-grown players and lesser-known overseas signings: "We simply cannot afford star players on inflated salaries," said Hamer. EDWARD BEVAN

At Oxford, April 15, 16, 17. GLAMORGAN drew with OXFORD UCCE.

At Lord's, April 22, 23, 24, 25. GLAMORGAN drew with MIDDLESEX.

GLAMORGAN v DERBYSHIRE

At Cardiff, April 28, 29, 30, May 1. Drawn. Glamorgan 12 pts. Derbyshire 7 pts. Toss: Glamorgan.

Rain cost the match 178 overs – including the whole of the third day – and ultimately Glamorgan their chance to press for victory as Derbyshire finished 159 runs adrift with seven wickets in hand. Centuries from Powell and the in-form Dalrymple, who together added 180 for the fourth wicket, and a maiden first-class fifty from Maynard helped Glamorgan to maximum batting points for the second game in succession before the declaration. Park compiled a resolute half-century in reply, but Derbyshire were undone by the pace and seam of Harrison and Harris, plus the spin of Croft, and were soon following on, 193 runs behind. Croft briefly tormented the visitors again in the second innings, but frequent interruptions by the weather meant Glamorgan were unable to ram home their advantage. The club was slightly embarrassed on the first day when groundstaff failed to manoeuvre the new Hovercover from the square following a break for rain. Fortunately, an engineer was on hand to rectify the mechanical fault, although play restarted ten minutes late.

Close of play: First day, Glamorgan 79-2 (Cosgrove 37, Powell 16); Second day, Derbyshire 37-2 (Park 20); Third day, No play.

Glamorgan

G. P. Rees c Redfern b Wagg	11	J. A. R. Harris not out		17
M. J. Cosgrove b Hunter	50			
B. J. Wright c Lawson b Wagg	6	B 5, l-b 3, n-b 10		18
M. J. Powell b Wagg	108			
*J. W. M. Dalrymple b Park	102	1/26 (1) 2/38 (3) (6 wkts dec, 116 overs)	403
T. L. Maynard not out	51	3/100 (2) 4/280 (5)	
†M. A. Wallace lbw b Park	40	5/303 (4) 6/371 (7)	

R. D. B. Croft, D. S. Harrison and G. J-P. Kruger did not bat.

Wagg 21–5–50–3; Hunter 22–6–46–1; Park 16–5–51–2; Clare 14–1–72–0; Lawson 23–1–77–0; Needham 11–0–60–0; Smith 9–1–39–0.

Derbyshire

S. D. Stubbings lbw b Harris	4	– not out	15
G. T. Park c Wright b Harrison	64	– c Dalrymple b Croft	6
W. W. Hinds lbw b Harris	12	– st Wallace b Croft	1
D. J. Redfern c Harrison b Harris	13	– b Croft	3
G. M. Smith c and b Croft	19	– not out	3
*†D. J. Pipe c Wright b Harrison	44		
G. G. Wagg b Harrison	1		
J. L. Clare lbw b Harrison	5		
J. Needham c Dalrymple b Croft	4		
M. A. K. Lawson not out	24		
I. D. Hunter c Maynard b Croft	8		
B 6, l-b 2, n-b 4	12	L-b 3, w 1, n-b 2	6

1/17 (1) 2/37 (3) 3/63 (4) 4/90 (5) (64.5 overs) 210   1/16 (2)   (3 wkts, 21 overs) 34
5/150 (2) 6/169 (6) 7/169 (7)   2/18 (3) 3/28 (4)
8/178 (8) 9/184 (9) 10/210 (11)

Harrison 18–3–60–4; Harris 14–2–54–3; Croft 21.5–5–45–3; Kruger 7–0–28–0; Dalrymple 4–0–15–0. *Second Innings*—Harris 3–0–7–0; Kruger 3–0–8–0; Croft 8–6–6–3; Dalrymple 7–1–10–0.

Umpires: N. G. Cowley and M. A. Gough.

At Canterbury, May 6, 7, 8, 9. GLAMORGAN lost to KENT by 204 runs.

GLAMORGAN v SURREY

At Cardiff, June 6, 7, 8, 9. Drawn. Glamorgan 9 pts, Surrey 11 pts. Toss: Glamorgan. County debut: R. J. Harris.

Mark Ramprakash's 105th first-class hundred was the highlight of a game long condemned to a draw by the loss of 144 overs to the weather on the first two days. His careful 138 from 271 balls questioned Dalrymple's decision to bowl first. Butcher marked his return to competitive cricket following a 12-month absence through injury with a fluent half-century, and later held three sharp chances at slip. In between, Cosgrove had given Glamorgan a rapid start with 11 boundaries in his fifty, but had Dalrymple not been badly dropped by Walters at second slip when he had seven, Glamorgan might have struggled to reach the follow-on target of 219. Instead, the captain ground out 72 in 162 balls and added 62 with Wright to allay fears, before Shantry and Kruger gave them a second batting point. Dernbach's six wickets rewarded his perseverance.

Close of play: First day, No play; Second day, Surrey 159-3 (Ramprakash 50, Murtaza Hussain 2); Third day, Glamorgan 136-4 (Dalrymple 18, Wright 9).

Surrey

S. A. Newman lbw b Harris	0	– b Kruger	7
M. J. Brown lbw b Kruger	40	– b Shantry	6
M. R. Ramprakash c Harris b Shantry	138	– c and b Croft	35
*M. A. Butcher b Shantry	65	– not out	27
Murtaza Hussain lbw b Kruger	5		
U. Afzaal c Powell b Shantry	13	– (5) not out	1
S. J. Walters lbw b Harris	2		
†J. N. Batty lbw b Shantry	42		
R. J. Harris c Croft b Kruger	4		
A. Nel not out	31		
J. W. Dernbach b Kruger	10		
B 7, l-b 8, w 3	18	B 2, l-b 4	6

1/0 (1) 2/58 (2) 3/156 (4) (99.3 overs) 368   1/7 (1) (3 wkts dec, 30 overs) 82
4/163 (5) 5/195 (6) 6/198 (7) 7/313 (3)   2/24 (2) 3/80 (3)
8/313 (8) 9/335 (9) 10/367 (11)

Harris 28–2–113–2; Shantry 25–7–73–4; Kruger 16.3–2–77–4; Cosgrove 9–1–36–0; Croft 18–4–41–0; Dalrymple 3–0–13–0. *Second Innings*—Harris 7–2–19–0; Kruger 4–2–3–1; Shantry 7–1–16–1; Croft 8–1–23–1; Dalrymple 4–0–15–0.

Glamorgan

G. P. Rees c Ramprakash b Nel	1	R. D. B. Croft c Butcher b Dernbach	2
M. J. Cosgrove c Brown b Dernbach	59	A. J. Shantry not out	23
W. D. Bragg c Batty b Dernbach	12	G. J-P. Kruger c Butcher b Harris	15
M. J. Powell b Dernbach	10	B 3, l-b 9, n-b 16	28
*J. W. M. Dalrymple c Nel b Dernbach	72		
B. J. Wright c Batty b Harris	27	1/28 (1) 2/62 (3) 3/88 (4) (85 overs) 271
†M. A. Wallace c Batty b Dernbach	13	4/115 (2) 5/177 (6) 6/215 (7)
J. A. R. Harris c Butcher b Murtaza Hussain	9	7/224 (8) 8/229 (9) 9/238 (5) 10/271 (11)

Nel 17–5–50–1; Harris 17–5–66–2; Murtaza Hussain 26–10–56–1; Dernbach 23–4–82–6; Afzaal 1–0–1–0; Walters 1–0–4–0.

Umpires: N. L. Bainton and J. H. Evans.

At Derby, June 11, 12, 13, 14. GLAMORGAN drew with DERBYSHIRE.

GLAMORGAN v NORTHAMPTONSHIRE

At Cardiff, June 16, 17, 18, 19. Drawn. Glamorgan 9 pts, Northamptonshire 8 pts. Toss: Glamorgan.
The loss of most of the second day denied Glamorgan the chance of a possible win, but there were question marks about Dalrymple's declaration, which set a weakened Northamptonshire side 326 in about two sessions. Since the visitors had declared 93 runs behind on first innings they could justifiably feel disappointed about Glamorgan's lack of adventure. Earlier, Cosgrove had retired hurt with an injured finger after scoring his second Championship hundred of the season out of only 142 while he was at the crease, and although he returned at the fall of the eighth wicket he did not face another ball. Powell's patient innings spanned 80 overs, and he was in sight of a century when he struck a full toss to square leg. Northamptonshire soon subsided to 80 for five, but were indebted to Wakely – tall and obdurate, but quick to pull – who reached a maiden first-class century from 224 balls. Although Rees and Dalrymple added a quick 149 second time round, Glamorgan were left to reflect on their captain's cautiousness when they finished only four wickets short of victory on the final day.

Close of play: First day, Northamptonshire 0-0 (Murphy 0, Peters 0); Second day, Northamptonshire 28-3 (Wakely 12, Boje 6); Third day, Glamorgan 59-1 (Rees 36, Wright 1).

Glamorgan

G. P. Rees c Murphy b Wigley	4	– not out		116
M. J. Cosgrove not out	102	– b Panesar		22
B. J. Wright b Wigley	6	– lbw b Boje		15
M. J. Powell c Willey b Hall	88	– lbw b Boje		2
*J. W. M. Dalrymple c Murphy b Wigley	1	– not out		70
†M. A. Wallace b Panesar	32			
J. A. R. Harris c Murphy b Willey	17			
R. D. B. Croft c Hall b Wigley	43			
D. A. Cosker c Murphy b Hall	10			
A. J. Shantry lbw b Wigley	1			
D. S. Harrison c Nelson b Hall	1			
W 1, n-b 2	3	L-b 1, n-b 6		7

1/19 (1) 2/29 (3) 3/144 (5)　　　　(92.1 overs) 308　　1/42 (2)　　(3 wkts dec, 59 overs) 232
4/202 (6) 5/233 (7) 6/291 (8)　　　　　　　　　　　　　2/79 (3) 3/83 (4)
7/306 (9) 8/307 (4) 9/307 (10) 10/308 (11)

In the first innings Cosgrove, when 102, retired hurt at 142 and resumed at 307-8.

Van der Wath 16–2–64–0; Wigley 20–3–78–5; Hall 12.1–3–37–3; Willey 11–1–37–1; Panesar 28–4–81–1; Boje 5–2–11–0. *Second Innings*—van der Wath 6–1–32–0; Wigley 10–3–42–0; Panesar 20–6–68–1; Boje 20–6–62–2; Hall 2–0–14–0; Wakely 1–0–13–0.

Northamptonshire

†D. Murphy lbw b Harris	2			
S. D. Peters c Dalrymple b Harrison	6	– (1) c Wallace b Harris		7
R. A. White lbw b Harris	2	– (2) lbw b Croft		12
A. G. Wakely not out	113	– (3) b Harris		0
*N. Boje lbw b Harrison	10	– (4) b Shantry		52
M. A. G. Nelson b Shantry	10	– (5) c Wallace b Shantry		38
A. J. Hall c and b Cosker	44	– (6) not out		17
D. J. Willey lbw b Croft	10	– not out		4
J. J. van der Wath b Harrison	26	– (7) c Wallace b Cosker		5
M. S. Panesar not out	0			
L-b 2	2	B 1, l-b 4		5

1/4 (1) 2/10 (2)　　　(8 wkts dec, 91.1 overs) 215　　1/10 (1)　　(6 wkts, 66.5 overs) 140
3/10 (3) 4/37 (5) 5/80 (6)　　　　　　　　　　　　　2/10 (3) 3/48 (2)
6/164 (7) 7/165 (8) 8/215 (9)　　　　　　　　　　　4/105 (5) 5/116 (4) 6/123 (7)

D. H. Wigley did not bat.

Harris 24–7–59–2; Harrison 23.1–6–71–3; Shantry 11–4–25–1; Croft 24–5–43–1; Cosker 9–2–15–1. *Second Innings*—Harris 9–3–37–2; Harrison 3–0–9–0; Croft 22–14–16–1; Cosker 23–10–46–1; Dalrymple 2.5–0–5–0; Shantry 7–2–22–2.

Umpires: M. J. D. Bodenham and J. W. Holder.

At Chelmsford, July 7, 8, 9, 10. GLAMORGAN drew with ESSEX.

GLAMORGAN v KENT

At Cardiff, July 15, 16, 17, 18. Kent won by an innings and 45 runs. Kent 22 pts, Glamorgan 4 pts. Toss: Glamorgan.

A career-best 270 not out from Key – surpassing the 221 he made for England against West Indies at Lord's in 2004 – paved the way for Kent to complete the double over Glamorgan and move top of Division Two. Key, who faced 339 balls, survived two chances in the slips, plus a convincing shout for leg-before and an appeal for caught behind, en route to Kent's highest individual score against Glamorgan, adding 180 with van Jaarsveld, who had previously held the record with an unbeaten 262 on the same ground in 2005. This time van Jaarsveld had to settle for 96 after lobbing an attempted reverse sweep to the wicketkeeper, while Kemp – caught at long-on – also fell in the nineties after putting on 215 with his captain before the declaration. Trailing by 240 on first innings, Glamorgan lost Rees – who on the first day had gone in to lunch on seven off 78 balls – first ball when he edged to slips, and bit by bit succumbed to Kent's varied attack. Despite the defiance of Powell, Tredwell's off-spin took four wickets, assisted by Key, who rounded off his game with three catches.

Close of play: First day, Glamorgan 295-8 (Cosker 17, Shantry 10); Second day, Kent 52-1 (Key 27, Jones 24); Third day, Kent 444-4 (Key 202, Kemp 53).

Glamorgan

G. P. Rees c van Jaarsveld b McLaren	80	– c Kemp b Parnell	0
H. H. Gibbs lbw b Cook	36	– lbw b Khan	4
B. J. Wright c Kemp b Cook	0	– c Tredwell b Parnell	10
M. J. Powell c Kemp b Parnell	30	– c Key b Tredwell	60
*J. W. M. Dalrymple lbw b McLaren	35	– c van Jaarsveld b Khan	24
†M. A. Wallace c Kemp b Khan	23	– c Key b Tredwell	4
J. A. R. Harris lbw b McLaren	4	– c Stevens b Tredwell	28
R. D. B. Croft c Jones b Cook	36	– lbw b McLaren	28
D. A. Cosker lbw b McLaren	25	– lbw b Khan	0
A. J. Shantry c Jones b Parnell	17	– c Key b Tredwell	6
G. J-P. Kruger not out	4	– not out	4
B 1, l-b 12, n-b 14	27	B 1, l-b 12, w 4, n-b 10	27

1/51 (2) 2/51 (3) 3/123 (4) (99.3 overs) 317 1/0 (1) 2/21 (2) (61.5 overs) 195
4/192 (1) 5/201 (5) 6/209 (7) 3/21 (3) 4/103 (5)
7/257 (6) 8/277 (8) 9/303 (10) 10/317 (9) 5/116 (6) 6/135 (4) 7/172 (8)
8/172 (9) 9/184 (7) 10/195 (10)

Parnell 20–6–61–2; Khan 15–1–62–1; McLaren 18.3–6–51–4; Cook 15–5–35–3; Stevens 3–1–14–0; Tredwell 27–8–71–0; Kemp 1–0–10–0. *Second Innings*—Parnell 12–3–44–2; Khan 11–3–33–2; Tredwell 20.5–7–48–4; Cook 10–5–10–0; McLaren 8–1–47–2.

Kent

J. L. Denly lbw b Harris	1
*R. W. T. Key not out	270
†G. O. Jones c Wallace b Kruger	68
M. van Jaarsveld c Wallace b Croft	96
D. I. Stevens c Cosker b Harris	12
J. M. Kemp c Rees b Harris	90
B 1, l-b 7, w 10, n-b 2	20

1/10 (1)   (5 wkts dec, 123.4 overs)   557
2/125 (3)   3/305 (4)
4/342 (5)   5/557 (6)   120 overs: 536-4

J. C. Tredwell, R. McLaren, W. D. Parnell, S. J. Cook and A. Khan did not bat.

Harris 29.4–5–118–3; Kruger 21–0–107–1; Shantry 18–2–74–0; Cosker 28–4–122–0; Croft 22–1–99–1; Wright 4–0–18–0; Dalrymple 1–0–11–0.

Umpires: V. A. Holder and R. T. Robinson.

At Bristol, July 31, August 1, 2, 3. GLAMORGAN drew with GLOUCESTERSHIRE.

GLAMORGAN v LEICESTERSHIRE

At Colwyn Bay, August 5, 6, 7, 8. Glamorgan won by an innings and 72 runs. Glamorgan 21 pts, Leicestershire 5 pts. Toss: Leicestershire. First-class debut: C. E. J. Thompson.

Glamorgan gained their first Championship win since defeating the same opposition towards the end of the previous season. Leicestershire, needing 253 to avoid an innings defeat, lost five for three in the final 20 minutes before lunch on the last day and were all out by two o'clock. It was Glamorgan's first four-day win by an innings since they defeated Derbyshire in 2003, and they owed much to a remarkable partnership of 197 between Croft and Shantry, only six runs short of Glamorgan's ninth-wicket record, set in 1929 by Joe Hills and Johnnie Clay against Worcestershire at Swansea. Shantry, whose top score in all first-team cricket had previously been 38 not out, also came within two runs of passing Clay's undefeated 101, still the highest score by a Glamorgan No. 10. Earlier, after Leicestershire had squandered a third-wicket alliance of 152 between Dippenaar and Ackerman, Glamorgan's left-handed opening pair of Rees and Bragg completed their second century stand in two Championship games. The middle order faltered, with Henderson taking six of the first seven wickets but, as the slow-left armer tired, Croft and Shantry ensured the last two wickets added 270. Croft then took three wickets as Leicestershire subsided quickly from 163 for four.

Close of play: First day, Glamorgan 45-0 (Rees 20, Bragg 21); Second day, Glamorgan 320-8 (Croft 15, Shantry 12); Third day, Leicestershire 77-2 (Dippenaar 18, Ackerman 7).

Leicestershire

G. P. Smith lbw b Harris	6	– b Dalrymple		20
C. E. J. Thompson c Wallace b Harrison	0	– lbw b Cosker		16
*H. H. Dippenaar b Cosker	85	– c Dalrymple b Croft		57
H. D. Ackerman b Harris	92	– lbw b Shantry		17
J. W. A. Taylor lbw b Harris	5	– st Wallace b Shantry		2
†T. J. New c Maynard b Dalrymple	45	– lbw b Croft		26
J. du Toit c Maynard b Dalrymple	42	– c Dalrymple b Croft		0
C. W. Henderson not out	10	– run out		2
N. L. Buck c Maynard b Dalrymple	0	– lbw b Cosker		0
A. J. Harris run out	0	– not out		3
H. F. Gurney c and b Cosker	8	– b Cosker		12
B 3, l-b 9, n-b 8	20	B 6, l-b 6, n-b 14		26

1/8 (1)   2/8 (2)   3/160 (4)   4/174 (5)   (84.3 overs)   313
5/215 (3)   6/274 (6)   7/299 (7)
8/299 (9)   9/304 (10)   10/313 (11)

1/25 (1)   2/57 (2)   (70 overs)   181
3/88 (4)   4/96 (5)
5/163 (6)   6/163 (7)   7/166 (8)
8/166 (9)   9/166 (3)   10/181 (11)

Harris 19–5–90–3; Harrison 14–3–54–1; Shantry 14–0–62–0; Croft 15–1–37–0; Cosker 15.3–4–47–2; Dalrymple 7–1–11–3. *Second Innings*—Harris 16–3–62–0; Harrison 5–4–4–0; Dalrymple 16–0–52–1; Cosker 12–8–12–3; Shantry 6–1–9–2; Croft 15–4–30–3.

Glamorgan

G. P. Rees c du Toit b Henderson	44	A. J. Shantry b Gurney	100
W. D. Bragg c Gurney b Henderson	80	D. S. Harrison not out	26
M. J. Powell b Henderson	40		
*J. W. M. Dalrymple b Gurney	40	B 16, l-b 21, w 5, n-b 10, p 5	57
T. L. Maynard c Smith b Henderson	38		
†M. A. Wallace c Taylor b Henderson	19	1/101 (1) 2/157 (2) (176.2 overs)	566
J. A. R. Harris lbw b Henderson	0	3/213 (4) 4/252 (3) 5/282 (6)	
R. D. B. Croft b Thompson	121	6/282 (7) 7/293 (5) 8/296 (9)	
D. A. Cosker c New b Buck	1	9/493 (10) 10/566 (8) 120 overs: 355-8	

Harris 32–7–109–0; Buck 26–3–81–1; Gurney 31–0–119–2; Henderson 67–16–152–6; Thompson 15.2–2–45–1; Taylor 4–0–17–0; Dippenaar 1–0–1–0.

Umpires: N. L. Bainton and V. A. Holder.

GLAMORGAN v MIDDLESEX

At Swansea, August 20, 21, 22. Glamorgan won by 22 runs. Glamorgan 18 pts, Middlesex 3 pts. Toss: Glamorgan.

A low-scoring thriller in which no batsman reached fifty was settled in Glamorgan's favour eight minutes into the extra half-hour on the third evening when Finn became the 30th player to fall to spin on a turning pitch. At 149 for seven in pursuit of 190, Middlesex were in the hunt, but Kartik was run out for the second time in the match, leaving Udal – back in the side after dropping himself for the previous game – to reflect on ten wickets and two unbeaten innings in vain. Glamorgan, ultimately boosted by nine wickets from their own veteran off-spinner, Croft, gained a 54-run advantage on first innings and, at 70 for two second time round, were building a substantial lead when they lost six for 12. A valuable 53 runs accrued from the last two wickets, before 47 from Malan, promoted by Middlesex to open the second innings, appeared to give his side hope. Twenty-two wickets fell on what turned out to be the final day. The only consolation for the visitors was Robson's seven catches – equalling the record for a fielder in a first-class match against Glamorgan.

Close of play: First day, Glamorgan 217-8 (Croft 18, Shantry 8); Second day, Middlesex 166-8 (Udal 32, Murtagh 13).

Glamorgan

G. P. Rees c Scott b Finn	40 – c Scott b Murtagh	26
W. D. Bragg c Shah b Berg	28 – c Robson b Finn	15
H. H. Gibbs c Robson b Udal	8 – c Robson b Kartik	20
M. J. Powell c Robson b Udal	29 – c Morgan b Udal	8
*J. W. M. Dalrymple c Malan b Kartik	40 – lbw b Kartik	2
J. Allenby c Kartik b Finn	7 – c Robson b Udal	1
†M. A. Wallace c Berg b Finn	6 – c Compton b Udal	4
J. A. R. Harris st Scott b Kartik	7 – c Robson b Udal	4
R. D. B. Croft lbw b Udal	21 – lbw b Udal	22
A. J. Shantry not out	11 – c Berg b Udal	21
D. A. Cosker c Robson b Udal	1 – not out	8
B 10, l-b 6, n-b 10	26	B 3, l-b 1	4

1/34 (2) 2/45 (3) 3/109 (4) (86.5 overs) 224
4/113 (1) 5/121 (6) 6/139 (7)
7/163 (8) 8/194 (5) 9/220 (9) 10/224 (11)

1/26 (1) 2/58 (3) (42.2 overs) 135
3/70 (1) 4/71 (4) 5/73 (5)
6/73 (6) 7/82 (7) 8/82 (8)
9/116 (10) 10/135 (9)

Murtagh 13–3–26–0; Finn 17–2–51–3; Berg 10–3–36–1; Udal 26.5–4–59–4; Kartik 20–9–36–2. *Second Innings*—Murtagh 8–1–36–1; Finn 5–0–32–1; Kartik 16–8–27–2; Udal 13.2–2–36–6.

Middlesex

S. D. Robson c Gibbs b Cosker	49	– (3) c Dalrymple b Cosker	3
N. R. D. Compton lbw b Shantry	7	– (1) c Wallace b Croft	13
O. A. Shah lbw b Allenby	11	– (4) c Bragg b Dalrymple	18
E. J. G. Morgan c Wallace b Cosker	16	– (5) lbw b Croft	17
D. J. Malan c Gibbs b Croft	11	– (2) c Gibbs b Croft	47
†B. J. M. Scott b Croft	2	– lbw b Cosker	18
G. K. Berg lbw b Cosker	19	– b Croft	8
M. Kartik run out	2	– run out	13
*S. D. Udal not out	34	– not out	16
T. J. Murtagh b Croft	14	– c Wallace b Croft	7
S. T. Finn lbw b Croft	1	– lbw b Cosker	1
L-b 2	2	B 4, l-b 2	6

1/14 (2) 2/49 (3) 3/80 (4) 4/89 (1)   (82.4 overs) 170
5/92 (6) 6/109 (5) 7/121 (7)
8/123 (8) 9/168 (10) 10/170 (11)

1/27 (1) 2/38 (3)   (54.2 overs) 167
3/77 (4) 4/98 (5)
5/99 (2) 6/125 (7) 7/129 (6) 8/149 (8)
9/158 (10) 10/167 (11)

Harris 18–4–35–0; Shantry 8–1–22–1; Allenby 7–4–8–1; Croft 25.4–7–47–4; Cosker 21–1–54–3; Dalrymple 3–2–2–0. *Second Innings*—Harris 8–1–26–0; Croft 22–3–65–5; Cosker 15.2–1–35–3; Dalrymple 9–0–35–1.

Umpires: R. J. Bailey and N. G. Cowley.

At Northampton, August 26, 27, 28, 29. GLAMORGAN drew with NORTHAMPTONSHIRE.

At Leicester, September 2, 3, 4, 5. GLAMORGAN drew with LEICESTERSHIRE.

GLAMORGAN v ESSEX

At Cardiff, September 10, 11, 12, 13. Drawn. Glamorgan 10 pts. Essex 9 pts. Toss: Glamorgan.
   Glamorgan came within one wicket of claiming an unexpected victory, but Essex's tenth pair survived the last 13 deliveries after five wickets had gone down for 16 runs in 15.2 overs as Croft and Cosker exploited a turning pitch. Croft was convinced he had Wright caught at short leg from the penultimate ball of the game, but umpire Sharp was unmoved. Essex never threatened a target of 320 after losing three early wickets, but Foster denied Glamorgan for 70 overs, sharing important partnerships with Pettini and Cook, who batted down the order after being off the field with a stomach disorder the previous day. Cosker returned a career-best in Essex's first innings, ending with match figures of 11 for 126 – the first ten-for of his 13-year career. Croft, meanwhile, wheeled away, taking his three wickets (including his 50th of the season) in one 14-ball burst. Pettini, dropped twice off Croft, anchored Essex's first effort, while Dalrymple ended two short of his fourth century of the season and one short of his thousand runs. Danish Kaneria's eventful game also included a ten-wicket haul, and a heated altercation during the final over when Rees accused him of time-wasting. In the first innings Rees – who was capped during the match – was given out lbw when he had 107 of his eventual six-hour 122, but was recalled after Sharp realised the ball had struck the bat first.
   Close of play: First day, Glamorgan 311; Second day, Essex 277-7 (Pettini 87, Masters 11); Third day, Glamorgan 279-9 (Dalrymple 89, Kruger 0).

Glamorgan

G. P. Rees b Napier	122	– c Maunders b Westley	38
M. J. Cosgrove b Napier	53	– c Foster b Napier	1
W. D. Bragg lbw b Danish Kaneria	0	– c Foster b Masters	47
M. J. Powell c Masters b Danish Kaneria	21	– b Westley	0
*J. W. M. Dalrymple b Danish Kaneria	44	– not out	98
J. Allenby b Danish Kaneria	5	– c Foster b Phillips	12
†M. A. Wallace st Foster b Danish Kaneria	5	– c Foster b Danish Kaneria	48
R. D. B. Croft c Foster b Masters	27	– run out	0
A. J. Shantry not out	9	– b Danish Kaneria	4
D. A. Cosker lbw b Danish Kaneria	0	– c Foster b Danish Kaneria	14
G. J-P. Kruger c Westley b Danish Kaneria	2	– c Foster b Napier	7
B 8, l-b 5, w 2, n-b 8	23	B 7, l-b 10, n-b 10	27

1/98 (2) 2/99 (3) 3/151 (4)   (93.3 overs) 311
4/220 (5) 5/228 (6) 6/240 (7)
7/292 (8) 8/302 (1) 9/303 (10) 10/311 (11)

1/20 (2) 2/79 (1)   (94 overs) 296
3/81 (4) 4/117 (3)
5/146 (6) 6/217 (7) 7/221 (8)
8/241 (9) 9/273 (10) 10/296 (11)

Masters 21–5–50–1; Wright 10–2–45–0; Napier 17–3–54–2; Danish Kaneria 34.3–4–111–7; Phillips 9–0–36–0; Westley 2–0–2–0. *Second Innings*—Masters 18–2–48–1; Napier 8–1–35–2; Danish Kaneria 39–6–108–3; Phillips 17–2–41–1; Westley 8–1–33–2; Wright 4–0–14–0.

Essex

J. K. Maunders lbw b Croft	44	– (2) c Allenby b Dalrymple	12
A. N. Cook c Allenby b Croft	57	– (6) c Rees b Shantry	17
T. Westley lbw b Croft	1	– (1) b Cosker	2
M. J. Walker c Rees b Cosker	25	– (3) c Cosgrove b Cosker	15
*M. L. Pettini b Cosker	90	– (4) c Rees b Cosker	37
†J. S. Foster lbw b Allenby	7	– (5) lbw b Croft	73
G. R. Napier c Dalrymple b Cosker	11	– c Cosgrove b Cosker	2
T. J. Phillips lbw b Cosker	20	– lbw b Croft	0
D. D. Masters b Cosker	11	– b Cosker	0
C. J. C. Wright not out	1	– not out	0
Danish Kaneria b Cosker	0	– not out	1
B 3, l-b 13, w 3, n-b 2	21	B 6, l-b 2, n-b 14	22

1/98 (1) 2/107 (2) 3/107 (3)   (103.4 overs) 288
4/171 (4) 5/194 (6) 6/207 (7)
7/253 (8) 8/279 (9) 9/288 (5) 10/288 (11)

1/9 (1)   (9 wkts, 101 overs) 181
2/18 (2) 3/38 (3)
4/106 (4) 5/164 (6) 6/178 (5)
7/178 (7) 8/180 (9) 9/180 (8)

Shantry 11–2–30–0; Allenby 9–1–31–1; Kruger 9–1–18–0; Croft 34–8–78–3; Cosker 31.4–6–91–6; Dalrymple 9–3–24–0. *Second Innings*—Croft 32–9–50–2; Cosker 36–19–35–5; Dalrymple 17–4–34–1; Cosgrove 4–1–8–0; Allenby 3–1–9–0; Kruger 6–0–28–0; Shantry 3–2–9–1.

Umpires: D. J. Millns and G. Sharp.

GLAMORGAN v GLOUCESTERSHIRE

At Cardiff, September 16, 17, 18, 19. Drawn. Glamorgan 12 pts, Gloucestershire 9 pts. Toss: Glamorgan.

For the second match in a row Glamorgan fell just one wicket short of victory which, on this occasion, would have taken them to joint-second in Division Two with one game left. Lewis was dismissed with seven balls remaining, but last man Banerjee survived one delivery and Kirby (who batted for 48 minutes in all) the last six, from Kruger. Gloucestershire had been set a generous 296 in what turned out to be 100 overs, and came within 15 of their goal, mainly thanks to Porterfield. He anchored the innings, and was still there at tea, when another 110 were needed with five wickets in hand. But once Croft finally ended Porterfield's five-hour vigil at 81, Gloucestershire were content to play for the draw. The two captains each reached 1,000 runs in the season – Dalrymple for the first time in his career – but the loss of 15.3 overs to bad light on the third day hampered Glamorgan's hopes of setting a larger target and also bowling that evening. On the first day, Glamorgan's openers had started brightly, putting on 141 in 32.2 overs, but it was left to their last-wicket pair to inch them past 400 and full batting points. Dawson mopped up, then added his first half-century for Gloucestershire.

Close of play: First day, Glamorgan 380-7 (Harris 12, Croft 4); Second day, Gloucestershire 251-7 (Dawson 26, Lewis 5); Third day, Glamorgan 171-8 (Croft 21, Cosker 2).

Glamorgan

G. P. Rees c Gidman b Franklin	88	– lbw b Dawson	43
M. J. Cosgrove c Kirby b Lewis	80	– c Porterfield b Kirby	1
W. D. Bragg lbw b Dawson	1	– c Adshead b Lewis	11
M. J. Powell b Kirby	84	– c Porterfield b Lewis	41
*J. W. M. Dalrymple lbw b Banerjee	0	– c Dawson b Kirby	6
J. Allenby lbw b Lewis	79	– c Taylor b Lewis	3
†M. A. Wallace c Adshead b Lewis	12	– b Dawson	25
J. A. R. Harris c Marshall b Dawson	18	– c Marshall b Kirby	10
R. D. B. Croft not out	22	– not out	21
D. A. Cosker lbw b Dawson	0	– not out	2
G. J-P. Kruger c Franklin b Dawson	6		
B 5, l-b 5, n-b 10	20	B 3, l-b 2, w 3	8

1/141 (2) 2/148 (3) 3/216 (1)   (109.4 overs) 410   1/18 (2)   (8 wkts dec, 62.3 overs) 171
4/225 (5) 5/337 (4) 6/353 (7)   2/49 (3) 3/82 (1)
7/376 (6) 8/390 (8) 9/390 (10) 10/410 (11)   4/93 (5) 5/103 (6) 6/138 (4)
                                                       7/140 (7) 8/156 (8)

Lewis 22–5–62–3; Franklin 15–3–58–1; Kirby 22–1–88–1; Marshall 5–2–30–0; Banerjee 16–3–66–1; Dawson 24.4–5–76–4; Taylor 5–0–20–0. *Second Innings*—Lewis 20–6–47–3; Kirby 16.3–1–44–3; Franklin 6–0–23–0; Dawson 18–0–47–2; Taylor 2–0–5–0.

Gloucestershire

Kadeer Ali b Allenby	42	– (7) b Kruger	19
W. T. S. Porterfield c Cosgrove b Kruger	0	– (1) c Allenby b Croft	81
H. J. H. Marshall lbw b Harris	5	– c Wallace b Harris	35
*A. P. R. Gidman c Wallace b Allenby	47	– c Rees b Croft	52
C. G. Taylor b Harris	0	– c Allenby b Dalrymple	24
J. E. C. Franklin lbw b Dalrymple	66	– lbw b Dalrymple	6
†S. J. Adshead lbw b Cosgrove	48	– (2) c Allenby b Harris	0
R. K. J. Dawson c Wallace b Harris	50	– c Bragg b Croft	15
J. Lewis b Kruger	5	– c Wallace b Dalrymple	28
V. Banerjee not out	6	– (11) not out	0
S. P. Kirby lbw b Harris	3	– (10) not out	7
L-b 12, n-b 2	14	B 5, l-b 2, w 1, n-b 6	14

1/4 (2) 2/13 (3) 3/94 (1) 4/95 (5)   (95.2 overs) 286   1/4 (2)   (9 wkts, 100 overs) 281
5/111 (4) 6/201 (7) 7/242 (6)   2/54 (3) 3/126 (4)
8/257 (9) 9/278 (8) 10/286 (11)   4/163 (5) 5/177 (6) 6/227 (1)
                                                          7/243 (8) 8/253 (7) 9/281 (9)

Harris 24.2–1–69–4; Kruger 18–3–61–2; Allenby 15–3–34–2; Cosker 15–4–43–0; Croft 13–2–32–0; Cosgrove 3–0–13–1; Dalrymple 7–0–22–1. *Second Innings*—Harris 12–1–56–2; Kruger 15–4–63–1; Allenby 3–1–8–0; Croft 38–8–67–3; Cosker 18–3–57–0; Dalrymple 14–3–23–3.

Umpires: N. A. Mallender and J. F. Steele.

At The Oval, September 23, 24, 25, 26. GLAMORGAN drew with SURREY. *Four batsmen score centuries as Glamorgan pass 700 for only the second time.*

GLOUCESTERSHIRE

Return of the messiah?

G<small>RAHAM</small> R<small>USSELL</small>

Sporting messiahs are perhaps more usually found in football, but there is no doubt that expectations were high when John Bracewell, who had coached the county to so much one-day success around the turn of the millennium, reappeared at Bristol as director of cricket after his stint with New Zealand.

Six Championship wins where there had been none the season before and a semi-final place in the Friends' Provident Trophy smacked of a considerable turnaround, but really it was no more than initial work in progress after a long period of underachievement and underinvestment. There was a frustrating search for consistency at the crease against the backdrop of a tightening financial situation. Players who might have been given another season found themselves jettisoned, and the only major new signing going into the winter was Surrey's Jon Batty, who agreed a three-year contract. Gloucestershire already had two keepers, the Steves Adshead and Snell, who shared the season between them. Adshead was by far the better bat and he hit two good hundreds, but he was out of contract and Snell had a season to run. It was a straight decision on economics: Adshead left and Batty, who turns 36 as the 2010 season begins, came in for the perceived extra stability and experience he could bring to the top order.

That is badly needed. The seam bowling, headed by Steve Kirby (64 wickets) and Jon Lewis (57) and with a solid back-up, was as good as any in the country, although allowance has to be made for some favourable early-season pitches at Nevil Road. Kirby was chosen for the England Lions against the Australians, and, like Lewis, finished in the top five of the national averages. That both of them stayed fit was a tribute to work put in by coach Stuart Barnes. The fielding under Chris Taylor, whose value as a coach was recognised by his appointment to England squads, was up to snuff, but the batting was a curate's egg.

The season began optimistically; in June Gloucestershire led the second division by 22 points, and were a game away from a Lord's final in the FPT. But from there it all went wrong. They lost to Sussex in a semi-final they thought they were winning, and their four-day results were even more disastrous. Victories at Cheltenham are a distant memory and, after being well beaten on the College Ground by Derbyshire and Northamptonshire, they lost back-to-back matches against two struggling sides, Leicestershire and Middlesex. A barren spell of seven games brought five defeats, a win and a draw. Bracewell threatened changes, but there was no one there. The batting had suffered a collective loss of confidence, none more so than Hamish Marshall. In eight matches he made 251 runs at just 19, before he rediscovered his form right at the end. There were wins by an innings over both Surrey and champions Kent, but they came too late, and the county finished fourth.

Only the new skipper, Alex Gidman, reached his 1,000 runs in the Championship as he put a devastatingly bad 2008 behind him; twice he bettered his career-best score, the pinnacle his 176 against Surrey. A chronic ankle weakness that virtually ruled him out of bowling led to surgery in the late autumn, but drawing on Bracewell's knowledge and drive he was a disciplined captain, particularly in his handling of the back-up seamers, Ian Saxelby, Anthony Ireland and, above all, New Zealander James Franklin.

Steve Kirby

Adam Davy, PA Photos

Franklin had a fine season, highlighted by his milestone match against Derbyshire at Cheltenham where he scored a hundred and took a hat-trick, something previously accomplished for Gloucestershire only by Mike Procter. He had to leave during the final game against Kent to join his country in the Champions Trophy in South Africa; having topped the county's averages and scored an unbeaten 104 on his last day, he signed a contract for 2010 before leaving.

The Pro40 League brought just two wins and, with their lack of batting power at the top, the Twenty20 passed the county by. However, it was marked by a frustrated protest from Grant Hodnett that was to end his Gloucestershire career. He had been under the same specialist as Marcus Trescothick for a stress illness and, after scoring a winning 60 at Northampton, he claimed he was undervalued and underused. He had made 49 on his debut in 2005, aged 23, and in 2007 had looked a settled first-team player, averaging close to 37 and hitting two hundreds.

The most significant departure, though, was Craig Spearman, who had been badly injured the year before when a ball flew into his visor. His swashbuckling strokeplay at the top of the order had been a driving force behind Gloucestershire's one-day success. He left a year early, taking with him the county's highest score of 341, set at Gloucester in 2004 when, after 128 years, W. G. Grace's 318 not out was at last surpassed. He was also one of the county's sharpest slip fielders since Wally Hammond.

While Bracewell was working on a five-year game plan to improve the side, off the field the club was busy with a £10m scheme to redesign Nevil Road to ensure it remains a venue for one-day internationals. There have been steady ground improvements over the past decade, but this was the big leap, with details of how it will be financed yet to be agreed. Members will be hoping it is not at the expense of the team.

GLOUCESTERSHIRE RESULTS

All first-class matches – Played 16: Won 6, Lost 6, Drawn 4.
County Championship matches – Played 16: Won 6, Lost 6, Drawn 4.

LV County Championship, 4th in Division 2; Friends Provident Trophy, s-f;
Pro40 League, 8th in Division 1; Twenty20 Cup, 6th in Midlands/Wales/West Division.

COUNTY CHAMPIONSHIP AVERAGES, BATTING AND FIELDING

Cap		M	I	NO	R	HS	100s	50s	Avge	Ct/St
2004	J. E. C. Franklin§	14	22	4	904	109	3	4	50.22	6
2004	A. P. R. Gidman	15	23	0	1,028	176	4	4	44.69	9
2004	S. J. Adshead	7	10	1	367	156*	2	0	40.77	22/1
2006	H. J. H. Marshall¶	16	26	2	844	158	1	5	35.16	13
2005	Kadeer Ali	16	28	4	834	90	0	4	34.75	10
2001	C. G. Taylor†	15	22	1	705	111	1	5	33.57	11
2008	R. K. J. Dawson	7	10	0	254	50	0	1	25.40	12
2002	C. M. Spearman	6	9	0	206	57	0	1	22.88	9
2008	W. T. S. Porterfield¶ . . .	9	16	1	341	81	0	2	22.73	17
1998	J. Lewis	15	22	6	358	61*	0	2	22.37	5
2008	I. D. Saxelby	9	13	3	168	60*	0	1	16.80	5
2005	S. D. Snell	9	14	1	215	85	0	1	16.53	28/2
2008	R. J. Woodman	6	10	1	144	32	0	0	16.00	3
2005	S. P. Kirby	16	22	8	157	27	0	0	11.21	2
2006	V. Banerjee	7	12	3	71	16	0	0	7.88	2
2007	A. J. Ireland¶	7	7	2	21	16	0	0	4.20	3

Also batted G. P. Hodnett¶ (cap 2005) (1 match) 31; G. M. Hussain (cap 2009) (1 match) 8, 8 (1 ct); T. P. Stayt (cap 2007) (1 match) 36.

† *Born in Gloucestershire.* § *Official overseas player.* ¶ *Other non-England-qualified player. Since 2004, Gloucestershire have awarded caps to all players making their first-class debut.*

BOWLING

	O	M	R	W	BB	5W/i	Avge
J. Lewis	426.3	110	1,146	57	5-73	1	20.10
S. P. Kirby	472.4	107	1,420	64	5-44	1	22.18
H. J. H. Marshall	104	24	360	16	4-24	0	22.50
J. E. C. Franklin	292.4	62	904	31	5-30	1	29.16
I. D. Saxelby	185.2	30	620	20	3-31	0	31.00
A. J. Ireland	167	34	664	21	6-31	1	31.61
V. Banerjee	200.3	38	667	21	4-58	0	31.76
R. K. J. Dawson	158.4	13	610	12	4-76	0	50.83

Also bowled: Kadeer Ali 4–0–15–0; A. P. R. Gidman 59.1–13–162–4; G. P. Hodnett 6–0–41–1; G. M. Hussain 22–1–107–2; T. P. Stayt 34–7–77–2; C. G. Taylor 86.2–22–242–6; R. J. Woodman 5–3–8–1.

COUNTY RECORDS

Highest score for:	341	C. M. Spearman v Middlesex at Gloucester	2004
Highest score against:	319	C. J. L. Rogers (Northamptonshire) at Northampton	2006
Leading run-scorer:	33,664	W. R. Hammond (avge 57.05)	1920–1951
Best bowling for:	10-40	E. G. Dennett v Essex at Bristol	1906
Best bowling against:	10-66	A. A. Mailey (Australians) at Cheltenham	1921
	10-66	K. Smales (Nottinghamshire) at Stroud	1956
Leading wicket-taker:	3,170	C. W. L. Parker (avge 19.43)	1903–1935
Highest total for:	695-9 dec	v Middlesex at Gloucester	2004
Highest total against:	774-7 dec	by Australians at Bristol	1948
Lowest total for:	17	v Australians at Cheltenham	1896
Lowest total against:	12	by Northamptonshire at Gloucester	1907

ADDRESS

County Ground, New Nevil Road, Bristol BS7 9EJ (0117 910 8000; **email** info@glosccc.co.uk).
Website www.glosccc.co.uk

OFFICIALS

Captain A. P. R. Gidman
Director of cricket J. G. Bracewell
President A. S. Brown
Chairman R. Body

Chief executive T. E. M. Richardson
Chairman, cricket committee A. M. Smith
Head groundsman S. Williams
Scorer K. T. Gerrish

Nevil Road, an international ground with permanent seating of less than 4,000, is transformed once
a year into an England venue: here, on a hot May day, for lukewarm West Indian opposition.

At The Oval, April 15, 16, 17, 18. GLOUCESTERSHIRE drew with SURREY.

GLOUCESTERSHIRE v ESSEX

At Bristol, April 21, 22, 23. Essex won by seven wickets. Essex 17 pts, Gloucestershire 3 pts. Toss: Essex.

A grassy wicket was supposed to encourage seam and swing, but an underlying dampness meant the ball came through slowly in a low-scoring match that was ultimately settled by the all-round tenacity of ten Doeschate. His five wickets on the first day outshone Marshall's cautious half-century – the only one of the match – and he then scored a careful 42 to give Essex, struggling at one point on 109 for seven, a small but handy first-innings lead. Gloucestershire had been hampered by a hamstring injury to Franklin, who was restricted to six overs, but appeared to be fighting back when Spearman and Kadeer Ali added 51 for their first wicket second time round. Instead, all ten wickets fell for 68 as Masters completed match figures of six for 28 from 28 overs and ten Doeschate extended his haul to eight. Foster completed nine dismissals (all catches) to equal the club record shared by Kenneth Gibson and David East, before Essex – set 98 – lurched to six for two. But Walker ensured there were no slip-ups, and victory was wrapped up shortly after lunch on the third day.

Close of play: First day, Essex 60-3 (Mickleburgh 11, Wright 6); Second day, Gloucestershire 115-9 (Banerjee 10, Kirby 0).

Gloucestershire

Kadeer Ali c Foster b Masters	6	– (2) c Foster b ten Doeschate ... 27
C. M. Spearman c Foster b Masters	11	– (1) lbw b Chambers ... 28
H. J. H. Marshall lbw b ten Doeschate	64	– c Foster b ten Doeschate ... 3
*A. P. R. Gidman c Foster b Wright	1	– lbw b Chambers ... 5
C. G. Taylor c Chopra b ten Doeschate	10	– c Foster b Chambers ... 16
J. E. C. Franklin c Foster b ten Doeschate	21	– (7) c Gallian b Masters ... 13
†S. D. Snell c Foster b ten Doeschate	18	– (6) b Masters ... 7
I. D. Saxelby lbw b Wright	10	– lbw b Masters ... 0
J. Lewis c Pettini b ten Doeschate	2	– b Wright ... 1
V. Banerjee b ten Doeschate	0	– c Foster b ten Doeschate ... 11
S. P. Kirby not out	6	– not out ... 2
L-b 4, n-b 2	6	L-b 2, w 4 ... 6

1/10 (1) 2/21 (2) 3/22 (4) 4/38 (5) (64.3 overs) 155
5/93 (6) 6/128 (7) 7/141 (3)
8/149 (9) 9/149 (10) 10/155 (8)

1/51 (2) 2/59 (1)   (49.1 overs) 119
3/61 (3) 4/75 (4)
5/86 (5) 6/87 (6) 7/87 (8) 8/88 (9)
9/110 (7) 10/119 (10)

Masters 16–8–16–3; Wright 15.3–5–38–2; ten Doeschate 18–1–62–5; Chambers 12–2–25–0; Middlebrook 1–0–6–0; Chopra 2–0–4–0. *Second Innings*—Masters 12–5–12–3; Wright 13–3–40–1; Chambers 13–1–30–3; ten Doeschate 11.1–0–35–3.

Essex

V. Chopra lbw b Franklin	15	– c Spearman b Kirby ... 1
J. E. R. Gallian lbw b Franklin	8	– c Spearman b Saxelby ... 11
J. C. Mickleburgh c Snell b Gidman	32	– lbw b Lewis ... 0
M. J. Walker lbw b Lewis	9	– not out ... 48
C. J. C. Wright c sub (G. P. Hodnett) b Saxelby	21	
*M. L. Pettini run out	8	– (5) not out ... 28
†J. S. Foster c Marshall b Lewis	0	
R. N. ten Doeschate c Saxelby b Gidman	42	
J. D. Middlebrook c Snell b Gidman	17	
D. D. Masters c sub (G. P. Hodnett) b Marshall	0	
M. A. Chambers not out	0	
B 6, l-b 11, w 2, n-b 6	25	B 5, l-b 7, w 1 ... 13

1/24 (1) 2/27 (2) 3/48 (4) 4/79 (5) (77.1 overs) 177
5/105 (6) 6/107 (7) 7/109 (3)
8/175 (8) 9/177 (10) 10/177 (9)

1/1 (1) 2/6 (3)   (3 wkts, 27 overs) 101
3/46 (2)

Lewis 23–7–39–2; Kirby 18–4–49–0; Saxelby 12–2–34–1; Franklin 6–3–7–2; Gidman 15.1–6–23–3; Banerjee 1–0–7–0; Marshall 2–1–1–1. *Second Innings*—Lewis 10–1–34–1; Kirby 7–2–14–1; Saxelby 5–3–16–1; Marshall 4–0–24–0; Taylor 1–0–1–0.

Umpires: J. W. Holder and J. W. Lloyds.

At Northampton, April 28, 29, 30, May 1. GLOUCESTERSHIRE beat NORTHAMPTONSHIRE by 44 runs.

GLOUCESTERSHIRE v LEICESTERSHIRE

At Bristol, May 6, 7, 8, 9. Gloucestershire won by ten wickets. Gloucestershire 21 pts, Leicestershire 2 pts. Toss: Gloucestershire. Championship debut: A. C. F. Wyatt.

Gloucestershire's first Championship win at Nevil Road for three years owed much to a career-best 159 from Gidman, their new captain, and a ball that conveniently went out of shape. Leicestershire were 83 without loss when the Tiflex ball was changed after protests from the home side and, with the replacement swinging more than its predecessor, the visitors quickly lost all ten wickets for 50. The damage was done by Ireland, the Zimbabwean Kolpak playing instead of the injured Franklin, who yorked Boyce first ball before going on to take six for 31. Although Gloucestershire were soon in trouble at 20 for three, Gidman employed his favourite cover-drive to turn the innings round. His first first-class century since August 2007, together with Snell's 85, formed the bulk of the 227 runs Gloucestershire reaped from the last four wickets. Boyce and New began with a defiant 127 in Leicestershire's second innings, but Lewis chipped away, and Gloucestershire reached their target of 72 by 2.30 on the final day, and went top of Division Two.

Close of play: First day, Gloucestershire 75-4 (Gidman 34, Kirby 4); Second day, Gloucestershire 361-7 (Snell 69, Stayt 30); Third day, Leicestershire 243-6 (Taylor 34).

Leicestershire

M. A. G. Boyce b Ireland		23	– c Snell b Lewis	85
T. J. New c Snell b Stayt		54	– c Snell b Kirby	41
H. H. Dippenaar b Ireland		0	– c Snell b Stayt	52
H. D. Ackerman lbw b Ireland		2	– st Snell b Taylor	10
J. W. A. Taylor c Lewis b Ireland		8	– c Snell b Ireland	35
*†P. A. Nixon c Porterfield b Ireland		0	– lbw b Lewis	8
W. A. White c Taylor b Lewis		14	– c Porterfield b Lewis	0
C. D. Crowe c Kadeer Ali b Woodman		0	– not out	41
A. J. Harris b Ireland		0	– c and b Lewis	9
I. E. O'Brien c Kadeer Ali b Kirby		23	– c Porterfield b Lewis	31
A. C. F. Wyatt not out		1	– b Kirby	0
B 4, w 2, n-b 2		8	B 4, l-b 13, n-b 2	19

1/83 (1) 2/83 (2) 3/86 (3) 4/89 (4)   (65 overs) 133   1/127 (2) 2/146 (1)   (112 overs) 331
5/89 (6) 6/95 (5) 7/95 (8) 8/96 (9)   3/165 (4) 4/212 (3)
9/128 (10) 10/133 (7)   5/237 (6) 6/243 (7) 7/257 (5)
                                                                 8/275 (9) 9/330 (10) 10/331 (11)

Lewis 17–7–22–1; Kirby 13–3–39–1; Ireland 14–4–31–6; Stayt 12–4–19–1; Gidman 7–1–14–0; Woodman 2–1–4–1. *Second Innings*—Ireland 21–3–78–2; Lewis 23–8–39–4; Kirby 23–5–70–2; Stayt 22–3–58–1; Taylor 12–4–44–1; Gidman 8–2–21–0; Woodman 3–2–4–0.

Gloucestershire

Kadeer Ali c Taylor b Harris	3	– (2) not out	38
W. T. S. Porterfield c Boyce b Wyatt	12	– (1) not out	32
H. J. H. Marshall b Taylor b O'Brien	0		
*A. P. R. Gidman c Ackerman b Crowe	159		
C. G. Taylor c Taylor b Wyatt	18		
S. P. Kirby c Ackerman b Crowe	27		
R. J. Woodman lbw b Crowe	6		
†S. D. Snell c O'Brien b Harris	85		
T. P. Stayt c New b O'Brien	36		
J. Lewis c Taylor b Harris	3		
A. J. Ireland not out	0		
B 20, l-b 14, w 8, n-b 2	44	B 2	2

1/7 (1) 2/8 (3) 3/20 (2) 4/70 (5)   (123.3 overs) 393
5/152 (6) 6/166 (7) 7/294 (4)
8/383 (9) 9/393 (8) 10/393 (10)   120 overs: 382-7

(no wkt, 15.1 overs) 72

O'Brien 32–8–78–2; Harris 30.3–8–85–3; Wyatt 20–6–44–2; White 10–2–31–0; Crowe 22–5–84–3; Taylor 7–1–20–0; New 2–0–17–0. *Second Innings*—Harris 5–1–15–0; Wyatt 7–0–39–0; Crowe 2–0–7–0; Nixon 1.1–0–9–0.

Umpires: B. Dudleston and R. A. Kettleborough.

At Chesterfield, June 6, 7, 8, 9. GLOUCESTERSHIRE drew with DERBYSHIRE.

At Weetwood, Leeds, June 11, 12, 13. GLOUCESTERSHIRE beat LEEDS/BRADFORD UCCE by two wickets.

GLOUCESTERSHIRE v MIDDLESEX

At Bristol, June 18, 19, 20. Gloucestershire won by nine wickets. Gloucestershire 20 pts, Middlesex 3 pts. Toss: Gloucestershire.

Gloucestershire opened up a 22-point lead in Division Two with a convincing win as they coaxed extra movement from a lively wicket under a good covering of grass. The ECB pitch inspector David Hughes ruled that Middlesex's first-day collapse to 153 was the result of efficient bowling rather than the vagaries of the surface. Four half-centuries in the Gloucestershire reply appeared to back up his judgment, though Burton's disciplined fast-medium brought him five for 68 against his former county. Buoyed by his fifty, Lewis then bowled Strauss, shouldering arms, for a duck as Middlesex resumed 189 runs in arrears. Udal and Silverwood prevented an innings defeat.

Close of play: First day, Gloucestershire 144-3 (Spearman 36, Taylor 12); Second day, Middlesex 129-5 (Dexter 33, Nash 5).

Middlesex

A. J. Strauss c Banerjee b Franklin	32	– b Lewis	0
N. R. D. Compton c Snell b Lewis	7	– b Lewis	17
O. A. Shah c Kadeer Ali b Kirby	25	– c Spearman b Banerjee	57
E. J. G. Morgan b Kirby	6	– lbw b Kirby	10
N. J. Dexter c Marshall b Lewis	6	– b Kirby	43
†D. C. Nash b Lewis	10	– (7) run out	38
G. K. Berg c Spearman b Ireland	29	– (8) c Snell b Lewis	8
*S. D. Udal c Taylor b Banerjee	8	– (9) c Snell b Ireland	27
C. E. W. Silverwood c Porterfield b Ireland	1	– (10) not out	26
S. T. Finn not out	24	– (6) b Kirby	1
D. A. Burton c Snell b Banerjee	1	– lbw b Banerjee	0
L-b 2, n-b 2	4	L-b 5, w 1	6

1/21 (2) 2/49 (1) 3/69 (4) 4/72 (3)   (50.5 overs) 153
5/80 (5) 6/99 (6) 7/123 (8) 8/125 (7)
9/130 (9) 10/153 (11)

1/0 (1) 2/45 (2)   (66.2 overs) 233
3/65 (4) 4/111 (3)
5/124 (6) 6/147 (5) 7/170 (8) 8/180 (7)
9/232 (9) 10/233 (11)

Lewis 13–2–34–3; Kirby 9–3–16–2; Franklin 10–2–33–1; Ireland 11–2–42–2; Banerjee 7.5–2–26–2. *Second Innings*—Lewis 14–3–54–3; Franklin 13–2–50–0; Kirby 14–5–30–3; Ireland 9–2–28–1; Banerjee 16.2–3–66–2.

Gloucestershire

Kadeer Ali lbw b Dexter	21	– (2) not out		8
W. T. S. Porterfield c Nash b Finn	53	– (1) c Strauss b Berg		4
H. J. H. Marshall c Nash b Berg	18	– not out		28
*C. M. Spearman c Nash b Burton	57			
C. G. Taylor lbw b Burton	40			
J. E. C. Franklin lbw b Burton	67			
†S. D. Snell c Berg b Udal	15			
J. Lewis c Dexter b Burton	54			
V. Banerjee c Nash b Udal	2			
S. P. Kirby not out	2			
A. J. Ireland c Morgan b Burton	1			
L-b 7, w 1, n-b 4	12	L-b 5		5

1/62 (1) 2/88 (2) 3/104 (3)   (100.2 overs) 342   1/11 (1)   (1 wkt, 9.5 overs)   45
4/193 (4) 5/200 (5) 6/225 (7)
7/328 (6) 8/339 (8) 9/339 (9) 10/342 (11)

Silverwood 20–3–68–0; Finn 21–2–69–1; Berg 17–3–65–1; Burton 18.2–2–68–5; Dexter 14–5–39–1; Udal 10–4–26–2. *Second Innings*—Finn 4–1–16–0; Shah 1–0–1–0; Berg 3.5–2–20–1; Silverwood 1–0–3–0.

Umpires: N. G. Cowley and V. A. Holder.

At Beckenham, June 30, July 1, 2, 3. GLOUCESTERSHIRE lost to KENT by 76 runs.

GLOUCESTERSHIRE v DERBYSHIRE

At Cheltenham, July 12, 13, 14, 15. Derbyshire won by 185 runs. Derbyshire 20 pts, Gloucestershire 3 pts. Toss: Derbyshire. County debut: W. L. Madsen.

The win that saw Derbyshire displace Gloucestershire at the top of Division Two was harsh on Franklin, who finished on the losing side despite taking Gloucestershire's first hat-trick for nine years (since Lewis at Trent Bridge) and hitting a maiden county hundred. But the home side, wasteful in the slips, had only themselves to blame. Rogers was dropped on four, while Greg Smith was missed on two before hitting a career-best 126 after Derbyshire had stumbled to 119 for five. Then, after Jones – loaned by Somerset to the club he had left in 2006 – helped bundle Gloucestershire out in 57 overs, the South African Wayne Madsen made the most of reprieves on 74 and 95 to make an unbeaten 170, the best by a batsman on first-class debut for Derbyshire. Franklin, who had removed Smith and Jones with the last two balls of Derbyshire's first innings and Rogers with his first of their second, resisted for just short of four hours, but the rest only Gidman reached fifty. Gloucestershire's coach, John Bracewell, warned of change.

Close of play: First day, Gloucestershire 10-0 (Kadeer Ali 5, Spearman 2); Second day, Derbyshire 126-3 (Madsen 71, Needham 5); Third day, Gloucestershire 148-4 (Gidman 39, Franklin 21).

Derbyshire

*C. J. L. Rogers b Lewis	81	– c Snell b Franklin	3
W. L. Madsen c Snell b Lewis	7	– not out	170
G. T. Park c Snell b Lewis	25	– c Snell b Lewis	9
D. J. Redfern c Marshall b Kirby	4	– lbw b Marshall	31
W. W. Hinds c Marshall b Kirby	0	– (6) b Kirby	54
G. M. Smith c Snell b Franklin	126	– (7) c Lewis b Ireland	34
†D. J. Pipe b Banerjee	22	– (8) not out	0
G. G. Wagg c Snell b Ireland	31		
T. D. Groenewald c Marshall b Franklin	26		
J. Needham not out	1	– (5) c Spearman b Kirby	5
P. S. Jones c Marshall b Franklin	0		
L-b 3	3	B 8, l-b 7, w 2	17

1/34 (2) 2/112 (3) 3/117 (4)   (88.4 overs) 326
4/117 (1) 5/119 (5) 6/183 (7)
7/231 (8) 8/321 (9) 9/326 (6) 10/326 (11)

1/3 (1)   (6 wkts dec, 89 overs) 323
2/28 (3) 3/117 (4)
4/126 (5) 5/243 (6) 6/321 (7)

Franklin 18.4–3–59–3; Kirby 14–3–50–2; Lewis 17–4–40–3; Ireland 14–2–79–1; Banerjee 19–0–84–1; Taylor 6–1–11–0. *Second Innings*—Lewis 11–3–24–1; Franklin 14–4–28–1; Kirby 19–5–58–2; Ireland 16–3–51–1; Banerjee 18–3–95–0; Taylor 2–0–9–0; Marshall 2–0–11–1; Gidman 7–2–32–0.

Gloucestershire

Kadeer Ali b Wagg	25	– (2) b Jones	44
C. M. Spearman c Pipe b Jones	7	– (1) c Pipe b Jones	27
H. J. H. Marshall run out	7	– b Groenewald	0
*A. P. R. Gidman lbw b Jones	55	– b Groenewald	60
C. G. Taylor c Pipe b Groenewald	6	– c Pipe b Groenewald	9
J. E. C. Franklin b Smith	14	– b Needham	109
†S. D. Snell b Jones	2	– c Rogers b Needham	13
J. Lewis c Needham b Jones	6	– c Rogers b Needham	0
S. P. Kirby c Hinds b Smith	9	– c Rogers b Wagg	16
V. Banerjee not out	5	– c Needham b Wagg	8
A. J. Ireland b Groenewald	16	– not out	2
L-b 5, w 1, n-b 6	12	L-b 9, w 1, n-b 2	12

1/21 (2) 2/34 (3) 3/74 (1) 4/89 (5)   (56.2 overs) 164
5/121 (6) 6/121 (4) 7/127 (8)
8/138 (9) 9/138 (7) 10/164 (11)

1/71 (2) 2/76 (3)   (95.4 overs) 300
3/76 (1) 4/91 (5)
5/185 (4) 6/213 (7) 7/213 (8)
8/261 (9) 9/276 (10) 10/300 (6)

Jones 18.2–6–44–4; Wagg 15.4–3–49–1; Groenewald 13.2–1–48–2; Smith 7–3–12–2; Needham 2–0–6–0. *Second Innings*—Jones 27–7–64–2; Wagg 33–4–96–2; Groenewald 20–4–64–3; Needham 14.4–3–51–3; Smith 1–0–16–0.

Umpires: B. Dudleston and P. Willey.

GLOUCESTERSHIRE v NORTHAMPTONSHIRE

At Cheltenham, July 20, 21, 22. Northamptonshire won by nine wickets. Northamptonshire 18 pts, Gloucestershire 3 pts. Toss: Northamptonshire.

    Career-best match figures of 12 for 73 from Lucas were too good for Gloucestershire, who lost all 20 wickets inside 77 overs to go down on the third day – despite the loss of the second to rain. Gidman blamed his side's inability to combat the swinging delivery of the Tiflex ball, but his coach, Bracewell, could not disguise his anger as Lucas's left-armers claimed six of the seven lbw decisions to befall the Gloucestershire batsmen, with 15 of their innings ending in single figures. Northamptonshire were in trouble themselves, slipping to eight for three, then 39 for four, but

Boje – caught off a no-ball on 42 – added a priceless 71 for the sixth wicket with Hall, and demonstrated how not to play across the line. His undefeated 87 was a quality display on a damp pitch, and Northamptonshire were denied an innings victory only by some late resistance from Dawson.

Close of play: First day, Northamptonshire 175-6 (Boje 57, van der Wath 6); Second day, No play.

Gloucestershire

Kadeer Ali c Boje b Lucas	0	– (2) b Lucas	6
W. T. S. Porterfield b Lucas	0	– (1) c Peters b Lucas	4
H. J. H. Marshall lbw b Lucas	6	– lbw b Lucas	0
*A. P. R. Gidman lbw b Lucas	8	– lbw b Lucas	7
C. G. Taylor c Wessels b Lucas	51	– lbw b Lucas	0
J. E. C. Franklin c Lucas b Hall	24	– c Wakely b Wigley	26
†S. D. Snell c Wessels b Hall	0	– lbw b Hall	1
R. K. J. Dawson c Wessels b van der Wath	21	– b van der Wath	44
J. Lewis not out	13	– not out	29
S. P. Kirby b van der Wath	0	– b Lucas	4
A. J. Ireland c Wakely b van der Wath	2	– lbw b Lucas	0
B 4, l-b 4, n-b 14	22	B 2, l-b 5, w 4, n-b 10	21

1/2 (2) 2/10 (4) 3/17 (3) 4/66 (6) (42.4 overs) 147
5/68 (7) 6/126 (5) 7/132 (8)
8/132 (1) 9/139 (10) 10/147 (11)

1/13 (1) 2/13 (3) (33.3 overs) 142
3/22 (2) 4/22 (5)
5/31 (4) 6/34 (7) 7/88 (6) 8/122 (8)
9/138 (10) 10/142 (11)

In the first innings Kadeer Ali, when 0, retired hurt at 2-0 and resumed at 126.

Van der Wath 14.4–4–47–3; Lucas 15–4–49–5; Hall 5–1–20–2; Wigley 5–1–16–0; Boje 1–0–2–0; Panesar 2–0–5–0. *Second Innings*—van der Wath 11–4–27–1; Lucas 10.3–1–24–7; Hall 6–0–45–1; Wigley 6–0–39–1.

Northamptonshire

S. D. Peters c sub (J. R. A. Campbell) b Franklin	1	– c Snell b Taylor	25
B. H. N. Howgego lbw b Kirby	0	– not out	28
R. A. White lbw b Franklin	0	– not out	5
A. G. Wakely lbw b Lewis	30		
†M. H. Wessels lbw b Lewis	23		
*N. Boje not out	87		
A. J. Hall c Lewis b Kirby	41		
J. J. van der Wath lbw b Franklin	16		
M. S. Panesar c Dawson b Kirby	0		
D. S. Lucas lbw b Kirby	0		
D. H. Wigley c Porterfield b Lewis	9		
B 4, l-b 10, w 2, n-b 9	25		

1/1 (2) 2/1 (1) 3/8 (3) 4/39 (5) (68.4 overs) 232
5/91 (4) 6/162 (7) 7/199 (8)
8/208 (9) 9/208 (10) 10/232 (11)

1/49 (1) (1 wkt, 17.2 overs) 58

Kirby 21–3–75–4; Franklin 20–3–60–3; Lewis 9.4–1–39–3; Ireland 10–3–30–0; Dawson 8–3–14–0. *Second Innings*—Kirby 2–0–10–0; Franklin 1–0–1–0; Ireland 3–0–21–0; Dawson 7–0–20–0; Taylor 4.2–1–6–1.

Umpires: D. J. Millns and R. T. Robinson.

GLOUCESTERSHIRE v GLAMORGAN

At Bristol, July 31, August 1, 2, 3. Drawn. Gloucestershire 11 pts, Glamorgan 11 pts. Toss: Glamorgan.

After three straight defeats without a single batting point, Gloucestershire – showing the benefit of several days' work in the nets – rode on Gidman's third hundred of the season to achieve a rare maximum haul of five. Bragg looked set for a maiden century in reply but was hit on the left hand by Franklin and sent to hospital, where X-rays revealed a chipped bone. He returned later, but was unable to add to his 92, falling second ball to become Lewis's fifth victim. In between, Gibbs made a refreshing 96 from 120 deliveries, sharing a breezy stand of 100 in 19 overs with Wallace, but with rain taking 66 overs out of the second day, Glamorgan declared 50 behind. That could have been the signal for the sides to agree a target, only for a tame draw to ensue.

Close of play: First day, Gloucestershire 337-5 (Gidman 122, Franklin 16); Second day, Glamorgan 35-0 (Rees 22, Bragg 12); Third day, Gloucestershire 19-0 (Woodman 14, Kadeer Ali 4).

Gloucestershire

Kadeer Ali c Bragg b Shantry	53	– (2) not out	67
R. J. Woodman c Wallace b Shantry	15	– (1) lbw b Harris	18
W. T. S. Porterfield c Dalrymple b Harris	22	– c Wallace b Harrison	31
H. J. H. Marshall b Kruger	43	– not out	27
*A. P. R. Gidman c Gibbs b Kruger	128		
C. G. Taylor c Dalrymple b Croft	37		
J. E. C. Franklin c Bragg b Harrison	16		
†S. J. Adshead c Wallace b Kruger	1		
I. D. Saxelby lbw b Harris	33		
J. Lewis not out	10		
S. P. Kirby not out	0		
B 8, l-b 6, w 6, n-b 22	42	B 8, l-b 9, n-b 8	25

1/27 (2) 2/86 (3)   (9 wkts dec, 101.1 overs) 400   1/39 (1)   (2 wkts, 68 overs) 168
3/118 (1) 4/195 (4)   2/114 (3)
5/313 (6) 6/337 (7) 7/343 (5) 8/347 (8) 9/399 (9)

Harris 18-1-91-2; Harrison 20-4-88-1; Shantry 13-3-38-2; Kruger 23.1-7-77-3; Croft 22-3-68-1; Dalrymple 5-0-24-0. *Second Innings*—Kruger 12-3-29-0; Harris 13-6-23-1; Croft 20-4-37-0; Harrison 12-1-34-1; Shantry 7-3-15-0; Dalrymple 4-0-13-0.

Glamorgan

G. P. Rees c Porterfield b Lewis	82	A. J. Shantry c Adshead b Lewis	4
W. D. Bragg c Porterfield b Lewis	92	D. S. Harrison not out	6
H. H. Gibbs c Adshead b Kirby	96	B 2, l-b 11, w 2, n-b 14	29
M. J. Powell c Porterfield b Lewis	0		
*J. W. M. Dalrymple lbw b Lewis	0	1/218 (1) (8 wkts dec, 94.1 overs) 350	
†M. A. Wallace c Gidman b Kirby	36	2/218 (4)	
J. A. R. Harris not out	5	3/224 (5) 4/324 (6) 5/337 (3)	
R. D. B. Croft c Adshead b Kirby	0	6/339 (8) 7/344 (9) 8/344 (2)	

G. J-P. Kruger did not bat.

Bragg, when 92, retired hurt at 181 and resumed at 344-7.

Kirby 20-3-58-3; Lewis 23-5-73-5; Franklin 15-0-94-0; Saxelby 14.1-5-50-0; Gidman 12-1-29-0; Taylor 7-2-22-0; Marshall 3-0-11-0.

Umpires: N. G. B. Cook and P. J. Hartley.

At Southend, August 5, 6, 7, 8. GLOUCESTERSHIRE beat ESSEX by ten wickets.

At Leicester, August 19, 20, 21, 22. GLOUCESTERSHIRE lost to LEICESTERSHIRE by 44 runs.

At Lord's, August 27, 28, 29, 30. GLOUCESTERSHIRE lost to MIDDLESEX by 180 runs.

GLOUCESTERSHIRE v SURREY

At Bristol, September 2, 3, 4, 5. Gloucestershire won by an innings and one run. Gloucestershire 22 pts, Surrey 2 pts. Toss: Gloucestershire. County debuts: A. Harinath, H. M. R. K. B. Heath.

After being put in, Surrey batted for two hours before bad light and rain ended the first day's play. In moving to 96 for one, Surrey showed no signs of the dismal collapse that would leave them all out for 183 next morning. With Ramprakash absent nursing a broken thumb, they lost nine wickets for 81 runs. Their fielding then matched their lack of application with the bat, as Gloucestershire took a tighter grip through big partnerships for the fourth and fifth wickets. Gidman led the way with a career-best 176, Marshall and Taylor contributing to stands of 173 and 197, before a declaration with a lead of 340. A drying pitch – on which the home side lost their top three for 88 – had been partly responsible for Surrey's poor first showing, and they put more determination into their second innings. Two late adhesive stands featuring Schofield came within a run of making Gloucestershire bat again. Instead, it became the first time since 1975 that Surrey had lost to them by an innings.

Close of play: First day, Surrey 96-1 (Batty 39, Harinath 18); Second day, Gloucestershire 224-3 (Marshall 72, Gidman 62); Third day, Surrey 136-3 (Harinath 44, Linley 2).

Surrey

†J. N. Batty c Adshead b Saxelby	43	– c Adshead b Marshall	40
M. J. Brown lbw b Franklin	37	– b Ireland	39
A. Harinath c Marshall b Kirby	18	– c Adshead b Kirby	44
*S. J. Walters c Adshead b Kirby	2	– lbw b Saxelby	1
U. Afzaal c Adshead b Franklin	23	– (6) c Gidman b Ireland	15
C. P. Schofield b Saxelby	5	– (7) c Taylor b Marshall	71
S. C. Meaker b Franklin	3	– (8) lbw b Marshall	2
A. J. Tudor not out	17	– (9) c Ireland b Taylor	33
H. M. R. K. B. Heath c Kadeer Ali b Ireland	1	– (10) not out	52
T. E. Linley c Kirby b Ireland	6	– (5) c Porterfield b Marshall	17
J. W. Dernbach c Franklin b Kirby	18	– b Kirby	6
B 1, l-b 5, n-b 4	10	B 9, l-b 10	19

1/70 (2) 2/102 (3) 3/104 (1) (58 overs) **183**   1/75 (1) 2/93 (2) (96.5 overs) **339**
4/112 (4) 5/127 (6) 6/136 (7) 7/137 (5)   3/128 (4) 4/143 (3)
8/138 (9) 9/150 (10) 10/183 (11)   5/170 (5) 6/170 (6) 7/177 (8)
                                                              8/249 (9) 9/332 (7) 10/339 (11)

Saxelby 12–1–64–2; Franklin 12–5–28–3; Kirby 17–7–32–3; Ireland 17–7–53–2. *Second Innings*— Kirby 18.5–5–48–2; Saxelby 13–1–59–1; Ireland 22–5–83–2; Franklin 14–3–46–0; Marshall 19–6–52–4; Taylor 12–2–32–1.

Gloucestershire

Kadeer Ali c Walters b Tudor	39	†S. J. Adshead st Batty b Heath	16
R. J. Woodman c Batty b Tudor	32	I. D. Saxelby not out	1
W. T. S. Porterfield b Linley	5	B 2, l-b 18, n-b 14	34
H. J. H. Marshall run out	84		
*A. P. R. Gidman c Brown b Heath	176	1/77 (2) 2/84 (1) (7 wkts dec, 116 overs) **523**
C. G. Taylor b Meaker	111	3/88 (3) 4/261 (4)
J. E. C. Franklin not out	25	5/458 (5) 6/492 (6) 7/521 (8)

A. J. Ireland and S. P. Kirby did not bat.

Dernbach 27–3–109–0; Linley 20–6–70–1; Tudor 26–3–109–2; Meaker 10–2–64–1; Heath 28–1–116–2; Schofield 1–0–6–0; Walters 4–0–29–0.

Umpires: N. G. Cowley and R. K. Illingworth.

At Cardiff, September 16, 17, 18, 19. GLOUCESTERSHIRE drew with GLAMORGAN.

GLOUCESTERSHIRE v KENT

At Bristol, September 23, 24, 25. Gloucestershire won by an innings and 23 runs. Gloucestershire 22 pts, Kent 4 pts. Toss: Gloucestershire. Championship debut: M. T. Coles.

In a desperate chase for the bonus points that could still, in theory, bring promotion, Gloucestershire's strategy was all too obvious. They prepared the greenest of pitches and pulled in the boundaries by ten yards; with the toss going their way, and overseas all-rounder Franklin on top form, they went on to beat Kent, already confirmed as Division Two champions. Gloucestershire collected maximum points, but results elsewhere meant they finished fourth. Franklin took five wickets on the first day and hit an unbeaten century on the second but didn't see out the game: New Zealand sent for him from South Africa. His replacement, Anthony Ireland, took two wickets in Kent's second innings. Runs had been a problem for Gloucestershire all season but, with wicketkeeper Adshead hitting a superb hundred to go alongside Franklin's, their first innings produced their highest score of the summer. Northeast became the first teenager to carry his bat for Kent, reaching his maiden hundred from 133 balls, and hitting 23 fours in all. Another Kentish 19-year-old, debutant seamer Matt Coles, from Maidstone, had already brought up a less welcome hundred of his own as Gloucestershire built their huge total.

Close of play: First day, Gloucestershire 21-0 (Kadeer Ali 12, Porterfield 5); Second day, Gloucestershire 439-5 (Franklin 104, Adshead 86).

Kent

S. A. Northeast c Porterfield b Lewis	7	– not out	128
*R. W. T. Key c Adshead b Lewis	50	– b Kirby	46
†G. O. Jones c Adshead b Franklin	44	– absent hurt	
D. I. Stevens lbw b Franklin	0	– c Adshead b Marshall	17
J. B. Hockley lbw b Franklin	7	– c Dawson b Lewis	10
J. M. Kemp c Dawson b Saxelby	21	– b Marshall	1
A. J. Blake c Franklin b Lewis	47	– (3) c Lewis b Saxelby	0
J. C. Tredwell c Kadeer Ali b Lewis	6	– (7) c Saxelby b Ireland	8
S. J. Cook not out	60	– (8) c Adshead b Ireland	0
M. T. Coles b Franklin	14	– (9) b Kirby	16
A. Khan lbw b Franklin	0	– (10) c Ireland b Lewis	29
L-b 2, n-b 6	8	B 4, l-b 2, n-b 4	10

1/20 (1) 2/101 (2) 3/106 (4)   (62 overs) 264 1/101 (2) 2/106 (3)   (56.3 overs) 265
4/107 (3) 5/122 (5) 6/139 (6) 7/181 (8)   3/140 (4) 4/155 (5)
8/214 (7) 9/248 (10) 10/264 (11)   5/158 (6) 6/173 (7) 7/179 (8)
                                                            8/222 (9) 9/265 (10)

Lewis 21–9–50–4; Franklin 13–3–30–5; Kirby 12.1–1–73–0; Saxelby 10.5–0–73–1; Marshall 4–0–20–0; Dawson 1–0–16–0. *Second Innings*—Lewis 12.3–2–45–2; Ireland 16–1–91–2; Kirby 12–1–54–2; Saxelby 5–1–16–1; Marshall 11–2–53–2.

Gloucestershire

Kadeer Ali lbw b Khan	25	S. P. Kirby not out	19
W. T. S. Porterfield lbw b Tredwell	42	A. J. Ireland lbw b Coles	0
H. J. H. Marshall c Jones b Stevens	87		
*A. P. R. Gidman c Tredwell b Cook	15	B 3, l-b 1, w 1, n-b 6	11
C. G. Taylor c Jones b Coles	69		
J. E. C. Franklin retired not out	104	1/52 (1) 2/136 (2) (123.4 overs) 552
†S. J. Adshead c Key b Tredwell	114	3/161 (4) 4/208 (3)
R. K. J. Dawson c Tredwell b Khan	18	5/295 (5) 6/462 (8) 7/468 (9)
I. D. Saxelby c Tredwell b Khan	5	8/512 (7) 9/543 (10)
J. Lewis c Hockley b Tredwell	43	10/552 (12) 120 overs: 523-8

Franklin retired not out at 439, after being called up by New Zealand, and was replaced by Ireland.

Khan 28–5–120–3; Cook 23–2–97–1; Stevens 10–2–55–1; Kemp 17–3–46–0; Coles 17.4–0–130–2; Tredwell 28–2–100–3.

Umpires: M. A. Gough and R. K. Illingworth.

HAMPSHIRE

One trophy is not enough

Pat Symes

Hampshire entered the season believing they had a team equipped to win all four competitions and, while they were successful in one, the Friends Provident Trophy, there was still a sense of being unfulfilled come the end of September. A good year might have been a great one. Mid-table finishes in the upper reaches of the Championship and the Pro40, and failure to reach finals day in the Twenty20 Cup, tended to dissipate the achievement of an emphatic victory over Sussex in the FPT final at Lord's.

Expectations at the Rose Bowl run high. Shane Warne might have gone, but his legacy is a fierce ambition which resides in Rod Bransgrove, the chairman, and Giles White, who had an impressive first full season as coach. Bransgrove is committed to turning the Rose Bowl into England's No. 1 cricket stadium outside Lord's, and White to building a side to challenge Durham's dominance.

While in previous years the batting had been unreliable, in 2009 it was the bowling that did not function consistently as a unit; in the Championship Hampshire beat just two teams – Worcestershire home and away, and Lancashire at Liverpool – and made sure of their Division One status only in the last fixture, at Headingley. A major reason for the decline in potency of the attack was the transformation of the Rose Bowl square. In its early years it had a reputation as a bowlers' paradise, particularly over the first session or two, but in 2009 it conspired to favour the batsmen. As a consequence, high-scoring draws predominated: of their Championship matches at Southampton, Hampshire won one, lost one and drew five.

Chris Tremlett managed only 14 first-class wickets, and departed for The Oval. The willing leg-spinner Imran Tahir took 52, but at 33 each, before leaving for Edgbaston. Left-arm pace bowler James Tomlinson, the previous year's discovery, found less swing and movement so that his 30 cost 40. Clearly there is a need to get the balance right.

By contrast the batting, even allowing for the decline and subsequent retirement of John Crawley, was stronger than at any time since Hampshire upped sticks from Northlands Road, and was reinforced by the signing of Neil McKenzie as a Kolpak. Nic Pothas, Michael Carberry, Jimmy Adams, Sean Ervine and Michael Lumb each scored more than 1,000 runs in all competitions, and in the Championship alone there were 14 centuries.

Adams and Carberry in the Championship – Adams and Lumb in the one-day matches – gave Hampshire numerous productive starts with three-figure opening stands. Lumb produced the summer's top score in the Twenty20 Cup with an unbeaten 124 from 69 balls against Essex, while Carberry and Adams profited from technical and physical improvements in the 2008 close season. Carberry was edging closer to Test selection when he broke a finger in August, but he was included in England's party to Bangladesh. Adams reached 50 on 20 occasions, but converted only three into centuries.

Most pleasing was the development of the younger players. Hamza Riazuddin, Danny Briggs, James Vince and Chris Wood all played for England Under-19s in the summer, while Liam Dawson, in his first full season, and David Griffiths continued their advancement and justified Hampshire's commitment to an academy programme under the auspices of Tony Middleton. His graduates are expected to form the nucleus of the team for years to come.

Michael Lumb

Clive Mason, Getty Images

While the rise of the younger players was a cause for satisfaction, the contribution made by Dominic Cork, aged 38 when the season ended, was important. Cork brought a belligerent edge to the dressing-room, missing since Warne, and his man-of-the-match performance in the Lord's final proved the shrewdness of his signing. Cork took 20 wickets in the FPT (35 in all limited-overs matches) and it was in the FPT that Hampshire enjoyed their finest moments, with big wins over Middlesex and Lancashire in the quarter- and semi-finals, plus the demolition of Sussex when the limping Pothas ushered his team to glory.

Duncan Fletcher, the former England coach hired to offer advice and assistance in a month-long watching brief, was at Lord's that day, and his knowledge and experience were valued by the captain, Dimitri Mascarenhas, and his players. But Fletcher could do little to help Hampshire in the Championship, and he had gone by the time they blew their chances of significant prize money in the Pro40 League with three successive defeats.

It was in the Twenty20, a format curiously undervalued by previous regimes, that Hampshire had the greatest regret. After emerging from a difficult group to reach the quarter-finals, they lost to Northamptonshire by 13 runs when their last four wickets fell at the same score.

Against this mixture of a playing season, the stadium development continued. The Rose Bowl staged its first England–Australia one-day international in front of 22,000, and its first Test is due in 2011. But the grand project is far from complete. Work started at the end of 2009 on a £48m scheme for two covered stands, a second entrance, and a full-size golf course. Crucial to the metamorphosis is a grant of £32m from Eastleigh council for the construction of a 175-room hotel on the site, an investment decision that provoked a group of rival hoteliers to seek a judicial review.

Despite the scheme's demands on their finances, Hampshire are not afraid to compete for the best available players: Ajantha Mendis was due to join for 2010, as is Shahid Afridi for the Twenty20 campaign. Hampshire will also hope that their gamble in recruiting Simon Jones and Kabir Ali was shrewd.

HAMPSHIRE RESULTS

All first-class matches – Played 17: Won 3, Lost 3, Drawn 11.
County Championship matches – Played 16: Won 3, Lost 3, Drawn 10.

LV County Championship, 6th in Division 1; Friends Provident Trophy, winners;
Pro40 League, 5th in Division 1; Twenty20 Cup, q-f.

COUNTY CHAMPIONSHIP AVERAGES, BATTING AND FIELDING

Cap		M	I	NO	R	HS	100s	50s	Avge	Ct/St
2003	N. Pothas	11	15	4	816	122*	1	6	74.18	24
2006	M. A. Carberry........	12	21	3	1,251	204	4	8	69.50	6
2006	J. H. K. Adams†.......	16	28	4	1,279	147	3	9	53.29	16
2005	S. M. Ervine¶.........	15	22	2	832	114	3	3	41.60	6
2008	M. J. Lumb..........	15	23	1	834	219	1	5	37.90	8
	C. C. Benham........	5	8	2	205	100	1	1	34.16	5
	L. A. Dawson........	14	21	4	536	69	0	4	31.52	10
1998	A. D. Mascarenhas‡...	10	11	2	254	108	1	0	28.22	4
	J. M. Vince.........	8	11	0	282	75	0	1	25.63	2
2002	J. P. Crawley	7	12	2	240	81*	0	1	24.00	6
2009	D. G. Cork	12	15	2	290	52	0	1	22.30	18
2009	Imran Tahir§	12	15	4	206	77*	0	1	18.72	4
2008	J. A. Tomlinson†	12	14	7	92	23	0	0	13.14	3
2004	C. T. Tremlett†.......	7	8	0	75	36	0	0	9.37	2
	T. G. Burrows	5	6	1	46	20	0	0	9.20	13/1
	D. A. Griffiths	9	12	3	36	20*	0	0	4.00	0

Also batted: D. J. Balcombe (2 matches) 10, 0; D. R. Briggs (3 matches) 36, 0, 1 (1 ct); M. J. North§
(1 match) 15. B. V. Taylor† (cap 2006) (1 match) did not bat.

† *Born in Hampshire.* ‡ *ECB contract.* § *Official overseas player.* ¶ *Other non-England-qualified player.*

BOWLING

	O	M	R	W	BB	5W/i	Avge
D. G. Cork................	287	69	767	27	5-14	1	28.40
Imran Tahir	487.4	81	1,711	52	7-140	4	32.90
D. A. Griffiths	255	47	949	28	4-48	0	33.89
J. A. Tomlinson	318.1	57	1,193	30	3-53	0	39.76
C. T. Tremlett	173	34	564	14	4-49	0	40.28
A. D. Mascarenhas	241	70	618	13	2-46	0	47.53
S. M. Ervine.............	233.3	55	793	13	3-22	0	61.00

Also bowled: J. H. K. Adams 15–0–66–1; D. J. Balcombe 44–7–174–4; D. R. Briggs
85.4–13–295–8; M. A. Carberry 43.1–3–242–2; L. A. Dawson 73–9–312–7; B. V. Taylor
21–4–52–1; J. M. Vince 10–0–37–0.

COUNTY RECORDS

Highest score for:	316	R. H. Moore v Warwickshire at Bournemouth ..	1937
Highest score against:	303*	G. A. Hick (Worcestershire) at Southampton ...	1997
Leading run-scorer:	48,892	C. P. Mead (avge 48.84)	1905–1936
Best bowling for:	9-25	R. M. H. Cottam v Lancashire at Manchester ...	1965
Best bowling against:	10-46	W. Hickton (Lancashire) at Manchester	1870
Leading wicket-taker:	2,669	D. Shackleton (avge 18.23).................	1948–1969
Highest total for:	714-5 dec	v Nottinghamshire at Southampton	2005
Highest total against:	742	by Surrey at The Oval	1909
Lowest total for:	15	v Warwickshire at Birmingham..............	1922
Lowest total against:	23	by Yorkshire at Middlesbrough..............	1965

ADDRESS

The Rose Bowl, Botley Road, West End, Southampton SO30 3XH (023 8047 2002; **email** enquiries@rosebowlplc.com). **Website** www.rosebowlplc.com

OFFICIALS

Captain A. D. Mascarenhas
Director of cricket T. M. Tremlett
Team manager G. W. White
Chairman R. G. Bransgrove

Group managing director G. D. W. Delve
Chairman, members committee D. Robinson
Head groundsman N. Gray
Scorer A. E. Weld

Growing your own

From A. J. L. "Ledger" Hill in 1896 to Shaun Udal in 2005 there was a barren spell of more than 100 years during which not a single Hampshire-born man played for England. The county did offer up a handful of Test players born outside its boundaries, such as Alec Kennedy, Lionel Tennyson, Johnny Arnold and George Brown, while Derek Shackleton's home in Todmorden was said to straddle the boundary between Yorkshire and Lancashire. Others came from abroad brandishing British passports.

It seemed strange that a county with a large population should rely so heavily on rejects from other counties (not least Phil Mead, who was rejected by Surrey) and, in post-war years, itinerant South Africans and West Indians, while Durham has turned out a steady stream of home-nurtured players for the national side since gaining first-class status in 1992. Only in the 1950s did Hampshire develop their own in any quantity: Peter Sainsbury, Mervyn Burden, Mike Barnard, Malcolm Heath and Jimmy Gray formed the basis of the first Hampshire side to win the Championship, in 1961.

But now, for the first time since then, Hampshire are making a conscious effort, through their academy system. It costs around £250,000 a year to run, and aims to identify (from the age of ten), improve and maintain county-standard cricketers. The rewards are already apparent. Tony Middleton, the academy director, and his assistant Jon Ayling (both Hampshire-born) have overseen the rise to first-class level of an encouraging number of players. Chris Tremlett (who has won three England caps), James Tomlinson, Jimmy Adams, Chris Benham and David Griffiths were among the first. During 2009 Michael Bates, Danny Briggs, Hamza Riazuddin, James Vince and Chris Wood all played for England Under-19s, while Liam Dawson was fast-tracked to the England Lions. They formed the nucleus of the Hampshire side that won the 2006 ECB Under-17 championship.

Some get away: one Under-16 prospect turned his back on Hampshire when a future as a seam-bowling all-rounder beckoned a few years ago. Jonny Wilkinson preferred rugby. PAT SYMES

HAMPSHIRE v WORCESTERSHIRE

At Southampton, April 15, 16, 17. Hampshire won by seven wickets. Hampshire 15 pts (after 3 pt penalty), Worcestershire 3 pts. Toss: Worcestershire. County debut: D. G. Cork.

Worcestershire's frail batting – forced to adjust to life without Graeme Hick, who had retired from county cricket in September 2008 – was twice exposed by a lively wicket offering bounce and movement. The match lasted three days, though it might have been two without rain on the first and third. Dominic Cork, on his Hampshire debut, exploited the conditions to take four for ten (including three in four balls) as Worcestershire, choosing to bat after a delayed start, were dismissed on the first afternoon. Kabir Ali and Imran Arif posed similar problems, but a mature 66 from the 19-year-old Dawson rescued Hampshire from 116 for seven and steered them to an important first-innings lead of 84. Worcestershire then plummeted to 53 for seven, but Solanki's patient 73, together with resistance from the lower order, meant Hampshire needed 106. Carberry, dropped at nought and again at 15 when Mitchell grassed a slip chance off Kabir, profited from the lapses to hit a cautious half-century. Mitchell took two wickets in an over, but Hampshire were not troubled. They were, however, docked points for being three overs behind the required total. Pothas, standing in as captain while Dimitri Mascarenhas was playing in the IPL, later admitted he should have speeded up his seam-dominated attack.

Close of play: First day, Hampshire 76-4 (Adams 33, Balcombe 3); Second day, Worcestershire 150-8 (Solanki 64).

Worcestershire

D. K. H. Mitchell c Lumb b Tremlett	31	– c Lumb b Cork	4
S. C. Moore c Cork b Balcombe	25	– b Tremlett	1
*V. S. Solanki c Pothas b Balcombe	6	– c Carberry b Tomlinson	73
B. F. Smith c Pothas b Dawson	21	– c Carberry b Balcombe	19
M. M. Ali c Dawson b Tomlinson	12	– c Ervine b Tomlinson	3
†S. M. Davies c Cork b Ervine	4	– c Cork b Ervine	8
G. J. Batty lbw b Cork	5	– c Crawley b Balcombe	0
Kabir Ali lbw b Cork	0	– lbw b Tomlinson	1
C. D. Whelan lbw b Cork	0	– c Pothas b Tremlett	47
M. S. Mason c Pothas b Cork	7	– b Cork	25
Imran Arif not out	0	– not out	4
B 2, l-b 10, w 3, n-b 6	21	B 1, l-b 1, w 2	4

1/41 (2) 2/50 (3) 3/91 (4)   (52.1 overs) 132   1/5 (2) 2/9 (1) 3/34 (4)   (68 overs) 189
4/101 (1) 5/112 (6) 6/120 (7)   4/39 (5) 5/48 (6) 6/52 (7)
7/124 (8) 8/124 (9) 9/132 (10)   7/53 (8) 8/150 (9) 9/163 (3)
10/132 (5)   10/189 (10)

Tremlett 13–4–18–1; Tomlinson 13.1–2–47–1; Balcombe 8–3–21–2; Cork 8–2–10–4; Ervine 8–4–13–1; Dawson 2–0–11–1. *Second Innings*—Tremlett 16–8–24–2; Cork 16–4–27–2; Balcombe 14–3–56–2; Tomlinson 15–5–53–3; Ervine 3–1–9–1; Dawson 4–0–18–0.

Hampshire

M. A. Carberry c Davies b Kabir Ali	4	– b Mitchell	58
J. H. K. Adams lbw b Imran Arif	49	– lbw b Batty	8
J. P. Crawley c Solanki b Mason	2	– not out	31
M. J. Lumb c Davies b Kabir Ali	0	– c Kabir Ali b Mitchell	0
S. M. Ervine c Mason b Whelan	28	– not out	8
D. J. Balcombe b Kabir Ali	10		
*†N. Pothas c Davies b Imran Arif	13		
L. A. Dawson c Kabir Ali b Mason	66		
D. G. Cork c Moore b Imran Arif	25		
C. T. Tremlett lbw b Imran Arif	0		
J. A. Tomlinson not out	0		
L-b 2, w 9, n-b 8	19	N-b 2	2

1/4 (1) 2/7 (3) 3/10 (4) 4/73 (5)   (63.4 overs) 216   1/38 (2)   (3 wkts, 33 overs) 107
5/91 (6) 6/111 (7) 7/116 (2)   2/99 (1) 3/99 (4)
8/207 (9) 9/214 (10) 10/216 (8)

Kabir Ali 18–3–74–3; Mason 17.4–6–47–2; Batty 7–1–17–0; Imran Arif 11–1–42–4; Whelan 10–2–34–1. *Second Innings*—Kabir Ali 5–0–23–0; Mason 5–1–13–0; Imran Arif 5–0–18–0; Batty 10–4–23–1; Whelan 7–1–30–0; Mitchell 1–1–0–2.

Umpires: N. J. Llong and D. J. Millns.

At Birmingham, April 22, 23, 24, 25. HAMPSHIRE drew with WARWICKSHIRE.

HAMPSHIRE v SUSSEX

At Southampton, April 29, 30, May 1, 2. Drawn. Hampshire 11 pts, Sussex 9 pts. Toss: Sussex.

Both teams settled for the pursuit of bonus points after the second day was washed out. On the first, Hampshire overcame a difficult start after being put in on a green-tinged pitch offering help to the bowlers. As conditions eased, Ervine and Pothas added 150 for the fifth wicket, with Ervine making his first Championship century at home – and only his second for Hampshire in his 54th match. Sussex's response was built around Prior's five-hour 140; coming in at 46 for three, he kept Sussex's deficit to just 14. With such a slender advantage, Hampshire had little alternative but to bat through the last two meaningless sessions. Openers Carberry and Adams put on 126, with Adams exploiting the absence of pressure to make his second fifty of the match. Carberry's 72 was his fourth half-century of the season, from just six innings.

Close of play: First day, Hampshire 341-8 (Dawson 22, Tomlinson 0); Second day, No play; Third day, Sussex 230-6 (Prior 112, Martin-Jenkins 12).

Hampshire

M. A. Carberry c Hodd b Martin-Jenkins	17	– lbw b Nash	72
J. H. K. Adams c Prior b Aga	61	– not out	55
M. J. Lumb c Prior b Wright	30	– b Hamilton-Brown	0
C. C. Benham c Hamilton-Brown b Martin-Jenkins	1	– not out	0
S. M. Ervine c Hamilton-Brown b Joyce	109		
*†N. Pothas c Prior b Collymore	74		
L. A. Dawson not out	27		
D. G. Cork c Prior b Collymore	2		
C. T. Tremlett c Hamilton-Brown b Wright	4		
J. A. Tomlinson not out	2		
B 11, l-b 8, w 4	23		

1/26 (1) 2/81 (3)	(8 wkts dec, 101.5 overs) 350	1/126 (1) (2 wkts dec, 50 overs) 127
3/89 (4) 4/145 (2)		2/127 (3)
5/295 (5) 6/317 (6) 7/321 (8) 8/341 (9)		

B. V. Taylor did not bat.

Collymore 26–8–64–2; Wright 21–7–54–2; Martin-Jenkins 22.5–5–69–2; Aga 17–1–82–1; Nash 9–0–38–0; Yardy 4–0–15–0; Joyce 2–0–9–1. *Second Innings*—Collymore 6–0–20–0; Martin-Jenkins 8–2–27–0; Aga 13–1–37–0; Wright 6–3–7–0; Yardy 5–0–11–0; Hamilton-Brown 10–2–22–1; Nash 2–1–3–1.

Sussex

*M. H. Yardy lbw b Cork	7	D. G. Wright c Pothas b Dawson	42
C. D. Nash c Adams b Tomlinson	33	R. G. Aga lbw b Dawson	24
E. C. Joyce b Cork	3	C. D. Collymore not out	0
M. W. Goodwin run out	7	B 1, l-b 9, n-b 14	24
M. J. Prior b Tomlinson	140		
†A. J. Hodd lbw b Cork	25	1/32 (1) 2/46 (2) 3/46 (3) (102 overs) 336
R. J. Hamilton-Brown b Tomlinson	15	4/97 (4) 5/171 (6) 6/209 (7)
R. S. C. Martin-Jenkins c Pothas b Taylor	16	7/252 (8) 8/281 (5) 9/336 (9) 10/336 (10)

Cork 22–4–83–3; Tomlinson 25–3–96–3; Taylor 21–4–52–1; Tremlett 10–2–33–0; Ervine 18–5–47–0; Carberry 4–0–12–0; Dawson 2–1–3–2.

Umpires: B. Dudleston and G. Sharp.

HAMPSHIRE v LOUGHBOROUGH UCCE

At Southampton, May 6, 7, 8. Drawn. Toss: Hampshire. First-class debuts: J. M. Vince; J. E. Ord. County debut: T. W. Parsons.

Loughborough's last pair, Michael Baer and Peter Groves, held on for the draw surrounded by a ring of close fielders. Hampshire had set the students 250 from what turned out to be 51 overs, and so long as Ashleigh Lynch was at the crease they were well placed. But his dismissal, run out for an enterprising 61, was the first of six wickets that fell for 46, prompting the nail-biting finish. Groves had earlier taken five wickets in Hampshire's first innings, the backbone of which was a fourth-wicket stand of 223 by Lumb and Benham, who finally scored a maiden hundred, against his old university. Loughborough's opening batsman Paul Borrington then held up Hampshire with a watchful 105, as did Gavin Baker with a career-best 66; Groves's livelier fifty came from just 51 balls.

Close of play: First day, Loughborough UCCE 24-0 (Borrington 11, Lynch 10); Second day, Hampshire 46-0 (Dawson 29, Adams 16).

Hampshire

L. A. Dawson c Evans b Groves	4	– c Baker b Groves		31
J. H. K. Adams lbw b Groves	4	– b Malan		67
J. P. Crawley lbw b Jones	14	– not out		54
*M. J. Lumb c Jones b Groves	172			
C. C. Benham lbw b Malan	111			
J. M. Vince b Baer	13	– (4) not out		6
†T. G. Burrows b Groves	32			
H. Riazuddin b Baker	3			
D. J. Balcombe b Groves	0			
D. A. Griffiths not out	9			
T. W. Parsons run out	0			
L-b 4, w 6, n-b 6	16	L-b 1, w 1		2

1/8 (2) 2/15 (1) 3/37 (3) 4/260 (5) (88.2 overs) 378   1/49 (1) (2 wkts dec, 45 overs) 160
5/297 (6) 6/359 (4) 7/367 (7)   2/154 (2)
8/369 (8) 9/373 (9) 10/378 (11)

Jones 14–4–65–1; Groves 15–4–72–5; Evans 4–0–31–0; Baker 13.2–1–87–1; Malan 25–6–48–1; Baer 13–0–48–1; Harinath 3–0–15–0; Lynch 1–0–8–0. *Second Innings*—Jones 10–3–31–0; Groves 11–4–33–1; Baker 7–2–16–0; Malan 9–0–35–1; Baer 8–0–44–0.

Loughborough UCCE

P. M. Borrington c Dawson b Riazuddin	105	– c Crawley b Riazuddin		33
*A. A. Lynch b Griffiths	20	– run out		61
J. E. Ord c Crawley b Griffiths	1	– c Adams b Balcombe		9
A. Harinath c Benham b Balcombe	10	– c Dawson b Balcombe		28
C. C. Malan lbw b Griffiths	24	– c Vince b Dawson		4
G. C. Baker b Dawson	66	– lbw b Parsons		20
R. F. Evans c Lumb b Balcombe	0	– c Burrows b Parsons		12
†D. Murphy c Lumb b Balcombe	0	– c Benham b Parsons		2
P. R. Groves c and b Dawson	52	– not out		7
H. D. Jones b Griffiths	0	– run out		2
M. Baer not out	0	– not out		4
L-b 5, n-b 6	11	B 2, l-b 8, w 2, n-b 2		14

1/47 (2) 2/53 (3) 3/79 (4) (78.2 overs) 289   1/55 (1) (9 wkts, 51 overs) 196
4/127 (5) 5/198 (1) 6/207 (7)   2/77 (3) 3/133 (4)
7/207 (8) 8/276 (6) 9/289 (9)   4/144 (2) 5/150 (5) 6/168 (6)
10/289 (10)   7/178 (8) 8/183 (7) 9/190 (10)

Griffiths 18.2–2–62–4; Balcombe 19–3–76–3; Dawson 12–1–53–2; Riazuddin 17–4–47–1; Parsons 9–2–24–0; Adams 3–0–22–0. *Second Innings*—Griffiths 10–3–28–0; Balcombe 15–3–38–2; Parsons 9–2–39–3; Riazuddin 5–0–25–1; Dawson 12–1–56–1.

Umpires: N. L. Bainton and M. A. Eggleston.

At Chester-le-Street, June 6, 7, 8. HAMPSHIRE lost to DURHAM by an innings and 110 runs.

HAMPSHIRE v NOTTINGHAMSHIRE

At Southampton, June 11, 12, 13, 14. Nottinghamshire won by 191 runs. Nottinghamshire 20 pts, Hampshire 5 pts. Toss: Nottinghamshire. Championship debut: J. M. Vince.

Nottinghamshire's third win of the season came with 17 overs to spare. The margin of victory hid how closely the contest had been fought over the first two and a half days. After gaining a narrow 31-run lead on a reliable surface, thanks mainly to a maiden fifty from Fletcher, who thumped three sixes and nine fours from 122 balls, Nottinghamshire slid to 26 for three (and then 47 for four) when Tomlinson grabbed three quick wickets. But Brown, sharing century stands with Voges and Read, took the match away from Hampshire. Brown's 148 was his first hundred since leaving Surrey in the close season. Read was just as forceful, enabling him to declare before the third-day close and setting Hampshire 412. The early loss of first-innings centurion Adams meant Hampshire had their sights set only on survival. Pattinson's control and pace prevented that, despite a promising 75 on Championship debut from 18-year-old James Vince – he struck Shreck for three consecutive fours – and a dogged innings at the death by Pothas.

Close of play: First day, Nottinghamshire 305-8 (Ealham 65, Pattinson 1); Second day, Hampshire 287-9 (Cork 21, Tomlinson 0); Third day, Hampshire 9-1 (Carberry 3, Tomlinson 0).

Nottinghamshire

W. I. Jefferson c Pothas b Ervine	12	– c Pothas b Tomlinson	2
B. M. Shafayat c Benham b Griffiths	20	– c Pothas b Tomlinson	11
M. A. Wagh c Ervine b Griffiths	21	– lbw b Imran Tahir	20
S. R. Patel c Pothas b Tomlinson	41	– c Vince b Tomlinson	0
A. C. Voges lbw b Imran Tahir	25	– lbw b Griffiths	49
A. D. Brown c Cork b Ervine	5	– c sub (L. A. Dawson) b Carberry	148
*†C. M. W. Read c Pothas b Ervine	16	– not out	116
M. A. Ealham not out	70	– not out	10
L. J. Fletcher b Imran Tahir	92		
D. J. Pattinson c Cork b Griffiths	12		
C. E. Shreck b Griffiths	5		
L-b 3, n-b 4	7	B 3, l-b 9, n-b 12	24

1/32 (2) 2/34 (1) 3/60 (3)   (103.2 overs) 326   1/5 (1)   (6 wkts dec, 86 overs) 380
4/123 (4) 5/125 (5) 6/146 (6)   2/16 (2) 3/26 (4)
7/147 (7) 8/299 (9) 9/320 (10) 10/326 (11)   4/47 (3) 5/157 (5) 6/343 (6)

Cork 15–5–36–0; Tomlinson 21.1–5–73–1; Ervine 13.5–7–22–3; Griffiths 16.2–4–48–4; Imran Tahir 34–5–130–2; Carberry 2–0–7–0; Adams 1–0–7–0. *Second Innings*—Cork 14–1–56–0; Tomlinson 15–4–60–3; Imran Tahir 29–8–103–1; Griffiths 15–2–67–1; Carberry 10–0–64–1; Adams 1–0–5–0; Vince 2–0–13–0.

Hampshire

M. A. Carberry c Jefferson b Fletcher	27	– lbw b Shreck	5
J. H. K. Adams c Shafayat b Patel	112	– c Read b Pattinson	6
M. J. Lumb st Read b Patel	43	– (4) c and b Patel	26
J. M. Vince c Jefferson b Ealham	13	– (5) c Voges b Fletcher	75
C. C. Benham c Jefferson b Fletcher	13	– (6) c Read b Fletcher	7
*†N. Pothas c Shafayat b Patel	36	– (7) not out	63
S. M. Ervine c Read b Fletcher	1	– (8) c Jefferson b Voges	21
D. G. Cork lbw b Ealham	26	– (9) c Read b Ealham	4
Imran Tahir c Ealham b Patel	0	– (11) c Voges b Pattinson	0
D. A. Griffiths c Brown b Patel	1	– b Pattinson	3
J. A. Tomlinson not out	3	– (3) c Shafayat b Pattinson	2
B 1, l-b 2, w 3, n-b 14	20	B 4, l-b 3, w 1	8

1/57 (1) 2/166 (3) 3/185 (4)   (90.4 overs) 295
4/211 (2) 5/238 (5) 6/254 (7)
7/266 (6) 8/266 (9) 9/287 (10) 10/295 (8)

1/8 (2) 2/14 (3)   (81.5 overs) 220
3/14 (1) 4/96 (4)
5/115 (6) 6/136 (5) 7/181 (8)
8/202 (9) 9/220 (10) 10/220 (11)

Pattinson 16–3–62–0; Shreck 14–1–59–0; Fletcher 16–3–56–3; Patel 28–10–81–5; Ealham 16.4–7–34–2. *Second Innings*—Fletcher 11–4–24–2; Pattinson 15.5–4–53–4; Patel 29–3–79–1; Shreck 11–4–22–1; Ealham 11–4–32–1; Voges 4–1–3–1.

Umpires: R. J. Bailey and J. F. Steele.

At Liverpool, June 17, 18, 19, 20. HAMPSHIRE beat LANCASHIRE by ten wickets.

At Taunton, July 10, 11, 12, 13. HAMPSHIRE drew with SOMERSET.

At Arundel, July 15, 16, 17, 18. HAMPSHIRE drew with SUSSEX.

HAMPSHIRE v WARWICKSHIRE

At Southampton, July 21, 22, 23, 24. Drawn. Hampshire 11 pts, Warwickshire 11 pts. Toss: Warwickshire.

A benign Rose Bowl pitch allowed both sides to amass substantial totals – though that looked unlikely when Warwickshire fell to 90 for five after choosing to bat. They had been 30 for none at the end of a truncated first day, but slumped next morning as cloud cover briefly gave the bowlers a helping hand. Trott led the recovery in easier conditions, profiting from dropped catches and finding a willing ally in Woakes who, after being dropped on 98 by Imran Tahir at midwicket, completed a maiden hundred. The pair had added 222 – a ground record for the eighth wicket – when Westwood declared. Hampshire promptly carried on in the same vein, the openers putting on 261 (an all-wicket record for the Rose Bowl) before Adams fell for 90. It meant that, between Botha's dismissal three overs before tea on the second day and Adams's departure late on the third, 118 overs yielded 483 runs and not one wicket. Carberry carried on to his first double-hundred, and Ervine ensured a narrow lead before falling to Frost, who in his 115th match picked up a maiden first-class victim with his off-spin.

Close of play: First day, Warwickshire 30-0 (Westwood 12, Frost 15); Second day, Warwickshire 383-7 (Trott 140, Woakes 77); Third day, Hampshire 309-1 (Carberry 183, Lumb 15).

Warwickshire

*I. J. Westwood c Tremlett b Tomlinson	13	– not out		14
T. Frost c Burrows b Tomlinson	15	– c Tremlett b Imran Tahir		3
I. R. Bell c Burrows b Tomlinson	7	– b Imran Tahir		0
I. J. L. Trott not out	184	– not out		0
J. O. Troughton c Burrows b Ervine	12			
†T. R. Ambrose c Burrows b Mascarenhas	4			
R. Clarke lbw b Mascarenhas	46			
A. G. Botha st Burrows b Dawson	40			
C. R. Woakes not out	131			
B 10, l-b 7, w 1, n-b 14	32	B 4, n-b 2		6

1/30 (2) 2/35 (1)   (7 wkts dec, 129 overs) 484   1/13 (2)   (2 wkts, 13.1 overs) 23
3/52 (3) 4/85 (5) 5/90 (6)   2/13 (3)
6/156 (7) 7/262 (8)   120 overs: 420-7

N. S. Tahir and W. B. Rankin did not bat.

Tremlett 30–5–101–0; Tomlinson 27–5–102–3; Ervine 20–2–97–1; Mascarenhas 18–2–63–2; Imran Tahir 28–0–91–0; Dawson 6–2–13–1. *Second Innings*—Imran Tahir 7–5–2–2; Dawson 6–3–7–0; Carberry 0.1–0–10–0.

Hampshire

M. A. Carberry c Clarke b Tahir	204	Imran Tahir c Botha b Westwood		8
J. H. K. Adams c Trott b Westwood	90	J. A. Tomlinson not out		7
M. J. Lumb c Trott b Rankin	20			
J. P. Crawley c Clarke b Rankin	14	B 7, l-b 11, w 2, n-b 14		34
L. A. Dawson c Troughton b Rankin	18			
S. M. Ervine c Westwood b Frost	82	1/261 (2) 2/333 (3) (135.1 overs) 505		
*A. D. Mascarenhas retired hurt	0	3/351 (1) 4/359 (4)		
†T. G. Burrows lbw b Woakes	0	5/376 (5) 6/387 (8) 7/461 (9)		
C. T. Tremlett b Botha	28	8/470 (10) 9/505 (6) 120 overs: 460-6		

Mascarenhas retired hurt at 378.

Rankin 27–1–117–3; Tahir 17–1–71–1; Woakes 17–1–67–1; Botha 35–4–111–1; Clarke 15–1–59–0; Westwood 15–2–39–2; Trott 4–0–11–0; Frost 5.1–1–12–1.

Umpires: P. J. Hartley and N. J. Llong.

HAMPSHIRE v LANCASHIRE

At Southampton, August 6, 7, 8, 9. Drawn. Hampshire 8 pts, Lancashire 12 pts. Toss: Hampshire. Championship debut: S. D. Parry.

For the second Championship match in a row the Rose Bowl was a bowler's nightmare. Two wickets fell on the rain-interrupted first day, only three on the third, and four on the fourth as the match drifted to a draw. There were four hundreds, and four further half-centuries, as batsmen took advantage of a placid pitch and two weakened attacks – Hampshire were without Cork and Tremlett, while Lancashire had neither Chapple nor Mahmood. After Adams began with a careful century, Hampshire were in some trouble when Newby took three wickets in as many overs, only for Ervine to make a Championship-best 114, hitting 15 fours and two sixes. Lancashire replied with interest: Laxman's century was his second in a week, while Tom Smith, who had recorded his best bowling figures in the previous match, now made his highest Championship score, as did du Plessis. Griffiths was the only bowler to trouble Lancashire, who stretched their lead to 231 before declaring on the fourth morning. However, Smith could not bowl after picking up a stomach injury, making Lancashire's attack even more threadbare, and Carberry accelerated to his fourth century in six first-class innings. John Crawley, 37, announced his retirement during the match against his former county, and in his final innings had reached 12 when he became a distinguished first Championship victim for slow left-armer Stephen Parry.

Close of play: First day, Hampshire 144-2 (Adams 82, Vince 4); Second day, Lancashire 106-1 (Smith 44, Loye 19); Third day, Lancashire 487-4 (Laxman 135, du Plessis 38).

Hampshire

M. A. Carberry c Chilton b Hogg	33	– not out	136
J. H. K. Adams lbw b Newby	107	– b Hogg	21
J. P. Crawley c Laxman b Hogg	21	– c Laxman b Parry	12
J. M. Vince c Sutton b Newby	23	– c Laxman b Keedy	9
L. A. Dawson c Sutton b Newby	3	– not out	23
S. M. Ervine c Smith b Hogg	114		
*A. D. Mascarenhas c Sutton b Hogg	21		
†T. G. Burrows c Laxman b Newby	0		
D. A. Griffiths b Keedy	0		
Imran Tahir b Smith	0		
J. A. Tomlinson not out	6		
L-b 3, w 2, n-b 4	9	B 16, l-b 4, n-b 8	28

1/65 (1) 2/133 (3) 3/183 (4)   (105.2 overs) 337   1/75 (2)   (3 wkts, 69 overs) 229
4/189 (5) 5/194 (2) 6/263 (7)   2/123 (3) 3/142 (4)
7/274 (8) 8/286 (9) 9/287 (10) 10/337 (6)

Hogg 29.2–8–74–4; Newby 30–4–105–4; Smith 26–6–84–1; Keedy 11–0–49–1; Parry 9–2–22–0. *Second Innings*—Hogg 11–3–39–1; Newby 12–2–30–0; Parry 13–3–38–1; Keedy 24–4–69–1; du Plessis 7–0–32–0; Laxman 2–1–1–0.

Lancashire

P. J. Horton c Imran Tahir b Griffiths	34	*†L. D. Sutton not out	30
T. C. Smith c Burrows b Griffiths	95	B 2, l-b 13, w 1, n-b 30	46
M. B. Loye lbw b Mascarenhas	61		
V. V. S. Laxman c Ervine b Griffiths	135	1/62 (1) (5 wkts dec, 144.1 overs) 568	
M. J. Chilton c Burrows b Griffiths	81	2/214 (2) 3/214 (3)	
F. du Plessis not out	86	4/430 (5) 5/487 (4) 120 overs: 430-4	

K. W. Hogg, S. D. Parry, O. J. Newby and G. Keedy did not bat.

Tomlinson 24–4–80–0; Mascarenhas 24–8–59–1; Imran Tahir 28–3–112–0; Griffiths 27–5–103–4; Dawson 19.1–1–100–0; Ervine 11–0–51–0; Adams 1–0–5–0; Carberry 6–0–34–0; Vince 4–0–9–0.

Umpires: S. A. Garratt and G. Sharp.

HAMPSHIRE v YORKSHIRE

At Basingstoke, August 11, 12, 13, 14. Yorkshire won by an innings and 22 runs. Yorkshire 21 pts, Hampshire 4 pts. Toss: Yorkshire.

Yorkshire's win, their first in 22 first-class matches stretching back to June 2008, sent Hampshire into the relegation zone. The dominant force, with bat and ball, was Rashid: his 117 not out, briefly a career-best, was followed by a match-winning spell as Hampshire's lower order capitulated. After starting their second innings 274 in arrears, the home side had looked comfortable at 230 for four with time dwindling. But once Ervine was run out going for a second leg-bye from a failed reverse sweep, Rashid took command, befuddling the tail with his leg-spin variations and cleaning up the last five wickets in 36 balls. Such an outcome seemed unlikely at the end of the second day, when Yorkshire led by 23 with three wickets standing. But Rashid and Shahzad, profiting from three dropped catches, put on 192 for the eighth wicket: Shahzad, who had claimed three victims in an over in Hampshire's first innings, recorded his first half-century. Yorkshire also owed a debt to Rudolph, whose patient 90 occupied 78 overs.

Close of play: First day, Yorkshire 13-0 (Rudolph 4, Sayers 5); Second day, Yorkshire 273-7 (Rashid 0, Shahzad 5); Third day, Hampshire 75-2 (Carberry 41, Vince 27).

Hampshire

M. A. Carberry c Bresnan b Shahzad	23	– c Brophy b Shahzad	70
J. H. K. Adams b Kruis	79	– b Bresnan	2
M. J. Lumb lbw b Bresnan	51	– lbw b Bresnan	0
J. M. Vince c Rudolph b Bresnan	18	– lbw b Hoggard	43
L. A. Dawson c Sayers b Kruis	1	– c Sayers b Rashid	50
S. M. Ervine c and b Hoggard	28	– run out	48
*A. D. Mascarenhas c Brophy b Shahzad	14	– c Brophy b Rashid	0
†T. G. Burrows lbw b Shahzad	16	– not out	8
C. T. Tremlett b Shahzad	0	– c Brophy b Rashid	0
Imran Tahir c Brophy b Bresnan	7	– st Brophy b Rashid	4
D. A. Griffiths not out	0	– b Rashid	0
B 5, l-b 2, w 2, n-b 4	13	B 12, l-b 8, w 1, n-b 6	27

1/32 (1) 2/119 (3) 3/153 (4)   (90.1 overs) 250
4/154 (5) 5/203 (6) 6/220 (2)
7/238 (7) 8/238 (9) 9/245 (8) 10/250 (10)

1/6 (2) 2/10 (3)   (79.5 overs) 252
3/107 (4) 4/136 (1)
5/230 (6) 6/230 (7) 7/239 (5)
8/239 (9) 9/247 (10) 10/251 (11)

Bresnan 19.1–6–45–3; Hoggard 17–5–38–1; Shahzad 22–4–72–4; Kruis 19–4–51–2; McGrath 9–1–24–0; Rashid 4–1–13–0. *Second Innings*—Hoggard 16–3–54–1; Bresnan 20–7–46–2; Shahzad 13–3–45–1; Kruis 10–1–39–0; Rashid 16.5–6–41–5; McGrath 4–2–7–0.

Yorkshire

J. A. Rudolph c Ervine b Imran Tahir	90		M. J. Hoggard c Mascarenhas b Tremlett	14
J. J. Sayers c Dawson b Griffiths	50		G. J. Kruis lbw b Imran Tahir	26
*A. McGrath c Burrows b Griffiths	0			
A. W. Gale c Dawson b Mascarenhas	8		B 18, l-b 16, w 3, n-b 14	51
J. M. Bairstow lbw b Imran Tahir	13			
†G. L. Brophy c Carberry b Griffiths	53		1/132 (2) 2/134 (3) (165 overs)	524
T. T. Bresnan run out	24		3/150 (4) 4/173 (5) 5/204 (1)	
A. U. Rashid not out	117		6/262 (7) 7/268 (6) 8/460 (9)	
A. Shahzad c Adams b Tremlett	78		9/488 (10) 10/524 (11) 120 overs: 354-7	

Mascarenhas 40–16–77–1; Tremlett 31–3–106–2; Ervine 27–10–67–0; Griffiths 32–5–117–3; Imran Tahir 33–7–116–3; Vince 2–0–7–0.

Umpires: B. Dudleston and V. A. Holder.

At Nottingham, August 19, 20, 21, 22. HAMPSHIRE drew with NOTTINGHAMSHIRE. *Michael Lumb scores 219 in a total of 654.*

HAMPSHIRE v SOMERSET

At Southampton, August 27, 28, 29, 30. Drawn. Hampshire 11 pts, Somerset 10 pts. Toss: Hampshire. First-class debut: D. R. Briggs.

After being left 17 overs to score 140, Hampshire were denied the chance of an important victory by bad light: on a cold, overcast day the umpires took the players off after only 11 balls of the final innings, much to the disappointment of the home side and a smattering of spectators. Adams's third century of the season – all scored at the Rose Bowl – provided the bedrock of Hampshire's substantial first-innings total on a pitch which offered some turn; both sides included three spinners, although Dawson was given only two overs. The later batsmen helped: Imran Tahir's half-century was his first in first-class cricket, while Cork's was his first for Hampshire. Tahir then found plenty of assistance in the pitch, taking seven wickets, although Trescothick almost prevented the follow-on with the seventh century of a prolific season. Cork chipped in with two wickets in successive balls. Somerset needed 155 just to force Hampshire to bat again, and looked in trouble at 152 for five when Trescothick edged an arm-ball to slip for 73 – a notable scalp for the debutant Danny Briggs, a left-arm spinner from the Isle of Wight, who finished with three wickets in a handy innings. However, Kieswetter struck some belligerent blows to eat into the time available, making 70 in 137 minutes, and Hampshire's hopes disappeared into the gloom. Langer was reported for showing dissent when given out caught at slip, and was later reprimanded by the ECB.

Close of play: First day, Hampshire 286-4 (Adams 113, Pothas 27); Second day, Somerset 98-3 (Trescothick 36, Thomas 8); Third day, Somerset 50-0 (Trescothick 26, Suppiah 20).

Hampshire

J. H. K. Adams b Willoughby	147	– not out	1
L. A. Dawson lbw b Banks	55		
M. J. Lumb c Trescothick b Banks	68	– (2) not out	3
J. M. Vince c Langer b Willoughby	4		
S. M. Ervine hit wkt b Banks	4		
†N. Pothas c Kieswetter b Willoughby	41		
*A. D. Mascarenhas lbw b Trego	31		
D. G. Cork c Suppiah b Waller	52		
Imran Tahir not out	77		
D. A. Griffiths c Willoughby b Banks	5		
D. R. Briggs c Banks b Suppiah	36		
B 10, l-b 13, w 1, n-b 4	28	L-b 5	5

1/104 (2) 2/235 (3) 3/240 (4)   (163 overs) 548   (no wkt, 1.5 overs) 9
4/249 (5) 5/326 (6) 6/337 (1)
7/422 (7) 8/430 (8) 9/468 (10)
10/548 (11)   120 overs: 351-6

Willoughby 35–12–117–3; Thomas 29–8–75–0; Banks 38–6–120–4; Waller 19–4–79–1; Trego 28–12–68–1; Suppiah 6–0–24–1; de Bruyn 8–1–42–0. *Second Innings*—Willoughby 1–0–1–0; Thomas 0.5–0–3–0.

Somerset

M. E. Trescothick b Imran Tahir	118	– c Cork b Briggs	73
A. V. Suppiah c and b Imran Tahir	35	– b Cork	21
*J. L. Langer c Cork b Imran Tahir	0	– c Vince b Imran Tahir	32
J. C. Hildreth c Mascarenhas b Imran Tahir	4	– lbw b Cork	4
A. C. Thomas c Pothas b Cork	15	– (9) b Briggs	11
Z. de Bruyn c Adams b Cork	0	– (5) c Pothas b Briggs	13
†C. Kieswetter c Pothas b Imran Tahir	94	– (6) c Dawson b Griffiths	70
P. D. Trego c Adams b Imran Tahir	20	– (7) c Adams b Imran Tahir	27
O. A. C. Banks not out	45	– (8) lbw b Ervine	6
M. T. C. Waller lbw b Imran Tahir	28	– c Pothas b Griffiths	18
C. M. Willoughby b Griffiths	0	– not out	5
B 6, l-b 4, n-b 24	34	B 1, l-b 2, w 1, n-b 10	14

1/76 (2) 2/78 (3) 3/86 (4) 4/129 (5) (106 overs) 393   1/52 (2) 2/117 (3)   (94 overs) 294
5/133 (6) 6/280 (1) 7/311 (7)   3/126 (4) 4/149 (5)
8/322 (8) 9/392 (10) 10/393 (11)   5/152 (1) 6/210 (7) 7/233 (8)
    8/261 (9) 9/278 (6) 10/294 (10)

Griffiths 19–2–74–1; Mascarenhas 10.5–2–31–0; Imran Tahir 35.1–6–140–7; Cork 16–5–39–2; Briggs 13–2–70–0; Dawson 2–0–8–0; Ervine 10.2–2–21–0. *Second Innings*—Ervine 11–2–36–1; Griffiths 12–2–25–2; Cork 16.2–4–48–2; Imran Tahir 36–9–120–2; Briggs 19–3–62–3.

Umpires: M. R. Benson and N. G. B. Cook.

At Worcester, September 9, 10, 11. HAMPSHIRE beat WORCESTERSHIRE by ten wickets.

HAMPSHIRE v DURHAM

At Southampton, September 15, 16, 17, 18. Drawn. Hampshire 10 pts, Durham 11 pts. Toss: Durham. First-class debut: S. G. Borthwick.

Champions Durham's push for their ninth win of a triumphant season was thwarted by rain on the first day and some determined Hampshire batting over the last two. Only 29 overs were possible on that opening day, after which Will Smith led Durham towards an imposing first-innings total with a disciplined 150, spread across almost six and a half hours and 325 balls. The slow and low pitch offered bowlers little help, but at 114 for four midway through the third day Hampshire still had plenty to do to reach the follow-on target of 290. It was then that Benham, playing only because Mascarenhas was away with the England one-day squad, hit his first Championship century in six years on the staff, in his 58th innings. A seventh-wicket stand of 78 between Pothas and Ervine made sure Durham had to bat again. Scott Borthwick, a leg-spinner making his debut, and slow left-armer Blackwell took eight wickets between them in marathon stints, but soon after Hampshire were all out, halfway between lunch and tea, the match was ended by bad light. Harmison took his 400th first-class wicket for Durham, and the 50th of his Championship season, when he had Cork caught behind.

Close of play: First day, Durham 95-1 (Di Venuto 61, Smith 11); Second day, Durham 435-9 (Borthwick 24); Third day, Hampshire 267-6 (Pothas 55).

Durham

M. J. Di Venuto lbw b Cork	62	– not out	8
K. J. Coetzer b Briggs	20	– not out	0
*W. R. Smith c Imran Tahir b Griffiths	150		
S. Chanderpaul b Briggs	4		
D. M. Benkenstein c Dawson b Briggs	24		
I. D. Blackwell c Adams b Imran Tahir	56		
†P. Mustard c Adams b Imran Tahir	35		
L. E. Plunkett lbw b Imran Tahir	37		
S. G. Borthwick not out	26		
M. Davies c Adams b Imran Tahir	0		
S. J. Harmison lbw b Griffiths	1		
B 3, l-b 5, w 2, n-b 14	24		

1/73 (2) 2/99 (1) 3/110 (4)   (132.4 overs) 439   (no wkt, 3.5 overs) 8
4/152 (5) 5/261 (6) 6/313 (7)
7/376 (8) 8/435 (3) 9/435 (10)
10/439 (11)   120 overs: 385-7

Cork 21–4–63–1; Griffiths 19.4–3–66–2; Briggs 38–5–126–3; Ervine 16–4–37–0; Imran Tahir 35–3–133–4; Dawson 3–1–6–0. *Second Innings*—Vince 2–0–8–0; Griffiths 1.5–1–0–0.

Hampshire

J. H. K. Adams c Harmison b Borthwick	57	Imran Tahir not out	0
L. A. Dawson c Mustard b Blackwell	29	D. R. Briggs c Plunkett b Blackwell	0
M. J. Lumb lbw b Blackwell	6		
J. M. Vince c Smith b Borthwick	8	B 7, l-b 3, n-b 4	14
C. C. Benham c Di Venuto b Borthwick	100		
*†N. Pothas b Blackwell	78	1/52 (2) 2/72 (3) 3/87 (4) (119.3 overs) 384
D. A. Griffiths b Plunkett	1	4/114 (1) 5/266 (5)
S. M. Ervine c Mustard b Blackwell	67	6/267 (7) 7/345 (6) 8/384 (9)
D. G. Cork c Mustard b Harmison	24	9/384 (8) 10/384 (11)

Harmison 21–5–78–1; Davies 14–3–36–0; Blackwell 39.3–9–110–5; Borthwick 27–2–95–3; Plunkett 14–4–49–1; Benkenstein 3–1–6–0; Smith 1–1–0–0.

Umpires: R. K. Illingworth and T. E. Jesty.

At Leeds, September 23, 24, 25, 26. HAMPSHIRE drew with YORKSHIRE.

KENT

Clambering back to base camp

MARK PENNELL

On the third morning of their penultimate Championship match, Kent finally clinched the Division Two title. Their supporters, having until 2009 enjoyed their four-day cricket exclusively in the top flight, fully expected Rob Key's powerful side to bounce straight back as champions; few expected to wait until September 17 to witness it.

Fittingly, it was leading scorer Martin van Jaarsveld who took Kent over the line. His trademark nurdled single to midwicket, one of 1,475 Championship runs at an impressive average of 70.23, brought a second batting point against Leicestershire – and an ECB cheque for £115,000: £90,000 for the players and £25,000 for the county.

Played out on another sublime St Lawrence pitch tended by the new head groundsman Andy Peirson, the final home Championship game petered out into a fifth draw, but Kent's eight wins – two more than any other side in the division – set them apart.

Yet celebrations remained subdued. "I look at the banner, and it says Division Two winners, so it won't go down as one of the great moments in my career," said Key, soon after lifting the trophy. "It's £90,000 for finishing tenth in my eyes, and is something we had to do in order to get back to Division One. I still want to win the Championship, and that means winning the first division. The hard work starts now, because there is a big difference in standard between the divisions."

A glance at Kent's averages these past two seasons shows up the gulf in class Key refers to. In winning Division Two, three batsmen – Key, van Jaarsveld and the supporters' player of the season Geraint Jones – all topped 1,000 Championship runs. Only van Jaarsveld had done so in Division One in 2008. Jones, who averaged 30 in the first division, reached 1,000 for the first time in the second, batting at No. 3 and averaging 51. Sam Northeast, aged 19, made a promising contribution, including his maiden hundred.

During 2009 Kent built the second and fourth highest totals in club history: 652 at Uxbridge against Middlesex, and 620 against a woeful Surrey attack at The Oval. In 2008, the county had only three times made it past 400. However, a modest return of 43 batting bonus points, 13 fewer than Glamorgan, pinpointed another moderate season in terms of first-innings batting.

If further pointers to a chasm in class were needed, Kent's bowlers provided them. Off-spinner James Tredwell bettered his modest 24 wickets at 51 apiece in Kent's relegation campaign with 69 at just 26, and an England call-up.

In the pace department, South Africa's Wayne Parnell prospered in his brief stints, taking 17 wickets in five appearances, while Azhar Mahmood topped the averages with 21 wickets at a frugal 18, without appearing at his best, or his fittest. The same could be said of Amjad Khan, who made his Test debut against West Indies in March, though this looked like being a one-off. He did not kick on, and took only 36 first-class wickets.

Robbie Joseph largely missed out with a shoulder problem and later required an operation, while persistent knee trouble forced the beneficiary Martin Saggers into retirement. Parnell and the injury-hit all-rounder Ryan McLaren, who underachieved with a highest score of 43 and best return of four for 51, were most unlikely to return – McLaren because he relinquished

James Tredwell

his Kolpak status by playing for South Africa. Strengthening the pace attack remained Kent's priority in their determination not to become the Championship's latest yo-yo county. They signed Stuart Clark, the highly rated Australian seamer, for the first half of 2010, and the Sri Lankan wrist-spinner Malinga Bandara for the second.

However, they had to face the season without Graham Ford, their popular director of cricket, who left after five seasons to concentrate on his post with the Dolphins in Durban. The former Kent academy coach and wicketkeeper Paul Farbrace ended his two-year stint as Sri Lanka's assistant to fill the void.

In September, supporters overwhelmingly sanctioned a slightly revised version of the controversial St Lawrence redevelopment, which nevertheless still included housing and a hotel. Having endured second-class facilities at their beloved yet increasingly dishevelled ground for long enough, they had little option.

Late-season cracks developed on the playing front too, where clinching promotion glossed over a patchy limited-overs campaign that started with promise only to fizzle out in a whimper. Successive Friends Provident Trophy wins over Middlesex, Scotland and Warwickshire gave a misleading impression because the Spitfires, beaten finalists in 2008, lost four of their eight Group B qualifiers to finish second-bottom and miss the knockout stages. A young, experimental side performed wonders to remain unbeaten in five Pro40 games, but lost out on the runners-up bonus in Division Two when three successive defeats dropped them to third.

Though worthy qualifiers for a third straight appearance at Twenty20 finals day, Kent saved their worst limited-overs performance for their Edgbaston semi-final. After topping a tough South Division with seven wins from ten and drubbing Durham in the quarter-finals, they stumbled to 31 for three, then served Somerset's Marcus Trescothick with buffet bowling. Key succinctly described his side's display as "rubbish".

KENT RESULTS

All first-class matches – Played 17: Won 8, Lost 3, Drawn 6.
County Championship matches – Played 16: Won 8, Lost 3, Drawn 5.

LV County Championship, winners in Division 2; Friends Provident Trophy, 4th in Group B;
Pro40 League, 3rd in Division 2; Twenty20 Cup, s-f.

COUNTY CHAMPIONSHIP AVERAGES, BATTING AND FIELDING

Cap		M	I	NO	R	HS	100s	50s	Avge	Ct/St
2005	M. van Jaarsveld¶	15	24	3	1,475	182	7	7	70.23	30
2001	R. W. T. Key	14	24	3	1,145	270*	4	3	54.52	15
2003	G. O. Jones	16	25	0	1,291	156	5	5	51.64	41/3
2006	J. M. Kemp¶	14	21	3	780	183	2	2	43.33	30
2008	J. L. Denly†	9	14	1	542	123	1	4	41.69	5
2005	D. I. Stevens	16	23	2	857	208	3	2	40.80	11
	S. A. Northeast†	10	18	2	603	128*	1	2	37.68	10
	W. D. Parnell§	5	6	1	183	90	0	2	36.60	0
	J. B. Hockley†	4	7	1	185	72	0	1	30.83	5
2007	J. C. Tredwell†	16	21	5	484	86*	0	4	30.25	12
	A. J. Blake†	4	5	0	125	47	0	0	25.00	1
2007	S. J. Cook	13	13	4	220	60*	0	1	24.44	0
2007	R. McLaren¶	7	8	1	127	44	0	0	18.14	1
	A. Khan	11	12	3	153	62*	0	1	17.00	2
2008	Azhar Mahmood¶	4	6	0	78	35	0	0	13.00	0
	P. S. Jones	3	4	0	26	16	0	0	6.50	1
	R. H. Joseph	4	5	2	11	9*	0	0	3.66	0
2001	M. J. Saggers	4	4	2	5	5*	0	0	2.50	0
	P. D. Edwards†	4	4	2	5	5	0	0	2.50	1

Also batted: M. T. Coles† (1 match) 14, 16; R. S. Ferley (2 matches) 17 (1 ct).

† *Born in Kent.* § *Official overseas player.* ¶ *Other non-England-qualified player.*

BOWLING

	O	M	R	W	BB	5W/i	Avge
Azhar Mahmood	130.3	38	382	21	5-39	1	18.19
M. J. Saggers...............	108.5	34	264	10	3-45	0	26.40
J. C. Tredwell	681.5	178	1,838	69	8-66	4	26.63
S. J. Cook	374.1	88	1,047	34	5-22	3	30.79
R. H. Joseph	97.2	9	373	12	6-55	1	31.08
W. D. Parnell...............	166.3	35	529	17	4-78	0	31.11
A. Khan...................	339.1	65	1,146	36	5-113	1	31.83
R. McLaren	164.5	37	608	19	4-51	0	32.00

Also bowled: A. J. Blake 4–0–15–0; M. T. Coles 17.4–0–130–2; J. L. Denly 25.7–7–60–0; P. D. Edwards 95–18–325–7; R. S. Ferley 75–15–189–7; P. S. Jones 80–19–240–4; J. M. Kemp 165.5–35–568–8; R. W. T. Key 22–5–59–1; S. A. Northeast 1–0–2–0; D. I. Stevens 68–13–256–2; M. van Jaarsveld 71.1–10–241–4.

COUNTY RECORDS

Highest score for:	332	W. H. Ashdown v Essex at Brentwood	1934
Highest score against:	344	W. G. Grace (MCC) at Canterbury	1876
Leading run-scorer:	47,868	F. E. Woolley (avge 41.77)	1906–1938
Best bowling for:	10-30	C. Blythe v Northamptonshire at Northampton..	1907
Best bowling against:	10-48	C. H. G. Bland (Sussex) at Tonbridge	1899
Leading wicket-taker:	3,340	A. P. Freeman (avge 17.64)................	1914–1936
Highest total for:	803-4 dec	v Essex at Brentwood	1934
Highest total against:	676	by Australians at Canterbury	1921
Lowest total for:	18	v Sussex at Gravesend	1867
Lowest total against:	16	by Warwickshire at Tonbridge	1913

ADDRESS

St Lawrence Ground, Old Dover Road, Canterbury CT1 3NZ (01227 456886; **email** kent@ecb.co.uk). **Website** www.kentccc.com

OFFICIALS

Captain R. W. T. Key
Team director P. Farbrace
High-performance director S. C. Willis
President A. A. Dunning
Chairman G. M. Kennedy

Acting chief executive J. A. Clifford
Chairman, cricket committee G. W. Johnson
Grounds co-ordinator A. Peirson
Scorer J. C. Foley

Return of the native

It took Paul Farbrace barely two hours to realise that the future lay at his leafy spiritual home in Canterbury rather than in tropical Colombo. Last September the former Kent and Middlesex wicketkeeper ended a two-year stint as assistant coach to the Sri Lankan national team, and returned home to replace the South African Graham Ford as Kent's head coach.

Farbrace, 42, was Kent's academy director for four years before linking up with Sri Lanka in 2007, and jumped at the chance to work again with Joe Denly, Sam Northeast, Alex Blake, James Goodman and James Tredwell, all players he helped blossom in Kent's age-group structure. "I was in England with the Sri Lankans for the Twenty20 World Cup when I received a call from Graham Johnson, Kent's chairman of cricket," said Farbrace. "He told me there was every possibility that Graham [Ford] might be moving on and asked if the job would be of interest to me."

Farbrace had been lured from Canterbury by the Sri Lankan coach Trevor Bayliss: they had met during a work exchange initiative linking Kent and New South Wales, a legacy of Steve Waugh's six-week stint as Kent's overseas player in 2002.

Though Sri Lanka did their utmost to retain Farbrace, the call of home proved too strong. "The opportunity to return was too tempting. I liked the sound of being tested, and needed to see if I could do it at this level. The Sri Lankan board matched all Kent had offered, but finances never came into it for me – if anything I'll probably be slightly worse off!"

A former coach to England women and the national Under-19 team, Farbrace feels he is prepared for his first stint at the helm of a Championship side. "I've picked up a lot more confidence working with Sri Lanka," he said. "And I now know I can make a difference to players at Test level and help improve their games. I feel I have far more patience and a greater understanding of what the job entails, as well as the knowledge that different characters like to be coached in different ways. There's an adage on the international circuit that says 'Good coaches coach technique, but great coaches coach people.' I think that's so very true."

MARK PENNELL

KENT v LOUGHBOROUGH UCCE

At Canterbury, April 15, 16, 17. Drawn. Toss: Loughborough UCCE. First-class debuts: M. T. Coles; R. F. Evans. County debut: P. D. Edwards.

Rain ended Kent's maiden first-class match against a non-Oxbridge university after just a day's play. There was time for Stevens to reach his first fifty in first-class games since June 2008 and to go on to a big unbeaten hundred. Phil Edwards became the first player born on the Isle of Sheppey to be picked for Kent, but neither he nor Matt Coles – another young local seamer – took the field.

Close of play: First day, Kent 499-5 (Stevens 193, Hockley 55); Second day, No play.

Kent

J. L. Denly b Groves	36	J. B. Hockley not out	55
*R. W. T. Key c Murphy b Groves	26	B 1, l-b 1, w 3, n-b 32	37
†G. O. Jones lbw b A. C. Evans	54		
M. van Jaarsveld c Murphy b R. F. Evans	34	1/71 (2) 2/82 (1) (5 wkts, 114 overs) 499	
D. I. Stevens not out	193	3/132 (4) 4/219 (3)	
S. A. Northeast b Malan	64	5/379 (6)	

J. C. Tredwell, R. S. Ferley, M. T. Coles and P. D. Edwards did not bat.

Jones 12–1–77–0; Groves 13–2–69–2; A. C. Evans 15–1–86–1; Baer 34–0–109–0; R. F. Evans 16–3–86–1; Malan 23–5–67–1; Harinath 1–0–3–0.

Loughborough UCCE

P. M. Borrington, P. L. Hayes, *A. A. Lynch, A. Harinath, C. C. Malan, †D. Murphy, R. F. Evans, P. R. Groves, H. D. Jones, M. Baer and A. C. Evans.

Umpires: S. J. O'Shaughnessy and J. F. Steele.

KENT v NORTHAMPTONSHIRE

At Canterbury, April 21, 22, 23, 24. Drawn. Kent 11 pts, Northamptonshire 10 pts. Toss: Kent. County debut: P. S. Jones. Championship debut: P. D. Edwards.

This high-scoring game lacked sparkle and imagination, and it meandered to a tame stalemate. Kent's new head groundsman, Andy Peirson, prepared a belter for his Championship debut, making Key's decision to bowl first without five of his top-flight seamers and an all-rounder all the more mysterious. Kent included Azhar Mahmood (signed on a limited-overs contract), Steffan Jones (on loan to his fourth county) and debutant Phil Edwards, took four sessions to winkle out workmanlike visitors while also attempting to master the new Tiflex Oxbridge ball. Boje scored 168 runs in total and batted nine and a half hours without adding to the entertainment value as Northamptonshire pottered along at around two and a half an over. Those turgid innings sandwiched Kent's brisker riposte, including centuries by Jones and van Jaarsveld. But only the diehards witnessed a final-day hundred by Peters and a maiden first-class wicket for Key in his 196th match. While Peters batted almost five hours for a determined 107, former prime minister Sir John Major addressed the annual lunch of the Hoppers Tie Club; only one of them received a standing ovation afterwards.

Close of play: First day, Northamptonshire 268-5 (Boje 77, Willey 19); Second day, Kent 257-3 (van Jaarsveld 70, Stevens 46); Third day, Northamptonshire 148-2 (Peters 62, Lucas 1).

Northamptonshire

S. D. Peters c G. O. Jones b P. S. Jones	32	– c Key b Tredwell	107
B. H. N. Howgego c Tredwell b Azhar Mahmood	18	– run out	5
R. A. White lbw b Azhar Mahmood	41	– c van Jaarsveld b Tredwell	70
*N. Boje c G. O. Jones b Tredwell	98	– (5) not out	70
†M. H. Wessels c G. O. Jones b Saggers	27	– (6) c van Jaarsveld b Tredwell	8
A. J. Hall lbw b Stevens	38	– (7) b Saggers	3
D. J. Willey c G. O. Jones b Saggers	31	– (8) b Key	47
J. J. van der Wath c Edwards b Azhar Mahmood	12		
D. S. Lucas b Azhar Mahmood	9	– (4) c G. O. Jones b Saggers	13
M. S. Panesar c Stevens b Tredwell	15	– (9) not out	2
D. H. Wigley not out	10		
L-b 4, w 2, n-b 18	24	B 7, l-b 6, w 2, n-b 8	23

1/32 (2) 2/98 (1) 3/100 (3)   (128.2 overs) 355   1/8 (2)   (7 wkts dec, 135 overs) 348
4/161 (5) 5/233 (6) 6/300 (7)   2/142 (3) 3/181 (4)
7/310 (4) 8/322 (8) 9/333 (9)   4/235 (1) 5/249 (6)
10/355 (10)   120 overs: 322-8   6/259 (7) 7/346 (8)

P. S. Jones 25–8–68–1; Saggers 23–8–48–2; Azhar Mahmood 23–6–73–4; Stevens 12–2–42–1; Edwards 14–1–31–0; Tredwell 30.2–9–84–2; van Jaarsveld 1–0–5–0. *Second Innings*—P. S. Jones 20–2–64–0; Azhar Mahmood 10–3–39–0; Edwards 16–2–54–0; Saggers 20–7–42–2; Tredwell 37–16–67–3; Denly 21–7–51–0; Stevens 2–1–4–0; Key 9–3–14–1.

Kent

J. L. Denly c Peters b Hall	27	P. D. Edwards lbw b Willey	0
*R. W. T. Key lbw b Lucas	2	M. J. Saggers b Willey	0
†G. O. Jones c and b Wigley	103		
M. van Jaarsveld c Hall b Panesar	107	L-b 7, w 1, n-b 10	18
D. I. Stevens c Wessels b Hall	73		
J. B. Hockley b Lucas	27	1/18 (2) 2/87 (1)	(107.4 overs) 417
Azhar Mahmood c Wigley b Hall	35	3/179 (3) 4/306 (5) 5/324 (4)	
J. C. Tredwell not out	15	6/361 (6) 7/393 (7) 8/412 (9)	
P. S. Jones c Peters b Panesar	10	9/413 (10) 10/417 (11)	

Van der Wath 6–0–26–0; Lucas 26–6–68–2; Wigley 19–0–96–1; Hall 20–2–89–3; Panesar 22–2–75–2; Boje 8–2–35–0; Willey 6.4–1–21–2.

Umpires: N. G. Cowley and B. Dudleston.

At Chelmsford, April 29, 30, May 1, 2. KENT beat ESSEX by 192 runs. *Kent win after following on.*

KENT v GLAMORGAN

At Canterbury, May 6, 7, 8, 9. Kent won by 204 runs. Kent 19 pts, Glamorgan 6 pts. Toss: Kent.

Having both fallen for ducks during a mixed first-innings show, Jones and van Jaarsveld combined for Kent's best stand against Glamorgan: 309 for the third wicket, in just 64 overs. That ensured a commanding 384-run lead and ample leeway for their strengthened attack. The 19-year-old South African Wayne Parnell, on home Championship debut, hit a first-innings 90 and took three wickets with his whippy left-arm seam, but it was the off-spinner Tredwell who proved the match-winner. He and Northeast, making his first Championship appearance since September 2007 after Denly pulled out with a migraine, also hit first-innings fifties. Then, on the final afternoon, bowling to a packed close field, Tredwell took a career-best eight for 66 (which was to remain the best return of the season) to claim his second ten-wicket match haul, as Glamorgan lost their last seven wickets for 41. Earlier, the former Kent batsman Bob Wilson had watched from the Harris Room as Jones (whose 133 was at the time a career-best) and van Jaarsveld broke his and Arthur Phebey's record for any Kent wicket against the Welsh – 304 at Blackheath in 1960.

Close of play: First day, Glamorgan 27-1 (O'Shea 14, Wright 6); Second day, Kent 30-0 (Northeast 15, Key 10); Third day, Kent 361-3 (van Jaarsveld 174, Hockley 6).

Kent

S. A. Northeast c Wallace b Kruger	87	– st Wallace b Croft	15
*R. W. T. Key lbw b Shantry	25	– c Wallace b Shantry	13
†G. O. Jones lbw b Shantry	0	– c Dalrymple b Harrison	133
M. van Jaarsveld lbw b Shantry	0	– lbw b Harrison	182
D. I. Stevens run out	3		
J. B. Hockley b Kruger	4	– (5) not out	19
J. C. Tredwell lbw b Dalrymple	59	– not out	2
W. D. Parnell c and b Croft	90	– (6) c Wright b Shantry	18
P. S. Jones c Rees b Croft	0		
R. H. Joseph not out	0		
M. J. Saggers run out	0		
B 4, l-b 7, w 3	14	B 9, l-b 14, w 4	27

1/63 (2) 2/63 (3) 3/65 (4) 4/76 (5)   (79.3 overs) 282   1/31 (1)   (5 wkts dec, 91 overs) 409
5/84 (6) 6/131 (1) 7/282 (8)   2/41 (2) 3/350 (3)
8/282 (9) 9/282 (7) 10/282 (11)   4/372 (4) 5/400 (6)

Harrison 15–0–66–0; Shantry 20–3–54–3; Kruger 15–4–42–2; Croft 17–2–66–2; Dalrymple
10.3–1–35–1; Wright 2–0–8–0. *Second Innings*—Kruger 15–1–66–0; Shantry 21–2–68–2; Harrison
18–0–100–2; Croft 26–2–96–1; Dalrymple 9–0–41–0; Wright 2–0–15–0.

Glamorgan

G. P. Rees c Hockley b Parnell	5	– c van Jaarsveld b Tredwell	25
M. P. O'Shea c Hockley b Joseph	50	– lbw b Tredwell	25
B. J. Wright c sub (M. T. Coles) b P. S. Jones	41	– b Tredwell	81
M. J. Powell b Saggers	65	– c and b Tredwell	1
*J. W. M. Dalrymple c Northeast b Tredwell	79	– c P. S. Jones b Tredwell	10
T. L. Maynard c Northeast b Tredwell	4	– c Key b P. S. Jones	4
†M. A. Wallace b Tredwell	1	– c sub (S. J. Cook) b Tredwell	0
R. D. B. Croft c Hockley b Saggers	17	– c G. O. Jones b Parnell	7
D. S. Harrison b Saggers	0	– b Tredwell	1
A. J. Shantry b Parnell	14	– c van Jaarsveld b Tredwell	0
G. J-P. Kruger not out	11	– not out	5
B 1, l-b 7, n-b 12	20	B 3, l-b 11, w 1, n-b 6	21

1/8 (1) 2/94 (2) 3/100 (3)   (95.4 overs) 307   1/39 (2) 2/99 (1)   (69 overs) 180
4/239 (5) 5/243 (6) 6/251 (7) 7/279 (4)   3/101 (4) 4/139 (5)
8/279 (9) 9/290 (8) 10/307 (10)   5/144 (6) 6/145 (7) 7/154 (8) 8/163 (9)
                                                           9/167 (10) 10/180 (3)

Parnell 25.4–6–97–2; Saggers 20–5–59–3; Joseph 15–3–50–1; P. S. Jones 6–0–30–1; Tredwell
24–8–54–3; van Jaarsveld 5–1–9–0. *Second Innings*—Joseph 10–0–32–0; Parnell 17–5–29–1;
Tredwell 28–7–66–8; van Jaarsveld 11–0–31–0; P. S. Jones 3–1–8–1.

Umpires: J. W. Lloyds and P. Willey.

At Leicester, June 6, 7, 8, 9. KENT drew with LEICESTERSHIRE.

KENT v ESSEX

At Tunbridge Wells, June 16, 17, 18, 19. Essex won by 122 runs. Essex 19 pts, Kent 3 pts. Toss:
Essex.

Key's return to lead Kent – after a frustrating time watching the majority of England's failed
World Twenty20 bid from the bench – coincided with their first Championship defeat of the
campaign, on a slow pitch at the Nevill. Essex, in trouble at 18 for three on the opening morning,

wriggled off the hook thanks to their captain Pettini, who passed 32 for the first time in 15 first-class innings, and a half-century from Napier. Masters, who learned his trade in Kent, then teamed up with fellow-seamer Napier to share eight wickets and skittle Kent in just over three hours. In the process, Masters claimed his 300th first-class wicket at an economy rate of under three an over. Pettini, not wanting to bat last on a deteriorating pitch, did not enforce the follow-on; he promptly hit a hundred, his first in the Championship for more than two and a half years, before declaring on the third afternoon to set Kent a mammoth target of 478. Denly's second hundred in successive games at Tunbridge Wells, coupled with van Jaarsveld's plucky 73, improved Kent's outside hopes of stealing a draw, until Danish Kaneria grabbed six for 92 to sweep Essex to victory with 15 overs remaining.

Close of play: First day, Kent 4-2 (Khan 1, Jones 3); Second day, Essex 109-3 (Chopra 38, Pettini 10); Third day, Kent 107-1 (Denly 74, Tredwell 4).

Essex

A. N. Cook lbw b Joseph	8	– c Jones b Cook	30
J. E. R. Gallian b Khan	1	– b Khan	14
V. Chopra b Joseph	3	– c van Jaarsveld b McLaren	63
M. J. Walker lbw b Cook	41	– c Jones b Cook	5
*M. L. Pettini c Tredwell b Kemp	55	– not out	101
†J. S. Foster lbw b Tredwell	36	– c Kemp b McLaren	37
R. N. ten Doeschate c Jones b McLaren	40	– c van Jaarsveld b McLaren	0
G. R. Napier not out	64	– not out	48
C. J. C. Wright c Kemp b McLaren	0		
D. D. Masters b McLaren	2		
Danish Kaneria b McLaren	12		
B 1, l-b 4, w 5, n-b 8	18	B 6, l-b 5, w 1, n-b 10	22

1/4 (2) 2/12 (1) 3/18 (3) 4/90 (4) (90.5 overs) 280
5/133 (5) 6/173 (6) 7/230 (7)
8/236 (9) 9/244 (10) 10/280 (11)

1/47 (2) (6 wkts dec, 99.4 overs) 320
2/47 (1) 3/57 (4)
4/152 (3) 5/230 (6) 6/230 (7)

Joseph 13.3–2–43–2; Khan 17–3–46–1; Cook 14–5–27–1; Tredwell 17–4–40–1; McLaren 17.2–1–80–4; Kemp 10–3–27–1; Stevens 2–0–12–0. *Second Innings*—Khan 22–5–58–1; Cook 22–6–56–2; McLaren 20–9–72–3; Tredwell 11–4–23–0; Kemp 14.4–3–58–0; Stevens 9–1–40–0; Denly 1–0–2–0.

Kent

J. L. Denly lbw b Masters	0	– c Masters b Cook	123
*R. W. T. Key lbw b Napier	0	– b Masters	21
A. Khan c Foster b Masters	18	– (10) b Danish Kaneria	16
†G. O. Jones c Foster b Masters	9	– b Danish Kaneria	28
M. van Jaarsveld c Foster b Napier	13	– lbw b Masters	73
D. I. Stevens c Chopra b Masters	6	– c Masters b Danish Kaneria	43
J. M. Kemp lbw b Napier	36	– lbw b Danish Kaneria	6
J. C. Tredwell b Napier	28	– (3) c Cook b Danish Kaneria	8
R. McLaren c Foster b ten Doeschate	1	– (8) b Danish Kaneria	2
S. J. Cook lbw b ten Doeschate	1	– (9) not out	8
R. H. Joseph not out	9	– c and b Napier	1
N-b 2	2	B 11, l-b 13, n-b 2	26

1/0 (1) 2/0 (2) 3/15 (4) 4/36 (3) (50.3 overs) 123
5/46 (6) 6/50 (5) 7/106 (8) 8/113 (9)
9/113 (7) 10/123 (10)

1/84 (2) 2/117 (3) (120.2 overs) 355
3/186 (4) 4/206 (1)
5/312 (5) 6/321 (7) 7/323 (8)
8/328 (6) 9/352 (10) 10/355 (11)

Masters 19–8–34–4; Napier 15–4–32–4; Wright 10.2–0–34–0; Danish Kaneria 4–0–19–0; ten Doeschate 2.3–0–4–2. *Second Innings*—Masters 34–14–78–2; Napier 15.2–4–54–1; Wright 11–2–36–0; ten Doeschate 16–2–62–0; Danish Kaneria 42–8–92–6; Walker 1–0–4–0; Cook 1–0–5–1.

Umpires: N. G. B. Cook and J. F. Steele.

KENT v GLOUCESTERSHIRE

At Beckenham, June 30, July 1, 2, 3. Kent won by 76 runs. Kent 18 pts, Gloucestershire 3 pts. Toss: Kent. First-class debut: G. M. Hussain.

Kent moved just nine points behind leaders Gloucestershire with a game in hand after a comfortable win in a surprisingly low-scoring game. Often praised by local boy Key as the best in the country, this Beckenham pitch produced tennis-ball bounce rather than genuine pace. In humid heat that approached 32°C, the ball swung throughout, and bowlers dominated to such an extent that only two batsmen hit half-centuries. Van Jaarsveld top-scored in each Kent innings on the fiery, ever-willing Kirby bent his back to take seven wickets in the match, including a second-innings five for 44. Cook bowled an ideal length for the conditions to take five for 22 as Kent secured a first-innings lead of 65, which they extended to 331 despite another slipshod second-innings batting performance. Azhar Mahmood proved Gloucestershire's nemesis second time around, stranding tailender Lewis – their only man to pass 50 – one short of his career-best.

Close of play: First day, Gloucestershire 69-2 (Kadeer Ali 18, Gidman 18); Second day, Kent 149-6 (Kemp 25, Khan 1); Third day, Gloucestershire 131-5 (Banerjee 0, Franklin 3).

Kent

S. A. Northeast c Snell b Franklin	10	– lbw b Kirby	30
*R. W. T. Key c Spearman b Lewis	33	– lbw b Kirby	12
†G. O. Jones b Kirby	46	– c Marshall b Kirby	4
M. van Jaarsveld c Franklin b Kirby	53	– c Snell b Kirby	62
D. I. Stevens c Snell b Franklin	31	– c Snell b Banerjee	3
J. M. Kemp c Lewis b Banerjee	40	– c Gidman b Banerjee	41
Azhar Mahmood c and b Banerjee	10	– c Gidman b Banerjee	4
J. C. Tredwell c Porterfield b Banerjee	3	– (9) c Hussain b Lewis	6
R. McLaren b Hussain	0	– (10) c Porterfield b Banerjee	42
S. J. Cook c Porterfield b Hussain	0	– (11) not out	40
A. Khan not out	0	– (8) lbw b Kirby	5
L-b 5	5	L-b 16, w 1	17

1/21 (1) 2/75 (2) 3/115 (3)   (74.2 overs) 231   1/25 (2) 2/37 (3)   (96 overs) 266
4/157 (4) 5/189 (5) 6/210 (7)   3/72 (1) 4/82 (5)
7/222 (8) 8/225 (9)   5/137 (4) 6/145 (7) 7/163 (8)
9/225 (10) 10/225 (6)   8/177 (6) 9/179 (9) 10/266 (10)

Lewis 13–2–27–1; Franklin 14–2–38–2; Hussain 14–1–73–2; Kirby 13–2–25–2; Banerjee 19.2–4–58–3; Marshall 1–0–5–0. *Second Innings*—Lewis 20–6–57–1; Franklin 17–4–57–0; Kirby 26–9–44–5; Banerjee 25–4–58–4; Hussain 8–0–34–0.

Gloucestershire

Kadeer Ali c van Jaarsveld b Tredwell	27	– (2) c Kemp b Tredwell	38
W. T. S. Porterfield c Kemp b Tredwell	19	– (1) c Key b Azhar Mahmood	11
H. J. H. Marshall c Kemp b Azhar Mahmood	4	– c van Jaarsveld b Azhar Mahmood	45
*A. P. R. Gidman c Stevens b Tredwell	28	– lbw b Tredwell	12
C. M. Spearman c van Jaarsveld b Cook	47	– lbw b Azhar Mahmood	13
J. E. C. Franklin c Kemp b Cook	7	– (7) b Tredwell	41
†S. D. Snell lbw b Cook	0	– (8) lbw b Azhar Mahmood	8
G. M. Hussain c Jones b Cook	8	– (9) c van Jaarsveld b Cook	8
J. Lewis c Kemp b Cook	7	– (10) not out	61
V. Banerjee c van Jaarsveld b Azhar Mahmood	0	– (6) c Key b Tredwell	1
S. P. Kirby not out	0	– c van Jaarsveld b Azhar Mahmood	0
B 6, l-b 10, w 3	19	B 6, l-b 5, w 6	17

1/43 (2) 2/48 (3) 3/92 (4)   (56.1 overs) 166   1/20 (1) 2/79 (2)   (82.3 overs) 255
4/101 (1) 5/134 (6) 6/136 (7) 7/151 (5)   3/107 (4) 4/123 (3)
8/164 (8) 9/166 (10) 10/166 (9)   5/128 (5) 6/150 (6) 7/161 (8)
                                         8/179 (9) 9/236 (7) 10/255 (11)

Khan 12–6–23–0; McLaren 5–1–18–0; Tredwell 16–4–52–3; Azhar Mahmood 12–3–35–2; Cook 11.1–3–22–5. *Second Innings*—Azhar Mahmood 16.3–5–39–5; Khan 5–1–29–0; Tredwell 34–9–84–4; Cook 16–3–45–1; McLaren 8–2–29–0; van Jaarsveld 3–0–18–0.

Umpires: M. J. D. Bodenham and J. W. Holder.

At The Oval, July 10, 11, 12, 13. KENT drew with SURREY. *Four Kent batsmen make hundreds in a total of 620 for seven declared.*

At Cardiff, July 15, 16, 17, 18. KENT beat GLAMORGAN by an innings and 45 runs.

KENT v DERBYSHIRE

At Canterbury, July 31, August 1, 2, 3. Kent won by three wickets. Kent 19 pts, Derbyshire 6 pts. Toss: Derbyshire.

With 19 balls remaining, Parnell and Tredwell stole the bye that gave Kent their first home victory over Derbyshire since 1993; the two-division Championship, however, meant this was in fact the first time the sides had met since 2000. Derbyshire secured a surprise 14-run lead at the mid-point after neither set of batsmen settled. But for a resilient unbeaten 86 from Tredwell, in just under four hours, Kent's position might have been even worse. A classy century from Rogers helped Derbyshire equal their first-innings total of 303, leaving Kent to score 318 in 74 overs. Key led from the front with his third century of the season, his first against Derbyshire; Jones then reached his hundred from 178 balls. Van Jaarsveld, who signed a three-year contract extension on the final day, led Kent to the brink of their fifth win of the campaign with a brisk 51 that also took him past 15,000 first-class runs.

Close of play: First day, Kent 49-1 (Key 13); Second day, Kent 249-8 (Tredwell 67, Cook 16); Third day, Derbyshire 236-4 (Hinds 16, Smith 18).

Derbyshire

*C. J. L. Rogers c Denly b McLaren	53	– st Jones b Tredwell	107
W. L. Madsen lbw b Cook	3	– run out	19
G. T. Park c Kemp b Tredwell	11	– lbw b Tredwell	53
D. J. Redfern c van Jaarsveld b Cook	29	– c Kemp b Cook	13
W. W. Hinds c Kemp b Tredwell	74	– b Kemp	16
G. M. Smith c Key b Tredwell	0	– c Jones b Parnell	44
†F. A. Klokker c Jones b Khan	13	– c Jones b Kemp	6
G. G. Wagg c Kemp b Tredwell	21	– c sub (C. D. Piesley) b Tredwell	23
T. D. Groenewald c Jones b Parnell	7	– c Jones b Kemp	3
J. Needham c Jones b Khan	20	– not out	2
P. S. Jones not out	53	– c Stevens b Tredwell	0
B 4, l-b 13, n-b 2	19	B 3, l-b 8, w 7, n-b 4	17

1/46 (2) 2/68 (1) 3/96 (3) (83.5 overs) 303   1/60 (2) 2/179 (3) (95 overs) 303
4/126 (4) 5/127 (6) 6/172 (7)   3/202 (1) 4/202 (4)
7/212 (5) 8/221 (8) 9/233 (9) 10/303 (10)   5/236 (5) 6/250 (7) 7/291 (6)
   8/296 (8) 9/300 (9) 10/303 (11)

Parnell 14–2–61–1; Khan 15.5–3–41–2; Cook 21–7–48–2; McLaren 11–2–44–1; Tredwell 22–5–92–4. *Second Innings*—Khan 22–3–72–0; Parnell 15–0–44–1; Cook 13–2–38–1; McLaren 8–2–38–0; Tredwell 32–5–93–4; Kemp 5–1–12–3.

Kent

J. L. Denly c Rogers b Groenewald	28	– b Jones	3
*R. W. T. Key c Klokker b Wagg	25	– c Redfern b Wagg	110
†G. O. Jones c Rogers b Groenewald	23	– c Madsen b Groenewald	100
M. van Jaarsveld c Hinds b Wagg	12	– c Smith b Wagg	51
D. I. Stevens c Rogers b Groenewald	8	– lbw b Groenewald	29
J. M. Kemp b Wagg	8	– c Klokker b Redfern	0
J. C. Tredwell not out	86	– not out	3
R. McLaren lbw b Wagg	29	– c Madsen b Groenewald	5
W. D. Parnell c Jones b Wagg	3	– not out	0
S. J. Cook c Redfern b Groenewald	34		
A. Khan lbw b Smith	1		
B 1, l-b 13, w 4, n-b 14	32	B 6, l-b 7, w 2, n-b 2	17

1/49 (1) 2/67 (2) 3/95 (4) 4/106 (5) (93 overs) 289
5/111 (3) 6/135 (6) 7/193 (8) 8/201 (9)
9/287 (10) 10/289 (11)

1/7 (1) (7 wkts, 70.5 overs) 318
2/182 (6) 3/265 (3)
4/279 (4) 5/289 (6) 6/307 (5) 7/317 (8)

Wagg 36–7–96–5; Jones 21–6–57–0; Groenewald 18–3–69–4; Smith 10–1–23–1; Needham
8–0–30–0. *Second Innings*—Wagg 15–0–87–2; Jones 13–1–56–1; Needham 13–1–54–0; Smith
8–1–24–0; Groenewald 12.5–1–52–3; Redfern 8–1–26–1; Park 1–0–6–0.

Umpires: S. A. Garratt and R. K. Illingworth.

KENT v MIDDLESEX

At Canterbury, August 5, 6, 7. Middlesex won by 47 runs. Middlesex 17 pts, Kent 3 pts. Toss:
Middlesex.

Middlesex won their first Championship match of the season, and first on Kent soil since 1983, as
Kartik undermined Kent's third-day run-chase with four for 53. Both first innings were completed
by 6 p.m. on the opening day. Middlesex, led for the first time in the Championship by acting-captain
Morgan, were shot out by 2.30, with the opening pair Khan and Azhar Mahmood taking three apiece,
to go with three run-outs. Then Murtagh and Kartik matched them as Kent disappointed a Canterbury
Week crowd by succumbing in under three hours for a paltry 141. Next-time round, Middlesex's
Berg improved his career-best for the second time in the match; his 98 was comfortably the highest
score of the game, despite a five-for from Tredwell, the first of
three in a row for him. At 201 for nine, Kent appeared woefully short until a last-wicket stand of 86
in 19 overs – Amjad Khan smashed an unbeaten 62 from 43 balls – put a gloss on an otherwise
dismal batting display.

Close of play: First day, Middlesex 50-1 (Robson 3, Shah 12); Second day, Kent 49-2 (Denly 24,
van Jaarsveld 7).

Middlesex

S. D. Robson run out	1	– c Jones b Azhar Mahmood	3
N. R. D. Compton c Jones b Khan	7	– c Jones b Tredwell	28
O. A. Shah b Khan	16	– c Kemp b Azhar Mahmood	16
*E. J. G. Morgan c van Jaarsveld b Azhar Mahmood	5	– b Khan	30
D. J. Malan run out	2	– c Jones b Tredwell	49
†B. J. M. Scott c Kemp b Cook	14	– c van Jaarsveld b Khan	0
G. K. Berg not out	57	– c Kemp b Tredwell	98
M. Kartik c Kemp b Azhar Mahmood	28	– c Khan b Tredwell	16
T. J. Murtagh c Northeast b Azhar Mahmood	4	– not out	11
C. E. W. Silverwood c Stevens b Khan	0	– c Denly b Tredwell	46
S. T. Finn run out	0	– lbw b Azhar Mahmood	0
B 6, l-b 3, n-b 12	21	B 2, l-b 11, w 4, n-b 6	23

1/5 (1) 2/30 (3) 3/33 (2) 4/39 (4) (36 overs) 155
5/42 (5) 6/70 (6) 7/122 (8) 8/138 (9)
9/139 (10) 10/155 (11)

1/32 (2) 2/50 (1) (93 overs) 320
3/57 (3) 4/117 (4)
5/117 (6) 6/209 (5) 7/257 (8)
8/258 (7) 9/319 (10) 10/320 (11)

Khan 12–1–41–3; Azhar Mahmood 13–2–46–3; Kemp 6–0–36–0; Cook 4–0–17–1; Tredwell 1–0–6–0. *Second Innings*—Khan 18–6–52–2; Azhar Mahmood 20–9–53–3; Cook 13–3–59–0; Tredwell 33–10–100–5; Stevens 1–1–0–0; Kemp 5–0–30–0; van Jaarsveld 3–0–13–0.

Kent

J. L. Denly c Silverwood b Finn	3	– c Kartik b Finn	25
*R. W. T. Key run out	1	– c Murtagh b Finn	0
†G. O. Jones c Malan b Murtagh	2	– c Morgan b Silverwood	16
M. van Jaarsveld lbw b Murtagh	9	– c Morgan b Berg	54
S. A. Northeast c Scott b Silverwood	12	– c Malan b Kartik	37
D. I. Stevens c Robson b Kartik	67	– lbw b Murtagh	4
J. M. Kemp c Malan b Kartik	3	– lbw b Berg	30
J. C. Tredwell b Finn	9	– (9) b Kartik	11
Azhar Mahmood c Scott b Murtagh	0	– (8) lbw b Kartik	0
S. J. Cook lbw b Kartik	17	– c Morgan b Murtagh	27
A. Khan not out	1	– not out	62
B 1, l-b 5, w 1, n-b 10	17	L-b 19, n-b 2	21

1/5 (2) 2/8 (1) 3/9 (3) 4/22 (4) (37 overs) 141
5/42 (5) 6/52 (7) 7/89 (8) 8/90 (9)
9/138 (10) 10/141 (6)

1/4 (2) 2/42 (3) (91.4 overs) 287
3/53 (1) 4/128 (4)
5/152 (6) 6/162 (5) 7/162 (8)
8/178 (9) 9/201 (7) 10/287 (10)

Murtagh 11–5–26–3; Finn 8–1–38–2; Silverwood 7–0–23–1; Berg 6–1–16–0; Kartik 5–0–32–3. *Second Innings*—Murtagh 22.4–6–70–2; Finn 13–2–62–2; Silverwood 9–2–27–1; Kartik 35–19–53–4; Berg 9–2–36–1; Malan 3–0–20–0.

Umpires: B. Dudleston and M. A. Gough.

At Northampton, August 11, 12, 13, 14. KENT beat NORTHAMPTONSHIRE by 238 runs.

KENT v SURREY

At Canterbury, August 28, 29, 30, 31. Kent won by six wickets. Kent 22 pts, Surrey 7 pts. Toss: Surrey. Championship debut: A. J. Blake.

Kent overcame an attack of the last-day jitters to secure their seventh Championship win of the summer, finishing off a battling Surrey with only three overs remaining. Played out on a benign pitch, Surrey's first-innings 423 owed much to Brown's 88 and Batty's painstaking 96. Yet Kent still took a 94-run lead thanks to Jones's career-best 156, a 111-ball hundred from Stevens and a thumping 92 in 79 balls from Kemp. Jones reached 1,000 runs in a season for the first time, the first full-time Kent keeper to do so since Godfrey Evans in 1952. Khan then took his match tally to eight wickets as Surrey – without Ramprakash, whose right thumb was broken by a first-innings lifter from Cook – were dismissed for 293. Set 200 from the 38 remaining overs, Northeast and Key put on 90 for the first wicket before Kent's middle order saw them home with 18 balls in hand.

Close of play: First day, Surrey 261-4 (Ramprakash 41, Spriegel 9); Second day, Kent 242-3 (Jones 102, Stevens 25); Third day, Surrey 148-5 (Schofield 33, Meaker 7).

Surrey

†J. N. Batty c Jones b Edwards	96	– lbw b Edwards	26
M. J. Brown c Jones b Khan	88	– c Blake b Tredwell	5
*S. J. Walters c Stevens b Khan	0	– (4) c Northeast b Tredwell	6
M. R. Ramprakash c van Jaarsveld b Cook	46	– absent hurt	
U. Afzaal c Jones b Edwards	3	– lbw b Tredwell	44
M. N. W. Spriegel lbw b Khan	49	– (3) b Edwards	6
C. P. Schofield c van Jaarsveld b Edwards	9	– (6) b Khan	36
S. C. Meaker c van Jaarsveld b Khan	23	– (7) not out	64
J. W. Dernbach c Northeast b Kemp	5	– (8) c Stevens b Kemp	16
T. E. Linley not out	35	– (9) c Tredwell b Khan	36
P. T. Collins b Khan	23	– (10) c Key b Khan	12
B 4, l-b 22, w 4, n-b 16	46	B 6, l-b 21, w 3, n-b 12	42

1/171 (2) 2/175 (3) 3/235 (1)   (129.3 overs) 423   1/38 (2) 2/38 (1)   (101.5 overs) 293
4/239 (5) 5/275 (4) 6/302 (7)   3/55 (4) 4/57 (3)
7/340 (8) 8/347 (9) 9/365 (6)   5/135 (5) 6/163 (6) 7/208 (8)
10/423 (11)   120 overs: 377-9   8/275 (9) 9/293 (10)

Khan 31.3–4–113–5; Cook 23–7–54–1; Edwards 21–6–72–3; Tredwell 38–9–100–0; Kemp 15–4–58–1; Stevens 1–1–0–0. *Second Innings*—Cook 19–5–62–0; Khan 17.5–5–49–3; Edwards 14–2–52–2; Tredwell 35–10–72–3; van Jaarsveld 6–1–11–0; Kemp 10–4–20–1.

Kent

S. A. Northeast c and b Spriegel	48	– c Walters b Meaker	28
*R. W. T. Key lbw b Dernbach	13	– lbw b Meaker	50
†G. O. Jones b Meaker	156	– st Batty b Afzaal	45
M. van Jaarsveld lbw b Schofield	28	– c Collins b Spriegel	19
D. I. Stevens c Walters b Schofield	112	– not out	35
J. M. Kemp run out	92	– not out	9
A. J. Blake b Schofield	1		
J. C. Tredwell c Spriegel b Linley	11		
S. J. Cook lbw b Meaker	2		
A. Khan lbw b Meaker	5		
P. D. Edwards not out	0		
B 6, l-b 16, w 6, n-b 16, p 5	49	L-b 2, w 6, n-b 6	14

1/21 (2) 2/112 (1) 3/193 (4)   (110.3 overs) 517   1/90 (1)   (4 wkts, 35 overs) 200
4/376 (3) 5/430 (5) 6/440 (7)   2/91 (2) 3/130 (4)
7/479 (8) 8/485 (9) 9/499 (10) 10/517 (6)   4/185 (3)

Dernbach 23–6–100–1; Collins 13–2–66–0; Linley 28–5–89–1; Meaker 22.3–2–114–3; Spriegel 5–0–31–1; Schofield 19–2–90–3. *Second Innings*—Dernbach 9–0–35–0; Collins 3–0–16–0; Linley 7–0–43–0; Meaker 4–0–29–2; Schofield 5–0–39–0; Spriegel 5–0–22–1; Afzaal 2–0–14–1.

Umpires: G. Sharp and P. Willey.

At Derby, September 2, 3, 4, 5. KENT drew with DERBYSHIRE.

At Uxbridge, September 9, 10, 11, 12. KENT beat MIDDLESEX by ten wickets. *Kent are promoted.*

KENT v LEICESTERSHIRE

At Canterbury, September 15, 16, 17, 18. Drawn. Kent 12 pts, Leicestershire 7 pts. Toss: Kent.

Kent secured the Division Two title on the third day, although Nixon, for three years their first-choice wicketkeeper but now playing as a specialist batsman for Leicestershire, ultimately denied them victory with a career-best unbeaten 173. First-day rain and cloud cover prompted Key's decision to bowl, and by tea Cook had his third five-for of the season (and Khan four for 46) as

Leicestershire capitulated in 57 overs. An easing pitch made for an end-of-season run-fest thereafter. Kent, through a van Jaarsveld single to midwicket, reached 250 for the second batting bonus point that clinched the title; van Jaarsveld went on to 146, his seventh Championship hundred of the summer, and 89 from Jones helped them canter along at four and a half an over. Leicestershire needed to score 305 simply to make Kent bat again – a task they readily achieved thanks to an opening stand of 204 between the stoic Nixon, who batted over seven hours, and Boyce. It was Leicestershire's best opening partnership against Kent, beating the 202 shared by Maurice Hallam and Gerry Lester at Grace Road in 1956.

Close of play: First day, No play; Second day, Kent 205-4 (van Jaarsveld 63, Khan 0); Third day, Leicestershire 97-0 (Nixon 37, Boyce 53).

Leicestershire

P. A. Nixon c van Jaarsveld b Khan	5	– not out	173
M. A. G. Boyce b Khan	8	– c Kemp b van Jaarsveld	98
*H. H. Dippenaar b Cook	54	– (4) not out	30
J. J. Cobb lbw b McLaren	8	– (3) c and b Tredwell	28
J. W. A. Taylor lbw b Cook	6		
†T. J. New c Jones b Cook	3		
J. G. E. Benning c van Jaarsveld b Khan	16		
J. K. H. Naik c Kemp b Khan	8		
W. A. White c Tredwell b Cook	8		
I. E. O'Brien c van Jaarsveld b Cook	0		
A. J. Harris not out	22		
L-b 5, w 3, n-b 2	10	B 5, l-b 7, w 1, n-b 8	21

1/14 (2) 2/21 (1) 3/35 (4) 4/52 (5)   (57 overs) 148   1/204 (2)   (2 wkts dec, 122 overs) 350
5/70 (6) 6/96 (7) 7/118 (3) 8/118 (8)   2/259 (3)
9/119 (10) 10/148 (9)

Cook 18–3–44–5; Khan 16–6–46–4; Stevens 2–1–3–0; McLaren 10–3–22–1; Kemp 11–2–28–0. *Second Innings*—Khan 20–2–74–0; Cook 22–8–41–0; Tredwell 34–11–80–1; McLaren 13–3–32–0; Kemp 10–4–29–0; van Jaarsveld 9–2–33–1; Key 9–1–32–0; Blake 4–0–15–0; Northeast 1–0–2–0.

Kent

S. A. Northeast b White	21	R. McLaren c New b Harris	44
*R. W. T. Key c Taylor b Harris	12	S. J. Cook not out	23
†G. O. Jones c Nixon b Harris	89		
M. van Jaarsveld c New b Benning	146	B 4, l-b 6, n-b 4	14
D. I. Stevens b Naik	18		
A. Khan c Cobb b White	16	1/32 (2) 2/75 (1) (100.4 overs) 453
J. M. Kemp lbw b White	8	3/153 (4) 4/203 (5) 5/249 (6)
A. J. Blake c and b Cobb	33	6/263 (7) 7/344 (4) 8/363 (8)
J. C. Tredwell c New b Harris	29	9/426 (9) 10/453 (10)

O'Brien 21–6–64–0; Harris 19.4–1–84–4; White 18–1–91–3; Benning 15–0–101–1; Naik 24–3–95–1; Cobb 3–1–8–1.

Umpires: J. H. Evans and P. J. Hartley.

At Bristol, September 23, 24, 25. KENT lost to GLOUCESTERSHIRE by an innings and 23 runs.

LANCASHIRE

Great expectations, mixed fortunes

ANDY WILSON

The most obvious failing in Peter Moores's first season as Lancashire's coach was in the management of expectations. Two wins from the first three Championship games, and fine form qualifying for the quarter-finals of the Friends Provident Trophy and Twenty20, raised unrealistic hopes for the thin squad he had inherited, whose limitations were then exposed. Seven straight draws in the second half of the Championship season left the county flirting dangerously with relegation for the second consecutive September.

So the fourth-place finish secured by victory in the final match, against Warwickshire at Old Trafford, was slightly misleading, but nonetheless a decent achievement. Only Durham in the first division managed more than Lancashire's four wins – two against Worcestershire – and only Durham and Somerset were harder to beat. Lancashire suffered just two defeats, coinciding with Andrew Flintoff's two Championship appearances.

As in 2008, it was an inability to build substantial first-innings totals that cost Lancashire vital bonus points, and left them chasing too many games. Thirty-five batting points was 11 more than in the previous season, but still ten fewer than any other first division county bar winless Worcestershire, and 21 behind Nottinghamshire.

The problems started at the top, with Paul Horton averaging less than 30 – a lean season that he put down partly to the lack of a regular opening partner. The promotion of Tom Smith, Moores's first selection shock, showed promise in the one-day competitions, but the signing of England Lions opener Stephen Moore from Worcestershire suggested the experiment would be shelved in first-class cricket.

One of the more heartening features of the season was Mal Loye's return to fitness then form in the second half of the summer; that made his decision to reject a new contract and rejoin Northamptonshire, for a combination of personal and financial reasons, more of a blow.

The two overseas batsmen, Ashwell Prince and V. V. S. Laxman (awarded his cap during his second stint at Old Trafford), were good value, with 1,354 runs between them at an average of 64. Lancashire hoped to have the Sri Lankan captain Kumar Sangakkara in 2010, subject to his country's ever-shifting arrangements; Prince's return was more definite. West Indies' unpredictable fast bowler Daren Powell signed as a Kolpak.

Mark Chilton's return as a first-team regular was welcomed by all who had been disappointed by his treatment the previous summer, when he played only half a dozen games, following his resignation as captain in 2007. His unbeaten century in the Headingley Roses match was arguably Lancashire's innings of the season, and he was voted player of the year.

But the lower middle order was a consistent disappointment. Faf du Plessis, who scored a century as good as Chilton's in a very different way to win the FPT quarter-final against Essex, again struggled in first-class cricket; Luke Sutton was as frustrated by his batting form as he was satisfied by his wicketkeeping; and Steven Croft, the 2008 player of the year, went a long way backwards.

Mark Chilton

Those failings were not so significant when Lancashire had strong bowling attacks at the start of the season. James Anderson took 11 wickets in his only Championship game, the opening victory at Sussex, then Sajid Mahmood completed ten in a match for the first time to secure a win at Worcester, set up by Glen Chapple's excellent all-round performance. But by the time champions-elect Durham arrived in mid-August, Kyle Hogg – who made enough handy contributions with bat and ball to keep his place for all but three Championship matches, in an overdue breakthrough season – was the unlikely spearhead of a seam attack completed by Oliver Newby and Tom Lungley, a loan signing from Derbyshire.

Fortunately Chapple, who started his first season as captain with a hamstring niggle then missed five matches in mid-summer with a foot problem, was back by September, and led from the front in the crucial last game against Warwickshire. Victory was sealed by Gary Keedy's second six-wicket haul of the year, which nudged the spinner ahead of Mahmood as the county's leading wicket-taker, with 42 Championship victims.

The highlights of Lancashire's impressive early one-day form were Horton's consistency as an opener and especially the fielding, which provoked comparisons from older members with Jack Bond's team who won the first two Sunday League titles in 1969 and 1970. Du Plessis was breathtaking at backward point, but even he did not better the boundary catches taken by Croft and Stephen Parry, in successive Twenty20 matches at Old Trafford.

As in the Championship, however, Lancashire were unable to last the course. A comprehensive home defeat by Hampshire in the FPT – which extended a miserable record of semi-final failures to nine in ten years – was followed by the emptiness of losing a bowl-out to Somerset in Old Trafford's indoor school in the Twenty20 quarter-final. That was a rare black mark for Moores, whose left-field selection of Chilton and Laxman for the bowl-out backfired. But his appointment proved popular with members and players alike, and a return to county cricket, close to his Macclesfield roots, seemed therapeutic for the former England coach.

Another new man in charge, head groundsman Matt Merchant, was named ECB groundsman of the year, breaking The Oval's seven-year stranglehold on the award.

LANCASHIRE RESULTS

All first-class matches – Played 17: Won 5, Lost 2, Drawn 10.
County Championship matches – Played 16: Won 4, Lost 2, Drawn 10.

LV County Championship, 4th in Division 1; Friends Provident Trophy, s-f;
Pro40 League, 5th in Division 2; Twenty20 Cup, q-f.

COUNTY CHAMPIONSHIP AVERAGES, BATTING AND FIELDING

Cap		M	I	NO	R	HS	100s	50s	Avge	Ct/St
2009	V. V. S. Laxman§......	11	16	3	857	135	4	4	65.92	15
	A. G. Prince§	5	10	2	497	135*	1	3	62.12	8
2003	M. B. Loye...........	13	21	3	983	151*	2	6	54.61	4
2002	M. J. Chilton	15	22	6	777	111*	1	6	48.56	14
1994	G. Chapple	11	14	2	390	89	0	3	32.50	3
	S. J. Croft†	8	12	2	317	79	0	2	31.70	6
	F. du Plessis¶........	13	20	3	531	86*	0	5	31.23	8
2007	P. J. Horton..........	16	29	2	776	173	1	4	28.74	16
	K. W. Hogg	13	13	1	307	69	0	2	25.58	2
2007	L. D. Sutton	16	21	6	377	45*	0	0	25.13	53/3
	T. C. Smith†.........	8	13	1	235	95	0	1	19.58	5
1998	A. Flintoff†‡.........	2	4	0	69	54	0	1	17.25	3
2007	S. I. Mahmood†	11	12	1	100	30*	0	0	9.09	6
2000	G. Keedy	16	16	7	63	18	0	0	7.00	0
	O. J. Newby†	12	11	1	64	15	0	0	6.40	2

Also batted: J. M. Anderson†‡ (cap 2003) (1 match) 9* (1 ct); K. R. Brown† (1 match) 3, 19;
T. Lungley (2 matches) 27*, 10 (2 ct); S. D. Parry† (2 matches) 2, 1 (1 ct).

† *Born in Lancashire.* ‡ *ECB contract.* § *Official overseas player.* ¶ *Other non-England-qualified player.*

BOWLING

	O	M	R	W	BB	5W/i	Avge
J. M. Anderson	51	15	109	11	6-56	2	9.90
G. Chapple................	335.4	87	884	35	6-19	2	25.25
S. I. Mahmood.............	306.3	59	1,118	38	6-30	2	29.42
K. W. Hogg	319.2	83	965	30	4-74	0	32.16
G. Keedy	487.5	83	1,457	42	6-50	3	34.69
O. J. Newby	274.1	35	1,058	25	4-105	0	42.32
T. C. Smith	181	41	572	13	6-46	1	44.00

Also bowled: K. R. Brown 8–0–37–2; S. J. Croft 16–3–83–2; F. du Plessis 54.1–1–199–4;
A. Flintoff 51.3–15–149–8; P. J. Horton 2–1–10–0; V. V. S. Laxman 13–4–26–1; T. Lungley
40–8–139–5; S. D. Parry 68–10–210–4.

COUNTY RECORDS

Highest score for:	424	A. C. MacLaren v Somerset at Taunton	1895
Highest score against:	315*	T. W. Hayward (Surrey) at The Oval	1898
Leading run-scorer:	34,222	E. Tyldesley (avge 45.20)	1909–1936
Best bowling for:	10-46	W. Hickton v Hampshire at Manchester	1870
Best bowling against:	10-40	G. O. B. Allen (Middlesex) at Lord's	1929
Leading wicket-taker:	1,816	J. B. Statham (avge 15.12)...................	1950–1968
Highest total for:	863	v Surrey at The Oval	1990
Highest total against:	707-9 dec	by Surrey at The Oval	1990
Lowest total for:	25	v Derbyshire at Manchester.................	1871
Lowest total against:	22	by Glamorgan at Liverpool	1924

ADDRESS

County Cricket Ground, Old Trafford, Manchester M16 0PX (0161 282 4000; **email** enquiries@lccc.co.uk). **Website** www.lccc.co.uk

OFFICIALS

Captain G. Chapple
Director of cricket M. Watkinson
Head coach P. Moores
President to be announced
Chairman M. Cairns

Chief executive J. Cumbes
Chairman, cricket committee G. Ogden
Head groundsman M. Merchant
Scorer A. West

The Flintoff factor

When Andrew Flintoff was given the devastating news that his comeback would be delayed until the late summer of 2010, he found solace in the possibility of fulfilling a career goal that had been on the back burner for the previous decade – helping Lancashire win that infamously elusive County Championship title. Flintoff admitted, when he signed a three-year contract to play one-day cricket in November 2009, that the contrast between his international and county records was a source of regret, even embarrassment. Then an exploratory operation revealed that while his battered left knee should heal sufficiently to reopen the possibility of first-class cricket, it would take six months longer than expected.

"I have enjoyed many highs with England over the years, but I have not had the same success with Lancashire, and that is something I want to address," said Flintoff, aware that he has been more of a jinx than a talisman in recent years. The 2009 season was typical, as his only two Championship matches – against Durham and Hampshire – were the only two Lancashire lost all summer. They have lost only seven of their 64 Championship games since 2006, all in the First Division; four of those defeats came in the 11 games which Flintoff played.

As so often with Flintoff, the statistics do not tell the whole story. He averages 35 with the bat and 29 with the ball for Lancashire in first-class cricket, but those unremarkable figures include some memorable performances, such as his century before lunch in a Roses Match in 1999, and plundering 34 off an Alex Tudor over the previous year.

Flintoff's county one-day record has been equally modest. In 2009 he played in the only loss of Lancashire's otherwise impressive Twenty20 qualifying campaign, before hitting 93 from 41 balls in his only other appearance, in victory at Derby. Lancashire have won only seven of the 16 limited-overs games in which Flintoff has played since 2004, with the eight losses including two semi-finals and the 2005 Twenty20 final.

Any reasons? One has to be that he has normally played for Lancashire when returning from injury, sometimes after a long period away, and his batting has always needed time in the middle. — ANDY WILSON

At Durham, April 11, 12, 13. LANCASHIRE beat DURHAM UCCE by 286 runs.

At Hove, April 21, 22, 23, 24. LANCASHIRE beat SUSSEX by eight wickets.

LANCASHIRE v NOTTINGHAMSHIRE

At Manchester, April 29, 30, May 1, 2. Drawn. Lancashire 7 pts, Nottinghamshire 11 pts. Toss: Lancashire. Championship debut: L. J. Fletcher.

Prince thwarted Nottinghamshire's hopes of two wins in two games through an unbroken stand of 191 with Chilton. It gave him 356 runs from his four Championship innings for Lancashire, at an average of 178 – compared with a less distinguished 123 in four innings for Nottinghamshire in late 2008. Lancashire had been in trouble on the fourth morning at 39 for three, still 139 behind; 20-year-old Luke Fletcher continued an impressive Championship debut, while Sidebottom had Horton caught behind by Shafayat, deputising for Read after he left for the birth of his first child. Voges, who narrowly missed a century for the second time in a week, stood in as captain. On his comeback after an Achilles injury ended his tour of the West Indies seven weeks earlier, Sidebottom showed no signs of rust. He took two for 13 in a seven-over spell on the first morning, establishing a supremacy that Nottinghamshire maintained throughout the rain-affected match.

Close of play: First day, Nottinghamshire 52-1 (Shafayat 12, Wagh 17); Second day, Nottinghamshire 263-6 (Read 48, Franks 22); Third day, Lancashire 1-0 (Smith 1, Horton 0).

Lancashire

P. J. Horton lbw b Sidebottom	6	– (2) c Shafayat b Sidebottom	14
T. C. Smith lbw b Sidebottom	4	– (1) lbw b Fletcher	7
A. G. Prince c Voges b Franks	74	– not out	135
F. du Plessis c Brown b Adams	24	– lbw b Fletcher	4
M. J. Chilton b Adams	7	– not out	56
S. J. Croft c Brown b Swann	31		
†L. D. Sutton c Read b Adams	12		
*G. Chapple c Read b Adams	4		
K. W. Hogg c Brown b Fletcher	0		
G. Keedy c Franks b Fletcher	3		
O. J. Newby not out	5		
L-b 11, w 4, n-b 4	19	L-b 8, n-b 6	14

1/6 (1) 2/22 (2) 3/86 (4) 4/96 (5)   (72.3 overs) 189   1/28 (1)   (3 wkts, 78.1 overs) 230
5/160 (3) 6/172 (6) 7/180 (8)   2/30 (2) 3/39 (4)
8/181 (9) 9/181 (7) 10/189 (10)

Sidebottom 18–9–48–2; Fletcher 15.3–8–30–2; Adams 19–4–49–4; Franks 13–3–41–1; Swann 7–2–10–1. *Second Innings*—Sidebottom 18–5–54–1; Adams 12–3–30–0; Fletcher 15–5–33–2; Franks 11–3–30–0; Swann 15–2–46–0; Voges 4–0–18–0; Brown 2.1–0–8–0; Hales 1–0–3–0.

Nottinghamshire

B. M. Shafayat c Croft b Newby	34	R. J. Sidebottom not out	11
A. D. Hales b Newby	17	L. J. Fletcher not out	8
M. A. Wagh b Chapple	17		
A. C. Voges lbw b Newby	95	B 4, l-b 9, n-b 4	17
A. D. Brown c Horton b Smith	21		
*†C. M. W. Read run out	63	1/29 (2) 2/63 (3) (9 wkts dec, 126 overs) 367
G. P. Swann c Horton b Chapple	0	3/95 (1) 4/151 (5)
P. J. Franks c Sutton b Hogg	51	5/215 (4) 6/218 (7) 7/301 (6)
A. R. Adams c du Plessis b Smith	33	8/317 (8) 9/350 (9) 120 overs: 355-9

Chapple 33–7–87–2; Hogg 26–8–52–1; Smith 28–9–75–2; Newby 29–3–98–3; Keedy 10–1–42–0.

Umpires: I. J. Gould and J. W. Lloyds.

At Worcester, May 6, 7, 8. LANCASHIRE beat WORCESTERSHIRE by six wickets.

LANCASHIRE v SOMERSET

At Manchester, June 6, 7, 8, 9. Drawn. Lancashire 9 pts, Somerset 10 pts. Toss: Lancashire.

For the second home match running, Lancashire chose to bat but fell short of a par total, although a washed-out first day meant the game was always likely to end in a draw. "Come on Lancs, give us something to cheer – you're as bad as Brown's government," one member shouted as they struggled to break Somerset's opening stand on the third day, after record losses for Labour in the European and local elections held on June 4. Newby obliged by dismissing Suppiah and Langer, and Trescothick's loss of patience against Keedy left him still looking for his first century against Lancashire, but the later batting did enough to ensure a first-innings lead of 57. Earlier, Stiff had returned career-best figures as he continued to relaunch his career with Somerset. But the appearance of Andrew Flintoff, who bowled several spells in the middle before play and during the lunch intervals in an attempt to prove his fitness after knee surgery, attracted more media attention than the match itself.

Close of play: First day, No play; Second day, Lancashire 281-9 (Newby 12, Keedy 0); Third day, Somerset 301-7 (Phillips 17, Thomas 11).

Lancashire

P. J. Horton c Kieswetter b Thomas	69	– (2) c Suppiah b Willoughby	68
T. C. Smith c Willoughby b Stiff	12	– (1) c Phillips b Stiff	0
M. B. Loye c Trego b Stiff	31	– lbw b de Bruyn	39
A. G. Prince c Suppiah b Trego	48	– c Trego b de Bruyn	34
M. J. Chilton c Langer b Trego	2	– c Langer b de Bruyn	15
F. du Plessis c Langer b Thomas	0	– c Langer b Suppiah	4
†L. D. Sutton c Kieswetter b Suppiah	20	– not out	6
*G. Chapple b Suppiah	55	– not out	4
S. I. Mahmood b Stiff	1		
O. J. Newby c Kieswetter b Stiff	15		
G. Keedy not out	2		
B 4, l-b 7, w 1, n-b 19	31	L-b 6, w 5, n-b 10	21

1/35 (2) 2/75 (3) 3/162 (4)   (82 overs) 286
4/166 (5) 5/171 (6) 6/178 (1) 7/206 (7)
8/217 (9) 9/281 (8) 10/286 (10)

1/0 (1)   (6 wkts, 61 overs) 191
2/106 (2) 3/122 (3)
4/159 (4) 5/172 (6) 6/176 (5)

Willoughby 11–3–30–0; Phillips 11–2–34–0; Thomas 17–4–80–2; Stiff 20–4–72–4; Trego 14–3–34–2; Suppiah 9–2–25–2. *Second Innings*—Stiff 6–2–21–1; Willoughby 13–4–38–1; Phillips 7–3–11–0; Thomas 7–1–11–0; Suppiah 13–3–45–1; Trego 6–2–12–0; de Bruyn 9–1–47–3.

Somerset

M. E. Trescothick st Sutton b Keedy	95	D. A. Stiff c Prince b Keedy	7
A. V. Suppiah b Newby	47	C. M. Willoughby c Chapple b Keedy	5
*J. L. Langer c Sutton b Newby	2		
J. C. Hildreth b du Plessis	60	B 4, l-b 5, n-b 8	17
†C. Kieswetter c Sutton b Chapple	45		
P. D. Trego b du Plessis	0	1/131 (2) 2/135 (3) (103.5 overs) 343
Z. de Bruyn c and b Chapple	7	3/179 (1) 4/250 (4)
B. J. Phillips not out	41	5/262 (6) 6/273 (7) 7/274 (5)
A. C. Thomas c Prince b Keedy	17	8/317 (9) 9/330 (10) 10/343 (11)

Mahmood 19–2–82–0; Chapple 24–7–45–2; Newby 16–4–58–2; Smith 15–3–49–0; Keedy 25.5–1–86–4; du Plessis 4–0–14–2.

Umpires: B. Dudleston and J. W. Holder.

At Chester-le-Street, June 11, 12, 13. LANCASHIRE lost to DURHAM by 138 runs.

LANCASHIRE v HAMPSHIRE

At Liverpool, June 17, 18, 19, 20. Hampshire won by ten wickets. Hampshire 20 pts, Lancashire 4 pts. Toss: Lancashire.

Imran Tahir took five of the last six wickets to spin Hampshire to their first Championship win against Lancashire since 1992, a sequence stretching back 18 matches. In 2008 he had taken 12 wickets at Old Trafford, on his first-class debut for Hampshire, but had to settle for a draw. Lancashire lost their last eight for 78 once Mascarenhas dismissed Flintoff, who took little consolation from regaining some batting confidence ahead of the Ashes as his county suffered a second consecutive defeat. Adams also made a crucial contribution by running out Laxman, who called for a risky second in the same over. When the game got under way a day late, Flintoff had volunteered to bat at No. 3 following Prince's departure, but edged stiffly to third slip immediately after launching Mascarenhas for a straight six in a lively opening session. Pothas and Vince coped impressively with Flintoff's hostility to build a solid base, while Mascarenhas denied him a hat-trick, batting aggressively and intelligently for his hundred.

Close of play: First day, No play; Second day, Hampshire 124-4 (Vince 34, Pothas 35); Third day, Lancashire 144-2 (Flintoff 36, Hogg 4).

Lancashire

P. J. Horton lbw b Mascarenhas	37	– (2) lbw b Tremlett	39
M. B. Loye lbw b Cork	18	– (1) lbw b Imran Tahir	55
A. Flintoff c Benham b Mascarenhas	12	– c Lumb b Mascarenhas	54
V. V. S. Laxman c Pothas b Tremlett	21	– (5) run out	1
F. du Plessis c Benham b Tremlett	6	– (6) c Adams b Imran Tahir	15
S. J. Croft c Pothas b Tremlett	7	– (7) c Adams b Imran Tahir	0
†L. D. Sutton lbw b Cork	25	– (8) c Benham b Tremlett	17
K. W. Hogg lbw b Tremlett	9	– (4) c Cork b Imran Tahir	16
*G. Chapple lbw b Cork	27	– not out	34
S. I. Mahmood not out	30	– c Pothas b Imran Tahir	0
G. Keedy lbw b Tomlinson	2	– c Cork b Imran Tahir	0
L-b 2, w 2, n-b 10	14	B 8, l-b 1, n-b 14	23

1/47 (2) 2/70 (3) 3/75 (1) 4/101 (4) (60.5 overs) 208
5/101 (5) 6/113 (6) 7/127 (8)
8/168 (7) 9/181 (9) 10/208 (11)

1/83 (2) 2/128 (1) (79.5 overs) 254
3/176 (3) 4/177 (5)
5/181 (4) 6/187 (7) 7/204 (6) 8/237 (8)
9/238 (10) 10/254 (11)

Tremlett 13–3–49–4; Tomlinson 9.5–0–54–1; Cork 16–4–43–3; Mascarenhas 15–4–46–2; Imran Tahir 7–2–14–0. *Second Innings*—Tremlett 11–3–35–2; Mascarenhas 16–2–43–1; Cork 8–1–17–0; Imran Tahir 32.5–4–108–6; Tomlinson 9–2–32–0; Carberry 3–1–10–0.

Hampshire

M. A. Carberry c Croft b Keedy	25	– not out	62
J. H. K. Adams c Sutton b Chapple	9	– not out	46
M. J. Lumb lbw b Hogg	16		
J. M. Vince c Sutton b Chapple	46		
C. C. Benham c Sutton b Keedy	1		
†N. Pothas b Hogg	86		
*A. D. Mascarenhas c Sutton b Mahmood	108		
D. G. Cork c Horton b Flintoff	5		
C. T. Tremlett c Croft b Flintoff	0		
J. A. Tomlinson c Sutton b Chapple	6		
Imran Tahir not out	24		
B 1, l-b 2, w 2, n-b 14	19	B 10	10

1/13 (2) 2/50 (3) 3/65 (1) 4/71 (5) (86.1 overs) 345
5/157 (4) 6/212 (6) 7/235 (8)
8/235 (9) 9/313 (10) 10/345 (7)

(no wkt, 23.1 overs) 118

Chapple 23–6–77–3; Mahmood 18.1–0–98–1; Hogg 9–0–48–2; Flintoff 17–2–60–2; Keedy 19–5–59–2. *Second Innings*—Chapple 5–1–19–0; Flintoff 3–1–12–0; Keedy 10–1–52–0; Mahmood 1–0–7–0; du Plessis 4.1–0–18–0.

Umpires: T. E. Jesty and P. Willey.

At Nottingham, June 30, July 1, 2, 3. LANCASHIRE drew with NOTTINGHAMSHIRE.

LANCASHIRE v WORCESTERSHIRE

At Manchester, July 10, 11, 12. Lancashire won by seven wickets. Lancashire 17 pts, Worcestershire 3 pts. Toss: Worcestershire.

Worcestershire briefly glimpsed their first win of the season, only to suffer their second demoralising three-day defeat by Lancashire, who consolidated their position in the top four. Solanki's decision to bat backfired as the home bowlers exploited extravagant swing. The visitors still secured an unlikely 27-run lead, thanks almost entirely to Mason. He conceded 14 runs from his first over, then five from his next 13, which included 11 maidens and five wickets from his final five of the day; next morning, he made that seven wickets as Lancashire went without batting points for the third time in seven games. But Worcestershire's batsmen failed to make the most of friendlier conditions in the second innings, apart from Moore, whose composed century went a long way to securing a move to Old Trafford for 2010. Keedy took four wickets despite a nasty gash on his spinning finger – he had dropped a weight on it in the gym. Lancashire needed 264, the highest total of the match, but Horton's best Championship score for 13 months ensured they knocked it off with ease.

Close of play: First day, Lancashire 119-8 (Chapple 22, Newby 11); Second day, Lancashire 39-0 (Loye 16, Horton 12).

Worcestershire

D. K. H. Mitchell c Laxman b Mahmood	0	– c Sutton b Mahmood	12
S. C. Moore b Newby	23	– b Hogg	107
*V. S. Solanki c Sutton b Chapple	35	– lbw b Hogg	9
B. F. Smith lbw b Hogg	16	– c Croft b Keedy	28
M. M. Ali lbw b Hogg	8	– c Laxman b Keedy	3
†S. M. Davies c Sutton b Mahmood	39	– run out	25
A. A. Noffke lbw b Chapple	5	– c Laxman b Mahmood	16
G. J. Batty c Sutton b Hogg	1	– c Sutton b Hogg	4
G. M. Andrew run out	9	– not out	19
C. D. Whelan not out	13	– c Horton b Keedy	3
M. S. Mason c and b Mahmood	15	– b Keedy	2
L-b 7, w 1	8	L-b 3, w 1, n-b 4	8

1/9 (1) 2/35 (2) 3/71 (3) 4/81 (4)   (57.3 overs) 172   1/33 (1) 2/54 (3)   (72.1 overs) 236
5/86 (5) 6/101 (7) 7/104 (8)   3/133 (4) 4/143 (5)
8/136 (6) 9/148 (9) 10/172 (11)   5/188 (6) 6/192 (2) 7/196 (8)
                                                                             8/219 (7) 9/230 (10) 10/236 (11)

Chapple 16–4–36–2; Mahmood 15.3–3–51–3; Newby 13–1–47–1; Hogg 12–6–26–3; Keedy 1–0–5–0. *Second Innings*—Chapple 9–2–29–0; Mahmood 16–3–42–2; Hogg 19–6–53–3; Newby 11–0–49–0; Keedy 17.1–2–60–4.

Lancashire

P. J. Horton c Solanki b Noffke	4	– (2) c Mitchell b Batty	77
M. B. Loye lbw b Mason	24	– (1) lbw b Mason	17
M. J. Chilton c Solanki b Noffke	13	– c Smith b Batty	45
V. V. S. Laxman lbw b Mason	19	– not out	64
S. J. Croft c Smith b Mason	9	– not out	40
K. W. Hogg lbw b Mason	1		
†L. D. Sutton c Batty b Mason	0		
*G. Chapple c Whelan b Mason	44		
S. I. Mahmood b Noffke	3		
O. J. Newby c Davies b Mason	14		
G. Keedy not out	1		
L-b 6, w 5, n-b 2	13	B 8, 1-b 7, n-b 6	21

1/18 (1) 2/38 (3) 3/54 (2) 4/71 (4)   (44 overs) 145   1/42 (1)   (3 wkts, 88.1 overs) 264
5/72 (5) 6/72 (7) 7/77 (6) 8/82 (9)   2/151 (2) 3/173 (3)
9/124 (10) 10/145 (8)

Noffke 16–3–48–3; Mason 17–11–39–7; Whelan 6–1–31–0; Andrew 5–0–21–0. *Second Innings*—Noffke 16–4–46–0; Mason 32–13–77–1; Batty 21–1–71–2; Andrew 11–0–26–0; Whelan 4.1–1–17–0; Ali 4–1–12–0.

Umpires: N. J. Llong and N. A. Mallender.

At Birmingham, July 15, 16, 17, 18. LANCASHIRE drew with WARWICKSHIRE.

LANCASHIRE v YORKSHIRE

At Manchester, July 31, August 1, 2, 3. Drawn. Lancashire 12 pts, Yorkshire 5 pts. Toss: Yorkshire.
    Rudolph and Gale secured a valuable draw by taking their third-wicket stand to 218 on the final day, breaking a Yorkshire record at Old Trafford set by Herbert Sutcliffe and Maurice Leyland in 1932. But the comfort with which they played on a placid pitch highlighted the slapdash first-day batting that had left the team in such a hole. Even Tom Smith admitted his career-best six for 46 owed something to the generosity of the Yorkshire batsmen; at least four gifted their wickets in a first innings wound up before tea. By the close, Smith and Horton had responded with an unbroken century opening stand and, after a rain-shortened second day, Loye and Laxman rammed home Lancashire's advantage with their own double-century third-wicket partnership. Rashid finally bowled Loye, for his first century since April 2007, to claim Yorkshire's only bonus point, in the 116th over, and Laxman collected 14 off the 120th to give Lancashire maximum batting points for the first time in the 20 Championship matches since their last trip to Leeds. When Sutton declared, 308 ahead, Yorkshire faced batting out 121 overs to save the game; they were two down on the third evening before Rudolph and Gale dug in.
    Close of play: First day, Lancashire 106-0 (Horton 61, Smith 40); Second day, Lancashire 219-2 (Loye 61, Laxman 23); Third day, Yorkshire 71-2 (Rudolph 33, Gale 17).

Yorkshire

J. A. Rudolph b Mahmood	14	– c Horton b Keedy	127
J. J. Sayers c Laxman b Smith	34	– c Laxman b Mahmood	1
*A. McGrath c Sutton b Smith	9	– lbw b Smith	14
A. W. Gale c Loye b Mahmood	54	– lbw b Smith	121
J. M. Bairstow c Chilton b Smith	5	– not out	52
†G. L. Brophy c Mahmood b Smith	15	– not out	21
T. T. Bresnan c Sutton b Smith	0		
A. U. Rashid c Sutton b Hogg	2		
R. M. Pyrah c Sutton b Smith	0		
A. Shahzad not out	26		
M. J. Hoggard c Sutton b Mahmood	1		
B 9, 1-b 2, w 2, n-b 8	21	B 8, 1-b 2, w 2, n-b 6	18

1/39 (1) 2/56 (3) 3/77 (2) 4/91 (5)   (52.3 overs) 181   1/9 (2)   (4 wkts, 104.4 overs) 354
5/115 (6) 6/115 (7) 7/121 (8)   2/39 (3) 3/257 (4)
8/122 (9) 9/158 (4) 10/181 (11)   4/299 (1)

Mahmood 14.3–3–57–3; Hogg 14–7–23–1; Smith 13–3–46–6; Newby 11–1–44–0. *Second Innings*—Mahmood 17–1–71–1; Hogg 13.5–15–0; Keedy 40–5–132–1; Smith 18–3–62–2; du Plessis 4–0–7–0; Newby 11.4–0–57–0; Horton 1–1–0–0.

Lancashire

P. J. Horton c Brophy b Bresnan	84	*†L. D. Sutton not out		30
T. C. Smith c Brophy b Hoggard	40	B 5, l-b 12, w 5, n-b 2		24
M. B. Loye b Rashid	146			
V. V. S. Laxman c Rudolph b Rashid	109	1/107 (2)	(5 wkts dec, 138 overs)	489
F. du Plessis c Sayers b Shahzad	18	2/156 (1) 3/381 (3)		
M. J. Chilton not out	38	4/402 (4) 5/426 (5)	120 overs: 400-3	

K. W. Hogg, S. I. Mahmood, O. J. Newby and G. Keedy did not bat.

Hoggard 29–7–86–1; Bresnan 34–11–90–1; Shahzad 30–6–107–1; Pyrah 17–1–58–0; Rashid 27–0–126–2; Sayers 1–0–5–0.

Umpires: M. R. Benson and J. W. Lloyds.

At Southampton, August 6, 7, 8, 9. LANCASHIRE drew with HAMPSHIRE.

LANCASHIRE v DURHAM

At Manchester, August 11, 12, 13, 14. Drawn. Lancashire 9 pts, Durham 9 pts. Toss: Durham. County debut: T. Lungley.

Blackwell recorded the best figures by a Durham spinner as the champions and table-leaders underlined their ability to prosper on all surfaces. Lancashire were in real trouble on the last day – four down, 269 behind – before Chilton and du Plessis saw them through to 4.30 when bad light ended play. Desperately short of seamers, Lancashire had signed Tom Lungley on a month's loan from Derbyshire, and hoped to negate the Durham attack with a dry pitch; Keedy, just called up by England Lions to play the Australians, celebrated with six first-day wickets, his best return for three years. But fellow slow left-armer Blackwell, whose last five-for was in 2004, responded with a career-best seven for 85, including five lbws; Lancashire were grateful to Laxman and a last-wicket stand of 52 by Keedy and Lungley which restricted the first-innings deficit to five. The spinners were nothing like as effective second time around. Di Venuto, dropped at slip on one, thwarted Keedy to set up Durham's fourth-morning declaration, and Blackwell was unable to capitalise on Onions's deadly opening burst.

Close of play: First day, Lancashire 0-0 (Horton 0, Parry 0); Second day, Lancashire 252-9 (Lungley 21, Keedy 16); Third day, Durham 256-5 (Benkenstein 48, Mustard 9).

Durham

M. J. Di Venuto c Hogg b Keedy	53	– (2) c Horton b Keedy	84
M. D. Stoneman lbw b Keedy	33	– (1) c du Plessis b Keedy	33
*W. R. Smith c Sutton b Parry	26	– c Sutton b Laxman	1
G. J. Muchall lbw b Lungley	39	– c Chilton b du Plessis	40
D. M. Benkenstein c Horton b Keedy	16	– run out	58
I. D. Blackwell c Chilton b Parry	29	– c Sutton b Parry	25
†P. Mustard c Chilton b Keedy	7	– not out	50
L. E. Plunkett c Parry b Keedy	28	– not out	10
C. D. Thorp c Chilton b Keedy	32		
G. Onions c Chilton b Lungley	0		
M. Davies not out	0		
B 2, l-b 1, n-b 4	7	B 9, l-b 8, n-b 2	19

1/87 (2) 2/88 (1) 3/149 (4)	(94.1 overs) 270	1/60 (1) (6 wkts dec, 104 overs)	320
4/167 (3) 5/187 (5) 6/207 (7)		2/65 (3) 3/153 (4)	
7/213 (6) 8/269 (9) 9/270 (10) 10/270 (8)		4/186 (2) 5/235 (6) 6/283 (5)	

Hogg 14–5–40–0; Newby 13–0–55–0; Lungley 13–6–36–2; Keedy 36.1–8–85–6; Parry 18–1–51–2. *Second Innings*—Hogg 3–2–4–0; Newby 5–0–23–0; Keedy 46–10–107–2; Parry 28–4–99–1; Laxman 7–3–13–1; Lungley 4–0–18–0; du Plessis 11–0–39–1.

Lancashire

P. J. Horton c Mustard b Thorp	0	– c Benkenstein b Onions	3
S. D. Parry lbw b Thorp	2	– c Onions b Thorp	1
M. B. Loye c Mustard b Blackwell	60	– c Mustard b Onions	0
V. V. S. Laxman c Plunkett b Benkenstein	87	– c Mustard b Onions	23
M. J. Chilton lbw b Blackwell	9	– not out	79
F. du Plessis lbw b Blackwell	0	– not out	54
*†L. D. Sutton lbw b Blackwell	0		
K. W. Hogg lbw b Blackwell	42		
T. Lungley not out	27		
O. J. Newby lbw b Blackwell	1		
G. Keedy c Stoneman b Blackwell	17		
B 6, l-b 12, n-b 2	20	B 1, n-b 2	3

1/1 (1) 2/16 (2) 3/101 (3) (101.5 overs) 265
4/119 (5) 5/119 (6) 6/123 (7)
7/207 (4) 8/207 (8) 9/213 (10) 10/265 (11)

1/4 (1) 2/4 (3) (4 wkts, 59.1 overs) 163
3/4 (2) 4/56 (4)

Onions 21–5–54–0; Thorp 17–2–40–2; Davies 6–2–21–0; Blackwell 38.5–10–85–7; Plunkett 9–1–30–0; Benkenstein 4–1–6–1; Smith 6–1–11–0. *Second Innings*—Onions 10–4–39–3; Thorp 12–3–43–1; Blackwell 25–8–56–0; Plunkett 2.1–1–4–0; Davies 10–2–20–0.

Umpires: M. J. D. Bodenham and N. A. Mallender.

At Leeds, August 19, 20, 21, 22. LANCASHIRE drew with YORKSHIRE.

LANCASHIRE v SUSSEX

At Manchester, September 2, 3, 4, 5. Drawn. Lancashire 8 pts, Sussex 8 pts. Toss: Lancashire. Championship debut: J. S. Gatting.

To Lancashire's considerable satisfaction, play was due to start promptly on the pitch that had been judged unfit for the previous night's Twenty20 international because of a muddy patch at the Statham End. But a short shower forced a 15-minute delay and set the tone for a deeply frustrating match, especially for Sussex, who squandered a couple of extra batting points by collapsing from 190 for three. Martin-Jenkins, taking off from the area deemed unsuitable for Twenty20 cricket, completed only the seventh five-wicket haul of his 15-year career on the second day when he grabbed four in 13 balls, starting with Lancashire captain Chapple, back after seven weeks off with a foot injury. Next day Joe Gatting, making his Championship debut on the ground where his uncle Mike was famously flummoxed by Shane Warne's ball of the (previous) century, was himself bowled by an inswinging yorker, but Yardy had Sussex on course to nibble away at the gap on one of their relegation rivals until fine last-day spells from Newby and Hogg caused them to lose seven for 50.

Close of play: First day, Lancashire 131-5 (du Plessis 10); Second day, Sussex 11-0 (Yardy 8, Gatting 3); Third day, Sussex 119-1 (Yardy 64, Joyce 39).

Lancashire

P. J. Horton c Yardy b Collymore	6	– not out		0
†L. D. Sutton c Rayner b Martin-Jenkins	17	– not out		0
M. B. Loye c Chawla b Rayner	58			
V. V. S. Laxman lbw b Smith	6			
M. J. Chilton c Yardy b Smith	26			
F. du Plessis c Joyce b Martin-Jenkins	54			
K. W. Hogg run out	6			
*G. Chapple c Rayner b Martin-Jenkins	39			
S. I. Mahmood lbw b Martin-Jenkins	0			
O. J. Newby c Rayner b Martin-Jenkins	3			
G. Keedy not out	4			
B 1, l-b 3, w 5, n-b 8	17			

1/10 (1) 2/50 (2) 3/71 (4) (87.4 overs) 236   (no wkt, 0.2 overs) 0
4/105 (3) 5/131 (5) 6/141 (7)
7/223 (8) 8/223 (9) 9/229 (6) 10/236 (10)

Collymore 16–5–44–1; Martin-Jenkins 14.4–4–43–5; Smith 21–8–47–2; Chawla 24–6–75–0; Rayner 12–1–23–1. *Second Innings*—Smith 0.2–0–0–0.

Sussex

*M. H. Yardy c Sutton b Newby	86	P. P. Chawla not out		32
J. S. Gatting b Mahmood	10	O. P. Rayner c Laxman b Newby		3
E. C. Joyce lbw b Mahmood	40	C. D. Collymore c and b Mahmood		4
M. W. Goodwin c Sutton b Mahmood	29	W 1, n-b 8		9
C. D. Hopkinson c Laxman b Hogg	19			
†A. J. Hodd c Laxman b Hogg	0	1/27 (2) 2/121 (3) 3/163 (4) (73.3 overs)		240
D. R. Smith lbw b Newby	8	4/190 (1) 5/191 (6) 6/200 (7)		
R. S. C. Martin-Jenkins lbw b Hogg	0	7/200 (5) 8/203 (8) 9/209 (10) 10/240 (11)		

Mahmood 24.3–4–87–4; Hogg 15–4–53–3; Chapple 15–5–38–0; Newby 15–1–49–3; Keedy 4–1–13–0.

Umpires: N. A. Mallender and D. J. Millns.

At Taunton, September 9, 10, 11, 12. LANCASHIRE drew with SOMERSET.

LANCASHIRE v WARWICKSHIRE

At Manchester, September 23, 24, 25. Lancashire won by ten wickets. Lancashire 21 pts, Warwickshire 3 pts. Toss: Warwickshire.

Chapple, whose spell against Kent had saved Lancashire from relegation 12 months earlier, effectively secured their safety again with six for 19, the second-best figures of his 18 seasons, and set up a convincing three-day victory that lifted them to a respectable fourth place in his first year as captain. Only Troughton and Carter, whose 59 came off 43 balls and included three sixes, offered much resistance after Warwickshire chose to bat and subsided inside 45 overs. Laxman, who needed a runner after suffering a back twinge on 61, completed his fourth century of the summer, adding 154 with the recalled Croft as Lancashire built a lead of 241. Then Keedy picked up six in an innings for the second time in three home games to nudge past Mahmood as the county's leading Championship wicket-taker of 2009. Warwickshire, who had started the match with a chance of climbing to second, ended up slipping out of the prize money to fifth, while Lancashire collected £35,000.

Close of play: First day, Lancashire 126-4 (Laxman 53, Croft 2); Second day, Lancashire 353-8 (Sutton 29, Mahmood 1).

Warwickshire

*I. J. Westwood c Sutton b Mahmood	11	– c Smith b Mahmood	30
A. G. Botha c Chilton b Chapple	5	– c Chilton b Mahmood	8
I. R. Bell c Smith b Hogg	5	– lbw b Hogg	9
I. J. L. Trott c Sutton b Chapple	1	– lbw b Keedy	44
J. O. Troughton c Horton b Chapple	48	– lbw b Keedy	27
†T. R. Ambrose c Horton b Hogg	3	– b Keedy	55
R. Clarke b Smith	1	– c Horton b Keedy	40
N. M. Carter c Laxman b Chapple	59	– b Keedy	0
C. R. Woakes c Sutton b Chapple	0	– not out	15
A. S. Miller c Horton b Chapple	0	– run out	0
W. B. Rankin not out	0	– b Keedy	2
L-b 3, n-b 10	13	B 6, l-b 6, n-b 2	14

1/16 (2) 2/26 (1) 3/29 (4) 4/37 (3)   (44.4 overs) 148
5/41 (6) 6/48 (7) 7/121 (8) 8/131 (9)
9/131 (10) 10/148 (5)

1/30 (2) 2/49 (3)   (74.2 overs) 244
3/53 (1) 4/103 (4)
5/162 (5) 6/215 (6) 7/215 (8)
8/236 (9) 9/242 (10) 10/244 (11)

Mahmood 12–1–61–1; Chapple 14.4–6–19–6; Hogg 8–3–29–2; Smith 10–1–36–1. *Second Innings*—Chapple 8–0–30–0; Mahmood 16–1–64–2; Hogg 12–2–56–1; Keedy 27.2–9–50–6; Smith 10–3–30–0; Croft 1–0–2–0.

Lancashire

P. J. Horton lbw b Woakes	3	– (2) not out	0
T. C. Smith c Westwood b Rankin	23	– (1) not out	4
M. B. Loye run out	13		
V. V. S. Laxman b Miller	113		
M. J. Chilton lbw b Clarke	19		
S. J. Croft b Miller	79		
†L. D. Sutton not out	45		
*G. Chapple lbw b Miller	14		
K. W. Hogg st Ambrose b Botha	23		
S. I. Mahmood lbw b Miller	1		
G. Keedy c Ambrose b Rankin	18		
B 10, l-b 16, w 6, n-b 6	38		

1/6 (1) 2/44 (2) 3/45 (3) 4/110 (5)   (126 overs) 389
5/264 (6) 6/282 (4) 7/296 (8)
8/352 (9) 9/353 (10) 10/389 (11)

(no wkt, 0.2 overs) 4

120 overs: 368-9

Woakes 26–6–80–1; Rankin 20–4–57–2; Miller 25–7–76–4; Carter 18–5–37–0; Botha 27–6–85–1; Clarke 10–2–28–1. *Second Innings*—Trott 0.2–0–4–0.

Umpires: P. J. Hartley and T. E. Jesty.

LEICESTERSHIRE

Starting afresh from the bottom

PAUL JONES

There is no question that Leicestershire embarked on the right course in placing the emphasis on the development of young players in 2009. The club had been heavily criticised in previous years for heading down the Kolpak route in the search of quality cricketers and a return to Division One of the Championship. However, recognising the need to develop their own youth players – and with plenty to choose from – they changed tack, in a move which was widely applauded.

Young sides need to grow up, though, and the Championship is an unforgiving environment in which to learn. The Grace Road hierarchy always accepted that blooding so many of their up-and-coming prospects would produce painful moments. So it proved, although nobody quite expected a first wooden spoon since 1962 as Leicestershire finished at the foot of the Championship.

The shortcomings were plain to see. Insufficient first-innings runs and wickets left Leicestershire chasing far too many games at the halfway stage. Five times they followed on yet, remarkably, the only one of those they lost was the last, when they imploded and fell to an innings defeat against promotion-chasing Northamptonshire.

That statistic should be enough to give supporters some optimism. They saw the batsmen dig in time and again to produce enough runs to save matches, underlining both ability and determination. The mystery was why they could not produce those runs in the first innings.

The bowling attack was beset by injury throughout. Much was expected of seamer Nadeem Malik, whose first season at the club in 2008 had been productive. But he was unable to cast off a back injury that struck pre-season, and did not bowl a ball in anger for the first team.

Senior coach Tim Boon had hoped that Malik would form a potent spearhead with overseas signing Iain O'Brien. That was not to come to fruition. Indeed, due to visa red tape at the start of the season and New Zealand calls later, O'Brien appeared in just seven Championship matches. That left the ageing seamer Andrew Harris to carry the attack for much of the year. Harris persisted gamely, but a genuine strike bowler was sorely missed; young hopes Alex Wyatt and Sam Cliff failed to make any meaningful progress due to lengthy absences through injury.

Leicestershire also lost the reliable medium-pace of all-rounder Jim Allenby from August onwards. Contract talks broke down in July, and Allenby subsequently moved to Glamorgan. That unhappy episode was followed by the resignation from the captaincy in mid-season of the redoubtable Paul Nixon, who had already stepped aside to allow Tom New to take over as

Mike Egerton, PA Photos

James Taylor

first-choice wicketkeeper; he then stood down as club captain, feeling he had been left out of decision-making while out of the first team.

Add in Leicestershire's erratic one-day form, and there was the risk of the season being a complete write-off. That was not the case. New performed behind the stumps with credit, particularly given the pressure of following a man given hero status at Grace Road. The England Under-19 fast bowler Nathan Buck broke into the Championship and one-day side at just 18, and off-spinner Jigar Naik progressed with ball and bat, despite a seven-week spell out with a broken arm.

Then there was James Taylor. Aged 19, he was Leicestershire's shining light – nothing less than a revelation – and he earned selection for England's Performance Programme over the winter. He had tasted first-team cricket in 2008 when still at Shrewsbury School and, while he had undoubtedly shown promise, there seemed much work to be done – as might be expected of someone so young. Injuries gave him an opportunity against Middlesex in the second Championship match; and how Taylor grasped it! His maiden first-class century helped save the game at Southgate, and from there his technique and sheer determination rarely let him down.

The diminutive Taylor finished with 1,207 first-class runs, a magnificent effort from a developing player – particularly one in a struggling side. He hit three centuries, including an outstanding unbeaten double against Surrey at The Oval, became the youngest Leicestershire player to make 1,000 Championship runs in a season, and won the Cricket Writers' Club and PCA awards for young cricketer of the year. But he remained splendidly level-headed, relishing every moment of playing county cricket. Others must follow his lead to offset the return to South Africa of H. D. Ackerman and Boeta Dippenaar.

Optimism was fired over the winter by the signing of the former England stalwart Matthew Hoggard, from Yorkshire, as captain. Initially, few considered Leicestershire serious contenders for his signature, but the management team set the pace and eventually captured their man, much to the delight of Leicestershire followers. Almost as encouraging was the recruitment of Andrew McDonald, the Australian all-rounder, whose medium-pace should be suited to English conditions. The addition of opener Will Jefferson, from Nottinghamshire, and batsman James Benning, from Surrey, also gave greater experience and depth to the squad.

Just how determined the club are to hang on to their talented young players can be gauged from the fact that Taylor, Buck, Greg Smith and Josh Cobb all signed new deals that will keep them at Grace Road until at least the end of 2012.

LEICESTERSHIRE RESULTS

All first-class matches – Played 18: Won 2, Lost 3, Drawn 13.
County Championship matches – Played 16: Won 2, Lost 3, Drawn 11.

LV County Championship, 9th in Division 2; Friends Provident Trophy, 4th in Group A;
Pro40 League, 8th in Division 2; Twenty20 Cup, 3rd in North Division.

COUNTY CHAMPIONSHIP AVERAGES, BATTING AND FIELDING

Cap		M	I	NO	R	HS	100s	50s	Avge	Ct/St
2009	J. W. A. Taylor	15	25	7	1,184	207*	3	6	65.77	8
	J. Allenby	5	8	2	328	96	0	4	54.66	3
2008	H. H. Dippenaar¶	15	28	4	1,074	143	2	8	44.75	4
2005	H. D. Ackerman¶	11	20	1	741	180	1	4	39.00	5
	C. D. Crowe†	2	4	2	76	41*	0	0	38.00	0
1994	P. A. Nixon	9	17	2	531	173*	1	2	35.40	10
2009	T. J. New	16	27	4	800	85*	0	6	34.78	28/1
	J. G. E. Benning	5	9	2	241	72	0	1	34.42	2
	J. H. K. Naik†	5	8	2	184	109*	1	0	30.66	1
	M. A. G. Boyce	14	27	2	638	98	0	4	25.52	4
2004	C. W. Henderson¶	10	13	2	241	79*	0	1	21.90	1
	J. J. Cobb†	12	23	0	445	95	0	3	19.34	4
	G. P. Smith†	5	10	1	174	46	0	0	19.33	2
	W. A. White	10	16	1	242	68	0	1	16.13	5
	N. L. Buck†	3	4	2	29	24*	0	0	14.50	0
	I. E. O'Brien§	7	9	1	110	31	0	0	13.75	1
	H. F. Gurney	8	9	5	53	24*	0	0	13.25	2
	A. J. Harris	16	19	3	143	22*	0	0	8.93	0
	G. W. Walker	3	4	0	21	13	0	0	5.25	0

Also batted: S. J. Cliff (1 match) 26; J. du Toit¶ (2 matches) 100*, 42, 0 (1 ct); C. E. J. Thompson (1 match) 0, 16; A. C. F. Wyatt (1 match) 1*, 0.

† *Born in Leicestershire.* § *Official overseas player.* ¶ *Other non-England-qualified player.*

BOWLING

	O	M	R	W	BB	5W/i	Avge
J. Allenby	101.3	29	238	10	3-70	0	23.80
I. E. O'Brien	181.2	38	547	21	6-39	2	26.04
W. A. White	170.3	18	728	18	3-91	0	40.44
A. J. Harris	395.1	79	1,439	35	5-26	1	41.11
C. W. Henderson	394.5	70	1,044	23	6-152	1	45.39
H. F. Gurney	189.5	30	726	15	5-82	1	48.40

Also bowled: J. G. E. Benning 112–20–384–7; N. L. Buck 74–13–241–2; S. J. Cliff 23–2–92–2; J. J. Cobb 10–1–31–1; C. D. Crowe 66–11–249–3; H. H. Dippenaar 8–0–35–0; J. du Toit 19–1–89–0; J. H. K. Naik 104–16–334–8; T. J. New 8–1–36–0; P. A. Nixon 1.1–0–9–0; J. W. A. Taylor 19–1–82–0; C. E. J. Thompson 15.2–2–45–1; G. W. Walker 50–8–159–2; A. C. F. Wyatt 27–6–83–2.

OFFICIALS

Captain 2009 – P. A. Nixon;
2010 – M. J. Hoggard
Senior coach T. J. Boon
Academy director P. Whitticase
Chairman R. C. N. Davidson

Chief executive K. D. Smith
Operations director P. Atkinson
Head groundsman A. Ward
Scorer G. A. York

COUNTY RECORDS

Highest score for:	309*	H. D. Ackerman v Glamorgan at Cardiff	2006
Highest score against:	341	G. H. Hirst (Yorkshire) at Leicester	1905
Leading run-scorer:	30,143	L. G. Berry (avge 30.32).	1924–1951
Best bowling for:	10-18	G. Geary v Glamorgan at Pontypridd	1929
Best bowling against:	10-32	H. Pickett (Essex) at Leyton	1895
Leading wicket-taker:	2,131	W. E. Astill (avge 23.18)	1906–1939
Highest total for:	701-4 dec	v Worcestershire at Worcester	1906
Highest total against:	761-6 dec	by Essex at Chelmsford	1990
Lowest total for:	25	v Kent at Leicester	1912
Lowest total against: {	24	by Glamorgan at Leicester	1971
	24	by Oxford University at Oxford	1985

ADDRESS

County Ground, Grace Road, Leicester LE2 8AD (0116 283 2128; **email** enquiries@ leicestershireccc.co.uk). **Website** www.leicestershireccc.co.uk

1,000 CHAMPIONSHIP RUNS IN A SEASON BY TEENAGERS

	M	I	NO	Runs	HS	100s	50s	Avge	Year
D. C. S. Compton (*Middx*).	23	32	2	1,345	177	2	10	44.83	1937
A. E. Fagg (*Kent*).	24	43	5	1,233	111	1	6	32.44	1934
J. W. A. Taylor (*Leics*).	**15**	**25**	**7**	**1,184**	**207***	**3**	**6**	**65.77**	**2009**
K. W. R. Fletcher (*Essex*)	28	48	3	1,181	94	0	5	26.24	1963
S. R. Tendulkar (*Yorks*).	16	25	2	1,070	100	1	7	46.52	1992
J. N. Crawford (*Surrey*).	28	40	4	1,064	148	1	5	29.55	1906
D. Bennett (*Middx*)	27	43	9	1,017	66	0	3	29.91	1953

Research: Philip Bailey

It was a group of some distinction that James Taylor joined when he became the seventh teenager to score 1,000 Championship (rather than first-class) runs in a season. Two of the all-time greats feature in the list, as well as the all-rounder often hailed as the finest schoolboy cricketer England has produced, Jack Crawford. Another teenage Leicestershire batsman, Les Berry, fell just one run short of the feat in 1925, but, in those low-scoring years of three-day games and uncovered pitches, he averaged 21. *Wisden* reported: "Increasing strength and experience should make Berry a thoroughly good batsman"; he remains the county's highest run-scorer.

To his front-foot play, Taylor seems to need only to add "increasing strength" in his off-side driving. His back-foot play will not be truly tested until he reaches England level, as fast bowlers are now so few in county cricket, especially the second division. But the excellence of Taylor's fielding – fast across the ground, quick hands – confirms his batting ability and suggests his promotion will not be long delayed.

LEICESTERSHIRE v LOUGHBOROUGH UCCE

At Leicester, April 11, 12, 13. Drawn. Toss: Leicestershire. First-class debuts: N. L. Buck, A. C. F. Wyatt, G. C. Baker, A. C. Evans, P. R. Groves, P. L. Hayes, A. A. Lynch, C. C. Malan, D. Murphy. County debut: W. A. White.

Rain on the first two days wrecked any chance of a competitive game, and – with the exception of Ackerman's 86 – Leicestershire took little from the match in terms of batting preparation ahead of the new season. Murphy and Baker both hit half-centuries for the students in an unbroken sixth-wicket stand of 136 on the final day when the sun made a belated appearance.

Close of play: First day, Leicestershire 78-4 (Ackerman 42, Taylor 5); Second day, Loughborough UCCE 35-0 (Hayes 6, Borrington 19).

Leicestershire

†T. J. New c Lynch b Jones	9	N. L. Buck lbw b Baer		0
J. Allenby lbw b Jones	7	H. F. Gurney not out		1
*H. H. Dippenaar b Baker	3	L-b 2, w 1, n-b 15		18
H. D. Ackerman lbw b Evans	86			
J. J. Cobb c Lynch b Jones	1	1/10 (1) 2/17 (3) (9 wkts dec, 52 overs)		183
J. W. A. Taylor c Murphy b Jones	14	3/21 (2) 4/51 (5)		
W. A. White st Murphy b Baer	43	5/102 (6) 6/173 (4) 7/181 (8)		
C. D. Crowe c Murphy b Evans	1	8/182 (9) 9/183 (7)		

A. C. F. Wyatt did not bat.

Jones 15–4–57–4; Baker 7–2–31–1; Groves 11–3–33–0; Evans 10–1–41–2; Baer 9–2–19–2.

Loughborough UCCE

P. L. Hayes c Buck b White	38	G. C. Baker not out		57
P. M. Borrington c Dippenaar b Buck	36	B 16, l-b 8, w 3, n-b 2		29
*A. A. Lynch c New b Allenby	15			
A. Harinath lbw b Wyatt	16	1/79 (1) 2/93 (2) (5 wkts dec, 90 overs)		264
C. C. Malan c and b Wyatt	4	3/117 (4) 4/128 (5)		
†D. Murphy not out	69	5/128 (3)		

P. R. Groves, H. D. Jones, M. Baer and A. C. Evans did not bat.

Gurney 17–6–45–0; Buck 14–4–35–1; White 13–4–42–1; Crowe 20–5–49–0; Wyatt 13–4–34–2; Allenby 7–3–11–1; Cobb 5–0–21–0; Dippenaar 1–0–3–0.

Umpires: S. J. Malone and P. Willey.

LEICESTERSHIRE v NORTHAMPTONSHIRE

At Leicester, April 15, 16, 17, 18. Drawn. Leicestershire 7 pts, Northamptonshire 11 pts. Toss: Leicestershire. First-class debut: D. J. Willey. County debut: A. J. Harris.

Leicestershire's batsmen made a poor start to the Championship season as they collapsed in the face of Northamptonshire's total of 387. Only Andrew Harris, playing for his fifth county, emerged with much credit among the bowlers, as the visitors recovered from 111 for five thanks to a sixth-wicket stand of 163 between the South African all-rounder Hall, who went on to an undefeated 124, and the debutant David Willey, son of the former England all-rounder and now first-class umpire, Peter, who represented both these counties. Van der Wath and Lucas then unhinged Leicestershire's fragile batting with four wickets each to force their neighbours to follow on, 204 behind, but Dippenaar's patient 68 not out allowed Leicestershire to get a foothold in the match, and Nixon helped him shepherd the home side to safety on the last day.

PLAYERS WHO HAVE APPEARED FOR FIVE COUNTIES

R. P. Davis ... Kent (1986–93), Warwicks (1994–95), Glos (1996–97), Sussex (1998), Leics (2001)
A. J. Harris .. **Derbys (1994–99), Notts (2000–08), Glos (2008), Worcs (2008), Leics (2009)**
I. J. Harvey .. Glos (1999–2006), Yorks (2004–05), Derby (2007), Hants (2008), Northants (2009)
M. J. North .. Durham (2004), Lancs (2005), Derbys (2006), Glos (2007–08), Hants (2009)

On April 15, 2009, Harris became the first person to play first-class cricket for five different counties. A week later, North became the second when he appeared for Hampshire. Davis did not play first-class for Sussex, or Harvey for Hampshire or Northamptonshire.

By the end of the 2009 season, another 20 cricketers had played first-class cricket for four counties: M. G. Bevan, W. Clarke, J. Cumbes, I. Dawood, J. M. de la Peña, V. C. Drakes, E. S. H. Giddins, M. Hayward, A. A. Jones, P. S. Jones, S. M. Katich, R. J. Logan, Mohammad Akram, A. A. Noffke, G. Parr, A. R. K. Pierson, Shoaib Akhtar, R. D. Stemp and D. H. Wigley.

Research: Philip Bailey

Close of play: First day, Northamptonshire 297-6 (Hall 95, van der Wath 11); Second day, No play; Third day, Leicestershire 150-8 (Allenby 50, Cliff 25).

Northamptonshire

S. D. Peters lbw b White	31	D. S. Lucas c Nixon b Cliff	15
B. H. N. Howgego lbw b Harris	24	M. S. Panesar c Nixon b White	24
R. A. White b Allenby	7	D. H. Wigley lbw b Henderson	0
*N. Boje lbw b Harris	9	B 18, l-b 10, w 6, n-b 14	48
†M. H. Wessels b Cliff	21		
A. J. Hall not out	124	1/66 (1) 2/73 (3) 3/75 (2) (115.5 overs) 387	
D. J. Willey c White b Harris	60	4/95 (4) 5/111 (5) 6/274 (7)	
J. J. van der Wath c Nixon b Harris	24	7/322 (8) 8/354 (9) 9/384 (10) 10/387 (11)	

Harris 29–6–106–4; Cliff 23–3–92–2; Allenby 20–6–47–1; White 17–5–54–2; Henderson 22.5–5–49–1; New 3–1–10–0; Cobb 1–0–1–0.

Leicestershire

T. J. New lbw b van der Wath	0	– (2) b van der Wath	11
M. A. G. Boyce c Wessels b van der Wath	4	– (1) c Hall b Wigley	25
H. H. Dippenaar c Wessels b Lucas	12	– not out	68
H. D. Ackerman lbw b van der Wath	0	– c Howgego b Hall	20
J. J. Cobb lbw b Lucas	1	– lbw b Hall	4
*†P. A. Nixon b Hall	31	– not out	39
J. Allenby not out	62		
W. A. White c Wessels b Lucas	6		
C. W. Henderson c Boje b Lucas	10		
S. J. Cliff b van der Wath	26		
A. J. Harris lbw b Wigley	17		
L-b 12, w 2	14	B 1, l-b 3, w 1, n-b 2	7

1/0 (1) 2/13 (2) 3/13 (4) 4/18 (3) (71.1 overs) 183   1/16 (2) (4 wkts, 63 overs) 174
5/19 (5) 6/72 (6) 7/102 (8) 8/118 (9)   2/53 (1) 3/94 (4)
9/151 (10) 10/183 (11)   4/104 (5)

Van der Wath 14–3–40–4; Lucas 19–5–46–4; Wigley 14.1–5–32–1; Panesar 16–6–30–0; Hall 6–1–20–1; Boje 2–0–3–0. *Second Innings*—van der Wath 10–3–19–1; Lucas 10–1–26–0; Panesar 18–3–57–0; Wigley 10–3–35–1; Willey 5–0–22–0; Hall 7–5–5–2; Boje 3–1–6–0.

Umpires: M. A. Gough and T. E. Jesty.

At Leicester, April 20, 21, 22. LEICESTERSHIRE drew with WEST INDIANS (see West Indian tour section).

At Southgate, April 28, 29, 30, May 1. LEICESTERSHIRE drew with MIDDLESEX.

At Bristol, May 6, 7, 8, 9. LEICESTERSHIRE lost to GLOUCESTERSHIRE by ten wickets.

LEICESTERSHIRE v KENT

At Leicester, June 6, 7, 8, 9. Drawn. Leicestershire 9 pts, Kent 9 pts. Toss: Leicestershire.
Rain wiped out the first two days, but when the skies finally cleared Leicestershire at last banked maximum batting points. Their previous three games had provided a paltry total of two points; twice they had been forced to follow on. Now Dippenaar anchored the innings with 89, and although he was frustrated not to hit a maiden hundred for his county, he received excellent support from Ackerman, who made 67, and New, 85 not out when the declaration came. Kent were left to chase only batting points and they achieved two in the time that remained, thanks to the highly disciplined Denly, who made his first Championship hundred of the season and added 181 for the second wicket with Jones, run out for an aggressive 87.
Close of play: First day, No play; Second day, No play; Third day, Leicestershire 351-6 (New 55, White 0).

Leicestershire

M. A. G. Boyce b McLaren	38		A. J. Harris lbw b Joseph	0
J. J. Cobb c Jones b Kemp	46		H. F. Gurney not out	0
H. H. Dippenaar c Denly b Cook	89			
H. D. Ackerman c Stevens b Cook	67		B 11, l-b 6, w 8, n-b 28	53
J. W. A. Taylor c Jones b Cook	0			
T. J. New not out	85		1/80 (1) (9 wkts dec, 110.3 overs)	403
*†P. A. Nixon lbw b McLaren	14		2/113 (2)	
W. A. White c Kemp b Cook	11		3/244 (4) 4/244 (5) 5/301 (3) 6/346 (7)	
C. W. Henderson b Cook	0		7/379 (8) 8/383 (9) 9/384 (10)	

Joseph 25.3–2–89–1; Saggers 15.5–3–53–0; Cook 26–8–78–5; McLaren 16–3–62–2; Tredwell 2–0–20–0; Kemp 13.1–3–49–1; Stevens 12–0–35–0.

Kent

J. L. Denly not out	116
S. A. Northeast c Nixon b Gurney	26
†G. O. Jones run out	87
*M. van Jaarsveld not out	13
B 4, l-b 8, w 3, n-b 8	23
1/57 (2) 2/238 (3) (2 wkts, 63.5 overs)	265

D. I. Stevens, J. M. Kemp, R. McLaren, J. C. Tredwell, S. J. Cook, M. J. Saggers and R. H. Joseph did not bat.

Harris 12–4–37–0; Gurney 17.5–6–55–1; Henderson 24–3–99–0; Taylor 3–0–10–0; White 7–0–52–0.

Umpires: N. G. Cowley and R. A. Kettleborough.

LEICESTERSHIRE v SURREY

At Leicester, June 16, 17, 18, 19. Drawn. Leicestershire 7 pts, Surrey 10 pts. Toss: Leicestershire.
Leicestershire's Championship season was neatly encapsulated in this match. A poor first-innings batting display (not helped when Jordan broke Naik's arm) left them fighting an uphill battle, after which they rose to the challenge and managed to force a draw, helped by the loss of more than half the play on the second day. Facing a deficit of 164, Leicestershire were indebted to Dippenaar's maiden century for them; he had endured a difficult first season in 2008, but generally looked far more settled in 2009. Recently installed as captain after Nixon was left out, Dippenaar put on 314 – an all-wicket record for either side in this fixture – in just under five hours with his compatriot

Ackerman, who took the lead role, hitting 24 fours in his 180 as Leicestershire made their way to safety. In the closing stages Meaker was banned from bowling (and later given three disciplinary points) after sending down two unintentional beamers to the diminutive Taylor; Newman completed the over. Surrey, fresh from ending their victory drought in the previous match at Northampton, might not have been able to force another win here, but two players will remember the game fondly: Dernbach bowled with control and hostility to take a career-best six for 47 in the first innings, while Michael Brown made his first century for his new county in Surrey's 329 – a total which might have been considerably higher had it not been for a maiden five-for from left-arm seamer Harry Gurney.

Close of play: First day, Surrey 121-1 (Brown 46, Ramprakash 29); Second day, Surrey 217-2 (Brown 82, Butcher 0); Third day, Leicestershire 181-2 (Dippenaar 50, Ackerman 50).

Leicestershire

M. A. G. Boyce b Dernbach	5	– lbw b Murtaza Hussain	29
J. J. Cobb c Schofield b Dernbach	1	– c Butcher b Murtaza Hussain	40
*H. H. Dippenaar c Batty b Murtaza Hussain	39	– c sub (A. Nel) b Afzaal	143
H. D. Ackerman c Batty b Jordan	21	– b Afzaal	180
J. Allenby c Schofield b Jordan	0	– c Batty b Afzaal	11
J. W. A. Taylor lbw b Jordan	16	– not out	23
†T. J. New c Batty b Dernbach	44	– not out	27
C. W. Henderson c Batty b Dernbach	12		
J. K. H. Naik lbw b Dernbach	7		
A. J. Harris c Butcher b Dernbach	13		
H. F. Gurney not out	0		
L-b 6, w 1	7	B 8, l-b 10, w 10, n-b 6	34

1/7 (1) 2/16 (2) 3/43 (4) 4/49 (5) (44.1 overs) 165
5/87 (3) 6/87 (6) 7/110 (8) 8/122 (9)
9/154 (10) 10/165 (7)

1/67 (1) (5 wkts dec, 147 overs) 487
2/90 (2) 3/404 (3)
4/412 (4) 5/421 (5)

Dernbach 14.1–3–47–6; Jordan 16–3–54–3; Meaker 7–0–32–0; Schofield 5–1–25–0; Murtaza Hussain 2–1–1–1. *Second Innings*—Dernbach 19–1–83–0; Jordan 22–5–80–0; Meaker 18–0–71–0; Murtaza Hussain 34–6–96–2; Schofield 31–5–66–0; Afzaal 18–1–51–3; Newman 3–0–10–0; Brown 2–0–12–0.

Surrey

S. A. Newman c Cobb b Henderson	40	Murtaza Hussain b Gurney	1
M. J. Brown c Henderson b Gurney	101	J. W. Dernbach not out	1
M. R. Ramprakash c New b Gurney	85	S. C. Meaker c New b Gurney	9
*M. A. Butcher c Cobb b Harris	7	B 6, l-b 14, n-b 2	22
U. Afzaal lbw b Allenby	29		
†J. N. Batty lbw b Allenby	0	1/58 (1) 2/216 (3) 3/231 (4) (115 overs) 329
C. P. Schofield c New b Harris	16	4/282 (5) 5/282 (6) 6/282 (2)
C. J. Jordan c New b Gurney	18	7/311 (8) 8/317 (7) 9/317 (9) 10/329 (11)

Harris 27–5–81–2; Gurney 31–8–82–5; Allenby 30–7–73–2; Henderson 26–2–71–1; Taylor 1–0–2–0.

Umpires: M. A. Gough and J. W. Lloyds.

At Derby, June 30, July 1, 2, 3. LEICESTERSHIRE drew with DERBYSHIRE.

LEICESTERSHIRE v MIDDLESEX

At Leicester, July 10, 11, 12. Leicestershire won by eight wickets. Leicestershire 18 pts, Middlesex 3 pts. Toss: Middlesex.

Leicestershire collected their first Championship win of the season after Middlesex – their closest rivals for the wooden spoon – collapsed dramatically for the second time in the match. They had already fallen apart in their first innings, skittled for 159 on a first day in which 16 wickets fell. Only Malan, who hit 11 fours, offered much resistance as the New Zealander O'Brien – who later joined Middlesex for 2010 – celebrated his 33rd birthday in style by taking six wickets as the ball swung.

Leicestershire threatened a collapse of their own – none of the first five batsmen dismissed reached double figures – but Cobb carried the innings with a resolute 95 before a last-wicket stand of 49 between Harris and Gurney stretched the lead to 85. It proved almost enough, as Middlesex's batting was ripped apart again. This time O'Brien shared the spoils with Harris, who took four wickets as the visitors were sent packing for a miserable 91. That left Leicestershire needing just seven to win but, reflecting the bulk of the game's batting efforts, they managed to lose two wickets before staggering home just before lunch on the third day.

Close of play: First day, Leicestershire 137-6 (Cobb 65, Walker 5); Second day, Middlesex 76-6 (Berg 7, Udal 0).

Middlesex

B. A. Godleman lbw b Allenby	12	– lbw b Harris	14
N. R. D. Compton lbw b O'Brien	4	– b O'Brien	0
O. A. Shah b O'Brien	12	– c New b Gurney	18
E. J. G. Morgan c Allenby b O'Brien	30	– c Boyce b Harris	1
D. J. Malan not out	67	– lbw b Allenby	13
†D. C. Nash c Allenby b Harris	9	– c Dippenaar b Allenby	14
G. K. Berg lbw b O'Brien	0	– c New b O'Brien	10
*S. D. Udal b O'Brien	0	– c New b Harris	5
M. Kartik b Gurney	11	– not out	2
T. J. Murtagh c and b Gurney	1	– c Dippenaar b Harris	4
S. T. Finn lbw b O'Brien	5	– lbw b O'Brien	1
L-b 8	8	B 4, l-b 3, w 2	9

1/15 (2) 2/27 (3) 3/37 (1) 4/75 (4)   (52.3 overs) 159   1/5 (2) 2/24 (1)   (40.2 overs) 91
5/84 (6) 6/101 (7) 7/101 (8)   3/32 (4) 4/50 (3)
8/131 (9) 9/141 (10) 10/159 (11)   5/64 (5) 6/76 (6) 7/84 (7) 8/84 (8)
                                         9/90 (10) 10/91 (11)

O'Brien 15.3–6–39–6; Harris 15–5–49–1; Allenby 10–4–17–1; Gurney 11–0–46–2; Walker 1–1–0–0. *Second Innings*—O'Brien 15.2–5–29–3; Harris 13–6–24–4; Gurney 9–2–30–1; Allenby 3–2–1–2.

Leicestershire

J. J. Cobb c Godleman b Murtagh	95	– c Nash b Finn	2
M. A. G. Boyce lbw b Finn	0	– b Murtagh	4
*H. H. Dippenaar b Finn	4	– not out	4
H. D. Ackerman c Berg b Finn	8	– not out	0
J. Allenby b Murtagh	2		
J. W. A. Taylor c Nash b Finn	5		
†T. J. New c Berg b Udal	42		
G. W. Walker c Morgan b Murtagh	5		
I. E. O'Brien lbw b Murtagh	20		
A. J. Harris b Berg	13		
H. F. Gurney not out	24		
B 14, l-b 10, n-b 2	26		

1/1 (2) 2/11 (3) 3/27 (4) 4/38 (5)   (70.2 overs) 244   1/2 (1) 2/6 (2)   (2 wkts, 4.1 overs) 10
5/53 (6) 6/126 (7) 7/138 (8)
8/188 (9) 9/195 (1) 10/244 (10)

Finn 24–5–76–4; Murtagh 17–1–70–4; Kartik 12–2–29–0; Berg 7.2–1–25–1; Udal 10–4–20–1. *Second Innings*—Finn 2.1–1–6–1; Murtagh 2–1–4–1.

Umpires: M. J. D. Bodenham and J. W. Lloyds.

LEICESTERSHIRE v ESSEX

At Leicester, July 21, 22, 23, 24. Drawn. Leicestershire 7 pts, Essex 12 pts. Toss: Leicestershire.

After the first day was washed out, Amla scored an attractive second century for Essex in his third and final Championship match for them, driving well, before falling to Allenby, who had earlier put him down – a relatively simple catch at first slip – when he had made 46. Matt Walker dropped anchor for his first century for his new county, putting on 158 with Foster, who missed a hundred of his own before ten Doeschate's first-ball dismissal triggered the declaration at 427. Then Leicestershire gave a characteristic first-innings batting display: Allenby, in what turned out to be his final match before joining Glamorgan, made a fortnight 71, and Taylor contributed a mature 88 – but apart from that no one exceeded 15 as the other nine batsmen managed only 58 runs between them. Taylor, who hit a six off Napier and 14 fours, was last out after a spirited tenth-wicket stand of 65 – the highest of the innings – with Gurney. Leicestershire still had to follow on, but fortunately for them bad weather had cut even more out of the game (only 47.1 overs were possible on the third day, and 70.2 on the fourth) and Boyce and Allenby easily steered them to a draw. O'Brien received an official reprimand from the ECB after querying his dismissal – he was given out caught behind but argued that the ball had hit the off stump without disturbing the bails.

Close of play: First day, No play; Second day, Essex 294-4 (Walker 67, Foster 10); Third day, Leicestershire 61-3 (Ackerman 8, Allenby 26).

Essex

V. Chopra lbw b O'Brien	5	R. N. ten Doeschate c Dippenaar b Allenby	0
J. K. Maunders c New b Gurney	56	L-b 19, w 2, n-b 2	23
H. M. Amla c New b Allenby	118		
M. J. Walker not out	116	1/10 (1) (6 wkts dec, 115.3 overs)	427
*M. L. Pettini b Walker	24	2/143 (2) 3/212 (3)	
†J. S. Foster c New b Allenby	85	4/269 (5) 5/427 (6) 6/427 (7)	

G. R. Napier, D. D. Masters, C. J. C. Wright and A. P. Palladino did not bat.

O'Brien 24–6–82–1; Harris 25–6–75–0; Gurney 22–1–96–1; Allenby 20.3–6–70–3; Walker 23–0–84–1; Cobb 1–0–1–0.

Leicestershire

J. J. Cobb c Walker b Palladino	14	– lbw b Masters	6
M. A. G. Boyce lbw b Palladino	4	– not out	45
*H. H. Dippenaar c Foster b Masters	7	– lbw b Palladino	9
H. D. Ackerman b Wright	15	– b Wright	19
J. Allenby c Foster b Masters	71	– not out	34
J. W. A. Taylor c Masters b ten Doeschate	88		
†T. J. New c Foster b Palladino	9		
G. W. Walker lbw b Palladino	0		
I. E. O'Brien c Foster b Wright	1		
A. J. Harris b Wright	0		
H. F. Gurney not out	8		
B 2, l-b 10, w 1, n-b 8	21	W 6, n-b 4	10

1/8 (2) 2/25 (3) 3/27 (1) 4/81 (4) (62.2 overs) 238
5/135 (5) 6/162 (7) 7/162 (8)
8/173 (9) 9/173 (10) 10/238 (6)

1/16 (1) (3 wkts, 26 overs) 123
2/30 (3) 3/62 (4)

Masters 18–6–49–2; Palladino 18–3–68–4; Wright 16–3–52–3; Napier 9–1–53–0; ten Doeschate 1.2–0–4–1. *Second Innings*—Masters 5–2–13–1; Palladino 7–3–26–1; Wright 7–1–38–1; ten Doeschate 4–0–33–0; Napier 3–1–13–0.

Umpires: S. A. Garratt and J. W. Holder.

At The Oval, July 31, August 1, 2, 3. LEICESTERSHIRE drew with SURREY. *James Taylor, 19, scores 207; Mark Ramprakash, 39, replies with 274.*

At Colwyn Bay, August 5, 6, 7, 8. LEICESTERSHIRE lost to GLAMORGAN by an innings and 72 runs.

LEICESTERSHIRE v DERBYSHIRE

At Leicester, August 11, 12, 13, 14. Drawn. Leicestershire 6 pts, Derbyshire 12 pts. Toss: Leicestershire.

At lunch on the final day Derbyshire were sitting pretty, with victory seemingly a formality. They had reduced Leicestershire to 224 for seven, still 77 runs shy of making the visitors bat again. But amazingly Leicestershire staved off defeat, as a county-record eighth-wicket stand of 195 between Taylor and Naik hindered Derbyshire's promotion drive. The ever-improving Taylor might have been expected to take the dominant role, but actually it was off-spinner Naik who led the way. Taylor was rock solid in making 94 while Naik, who came to prominence in 2006 as the first Leicester-born Asian to play for the county's first team, produced an exceptional innings on the way to his maiden first-class century. He played with great sense, and was happy to take the attack to the bowlers when the opportunity arose. Naik, whose highest score in nine previous first-class matches was 16 not out, took advantage of some wayward bowling to hit 19 fours in his unbeaten 109, which lasted 202 balls. "We applied ourselves at the crease and spoke to each other at every opportunity," he said afterwards. "We set ourselves small targets and tried not to get too far ahead of ourselves." Until this, Derbyshire had held the upper hand throughout. They dismissed Leicestershire for an inadequate 177 – the on-loan Steffan Jones started the slide with two wickets in three balls in his second over – before Rogers set up the prospect of victory, overcoming a sticky start to reach a high-class 163 in his side's big total.

Close of play: First day, Derbyshire 67-1 (Rogers 29, Park 11); Second day, Derbyshire 277-2 (Rogers 122, Smith 74); Third day, Leicestershire 154-2 (Boyce 72, Ackerman 29).

Leicestershire

G. P. Smith c Park b Groenewald	20	– c sub (R. McCarroll) b Jones	0
M. A. G. Boyce c Park b Jones	0	– c Pipe b Jones	80
*H. H. Dippenaar c Pipe b Jones	0	– c Park b Redfern	37
H. D. Ackerman c Rogers b Smith	17	– c Smith b Groenewald	29
J. W. A. Taylor lbw b Lawson	45	– b Smith	94
†T. J. New c Park b Smith	17	– c Pipe b Lawson	19
W. A. White c sub (E. P. Jones) b Smith	1	– run out	4
C. W. Henderson lbw b Lawson	16	– c Pipe b Park	9
J. K. H. Naik b Jones	5	– not out	109
N. L. Buck not out	24	– not out	5
A. J. Harris c Groenewald b Jones	7		
B 1, l-b 10, w 4, n-b 10	25	B 8, l-b 13, w 1, n-b 16, p 5	43

1/9 (2) 2/9 (3) 3/36 (4) 4/63 (1)   (68.1 overs) 177   1/0 (1)   (8 wkts, 137 overs) 429
5/100 (6) 6/107 (7) 7/128 (5)   2/107 (3) 3/162 (4)
8/145 (8) 9/147 (9) 10/177 (11)   4/162 (2) 5/198 (6) 6/209 (7)
                                           7/224 (8) 8/419 (5)

Wagg 12.1–3–36–0; Jones 19.1–5–43–4; Smith 12–2–31–3; Groenewald 13.5–5–34–1; Lawson 10–4–20–2; Madsen 1–0–2–0. *Second Innings*—Jones 34–8–92–2; Groenewald 30–6–97–1; Park 10–1–32–1; Smith 26–8–72–1; Lawson 28–5–78–1; Redfern 7–1–31–1; Madsen 2–1–1–0.

Derbyshire

*C. J. L. Rogers c Taylor b White	163	P. S. Jones c Boyce b Henderson	19
W. L. Madsen lbw b Henderson	19	M. A. K. Lawson not out	14
G. T. Park b Naik	41	L-b 5, w 9, n-b 22	36
G. M. Smith b Harris	95		
W. W. Hinds c White b Naik	40	1/49 (2) (8 wkts dec, 130 overs) 478
D. J. Redfern c New b White	19	2/132 (3) 3/321 (4)
†D. J. Pipe not out	32	4/352 (1) 5/399 (6) 6/414 (5)
T. D. Groenewald lbw b Henderson	0	7/414 (8) 8/450 (9) 120 overs: 435-7

G. G. Wagg did not bat.

Harris 24–4–78–1; Buck 21–4–87–0; White 20–2–89–2; Henderson 36–6–93–3; Naik 29–0–126–2.

Umpires: R. J. Bailey and J. W. Holder.

LEICESTERSHIRE v GLOUCESTERSHIRE

At Leicester, August 19, 20, 21, 22. Leicestershire won by 44 runs. Leicestershire 21 pts, Gloucestershire 3 pts. Toss: Leicestershire.

Leicestershire secured their second Championship victory of the season, and it was no surprise to find Taylor at the heart of it. He hit an unbeaten 83 in the first innings, steering his side to 368, one of their better efforts of the season. It followed a gritty 57 from Nixon, restored to the Championship side after more than two months, and an attractive 72 from Cobb, assured of a place now that H. D. Ackerman had returned home to South Africa. Then Harris's five wickets, which included a spell of three for none in ten balls, dismantled the Gloucestershire reply – but the game almost turned against Leicestershire after Dippenaar decided not to enforce the follow-on. Marshall, an unlikely bowling hero, ran through the home batting with his wobbly medium-pacers, and his career-best four for 24 left the game in the balance as Leicestershire were shot out for 133. Gloucestershire had plenty of time to chase 364 and, although they lost wickets regularly, a seventh-wicket stand of 98 between Franklin and Dawson had home supporters fretting. But the wicket of Dawson proved the decisive breakthrough and, although Franklin finished unbeaten on 97, surviving more than five hours until past tea on the final day, his valiant effort was in vain.

Close of play: First day, Leicestershire 332-8 (Taylor 76, Henderson 13); Second day, Leicestershire 49-5 (Taylor 9, Benning 11); Third day, Gloucestershire 133-5 (Franklin 0, Adshead 7).

Leicestershire

P. A. Nixon c Dawson b Franklin	57	– b Kirby	0
G. P. Smith lbw b Kirby	32	– c Adshead b Kirby	1
*H. H. Dippenaar c Gidman b Lewis	7	– b Saxelby	12
J. J. Cobb c Gidman b Dawson	72	– b Marshall	11
J. W. A. Taylor not out	83	– lbw b Saxelby	24
†T. J. New c Adshead b Dawson	0	– lbw b Marshall	0
J. G. E. Benning b Kirby	37	– c Taylor b Marshall	25
W. A. White b Kirby	23	– c Franklin b Saxelby	3
J. K. H. Naik lbw b Lewis	4	– not out	21
C. W. Henderson c Marshall b Kirby	34	– c Woodman b Marshall	3
A. J. Harris b Lewis	2	– lbw b Lewis	18
L-b 7, w 6, n-b 4	17	B 10, l-b 3, n-b 2	15

1/51 (2) 2/72 (3) 3/175 (4)   (103.4 overs) 368   1/1 (2) 2/14 (1)   (55.3 overs) 133
4/179 (1) 5/182 (6) 6/228 (7)   3/14 (3) 4/33 (4)
7/281 (8) 8/292 (9) 9/366 (10) 10/368 (11)   5/33 (6) 6/77 (7) 7/82 (8) 8/82 (5)
                                         9/95 (10) 10/133 (11)

Lewis 18.4–3–68–3; Franklin 19–6–62–1; Saxelby 16–1–41–0; Kirby 21–6–78–4; Gidman 1–0–9–0; Dawson 21–0–82–2; Taylor 7–1–21–0. *Second Innings*—Kirby 14–4–48–2; Lewis 8.3–3–10–1; Saxelby 15–4–31–3; Dawson 1–0–7–0; Marshall 17–6–24–4.

Gloucestershire

Kadeer Ali b Harris	13	– (2) b Henderson	48
R. J. Woodman c New b White	31	– (1) lbw b Harris	5
H. J. H. Marshall lbw b Harris	0	– b White	36
*A. P. R. Gidman b Harris	0	– lbw b Harris	10
C. G. Taylor b Naik	50	– run out	19
J. E. C. Franklin lbw b Henderson	12	– not out	97
†S. J. Adshead lbw b Harris	0	– b White	18
R. K. J. Dawson c and b White	14	– lbw b Benning	49
I. D. Saxelby b Harris	0	– lbw b Henderson	17
J. Lewis run out	0	– c Smith b Naik	1
S. P. Kirby not out	13	– b Naik	0
L-b 2, w 1, n-b 2	5	B 8, l-b 9, w 2	19

1/18 (1) 2/26 (3) 3/26 (4) 4/77 (2)   (50.1 overs) 138   1/18 (1) 2/76 (3)   (134 overs) 319
5/111 (6) 6/111 (5) 7/112 (7)   3/96 (4) 4/122 (5)
8/112 (9) 9/117 (10) 10/138 (8)   5/122 (2) 6/169 (7) 7/267 (8)
                                         8/301 (9) 9/304 (10) 10/319 (11)

Harris 12–4–26–5; Henderson 19–4–48–1; White 8.1–0–28–2; Benning 9–2–26–0; Naik 2–0–8–1. *Second Innings*—Harris 22–4–65–2; Benning 23–6–50–1; Henderson 43–6–106–2; White 22–4–49–2; Naik 24–10–32–2.

Umpires: T. E. Jesty and R. T. Robinson.

At Chelmsford, August 26, 27, 28, 29. LEICESTERSHIRE drew with ESSEX.

LEICESTERSHIRE v GLAMORGAN

At Leicester, September 2, 3, 4, 5. Drawn. Leicestershire 9 pts, Glamorgan 8 pts. Toss: Glamorgan. First-class debut: C. P. Ashling.

Even by their own disappointing standards, Leicestershire's first innings threatened to become a complete shambles: after a decent start on the truncated first day they crashed to 95 for seven before the tail wagged vigorously. White and Henderson led the counter-attack, putting on 120 in 31 overs, then Henderson added a further 52 with O'Brien as Leicestershire reached the lofty heights of 282. Promotion-chasing Glamorgan began well, and at 146 for three looked likely to claim the lead – but they fluffed their lines, losing four wickets for eight runs before recovering slightly to 218. With the captains unable to agree a run-chase on the final day, the last word went to Taylor, whose unbeaten 96 would surely have been converted to his fourth century of the first-class season had time allowed. It was another mature performance from the teenager, who arrived at the crease with his side in a spot of bother at 62 for three. Had Taylor fallen cheaply Leicestershire might have faced a nervy final afternoon but, not for the first time, he showed his unflappable nature and sheer hunger for runs.

Close of play: First day, Leicestershire 39-1 (Nixon 23, Dippenaar 16); Second day, Leicestershire 269-9 (Henderson 71, Harris 1); Third day, Leicestershire 21-0 (Nixon 7, Boyce 13).

Leicestershire

P. A. Nixon b Kruger	32	– st Wallace b Croft	29
M. A. G. Boyce b Kruger	0	– run out	22
*H. H. Dippenaar c and b Kruger	24	– c Dalrymple b Ashling	8
J. J. Cobb c Wallace b Harris	5	– c and b Dalrymple	34
J. W. A. Taylor b Harris	19	– not out	96
†T. J. New lbw b Harris	4	– c Rees b Dalrymple	12
J. G. E. Benning lbw b Ashling	9	– lbw b Cosgrove	6
W. A. White b Dalrymple	68	– not out	38
C. W. Henderson not out	79		
I. E. O'Brien lbw b Ashling	28		
A. J. Harris lbw b Harris	4		
B 1, l-b 7, n-b 2	10	B 5, l-b 9	14
	—		—
	282	(6 wkts, 92 overs)	259

1/2 (2) 2/57 (1) 3/62 (3) 4/64 (4)   (93 overs) 282   1/53 (2)   (6 wkts, 92 overs) 259
5/68 (6) 6/87 (7) 7/95 (5) 8/215 (8)   2/56 (1) 3/62 (3)
9/267 (10) 10/282 (11)   4/160 (4) 5/182 (6) 6/201 (7)

Harris 31–8–85–4; Kruger 27–8–66–3; Ashling 15–2–66–2; Croft 10–2–27–0; Cosgrove 5–2–16–0; Dalrymple 5–1–14–1. *Second Innings*—Harris 12–3–17–0; Kruger 13–0–45–0; Croft 31–9–52–1; Ashling 13–1–50–1; Dalrymple 19–3–62–2; Cosgrove 4–0–19–1.

Glamorgan

G. P. Rees b O'Brien	2	R. D. B. Croft not out	40
W. D. Bragg c New b White	20	G. J-P. Kruger c Boyce b O'Brien	0
M. J. Cosgrove lbw b Harris	12	C. P. Ashling b Henderson	12
M. J. Powell lbw b Benning	61	B 4, l-b 11, w 1, n-b 2	18
*J. W. M. Dalrymple lbw b Benning	37		
T. L. Maynard lbw b Henderson	2	1/2 (1) 2/37 (3) 3/64 (2) (75.5 overs) 218
†M. A. Wallace c Benning b Henderson	14	4/146 (5) 5/147 (4) 6/151 (6)
J. A. R. Harris b Benning	0	7/154 (8) 8/186 (7) 9/187 (10) 10/218 (11)

O'Brien 20–2–52–2; Harris 13–1–53–1; White 9–2–24–1; Henderson 19.5–5–31–3; Benning 14–3–43–3.

Umpires: N. L. Bainton and M. J. D. Bodenham.

At Canterbury, September 15, 16, 17, 18. LEICESTERSHIRE drew with KENT.

At Northampton, September 23, 24, 25. LEICESTERSHIRE lost to NORTHAMPTONSHIRE by an innings and 196 runs. *Leicestershire finish bottom of Division Two.*

MIDDLESEX

Old failings, new coach

NORMAN DE MESQUITA

The 2009 season was very nearly a record-breaking one, but for all the wrong reasons. After another frustrating year it was only by two points that Middlesex avoided what would have been a first bottom place in the Championship, and no county in Division Two suffered as many as their seven defeats.

It was suggested in these pages last year that success in the 2008 Twenty20 Cup had only masked what was wrong, and 2009 did not even have the consolation of Twenty20 success. Losing several members of the victorious side was a significant factor, as was recognised when the club signed Adam Gilchrist to bring his aggressive batting to the group stage for 2010. Second in the lower division of the Pro40 League represented a modicum of consolation, although it did not bring promotion because the competition was not continuing in the same form.

Following the unsettling shuffling of three captains in 2008, Shaun Udal was official captain for the whole season and reappointed for 2010. But there was a change of coach, with Toby Radford leaving suddenly in July, believing his authority had been undermined. There was a feeling when Radford was appointed in 2007 that he might be lacking in experience and, as a result, authority – and so it proved. Richard Scott, the second-team coach, stepped in and, by the winter, had been appointed permanently, with the former England seamer Richard Johnson as his assistant.

"Many former players and current coaches spoke to me about the positions," said the county's director of cricket, Angus Fraser. "But, as the 2009 season progressed, it became clear to me that Richard Scott was the right man for the job. Unlike many modern coaches who like the sound of their own voice, believe everything they say is correct and want to be the star of the show, Richard sits back, listens and works quietly with a player. As for Richard Johnson, while most professional coaches are former batsmen, I wanted Middlesex's assistant coach to have a fast-bowling pedigree."

Once again it was the inconsistency of the batting which was the main problem. The leading Middlesex man in the Championship averages (ignoring Australia's Phillip Hughes and England's Andrew Strauss, who appeared in only a handful of matches) was Owais Shah, who in eight Championship appearances hit 591 runs at 42, as he dropped out of England's Test and one-day teams. Shah, in fact, was a constant disappointment, all too often wasting a good start with a bizarre choice of shot or lacking concentration in the field. Then came Neil Dexter, but he missed much of the season because of injury. Dawid Malan passed fifty eight times, but did not once go on to make a century. Eoin Morgan scored only 413 Championship runs, although his poor form did not seem to affect his selection for the England one-day squad.

Stephen Pond, PA Photos

Steven Finn

There was a welcome rediscovery of form by Nick Compton, and the young Sydneysider Sam Robson proved to be a late-season find; his opening partnership with Compton became consistent and reliable. So it was a sore blow when, in October, Compton turned down an improved contract and left for what he called a "fresh start" with Somerset. He followed Billy Godleman, who had found runs hard to come by, thought a change of scene might help, and joined Essex. The gap was only partly plugged by signing Scott Newman from Surrey.

A plus was the development of Gareth Berg. He started the year as a fringe player but, by mid-August, had established himself as a key member of the side, with significant improvement in both his batting and bustling seam bowling. He played two important innings in the county's first Championship win of the season, at Canterbury.

But Murali Kartik also departed for Somerset, and it is hard to see who will share the spin attack with Udal in 2010. Voted player of the year for the third successive time, Tim Murtagh had 60 Championship victims at 25.35, which proved invaluable. He had strong support from Steven Finn, who took 53 wickets, mostly top-order batsmen, at 30.64 – a notable achievement for a 20-year-old. While it may seem churlish to be critical, Finn did seem to be a one-spell bowler and might have done even better had he not tended to bowl too short in his later stints. The stamina of Makhaya Ntini – expected to arrive from South Africa as a Kolpak – and of the new overseas player, Iain O'Brien, from New Zealand, should save Finn from being overbowled.

As in previous years, the appearances of Chris Silverwood and Alan Richardson were limited by injury and, at the end of the season, both departed. David Nash also decided the time had come to end his 23-year association with the club and announced his retirement. His ebullient presence will be missed. Towards the end of the season, the 21-year-old Lancastrian John Simpson burst upon the scene with some excellent batting performances. His wicketkeeping is still a work in progress, but his new position as first choice was confirmed in the winter, when a loan deal with Worcestershire was agreed for Ben Scott, whose keeping (and especially batting) fell below his previous high standards.

So 2009 was clearly a disappointment. Things could have been better had luck gone the county's way in early-season fixtures, and a pair of wins in August took them within sight of promotion. But it was too little too late. Still, the promising form shown by younger players such as Adam London, Dan Housego and Kabir Toor holds out a great deal of hope under new direction.

MIDDLESEX RESULTS

All first-class matches – Played 16: Won 2, Lost 7, Drawn 7.
County Championship matches – Played 16: Won 2, Lost 7, Drawn 7.

LV County Championship, 8th in Division 2; Friends Provident Trophy, q-f;
Pro40 League, 2nd in Division 2; Twenty20 Cup, 6th in South Division.

COUNTY CHAMPIONSHIP AVERAGES, BATTING AND FIELDING

Cap		M	I	NO	R	HS	100s	50s	Avge	Ct/St
	P. J. Hughes§	3	5	1	574	195	3	2	143.50	4
2001	A. J. Strauss‡	3	5	0	295	150	1	1	59.00	2
2000	O. A. Shah‡	8	16	2	591	159	2	2	42.21	5
	N. J. Dexter¶	10	19	2	709	146	2	2	41.70	15
	D. J. Malan	15	28	3	930	88	0	8	37.20	19
	S. D. Robson¶	7	13	0	441	110	1	2	33.92	12
2006	N. R. D. Compton	14	28	2	860	178	2	3	33.07	8
	G. K. Berg¶	13	23	2	668	98	0	7	31.80	9
	J. A. Simpson	3	6	0	170	87	0	1	28.33	5
	A. B. London	4	8	1	190	68	0	2	27.14	1
2008	E. J. G. Morgan	10	18	1	413	114*	1	1	24.29	12
2007	M. Kartik§	10	19	5	336	62*	0	2	24.00	1
2008	S. D. Udal	14	24	4	398	55	0	1	19.90	4
2000	D. C. Nash	5	8	0	152	43	0	0	19.00	16
2008	T. J. Murtagh	13	20	6	249	51*	0	1	17.78	2
	B. A. Godleman†	5	9	0	160	48	0	0	17.77	3
2006	C. E. W. Silverwood . . .	5	8	1	113	46	0	0	16.14	2
	D. M. Housego	3	6	0	86	34	0	0	14.33	2
2005	A. Richardson	6	7	4	40	18*	0	0	13.33	5
2007	B. J. M. Scott†	8	14	1	167	44	0	0	12.84	18/2
2009	S. T. Finn	14	22	4	107	24*	0	0	5.94	4
	D. A. Burton.	2	4	2	3	2*	0	0	1.50	0

D. Evans (1 match) did not bat.

† *Born in Middlesex.*   ‡ *ECB contract.*   § *Official overseas player.*   ¶ *Other non-England-qualified player.*

BOWLING

	O	M	R	W	BB	5W/i	Avge
M. Kartik	317.1	103	755	33	5-65	1	22.87
T. J. Murtagh	443	81	1,521	60	7-82	3	25.35
S. D. Udal	368.5	67	1,007	37	6-36	2	27.21
S. T. Finn	418.3	64	1,624	53	5-57	1	30.64
G. K. Berg	249.1	46	886	23	5-55	2	38.52
A. Richardson	222.2	53	618	11	3-52	0	56.18

Also bowled: D. A. Burton 53.2–3–249–8; N. R. D. Compton 2–0–5–0; N. J. Dexter 88–25–266–6; D. Evans 42–3–190–3; D. M. Housego 1.1–0–17–0; P. J. Hughes 3–0–9–0; A. B. London 8–0–39–0; D. J. Malan 96.4–10–358–7; S. D. Robson 2–0–5–0; O. A. Shah 1–0–1–0; C. E. W. Silverwood 115–21–355–4; A. J. Strauss 2–1–10–0.

COUNTY RECORDS

Highest score for:	331*	J. D. Robertson v Worcestershire at Worcester .	1949
Highest score against:	341	C. M. Spearman (Gloucestershire) at Gloucester	2004
Leading run-scorer:	40,302	E. H. Hendren (avge 48.81)	1907–1937
Best bowling for:	10-40	G. O. B. Allen v Lancashire at Lord's	1929
Best bowling against:	9-38	R. C. Robertson-Glasgow (Somerset) at Lord's .	1924
Leading wicket-taker:	2,361	F. J. Titmus (avge 21.27)	1949–1982
Highest total for:	642-3 dec	v Hampshire at Southampton	1923
Highest total against:	850-7 dec	by Somerset at Taunton	2007
Lowest total for:	20	v MCC at Lord's	1864
Lowest total against: {	31	by Gloucestershire at Bristol	1924
	31	by Glamorgan at Cardiff	1997

ADDRESS

Lord's Cricket Ground, London NW8 8QN (020 7289 1300; **email** enquiries@middlesexccc.com).
Website www.middlesexccc.com

OFFICIALS

Captain S. D. Udal

Managing director of cricket A. R. C. Fraser
First-team coach R. J. Scott
President P. H. Parfitt

Chairman I. N. Lovett
Secretary/chief executive V. J. Codrington
Head groundsman M. J. Hunt
Scorer D. K. Shelley

A visit from the Royals

This charity match, for the inaugural British Asian Cup, pitted the 2008 English Twenty20 Cup-winners against the first champions of the Indian Premier League. Rajasthan Royals ran up an imposing total on a rainy evening, boosted by a late burst from Dimitri Mascarenhas, who hit 32 from 16 balls before opening the bowling and striking twice to set Middlesex's run-chase on its heels. Sohail Tanvir added the important wickets of Eoin Morgan and Tyron Henderson, and Middlesex never looked like getting the runs after that. Rajasthan's player/coach Shane Warne chimed in with possibly his last wicket at Lord's, when he lured Dawid Malan down the track with a googly and Naman Ojha completed the stumping. Justin Langer, playing his first match for the Royals, was out second ball. Despite a crowd of around 20,000, reports claimed MCC lost around £18,000, after making an agreed £50,000 donation to the British Asian Trust.

At Lord's, July 6 (floodlit). **Rajasthan Royals won by 46 runs**. Toss: Middlesex. **Rajasthan Royals 162-5** (20 overs) (S. A. Asnodkar 41, M. Kaif 41, A. D. Mascarenhas 32*); **Middlesex 116-7** (20 overs) (D. J. Malan 34; Sohail Tanvir 3-20). *Man of the Match:* A. D. Mascarenhas.

MIDDLESEX v GLAMORGAN

At Lord's, April 22, 23, 24, 25. Drawn. Middlesex 11 pts, Glamorgan 11 pts. Toss: Middlesex. County debuts: P. J. Hughes; G. J-P. Kruger.

Udal's first decision as Middlesex captain in 2009 – to field first – did not meet with universal approval, but his reasoning made sense: most Lord's pitches, he said, offered help to the bowlers only in the first hour of the day. But Middlesex bowled too short, only one early wicket fell, and Cosgrove and Wallace helped themselves to centuries as Glamorgan passed 500. Hughes, the Australian opener signed as an overseas replacement for the unavailable Kartik, marked his debut with a century that featured exuberant strokes either side of point; he was restrained only by Croft's off-spin as his hundred, made in a little over three hours, approached. The two first innings, however, were not completed until well into the third day. Glamorgan batted long enough for Dalrymple to score a hundred against his former county, but there was too little time for either side to force a win. Play was late starting on the third day because of a lack of bails. To compound matters, the groundstaff were on their mid-morning break, and it was some time before umpire Garratt found them and the missing woodwork.

Close of play: First day, Glamorgan 351-6 (Wallace 58, Croft 23); Second day, Middlesex 174-1 (Hughes 100, Dexter 43); Third day, Glamorgan 94-4 (Dalrymple 22, Shantry 3).

Glamorgan

G. P. Rees c Scott b Murtagh	6	– lbw b Murtagh	9
M. J. Cosgrove lbw b Dexter	120	– c Berg b Murtagh	8
B. J. Wright c Murtagh b Udal	38	– b Berg	28
M. J. Powell lbw b Malan	51	– lbw b Richardson	24
*J. W. M. Dalrymple c Morgan b Evans	28	– not out	112
T. L. Maynard c Scott b Dexter	16	– (7) lbw b Evans	0
†M. A. Wallace c Dexter b Udal	128	– (8) b Evans	17
R. D. B. Croft b Murtagh	42	– (9) c Richardson b Dexter	52
D. S. Harrison c Udal b Berg	51		
A. J. Shantry c Richardson b Udal	1	– (6) c Malan b Udal	20
G. J-P. Kruger not out	4		
B 5, l-b 14, w 1	20	B 2, n-b 6	8

1/10 (1) 2/86 (3) 3/185 (4) (140.3 overs) 505
4/250 (5) 5/260 (2) 6/281 (6)
7/381 (8) 8/498 (9) 9/500 (7)
10/505 (10) 120 overs: 436-7

1/17 (2) (8 wkts dec, 89.5 overs) 278
2/17 (1) 3/65 (3)
4/82 (4) 5/127 (6) 6/128 (7)
7/154 (8) 8/278 (9)

Murtagh 30–3–103–2; Richardson 30–8–54–0; Evans 22–1–121–1; Berg 20–3–65–1; Udal 22.3–0–87–3; Malan 5–0–19–1; Dexter 11–4–37–2. *Second Innings*—Murtagh 12–2–38–2; Richardson 24–5–72–1; Berg 15–4–46–1; Evans 20–2–69–2; Udal 14–2–28–1; Dexter 4.5–0–23–1.

Middlesex

B. A. Godleman c and b Harrison	23	– c Wallace b Harrison	3
P. J. Hughes b Kruger	118	– not out	65
N. J. Dexter c Powell b Kruger	72	– c Maynard b Harrison	0
E. J. G. Morgan lbw b Harrison	26	– b Shantry	8
D. J. Malan c Cosgrove b Harrison	88	– not out	13
†B. J. M. Scott lbw b Kruger	14		
G. K. Berg c Powell b Kruger	3		
*S. D. Udal lbw b Dalrymple	20		
T. J. Murtagh not out	23		
A. Richardson not out	3		
B 8, l-b 9, w 5, n-b 2	24	L-b 2, w 1, n-b 2	5

1/67 (1) 2/221 (2) (8 wkts dec, 105 overs) 414
3/226 (3) 4/261 (4)
5/293 (6) 6/311 (7) 7/349 (8) 8/404 (5)

1/22 (1) (3 wkts, 28 overs) 94
2/22 (3) 3/31 (4)

D. Evans did not bat.

Shantry 22–3–69–0; Kruger 20–3–85–4; Harrison 25–3–117–3; Croft 28–6–79–0; Cosgrove 4–1–12–0; Dalrymple 6–0–35–1. *Second Innings*—Kruger 7–0–42–0; Harrison 10–1–26–2; Croft 5–1–7–0; Shantry 4–1–8–1; Cosgrove 2–0–9–0.

Umpires: S. A. Garratt and I. J. Gould.

MIDDLESEX v LEICESTERSHIRE

At Southgate, April 28, 29, 30, May 1. Drawn. Middlesex 12 pts, Leicestershire 8 pts. Toss: Middlesex. Championship debut: I. E. O'Brien.

Hughes continued to show excellent form with his second century in two matches, adding 244 in 53 overs with Strauss, who made 150 from 167 balls in a rare county appearance. Morgan then cracked the third hundred of the innings and put on an undefeated 110 for the eighth wicket with Murtagh. Only New and Cobb passed fifty as Leicestershire followed on, 235 behind, but an impressive maiden century from Taylor eased the visitors to safety on this fast-scoring ground. The match was notable for Middlesex using five wicketkeepers. Scott started but fell ill; Morgan kept for most of the third morning, until David Nash arrived from a second-team game at Beckenham. But next day he was injured in the warm-ups, and Dexter took over until John Simpson, too, was seconded from Beckenham.

Close of play: First day, Middlesex 281-2 (Hughes 99, Dexter 24); Second day, Leicestershire 161-5 (Cobb 23, Taylor 3); Third day, Leicestershire 177-2 (Dippenaar 85, Ackerman 45).

Middlesex

A. J. Strauss c Nixon b White	150	*S. D. Udal b White	0
B. A. Godleman lbw b Harris	1	T. J. Murtagh not out	51
P. J. Hughes c Nixon b Harris	139	B 5, l-b 1, n-b 2	8
N. J. Dexter c Nixon b O'Brien	27		
E. J. G. Morgan not out	114	1/2 (2) 2/246 (1) (7 wkts dec, 113 overs) 493	
D. J. Malan b Harris	0	3/294 (4) 4/354 (3)	
†B. J. M. Scott c Nixon b White	3	5/354 (6) 6/383 (7) 7/383 (8)	

S. T. Finn and A. Richardson did not bat.

O'Brien 24–2–116–1; Harris 23–4–105–3; White 20–1–94–3; Crowe 42–6–158–0; Taylor 1–0–5–0; New 3–0–9–0.

Leicestershire

M. A. G. Boyce c Scott b Finn	27	– lbw b Murtagh	1
T. J. New c Dexter b Udal	66	– c Malan b Udal	43
H. H. Dippenaar lbw b Finn	0	– lbw b Murtagh	93
H. D. Ackerman lbw b Richardson	29	– b Murtagh	60
J. J. Cobb c Finn b Richardson	60	– lbw b Murtagh	0
*†P. A. Nixon c Richardson b Finn	8	– c sub (J. A. Simpson) b Malan	31
J. W. A. Taylor c sub (D. C. Nash) b Dexter	9	– not out	122
W. A. White b Murtagh	32	– c sub (J. A. Simpson) b Murtagh	19
C. D. Crowe lbw b Malan	10	– not out	25
I. E. O'Brien c and b Malan	2		
A. J. Harris not out	0		
L-b 4, w 1, n-b 10	15	B 3, l-b 3	6

1/49 (1) 2/55 (3) 3/125 (2)	(84.1 overs) 258	1/2 (1) (7 wkts dec, 135 overs) 400
4/125 (4) 5/151 (6) 6/206 (5)		2/81 (2) 3/196 (3)
7/212 (7) 8/241 (9) 9/243 (10) 10/258 (8)		4/196 (5) 5/205 (4)
		6/313 (6) 7/355 (8)

Richardson 22–11–42–2; Murtagh 15.1–4–60–1; Udal 20–4–54–1; Malan 7–2–21–2; Finn 14–1–56–3; Dexter 6–1–21–1. *Second Innings*—Murtagh 32–8–83–5; Richardson 22–5–58–0; Finn 21–1–107–0; Udal 34–6–91–1; Dexter 8–1–14–0; Malan 14–2–28–1; Strauss 2–1–10–0; Hughes 2–0–3–0.

Umpires: N. G. B. Cook and N. J. Llong.

At The Oval, May 6, 7, 8, 9. MIDDLESEX drew with SURREY.

At Chelmsford, June 6, 7, 8, 9. MIDDLESEX drew with ESSEX.

At Richmond, June 11, 12, 13 (not first-class). **Middlesex won by 201 runs.** Toss: Middlesex. **Middlesex 353-5 dec** (B. A. Godleman 107, B. J. M. Scott 88, D. M. Housego 62*, K. S. Toor 35*) and 165-5 dec (S. D. Robson 49, B. J. M. Scott 52*, D. M. Housego 30); **Cardiff UCCE 161** (R. Bishop 39, S. R. Benton 39; S. Tailor 3-45, A. B. London 3-26) and 156 (S. M. Ransley 30, S. M. Moore 37*; D. A. Burton 3-31). *County debuts:* T. R. G. Hampton, A. B. London, J. A. Simpson, S. Tailor, K. S. Toor.

Only one player, Sam Robson, remained from Middlesex's eleven against Essex the previous week. Godleman scored a four-hour century and added 161 with Scott. Middlesex allowed Cardiff to have a full bowling substitute, Stefan Kelly, after Tom Allin was injured. Set 358 to win, Cardiff crashed to 22-4; Stuart Ransley and Sean Moore added 64, the highest stand of the innings, for their ninth and last wicket.

At Bristol, June 18, 19, 20. MIDDLESEX lost to GLOUCESTERSHIRE by nine wickets.

MIDDLESEX v SURREY

At Lord's, June 30, July 1, 2, 3. Drawn. Middlesex 10 pts, Surrey 10 pts. Toss: Middlesex. First-class debut: S. J. King.

Surrey's uninspiring second-innings score might suggest Middlesex could have won had they declared earlier – the eventual target was 240 in 44 overs, and Surrey made a poor start when Batty fell second ball – but actually they were never really in a position to do so on a slow pitch. Earlier, Shah showed his mettle with an innings of admirable patience, lasting more than five and a half hours and containing 23 fours, many from sweet drives. He received good support from Godleman, who took 71 balls to reach double figures, and Malan. The experienced pair of Nash and Udal pushed the score even higher, but overall the runs came at less than three an over. Surrey were equally restrained, although there was a certain inevitability about Ramprakash making a fourth century against his former county (after this game he had 1,058 runs against them in eight matches, at an average of 105.80); he had hit 17 fours from 306 balls when Kartik's deceptive change of pace trapped him in front. For all that Phillip Hughes had contributed with the bat, Middlesex looked a more rounded side with Kartik back purveying his slow left-arm variations. Surrey gave a debut to Simon King, a 21-year-old off-spinner, who polished off Middlesex's first innings with three quick wickets – two of them smart slip catches for Butcher – after a rather expensive start.

Close of play: First day, Middlesex 269-5 (Malan 32); Second day, Surrey 186-2 (Ramprakash 64, Butcher 48); Third day, Middlesex 38-0 (Godleman 18, Compton 13).

Middlesex

B. A. Godleman run out	48	– c Jordan b Tudor	21
N. R. D. Compton lbw b Nel	2	– not out	100
O. A. Shah c Walters b Nel	159	– c sub (C. P. Murtagh) b Murtaza Hussain	61
N. J. Dexter c Tudor b Murtaza Hussain	14	– (7) not out	8
D. J. Malan c Batty b Nel	54	– (6) c Walters b Afzaal	30
S. T. Finn lbw b Jordan	5		
†D. C. Nash c Brown b King	43		
G. K. Berg c Jordan b Nel	0		
*S. D. Udal c Butcher b King	33	– (4) c Butcher b Murtaza Hussain	2
M. Kartik not out	8	– (5) st Batty b Afzaal	4
C. E. W. Silverwood c Butcher b King	7		
B 4, l-b 3, w 1, n-b 4	12	B 2, l-b 5, w 3, n-b 10	20

1/3 (2) 2/160 (1) 3/186 (4) (130.3 overs) 385 1/50 (1) (5 wkts dec, 67.5 overs) 246
4/259 (3) 5/269 (6) 6/304 (5) 2/170 (3) 3/173 (4)
7/304 (8) 8/360 (7) 9/371 (9) 4/178 (5) 5/233 (6)
10/385 (11)

120 overs: 350-7

Nel 27–9–59–4; Jordan 29–9–81–1; Tudor 23–3–76–0; Walters 5–1–14–0; King 16.3–0–61–3; Murtaza Hussain 25–2–75–1; Afzaal 5–1–12–0. *Second Innings*—Nel 11–6–15–0; Jordan 11–5–24–0; King 6–0–34–0; Tudor 11–6–37–1; Afzaal 13.5–0–60–2; Murtaza Hussain 15–1–69–2.

Surrey

†J. N. Batty c Malan b Berg	24	– c Kartik b Finn	0
M. J. Brown c Nash b Dexter	44	– lbw b Finn	13
M. R. Ramprakash lbw b Kartik	136	– not out	49
*M. A. Butcher c Udal b Silverwood	49	– (6) lbw b Udal	2
U. Afzaal c Berg b Finn	58	– c Malan b Kartik	1
S. J. Walters lbw b Kartik	6	– (4) lbw b Kartik	3
C. J. Jordan not out	34	– not out	30
A. J. Tudor c Berg b Kartik	0		
Murtaza Hussain c Udal b Kartik	13		
A. Nel c Compton b Finn	9		
S. J. King c Nash b Kartik	0		
B 8, l-b 4, w 3, n-b 4	19	L-b 1	1

1/62 (1) 2/87 (2) 3/188 (4)   (134.2 overs) 392   1/0 (1) 2/23 (2)   (5 wkts, 40 overs) 99
4/297 (5) 5/326 (6) 6/349 (3)   3/34 (4) 4/40 (5)
7/349 (8) 8/378 (9) 9/391 (10)   5/55 (6)
10/392 (11)   120 overs: 354-7

Finn 26–5–120–2; Silverwood 22–6–61–1; Berg 15–0–42–1; Dexter 4–2–10–1; Kartik 39.2–12–65–5; Udal 26–1–72–0; Malan 2–0–10–0. *Second Innings*—Finn 12–5–29–2; Silverwood 5–1–15–0; Kartik 14–5–26–2; Udal 7–0–24–1; Malan 2–0–4–0.

Umpires: M. R. Benson and B. Dudleston.

At Lord's, July 6. MIDDLESEX lost to RAJASTHAN ROYALS by 46 runs (see page 704).

At Leicester, July 10, 11, 12. MIDDLESEX lost to LEICESTERSHIRE by eight wickets.

At Derby, July 21, 22, 23, 24. MIDDLESEX drew with DERBYSHIRE.

MIDDLESEX v NORTHAMPTONSHIRE

At Lord's, July 31, August 1, 2, 3. Northamptonshire won by 35 runs. Northamptonshire 19 pts, Middlesex 7 pts. Toss: Northamptonshire.

If ever a dropped catch changed the course of a match, this was it. Northamptonshire, 72 behind on first innings after Middlesex's openers put on 167, were only just in front in their second innings, with five wickets down, when Shah missed a straightforward slip chance from an attempted drive by Wessels against Kartik. Suddenly the balance shifted. Northamptonshire, who would effectively have been seven for six – with Panesar in next – if the catch had stuck, regrouped: the reprieved Wessels took his score from 17 to 57, and put on 82 for the sixth wicket with Hall. Some lusty blows by van der Wath, who clubbed a six and 12 fours in his 85, then left Middlesex contemplating a far from straightforward target of 222 in 71 overs. Four of the top five fell for single figures, two of them to Panesar after Lucas made early inroads, and there was no comeback from 66 for five, even though Udal defied the bowlers for 94 balls.

Close of play: First day, Northamptonshire 288-9 (Lucas 0, Wigley 6); Second day, Middlesex 310-6 (Udal 2, Kartik 5); Third day, Northamptonshire 225-7 (van der Wath 40, Panesar 5).

Northamptonshire

Batsman	First Innings		Second Innings	
S. D. Peters	lbw b Finn	13	lbw b Finn	25
B. H. N. Howgego	c Morgan b Finn	47	c Scott b Murtagh	6
R. A. White	c Malan b Finn	51	lbw b Murtagh	1
A. G. Wakely	lbw b Udal	61	c and b Udal	24
†M. H. Wessels	c Kartik b Richardson	19	c Malan b Murtagh	57
*N. Boje	c Finn b Murtagh	55	c Robson b Udal	2
A. J. Hall	c Shah b Murtagh	11	c Scott b Richardson	48
J. J. van der Wath	c Shah b Richardson	7	c Shah b Kartik	85
M. S. Panesar	c Kartik b Richardson	2	c Kartik b Richardson	14
D. S. Lucas	lbw b Murtagh	0	c Scott b Murtagh	8
D. H. Wigley	not out	6	not out	5
Extras	L-b 8, n-b 8	16	B 5, l-b 10, w 1, n-b 2	18

1/19 (1) 2/106 (2) 3/119 (3)   (96.5 overs) 288
4/157 (5) 5/254 (4) 6/262 (6)
7/280 (8) 8/280 (7) 9/282 (9) 10/288 (10)

1/19 (2) 2/25 (3)   (103 overs) 293
3/37 (1) 4/75 (4)
5/79 (6) 6/161 (5) 7/211 (7)
8/273 (9) 9/284 (10) 10/293 (8)

Murtagh 22.5–5–63–3; Finn 18–3–41–3; Kartik 19–5–52–3; Udal 11–3–28–1; Malan 3–0–16–0; Robson 2–0–5–0. *Second Innings*—Murtagh 26–4–51–4; Finn 17–1–89–1; Kartik 23–8–38–1; Richardson 21–3–52–2; Udal 16–0–48–2.

Middlesex

Batsman	First Innings		Second Innings	
S. D. Robson	c Wessels b van der Wath	75	lbw b Lucas	9
N. R. D. Compton	c Boje b Wigley	82	c Wessels b Lucas	32
O. A. Shah	b Lucas	24	lbw b Lucas	4
E. J. G. Morgan	lbw b Boje	71	lbw b Panesar	6
D. J. Malan	c Howgego b Boje	10	lbw b Panesar	5
†B. J. M. Scott	b van der Wath	20	lbw b Boje	23
*S. D. Udal	b Hall	3	b van der Wath	55
M. Kartik	not out	28	c Wessels b van der Wath	16
T. J. Murtagh	lbw b van der Wath	9	c White b van der Wath	1
S. T. Finn	c Hall b van der Wath	3	not out	14
A. Richardson	lbw b Hall	11	lbw b Lucas	4
Extras	B 2, l-b 6, n-b 16	24	B 2, l-b 4, w 1, n-b 10	17

1/167 (2) 2/181 (1) 3/200 (3)   (87.5 overs) 360
4/213 (5) 5/298 (6) 6/304 (4)
7/316 (7) 8/335 (9) 9/345 (10) 10/360 (11)

1/25 (1) 2/29 (3)   (63 overs) 186
3/52 (1) 4/61 (5) 5/66 (4)
6/109 (6) 7/150 (8) 8/163 (7)
9/164 (9) 10/186 (11)

Van der Wath 22–1–107–4; Lucas 13–2–51–1; Panesar 9–1–31–0; Hall 13.5–2–44–2; Wigley 12–0–61–1; Boje 18–3–58–2. *Second Innings*—Lucas 14–3–38–4; van der Wath 14–4–38–3; Panesar 12–0–34–2; Wigley 5–1–21–0; Hall 7–2–15–0; Boje 11–2–34–1.

Umpires: J. W. Holder and V. A. Holder.

At Canterbury, August 5, 6, 7. MIDDLESEX beat KENT by 47 runs.

MIDDLESEX v ESSEX

At Lord's, August 11, 12, 13, 14. Essex won by five wickets. Essex 19 pts (after 1 pt penalty), Middlesex 7 pts. Toss: Essex.

Much was made later in the season of Derbyshire's supposed generosity in setting a target that Essex reached to clinch promotion in the final round of matches, but the declaration by Middlesex's stand-in captain Morgan in this game was arguably even more munificent. Essex took suitable advantage, chasing down 241 with two overs to spare. They were led home by Cook, whose 66 came off 79 balls and included ten fours. He had strong support from Bopara (whose return to something like form after a demoralising run against Australia was not enough to save his place for the final

Ashes Test) and ten Doeschate, who smashed 40 from 20 balls, and an Essex win was rarely in doubt. Middlesex should really have put the match beyond Essex before this: after Robson completed a careful maiden century to underpin a total of 356, three quick wickets from Murtagh spoiled the start of Essex's first innings, and later they were 256 for seven – still 100 behind – before Walker, who hit his second century after leaving Kent, batted for almost seven hours and orchestrated a recovery that restricted the eventual lead to just 11.

Close of play: First day, Middlesex 280-6 (Berg 43, Kartik 5); Second day, Essex 107-4 (Walker 35, Foster 40); Third day, Middlesex 47-3 (Shah 9, Finn 3).

Middlesex

S. D. Robson lbw b Palladino 110	– c Cook b Danish Kaneria	12
N. R. D. Compton c Bopara b Napier 16	– lbw b Danish Kaneria.............	13
O. A. Shah lbw b Napier 8	– lbw b Masters.................	10
*E. J. G. Morgan c Foster b Napier 4	– lbw b Danish Kaneria.............	8
D. J. Malan c Cook b Danish Kaneria 73	– (6) not out....................	87
†B. J. M. Scott lbw b Danish Kaneria 0	– (7) lbw b Danish Kaneria.........	44
G. K. Berg lbw b ten Doeschate............... 66	– (8) st Foster b Cook	29
M. Kartik c Foster b ten Doeschate 22	– (9) not out....................	5
T. J. Murtagh lbw b Danish Kaneria 20		
S. T. Finn st Foster b Danish Kaneria 7	– (5) c Walker b Danish Kaneria......	9
A. Richardson not out 3		
B 4, l-b 17, w 2, n-b 4 27	B 2, l-b 4, n-b 6	12

1/26 (2) 2/44 (3) 3/64 (4)   (118.5 overs) 356   1/22 (1)   (7 wkts dec, 69.5 overs) 229
4/207 (5) 5/207 (6) 6/262 (1)   2/31 (2) 3/43 (4)
7/307 (8) 8/340 (9) 9/340 (7) 10/356 (10)   4/55 (3) 5/59 (5)
                                                               6/157 (7) 7/205 (8)

Masters 27–9–61–0; Palladino 18–3–64–1; Napier 23–8–63–3; ten Doeschate 22–6–51–2; Danish Kaneria 23.5–2–74–4; Bopara 5–2–22–0. *Second Innings*—Masters 16–4–39–1; Napier 11–3–26–0; Danish Kaneria 26–6–76–5; Palladino 8–2–28–0; ten Doeschate 6–1–21–0; Bopara 1–0–6–0; Cook 1–0–3–1; Pettini 0.5–0–24–0.

Essex

J. K. Maunders c Morgan b Murtagh 23		
A. N. Cook lbw b Murtagh 4	– b Kartik	66
R. S. Bopara c Kartik b Murtagh 1	– not out	52
M. J. Walker c Compton b Kartik 150	– c Compton b Kartik	12
*M. L. Pettini lbw b Murtagh................... 1	– (1) c Scott b Murtagh...........	37
†J. S. Foster run out 72	– c Berg b Richardson.............	10
R. N. ten Doeschate lbw b Murtagh............ 18	– (5) b Kartik.................	40
G. R. Napier lbw b Murtagh.................. 3	– (7) not out.................	13
D. D. Masters not out....................... 35		
A. P. Palladino c Malan b Kartik 0		
Danish Kaneria st Scott b Kartik 7		
B 10, l-b 10, w 1, n-b 10 31	L-b 7, w 2, n-b 2..........	11

1/9 (2) 2/15 (3) 3/30 (1) 4/32 (5)   (114.4 overs) 345   1/100 (1)   (5 wkts, 43 overs) 241
5/195 (6) 6/244 (7) 7/256 (8)   2/108 (2) 3/136 (4)
8/333 (4) 9/333 (10) 10/345 (11)   4/212 (5) 5/227 (6)

Murtagh 29–11–84–6; Finn 24–6–69–0; Richardson 19–2–71–0; Berg 16–4–46–0; Kartik 26.4–11–55–3. *Second Innings*—Murtagh 14–0–71–1; Finn 4–0–31–0; Kartik 18–4–84–3; Richardson 7–0–48–1.

Umpires: N. L. Bainton and P. Willey.

At Swansea, August 20, 21, 22. MIDDLESEX lost to GLAMORGAN by 22 runs.

MIDDLESEX v GLOUCESTERSHIRE

At Lord's, August 27, 28, 29, 30. Middlesex won by 180 runs. Middlesex 20 pts, Gloucestershire 4 pts. Toss: Middlesex. First-class debut: A. B. London.

Needing a daunting 406 to win, Gloucestershire were never in the hunt, and it was the bowling of Berg which was mainly instrumental in dismissing them. His first five-for followed a match-winning 98 at Canterbury, and confirmed his emergence as a genuine all-rounder. There was also an encouraging debut from 20-year-old Adam London, who during his 68 from 173 balls looked a young batsman with an excellent technique. After another late flourish from Udal pushed Middlesex to 342, Gloucestershire struggled from the start: only Taylor, who hit 13 fours before falling to a superb catch by Berg at cover, passed 20 in their first innings. Murtagh and Finn again produced fine opening spells before Kartik took three late wickets, although the last pair saved the follow-on. Kartik proved a surprise last as stand-in opener for the injured Robson in Middlesex's second innings, putting on 128 with Compton. This win, only Middlesex's second in the Championship, rather surprisingly gave them an outside chance of promotion.

Close of play: First day, Middlesex 307-6 (Dexter 46, Udal 23); Second day, Gloucestershire 196-9 (Lewis 18, Kirby 6); Third day, Gloucestershire 55-3 (Kadeer Ali 20, Taylor 16).

Middlesex

S. D. Robson c Dawson b Kirby	83				
N. R. D. Compton c Taylor b Marshall	28	– c Saxelby b Marshall	83		
A. B. London b Marshall	68	– run out	11		
D. J. Malan c Marshall b Saxelby	38	– b Taylor	20		
N. J. Dexter c Adshead b Saxelby	51	– not out	39		
†B. J. M. Scott lbw b Saxelby	6	– c Dawson b Saxelby	22		
G. K. Berg c Adshead b Kirby	5	– c Adshead b Kirby	7		
*S. D. Udal c Saxelby b Kirby	45	– c Gidman b Kirby	26		
M. Kartik c Kadeer Ali b Kirby	1	– (2) st Adshead b Dawson	57		
T. J. Murtagh not out	3				
S. T. Finn run out	4				
L-b 10	10	L-b 6, n-b 2	8		

1/46 (2) 2/142 (1) 3/226 (3) (104.4 overs) 342
4/226 (4) 5/244 (6) 6/263 (7)
7/321 (5) 8/326 (9) 9/335 (8) 10/342 (11)

1/128 (2) (7 wkts dec, 71.1 overs) 273
2/150 (3) 3/155 (1)
4/184 (4) 5/226 (6) 6/237 (7) 7/273 (8)

Lewis 21–6–64–0; Franklin 18–6–44–0; Kirby 21–4–77–4; Saxelby 21.4–3–58–3; Marshall 17–5–52–2; Dawson 4–0–23–0; Taylor 2–0–14–0. *Second Innings*—Saxelby 16.2–5–51–1; Kirby 14.1–3–41–2; Lewis 5–0–24–0; Dawson 13–0–60–1; Franklin 10–2–35–0; Marshall 8–1–32–1; Taylor 5–1–24–1.

Gloucestershire

Kadeer Ali c Scott b Murtagh	4	– (2) c Compton b Berg	48		
R. J. Woodman c Malan b Finn	9	– (1) lbw b Murtagh	4		
H. J. H. Marshall c Malan b Murtagh	17	– c Scott b Murtagh	0		
*A. P. R. Gidman b Murtagh	0	– lbw b Finn	7		
C. G. Taylor c Finn b Kartik	65	– c Scott b Finn	25		
J. E. C. Franklin b Finn	16	– not out	80		
†S. J. Adshead c Robson b Kartik	14	– b Berg	0		
R. K. J. Dawson b Berg	0	– c Malan b Berg	35		
I. D. Saxelby lbw b Kartik	17	– c Scott b Berg	0		
J. Lewis not out	20	– c Scott b Berg	4		
S. P. Kirby c Dexter b Murtagh	18	– c Dexter b Murtagh	9		
B 4, l-b 11, w 1, n-b 14	30	B 1, l-b 8, n-b 4	13		

1/10 (1) 2/28 (3) 3/28 (4) 4/77 (2) (70.3 overs) 210
5/107 (6) 6/148 (7) 7/149 (8)
8/149 (5) 9/178 (9) 10/210 (11)

1/4 (1) 2/4 (3) (60.5 overs) 225
3/21 (4) 4/73 (5) 5/118 (2)
6/118 (7) 7/196 (8) 8/196 (9)
9/204 (10) 10/225 (11)

Murtagh 16.3–3–61–4; Finn 17–4–47–2; Udal 6–2–10–0; Berg 12–5–28–1; Dexter 2–1–5–0;
Kartik 17–4–44–3. *Second Innings*—Murtagh 18.5–2–83–3; Finn 14–3–52–2; Berg 14–1–55–5;
Kartik 1–0–4–0; Udal 9–4–12–0; Malan 2–0–7–0; London 2–0–3–0.

Umpires: M. J. D. Bodenham and R. K. Illingworth.

At Northampton, September 2, 3, 4. MIDDLESEX lost to NORTHAMPTONSHIRE by six wickets.

MIDDLESEX v KENT

At Uxbridge, September 9, 10, 11, 12. Kent won by ten wickets. Kent 22 pts, Middlesex 5 pts.
Toss: Kent.

The only surprises on the first day, as Kent cruised to 390 for four, came when a wicket fell. The
visitors took full advantage of winning the toss in batsman-friendly conditions, eventually calling a
halt at 652 – their second-highest total, and the biggest in 37 first-class matches at Uxbridge, beating
Worcestershire's 627 for six in 1998. Stevens reached his second double-century, but inside-edged
an attempted cut just after equalling his career-best 208 against Glamorgan in 2005: he hit 34 fours

HIGHEST TOTALS FOR KENT

803-4 dec	v Essex at Brentwood	1934
652-7 dec	**v Middlesex at Uxbridge**	**2009**
621-6 dec	v Essex at Tonbridge	1922
620-7 dec	**v Surrey at The Oval**	**2009**
616-6 dec	v Oxford University at Oxford	1982
616-7 dec	v Somerset at Canterbury	1996
615	v Derbyshire at Derby	1908
615	v Lancashire at Tunbridge Wells	2004
610	v Hampshire at Bournemouth	1906

from 255 balls in 348 minutes, and shared stands of 193 with van Jaarsveld and 228 with Kemp. All
this left Middlesex needing their highest total of the season just to avoid following on, which they
failed to do in spite of the efforts of Dexter and Berg, who put on 119. Dexter's first century for
Middlesex compensated for missing much of the season through injury and illness, and he made his
former county pay further in the follow-on with another hundred, becoming the first to score twin
centuries for Middlesex since Ben Hutton at Southgate in 2004, also against Kent. Still it was not
enough: Dexter's only significant support in the second innings came from Malan, with whom he
added 202, and Kent were left just 31 to win, which they attained when Key hoisted Housego's first
ball in first-class cricket for six.

Close of play: First day, Kent 390-4 (Stevens 129, Kemp 16); Second day, Middlesex 109-4
(Dexter 27, Simpson 12); Third day, Middlesex 89-3 (Malan 16, Dexter 39).

Kent

S. A. Northeast c Simpson b Murtagh	84	– not out	19
*R. W. T. Key c and b Silverwood	46	– not out	17
†G. O. Jones b Murtagh	20		
M. van Jaarsveld c London b Finn	86		
D. I. Stevens b Malan	208		
J. M. Kemp not out	138		
J. C. Tredwell c Dexter b Udal	19		
Azhar Mahmood c Compton b Udal	29		
L-b 9, n-b 8, p 5	22		

1/116 (2) 2/145 (1)   (7 wkts dec, 153 overs) 652   (no wkt, 5.1 overs) 36
3/156 (3) 4/349 (4)
5/577 (5) 6/608 (7) 7/652 (8)   120 overs: 503-4

S. J. Cook, R. S. Ferley and A. Khan did not bat.

Murtagh 24–2–114–2; Finn 21–3–88–1; Berg 23–3–102–0; Udal 37–3–115–2; Silverwood 22–2–73–1; Dexter 8–0–41–0; Malan 15–0–82–1; London 3–0–23–0. *Second Innings*—Murtagh 2–0–16–0; Silverwood 2–0–11–0; London 1–0–3–0; Housego 0.1–0–6–0.

Middlesex

A. B. London lbw b Tredwell	7	– lbw b Azhar Mahmood	0
N. R. D. Compton b Azhar Mahmood	30	– b Cook	9
D. M. Housego lbw b Azhar Mahmood	20	– b Cook	19
D. J. Malan b Tredwell	3	– lbw b Ferley	80
N. J. Dexter c Key b Khan	146	– c Kemp b Tredwell	118
†J. A. Simpson c Northeast b Azhar Mahmood	18	– st Jones b Ferley	14
G. K. Berg b Ferley	67	– c Khan b Ferley	3
*S. D. Udal c Northeast b Khan	1	– c van Jaarsveld b Tredwell	14
T. J. Murtagh lbw b van Jaarsveld	22	– not out	35
C. E. W. Silverwood st Jones b van Jaarsveld	10	– lbw b Tredwell	14
S. T. Finn not out	10	– run out	0
B 8, l-b 4, n-b 10	22	B 10, l-b 6, n-b 4	20

1/29 (1) 2/57 (2) 3/68 (4) 4/72 (3)   (110 overs) 356
5/128 (6) 6/247 (7) 7/257 (8)
8/314 (9) 9/328 (10) 10/356 (5)

1/0 (1) 2/28 (3)   (116 overs) 326
3/33 (2) 4/235 (5)
5/243 (4) 6/255 (7) 7/264 (6) 8/286 (8)
9/313 (10) 10/326 (11)

Khan 13–0–64–2; Cook 6–0–19–0; Tredwell 44–7–127–2; Ferley 18–2–59–1; Azhar Mahmood 22–5–60–3; van Jaarsveld 7–1–15–2. *Second Innings*—Azhar Mahmood 14–5–37–1; Khan 12–0–43–0; Cook 13–1–42–2; van Jaarsveld 5–0–17–0; Tredwell 34–11–82–3; Ferley 33–9–73–3; Stevens 1–1–0–0; Kemp 4–0–16–0.

Umpires: J. W. Holder and T. E. Jesty.

MIDDLESEX v DERBYSHIRE

At Uxbridge, September 15, 16, 17, 18. Drawn. Middlesex 9 pts, Derbyshire 12 pts. Toss: Derbyshire.
With more than 70 overs lost to rain on the first day, Derbyshire did not complete their first innings until tea on the second. Madsen extended his third century of the season to 167, made from 237 balls in 322 minutes with two driven sixes off Kartik to add to 18 fours, but Compton replied in kind on a typically amiable pitch with his highest score since making 190 against Durham in 2006. He batted five minutes longer than Madsen, hit 19 fours and two sixes, and his stand of 135 with the in-form Berg was the biggest of the innings. Middlesex batted deep into the third day but Derbyshire, still in with a faint chance of promotion, went for the runs and set a target of 330 in what became 85 overs. Housego and Malan started brightly, but 135 for two in the 40th over turned into 149 for seven in the 49th, and it looked all over. However, London defied a broken little finger to bat for nearly two hours before becoming the fifth victim of Greg Smith's seldom-seen off-spin with 16 balls still remaining – and Murtagh and Burton survived, boosting Middlesex's chances of avoiding a first-ever wooden spoon, which they did when Leicestershire slumped to a heavy defeat in their final match.
Close of play: First day, Derbyshire 72-1 (Madsen 26, Park 9); Second day, Middlesex 75-2 (Compton 42); Third day, Derbyshire 196-2 (Rogers 75, Smith 3).

Derbyshire

*C. J. L. Rogers c Simpson b Murtagh	25	– not out	112
W. L. Madsen c Housego b Burton	167	– c Kartik b Udal	89
G. T. Park b Burton	28	– b Malan	3
G. M. Smith b Kartik	62	– not out	42
W. W. Hinds c Simpson b Burton	28		
J. L. Sadler not out	12		
†D. J. Pipe not out	38		
B 5, l-b 14, w 2, n-b 20	41	B 20, l-b 11, w 2, n-b 2	35

1/46 (1) 2/142 (3) (5 wkts dec, 90 overs) 401 1/181 (2) (2 wkts dec, 54.1 overs) 281
3/271 (4) 4/350 (2) 5/351 (5)   2/193 (3)

G. G. Wagg, T. D. Groenewald, M. A. K. Lawson and P. S. Jones did not bat.

Murtagh 22–2–83–1; Burton 22–1–121–3; Berg 13–2–45–0; Kartik 19–3–72–1; Udal 14–1–61–0.
Second Innings—Murtagh 6–2–21–0; Burton 13–0–60–0; Berg 6–0–35–0; Kartik 5–0–25–0;
Udal 6–0–27–1; Malan 15–0–66–1; Dexter 2.1–0–5–0; Housego 1–0–11–0.

Middlesex

D. M. Housego lbw b Jones	4	– b Groenewald	34
N. R. D. Compton b Groenewald	178	– lbw b Groenewald	8
D. J. Malan run out	21	– c Pipe b Smith	52
N. J. Dexter c Rogers b Jones	13	– b Park	34
†J. A. Simpson c Pipe b Smith	9	– lbw b Smith	1
G. K. Berg c Madsen b Jones	70	– b Smith	0
*S. D. Udal b Jones	20	– (8) b Smith	0
M. Kartik c Jones b Smith	1	– (9) c Rogers b Lawson	22
T. J. Murtagh c Jones b Wagg	14	– (10) not out	18
D. A. Burton not out	2	– (11) not out	0
A. B. London not out	4	– (7) lbw b Smith	65
L-b 5, n-b 12	17	B 5, l-b 10, n-b 10	25

1/9 (1) 2/75 (3) (9 wkts dec, 87 overs) 353 1/34 (2) (9 wkts, 85 overs) 259
3/105 (4) 4/122 (5) 5/257 (6)   2/59 (1) 3/135 (4)
6/280 (7) 7/295 (8) 8/341 (9)   4/136 (5) 5/142 (6) 6/143 (3)
9/349 (2)   7/149 (8) 8/206 (9) 9/254 (7)

Wagg 26–3–97–1; Jones 19–4–69–4; Smith 18–1–73–2; Groenewald 12–3–60–1; Lawson
10–1–41–0; Park 2–0–8–0. *Second Innings*—Jones 14–3–36–0; Wagg 19–2–61–0; Lawson
12–3–32–1; Smith 23–7–65–5; Groenewald 14–4–42–2; Park 3–0–8–1.

Umpires: R. T. Robinson and P. Willey.

NORTHAMPTONSHIRE

Conspiracy and coincidence

ANDREW RADD

For older supporters still smarting from Colin Ingleby-Mackenzie's declaration at Bournemouth in 1965, which arguably cost Northamptonshire that still-awaited first Championship title, the events of late September 2009 reopened many wounds. One of the largest victories in the club's history, over Leicestershire in the final round of matches, left Northamptonshire in line for promotion from the second division with a day of the season remaining. Only a win for Essex, from an unpromising position at Derby, could deny them.

Cue Derbyshire's decision to set a last-afternoon target, a televised successful run-chase which prompted a mixture of disappointment and disbelief around Wantage Road – and, a little later, enough conspiracy theories (relating mostly to Chris Rogers's departure from Northamptonshire in 2007, and the home game against Derbyshire in July which was allowed to drift to a draw) to keep the film director Oliver Stone in business for a year or two.

To his credit, head coach David Capel declined to get involved in the post-Derby post mortem. "If things had gone differently for us against Surrey [who played out a dogged final day at The Oval to earn a draw] and Essex [who triumphed with a ball to spare at Chelmsford] it would have been in our own hands," he said, "and we wouldn't have been relying on Derbyshire." It might also have helped if Nicky Boje had not lost the toss in every home Championship match.

Instead, Capel emphasised the season's pluses. Six Championship victories constituted Northamptonshire's best effort since they were last promoted in 2003, and they also reached Twenty20 Cup finals day for the first time. Sussex dashed hopes of a first major limited-overs title in 17 years, with a seven-wicket semi-final victory, admittedly with only two balls to spare.

Fully fit, and free from the distractions that delayed his debut the previous summer (when his eligibility was initially in doubt following his appearances in the unauthorised Indian Cricket League), Andrew Hall did most to bring about the overall improvement. The leading run-scorer and a reliable member of the seam attack in Championship cricket, he also shone in the shorter game, and demonstrated whole-hearted commitment throughout. Hall, Johan van der Wath and short-term signing Ian Harvey were a formidable trio of all-rounders to boost the Twenty20 campaign, which also featured some eye-catching efforts from 19-year-old David Willey.

The emergence of Willey, a product of Northamptonshire's academy (run by former captain David Ripley), delighted those followers desperate to see some local talent in the first team again. He was the first Northamptonshire-born cricketer to make the side since Tim Roberts in 2005, and launched his first-class career by hitting an impressive 60 in a match between his

Sean Dempsey, PA Photos

Andrew Hall

father Peter's two counties – Northamptonshire and Leicestershire. Northants Cricket's new "player pathway" envisages the recruitment of more home-grown youngsters: a welcome (if perhaps overdue) statement of intent. The other notable effort from a younger player was Alex Wakely's maiden Championship century, at Cardiff in June. Following a miserable 2008, Wakely re-emerged as a rising star.

The team achieved what it did without David Sales who, after not missing a four-day match since June 2002, was ruled out for the entire summer by a knee injury that necessitated reconstructive surgery. It was a bitter disappointment for Northamptonshire's most consistent scorer of recent seasons, but he expressed his determination to be back in harness for 2010. On the subject of happy returns, Mal Loye opted to re-sign for his native county on a two-year contract, wishing to end his playing career on home soil. A top order boasting Stephen Peters (the only batsman apart from Hall to reach 1,000 runs in the Championship), Rob White, Niall O'Brien, Loye and a fit-again Sales ought to prove potent and popular.

Spin bowling no longer rules at Northampton. Boje, who led the side purposefully from start to finish and agreed to stay for another season, was easily the pick of the slow men. But Monty Panesar's oft-stated desire to regain his Test place following his batting heroics in the Ashes opener at Cardiff did not translate into county wickets – he managed only 18 in 13 Championship matches, and was left out of the final game. It was a far cry from Allan Lamb's usual response to being dropped by England, which generally involved a match-winning performance or two until the selectors saw sense. After the season Northamptonshire – worried at covering Panesar's salary after he lost his England contract – allowed him to join Sussex. Graeme White, another slow left-armer, grew frustrated at the lack of opportunities and moved to Nottinghamshire, while the off-spinner James Middlebrook arrived from Essex.

Of the seamers, Hall, van der Wath, David Lucas and David Wigley all had their moments. Left-armer Lucas enjoyed far and away his most successful season as he turned 31. Skilfully controlled swing, reminiscent of Paul Taylor at his best, brought 60 first-class wickets, including 12 for 73 in the win over Gloucestershire at Cheltenham, the best match return for Northamptonshire since Anil Kumble claimed 13 Hampshire wickets at Northampton in 1995. Lucas was Hall's only serious rival for the player of the year.

Lower down the age scale, 17-year-old Robert Keogh from Dunstable impressed club officials as a batsman/off-spinner, and earned a place on the academy for 2010, as did a promising young fast bowler from Norfolk named... Oliver Stone. Coincidence? Some would doubtless have you believe otherwise.

NORTHAMPTONSHIRE RESULTS

All first-class matches – Played 17: Won 6, Lost 5, Drawn 6.
County Championship matches – Played 16: Won 6, Lost 4, Drawn 6.

LV County Championship, 3rd in Division 2; Friends Provident Trophy, 5th in Group D;
Pro40 League, 4th in Division 2; Twenty20 Cup, s-f.

COUNTY CHAMPIONSHIP AVERAGES, BATTING AND FIELDING

Cap		M	I	NO	R	HS	100s	50s	Avge	Ct/St
2009	A. J. Hall¶	16	25	2	1,161	159	2	6	50.47	16
2007	S. D. Peters.	14	25	1	1,050	175	3	5	43.75	12
2008	N. Boje¶.	15	25	4	801	98	0	8	40.05	7
2008	R. A. White	16	29	4	986	193	1	7	39.44	11
	M. H. Wessels¶	14	23	0	804	109	1	6	34.95	25/1
2009	J. J. van der Wath¶.	13	19	1	452	85	0	3	25.11	4
	N. J. O'Brien	8	14	0	346	128	1	0	24.71	32/1
	A. G. Wakely	11	18	1	394	113*	1	1	23.17	9
	D. J. Willey†	9	15	1	310	60	0	1	22.14	2
	B. H. N. Howgego	5	9	1	164	47	0	0	20.50	3
2009	D. S. Lucas.	15	23	7	290	55*	0	1	18.12	5
	M. A. G. Nelson	3	5	0	88	38	0	0	17.60	2
2006	M. S. Panesar‡	13	20	5	182	38	0	0	12.13	0
	D. H. Wigley	11	14	8	58	10*	0	0	9.66	5
	L. M. Daggett.	5	4	0	3	2	0	0	0.75	1

Also batted: J. A. Brooks (2 matches) 0*, 10* (1 ct); S. P. Crook (2 matches) 16, 55, 13 (2 ct); P. W. Harrison (2 matches) 32, 3, 18; D. Murphy (2 matches) 14, 14, 2 (7 ct); G. G. White (1 match) 0, 29*.

† *Born in Northamptonshire.*   ‡ *ECB contract.*   ¶ *Other non-England-qualified player.*

BOWLING

	O	M	R	W	BB	5W/i	Avge
D. S. Lucas	393.3	83	1,224	58	7-24	3	21.10
A. J. Hall	310.2	76	911	40	5-29	1	22.77
J. J. van der Wath	364.3	75	1,237	50	5-71	1	24.74
N. Boje	311	81	891	30	4-59	0	29.70
D. H. Wigley	284.1	54	1,090	30	6-72	2	36.33
M. S. Panesar.	412.1	89	1,070	18	3-55	0	59.44

Also bowled: J. A. Brooks 50–5–184–7; S. P. Crook 48–8–193–6; L. M. Daggett 88–15–311–8; A. G. Wakely 11–0–64–0; M. H. Wessels 1–1–0–0; G. G. White 4–0–13–0; D. J. Willey 42.4–4–185–4.

COUNTY RECORDS

Highest score for:	331*	M. E. K. Hussey v Somerset at Taunton	2003
Highest score against:	333	K. S. Duleepsinhji (Sussex) at Hove	1930
Leading run-scorer:	28,980	D. Brookes (avge 36.13)	1934–1959
Best bowling for:	10-127	V. W. C. Jupp v Kent at Tunbridge Wells.	1932
Best bowling against:	10-30	C. Blythe (Kent) at Northampton	1907
Leading wicket-taker:	1,102	E. W. Clark (avge 21.26).	1922–1947
Highest total for:	781-7 dec	v Nottinghamshire at Northampton	1995
Highest total against:	673-8 dec	by Yorkshire at Leeds	2003
Lowest total for:	12	v Gloucestershire at Gloucester	1907
Lowest total against:	33	by Lancashire at Northampton.	1977

ADDRESS

County Ground, Wantage Road, Northampton NN1 4TJ (01604 514455; **email** reception@nccc.co.uk). **Website** www.northantscricket.com

OFFICIALS

Captain N. Boje
First-team coach D. J. Capel
Director of academy D. Ripley
President Lord Naseby

Chairman M. Lawrence
Chief executive M. J. Tagg
Head groundsman P. Marshall
Scorer A. C. Kingston

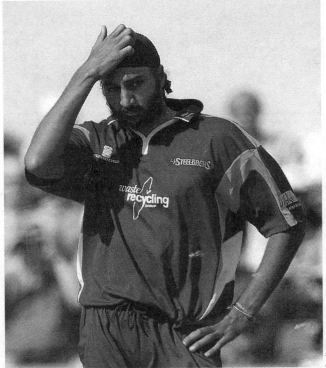

Career heading south: after a difficult 2009, Monty Panesar aimed to revive his fortunes by moving to Sussex.

At Northampton, April 11, 12, 13 (not first-class). **Drawn.** Toss: Cardiff UCCE. **Cardiff UCCE 141-5 dec.** (M. A. Jones 58; R. A. G. Cummins 3-21); **Northamptonshire 183-5 dec.** (R. A. White 43, D. S. Bendon 53*, Extras 40). *County debuts: D. S. Bendon, J. A. Brooks, R. A. G. Cummins, J. W. Johnson, D. J. Willey.*

There was no play on the first two days.

At Leicester, April 15, 16, 17, 18. NORTHAMPTONSHIRE drew with LEICESTERSHIRE.

At Canterbury, April 21, 22, 23, 24. NORTHAMPTONSHIRE drew with KENT.

NORTHAMPTONSHIRE v GLOUCESTERSHIRE

At Northampton, April 28, 29, 30, May 1. Gloucestershire won by 44 runs. Gloucestershire 19 pts, Northamptonshire 3 pts. Toss: Gloucestershire.

After dominating for three days, Gloucestershire were made to work hard for their first Championship victory for 20 months as Northamptonshire belatedly discovered their fighting spirit in pursuit of an unlikely target of 371. Injuries to Saxelby, Gidman and Franklin, which obliged 51-year-old coach John Bracewell to come on as a substitute fielder (another sub, Craig Spearman, took four good catches at slip), put heavy responsibility on to the remaining bowlers. They proved equal to the task, although it took three quick wickets with the second new ball to settle the issue after Northamptonshire – reeling at 102 for five on the third afternoon – rallied strongly. Hall put on 116 with Willey, who drove well through the covers, and 65 with Crook, but he finally fell to the fifth ball of a new spell from Gidman, who was cautiously testing out his back after an earlier spasm. Wigley made the most of van der Wath's absence to return career-best bowling figures, but Kirby's pace and the probing left-arm spin of Banerjee (who comfortably outshone Panesar) gave Gloucestershire a substantial lead, which they consolidated after the loss of Porterfield to the first ball of their second innings – the first of five catches for his Ireland team-mate O'Brien.

Close of play: First day, Gloucestershire 287-8 (Saxelby 54, Banerjee 5); Second day, Gloucestershire 105-1 (Kadeer Ali 24, Marshall 68); Third day, Northamptonshire 200-5 (Hall 50, Willey 43).

Gloucestershire

Kadeer Ali b Lucas	9	– (2) c White b Wigley	45
W. T. S. Porterfield c O'Brien b Wigley	25	– (1) c O'Brien b Lucas	0
H. J. H. Marshall c Wessels b Hall	12	– b Boje	69
*A. P. R. Gidman c Hall b Wigley	39	– (8) c O'Brien b Lucas	1
C. G. Taylor c Wakely b Wigley	32	– (4) c O'Brien b Wigley	55
J. E. C. Franklin b Boje	38	– c O'Brien b Hall	11
†S. D. Snell c Wessels b Wigley	47	– (5) c Crook b Wigley	11
J. Lewis lbw b Boje	0	– (7) c Hall b Panesar	0
I. D. Saxelby not out	60	– (11) not out	5
V. Banerjee c Wakely b Wigley	6	– (9) c O'Brien b Lucas	16
S. P. Kirby b Wigley	0	– (10) lbw b Lucas	3
B 5, l-b 14, w 1, n-b 6	26	B 2, l-b 8, w 11	21

1/17 (1) 2/37 (2) 3/57 (3) 4/135 (5) (101 overs) 294
5/136 (4) 6/213 (6) 7/213 (8)
8/262 (7) 9/294 (10) 10/294 (11)

1/0 (1) 2/107 (3) (67.4 overs) 237
3/140 (2) 4/152 (5)
5/192 (6) 6/193 (7) 7/207 (8)
8/207 (4) 9/222 (10) 10/237 (9)

Crook 15–2–62–0; Lucas 17–3–32–1; Wigley 25–5–72–6; Hall 15–5–22–1; Panesar 13–2–49–0; Willey 5–0–19–0; Boje 11–4–19–2. *Second Innings*—Lucas 12.4–3–39–4; Wigley 20–3–80–3; Panesar 17–2–49–1; Crook 6–1–23–0; Boje 7–3–23–1; Hall 5–0–13–1.

Northamptonshire

R. A. White c Kirby	26 – c Snell b Marshall	23
†N. J. O'Brien lbw b Lewis	13 – lbw b Lewis	9
A. G. Wakely c sub (C. M. Spearman) b Kirby	4 – b Lewis	1
*N. Boje c sub (C. M. Spearman) b Banerjee	58 – (5) c Taylor b Banerjee	17
M. H. Wessels lbw b Banerjee	23 – (4) c Snell b Kirby	50
A. J. Hall c Snell b Lewis	5 – lbw b Gidman	91
D. J. Willey c sub (C. M. Spearman) b Banerjee	3 – c Porterfield b Banerjee	47
S. P. Crook b Kirby	16 – b Lewis	55
D. S. Lucas c Kadeer Ali b Banerjee	2 – c sub (C. M. Spearman) b Kirby	13
M. S. Panesar lbw b Kirby	0 – not out	5
D. H. Wigley not out	0 – c Porterfield b Kirby	0
L-b 3, n-b 8	11 B 1, l-b 8, n-b 6	15

1/48 (1) 2/48 (2) 3/74 (3) 4/117 (5) (60.1 overs) 161
5/128 (6) 6/142 (4) 7/151 (7)
8/161 (8) 9/161 (9) 10/161 (10)

1/17 (2) 2/25 (3)   (89.5 overs) 326
3/60 (1) 4/98 (5)
5/102 (4) 6/218 (7) 7/283 (6)
8/321 (9) 9/321 (8) 10/326 (11)

Franklin 8–2–23–0; Kirby 14.1–2–41–4; Lewis 12–5–24–2; Banerjee 21–5–62–4; Taylor 5–2–8–0. *Second Innings*—Lewis 23–5–85–3; Kirby 20.5–3–76–3; Marshall 2–0–19–1; Banerjee 32–6–90–2; Kadeer Ali 4–0–15–0; Franklin 2–0–14–0; Taylor 2–0–7–0; Gidman 4–0–11–1.

Umpires: R. J. Bailey and K. Coburn.

NORTHAMPTONSHIRE v ESSEX

At Northampton, May 6, 7, 8, 9. Northamptonshire won by eight wickets. Northamptonshire 21 pts, Essex 4 pts. Toss: Essex.

Essex were left chasing the game following a first-day batting collapse, and Northamptonshire never loosened their grip once Hall, who had an outstanding match, had broken the 94-run opening stand between Chopra and Mickleburgh. Hall finished with five for 29, his best first-class figures in England. The late arrival of Panesar, released from the England squad for the Lord's Test against West Indies, had little bearing on proceedings as Essex lost their last nine wickets for 83, and Northamptonshire secured a formidable lead through White, Wessels (who survived being bowled by a Napier no-ball) and the ubiquitous Hall. The quick loss of their openers late on the second day left Essex in deep trouble, and it took a gritty innings from Foster, who hit a six and 11 fours from 169 balls, to keep his side afloat. Had Hall managed to hold a sharp return chance offered by Foster before he had scored, the match would surely have been over much earlier. As it was, Northamptonshire galloped to their modest target with White hoisting Walker for six to wrap it up.

Close of play: First day, Northamptonshire 63-1 (White 39); Second day, Essex 41-2 (Walker 15, Pettini 6); Third day, Northamptonshire 16-0 (White 9, O'Brien 7).

Essex

V. Chopra c Crook b Hall	42 – c O'Brien b Crook	0
J. C. Mickleburgh c Boje b Hall	62 – b Lucas	16
M. J. Walker c White b Wigley	16 – b Panesar	35
*M. L. Pettini c White b Wigley	3 – lbw b Wigley	29
†J. S. Foster c Hall b Boje	38 – c White b Crook	84
R. N. ten Doeschate c O'Brien b Crook	10 – c Nelson b Boje	45
J. D. Middlebrook c O'Brien b Hall	18 – c O'Brien b Crook	19
G. R. Napier c Willey b Boje	7 – lbw b Crook	16
C. J. C. Wright c Wigley b Hall	2 – not out	16
Danish Kaneria lbw b Hall	0 – c Wigley b Crook	17
M. A. Chambers not out	0 – lbw b Hall	5
L-b 13, w 2, n-b 8	23 B 6, l-b 11, w 1, n-b 8	26

1/94 (1) 2/138 (2) 3/138 (3)   (76.1 overs) 221
4/153 (4) 5/182 (6) 6/199 (5)
7/211 (7) 8/221 (8) 9/221 (9) 10/221 (10)

1/2 (1) 2/30 (2)   (108.4 overs) 308
3/78 (3) 4/102 (4)
5/177 (6) 6/227 (7) 7/264 (5)
8/275 (8) 9/301 (10) 10/308 (11)

Crook 12–2–37–1; Lucas 13–4–27–0; Daggett 8–1–31–0; Wigley 17–4–61–2; Hall 13.1–4–29–5; Panesar 4–0–9–0; Boje 9–2–14–2. *Second Innings*—Crook 15–3–71–5; Lucas 21–8–59–1; Wigley 22–7–66–1; Panesar 27–11–33–1; Hall 15.4–4–42–1; Boje 8–2–20–1.

Northamptonshire

R. A. White c Foster b Wright	70	– not out	76
†N. J. O'Brien c Wright b Napier	23	– c Mickleburgh b Middlebrook	29
M. H. Wessels b Danish Kaneria	84	– c ten Doeschate b Danish Kaneria	24
*N. Boje c Middlebrook b Wright	0	– not out	34
M. A. G. Nelson c Chopra b Napier	27		
A. J. Hall c ten Doeschate b Middlebrook	58		
D. J. Willey c Foster b Napier	30		
S. P. Crook c Pettini b Wright	13		
D. S. Lucas lbw b Danish Kaneria	13		
M. S. Panesar b Napier	4		
D. H. Wigley not out	4		
B 5, l-b 6, n-b 17	28	B 4, l-b 2, w 1, n-b 6	13

1/63 (2) 2/122 (1) 3/122 (4) (91.5 overs) 354 1/81 (2) (2 wkts, 39.2 overs) 176
4/195 (5) 5/245 (3) 6/311 (6) 2/113 (3)
7/326 (8) 8/340 (7) 9/350 (9) 10/354 (10)

Panesar replaced L. M. Daggett after being released from the England squad.

Napier 23.5–5–107–4; Wright 22–2–77–3; Chambers 15–4–59–0; Danish Kaneria 18–5–46–2; ten Doeschate 9–1–49–0; Middlebrook 4–2–5–1. *Second Innings*—Napier 7–0–37–0; Wright 8–1–37–0; Danish Kaneria 15–3–44–1; Chambers 2–0–20–0; Middlebrook 6–1–21–1; Walker 1.2–0–11–0.

Umpires: N. G. B. Cook and G. Sharp.

NORTHAMPTONSHIRE v SURREY

At Northampton, June 11, 12, 13, 14. Surrey won by an innings and 95 runs. Surrey 21 pts, Northamptonshire 3 pts. Toss: Surrey. County debut: D. Murphy.

To the relief of Surrey's players, supporters and management alike, they ended a sequence of 19 Championship matches since September 2007 without a victory, winning early on the final morning thanks largely to outstanding individual performances from two Northamptonshire old boys – fittingly, perhaps, since the annual players' reunion took place during this match. Butcher's decision to bowl first on a Wantage Road pitch tinged with green paid handsome dividends as Nel's hostility and skilful use of the conditions undid his former county on the opening day. Then Afzaal, who left Northamptonshire at the end of 2007, hit the first double-century of his career after the home seamers had threatened to retrieve the situation by reducing Surrey to 94 for four. Afzaal's innings spanned 554 minutes and 427 balls, and featured two sixes and 27 fours; he added 149 for the seventh wicket with Ryan Harris, the Queensland all-rounder who, despite needing a runner because of a knee injury, attacked the bowling with relish and narrowly missed out on a maiden first-class century. Trailing by 321, Northamptonshire struggled against Schofield's leg-spin and would have capitulated with a full day to spare but for Peters, seventh out after an admirably resilient innings.

Close of play: First day, Surrey 113-4 (Afzaal 22, Batty 13); Second day, Surrey 428-7 (Afzaal 156, Murtaza Hussain 17); Third day, Northamptonshire 189-7 (van der Wath 9, Lucas 4).

Northamptonshire

S. D. Peters c Ramprakash b Dernbach	59	– c Butcher b Schofield		78
R. A. White c Batty b Nel	6	– c Batty b Nel		8
M. A. G. Nelson c Batty b Nel	12	– lbw b Dernbach		1
*N. Boje c Batty b Dernbach	4	– c Brown b Schofield		15
D. J. Willey c Harris b Nel	4	– lbw b Schofield		1
A. J. Hall b Harris	23	– c Newman b Murtaza Hussain		45
†D. Murphy c Batty b Nel	14	– b Dernbach		14
J. J. van der Wath c sub (S. J. Walters) b Nel	28	– c Afzaal b Schofield		35
D. S. Lucas b Nel	0	– lbw b Schofield		4
M. S. Panesar c Batty b Dernbach	38	– not out		6
D. H. Wigley not out	2	– c Nel b Murtaza Hussain		1
B 4, l-b 10, w 1, n-b 4	19	B 7, l-b 6, w 1, n-b 4		18

1/31 (2) 2/55 (3) 3/66 (4) 4/97 (1) (59.2 overs) 209
5/107 (5) 6/123 (6) 7/145 (7)
8/147 (9) 9/205 (8) 10/209 (10)

1/28 (2) 2/33 (3) (76.4 overs) 226
3/57 (4) 4/65 (5)
5/141 (6) 6/162 (7) 7/184 (1)
8/194 (9) 9/223 (8) 10/226 (11)

Nel 19–3–36–6; Harris 16.5–1–69–1; Dernbach 16.3–3–74–3; Murtaza Hussain 7–2–16–0. *Second Innings*—Nel 14–3–37–1; Dernbach 12–2–56–2; Schofield 21–5–40–5; Murtaza Hussain 27.4–3–72–2; Afzaal 2–1–8–0.

Surrey

S. A. Newman c Murphy b van der Wath	10	A. Nel b Wigley		6
M. J. Brown b Lucas	12	J. W. Dernbach c White b van der Wath		19
M. R. Ramprakash b Wigley	17			
*M. A. Butcher c van der Wath b Wigley	32	B 8, l-b 15, w 5, n-b 6, p 5		39
U. Afzaal not out	204			
†J. N. Batty c Murphy b Lucas	48			
C. P. Schofield c Peters b Lucas	15	1/21 (2) 2/24 (1) 3/73 (4)	(164 overs)	530
R. J. Harris lbw b Wigley	94	4/94 (3) 5/224 (6) 6/244 (7)		
Murtaza Hussain c Murphy b Boje	34	7/393 (8) 8/462 (9) 9/471 (10)		
		10/530 (11)	120 overs:	399-7

Van der Wath 22–5–76–2; Lucas 26–5–83–3; Wigley 35–4–134–4; Hall 22–6–55–0; Panesar 28–9–69–0; Boje 26–8–66–1; Willey 5–2–19–0.

Umpires: S. A. Garratt and V. A. Holder.

At Cardiff, June 16, 17, 18, 19. NORTHAMPTONSHIRE drew with GLAMORGAN.

NORTHAMPTONSHIRE v DERBYSHIRE

At Northampton, July 7, 8, 9, 10. Drawn. Northamptonshire 11 pts, Derbyshire 12 pts. Toss: Derbyshire.

A combination of poor weather – which allowed only eight overs on the opening day – and the two sides' inability to agree a formula for overcoming that loss of play killed off any prospect of a positive result. Nearly three months later, as Essex successfully chased a target at Derby to deny Northamptonshire promotion, some supporters were heard to wonder whether this disappointing contest might have had any bearing on the events of the Championship season's final afternoon. Hayward made early inroads, and then Needham's off-spin proved dangerous, but otherwise the Derbyshire attack lacked bite; Peters was the main beneficiary, extending his 20th first-class century to 175 before van der Wath clobbered 82 from 71 balls, with six sixes and seven fours. After that Redfern, just 19, again underlined his outstanding potential, but missed out on a maiden century when Boje bowled him. Redfern put on 237 for the fourth wicket with Hinds, who hit 20 fours and five sixes, as Derbyshire extended their innings well into the final day.

Close of play: First day, Northamptonshire 23-1 (Peters 11, White 10); Second day, Derbyshire 11-0 (Rogers 7, Stubbings 2); Third day, Derbyshire 371-4 (Hinds 133, Smith 0).

Northamptonshire

S. D. Peters c Rogers b Hayward	175	– not out	64
B. H. N. Howgego c Rogers b Hayward	0	– lbw b Smith	36
R. A. White lbw b Hayward	18	– not out	1
A. G. Wakely c Stubbings b Hayward	4		
†M. H. Wessels lbw b Smith	27		
*N. Boje c and b Needham	30		
A. J. Hall b Pipe b Needham	52		
D. J. Willey st Pipe b Needham	5		
J. J. van der Wath c Hayward b Hunter	82		
D. S. Lucas not out	12		
B 1, l-b 7, n-b 20	28	W 1, n-b 2	3

1/1 (2) 2/38 (3)   (9 wkts dec, 96.4 overs) 433   1/98 (2)   (1 wkt, 41 overs) 104
3/54 (4) 4/89 (5) 5/143 (6)
6/250 (7) 7/292 (8) 8/369 (1) 9/433 (9)

D. H. Wigley did not bat.

Hayward 22–2–99–4; Hunter 15.4–2–90–1; Clare 18–3–92–0; Smith 20–3–81–1; Needham 16–2–47–3; Hinds 2–1–4–0; Park 3–0–12–0. *Second Innings*—Clare 6–2–15–0; Hunter 6–1–17–0; Smith 9–1–32–1; Needham 14–2–25–0; Redfern 6–0–15–0.

Derbyshire

*C. J. L. Rogers lbw b Hall	49	I. D. Hunter b Lucas	7
S. D. Stubbings lbw b van der Wath	42		
G. T. Park c Wessels b van der Wath	33	B 3, l-b 5, w 6, n-b 6	20
D. J. Redfern b Boje	95		
W. W. Hinds lbw b van der Wath	148		(9 wkts dec, 135.5 overs) 502
G. M. Smith b Wigley	22	1/82 (1)	
†D. J. Pipe c Howgego b Lucas	63	2/132 (3) 3/133 (2)	
J. L. Clare c Hall b Wigley	6	4/370 (4) 5/400 (5) 6/433 (6)	
J. Needham not out	17	7/451 (8) 8/492 (7) 9/502 (10)	
		120 overs: 451-7	

M. Hayward did not bat.

Van der Wath 26–3–97–3; Lucas 19.5–5–64–2; Wigley 25–7–96–2; Hall 20–8–52–1; Boje 32–8–111–1; Wakely 9–0–45–0; Willey 4–0–29–0.

Umpires: M. R. Benson and P. J. Hartley.

At Cheltenham, July 20, 21, 22. NORTHAMPTONSHIRE beat GLOUCESTERSHIRE by nine wickets. *David Lucas takes 12 for 73 in the match.*

At Northampton, July 24, 25, 26. NORTHAMPTONSHIRE lost to AUSTRALIANS by 135 runs (see Australian tour section).

At Lord's, July 31, August 1, 2, 3. NORTHAMPTONSHIRE beat MIDDLESEX by 35 runs.

NORTHAMPTONSHIRE v KENT

At Northampton, August 11, 12, 13, 14. Kent won by 238 runs. Kent 18 pts, Northamptonshire 4 pts. Toss: Kent.

Kent's promotion challenge received a substantial boost with victory in a match that featured, by way of an intriguing sub-plot, the efforts of Key and Panesar to impress the England selectors ahead of the final and decisive Ashes Test at The Oval. Key hit 90 from 134 balls on the opening day, but then his side lost seven wickets for 74, while Panesar accounted for van Jaarsveld – caught in the covers via silly point's leg – and Cook. The visitors claimed a narrow but psychologically significant lead thanks to Tredwell, who passed 50 wickets for the season, and built on it through a century partnership between Jones and van Jaarsveld, after Key (to his obvious frustration) had departed cheaply and Denly had reached his half-century with a six that broke a committee-room window. Northamptonshire were left to score 329 on the final day, and never threatened to get close, succumbing to Tredwell's off-spin for the second time. His match return of ten for 100 secured Kent's sixth win of the season, and only Kent old boy O'Brien offered any meaningful resistance.

Close of play: First day, Northamptonshire 38-1 (O'Brien 11, White 13); Second day, Northamptonshire 147-5 (Wessels 47, Hall 0); Third day, Kent 220-2 (Jones 85, van Jaarsveld 52).

Kent

J. L. Denly c White b Lucas	15	– c White b Boje	59
*R. W. T. Key lbw b Hall	90	– c Wessels b Lucas	15
†G. O. Jones c Lucas b Wigley	11	– b Boje	93
M. van Jaarsveld c Wakely b Panesar	19	– not out	100
S. A. Northeast lbw b van der Wath	35	– c and b Boje	3
D. I. Stevens b van der Wath	20	– c Wigley b Boje	1
J. M. Kemp lbw b Hall	12	– not out	18
J. C. Tredwell c Wakely b Boje	10		
S. J. Cook c Wessels b Panesar	6		
R. S. Ferley c O'Brien b van der Wath	17		
P. Edwards not out	0		
L-b 4, w 1, n-b 4	9	L-b 5, w 2, n-b 6	13

1/24 (1) 2/63 (3) 3/100 (4)   (80.4 overs) 244   1/32 (2)   (5 wkts dec, 88.4 overs) 302
4/170 (2) 5/196 (6) 6/197 (5)   2/117 (1) 3/237 (3)
7/212 (7) 8/219 (9) 9/239 (8) 10/244 (10)   4/251 (5) 5/255 (6)

Van der Wath 12.4–2–32–3; Lucas 13–2–47–1; Wigley 10–3–31–1; Panesar 22–6–56–2; Boje 11–1–53–1; Hall 12.5–5–21–2. *Second Innings*—van der Wath 16–5–43–0; Lucas 7–2–42–1; Panesar 21.4–1–71–0; Hall 12.5–5–24–0; Boje 20–2–59–4; Wigley 11–1–52–0; Wakely 1–0–6–0.

Northamptonshire

S. D. Peters c Jones b Cook	8	– lbw b Cook	1
†N. J. O'Brien c Kemp b Edwards	16	– c and b Ferley	41
R. A. White c Kemp b Edwards	21	– c Tredwell b Cook	11
A. G. Wakely c Key b Tredwell	33	– lbw b Tredwell	4
M. H. Wessels c Jones b Tredwell	74	– c Stevens b Tredwell	4
*N. Boje b Ferley	9	– lbw b Ferley	6
A. J. Hall c Northeast b Tredwell	19	– lbw b Tredwell	2
J. J. van der Wath c Northeast b Tredwell	2	– c Jones b Tredwell	7
M. S. Panesar b Cook	2	– c van Jaarsveld b Tredwell	7
D. S. Lucas c Northeast b Tredwell	13	– not out	2
D. H. Wigley not out	8	– c Jones b van Jaarsveld	0
B 4, l-b 7, n-b 2	13	B 2, l-b 3	5

1/16 (1) 2/53 (3) 3/56 (2)   (73.4 overs) 218   1/6 (1) 2/38 (3)   (46.1 overs) 90
4/115 (4) 5/138 (6) 6/169 (7)   3/45 (4) 4/51 (5)
7/171 (8) 8/180 (9) 9/205 (10) 10/218 (5)   5/71 (6) 6/74 (7) 7/74 (2)
                                           8/87 (9) 9/90 (8) 10/90 (11)

Cook 21–2–63–2; Edwards 12–3–26–2; Tredwell 24.4–3–68–5; Ferley 9–0–29–1; Kemp 7–0–21–0. *Second Innings*—Cook 8–3–18–2; Edwards 2–0–6–0; Tredwell 20–10–32–5; Ferley 15–4–28–2; van Jaarsveld 1.1–0–1–1.

Umpires: D. J. Millns and R. T. Robinson.

At Chesterfield, August 19, 20, 21. NORTHAMPTONSHIRE beat DERBYSHIRE by two wickets.

NORTHAMPTONSHIRE v GLAMORGAN

At Northampton, August 26, 27, 28, 29. Drawn. Northamptonshire 11 pts, Glamorgan 11 pts. Toss: Glamorgan.

The batting of Peters, Gibbs and Allenby illuminated an otherwise less than sparkling match, which never fully recovered from the loss of half the opening day's play to rain. Glamorgan's decision to bowl first on a well-grassed pitch looked sound after their seam attack made early breakthroughs, but Peters and Hall settled to add 191, giving promotion-chasing Northamptonshire a chance of maximum batting points. They failed to get them, though, losing the last five wickets for 38, and Glamorgan's reply began positively, with Gibbs hitting seven fours before perishing against Panesar, who claimed his best Championship figures of a disheartening season. Powell dropped anchor for 55 from 171 deliveries, but Allenby's identical score occupied just 50 balls, with ten fours, while both Wallace and Shantry also played attractively. But time was already running out, unless either Glamorgan claimed early wickets on the final morning or the teams were prepared to manufacture a result. In the event neither scenario unfolded, and Northamptonshire opted to occupy the crease throughout the final day, with Peters (again) and Wessels making solid contributions against the testing off-spin of Croft and Dalrymple.

Close of play: First day, Northamptonshire 224-4 (Peters 124, Hall 48); Second day, Glamorgan 149-3 (Powell 30, Dalrymple 5); Third day, Northamptonshire 19-1 (Peters 6, Wakely 4).

Northamptonshire

S. D. Peters c Rees b Croft	163	– st Wallace b Croft	86
R. A. White c Rees b Harris	0	– lbw b Harris	9
A. G. Wakely b Kruger	5	– c Rees b Croft	29
†M. H. Wessels c Wallace b Allenby	39	– b Dalrymple	92
*N. Boje run out	5	– lbw b Croft	4
A. J. Hall lbw b Allenby	89	– c Powell b Harris	25
D. J. Willey c Rees b Croft	8	– b Dalrymple	16
M. S. Panesar lbw b Croft	0	– lbw b Croft	4
D. S. Lucas b Harris	16	– not out	25
D. H. Wigley c Gibbs b Harris	10	– not out	3
J. A. Brooks not out	10		
L-b 3, w 2	5	B 8, l-b 7, n-b 4	19

1/3 (2) 2/16 (3) 3/84 (4) 4/98 (5)   (88.2 overs) **350**   1/11 (2)   (8 wkts dec, 92 overs) **312**
5/289 (6) 6/312 (1) 7/312 (8)   2/116 (3) 3/144 (1)
8/313 (7) 9/333 (10) 10/350 (9)   4/152 (5) 5/203 (6) 6/240 (7)
                                                                  7/253 (8) 8/309 (4)

Harris 17.2–2–92–3; Kruger 19–4–66–1; Shantry 11–0–68–0; Allenby 18–3–54–2; Croft 18–1–53–3; Dalrymple 5–0–14–0. *Second Innings*—Harris 17–2–60–2; Kruger 12–0–51–0; Shantry 4–0–28–0; Allenby 7–2–18–0; Croft 32–4–71–4; Dalrymple 15–3–46–2; Bragg 5–0–23–0.

Glamorgan

G. P. Rees lbw b Hall	31	A. J. Shantry lbw b Panesar	32
W. D. Bragg c Boje b Lucas	28	G. J-P. Kruger not out	5
H. H. Gibbs st Wessels b Panesar	42		
M. J. Powell c Wessels b Brooks	55	B 8, l-b 14, n-b 4	26
*J. W. M. Dalrymple lbw b Boje	27		
J. Allenby b Wigley	55	1/71 (1) 2/77 (2) (122.3 overs) **383**
†M. A. Wallace b Panesar	42	3/137 (3) 4/196 (5) 5/212 (4)
J. A. R. Harris c Wessels b Hall	26	6/299 (6) 7/317 (7) 8/338 (9)
R. D. B. Croft b Brooks	14	9/365 (8) 10/383 (10) 120 overs: 374-9

Lucas 24–3–88–1; Brooks 24–4–70–2; Wigley 18–4–78–1; Panesar 33.3–12–55–3; Hall 14–5–33–2; Boje 9–0–37–1.

Umpires: N. L. Bainton and M. A. Gough.

NORTHAMPTONSHIRE v MIDDLESEX

At Northampton, September 2, 3, 4. Northamptonshire won by six wickets. Northamptonshire 18 pts, Middlesex 5 pts. Toss: Middlesex. First-class debut: J. A. Simpson.

Northamptonshire won at a canter with a full day to spare, and climbed to second place in the division. But a sickening injury to Udal on the second morning threatened to overshadow everything else. Middlesex's captain was knocked unconscious after being struck on the back of the head by a bouncer from van der Wath, and play was halted for nearly half an hour while he received treatment. Not surprisingly, he took no further part in the match. Five stoppages for rain and bad light had made life difficult for Middlesex on the first day, and they were indebted to their new Lancashire-born wicketkeeper John Simpson, 21, whose level-headed approach took him to within 13 runs of a century on debut. Berg, a former Northamptonshire League player who appeared for the county's second team in 2004 without earning a contract, then made his point with ball and bat, but the outcome was settled by Lucas and van der Wath, who reduced Middlesex to 29 for five in their second innings. Berg's magnificent 118-ball counter-attack, and two wickets for Kartik in his first over, couldn't deny Northamptonshire.

Close of play: First day, Middlesex 205-6 (Simpson 60, Udal 0); Second day, Middlesex 17-3 (London 4, Malan 4).

Middlesex

N. R. D. Compton c O'Brien b van der Wath	4	– c O'Brien b Lucas	5
A. B. London c Peters b Hall	31	– c O'Brien b van der Wath	4
D. M. Housego c Wessels b van der Wath	9	– c O'Brien b Lucas	0
D. J. Malan c Wessels b Lucas	39	– (5) lbw b Panesar	26
N. J. Dexter c Boje b Daggett	30	– (6) c O'Brien b Lucas	1
†J. A. Simpson b Daggett	87	– (7) c O'Brien b Hall	41
G. K. Berg run out	18	– (8) not out	94
*S. D. Udal retired hurt	4	– absent hurt	
M. Kartik c Lucas b van der Wath	7	– c and b van der Wath	29
T. J. Murtagh c Wessels b Daggett	2	– lbw b Lucas	0
S. T. Finn not out	1	– (4) b van der Wath	0
B 9, l-b 6, w 2, n-b 2	19	B 3, l-b 4	7

1/4 (1) 2/21 (3) 3/97 (2) 4/97 (4)   (75 overs) 251   1/6 (1) 2/8 (3) 3/9 (4)   (59 overs) 207
5/148 (5) 6/202 (7) 7/230 (9)   4/18 (2) 5/29 (6) 6/47 (5)
8/248 (10) 9/251 (6)   7/147 (7) 8/200 (9) 9/207 (10)

In the first innings Udal retired hurt at 210.

Van der Wath 23–7–75–3; Lucas 11–4–35–1; Daggett 16–3–47–3; Panesar 8–1–31–0; Hall 16–3–42–1; Boje 1–0–6–0. *Second Innings*—Lucas 15–3–43–4; van der Wath 14–5–32–3; Panesar 7–0–26–1; Daggett 7–1–25–0; Hall 10–0–44–1; Boje 6–2–30–0.

Northamptonshire

S. D. Peters c Compton b Murtagh	0	– c Dexter b Murtagh	73
†N. J. O'Brien c Malan b Finn	1	– c Simpson b Finn	0
A. G. Wakely b Murtagh	9	– lbw b Kartik	13
M. H. Wessels c Compton b Finn	6	– lbw b Kartik	0
R. A. White b Berg	47	– not out	85
*N. Boje c Kartik b Berg	51	– not out	30
A. J. Hall c Housego b Berg	38		
J. J. van der Wath b Berg	31		
D. S. Lucas not out	25		
M. S. Panesar c Dexter b Berg	7		
L. M. Daggett c Simpson b Berg	1		
B 4, l-b 6, w 1, n-b 12	23	B 5, l-b 2, w 2, n-b 10	19

1/2 (1) 2/2 (2) 3/14 (4) 4/40 (3)   (58 overs) 239   1/4 (2)   (4 wkts, 45.4 overs) 220
5/88 (5) 6/145 (7) 7/194 (8) 8/205 (6)   2/65 (3) 3/65 (4)
9/231 (10) 10/239 (11)   4/121 (1)

Murtagh 13–4–35–2; Finn 13–2–82–3; Berg 16–1–68–5; Kartik 12–3–31–0; Dexter 4–2–13–0. *Second Innings*—Murtagh 12–1–47–1; Finn 8–1–62–1; Kartik 16–4–39–2; Berg 6–1–43–0; London 2–0–10–0; Malan 1.4–0–12–0.

Umpires: S. A. Garratt and J. F. Steele.

At The Oval, September 9, 10, 11, 12. NORTHAMPTONSHIRE drew with SURREY.

At Chelmsford, September 15, 16, 17, 18. NORTHAMPTONSHIRE lost to ESSEX by four wickets.

NORTHAMPTONSHIRE v LEICESTERSHIRE

At Northampton, September 23, 24, 25. Northamptonshire won by an innings and 196 runs. Northamptonshire 22 pts, Leicestershire 3 pts. Toss: Leicestershire.

The margin of victory – Northamptonshire's fifth-highest by an innings in the Championship since they joined in 1905 – neither flattered the home side nor did their old local rivals an injustice. Despite missing Dippenaar and Iain O'Brien, Leicestershire were out of the blocks swiftly, and reduced Northamptonshire to 44 for four after putting them in, before Wessels helped stop the rot and paved the way for Rob White (226 balls, four sixes, 27 fours) and Hall (182 balls, 23 fours) to add 268, a county sixth-wicket record against Leicestershire. It was White's first century of the summer and Hall's second, the other having also come against Leicestershire, in the first match of the season. The final session produced 212 runs from 32 overs – Northamptonshire gained maximum batting points in 88 – and Boje continued the onslaught on the second morning. After that Leicestershire appeared to have little stomach for the fight once Smith and Nixon fell to excellent catches by Wakely at short leg. Following on for the fifth time in the season – 382 adrift this time – wooden-spoonists Leicestershire had no answer to Lucas, who swung the ball skilfully to finish the match with four sessions to spare. But Northamptonshire's players and followers could only watch helplessly on television as Essex beat Derbyshire the following day to snatch the final promotion spot, by one point.

Close of play: First day, Northamptonshire 465-6 (Hall 138, Boje 14); Second day, Leicestershire 30-2 (Nixon 7).

Northamptonshire

S. D. Peters c New b Gurney	3		J. J. van der Wath b Henderson	30
†N. J. O'Brien c Taylor b Harris	6		D. S. Lucas not out	5
P. W. Harrison c New b Benning	18			
A. G. Wakely c New b Benning	5		B 5, l-b 9, w 1, n-b 11	26
M. H. Wessels lbw b Henderson	65			
R. A. White c White b Harris	193		1/9 (2) (8 wkts dec, 116.2 overs)	600
A. J. Hall c and b White	159		2/13 (1) 3/33 (3) 4/44 (4)	
*N. Boje not out	90		5/153 (5) 6/421 (6) 7/562 (7) 8/595 (9)	

L. M. Daggett did not bat.

Harris 23–1–150–2; Gurney 22–3–131–1; White 18.2–1–115–1; Benning 15–3–53–2; Henderson 33–6–116–2; Cobb 5–0–21–0.

Leicestershire

P. A. Nixon c Wakely b Boje	52	– c O'Brien b Lucas	8
*M. A. G. Boyce c Peters b Daggett	20	– c O'Brien b Lucas	12
G. P. Smith c Wakely b Hall	26	– (4) lbw b Lucas	9
J. J. Cobb c O'Brien b Hall	0	– (5) b van der Wath	1
J. W. A. Taylor c Peters b Hall	0	– (6) not out	30
†T. J. New not out	46	– (7) b Lucas	0
J. G. E. Benning c Wakely b van der Wath	19	– (8) c Lucas b Boje	72
W. A. White lbw b Lucas	4	– (10) c Wessels b Lucas	0
C. W. Henderson c O'Brien b van der Wath	10	– b Lucas	42
A. J. Harris st O'Brien b Boje	20	– (3) c O'Brien b Lucas	4
H. F. Gurney b Hall	0	– b van der Wath	0
B 4, l-b 9, w 4, n-b 4	21	L-b 6, n-b 2	8

1/51 (2) 2/106 (3) 3/106 (1)   (60.4 overs) 218   1/26 (2) 2/30 (3)   (56.4 overs) 186
4/106 (4) 5/111 (5) 6/151 (7)   3/31 (1) 4/40 (4)
7/156 (8) 8/169 (9) 9/209 (10)   5/44 (5) 6/45 (7) 7/131 (8)
10/218 (11)   8/183 (9) 9/183 (10) 10/186 (11)

Van der Wath 16–4–49–2; Lucas 12–1–50–1; Daggett 10–1–51–1; Hall 9.4–0–41–4; Boje 13–7–14–2. *Second Innings*—van der Wath 17.4–2–78–2; Lucas 16–4–45–7; Hall 9–4–22–0; Boje 11–5–10–1; Daggett 3–0–25–0.

Umpires: N. J. Llong and G. Sharp.

NOTTINGHAMSHIRE

Silver-plating masks the flaws

SIMON CLEAVES

If 2008 was a summer of tantalising possibilities for Nottinghamshire, 2009 represented the point at which frustration took over from hope, and the key question became "what now?" On the face of it, their finishing position in the Championship suggested some improvements – runners-up again, with 11 more points than the previous year, and a total of 56 batting bonus points, the most in Division One.

Those numbers, however, do little to mask the fact that, after a vibrant start to the campaign, the team did not so much stall as run into a brick wall in late June, the start of a three-month spell without a win in all competitions. That came to an end in the final Championship match, when they roused themselves to beat Sussex and secure second spot (and the cheque for £225,000 that went with it). Observers spent most of the period wondering how on earth they were maintaining a notional challenge for the title, especially as Durham twice thrashed them by an innings, demonstrating their superiority in all departments.

But while Nottinghamshire weren't winning in the Championship, those Durham games were their only defeats, and a run of seven straight draws proved enough to keep them ahead of the chasing pack. The habit of winning had slipped, however, and it was in the shorter forms of the game that the squad's shortcomings were really highlighted.

While the specialist batsmen were fragile all summer, in limited-overs cricket there was no time for the middle and lower order to rescue the situation, as they did time and time again in the Championship. The veteran Ali Brown failed to have much impact with the one-day unit, which was seen as his primary role when signed from Surrey, but he was a linchpin at No. 6 in four-day cricket. He was the second-highest scorer behind the captain Chris Read, who took his batting to new levels and finished sixth in the national averages with 1,203 at 75.

With low totals to defend, Nottinghamshire's inadequacies in the field were highlighted: few were capable of the athleticism and sharp reflexes required by the modern game. Samit Patel was actually one of the better performers in this regard, despite a public dressing-down by the England selectors over his fitness. But it was clear that his confidence was badly affected, and he endured a miserable season with the bat, managing only five half-centuries in all competitions. His promotion to front-line spinner in the absence of Graeme Swann was a tough assignment, as he was unable to provide the same consistent threat; and Jason Brown, supposed to be Swann's like-for-like replacement, took just three wickets all year. The 2010 season will be a defining one for Patel, a talented cricketer who needs to marry his ability to some basic discipline off the field.

Mike Egerton, PA Photos

Luke Fletcher

Patel's poor run meant the top-order batting became even weaker. Six different opening partnerships were tried in the Championship and the first wicket averaged just 22, worse even than in 2008. They passed 50 on only three occasions, with the common factor in all three stands being the former MCC Young Cricketer Alex Hales. Signed in 2007, his aggressive strokeplay had the pundits purring as he hit an unbeaten 150 against Worcestershire in the Pro40. It was the second-highest score by a Nottinghamshire batsman in one-day games – and they still managed to lose.

Director of cricket Mick Newell described Hales's performance as "the innings of the summer", and he can expect more regular first-team cricket next year. If Hales, a 6ft 4in right-hander, continues to produce the goods it will lessen the burden on Mark Wagh, who hit three Championship hundreds but was also dismissed for single figures on nine occasions, and on the overseas batsman, with Newell moving swiftly to secure the return of the prolific David Hussey. This is bound to have an uplifting effect on the field and in the dressing-room. Despite being available for only a month in 2009, Hussey hit two Championship hundreds and blazed 120 from 61 balls against Somerset in the Pro40, including ten sixes. His fellow-Australian Adam Voges, while a consistent scorer, did not dominate opposition bowlers in the same way.

One positive to come from such a stagnant second half of the summer was that the areas requiring improvement became clear early on. Somerset's Neil Edwards will perhaps provide an answer to the opening conundrum, and he was joined by Northamptonshire's left-arm spinner Graeme White and Lancashire's Steven Mullaney. Both have been signed with a view to freshening up the one-day line-up, and as all-rounders will go some way to filling the massive hole left by Mark Ealham, who retired at the age of 40 after a hugely distinguished career. The likes of Luke Fletcher with the ball and Paul Franks with the bat will also need to step up.

Fletcher's emergence and the quality of Andre Adams together covered for nightmare campaigns suffered by Charlie Shreck and Darren Pattinson. Both struggled with injury, and Shreck will need a smooth recovery from major knee and shoulder surgery to be ready in time for the new campaign. A fully fit Shreck, in combination with Ryan Sidebottom, England permitting, would revitalise the new-ball attack. Combine that with Hussey's game-changing ability and Read's excellence with bat and gloves, and Nottinghamshire might have a team capable of challenging once more. Whether they can overcome the excellence of Durham – and string together a coherent one-day strategy – is another question.

NOTTINGHAMSHIRE RESULTS

All first-class matches – Played 17: Won 4, Lost 2, Drawn 11.
County Championship matches – Played 16: Won 4, Lost 2, Drawn 10.

LV County Championship, 2nd in Division 1; Friends Provident Trophy, q-f;
Pro40 League, 9th in Division 1; Twenty20 Cup, 4th in North Division.

COUNTY CHAMPIONSHIP AVERAGES, BATTING AND FIELDING

Cap		M	I	NO	R	HS	100s	50s	Avge	Ct/St
2004	D. J. Hussey§	3	5	0	407	189	2	1	81.40	5
2008	A. C. Voges§	8	10	1	697	139	1	6	77.44	8
1999	C. M. W. Read	16	22	6	1,203	125	4	6	75.18	46/4
1999	P. J. Franks†	4	4	0	167	64	0	2	41.75	1
	A. D. Brown	16	24	3	849	148	1	6	40.42	18
2004	M. A. Ealham	14	20	7	493	70*	0	2	37.92	6
2007	M. A. Wagh	15	24	2	814	147	3	2	37.00	4
	A. D. Hales.	6	10	0	358	78	0	3	35.80	2
2008	S. R. Patel‡.	15	23	0	712	95	0	4	30.95	7
2007	A. R. Adams¶	11	13	1	300	84	0	1	25.00	13
	M. J. Wood.	6	9	1	200	86	0	1	25.00	0
	L. J. Fletcher†	8	8	3	121	92	0	1	24.20	0
	B. M. Shafayat†	13	21	0	485	69	0	2	23.09	13
	S. A. Newman	7	11	0	249	87	0	1	22.63	3
2004	R. J. Sidebottom‡.	7	9	3	100	46	0	0	16.66	1
2008	D. J. Pattinson	8	8	0	102	59	0	1	12.75	1
	W. I. Jefferson	3	5	0	48	21	0	0	9.60	5
2006	C. E. Shreck	11	12	7	28	12*	0	0	5.60	1

Also batted: S. C. J. Broad†‡ (1 match) 60 (2 ct); A. Carter (1 match) 4; A. Patel† (1 match) 0, 37 (2 ct); G. P. Swann‡ (cap 2005) (2 matches) 26, 0 (1 ct).

† *Born in Nottinghamshire.*   ‡ *ECB contract.*   § *Official overseas player.*   ¶ *Other non-England-qualified player.*

BOWLING

	O	M	R	W	BB	5W/i	Avge
R. J. Sidebottom	260.2	70	760	31	5-59	2	24.51
L. J. Fletcher	245.3	62	800	29	4-38	0	27.58
A. R. Adams	409	103	1,224	43	4-39	0	28.46
M. A. Ealham	387	117	983	28	5-31	1	35.10
S. R. Patel	473.2	83	1,531	32	6-84	2	47.84
C. E. Shreck	363.2	77	1,281	21	4-63	0	61.00
D. J. Pattinson	219.5	40	872	10	4-53	0	87.20

Also bowled: S. C. J. Broad 48–12–106–7; A. D. Brown 23.1–2–83–1; A. Carter 24–5–96–1; P. J. Franks 116–33–323–9; A. D. Hales 40–6–140–3; D. J. Hussey 5–2–18–0; S. A. Newman 6–1–25–0; C. M. W. Read 1–0–2–0; B. M. Shafayat 8–1–32–1; G. P. Swann 55–14–127–6; A. C. Voges 33.3–2–100–3.

COUNTY RECORDS

Highest score for:	312*	W. W. Keeton v Middlesex at The Oval	1939
Highest score against:	345	C. G. Macartney (Australians) at Nottingham . . .	1921
Leading run-scorer:	31,592	G. Gunn (avge 35.69)	1902–1932
Best bowling for:	10-66	K. Smales v Gloucestershire at Stroud.	1956
Best bowling against:	10-10	H. Verity (Yorkshire) at Leeds	1932
Leading wicket-taker:	1,653	T. G. Wass (avge 20.34)	1896–1920
Highest total for:	791	Nottinghamshire v Essex at Chelmsford	2007
Highest total against:	781-7 dec	by Northamptonshire at Northampton	1995
Lowest total for:	13	v Yorkshire at Nottingham	1901
Lowest total against:	{ 16	by Derbyshire at Nottingham.	1879
	{ 16	by Surrey at The Oval	1880

ADDRESS

County Cricket Ground, Trent Bridge, Nottingham NG2 6AG (0115 982 3000; **email** administration@nottsccc.co.uk). **Website** www.nottsccc.co.uk

OFFICIALS

Captain C. M. W. Read
Director of cricket M. Newell
Chairman P. G. Wright
Chief executive D. M. Brewer

Chairman, cricket committee P. G. Wright
Head groundsman S. Birks
Scorer L. B. Hewes

An open secret?

Trent Bridge has become known as a swing-bowler's paradise, and in recent seasons Nottinghamshire's opening batsmen have struggled to find an answer to the problems posed by the new ball. Statistics show that the home side's opening partnership has been outscored by the opposition's in each of the past four seasons, and you have to go back to August 2005 to find the last century partnership from Nottinghamshire's top two.

Some might argue that the ball has swung more with every new stand that has been built at Trent Bridge. But both Darren Bicknell and Jason Gallian – the pair responsible for that last century partnership, 115 against Middlesex – believe it has more to do with a change in mentality in the modern-day player.

Gallian, who retired in 2009, said: "The game has changed dramatically in the last four or five years, and players are going out to score at least four runs an over straight away. The first session of a Championship match has always been pretty crucial in terms of getting the shine off the ball, but now batsmen want to do that by hitting it against the boundary boards. I think a lot of that is down to Twenty20 cricket, which is seen as the way forward, and young players are gearing themselves towards that style of play – which might come at a cost."

While Gallian spent his last two seasons at Essex, Bicknell has been able to watch plenty of action at Trent Bridge following his retirement, as he still lives in the area. He said: "I don't believe it's become any harder for batsmen – and, frankly, it's up to them to adjust their game to the situation. Jason and I were pretty phlegmatic and prepared to tough it out. Perhaps that's something that comes with experience, but they have to be patient and show some discipline. There's a skill to playing the ball late, and they have to remember that it doesn't matter how you score the runs, as long as you put the totals on the board."   SIMON CLEAVES

NOTTINGHAMSHIRE v WORCESTERSHIRE

At Nottingham, April 21, 22, 23, 24. Nottinghamshire won by an innings and five runs. Nottinghamshire 21 pts, Worcestershire 5 pts. Toss: Nottinghamshire. County debut: A. A. Noffke.

Nottinghamshire's push for the Championship in 2008 foundered on a lack of runs at home, where their highest first-innings total was 268 and no one made a century until July. Supporters were therefore delighted to see Read, with his 13th first-class hundred, open the club's 2009 account at the earliest possible opportunity. He might have been beaten to it by Patel and Voges, but Patel was run out by yards after chancing a ridiculous single to Solanki at mid-off, and Voges was caught behind down the leg side. Even so, Nottinghamshire gained maximum batting points at home for the first time since July 2007, and a total of 505 proved a match-winner. Broad, making his only county appearance of the summer in any competition, followed a lovely batting cameo with his first Nottinghamshire five-for, generating pace and bounce that proved beyond anyone else. And, after the visitors lost their last four first-innings wickets for 24 to miss the follow-on target by two, Nottinghamshire wrapped up an innings victory before tea on the final day.

Close of play: First day, Nottinghamshire 334-5 (Read 69, Swann 19); Second day, Worcestershire 140-4 (Mitchell 52, Davies 14); Third day, Worcestershire 24-3 (Solanki 0, Smith 8).

Nottinghamshire

M. A. Wagh c Davies b Mason	19		A. R. Adams st Davies b Batty	4
B. M. Shafayat c Mitchell b Imran Arif	14		D. J. Pattinson run out	19
S. R. Patel run out	95			
A. C. Voges c Davies b Mason	99		B 5, l-b 8, w 2, n-b 4	19
A. D. Brown lbw b Whelan	4			
*†C. M. W. Read c Mason b Whelan	125		1/23 (1) 2/46 (2) 3/186 (3) (138.1 overs)	505
G. P. Swann c Davies b Mason	26		4/199 (5) 5/312 (4)	
S. C. J. Broad b Whelan	60		6/351 (7) 7/455 (8) 8/460 (6)	
M. A. Ealham not out	21		9/468 (10) 10/504 (11) 120 overs: 422-6	

Noffke 25–8–73–0; Mason 26–9–83–3; Imran Arif 26.4–120–1; Whelan 27–1–116–3; Batty 33.1–6–90–1; Ali 1–0–10–0.

Worcestershire

D. K. H. Mitchell c Brown b Swann	80	– c Read b Ealham	9
S. C. Moore lbw b Broad	8	– lbw b Adams	4
*V. S. Solanki c Brown b Broad	50	– (4) c Broad b Swann	64
B. F. Smith c Adams b Broad	0	– (5) b Adams	24
M. M. Ali c and b Broad	3	– (6) c Read b Ealham	8
†S. M. Davies c Adams b Patel	126	– (7) c Read b Broad	11
G. J. Batty c Read b Broad	22	– (8) lbw b Broad	3
A. A. Noffke c Shafayat b Swann	39	– (9) lbw b Patel	13
C. D. Whelan lbw b Patel	2	– (3) lbw b Adams	0
M. S. Mason c and b Swann	4	– not out	1
Imran Arif not out	1	– c Patel b Swann	3
B 5, w 2, n-b 12	19	B 3, l-b 1, n-b 2	6

1/11 (2) 2/111 (3)		(134.4 overs) 354	1/8 (2) 2/8 (3) 3/16 (1) (67.2 overs) 146
3/111 (4) 4/115 (5) 5/209 (1)			4/49 (5) 5/64 (6) 6/83 (7)
6/257 (7) 7/330 (8) 8/344 (6)			7/89 (8) 8/120 (9) 9/142 (4) 10/146 (11)
9/344 (9) 10/354 (10)		120 overs: 317-6	

Broad 31–5–79–5; Pattinson 12–0–45–0; Ealham 22–5–63–0; Adams 27–9–71–0; Swann 22.4–6–52–3; Patel 20–6–39–2. *Second Innings*—Broad 17–7–27–2; Adams 21–6–59–3; Ealham 10–4–19–2; Patel 9–3–18–1; Swann 10.2–5–19–2.

Umpires: R. J. Bailey and R. A. Kettleborough.

At Manchester, April 29, 30, May 1, 2. NOTTINGHAMSHIRE drew with LANCASHIRE.

NOTTINGHAMSHIRE v SOMERSET

At Nottingham, May 6, 7, 8, 9. Nottinghamshire won by six wickets. Nottinghamshire 19 pts, Somerset 3 pts. Toss: Somerset.

The formidable seam attack that had sustained Nottinghamshire for several years unveiled its newest member, as the 20-year-old Luke Fletcher took seven wickets in his first home Championship appearance. A strongly built, hit-the-deck bowler born and bred in Nottingham, Fletcher struck with his fourth ball and demonstrated excellent control throughout to help skittle Somerset for 138 before tea after they had won the toss. In reply, Nottinghamshire slipped to 55 for three by stumps, but only Willoughby offered a consistent threat, and they secured a 123-run lead thanks largely to a fifth-wicket century stand between Voges and Brown. Momentum swung Somerset's way after Trescothick made 98 and a wagging tail added 190 for the last five wickets to leave the hosts needing 261. At 112 for three going into the final day, the game was in the balance. But Voges continued his early-season form in another successful partnership with Brown to snuff out Somerset's hopes, and Brown finished the match in style with a six over extra cover shortly after lunch.

Close of play: First day, Nottinghamshire 55-3 (Shafayat 19, Voges 8); Second day, Somerset 137-3 (Trescothick 66, Langer 26); Third day, Nottinghamshire 112-3 (Patel 18, Voges 10).

Somerset

M. E. Trescothick c Adams b Fletcher	13	– c Shafayat b Fletcher	98
A. V. Suppiah c Read b Fletcher	0	– c Read b Adams	14
*J. L. Langer c Ealham b Adams	11	– (5) c Read b Ealham	35
J. C. Hildreth b Fletcher	2	– b Ealham	18
Z. de Bruyn c Read b Sidebottom	64	– (6) b Fletcher	54
†C. Kieswetter lbw b Adams	5	– (7) c Read b Ealham	52
P. D. Trego c Read b Adams	4	– (8) b Fletcher	23
O. A. C. Banks b Sidebottom	28	– (3) lbw b Sidebottom	4
B. J. Phillips lbw b Sidebottom	0	– c Shafayat b Adams	39
D. A. Stiff c Adams b Fletcher	9	– st Read b Patel	21
C. M. Willoughby not out	0	– not out	0
L-b 2	2	L-b 23, w 2	25

1/0 (2) 2/13 (1) 3/17 (4) 4/43 (3)　　(59.4 overs) 138
5/53 (6) 6/61 (7) 7/129 (8) 8/129 (9)
9/130 (5) 10/138 (10)

1/50 (2) 2/59 (3)　　(99 overs) 383
3/92 (4) 4/153 (5)
5/193 (1) 6/287 (7) 7/304 (6)
8/325 (8) 9/373 (10) 10/383 (9)

Sidebottom 19–7–32–3; Fletcher 16.4–8–38–4; Ealham 13–4–36–0; Adams 11–3–30–3. *Second Innings*—Sidebottom 21–3–86–1; Fletcher 22–3–71–3; Adams 23–3–70–2; Ealham 21–4–74–3; Patel 12–1–59–1.

Nottinghamshire

B. M. Shafayat c Kieswetter b Willoughby	19	– c Kieswetter b Stiff	32
A. D. Hales lbw b Willoughby	0	– c Langer b Stiff	28
M. A. Wagh c Hildreth b Phillips	10	– lbw b Willoughby	14
S. R. Patel lbw b Willoughby	11	– lbw b Willoughby	35
A. C. Voges lbw b Willoughby	63	– not out	73
A. D. Brown c Hildreth b Trego	63	– not out	63
*†C. M. W. Read c Phillips b Willoughby	41		
M. A. Ealham c Langer b Trego	5		
A. R. Adams b Trego	24		
R. J. Sidebottom c Hildreth b Stiff	13		
L. J. Fletcher not out	0		
L-b 2, w 8, n-b 2	12	B 6, l-b 4, w 6	16

1/1 (2) 2/20 (3) 3/37 (4) 4/56 (1)　　(82.5 overs) 261
5/175 (5) 6/183 (6) 7/189 (8)
8/231 (9) 9/261 (10) 10/261 (7)

1/51 (2)　　(4 wkts, 71.1 overs) 261
2/78 (1) 3/79 (3)
4/137 (4)

Willoughby 28.5–7–81–5; Phillips 15–6–30–1; Stiff 20–3–63–1; Trego 12–3–53–3; de Bruyn 2–0–13–0; Banks 3–0–13–0; Suppiah 2–0–6–0. *Second Innings*—Willoughby 24–5–89–2; Stiff 19–7–57–2; Phillips 10–1–40–0; Banks 6.1–1–22–0; Trego 4–0–21–0; de Bruyn 8–3–22–0.

Umpires: M. J. D. Bodenham and T. E. Jesty.

At Birmingham, June 6, 7, 8, 9. NOTTINGHAMSHIRE drew with WARWICKSHIRE.

At Southampton, June 11, 12, 13, 14. NOTTINGHAMSHIRE beat HAMPSHIRE by 191 runs.

At Oxford, June 18, 19, 20. NOTTINGHAMSHIRE drew with OXFORD UCCE.

NOTTINGHAMSHIRE v LANCASHIRE

At Nottingham, June 30, July 1, 2, 3. Drawn. Nottinghamshire 11 pts, Lancashire 9 pts. Toss: Nottinghamshire.

While Richard Hadlee and Clive Rice took Nottinghamshire to unparalleled heights in the 1980s, not every overseas import has proved quite as useful in the years that followed. Things changed in 2004 when the unknown David Hussey arrived from Australia and proceeded to pound county attacks to dust for four seasons. His belated international recognition – and the money on offer from the Indian Premier League – ruled him out in 2008, but when Voges, his replacement, was called up for Australia A duty, Hussey returned. Nottinghamshire were in a spot of bother at 94 for three, but from the moment Hussey smashed his third ball through midwicket for four his 15th Championship century at Trent Bridge felt inevitable. Loye held out for 191 balls in Lancashire's first innings, but Ealham winkled out five batsmen to secure a 103-run lead, which was extended by Wagh's second hundred of the season and more quick runs from Hussey, who finished with 200 in the match, from only 223 balls. Set 393 to win in a day plus six overs, Lancashire lost three early wickets before heavy rain intervened.

Close of play: First day, Nottinghamshire 369-9 (Sidebottom 35, Shreck 10); Second day, Lancashire 237-6 (Sutton 25, Chapple 39); Third day, Lancashire 22-1 (Brown 11, Hogg 11).

Nottinghamshire

W. I. Jefferson c Sutton b Newby	11	– b Newby	2
B. M. Shafayat lbw b Newby	14	– c sub (M. Baer) b Keedy	30
M. A. Wagh c Laxman b Croft	40	– c Chilton b Hogg	131
S. R. Patel c Sutton b Croft	25	– lbw b Hogg	1
D. J. Hussey c Hogg b Brown	126	– b Chapple	74
A. D. Brown c Sutton b Brown	54	– c Sutton b Chapple	7
*†C. M. W. Read lbw b Keedy	1	– not out	21
M. A. Ealham c Sutton b Chapple	18	– c Sutton b Keedy	5
R. J. Sidebottom b Newby	46	– not out	0
D. J. Pattinson lbw b Chapple	4		
C. E. Shreck not out	12		
B 9, l-b 13, w 5, n-b 10	37	B 8, l-b 5, w 1, n-b 4	18

1/12 (1) 2/41 (2) 3/94 (3) (101.3 overs) 388 1/11 (1) (7 wkts dec, 67 overs) 289
4/116 (4) 5/286 (6) 6/295 (7) 2/72 (2) 3/79 (4)
7/305 (5) 8/340 (8) 9/354 (10) 10/388 (9) 4/220 (5) 5/230 (6)
  6/275 (3) 7/280 (8)

Chapple 28–6–82–2; Newby 22.3–5–68–3; Hogg 15–1–58–0; Croft 6–0–42–2; Keedy 23–4–76–1; Horton 1–0–10–0; Brown 6–0–30–2. *Second Innings*—Chapple 16–2–69–2; Newby 6–0–32–1; Keedy 27–1–98–2; Hogg 13–1–49–2; Croft 3–0–21–0; Brown 2–0–7–0.

Lancashire

P. J. Horton c Brown b Pattinson	9	– (2) run out		0
K. R. Brown lbw b Ealham	3	– (1) c Hussey b Sidebottom		19
M. B. Loye b Patel	84	– (4) not out		31
V. V. S. Laxman c Shafayat b Ealham	30			
M. J. Chilton lbw b Ealham	5	– not out		7
S. J. Croft lbw b Shreck	25			
†L. D. Sutton c Read b Sidebottom	34			
*G. Chapple b Sidebottom	55			
K. W. Hogg not out	17	– (3) b Pattinson		34
O. J. Newby b Ealham	4			
G. Keedy c and b Ealham	0			
B 1, l-b 6, w 2, n-b 10	19	B 4, n-b 2		6

1/9 (1) 2/31 (2) 3/112 (4) 4/126 (5) (107 overs) 285   1/1 (2) 2/45 (1) (3 wkts, 33 overs) 97
5/158 (3) 6/186 (6) 7/261 (7)   3/68 (3)
8/274 (8) 9/283 (10) 10/285 (11)

Sidebottom 26–8–59–2; Pattinson 18–7–55–1; Shreck 27–5–87–1; Ealham 18–6–31–5; Patel 18–4–46–1. *Second Innings*—Sidebottom 8–1–23–1; Pattinson 8–1–25–1; Shreck 9–0–32–0; Ealham 3–2–10–0; Patel 3–0–3–0; Hussey 2–2–0–0.

Umpires: R. A. Kettleborough and G. Sharp.

NOTTINGHAMSHIRE v DURHAM

At Nottingham, July 15, 16, 17, 18. Durham won by an innings and 102 runs. Durham 20 pts, Nottinghamshire 2 pts. Toss: Nottinghamshire.

An apparently appetising clash between the two unbeaten sides in Division One instead served as a demonstration of the all-round strength of the defending champions, who won seven balls into the final day after rain stole most of the third. While three wickets on the first morning seemed to justify Read's decision to insert Durham, a partnership of 193 between Smith and Benkenstein, skippers present and past, proved invaluable – even more so when Harmison, replacing Claydon after being released from England duty, softened up the Nottinghamshire openers with a spell of 8–7–1–1, with Wood fending a throat ball to short leg. Desperate to score while Harmison was resting, the middle order succumbed to some rash strokes and, although Brown and Read took on Harmison in his second spell, Blackwell and Plunkett mopped up the innings. Following on 185 behind, Nottinghamshire ran up the white flag to register 83, their lowest total since 2003, as Harmison ran riot. Of the many soft dismissals, that of Adams – stepping away from his stumps and slicing to point – was the worst.

Close of play: First day, Durham 257-5 (Claydon 1); Second day, Nottinghamshire 171; Third day, Nottinghamshire 79-9 (Ealham 17, Shreck 0).

Durham

M. J. Di Venuto lbw b Sidebottom	22	C. D. Thorp lbw b Sidebottom		5
M. D. Stoneman c and b Adams	24	M. Davies not out		1
*W. R. Smith c Read b Ealham	87			
G. J. Muchall c Read b Adams	10	B 1, l-b 9, n-b 2		12
D. M. Benkenstein b Ealham	105			
M. E. Claydon c Hussey b Adams	3	1/44 (1) 2/51 (2) 3/63 (4) (122.5 overs) 356		
I. D. Blackwell c Adams b Sidebottom	38	4/256 (5) 5/257 (3)		
†P. Mustard c Read b Sidebottom	40	6/269 (6) 7/316 (7) 8/348 (9)		
L. E. Plunkett c Wagh b Ealham	9	9/350 (8) 10/355 (10) 120 overs: 348-8		

S. J. Harmison replaced Claydon after being released from the England squad.

Sidebottom 27.5–5–65–4; Shreck 31–6–112–0; Ealham 22–5–40–3; Adams 26–4–80–3; Patel 15–3–39–0; Hussey 1–0–10–0.

Nottinghamshire

M. J. Wood c Stoneman b Harmison	12	– c Mustard b Davies	9
B. M. Shafayat lbw b Thorp	16	– c Mustard b Harmison	12
M. A. Wagh c Di Venuto b Thorp	1	– c Benkenstein b Davies	6
S. R. Patel c Thorp b Plunkett	7	– c Smith b Harmison	14
D. J. Hussey c Mustard b Plunkett	9	– lbw b Thorp	9
A. D. Brown b Blackwell	36	– c Davies b Harmison	5
*†C. M. W. Read lbw b Blackwell	48	– c Mustard b Harmison	4
M. A. Ealham c Blackwell b Plunkett	24	– not out	17
A. R. Adams c Benkenstein b Blackwell	6	– c Plunkett b Harmison	2
R. J. Sidebottom c Mustard b Plunkett	3	– c Stoneman b Harmison	0
C. E. Shreck not out	1	– c Thorp b Blackwell	4
L-b 3, w 3, n-b 2	8	L-b 1	1

1/14 (1) 2/17 (3) 3/33 (4) 4/47 (5) (62.2 overs) 171
5/54 (2) 6/135 (6) 7/158 (7)
8/166 (9) 9/168 (8) 10/171 (10)

1/9 (1) 2/19 (3) (32.4 overs) 83
3/38 (2) 4/51 (5)
5/55 (4) 6/60 (6) 7/66 (7) 8/68 (9)
9/76 (10) 10/83 (11)

Claydon 2–2–0–0; Davies 12–5–31–0; Harmison 16–7–45–1; Thorp 11–4–30–2; Plunkett 13.2–1–56–4; Blackwell 8–3–6–3. *Second Innings*—Harmison 13–5–20–6; Davies 7–2–13–2; Thorp 9–2–33–1; Blackwell 3.4–0–16–1.

Umpires: S. A. Garratt and P. J. Hartley.

At Scarborough, July 21, 22, 23, 24. NOTTINGHAMSHIRE drew with YORKSHIRE.

At Taunton, July 31, August 1, 2, 3. NOTTINGHAMSHIRE drew with SOMERSET.

At Horsham, August 5, 6, 7, 8. NOTTINGHAMSHIRE drew with SUSSEX.

NOTTINGHAMSHIRE v WARWICKSHIRE

At Nottingham, August 11, 12, 13, 14. Drawn. Nottinghamshire 11 pts, Warwickshire 8 pts. Toss: Warwickshire. Championship debut: S. Sreesanth.

Nottinghamshire began the match 30 points behind leaders Durham and without a win in five games, but they were in control at the halfway stage thanks to Read's third hundred of the season and some productive swing bowling from Shreck and Sidebottom. In testing conditions, Read rescued Nottinghamshire from 141 for five with a selection of cuts, pulls and wristy drives and, when Warwickshire – after being 94 for seven – were dismissed for 219 and asked to follow on, the game appeared there for the taking. Instead, Bell and Trott took their chance in front of the England selectors, adding 188 – a club record for the third wicket against Nottinghamshire – and showing increasing assurance on a pitch that went flatter by the hour. Trott was the more aggressive, reaching three figures from 136 balls as he passed 1,000 Championship runs for the season, while Bell demonstrated a tighter technique until a quicker ball from Adams had his push to leg. A nominal declaration set Nottinghamshire 302 from 42 overs, which they chose not to pursue.

Close of play: First day, Warwickshire 24-0 (Westwood 7, Botha 16); Second day, Warwickshire 214-9 (Sreesanth 25, Rankin 3); Third day, Warwickshire 298-3 (Bell 92, Tahir 6).

Nottinghamshire

S. A. Newman lbw b Tahir	5	– lbw b Rankin	0
M. J. Wood c Westwood b Tahir	14	– not out	39
M. A. Wagh b Tahir	10	– not out	28
A. C. Voges c Bell b Sreesanth	68		
S. R. Patel lbw b Clarke	47		
A. D. Brown c Clarke b Sreesanth	0		
*†C. M. W. Read b Tahir	110		
M. A. Ealham c Clarke b Sreesanth	37		
A. R. Adams c Clarke b Rankin	32		
R. J. Sidebottom c Woakes b Clarke	12		
C. E. Shreck not out	4		
B 4, l-b 10, n-b 35	49	N-b 4	4

1/9 (1) 2/32 (2) 3/43 (3) 4/141 (4)   (84.1 overs) 388   1/0 (1)   (1 wkt, 25 overs) 71
5/141 (6) 6/224 (5) 7/308 (8)
8/366 (7) 9/366 (9) 10/388 (10)

Rankin 15–2–92–1; Tahir 20–1–89–4; Sreesanth 14–1–65–3; Woakes 16–0–76–0; Trott 4–0–7–0; Clarke 5.1–2–15–2; Botha 10–0–30–0. *Second Innings*—Rankin 6–2–19–1; Tahir 5–2–16–0; Woakes 5–1–14–0; Sreesanth 4–1–7–0; Westwood 2–0–6–0; Botha 2–0–2–0; Clarke 1–0–7–0.

Warwickshire

*I. J. Westwood c Adams b Shreck	12	– c Voges b Ealham	11
A. G. Botha c Adams b Shreck	19	– c Patel b Adams	64
I. R. Bell c Read b Sidebottom	1	– lbw b Adams	126
I. J. L. Trott c Voges b Shreck	1	– lbw b Sidebottom	121
J. O. Troughton lbw b Sidebottom	9	– (6) c Read b Adams	15
†T. R. Ambrose lbw b Sidebottom	1	– (7) not out	32
R. Clarke run out	67	– (8) b Shreck	62
C. R. Woakes b Adams	22	– (9) not out	1
N. S. Tahir c Voges b Ealham	24	– (5) c Read b Adams	22
S. Sreesanth not out	30		
W. B. Rankin b Shreck	3		
L-b 10, n-b 6	16	B 4, l-b 9, w 1, n-b 2	16

1/35 (1) 2/36 (2) 3/36 (3) 4/48 (5)   (75.3 overs) 219   1/53 (1)   (7 wkts dec, 144 overs) 470
5/64 (4) 6/66 (6) 7/94 (8) 8/163 (9)   2/101 (2) 3/289 (4)
9/202 (7) 10/219 (11)   4/334 (5) 5/355 (3) 6/370 (6) 7/465 (8)

Sidebottom 20–7–37–3; Shreck 21.3–7–63–4; Adams 14–2–47–1; Ealham 13–3–41–1; Patel 6–0–19–0; Voges 1–0–2–0. *Second Innings*—Sidebottom 28–6–97–1; Shreck 31–9–109–1; Adams 30–10–86–4; Ealham 26–16–46–1; Patel 23–3–97–0; Voges 6–0–22–0.

Umpires: R. K. Illingworth and R. A. Kettleborough.

NOTTINGHAMSHIRE v HAMPSHIRE

At Nottingham, August 19, 20, 21, 22. Drawn. Nottinghamshire 10 pts, Hampshire 12 pts. Toss: Hampshire.

Needing to inject some spark into their title challenge, Nottinghamshire produced a wicket so green supporters may have felt transported back to the 1980s. Mascarenhas's decision to bat thus came as a surprise, but his instincts proved correct. On a largely lifeless pitch, Carberry looked immovable until a lifting delivery from Andre Adams broke a finger and ended his season; Lumb hit a maiden double-century, his first three-figure score in the Championship for 12 months; and Ervine helped himself to easy runs as the bowlers flagged. A familiar batting collapse then left Nottinghamshire struggling on 48 for four, but Read, shouldering the responsibility once again, guided his side past 400 with his fourth century of the season as Ealham and Adams helped him add

179 for the last three wickets. Even so, a deficit of 247 meant Hampshire enforced the follow-on, only for Wagh's third hundred of the campaign – a chanceless, graceful innings – to steer the hosts to safety. The result helped neither team: Nottinghamshire's chances of overtaking Durham were disappearing, and Hampshire were still in the relegation battle.

Close of play: First day, Hampshire 345-3 (Lumb 103, Burrows 7); Second day, Nottinghamshire 48-4 (Patel 0, Shafayat 0); Third day, Nottinghamshire 407.

Hampshire

M. A. Carberry retired hurt	86	Imran Tahir lbw b Patel	0
J. H. K. Adams b Adams	55	D. A. Griffiths not out	20
M. J. Lumb c Read b Patel	219		
J. M. Vince c Newman b Patel	27	B 7, l-b 7, n-b 18	32
L. A. Dawson lbw b Adams	43		
†T. G. Burrows c Shafayat b Shreck	20	1/146 (2) (8 wkts dec, 161 overs)	654
S. M. Ervine c Newman b Shafayat	104	2/226 (4) 3/331 (5)	
*A. D. Mascarenhas not out	48	4/366 (6) 5/574 (3) 6/598 (7)	
D. G. Cork lbw b Patel	0	7/599 (9) 8/612 (10)	120 overs: 424-4

Carberry retired hurt at 163.

Shreck 27–5–115–1; Pattinson 22–1–144–0; Adams 35–7–108–2; Patel 48–6–199–4; Ealham 21–6–42–0; Shafayat 8–1–32–1.

Nottinghamshire

S. A. Newman c Burrows b Cork	25	– c Burrows b Griffiths	0
M. J. Wood c Adams b Griffiths	10	– lbw b Mascarenhas	17
M. A. Wagh lbw b Imran Tahir	8	– not out	136
D. J. Pattinson lbw b Imran Tahir	0		
S. R. Patel lbw b Ervine	35	– (4) c Lumb b Imran Tahir	48
B. M. Shafayat c Burrows b Griffiths	69	– (5) b Imran Tahir	6
A. D. Brown lbw b Imran Tahir	39	– (6) not out	37
*†C. M. W. Read not out	119		
M. A. Ealham c Adams b Griffiths	32		
A. R. Adams c Lumb b Imran Tahir	46		
C. E. Shreck b Griffiths	2		
B 1, l-b 10, w 1, n-b 10	22	B 12, l-b 6, n-b 4, p 5	27
1/29 (2) 2/46 (3) 3/46 (4) (114.1 overs)	407	1/0 (1) 2/48 (2) (4 wkts, 79 overs)	271
4/48 (1) 5/126 (5) 6/183 (6) 7/228 (7)		3/158 (4)	
8/297 (9) 9/394 (10) 10/407 (11)		4/183 (5)	

Griffiths 28.1–4–144–4; Mascarenhas 18–6–42–0; Imran Tahir 36–7–106–4; Cork 17–3–48–1; Ervine 10–1–41–1; Dawson 5–0–15–0. *Second Innings*—Griffiths 16–2–51–1; Mascarenhas 10–2–43–1; Cork 10–1–40–0; Imran Tahir 29–6–79–2; Ervine 14–5–35–0.

Umpires: N. L. Bainton and I. J. Gould.

At Worcester, August 25, 26, 27, 28. NOTTINGHAMSHIRE drew with WORCESTERSHIRE.

NOTTINGHAMSHIRE v YORKSHIRE

At Nottingham, September 3, 4, 5, 6. Drawn. Nottinghamshire 11 pts, Yorkshire 9 pts. Toss: Nottinghamshire.

For the second home game in succession Nottinghamshire prepared a greentop, but this time – initially, at least – the ploy worked. Pattinson, who had been struggling with injury and form all season, and Shreck found enough life and sideways movement to leave Yorkshire in trouble. The hosts opened up a 96-run lead after the openers put on 76 and Franks clubbed 15 fours in his 69-ball 64, but Yorkshire's response was resolute. Rudolph and Sayers dug in to put on 244, the county's highest opening stand in over eight years, and at the end of day three Yorkshire were 173 ahead.

Given their precarious position in the table, they needed at least to consider setting up a run-chase, but McGrath proved unable to agree a target with Read, and Yorkshire batted out the final day to take four points rather than gamble on winning the additional ten – a dismal demonstration of a safety-first attitude.

Close of play: First day, Yorkshire 220-8 (Wainwright 16, Hoggard 4); Second day, Nottinghamshire 301-7 (Franks 46, Ealham 10); Third day, Yorkshire 269-2 (McGrath 18, Gale 5).

Yorkshire

J. A. Rudolph b Pattinson	42	– c Ealham b Franks	149
J. J. Sayers b Franks	53	– b Franks	86
*A. McGrath c Ealham b Shreck	0	– b Franks	40
A. W. Gale c Read b Pattinson	5	– b Pattinson	9
J. M. Bairstow lbw b Ealham	49	– c Brown b Hales	82
†G. L. Brophy c Read b Franks	0	– c Patel b Patel	29
A. Shahzad c Read b Shreck	19	– b Hales	45
R. M. Pyrah lbw b Shreck	9	– not out	50
D. J. Wainwright c Brown b Franks	37	– c and b Brown	6
M. J. Hoggard not out	12	– not out	0
G. J. Kruis c Read b Ealham	1		
B 4, l-b 16, w 5, n-b 4	29	B 10, l-b 6, w 5, n-b 2	23

1/72 (1) 2/73 (3) 3/100 (4)   (111.3 overs) 256
4/132 (2) 5/132 (6) 6/174 (5)
7/192 (7) 8/199 (8) 9/255 (9) 10/256 (11)

1/244 (1)   (8 wkts dec, 174 overs) 519
2/254 (2) 3/284 (4)
4/304 (3) 5/384 (6) 6/427 (5)
7/504 (7) 8/515 (9)

Shreck 33–10–57–3; Pattinson 29–6–74–2; Franks 20–7–52–3; Ealham 22.3–11–38–2; Patel 7–1–15–0. *Second Innings*—Shreck 27–7–88–0; Pattinson 25–6–69–1; Ealham 19–5–46–0; Franks 30–12–71–3; Patel 36–9–123–1; Hales 20–4–63–2; Newman 6–1–25–0; Read 1–0–2–0; Brown 10–2–16–1.

Nottinghamshire

S. A. Newman c Gale b Hoggard	79	M. A. Ealham lbw b Kruis	36
A. D. Hales c and b Pyrah	35	D. J. Pattinson b Shahzad	3
M. A. Wagh b Brophy b Pyrah	0	C. E. Shreck not out	0
S. R. Patel c Bairstow b Shahzad	7	B 8, l-b 8, w 2, n-b 2	20
B. M. Shafayat b Hoggard	66		
A. D. Brown b Wainwright	0	1/76 (2) 2/78 (3) (85.2 overs) 352
*†C. M. W. Read st Brophy b Wainwright	42	3/101 (4) 4/152 (1) 5/153 (6) 6/231 (7)
P. J. Franks c and b Shahzad	64	7/279 (5) 8/345 (9) 9/349 (8) 10/352 (10)

Hoggard 17–5–60–2; Shahzad 22.2–1–101–3; Kruis 17–0–73–1; Pyrah 17–3–53–2; Wainwright 12–4–49–2.

Umpires: M. A. Gough and P. Willey.

At Chester-le-Street, September 9, 10, 11, 12. NOTTINGHAMSHIRE lost to DURHAM by an innings and 52 runs.

NOTTINGHAMSHIRE v SUSSEX

At Nottingham, September 23, 24, 25, 26. Nottinghamshire won by 35 runs. Nottinghamshire 20 pts, Sussex 4 pts. Toss: Sussex. Championship debut: A. Patel.

Nottinghamshire claimed their first win in any form of cricket for three months to secure second place and a £225,000 windfall. Since they had suffered in 2006 at the hands of Sussex who came to Trent Bridge for the final game of the season, won the title and sent Nottinghamshire down, there was a symmetrical feel to the occasion as the visitors found themselves relegated at the end of day two. Needing a win with maximum points, and for one of Lancashire, Yorkshire or Hampshire to be thrashed, Sussex had to concede defeat when they lost their last six wickets inside 15 overs for 41 runs to waste Nash's fourth century of the summer. Their collapse gave Nottinghamshire an 85-run lead, which was stretched to 371 thanks to another half-century from Read, who put on 80 for the seventh wicket with Akhil Patel, Samit's younger brother. A left-handed batsman and chinaman bowler, Akhil hit seven fours as he eased into Championship cricket following a first-innings duck. On an entertaining final day, Sussex got off to a solid start before slumping to Samit Patel's left-arm spin. Dwayne Smith smashed six sixes in a brutal 54-ball innings to raise hopes, but he was last out as the Patels combined – Akhil holding the catch on the midwicket boundary to give Samit career-best figures.

Close of play: First day, Nottinghamshire 294-8 (Read 78, Fletcher 0); Second day, Nottinghamshire 4-1 (Hales 0, Fletcher 0); Third day, Nottinghamshire 236-7 (Read 64, Ealham 23).

Nottinghamshire

B. M. Shafayat c Yardy b Smith	45	– lbw b Collymore	4
A. D. Hales lbw b Lewry	33	– b Chawla	38
M. A. Wagh b Chawla	67	– (4) lbw b Smith	2
S. R. Patel lbw Martin-Jenkins	21	– (5) c Martin-Jenkins b Smith	54
A. Patel lbw b Smith	0	– (6) c Hodd b Nash	37
A. D. Brown c Hamilton-Brown b Martin-Jenkins	10	– (7) lbw b Smith	1
*†C. M. W. Read lbw b Collymore	88	– (8) c Collymore b Smith	83
M. A. Ealham lbw b Chawla	13	– (9) lbw b Lewry	24
A. R. Adams b Chawla	3	– (10) c Yardy b Lewry	25
L. J. Fletcher not out	19	– (3) lbw b Collymore	0
C. E. Shreck b Smith	0	– not out	0
B 9, l-b 16, n-b 4	29	B 13, l-b 2, w 1, n-b 2	18

1/70 (2) 2/86 (1) 3/137 (4)   (105 overs) 328
4/138 (5) 5/163 (6) 6/239 (3) 7/277 (8)
8/293 (9) 9/319 (7) 10/328 (11)

1/4 (1) 2/4 (3)   (90.3 overs) 286
3/15 (4) 4/86 (5) 5/106 (2)
6/107 (7) 7/187 (6) 8/244 (9)
9/286 (10) 10/286 (8)

Lewry 9–1–40–1; Collymore 24–5–59–1; Martin-Jenkins 19–3–69–2; Smith 27–7–73–3; Chawla 26–8–62–3. *Second Innings*—Collymore 15–3–41–2; Lewry 12–3–53–2; Smith 25.3–7–58–4; Martin-Jenkins 9–2–32–0; Chawla 18–3–55–1; Hamilton-Brown 4–0–8–0; Nash 7–0–24–1.

Sussex

*M. H. Yardy c Read b Fletcher	21	– b Ealham	48
C. D. Nash c Brown b S. R. Patel	135	– lbw b Fletcher	70
J. S. Gatting c Adams b Fletcher	12	– c Wagh b Fletcher	70
M. W. Goodwin c S. R. Patel b Shreck	20	– c Ealham b S. R. Patel	9
R. J. Hamilton-Brown lbw b S. R. Patel	1	– c Read b S. R. Patel	4
†A. J. Hodd b Adams	12	– lbw b Ealham	11
R. S. C. Martin-Jenkins c Read b Adams	1	– c Brown b S. R. Patel	15
D. R. Smith c A. Patel b Adams	5	– c A. Patel b S. R. Patel	80
P. P. Chawla st Read b S. R. Patel	16	– st Read b S. R. Patel	8
C. D. Collymore b Adams	9	– c Hales b S. R. Patel	3
J. D. Lewry not out	0	– not out	1
B 1, l-b 8, w 2	11	B 5, l-b 10, n-b 2	17

1/74 (1) 2/104 (3) 3/156 (4)   (75.1 overs) 243
4/161 (5) 5/202 (6) 6/208 (7)
7/218 (2) 8/218 (8) 9/243 (10) 10/243 (9)

1/114 (1) 2/145 (2)   (75.1 overs) 336
3/170 (4) 4/176 (5)
5/199 (6) 6/224 (7) 7/278 (3)
8/303 (9) 9/309 (10) 10/336 (8)

Shreck 13–3–51–1; Fletcher 15–1–43–2; Adams 22–7–63–4; Ealham 11–3–37–0; S. R. Patel 14.1–3–40–3. *Second Innings*—Shreck 5–1–26–0; Fletcher 21–3–93–2; Adams 11–1–59–0; S. R. Patel 24.1–1–84–6; Ealham 14–2–59–2.

Umpires: N. G. B. Cook and R. T. Robinson.

SOMERSET

Once more the nearly men

DAVID FOOT

There was so much going for Somerset in 2009 and yet, in the strictest sense, they ended with nothing: certainly not a title, or the kind of acclaim that at times they appeared to deserve amid the miscalculations and highlights which deceptively cheered their noisy, good-natured regional followers.

The county's physical strength mostly looked adequate, even if they lacked a seam bowler to compensate for Andrew Caddick's withdrawal from the first-class game he had served on England's and Somerset's behalf with distinction and memorable feats of stamina and wicket-taking. As for the necessary mental fibre, this was again a more elusive quality. The county continues to wear its hints of grandeur with sheepish unease. Players freeze at the wrong moments.

Throughout the season Marcus Trescothick, imperiously assured and with past cares cast aside – except when he returned home early from the inaugural Champions League in India – set the zestful Taunton mood and upped the local pulse-rate. He was by some distance the leading scorer in the country, fifth in the national averages and threatening to top 3,000 runs in all matches (in the end he fell just 66 short). On occasions it even seemed to be coming too easily to him. His Test career might have been over, but the fluent strokemaking was as uplifting as ever. Justin Langer, a natural leader by example who clearly liked the ambience of the West Country, would soon be on his way back to Australia, and Trescothick was ready and eager to take over as the captain of his native county.

It is true that he often dominated the batting and, with his exciting rattle of early runs, the direction of the match. Yet his days of aesthetic skill and intrepid brio also rubbed off on others who, at times, increasingly emerged to parade their gifts of wristy wonderment and improvised aggression. Into this burgeoning category stepped Arul Suppiah and Craig Kieswetter. Both passed 1,000 runs for the first time and fashioned career-best innings. They could have exceptional futures.

Suppiah, born in Malaysia, actually made his Somerset debut in 2002. He arrived by way of Millfield and Kolpak, was sensitively integrated into first-team cricket. His repertoire is good to the eye; some of the most handsome stands in 2009 featured him.

Kieswetter, another Millfield graduate, decided he had a better future in this country than his native South Africa, where his progress had been meticulously monitored. From the 2010 season he is qualified to play for England; it should not necessarily be discounted as premature ambition. Despite the resurgence of Trescothick, many Somerset supporters would nominate Kieswetter as the revelation of the summer. As a batsman he can naturally blend to the needs of the team. He can defend or, perhaps more happily, attack. There is an ability to improvise; in the one-day matches he is an obvious opener. His wicketkeeping as yet poses one or two questions. He has pulled off some outstandingly agile catches – and has also probably put down too many. But, once considered a fallible keeper, he grew markedly in stature and intuition, and worked assiduously to improve. Here is true talent – and Somerset, with their envied, opportunistic traits, seem lucky to have found him.

Arul Suppiah

Stu Forster, Getty Images

James Hildreth, not so long ago another player of undeniable promise, should also have recorded 1,000 runs. It was certainly expected of him after a dazzling early-season triple-hundred (on April 18 – the earliest of any English season). Then his form too often wavered. And he accepted that there were a few technical flaws to sort out. Langer rightly persisted with him: mark Hildreth down for a timely revival in 2010, as here is a player with an attractive armoury of shots. He has been around now long enough to dispense with that "promising" tag. Like Hildreth, Peter Trego – his stunning 54-ball hundred which won the match against Yorkshire won't easily be forgotten – and Zander de Bruyn had relatively modest returns.

As for Somerset's bowling, the county's perceptive director of cricket, Brian Rose, and head coach Andy Hurry have at times struggled to find the most effective balance. It hasn't been easy anticipating just how cussed the Taunton pitch would be. It has been ceaselessly maligned, underscored by the mountainous statistics that are apt to drive bowlers to distraction as batsmen, often from the opposition, bolster their averages. Efforts to examine and rectify the balance of bat and ball will doubtless be tirelessly pursued.

Somerset relied on the reassuring accuracy of Charl Willoughby's swing. He rarely sent down an untidy over, though he badly needed more support. Other bowlers, such as Ben Phillips and David Stiff, worked hard for meagre rewards, and Alfonso Thomas was of especial value in bowling with economy at the end of one-day matches, when liberties couldn't be risked. The arrival of the Indian slow left-armer Murali Kartik will mean additional variety, while Nick Compton, also coming from Lord's, will replace Langer at the top of the order.

Somerset are historically familiar enough with unfulfilled endeavour. They ended third in the Championship, wantonly wrecked their chances of carrying off the Pro40 title, and had to be satisfied with reaching the final of the Twenty20 Cup. At times they got the one-day tactics right, but then lost their way. This year they have signed the heavyweight 20Twenty players Cameron White and Kieron Pollard. As a seemingly exasperated Rose said: "We've had enough of being cricket's nearly men."

SOMERSET RESULTS

All first-class matches – Played 16: Won 3, Lost 1, Drawn 12.
County Championship matches – Played 16: Won 3, Lost 1, Drawn 12.

LV County Championship, 3rd in Division 1; Friends Provident Trophy, q-f;
Pro40 League, 2nd in Division 1; Twenty20 Cup, finalists.

COUNTY CHAMPIONSHIP AVERAGES, BATTING AND FIELDING

Cap		M	I	NO	R	HS	100s	50s	Avge	Ct/St
1999	M. E. Trescothick†.....	16	26	2	1,817	146	8	9	75.70	21
2009	C. Kieswetter¶.......	16	24	3	1,242	153	4	7	59.14	48
2009	A. V. Suppiah.........	16	26	1	1,201	151	3	6	48.04	18
2007	J. C. Hildreth	15	23	2	934	303*	2	4	44.47	10
2007	J. L. Langer§	15	21	2	831	122*	2	4	43.73	17
2007	P. D. Trego†..........	16	23	5	610	103*	1	5	33.88	5
	B. J. Phillips..........	7	8	2	190	84	0	1	31.66	4
	O. A. C. Banks¶......	6	7	2	156	53	0	1	31.20	1
2008	Z. de Bruyn¶	16	25	3	686	106	1	6	31.18	3
2008	A. C. Thomas¶.......	14	15	3	338	70	0	3	28.16	2
	D. A. Stiff..........	10	14	5	193	49	0	0	21.44	0
	M. T. C. Waller	4	6	1	67	28	0	0	13.40	1
2007	C. M. Willoughby¶ ...	16	13	4	40	23	0	0	4.44	4

Also batted: J. C. Buttler† (1 match) 30; A. R. Caddick (cap 1992) (5 matches) 1, 3, 11* (1 ct); W. J. Durston† (1 match) 0, 54*; M. K. Munday (1 match) 1. M. L. Turner (1 match) did not bat (1 ct).

† *Born in Somerset.* § *Official overseas player.* ¶ *Other non-England-qualified player.*

BOWLING

	O	M	R	W	BB	5W/i	Avge
C. M. Willoughby	555.4	161	1,621	54	5-56	3	30.01
D. A. Stiff	268.2	33	1,120	31	5-91	1	36.12
A. C. Thomas	401.1	77	1,317	35	5-53	1	37.62
B. J. Phillips	158.1	37	456	12	4-46	0	38.00
A. V. Suppiah	212.5	47	682	15	3-58	0	45.46
P. D. Trego	256.5	57	889	19	3-53	0	46.78
A. R. Caddick	131.1	24	525	10	3-53	0	52.50

Also bowled: O. A. C. Banks 111.1–15–456–7; Z. de Bruyn 136–23–541–7; W. J. Durston 2–0–13–0; M. K. Munday 25.1–0–114–4; M. E. Trescothick 5–2–10–0; M. L. Turner 30–4–111–2; M. T. C. Waller 82.4–11–320–5.

COUNTY RECORDS

Highest score for:	342	J. L. Langer v Surrey at Guildford............	2006
Highest score against:	424	A. C. MacLaren (Lancashire) at Taunton	1895
Leading run-scorer:	21,142	H. Gimblett (avge 36.96)....................	1935–1954
Best bowling for:	10-49	E. J. Tyler v Surrey at Taunton	1895
Best bowling against:	10-35	A. Drake (Yorkshire) at Weston-super-Mare....	1914
Leading wicket-taker:	2,165	J. C. White (avge 18.03)	1909–1937
Highest total for:	850-7 dec	v Middlesex at Taunton	2007
Highest total against:	811	by Surrey at The Oval	1899
Lowest total for:	25	v Gloucestershire at Bristol	1947
Lowest total against:	22	by Gloucestershire at Bristol	1920

ADDRESS

County Ground, St James's Street, Taunton TA1 1JT (0845 337 1875; **email** info@somersetcountycc.co.uk). **Website** www.somersetcricketclub.co.uk

OFFICIALS

Captain 2009 – J. L. Langer;
  2010 – M. E. Trescothick
Director of cricket B. C. Rose
Head coach A. Hurry
Development director J. I. D. Kerr
President R. C. Kerslake

Chairman A. J. Nash
Chief executive R. A. Gould
Chairman, cricket committee V. J. Marks
Head groundsman P. Frost
Scorer G. A. Stickley

Twenty20 reality check

Somerset's players and coaching staff returned from the inaugural Champions League Twenty20 in India last October admitting that the counties have a gulf to close when it comes to competing against the world's best club sides.

A thrilling opening victory over one of the tournament favourites, the IPL champions Deccan Chargers, inspired largely by the all-round skills of Alfonso Thomas, promised much for the remainder of the competition. But from then on, like the other English representatives Sussex, Somerset found themselves out of their depth and, though they did reach the Super Eights stage, heavy defeats by Trinidad and Tobago, South Africa's Eagles and eventual winners New South Wales provided a stark reality check.

The early return of Marcus Trescothick, with a recurrence of his stress problems, after the first two games was a blow. But Somerset's director of cricket Brian Rose and coach Andy Hurry were honest enough to admit that the strength of the opposition and the tactics they employed had come as a real eye-opener. While Somerset could hardly hope to match the pace of the NSW attack, Rose developed a deep admiration for the approach of Trinidad and Tobago, who proved the surprise packets of the tournament and reached the final. "I thought they were the outstanding fielding side in the competition," said Rose, "and also demonstrated the increasing role spin bowling is playing in Twenty20 cricket."

Somerset looked flat in the field compared to their opponents, which may have been due to the tournament coming at the end of a long domestic season in which they had challenged strongly in all four competitions. Most of the other Champions League sides also fielded a greater number of experienced Test players than Somerset, who had only Trescothick and skipper Justin Langer, for whom the tournament signalled the end of an illustrious playing career.

But Rose warns: "Until English sides work out a way of scoring big runs against top international bowlers in the six overs of fielding restrictions, we shall remain second-best."   RICHARD LATHAM

SOMERSET v WARWICKSHIRE

At Taunton, April 15, 16, 17, 18. Drawn. Somerset 12 pts, Warwickshire 10 pts. Toss: Somerset. Championship debut: O. A. C. Banks.

There were familiar murmurs of "here we go again" as the runs mounted and the bowlers, not always at their best, were inclined to struggle. Bell set the mood, batting as if determined to illustrate the folly of the Test selectors in rejecting his hopes for the No. 3 place. He had Troughton, Ambrose and Woakes to reinforce the supremacy of bat over ball. Then the point was made in exquisite style by Somerset's Hildreth. His triple-hundred, the earliest ever scored in an English season, mocked the aberrations and inconsistencies of the previous summer, as he sailed past 5,000 first-class runs. He remained undefeated, as did Kieswetter with his maiden Championship century. Both young batsmen paraded an attractive repertoire of shots, encouraging for their county, even if the match sustained an imbalance and gave the bowlers a frustrating time. One was left to sympathise with them, though the towering Phillips, once of Kent and Northamptonshire, and Woakes did their best to buck the trend. There was, however, not much chance of a positive result.

Close of play: First day, Warwickshire 189-3 (Bell 84, Troughton 58); Second day, Somerset 70-0 (Trescothick 27, Suppiah 31); Third day, Somerset 454-4 (Hildreth 191, Kieswetter 53).

Warwickshire

D. L. Maddy b Phillips	17	– c Turner b Suppiah	36
T. Frost c Kieswetter b Phillips	7	– not out	46
I. R. Bell c Kieswetter b Phillips	172	– not out	13
I. J. L. Trott lbw b Phillips	0		
J. O. Troughton c Phillips b Willoughby	77		
*†T. R. Ambrose b Banks	57		
R. Clarke c Kieswetter b Turner	0		
N. M. Carter lbw b Willoughby	21		
C. R. Woakes c Langer b Willoughby	63		
A. G. Botha c de Bruyn b Turner	15		
J. E. Anyon not out	15		
B 24, l-b 19, w 11, n-b 2	56	B 1, l-b 4, w 2, n-b 6	13

1/12 (2) 2/66 (1) 3/66 (4)   (129.4 overs) 500   1/71 (1)   (1 wkt, 38 overs) 108
4/220 (5) 5/361 (3) 6/362 (7)
7/385 (6) 8/399 (8) 9/433 (10)
10/500 (9)   120 overs: 464-9

Willoughby 31.4–7–87–3; Phillips 28–9–100–4; Turner 21–3–82–2; Trego 13–2–56–0; de Bruyn 16–3–44–0; Banks 20–2–88–1. *Second Innings*—Willoughby 5–2–10–0; Phillips 4–1–6–0; Turner 9–1–29–0; Banks 6–3–9–0; Suppiah 6–1–34–1; Trescothick 5–2–10–0; Trego 3–1–5–0.

Somerset

M. E. Trescothick c Maddy b Woakes	52
A. V. Suppiah c Frost b Anyon	38
*J. L. Langer lbw b Woakes	76
J. C. Hildreth not out	303
Z. de Bruyn c Clarke b Woakes	4
†C. Kieswetter not out	150
B 17, l-b 8, w 4, n-b 20	49

1/104 (1) 2/118 (2)   (4 wkts dec, 154.1 overs) 672
3/343 (3) 4/354 (5)   120 overs: 469-4

P. D. Trego, B. J. Phillips, O. A. C. Banks, M. L. Turner and C. M. Willoughby did not bat.

Carter 11–1–44–0; Woakes 27–4–107–3; Anyon 33–6–124–1; Botha 41–6–178–0; Maddy 7.1–0–31–0; Clarke 22–0–99–0; Trott 13–1–64–0.

Umpires: R. K. Illingworth and R. A. Kettleborough.

At Taunton Vale, April 22, 23, 24 (not first-class). **Somerset won by 359 runs.** Toss: Cardiff UCCE. **Somerset 342-6 dec** (N. J. Edwards 72, P. D. Trego 135*, A. C. Thomas 46, Extras 37) **and 452-4 dec** (N. J. Edwards 140, A. V. Suppiah 193, W. J. Durston 45, P. D. Trego 31*); **Cardiff UCCE 281-8 dec** (R. Bishop 74, S. M. Ransley 40, T. W. Allin 51*, Extras 40; D. A. Stiff 4-60) **and 154** (R. Bishop 38, M. Crump 32; D. A. Stiff 5-50). *County debuts:* J. C. Buttler, D. A. Stiff, M. T. C. Waller.

It was hardly the most challenging of early-season run-outs for Somerset. The zestful Trego and Edwards scored good-looking hundreds, while Suppiah nearly reached a double with wristy freedom. The tall David Stiff had every reason to be pleased with his nine wickets. Cardiff's best batting came from Ryan Bishop.

SOMERSET v DURHAM

At Taunton, April 28, 29, 30, May 1. Drawn. Somerset 6 pts, Durham 12 pts. Toss: Somerset.

Somerset were shamefacedly bowled out for 69 in their first innings, a reflection of fumbling batting that lasted just over two hours and occupied a token 28 overs. Six batsmen failed to score, and the county were saved from greater ignominy by Langer's fighting, undefeated 35 from No. 3. Bowling from the River End, Onions excelled with his six for 31. "He seems to have gained a yard of pace this season," said Trescothick. "I found it difficult to pick the ball up." The Taunton pitch was a disloyal friend to Somerset after their being so spoilt over recent years. Durham, who had been put in, amassed 543, substantially due to Benkenstein's Championship-best 181, with Di Venuto, Muchall and Blackwell, against his former county, also weighing in against a moderate attack for whom the newcomer Stiff, in particular, suffered. When Somerset followed on, there were hundreds from Trescothick, Langer and Kieswetter, and West Country spectators could breathe easily once more.

Close of play: First day, Durham 372-6 (Benkenstein 110); Second day, Somerset 83-1 (Trescothick 32, Hildreth 22); Third day, Somerset 178-1 (Trescothick 90, Hildreth 52).

Durham

M. J. Di Venuto c Trescothick b Willoughby	53	M. E. Claydon b Banks	38
M. D. Stoneman c Kieswetter b Stiff	38	S. J. Harmison not out	10
*W. R. Smith lbw b Thomas	7		
G. J. Muchall c Trescothick b Banks	68	B 13, l-b 11, w 12, n-b 26	62
D. M. Benkenstein c Suppiah b Thomas	181		
I. D. Blackwell c Hildreth b Trego	50	1/98 (1) 2/119 (3)	(134.5 overs) 543
G. Onions b Trego	0	3/119 (2) 4/285 (4)	
†P. Mustard run out	4	5/366 (6) 6/372 (7) 7/382 (8) 8/450 (9)	
C. D. Thorp c Kieswetter b Stiff	32	9/521 (10) 10/543 (5)	120 overs: 447-7

Willoughby 31–10–75–1; Thomas 21.5–5–86–2; Stiff 25–4–134–2; Trego 26–6–73–2; de Bruyn 9–0–53–0; Banks 15–0–75–2; Suppiah 7–1–23–0.

Somerset

M. E. Trescothick b Onions	12	– c Muchall b Onions	105
A. V. Suppiah c and b Onions	12	– lbw b Claydon	29
*J. L. Langer not out	35	– (4) not out	122
J. C. Hildreth lbw b Onions	0	– (3) b Thorp	71
Z. de Bruyn c Mustard b Harmison	0	– c Muchall b Claydon	6
†C. Kieswetter c Thorp b Onions	0	– c Mustard b Blackwell	106
P. D. Trego c Mustard b Onions	0	– not out	21
O. A. C. Banks c Di Venuto b Thorp	4		
A. C. Thomas b Thorp	2		
D. A. Stiff b Thorp	0		
C. M. Willoughby c Smith b Onions	0		
L-b 4	4	B 3, l-b 16, n-b 6	25

1/12 (1) 2/39 (2) 3/39 (4) 4/40 (5)	(28.2 overs)	69	1/49 (2) (5 wkts, 129 overs) 485
5/49 (6) 6/49 (7) 7/54 (8) 8/66 (9)			2/196 (1) 3/223 (3)
9/66 (10) 10/69 (11)			4/238 (5) 5/435 (6)

Onions 14.2–4–31–6; Harmison 8–2–29–1; Thorp 6–2–5–3. *Second Innings*—Onions 29–5–110–1; Thorp 29–9–80–1; Harmison 27–7–100–0; Claydon 23–3–95–2; Blackwell 21–2–81–1.

Umpires: R. A. Kettleborough and R. T. Robinson.

At Nottingham, May 6, 7, 8, 9. SOMERSET lost to NOTTINGHAMSHIRE by six wickets.

At Manchester, June 6, 7, 8, 9. SOMERSET drew with LANCASHIRE.

At Leeds, June 11, 12, 13, 14. SOMERSET beat YORKSHIRE by four wickets.

At Hove, June 16, 17, 18, 19. SOMERSET beat SUSSEX by 35 runs.

SOMERSET v YORKSHIRE

At Taunton, June 30, July 1, 2, 3. Somerset won by four wickets. Somerset 20 pts, Yorkshire 8 pts. Toss: Yorkshire.

Nothing is more demanding for a visiting captain to Taunton, with its notoriously flat pitch, than calculating when to risk a final-day declaration. McGrath got it slightly wrong, but it was not so much to do with his arithmetic as the aggressive brilliance of the Somerset batsmen. Set 476, they carved and clubbed in a style that was always more transfixing than mere slogging. In the end it was a team conquest, and in particular a daring, dazzling triumph for Trego, whose hundred came from

---

HIGHEST FOURTH-INNINGS CHAMPIONSHIP TOTALS TO WIN

502-6	Middlesex v Nottinghamshire at Nottingham	1925
479-6	**Somerset v Yorkshire at Taunton**	**2009**
461-3	Nottinghamshire v Worcestershire at Worcester	2001
455-8	Sussex v Gloucestershire at Hove	1999
453-9	Durham v Somerset at Taunton	2004
449-9	Worcestershire v Somerset at Bath	1996
446-8	Hampshire v Gloucestershire at Southampton (Northlands Road)	1990
442-6	Essex v Derbyshire at Derby	1992

---

54 balls. He called it the best innings of his life, and surely no one would disagree. It was the second-highest successful chase in a Championship match, and the biggest since 1925, and brought Somerset a third successive victory. The finish deserved a larger crowd. Trescothick, at his finest, began the beefy second-innings score. Suppiah, neat as ever, fashioned his highest first-class score. Stiff, once with Yorkshire and hardly renowned for his batting, was successfully promoted up the order; and the rest was left to Trego. One could only sympathise with Hoggard who, despite eight hard-earned wickets, finished on the losing side after Yorkshire had looked poised for their first win in a year. For Somerset, Caddick came in for his first match of the season; he failed to take a wicket, though would have taken two had he not overstepped and a chance been held in the gully. Just as the previous summer here, Rudolph scored a thoroughly notable hundred, so nearly a double, and was out for a duck in the second innings. It was later the turn of his opening partner, Sayers, for a century as Yorkshire built what had looked like an unassailable total.

Close of play: First day, Yorkshire 375-7 (Shahzad 5); Second day, Somerset 326-9 (Stiff 6, Willoughby 6); Third day, Yorkshire 329-5 (Bairstow 54).

Yorkshire

J. A. Rudolph b Stiff	191	– c Trescothick b Willoughby	0
J. J. Sayers b Thomas	8	– b de Bruyn	152
*A. McGrath c Kieswetter b Trego	40	– b Willoughby	25
A. Lyth c Hildreth b de Bruyn	36	– c Kieswetter b Stiff	71
A. W. Gale c Trescothick b Willoughby	17	– c Trescothick b Thomas	16
†J. M. Bairstow c Kieswetter b Thomas	39	– not out	66
Azeem Rafiq c Kieswetter b Thomas	4		
A. Shahzad not out	27	– (7) not out	16
M. J. Hoggard c Thomas b Stiff	26		
S. A. Patterson c Kieswetter b Stiff	8		
J. E. Lee c Trescothick b Stiff	2		
B 13, l-b 11, w 8, n-b 8	40	B 1, l-b 3, w 3, n-b 10	17

1/24 (2) 2/104 (3) 3/222 (4) (112 overs) 438
4/267 (5) 5/338 (1) 6/370 (7)
7/375 (6) 8/409 (9) 9/436 (10) 10/438 (11)

1/0 (1) (5 wkts dec, 96.5 overs) 363
2/58 (3) 3/181 (4)
4/221 (5) 5/329 (2)

Willoughby 23–3–78–1; Thomas 24–3–65–3; Caddick 20–2–94–0; Stiff 19–2–92–4; Trego 13–4–30–1; Suppiah 8–4–28–0; de Bruyn 5–1–27–1. *Second Innings*—Willoughby 19–6–39–2; Thomas 13–1–63–1; Caddick 15–4–45–0; Suppiah 27.5–4–99–0; Trego 6–0–34–0; Stiff 11–0–52–1; de Bruyn 5–0–27–1.

Somerset

M. E. Trescothick c and b Lee	146	– b Hoggard	96
A. V. Suppiah c Sayers b Hoggard	17	– c McGrath b Azeem Rafiq	131
*J. L. Langer lbw b Patterson	4	– (5) c Bairstow b Patterson	24
J. C. Hildreth b Shahzad	51	– (3) b Hoggard	18
Z. de Bruyn c Gale b Lee	31	– (8) not out	27
†C. Kieswetter b Shahzad	28	– b Azeem Rafiq	17
P. D. Trego lbw b Hoggard	7	– not out	103
A. C. Thomas c Bairstow b Hoggard	13		
D. A. Stiff not out	6	– (4) c Bairstow b Hoggard	49
A. R. Caddick b Hoggard	1		
C. M. Willoughby c Bairstow b Hoggard	6		
L-b 15, w 1	16	B 1, l-b 7, w 2, n-b 4	14

1/51 (2) 2/64 (3) 3/144 (4) (79.4 overs) 326
4/215 (5) 5/277 (6) 6/287 (7)
7/313 (8) 8/315 (1) 9/316 (10) 10/326 (11)

1/187 (1) (6 wkts, 85.3 overs) 479
2/246 (2) 3/292 (3)
4/307 (4) 5/338 (6) 6/414 (5)

Hoggard 19.4–2–82–5; Shahzad 20–3–57–2; Patterson 14–2–55–1; Lee 13–1–63–2; Azeem Rafiq 13–0–54–0. *Second Innings*—Hoggard 24–0–118–3; Shahzad 19–1–119–0; Patterson 21–2–98–1; Lee 6–0–50–0; Azeem Rafiq 14.3–0–72–2; Rudolph 1–0–14–0.

Umpires: T. E. Jesty and D. J. Millns.

SOMERSET v HAMPSHIRE

At Taunton, July 10, 11, 12, 13. Drawn. Somerset 12 pts, Hampshire 8 pts. Toss: Hampshire.

This was a dogged recovery by Hampshire, gratifying to them in the way they thwarted Somerset after an innings defeat looked possible, but hardly entertaining for the home spectators; Crawley batted nearly six hours for 81 while guiding his side to safety, with plenty of single-minded support in the second innings. The Taunton pitch predictably offered little to the bowlers. Somerset had scorched to more than 500 at the outset, with Hildreth eloquently ending a relatively nondescript sequence. Later, Stiff managed a career-best five for 91. The moments of elevating cricket, such as Carberry's fine hundred, were partly obscured as the match petered out. Somerset, 21 points behind leaders Durham before the game, and still fancied in the chase, had hoped for a better reward after effortlessly constructing their early total.

Close of play: First day, Somerset 368-6 (Hildreth 124, Thomas 5); Second day, Hampshire 83-0 (Carberry 49, Adams 30); Third day, Hampshire 122-3 (Crawley 14, Dawson 21).

Somerset

M. E. Trescothick c Crawley b Mascarenhas	22	A. R. Caddick b Ervine 3
A. V. Suppiah c Crawley b Tremlett	52	C. M. Willoughby not out 0
*J. L. Langer lbw b Tomlinson	30	
J. C. Hildreth c Mascarenhas b Tomlinson .	155	B 4, l-b 2, n-b 30 36
Z. de Bruyn c Crawley b Tomlinson	24	___
†C. Kieswetter c Crawley b Imran Tahir....	43	1/38 (1) 2/81 (3) (127.4 overs) 510
P. D. Trego c sub (T. G. Burrows) b Tremlett	50	3/147 (2) 4/182 (5) 5/282 (6)
A. C. Thomas c Tomlinson b Ervine......	70	6/358 (7) 7/445 (4) 8/498 (9)
D. A. Stiff st sub (T. G. Burrows) b Dawson	25	9/505 (10) 10/510 (8) 120 overs: 482-7

Mascarenhas 33–9–87–1; Tremlett 25–1–111–2; Tomlinson 27–4–119–3; Imran Tahir 30–0–141–1; Ervine 7.4–1–39–2; Dawson 5–1–7–1.

Hampshire

M. A. Carberry c Willoughby b Stiff	123	– c and b Suppiah 52
J. H. K. Adams c Trescothick b Willoughby	33	– lbw b Caddick 28
M. J. Lumb c Suppiah b Thomas	11	– lbw b Suppiah 3
J. P. Crawley c Trescothick b Stiff	2	– not out 81
L. A. Dawson c de Bruyn b Stiff	0	– lbw b Trego 69
S. M. Ervine c Hildreth b Suppiah	10	– lbw b Suppiah 58
*A. D. Mascarenhas c Trescothick b Stiff	0	
†N. Pothas c Hildreth b Stiff	15	– (7) not out..................... 49
C. T. Tremlett c Trescothick b Suppiah	7	
J. A. Tomlinson not out	14	
Imran Tahir c Kieswetter b Thomas............	33	
L-b 4, w 2, n-b 10.....................	16	L-b 2, n-b 15 17
		___

1/89 (2) 2/126 (3) 3/157 (4)   (61.3 overs) 264   1/51 (2)   (5 wkts dec, 121 overs) 357
4/157 (5) 5/185 (6) 6/186 (7)   2/68 (3) 3/87 (1)
7/204 (8) 8/208 (1) 9/216 (9) 10/264 (11)   4/185 (5) 5/273 (6)

Willoughby 14–5–48–1; Caddick 11–1–60–0; Stiff 15–1–91–5; Trego 1–0–12–0; Thomas 10.3–4–22–2; Suppiah 10–5–27–2. *Second Innings*—Willoughby 25–6–85–0; Thomas 22–8–59–0; Suppiah 24–7–58–3; Caddick 22–6–68–1; Stiff 13–3–46–0; Trego 11–2–33–1; de Bruyn 4–1–6–0.

Umpires: N. L. Bainton and R. T. Robinson.

At Worcester, July 21, 22, 23, 24. SOMERSET drew with WORCESTERSHIRE.

SOMERSET v NOTTINGHAMSHIRE

At Taunton, July 31, August 1, 2, 3. Drawn. Somerset 12 pts, Nottinghamshire 10 pts. Toss: Somerset. County debut: S. A. Newman.

Maybe there was too much batting talent and canny attitude on view for risk-taking declarations from two teams anxiously eyeing Durham's strong position above them. It was really Read who defiantly averted any Nottinghamshire follow-on fears by crafting an elegant near-century from No. 8. Somerset, formidable in the middle order, had set the pattern in the singularly good-natured conditions. Trescothick, briefly continuing his free-scoring form, became the first batsman to pass 1,000 first-class runs for the season. In the second innings he was out for 99, from his fourth dismissal of the summer in the late nineties. Some of the most threatening bowling came from the left-arm swing of Sidebottom, as if pressing for his Test recall, and Somerset's Willoughby. Caddick picked up three wickets and announced that he would retire at season's end. Once again, Langer shaped like a batsman who had departed the Test scene too quickly, while Suppiah's exhibition of strokeplay in the second innings was not only his most productive, but his best.

Close of play: First day, Somerset 316-5 (de Bruyn 62, Trego 13); Second day, Nottinghamshire 77-3 (Newman 46, Sidebottom 3); Third day, Somerset 29-0 (Trescothick 6, Suppiah 23).

Somerset

M. E. Trescothick c Brown b Adams	37	– c Pattinson b Patel	99
A. V. Suppiah c Read b Sidebottom	51	– b Voges	151
*J. L. Langer lbw b Sidebottom	79		
Z. de Bruyn c Voges b Sidebottom	74	– not out	28
W. J. Durston c Read b Waller	0	– (3) not out	54
†C. Kieswetter c Read b Ealham	67		
P. D. Trego not out	66		
A. C. Thomas c Read b Ealham	6		
M. T. C. Waller lbw b Sidebottom	1		
A. R. Caddick not out	11		
B 2, l-b 3, n-b 4	9	B 4, l-b 2, n-b 6	12

1/45 (1) 2/167 (2)   (8 wkts dec, 100.4 overs) 401   1/229 (1)   (2 wkts dec, 97.3 overs) 344
3/172 (3) 4/172 (5)   2/276 (2)
5/280 (6) 6/361 (4) 7/382 (8) 8/389 (9)

C. M. Willoughby did not bat.

Sidebottom 26.4–6–106–5; Pattinson 11–0–82–0; Adams 21–3–86–1; Ealham 23–5–62–2; Franks 15–3–52–0; Voges 1–0–1–0. *Second Innings*—Sidebottom 8–2–28–0; Adams 11–2–22–0; Pattinson 16–1–73–0; Franks 15–5–37–0; Ealham 7–0–12–0; Patel 27–1–113–1; Voges 11.3–0–41–1; Brown 2–0–12–0.

Nottinghamshire

S. A. Newman lbw b Suppiah	87	M. A. Ealham not out	64
M. J. Wood c Suppiah b Caddick	9	A. R. Adams c Suppiah b Thomas	6
P. J. Franks c Kieswetter b Willoughby	4	D. J. Pattinson b Willoughby	1
A. C. Voges c Suppiah b Caddick	10	B 4, l-b 6, w 1, n-b 14	25
R. J. Sidebottom lbw b Willoughby	5		
S. R. Patel c Kieswetter b Caddick	19	1/24 (2) 2/37 (3) 3/73 (4) (92.3 overs) 356
A. D. Brown c Kieswetter b Waller	28	4/97 (5) 5/147 (1) 6/147 (6)
*†C. M. W. Read c Waller b Willoughby	98	7/222 (7) 8/338 (8) 9/345 (10) 10/356 (11)

Willoughby 22.3–6–71–4; Caddick 20–2–96–3; Thomas 23–3–83–1; Suppiah 7–1–12–1; Waller 11–2–37–1; Trego 7–0–34–0; Durston 2–0–13–0.

Umpires: N. G. Cowley and N. J. Llong.

At Birmingham, August 5, 6, 7, 8. SOMERSET drew with WARWICKSHIRE.

SOMERSET v SUSSEX

At Taunton, August 19, 20, 21, 22. Drawn. Somerset 10 pts, Sussex 10 pts. Toss: Sussex.

Here at county headquarters, where scoring statistics soar and batsmen are understandably reluctant to depart, Sussex were playing for the second time in a week – and glad to be batting first. They eventually declared at a monopolistic 742 for five, the highest in their history, beating 705 for eight against Surrey at Hastings in 1902. In the process, Goodwin finished undefeated on 344, a memorably polished exhibition, even if he survived a few chances, two at the wicket, and might have been out before he had scored. In all the summers of Ranji, Fry, Duleep and Dexter, no Sussex batsman had ever scored more in an innings, Goodwin surpassing his own county record of 335 not out set against Leicestershire six years earlier. At his side he had Nash and Hopkinson, each with a career-best hundred and, for Hopkinson, the opportunity to share a county-record fourth-wicket stand. For Somerset, patience and even good nature may have slightly wavered. Some of the home fans became critical of Langer for delaying the use of young leg-spinner Max Waller. The captain threw his cap

CHAMPIONSHIP SCORING AT COUNTY GROUNDS, 2000–9

	Matches	Total runs	Total wickets	Runs per wicket
Taunton	73	79,487	1,913	**41.55**
The Oval	62	66,666	1,750	38.09
Lord's	59	61,289	1,673	36.63
Birmingham	78	78,379	2,152	36.42
Chelmsford	57	60,557	1,707	35.47
Northampton	80	81,108	2,295	35.34
Cardiff	54	52,723	1,494	35.28
Canterbury	63	63,857	1,844	34.62
Bristol	55	52,972	1,594	33.23
Derby	74	70,855	2,137	33.15
Leeds	59	54,011	1,639	32.95
Nottingham	80	75,392	2,292	32.89
Hove	60	61,661	1,885	32.71
Worcester	72	69,300	2,153	32.18
Leicester	75	70,613	2,194	32.18
Manchester	64	55,775	1,773	31.45
Southampton	70	63,493	2,131	29.79
Chester-le-Street	74	65,990	2,320	28.44

down in a gesture of frustration, saying later: "I don't blame the supporters, but I was doing the best I could in the circumstances." Somerset predictably sailed past 500 themselves, as Suppiah and Kieswetter took their turn to score more centuries. After all the handsome strokes and the excesses, there was no prospect of a result, especially after play was lost to rain on the third day.

Close of play: First day, Sussex 326-3 (Goodwin 96, Hopkinson 7); Second day, Somerset 126-0 (Trescothick 55, Suppiah 61); Third day, Somerset 164-0 (Trescothick 71, Suppiah 80).

Sussex

*M. H. Yardy c Kieswetter b Willoughby	15	†A. J. Hodd not out	18
C. D. Nash c Suppiah b Thomas	157	B 12, l-b 5, w 3, n-b 8	28
E. C. Joyce lbw b Trego	37		
M. W. Goodwin not out	344	1/44 (1) (5 wkts dec, 164 overs)	742
C. D. Hopkinson b Suppiah	139	2/142 (3) 3/313 (2)	
D. R. Smith b Suppiah	4	4/676 (5) 5/680 (6) 120 overs: 446-3	

R. S. C. Martin-Jenkins, O. P. Rayner, Yasir Arafat and C. D. Collymore did not bat.

Willoughby 28–8–96–1; Thomas 27–4–97–1; Banks 21–3–114–0; Suppiah 19–1–117–2; Trego 18–3–71–1; de Bruyn 18–0–83–0; Waller 33–1–147–0.

Somerset

M. E. Trescothick c Joyce b Smith	73	M. T. C. Waller not out	3
A. V. Suppiah lbw b Rayner	133		
J. C. Hildreth c Hodd b Smith	11	B 12, l-b 12, w 7, n-b 12	43
Z. de Bruyn c Goodwin b Rayner	3		
†C. Kieswetter not out	135	1/169 (1) 2/192 (3) (6 wkts, 133 overs)	521
P. D. Trego c Hopkinson b Rayner	67	3/203 (4) 4/280 (2)	
O. A. C. Banks lbw b Rayner	53	5/411 (6) 6/511 (7) 120 overs: 422-5	

*J. L. Langer, A. C. Thomas and C. M. Willoughby did not bat.

Yasir Arafat 22–4–98–0; Collymore 6–2–20–0; Rayner 52–7–186–4; Martin-Jenkins 6–2–19–0; Smith 36–15–91–2; Nash 3–0–6–0; Yardy 6–0–64–0; Goodwin 2–0–13–0.

Umpires: R. A. Kettleborough and G. Sharp.

At Southampton, August 27, 28, 29, 30. SOMERSET drew with HAMPSHIRE.

At Chester-le-Street, September 1, 2, 3, 4. SOMERSET drew with DURHAM.

SOMERSET v LANCASHIRE

At Taunton, September 9, 10, 11, 12. Drawn. Somerset 12 pts, Lancashire 8 pts. Toss: Somerset. First-class debut: J. C. Buttler.

Lancashire batted largely untroubled through the last day, an anti-climactic one for Somerset, who went wicketless while Durham were thrashing Nottinghamshire to retain the title. Centuries from Loye and Laxman nullified the home county's aspirations. Surprisingly put in by Trescothick, captaining in the absence of Langer, Lancashire leaned on Horton's dominant career-best innings. Willoughby, ever reliable with his swing bowling, once more passed 50 wickets for the season, while Phillips was justly rewarded with four economically earned victims. Somerset's sturdy batting riposte brought Trescothick his eighth hundred of the Championship summer, though the graceful Suppiah was dismissed five short of three figures. Again the Taunton crowd feasted on an array of aggression and good-looking control as Kieswetter went to 1,000 Championship runs for the first time with his highest score to date. With Trego he creamed 183 in 35 overs, a sixth-wicket record by Somerset against Lancashire. Debutant Jos Buttler, a 19-year-old student from King's College, Taunton, and *Young Wisden* Schools Cricketer of the Year, marked his arrival with a neat little innings; his wicketkeeping skills may not be needed much, however, with Kieswetter around.

Close of play: First day, Lancashire 297-5 (Horton 155, Hogg 69); Second day, Somerset 266-3 (de Bruyn 36, Buttler 13); Third day, Lancashire 87-2 (Loye 23, Laxman 16).

Lancashire

P. J. Horton c Kieswetter b Willoughby	173	– (2) c Kieswetter b Stiff	32
†L. D. Sutton c Kieswetter b Phillips	26	– (1) c Kieswetter b Thomas	16
M. B. Loye lbw b Willoughby	14	– not out	151
V. V. S. Laxman c Kieswetter b Willoughby	12	– not out	113
M. J. Chilton c Kieswetter b Phillips	0		
F. du Plessis c Kieswetter b Phillips	1		
K. W. Hogg c Trescothick b Willoughby	69		
*G. Chapple lbw b Willoughby	0		
S. I. Mahmood c Suppiah b Thomas	9		
O. J. Newby c Kieswetter b Phillips	13		
G. Keedy not out	3		
B 10, l-b 8, w 6	24	N-b 2	2

1/58 (2) 2/99 (3) 3/119 (4)   (105.1 overs) 344   1/27 (1)   (2 wkts, 111 overs) 314
4/128 (5) 5/153 (6) 6/303 (7)   2/67 (2)
7/303 (8) 8/318 (9) 9/330 (1) 10/344 (10)

Willoughby 28-6-109-5; Thomas 22-2-58-1; Phillips 19.1-6-46-4; Stiff 15-2-47-0; Trego 9-1-34-0; Suppiah 4-0-7-0; de Bruyn 8-3-25-0. *Second Innings*—Willoughby 23.5-5-64-0; Thomas 19-6-42-1; Stiff 18-1-70-1; Phillips 10-0-27-0; Suppiah 28-3-75-0; Trego 7-1-24-0; de Bruyn 6-2-12-0.

Somerset

*M. E. Trescothick b Mahmood	102	D. A. Stiff c Sutton b Keedy	0
A. V. Suppiah b Chapple	95		
Z. de Bruyn c Laxman b Hogg	71	B 9, l-b 5, n-b 6	20
J. C. Hildreth b Mahmood	5		
J. C. Buttler c Sutton b Chapple	30	1/193 (1) (8 wkts dec, 137.1 overs) 557	
†C. Kieswetter c du Plessis b Newby	153	2/221 (2) 3/230 (4)	
P. D. Trego c Mahmood b Keedy	80	4/299 (5) 5/350 (6) 6/533 (7)	
B. J. Phillips not out	1	7/557 (6) 8/557 (9) 120 overs: 460-5	

A. C. Thomas and C. M. Willoughby did not bat.

Chapple 28-11-81-2; Mahmood 28-6-96-2; Keedy 36.1-3-143-2; Newby 17-4-88-1; Hogg 19-5-91-1; Laxman 2-0-5-0; du Plessis 7-0-39-0.

Umpires: M. J. D. Bodenham and V. A. Holder.

SOMERSET v WORCESTERSHIRE

At Taunton, September 16, 17, 18, 19. Drawn. Somerset 8 pts, Worcestershire 12 pts. Toss: Worcestershire. First-class debut: O. B. Cox.

It looked as though the visitors – already relegated – might win their first game of the season after Mitchell had brought substance to their determined total with his unruffled innings just short of 300 on this familiar flat cliché of a pitch. He hit a six and 54 fours, most to the short western boundary, and shared a stand of 124 with 17-year-old schoolboy Ben Cox. Somerset were 291 behind on first innings but salvaged their ninth consecutive draw – not the way they intended to commemorate Langer's last Championship match. The final walk from the crease was warmly acknowledged; his disciplined qualities had introduced additional resolve to the side. Trescothick had hoped for a battery of late runs to take him nearer the elusive 2,000 mark. The centurion was in fact de Bruyn, compensating for some patchy form. Somerset's second innings eased past 500, with the best bowling coming from their former seamer Andrew. However mutually generous Langer's farewell, he was not inhibited about criticising Somerset's first-innings batting form. Kieswetter and Suppiah were awarded their county caps during the match.

Close of play: First day, Worcestershire 408-4 (Mitchell 232, Wheeldon 87); Second day, Somerset 184-3 (Hildreth 19, de Bruyn 15); Third day, Somerset 203-4 (de Bruyn 20, Kieswetter 10).

Worcestershire

D. K. H. Mitchell b Trego	298	M. S. Mason b Trego	4
S. C. Moore c Kieswetter b Stiff	32	J. D. Shantry b Stiff	1
*V. S. Solanki c Trescothick b Willoughby	15		
M. M. Ali c Kieswetter b Willoughby	1	B 5, l-b 14, n-b 16	35
A. N. Kervezee c Suppiah b Stiff	19		
D. A. Wheeldon c Phillips b Thomas	87	1/73 (2) 2/109 (3) (141.2 overs) 571	
G. M. Andrew c de Bruyn b Thomas	0	3/111 (4) 4/191 (5) 5/409 (6)	
†O. B. Cox b Trego	61	6/415 (7) 7/539 (1) 8/542 (8)	
R. A. Jones not out	18	9/548 (10) 10/571 (11) 120 overs: 504-6	

Willoughby 35–9–126–2; Thomas 23–5–104–2; Phillips 26–6–74–0; Stiff 17.2–0–102–3; Trego 20–4–89–3; Suppiah 20–6–57–0.

Somerset

M. E. Trescothick st Cox b Ali	72	– c Mitchell b Mason	0
A. V. Suppiah b Andrew	22	– c Cox b Andrew	83
*J. L. Langer c Wheeldon b Shantry	46	– c Ali b Andrew	64
J. C. Hildreth c Solanki b Mason	24	– c Cox b Jones	18
Z. de Bruyn c Cox b Jones	15	– c Solanki b Andrew	106
†C. Kieswetter lbw b Mason	1	– c Kervezee b Andrew	90
P. D. Trego c Ali b Mason	0	– lbw b Andrew	9
B. J. Phillips c Jones b Shantry	18	– c Solanki b Andrew	84
A. C. Thomas c Cox b Andrew	38	– not out	54
D. A. Stiff not out	30	– not out	0
C. M. Willoughby c Shantry b Andrew	1		
L-b 6, w 3, n-b 4	13	B 5, l-b 6, w 2, n-b 2	15

1/45 (2) 2/143 (3) 3/161 (1)	(78.3 overs) 280	1/0 (1) (8 wkts, 133 overs) 523
4/189 (5) 5/189 (4) 6/189 (7)		2/142 (2) 3/163 (3)
7/190 (6) 8/239 (9) 9/247 (8) 10/281 (11)		4/175 (4) 5/342 (6) 6/366 (7)
		7/398 (5) 8/523 (8)

Mason 24–9–60–3; Jones 11–1–42–1; Andrew 17.3–3–75–3; Shantry 16–4–65–2; Ali 10–2–32–1. *Second Innings*—Mason 14–5–28–1; Jones 29–3–142–1; Ali 26–3–136–0; Andrew 30–4–117–5; Shantry 21–6–61–1; Mitchell 6–1–11–0; Solanki 7–2–17–0.

Umpires: D. J. Millns and G. Sharp.

SURREY

Buildings for the future

DAVID LLEWELLYN

Off-field improvements at The Oval were not echoed on the field in 2009. While the Surrey administration rejoiced in being given the go-ahead to build a 168-bedroom hotel at the Pavilion End, together with a stand that will increase capacity to 25,000, the county side was regularly being demolished. Some members believe that the team does not receive much interest or attention from the administrators because the half-dozen international match-days generate so much more income than around 35 days of county cricket. However, the county side certainly does need help, because, by anyone's standards – not least their own – Surrey's performance in all competitions was second-rate.

They finished seventh in the County Championship's second division, recording a solitary victory (their only one in two seasons); they were bottom of the second tier of the Pro40, missed the knockout stages of the Friends Provident, and in the Twenty20 Cup – a competition they dominated in its early years – managed just two wins. The only bright spot was that Surrey won the Second Eleven Championship.

True, the first team was shorn of the astute captaincy of Mark Butcher for all but five games (the lone Championship win, an innings victory over Northamptonshire, came under his command). Mark Ramprakash sat out the opening two matches while serving a ban for dissent late in 2008, and missed the last three with a fractured thumb. The enforced absence of this key pair was a significant factor, but a team is more than just two batsmen.

The maths was fairly straightforward: to win a match you had to bowl a side out twice. That meant, for a return to the top flight to be seriously contemplated, the bowling attack had to aim to take 320 Championship wickets. The 21 bowlers employed by Surrey in 2009 managed just over half that – 184 – and only once did they bowl a side out twice. Lack of penetration has been an annual complaint in recent years.

Jade Dernbach was going well until he picked up an injury and chose, probably unwisely, to play on. He did collect two six-wicket hauls, although neither won a match, and he was Surrey's leading wicket-taker with 37 (Alec Bedser's view of such a statistic is probably unprintable). Andre Nel did a manful job until sidelined by a freak elbow injury with five games remaining, but no one else was able to step up when he dropped out. The desperate late signings of Richard Logan, Jimmy Anyon and the Sri Lankan Test slow left-armer Rangana Herath produced pitiful returns. Pedro Collins contributed next to nothing and was released, along with Alex Tudor. Chris Schofield (who looked more like a batsman who could bowl a bit than a specialist leg-spinner who bats), ploughed a lone furrow on the spinning front, although Simon King, a Surrey-born off-spinner, looked promising before being moved aside for

Rory Hamilton-Brown

Herath. Stuart Meaker, who picked up three disciplinary points (taking his running total to six, just three off an automatic ban) for the second of two beamers at Leicester, clearly needs more game time in order to master control of undoubted pace; it is also vital that Chris Jordan sharpens up and gets fitter.

The batting was not that great, either. Early on Surrey took a firm line with James Benning, sending him out on loan to underachieve elsewhere, in his case Leicestershire, for whom he signed during the winter. Scott Newman was also banished on loan, to Trent Bridge, for unspecified reasons; he joined Middlesex for 2010. Of those left only Usman Afzaal and "Old Reliable", Ramprakash, passed 1,000 runs for the season, although Michael Brown, in his first season since leaving Hampshire, just missed out. Ramprakash, who got there despite missing those five games, topped the national averages once again; Afzaal was 20 places lower, but was still able to boast an impressive 57.68. But apart from Butcher, who averaged 41 before he lost the battle of his wounded knee and retired, no one else made a significant contribution.

Stand-in captain Stewart Walters did score his maiden first-class hundred, following it up next innings with an even bigger one, but his overall performance was below par; Matthew Spriegel also registered his first century, while showing signs that he could become a consistent performer. Arun Harinath scored his maiden Championship fifty in only his fifth innings.

Jon Batty rounded off another consistent season with a couple of hundreds, although he fell just short of four figures. What he made of the signing from Worcestershire of Steve Davies, the 23-year-old England wicketkeeper, was perhaps clear from Batty's move to Gloucestershire, after making 120 in his final innings for the county he captained in 2004.

Gus Mackay, the managing director of Surrey cricket, and his professional cricket manager Chris Adams clearly had some thinking to do after the season. After their conclave, the white smoke emerging from The Oval anointed a new captain: Rory Hamilton-Brown, just 22, was lured back to Surrey from Sussex, where he had decamped in 2008 in search of regular cricket. Although he did make two centuries in 2009, by the time he rejoined Surrey Hamilton-Brown had played only eight first-class matches, so his elevation carried a whiff of desperation, for all Adams's encouraging words. Time will tell.

Adams also recruited his new overseas player from Sussex, snapping up the young Indian leg-spinner Piyush Chawla. Another returnee is off-spinner Gareth Batty, like Davies signed from Worcestershire, while Surrey liked to think they could finally get the best from Hampshire's Chris Tremlett.

SURREY RESULTS

All first-class matches – Played 16: Won 1, Lost 4, Drawn 11.
County Championship matches – Played 16: Won 1, Lost 4, Drawn 11.

LV County Championship, 7th in Division 2; Friends Provident Trophy, 5th in Group C;
Pro40 League, 9th in Division 2; Twenty20 Cup, 5th in South Division.

COUNTY CHAMPIONSHIP AVERAGES, BATTING AND FIELDING

Cap		M	I	NO	R	HS	100s	50s	Avge	Ct/St
2002	M. R. Ramprakash	11	17	2	1,350	274	5	4	90.00	5
2009	U. Afzaal	16	28	6	1,269	204*	3	7	57.68	3
1996	M. A. Butcher†	5	8	2	251	65	0	2	41.83	10
	M. J. Brown	16	28	1	992	120	2	4	36.74	7
2001	J. N. Batty	16	26	0	937	120	2	1	36.03	46/4
	C. P. Schofield	14	21	3	644	144	1	3	35.77	7
	S. J. Walters¶	11	18	0	573	188	2	1	31.83	15
	C. J. Jordan	8	10	3	213	42	0	0	30.42	0
	A. Harinath†	3	6	0	165	57	0	1	27.50	0
2005	S. A. Newman†	5	8	0	217	124	1	0	27.12	2
	S. C. Meaker	5	9	1	214	72	0	2	26.75	0
	M. N. W. Spriegel†	6	11	0	294	100	1	2	26.72	7
1999	A. J. Tudor	4	6	2	83	33	0	0	20.75	1
	H. M. R. K. B. Herath§ .	3	5	1	80	52*	0	1	20.00	0
	T. E. Linley	5	6	1	98	36	0	0	19.60	1
	Murtaza Hussain¶	7	8	1	111	34	0	0	15.85	0
	A. Nel¶	9	10	2	117	32	0	0	14.62	3
	J. W. Dernbach¶	14	19	6	138	19	0	0	10.61	1
	P. T. Collins¶	5	8	3	49	23	0	0	9.80	1
	L. J. Evans	2	4	0	23	9	0	0	5.75	0

Also batted: J. E. Anyon (1 match) 0*, 1*; J. G. E. Benning (2 matches) 0, 5, 36; G. D. Elliott§ (1 match) 1, 22 (2 ct); R. J. Harris§ (2 matches) 4, 94 (1 ct); S. J. King† (2 matches) 0, 8; R. J. Logan (1 match) 0, 6; C. P. Murtagh (2 matches) 15, 14* (2 ct).

† *Born in Surrey.*   § *Official overseas player.*   ¶ *Other non-England-qualified player.*

BOWLING

	O	M	R	W	BB	5W/i	Avge
A. Nel	260.4	69	754	27	6-36	1	27.92
P. T. Collins	137.2	25	504	16	5-75	1	31.50
J. W. Dernbach	395.2	67	1,436	37	6-47	2	38.81
Murtaza Hussain	271	47	825	19	4-70	0	43.42
S. C. Meaker	110.4	11	498	10	3-114	0	49.80
C. J. Jordan	208.2	36	764	13	4-84	0	58.76
C. P. Schofield	363.5	35	1,357	22	5-40	1	61.68

Also bowled: U. Afzaal 87.5–6–348–7; J. E. Anyon 7–0–59–0; J. G. E. Benning 15–2–52–2; M. J. Brown 3–0–20–0; G. D. Elliott 2–0–15–0; R. J. Harris 33.5–6–135–3; H. M. R. K. B. Herath 108.2–8–431–8; S. J. King 39.3–2–156–4; T. E. Linley 131–23–442–8; R. J. Logan 30–6–101–2; S. A. Newman 3–0–10–0; M. N. W. Spriegel 44.4–2–205–2; A. J. Tudor 100–18–417–4; S. J. Walters 19–2–75–0.

OFFICIALS

Captain 2009 – M. A. Butcher;
        2010 – R. J. Hamilton-Brown
Professional cricket manager C. J. Adams
Batting coach G. P. Thorpe
Bowling coach M. P. Bicknell
Coach/consultant A. J. Stewart

President D. T. Watts
Chairman D. P. Stewart
Chief executive P. C. J. Sheldon
Chairman of cricket R. Harman
Head groundsman W. H. Gordon
Scorer K. R. Booth

COUNTY RECORDS

Highest score for:	357*	R. Abel v Somerset at The Oval	1899
Highest score against:	366	N. H. Fairbrother (Lancashire) at The Oval	1990
Leading run-scorer:	43,554	J. B. Hobbs (avge 49.72)	1905–1934
Best bowling for:	10-43	T. Rushby v Somerset at Taunton.	1921
Best bowling against:	10-28	W. P. Howell (Australians) at The Oval.	1899
Leading wicket-taker:	1,775	T. Richardson (avge 17.87)	1892–1904
Highest total for:	811	v Somerset at The Oval.	1899
Highest total against:	863	by Lancashire at The Oval	1990
Lowest total for:	14	v Essex at Chelmsford	1983
Lowest total against:	16	by MCC at Lord's.	1872

ADDRESS

The Oval, Kennington, London SE11 5SS (0871 246 1100; **email** enquiries@surreycricket.com).
Website www.surreycricket.com

Rory, Rory, bring us some glory

Desperate times call for desperate measures. And the signing of the inexperienced Rory Hamilton-Brown, aged 22, as Surrey's captain on a three-year contract worth somewhere in the region of £400,000–450,000 certainly smacks of desperation. It is Surrey's professional cricket manager Chris Adams's first major signing, and *prima facie* a major gamble. Hamilton-Brown's primary brief is to take Surrey back to the first division of the Championship; failure to do so would almost certainly cost Adams his performance-related £90,000-a-year job.

Hamilton-Brown, the 40th captain in Surrey's history, is the least experienced in over 60 years, with just eight first-class matches to his name. Neither Swainson Akroyd (1869) nor Nigel Bennett (1946) had played any first-class cricket when they were appointed, while William Collyer (1867) with six matches, and John Gregory (1871) with seven (three of them for Middlesex) edge Hamilton-Brown into fifth. None set the world alight with their cricket.

Adams, though, has faith. Hamilton-Brown, who will be the youngest captain in the 2010 Championship, caught his eye in early 2008, after he had been released by Surrey to join Adams at Sussex. So when Adams describes him as a "super-talented cricketer" possessed of "charisma, intelligence and the ability to get people to follow [him]," he speaks from first-hand knowledge.

Hamilton-Brown led England Under-15s and, more significantly, England Under-19s. And there are signs of a prodigious talent as a middle-order batsman – he scored his maiden Championship hundred against Yorkshire at Hove last season. He is also a promising off-spinner. As a product of the Surrey academy before moving to Hove he will have the advantage of knowing most of his new squad. DAVID LLEWELLYN

At The Oval, April 10, 11, 12 (not first-class). **Drawn.** Toss: Leeds/Bradford UCCE. **Surrey 220-4 dec** (M. J. Brown 102, C. P. Murtagh 64*; T. S. Roland-Jones 3-57) **and 55-1; Leeds/Bradford UCCE 247** (C. Dougherty 35, A. G. Burton 46, C. G. Prowting 53, Extras 37; S. J. King 3-39). *County debuts:* R. S. G. Anderson, M. J. Brown, R. J. Burns, S. J. King, T. E. Linley, C. E. J. Thompson.

The captain, Michael Brown, hit 102 from 135 balls and was one of six players making their Surrey debut; another was Ricky Anderson, who had left Northamptonshire in 2004. The weather was reluctant to leave this match alone, but there was time for Christopher Prowting, the students' captain and wicketkeeper, to steer his side to a modest first-innings lead.

SURREY v GLOUCESTERSHIRE

At The Oval, April 15, 16, 17, 18. Drawn. Surrey 7 pts, Gloucestershire 10 pts. Toss: Gloucestershire. County debuts: L. J. Evans, A. Nel.

The rescue of a cat, apparently trapped in the narrowest of gaps between the committee balcony and the adjoining Bedser Stand, proved the high point of a blank third day. It subsequently transpired that the creature was able to go in and out at will, so the efforts of Surrey president Mike Soper (he took the head end, members of the groundstaff the rear, as they freed the cat in a 20-minute operation) were pointless. It was the weather, rather than their own efforts, that saw Surrey out of the tight place in which they found themselves after Kadeer Ali shared century stands with Marshall and Gidman. Eventually, Nel and Dernbach showed some teeth to engineer a Gloucestershire collapse from 247 for two but, without the banned Mark Ramprakash (see *Wisden 2009*, page 736) and the injured Mark Butcher, Surrey followed on 173 adrift; it would have been more but for Afzaal's dogged four-hour vigil. Brown, captaining Surrey on his first Championship appearance for them – something that had not happened since 1946, when Nigel Bennett led Surrey out after the war – helped claw back some self-respect second time around.

Close of play: First day, Gloucestershire 321-8 (Lewis 27, Banerjee 16); Second day, Surrey 18-3 (Afzaal 3, Batty 2); Third day, No play.

Gloucestershire

C. M. Spearman lbw b Nel	0	V. Banerjee c Jordan b Nel		16
Kadeer Ali lbw b Benning	90	S. P. Kirby b Dernbach		0
H. J. H. Marshall b Nel	76			
*A. P. R. Gidman c Batty b Benning	69	L-b 9, w 3, n-b 7		19
C. G. Taylor lbw b Nel	9			
J. E. C. Franklin c Spriegel b Dernbach	11	1/0 (1) 2/126 (3)	(101.3 overs)	333
†S. D. Snell b Dernbach	4	3/247 (2) 4/250 (4) 5/265 (5)		
I. D. Saxelby b Dernbach	0	6/276 (7) 7/276 (8)		
J. Lewis not out	39	8/283 (6) 9/326 (10) 10/333 (11)		

Nel 22–6–52–4; Dernbach 18.3–1–79–4; Jordan 12–3–46–0; Benning 7–1–25–2; Murtaza Hussain 23–7–61–0; Schofield 18–1–60–0; Spriegel 0–1–0–1.

Surrey

*M. J. Brown b Franklin	8	– (2) not out	35
L. J. Evans b Franklin	1	– (1) c Snell b Lewis	9
M. N. W. Spriegel lbw b Lewis	0	– c Spearman b Taylor	4
U. Afzaal c Franklin b Saxelby	65	– not out	10
†J. N. Batty b Kirby	11		
J. G. E. Benning lbw b Kirby	0		
C. J. Jordan c Spearman b Franklin	7		
C. P. Schofield b Banerjee	29		
Murtaza Hussain c Kadeer Ali b Saxelby	8		
A. Nel b Banerjee	9		
J. W. Dernbach not out	9		
B 2, l-b 4, w 1, n-b 6	13	L-b 4, n-b 2	6

1/10 (2) 2/11 (1) 3/11 (3) 4/35 (5) (61.5 overs) 160
5/35 (6) 6/46 (7) 7/91 (8) 8/108 (9)
9/133 (10) 10/160 (4)

1/20 (1) (2 wkts, 30 overs) 64
2/24 (3)

Lewis 12–2–28–1; Franklin 12–3–23–3; Kirby 14–5–44–2; Saxelby 10.5–2–33–2; Banerjee 13–4–26–2. *Second Innings*—Lewis 4–0–13–1; Franklin 3–0–7–0; Banerjee 12–4–29–0; Taylor 11–6–11–1.

Umpires: S. A. Garratt and N. A. Mallender.

At Derby, April 22, 23, 24, 25. SURREY lost to DERBYSHIRE by five wickets.

SURREY v MIDDLESEX

At The Oval, May 6, 7, 8, 9. Drawn. Surrey 10 pts, Middlesex 11 pts. Toss: Surrey. Championship debut: G. D. Elliott.

In a thrilling finish, Richardson was run out off the last ball to leave Surrey one wicket – and Middlesex two runs – from victory. The frantic final session saw Middlesex launch themselves spectacularly at a target of 186 from 25 overs, but four wickets each for spinners Murtaza Hussain, who claimed eight in the match, and Schofield managed to contain the Middlesex batsmen – just. The assault was led by Hughes, playing his last first-class game before joining the touring Australians: he smashed 57 from 46 balls, meaning he had passed fifty in all his five Championship innings. Earlier, Ramprakash, back after his two-match ban, hit his third hundred against his former employers, earning Surrey their first batting points of the season in the process. But he was upstaged by Hughes, whose third hundred in successive Championship matches fell five short of a maiden double. There was also a lusty 86 from Dawid Malan.

Close of play: First day, Surrey 290-5 (Ramprakash 126, Schofield 14); Second day, Middlesex 200-2 (Hughes 134, Morgan 7); Third day, Surrey 60-1 (Brown 27, Ramprakash 31).

Surrey

S. A. Newman c Malan b Finn	22	– c Hughes b Murtagh	2
*M. J. Brown c Scott b Murtagh	7	– c Hughes b Udal	73
M. R. Ramprakash c Richardson b Finn	133	– c Hughes b Murtagh	37
U. Afzaal b Udal	82	– c Dexter b Udal	6
†J. N. Batty lbw b Murtagh	29	– c Dexter b Udal	30
G. D. Elliott c Dexter b Richardson	1	– c Morgan b Finn	22
C. P. Schofield c Godleman b Finn	47	– c Hughes b Udal	20
Murtaza Hussain c Scott b Murtagh	0	– not out	26
A. Nel c Dexter b Udal	32	– b Udal	2
J. W. Dernbach not out	16	– c Dexter b Finn	4
S. C. Meaker b Richardson	3	– c Godleman b Udal	15
L-b 12, n-b 4	16	L-b 1, n-b 4	5

1/25 (2) 2/31 (1) 3/174 (4)   (131.2 overs) 388
4/254 (5) 5/263 (6) 6/318 (3)
7/319 (8) 8/355 (7) 9/373 (9)
10/388 (11)   120 overs: 365-8

1/2 (1) 2/82 (3)   (86.1 overs) 242
3/90 (4) 4/136 (5)
5/159 (2) 6/193 (7) 7/197 (6)
8/200 (9) 9/209 (10) 10/242 (11)

Murtagh 31–5–97–3; Richardson 25.2–6–64–2; Finn 26–2–111–3; Dexter 15–6–26–0; Udal 22–8–47–2; Malan 9–0–20–0; Compton 2–0–5–0; Hughes 1–0–6–0. *Second Innings*—Murtagh 10–0–45–2; Richardson 6–2–20–0; Udal 33.1–12–74–6; Malan 10–5–24–0; Finn 22–4–58–2; Dexter 5–1–20–0.

Middlesex

B. A. Godleman c Elliott b Nel	37	– (6) st Batty b Schofield	1
P. J. Hughes c Batty b Dernbach	195	– c Batty b Schofield	57
N. J. Dexter c Batty b Murtaza Hussain	8	– (5) b Schofield	28
E. J. G. Morgan c Batty b Dernbach	13	– (3) c Ramprakash b Murtaza Hussain	41
D. J. Malan c Brown b Nel	86	– (4) b Schofield	1
N. R. D. Compton lbw b Murtaza Hussain	23	– (1) b Murtaza Hussain	28
†B. J. M. Scott c Newman b Murtaza Hussain	0	– not out	1
*S. D. Udal b Meaker	36	– b Murtaza Hussain	6
T. J. Murtagh c Batty b Meaker	5		
S. T. Finn c Elliott b Murtaza Hussain	1	– (9) lbw b Murtaza Hussain	0
A. Richardson not out	0	– (10) run out	1
B 5, l-b 15, w 6, n-b 15	41	B 5, l-b 4, w 1, n-b 10	20

1/165 (1) 2/178 (3) 3/223 (4)   (124.1 overs) 445   1/93 (1)   (9 wkts, 25 overs) 184
4/317 (2) 5/377 (6) 6/377 (7)   2/99 (2) 3/107 (4)
7/415 (5) 8/433 (9) 9/439 (10)   4/169 (3) 5/175 (6) 6/176 (5)
10/445 (8)   120 overs: 433-7   7/183 (8) 8/183 (9) 9/184 (10)

Nel 20–3–78–2; Dernbach 17–2–52–2; Murtaza Hussain 44–11–101–4; Meaker 20.1–1–86–2; Elliott 2–0–15–0; Schofield 19–0–85–0; Afzaal 2–0–8–0. *Second Innings*—Murtaza Hussain 13–0–70–4; Nel 4–0–45–0; Schofield 6–0–49–4; Meaker 2–0–11–0.

Umpires: J. H. Evans and D. J. Millns.

At Cardiff, June 6, 7, 8, 9. SURREY drew with GLAMORGAN.

At Northampton, June 11, 12, 13, 14. SURREY beat NORTHAMPTONSHIRE by an innings and 95 runs.

At Leicester, June 16, 17, 18, 19. SURREY drew with LEICESTERSHIRE.

At Lord's, June 30, July 1, 2, 3. SURREY drew with MIDDLESEX.

SURREY v KENT

At The Oval, July 10, 11, 12, 13. Drawn. Surrey 9 pts, Kent 12 pts. Toss: Surrey.

Each side made a modest piece of history in this fixture, played out on a true Oval pitch. Kent became the first team to boast four individual hundreds in an innings against Surrey (though it would happen again before the season was out), while Murtaza Hussain's eye-watering two for 208 was the most expensive Championship return in Surrey history: their only costlier figures were John McMahon's four for 210 against Don Bradman's invincible 1948 Australians. One of the quartet of centurions was van Jaarsveld, whose record against Surrey was staggering. His third successive hundred at The Oval was also his fifth in seven matches against his favourite opponents, and it took his average against them to 94.87. Van Jaarsveld and his fellow-South African Kemp added 214 for the fifth wicket, while Key and Denly's 247 was a record opening stand for Kent against Surrey; Kent's 620 for seven declared was then their third-highest total. The in-form Ramprakash, dismissed in the eighties, was left in the shade as the visitors established a lead of 234, though Surrey hung on for the draw.

Close of play: First day, Surrey 342-8 (Schofield 34, Murtaza Hussain 7); Second day, Kent 152-0 (Denly 79, Key 71); Third day, Kent 509-5 (Kemp 121, Tredwell 16).

Surrey

†J. N. Batty c Kemp b Tredwell	44	– b McLaren	48
M. J. Brown run out	55	– c Key b Tredwell	25
M. R. Ramprakash c van Jaarsveld b Kemp	86	– c Key b Tredwell	5
*M. A. Butcher c Key b McLaren	9	– not out	60
U. Afzaal c van Jaarsveld b Khan	46	– not out	24
S. J. Walters b Parnell	12		
C. J. Jordan c Jones b Tredwell	28		
C. P. Schofield c McLaren b Khan	54		
A. J. Tudor c Kemp b Tredwell	0		
Murtaza Hussain c Jones b Khan	24		
P. T. Collins not out	1		
B 5, l-b 12, n-b 10	27	B 1, l-b 3, n-b 4	8

1/105 (1) 2/114 (2) 3/137 (4)   (115 overs) 386   1/40 (2)   (3 wkts, 62 overs) 170
4/255 (3) 5/271 (6) 6/275 (5)   2/48 (3) 3/104 (1)
7/329 (7) 8/329 (9) 9/385 (10) 10/386 (8)

Parnell 16–3–59–1; Khan 18–5–56–3; Stevens 2–1–1–0; McLaren 24–3–87–1; Cook 21–5–66–0; Tredwell 25–4–76–3; van Jaarsveld 6–2–10–0; Kemp 3–1–14–1. *Second Innings*—Khan 7–3–14–0; McLaren 6–1–26–1; Tredwell 23–7–42–2; van Jaarsveld 12–3–52–0; Cook 7–1–12–0; Denly 3–0–7–0; Key 4–1–13–0.

Kent

J. L. Denly run out	123	R. McLaren not out	4
*R. W. T. Key run out	123	B 10, l-b 4, w 1, n-b 2	17
†G. O. Jones c Batty b Collins	0		
M. van Jaarsveld lbw b Tudor	110	1/247 (1) (7 wkts dec, 154.2 overs) 620
D. I. Stevens c Batty b Collins	0	2/252 (3) 3/265 (2)
J. M. Kemp c Walters b Murtaza Hussain	183	4/269 (5) 5/483 (4)
J. C. Tredwell c Walters b Murtaza Hussain	60	6/606 (7) 7/620 (6) 120 overs: 468-4

W. D. Parnell, A. Khan and S. J. Cook did not bat.

Jordan 22–2–93–0; Collins 32–7–107–2; Walters 2–1–5–0; Tudor 27–5–110–1; Murtaza Hussain 54.2–4–208–2; Schofield 4–0–18–0; Afzaal 13–0–65–0.

Umpires: R. J. Bailey and J. F. Steele.

SURREY v ESSEX

At Guildford, July 15, 16, 17, 18. Drawn. Surrey 11 pts, Essex 10 pts. Toss: Essex. Championship debut: T. E. Linley.

With Mark Butcher absent through injury, Stewart Walters celebrated his first Championship game in charge with a maiden first-class hundred – in his 31st innings. It proved timely, lifting Surrey clear of trouble after they slipped to 66 for three in reply to Essex's 401; Walters and Afzaal added 222 for the fourth wicket. Ramprakash, however, failed to score from any of his 16 balls, only his second duck in his last 102 first-class innings, though Walters was able to declare, eight down, once the fourth batting point was in the bag. Essex too had made an uncertain start, also stumbling to 66 for three, and were 116 for five when ten Doeschate strode to the crease. He was given two lives early on, and reached his hundred from 140 balls. Despite promising performances from right-arm seamers Tim Linley – on Championship debut – and Chris Jordan, it was the weather that ultimately had the upper hand, ensuring that Surrey suffered their fourth consecutive draw.

Close of play: First day, Essex 317-7 (ten Doeschate 105, Middlebrook 5); Second day, Surrey 219-3 (Walters 86, Afzaal 80); Third day, Surrey 288-4 (Walters 111).

Essex

V. Chopra lbw b Dernbach	2	– c and b Schofield	85
J. K. Maunders c Batty b Jordan	31	– lbw b Dernbach	0
H. M. Amla c Batty b Jordan	26	– not out	81
M. J. Walker c Batty b Linley	27	– c Walters b Linley	21
*M. L. Pettini c Batty b Jordan	10	– not out	9
†J. S. Foster c Murtagh b Nel	48		
R. N. ten Doeschate not out	159		
G. R. Napier c Murtagh b Linley	43		
J. D. Middlebrook c Ramprakash b Jordan	16		
D. D. Masters c Batty b Linley	9		
A. P. Palladino c Dernbach b Linley	5		
B 1, l-b 1, w 9, n-b 8	25	B 2, w 1, n-b 2	5

1/10 (1) 2/61 (3) 3/66 (2) 4/88 (5) (123.5 overs) 401
5/116 (4) 6/214 (6) 7/297 (8)
8/358 (9) 9/383 (10) 10/401 (11)   120 overs: 391-9

1/9 (2)   (3 wkts, 54.1 overs) 201
2/150 (1) 3/187 (4)

Nel 31–6–87–1; Dernbach 25–3–74–1; Linley 22.5–1–77–4; Jordan 26–3–84–4; Schofield 19–1–71–0. *Second Innings*—Nel 7–2–22–0; Dernbach 8–1–25–1; Jordan 3–1–10–0; Schofield 19–0–78–1; Afzaal 13–1–54–0; Linley 4.1–1–10–1.

Surrey

†J. N. Batty c Maunders b Napier	30	A. Nel c Chopra b Middlebrook	0
M. J. Brown c Walker b Palladino	17	J. W. Dernbach not out	0
M. R. Ramprakash c Foster b Masters	0	B 8, l-b 7, w 2	17
*S. J. Walters c Walker b Masters	142		
U. Afzaal c Chopra b Masters	116	1/28 (2) (8 wkts dec, 118.3 overs) 352
C. P. Murtagh c Maunders b Masters	15	2/29 (3) 3/66 (1)
C. J. Jordan b Napier	8	4/288 (5) 5/328 (6) 6/335 (4)
C. P. Schofield not out	7	7/350 (7) 8/351 (9)

T. E. Linley did not bat.

Masters 39–16–86–4; Palladino 31–8–72–1; ten Doeschate 11–4–44–0; Napier 14.3–2–59–2; Middlebrook 23–1–76–1.

Umpires: N. G. Cowley and R. A. Kettleborough.

SURREY v LEICESTERSHIRE

At The Oval, July 31, August 1, 2, 3. Drawn. Surrey 10 pts, Leicestershire 8 pts. Toss: Leicestershire. Championship debut: N. L. Buck.

This match was notable for double-hundreds from batsmen aged 20 years apart: one from a cub in the spring of his career; the other from a lion in the winter of his. James Taylor, aged 19, became the first teenager to score a double-hundred for Leicestershire, batting seven hours in all, while Mark Ramprakash, who turned 40 before the end of the season, scored his tenth double for Surrey, and the

YOUNGEST DOUBLE-CENTURIONS IN ENGLAND

Years	Days			
18	13	W. G. Grace (224*)	England v Surrey at The Oval	1866
18	237	D. J. Sales (210*)	Northamptonshire v Worcestershire at Kidderminster	1996
19	19	G. A. Hick (230)	Zimbabweans v Oxford University at Oxford	1985
19	95	E. J. Craig (208*)	Cambridge Univ. v L. C. Stevens' XI at Eastbourne	1961
19	**207**	**J. W. A. Taylor (207*)**	**Leicestershire v Surrey at The Oval**	**2009**
19	235	D. N. Moore (206)	Gloucestershire v Oxford University at Oxford	1930
19	250	D. Nicholls (211)	Kent v Derbyshire at Folkestone	1963
19	308	R. A. Young (220)	Sussex v Essex at Leyton	1905

15th of his career. But statistics were all that could be salvaged from a match so dominated by the bat that just nine wickets fell for 1,224 runs over four days. Taylor and du Toit put on 230 in an unbroken sixth-wicket stand, but that was eclipsed by Ramprakash and Surrey's acting-captain, Walters, who added a colossal 404, the highest third-wicket stand at The Oval, and the best for any wicket against Leicestershire, surpassing the 403 set by Graham Gooch and Paul Prichard for Essex in 1990. Walters's 188 was his second hundred ever, straight after his first. In the circumstances, Nathan Buck, an 18-year-old Leicester-born seam bowler, did not fare too badly on debut, and took a notable maiden Championship wicket.

BATSMEN'S MATCHES

Highest runs per wicket in first-class matches in the UK containing 1,000 runs or more:

189.14	1,324 for 7	Cambridge Univ. (594-4 dec) v West Indians (730-3) at Cambridge....	1950
146.50	1,172 for 8	Warwicks (303-2 and 390-4 dec) v Worcs (395-4 and 84-0) at Birmingham	1978
136.00	**1,224 for 9**	**Leics (593-5 dec and 23-0) v Surrey (608-4 dec) at The Oval**	**2009**
127.61	1,659 for 13	Middx (600-4 dec and 209-2) v Somerset (850-7 dec) at Taunton......	2007
120.21	1,683 for 14	Glam (584-3 dec and 256-3 dec) v Middx (435-4 dec and 408-4) at Southgate	2005
114.81	**1,263 for 11**	**Sussex (742-5 dec) v Somerset (521-6) at Taunton**	**2009**
114.20	1,142 for 10	Somerset (553-5 dec) v Yorks (589-5) at Bath	2001
113.83	1,366 for 12	Durham (556-8 dec) v Warwicks (810-4 dec) at Birmingham	1994
103.20	1,032 for 10	Warwicks (511-3 dec) v Notts (521-7) at Birmingham..............	1931

Research: Philip Bailey

Close of play: First day, Leicestershire 291-4 (Taylor 53, New 16); Second day, Leicestershire 593-5 (Taylor 207, du Toit 100); Third day, Surrey 311-2 (Ramprakash 174, Walters 84).

Leicestershire

G. P. Smith c Batty b Dernbach................	46	– not out	14
M. A. G. Boyce run out	0	– not out	8
*H. H. Dippenaar c Walters b Dernbach	86		
H. D. Ackerman c Walters b Schofield	75		
J. W. A. Taylor not out	207		
†T. J. New c Batty b Linley	53		
J. du Toit not out	100		
B 4, l-b 15, w 5, n-b 2	26	W 1	1

1/1 (2) 2/140 (3)   (5 wkts dec, 157.2 overs) 593   (no wkt, 9 overs) 23
3/153 (1) 4/258 (4)
5/363 (6)   120 overs: 380-5

C. W. Henderson, N. L. Buck, A. J. Harris and H. F. Gurney did not bat.

Dernbach 30–9–92–2; Nel 30–6–113–0; Jordan 26.2–2–104–0; Linley 27–5–98–1; Schofield 36–2–123–1; Walters 4–0–14–0; Afzaal 4–0–30–0. *Second Innings*—Dernbach 4–0–10–0; Schofield 4–1–5–0; Brown 1–0–8–0.

Surrey

†J. N. Batty b Harris	0	C. P. Murtagh not out	14
M. J. Brown c Ackerman b Henderson	46	B 4, l-b 7, w 3, n-b 2	16
M. R. Ramprakash b Buck	274		
*S. J. Walters c Ackerman b Henderson 188		1/0 (1) 2/75 (2) (4 wkts dec, 167 overs) 608	
U. Afzaal not out.....................	70	3/479 (3) 4/563 (4) 120 overs: 412-2	

C. P. Schofield, C. J. Jordan, A. Nel, J. W. Dernbach and T. E. Linley did not bat.

Harris 21–2–96–1; Buck 27–6–73–1; Gurney 26–6–99–0; Henderson 64–11–178–2; du Toit 19–1–89–0; Taylor 3–0–28–0; Dippenaar 7–0–34–0.

Umpires: I. J. Gould and J. F. Steele.

SURREY v DERBYSHIRE

At Whitgift School, Croydon, August 6, 7, 8, 9. Drawn. Surrey 11 pts, Derbyshire 10 pts. Toss: Surrey.

Even before the match started, the news was not good: after 18 years as a Surrey player, Mark Butcher, the club captain, announced his enforced retirement through injury, so ending a long association between the Butcher family and the county. (His father Alan began his Surrey career in 1971 and his brother Gary first played for them in 1999.) And before the game had dribbled to a draw, Surrey's sixth on the trot, they confirmed the loan signing of seamer James Anyon from Warwickshire in a bid to bolster their blunt attack. On the last day, Derbyshire, chasing 349 from a minimum of 77 overs, were struggling at 170 for five; but with nigh on two hours remaining, Surrey failed to claim another wicket. They were thwarted chiefly by a dogged, unbeaten hundred from Madsen, a 25-year-old South African who now had two hundreds from four Championship matches. Earlier, Ramprakash hit a hundred of his own, the 108th of his career, taking him to 16th in the list of first-class century-makers, level with Zaheer Abbas. Ramprakash had fallen 20 short of three figures in the first innings, when he became a victim of Groenewald's first six-for.

Close of play: First day, Surrey 308-3 (Walters 14, Afzaal 18); Second day, Derbyshire 169-2 (Rogers 80, Smith 48); Third day, Surrey 195-3 (Ramprakash 76, Afzaal 21).

Surrey

†J. N. Batty c Smith b Hayward	48	– c Rogers b Jones	30
M. J. Brown b Madsen b Hayward	120	– c Klokker b Wagg	56
M. R. Ramprakash b Groenewald	80	– not out	134
*S. J. Walters lbw b Groenewald	28	– c Rogers b Wagg	0
U. Afzaal c Hinds b Wagg	24	– c Park b Wagg	85
M. N. W. Spriegel b Wagg	9		
C. P. Schofield lbw b Groenewald	4	– (6) not out	0
S. J. King b Groenewald	8		
J. W. Dernbach c Rogers b Groenewald	2		
P. T. Collins c Wagg b Groenewald	4		
A. Nel not out	1		
L-b 12, n-b 22	34	B 4, l-b 7, w 2, n-b 2	15

1/113 (1) 2/275 (2) 3/275 (3)   (108.1 overs)   362   1/63 (1)   (4 wkts dec, 68 overs)   320
4/316 (5) 5/336 (4) 6/342 (6)   2/152 (2)
7/342 (7) 8/346 (9) 9/350 (10) 10/362 (8)   3/152 (4) 4/308 (5)

Wagg 33–4–126–2; Hayward 18–5–44–2; Jones 17–2–73–0; Groenewald 24.1–5–50–6; Smith 8–0–27–0; Redfern 3–1–7–0; Hinds 4–0–18–0; Madsen 1–0–5–0. *Second Innings*—Wagg 23–3–109–3; Groenewald 15–1–68–0; Hayward 9–0–51–0; Madsen 4–1–8–0; Jones 13–1–53–1; Smith 4–0–20–0.

Derbyshire

*C. J. L. Rogers c Batty b Collins	80	– c Batty b Nel	0
W. L. Madsen lbw b Dernbach	1	– not out	108
G. T. Park c Walters b Collins	15	– c Spriegel b King	5
G. M. Smith c Batty b Nel	54	– c Schofield b Collins	49
W. W. Hinds c Schofield b Nel	5	– c Brown b Afzaal	8
D. J. Redfern not out	55	– c Afzaal b Nel	13
†F. A. Klokker b Dernbach	2	– not out	32
G. G. Wagg c Ramprakash b Collins	71		
T. D. Groenewald b Nel	1		
P. S. Jones c Batty b Nel	5		
M. Hayward b Dernbach	2		
B 4, l-b 7, n-b 32	43	B 2, l-b 5, n-b 10	17

1/8 (2) 2/47 (3) 3/169 (1)   (87.5 overs)   334   1/0 (1) 2/30 (3)   (5 wkts, 78 overs)   232
4/178 (5) 5/185 (4) 6/209 (7)   3/120 (4)
7/314 (8) 8/315 (9) 9/331 (10) 10/334 (11)   4/153 (5) 5/170 (6)

Nel 24–9–83–4; Dernbach 19.5–5–73–3; Collins 18–1–76–3; Walters 3–0–9–0; Schofield 15–2–50–0; Spriegel 8–0–32–0. *Second Innings*—Nel 13–4–28–2; Collins 11–4–21–1; Schofield 22–4–80–0; King 17–2–61–1; Dernbach 11–4–25–0; Afzaal 2–0–9–1; Spriegel 2–1–1–0.

Umpires: M. J. D. Bodenham and R. T. Robinson.

At Colchester, August 19, 20, 21, 22. SURREY lost to ESSEX by nine wickets.

At Canterbury, August 28, 29, 30, 31. SURREY lost to KENT by six wickets.

At Bristol, September 2, 3, 4, 5. SURREY lost to GLOUCESTERSHIRE by an innings and one run.

SURREY v NORTHAMPTONSHIRE

At The Oval, September 9, 10, 11, 12. Drawn. Surrey 10 pts, Northamptonshire 12 pts. Toss: Surrey. County debut: J. E. Anyon.

Surrey had re-signed Alex Tudor for his fast bowling, but it was his slow batting which helped prevent what would have been a fourth successive Championship defeat. While the House of Tudor reigned for a total of 118 years, the 31-year-old Alex commanded the crease for a dogged 115 minutes to force a draw. Just six balls into the last day, Surrey had effectively been three for four, but thanks chiefly to the cussedness of Spriegel, Schofield and Tudor, they lost only five more second-innings wickets in 84 overs, by when the draw was secure. Earlier, Batty's hundred, his first of the season, at least meant Northamptonshire did not quite take the game away, although they still managed a 116-run first-innings advantage: Wessels reached a whirlwind 94-ball hundred and O'Brien a more stately one from 150 deliveries.

Close of play: First day, Surrey 305-5 (Batty 110, Schofield 20); Second day, Northamptonshire 331-4 (White 63, Boje 15); Third day, Surrey 116-3 (Harinath 13, Afzaal 9).

Surrey

†J. N. Batty c Peters b van der Wath	110	– c Hall b Boje	37
M. J. Brown c O'Brien b van der Wath	31	– c Hall b Panesar	42
A. Harinath c Wessels b Daggett	20	– c O'Brien b Daggett	14
*S. J. Walters c Lucas b Boje	40	– lbw b Boje	4
U. Afzaal c Peters b van der Wath	62	– b Boje	31
M. N. W. Spriegel b Lucas	3	– lbw b Daggett	56
C. P. Schofield b Hall	57	– b Daggett	36
A. J. Tudor c Wessels b Boje	13	– not out	20
H. M. R. K. B. Herath c Hall b Boje	10	– c Wessels b Boje	9
J. W. Dernbach lbw b Hall	2	– lbw b Panesar	4
J. E. Anyon not out	0	– not out	1
B 10, l-b 4, w 8, n-b 6	28	B 12, l-b 14, w 2	28

1/50 (2) 2/80 (3) 3/153 (4) (116.1 overs) 376
4/257 (5) 5/274 (6) 6/320 (1)
7/353 (8) 8/366 (9) 9/375 (7) 10/376 (10)

1/80 (2) (9 wkts dec, 136 overs) 282
2/84 (1) 3/98 (4)
4/119 (3) 5/171 (5) 6/230 (6)
7/247 (7) 8/262 (9) 9/269 (10)

Van der Wath 23–3–84–3; Lucas 22–2–75–1; Daggett 19–4–53–1; Panesar 20–3–56–0; Boje 23–7–61–3; Hall 9.1–3–33–2. *Second Innings*—Lucas 10–1–26–0; van der Wath 13.5–5–16–0; Boje 43–14–75–4; Panesar 51–14–85–2; Hall 3–0–15–0; Daggett 15–1–39–3; Wessels 1–1–0–0.

Northamptonshire

S. D. Peters c Spriegel b Dernbach	2	M. S. Panesar c Afzaal b Herath	1
†N. J. O'Brien c Walters b Schofield	128	L. M. Daggett lbw b Herath	0
A. G. Wakely b Dernbach	0		
M. H. Wessels run out	109	B 12, l-b 3, w 2, n-b 4	21
R. A. White c Batty b Herath	66		
*N. Boje c Batty b Dernbach	49	1/28 (1) 2/28 (3) 3/187 (4) (126 overs) 492
A. J. Hall lbw b Schofield	59	4/304 (2) 5/342 (5) 6/405 (6)
J. J. van der Wath not out	50	7/467 (7) 8/478 (9) 9/488 (10)
D. S. Lucas c Spriegel b Herath	7	10/492 (11) 120 overs: 487-8

Dernbach 20–3–82–3; Tudor 13–1–85–0; Anyon 7–0–59–0; Herath 47–6–151–4; Schofield 36–4–82–2; Spriegel 3–0–18–0.

Umpires: N. L. Bainton and N. G. B. Cook.

SURREY v GLAMORGAN

At The Oval, September 23, 24, 25, 26. Drawn. Surrey 10 pts, Glamorgan 11 pts. Toss: Surrey.

The Surrey attack was brutally exposed on another good batting pitch when, for the second time in 2009, four opponents scored centuries in one innings. Surrey made a respectable 430, but that was soon dwarfed by Glamorgan's mammoth total, just 16 short of their highest ever. Their 702 for eight declared contained the county's largest stand against Surrey, 315 by Rees and Cosgrove, and their highest for the sixth wicket against anyone, 240 by Wallace and Allenby. It was also the tenth time in 14 Championship games that Surrey had conceded more than 400 in an innings. With Afzaal and Spriegel having already scored hundreds, the game provided the first instance of five different left-handed centurions (Allenby and Batty were the right-handed exceptions). Batty's effort, his last before joining Gloucestershire, staved off defeat. In a run-packed game, Kruger's match return of nine for 121 was outstanding. Surrey could perhaps take solace in a first Championship fifty for Harinath and a maiden first-class hundred for Spriegel, in his 21st match.

Close of play: First day, Surrey 334-4 (Afzaal 170, Spriegel 71); Second day, Glamorgan 271-0 (Rees 109, Cosgrove 145); Third day, Surrey 24-1 (Batty 7, Logan 0).

Surrey

†J. N. Batty c Wallace b Kruger	13	– b Harris	120
M. J. Brown b Harris	9	– b Kruger	17
A. Harinath c Allenby b Croft	57	– (4) b Kruger	12
*S. J. Walters lbw b Kruger	7	– (5) c Dalrymple b Harris	82
U. Afzaal b Kruger	170	– (9) not out	2
M. N. W. Spriegel c Cosker b Croft	100	– c sub (T. L. Maynard) b Harris	0
C. P. Schofield b Kruger	8	– lbw b Croft	21
C. J. Jordan c Wallace b Kruger	42	– not out	37
H. M. R. K. B. Herath c Wallace b Kruger	8		
R. J. Logan lbw b Cosker	0	– (3) c Wallace b Kruger	6
J. W. Dernbach not out	4		
B 2, l-b 6, w 2, n-b 2	12	B 4, l-b 1, n-b 2, p 5	12

1/23 (2) 2/23 (1) 3/51 (4)   (122.4 overs) 430   1/20 (2)   (7 wkts, 104 overs) 309
4/154 (3) 5/335 (5) 6/349 (7)   2/41 (3) 3/63 (4)
7/400 (6) 8/425 (8) 9/426 (9)   4/237 (5) 5/237 (6) 6/256 (1) 7/302 (7)
10/430 (10)   120 overs: 425-8

Harris 23–6–88–1; Kruger 26–5–93–6; Allenby 13–4–39–0; Cosgrove 8–1–31–0; Croft 34–4–107–2; Cosker 17.4–3–54–1; Dalrymple 1–0–10–0. *Second Innings*—Harris 19–4–70–3; Kruger 12–2–28–3; Cosker 26–8–70–0; Croft 35–6–91–1; Allenby 3–0–8–0; Dalrymple 5–1–18–0; Cosgrove 4–0–14–0.

Glamorgan

G. P. Rees c Batty b Logan	154	R. D. B. Croft not out	1
M. J. Cosgrove run out	175		
W. D. Bragg c Walters b Jordan	33	B 10, l-b 17, w 3, n-b 2	32
M. J. Powell c Walters b Logan	12		
*J. W. M. Dalrymple b Jordan	4	1/315 (2) (8 wkts dec, 145.2 overs) 702
J. Allenby b Herath	137	2/368 (1) 3/400 (4)
†M. A. Wallace lbw b Herath	139	4/400 (5) 5/405 (5) 6/645 (7)
J. A. R. Harris c Batty b Schofield	15	7/692 (8) 8/702 (6) 120 overs: 531-5

D. A. Cosker and G. J-P. Kruger did not bat.

Dernbach 26–2–106–0; Logan 30–6–101–2; Jordan 16–1–85–2; Herath 33.2–1–164–2; Schofield 31–1–176–1; Spriegel 9–1–43–0.

Umpires: J. W. Holder and D. J. Millns.

SUSSEX

Running on empty

BRUCE TALBOT

Two trophies, a Lord's final and a pioneering end-of-season trip to India. The most successful era in Sussex's history, thought to be coming to an end following Mushtaq Ahmed's retirement, continued – but all this one-day success was overshadowed by relegation from the first division of the Championship after eight years.

In the end Sussex surrendered their top-flight place with barely a whimper. Although they had a squad of 24, six more than when they won the first of their three Championships in 2003, the workload as they chased one-day honours while trying to keep their place in the first division was never evenly shared. Five players had just nine games between them in all competitions, and by September several key individuals were running on empty. Sussex lost their last three Championship matches, two of them at Hove, and needed a favour from Durham to retain the Pro40 title on the final day of the season.

Sussex had expected another difficult four-day campaign after surviving by only five points in 2008. The squad looked stronger, however, after Ed Joyce joined from Middlesex, hoping a change of county would help him win back his England place. But they won only two games – both against whipping-boys Worcestershire – and lost four at Hove, a fortress under former captain Chris Adams. By the end of the season the players were fed up with its moribund square.

Sussex might have scored just one fewer century than the 19 of champions Durham, but batting depth was lacking. There were a dozen occasions when the side squandered strong positions or folded spectacularly, such as the final two home games against Warwickshire and Yorkshire.

Another problem was an inability to bowl teams out. The leading wicket-taker was the young Indian leg-spinner Piyush Chawla, even though he played just six Championship matches. But just as he was shaping up as the new Mushtaq Ahmed – he could bat too, as he proved with a century at Worcester – he was lured by Surrey. Corey Collymore was consistent without ever threatening to run through a side, but Jason Lewry retired after a season ravaged by illness and injury. It was an anti-climactic end to a magnificent 15-year career during which his left-arm swing took more than 600 first-class wickets; Lewry might have played for England but for his lack of self-confidence.

There were some positives. Chris Nash finished just short of 1,300 Championship runs and earned a place in the England Performance squad, while Rory Hamilton-Brown's unbeaten 171 against Yorkshire confirmed his potential. He had been expected to play a big part in 2010, until a surprise return to The Oval as captain.

Mike Yardy captained well in his first season, and passed 1,000 runs. The big surprise was Murray Goodwin's poor form, although it was his benefit year. There was one spectacular contribution, when he broke his own county record by scoring 344 not out at Taunton, but 26 further Championship innings produced only 456 runs.

Thembs Hadebe, AP/PA

Dwayne Smith

If the Championship was a disappointment, ample compensation came in one-day cricket. A year after winning only two group games, Sussex took the Twenty20 Cup for the first time with an impressive demolition of Somerset in the final, fired by another spectacular contribution from the West Indian all-rounder Dwayne Smith: this won them a lucrative trip to India for the inaugural Twenty20 Champions League. Sussex had depth in batting, even when Matt Prior was away with England, and bowling their opponents could only admire. The spinners came into their own at Hove, where Sussex were unbeaten in one-day games. With these home conditions in mind, Monty Panesar was signed on a three-year deal.

Joyce was the star of the Friends Provident campaign with three centuries, including a brilliant 146 in the semi-final win over Gloucestershire. A week before meeting Hampshire at Lord's Sussex beat them in the Pro40 League, but on the big day Sussex had no answer to Dominic Cork's new-ball burst. It was their worst one-day performance of the summer.

Sussex were confident of retaining their Pro40 title and, although they ultimately did so only thanks to Somerset's unexpected last-day defeat, they still won more games than anyone else.

Sussex allowed Tom Smith to join Middlesex, and will be able to engage Dwayne Smith only as an overseas player in 2010, probably for the Twenty20 Cup. Carl Hopkinson is to concentrate on his role as fielding coach. Left-arm Chris Liddle was awarded a new contract after missing the season with an ankle injury, and Sussex are hoping that either he or Ragheb Aga come through to boost the seam attack. There are plenty of promising young batsmen at Hove, such as Joe Gatting and Luke Wells, son of the former captain Alan – but it has been too long since a fast bowler came through the ranks.

Off the pitch the redevelopment of Hove, first discussed in the early 1990s, finally began with the demolition of the Gilligan Stand, surely the biggest eyesore on the circuit, during the winter. The £8m scheme also includes a revamp of the pavilion and the floodlights, and a new double-decker stand in the south-west corner. The whole project, which will give Hove a permanent capacity of 7,000, should be completed by 2011, belatedly providing facilities which reflect the club's winning of ten trophies in nine years.

SUSSEX RESULTS

All first-class matches – Played 17: Won 2, Lost 6, Drawn 9.
County Championship matches – Played 16: Won 2, Lost 6, Drawn 8.
LV County Championship, 8th in Division 1; Friends Provident Trophy, finalists;
Pro40 League, winners in Division 1; Twenty20 Cup, winners.

COUNTY CHAMPIONSHIP AVERAGES, BATTING AND FIELDING

Cap		M	I	NO	R	HS	100s	50s	Avge	Ct/St
2008	C. D. Nash†	14	25	3	1,298	157	4	6	59.00	3
2007	L. J. Wright‡	8	13	2	527	118*	2	3	47.90	1
2003	M. J. Prior‡..........	5	8	0	362	140	1	2	45.25	12
2009	E. C. Joyce	14	23	1	936	183	3	3	42.54	12
2005	M. H. Yardy..........	16	28	3	1,046	152	2	5	41.84	13
2008	C. D. Hopkinson†	9	13	1	443	139	2	0	36.91	2
	R. J. Hamilton-Brown ..	4	7	1	205	171*	1	0	34.16	5
2001	M. W. Goodwin¶......	16	27	3	800	344*	1	2	33.33	6
	J. S. Gatting†	3	5	0	158	70	0	1	31.60	2
2009	P. P. Chawla§.........	6	10	3	206	102*	1	0	29.42	2
	D. G. Wright§.........	3	4	1	88	42	0	0	29.33	0
	A. J. Hodd†	15	22	3	489	101	1	2	25.73	23/3
	Yasir Arafat§	5	5	0	108	37	0	0	21.60	0
	D. R. Smith¶	9	14	0	261	80	0	2	18.64	1
2000	R. S. C. Martin-Jenkins .	12	16	2	259	67	0	1	18.50	5
	O. P. Rayner..........	10	11	1	173	60	0	1	17.30	14
1996	J. D. Lewry†..........	6	10	4	51	25	0	0	8.50	0
	C. D. Collymore¶......	14	17	5	89	23	0	0	7.41	2

Also batted: R. G. Aga¶ (2 matches) 1*, 2, 24; R. J. Kirtley† (2 matches) 33, 2*, 10 (2 ct); P. S. E. Sandri¶ (1 match) 0*; T. M. J. Smith† (1 match) 10, 1; M. A. Thornely (1 match) 8, 19 (1 ct).

† *Born in Sussex.*   ‡ *ECB contract.*   § *Official overseas player.*   ¶ *Other non-England-qualified player.*

BOWLING

	O	M	R	W	BB	5W/i	Avge
P. P. Chawla	341.5	72	981	36	6-52	4	27.25
D. R. Smith	301	84	814	25	4-58	0	32.56
C. D. Collymore	396	102	1,104	33	4-66	0	33.45
L. J. Wright	210.1	35	710	21	5-66	2	33.80
R. S. C. Martin-Jenkins	275.4	74	781	23	5-43	1	33.95
O. P. Rayner	294.3	48	870	20	4-186	0	43.50
Yasir Arafat................	151	24	621	12	3-83	0	51.75
J. D. Lewry	159.1	39	535	10	2-53	0	53.50

Also bowled: R. G. Aga 37–2–147–1; M. W. Goodwin 2–0–13–0; R. J. Hamilton-Brown 37–6–109–3; A. J. Hodd 1.4–0–7–0; E. C. Joyce 2–0–9–1; R. J. Kirtley 50.5–6–177–5; C. D. Nash 114.4–22–394–7; P. S. E. Sandri 14–2–80–0; T. M. J. Smith 12.4–1–70–0; D. G. Wright 83.5–33–187–5; M. H. Yardy 69–4–320–4.

COUNTY RECORDS

Highest score for:	344*	M. W. Goodwin v Somerset at Taunton	2009
Highest score against:	322	E. Paynter (Lancashire) at Hove	1937
Leading run-scorer:	34,150	J. G. Langridge (avge 37.69)................	1928–1955
Best bowling for:	10-48	C. H. G. Bland v Kent at Tonbridge	1899
Best bowling against:	9-11	A. P. Freeman (Kent) at Hove	1922
Leading wicket-taker:	2,211	M. W. Tate (avge 17.41)	1912–1937
Highest total for:	742-5 dec	v Somerset at Taunton.	2009
Highest total against:	726	by Nottinghamshire at Nottingham	1895
Lowest total for: {	19	v Surrey at Godalming.....................	1830
	19	v Nottinghamshire at Hove	1873
Lowest total against:	18	by Kent at Gravesend......................	1867

ADDRESS

County Ground, Eaton Road, Hove BN3 3AN (01273 827100; **email** info@sussexcricket.co.uk).
Website www.sussexcricket.co.uk

OFFICIALS

Captain M. H. Yardy
Professional cricket manager M. A. Robinson
Cricket performance manager K. Greenfield
President B. Bedson
Chairman J. R. May

Chief executive D. Brooks
Chairman, cricket committee J. R. T. Barclay
Head groundsman A. Mackay
Scorer M. J. Charman

No champagne super over

It is a measure of the general indifference in Britain to the inaugural Champions League Twenty20 that infinitely more column inches were devoted to Marcus Trescothick's early return home than to the performances in the competition itself of either his Somerset side or Sussex.

When the IPL commissioner Lalit Modi suggested that the tournament might be staged in England, it was surely just a soundbite. Would he expect, say, Victoria Bushrangers v Cape Cobras at Leicester to attract any sort of crowd? India is the natural home of this competition. The only first-round match-day which did not feature an IPL team still attracted around 10,000 for Sussex's game against the Diamond Eagles in Delhi. They saw the closest match of the tournament, which was ultimately decided by a "super over", perhaps the one enduring legacy of Sir Allen Stanford's dalliance with the game. Unfortunately, Dwayne Smith and Rory Hamilton-Brown played millionaire shots, and Sussex were heading home after two defeats.

Mark Robinson called it the most rewarding experience of his career, as he could pick the brains of rival coaches, although his main conclusion was depressingly familiar: English counties will struggle to compete at this rarefied level, he felt, because the demands of the domestic schedule precluded them from reaching the standards of fitness and fielding of the other teams, particularly those from Australia and South Africa.

It didn't help that Sussex went into their opening game, against New South Wales, without four automatic selections. Their batting was exposed as far too lightweight by the pace of Brett Lee and Doug Bollinger on the slow Delhi pitch.

Mike Yardy and Luke Wright, who spent just 48 hours in India after arriving late because of a virus, returned against the Eagles, but there was to be no champagne super over, although a participation fee of £314,000 helped cushion the blow, and the whole Indian experience will have been invaluable for the younger members of the squad. — BRUCE TALBOT

At Cambridge, April 15, 16, 17. SUSSEX drew with CAMBRIDGE UCCE.

SUSSEX v LANCASHIRE

At Hove, April 21, 22, 23, 24. Lancashire won by eight wickets. Lancashire 19 pts, Sussex 5 pts. Toss: Sussex. Championship debut: T. M. J. Smith.

Sussex had no answer to Anderson's sustained excellence as, unusually for Hove, the ball swung throughout. He claimed career-best match figures of 11 for 109, although it was left-arm spinner Keedy who bowled the decisive spell late on the third day, removing Goodwin, Prior and Joyce as Sussex's folly in playing only four specialist batsmen was exposed. The consolation for Sussex was Luke Wright, who also took a career-best in Lancashire's first innings, adding control to his raw pace. That enabled Sussex to restrict their deficit to just ten, but their position would have been even stronger had they not dropped four catches behind the wicket. Sussex lost their last five for 17 on the final morning and Lancashire cruised to a target of 158 after an early wobble. For the first time since the end of 2007 no one made a hundred in a Championship game at Hove, although Joyce, on his home Sussex debut, and Chilton showed the technique to cope with the moving ball.

Close of play: First day, Sussex 247-5 (Joyce 89, Martin-Jenkins 52); Second day, Lancashire 209-4 (Chilton 72, Croft 59); Third day, Sussex 148-5 (L. J. Wright 35).

Sussex

*M. H. Yardy lbw b Anderson	35	– b Anderson	22
C. D. Nash c Sutton b Anderson	22	– c Sutton b Anderson	13
E. C. Joyce b Anderson	90	– lbw b Keedy	55
M. W. Goodwin c Prince b Chapple	11	– st Sutton b Keedy	20
†M. J. Prior c Horton b Chapple	4	– lbw b Keedy	0
L. J. Wright c and b Anderson	6	– c Sutton b Anderson	35
R. S. C. Martin-Jenkins b Anderson	67	– c Sutton b Anderson	13
T. M. J. Smith lbw b Anderson	10	– c Horton b Anderson	1
D. G. Wright lbw b Chapple	4	– c Chilton b Keedy	1
R. G. Aga not out	1	– c Chilton b Keedy	2
C. D. Collymore lbw b Chapple	0	– not out	1
B 19, l-b 14, w 4, n-b 2	39	L-b 4	4

1/43 (2) 2/116 (1) 3/132 (4)   (120 overs) 289   1/24 (2) 2/45 (1)   (61.5 overs) 167
4/142 (5) 5/160 (6) 6/250 (3)   3/95 (4) 4/95 (5) 5/148 (3)
7/271 (8) 8/276 (9) 9/284 (7) 10/289 (11)   6/150 (6) 7/156 (8) 8/163 (7)
                                         9/166 (10) 10/167 (9)

Anderson 32–11–56–6; Chapple 31–6–69–4; Mahmood 19–6–48–0; Smith 28–10–58–0; Keedy 5–0–15–0; Croft 3–2–6–0; du Plessis 2–0–4–0. *Second Innings*—Anderson 19–4–53–5; Chapple 11–2–24–0; Mahmood 6–2–18–0; Smith 3–0–16–0; Keedy 20.5–4–45–5; du Plessis 2–0–7–0.

Lancashire

P. J. Horton lbw b Collymore	1	– (2) c Goodwin b Collymore	4
T. C. Smith c Prior b Collymore	0	– (1) c Nash b Collymore	5
A. G. Prince b L. J. Wright	56	– not out	91
F. du Plessis c Prior b Martin-Jenkins	6	– not out	58
M. J. Chilton lbw b Martin-Jenkins	89		
S. J. Croft c Joyce b L. J. Wright	59		
†L. D. Sutton c Prior b L. J. Wright	20		
*G. Chapple c Prior b Martin-Jenkins	4		
S. I. Mahmood lbw b L. J. Wright	26		
G. Keedy c Prior b L. J. Wright	7		
J. M. Anderson not out	9		
B 4, l-b 9, w 1, n-b 8	22	L-b 2	2

1/1 (2) 2/2 (1) 3/31 (4) 4/102 (3)   (113.5 overs) 299   1/7 (2)   (2 wkts, 41.4 overs) 160
5/209 (6) 6/253 (5) 7/257 (7)   2/12 (1)
8/273 (8) 9/284 (10) 10/299 (9)

Collymore 27–7–73–2; D. G. Wright 21–10–43–0; Martin-Jenkins 25–10–50–3; Aga 7–0–28–0; L. J. Wright 27.5–8–80–5; Smith 4–1–11–0; Nash 2–1–1–0. *Second Innings*—Collymore 7–3–11–2; D. G. Wright 9–3–19–0; Martin-Jenkins 8–4–23–0; L. J. Wright 5–0–27–0; Smith 8.4–0–59–0; Nash 4–0–19–0.

Umpires: P. J. Hartley and R. K. Illingworth.

At Southampton, April 29, 30, May 1, 2. SUSSEX drew with HAMPSHIRE.

SUSSEX v DURHAM

At Hove, May 6, 7, 8, 9. Drawn. Sussex 11 pts, Durham 11 pts. Toss: Durham.

A benign pitch proved frustrating, although both sides squandered opportunities to wrest control. Benkenstein, dropped on 19, led Durham's recovery with his second hundred in successive matches at Hove and added 148 for the seventh wicket with Plunkett, who ran out of partners with a maiden century in sight and later capped a fine match with six wickets. Durham then exploited a pitch freshened up by a brief shower to reduce Sussex from 81 without loss to 109 for five, but Luke Wright and Hodd counter-attacked impressively with 150 in 38 overs. Hodd duly completed his third first-class hundred, before Damien Wright, defying the discomfort of a side strain which prevented him from bowling in the second innings, ensured first-innings parity. Di Venuto made a century against his former county after a reprieve on seven when a ball from Martin-Jenkins hit his stumps without dislodging the bails. Durham delayed setting a target until the final afternoon and must have regretted it when they reduced Sussex, asked to make 317 in just 56 overs, to 105 for five. But Hodd and the resourceful Nash batted 26 overs to save the game. An unwell Nigel Cowley was replaced by Surrey Championship umpire Roger Croft, who was watching from the pavilion, until Steven Garratt arrived.

Close of play: First day, Durham 318-7 (Plunkett 65, Thorp 8); Second day, Sussex 269-6 (Hodd 84, Martin-Jenkins 3); Third day, Durham 164-2 (Di Venuto 75, Muchall 51).

Durham

M. J. Di Venuto c Hodd b D. G. Wright	20	– (2) c Hodd b Martin-Jenkins 103
M. D. Stoneman b D. G. Wright	2	– (1) c Hodd b Rayner. 24
*W. R. Smith lbw b Martin-Jenkins	12	– run out 7
G. J. Muchall c Hodd b L. J. Wright	24	– not out 106
D. M. Benkenstein c Nash b D. G. Wright	136	– c sub (C. D. Hopkinson) b L. J. Wright 7
I. D. Blackwell lbw b Collymore	2	– not out 39
†P. Mustard lbw b Martin-Jenkins	32	
L. E. Plunkett not out	94	
C. D. Thorp c Yardy b Rayner	29	
M. E. Claydon b L. J. Wright.	6	
S. J. Harmison c Hodd b Rayner	0	
B 5, l-b 10, w 2, n-b 6	23	B 3, l-b 4, w 4, n-b 2 13

1/10 (2) 2/37 (3) 3/41 (1)   (115.5 overs) 380   1/39 (1)   (4 wkts dec, 95 overs) 299
4/101 (4) 5/104 (6) 6/162 (7)   2/67 (3) 3/196 (2)
7/310 (5) 8/369 (9) 9/377 (10) 10/380 (11)   4/211 (5)

Collymore 18–4–74–1; D. G. Wright 26.5–10–64–3; Martin-Jenkins 18.1–5–65–2; Rayner 18.5–1–51–2; L. J. Wright 26–3–82–2; Hamilton-Brown 2–1–2–0; Nash 6–0–27–0. *Second Innings*—Collymore 16–4–52–0; Martin-Jenkins 22.7–52–1; L. J. Wright 14–4–38–1; Rayner 27–2–83–1; Hamilton-Brown 6–1–28–0; Yardy 2–0–8–0; Nash 8–1–31–0.

Sussex

*M. H. Yardy b Claydon	51	– c Plunkett b Harmison	12
C. D. Nash b Plunkett	40	– not out	85
E. C. Joyce c Mustard b Claydon	0	– b Thorp	3
M. W. Goodwin c Mustard b Plunkett	0	– lbw b Claydon	21
R. J. Hamilton-Brown c Mustard b Plunkett	0	– c Benkenstein b Plunkett	12
L. J. Wright c Muchall b Blackwell	67	– c Muchall b Plunkett	4
†A. J. Hodd lbw b Plunkett	101	– not out	21
R. S. C. Martin-Jenkins c Mustard b Claydon	3		
O. P. Rayner c Mustard b Harmison	25		
D. G. Wright not out	41		
C. D. Collymore lbw b Claydon	4		
B 1, l-b 13, w 3, n-b 14	31	L-b 7, w 2, n-b 2	11

1/81 (2) 2/90 (3) 3/95 (4) 4/97 (5) (98 overs) 363 1/13 (1) (5 wkts, 50 overs) 169
5/109 (1) 6/259 (6) 7/282 (8)   2/16 (3) 3/71 (4)
8/310 (7) 9/332 (9) 10/363 (11)   4/92 (5) 5/105 (6)

Harmison 23–2–59–1; Thorp 14–5–48–0; Plunkett 24–1–105–4; Claydon 20–1–90–4; Blackwell 13–3–30–1; Benkenstein 4–0–17–0. *Second Innings*—Harmison 13–3–41–1; Thorp 10–3–29–1; Plunkett 13–2–36–2; Claydon 6–0–29–1; Blackwell 7–0–16–0; Smith 1–0–11–0.

Umpires: N. G. Cowley and J. W. Holder.
Cowley was replaced by J. R. Croft on the 3rd day and S. A. Garratt on the 4th day.

At Leeds, June 6, 7, 8, 9. SUSSEX drew with YORKSHIRE.

At Worcester, June 11, 12, 13, 14. SUSSEX beat WORCESTERSHIRE by ten wickets.

SUSSEX v SOMERSET

At Hove, June 16, 17, 18, 19. Somerset won by 35 runs. Somerset 21 pts, Sussex 3 pts. Toss: Somerset. First-class debut: M. T. C. Waller.

All bar Lewry of the Sussex side boasted a first-class hundred but only opener Nash showed the necessary application on an over-prepared pitch offering seam movement. A fluctuating contest on day one turned Somerset's way the next morning when their last pair flayed 53 in 5.2 overs, before Thomas took three wickets in 12 balls to undermine Sussex's reply. Langer did not enforce the follow-on, and leg-spinner Chawla, on his Hove debut, took his tally to 19 wickets in two games, while Dwayne Smith bowled unchanged into a howling gale for 17 overs on the third day to offer excellent support. Nash and night-watchman Lewry added 60 for the fifth wicket to give Sussex hope of chasing 349, but resistance was only sporadic after Nash went for 134, then a career-best. Earlier, Trescothick had scored his second hundred of the season with a fluency only Nash could emulate.

Close of play: First day, Somerset 314-9 (Trego 50, Willoughby 12); Second day, Somerset 52-1 (Suppiah 24, Hildreth 17); Third day, Sussex 169-4 (Nash 111, Lewry 4).

Somerset

M. E. Trescothick run out	109	– c Martin-Jenkins b Wright	11
A. V. Suppiah lbw b Chawla	49	– c Prior b Chawla	50
J. C. Hildreth b Chawla	2	– b Smith	23
Z. de Bruyn c Hodd b Chawla	50	– c Yardy b Chawla	5
*J. L. Langer b Chawla	4	– c Joyce b Smith	33
†C. Kieswetter c Prior b Chawla	1	– c Yardy b Smith	7
P. D. Trego not out	92	– lbw b Chawla	5
A. C. Thomas b Nash	4	– b Chawla	22
M. T. C. Waller b Lewry	15	– b Chawla	2
D. A. Stiff b Lewry	4	– not out	14
C. M. Willoughby run out	23	– b Chawla	0
B 5, l-b 8, w 1	14	L-b 5, w 1	6

1/138 (2) 2/140 (3) 3/191 (1)   (106.2 overs) 367
4/202 (5) 5/212 (6) 6/235 (4)
7/240 (8) 8/284 (9) 9/298 (10) 10/367 (11)

1/21 (1) 2/82 (3)   (59.3 overs) 178
3/88 (2) 4/97 (4)
5/112 (6) 6/127 (7) 7/140 (5)
8/153 (9) 9/170 (8) 10/178 (11)

Lewry 20–7–82–2; Martin-Jenkins 9–2–30–0; Smith 13–1–31–0; Wright 15.2–2–54–0; Chawla 35–7–118–5; Nash 14–5–39–1. *Second Innings*—Lewry 7–0–33–0; Wright 8–1–24–1; Smith 23–4–64–3; Chawla 21.3–4–52–6.

Sussex

*M. H. Yardy c Langer b Thomas	5	– lbw b Willoughby	6
C. D. Nash lbw b Thomas	4	– c Kieswetter b Thomas	134
E. C. Joyce c Trescothick b Willoughby	45	– (4) b Trego	30
M. W. Goodwin lbw b Thomas	0	– (3) lbw b Thomas	5
M. J. Prior c Hildreth b Thomas	59	– c Suppiah b Waller	11
L. J. Wright c Suppiah b Thomas	10	– (7) c Suppiah b Willoughby	11
†A. J. Hodd c Kieswetter b Stiff	11	– (8) lbw b Thomas	2
D. R. Smith lbw b Waller	30	– (9) lbw b Willoughby	24
R. S. C. Martin-Jenkins not out	17	– (10) c Trescothick b Willoughby	27
P. P. Chawla lbw b Stiff	0	– (11) not out	27
J. D. Lewry b Waller	0	– (6) b Stiff	25
B 2, l-b 2, w 8, n-b 4	16	L-b 8, w 1, n-b 2	11

1/4 (2) 2/9 (1) 3/9 (4) 4/104 (5)   (65.4 overs) 197
5/130 (3) 6/130 (6) 7/175 (8)
8/196 (7) 9/196 (10) 10/197 (11)

1/28 (1) 2/40 (3)   (88.5 overs) 313
3/134 (4) 4/158 (5)
5/218 (6) 6/222 (2) 7/227 (8)
8/247 (7) 9/270 (9) 10/313 (10)

Willoughby 20–9–43–1; Thomas 18–6–53–5; Trego 2–0–8–0; de Bruyn 4–0–19–0; Stiff 11–1–43–2; Waller 10.4–2–27–2. *Second Innings*—Willoughby 24.5–6–80–4; Thomas 25–3–99–3; Stiff 15–0–49–1; Waller 9–2–30–1; Trego 7–1–25–1; de Bruyn 8–2–22–0.

Umpires: R. J. Bailey and S. A. Garratt.

At Hove, June 24, 25, 26, 27. SUSSEX drew with AUSTRALIANS (see Australian tour section).

At Birmingham, July 7, 8, 9, 10. SUSSEX drew with WARWICKSHIRE.

SUSSEX v HAMPSHIRE

At Arundel, July 15, 16, 17, 18. Drawn. Sussex 12 pts, Hampshire 10 pts. Toss: Sussex.
Only 9.1 overs were possible on the third day, and Hampshire refused Sussex's offer to set up a run-chase, condemning a decent-sized last-day crowd to watch a battle for bonus points. On the day Flintoff announced he was retiring from Test cricket, Wright strengthened his claims as England's next all-rounder by scoring his sixth first-class hundred – though first in the Championship – after flogging

three sixes when he only had last man Lewry for company. Rayner showed impressive resolve to compile his first Championship half-century, and Goodwin made his highest score to date of what until then had been a wretched season, although Imran Tahir's googly proved hard to pick. After Carberry had made his second hundred in successive games, Hampshire lost five wickets for 51 during an inspired wicket-to-wicket spell by Collymore on the final morning that brought him his best figures of the season, but Cork's cussed approach ended Sussex's faint hopes of enforcing the follow-on.

Close of play: First day, Sussex 330-7 (Wright 53, Rayner 15); Second day, Hampshire 213-2 (Lumb 38, Crawley 13); Third day, Hampshire 227-2 (Lumb 45, Crawley 20).

Sussex

*M. H. Yardy lbw b Tomlinson	5	– not out	47
C. D. Nash c Carberry b Imran Tahir	57	– c Cork b Tomlinson	37
E. C. Joyce lbw b Tomlinson	2	– c Burrows b Imran Tahir	43
M. W. Goodwin c Dawson b Mascarenhas	65	– not out	3
C. D. Hopkinson c Burrows b Imran Tahir	49		
L. J. Wright c Carberry b Imran Tahir	104		
†A. J. Hodd c Burrows b Imran Tahir	11		
Yasir Arafat lbw b Tomlinson	37		
O. P. Rayner c Imran Tahir b Mascarenhas	60		
C. D. Collymore lbw b Imran Tahir	0		
J. D. Lewry not out	9		
B 4, l-b 2, w 2, n-b 34	42	B 4, n-b 4	8

1/20 (1) 2/26 (3) 3/96 (2)   (117.2 overs) 441   1/49 (2)   (2 wkts dec, 32.1 overs) 138
4/187 (4) 5/205 (5) 6/253 (7)   2/135 (3)
7/312 (8) 8/397 (9) 9/404 (10) 10/441 (6)

Tomlinson 27–6–108–3; Cork 21–6–54–0; Ervine 12–1–68–0; Mascarenhas 20–6–57–2; Imran Tahir 36.2–4–140–5; Dawson 1–0–8–0. *Second Innings*—Tomlinson 6–0–27–1; Cork 3–0–15–0; Imran Tahir 6–0–29–1; Ervine 7–2–22–0; Dawson 9–0–41–0; Carberry 1–1–0–0; Mascarenhas 0.1–0–0–0.

Hampshire

M. A. Carberry c Joyce b Rayner	112	Imran Tahir not out	25
J. H. K. Adams c and b Rayner	33	J. A. Tomlinson c Goodwin b Rayner	0
M. J. Lumb c Yardy b Collymore	46		
J. P. Crawley lbw b Collymore	26	B 2, l-b 7, w 1, n-b 12	22
L. A. Dawson c Rayner b Lewry	5		
S. M. Ervine b Collymore	17	1/107 (2) 2/183 (1) (119.1 overs) 346
*A. D. Mascarenhas lbw b Collymore	22	3/228 (3) 4/237 (5)
†T. G. Burrows lbw b Wright	2	5/239 (4) 6/278 (6) 7/279 (7)
D. G. Cork c Nash b Yasir Arafat	36	8/297 (8) 9/325 (9) 10/346 (11)

Yasir Arafat 20–2–89–1; Lewry 14–0–60–1; Collymore 29–10–66–4; Rayner 31.1–9–61–3; Wright 17–3–41–1; Yardy 5–0–19–0; Nash 3–2–1–0.

Umpires: M. A. Gough and N. A. Mallender.

At Chester-le-Street, July 31, August 1, 2, 3. SUSSEX lost to DURHAM by nine wickets.

SUSSEX v NOTTINGHAMSHIRE

At Horsham, August 5, 6, 7, 8. Drawn. Sussex 8 pts, Nottinghamshire 12 pts. Toss: Nottinghamshire. Championship debut: P. S. E. Sandri.

Nottinghamshire's seamers did their best to set up victory, but the lack of a front-line spinner – and the loss of half the third day to rain – cost them. The ball swung at the start to justify Read's decision to insert, but Joyce led a recovery with the second-highest score by a Sussex batsman at Cricketfield Road, while that noted rabbit Collymore survived for a session for his career-best (he had never passed 20 in 114 previous first-class matches). Thereafter the pitch flattened out, and Voges – who ruined South African seamer Pepler Sandri's Championship debut by flaying five boundaries off him in six balls – scored his first hundred for Nottinghamshire. In the absence of Yasir

Arafat, Sussex's seam attack lacked bite, condemning their batsmen to a rearguard action on the last day after Nottinghamshire had taken a lead of 222. Nash batted attractively on his home ground, but it needed a more obdurate response from Hopkinson and Wright to secure a draw. Both Joyce and Newman were reprimanded for dissent.

Close of play: First day, Sussex 309-9 (Collymore 23, Sandri 0); Second day, Nottinghamshire 231-2 (Wood 85, Voges 27); Third day, Nottinghamshire 429-4 (Voges 117, Brown 2).

Sussex

*M. H. Yardy b Adams	22	– c Read b Shreck	24
C. D. Nash b Shreck	4	– lbw b Adams	87
E. C. Joyce lbw b Voges	183	– c and b Patel	17
M. W. Goodwin b Adams	11	– b Patel	2
C. D. Hopkinson c Read b Fletcher	15	– not out	47
L. J. Wright c Read b Fletcher	4	– not out	59
†A. J. Hodd lbw b Adams	0		
R. S. C. Martin-Jenkins c Brown b Fletcher	4		
O. P. Rayner lbw b Patel	22		
C. D. Collymore hit wkt b Shreck	23		
P. S. E. Sandri not out	0		
B 4, l-b 2, w 9, n-b 6	21	B 2, l-b 5, n-b 6	13

1/9 (2) 2/43 (1) 3/76 (4) 4/120 (5) (98.5 overs) 309
5/127 (6) 6/128 (7) 7/144 (8)
8/204 (9) 9/308 (3) 10/309 (10)

1/62 (1) (4 wkts, 69 overs) 249
2/128 (3) 3/140 (2)
4/140 (4)

Shreck 22.5–1–92–2; Fletcher 19–5–58–3; Adams 26–10–64–3; Ealham 18–3–64–0; Patel 12–5–23–1; Voges 1–0–2–1. *Second Innings*—Shreck 15–4–55–1; Adams 13–3–43–1; Patel 18–7–40–2; Ealham 9–3–31–0; Fletcher 8–1–50–0; Voges 5–1–11–0; Brown 1–0–12–0.

Nottinghamshire

S. A. Newman b Rayner	25	M. A. Ealham not out	9
M. J. Wood lbw b Wright	86	B 3, l-b 10, w 10, n-b 18	41
M. A. Wagh b Martin-Jenkins	73		
A. C. Voges lbw b Rayner	139	1/48 (1) (6 wkts dec, 134 overs) 531
S. R. Patel c Goodwin b Martin-Jenkins	91	2/180 (3) 3/239 (2)
A. D. Brown c Joyce b Rayner	42	4/407 (5) 5/478 (4)
*†C. M. W. Read not out	25	6/501 (6) 120 overs: 443-4

A. R. Adams, L. J. Fletcher and C. E. Shreck did not bat.

Collymore 27–8–73–0; Sandri 14–2–80–0; Rayner 26–1–110–3; Wright 19–5–68–1; Martin-Jenkins 31–7–104–2; Yardy 13–0–61–0; Nash 4–0–22–0.

Umpires: P. J. Hartley and R. K. Illingworth.

SUSSEX v WORCESTERSHIRE

At Hove, August 11, 12, 13. Sussex won by eight wickets. Sussex 18 pts (after 1 pt penalty), Worcestershire 5 pts. Toss: Sussex. Championship debut: M. Ahmed.

Sussex won their first Championship game at Hove since 2007, but had Worcestershire's attack been able to offer Mason some support it might have been different. There was lateral movement and good carry on a grassy pitch, and Mason, who once played club cricket in Sussex, took his second seven-wicket haul of the season. Earlier, Sussex's seamers had relished first use of the conditions, and Wright claimed only the second five-for of his senior career. But it was a typically gutsy half-century from No. 8 by Hodd which halted Mason's charge and gave Sussex a small but important first-innings lead. In response, Worcestershire's batting frailties were such that their advantage was negligible until Davies and the tail wagged furiously, setting what might have been a tricky target of 212. Mason quickly took his eighth wicket of the game, but he retreated to the outfield exhausted, and Nash took advantage to reach an aggressive second hundred of the season. Sussex were deducted a point for a slow over-rate for the first time.

Close of play: First day, Sussex 48-2 (Yardy 24, Rayner 8); Second day, Worcestershire 71-4 (Ali 2).

Worcestershire

D. K. H. Mitchell c Wright b Yasir Arafat	12	– lbw b Martin-Jenkins	13
S. C. Moore lbw b Martin-Jenkins	28	– c Goodwin b Wright	18
*V. S. Solanki b Wright	19	– lbw b Yasir Arafat	31
B. F. Smith c Yardy b Yasir Arafat	32	– lbw b Yasir Arafat	5
M. M. Ali b Collymore	22	– b Yasir Arafat	3
†S. M. Davies c Hodd b Wright	25	– c Joyce b Rayner	67
G. J. Batty c Hodd b Wright	46	– lbw b Collymore	22
G. M. Andrew c Collymore b Wright	4	– b Collymore	1
M. S. Mason b Hodd b Yasir Arafat	25	– b Wright	28
Imran Arif c Martin-Jenkins b Wright	27	– b Rayner	35
M. Ahmed not out	0	– not out	0
B 2, l-b 10, n-b 4	16	L-b 4, n-b 8	12

1/36 (1) 2/50 (2) 3/84 (3) 4/121 (5)   (82 overs) 256
5/139 (4) 6/154 (6) 7/160 (8) 8/204 (9)
9/245 (10) 10/256 (7)

1/22 (1) 2/48 (2)   (57.2 overs) 235
3/64 (4) 4/71 (3)
5/74 (5) 6/108 (7) 7/110 (8)
8/155 (9) 9/226 (10) 10/235 (6)

Yasir Arafat 22–4–83–3; Collymore 14–2–45–1; Martin-Jenkins 20–7–45–1; Wright 22–6–66–5; Rayner 4–2–5–0. *Second Innings*—Yasir Arafat 19–1–98–3; Collymore 9–3–32–2; Martin-Jenkins 14–5–23–1; Wright 11–0–61–2; Rayner 4.2–0–17–2.

Sussex

*M. H. Yardy b Mason	29	– c Solanki b Mason	6
C. D. Nash c Davies b Mason	10	– not out	100
E. C. Joyce b Andrew	2	– c Imran Arif b Batty	53
O. P. Rayner lbw b Mason	8		
M. W. Goodwin c Smith b Mason	21	– (4) not out	40
C. D. Hopkinson c Solanki b Mason	19		
L. J. Wright c Mitchell b Mason	38		
†A. J. Hodd c Mitchell b Mason	73		
Yasir Arafat c Davies b Batty	32		
R. S. C. Martin-Jenkins c Smith b Andrew	18		
C. D. Collymore not out	4		
B 13, l-b 9, w 2, n-b 2	26	L-b 5, w 2, n-b 6	13

1/17 (2) 2/32 (3) 3/51 (4) 4/54 (1)   (85.1 overs) 280
5/91 (5) 6/101 (6) 7/170 (7)
8/248 (9) 9/266 (8) 10/280 (10)

1/10 (1)   (2 wkts, 38.5 overs) 212
2/119 (3)

Mason 30–9–60–7; Imran Arif 12–1–60–0; Andrew 22.1–6–73–2; Ahmed 4–0–31–0; Batty 8–2–17–1; Mitchell 9–2–17–0. *Second Innings*—Mason 4–1–17–1; Andrew 12.5–1–60–0; Imran Arif 6–0–52–0; Batty 9–2–32–1; Ahmed 5–0–42–0; Ali 2–1–4–0.

Umpires: M. R. Benson and J. W. Lloyds.

At Taunton, August 19, 20, 21, 22. SUSSEX drew with SOMERSET. *Murray Goodwin hits an unbeaten 344 in a total of 742 for five declared; both are Sussex records.*

At Manchester, September 2, 3, 4, 5. SUSSEX drew with LANCASHIRE.

SUSSEX v WARWICKSHIRE

At Hove, September 9, 10, 11, 12. Warwickshire won by an innings and two runs. Warwickshire 20 pts, Sussex 4 pts. Toss: Sussex.

Sussex's plight near the bottom of the table deepened after they were comprehensively outplayed, and they dropped one place to eighth. They failed to take advantage of batting first, with only Joyce showing the necessary application. He held the innings together with his first first-class century at

Hove. Warwickshire found that a desperately slow pitch, even by Hove standards, inhibited their strokeplayers too, but their no-risk strategy paid off. Bell showed his class with his fourth hundred of the season, and five others reached 50. Sussex got bogged down by Botha's left-arm spin when they replied 174 behind; only 34 runs were scored during the final session on the third day, when Nash reached 1,000 Championship runs in a season for the first time. Hodd resisted stoically for 168 balls, but the last eight wickets fell for 59 as Botha, having gone 23 overs without success, was rewarded for his perseverance with his first five-for in two years.

Close of play: First day, Warwickshire 15-2 (Westwood 11, Bell 2); Second day, Warwickshire 302-5 (Troughton 28, Ambrose 40); Third day, Sussex 113-3 (Hodd 20, Kirtley 0).

Sussex

*M. H. Yardy c Ambrose b Rankin	29	– lbw b Tahir	27
C. D. Nash b Tahir	16	– lbw b Woakes	44
E. C. Joyce lbw b Woakes	107	– (8) lbw b Botha	2
M. W. Goodwin b Botha	32	– c Ambrose b Rankin	16
C. D. Hopkinson b Botha	8	– (6) lbw b Botha	1
†A. J. Hodd c Westwood b Tahir	0	– (3) c Trott b Rankin	33
D. R. Smith c Sreesanth b Botha	0	– c Ambrose b Rankin	8
R. S. C. Martin-Jenkins c Trott b Tahir	12	– (9) not out	10
P. P. Chawla c Bell b Botha	6	– (10) c Westwood b Botha	9
O. P. Rayner lbw b Woakes	22	– (11) c Westwood b Botha	2
R. J. Kirtley not out	2	– (5) lbw b Botha	10
B 8, l-b 6, w 2, n-b 4	20	L-b 4, w 2, n-b 4	10

1/31 (2) 2/84 (1) 3/149 (4)   (89.2 overs) 254
4/185 (5) 5/186 (6) 6/187 (7)
7/218 (8) 8/225 (9) 9/238 (3) 10/253 (10)

1/70 (2) 2/79 (1)   (82 overs) 172
3/113 (4) 4/133 (5)
5/137 (6) 6/139 (3) 7/148 (7) 8/150 (8)
9/166 (10) 10/172 (11)

Sreesanth 15–4–41–0; Tahir 18–4–48–3; Rankin 14–2–54–1; Woakes 11.2–3–34–2; Botha 31–10–63–4. *Second Innings*—Sreesanth 10–4–32–0; Tahir 11–4–28–1; Woakes 18–10–30–1; Botha 36–15–51–5; Rankin 7–1–27–3.

Warwickshire

*I. J. Westwood lbw b Smith	57	R. Clarke not out	52
A. G. Botha lbw b Rayner	1	S. Sreesanth lbw b Kirtley	0
N. S. Tahir run out	0	W. B. Rankin c Kirtley b Chawla	1
I. R. Bell c sub (R. J. Hamilton-Brown) b Chawla	104	B 9, l-b 7, w 2, n-b 4	22
I. J. L. Trott lbw b Chawla	56		
J. O. Troughton b Kirtley	85	1/8 (2) 2/10 (3) 3/120 (1) (140.5 overs) 428
†T. R. Ambrose c sub (R. J. Hamilton-Brown) b Nash	50	4/212 (4) 5/239 (5)
C. R. Woakes lbw b Chawla	0	6/336 (7) 7/337 (8) 8/413 (6)
		9/413 (10) 10/428 (11) 120 overs: 336-6

Chawla 57.5–12–151–4; Rayner 21–5–47–1; Kirtley 20–3–59–2; Martin-Jenkins 11–0–33–0; Smith 24–7–81–1; Nash 5–1–28–1; Yardy 2–0–13–0.

Umpires: J. H. Evans and M. A. Gough.

SUSSEX v YORKSHIRE

At Hove, September 16, 17, 18, 19. Yorkshire won by 156 runs. Yorkshire 20 pts, Sussex 7 pts. Toss: Yorkshire.

Sussex were left staring at relegation after yet another depressing batting collapse. Chasing 240 in 42 overs to win on a wearing pitch, they lost all ten wickets for 46 in 20 overs, with Hoggard taking the second hat-trick of his career when his off-cutters proved too good for Hodd, Smith and Chawla. Sussex had looked the more likely winners until a last-wicket stand of 38 left them having to score at almost a run a ball. Like Sussex collapses, Yorkshire lower-order revivals had been a theme of the season, and in the first innings Nos 8 and 9, Shahzad and Wainwright, put on 157 in 43 overs. Still, their 403 was no more than par, and on the third day Hamilton-Brown led a bold counter-attack against the spinners, his maiden Championship hundred including 101 from 96 balls on the third morning. Yet Sussex's lead was modest after another collapse. In Yorkshire's second innings, Chawla bowled his leg-spin with impressive control, becoming his county's leading wicket-taker in only his fifth game of the season. But in the end a pitch designed with him in mind proved too much of a handicap to Sussex's batsmen.

Close of play: First day, Yorkshire 274-7 (Shahzad 35, Wainwright 39); Second day, Sussex 233-4 (Goodwin 44, Hamilton-Brown 32); Third day, Yorkshire 147-2 (Rudolph 70, McGrath 5).

Yorkshire

J. A. Rudolph lbw b Lewry	0	– b Chawla 70
J. J. Sayers st Hodd b Chawla	10	– c Hodd b Collymore 31
A. Lyth lbw b Collymore	50	– b Yardy 31
*A. McGrath c Hodd b Chawla	25	– c Hamilton-Brown b Chawla 37
A. W. Gale c Gatting b Hamilton-Brown	60	– c Hodd b Chawla 22
J. M. Bairstow lbw b Chawla	0	– lbw b Smith 2
†G. L. Brophy b Chawla	34	– c Gatting b Chawla 30
A. Shahzad lbw b Hamilton-Brown	88	– c Yardy b Chawla 0
D. J. Wainwright not out	85	– not out 14
Azeem Rafiq lbw b Smith	0	– b Smith 0
M. J. Hoggard b Nash	17	– b Lewry 26
B 8, l-b 11, w 1, n-b 14	34	B 14, l-b 5, n-b 2 21

1/0 (1) 2/41 (2) 3/75 (3) 4/96 (4)   (136 overs) 403   1/55 (2) 2/106 (3)   (98.1 overs) 284
5/104 (6) 6/164 (7) 7/209 (5)   3/147 (1) 4/185 (5)
8/366 (8) 9/368 (10) 10/403 (11)   120 overs: 346-7   5/188 (6) 6/220 (4) 7/220 (8)
                                                            8/245 (7) 9/246 (10) 10/284 (11)

Lewry 23–6–51–1; Collymore 21–5–69–1; Smith 19–4–60–1; Chawla 46–9–115–4; Hamilton-Brown 15–2–49–2; Nash 9–2–29–1; Yardy 3–1–11–0. *Second Innings*—Lewry 9.1–2–27–1; Collymore 10–2–31–1; Chawla 41–10–112–5; Smith 32–9–75–2; Yardy 6–1–20–1.

Sussex

*M. H. Yardy c Lyth b Shahzad	58	– (5) not out 13
C. D. Nash c Sayers b Wainwright	42	– c Brophy b Shahzad 26
J. S. Gatting lbw b Hoggard	46	– (1) c Sayers b Hoggard 20
M. W. Goodwin b Wainwright	63	– c Brophy b Wainwright 5
C. D. Hopkinson lbw b Shahzad	0	– (6) b Wainwright 6
R. J. Hamilton-Brown not out	171	– (3) run out 2
†A. J. Hodd c Rudolph b Shahzad	22	– c Brophy b Hoggard 2
D. R. Smith c and b Shahzad	11	– b Hoggard 0
P. P. Chawla c Rudolph b Wainwright	6	– c Bairstow b Hoggard 0
C. D. Collymore lbw b Wainwright	6	– lbw b Wainwright 0
J. D. Lewry lbw b Wainwright	0	– b Wainwright 0
B 4, l-b 12, n-b 2, p 5	23	B 4, l-b 5 9

1/68 (2) 2/130 (3) 3/165 (1)   (119.5 overs) 448   1/37 (1) 2/39 (3)   (25.3 overs) 83
4/165 (5) 5/293 (4) 6/392 (7)   3/46 (4) 4/64 (2)
7/408 (8) 8/420 (9) 9/448 (10) 10/448 (11)   5/71 (6) 6/80 (7) 7/80 (8)
                                                         8/80 (9) 9/81 (10) 10/83 (11)

Shahzad 29–7–84–4; Hoggard 26–5–70–1; Wainwright 31.5–4–134–5; Azeem Rafiq 29–2–128–0; McGrath 4–1–11–0. *Second Innings*—Shahzad 9–0–33–1; Hoggard 8–3–29–4; Wainwright 8.3–4–12–4.

Umpires: R. J. Bailey and J. W. Lloyds.

At Nottingham, September 23, 24, 25, 26. SUSSEX lost to NOTTINGHAMSHIRE by 35 runs. *Sussex are relegated.*

WARWICKSHIRE

Consolidation... and demolition

Paul Bolton

Warwickshire enjoyed a solid season of quiet consolidation, their second under director of cricket Ashley Giles. They retained their place in Division One of the Championship, and won the second division in the final year of the Pro40.

Until they lost their final Championship match, Warwickshire were contenders to finish a distant second to champions Durham, but that would have been a flattering position. They proved difficult to beat – the only defeats came against Durham (twice) and Lancashire – but some attritional cricket produced just three wins, against the two relegated counties. Indeed, Warwickshire were relegation candidates themselves until the final month.

Edgbaston's bland pitches produced six turgid draws, mostly played out before pitifully small crowds. An unbalanced fixture list, caused by Warwickshire's over-optimistic hopes that they would start building work before the end of the summer, meant a run of six consecutive home games, which condemned an inexperienced seam attack to some hard labour.

The indications from the final month were that Chris Woakes, Boyd Rankin and Naqaash Tahir emerged stronger from the experience. After they prospered in the late run of away matches, Warwickshire might be encouraged to prepare pitches offering their seamers more help in the future. Woakes took eight wickets in the match for England Lions against the West Indians on a green seamer at Derby, and nine when groundsman Steve Rouse produced a result pitch for the local derby against Worcestershire. In between, Woakes struggled for wickets, but he made the most of the batsman-friendly conditions by developing his batting sufficiently to be considered a genuine all-rounder.

Rankin stayed fit and produced some genuinely hostile spells, while Tahir gave a welcome reminder of his talents by ending the season with a flourish, swinging the ball late. Until mid-season Warwickshire were uncertain whether to renew Tahir's contract, but interest from Kent and Worcestershire persuaded them to give him one last chance. He responded impressively and committed himself to a new two-year contract.

Edgbaston's pitches proved a graveyard for spinners, which meant that the New Zealand off-break bowler Jeetan Patel made little impression, apart from a maiden century against Yorkshire, before a knee injury cut short his stint. Patel's replacement Sreesanth, the Indian fast bowler, fared a little better, without providing a lasting solution to Warwickshire's overseas problem.

Ian Salisbury's decision to become Surrey's second-team coach left Ant Botha as the senior spinner for most of the season. He was troubled by tennis elbow, but plugged away uncomplainingly, and was a nine-wicket match-winner in the crucial win over Sussex at Hove when he eventually found a pitch that suited him. Botha also opened the batting for the final month of the

season to fill the gaps left by Darren
Maddy, who played only two matches
before suffering a knee ligament
injury, and Tony Frost, who returned
to his groundstaff job after struggling
to reproduce his 2008 form. Navdeep
Poonia, the Scotland opener, lost form
so wretchedly that he was released
before the end of the season.

Chris Woakes

Ian Westwood also struggled to
combine the increased demands of
opening the batting with leading the
side. While his captaincy was usually
assured, Westwood had a prolonged
lean spell – ten single-figure scores in
17 first-class innings, and only one
higher than 22 – although his only century helped Warwickshire complete
their first double over Worcestershire since 1933.

The shortcomings of the various opening combinations were more than
compensated for by the availability of Ian Bell, before he was recalled by
England, and another outstanding season from Jonathan Trott. Bell did not
sulk during his lengthy absence from international cricket, and forced his way
back into England contention through weight of runs. Trott also scored heavily
in all formats, including a Twenty20 Cup record aggregate of 525 runs, and
his match-shaping century on Test debut at The Oval surprised few at
Edgbaston – least of all Giles, one of England's part-time selectors.

Jim Troughton made a maiden double-century in April, but lost form so
badly that he scored only 108 runs in ten innings before a century in the defeat
at Durham. Tim Ambrose, who shared a county-record fifth-wicket stand with
Troughton against Hampshire, also had an uneven season after being discarded
by England. There were middle-order contributions from Rikki Clarke,
who held some outstanding slip catches, and useful all-round performances
from Steffan Piolet and Keith Barker, a former Rochdale footballer, in one-
day cricket.

The season was due to be the last for the ramshackle Edgbaston pavilion,
built in the 1890s, but demolition, due to start in September, was delayed by
determined opposition from local residents, who had successfully blocked
plans for permanent floodlights in 2000.

Giles has some work to do on building a title-winning squad, despite the
capture of Essex batsman Varun Chopra and the leg-spinner Imran Tahir as
his new overseas player. He was less successful in attempts to recruit the
Worcestershire trio of Stephen Moore, Gareth Batty and Kabir Ali, and the
Yorkshire all-rounder Ajmal Shahzad. Giles also lost his right-hand man,
bowling coach Allan Donald, who decided to return to South Africa for family
reasons. Donald subsequently had a change of heart, and reapplied for his old
job, but he did not make the short list. Warwickshire replaced him with Graeme
Welch, a member of their 1994 treble-winning side.

WARWICKSHIRE RESULTS

All first-class matches – Played 18: Won 4, Lost 3, Drawn 11.
County Championship matches – Played 16: Won 3, Lost 3, Drawn 10.

LV County Championship, 5th in Division 1; Friends Provident Trophy, 3rd in Group B;
Pro40 League, winners in Division 2; Twenty20 Cup, q-f.

COUNTY CHAMPIONSHIP AVERAGES, BATTING AND FIELDING

Cap		M	I	NO	R	HS	100s	50s	Avge	Ct/St
2005	I. J. L. Trott	14	20	5	1,207	184*	4	5	80.46	10
2001	I. R. Bell†‡..........	13	21	3	986	172	4	4	54.77	10
	J. S. Patel§	3	4	1	131	120	1	0	43.66	1
2002	J. O. Troughton	16	21	0	823	223	2	3	39.19	10
	R. Clarke	13	17	1	619	112	1	5	38.68	22
2007	T. R. Ambrose‡	16	21	1	686	153	2	4	34.30	37/2
2009	C. R. Woakes†	16	21	7	480	131*	1	1	34.28	3
2008	I. J. Westwood†	14	23	3	605	133	1	4	30.25	10
	A. G. Botha¶	14	19	2	444	64	0	2	26.11	5
2005	N. M. Carter.........	9	13	0	318	67	0	2	24.46	0
1999	T. Frost.............	13	20	1	463	94	0	2	24.36	7
	N. S. Tahir†	10	13	3	145	24	0	0	16.11	1
	S. Sreesanth§	5	7	2	74	30*	0	0	14.80	3
	W. B. Rankin¶	12	12	4	18	7	0	0	2.25	2

Also batted: J. E. Anyon (2 matches) 15*, 14*; K. H. D. Barker (1 match) 0; A. Javid† (1 match) 8, 21 (1 ct); D. L. Maddy (cap 2007) (2 matches) 17, 36, 8 (2 ct); A. S. Miller (2 matches) 0, 0. N. A. Newport (1 match) did not bat.

† *Born in Warwickshire.*   ‡ *ECB contract.*   § *Official overseas player.*   ¶ *Other non-England-qualified player.*

BOWLING

	O	M	R	W	BB	5W/i	Avge
N. S. Tahir................	232.5	55	711	30	5-67	1	23.70
S. Sreesanth...............	109.3	21	418	13	5-93	1	32.15
W. B. Rankin..............	316.1	54	1,164	35	5-85	1	33.25
C. R. Woakes..............	415.5	91	1,354	37	5-40	1	36.59
A. G. Botha...............	316.3	61	941	23	5-51	1	40.91
N. M. Carter	190	30	704	16	5-37	1	44.00

Also bowled: J. E. Anyon 44.2–7–199–2; K. H. D. Barker 14–1–54–0; I. R. Bell 10–1–43–0; R. Clarke 146.1–21–567–9; T. Frost 5.1–1–12–1; D. L. Maddy 31.1–8–100–1; A. S. Miller 61–12–184–7; J. S. Patel 94–4–399–6; I. J. L. Trott 77.2–9–281–4; I. J. Westwood 19–2–49–2.

COUNTY RECORDS

Highest score for:	501*	B. C. Lara v Durham at Birmingham.........	1994
Highest score against:	322	I. V. A. Richards (Somerset) at Taunton.......	1985
Leading run-scorer:	35,146	D. L. Amiss (avge 41.64).................	1960–1987
Best bowling for:	10-41	J. D. Bannister v Combined Services at	
		Birmingham.........................	1959
Best bowling against:	10-36	H. Verity (Yorkshire) at Leeds	1931
Leading wicket-taker:	2,201	W. E. Hollies (avge 20.45)	1932–1957
Highest total for:	810-4 dec	v Durham at Birmingham	1994
Highest total against:	887	by Yorkshire at Birmingham.................	1896
Lowest total for:	16	v Kent at Tonbridge.......................	1913
Lowest total against:	15	by Hampshire at Birmingham	1922

ADDRESS

County Ground, Edgbaston, Birmingham B5 7QU (0121 446 4422; **email** info@edgbaston.com).
Website www.edgbaston.com

OFFICIALS

Captain I. J. Westwood
Director of cricket A. F. Giles
Bowling coach G. Welch
President Earl of Aylesford

Chairman W. N. Houghton
Chief executive C. Povey
Head groundsman S. J. Rouse
Scorer D. E. Wainwright

Trott's debt to Giles

Jonathan Trott owes a debt of gratitude to Ashley Giles – not, as Mark Ramprakash suggested, for pushing him into the England team, but for making him appreciate what was required to become an international-class batsman.

Trott's career appeared at a crossroads in 2007, after he had mustered just two half-centuries in a wretched County Championship season that also saw Warwickshire relegated. But Giles's surprise appointment as director of cricket, replacing Mark Greatbatch, has been the making of Trott. He has scored heavily in all forms of cricket since, including a superb century on Test debut in the pressure-cooker of the Ashes decider at The Oval in 2009, a season that also brought him a record Twenty20 Cup aggregate of 525 runs.

"If I hadn't had the 2007 season I don't think I'd be where I am now," said Trott. "That made me think about my game, and I realised that I was relying on talent to get me through rather than hard work. Ashley's arrival as coach has also been a big help. He went through a lot of setbacks in his career, some of them that I can't relate to, but he always came out the other side. He sat me down soon after he took over and set me some goals and checkpoints that have helped me.

"When I first came to Warwickshire Nick Knight used to talk about making sure you ticked all the boxes, and I hadn't a clue what he was talking about. But now I understand. I used to go to the nets and hit ball after ball without knowing what I was doing. Now I know exactly what I need to do in my preparation to be able to go into a game."

Giles has also played his part in helping Trott mature as a player and person. "I have been guilty of being a bit too wrapped up in my own game and sometimes I need to take a step back," admitted Trott. "I need to manage myself and I need people around me to say when I am doing something wrong – and Ashley has been very good in helping me with that."

Trott's match-winning batting in the Oval Test was not simply a product of his upbringing in South African cricket.   PAUL BOLTON

At Taunton, April 15, 16, 17, 18. WARWICKSHIRE drew with SOMERSET.

WARWICKSHIRE v HAMPSHIRE

At Birmingham, April 22, 23, 24, 25. Drawn. Warwickshire 12 pts, Hampshire 9 pts. Toss: Hampshire. County debut: M. J. North. Championship debut: A. S. Miller.

Lumb, who was not in Hampshire's original side, saved them with a dogged half-century on the final day. Lumb was dropped after bagging a pair against Worcestershire, but Hampshire were given special dispensation for him to replace North, briefly playing for his fifth county before being drafted into Australia's one-day squad on the second day. Batsmen prospered on a slow pitch, with Pothas's bustling hundred helping Hampshire recover from a first-day wobble against Andy Miller, a former England Under-19 seamer. Warwickshire also stuttered before Troughton and Ambrose compiled a county-record fifth-wicket stand of 335, surpassing 322 by Brian Lara and Keith Piper during Lara's 501 not out against Durham in 1994. Troughton completed his maiden double-century, which included four leg-side sixes off Dawson, who had dropped him on 99. Hampshire turned to their occasional bowlers to break the partnership, but further punishment was inflicted by Clarke, who hit his first century for Warwickshire, from only 78 balls. Hampshire batted out the final day helped by four dropped catches, two off Pothas before he had reached 21.

Close of play: First day, Hampshire 310-7 (Pothas 83, Tremlett 15); Second day, Warwickshire 224-4 (Troughton 100, Ambrose 47); Third day, Hampshire 61-0 (Carberry 38, Adams 22).

Hampshire

M. A. Carberry c Ambrose b Miller	77	–	c Clarke b Botha	65
J. H. K. Adams c Clarke b Rankin	1	–	c Rankin b Botha	39
J. P. Crawley c Clarke b Miller	30	–	c Clarke b Botha	6
M. J. North c Ambrose b Maddy	15			
S. M. Ervine lbw b Rankin	30	–	c Clarke b Rankin	21
*†N. Pothas not out	122	–	not out	65
L. A. Dawson c Troughton b Clarke	22	–	lbw b Botha	2
D. G. Cork c Bell b Miller	5	–	not out	7
C. T. Tremlett b Woakes	36			
D. J. Balcombe lbw b Rankin	0			
J. A. Tomlinson c Maddy b Clarke	8			
M. J. Lumb (did not bat)		–	(4) b Rankin	84
B 4, l-b 8, w 5, n-b 16	33		B 5, l-b 4, w 1, n-b 2	12

1/24 (2) 2/115 (1) 3/121 (3)   (123.5 overs) 379   1/95 (2)   (6 wkts, 103 overs) 301
4/167 (4) 5/183 (5) 6/239 (7) 7/271 (8)   2/103 (3) 3/140 (1)
8/337 (9) 9/340 (10) 10/375 (11)   120 overs: 372-9   4/177 (5) 5/264 (4) 6/279 (7)

Lumb replaced North, who had been called up by Australia.

Woakes 33–9–89–1; Rankin 25–7–64–3; Miller 27–5–79–3; Clarke 11.5–0–63–2; Maddy 19–7–48–1; Bell 3–0–7–0; Botha 5–0–13–0. *Second Innings*—Woakes 18–4–49–0; Rankin 24–5–72–2; Botha 42–7–103–4; Miller 9–0–29–0; Clarke 5–1–14–0; Maddy 5–1–21–0.

Warwickshire

D. L. Maddy c Ervine b Cork	8		C. R. Woakes not out	8
T. Frost run out	4			
I. J. L. Trott c Cork b Tomlinson	22		B 1, l-b 7, n-b 12	20
J. O. Troughton c Cork b Carberry	223			
I. R. Bell c Cork b Tremlett	29		1/12 (1) (8 wkts dec, 148.5 overs) 630	
*†T. R. Ambrose b Adams	153		2/12 (2) 3/54 (3)	
R. Clarke c Ervine b Dawson	112		4/120 (5) 5/455 (6) 6/476 (4)	
A. G. Botha c Carberry b Dawson	51		7/614 (8) 8/630 (7) 120 overs: 454-4	

A. S. Miller and W. B. Rankin did not bat.

Cork 19–4–55–1; Tremlett 24–5–87–1; Balcombe 22–1–97–0; Tomlinson 29–3–104–1; Ervine 17–3–50–0; Dawson 8.5–0–75–2; Carberry 17–1–105–1; Adams 12–0–49–1.

Umpires: J. H. Evans and R. T. Robinson.

WARWICKSHIRE v YORKSHIRE

At Birmingham, May 6, 7, 8, 9. Drawn. Warwickshire 9 pts, Yorkshire 11 pts. Toss: Yorkshire. Championship debut: J. S. Patel.

A slow pitch proved demoralising for bowlers but a delight for statisticians as two more county records tumbled at Edgbaston. Sayers, who had not reached 50 in his last 26 first-class innings, and McGrath, with a maiden double-century to go with the unbeaten 188 he made here two years earlier, established Yorkshire's record third-wicket partnership when they added 346 in 98 overs, eclipsing the 323 by Herbert Sutcliffe and Maurice Leyland against Glamorgan at Huddersfield in 1928. Trott and Patel, the New Zealand off-spinner making his Championship debut, then erased an 84-year-old Warwickshire record – held by George Stephens and Arthur Croom, who had put on 154 against Derbyshire – when they helped themselves to a ninth-wicket stand of 233. Patel's entertaining hundred was the first of his career and the first for Warwickshire from a No. 10; Durham, Kent and Leicestershire were now the only counties for whom a No. 10 had not hit a century. Patel had earlier claimed his first Championship wicket by removing the obdurate Sayers, whose innings lasted more than nine hours. Vaughan, battling in vain to catch the eye of the England selectors, managed 16, and sat out the second innings because of a hamstring niggle. Warwickshire saved the follow-on only during the stand on the final morning between Trott and Patel, after which the match fizzled out.

HIGHEST FIRST-CLASS SCORES FOR WARWICKSHIRE BY NUMBERS 10 AND 11

120	J. S. Patel v Yorkshire at Birmingham	**2009**
91	A. Richardson v Hampshire at Birmingham	2002
84	W. A. Bourne v Oxford University at Birmingham	1973
83	A. F. Giles v Worcestershire at Worcester	1996
82	N. M. Carter v Kent at Birmingham	2005
75	A. F. Giles v Hampshire at Birmingham	1998
74*	J. H. Mayer v Surrey at The Oval	1927
67*	F. R. Santall v Derbyshire at Derby	1923
66	S. J. Rouse v Surrey at Birmingham	1976
65	A. F. Giles v Kent at Birmingham	1996

Note: All batted at No. 10 apart from Richardson and Mayer.

Research: Philip Bailey

Close of play: First day, Yorkshire 258-2 (Sayers 114, McGrath 46); Second day, Warwickshire 81-1 (Westwood 24, Bell 33); Third day, Warwickshire 422-8 (Trott 140, Patel 89).

Yorkshire

J. A. Rudolph c Ambrose b Clarke	62	– c Frost b Clarke	30
J. J. Sayers c Clarke b Patel	173	– c Ambrose b Woakes	14
M. P. Vaughan c Troughton b Woakes	16		
*A. McGrath b Carter	211	– (3) not out	53
A. W. Gale c Patel b Carter	12		
†G. L. Brophy not out	40	– (4) lbw b Clarke	0
A. U. Rashid c Trott b Carter	0	– (5) not out	58
Naved-ul-Hasan c Ambrose b Carter	32		
A. Shahzad c Ambrose b Trott	5		
G. J. Kruis not out	1		
B 5, l-b 10, w 1, n-b 32	48	B 1, l-b 5, w 1	7

1/93 (1) 2/124 (3) (8 wkts dec, 167.4 overs) 600 1/49 (2) (3 wkts dec, 42 overs) 162
3/470 (2) 4/505 (5) 5/514 (4) 2/63 (1) 3/63 (4)
6/514 (7) 7/578 (8) 8/597 (9)
120 overs: 370-2

M. J. Hoggard did not bat.

Woakes 28–10–68–1; Rankin 27–6–85–0; Carter 30.4–4–129–4; Patel 36–1–150–1; Clarke 25–8–64–1; Trott 16–2–62–1; Bell 5–0–27–0. *Second Innings*—Woakes 10–2–29–1; Rankin 9–1–48–0; Carter 2–0–5–0; Clarke 8–2–28–2; Patel 11–1–40–0; Trott 2–0–6–0.

Warwickshire

*I. J. Westwood lbw b Naved-ul-Hasan	41	– not out	19
T. Frost c Rudolph b Kruis	8	– c Brophy b Kruis	5
I. R. Bell c Shahzad b Kruis	37	– not out	30
I. J. L. Trott not out	161		
J. O. Troughton lbw b Naved-ul-Hasan	0		
†T. R. Ambrose c Brophy b Naved-ul-Hasan	0		
R. Clarke b Shahzad	9		
N. M. Carter b Rashid	32		
C. R. Woakes b Rashid	30		
J. S. Patel c McGrath b Shahzad	120		
W. B. Rankin lbw b Hoggard	0		
B 16, l-b 16, n-b 12	44	B 2, l-b 1, w 1, n-b 2	6

1/12 (2) 2/90 (3) 3/119 (1)   (122.1 overs) 482   1/11 (2)   (1 wkt, 16 overs) 60
4/119 (5) 5/121 (6) 6/138 (7)/193 (8)
8/241 (9) 9/474 (10) 10/482 (11)   120 overs: 474-9

Hoggard 16.1–2–67–1; Kruis 22–3–89–2; Rashid 22–6–89–2; Naved-ul-Hasan 27–5–102–3; Shahzad 21–2–72–2; McGrath 14–4–31–0. *Second Innings*—Hoggard 3–1–5–0; Kruis 6–1–25–1; Rashid 5–0–19–0; Shahzad 2–0–8–0.

Umpires: R. K. Illingworth and N. J. Llong.

WARWICKSHIRE v NOTTINGHAMSHIRE

At Birmingham, June 6, 7, 8, 9. Drawn. Warwickshire 11 pts, Nottinghamshire 11 pts. Toss: Nottinghamshire. First-class debut: K. H. D. Barker.

Wagh enjoyed his return to Edgbaston, enlivening a rain-affected draw with a century in his first Championship innings against his former employers. Wagh left Warwickshire at the end of the 2006 season; disillusioned with life at Edgbaston, he had described the club as "a political monstrosity" in his book *Pavilion to Crease… and Back.* Wagh's unfettered strokeplay on another flat pitch was a reminder of his rich talents and he did not give a chance until he had completed the 26th first-class century of his career. The loss of the first two days to rain meant this became a battle for bonus points, but Nottinghamshire missed out on the chance of a fifth batting point when the umpires halted play for bad light shortly after Ealham had hit Anyon for six. Voges passed 50 for the fifth successive Championship innings after Warwickshire had been made to toil by the lively Fletcher, whose figures would have been better had Wagh not dropped Carter at long leg. Carter's brutal cameo lit up proceedings after Warwickshire, who earlier handed a first-class debut to the 22-year-old Keith Barker following some impressive displays in the Twenty20 Cup, were forced to retrench following a mid-innings slump.

Close of play: First day, No play; Second day, No play; Third day, Warwickshire 367-7 (Troughton 63, Woakes 32).

Warwickshire

*I. J. Westwood c Jefferson b Fletcher	73	J. S. Patel not out	3
T. Frost c Read b Ealham	37	J. E. Anyon not out	14
I. R. Bell c Wagh b Patel	60		
I. J. L. Trott c Read b Fletcher	37	B 5, l-b 8, n-b 12	25
J. O. Troughton b Shreck	73		
†T. R. Ambrose c Voges b Patel	0	1/87 (2) (9 wkts dec, 104.2 overs) 402
K. H. D. Barker b Fletcher	0	2/143 (1) 3/220 (3)
N. M. Carter c Shreck b Pattinson	47	4/224 (4) 5/239 (6) 6/242 (7)
C. R. Woakes c Brown b Fletcher	33	7/313 (8) 8/382 (5) 9/384 (9)

Shreck 26–5–95–1; Pattinson 19–4–84–1; Fletcher 24.2–4–115–4; Ealham 18–5–46–1; Patel 17–3–49–2.

Nottinghamshire

W. I. Jefferson c Frost b Patel 21	M. A. Ealham not out 14
B. M. Shafayat c Ambrose b Anyon 20	
M. A. Wagh c Ambrose b Carter 147	B 8, l-b 3, n-b 4 15
S. R. Patel c Ambrose b Woakes 4	
A. C. Voges c Ambrose b Patel 76	1/36 (2) 2/64 (1) (6 wkts, 77.2 overs) 376
A. D. Brown run out 64	3/68 (4) 4/216 (5)
*†C. M. W. Read not out 15	5/340 (6) 6/353 (3)

L. J. Fletcher, C. E. Shreck and D. J. Pattinson did not bat.

Woakes 17–0–68–1; Carter 16–3–51–1; Anyon 11.2–1–75–1; Barker 14–1–54–0; Patel 14–0–97–2; Trott 5–0–20–0.

Umpires: G. Sharp and P. Willey.

At Durham, June 11, 12, 13. WARWICKSHIRE beat DURHAM UCCE by 74 runs.

WARWICKSHIRE v DURHAM

At Birmingham, June 16, 17, 18, 19. Durham won by ten wickets. Durham 22 pts, Warwickshire 4 pts. Toss: Durham.

The hostility of Onions and Harmison, who between them took 16 for 230 on a slow pitch raked at both ends in an attempt to nullify them, inflicted a first Championship defeat on Warwickshire in 21 games under Ashley Giles, their director of cricket. Harmison took five for 18 in two hostile spells at the end of the third day, and struck Frost on the helmet, Bell on the hand and Woakes on the forearm. Onions sealed victory with his best figures since taking eight for 101 at Edgbaston in 2007, including his 50th first-class wicket of a profitable summer. Only Bell showed much appetite for the fight, and Warwickshire, who narrowly failed to avoid the follow-on, folded in each innings after he departed. Blackwell applied himself sensibly for his first Championship century for Durham, although he was helped by Warwickshire putting down five catches on the first day. Victory took Durham to the top of the table, never to be dislodged.

Close of play: First day, Durham 322-6 (Blackwell 107, Stoneman 21); Second day, Durham 403-7 (Blackwell 139, Thorp 4); Third day, Warwickshire 264-9 (Botha 20, Rankin 4).

Durham

M. J. Di Venuto lbw b Woakes 40	– (2) not out 13
M. D. Stoneman c Rankin b Woakes 64	
*W. R. Smith lbw b Woakes 1	– (1) not out 9
G. J. Muchall lbw b Woakes 39	
D. M. Benkenstein c Troughton b Carter 14	
I. D. Blackwell b Rankin 158	
†P. Mustard c Bell b Patel 24	
G. R. Breese c Troughton b Carter 48	
C. D. Thorp st Ambrose b Patel 7	
G. Onions not out 1	
S. J. Harmison c Bell b Patel 1	
B 13, l-b 11, w 8, n-b 4 36	

1/31 (3) 2/97 (4) 3/114 (1) 4/120 (5) (125 overs) 433   (no wkt, 4 overs) 22
5/206 (7) 6/304 (8) 7/397 (2)
8/420 (9) 9/430 (6) 10/433 (11)   120 overs: 415-7

In the first innings Stoneman, when 17, retired hurt at 23 and resumed at 304.

Woakes 32–7–105–4; Rankin 24–5–68–1; Carter 23–5–90–2; Patel 33.2–2–112–3; Trott 1–1–0–0; Botha 12–2–34–0. *Second Innings*—Woakes 2–0–6–0; Rankin 2–0–16–0.

Warwickshire

*I. J. Westwood b Onions	8	– c sub (S. G. Borthwick) b Blackwell .	8
T. Frost c Breese b Benkenstein	56	– c Mustard b Onions	3
I. R. Bell c Di Venuto b Blackwell	79	– b Onions	57
I. J. L. Trott b Harmison	25	– c Thorp b Onions	32
J. O. Troughton c Muchall b Harmison	16	– lbw b Onions	5
†T. R. Ambrose c Mustard b Harmison	10	– c Benkenstein b Harmison	9
A. G. Botha not out	29	– not out	34
N. M. Carter lbw b Blackwell	0	– c Benkenstein b Harmison	23
C. R. Woakes c Thorp b Harmison	24	– c Mustard b Onions	1
J. S. Patel c Breese b Harmison	6	– b Onions	2
W. B. Rankin b Onions	7	– c Thorp b Onions	2
B 1, l-b 10, w 5	16	L-b 1	1

1/17 (1) 2/146 (2) 3/168 (3)   (92.1 overs) 276   1/3 (2) 2/28 (1)   (78 overs) 177
4/197 (4) 5/200 (5) 6/211 (6)   3/100 (3) 4/101 (4)
7/212 (8) 8/253 (9) 9/259 (10) 10/276 (11)   5/106 (5) 6/119 (6) 7/153 (8) 8/157 (9)
    9/163 (10) 10/177 (11)

Onions 22.1–2–89–2; Harmison 20–6–44–5; Thorp 11–2–25–0; Blackwell 25–7–47–2; Breese 9–2–43–0; Benkenstein 5–1–17–1. *Second Innings*—Onions 22–9–38–7; Harmison 17–5–59–2; Thorp 6–1–19–0; Blackwell 25–4–53–1; Breese 8–4–7–0.

Umpires: N. L. Bainton and R. A. Kettleborough.

WARWICKSHIRE v ENGLAND XI

At Birmingham, July 1, 2, 3. Drawn. Toss: Warwickshire.

England's decision to limber up for the Ashes with a three-day match against county opposition was a qualified success. Warwickshire's inexperienced attack was competitive, but without Bell, who was captaining England Lions against the Australians, their batting proved less so. Warwickshire's decision to charge members was unpopular, and there were boos from disgruntled spectators who felt short-changed when the captains shook hands on a draw at the earliest opportunity, after barely three hours' cricket on a rain-delayed final day. Cook made best use of a greenish pitch that played better than it looked. But, on the day it was revealed he had missed the team bus on an England visit to the Ypres trenches the previous week, Flintoff survived just 16 balls before edging Tahir to second slip. Warwickshire then crumpled against Anderson's pace and swing and Panesar's spin. England opted for more batting practice, but Pietersen missed out again. Bopara completed a fluent fourth first-class century in as many matches, before retiring to allow Prior an extended net. England, or England XIs, had played against counties in the distant past, but they were usually festival games.

Close of play: First day, Warwickshire 31-1 (Frost 3, Trott 18); Second day, England XI 185-2 (Bopara 88, Collingwood 21).

England XI

*A. J. Strauss c Clarke b Tahir	31	– c and b Woakes	61
A. N. Cook c Ambrose b Trott	124		
R. S. Bopara c Javid b Rankin	43	– (2) retired out	104
K. P. Pietersen c Frost b Clarke	1	– (3) c Clarke b Rankin	6
P. D. Collingwood b Barker	16	– (4) not out	79
†M. J. Prior c Trott b Tahir	10	– (5) not out	50
A. Flintoff c Clarke b Tahir	19		
S. C. J. Broad not out	22		
G. P. Swann c Tahir b Clarke	14		
L-b 5, w 2, n-b 3	10	L-b 16, w 1, n-b 2	19

1/61 (1) 2/162 (3)   (8 wkts dec, 78 overs) 290   1/109 (1)   (3 wkts dec, 76 overs) 319
3/172 (4) 4/213 (2) 5/229 (5)   2/125 (3) 3/208 (2)
6/243 (6) 7/255 (7) 8/290 (9)

J. M. Anderson and M. S. Panesar did not bat.

Woakes 16–1–50–0; Rankin 11–0–60–1; Tahir 15–2–54–3; Barker 15–2–51–1; Clarke 13–2–46–2; Trott 7–1–21–1; Javid 1–0–3–0. *Second Innings*—Woakes 14–4–32–1; Rankin 13–0–55–1; Tahir 10–2–26–0; Clarke 5–0–27–0; Barker 12–2–44–0; Trott 10–0–44–0; Javid 12–0–75–0.

Warwickshire

*I. J. Westwood c Prior b Anderson	2	– c Prior b Broad 5
T. Frost lbw b Flintoff	14	
I. J. L. Trott c Prior b Anderson	19	– (2) not out 14
J. O. Troughton c Prior b Flintoff	5	– (3) run out 0
A. Javid c Swann b Anderson	4	– (4) c Strauss b Flintoff 3
†T. R. Ambrose b Anderson	7	– (5) not out 4
R. Clarke c Flintoff b Anderson	12	
C. R. Woakes c Strauss b Panesar	13	
K. H. D. Barker b Panesar	5	
N. S. Tahir not out	7	
W. B. Rankin c Bopara b Panesar	1	
B 8, l-b 5	13	L-b 1 1

1/2 (1) 2/38 (3) 3/48 (2) 4/49 (4)   (45.4 overs) 102   1/13 (1)   (3 wkts, 12 overs) 27
5/59 (6) 6/64 (5) 7/75 (7) 8/81 (9)   2/13 (3) 3/18 (4)
9/96 (8) 10/102 (11)

Anderson 13–2–34–5; Broad 11–4–18–0; Flintoff 9–3–16–2; Swann 5–1–11–0; Panesar 7.4–4–10–3. *Second Innings*—Anderson 4–1–6–0; Broad 4–1–16–1; Flintoff 4–3–4–1.

Umpires: A. Hicks and R. K. Illingworth.

WARWICKSHIRE v SUSSEX

At Birmingham, July 7, 8, 9, 10. Drawn. Warwickshire 11 pts, Sussex 12 pts. Toss: Sussex.

Sussex briefly scented their first win at Edgbaston since 1982 when their new-ball attack reduced Warwickshire to 16 for three on a helpful pitch, which started damp after days of heavy rain. But they were let down by their back-up seamers who were punished for dropping too short by an in-form Trott; he reached 150 for the eighth time in a chanceless innings of assured strokeplay. Solid batting down the order, including a last-wicket stand of 65 between Woakes and Tahir, in his first Championship appearance of the season, insured Warwickshire against defeat. Trott then pocketed – quite literally – a catch at short leg when the ball lodged in his right trouser pocket as he jumped to take evasive action from Joyce's full-blooded sweep off Botha. On a final day that was all about bonus-point accumulation after the captains failed to agree on a contrived finish, Hopkinson followed up a century against the Australians with another, in his first Championship start of the season.

Close of play: First day, Warwickshire 5-1 (Westwood 5, Bell 0); Second day, Warwickshire 349-9 (Woakes 12, Tahir 1); Third day, Sussex 276-4 (Hopkinson 64, Wright 59).

Warwickshire

*I. J. Westwood c Rayner b Collymore	5	– c Yardy b Collymore 4
T. Frost b Yasir Arafat	0	– c Rayner b Smith 17
I. R. Bell c Hodd b Collymore	2	– not out 55
I. J. L. Trott c Hodd b Wright	166	– not out 9
J. O. Troughton st Hodd b Rayner	18	
†T. R. Ambrose c Rayner b Yasir Arafat	28	
R. Clarke c Joyce b Wright	36	
A. G. Botha b Yasir Arafat	46	
N. M. Carter c Hopkinson b Wright	17	
C. R. Woakes not out	49	
N. S. Tahir c and b Rayner	22	
L-b 5, w 1, n-b 12	18	B 5, l-b 1, n-b 6 12

1/5 (2) 2/7 (1) 3/16 (3) 4/71 (5)   (115.1 overs) 407   1/11 (1)   (2 wkts dec, 33.4 overs) 97
5/140 (6) 6/212 (7) 7/308 (8)   2/70 (2)
8/329 (4) 9/342 (9) 10/407 (11)

Yasir Arafat 28–7–106–3; Collymore 20–6–54–2; Smith 9–1–45–0; Wright 26–2–94–3; Rayner 29.1–6–82–2; Nash 3–0–21–0. *Second Innings*—Yasir Arafat 6–0–19–0; Collymore 6–1–9–1; Nash 8–0–34–0; Smith 9–1–15–1; Rayner 3–1–7–0; Hodd 1.4–0–7–0.

Sussex

*M. H. Yardy c Ambrose b Tahir	57	Yasir Arafat lbw b Carter		11
C. D. Nash c Botha b Tahir	31			
E. C. Joyce c Trott b Botha	29	B 3, l-b 12, w 1, n-b 14		30
M. W. Goodwin c Woakes b Tahir	22			
C. D. Hopkinson c Botha b Trott	119	1/55 (2) (8 wkts dec, 117.2 overs)		429
L. J. Wright c Frost b Tahir	71	2/99 (3) 3/148 (4)		
†A. J. Hodd not out	59	4/151 (1) 5/303 (6) 6/390 (5)		
D. R. Smith c Clarke b Trott	0	7/390 (8) 8/429 (9)		

O. P. Rayner and C. D. Collymore did not bat.

Woakes 14–1–67–0; Carter 22.2–1–96–1; Tahir 28–7–83–4; Botha 29–5–84–1; Clarke 10–1–54–0; Trott 12–2–26–2; Westwood 2–0–4–0.

Umpires: B. Dudleston and P. Willey.

WARWICKSHIRE v LANCASHIRE

At Birmingham, July 15, 16, 17, 18. Drawn. Warwickshire 12 pts, Lancashire 9 pts. Toss: Warwickshire.

A slow pitch and the loss of the opening day contributed to another dreary draw at Edgbaston, brightened only by Bell's 25th first-class century. He had been released from England's Test squad at Lord's on the scheduled opening day of this match and hid his disappointment by passing 50 for the fifth time in six Championship innings. Warwickshire's first innings stretched into the final morning, when they declared with maximum batting points. Lancashire then failed to collect full batting points for the 27th time in 28 matches. Even though there was no prospect of a positive result, the sides agreed to play into the final hour to collect as many bonus points as they could. Tahir and Botha profited from some timid batting as Lancashire surrendered their last five wickets in six overs.

Close of play: First day, No play; Second day, Warwickshire 256-4 (Trott 69, Ambrose 13); Third day, Warwickshire 370-8 (Woakes 24, Tahir 1).

Warwickshire

*I. J. Westwood c Smith b Hogg	60	C. R. Woakes not out		37
T. Frost lbw b Hogg	1	N. S. Tahir not out		18
I. R. Bell c Sutton b Newby	106	L-b 3, w 2, n-b 6		11
I. J. L. Trott b Mahmood	79			
J. O. Troughton c Loye b Keedy	2	1/2 (2) (8 wkts dec, 117.1 overs)		403
†T. R. Ambrose c Chilton b Newby	28	2/132 (1) 3/210 (3)		
R. Clarke c du Plessis b Newby	54	4/227 (5) 5/274 (6) 6/281 (4)		
A. G. Botha c Sutton b Hogg	7	7/317 (8) 8/365 (7)		

W. B. Rankin did not bat.

Mahmood 26.1–4–104–1; Hogg 27–4–80–3; Smith 10–1–45–0; Newby 17–4–62–3; Keedy 36–6–104–1; du Plessis 1–0–5–0.

Lancashire

P. J. Horton c Troughton b Woakes	43	S. I. Mahmood b Tahir		7
T. C. Smith lbw b Tahir	5	O. J. Newby b Tahir		6
M. B. Loye c Ambrose b Rankin	29	G. Keedy not out		1
V. V. S. Laxman c Trott b Tahir	9	L-b 19, w 5, n-b 2		26
M. J. Chilton c Westwood b Botha	85			
J. du Plessis c Tahir b Botha	79	1/16 (2) 2/81 (1) 3/93 (3) (81 overs)		317
*†L. D. Sutton c Trott b Botha	26	4/101 (4) 5/244 (6) 6/298 (7)		
K. W. Hogg c Clarke b Botha	1	7/299 (8) 8/302 (5) 9/310 (9) 10/317 (10)		

Tahir 17–5–55–4; Rankin 13–4–33–1; Clarke 10–1–36–0; Woakes 15–3–51–1; Botha 17–2–86–4; Trott 9–1–37–0.

Umpires: T. E. Jesty and J. F. Steele.

At Southampton, July 21, 22, 23, 24. WARWICKSHIRE drew with HAMPSHIRE.

At Worcester, July 31, August 1, 2, 3. WARWICKSHIRE beat WORCESTERSHIRE by nine wickets.

WARWICKSHIRE v SOMERSET

At Birmingham, August 5, 6, 7, 8. Drawn. Warwickshire 8 pts, Somerset 10 pts. Toss: Warwickshire. First-class debut: N. A. Newport.

Trescothick dominated another rain-ruined Edgbaston draw by making two centuries in a match for the second time. The previous instance was also at Edgbaston, for England against West Indies in 2004. Trescothick's first century was the better since it came after Somerset had been inserted on a green pitch, though the wicket promised more to the bowlers than it delivered. Trescothick, dropped by Frost at first slip on 87, pummelled the bowling and with Langer added 175, Somerset's best second-wicket stand against Warwickshire. Langer's tea-time declaration on the third day came around the time Trott arrived after being released from England's Test squad at Headingley. Trott replaced Nathan Newport, son of the former England swing bowler Phil, who had been recruited from Birmingham League club Barnt Green and became a footnote in the scorecard on an unusual debut. Trott timed the ball superbly, but Warwickshire were dismissed for their lowest first-innings total of the Championship season at home. Trescothick then eased to another century at a run a ball as the match drifted.

Close of play: First day, No play; Second day, Somerset 226-2 (Trescothick 104, Hildreth 22); Third day, Warwickshire 156-3 (Frost 71, Trott 40).

Somerset

M. E. Trescothick lbw b Rankin	108	– not out		107
A. V. Suppiah c Ambrose b Rankin	7	– c Clarke b Rankin		8
*J. L. Langer c Ambrose b Woakes	69			
J. C. Hildreth not out	86	– (3) c sub (C. S. Macleod) b Carter		11
Z. de Bruyn c Ambrose b Rankin	0	– (4) lbw b Botha		9
†C. Kieswetter c Frost b Woakes	6	– (5) b Trott		5
P. D. Trego c Clarke b Woakes	1	– (6) not out		4
B. J. Phillips c Clarke b Woakes	7			
A. C. Thomas c Ambrose b Clarke	10			
B 9, l-b 10, w 2, n-b 8	29	B 4, l-b 1, w 1, n-b 6		12

1/17 (2) 2/192 (3)   (8 wkts dec, 79.1 overs) 323   1/23 (2)   (4 wkts dec, 37 overs) 156
3/230 (1) 4/234 (5)   2/53 (3) 3/125 (4)
5/269 (6) 6/279 (7) 7/295 (8) 8/323 (9)   4/150 (5)

A. R. Caddick and C. M. Willoughby did not bat.

Rankin 17–2–71–3; Tahir 11–2–37–0; Carter 23–2–99–0; Woakes 25–6–89–4; Clarke 3.1–0–8–1. *Second Innings*—Rankin 7–2–34–1; Tahir 7–2–18–0; Carter 3–0–21–1; Woakes 4–2–8–0; Clarke 6–0–26–0; Botha 7–0–34–1; Trott 3–1–10–1.

Warwickshire

*I. J. Westwood lbw b Willoughby	0	C. R. Woakes c Kieswetter b Willoughby	13
N. M. Carter c Langer b Thomas	24	N. S. Tahir c Suppiah b Willoughby	23
J. O. Troughton c Trescothick b Willoughby	11	W. B. Rankin not out	0
T. Frost c Kieswetter b Thomas	94	B 5, l-b 6, w 2, n-b 2	15
I. J. L. Trott c Trescothick b Caddick	79		
†T. R. Ambrose c Langer b Thomas	0	1/0 (1) 2/24 (3) 3/61 (2) (66.2 overs)	261
R. Clarke c Kieswetter b Thomas	0	4/203 (4) 5/207 (6) 6/207 (7)	
A. G. Botha b Caddick	2	7/210 (8) 8/233 (5) 9/252 (9) 10/261 (10)	

Trott replaced N. A. Newport after being released from the England squad.

Willoughby 13.2–4–37–4; Caddick 18–4–67–2; Thomas 21–2–72–4; Phillips 8–1–42–0; Trego 4–0–22–0; de Bruyn 2–0–10–0.

Umpires: M. R. Benson and N. A. Mallender.

At Nottingham, August 11, 12, 13, 14. WARWICKSHIRE drew with NOTTINGHAMSHIRE.

At Chester-le-Street, August 19, 20, 21. WARWICKSHIRE lost to DURHAM by eight wickets.

At Scarborough, August 26, 27, 28, 29. WARWICKSHIRE drew with YORKSHIRE.

WARWICKSHIRE v WORCESTERSHIRE

At Birmingham, September 2, 3, 4, 5. Warwickshire won by an innings and 18 runs. Warwickshire 22 pts, Worcestershire 3 pts. Toss: Worcestershire.

Warwickshire completed their first double over Worcestershire since 1933, outplaying their neighbours in all departments. Worcestershire failed to make the most of bowling first on a pitch that began so green that it was difficult to distinguish from the rest of the square, and they were punished by Westwood, who made a swashbuckling first century of the season. Richard Jones, with a maiden five-wicket haul, and Mason did their best to redeem things, but Worcestershire's back-up bowling was poor. Though Trott – returning from his triumphant Test debut – narrowly missed out on a third century in successive first-class matches, he helped to bat Warwickshire into an impregnable position. Worcestershire's brittle batting was then exploited by Woakes with a burst of five wickets in 40 balls, a performance that helped gain him his county cap. Woakes followed up with four more wickets when Worcestershire followed on; only Moore and Davies offered prolonged resistance. Defeat pushed Worcestershire to the brink of relegation, a grim situation made worse by news that Kabir Ali, the former England seam bowler, had requested to speak to other counties.

Close of play: First day, Warwickshire 179-1 (Westwood 101, Bell 32); Second day, Worcestershire 11-0 (Mitchell 10, Moore 1); Third day, Worcestershire 123-3 (Solanki 10, Ali 10).

Warwickshire

*I. J. Westwood run out	133	N. S. Tahir c Mason b Jones	15
A. G. Botha b Jones	22	S. Sreesanth not out	23
I. R. Bell lbw b Imran Arif	36	W. B. Rankin c Solanki b Jones	0
I. J. L. Trott c Smith b Jones	93	B 16, l-b 19, w 5, n-b 6	46
J. O. Troughton c Davies b Mason	22		
T. Frost c Moore b Andrew	24	1/79 (2) 2/188 (3) 3/255 (1) (117 overs)	443
†T. R. Ambrose c Mitchell b Jones	8	4/301 (5) 5/344 (6) 6/361 (7)	
C. R. Woakes c Solanki b Jones	21	7/382 (4) 8/399 (8) 9/426 (9) 10/443 (11)	

Mason 26–7–59–1; Imran Arif 25–3–112–1; Andrew 23–1–104–1; Jones 29–6–100–6; Mitchell 10–2–16–0; Ali 4–1–17–0.

Worcestershire

	First Innings		Second Innings	
D. K. H. Mitchell c Ambrose b Woakes	30	– c Trott b Woakes	25
S. C. Moore run out	5	– c Bell b Rankin	63
*V. S. Solanki lbw b Woakes	27	– b Woakes	10
B. F. Smith b Woakes	4	– c Troughton b Woakes	0
M. M. Ali c Bell b Woakes	0	– c Bell b Sreesanth	11
†S. M. Davies c Bell b Woakes	8	– b Sreesanth	62
A. N. Kervezee c Botha b Tahir	33	– c Westwood b Sreesanth	12
G. M. Andrew c Ambrose b Sreesanth	0	– c Trott b Botha	23
R. A. Jones lbw b Tahir	24	– c Sreesanth b Rankin	12
M. S. Mason not out	8	– not out	8
Imran Arif b Rankin	1	– b Woakes	6
L-b 6, n-b 8	14	B 9, l-b 13, w 1, n-b 16	39
	—		—
	154		271

1/29 (2) 2/45 (1) 3/63 (4) 4/71 (5)   (48.1 overs) 154
5/83 (6) 6/90 (3) 7/97 (8) 8/142 (9)
9/153 (7) 10/154 (11)

1/91 (1) 2/91 (2)   (82.4 overs) 271
3/95 (4) 4/124 (5)
5/124 (3) 6/155 (7) 7/226 (8)
8/247 (9) 9/264 (6) 10/271 (11)

Sreesanth 15–3–45–1; Tahir 12–3–25–2; Rankin 9.1–1–38–1; Woakes 12–5–40–5. *Second Innings*—Tahir 14–3–32–0; Rankin 22–1–93–2; Sreesanth 16–3–56–3; Woakes 19.4–4–43–4; Trott 3–1–9–0; Botha 8–2–16–1.

Umpires: J. W. Lloyds and R. T. Robinson.

At Hove, September 9, 10, 11, 12. WARWICKSHIRE beat SUSSEX by an innings and two runs.

At Manchester, September 23, 24, 25. WARWICKSHIRE lost to LANCASHIRE by ten wickets.

WORCESTERSHIRE

The only way is down

JOHN CURTIS

It was a season of upheaval: relegation from the first division of the Championship was followed by the loss of several key players. Worcestershire had begun the post-Graeme Hick era with a misplaced confidence that their squad was good enough for the top flight, although there was little evidence to suggest they could defy the pre-season forecasts that they would finish in the bottom two, even before injuries ravaged the bowling attack.

And so, for the third time since the start of the new millennium, Worcestershire made an instant return to the second tier after gaining promotion. But 2009 was by far the most disappointing campaign of the three: no Championship games were won, for only the second time in their history, and they often looked completely out of their depth. Only in the final match did they pass the lowest number of points in a season – Glamorgan's 88.5 in 2005 – since the Championship was split into two divisions.

After those previous demotions Worcestershire mounted a serious challenge to regain their top-table place, but the departure of the spine of their team suggested this was unlikely in 2010. Opener Stephen Moore – the leading first-class run-scorer of 2008 – headed for Lancashire, while wicketkeeper Steve Davies, who toured South Africa with England, and off-spinner Gareth Batty both joined Surrey. Then came the news that Kabir Ali wanted out: at first Worcestershire refused to release him unless they received £60,000 compensation, but when that put off potential suitors Kabir failed to turn up for winter training. Eventually, he followed Simon Jones to Hampshire.

None of them publicly explained why so many experienced performers wanted to leave New Road at the same time. But the issue clearly runs far deeper than the chance of lucrative contracts elsewhere, as Worcestershire have always been among the best payers, even if they have had to operate with smallish squads. Members' concern was such that nearly 400 packed the annual forum in the new Graeme Hick Pavilion in August, and there were calls for director of cricket Steve Rhodes to resign.

The departing players are believed to have expressed concerns at the lack of ambition, and the practice and rehabilitation facilities at New Road (Worcestershire are alone in not having an indoor school). Of the leavers, only Davies lived up to his potential during the upheaval: he topped the batting averages in four-day and limited-overs cricket, and deservedly won the player of the year award. Worcestershire also released his understudy Josh Knappett, but signed Ben Cox, 17, on a four-year deal following a successful debut at Taunton in September after being given time off school. Ben Scott, the former England A wicketkeeper, was signed on loan from Middlesex to allow Cox to complete his A-levels.

Moore struggled to reproduce his 2008 form, although ironically he did make one fine century at New Road – for the England Lions against the Australians. Batty had a disastrous time in four-day cricket, claiming only nine wickets at 78. He was eventually left out, and replaced as vice-captain by opening batsman Daryl Mitchell.

Worcestershire had pinned their faith on a pace attack spearheaded by Kabir and Simon Jones, who in 2008 took 101 Championship wickets between them despite a history of injuries. But Jones did not bowl a single ball after further knee troubles, while Kabir suffered an early-season hamstring injury and then a recurrence of back problems, and was restricted to only four Championship games.

Daryl Mitchell

Stu Forster, Getty Images

Worcestershire's overseas player, the 32-year-old Australian Ashley Noffke, also failed to fire with the ball although he did play some useful innings. Of the pacemen, only the bowling coach Matt Mason performed consistently, although Richard Jones and Chris Whelan showed promise.

As the attack often lacked experience, the batsmen needed to excel – but their batting bonus-point tally (30) was the lowest in either division. Only Mitchell passed 1,000 first-class runs for Worcestershire largely thanks to a career-best 298 in the penultimate game, at Taunton. Davies was consistent, but there were only occasional flashes of brilliance from Vikram Solanki, who had to combine captaining an underperforming side with the chairmanship of the Professional Cricketers' Association. Moeen Ali failed to make progress, while Ben Smith managed only three Championship half-centuries in his benefit year, and was dropped. Promising youngsters Alexei Kervezee and David Wheeldon are likely to be given extended chances in 2010.

The only crumb of comfort was a successful run in the Pro40, with Davies outstanding as an opening bat, before defeat by Somerset in the penultimate game ended Worcestershire's hopes of a second title in three years. A dismal home surrender for 58 all out against Ireland ended any hopes of reaching the Friends Provident quarter-finals after some impressive early performances, including two wins over Hampshire, the eventual winners. And Worcestershire again failed to come to terms with Twenty20 cricket, making another early exit.

Rhodes was looking to recruit new blood during the winter, but admitted he would rather pin faith in the current crop of youngsters than recruit average players. He started by making two bold overseas signings: the prolific Australian opener Phil Jaques, who averaged 56 in two part-seasons for the county in 2006 and 2007, returns for the first part of the summer. He will then give way to the highly rated all-rounder Shakib Al Hasan, the first Bangladeshi to be an English county's overseas player.

WORCESTERSHIRE RESULTS

All first-class matches – Played 17: Won 0, Lost 10, Drawn 7.
County Championship matches – Played 16: Won 0, Lost 10, Drawn 6.

LV County Championship, 9th in Division 1; Friends Provident Trophy, 3rd in Group A;
Pro40 League, 3rd in Division 1; Twenty20 Cup, 4th in Midlands/Wales/West Division.

COUNTY CHAMPIONSHIP AVERAGES, BATTING AND FIELDING

Cap/Colours		M	I	NO	R	HS	100s	50s	Avge	Ct/St
2005	S. M. Davies†........	14	26	2	952	126	2	4	39.66	39/2
2008	G. M. Andrew	9	16	5	391	92*	0	3	35.54	0
1998	V. S. Solanki	15	28	1	953	206*	1	4	35.29	13
2005	D. K. H. Mitchell†	16	30	0	1,022	298	1	5	34.06	17
2007	M. M. Ali	16	30	2	803	153	2	3	28.67	4
2009	A. A. Noffke§........	6	9	0	258	89	0	2	28.66	0
2009	D. A. Wheeldon	4	5	0	138	87	0	1	27.60	3
2003	S. C. Moore	14	27	0	738	107	1	5	27.33	5
2009	A. N. Kervezee¶.......	8	14	0	381	66	0	2	27.21	2
2002	B. F. Smith........	13	26	2	565	80*	0	3	23.54	9
2007	R. A. Jones†.........	7	11	2	209	53*	0	1	23.22	3
2008	C. D. Whelan	11	17	3	205	47	0	0	14.64	1
2002	Kabir Ali	4	7	1	81	30*	0	0	13.50	2
2008	Imran Arif§	8	13	7	81	35	0	0	13.50	4
2002	M. S. Mason.........	14	23	6	207	28	0	0	12.17	6
2002	G. J. Batty	10	16	0	175	46	0	0	10.93	8
2009	J. D. Shantry..........	4	5	1	12	6	0	0	3.00	2

Also batted: O. B. Cox† (colours 2009) (1 match) 61 (4 ct, 1 st); J. P. T. Knappett (colours 2007) (1 match) 4*, 1 (5 ct); M. Ahmed (colours 2009) (1 match) 0*, 0*.

† *Born in Worcestershire.* § *Official overseas player.* ¶ *Other non-England-qualified player.*

In 2002, Worcestershire replaced caps with colours awarded to all players making their Championship debut.

BOWLING

	O	M	R	W	BB	5W/i	Avge
M. S. Mason	418.4	125	1,186	43	7-39	2	27.58
R. A. Jones	174	25	745	22	6-100	1	33.86
Kabir Ali	97	10	416	11	6-68	1	37.81
G. M. Andrew	249.3	37	964	22	5-117	1	43.81
A. A. Noffke	158	38	452	10	4-92	0	45.20
C. D. Whelan	223	20	1,040	22	5-95	1	47.27
Imran Arif	172.5	18	969	17	5-93	1	57.00

Also bowled: M. Ahmed 9–0–73–0; M. M. Ali 94.1–15–461–7; G. J. Batty 218.1–33–707–9; D. K. H. Mitchell 90–13–252–9; J. D. Shantry 127.1–31–382–8; V. S. Solanki 12–2–36–0.

COUNTY RECORDS

Highest score for:	405*	G. A. Hick v Somerset at Taunton............	1988
Highest score against:	331*	J. D. Robertson (Middlesex) at Worcester......	1949
Leading run-scorer:	34,490	D. Kenyon (avge 34.18)....................	1946–1967
Best bowling for:	9-23	C. F. Root v Lancashire at Worcester	1931
Best bowling against:	10-51	J. Mercer (Glamorgan) at Worcester	1936
Leading wicket-taker:	2,143	R. T. D. Perks (avge 23.73).................	1930–1955
Highest total for:	701-6 dec	v Surrey at Worcester	2007
Highest total against:	701-4 dec	by Leicestershire at Worcester...............	1906
Lowest total for:	24	v Yorkshire at Huddersfield.................	1903
Lowest total against:	30	by Hampshire at Worcester	1903

ADDRESS

County Ground, New Road, Worcester WR2 4QQ (01905 748474; **email** info@wccc.co.uk). Website www.wccc.co.uk

OFFICIALS

Captain V. S. Solanki
Director of cricket S. J. Rhodes
Academy director D. B. D'Oliveira
President K. T. Mills

Chairman J. M. Price
Chief executive M. S. Newton
Head groundsman T. R. Packwood
Scorers N. D. Smith; D. Pugh

RELEGATION/PROMOTION IN THE CHAMPIONSHIP, 2000–09

	Relegated	W	L	D	Pts	**Promoted**	W	L	D	Pts
2000	Hampshire	3	9	4	112	Northamptonshire	7	4	5	188
	Durham	2	9	5	112	Essex	5	2	9	165
	Derbyshire	2	6	8	111	Glamorgan	5	3	8	160
2001	Northamptonshire	2	5	9	148	Sussex	9	3	4	208
	Glamorgan	2	5	7	133†	Hampshire	7	2	7	192
	Essex	2	7	7	116	Warwickshire	5	1	10	185.75
2002	Hampshire	2	5	9	131	Essex	10	3	3	219
	Somerset	1	7	8	126.75	Middlesex	7	3	6	211.75
	Yorkshire	2	8	6	124.75	Nottinghamshire	8	5	3	201.25
2003	Essex	3	5	7	156‡	**Worcestershire**	10	1	5	245.75
	Nottinghamshire	2	8	6	132	Northamptonshire	10	2	4	237
	Leicestershire	1	6	9	126.5	Gloucestershire	5	2	9	190
2004	**Worcestershire**	3	6	7	161	Nottinghamshire	9	2	5	252
	Lancashire	2	4	10	154	Hampshire	9	2	5	228
	Northamptonshire	1	4	11	134	Glamorgan	5	2	9	196.5
2005	Surrey	4	3	9	180.5	Lancashire	7	3	6	212
	Gloucestershire	1	10	5	104	Durham	6	2	8	205
	Glamorgan	1	14	1	88.5	Yorkshire	5	1	10	200.5
2006	Nottinghamshire	4	7	5	153	Surrey	10	2	4	262
	Middlesex	1	7	8	133.5	**Worcestershire**	8	4	4	229
2007	Warwickshire	2	5	9	139	Somerset	10	1	5	266
	Worcestershire	1	8	5	95§	Nottinghamshire	6	3	7	214.5
2008	Kent	4	6	6	154	Warwickshire	5	0	11	213
	Surrey	0	5	10	124	**Worcestershire**	6	2	7	196†
2009	Sussex	2	6	8	143	Kent	8	3	5	219
	Worcestershire	0	10	6	94	Essex	6	3	7	194

† One match abandoned.   ‡ One match tied.   § Two matches abandoned.

At Oxford, April 11, 12, 13. WORCESTERSHIRE drew with OXFORD UCCE.

At Southampton, April 15, 16, 17. WORCESTERSHIRE lost to HAMPSHIRE by seven wickets.

At Nottingham, April 21, 22, 23, 24. WORCESTERSHIRE lost to NOTTINGHAMSHIRE by an innings and five runs.

At Leeds, April 28, 29, 30, May 1. WORCESTERSHIRE drew with YORKSHIRE.

WORCESTERSHIRE v LANCASHIRE

At Worcester, May 6, 7, 8. Lancashire won by six wickets. Lancashire 20 pts, Worcestershire 3 pts.
Toss: Worcestershire.

Deprived of Simon Jones, Kabir Ali and Ashley Noffke through injury, Solanki decided to bat first, only for the move to backfire in conditions conducive to swing and seam: ultimately, it was his opposite number, Chapple, who starred in Lancashire's unexacting three-day win. His initial spell of three for 11 in nine overs set the tone, before he returned to break the fifth-wicket resistance of Davies and Moeen Ali. Chapple then overshadowed Whelan's maiden five-for with a spritely 89, adding 123 for the eighth wicket with Hogg to turn the game decisively in Lancashire's favour. Moore reached his first half-century of the summer before Ben Smith and Moeen Ali put on 102 as Worcestershire rallied to 223 for three second time round. But Mahmood bowled with hostility to claim a career-best six for 75 – including Batty, his 200th first-class victim, for a second duck – and ten wickets in a match for the first time. With the last seven wickets falling for 78, Lancashire were left needing only 122 for victory.

Close of play: First day, Lancashire 172-5 (Chilton 51, Sutton 8); Second day, Worcestershire 129-3 (Smith 14, Ali 6).

Worcestershire

D. K. H. Mitchell lbw b Chapple	9	– c Smith b Hogg	20
S. C. Moore c Chilton b Chapple	0	– b Hogg	53
*V. S. Solanki c Sutton b Mahmood	22	– b Mahmood	35
B. F. Smith c Prince b Chapple	1	– lbw b Smith	43
M. M. Ali c Sutton b Chapple	35	– c Chapple b Mahmood	80
†S. M. Davies lbw b Chapple	48	– c Prince b Mahmood	9
G. J. Batty b Chapple	0	– lbw b Mahmood	0
G. M. Andrew c and b Mahmood	14	– b Keedy	30
C. D. Whelan c Prince b Mahmood	7	– c Sutton b Mahmood	7
M. S. Mason c Sutton b Mahmood	9	– c Croft b Mahmood	14
Imran Arif not out	4	– not out	0
B 8, l-b 9, w 1	18	B 1, l-b 7, n-b 2	10

1/1 (2) 2/26 (1) 3/28 (4) 4/36 (3)   (47.3 overs) 167
5/124 (6) 6/124 (7) 7/133 (5)
8/142 (9) 9/156 (10) 10/167 (8)

1/42 (1) 2/81 (2)   (103.1 overs) 301
3/121 (3) 4/223 (4)
5/236 (6) 6/236 (7) 7/259 (5)
8/267 (9) 9/301 (8) 10/301 (10)

Chapple 17–9–34–6; Mahmood 17.3–5–65–4; Hogg 7–0–23–0; Smith 5–0–28–0; Croft 1–1–0–0. *Second Innings*—Chapple 23–6–54–0; Mahmood 28.1–7–75–6; Hogg 20–3–77–2; Keedy 17–5–44–1; Smith 15–2–43–1.

Lancashire

P. J. Horton lbw b Whelan	5	– (2) c Smith b Imran Arif	24
T. C. Smith lbw b Whelan	22	– (1) b Whelan	18
A. G. Prince c Davies b Whelan	18	– c Mitchell b Batty	21
F. du Plessis c Davies b Imran Arif	10	– c Davies b Andrew	34
M. J. Chilton c Mitchell b Mason	55	– not out	11
S. J. Croft lbw b Mason	43	– not out	9
†L. D. Sutton b Mason	9		
K. W. Hogg b Whelan	60		
*G. Chapple c Mason b Imran Arif	89		
S. I. Mahmood c Moore b Whelan	0		
G. Keedy not out	1		
B 6, l-b 9, w 4, n-b 16	35	B 2, l-b 3	5

1/18 (1) 2/44 (3) 3/59 (2) 4/73 (4)   (90 overs) 347   1/27 (1)   (4 wkts, 33.5 overs) 122
5/141 (6) 6/178 (5) 7/181 (7) 8/304 (8)   2/47 (2) 3/91 (3)
9/340 (10) 10/347 (9)   4/107 (4)

Mason 24–8–76–3; Whelan 25–2–95–5; Imran Arif 10–0–65–2; Andrew 5–0–32–0; Batty 20–3–49–0; Mitchell 6–1–15–0. *Second Innings*—Mason 6–3–16–0; Whelan 6–2–11–1; Imran Arif 8–0–40–1; Andrew 8–1–35–1; Batty 5.5–1–15–1.

Umpires: R. T. Robinson and J. F. Steele.

WORCESTERSHIRE v SUSSEX

At Worcester, June 11, 12, 13, 14. Sussex won by ten wickets. Sussex 22 pts, Worcestershire 4 pts. Toss: Worcestershire. County debut: P. P. Chawla.

Indian leg-spinner Piyush Chawla began his stint at Sussex with a maiden century and six second-innings wickets to earn them their first Championship win for 11 months. On a damp pitch Worcestershire were reliant on Ben Smith's fluency and a competition-best from Noffke to inch them towards respectability, but Sussex then took advantage of easing conditions to achieve maximum batting points for the first time in five attempts in 2009. Yardy's second hundred in four days was also his highest Championship score for three years, before Chawla – deputising for Yasir Arafat, on duty with Pakistan – cracked an 82-ball century including six sixes, adding 105 for the ninth wicket with Kirtley against a demoralised attack. Mitchell and Moeen Ali put on 208 in 62 overs as Worcestershire threatened to escape with a draw, but when Moeen gloved Kirtley's leg-side loosener, the door was open for Chawla, who wheeled through 51 overs, to settle the matter.

Close of play: First day, Sussex 17-0 (Yardy 5, Nash 12); Second day, Sussex 409-5 (Hodd 24, Smith 49); Third day, Worcestershire 120-3 (Mitchell 52, M. M. Ali 26).

Worcestershire

D. K. H. Mitchell b Collymore	19	– c Joyce b Chawla	99
S. C. Moore lbw b Kirtley	0	– b Kirtley	6
*V. S. Solanki b Collymore	15	– lbw b Chawla	33
B. F. Smith run out	80	– lbw b Chawla	1
M. M. Ali c Hodd b Martin-Jenkins	5	– c Hodd b Kirtley	124
†S. M. Davies c Joyce b Chawla	15	– b Nash	35
A. A. Noffke st Hodd b Chawla	89	– lbw b Chawla	0
G. J. Batty c Hodd b Smith	17	– c Kirtley b Chawla	3
Kabir Ali c Hodd b Smith	10	– lbw b Chawla	9
C. D. Whelan c Chawla b Collymore	19	– b Smith	24
M. S. Mason not out	7	– not out	22
B 5, l-b 2, w 1, n-b 4	12	B 10, l-b 14, w 8, n-b 4	36

1/0 (2) 2/23 (3) 3/64 (1) 4/91 (5)   (89.3 overs) 288   1/6 (2) 2/59 (3)   (130.1 overs) 392
5/118 (6) 6/176 (4) 7/216 (8)   3/73 (4) 4/281 (5)
8/234 (9) 9/262 (10) 10/288 (7)   5/297 (1) 6/297 (7) 7/305 (8) 8/344 (9)
9/346 (6) 10/392 (10)

Collymore 17–5–42–3; Kirtley 17–2–57–1; Martin-Jenkins 12–3–41–1; Smith 20–8–44–2; Chawla 21.3–2–89–2; Yardy 2–0–8–0. *Second Innings*—Collymore 12–2–37–0; Kirtley 13.5–1–61–2; Smith 18.2–6–46–1; Chawla 51–11–152–6; Martin-Jenkins 8–1–18–0; Yardy 9–1–19–0; Nash 18–7–35–1.

Sussex

*M. H. Yardy c Davies b Whelan	152	– not out	34
C. D. Nash run out	52	– not out	25
E. C. Joyce c M. M. Ali b Kabir Ali	21		
M. W. Goodwin c Davies b Whelan	16		
M. J. Prior c Solanki b Whelan	82		
†A. J. Hodd lbw b Noffke	43		
D. R. Smith c Batty b Noffke	77		
R. S. C. Martin-Jenkins c Moore b Noffke	20		
P. P. Chawla not out	102		
R. J. Kirtley c Davies b Noffke	33		
C. D. Collymore not out	1		
B 3, l-b 11, w 1, n-b 6	21	B 1, l-b 1	2

1/93 (2) 2/144 (3)   (9 wkts dec, 141 overs) 620   (no wkt, 10 overs)   61
3/196 (4) 4/315 (1)
5/343 (5) 6/458 (6) 7/467 (7)
8/492 (8) 9/597 (10)
               120 overs: 497-8

Kabir Ali 22–1–79–1; Mason 27–2–112–0; Noffke 27–3–92–4; Batty 29–5–123–0; Whelan 26–1–151–3; Mitchell 7–0–19–0; M. M. Ali 3–0–30–0. *Second Innings*—Kabir Ali 3–0–22–0; Mason 2–0–14–0; Whelan 2–0–10–0; Batty 2–0–9–0; Mitchell 1–0–4–0.

Umpires: J. W. Holder and R. A. Kettleborough.

WORCESTERSHIRE v YORKSHIRE

At Worcester, June 16, 17, 18, 19. Drawn. Worcestershire 11 pts, Yorkshire 12 pts. Toss: Worcestershire.

In what turned out to be his final Championship appearance, Vaughan made his highest first-class score for nearly a year in front of the national selector, Geoff Miller, only to announce his retirement two weeks later. The plaudits went instead to younger men. Mitchell and Moore began with Worcestershire's first century opening stand of the season, before Davies made a hundred on his 23rd birthday, while rumours circulated about a move to Surrey despite Worcestershire's offer of a three-year contract. Yorkshire were rescued from 108 for five when Gale, whose first Championship half-century of the summer turned into the fifth hundred of his career, added 170 with Bresnan. Azeem Rafiq, who hit three sixes in a 36-ball fifty and went on to a maiden first-class hundred from 92 balls, put on 150 for the ninth wicket with Hoggard. In all, Yorkshire's last five wickets added 408 to establish a lead of 101, but the loss of nearly two-thirds of the second day to rain meant they eventually ran out of time to force a result, with Moore's second fifty of the game ensuring the draw. Worcestershire's injury-hit fast bowler Simon Jones was ruled out for the rest of the season with his troublesome knee.

Close of play: First day, Worcestershire 319-5 (Davies 75, Noffke 24); Second day, Yorkshire 55-1 (Sayers 25, Vaughan 21); Third day, Yorkshire 413-8 (Azeem Rafiq 62, Hoggard 15).

Worcestershire

D. K. H. Mitchell b Azeem Rafiq	68	– lbw b Azeem Rafiq	32
S. C. Moore lbw b Hoggard	60	– b Kruis	52
*V. S. Solanki c Bairstow b Shahzad	1	– c Rudolph b Azeem Rafiq	48
B. F. Smith c Rudolph b Kruis	15	– not out	48
M. M. Ali b Kruis	55	– not out	14
†S. M. Davies c Bairstow b Kruis	112		
A. A. Noffke lbw b Shahzad	35		
G. J. Batty c Rudolph b Bresnan	25		
Kabir Ali c Azeem Rafiq b Hoggard	3		
C. D. Whelan b Sayers b Bresnan	5		
M. S. Mason not out	11		
B 8, l-b 14, w 1, n-b 2	25	L-b 6, w 1, n-b 2	9

1/104 (2) 2/105 (3) 3/147 (4) (121.3 overs) 415   1/67 (1) (3 wkts dec, 57 overs) 203
4/173 (1) 5/265 (5) 6/346 (7)   2/95 (2) 3/176 (3)
7/375 (6) 8/389 (9) 9/400 (8)
10/415 (10)   120 overs: 411-9

Hoggard 29–3–88–2; Bresnan 23.3–8–58–2; Shahzad 25–3–93–2; Kruis 20–5–65–3; Azeem Rafiq 19–5–62–1; Rudolph 5–0–27–0. *Second Innings*—Bresnan 4–0–19–0; Shahzad 13–2–43–0; Azeem Rafiq 22–0–82–2; Kruis 7–1–15–1; Rudolph 8–0–24–0; Sayers 2–0–3–0; Gale 1–0–11–0.

Yorkshire

J. A. Rudolph c Davies b Mason	9	M. J. Hoggard not out	56
J. J. Sayers c Batty b Noffke	44	G. J. Kruis b M. M. Ali	16
M. P. Vaughan c Batty b Whelan	43		
*A. McGrath c Davies b Whelan	6	L-b 16, w 1, n-b 8	25
A. W. Gale c Mason b Batty	101		
†J. M. Bairstow c Mitchell b Whelan	0	1/15 (1) 2/97 (3) 3/107 (4) (131 overs) 516
T. T. Bresnan c Mitchell b Kabir Ali	97	4/107 (2) 5/108 (6) 6/278 (7)
A. Shahzad lbw b Whelan	19	7/328 (8) 8/334 (5) 9/484 (9)
Azeem Rafiq c Mason b Batty	100	10/516 (11) 120 overs: 463-8

Kabir Ali 25–2–127–1; Mason 22–8–67–1; Noffke 28–8–77–1; Whelan 25–4–130–4; Batty 25–5–79–2; Mitchell 4–1–11–0; M. M. Ali 2–0–9–1.

Umpires: B. Dudleston and J. H. Evans.

At Chester-le-Street, June 30, July 1, 2, 3. WORCESTERSHIRE lost to DURHAM by five wickets.

At Manchester, July 10, 11, 12. WORCESTERSHIRE lost to LANCASHIRE by seven wickets.

WORCESTERSHIRE v SOMERSET

At Worcester, July 21, 22, 23, 24. Drawn. Worcestershire 7 pts, Somerset 12 pts. Toss: Worcestershire.
Justin Langer passed Sir Donald Bradman's total of 28,067 first-class runs on the third morning to become the highest-scoring Australian, but the loss of more than 150 overs – including the whole of the opening day – enabled Worcestershire to escape with a draw after following on. Langer, who added 169 for the second wicket with Trescothick after Somerset had been put in on a green pitch, reached the milestone in his 615th innings – 277 more than Bradman – on his way to his 86th first-class hundred, and later said Bradman "has had a place in my heart since I started walking". Kieswetter's run-a-ball 59, including four sixes, took Somerset to full batting points in the 81st over. But no Worcestershire batsman reached fifty first time round, and – after the openers departed either side of lunch on the final day – it was left to Solanki, who batted with great fluency for 93 from 89 balls, and Smith to frustrate the visitors in the second innings.

Close of play: First day, No play; Second day, Somerset 312-3 (Langer 89, Kieswetter 0); Third day, Worcestershire 164-6 (Davies 40, Andrew 5).

Somerset

M. E. Trescothick c Davies b Mason	142	D. A. Stiff not out		0
A. V. Suppiah lbw b Mason	47			
*J. L. Langer c Smith b Mason	107	B 8, l-b 21, w 12, n-b 6		47
P. D. Trego c Batty b Mitchell	1			
†C. Kieswetter not out	59	1/140 (2)	(6 wkts dec, 87.3 overs)	428
J. C. Hildreth b Andrew	16	2/309 (1) 3/312 (4)		
Z. de Bruyn c Batty b Mitchell	9	4/363 (3) 5/391 (6) 6/425 (7)		

A. C. Thomas, A. R. Caddick and C. M. Willoughby did not bat.

Mason 28–6–111–3; Whelan 10–0–67–0; Andrew 26–2–111–1; Jones 4.3–0–29–0; Batty 12–1–56–0; Mitchell 7–0–25–2.

Worcestershire

D. K. H. Mitchell b Caddick	20	– c Kieswetter b Willoughby		4
S. C. Moore lbw b Willoughby	7	– c Kieswetter b Thomas		17
*V. S. Solanki c Hildreth b Stiff	12	– b de Bruyn		93
B. F. Smith c Suppiah b Trego	38	– not out		80
M. M. Ali c Langer b Willoughby	0	– c Caddick b Caddick		16
†S. M. Davies c Langer b Suppiah	44	– not out		7
G. J. Batty c Kieswetter b Thomas	4			
G. M. Andrew not out	43			
R. A. Jones lbw b Suppiah	0			
C. D. Whelan c Kieswetter b Caddick	12			
M. S. Mason c Kieswetter b Caddick	4			
B 1, l-b 1, w 7, n-b 32	41	L-b 4, n-b 4		8

1/7 (2) 2/49 (3) 3/60 (1) 4/73 (5) (62.1 overs) 225   1/4 (1) 2/40 (2) (4 wkts, 56 overs) 225
5/109 (4) 6/131 (7) 7/180 (6)   3/176 (3)
8/180 (9) 9/217 (10) 10/225 (11)   4/209 (5)

Willoughby 16–5–45–2; Thomas 11–3–34–1; Stiff 5–0–38–1; Caddick 14.1–3–53–3; Trego 5–0–25–1; Suppiah 11–3–28–2. *Second Innings*—Willoughby 14–6–40–1; Caddick 11–2–42–1; Thomas 6–0–31–1; Stiff 10–0–47–0; Trego 4–1–29–0; de Bruyn 6–1–31–1; Suppiah 5–4–1–0.

Umpires: M. R. Benson and P. Willey.

WORCESTERSHIRE v WARWICKSHIRE

At Worcester, July 31, August 1, 2, 3. Warwickshire won by nine wickets. Warwickshire 20 pts, Worcestershire 3 pts. Toss: Worcestershire.

Warwickshire took advantage of another woeful performance from Worcestershire, who were bowled out twice in three and a half sessions, to register their first Championship victory of the season. Richard Jones claimed a career-best four for 66, and Mason was persevering, but Worcestershire's inexperienced attack failed to take advantage of a green-tinged pitch, allowing Warwickshire to recover from 160 for five after the out-of-form Ambrose was dropped at square leg before he had scored. Instead, Ambrose and Clarke put on 116 for the sixth wicket, before Worcestershire collapsed from 69 for one to 111 all out in the space of 20 overs, thanks to a mixture of inept shot selection and accurate swing bowling from Woakes and Carter. Following on, Worcestershire fared better while Moore and Solanki were adding 121 for the second wicket, but another slump – this time nine for 104 in 41 overs to Tahir and Rankin – meant the loss of the second day to rain did not inconvenience Warwickshire.

Close of play: First day, Worcestershire 2-0 (Mitchell 1, Moore 1); Second day, No play; Third day, Worcestershire 206-6 (Ali 24, Andrew 3).

Warwickshire

*I. J. Westwood c Solanki b Andrew	22	– not out	18
N. M. Carter b Imran Arif	13	– c Imran Arif b Mason	4
I. J. L. Trott c Davies b Jones	67	– not out	16
J. O. Troughton c Mitchell b Jones	6		
T. Frost c Davies b Mason	37		
†T. R. Ambrose c Mitchell b Mason	63		
R. Clarke b Jones	50		
A. G. Botha c Davies b Andrew	18		
C. R. Woakes c Mitchell b Andrew	2		
N. S. Tahir not out	5		
W. B. Rankin b Jones	1		
L-b 11, w 2, n-b 12	25	L-b 1, n-b 8	9

1/22 (2) 2/56 (1) 3/79 (4) 4/154 (5) (79.1 overs) 309
5/160 (3) 6/276 (6) 7/292 (7)
8/295 (9) 9/298 (8) 10/309 (11)

1/9 (2)   (1 wkt, 8.5 overs) 47

Mason 21–4–51–2; Imran Arif 15–1–78–1; Andrew 14–2–57–3; Jones 20.1–4–66–4; Mitchell 6–0–19–0; Ali 2–0–24–0; Solanki 1–0–3–0. *Second Innings*—Mason 4–0–13–1; Imran Arif 4–1–28–0; Jones 0.5–0–5–0.

Worcestershire

D. K. H. Mitchell c Ambrose b Rankin	6	– c Clarke b Tahir	0
S. C. Moore c Clarke b Woakes	28	– c Clarke b Tahir	88
*V. S. Solanki c Ambrose b Woakes	27	– c Troughton b Rankin	46
B. F. Smith lbw b Carter	1	– b Rankin	2
M. M. Ali b Carter	6	– c Ambrose b Tahir	47
†S. M. Davies lbw b Carter	19	– c Ambrose b Rankin	0
A. N. Kervezee lbw b Woakes	0	– c Ambrose b Carter	26
G. M. Andrew lbw b Woakes	1	– c Ambrose b Tahir	14
R. A. Jones lbw b Carter	4	– lbw b Tahir	3
M. S. Mason c Ambrose b Woakes	2	– c Botha b Rankin	0
Imran Arif not out	0	– not out	0
L-b 7, n-b 12	19	B 2, l-b 4, n-b 12	18

1/8 (1) 2/69 (3) 3/70 (4) 4/70 (2) (37.5 overs) 111
5/76 (5) 6/76 (7) 7/77 (8) 8/88 (9)
9/105 (6) 10/111 (10)

1/19 (1) 2/140 (3) (73.5 overs) 244
3/144 (2) 4/152 (4)
5/152 (6) 6/198 (7) 7/229 (8)
8/233 (9) 9/234 (10) 10/244 (5)

Rankin 7–0–31–1; Tahir 5–3–6–0; Woakes 13.5–4–30–4; Carter 12–2–37–5. *Second Innings*—Rankin 20–7–56–4; Tahir 19.5–5–67–5; Woakes 10–1–35–0; Carter 14–5–46–1; Trott 5–0–25–0; Clarke 5–3–9–0.

Umpires: N. L. Bainton and G. Sharp.

At Hove, August 11, 12, 13. WORCESTERSHIRE lost to SUSSEX by eight wickets.

WORCESTERSHIRE v NOTTINGHAMSHIRE

At Worcester, August 25, 26, 27, 28. Drawn. Worcestershire 10 pts, Nottinghamshire 8 pts. Toss: Nottinghamshire. First-class debut: J. D. Shantry. Championship debut: J. Carter.

A gripping run-chase eventually came to nothing after Nottinghamshire, needing a win to maintain pressure on Durham at the top of the table, fell seven short of victory after being set an apparently conservative 358 in 74 overs. At 170 for five, Nottinghamshire were struggling, but Brown and Read together added 115 and, when two overs of part-time off-spin from Moeen Ali disappeared for 31, the chase was on. But the requirement of 21 off Andrew's final over – reduced to ten off three balls – proved too much. Earlier, Worcestershire, after claiming only their second first-innings lead of a miserable summer thanks to Andrew's maiden half-century and Imran Arif's best performance of the season, moved into a position of strength when Davies and Moeen Ali put on 142 after the second innings had started badly. But Worcestershire played the game under a cloud. Both Davies – who equalled the club record of six catches in an innings, but crucially dropped Brown on 55 – and Batty confirmed they were signing three-year deals with Surrey, while the director of cricket, Steve Rhodes, faced calls to resign at an angry forum attended by 300 club members at the end of the first day's play.

Close of play: First day, Worcestershire 314-7 (Andrew 77, Jones 27); Second day, Nottinghamshire 9-1 (Hales 4, Wagh 1); Third day, Worcestershire 176-5 (Ali 59).

Worcestershire

D. K. H. Mitchell c Read b Ealham	53	– c Read b Adams	10
S. C. Moore c Read b Adams	0	– c Read b Adams	11
*V. S. Solanki c Brown b Adams	30	– lbw b Adams	0
B. F. Smith c Read b Shreck	52	– b Shreck	10
M. M. Ali b Adams	0	– not out	84
†S. M. Davies c Adams b Shreck	9	– c Shafayat b Carter	76
A. N. Kervezee lbw b Shreck	34	– c Newman b Shreck	30
G. M. Andrew not out	92	– not out	5
R. A. Jones b Ealham	31		
Imran Arif b Adams	0		
J. D. Shantry lbw b Ealham	0		
B 5, l-b 14, n-b 14	33	B 4, w 2, n-b 10	16

1/2 (2) 2/51 (3) 3/140 (4)   (105.5 overs) 334   1/16 (2)   (6 wkts dec, 52 overs) 242
4/141 (5) 5/152 (6) 6/181 (1)   2/16 (3) 3/33 (1)
7/240 (7) 8/324 (9) 9/333 (10) 10/334 (11)   4/34 (4) 5/176 (6) 6/229 (7)

Shreck 23–2–102–3; Adams 29–9–81–4; Carter 18–5–68–0; Ealham 25.5–13–40–3; Patel 10–3–24–0. *Second Innings*—Shreck 20–4–90–2; Adams 17–1–79–3; Ealham 7–1–31–0; Carter 6–0–28–1; Patel 2–0–10–0.

Nottinghamshire

S. A. Newman c Mitchell b Imran Arif	3	– c Davies b Andrew	0
A. D. Hales c Mitchell b Imran Arif	12	– c Davies b Jones	55
M. A. Wagh c Davies b Imran Arif	49	– c Davies b Andrew	0
S. R. Patel c Kervezee b Imran Arif	46	– c Davies b Jones	55
B. M. Shafayat c Davies b Shantry	0	– c Davies b Jones	30
A. D. Brown not out	46	– c Shantry b Andrew	84
*†C. M. W. Read b Andrew	9	– not out	70
M. A. Ealham c Imran Arif b Shantry	17	– c Davies b Jones	10
A. R. Adams c Moore b Jones	6	– not out	29
C. E. Shreck lbw b Jones	0		
A. Carter c and b Imran Arif	4		
B 8, l-b 11, w 2, n-b 6	27	L-b 10, w 6, n-b 2	18

1/7 (1) 2/22 (2) 3/88 (4) 4/105 (5)   (54.5 overs) 219   1/15 (1) 2/15 (3) (7 wkts, 74 overs) 351
5/143 (3) 6/158 (7) 7/182 (8)   3/94 (4) 4/144 (2)
8/200 (9) 9/202 (10) 10/219 (11)   5/170 (5) 6/285 (6) 7/298 (8)

Andrew 13–3–35–1; Imran Arif 20.5–4–93–5; Shantry 14–2–53–2; Jones 7–3–19–2. *Second Innings*—Imran Arif 18–3–72–0; Andrew 21–3–97–3; Jones 18–2–105–4; Shantry 11–3–30–0; Ali 6–1–37–0.

Umpires: J. H. Evans and T. E. Jesty.

At Birmingham, September 2, 3, 4, 5. WORCESTERSHIRE lost to WARWICKSHIRE by an innings and 18 runs.

WORCESTERSHIRE v HAMPSHIRE

At Worcester, September 9, 10, 11. Hampshire won by ten wickets. Hampshire 21 pts, Worcestershire 3 pts. Toss: Worcestershire.

For the first time in three years after the floods of 2007 and 2008, a match was played to its conclusion at New Road in September. But there was little cause for celebration as Worcestershire's relegation was confirmed before tea on the third day after another dismal batting performance. Adams and Pothas made light of a well-grassed pitch to put on 161 for Hampshire's fifth wicket, before Cork shepherded the tail effectively to earn them four batting points. Mitchell and Moore began with 70 in reply, but Worcestershire then lost all ten wickets in 39 overs and, following on, quickly slumped to six for three. The damage was done by Cork, who finished with five for 14, his best figures for Hampshire, to take his overall analysis against Worcestershire in two victories in 2009 to 12 for 81 from 50 overs. He was well supported by seven wickets from Imran Tahir; Kervezee's half-century and a career-best from Jones narrowly averted an innings defeat.

Close of play: First day, Hampshire 357-8 (Cork 28, Tomlinson 16); Second day, Worcestershire 102-4 (Ali 31, Davies 31).

Hampshire

J. H. K. Adams lbw b Ali	91	– not out	7
L. A. Dawson c Davies b Jones	37	– not out	0
M. J. Lumb c Smith b Shantry	11		
J. M. Vince c Davies b Whelan	16		
S. M. Ervine c Davies b Jones	14		
†N. Pothas c Solanki b Shantry	93		
*A. D. Mascarenhas b Ali	2		
D. G. Cork c Jones b Ali	43		
Imran Tahir c Mitchell b Mason	28		
J. A. Tomlinson b Ali	23		
D. A. Griffiths not out	4		
B 6, l-b 6, w 7, n-b 2	21		

1/50 (2) 2/73 (3) 3/95 (4) (107.1 overs) 383   (no wkt, 1.3 overs) 7
4/119 (5) 5/280 (1) 6/280 (6)
7/283 (7) 8/322 (9) 9/378 (10) 10/383 (8)

Mason 26-5-78-1; Jones 26-2-104-2; Shantry 25-7-68-2; Whelan 14-1-78-1; Mitchell 5-1-14-0; Ali 11.1-5-29-4. *Second Innings*—Shantry 1-0-3-0; Jones 0.3-0-4-0.

Worcestershire

D. K. H. Mitchell c Cork b Tomlinson	37	– lbw b Cork	0
S. C. Moore b Tomlinson	35	– c Lumb b Tomlinson	28
*V. S. Solanki c Cork b Griffiths	8	– lbw b Cork	3
B. F. Smith c Adams b Cork	9	– c Adams b Cork	0
M. M. Ali lbw b Mascarenhas	12	– c Dawson b Cork	37
†S. M. Davies c Lumb b Imran Tahir	24	– c Adams b Cork	31
A. N. Kervezee lbw b Imran Tahir	5	– c Mascarenhas b Imran Tahir	54
R. A. Jones lbw b Imran Tahir	1	– c Cork b Imran Tahir	36
C. D. Whelan c Pothas b Griffiths	1	– not out	21
M. S. Mason lbw b Imran Tahir	0	– c Pothas b Griffiths	4
J. D. Shantry not out	5	– c Lumb b Imran Tahir	0
B 1, l-b 5, w 6, n-b 10	22	L-b 4, n-b 4, p 5	13

1/70 (1) 2/81 (3) 3/89 (2) 4/111 (5) (57 overs) 159   1/0 (1) 2/6 (3) 3/6 (4) (58.2 overs) 227
5/111 (4) 6/131 (7) 7/135 (8) 8/150 (9)   4/58 (2) 5/103 (6)
9/150 (6) 10/159 (10)   6/128 (5) 7/198 (7) 8/218 (8)
   9/223 (10) 10/227 (11)

Cork 12-4-30-1; Mascarenhas 12-5-21-1; Ervine 2-0-17-0; Tomlinson 11-4-28-2; Griffiths 14-4-39-2; Imran Tahir 6-0-18-4. *Second Innings*—Cork 14-7-14-5; Mascarenhas 2-0-5-0; Griffiths 11-0-69-1; Tomlinson 15-2-55-1; Imran Tahir 12.2-5-44-3; Ervine 4-0-31-0.

Umpires: B. Dudleston and N. A. Mallender.

At Taunton, September 16, 17, 18, 19. WORCESTERSHIRE drew with SOMERSET.

WORCESTERSHIRE v DURHAM

At Worcester, September 23, 24, 25, 26. Drawn. Worcestershire 9 pts, Durham 12 pts. Toss: Worcestershire.

Worcestershire, doomed to relegation, battled hard on the final day to stave off defeat, but a draw still meant they went through the Championship without a win for the first time since 1928; Durham, already champions, could also celebrate their first unbeaten season. On the opening day, Worcestershire recovered from 197 for six thanks chiefly to the first of two fifties from Andrew; when they reached 350, they passed the lowest points tally since the competition split into two divisions – Glamorgan's 88.5 in 2005. Against a limited attack, Di Venuto hit his sixth hundred of the summer, matching the Durham record set by Paul Collingwood in 2005, and becoming the first Durham player to pass 1,500 Championship runs in a season. Chanderpaul's sixth double-hundred, which came in eight hours 22 minutes, became progressively slower: his first century took 151 balls and his second 231. Needing 278 to avoid an innings defeat, Worcestershire lost five for 169, despite Harmison's absence on the final day with a sore knee. But Davies bludgeoned 97 from 75 balls in his last Championship innings before joining Surrey, and then Andrew and Jones added 119.

Close of play: First day, Worcestershire 347-9 (Whelan 23, Shantry 2); Second day, Durham 390-3 (Chanderpaul 100, Benkenstein 91); Third day, Worcestershire 41-1 (Mitchell 22, Solanki 0).

Worcestershire

D. K. H. Mitchell lbw b Benkenstein	67	– c Mustard b Plunkett	26
S. C. Moore c Chanderpaul b Davies	23	– lbw b Blackwell	16
*V. S. Solanki b Plunkett	4	– lbw b Plunkett	31
M. M. Ali c Benkenstein b Plunkett	19	– lbw b Plunkett	25
A. N. Kervezee c Di Venuto b Benkenstein	46	– c Mustard b Claydon	48
†S. M. Davies c Chanderpaul b Claydon	31	– c sub (S. G. Borthwick) b Plunkett	97
D. A. Wheeldon c Claydon b Harmison	14	– c Di Venuto b Blackwell	30
G. M. Andrew b Plunkett	77	– not out	59
R. A. Jones lbw b Davies	27	– not out	53
C. D. Whelan not out	23		
J. D. Shantry c Mustard b Plunkett	6		
B 3, l-b 10, w 4, n-b 2	19	B 14, l-b 9, w 2	25

1/48 (2) 2/54 (3) 3/116 (4)   (98.5 overs) 356   1/41 (2) 2/55 (1) (7 wkts, 91 overs) 410
4/120 (1) 5/197 (5) 6/197 (6)   3/93 (4) 4/128 (3)
7/226 (7) 8/304 (9) 9/334 (8) 10/356 (11)   5/169 (5) 6/286 (6) 7/291 (7)

Harmison 22–9–47–1; Davies 20–3–71–2; Plunkett 26.5–4–104–4; Claydon 14–2–57–1; Benkenstein 9–2–38–2; Blackwell 7–2–26–0. *Second Innings*—Davies 19–3–64–0; Claydon 12–3–53–1; Plunkett 29–1–132–4; Blackwell 27–2–124–2; Benkenstein 2–1–5–0; Smith 2–0–9–0.

Durham

M. J. Di Venuto b Ali	113	M. E. Claydon c Davies b Whelan	10
K. J. Coetzer c Jones b Andrew	44	M. Davies not out	16
*W. R. Smith c Davies b Shantry	28	B 3, l-b 13, w 3, n-b 8	27
S. Chanderpaul not out	201		
D. M. Benkenstein c Davies b Andrew	109	1/124 (2) (8 wkts dec, 172.1 overs) 634
I. D. Blackwell lbw b Jones	9	2/185 (1) 3/207 (3)
†P. Mustard c Davies b Jones	25	4/433 (5) 5/444 (6) 6/480 (7)
L. E. Plunkett c Wheeldon b Mitchell	52	7/583 (8) 8/600 (9) 120 overs: 470-5

S. J. Harmison did not bat.

Andrew 41–11–121–2; Jones 28–4–129–2; Shantry 39.1–9–102–1; Whelan 28–2–94–1; Ali 21–1–104–1; Mitchell 11–1–52–1; Solanki 4–0–16–0.

Umpires: N. L. Bainton and J. F. Steele.

YORKSHIRE

Another great escape

DAVID WARNER

It was the same old story for Yorkshire: another season, another great escape. The only variation this time was that although they once again narrowly preserved their first division status in the County Championship, their showing in all one-day cricket was much flatter than in 2008, when they were pepped up by the now-retired Darren Gough.

Yorkshire eventually finished seventh, as they had the previous year, following two successive sixth places, emphasising how much of a struggle life has been since they gained promotion in 2005.

Avoiding the drop in the Championship at least released some of the pressure on Martyn Moxon, the director of professional cricket. Image is everything these days, and Yorkshire would have felt distinctly uncomfortable if their new £21m pavilion and media centre – due to be opened in May 2010 – had served a second division team.

The strain Moxon was under surfaced early in May, when he lost his cool following the Friends Provident Trophy defeat by Surrey at Headingley, and chased after a spectator who had accused the players of having an attitude problem, a charge Moxon strenuously denied. As the season wore on, his future was discussed at management board level, but he survived, and his unshakeable belief that Yorkshire were good enough to remain in the top tier proved to be sound, although it was a close-run thing. They did not win a home match all season – their last one was in the first game of 2008 – and their morale-boosting second victory did not arrive until they dramatically turned the tables on Sussex at Hove in the penultimate match. Their first success, at Basingstoke in mid-August, ended a record winless sequence of 21 first-class matches.

Matters were not helped by the Michael Vaughan situation. At England's behest he batted at No. 3, when it would have suited Yorkshire better for him to have opened, allowing Jacques Rudolph to drop down the order. Vaughan's presence also squeezed out the up-and-coming Adam Lyth. There was a feeling that if Vaughan made runs he would be recalled by England and that if he didn't he would retire, so Yorkshire would lose out either way. In the end Vaughan made a low-key exit with an absence of fanfare when he stepped down from the Twenty20 match against Derbyshire on June 28, a newspaper having revealed earlier in the day that the end was nigh.

Yorkshire's main handicap, however, stemmed from a thin pace attack, which was rendered even less penetrative on docile pitches, none being worse than Headingley, where five of the six matches ended in draws (as did both games at Scarborough). Three pitches were resurfaced over the winter in an attempt to spice things up. Matthew Hoggard, consistent rather than explosive

– apart from his hat-trick at Hove – led the way with 43 wickets, closely followed by the rapidly improving Ajmal Shahzad, who had several other counties interested in him before he signed a new three-year deal and was called up for England's tour of Bangladesh. Hoggard, though, was controversially released after the season ended. He claimed he had been sacked, but Yorkshire insisted he had rejected a lucrative two-year contract with the option of a third based on performance.

Ajmal Shahzad

Vaughn Ridley, SWPIX.com

Tim Bresnan, so reliable in previous seasons, was often lost to England; Naved-ul-Hasan arrived late and departed early (this time for good); and the popular Deon Kruis bade farewell after five seasons, the first of which was easily his best. Even though the Australian Ryan Harris has been signed for his sharp pace, the attack will continue to look worryingly under-strength unless a couple of the youngsters burst through.

Adil Rashid was slow out of the traps with bat and ball, but suddenly peaked to score a century and take a five-for against both Hampshire and Lancashire, the only player in Yorkshire's history to achieve this in consecutive matches. Like Bresnan, his county season ended early: they both missed the last four Championship matches after joining England's one-day squad. Once again, David Wainwright stepped into the breach. In 2008 his unbeaten century in the last match staved off relegation; this time he made another one to save the day against Warwickshire, then added 85 not out and nine wickets with his left-arm spin in the destruction of Sussex.

The individual parts of the batting were often better than the total. Rudolph, although better suited to a middle-order spot, still enjoyed his best Championship season to date, finishing with 1,334 runs at 51.30. His opening partner, Joe Sayers, saved his career in style, also passing 1,000 runs. Five others averaged more than 40, including Jonathan Bairstow, a chip off the old block (his father David was a Yorkshire stalwart and former captain). Bairstow junior hit an unbeaten 82 on debut, and followed with five more fifties.

However, it was a tough season all round for Anthony McGrath, the captain, who uncomplainingly struggled to get his team to gel, and also lost his own form after a fine start. He stood down, and was replaced by Andrew Gale, who at 27 was Yorkshire's youngest official captain since Brian Sellers in 1933.

The one-day season began promisingly with wins over Durham and Sussex, but then faded into oblivion, as Yorkshire failed to reach the quarter-finals of the FPT or the Twenty20 Cup. In the later stages of the Pro40 League, they increasingly turned to youth in a bid to unearth one or two gems for 2010.

YORKSHIRE RESULTS

All first-class matches – Played 17: Won 2, Lost 2, Drawn 13.
County Championship matches – Played 16: Won 2, Lost 2, Drawn 12.

LV County Championship, 7th in Division 1; Friends Provident Trophy, 3rd in Group C;
Pro40 League, 7th in Division 1; Twenty20 Cup, 5th in North Division.

COUNTY CHAMPIONSHIP AVERAGES, BATTING AND FIELDING

Cap		M	I	NO	R	HS	100s	50s	Avge	Ct/St
2008	A. U. Rashid†	7	9	4	387	157*	2	1	77.40	4
2007	J. A. Rudolph¶	16	27	1	1,334	198	4	6	51.30	13
	J. M. Bairstow†	12	19	6	592	84*	0	6	45.53	21
	D. J. Wainwright†	9	12	4	356	102*	1	1	44.50	0
2008	G. L. Brophy	13	21	5	709	99	0	6	44.31	35/2
2007	J. J. Sayers†	16	27	1	1,103	173	2	5	42.42	15
	A. Shahzad†	13	17	6	445	88	0	2	40.45	4
2008	A. W. Gale†	16	25	1	828	121	2	4	34.50	6
1999	A. McGrath†	16	26	1	825	211	2	2	33.00	10
	A. Lyth†	4	7	0	220	71	0	2	31.42	1
2006	T. T. Bresnan†	10	14	2	372	97	0	1	31.00	5
	Azeem Rafiq	4	5	0	117	100	1	0	23.40	1
1995	M. P. Vaughan‡	5	7	0	147	43	0	0	21.00	0
	R. M. Pyrah†	3	4	1	59	50*	0	1	19.66	3
2006	G. J. Kruis¶	9	9	2	131	37	0	0	18.71	1
	Naved-ul-Hasan§	4	6	0	93	32	0	0	15.50	0
2000	M. J. Hoggard†	15	16	3	195	56*	0	1	15.00	5

Also batted: J. E. Lee† (1 match) 2 (1 ct); S. A. Patterson† (3 matches) 3, 4*, 8.

† *Born in Yorkshire.* ‡ *ECB contract.* § *Official overseas player.* ¶ *Other non-England-qualified player.*

BOWLING

	O	M	R	W	BB	5W/i	Avge
D. J. Wainwright	244.2	50	797	26	5-134	1	30.65
A. U. Rashid	242.4	37	818	26	5-41	2	31.46
M. J. Hoggard	466.1	100	1,467	43	5-56	2	34.11
A. Shahzad	409.5	81	1,376	40	4-72	0	34.40
G. J. Kruis	252.1	56	816	22	3-51	0	37.09
T. T. Bresnan	352.4	91	909	24	4-116	0	37.87
Naved-ul-Hasan	124	23	412	10	3-102	0	41.20
Azeem Rafiq	124.3	9	487	10	3-34	0	48.70

Also bowled: G. L. Brophy 1–1–0–0; A. W. Gale 1–0–1–0; J. E. Lee 19–1–113–2; A. Lyth 19–9–38–1; A. McGrath 106–24–279–3; S. A. Patterson 96–18–368–3; R. M. Pyrah 60–7–213–4; J. A. Rudolph 25–0–111–0; J. J. Sayers 10.5–0–32–3.

COUNTY RECORDS

Highest score for:	341	G. H. Hirst v Leicestershire at Leicester	1905
Highest score against:	318*	W. G. Grace (Gloucestershire) at Cheltenham	1876
Leading run-scorer:	38,558	H. Sutcliffe (avge 50.20)	1919–1945
Best bowling for:	10-10	H. Verity v Nottinghamshire at Leeds	1932
Best bowling against:	10-37	C. V. Grimmett (Australians) at Sheffield	1930
Leading wicket-taker:	3,597	W. Rhodes (avge 16.02)	1898–1930
Highest total for:	887	v Warwickshire at Birmingham	1896
Highest total against:	681-7 dec	by Leicestershire at Bradford	1996
Lowest total for:	23	v Hampshire at Middlesbrough	1965
Lowest total against:	13	by Nottinghamshire at Nottingham	1901

ADDRESS

Headingley Cricket Ground, Leeds LS6 3BU (0113 278 7394; **email** cricket@yorkshireccc.com).
Website www.yorkshireccc.com

OFFICIALS

Captain 2009 – A. McGrath;
2010 – A. W. Gale
Director of cricket M. D. Moxon
Batting coach K. Sharp
Bowling coach S. Oldham

President R. Illingworth
Chief executive S. Regan
Director of cricket operations I. Dews
Head groundsman A. W. Fogarty
Scorer J. T. Potter

Hoggy's sad farewell

There was little goodwill on either side when Yorkshire parted company with Matthew Hoggard at the end of the 2009 season. Hoggard, the sixth-most successful bowler in England's history with 248 Test wickets, claimed he had been sacked, but the club insisted he had been released because he had refused to sign "an extremely competitive" two-year contract with the option of a third year based on performance.

Had Hoggard belonged to an earlier generation of first-class cricketers, he would probably have signed the new contract offered to him in April, when he was already aware that his England days were behind him. Nowadays, however, the financial rewards of representing one's country are so much higher than they used to be that players would no doubt like to feel their earning powers remain just as great when they return to their counties. Hoggard wanted a three-year contract and stuck to his guns, but a modest 43 Championship wickets during the summer weakened his bargaining power and, after Yorkshire had made sure of retaining the up-and-coming Ajmal Shahzad, they showed their senior pace bowler the door. He joined Leicestershire, as captain.

Another sign of the times was that the news of Hoggard's "sacking" was revealed by the player himself in the national newspaper in which he had been a regular columnist during his England days. Earlier in the summer, the imminent closure of Michael Vaughan's playing career was also made public in similar circumstances. Such headline-making disclosures would once have come from the regular cricket correspondent – often earning the wrath of the county concerned – but, increasingly, top players have a foot in both camps.

Hoggard's departure was a reminder that Yorkshire have a long tradition of star players departing in acrimonious circumstances. The difference was that this case was mainly about money, whereas some famous names from the past have left for other reasons: Brian Close because the county felt he was against one-day cricket; and Ray Illingworth – who like Hoggard headed south to take up the reins at Leicester – because he wanted the security of a longer contract.   DAVID WARNER

At Cambridge, April 11, 12, 13. YORKSHIRE drew with CAMBRIDGE UCCE.

At Chester-le-Street, April 22, 23, 24, 25. YORKSHIRE drew with DURHAM.

YORKSHIRE v WORCESTERSHIRE

At Leeds, April 28, 29, 30, May 1. Drawn. Yorkshire 9 pts, Worcestershire 10 pts. Toss: Worcestershire. Championship debuts: A. N. Kervezee, D. A. Wheeldon.

Although there was some seam movement on a slow pitch, the only swing came from a crane working behind the sightscreen at the Kirkstall Lane End on the construction of Headingley's new £21m pavilion and media centre. Rain and bad light took too many chunks out of the game for a positive result, but batsmen on both sides dug in for records. Rudolph, after helping Sayers to Yorkshire's first three-figure opening partnership since May 2007 – same opponents, same ground – then put on 237 with McGrath (Yorkshire's best for the third wicket against Worcestershire). Mysteriously, Rudolph and Gale did not push for a fifth batting point when only a further 33 runs were needed from nine overs: they finished nine adrift. Rudolph finally departed two short of a double-century, neatly stumped down the leg side off Mitchell's medium-pace. Any thoughts of bowling out the opposition once, let alone twice, soon vanished as Solanki and Moeen Ali amassed 317, Worcestershire's first stand of over 300 against Yorkshire. Dropped twice, Solanki converted his fourth consecutive half-century into an unbeaten 206 – in all he faced 326 balls in 576 minutes, and hit 23 fours and two sixes – while Moeen Ali extended his maiden century to 153. The only previous Worcestershire player to score a hundred in a Championship match at Headingley was Dick Richardson in 1962.

Close of play: First day, Yorkshire 123-1 (Rudolph 73, Vaughan 0); Second day, Yorkshire 394-3 (Rudolph 194, Gale 14); Third day, Worcestershire 100-2 (Solanki 66, Ali 15).

Yorkshire

J. A. Rudolph st Davies b Mitchell	198	A. Shahzad not out	20
J. J. Sayers c Davies b Whelan	49	L-b 1, w 7, n-b 6	14
M. P. Vaughan c Davies b Noffke	5		
*A. McGrath c Batty b Mitchell	120	1/123 (2) (6 wkts dec, 136 overs)	460
A. W. Gale c Ali b Mitchell	21	2/130 (3) 3/367 (4)	
†G. L. Brophy b Mitchell	16	4/405 (5) 5/405 (1)	
T. T. Bresnan not out	17	6/426 (6) 120 overs:	391-3

D. J. Wainwright, S. A. Patterson and M. J. Hoggard did not bat.

Noffke 29–6–77–1; Mason 31–8–75–0; Whelan 21–1–105–1; Imran Arif 12–0–75–0; Batty 26–2–78–0; Mitchell 17–3–49–4.

Worcestershire

D. K. H. Mitchell lbw b Shahzad	10
A. N. Kervezee c Sayers b Hoggard	2
*V. S. Solanki not out	206
M. M. Ali c Brophy b Shahzad	153
†S. M. Davies not out	20
B 1, l-b 6, w 5, n-b 2	14

1/3 (2) 2/39 (1)   (3 wkts dec, 116 overs)   405
3/356 (4)

D. A. Wheeldon, G. J. Batty, A. A. Noffke, C. D. Whelan, M. S. Mason and Imran Arif did not bat.

Hoggard 21–4–60–1; Bresnan 28–6–94–0; Patterson 22–6–92–0; Shahzad 22–8–64–2; McGrath 8–1–31–0; Wainwright 13–2–52–0; Rudolph 2–0–5–0.

Umpires: P. J. Hartley and V. A. Holder.

At Birmingham, May 6, 7, 8, 9. YORKSHIRE drew with WARWICKSHIRE. *Joe Sayers (173) and Anthony McGrath (211) share a partnership of 346.*

YORKSHIRE v SUSSEX

At Leeds, June 6, 7, 8, 9. Drawn. Yorkshire 8 pts, Sussex 8 pts. Toss: Yorkshire. First-class debut: Azeem Rafiq. Championship debut: D. R. Smith.

Although 65 overs were lost to a wet outfield on the first day, there was still an exciting climax thanks to a bold declaration which set Sussex 281 in 71 overs. An unruffled century from Yardy (his first in the Championship since September 2007) put them on course until a collapse left them needing 29 from as many deliveries with two wickets remaining; neither side could finish the job. The 18-year-old off-spinner Azeem Rafiq – the unwitting cause of Yorkshire's removal from the Twenty20 Cup in 2008 when he was played before being properly registered – enjoyed a successful first-class debut, claiming a wicket with his fifth ball and finishing with five wickets in the match. Joyce kept Sussex afloat in the first innings with a workmanlike five-hour century, after Brophy's positive approach had similarly baled Yorkshire out after slumping to 110 for seven. Rudolph and McGrath later batted enterprisingly, as did Vaughan, although he was forced to leave the field on the final afternoon when his troublesome right knee flared up, effectively ending his fading hopes of Ashes action.

Close of play: First day, Yorkshire 58-2 (Sayers 15, McGrath 24); Second day, Sussex 78-3 (Joyce 38, Prior 18); Third day, Yorkshire 152-2 (Rudolph 86, McGrath 1).

Yorkshire

J. A. Rudolph c Rayner b Collymore	15	– b Collymore	89
J. J. Sayers b Martin-Jenkins	29	– lbw b Collymore	15
M. P. Vaughan c Rayner b Collymore	0	– c Prior b Smith	39
*A. McGrath c Rayner b Collymore	24	– c Goodwin b Yardy	58
A. W. Gale c Martin-Jenkins b Lewry	11	– b Smith b Lewry	25
†G. L. Brophy not out	75	– (7) not out	7
T. T. Bresnan c Hodd b Martin-Jenkins	7	– (8) c Thornely b Yardy	7
Naved-ul-Hasan lbw b Martin-Jenkins	1	– (6) c Rayner b Yardy	6
D. J. Wainwright c Martin-Jenkins b Collymore	36	– not out	1
Azeem Rafiq c Rayner b Smith	13		
G. J. Kruis c Joyce b Smith	0		
B 1, l-b 11, w 2	14	B 7, l-b 11, w 1, n-b 6	25

1/19 (1) 2/19 (3) 3/58 (4) 4/75 (5) (94.5 overs) 225
5/95 (2) 6/108 (7) 7/110 (8)
8/206 (9) 9/225 (10) 10/225 (11)

1/67 (2) (7 wkts dec, 67 overs) 272
2/150 (3) 3/162 (1)
4/223 (5) 5/250 (6)
6/254 (4) 7/265 (8)

Lewry 27–8–66–1; Collymore 27–9–68–4; Martin-Jenkins 18–5–38–3; Smith 9.5–4–22–2; Rayner 13–4–19–0. *Second Innings*—Lewry 17–4–67–1; Collymore 18–2–54–2; Rayner 16–4–56–0; Smith 14–2–62–1; Yardy 2–0–15–3.

Sussex

*M. H. Yardy lbw b Kruis	8	– c Sayers b Wainwright	110
M. A. Thornely lbw b Naved-ul-Hasan	8	– b Naved-ul-Hasan	19
E. C. Joyce not out	100	– lbw b Azeem Rafiq	24
M. W. Goodwin c Sayers b McGrath	0	– c Bresnan b Azeem Rafiq	19
M. J. Prior c Sayers b Kruis	20	– not out	46
†A. J. Hodd lbw b Bresnan	1	– b Wainwright	7
D. R. Smith c Kruis b Bresnan	0	– b Naved-ul-Hasan	14
R. S. C. Martin-Jenkins b Azeem Rafiq	33	– b Wainwright	3
O. P. Rayner c Gale b Azeem Rafiq	4	– not out	2
C. D. Collymore c Gale b Azeem Rafiq	11	– not out	2
J. D. Lewry b Naved-ul-Hasan	12		
B 1, l-b 13, w 2, n-b 4	20	B 5, l-b 3, w 1, n-b 2	11

1/9 (1) 2/34 (2) 3/43 (4) 4/89 (5) (82.3 overs) 217
5/90 (6) 6/94 (7) 7/150 (8) 8/162 (9)
9/192 (10) 10/217 (11)

1/69 (2) (8 wkts, 70.5 overs) 257
2/114 (3) 3/170 (4)
4/203 (1) 5/211 (6)
6/241 (7) 7/252 (8) 8/252 (5)

Bresnan 24–9–44–2; Kruis 17–7–36–2; Naved-ul-Hasan 19.3–3–59–2; McGrath 9–3–26–1; Azeem Rafiq 11–0–34–3; Wainwright 2–0–4–0. *Second Innings*—Bresnan 18–4–44–0; Kruis 12–2–40–0; Naved-ul-Hasan 9.5–1–45–2; McGrath 5–0–19–0; Wainwright 10–1–46–3; Azeem Rafiq 16–2–55–2.

Umpires: T. E. Jesty and R. T. Robinson.

YORKSHIRE v SOMERSET

At Leeds, June 11, 12, 13, 14. Somerset won by four wickets. Somerset 18 pts, Yorkshire 5 pts. Toss: Yorkshire. First-class debut: J. M. Bairstow.

An absorbing match ended with Somerset gaining their first victory of the season – leaving Yorkshire winless since their success at Taunton a year earlier. Yorkshire twice looked set to take command, but fell short both times: in the first innings too many batsmen got out when set, then they lacked pace-bowling support to back up Hoggard, who enjoyed a splendid four-wicket burst with the new ball, including Trescothick and Langer in his first over, a double-wicket maiden. These two former Test stars did not capitulate so easily in both innings, set about their target of 296, and once they did depart de Bruyn took his side home, ending Yorkshire's run of nine successive Championship draws. Jonathan Bairstow, the 19-year-old son of the former Yorkshire and England wicketkeeper David, looked a class act on debut, and might even have reached a century had he not run out of partners. Bairstow, the first recipient of the *Young Wisden* Schools Cricketer of the Year award in 2008, also kept wicket in the second innings after Brophy injured his hand.

Close of play: First day, Yorkshire 269-8 (Shahzad 2, Wainwright 0); Second day, Yorkshire 26-1 (Sayers 4, Hoggard 0); Third day, Somerset 88-1 (Trescothick 58, Langer 10).

Yorkshire

J. A. Rudolph b Thomas	14	– c Trego b Willoughby	22
J. J. Sayers c Langer b Willoughby	60	– c Langer b Trego	18
*A. McGrath c Kieswetter b Stiff	16	– (4) b Thomas	9
A. W. Gale lbw b Trego	35	– (5) c Trego b Munday	30
J. M. Bairstow b Munday	28	– (6) not out	82
†G. L. Brophy c and b Thomas	33	– (7) lbw b Stiff	14
T. T. Bresnan c Willoughby b Munday	48	– (8) c Trescothick b Stiff	7
Naved-ul-Hasan b Willoughby	10	– (9) c Langer b Willoughby	22
A. Shahzad not out	8	– (10) c Trego b Willoughby	4
D. J. Wainwright c Trescothick b Thomas	1	– (11) c Trescothick b Munday	23
M. J. Hoggard c Kieswetter b Willoughby	1	– (3) c Kieswetter b Thomas	4
B 5, l-b 12, w 2, n-b 4	23	B 4, l-b 1, w 6, n-b 2	13

1/35 (1) 2/72 (3) 3/111 (2)		(99.3 overs) 277
4/166 (4) 5/166 (5) 6/248 (6)		
7/261 (8) 8/269 (7) 9/274 (10) 10/277 (11)		

1/26 (1) 2/33 (3)		(78.1 overs) 248
3/49 (4) 4/87 (5)		
5/92 (2) 6/111 (7) 7/133 (8)		
8/181 (9) 9/193 (10) 10/248 (11)		

Stiff 17–2–47–1; Willoughby 23.3–11–30–3; Thomas 20–1–48–3; Munday 16–0–68–2; de Bruyn 7–2–27–0. *Second Innings*—Willoughby 24–9–46–3; Stiff 12–1–49–2; Thomas 21–4–78–2; Munday 9.1–0–46–2; Trego 12–3–24–1.

Somerset

M. E. Trescothick c Brophy b Hoggard	0	– c Bairstow b Wainwright	78
A. V. Suppiah lbw b Wainwright	20	– b Shahzad	15
*J. L. Langer c Brophy b Hoggard	0	– c Bairstow b Naved-ul-Hasan	46
J. C. Hildreth c McGrath b Hoggard	20	– c Rudolph b Wainwright	5
Z. de Bruyn lbw b Hoggard	0	– not out	70
†C. Kieswetter c Brophy b Shahzad	83	– c Bairstow b Bresnan	25
P. D. Trego c Gale b Hoggard	3	– c Bairstow b Shahzad	23
A. C. Thomas not out	64	– not out	12
D. A. Stiff c McGrath b Wainwright	28		
M. K. Munday c McGrath b Wainwright	1		
C. M. Willoughby b Shahzad	0		
B 2, l-b 9	11	B 5, l-b 15, n-b 2	22

1/0 (1) 2/0 (3) 3/26 (4) 4/30 (5) (74.5 overs) 230
5/84 (2) 6/97 (7) 7/149 (6) 8/215 (9)
9/219 (10) 10/230 (11)

1/36 (2) (6 wkts, 85.3 overs) 296
2/131 (1) 3/139 (4)
4/179 (3) 5/221 (6) 6/274 (7)

Hoggard 16–3–56–5; Naved-ul-Hasan 15–1–47–0; Shahzad 14.5–3–41–2;
Wainwright 17–4–49–3. *Second Innings*—Hoggard 14–1–52–0; Naved-ul-Hasan 17–3–57–1;
Shahzad 15.3–3–45–2; Bresnan 20–4–55–1; Rudolph 1–0–1–0; Wainwright 18–0–66–2.

Umpires: K. Coburn and P. J. Hartley.

At Worcester, June 16, 17, 18, 19. YORKSHIRE drew with WORCESTERSHIRE. *Michael Vaughan's last first-class match before retirement.*

At Taunton, June 30, July 1, 2, 3. YORKSHIRE lost to SOMERSET by four wickets. *Yorkshire set a county record of 18 first-class matches without a win.*

YORKSHIRE v DURHAM

At Leeds, July 10, 11, 12, 13. Drawn. Yorkshire 10 pts, Durham 7 pts. Toss: Durham.
    Steve Harmison, ignored for the first Ashes Test, vented his fury on Yorkshire instead with a dynamic exhibition on a mainly flat pitch which brought him five wickets, including three for two in 15 balls during a hostile burst on the second morning. In many respects it was typical Harmison: sharply lifting deliveries from back of a length, on this occasion homing in on the batsman rather than second slip. McGrath threw his bat away in pain after being rapped on the fingers. "He had to thrash himself to get anything out of the wicket," said Durham's head coach Geoff Cook of Harmison, who was added to the Ashes squad after this display. But despite being reduced to 93 for five, Yorkshire still secured a first-innings lead of 135 thanks to a courageous knock from Gale, who fought valiantly for almost five hours, resisting the urge to play his normal attacking game. Yorkshire's hopes of a first win of the season faded as Durham (captained again by Benkenstein, as Will Smith was absent owing to family illness) showed far more resilience in their second innings. Mustard and Plunkett put on 147, beating their own county eighth-wicket record also made here in 2008 – by four runs. Set 287 in a minimum of 55 overs, Yorkshire dipped to 68 for four before holding firm for the draw which extended their record winless streak to 19 first-class matches.
    Close of play: First day, Yorkshire 64-1 (Sayers 34, McGrath 13); Second day, Durham 26-1 (Di Venuto 13, Davies 1); Third day, Durham 288-7 (Mustard 29, Plunkett 6).

Durham

M. J. Di Venuto b Rashid	29	– (2) b Bresnan		84
M. D. Stoneman run out	22	– (1) b Rashid		12
K. J. Coetzer c Bairstow b Shahzad	0	– (4) b Hoggard		38
G. J. Muchall lbw b Shahzad	0	– (5) lbw b Hoggard		15
*D. M. Benkenstein c Bairstow b Hoggard	62	– (6) lbw b Rashid		36
I. D. Blackwell b Rashid	12	– (7) c Bairstow b Shahzad		32
†P. Mustard c Rudolph b Naved-ul-Hasan	7	– (8) c and b Bresnan		85
L. E. Plunkett lbw b Shahzad	3	– (9) c Hoggard b Naved-ul-Hasan		65
M. E. Claydon c Bairstow b Hoggard	20	– (10) not out		1
S. J. Harmison lbw b Rashid	0			
M. Davies not out	0	– (3) c Bairstow b Hoggard		6
B 5, l-b 4, n-b 14	23	B 20, l-b 14, w 1, n-b 12		47

1/47 (2) 2/53 (3) 3/55 (4) 4/62 (1)   (70.2 overs) 178
5/82 (6) 6/101 (7) 7/128 (8)
8/171 (9) 9/176 (10) 10/178 (5)

1/20 (1)   (9 wkts dec, 147.4 overs) 421
2/39 (3)
3/148 (6) 4/158 (2) 5/178 (5) 6/231 (7)
7/268 (6) 8/415 (8) 9/421 (9)

Hoggard 17.2–6–36–2; Bresnan 13–3–24–0; Shahzad 12–3–39–3; Naved-ul-Hasan 10–1–38–1; Rashid 18–4–32–3. *Second Innings*—Bresnan 29–1–69–2; Hoggard 29–9–67–3; Rashid 43–7–124–2; Shahzad 18–3–55–1; Naved-ul-Hasan 25.4–9–64–1; Rudolph 3–0–8–0.

Yorkshire

J. A. Rudolph c Mustard b Claydon	5	– c Plunkett b Blackwell		39
J. J. Sayers c Stoneman b Harmison	37	– c Stoneman b Plunkett		14
*A. McGrath c Coetzer b Harmison	19	– lbw b Plunkett		0
A. Lyth c Mustard b Harmison	4	– c Muchall b Blackwell		2
A. W. Gale b Blackwell	84	– not out		24
†J. M. Bairstow c Plunkett b Davies	8	– not out		9
T. T. Bresnan c Coetzer b Harmison	36			
A. U. Rashid lbw b Blackwell	32			
Naved-ul-Hasan c Stoneman b Harmison	22			
A. Shahzad not out	41			
M. J. Hoggard c Di Venuto b Blackwell	0			
B 1, l-b 9, w 1, n-b 14	25	B 8, l-b 2		10

1/9 (1) 2/71 (3) 3/74 (2) 4/77 (4)   (104 overs) 313
5/93 (6) 6/147 (7) 7/198 (8) 8/229 (9)
9/313 (5) 10/313 (11)

1/47 (2)   (4 wkts, 50.3 overs) 98
2/51 (3) 3/63 (1)
4/68 (4)

Harmison 25–6–60–5; Claydon 21–4–76–1; Plunkett 19–4–68–0; Davies 13–6–33–1; Blackwell 26–4–66–3. *Second Innings*—Harmison 11–3–22–0; Claydon 3–0–17–0; Blackwell 21–10–23–2; Plunkett 11–4–22–2; Davies 3.3–2–4–0; Benkenstein 1–1–0–0.

Umpires: M. A. Gough and G. Sharp.

YORKSHIRE v NOTTINGHAMSHIRE

At Scarborough, July 21, 22, 23, 24. Drawn. Yorkshire 8 pts, Nottinghamshire 11 pts. Toss: Nottinghamshire.

Coverage of a nearby funeral service was somehow picked up by the Scarborough club's public-address system, and some readings were broadcast during the first morning's play. It was later on, however, that Yorkshire needed divine intervention if they were to end their record run of first-class matches without a win, despite a promising start. Nothing happened. Hoggard and Bresnan, with his best figures of the season, reduced Nottinghamshire to 125 for six early on the second day after rain allowed only 34 overs on the first, but then the bowling was torn to shreds by Hussey. In the last match of a brief return as an overseas locum, he plundered 26 fours and seven sixes, while his partnership of 147 with Franks was Nottinghamshire's best for the seventh wicket against Yorkshire. It was Hussey's 35th first-class century, and 21st for Nottinghamshire. Adams (who thrashed eight sixes, and faced only 57 balls for his 84) and Sidebottom further twisted the knife with a last-wicket stand of 93, then they struck with the ball as well, sharing nine wickets. Bairstow further enhanced his reputation with a stylish and patient career-best, while his more experienced colleagues were undone. Yorkshire followed on, but were saved from defeat in a rain-hit match by Gale, who deprived himself of a century with a dreadful stroke – top-edging a long-hop – when one short.

Close of play: First day, Nottinghamshire 101-5 (Hussey 59, Read 7); Second day, Yorkshire 25-2 (Sayers 9, Wainwright 0); Third day, Yorkshire 14-1 (Sayers 2).

Nottinghamshire

M. J. Wood c Rashid b Bresnan	4	L. J. Fletcher lbw b Kruis	0
B. M. Shafayat lbw b Hoggard	7	A. R. Adams c Brophy b Kruis	84
M. A. Wagh c Brophy b Bresnan	6	R. J. Sidebottom not out	10
D. J. Hussey c Sayers b Rashid	189	L-b 4, w 10	14
S. R. Patel c Sayers b Bresnan	8		
A. D. Brown c Rashid b Bresnan	5	1/11 (1) 2/15 (2) 3/33 (3) (96.1 overs) 395
*†C. M. W. Read b Hoggard	20	4/43 (5) 5/84 (6) 6/125 (7)
P. J. Franks b Rashid	48	7/272 (8) 8/273 (9) 9/302 (4) 10/395 (10)

Hoggard 21–5–57–2; Bresnan 30–5–116–4; Kruis 19.1–3–79–2; Rashid 14–0–97–2; Wainwright 12–3–42–0.

Yorkshire

J. A. Rudolph lbw b Sidebottom	0	– c Hussey b Sidebottom	12
J. J. Sayers c Read b Adams	17	– c Adams b Sidebottom	36
*A. McGrath b Adams	15	– lbw b Adams	9
D. J. Wainwright c Hussey b Adams	29		
A. W. Gale c Hussey b Adams	6	– (4) c Sidebottom b Franks	99
J. M. Bairstow not out	84	– (5) c Adams b Sidebottom	4
†G. L. Brophy c Patel b Sidebottom	5	– (6) not out	51
T. T. Bresnan c Brown b Sidebottom	7	– (7) not out	16
A. U. Rashid c Brown b Sidebottom	4		
M. J. Hoggard c Wagh b Franks	11		
G. J. Kruis c Adams b Sidebottom	37		
L-b 4, n-b 12	16	B 1, n-b 4	5

1/0 (1) 2/25 (3) 3/61 (2) 4/72 (4) (80.5 overs) 231	1/14 (1) (5 wkts dec, 75 overs) 232
5/73 (5) 6/81 (7) 7/97 (8) 8/105 (9)	2/31 (3) 3/117 (2)
9/149 (10) 10/231 (11)	4/131 (5) 5/182 (4)

Sidebottom 21.5–7–59–5; Fletcher 19–8–44–0; Adams 20–9–39–4; Franks 11–1–50–1; Patel 7–0–27–0; Hussey 2–0–8–0. *Second Innings*—Sidebottom 18–4–66–3; Adams 21–8–57–1; Fletcher 9–3–20–0; Patel 13–1–46–0; Franks 13–2–35–1; Brown 1–0–6–0.

Umpires: N. L. Bainton and J. F. Steele.

At Manchester, July 31, August 1, 2, 3. YORKSHIRE drew with LANCASHIRE.

At Basingstoke, August 11, 12, 13, 14. YORKSHIRE beat HAMPSHIRE by an innings and 22 runs. *Yorkshire win for the first time in 22 first-class matches.*

YORKSHIRE v LANCASHIRE

At Leeds, August 19, 20, 21, 22. Drawn. Yorkshire 11 pts, Lancashire 8 pts. Toss: Lancashire.

In his last county match of the season before joining England's one-day squad, Rashid entered Yorkshire's record books as their only player to score a century and take five wickets in consecutive first-class matches – a feat all the more remarkable as he was still only 21. But despite his fine performance – and good support from Bresnan, another about to be lost to England – the combination of time stolen by the weather, a benign pitch and a couple of dropped catches on the final morning meant that Yorkshire never looked like winning a match they had once been in danger of losing. After the early loss of their openers, Lancashire recovered thanks to a determined unbeaten century from Chilton, which he reached with the last man at the crease, and the total looked much healthier when Tom Lungley (on loan from Derbyshire) helped reduce Yorkshire to 72 for five with an excellent spell of 10–1–28–3. The tables were turned when Brophy and Rashid put on 168 – a record for either side for the seventh wicket in a Championship Roses match, and Yorkshire's highest in any match at Headingley – but neither would have survived that long if catches had been held. Brophy narrowly missed a century, while Rashid overhauled his career-best, set a week earlier at Basingstoke. Two wickets went down before Lancashire erased the deficit, but Loye and Laxman made the match safe.

Close of play: First day, Lancashire 226-7 (Chilton 73, Lungley 6); Second day, Yorkshire 131-5 (Brophy 13, Bresnan 46); Third day, Yorkshire 386-7 (Rashid 136, Shahzad 24).

Lancashire

P. J. Horton c Bairstow b Hoggard	....	2 – (2) c Brophy b Rashid	28
S. J. Croft c Brophy b Bresnan	....	0 – (1) c Brophy b Bresnan	15
M. B. Loye c Bresnan b Rashid	....	24 – not out	84
V. V. S. Laxman c Hoggard b Rashid	....	50 – not out	65
M. J. Chilton not out	....	111	
F. du Plessis lbw b Wainwright	....	32	
*†L. D. Sutton c Brophy b Bresnan	....	4	
K. W. Hogg c sub (Azeem Rafiq) b Rashid	......	29	
T. Lungley c Bairstow b Bresnan	....	10	
O. J. Newby b Rashid	....	2	
G. Keedy c Sayers b Rashid	....	4	
B 3, l-b 3, n-b 2	....	8	L-b 3, w 1 4

1/2 (2) 2/2 (1) 3/65 (3) 4/92 (4)   (122.2 overs) 276   1/23 (1) 2/65 (2) (2 wkts, 72 overs) 196
5/144 (6) 6/159 (7) 7/213 (8)
8/241 (9) 9/252 (10) 10/276 (11)   120 overs: 266-9

Hoggard 18–7–40–1; Bresnan 31–13–46–3; Shahzad 18–7–48–0; Rashid 34.2–7–97–5; Wainwright 21–5–39–1. *Second Innings*—Hoggard 10–2–24–0; Bresnan 11–2–30–1; Rashid 24–5–55–1; Wainwright 19–3–67–0; Shahzad 5–3–13–0; Sayers 3–0–4–0.

Yorkshire

J. A. Rudolph c du Plessis b Hogg	....	0	D. J. Wainwright st Sutton b Keedy 1
J. J. Sayers lbw b Lungley	....	17	M. J. Hoggard c Horton b Keedy 8
*A. McGrath c Croft b Lungley	....	17	
A. W. Gale c and b Lungley	....	6	B 5, l-b 6, n-b 20 31
J. M. Bairstow c and b Newby	....	15	
†G. L. Brophy c Sutton b Keedy	....	99	1/0 (1) 2/27 (3) 3/35 (4) (141.2 overs) 429
T. T. Bresnan c Lungley b Newby	....	14	4/68 (5) 5/72 (2) 6/144 (7)
A. U. Rashid not out	....	157	7/312 (6) 8/412 (9) 9/413 (10)
A. Shahzad c Loye b du Plessis	....	32	10/429 (11) 120 overs: 373-7

Hogg 33–10–75–1; Newby 24–4–102–2; Lungley 23–2–85–3; Keedy 46.2–11–104–3; Croft 2–0–12–0; du Plessis 11–1–33–1; Laxman 2–0–7–0.

Umpires: J. H. Evans and V. A. Holder.

YORKSHIRE v WARWICKSHIRE

At Scarborough, August 26, 27, 28, 29. Drawn. Yorkshire 10 pts, Warwickshire 10 pts. Toss: Yorkshire.

During a fluctuating match, both sides sniffed the victory that would have taken them away from the relegation zone, but neither could press home the advantage. Warwickshire recovered from 53 for four on the rain-hit first day to reach 320, while Yorkshire staged an even better comeback, from 99 for seven to 328. They lost two wickets in the first over, including Rudolph for his second successive golden duck. Ambrose, who put on 110 with Carter, had made the most of easing batting conditions, but Yorkshire's early problems stemmed – according to the watching Dickie Bird – from using the heavy roller, the effects of which had worn off by the time Wainwright helped Brophy add

144 after two destructive spells from Sreesanth. In 2008 Wainwright had saved Yorkshire from relegation with a maiden century from No. 10 at Hove in the last match of the season; this time, one place higher, he strode to the rescue again, his 102 coming off 149 balls with 14 fours. His technique and calmness under pressure suggested he deserved further promotion. Yorkshire might just have sneaked home if Westwood and Troughton had been snapped up early in the second innings, but the chances went down. Rudolph had time to complete 1,000 Championship runs for the season.

Close of play: First day, Warwickshire 53-4 (Frost 4, Ambrose 0); Second day, Yorkshire 100-7 (Brophy 28, Wainwright 0); Third day, Warwickshire 111-2 (Westwood 58, Bell 4).

Warwickshire

*I. J. Westwood c Sayers b Shahzad	1	– c Pyrah b Shahzad	58
A. G. Botha b Kruis	13	– c Pyrah b McGrath	33
I. R. Bell b Shahzad	23	– (4) lbw b Wainwright	35
J. O. Troughton c Bairstow b Shahzad	9	– (5) b Hoggard	40
T. Frost b Wainwright	35	– (6) c Brophy b Pyrah	48
†T. R. Ambrose c McGrath b Kruis	113	– (7) lbw b Wainwright	33
R. Clarke c Brophy b Wainwright	22	– (8) b Sayers	23
N. M. Carter c McGrath b Pyrah	67	– (9) c Rudolph b Sayers	11
C. R. Woakes c Bairstow b Kruis	9	– (10) not out	6
N. S. Tahir not out	5	– (3) b Shahzad	0
S. Sreesanth b Shahzad	11	– c Brophy b Sayers	1
B 4, l-b 7, w 1	12	B 9, l-b 15, w 1	25

1/1 (1) 2/28 (2) 3/48 (3) 4/53 (4)   (81.4 overs) 320
5/138 (5) 6/178 (7) 7/288 (6)
8/300 (9) 9/304 (8) 10/320 (11)

1/96 (2) 2/97 (3)   (108.5 overs) 313
3/116 (1) 4/159 (4)
5/229 (5) 6/256 (6) 7/288 (8) 8/304 (9)
9/310 (7) 10/313 (11)

Hoggard 18–3–51–0; Shahzad 17.4–3–78–4; Kruis 23–8–68–3; Wainwright 14–0–74–2; Pyrah 9–1–38–1. *Second Innings*—Hoggard 20–9–42–1; Shahzad 19–3–57–2; Pyrah 17–2–64–1; Kruis 12–5–24–0; Wainwright 30–8–71–2; McGrath 6–1–11–1; Sayers 4.5–0–20–3.

Yorkshire

J. A. Rudolph c Troughton b Sreesanth	0	– not out	21
J. J. Sayers c Bell b Tahir	21	– not out	4
*A. McGrath c Ambrose b Sreesanth	0		
A. W. Gale c Woakes b Tahir	23		
J. M. Bairstow c Frost b Carter	4		
†G. L. Brophy c Clarke b Botha	85		
A. Shahzad c Westwood b Sreesanth	13		
R. M. Pyrah c Frost b Sreesanth	0		
D. J. Wainwright not out	102		
M. J. Hoggard c Ambrose b Tahir	18		
G. J. Kruis c Ambrose b Sreesanth	30		
L-b 5, w 3, n-b 24	32	W 1, n-b 4	5

1/0 (1) 2/0 (3) 3/47 (4) 4/50 (2)   (86.2 overs) 328
5/67 (5) 6/95 (7) 7/99 (8) 8/243 (6)
9/291 (10) 10/328 (11)

(no wkt, 8 overs) 30

Sreesanth 15.2–3–93–5; Tahir 21–7–59–3; Carter 15–2–49–1; Woakes 19–5–63–0; Clarke 4–0–20–0; Botha 12–2–39–1. *Second Innings*—Sreesanth 4–1–17–0; Tahir 2–1–4–0; Bell 2–1–9–0.

Umpires: R. J. Bailey and N. A. Mallender.

At Nottingham, September 3, 4, 5, 6. YORKSHIRE drew with NOTTINGHAMSHIRE.

At Hove, September 16, 17, 18, 19. YORKSHIRE beat SUSSEX by 156 runs. *Matthew Hoggard takes a hat-trick as Sussex collapse on the final afternoon.*

YORKSHIRE v HAMPSHIRE

At Leeds, September 23, 24, 25, 26. Drawn. Yorkshire 10 pts, Hampshire 11 pts. Toss: Yorkshire.

Yorkshire went into the match needing five points to guarantee their first division survival, while Hampshire required only three. After being put in, Hampshire acquired the points they needed on the second morning, and Yorkshire's own safety was confirmed when news filtered through that Sussex had failed to take enough batting points from their final game. This match began with sections of the crowd hurling abuse at the umpires for ruling that it was too dark for play on the first morning, and it ended with a standing ovation for Deon Kruis, the South African Kolpak paceman, who was leaving Headingley after five seasons. Rudolph and Sayers, Yorkshire's only players to top 1,000 runs, put on 162 for the first wicket – their fourth century opening stand of the season – while Lumb hit 81 and 64 against his former team-mates, which enabled him to reach 1,000 too. After their earlier frustrations, Yorkshire's supporters sat patiently through the final crystal-clear day as the game meandered to a draw on a pitch which got slower and slower.

Close of play: First day, Hampshire 227-4 (Lumb 72, Pothas 4); Second day, Yorkshire 169-1 (Sayers 74, Wainwright 0); Third day, Hampshire 41-0 (Adams 16, Dawson 16).

Hampshire

J. H. K. Adams b Kruis	51	– b Wainwright	72
L. A. Dawson c Gale b Wainwright	45	– c Shahzad b Kruis	35
M. J. Lumb c McGrath b Shahzad	81	– c Brophy b Lyth	64
C. C. Benham c McGrath b Shahzad	16	– not out	67
S. M. Ervine c Brophy b McGrath	26	– not out	18
†N. Pothas c Brophy b Kruis	38		
*A. D. Mascarenhas c McGrath b Hoggard	8		
D. G. Cork not out	42		
J. A. Tomlinson b Shahzad	14		
D. A. Griffiths b Kruis	0		
D. R. Briggs c Rudolph b Shahzad	1		
B 8, l-b 13, w 2, n-b 6	29	B 15, l-b 3, w 2, n-b 8	28

1/95 (2) 2/110 (1) 3/152 (4)   (115.3 overs) 351   1/105 (2)   (3 wkts dec, 98 overs) 284
4/219 (5) 5/260 (3) 6/275 (7)   2/142 (1) 3/262 (3)
7/311 (6) 8/345 (9) 9/346 (10) 10/351 (11)

Hoggard 27–6–115–1; Shahzad 29.3–9–75–4; Kruis 23–8–51–3; McGrath 20–4–46–1; Wainwright 16–6–43–1. *Second Innings*—Hoggard 11–3–31–0; Shahzad 19–9–38–1; Kruis 14–5–50–1; McGrath 15–2–39–0; Wainwright 20–6–49–1; Lyth 20–9–38–1; Rudolph 5–0–32–0; Brophy 1–1–0–0.

Yorkshire

J. A. Rudolph c Tomlinson b Briggs	68	M. J. Hoggard c Benham b Ervine	0
J. J. Sayers c Tomlinson b Cork	95	G. J. Kruis c Cork b Briggs	20
D. J. Wainwright c Briggs b Mascarenhas	21		
A. Lyth c Adams b Griffiths	26	L-b 6, w 6, n-b 26	38
*A. McGrath c Dawson b Tomlinson	25		
A. W. Gale c Pothas b Tomlinson	1	1/162 (1) 2/209 (3) (109.4 overs) 348
J. M. Bairstow not out	50	3/231 (2) 4/259 (5)
†G. L. Brophy c Pothas b Griffiths	0	5/273 (6) 6/273 (4) 7/277 (8)
A. Shahzad c Pothas b Ervine	4	8/317 (9) 9/319 (10) 10/348 (11)

Griffiths 23–7–73–2; Mascarenhas 22–8–44–1; Cork 19–7–44–1; Tomlinson 21–4–83–2; Briggs 15.4–3–37–2; Ervine 9–0–61–2.

Umpires: M. J. D. Bodenham and N. G. Cowley.

FRIENDS PROVIDENT TROPHY, 2009

REVIEW BY STEVE JAMES

With its group stages done and dusted by May 20, its semi-finals taking place just days before the first Ashes Test and its final then sandwiched between a historic England victory at Lord's and a drawn third Test at Birmingham, the 2009 Friends Provident Trophy was always destined for relative anonymity. That much was expected.

What was not expected was its death as a 50-over competition. That shocking, unfathomable news came in late August when the ECB announced there would be no domestic 50-over cricket from 2010, despite both the 2011 and 2015 World Cups being confirmed as having that format. The FPT had long been flawed – crammed into the early season with its generally sporting pitches – but this was a ridiculous decision based purely on commercial considerations. The change to a 40-over Sunday competition was supposedly vindicated by spectator feedback: no matter that in a poll conducted by the Professional Cricketers' Association 83% of their membership voted that domestic one-day cricket should mirror international cricket.

Mission accomplished: Hampshire captain Dimitri Mascarenhas holds the Friends Provident Trophy.

At least in 2009 the early-season weather was kinder. And the 2009 tournament also saw the introduction of the batting powerplay – a block of five overs in which only three fielders were allowed outside the semi-circles, and whose timing was chosen by the batting side, usually late in the innings. The net result was more centuries (37) than the previous year (32), and, fortunately, some of them at least hinted at talent for which England might find some future use. The most significant was probably the 138 not out made by opener Craig Kieswetter to see Somerset home against Warwickshire. For a 21-year-old to display such maturity, allied to some thrilling strokeplay, was hugely impressive. Kieswetter also made 106 in defeat against Sussex in the quarter-final. A South African, he qualifies for England in February 2010.

Middlesex's Irish southpaw Eoin Morgan also made an eye-catching 161 against Kent (in a partnership of 277 with Nick Compton, who hit 131), full of the sort of scoops, sweeps and deflections that earned subsequent selection for England's Twenty20 and one-day international squads. But this match highlighted the perennial problem of tiredness. This was Kent's 11th day of cricket in 13, and it took special toll on their 19-year-old South African overseas bowler Wayne Parnell, later to be such a shining star in the Twenty20 World Cup. He returned wearily woeful figures of 10–1–75–1. Many a young English fast bowler will have nodded gravely in recognition.

Sometimes the old sweats know best how to pace themselves. That is certainly true of Hampshire's Dominic Cork, aged 37. He finished as the tournament's leading wicket-taker (with 20, matching Surrey's Chris Schofield and Somerset's Alfonso Thomas), but more importantly he snared the match award in the final with an ebullient four for 41. From the moment Cork bowled the tournament's most prolific run-scorer, Ed Joyce, so revitalised after a move from Middlesex, you sensed it was not to be Sussex's day.

In days of yore these bright finals were held in September and it was de rigueur to bowl first. But a bright sunny morning in late July persuaded Sussex skipper Michael Yardy to bat. His opposite number Dimitri Mascarenhas would have done likewise. Only one man on either side declared it prudent to bowl first – former England coach Duncan Fletcher, on a month's consultancy work with Hampshire. Fletcher's role might only have been small – he did persuade Mascarenhas, against his original inclination, that wicketkeeper Nic Pothas should continue batting with a recurrence of a groin injury, finishing 35 not out – but his coaching Midas touch is clear. The University of Cape Town, Western Province, Glamorgan and now Hampshire have all collected silverware in their first seasons of contact with him.

Fletcher's Midas touch was clear

And Fletcher was right. There was some dampness in the pitch, which Cork duly exploited. Yardy's typically quirky innings of 92 not out was heroic, but only in salvage terms. Hampshire never looked troubled in pursuit of 222. Three youngish left-handers shone: Jimmy Adams, with a new baseball-style backlift acquired during a winter in Australia, made a half-century; the firm-handed Michael Lumb (having made a fine century in the quarter-final against Middlesex and 76 in the semi at Lancashire) ratified his previous day's selection in England's 30-man Champions Trophy squad with 38; and the muscular Michael Carberry briefly showed the form of a man in a purple patch, following Championship scores of 123, 52, 112 and 204 with a quickfire 30.

If victory by six wickets with 57 balls to spare was a cakewalk, Hampshire's progress from Group A (there were four randomly picked groups of five in 2009) was not necessarily so. They lost twice to Worcestershire who, remarkably, failed to qualify by losing at home to Ireland in their last match. Somerset, with Marcus Trescothick also in sublime form, were far the most impressive qualifiers, remaining unbeaten in Group B, with one no result. Gloucestershire's progress, as winners of Group C, obviously surprised their administrators: the quarter-finals were scheduled for the day before Bristol hosted a one-day international against West Indies. After talk of a relocation (maybe to Cardiff), the match was eventually played two and a half weeks later.

There were other oddities. Middlesex asked for a replay after a miscalculation in their rain-affected group match against Somerset. Umpires Peter Willey and Michael Gough allocated Somerset 19 overs of powerplays in their adjusted

41-over chase of 290 when it should have been only 16. Somerset duly won, the umpires admitted error, but the ECB refused to order a replay.

And there was a significant sanction against Glamorgan. They were penalised after the pitch for their match against Essex was deemed "poor", and the degree of turn for the spinners (Danish Kaneria took four for 16 as Glamorgan were dismissed for 124) considered "excessive". With judgment coming just 51 days before the newly developed Swalec Stadium hosted the first Ashes Test, it sent the whole country into jittery apprehension. But all was well that ended well. Not so for Glamorgan, though: in the last three years of this competition they have won just four matches from 34.

FINAL GROUP TABLES

Group A

	Played	Won	Lost	Tied	No result	Points	NRR
HAMPSHIRE.............	8	5	2	0	1	11	0.34
NOTTINGHAMSHIRE.....	8	5	3	0	0	10	0.42
Worcestershire	8	4	3	0	1	9	0.29
Leicestershire	8	2	4	0	2	6	−0.64
Ireland	8	1	5	0	2	4	−0.75

Group B

	Played	Won	Lost	Tied	No result	Points	NRR
SOMERSET.............	8	7	0	0	1	15	2.00
MIDDLESEX.............	8	4	4	0	0	8	0.14
Warwickshire	8	3	3	1	1	8	0.47
Kent	8	3	4	1	0	7	−0.41
Scotland	8	1	7	0	0	2	−1.78

Group C

	Played	Won	Lost	Tied	No result	Points	NRR
GLOUCESTERSHIRE	8	5	2	0	1	11	0.45
SUSSEX.................	8	4	3	0	1	9	0.12
Yorkshire	8	4	4	0	0	8	−0.15
Durham.................	8	3	5	0	0	6	−0.63
Surrey..................	8	3	5	0	0	6	0.30

Group D

	Played	Won	Lost	Tied	No result	Points	NRR
LANCASHIRE	8	6	2	0	0	12	0.63
ESSEX..................	8	5	2	0	1	11	0.41
Derbyshire	8	3	4	0	1	7	−0.30
Glamorgan	8	2	5	0	1	5	−0.78
Northamptonshire..........	8	1	4	0	3	5	−0.16

Where two or more teams finished with an equal number of points, the positions were decided by (a) most wins, (b) most points in head-to-head matches, (c) net run-rate (runs scored per over minus runs conceded per over), (d) most wickets taken per balls bowled in matches achieving a result.

Prize money

£150,000 for winners: HAMPSHIRE.
£100,000 for runners-up: SUSSEX.
£25,000 for losing semi-finalists: GLOUCESTERSHIRE, LANCASHIRE.
£10,000 for losing quarter-finalists: ESSEX, MIDDLESEX, NOTTINGHAMSHIRE, SOMERSET.

FRIENDS PROVIDENT TROPHY AVERAGES, 2009

BATTING

(Qualification: 200 runs, average 50.00)

		M	I	NO	R	HS	100s	50s	Avge	SR	4	6
1	Z. de Bruyn (*Somerset*) ...	9	6	2	388	96	0	5	97.00	94.17	29	8
2	F. du Plessis (*Lancs*)	10	8	3	412	113*	2	2	82.40	106.45	36	8
3	†J. H. K. Adams (*Hants*) ...	5	5	1	327	78	0	4	81.75	93.69	33	4
4	M. R. Ramprakash (*Surrey*)	6	6	1	373	121	3	0	74.60	93.48	26	10
5	†M. H. Yardy (*Sussex*).....	10	8	2	399	92*	0	5	66.50	86.73	36	0
6	†S. A. Newman (*Surrey*) ...	7	7	0	463	177	2	2	66.14	90.78	45	8
7	C. Kieswetter (*Somerset*)..	8	8	2	395	138*	2	0	65.83	95.87	45	6
8	I. R. Bell (*Warwicks*)	7	6	2	260	108	1	2	65.00	76.69	29	0
9	H. D. Ackerman (*Leics*) ...	5	5	1	243	118*	1	1	60.75	86.78	28	1
10	†E. C. Joyce (*Sussex*)	11	10	1	546	146	3	1	60.66	81.98	42	6
11	†M. E. Trescothick (*Som*) ..	9	9	1	476	144	1	4	59.50	116.95	61	3
12	N. R. D. Compton (*Middx*)	5	5	1	236	131	1	0	59.00	88.38	23	0
13	C. J. Borgas (*Scotland*) ...	7	6	1	289	78*	0	3	57.80	68.16	19	4
14	M. J. Chilton (*Lancs*).....	10	10	3	404	101*	1	1	57.71	80.63	27	3
15	V. Chopra (*Essex*)	9	8	0	460	99	0	5	57.50	71.76	46	1
16	†M. A. Carberry (*Hants*) ..	10	9	3	337	121*	1	0	56.16	91.08	31	3
17	C. C. Benham (*Hants*)	10	8	2	333	108*	1	1	55.50	78.72	25	2
18	J. W. A. Taylor (*Leics*)...	7	6	1	260	101	1	0	52.00	75.58	19	4
19	J. L. Denly (*Kent*)	8	8	1	363	115	1	1	51.85	75.78	29	6
20	G. W. Flower (*Essex*).....	9	8	4	207	54	0	1	51.75	80.85	18	1
21	M. W. Goodwin (*Sussex*)..	10	9	1	406	144	1	2	50.75	94.19	38	3

† *Left-handed batsman.*

BOWLING

(Qualification: 10 wickets, average 25.00)

		Style	O	M	R	W	BB	4W/i	Avge	SR	ER
1	C. D. Whelan (*Worcs*)......	RFM	32	0	155	11	4-27	1	14.09	17.45	4.84
2	C. P. Schofield (*Surrey*).....	LBG	73	2	307	20	5-32	1	15.35	21.90	4.20
3	A. D. Mascarenhas (*Hants*)..	RM	45	3	190	11	4-39	1	17.27	24.54	4.22
4	D. G. Cork (*Hants*)	RFM	85.4	6	352	20	4-18	3	17.60	25.70	4.10
5	S. R. Patel (*Notts*)	SLA	63	3	249	14	6-13	1	17.78	27.00	3.95
6	A. C. Thomas (*Somerset*) ...	RFM	67	1	361	20	4-22	1	18.05	20.10	5.38
7	G. J. Kruis (*Yorks*).........	RFM	68.1	8	253	13	3-24	0	19.46	31.46	3.71
8	D. D. Masters (*Essex*)......	RFM	80	16	259	13	3-19	0	19.92	36.92	3.23
9	P. Connell (*Ireland*)........	RFM	39	0	241	12	5-19	2	20.08	19.50	6.17
10	Imran Tahir (*Hants*)	LBG	50	1	201	10	3-38	0	20.10	30.00	4.02
11	A. G. Botha (*Warwicks*)	SLA	47.5	1	225	11	3-27	0	20.45	26.09	4.70
12	G. J. Batty (*Worcs*)	OB	62	4	225	11	5-35	1	20.45	33.81	3.62
13	P. D. Trego (*Somerset*)	RFM	69.2	4	374	18	4-17	3	20.77	23.11	5.39
14	G. Chapple (*Lancs*)........	RFM	61.4	10	250	12	3-46	0	20.83	30.83	4.05
15	B. V. Taylor (*Hants*)	RM	73.2	1	342	16	3-37	0	21.37	27.50	4.66
16	G. M. Smith (*Derbys*)	RM/OB	54	1	279	13	4-53	1	21.46	24.92	5.16
17	J. Lewis (*Glos*)	RFM	79	7	371	17	4-34	2	21.82	27.88	4.69
18	J. E. C. Franklin (*Glos*)	LFM	50.3	3	241	11	3-18	0	21.90	27.54	4.77
19	S. I. Mahmood (*Lancs*)	RFM	84.5	7	378	17	3-17	0	22.23	29.94	4.45
20	Danish Kaneria (*Essex*).....	LBG	66.1	4	293	13	5-32	2	22.53	30.53	4.42
21	R. M. Pyrah (*Yorks*)........	RM	71	3	387	17	4-54	1	22.76	25.05	5.45
22	G. Keedy (*Lancs*)	SLA	81	1	366	16	4-43	2	22.87	30.37	4.51

Full scores of these matches are available at: www.cricinfo.com/db/ARCHIVE/2009/ENG_
LOCAL/FPT/ and www.cricketarchive.co.uk/Archive/Seasons/ENG/2009_ENG_Friends_
Provident_Trophy_2009.html.

GROUP A

At Southampton, April 19. **Worcestershire won by 53 runs.** Toss: Worcestershire. **Worcestershire 320-8** (50 overs) (V. S. Solanki 35, S. M. Davies 50, M. M. Ali 125, B. F. Smith 70; C. T. Tremlett 3-76); **Hampshire 267** (48.1 overs) (M. J. Lumb 61, J. P. Crawley 100, M. A. Carberry 34; G. J. Batty 5-35). *Worcestershire 2 pts.*

Moeen Ali made his highest one-day score, from 109 balls with nine fours and three sixes – one of them at 93 when Billy Taylor held the ball on the boundary but toppled over the ropes; Ben Smith helped Moeen add 164 for the fourth wicket. Gareth Batty dismissed Michael Lumb to break Hampshire's first-wicket stand of 116 in 21 overs and went on to a career-best; opener John Crawley was eighth out for what proved to be his last hundred for Hampshire before retiring.

At Nottingham, April 19. **Nottinghamshire won by eight wickets.** Toss: Nottinghamshire. **Leicestershire 155** (45.4 overs) (H. H. Dippenaar 34, J. W. A. Taylor 44*; G. P. Swann 3-24); **Nottinghamshire 159-2** (30 overs) (M. A. Wagh 68*, A. D. Hales 52). *Nottinghamshire 2 pts. County debut:* A. D. Brown (Nottinghamshire).

Only four Leicestershire batsmen made double figures as 108-3 became 155 all out. Graeme Swann proved his fitness after elbow surgery; he said the operation allowed him to bowl without pain for the first time in four years. Mark Wagh and Alex Hales added 106 for the second wicket, and Nottinghamshire raced to their target in 20 overs to spare.

At Belfast, April 26. **Worcestershire won by 52 runs.** Reduced to 33 overs a side. Toss: Worcestershire. **Worcestershire 180-8** (33 overs) (S. M. Davies 47; W. K. McCallan 3-26); **Ireland 128-9** (33 overs) (P. R. Stirling 51). *Worcestershire 2 pts.*

Ireland were brought back to reality after their World Cup Qualifiers success in South Africa seven days earlier. Missing seven of their winning squad and choosing to play without a professional, the Irish batsmen had no answer to a pacy opening burst by Gareth Andrew and Ashley Noffke. Only 18-year-old Paul Stirling reached 50, despite Worcestershire using eight bowlers.

At Leicester, April 26. **Hampshire won by four wickets.** Toss: Leicestershire. **Leicestershire 238-6** (50 overs) (M. A. G. Boyce 80, H. H. Dippenaar 65; L. A. Dawson 4-48); **Hampshire 242-6** (48.1 overs) (M. A. Carberry 39, C. C. Benham 79, L. A. Dawson 35). *Hampshire 2 pts. County debut:* I. E. O'Brien (Leicestershire).

All-rounder Liam Dawson helped steer Hampshire to a comfortable victory. He took four wickets with left-arm spin and hit 35 from 38 balls, giving excellent support to Chris Benham, whose 79 was the mainstay of the Hampshire reply. Leicestershire's total was some way below par, only opener Matthew Boyce and Boeta Dippenaar building innings as Dawson plucked out the middle order. Carl Crowe, whose previous one-day game for Leicestershire was in September 2002, took the wicket of Michael Carberry, which brought Dawson to join Benham in a stand of 73.

At Southampton, May 3. **Hampshire won by 46 runs.** Toss: Hampshire. **Hampshire 300-5** (50 overs) (J. H. K. Adams 45, S. M. Ervine 43, C. C. Benham 108*, N. Pothas 57*); **Leicestershire 254** (49.2 overs) (J. W. A. Taylor 41, H. H. Dippenaar 34, P. A. Nixon 50; B. V. Taylor 3-46, S. M. Ervine 3-50). *Hampshire 2 pts.*

Chris Benham and Nic Pothas put on 177, a county record for the sixth wicket, as Hampshire completed a seven-day double over Leicestershire. Benham's runs came from 103 balls. Pothas needed a runner after pulling a hamstring half way through his innings; reserve keeper Tom Burrows substituted when Hampshire fielded, and Dominic Cork took the captaincy and the new ball. Leicestershire were always behind the clock, and lingering hopes faded with the dismissal of Paul Nixon.

At Nottingham, May 3. **Nottinghamshire won by 134 runs.** Toss: Nottinghamshire. **Nottinghamshire 346-9** (50 overs) (A. D. Brown 89, A. D. Hales 106, A. C. Voges 48, W. I. Jefferson 57*; P. Connell 4-71); **Ireland 212-9** (50 overs) (J. P. Bray 41, A. R. White 50*; M. A. Ealham 4-40, S. R. Patel 3-30). *Nottinghamshire 2 pts. County debut:* J. F. Brown (Nottinghamshire).

After a mighty scare against Ireland in 2008, Nottinghamshire racked up their highest limited-overs total thanks to a brilliant maiden century by 20-year-old Alex Hales, who combined with Ali Brown – almost twice his age – to put on 150 for the second wicket; Hales hit nine fours and a six from 92 balls; Brown whacked two sixes and 13 fours off just 57. With no one able to replicate that weight of stroke, Ireland finished well short; Mark Ealham and Samit Patel both profited.

At Leicester, May 4. **Leicestershire won by seven wickets.** Reduced to 31 overs a side. Toss: Leicestershire. **Ireland 197-5** (31 overs) (P. R. Stirling 80, K. J. O'Brien 67*); **Leicestershire 201-3** (29 overs) (H. D. Ackerman 118*, J. W. A. Taylor 48). *Leicestershire 2 pts.*

Rain reduced the match, which Leicestershire eventually won decisively, though they endured some uncomfortable moments. Paul Stirling's career-best 80 and Kevin O'Brien's run-a-ball 67* took Ireland to a useful total after being put in. H. D. Ackerman repeated his century against the Irish from the year before and ensured Leicestershire stayed ahead of the required rate. He and the enterprising James Taylor added 107.

At Worcester, May 4. **Worcestershire won by ten wickets** (D/L method). Reduced initially to 43 overs a side. Toss: Worcestershire. **Nottinghamshire 188-8** (40 overs) (M. A. Wagh 85, M. A. Ealham 42*; A. A. Noffke 3-37); **Worcestershire 138-0** (23.1 overs) (V. S. Solanki 49*, S. M. Davies 82*). *Worcestershire 2 pts.*

Steve Davies and Vikram Solanki made light of a revised target of 138 in 26 overs after rain interrupted both innings. Earlier, Ashley Noffke marked his first home match at New Road by picking up two wickets in his first over; Mark Wagh's anchor innings and a late bash by Mark Ealham helped Nottinghamshire to recover.

At Eglinton, May 10. **Ireland v Hampshire. Abandoned.** *Ireland 1 pt, Hampshire 1 pt.*

At Nottingham, May 10. **Nottinghamshire won by four wickets.** Toss: Nottinghamshire. **Worcestershire 209-8** (50 overs) (M. M. Ali 58, D. K. H. Mitchell 59); **Nottinghamshire 211-6** (44.3 overs) (M. A. Wagh 52, S. R. Patel 45, A. C. Voges 35*, P. J. Franks 37*). *Nottinghamshire 2 pts.*

The Nottinghamshire attack applied pressure from the outset, and although half-centuries from Moeen Ali and Daryl Mitchell pushed Worcestershire past 200, it was not enough to defend. Despite a wobble in the middle of the Nottinghamshire chase, after Mark Wagh had hit his third fifty in four innings, Adam Voges and Paul Franks put them back on top of the group with 61 in 12 overs.

At Southampton, May 12. **Hampshire won by six wickets.** Toss: Nottinghamshire. **Nottinghamshire 202** (49.1 overs) (W. I. Jefferson 93, P. J. Franks 50; A. D. Mascarenhas 4-39, D. G. Cork 3-13, B. V. Taylor 3-40); **Hampshire 203-4** (43.2 overs) (M. J. Lumb 57, S. M. Ervine 34, M. A. Carberry 42*, C. C. Benham 30). *Hampshire 2 pts.* County debut: D. R. Briggs (Hampshire).

Dimitri Mascarenhas, back in charge after IPL duty with the Rajasthan Royals, took three early wickets, and Nottinghamshire, 50-6 after winning the toss, were indebted to Will Jefferson and Paul Franks, who added 94 for the seventh wicket. Hampshire's top five batsmen all contributed towards a comfortable win. For Nottinghamshire, only Ryan Sidebottom (2-39 in ten overs) made much impression with the ball.

At Worcester, May 12. **Leicestershire won by 18 runs.** Toss: Leicestershire. **Leicestershire 282-3** (50 overs) (M. A. G. Boyce 32, H. D. Ackerman 63, J. W. A. Taylor 101, H. H. Dippenaar 63*); **Worcestershire 264** (48.2 overs) (S. M. Davies 62, S. C. Moore 51, B. F. Smith 54, D. K. H. Mitchell 30; C. W. Henderson 3-44). *Leicestershire 2 pts.*

Former Worcestershire academy player James Taylor was the dominant figure, hitting a maiden one-day century and making two smart run-outs. His 109-ball innings on a flat pitch contained seven fours and a six, and he shared partnerships of 90 with H. D. Ackerman and 121 with Boeta Dippenaar. Steve Davies made a fluent 62, and the game was in the balance when Ben Smith and Daryl Mitchell added 71. But Taylor's run-out of Mitchell at 214-5 proved the turning point, and a late onslaught by Ashley Noffke could not deny Leicestershire.

At Dublin, May 14. **Ireland v Leicestershire. Abandoned.** *Ireland 1 pt, Leicestershire 1 pt.*

At Worcester, May 14. **Worcestershire won by 108 runs.** Toss: Worcestershire. **Worcestershire 246-8** (50 overs) (S. M. Davies 34, M. M. Ali 31, G. J. Batty 31, I. D. Fisher 31*; B. V. Taylor 3-37); **Hampshire 138** (38.5 overs) (C. C. Benham 42; C. D. Whelan 4-27). *Worcestershire 2 pts.*

In dank conditions, Ashley Noffke and Matt Mason reduced Hampshire to 28-4. Chris Whelan wrapped up the tail with three wickets in three overs to finish with his best one-day figures. All but one of the Worcestershire batsmen made double figures, and Ian Fisher produced a final fillip off 17 deliveries.

At Dublin, May 16. **Nottinghamshire won by two wickets.** Reduced to 34 overs a side. Toss: Nottinghamshire. **Ireland 140-8** (34 overs) (S. R. Patel 6-13); **Nottinghamshire 141-8** (33.5 overs) (A. D. Brown 32, W. I. Jefferson 31). *Nottinghamshire 2 pts.*

Samit Patel claimed career-best figures of 6-13 from seven overs, but the Nottinghamshire batsmen also found scoring difficult on a slow, low pitch. They still needed eight off the last over bowled by Andrew White and, after four singles off the first four balls, Paul Franks struck the fifth for four.

At Leicester, May 16. **No result.** Reduced to 31 overs a side. Toss: Worcestershire. **Worcestershire 67-1** (8 overs) (V. S. Solanki 43*) **v Leicestershire.** *Leicestershire 1 pt, Worcestershire 1 pt.*

After a delayed start, Vikram Solanki hit six fours and a six off 28 deliveries before rain returned.

At Southampton, May 18 (day/night). **Hampshire won by 77 runs.** Toss: Hampshire. **Hampshire 316-2** (50 overs) (S. M. Ervine 167*, M. A. Carberry 121*); **Ireland 239-9** (50 overs) (K. J. O'Brien 94, A. R. Cusack 41; D. G. Cork 4-20). *Hampshire 2 pts.*

Sean Ervine, who holds an Irish passport, hit a chanceless 167, the best one-day score at the Rose Bowl and the highest individual innings for Hampshire in a 50-over match. Ervine, who struck four sixes and 20 fours from 140 balls, and Michael Carberry, with three sixes and 11 fours from 124, added an unbroken 260 in 35 overs, Hampshire's best 50-over partnership for any wicket. Kevin O'Brien smacked six sixes in a valiant 94 for Ireland.*

At Leicester, May 19. **Nottinghamshire won by nine runs** (D/L method). Toss: Nottinghamshire. **Nottinghamshire 149-3** (35.3 overs) (M. A. Wagh 40, S. R. Patel 48*); **Leicestershire 67-5** (10 overs). *Nottinghamshire 2 pts.*

After rain halted the Nottinghamshire innings, Duckworth/Lewis set Leicestershire a target of 77 in ten overs. A break of more than four hours between innings meant there were few spectators to see them stifled by the spin of Samit Patel and Adam Voges.

At Nottingham, May 20. **Hampshire won by ten wickets.** Toss: Nottinghamshire. **Nottinghamshire 145** (46.1 overs) (M. A. Ealham 33*; D. G. Cork 4-18); **Hampshire 149-0** (29.1 overs) (M. J. Lumb 72*, J. H. K. Adams 73*). *Hampshire 2 pts.*

Dominic Cork held a return catch to remove Mark Wagh with the first ball of the match. Nottinghamshire collapsed to 68-7 before Mark Ealham steered them past their lowest score in this competition, 121, made in 2008 against Warwickshire. Michael Lumb and Jimmy Adams cruised to the meagre target with 125 balls to spare. Thankfully for Nottinghamshire, Ireland's shock defeat of Worcestershire gifted them an unexpected place in the quarter-finals along with Hampshire.

At Worcester, May 20. **Ireland won by 94 runs.** Toss: Worcestershire. **Ireland 152** (48.5 overs) (D. T. Johnston 39, W. K. McCallan 40; C. D. Whelan 3-22); **Worcestershire 58** (20.3 overs) (P. Connell 5-19). *Ireland 2 pts.*

Steve Rhodes, Worcestershire's director of cricket, made a public apology to supporters and admitted "harsh words" had been exchanged in the dressing-room after they were shot out for their lowest List A total. New Zealand-born paceman Peter Connell inflicted the early damage with five wickets in 14 balls, and the last four batsmen fell for eight runs. Ireland had earlier been reduced to 75-6, but a determined stand of 57 from Kyle McCallan and Trent Johnston took them to 152. Worcestershire lost their chance of a quarter-final place, while Ireland moved on to the World Twenty20 in good heart.

GROUP B

At Birmingham, April 19. **Somerset won by eight wickets.** Toss: Somerset. **Warwickshire 271-9** (50 overs) (I. R. Bell 108, J. O. Troughton 53; A. C. Thomas 3-65, Z. de Bruyn 3-30); **Somerset 272-2** (46 overs) (C. Kieswetter 138*, Z. de Bruyn 73*). *Somerset 2 pts. County debuts: K. H. D. Barker, S. A. Piolet (both Warwickshire).*

Craig Kieswetter followed up his maiden first-class century – made against Warwickshire at Taunton the previous day – with a match-winning 138, from 131 balls with three sixes and 14 fours. He shared a third-wicket stand of 188 with Zander de Bruyn, whose medium-pace had earlier undermined Warwickshire's middle order. Ian Bell's hundred stabilised the home side's innings; Keith Barker, a former Rochdale footballer, gave him useful support on debut with 28 in a seventh-wicket stand of 70.*

At Lord's, April 26. **Middlesex won by 162 runs.** Toss: Middlesex. **Middlesex 302-7** (50 overs) (B. A. Godleman 82, P. J. Hughes 74, N. R. D. Compton 38, E. J. G. Morgan 33, G. K. Berg 33; J. D. Nel 3-62); **Scotland 140** (37.1 overs) (G. M. Hamilton 30, K. J. Coetzer 45). *Middlesex 2 pts.*
    Middlesex were too strong for the Scots, and only Dewald Nel made any inroads, although he proved expensive. Phillip Hughes and Billy Godleman enjoyed an opening partnership of 147, Godleman hitting his highest List A score.

At Taunton, April 26. **Somerset won by 110 runs.** Reduced to 38 overs a side. Toss: Kent. **Somerset 291-3** (38 overs) (M. E. Trescothick 70, J. C. Hildreth 67, Z. de Bruyn 71*, P. D. Trego 73*); **Kent 181** (33.1 overs) (J. L. Denly 43, G. O. Jones 43*; O. A. C. Banks 3-40, A. C. Thomas 3-38). *Somerset 2 pts. County debut:* W. W. Lee (Kent).
    Invited to bat, Somerset displayed plenty of evidence of their formidable batting strength, with Peter Trego in an especial hurry: he whacked five sixes and six fours from 36 deliveries. His onslaught put the total well out of reach of Kent. The track offered little for the bowlers, but Alfonso Thomas and Omari Banks both claimed a trio of victims.

At Southgate, May 3. **Kent won by six wickets.** Toss: Middlesex. **Middlesex 133** (36.4 overs) (J. C. Tredwell 6-27); **Kent 137-4** (37.2 overs) (J. L. Denly 32, D. I. Stevens 37*). *Kent 2 pts.*
    James Tredwell demolished the Middlesex batting with 6-27, the first time he had taken more than four in a one-day game. Not even Phillip Hughes – he and Ben Scott were alone in passing 20 – could save them. Kent took their time, but were always in control.

At Birmingham, May 3. **Warwickshire won by seven wickets.** Toss: Warwickshire. **Scotland 182** (48.3 overs) (G. M. Hamilton 51, C. J. Borgas 59); **Warwickshire 183-3** (30.4 overs) (I. J. L. Trott 33, N. M. Carter 65, I. R. Bell 51*). *Warwickshire 2 pts. County debut:* J. S. Patel. *Scotland debuts:* C. J. Borgas, M. A. Parker.
    Neil Carter's opening assault – his 65 came from just 38 balls and included four sixes – and Ian Bell's calm fifty together sealed a facile win for Warwickshire. Former England all-rounder Gavin Hamilton, in his first game as Scotland's captain, made a half-century, as did the South Australian batsman Cameron Borgas on his debut as their overseas player.

At Canterbury, May 4. **Kent won by four wickets** (D/L method). Toss: Kent. **Scotland 227-7** (50 overs) (G. M. Hamilton 75, C. J. Borgas 65; R. H. Joseph 3-55); **Kent 206-6** (42.2 overs) (J. L. Denly 97*, M. van Jaarsveld 37). *Kent 2 pts.*
    The loss of six overs to rain improved Scotland's chances of an upset before Joe Denly's solid 129-ball innings helped a jittery Kent reach their revised target of 206 from 44 overs with ten balls to spare. Scotland's respectable total was built around a third-wicket stand of 84 between Gavin Hamilton and Cameron Borgas.

At Bath, May 4. **Somerset won by eight wickets.** Toss: Somerset. **Middlesex 65** (24.1 overs) (G. K. Berg 30; P. D. Trego 4-17, B. J. Phillips 3-23); **Somerset 66-2** (8.3 overs) (C. Kieswetter 36*). *Somerset 2 pts.*
    Bath, which contentiously lost its festival in 2006, deserved rather more play than this for its nominal compromise fixture. Those with long memories were left to regret the lack of atmosphere in this early visit, only nine days after the last rugby match on the shared ground. Somerset, with an eye on the clouds, shot past Middlesex's threadbare total in just eight and a half overs. Peter Trego excelled with his swing bowling and was twice on a hat-trick. Gareth Berg alone made double figures as the Middlesex batting failed for the second day running.

At Canterbury, May 10. **Kent won by four wickets.** Toss: Warwickshire. **Warwickshire 218** (49.2 overs) (I. J. L. Trott 53, J. O. Troughton 62; W. D. Parnell 3-27, R. S. Ferley 3-34); **Kent 219-6** (41.5 overs) (J. L. Denly 49, G. O. Jones 35, J. M. Kemp 45*). *Kent 2 pts.*
    Justin Kemp kept his expansive shots under wraps during an unbeaten 52-ball 45 that steered Kent to a third straight win with eight overs to spare. Left-arm paceman Wayne Parnell, warming up before South Africa's ICC World Twenty20 campaign, bowled Neil Carter and Ian Bell in successive overs to restrict Warwickshire to a total which hardly caused Kent or Kemp to break sweat.*

At Canterbury, May 11. **Middlesex won by 80 runs.** Toss: Middlesex. **Middlesex 322-5** (50 overs) (N. R. D. Compton 131, E. J. G. Morgan 161); **Kent 242** (45.4 overs) (G. O. Jones 57, J. M. Kemp 69; C. E. W. Silverwood 3-26). *Middlesex 2 pts.*

A record Middlesex one-day stand of 277 between a graceful Nick Compton and an impudent Eoin Morgan lifted them to their highest 50-over total – although it was exceeded within a week. They came together at 31-2 after Owais Shah, back from sitting on the bench for the Delhi Daredevils in the IPL, was out for a second-ball duck. Compton and Morgan, who became the first pair to score centuries in the same one-day game against Kent, reached a crescendo by pilfering 64 powerplay runs as both set personal-bests. Kent were flagging once Chris Silverwood removed Rob Key and Martin van Jaarsveld to reduce them to 40-3.

At Taunton, May 11. **Somerset won by 151 runs.** Toss: Scotland. **Somerset 403-3** (50 overs) (M. E. Trescothick 144, J. C. Hildreth 151, P. D. Trego 74*); **Scotland 252-9** (50 overs) (G. M. Hamilton 62, R. R. Watson 67, N. F. I. McCallum 50; P. D. Trego 3-43, A. C. Thomas 3-46). *Somerset 2 pts.*

Somerset romped to their highest total in 50-over cricket as Marcus Trescothick and James Hildreth added 270 for the second wicket in an awesome display of aggression. Trescothick's 144 came from just 108 deliveries, Hildreth's career-best 151 from 141; both hit 13 fours, while Trescothick added a couple of sixes. Peter Trego faced just 39 balls for his 74, and hit four sixes. Jan Stander came in for particularly brutal treatment. Scotland gained some consolation by hitting a respectable total, even if the result was never in doubt.*

MOST EXPENSIVE BOWLING FIGURES IN LIST A GAMES

10–0–113–0	M. L. Lewis	Australia v South Africa at Johannesburg	2005-06
9–0–108–3	S. D. Thomas	Glamorgan v Surrey at The Oval	2002
10–0–107–0	J. W. Dernbach	Surrey v Essex at The Oval	2008
12–0–107–2	C. C. Lovell	Cornwall v Warwickshire at St Austell	1996
12–0–106–2	D. A. Gallop	Oxfordshire v Warwickshire at Birmingham	1984
10–0–106–1	**J. H. Stander**	**Scotland v Somerset at Taunton**	**2009**
12–0–105–1	S. R. Porter	Oxfordshire v Warwickshire at Birmingham	1984
12–1–105–2	M. C. Snedden	New Zealand v England at The Oval	1983
10–0–105–0	**T. G. Southee**	**New Zealand v India at Christchurch**	**2008-09**
12–0–103–3	J. P. Govett	Berkshire v Leicestershire at Leicester	1996
11–0–103–5	P. D. Heger	G. A. Minkley's XI v R. G. Pollock's XI at Port Elizabeth	1969-70
11–0–103–0	G. Welch	Warwickshire v Lancashire at Birmingham	1995
12–2–101–0	K. Donohue	Devon v Somerset at Torquay	1990
11–0–101–2	A. Weir	Eastern Transvaal Country Districts v Natal at Witbank	1991-92

At Birmingham, May 12. **Warwickshire won by six wickets.** Toss: Middlesex. **Middlesex 165** (47.3 overs) (E. J. G. Morgan 62, D. J. Malan 43; N. M. Carter 3-40); **Warwickshire 166-4** (35.4 overs) (N. M. Carter 56, I. R. Bell 60*). *Warwickshire 2 pts.*

Ian Bell, given permission to play before travelling to Durham to join the England squad, made the most of the opportunity by scoring an unbeaten 60 from 82 balls after Neil Carter had softened up the bowling with another rapid fifty. Eoin Morgan again top-scored for Middlesex but needed two more balls – 95 – to complete his fifty than it took him to make a century the previous day. Tim Ambrose claimed a one-day Warwickshire record of seven dismissals: five catches and two stumpings.

At Edinburgh, May 14. **Middlesex won by 138 runs.** Toss: Middlesex. **Middlesex 280-4** (50 overs) (N. R. D. Compton 44*, O. A. Shah 42, E. J. G. Morgan 55, S. D. Udal 79*, N. J. Dexter 37*); **Scotland 142** (34.3 overs) (R. R. Watson 47; S. D. Udal 3-32). *Middlesex 2 pts.*

After four defeats on the road, the Scots were outplayed in all departments. Shaun Udal, dropped six times, rode his luck to bludgeon his best one-day score with three sixes and five fours off 46 balls – and he followed this with three wickets. A second-wicket stand of 53 between Ryan Watson and Fraser Watts was the only redeeming feature of an insipid Scottish batting display.

At Taunton, May 14. **No result.** Toss: Warwickshire. **Somerset 135-2** (22 overs) (M. E. Trescothick 84*, J. C. Hildreth 33) **v Warwickshire.** *Somerset 1 pt, Warwickshire 1 pt.*

Marcus Trescothick was going strongly with 13 boundaries from 69 balls when the rain arrived. It was not the perfect day to welcome back West Indian favourite Joel Garner for the official opening of eponymous gates at the ground.

At Canterbury, May 16. **Somerset won by 45 runs.** Toss: Somerset. **Somerset 296** (50 overs) (M. E. Trescothick 56, Z. de Bruyn 72, J. L. Langer 77; W. D. Parnell 3-43, S. J. Cook 3-29); **Kent 251-9** (50 overs) (M. van Jaarsveld 132*; P. D. Trego 4-56, A. C. Thomas 3-48). *Somerset 2 pts. County debut:* M. T. C. Waller (Somerset).

Martin van Jaarsveld equalled his previous best, but his unbeaten century came in a losing cause as he watched his partners fall to Peter Trego and Alfonso Thomas. The Somerset batsmen cashed in on a sublime track until they lost six for 20 in five overs, but victory secured progress to the quarter-finals.

At Edinburgh, May 16. **Warwickshire won by 50 runs** (D/L method). Toss: Scotland. **Warwickshire 242-6** (50 overs) (J. O. Troughton 77, A. G. Botha 37*, K. H. D. Barker 30*); **Scotland 187** (43.4 overs) (G. M. Hamilton 30, C. J. Borgas 35; A. G. Botha 3-27). *Warwickshire 2 pts.*

Scotland's run-chase was bizarrely interrupted by a visiting supporter who came on to the field of play, helped himself to a bail, and legged it over the perimeter wall and into the Edinburgh afternoon. Neil McCallum, who had made a run-a-ball 22, was dismissed as soon as a replacement was found, and the Scots fell 50 short of their revised target of 238 from 48 overs. Scotland skipper Gavin Hamilton called the chap an "idiot" who upset the momentum of their chase when they were going strongly at 131-3. Earlier, Jim Troughton held the Warwickshire innings together with a patient 77.

At Lord's, May 17. **Somerset won by five wickets** (D/L method). Toss: Somerset. **Middlesex 341-7** (50 overs) (P. J. Hughes 119, O. A. Shah 82, N. J. Dexter 65*; P. D. Trego 4-65); **Somerset 293-5** (39.1 overs) (M. E. Trescothick 62, C. Kieswetter 40, Z. de Bruyn 70, J. L. Langer 78*; S. T. Finn 3-67). *Somerset 2 pts.*

Middlesex made their highest score in one-day cricket thanks largely to Phillip Hughes and Owais Shah, who added 151 for the second wicket. Hughes hit two sixes and 12 fours off 112 balls to reach his maiden List A century. But rain in the interval reduced the Somerset reply by two overs, and a further shower led to a revised target of 290 in 41 overs – in practice 81 off 56 deliveries – which made it a shade too easy for Justin Langer, who saw Somerset home with time to spare. They also benefited from three extra powerplay overs due to a miscalculation by umpires Peter Willey and Michael Gough, which led to a complaint from Middlesex. However, the ECB "decided to uphold the precedent that umpire errors cannot form the basis to declare a match null and void". The official statement added: "ECB has great sympathy for the position in which Middlesex CCC has been placed but a replay cannot be ordered in these circumstances."

At Lord's, May 18. **Middlesex won by four wickets.** Toss: Middlesex. **Warwickshire 276-7** (50 overs) (I. J. L. Trott 120, N. M. Carter 68, I. J. Westwood 33); **Middlesex 278-6** (49.3 overs) (P. J. Hughes 63, O. A. Shah 63, N. J. Dexter 69*; A. G. Botha 3-47). *Middlesex 2 pts.*

As on the day before, the major contributions came from Phillip Hughes – playing his last game before returning to Australia for a pre-Ashes boot camp – Owais Shah and Neil Dexter. Despite a blistering start by Neil Carter, Warwickshire ended with a total just below par; Jonathan Trott was dismissed from the last ball of the innings, having hit ten fours from 142 balls.

At Edinburgh, May 18. **Scotland won by nine wickets** (D/L method). Reduced to 37 overs a side. Toss: Scotland. **Kent 65-4** (19.5 overs); **Scotland 80-1** (14.5 overs) (D. F. Watts 45). *Scotland 2 pts.*

The Scots traditionally claim at least one county scalp during these jousts, and they took advantage of the elements to claim a first-ever win over Kent. Chasing 77 in 18 overs, Fraser Watts led the way with 45 from 38 balls, hitting two sixes and six fours; Gavin Hamilton and Ryan Watson completed the task, giving Hamilton his first victory since replacing Watson as captain. Kent's hopes of setting a stiff target were upset by Sean Weeraratna, who removed Joe Denly and Martin van Jaarsveld.

At Edinburgh, May 20. **Somerset won by 37 runs.** Toss: Scotland. **Somerset 220-8** (50 overs) (C. Kieswetter 42, A. V. Suppiah 48, J. L. Langer 39; J. H. Stander 3-45); **Scotland 183** (46.2 overs) (C. J. Borgas 78*; Z. de Bruyn 3-24, A. C. Thomas 4-22). *Somerset 2 pts.*

Scotland could – and probably should – have won again after a fine display in the field. There was little chance of Somerset matching their 403-3 achieved at Taunton nine days earlier as wickets fell at regular intervals to a hungry fielding side. However, a series of soft Scots dismissals saw Cameron Borgas stranded.

At Birmingham, May 20. **Tied** (D/L method). Toss: Warwickshire. **Kent 265** (49.2 overs) (J. L. Denly 115, J. B. Hockley 50; S. A. Piolet 3-53); **Warwickshire 241-6** (46.5 overs) (I. J. L. Trott 36,

N. M. Carter 37, J. O. Troughton 67, T. R. Ambrose 36*; S. J. Cook 4-37). *Warwickshire 1 pt, Kent 1 pt.*

Warwickshire missed out on a place in the quarter-finals after a downpour halted play with them needing 25 from 19 balls. Despite urgent mopping up, play could not resume, and Duckworth/Lewis put the scores level. Middlesex, who like Warwickshire ended on eight points, went through by virtue of one more win. Joe Denly, hitting his third and highest one-day century, added 116 for the sixth wicket with James Hockley. After Jim Troughton had raced to his fourth half-century in six innings, Warwickshire stumbled when Simon Cook took three wickets in six balls, but Tim Ambrose and Keith Barker hammered 55 before the rain arrived.

GROUP C

At Chester-le-Street, April 19. **Yorkshire won by 80 runs.** Toss: Durham. **Yorkshire 268-7** (50 overs) (J. A. Rudolph 73, M. P. Vaughan 43, G. L. Brophy 66*); **Durham 188** (41 overs) (D. M. Benkenstein 68; T. T. Bresnan 3-28, G. J. Kruis 3-28). *Yorkshire 2 pts.*

Four South Africans dominated, with Yorkshire's trio upstaging Dale Benkenstein, who attempted to revive Durham after their reply was strangled by Deon Kruis. Jacques Rudolph had built the platform for Yorkshire, and Gerard Brophy's unbeaten 48-ball knock gave crucial impetus. The non-South African Michael Vaughan showed glimpses of form, stroking six boundaries from 44 deliveries.

At Bristol, April 19. **Gloucestershire won by seven wickets.** Toss: Gloucestershire. **Sussex 227** (49.5 overs) (M. J. Prior 50, L. J. Wright 40, M. H. Yardy 58; V. Banerjee 3-47); **Gloucestershire 228-3** (46.2 overs) (A. P. R. Gidman 43, C. M. Spearman 69*, C. G. Taylor 68*). *Gloucestershire 2 pts. County debut: D. G. Wright (Sussex).*

John Bracewell's new era as coach got off to a good start as Gloucestershire made a well-paced reply to a patchy Sussex innings, which needed Mike Yardy's fifty to set a challenge. In the event, Craig Spearman and Chris Taylor were untroubled in their stand of 122. Vikram Banerjee, making his List A debut five years after his first-class debut (for Cambridge in the 2004 Varsity Match), claimed three wickets: Matt Prior and, off consecutive deliveries, Rory Hamilton-Brown and Robin Martin-Jenkins. For Sussex, Will Beer and Joe Gatting were also making their one-day debuts.

At Bristol, April 26. **Gloucestershire won by 128 runs.** Toss: Surrey. **Gloucestershire 268-9** (50 overs) (W. T. S. Porterfield 74, A. P. R. Gidman 31, C. G. Taylor 63, J. Lewis 32; A. Nel 3-39); **Surrey 140** (38.2 overs) (U. Afzaal 36; I. D. Saxelby 4-31). *Gloucestershire 2 pts. County debut: G. D. Elliott (Surrey).*

Will Porterfield had been due to captain Ireland in the FPT, but Gloucestershire called him up when Craig Spearman was injured, and he responded with the day's top score, from 84 deliveries. A late surge by Chris Taylor and Jon Lewis, who added 60 for the seventh wicket, left Surrey regretting their decision to bowl and, when Mark Ramprakash fell for a fifth-ball duck, it was clear they were going to struggle. Ian Saxelby, a right-arm seamer whose uncles Mark and Kevin played for Nottinghamshire, kept a tight line on his List A debut.

At Leeds, April 26. **Yorkshire won by 14 runs.** Toss: Sussex. **Yorkshire 227-5** (50 overs) (M. P. Vaughan 82, G. L. Brophy 68*, A. Shahzad 43*; R. S. C. Martin-Jenkins 3-49); **Sussex 213** (48.4 overs) (M. W. Goodwin 45, L. J. Wright 46, Extras 30; T. T. Bresnan 4-35). *Yorkshire 2 pts.*

Michael Vaughan helped Yorkshire recover from three early wickets and the handicap of a slow pitch and outfield. He hit four fours and three sixes, putting on 117 for the fourth wicket with Gerard Brophy, who ran all but eight of his runs. Vaughan, bowled by Robin Martin-Jenkins, awaited confirmation from the umpire that his off bail had not been dislodged by wicketkeeper Matt Prior's gloves. Tim Bresnan dismissed the Sussex openers before Murray Goodwin and Luke Wright briefly revived hopes with a stand of 90. Brophy added four catches and a stumping.

At Chester-le-Street, May 3. **Durham won by one run.** Toss: Durham. **Durham 266-7** (50 overs) (P. Mustard 61, D. M. Benkenstein 77*, L. E. Plunkett 30); **Surrey 265-6** (50 overs) (S. A. Newman 70, M. R. Ramprakash 109*; I. D. Blackwell 3-43). *Durham 2 pts.*

Surrey looked to be sailing home as Mark Ramprakash completed a classic century by hitting the last two balls of a Liam Plunkett over for four and six. The target was 16 off three overs with six wickets left. Five were still needed from the last, bowled by Ian Blackwell, and it came down to two off two balls. Ramprakash could only watch as Grant Elliott was caught at mid-off and Jon Batty at deep midwicket.

At Leeds, May 3. **Gloucestershire won by 28 runs.** Toss: Gloucestershire. **Gloucestershire 269** (49 overs) (Kadeer Ali 63, W. T. S. Porterfield 37, C. M. Spearman 92; R. M. Pyrah 4-54); **Yorkshire 241-8** (50 overs) (A. W. Gale 33, J. A. Rudolph 118, J. J. Sayers 30; J. Lewis 3-46). *Gloucestershire 2 pts.*

Unruffled batting from Craig Spearman and Kadeer Ali, followed by tight bowling and astute field placings, earned Gloucestershire a well-merited victory, despite Jacques Rudolph batting for all but two balls of Yorkshire's reply. However, Rudolph never controlled events sufficiently to keep up with the rate, and the target was out of range before the end. Gloucestershire might have made more, but Richard Pyrah wrapped up the innings with four wickets in 11 balls. Simon Guy took a catch and made a stumping on his return to Yorkshire three months after undergoing surgery to remove a cerebral abscess.

At Chester-le-Street, May 4. **Sussex won by eight wickets.** Toss: Durham. **Durham 192** (48.2 overs) (W. R. Smith 65; R. J. Hamilton-Brown 3-37); **Sussex 193-2** (43.2 overs) (E. C. Joyce 103*, J. S. Gatting 48). *Sussex 2 pts.*

In cold, gloomy conditions, Durham were throttled by three spinners – Rory Hamilton-Brown, Will Beer and Mike Yardy – on a sluggish pitch. Their modest total allowed Sussex to pick off the runs at leisure. Ed Joyce and Joe Gatting put on 117 for the first wicket, Joyce eventually bringing up his first hundred since joining Sussex with the winning hit.

At Leeds, May 4. **Surrey won by 63 runs** (D/L method). Reduced to 47 overs a side. Toss: Surrey. **Surrey 184-7** (47 overs) (M. N. W. Spriegel 56*, G. C. Wilson 34); **Yorkshire 104** (30.2 overs) (Naved-ul-Hasan 49; J. W. Dernbach 3-23, C. P. Schofield 3-16, G. D. Elliott 4-14). *Surrey 2 pts.*

Martyn Moxon, Yorkshire's director of cricket, was so distraught at the squandering, before an interruption for rain, of five wickets for four runs that he confronted an elderly supporter who had complained loudly about the team's attitude. "I tried to explain to him it wasn't about attitude," Moxon said. "It was that we didn't bat well enough." Yorkshire were cantering at 63-1 but the introduction of Chris Schofield and Grant Elliott created panic. Naved-ul-Hasan, the pinch-hitter, was denied the strike by slow batting from Michael Vaughan, and when Vaughan departed the rest quickly followed. Rain intervened at 86-7 and, on the resumption, Yorkshire needed an impossible 82 off 4.5 overs.

At Bristol, May 10. **Gloucestershire won by 148 runs.** Toss: Gloucestershire. **Gloucestershire 301-8** (50 overs) (H. J. H. Marshall 56, W. T. S. Porterfield 68, C. G. Taylor 71, S. J. Adshead 39*); **Durham 153** (40.3 overs) (G. R. Breese 47; J. E. C. Franklin 3-18, A. J. Ireland 3-12). *Gloucestershire 2 pts.*

Hamish Marshall and Will Porterfield put on 116 for the second wicket, and Chris Taylor made his third half-century in four FPT innings, at a run a ball. Durham never got going, and were well beaten.

At Hove, May 10. **Sussex won by two runs.** Toss: Sussex. **Sussex 313-7** (50 overs) (J. S. Gatting 34, M. W. Goodwin 144, M. H. Yardy 59, R. J. Hamilton-Brown 43; P. T. Collins 3-56); **Surrey 311-6** (50 overs) (S. A. Newman 130, M. J. Brown 66, S. J. Walters 49, G. D. Elliott 30*). *Sussex 2 pts.*

Chris Adams, returning to Hove for the first time since becoming Surrey coach, was given a reminder of the skill of Murray Goodwin, who powered to his ninth one-day hundred for Sussex. He went to three figures off 99 balls, and hit two sixes and 16 fours in all, adding 135 for the fourth wicket with Mike Yardy. Scott Newman and Michael Brown responded with an opening partnership of 154 – an all-wicket record for Surrey against Sussex. Newman struck three sixes and ten fours from 126 balls. The later batsmen struggled to match the run-rate: 15 were needed off the final over; five from the last ball, when James Kirtley delivered the perfect yorker to thwart Grant Elliott.

At Bristol, May 11. **Gloucestershire won by three wickets.** Toss: Gloucestershire. **Yorkshire 217-9** (50 overs) (A. McGrath 67, R. M. Pyrah 67; J. Lewis 4-43, J. E. C. Franklin 3-38); **Gloucestershire 221-7** (49.2 overs) (W. T. S. Porterfield 34, J. E. C. Franklin 51*, S. J. Adshead 56; G. J. Kruis 3-45, D. J. Wainwright 3-33). *Gloucestershire 2 pts.*

David Wainwright's left-arm spin brought three wickets in seven balls at no cost, but Gloucestershire marched on to a fifth straight win. All the batsmen struggled on a slow wicket until James Franklin and Steve Adshead added 106 for the seventh wicket in 18 overs. Yorkshire were 49-5 before Richard Pyrah and Anthony McGrath put on 115.

At Hove, May 11. Sussex won by 56 runs. Toss: Sussex. **Sussex 313-6** (50 overs) (E. C. Joyce 127, J. S. Gatting 50); **Durham 257** (46.5 overs) (M. J. Di Venuto 32, P. Mustard 92, W. R. Smith 30; R. J. Kirtley 6-50). *Sussex 2 pts.*

The pitch on which 624 runs were scored the previous day again favoured the batsmen. Ed Joyce hit his second century of the competition against Durham, sharing an opening partnership of 110 with Joe Gatting. Durham were in the hunt until James Kirtley's devastating mix of yorkers and slower balls gave him a career-best return.

At The Oval, May 13. Surrey won by 164 runs. Toss: Gloucestershire. **Surrey 306-6** (50 overs) (M. J. Brown 34, M. R. Ramprakash 121, U. Afzaal 34, M. N. W. Spriegel 64); **Gloucestershire 142** (33.3 overs) (W. T. S. Porterfield 42). *Surrey 2 pts.*

A peerless hundred by Mark Ramprakash led to a dominant total. He struck three sixes and nine fours, adding 94 with Usman Afzaal and 96 with Matthew Spriegel. The shame was that at an overcast Oval there were so few to witness it. Gloucestershire lost their last seven wickets for 33, and with them their unbeaten record in the competition.

At Leeds, May 13. Yorkshire won by two wickets. Toss: Durham. **Durham 166** (49.3 overs) (G. J. Muchall 31; R. M. Pyrah 3-23); **Yorkshire 167-8** (49.2 overs) (J. J. Sayers 51, R. M. Pyrah 42*; I. D. Blackwell 3-26). *Yorkshire 2 pts.*

Richard Pyrah, having claimed three cheap wickets, snatched the game from Durham's grasp by adding 37 for the ninth wicket with David Wainwright, who had also bowled tightly. Yorkshire lost Jacques Rudolph first ball but Joe Sayers anchored the innings until Pyrah took control. The victory ended Yorkshire's run of three defeats.

At The Oval, May 15. Durham won by 60 runs. Toss: Durham. **Durham 287-4** (50 overs) (K. J. Coetzer 61, W. R. Smith 77, I. D. Blackwell 57, D. M. Benkenstein 45*); **Surrey 227** (47.2 overs) (S. A. Newman 53, M. R. Ramprakash 36, U. Afzaal 58, C. P. Schofield 31; G. R. Breese 3-42). *Durham 2 pts. County debut: B. A. Stokes (Durham).*

Ben Stokes, born in New Zealand on June 6, 1991 – the day Mark Ramprakash started his Test career – marked his debut by bowling Ramprakash with his third legitimate delivery. Stokes, who just had time to reach double figures in the Durham innings, also dismissed Matthew Spriegel. Surrey, ruled out of the knockout stages by this defeat, had no answer to Durham's batting firepower. Durham, already eliminated, at least ended their high-mileage tour on a high: they had been on the road for four matches in six days while Riverside hosted a Test.

At Hove, May 15 (day/night). No result. Toss: Gloucestershire. **Gloucestershire 306-9** (50 overs) (H. J. H. Marshall 32, W. T. S. Porterfield 31, A. P. R. Gidman 35, C. M. Spearman 67, J. E. C. Franklin 48, S. J. Adshead 66*) **v Sussex.** *Sussex 1 pt, Gloucestershire 1 pt.*

Sussex were prevented from starting their reply by rain during the interval. For the third game running at Hove the side batting first scored more than 300, with the resourceful James Franklin featuring in key stands with Craig Spearman and Steve Adshead, who both made forceful half-centuries.

At Hove, May 18. Sussex won by 60 runs. Toss: Sussex. **Sussex 269-7** (50 overs) (E. C. Joyce 47, M. H. Yardy 68; R. M. Pyrah 3-65); **Yorkshire 209** (47.3 overs) (M. P. Vaughan 66, A. McGrath 53; Yasir Arafat 3-44, C. D. Nash 4-40). *Sussex 2 pts.*

Chris Nash an unlikely hero as Sussex secured a quarter-final spot. He claimed career-best figures with his little-used off-breaks as Yorkshire folded after Anthony McGrath and Michael Vaughan had given them hope on a slow pitch with a third-wicket stand of 102. All the Sussex batsmen made contributions, led by Mike Yardy, and 77 came off the last ten overs. Yasir Arafat took his 300th List A wicket.

At The Oval, May 19. Surrey won by 79 runs (D/L method). Toss: Sussex. **Surrey 241-7** (39 overs) (M. J. Brown 33, M. R. Ramprakash 102); **Sussex 162** (30 overs) (J. S. Gatting 37, C. B. Keegan 38; C. P. Schofield 5-32). *Surrey 2 pts. County debut: C. B. Keegan.*

The weather limited proceedings to 39 overs per side, but could not reduce Mark Ramprakash's appetite for runs. He scored his third hundred in six Trophy innings, and was going strongly when he was run out after cracking five sixes and five fours off 94 deliveries. Chad Keegan clobbered three sixes in an over from Usman Afzaal, but by then Chris Schofield had wrenched the heart out of the Sussex reply with the second five-for of his one-day career. With limited interest in the game – Sussex had already qualified for the knockout stage and Surrey could not – tickets were given to children from 100 schools.

At Chester-le-Street, May 20. **Durham won by four wickets.** Toss: Durham. **Gloucestershire 254-8** (50 overs) (C. G. Taylor 36, J. E. C. Franklin 85, S. J. Adshead 87; N. Killeen 5-48); **Durham 255-6** (48.1 overs) (P. Mustard 57, K. J. Coetzer 36, I. D. Blackwell 64, D. M. Benkenstein 44; V. Banerjee 3-60). *Durham 2 pts.*

Following noon starts in the three other ties at Riverside, this started at 10.45, and Gloucestershire found batting tricky in the first hour. They were revived from 72-5 by a sixth-wicket stand of 175 between James Franklin and Steve Adshead. Neil Killeen, in his first appearance of the season, took three wickets in the 49th over to complete a five-wicket haul. Durham's well-paced reply saw them home decisively, but they had no chance of further progress. Gloucestershire had already booked a home quarter-final, which gave them a headache as their Bristol headquarters were needed for England's one-day international against West Indies the following day.

At The Oval, May 20. **Yorkshire won by four wickets.** Toss: Surrey. **Surrey 329-8** (50 overs) (S. A. Newman 177, M. J. Brown 31, S. J. Walters 85; G. J. Kruis 3-24, Naved-ul-Hasan 3-75); **Yorkshire 330-6** (49.4 overs) (J. A. Rudolph 37, M. P. Vaughan 74, A. Lyth 83, A. U. Rashid 35*, Naved-ul-Hasan 53*). *Yorkshire 2 pts.*

A dead match came to life in a thunderous finish as Naved-ul-Hasan brought victory by smashing a six and three fours off the first four balls of the final over, bowled by Andre Nel. Scott Newman dominated the Surrey innings with a career-best 177 off 156 deliveries, with four sixes and 19 fours. Stewart Walters contributed 85 and shared a second-wicket stand of 211 with Newman, before five wickets fell for one run. Brisk half-centuries by Michael Vaughan and Adam Lyth set the stage for the dramatic finale.

GROUP D

At Chelmsford, April 19. **Essex won by seven wickets.** Toss: Northamptonshire. **Northamptonshire 281** (50 overs) (R. A. White 47, N. Boje 56, M. H. Wessels 57, S. P. Crook 72); **Essex 282-3** (48.2 overs) (M. L. Pettini 57, V. Chopra 76, M. J. Walker 69*, G. W. Flower 42*). *Essex 2 pts. County debut:* L. M. Daggett (Northamptonshire).

Essex began their defence of the title without Ravi Bopara, Graham Napier (both at the IPL), Danish Kaneria (awaiting a new visa) and Alastair Cook, nursing a broken finger. A mid-order revival by Northamptonshire, encouraged by Steven Crook's career-best, appeared to set a stiff test, but Essex paced their reply perfectly as Mark Pettini and Varun Chopra formed a platform on which veterans Matt Walker, newly arrived from Kent, and Grant Flower, hero of the 2008 Trophy final, built 88 in 12 overs.

At Manchester, April 19. **Lancashire won by 80 runs.** Toss: Glamorgan. **Lancashire 241-6** (50 overs) (T. C. Smith 66, F. du Plessis 66; D. S. Harrison 3-44); **Glamorgan 161** (40.2 overs) (B. J. Wright 34, M. A. Wallace 60; K. W. Hogg 3-21, S. I. Mahmood 3-17). *Lancashire 2 pts.*

Peter Moores's first competitive game as Lancashire's coach, and Glen Chapple's as captain, produced a comfortable win in spring sunshine, helped by surprise appearances from James Anderson, made available at the last moment by England, and Francois du Plessis, who had only arrived from South Africa the previous day. He jointly top-scored with Tom Smith, promoted to open in the most notable move by Moores. Glamorgan, under their new captain Jamie Dalrymple, were undone by Sajid Mahmood and Kyle Hogg.

At Derby, April 26. **Derbyshire won by four wickets.** Toss: Derbyshire. **Glamorgan 205-9** (50 overs) (M. J. Powell 32, J. W. M. Dalrymple 75*; T. D. Groenewald 3-33); **Derbyshire 206-6** (46 overs) (D. J. Redfern 53, D. S. Stubbings 32, G. T. Park 43*). *Derbyshire 2 pts. County debut:* T. D. Groenewald (Derbyshire).

Spin bowlers kept a firm grip on the run-rate throughout the match. Jake Needham and Mark Lawson conceded 64 in their 20 overs and took three wickets as Jamie Dalrymple held the Glamorgan innings together. Derbyshire were 85 without loss in the 19th over, but Dean Cosker and Dalrymple allowed just 55 from their 20 overs and shared four wickets. Wobbling on 108-4, Derbyshire were steadied by Garry Park's diligent 81-ball 43.*

At Northampton, April 26. **Lancashire won by six wickets.** Toss: Lancashire. **Northamptonshire 240** (47.3 overs) (A. J. Hall 81, M. H. Wessels 45; S. I. Mahmood 3-38, T. C. Smith 3-52); **Lancashire 241-4** (44.5 overs) (P. J. Horton 100, M. J. Chilton 41, S. J. Croft 35*). *Lancashire 2 pts.*

Paul Horton's maiden one-day century, from 108 balls, put Lancashire on course for victory with plenty to spare. Ashwell Prince's golden duck was a minor blip as Mark Chilton shared a third-wicket stand of 120 with Horton. Northamptonshire earlier committed the cardinal sin of failing to bat out their overs. Andrew Hall and Riki Wessels caught the eye, but Sajid Mahmood and Gary Keedy (1-31) gave little away.

At Chelmsford, May 3. **Glamorgan won by eight wickets.** Toss: Glamorgan. **Essex 297-6** (50 overs) (J. E. R. Gallian 38, V. Chopra 99, G. W. Flower 54, G. R. Napier 42); **Glamorgan 299-2** (46.1 overs) (G. P. Rees 123*, M. J. Cosgrove 72, M. J. Powell 33, T. L. Maynard 59*). *Glamorgan 2 pts.*

Mark Cosgrove struck 72 from 36 balls to give Glamorgan an explosive start to their chase. He pulled a muscle hitting one of three sixes and continued with a runner – little used, since 58 of his runs came in boundaries – and was eventually out with the score on 80. Gareth Rees then took over, reaching his maiden one-day hundred and adding 133 with Tom Maynard. Graham Napier, who had just returned from the IPL, belted 42 from 18 deliveries, but this was Glamorgan's day. It was only their third 50-over victory in 29 matches.

At Manchester, May 3. **Lancashire won by eight wickets.** Toss: Lancashire. **Derbyshire 240-6** (50 overs) (S. D. Stubbings 50, W. W. Hinds 95); **Lancashire 241-2** (46.3 overs) (P. J. Horton 111*, M. J. Chilton 101*). *Lancashire 2 pts.*

Paul Horton and Mark Chilton put on 202, a competition record for Lancashire's third wicket. Horton, after his maiden hundred a week earlier, became the fourth Lancashire batsman to score a century in consecutive one-day games. Chilton, who had gone almost five years since his last hundred, had earlier run out Stuart Law, making his first return to Old Trafford in Derbyshire's colours. Playing despite a broken finger, Law made 18. Steve Stubbings and Wavell Hinds added 104, but Derbyshire's total was inadequate.

At Derby, May 4. **Essex won by six wickets.** Reduced to 43 overs a side. Toss: Essex. **Derbyshire 192-7** (43 overs) (W. W. Hinds 81, G. M. Smith 38*; G. R. Napier 3-35); **Essex 194-4** (40.1 overs) (V. Chopra 69, M. J. Walker 37). *Essex 2 pts.*

Derbyshire, after a delayed start, struggled to 12-2 from ten overs. Wavell Hinds played with authority and was helped by Greg Smith, but the innings never really gathered momentum. Enjoying the better of the conditions, Varun Chopra and Matt Walker shared 103 in 22 overs, before Graham Napier ended it with a flourish, striking 28 off 15, having earlier taken three wickets in six balls.

At Northampton, May 4. **Northamptonshire won by 35 runs.** Reduced to 39 overs a side. Toss: Glamorgan. **Northamptonshire 200-9** (39 overs) (M. H. Wessels 39, N. Boje 32, S. P. Crook 42; D. S. Harrison 3-31, D. A. Cosker 3-26); **Glamorgan 165-8** (39 overs) (M. J. Powell 30, D. A. Cosker 50*; A. J. Hall 4-14). *Northamptonshire 2 pts.*

Glamorgan hit trouble when Lee Daggett took two wickets in an over to leave them 44-3. Dean Cosker – earlier the pick of their bowlers – lifted them from 95-8 with a late flourish, but Andrew Hall had already ripped out the middle order. It was Northamptonshire's first victory in any competition since July 2008.

At Chelmsford, May 10. **Essex won by six wickets.** Toss: Lancashire. **Lancashire 157** (44.4 overs) (A. G. Prince 44, L. D. Sutton 31*, S. D. Parry 31; D. D. Masters 3-19); **Essex 160-4** (44.1 overs) (V. Chopra 72, M. J. Walker 34). *Essex 2 pts.*

The Lancashire batsmen failed to cope with a pitch offering bounce, and only a ninth-wicket stand of 74 between Luke Sutton and Stephen Parry – on his List A debut – detained Essex. Varun Chopra made his fourth successive fifty in the competition during a partnership of 82 for the third wicket with Matt Walker. Ravi Bopara, who volunteered to play between Tests, was dismissed for two.

At Northampton, May 10. **Derbyshire won by 21 runs.** Toss: Northamptonshire. **Derbyshire 286-9** (50 overs) (C. J. L. Rogers 42, S. G. Law 95, W. W. Hinds 57; L. M. Daggett 4-51); **Northamptonshire 265** (49.2 overs) (M. H. Wessels 35, N. J. O'Brien 45, M. A. G. Nelson 74). *Derbyshire 2 pts.*

Stuart Law was effectively the difference between the two sides. He laid the foundations for Derbyshire's substantial total with 95 off 113 balls and shared a century stand with Wavell Hinds, before Graham Wagg struck three sixes from nine deliveries. Riki Wessels and Niall O'Brien replied positively, but wickets fell regularly until Mark Nelson, with a maiden half-century, and David Willey added 60 for the seventh wicket, by when it was too late.

At Cardiff, May 12 (day/night). **Essex won by seven wickets.** Toss: Glamorgan. **Glamorgan 124** (46.2 overs) (B. J. Wright 40*; D. D. Masters 3-21, Danish Kaneria 4-16); **Essex 127-3** (25.5 overs) (V. Chopra 37, G. R. Napier 41). *Essex 2 pts.*

   Glamorgan were penalised two points for a "poor" surface a couple of months before the Ashes series was due to start on this ground. It was the first one-day pitch prepared by Keith Exton, who had won plaudits for Oakham School's square. Glamorgan appealed against the penalty, but eight days later withdrew and accepted their punishment, which applies in 2010. At one stage Glamorgan were 57-7, Danish Kaneria having taken four for two in 18 deliveries. There were no such demons for the Essex batsmen.

At Manchester, May 12. **Lancashire won by six wickets.** Toss: Lancashire. **Northamptonshire 211-9** (50 overs) (N. Boje 50, A. G. Wakely 32, D. S. Lucas 32*, Extras 33); **Lancashire 213-4** (47.3 overs) (P. J. Horton 46, A. G. Prince 78, F. du Plessis 40*). *Lancashire 2 pts.*

   Lancashire bounced back convincingly from their first defeat of the season two days earlier. Ashwell Prince made his best one-day score for them after a good collective performance by the four seamers. Another South African, Nicky Boje, was Northamptonshire's top scorer after they slipped to 97-5.

At Derby, May 13 (day/night). **Lancashire won by 114 runs** (D/L method). Toss: Derbyshire. **Lancashire 296-8** (50 overs) (T. C. Smith 59, M. J. Chilton 32*, F. du Plessis 112; G. M. Smith 4-53); **Derbyshire 175** (38.4 overs) (C. J. L. Rogers 68, G. T. Park 37*; G. Keedy 4-43). *Lancashire 2 pts.*

   Francois du Plessis hit his first century for Lancashire, his 112 coming off 86 balls and including 12 fours. Derbyshire were set a revised target of 290 from 48 overs, and never threatened to make it once Chris Rogers became the first of Gary Keedy's four victims. A six by Graham Wagg landed on the sponsored car belonging to former Derbyshire captain Dominic Cork, who was working as a television commentator.

At Derby, May 15 (day/night). **Derbyshire v Northamptonshire. Abandoned.** *Derbyshire 1 pt, Northamptonshire 1 pt.*

At Cardiff, May 15 (day/night). **Lancashire won by eight wickets** (D/L method). Reduced to 31 overs a side. Toss: Lancashire. **Glamorgan 172-8** (31 overs) (M. P. O'Shea 49, M. J. Cosgrove 68; O. J. Newby 4-41); **Lancashire 208-2** (28 overs) (P. J. Horton 34, T. C. Smith 87*, M. J. Chilton 58*). *Lancashire 2 pts.*

   In contrast to the pitch three days earlier, this strip was marked "above average". Glamorgan were well placed at 122-1 when rain intervened, but after the match had been reduced to 31 overs a side, they lost their way in the remaining ten overs, seven wickets falling for 50. Tom Smith, dropped three times, went on to his highest one-day score, adding 132 with Mark Chilton as Lancashire eased to their increased target of 208.

At Northampton, May 17. **No result** (D/L method). Reduced to 31 overs a side. Toss: Essex. **Northamptonshire 124-4** (18 overs) (R. A. White 51; C. J. C. Wright 3-22) **v Essex.** *Northamptonshire 1 pt, Essex 1 pt.*

   Essex were left needing one point from their two remaining matches to qualify for the quarter-finals after rain allowed only 18 overs at Wantage Road.

At Chelmsford, May 18 (day/night). **Derbyshire won by three wickets.** Reduced to 49 overs a side. Toss: Essex. **Essex 192** (44.3 overs) (V. Chopra 42, J. S. Foster 71; G. M. Smith 3-50); **Derbyshire 195-7** (46.2 overs) (G. M. Smith 43, S. G. Law 62*, D. J. Redfern 47; Danish Kaneria 5-32). *Derbyshire 2 pts.*

   Four maidens in the opening ten overs kept Essex in check, and only James Foster prospered. Derbyshire lost half their side for 79, but Stuart Law returned to haunt his first county. He added 106 with Dan Redfern and defied the wiles of Danish Kaneria to usher in victory.

At Swansea, May 19. **Glamorgan v Northamptonshire. Abandoned.** *Glamorgan 1 pt, Northamptonshire 1 pt.*

At Cardiff, May 20. **Glamorgan won by five wickets.** Toss: Glamorgan. **Derbyshire 211** (49.1 overs) (C. J. L. Rogers 59, G. T. Park 38); **Glamorgan 212-5** (47.2 overs) (J. W. M. Dalrymple 78*, B. J. Wright 65). *Glamorgan 2 pts.*

Jamie Dalrymple and Ben Wright shared a stand of 135 for the fifth wicket, surpassing a county record that had stood for 40 years, to give Glamorgan their second win in the competition. Derbyshire collapsed from 114-1 with the departure of Chris Rogers, and lost their last five wickets for 19.

At Manchester, May 20. **Essex won by five wickets** (D/L method). Toss: Essex. **Lancashire 214-7** (50 overs) (P. J. Horton 41, M. J. Chilton 39, F. du Plessis 51); **Essex 207-5** (45.3 overs) (A. N. Cook 65, V. Chopra 65, M. J. Walker 35*). *Essex 2 pts.*

Essex's target was revised to 207 off 46 overs, and half-centuries from Alastair Cook and Varun Chopra, who shared a second-wicket stand of 124, helped guide them home; the experience of Matt Walker was also important in a tight finish. Lancashire were already guaranteed to head the group and so take home advantage in the last eight. Essex also reached the quarter-finals.

QUARTER-FINALS

At Southampton, May 23. **Hampshire won by 44 runs.** Toss: Hampshire. **Hampshire 310-4** (50 overs) (M. J. Lumb 100, J. H. K. Adams 76, S. M. Ervine 34, M. A. Carberry 42*, L. A. Dawson 51*); **Middlesex 266** (49.2 overs) (S. D. Robson 48, N. J. Dexter 79; B. V. Taylor 3-44).

Michael Lumb and Jimmy Adams laid the foundations for Hampshire's commanding total with an opening stand of 156. Lumb, who went to his second one-day hundred, from 97 deliveries, was stumped next ball. Liam Dawson, on the way to his maiden fifty, outpaced Michael Carberry. Middlesex were in with a chance at 207-3, but lost four wickets in 18 balls during their batting powerplay.

At Taunton, May 23. **Sussex won by six wickets.** Toss: Somerset. **Somerset 285-8** (50 overs) (C. Kieswetter 106, Z. de Bruyn 96; Yasir Arafat 3-52); **Sussex 288-4** (49.1 overs) (E. C. Joyce 74, C. D. Nash 41, M. W. Goodwin 93, M. H. Yardy 57*).

Somerset, undefeated in the group stage, went down in the last over. They suffered a bad start when Marcus Trescothick was out first ball, and Craig Kieswetter might have been caught in the slips before he had scored, but confidence and strokes soared as he went on to a memorable hundred, finding calm support from Zander de Bruyn in a stand of 167. Sussex had the man for a tight run-chase in Murray Goodwin: he shared two partnerships of 89, with Ed Joyce and Mike Yardy, who saw his side home.

At Manchester, May 23. **Lancashire won by 67 runs.** Toss: Essex. **Lancashire 262-6** (50 overs) (A. G. Prince 40, M. J. Chilton 43, F. du Plessis 113*); **Essex 195** (44 overs) (G. W. Flower 44, R. N. ten Doeschate 41; G. Keedy 4-45).

A magnificent innings from Francois du Plessis that trumped his own record for the fastest century of the summer, knocked out the holders, who had already beaten Lancashire twice in the group stages. He was cautious at first, having come in at 86-3 in the 27th over, but became irresistible in the closing overs as he raced from 50 to 100 in 19 balls to complete a century from 71, five fewer than it had taken him at Derby ten days earlier. He ended with seven sixes as Lancashire scored 121 off the last 12 overs – 63 off the batting powerplay and 23 from the last over, bowled by Chris Wright. Amid the carnage, David Masters emerged with figures of 10–4–14–2. The Essex batsmen failed to mount a challenge.

At Bristol, June 16. **Gloucestershire won by six wickets.** Toss: Nottinghamshire. **Nottinghamshire 189** (44.2 overs) (C. M. W. Read 57, M. A. Ealham 33, A. R. Adams 30; J. Lewis 4-34, S. P. Kirby 3-33); **Gloucestershire 190-4** (37.3 overs) (W. T. S. Porterfield 36, C. M. Spearman 50*, C. G. Taylor 40).

This match was played more than three weeks after the other ties because Gloucestershire's headquarters had been booked for a one-day international on May 24. Jon Lewis and Steve Kirby reduced the visitors to 9-3 and went on to share seven wickets; only Chris Read offered any resistance. The target did not stretch Craig Spearman who, unhurried, took Gloucestershire into the final four.

SEMI-FINALS

LANCASHIRE v HAMPSHIRE

At Manchester, July 5. Hampshire won by 64 runs. Toss: Lancashire.

The key figure in a comfortable victory that secured Hampshire a third Lord's final in five years – and condemned Lancashire to a ninth semi-final defeat since their last cup win in 1998 – was Jimmy Adams. He and Lumb shared an opening stand of 159 inside 25 overs after Lancashire opted to field. However, with Lancashire's bowling improving, Hampshire failed to make the most of the flying start. Adams then held two brilliant catches at crucial stages as Lancashire's run-chase was beginning to build momentum. First, he snapped up du Plessis, who had been Lancashire's quarter-final hero (and had earlier taken an excellent catch to dismiss Adams), but it was his spectacular diving effort at short extra cover to remove Laxman that settled the outcome. Much was made of the presence at Old Trafford of Duncan Fletcher, who was beginning a month's coaching consultancy with Hampshire; Lancashire were playing in their first semi-final under Peter Moores, another former England coach.

Man of the Match: J. H. K. Adams.

Hampshire

M. J. Lumb c Chapple b Mahmood	76	C. T. Tremlett not out		3
J. H. K. Adams c du Plessis b Mahmood	78	Imran Tahir c Keedy b Chapple		5
M. A. Carberry lbw b Keedy	12			
S. M. Ervine b Keedy	12			
C. C. Benham c Sutton b Chapple	29	L-b 9, w 3, n-b 4		16
L. A. Dawson lbw b Keedy	6			
†N. Pothas b Hogg	15	1/159 (2) 2/168 (1) 3/180- (48.4 overs)	271
*A. D. Mascarenhas c Hogg b Mahmood	13	(3) 4/203 (4) 5/215 (6)	
D. G. Cork c Sutton b Chapple	6	6/236 (5) 7/247 (7) 8/262 (9)	
		9/262 (8) 10/271 (11)	

Chapple 9.4–2–46–3; Hogg 9–0–37–1; Mahmood 9–0–56–3; Croft 2–0–19–0; du Plessis 9–0–55–0; Keedy 10–0–49–3.

Lancashire

P. J. Horton c Lumb b Mascarenhas	5	K. W. Hogg b Tremlett		2
M. B. Loye lbw b Imran Tahir	31	S. I. Mahmood b Tremlett		12
V. V. S. Laxman c Adams b Dawson	54	G. Keedy not out		2
M. J. Chilton c Carberry b Ervine	18	L-b 9, w 4, n-b 2		15
F. du Plessis c Adams b Ervine	5			
S. J. Croft b Imran Tahir	33	1/5 (1) 2/78 (2) 3/108 (4) (45.4 overs)	207
†L. D. Sutton lbw b Mascarenhas	22	4/117 (5) 5/123 (3) 6/170 (7)	
*G. Chapple st Pothas b Imran Tahir	8	7/189 (8) 8/191 (6) 9/199 (9) 10/207 (10)	

Cork 4–0–19–0; Mascarenhas 8–1–35–2; Tremlett 7.4–0–44–2; Imran Tahir 10–0–38–3; Ervine 8–0–28–2; Dawson 8–1–34–1.

Umpires: P. J. Hartley and R. A. Kettleborough.

SUSSEX v GLOUCESTERSHIRE

At Hove, July 5. Sussex won by 34 runs. Toss: Gloucestershire.

A raucous crowd of 6,500, watching the first semi-final on Sussex soil for 16 years, cheered their team on to Lord's for their second final in four seasons, and tenth in all. The outcome, though, was in the balance until the 41st over of Gloucestershire's reply, when Yardy brought himself back into the attack and removed the increasingly threatening Gidman for a career-best 116. Sussex couldn't believe their luck when Gidman, believing a pitch that had been glued on was damp, chose to bowl. Joyce took advantage with his highest one-day score as Sussex made their largest limited-overs total at Hove, despite scoring just 57 in the last ten overs. Only fatigue stopped Joyce, who hit his third hundred of the tournament, from batting through. Goodwin helped add 144 in 20 overs for the third wicket, and Sussex should have made in excess of 350. Gidman nearly made amends for his blunder as he and Marshall kept pace with the rate in a stand of 155 in 25, but Joyce's alert fielding ran out Marshall – and the last six Gloucestershire wickets fell in 7.2 overs.

Man of the Match: E. C. Joyce.

Sussex

E. C. Joyce run out	146		Yasir Arafat not out	9
C. D. Nash b Kirby	32		†A. J. Hodd not out	10
L. J. Wright c Franklin b Dawson	36		L-b 5, w 5	10
M. W. Goodwin b Lewis	60			
D. R. Smith c Marshall b Dawson	6		1/62 (2) 2/118 (3) (7 wkts, 50 overs)	326
R. J. Hamilton-Brown run out	6		3/262 (4) 4/270 (5)	
*M. H. Yardy c Adshead b Lewis	11		5/288 (6) 6/305 (1) 7/310 (7)	

W. A. T. Beer and R. J. Kirtley did not bat.

Lewis 10–0–58–2; Franklin 6–0–53–0; Kirby 9–0–61–1; Banerjee 7–0–51–0; Dawson 10–0–50–2; Gidman 2–0–16–0; Taylor 6–0–32–0.

Gloucestershire

Kadeer Ali lbw b Kirtley	5		J. Lewis b Yasir Arafat	2
H. J. H. Marshall run out	57		S. P. Kirby st Hodd b Yardy	0
*A. P. R. Gidman c Hodd b Yardy	116		V. Banerjee not out	0
C. M. Spearman lbw b Hamilton-Brown	2		B 11, l-b 6, w 21	38
C. G. Taylor b Yasir Arafat	25			
J. E. C. Franklin c Wright b Yardy	34		1/8 (1) 2/163 (2) 3/170 (4) (47.4 overs)	292
†S. J. Adshead st Hodd b Nash	1		4/219 (5) 5/252 (3) 6/255 (7)	
R. K. J. Dawson c Hamilton-Brown b Yardy	12		7/276 (8) 8/284 (9) 9/292 (6) 10/292 (10)	

Yasir Arafat 9–0–32–2; Kirtley 6–0–50–1; Wright 3–0–21–0; Smith 4–0–24–0; Yardy 8.4–0–54–4; Beer 7–0–33–0; Hamilton-Brown 7–0–44–1; Nash 3–0–17–1.

Umpires: R. J. Bailey and R. K. Illingworth.

FINAL

HAMPSHIRE v SUSSEX

Paul Weaver

At Lord's, July 25. Hampshire won by six wickets. Toss: Sussex.

The 50-over game, fighting for survival in the domestic schedule at the time, was in urgent need of a compelling commercial, but this wasn't it. Hampshire, in their third final in five seasons, repeated their success of 2005, winning with almost ten overs to spare. So once again Friends Provident, like Cheltenham & Gloucester, who came before, produced a disappointing paean for county cricket's big day at Lord's, and the nostalgic continued to recall the twilight thrillers presided over by Gillette and NatWest. Dominic Cork, two weeks short of his 38th birthday and now with his third county – he had helped Derbyshire win the Benson and Hedges Cup here 16 years earlier – still had enough hoary skill and big-match temperament to swagger on an important stage.

Sussex, who had beaten Cork's Lancashire in the 2006 final, won the toss and Yardy decided to bat. But their total of 219 for nine was probably 30 short of par on a good pitch, despite the experience and depth of their batting: Yasir Arafat, with four first-class centuries to his name, batted at No. 9, and Martin-Jenkins, who once scored a Championship double-hundred, at No. 10. They were undone by a fine opening spell from Cork, from the Nursery End, and by the niggardly Mascarenhas. Cork's burst, in particular, was decisive. In his fourth over he bowled Joyce, who had

Prior notice: Jimmy Adams and Dominic Cork exult at the downfall of Matt Prior.

been the tournament's most successful batsman: Joyce got an inside edge to a delivery he was trying to leave. Prior, making a rare appearance for his county, came in next, which meant that Wright, who had prospered at first drop, was moved back to No. 6. The disruption did not help.

Prior was perhaps fortunate to survive an lbw shout from the rampant Cork from the first delivery he received; he edged the second to wicketkeeper Nic Pothas. Four overs later, Cork brought one back up the hill to have Nash leg-before. His opening spell was 7–1–23–3. And when Tremlett's direct hit from mid-off surprised Goodwin, Sussex were 43 for four in the 14th over.

Yardy played a captain's innings to score an unbeaten 92 from 127 deliveries, and received support from Dwayne Smith and Hamilton-Brown. But their total looked more respectable than challenging. It was put in perspective by an opening stand of 93 between Lumb and Adams. Hampshire lost four wickets in 11 overs as Wright bustled in to take three, but they looked discomfited only when Pothas aggravated a groin strain. Denied a runner, he was about to retire hurt when frantic signals from the dressing-room urged him to continue. Pothas, now on one leg, opted for the aerial route, striking three lofted fours and a pulled six, and imparted confidence to Benham, who swept the winning boundary past a sprawling square leg. This was the tenth time Sussex had appeared in this final, a record bettered only by Warwickshire and Lancashire; they have now won five and lost five.

Man of the Match: D. G. Cork.   *Attendance:* 21,110.

Sussex

E. C. Joyce b Cork	15		Yasir Arafat c Pothas b Mascarenhas	9
C. D. Nash lbw b Cork	21		R. S. C. Martin-Jenkins c Benham b Cork	4
†M. J. Prior c Pothas b Cork	0		R. J. Kirtley not out	3
M. W. Goodwin run out	1		L-b 9, w 4, n-b 2	15
*M. H. Yardy not out	92			
L. J. Wright b Tremlett	7		1/30 (1) 2/30 (3) 3/39–(9 wkts, 50 overs)	219
D. R. Smith c Carberry b Imran Tahir	20		(2) 4/43 (4) 5/77 (6)	
R. J. Hamilton-Brown c Mascarenhas			6/111 (7) 7/171 (8)	
b Imran Tahir	32		8/186 (9) 9/203 (10)	

Cork 10–1–41–4; Mascarenhas 9–0–27–1; Imran Tahir 10–0–50–2; Tremlett 10–0–40–1; Ervine 6–0–31–0; Dawson 5–0–21–0.

Hampshire

M. J. Lumb c Prior b Wright	38	†N. Pothas not out	35
J. H. K. Adams lbw b Wright	55	L-b 2, w 5, n-b 4	11
M. A. Carberry c and b Yasir Arafat	30		
S. M. Ervine c Nash b Wright	15	1/93 (2) 2/110 (1) (4 wkts, 40.3 overs) 221	
C. C. Benham not out	37	3/137 (3) 4/154 (4)	

L. A. Dawson, *A. D. Mascarenhas, D. G. Cork, C. T. Tremlett and Imran Tahir did not bat.

Kirtley 5–0–26–0; Yasir Arafat 10–0–54–1; Martin-Jenkins 4–0–21–0; Wright 9–1–50–3; Nash 3–0–15–0; Hamilton-Brown 3.3–0–27–0; Yardy 6–1–26–0.

Umpires: N. J. Llong and N. A. Mallender.

WINNERS 1963–2009

Gillette Cup

		Man of the Match
1963	SUSSEX* beat Worcestershire by 14 runs.	N. Gifford†
1964	SUSSEX* beat Warwickshire* by eight wickets.	N. I. Thomson
1965	YORKSHIRE beat Surrey* by 175 runs.	G. Boycott
1966	WARWICKSHIRE* beat Worcestershire by five wickets.	R. W. Barber
1967	KENT* beat Somerset by 32 runs.	M. H. Denness
1968	WARWICKSHIRE beat Sussex* by four wickets.	A. C. Smith
1969	YORKSHIRE beat Derbyshire* by 69 runs.	B. Leadbeater
1970	LANCASHIRE* beat Sussex by six wickets.	H. Pilling
1971	LANCASHIRE* beat Kent by 24 runs.	Asif Iqbal†
1972	LANCASHIRE* beat Warwickshire by four wickets.	C. H. Lloyd
1973	GLOUCESTERSHIRE* beat Sussex by 40 runs.	A. S. Brown
1974	KENT* beat Lancashire by four wickets.	A. P. E. Knott
1975	LANCASHIRE* beat Middlesex by seven wickets.	C. H. Lloyd
1976	NORTHAMPTONSHIRE* beat Lancashire by four wickets.	P. Willey
1977	MIDDLESEX* beat Glamorgan by five wickets.	C. T. Radley
1978	SUSSEX* beat Somerset by five wickets.	P. W. G. Parker
1979	SOMERSET beat Northamptonshire* by 45 runs.	I. V. A. Richards
1980	MIDDLESEX* beat Surrey by seven wickets.	J. M. Brearley

NatWest Trophy

1981	DERBYSHIRE* beat Northamptonshire by losing fewer wickets with the scores level	G. Cook†
1982	SURREY* beat Warwickshire by nine wickets.	D. J. Thomas
1983	SOMERSET beat Kent* by 24 runs.	V. J. Marks
1984	MIDDLESEX beat Kent* by four wickets.	C. T. Radley
1985	ESSEX beat Nottinghamshire* by one run.	B. R. Hardie
1986	SUSSEX* beat Lancashire by seven wickets.	D. A. Reeve
1987	NOTTINGHAMSHIRE* beat Northamptonshire by three wickets.	R. J. Hadlee
1988	MIDDLESEX* beat Worcestershire by three wickets.	M. R. Ramprakash
1989	WARWICKSHIRE beat Middlesex* by four wickets.	D. A. Reeve
1990	LANCASHIRE* beat Northamptonshire by seven wickets.	P. A. J. DeFreitas
1991	HAMPSHIRE* beat Surrey by four wickets.	R. A. Smith
1992	NORTHAMPTONSHIRE* beat Leicestershire by eight wickets.	A. Fordham
1993	WARWICKSHIRE* beat Sussex by five wickets.	Asif Din
1994	WORCESTERSHIRE* beat Warwickshire by eight wickets.	T. M. Moody
1995	WARWICKSHIRE beat Northamptonshire* by four wickets.	D. A. Reeve
1996	LANCASHIRE beat Essex* by 129 runs.	G. Chapple
1997	ESSEX* beat Warwickshire by nine wickets.	S. G. Law
1998	LANCASHIRE* beat Derbyshire by nine wickets.	I. D. Austin
1999	GLOUCESTERSHIRE beat Somerset* by 50 runs.	R. C. Russell
2000	GLOUCESTERSHIRE* beat Warwickshire by 22 runs (D/L method).	A. A. Donald†

Cheltenham & Gloucester Trophy

2001	SOMERSET* beat Leicestershire by 41 runs.	K. A. Parsons
2002	YORKSHIRE beat Somerset* by six wickets.	M. T. G. Elliott
2003	GLOUCESTERSHIRE* beat Worcestershire by seven wickets.	I. J. Harvey
2004	GLOUCESTERSHIRE† beat Worcestershire by eight wickets.	V. S. Solanki†
2005	HAMPSHIRE beat Warwickshire* by 18 runs.	S. M. Ervine
2006	SUSSEX beat Lancashire* by 15 runs.	R. J. Kirtley

Friends Provident Trophy

2007	DURHAM beat Hampshire* by 125 runs.	O. D. Gibson
2008	ESSEX beat Kent* by five wickets.	G. W. Flower
2009	HAMPSHIRE beat Sussex* by six wickets	D. G. Cork

* Won toss.   † On losing side.

FIRST-CLASS COUNTIES' RECORDS 1963–2009

	Rounds reached					Matches		
	W	F	SF	QF	P	W	L	NR
Derbyshire	1	3	5	14	122*	59	58	5
Durham	1	1	2	3	91	42	48	1
Essex	3	4	8	19	135	79	53	3
Glamorgan	0	1	4	16	126	53	65	8
Gloucestershire	5	5	10	21	139	84	49	6
Hampshire	3	4	13	24	148†	91	52	4
Kent	2	6	9	19	138†	79	55	3
Lancashire	7	11	20	27	164	111	49	4
Leicestershire	0	2	5	18	127	64	57	6
Middlesex	4	6	13	24	147	89	54	4
Northamptonshire	2	7	10	23	142	74	61	7
Nottinghamshire	1	2	3	15	125	66	53	6
Somerset	3	7	12	22	144†	86	51	6
Surrey	1	4	12	26	145*	81	60	4
Sussex	5	10	14	22	147	87	54	6
Warwickshire	5	12	21	26	164†	104	53	6
Worcestershire	1	6	12	18	137	77	54	6
Yorkshire	3	3	11	22	137	77	54	6

Durham's record includes their matches before 1992, when they were a Minor County.
* Derbyshire and Surrey totals each include a bowling contest after their first-round matches were abandoned in 1991; Derbyshire lost to Hertfordshire and Surrey beat Oxfordshire.
† One match tied.
There were no semi-finals or quarter-finals in 2006, or quarter-finals in 2007.

Records for the knockout competition, in its various guises, can be found in *Wisden 2006* (pages 853–7). Past winners of the Benson and Hedges Cup (1972–2002) can be found in relevant *Wisdens*, including page 857 of *Wisden 2006*.

TWENTY20 CUP, 2009

Review by Paul Edwards

Finals Day Reports by Vic Marks

Anyone wishing to trace the moment when the Sussex director of cricket Mark Robinson began to plan his side's victory in the 2009 Twenty20 Cup will need to go back exactly 12 months. As the Middlesex players frolicked round the Rose Bowl that hot Saturday evening and pondered – mistakenly as it turned out – the riches to be gained from their Champions League involvement, Robinson watched them, as he himself puts it, "with jealous eyes". In the 21st century, Sussex had become a team that expected to win things, and it was painful not to be involved in what is now one of the county game's great showpiece occasions. "We'd got to finals day in 2007 with what I saw as a dream team," said Robinson. "We had a great day but we didn't win it. In 2008 we bombed and hardly

won a Twenty20 game all season. Watching finals day without us being there really hurt me, and success often comes from failure." As the 2009 season drew to a close, though, it was the Sharks' turn to eye a share of the $6m pot on offer in India.

Mike Yardy's team secured the Twenty20 Cup with some ease. Five successive victories in June enabled them to qualify from the South Group as runners-up to Kent, and their 38-run defeat of Warwickshire in the quarter-final rarely had the Hove faithful shifting uneasily in their deckchairs. Sussex's finals-day wins over Northamptonshire – already denied Champions League involvement because of the ICL connections of some of their players – and Somerset were straightforward by the standards established on previous such occasions.

The reasons for this dominance cannot be explained by the talents of one or two players, but rather by the complementary qualities of all 11 members of the Sussex team. Winning a Twenty20 game often hinges on a side's ability to maintain a run-rate even when it is losing wickets, or a bowler's capacity to take over from a team-mate and deliver one tight over when the game is in the hazard. It was in these respects that Sussex were superior in 2009.

Three Sussex bowlers finished among the top 12 wicket-takers in 2009, but Yardy often had eight bowling options. Four of them, including the very promising leg-spinner Will Beer, were purveyors of the slow stuff, increasingly highly prized in the short game. James Kirtley, who took 17 wickets, or Yasir Arafat, who claimed 15, were important, but the Sussex cause did not collapse if they were collared. A quick-thinking captain such as Yardy was always alert to the need for a change. Quick-learning players can be useful too: Andrew

Julian Finney, Getty Images

Trophy boys: Mike Yardy and his Sussex team-mates celebrate winning the Twenty20 Cup.

Hodd noted Tillekeratne Dilshan's unconventional strokeplay in the Twenty20 World Cup and successfully played the "Dilscoop" (or "starfish") over the wicketkeeper's head. James Langridge would probably not have approved, though Ranji might.

Sussex's batting was also a team effort: if there was no one as dominant as Warwickshire's Jonathan Trott, whose 525 runs included five fifties and made him the heaviest scorer in any of the seven Twenty20 Cups, there were five who made 199 runs or more, while Dwayne Smith racked up 338. Such strength in depth leads to success.

Sussex had plenty of rivals as competition favourites during the group matches, which were split into two unequal periods in order to accommodate the Twenty20 World Cup. Kent topped the South Group and appeared a good bet to repeat their 2007 triumph until blasted out of finals day by a thunderous half-century from Marcus Trescothick. Hampshire, helped by Michael Lumb's 442 runs, reached the last eight but, in the strongest group, Essex were unlucky to lose out. However, Middlesex, the cup-holders, and Surrey were in shocking form, winning just two matches each. Middlesex lost their first seven games.

In the North Group, Lancashire were the form horses, raising hopes in the Rossendale valley and elsewhere that the Old Trafford side would win its first top-flight trophy since 1998. Eight wins and a solitary defeat against Leicestershire on a golden June evening in Aigburth allowed Glen Chapple's well-balanced and confident side to cruise into the quarter-finals with more points than any team in the country. Few players stood out – the Sussex paradigm again – but none needed to when everyone was chipping in. However, the Manchester weather then intervened, preventing any play on the three days eventually allotted for the quarter-final and forcing Lancashire and Somerset to settle the tie by means of a bowl-out in Old Trafford's Indoor School.

Adept at hitting the stumps when batsmen were in the way, Lancashire's cricketers were flummoxed when required to hit an unprotected set. Somerset won 5–1, with the last pair of bowlers not required to display their skill. (In general, the 2009 Twenty20 Cup was blessed with excellent weather: only four of the 97 scheduled matches – two of which involved Lancashire – did not reach a result.) Of the other sides in the group, only Durham, helped by Mitch Claydon's 17 wickets, and Leicestershire, bolstered by Jim Allenby's 432 runs, looked capable of making much progress. As it was, Durham were swept aside by Kent in the quarter-final at Canterbury.

In the felicitously named Midlands/Wales/West Group, Northamptonshire were outsiders who soon proved themselves capable of mixing it with the thoroughbreds. The Steelbacks (christened the Steelboks by an unkind wit because of their South African connections) won seven of their group matches and reached finals day courtesy of a fine victory over Hampshire. Four of the competition's top 16 wicket-takers came from, if not originated in, Northamptonshire: Andrew Hall, Johan van der Wath, the invaluable Ian Harvey, now representing his fifth county, and the captain, Nicky Boje.

Warwickshire, aided by Trott's batting – soon to be enlisted in a greater cause – and by the medium-paced bowling of Keith Barker, also won seven games, but came up against Sussex in the quarter-final where Chris Nash's clean hitting and Rory Hamilton-Brown's off-spin were decisive. Somerset finished third, squeezed into the quarter-finals and, as ever, hosted some of the noisiest and best-natured limited-overs matches in England: despite the curious pro-liferation of pavilions, a summer evening at a packed

Slightly less biff, bang and whack

Taunton still has an atmosphere all its own. Worcestershire put aside their four-day travails to win half their Twenty20 games, but Gloucestershire and Glamorgan were the whipping boys of the group.

The 2009 competition proved yet again that the Twenty20 Cup is now an established part of the English summer. Most of the players enjoy it – although thankfully nearly all insist the Championship is their priority – and the suits at county clubs look at the attendance figures and adore it. What was once, in the words of Lancashire's head coach Peter Moores, a "biff–bang–whack" affair is now taken very seriously by coaches as a format demanding specific skills.

In fact, there was slightly less biff, bang and whack in 2009: the average number of runs per over was 7.66, the lowest in Twenty20 history. No longer was the bowler, in Gideon Haigh's phrase, merely "the fall guy in a comic routine stoically awaiting the inevitable custard pie". Slow bouncers, cunning yorkers and even the humble jaffa, which pitches on leg and hits the top of off, all allowed the infantry to get some of their own back on their hitherto bullying officers. Success was not limited to one discipline: of the 41 to take ten or more wickets, 13 bowled spin; and of the select six to take 12 wickets at an economy-rate of under 6.50, three were slow bowlers and three not.

Twenty20 threw up other curious statistical features in 2009. Batting first, for example, offered negligible advantage: 47 of the 93 results favoured the side taking first knock. And it was only slightly more useful to win the toss; 49 went the way of teams whose captains had called correctly. (Oddly, 22 of 29 matches in the Midlands/Wales/West Group were won by the side winning the toss, while in the North, it was the reverse: here, losing the toss led to victory in 20 of 29 games.)

The 2009 event was, then, a success, and fresh trends will develop as yet more thought is given to the game's shortest form. But that success was no reason to argue that the English game needed yet more of the same – as was briefly planned in the ECB's now abandoned scheme to run a second 20-over competition beside its older brother. In 2010, a revamped Twenty20 Cup will see two nine-team pools, with the top four from each contesting the quarter-finals. This change will mean that the format for the competition will have been tinkered with on four occasions in eight seasons; each has increased the number of matches. The winners of the 2010 Twenty Cup will have played 19 games when they hoist the trophy aloft at the Rose Bowl. That is enough; indeed, it may turn out to be a little more than enough. Shrewd entertainers always leave the customer wanting more.

Prize money

£80,000 for winners: SUSSEX.
£50,000 for runners-up: SOMERSET.
£40,000 for losing semi-finalists: KENT, NORTHAMPTONSHIRE.
£5,000 for losing quarter-finalists: DURHAM, HAMPSHIRE, LANCASHIRE, WARWICKSHIRE.

The following awards, worth £1,500 each, were made at the end of the group stages.

Most runs: I. J. L. Trott (Warwickshire) 469.
Most sixes: J. Allenby (Leicestershire) 20.
Best strike-rate (minimum 72 balls faced): M. J. Lumb (Hampshire) 160.00.
Best all-rounder: J. W. M. Dalrymple (Glamorgan).
Best wicketkeeper: C. Kieswetter (Somerset).
Most wickets: M. E. Claydon (Durham) 16.
Best economy-rate (minimum 72 balls bowled): D. J. Willey (Northamptonshire) 4.85.

Note: Performances in the quarter-finals, semi-finals and final had no bearing on these awards.

Match-award winners received £1,500 in the final, £500 in the semi-finals, £250 in the quarter-finals and £200 in group games.

All attendance figures supplied by the ECB.

FINAL GROUP TABLES

Midlands/Wales/West

	Played	Won	Lost	No result	Points	NRR
NORTHAMPTONSHIRE.......	10	7	2	1	15	0.58
WARWICKSHIRE............	10	7	3	0	14	0.23
SOMERSET	10	6	3	1	13	0.41
Worcestershire...............	10	5	5	0	10	0.58
Glamorgan...................	10	2	8	0	4	−1.03
Gloucestershire	10	2	8	0	4	−0.66

North Group

	Played	Won	Lost	No result	Points	NRR
LANCASHIRE	10	8	1	1	17	1.11
DURHAM..................	10	5	4	1	11	0.15
Leicestershire................	10	5	5	0	10	−0.04
Nottinghamshire.............	10	4	6	0	8	0.00
Yorkshire...................	10	4	6	0	8	−0.47
Derbyshire	10	3	7	0	6	−0.61

South Group

	Played	Won	Lost	No result	Points	NRR
KENT	10	7	2	1	15	0.63
SUSSEX	10	7	3	0	14	0.31
HAMPSHIRE	10	6	4	0	12	0.85
Essex	10	5	4	1	11	0.15
Surrey	10	2	8	0	4	−0.66
Middlesex	10	2	8	0	4	−1.18

Where two or more counties finished with an equal number of points, the positions were decided by (a) most points in head-to-head matches (b) net run-rate (runs scored per over minus runs conceded per over) (c) most wickets taken per balls bowled in matches achieving a result.

TWENTY20 CUP AVERAGES, 2009

BATTING

(Qualification: 200 runs, average 30.00)

		M	I	NO	R	HS	100s	50s	Avge	SR	4	6
1	I. J. L. Trott (*Warwicks*)	11	11	3	525	86*	0	5	65.62	132.24	63	11
2	D. I. Stevens (*Kent*)........	11	11	5	356	77	0	4	59.33	144.12	31	15
3	Z. de Bruyn (*Somerset*)	12	10	3	391	83*	0	3	55.85	112.68	30	8
4	P. D. Trego (*Somerset*)	12	8	3	241	58*	0	1	48.20	154.48	21	11
5	†A. N. Cook (*Essex*)	8	8	1	337	100*	1	2	48.14	144.01	36	8
6	J. Allenby (*Leics*)	10	10	1	432	110	1	3	48.00	139.80	38	20
7	†M. J. Lumb (*Hants*)........	11	11	1	442	124*	1	3	44.20	160.72	60	13
8	C. D. Nash (*Sussex*)........	10	8	3	216	56*	0	1	43.20	151.04	22	7
9	†W. W. Hinds (*Derbys*)......	10	10	3	299	66	0	1	42.71	112.83	20	6
10	†A. W. Gale (*Yorks*)	10	10	1	383	91	0	3	42.55	133.91	53	6
11	M. L. Pettini (*Essex*)	10	10	1	334	87	0	2	37.11	137.44	45	7
12	S. J. Croft (*Lancs*)	9	9	2	259	83*	0	1	37.00	134.89	31	8
13	M. van Jaarsveld (*Kent*)	12	10	1	326	75*	0	3	36.22	138.72	46	4
14	D. M. Benkenstein (*Durham*)	10	10	2	276	53	0	1	34.50	123.76	19	12
15	M. W. Goodwin (*Sussex*) ...	10	10	2	273	80*	0	2	34.12	107.90	35	2
16	D. R. Smith (*Sussex*)........	13	13	3	338	69*	0	2	33.80	126.59	25	12
17	S. C. Moore (*Worcs*)........	10	10	1	294	62*	0	1	32.66	124.05	26	5
18	†M. E. Trescothick (*Somerset*)	12	11	1	323	69*	0	3	32.30	159.90	43	11
19	M. R. Ramprakash (*Surrey*) .	8	8	1	225	73	0	2	32.14	136.36	21	6
20	J. W. M. Dalrymple (*Glam*) .	10	10	0	318	63	0	3	31.80	110.80	41	2
21	†U. Afzaal (*Surrey*).........	9	9	1	251	98*	0	2	31.37	147.64	27	4

		M	I	NO	R	HS	100s	50s	Avge	SR	4	6
22	I. J. Harvey (*Northants*)	10	10	1	279	64	0	1	31.00	139.50	42	4
23	C. Kieswetter (*Somerset*)....	12	11	3	248	84	0	2	31.00	140.11	22	10
24	W. I. Jefferson (*Notts*)......	10	9	2	216	75	0	1	30.85	122.03	24	5
25	†M. A. Carberry (*Hants*).....	11	10	0	307	62	0	2	30.70	104.06	28	8

† *Left-handed batsman.*

BOWLING

(Qualification: 12 wickets)

		Style	O	M	R	W	BB	4W/i	Avge	SR	ER
1	R. J. Kirtley (*Sussex*)	RFM	27	2	185	17	3-9	0	10.88	9.52	6.85
2	I. J. Harvey (*Northants*)	RM	22	0	138	12	4-18	1	11.50	11.00	6.27
3	B. W. Harmison (*Durham*)....	RFM	24	0	180	14	3-20	0	12.85	10.28	7.50
4	N. Boje (*Northants*)	SLA	27	0	159	12	3-14	0	13.25	13.50	5.88
5	Yasir Arafat (*Sussex*)	RFM	34.3	3	210	15	2-13	0	14.00	13.80	6.08
6	M. E. Claydon (*Durham*)	RFM	37.5	0	254	17	5-26	1	14.94	13.35	6.71
7	S. P. Kirby (*Glos*)...........	RFM	29.1	1	214	14	3-29	0	15.28	12.50	7.33
8	S. M. Ervine (*Hants*)........	RFM	29	0	220	13	4-16	1	16.92	13.38	7.58
9	A. C. Thomas (*Somerset*)	RFM	40.2	0	310	18	3-31	0	17.22	13.44	7.68
10	K. H. D. Barker (*Warwicks*) ...	LM	35	0	283	16	4-19	1	17.68	13.12	8.08
11	J. S. Patel (*Warwicks*)	OB	37.4	0	270	15	3-15	0	18.00	15.06	7.16
12	A. J. Hall (*Northants*)	RFM	41.1	1	267	14	4-19	1	19.07	17.64	6.48
13	M. H. Yardy (*Sussex*)	SLA	47.1	0	254	13	3-21	0	19.53	21.76	5.38
14	Azhar Mahmood (*Kent*)	RFM	45.1	0	328	16	3-16	0	20.50	16.93	7.26
15	J. C. Tredwell (*Kent*)	OB	42	0	271	13	3-18	0	20.84	19.38	6.45
16	J. J. van der Wath (*Northants*) .	RFM	40	1	311	13	3-23	0	23.92	18.46	7.77
17	C. P. Schofield (*Surrey*)	LBG	34.5	0	298	12	3-21	0	24.83	17.41	8.55

LEADING WICKETKEEPERS

Dismissals	Matches		
13 (7 ct, 6 st)	12	G. O. Jones (*Kent*)	
13 (8 ct, 5 st)	12	C. Kieswetter (*Somerset*)	
9 (7 ct, 2 st)	9	T. R. Ambrose (*Warwicks*)	
9 (9 ct)	10	P. A. Nixon (*Leics*)	
9 (4 ct, 5 st)	10	M. A. Wallace (*Glam*)	
7 (2 ct, 5 st)	5	N. J. O'Brien (*Northants*)	
7 (7 ct)	9	C. M. W. Read (*Notts*)	
7 (7 ct)	9	G. D. Cross (*Lancs*)	

LEADING FIELDERS

	Ct	M	
	11	10	W. R. Smith (*Durham*)
	10	10	C. J. L. Rogers (*Derbys*)
	9	10	G. J. Batty (*Worcs*)
	9	13	R. J. Hamilton-Brown (*Sussex*)
	8	10	W. A. White (*Leics*)
	8	11	J. O. Troughton (*Warwicks*)
	8	11	C. C. Benham (*Hants*)
	8	11	L. A. Dawson (*Hants*)

Full scores of these matches are available at: www.cricinfo.com/db/ARCHIVE/2009/ENG_LOCAL/TWENTY-20/ and www.cricketarchive.co.uk/Archive/Seasons/ENG/2009_ENG_Twenty20_Cup_2009.html

MIDLANDS/WALES/WEST GROUP

At Cardiff, May 25 (floodlit). **Somerset won by one run.** Toss: Somerset. **Somerset 113-6** (20 overs) (Z. de Bruyn 70*); **Glamorgan 112-9** (20 overs) (M. T. C. Waller 3-17). Somerset 2 pts. *Man of the Match:* Z. de Bruyn. *Attendance:* 2,478.

Needing only 20 from four overs with six wickets in hand, Glamorgan squandered the opportunity. Ben Wright and Mark Wallace put on 63, but when Wallace was caught on the midwicket boundary, panic ensued, with batsmen choosing the aerial route instead of accumulation; the last four wickets fell for nine runs. Zander de Bruyn held the Somerset innings together after Marcus Trescothick and James Hildreth were out in the first over. Somerset won despite making their lowest Twenty20 total.

Northampton, May 25. **Northamptonshire won by 17 runs.** Toss: Northamptonshire. **Northamptonshire 176-6** (20 overs) (R. A. White 40, N. J. O'Brien 42, N. Boje 45); **Warwickshire 159-8**

(20 overs) (J. O. Troughton 53; I. J. Harvey 4-18). *Northamptonshire 2 pts. Man of the Match:* I. J. Harvey. *Attendance:* 3,667. *County debut:* I. J. Harvey.

Australian all-rounder Ian Harvey appeared for his fourth county in Twenty20, turning out for Northamptonshire after previous stints with Gloucestershire, Yorkshire and Hampshire. He hit a couple of early boundaries and then, as fifth change, claimed four wickets – including Jim Troughton, whose 53 came off 39 balls. Warwickshire never really recovered from that blow. Northamptonshire were given a flying start by Rob White, who hit 40 from just 15 deliveries.

At Worcester, May 25. **Worcestershire won by 23 runs.** Toss: Worcestershire. **Worcestershire 145-7** (20 overs) (D. K. H. Mitchell 32, A. A. Noffke 34; S. P. Kirby 3-41); **Gloucestershire 122** (17.4 overs) (I. D. Fisher 3-16). *Worcestershire 2 pts. Man of the Match:* I. D. Fisher. *Attendance:* 2,936. *County debut:* G. M. Hussain (Gloucestershire).

Worcestershire spinner Ian Fisher took the first hat-trick of his career, against his former county, dismissing Steve Adshead, debutant Gemaal Hussain and Ian Saxelby to secure an unexpected win. Ashley Noffke's 34 off 20 balls helped Worcestershire to reach a modest total with Hussain, who had been playing for Alvaston and Boulton in Derby, returning 2-17 in his four overs. Gloucestershire seemed in control as openers Hamish Marshall and Will Porterfield put on 41 in five overs, but they were gradually pegged back; then Fisher made his decisive contribution.

At Cardiff, May 27 (floodlit). **Glamorgan won by 39 runs.** Toss: Gloucestershire. **Glamorgan 166-6** (20 overs) (J. W. M. Dalrymple 43, M. J. Cosgrove 52); **Gloucestershire 127** (19 overs) (J. Lewis 30*; R. E. Watkins 5-16). *Glamorgan 2 pts. Men of the Match:* M. J. Cosgrove and R. E. Watkins. *Attendance:* 1,037.

Ryan Watkins recorded the best figures for Glamorgan, and Mark Cosgrove (4–0–11–2) the most economical, as Glamorgan eased home. Gloucestershire lost eight wickets for 34 runs after an opening stand of 35, and would have been further embarrassed had Jon Lewis and Steve Kirby not put on 55 for the last wicket. Watkins had a spell of four for four in nine balls. Glamorgan's openers, Jamie Dalrymple and Cosgrove, had earlier put on 86.

At Taunton, May 27 (floodlit). **Somerset won by five wickets.** Toss: Somerset. **Warwickshire 187-5** (20 overs) (J. L. Trott 42, J. O. Troughton 50, I. J. Westwood 49*, A. G. Botha 35*); **Somerset 190-5** (19.4 overs) (Z. de Bruyn 72, J. C. Hildreth 39). *Somerset 2 pts. Man of the Match:* Z. de Bruyn. *Attendance:* 3,262.

What pleased Justin Langer was the growing composure of his players as they made sure of another last-over win. He also had a special word for Zander de Bruyn who had again demonstrated that Twenty20 does not always need a flailing and reckless bat. His was the innings that kept Somerset on course after some lively batting from Warwickshire. Somerset spectators noted two more wickets from promising, if inexperienced, leg-spinner Max Waller.

At Northampton, May 29 (floodlit). **Northamptonshire won by 40 runs.** Toss: Northamptonshire. **Northamptonshire 195-3** (20 overs) (I. J. Harvey 64, R. A. White 36, M. H. Wessels 55*); **Glamorgan 155-9** (20 overs) (M. J. Cosgrove 40; J. J. van der Wath 3-23, I. J. Harvey 3-24). *Northamptonshire 2 pts. Man of the Match:* I. J. Harvey. *Attendance:* 4,206.

Nicky Boje's tactic of delaying Ian Harvey's entry into the attack paid dividends as he picked up the key wickets of Jamie Dalrymple, Mark Wallace and Robert Croft. Harvey also crashed 64 from 37 balls in a great opening partnership with Rob White. Hard hitting from Riki Wessels and Johan van der Wath drove Northamptonshire close to 200, and the visitors wilted once Mark Cosgrove's brilliant 40 – lasting 22 balls – was ended by Boje.

At Taunton, May 29 (floodlit). **Gloucestershire won by 21 runs.** Toss: Gloucestershire. **Gloucestershire 162-8** (20 overs) (C. M. Spearman 51; A. C. Thomas 3-31); **Somerset 141-5** (20 overs) (J. L. Langer 33, P. D. Trego 44*). *Gloucestershire 2 pts. Man of the Match:* C. M. Spearman. *Attendance:* 8,022.

Not for the first time, things suddenly went wrong for Somerset against their rivals, prompting a shock response from a packed ground. Gloucestershire's total might not have seemed imposing, but Somerset's batting lost its recent poise, and there was a significant discomfort facing the slow bowlers. Craig Spearman was one of the few to shape decently as a batsman. Somerset timed their reply badly – meaning that Peter Trego's late vigour was in vain.

At Birmingham, May 29 (floodlit). **Warwickshire won by seven wickets.** Toss: Worcestershire. **Worcestershire 148-8** (20 overs) (S. M. Davies 73, D. K. H. Mitchell 35; K. H. D. Barker 4-19);

Warwickshire 149-3 (18.2 overs) (J. O. Troughton 58, I. J. L. Trott 53*). *Warwickshire 2 pts. Man of the Match:* K. H. D. Barker. *Attendance:* 8,044.

Former professional footballer Keith Barker continued a promising start to his cricket career by taking four wickets, including Vikram Solanki with his first ball. Tim Ambrose held four catches. Steve Davies's first Twenty20 half-century gave Worcestershire a defendable target, but they squandered the initiative with some ragged fielding. Jim Troughton made his third successive Twenty20 fifty, finishing on the winning side for the first time.

At Cardiff, May 30 (floodlit). **Warwickshire won by six wickets.** Toss: Warwickshire. **Glamorgan 129-8** (20 overs) (J. W. M. Dalrymple 50; N. M. Carter 3-16); **Warwickshire 133-4** (19.1 overs) (I. J. L. Trott 55, I. R. Bell 42). *Warwickshire 2 pts. Man of the Match:* N. M. Carter. *Attendance:* 4,253.

Glamorgan suffered a third defeat in six days after another poor batting performance; Jamie Dalrymple was alone in passing 13. Neil Carter restricted Glamorgan at the start and finish of their innings, and struck three boundaries in the first over of Warwickshire's reply. Jonathan Trott and Ian Bell then shared a third-wicket stand of 71 in 11 overs.

At Worcester, May 30. **Northamptonshire won by six wickets.** Toss: Worcestershire. **Worcestershire 140-5** (20 overs) (S. C. Moore 62*; D. J. Willey 3-9); **Northamptonshire 142-4** (19 overs) (N. J. O'Brien 48*, J. J. van der Wath 29*). *Northamptonshire 2 pts. Man of the Match:* J. J. van der Wath. *Attendance:* 3,977.

Graeme Hick opened the £2m pavilion named in his honour, but Worcestershire could not mark the occasion with a victory. Stephen Moore made his highest Twenty20 score, off 52 balls, but David Willey's 3-9 in three overs kept Worcestershire in check. Northamptonshire also found runs hard to come by and required 48 off four overs; Johan van der Wath's unbeaten 29 off 11 balls, including three sixes, saw them home.

At Bristol, June 1 (floodlit). **Worcestershire won by 13 runs.** Toss: Worcestershire. **Worcestershire 188-5** (20 overs) (V. S. Solanki 51, S. M. Davies 50, S. C. Moore 33, B. F. Smith 41*); **Gloucestershire 175-8** (20 overs) (H. J. H. Marshall 41, A. P. R. Gidman 64). *Worcestershire 2 pts. Man of the Match:* V. S. Solanki. *Attendance:* 3,027.

An opening stand of 102 in ten overs by Vikram Solanki and Steven Davies gave Worcestershire an ideal start, though both fell to Steve Kirby in four balls. Gloucestershire's second-wicket pair of Alex Gidman (dropped twice) and Hamish Marshall (held at long-on) then took 44 off ten overs to keep the game close. Worcestershire's generally sharp fielding, highlighted by a full-length diving catch by Solanki to dismiss Craig Spearman, gave them two victories over Gloucestershire in a week.

At Taunton, June 1 (floodlit). **Somerset won by ten wickets.** Toss: Somerset. **Glamorgan 128-7** (20 overs) (J. W. M. Dalrymple 56); **Somerset 132-0** (14.4 overs) (M. E. Trescothick 69*, C. Kieswetter 57*). *Somerset 2 pts. Man of the Match:* M. E. Trescothick. *Attendance:* 4,985.

It took Marcus Trescothick and Craig Kieswetter, untroubled and very much in charge, just 14.4 overs to complete a rout; Somerset were hardly extended. Apart from Jamie Dalrymple there was little sign of determined batting from Glamorgan. This was not a journey across the Severn that they much enjoyed; Robert Croft, who came in for some rough treatment from Kieswetter, also came in for some rough treatment from the Taunton crowd.

At Birmingham, June 1 (floodlit). **Northamptonshire won by 24 runs.** Toss: Northamptonshire. **Northamptonshire 155-7** (20 overs) (R. A. White 59); **Warwickshire 131-6** (20 overs) (I. J. L. Trott 44). *Northamptonshire 2 pts. Man of the Match:* D. J. Willey. *Attendance:* 3,759.

Warwickshire appeared on course for victory, but their chase juddered to a halt after Jonathan Trott holed out to long-on. They managed only 39 in their last nine overs against accurate bowling led by the inexperienced left-armer David Willey, whose four overs yielded just 17 runs and included two wickets. Rob White's measured 50 gave Northamptonshire a total their bowlers expertly defended.

At Bristol, June 3 (floodlit). **Northamptonshire won by ten runs.** Toss: Northamptonshire. **Northamptonshire 162** (19.5 overs) (I. J. Harvey 48, M. H. Wessels 37; S. P. Kirby 3-29, J. Lewis 4-37); **Gloucestershire 152-7** (20 overs) (H. J. H. Marshall 42, G. P. Hodnett 30, A. P. R. Gidman 40). *Northamptonshire 2 pts. Man of the Match:* I. J. Harvey. *Attendance:* 2,555.

Chasing 163, Gloucestershire took 64 off the first six overs, with Hamish Marshall smacking 42. He was stumped giving Andrew Hall the charge and, with six more wickets following, Gloucestershire fell 11 runs short of a first home win. Jon Lewis took four wickets in six balls for the home side, but 48 from their old boy Ian Harvey kept Northamptonshire in front.

At Worcester, June 3 (floodlit). Worcestershire won by eight runs. Toss: Worcestershire. **Worcestershire 165-6** (20 overs) (S. M. Davies 33, B. F. Smith 35*; A. V. Suppiah 3-25); **Somerset 157** (20 overs) (M. E. Trescothick 52, Z. de Bruyn 30, P. D. Trego 58*; G. J. Batty 3-21). *Worcestershire 2 pts. Man of the Match:* G. J. Batty. *Attendance:* 2,682.

Somerset seemed sure of success, but lost their last six wickets in 21 balls for 20 runs with Gareth Batty taking his best Twenty20 figures. Steve Davies's 33 off 22 balls, coupled with Ben Smith's 35, set a challenging target. Marcus Trescothick's 35-ball 52 gave Somerset the initiative, but Peter Trego, unable to find anyone to stay with him, was stranded on 58 from 31 deliveries.*

At Cardiff, June 4 (floodlit). Worcestershire won by 29 runs. Toss: Worcestershire. **Worcestershire 164-6** (20 overs) (V. S. Solanki 34, S. C. Moore 42, M. M. Ali 41); **Glamorgan 135** (20 overs) (B. J. Wright 30, M. J. Powell 30; G. M. Andrew 3-19). *Worcestershire 2 pts. Man of the Match:* G. Batty. *Attendance:* 2,041.

After Glamorgan's fifth defeat in six games ended any realistic chance of reaching the quarter-finals, director of cricket Matthew Maynard was critical of the middle order for not building partnerships. Jamie Dalrymple and Mark Cosgrove again gave them a decent base, but three wickets fell for one run. Vikram Solanki had given Worcestershire a rousing start, before Stephen Moore and Moeen Ali consolidated with a 78-run partnership for the third wicket.

At Northampton, June 4 (floodlit). Somerset won by 30 runs. Toss: Somerset. **Somerset 163-3** (20 overs) (Z. de Bruyn 83*, P. D. Trego 34*); **Northamptonshire 133-9** (20 overs) (I. J. Harvey 30; C. M. Willoughby 4-29). *Somerset 2 pts. Man of the Match:* Z. de Bruyn. *Attendance:* 3,359.

After five straight wins, Northamptonshire tasted defeat for the first time. The match had begun well for them, with Andrew Hall removing Marcus Trescothick in the second over, but Zander de Bruyn shouldered responsibility and hit an unbeaten 83 from 52 balls. Peter Trego supplied vital late momentum. Once Charl Willoughby reduced them to 69-5, the Steelbacks were not seriously in the hunt. Trego conceded just 20 in his four overs to add to his belligerent 34 off 21 balls.*

At Birmingham, June 4 (floodlit). Warwickshire won by four wickets. Toss: Warwickshire. **Gloucestershire 135-7** (20 overs) (G. P. Hodnett 39); **Warwickshire 139-6** (19 overs) (I. J. Westwood 44*). *Warwickshire 2 pts. Man of the Match:* I. J. Westwood. *Attendance:* 4,034.

Inexperienced seamers Keith Barker and Steffan Piolet stifled Gloucestershire with combined figures of 8–0–40–3, despite attempts by Grant Hodnett and Craig Spearman to break the shackles. Ian Westwood saw Warwickshire home with 44 from 37 balls after Jonathan Trott's early aggression had taken a chunk out of a moderate target.

At Bristol, June 22 (floodlit). Warwickshire won by seven wickets. Toss: Warwickshire. **Gloucestershire 141** (19.4 overs) (D. O. Brown 33; R. Clarke 3-20, A. G. Botha 3-31, J. S. Patel 3-15); **Warwickshire 144-3** (16.1 overs) (I. J. L. Trott 73*, I. R. Bell 42). *Warwickshire 2 pts. Man of the Match:* I. J. L. Trott. *Attendance:* 2,368.

Slipshod fielding saw Gloucestershire beaten for the sixth time in seven games. Jonathan Trott, who made an unbeaten 73, was missed at backward point and at the wicket. Ian Bell's 42 came off 22 balls as Warwickshire ran out winners with time to spare. Hamish Marshall, caught at midwicket, and David Brown, held on the boundary, were the pick of the Gloucestershire batsmen before Jeetan Patel claimed three wickets in four balls in the 20th over.

At Northampton, June 23 (floodlit). Gloucestershire won by two wickets. Toss: Northamptonshire. **Northamptonshire 133** (20 overs) (I. J. Harvey 43; G. M. Hussain 3-22); **Gloucestershire 134-8** (19.5 overs) (G. P. Hodnett 60; N. Boje 3-23). *Gloucestershire 2 pts. Man of the Match:* G. P. Hodnett. *Attendance:* 3,876.

Kadeer Ali guided Gloucestershire to a surprise victory, hitting a six and a four in his unbeaten 21, but the batting honours belonged to Grant Hodnett with 60 from 46 balls after William Porterfield fell to the first ball of the innings. Hodnett's dismissal, with 36 still needed, gave group leaders Northamptonshire hope, but Kadeer was equal to the task. Earlier, Ian Harvey, facing another former employer, was alone in scoring freely against a disciplined attack.

At Taunton, June 23 (floodlit). Somerset won by seven wickets. Toss: Somerset. **Worcestershire 176-8** (20 overs) (S. C. Moore 40, M. M. Ali 36, B. F. Smith 44); **Somerset 177-3** (19 overs) (M. E.

Trescothick 34, J. L. Langer 44, J. C. Hildreth 48*, C. Kieswetter 31*). *Somerset 2 pts. Man of the Match:* J. C. Hildreth. *Attendance:* 5,864.

Watched by a crowd of just under 6,000, Somerset won with an over to spare. Worcestershire had relied on the jaunty batting of Stephen Moore and Ben Smith, helped by some poor fielding. Most of Somerset's early batsmen hit assured form, and the target was always within reach.

At Birmingham, June 23 (floodlit). **Warwickshire won by four wickets.** Toss: Warwickshire. **Glamorgan 148-7** (20 overs) (J. W. M. Dalrymple 63, M. J. Powell 39*; R. Clarke 2-31); **Warwickshire 149-6** (18.5 overs) (I. J. L. Trott 33, R. Clarke 24*). *Warwickshire 2 pts. Man of the Match:* R. Clarke. *Attendance:* 5,696.

Jonathan Trott, who moved into the top ten of career Twenty20 run-scorers during his quickfire 33 from 17 balls, set up Warwickshire's well-paced run-chase. Jamie Dalrymple struck 63 from 42 balls but found little support, and Glamorgan's total quickly looked inadequate as Garnett Kruger and David Harrison conceded 51 in four overs.

At Worcester, June 24 (floodlit). **Worcestershire won by 101 runs.** Toss: Worcestershire. **Worcestershire 222-4** (20 overs) (V. S. Solanki 100, S. M. Davies 32, S. C. Moore 49); **Glamorgan 121-6** (20 overs) (R. D. B. Croft 52*). *Worcestershire 2 pts. Man of the Match:* V. S. Solanki. *Attendance:* 2,707.

Vikram Solanki's century, which came from just 47 balls and contained 14 fours and two sixes, was nevertheless the second-slowest of the four Twenty20 hundreds hit by Worcestershire batsmen. Steve Davies, with 32 from 18 balls, and Stephen Moore, 49 from 30, gave Solanki excellent support against a ragged Glamorgan bowling and fielding display. The loss of three wickets in the first three overs ended Glamorgan's hopes of reaching their sizeable target, and only Robert Croft's unbeaten half-century ensured respectability.

At Taunton, June 25 (floodlit). **No result.** Toss: Northamptonshire. **Northamptonshire 49-0** (5 overs) **v Somerset.** *Somerset 1 pt, Northamptonshire 1 pt.*

At Cardiff, June 26 (floodlit). **Northamptonshire won by 20 runs.** Toss: Northamptonshire. **Northamptonshire 157-7** (20 overs) (M. H. Wessels 66*; J. A. R. Harris 4-23); **Glamorgan 137-9** (20 overs) (J. W. M. Dalrymple 33; N. Boje 3-14). *Northamptonshire 2 pts. Man of the Match:* M. H. Wessels. *Attendance:* 3,895.

The day after their heaviest Twenty 20 defeat, Glamorgan produced another poor performance in front of a large home crowd. They were well placed at 67-1 in the ninth over, but then lost wickets regularly. Batting first, Northamptonshire slumped to 24-3, but Riki Wessels, who scored 66* from 44 balls, ensured they set a defendable target by helping add 97 from the last ten overs. Victory took Northamptonshire to the quarter-finals.

At Bristol, June 26 (floodlit). **Somerset won by three wickets.** Toss: Somerset. **Gloucestershire 173** (19.3 overs) (K. Ali 33, H. J. H. Marshall 36, W. T. S. Porterfield 32; A. C. Thomas 3-31); **Somerset 175-7** (19 overs) (C. Kieswetter 84, P. D. Trego 49). *Somerset 2 pts. Man of the Match:* C. Kieswetter. *Attendance:* 7,761.

At 23-4 in the sixth over, Somerset's hopes of a quarter-final place looked bleak. Then Craig Kieswetter, at No. 5, delighted a capacity crowd with a thrilling 84 from 42 balls, his fifty coming from 27. He hit four sixes and eight fours, prompting his captain Justin Langer to hail him a Test match superstar in the making. Peter Trego (49 from 26) shared in Somerset's fightback. Gloucestershire had raced to 100-1 in eight overs, but were tied down by the spinners.

At Worcester, June 26 (floodlit). **Warwickshire won by seven wickets.** Toss: Warwickshire. **Worcestershire 162-6** (20 overs) (M. M. Ali 46, B. F. Smith 30, A. A. Noffke 32); **Warwickshire 166-3** (19.1 overs) (I. J. L. Trott 86*, N. M. Carter 45). *Warwickshire 2 pts. Man of the Match:* I. J. L. Trott. *Attendance:* 4,017.

Jonathan Trott's fourth half-century of the tournament ended Worcestershire's hopes of qualification, and took him past 400 Twenty20 runs for the summer. He hit 86 off 62 balls with nine fours and three sixes as Warwickshire completed a double over their neighbours. Trott shared an opening stand of 105 in 12 overs with Neil Carter, effectively settling the contest. Worcestershire had struggled for momentum after losing three early wickets; Moeen Ali's brisk 46 and a late flurry of 32 off 20 balls from Ashley Noffke kept them afloat a while longer.

At Bristol, June 28. **Glamorgan won by six wickets.** Toss: Gloucestershire. **Gloucestershire 148-7** (20 overs) (J. E. C. Franklin 44, D. O. Brown 56; R. E. Watkins 3-23); **Glamorgan 151-4** (18.3 overs) (B. J. Wright 55*, T. L. Maynard 49*). *Glamorgan 2 pts. Man of the Match:* B. J. Wright. *Attendance:* 2,795.

With neither side able to progress, the only issue at stake was who would finish bottom of the group. Chasing 149, Glamorgan slipped to 54-4 before Ben Wright, who faced 39 balls, and Tom Maynard, 30 balls, shared an unbroken stand of 97 to leave Gloucestershire "hurt and disappointed" according to their captain, Alex Gidman.

At Northampton, June 28. **Northamptonshire won by seven wickets.** Toss: Worcestershire. **Worcestershire 109-9** (20 overs) (A. J. Hall 4-19); **Northamptonshire 110-3** (18 overs) (S. D. Peters 61*). *Northamptonshire 2 pts. Man of the Match:* A. J. Hall. *Attendance:* 3,695.

Northamptonshire finished top of the group thanks to Andrew Hall and Stephen Peters. Hall demolished Worcestershire's middle order with 4-19 after Johan van der Wath secured the vital wicket of Vikram Solanki early on. Peters guided Northamptonshire to victory with two overs to spare, adding an unbroken 66 with Alex Wakely.

At Birmingham, June 28. **Warwickshire won by one run.** Toss: Somerset. **Warwickshire 193-6** (20 overs) (I. J. L. Trott 38, J. O. Troughton 62, R. Clarke 51*); **Somerset 192-7** (20 overs) (M. E. Trescothick 39, J. L. Langer 33, Z. de Bruyn 40, C. Kieswetter 39; J. S. Patel 3-23). *Warwickshire 2 pts. Man of the Match:* J. S. Patel. *Attendance:* 8,278.

Both teams had qualified for the knockouts, but the game was still competitive. Jonathan Trott established a record for most runs in a Twenty20 Cup season, his 27-ball 38 taking him to 469, five more than Justin Langer, also playing in the match, made for Somerset in 2006. Jim Troughton's best score of the campaign and Rikki Clarke's belligerent half-century helped Warwickshire to their highest total of the tournament. It proved just enough: Jeetan Patel conceded only five singles in a nerveless final over that culminated in Ben Phillips being run out attempting a second that would have tied the match.

NORTH GROUP

At Nottingham, May 25. **Durham won by one wicket.** Toss: Durham. **Nottinghamshire 163-6** (20 overs) (W. I. Jefferson 75, C. M. W. Read 43*; N. Killeen 3-21); **Durham 167-9** (20 overs) (I. D. Blackwell 59, D. M. Benkenstein 53; D. J. Pattinson 3-34). *Durham 2 pts. Man of the Match:* I. D. Blackwell. *Attendance:* 6,516. *County debut:* K. J. O'Brien (Nottinghamshire).

A raucous crowd saw Durham squeeze home off the final ball in a game of fluctuating fortunes. Nottinghamshire recovered from 49-4 to make a challenging total thanks to Will Jefferson's Twenty20 best and Chris Read, who helped add 97 from the final ten overs. Durham then stumbled to 27-4 before Ian Blackwell and Dale Benkenstein put them back on track. The scores were level at the start of the final over, bowled by Mark Ealham; he bowled five dot balls, one removing Gordon Muchall lbw, while Graham Onions was run out attempting a suicidal single. Mitch Claydon hit the last ball through midwicket to clinch the win.

At Leeds, May 25. **Yorkshire won by three wickets.** Toss: Leicestershire. **Leicestershire 148-3** (20 overs) (H. D. Ackerman 66*, J. W. A. Taylor 31, P. A. Nixon 31); **Yorkshire 149-7** (19.5 overs) (A. McGrath 30, M. P. Vaughan 35). *Yorkshire 2 pts. Man of the Match:* A. Shahzad. *Attendance:* 4,120. *County debut:* A. Roberts (Leicestershire).

Yorkshire included Naved-ul-Hasan (who had received a termination agreement from the Indian Cricket League just two hours earlier) and introduced their new video screen and scoreboard – the largest in the country. It registered a narrow home win, thanks to Ajmal Shahzad; he hit consecutive balls for six and four in the penultimate over, which began with 22 still required. H. D. Ackerman batted throughout for Leicestershire, but could never cut loose against accurate bowling.

At Chester-le-Street, May 26 (floodlit). **Derbyshire won by 59 runs.** Toss: Durham. **Derbyshire 175-6** (20 overs) (C. J. L. Rogers 50, G. T. Park 50, S. G. Law 42); **Durham 116** (15.3 overs) (K. J. Coetzer 31; T. Lungley 3-16). *Derbyshire 2 pts. Man of the Match:* G. T. Park. *Attendance:* 2,625.

This was the match in which Stuart Law pioneered the Mongoose bat, with a short, fat body and long handle. He was on 32 when he sent for it with two overs of Derbyshire's innings left, adding four singles and a stratospheric six over midwicket from a full toss. Garry Park, on his first return to the club he left for greater opportunities, took two wickets and hit a 33-ball 50. Durham's batting was woeful.

At Manchester, May 26 (floodlit). **Lancashire won by six wickets.** Toss: Yorkshire. **Yorkshire 105-8** (20 overs) (M. P. Vaughan 36; S. D. Parry 3-20); **Lancashire 107-4** (15.3 overs) (A. G. Prince 44). *Lancashire 2 pts. Man of the Match:* A. G. Prince. *Attendance:* 6,295.

A stunning catch by Steven Croft in front of the pavilion at deep midwicket to dismiss Michael Vaughan for his Twenty20 best was the highlight for a large crowd. The attendance was Lancashire's best of the season so far but more than 10,000 down on the equivalent fixture in 2008. Left-arm spinner Stephen Parry took three wickets on Twenty20 debut. Croft (21 from ten balls) and Ashwell Prince ensured a comfortable win.

At Manchester, May 28 (floodlit). **Lancashire won by 11 runs.** Toss: Nottinghamshire. **Lancashire 151-6** (20 overs) (F. du Plessis 31, A. G. Prince 30*); **Nottinghamshire 140-7** (20 overs) (S. R. Patel 35, C. M. W. Read 58*; T. C. Smith 3-20). *Lancashire 2 pts. Man of the Match:* C. M. W. Read. *Attendance:* 2,871.

Stephen Parry took a catch at third man to rank alongside Steven Croft's 48 hours previously. Parry dismissed Adam Voges, although an intelligent innings by Chris Read produced a tighter contest than seemed possible when Nottinghamshire slumped to 19-5. Parry jumped high to take the catch, threw the ball into the air as he toppled over the boundary, then returned to the field to complete the dismissal. Voges was the biter bit: he produced a similar effort for Australia during the winter. Lancashire put videos of Parry and Croft's catches on YouTube and asked their supporters to vote on which was the better.

At Leicester, May 28 (floodlit). **Derbyshire won by eight wickets.** Toss: Leicestershire. **Leicestershire 127-9** (20 overs) (J. W. A. Taylor 40; T. Lungley 5-27); **Derbyshire 129-2** (19 overs) (C. J. L. Rogers 58, G. M. Smith 47*). *Derbyshire 2 pts. Man of the Match:* T. Lungley. *Attendance:* 2,609.

Derbyshire's first Twenty20 five-for, by Tom Lungley, left them needing a modest 128. Skipper Chris Rogers led by example with a 36-ball 58 (with eight fours and three sixes) against the side he served briefly in 2005. Greg Smith finished the job with 47 and Derbyshire secured an eight-wicket victory with an over to spare.*

At Derby, May 29 (floodlit). **Nottinghamshire won by eight wickets.** Toss: Nottinghamshire. **Derbyshire 158-5** (20 overs) (G. M. Smith 52, W. W. Hinds 66); **Nottinghamshire 159-2** (15.1 overs) (G. P. Swann 90*, A. C. Voges 45*). *Nottinghamshire 2 pts. Man of the Match:* G. P. Swann. *Attendance:* 4,206.

After problems with the setting sun – despite a mobile screen suspended from a crane – Greg Smith and Wavell Hinds scored 115 in 11.5 overs. Hinds fell to a disputed catch by Darren Pattinson in front of the pavilion that frayed tempers. The umpires later told Graeme Swann and Graham Wagg to calm down. There was no arguing about the quality of Swann's 47-ball 90, which brought a comfortable victory; only Mark Ealham, who hit 91 v Yorkshire in 2004, had made more for Nottinghamshire.*

At Chester-le-Street, May 29 (floodlit). **Leicestershire won by seven wickets.** Toss: Durham. **Durham 144-8** (20 overs) (K. J. Coetzer 39*, G. R. Breese 37; A. C. F. Wyatt 3-14); **Leicestershire 148-3** (20 overs) (J. Allenby 53, P. A. Nixon 53*). *Leicestershire 2 pts. Man of the Match:* P. A. Nixon. *Attendance:* 3,767.

Durham again batted poorly, slipping from 35-0 after five overs to 55-5 by the 11th; the accuracy of 18-year-old seamer Alex Wyatt and off-spinner Jigar Naik caused the problems. Only Gareth Breese, at No. 8, struck with authority, making 37 from 15 balls. In his only game for Durham in the 2009 Twenty20, Paul Collingwood hit nine from 12 balls, then bowled the last over when Leicestershire needed ten. Jacques du Toit hit the penultimate ball for a straight six to level the scores and lofted the last ball over extra cover for four. Paul Nixon's improvisations produced 53 from 39 balls.*

At Leeds, May 29 (floodlit). **Lancashire won by five wickets.** Toss: Yorkshire. **Yorkshire 111-8** (20 overs) (J. A. Rudolph 38; S. I. Mahmood 2-17); **Lancashire 112-5** (19.1 overs) (S. J. Croft 40*). *Lancashire 2 pts. Man of the Match:* S. I. Mahmood. *Attendance:* 10,397.

Jacques Rudolph got the bird when his throw from near the boundary killed a pigeon flying across the outfield. Yorkshire got the bird from the home fans in a healthy crowd, who saw an insipid performance in which they were always second best. Completing a Roses double was easy work for Lancashire, who were never stretched, despite the game going to the final over.

At Chesterfield, May 31. **Yorkshire won by eight wickets.** Toss: Derbyshire. **Derbyshire 131-6** (20 overs) (W. W. Hinds 43); **Yorkshire 134-2** (16.1 overs) (A. W. Gale 79*). *Yorkshire 2 pts. Man of the Match:* A. W. Gale. *Attendance:* 3,989.

At a packed Queen's Park, Derbyshire never mastered Deon Kruis, Naved-ul-Hasan or Tim Bresnan, who between them took 5-66 from 12 overs. Andrew Gale made light of an inadequate total, hitting three sixes and eight fours from 59 balls. Yorkshire won with 23 balls to spare.

At Chester-le-Street, May 31. **Durham won by eight runs.** Toss: Nottinghamshire. **Durham 177-4** (20 overs) (M. J. Di Venuto 55, D. M. Benkenstein 48*); **Nottinghamshire 169** (19.4 overs) (A. C. Voges 33, W. I. Jefferson 42; M. E. Claydon 5-26). *Durham 2 pts. Man of the Match:* M. E. Claydon. *Attendance:* 4,918.

In his 16th Twenty20 innings for Durham, Michael Di Venuto made his first fifty; Dale Benkenstein's 48 from 18 balls included five sixes. Mitch Claydon became only the second bowler to take five wickets for Durham in a Twenty20 game (the first was Paul Collingwood against Derbyshire in 2008) when, with Nottinghamshire needing ten from the last over and two wickets left, he bowled Luke Fletcher and Mark Ealham.*

At Leicester, May 31. **Lancashire won by seven wickets.** Toss: Lancashire. **Leicestershire 147-3** (20 overs) (J. Allenby 71*, H. H. Dippenaar 39*); **Lancashire 151-3** (16.3 overs) (F. du Plessis 78*). *Lancashire 2 pts. Man of the Match:* F. du Plessis. *Attendance:* 3,589.

Lancashire's run-chase was faltering at 47-3, but the experience of Ashwell Prince (29) and the flair of his fellow South African Faf du Plessis turned the game back in their favour. Du Plessis picked the bowling apart with a thrilling 78* containing 13 fours and two sixes.*

At Manchester, June 2 (floodlit). **Lancashire won by 38 runs.** Toss: Derbyshire. **Lancashire 165-7** (20 overs) (P. J. Horton 41, T. C. Smith 32, A. G. Prince 38*; G. T. Park 3-23); **Derbyshire 127-9** (20 overs) (W. W. Hinds 32; S. I. Mahmood 4-29). *Lancashire 2 pts. Man of the Match:* S. I. Mahmood. *Attendance:* 4,331.

Lancashire moved four points clear at the top of the North Group, Sajid Mahmood removing Derbyshire's faint hopes of chasing down a big total with Twenty20-best figures of 4-29. Garry Park, who had kept wicket for Durham, was the pick of Derbyshire's attack, claiming three wickets with his medium-pace.

At Leeds, June 2 (floodlit). **Yorkshire won by two wickets.** Toss: Durham. **Durham 116-8** (20 overs) (D. M. Benkenstein 36); **Yorkshire 117-8** (20 overs) (A. McGrath 34). *Yorkshire 2 pts. Man of the Match:* T. T. Bresnan. *Attendance:* 4,602.

After collapsing from 67-2 to 85-7, largely through poor shot selection, Yorkshire would almost certainly have lost had Mitch Claydon, with the sun in his eyes, not dropped an otherwise easy chance on the square-leg boundary from Tim Bresnan. In a frenzied finish Bresnan went on to scamper the winning run off the final ball. The bowling was of a high standard throughout, the best coming from Naved-ul-Hasan, who conceded only a single in the 16th over, and two runs in the 18th, to peg back Durham.

At Leicester, June 3 (floodlit). **Leicestershire won by 70 runs.** Toss: Nottinghamshire. **Leicestershire 205-2** (20 overs) (M. A. G. Boyce 34, J. Allenby 110, J. W. A. Taylor 41*); **Nottinghamshire 135** (18.3 overs) (H. F. Gurney 3-21, W. A. White 3-27, J. Allenby 3-25). *Leicestershire 2 pts. Man of the Match:* J. Allenby. *Attendance:* 2,686.

Jim Allenby became only the second Leicestershire batsman, after Darren Maddy, to hit a Twenty20 century. His stirring 110 included seven fours and eight sixes and came from 58 balls. Leicestershire's total of 205-2 was their best at home; 61 came from the final four overs. Nottinghamshire were never in contention, and three wickets each for Allenby, Harry Gurney and Wayne White settled the issue.

At Derby, June 4 (floodlit). **Leicestershire won by 14 runs.** Toss: Leicestershire. **Leicestershire 144-6** (20 overs) (M. A. G. Boyce 33, J. Allenby 31; G. T. Park 3-29); **Derbyshire 130-5** (20 overs) (G. M. Smith 43). *Leicestershire 2 pts. Man of the Match:* J. Allenby. *Attendance:* 1,585.

Tidy bowling restricted Leicestershire, who could add only 29 in the last five overs. Derbyshire, however, fading fast from the competition, suffered a fourth consecutive defeat, undone by timid batting. The expected spurt in the run-rate never appeared, and Leicestershire's four main bowlers gave little away. Jim Allenby won his second match award in 24 hours.

At Manchester, June 4 (floodlit). **Lancashire won by six wickets.** Toss: Durham. **Durham 123-6** (20 overs) (G. J. Muchall 50*); **Lancashire 124-4** (19.1 overs) (T. C. Smith 57*, F. du Plessis 36). *Lancashire 2 pts. Man of the Match: T. C. Smith. Attendance: 4,721.*

Lancashire kept the competition's only 100% record with a sixth consecutive win, set up by their three spinners and completed by an intelligent unbeaten half-century from Tom Smith, who continued to make a success of his promotion to opener.

At Leeds, June 4 (floodlit). **Yorkshire won by eight wickets.** Toss: Nottinghamshire. **Nottinghamshire 155-6** (20 overs) (W. I. Jefferson 36, A. C. Voges 82*; Naved-ul-Hasan 4-23); **Yorkshire 156-2** (18 overs) (A. W. Gale 91, M. P. Vaughan 41*). *Yorkshire 2 pts. Man of the Match: A. W. Gale. Attendance: 4,400.*

A record Twenty20 stand for Yorkshire of 129 between Andrew Gale and Michael Vaughan helped them canter home; Gale hit 12 fours and two sixes off 55 balls. Adam Voges also faced 55 for his 82* with five fours and four sixes. In all he smashed 26 off one over from Bresnan: 226446. Naved-ul-Hasan's figures were the second-best for Yorkshire, behind Richard Pyrah's 4-20 v Durham in 2008.

At Liverpool, June 22 (floodlit). **Leicestershire won by eight runs.** Toss: Leicestershire. **Leicestershire 146-5** (20 overs) (J. Allenby 69); **Lancashire 138** (19.5 overs) (S. J. Croft 40, M. J. Chilton 34; I. E. O'Brien 5-23). *Leicestershire 2 pts. Man of the Match: I. E. O'Brien. Attendance: 3,842.*

The first Twenty20 fixture at a Lancashire outground was a sell-out even before Andrew Flintoff was given permission to play by the ECB. But the beer tents had run dry before the match ended, and it was Leicestershire who were inspired by the occasion, with Iain O'Brien taking five wickets, including Flintoff, to maintain hopes of reaching the quarter-finals. Jim Allenby, the only other bowler to take five wickets in a Twenty20 match for Leicestershire, played the crucial innings, with 69 off 45 balls.

At Nottingham, June 22 (floodlit). **Nottinghamshire won by 11 runs.** Toss: Nottinghamshire. **Nottinghamshire 165-4** (20 overs) (A. D. Brown 66, M. J. Wood 45, S. R. Patel 32*); **Yorkshire 154-8** (20 overs) (A. W. Gale 76). *Nottinghamshire 2 pts. Man of the Match: A. D. Brown. Attendance: 5,626.*

Having hit only 29 runs in the first six group games, Ali Brown announced his return to form in style, hitting four sixes and five fours in his 32-ball 66; he was supported by a brisk 45 from Matthew Wood. Yorkshire relied on Andrew Gale, but no one stuck around to help him, and they were unable to rebuild after he fell in the 14th over.

At Derby, June 23 (floodlit). **Durham won by six wickets.** Toss: Durham. **Derbyshire 153-6** (20 overs) (S. G. Law 59); **Durham 154-4** (18 overs) (D. A. Warner 50, P. Mustard 52). *Durham 2 pts. Man of the Match: D. A. Warner. Attendance: 1,987. County debuts: M. Hayward (Derbyshire); D. A. Warner.*

Stuart Law's half-century led Derbyshire to a reasonable, though not dominant, total. David Warner and Phil Mustard sped to 96 in nine overs, ensuring Durham had no need of further heroics. Certainly there were none from Derbyshire's impotent bowling, and they lost by a distance.

At Chester-le-Street, June 24 (floodlit). **Durham won by 41 runs.** Toss: Yorkshire. **Durham 131-7** (20 overs) (T. T. Bresnan 3-26); **Yorkshire 90-9** (20 overs) (B. W. Harmison 3-20). *Durham 2 pts. Man of the Match: B. W. Harmison.*

Yorkshire's tenth-wicket pair saved them from the lowest total in seven seasons of English Twenty20 cricket. They were five short of Sussex's 67 against Hampshire at Hove in 2004 when last man Deon Kruis joined Adil Rashid. Chasing what looked a modest target, even on a slow pitch, Yorkshire never recovered from two run-outs in the first three overs. Nor were they helped by Jacques Rudolph – captain in the absence of Anthony McGrath with a whiplash injury – putting Durham in on a glorious evening, only for the sky to cloud over at the interval.

At Nottingham, June 24 (floodlit). **Nottinghamshire won by nine wickets.** Toss: Leicestershire. **Leicestershire 123-7** (20 overs) (M. A. G. Boyce 32; R. J. Sidebottom 3-16); **Nottinghamshire 124-1** (14.3 overs) (M. J. Wood 43*, A. D. Brown 72). *Nottinghamshire 2 pts. Man of the Match: A. D. Brown. Attendance: 5,861.*

Nerveless bowling from Ryan Sidebottom ensured Nottinghamshire had a straightforward chase. His 3-16 equalled his Twenty20 best and included a stunning catch by wicketkeeper Chris Read in the final over. A ten-wicket humiliation seemed on the cards for Leicestershire as Matthew Wood and Ali Brown put on a club record 119, but Brown's dismissal at least prevented that.

At Derby, June 25 (floodlit). **Lancashire won by 56 runs.** Toss: Lancashire. **Lancashire 220-5** (20 overs) (V. V. S. Laxman 63, A. Flintoff 93); Derbyshire 164-7 (20 overs) (C. J. L. Rogers 52, G. M. Smith 56). *Lancashire 2 pts. Man of the Match:* A. Flintoff. *Attendance:* 3,182.

This match brought rather better news for England than Derbyshire, with Andrew Flintoff showing his power to blast Lancashire into the quarter-finals. He came in at 70-3 in the seventh over and hit 93 from 41 balls, including six sixes and nine fours; he took 26 from one Nantie Hayward over, which, with five wides, yielded 31 in all. A total of 220 was far too much for Derbyshire, who lost all five home games in the 2009 competition.

At Chester-le-Street, June 26 (floodlit). **Durham v Lancashire. Abandoned.** *Durham 1 pt, Lancashire 1 pt.*

At Leicester, June 26 (floodlit). **Leicestershire won by 11 runs.** Toss: Yorkshire. **Leicestershire 164-6** (20 overs) (J. Allenby 32, J. du Toit 39, P. A. Nixon 32); Yorkshire 153-6 (20 overs) (A. W. Gale 43, J. A. Rudolph 61). *Leicestershire 2 pts. Man of the Match:* C. W. Henderson. *Attendance:* 3,600.

Few knew it at the time, but this was Michael Vaughan's last appearance for Yorkshire before retirement, and it came in a losing cause. Set 165 to win, Yorkshire seemingly had the game at their mercy when Andrew Gale and Jacques Rudolph put on 104 for the first wicket inside 12 overs. But they lost wickets at crucial times, including Vaughan for 17, and against accurate bowling they faltered.

At Nottingham, June 26 (floodlit). **Nottinghamshire won by eight wickets.** Toss: Nottinghamshire. **Derbyshire 165-6** (20 overs) (G. G. Wagg 62, W. W. Hinds 45*); M. A. Ealham 3-20); **Nottinghamshire 166-2** (16.4 overs) (M. J. Wood 34, A. D. Brown 65, W. I. Jefferson 31*). *Nottinghamshire 2 pts. Man of the Match:* A. D. Brown. *Attendance:* 8,653.

Ali Brown's turnaround in form continued with his third half-century as Nottinghamshire cruised to victory. Mark Ealham, another England veteran to enjoy a move to Trent Bridge, also played a key role, bowling a double-wicket maiden in the fifth over, on his way to 3-20. Matthew Wood then hit six fours from 16 balls to provide the platform for Brown to push on.

At Leicester, June 28. **Durham won by six wickets.** Toss: Leicestershire. **Leicestershire 133-8** (20 overs) (H. H. Dippenaar 63; M. E. Claydon 3-14, B. W. Harmison 3-28); **Durham 137-4** (16.2 overs) (D. A. Warner 44, D. M. Benkenstein 33*; C. W. Henderson 3-32). *Durham 2 pts. Man of the Match:* M. E. Claydon. *Attendance:* 3,800.

This match was in essence a knockout: the winners would progress to the quarter-finals along with Lancashire, but defeat would spell elimination. Australian opener David Warner hit 44 from 18 deliveries as Durham easily overhauled a modest target.

At Nottingham, June 28. **Lancashire won by nine wickets.** Toss: Nottinghamshire. **Nottinghamshire 173-7** (20 overs) (S. R. Patel 37, D. J. Hussey 55); **Lancashire 175-1** (18 overs) (V. V. S. Laxman 78*, S. J. Croft 83*). *Lancashire 2 pts. Man of the Match:* S. J. Croft. *Attendance:* 7,067.

Nottinghamshire's recently productive opening partnership of Matthew Wood and Ali Brown made just 27, but No. 5 David Hussey hit four sixes in a 31-ball 55. Lancashire's second-wicket pair of Steven Croft and V. V. S. Laxman then manoeuvred the ball expertly – and in all cleared the ropes five times in their stand of 162 – to set a club record partnership for any wicket in the Twenty20 Cup.

At Leeds, June 28. **Derbyshire won by 37 runs.** Toss: Yorkshire. **Derbyshire 164-5** (20 overs) (C. J. L. Rogers 37, W. W. Hinds 49*, G. T. Park 42); Yorkshire 127 (19.5 overs) (J. Needham 4-21). *Derbyshire 2 pts. Man of the Match:* J. Needham. *Attendance:* 2,565.

Newspaper claims that Michael Vaughan would announce his retirement a couple of days later led to urgent lunchtime talks with chief executive Stuart Regan, resulting in Vaughan pulling out and denying home supporters a chance to say farewell in a competitive game. Once again, Yorkshire's batting collapsed after a good start, Jake Needham's off-spin doing most damage with three wickets in four balls. Neither side could make the last eight before the game began.

SOUTH GROUP

At Southampton, May 25. **Hampshire won by nine wickets.** Toss: Sussex. **Sussex 133-8** (20 overs) (D. R. Smith 63; D. G. Cork 3-30, H. Riazuddin 3-15); **Hampshire 137-1** (16.1 overs) (J. H. K. Adams 68*, S. M. Ervine 42*). *Hampshire 2 pts. Man of the Match:* H. Riazuddin. *Attendance:* 3,956.

Sussex were undermined by Hamza Riazuddin, who took three wickets in eight deliveries, including Luke Wright first ball. They never recovered, although Dwayne Smith, newly arrived from the IPL, offered mid-innings resistance. Hampshire made light of their target, Jimmy Adams and Sean Ervine putting on 110 in 13 overs for the second wicket.*

At Canterbury, May 25. **No result.** Toss: Essex. **Essex 187-7** (20 overs) (M. L. Pettini 31, A. N. Cook 80); **Kent 16-0** (3.2 overs). *Kent 1 pt, Essex 1 pt. Attendance:* 3,644.

Alastair Cook's competition-best 80 from 56 balls counted for nought when bad light, followed by rain, stopped play 20 balls into Kent's reply. The weather left Essex frustrated, and a weakened home attack, without both Ryan McLaren and Wayne Parnell, somewhat relieved.

At Lord's, May 25. **Surrey won by 57 runs.** Toss: Surrey. **Surrey 186-1** (20 overs) (U. Afzaal 98*, M. R. Ramprakash 61*); **Middlesex 129-7** (20 overs) (T. Henderson 32; C. P. Schofield 3-31). *Surrey 2 pts. Man of the Match:* U. Afzaal. *Attendance:* 10,890.

Middlesex made the worst possible start to the defence of their Twenty20 title, with Usman Afzaal and Mark Ramprakash scoring at will in a second-wicket stand of 139 against an under-strength attack. Missing six of the team who defeated Kent in the 2008 final, Middlesex were outclassed. The only disappointment for Surrey was Afzaal not quite making his century; his 98 came from 59 balls with eight fours and two sixes.*

At The Oval, May 26 (floodlit). **Sussex won by 21 runs.** Toss: Sussex. **Sussex 184-9** (20 overs) (C. D. Nash 40, L. J. Wright 58); **Surrey 163-9** (20 overs) (S. A. Newman 38, S. J. Walters 34; M. H. Yardy 3-21). *Sussex 2 pts. Man of the Match:* L. J. Wright. *Attendance:* 8,541.

The big switch-on of Surrey's new floodlights saw the home team left in the shade, first by Nash's 16-ball innings, which contained two sixes off fast bowler Andre Nel, and then by Luke Wright's 46-ball onslaught. Surrey's reply began with two maidens before Scott Newman and Mark Ramprakash picked up speed; but both fell to the left-arm spin of Michael Yardy, who finished with three wickets and two catches.

At Lord's, May 27 (floodlit). **Kent won by 62 runs.** Toss: Kent. **Kent 191-3** (20 overs) (M. van Jaarsveld 75*, G. O. Jones 30, D. I. Stevens 59*); **Middlesex 129-8** (20 overs). *Kent 2 pts. Man of the Match:* D. I. Stevens. *Attendance:* 6,034.

This was the first match staged under the new permanent Lord's floodlights, but the combination of a cold evening and the counter-attraction of Manchester United appearing on TV in the Champions League final kept the attendance down. Those who did get to Lord's might have wished they had stayed away: once again Middlesex were let down by an inept batting display.

At The Oval, May 27 (floodlit). **Surrey won by one run.** Toss: Surrey. **Surrey 125-8** (20 overs) (S. J. Walters 30); **Hampshire 124-9** (20 overs) (C. C. Benham 39). *Surrey 2 pts. Man of the Match:* G. D. Elliott. *Attendance:* 6,813.

Everything boiled down to the very last ball. Ten had already come from Jade Dernbach's first five deliveries, and Hamza Riazuddin, needing a four, cut hard at the final ball. But a desperate dive by James Benning restricted the batsmen to two runs, so earning Surrey a second victory of the tournament. Both teams suffered poor starts: Surrey lost Usman Afzaal to the third ball of the innings, while the Hampshire openers also made ducks. Grant Elliott, Surrey's New Zealand all-rounder, had figures of 4–0–13–2.

At Hove, May 28 (floodlit). **Essex won by 17 runs.** Toss: Essex. **Essex 148** (19.4 overs) (M. L. Pettini 31, R. S. Bopara 45); **Sussex 131** (19.1 overs) (D. R. Smith 30; G. R. Napier 3-21, C. J. C. Wright 4-24). *Essex 2 pts. Man of the Match:* C. J. C. Wright. *Attendance:* 3,558.

Sussex looked to be in control after a competition-record five run-outs – including Ravi Bopara, beaten by Dwayne Smith's direct hit from 50 yards. Essex's total seemed 20 below par, and at 75-3 in the 11th over Sussex were on course. But then Smith was dismissed, and they could not manage another boundary; Chris Wright became the sixth Essex player to take four wickets in a Twenty20 innings.

At Chelmsford, May 29 (floodlit). **Essex won by four wickets.** Toss: Surrey. **Surrey 165-5** (20 overs) (S. A. Newman 81*); **Essex 169-6** (19.5 overs) (A. N. Cook 39, R. S. Bopara 53, M. J. Walker 30). *Essex 2 pts. Man of the Match:* S. A. Newman. *Attendance:* 6,235.

A sell-out crowd witnessed a tight contest which Essex won with a ball to spare. Scott Newman batted throughout for Surrey, hitting 81* from 60 balls, including 11 boundaries, but it was Ravi Bopara's 38-ball half-century, containing successive sixes off Andre Nel, that swung the match. Ten came from the 19th over, bowled by Nel, leaving his former county to get just three from the last.

At Canterbury, May 29 (floodlit). **Kent won by four wickets.** Toss: Middlesex. **Middlesex 104-6** (20 overs) (T. Henderson 31*); **Kent 107-6** (18.2 overs) (R. McLaren 31; A. Richardson 3-29). *Kent 2 pts. Man of the Match:* R. H. Joseph. *Attendance:* 3,155.

Kent avenged their defeat in the 2008 final with a comfortable win over a feeble Middlesex, who never recovered from losing Nick Compton and Owais Shah in Robbie Joseph's two fiery opening overs. Former Kent favourite Tyron Henderson top-scored with a relatively painstaking 31 from 37 balls as Middlesex crept past 100 in the final over. Fellow South Africans Martin van Jaarsveld and Ryan McLaren led Kent's successful, low-key pursuit.

At Hove, May 29 (floodlit). **Sussex won by eight wickets.** Toss: Hampshire. **Hampshire 122-7** (20 overs) (M. A. Carberry 36); **Sussex 128-2** (17.1 overs) (C. D. Nash 56*, D. R. Smith 31*). *Sussex 2 pts. Man of the Match:* C. D. Nash. *Attendance:* 5,917.

Sussex were again outstanding in the field, this time making no mistake in pursuit of a lowish total; Chris Nash struck only his second Twenty20 half-century and sealed victory with the only six of the innings. He added 73 in seven overs with Dwayne Smith, whose medium-pace had earlier claimed two wickets in four balls as Hampshire's poor shot selection on a slow surface was exposed.

At Southampton, May 31. **Hampshire won by 18 runs.** Toss: Hampshire. **Hampshire 191-6** (20 overs) (M. J. Lumb 54, J. H. K. Adams 44); **Surrey 173-8** (20 overs) (M. R. Ramprakash 73). *Hampshire 2 pts. Man of the Match:* M. R. Ramprakash. *Attendance:* 5,254.

Hampshire openers Michael Lumb and Jimmy Adams put on 92 in just nine overs; Jade Dernbach's only over cost 19, and Andre Nel conceded 17 off the penultimate. Mark Ramprakash kept Surrey in contention in a 47-ball innings, but he was sixth out at 168, and the challenge died with his departure.

At Canterbury, May 31. **Kent won by five wickets.** Toss: Sussex. **Sussex 132-7** (20 overs) (M. W. Goodwin 39, Yasir Arafat 43; Azhar Mahmood 3-16); **Kent 133-5** (17 overs) (M. van Jaarsveld 39, G. O. Jones 56). *Kent 2 pts. Man of the Match:* G. O. Jones. *Attendance:* 3,042.

A three-wicket return by one-day maestro Azhar Mahmood left Kent with a modest run-chase, which they achieved comfortably. Azhar removed big-hitting Dwayne Smith, had Ed Joyce caught behind three balls later and at the death dismissed the dangerous Yasir Arafat. Geraint Jones's 56 from 39 balls ensured victory, though he was dropped on 44 when Chris Nash and Smith collided at long leg. Nash went to hospital for treatment to a badly gashed shin.

At Chelmsford, June 1 (floodlit). **Essex won by 36 runs.** Toss: Essex. **Essex 205-4** (20 overs) (M. L. Pettini 40, A. N. Cook 77, G. W. Flower 61); **Kent 169-7** (20 overs) (J. L. Denly 32, M. van Jaarsveld 33; G. W. Flower 3-26). *Essex 2 pts. Man of the Match:* G. W. Flower. *Attendance:* 4,800. *County debut:* M. A. Hardinges (Essex).

Explosive Essex batting set county partnership records for the first two wickets: Alastair Cook shared stands of 90 with Mark Pettini for the first and 89 with Grant Flower for the second. Cook hit a 55-ball 77 that included two sixes, but was outpaced by Flower, whose 61 came from 30 balls. In reply, Joe Denly and Martin van Jaarsveld struck six successive fours, but Kent's challenge fell away as Flower took over: in all he had a hand in six Kent wickets, holding three catches and taking 3-26.

At Hove, June 1 (floodlit). **Sussex won by seven wickets.** Toss: Middlesex. **Middlesex 116** (19.3 overs) (G. K. Berg 33; M. H. Yardy 3-22, R. J. Hamilton-Brown 3-15); **Sussex 120-3** (16.3 overs) (R. J. Hamilton-Brown 69*). *Sussex 2 pts. Man of the Match:* R. J. Hamilton-Brown. *Attendance:* 2,955.

The holders slumped to a fourth successive defeat after wasting a useful toss. They were undermined by the Sussex spinners who had combined figures of 10-0-63-7, Rory Hamilton-Brown's off-breaks claiming three wickets for the first time. He followed up by hitting ten fours and a six as Sussex eased to a bloodless victory with time to spare.

At Uxbridge, June 2 (floodlit). **Hampshire won by 56 runs.** Toss: Hampshire. **Hampshire 181-6** (20 overs) (M. A. Carberry 56, S. M. Ervine 53); **Middlesex 125** (19 overs) (B. A. Godleman 34; L. A. Dawson 3-25, S. M. Ervine 4-16). *Hampshire 2 pts. Man of the Match:* S. M. Ervine. *Attendance:* 2,802.

Sean Ervine's 53 came only from 26 balls and, with Middlesex giving yet another abysmal batting display, there was little doubt about the outcome as soon as they were reduced to 33-2. Five defeats in five outings meant Middlesex were unlikely to progress beyond the group stage.

At Chelmsford, June 3 (floodlit). **Sussex won by eight wickets.** Toss: Essex. **Essex 126-7** (20 overs) (D. R. Smith 3-19); **Sussex 130-2** (18.2 overs) (M. W. Goodwin 64*). *Sussex 2 pts. Man of the Match:* M. W. Goodwin. *Attendance:* 4,881.

Controlled bowling and superb fielding ensured Sussex dictated the Essex innings, as Dwayne Smith took a wicket in each of his first three overs. Only once did Essex manage as many as ten from an over – though that was when a useful 22 came off one from Robin Martin-Jenkins. Murray Goodwin added to a fine Sussex team performance with a well-fashioned 64 from 54 deliveries. His opening stand of 74 in nine overs with Rory Hamilton-Brown made victory a formality.*

At Southampton, June 4 (floodlit). **Hampshire won by 75 runs.** Toss: Hampshire. **Hampshire 219-2** (20 overs) (M. J. Lumb 124*, M. A. Carberry 62); **Essex 144** (18.4 overs) (M. J. Walker 50; S. M. Ervine 3-19). *Hampshire 2 pts. Man of the Match:* M. J. Lumb. *Attendance:* 4,767.

Michael Lumb's 124 from 69 balls and with 14 fours and four sixes was the fourth-highest innings in all Twenty20 cricket – and Hampshire's first century. Lumb and Michael Carberry added 170 for the second wicket (also the fourth-best, for any wicket, in all Twenty20 games). Essex, reduced to 15-3 in the fourth over by Dominic Cork and Hamza Riazuddin, never threatened to reach a mountainous target.*

At Hove, June 4 (floodlit). **Sussex won by two runs** (D/L method). Toss: Kent. **Sussex 131-3** (20 overs) (D. R. Smith 69*); **Kent 61-0** (11 overs) (J. L. Denly 32*). *Sussex 2 pts. Man of the Match:* D. R. Smith. *Attendance:* 4,415.

Kent had only themselves to blame for losing after a generator problem had knocked out the floodlights at the Sea End. Despite knowing that the fading light would bring Duckworth/Lewis into play, Joe Denly and Darren Stevens batted too cautiously and slipped behind the par score for the first time at the end of the tenth over. Michael Yardy promptly brought back Robin Martin-Jenkins, whose pace was considered too fast by the umpires. Sussex had been indebted to Dwayne Smith and to Yardy who, in seamer-friendly conditions, added 58 in six overs.

At Chelmsford, June 22 (floodlit). **Essex won by eight wickets.** Toss: Middlesex. **Middlesex 148** (19.2 overs) (E. J. G. Morgan 31, D. J. Malan 31; Danish Kaneria 3-21); **Essex 151-2** (19 overs) (M. L. Pettini 80*, M. J. Walker 34*). *Essex 2 pts. Man of the Match:* M. L. Pettini. *Attendance:* 5,998.

A career-best 80 by Mark Pettini allowed Essex to rediscover the winning thread after two successive defeats. His 57-ball innings, which included a six and ten fours, secured victory with an over to spare. Only a 60-run sixth-wicket stand between Eoin Morgan and Dawid Malan afforded Middlesex respectability.*

At Tunbridge Wells, June 22 (floodlit). **Kent won by eight runs.** Toss: Kent. **Kent 182-4** (20 overs) (R. W. T. Key 58*, D. I. Stevens 56); **Hampshire 174-7** (20 overs) (M. J. Lumb 59, M. A. Carberry 39, C. C. Benham 36). *Kent 2 pts. Man of the Match:* D. I. Stevens. *Attendance:* 4,325.

Rob Key hit his first half-century of the summer in all cricket and helped Kent zip along at nine an over. Key batted throughout, but was outshone by Darren Stevens, whose majestic 27-ball 56 included six sixes; they added 78 in seven overs. In reply, Michael Lumb's 59 from 33 balls gave Hampshire a sound base, and when Chris Benham helped plunder 19 off the 18th over, from James Tredwell, a Hampshire win was possible. But Michael Carberry, who hit a cameo 39, and Dimitri Mascarenhas were run out in the penultimate over, leaving Benham too much to do.

At Hove, June 22 (floodlit). **Sussex won by six wickets.** Toss: Surrey. **Surrey 123** (20 overs) (R. S. C. Martin-Jenkins 3-17); **Sussex 125-4** (16.5 overs) (M. W. Goodwin 38, L. J. Wright 31). *Sussex 2 pts. Man of the Match:* R. S. C. Martin-Jenkins. *Attendance:* 5,270.

Sussex coasted to a fourth successive win after Surrey struggled against their four spinners, who between them took 5-60 from 12 overs. One of the four, India leg-spinner Piyush Chawla, making his competition debut, had figures of 4–0–17–2, while Michael Yardy took 2-14 from his four overs.

Openers Murray Goodwin and Luke Wright, reprising his World Twenty20 role, set up a comfortable victory by putting on 71 in ten overs.

At Southampton, June 23 (floodlit). **Hampshire won by 28 runs.** Toss: Hampshire. **Hampshire 183-6** (20 overs) (M. J. Lumb 93); **Middlesex 155-5** (20 overs) (B. A. Godleman 57, O. A. Shah 45). *Hampshire 2 pts. Man of the Match:* M. J. Lumb. *Attendance:* 5,401.

Michael Lumb, already the scorer of a century in the competition, was seven short of another when he was stumped by Ben Scott off a wide from Gareth Berg's medium-pace. Billy Godleman and Owais Shah kept Middlesex hopes alive with a second-wicket stand of 97, but the champions slumped to a seventh successive defeat.

At The Oval, June 24 (floodlit). **Kent won by one run.** Toss: Kent. **Kent 168-6** (20 overs) (R. W. T. Key 44, M. van Jaarsveld 54); **Surrey 167** (19.4 overs) (J. G. E. Benning 38, U. Afzaal 62). *Kent 2 pts. Man of the Match:* M. van Jaarsveld. *Attendance:* 13,432.

The second dramatic final-over finish of the season at The Oval was watched by a substantial crowd. This time it was the visitors who won, ending Surrey's chances of reaching the quarter-finals. The fractious last over began with Surrey nine down and needing eight runs – it would have been 14 but Kent were penalised six runs for not bowling their overs in time. Andre Nel squirted four past third man, then took a quick single, but barged into the bowler, Ryan McLaren. Kent captain Rob Key barked angrily at batsman and umpire. Next ball Jade Dernbach was run out and Kent had won. Earlier Martin van Jaarsveld had helped Kent reach three figures in ten overs, sharing in a stand of 92 with Key.

At The Oval, June 25 (floodlit). **Essex won by 84 runs.** Toss: Essex. **Essex 210-3** (20 overs) (M. L. Pettini 87, A. N. Cook 100*); **Surrey 126** (15.2 overs) (U. Afzaal 30). *Essex 2 pts. Man of the Match:* A. N. Cook. *Attendance:* 14,266.

Alastair Cook reached a maiden Twenty20 hundred when, from the penultimate ball of the Essex innings, he was dropped by Chris Schofield. Cook's 57-ball innings contained 11 fours and four sixes, and thrilled another big crowd. He was supported by his captain and fellow-opener Mark Pettini, who made 80 for the second match running; they put on 169, bettering the Essex first-wicket record of 90 they had established three weeks earlier, and just six short of the Twenty20 best set by Graeme Hick and Vikram Solanki for Worcestershire in 2007. The Surrey batting fell woefully short, stand-in captain Usman Afzaal top-scoring with 30.

At Southampton, June 26 (floodlit). **Kent won by seven wickets.** Toss: Hampshire. **Hampshire 131-7** (20 overs) (A. D. Mascarenhas 45*); **Kent 132-3** (17.5 overs) (G. O. Jones 35*, D. I. Stevens 62*). *Kent 2 pts. Man of the Match:* D. I. Stevens. *County debut:* T. E. Linley (Surrey). *Attendance:* 8,256.

Hampshire subsided to 42-6 before Dimitri Mascarenhas engineered a partial recovery. Kent were 30-3 and would have been 35-4 had Dominic Cork at slip not put down Geraint Jones off Mascarenhas. Jones and the more aggressive Darren Stevens made the most of the escape, together fashioning a match-winning stand of 102 for the fourth wicket. The Kent bowlers had shared the wickets – all six took at least one – and the runs: three bowled three overs for 17 runs and a fourth three for 16. Kent were guaranteed a quarter-final place, while Hampshire still had work to do.

At Lord's, June 26 (floodlit). **Middlesex won by 23 runs.** Toss: Middlesex. **Middlesex 166-5** (20 overs) (N. J. Dexter 73, O. A. Shah 49); **Essex 143** (19.2 overs) (V. Chopra 51; T. Henderson 3-34). *Middlesex 2 pts. Man of the Match:* N. J. Dexter. *Attendance:* 19,437.

At last, at long last. Middlesex eventually made a total in excess of 150, and eventually they won. Unfortunately it followed seven defeats and was far too late to salvage anything other than a little self-respect from the campaign. Owais Shah hinted at what might have been if Middlesex had been able to retain the side that did so well in 2008.

At The Oval, June 27. **Middlesex won by seven wickets.** Toss: Surrey. **Surrey 160-5** (20 overs) (M. J. Brown 77); **Middlesex 162-3** (18.2 overs) (O. A. Shah 61*, D. J. Malan 38). *Middlesex 2 pts. Man of the Match:* O. A. Shah. *Attendance:* 10,885. *County debut:* T. E. Linley (Surrey).

After seven straight defeats came a second win on the trot for Middlesex. Once again Owais Shah was to the fore, thumping a 41-ball 61 that contained three sixes and four fours. Shah and Dawid Malan put on exactly 100 inside 11 overs as they overhauled a Surrey total which had owed everything to a first-wicket stand of 76 between Michael Brown, who scored a half-century in his first Twenty20 appearance of the season, and Chris Jordan (28).*

At Chelmsford, June 28. **Hampshire won by six wickets.** Toss: Essex. **Essex 149-6** (20 overs) (G. R. Napier 47, R. N. ten Doeschate 43; S. M. Ervine 3-26); **Hampshire 153-4** (19.1 overs) (M. A. Carberry 39, S. M. Ervine 39*; G. W. Flower 3-25). *Hampshire 2 pts. Man of the Match:* S. M. Ervine. *Attendance:* 5,838.

This was a crunch game: the winners would progress and the losers would be out. In front of another healthy crowd, Graham Napier hit a cameo 47 from 33 balls, including three sixes, but it was not enough. The defining moment came in the 15th over of Hampshire's reply, when Dimitri Mascarenhas was dropped by James Middlebrook. He and Sean Ervine shared an unbroken 66-run match-winning partnership.

At Beckenham, June 28. **Kent won by 16 runs.** Toss: Kent. **Kent 184-7** (20 overs) (M. van Jaarsveld 64, G. O. Jones 47; M. N. W. Spriegel 4-33); **Surrey 168-9** (20 overs) (R. McLaren 4-37). *Kent 2 pts. Man of the Match:* M. van Jaarsveld. *Attendance:* 5,422. *County debut:* S. J. King (Surrey).

Kent already had a place in the knockout stages, but a comfortable win over an experimental Surrey side containing two cup debutants in Simon King and Laurie Evans ensured they remained unbeaten at home and gained a home tie in the quarters. After the loss of both openers, Kent regrouped with a 96-run third-wicket stand in nine overs between Martin van Jaarsveld and Geraint Jones. Van Jaarsveld's third fifty of the tournament came from 34 balls; Jones paced 30 for his 47. Surrey's inexperienced top six all made it into the twenties, but none reached 30. The wily Ryan McLaren returned career-best Twenty20 figures of 4-37.

At Lord's, June 28. **Sussex won by six wickets.** Toss: Middlesex. **Middlesex 127-8** (20 overs) (G. K. Berg 30*); **Sussex 130-4** (19 overs) (D. R. Smith 33, E. C. Joyce 41*, C. D. Nash 35*). *Sussex 2 pts. Man of the Match:* C. D. Nash. *Attendance:* 9,807.

The formula held once again: whenever Middlesex failed to make 150, they would lose. Another shoddy batting performance gave Sussex far too little to do. Joyce, who led Middlesex to their 2008 Twenty20 success, took delight in playing a significant role in this win.

QUARTER-FINALS

At Canterbury, July 27. **Kent won by 56 runs.** Toss: Kent. **Kent 149-7** (20 overs) (J. L. Denly 31; B. W. Harmison 3-24); **Durham 93** (17.2 overs) (D. M. Benkenstein 47; J. C Tredwell 3-18). *Man of the Match:* J. C. Tredwell. *Attendance:* 7,071.

Kent, appearing in the knockouts for the fourth year running, won emphatically to reach a third consecutive finals day. Durham gambled by opening with Ian Blackwell's left-arm spin, but in eight overs Rob Key and Joe Denly raced to a first-wicket stand of 69, Kent's best of the campaign. Blackwell's first over cost 11, but he recovered his poise and conceded just ten from his remaining three. Kent's canny attack were never pressured once Wayne Parnell dismissed openers Phil Mustard and David Warner (who had flown in from Australia for the occasion) for ducks.

At Hove, July 27 (floodlit). **Sussex won by 38 runs.** Toss: Warwickshire. **Sussex 152-9** (20 overs) (L. J. Wright 38); **Warwickshire 114** (19 overs) (I. J. L. Trott 56; R. J. Hamilton-Brown 4-15). *Man of the Match:* R. J. Hamilton-Brown. *Attendance:* 6,773.

Rory Hamilton-Brown won the match award for his career-best 4-15, but as decisive a contribution came from No. 7 Chris Nash, who smashed 29 off 14 balls to regain the momentum. Jonathan Trott's fifth half-century of the tournament took his aggregate to a record 525 runs, but when he was the second to fall in Hamilton-Brown's first over, Warwickshire's hopes departed with him.

At Manchester, July 28, 29, 30. **Lancashire v Somerset. Abandoned. Somerset won 5–1 in a bowl-out.**

Despite the ECB granting the counties' request for a second reserve day in an attempt to decide the game on the field, heavy rain meant that the place at finals day would be won and lost in a bowl-out held in Old Trafford's indoor school. Somerset won comfortably, Alfonso Thomas hitting the stumps with both of his deliveries. Lancashire's five bowlers, only four of whom were required, included V. V. S. Laxman.

At Northampton, July 29, 30 (floodlit). **Northamptonshire won by 13 runs.** Toss: Hampshire. **Northamptonshire 134-6** (20 overs) (A. J. Hall 39*); **Hampshire 121** (19.4 overs) (A. D. Mascarenhas 36; A. J. Hall 3-25). *Man of the Match:* A. J. Hall. *Attendance:* 5,000.

Northamptonshire reached finals day for the first time, at the expense of Hampshire, newly crowned Friends Provident Trophy champions. After rain washed out the scheduled day, an

enthusiastic crowd saw Northamptonshire crumble to 5-2 and 40-4, only for Andrew Hall to stage a
spirited recovery with 39* from 24 balls. Hampshire still seemed favourites, even after the early loss
of Jimmy Adams, but the experience of Hall and an outstanding spell from Lee Daggett (4–0–19–2)
pegged them back. They were in contention while Dimitri Mascarenhas was there, but once he was
bowled by Johan van der Wath, the last three wickets fell without addition.

SEMI-FINALS

NORTHAMPTONSHIRE v SUSSEX

At Birmingham, August 15. Sussex won by seven wickets. Toss: Sussex.

Sussex won a humdrum match with ease, to the relief of their own supporters and, quite probably, the ECB. Lalit Modi, chairman of the IPL, had already declared that if Northamptonshire reached the finals of the Twenty20 Cup they would not be allowed to participate in the lucrative Champions League because of the ICL connections of so many of their players. Perhaps that explained the lacklustre performance by Northamptonshire. The top six all made double figures, but no one reached 35; Hall was too low at No. 8. Sussex were disciplined in the field and always in control. They were quick to recognise that the pitch offered encouragement to slow bowling. Yardy's utilitarian darts and Beer's promising wrist-spinners were equally effective. The modest target of 137 allowed Goodwin to play the measured innings of a cagey veteran. Minimising risks, he was still there at the end with time to decelerate as he approached the finishing line. He received a little help from Wright and Hamilton-Brown. Supposedly one of the most stressful fixtures in the domestic calendar, given the potential prizes in India, this had been a breeze for Sussex – and a bit of a bore for neutral onlookers.

Man of the Match: M. W. Goodwin.
Attendance (for all three matches on finals day): 19,210.

Northamptonshire

		B	4	6
I. J. Harvey *b 11*	21	15	4	0
R. A. White *run out*	20	21	1	0
†N. J. O'Brien *st 8 b 6*	24	24	0	1
A. G. Wakely *c 9 b 10*	10	11	0	0
*N. Boje *not out*	34	29	4	0
M. H. Wessels *b 9*	10	11	0	0
J. J. van der Wath *b 9*	9	7	1	0
A. J. Hall *not out*	5	2	1	0
B 3	3			

(20 overs) 136-6

1/23 2/54 3/69 4/85 5/112 6/130

D. J. Willey, M. S. Panesar and L. M. Daggett did not bat.

Wright 3–0–23–0; Yasir Arafat 4–0–28–2; Kirtley 3–0–22–1; Smith 1–0–6–0; Yardy 4–0–23–1; Beer 4–0–26–1; Hamilton-Brown 1–0–5–0.

Sussex

		B	4	6
M. W. Goodwin *not out*	80	67	10	0
L. J. Wright *c 2 b 8*	18	13	2	1
R. J. Hamilton-Brown *b 8*	29	30	0	1
D. R. Smith *c 3 b 7*	2	3	0	0
E. C. Joyce *not out*	4	5	0	0
L-b 2, w 2	4			

(19.4 overs) 137-3

1/30 2/121 3/126

*M. H. Yardy, C. D. Nash, †A. J. Hodd, Yasir Arafat, W. A. T. Beer and R. J. Kirtley did not bat.

Van der Wath 4–0–34–1; Hall 3.4–0–20–2; Harvey 2–0–11–0; Daggett 3–0–27–0; Boje 2–0–15–0; Panesar 3–0–12–0; Willey 2–0–16–0.

Umpires: R. K. Illingworth and R. A. Kettleborough.   Third umpire: I. J. Gould.

KENT v SOMERSET

At Birmingham, August 15. Somerset won by seven wickets. Toss: Somerset.

This match was decided and decorated by a glorious innings of 56 from 32 balls by Marcus Trescothick. With Somerset needing a relatively modest 146, he cracked the last four balls of Amjad Khan's opening over to the boundary, and the pattern was set. In a week when there had been speculation, eventually doused by the man himself, that Trescothick might be approached to play in the final Test at The Oval, he batted with massive assurance. The Kent seamers could not bowl to

On song: Marcus Trescothick in his match-winning innings against Kent.

him, as he despatched them over the infield time and time again in the first six overs. When Tredwell, the off-spinner, dismissed Trescothick, Somerset were well on course. Their target would have been smaller still but for a spirited innings of 77 from Stevens. He rescued Kent, who had sunk to 31 for three after a fine opening burst from Thomas. Stevens was especially severe on Suppiah, the left-arm spinner given the burden of the final over by his captain Langer, which yielded 20 runs. At the time it seemed a critical error, but once Trescothick set to work it became an irrelevance.

Man of the Match: M. E. Trescothick.

Kent

		B	4	6
J. L. Denly *b 9*	0	3	0	0
*R. W. T. Key *b 7*	34	38	2	0
M. van Jaarsveld *lbw b 9*	10	7	2	0
†G. O. Jones *b 11*	6	9	1	0
D. I. Stevens *run out*	77	51	7	2
J. M. Kemp *not out*	15	12	1	0
L-b 3	3			

(20 overs) 145-5

1/2 2/22 3/31 4/93 5/145

Azhar Mahmood, W. D. Parnell, J. C. Tredwell, S. J. Cook and A. Khan did not bat.

Thomas 4–0–26–2; Willoughby 4–0–20–1; Phillips 3–0–22–0; Suppiah 4–0–35–0; Trego 4–0–28–1; Waller 1–0–11–0.

Somerset

		B	4	6
M. E. Trescothick *c 7 b 9*	56	32	8	2
*J. L. Langer *c 3 b 9*	17	12	3	0
J. C. Hildreth *b 7*	36	32	3	1
Z. de Bruyn *not out*	33	35	1	1
†C. Kieswetter *not out*	2	3	0	0
N-b 2	2			

(18.5 overs) 146-3

1/73 2/84 3/141

A. V. Suppiah, P. D. Trego, B. J. Phillips, A. C. Thomas, M. T. C. Waller and C. M. Willoughby did not bat.

Khan 1–0–16–0; Parnell 4–0–31–0; Cook 4–0–25–0; Stevens 3–0–21–0; Azhar Mahmood 2.5–0–28–1; Tredwell 4–0–25–2.

Umpires: R. J. Bailey and I. J. Gould.   Third umpire: R. K. Illingworth.

FINAL

SOMERSET v SUSSEX

At Birmingham, August 15 (floodlit). Sussex won by 63 runs. Toss: Somerset.

There would be no gnawed fingernails at Edgbaston. The final of the Twenty20 Cup was as one-sided as both semi-finals, and Sussex defeated Somerset in a rush. Needing 173, Somerset lost their last six wickets for five runs, almost catching the podium-erectors for the presentations by surprise.

The crucial innings was played by Dwayne Smith, the West Indian all-rounder, who hit 59 from 26 balls after Sussex had been sent in by Langer. Smith pillaged 18 in one over from Phillips and struck the ball with astonishing power, enabling Sussex to make the highest score of the day on a pitch showing signs of wear, especially when the spinners were bowling. Smith also fielded brilliantly and bowled his one over for just three runs, making him the automatic choice for the match award.

There were also skilful, skittish innings from two young Englishmen, Hamilton-Brown and Nash, to ensure that Somerset would have to produce something special to win. At the start of their chase, Trescothick struck the ball with the authority he had shown earlier in the day, waving sixes over extra cover and midwicket. He had raced to 33 from just 14 balls when he skied an off-side drive towards the point boundary, where Hamilton-Brown ran in and calmly accepted a vital catch.

Sussex celebrated Trescothick's dismissal as if the game were won. In effect it was. As in the semi-final, Yardy, who had led his county shrewdly throughout the day, and Beer combined effectively in the middle of the innings as Somerset grew ever more desperate. The only threat came from Trego who thrashed 27 from 14 balls before Kirtley enjoyed a double-wicket maiden. Sussex received £80,000 for their efforts, but both sides were conscious of a greater purse on the horizon: the prize fund for the Champions League scheduled for India in October was $6m.

Man of the Match: D. R. Smith.

Sussex

		B	4	6
M. W. Goodwin *c 5 b 11*	7	5	1	0
L. J. Wright *run out*	20	20	2	0
R. J. Hamilton-Brown *lbw b 10*	25	22	4	0
D. R. Smith *st 5 b 10*	59	26	7	3
E. C. Joyce *b 6*	4	6	0	0
*M. H. Yardy *b 7*	4	6	0	0
C. D. Nash *b 9*	28	22	3	0
Yasir Arafat *not out*	20	13	3	0
B 1, l-b 1, w 3	5			

(20 overs) 172-7

1/16 2/48 3/67 4/80 5/122 6/126 7/172

†A. J. Hodd, W. A. T. Beer and R. J. Kirtley did not bat.

Thomas 4–0–37–1; Willoughby 4–0–27–1; Phillips 3–0–36–0; Trego 4–0–26–1; Waller 3–0–33–2; Suppiah 2–0–11–1.

Somerset

		B	4	6
M. E. Trescothick *c 3 b 11*	33	15	3	3
*J. L. Langer *b 8*	15	14	2	0
Z. de Bruyn *c 6 b 2*	22	32	1	0
J. C. Hildreth *c 3 b 10*	1	7	0	0
†C. Kieswetter *st 9 b 10*	1	8	0	0
P. D. Trego *c 4 b 3*	27	14	2	2
A. V. Suppiah *c 1 b 11*	2	5	0	0
B. J. Phillips *c 3 b 11*	1	4	0	0
A. C. Thomas *c 6 b 8*	0	4	0	0
M. T. C. Waller *run out*	0	0	0	0
C. M. Willoughby *not out*	0	1	0	0
L-b 5, w 2	7			

(17.2 overs) 109

1/43 2/51 3/57 4/63 5/104 6/108 7/109 8/109 9/109

Wright 3–0–25–1; Yasir Arafat 2.2–0–14–2; Kirtley 2–1–9–3; Smith 1–0–3–0; Yardy 4–0–17–0; Beer 4–0–29–2; Hamilton-Brown 1–0–7–1.

Umpires: R. K. Illingworth and R. A. Kettleborough. Third umpire: R. J. Bailey.

WINNERS 2003–2009

2003: Surrey beat Warwickshire by nine wickets. 2004: Leicestershire beat Surrey by seven wickets. 2005: Somerset beat Lancashire by seven wickets. 2006: Leicestershire beat Nottinghamshire by four runs. 2007: Kent beat Gloucestershire by four wickets. 2008: Middlesex beat Kent by three runs. 2009: Sussex beat Somerset by 63 runs.

NATWEST PRO40 LEAGUE, 2009

REVIEW BY ANDREW McGLASHAN

When the Pro40 began in July, it was expected to be the dying gasp of a format that had first drawn breath as John Player's County League in 1969. However, before the season was done, the 40-over game was firmly back on the agenda after the ECB decided to ditch the 50-over version from the domestic game instead.

The ECB said they wanted to look at ways of reinvigorating one-day cricket in the wake of Twenty20. However, it didn't say much about their commitment to England's 2011 and 2015 World Cup aims. Developments will be watched with interest to see what the future holds for the 50-over game, which has long been cricket's cash cow.

On the field, Sussex retained their Division One title on a thrilling final day of the season. They had triumphed in 2008 when Murray Goodwin hit the final ball against Nottinghamshire for six, but this time had to rely on Durham doing them a favour against Somerset – who would have pipped them with a victory – after Mike Yardy's team lost heavily against Worcestershire. Those Sussex players who could stand the tension watched the big screen from the balcony at New Road as pictures were beamed from Taunton. When Durham hit the winning runs, Sussex celebrations could start, and their standing as the one-day team of the season was confirmed.

Ed Joyce continued his productive one-day season with 395 runs, well supported by the flashing blade of Dwayne Smith, whose 211 came at a strike-rate of 166. Smith was rarely far from the action, as he claimed the season's bowling highlight with four wickets in an over against Nottinghamshire, including a hat-trick. He finished with six for 29, the best of the tournament, and also led Sussex's slick fielding outfit.

However, Sussex had to wait until their end-of-season dinner before getting their hands on the trophy. With the winners uncertain until late on the last day of the season, the cup was sitting in Bristol, supposedly ready to be driven either to Taunton (for Somerset) or Worcester (for Sussex). But by the time the result came through from Worcester, it was too late. In less straitened times, the ECB would have had a helicopter on standby.

Worcestershire had also pushed hard for the title until defeat by Somerset ended their hopes and meant a harrowing season would finish without a silver lining. At the foot of the first division, Nottinghamshire took the wooden spoon after crashing to 57 all out, their lowest one-day total, on the final day against Gloucestershire. This time, though, there was no relegation looming. Despite 40-over cricket surviving, the new tournament will be formed of three groups of seven.

They think it's all over... Members of the Sussex squad watch anxiously as the big screen shows Somerset stumbling to defeat by Durham, so confirming Sussex as Pro40 champions. Michael Thornely, Will Beer, Ragheb Aga, Chad Keegan, Chris Pickett (team analyst), Jason Lewry and Dwayne Smith gear themselves up to celebrate.

Division Two was won up by Warwickshire, who leapfrogged Middlesex with a final-ball victory against Lancashire. However, the lack of promotion and relegation brought a sense of irrelevance to much of the season, and most counties took the chance to blood youngsters. The two-division Championship has produced a reluctance to try them when so much is at stake, so the Pro40 was a valuable opportunity to assess bench strength and talent coming through.

A number of batsmen grabbed their chance to shine. Middlesex's Nick Compton was the overall leading scorer with 458 runs, but it was the appearance of new names that caught the eye. Hampshire's James Vince displayed a confidence beyond his 18 years, possessing the ability to hit straight as well as employ sweeps and paddles. Alex Hales, the tall Nottinghamshire batsman, made the highest individual score, though his unbeaten 150 against Worcestershire came in a losing cause.

However, at a time when cricket is more and more about hitting the ball further and harder, English batsmen showed a worrying inability to clear the boundary. Kent's Darren Stevens managed ten sixes in the second division, while in the first Essex's James Foster hit 12; his tally, though, was boosted by five in a row against Durham leg-spinner Scott Borthwick. Ironically, or perhaps tellingly, Foster had just been dropped by England because of concerns about his hitting power.

Marcus Trescothick, one of few players in the current generation who can regularly clear the ropes, also slammed 12 sixes, but, from those around England's current set-up, Steven Davies hit just a lone six in his 390 runs, while Jonathan Trott didn't manage any, despite scoring 275 runs at 91.66 and earning an international recall. Owais Shah launched seven, but was dropped after the Champions Trophy. By comparison, Dwayne Smith managed 14 sixes in seven innings, and David Hussey ten in his extraordinary 120 not out from 61 balls.

On the firm pitches of the summer's second half, teams scored at a healthy 5.72 runs per over, meaning the average Pro40 score across both divisions was 228.8, only 24 fewer than in the 50-over Friends Provident. But as well as scoring quickly, there is also the need to build hundreds – another area where the English game suffers – and six counties didn't manage a single three-figure score. Alistair Cook, remodelling his technique after the Ashes, scored in four innings as many hundreds as anyone.

The bowling, too, highlighted the long-standing dominance of the English diet of medium-pace and orthodox spin. Just as there is a lack of natural six-hitters in the domestic game, so there is a dearth of strike bowlers. Ben Phillips, James Kirtley and Gareth Andrew were the leading wicket-takers with 14 apiece, but none could be called an out-and-out strike bowler.

One positive from the bowling front, however, was the appearance of a triumvirate of young leg-spinners. Borthwick, despite his punishment from Foster, kept his spirits high, while Max Waller played five matches for Somerset and Will Beer four for Sussex. Yet when the crunch came, and Sussex faced their final match, they dropped Beer in favour of Indian wrist-spinner Piyush Chawla.

The decision to retain 40 overs rather than 50 didn't go down well with many players, who couldn't see sense in not replicating the international format at domestic level. However, most chief executives were delighted at the move to retain a version that brings a regular stream of income.

Crowds remained good, although it should not be forgotten that the Pro40 was held largely during school holidays when the weather tends to be warmer. Forty-over cricket will now be played in April and May: that will test the loyalty of even the most enthusiastic supporters.

Prize money

NATWEST PRO40 LEAGUE

Division One

	M	W	L	T	NR	Pts	Net run-rate
1 – Sussex (**1**)................	8	6	2	0	0	12	1.25
2 – Somerset (**6**)..............	8	5	2	0	1	11	1.14
3 – Worcestershire (**7**).........	8	5	2	0	1	11	−0.33
4 – Essex (*1*).................	8	5	3	0	0	10	0.33
5 – Hampshire (**2**).............	8	4	4	0	0	8	0.23
6 – Durham (**3**)................	8	4	4	0	0	8	−0.35
7 – Yorkshire (**2**).............	8	2	5	0	1	5	−0.18
8 – Gloucestershire (**5**)........	8	2	5	0	1	5	−0.36
9 – Nottinghamshire (**4**)........	8	0	6	0	2	2	−2.41

Division Two

	M	W	L	T	NR	Pts	Net run-rate
1 – Warwickshire (6)	8	5	0	1	2	13	1.28
2 – Middlesex (**9**)	8	5	1	0	2	12	0.99
3 – Kent (4)	8	4	3	0	1	9	−0.63
4 – Northamptonshire (**9**)	8	3	2	1	2	9	0.60
5 – Lancashire (**8**)	8	3	3	0	2	8	−0.19
6 – Glamorgan (3)	8	2	4	0	2	6	−0.36
7 – Derbyshire (8)	8	2	4	0	2	6	−0.57
8 – Leicestershire (7)	8	2	5	0	1	5	−0.23
9 – Surrey (5)	8	2	6	0	0	4	−0.77

2008 positions are shown in brackets: Division One in bold; Division Two in italics.

Where two or more counties finished with an equal number of points, the positions were decided by (a) most wins (b) most points in head-to-head matches (c) net run-rate (runs scored per over minus runs conceded per over).

NATWEST PRO40 AVERAGES, 2009

BATTING

(Qualification: 200 runs, average 40.00)

		M	I	NO	R	HS	100s	50s	Avge	SR	4	6
1	J. S. Foster (*Essex*)	8	6	3	279	83*	0	3	93.00	126.81	20	12
2	I. J. L. Trott (*Warwicks*)	7	5	2	275	86	0	3	91.66	79.94	30	0
3	N. R. D. Compton (*Middx*) . .	8	8	3	458	121	2	2	91.60	86.90	46	3
4	O. A. Shah (*Middx*)	5	4	1	266	130	1	1	88.66	106.40	27	7
5	†A. N. Cook (*Essex*)	4	4	1	235	104*	2	0	78.33	100.00	24	2
6	I. R. Bell (*Warwicks*)	6	5	1	310	105	1	2	77.50	96.27	38	1
7	†C. J. L. Rogers (*Derbys*)	5	5	1	287	111*	1	1	71.75	96.30	39	1
8	†J. A. Rudolph (*Yorks*)	7	7	1	421	95	0	5	70.16	86.80	34	6
9	Z. de Bruyn (*Somerset*)	8	8	3	324	109*	1	2	64.80	89.75	29	3
10	†N. J. O'Brien (*Northants*) . . .	5	5	1	254	82	0	3	63.50	125.74	35	6
11	T. L. Maynard (*Glam*)	7	6	1	315	108	1	2	63.00	125.00	36	5
12	V. Chopra (*Essex*)	5	5	1	231	101*	1	2	57.75	78.83	18	0
13	†E. C. Joyce (*Sussex*)	8	8	1	395	94	0	3	56.42	84.40	42	0
14	†S. M. Davies (*Worcs*)	8	7	0	390	106	2	1	55.71	127.86	65	1
15	A. D. Hales (*Notts*)	5	5	1	215	150*	1	0	53.75	118.13	22	8
16	†P. Mustard (*Durham*)	8	8	0	416	102	1	3	52.00	108.05	46	8
17	J. M. Vince (*Hants*)	6	6	1	257	93	0	2	51.40	100.39	29	0
18	†M. E. Trescothick (*Somerset*)	8	8	1	318	80*	0	1	45.42	134.74	46	12
19	M. J. Brown (*Surrey*)	7	7	0	305	87	0	4	43.57	89.70	32	3
20	J. W. A. Taylor (*Leics*)	8	8	1	296	95	0	3	42.28	81.09	25	2
21	†A. W. Gale (*Yorks*)	7	7	1	245	83	0	2	40.83	81.93	30	3
22	†N. M. Carter (*Warwicks*)	8	6	1	201	103*	1	1	40.20	146.71	28	9

† *Left-handed batsman.*

BOWLING

(Qualification: 8 wickets, average 25.00)

		Style	O	M	R	W	BB	4W/i	Avge	SR	ER
1	N. Boje (*Northants*)	SLA	35	2	164	13	3-49	0	12.61	16.15	4.68
2	B. J. Phillips (*Somerset*)	RFM	47	3	196	14	3-24	0	14.00	20.14	4.17
3	A. C. Thomas (*Somerset*)	RFM	37.1	3	194	13	4-18	1	14.92	17.15	5.21
4	D. S. Lucas (*Northants*)	LFM	24	1	122	8	4-28	1	15.25	18.00	5.08
5	D. R. Smith (*Sussex*)	RM	33	4	143	9	6-29	1	15.88	22.00	4.33
6	I. J. L. Trott (*Warwicks*)	RM	25	0	132	8	3-36	0	16.50	18.75	5.28

		Style	O	M	R	W	BB	4W/i	Avge	SR	ER
7	I. D. Blackwell (*Durham*).....	SLA	33	1	173	10	4-36	1	17.30	19.80	5.24
8	T. J. Murtagh (*Middx*)	RFM	32.2	0	156	9	3-43	0	17.33	21.55	4.82
9	S. D. Parry (*Lancs*)	SLA	49	0	196	11	2-12	0	17.81	26.72	4.00
10	G. K. Berg (*Middx*).........	RFM	36	3	163	9	3-18	0	18.11	24.00	4.52
11	C. M. Willoughby (*Somerset*) .	LFM	42.4	1	211	11	3-36	0	19.18	23.27	4.94
12	S. Sreesanth (*Warwicks*)......	RFM	36.3	3	174	9	3-36	0	19.33	24.33	4.76
13	S. A. Piolet (*Warwicks*)	RM	31.5	0	186	9	3-34	0	20.66	21.22	5.84
14	T. J. Phillips (*Essex*)........	SLA	45	0	252	12	5-38	1	21.00	22.50	5.60
15	C. W. Henderson (*Leics*)	SLA	43	2	190	9	3-30	0	21.11	28.66	4.41
16	R. J. Kirtley (*Sussex*)	RFM	51	3	299	14	5-26	2	21.35	21.85	5.86
17	N. M. Carter (*Warwicks*)	LFM	39	4	171	8	3-18	0	21.37	29.25	4.38
18	S. D. Udal (*Middx*)..........	OB	46	0	220	10	2-31	0	22.00	27.60	4.78
19	G. M. Andrew (*Worcs*).......	RFM	54	1	331	14	5-31	1	23.64	23.14	6.12
20	G. R. Napier (*Essex*).........	RFM	46.2	2	286	12	4-33	1	23.83	23.16	6.17

Full scores of these matches are available at: www.cricketarchive.co.uk/Archive/Seasons/ENG/ 2009_ENG_NatWest_Pro40_League_2009.html or www.cricinfo.com/db/ARCHIVE/2009/ENG_ LOCAL

DIVISION ONE

At Chelmsford, July 13 (day/night). **Sussex won by four wickets.** Toss: Essex. **Essex 263-8** (40 overs) (H. M. Amla 111, J. S. Foster 65); **Sussex 267-6** (38.2 overs) (E. C. Joyce 91, M. W. Goodwin 41, D. R. Smith 60*). *Sussex 2 pts.*

Hashim Amla struck a sublime century on his one-day debut for Essex. He faced 107 deliveries and hit one six and eight fours; he also twice collected five runs thanks to overthrows. But his efforts ended in defeat as Sussex began the defence of their title in style. After Ed Joyce and Murray Goodwin laid a firm base, Dwayne Smith blasted 60 from 34 balls, completing victory with a six.

At Worcester, July 15 (day/night). **Worcestershire won by 12 runs.** Toss: Worcestershire. **Worcestershire 190-9** (40 overs) (S. M. Davies 46, D. K. H. Mitchell 49); **Yorkshire 178** (40 overs) (J. A. Rudolph 68, A. Lyth 30; G. M. Andrew 5-31, M. M. Ali 3-32). *Worcestershire 2 pts.*

Gareth Andrew's first one-day five-for gave Worcestershire an unexpected victory after they were restricted to a modest total. The Yorkshire openers put on 57 in ten overs, but Andrew picked up three quick wickets after coming on first change and then polished off the tail. Moeen Ali also took a career-best with his occasional off-spin, and ran out Jacques Rudolph. Worcestershire had struggled after losing Vikram Solanki to the first ball, and were grateful for Daryl Mitchell's dogged 49.

At Cheltenham, July 17. **No result.** Toss: Worcestershire. **Gloucestershire 217-3** (32.4 overs) (Kadeer Ali 100*, J. E. C. Franklin 47, H. J. H. Marshall 38*) v **Worcestershire.** *Gloucestershire 1 pt, Worcestershire 1 pt.*

Batting under dark clouds, Kadeer Ali just beat the rain to reach his hundred, with two sixes and 11 fours.

At Cheltenham, July 19. **Gloucestershire won by six wickets** (D/L method). Reduced to 20 overs a side. Toss: Gloucestershire. **Essex 191-5** (18 overs) (R. N. ten Doeschate 88, G. W. Flower 34*); **Gloucestershire 193-4** (17.3 overs) (W. T. S. Porterfield 97*, J. E. C. Franklin 60). *Gloucestershire 2 pts.*

After a delayed start, Ryan ten Doeschate whacked half a dozen huge sixes from 43 balls. He holed out from the final ball of the Essex innings, which had been interrupted by a further shower, causing Gloucestershire's target to be revised, marginally, to 193 from 18 overs. They slipped to 39-2 before Will Porterfield and James Franklin added 135. Porterfield, who struck three sixes and 12 fours from 53 balls, was denied his hundred when Chris Taylor hit the winning run.

At Nottingham, July 19. **No result.** Toss: Somerset. **Nottinghamshire 247-5** (26 overs) (M. J. Wood 91, D. J. Hussey 120*; A. C. Thomas 3-48); **Somerset 71-3** (9 overs) (M. E. Trescothick 34). *Nottinghamshire 1 pt, Somerset 1 pt.*

An astonishing innings from David Hussey ultimately counted for nothing as rain rescued Somerset from almost certain defeat: one more over would have brought a result. A two-hour delay left Nottinghamshire to face 26 overs; Hussey played out a maiden from Ben Phillips before launching

ten sixes and six fours from 61 balls – his second fifty coming from 15 as he smacked Arul Suppiah for three consecutive sixes. Matthew Wood supported him in a club record third-wicket stand of 204. After more rain, Somerset's target was revised to 213 from 23 overs. Marcus Trescothick attacked briefly, but when he was run out at 51-2, it seemed a lost cause for Somerset – until the rain returned. If there had been a tenth over, Somerset would have needed 27 more, without losing another wicket.

At Arundel, July 19. **Sussex won by four runs.** Toss: Hampshire. **Sussex 224-9** (40 overs) (M. W. Goodwin 39, M. H. Yardy 31); **Hampshire 220-8** (40 overs) (M. A. Carberry 55, A. D. Mascarenhas 76, D. G. Cork 35*; R. J. Kirtley 4-38). *Sussex 2 pts.*

   Six days before they met in the Friends Provident final, Sussex held off a late Hampshire rally led by Dimitri Mascarenhas. They were indebted to James Kirtley, who had Mascarenhas caught at long-off in the penultimate over, which cost just five runs. Dominic Cork needed five from the last two balls, but failed to score. Batsmen on both sides struggled for momentum on a slow pitch, with players keeping an eye on the impending confrontation at Lord's.

At Scarborough, July 19. **Yorkshire won by 13 runs** (D/L method). Toss: Yorkshire. **Yorkshire 199-7** (37 overs) (A. W. Gale 83, J. A. Rudolph 30, Naved-ul-Hasan 42; G. R. Breese 3-34); **Durham 154** (29.4 overs) (P. Mustard 55, I. D. Blackwell 37; Naved-ul-Hasan 3-44). *Yorkshire 2 pts.*

   Andrew Gale was run out by a direct hit from Gareth Breese to end a belligerent innings, but it was Naved-ul-Hasan, who made a ferocious 42 from 15 balls, with five sixes and two fours, and followed it up with three wickets, who was chiefly responsible for Yorkshire ending a run of ten winless matches in all competitions. Durham got away to a rousing start thanks to Phil Mustard and Ian Blackwell, but rain at 118-4 left a revised target of 168 from 30 overs, and the task of scoring 50 from 7.3 overs proved too much.

At Cheltenham, July 24. **Durham won by one run.** Toss: Durham. **Durham 206** (39.4 overs) (B. W. Harmison 47, K. J. Coetzer 63; S. P. Kirby 4-32); **Gloucestershire 205** (39.1 overs) (W. T. S. Porterfield 62, R. K. J. Dawson 31, J. Lewis 54; I. D. Blackwell 4-36). *Durham 2 pts.*

   Gloucestershire's middle order flopped to 105-7 before Jon Lewis hit a lusty half-century in a stand of 80 with Richard Dawson. When Lewis was out with 22 still needed, Alex Gidman returned with a runner, having retired hurt after being hit in the face by a short ball from Mitch Claydon. The last over began with Gloucestershire, nine down, just two from victory, but Gidman could only watch as Steve Kirby edged Liam Plunkett's first ball to the wicketkeeper. Kirby had earlier claimed four wickets in Durham's low-key innings.

At Southampton, August 5 (day/night). **Hampshire won by five wickets.** Toss: Yorkshire. **Yorkshire 232-6** (40 overs) (A. W. Gale 54, J. A. Rudolph 79, G. L. Brophy 34); **Hampshire 233-5** (40 overs) (M. J. Lumb 53, J. H. K. Adams 44, M. A. Carberry 39, S. M. Ervine 41, A. D. Mascarenhas 34). *Hampshire 2 pts.*

   After Michael Lumb and Jimmy Adams established a firm base by putting on 95 for Hampshire's first wicket, ten were needed off the last over, from Matthew Hoggard. Hampshire lost Sean Ervine to a run out, leaving the new batsman, Liam Dawson, to steal three from two balls, which he managed with a two and a single. Jacques Rudolph anchored the Yorkshire innings – he was fifth out at 207 – but the rest failed to kick on around him.

At Chester-le-Street, August 6 (day/night). **Durham won by 145 runs.** Toss: Durham. **Durham 274-6** (40 overs) (P. Mustard 92, I. D. Blackwell 36, B. W. Harmison 30, D. M. Benkenstein 51*, K. J. Coetzer 31*); **Worcestershire 129** (30.1 overs) (S. M. Davies 36, S. C. Moore 33; I. D. Blackwell 3-11). *Durham 2 pts.*

   In front of almost 4,000 spectators for Durham's only floodlit match of the tournament, openers Phil Mustard and Ian Blackwell put on 71 in eight overs. Mustard made a run-a-ball 92, and Dale Benkenstein 51 from 34 deliveries, as Durham reached what was then their highest 40-over total at Riverside. They handed a one-day debut to 19-year-old Scott Borthwick, whose leg-breaks accounted for two of the seven wickets that fell to spin as Worcestershire crumbled from 89-2.*

At Southend, August 9. **Essex won by 34 runs.** Toss: Essex. **Essex 224-8** (40 overs) (V. Chopra 51, R. N. ten Doeschate 64*, A. Carter 3-32); **Nottinghamshire 190** (36.4 overs) (A. D. Brown 36, S. R. Patel 58; Danish Kaneria 3-28). *Essex 2 pts.*

   Ryan ten Doeschate and Mervyn Westfield added 55 in six overs for the eighth wicket to give Essex a fillip after Andy Carter captured three wickets on his List A debut. Nottinghamshire were up with the rate at the halfway stage, but the dismissal of Samit Patel by ten Doeschate at 172-7 ended their hopes. James Foster caught the first four batsmen and added a stumping as Danish Kaneria mopped up the tail.

At Taunton, August 9. **Somerset won by five wickets.** Toss: Yorkshire. **Yorkshire 208** (39.4 overs) (A. W. Gale 32, J. A. Rudolph 95; Z. de Bruyn 4-20); **Somerset 211-5** (36.5 overs) (M. E. Trescothick 39, C. Kieswetter 37, J. C. Hildreth 62*, A. V. Suppiah 32*). *Somerset 2 pts.*

Jacques Rudolph monopolised the Yorkshire innings and was last out – the fourth victim for Zander de Bruyn – attempting a six for his hundred. There were a few scares when Somerset wobbled on 91-4 after an opening stand of 77, but James Hildreth and Arul Suppiah calmed the nerves. The batsmen went after Adil Rashid; in revenge, he got rid of Marcus Trescothick with a one-handed catch short on the leg side, one of the best seen at the ground all season.

At Horsham, August 9. **Sussex won by nine wickets.** Toss: Gloucestershire. **Gloucestershire 189** (39.5 overs) (J. E. C. Franklin 36, H. J. H. Marshall 50; R. J. Kirtley 3-29, Yasir Arafat 3-30); **Sussex 192-1** (26.1 overs) (E. C. Joyce 66*, L. J. Wright 95*). *Sussex 2 pts.*

Yasir Arafat took the first hat-trick of his one-day career to finish off Gloucestershire; they never recovered after James Kirtley dismissed the top three with 35 on the board. Luke Wright then thrilled the crowd of 4,000 with some spectacular strokeplay as he brought up his fifty entirely in boundaries. Ed Joyce proved the perfect foil in their partnership of 136.

At Bristol, August 13 (day/night). **Somerset won by eight wickets.** Toss: Gloucestershire. **Gloucestershire 116** (28.2 overs) (S. J. Adshead 34; A. C. Thomas 4-18, B. J. Phillips 3-24, M. L. Turner 3-27); **Somerset 119-2** (18.4 overs) (M. E. Trescothick 80*). *Somerset 2 pts.*

For Gloucestershire, there was an unwelcome sense of déjà vu about the start of this game; as at Horsham four days before, they chose to bat, only to lose three quick wickets – and never really recover. Here, two batsmen fell in the first over, from Alfonso Thomas, and another in the second, from Ben Phillips. Marcus Trescothick, with four sixes and 11 fours from 61 balls, showed the pitch was blameless. The Bristol Evening Post had earlier reported that Trescothick was ruling out an Ashes comeback after a dream: "I couldn't get my England kit out of my bag! The other players were waiting for me on the pitch to do a team photo so I was in a right panic. I woke up in a cold sweat. Perhaps that told me something." His powerful hitting ended the game soon after 8 p.m., giving everyone an early night.

At Taunton, August 17 (day/night). **Somerset won by 49 runs.** Toss: Somerset. **Somerset 238-5** (40 overs) (M. E. Trescothick 36, C. Kieswetter 45, J. C. Hildreth 45, Z. de Bruyn 73); **Sussex 189** (36.4 overs) (E. C. Joyce 94; B. J. Phillips 3-34). *Somerset 2 pts.*

Somerset avenged their defeat in the Twenty20 Cup final two days earlier, despite their batsmen failing to amass a daunting total. There were, however, useful contributions from the top four, including a perky knock by Zander de Bruyn. In experimental mood, Somerset opened the bowling with spinner Arul Suppiah, who took two wickets in his second over. Ed Joyce anchored the Sussex innings – he was last out – but received little support. Michael Yardy was unlucky: he lost his balance and was stumped first ball, one of four victims for the wicketkeeper, Craig Kieswetter. Somerset's win took them to the top, one point ahead of Sussex at the halfway stage of the competition.

At Chester-le-Street, August 23. **Hampshire won by 23 runs** (D/L method). Toss: Durham. **Durham 207-5** (36 overs) (P. Mustard 50, W. R. Smith 39, S. Chanderpaul 54); **Hampshire 87-1** (11 overs) (M. J. Lumb 57*). *Hampshire 2 pts.*

After several weather interruptions – when Durham were 145-3 after 28 overs, during the interval, and again in the third over of the reply – Hampshire faced a target of 163 in 24 overs. Michael Lumb's 43-ball fifty put them well ahead of the requirement when bad light ended play.

At Colchester, August 23. **Worcestershire won by three wickets.** Toss: Essex. **Essex 247-5** (40 overs) (V. Chopra 62, J. K. Maunders 30, G. W. Flower 43, J. S. Foster 52*); **Worcestershire 248-7** (40 overs) (V. S. Solanki 62, S. M. Davies 61, D. K. H. Mitchell 50*; T. J. Phillips 3-49). *Worcestershire 2 pts. County debut: J. D. Shantry (Worcestershire).*

Varun Chopra hit five boundaries from his first 22 balls and then went 26 overs without managing another; James Foster lifted the tempo as 98 came off the last ten overs. Vikram Solanki and Steve Davies added 103 for Worcestershire's first wicket, and with 12 required from the final over, Daryl

Mitchell saw them home off the last ball. Jack Shantry, the brother of Glamorgan's Adam and whose father played for Gloucestershire – all three left-arm seamers – took the early wicket of Ravi Bopara.

At Southampton, August 25. **Hampshire won by three wickets.** Toss: Gloucestershire. **Gloucestershire 184-8** (40 overs) (W. T. S. Porterfield 47, C. G. Taylor 44; D. A. Griffiths 4-29); **Hampshire 185-7** (37.1 overs) (J. H. K. Adams 79, S. M. Ervine 37; I. D. Saxelby 3-20). *Hampshire 2 pts. County debut: D. A. Payne (Gloucestershire).*

Hampshire pace bowler David Griffiths celebrated his Pro40 debut by taking four wickets in two hostile spells. Opener Jimmy Adams shared in stands of 54 and 56 with James Vince and Sean Ervine to guide Hampshire to victory.

At Hove, August 28. **Sussex won by 193 runs.** Toss: Sussex. **Sussex 277-6** (40 overs) (R. J. Hamilton-Brown 39, E. C. Joyce 49, M. W. Goodwin 77, D. R. Smith 54); **Durham 84** (24.1 overs) (R. J. Kirtley 5-26). *Sussex 2 pts.*

A partisan crowd of almost 4,000 were not complaining, despite an embarrassingly one-sided contest. Murray Goodwin laid a sound platform and Dwayne Smith smashed four sixes to set an imposing total. Durham were torpedoed by James Kirtley's new-ball burst as he became the first Sussex bowler to take four or more wickets ten times in the one-day league.

At Nottingham, August 29. **Worcestershire won by seven wickets.** Toss: Nottinghamshire. **Nottinghamshire 282-7** (40 overs) (A. D. Hales 150*, K. J. O'Brien 42); **Worcestershire 286-3** (37.5 overs) (S. M. Davies 106, S. C. Moore 87*, B. F. Smith 40*). *Worcestershire 2 pts.*

Despite blasting 150 – only Paul Johnson, whose 167* came against Kent in 1993, had made more for Nottinghamshire – the 20-year-old Alex Hales ended on the losing side. He faced 102 deliveries and hit eight sixes and 13 fours in a stunning announcement of his talent. But with the home attack badly out of sorts, Worcestershire never looked troubled by their lofty target. Steve Davies eased to 106 from 78 balls and shared a second-wicket partnership of 169 with Stephen Moore.*

At Scarborough, August 30. **Sussex won by 38 runs** (D/L method). Toss: Yorkshire. **Yorkshire 254-2** (40 overs) (J. A. Rudolph 68, A. Lyth 109*, A. McGrath 48*); **Sussex 231-5** (31.3 overs) (J. S. Gatting 99*, D. R. Smith 58). *Sussex 2 pts.*

Adam Lyth scored his maiden one-day century, on his home ground at North Marine Road; he faced 95 deliveries and struck four sixes and eight fours. But his innings was overshadowed by a violent assault from Dwayne Smith, who thrashed 58 from 22 balls, with five sixes and five fours, including 26 off one over from Richard Pyrah. His blast made sure Sussex were ahead when the bad weather set in, leaving Joe Gatting tantalisingly close to his first limited-overs hundred.

At Worcester, August 31. **Worcestershire won by seven wickets.** Toss: Worcestershire. **Hampshire 220-6** (40 overs) (J. H. K. Adams 33, J. M. Vince 44, S. M. Ervine 60*, N. Pothas 36); **Worcestershire 222-3** (29.3 overs) (V. S. Solanki 82*, S. M. Davies 100). *Worcestershire 2 pts.*

The Surrey-bound Steve Davies gave another demonstration of what Worcestershire would be missing with a second successive hundred. He helped his side romp to victory with ten overs to spare. Davies reached three figures from 65 balls with 16 fours as he and Vikram Solanki plundered 173 in 19.2 overs. Dominic Cork was unable to bowl for Hampshire after being struck on the nose while batting and needing stitches, further weakening a depleted attack.

At Nottingham, September 2 (day/night). **No result.** Toss: Nottinghamshire. **Yorkshire 63-2** (13.1 overs) (A. Lyth 30) **v Nottinghamshire.** *Nottinghamshire 1 pt, Yorkshire 1 pt.*

Bad weather had been forecast, and heavy rain arrived after less than an hour's play.

At Chelmsford, September 3 (day/night). **Essex won by seven wickets.** Toss: Hampshire. **Hampshire 246-5** (40 overs) (J. M. Vince 93, L. A. Dawson 69*); **Essex 249-3** (38.5 overs) (A. N. Cook 104, V. Chopra 101*). *Essex 2 pts.*

At 18 years and 173 days, James Vince became the youngest Hampshire player to score a one-day fifty; he was seven short of his hundred when he fell victim to a clever leg-side stumping by James Foster. Another talented teenager, Liam Dawson, joined Vince in a fifth-wicket stand of 140 in 18 overs. Despite the loss of power from one of the eight floodlight pylons, Alastair Cook and Varun Chopra put on 192 to set an Essex third-wicket record for the League. Cook reached his hundred from 100 balls; Chopra needed six more.

J. M. Vince st Foster b Napier 93. Only there was a little more to it than that... Essex's James Foster, standing up to the brisk Graham Napier (1), collects the ball after it goes through the legs of Hampshire's James Vince (2). Sprawled on the ground (3), Foster somehow springs back (4) to find Vince short of his ground.

At Chester-le-Street, September 5. **Essex won by seven wickets.** Toss: Essex. **Durham 276-6** (40 overs) (P. Mustard 102, I. D. Blackwell 59); **Essex 279-3** (36.5 overs) (A. N. Cook 104*, G. R. Napier 63, J. S. Foster 83*). *Essex 2 pts.*

Essex needed 33 from four overs when James Foster hit five consecutive leg-side sixes off Scott Borthwick's leg-spin; the sixth ball of the over was fired wide of leg stump and went to the boundary to complete the match. In all, 35 runs came from five legitimate balls. In a high-scoring contest – Durham improved their highest 40-over score at Riverside for the second time in a month – both Alastair Cook and Phil Mustard made centuries at around a run a ball. If Mustard hoped to nudge the England one-day selectors, he was swiftly reminded of the competition: Foster's whirlwind 83 came from just 38 deliveries.

At Hove, September 7 (day/night). **Sussex won by 152 runs.** Toss: Nottinghamshire. **Sussex 254** (40 overs) (R. J. Hamilton-Brown 49, E. C. Joyce 42, M. W. Goodwin 39, M. H. Yardy 34; A. C. Voges 3-25); **Nottinghamshire 102** (21.3 overs) (A. D. Hales 33; D. R. Smith 6-29). *Sussex 2 pts.* County debut: J. T. Ball (Nottinghamshire).

Although the talismanic Dwayne Smith may have disappointed the crowd by hitting only a couple of balls out of the ground, he more than made up for it with a devastating bowling spell that brought four wickets in an over including the first hat-trick of his career. He finished with the joint fifth-best one-day league analysis by a Sussex bowler as a young Nottinghamshire side offered feeble resistance.

At Taunton, September 8 (day/night). **Essex won by two wickets.** Toss: Essex. **Somerset 205** (39.2 overs) (M. E. Trescothick 42, C. Kieswetter 36, Z. de Bruyn 33; T. J. Phillips 5-38); **Essex 206-8** (39.1 overs) (J. K. Maunders 78, J. S. Foster 38, T. J. Phillips 41). *Essex 2 pts.*

It was a bad day for the fielders, with too many catches put down by both sides. John Maunders, whose innings steadied Essex, was dropped three times. Somerset batted modestly as Tim Phillips took five wickets, and he went on to score invaluable runs. There was nothing wrong with the accurate bowling of Charl Willoughby and Alfonso Thomas – they both took 2-28 – but Essex kept their cool to win in the final over.

At Leeds, September 10 (day/night). **Yorkshire won by eight wickets.** Toss: Gloucestershire. **Gloucestershire 172** (39.4 overs) (J. E. C. Franklin 55; S. A. Patterson 3-35, J. E. Lee 3-43); **Yorkshire 173-2** (31.1 overs) (J. A. Rudolph 72*, J. J. Sayers 55). *Yorkshire 2 pts.*

Only James Franklin managed to settle against Yorkshire's quintet of uncapped bowlers, among whom Lee Hodgson claimed his first two wickets for the club. Gloucestershire's total soon began to appear very modest as openers Jacques Rudolph and Joe Sayers put on 121 inside 22 overs, Rudolph recording his fifth half-century in seven matches.

At Chester-le-Street, September 13. **Durham won by four runs.** Reduced to 35 overs a side. Toss: Durham. **Durham 224-6** (35 overs) (P. Mustard 61, B. W. Harmison 67); **Nottinghamshire 220-9** (35 overs) (M. A. Wagh 56, S. R. Patel 36, L. J. Fletcher 40*). *Durham 2 pts.*

Ben Harmison, not needed in the Durham side that secured the Championship the day before, produced a fine performance, hitting 67 from 64 balls and putting the shackles on Nottinghamshire's reply with a five-over spell of 2-14. Luke Fletcher spoilt Harmison's figures with two sixes. And with 12 needed off the last two balls, Fletcher drove Will Gidman over the rope at long-on. But he could manage only a single from the final ball.

At Southampton, September 13. **Somerset won by six wickets.** Toss: Hampshire. **Hampshire 205-7** (40 overs) (C. C. Benham 42, L. A. Dawson 34, A. D. Mascarenhas 43*; C. M. Willoughby 3-36); **Somerset 207-4** (33 overs) (M. E. Trescothick 44, C. Kieswetter 81). *Somerset 2 pts.*

Craig Kieswetter made the most of being dropped off a skier on two as Somerset cruised to victory with seven overs to spare. He put on 78 for the first wicket with Marcus Trescothick and 87 for the third with Zander de Bruyn before being dismissed with 21 needed. Charl Willoughby had curbed Hampshire's expectations by taking the first three wickets.

At Worcester, September 14 (day/night). **Somerset won by 84 runs.** Toss: Somerset. **Somerset 236-5** (40 overs) (M. E. Trescothick 30, Z. de Bruyn 109*, J. L. Langer 45; G. M. Andrew 3-49); **Worcestershire 152** (36.2 overs) (S. C. Moore 40). *Somerset 2 pts.*

Zander de Bruyn's maiden one-day century in county cricket ended Worcestershire's hopes of winning the League for the second time in three seasons – and kept alive Somerset's own aspirations. They were struggling at 52-3 after an impressive opening spell by Gareth Andrew, but de Bruyn retrieved the situation with a run-a-ball innings, aided by a runner after he suffered a groin injury. Justin Langer, the foil in a fourth-wicket stand of 128 in 24 overs, took 57 deliveries to find the boundary. Worcestershire never threatened to mount a serious reply once Alfonso Thomas removed openers Steve Davies and Vikram Solanki cheaply.

At Southampton, September 19. **Hampshire won by 142 runs.** Toss: Hampshire. **Hampshire 281-6** (40 overs) (M. J. Lumb 61, J. H. K. Adams 73, J. M. Vince 55, S. M. Ervine 31); **Nottinghamshire 139** (32.4 overs) (S. M. Ervine 3-23, Imran Tahir 3-30). *Hampshire 2 pts.*

Nottinghamshire were without ten senior players, and their inexperienced replacements were overwhelmed. Openers Jimmy Adams and Michael Lumb put on 100 for Hampshire, before Adams and James Vince added 98 for the second wicket. Brothers Samit and Akhil Patel bowled tidily, briefly in tandem; later, their batting partnership was also brief – ending in a less than fraternal run-out muddle that typified Nottinghamshire's misfortunes.

At Nottingham, September 27. **Gloucestershire won by nine wickets.** Toss: Nottinghamshire. **Nottinghamshire 57** (18.5 overs) (A. Patel 41; A. J. Ireland 3-10, D. A. Payne 3-10); **Gloucestershire 58-1** (7.3 overs) (Kadeer Ali 30*). *Gloucestershire 2 pts.* County debuts: B. T. McGuire (Nottinghamshire); C. D. J. Dent (Gloucestershire).

The previous day Nottinghamshire had finished as runners-up in the Championship, but their ignominious limited-overs season now reached its nadir. On the final afternoon of the summer, they were despatched inside 19 overs for their lowest one-day total. Their previous low of 66 came 40 years earlier, when they played at Bradford in the inaugural season of the 40-over League, known at the time as John Player's County League. On a used, two-paced pitch, the batsmen utterly failed to adjust, and apart from Akhil Patel, who hit two sixes and five fours, only four got off the mark. Kadeer Ali encountered no demons in the pitch, and the match was wrapped up in just over two hours.

At Taunton, September 27. **Durham won by two wickets.** Toss: Somerset. **Somerset 242-7** (40 overs) (Z. de Bruyn 55, J. C. Hildreth 49, A. V. Suppiah 52*); **Durham 243-8** (39.4 overs) (P. Mustard 49, G. J. Muchall 63, G. R. Breese 38*; B. J. Phillips 3-34). *Durham 2 pts.*

Everything should have gone Somerset's way. They won the toss, while rivals Sussex went down surprisingly against Worcestershire, so victory would have given Somerset the title. But in a match of too many flaws and – in Somerset's view – not enough runs for comfort, the excitement was encapsulated in the final over when Durham again demonstrated their confidence, winning with two balls left. Local hopes ran highest when Zander de Bruyn, James Hildreth and Arul Suppiah were at the wicket. Durham had a few blips, but Phil Mustard – who just missed out on his sixth Pro40 score of 50-plus – and Gordon Muchall were the mainstays. For Somerset, it had been a long and wearying summer. And it showed. Justin Langer left with a warm ovation, but no silverware.

At Worcester, September 27. **Worcestershire won by 49 runs.** Toss: Worcestershire. **Worcestershire 214-6** (40 overs) (S. M. Davies 33, M. M. Ali 51, B. F. Smith 36); **Sussex 165** (34.5 overs) (M. W. Goodwin 32, P. P. Chawla 32; I. D. Fisher 3-18, G. J. Batty 3-45). *Worcestershire 2 pts.*

Sussex retained their crown, but only after the players spent an agonising 35 minutes on the New Road balcony following events at Taunton on a big screen. Eventually, Somerset's defeat allowed the celebrations to begin. Sussex brought the agony on themselves with a feeble batting display; in mitigation there was some sharp fielding and catching, particularly by Daryl Mitchell. Steve Davies hit a rapid 33 in his final innings for Worcestershire, and two more departing players – spinners Gareth Batty and Ian Fisher – shared six wickets to end a dismal season with victory. For Sussex, there was champagne, but no presentation: the trophy was still at Bristol, theoretically within reach of both Worcester and Taunton but, with the authorities no longer prepared to lash out on helicopters, not in reality.

At Leeds, September 27. **Essex won by seven wickets.** Toss: Essex. **Yorkshire 187-7** (40 overs) (J. E. Root 63, A. McGrath 34, G. S. Ballance 33; G. R. Napier 4-33); **Essex 189-3** (33.3 overs) (M. L. Pettini 101*). *Essex 2 pts.* County debut: J. E. Root (Yorkshire).

The day after Essex secured promotion in the Championship, skipper Mark Pettini had a sufficiently clear head to canter to a match-winning unbeaten century after the equally focused Graham Napier had captured four wickets, including that of 18-year-old Joe Root, who lived up to his growing reputation by remaining firmly embedded until the 37th over.

DIVISION TWO

At Birmingham, July 14 (day/night). **No result.** Toss: Warwickshire. **Middlesex 10-0** (2 overs) **v Warwickshire.** *Warwickshire 1 pt, Middlesex 1 pt. County debut: J. E. Ord (Warwickshire).*

James Ord, the grandson of former Warwickshire batsman Jimmy Ord, made a 330-mile round trip for a debut that lasted just two overs. Ord was batting in a Second Eleven Trophy game at Chester-le-Street when he was summoned to Edgbaston to replace Ian Westwood who had been taken ill. He arrived in Birmingham just 50 minutes before the start of play and touched the ball only once before the match was abandoned. Warwickshire hired a driver to take him back to Durham that night. The following morning Ord's odyssey culminated in a third-ball duck in a Second Eleven Championship match at Riverside.

At Derby, July 17 (day/night). **Derbyshire v Northamptonshire. Abandoned.** *Derbyshire 1 pt, Northamptonshire 1 pt.*

At Manchester, July 19. **Lancashire v Derbyshire. Abandoned.** *Lancashire 1 pt, Derbyshire 1 pt.*

At Northampton, July 19. **No result.** Reduced to 30 overs a side. Toss: Northamptonshire. **Leicestershire 175-5** (30 overs) (J. Allenby 43, J. C. Cobb 43); **Northamptonshire 37-1** (4.2 overs). *Northamptonshire 1 pt, Leicestershire 1 pt.*

The rain returned with Northamptonshire slight favourites after making a promising start in their quest for 122 from 17 overs. Jim Allenby and Josh Cobb had earlier added 61 in Leicestershire's weather-interrupted innings before both were dismissed by Nicky Boje.

At Guildford, July 19. **Middlesex won by nine wickets.** Toss: Middlesex. **Surrey 213-7** (40 overs) (M. J. Brown 57, C. P. Schofield 48*, G. C. Wilson 42; T. J. Murtagh 3-43); **Middlesex 217-1** (35.1 overs) (N. R. D. Compton 87*, D. J. Malan 60, O. A. Shah 57*). *Middlesex 2 pts.*

Nick Compton shared an opening partnership of 118 with Dawid Malan and an unbroken stand of 99 with Owais Shah to see Middlesex home with ease. The Surrey attack failed to take a wicket, captain Stewart Walters claiming the only one when Malan was run out. Surrey old-boy Tim Murtagh gained some satisfaction with three victims, including his younger brother Chris, bowled third ball for a single.

At Birmingham, July 19. **No result.** Toss: Warwickshire. **Glamorgan 90-2** (18.3 overs) (H. H. Gibbs 47*, J. W. M. Dalrymple 37*) **v Warwickshire.** *Warwickshire 1 pt, Glamorgan 1 pt.*

Warwickshire suffered their second no result at Edgbaston in five days. Herschelle Gibbs had just started to accelerate when a deluge descended. Shortly after play was abandoned, spectators were treated to the bizarre sight of groundsman Steve Rouse watering the pitch for the Test match, even though the rest of the playing area had become a lake; the strip had become very dry after being covered during ten days of cricket in a fortnight.

At Cardiff, July 21 (day/night). **Glamorgan v Kent. Abandoned.** *Glamorgan 1 pt, Kent 1 pt.*

At Manchester, July 22 (day/night). **Lancashire won by eight runs.** Toss: Lancashire. **Lancashire 221-7** (40 overs) (T. C. Smith 54, P. J. Horton 84); **Surrey 213-6** (40 overs) (M. J. Brown 87, S. J. Walters 63). *Lancashire 2 pts.*

Surrey were well on course while Michael Brown and Stewart Walters were adding 146 in 27 overs for the second wicket under the floodlights on a chilly and damp evening. But the innings lost momentum after both fell in consecutive overs to Stephen Parry's left-arm spin. Surrey required 12 from the last over, and were stifled by two wickets for Tom Smith. He had earlier shared a stand of 129 with Paul Horton before being brilliantly run out by Chris Schofield.

At Northampton, August 4 (day/night). **Lancashire won by eight wickets** (D/L method). Reduced to 35 overs a side. Toss: Lancashire. **Northamptonshire 102-7** (21 overs) (J. J. van der Wath 35*; K. W. Hogg 3-18); **Lancashire 91-2** (11.5 overs) (T. C. Smith 43, V. V. S. Laxman 38*). *Lancashire 2 pts.*

Poor weather continued to dog these sides; the match was cut to 35 overs before the start, and interruptions to each innings reduced Lancashire's target to 88 from 18 overs. Tom Smith and V. V. S. Laxman made the recalculation appear lenient in an aggressive opening stand of 72. In fact, Northamptonshire were effectively out of the game from the start when Kyle Hogg claimed three top-order wickets to leave them reeling at 25-5.

At Whitgift School, Croydon, August 5. **Derbyshire won by four wickets.** Toss: Surrey. **Surrey 282-5** (40 overs) (M. J. Brown 51, U. Afzaal 43, C. P. Schofield 66, L. J. Evans 36*); **Derbyshire 286-6** (39.1 overs) (C. J. L. Rogers 49, G. T. Park 64, G. M. Smith 77, J. L. Sadler 33*). *Derbyshire 2 pts.*

Surrey lost their third Pro40 game on the trot despite setting an imposing target. Michael Brown raced to his third fifty in successive innings, from just 33 balls, and there was a useful contribution from Laurie Evans, making his List A debut on his old school ground. The Derbyshire batsmen then responded in kind. Greg Smith also reached 50 in 33 balls, going on to 77 from 52, with three sixes. Against a blunt Surrey attack, Derbyshire made their highest successful run-chase in the League.

At Colwyn Bay, August 9. **Northamptonshire won by six runs.** Toss: Northamptonshire. **Northamptonshire 268-7** (40 overs) (S. D. Peters 69, N. J. O'Brien 82, R. A. White 35, N. Boje 43; R. D. B. Croft 4-43); **Glamorgan 262-8** (40 overs) (G. P. Rees 73, T. L. Maynard 108; J. J. van der Wath 3-55, N. Boje 3-49). *Northamptonshire 2 pts.*

Twenty-year-old Tom Maynard emulated his father Matthew's feat of scoring a one-day hundred at Colwyn Bay, but he fell in the penultimate over and could not bring victory. Maynard struck his century from just 57 balls, with four sixes and 13 fours, so beating Glamorgan's record for the fastest League century, held by his father since 1997. Stephen Peters and Niall O'Brien put on 153 for Northamptonshire's first wicket before Robert Croft applied the brakes with a spell of 4-11 in 17 balls.

At Canterbury, August 9. **Kent won by 12 runs.** Toss: Kent. **Kent 258-4** (40 overs) (J. L. Denly 66, G. O. Jones 73, D. I. Stevens 75*); **Middlesex 246** (38.3 overs) (N. R. D. Compton 33, O. A. Shah 130, B. J. M. Scott 30; W. W. Lee 3-39, M. T. Coles 3-50). *Kent 2 pts.*

An inexperienced Kent side landed victory despite a sumptuous 94-ball 130 from Shah that contained four sixes and 14 fours. Once he was eighth out with 23 needed, Kent quickly wrapped up the innings. Four players were making their List A debuts: the opening bowler Philip Edwards was Kent's first cricketer from the Isle of Sheppey, while 19-year-old Matt Coles took three wickets with his medium-pace; for Middlesex, David Burton was appearing three years after his first-class debut (for Gloucestershire), while John Simpson, 21, had played in the Lancashire League aged ten.

At Birmingham, August 9. **Warwickshire won by nine wickets.** Toss: Warwickshire. **Leicestershire 158-8** (40 overs) (M. A. G. Boyce 32, C. E. J. Thompson 39*; N. M. Carter 3-22); **Warwickshire 161-1** (22.4 overs) (I. J. L. Trott 73*, N. M. Carter 63). *Warwickshire 2 pts. County debut:* D. Masters (Leicestershire), S. Sreesanth (Warwickshire).

Recalled from his day job as radio presenter for BBC Leicester, Charlie Dagnall chose a bad time to return to county cricket after a four-year absence. Playing for one erstwhile employer against another, he ran into an onslaught from Neil Carter and Jonathan Trott, whose opening stand of 114 from 74 balls put Warwickshire on course for a simple win; Dagnall's five overs cost 34. The late withdrawal of Boeta Dippenaar with a back spasm forced an already injury-depleted Leicestershire to field a team of uncapped players. Triallist all-rounder Chris Thompson and seamer Daniel Masters, younger brother of Essex's David, made some impression in difficult circumstances.

At The Oval, August 12 (day/night). **Surrey won by eight wickets** (D/L method). Toss: Glamorgan. **Glamorgan 192-5** (37 overs) (W. D. Bragg 36, J. W. M. Dalrymple 39, M. A. Wallace 42*); **Surrey 156-2** (20.4 overs) (M. J. Brown 35, S. J. Walters 67*). *Surrey 2 pts. County debut:* J. Allenby (Glamorgan).

Stewart Walters led from the front, hitting 67 from 58 balls as Surrey reached their revised target of 153 in 24 overs with time to spare. Mark Ramprakash, the focus of speculation about a Test recall, contributed a cameo run-a-ball 24 after Glamorgan's innings was curtailed by rain.*

At Lord's, August 16. **Middlesex won by 27 runs.** Toss: Middlesex. **Middlesex 201-7** (40 overs) (N. R. D. Compton 46, O. A. Shah 43); **Leicestershire 174** (37.2 overs) (J. W. A. Taylor 50; O. A. Shah 4-11). *Middlesex 2 pts. County debut:* J. G. E. Benning (Leicestershire).

The match-winner for Middlesex was Owais Shah – and not just with the bat. His occasional off-breaks, which had previously brought 18 wickets in 297 List A games, realised four in 20 balls. Whether Shaun Udal, his captain, was inspired or saw Shah, Middlesex's seventh bowler, as a last chance, he responded with a career-best, twice hitting the stumps – including James Taylor for 50 – and twice enabling Ben Scott to make smart stumpings. "Are you Warnie in disguise?" sang spectators.

At Leicester, August 18 (day/night). **Kent won by three wickets.** Toss: Leicestershire. **Leicestershire 209-8** (40 overs) (J. W. A. Taylor 95, H. H. Dippenaar 47; Azhar Mahmood 4-41); **Kent 211-7** (39.4 overs) (S. A. Northeast 39, J. M. Kemp 38). *Kent 2 pts.*

Wicketkeeper Paul Dixey, 21, making his first Pro40 appearance in place of the rested Geraint Jones, became a hero with the bat when he drilled the third and fourth balls of the final over, bowled by James Benning, for six and four to give Kent victory. For Leicestershire, James Taylor, the youngest of 11 players in the match aged 25 or under, shone brightly until he was brilliantly run out by a hit direct from Justin Kemp for 95.

At Cardiff, August 19 (day/night). **Middlesex won by 63 runs.** Toss: Middlesex. **Middlesex 254-3** (40 overs) (D. J. Malan 53, N. R. D. Compton 121, O. A. Shah 36); **Glamorgan 191** (35.2 overs) (G. P. Rees 58, T. L. Maynard 69). *Middlesex 2 pts.*

Nick Compton and Dawid Malan took advantage of some toothless bowling from the Glamorgan seamers in an opening stand of 105. Middlesex would have scored even more had Robert Croft and Dean Cosker not restricted them in mid-innings. A partnership of 89 between Gareth Rees and Tom Maynard gave Glamorgan a glimmer of hope, but when Maynard was run out they folded, the last five wickets falling for 13.

At Chesterfield, August 23. **Kent won by four wickets.** Toss: Derbyshire. **Derbyshire 259-8** (40 overs) (C. J. L. Rogers 88, J. L. Sadler 38, J. L. Clare 34; P. D. Edwards 3-57); **Kent 260-6** (38.2 overs) (J. B. Hockley 37, A. J. Blake 80, D. I. Stevens 52, Azhar Mahmood 51). *Kent 2 pts.*

Alex Blake's one-day best left Kent needing 87 from ten overs. Darren Stevens and Azhar Mahmood, each slamming a fifty containing three sixes, then helped steer them home with ten overs to spare. On a slow and low pitch, Derbyshire should have been able to defend a total built around Chris Rogers and a final flurry by Jon Clare and Tim Groenewald: 75 came from their last six overs.

At Leicester, August 23. **Leicestershire won by 76 runs.** Toss: Leicestershire. **Leicestershire 222-6** (40 overs) (J. G. E. Benning 89, T. J. New 50); **Lancashire 146** (27.2 overs) (P. J. Horton 34, F. du Plessis 30; C. W. Henderson 3-30, J. K. H. Naik 3-21). *Leicestershire 2 pts.*

Leicestershire won comfortably after James Benning and Tom New laid the foundations with an opening stand of 118. Lancashire were spun out by the slow left-arm of Claude Henderson and Jigar Naik's off-breaks.

At Lord's, August 26 (day/night). **No result.** Toss: Lancashire. **Middlesex 112-3** (26.1 overs) (N. R. D. Compton 52*) **v Lancashire.** *Middlesex 1 pt, Lancashire 1 pt.*

The new permanent floodlights at Lord's were hardly given a chance to shine, thanks to persistent rain.

At Canterbury, August 27 (day/night). **Kent won by eight runs** (D/L method). Reduced to 27 overs a side. Toss: Surrey. **Kent 167-6** (27 overs) (S. A. Northeast 69); **Surrey 110-5** (19.4 overs) (C. P. Schofield 42*). *Kent 2 pts. County debut: T. M. J. Smith (Surrey).*

Bad light forced the umpires to abandon play after strong winds ruled out the use of the retractable floodlight pylons on safety grounds. In the gathering gloom, Surrey were unable to get ahead of the asking-rate, despite the efforts of Chris Schofield, whose 42 came from 33 balls. Sam Northeast, replacing Joe Denly who was on England duty, made his one-day best, from 67 deliveries.*

At Northampton, August 31. **Tied.** Toss: Warwickshire. **Northamptonshire 212-6** (40 overs) (A. J. Hall 104*, N. Boje 44; S. A. Piolet 3-34); **Warwickshire 212-9** (40 overs) (I. R. Bell 65, J. O. Troughton 33; L. M. Daggett 3-44). *Northamptonshire 1 pt, Warwickshire 1 pt.*

Andrew Hall thwarted Warwickshire by denying them the single they needed from two balls; from the last he ran out Steffan Piolet to secure the tie. Earlier, Hall hit two sixes and eight fours from 115 balls, adding 100 in 19 overs with Nicky Boje. Ian Bell and Jim Troughton put Warwickshire on course until Boje accounted for both, but Tim Ambrose and Rikki Clarke – reprieved by the third umpire when Monty Panesar claimed a catch at mid-on – kept them in the hunt.

At Manchester, September 6. **Lancashire won by 25 runs** (D/L method). Toss: Kent. **Kent 162** (40 overs) (J. M. Kemp 44; S. J. Mullaney 3-36); **Lancashire 80-1** (17.4 overs) (P. J. Horton 51). *Lancashire 2 pts.*

Kent's unbeaten run came to an emphatic end in an abridged match, with rain removing any chance of their rescuing a poor batting performance. Steven Mullaney was Lancashire's key man, taking three wickets and two catches, one on the run at long-on to dismiss Azhar Mahmood. That was typical of a fine team fielding performance, with Paul Horton taking a stunning one-handed catch at midwicket to give Mullaney the wicket of Justin Kemp. Horton's 55-ball innings ensured Lancashire were well ahead when the weather closed in.

At Leicester, September 6. **Leicestershire won by 23 runs.** Toss: Leicestershire. **Leicestershire 217-8** (40 overs) (T. J. New 34, J. du Toit 31, H. H. Dippenaar 49, W. A. White 46*); **Glamorgan 194** (39.5 overs) (W. D. Bragg 78, T. L. Maynard 39; W. A. White 4-36). *Leicestershire 2 pts.*

Wayne White produced career-best performances with bat and ball to give Leicestershire a second consecutive victory. White's run-a-ball 46* helped them to a competitive total, and four wickets for his medium-pace left Glamorgan well short; his dismissal of Tom Maynard at 125-3 proved the tipping point.

At Birmingham, September 6. **Warwickshire won by 110 runs.** Toss: Derbyshire. **Warwickshire 246-6** (40 overs) (I. J. L. Trott 36, I. R. Bell 105, R. Clarke 33*, A. G. Botha 32*); **Derbyshire 136** (29.3 overs) (G. M. Smith 35, G. G. Wagg 35; N. M. Carter 3-18, S. Sreesanth 3-36). *Warwickshire 2 pts. County debut: C. F. Hughes (Derbyshire).*

Ian Bell reached 50 from 42 deliveries, but needed treatment for a back spasm before completing his 97-ball century. The Derbyshire bowlers suffered at the hands of their former colleagues Rikki Clarke and Ant Botha, before Neil Carter effectively sealed the win with a three-wicket opening burst. This was the final game at Edgbaston before the Victorian pavilion was due to be demolished.

At Derby, September 11 (day/night). **Derbyshire won by nine wickets.** Toss: Leicestershire. **Leicestershire 194-8** (40 overs) (J. G. E. Benning 61, W. A. White 34; T. D. Groenewald 3-33); **Derbyshire 198-1** (34.4 overs) (C. J. L. Rogers 111*, W. L. Madsen 42, G. M. Smith 37*). *Derbyshire 2 pts.*

For once, Derbyshire controlled a one-day match. Tim Groenewald set the tone with two wickets in the first six overs, and Leicestershire never broke free. Chris Rogers, who scored his first List A hundred for Derbyshire, shared two stands of 99.

At Canterbury, September 13. **Warwickshire won by 59 runs.** Toss: Kent. **Warwickshire 283-6** (40 overs) (N. M. Carter 103 retired hurt, J. O. Troughton 53, T. R. Ambrose 46); **Kent 224** (35.2 overs) (G. O. Jones 63, D. I. Stevens 46, J. C. Tredwell 45; A. G. Botha 3-72). *Warwickshire 2 pts.*

Kent's young seam attack were spared further punishment once Neil Carter, having clubbed a 64-ball century, slipped a disc as he was backing up and was forced to retire. He had taken advantage of a short boundary to smite six sixes and 13 fours. Kent, already without Joe Denly on England duty, paid the price for resting Rob Key and Martin van Jaarsveld: they lost three early wickets, and their run-chase never gathered steam. The teams were now equal on points in second and third places, but Warwickshire had a game in hand.

At Uxbridge, September 13. **Middlesex won by 50 runs.** Toss: Derbyshire. **Middlesex 242-6** (40 overs) (N. R. D. Compton 107, D. J. Malan 32, N. J. Dexter 31); **Derbyshire 192** (37.4 overs) (D. J. Redfern 32, T. D. Groenewald 31*). *Middlesex 2 pts.*

Nick Compton, who faced 117 balls, dominated proceedings from the start. Derbyshire were never up with the rate against the crafty Middlesex bowlers, with four taking two wickets each. Leg-spinner Kabir Toor, 19, also picked up a wicket on List A debut. The win took Middlesex to the top of the division.

At Northampton, September 13. **Northamptonshire won by eight wickets.** Toss: Northamptonshire. **Surrey 134** (35.2 overs) (H. M. R. K. B. Herath 39; D. S. Lucas 3-32); **Northamptonshire 135-2** (15.3 overs) (N. J. O'Brien 81*). *Northamptonshire 2 pts. County debut: P. W. Harrison (Northamptonshire).*

Niall O'Brien settled a thoroughly one-sided affair by powering Northamptonshire to their modest target with a spectacular 46-ball innings including three sixes and 12 fours. He and Andrew Hall added 65 in just seven overs as Surrey capitulated. Johan van der Wath and David Lucas had them reeling at 46-5 after Nicky Boje opted to bowl first; only Rangana Herath offered any resistance.

At Cardiff, September 14 (day/night). **Glamorgan won by 27 runs.** Toss: Glamorgan. **Glamorgan 219** (39.1 overs) (M. J. Cosgrove 73); **Lancashire 192** (37.4 overs) (V. V. S. Laxman 31, S. J. Croft 50). *Glamorgan 2 pts. County debut: N. A. James (Glamorgan).*

Glamorgan, without several first-team players, surprised a full-strength Lancashire team by winning their first Pro40 game of the summer. After Mark Cosgrove's opening salvo, Glamorgan lost their way, with five wickets falling for 19. Lancashire also enjoyed a rapid start, but against an accurate attack their last seven wickets fell for 63, which included three run-outs. Lancashire could no longer win the second division title.

At The Oval, September 16 (day/night). **Warwickshire won by nine wickets.** Toss: Surrey. **Surrey 200-8** (40 overs) (M. J. Brown 56, U. Afzaal 44; I. J. L. Trott 3-36); **Warwickshire 201-1** (35 overs) (I. J. L. Trott 79*, I. R. Bell 90*). *Warwickshire 2 pts. County debut: R. J. Logan (Surrey).*

Surrey went down to their second nine-wicket defeat of the tournament. Jonathan Trott picked up three wickets before sharing an unbroken partnership of 169 with Ian Bell as Warwickshire cruised to victory. Maintaining his sizzling 40-over form, Bell reached his fifty from 45 balls, in all stroking 11 boundaries off the ineffectual Surrey attack.

At Uxbridge, September 19. **Middlesex won by 78 runs.** Toss: Middlesex. **Middlesex 220-8** (40 overs) (T. Henderson 55, J. A. Simpson 32; G. G. White 3-30); **Northamptonshire 142** (36.2 overs) (R. A. White 58; G. K. Berg 3-18). *Middlesex 2 pts. County debut: R. I. Newton (Northamptonshire).*

Tyron Henderson smashed 55 from 36 balls to give Middlesex the impetus they needed after the early loss of Nick Compton. Northamptonshire never looked in with a chance of victory. Middlesex would win the second division if Warwickshire failed to beat Lancashire the following weekend.

At Derby, September 27. **Glamorgan won by five wickets.** Toss: Derbyshire. **Derbyshire 214-9** (40 overs) (G. T. Park 49; D. S. Harrison 3-55); **Glamorgan 215-5** (38.5 overs) (J. Allenby 60, T. L. Maynard 69*). *Glamorgan 2 pts.*

Tom Maynard's unbeaten 69 from 61 balls gave colour to a largely featureless match and carried Glamorgan home with ease. For Derbyshire, eight batsmen made double figures but nobody settled for long enough to build a testing total. Jamie Pipe was given the captaincy and kept wicket for the last time before retiring to become the club's physiotherapist.

At Canterbury, September 27. **Northamptonshire won by 99 runs.** Toss: Northamptonshire. **Northamptonshire 244-6** (40 overs) (S. D. Peters 47, N. J. O'Brien 72, R. A. White 70*); **Kent 145** (31.5 overs) (J. B. Hockley 55, Azhar Mahmood 36; D. S. Lucas 4-28, G. G. White 3-42). *Northamptonshire 2 pts.*

Kent missed the chance to take the £25,000 runners-up cheque after suffering their second-biggest one-day defeat by Northamptonshire. Kent old-boy Niall O'Brien top-scored with 72 from 52 balls to set a target well beyond Kent's compass. Only James Hockley offered much resistance, hitting his highest score since 2002, the last year he played for Kent before his reappearance in 2009.

At Manchester, September 27. **Warwickshire won by three wickets.** Toss: Lancashire. **Lancashire 166** (39.5 overs) (S. J. Croft 70, G. D. Cross 34; K. H. D. Barker 3-25); **Warwickshire 167-7** (40 overs) (I. J. L. Trott 86). *Warwickshire 2 pts. County debut: L. A. Procter (Lancashire).*

Warwickshire stumbled rather than surged over the line to clinch the Division Two title, losing two wickets in the last over to leave Rikki Clarke having to scramble a single off the last ball. They had needed only five from the over, mainly thanks to opener Jonathan Trott, but his dismissal from the first ball, heaving to deep midwicket, was followed by the run-out of Ant Botha. Warwickshire were indebted to their seamers: Keith Barker's medium-pace proved awkward on a slow pitch, though Chris Woakes was the pick, claiming 1-19 from eight overs.

At Leicester, September 27. **Surrey won by four wickets.** Toss: Surrey. **Leicestershire 225-4** (40 overs) (J. G. E. Benning 47, J. W. A. Taylor 83*, P. A. Nixon 44*); **Surrey 228-6** (39.1 overs) (M. N. W. Spriegel 81*, T. M. J. Smith 65). *Surrey 2 pts. County debut: T. J. Lancefield (Surrey).*

Leicestershire looked on course for a win when they reduced Surrey to 94-5. But a carefully compiled partnership of 123 between Matthew Spriegel and Tom Smith turned the game Surrey's way, Spriegel sealing victory with a one-day best 81. Earlier, James Taylor hit his third fifty of the campaign; he and Paul Nixon had put on 86 for the fourth wicket when Nixon was forced to retire hurt after being struck on the calf by a shy at the stumps.*

A list of past winners appeared on page 855 of Wisden 2009.

THE UNIVERSITIES, 2009

Ralph Dellor and Stephen Lamb

Once again the standing of university cricket was the subject of debate, but first-class status was nevertheless retained for Oxford, Cambridge, Durham and Loughborough University Centres of Cricket Excellence. However, according to Mike Gatting, managing director of cricket partnerships at the ECB, the situation is being constantly reviewed.

Chris Scott, who runs the **Cambridge UCCE**, looks at the honours board in the Fenner's pavilion knowing the days of Dewes and Doggart, May and Dexter have long gone. He does not expect his charges to compete with the first-class counties in the three matches to which they are now restricted, but he does expect Cambridge to provide good pitches, decent facilities and a good game of cricket to supply the counties with some worthwhile early-season practice. He thinks that aim was achieved in the first two matches, while the third, in June, came at just the right time for their opponents, Essex. They had been involved with Twenty20 and welcomed the chance to ease back into four-innings cricket.

Such matches also allow Scott's players to put themselves in the shop window. He believes the loss of first-class status would be a disaster for English cricket, since without UCCEs talented young players would have to decide between cricket and further education at a time when their suitability for a career in cricket had not been fully tested. He sees the role of the UCCEs as providing a means of continuing in education while not losing any ground in cricket. It means that players such as Jamie Dalrymple from Oxford, Monty Panesar from Loughborough and Andrew Strauss from Durham have all been able to play first-class cricket while continuing their education.

Cambridge UCCE had a number of players in 2009 who may well go on to gain contracts with counties, as did **Oxford**. Graham Charlesworth, the coach at The Parks, believes MCC's backing for the UCCEs has given university cricket a genuine boost and allowed for competitive cricket. If first-class status is slightly anomalous, he sees no reason for removing what is part of the heritage of the English game. He agrees with the notion that it gives students the chance to measure their game against the best opponents, to see if they are likely to make it at the higher level, and he reports that the counties Oxford play are keen to continue the fixtures.

He also raises another interesting point. Oxbridge degrees are attractive to employers, while university cricketers tend to obtain life skills that will help them decide whether they go into professional sport or become leaders of business. If they follow the latter path, they might well become the head of a major business organisation and their interest in the game, nurtured by playing first-class cricket at university, could well result in them being more amenable to offering sponsorship opportunities.

At **Loughborough**, Graham Dilley claims the establishment of the UCCEs has been one of the most important development tools for English cricket. He says that a glance through county staffs reveals how many players have gone through the university system. That, of course, poses the question of how many of those players were already attached to counties before going to university, and to what extent their development into regular county players was enhanced by their time as students.

In 2009 no UCCE side beat a first-class county. Loughborough held their own in their fixture against Hampshire, with opener Paul Borrington making a century. But it is impossible to know how much that performance owed to his time at Loughborough and how much to development with his father Tony's old county, Derbyshire.

Loughborough, Oxford and Cambridge drew all their first-class matches, while **Durham** lost all theirs. Of the UCCEs without first-class status, **Leeds/Bradford** nearly embarrassed a sub-strength Gloucestershire, who eventually sneaked home by two wickets; they drew their other two county games. **Cardiff** drew one but lost two heavily.

But university cricket is not all about the matches against first-class counties. The MCC UCCE Championship saw Leeds/Bradford finish top, with Cardiff second, after winning four and three matches on first innings respectively. Durham occupied last place by virtue of losing four of their five matches on first innings. It has been a sad demise for the institution that has so recently produced two England captains in Nasser Hussain and Andrew Strauss, and a host of first-class and international players. In the play-off match at Lord's, Cardiff beat Leeds/Bradford by three wickets, and Cardiff beat Oxford by the same margin to win the British Universities and Colleges one-day title.

The fact that none of the UCCE Championship matches resulted in an outright win, and has not done so in many years, has led the *éminence grise* of Durham University cricket, Grenville Holland, to propose radical changes to the way the competition is structured. In order to regenerate what he describes as a stale tournament needing stimulation, he proposes a change to the points system.

He assumes two full days of cricket with a minimum of 240 overs, of which no more than 50 can be bowled in each first innings. In the second innings, 140 overs would be available across the two innings, with the batting team determining the timing of a declaration – mindful that without second-innings bonus points everything depends on the result. He proposes ten points for a winning draw, based on overall runs per over, and 25 points for an outright win. Bonus points and penalties from the first innings would be taken into account. When rain intervenes, games could be scaled down using the Duckworth/Lewis method.

It is an interesting proposition that could gain momentum should the focus of attention change from first-class matches against the counties to the UCCE Championship. Of course, matches between the UCCEs and the counties do not have to be labelled as first-class to serve the same purpose as they do now, namely to give the students a measure of their prowess and the counties meaningful practice. There is certainly strong evidence to suggest that the Varsity Match does not deserve first-class status when ten of the players in the 2009 fixture were making their first-class debuts, and three had appeared only in that fixture before. But, as Charlesworth says, the fixture has been going for some 150 years and is part of the tradition of the game, so what good reason is there to change it?

Support of the UCCEs is not the extent of MCC's involvement with university cricket. A new venture for 2009 was the introduction of a UCCE select side playing in the Second Eleven Championship, coached by Clive Radley. The side comprises the best of the UCCE players who are not contracted to counties, to give further opportunities to attract the attention of counties and to give such players meaningful cricket after coming down from university for the summer vacation. It also helps to develop the relationship between the universities and the counties, allowing young players to seek advice about going to university from those already there. The university side played nine matches and drew five, losing the other four.

Whatever the outcome of the ongoing consultations about the structure and status of university cricket, it has a definite role to play in the landscape of the game in England. A high proportion of young cricketers now go to university, and so it is imperative that the correct cricketing environment is provided when they get there, so that their cricket can progress along with their education.

Additional reporting by Grenville Holland.

OXFORD

President: F. W. Neate (Brasenose)
Chairman: Dr F. R. Porter (St Cross College)
Head Coach: G. M. Charlesworth

Oxford UCCE Captain: R. J. H. Lett (Millfield School and Oxford Brookes)
Oxford University Captain: A. H. Ball (Eton and St Catherine's College)
Oxford UCCE Captain for 2010: R. Sharma (Auckland GS, Auckland U. and Mansfield)
Oxford University Captain for 2010: to be announced

OXFORD UCCE/UNIVERSITY RESULTS

First-class matches – Played 4: Drawn 3, Lost 1.

OXFORD UCCE v WORCESTERSHIRE

At Oxford, April 11, 12, 13. Drawn. Toss: Worcestershire. First-class debuts: Morteza Ali, R. G. Coughtrie, M. F. Khalid, J. Martin, M. J. Milligan, R. Sharma, M. J. C. Watson, E. G. C. Young; D. A. Wheeldon. County debut: I. D. Fisher.

With such an early start to the season the weather was always likely to play a major role. The first day was lost completely and the second limited to 38 overs. In the time available Mitchell recorded what was then his highest first-class score, while Ben Smith got his season off to a decent start. The two wickets to fall went to the Auckland-born Rajiv Sharma, who proceeded to compile a useful half-century as the students generally negotiated the remainder of the match without alarm.

Close of play: First day, No play; Second day, Worcestershire 125-1 (Mitchell 44, Solanki 27).

Worcestershire

D. K. H. Mitchell not out.	140
D. A. Wheeldon c Coughtrie b Sharma. . . .	22
*V. S. Solanki c Coughtrie b Sharma	27
B. F. Smith not out	61
B 4, l-b 7, w 9, n-b 28	48

1/51 (2) 2/133 (3) (2 wkts dec, 75 overs) 298

M. M. Ali, G. J. Batty, †J. P. T. Knappett, G. M. Andrew, I. D. Fisher, C. D. Whelan and Imran Arif did not bat.

Milligan 12–1–58–0; Khalid 12–1–57–0; Sharma 25–8–58–2; Bradshaw 16–3–49–0; Young 3–0–22–0; Ryan 6–0–38–0; Watson 1–0–5–0.

Oxford UCCE

†R. G. Coughtrie c Mitchell b Andrew	4	E. G. C. Young not out	0
J. Martin c and b Batty	38	B 4, l-b 9	13
R. Sharma not out	58		
*R. J. H. Lett c Whelan b Imran Arif	26	1/9 (1) 2/102 (2) (4 wkts dec, 41 overs) 143	
D. P. Bradshaw lbw b Imran Arif	4	3/135 (4) 4/143 (5)	

M. J. C. Watson, L. C. Ryan, Morteza Ali, M. J. Milligan and M. F. Khalid did not bat.

Imran Arif 12–3–44–2; Andrew 8–1–27–1; Whelan 9–4–27–0; Batty 9–4–17–1; Fisher 3–0–15–0.

Umpires: M. J. D. Bodenham and P. J. Hartley.

OXFORD UCCE v GLAMORGAN

At Oxford, April 15, 16, 17. Drawn. Toss: Oxford UCCE. First-class debut: M. F. Lewis, D. T. Smith, C. J. Swainland.

It is always a sign of belief in their own ability when a university side wins the toss and elects to bat against a first-class county. However, after Shantry and Harris reduced Oxford to 41 for four, that confidence was justified only by Mark Lewis, a 21-year-old on Warwickshire's books, who marked his first-class debut with an accomplished innings of 74 not out as the six Glamorgan bowlers combined to dismiss the students cheaply. Glamorgan's reply was not totally convincing, but before either side could gain the upper hand the rain set in to wash out the second and third days.

Close of play: First day, Glamorgan 74-2 (Rees 33, Powell 0); Second day, No play.

Oxford UCCE

†C. J. Swainland c Rees b Shantry	2	D. T. Smith c Rees b Croft	6
J. Martin b Harrison.	8	L. C. Ryan b Dalrymple	21
R. Sharma c Maynard b Shantry	10	M. J. Milligan lbw b Dalrymple	2
*R. J. H. Lett c Wallace b Harris.	9	L-b 5, w 2	7
D. P. Bradshaw b Cosgrove.	38		
M. F. Lewis not out	74	1/3 (1) 2/21 (2) 3/25 (3) (70.3 overs) 208	
E. G. C. Young c Powell b Harris	9	4/41 (4) 5/75 (5) 6/89 (7)	
M. J. C. Watson lbw b Croft	22	7/167 (8) 8/177 (9) 9/204 (10) 10/208 (11)	

Harrison 13–3–38–1; Shantry 12–1–31–2; Harris 14–3–57–2; Cosgrove 7–1–14–1; Croft 17–2–46–2; Dalrymple 7.3–2–17–2.

Glamorgan

G. P. Rees not out	....	33
M. J. Cosgrove c Martin b Milligan	......	23
B. J. Wright lbw b Ryan	....	8
M. J. Powell not out	....	0
B 2, l-b 4, w 2, n-b 2	....	10

1/43 (2) 2/65 (3)   (2 wkts, 30 overs)   74

*J. W. M. Dalrymple, T. L. Maynard, †M. A. Wallace, R. D. B. Croft, J. A. R. Harris, D. S. Harrison and A. J. Shantry did not bat.

Milligan 11–4–17–1; Sharma 7–1–16–0; Bradshaw 7–1–18–0; Ryan 3–0–12–1; Watson 2–1–5–0.

Umpires: I. Dawood and B. Dudleston.

OXFORD UCCE v NOTTINGHAMSHIRE

At Oxford, June 18, 19, 20. Drawn. Toss: Nottinghamshire. First-class debut: A. Carter. County debut: A. Patel.

A fine hundred by Jefferson, with useful contributions from the middle order, enabled Nottinghamshire's acting-captain Franks to declare, giving his bowlers 12 overs before the close of the first day to attack the university batsmen. They claimed one success before finishing the job on day two. A succession of batsmen got in, with eight passing 20, yet none went beyond 31. Nottinghamshire's bowling was equally indisciplined with 24 no-balls helping make extras top score. Matthew Watson took four wickets with his leg-breaks in the Nottinghamshire second innings as they extended their lead, setting the students a nominal 388 to win. But after two early wickets Sharma and Robin Lett, whose unbeaten 76 came from 70 balls, combined in a lively century partnership to deny the bowlers further inroads.

Close of play: First day, Oxford UCCE 42-1 (Martin 23, Sharma 11); Second day, Nottinghamshire 104-3 (Shafayat 13, Franks 1).

Nottinghamshire

M. J. Wood c Lett b Strachan	....	23	– c Abel b Watson.................	47
†B. M. Shafayat c Ryan b Bradshaw	....	15	– (3) not out......................	90
W. I. Jefferson c and b Ryan	....	133		
S. R. Patel c and b Young	....	45	– (6) b Watson....................	37
*P. J. Franks c Ball b Young	....	33	– lbw b Watson...................	1
K. J. O'Brien b Ryan	....	13	– (4) c Ball b Watson.............	5
A. D. Hales not out	....	53	– (2) c Martin b Lett	36
A. Patel c and b Ryan	....	4	– (7) not out......................	69
M. H. A. Footitt not out	....	9		
B 6, l-b 2, w 2, n-b 8	....	18	L-b 2, n-b 6	8

1/32 (2) 2/55 (1)   (7 wkts dec, 102 overs) 346   1/77 (2)   (5 wkts dec, 70 overs) 293
3/141 (4) 4/217 (5)   2/94 (1) 3/102 (4)
5/239 (6) 6/312 (3) 7/332 (8)   4/104 (5) 5/163 (6)

A. Carter and J. F. Brown did not bat.

Bradshaw 10–2–32–1; Strachan 8–2–34–1; Sharma 9–1–26–0; Ryan 29–5–89–3; Lett 7–0–28–0; Watson 14–0–55–0; Young 25–5–74–2. *Second Innings*—Bradshaw 5–0–29–0; Strachan 10–0–40–0; Sharma 3–0–13–0; Young 16–3–55–0; Lett 10–1–39–1; Watson 17–4–78–4; Ryan 9–1–37–0.

Oxford UCCE

A. H. Ball c Jefferson b Footitt	2	– c S. R. Patel b Carter	0
J. Martin lbw b Franks	30	– c Jefferson b O'Brien	19
R. Sharma b Franks	21	– not out	40
*R. J. H. Lett c Hales b O'Brien	27	– not out	76
D. P. Bradshaw run out	22		
E. Abel b Footitt	26		
E. G. C. Young c O'Brien b Footitt	31		
†R. G. Coughtrie lbw b S. R. Patel	27		
L. C. Ryan lbw b Carter	0		
M. J. C. Watson not out	21		
J. P. Strachan c S. R. Patel b A. Patel	0		
B 7, l-b 14, n-b 24	45	B 8, l-b 2, n-b 6	16

1/8 (1) 2/66 (2) 3/77 (3) 4/122 (4) (75.5 overs) 252 1/9 (1) 2/44 (2) (2 wkts, 38 overs) 151
5/123 (5) 6/165 (6) 7/202 (7)
8/208 (9) 9/251 (8) 10/252 (11)

Footitt 16–5–58–3; Carter 19–7–41–1; Franks 14–1–73–2; Brown 1–0–4–0; O'Brien 9–4–9–1; A. Patel 10.5–2–34–1; S. R. Patel 6–2–12–1. *Second Innings*—Franks 11–3–32–0; Carter 10–3–27–1; O'Brien 5–0–24–1; S. R. Patel 5–1–15–0; A. Patel 4–1–12–0; Shafayat 3–0–31–0.

Umpires: R. K. Illingworth and P. J. Nero.

CAMBRIDGE

President: Professor A. D. Buckingham (Pembroke)
Head Coach: C. W. Scott

Cambridge UCCE and Cambridge University Captain: A. S. Ansari (Hampton School and Trinity Hall)
Cambridge UCCE Captain for 2010: A. J. Wheater (Millfield and Anglia Ruskin University)
Cambridge University Captain for 2010: A. S. Ansari (Hampton School and Trinity Hall)

CAMBRIDGE UCCE/UNIVERSITY RESULTS

First-class matches – Played 4: Won 1, Drawn 3.

CAMBRIDGE UCCE v YORKSHIRE

At Cambridge, April 11, 12, 13. Drawn. Toss: Cambridge UCCE. First-class debuts: C. M. Grammer, J. D. S. Lotay, A. Sen, R. J. J. Woolley. County debut: L. J. Hodgson.

After a washout on day one turned this into a two-day match, Cambridge inserted a near full-strength Yorkshire side; Manchester-born debutant Robert Woolley struck in his first over, dismissing experienced South African Test batsman Rudolph for a distinguished first scalp. Woolley took two more wickets and held three catches before Yorkshire declared on their overnight total, after Gale had just missed his century. Cambridge's response was frail, as Hoggard and Patterson swept away the top order, with the exception of their former captain Nicholas Lee, who was last out having come in at No. 3. Yorkshire's openers took some further batting practice before the fall of Rudolph a second time signalled the end of proceedings.

Close of play: First day, No play; Second day, Yorkshire 346-9 (Patterson 30, Hoggard 0).

Yorkshire

J. A. Rudolph c Lee b Woolley	1	– b Brathwaite	31
J. J. Sayers c Woolley b Rosenberg	22	– not out	25
*A. McGrath c Gray b Rosenberg	46		
A. W. Gale lbw b Lotay	93		
A. Lyth c Woolley b Mohammad Amin	20		
†G. L. Brophy b Woolley	39		
L. J. Hodgson c Woolley b Brathwaite	32		
D. J. Wainwright c Gray b Woolley	22		
A. Shahzad c Ansari b Lotay	6		
S. A. Patterson not out	30		
M. J. Hoggard not out	0		
B 8, l-b 1, w 6, n-b 20	35	B 3, l-b 1, n-b 4	8

1/1 (1) 2/89 (2) 3/96 (3) (9 wkts dec, 97 overs) 346   1/64 (1) (1 wkt dec, 14.5 overs) 64
4/182 (5) 5/242 (4)
6/274 (6) 7/304 (8) 8/304 (7) 9/346 (9)

Brathwaite 26–5–86–1; Woolley 23–7–71–3; Rosenberg 16–4–56–2; Mohammad Amin 15–1–64–1; Grammer 1–0–10–0; Ansari 3–0–21–0; Lotay 13–3–29–2. *Second Innings*—Brathwaite 7.5–2–20–1; Woolley 7–0–40–0.

Cambridge UCCE

C. M. Grammer b Hoggard	4	R. J. J. Woolley c Sayers b Patterson	17
A. Sen lbw b Patterson	17	R. M. R. Brathwaite lbw b Patterson	0
N. T. Lee c McGrath b Patterson	72	Mohammad Amin not out	2
*A. S. Ansari c Rudolph b Hoggard	1	L-b 8, n-b 5	13
E. C. Ballard lbw b McGrath	0		
M. C. Rosenberg b McGrath	0	1/8 (1) 2/39 (2) 3/48 (4) (59.1 overs) 155	
†S. K. Gray c Brophy b Hoggard	6	4/49 (5) 5/49 (6) 6/56 (7)	
J. D. S. Lotay c Brophy b Shahzad	23	7/114 (8) 8/136 (9) 9/136 (10) 10/155 (3)	

Hoggard 13–7–19–3; Shahzad 13–5–29–1; Patterson 14.1–4–41–4; Hodgson 10–3–30–0; McGrath 3–2–1–2; Wainwright 6–0–27–0.

Umpires: S. A. Garratt and M. A. Gough.

CAMBRIDGE UCCE v SUSSEX

At Cambridge, April 15, 16, 17. Drawn. Toss: Cambridge UCCE. First-class debuts: U. S. Chandra; J. S. Gatting. County debut: E. C. Joyce.

Joe Gatting, nephew of the former England captain Mike, flourished on first-class debut, hitting an impressive and entertaining 152 that dominated the Sussex innings after they were put in. Gatting, who is the son of the former Arsenal and Brighton & Hove Albion footballer Steve, scored at almost a run a ball, with four sixes and 11 fours. Wright and Hamilton-Brown also made rapid centuries before Sussex declared at stumps on day one, having scored at nearly five runs an over. The weather prevented any more than 18 overs in the remainder of the match, which perhaps saved Cambridge from an embarrassing outcome.

Close of play: First day, Sussex 527-7 (Hamilton-Brown 106); Second day, Cambridge UCCE 36-3 (Lee 17, Ansari 7).

Sussex

*M. H. Yardy c Gray b Chandra	50	R. S. C. Martin-Jenkins c Gray b Ansari	40
C. D. Nash c Grammer b Woolley	23		
J. S. Gatting c Bott b Baker	152	B 4, l-b 3, w 7, n-b 17	31
E. C. Joyce st Gray b Lotay	9		
L. J. Wright c and b Lotay	106	1/82 (2) (7 wkts dec, 106.5 overs) 527	
R. J. Hamilton-Brown not out	106	2/99 (1) 3/124 (4)	
†A. J. Hodd c Bott b Lotay	10	4/307 (5) 5/385 (3) 6/424 (7) 7/527 (8)	

O. P. Rayner, R. G. Aga and R. J. Kirtley did not bat.

Brathwaite 21–3–84–0; Woolley 16–2–67–1; Chandra 19–0–112–1; Lotay 30–5–147–3; Baker 18–0–96–1; Ansari 2.5–0–14–1.

Cambridge UCCE

M. D. Bott c Hodd b Aga	10
A. Sen c Hodd b Kirtley	1
N. T. Lee not out	17
C. M. Grammer c Rayner b Aga	0
*A. S. Ansari not out	7
L-b 1	1

1/1 (2) 2/15 (1)   (3 wkts, 18 overs) 36
3/15 (4)

J. D. S. Lotay, †S. K. Gray, R. J. J. Woolley, F. B. Baker, R. M. R. Brathwaite and U. S. Chandra did not bat.

Kirtley 6–3–8–1; Aga 7–4–8–2; Wright 3–0–7–0; Martin-Jenkins 2–0–12–0.

Umpires: N. G. Cowley and G. D. Lloyd.

CAMBRIDGE UCCE v ESSEX

At Cambridge, June 11, 12, 13. Drawn. Toss: Cambridge UCCE. First-class debuts: F. A. Brown, A. J. P. Joslin, P. T. Turnbull.

A century from the experienced opener, Gallian, who put on 118 with Maunders and 168 with Chopra, held some stern lessons for the student attack as Essex cruised to a substantial total before declaring. Mohammad Amin, a medium-pacer from Gujranwala who had appeared for three county Second Elevens, including Essex, struck three times but also leaked runs, while the tall opening bowler Ruel Brathwaite, who represented West Indies against England Lions in a one-day game in 2007, continued to show promise. Lee again prospered in Cambridge's response, while Chris Grammer made a solid half-century. Cambridge declared 103 runs behind Essex, and after being set a token 292, safely achieved a draw.

Close of play: First day, Essex 316-3 (Walker 13, Mickleburgh 3); Second day, Essex 11-0 (Mickleburgh 7, Wheater 0).

Essex

J. K. Maunders c Gray b Woolley	61		
*J. E. R. Gallian b Mohammad Amin	125		
V. Chopra c Turnbull b Mohammad Amin	88		
M. J. Walker c Gray b Brathwaite	21	– (3) not out	50
J. C. Mickleburgh c Gray b Brathwaite	18	– (1) c Woolley b Brathwaite	48
J. D. Middlebrook not out	9	– (4) c Joslin b Grammer	45
T. J. Phillips c Brown b Mohammad Amin	11		
†A. J. Wheater (did not bat)		– (2) lbw b Turnbull	36
L-b 7, w 3, n-b 22	32	L-b 1, n-b 8	9

1/118 (1) 2/286 (2)   (6 wkts dec, 91.3 overs) 365
3/305 (3) 4/339 (4)
5/340 (5) 6/365 (7)

1/83 (2)   (3 wkts dec, 52.4 overs) 188
2/114 (1) 3/188 (4)

M. S. Westfield, A. P. Palladino and M. A. Chambers did not bat.

Brathwaite 23–3–70–2; Woolley 21.5–4–89–1; Turnbull 19–4–60–0; Mohammad Amin 9.3–0–63–3; Brown 16–2–65–0; Lotay 2.1–0–11–0. *Second Innings*—Brathwaite 14–3–38–1; Woolley 8–1–28–0; Mohammad Amin 6–1–25–0; Turnbull 12–2–43–1; Brown 7–1–24–0; Grammer 5.4–1–29–1.

Cambridge UCCE

F. A. Brown c Gallian b Palladino	1		
C. M. Grammer b Phillips	64	– b Middlebrook	29
A. J. P. Joslin c Gallian b Middlebrook	29	– c Walker b Phillips	33
†S. K. Gray c Wheater b Chambers	19	– not out	3
*N. T. Lee not out	79	– not out	1
E. C. Ballard lbw b Westfield	33		
J. D. S. Lotay c Gallian b Middlebrook	21	– (1) c Wheater b Palladino	0
R. J. J. Woolley b Middlebrook	1		
P. T. Turnbull not out	0		
B 8, l-b 5, n-b 2	15	B 1, l-b 1, w 1, n-b 2	5

1/3 (1) 2/73 (3) 3/107 (6) (7 wkts dec, 80 overs) 262
4/153 (2) 5/213 (6)
6/258 (7) 7/262 (8)

1/0 (1) 2/67 (3) (3 wkts, 31 overs) 71
3/67 (2)

R. M. R. Brathwaite and Mohammad Amin did not bat.

Chambers 10–3–26–1; Palladino 11–5–36–1; Westfield 18–8–35–1; Middlebrook 24–5–80–3; Phillips 17–2–72–1. *Second Innings*—Palladino 6–2–8–1; Westfield 4–0–22–0; Middlebrook 11–5–22–1; Chopra 5–1–11–0; Phillips 5–1–6–1.

Umpires: M. J. D. Bodenham and P. J. Nero.

DURHAM

Head Coach: G. Fowler
Durham UCCE Captain: P. J. Foster
Durham UCCE Captain for 2010: T. Westley

DURHAM UCCE RESULTS

First-class matches – Played 3: Lost 3.

DURHAM UCCE v LANCASHIRE

At Durham, April 11, 12, 13. Lancashire won by 286 runs. Toss: Lancashire. First-class debut: J. J. Atkinson. County debut: A. G. Prince.

Lancashire achieved a comprehensive victory in a match they dominated throughout. Their large first-innings total was based on hundreds from Horton and Chilton, a former Durham University captain, before the students were swept away by an eager Lancashire attack led by Hogg, with four wickets. Tom Smith, promoted from No. 9 to open, hit a maiden first-class hundred before the declaration set Durham 470. Despite a splendidly defiant hundred by Paul Dixey, a wicketkeeper on Kent's books, the students were dismissed cheaply for a second time, with four wickets falling to Newby.

Close of play: First day, Lancashire 362-6 (Sutton 36, Smith 28); Second day, Lancashire 69-1 (Smith 32, Croft 19).

Lancashire

P. J. Horton st Dixey b Gale	105			
M. B. Loye retired hurt	13			
A. G. Prince c Smith b Foster	11	– (1) lbw b Buttleman	18	
S. J. Croft c Paget b Buttleman	1	– (3) st Dixey b Paget	42	
M. J. Chilton retired out	114			
K. R. Brown c Foster b Williams	18	– (4) b Paget	0	
*†L. D. Sutton not out	53	– (5) c Dixey b Glover	8	
K. W. Hogg c Atkinson b Paget	25	– (6) not out	1	
T. C. Smith not out	51	– (2) not out	104	
B 5, l-b 4, w 4	13	B 6, l-b 4	10	

1/50 (3) 2/51 (4)   (6 wkts dec, 121.5 overs) 404   1/27 (1)   (4 wkts dec, 57 overs) 183
3/217 (1) 4/266 (5)   2/145 (3) 3/145 (4)
5/276 (6) 6/319 (8)   4/170 (5)

G. Keedy and O. J. Newby did not bat.

In the first innings Loye retired hurt at 26-0.

Williams 16–5–37–1; Glover 21–7–75–0; Foster 30–6–101–1; Buttleman 17–3–58–1; Gale 23.5–2–67–1; Paget 14–1–57–1. *Second Innings*—Williams 7–1–27–0; Glover 14–3–33–1; Foster 16–5–31–0; Buttleman 7–0–37–1; Gale 3–0–18–0; Paget 9–0–26–2; Johnston 1–0–1–0.

Durham UCCE

P. R. A. Johnston lbw b Hogg	0	– c Chilton b Newby	8	
J. J. Atkinson lbw b Smith	16	– run out	0	
G. P. Smith c Sutton b Hogg	0	– lbw b Newby	3	
†P. G. Dixey c Smith b Newby	8	– c Brown b Chilton	103	
C. F. D. Morgan c Brown b Newby	38	– b Newby	2	
J. E. L. Buttleman c Prince b Hogg	0	– c Sutton b Keedy	20	
C. D. Paget lbw b Hogg	0	– (8) b Newby	3	
*P. J. Foster c Brown b Croft	13	– (7) b Croft	2	
R. E. M. Williams c and b Smith	21	– c Brown b Chilton	31	
J. C. Glover c Sutton b Keedy	10	– c Brown b Keedy	2	
D. J. Gale not out	0	– not out	0	
L-b 4, w 1, n-b 3	8	B 2, l-b 2, n-b 5	9	

1/0 (1) 2/0 (3) 3/13 (4) 4/52 (2)   (63.4 overs) 118   1/1 (2) 2/11 (1)   (72.2 overs) 183
5/62 (6) 6/62 (7) 7/77 (8) 8/92 (5)   3/12 (3) 4/14 (5)
9/114 (10) 10/118 (9)   5/56 (6) 6/79 (7) 7/88 (8) 8/168 (9)
                                                   9/183 (10) 10/183 (4)

Hogg 11–5–22–4; Newby 12–4–28–2; Keedy 26–14–23–1; Smith 8.4–2–20–2; Croft 6–0–21–1. *Second Innings*—Hogg 8–3–13–0; Newby 11–4–21–4; Keedy 30–10–60–2; Smith 10–2–31–0; Croft 8–1–51–1; Chilton 5.2–3–3–2.

Umpires: J. H. Evans and A. Hicks.

DURHAM UCCE v DURHAM

At Durham, April 15, 16, 17. Durham won by ten wickets. Toss: Durham.

At 122 for one with Greg Smith and Tom Westley both going well, the UCCE were in good shape, only for nine wickets to fall for 32, strangled by Durham's experienced spinners. John Glover hit back, taking the first five Durham wickets to fall as the county champions were reduced to 77 for seven, but some judicious batting from Will Smith, a former captain of the university, and lusty lower-order blows helped acquire a slender but decisive first-innings lead. When the students were dismissed cheaply a second time, Durham needed only 59 to win.

Close of play: First day, Durham UCCE 102-1 (Westley 57, Smith 39); Second day, Durham 172-9 (Blackwell 44, S. J. Harmison 0).

Durham UCCE

P. R. A. Johnston c Breese b Claydon	0	– c Stoneman b S. J. Harmison 0
G. P. Smith c Mustard b Plunkett	51	– c Mustard b Blackwell 3
T. Westley lbw b Breese	79	– c Mustard b Claydon 2
†P. G. Dixey c Stoneman b Plunkett	4	– b Plunkett 18
C. F. D. Morgan b Plunkett	1	– c B. W. Harmison b Blackwell...... 4
J. E. L. Buttleman c Stoneman b Breese	2	– c Mustard b Blackwell 8
C. D. Paget run out	0	– c Mustard b Plunkett 2
*P. J. Foster c Muchall b Blackwell	5	– b Breese 24
R. E. M. Williams b Breese	2	– c Stoneman b Breese 9
J. C. Glover b Breese	1	– run out 14
D. J. Gale not out	0	– not out 11
L-b 6, w 1, n-b 2	9	B 2, l-b 1, w 6 9

1/1 (1) 2/122 (2) 3/126 (4) (71.1 overs) 154
4/138 (5) 5/141 (6) 6/146 (3)
7/147 (7) 8/151 (8) 9/153 (9) 10/154 (10)

1/0 (1) 2/8 (3) 3/25 (2) (44.4 overs) 104
4/29 (4) 5/38 (6) 6/41 (5)
7/43 (7) 8/74 (8) 9/79 (9)
10/104 (10)

S. J. Harmison 11–3–40–0; Claydon 12–8–11–1; B. W. Harmison 6–1–19–0; Plunkett 17–5–42–3; Benkenstein 7–3–16–0; Blackwell 9–6–10–1; Breese 9.1–5–10–4. *Second Innings*—S. J. Harmison 5–3–7–1; Claydon 5–1–18–1; Blackwell 17.4–8–42–3; Plunkett 6–1–18–2; Breese 11–4–16–2.

Durham

M. D. Stoneman c Paget b Glover	6 – not out 35
†P. Mustard c Gale b Glover	12 – not out 23
G. J. Muchall b Johnston b Glover	13
D. M. Benkenstein c Williams b Glover	1
B. W. Harmison b Glover	0
*W. R. Smith c Westley b Buttleman	63
G. R. Breese c Dixey b Foster	14
L. E. Plunkett c Dixey b Foster	8
I. D. Blackwell c Foster b Williams	46
M. E. Claydon c Westley b Paget	0
S. J. Harmison not out	25
L-b 11, w 1	12 L-b 2, w 1 3

1/9 (1) 2/20 (2) 3/24 (4) 4/35 (5) (56.1 overs) 200
5/40 (3) 6/63 (7) 7/77 (8) 8/170 (6)
9/171 (10) 10/200 (9)

(no wkt, 11.4 overs) 61

Williams 11.1–1–51–1; Glover 11–0–38–5; Foster 12–3–40–2; Buttleman 9–3–12–1; Paget 7–0–35–1; Gale 6–1–13–0. *Second Innings*—Williams 2–0–18–0; Glover 4–0–18–0; Foster 4–2–10–0; Paget 1.4–0–13–0.

Umpires: S. C. Gale and J. W. Holder.

DURHAM UCCE v WARWICKSHIRE

At Durham, June 11, 12, 13. Warwickshire won by 74 runs. Toss: Warwickshire. First-class debuts: G. M. Harper; A. Javid, S. A. Piolet. County debut: S. H. Choudhry.

Four wickets for the debutant George Harper, a Minnesota-born left-arm seamer, and three for the on-song Robbie Williams, meant an admittedly sub-strength Warwickshire were bowled out for a modest total, despite Frost's hundred. However, another first-class debutant, Steffan Piolet, returned the remarkable figures of 18–11–17–6 to destroy the students' batting with gentle medium-pace. Five wickets fell as Warwickshire extended their lead to 241 before declaring. Paul Johnston did his best to organise some sort of resistance, but it was to no avail as Tahir and Piolet took four wickets each; five student batsmen returned to the pavilion without scoring, including Harper and Glover for pairs.

JUST GIVE ME THE BALL...

Best match figures by players on first-class debut since 1918 (British Isles only):

F. Fee	14-100 (7-56 and 7-44)	Ireland v MCC at Dublin	1956
V. R. Price	14-112 (6-82 and 8-30)	Oxford U. v Gentlemen of England at Oxford	1919
R. V. Webster	11-100 (7-56 and 4-44)	Scotland v MCC at Greenock	1961
S. A. Piolet	**10-43 (6-17 and 4-26)**	**Warwickshire v Durham UCCE at Durham**	**2009**
H. R. A. Kelleher	10-73 (5-23 and 5-50)	Surrey v Worcestershire at The Oval	1955
G. N. Francis	10-83 (4-50 and 6-33)	West Indians v Sussex at Hove	1923
J. G. Saunders	10-102 (5-50 and 5-52)	Oxford University v Lancashire at Oxford	1966
G. T. S. Stevens	10-136 (7-104 and 3-32)	Middlesex v Hampshire at Lord's	1919
A. Jessup	10-137 (5-43 and 5-94)	Oxford U. v Free Foresters at Oxford	1950

Research: Philip Bailey

Close of play: First day, Warwickshire 103-5 (Frost 50, Choudhry 4); Second day, Durham UCCE 97-9 (Williams 8, Gale 5).

Warwickshire

N. S. Poonia c Williams b Harper	6	– c Johnston b Williams	0
*T. Frost c Paget b Williams	105	– c Dixey b Foster	16
S. A. Piolet lbw b Foster	5	– not out	26
A. Javid c and b Foster	7	– c Dixey b Glover	12
†R. M. Johnson c Westley b Williams	22	– c and b Foster	11
K. H. D. Barker c Dixey b Williams	0	– c Foster b Buttleman	23
S. H. Choudhry c Atkinson b Foster	75		
C. S. MacLeod c Dixey b Harper	26		
N. S. Tahir c Gale b Harper	0		
J. E. Anyon c Dixey b Harper	9		
A. S. Miller not out	1		
L-b 8, w 1	9	B 1, w 3, n-b 2	6

1/27 (1) 2/32 (3) 3/48 (4) 4/75 (5) (98.5 overs) 265
5/85 (6) 6/208 (2) 7/244 (8)
8/250 (9) 9/264 (7) 10/265 (10)

1/0 (1) (5 wkts dec, 17.1 overs) 94
2/21 (2) 3/38 (4)
4/60 (5) 5/94 (6)

Williams 22–8–51–3; Glover 20–5–41–0; Foster 22–7–36–3; Harper 14.5–3–49–4; Buttleman 10–2–28–0; Gale 4–0–15–0; Paget 6–0–37–0. *Second Innings*—Williams 3–2–8–1; Glover 6–1–28–1; Foster 6–0–50–2; Buttleman 2.1–0–7–1.

Durham UCCE

C. D. Paget c Johnson b Tahir	18	– c MacLeod b Anyon	4
P. R. A. Johnston c MacLeod b Miller	18	– c Johnson b Anyon	73
T. Westley c Johnson b MacLeod	35	– c Johnson b Piolet	26
†P. G. Dixey b Piolet	9	– lbw b Piolet	0
J. J. Atkinson b Piolet	3	– c Johnson b Piolet	2
J. E. L. Buttleman lbw b Piolet	0	– lbw b Piolet	33
*P. J. Foster c Johnson b Piolet	0	– b Tahir	4
G. M. Harper lbw b Piolet	0	– c MacLeod b Tahir	0
J. C. Glover b Piolet	0	– c Johnson b Tahir	0
R. E. M. Williams not out	22	– c Javid b Tahir	0
D. J. Gale not out	11	– not out	0
W 2	2	B 4, l-b 5, w 2, n-b 14	25

1/29 (2) 2/49 (1) 3/66 (4) (9 wkts dec, 61 overs) 118
4/78 (5) 5/78 (6) 6/80 (7)
7/80 (8) 8/84 (9) 9/84 (3)

1/18 (1) 2/82 (3) (48.3 overs) 167
3/82 (4) 4/96 (5)
5/131 (2) 6/162 (7) 7/167 (8) 8/167 (9)
9/167 (6) 10/167 (10)

Anyon 8–3–15–0; Barker 8–2–10–0; Miller 13–4–33–1; Choudhry 1–0–11–0; Tahir 7–0–22–1; Piolet 18–11–17–6; MacLeod 6–2–10–1. *Second Innings*—Miller 9–2–32–0; Anyon 13–3–38–2; Barker 4–1–16–0; Tahir 9.3–3–30–4; Piolet 9–2–26–4; MacLeod 4–0–16–0.

Umpires: M. A. Gough and R. K. Illingworth.

LOUGHBOROUGH

Cricket Performance Manager: Miss S. Briggs
Head Coach: G. R. Dilley
Assistant Coach: Miss N. J. Shaw
Loughborough UCCE Captain: A. A. Lynch
Loughborough UCCE Captain for 2010: to be announced

LOUGHBOROUGH UCCE RESULTS

First-class matches – Played 3: Drawn 3.

At Leicester, April 11, 12, 13. LOUGHBOROUGH UCCE drew with LEICESTERSHIRE.

At Canterbury, April 15, 16, 17. LOUGHBOROUGH UCCE drew with KENT.

At Southampton, May 6, 7, 8. LOUGHBOROUGH UCCE drew with HAMPSHIRE.

OTHER UCCEs, 2009

Note: Matches in this section were not first-class.

CARDIFF UCCE

At Northampton, April 11, 12, 13. CARDIFF UCCE drew with NORTHAMPTONSHIRE.

At Taunton, April 22, 23, 24. CARDIFF UCCE lost to SOMERSET by 359 runs.

At Richmond, June 11, 12, 13. CARDIFF UCCE lost to MIDDLESEX by 201 runs.

LEEDS/BRADFORD UCCE

At The Oval, April 10, 11, 12. LEEDS/BRADFORD UCCE drew with SURREY.

At Derby, May 6, 7, 8. LEEDS/BRADFORD UCCE drew with DERBYSHIRE.

At Weetwood, Leeds, June 11, 12, 13. **Gloucestershire won by two wickets.** Toss: Leeds/Bradford UCCE. **Leeds/Bradford UCCE 278** (J. R. Moorhouse 83, J. A. Hawley 60) **and 159; Gloucestershire 203 and 235-8** (S. D. Snell 98; D. A. Woods 5-58). *County debuts:* C. D. J. Dent, M. J. Wilson.
    Half-centuries from James Moorhouse and James Hawley rescued the students after they had slipped to 114-5, and Leeds/Bradford had high hopes of an unlikely win when Gloucestershire conceded a first-innings lead of 75. But although seven Leeds/Bradford batsmen reached double figures second time round, none made more than 36, and the county team were left chasing 235. At 144-5, the game was in the balance, with Daniel Woods, a slow left-armer from Stockport, bowling well. But 98 from stand-in captain Snell ensured Gloucestershire scraped over the line.

THE UNIVERSITY MATCHES, 2009

At Cambridge, June 10 (not first-class). **No result**. Toss: Cambridge University. **Oxford University 78-2** (7 overs); **Cambridge University 28-3** (3 overs).

Rain, which had already reduced the game to seven overs a side, returned to ruin the second Twenty20 match between the two universities just three overs into Cambridge's reply; Cambridge retained the trophy.

At Lord's, July 4 (not first-class). **Oxford University won by six wickets.** Toss: Cambridge University. **Cambridge University 123** (40.1 overs) (J. P. Strachan 4-30); **Oxford University 124-4** (28.5 overs).

Cambridge were blown away by the new-ball pairing of the Cape Town-born Jonty Strachan and the economical Aukland-born Rajiv Sharma (10–4–11–2), and never properly recovered from 24 for five. Set 124, Oxford rode on the back of a second-wicket stand of 70 between wicketkeeper Dan King and Sharma to take a 9–6 lead in the one-day Varsity series.

CAMBRIDGE UNIVERSITY v OXFORD UNIVERSITY

At Cambridge, July 7, 8, 9, 10. Cambridge University won by ten wickets. Toss: Cambridge University. First-class debuts: A. Ashok, P. P. Ashton, M. P. Cook, E. G. Pearson, T. J. W. Probert; T. E. Bryan, N. J. S. Buchanan, D. A. King, W. A. Klopper, D. C. Pascoe.

The 164th Varsity Match ended in a comprehensive win for Cambridge, their first in this contest for 17 years, after Oxford failed to recover from a below-par first-innings total. The omens did not look good for the Dark Blues, put in on a green Fenner's pitch, when Brendan McKerchar was run out by a direct hit from Ed Pearson just three balls into the game. By the time rain ended play early on the first day, Oxford had slipped to 42 for four, with no answers to Cambridge's opening attack of Brathwaite and Thomas Probert. Day two brought no respite, and three wickets fell to the slow left arm of Francis Brown as Oxford subsided. Centuries for Cambridge followed from Anand Ashok and the captain, Akbar Ansari, who continued the brilliant form he showed in last year's game at Oxford before he was last out. By then Cambridge had a lead of 187, and a double strike from Brathwaite – including McKerchar for a pair – soon had Oxford in trouble again. Although Kruger resisted stoutly, Brathwaite finished with five wickets; Oxford's 226 left a target of just 40, which Cambridge passed without loss in under nine overs.

Close of play: First day, Oxford University 42-4 (Kruger 14, Hill 6); Second day, Cambridge University 155-2 (Ashok 93, Ansari 34); Third day, Oxford University 124-4 (Kruger 67, Pascoe 15).

Oxford University

B. T. McKerchar run out	0	– b Brathwaite	0
†D. A. King lbw b Probert	1	– c Sen b Brathwaite	1
R. Sharma lbw b Brathwaite	12	– b Brathwaite	38
N. Kruger c and b Probert	26	– lbw b Grammer	98
*A. H. Ball b Brathwaite	5	– c Sen b Ashok	0
C. M. M. Hill lbw b Brown	19	– (7) c Sen b Brown	29
W. A. Klopper c Sen b Brown	18	– (8) lbw b Ansari	6
D. C. Pascoe c Grammer b Ansari	37	– (6) b Grammer	30
T. E. Bryan c Ashton b Brown	1	– lbw b Brathwaite	16
N. J. S. Buchanan b Brathwaite	7	– not out	1
J. P. Strachan not out	13	– lbw b Brathwaite	0
L-b 11, n-b 2	13	L-b 5, n-b 2	7

1/0 (1) 2/1 (2) 3/15 (3) 4/27 (5)   (73.3 overs) 152
5/57 (4) 6/86 (6) 7/91 (7) 8/105 (9)
9/116 (10) 10/152 (8)

1/0 (1) 2/9 (2)   (79.5 overs) 226
3/77 (3) 4/92 (5) 5/163 (6)
6/182 (4) 7/189 (8) 8/224 (7)
9/226 (9) 10/226 (11)

Brathwaite 30–9–76–3; Probert 21–13–20–2; Brown 17–6–26–3; Ansari 5.3–1–19–1. *Second Innings*—Brathwaite 20.5–6–54–5; Probert 7–2–23–0; Brown 5–1–21–1; Ansari 21–2–64–1; Ashok 7–3–15–1; Cook 3–0–9–0; Grammer 16–3–35–2.

Cambridge University

C. M. Grammer c King b Sharma	2	– not out	14
A. Ashok lbw b Pascoe	112	– not out	19
†A. Sen c Kruger b Buchanan	16		
*A. S. Ansari c Sharma b Pascoe	132		
F. A. Brown lbw b Sharma	30		
S. K. MacLennan c Kruger b Strachan	3		
E. G. Pearson c King b Sharma	0		
P. P. Ashton lbw b Sharma	4		
M. P. Cook c Ball b Strachan	3		
R. M. R. Brathwaite b Sharma	2		
T. J. W. Probert not out	0		
B 8, l-b 7, w 6, n-b 14	35	L-b 4, w 6	10

1/16 (1) 2/78 (3) 3/180 (2)   (115.5 overs) 339   (no wkt, 8.3 overs) 43
4/265 (5) 5/270 (6) 6/271 (7)
7/283 (8) 8/298 (9) 9/303 (10) 10/339 (4)

Sharma 23–5–81–5; Strachan 21–7–48–2; Bryan 1–0–6–0; Buchanan 10–1–30–1; Pascoe 27.5–3–79–2; Klopper 29–5–76–0; Hill 4–1–4–0. *Second Innings*—Sharma 4.3–1–16–0; Strachan 3–0–14–0; Buchanan 1–0–9–0.

Umpires: S. A. Garratt and V. A. Holder.

This was the 164th University Match, a first-class fixture dating back to 1827. Cambridge have won 57 and Oxford 53, with 54 drawn. It was played at Lord's until 2000.

MCC UNIVERSITIES CHAMPIONSHIP, 2009

	Played	Won	Lost	1st-inns wins	1st-inns losses	Drawn/ no result	Bonus points	Points
Leeds/Bradford	5	0	0	4	0	1	35	80
Cardiff	5	0	0	3	1	1	41	76
Oxford	5	0	0	2	2	1	36	61
Cambridge	5	0	0	2	3	0	38	58
Loughborough	5	0	0	0	1	4	17	37
Durham	5	0	0	0	4	1	28	33

Outright win = 17 pts; 1st-innings win in a drawn match = 10 pts; no result on 1st innings = 5 pts; abandoned = 5 pts. Up to six bonus points for batting and bowling were available (four in the first innings and two in the second).

WINNERS

2001	Loughborough	2004	Oxford	2007	Cardiff/Glamorgan
2002	Loughborough	2005	Loughborough	2008	Loughborough
2003	Loughborough	2006	Oxford	2009	Leeds/Bradford

MCC UNIVERSITIES CHALLENGE FINAL

At Lord's, June 29 (not first-class). **Cardiff won by three wickets.** Toss: Leeds/Bradford. **Leeds/Bradford 236-7** (50 overs) (D. G. H. Snell 63, A. J. Blake 70; T. W. Allin 3-45); **Cardiff 240-7** (48 overs) (R. Bishop 30, B. L. Wadlan 88*; D. A. Woods 3-30).

A fine all-round performance from Tom Allin helped steer Cardiff to victory. He had a hand in dismissing four of the top six after Leeds/Bradford chose to bat. He removed opener Christopher Dougherty for five, ran out Duncan Snell for a brisk 63 and then dismissed Bradley Kruger and James Moorhouse, both for 12. Needing 237, Cardiff had slipped to a precarious 145-7 when Allin joined Bradley Wadlan in an unbeaten match-winning stand worth 95 in 14 overs. Wadlan faced just 73 balls for his 88, while Allin ended with 28 not out. Earlier, Alex Blake had crashed 70 from 62.

MCC IN 2009

Pink balls, and pink trousers

STEPHEN FAY

The scramble to secure the future of Test cricket reached critical mass at Lord's during 2009. MCC's World Cricket Committee, the sport's own think tank, proposed a world championship as a way of reviving Test cricket. MCC also commissioned a survey into declining Test attendances in India, South Africa and New Zealand. Its conclusions fuelled their campaign to make Tests more accessible by starting them later in the day and finishing play under floodlights. John Stephenson, MCC's head of cricket, travelled the world making the case for the pink cricket ball, which may be more visible under lights when players are wearing whites.

There is an element of self-interest involved, of course: MCC members expect 10–12 days' Test and international cricket each summer, and consequently a guarantee of two Tests a year is a crucial preliminary condition for going ahead with the bold and ambitious development "Masterplan" for Lord's.

The opportunity to experiment with the pink ball under lights was the main reason MCC transferred the first game of the 2010 season, the traditional pipe-opener against the champion county, to Abu Dhabi. Another reason was the ECB's decision to schedule the match to start on April 3 – "far too early for Lord's", said Stephenson. Relations between MCC and the ECB were strained. The counties are not keen on the pink ball, and the ECB has been stubbornly reluctant to concede two Tests a year to Lord's, refusing even to confirm the Ashes Test in 2013. MCC's chief executive, Keith Bradshaw, resigned from the ECB's board of directors during 2009 because of "conflicts of interest".

Estimated costs of the redevelopment plan rose to £400m, and there are other preliminary conditions to be met. MCC's share of the profit from the development of four blocks of flats at the Nursery End has to be large enough to enable the project to begin, with the rebuilding of the Edrich and Compton Stands. Not least among the conditions is the consent of the members to go ahead with the plans to increase capacity to 37,000 and to turn Lord's into a building site for a generation: this might prove more difficult than getting planning permission from Westminster Council.

Some things don't change. Among contributions to a sprightly conversational website for members was a query about the propriety of wearing pink trousers in the Pavilion, and a report of a sighting of a woman sitting in front of the Pavilion with a number of tattoos on her bare back.

More active members played in 441 out-matches in 2009, winning 175, losing 126 and drawing 73, with a further 66 abandoned or cancelled. Women's teams played a further 25, winning and losing ten and drawing two, with three abandoned.

MCC v DURHAM

At Lord's, April 9, 10, 11, 12. Drawn. Toss: MCC. County debut: I. D. Blackwell.

The English season opened under gloomy skies, and there was no relief from the looming towers of the new Lord's floodlights, which were not yet in use. Barely a third of the scheduled play survived. On the first day, Key invited county champions Durham to bat, and their openers, Di Venuto and Stoneman, shared a century stand before Bresnan (a late replacement for the injured Middlesex fast bowler Steven Finn) dismissed both in 15 balls after lunch. Two more quick wickets fell before Blackwell, who had lost ten kilos since leaving Somerset during the winter, joined his new captain, Will Smith. Blackwell cut and hooked his way to 102 in 109 balls on county debut as they put on 170 together. After a third-day washout, play resumed at one o'clock on the final afternoon, finally offering Vaughan and Bell a chance to show why they should be recalled to the England side. But both perished for 12, against Australian bowlers with British passports: Vaughan edged a square-cut at a short ball from Claydon, and Bell followed during Thorp's second spell of 5–3–5–3. Only Worcestershire opener Moore passed 20 before bad light closed in again to halt MCC's collapse.

Close of play: First day, Durham 244-4 (Smith 43, Blackwell 63); Second day, Durham 311-4 (Smith 71, Blackwell 102); Third day, No play.

Durham

M. J. Di Venuto c Bell b Bresnan	53	I. D. Blackwell not out	102
M. D. Stoneman b Bresnan	49	B 2, l-b 12, w 3, n-b 2	19
*W. R. Smith not out	71		
G. J. Muchall c Foster b Woakes	5	1/104 (1) 2/113 (2) (4 wkts dec, 89 overs)	311
D. M. Benkenstein c Kabir Ali b Mahmood	12	3/128 (4) 4/141 (5)	

†P. Mustards, L. E. Plunkett, C. D. Thorp, G. Onion and M. E. Claydon did not bat.

Kabir Ali 20–2–69–0; Mahmood 18–3–68–1; Bresnan 25–6–56–2; Woakes 20–2–76–1; Rashid 6–0–28–0.

MCC

S. C. Moore c Mustard b Thorp	45	T. T. Bresnan lbw b Onions	0
*R. W. T. Key c Plunkett b Thorp	5	Kabir Ali not out	0
M. P. Vaughan c Mustard b Claydon	12	B 3, l-b 4, w 1, n-b 2	10
I. R. Bell c Mustard b Thorp	12		
T. Westley not out	18	1/18 (2) 2/50 (3) (7 wkts, 47 overs)	126
†J. S. Foster lbw b Thorp	4	3/76 (1) 4/77 (4)	
A. U. Rashid b Plunkett	20	5/81 (6) 6/124 (7) 7/125 (8)	

C. R. Woakes and S. I. Mahmood did not bat.

Onions 14–2–42–1; Thorp 13–5–15–4; Plunkett 12–2–41–1; Claydon 7–2–14–1; Benkenstein 1–0–7–0.

Umpires: N. L. Bainton and J. W. Lloyds.

THE MINOR COUNTIES, 2009

Philip August

Buckinghamshire became champions for the tenth time, though it was their first title since 1987. They blended a team of experience and youth under the astute leadership of Jason Harrison, and led the Eastern Division from the first match. Cheshire, who were Western champions, won their last match to overtake Cornwall, leaders until the final round, who were stranded as the rain poured down in Wales. It was cruel for Cornwall, who had challenged all season by playing purposeful cricket. They and Wales are the only sides yet to win an honour – but Cornwall had been trying for 94 years longer.

The Championship final proved the wisdom of having a four-day game: with no interruption except a few minutes lost for bad light, Buckinghamshire had to winkle Cheshire out, and it took until mid-afternoon on the last day. Given less than a fortnight's notice, Slough produced a pitch on a much-used square that would have done justice to any on the subcontinent: it was devoid of grass, but rewarded bowlers with pace and eventually took spin, and provided good cricket conditions.

A crowded schedule meant the knockout final could not be staged at Lord's, and county champions Durham, a Minor County themselves until 1992, hosted the game between Norfolk and Staffordshire. Heavy rain did not allow a start until early afternoon – and then only thanks to the efforts of the Riverside groundstaff. Such a delay penalises the side batting second, who know they will have only a few overs to face in the evening, and Staffordshire, chasing 258, stumbled to 26 for four when bad light ended play in the tenth over; to all intents and purposes the game was lost.

Buckinghamshire

In Championship cricket, 2009 was the year of the spinner. Of the seven bowlers to take 30 wickets or more, six were spinners. Richard Logan of Berkshire was the exception, and late in the season he was called up by Surrey – his fourth first-class county.

Chris Metters, aged 18, a slow left-armer from Devon, won the Frank Edwards Trophy, with 34 wickets at 17 each. Sam Cherry took 40 wickets with his off-spin for Buckinghamshire, but the leading wicket-taker with 41 in five matches was George Walker, a left-arm spinner from Norfolk. Walker was recalled by Leicestershire in mid-season but later returned to Norfolk and took 16 for 96 in the match against Cambridgeshire. The senior spinners were also to the fore: in June, when Lincolnshire followed on against Norfolk, Chris Brown shared all 89.1 overs with Walker, each taking nine wickets in the game; Nathan Dumelow of Cheshire and Andy Gray of Shropshire also prospered.

Hassan Adnan of Suffolk had a batting average of 127, leaving his nearest rival, Gary Scott from Northumberland, trailing at 73. Adnan hit four hundreds and four fifties in his ten innings, but the Wilfred Rhodes Trophy went to

Scott, since those with more than 40 first-class appearances are ineligible: Adnan's total stands at 127, including 65 for Derbyshire.

Since the ECB introduced an incentive scheme encouraging counties to select sides with an average age below 26, teams have continued to become younger. Wales blooded wicketkeeper Tom Baker, aged 15, and Bedfordshire the 16-year-old James Kettleborough, who scored 66 not out and 44 on his debut. Another young Bedfordshire batsman, Oliver Swann, aged 17, was five short of a century on debut when he ran out of partners; he added two more fifties in his next three innings.

At the other end of the age range, some stalwarts of Minor County cricket achieved significant milestones. At the age of 49, Keith Arnold became Oxfordshire's leading wicket-taker when he claimed his 671st victim, surpassing David Laity's 670; Ajaz Akhtar, aged 41, moved second on the Cambridgeshire list with 418, ahead of Derek Wing, but some way behind C. J. Smith's 573; and the 46-year-old Phil Caley had become Suffolk's leading run-scorer, with 9,269, when he retired at the end of the season. The enthusiasm and knowledge of such senior players help improve and educate their protégés.

MINOR COUNTIES CHAMPIONSHIP, 2009

Eastern Division	P	W	L	D	A	Bonus points Batting	Bonus points Bowling	Total Points
Buckinghamshire	6	3	0	3	0	15	24	99
Suffolk	6	2	0	3	1	19	16	85
Norfolk	6	2	1	3*	0	13	22	83
Hertfordshire	6	2	0	4	0	20	16	82§
Northumberland	6	2	1	3	0	15	21	80
Staffordshire	6	1	1	3	1	10	17	59§
Cumberland	6	1	2	3	0	7	23	58
Cambridgeshire	6	0	1	5	0	14	18	52
Bedfordshire	6	1	5	0	0	8	20	44
Lincolnshire	6	0	3	3	0	11	21	44

Western Division	P	W	L	D	A	Bonus points Batting	Bonus points Bowling	Total Points
Cheshire	6	3	0	2	1	19	20	101
Cornwall	6	3	1	1	1	15	16	89
Oxfordshire	6	2	1	3	0	17	24	85
Dorset	6	3	1	1	1	6	19	83
Shropshire	6	2	1	3	0	13	17	74
Berkshire	6	1	2	3	0	17	22	67
Devon	6	1	2	3	0	11	24	63
Wiltshire	6	1	3	2	0	14	21	59
Wales	6	1	2	2	1	15	12	55§
Herefordshire	6	0	4	2	0	14	23	43§

Final: Buckinghamshire beat Cheshire by 117 runs.

Win = 16 points; draw = 4 points; abandoned = 6 points.

* *Norfolk received 8 points batting second against Staffordshire in a drawn match with scores level.*
§ *Two points deducted for a slow over-rate.*

Buckinghamshire's success was all the more pleasing given that seven players had appeared for the county's junior sides. They included Sam Cherry, who took five five-fors, and 20-year-old Richard Hopwood, who became only the second player to score two centuries in a match for the county, with 131 and 100 against Lincolnshire. All-rounder Mark Hardinges proved a valuable acquisition, but was unavailable for the Championship final, as was promising wicketkeeper David Cranfield-Thompson, but the squad had quality in depth. Wins with maximum points against Northumberland and Lincolnshire in their first two matches, as well as full bowling bonus points in every game, meant they always looked like champions.

Justin Bishop was **Suffolk's** first new captain for over a decade after Phil Caley retired, but not before he reached 9,269 runs and became the county's leading run-scorer. Rain interrupted three games, but did not seem to inconvenience their batsmen, with Hassan Adnan scoring over 700 runs, including two hundreds against Hertfordshire, when Martyn Cull also hit 208 not out. Tom Huggins and Ben France were two more to score heavily. Bishop was the top bowler, but with only 15 wickets; the fact that no one secured fewer bowling points in the Eastern Division reveals where their weakness lay.

The highlight of **Norfolk's** season was a fifth victory in the knockout trophy, but they spurned an opportunity to challenge for the Eastern title. Set a generous 243 by Bedfordshire in the fourth round of games, wickets fell to a succession of rash shots, frustrating Trevor Ward, who might have steered his side to victory, given some sensible support. The combination of Ward's experience, the cavalier style of Ben Patston, the reliable batting of James Spelman and Chris Borrett, plus the 72 wickets of spinners George Walker and Chris Brown, meant Norfolk had a side capable of doing better.

Hertfordshire's young team started to fulfil their potential, yet failed to win friends with their over-exuberant attitude on the field. They had the advantage of playing their penultimate match after everyone else in order to help Norfolk with their festival. Needing a win to retain a realistic chance of the title, they set Norfolk an absurd 397 at seven an over, and the result unsurprisingly was a draw. James Hewitt scored two hundreds in that game, but their attack lacked a cutting edge.

Runs from Gary Scott, Adam Cragg and Mark Dale helped **Northumberland** punch above their weight, and all-rounder Marc Symington, who scored two undefeated hundreds against Hertfordshire, enjoyed another top-quality season. In nine innings, four unbeaten, Symington scored 366 runs; he also took 16 wickets at 21.68. In five matches, captain Phil Nicholson took 20 catches behind the stumps; he also played his 100th Championship game.

Staffordshire struggled with availabilities and injuries in Championship cricket following their run in the knockout Trophy; key players were absent for the final at Chester-le-Street, which resulted in a heavy defeat by Norfolk. Liam Hughes, aged 21, scored 184 not out on his Championship debut, against Norfolk, but the side badly missed the all-round ability of Mo Sheikh who was unable to play a single Championship game.

Another difficult season for **Cumberland** ended on a high note with a resounding victory over Bedfordshire. Gary Pratt and Marcus Sharp captained the side but were rarely able to pick a settled team. James Smith (130 not out) and James Beaumont (77 not out) put on a record unbeaten 204 for the seventh wicket against Cambridgeshire, but a meagre total of seven batting bonus points highlighted a problem area.

Cambridgeshire failed to win a match, drawing the first five, but losing inside two days to Norfolk in their last game. A few individual performances stood out, such as David Williams's seven for 47 in the defeat, but their cricket seemed to lack purpose.

Derek Randall coached an improving young **Bedfordshire** side, but poor first-innings batting meant they were too often out of a match by the end of the opening day. The one exception was their only victory, when spinners Andy Roberts and 19-year-old Tom Brett bowled out Norfolk against the odds. Ollie Clayson captained the side in the absence of the injured Jon Walford, and scored five fifties in ten innings. After four years without a win in the one-day competition they reached the semi-final, when they lost to Staffordshire.

Lincolnshire finished bottom with three losses and three draws. They were able to field almost the same side that won the division the year before, but Robert Cook, the appointed captain, was unable to play any Championship cricket due to professional rugby commitments, and wicketkeeper Oliver Burford took on the role. The side never seriously challenged in a Championship game, though they won their group in the knockout trophy before losing a close quarter-final to Norfolk.

Cheshire continued their domination of the Western Division with their fourth title in the nine years of the three-day Championship; they were the only side in the division to be undefeated. A complete washout of their fourth match, against Dorset, effectively meant they needed to win their last two games to overtake Cornwall. A comprehensive defeat of Wales and a five-wicket victory against Shropshire, when Adam Syddall took eight for 83, ensured they did. Syddall, with 25 wickets, and Nathan Dumelow, with 30, were the key bowlers, and Ben Spendlove with 731 runs was the second-highest run-scorer in the competition. Chris Tipper, aged 19, hit 219 against Herefordshire, and Rick Moore averaged 35 opening the innings. Wicketkeeper Matt Dawson topped the stumpers' table with 21 victims.

Frustration is the word that sums up **Cornwall's** season. Going to Wales for the last match, they led Cheshire by five points, but heavy rain at Pontarddulais permitted only 4.2 overs, while their challengers had time to win. Their season, however, did not lack excitement. Keith Parsons and Gary Thomas put on a record 272 for the fifth wicket against Cheshire at Falmouth. Against Herefordshire, 20-year-old Dan Davis, in his second game, scored 153, and followed this with 93 and 114 against Oxfordshire. Captain Tom Sharp (six for 24) and Chris Hunkin (four for 20) bowled Wiltshire out for 98 to set up a ten-wicket victory. Sharp also took six for 27 as Devon, who were 19 for seven at one stage, scrambled to 73 in their second innings, leaving Cornwall just enough time to chase 94 as seven wickets fell. Thomas made his 100th Championship appearance during the season and shared another record as he and Davis added 150 for the sixth wicket against Oxfordshire.

A third consecutive semi-final defeat in the knockout trophy was a disappointment for **Oxfordshire**, but a successful Championship season followed, and a number of young players were given debuts. However, at 49, Keith Arnold still topped the county's bowling averages; Daniel Rowe and Paul McMahon gave him good support. Damian Shirazi, who moved from Wiltshire, was the leading run-scorer, hitting 110 on his county debut in a one-day game against Bedfordshire.

Wins against Oxfordshire and Berkshire in their first three games gave **Dorset** hope of challenging for the title, but a washout in the next match at Cheshire and defeat by Shropshire put them out of the running. At Dean Park in the last match they narrowly beat Wiltshire, despite conceding a first-innings deficit of 173, after Nick Park scored 219 and added 157 for the last wicket with David Kidner. Wiltshire were 242, but captain Tom Hicks took six for 82 with his off-spin to give Dorset victory by four runs in an enthralling game.

If **Shropshire** had beaten Cheshire in the last match they would have been champions of the west, but a tame display saw them lose by five wickets, and a mid-table finish was a true reflection of their season. Jono Whitney was the top-scorer and Andy Gray again headed the bowling; he has taken 106 wickets for the county in all cricket in his three seasons. Ed Foster and Richard Oliver hit maiden centuries, and 17-year-old Alex Blofield made his debut.

Berkshire finished the season far better than they started: after four games the 2008 champions were bottom of the table. New professional Richard Logan topped both batting and bowling averages, his eight for 56 against Devon the highlight, but no other bowler managed a five-for. James Morris (156) and captain Bjorn Mordt (123 not out) broke a 74-year-old record for the seventh wicket when they put on 185 against Oxfordshire.

By beating Herefordshire in their last match, **Devon** avoided experiencing two consecutive seasons without a Championship win, but all except one of their games were interrupted by the weather. They were a side in transition, and Bobby Dawson stood down as captain at the end of the season after seven years which brought success in both the Championship and knockout Trophy. Dawson had a fine season with the bat, but with the exception of Chris Metters – only the second Devon bowler to win the Frank Edwards Trophy – the attack lacked real penetration despite collecting maximum bowling points. Their only win came when Dawson and David Lye rescued the side from 29 for four, and set a fifth-wicket record of 286.

James Hibberd took over as captain of **Wiltshire** and had instant success in winning their group of the knockout Trophy before being beaten by Oxfordshire in the quarter-final. In the Championship they rose off the bottom, thanks to a single win against Herefordshire, but despite that modest improvement Hibberd decided to stand down at the end of the season. Wes Durston, Greg Lamb, Eddie Abel and Michael Coles all scored centuries, but there was no outstanding bowler. Andy Caddick made one appearance, taking five wickets in 43 overs as he aimed for fitness in his final first-class season.

Wales, whose only victory came against Devon when the captains co-operated to create a meaningful last day, shared several players with the Glamorgan first team. Tom Maynard played in four games and scored three centuries, two against Wiltshire when he featured in a record third-wicket stand of 191 with Huw Waters.

For the fourth consecutive season **Herefordshire** were bottom of the Western Division. Their last win in the Championship was in 2005. Chris Boroughs was again captain, a position he has held since 2002, and his batting was outstanding.

LEADING AVERAGES, 2009

BATTING

(Qualification: 300 runs in 5 completed innings, average 40.00)

	M	I	NO	Runs	HS	100s	Avge
Hassan Adnan (*Suffolk*)	5	10	4	763	125	4	127.16
G. M. Scott (*Northumberland*)	5	10	2	590	176*	3	73.75
B. L. Spendlove (*Cheshire*)	7	11	1	731	148	2	73.10
C. L. Tipper (*Cheshire*)	4	6	0	422	219	1	70.33
R. I. Dawson (*Devon*)	6	9	2	429	121	2	61.28
A. D. Cragg (*Northumberland*)	5	7	1	363	101*	1	60.50
A. S. Lewis (*Hertfordshire*)	6	10	2	482	171*	1	60.25
T. R. Ward (*Norfolk*)	6	11	3	476	89*	0	59.50
D. F. Davis (*Cornwall*)	6	8	0	472	153	2	59.00
M. G. Cull (*Suffolk*)	5	10	2	471	208*	1	58.87
A. G. Burton (*Cambridgeshire*)	3	6	0	340	133	2	56.66
B. J. France (*Suffolk*)	5	10	1	494	102	1	54.88
N. G. E. Walker (*Hertfordshire*)	6	10	2	432	121	2	54.00
B. J. Patston (*Norfolk*)	3	6	0	321	107	1	53.50
R. J. Hopwood (*Buckinghamshire*)	7	14	2	635	131	2	52.91
N. J. Ferraby (*Cambridgeshire*)	4	8	2	316	131*	1	52.66
K. A. Parsons (*Cornwall*)	6	8	1	350	175	1	50.00
O. J. Clayson (*Bedfordshire*)	5	10	1	442	88	0	49.11
T. B. Huggins (*Suffolk*)	5	10	0	490	150	3	49.00
N. G. Park (*Dorset*)	6	10	0	482	219	2	48.20
V. Atri (*Lincolnshire*)	5	10	3	326	100*	1	46.57
C. R. Borrett (*Norfolk*)	6	10	3	321	89*	0	45.85
M. C. Dobson (*Lincolnshire*)	4	8	0	365	108	2	45.62
G. D. Freear (*Cambridgeshire*)	5	10	0	446	107	1	44.60
J. M. Spelman (*Norfolk*)	5	10	1	401	104	1	44.55
C. W. Boroughs (*Herefordshire*)	6	11	1	439	135	1	43.90
G. J. Pratt (*Cumberland*)	6	11	1	434	149	2	43.40
M. A. P. Dale (*Northumberland*)	5	8	0	332	87	0	41.50
F. I. Qureshi (*Buckinghamshire*)	4	8	0	330	162	1	41.25
P. G. Cook (*Lincolnshire*)	6	10	1	371	63*	0	41.22
D. J. R. Exall (*Herefordshire*)	6	11	3	320	98*	0	40.00

BOWLING

(Qualification: 15 wickets, average 30.00)

	O	M	R	W	BB	5W/i	Avge
C. L. Metters (*Devon*)	177	33	582	34	6-41	2	17.11
T. G. Sharp (*Cornwall*)	195.5	51	469	27	6-24	3	17.37
M. A. Hardinges (*Buckinghamshire*)	166.5	52	499	27	4-40	0	18.48
S. A. Cherry (*Buckinghamshire*)	274	57	749	40	5-57	5	18.72
G. W. Walker (*Norfolk*)	271.1	56	793	41	9-48	5	19.34
R. J. Logan (*Berkshire*)	192.5	40	691	34	8-56	2	20.32
S. A. Taylor (*Shropshire*)	157	30	485	23	4-31	0	21.08
A. R. Roberts (*Bedfordshire*)	89	16	381	18	6-39	1	22.04
M. J. Symington (*Northumberland*)	108.2	23	347	16	5-28	1	21.68
D. O. Conway (*Cumberland*)	137.4	31	463	21	6-39	1	22.04
Ajaz Akhtar (*Cambridgeshire*)	203.1	60	489	22	4-58	0	22.22
T. C. Hicks (*Dorset*)	121.1	30	357	16	6-82	1	22.31
G. R. Willott (*Staffordshire*)	151.1	39	483	21	6-73	1	23.00
K. A. Arnold (*Oxfordshire*)	168	45	461	20	4-72	0	23.05
G. M. Harper (*Buckinghamshire*)	109	18	424	18	5-43	1	23.55
C. T. Griffiths (*Herefordshire*)	108	21	408	17	5-98	2	24.00
A. K. D. Gray (*Shropshire*)	207.5	23	733	30	7-97	2	24.43
C. Brown (*Norfolk*)	270.5	53	802	31	5-16	2	25.87
A. J. Syddall (*Cheshire*)	182	27	669	25	8-83	2	26.76
N. R. C. Dumelow (*Cheshire*)	244.5	60	814	30	5-96	2	27.13
D. T. Rowe (*Oxfordshire*)	145.5	34	578	20	4-56	0	28.90
P. J. McMahon (*Oxfordshire*)	262	52	809	27	6-103	2	29.96

CHAMPIONSHIP FINAL

At Slough CC, September 6, 7, 8, 9. **Buckinghamshire won by 117 runs.** Toss Buckinghamshire. **Buckinghamshire 369-5** (F. I. Qureshi 162, R. J. Hopwood 35, J. C. Harrison 101, P. R. Sawyer 39) and **336** (F. I. Qureshi 32, R. J. Hopwood 73, P. R. Sawyer 50, S. A. Cherry 52*; D. O. Berry 4-56). Cheshire **305** (W. M. Goodwin 44, R. A. L. Moore 62, B. L. Spendlove 41, A. J. Hall 54*; S. F. Stanway 4-74) and **283** (W. M. Goodwin 40, R. A. L. Moore 33, B. L. Spendlove 91, D. O. Berry 50*; S. A. Cherry 5-85). *Man of the Match:* F. I. Qureshi.

Buckinghamshire batted with more caution than ambition, and a second-wicket stand of 231 between Fahim Qureshi and captain Jason Harrison saw them to a par score in their allotted 90 overs. Three of Cheshire's top four scored over 40, but the tail could not survive to support skipper Andrew Hall, at No. 5. The dry pitch did not deteriorate as much as had been predicted, and Buckinghamshire set about batting Cheshire out of the game: their lead was 400 when they were all out in the 110th over. Richard Moore and Warren Goodwin put on 88 for the first wicket, but both fell late on the third day. On the last morning, Cheshire slumped to 172-7 before Ben Spendlove and Dan Berry put on 97 for the eighth wicket. But Buckinghamshire off-spinners Sam Cherry and Zaheer Sher (who took 2-59) bowled with great control to see them home.

RECENT MINOR COUNTIES CHAMPIONS

1990	Hertfordshire	1998	Staffordshire	2004	{ Bedfordshire / Devon
1991	Staffordshire	1999	Cumberland		
1992	Staffordshire	2000	Dorset	2005	{ Cheshire / Suffolk
1993	Staffordshire	2001	{ Cheshire / Lincolnshire		
1994	Devon			2006	Devon
1995	Devon	2002	{ Herefordshire / Norfolk	2007	Cheshire
1996	Devon			2008	Berkshire
1997	Devon	2003	Lincolnshire	2009	Buckinghamshire

A full list of previous Champions can be found on pages 915–16 of Wisden 2008.

MCCA KNOCKOUT TROPHY FINAL

At Chester-le-Street, July 22, 23. **Norfolk won by 104 runs.** Toss: Norfolk. **Norfolk 257-6** (50 overs) (C. J. Rogers 91, B. J. Patston 65, J. M. Spelman 43*), **Staffordshire 153** (40.3 overs) (R. P. Harvey 36, P. S. J. Goodwin 32; M. P. Eccles 5-34). *Man of the Match*: M. P. Eccles.

After a late start, Norfolk quickly dominated through Carl Rogers and Ben Patston, who rattled up an opening stand of 109 in 89 minutes; Patston was eventually bowled for 65 from 57 balls, including three sixes and seven fours. Despite a tight ten-over spell from Craig Barker in which he conceded only 36 and had Trevor Ward and Stephen Gray caught behind, Norfolk set a challenging target. When bad light ended play 9.3 overs into their reply, Staffordshire were reeling at 26-4, three of the wickets falling to opening bowler Michael Eccles. On the reserve day the game drifted towards its inevitable conclusion, though the last three wickets did manage to add 55 runs.

WINNERS 1983–2009

1983	Cheshire	1992	Devon	2001	Norfolk	
1984	Hertfordshire	1993	Staffordshire	2002	Warwickshire Board XI	
1985	Durham	1994	Devon	2003	Cambridgeshire	
1986	Norfolk	1995	Cambridgeshire	2004	Berkshire	
1987	Cheshire	1996	Cheshire	2005	Norfolk	
1988	Dorset	1997	Norfolk	2006	Northumberland	
1989	Cumberland	1998	Devon	2007	Suffolk	
1990	Buckinghamshire	1999	Bedfordshire	2008	Devon	
1991	Staffordshire	2000	Herefordshire	2009	Norfolk	

Staged as the ECB 38-County Competition from 1999 to 2002.

SECOND ELEVEN CHAMPIONSHIP, 2009

Michael Vockins

For the first time, the Championship was split into two divisions. MCC Universities replaced Scotland A, and the 20 teams competed in two groups of ten, each playing nine three-day games.

Yorkshire won five – more than any other county in 2009 – but trailed Lancashire by a single point in the North Division. Surrey, who like Lancashire had four victories, topped the South. The three-day final between these two counties was drawn, but Surrey claimed the title on first-innings lead. In one of the leanest periods in their history, the success was a welcome, if modest, lift at The Oval.

The new format won praise from those most closely connected with this level of the game, though some counties wanted to play more matches, and for them to count towards the Championship. Many would also like to see four-day cricket to mirror the County Championship as a better preparation for the step up to first-class cricket.

The number of younger players making their way in the game through the Second Eleven Championship was encouraging, although there were occasional frustrations caused by the mismatch of a youthful side coming up against an older, more experienced team. With many counties using 30 or more players, secretariats were kept busy with registration paperwork.

Registration had rather more serious repercussions for Leicestershire and Worcestershire, when in December they were found guilty of fielding an ineligible player. Chris Thompson, who made his first-class debut for Leicestershire at Colwyn Bay in August, played second-eleven cricket for both counties during the summer while still on Surrey's books. Leicestershire and Worcestershire were fined £1,000, £500 of which was suspended for 12 months, and docked half the points they gained while Thompson was playing for them.

Somerset were in trouble, too. Their Kolpak player, Omari Banks – the first player from the tiny Leeward island of Anguilla to play Test cricket – was seen scoring the ball with his thumbnails and fingernails during the game against Essex. The umpires promptly awarded five penalty runs to Essex and reported the incident to the ECB. Banks was banned for three matches for ball-tampering, while Somerset were deducted all points from the game and fined £500, plus another £500 in costs. An ECB statement berated Somerset: "These penalties reflected the panel's view that the club had not taken adequate measures to prevent the offence occurring. The panel also expressed the view that they would expect the club to write to all the players, strongly reminding them of the law and the seriousness with which any breach is regarded." Banks admitted the offence, saying he acted out of boredom.

The new north–south structure of the championship mirrors the long-established east–west format of the Minor Counties Championship. Unfortunately, the first play-off final also reflected the pattern of some Minor Counties finals in which the side winning the toss had the sole intention of batting their opponents out of the game. In 2010, however, the final is a four-day game (matching the Minor Counties, again), increasing the likelihood of a decisive result. Perhaps a more far-reaching innovation is the introduction of a new knockout competition, starting in 2010, of 40 overs a side, spread over two innings for each team. This was considered as a possible format for the first-class counties' 40-over tournament, so influential figures will be keeping an eye on progress.

In the 50-over Trophy, Yorkshire beat Lancashire by two wickets in a low-scoring final at Scarborough. It was a double disappointment for Lancashire who, three days earlier, had lost the Championship final. Yorkshire comfortably beat Hampshire in the semi-finals, and Lancashire outplayed Sussex, who had earlier won seven of their nine games in the South Division.

SECOND ELEVEN CHAMPIONSHIP, 2009

North Division

	P	W	L	D	Bonus Points Bat	Bowl	Pen	Total Points
Lancashire (14)	9	4	0	5	30	28	0	134
Yorkshire (5)	9	5	0	4	21	26	0	133
Nottinghamshire (9)	9	4	1	4	23	36	0	131
Durham (1)	9	3	1	5	28	30	0	120
Worcestershire (4)	9	2	5	2	18	30	−10.5	73.5
Derbyshire (16)	9	1	2	6	21	12	0	71
MCC Young Cricketers (20)	9	1	3	5	12	20	0	66
Leicestershire (18)	9	0	3	6	15	27	−10	56
Glamorgan (17)	9	0	2	7	10	18	−1.5	54.5
Warwickshire (10)	9	0	3	6	6	23	0	53

South Division

	P	W	L	D	Bonus Points Bat	Bowl	Pen	Total Points
Surrey (6)	9	4	0	5	28	33	0	137
Hampshire (15)	9	4	0	5	24	22	0	122
Middlesex (2)	9	2	2	5	30	33	0	111
Sussex (7)	9	3	2	4	25	23	−1	105
Kent (8)	9	2	2	5	26	29	0	103
Gloucestershire (12)	9	3	1	5	12	25	0	99
Somerset (3)	9	2	2	5	26	29	−11	92
Essex (11)	9	1	3	5	30	25	−2	87
Northamptonshire (13)	9	0	5	4	23	30	−1.5	67.5
MCC Universities (–)	9	0	4	5	18	27	0	65

2008 positions are shown in brackets.

Win = 14 pts; draw = 4 pts.

Somerset were deducted all 11 points gained against Essex for ball-tampering.
Leicestershire and Worcestershire were deducted half the points gained in matches in which they fielded an ineligible player.
Essex, Glamorgan, Northamptonshire and Sussex were deducted points for a slow over-rate.

Lancashire owed their position at the head of the North Division to their total of 30 batting points. Steven Mullaney's 620 runs included 207 against Worcestershire – one of eight double-centuries scored in the Second Eleven Championship in a summer when batsmen generally prospered. Karl Brown was another high scorer, and Luke Procter won a two-year contract by merit of his batting. Gary Montgomery, a left-arm seamer, had two five-fors, and also won a full-time contract after being a professional goalkeeper with three league clubs.

Yorkshire won more games than any other county. Jonathan Bairstow (202 not out) and Joe Root (163 not out) shared an unbroken fourth-wicket partnership of 358 against Leicestershire. Bairstow scored two more centuries and two fifties in five innings, making an irrefutable case to move up a grade. Fast-medium James Lee's 29 wickets included two five-fors.

Akhil Patel hit three hundreds for **Nottinghamshire**, and Alex Hales made 246 – the season's highest score – against Derbyshire. Andy Carter, signed from the Lincolnshire Premier League in 2008, was comfortably the top wicket-taker in the Championship with 55 at 11.94, twice claiming ten in a match; his 14 for 99 against Warwickshire was a club record.

Durham had batsmen and bowlers challenging for places to support their successful first team. Runs flowed from the bats of Paul Muchall (younger brother of Gordon), Karl Turner and Kyle Coetzer, who hit a double-hundred against Glamorgan. Chris Rushworth and Luke Evans led the attack, while leg-spinner Scott Borthwick added variety.

David Wheeldon, with 493 runs, was **Worcestershire's** leading scorer, ahead of Matthew Pardoe, with 374. Imran Arif and Jack Shantry took most wickets, and pace bowler Chris Russell had a good first season. Those who saw 17-year-old wicketkeeper-batsman Ben Cox's performances were wholly unsurprised that he gained a first-class debut in September.

Derbyshire valued the 475 runs scored by 18-year-old Chesney Hughes, from Anguilla; he also claimed 11 wickets with his slow left-arms. He, off-spinner Jake Needham and leggie Mark Lawson provided a varied spin combination. Tom Poynton was impressive behind the stumps.

Jackson Thompson hit **MCC Young Cricketers'** only century, but Ned Eckersley's innings of 97 against Durham and 72 against Worcestershire – which set up their sole victory – were just as important. Zimbabwean medium-pacer Glenn Querl was their leading wicket-taker, with 20.

Tom New, Chris Thompson and the veteran Paul Nixon all made centuries for **Leicestershire**, but overall, batsmen found runs hard to come by. Pacemen Daniel Masters (younger brother of Essex's David) and Kieron Garside led the attack, and were well supported by keeper Joel Pope.

Glamorgan failed to record a win. Will Bragg scored heavily early in the summer and was promoted to the first team. Batsman Nick James won a contract for 2010, as did Cardiff-born Aneurin Norman, a promising all-rounder from Millfield School.

Wicketkeeper-batsman Richard Johnson performed well for **Warwickshire**. Paul Best, a left-arm spinning all-rounder aged just 18, captained the side in a manner well beyond his years.

At the top of the South Division, **Surrey** had Laurie Evans to thank for 655 runs, and Chris Murtagh for 445. Off-spinner Simon King captured 25 wickets at 21.64, and fast bowler Stuart Meaker bagged 13 at 13.07; Timothy Linley, James Ormond, Tom Smith and Alex Tudor also took wickets economically. Five squad members were awarded emerging-player contracts: batsmen Tom Lancefield and Seren Waters, leg-spinner Muhunthan Harinath, and pace bowlers Tom Jewell and George Edwards.

Like Surrey, **Hampshire** won four games but could not match them for bowling points: only seamer Tom Parsons managed a five-for. David Balcombe claimed 18 wickets and David Griffiths 16, while left-arm spinner Danny Briggs took 13. Luke Towers, from Western Australia, scored 553 runs and notched up an undefeated double-hundred against Middlesex; Southampton-born Matthew Kleinveldt was just behind him with 542.

Dan Housego was the leading run-scorer for **Middlesex** with 570; John Simpson hit 463 and added 18 victims behind the stumps. Adam London scored four fifties in his total of 428. Josh Davey was another consistent batsman with 301 runs; he also took 15 wickets with his medium-pace. Left-arm spinner Ravi Patel led with 22.

Joe Gatting (nephew of former England captain Mike) scored 669 runs for **Sussex**, with two centuries and two fifties, winning promotion to the first team. Another familiar name was Luke Wells, whose father Alan was captain in the 1990s; Luke made 361 runs in four games with a top score of 133 not out. Leg-spinner Will Beer and off-spinner Ollie Rayner both took 20 wickets, Beer at just 13.55 each; Rayner added 324 runs to his all-round account.

Alex Blake of **Kent** was the heaviest scorer in the Championship with 746. James Hockley returned seven years after his last appearance, and totalled 429. Kent's leading wicket-taker with 21 was off-spinner Charlie Hemphrey who also hit 389 runs. Fabian Cowdrey – son of Chris and grandson of Colin – made a notable debut at the age of 16: appearing as a full substitute in the game against Surrey at Charterhouse in August, he top-scored from No. 10 with 42 in his only innings.

Gloucestershire fielded a staggering 40 players over the summer. Two newcomers who won contracts for 2010 were Chris Dent, after hitting two centuries in six innings, and pace bowler Gemaal Hussain whose 18 wickets cost only 19 each.

Runs for **Somerset** came chiefly from opener Chris Jones and the experienced Wes Durston; leg-spinner Michael Munday was the fourth-highest wicket-taker of the season.

Essex endeavoured to bring on younger players such as Adam Wheater and 16-year-old Ben Foakes; both made maiden centuries, though old hand Grant Flower scored most runs.

For **Northamptonshire**, who failed to record a victory, Nathan Hawkes hit a maiden hundred, and pace bowlers Jack Brooks and Bud Bailey showed consistent form.

MCC Universities found their first season in the Championship something of a struggle, but individual players benefited from the experience. Leading run-maker Robin Lett (Oxford) made two centuries, and Duncan Snell (Leeds/Bradford) was also consistent. Seam bowler Gavin Baker (Loughborough) claimed 24 wickets, and Bradley Kruger (Leeds/Bradford) took eight for 45 against Middlesex. Most of the players have links with a first-class county and, with MCC's support and encouragement for university cricket, their time may well come.

LEADING AVERAGES, 2009

BATTING

(Qualification: 400 runs in 6 completed innings, average 40.00)

	M	I	NO	R	HS	100s	Avge
G. W. Flower (*Essex*)	7	10	3	529	119	2	75.57
A. J. Blake (*Kent*)	7	12	1	746	206	3	67.81
C. P. Murtagh (*Surrey*)	5	9	2	445	154*	1	63.57
W. J. Durston (*Somerset*)	7	13	2	667	165*	2	60.63
L. J. Evans (*Surrey*)	8	13	2	655	148	1	59.54
A. D. Hales (*Nottinghamshire*)	5	8	0	423	246	1	52.87
S. J. Mullaney (*Lancashire*)	9	13	1	620	207	2	51.66
J. S. Gatting (*Sussex*)	7	13	0	669	141	2	51.46
C. F. Hughes (*Derbyshire*)	9	14	4	475	88	0	47.50
J. A. Simpson (*Middlesex*)	7	12	2	463	118	1	46.30
G. S. Ballance (*Yorkshire*)	9	12	1	502	212	1	45.63
K. R. Brown (*Lancashire*)	9	14	2	547	130*	1	45.58
D. A. Wheeldon (*Worcestershire*)	7	11	0	493	138	1	44.81
C. R. Jones (*Somerset*)	9	17	1	704	137	2	44.00
R. J. H. Lett (*MCCU, Somerset*)	9	15	1	599	113	2	42.78
A. Patel (*Nottinghamshire*)	9	15	1	599	136	3	42.78
T. Westley (*Essex*)	6	10	0	426	113	1	42.60
E. J. Eckersley (*MCC YC*)	7	13	2	461	97	0	41.90

BOWLING

(Qualification: 20 wickets)

	O	M	R	W	BB	5W/i	Avge
A. Carter (*Nottinghamshire*)	219.2	53	657	55	7-43	6	11.94
J. E. Lee (*Yorkshire*)	119.3	25	389	29	5-33	2	13.41
W. A. T. Beer (*Sussex*)	104.3	27	271	20	6-38	1	13.55
G. S. Montgomery (*Lancs, Leics, Warks*) .	211.5	47	650	38	7-29	3	17.10
T. M. J. Smith (*Sussex, Surrey*)	189.5	32	484	24	5-74	2	20.16
S. J. King (*Surrey*)	172.1	23	541	25	5-56	2	21.64
Imran Arif (*Worcestershire*)	208.5	46	729	32	7-53	2	22.78
M. H. A. Footitt (*Nottinghamshire*)	214.3	51	621	25	5-32	1	24.84
O. P. Rayner (*Sussex*)	196	47	514	20	5-60	1	25.70
R. H. Patel (*Middlesex*)	170.4	34	580	22	5-65	1	26.36
S. C. Kerrigan (*Lancashire*)	293.5	60	780	26	6-58	2	30.00
C. R. Humphrey (*Kent*)	187.3	29	665	21	8-51	1	31.66
M. K. Munday (*Somerset*)	237.1	21	992	31	7-109	1	32.00
G. C. Baker (*MCC Universities*)	211.5	37	780	24	4-42	0	32.50
M. S. Westfield (*Essex*)	196	36	718	22	5-80	1	32.63
R. G. Querl (*MCC YC*)	212	43	690	20	5-35	1	34.50

CHAMPIONSHIP FINAL

At Manchester, September 16, 17, 18. **Drawn.** Toss: Surrey. **Surrey 500-8 dec** (151 overs) (S. R. Waters 53, J. N. Batty 70, J. J. Roy 50, C. J. Jordan 135, T. M. J. Smith 88*); **Lancashire 438** (123.4 overs) (K. R. Brown 83, G. D. Cross 65, S. J. Mullaney 77, A. Shankar 79, C. L. Tipper 45; T. M. J. Smith 5-90).

Surrey's total owed much to the seventh-wicket stand of 170 between Chris Jordan and Tom Smith, who was on loan from Sussex. Nineteen-year-old Seren Waters made a half-century, and Surrey's captain, the experienced Jon Batty, 70. Smith's left-arm spin then accounted for four of the last five Lancashire wickets as they folded from 414-5. Opener Karl Brown had batted well, and there were useful contributions down the order, but Surrey claimed first-innings advantage and with it the title.

SECOND ELEVEN TROPHY, 2009

Semi-finals

At Horsham, September 7. **Lancashire won by 149 runs.** Toss: Lancashire. **Lancashire 258-8** (50 overs) (K. R. Brown 56, S. J. Croft 40, G. D. Cross 58, S. D. Parry 50*); **Sussex 109** (27.3 overs) (O. J. Newby 5-15, S. D. Parry 3-21).

A devastating spell by Oliver Newby reduced Sussex to 48-5, and Stephen Parry, following his undefeated fifty, ended a one-sided match with three wickets.

At Leeds, September 7. **Yorkshire won by four wickets.** Toss: Hampshire. **Hampshire 180** (44.3 overs) (J. M. Vince 35, M. C. Kleinveldt 40; Azeem Rafiq 5-33); **Yorkshire 181-6** (44 overs) (A. Lyth 52).

Azeem Rafiq came on as third change, and Hampshire plummeted from 110-4. Adam Lyth anchored Yorkshire's reply.

Final

At Scarborough, September 21. **Yorkshire won by two wickets.** Toss: Lancashire. **Lancashire 142** (42.1 overs) (T. C. Smith 46, L. A. Procter 41); **Yorkshire 143-8** (36.5 overs) (J. E. Lee 39*; O. J. Newby 3-35, S. C. Kerrigan 3-37).

Lancashire slumped to 11-4 before Luke Procter joined Tom Smith to add 67, the biggest stand of the match. James Lee, who took two of the early wickets, came in to bat with the score on 85-6 and carried Yorkshire to a narrow victory.

A list of past winners of the Second Eleven Championship can be found on page 883 of Wisden 2009.

LEAGUE CRICKET, 2009

GEOFFREY DEAN

The most astonishing performance of the season came in the first, baking week of July in the **Kent League**. After being put in by visiting Gore Court on a belter, Hartley amassed 540 for one from 55 overs, with Kent batsman James Hockley batting right through for a chanceless 283 from 170 balls. He hit 47 fours and 11 sixes, putting on 261 with Trinidadian professional Justin Guillen and 279 with Matthew Walker of Essex, who both made 104. Daniel Forster, a Victorian off-spinner, went for 130 in his 11 overs; later, he made 88 – one of only two players in double figures for Gore Court as they succumbed by 340 runs in their 29th over. The match established league records for highest team score, individual score, margin of victory and stands for the first and second wicket.

Hartley captain Andy Tutt said it was a decent attack, featuring first-class players Alamgir Sheriyar (whose 11 overs cost 74) and Philip Edwards (15 overs for 113). "But James was devastating – apart from cutting and pulling anything short, he hardly played a cross-batted shot. The outfield was incredibly quick, with one straight boundary of 65 yards, but the other three were 70 to 75. There was no part where our batsmen took the mickey. Some of their fielders asked why didn't I declare, but we'd been put in, I was aware something special was taking place, and I wanted to be part of it. To win, we needed to bowl them out, as it wasn't limited-overs, and I thought the longer they fielded, the more it might affect their batting."

In a season where – highly unusually – not one Kent League match was abandoned to rain, Hartley were pipped to the title by Bromley, who beat them by three runs in August. On the last day, Gore Court gained the victory they needed to avoid relegation in their return match with Hartley; fortunately for them, Hockley was absent.

Fittingly, in the year that Durham retained the County Championship at Chester-le-Street, the town's club side ended South Northumberland's six-year reign as kings of the **North-East Premier League**; they also won the ECB's National Club Championship. Visiting Gosforth in July, they inflicted South Northumberland's first defeat for 14 months, thanks to Luke Evans, who took six for 13. Other heroes of Chester-le-Street's campaign were off-spinner Richard Waite, whose 36 victims included seven against Stockton, and Andrew Smith, with 825 runs at 51.

Though South Northumberland's remarkable run ended, Bracebridge Heath did win a seventh successive title in **Lincolnshire**, with over 800 runs from Paul Cook, while St Just became champions of **Cornwall** for the sixth year running. Ealing won their fifth consecutive **Middlesex League**, and were unbeaten until the end of August; former Middlesex slow left-armer Chris Peploe contributed 49 wickets.

Dan Wilson, a 25-year-old Queenslander, set a **Yorkshire League** record of 1,542 runs to help York to their fourth title in six years. St Annes, the **Northern**

A win on aggregate

NEIL PRISCOTT

For the Ashes series of 2009, read the West of England Premier League: it was a good year, but by no means a vintage one.

The major success was the adoption of an aggregate points system for the first time (rather than ranking teams on average points per match played, excluding abandoned games). It encouraged the playing of more cricket, as the League administrators had hoped. In the past, teams have been minded to protect their average point score in adverse weather conditions, and perhaps wouldn't go the extra mile to ensure play. With teams eager to get on the park, the League was off to a good start.

It finished well, too. With no dominant side in the ten-team division, the title was up for grabs on the last day of the season. In a compelling finale, former Somerset all-rounder Keith Parsons captained Taunton St Andrews to victory over Bridgwater by 4.30 p.m., but had a nervous three-hour wait on the outcome of the Bath–Frocester match. Frocester, near Stonehouse, were in pole position before the start of play, but a 37-run defeat by outgoing champions Bath ensured the champagne corks would be popping in Somerset, not Gloucestershire.

The champagne wasn't vintage, though, for two main reasons: poor pitches and a few too many dull, drawn matches. Substandard pitches are probably the League's Achilles heel. In what is rightly considered the strongest level of competition in the whole of the West Country, and with two increasingly supportive counties in Somerset and Gloucestershire, the fact that the general level of playing surface is poor does little to help the development of the next generation of talent for the first-class game.

In general, the wickets play low and slow and are conducive to medium-pace seam with a swinging Dukes ball. You'll be lucky, therefore, to see a game that features quick scoring or fast, intimidating bowling. And while the ball might swing or seam, the pitches do not make it easy for the team bowling second to take ten wickets in the maximum 55-over allocation. Here we get to the other vexing issue: the draw.

The draw is a divisive issue for most local players in the West of England Premier League. The principle of being required to take all ten wickets bowling second to win is applauded but, when the reality is to witness chasing teams blocking for the draw with 40 overs to go, perhaps consideration should be given to removing the draw from the equation. The League might also benefit from reducing the maximum number of overs per bowler from 16, as some teams rely on using a few experienced bowlers, at the expense of giving youth a chance.

Taunton and Taunton Deane gained promotion, to increase the Somerset bias of the top division in 2010. This is a strong, improving and competitive league, which would be further improved with investment in pitches.

League champions, owed much to Sri Lankan Dinuka Hettiarachchi's 87 victims and Atiq-uz-Zaman's 792 runs. Neston's Jack Smith amassed 1,148 runs, a record for the **Cheshire League**, while former Worcestershire all-rounder Roger Sillence masterminded Longton's push for the **North Staffs & South Cheshire** title with 48 wickets.

Paul Burman was instrumental in Lutterworth's **Leicestershire League** triumph with 60 victims, four of them in successive balls in a crucial victory over Ashby Hastings in September. Knowle & Dorridge won their first **Birmingham League** without any of their batsmen managing a hundred, though Nick James combined 542 runs with 33 wickets, while Atiq-ur-Rehman Chisti and Luke Parker also passed 400 runs. James's form was trumped by former Warwickshire all-rounder Dougie Brown, who collected 482 runs and 53 wickets for Barnt Green. Carl Simon, a West Indian, claimed 64 victims to help Preston Nomads retain the **Sussex League**.

Misdemeanours on and off the field were an issue. Steve Smith, the captain of **North Wales League** champions Llandudno, was banned for life (which became eight weeks on appeal) and five team-mates disciplined after remarks made about other clubs, players and league officials appeared on the social networking site Facebook. Llandudno were fined £50 for bringing the game into disrepute. Widnes's former Pakistan bowler, Ata-ur-Rehman, and Alderley Edge's Sohail Rauf were suspended for the rest of the season – reduced to six and four weeks respectively – after guesting for clubs outside the Cheshire League. Widnes were also docked 128 points, reduced to 60, which led to relegation. In the **Southern League**, the management committee warned players and captains about their responsibilities under the spirit of cricket, after a series of disciplinary and behavioural incidents in all three divisions.

Chris Aspin writes: On the last afternoon of the **Lancashire League** season in September, David Lloyd – the former Lancashire and England batsman and now a commentator for Sky – turned out for Accrington at the age of 62, and struck the four runs needed to beat Lowerhouse and give his old club their second successive championship. "This is certainly more interesting than watching the England cricket team at the minute," said Lloyd. Accrington's success was highly unexpected: Haslingden, who headed the table for much of the season, lost their last three matches and finished four points adrift. Ramsbottom won the Worsley Cup final for the seventh time, beating Todmorden by five runs.

For financial reasons, Haslingden broke with tradition. Instead of signing an overseas professional, they turned to Phil Hayes, a 23-year-old chemistry student at Loughborough, who had shone for Ramsbottom in 2008. He made 806, including ten fifties, and the only more successful pro was West Indian Test batsman Brendan Nash, who topped the averages with 874 at 72 for East Lancashire. As the credit squeeze tightens and the bureaucracy surrounding overseas recruits grows more frustrating, others are likely to follow Haslingden's lead.

Two brothers from Burnley, Vishal and Bharat Tripathi, achieved a remarkable double. Vishal was the league's leading run-scorer with 932 runs, and Bharat the joint-leading wicket-taker with 76 wickets at 14, a club record. Professionals Anwar Ali of Colne and Enfield's Zimbabwean, Gary Brent, matched his 76 wickets.

With several pros arriving late, being called up in mid-season or returning home early, the amateurs took most of the honours. Just behind Vishal Tripathi, Graham Knowles made 925 runs for Haslingden and Simon Newbitt 892 for Todmorden. Accrington's leading batsman was David Lloyd's son Graham, with 842 runs, and their best bowler David Ormerod with 66. Among the pros, South Africa's Robin Peterson took 44 at eight apiece in ten games for Nelson to head the averages, and Andrew Payne took seven for four for Rawtenstall against Colne on the last day of the season.

Haslingden set a league record with 362 for three against Bacup, including an unbeaten 150 off 82 balls by Steve Dearden, who struck ten sixes and nine fours. They had already scored 323 for five at Rishton. One to watch was the 15-year-old Alex Coleman, who made 56 for Haslingden against Lowerhouse.

In the **Central Lancashire League**, Monton & Weaste and Norden ended the season with identical numbers of wins, losses, draws and points. For the first time ever, the tie-breaker of most away wins was used, and Monton & Weaste came out on top. They had already won the Lees Wood Cup final against Rochdale.

The season will be remembered for the huge number of runs scored, especially when Norden visited Royton. Spectators saw an astonishing display as Norden's South African professional, Jean Symes, scored the highest innings since the league was formed in 1892, an undefeated 268 out of 381 for three, striking 28 fours and 16 sixes; he gave only one chance, at 130, in 49 overs. Symes hit another three centuries and seven fifties, amassing 1,332 runs at 83. Even more prolific was another South African, Wayne Madsen with 1,858 for Unsworth at 103.22, including six centuries and ten fifties, plus 66 wickets at 15. Professionals Kyle Smit of Littleborough and Luke Procter of Royton both captured 79 wickets and topped 1,000 runs. Paul Green of Monton & Weaste raised the amateur run record to 1,670 at 98.

ECB PREMIER LEAGUE TABLES, 2009

Birmingham & District Premier Cricket League

	P	W	L	Pts
Knowle & Dorridge	22	14	3	374
Wolverhampton	22	11	5	291
Walmley	22	8	7	263
Kenilworth Wardens	22	7	5	255
Himley	22	8	8	253
Shrewsbury	22	7	6	247
Kidderminster Victoria	22	8	9	241
Barnt Green	22	7	10	237
Walsall	22	4	5	228
Moseley	22	7	11	220
Leamington	22	5	11	202
Bromsgrove	22	3	9	182

Cheshire County Cricket League

	P	W	L	Pts
Oulton Park	22	12	4	389
Bowdon	22	11	4	366
Nantwich	22	10	6	353
Alderley Edge	22	11	6	352
Neston	22	10	4	349
Hyde	22	7	7	308
Didsbury	22	7	9	287
Chester Boughton Hall	22	5	12	283
Oxton	22	6	8	279
Toft	22	7	14	268
Widnes	22	9	7	244
Macclesfield	22	2	16	203

Cornwall Premier League

	P	W	L	Pts
St Just	21	11	2	310
Werrington	21	11	2	299
Truro	21	10	4	271
St Austell	21	7	8	240
Falmouth	21	5	8	216
Newquay	21	6	9	193
Paul	21	5	10	182
Callington	21	2	14	144

Derbyshire Premier League

	P	W	L	Pts
Ockbrook & Borrowash	22	15	1	448
Sandiacre Town	22	13	2	421
Chesterfield	22	6	2	340
Spondon	22	10	5	332
Lullington Park	22	8	4	320
Dunstall	22	8	5	306
Ilkeston Rutland	22	3	9	221
Alfreton	22	3	5	220
Alvaston & Boulton	22	4	11	217
Quarndon	22	3	7	206
Rolls Royce, Derby	22	3	12	193
Aston-on-Trent	22	1	14	137

Devon Cricket League

	P	W	L	Pts
Sidmouth	18	11*	0	291
Plympton	18	8†	3	225
Bovey Tracey	18	5	5	207
Bradninch	18	6	7	189
North Devon	18	5	7	186
Budleigh Salterton	18	3*	5	182
Exeter	18	5	5	176
Plymouth	18	4*	5	174
Torquay	18	3†	6	167
Sandford	18	2*	9	151

Plus one tie.   †Plus two ties.

East Anglian Premier Cricket League

	P	W	L	Pts
Vauxhall Mallards	22	15	1	437
Norwich	22	9	5	351
Swardeston	22	10	8	350
Cambridge Granta	22	9	5	337
Saffron Walden	22	7	7	299
Clacton-on-Sea	22	6	6	295
Bury St Edmunds	22	4	6	293
Great Witchingham	22	7	9	285
Fakenham	22	7	8	278
Horsford	22	6	9	274
Halstead	22	5	12	206
Godmanchester	22	4	13	199

Essex Premier League

	P	W	L	Pts
Brentwood	18	13	1	290
Wanstead	18	7*	5	228
Woodford Wells	18	7	5	219
Chelmsford	18	7	7	216
Hainault & Clayhall	18	7	5	208
Colchester & East Essex	18	7	8	205
Upminster	18	6	9	192
Gidea Park & Romford	18	5	8	176
South Woodford	18	4*	9	170
Ardleigh Green	18	4	10	138

Plus one tie.

Home Counties Premier Cricket League

	P	W	L	Pts
Henley	18	9	3	318
Banbury	18	7	3	282
High Wycombe	18	7	3	275
Tring Park	18	7	5	263
Radlett	18	6	4	254
Potters Bar	18	6	8	244
Welwyn Garden City	18	6	6	235
Oxford	18	4	5	217
Slough	18	0	6	151
Farnham Royal	18	1	10	150

Kent Cricket League

	P	W	L	Pts
Bromley	18	13	0	286
Hartley	18	11	4	246
Tunbridge Wells	18	10	6	229
Bickley Park	18	9	8	207
Bexley	18	7	7	172
Sevenoaks Vine	18	6	10	167
St Lawrence & Highland Court	18	5	9	156
Gore Court	18	5	10	146
Blackheath	18	6	9	144
Beckenham	18	2	11	129

Leicestershire County Cricket League

	P	W	L	Pts
Lutterworth	22	15	3	421
Barrow Town	22	14	3	419
Loughborough Town	22	13	5	399
Kibworth	22	10	5	346
Market Harborough	22	12	7	333
Ashby Hastings	22	8	8	302
Leicester Ivanhoe	22	8	8	285
Stoughton & Thurnby	22	6	9	280
Syston Town	22	7	12	256
Sileby Town	22	6	12	255
Hinckley Town	22	6	12	240
Illston Abey	22	0	21	75

Lincolnshire Cricket Board Premier League

	P	W	L	Pts	Avge
Bracebridge Heath	**19**	**13**	**0**	**340**	**17.89**
Skegness	19	11	1	298	15.68
Louth	18	10	1	274	15.22
Sleaford	20	9	8	242	12.10
Lindum	20	8	7	236	11.80
Grimsby Town	20	7	8	226	11.30
Woodhall Spa	21	6	10	229	10.90
Market Deeping	19	7	9	205	10.78
Nettleham	21	6	11	212	10.09
Bourne	20	5	9	197	9.85
Caistor	19	2*	11	137	7.21
Messingham	20	3*	12	143	7.15

* Plus one tie.

Liverpool & District Cricket Competition

	P	W	L	Pts
Bootle	26	18	2	479
New Brighton	26	15	7	412
Ormskirk	26	14	5	410
Lytham	26	13	6	375
Colwyn Bay	26	12	9	352
Wallasey	26	12	11	340
Northop Hall	26	8	10	278
Northern	26	8	8	273
Hightown	26	8	13	268
Newton-le-Willows	26	7	12	249
Prestatyn	26	8	12	246
Southport & Birkdale	26	7	16	239
Fleetwood Hesketh	26	5	14	222
Formby	26	4	14	199

Middlesex County Cricket League

	P	W	L	Pts
Ealing	18	11	1	134
Teddington	18	11	5	115
Finchley	18	9	4	104
Hampstead	18	7	2	88
Eastcote	18	6	7	71
Stanmore	18	6	8	67
Brondesbury	18	4	6	57
Shepherds Bush	18	4	8	49
Winchmore Hill	18	2	9	36
Richmond	18	0	10	17

Northamptonshire Cricket League

	P	W	L	Pts
Finedon Dolben	22	15	2	471
Northampton Saints	22	13	3	438
Rushden Town	22	12	4	421
Old Northamptonians	22	11	6	383
Wollaston	22	9	6	353
Peterborough Town	22	9	8	338
Northants Cricket Academy	22	5	7	288
Stony Stratford	22	6	11	280
Rushton	22	5	8	277
Burton Latimer	22	5	9	273
Brixworth	22	1	13	173
Desborough Town	22	1	15	138

North East Premier Cricket League

	P	W	L	Pts
Chester-le-Street	22	14	0	485
Blaydon	22	13	2	409
South Northumberland	22	12	3	407
Benwell Hill	22	9	6	332
South Shields	22	8	8	289
Sunderland	22	7	7	274
Gateshead Fell	22	7	6	270
Durham Cricket Academy	22	6	8	253
Stockton	22	5	11	242
Tynemouth	22	3	11	177
Newcastle	22	2	12	173
Norton	22	2	14	148

†Northern Cricket League

	P	W	L	Pts
St Annes	24	13	3	226
Preston	24	11	4	215
Chorley	24	10	7	187
Netherfield	24	7	4	180
Morecambe	24	7	5	177
Barrow	24	9	8	164
Blackpool	24	5	4	161
Kendal	24	6	9	144
Leyland	24	4	9	129
Fleetwood	24	5	9	125
Darwen	24	4	8	125
Carnforth	24	3	9	120
Lancaster	24	4	9	117

† ECB-approved but not a Premier League.

North Staffs & South Cheshire League

	P	W	L	Pts
Longton	22	11	6	320
Little Stoke	22	9	4	302
Stone	22	9	4	282
Porthill Park	22	10	7	279
Wood Lane	22	9	6	273
Knypersley	22	9	5	263
Burslem	22	8	8	259
Audley	22	5	9	219
Hem Heath	22	4	8	202
Moddershall	22	5	10	194
Leycett	22	4	8	189
Leek	22	3	11	175

North Wales Premier League

	P	W	L	Pts
Llandudno	22	**13**	**2**	**398**
Mochdre	22	12	5	397
Pontblyddyn	22	11	5	325
Bangor	22	10	6	321
Mold	22	9	10	313
Connah's Quay	22	8	4	312
Llanrwst	22	8	6	305
Menai Bridge	22	4	6	256
Brymbo	22	6	9	238
Hawarden Park	22	4	11	233
Chirk	22	4	12	193
Bethesda	22	1	14	118

Nottinghamshire Cricket Board Premier League

	P	W	L	Pts
Clifton Village	22	**7**	**3**	**325**
Caythorpe	22	13	3	320
Cuckney	22	9	5	302
West Indian Cavaliers	22	9	4	295
Papplewick & Linby	22	12	4	290
Mansfield Hosiery Mills	22	8	7	270
Wollaton	22	8	7	265
Welbeck Colliery	22	6	8	228
Kimberley Institute	22	4	9	180
Attenborough	22	3	13	151
Farnsfield	22	2	11	150
Plumtree	22	4	11	147

Southern Premier Cricket League

	P	W	L	Pts
Havant	16	**9***	**1**	**290**
South Wiltshire	16	10	5	250
Hampshire Academy	16	8	7	222
Bournemouth	16	8	6	221
Totton & Eling	16	7	7	218
Alton	16	8	5	216
Bashley	16	7	5	215
Lymington	16	5	10	156
St Cross Symondians	16	3*	10	141
Andover	16	2	11	127

South Wales Cricket League

	P	W	L	Pts	Avge
Cardiff	16	13	1	308	19.25
Newport	18	11	6	290	16.11
St Fagans	17	11	5	268	15.76
Usk	18	12	5	275	15.27
Sully Centurions	16	9	5	243	15.18
Sudbrook	17	7	5	241	14.17
Pentyrch	16	4	9	163	10.18
Penarth	17	3	9	167	9.82
Abergavenny	16	5	5	154	9.62
Croesyceiliog	14	1	8	98	7.00
Tondu	14	1	10	95	6.78
Blackwood Town	15	1	10	100	6.66

Surrey Championship

	P	W	L	Pts
Sutton	18	**12**	**3**	**142**
Reigate Priory	18	12	4	135
Sunbury	18	8	8	95
Cobham Avorians	18	8	8	89
Wimbledon	18	7	5	88
Guildford	18	6	8	82
Malden Wanderers	18	5	10	64
Banstead	18	5	8	63
Weybridge	18	5	8	59
Spencer	18	4	10	56

Sussex Cricket League

	P	W	L	Pts
Preston Nomads	19	**15**	**2**	**488**
East Grinstead	19	11*	4	412
Brighton & Hove	19	11	5	397
Horsham	19	10	4	380
Sussex Development XI	10	5	4	†355
Eastbourne	19	8*	8	312
Cuckfield	19	7	7	308
Hastings & St Leonard's Priory	19	6	7	286
Three Bridges	19	5	9	250
Haywards Heath	19	3	14	191
Lewes Priory	19	1	18	150

* *Plus tie.*

† *Sussex Development XI played only ten games; their actual points total was multiplied by 1.9.*

West of England Premier League

	P	W	L	Pts
Taunton St Andrews	18	**9**	**1**	**371**
Weston-super-Mare	18	9	2	361
Frocester	18	8	3	350
Bath	18	8	5	312
Corsham	18	4	6	283
Bridgwater	18	4	5	281
Glastonbury	18	5	6	265
Bristol	18	4	7	242
Knowle	18	3	9	212
Downend	18	1	11	124

Yorkshire ECB County Premier League

	P	W	L	Pts
York	26	**15**	**1**	**160**
Scarborough	26	12	2	150
Yorkshire Academy	26	13	3	149
Castleford	26	14	5	127
Barnsley	26	13	4	117
Cleethorpes	26	6	7	99
Doncaster Town	26	8	7	94
Driffield Town	26	7	10	84
Rotherham Town	26	6	13	78
Sheffield Collegiate	26	5	12	71
Appleby Frodingham	26	7	13	66
Harrogate	26	4	13	54
Sheffield United	26	4	12	51
Hull & YPI	26	4	16	47

The following leagues do not have ECB Premier League status:

LANCASHIRE LEAGUES

Lancashire League

	P	W	L	Pts
Accrington	**26**	**17**	**8**	**213**
Haslingden	26	16	8	209
Todmorden	26	15	8	203
East Lancs	26	12	9	186
Nelson	26	13	11	171
Church	26	12	12	167
Enfield	26	13	10	166
Burnley	26	12	11	162
Ramsbottom	26	10	12	153
Colne	26	10	12	145
Lowerhouse	26	9	14	144
Rishton	26	9	15	137
Bacup	26	8	16	121
Rawtenstall	26	7	17	106

Central Lancashire League

	P	W	L	Pts
Monton & Weaste	**30**	**22**	**5**	**112**
Norden	30	22	5	112
Heywood	30	19	6	98
Middleton	30	15	9	89
Littleborough	30	15	11	82
Unsworth	30	13	10	82
Rochdale	30	14	12	81
Walsden	30	14	12	77
Crompton	30	13	11	73
Milnrow	30	10	16	63
Werneth	30	10	15	63
Royton	30	9	16	58
Clifton	30	10	16	56
Ashton	30	7	21	46
Radcliffe	30	5	19	38
Oldham	30	5	19	36

Monton & Weaste were champions by virtue of winning more away games than Norden.

OTHER LEAGUE WINNERS, 2009

Airedale & Wharfedale	Beckwithshaw
Bolton Association	Walshaw
Bolton League	Farnworth
Bradford	Baildon
Cambridgeshire	Burwell
Central Yorkshire	Methley
Durham County	Kimblesworth
Durham Senior	Hetton Lyons
Hertfordshire	Knebworth Park
Huddersfield	Scholes
Lancashire County	Denton West
Merseyside	Old Xaverians
Norfolk Alliance	Downham Town
North Essex	Mistley
N. Lancs & Cumbria	Furness
Northumberland & Tyneside Senior	Swalwell
North Yorks & South Durham	Marton
Pembrokeshire	Cressely
Quaid-e-Azam	Keighley RZM
Ribblesdale	Baxenden
Saddleworth	Bamford Fieldhouse
Shropshire	Oswestry
South Wales Association	Ammanford
South Yorkshire	Treeton
Two Counties	Copdock & Old Ipswichians
Warwickshire	Bablake Old Boys
West Wales	Aberystwyth
Worcestershire	Pershore
York Senior	Woodhouse Grange

CLUB CHAMPIONSHIP AND COCKSPUR CUP, 2009

Paul Edwards

After reaching the last eight of the national knockout three times when the winners received serious prize money, Chester-le-Street finally secured recreational cricket's most prestigious trophy on a day when each member of the victorious side was given nothing more than a tankard and a cricket bat. This made no obvious difference to the pleasure of the Ropery Lane players, whose win against Spencer, from Wandsworth in south-west London, was well earned and properly celebrated. But the delight of Quentin Hughes and his side had a wider resonance: it demonstrated to the ECB that a competition of the quality of the national knockout can lose both its sponsor, Cockspur Rum, and its glitzy prizes, and yet still be regarded by very many clubs as the supreme test of over-limit cricket.

All of which threw into even sharper relief the ECB's short-lived decision to kill off the 40-year-old trophy in the autumn of 2008. "We weren't sure how much the clubs wanted to continue with a 45-over competition," said Paul Bedford, head of non-first-class operations, as he watched Chester-le-Street and Spencer contest the final at the County Ground in Derby. "But by the end of last September the clubs had written in and said we value it immensely. I like to think we listened to them." The best cricket clubs in the country may like to think that the abolition of the national knockout will never again be contemplated without extensive consultation.

However, while 253 clubs showed their enthusiasm for the more traditional format of limited-overs cricket by entering the slimmed-down national knockout in 2009, more than twice that number contested the Twenty20 trophy, to which Cockspur Rum had transferred their allegiance. All told, 541 signed up for this competition.

Nine days after Chester-le-Street's victory, four clubs – Bournemouth (Dorset), Cuckney (Nottinghamshire), Ockbrook & Borrowash (Derbyshire) and Reigate Priory (Surrey) – gathered, also at Derby, on a crisp early-autumn morning for recreational cricket's own Twenty20 finals day. Like its more illustrious cousin, this version (also televised) had plenty of razzamatazz, thanks to a venue that could not have been more welcoming. Before a ball had been bowled, a lot of shrewd money was being put on Cuckney and Ockbrook, but at the end of the hectic nine-hour spectacular, it was Bournemouth's Craig de Weymarn who collected the trophy. He and his players could look forward to an autumn holiday in Barbados, courtesy of sponsors who had taken a hard-headed business decision to support a very fashionable brand. "The Twenty20 revolution has just taken over cricket," said Cockspur's sponsorship consultant Omar Khan. "But it was never our intention to endanger the national knockout because it's a very valued format."

The upshot is that clubs now have two national competitions – and at least one reliable venue happy to host both finals. (Until 2008, Lord's had always staged the 45-over final.) This may have arisen more by accident than design, but providing the longer format can survive, top-class club cricketers will be happy.

ECB NATIONAL CLUB CHAMPIONSHIP FINAL

CHESTER-LE-STREET v SPENCER

At Derby, September 19. Chester-le-Street won by 24 runs. Toss: Chester-le-Street.

The choice of a man of the match can sometimes seem whimsical. No one, however, could dispute the selection of Chester-le-Street captain Quentin Hughes after his side defeated Spencer on a balmy afternoon in Derby. Hughes, who led Cambridge in the 1999 Varsity Match, has the nickname "Q", but there was nothing gimmicky or newfangled about his strokeplay as he rescued his side from a parlous 101 for seven in the 31st over, taking them to a very defendable 175 for nine. Instead, his unbeaten 76, which contained a solitary four, was full of nous and craft. His accurate off-spin then dismissed three Spencer batsmen, all showing the impetuosity Hughes had eschewed in his 99-ball innings. Neil Baker and Luke Billingham both made 35 as Spencer, from the Surrey Championship's Premier League, recovered from 45 for four in the 22nd over. But the departure of Baker at 93 for five – brilliantly run out by Andrew Smith when the exertions of trying to run three from successive balls proved too great – was crucial. Chester-le-Street's experienced attack closed out the game rather more easily than the margin might suggest; the result was hard on Jim Birt, whose three for 17 had drawn first blood for Spencer.

Man of the Match: Q. J. Hughes.

Chester-le-Street

S. J. Birtwisle lbw b Birt	11		A. Tye c Byrne b Billingham	10
A. Mustard c Byrne b Birt	5		A. Bell c Byrne b Birt	17
A. L. Smith c Mawson b Turk	27		†D. Wilson not out	3
R. P. Waite c and b Abid Jafri	10		L-b 4, w 3	7
*Q. J. Hughes not out	76			
J. W. Coxon c and b Billingham	2		1/15 (2) 2/20 (1) (9 wkts, 45 overs)	175
L. Simpson b Turk	6		3/31 (4) 4/74 (3) 5/79 (6)	
A. Birbeck st Baker b Byrne	1		6/92 (7) 7/101 (8) 8/127 (9) 9/163 (10)	

Radloff 7–0–33–0; Birt 9–3–17–3; Abid Jafri 3–0–12–1; Turk 9–0–41–2; Billingham 8–0–31–2; Byrne 9–0–37–1.

Spencer

A. D. Mawson c Tye b Hughes	17		P. W. Turk b Tye	2
C. Thomas c Mustard b Hughes	9		Abid Jafri b Birtwisle	5
*†N. Baker run out	35		J. Birt lbw b Birtwisle	4
J. Lawrence st Wilson b Hughes	0		B 5, l-b 3, w 6, n-b 2	16
P. Jason b Waite	5			
C. Radloff b Birtwisle	19		1/28 (1) 2/28 (2) 3/32 (4) (43 overs)	151
L. Billingham not out	35		4/45 (5) 5/93 (3) 6/110 (6)	
P. Byrne b Waite	4		7/125 (8) 8/1 9 (9) 9/146 (10) 10/151 (11)	

Tye 8–1–19–1; Simpson 7–1–20–0; Hughes 9–3–15–3; Waite 9–1–37–2; Bell 4–0–21–0; Birtwisle 6–0–31–3.

Umpires: J. Anning and P. K. Baldwin.

A list of winners from the start of the competition in 1969 appears in Wisden 2005, page 941.

COCKSPUR CUP FINALS DAY

Semi-finals

At Derby, September 28. **Bournemouth won by 15 runs.** Toss: Reigate Priory. **Bournemouth 162-4** (20 overs) (N. G. Park 46, M. A. House 65*); **Reigate Priory 147-7** (20 overs) (J. P. A. Gale 34*).

At Derby, September 28 (floodlit). **Cuckney won by 66 runs.** Toss: Cuckney. **Cuckney 180-4** (20 overs) (R. A. Stroh 95); **Ockbrook & Borrowash 114** (18.4 overs) (C. Ault 35; T. G. J. A. Ullyott 4-16, R. A. Bostock 3-20).

Final

At Derby, September 28 (floodlit). **Bournemouth won by six wickets.** Toss: Cuckney. **Cuckney 152-7** (20 overs) (R. A. Stroh 50, T. G. J. A. Ullyott 53; E. G. Denham 3-39); **Bournemouth 153-4** (18.3 overs) (N. G. Park 58, M. A. House 34).

NPOWER VILLAGE CUP, 2009

BENJ MOOREHEAD

As the 222nd and last game of the 2009 Village Cup neared its climax, the result was still unclear. The final, held at Lord's in mid-September, ebbed and flowed, and with two overs to go it was deliciously poised: Streethouse, a former mining community in West Yorkshire, needed 19 with five wickets left. They reduced that to 16 before Mark Beddis, a left-arm seamer playing for Glynde & Beddingham, hit the stumps twice to shift the momentum decisively south. Glynde, whose history stretches back to the 18th century, became the first Sussex club to win "the Village".

But Beddis is no southerner. In fact, he's something of a Ryan Sidebottom: a left-armer possessed of a Yorkshire accent and flowing hair. And like Sidebottom, Beddis, who hails from Hull, has tasted greatest success away from God's own county. His team-mates, though, come from Glynde, a pretty East Sussex village tucked underneath the looming Sussex Downs, or thereabouts. A mile away is the Glyndebourne Opera House, where many of the team have worked part-time.

The Streethouse contingent might have had further to travel, but they seemed to outnumber their opponents' supporters. "Nobody seems to be back at home when we have an away fixture," said Richard Vigars, the club captain. "Burglar's paradise, they call it." Vigars, an accurate medium-pacer and dangerous No. 7, was outstanding throughout the competition. He dragged his side to Lord's by overcoming Stockton, of Warwickshire, in the semi-final, taking five wickets and guiding the tail to a one-wicket win. With three balls left and two runs needed, the Streethouse No. 11 had been in tears, so dismayed was he at the circumstances.

This was also the summer of the Glynde opening bats, Joe Adams and Dominic Shepheard. Together they scored 1,023 runs – more than half Glynde's total – in eight games. They proved quite an all-round partnership, sharing 32 wickets and both making fifties in the easy semi-final defeat of Cresselly that ended Welsh hopes of a Lord's final. Cresselly, a Pembrokeshire village of fewer than 100 residents, had beaten Miskin Manor in a Welsh derby that had the local press abuzz. Among those who made the 600-mile round trip to Glynde was Don Twigg, 79, a former umpire from the Pembrokeshire leagues. "I've never travelled so far in my life," he said.

The season was not without controversy: Oxford Downs pulled out after it emerged that they had fielded an ineligible player in the victory over Aston Rowant. The organisers, *The Wisden Cricketer*, agreed the eligibility rules were ambiguous and that there had been no wilful deception; Downs were offered a replay, but chose not to take up the offer. The rules for the 2010 competition have been redrafted to remove any ambiguity.

For much of the competition it seemed nothing could stop Stockton and their captain, Owen Edwards, who lashed a 39-ball 113 against Gretton as 241 cascaded from the last 20 overs, and 136 against Old CC, including 106 in boundaries. Also buried in the obscurity of the earlier rounds were moments that will go down in the folklore of the clubs concerned: Martley's Peter Gardner hitting leg stump with his hat-trick ball, only for the bail to stick in its groove; Apperley's chairman Brian Leeke coming out of retirement at the age of 72; and the unintentional swimmer at Eynsford, in Kent... This happened when a spectator, trying to stop the ball rolling into the River Darent, tripped and somehow managed to throw the ball back before splashing into the water. Proof, then, that village cricket isn't immune to Twenty20 athleticism, even if it doesn't always work out quite as intended.

FINAL

GLYNDE & BEDDINGHAM v STREETHOUSE

At Lord's, September 14. Glynde & Beddingham won by six runs. Toss: Streethouse.

The game seemed to be fizzling out when, after 23 overs, Streethouse were 98 for five in pursuit of 208. But in the 31st over, opener Paul Langley, whose previous 18 scoring shots had been singles, unexpectedly struck the ball into the crowd. The tempo had changed. The left-handed Richard Vigars then hit with the spin as three of Ollie Bailey's leg-breaks disappeared into the nearby Tavern stand; 18 balls had produced 38 runs. Roars of Yorkshire delight penetrated even the thick glass of the media centre. But left-arm fast bowler Mark Beddis bowled both Vigars and Langley in the penultimate over, and 16 from the last six balls proved too many for a pair new to the crease. That Glynde had made a decent total was partly down to an imposing innings by opener Joe Adams, equally as happy on the front foot as the back. The crucial contribution, though, was a pugnacious 41 by little Dominic Harris. It might never have been: he was dropped at long-on and then, on 15, smartly stumped by wicketkeeper Langley. The square-leg umpire had no hesitation, but his colleague ruled it a no-ball. In such a close contest, the call might well have been crucial.

Man of the Match: J. Adams.

Glynde & Beddingham

J. Adams b Vigars	79		D. Tranter b Vigars		0
D. Shepheard c Langley b Bellwood	4		M. Beddis not out		2
C. Smith c and b Bland	32				
R. Mouland lbw b Vigars	10		B 1, l-b 2, w 6, n-b 2		11
O. Bailey b Hughes	13				
D. Harris lbw b Hughes	41		1/10 (2) 2/80 (3)	(9 wkts, 40 overs)	207
*A. Davies not out	12		3/129 (4) 4/134 (1)		
C. Blunt b Hughes	0		5/167 (5) 6/200 (6) 7/200 (8)		
†S. Mouland c Langley b Vigars	3		8/205 (9) 9/205 (10)		

Vigars 9–1–60–4; Bellwood 5–2–24–1; Bland 9–2–32–1; Rhodes 8–0–55–0; Hughes 9–0–33–3.

Streethouse

J. G. Hughes c S. Mouland b Shepheard	4		P. A. Haselden not out		4
†P. C. Langley b Beddis	68		S. Bellwood not out		4
C. J. Geldart c S. Mouland b Tranter	34		B 4, l-b 12, w 6, n-b 9		31
M. Rhodes lbw b Tranter	0				
M. Robinson b Shepheard	5		1/4 (1) 2/60 (3)	(7 wkts, 40 overs)	201
P. MacMullan b Adams	10		3/61 (4) 4/72 (5)		
*R. Vigars b Beddis	41		5/98 (6) 6/191 (7) 7/192 (2)		

G. Rhodes and S. A. Bland did not bat.

Shepheard 9–0–34–2; Beddis 7–1–34–2; Tranter 8–0–36–2; Bailey 8–0–52–0; Adams 8–1–29–1.

Umpires: P. Hinstridge and C. Jones.

A list of winners from the start of the competition in 1972 appears in Wisden 2005, *page 944.*

ENGLAND UNDER-19 v BANGLADESH UNDER-19

PATRICK KIDD

Under-19 Tests (2): England 1, Bangladesh 0
Under-19 one-day internationals (5): England 1, Bangladesh 2
Under-19 Twenty20 internationals (2): England 1, Bangladesh 0

"If you are 1–0 up and you lose 2–1, there are very few positives you can take out of it." So said Andy Pick, the England Under-19 head coach, after watching his team throw away a winning position in their five-match one-day international series with Bangladesh; but the scoreline could easily have been 2–1 in England's favour. Bangladesh won the final match at Hove by one wicket, and there were enough glimpses of talent in a young England side to ensure that the mood was not all doom and gloom ahead of the eighth Under-19 World Cup in New Zealand early in 2010.

England won the two-match Test series 1–0, and it would have been even more decisive had the weather been kinder. They also won the first Twenty20 youth international played in England, with the second match a victim of the rain that also caused two of the one-day internationals to be abandoned.

Bangladesh's stars were Mominul Haque – dubbed "Minimal" as he stood barely taller than the stumps – who averaged 54 in the Tests, Anamul Haque, who had three fifties on the tour, and Sabbir Rahman, a talented leg-spinner.

Yet if Bangladesh relied heavily on all their spin bowlers to frustrate the England batsmen and win the last two one-day internationals, the home team showed that spin was no longer just an Asian art. Azeem Rafiq's off-spin and Scott Borthwick's leg-breaks led England's most impressive slow bowling.

For Rafiq, who took over the captaincy from Hamza Riazuddin after the Tests, it was good to be grabbing attention for the right reasons. In 2008, Yorkshire were thrown out of the Twenty20 Cup because Rafiq, who had been born in Pakistan but schooled in Barnsley, had not been properly registered as an eligible player for a match against Nottinghamshire. (He had already captained England Under-15, although it later emerged that he did not have a British passport.) Rafiq thought he had benefited from the unfortunate episode. "It made me grow up a lot quicker than I imagined," he said. "Those two weeks [of attention] forced me to mature a lot. Looking back now, I feel stronger as a person and as a cricketer because of it."

On the batting front, Sam Northeast and Josh Cobb each made more than 250 runs from just two Test innings; Northeast, the outstanding batsman on either side, also added almost 250 more from four limited-overs innings. He first came to attention when, aged 13, he made 19 hundreds in a term for Wellesley House, his prep school in Broadstairs. He continued to develop at Harrow and, after making his maiden first-class hundred in the final Championship match of 2009, there are plenty who believe that when people talk fondly in future of "Northeast of Kent" they will not be referring to somewhere such as Amsterdam.

Cobb could have played more for the Under-19s but for a new understanding between the ECB and the counties that gave priority to first-team cricket rather than age-group national service. Cobb proved the worth of this by making 95 on his return to Leicestershire two days after playing for England Under-19.

Defeats by Bangladesh are nothing new for England at age-group level. They have met three times in the Under-19 World Cup and twice – including the opening round of the 1998 tournament, which England went on to win – Bangladesh came out on top. England also lost 3–0 on a humbling winter tour to Bangladesh in 2005 in which they lost 11 matches. (They would also come unstuck on the return trip to Bangladesh, in October and November, losing the one-day series 5–2.)

Bangladesh's success at junior level may ultimately bring them reward in full internationals. Twelve members of the Bangladesh Under-19 sides who played England in 2004 and 2005 have stepped up to Test cricket, compared with only Alastair Cook and Ravi Bopara of those who competed against them, with Joe Denly, Luke Wright and Samit Patel playing one-day internationals.

It is with an eye on the future that Pick urged the England class of 2009 to look back on their defeat by Bangladesh and learn from it, especially the experience of playing top-quality spin bowlers, who provided the bulk of Bangladesh's attack. "The development of the players is more important than the result," Pick said. "If they are going to play at the top level, they are going to play 50% of their cricket on the subcontinent. That was very much subcontinent cricket at Hove. Our lads have never seen anything like that before. I asked them to lock away that experience because down the line they could well benefit from it."

> "Our lads have never seen anything like that before"

Pick helped select the Under-19 squad for the autumn tour to Bangladesh (see page 1093), but he handed over the coaching reins, which he had held since 2003, to Mick Newell, the director of cricket at his old county, Nottinghamshire. Newell in turn was to be replaced by Mark Robinson, the Sussex cricket manager, for the 2010 Under-19 World Cup. Pick is now the ICC development performance manager for the Americas.

Selection for the autumn and winter was helped by potential candidates – under the catchy name of the Elite Player Development Under-19 XI – playing a series of five matches against county second teams. They beat Leicestershire 2–1 and then drew 1–1 with Nottinghamshire, with Luke Wells, of Sussex, sparing the teenagers' blushes by making 47 not out in a one-wicket win in the final game as they chased only 103.

BANGLADESH UNDER-19 TOURING PARTY

Mahmudul Hasan (*captain*), Amit Majumder (*vice-captain*), Abu Jayed, Abul Hasan, Alauddin Babu, Anamul Haque, Asif Ahmed, Imamul Hossain, Mominul Haque, Noor Hossain, Nurul Hasan, Sabbir Rahman, Saikat Ali, Shaker Ahmed, Shohag Raza. *Coach:* Minhazul Abedin. *Manager:* Tanjeeb Ahsan.

Note: Matches in this section were not first-class.

At Loughborough, July 3, 4. **Drawn.** Toss: Bangladesh Under-19. **Bangladesh Under-19 174** (54.5 overs) (Saikat Ali 57; R. H. Patel 5-34) and **106-3** (33 overs); **England Under-18 233-7 dec** (64 overs) (J. E. Root 87, L. A. Perry 54).

Ravi Patel, a slow left-arm bowler from Middlesex, ended a fourth-wicket stand of 66 before running through the Bangladesh lower order. Joe Root, of the Yorkshire Academy, was selected for the Under-19 winter tour to Bangladesh on the back of his three-hour innings.

ENGLAND v BANGLADESH

First Under-19 Test

At Scarborough, July 6, 7, 8. England Under-19 won by ten wickets. Toss: England Under-19.

Josh Cobb, of Leicestershire, made quite an impression in what was his first and last Under-19 Test. Called up a month before his 19th birthday, he became the seventh England batsman to make a double-hundred in a youth Test, following the likes of Marcus Trescothick and Bilal Shafayat. But early success is no guarantee of a long international career: the four Under-19 batsmen to have scored more than Cobb's 220 – Clinton Peake (Australia), Mathew Dowman, Kevin Sharp and Gordon Muchall (England) – have not set the world alight. Those who watched Cobb's splendid five-and-a-half-hour innings, though, will hope he can go on to greater things. Bangladesh used nine bowlers in an attempt to shift him, but it was the opening bowler, Alauddin Babu, who, late in the day, eventually succeeded. Cobb put on 139 for the first wicket with Jaik Mickleburgh and, after wickets had fallen too frequently, 109 for the seventh with Hamza Riazuddin, the captain. When Cobb fell, Riazuddin took the total past 500. By stumps on the second day, Durham leg-spinner Scott Borthwick had taken four wickets to reduce Bangladesh to 265 for nine, still 88 shy of avoiding the follow-on, and he added a fifth next morning. When Bangladesh followed on, another northern spinner completed the deal: Yorkshire's Azeem Rafiq took six for 90 in 30 overs of off-spin as the tourists were bowled out for 276. A third-wicket stand of 97 between Saikat Ali and Mominul Haque held England up before Rafiq ran through the lower order. With only 45 needed, Cobb concluded a triumphant debut with 31 not out from 18 deliveries.

Close of play: First day, England Under-19 422-8 (Riazuddin 36, Wood 3); Second day, Bangladesh Under-19 265-9 (Sabbir Rahman 52, Abu Jayed 4).

England Under-19

J. J. Cobb c Mahmudul Hasan b Alauddin Babu . . .	220	– (2) not out	31
J. C. Mickleburgh hit wkt b Sabbir Rahman	57		
J. M. Vince c Saikat Ali b Sabbir Rahman.	22	– (1) not out	16
J. W. A. Taylor c Mahmudul Hasan b Mominul Haque .	21		
L. W. P. Wells c Anamul Haque b Alauddin Babu .	0		
S. G. Borthwick c Amit Majumder b Sabbir Rahman	14		
Azeem Rafiq c Saikat Ali b Shaker Ahmed	28		
*H. Riazuddin c Amit Majumder b Mominul Haque	95		
†T. Poynton b Alauddin Babu	0		
C. P. Wood c Mahmudul Hasan b Alauddin Babu .	14		
N. L. Buck not out	9		
B 5, l-b 7, w 5, n-b 5	22		

1/139 (2) 2/168 (3) 3/205 (4)   (121.4 overs) 502   (no wkt, 6.2 overs) 47
4/206 (5) 5/250 (6) 6/300 (7)
7/409 (1) 8/417 (9) 9/436 (10) 10/502 (8)

Abu Jayed 15–3–77–0; Alauddin Babu 17–2–73–4; Saikat Ali 2–0–14–0; Shaker Ahmed 20–2–77–1; Noor Hossain 12–0–61–0; Sabbir Rahman 30–5–76–3; Mahmudul Hasan 11–3–34–0; Mominul Haque 12.4–2–65–2; Amit Majumder 2–0–13–0. *Second Innings*—Alauddin Babu 2–0–9–0; Saikat Ali 2–0–25–0; Shaker Ahmed 1.2–0–7–0; Noor Hossain 1–0–6–0.

Bangladesh Under-19

Amit Majumder c Cobb b Wood	2	– c Vince b Wood	4
Saikat Ali c Buck b Borthwick	33	– b Azeem Rafiq	58
Asif Ahmed c Vince b Azeem Rafiq	23	– lbw b Buck	0
Mominul Haque c Cobb b Buck	90	– lbw b Azeem Rafiq	80
†Anamul Haque c sub b Buck	31	– b Azeem Rafiq	39
*Mahmudul Hasan lbw b Wood	5	– c Vince b Azeem Rafiq	46
Sabbir Rahman c Azeem Rafiq b Borthwick	57	– c Borthwick b Azeem Rafiq	4
Noor Hossain b Borthwick	2	– c Taylor b Azeem Rafiq	12
Alauddin Babu c and b Borthwick	6	– b Buck	24
Shaker Ahmed b Borthwick	2	– b Wood	1
Abu Jayed not out	4	– not out	0
L-b 6, n-b 9	15	B 4, l-b 1, w 1, n-b 2	8

1/8 (1) 2/62 (3) 3/103 (2)   (70.4 overs) 270   1/4 (1) 2/5 (3)   (83.5 overs) 276
4/186 (5) 5/195 (4) 6/204 (6)   3/106 (2) 4/175 (4)
7/221 (8) 8/247 (9) 9/253 (10) 10/270 (7)   5/190 (6) 6/194 (7) 7/236 (8)
                               8/251 (9) 9/276 (9) 10/276 (10)

Wood 19–3–59–2; Buck 12–1–38–2; Azeem Rafiq 21–2–89–1; Riazuddin 1–0–8–0; Borthwick 17.4–4–70–5. *Second Innings*—Wood 15.5–5–44–2; Buck 15–4–31–2; Vince 4–0–24–0; Borthwick 13–0–64–0; Azeem Rafiq 30–7–90–6; Wells 6–1–18–0.

Umpires: N. G. Cowley and M. A. Gough.

ENGLAND v BANGLADESH

Second Under-19 Test

At Derby, July 12, 13, 14, 15. Drawn. Toss: Bangladesh Under-19.

Bangladesh held out for a draw to prevent a clean sweep by England, although rain on the third afternoon also played its part. Set 375 in a day, Bangladesh were reeling at 133 for seven, five of them falling to Azeem Rafiq's off-spin, but Alauddin Babu and Sabbir Rahman frustrated England for 15 overs. Babu then fell for 28, but the captains shook hands on a draw four overs later. After Josh Cobb's 220 in the First Test, it was the turn of another debutant England opener to score heavily – this time with twin hundreds. In one of four changes, Cobb had been replaced by Kent's Sam Northeast, who batted for just over 200 minutes in each innings, so becoming the fourth England Under-19 batsman to make two centuries in a Test, after Mark Ramprakash in 1986, Bilal Shafayat in 2002 and Varun Chopra in 2006. In the first innings Northeast made 107, sharing a third-wicket stand of 149 with David Willey, son of the former England Test player Peter. Ben Stokes, a New Zealand-born Durham batsman, made 72 as England reached 392. Hamza Riazuddin dismissed the Bangladesh openers, but they built enough modest partnerships to squeak past 300. Northeast increased the pressure with a bigger and brisker hundred – his 149 came from 176 balls – to put England in a strong position. They had a lead of 341 when Northeast fell, and would have wanted to give the bowlers a shot at Bangladesh that evening, but only five more overs were possible before the rain came. A delayed start on the final morning further reduced the time they had to bowl Bangladesh out.

Close of play: First day, England Under-19 338-7 (Riazuddin 18, Poynton 1); Second day, Bangladesh Under-19 209-5 (Anamul Haque 45, Sabbir Rahman 2); Third day, England Under-19 284-3 (Willey 20, Stokes 17).

England Under-19

S. A. Northeast c Amit Majumder			
b Mahmudul Hasan . 107	– c Mominul Haque b Abul Hasan 149
J. K. Manuel b Abul Hasan 0	– st Anamul Haque b Noor Hossain . . . 54
J. M. Vince c Anamul Haque b Abu Jayed 21	– c and b Imamul Hossain. 37
D. J. Willey c Alauddin Babu b Noor Hossain . . 65	– not out 20
B. A. Stokes c Sabbir Rahman b Mahmudul Hasan 72	– not out 17
L. W. P. Wells run out 8	
Azeem Rafiq lbw b Saikat Ali 22	
*H. Riazuddin st Anamul Haque b Mahmudul Hasan 38	
†T. Poynton lbw b Abul Hasan 1	
C. P. Wood b Sabbir Rahman 30	
N. L. Buck not out 0	
B 7, l-b 5, w 4, n-b 12 28	B 2, l-b 4, w 1. 7

1/5 (2) 2/57 (3) 3/206 (4) (115.1 overs) 392	1/129 (2) (3 wkts dec, 60 overs) 284
4/227 (1) 5/247 (6) 6/294 (5)	2/220 (3) 3/251 (1)
7/327 (7) 8/342 (9) 9/389 (10) 10/392 (8)	

Abu Jayed 18–4–75–1; Abul Hasan 20–4–58–2; Alauddin Babu 19–3–86–0; Sabbir Rahman 19–2–63–1; Mahmudul Hasan 25.1–7–47–3; Noor Hossain 11–1–40–1; Mominul Haque 1–0–1–0; Saikat Ali 2–0–10–1. *Second Innings*—Abul Hasan 6–0–35–1; Abu Jayed 6–0–31–0; Alauddin Babu 9–0–49–0; Mahmudul Hasan 12–1–49–0; Sabbir Rahman 13–1–39–0; Noor Hossain 12–2–61–1; Imamul Hossain 2–0–14–1.

Bangladesh Under-19

Saikat Ali c Azeem Rafiq b Riazuddin 45	– (2) c Wells b Buck 12
Amit Majumder lbw b Riazuddin 29	– (1) lbw b Azeem Rafiq. 35
Imamul Hossain lbw b Willey 8	– b Azeem Rafiq 21
Mominul Haque c Poynton b Azeem Rafiq 32	– c Wood b Wells 13
†Anamul Haque c Riazuddin b Buck. 71	– c Poynton b Azeem Rafiq. 0
*Mahmudul Hasan lbw b Wells. 26	– c and b Azeem Rafiq 0
Sabbir Rahman c Riazuddin b Wood 7	– not out 51
Noor Hossain b Willey. 12	– lbw b Azeem Rafiq 22
Alauddin Babu not out 24	– c Riazuddin b Willey 28
Abul Hasan c and b Willey 6	– not out 0
Abu Jayed c Manuel b Buck 6	
B 10, l-b 10, w 1, n-b 15 36	B 6, l-b 5, w 2, n-b 9 22

1/68 (2) 2/89 (1) 3/118 (3) (96.4 overs) 302	1/28 (2) 2/69 (1) (8 wkts, 76 overs) 204
4/146 (4) 5/202 (6) 6/232 (7)	3/76 (3) 4/76 (5)
7/266 (5) 8/296 (8) 9/278 (10) 10/302 (11)	5/80 (6) 6/103 (4) 7/133 (8) 8/192 (9)

Wood 25–4–74–1; Buck 17.4–3–52–2; Riazuddin 18–7–43–2; Azeem Rafiq 20–7–59–1; Willey 13–1–45–3; Wells 3–0–9–1. *Second Innings*—Buck 11–1–31–1; Wood 9–3–24–0; Willey 8–2–13–1; Riazuddin 5–1–23–0; Azeem Rafiq 28–7–77–5; Wells 15–7–25–1.

Umpires: J. W. Holder and D. J. Millns.

At Leicester, July 18. **First Under-19 one-day international: England won by 84 runs.** Toss: Bangladesh. **England 282-7** (50 overs) (S. A. Northeast 123, J. K. Manuel 54; Mahmudul Hasan 3-40); **Bangladesh 198** (49.5 overs) (Amit Majumder 30, Asif Ahmed 51, Alauddin Babu 40*).
Sam Northeast's 123 was the fourth-highest score by an England batsman in an Under-19 one-day international after Billy Godleman's 149 against Pakistan in 2007, Anurag Singh's 130* against West Indies in 1995 and Mike Gatting's 128 against West Indies in 1976. Northeast put on 113 for the first wicket with Jack Manuel in 18 overs and added 89 for the third wicket with Luke Wells, son of the former Sussex, Kent and England player Alan. Bangladesh fell from 48-1 to 51-4 in the space of eight balls.*

At Leicester, July 19. **Second Under-19 one-day international: No result.** Toss: Bangladesh. **Bangladesh 269-6** (50 overs) (Anamul Haque 78, Mominul Haque 57, Alauddin Babu 41*); **England 18-0** (3.3 overs).

Anamul Haque was the linchpin of the innings, with 78 in 130 minutes, but it was Alauddin Babu's late 41 from 18 balls, with three sixes, that put Bangladesh in a commanding position before the weather intervened.

At Northampton, July 21. **Third Under-19 one-day international: Abandoned.**
Heavy rain prevented any play.

At Hove, July 23. **Fourth Under-19 one-day international: Bangladesh won by 53 runs.** Toss: Bangladesh. **Bangladesh 192** (46.2 overs) (Anamul Haque 53, Noor Hossain 33); **England 139** (45 overs) (S. A. Northeast 41).

The Bangladeshi spinners strangled the life out of England's run-chase, bowling all but six overs. Bangladesh slipped from 96-3 to 98-6 in eight balls before Noor Hossain and Sabbir Rahman added 60 to steer them towards a defendable total. Sam Northeast passed 500 runs in youth one-day internationals, but no one else put together a score.

At Hove, July 24. **Fifth Under-19 one-day international: Bangladesh won by one wicket.** Toss: England. **England 196-8** (50 overs) (S. A. Northeast 62); **Bangladesh 197-9** (49 overs) (Anamul Haque 34, Mahmudul Hasan 70; D. R. Briggs 3-23).

Another fine innings by Sam Northeast, playing the 19th and final youth international of his career, took him past Ian Bell, Varun Chopra and Stephen Peters in the list of England run-scorers in Under-19 one-day matches; only Billy Godleman and Samit Patel were ahead of him. It was not enough, though, as Bangladesh won the match and the series in a thrilling finale. They were 59-4 when Mahmudul Hasan, the captain, came out to bat. They needed only 15 more when he was eighth out in the 47th over, but Abul Hasan was run out with the scores level, and there might have been a tie if England had hit the stumps as Bangladesh stole a risky single next ball.

At Sleaford, July 28. **First Under-19 Twenty20 international: England won by five wickets.** Toss: England. **Bangladesh 154-8** (20 overs) (Amit Majumder 74); **England 156-5** (18 overs) (J. K. Manuel 36, J. C. Buttler 33, A. J. Wheater 43*).

Amit Majumder's 74 from 45 balls was the highest score in youth Twenty20s, surpassing Jaik Mickleburgh's 55 for England against South Africa in January 2009, which was the only previous fifty in this format. Two of England's five wickets were stumped by Nurul Hasan off Sabbir Rahman's leg-spin; Adam Wheater guided them home with 43 from 33 balls.*

At Sleaford, July 29. **Second Under-19 Twenty20 international: Abandoned.**
The game was called off in late afternoon, giving England a 1–0 win in what was only the second series of youth Twenty20 internationals. England had lost the first, against South Africa at the beginning of the year, 2–0.

YOUTH CRICKET, 2009

Patrick Kidd

Where does the balance lie between too much caution and not enough? The 2009 youth season was bookended by directives from the ECB affecting safety and fitness. In March, it was decided that parents would no longer be allowed to give children under 18 permission to bat bare-headed. All under-18 batsmen must now wear helmets, as must wicketkeepers, although face-masks remain optional.

At the end of the season the ECB issued new directives for young fast bowlers. Those at the start of their school careers will be allowed to bowl an extra two overs per day (up from eight to ten for under-13s and from ten to 12 for under-14s and under-15s); under-18 and under-19 players will have a reduction, from 21 overs in a day to 18. Those at under-16 and under-17 level are permitted 18 overs, as before, but get an increase to seven overs per spell. Kevin Shine, the ECB's fast-bowling coach, said: "It is clear that our young bowlers need to bowl more so that they can develop match-winning abilities and habits."

The ECB also launched Stix, a social networking area on their website for children to discuss the game, find clubs, learn about their favourite players and receive coaching tips. In a campaign fronted by Monty Panesar, children were encouraged to film their street cricket games and submit them to the ECB, with Test tickets for the best film.

England Under-18 won all three of their 50-over matches on a tour to Scotland. Jos Buttler, of Somerset, made 103 not out in the opening game against Scotland Lions while the third match, against a Scottish Development XI, was over so early that the sides fitted in a Twenty20 "beer match". David Payne, of Gloucestershire, took four for nine as the Scots were dismissed for 54, which England passed in five overs. The Under-18s later drew a two-day game against Bangladesh Under-19s at Loughborough, with Ravi Patel, of Middlesex, taking five for 34.

Kent did the double in the ECB's Under-17 tournaments, beating Durham in the final of both the Championship and the Cup. In the Cup final at Caythorpe in Nottinghamshire (where Eddie Hemmings, the former England spin bowler, is groundsman), Durham's openers put on 68 in 13 overs, but wickets tumbled as Kent's spinners took hold.

Fabian Cowdrey, the son and grandson of England captains in Chris and Colin Cowdrey, took five for 21 in six overs and effected a run-out as Durham were skittled for 216. Kent won with four and a half overs to spare. Cowdrey had been a key player ten days earlier, too, making 41 and taking three wickets in the Championship final win, which was founded on a century by Daniel Bell-Drummond.

Kent also reached the finals of the Under-15 Championship, joining Wales, Lancashire and Nottinghamshire but, with rain spoiling the final day of the three, Wales regained the title they won in 2007. The first ever Roses final in an ECB age-group competition was won by Yorkshire, who beat Lancashire in the Under-15 County Cup by 135 runs after dismissing them for 65 in 28 overs.

London & East won the inaugural ECB Under-16 Regional Festival. Bell-Drummond made an unbeaten 80 in their first victory against the Midlands, and Adam Rossington added an unbeaten hundred and Bell-Drummond 64 as they beat the North by six wickets. South & West won the Under-17 Regional Festival, beating London & East in the final.

Ten England Under-16 players were invited to attend the opening day of the match between England Lions and Australia at Worcester, where they received a coaching session from Richard Halsall, the England senior side's fielding coach, and a talk by John Buchanan, the former Australian national coach.

Winners of age-group competitions: Under-17 County Championship: **Kent**. Under-17 County Cup: **Kent**. Under-15 County Championship: **Wales**. Under-15 County Cup: **Yorkshire**. ESCA National Under-15 Twenty20: **Shrewsbury School**. Under-14 County Cup: **Surrey**. Under-13 County Cup: **Yorkshire and Northamptonshire** (shared after washout). Under-13 David English Schools Cup: **Whitgift**. ESCA/Bunbury Under-11 Schools Cup: **Exeter Junior School**.

SCHOOLS CRICKET, 2009

Review by Douglas Henderson

For the first time for several years, few involved with schools cricket could complain about the weather... There were of course the usual gripes about the iniquities of the public examination system, but at least the sun shone on much, if not quite all, of the UK. Most schools had completed the majority of their fixture list before the rains of July and August, by when school seasons are usually over. An unexpected hazard for 2009 was the advent of swine flu, which caused cancellations for several schools.

Of greater concern, for this reviewer at least, is the continued drift towards "making more noise". It could be argued this is technically illegal. Although "The Spirit of the Game" is a preamble to the Laws rather than a part of them, Law 42 is explicit: "The responsibility lies with the captains for ensuring that play is conducted within the spirit and traditions of the game, as described in The Preamble – The Spirit of Cricket, as well as within the Laws." The preamble is clear that players should not "indulge in cheating or any sharp practice, for instance... seek to distract an opponent either verbally or by harassment with persistent clapping or unnecessary noise under the guise of enthusiasm and motivation of one's own side." There have been schools matches in which the fielding side scarcely pauses for breath during their opponents' innings; their hands must have been sore, too.

Another dubious practice is surreptitious coaching from beyond the boundary. Bob Woolmer famously tried this with Hansie Cronje and a radio earpiece in the 1999 World Cup. They were in breach of the tournament's regulations rather than the Laws, but it has long been the convention not to intervene once the players cross the boundary rope. One or two schools' coaches have come close to captaining via the fielder at third man, or openly gesturing where others should be standing. Wiser to let captains learn from their mistakes.

Schools Twenty20 cricket continues to develop and, as with the professional version, there are fears that it will take over from longer forms of the game. One school's cricket master was summoned by his headmaster and director of studies and told that all matches, even on a Saturday afternoon, should be of 20 overs until after the exam season – effectively the end of term in many cases. The shortest format of the game has advantages for a competitive midweek game that minimises interference with academic work, but is hardly the basis for developing young cricketers.

The 2009 season saw some new initiatives: Michael Harrison at St George's Weybridge formed a league in his area for normal term-time fixtures involving nine schools. Called the 50/40 league, 50-over games were played on Saturdays, 40-over games midweek. It was extremely successful, with Hampton emerging as inaugural winners. Another was an elaborate Twenty20 competition in the strong western schools circuit. Organised by John Bobby of Clifton College, it encompassed schools from Taunton to Cheltenham, from Bath to Bristol. The first winners were King's Taunton, who beat Clifton in the overall final.

Oli Wilkin of Merchant Taylors', Northwood, bowling against Westminster, when he took eight for 14 and hit 121.

King's, indeed, proved the most successful school in the country in 2009. They finished on the same win percentage as Winchester, 88.24%, but lost only one match to Winchester's two. West Buckland enjoyed one of their best seasons ever to come third with an 84.62% record, while some more familiar names in the top-team lists – Oratory, Shrewsbury, Monmouth, Haberdashers' Aske's, Sedbergh and Hampton – also topped the 80% mark. Bancroft's just missed that, but again played a huge number of matches, 24, pipped only by Stowe's 25.

The Leys and Manchester Grammar School were the only unbeaten sides, though Manchester nearly lost that record in an extraordinary game. Denstone needed two to win with two balls and three wickets left. The striker guided the ball to third man and scampered two runs to win the match with a ball to spare, or so he and his partner believed. They met in the middle to congratulate each other, unaware that an umpire had called one short. The striker, somewhat controversially, was given run out, leaving the new batsman one ball to score one run. With ten men round the bat, he was stumped and, as it was a 50-over match, the result was a tie.

Aaron West, Brentwood's captain, scored most runs with 1,290, closely followed by Stamford's Shaan Masood-Khan with 1,237. Four more – Nigel Jacob of Bancroft's, Michael Baxter from Gordonstoun, Tom Elliott of Tonbridge and Cheltenham's Charles Wootton – topped 1,000. Masood-Khan, with 202, scored one of two double-hundreds in 2009, the other coming from Ben Shepperson of Culford, who made 205 not out against the Gentlemen of Suffolk.

In recent years it has become extremely difficult to take large numbers of wickets in a season. ECB restrictions on bowlers of medium-pace and faster – permitted no more than seven overs per spell and 21 in total – have combined with the exponential growth of limited-overs cricket (where bowlers are usually confined to ten overs or fewer) to reduce opportunities. Spinners attending a school that still favours declaration games have a distinct advantage.

Three players achieved an eight-wicket haul in 2009: Oli Wilkin of Merchant Taylors' Northwood, Jake Lintott from Queen's Taunton, and William Culhane of City of London Freemen's. Twelve others managed seven. Wilkin and Lintott each enjoyed phenomenal all-round games: against Westminster, Wilkin took eight for 14 and scored 121; Lintott combined eight for 45 and an innings of 145 against Queen's Taunton Old Boys.

Wisden's table of leading bowling averages has a qualification of 25 wickets, but if that is lowered a little, two young Scots pace bowlers, Lyle Hill and Haris Chaudry, leap to the top with remarkable figures. Both were aged just 14 and came from Glasgow Academy: Hill snapped up 13 wickets at 4.76; Chaudhry 19 at 6.36. Hill went on to play for Scotland's Under-15 side. Such averages occur sometimes if, say, a young leg-spinner comes up against a weakened team during the exam season. However, these two played all season, if a rather meagre one of only seven matches. All told, 18 bowlers took ten wickets or more at an average below ten. William Culhane claimed most wickets with 56 (and a best of eight for 18); Malvern's Will Meredith took 53. Nine others achieved 40 or more.

In early September, Jos Buttler (King's Taunton) made his first-class debut for Somerset, while Ben Cox, Bromsgrove's wicketkeeper-batsman, appeared for Worcestershire against Somerset a week later, stumping Marcus Trescothick and hitting 61 in his maiden first-class innings. In August, Cox had played for Worcestershire against Warwickshire in the Second Eleven Championship. In the Warwickshire team were Cox's Bromsgrove team-mate Jonathon Webb and, as captain, Paul Best, a slow left-armer and batsman from Bablake. Others to represent county second teams during the summer were Jake Lintott (Queen's Taunton), Shiv Thakor (Uppingham), Adam Dibble (Taunton), Uzair Qureishi (Marlborough), Aaron West (Brentwood) and Muhunthan Harinath (Tiffin).

Talented players are always in demand, and increasingly many have to choose between a school first eleven on the one hand, and a county second team, a county academy or a league club on the other. Those who prefer the county/club path inevitably play fewer schools matches – and so are less likely

Stu Forster, Getty Images

Jos Buttler of King's College Taunton, the third *Young Wisden* Schools Cricketer of the Year.

to feature in *Wisden's* tables of leading batsmen and bowlers. This particularly applied to Bablake's Paul Best, who played far more for Stratford Town, topping both their batting and bowling averages.

However, the third *Young Wisden* Schools Cricketer of the Year is Jos Buttler of King's College Taunton. Like Best, he missed a few games because of England Under-19 commitments, and he also broke his thumb, which put him out for three weeks. He first represented Somerset seconds, as a wicketkeeper-batsman, in September 2006, three days after his 16th birthday. He played again in 2007, and was a regular in 2008, when he made 145 against Hampshire; he also hit a double-hundred for King's.

In 2009, he scored at more than a run a ball in every innings for King's and hit another century against Hampshire seconds, as well as being one of only two schoolboys (the other was Ben Cox) to play first-class cricket. He hit 30 against Lancashire, but it was Craig Kieswetter who kept wicket. Somerset's faith in Buttler was clear from their decision to include him in the squad for the Twenty20 Champions League in India in October, where he had the privilege of playing against New South Wales and facing Brett Lee.

Douglas Henderson is the current editor of Schools Cricket Online at www.schoolscricketonline.co.uk

ETON v HARROW

At Lord's, June 27. No result. Toss: Harrow.

An apocalyptic storm ended Harrow's bid for a fifth successive victory, but it already looked doomed. Only one of their previous Lord's eleven remained, while Eton's experienced top four batted steadily, accelerating after lunch when left-hander Rory Cox, sporting a Foreign Legion-style neck-cloth, hit a couple of sixes off Yunus Sert's off-spin and Nico Fitzroy battered 31 off 17 balls. Ted Morrison gave Harrow an unexpected bonus by bowling nine wides (14 including byes run off them) in two overs; even so, the batsmen began to slip behind the asking-rate. Captain Tom Tennant, son of the cricket writer Ivo, stood firm, reaching fifty with a six into the Tavern Stand. He was the game's top scorer when the teams went off amid claps of thunder. As lightning flashed and hail spattered the outfield, it was mistakenly announced that the match would be decided by the Duckworth/Lewis method, which would have given it to Eton; as the ground flooded, it was declared a draw.

Eton

*W. G. R. Vanderspar c Pearson-Jones	
b Bunting.	40
I. H. Hobson c Sert b Smith.	53
R. D. Cox st Spencer b Smith	67
A. S. Sangha c Pratt b Bunting	55
N. A. C. Fitzroy b Bunting	31
E. W. C. Gross run out	11

†J. M. MacDonagh run out	0
J. R. J. Hopton not out.	0
L-b 3, w 8	11
1/79 (1) 2/118 (2) (7 wkts, 55 overs) 268	
3/215 (3) 4/249 (4)	
5/264 (5) 6/265 (7) 7/268 (6)	

F. P. G. D. Barber, E. G. J. Morrison and J. F. M. Priest did not bat.

Pratt 11–2–37–0; Faber 8–0–35–0; Bunting 9–0–51–3; Pearson-Jones 6–0–24–0; Smith 10–1–49–2; Sert 11–0–69–0.

Harrow

C. J. Baird c Cox b Hobson.	28
*T. S. A. Tennant not out	72
A. C. Smith c sub (A. Gibson) b Hobson ..	17
T. W. Pearson-Jones run out	14
C. D. Berrill c Cox b Hopton.	2
Y. M. Sert not out	6
W 19	19

1/77 (1) 2/116 (3)   (4 wkts, 39.1 overs) 158
3/138 (4) 4/142 (5)

†A. C. Spencer, H. C. J. Cousens, G. M. O. Bunting, D. T. P. Pratt and T. M. N. Faber did not bat.

Morrison 2.1–0–17–0; Priest 8–2–33–0; Sangha 8–2–14–0; Barber 11–0–50–0; Hobson 7–0–35–2; Hopton 3–0–9–1.

Umpires: M. L. Brown and D. J. A. Edwards.

Of the 171 matches played between the two schools since 1805, Eton have won 55, Harrow 49 and 67 have been drawn. Matches during the two world wars are excluded from the reckoning. The fixture was reduced from a two-day, two-innings-a-side match to one day in 1982, and became a limited-overs fixture from 1999. Fifty-two centuries have been scored, the highest being 183 by D. C. Boles of Eton in 1904; M. C. Bird of Harrow is the only batsman to have made two hundreds in a match, in 1907. The highest score since the First World War is 161 not out by M. K. Fosh of Harrow in 1975, Harrow's last victory before 2000. A full list of results and centuries can be found on www.wisden.com.

Schools who wish to be considered for inclusion in *Wisden* should email the deputy editor: hugh.chevallier@wisden.com. State schools and girls' schools are especially welcome.

Note: The following tables cover only those schools listed in the Schools A–Z section.

LEADING BATSMEN IN SCHOOLS CRICKET

(Qualification: 500 runs at 60.00)

	I	NO	Runs	HS	100s	Avge
A. S. T. West (*Brentwood School*)	19	8	1,290	153*	5	117.27
A. M. Rossington (*Mill Hill School*)	11	5	695	119*	2	115.83
U. A. Qureshi (*Marlborough College*)	13	5	846	123*	1	105.75
S. Masood-Khan (*Stamford School*)	17	5	1,237	202	3	103.08
J. P. P. Cornick (*KES, Birmingham*)	15	6	894	138*	3	99.33
M. W. Baxter (*Gordonstoun School*)	15	2	1,097	175	5	84.38
N. Jacob (*Bancroft's School*)	21	7	1,169	148*	3	83.50
A. D. P. Gravell (*Ipswich School*)	15	4	910	120*	6	82.72
B. R. Wright (*Framlingham College*)	13	3	800	102	2	80.00
S. G. Rivers (*Reigate Grammar School*)	12	5	540	122*	1	77.14
M. W. Weightman (*Loughborough GS*)	12	2	771	127*	4	77.10
J. W. Evans (*Ellesmere College*)	11	2	684	128	3	76.00
R. Amin (*Gordonstoun School*)	13	6	531	101	1	75.85
F. K. Cowdrey (*Tonbridge School*)	19	8	831	109*	2	75.54
M. A. Wellings (*Lancaster RGS*)	13	4	679	150	2	75.44
O. J. Alsop (*Dauntsey's School*)	15	4	801	114*	3	72.81
J. Clark (*Sedbergh School*)	12	3	625	144*	2	69.44
B. T. Creese (*Perse School*)	9	0	613	120	3	68.11
C. A. J. Meschede (*King's College, Taunton*)	13	4	608	143	3	67.55
W. A. C. Sargent (*University College School*)	11	2	607	111	1	67.44
M. Lenygon (*King's College, Taunton*)	14	4	671	135	3	67.10
J. R. Biddle (*Kimbolton School*)	16	5	737	103*	1	67.00
J. Harrison-Dring (*Dover College*)	13	4	600	94	0	66.66
M. L. Shirt (*Brentwood School*)	16	2	932	111	3	66.57
M. N. Healy (*King's School, Canterbury*)	12	4	528	133	1	66.00
T. P. A. Davies (*Monkton Combe School*)	13	3	659	109*	2	65.90
W. G. R. Vanderspar (*Eton College*)	15	2	838	117	4	64.46
T. R. McCormick-Cox (*KES, Southampton*)	11	3	515	159*	1	64.37
T. C. Elliott (*Tonbridge School*)	19	2	1,091	157	5	64.17
K. C. Smith (*Merchiston Castle School*)	12	4	510	108*	2	63.75
S. J. de la Haye (*Victoria College, Jersey*)	15	2	822	113	2	63.23
R. T. Osmond (*Oundle School*)	17	3	884	108	4	63.14
K. S. Bansal (*Worksop College*)	10	1	567	94	0	63.00
C. J. Parsons (*Ardingly College*)	12	0	747	179	1	62.25
J. C. Buttler (*King's College, Taunton*)	10	1	554	124	1	61.55
G. O. James (*Bancroft's School*)	18	4	850	93*	0	60.71
O. J. Hairs (*Merchiston Castle School*)	12	1	665	121*	2	60.45

LEADING BOWLERS IN SCHOOLS CRICKET

(Qualification: 25 wickets at 14.00)

	O	M	R	W	BB	Avge
B. W. Kemp (*St Edmund's, Canterbury*)	69.5	7	227	28	4-11	8.10
N. A. T. Watkins (*Abingdon School*)	129	24	314	36	6-10	8.72
E. L. J. Easthope (*Dover College*)	91	22	229	26	5-24	8.80
E. E. Brock (*Oratory School*)	173	29	413	46	7-32	8.97
R. H. Patel (*Merchant Taylors', Northwood*)	116	29	314	32	7-8	9.81
A. C. Fisken (*Westminster School*)	126.5	15	462	45	6-11	10.26
M. J. Palmer (*Belfast Royal Academy*)	88.3	13	310	29	4-21	10.68
J. W. Howe (*St John's, Leatherhead*)	74	7	279	26	4-20	10.73
M. J. Faasen (*Gordonstoun School*)	114	23	346	32	5-5	10.81
A. J. Clarke (*Pocklington School*)	117.3	29	325	30	5-9	10.83
J. H. D. Hong (*Ardingly College*)	106.5	17	285	26	5-33	10.96
F. A. Seccombe (*Royal Hospital School*)	80	11	315	28	7-34	11.25
C. G. Roper (*Colston's School*)	122.2	17	432	38	4-10	11.36
O. J. Alsop (*Dauntsey's School*)	123	25	390	34	5-29	11.47
S. J. Lister (*Barnard Castle School*)	80.5	11	287	25	5-9	11.48
R. M. Collier (*Chigwell School*)	91	15	301	26	5-16	11.57
J. Leach (*Shrewsbury School*)	142.2	25	408	35	4-12	11.65
A. M. Stanley (*St George's, Weybridge*)	82	11	308	26	5-42	11.84
O. Wilkin (*Merchant Taylors', Northwood*)	116.3	29	319	26	8-14	12.26
J. B. Lintott (*Queen's College, Taunton*)	149.2	30	494	40	8-51	12.35
A. D. W. Tinsley (*Radley College*)	88	15	334	27	4-23	12.37
J. H. Lomas (*King's School, Macclesfield*)	176.4	34	536	43	7-45	12.46
R. S. Patel (*Bancroft's School*)	104.5	14	378	30	4-32	12.60
J. Oughtred (*Oundle School*)	193.2	49	456	36	5-10	12.66
M. J. Payne (*Bradfield College*)	127.3	18	382	30	4-29	12.73
R Patel (*Colfe's School*)	86	22	337	26	5-46	12.96
M. W. Shore (*Enfield Grammar School*)	81	3	416	32	3-10	13.00
W. J. D. Culhane (*City of London Freemen's School*)	205.5	24	730	56	8-18	13.03
A. Price (*Wellingborough School*)	100	15	381	29	5-33	13.13
M. G. Jay (*Dover College*)	134	28	356	27	4-13	13.18
J. R. Wilson (*Rossall School*)	90	13	334	25	4-19	13.36
K. J. Gammell (*Fettes College*)	92	11	336	25	6-29	13.44
M. J. Scarr (*Monmouth School*)	114.2	20	406	30	4-20	13.53
J. Leather (*St Albans School*)	114	11	380	28	4-30	13.57
B. G. C. Scott (*St George's, Weybridge*)	127.2	23	412	30	4-43	13.73
S. J. Holland (*King's College School, Wimbledon*)	105.3	15	373	27	5-20	13.81
J. I. B. A. Adkins (*Duke of York's RMS*)	83.5	3	415	30	6-24	13.83
J. C. Richards (*Lord Wandsworth College*)	97.1	15	346	25	7-34	13.84
M. Harinath (*Tiffin School*)	163	29	556	40	6-30	13.90

OUTSTANDING SEASONS, 2009

(Qualification: 10 matches)

	P	W	L	T	D	A	%W
King's College, Taunton	17	15	1	0	1	0	88.24
Winchester College	17	15	2	0	0	2	88.24
West Buckland School	13	11	2	0	0	0	84.62
Oratory School	18	15	1	1	1	0	83.33
Shrewsbury School	16	13	2	0	1	0	81.25
Monmouth School	16	13	3	0	0	0	81.25
Haberdashers' Aske's Boys' School	20	16	2	0	2	3	80.00
Sedbergh School	15	12	3	0	0	4	80.00
Hampton School	10	8	2	0	0	5	80.00
Bancroft's School	24	19	2	0	3	0	79.17

	P	W	L	T	D	A	%W
St George's, Weybridge	19	15	4	0	0	0	78.95
Abingdon School..........................	14	11	1	0	2	0	78.57
King Edward VI School, Southampton.........	13	10	3	0	0	0	76.92
King's School, Canterbury	13	10	2	0	1	1	76.92
Ryde School with Upper Chine..............	13	10	3	0	0	0	76.92
Cheltenham College	20	15	4	0	1	1	75.00

Note: The Leys School, who won six and drew five of their 11 matches, and Manchester Grammar School, who won eight, tied one and drew seven of their 16, were the only two schools reporting an unbeaten season.

SCHOOLS A–Z

(Qualification for averages: 150 runs or ten wickets)

In the results line, A = abandoned without a ball bowled. An asterisk next to a name indicates captain. Schools provide their own reports and averages.

Abingdon School
P14 W11 L1 D2

Master i/c D. C. Shirazi

Abingdon had a very positive year, winning 78% of their games. Nathaniel Watkins scored 432 runs and took 36 wickets, while Joshua Smith combined his 409 runs with 20 dismissals behind the stumps. Matthew Pursell also had a fine year, collecting 24 wickets.

Batting N. A. T. Watkins* 432 at 48.00; J. W. G. Smith 409 at 45.44; J. H. Edwards 290 at 32.22; M. W. Pursell 289 at 26.27; J. P. T. Manasseh 190 at 21.11.

Bowling N. A. T. Watkins 36 at 8.72; M. W. Pursell 24 at 11.79; J. W. Bartlett 13 at 13.23; T. R. Deeks 18 at 16.72.

Aldenham School
P11 W7 L4 A1

Master i/c M. I. Yeabsley
Coach D. J. Goodchild

The team was strongly led by Tom Pettet, who had an excellent season with both bat and ball. Bhasker Patel took 16 wickets, ensuring he left with over 60 victims. The highlight of the season was beating MCC for a second year running.

Batting T. S. Pettet* 362 at 60.33; G. P. Copley 206 at 25.75; W. E. C. Collier 163 at 23.28; B. S. Weinberg 156 at 19.50.

Bowling S. Shah 14 at 10.14; B. Patel 16 at 13.50; T. R. Bayley 10 at 14.40; T. S. Pettet 17 at 16.76.

Alleyn's School
P14 W6 L8 A3

Master i/c R. N. Ody
Coach P. H. Edwards

The school enjoyed a most successful first half of the season, but latter results were not as good. Jake Asghar was a most dependable captain. Matthew Syrett topped both the batting and bowling averages – a fine achievement.

Batting M. A. S. Syrett 447 at 40.63; J. M. Asghar* 297 at 27.00; H. E. Stones 236 at 23.60; J. H. Gallagher-Powell 208 at 18.90.

Bowling M. A. S. Syrett 22 at 13.18; D. L. Forde 11 at 19.54; J. M. Asghar 16 at 20.68.

Ampleforth College
P13 W5 L4 D4 A3

Master i/c G. D. Thurman

The first team played exciting cricket. Captained by George Hattrell, the school enjoyed their year and entertained those who watched. Peter Lydon led the batting, averaging over 43, and William Prest also did well.

Batting P. T. M. Lydon 519 at 43.25; W. D. Prest 331 at 25.46; C. G. Blakiston Houston 254 at 25.40; H. I. Adams-Cairns 165 at 20.62; H. G. Barnard 196 at 17.81; G. P. J. Hattrell* 218 at 16.76.

Bowling G. P. J. Hattrell 12 at 16.66; H. G. Wadsworth 16 at 19.06; C. G. Blakiston Houston 15 at 23.93; P. T. M. Lydon 14 at 27.78; J. A. Butler 14 at 30.07.

Ardingly College
P12 W5 L7

Master i/c R. A. F. King
Coach C. E. Waller

A very young side had mixed fortunes. There were victories against Seaford College, Caterham, the Old Boys, Sussex Martlets, XL Club and King's Bruton, and a winning draw against St Peter's, York. Opening batsman Chris Parsons was outstanding.

Batting C. J. Parsons 747 at 62.25; H. W. Tye 317 at 31.70; B. S. H. Carter 236 at 29.50; H. O. Sims 311 at 25.91; J. D. H. Hong* 168 at 16.80; J. S. Howard 157 at 13.08.
Bowling J. D. H. Hong 26 at 10.96; J. S. Howard 24 at 20.50; C. J. Parsons 24 at 23.87.

Arnold School
P9 W3 L4 D2

Master i/c M. L. Evans   **Coach** A. J. McKeown

Some very good cricket was played by the first team, with a good mixture of youth and experience making up the squad. The major highlights were a first-ever win over MCC and Nathan Bolus's magnificent 130 not out away at Cheadle Hulme.
Batting B. H. Perkins 156 at 26.00; T. J. Hessey 223 at 24.77; N. J. Bolus 170 at 24.28.
Bowling T. J. Hessey 11 at 18.54.

Ashville College
P13 W4 L7 D2 A2

Master i/c J. Goldthorp

Ashville started the season with limited success, winning only one game in the first half of term. However, after a week's break, the team came back strongly and showed signs of their true potential. The majority of the squad will still be at school in 2010, so the experience should help ensure more success.
Batting M. R. J. Johnson 536 at 59.55; N. P. Hammond* 411 at 45.66; M. D. McKee 239 at 23.90; O. P. Mitchell 241 at 20.08.
Bowling N. P. Hammond 24 at 16.54; E. J. Goodall 16 at 23.81; M. R. J. Johnson 14 at 24.64; R. M. B. Simms 12 at 33.00.

Bancroft's School
P24 W19 L2 D3

Master i/c J. K. Lever

Bancroft's strength produced another excellent season, the highlight being Nigel Jacob breaking the school's record aggregate for runs. Also in fine form were all-rounders Gareth James and Rahul Patel, with solid support from Rishabh Shah and spin bowler Neville Jacob.
Batting N. Jacob 1,169 at 83.50; G. O. James 850 at 60.71; R. S. Shah 714 at 54.92; A. R. Patel* 592 at 32.88; R. S. Patel 297 at 22.84.
Bowling R. S. Patel 30 at 12.60; N. P. Jacob 28 at 15.53; G. O. James 24 at 17.66; S. A. Khan 25 at 17.68; N. Jacob 13 at 18.23; R. S. Shah 26 at 18.69; A. Bothra 26 at 24.42.

Barnard Castle School
P13 W7 L1 T2 D3 A3

Master i/c B. C. Usher   **Coach** J. W. Lister

Steve Lister concluded his three-year stint as captain in some style, losing just once, against a strong Sedbergh side. John Huck scored most runs and also kept tidily. The all-round capabilities of James Sutton and Tom Chapman will also be missed in 2010.
Batting S. J. Lister* 393 at 49.12; J. R. Huck 403 at 44.77; J. R. Sutton 159 at 31.80.
Bowling J. R. Sutton 24 at 10.25; S. J. Lister 25 at 11.48; G. J. Upton 10 at 14.70; B. P. Upton 14 at 16.57; T. J. Chapman 19 at 18.52.

Bedford Modern School
P15 W5 L6 D4

Master i/c N. J. Chinneck

A very mixed season contained some good performances, while other matches were lost because of a lack of application, especially in the batting. Alastair Craig, the captain, missed the first half of the season through injury, but his return sparked considerable improvement.
Batting A. J. Craig* 403 at 67.16; C. D. Wood 284 at 40.57; G. R. Thurstance 443 at 34.07; B. Naik 283 at 21.76; J. Nicklin 165 at 15.00.
Bowling F. R. Wilson 12 at 16.41; G. R. Thurstance 23 at 23.86; N. J. O'Quinn 14 at 24.64; A. J. Walker 17 at 27.64.

Bedford School
P22 W11 L8 D3

Master i/c P. Sherwin   **Coach** D. W. Randall

Bedford experienced a season of mixed fortunes, with excellent victories over Rugby, Oakham and Haileybury tempered by disappointing defeats by Harrow and St Edward's. James Kettleborough, Sam Kumar and Christian Davis were the prominent performers.
Batting S. Kumar 836 at 46.44; J. M. Kettleborough 771 at 35.04; W. P. Aitkenhead 372 at 31.00; W. Gallimore 214 at 26.75; C. A. L. Davis 457 at 24.05; C. G. Smart 297 at 21.21; J. E. Cook* 371 at 19.52.

Bowling W. Gallimore 16 at 18.68; C. A. L. Davis 31 at 19.06; S. Kumar 21 at 23.80; T. H. Rhodes 15 at 31.13; M. W. Edmunds 13 at 34.38; J. E. Cook* 10 at 36.80; C. G. Smart 11 at 52.54.

Beechen Cliff School
P12 W3 L8 D1
Master i/c E. J. Wilmot   **Coach** M. Thorburn
An inconsistent season left a disappointing win/loss ratio, but the players showed signs of improvement as the season progressed, highlighted by Jordan Price's hat-trick at Prior Park. The team enjoyed a tour to the Caribbean where cricketing skills were enhanced.
Batting J. Price 248 at 27.55; R. Holton 272 at 27.20; N. Carlin 157 at 26.16; C. E. Mackenzie 205 at 25.62; J. J. N. Hamilton 225 at 20.45; M. Watters 153 at 17.00.
Bowling J. P. Addey 16 at 16.56; C. E. Mackenzie 15 at 17.60; J. Price 18 at 19.16; J. J. N. Hamilton 13 at 22.30.

Belfast Royal Academy
P9 W3 L5 D1
Master i/c W. I. McGonigle   **Coaches** M. C. W. Harte/J. A. McCombe
A young team gained valuable experience that should translate into success in 2010. Stephen Bunting captained Ulster Schools and was selected for the Ireland Under-19 squad. Matthew Palmer bowled with considerable skill and guile.
Batting P. N. Black 196 at 28.00.
Bowling M. J. Palmer* 29 at 10.68; R. J. R. Martin 15 at 22.60.

Berkhamsted School
P13 W7 L4 D2
Master i/c D. J. Gibson   **Coach** G. R. A. Campbell
The first team worked hard at their game and produced some excellent cricket; the win against local rivals St Albans was particularly pleasing. Tom Sambrook performed well with bat and ball, and Jeremy O'Neill's contribution as captain, keeper and top-order batsman was outstanding.
Batting T. S. Sambrook 431 at 47.88; J. S. O'Neill* 354 at 27.23; E. H. G. Gilder 247 at 20.58; A. R. A. Joyce 255 at 19.61.
Bowling T. Baker 15 at 13.46; C. D. King 18 at 15.00; C. D. Richardson 12 at 20.91; T. S. Sambrook 13 at 21.15.

Birkenhead School
P13 W3 L10 A1
Master i/c P. N. Lindberg   **Coach** B. T. P. Donelan
Following the departure of the majority of the highly successful 2008 side, this was expected to be a very difficult season. So it proved, as a youthful, inexperienced team struggled to score enough runs or dismiss top batsmen.
Batting T. F. Horrocks 229 at 20.81; A. M. F. Hind 223 at 20.27; A. J. Davis 185 at 16.81.
Bowling T. J. Bills 18 at 15.94; A. J. Davis 13 at 25.23; M. J. Lennon 10 at 25.80.

Bishop's Stortford College
P9 W3 L6
Master i/c M. Drury   **Coach** J. Kirton
This was not one of the better seasons at the College. In several fixtures the team were unable to capitalise on their initial hard work, but instead relaxed and allowed the match to slip away.
Batting W. Parker 340 at 48.57; H. Gerard 245 at 35.00; M. Silkstone 279 at 31.00.
Bowling No one took ten wickets. The leading bowler was F. Hiard, who took nine at 19.66.

Bloxham School
P11 W5 L2 T1 D3 A2
Master i/c R. W. F. Hastings   **Coach** A. D. Jones
The best season for many years saw much positive cricket played and a number of fine individual performances. Sam Ryan and Jon Best both scored outstanding centuries and Joseph Cooper led the bowling attack with pace and swing.
Batting J. R. Best 378 at 37.80; S. E. Ryan* 324 at 32.40.
Bowling J. M. Cooper 15 at 17.00; H. A. Loxton 13 at 21.92.

Blundell's School
P16 W6 L8 T1 D1
Master i/c R. J. Turner   **Coach** C. L. L. Gabbitass
Captained by Sam Smith, Blundell's had an inconsistent season. There were many notable performances, though, and leavers Smith, Will Denford and Justin Williams made fine all-round contributions. Zac Bess and Cameron Grainger are young players to look out for.
Batting J. G. Williams 291 at 29.10; S. J. Smith* 347 at 24.78.
Bowling S. J. Smith 14 at 22.07; Z. G. Bess 16 at 23.18.

Rehan Hassan, a 14-year-old leg-spinner from Brentwood, claimed 46 wickets and played for England Under-15s. Bancroft's Nigel Jacob hit 1,169 runs at 83.50.

Bradfield College

P16 W9 L6 D1 A1

Master i/c D. J. Clark   **Coach** J. R. Wood

After a poor start, the team played some excellent cricket in the second half of the season, with Tom Jewell leading superbly. His 707 runs and 23 wickets were essential to the team's overall success. Michael Payne's off-breaks earned him 30 wickets, and the hard-hitting Shelvin Gumbs scored quickly, with Rob Furness the leading pace bowler. The high point was success in the National Schools Twenty20 Plate final held at the beautiful Wormsley ground.

Batting T. M. Jewell* 707 at 54.38; S. S. E. Gumbs 584 at 44.92; R. Wijeratne 298 at 37.25; M. J. Payne 382 at 34.72; J. J. Gaffney 194 at 32.33; F. M. J. Walker 253 at 18.07.

Bowling M. J. Payne 30 at 12.73; T. M. Jewell 23 at 22.69; G. E. Graham 14 at 26.00; R. C. E. Furness 18 at 28.05; J. J. Gaffney 10 at 40.70.

Bradford Grammar School

P13 W6 L5 D2 A3

Master i/c A. G. Smith   **Coach** S. A. Kellett

The aggressive batting of captain Khawer Ayub set up four early-season victories. However, after an excellent win over MCC, the season was disrupted by weather and exams, leaving just an emphatic 234-run win against Pocklington to close the campaign.

Batting M. A. Asif 466 at 42.36; K. Ayub* 373 at 37.30; S. Rashid 386 at 35.09; U. A. Khan 168 at 28.00; A. E. Browne 155 at 19.37.

Bowling G. Hussain 12 at 13.16; J. M. Thornton 17 at 17.41; M. A. Asif 10 at 25.90; W. P. F. Vickers 11 at 29.81.

Brentwood School

P19 W13 L1 D5

Master i/c B. R. Hardie

Brentwood had their most successful season in recent times. The captain, Aaron West, broke the school's batting record set by Max Shirt in 2008. His total was the highest reported by schools in 2009.

Batting A. S. T. West* 1,290 at 117.27; M. L. Shirt 932 at 66.57; C. Sutherland 259 at 32.37; B. Akram 321 at 29.18; E. Allen 224 at 24.88; E. W. Nation 307 at 20.46; M. Watson 162 at 16.20.

Bowling A. S. T. West 26 at 15.00; R. Hassan 46 at 16.02; B. Akram 26 at 19.88; H. Owers 11 at 27.63; T. Moore 13 at 30.23.

Brighton College
P14 W8 L5 D1

Master i/c N. J. Buoy
Coach J. Appleton

Early-season wins over local rivals Eastbourne, Ardingly and St Bede's, a convincing victory against Harrow, and festival success versus Oakham and Sedbergh were the season's high spots. Playing the England Women's Eleven was an excellent occasion, as was the triumph in the Hampshire and Sussex regional Twenty20.

Batting A. H. Davies 613 at 55.72; H. B. Richards 259 at 37.00; J. W. C. Chapman 450 at 32.14; M. E. C. Chapman* 388 at 29.84; J. N. Thornely 266 at 26.60; B. J. Bridson 179 at 19.88.
Bowling F. C. Jordan 22 at 17.09; A. Hamid 15 at 17.86; M. E. C. Chapman 14 at 17.92; A. J. Rawstrone 13 at 24.38; A. M. Skan 18 at 24.88.

Bristol Grammar School
P15 W4 L10 D1 A3

Master i/c R. S. Jones
Coach K. R. Blackburn

A crisis of confidence among the batsmen meant the side seldom scored enough runs to be competitive, despite boasting a sound seam attack, wholeheartedly led by captain Stuart MacArthur.
Batting A. Moeller 171 at 21.37; W. F. Godfrey 259 at 18.50.
Bowling G. F. J. Bacon 20 at 18.35; S. M. MacArthur* 24 at 18.45; L. C. Luscombe 19 at 23.89; S. A. Brewer 12 at 32.00.

Bromsgrove School
P14 W6 L4 D4 A2

Master i/c C. J. Munn
Coach P. Greetham

Bromsgrove School revelled in a short but successful season with notable victories against Loughborough GS, Monmouth and Magdalen College School. Special mention must go to promising academy players Jonathon Webb (Warwickshire) and Benjamin Cox (Worcestershire). Both played in the Second Eleven Championship; Cox made his first-class debut in September.
Batting G. M. Macleod 249 at 83.00; O. B. Cox 443 at 73.83; J. P. Webb* 262 at 32.75; A. J. Morris 187 at 15.58.
Bowling M. J. Cox 16 at 14.00; M. M. Nawaz 23 at 17.00; J. P. Webb 15 at 19.13; M. Wyres 19 at 21.94.

Bryanston School
P14 W7 L5 D2

Master i/c B. J. Lawes

Bryanston had a pleasing season with plenty of close games. Dean Pearce, James Ladd-Gibbon and Jack Peck all performed admirably in their final campaign. Oliver d'Erlanger-Bertrand proved to be the star batsman, while Mitch Wilson made his debut for Gloucestershire's first team (v Leeds/Bradford UCCE) the day after his 17th birthday.
Batting O. A. d'Erlanger-Bertrand 476 at 36.61; H. E. Waterton 358 at 29.83; D. W. Pearce* 305 at 27.72; J. H. W. Ladd-Gibbon 211 at 19.18; J. A. W. Peck 201 at 18.27; M. J. Wilson 232 at 17.84; J. J. R. Weld 172 at 14.33.
Bowling M. J. Wilson 23 at 19.30; J. A. W. Peck 15 at 22.13; J. H. W. Ladd-Gibbon 17 at 22.70; D. W. Pearce 13 at 26.53; S. G. Fry 10 at 30.30.

Canford School
P12 W7 L4 D1

Master i/c D. King
Coach M. Griggs

Canford enjoyed success in a season where several junior players made significant contributions, boding well for 2010. However, expectation is tempered by the knowledge that the team must cope without master-in-charge David King, who has been most influential.
Batting T. W. E. Darby* 365 at 45.62; J. C. Hadley 367 at 33.36; B. C. W. Upton 314 at 26.16; W. J. Connor 230 at 23.00.
Bowling T. W. E. Darby 14 at 15.85; R. C. Triniman 13 at 18.76; R. A. G. Graham 15 at 19.33; J. R. A. Taylor 13 at 20.00; J. D. T. Marsh 12 at 22.25.

Charterhouse
P18 W12 L5 D1

Master i/c M. P. Bicknell

An excellent summer: the team beat Eton and Harrow in the same season for the first time, and came a close second in the Cowdrey Cup. Ben Jeffery struck a six off his last ball to pass Peter May's total of runs and become the school's fourth-highest scorer.
Batting B. A. Jeffery 786 at 52.40; J. H. M. Rumball* 538 at 33.62; T. C. A. Kimmins 369 at 28.38; S. T. de Soysa 380 at 20.00; C. E. R. Kimmins 215 at 19.54; A. D. Gloak 280 at 18.66; J. W. S. Kinsey 185 at 18.50.

Bowling T. C. G. Bray 29 at 14.86; A. D. Gloak 32 at 15.25; C. E. R. Kimmins 21 at 17.00; B. E. N. Rinck 27 at 19.00; J. W. S. Kinsey 18 at 24.27.

Cheadle Hulme School   P10 W4 L2 D4 A3
Master i/c J. C. Winter
Fifteen-year-old Matthew Winter made a significant impact with the bat, while Matt Marfani, Chris Winter and Jack Langley all scored important runs. Michael Anderson, Akshat Agarwal, Marfani and Chris Winter shared the wickets in a season of close games and exciting finishes, typified by the five run defeat – chasing 248 – at Millfield.
Batting M. A. Marfani 399 at 49.87; C. J. Winter* 265 at 37.85; M. J. Winter 356 at 35.60; J. F. Langley 267 at 33.37.
Bowling M. R. Anderson 21 at 14.80; M. A. Marfani 13 at 22.46; A. Agarwal 13 at 22.92; C. J. Winter 14 at 27.57.

Cheltenham College   P20 W15 L4 D1 A1
Master i/c M. W. Stovold   **Coach** M. P. Briers
An excellent season, with wicketkeeper-batsman Charles Wootton scoring over 1,000 runs, including three centuries and a 99. The side contained strength in depth and was well marshalled by Chris Butlin.
Batting C. P. J. Wootton 1,072 at 53.60; T. A. Newman 703 at 50.21; A. M. Mason 390 at 32.50; C. J. Butlin* 613 at 32.26; A. J. Henniker-Gotley 233 at 25.88; M. H. Delamain 276 at 18.40; J. W. Croft 164 at 18.22.
Bowling L. J. Watkins 31 at 15.67; C. C. Scott 21 at 21.85; D. A. Scott 18 at 22.05; M. H. Delamain 18 at 25.16; O. W. Matthews 16 at 34.37.

Chigwell School   P13 W6 L4 D3
Master i/c F. A. Griffith
Some outstanding victories were achieved despite the loss of key players from 2008. The best was the four-wicket victory against MCC. Skipper Daniel Majeed scored 125, his second hundred of the season, and finished the top batsman by some distance. Richard Collier also had a productive all-round season.
Batting D. Majeed* 589 at 58.90; C. D. A. Briggs 244 at 30.50; R. M. Collier 263 at 29.22; P. J. Valentine 198 at 24.75; D. J. Holdsworth 186 at 20.66; G. E. Slade 168 at 18.66.
Bowling R. M. Collier 26 at 11.57; T. J. Gibbs 15 at 13.80; C. N. Stephens 10 at 18.30; D. Majeed 14 at 21.42.

Chislehurst and Sidcup Grammar School   P7 W3 L4 A2
Master i/c R. P. Kearney   **Coach** I. B. Willmott
The players showed great dedication to their cricket and gained some excellent results. Good performances were shared throughout the season, highlighting a new depth and quality within the squad.
Batting M. S. Kilbey 198 at 33.00.
Bowling No one took ten wickets. The leading bowler was J. E. Green who took eight at 14.00.

Christ College, Brecon   P10 W3 L7 A1
Master i/c C. J. Webber   **Coach** P. Brett
A side with no great depth of talent pulled together effectively as a team and produced some solid performances. Sixteen-year-old Will Burton had a fine season, hitting three unbeaten centuries.
Batting T. W. Burton 410 at 82.00; D. R. Rich* 301 at 33.44; J. W. K. Spencer 243 at 30.37; R. Jones 150 at 18.75.
Bowling T. M. G. Trumper 10 at 17.90; J. W. K. Spencer 14 at 19.35.

Christ's College, Finchley   P10 W2 L2 D6 A4
Master i/c S. S. Goldsmith
An enthusiastic team faced a demanding fixture list; they were unable to convert chances into winning positions, and results were disappointing. Frail batting proved particularly costly, with no one averaging above 27.00.
Batting R. V. Thakkar 162 at 27.00; R. M. Tanna 188 at 23.50; W. H. Rizvi* 222 at 22.20; K. R. Nirban 152 at 16.88.
Bowling W. H. Rizvi 16 at 14.25; P. H. Pujara 13 at 14.38.

Christ's Hospital
Master i/c H. P. Holdsworth

P17 W8 L8 D1 A2
Coach T. E. Jesty

Christ's Hospital began and ended the season in fine form, but in between too many games were lost. The captain, Matthew Bassett, overtook Nick Konig and Dennis Silk to become the leading run-maker in the school's history. Records date back to 1884.

Batting M. A. Bassett* 550 at 34.37; J. O. Launchbury 316 at 26.33; J. H. Noble 338 at 24.14; A. P. Marsh 402 at 23.64; A. D. Satterfield 378 at 23.62; S. J. Clark 256 at 16.00.

Bowling M. F. Haywood 21 at 15.57; A. W. Nichols 29 at 17.79; S. G. Whittingham 16 at 22.93; S. P. Streeting 12 at 28.33; A. P. Marsh 20 at 29.45.

City of London Freemen's School
Master i/c J. G. Moore

P18 W11 L4 D3 A1
Coach N. M. Stewart

A successful tour to Dubai meant cricket in all three terms, and this was reflected in the performances. Pleasing wins against RGS Guildford, Reed's and St Peter's York were the highlights. William Culhane's off-spin offered control and penetration; his 56 victims made him the top wicket-taker in schools cricket. James Brooks held sway with the bat.

Batting J. E. L. Brooks* 600 at 40.00; J. A. Godfrey 527 at 32.93; F. H. Davies 592 at 31.15; J. P. Ray 260 at 26.00; J. J. Lewis-Oliver 330 at 23.57; J. D. E. Hutter 269 at 19.21; M. J. Hall 163 at 14.81.

Bowling W. J. D. Culhane 56 at 13.03; F. H. Davies 20 at 19.80; J. J. Lewis-Oliver 21 at 21.95; M. Dawes 13 at 23.61.

Clayesmore School
Master i/c D. I. Rimmer

P11 W6 L3 D2 A2
Coach P. M. Warren

Under the thoughtful, mature captaincy of Peter Merrell, and with new talent in the squad, this was a more successful season. Once again Toby Sutton proved an invaluable all-rounder; useful runs also came from Lewis Brown and, later on, 14-year-old wicketkeeper-batsman Lewis McManus.

Batting T. J. Sutton 450 at 90.00; L. S. Brown 259 at 43.16.

Bowling T. J. Sutton 12 at 16.50; P. J. Merrell* 18 at 17.77; H. H. Cossins 12 at 26.33.

Clifton College
Master i/c J. C. Bobby

P13 W8 L5 A1
Coach P. W. Romaines

With a young but talented squad much was expected for the season. The highlights were a nail-biting win at Marlborough and a convincing seven-wicket victory over Westminster College, Adelaide. A pre-season tour of Barbados is planned for Easter 2010, and with only one leaver there is considerable optimism.

Batting G. R. M. Kinsey 243 at 48.60; L. E. V. Durrans 321 at 40.12; J. E. V. Barnes 164 at 27.33; C. A. M. Walker 265 at 24.09.

Bowling M. W. Cornish 18 at 17.72; C. A. M. Walker 16 at 23.62; J. F. Daniel 12 at 26.08; R. E. Miller 13 at 27.38.

Colfe's School
Master i/c G. S. Clinton

P13 W7 L3 D3 A3

A youthful side produced very encouraging results. With the junior teams boasting a number of county representatives, the future for the senior side looks bright.

Batting R. Clayton* 309 at 30.90; J. Potter 297 at 24.75; D. Patel 235 at 23.50.

Bowling R. Patel 26 at 12.96; R. Clayton 16 at 13.62.

Colston's School
Master i/c T. A. H. Williams

P16 W5 L8 D3
Coach D. V. Lawrence

After a highly successful tour of Grenada, the side struggled to fulfil their potential. The team was led by Chris Roper, who was top of both sets of averages.

Batting C. G. Roper* 492 at 49.20; O. King-Sorrell 242 at 30.25; C. Foley 188 at 23.50; M. Thatcher 198 at 22.00.

Bowling C. G. Roper 38 at 11.36; B. Ferrett 22 at 13.72; M. A. Hurrell 16 at 23.87; C. Foley 10 at 24.10.

Run machines: Wicketkeeper-batsman Charles Wootton scored 1,072 runs for Cheltenham College, while Dauntsey's Owen Alsop added 34 wickets to over 800 runs.

Cranbrook School   P17 W7 L7 D3
Master i/c A. J. Presnell
A very inexperienced side performed with great character. The potential for success in 2010 became clear towards the end of the season, with satisfying wins and solid all-round form.
Batting T. Walker 288 at 28.80; S. Underwood 312 at 24.00; E. Berger 285 at 21.92.
Bowling D. Gordon 13 at 20.61; R. Smith* 13 at 22.84; E. Berger 16 at 24.37; A. Welchman 11 at 28.45.

Cranleigh School   P17 W8 L6 D3
Master i/c J. S. Ross   **Coach** S. D. Welch
The season was always likely to be a transitional period following several highly successful summers. A young side, ably led by Robert Cowdrey, enjoyed eight admirable victories, including wins over Eastbourne, Radley, St Paul's and St John's.
Batting D. I. Allan 461 at 27.11; J. C. Austin 359 at 23.93; M. Burgess 167 at 20.87; O. J. Davies 239 at 19.91; W. M. Langmead 216 at 19.63; C. Jason 239 at 17.07; R. C. Cowdrey* 287 at 16.88; W. P. F. Jordan 189 at 11.11.
Bowling J. G. Richards 12 at 19.08; H. Adolphus 16 at 23.50; O. J. Davies 17 at 23.64; O. J. Cross 18 at 23.72; D. I. Allan 14 at 25.35; S. G. R. Wilson 13 at 33.38.

Culford School   P17 W11 L2 D4
Master i/c A. H. Marsh
Culford relished a highly successful season, with teamwork to the fore. Mature captaincy from Alex Lee helped develop a strong spirit. Powerful batting from, in particular, Patrick Kearney and Ben Shepperson was the key to either chasing effectively or setting stiff targets. The bowling was a desirable blend of seam, swing and spin. Eight of the squad return for 2010.
Batting B. Shepperson 692 at 57.66; P. Kearney 528 at 44.00; A. J. Lee* 329 at 27.41; F. Preston 287 at 23.91; C. J. Recaldin 336 at 22.40; T. W. Beaumont 210 at 19.09.
Bowling A. J. Lee 21 at 13.04; P. Kearney 20 at 16.25; J. Shepherd 25 at 18.88; B. Shepperson 18 at 29.00; T. E. Singer 10 at 37.10.

Dame Allan's School
P6 W2 L4 A1

Master i/c J. A. Benn   **Coach** W. P. Hudson

Although team spirit was high, the side lacked consistency on the field. The batting and bowling were often proficient, but rarely in the same match. John Richardson, the skipper, was the most reliable performer with his off-spinners. Assad Mohammed was the best of the batsmen.

Batting No one scored 150 runs. The leading batsman was A. Mohammed who hit 105 at 26.25.

Bowling J. D. Richardson* 14 at 9.28.

Dauntsey's School
P16 W9 L7 A1

Master i/c A. J. Palmer   **Coach** S. Cloete

A successful two-week tour to St Kitts and Nevis preceded another strong campaign in which the team finished joint-top of the Peak Sports League; a third successive year as winners. Owen Alsop topped both averages and scored three centuries in June. Fourteen-year-old Jack Mynott, in only his second outing, became the youngest player to score a century for the first team.

Batting O. J. Alsop 801 at 72.81; H. G. M. Dixon 428 at 30.57; J. F. Page 374 at 24.93; W. J. E. Caiger 342 at 22.80; B. D. Rostand 169 at 21.12.

Bowling O. J. Alsop 34 at 11.47; J. R. Duckworth 15 at 17.53; V. S. Patel* 22 at 23.13; C. I. Blewitt 13 at 32.53; J. F. Page 15 at 32.66.

Dean Close School
P13 W3 L10

Master i/c B. P. Price   **Coach** R. J. Cunliffe

Although the side was disappointed to record only three victories, it was a very agreeable season. Several exciting games went down to the last over. Liam Brignull led the side exceptionally well, and most members of the squad made a telling contribution.

Batting B. J. Andrew 380 at 38.00; L. R. Brignull* 454 at 37.83; S. P. Slabbert 338 at 30.72; M. Penny 229 at 25.44.

Bowling R. C. Bamforth 16 at 26.56.

Denstone College
P13 W8 L1 T1 D3

Master i/c J. R. Morris

A magnificent season was built around a strong all-round team performance. Ben Young guided the team in fine style, while Chris Beech hit two centuries. Brothers James and Jack Warren shared the wickets and contained the opposition well.

Batting C. J. Beech 502 at 45.63; T. J. Bamford 456 at 38.00; G. F. Roe 173 at 34.60; B. J. Young* 311 at 25.91; J. J. Moran 203 at 25.37; J. G. M. Bamford 175 at 19.44.

Bowling J. S. Warren 19 at 14.00; J. J. Warren 19 at 17.89; C. J. Beech 16 at 19.18; B. J. Young 10 at 20.30; J. J. Moran 12 at 27.50.

Dr Challoner's Grammar School
P13 W9 L1 D3

Master i/c D. J. Colquhoun

This was one of the best seasons in recent times. Jack Shiel led the way with the bat, scoring 520 runs. A high spot for Tom Crick was a spell of four for nought to win the game against Watford GS. All-rounder Ali Birkby's bowling was always reliable.

Batting J. J. Shiel 520 at 43.33; A. F. Birkby 316 at 39.50; A. T. Wilson 151 at 37.75; S. A. Westaway 180 at 25.71; J. A. Suter* 210 at 21.00.

Bowling S. S. Rogers 16 at 13.87; T. L. Crick 24 at 13.95; A. F. Birkby 15 at 15.00; M. J. Rance 14 at 22.57.

Dollar Academy
P13 W7 L4 D2

Master i/c J. G. A. Frost

Narrow defeats by Fettes College and Stewart's Melville were a disappointment for this talented and capable team. An excellent win against a strong Gordonstoun side was the highlight. Calum Watson was the pick of the bowling attack.

Batting K. A. Bostic* 247 at 35.28; P. A. Ross 302 at 33.55; J. J. Ross 325 at 29.54.

Bowling S. D. Weir 15 at 12.53; C. M. Watson 23 at 12.56; J. J. Ross 14 at 19.00.

Dover College
P13 W7 L5 D1

Master i/c G. R. Hill

An inexperienced team won over half their matches and prospects for 2010 are high, with nine of the side returning. Top moments were the ten-wicket defeat of the Band of Brothers, a two-wicket win against the XL Club and a hat-trick by Matthew Jay against St Lawrence.

Batting J. Harrison-Dring 600 at 66.66; M. G. Jay 227 at 28.37; E. L. J. Easthope 150 at 21.42.
Bowling E. L. J. Easthope 26 at 8.80; M. G. Jay 27 at 13.18; J. G. R. Woods 15 at 24.26.

Downside School   P7 W1 L5 D1
Master i/c A. C. Woodin   **Coach** P. Lawrence
Ben Tatham's 116 not out against MCC was the outstanding feature of a rather disappointing summer. The core of the team remains for 2010 when Tom Doe and Freddie Mercer should both be prominent.
Batting B. G. P. Tatham* 164 at 41.00; T. B. Doe 210 at 30.00.
Bowling No one took ten wickets. The leading bowler was F. A. M. Mercer who took nine at 28.00.

Duke of York's Royal Military School   P14 W10 L4 A3
Master i/c S. Salisbury
A productive season with contributions from everyone at some point. Jack Adkins, promoted from the Under-15s, performed exceptionally well as the team's sole spinner. Michael Thompson, the captain, and Harry Catmur provided the bulk of the runs. The fielding was exceptional. With eight boys returning, 2010 should bring success.
Batting H. S. C. C. Catmur 432 at 36.00; M. P. Thompson* 405 at 33.75.
Bowling J. I. B. A. Adkins 30 at 13.83; T. S. Kaye 20 at 16.80; J. M. Boxall 12 at 17.00; M. P. Thompson 15 at 23.60.

Dulwich College   P20 W13 L4 D3
Master i/c D. J. Cooper   **Coach** C. W. J. Athey
An excellent season saw the post-war record for victories (12) broken. The team reached the final of the national Twenty20 competition for the third year in succession, but lost to Millfield. The batting contributed to some highly entertaining cricket and was generally better than the bowling. The most interesting scalp of the summer was possibly that of the triumphant England Women's World Cup squad.
Batting A. T. Alleyne 813 at 54.20; W. A. MacVicar 764 at 44.94; T. E. Eadon 662 at 34.84; M. J. Keyte 162 at 27.00; S. A. R. Northcote-Green 413 at 24.29; T. J. Deasy 461 at 24.26; A. J. Corbin 485 at 24.25; J. F. Kelleher 215 at 23.88; A. J. Paton* 237 at 14.81.
Bowling T. E. Eadon 16 at 14.37; S. A. R. Northcote-Green 27 at 20.51; A. J. Corbin 27 at 21.18; W. A. MacVicar 24 at 23.83; H. F. Cullum 12 at 25.91; A. T. Alleyne 19 at 27.84; P. Patel 10 at 30.80.

Durham School   P16 W6 L5 T1 D4 A5
Master i/c M. B. Fishwick
An enjoyable and rewarding season from an inexperienced side. The high point was the final match when Durham took the last three Malvern wickets to tie. Sixteen-year-old Ross Burdon won the Hirsch Trophy for the best cricketer.
Batting R. Burdon 453 at 34.84; M. Turns* 202 at 33.66; L. Hall 411 at 29.35; J. Ritzema 434 at 27.12; T. H. Temple 282 at 25.63; A. J. Elliott 190 at 17.27.
Bowling A. Elliott 19 at 14.31; L. Hall 19 at 22.36; R. Burdon 21 at 22.95.

Eastbourne College   P19 W8 L9 D2
Master i/c M. J. Banes   **Coach** A. C. Waller
Effectively skippered by Ollie Smith, who scored two centuries, the side had its finest day with a victory over Christ's College, New Zealand, who were otherwise unbeaten on tour. Four Under-16 batsmen gained valuable experience and Ben Barter, with 32, took most wickets.
Batting O. L. Smith* 592 at 37.00; J. Hughes 399 at 26.60; P. J. Wooldridge 421 at 24.76; W. J. Wheeler 341 at 21.31; H. J. H. Finzel 356 at 20.94; O. P. Smith 218 at 18.16; S. C. Garratt 300 at 16.66; B. J. Barter 178 at 14.83.
Bowling P. J. Wooldridge 10 at 14.40; B. J. Barter 32 at 16.71; O. L. Smith 23 at 22.52; S. C. Garratt 25 at 23.32; H. J. H. Finzel 10 at 27.80; A. J. Hinchliffe 13 at 34.69.

The Edinburgh Academy   P14 W5 L8 D1
Master i/c M. J. D. Allingham
The team was skilfully captained by Bertie Allison, despite losing every toss bar one! There were some fine victories in the second half of the season, with the lower-order batsmen playing a key role.
Batting A. J. H. Colam 209 at 41.80; A. R. M. Muir 287 at 24.75; F. R. S. Gillies 210 at 21.00; N. C. G. Hunt 223 at 15.92; J. D. Munro 178 at 14.83.

Bowling R. J. S. Cumming 15 at 16.93; J. D. Munro 10 at 20.90; P. Scott Reid 11 at 21.27; A. C. S. Murray 14 at 22.35; C. J. R. W. Simpson 16 at 22.75; N. C. G. Hunt 17 at 23.23.

Elizabeth College, Guernsey   P12 W6 L6 A1
Master i/c M. E. Kinder
The side failed to do itself justice. The outstanding moment was a thrilling last-ball one-wicket win against Victoria College, Jersey, with Elizabeth's score 263-9. At the Shrewsbury School Silk Trophy, Elizabeth trounced Melbourne GS by eight wickets, with William Thompson 102 and Tim Ravenscroft 51, both not out.
Batting T. J. Ravenscroft 320 at 40.00; W. G. Thompson 230 at 28.75; A. E. Hindle 168 at 24.00; J. D. Clark* 174 at 21.75.
Bowling B. J. McVey 11 at 18.90; M. L. Ellis 13 at 20.38.

Ellesmere College   P11 W6 L5 A3
Master i/c P. J. Hayes   **Coach** R. Jones
The captain, Jordan Evans, hit three centuries and inspired a young side to five consecutive wins. The season's high point was an unbeaten partnership of 149 from the final 11 overs between Evans (69) and 15-year-old Matthew Macintosh (85) to defeat the Gentlemen of Shropshire.
Batting J. W. Evans* 684 at 76.00; M. R. Macintosh 265 at 29.44; J. M. Maddock-James 188 at 26.85.
Bowling A. J. Owen 13 at 22.84.

Eltham College   P17 W10 L6 D1
Master i/c E. T. Thorogood   **Coaches** R. W. Hills/D. DeBeer
Eltham revelled in a good season under captain James Pearse, winning over half of their matches. Six of this year's team return for 2010, after touring Australia at Christmas. The side will be captained by David Voisey.
Batting J. Pearse* 516 at 43.00; R. Fleming 403 at 40.30; D. Voisey 325 at 32.50.
Bowling J. Robertson 10 at 11.20; D. Giles 13 at 18.38; E. J. Whyte 15 at 27.66; T. Scorgie 22 at 28.00; J. Pearse 11 at 32.81.

Emanuel School   P12 W7 L4 D1
Master i/c P. A. King   **Coaches** M. G. Stear/M. L. Roberts
The most successful season in over a decade started with a very pleasing pre-season tour to Gibraltar, and included victories against a number of local rivals. The captain, Abdul Sheikh, capped the season off with 109 not out while leading his team to victory over MCC.
Batting A. A. Sheikh* 326 at 36.22; J. W. Lampier 357 at 29.75; S. M. Hawley 292 at 29.20; T. G. Lampier 216 at 21.60.
Bowling V. N. Patel 14 at 12.28; H. Thaker 19 at 14.47; A. A. Sheikh 13 at 14.76; T. I. N. Dunbar 17 at 15.76.

Enfield Grammar School   P14 W2 L8 D4
Master i/c M. S. Alder
A youthful and inexperienced side worked hard but found life difficult, well though Matthew Shore batted and bowled. A successful tour to Barbados in the summer break has strengthened the side, and prospects for 2010 are enhanced.
Batting M. W. Shore 281 at 20.07; C. Cameron* 192 at 17.45.
Bowling M. W. Shore 32 at 13.00; J. C. Smith 18 at 22.44; T. M. Ansari 13 at 29.15.

Eton College   P18 W12 L4 T1 D1
Master i/c N. A. Leamon   **Coach** J. M. Rice
Batting W. G. R. Vanderspar* 838 at 64.46; R. D. Cox 597 at 49.75; E. W. C. Gross 322 at 46.00; A. S. Sangha 398 at 44.22; I. H. Hobson 503 at 38.69.
Bowling E. W. C. Gross 10 at 17.70; A. S. Sangha 23 at 18.82; J. F. M. Priest 12 at 20.16; E. G. J. Morrison 24 at 20.50; F. P. D. G. Barber 22 at 24.68; I. H. Hobson 19 at 25.78; J. R. J. Hopton 14 at 32.92.

Felsted School
P18 W7 L5 D6

Master i/c C. S. Knightley   Coach N. J. Lockhart

Felsted enjoyed their summer, with wins against Bishop's Stortford HS, Uppingham, Haileybury, Colchester RGS, Eltham, Gentlemen of Essex and Hunter Valley, Australia. A tour to Australia is planned for December; nine of the squad return for 2010.

Batting J. E. L. Buttleman 758 at 54.14; H. C. Hebron 176 at 44.00; B. W. Blackwell* 566 at 35.37; A. J. Marjoribanks 325 at 32.50; A. H. J. Ross 351 at 29.25; J. A. Wells 390 at 26.00; M. J. Houlder 274 at 24.90; O. Ekers 363 at 24.20.

Bowling A. J. Marjoribanks 29 at 22.48; H. C. Hebron 19 at 24.84; R. C. Howell 22 at 25.81; B. W. Blackwell 24 at 27.87.

Fettes College
P13 W9 L3 D1

Master i/c C. S. Thomson   Coach A. B. Russell

Another splendid season which yielded nine victories from 13 games. Four-year veteran Sam Hunt captained the side effectively and contributed 439 runs, with valuable support coming from Hector Cottam with 344. Kit Gammell was the top wicket-taker with 25.

Batting D. W. Murphy 199 at 39.80; C. S. C. Hunt* 439 at 36.58; H. G. I. Cottam 344 at 34.40; H. R. Edwards 153 at 30.60; W. D. R. Philip 225 at 18.75.

Bowling K. J. Gammell 25 at 13.44; A. G. B. Boisseau 17 at 14.88; W. D. R. Philip 17 at 15.41; C. N. Giffin 17 at 16.88; J. P. M. Dingwall 10 at 26.20.

Forest School
P16 W7 L9 A0

Master i/c S. Turner

An inexperienced first team acquitted themselves well, winning seven of their 16 games. Joel Coppeard led by example, and Jehanshar Akbar, a young leg-spinner, took five for 35 against MCC. Every team member played a part.

Batting J. L. T. Coppeard* 323 at 35.88; J. J. Das 268 at 24.36; P. Chand-Bajpai 262 at 23.81; G. N. Summers 164 at 11.71.

Bowling M. E. J. Cheeseman 12 at 17.08; J. Akbar 28 at 19.60; J. L. T. Coppeard 20 at 20.60; G. N. Summers 12 at 36.83.

Framlingham College
P13 W6 L5 D2

Master i/c P. W. Jarvis

The 2009 season saw further improvement. The team learned how to build pressure in the field and form partnerships when batting. Their hard work paid off with a superb win over Felsted in the summer's last game. They were captained ably by Ben Gowing, and the player of the season was Ben Wright.

Batting B. R. Wright 800 at 80.00; C. A. J. Garrard 176 at 35.20; R. Bridgstock 315 at 31.50; T. D. Over 267 at 29.66; B. W. Gowing* 353 at 29.41.

Bowling D. Whitehouse 10 at 13.30; C. P. Rowles 18 at 25.44; S. J. P. Bennett-King 10 at 38.80.

George Watson's College
P13 W7 L5 D1 A1

Master i/c I. Geddes   Coach M. J. Leonard

The team had a solid season without quite fulfilling their potential. Highlights included the batting of Jack Kennedy and Scott Mullins in the stunning win over MCC, and reaching the Lothian Schools' Cup final after a nail-biting semi-final.

Batting T. D. Barrett 228 at 57.00; A. D. Chalmers 309 at 30.90; S. R. H. Mullins 301 at 30.10; J. Kennedy 253 at 23.00.

Bowling A. D. Chalmers 14 at 17.42; H. K. Peddie* 14 at 18.50; F. J. Sands 11 at 30.54.

Giggleswick School
P12 W7 L4 D1

Master i/c D. Muckalt   Coach M. J. F. Shrimpton

Giggleswick had their most successful season for several years. Four centuries were scored: three by Andrew McCracken and one by Christopher Gemmell. The captain, Eddie Read, performed well with both bat and ball.

Batting A. J. McCracken 484 at 53.77; C. P. Gemmell 237 at 47.40; E. A. Read* 288 at 28.80.

Bowling E. A. Read 24 at 9.54; C. P. Gemmell 11 at 15.36; A. J. McCracken 10 at 18.60.

The Glasgow Academy
P7 W3 L3 D1 A1

Master i/c S. G. Weston   Coach V. Hariharan

Two talented 14-year-old quick bowlers, Lyle Hill and Haris Chaudhry, provided the high spots and gave the bowling strength. Hill went on to play for the Scotland Under-15 team.

Batting No one scored 150 runs. The leading batsman was L. H. Hill, who hit 78 at 15.60.

Bowling L. H. Hill 13 at 4.76; H. M. Chaudhry 19 at 6.36.

The High School of Glasgow
P13 W5 L6 D2 A1

Master i/c D. N. Barrett   Coaches N. R. Clarke/K. J. A. Robertson

A very encouraging campaign contained almost twice as many games played as in 2008. There were wins against all the other Glasgow independent schools. Connor McInteer was very successful with the ball, taking seven for 12 in one match, including a hat-trick.

Batting C. L. McInteer 174 at 19.33.

Bowling A. R. I. Umeed 11 at 12.00; C. L. McInteer 22 at 14.13; E. O. Allan* 19 at 19.26; K. K. Majhu 15 at 19.26; M. R. Ralston 10 at 29.60.

Glenalmond College
P13 W6 L4 D3 A4

Master i/c A. Norton

With many returning from 2008, this was perhaps a slightly disappointing season. Inconsistency from the middle order and in the out-cricket meant some potential victories slipped away, despite some admirable performances from the bowlers.

Batting C. D. Martin 312 at 34.66; T. S. J. Robertson 273 at 27.30; B. P. D. King 178 at 19.77; N. M. Fenton 166 at 15.09.

Bowling C. D. Martin 13 at 8.69; G. H. C. Smith 11 at 12.36; B. P. D. King 17 at 16.64; S. C. D. Shillington 12 at 16.83; T. S. J. Robertson 11 at 25.72.

Gordonstoun School
P15 W9 L3 D3 A1

Master i/c C. J. Barton   Coach K. Foster

The dry Morayshire summer led to very flat North Lawn wickets on which Michael Baxter excelled, scoring 1,097 runs. He was ably assisted by the economical left-arm spin of Michael Faasen, who took 32 wickets. The youthful side were defeated on only three occasions, which augurs well for 2010.

Batting M. W. Baxter 1,097 at 84.38; R. Amin 531 at 75.85; M. J. Faasen 368 at 36.80; A. W. Patrick 302 at 25.16; F. Amin 199 at 19.90.

Bowling M. J. Faasen 32 at 10.81; A. W. Patrick 11 at 10.90; F. Amin 13 at 14.84; J. R. Barton 10 at 16.10; R. Amin 17 at 23.94; M. W. Baxter 10 at 30.80.

Haberdashers' Aske's Boys' School
P20 W16 L2 D2 A3

Master i/c S. D. Charlwood   Coaches D. H. Kerry/D. I. Yeabsley

Outstanding episodes in a fine season included wins against Merchant Taylors' and Bancroft's, while the annual Devon tour produced three narrow victories on consecutive days. The side was skilfully led by Lewis Jenkins, with contributions from everyone, notably all-rounder Kushal Patel, wicketkeeper-batsman Nishanth Selvakumar and our trio of spinners, Tom Edrich (grandson of Bill), Amish Parekh and Seb Schusman, who claimed 78 wickets between them.

Batting L. G. Jenkins* 693 at 43.31; N. N. Selvakumar 402 at 30.92; N. K. Malde 417 at 27.80; J. P. Miller 345 at 26.53; B. A. Letts 310 at 25.83; K. A. Patel 408 at 24.00; T. W. Edrich 210 at 23.33.

Bowling K. A. Patel 36 at 16.13; S. A. Schusman 25 at 16.16; T. W. Edrich 27 at 18.96; A. Parekh 26 at 19.15; H. Malde 16 at 21.87; K. Patel 14 at 22.92.

Haileybury
P15 W8 L5 D2

Master i/c M. J. Cawdron   Coach G. P. Howarth

This was a successful season for the young Haileybury side, ably captained by Sam Anthony. With only three leaving and a squad that matured throughout the year, the next few campaigns should be exciting.

Batting S. P. Anthony* 432 at 48.00; B. L. Lane 376 at 47.00; S. W. Billings 579 at 44.53; T. H. Billings 350 at 26.92; C. E. Stewart 332 at 25.53; L. R. Anthony 154 at 22.00.

Bowling S. J. Boothby 15 at 16.40; S. P. Anthony 16 at 26.06; B. R. Carter 11 at 27.90; L. R. Anthony 11 at 30.00; B. L. Lane 15 at 30.06.

Hampton School

P10 W8 L2 A5

Master i/c D. E. Peel   **Coach** A. M. Banerjee

An extremely productive season, with all Saturday matches won and a first-ever victory against Harrow the highlight. Ian Prowse was a high-class captain and opening batsman, and Zafar Ansari's left-arm spin was the match-winner on several occasions.

Batting I. R. Prowse* 468 at 52.00; Z. S. Ansari 265 at 44.16; N. T. Prowse 282 at 40.28.

Bowling Z. S. Ansari 23 at 9.95; B. Chohan 14 at 15.21; I. R. Prowse 12 at 15.58.

Harrow School

P16 W6 L8 D2

Master i/c S. J. Halliday   **Coach** S. A. Jones

After losing nine players from 2008, Harrow were rebuilding. Douglas Pratt carried an attack that included four spinners, while Tom Pearson-Jones was a quality batsman. High spots were an excellent performance at Lord's against Eton and last-ball wins versus MCC and Bedford.

Batting T. W. Pearson-Jones 452 at 45.20; Y. M. Sert 366 at 33.27; A. C. Spencer 292 at 32.44; A. C. Smith 377 at 25.13; C. D. Berrill 315 at 21.00; H. C. J. Cousens 265 at 20.38; T. S. A. Tennant* 277 at 19.78; C. J. Baird 254 at 19.53.

Bowling D. T. P. Pratt 27 at 18.81; T. W. Pearson-Jones 13 at 19.84; A. C. Smith 23 at 24.78; Y. M. Sert 15 at 36.86.

The Harvey Grammar School

P17 W7 L8 D2 A2

Master i/c N. Bristow   **Coach** P. M. Castle

The squad comprised a good mix of youth and experience and played some enterprising cricket. The climax was a first-ever victory over MCC when, with real purpose, the team chased a total of 220 to win by six wickets.

Batting J. A. Keeler 326 at 40.75; T. D. Payne 543 at 33.93; B. A. Tosland 157 at 26.16; J. M. Hemphrey 299 at 23.00; D. M. Lodge 365 at 22.81.

Bowling N. S. Inglestone 21 at 14.47; J. M. Hemphrey 22 at 15.59; D. M. Lodge 17 at 18.29; J. A. Metcalfe* 11 at 23.90.

Highgate School

P17 W7 L8 D2

Master i/c A. G. Tapp   **Coach** S. Patel

The team won the Middlesex Under-19 cup. Captain and Middlesex player Will Nicoll ended his school career having taken 100 wickets and scored over 1,000 runs. Under-14 Middlesex player Charlie Yorke-Starkey showed great promise in his five matches.

Batting W. J. R. Nicoll* 576 at 38.40; S. C. Little 294 at 18.37; A. P. Thomas 194 at 13.85; L. E. B. Masefield 186 at 13.28.

Bowling L. E. B. Masefield 29 at 14.20; W. J. R. Nicoll 32 at 16.84; R. A. Blackshaw 13 at 22.84; J. L. Harris 10 at 23.50; A. P. Thomas 14 at 25.35.

Hurstpierpoint College

P21 W11 L9 D1

Master i/c G. J. Haines   **Coach** N. J. K. Creed

An excellent season for Hurstpierpoint, rapidly regaining their reputation for top-flight cricket. Alex Pearce's 666 runs included a century. Josiah Menzies and Jack Parsons were the mainstays of the bowling.

Batting R. J. Noble 201 at 50.25; A. N. Pearce 666 at 47.57; J. C. Stone 314 at 31.40; J. J. Levene 347 at 23.13; J. S. Thompson 410 at 22.77; J. Parsons 193 at 19.30.

Bowling J. W. Menzies 21 at 14.80; J. T. Wright 17 at 21.58; R. J. Noble 19 at 23.05; J. Parsons 21 at 25.23; J. J. Levene 11 at 34.27.

Hymers College

P8 W3 L1 D4 A2

Master i/c G. Tipping

An agreeable season with good all-round performances from all players. Neeladri Dutta, the captain, showed maturity and good tactical awareness. A special moment for Calum Robertson was his 133 against Scarborough College.

Batting G. W. Lound 305 at 43.57; C. S. F. Robertson 204 at 34.00.

Bowling N. M. Dutta* 16 at 13.62; U. bin Mansoor 11 at 19.63.

Ipswich School

Master i/c A. K. Golding

P15 W6 L4 D5
Coach R. E. East

The team batted well to secure six wins. The run-scoring was dominated by Archie Gravell who hit six centuries, and 13 in his first-team career. Ashwin Thurairaj, who returns for 2010, scored two hundreds. Harry Cook bowled with good pace for a Year 11.

Batting A. D. P. Gravell* 910 at 82.72; A. Thurairaj 558 at 46.50; J. B. G. Crame 362 at 36.20; S. B. J. Ward 394 at 26.26; H. W. M. Gravell 218 at 24.22; T. C. Sinclair 150 at 21.42.

Bowling H. J. Cook 17 at 19.76; L. J. Catlow 26 at 21.65; M. A. Heal-Cohen 14 at 24.71.

John Lyon School

Master i/c I. R. Parker

P18 W5 L10 D3
Coach C. T. Peploe

After a very disappointing start the boys rallied, winning four and drawing two of their last seven games. High points included chasing 241 at Reading Blue Coat School and Hassaan Mohamed's 101 versus MCC.

Batting H. H. Mohamed 443 at 31.64; A. K. Patel 486 at 30.37; S. Dhami 275 at 27.50; F. G. Grist 243 at 22.09; K. Patel* 226 at 17.38; T. Obeysekera 267 at 16.68.

Bowling D. Barchha 11 at 21.81; A. I. DeAlwis 10 at 22.80; A. C. Sloan 19 at 23.47; B. M. Makwana 19 at 26.47; A. K. Patel 10 at 27.00.

The Judd School

Master i/c D. W. Joseph

P16 W11 L4 D1

Sam Spink led the side adroitly in what proved to be a very successful season. Many of the team return for 2010, including leading all-rounder Michael Thompson and spinner Will Needham.

Batting C. M. Williams 190 at 38.00; S. P. Spink* 220 at 31.42; M. R. Thompson 313 at 28.45; T. D. Williams 249 at 22.63; T. J. Dowding 154 at 17.11.

Bowling W. E. Needham 21 at 11.76; W. Bryce-Borthwick 14 at 14.28; S. E. Treleaven 10 at 17.30; M. R. Thompson 14 at 18.42; R. J. Pulsford 12 at 22.16.

Kimbolton School

Master i/c T. Webley

P17 W9 L6 D2 A1
Coach P. S. Coverdale

Kimbolton enjoyed a highly successful season with impressive victories over Wellingborough, Highgate and the XL Club. The team progressed significantly over the term ending with a fantastic display at the Castle Festival. Skipper James Biddle ended his first-team career with 1,725 runs.

Batting J. R. Biddle* 737 at 67.00; G. F. Richards 323 at 35.88; G. M. Kooner 361 at 30.08; D. A. Wright 150 at 18.75.

Bowling G. M. Kooner 19 at 17.00; J. R. Biddle 13 at 17.69; R. G. Craze 10 at 19.20; W. J. Kirkpatrick 14 at 28.42.

King Edward VI College, Stourbridge

Master i/c M. L. Ryan

P8 W5 L2 D1 A3

There were some outstanding individual performances that do not shine through in total runs scored or wickets taken. Once again, the weather intervened, preventing a full programme of matches for a team of considerable all-round ability. Mark Ryan retires after 37 years in post.

Batting A. D. Biddle 300 at 60.00; M. Tromans 172 at 34.40; D. J. Cooper 232 at 33.14.

Bowling P. S. Grewal 12 at 13.75.

King Edward VI School, Southampton

Master i/c M. G. M. Mixer

P13 W10 L3
Coach C. R. Surry

Brothers Tom and Simon McCormick-Cox, along with Jamie Cook, played a big part in one of the most successful seasons in recent times. A five-for in the final game saw Duncan Jones surpass Ali Pennycuick as top wicket-taker.

Batting T. R. McCormick-Cox* 515 at 64.37; S. J. McCormick-Cox 444 at 49.33; J. E. Cook 420 at 42.00; J. E. D. Fox 243 at 27.00; J. S. Higginson 200 at 25.00; A. M. Wilkinson 230 at 23.00; S. M. Knott 185 at 20.55.

Bowling D. E. M. Jones 23 at 11.17; A. R. Pennycuick 18 at 16.55; C. P. R. Ratcliffe 16 at 17.93; M. W. Oliver 11 at 27.54.

King Edward VII and Queen Mary's School, Lytham

P14 L8 D6 A3

Master i/c J. A. Liggett   **Coach** A. Uz Zaman

The 2009 season proved difficult for a young team. Although there were no victories there was 100% commitment. Two outstanding players were the captain Lewis Williams and opener Kenji King. The climax of the season was Williams's 118 not out against Cheadle Hulme School, with 18 off the last over to bring the totals level.

Batting L. J. Williams* 420 at 32.30; K. S. O'Hanlon 172 at 19.11; K. D. R. King 224 at 16.00; P. D. Mackay 207 at 15.92.

Bowling K. D. R. King 16 at 21.25; L. J. Williams 16 at 25.00; W. Arshad 11 at 29.63.

King Edward's School, Bath

P11 W6 L3 D2

Master i/c P. J. McComish   **Coach** M. R. Howarth

KES remain unbeaten in the Bath section of the Western Schools Twenty20 competition over two seasons, losing only in the semi-finals to King's Taunton. The team also shared the Peak Sports League title. The top individual performance came from Sam Mount (Year 11) who in consecutive innings in June scored 116, 99 and 145 not out.

Batting S. A. Mount 467 at 58.37; W. H. Wales 335 at 37.22; J. W. Collier 308 at 34.22; A. J. M. McLaughlin 254 at 31.75; W. A. Robinson* 189 at 18.90.

Bowling O. W. Metcalfe 14 at 13.21; W. A. Robinson 12 at 29.33.

King Edward's School, Birmingham

P15 W7 L5 T1 D2 A3

Master i/c L. M. Roll   **Coach** D. Collins

A flurry of wins at the end of the season rounded off a very encouraging summer. The team batted around the talented Jack Cornick, who came within 60 runs of the school record.

Batting J. P. P. Cornick 894 at 99.33; H. K. Ismail 331 at 27.58; S. C. Gateley* 331 at 25.46; R. Maini 266 at 22.16.

Bowling E. R. Botha 19 at 14.78; H. K. Ismail 19 at 20.84; S. J. B. Hobbs 10 at 34.80.

King Henry VIII School

P14 W7 L6 T1 A1

Master i/c A. M. Parker

The 2009 season proved a very positive experience with boys from four age groups making up the squad. Three Under-15s, Steve Abbey, Sam Lucas and Josh DeSouza, coped well, and should bring considerable strength to the team in the coming seasons.

Batting S. R. Lucas 174 at 34.80; A. Fisher* 372 at 28.61; S. A. Ballinger 358 at 23.86; S. D. Abbey 153 at 21.85; D. A. S. Kaliray 178 at 14.83.

Bowling K. S. Punian 21 at 13.09; S. D. Sykes 22 at 15.00; D. A. S. Kaliray 15 at 15.40; S. A. Ballinger 14 at 15.92; J. DeSouza 13 at 18.15; A. S. Kalsi 11 at 29.81.

King's College, Taunton

P17 W15 L1 D1

Master i/c A. Jones   **Coach** P. D. Lewis

A very talented and effective side remained unbeaten in 50-overs matches, and were deserved champions of the Western Schools Twenty20. Captain Jos Buttler was superb, with Craig Meschede, Nick Evans, Alex Barrow, Miles Lenygon and Nathan Smith all making significant contributions.

Batting C. A. J. Meschede 608 at 67.55; M. Lenygon 671 at 67.10; J. C. Buttler* 554 at 61.55; N. P. Evans 637 at 53.08; A. W. R. Barrow 446 at 49.55; T. Barrett 168 at 33.60; E. H. Kean 190 at 31.66.

Bowling C. A. J. Meschede 25 at 14.80; N. A. Smith 30 at 15.00; M. Lenygon 26 at 15.07; C. A. J. Morris 14 at 16.71; T. Barrett 19 at 23.47; A. W. R. Barrow 15 at 24.06.

King's College School, Wimbledon

P13 W6 L6 D1 A1

Master i/c T. P. Howland   **Coach** G. P. Butcher

A very agreeable term of cricket, with Sam Holland and Tim Rawlinson demonstrating the value of good spinners.

Batting H. A. M. Palengat 307 at 27.90; D. C. A. Newton* 191 at 27.28; M. E. S. Rawlinson 150 at 25.00; T. C. Rawlinson 328 at 23.42; E. C. Goldsmith 270 at 22.50; H. O. Jones 197 at 19.70; A. Thiruchandran 155 at 17.22.

Bowling S. J. Holland 27 at 13.81; T. C. Rawlinson 21 at 17.85; M. A. Sheikh 10 at 26.50.

Jack Cornick came within a squeak of averaging 100 for King Edward's, Birmingham. Slow left-armer James Lomas, of King's, Macclesfield, grabbed 43 wickets and captained shrewdly.

The King's School, Canterbury
P13 W10 L2 D1 A1

Master i/c R. C. White   **Coach** A. G. E. Ealham

Five centuries were scored by four different players; on three other occasions matches finished with players unbeaten in the nineties. The strong bowling attack was backed up by excellent catching close to the wicket. Patrick Mitchell, the captain, set a fine example with bat and ball.

Batting M. N. Healy 528 at 66.00; C. A. R. MacLeod 293 at 58.60; J. S. Masters 293 at 41.85; L. S. Kock 193 at 38.60; P. D. B. Mitchell* 311 at 31.10; W. D. Chilcott 176 at 22.00.

Bowling O. E. Robinson 10 at 8.90; W. D. Chilcott 23 at 14.69; K. Premnath 22 at 15.81; L. M. Anglin 10 at 15.90; P. D. B. Mitchell 15 at 21.66; T. J. Dixey 11 at 23.09.

The King's School, Chester
P19 W8 L9 D2 A2

Masters i/c S. Neal/T. R. Hughes   **Coaches** N. R. Walker/E. D. I. L. de Silva

Two undefeated centuries secured important wins. Glenn Coppack's 100 helped achieve a thrilling last-over success against MCC, and Oliver Thompson's 109 set up victory over Birkenhead. With most of this talented side returning, prospects for 2010 are sound.

Batting M. J. Torr 441 at 33.92; G. M. Coppack 507 at 29.82; O. E. J. Thompson 399 at 28.50; A. J. Dunbavand 309 at 25.75; H. F. J. Peel 248 at 20.66; A. W. Leech* 185 at 18.50; J. S. Benson 222 at 14.80.

Bowling J. L. A. F. Oldman 19 at 11.68; M. J. Torr 23 at 19.26; A. W. Leech 13 at 25.30; J. S. Benson 15 at 26.66; A. A. Thomas 22 at 27.00; O. E. J. Thompson 15 at 39.00.

The King's School, Ely
P11 W2 L9

Master i/c K. G. Shaw   **Coach** G. R. Cowdrey

A difficult year of transition for the first team, with their only wins coming against the Cowdrey XI and the Enzymes. Nicholas Seaman captained the side and won the batting award, while Freddy Steele led the bowling and fielding with skill and determination.

Batting F. A. Steele 237 at 23.70; N. H. P. Seaman* 179 at 19.88; S. A. Montague-Fuller 153 at 17.00; S. R. Frost 157 at 15.70.

Bowling F. A. Steele 15 at 16.33; L. C. T. Pratten 11 at 21.09; T. C. G. Sweeney 10 at 21.60; N. H. P. Seaman 10 at 27.60.

The King's School in Macclesfield   P21 W8 L6 T1 D2 A4
Master i/c S. Moores
Jimmy Lomas, who astutely guided a very young side, was the most successful bowler, with 43
wickets. Alex Thomson and Andrew Hodgson (both in Year 10) performed well with the bat.
Batting A. T. Thomson 419 at 32.23; A. J. Hodgson 330 at 30.00; J. O. Stanley 296 at 29.60; J. H.
Lomas* 313 at 26.08; T. S. Foreman 197 at 17.90; B. J. Marsden 165 at 13.75.
Bowling J. H. Lomas 43 at 12.46; J. Marsden 19 at 15.68; A. J. Hodgson 10 at 16.40; J. O. Stanley
12 at 16.50; S. J. T. Stockwin 16 at 21.68; T. S. Foreman 10 at 25.80.

King's School, Rochester   P12 W4 L7 D1 A1
Master i/c W. E. Smith   **Coach** C. H. Page
This was an indifferent year, but some sound cricket was played and, it is hoped, many lessons
learned. Chetan Belliappa completed his fifth year in the first team with ten more wickets and some
outstanding batting. This remains a young side with much potential.
Batting C. Belliappa 433 at 39.36; A. Poddar 229 at 28.62; H. F. J. Ashdown* 306 at 27.81.
Bowling J. F. W. Kemsley 12 at 14.66; D. A. W. Ashdown 14 at 17.42; C. Belliappa 10 at 24.80;
H. F. J. Ashdown 13 at 28.00.

The King's School, Tynemouth   P9 W2 L5 D2
Masters i/c W. Ryan/P. J. Nicholson
The high point of the summer was a successful two-week tour to Barbados in July. Martin Fearon,
the captain, was the outstanding player in a promising team. He was selected for Durham Second XI
and was a member of their Academy.
Batting R. M. Fearon* 193 at 38.60.
Bowling R. M. Fearon 11 at 13.45.

King's School, Worcester   P21 W10 L7 D4 A1
Master i/c D. P. Iddon   **Coach** A. A. D. Gillgrass
Impressive bowling from Tom Bird and Sean Robinson often recovered a situation caused by brittle
middle-order batting. Liam Gwynne gave top-class all-round support with 917 runs and 26 wickets.
Batting L. Gwynne* 917 at 50.94; O. G. Meadows 426 at 22.42; J. M. Ellis 288 at 22.15; H. W.
Iddon 151 at 21.57; S. Harris 280 at 18.66; H. H. Patel 165 at 18.33; T. M. Bird 192 at 14.76.
Bowling T. M. Bird 32 at 17.06; S. A. Robinson 27 at 17.25; O. J. Kitching 15 at 17.33; L. Gwynne
26 at 19.00; M. A. Marskell 18 at 28.00.

Kingston Grammar School   P11 W3 L2 D6 A1
Master i/c J. E. K. Schofield
It was a solid season for a team with several Year 11s in the ranks. It proved an important and
difficult learning curve for many, especially against our four most powerful opponents. Three draws
and only one defeat bodes well for the future.
Batting T. R. A. Huxford* 280 at 40.00.
Bowling B. M. D. Hunter 16 at 14.12; O. T. Park 14 at 15.57.

Kingswood School   P12 W6 L5 D1
Master i/c G. D. Opie
The side was captained positively by Alex Ockwell and did well to become joint winners of the Peak
Sports League. Euan Gordon enjoyed a fine season with the bat. Somerset's Harry Rouse, aged 15,
showed his all-round class.
Batting E. Gordon 521 at 52.10; A. A. Ockwell* 280 at 31.11; H. P. Rouse 356 at 29.66; N. G.
Prettejohn 241 at 24.10.
Bowling W. H. Samler 13 at 14.92; N. A. J. Gerrish 13 at 15.38; O. G. Canning 20 at 15.95; N. G.
Prettejohn 17 at 17.23; M. A. T. Ticehurst 11 at 23.36; H. P. Rouse 13 at 29.61.

Kirkham Grammar School   P11 W3 L8 A4
Master i/c M. A. Whalley   **Coach** N. S. Passenger
Kirkham's youthful squad competed well on a tough circuit and narrowly lost a number of matches,
most notably against Bury GS, Arnold and MCC. However, the side won the Rossall Twenty20
tournament. Adam Galley was the leading batsman, with Kieran Marmion heading the bowlers.
Batting A. Galley 261 at 43.50.
Bowling K. Marmion 12 at 15.33.

Lancaster Royal Grammar School

P14 W6 L2 D6 A3

Master i/c I. W. Ledward   **Coach** I. D. Whitehouse

A reasonably productive season for a young side; the highlight was rejoining the RGS Festival and finishing second. Run-scoring was dominated by Michael Wellings and Jamie Hirst, while Alex Metcalfe is maturing as an opening bat with a very useful line in leg-spin.

Batting M. A. Wellings 679 at 75.44; J. S. Hirst 318 at 45.42; B. N. Barrow* 273 at 30.33; A. R. Metcalfe 223 at 22.30; M. A. Walling 234 at 19.50.

Bowling G. C. Bagguley 10 at 12.30; C. E. Rossiter 11 at 13.45; A. R. Metcalfe 17 at 16.11.

Lancing College

P13 W8 L4 D1

Master i/c R. J. Davies   **Coach** C. M. Mole

Solid batting underpinned a successful season, especially Jamie Betts's contribution in his first year in the side. For the third year running, the bulk of the wickets were taken by leg-spinner John McLean, backed up by Will Dawson and Jack Bradshaw.

Batting A. J. Harvey 255 at 51.00; J. E. R. Betts 334 at 30.36; H. J. C. Longden 230 at 25.55; W. A. Dawson 211 at 23.44; G. R. T. Holman 213 at 21.30; S. Crosby 210 at 21.00; A. J. N. Edgell* 174 at 13.38.

Bowling W. A. Dawson 14 at 19.64; J. R. J. McLean 24 at 20.12; J. D. H. Bradshaw 10 at 38.50.

Latymer Upper School

P10 W3 L7 A1

Master i/c G. E. Cooper   **Coaches** T. Biddle/B. Taylor

With most of the key players from 2008 still in the side, expectations were high. But the season fizzled out with four defeats in cricket week. Earlier, the team had won three and lost three, with two games they should have won slipping away. Although there were some good individual performances, this set of players should have achieved more.

Batting D. A. White 334 at 33.40; J. Ponnusamy* 175 at 19.44; T. R. C. Skinner 152 at 19.00.

Bowling A. E. Manning 12 at 19.08; J. Fogarty 10 at 27.20.

The Grammar School at Leeds

P15 W3 L10 D2

Master i/c S. H. Dunn

Despite several heavy defeats on the tough northern HMC circuit, an inexperienced side began to gel and show real promise for 2010. The bowling of James Wainman and Amrit Bhogal were the mainstays of a solid attack, supported by Luke Johnson's off-spin and the medium-pace of Rishi Patel.

Batting J. Habergham 334 at 23.85; A. Windle* 266 at 17.73.

Bowling R. Patel 19 at 14.84; J. Wainman 23 at 15.95; A. Bhogal 24 at 18.70; L. Johnson 10 at 23.70.

Leicester Grammar School

P8 W3 L5

Master i/c L. Potter

The team thrived after a poor start against Trent College in the first fixture. Playing at the new school fields in Great Glen has improved standards, typified by the classy all-round skills of Ross Clarke. Since he and other developing youngsters are available, there is real excitement for next season.

Batting R. Clarke 238 at 39.66.

Bowling R. Clarke 10 at 19.10.

The Leys School

P11 W6 D5

Master i/c B. A. Barton   **Coach** J. D. R. Benson

This highly talented team remained undefeated throughout the regular season, as well as reaching the last eight of the independent schools' Twenty20 cup. Adam Webster was fundamental to this success, along with Nicolaas Viljoen, both in their fourth season in the side. James Latham was the stand-out performer in a group of promising Year 11s, and Andrew Laws represented Cambridgeshire during the summer.

Batting J. M. Latham 391 at 48.87; A. J. Webster* 366 at 36.60; N. J. Viljoen 241 at 34.42; A. Laws 183 at 30.50; M. T. Horsford 246 at 27.33; P. D. Miller 155 at 22.14.

Bowling N. J. Viljoen 19 at 16.05; A. J. Webster 13 at 16.84; A. Laws 12 at 26.00; G. J. H. Banfield 11 at 26.63.

Lord Wandsworth College

P11 W7 L4

Master i/c A. L. Eysele   **Coach** C. C. Hicks

A season that started with five consecutive wins should have been an excellent one. But form ebbed away. However, Tom Grimes was an outstanding captain, and Jamie Richards an invaluable all-rounder. Andrew House offers hope for the future.

Batting J. C. Richards 388 at 48.50; A. C. House 438 at 39.81; T. D. Grimes* 344 at 34.40; C. J. Arundel 216 at 24.00.

Bowling J. C. Richards 25 at 13.84; S. L. Taylor 11 at 23.27; T. M. Dixon 11 at 25.63.

Loughborough Grammar School

P14 W9 L4 D1

Master i/c H. T. Tunnicliffe   **Coach** M. I. Gidley

A gratifying season with nine wins from 14 games. Martin Weightman was outstanding, scoring four hundreds and topping the averages; he picked up vital wickets too. He was ably supported by batsmen Tom Foulds, John Orchiston and Tom Burton. The bowling was a collective effort with Burton the leading wicket-taker.

Batting M. W. Weightman 771 at 77.10; T. Foulds 471 at 47.10; J. D. Orchiston 307 at 38.37; T. R. H. Burton 293 at 36.62; C. F. Kindleysides 330 at 27.50; J. A. Williamson 203 at 25.37; J. W. Purvis 171 at 24.42.

Bowling S. A. Patel 11 at 19.00; A. J. Morris 12 at 23.08; T. R. H. Burton 16 at 24.12; T. Foulds 11 at 26.81; M. W. Weightman 12 at 27.41.

Magdalen College School

P18 W6 L10 D2

Master i/c R. G. Gilbert

A worrying lack of consistency with bat and ball left a feeling of disappointment. The only exception was David Bunn, who scored three hundreds in six innings. However, there was an opportunity to blood some younger players who should perform well in coming seasons.

Batting D. Bunn 320 at 53.33; J. A. Forrest* 265 at 29.44; G. L. Rendall 427 at 28.46; E. A. Shaw 266 at 19.00; H. F. Anderson-Elliott 266 at 17.73; O. L. Dolton 195 at 16.25.

Bowling D. Bunn 12 at 17.33; H. F. Anderson-Elliott 22 at 20.59; J. A. Forrest 22 at 21.95; I. A. Khan 19 at 26.31; H. L. Anderson-Elliott 13 at 30.61.

Malvern College

P18 W6 L7 T1 D4 A4

Master i/c T. P. Newman   **Coach** T. W. Roberts

This was not a vintage year for the College, winning just six games. Nevertheless, there were some fine performances, notably two hundreds by the captain, Jonty Hylands, and one from Odge Davey. Will Meredith bowled his left-arm spin beautifully, collecting 53 wickets at 14 each.

Batting J. Hylands* 669 at 39.35; O. J. Davey 574 at 35.87; S. P. Harwood 491 at 35.07; S. G. Coffey 214 at 26.75; C. W. F. Lacey 300 at 21.42; H. T. B. Sinclair 294 at 19.60; G. Lacey 172 at 13.23.

Bowling W. Meredith 53 at 14.62; H. T. B. Sinclair 16 at 19.37; O. R. Barnett 19 at 24.00; W. T. R. Jones 11 at 27.54; S. P. Harwood 17 at 32.41.

The Manchester Grammar School

P16 W8 T1 D7 A2

Master i/c D. A. Moss

An unbeaten season was illuminated by some very close matches, including a tie against Denstone and a last-ball, one-wicket win over QEGS Wakefield. Outstanding moments were the back-to-back victories against Shrewsbury and Sedbergh. Captain and top all-rounder Charles Reid was the key performer.

Batting C. T. Reid* 535 at 41.15; D. T. Brown 358 at 29.83; E. C. Bullock 401 at 28.64; A. T. Platts 407 at 27.13; S. Qasim 192 at 21.33; A. A. Sheikh 211 at 19.18.

Bowling C. T. Reid 31 at 16.22; D. T. Brown 23 at 16.56; M. R. Tully 18 at 17.11; J. J. Brierley 24 at 19.62; C. D. Wyche 15 at 20.80.

Marlborough College

P15 W7 L4 T1 D3 A2

Master i/c N. E. Briers   **Coach** R. M. Ratcliffe

There were impressive wins against Radley, Sherborne (twice), Portsmouth GS, Haileybury, Free Foresters and MCC. Uzair Qureshi scored 123 not out against Rugby in the two-day Colours Match, which ended in a draw. He is in the England Under-17 development squad and has played for Gloucestershire Seconds.

Batting U. A. Qureshi 846 at 105.75; H. A. C. Pike 567 at 43.61; A. L. de V. Kidwell 446 at 34.30; P. J. Malovany 295 at 29.50.
Bowling J. R. Lowe 17 at 17.00; T. G. B. Pascoe 19 at 23.94; A. L. M. Cary 23 at 28.21.

Merchant Taylors' School, Crosby   P14 W8 L4 D2
Master i/c Rev. D. A. Smith   **Coach** S. P. Sutcliffe
Satisfying wins came at home to Birkenhead, away at King's Chester, and in a close, low-scoring game at KEQMS Lytham. Honourable draws were fought out with King's Macclesfield and Stonyhurst. Laurence Armstrong finished as leading batsman and, other than Jordan Bell, no one took more wickets; James Morrissey proved a strong all-rounder.
Batting L. T. E. Armstrong* 351 at 31.90; R. E. Metcalf 209 at 26.12; A. P. D. Rigby 275 at 22.91; J. J. Morrissey 212 at 19.27; P. J. Reade 150 at 15.00.
Bowling J. G. Bell 22 at 13.90; L. T. E. Armstrong 18 at 17.33; S. J. Kennedy 10 at 20.30; J. R. Firth 10 at 23.10; J. J. Morrissey 17 at 23.47.

Merchant Taylors' School, Northwood   P12 W6 L2 D4
Master i/c A. J. Booth   **Coach** H. C. Latchman
This was a transitional season, with many players new to the team. Highlights were wins against MCC and St Paul's; the two defeats came in low-scoring run-chases. Ravi Patel twice took seven wickets and, against Westminster, Oli Wilkin scored 121 and grabbed eight for 14.
Batting W. M. Magie 411 at 51.37; O. Wilkin 498 at 49.80; R. H. Patel 226 at 28.25; R. R. Patel* 273 at 27.30.
Bowling R. H. Patel 32 at 9.81; O. Wilkin 26 at 12.26.

Merchiston Castle School   P13 W9 L1 T1 D2 A4
Master i/c C. W. Swan   **Coach** S. C. Gilmore
In nine matches against other schools, Merchiston won eight and lost one, making this a fine season. The Lothian Schools' Cup was won for the fifth time in eight years. Runs came at 5.8 per over, reflecting the positive nature of the batting.
Batting K. M. Smith 510 at 63.75; O. J. Hairs 665 at 60.45; D. D. D. Duff 285 at 57.00; P. A. Baker 330 at 30.00; P. Hewat 201 at 25.12.
Bowling R. Patel 12 at 18.08; P. A. Towers 13 at 20.46; P. A. Baker 13 at 20.53; A. Maxwell 11 at 24.18; K. M. Smith 16 at 24.81; O. J. Hairs 12 at 31.00.

Mill Hill School   P13 W7 L6
Master i/c I. J. F. Hutchinson
Another solid season in which the side, when at full strength, proved highly competitive. The prolific batsman Adam Rossington and all-rounder Fred Daeche-Marshall were the outstanding performers in a squad that blended youth and experience.
Batting A. M. Rossington 695 at 115.83; F. Daeche-Marshall* 230 at 46.00.
Bowling F. Daeche-Marshall 10 at 14.80; N. P. S. Hughes 20 at 16.00; M. G. E. Hughes 12 at 17.00.

Millfield School   P16 W8 L7 D1 A3
Master i/c R. M. Ellison   **Coaches** M. R. Davis/R. L. Cook
A batting and bowling rotation system was operated: each match was adapted to help develop players. Tough fixtures proved challenging, but success in the National Twenty20 competition compensated for defeats by Tonbridge and King's Taunton.
Batting S. Agarwal 622 at 51.83; R. L. Jenkins* 388 at 38.80; J. A. McKinnon 331 at 36.77; J. M. Lawrence 388 at 35.27; H. M. Thomas 174 at 34.80; J. Pinn 271 at 33.87; C. J. Haggett 293 at 26.63; T. P. Wheater 186 at 26.57; C. P. Ellison 224 at 22.40; D. J. Bell-Drummond 191 at 21.22.
Bowling D. J. Bell-Drummond 14 at 22.42; A. J. Norman 17 at 23.47; S. Agarwal 13 at 23.84; T. P. Wheater 13 at 26.76; C. J. Haggett 16 at 31.00; C. P. Ellison 10 at 38.90.

Monkton Combe School   P17 W7 L8 D2
Master i/c P. R. Wickens   **Coaches** M. B. Abington/N. D. Botton
Until the last three games, when the batting was brittle, the team played positive cricket and were joint champions of the Bath Schools League. Toby Davies scored heavily, as did Ed Vickers. Ben Stupples and Richard Madgwick proved valuable all-rounders.
Batting T. P. A. Davies* 659 at 65.90; E. J. Vickers 389 at 27.78; R. J. Madgwick 262 at 23.81; B. Stupples 277 at 17.31; M. J. Morley 212 at 13.25; H. Farley 155 at 11.07.

Bowling J. Adams 11 at 21.18; P. Du Boulay 20 at 23.05; T. P. A. Davies 16 at 23.06; B. Stupples 21 at 23.19; M. Paynter 16 at 24.93; R. J. Madgwick 18 at 29.50.

Monmouth School
P16 W13 L3 A3

Master i/c A. J. Jones   **Coach** G. I. Burgess

Monmouth had a very successful season. The captain Seb Warwick featured brilliantly with the bat, scoring four centuries. Four boys represented Wales Minor Counties during the season, and Oli James played for Glamorgan seconds.

Batting J. S. T. Denning 358 at 59.66; S. E. Warwick* 731 at 56.23; O. R. James 470 at 47.00; M. J. L. Scarr 543 at 38.78; M. Lovett 242 at 24.20; C. Lawler 327 at 23.35.

Bowling M. J. L. Scarr 30 at 13.53; J. S. T. Denning 29 at 14.03; O. R. James 19 at 14.36; M. Evans 17 at 19.11; M. Lovett 16 at 19.81.

Newcastle-under-Lyme School
P10 W5 L4 D1

Master i/c G. M. Breen   **Coach** A. Hill

The first team won half their matches, thanks largely to disciplined bowling and fielding. Although both Benjamin Wright and Stephen Shirley enjoyed excellent all-round seasons, others found form only towards the end. Against Denstone in May, after bowling 67 overs, the side were bundled out for 45, their lowest total.

Batting S. W. Shirley 199 at 33.16; B. D. J. Wright* 255 at 28.33; M. S. Cope 170 at 21.25.

Bowling B. D. J. Wright 21 at 11.52; S. W. Shirley 14 at 14.07; A. S. Jheeta 17 at 15.76; S. M. Cooper 10 at 25.10; P. Nalwaya 12 at 25.41.

Nottingham High School
P13 W5 L7 T1 A2

Master i/c S. A. J. Boswell   **Coach** I. Rose

Ben Storey captained a young and talented side extremely well. He led by example with the bat and scored his runs freely. Principal support came from vice-captain Alpesh Tosar in the middle order.

Batting B. I. Storey* 646 at 58.72; A. D. Tosar 261 at 32.62; S. J. Johnson 201 at 22.33; G. R. McCarthy 246 at 20.50; J. S. Godrich 212 at 19.27; P. Sidhu 151 at 15.10.

Bowling L. G. Robinson 16 at 20.37; A. D. Cobbett 12 at 22.25; S. J. Johnson 11 at 27.45.

Oakham School
P19 W2 L10 D7

Master i/c F. C. Hayes   **Coach** P. A. J. DeFreitas

At first glance a disastrous season, with ten defeats the most on record. But this was a year of intentional rebuilding with the next two or three seasons in mind. All the high performers were Years 10 and 11, and they should challenge past records.

Batting T. C. Fell 510 at 30.00; C. A. French 386 at 29.69; W. H. R. Edwards 544 at 28.63; A. T. A. Martin 307 at 27.90; G. Maybury 213 at 26.62; B. D. Jacobs-Farnsworth 290 at 19.33; J. A. D. McCormack 238 at 15.86.

Bowling A. T. A. Martin 12 at 19.08; C. A. French 30 at 22.26; T. C. Fell 16 at 24.81; G. Maybury 19 at 29.00; D. C. Selmes 10 at 29.30; J. C. Keywood 11 at 44.54.

The Oratory School
P18 W15 L1 T1 D1

Master i/c S. C. B. Tomlinson

Another outstanding season; the team remained unbeaten in 11.30 a.m. starts. There were many high points, including victories over Bradfield, Bedford Modern, Felsted and a tied match versus Warwickshire Under-17s. Strong individual performances came from the left-arm spinner Euan Brock and the ever-improving wicketkeeper Tom Huysinga.

Batting E. E. Brock* 530 at 44.16; T. J. Huysinga 260 at 28.88; T. Q. McGeer 244 at 22.18; J-C. T. Arnold 266 at 20.46; C. G. M. Whittaker 169 at 14.08; B. J. Mitchell 162 at 13.50.

Bowling E. E. Brock 46 at 8.97; T. Q. McGeer 18 at 14.27; H. O. Perryment 24 at 17.91.

Oundle School
P20 W13 L5 D2

Master i/c J. R. Wake   **Coach** van der Merwe Genis

Oundle achieved 13 victories, the fourth-highest total since 1877, and a 65% win ratio was the second-best since the Second World War. Outstanding contributions came from captain elect Rory Osmond and all-rounder Jack Oughtred; both boys, along with Harry Ramsden, were selected for ESCA v MCC Schools at Lord's.

Batting R. T. Osmond 884 at 63.14; J. Oughtred 472 at 39.33; J. G. T. Johansen 515 at 34.33; T. M. A. Bishop 353 at 25.21; H. D. Ramsden 297 at 17.47; G. H. Hodgkinson 270 at 16.87.

All action: captain and left-arm spinner Euan Brock fires in another delivery on course to 46 wickets at 8.97 for The Oratory School.

Bowling J. Oughtred 36 at 12.66; W. P. Street 22 at 22.00; H. D. Ramsden 30 at 22.76; A. J. C. Cossor 14 at 23.85; T. E. Spencer* 12 at 36.91.

The Perse School

Master i/c E. W. H. Wiseman   P11 W7 L1 D3
                                                             Coach D. C. Collard

The Perse had another excellent season, winning seven matches and losing just once, to a strong MCC side. Ben Creese top-scored with 613, including three centuries, while Alex Hooley and Peter Richer both averaged over 50.

Batting B. T. Creese 613 at 68.11; P. G. Richer 439 at 54.87; A. J. Hooley* 309 at 51.50; A. P. Stafford 260 at 43.33.
Bowling F. T. Clamp 17 at 21.94; A. J. Hooley 11 at 22.27; I. Baksh 10 at 24.40; H. D. Picton-Turbervill 10 at 29.50.

Plymouth College

Master i/c S. Vorster   P11 W4 L5 D2 A2
                                                             Coach J. R. Mears

A new cricket master and a new coach brought a greater intensity to performances. Although the win/loss record appears modest, significant progress was evident under the strong captaincy of Sam Cload.

Batting T. D. Watkins 399 at 79.80; G. Stephenson 281 at 70.25; J. D. Libby 390 at 65.00; J. Luffman 259 at 43.16; S. C. W. Cload* 164 at 23.42.
Bowling O. Mulberry 16 at 11.25; A. J. Hill 10 at 12.80.

Pocklington School   P16 W8 L6 D2
Master i/c D. Watton

A good season with eight wins and five very narrow defeats. Highlights were Chris Suddaby's 101 against Leeds GS and his seven for 88 versus Bradford GS.
Batting C. J. Suddaby 447 at 34.38; A. J. Clarke 343 at 26.38; W. D. Axup 221 at 24.55; R. J. Cawood 287 at 17.93; F. J. Deas 231 at 16.50; J. D. Green* 150 at 15.00; R. W. T. Moorhouse 238 at 14.87; H. G. Laverack 201 at 14.35.
Bowling A. J. Clarke 30 at 10.83; C. J. Suddaby 37 at 14.97; R. W. T. Moorhouse 15 at 15.33; W. A. Axup 14 at 18.64; P. D. Massie 14 at 18.78; J. D. Green 13 at 21.38.

Portsmouth Grammar School   P15 W9 L4 D2
Master i/c S. J. Curwood   **Coach** R. J. Maru

Robert Gibson was the stand-out individual with a batting average of 40, as well as taking 20 wickets. Other notable performers were opening bowler Cameron Prentice, also with 20 wickets, and Chris Stone, who contributed solidly at the top of the order.
Batting R. Gibson 282 at 40.28; C. Stone 235 at 39.16; A. Winfield 266 at 29.55; J. George 170 at 28.33; N. Hodgson* 217 at 24.11.
Bowling R. Gibson 20 at 15.05; C. Prentice 20 at 15.15; C. Harding 10 at 24.70; R. Tusler 11 at 31.18.

Prior Park College   P8 W3 L4 D1
Master i/c S. J. Capon   **Coach** M. D. Browning

There were a few outstanding team performances and some impressive victories, but consistency proved elusive. High points were the batting of Seth Tapsfield and the bowling of Edward Robinson. Eight of the team are available for 2010.
Batting B. S. Tapsfield 445 at 74.16; A. J. Barnes 250 at 41.66; H. A. Polson 161 at 32.20; E. J. M. Singleton 157 at 19.62.
Bowling E. G. Robinson 17 at 8.70; J. C. B. Harper 10 at 19.90.

Queen Elizabeth Grammar School, Wakefield   P9 W3 L4 D2 A3
Master i/c I. A. Wolfenden

Despite losing several fixtures to the weather, a young squad completed an encouraging season with victories over Leeds GS, Silcoates College and Bradford GS.
Batting T. Pickles 173 at 28.83; J. R. B. Sleightholme 229 at 25.44; S. P. Douglas 195 at 24.37.
Bowling R. J. Knowles 13 at 13.15; S. P. Douglas 11 at 18.63; J. R. B. Sleightholme 11 at 22.36.

Queen Elizabeth's Hospital   P11 W6 L4 D1 A3
Master i/c P. E. Joslin   **Coach** D. C. Forder

An enjoyable season in which Mike Willmott hit most runs and took most wickets. Jordan van Laun, the captain, could rely on a solid bowling attack with main contributions from Jo Barnsley, Alex Davis and 14-year-old Bobby Naeem.
Batting M. T. Willmott 319 at 53.16.
Bowling A. J. Davis 13 at 10.38; B. A. Naeem 10 at 10.80; J. W. Barnsley 15 at 10.86; M. T. Willmott 17 at 12.70.

Queen's College, Taunton   P18 W8 L7 D3
Master i/c A. S. Free   **Coach** D. R. Bates

An encouraging season for a youthful side excellently led by Joe Sibley. Jake Lintott was outstanding with both bat and ball; William Tanner and William Steward were other notable run-scorers.
Batting J. B. Lintott 726 at 45.37; W. E. Steward 515 at 34.33; W. M. Tanner 396 at 30.46; J. A. L. Sibley* 312 at 24.00; J. S. A. Kohler 269 at 17.93; G. H. Musgrave 192 at 12.80.
Bowling J. B. Lintott 40 at 12.35; E. K. Khodabandehloo 16 at 15.25.

Jake Lintott headed both averages for Queen's, Taunton, and turned out for Somerset seconds. The Royal Hospital's Jed Cawkwell set a new aggregate run record with 719.

Radley College

P18 W8 L8 D2

Master i/c J. R. W. Beasley   **Coach** A. R. Wagner

An exceedingly young side showed its inexperience but, ably led by Henry Mills through example and spirit, they managed an even record of wins and losses, and played with great heart.

Batting H. T. Mills* 548 at 36.53; N. R. T. Gubbins 363 at 36.30; A. G. Hearne 525 at 35.00; W. W. J. Marriott 338 at 26.00; J. M. Wynne-Griffith 353 at 25.21; H. A. Freyne 188 at 18.80; N. G. M. Ramsay 168 at 15.27.

Bowling A. D. W. Tinsley 27 at 12.37; W. W. J. Marriott 21 at 18.66; W. R. Langton 18 at 23.11; A. G. Hearne 15 at 25.26; N. G. M. Ramsay 21 at 25.52.

Ratcliffe College

P12 W4 L6 T1 D1 A3

Master i/c R. M. Hughes   **Coach** E. O. Woodcock

After a promising start, including three wins and a tie, Ratcliffe lost some momentum and focus after the exam break, winning only one more game. The captain Luke Welch provided leadership with the ball, while Tom Smith was leading run-scorer.

Batting T. R. Smith 346 at 57.66; M. K. Phillips 322 at 40.25; H. F. G. Spillane 304 at 27.63; J. H. Mason 157 at 22.42.

Bowling L. A. B. Welch* 19 at 14.57; M. Noss 11 at 19.09; J. S. Charnock 15 at 29.40.

Reed's School

P17 W4 L6 T1 D6 A2

Master i/c M. R. Dunn   **Coach** K. T. Medlycott

A promising side, led by Will Clapp, matured as the season developed and successfully chased big totals on a number of occasions. Simon Sweeney and Toby Tarrant formed a hostile opening attack; Alex Redmayne excelled as wicketkeeper-batsman.

Batting A. J. S. Redmayne 483 at 30.18; A. J. Robinson 281 at 28.10; T. D. Chalcraft 436 at 27.25; W. G. A. Clapp* 430 at 26.87; S. A. C. Sweeney 251 at 19.30.

Bowling P. N. Oldreive 19 at 22.63; S. A. C. Sweeney 14 at 24.14; W. G. A. Clapp 31 at 26.70; T. C. Tarrant 24 at 27.04.

Reigate Grammar School

P16 W11 L5 A1

Master i/c E. M. Wesson   **Coach** J. E. Benjamin

A season of considerable success, inspired by the crackerjack batting of Simon Rivers, included a fine run of eight wins. Guy Duhig marshalled the side ably, while Will Irving, Will Fry and Simon Hope were consistent throughout.

Batting S. G. Rivers 540 at 77.14; W. C. F. Fry 401 at 40.10; W. G. O. Irving 379 at 31.58; G. P. Duhig* 271 at 24.63; H. P. Elsey 236 at 23.60.
Bowling W. G. O. Irving 24 at 16.75; T. S. Chellis 18 at 17.38; T. G. Flack 14 at 20.07; S. J. Hope 14 at 21.07; S. G. Rivers 16 at 23.06; N. E. Gunning 12 at 31.66.

Repton School
P17 W12 L2 D3

Master i/c F. P. Watson
Coach H. B. Dytham

The depth of batting and bowling underpinned another fine season. Chris Murrall hit the only hundred, but eight others passed fifty. Joshua Moore and Matthew Sanderson offered a spin-bowling combination that turned many games.
Batting S. R. Graham 276 at 55.20; M. W. Sanderson 325 at 36.11; T. M. Cosford 340 at 34.00; C. G. Murrall 418 at 32.15; H. G. Siddique* 427 at 28.46; E. Ikin 323 at 26.91; L. Lacey 185 at 20.55.
Bowling J. J. Moore 37 at 14.72; M. W. Sanderson 26 at 17.07; A. Ahmed 13 at 20.30; L. Lacey 15 at 22.86; T. M. Cosford 12 at 23.50.

Rossall School
P11 W4 L5 D2 A2

Master i/c T. L. N. Root

A youthful eleven battled well all season. James Wilson performed admirably with the ball, and the emergence of 14-year-old Luke Williams provided great excitement. Twelve of the squad of 14 return next year.
Batting L. C. W. Williams 262 at 32.75; J. A. Morrison 191 at 21.22; M. C. Dryden 215 at 19.54; J. R. Wilson 198 at 18.00; C. J. Metcalfe 201 at 16.75; A. Alonso* 152 at 13.81.
Bowling J. R. Wilson 25 at 13.36; A. Hazarika 13 at 14.15; L. C. W. Williams 15 at 17.06; C. J. Metcalfe 10 at 38.30.

The Royal Grammar School, Guildford
P17 W7 L9 D1

Master i/c S. B. R. Shore
Coach M. A. Lynch

After a disappointing season with the bat, team spirits were raised by the retention of top spot at the RGS Festival, held at High Wycombe, with four straight wins. Here Nick Cooper's two centuries and a 90, together with a hundred from captain Ed Sutton, fulfilled our potential. The bowling was sound all summer.
Batting N. G. R. Cooper 580 at 38.66; C. D. Hughes 261 at 23.72; E. J. Sutton* 284 at 21.84; P. N. A. Bennett 208 at 20.80; A. D. Z. Brown 243 at 20.25; D. T. W. Vincent 167 at 18.55.
Bowling O. R. Markham 17 at 14.35; M. P. Dawe 18 at 15.50; H. G. Peters 15 at 16.46; G. J. P. Neal-Smith 17 at 22.47; O. J. Hickman 10 at 28.10.

The Royal Grammar School, Worcester
P20 W10 L9 D1 A2

Master i/c M. D. Wilkinson
Coach P. J. Newport

An inconsistent season included two excellent wins over King's Worcester, by two and 52 runs. Ollie Flower and Sam Roberts held the batting together, but only captain James Ganderton and Ali Pollock (Year 10) bowled with any dependability. Andrew Curtis shows all-round potential.
Batting S. L. Roberts 752 at 53.71; O. Flower 671 at 35.31; A. Pollock 341 at 28.41; O. J. Steele 338 at 26.00; A. S. N. Curtis 400 at 25.00; D. A. Hagger 323 at 24.84; T. J. P. Williams 182 at 16.54.
Bowling A. S. N. Curtis 27 at 18.22; J. M. J. Ganderton* 31 at 18.80; D. S. M. Keir 18 at 22.11; A. Pollock 25 at 22.52; J. A. Watkins 19 at 26.47; W. Short 12 at 52.08.

Royal Hospital School
P15 W10 L2 D3 A1

Master i/c T. D. Topley
Coach D. W. Hawkley

Jed Cawkwell provided a record number of runs in a highly successful and enjoyable season, resulting in ten fine victories. Matt Drury and Freddie Seccombe also scored centuries. The youthful Reece Topley and skipper Cawkwell led an aggressive bowling attack which frequently paved the way for spinner Seccombe to polish off the tail.
Batting J. L. O. Cawkwell* 719 at 59.91; M. G. Drury 470 at 39.16; F. A. Seccombe 326 at 29.63.
Bowling J. L. O. Cawkwell 24 at 11.08; F. A. Seccombe 28 at 11.25; R. J. W. Topley 23 at 11.56; J. W. Pile 13 at 19.30.

Rugby School
P14 W5 L5 D4

Master i/c M. J. Semmence
Coach G. B. Brent

Following a slow start the team finished the season strongly. A tour of India is planned for December; nine of the squad return for 2010.

Batting J. L. Moxham* 460 at 35.38; T. W. Dowdeswell 155 at 31.00; G. R. Mackenzie 334 at 25.69; W. L. Weaving 151 at 25.16; C. L. Wedgwood 299 at 24.91; C. T. Cutter 262 at 23.81.
Bowling J. M. Barker 18 at 17.27; T. H. Clarke 18 at 19.83; C. T. Cutter 13 at 28.84; J. B. Kings 12 at 35.00.

Rydal Penrhos
P10 W1 L8 D1

Master i/c M. T. Leach

Jack Coates, the captain, led the team with confidence and involved several younger players to good effect. It is hoped this will see results improve. Joe Parry, the wicketkeeper, again performed very competently in his final year.

Batting J. Coates* 233 at 29.12.
Bowling No one took ten wickets. The leading bowler was D. J. M. Parry who took eight at 29.25.

Ryde School with Upper Chine
P13 W10 L3

Master i/c C. Sutton

Ryde School experienced one of their most successful seasons for decades, with a win ratio of 76.92%. There were some outstanding individual performances and, with only one player leaving, 2010 looks very exciting.

Batting C. J. Mitchell 512 at 73.14; D. A. Gordon* 405 at 45.00; J. S. Cutting 396 at 44.00; T. A. Jackson 158 at 31.60; C. G. Grant 154 at 17.11.
Bowling T. A. Jackson 21 at 16.19; D. A. Gordon 15 at 18.26; B. R. McEwen 11 at 21.72.

St Albans School
P20 W14 L4 D2 A1

Master i/c C. C. Hudson
Coach M. C. Ilott

Over two seasons, Jack Reynolds captained the side to 27 victories, a school record. Only Bancroft's have proved a thorn in his side. Twenty20 games constituted 40% of matches, including one against MCC.

Batting C. K. Dobson 534 at 38.14; H. J. J. Stairmand 192 at 21.33; J. S. Reynolds* 280 at 20.00; D. A. C. Jayawardena 212 at 17.66; R. D. Leather 258 at 16.12; A. Rajah 207 at 15.92; J. E. B. Scott 153 at 15.30; A. C. A. Reed 184 at 14.15.
Bowling J. Leather 28 at 13.57; V. A. G. Stairmand 30 at 14.93; H. J. J. Stairmand 19 at 15.26; R. A. F. Grant 14 at 18.35; J. S. Reynolds 17 at 21.17; C. K. Dobson 16 at 22.06.

St Edmund's School, Canterbury
P11 W8 L3 A3

Master i/c A. R. Jones

A frustrating season, impeded by a shorter term and longer examination period, allied to cancellations for poor weather and swine flu, allowed just 11 matches. However, the side built effectively on last year's foundations, winning eight fixtures, and secured the County Cup. The outstanding performer was Ben Kemp who, in Year 11, captured 28 wickets at 8.10. With several good youngsters coming through, we expect another strong season in 2010.

Batting B. J. Pape 414 at 41.40; B. W. T. Easter* 255 at 36.42; H. J. Callaway 210 at 30.00; R. J. Stone 163 at 20.37.
Bowling B. W. Kemp 28 at 8.10; B. W. T. Easter 12 at 14.91; B. J. Clarke 15 at 15.73; A. J. Higson 11 at 18.63.

St Edward's School, Oxford
P22 W10 L4 D8 A2

Master i/c R. W. J. Howitt
Coach R. E. Jones

Ten victories made it one of the school's most successful seasons. It was very much a team effort: Jay Webster captained the side superbly and scored 650 runs, Giles Blanchard was the top run-scorer with 803, and leg-spinner Daryl Johnson bowled fantastically well to snare 47 victims. Olly Hargreaves and Matthew Holyland proved excellent all-rounders.

Batting G. W. Blanchard 803 at 53.53; J. P. Webster* 650 at 34.21; M. J. Holyland 503 at 33.53; O. P. Hargreaves 453 at 23.84; J. L. Joyce 205 at 22.77; A. D. Smith 361 at 20.05; H. A. Coles 301 at 17.70; J. R. Fraser 150 at 12.50.
Bowling J. R. Fraser 18 at 17.38; M. J. Holyland 38 at 18.65; D. E. R. Johnson 47 at 21.06; J. P. Webster 18 at 27.55; O. P. Hargreaves 21 at 28.85.

St George's College, Weybridge
P19 W15 L4

Master i/c M. T. Harrison   Coach J. R. P. Heath

Eight consecutive wins, not a game lost to rain, and a very stable side set up a record-breaking season. Only 12 players, outstandingly led by Christoph Kent, were used in 19 games. The averages reflect a genuine team effort. All but two players return next season.

Batting R. G. F. Snowball 308 at 34.22; S. W. Gorvin 477 at 29.81; J. D. McKinlay 427 at 25.11; A. M. Stanley 275 at 25.00; S. M. Cox 331 at 23.64; T. P. Cross 349 at 20.52; W. R. Grant 238 at 18.30.

Bowling A. M. Stanley 26 at 11.84; B. G. C. Scott 30 at 13.73; A. K. Colville 24 at 16.16; N. W. Kent 28 at 18.42; R. G. F. Snowball 12 at 19.16; C. W. Kent* 24 at 21.45.

St John's School, Leatherhead
P17 W9 L8

Master i/c G. I. Macmillan   Coach I. Trott

Overall, with a strong team ethic and powerful bowling, a youthful side had a gratifying season. The outstanding performer was all-rounder Adam Dyson, while Joshua Howe bowled exceptional leg-spin to grab 26 wickets.

Batting A. A. Dyson 708 at 47.20; J. A. Pickering 163 at 40.75; S. P. Burgess* 328 at 25.23.

Bowling J. W. Howe 26 at 10.73; E. P. C. Davies 11 at 17.00; A. A. Dyson 25 at 17.12; T. L. J. Davies 11 at 19.90; W. J. Lander 19 at 20.31; O. J. Glanville 10 at 29.20.

St Lawrence College
P7 W1 L5 D1 A4

Master i/c T. Moulton

This was an inexperienced squad with eight of the side returning in 2010. Ryan Jones prospered as an attacking opening batsman and was well supported by Robbie Newbery. Otherwise, the batting was brittle. Danny Whittle, Will Bowra and Tom Eccles were promising bowlers.

Batting R. A. Jones 202 at 28.85; R. Newbery 151 at 25.16.

Bowling No one took ten wickets. The leading bowler was D. Whittle*, who took six at 30.83.

St Paul's School
P15 W5 L8 D2

Master i/c M. G. Howat   Coach A. G. J. Fraser

After an inconsistent start, St Paul's finished strongly, winning four of their last five games. The captain, Oliver Ratnatunga, completed four years in the first team.

Batting S. J. Cato 410 at 37.27; O. M. Ratnatunga* 354 at 35.40; H. W. Browne 263 at 29.22; T. A. Crewe 214 at 21.40; J. N. Harris 228 at 19.00; A. J. Foster 156 at 17.33.

Bowling J. I. Bomford 15 at 15.26; O. M. Ratnatunga 18 at 17.16; S. J. Cato 14 at 20.42; G. L. Barr-Smith 11 at 28.00; H. W. Browne 11 at 32.90.

St Peter's School, York
P15 W6 L2 D7 A1

Master i/c D. Kirby

St Peter's had a fine season, remaining unbeaten in inter-school matches. The captain, Paul Steadman, made an impressive all-round contribution. The batting had depth, and spin bowlers Harry Booth and Will Peet were effective.

Batting P. C. Steadman* 709 at 59.08; W. Stephen 221 at 27.62; J. J. Halstead 306 at 25.50; J. North 173 at 24.71; H. T. R. Booth 283 at 21.76; J. W. B. Hepworth 250 at 20.83; O. C. Burdass 230 at 16.42.

Bowling P. C. Steadman 19 at 14.89; H. T. R. Booth 32 at 20.18; D. T. Snook 19 at 29.26; W. T. Peet 16 at 30.75.

Sedbergh School
P15 W12 L3 A4

Master i/c C. P. Mahon   Coach D. J. Fallows

An experienced side enjoyed a satisfying season, with notable wins against Durham Academy, Lancaster RGS and Oakham. The side was effectively guided by Jordan Clark, who became the first Sedberghian to score 3,000 first-team runs. The season finished with a successful tour to the Caribbean where the highlight was victory against Trinidad and Tobago Under-17 in the Sir Garfield Sobers' Festival.

Batting J. Clark* 625 at 69.44; D. W. Bell 584 at 48.66; W. Chapples 321 at 40.12; H. E. Wilson 163 at 27.16; T. A. Benn 181 at 20.11; T. P. Forster 192 at 19.20.

Bowling J. Harrison 24 at 13.62; J. Clark 26 at 17.11; S. D. Bell 17 at 21.17; J. J. McCluskie 14 at 24.42; W. Chapples 14 at 28.21.

Sevenoaks School
P19 W8 L11 A1
Master i/c C. J. Tavaré   **Coach** P. J. Hulston
The notable points of the season were a run of six straight wins before half-term, Max Thorpe's 597 runs in his first full season (including an exceptionally powerful 119 against City of London Freemen's) and Ed Woodhouse-Darry's 33 wickets with well-flighted leg-spin.
Batting M. C. Thorpe 597 at 35.11; K. M. Ramji 278 at 23.16; B. A. Richardson 286 at 22.00; A. P. Kirkpatrick* 212 at 21.20; D. W. Makepeace 200 at 16.66; C. C. Farrant 185 at 12.33.
Bowling B. A. Richardson 10 at 15.40; E. T. Woodhouse-Darry 33 at 15.45; T. G. Farrant 14 at 22.35; C. B. Carter Leno 11 at 25.36; J. Nanavati 12 at 29.83; C. C. Farrant 13 at 31.23; A. P. Kirkpatrick 10 at 33.70.

Sherborne School
P17 W10 L5 D2 A2
Master i/c R. W. Hill   **Coach** A. Willows
A splendid season for a young team, well captained by all-rounder Will Peatfield. Theo Cooke was the leading wicket-taker and South African Jimmy Crowson scored over 700 runs in all competitions. Theo Grainzevelles was voted young cricketer of the season.
Batting J. A. J. Crowson 426 at 35.50; W. A. Peatfield* 308 at 28.00; T. Grainzevelles 388 at 24.25; F. E. Taylor 173 at 21.62; T. S. C. Cooke 315 at 21.00; J. A. Hamshaw-Thomas 159 at 17.66; C. J. Peatfield 175 at 17.50; W. M. Smibert 162 at 16.20.
Bowling T. S. C. Cooke 27 at 18.44; T. Grainzevelles 12 at 19.83; J. A. Hamshaw-Thomas 17 at 24.29; W. J. G. Marks 17 at 28.23; W. A. Peatfield 15 at 31.93.

Shrewsbury School
P16 W13 L2 D1
Master i/c A. S. Barnard   **Coach** A. P. Pridgeon
Another vintage season. A very strong unit, lead by Joe Leach (Worcestershire Academy), lost only two matches all season. They won the Silk Trophy for only the second time, and lost to Millfield in the National Twenty20 semi-finals.
Batting J. Leach* 586 at 58.60; S. G. Leach 411 at 45.66; D. W. Holden 508 at 39.07; D. L. Lloyd 391 at 35.54; A. D. Blofield 290 at 26.36; B. Williams 287 at 26.09; T. J. Home 227 at 25.22.
Bowling H. R. C. Dawson 24 at 11.00; J. Leach 35 at 11.65; R. F. Griffiths 18 at 14.50; A. D. Blofield 22 at 15.22; T. E. Welti 15 at 17.00; D. L. Lloyd 12 at 20.16.

Silcoates School
P10 W3 L6 D1 A2
Master i/c G. M. Roberts   **Coach** E. R. Hudson
A pleasing season for a very hard-working and enthusiastic group of young cricketers. The high point came in the 21-run victory against Leeds GS, when Silcoates bowled and fielded superbly to defend a small total.
Batting A. R. Carter 193 at 24.12; Y. Patel* 174 at 21.75.
Bowling S. E. Wright 14 at 17.35; T. Duczenko 14 at 17.50.

Simon Langton Grammar School
P8 W3 L5 A2
Master i/c R. H. Green
A total of 24 different players represented the first team this season, mainly owing to exam clashes. Three consecutive wins brought the Kent Schools CA Under-19 League (East) title. In three defeats, the margin was six runs or fewer.
Batting J. M. Blower* 176 at 35.20.
Bowling J. M. C. Pearson 15 at 8.60.

Solihull School
P12 W6 L5 D1 A2
Master i/c C. H. Jones   **Coach** D. L. Hemp
Edward Sykes captained the team and Christopher Williamson assisted him as vice-captain. The most notable success was a first victory against MCC in 25 years. Several young players made impressive debuts, which bodes well.
Batting D. Harding 404 at 50.50; J. Lucas 257 at 25.70.
Bowling T. Haley 11 at 8.72.

Stamford School
P19 W11 L6 D2
Master i/c D. G. Colley   **Coach** E. J. Wilson
An excellent winning campaign, dominated by outstanding batting displays from Shaan Masood-Khan. His five centuries included a magnificent 202 at Gresham's, contributing to a record team score of 354 for three in 50 overs.

Batting S. Masood-Khan 1,237 at 103.08; J. Bolus 501 at 29.47; O. F. Lindley* 357 at 27.46; T. Williams 308 at 25.66; B. J. P. Mahlanga 334 at 22.26; T. P. Anders 158 at 15.80.
Bowling O. F. Lindley 27 at 15.59; V. K. Spurr 26 at 15.73; G. Hook 22 at 17.22; S. Masood-Khan 33 at 19.48.

Stockport Grammar School
P8 W3 L5

Masters i/c R. Young/R. Bowden
Coach D. J. Makinson

Early defeats were due to flimsy batting, but there was all-round improvement as the season progessed. Key contributors were James Needham, Matthew Barker, Johnny Marshall, Tom Isherwood, Josh Higginbotham-Jones, Rick Topham and Azeem Shahid.
Batting M. Barker 157 at 22.42.
Bowling J. Needham* 12 at 17.41.

Stowe School
P25 W7 L11 D7 A2

Master i/c J. A. Knott
Coach C. J. Townsend

Will Scholfield topped batting and bowling averages in his final year. John Gurney was awarded a place at the Leicestershire Academy. Three Year 9s played: Jake Olley, Harry Martin and Ben Duckett, who was invited to the Academy at Northamptonshire.
Batting W. S. Scholfield 518 at 39.84; J. A. Olley 180 at 25.71; C. E. K. Morris 331 at 20.68; W. H. Richardson 278 at 17.37; B. T. Sutton 366 at 16.63; M. C. Platts-Martin 364 at 16.54; O. J. Tett* 158 at 15.80; J. H. Gurney 201 at 13.40.
Bowling W. S. Scholfield 21 at 17.14; J. K. W. Sainsbury-Bow 15 at 19.80; J. H. Gurney 26 at 23.03; A. J. D. Blayney 10 at 24.80; O. J. Tett 20 at 29.70; C. E. K. Morris 12 at 30.58.

Strathallan School
P13 W6 L5 T1 D1 A2

Master i/c R. H. Fitzsimmons
Coach I. L. Philip

An up-and-down season in terms of results, but some players made major strides. Toby Culham was the heaviest scorer, including a superb 114 against MCC. Fourteen-year-old Nick Farrar came into his own as an all-rounder, bowling with genuine pace. Robbie Cachia, in his final year, was the leading wicket-taker.
Batting T. P. D. Culham 453 at 37.75; F. R. J. Coleman* 207 at 34.50; A. A. Whitelaw 253 at 25.30; C. D. R. Donald 240 at 24.00; N. A. G. Farrar 233 at 21.18; J. D. King 197 at 19.70.
Bowling R. F. Cachia 26 at 15.07; N. A. G. Farrar 16 at 16.62; T. P. D. Culham 15 at 19.33; J. D. King 11 at 22.09; D. J. P. O'Reilly 10 at 35.30.

Sutton Valence School
P16 W11 L4 T1

Masters i/c W. D. Buck/V. J. Wells
Coach V. J. Wells

A tally of 11 wins, allied to a good run in the National Twenty20 (defeated by Bradfield in the Plate Final), was a fitting return for this young, attacking side (only two players go in 2010). With four representatives in the Kent Under-18 set-up and one participating for Leeward Islands, five batsmen exceeded 300 runs – including three centuries from Chris Vernon – the best of which (135) helped chase down 275 in a tied game with Eton.
Batting H. A. Walsh 413 at 82.60; A. D. Neale 344 at 49.14; B. J. B. McMenemy 192 at 48.00; C. R. Vernon 632 at 42.13; T. J. Griffin* 390 at 35.45; B. A. Regan 324 at 32.40; M. N. Murray 260 at 23.63.
Bowling A. D. Neale 28 at 15.17; A. B. Carter 16 at 16.43; H. A. Walsh 13 at 25.46; T. J. Griffin 10 at 27.40.

Taunton School
P14 W10 L3 D1

Master i/c S. T. Hogg
Coach H. K. C. Todd

Expertly captained by quick bowling all-rounder Adam Dibble, an inexperienced side enjoyed a rewarding season. Luke Bess and Thomas Abell proved to be extremely reliable opening batsmen, with 15-year-old Abell recording three fine centuries. Dibble and William Gater were impressive with the new ball and formed the basis of a powerful, quick-scoring, middle order.
Batting T. B. Abell 710 at 59.16; W. H. Gater 276 at 34.50; A. J. Dibble* 344 at 34.40; L. F. Bess 411 at 34.25; N. E. Neubert 187 at 26.71.
Bowling M. O. Abell 17 at 8.58; A. J. Dibble 16 at 12.00; R. P. Glover 13 at 16.53; G. A. Cook 16 at 16.93; W. H. Gater 17 at 20.52.

Adam Dibble, who captained another powerful Taunton side, also shouldered all-rounder duties.
Influential leg-spinner Alex Fiskin snared 45 victims for Westminster, from only 126.5 overs.

Tiffin School
P15 W4 L5 D6

Master i/c M. J. Williams

This was a highly agreeable season with a whole string of closely fought matches. The first year of
the new 50/40 league, embracing a number of the Surrey schools, proved highly successful. Tiffin's
season was based on fine team performances and the excellence of its two all-rounders, Muhunthan
Harinath and Alistair Watkins.

Batting M. Harinath 359 at 32.63; A. G. Watkins 382 at 27.28; K. Gor 349 at 26.84; V. K.
Mallikaaratchi 270 at 22.50; B. Khan 303 at 21.64; M. Khan 203 at 18.45.

Bowling M. Harinath 40 at 13.90; A. G. Watkins 27 at 17.77; R. R. Street 10 at 24.80; A. Thapar 14
at 27.50.

Tonbridge School
P19 W13 L2 D4

Master i/c D. R. Walsh   **Coaches** A. R. Whittall/J. P. Arscott

This was a fantastic season for Tonbridge, winning the Cowdrey Cup, and beating Millfield in the
final match. Principal among the batsmen were Tom Elliott (who scored over 1,000 runs, making
him the third-highest scorer in the school's history) and Fabian Cowdrey, son of Christopher and
grandson of Colin. Cowdrey also spearheaded the bowling, taking 41 wickets. Hugo Snape was an
outstanding captain.

Batting F. K. Cowdrey 831 at 75.54; T. C. Elliott 1,091 at 64.17; J. J. Payne 539 at 35.93; T. J.
Spurling 272 at 30.22; C. F. Munton 262 at 29.11; C. J. A. Paget 256 at 28.44; H. D. M. Snape* 243
at 22.09; T. P. W. Harvey 191 at 17.36; J. S. Baillie 176 at 16.00.

Bowling F. K. Cowdrey 41 at 15.95; C. J. A. Paget 10 at 16.70; T. P. W. Harvey 27 at 17.37;
A. Patel 27 at 21.66; H. D. M. Snape 14 at 25.57; T. C. Elliott 17 at 28.94.

Truro School
P9 W3 L6

Master i/c A. D. Lawrence

Batting C. Purchase 227 at 45.40; M. Manuell* 280 at 35.00.

Bowling M. Manuell 10 at 12.90.

University College School
P14 W5 L7 D2

Master i/c S. M. Bloomfield   **Coach** W. G. Jones

Adam Sargent, the captain, led by example with forthright batting and fostered a healthy team spirit.
This, together with a varied bowling attack, suitable for all conditions, saw a young side achieve five
notable victories over Berkhamsted, Highgate, St. Benedict's, KEQMS Lytham and Birkenhead.

Batting W. A. C. Sargent* 607 at 67.44; B. N. Brodie 280 at 23.33; T. B. Bradshaw 158 at 19.75.

Bowling G. S. Bennetts 11 at 17.63; O. G. Chapman 17 at 21.47; J. S. Mills 22 at 23.00; E. J. Lowe
14 at 26.35.

Uppingham School

P15 W5 L4 D6

Master i/c C. P. Simmons

Coach T. R. Ward

Uppingham had solid success with a predominantly Under-16 team. Fifteen-year-old Shiv Thakor continued to progress, hitting centuries against Bedford and Stamford.

Batting S. J. Thakor 668 at 47.71; H. C. D. Hughes 274 at 22.83; T. W. Hamilton 292 at 22.46; G. T. G. Weller 173 at 19.22; T. C. Moxon 162 at 18.00.

Bowling A. W. S. Salloway 20 at 22.50; P. E. D. Morrissey 21 at 24.52; F. G. W. Lewis 13 at 28.61; S. J. Thakor 14 at 35.21; G. T. G. Weller 10 at 42.10.

Victoria College, Jersey

P15 W4 L6 D5

Master i/c M. D. Smith

Coach C. E. Minty

Eight Under-16s in the team gained valuable experience for the future. Captain Sam de la Haye guided the team effectively and scored over 800 runs, including two centuries. He was ably assisted by younger brother Tim, who scored his first hundred, against King's Worcester. Daniel McAviney also hit a maiden hundred, against the President's XI. Corne Bodenstein was the top wicket-taker with 21, including three in a win over Elizabeth College.

Batting S. J. de la Haye* 822 at 63.23; C. P. F. Bisson 258 at 43.00; T. N. de la Haye 330 at 33.00; R. N. Sinel 159 at 26.50; D. McAviney 236 at 26.22; J. R. Borg 306 at 20.40; C. J. Bodenstein 173 at 17.30.

Bowling C. J. Bodenstein 21 at 15.95; A. M. McGuire 16 at 21.43; S. Blackburn 14 at 22.85; A. X. Noel 14 at 23.28; T. N. de la Haye 16 at 30.62.

Warwick School

P17 W5 L10 D2

Master i/c G. A. Tedstone

Coach S. R. G. Francis

This was a development year for a youthful side who showed promise for the next two years. The captain, Joe Melly, played the major part, scoring the only century and taking six for 12, the only time anyone managed five wickets. Peter Walters bowled superbly, as did next year's captain Thomas Edwards.

Batting J. P. Melly* 476 at 31.73; L. W. Bywater 250 at 25.00; M. S. Gill 234 at 23.40; T. A. Williams 283 at 21.76; O. J. Lunel 216 at 21.60; B. J. Howard 150 at 21.42; E. H. F. Russ 255 at 21.25; J. G. J. Cumberland 264 at 16.50.

Bowling P. J. Walters 15 at 22.00; J. P. Melly 20 at 24.80; O. J. Lunel 13 at 27.15; T. O. J. Edwards 15 at 28.00; J. M. Atkins 17 at 29.82.

Wellingborough School

P13 W5 L5 D3

Master i/c S. M. Adams

Coach N. L. Knight

The results – as many wins as defeats – were as expected given the number of inexperienced players. Zak Harvey hit two hundreds and averaged of 58, but he could not always mask the lack of depth in the bowling.

Batting Z. D. Harvey* 643 at 58.45; J. W. Johnson 422 at 32.46; P. Patel 248 at 22.54; A. C. Waring 156 at 19.50; J. Collins 176 at 16.00.

Bowling A. Price 29 at 13.13; P. Patel 18 at 23.61; A. C. Waring 15 at 27.46; W. C. Knibbs 10 at 30.50.

Wellington College

P18 W9 L8 D1

Master i/c G. D. Franklin

The season finished on a high, winning the BOWS Festival at a sun-drenched Brighton. Mickey Barkett guided the side with maturity, and his twin, Alec, spearheaded the bowling. Promising all-rounders Tom Wood, Will Leith and Angus Boobbyer return next year.

Batting W. R. G. Leith 510 at 36.42; A. T. Boobbyer 454 at 32.42; M. W. A. Tulley 221 at 31.57; T. J. Wood 458 at 30.53; J. B. Rendell 453 at 30.20; M. Barkett* 310 at 20.66; A. Barkett 260 at 20.00; J. P. P. Brooks 217 at 18.08.

Bowling A. Barkett 40 at 16.15; A. T. Boobbyer 29 at 22.27; T. J. Wood 16 at 29.62; W. R. G. Leith 17 at 33.00.

Wellington School

P9 W3 L6 A2

Master i/c M. H. Richards

Coach J. M. Wyatt

Following a good winter training programme, the season, which promised much at the outset, proved a disappointment. However, with only two departures, the outlook is positive.

Batting M. C. M. Capaldi* 280 at 31.11; C. F. Davies 189 at 27.00; J. E. Brown 165 at 23.57.

Bowling L. R. Corbin-O'Grady 10 at 9.40; M. C. M. Capaldi 10 at 25.90.

Wells Cathedral School
P13 W5 L7 D1 A3

Master i/c R. J. Newman   **Coach** C. R. Keast

Although the batting lacked real consistency throughout the summer, strong leadership from Harry New and reliable seam bowling from Harry Keevil allowed the side to edge some very tense limited-overs games.

Batting D. C. Gray 279 at 23.25; H. P. New* 184 at 20.44; T. A. Farnon 192 at 17.45; H. G. Keevil 154 at 17.11; S. A. Moss 196 at 16.33; N. C. Jarman 159 at 14.45.

Bowling H. G. Keevil 12 at 16.75; T. A. Farnon 12 at 29.41.

West Buckland School
P13 W11 L2

Master i/c D. R. Ford   **Coach** M. T. Brimson

A young and talented side ended the school's most successful season by winning their last five matches. All the players contributed, but it was excellent batting from Tom Mitcham and Craig Overton that proved crucial.

Batting C. Overton 440 at 55.00; T. M. Mitcham 568 at 47.33; C. Wood 234 at 23.40; J. Overton 185 at 23.12.

Bowling W. H. Popplewell* 15 at 9.66; J. Popplewell 16 at 15.43; J. G. Bentley 16 at 19.06; R. F. L. Merchant 14 at 23.50; S. James 12 at 24.00.

Westminster School
P17 W12 L4 D1

Master i/c J. D. Kershen   **Coaches** J. R. Hall/P. N. Weekes

A record-breaking summer saw the team retain the London Schools' Under-19 Cup and win 12 games, unsurpassed in the school's history. All-rounders Jeremy Holt, Keval Patel and Alex Fisken were the main contributors, ably supported by Oliver Wood, Alex Stewart, Oliver Jones and wicketkeeper Harry McNeill Adams.

Batting J. D. Z. W. Holt 489 at 44.45; O. W. G. Wood 288 at 26.18; K. A. Patel* 323 at 24.84; H. G. McNeill Adams 294 at 22.61; A. C. Fisken 227 at 17.46.

Bowling A. C. Fisken 45 at 10.26; A. D. Stewart 19 at 14.26; J. D. Z. W. Holt 15 at 17.60; K. A. Patel 30 at 19.30; O. W. Jones 15 at 19.86.

Whitgift School
P9 W5 L3 D1 A1

Master i/c D. M. Ward   **Coach** N. M. Kendrick

Following some high-profile departures from the 2008 squad, an inexperienced Whitgift side managed notable wins against Brighton and Charterhouse. The all-round competitiveness of Elliot Daly and the excellent spin of Freddie van den Bergh galvanised the team into a strong unit. With ten of the side available next year, the outlook is encouraging.

Batting H. Ledger 215 at 43.00; E. F. Daly 296 at 42.28; T. C. J. Woodrow 205 at 34.16; M. J. Laidman 169 at 21.12.

Bowling F. O. E. van den Bergh 17 at 16.47; E. F. Daly 10 at 22.30.

Winchester College
P17 W15 L2 A2

Master i/c C. J. Good   **Coaches** B. L. Reed/P. Gover

A record-breaking season for the first team brought 15 wins from 17 matches (including all home games), as well as the John Harvey Cup. There were top-quality performances from Ben Stevens, Christian Portz and Luke Squire-Smith throughout the season.

Batting C. P. Portz 814 at 50.87; B. D. H. Stevens 753 at 50.20; A. M. Portz 374 at 31.16; O. C. H. Mills 262 at 26.20; T. P. G. Walsh 220 at 22.00; P. J. Fuller* 288 at 20.57.

Bowling L. J. Squire-Smith 32 at 15.84; C. T. Bowden 13 at 16.07; B. D. H. Stevens 33 at 17.27; J. R. Taylor 13 at 17.30; C. P. Portz 10 at 20.00; A. M. Portz 13 at 27.69; T. P. G. Walsh 19 at 29.10.

Wolverhampton Grammar School
P12 L9 D3 A3

Master i/c N. H. Crust   **Coach** T. King

Although positive results were hard to come by, the team, under the enthusiastic leadership of Tom Meek, played fair cricket against some strong opponents. The batting was frail, but the side bowled and fielded well on many occasions.

Batting T. J. Meek* 239 at 23.90; D. J. Powner 176 at 22.00.

Bowling B. C. Willis 16 at 20.56; M. McEwen 17 at 21.47; M. I. Jones 11 at 22.63.

Woodbridge School   P11 W3 L3 D5 A3
Master i/c D. A. Brous

The season saw a determined, spirited effort from the team. Benjamin Havard and Edward Feldman dominated with the ball, Marmaduke Hatfield with the bat, and Joseph Youngs was easily the best all-rounder. The squad can look forward to continued development in 2010.

Batting J. G. Cousins 177 at 19.66; M. T. C. Hatfield 208 at 18.90; J. J. Youngs 220 at 18.33; T. J. B. Dobree 196 at 17.81.

Bowling E. S. Feldman 15 at 24.60; J. J. Youngs 12 at 31.66; B. J. Havard 12 at 33.25.

Woodhouse Grove School   P16 W10 L2 D4 A2
Master i/c R. I. Frost

Woodhouse Grove exceeded expectations with ten victories, including a first-ever win against MCC. Dalton Polius returned to St Lucia after two very successful seasons to captain the Windward Islands Under-19 team. Daniel Allen represented Yorkshire Schools at Under-19 level.

Batting D. Polius 595 at 59.50; O. J. Hardaker 573 at 35.81; D. J. T. Allen* 455 at 30.33; C. T. Fairbank 412 at 24.23; L. C. Dissanayaka 176 at 22.00; Z. J. P. Wheatley 229 at 20.81.

Bowling L. C. Dissanayaka 24 at 17.04; B. T. Weaving 13 at 17.07; R. C. Sharrocks 19 at 18.21; J. A. Frost 16 at 20.56; Z. J. P. Wheatley 10 at 21.70; A. G. S. Hewitt 11 at 27.09.

Worksop College   P16 W7 L4 T1 D4 A2
Master i/c I. C. Parkin   **Coach** A. Kettleborough

This was a talented but youthful squad, which explains the up-and-down nature of the season. Karanjit Bansal batted with flair, and represented Lincolnshire. Adam Dobb and Brett Hutton continued to improve and played for the Midlands, while Will Root played for Yorkshire seconds. The Yorkshire independent schools Twenty20 was retained.

Batting K. S. Bansal* 567 at 63.00; M. Smallwood 238 at 39.66; C. J. Smith 349 at 31.72; B. Hutton 260 at 26.00; W. R. Root 283 at 25.72; A. Dobb 282 at 23.50.

Bowling A. Dobb 17 at 19.76; B. Hutton 16 at 20.31; J. Smith 14 at 20.64; K. S. Bansal 15 at 29.20.

Worth School   P13 W7 L5 D1 A1
Master i/c R. Chaudhuri

Worth had a decent season, winning more than half their games; the highlight was the defeat of a good MCC side. Matthew Donegan was again the highest run-getter, helped purposefully by Christopher Adlam and Benjamin Wright. Greg Russell was the leading wicket-taker, well supported by Thomas Prower and Theodore Rivers.

Batting C. S. Adlam 350 at 38.88; B. P. Wright 385 at 38.50; E. J. C. Watson 279 at 34.87; M. J. P. Donegan 368 at 33.45.

Bowling G. A. Russell 19 at 17.89; B. P. Wright 17 at 23.05; T. L. Rivers 15 at 24.06; T. F. A. Prower 15 at 30.46.

Wrekin College   P15 W6 L5 D4 A3
Master i/c M. de Weymarn   **Coach** P. C. Lloyd

A young and inexperienced squad had a tough time early on. However, under the determined leadership of James Hammond, the side later blossomed, with four consecutive wins and two winning draws. Tom Saunders (Year 11) and James Shaw (Year 10) showed real promise.

Batting J. B. Hammond* 668 at 47.71; T. A. J. Saunders 370 at 33.63; M. L. Swift 262 at 20.15; J. Shaw 198 at 18.00; R. J. Graham 158 at 14.36.

Bowling S. C. Crockett 15 at 13.66; J. Shaw 24 at 16.83; J. B. Hammond 15 at 19.53; H. D. P. Yiend 17 at 23.52.

Wycliffe College   P13 W4 L8 D1 A1
Master i/c M. J. Kimber

James Gilchriest captained with enterprise and scored 498 runs. Ben Rodgers hit his maiden century and, with a total of 19, Archie Trow was the leading wicket-taker for the second year running.

Batting J. Gilchriest* 498 at 45.27; B. J. Rodgers 167 at 23.85; R. C. Fisher 275 at 22.91.

Bowling B. J. Rodgers 14 at 24.85; R. W. J. Woodmason 14 at 26.64; A. B. Trow 19 at 27.94; E. C. H. Price 12 at 34.75.

WOMEN'S CRICKET, 2009

SARAH POTTER

ENGLAND v AUSTRALIA, 2009

Test match (1): England 0, Australia 0
One-day internationals (5): England 4, Australia 0
Twenty20 international (1): England 0, Australia 1

Of the 14 players in England's squad for this series, only Claire Taylor was born when their predecessors last defeated Australia in a bilateral one-day series, back in 1976. With the Ashes, the World Cup and the World Twenty20 already in the trophy cabinet, England's class of 2009 had the confidence and poise to overhaul that 33-year-old record.

Oddly, the so-called "Ashes Summer", which included five one-day internationals and a single Test match at Worcester, began four days after the ICC's World Twenty20 competition with yet another Twenty20 international, in Derby. Unsurprisingly, it was a flat, rather meaningless affair. It was most notable for Australia's changing of the guard. Before setting out for England, Karen Rolton had announced that she would stand down as captain after the World Twenty20. Her successor, wicketkeeper Jodie Fields, began her reign with a 34-run victory, in which Rolton, restored to the ranks, was the top scorer.

England's leader, Charlotte Edwards, who had been made an MBE in June, was ill – but hardly missed – for the first two 50-over internationals at Chelmsford, in which Nicky Shaw captained the side to comprehensive victories. While Australia's batting misfired in the sunshine, Sarah Taylor sparkled; the young opener struck 68 and 120 in those two games to restore England's recent sense of dominance and self-belief.

Perhaps it was this relatively new-found psychological steeliness that enabled England to win the next two matches – and the series – in last-ball thrillers. Overnight thunderstorms reduced the game in Stratford-upon-Avon to 29 overs a side. Australia squandered the chance to stay in the series when Alex Blackwell allowed Laura Marsh's last-gasp heave to the leg-side boundary, off a Shelley Nitschke full toss, to slip through her buttery fingers for England to scramble the two runs needed for victory. In the fourth game at Wormsley, "Boggy" (as Marsh is nicknamed by her team-mates) spared the 600 or so spectators the added drama of an offered catch and hit the winning single behind point off the final delivery, bowled by Rene Farrell. Suddenly, England had beaten Australia in four successive one-day internationals; they had never managed more than two before.

Sir Paul Getty's ground on the Wormsley Estate had never seen anything like it. A pink ball was used for the first time in an international fixture in England, and the crowd were encouraged to celebrate "Pink Sunday", a fund-raising day for the Breast Cancer Campaign, by wearing clothes of the appropriate colour.

World leaders? On their visit to Downing Street, Charlotte Edwards and Nicky Shaw show off the spoils of a successful few months.

There was no whitewash, though, as rain and hailstones caused the abandonment of the final one-day game at Lord's. Australia's 100 for seven from 31 overs between showers looked inadequate but, with England struggling at six for two before the heavens opened again, another home victory was by no means inevitable.

Australia stopped haemorrhaging defeats by drawing the one-off four-day Ashes Test at Worcester. Fields established her authority with an astonishing fightback, adding 229 with Rachael Haynes after England reduced them to 28 for five on the first morning. But although Australia held the advantage, England held the Ashes, and so the draw was enough for Edwards's side to claim their third major prize in four months, a historic clean sweep.

Not since the 1950s has an England cricket team been so dominant on the world stage. Even the beleaguered prime minister, Gordon Brown, found time to recognise the team's achievements by hosting an official reception at Downing Street. With two gleaming world cups and the Ashes trophy on show, even the gloom of the global recession was momentarily lifted in the nation's corridors of power.

AUSTRALIAN TOURING PARTY

J. M. Fields (*captain*), A. J. Blackwell (*vice-captain*), S. J. Andrews, J. E. Cameron, L. K. Ebsary, R. M. Farrell, R. L. Haynes, S. Nitschke, E. A. Osborne, E. A. Perry, K. E. Pike, L. J. Poulton, K. L. Rolton, L. C. Sthalekar. *Coach:* R. J. McInnes. *Assistant coach:* C. L. Fitzpatrick.

Fields was appointed captain to succeed Rolton, who stepped down after the preceding Women's World Twenty20 tournament.

Note: Matches in this section were not first-class.

Details of Australia's matches in the Women's World Twenty20 tournament in June can be found on page 560.

At Derby, June 25. **Twenty20 international: Australia won by 34 runs.** Toss: Australia. **Australia 151-3** (20 overs) (L. J. Poulton 33, S. Nitschke 32, K. L. Rolton 43*); **England 117-6** (20 overs) (S. C. Taylor 31). *Player of the Match:* S. Nitschke.
Australia began the Ashes section of their tour by defeating the World Twenty20 champions.

At Chelmsford, June 29. **First one-day international: England won by nine wickets.** Toss: Australia. **Australia 133** (49.4 overs) (R. M. Farrell 39*; H. L. Colvin 3-27); **England 134-1** (27.1 overs) (S. J. Taylor 68, C. M. G. Atkins 48*). *Player of the Match:* S. J. Taylor.
Six of Australia's top seven failed to open decently as they slumped to 57-7 in the 23rd over after choosing to bat. In reply, Sarah Taylor and Caroline Atkins opened with 119 in 25 overs as England galloped home.

At Chelmsford, June 30. **Second one-day international: England won by 55 runs.** Toss: England. **England 259-6** (50 overs) (S. J. Taylor 120, S. C. Taylor 42, B. L. Morgan 41, E-J. C-L. R. C. Rainford-Brent 30*); **Australia 204** (43.4 overs) (S. Nitschke 47, L. C. Sthalekar 43, K. L. Rolton 32, L. K. Ebsary 38; N. J. Shaw 3-39, L. A. Marsh 3-33). *Player of the Match:* S. J. Taylor.
Sarah Taylor, still only 20, scored her third one-day international century. She made 120 at a run a ball with 12 fours, before acting-captain Nicky Shaw and Laura Marsh shared six wickets in another comfortable victory.

At Stratford-upon-Avon, July 3. **Third one-day international: England won by two wickets.** Reduced to 29 overs a side. Toss: England. **Australia 150-8** (29 overs) (L. C. Sthalekar 38, L. K. Ebsary 40); **England 151-8** (29 overs) (C. M. G. Atkins 35). *Player of the Match:* L. C. Sthalekar.
England made sure of the series with a third win, but this time they had to fight much harder, their ninth-wicket pair securing victory off the very last ball, when Laura Marsh was dropped. In a rain-shortened match, Lisa Sthalekar and Lauren Ebsary added 79 for Australia's fourth wicket.

At Wormsley, July 5. **Fourth one-day international: England won by two wickets.** Toss: Australia. **Australia 225-7** (50 overs) (S. Nitschke 71, K. L. Rolton 52); **England 226-8** (50 overs) (C. M. Edwards 65, L. S. Greenway 50; S. J. Andrews 4-50). *Player of the Match:* S. Nitschke.
For the second game running, England's ninth-wicket pair scored the winning run off the final ball. Shelley Nitschke led Australia's recovery after Katherine Brunt struck twice in the first three balls of the match. But Charlotte Edwards, back at the helm, shared a fifth-wicket stand of 113 in 25 overs with Lydia Greenway, which ultimately ensured England's winning run continued.

At Lord's, July 7. **Fifth one-day international: No result.** Toss: Australia. **Australia 100-7** (31 overs) (L. A. Marsh 3-11); **England 6-2** (2.4 overs). *One-day international debut:* R. L. Haynes. *Player of the Series:* S. J. Taylor.
Rain interrupted Australia's innings twice and then ended it, with England's target being revised to 115 in 31 overs by the Duckworth/Lewis method. Both openers fell in the 16 balls possible before the rain returned. England took the series 4–0.

ENGLAND v AUSTRALIA

Test Match

At Worcester, July 10, 11, 12, 13. Drawn. Toss: Australia. Test debuts: L. K. Ebsary, R. M. Farrell, R. L. Haynes, L. J. Poulton.
While the men played the opening Ashes Test at the novel venue of Cardiff, 60-odd miles away, the women returned to New Road, where England had won their first series victory over Australia

for 42 years in 2005. They needed only a draw to take the trophy for the third time running, having won a one-off Test at Bowral in February 2008. On the first morning it looked as if England's all-conquering form would sweep them to an easy victory: Katherine Brunt's venomous opening burst reduced Australia to 28 for five in the 15th over. Then, in the game's pivotal moment, Claire Taylor dropped the new captain, Jodie Fields, on 21. That would have been 48 for six, but Fields scored 139, with 21 fours, and added 229, the fifth-highest partnership in all women's Tests, with left-handed debutant Rachael Haynes, who narrowly missed her own century. Brunt trapped Fields in the end, and finished with six wickets for the first time in Tests. But her excellence was not matched by England's batsmen; it took a dogged 58 in 262 balls from Beth Morgan and a wagging tail to keeping their first-innings deficit down to 41. Australia were looking for quick runs when they batted again, and Alex Blackwell struck the game's only six on her way to 68. But rain robbed the match of a potentially exciting conclusion by washing out 26 overs on the final day. Set 273 to win, England lost Claire Taylor – tired after her limited-overs exertions – cheaply for the second time, and closed on 106 for three. Charlotte Edwards hit ten fours in an unbeaten fifty.

Player of the Match: J. M. Fields.

Close of play: First day, Australia Women 271-7 (Perry 4); Second day, England 116-5 (Morgan 23, Gunn 34); Third day, Australia 128-1 (Blackwell 59, Rolton 31).

Australia

S. Nitschke c Atkins b Shaw	15	– (2) lbw b Marsh	25
A. J. Blackwell c S. J. Taylor b Brunt	0	– (1) c and b Brunt	68
K. L. Rolton lbw b Brunt	0	– run out	31
L. C. Sthalekar lbw b Brunt	6	– (5) run out	7
*†J. M. Fields lbw b Brunt	139	– (7) b Marsh	9
L. J. Poulton b Brunt	1	– run out	23
R. L. Haynes b Marsh	98	– (9) st S. J. Taylor b Colvin	16
E. A. Perry not out	18	– (10) c Morgan b Colvin	6
L. K. Ebsary lbw b Brunt	3	– (4) b Shaw	21
R. M. Farrell b Shaw	8	– (8) c Greenway b Colvin	4
S. J. Andrews c S. J. Taylor b Shaw	11	– not out	4
B 1, l-b 9	10	B 10, l-b 6, w 1	17

1/1 (2) 2/5 (3) 3/19 (4) 4/23 (1)   (113.3 overs) 309
5/28 (6) 6/257 (5) 7/271 (7)
8/280 (9) 9/297 (10) 10/309 (11)

1/49 (2) 2/130 (3)   (70.1 overs) 231
3/150 (1) 4/164 (5)
5/171 (4) 6/191 (7) 7/204 (8)
8/206 (6) 9/224 (9) 10/231 (10)

Brunt 26–10–69–6; Shaw 21.3–4–67–3; Gunn 12–2–41–0; Marsh 27–7–61–1; Colvin 16–3–37–0; Atkins 3–0–13–0; Morgan 8–4–11–0. *Second Innings*—Brunt 18–2–64–1; Shaw 17–4–34–1; Marsh 19–3–43–2; Colvin 12.1–0–59–3; Morgan 2–0–11–0; Atkins 2–0–4–0.

England

C. M. G. Atkins lbw b Farrell	2	– lbw b Andrews	0
L. S. Greenway c Andrews b Farrell	5	– c and b Perry	23
S. C. Taylor c Poulton b Ebsary	10	– b Sthalekar	12
*C. M. Edwards b Perry	10	– not out	53
B. L. Morgan b Sthalekar	58	– not out	9
†S. J. Taylor lbw b Nitschke	21		
J. L. Gunn c Fields b Ebsary	41		
K. H. Brunt b Farrell	27		
N. J. Shaw b Haynes	13		
H. L. Colvin not out	17		
L. A. Marsh b Andrews	38		
B 4, l-b 14, w 3, n-b 5	26	B 5, l-b 1, w 3	9

1/2 (1) 2/11 (2) 3/28 (3) 4/28 (4)   (129.3 overs) 268
5/59 (6) 6/136 (7) 7/183 (8) 8/209 (9)
9/209 (5) 10/268 (11)

(3 wkts, 53 overs) 106
1/1 (1) 2/37 (3) 3/39 (2)

Farrell 30–14–32–3; Andrews 20.3–8–32–1; Perry 12–1–49–1; Ebsary 14–4–35–2; Sthalekar 26–14–41–1; Nitschke 19–4–46–1; Haynes 4–4–0–1; Poulton 4–0–15–0. *Second Innings*—Farrell 7–6–4–0; Andrews 13–5–22–1; Ebsary 2–0–8–0; Sthalekar 13–4–19–1; Perry 8–2–14–1; Nitschke 5–0–20–0; Haynes 5–3–13–0.

Umpires: N. G. B. Cook and T. E. Jesty. Referee: D. T. Jukes.

ENGLISH WOMEN'S CRICKET, 2009

The women's County Championship was expanded and revamped in 2009. There was no festival week at Taunton, and all matches took place on a home and away basis between May and September. The Netherlands and Ireland joined the five-division tournament.

Kent won their third title in four seasons after winning all their ten games. They needed only one bonus point in their last match, against defending champions Sussex, but captain Charlotte Edwards, with 71, and her England colleague Lydia Greenway, with 89 not out, ensured victory with a convincing seven wickets and six overs to spare.

In Division Two, Yorkshire also won all ten games, to ensure their second successive promotion; they replaced Surrey in the top flight. Perennial county champions a decade ago, Yorkshire confirmed their revival by winning the Under-17 and Under-13 Championship finals, beating Sussex and Surrey respectively. Sussex defeated Wales in the Under-15 final. Surrey won the inaugural County Twenty20 Cup at the end of July, though the tournament was badly affected by rain.

The top domestic competition, the Super Fours, was called off because of the hectic international calendar, but the Emeralds won the Junior Super Fours.

The National Knockout Cup was scrapped in 2009. The Premier League – the leading tournament for clubs – had a new winner when Hayes Hurricanes, the Southern Division champions, defeated their Northern counterparts, Ransome & Marles, by a whopping 214 runs. Hayes fielded several Kent players, including Greenway, England's stylish left-hander, who scored 74, and Charlotte Anneveld, the leading wicket-taker in the County Championship, who claimed three for 13 as the Nottinghamshire side were dismissed for 52.

Leeds & Broomfield overcame Twickenham, at East Molesey in mid-September, to win the inaugural Women's Cricket Southern League Super Eight Twenty20.

Note: Matches in this section were not first-class.

LV= COUNTY CHAMPIONSHIP, 2009

50-over league

Division One	Played	Won	Lost	Abandoned	Bonus points Batting	Bowling	Points
Kent..............	10	10	0	0	0	0	200
Sussex............	10	8	2	0	2	1	163
Nottinghamshire	10	6	4	0	9	8	137
Somerset	10	3	7	0	6	8	74
Berkshire..........	10	2	8	0	10	20	70
Surrey	10	1	9	0	15	15	50

Division Two	Played	Won	Lost	Abandoned	Bonus points Batting	Bonus points Bowling	Points
Yorkshire..........	10	10	0	0	0	0	200
Middlesex	10	7	3	0	5	9	154
Essex	10	4	6	0	11	12	103
Cheshire	10	4	6	0	6	13	99
Warwickshire	10	4	6	0	6	9	95
Lancashire.........	10	1	9	0	6	16	42

Division Three	Played	Won	Lost	Abandoned	Bonus points Batting	Bonus points Bowling	Points
Worcestershire	10	7	3	0	2	9	151
Devon	10	7	2	1	3	2	150
Staffordshire	10	6	1	3	0	0	135
Scotland...........	10	4	5	1	5	9	99
Hampshire..........	10	2	8	0	9	7	56
Derbyshire.........	10	1	8	1	8	14	47

Division Four	Played	Won	Lost	Abandoned	Bonus points Batting	Bonus points Bowling	Points
Wales.............	10	9	1	0	2	3	185
Durham	10	8	2	0	3	2	165
Hertfordshire.......	10	7	3	0	3	8	151
Northamptonshire ...	10	4	6	0	6	19	105
Cornwall	10	1	9	0	6	24	50
Norfolk	10	1	9	0	4	15	39

Win = 20 pts; abandoned = 5 pts. Winning teams do not receive bonus points; up to four batting points and four bowling are available to losing teams and to both sides in an uncompleted match.

Division Five

North and East Cumbria 65 pts, Ireland 64 pts, Suffolk 45 pts, Northumberland 44 pts, Leicestershire 0 pt.
South and West Netherlands 85 pts, Gloucestershire 84 pts, Shropshire 68 pts, Oxfordshire 50 pts, Dorset 32 pts, Wiltshire 12 pts.

COUNTY TWENTY20 CUP, 2009

Division One Surrey 5 pts, Kent 3 pts, Berkshire 2 pts, Sussex 2 pts.
Division Two Somerset 5 pts, Lancashire 3 pts, Yorkshire 3 pts, Warwickshire 1 pt.
Division Three Essex 5 pts, Cheshire 3 pts, Middlesex 2 pts, Derbyshire 2 pts.
Division Four Devon 4 pts, Staffordshire 4 pts, Worcestershire 4 pts, Scotland 0 pt.
Division Five Northamptonshire 4 pts, Hampshire 4 pts, Norfolk 2 pts, Hertfordshire 2 pts.
Division Six Durham 0 pt, Gloucestershire 0 pt, Wales 0 pt, Wiltshire 0 pt (all games abandoned).
Division Seven Cumbria 0 pt, Dorset 0 pt, Northumberland 0 pt, Shropshire 0 pt (all games abandoned).
Division Eight Oxfordshire 6 pts, Suffolk 4 pts, Buckinghamshire 2 pts, Cambridgeshire–Huntingdonshire 0 pt.

ECB PREMIER LEAGUE FINAL, 2009

At Great Oakley, September 20. **Hayes Hurricanes won by 214 runs**. Toss: Hayes Hurricanes.
Hayes Hurricanes 266-9 (50 overs) (L. Penny 52, K. M. Leng 38, L. S. Greenway 74, Extras 54; S. B. Odedra 4-62); **Ransome & Marles 52** (20.3 overs) (C. A. Anneveld 3-13).

Lydia Greenway led Hayes Hurricanes' solid batting, which was boosted by 44 wides. In reply, only England's Jenny Gunn reached double figures for Ransome & Marles as the match ended with nearly 30 overs to spare.

CRICKET IN IRELAND, 2009

Going it alone

IAN CALLENDER

In the year when Ireland qualified for their second successive World Cup, the defining moment came a month after the season finished, when Cricket Ireland announced that they would not be taking part in the English 40-over competition in 2010. Although primarily a financial decision – the 12-match programme was set to cost €120,000, which CI's chief executive Warren Deutrom thought could be better spent – the subtext was that Ireland were ready to go it alone, bringing to an end 30 years of county competition.

When Ireland played Middlesex in 1980 in their first-ever Gillette Cup match, it was one of just six games the team played that year (they were captained on that memorable day at Lord's by slow left-armer and Ireland legend Dermott Monteith, who sadly died in December). In 2009, Ireland contested 38 matches, winning 17; a further three were abandoned without a ball bowled. This year they could in theory have as many as 56 fixtures. With only six full-time professionals, four of them attached to counties, something had to give. In recent years, it was essentially an Ireland A team that played in the Friends Provident Trophy, but with around six fixtures against Second Elevens this year the link with county cricket should not be lost.

The year started with a defeat, by Zimbabwe A at Benoni, in the first of three warm-up games for the World Cup qualifying competition, which was played in and around Johannesburg. Victories over Afghanistan and the UAE set the Irish up for the first game of the tournament proper, against Scotland. They started impressively: after being set 233, captain William Porterfield made a century and put on 131 with Eoin Morgan, and Ireland coasted home with 74 balls to spare.

Kevin O'Brien added an undefeated century against Oman and, after Uganda were brushed aside, Ireland completed another emphatic win over previously unbeaten Canada. Victory over Namibia sent the Irish into the Super Eights with a 100% record, so it was a huge surprise when they then lost to Afghanistan by 22 runs. The slow, turning pitch favoured a team that had four spinners, while no one outside Ireland's top six had batted in the tournament's first phase, and it showed as they slumped from 186 for five to 196 all out.

Ireland bounced back with a straightforward win over UAE, and went into their match against the Netherlands knowing victory would ensure a place in the 2011 World Cup finals. Batting second for the seventh time out of eight, Porterfield and Morgan set up a six-wicket win.

With qualification assured, coach Phil Simmons rested four players for the last round-robin game before the final. One of them was Morgan who, much to Simmons's displeasure, had been making plans to return to Middlesex from the morning of the Afghanistan defeat. It was never Morgan's intention to play in the final: Simmons had agreed he could rejoin his county once World Cup qualification was assured. Morgan was subsequently named in England's squad for the World Twenty20 in June, and so the game against the Dutch was his 63rd, and probably last, for his native country. He made 2,075 runs, including Ireland's record score of 209 not out against the UAE in February 2007.

The World Cup Qualifier final at Centurion highlighted the gulf in class between Ireland and the rest of the Associate nations. Trent Johnston took five for 14 in his ten overs to reduce Canada to 88 for six and, although they recovered to 185, Ireland passed that with something to spare. Porterfield finished the tournament as he started it, with a century, and in all made 515 runs at 57.22.

Seven days after their prolonged celebrations in Pretoria, Ireland were playing Worcestershire in their first FPT game. Without seven of their squad from South Africa they lost by 52 runs, and it got no better the following weekend when they conceded 346 at Trent Bridge and then failed to defend 197 in 31 overs against Leicestershire.

The home games against Hampshire and Leicestershire fell victim to the weather, before Nottinghamshire won by two wickets off the penultimate ball in Dublin. At the Rose Bowl, Ireland's bowlers had no answer to Sean Ervine and Michael Carberry (Hampshire racked up 316 for two), but everything came right two days later at New Road. Ireland's 152 seemed to offer little chance of victory, but Peter Connell, a teacher who had moved from New Zealand in 2006, took five for 19 as Worcestershire were humbled for 58, their lowest one-day total. It was the first time Ireland had bowled a county out for under 100. If it is to be their last county action, at least they bowed out on a winning note.

The players had only a week's break before they were back in England for six warm-up games for the World Twenty20. In the tournament proper, a six-wicket win over Bangladesh was enough to take Ireland into the Super Eights and, although they then lost to New Zealand, Sri Lanka (by only nine runs) and eventual winners Pakistan, the Irish left the tournament with heads held high. Even so, they were still forced to qualify for the next World Twenty20, in an eight-team competition in Abu Dhabi and Dubai in February 2010, and did so.

Ireland began the defence of the Intercontinental Cup they won in 2008 with a draw against Kenya. The teams then played three one-day internationals in Clontarf: Ireland won all three, though two were close. Rain on the final day in Aberdeen washed away a probable Intercontinental Cup victory over Scotland. Ireland have four more I-Cup matches to play in 2010, and they may need to win all of them to reach their fourth successive final.

The grand finale to the season came at Stormont with the visit of England, fresh (or rather stale) from their Ashes success. In front of 5,000 spectators, Johnston again led the way as England were restricted to 203 for nine. Rain during the interval reduced Ireland's target to 116 from 20 overs. They reached 64 for two by the ninth over, but lost their next seven wickets for 30 and, after Morgan (fielding as a substitute for his new team) denied his former captain

Johnston a six with a spectacular piece of fielding, England just hung on. Johnston won the match award on his 100th international appearance: he was the ninth to reach this landmark for Ireland.

Porterfield, the ICC's Associate Player of the Year, scored 1,028 runs in his 24 matches, and his average of 42.83 was 18 higher than in 2008. He was one of three batsmen (Morgan and Kevin O'Brien were the others) to pass 2,000 runs for Ireland during the year, while Alex Cusack and Gary Wilson both reached 1,000. Of the 23 players used during 2009, two were new caps: Andrew Britton, a pace bowler from Donemana, and Nigel Jones, a New Zealand-born batting all-rounder.

On the domestic front, Leinster won the Bob Kerr Irish Senior Cup for the first time, but they avoided relegation by only four points. Clontarf completed the league and cup double for the second time in three years. The league titles in the Northern and North West unions were both shared. Instonians, who also won the Challenge Cup for the first time since 1964, tied with Waringstown at the top of the Premier Division, while Limavady and Strabane could not be separated in the North West.

Winners of Irish Leagues and Cups
Bob Kerr Irish Senior Cup Leinster. **Leinster Major League** Clontarf. **Leinster Short League** Railway Union. **Leinster Cup** Clontarf. **Munster League** Cork Harlequins. **Munster Cup** Cork Harlequins. **Northern Union League** Instonians and Waringstown *(shared)*. **Northern Union Cup** Instonians. **North West League** Limavady and Strabane *(shared)*. **North West Cup** Donemana.

Note: Matches in this section were not first-class.

ONE-DAY INTERNATIONALS IN IRELAND IN 2009

At Dublin, July 9. **First one-day international: Ireland won by three wickets.** Toss: Kenya. **Kenya 214-9** (50 overs) (D. O. Obuya 41, K. O. Otieno 79; A. R. Cusack 3-37, W. K. McCallan 4-30); **Ireland 215-7** (48.5 overs) (W. T. S. Porterfield 81, A. R. Cusack 30; T. M. Odoyo 4-33).

Ireland's captain William Porterfield anchored his side's run-chase with 81 from 111 balls, with 11 fours, but it was left to the seasoned eighth-wicket pair of Trent Johnston and Kyle McCallan, who added 13, to ease their side over the finishing line with seven balls to spare. Kenya's challenging total owed much to an opening stand of 80 between David Obuya and his brother Kennedy Otieno, but the middle order misfired against McCallan's tight off-spin. No match awards were made in this series.

At Dublin, July 11. **Second one-day international: Ireland won by 52 runs** (D/L method). Toss: Kenya. **Kenya 175** (45.2 overs) (A. Obanda 59, N. Odhiambo 40*; W. B. Rankin 3-40); **Ireland 104-1** (21 overs) (W. T. S. Porterfield 49, G. C. Wilson 51*).

Kenya's modest total owed almost everything to Alex Obanda, who made 59 from 78 balls, and No. 9 Nehemiah Odhiambo (40 from 48). With rain threatening, Ireland set off at a fair lick, and were well ahead of the Duckworth/Lewis par score (52) when the weather did eventually close in.

At Dublin, July 12. **Third one-day international: Ireland won by four runs** (D/L method). Toss: Kenya. **Ireland 256-7** (50 overs) (P. R. Stirling 84, J. F. Mooney 42); **Kenya 240-6** (46 overs) (M. A. Ouma 61, A. Obanda 41, C. O. Obuya 78*). *One-day international debut: S. A. Britton (Ireland).*

Ireland secured a clean sweep, but it was a close-run thing: an aggressive 78 off 69 balls from Collins Obuya threatened to give Kenya a consolation victory – but ten from the final over, bowled by Kevin O'Brien, proved beyond them. A shower interrupted the Kenyan reply after 4.2 overs, and their target was revised to 245 from 46 overs. Earlier, 18-year-old Paul Stirling made 84 from 92 balls.*

IRELAND v ENGLAND

Only One-Day International

At Belfast, August 27. England won by three runs (D/L method). Toss: England. One-day international debuts: J. L. Denly, A. U. Rashid, I. J. L. Trott.

As Ireland chased a reduced target of 116 from 20 overs after a three-hour rain delay, England's blushes were saved by an Irishman. With two balls left, and nine runs still needed, Johnston blasted Shah for what looked a six all the way. Then Eoin Morgan, fielding as substitute for Swann, leapt up at long-on and took a fine catch except that, realising his momentum would carry him over the rope, he threw the ball back into the field of play; the batsmen ran two, but the umpires called one short, leaving an impossible eight to win off the last delivery. Although Johnston creamed that through the covers for four, it was too late. Dublin-born Morgan played 23 one-day internationals for Ireland, the last of them in April 2009, before being selected for England. Earlier Denly, in his first one-day international, had anchored England's innings with a restrained 67 from 111 balls, containing only three fours. He needed to be watchful after Johnston, in his 100th match overall for Ireland, took two cheap wickets, including that of Trott, whose first one-day international proved far less fruitful than his Test debut. Five days earlier he had made a century in the nerve-wracking Ashes decider: now he, and several of the side who had defeated Australia, were forced to fly to Ireland by fixture-scheduling that was insensitively over-commercial. It was no coincidence that England's best performers were the fresh players who had been involved in the Ashes: Shah, whose death bowling on a very slow pitch was vital, and Denly... and the substitute Morgan. During the rain delay, the crowd were entertained by a pair of Irish musicians together known as The Duckworth Lewis Method; the mathematical calculations of the original pair proved rather less palatable to home supporters.

Man of the Match: D. T. Johnston.

England

R. S. Bopara c Stirling b Johnston	0	T. T. Bresnan not out		14
J. L. Denly lbw b Johnston	67	R. J. Sidebottom not out		5
I. J. L. Trott lbw b Johnston	0	L-b 3, w 7		10
†M. J. Prior c West b Botha	29			
*P. D. Collingwood c N. J. O'Brien b West	9	1/2 (1) 2/6 (3)	(9 wkts, 50 overs)	203
O. A. Shah c K. J. O'Brien b Cusack	21	3/59 (4) 4/92 (5)		
L. J. Wright c Mooney b Johnston	36	5/128 (6) 6/135 (2)		
A. U. Rashid c K. J. O'Brien b Cusack	7	7/177 (7) 8/183 (8)		
G. P. Swann b Botha	5	9/185 (9)	10 overs: 20-2	

Johnston 10–2–26–4; K. J. O'Brien 6–1–22–0; Cusack 8–0–41–2; Botha 10–0–38–2; West 10–0–33–1; McCallan 6–0–40–0.

Ireland

*W. T. S. Porterfield c Collingwood b Bresnan	4	R. M. West c Bresnan b Shah		0
†N. J. O'Brien c Collingwood b Bresnan	12	A. R. Cusack b Shah		0
P. R. Stirling c and b Rashid	30	W. K. McCallan not out		5
A. C. Botha lbw b Swann	15	B 1, l-b 8, w 3		12
K. J. O'Brien b Collingwood	4			
J. F. Mooney st Prior b Shah	9	1/8 (1) 2/25 (2)	(9 wkts, 20 overs)	112
D. T. Johnston not out	20	3/64 (4) 4/66 (3) 5/82 (5) 6/86 (6)		
A. R. White run out	1	7/89 (8) 8/93 (9) 9/94 (10)	4 overs: 28-2	

Sidebottom 3–0–19–0; Bresnan 2–0–10–2; Swann 4–0–21–1; Rashid 4–0–16–1; Collingwood 4–0–22–1; Shah 3–0–15–3.

Umpires: Asad Rauf and P. K. Baldwin.
Referee: R. S. Madugalle.

CRICKET IN SCOTLAND, 2009

Green shoots defy chill winds

WILLIAM DICK

Green shoots of recovery were in evidence by the end of a year which offered great riches, but instead descended into deep depression. A new professional era arrived with three players – opener and captain Ryan Watson, and fast bowlers Dewald Nel and Gordon Goudie – being placed on full-time contracts in time for the World Cup qualifying tournament in South Africa in April. However, Scotland's campaign there was often amateurish and sometimes downright shambolic.

The cause was not helped by Watson's spectacular loss of form, which was as untimely as it was harmful: he managed only 72 runs from ten increasingly painful appearances. An injury to Goudie also set back Scotland's prospects of a third World Cup in 2011, as he had to fly home with a badly damaged shoulder which was to keep him on the sidelines for six months.

The Scots had travelled to South Africa confident of securing one of the four available World Cup places – but in the end they missed out, and were left clinging to the consolation of keeping official one-day international status, which they managed only thanks to a nervy win over the UAE in the final qualifying match. A heavy defeat by Ireland on the opening day set the tone for two weeks of abject underachievement, during which Canada, Kenya and Afghanistan (twice) also proved too good for Watson's disjointed side.

The selectors, having stuck with Watson and Gavin Hamilton as the opening pair for the first five matches, then appeared to lose the plot as the combination was changed for each of the remaining five games, while bemused onlookers searched in vain for a coherent game plan.

After failing in their quest for qualification and thus losing out on an estimated £2.5m, Scotland returned home to think again… but there was no knee-jerk reaction. To the surprise of many, Watson retained his position as captain for the start of the Friends Provident Trophy campaign, against Middlesex. The reprieve proved short-lived, as he chose to stand down after yet another failure. As he trudged off at Lord's for the last time as skipper, comparisons were made with the departure from the same stage of Ian Botham after the 1981 Test against Australia.

Alas, despite being freed from the cares of captaincy, Watson – a player memorably capable of scoring a century from 43 balls against Somerset in 2003 – failed to recapture his best form in the manner of England's Ashes hero. With Hamilton as captain (a surprise but potentially inspired choice), Scotland did manage to claim their customary county scalp, beating Kent in a rain-shortened game in Edinburgh.

If the World Cup Qualifiers and Watson's sad demise were not bad enough, worse was to come with John Blain's controversial departure from the squad on the eve of the World Twenty20 in England in June. This followed a misunderstanding and then a bitter disagreement with Hamilton over team tactics. Blain, a sportsman of the highest professional standards and a proud Scot of unwavering integrity, felt sufficiently isolated and let down to walk away from an international career which had seen him earn 117 caps and take 188 wickets – the second-highest in Scotland's history. Hamilton, meanwhile, believing his authority had been undermined, proceeded to tell the world's media that his old pal would never play for Scotland again.

Both Blain and Hamilton have been fine ambassadors for Scottish cricket since they first made their marks as talented teenagers. It is therefore a matter of deep regret that no one at Cricket Scotland appears to have tried to bring Blain back into the fold. In the meantime, Yorkshire are cashing in on Scotland's loss, having promoted Blain to captain and coach their Second Eleven as reward for guiding the Academy side to its most successful season. Blain's departure deprived Scotland of their planned new-ball pair for the World Twenty20, since Nel had also been ruled out with a broken finger.

The Scots still gave New Zealand a real fright in what became a seven-over thrash at The Oval, amassing 89 for four. They might have created an upset to match the Netherlands' defeat of England had they placed a little more faith in their spinners. Scotland were subsequently humbled by South Africa, but not before Kyle Coetzer had clasped the catch of the tournament to dismiss Mark Boucher.

Scotland's Under-19s suffered their share of disappointment when they failed to claim a place at the 2010 Youth World Cup, losing out on net run-rate to Ireland and a Netherlands side inspired almost singlehandedly by Worcestershire's Alexei Kervezee.

So where are those elusive green shoots? Towards the end of the domestic season, a remoulded Scotland – now captained by Gordon Drummond as Hamilton has given up four-day cricket – launched their Intercontinental Cup campaign with victory over Canada at Aberdeen. A century from Qasim Sheikh helped them claim first-innings points against Ireland, although in the end only rain denied the Irish a probable victory. Goudie returned to fitness and claimed four wickets in each innings against Ireland before celebrating a memorable five-for in the one-day international against Australia at The Grange, although, predictably enough, he couldn't prevent the Aussies winning by a distance.

Cricket Scotland announced that Majid Haq would join Goudie and Nel on professional contracts in 2010, Watson having rejected a new deal, and an additional four players will have full-time status for the summer months.

Domestically, league reconstruction was voted through by the 30 Scottish National Cricket League clubs, meaning the current three-division set-up will be replaced by a 14-team "Premiership" and a "Championship" of 16 teams from 2011. The rationale for change hinged on the perceived need for "whole club development" and a greater emphasis on quality coaching. Whether this will lead to an improvement in standards across the board remains to be seen.

Two of Scotland's finest servants – former captain and leading wicket-taker Craig Wright, and Colin Smith, the country's most successful wicketkeeper –

announced their retirements during 2009. With 375 caps and numerous "c Smith b Wright" dismissals between them, this pair will not be easy to replace in the national side.

Winners of Scottish Leagues and Cups
Premier Division Aberdeenshire. **First Division** Dunfermline. **Second Division** Falkland. **Scottish Cup** Aberdeenshire. **Murgitroyd Twenty20 Cup** Greenock.

ONE-DAY INTERNATIONALS IN SCOTLAND IN 2009

At Aberdeen, July 7. **First one-day international: Canada won by six wickets.** Toss: Canada. **Scotland 286-4** (50 overs) (G. M. Hamilton 119, D. F. Watts 101); **Canada 287-4** (48.4 overs) (Rizwan Cheema 47, S. Jyoti 117, A. Bagai 92*). *One-day international debuts:* S. J. Chalmers, A. C. Evans, M. J. Petrie (Scotland); S. Keshvani (Canada).

Gavin Hamilton, who scored a century in his first one-day international as captain, and Fraser Watts, with his maiden one-day hundred, put on 203 for the first wicket (easily a Scottish record) in 40 overs – but they were trumped by the Canadians, for whom Sandeep Jyoti and captain Ashish Bagai put on 146. Jyoti, whose previous-highest score was 33, went on to 117, and Bagai was still there at the end. No match awards were made in this series.

At Aberdeen, July 8. **Second one-day international: Scotland won by five wickets.** Toss: Canada. **Canada 250-9** (50 overs) (Z. E. Surkari 33, A. Bagai 31, S. Dhaniram 92, Khurram Chauhan 35*; G. D. Drummond 4-41); **Scotland 253-5** (47.2 overs) (G. M. Hamilton 59, R. R. Watson 74, N. F. I. McCallum 79*).

Scotland levelled the short series after another closely fought game, their victory owing much to a fine innings from Neil McCallum, who faced only 67 balls and hit 12 fours; he and Ryan Watson put on 86 for the fourth wicket. Scotland's openers were rather less successful than in the first game: this time Fraser Watts was run out without facing in the opening over. Earlier, Canada had recovered from 96-5 thanks to Sunil Dhaniram, who faced 88 balls and hit eight fours.

At Aberdeen, August 22. **First one-day international: Ireland won by 96 runs.** Toss: Scotland. **Ireland 205-9** (50 overs) (W. T. S. Porterfield 50, A. C. Botha 33, A. R. White 32); **Scotland 109** (40.3 overs) (G. M. Hamilton 36; R. M. West 4-26).

A dismal Scottish batting performance – skipper Gavin Hamilton aside, no one managed more than 12 – presented Ireland with a thumping victory. On a pitch freshened up by recent rain the Irish total featured 50 from 76 balls from their own captain, William Porterfield, and some useful lower-order contributions after three quick wickets left them in a spot of bother at 103-5.

At Aberdeen, August 23. **Second one-day international: Scotland v Ireland. Abandoned.**
Persistent light drizzle eventually forced an abandonment, giving Ireland the series 1–0.

At Edinburgh, August 28. **Only one-day international: Australia won by 189 runs.** Toss: Scotland. **Australia 345** (50 overs) (S. R. Watson 68, D. J. Hussey 111, A. C. Voges 72; G. Goudie 5-73); **Scotland 156** (39.3 overs) (G. M. Hamilton 38; S. R. Watson 3-30). *One-day international debuts:* D. P. Nannes, T. D. Paine (Australia). *Man of the Match:* D. J. Hussey.

Australia warmed up for their one-day series against England by teaching the Scots a lesson, although the main contributors, David Hussey and Adam Voges, played no part in the thrashings that followed down south. Hussey, who made his first one-day international hundred, faced 83 balls, hitting eight fours and six sixes, four of them off Majid Haq, whose ten overs of off-spin cost 75. West of Scotland seamer Gordon Goudie wrapped up the innings with two wickets in each of the 48th and 50th overs, to finish with only the second five-for by a Scotland bowler in one-day internationals, after John Blain's 5-22 against the Netherlands in Dublin in 2008. Scotland began with an opening stand of 51 in 9.2 overs, but lost wickets regularly after that. Dirk Nannes made his one-day international debut for Australia after playing for the Netherlands in the World Twenty20 earlier in the English season.

CRICKET IN THE NETHERLANDS, 2009

Putting the stamp on a Dutch triumph

DAVID HARDY

Kervezee, Reekers, Zuiderent, de Grooth, Borren, ten Doeschate, van Bunge, Schiferli, Smits, Seelaar and Nannes: 11 names to conjure with. No longer is the win over the 1964 Australians on a matting wicket in The Hague the finest hour for Dutch cricket. That has become a damp evening in early June 2009 when, in the World Twenty20 and at Lord's, the game's headquarters, the Netherlands defeated England in front of a thousand or more increasingly vociferous members of the Orange army. Who would have thought it possible? And this from a country with just 5,000 or so cricketers and, as at June 5, only five grass squares. The Dutch did virtually everything right, and England, save for a convincing opening partnership, everything wrong. All the Dutch bowlers were disciplined, the ground fielding near faultless and catches held. And, as Peter Drinnen, the Netherlands coach reflected later, he had never seen the Dutch batsmen so pumped up. Tom de Grooth, who won the match award, played the innings of his life.

But the XI who fought that and the next match, against Pakistan, will not play together again. Shortly afterwards Australia called up Dirk Nannes – born in Melbourne of Dutch parents and the owner of a Dutch passport – so depriving Drinnen of his valued services: he is consistently as fast and awkward as Brett Lee, but he may be bowling *at* the Netherlands in the next World Cup. Nannes's tally of international matches for them is stuck at two, presumably for ever. Another unlikely to be seen again is Darron Reekers, the archetypal pinch hitter who once struck six sixes in an over in the Dutch *Hoofdklasse*. He

retired from the national team with a strike-rate in one-day internationals of 116. Both men are proving difficult to replace.

The national team's preparations in 2009 were very organised: a boot camp at home was followed by a successful extended stay in South Africa, culminating in qualification for the 2011 World Cup. The size of the back-room staff is beginning to acquire England proportions, but the focus of coach, captain Jeroen Smits and staff never wavered: the Dutch ship was a happy one. Pakistan's spin bowlers proved too good in the next group game, but history had been made – and recorded by the issue of a celebratory postage stamp.

Even though the Twenty20 euphoria was short-lived, it masked the year's other major achievement: qualification for a third successive World Cup. This was a struggle, but victory over Canada in the last match of the Super Eights – after Essex had recalled Ryan ten Doeschate – was enough. Alexei Kervezee (who *was* allowed by Worcestershire to complete the tournament) and Mudassar Bukhari set the Dutch on course with an opening stand of 167. Kervezee later enjoyed a decent first season at Worcestershire, averaging 27.21 in first-class matches; ten Doeschate struck two hundreds and averaged more than 45 in the County Championship.

The other international matches in 2009 were less successful, partly because an under-strength team contested the four-day Intercontinental Cup. Despite home advantage, the Dutch only just salvaged a draw against Canada. Then, near the end of a long season and with the team showing signs of fatigue, they lost to Afghanistan, and again in the second of two one-day internationals. In that game, ten Doeschate became the third-fastest to 1,000 runs in one-day internationals. Only Viv Richards and Kevin Pietersen had needed fewer than his 23 innings.

The year saw three CEOs at the helm of the Dutch National Cricket Association: former Somerset fast bowler Andre van Troost, appointed in 2008, returned to the business world after only a few months; Jan Zwart then filled the post until the appointment, towards the end of the year, of ex-Warwickshire administrator Richard Cox. He was the fourth CEO in less than two years, and the first non-Dutch. Meanwhile, the most significant addition to the staff was the arrival of Marike Dickmann, with a remit to develop junior cricket.

In the spring an ambitious plan to restructure the game in the Netherlands was launched under the banner "broaden the base and strengthen the top". A strengthening of the top has now been addressed by reshuffling the top two echelons of the league pyramid into three leagues of eight (*Topklasse, Hoofdklasse* and *Eerste Klasse*), but there has been little evidence of a broadening of the base. Two issues of particular importance to the ICC remain unresolved: the introduction of two-day cricket and of contracts for national team members. The Netherlands is now the only leading Associate Member without such contracts and, with a very busy programme in 2010, this is going to become crucial.

The rejigging of the top leagues produced an almighty scramble at the end of the season to avoid relegation. In the end, VVV of Amstelveen, HBS of The Hague (for the first time in their 125-year history) and (after a best-of-three play-off against Rood en Wit of Haarlem) Voorburg CC, for whom Tim de Leede came out of retirement halfway through the season, all dropped down. At the top, Excelsior of Schiedam clamed their seventh title in 18 seasons, beating closest rivals VRA of Amstelveen in the play-off final. In 2010, Excelsior and Voorburg will be playing on grass pitches – bringing the total to seven in the Netherlands.

The Dutch women's team played in Division Five (South and West) of the English County Championship with great success, heading the table and earning a play-off place for promotion to Division Four. The game was scheduled for September 2009, but the weather scuppered that; the plan is to stage the play-off early in the 2010 season. In the European Championships in Ireland, the women maintained their world ranking of ten, two places higher than the men, who will also be facing county opposition in 2010, when they enter the new 40-over tournament.

Jeroen Smits had asked for such an invitation after the Lord's win – one of many significant contributions to the national team's cause, though sadly one of his last. In October 2009, at the age of 37, he announced his retirement after 140 matches, 43 as captain. He made his debut in 1992, but his limitations as a batsman curtailed his appearances, especially early in his career. He came into his own, however, on stepping up to the captaincy during the 2007 World Cup; in his two years as an outstanding leader, he helped make the set-up far more methodical. He was also an excellent wicketkeeper and will be sorely missed.

But the end of 2009 brought an even bigger concern: the number of active cricketers in the Netherlands is not increasing. In other words, the base is not being broadened. The total hovers at about 5,000, of whom only 1,000 or so are juniors. The pool of real talent is very small. The Under-19s almost qualified for their World Cup in early 2010, but none of the younger national teams showed significant progress. Batting, or rather compiling big scores, is a problem for Dutch players. It is partly a mental issue, but more grass wickets and much cricket at a higher level can only help.

ONE-DAY INTERNATIONALS IN THE NETHERLANDS IN 2009

At Amstelveen, July 11. **First one-day international: Netherlands won by 50 runs.** Toss: Canada. **Netherlands 237-7** (50 overs) (A. N. Kervezee 75, R. N. ten Doeschate 35, P. W. Borren 50); **Canada 187** (39 overs) (Rizwan Cheema 94; E. Schiferli 4-44). *One-day international debut: M. Z. Zahir (Canada).*

A fine innings from 19-year-old Alexei Kervezee, who faced 111 balls, took the Dutch to a total that proved beyond Canada's reach, despite Rizwan Cheema's typically forceful 94, which came from only 69 balls and contained 13 fours and three sixes. Canada were 137-2 before he fell, but with Edgar Schiferli bowling quick and straight (his four wickets needed no assistance from the field) the last seven wickets added only 50, the next-highest score being Sunil Dhaniram's 17. Holland's Nick Statham played his third one-day international more than six years after his second, but made a duck – as he had in his previous game, when he was Wasim Akram's 500th wicket in one-day internationals during the 2002-03 World Cup. There were no match awards in this series.

At Amstelveen, July 12. **Second one-day international: Netherlands v Canada. Abandoned.**
The Dutch took the series 1–0 after this match was washed out.

At Amstelveen, August 30. **First one-day international: Netherlands won by eight runs.** Toss: Afghanistan. **Netherlands 188** (47 overs) (Mudassar Bukhari 38, R. N. ten Doeschate 58; Shapoor Zadran 4-24); **Afghanistan 180** (49.5 overs) (Noor Ali 34, Extras 32; E. Schiferli 3-36, R. N. ten Doeschate 4-35). *One-day international debuts: Ahmed Shah, Mirwais Ashraf, Mohammad Shahzad, Shapoor Zadran (Afghanistan). Man of the Match: R. N. ten Doeschate.*

A fine all-round performance from Ryan ten Doeschate lifted the Netherlands to victory over a spirited Afghan side playing their first bilateral one-day series. First ten Doeschate steadied the Dutch innings after the debutant left-arm fast bowler Shapoor Zadran had taken four wickets to reduce them to 52-4, then he wrapped up the Afghan reply with three wickets in nine balls. They had been 152-6 in the 44th over, needing only 37 more from 39 deliveries.

At Amstelveen, September 1. **Second one-day international: Afghanistan won by six wickets.** Toss: Netherlands. **Netherlands 231-7** (50 overs) (E. S. Szwarczynski 65, R. N. ten Doeschate 98*; Nowroz Mangal 3-35); **Afghanistan 232-4** (46.4 overs) (Mohammad Shahzad 110, Asghar Stanikzai 30, Samiullah Shenwari 39*). *One-day international debut: Shafiqullah (Afghanistan). Man of the Match: Mohammad Shahzad.*

Afghanistan levelled the short series with a fine win which owed much to Mohammad Shahzad, who scored Afghanistan's first official one-day international hundred in their third match (his own second). He faced 111 balls and hit 11 fours, and was out with victory all but in the bag. Earlier, Ryan ten Doeschate just missed a hundred of his own: he needed four from the last ball of the innings, but could manage only two to long-on.

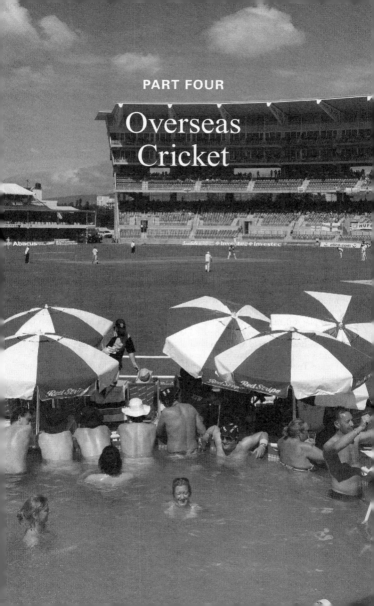

PART FOUR

Overseas Cricket

WORLD CRICKET IN 2009

Test cricket hits back

Simon Wilde

After two years dominated by the rise of 20-over cricket – both Twenty20 internationals and the Indian Premier League – Test cricket enjoyed something of a renaissance in 2009. Another Ashes series in England produced rare drama, and there were many other exciting finishes around the world. Five-day cricket showed that it retained the capacity to be the most richly absorbing format of all.

There were also encouraging signs that Test cricket might be made into a more accessible product in the future. The ICC's resolve to establish a more structured world Test championship, culminating in a showpiece final, hardened to the point where it appeared to be only a matter of time before such an event was introduced. A committee chaired by David Richardson, the ICC's general manager, was set up to review various proposals as to how the present system – a world Test rankings in which the No. 1 team holds a mace as a symbol of their supremacy – might be improved upon.

The biggest challenge was to develop a programme which did not unduly interfere with icon series, such as the Ashes, that were commercially too valuable and too popular to disrupt. Richardson's group also had to determine how play-off matches among the top four sides – or more likely the top two sides to start with – would be decided in the event of a draw. Preliminary discussions were held with England about the feasibility of staging a final at Lord's – widely agreed to be the best venue – in 2012, the first year of the next Future Tours Programme but also when London is due to stage the Olympic Games.

Regular Test championship play-offs were seen as one means of generating wider interest in, and attendance at, Test matches. Another was floodlit cricket played after regular hours of work. Some regions were particularly eager to embrace day/night Tests, and David Morgan, the ICC president, said he would be "surprised and disappointed" if floodlit Test cricket had not been introduced within two years.

The main stumbling block was finding a suitable colour of ball that would be visible under floodlights and last a minimum of 80 overs. MCC's trials with pink balls hit difficulties, but they were due to be used in a four-day match between MCC and Durham – in Abu Dhabi, rather than Lord's – in April 2010.

A further indication that patience was running out with the existing Test schedule came when ICC members agreed in principle that the next Future Tours Programme should relieve teams of the obligation to play every other side home and away. This was a decision specifically designed to avoid weaker sides such as Bangladesh being required to undertake tours against the bigger nations that were commercially unviable and of little cricketing value to players.

Often criticised for its prevarication, the ICC also instigated the most radical change to the way Test cricket had been played since the introduction of the helmet in the late 1970s. After a period of experimentation and refinement, it decided to adopt the Umpire Decision Review System (UDRS), which allowed each team to challenge an umpiring decision if they thought it was wrong, up to a limit of two incorrect challenges per innings. Adjudication was to be by a third umpire armed with TV replays and technological aids.

In an important improvement on what had happened during the trials, the third umpire was allowed to view the predictive element of the Hawk-Eye ball-tracking device to resolve whether the ball would have gone on to hit the stumps in the case of lbw appeals. The Snickometer device was excluded as too time-consuming, while the expensive infra-red Hot Spot was left to availability and affordability. There had to be conclusive evidence for the on-field umpire's decision to be overturned.

TEST MATCHES IN 2009

	Played	Won	Lost	Drawn	% won	% lost	% drawn
Bangladesh	3	2	1	0	**66.66**	33.33	0.00
Australia	13	7	3	3	**53.85**	23.08	23.08
India...............	6	3	0	3	**50.00**	0.00	50.00
Sri Lanka	11	5	2	4	**45.45**	18.18	36.36
England	14	5	2	7	**35.71**	14.29	50.00
South Africa.........	6	1	4	1	**16.66**	66.66	16.66
New Zealand	8	1	4	3	**12.50**	50.00	37.50
Pakistan	9	1	4	4	**11.11**	44.44	44.44
West Indies	12	1	6	5	**8.33**	50.00	41.66
Totals...............	41	26	26	15	**63.41**	63.41	36.59

Zimbabwe did not play any Test matches in 2009.

After the UDRS started in November, most of the early challenges related to lbws, and it was revealing that the players were more often proved wrong than right in their challenges, even allowing for the fact that towards the end of an innings sides would use up their remaining challenges on rather speculative appeals.

The early signs from the Tests that used the UDRS in New Zealand, Australia and South Africa were that it worked well enough, with umpires being spared the embarrassment of making a bad mistake that then had to stand, and the onus falling on the players – previously free to appeal indiscriminately – to use their good judgment. There was an element of self-policing to the whole process, which promised one unexpected by-product: that dissent by players towards officialdom might be reduced.

Inevitably there were teething problems – wrangling over who should pay for the extra technology meant India did not use the system for their series with Sri Lanka – but players, umpires and spectators seemed broadly content, although those among the crowd were entitled to be shown more replays on the big screen after a review had been resolved. In the past, big-screen replays

Paul Gilham, Getty Images

Sign of the times: Graeme Smith signals that he wants to challenge the umpire's decision. Mark Boucher and Jean-Paul Duminy seem to back up the query.

were limited in number to prevent riots in one-day games; but this was hardly going to happen at most Tests.

On-field umpire Mark Benson's sudden withdrawal midway through a Test in Australia after a difficult day sparked concerns that he was walking out in protest at having been wrongly overruled by Asad Rauf, the third official, but publicly he cited health issues. By the year's end, it seemed certain that the system was here to stay.

It became apparent that the review system was good news for spin bowlers. With Hawk-Eye showing just how many of a spinner's deliveries were hitting the stumps, umpires had already become more inclined to accept their lbw appeals, and now spinners had a second chance through the reviews. In 2009, spinners took 23.8% of their Test wickets through lbws, their highest percentage in any calendar year, while 2000–09 was the first decade in five in which spin bowlers had taken a greater proportion of their wickets lbw (18.4%) than fast bowlers (17.3%).

Orthodox finger-spinners who did not possess a *doosra* had been thought an endangered species, but they had a very good year in 2009, providing eight of the 18 instances of a bowler taking eight or more wickets in a Test – four by slow left-armers, four by off-spinners. Three of the latter were the work of Graeme Swann, who became the first England spinner to take 50 wickets in a calendar year. Of his 54 victims, 22 fell to lbws. By the end of the year, his career tally in 14 games of 27 leg-befores left him third among England spinners behind Jim Laker (32 out of 193 wickets) and his sometime team-mate Monty Panesar (31 out of 126).

The potency of off-spin had been enhanced by the greater number of left-handed batsmen in the game. Left-handers were now playing more than 30% of all Test innings, compared to 18.5% during the 1970s.

ONE-DAY INTERNATIONALS IN 2009

(excluding Zimbabwe, Bangladesh and Associate matches)

	Played	Won	Lost	NR	% won	% lost
India..............	31	17	10	4	**62.96**	37.03
Australia............	38	22	14	2	**61.11**	38.88
South Africa..........	16	9	7	0	**56.25**	43.75
New Zealand..........	24	10	11	3	**47.61**	52.38
England..............	21	10	11	0	**47.61**	52.38
Sri Lanka.............	24	10	13	1	**43.47**	56.52
Pakistan.............	20	8	12	0	**40.00**	60.00
West Indies..........	18	4	12	2	**25.00**	75.00
Totals...............	96	90	90	6		

The % won and lost excludes no-results.

For all that, cricket remained predominantly a batsman's game, whatever the format. In Tests, the overall average of runs per wicket was 37.84, the second-highest figure on record in years when eight or more Tests were played, behind only the average for 1989. The overall scoring-rate of 3.37 runs per over was also the second-highest in history, a touch behind 2005's rate of 3.38. India's opener Virender Sehwag again set the pace with a personal rate of 109 runs per 100 balls. Sehwag's spectacular 293 in Mumbai included a double-century from just 168 balls, the second-fastest on record. Another opener, the West Indian captain Chris Gayle, took a hundred off Australia at Perth in 70 balls, the fifth-swiftest in Tests.

HIGHEST RUNS PER WICKET BY YEAR IN TESTS

Year	Tests	Runs	Wkts	RPW	Year	Tests	Runs	Wkts	RPW
1989	21	22,687	574	39.52	2004	51	57,064	1,605	35.55
2009	**41**	**47,381**	**1,252**	**37.84**	2007	31	33,340	945	35.28
2003	44	48,944	1,347	36.33	1985	26	26,080	747	34.91
1973	22	23,521	661	35.58	2006	46	50,043	1,446	34.60
1964	24	24,656	693	35.57	1983	30	28,821	840	34.31

Minimum 20 Tests in the year.   *Research: Andrew Samson*

There were 11 Test totals in excess of 600 (of which four went beyond 700), a record by three for a calendar year. There were eight totals of 350 or more in one-day internationals, seven of them conceded by front-line teams (another record). In an extraordinary match at Rajkot, India only narrowly managed to defend a score of 414 for eight; thanks to 160 off 124 balls from Tillekeratne Dilshan, Sri Lanka fell just three runs short. India passed 350 on four occasions in all, as well as failing by only three runs themselves to match Australia's 350 for four at Hyderabad. Dilshan had a notable personal year, hitting the most hundreds in Tests (six) and one-day internationals (four), as well as the highest score in a Twenty20 international – an unbeaten 96 against West Indies in the

A man for all formats: Sri Lanka's Tillekeratne Dilshan was in the form of his life, as in the Mumbai Test in December.

World Twenty20 semi-final. His duck in the final against Pakistan had much to do with Sri Lanka's eventual defeat.

Further evidence of the bat's dominance was that the year failed to provide one instance of a bowler taking ten wickets in a match, the first time this had happened since 1970. The best match figures of nine for 107 were provided by Pakistan fast bowler Mohammad Asif, playing at Wellington in only his second match back in Test cricket after a ban for testing positive for nandrolone. There were just seven innings returns of six or more wickets, and only one of seven (by Danish Kaneria, Pakistan's leg-spinner, and he conceded 168 runs in doing so against New Zealand), evidence that bowlers were struggling to run through opposing line-ups and that on unhelpful, too-durable pitches the bowling workload had to be shared.

ALL ONE-DAY INTERNATIONALS IN 2009

	Played	Won	Lost	NR	% won	% lost
Ireland	8	7	1	0	**87.50**	12.50
Netherlands	6	5	1	0	**83.33**	16.66
Bangladesh	19	14	5	0	**73.68**	26.31
Afghanistan	3	2	1	0	**66.66**	33.33
South Africa	18	11	7	0	**61.11**	38.88
India.	31	17	10	4	**62.96**	37.03
Australia	39	23	14	2	**62.16**	37.83
England	22	11	11	0	**50.00**	50.00
Zimbabwe	27	13	14	0	**48.14**	51.85
New Zealand	24	10	11	3	**47.61**	52.38
Sri Lanka	27	12	14	1	**46.15**	53.84
Canada.	8	3	4	1	**42.85**	57.14
Pakistan	20	8	12	0	**40.00**	60.00
West Indies	21	4	15	2	**21.05**	78.94
Scotland.	7	1	6	0	**14.28**	85.71
Kenya	18	2	15	1	**11.76**	88.23
Bermuda	2	0	2	0	**0.00**	100.00
Totals.	150	143	143	7		

The % won and lost excludes no-results.

Lower-order batsmen continued to flourish. Indeed, rarely can there have been a year when they wielded such influence, as several last-wicket pairs blocked out for draws. The efforts with the bat of England's bowling specialists played a large part in Australia being relieved of the Ashes: Swann scored 249 runs in the five-match series and Stuart Broad 234. England's average for the last five wickets was better than any other side's during 2009.

There were other twists. Pakistan, whose ability to host matches was struck a devastating blow by the terrorist attack on the Sri Lanka team in Lahore in March, subsequently botched a number of fourth-innings run-chases. But Pakistan did not stumble in probably the most important, and certainly the most valuable, run-chase of all – in the World Twenty20 final at Lord's against Sri Lanka, a moving rematch between the teams caught up in the horror of Lahore. With their future so uncertain, Pakistan had the backing of most neutrals, and the support they received encouraged plans for them to stage two "home" Tests against Australia in England in 2010.

In an effort to combat tracks not only being too favourable for batting but too lifeless to produce an entertaining spectacle, the ICC issued new instructions stating that Test pitches could be marked down for failing to provide a good and fair contest. The speed with which some balls such as the Kookaburra went soft was also a factor in bowlers being dealt such a difficult hand.

Ironically, the year saw a number of controversies over poor pitches and playing conditions. The Test between West Indies and England at the Sir Vivian Richards Stadium in Antigua was abandoned after only ten balls because West Indies' opening bowlers found themselves unable to run up properly over an outfield laid on a heavy base of sand. The outfield had been recently relaid to improve drainage. As a consequence the stadium was suspended from staging internationals for 12 months. A Twenty20 international at Old Trafford was abandoned because the drainage system failed to work adequately, and a one-dayer at the Feroz Shah Kotla stadium in Delhi, earmarked to stage matches at the 2011 World Cup, was called off after 23.3 overs due to "extremely variable bounce".

TWENTY20 INTERNATIONALS IN 2009

	Played	Won	Lost	NR	% won	% lost
Pakistan	11	9	2	0	81.81	18.18
South Africa	12	8	4	0	66.66	33.33
West Indies	8	5	3	0	62.50	37.50
Sri Lanka	13	7	6	0	53.84	46.15
New Zealand	12	6	6	0	50.00	50.00
Netherlands	2	1	1	0	50.00	50.00
India.................	10	4	6	0	40.00	60.00
England	9	3	5	1	37.50	62.50
Australia	9	3	5	1	37.50	62.50
Ireland	5	1	4	0	20.00	80.00
Scotland..............	2	0	2	0	0.00	100.00
Bangladesh	3	0	3	0	0.00	100.00
Totals................	48	47	47	1		

The % won and lost excludes no-results.

Australia's decline since the retirement of many of their great players was another reason why play-offs to decide the best Test team looked an attractive idea. Australia still won more Tests in the year than anyone else (besides winning the Champions Trophy), but the loss of the Ashes was their third series defeat in five, and cost them the place they had held at the top of the ICC's world Test rankings since they were officially introduced in June 2003. Australia fell to fourth, and were displaced at the top by South Africa. They in turn stayed at No. 1 for four months until India went top for the first time following a 2–0 home win over Sri Lanka. This was one of only two Test series played by India, who also won 1–0 in New Zealand. But it was enough.

RELIANCE MOBILE ICC TEST CHAMPIONSHIP

(As at January 27, 2010)

		Matches	Points	Rating
1	India	35	4,359	125
2	South Africa	35	4,197	120
3	Australia	39	4,586	118
4	Sri Lanka	31	3,574	115
5	England	44	4,712	107
6	New Zealand	29	2,337	81
7	Pakistan	25	2,008	80
8	West Indies	29	2,224	77
9	Bangladesh	22	264	12

RELIANCE MOBILE ICC ONE-DAY CHAMPIONSHIP

(As at December 31, 2009)

		Matches	Points	Rating
1	Australia	39	5,080	130
2	India	41	5,046	123
3	South Africa	26	3,085	119
4	New Zealand	25	2,789	112
5	England	33	3,606	109
6	Pakistan	28	3,012	108
7	Sri Lanka	35	3,686	105
8	West Indies	21	1,589	76
9	Bangladesh	28	1,548	55
10	Zimbabwe	32	823	26
11	Ireland	6	152	25
12	Kenya	14	28	2

RELIANCE MOBILE ICC RANKINGS

Introduced in 1987, the Rankings have been backed by various sponsors, but were taken over by the International Cricket Council in January 2005. They rank cricketers on a scale up to 1,000 on their performances in Tests. The rankings take into account playing conditions, the quality of the opposition and the result of the matches. In August 1998, a similar set of rankings for one-day internationals was added.

The leading ten batsmen and bowlers in the Test Rankings on January 27, 2010, were:

Rank	Batsmen	Points	Rank	Bowlers	Points
1	G. Gambhir (*India*)	882	1	D. W. Steyn (*South Africa*)	852
2	G. C. Smith (*South Africa*)	843	2	M. G. Johnson (*Australia*)	780
3	D. P. M. D. Jayawardene (*SL*)	836	3	Mohammad Asif (*Pakistan*)	757
4	K. C. Sangakkara (*Sri Lanka*)	835	4	M. Muralitharan (*Sri Lanka*)	752
5	M. J. Clarke (*Australia*)	805	5	G. P. Swann (*England*)	732
6	V. Sehwag (*India*)	797	6	Zaheer Khan (*India*)	715
7	R. T. Ponting (*Australia*)	783	7	M. Morkel (*South Africa*)	691
8	J. H. Kallis (*South Africa*)	773	8	Harbhajan Singh (*India*)	679
9	S. R. Tendulkar (*India*)	772	9	S. C. J. Broad (*England*)	673
10	S. Chanderpaul (*West Indies*)	765	10	M. Ntini (*South Africa*)	671

The leading ten batsmen and bowlers in the One-Day International Rankings on December 31, 2009, were:

Rank	Batsmen	Points	Rank	Bowlers	Points
1	M. S. Dhoni (*India*)	825	1	D. L. Vettori (*New Zealand*) . .	719
2	M. E. K. Hussey (*Australia*) . .	801	2	Shakib Al Hasan (*Bangladesh*)	716
3	A. B. de Villiers (*South Africa*)	749	3	R. W. Price (*Zimbabwe*)	701
4	S. R. Tendulkar (*India*)	741	4	K. D. Mills (*New Zealand*) . . .	685
5	R. T. Ponting (*Australia*)	738	5	K. M. D. N. Kulasekara (*SL*) . .	662
6	C. H. Gayle (*West Indies*)	736	6	{ S. E. Bond (*New Zealand*)	652
7	S. Chanderpaul (*West Indies*) .	733		{ Harbhajan Singh (*India*)	652
8	G. C. Smith (*South Africa*) . . .	729	8	S. C. J. Broad (*England*)	646
9	Yuvraj Singh (*India*)	712	9	{ J. M. Anderson (*England*)	638
10	V. Sehwag (*India*)	701		{ D. W. Steyn (*South Africa*) . . .	638

In October 2008, the ICC launched a set of rankings for women cricketers, based on one-day international performances because of the paucity of women's Test cricket. The ICC said it hoped to raise the profile of the women's game by identifying where the leading players stood, and to add further competition and context to their achievements.

The leading ten batsmen and bowlers in the Women's One-Day International Rankings on December 31, 2009, were:

Rank	Batsmen	Points	Rank	Bowlers	Points
1	M. Raj (*India*)	758	1	H. L. Colvin (*England*)	719
2	S. C. Taylor (*England*)	744	2	J. Goswami (*India*)	713
3	S. J. Taylor (*England*)	732	3	L. C. Sthalekar (*Australia*). . . .	693
4	S. Nitschke (*Australia*)	656	4	S. Nitschke (*Australia*)	640
5	L. C. Sthalekar (*Australia*). . . .	643	5	K. H. Brunt (*England*)	633
6	K. L. Rolton (*Australia*).	636	6	R. Dhar (*India*)	604
7	N. J. Browne (*New Zealand*) . .	604	7	N. J. Shaw (*England*).	599
8	C. M. Edwards (*England*)	603	8	L. A. Marsh (*England*).	598
9	S. R. Taylor (*West Indies*)	545	9	N. J. Browne (*New Zealand*) . .	597
10	C. M. G. Atkins (*England*) . . .	541	10	I. T. Guha (*England*)	589

INTERNATIONAL AVERAGES, 2009

The averages in this section refer to the calendar year 2009.

TEST AVERAGES

BATTING

(Qualification: 300 runs, average 35.00)

	T	I	NO	R	HS	100s	Avge	SR	Ct/St
M. S. Dhoni (I)..............	5	6	2	369	110	2	92.25	59.22	21/1
†G. Gambhir (I)..............	5	9	1	727	167	4	90.87	51.89	2
R. Dravid (I)................	6	10	1	747	177	2	83.00	48.60	8
T. T. Samaraweera (SL).......	11	20	3	1,234	231	4	72.58	58.34	3
V. Sehwag (I)...............	6	9	0	631	293	2	70.11	108.98	6
S. R. Tendulkar (I)..........	6	9	1	541	160	2	67.62	55.83	4
V. V. S. Laxman (I).........	6	9	2	471	124*	1	67.28	49.42	6
S. R. Watson (A)............	7	12	1	716	120*	1	65.09	54.32	9
T. M. Dilshan (SL)...........	11	18	1	1,097	162	6	64.52	82.66	16
Younis Khan (P)	5	7	0	444	313	1	63.42	53.42	1
D. P. M. D. Jayawardene (SL)...	11	20	1	1,194	275	3	62.84	52.20	13
R. R. Sarwan (WI)	9	14	0	850	291	4	60.71	58.17	4
†D. L. Vettori (NZ)	8	14	1	779	140	3	59.92	67.09	11
A. B. de Villiers (SA)	6	11	1	572	163	2	57.20	53.40	9
Umar Akmal (P)..............	4	8	0	457	129	1	57.12	66.52	3
†K. C. Sangakkara (SL)........	11	20	1	1,083	137	4	57.00	54.72	4
L. R. P. L. Taylor (NZ)	8	14	0	782	151	2	55.85	58.44	20
M. J. Clarke (A).............	13	23	4	1,042	138	3	54.84	55.60	14
†A. J. Strauss (E)	14	24	2	1,172	169	4	53.27	54.13	9
†P. J. Hughes (A).............	5	9	0	472	160	2	52.44	58.56	3
†J. D. Ryder (NZ)	5	9	0	454	201	2	50.44	55.36	2
†C. H. Gayle (WI)	10	16	1	739	165*	4	49.26	67.73	5
J. H. Kallis (SA)............	6	11	0	532	120	2	48.36	50.18	12
†S. M. Katich (A)............	13	23	0	1,111	122	2	48.30	50.91	12
P. D. Collingwood (E)........	14	21	2	915	161	2	48.15	48.10	19
K. P. Pietersen (E)	11	17	1	760	102	1	47.50	58.28	2
R. S. Bopara (E)............	7	10	0	460	143	3	46.00	53.30	4
†A. N. Cook (E).............	14	24	3	960	160	3	45.71	48.38	13
G. P. Swann (E).............	12	14	4	452	85	0	45.20	85.93	6
Kamran Akmal (P)...........	9	15	2	581	158*	1	44.69	73.73	34/3
B. J. Haddin (A)............	12	18	2	706	121	1	44.12	65.67	46/2
M. J. Prior (E)	13	20	3	740	131*	1	43.52	72.69	25/2
H. A. P. W. Jayawardene (SL)..	8	13	3	419	154*	1	41.90	58.60	17/4
†M. J. North (A).............	11	18	1	701	125*	3	41.23	47.52	8
T. M. Dowlin (WI)...........	4	8	0	328	95	0	41.00	47.19	4
Mohammad Yousuf (P)	7	14	0	566	112	1	40.42	48.21	3
R. T. Ponting (A)............	13	23	1	853	150	1	38.77	67.48	20
A. D. Mathews (SL)..........	7	11	1	379	99	0	37.90	59.68	2
†B. P. Nash (WI)	10	16	0	585	109	1	36.56	40.93	4
†M. E. K. Hussey (A)	13	23	1	804	121	1	36.54	44.22	13
Shoaib Malik (P)	7	11	1	364	134	1	36.40	48.46	6
†S. Chanderpaul (WI)	9	14	1	466	147*	1	35.84	37.13	1

† Left-handed batsman.

BOWLING

(Qualification: 10 wickets)

	Style	O	M	R	W	BB	5Wli	Avge	SR
Mahmudullah (B)	OB	62.4	9	191	12	5-51	1	15.91	31.33
K. M. D. N. Kulasekara (SL) . . .	RFM	133.4	25	422	20	4-21	0	21.10	40.10
D. J. G. Sammy (WI)	RM	103.1	19	308	14	5-55	2	22.00	44.21
Mohammad Asif (P)	RFM	169.4	41	500	22	5-67	1	22.72	46.27
Shakib Al Hasan (B)	SLA	159.1	39	432	18	5-70	1	24.00	53.05
D. E. Bollinger (A)	LFM	162.2	32	481	20	5-70	1	24.05	48.70
M. G. Johnson (A)	LF	502.5	89	1,728	63	5-69	2	27.42	47.88
G. P. Swann (E)	OB	518	111	1,508	54	5-54	4	27.92	57.55
S. C. J. Broad (E)	RFM	421.3	84	1,333	47	6-91	3	28.36	53.80
G. Onions (E)	RFM	196.1	35	713	25	5-38	1	28.52	47.08
D. J. Bravo (WI)	RFM	94.1	16	319	11	4-42	0	29.00	51.36
K. A. J. Roach (WI)	RF	180.4	39	586	20	6-48	1	29.30	54.20
P. M. Siddle (A)	RFM	432	116	1,320	45	5-21	2	29.33	57.60
Harbhajan Singh (I)	OB	306	47	875	29	6-63	1	30.17	63.31
B. W. Hilfenhaus (A)	RFM	328.5	75	1,040	34	4-60	0	30.58	58.02
M. T. T. Mirando (SL)	LFM	180.1	22	652	20	5-83	1	32.60	54.05
D. W. Steyn (SA)	RF	205	35	723	22	4-56	0	32.86	55.90
P. L. Harris (SA)	SLA	291.4	61	862	26	6-127	2	33.15	67.30
Zaheer Khan (I)	LFM	219.3	42	765	23	5-65	2	33.26	57.26
Danish Kaneria (P)	LBG	253.5	35	833	25	7-168	2	33.32	60.92
H. M. R. K. B. Herath (SL)	SLA	388	57	1,150	34	5-99	4	33.82	64.94
J. M. Anderson (E)	RFM	440.5	100	1,355	40	5-80	2	33.87	66.12
C. S. Martin (NZ)	RFM	312.1	65	1,018	30	4-52	0	33.93	62.43
N. M. Hauritz (A)	OB	318.2	59	958	28	5-101	1	34.21	68.21
J. E. Taylor (WI)	RF	156.2	30	533	14	5-11	1	38.07	67.00
D. L. Vettori (NZ)	SLA	409.5	110	1,055	27	4-58	0	39.07	91.07
Umar Gul (P)	RFM	244	33	946	24	6-135	1	39.41	61.00
I. E. O'Brien (NZ)	RFM	335.4	61	1,220	30	4-35	0	40.66	67.13
M. Morkel (SA)	RF	185.4	23	610	15	3-78	0	40.66	74.26
S. J. Benn (WI)	SLA	385.4	70	1,117	27	5-155	1	41.37	85.70
Mohammad Aamer (P)	LFM	226	49	747	18	5-79	1	41.50	75.33
Saeed Ajmal (P)	OB	270.4	43	761	18	4-87	0	42.27	90.22
A. Flintoff (E)	RF	191.1	37	568	13	5-92	1	43.69	88.23
F. H. Edwards (WI)	RF	181	16	711	16	6-92	1	44.43	67.87
B. A. W. Mendis (SL)	OB/ LBG	267.5	45	820	18	4-71	0	45.55	89.27
M. Muralitharan (SL)	OB	374.5	52	1,195	26	4-73	0	45.96	86.50
I. Sharma (I)	RFM	127.2	21	469	10	4-73	0	46.90	76.40
J. S. Patel (NZ)	OB	154	20	569	11	4-78	0	51.72	84.00
M. Ntini (SA)	RFM	219	49	741	13	3-52	0	57.00	101.07

MOST DISMISSALS BY A WICKETKEEPER

Dis			Dis		
48 (46 ct, 2 st)	12	B. J. Haddin (A)	27 (25 ct, 2 st)	13	M. J. Prior (E)
37 (34 ct, 3 st)	9	Kamran Akmal (P)	22 (21 ct, 1 st)	5	M. S. Dhoni (I)
34 (33 ct, 1 st)	8	B. B. McCullum (NZ)	21 (17 ct, 4 st)	8	H. A. P. W. Jayawardene (SL)
28 (28 ct)	10	D. Ramdin (WI)	20 (19 ct, 1 st)	6	M. V. Boucher (SA)

MOST CATCHES IN THE FIELD

Ct	T		Ct	T	
20	8	L. R. P. L. Taylor (NZ)	16	11	T. M. Dilshan (SL)
20	13	R. T. Ponting (A)	14	13	M. J. Clarke (A)
19	14	P. D. Collingwood (E)			

ONE-DAY INTERNATIONAL AVERAGES

BATTING

(Qualification: 500 runs, average 35.00)

	M	I	NO	R	HS	100s	50s	Avge	SR	4	6
M. S. Dhoni (I)	29	24	7	1,198	124	2	9	70.47	85.57	79	18
†S. Chanderpaul (WI)	14	12	3	531	112*	1	3	59.00	77.29	43	5
T. M. Dilshan (SL)	19	19	1	1,000	160	4	2	55.55	103.19	130	8
A. B. de Villiers (SA)	17	17	3	762	121	1	6	54.42	92.81	66	6
S. R. Tendulkar (I)	21	20	2	972	175	3	3	54.00	94.00	108	13
†Shakib Al Hasan (B)	19	17	4	671	105*	2	4	51.61	106.17	61	14
S. R. Watson (A)	24	24	4	1,013	136*	3	3	50.65	84.48	105	20
P. D. Collingwood (E)....	19	18	4	705	105*	1	4	50.35	83.92	53	16
†M. E. K. Hussey (A)	33	31	7	1,166	83*	0	11	48.58	90.80	81	16
C. J. Ferguson (A)........	25	22	9	599	71*	0	5	46.07	85.08	58	0
V. Sehwag (I)	20	19	1	810	146	3	3	45.00	136.59	114	20
J. H. Kallis (SA)	12	12	0	538	81	0	5	44.83	81.76	53	4
H. Masakadza (Z)	27	27	2	1,087	178*	3	5	43.48	88.08	118	19
M. J. Clarke (A)	23	23	3	868	100*	1	8	43.40	69.49	79	1
†S. H. T. Kandamby (SL)...	21	21	5	686	93*	0	5	42.87	77.33	62	0
R. T. Ponting (A)........	29	29	1	1,198	126	2	9	42.78	81.11	121	12
G. D. Elliott (NZ)	21	17	5	507	115	1	2	42.25	77.40	32	3
B. R. M. Taylor (Z).......	17	17	3	590	118*	1	5	42.14	84.04	31	13
M. J. Guptill (NZ)........	22	21	3	738	122*	1	6	41.00	82.00	62	15
†G. Gambhir (I)	27	23	2	848	150*	2	5	40.38	92.57	77	5
†W. U. Tharanga (SL)......	13	13	0	523	118	1	4	40.23	82.36	53	8
†C. H. Gayle (WI)	15	15	1	553	135	1	2	39.50	117.65	56	27
†Yuvraj Singh (I)	23	21	1	783	131	2	5	39.15	95.95	88	21
†G. C. Smith (SA)........	13	13	0	502	141	1	4	38.61	96.35	64	3
†S. K. Raina (I)	27	21	5	605	68	0	5	37.81	101.51	41	24
B. J. Haddin (A)	20	20	1	716	109	1	5	37.68	88.61	64	16
C. L. White (A)	26	22	3	682	105	1	5	35.89	77.76	54	13
†K. C. Sangakkara (SL)	27	27	1	919	90	0	8	35.34	80.33	81	7

† *Left-handed batsman.*

BOWLING

(Qualification: 20 wickets, average 35.00)

	Style	O	M	R	W	BB	4W/i	Avge	SR	ER
Abdur Razzak (B)	SLA	70.4	2	332	22	5-29	2	15.09	19.27	4.69
R. W. Price (Z)	SLA	238.1	25	907	44	4-22	1	20.61	32.47	3.80
W. D. Parnell (SA)	LFM	79.3	7	462	22	5-48	3	21.00	21.68	5.81
S. R. Watson (A)	RFM	124	4	621	29	3-29	0	21.41	25.65	5.00
A. G. Cremer (Z)	LBG	157.5	9	709	33	6-46	3	21.48	28.69	4.49
S. C. J. Broad (E)...........	RFM	129.3	6	731	32	4-39	3	22.84	24.28	5.64
Shakib Al Hasan (B)	SLA	170.3	28	595	26	3-8	0	22.88	39.34	3.48
J. M. Anderson (E)	RFM	161.3	9	803	34	5-23	2	23.61	28.50	4.97
B. Lee (A)	RF	104.1	7	501	21	5-49	1	23.85	29.76	4.80
Umar Gul (P)..............	RFM	134.4	9	689	27	4-58	1	25.51	29.92	5.11
Saeed Ajmal (P)............	OB	152.1	3	604	23	4-33	1	26.26	39.69	3.96
D. W. Steyn (SA)...........	RF	139.2	10	709	26	4-27	2	27.26	32.15	5.08
K. M. D. N. Kulasekara (SL)...	RFM	186	14	934	34	3-13	0	27.47	32.82	5.02
M. T. T. Mirando (SL).......	LFM	126	8	618	22	3-29	0	28.09	34.36	4.90
K. D. Mills (NZ)	RFM	182.4	14	907	32	4-35	1	28.34	34.25	4.96
D. L. Vettori (NZ)	SLA	169.1	10	688	24	4-20	1	28.66	42.29	4.06
N. M. Hauritz (A)	OB	238	10	1,025	35	4-29	1	29.28	40.80	4.30

	Style	O	M	R	W	BB	4W/i	Avge	SR	ER
M. Muralitharan (SL)	OB	135.5	5	648	22	3-19	0	29.45	37.04	4.77
Shahid Afridi (P)...........	LBG	181.5	4	807	27	6-38	1	29.88	40.40	4.43
M. G. Johnson (A)...........	LF	261.4	14	1,383	46	4-34	1	30.06	34.13	5.28
A. Nehra (I)................	LFM	157.3	6	933	31	4-55	1	30.09	30.48	5.92
P. Utseya (Z)	OB	194.5	12	793	25	4-46	1	31.72	46.76	4.07
B. A. W. Mendis (SL)	OB/	164	3	800	24	3-15	0	33.33	41.00	4.87
	LBG									
I. Sharma (I)...............	RFM	153.5	7	969	29	4-57	1	33.41	31.82	6.29
Harbhajan Singh (I).........	OB	206.5	4	1,036	31	5-56	1	33.41	40.03	5.00
J. R. Hopes (A)	RFM	199.1	9	910	27	3-32	0	33.70	44.25	4.56

MOST DISMISSALS BY A WICKETKEEPER

Dis		M		Dis		M	
39	(34 ct, 5 st)	27	K. C. Sangakkara (SL)	19	(18 ct, 1 st)	15	D. Ramdin (WI)
37	(26 ct, 11 st)	29	M. S. Dhoni (I)	19	(16 ct, 3 st)	16	M. V. Boucher (SA)
27	(22 ct, 5 st)	20	Kamran Akmal (P)	19	(14 ct, 5 st)	19	Mushfiqur Rahim (B)
24	(20 ct, 4 st)	15	T. D. Paine (A)	19	(18 ct, 1 st)	19	M. J. Prior (E)
23	(22 ct, 1 st)	20	B. J. Haddin (A)	19†	(19 ct)	20	B. B. McCullum (NZ)

† *McCullum also made one catch in the field in four matches when not keeping wicket.*

MOST CATCHES IN THE FIELD

Ct	M		Ct	M	
22	24	L. R. P. L. Taylor (NZ)	13	27	S. K. Raina (I)
18	33	M. E. K. Hussey (A)	12	17	J-P. Duminy (SA)
14	30	N. M. Hauritz (A)	12	27	H. Masakadza (Z)
13	26	C. L. White (A)			

TWENTY20 INTERNATIONAL AVERAGES

BATTING

(Qualification: 150 runs, average 25.00)

	M	I	NO	R	HS	50s	Avge	SR	4	6
L. L. Bosman (SA)...............	2	2	0	152	94	2	76.00	200.00	10	13
Younis Khan (P)................	7	6	3	172	50	1	57.33	139.83	11	3
†C. H. Gayle (WI)	5	5	1	193	88	2	48.25	134.02	21	8
†K. C. Sangakkara (SL)...........	12	12	2	434	78	5	43.40	135.20	44	7
T. M. Dilshan (SL).............	12	12	1	471	96*	5	42.81	141.44	66	6
B. B. McCullum (NZ)	12	12	2	417	69*	4	41.70	122.28	39	11
J. H. Kallis (SA)..............	7	7	1	249	64	2	41.50	125.12	30	4
†Yuvraj Singh (I)	10	10	2	302	67	3	37.75	158.94	19	20
†J-P. Duminy (SA)..............	12	12	4	284	78	2	35.50	124.01	24	6
†G. C. Smith (SA)	8	8	0	278	88	1	34.75	136.27	32	11
L. M. P. Simmons (WI)	6	6	1	173	77	1	34.60	122.69	23	1
†D. A. Warner (A)	8	8	0	273	89	2	34.12	139.28	26	9
Shahid Afridi (P)	11	10	2	272	54*	3	34.00	139.48	23	7
K. P. Pietersen (E)	6	6	0	195	58	1	32.50	143.38	20	6
D. J. Bravo (WI)...............	7	6	1	162	66*	2	32.40	138.46	13	6
C. L. White (A)	6	6	1	157	55	1	31.40	140.17	8	8
D. J. Hussey (A)...............	9	9	1	236	88*	1	29.50	142.16	11	14
Kamran Akmal (P)...............	11	11	1	286	59*	2	28.60	124.34	26	11
L. R. P. L. Taylor (NZ)	9	9	1	203	60	1	25.37	114.68	14	7
†G. Gambhir (I)	10	10	0	253	55	2	25.30	123.41	32	2
A. B. de Villiers (SA)............	11	11	2	227	79*	1	25.22	142.76	21	7

† *Left-handed batsman.*

BOWLING

(Qualification: 8 wickets, average 30.00)

	Style	O	M	R	W	BB	4W/i	Avge	SR	ER
Umar Gul (P)	RFM	34.3	0	208	19	5-6	2	10.94	10.89	6.02
Shahid Afridi (P)	LBG	42.3	1	226	18	4-11	1	12.55	14.16	5.31
Saeed Ajmal (P)	OB	42.5	0	242	19	4-19	1	12.73	13.52	5.64
B. A. W. Mendis (SL).........	OB/	34	0	189	14	3-9	0	13.50	14.57	5.55
	LBG									
D. L. Vettori (NZ).	SLA	27	0	152	9	2-11	0	16.88	18.00	5.62
W. K. McCallan (Ireland).......	OB	19.3	0	137	8	2-26	0	17.12	14.62	7.02
W. D. Parnell (SA)	LFM	28.5	0	192	11	4-13	1	17.45	15.72	6.65
N. L. McCullum (NZ).	OB	24.2	0	159	9	3-15	0	17.66	16.22	6.53
S. C. J. Broad (E)	RFM	23	0	163	9	3-17	0	18.11	15.33	7.08
R. E. van der Merwe (SA)	SLA	34	0	221	12	2-14	0	18.41	17.00	6.50
A. R. Cusack (Ireland)	RM	17	0	153	8	4-18	1	19.12	12.75	9.00
D. W. Steyn (SA)	RF	41	0	315	16	3-38	0	19.68	15.37	7.68
D. J. Bravo (WI)	RFM	25	0	218	11	4-38	1	19.81	13.63	8.72
I. G. Butler (NZ).	RFM	40	0	332	16	3-19	0	20.75	15.00	8.30
M. Muralitharan (SL)	OB	31	0	188	9	3-29	0	20.88	20.66	6.06
S. L. Malinga (SL)	RF	46.4	0	360	17	3-17	0	21.17	16.47	7.71
K. D. Mills (NZ).	RFM	21.4	0	173	8	2-12	0	21.62	16.25	7.98
Zaheer Khan (I)	LFM	26.4	0	207	9	4-19	1	23.00	17.77	7.76
A. D. Mathews (SL)	RFM	28.1	0	224	9	3-16	0	24.88	18.77	7.95
Mohammad Aamer (P)........	LFM	34	2	251	9	2-21	0	27.88	22.66	7.38
J. A. Morkel (SA)............	RFM	29.4	1	268	9	2-15	0	29.77	19.77	9.03

MOST DISMISSALS BY A WICKETKEEPER

Dis		M			Dis		M	
13	(4 ct, 9 st)	11	Kamran Akmal (P)		6	(3 ct, 3 st)	5	J. S. Foster (E)
10	(6 ct, 4 st)	12	K. C. Sangakkara (SL)		6	(6 ct)	7	D. Ramdin (WI)
6	(4 ct, 2 st)	4	N. J. O'Brien (Ireland)					

MOST CATCHES IN THE FIELD

Ct	M		Ct	M	
9	11	A. B. de Villiers (SA)	6†	8	B. B. McCullum (NZ)
7	11	J. Botha (SA)	6	9	J. D. P. Oram (NZ)
7	12	J. A. Morkel (SA)	6	11	Shoaib Malik (P)
6	7	A. D. S. Fletcher (WI)	6	12	J-P. Duminy (SA)

† *McCullum also made two catches in four matches as wicketkeeper.*

INDEX OF TEST MATCHES

Eight earlier 2008-09 Test series – India v Australia, Bangladesh v New Zealand, South Africa v Bangladesh, Australia v New Zealand, New Zealand v West Indies, India v England, Australia v South Africa, and Bangladesh v Sri Lanka – appeared in *Wisden 2009*.

THE WOMEN'S WORLD CUP, 2008-09

Jenny Roesler

1. England   *2. New Zealand*   *3. India*   *4. Australia*

For the hardy perennial that is women's cricket, 2009 was the time to bloom. The ICC had lovingly tended a promising crop since taking over four years earlier, and their first global show came with the World Cup in March.

The players had been working hard out of sight – the odd peep around the curtain with the Ashes and Twenty20 games notwithstanding – but could they impress in Australia? Virgin viewers such as Wasim Akram, commentating on television, proved useful test subjects. He found himself singing their praises, if with a cautionary chorus. "I've been impressed by the standard of the cricket ability," Wasim said. "They've got every shot. But I haven't seen anyone attacking the spinners, playing with the spin, using their feet, apart from a few of the seniors." He would also like to see more pace, naturally, though his solution – longer matches – is unlikely: for commercial reasons, women's cricket will stay short and needs to be sleeker still, particularly for the unforgiving cameras. And although Wasim lavishly praised the fielding of Australia, England and New Zealand as "mind-blowing", uncharacteristic errors sometimes embarrassed players.

Still, the eight-team competition had almost everything: records were smashed and expectations dashed. The general lack of close games was hardly noticed, even when poor shot selection or wayward bowling were occasional culprits. Undoubtedly, the standard had much improved from the last World Cup, in South Africa in 2005, just before the ICC took charge of the women's game. There was controversy, too, when England's Jenny Gunn was reported for a suspect bowling action in the opening game against Sri Lanka. She had already been suspended from Australian domestic cricket (where she played for Western Australia), but was allowed to continue bowling in the World Cup, and the ICC cleared her action before the start of the Super Six phase.

It was one of the few dents in an otherwise polished campaign from a confident **England**. The world's No. 1 batsman, Claire Taylor, was the tournament's leading scorer with 324 runs at 64.80, starting with a century against Sri Lanka, while the steady Caroline Atkins complemented Sarah Taylor's flair in an influential opening partnership. The spin trio of the delightfully flightful Holly Colvin, the seamer-turned-slow Laura Marsh (the leading wicket-taker, with 16) and captain Charlotte Edwards accounted for three-fifths of England's wickets. The team collected a record-equalling 17 consecutive wins upon beating West Indies to secure a place in the final for the first time since 1993. The winning streak came to a thudding end courtesy of Australia, who mauled them in the last Super Six match – but it may have actually done them a good turn, by shocking them out of any complacency in the final.

On top of the world: England captain Charlotte Edwards and player of the tournament Claire Taylor hold the Women's World Cup.

They would not meet the favourites, **Australia**, in that final. It wasn't quite Steve Harmison's wide, but a dropped slip catch off the first ball Australia bowled, against New Zealand, summed up their campaign: unexpectedly toothless when most needing bite. Their great slight hope – the bouncy and bright pin-up Ellyse Perry – seemed deflated, and only Shelley Nitschke shone consistently, with 275 runs and seven wickets. Australia could not live up to the overall hype of the most exposed World Cup yet, in which seven matches held at North Sydney Oval were both streamed live via the ESPN Star Sports website and broadcast to all participating nations (as well as several others). As Australia's hopes faded the home media, who had given them such an opening fanfare, packed up their trumpets and sloped off quietly. Australia were cowed into fourth place – a ranking set to rankle until the next World Cup – when they were beaten for the second time in the tournament by India, their whipping girls in a one-day series a few months before.

India belied some shocking pre-tournament form to canter forward menacingly on the back of some silken batting from Mithali Raj, Anjum Chopra and recent newcomer Anagha Deshpande – only to slip back into the pack when fielding fluffs cost them against New Zealand in a must-win match.

It was **New Zealand** who rode deservedly into the final, slipping up only against England in the Super Sixes. Though Australia had pipped them to the trans-Tasman Rose Bowl for the ninth time running shortly before the World Cup, New Zealand's warrior-like side exacted bloody revenge in a rain-affected opener. Feisty all-rounder Kate Pulford, newly returned to international cricket after a five-year absence, celebrated her comeback with three Australian wickets. Prone to batting slips despite their considerable depth, New Zealand had their best match against Pakistan, when Suzie Bates, with a freakishly good 168, and captain Haidee Tiffen, with a maiden international century, shared a world-record second-wicket stand of 262. New Zealand flayed nine sixes – the most in any women's one-day international – on an admittedly small Drummoyne Oval.

Bottom-ranked **Pakistan** played above themselves throughout, joyously so. They arrived in the shadow of the Lahore terrorist attack, but bloggers declared them "our country's silver lining" when their first-ever victory against Sri Lanka landed them in the Super Sixes, where they beat West Indies; though they lost the rematch in the play-offs, they finished a dreamy sixth.

West Indies also surpassed expectations. Last-ditch tours of Europe and Sri Lanka had salvaged their eligibility for Sydney, if not their credibility; they had played no international cricket for the previous three years. Recapturing fifth place was thus a credit to a young side and the enthusiasm of their coach, former Test batsman Sherwin Campbell. With better support, he could help them achieve much more.

Though the impressive technique of Pakistan and West Indies often surprised, their mental fallibility did not; collapses were all too common for the bottom quartet. **Sri Lanka** and **South Africa** sorely disappointed, without a single win in their groups.

In a shake-up of automatic qualification, sides below the top four will have to re-qualify for the next World Cup, forcing them to play more cricket. Unsurprisingly, the more matches a team had played, the better its prospects – exemplified by a ruthless England. The ECB and the Cricket Foundation had become the most understanding employers in women's cricket, providing ambassadorial contracts which meant abundant time for training and playing.

Such superior experience allowed England to hold their nerve against New Zealand in the final, and claim the World Cup for the third time. If the tournament had favoured spinners on the autumn pitches – which still allowed batsmen fair expression – the final belonged to the pace of England's Nicky Shaw, a last-minute selection after Gunn was injured. She claimed a career-best four wickets and was at the crease when the winning run came. "I began the day crying, I ended it crying, but we won a World Cup in between," Shaw said. A Champions League-style confetti burst and champagne shower closed a coquettishly brief fortnight, leaving many wanting more. The brevity compared well to the men's bloatfest of 2007.

England had achieved something their men hadn't in 15 attempts – winning an ICC trophy. Ominously, Edwards warned they had not played their best. It wasn't a boast: they failed to complete a perfect game, but still won comfortably. Their glittering gold-and-silver spoils – ultimately forged through the dedication allowed by superior support and funding – flashed warnings to every other board. The ECB's long-held faith since taking over the game in 1998 had finally been repaid.

What about the ICC? While the recent introduction of player rankings had helped media new to the game, team rankings had looked outdated. England were insulted by being listed fourth, having won their last four series. Placing the final at North Sydney was no snub, however. Even the players recognised the SCG, at ten times the cost, would have been a hollow extravagance, while the picturesque North Sydney Oval oozed charm and intimacy, not least for television. The introduction of Super Sixes and axing of the semi-finals made for a pleasingly ruthless format, which ultimately rewarded the most consistent sides with places in the final. The top four teams, who play the most cricket and have the best set-ups, were the only realistic contenders; nevertheless, the finalists were not predictable.

Overall, the ICC earned praise for structure, execution and foresight. With benevolent custodians and more support than ever before, the World Cup provided a largely representative snapshot of women's cricket, with the bigger picture looking ever more exciting.

Note: Matches in this section were not first-class.

GROUP A

At North Sydney Oval, Sydney, March 8, 2009. **New Zealand won by 13 runs** (D/L method). Toss: Australia. **New Zealand 205** (48 overs) (H. M. Tiffen 57, A. E. Satterthwaite 38; E. A. Perry 3-40); **Australia 132-6** (33 overs) (K. L. Pulford 3-32). *New Zealand 2 pts. Player of the Match:* K. L. Pulford.

New Zealand lost their last seven wickets for 34 in 44 balls, but all-rounder Kate Pulford fought back with three top-order wickets in four overs. Hosts and reigning world champions Australia were 14 short of a D/L target of 146 when a second rain-break ended their innings.

At No. 1 Sports Ground, Newcastle, March 8, 2009. **West Indies won by two wickets.** Toss: South Africa. **South Africa 116** (45.2 overs) (A. E. Smith 46; S. R. Taylor 4-17); **West Indies 117-8** (48.4 overs). *West Indies 2 pts. One-day international debut:* D. van Niekerk (South Africa). *Player of the Match:* S. R. Taylor.

Once opener Alicia Smith was run out, South Africa lost their last seven wickets for 22; 17-year-old off-spinner Stafanie Taylor claimed four wickets in 14 balls.

At No. 1 Sports Ground, Newcastle, March 10, 2009. **Australia won by 61 runs.** Toss: Australia. **Australia 258-4** (50 overs) (S. Nitschke 87, K. L. Rolton 96*; A. E. Smith 3-42); **South Africa 197** (49.3 overs) (T. Chetty 58, C-Z. Brits 36, M. du Preez 37; S. Nitschke 3-43). *Australia 2 pts. One-day international debut:* M. Kapp (South Africa). *Player of the Match:* S. Nitschke.

Australian captain Karen Rolton was stranded four short of her ninth one-day international hundred in the final over. Shelley Nitschke followed up her 87 with three wickets from her left-arm spin to put Australia back on course.

At Bankstown Oval, Sydney, March 10, 2009. **New Zealand won by 56 runs.** Toss: New Zealand. **New Zealand 192-8** (50 overs) (A. E. Satterthwaite 37, A. L. Mason 38, S. J. Tsukigawa 41*); **West Indies 136-8** (50 overs) (S. R. Taylor 38, P. Y. Lavine 40; A. L. Mason 3-26, L. R. Doolan 3-21). *New Zealand 2 pts. Player of the Match:* S. J. Tsukigawa.

Missing their captain, Haidee Tiffen, New Zealand needed a blast of 41 from 35 balls from Sarah Tsukigawa to reach a defensible total.

At Drummoyne Oval, Sydney, March 12, 2009. **Australia won by 47 runs.** Toss: West Indies. **Australia 211-7** (50 overs) (S. Nitschke 45, J. M. Fields 42, A. J. Blackwell 46*, E. A. Perry 36); **West Indies 164-7** (50 overs) (S. R. Taylor 32, D. J. S. Dottin 51). *Australia 2 pts. Player of the Match:* E. A. Perry.

Both sides reached the Super Sixes, but Australia pulled ahead; Ellyse Perry scored a run-a-ball 36 and claimed two wickets.

At Bradman Oval, Bowral, March 12, 2009. **New Zealand won by 199 runs.** Toss: South Africa. **New Zealand 250-5** (50 overs) (A. E. Satterthwaite 73, S. J. McGlashan 88*, N. J. Browne 51*); **South Africa 51** (22.1 overs) (S. W. Bates 4-7, A. L. Mason 4-2). *New Zealand 2 pts. One-day international debut*: Y. van der Westhuizen (South Africa). *Player of the Match*: A. E. Satterthwaite.

New Zealand completed a clean sweep of their group, while South Africa were whitewashed, succumbing for their lowest one-day total; only captain Cri-Zelda Brits (25) reached double figures. Suzie Bates and Aimee Mason had career-best returns. Three individual New Zealand innings matched or out-scored the entire South African XI; Sara McGlashan and Nicola Browne added 139*, a sixth-wicket record in women's one-day internationals.

New Zealand 6 pts, Australia 4 pts, West Indies 2 pts, South Africa 0 pts. New Zealand, Australia and West Indies qualified for the Super Six stage.

GROUP B

At Manuka Oval, Canberra, March 7, 2009. **England won by 100 runs.** Toss: Sri Lanka. **England 277-5** (50 overs) (S. J. Taylor 38, C. M. G. Atkins 50, S. C. Taylor 101, L. S. Greenway 32*); **Sri Lanka 177-7** (50 overs) (S. P. de Alwis 37; L. A. Marsh 3-31). *England 2 pts. Player of the Match*: S. C. Taylor.

England opened their campaign with a convincing victory after Claire Taylor scored her eighth one-day international century; she hit ten fours in 95 balls. England seamer Jenny Gunn and Sri Lankan off-spinner Rose Fernando were subsequently reported for suspect actions.

At Bradman Oval, Bowral, March 7, 2009. **India won by ten wickets.** Toss: India. **Pakistan 57** (29 overs) (R. Dhar 3-7); **India 58-0** (10 overs). *India 2 pts. One-day international debut*: H. Kaur (India). *Player of the Match*: R. Dhar.

India reduced Pakistan to 25-7; despite a slight recovery, the entire match lasted only 39 overs. Opening bowler Rumeli Dhar had figures of 8–5–7–3.

At Manuka Oval, Canberra, March 9, 2009. **Pakistan won by 57 runs.** Toss: Pakistan. **Pakistan 161-7** (50 overs); **Sri Lanka 104** (39.4 overs) (H. A. S. D. Siriwardene 58; Qanita Jalil 3-33). *Pakistan 2 pts. One-day international debut*: Sukhan Faiz (Pakistan). *Player of the Match*: Qanita Jalil.

Pakistan bounced back with their first World Cup win (they lost all five games on their previous appearance in 1997-98). Qanita Jalil struck three times in her first four overs, and later Sri Lanka's last five wickets fell for 13.

At North Sydney Oval, Sydney, March 10, 2009. **England won by nine wickets.** Toss: England. **India 169** (48.4 overs) (A. A. Deshpande 32, M. Raj 59, A. Sharma 33; J. L. Gunn 3-50, H. L. Colvin 3-22); **England 172-1** (38.4 overs) (C. M. G. Atkins 69*, S. C. Taylor 69*). *England 2 pts. Player of the Match*: C. M. G. Atkins.

England might have won even more easily but for India's Nos 10 and 11, Amita Sharma and Gouher Sultana, who added 43, a last-wicket record in women's one-day internationals.

At North Sydney Oval, Sydney, March 12, 2009. **England won by eight wickets.** Toss: Pakistan. **Pakistan 78** (39.5 overs) (L. A. Marsh 5-15); **England 82-2** (23.1 overs) (C. M. Edwards 32*). *England 2 pts. Player of the Match*: L. A. Marsh.

Off-spinner Laura Marsh's 5-15 was the best return of the tournament. Only the openers reached double figures as Pakistan failed to reach 100 for the second time in their three group games; England completed their third successive crushing win shortly after lunch.

At Bankstown Oval, Sydney, March 12, 2009. **India won by 35 runs.** Toss: India. **India 137-7** (50 overs) (M. Raj 75*); **Sri Lanka 102** (44.2 overs) (A. Sharma 3-19). *India 2 pts. Player of the Match*: M. Raj.

India were a shaky 78-7 before captain Jhulan Goswami joined leading batsman Mithali Raj to add 59 in the last ten overs.

England 6 pts, India 4 pts, Pakistan 2 pts, Sri Lanka 0 pts. England, India and Pakistan qualified for the Super Six stage.

SUPER SIX

At North Sydney Oval, Sydney, March 14, 2009. **India won by 16 runs.** Toss: Australia. **India 234-5** (50 overs) (A. A. Deshpande 45, A. Chopra 76, M. Raj 44, A. Sharma 31*; L. C. Sthalekar 3-52); **Australia 218-7** (50 overs) (A. J. Blackwell 54, J. M. Fields 43, L. K. Ebsary 39*). *India 2 pts. Player of the Match:* A. Chopra.
Australia's unhappy campaign continued as they suffered only their sixth defeat by India in 33 one-day internationals. After Anjum Chopra set up the innings, India scored 73 in the last seven overs.

At Bankstown Oval, Sydney, March 14, 2009. **England won by 31 runs.** Toss: England. **England 201-5** (50 overs) (C. M. G. Atkins 36, C. M. Edwards 57, B. L. Morgan 37*); **New Zealand 170** (48.4 overs) (H. M. Tiffen 53; C. M. Edwards 4-37). *England 2 pts. Player of the Match:* C. M. Edwards.
Charlotte Edwards led England to the top of the table through this victory over the only other unbeaten team.

At Drummoyne Oval, Sydney, March 14, 2009. **Pakistan won by four wickets.** Toss: Pakistan. **West Indies 132-9** (50 overs) (S. R. Taylor 55; Almas Akram 3-7); **Pakistan 134-6** (47.5 overs) (Armaan Khan 43*). *Pakistan 2 pts. Player of the Match:* Almas Akram.
Both sides struggled to 55-5, but Armaan Khan's 43 in 48 balls made Pakistan's recovery decisive.*

At Bankstown Oval, Sydney, March 16, 2009. **Australia won by 107 runs.** Toss: Australia. **Australia 229-6** (50 overs) (S. Nitschke 56, L. J. Poulton 47, L. K. Ebsary 51, J. M. Fields 36); **Pakistan 122** (45.1 overs) (Asmavia Iqbal 36). *Australia 2 pts. Player of the Match:* S. Nitschke.
Australia started off with a century opening partnership and made no mistakes, keeping their hopes alive.

At Drummoyne Oval, Sydney, March 17, 2009. **England won by 146 runs.** Toss: England. **England 236-8** (50 overs) (S. J. Taylor 78, C. M. G. Atkins 50, S. C. Taylor 65; S. F. Daley 3-31); **West Indies 90** (38.2 overs) (L. A. Marsh 3-17). *England 2 pts. Player of the Match:* S. J. Taylor.
Sarah Taylor and Caroline Atkins opened with 134 before Claire Taylor hit 65 from 56 balls. Though none of their team-mates reached double figures, England had no difficulty maintaining their 100% record. It was their 17th successive one-day international win (excluding three washed out games) since February 2008, and saw them into their first World Cup final for 16 years.

At North Sydney Oval, Sydney, March 17, 2009. **New Zealand won by five wickets.** Toss: India. **India 207** (49.4 overs) (A. Chopra 52, R. Malhotra 59*); **New Zealand 210-5** (47.4 overs) (K. L. Pulford 71, S. W. Bates 47*). *New Zealand 2 pts. Player of the Match:* K. L. Pulford.
Kate Pulford survived a dropped catch and a run-out chance to set up a vital win for New Zealand with 71 in 88 balls; by contrast with India's sloppy fielding, New Zealand pulled off four run-outs.

At North Sydney Oval, Sydney, March 18, 2009. **Australia won by eight wickets.** Toss: England. **England 161** (49.3 overs) (S. C. Taylor 49; S. J. Andrews 3-35); **Australia 163-2** (33.5 overs) (S. Nitschke 37, L. J. Poulton 38, K. L. Rolton 41*, A. J. Blackwell 38*). *Australia 2 pts. Player of the Match:* S. Nitschke.
Too late to rescue their own prospects Australia inflicted England's first defeat. England lost their last seven wickets for 55, and 161 was their lowest all-out total since their last defeat, by New Zealand in February 2008; in reply, Australian openers Shelley Nitschke and Leah Poulton raced to 79 by the 15th over, and victory came with 16 overs to spare.

At Bankstown Oval, Sydney, March 19, 2009. **India won by eight wickets.** Toss: West Indies. **West Indies 84** (44.4 overs) (P. Roy 4-14); **India 86-2** (17.5 overs) (S. Naik 39*, M. Raj 34*). *India 2 pts. One-day international debut:* P. G. Raut (India). *Player of the Match:* P. Roy.
India won with 32 overs in hand after leg-spinner Priyanka Roy took a career-best 4-14. Five West Indians went for ducks.

At Drummoyne Oval, Sydney, March 19, 2009. **New Zealand won by 223 runs.** Toss: New Zealand. **New Zealand 373-7** (50 overs) (H. M. Tiffen 100, S. W. Bates 168, N. J. Browne 33*); **Pakistan**

150 (48.1 overs) (Nain Abidi 52; L. R. Doolan 3-30). *New Zealand 2 pts. Player of the Match:* S. W. Bates.

Haidee Tiffen and Suzie Bates ensured New Zealand's place in the final by adding 262 for the second wicket, the second-highest stand in all women's one-day internationals after 268 for the first wicket by Sarah Taylor and Caroline Atkins for England v South Africa at Lord's in August 2008. Bates hit 168 – the third-highest innings in a women's one-day international – in just 105 balls, with six sixes and 19 fours, outscoring Pakistan single-handed. Tiffen's maiden hundred came from a more sedate 128 balls, with only three fours.

FINAL SUPER SIX TABLE

	Played	Won	Lost	Points	Net run-rate
NEW ZEALAND	5	4	1	8	1.18
ENGLAND	5	4	1	8	1.15
India	5	3	2	6	1.10
Australia	5	3	2	6	0.85
Pakistan..............	5	1	4	2	-2.58
West Indies	5	0	5	0	-1.55

Each team carried forward its results against the two fellow qualifiers from its group, then played the other three qualifiers in the Super Six phase.

Win = 2 pts. Where teams were tied on points, their position was determined on net run-rate, calculated by subtracting runs conceded per over from runs scored per over.

Seventh-place Play-off

At North Sydney Oval No. 2, Sydney, March 14, 2009. **South Africa won by nine wickets.** Toss: Sri Lanka. **Sri Lanka 75** (39 overs) (D. van Niekerk 3-11); **South Africa 76-1** (28.3 overs) (T. Chetty 41*, C-Z. Brits 31*). *Player of the Match:* D. van Niekerk.

South Africa finally chalked up a win in the battle over the wooden spoon; they reduced Sri Lanka to 35-5 before 15-year-old leg-spinner Dane van Niekerk cleaned up, and their batsmen swept home with 21 overs to spare.

Fifth-place Play-off

At Drummoyne Oval, Sydney, March 21, 2009. **West Indies won by three wickets.** Toss: Pakistan. **Pakistan 131** (46.3 overs) (Bismah Maroof 33; S. F. Daley 4-29); **West Indies 135-7** (46.3 overs). *Player of the Match:* S. F. Daley.

West Indies regained fifth place after left-arm seamer Shanel Daley snatched three Pakistan wickets in as many overs before opening the reply.

Third-place Play-off

At Bankstown Oval, Sydney, March 21, 2009. **India won by three wickets** (D/L method). Reduced to 46 overs a side. Toss: Australia. **Australia 142** (44.4 overs) (K. L. Rolton 52, L. C. Sthalekar 30); **India 145-7** (43.5 overs) (L. C. Sthalekar 3-27). *Player of the Match:* R. Dhar.

Australia had already lost both openers at 8-2 before a rain-break, and later declined to 63-5 before captain Karen Rolton's fightback. Chasing a revised target of 143 from 46 overs, India were seen home by their captain, Jhulan Goswami (18), and Rumeli Dhar, who followed up two wickets with 24* in 27 balls.*

FINAL

ENGLAND v NEW ZEALAND

At North Sydney Oval, Sydney, March 22, 2009. England won by four wickets. Toss: New Zealand.
   The star of the World Cup final didn't even know she was playing until minutes before the start. Vice-captain Nicky Shaw was recalled when Jenny Gunn pulled out unfit, and burst forth with a career-best four for 34 "to prove a point" – though she rightly gave credit to Katherine Brunt's

Halfway there: Nicky Shaw claims the wicket of Nicola Browne to end the New Zealand innings.

pressure-building opening spell. Haidee Tiffen said later she didn't regret choosing to bat in swinging conditions, but once England made the breakthrough – a blinding gully catch by Claire Taylor to remove Kate Pulford – the New Zealanders panicked against the moving ball. They wobbled to 101 for seven before Lucy Doolan and Nicola Browne added 63, which eventually lifted the total to 166. It looked far from enough while Caroline Atkins and Sarah Taylor were trampling their way to another strong opening stand, 74 in 17 overs, helped by short and loose bowling. Then New Zealand's two off-spinners kicked up and the batting trembles kicked in. Sarah Taylor clipped to midwicket in Doolan's second over; Aimee Mason bowled the player of the tournament, Claire Taylor; and Doolan went on to shoot down Atkins, taken at point, and captain Charlotte Edwards, judged caught behind against the evidence. New Zealand kept up the attack, but England's later batsmen held their nerve; Holly Colvin caressed the winning run, with Shaw her fitting accomplice as Edwards burst into tears on the boundary.

Player of the Match: N. J. Shaw. *Player of the Series:* S. C. Taylor.

New Zealand

K. L. Pulford c S. C. Taylor b Guha	8	L. R. Doolan st S. J. Taylor b Marsh	48
*H. M. Tiffen c S. J. Taylor b Shaw	30	S. F. M. Devine lbw b Edwards	0
S. W. Bates c Atkins b Shaw	2	†R. H. Priest not out	0
A. E. Satterthwaite c S. J. Taylor b Shaw	0	L-b 2, w 15	17
S. J. McGlashan c Greenway b Colvin	21		
A. L. Mason b Marsh	13	1/26 (1) 2/49 (3) 3/49 (4) (47.2 overs) 166	
N. J. Browne lbw b Shaw	25	4/62 (2) 5/74 (5) 6/92 (6)	
S. J. Tsukigawa c S. J. Taylor b Brunt	2	7/101 (8) 8/164 (9) 9/166 (10) 10/166 (7)	

Brunt 10–3–33–1; Guha 5–0–24–1; Shaw 8.2–0–34–4; Colvin 10–1–26–1; Marsh 10–3–34–2; Edwards 4–1–13–1.

England

†S. J. Taylor c Tiffen b Doolan	39	H. L. Colvin not out	5
C. M. G. Atkins c Devine b Doolan	40		
S. C. Taylor b Mason	21	L-b 1, w 17	18
*C. M. Edwards c Priest b Doolan	10		
L. S. Greenway c Satterthwaite b Mason	8	1/74 (1) 2/109 (3) (6 wkts, 46.1 overs)	167
B. L. Morgan run out	9	3/111 (2) 4/121 (4)	
N. J. Shaw not out	17	5/139 (5) 6/149 (6)	

L. A. Marsh, K. H. Brunt and I. T. Guha did not bat.

Devine 9–0–30–0; Pulford 3–0–17–0; Browne 7–1–24–0; Bates 4.1–0–21–0; Doolan 10–4–23–3; Tsukigawa 4–1–23–0; Mason 9–0–28–2.

Umpires: S. J. Davis and B. G. Jerling.
Third umpire: T. H. Wijewardene. Referee: B. L. Aldridge.

WOMEN'S WORLD CUP WINNERS

1973	*ENGLAND (279-3) beat Australia (187-9) by 92 runs	Birmingham
1977-78	*AUSTRALIA (100-2) beat England (96-8) by eight wickets	Hyderabad
1981-82	AUSTRALIA (152-7) beat England (151-5) by three wickets	Christchurch
1988-89	AUSTRALIA (129-2) beat England (127-7) by eight wickets	Melbourne
1993	ENGLAND (195-5) beat New Zealand (128) by 67 runs	Lord's
1997-98	AUSTRALIA (165-5) beat New Zealand (164) by five wickets	Calcutta
2000-01	NEW ZEALAND (184) beat Australia (180) by four runs	Lincoln
2004-05	AUSTRALIA (215-4) beat India (117) by 98 runs	Centurion
2008-09	ENGLAND (167-6) beat New Zealand (166) by four wickets	North Sydney

* The first two Women's World Cups were played solely as a round-robin league, but in both the last scheduled match was between England and Australia and decided the title.

ICC CHAMPIONS TROPHY, 2009-10

RICHARD HOBSON

1. Australia   2. New Zealand   3= England and Pakistan

Against prediction and precedent the sixth ICC Champions Trophy was justly declared a resounding success. The format mirrored that of the inaugural World Cup in 1975, confirming that the simplest ideas are often the best, and that less means more where global events are concerned. Australia retained the prize secured three years earlier, and Ricky Ponting, the man of the tournament as well as the winning captain, joined the ICC president David Morgan in praising the short, sharp design. Clearly the ICC had learned something from the never-ending 2007 World Cup in the West Indies.

The competition was condensed into 14 days, with eight teams, all housed in the same Johannesburg hotel, contesting 15 matches at two venues less than an hour apart, even allowing for some untimely roadworks. Such a structure could absorb the loss in the first phase of South Africa, the hosts, and India, the most lucrative commercial outfit. England and New Zealand confounded expectations by qualifying for the semi-finals alongside Australia, unbeaten throughout, and Pakistan, who mixed brilliance with inexplicable lapses.

This was the first major 50-over competition since the groundbreaking World Twenty20 in South Africa two years earlier and the equally successful follow-up in England, so the future of the longer one-day format became the hottest topic during the build-up. Captains seemed to have diplomatic answers prepared for public consumption, while the ICC insisted that 50 overs would remain until at least the 2015 World Cup – give or take the odd tweak to the playing conditions – because of existing contracts with television and sponsors. Nevertheless, a feeling persisted of a format on trial.

It had taken no little determination from the ICC, doubtless concerned about the financial losses from cancellation, to get the event on at all. A year had passed since security fears over the original location of Pakistan forced a postponement. Only in January was it eventually switched, with unease over the weather in Sri Lanka – who could forget the 2002 Champions Trophy in Colombo which failed to yield a champion? – persuading officialdom to ignore the designated reserve location and head to South Africa instead.

They did well to find space in the calendar. Things were so tight that Ponting and Andrew Strauss gave their arrival press conferences the day after the tournament had started. And the cricket? Well, relief and brevity hid the truth. Few matches were particularly tight, and the pitches at the Wanderers overemphasised the importance of the toss. The neutral games – India v Pakistan being a memorably raucous exception – attracted crowds that ranged from average to poor. A dispute over contracts between the West Indies Cricket Board and their players meant that one of the sides was barely a second eleven. Even Australia were a depleted team in transition.

Gareth Copley, PA Photos

The quality of mercy... Daniel Vettori and Paul Collingwood shake hands after Vettori withdraws his appeal for Collingwood's dismissal.

To win without the injured Michael Clarke, Nathan Bracken and Brad Haddin represented an enormous triumph for Ponting. His own form was sublime, and Shane Watson, having started with a golden duck and a seven-ball zero, ended with unbeaten hundreds in the semi-final and final. It was probably the biggest personal turnaround at a major cricket event. Australia could also call upon penetrating rather than defensive bowlers. Peter Siddle supported Brett Lee and Mitchell Johnson, while Nathan Hauritz prospered with flight and an attacking line, despite lacking the variety of Ajantha Mendis or Saeed Ajmal.

Three years ago, *Wisden* said that New Zealand "again punched above their weight" as they reached the semi-final. They went one round further this time; perhaps they are just heavier than they look, Jesse Ryder notwithstanding. The hefty Ryder was among three New Zealanders who had to be replaced during the tournament – Daryl Tuffey and Jacob Oram were the other two – but the loss of the outstanding Vettori for the final proved an injury too far.

England's progress to the semi-finals was at least as surprising, given their 6–1 defeat by Australia in the preceding NatWest Series. Graeme Swann joked that the side were on a roll after winning the final game back home, but his humour shielded the uncomfortable truth: they expected elimination straight away. Instead, with Paul Collingwood reinvigorated and Eoin Morgan dealing fearlessly with contrasting challenges, they beat Sri Lanka and South Africa inside three heady days. Accepting a definition of "news" as being something out of the ordinary, it was quite right that very good batting drew most attention. But James Anderson's role was scarcely less important. Unfortunately for England, the upturn did not even flatline. They immediately dipped against New Zealand and were crushed by Australia in the semi-final.

Sportsmanship became a recurring topic, with incidents in all three of England's Group B games. In the first, Strauss opted to recall Angelo Mathews of Sri Lanka when the batsman was run out following a collision with Graham Onions, who did not appear to have deliberately impeded his opponent. But Strauss went from saint to devil two days later as he supported the umpires in denying a cramping Graeme Smith the use of a runner at a critical stage of a critical game against South Africa. The law stating that any request must be adjudicated by the umpires had become vaguely applied, and Smith called for consistency and clarification. It came a day later when the ICC backed the on-field officials in denying a runner to a batsman with cramp.

Then Vettori chose to recall Collingwood after he had casually walked to the middle of the pitch at the end of an over without making his ground, allowing the wicketkeeper Brendon McCullum to throw down the stumps. McCullum had the law on his side, if not the spirit. Given the importance of wickets in what would always be a low-scoring game, as well as Collingwood's refusal to reverse a broadly similar decision in a one-day meeting between the sides a year earlier, this call was especially magnanimous. "The spirit of cricket is at the forefront of everyone's mind at the moment," Vettori said. Whether that spirit would have been as evident if the World Cup had been at stake was a moot point.

Beyond cricket, the tournament will be remembered for a dossier attributed to India's coach Gary Kirsten encouraging sex for players as a way of raising testosterone levels and becoming more aggressive on tour. By the time the devoutly Christian Kirsten issued an earnest statement identifying Paddy Upton, the team's mental-conditioning expert, as the author, the story had become the talk of the event and a godsend to tabloid and broadsheet newspapers alike. Most saw the funny side of a genuinely embarrassing leak, though on the field India were a shadow of the team they can be. Draw your own conclusions.

NATIONAL SQUADS

* Captain.   ‡ Did not play in ICC Champions Trophy.

Australia *R. T. Ponting, ‡N. W. Bracken, ‡M. J. Clarke, C. J. Ferguson, N. M. Hauritz, ‡B. W. Hilfenhaus, J. R. Hopes, M. E. K. Hussey, M. G. Johnson, B. Lee, T. D. Paine, P. M. Siddle, ‡A. C. Voges, S. R. Watson, C. L. White. *Coach:* T. J. Nielsen.
    B. J. Haddin was originally selected, but withdrew after finger surgery and was replaced by Paine.
‡D. E. Bollinger was called up to replace Bracken, who injured his knee during the tournament;
‡D. J. Hussey was called up to replace Clarke, who suffered back problems.

England *A. J. Strauss, J. M. Anderson, R. S. Bopara, T. T. Bresnan, S. C. J. Broad, P. D. Collingwood, J. L. Denly, E. J. G. Morgan, G. Onions, M. J. Prior, ‡A. U. Rashid, O. A. Shah, R. J. Sidebottom, G. P. Swann, L. J. Wright. *Coach:* A. Flower.
    A. Flintoff was originally selected but withdrew to undergo knee surgery and was replaced by Onions. S. M. Davies was called up to replace Prior, who fell ill during the tournament.

India *M. S. Dhoni, R. Dravid, G. Gambhir, Harbhajan Singh, K. D. Karthik, V. Kohli, P. Kumar, A. Mishra, A. M. Nayar, A. Nehra, Y. K. Pathan, S. K. Raina, I. Sharma, R. P. Singh, S. R. Tendulkar. *Coach:* G. Kirsten.
    Yuvraj Singh was originally selected but withdrew with a broken finger and was replaced by Kohli.

New Zealand *D. L. Vettori, S. E. Bond, N. T. Broom, I. G. Butler, ‡B. J. Diamanti, G. D. Elliott, M. J. Guptill, G. J. Hopkins, B. B. McCullum, K. D. Mills, ‡J. D. P. Oram, J. S. Patel, J. D. Ryder, L. R. P. L. Taylor, D. R. Tuffey. *Coach:* A. J. Moles.

A. J. Redmond was called up to replace Ryder, who suffered a groin injury during the tournament; J. E. C. Franklin was called up to replace Oram (hamstring); ‡I. E. O'Brien was called up to replace Tuffey (hand).

Pakistan *Younis Khan, ‡Fawad Alam, ‡Iftikhar Anjum, Imran Nazir, Kamran Akmal, Misbah-ul-Haq, Mohammad Aamer, Mohammad Asif, Mohammad Yousuf, Naved-ul-Hasan, Saeed Ajmal, Shahid Afridi, Shoaib Malik, Umar Akmal, Umar Gul. *Coach:* Intikhab Alam.

South Africa *G. C. Smith, H. M. Amla, J. Botha, M. V. Boucher, A. B. de Villiers, J-P. Duminy, H. H. Gibbs, J. H. Kallis, J. A. Morkel, ‡M. Ntini, W. D. Parnell, ‡R. J. Peterson, D. W. Steyn, ‡L. L. Tsotsobe, R. E. van der Merwe. *Coach:* J. M. Arthur.

Sri Lanka *K. C. Sangakkara, T. M. Dilshan, S. T. Jayasuriya, D. P. M. D. Jayawardene, S. H. T. Kandamby, ‡C. K. Kapugedera, K. M. D. N. Kulasekara, S. L. Malinga, A. D. Mathews, B. A. W. Mendis, M. T. T. Mirando, M. Muralitharan, ‡K. T. G. D. Prasad, T. T. Samaraweera, ‡W. U. Tharanga. *Coach:* T. H. Bayliss.

West Indies *F. L. Reifer, D. E. Bernard, T. L. Best, R. T. Crandon, T. M. Dowlin, A. D. S. Fletcher, ‡K. R. McClean, N. O. Miller, K. O. A. Powell, D. M. Richards, K. A. J. Roach, D. J. G. Sammy, D. S. Smith, G. C. Tonge, C. A. K. Walton. *Coach:* J. Dyson.

D. B. Powell was named in the original squad but failed to recover from a groin injury and was replaced by McClean.

Note: Matches in this section were not first-class.

GROUP A

PAKISTAN v WEST INDIES

At Johannesburg, September 23, 2009 (day/night). Pakistan won by five wickets. Pakistan 2 pts. Toss: West Indies. One-day international debut: C. A. K. Walton.

Inexperienced players came to the fore in a contest that ultimately showed how West Indies lacked the depth to overcome the absence of senior men embroiled in a dispute with their board. Mohammad Aamer, a 17-year-old left-arm seamer, found the perfect line and length in helping Umar Gul to reduce West Indies to 47 for seven on a juicy surface. Chadwick Walton added a first-ball duck on one-day international debut to the one he collected in his first Test (though he later took four catches behind the wicket). Miller's breezy half-century took the score into three figures. Gavin Tonge, largely unknown outside the Caribbean, then checked Pakistan with four wickets for 18 runs in a nine-over opening spell. But Umar Akmal, 19-year-old brother of wicketkeeper Kamran, responded maturely and confidently, unfazed even after being struck by Best's worst, a beamer.

Man of the Match: Umar Akmal.

West Indies

D. M. Richards c and b Mohammad Aamer	1
A. D. S. Fletcher c Imran Nazir b Naved-ul-Hasan	7
D. S. Smith c Umar Akmal b Umar Gul	18
T. M. Dowlin c Kamran Akmal b Mohammad Aamer	0
*F. L. Reifer c Misbah-ul-Haq b Umar Gul	7
D. E. Bernard b Mohammad Aamer	0
D. J. G. Sammy b Saeed Ajmal	25
†C. A. K. Walton lbw b Umar Gul	0

N. O. Miller c Shoaib Malik b Shahid Afridi	51
T. L. Best st Kamran Akmal b Saeed Ajmal	8
G. C. Tonge not out	4
W 5, n-b 1	6
1/2 (1) 2/11 (2) 3/14 (4) (34.3 overs)	133
4/36 (3) 5/43 (6) 6/47 (5)	
7/47 (8) 8/85 (7) 9/121 (10)	
10/133 (9) 10 overs: 31-3	

Mohammad Aamer 7–1–24–3; Naved-ul-Hasan 7–0–26–1; Umar Gul 8–2–28–3; Shahid Afridi 8.3–0–39–1; Saeed Ajmal 4–0–16–2.

Pakistan

Imran Nazir b Tonge	5	*Shahid Afridi not out	17
†Kamran Akmal c Walton b Tonge	5	L-b 2, w 9, n-b 3	14
Shoaib Malik c Walton b Tonge	23		
Mohammad Yousuf c Walton b Tonge	23	1/5 (1) 2/21 (2)	(5 wkts, 30.3 overs) 134
Misbah-ul-Haq c Walton b Bernard	6	3/54 (3) 4/61 (4)	
Umar Akmal not out	41	5/76 (5)	
			10 overs: 35-2

Naved-ul-Hasan, Umar Gul, Mohammad Aamer and Saeed Ajmal did not bat.

Sammy 7–0–29–0; Tonge 10–3–25–4; Best 6.3–0–50–0; Bernard 7–0–28–1.

Umpires: S. J. Davis and D. J. Harper.
Third umpire: S. J. A. Taufel.   Referee: J. Srinath.

AUSTRALIA v WEST INDIES

At Johannesburg, September 26, 2009. Australia won by 50 runs. Australia 2 pts. Toss: West Indies.
On paper a huge mismatch, the game was decided at the back end of both innings. Australia were indebted to Johnson, who crashed an unbeaten 73 from 47 balls after momentum generated by Ponting had been slowed. Sixty-nine runs came in the five batting powerplay overs, but Fletcher and Dowlin laid a strong platform for the reply, and West Indies needed a plausible 119 from 18 overs with seven wickets in hand at the final drinks break. They were unable to accelerate, however. Reifer's painful innings, from 56 balls, was symptomatic of problems against the pace of Lee and Johnson, and Watson and Hauritz reaped the benefits. Richards dislocated his shoulder while fielding.
Man of the Match: M. G. Johnson.

Australia

S. R. Watson b Roach	0	B. Lee run out	25
†T. D. Paine c Walton b Bernard	33	N. M. Hauritz not out	7
*R. T. Ponting st Walton b Miller	79	L-b 7, w 9, n-b 7	23
M. E. K. Hussey c Fletcher b Bernard	6		
C. J. Ferguson b Roach	20	1/0 (1) 2/85 (2)	(8 wkts, 50 overs) 275
C. L. White b Miller	4	3/120 (4) 4/148 (3)	
J. R. Hopes c Walton b Sammy	5	5/162 (6) 6/164 (5)	
M. G. Johnson not out	73	7/171 (7) 8/241 (9)	10 overs: 57-1

P. M. Siddle did not bat.

Roach 10–0–73–2; Tonge 10–1–55–0; Sammy 10–0–53–1; Bernard 10–0–63–2; Miller 10–1–24–2.

West Indies

D. S. Smith c Paine b Siddle	17	G. C. Tonge not out	0
A. D. S. Fletcher run out	54	D. M. Richards absent hurt	
T. M. Dowlin c Paine b Lee	55		
†C. A. K. Walton b Hopes	0	B 1, l-b 18, w 16, n-b 1	36
*F. L. Reifer c Hauritz b Watson	28		
D. E. Bernard b Siddle	8	1/38 (1) 2/124 (2)	(46.5 overs) 225
D. J. G. Sammy c Hussey b Watson	20	3/128 (4) 4/170 (3) 5/187 (6)	
N. O. Miller c Ponting b Hauritz	4	6/215 (7) 7/219 (5) 8/225 (8)	
K. A. J. Roach c Johnson b Hauritz	3	9/225 (9)	10 overs: 61-1

Lee 8–0–41–1; Siddle 8–1–37–2; Johnson 10–0–44–0; Watson 7–0–34–2; Hauritz 7.5–0–23–2; Hopes 6–1–27–1.

Umpires: Asad Rauf and A. L. Hill.
Third umpire: B. F. Bowden.   Referee: J. J. Crowe.

INDIA v PAKISTAN

At Centurion, September 26, 2009 (day/night). Pakistan won by 54 runs. Pakistan 2 pts. Toss: Pakistan.

After the sides' memorable meeting here during the 2003 World Cup, expectations were high and supporters of both teams mingled easily on the grassy banks making up two-thirds of the ground. Against a cacophonous backdrop, Pakistan emerged the stronger thanks to a fourth-wicket stand of 206 between Shoaib Malik and Mohammad Yousuf. Dhoni, India's captain, said that he felt three bowlers short as the partnership evolved from consolidation, through gentle acceleration

---

HIGHEST ONE-DAY INTERNATIONAL TOTALS WITHOUT A SIX

	Fours		
321-8	28	South Africa v Pakistan at Nairobi...............................	1996-97
309-5	34	India v Australia at Kochi.......................................	1997-98
307-6	**33**	**Sri Lanka v India at Colombo (RPS)**...........................	**2009-10**
302-9	**35**	**Pakistan v India at Centurion**................................	**2009-10**

Research: Nirav Malavi

---

to ferocious hitting by Malik, whose second fifty came from 27 balls. Passing 5,000 one-day international runs, Malik struck 128 from 126 balls in all. Pakistan's total was only the fourth of 300 or more not to include a six. The Indian innings faltered on two needless run-outs: Gambhir sent back by Dravid, and Dravid himself, with 67 needed from 49 balls, called for an impossible third run by Harbhajan Singh. A pitch invasion at the finish prompted the ICC to review its security operation.

Man of the Match: Shoaib Malik.

Pakistan

Imran Nazir c Harbhajan Singh b Nehra	20	Mohammad Aamer c Kohli b Sharma	0	
†Kamran Akmal b Nehra	19	Saeed Ajmal not out	0	
*Younis Khan c Dhoni b R. P. Singh	20			
Shoaib Malik c Pathan b Harbhajan Singh	128	L-b 1, w 12	13	
Mohammad Yousuf b Nehra	87			
Shahid Afridi c Dhoni b Pathan	4	1/29 (1) 2/53 (2) (9 wkts, 50 overs)	302	
Umar Akmal c Dhoni b Nehra	0	3/65 (3) 4/271 (5)		
Naved-ul-Hasan not out	11	5/278 (6) 6/289 (7) 7/300 (4)		
Umar Gul c Raina b Sharma	0	8/301 (9) 9/302 (10) 10 overs: 53-2		

Nehra 10–0–55–4; R. P. Singh 9–1–59–1; Sharma 8–2–39–2; Kohli 3–0–21–0; Pathan 10–0–56–1; Harbhajan Singh 10–0–71–1.

India

G. Gambhir run out	57	R. P. Singh c Mohammad Yousuf b Naved-ul-Hasan	2	
S. R. Tendulkar c Kamran Akmal b Mohammad Aamer	8	I. Sharma b Naved-ul-Hasan	0	
R. Dravid run out	76	A. Nehra not out	0	
V. Kohli c Umar Gul b Shahid Afridi	16	L-b 4, w 11, n-b 7	22	
*†M. S. Dhoni lbw b Shahid Afridi	3			
S. K. Raina lbw b Saeed Ajmal	46	1/23 (2) 2/90 (1) (44.5 overs)	248	
Y. K. Pathan c sub (Misbah-ul-Haq) b Mohammad Aamer	5	3/126 (4) 4/133 (5) 5/205 (6)		
Harbhajan Singh b Saeed Ajmal	15	6/218 (7) 7/238 (3) 8/243 (9)		
		9/244 (10) 10/248 (8) 10 overs: 65-1		

Mohammad Aamer 8–0–46–2; Naved-ul-Hasan 9–0–48–2; Umar Gul 6–0–55–0; Saeed Ajmal 8.5–0–31–2; Shahid Afridi 10–0–39–2; Shoaib Malik 3–0–25–0.

Umpires: S. J. Davis and S. J. A. Taufel.
Third umpire: I. J. Gould.   Referee: R. S. Mahanama.

AUSTRALIA v INDIA

At Centurion, September 28, 2009 (day/night). No result. Australia 1 pt, India 1 pt. Toss: Australia.

After the early loss of Watson, Australia took control and were heading towards a total of around 300 when the predicted storms soaked the ground, guaranteeing Pakistan a semi-final spot. Ponting added 84 with Paine and 88 with Hussey as India's pace attack, with the exception of Nehra, again lacked menace. Hussey was the pick of the batsmen, stroking his fifty from 45 balls, although it took a brilliant long throw by Gambhir to run out the fluent Ponting.

Australia

S. R. Watson c Harbhajan Singh b Nehra . .	0	C. J. Ferguson not out	2
†T. D. Paine c Harbhajan Singh b Mishra. . .	56	B 1, l-b 1, w 7	9
*R. T. Ponting run out	65		
M. E. K. Hussey c Tendulkar b Sharma . . .	67	1/3 (1) 2/87 (2) (4 wkts, 42.3 overs)	234
C. L. White not out	35	3/175 (3) 4/227 (4) 10 overs: 49-1	

J. R. Hopes, M. G. Johnson, B. Lee, N. M. Hauritz and P. M. Siddle did not bat.

Nehra 8–1–38–1; Kumar 8–0–34–0; Sharma 7.3–0–53–1; Mishra 9–0–45–1; Harbhajan Singh 9–0–54–0; Raina 1–0–8–0.

India

G. Gambhir, S. R. Tendulkar, R. Dravid, V. Kohli, *†M. S. Dhoni, S. K. Raina, Harbhajan Singh, A. Mishra, P. Kumar, I. Sharma and A. Nehra.

Umpires: B. F. Bowden and I. J. Gould.
Third umpire: Asad Rauf. Referee: J. J. Crowe.

AUSTRALIA v PAKISTAN

At Centurion, September 30, 2009. Australia won by two wickets. Australia 2 pts. Toss: Australia.

Having made elementary mistakes, Pakistan, who could afford to lose because they were already sure of their semi-final place, recovered spectacularly to take the contest to the last ball, before Lee and Hauritz scampered a winning bye. In fact, a tie would have been enough to secure Australia's own passage into the last four. The Pakistan innings was one-paced – Younis Khan faced 49 balls for his 18 – and Hussey and Ponting progressed serenely in reply until Umar Gul's diving catch removed Ponting and set in train the loss of six wickets for 47 runs. Saeed Ajmal and Naved-ul-Hasan stepped up, but Lee's experience saw Australia home with four required from the last over, from Gul. This was Mohammad Asif's first international since being banned by the PCB for testing positive for nandrolone.

Man of the Match: M. E. K. Hussey.

Pakistan

†Kamran Akmal b Watson	44	Naved-ul-Hasan not out.	7
Shahid Afridi c Hopes b Johnson	15		
*Younis Khan c Johnson b Hopes.	18	W 6	6
Shoaib Malik c Ponting b Johnson	27		
Mohammad Yousuf c White b Lee	45	1/30 (2) 2/75 (1) (6 wkts, 50 overs)	205
Misbah-ul-Haq hit wkt b Watson	41	3/89 (3) 4/123 (4)	
Umar Akmal not out	2	5/186 (5) 6/198 (6) 10 overs: 45-1	

Umar Gul, Mohammad Asif and Saeed Ajmal did not bat.

Lee 10–0–30–1; Siddle 5–0–24–0; Johnson 10–0–45–2; Watson 8–0–32–2; Hopes 10–0–50–1; Hauritz 7–1–24–0.

Australia

S. R. Watson c Kamran Akmal b Umar Gul	24	B. Lee not out	12
†T. D. Paine lbw b Shahid Afridi	29	N. M. Hauritz not out	9
*R. T. Ponting c Umar Gul b Shoaib Malik .	32		
M. E. K. Hussey b Naved-ul-Hasan	64	B 1, w 12, n-b 1................	14
C. J. Ferguson b Saeed Ajmal	7		
C. L. White b Mohammad Asif .	5	1/44 (1) 2/59 (2) (8 wkts, 50 overs) 206	
J. R. Hopes c Younis Khan		3/140 (3) 4/157 (5)	
b Mohammad Asif .	1	5/174 (4) 6/175 (7)	
M. G. Johnson b Saeed Ajmal........	9	7/176 (6) 8/187 (8) 10 overs: 50-1	

P. M. Siddle did not bat.

Umar Gul 9–1–38–1; Mohammad Asif 8–0–34–2; Shahid Afridi 10–0–47–1; Naved-ul-Hasan 9–2–39–1; Saeed Ajmal 10–1–31–2; Shoaib Malik 4–0–16–1.

Umpires: B. F. Bowden and A. L. Hill.
Third umpire: I. J. Gould.   Referee: J. Srinath.

INDIA v WEST INDIES

At Johannesburg, September 30, 2009 (day/night). India won by seven wickets. India 2 pts. Toss: India. One-day international debut: R. T. Crandon.

West Indies never recovered from the new-ball burst of Kumar and Nehra, but India, highly fancied before the start of the competition, were eliminated when Australia narrowly beat Pakistan at Centurion, to the disappointment of the Indian players who were monitoring television coverage in their dressing-room. The feature of another low first innings at the Wanderers was Dhoni's first wicket in a one-day international – "It was swinging a bit, so I thought why not give myself a bowl?" – while he gave the gloves to Karthik. Kohli's unbeaten 79 came from 104 balls, by when the inquests back home were just about beginning.

Man of the Match: V. Kohli.

West Indies

†A. D. S. Fletcher c Dravid b Kumar	0	N. O. Miller not out...................	17
K. O. A. Powell c Dhoni b Nehra	5	K. A. J. Roach c Gambhir b Harbhajan Singh	4
D. S. Smith c Dhoni b Nehra............	21	G. C. Tonge c and b Kumar	5
T. M. Dowlin b Dhoni.................	14	L-b 4, w 7, n-b 1	12
*F. L. Reifer c Karthik b Kumar	1		
D. E. Bernard c Dravid b Mishra.........	22	1/0 (1) 2/26 (2) 3/27 (3) (36 overs) 129	
D. J. G. Sammy c Mishra b Nehra........	23	4/31 (5) 5/57 (4) 6/89 (6) 7/99 (7) 8/102 (8)	
R. T. Crandon b Harbhajan Singh........	5	9/122 (10) 10/129 (11) 10 overs: 30-3	

Kumar 9–3–22–3; Nehra 8–1–31–3; Nayar 3–0–17–0; Dhoni 2–0–14–1; Harbhajan Singh 8–2–14–2; Mishra 6–0–27–1.

India

K. D. Karthik c Dowlin b Tonge........	34
G. Gambhir b Roach	6
R. Dravid run out	4
V. Kohli not out....................	79
A. M. Nayar not out	0
W 3, n-b 4	7

1/7 (2) 2/12 (3)   (3 wkts, 32.1 overs) 130
3/104 (1)   10 overs: 34-2

*†M. S. Dhoni, S. K. Raina, Harbhajan Singh, A. Mishra, P. Kumar and A. Nehra did not bat.

Roach 6–1–27–1; Tonge 10–0–36–1; Sammy 10–1–25–0; Bernard 3–0–22–0; Miller 3.1–0–20–0.

Umpires: Aleem Dar and S. J. A. Taufel.
Third umpire: D. J. Harper.   Referee: J. J. Crowe.

GROUP B

SOUTH AFRICA v SRI LANKA

At Centurion, September 22, 2009 (day/night). Sri Lanka won by 55 runs (D/L method). Sri Lanka 2 pts. Toss: South Africa.

Having finished as the leading run-scorer at the World Twenty20 in June, Dilshan resumed as though intent on completing a personal double. His 106 from 92 balls set up Sri Lanka for a success that was all but secured when heavy rain hit the ground. Given every chance to play his favourite shots square of the wicket, and unfurling his "starfish" or "Dilscoop" early on, Dilshan dominated a second-wicket stand of 158 with Sangakkara before deft placement by Jayawardene gave the total a formidable look. Smith's decision to bat second against an attack boasting Mendis and Muralitharan was questionable. Mendis duly baffled South Africa's captain when his very first ball skidded on, and Kallis and Duminy soon followed from successive deliveries.
Man of the Match: T. M. Dilshan.

Sri Lanka

T. M. Dilshan c Morkel b Steyn	106	K. M. D. N. Kulasekara run out	1
S. T. Jayasuriya lbw b Steyn	10	M. Muralitharan not out	0
*†K. C. Sangakkara c and b Duminy	54	L-b 5, w 5, n-b 3	13
D. P. M. D. Jayawardene c Duminy b Parnell	77		
T. T. Samaraweera c van der Merwe b Parnell	37	1/16 (2) 2/174 (3) (8 wkts, 50 overs)	319
		3/181 (1) 4/297 (4)	
A. D. Mathews b Steyn	15	5/297 (5) 6/314 (7)	
S. H. T. Kandamby c Duminy b Parnell	6	7/317 (8) 8/319 (6) 10 overs: 70-1	

S. L. Malinga and B. A. W. Mendis did not bat.

Steyn 9–2–47–3; Parnell 10–0–79–3; Kallis 7–0–43–0; Morkel 4–0–39–0; Botha 9–0–53–0; van der Merwe 10–0–42–0; Duminy 1–0–11–1.

South Africa

*G. C. Smith b Mendis	58	J. Botha c Mathews b Malinga	21
H. M. Amla b Mathews	2	R. E. van der Merwe not out	3
J. H. Kallis c Mathews b Mendis	41	W 2	2
A. B. de Villiers c Jayawardene b Malinga	24		
J-P. Duminy b Mendis	0	1/9 (2) 2/90 (1) (7 wkts, 37.4 overs)	206
†M. V. Boucher lbw b Mathews	26	3/113 (3) 4/113 (5)	
J. A. Morkel not out	29	5/142 (4) 6/163 (6) 7/198 (8) 10 overs: 61-1	

W. D. Parnell and D. W. Steyn did not bat.

Malinga 7.4–0–43–2; Kulasekara 7–0–44–0; Mathews 8–1–43–2; Muralitharan 8–0–46–0; Mendis 7–0–30–3.

Umpires: I. J. Gould and S. J. A. Taufel.
Third umpire: S. J. Davis. Referee: J. J. Crowe.

SOUTH AFRICA v NEW ZEALAND

At Centurion, September 24, 2009. South Africa won by five wickets. South Africa 2 pts. Toss: South Africa.

De Villiers batted with a command and fluency of his own to assuage concern among a holiday crowd that South Africa were about to choke yet again at a major tournament. At 138 for four, chasing 215, the possibility grew of a second defeat on a pitch that became increasingly awkward through the day. Important innings from Boucher and Morkel gave de Villiers the support he needed, and New Zealand were left to regret the omission of a second spinner. South Africa's slow bowlers, van der Merwe and Botha, had kept tight control of New Zealand, despite a battling 72 by Taylor, before Parnell made a mockery of the batting powerplay as the last five wickets fell in 18 balls.
Man of the Match: W. D. Parnell.

New Zealand

†B. B. McCullum c Duminy b Botha	44	D. R. Tuffey c Duminy b Parnell	4
J. D. Ryder c van der Merwe b Parnell	8	S. E. Bond c de Villiers b Steyn	0
M. J. Guptill c Amla b Parnell	21		
L. R. P. L. Taylor lbw b Parnell	72	B 4, l-b 5, w 1, n-b 1	11
G. D. Elliott b van der Merwe	39		
N. T. Broom lbw b van der Merwe	1	1/12 (2) 2/58 (3) 3/92 (1) (47.5 overs) 214	
G. J. Hopkins c Duminy b Parnell	13	4/163 (5) 5/171 (6) 6/203 (7)	
K. D. Mills c de Villiers b Steyn	0	7/204 (8) 8/209 (4)	
*D. L. Vettori not out	1	9/213 (10) 10/214 (11) 10 overs: 36-1	

Steyn 9.5–1–32–2; Parnell 8–0–57–5; Kallis 8–0–24–0; Morkel 3–0–13–0; Botha 9–1–44–1; van der Merwe 10–1–35–2.

South Africa

*G. C. Smith c Vettori b Tuffey	7	J. A. Morkel not out	19
H. M. Amla lbw b Vettori	38	L-b 2, w 4, n-b 2	8
J. H. Kallis c McCullum b Bond	36		
A. B. de Villiers not out	70	1/22 (1) 2/74 (3) (5 wkts, 41.1 overs) 217	
J-P. Duminy c McCullum b Mills	11	3/108 (2) 4/138 (5)	
†M. V. Boucher c McCullum b Tuffey	28	5/180 (6) 10 overs: 45-1	

J. Botha, R. E. van der Merwe, W. D. Parnell and D. W. Steyn did not bat.

Mills 8.1–0–45–1; Bond 10–0–51–1; Tuffey 9–1–52–2; Vettori 10–1–34–1; Ryder 2–0–15–0; Guptill 1–0–13–0; Elliott 1–0–5–0.

Umpires: Aleem Dar and Asad Rauf.
Third umpire: D. J. Harper.   Referee: R. S. Mahanama.

ENGLAND v SRI LANKA

At Johannesburg, September 25, 2009 (day/night). England won by six wickets. England 2 pts. Toss: England.

England must have surprised even themselves with the vigour of this response after the crushing NatWest Series defeat by Australia. Anderson, bowling superbly with the new ball, and Onions reduced Sri Lanka to 17 for four on a pitch which greatly favoured the side bowling first. The batsmen then matched that controlled aggression in an all-round performance which had "fresh start" stamped through it. Strauss also earned praise for sportsmanship in withdrawing a run-out appeal against Mathews after the batsman collided with Onions while attempting a very tight second run. Flower, the England team director, admitted subsequently that he would not have made the same generous call. Having rescued the innings in tandem with Kandamby, Mathews lasted only three more balls after that reprieve, but the early loss of both England openers suggested that their recovery might bring reward. Instead, Shah batted steadily, Collingwood thrillingly took on Malinga, and Muralitharan, lacking his usual fizz, was played on merit rather than reputation. Morgan needed the full width of his bat early on, but finished his most convincing performance for England with 62 not out from 83 balls.

Man of the Match: P. D. Collingwood.

Sri Lanka

T. M. Dilshan c Morgan b Anderson	2	S. L. Malinga b Broad	0
S. T. Jayasuriya c Prior b Onions	0	B. A. W. Mendis c Strauss b Anderson	5
*†K. C. Sangakkara c Strauss b Onions	1		
D. P. M. D. Jayawardene lbw b Anderson	9	L-b 4, w 21	25
T. T. Samaraweera c Collingwood b Broad	30		
S. H. T. Kandamby run out	53	1/7 (2) 2/7 (1) 3/17 (4) (47.3 overs) 212	
A. D. Mathews c Prior b Wright	52	4/17 (3) 5/81 (5) 6/163 (6)	
K. M. D. N. Kulasekara not out	17	7/176 (7) 8/197 (9)	
M. Muralitharan b Broad	18	9/197 (10) 10/212 (11) 10 overs: 43-4	

Anderson 9.3–2–20–3; Onions 10–0–58–2; Broad 10–0–49–3; Wright 6–0–34–1; Collingwood 8–0–24–0; Swann 4–0–23–0.

England

*A. J. Strauss c Kandamby b Kulasekara ...	9	†M. J. Prior not out	28
J. L. Denly lbw b Kulasekara	5	L-b 7, w 11, n-b 1	19
O. A. Shah c Sangakkara b Muralitharan ..	44		
P. D. Collingwood b Malinga	46	1/9 (2) 2/19 (1) (4 wkts, 45 overs)	213
E. J. G. Morgan not out................	62	3/82 (4) 4/158 (3) 10 overs: 36-2	

L. J. Wright, S. C. J. Broad, G. P. Swann, J. M. Anderson and G. Onions did not bat.

Malinga 9–0–43–1; Kulasekara 9–1–42–2; Mathews 8–2–26–0; Mendis 9–0–35–0; Muralitharan 10–0–60–1.

Umpires: Aleem Dar and B. F. Bowden.
Third umpire: A. L. Hill.   Referee: J. Srinath.

NEW ZEALAND v SRI LANKA

At Johannesburg, September 27, 2009. New Zealand won by 38 runs. New Zealand 2 pts. Toss: Sri Lanka.

Ryder withdrew from the tournament after pulling a groin muscle during his innings of 74 from 58 balls, which included a 28-ball fifty. New Zealand lost four wickets for 15 runs after his opening stand of 125 with McCullum, but the dogged Guptill shepherded his side towards recovery, and the lower order established a winning total with a late flourish. Sri Lanka's decision to omit Muralitharan for an extra pace bowler backfired and, when a quicker ball from Vettori removed Jayawardene to end a brisk seventh-wicket stand with Kulasekara, the final sting was drawn from the reply.

Man of the Match: D. L. Vettori.

New Zealand

†B. B. McCullum c Dilshan b Mathews ...	46	J. E. C. Franklin not out...............	28
J. D. Ryder c Sangakkara b Kulasekara....	74	K. D. Mills not out..................	18
M. J. Guptill b Malinga	66		
L. R. P. L. Taylor c Jayawardene		B 3, l-b 2, w 8, n-b 3	16
b Jayasuriya..	4		
G. D. Elliott lbw b Mathews	0	1/125 (2) 2/128 (1) (7 wkts, 50 overs)	315
N. T. Broom c Jayawardene b Jayasuriya..	15	3/133 (4) 4/140 (5)	
*D. L. Vettori c sub (C. K. Kapugedera)		5/161 (6) 6/230 (7)	
b Jayasuriya..	48	7/284 (3) 10 overs: 76-0	

D. R. Tuffey and S. E. Bond did not bat.

Kulasekara 7–0–52–1; Mirando 7–0–50–0; Malinga 10–0–85–1; Mendis 9–1–49–0; Mathews 6–0–33–2; Jayasuriya 10–0–39–3; Kandamby 1–0–2–0.

Sri Lanka

T. M. Dilshan c sub (J. S. Patel) b Mills ...	41	S. L. Malinga c Taylor b Mills	15
S. T. Jayasuriya c Mills b Tuffey	24	B. A. W. Mendis c Vettori b Tuffey	3
*†K. C. Sangakkara c Taylor b Franklin	11		
D. P. M. D. Jayawardene b Vettori	77	L-b 2, w 5, n-b 1	8
T. T. Samaraweera c Broom b Vettori.....	17		
S. H. T. Kandamby run out	11	1/66 (2) 2/67 (1) 3/85 (3) (46.4 overs)	277
A. D. Mathews c Guptill b Franklin	2	4/114 (5) 5/137 (6) 6/141 (7)	
K. M. D. N. Kulasekara not out..........	57	7/219 (4) 8/243 (9)	
M. T. T. Mirando c Guptill b Mills	11	9/262 (10) 10/277 (11) 10 overs: 69-2	

Mills 10–0–69–3; Bond 9–0–82–0; Tuffey 8.4–1–39–2; Franklin 9–0–40–2; Vettori 10–0–45–2.

Umpires: I. J. Gould and D. J. Harper.
Third umpire: Aleem Dar.   Referee: J. Srinath.

SOUTH AFRICA v ENGLAND

At Centurion, September 27, 2009 (day/night). England won by 22 runs. England 2 pts. Toss: England.

England reached the last four courtesy of a fine all-round batting performance, taking advantage of a belter after winning the toss yet again. However, a towering 141 from 134 balls by Smith took South Africa close to the win required by his own side to avoid elimination on home soil. With 69 needed from six overs, he was denied a runner having complained of cramp. While Strauss took the brunt of criticism for what was deemed poor sportsmanship, the decision rested with the umpires, and the issue

---

FASTEST ONE-DAY INTERNATIONAL FIFTIES FOR ENGLAND

Balls

24	P. D. Collingwood......	v New Zealand at Napier......................	2007-08
26	**E. J. G. Morgan**......	**v South Africa at Centurion**................	**2009-10**
28	A. Flintoff............	v Sri Lanka at Nottingham...................	2002
30	C. M. Old	v India at Lord's...........................	1975
31	A. D. Brown	v South Africa at Leeds	1998
32	I. T. Botham	v Australia at Perth........................	1986-87
32	A. J. Stewart	v Sri Lanka at Ballarat.....................	1991-92
32	V. S. Solanki	v Zimbabwe at Bulawayo	2004-05

---

became a smokescreen for flaws elsewhere. South Africa had crumbled from 206 for three when Swann worked over Duminy, and the return of Anderson for the 41st over checked even Smith. England's 323 for eight was their highest in a one-day international against South Africa and the total of 12 sixes their best against any side. Shah hit six of them, succumbing only when he reverted to caution in search of his hundred, reaching 98 from 89 balls and adding 163 with Collingwood. Morgan matched his Middlesex colleague for audacity with a series of orthodox and reverse shots; his unbeaten 67 from 34 balls included England's second-fastest one-day fifty, from 26 balls. He had also kept wicket competently as Matt Prior had a virus.

Man of the Match: O. A. Shah.

In a class of his Eoin... Mark Boucher watches as Morgan races to a 26-ball half-century.

England

*A. J. Strauss c Boucher b Parnell	25		G. P. Swann not out	8
J. L. Denly c Duminy b Kallis	21		J. M. Anderson not out	2
O. A. Shah c Boucher b Botha	98		B 1, l-b 4, w 5, n-b 1	11
P. D. Collingwood b Parnell	82			
†E. J. G. Morgan run out b Steyn	67		1/48 (2) 2/59 (1)	(8 wkts, 50 overs) 323
L. J. Wright run out	8		3/222 (3) 4/262 (4)	
R. S. Bopara c Morkel b Botha	1		5/291 (6) 6/295 (7)	
S. C. J. Broad b Parnell	0		7/297 (8) 8/320 (5)	10 overs: 48-1

G. Onions did not bat.

Steyn 10–0–59–1; Parnell 10–2–60–3; Kallis 3–0–14–1; Morkel 6–0–45–0; van der Merwe 9–0–67–0; Botha 9–0–56–2; Duminy 3–0–17–0.

South Africa

*G. C. Smith c Shah b Broad	141		W. D. Parnell not out	10
H. H. Gibbs c Wright b Anderson	22		D. W. Steyn not out	17
J. H. Kallis c Denly b Broad	12			
A. B. de Villiers c Denly b Collingwood	36		L-b 8, w 5, n-b 1	14
J-P. Duminy b Swann	24			
†M. V. Boucher b Anderson	8		1/42 (2) 2/64 (3)	(9 wkts, 50 overs) 301
J. A. Morkel run out	17		3/142 (4) 4/206 (5)	
J. Botha c Onions b Broad	0		5/230 (6) 6/255 (7) 7/255 (8)	
R. E. van der Merwe b Anderson	0		8/263 (9) 9/274 (1)	10 overs: 55-1

Anderson 10–0–42–3; Onions 7–0–52–0; Broad 10–0–67–3; Wright 5–0–31–0; Collingwood 10–0–58–1; Swann 8–0–43–1.

Umpires: S. J. Davis and A. L. Hill.
Third umpire: B. F. Bowden. Referee: R. S. Mahanama.

ENGLAND v NEW ZEALAND

At Johannesburg, September 29, 2009 (day/night). New Zealand won by four wickets. New Zealand 2 pts. Toss: New Zealand.

On a pitch at best only marginally fit for the occasion, New Zealand allowed England scant room for recovery once Mills and Bond exploited the new ball. England appeared to be stuck in the aggressive mode that served them so well against South Africa two days earlier; conditions demanded a more watchful approach this time. Things would have been worse had Vettori not recalled Collingwood when the batsman was run out by a throw from McCullum having left the crease before making his ground after the last ball of the 11th over. It was a particularly generous decision by the New Zealand captain given that Collingwood had refused to spare Elliott at The Oval in 2008 when the batsman collided with Sidebottom attempting to complete a run. Elliott took revenge here as his wobbly medium-pace kept the pressure on England, assisted by horribly uneven bounce. An opening stand of 84 between McCullum and Guptill set New Zealand well on their way, though McCullum twice survived strong lbw appeals from Sidebottom in the early overs. While an incisive spell by Broad made late inroads, the target was only a few good blows away.

Man of the Match: G. D. Elliott.

England

*A. J. Strauss c McCullum b Mills	0		R. J. Sidebottom c Taylor b Vettori	20
J. L. Denly b Bond	5		J. M. Anderson not out	4
O. A. Shah c McCullum b Bond	3			
P. D. Collingwood c Taylor b Elliott	40		B 4, l-b 4, w 9, n-b 2	19
†E. J. G. Morgan c Taylor b Butler	9			
R. S. Bopara b Bond	30		1/0 (1) 2/10 (2) 3/13 (3)	(43.1 overs) 146
L. J. Wright c McCullum b Elliott	4		4/50 (5) 5/80 (4) 6/90 (7)	
S. C. J. Broad c and b Elliott	1		7/95 (8) 8/109 (9)	
G. P. Swann c McCullum b Elliott	11		9/117 (6) 10/146 (10)	10 overs: 23-3

Mills 10–2–19–1; Bond 10–2–21–3; Franklin 6–0–31–0; Butler 8–1–34–1; Elliott 8–0–31–4; Vettori 1.1–0–2–1.

New Zealand

†B. B. McCullum c Bopara b Broad	48	J. E. C. Franklin not out	2
M. J. Guptill c Swann b Anderson	53		
N. T. Broom c Morgan b Sidebottom	17	L-b 7, w 4	11
L. R. P. L. Taylor c Swann b Broad	1		
G. D. Elliott c Morgan b Broad	3	1/84 (1) 2/113 (2) (6 wkts, 27.1 overs)	147
G. J. Hopkins c Morgan b Broad	2	3/114 (4) 4/118 (5)	
*D. L. Vettori not out	10	5/130 (6) 6/140 (3) 10 overs: 66-0	

K. D. Mills, I. G. Butler and S. E. Bond did not bat.

Anderson 10–0–53–1; Sidebottom 6–0–32–1; Broad 8.1–1–39–4; Collingwood 3–0–16–0.

Umpires: Asad Rauf and D. J. Harper.
Third umpire: Aleem Dar.   Referee: R. S. Mahanama.

FINAL GROUP TABLES

Group A	Played	Won	Lost	No result	Points	Net run-rate
AUSTRALIA	3	2	0	1	5	0.51
PAKISTAN	3	2	1	0	4	0.99
India	3	1	1	1	3	0.29
West Indies	3	0	3	0	0	−1.53

Group B	Played	Won	Lost	No result	Points	Net run-rate
NEW ZEALAND	3	2	1	0	4	0.78
ENGLAND	3	2	1	0	4	−0.48
Sri Lanka	3	1	2	0	2	−0.08
South Africa	3	1	2	0	2	−0.17

Win = 2 pts, no-result = 1 pt. Net run-rate is calculated by subtracting runs conceded per over from runs scored per over.

SEMI-FINALS

AUSTRALIA v ENGLAND

At Centurion, October 2, 2009 (day/night). Australia won by nine wickets. Toss: England. One-day international debut: S. M. Davies.

England's unexpectedly bright start to the Champions Trophy might as well never have happened. Australia were even more dominant than in the recent NatWest Series, ending the game in complete control as Watson and Ponting built a partnership of 252, a national record for any wicket. It ended only with the conclusion of the game, leaving the increasingly forceful Watson on 136 from 132 balls with ten fours and seven leg-side sixes, and Ponting, who cruised from first to last and passed 12,000 one-day international runs along the way, on 111 from 115 balls. England barely mustered an appeal, let alone created a chance to hand; it was therefore a low-key debut for their stand-in wicketkeeper, Steve Davies, called up to replace the virus-stricken Matt Prior. England's own innings imploded as batsmen either tried to be too aggressive too soon or fell when they sought to press on having made a start. Bresnan, warned by the management for posting rude messages on the social networking site Twitter the day before, rebuilt the innings alongside Wright, but the 107-run stand for the seventh wicket merely served to underline earlier mistakes.

Man of the Match: S. R. Watson.

England

*A. J. Strauss c Hopes b Siddle	14	J. M. Anderson not out	5
J. L. Denly c Paine b Siddle	36	G. Onions run out	1
O. A. Shah c Paine b Lee	0		
P. D. Collingwood c Paine b Johnson	34	W 6, n-b 1	7
E. J. G. Morgan c Paine b Watson	9		
†S. M. Davies b Watson	5	1/15 (1) 2/16 (3) 3/71 (4)	(47.4 overs) 257
L. J. Wright c Paine b Siddle	48	4/91 (2) 5/100 (6) 6/101 (5)	
T. T. Bresnan b Lee	80	7/208 (7) 8/245 (9)	
G. P. Swann run out	18	9/251 (8) 10/257 (11)	10 overs: 68-2

Lee 9–0–46–2; Siddle 10–0–55–3; Hopes 4–0–28–0; Johnson 10–1–61–1; Watson 8.4–1–35–2; Hauritz 6–0–32–0.

Australia

S. R. Watson not out	136	L-b 2, w 5	7
†T. D. Paine c Davies b Onions	4		
*R. T. Ponting not out	111	1/6 (2)	(1 wkt, 41.5 overs) 258
			10 overs: 63-1

M. E. K. Hussey, C. J. Ferguson, C. L. White, J. R. Hopes, M. G. Johnson, B. Lee, N. M. Hauritz and P. M. Siddle did not bat.

Anderson 8.5–0–48–0; Onions 8–0–47–1; Bresnan 8–0–51–0; Collingwood 8–0–50–0; Swann 5–0–31–0; Wright 3–0–18–0; Shah 1–0–11–0.

Umpires: Aleem Dar and B. F. Bowden.
Third umpire: A. L. Hill. Referee: J. J. Crowe.

NEW ZEALAND v PAKISTAN

At Johannesburg, October 3, 2009 (day/night). New Zealand won by five wickets. Toss: Pakistan. One-day international debut: A. J. Redmond.

In a tale of two captains, Vettori played a timely innings to add to his three earlier wickets, while Younis Khan was left to rue a dropped catch which might have been the contest's single most important moment. Concerned at further damaging a finger he broke during a warm-up game, Younis spilt a simple chance at short extra cover from Elliott on 42 when New Zealand were 165 for four. The batting powerplay soon followed and Elliott, himself playing with a broken thumb, accelerated to stretch his fifth-wicket stand with Vettori to a decisive 104. Victory arrived with 13 balls to spare. Pakistan had not produced a partnership of such magnitude after Umar Akmal's burgeoning fifty was ended by a rare poor lbw call from umpire Taufel. They never dominated New Zealand's pace attack, with Butler returning four for 44, his best figures in one-day internationals.

Man of the Match: D. L. Vettori.

Pakistan

Imran Nazir c Taylor b Bond	28	Mohammad Aamer not out	19
†Kamran Akmal c Redmond b Butler	24	Saeed Ajmal not out	14
Shoaib Malik c Taylor b Butler	2		
*Younis Khan c Taylor b Vettori	15	L-b 6, w 5, n-b 2	13
Mohammad Yousuf b Mills	45		
Umar Akmal lbw b Vettori	55	1/46 (1) 2/61 (3)	(9 wkts, 50 overs) 233
Shahid Afridi c McCullum b Butler	4	3/69 (2) 4/86 (4)	
Naved-ul-Hasan b Guptill b Vettori	8	5/166 (5) 6/181 (6) 7/183 (7)	
Umar Gul c Broom b Butler	6	8/192 (9) 9/198 (8)	10 overs: 46-1

Mills 10–0–46–1; Bond 10–1–54–1; Butler 10–0–44–4; Franklin 8–0–33–0; Vettori 10–2–43–3; Elliott 2–0–7–0.

New Zealand

†B. B. McCullum c Shahid Afridi		
b Mohammad Aamer .	17	
A. J. Redmond c and b Saeed Ajmal	31	
M. J. Guptill c Naved-ul-Hasan b Umar Gul	11	
L. R. P. L. Taylor b Shahid Afridi	38	
G. D. Elliott not out	75	
*D. L. Vettori st Kamran Akmal		
b Saeed Ajmal .	41	

N. T. Broom not out		3
B 2, l-b 6, w 6, n-b 4		18
1/22 (1) 2/43 (3) (5 wkts, 47.5 overs)		234
3/71 (2) 4/126 (4)		
5/230 (6) 10 overs: 44-2		

J. E. C. Franklin, K. D. Mills, I. G. Butler and S. E. Bond did not bat.

Mohammad Aamer 10–2–32–1; Naved-ul-Hasan 8–0–57–0; Umar Gul 8.5–0–48–1; Saeed Ajmal 8–0–39–2; Shahid Afridi 10–0–41–1; Shoaib Malik 3–0–9–0.

Umpires: I. J. Gould and S. J. A. Taufel.
Third umpire: D. J. Harper.   Referee: J. Srinath.

FINAL

AUSTRALIA v NEW ZEALAND

At Centurion, October 5, 2009 (day/night). Australia won by six wickets. Toss: New Zealand.
Ponting praised the contributions of less-heralded members of a side who retained the trophy with 28 balls to spare. Siddle, named ICC Emerging Player of the Year at the awards ceremony during the competition, was the pick of the bowlers, while Watson added an unbeaten 105 from 129 balls to his unbeaten 136 in the semi-final three days earlier. He found good support from White, enjoying his best period as an Australian player, during a careful third-wicket stand worth 128. Paine and Ponting had fallen inside the first three overs, with Bond and Mills bowling brilliant spells. At that point, New Zealand were entitled to feel they could defend a target of 201, eked out against consistent bowling with a line-up missing Vettori, the captain, because of hamstring trouble. But his deputy, McCullum, dropped a skyer from White at short fine leg with the total on 41 in the 18th over. Watson, as he had against England, again scored heavily through the leg side, hitting four sixes in that region to win the match award for the second consecutive Champions Trophy final.
Man of the Match: S. R. Watson.   *Man of the Series:* R. T. Ponting.

New Zealand

*†B. B. McCullum c Paine b Siddle	0	
A. J. Redmond st Paine b Hauritz	26	
M. J. Guptill c and b Hauritz	40	
L. R. P. L. Taylor c Hussey b Johnson	6	
G. D. Elliott lbw b Lee	9	
N. T. Broom run out	37	
J. E. C. Franklin b Lee	33	
K. D. Mills run out	12	
I. G. Butler lbw b Hauritz	6	

J. S. Patel not out		16
S. E. Bond not out		3
B 1, l-b 2, w 9		12
1/5 (1) 2/66 (2) (9 wkts, 50 overs)		200
3/77 (3) 4/81 (4)		
5/94 (5) 6/159 (6) 7/166 (7)		
8/174 (9) 9/187 (8) 10 overs: 22-1		

Lee 10–1–45–2; Siddle 10–1–30–1; Johnson 10–1–35–1; Watson 10–0–50–0; Hauritz 10–0–37–3.

Australia

S. R. Watson not out 105		
†T. D. Paine c Taylor b Bond	1	
*R. T. Ponting lbw b Mills	1	
C. L. White b Mills	62	
M. E. K. Hussey c Patel b Mills	11	

J. R. Hopes not out		22
L-b 3, w 1		4
1/2 (2) 2/6 (3) (4 wkts, 45.2 overs)		206
3/134 (4) 4/156 (5) 10 overs: 18-2		

C. J. Ferguson, M. G. Johnson, B. Lee, N. M. Hauritz and P. M. Siddle did not bat.

Mills 10–2–27–3; Bond 10–2–34–1; Butler 9–0–50–0; Franklin 9–0–42–0; Patel 6.2–0–44–0; Elliott 1–0–6–0.

Umpires: Aleem Dar and I. J. Gould.
Third umpire: Asad Rauf. Referee: R. S. Mahanama.

All or nothing: Shane Watson smashes a six en route to a second successive hundred; he began the tournament with two ducks.

CHAMPIONS TROPHY WINNERS

1998-99	South Africa		2004	West Indies
2000-01	New Zealand		2006-07	Australia
2002-03	India and Sri Lanka (shared)		2009-10	Australia

AUSTRALIAN CRICKET, 2009

The aura disappears

PETER ENGLISH

During the Ashes series there was much discussion about whether Australia had lost their "aura", but by the end of another bumpy year for Ricky Ponting the suggestion first raised by Andrew Strauss was universally accepted. Even Ponting had grown to understand that his young band of willing-but-not-yet-able men were no longer guaranteed final-day victories, and that emerging players were not capable of top-level consistency. Each time Australia moved forward they were pushed back, becoming agitated whenever it was the opposition doing the intimidating.

Ponting was defiant in wanting to steer the new generation, which three years after losing Shane Warne, Glenn McGrath and Justin Langer was still stuttering in transition, and he remained the right choice despite regular calls – mostly from rent-a-quote former players – for his removal. In the unfamiliar uncertainty, Australia needed to be thankful that Ponting, who had grown as a person and a leader while missing the astute tactical nous of his predecessors, was staying on. However, the downturn in team results matched Ponting's

AUSTRALIA IN 2009

	Played	Won	Lost	Drawn/No result
Tests	13	7	3	3
One-day internationals	39	23	14	2
Twenty20 internationals	9	3	5	1

DECEMBER JANUARY	3 Tests, 5 ODIs and 2 T20Is (h) v South Africa	(see *Wisden 2009*, page 1005)
FEBRUARY	5 ODIs and 1 T20I (h) v New Zealand	(page 1037)
MARCH	3 Tests and 2 T20Is (a) v South Africa	(page 1250)
APRIL MAY	5 ODIs and 1 T20I (in UAE) v Pakistan	(page 1215)
JUNE	World Twenty20 (in England)	(page 527)
JULY AUGUST SEPTEMBER	5 Tests, 7 ODIs and 2 T20Is (a) v England; 1 ODI (a) v Scotland	(page 479)
OCTOBER	Champions Trophy (in South Africa)	(page 1015)
NOVEMBER	7 ODIs (a) v India	(page 1107)
DECEMBER	3 Tests (h) v West Indies	(page 1044)
JANUARY	3 Tests, 5 ODIs and 1 T20I (h) v Pakistan	(page 1055)

For a review of Australian domestic cricket from the 2008-09 season, see page 1073.

Ryan Pierse, Getty Images

United front? Captain Ricky Ponting, vice-captain Michael Clarke and coach Tim Nielsen.

form, and it was sad that Australia's second-greatest batsman was no longer the team's most consistent contributor. His output, in the year he turned 35, was 853 Test runs at 38.77, the second time since 2007 he had delivered an annual mean of less than 40.

Losing the Ashes for the second time was something Ponting could deal with, in public at least, but by the end of the year he could not cope with the pace of Kemar Roach, the 21-year-old West Indian, and in the Perth Test was forced to retire hurt for the first time in his career. Roach, who arrived in Australia having played only two Tests against Bangladesh, had backed up his well-publicised belief that he had Ponting's number by dismissing him three times in the series as well as tenderising the captain's left elbow.

There was high-level support for Ponting, even after he became the first Australian captain since 1890 to lose two Ashes series in England. Cricket Australia's chief executive James Sutherland and the chairman Jack Clarke both felt the criticism was unfair. "Ricky's had a very, very good series," said Sutherland. "He's been under incredible pressure… I thought the dignity and poise that he showed in defeat was something that all Australians should be very proud of." By New Year's Eve he was the most successful captain in Test history with 42 wins, one more than Steve Waugh, but Ponting's most memorable moments of 2009 were the most painful. There was the split lip while fielding at The Oval, then trying to remain expressionless as another England captain lifted the urn, and walking off the WACA, accompanied by the team physio, with a throbbing elbow.

The year began with a dream run, by Australia's current standards, with three successive Test wins against South Africa in a worthy home-and-away battle over the No. 1 ranking. In between those contests Australia's inconsistency began, with a 4–1 one-day defeat by South Africa and the heavy patriotic blow of a draw with New Zealand in the one-day Chappell–Hadlee Series: Ponting had been called back from a supposed rest, with the host broadcaster Channel 9 adding their weight to the decision, after New Zealand had taken a 2–0 lead. The 2–1 Test success in South Africa was the postcard experience in a year dotted with troughs. Even after the Ashes, the memories of Johannesburg and Durban were still being promoted by the selectors as proof of the way the side could play all the time. However, young players, particularly bowlers, do not perform on plateaux.

Despite never being in front during the Ashes, the Australian players, selectors and administrators comforted themselves in a blanket of statistics. Forget the overall result; they were on top in those essential areas of most century-makers and leading wicket-takers. It was, they said with unblinking sincerity, only the big moments that had been the problem. What was harder to ignore was the drop to No. 4 in the world Test rankings, the lowest Australia had been since the table was introduced. South Africa, India and Sri Lanka were above them, with England just below.

After exiting the World Twenty20 in the first round and losing the Ashes, Australia's focus turned to winning something – anything – in the United Kingdom. They brushed off Scotland, and soon felt better after wiping England out 6–1 before retaining the Champions Trophy in South Africa. A 4–2 success in India followed, Ponting rating the injury-hit triumph as the most satisfactory one-day series of his career. A 3–0 win was expected in the Tests against West Indies, whose factions had come together after another divisive strike, but after a three-day victory at Brisbane the hosts were suddenly behind for much of the game in Adelaide and just held on to win by 35 runs at Perth. It was not the convincing performance expected against the eighth-ranked side, although Australia did beat Pakistan at Melbourne in a ruthless display that gave them seven wins, three defeats and three draws for the year.

The opener Simon Katich was the most prolific batsman, continuing his renaissance with 1,111 runs, while Michael Clarke was the go-to man instead of Ponting. Although Clarke's total of 1,042 runs at 54.84 with three hundreds confirmed his rise into one of the world's leading performers, his A-list lifestyle and public coveting of the leadership created doubts over his virtual birthright to be Ponting's successor. As the team peered towards England's visit late in 2010, the selectors started to plan ahead, happy with the emergence of Marcus North, Peter Siddle and Ben Hilfenhaus, and convinced that the unconvincing Michael Hussey would make it through another season.

Workload remained a major issue: at Perth in December the only bowlers from the Ashes tour who were fit to play against West Indies were Mitchell Johnson and Nathan Hauritz. Siddle, Hilfenhaus, Brett Lee and Stuart Clark, as well as the limited-overs regular Nathan Bracken, were unavailable, despite a careful resting policy that even extended to the coach Tim Nielsen, who left England during the one-day series for a holiday, leaving Troy Cooley in charge. Once again Nielsen, a wicketkeeper with a modest first-class background, was unable to lift the side when they were behind against major teams. Like the players, Nielsen was not at his best at the big moments.

Ponting cut down his commitments by retiring from Twenty20 internationals, a format he had never embraced, and left with a warning for those wanting to downgrade the status of Tests: "I've made no secret that I'm a bit worried about some of the attitudes of younger players," he said, "with the amount of money that's around in Champions League and IPL." Nobody wanted to talk about less Twenty20, though, and Cricket Australia announced plans for an expanded region-based domestic tournament in 2011-12.

500 RUNS AND 50 WICKETS IN A CALENDAR YEAR

	Tests	Runs	Avge	Wickets	Avge	Year
I. T. Botham (England).............	12	597	39.80	66	18.19	1978
Kapil Dev (India)	17	619	30.95	74	22.95	1979
I. T. Botham (England).............	13	629	28.59	62	25.54	1981
Kapil Dev (India)	18	579	22.26	75	23.18	1983
S. M. Pollock (South Africa)	14	593	29.65	69	20.44	1998
S. M. Pollock (South Africa)	13	573	52.09	55	21.38	2001
A. Flintoff (England/World).........	14	709	30.82	68	24.41	2005
D. L. Vettori (New Zealand)........	14	672	35.36	54	26.12	2008
M. G. Johnson (Australia)	**13**	**500**	**33.33**	**63**	**27.42**	**2009**

Andrew Hilditch, the chairman of selectors, was reappointed for two years after a unanimous board decision, despite some thundering calls for him to be replaced and recommendations from inside Cricket Australia that a full-time selector be appointed. The panel, which also included David Boon, Jamie Cox and Merv Hughes, remained unchanged through a sequence of inconsistent and contentious decisions. The biggest mistake was the unbalanced Ashes squad, a 17-man unit which did not have a specialist opener as back-up and included the bits-and-pieces all-rounder Andrew McDonald, who did not play a Test. The exclusion of Hauritz, the only specialist spinner, for the Oval Test was baffling: the decision effectively handed over the Ashes. Other problems came with Phillip Hughes's sudden aversion to the short ball, leading to him being dropped after two Tests and Shane Watson, a batting all-rounder, being pushed up to open. It was a strange move that would eventually mature in the Australian summer, when Watson scored six fifties in seven Tests before finally reaching three figures during a run that was painful and comical.

Keeping faith with Mitchell Johnson in England was another major error, as Australia lost the two matches in which he was at his worst, at Lord's and The Oval. Johnson is a soft soul with a confusing bowling demeanour and an uncanny knack of taking wickets consistently while delivering full, wide and short. He did the Test double of 50 wickets and 500 runs in 2009 without being on song for half of it. "He bowls a lot of dross," said the former Test leg-spinner Kerry O'Keeffe, "but gets lots of wickets." Johnson was a rather surprised recipient of the ICC's Player of the Year just after his Ashes slump, but by late December he was looking more like a destroyer again, and led the world with 63 wickets at 27.42 in 2009.

At board level Matthew Hayden, who retired in January after 8,625 runs at 50.73 in 103 Tests, was appointed as Allan Border's replacement as

Kirsty Wigglesworth, AP/PA

Sin of omission: the exclusion of Nathan Hauritz from the Oval Test team played into English hands.

Queensland's delegate in August, and was soon employing the type of convoluted corporate-speak preferred by effusive chief executives. It takes a lot for Cricket Australia to lose faith in its employed, and an old fishing mate of Hayden's was the only high-profile figure who was sacked. Andrew Symonds's spiral started in 2008 when he wet a line instead of attending a team meeting, and continued with a pub altercation on his Test return, a knee injury, a radio interview in which he called New Zealand's Brendon McCullum a "lump of shit", and a ban from the South African tour. He returned to the limited-overs side in the UAE, after committing to a personalised contract that included the condition not to drink in public, which is easier to do in the Middle East than in London. He was sent home two days before Australia's opening World Twenty20 match after heading to a pub to watch a rugby league game on television and sipping a couple of beers. Ponting spoke about the decision while wearing the team's alcohol-sponsored cap – and Symonds, whose Cricket Australia contract was taken by Shaun Tait, restricted himself to lucrative Twenty20 games.

Having four of the future breed – Johnson, Watson, Brad Haddin and Doug Bollinger – reported to the referee in consecutive Tests against West Indies showed that the unruly elements of the team had not been eliminated with Symonds's disgruntled departure. The players were increasingly grumpy when threatened by the opposition, but even wins didn't necessarily create harmony, with Clarke and Katich having to be pulled apart in the SCG dressing-room following the victory over South Africa in January. Clarke wanted to go to dinner around 11 p.m., leaving Katich angry that the vice-captain was departing before the singing of the team song. The confrontation marked the start of a period that was out of tune with Australia's modern success, and nobody was sure when the winning feeling would return against top-rate opposition.

CHAPPELL–HADLEE SERIES, 2008-09

Daniel Brettig

One-day internationals (5): Australia 2, New Zealand 2
Twenty20 international (1): Australia 1, New Zealand 0

Australia had begun their home summer by brushing New Zealand aside with some contempt in two Tests in November. That they ended it thanking the rain for sparing them the ignominy of a third successive series defeat gave some indication of the tribulations in between. There was little doubt that the New Zealanders were buoyed as they watched South Africa scoop both Test and limited-overs laurels, and in the early exchanges they were as confident as the Australians were timid.

The on-field demeanour of the two teams made a mockery of Australian vice-captain Michael Clarke's pre-series boast that defeat by New Zealand was "unthinkable". At 2–0 up, Daniel Vettori's men were on the brink of forcing Clarke to eat his words, and also scented their first series win of any kind in Australia since Richard Hadlee's 1985-86 romp through a team gutted by the South African rebel tour. But the Australians were able to summon some overdue verve in the third and fourth games, helped by the call-up of the poised young South Australian batsman Callum Ferguson and the shift of Brad Haddin to the top of the order in place of the overawed David Warner. The Brisbane rain robbed the series of a decider, although Australia gained some measure of solace from a narrow win in the Twenty20 match that followed.

Apart from Ferguson and Haddin, the Australians were grateful for the runs of Mike Hussey, while Clarke played with a sturdiness that eluded Ricky Ponting, whose return of 38 runs in four innings was symptomatic of a captain fatigued by the unaccustomed weight of leading a losing team. The selectors had wanted to rest him from the second and third games, but he insisted on returning for the third one. "There is never a good time to be rested from the Australian side," he said. "The selection panel were determined to rest me no matter what. There had been suggestions I have a break earlier, but I did not think there was ever an appropriate opportunity and I am not sure there ever will be a good time to do it."

Among the bowlers, Nathan Bracken, James Hopes and Mitchell Johnson all had moments without ever showing true menace, a characteristic wholly absent from the Australian attack once Shaun Tait was cut down by a recurring hamstring problem just one game into his international comeback. Tait lost his national contract after that, only to get it back when Andrew Symonds's was torn up.

New Zealand could look back on the series with some satisfaction, if not the full-bodied glow that would have come with an overall victory. Vettori led his side ably, although his share of the wickets was smaller than usual. He was well supported by Kyle Mills and Iain O'Brien, the best-performing bowlers on either side. Johannesburg-born Grant Elliott maintained Australia's dislike

for things South African by playing two of the best innings of the series. Ross
Taylor and Martin Guptill also offered glimpses of class, suggesting that New
Zealand would be difficult opponents when the two sides next locked horns.

NEW ZEALAND TOURING PARTY

D. L. Vettori (*captain*), T. A. Boult, N. T. Broom, C. D. Cumming, B. J. Diamanti, G. D. Elliott,
P. G. Fulton, M. J. Guptill, B. B. McCullum, K. D. Mills, I. E. O'Brien, J. S. Patel, T. G. Southee,
L. R. P. L. Taylor. *Coach:* A. J. Moles.
    J. D. Ryder was originally selected, but failed to recover from a shoulder injury and was replaced
by Cumming. G. J. Hopkins joined the squad as wicketkeeping cover for B. B. McCullum. I. G.
Butler, J. E. C. Franklin, N. L. McCullum and P. D. McGlashan flew in for the Twenty20 international
which ended the series, replacing Boult, Cumming, Diamanti, Fulton, Hopkins, Mills (leg injury)
and Patel.

Note: Matches in this section were not first-class.

At Canberra, January 29, 2009. **Prime Minister's XI won by six wickets.** Toss: Prime Minister's
XI. **New Zealanders 271-5** (50 overs) (B. B. McCullum 114, P. G. Fulton 53, L. R. P. L. Taylor 38;
C. J. McKay 3-52); **Prime Minister's XI 272-4** (47.5 overs) (C. J. Ferguson 30, G. J. Bailey 107*,
J. L. Langer 72).
    *Tasmania's George Bailey and the former Australian batsman Justin Langer added 153 in 30
overs to help the PM's XI to victory. Former Australia Under-19 player Ryan Carters kept wicket
during the PM's XI innings while McCullum rested after his century (he had injured his hip a few
days previously).*

AUSTRALIA v NEW ZEALAND

First One-Day International

At Perth, February 1, 2009 (day/night). New Zealand won by two wickets. Toss: Australia.
    The helplessness that gripped Australia's cricket towards the end of the South African series was
still in painful evidence as New Zealand scrambled to victory. Both openers popped off-side catches
after being tied down by the crafty Mills, and things took on a farcical air when both Ponting and
Clarke ran themselves out by misjudging the strength of Kiwi arms. From 54 for five, Australia did
well to cobble together 181, a total which at least looked vaguely challenging when McCullum
squeezed Tait on to his pads but was given lbw to the second ball of the reply. New Zealand's
innings developed in similarly uncertain fashion, though with the benefit of knowing the modest
target. Taylor anchored much of the pursuit. Broom's gritty contribution ended when he was bowled
by Clarke – a straightforward-looking dismissal until replays showed Haddin's gloves creeping
ahead of the stumps to take the ball (which should have been called a no-ball under Law 40.3). The
New Zealanders' irritation at this was nothing next to the Australians' self-righteous fury at being
accused of dishonesty. As for the truth, only Haddin knows.
    Man of the Match: K. D. Mills.

Australia

S. E. Marsh c Fulton b Mills	15	N. W. Bracken lbw b Southee 0
D. A. Warner c Fulton b Mills.	7	S. W. Tait not out 9
*R. T. Ponting run out.	5	
M. J. Clarke run out.	12	W 2 2
D. J. Hussey c McCullum b Patel	13	
M. E. K. Hussey c Elliott b O'Brien	49	1/20 (1) 2/23 (2) 3/27 (3) (48.4 overs) 181
†B. J. Haddin b Mills.	31	4/51 (4) 5/54 (5) 6/115 (7)
J. R. Hopes c Vettori b O'Brien	18	7/152 (6) 8/153 (8) 9/154 (10)
M. G. Johnson b Mills.	20	10/181 (9) 10 overs: 26-2

Mills 9.4–0–35–4; Southee 10–0–34–1; O'Brien 10–1–43–2; Vettori 10–0–22–0; Patel
9–0–47–1.

New Zealand

†B. B. McCullum lbw b Tait	0	T. G. Southee b Bracken	3	
M. J. Guptill b Bracken	13	J. S. Patel not out	2	
P. G. Fulton c and b Johnson	7	B 3, l-b 9, w 11	23	
L. R. P. L. Taylor c Clarke b Bracken	64			
G. D. Elliott c M. E. K. Hussey b Hopes	8	1/0 (1) 2/25 (2)	(8 wkts, 50 overs)	182
N. T. Broom b Clarke	29	3/25 (3) 4/64 (5)		
K. D. Mills b Tait	26	5/106 (6) 6/168 (7)		
*D. L. Vettori not out	7	7/170 (4) 8/178 (9)	10 overs: 25-1	

I. E. O'Brien did not bat.

Tait 10–1–40–2; Bracken 10–3–35–3; Johnson 10–2–34–1; Hopes 10–1–23–1; Clarke 6–0–18–1; D. J. Hussey 4–0–20–0.

Umpires: S. A. Bucknor and B. N. J. Oxenford.
Third umpire: P. R. Reiffel.   Referee: R. S. Mahanama.

AUSTRALIA v NEW ZEALAND

Second One-Day International

At Melbourne, February 6, 2009 (day/night). New Zealand won by six wickets. Toss: New Zealand. One-day international debut: C. J. Ferguson.

New Zealand secured a 2–0 lead in the five-match series by comfortably overhauling a modest target. Australia's form had deserted them in previous games, but here it was lack of confidence and tactical nous that proved their undoing, resulting in a fifth consecutive defeat. After three early wickets, Clarke and Mike Hussey sauntered along at around four an over, putting on 133 in 28 overs before Hussey was out at the end of the 46th. They had played themselves cautiously back into touch, but left their team with an unremarkable score given that only five wickets went down. This became uncomfortably clear as New Zealand started their chase on a good pitch that offered little to any bowler. McCullum both passed 40, then Elliott unleashed some handsome strokes to finish the match off. All of them batted with the urgency demanded by the run-rate which, thanks to the earlier dithering, was not too much at all. Clarke admitted his error while sheepishly accepting the match award.

Man of the Match: M. J. Clarke.

Australia

D. A. Warner c Vettori b Mills	2	C. J. Ferguson not out	6	
*M. J. Clarke b O'Brien	98	L-b 2, w 3	5	
†B. J. Haddin c McCullum b Southee	12			
D. J. Hussey run out	10	1/4 (1) 2/35 (3)	(5 wkts, 50 overs)	225
M. E. K. Hussey c Vettori b O'Brien	75	3/63 (4) 4/196 (5)		
C. L. White not out	17	5/206 (2)	10 overs: 35-2	

J. R. Hopes, M. G. Johnson, N. W. Bracken and B. W. Hilfenhaus did not bat.

Mills 10–1–37–1; Southee 10–0–57–1; O'Brien 10–0–48–2; Vettori 10–0–35–0; Patel 8–0–38–0; Elliott 2–0–8–0.

New Zealand

†B. B. McCullum c M. E. K. Hussey b Hopes	43	N. T. Broom not out	26	
M. J. Guptill c White b Bracken	8	L-b 8, w 12	20	
P. G. Fulton c Haddin b Hopes	21			
L. R. P. L. Taylor c Haddin b Johnson	47	1/21 (2) 2/62 (3)	(4 wkts, 48.5 overs)	226
G. D. Elliott not out	61	3/104 (1) 4/176 (4)	10 overs: 42-1	

K. D. Mills, *D. L. Vettori, T. G. Southee, J. S. Patel and I. E. O'Brien did not bat.

Bracken 9–1–34–1; Hilfenhaus 9.5–1–58–0; Johnson 10–0–43–1; Clarke 5–0–21–0; Hopes 10–1–30–2; White 3–0–18–0; D. J. Hussey 2–0–14–0.

Umpires: S. A. Bucknor and P. R. Reiffel.
Third umpire: R. J. Tucker. Referee: R. S. Mahanama.

AUSTRALIA v NEW ZEALAND

Third One-Day International

At Sydney, February 8, 2009 (day/night). Australia won by 32 runs. Toss: New Zealand.

New Zealand preferred their team plan – bowl first – to the conventional wisdom that dictates doing the opposite at the SCG. They paid the appropriate penalty with a defeat that allowed Australia back into the series. Handed the chance to bat on a blameless surface and under sunny skies, local boys Haddin and Clarke provided the launch pad with 135 in less than 24 overs. Haddin went on to his first one-day international century, hitting eight fours and three sixes from 114 balls in all. There was a minor stumble in the middle overs – Ponting, returning early from an enforced break insisted upon by the selectors, made just 16 – before Mike Hussey and Callum Ferguson, in only his second match, stroked the ball around in their contrasting styles to ensure a total above 300. New Zealand's reply was speckled with regular wickets, but they kept up with the steep asking-rate for much of the journey thanks to an exceptional maiden international century by Elliott. His eighth-wicket stand of 69 with McCullum, batting down the order after being struck on the shoulder earlier while standing up to Mills, kept the Australians on edge almost to the end.

Man of the Match: B. J. Haddin.

Australia

†B. J. Haddin run out	109	N. W. Bracken not out	3
M. J. Clarke c Guptill b Elliott	64	B. W. Hilfenhaus not out	0
*R. T. Ponting c Mills b Elliott	16		
D. J. Hussey c McCullum b O'Brien	7	B 1, w 3	4
C. L. White c Vettori b O'Brien	10		
M. E. K. Hussey c Taylor b Mills	51	1/135 (2) 2/0169(3) (9 wkts, 50 overs)	301
C. J. Ferguson lbw b Vettori	28	3/187 (4) 4/200 (1)	
J. R. Hopes b O'Brien	8	5/212 (5) 6/274 (7) 7/297 (8)	
M. G. Johnson c Patel b Mills	1	8/297 (6) 9/299 (9)	10 overs: 44–0

Mills 9–0–59–2; Southee 10–0–52–0; Vettori 10–0–52–1; O'Brien 10–1–68–3; Elliott 8–0–44–2; Patel 3–0–25–0.

New Zealand

M. J. Guptill c Ferguson b Bracken	6	J. S. Patel b Bracken	9
P. G. Fulton c White b Hopes	40	I. E. O'Brien not out	0
L. R. P. L. Taylor lbw b Hilfenhaus	8		
G. D. Elliott c M. E. K. Hussey b Hopes	115	B 4, l-b 11, w 8	23
N. T. Broom c Hilfenhaus b White	15		
K. D. Mills c Bracken b D. J. Hussey	2	1/12 (1) 2/16 (3) 3/96 (2) (47.3 overs)	269
*D. L. Vettori c Clarke b White	2	4/149 (5) 5/152 (6) 6/157 (7)	
T. G. Southee c Haddin b Johnson	17	7/183 (8) 8/252 (4) 9/262 (9)	
†B. B. McCullum c Ponting b Hilfenhaus	36	10/269 (10)	10 overs: 31–2

Bracken 8.3–1–65–2; Hilfenhaus 9–1–44–2; Johnson 10–2–35–1; Hopes 10–0–49–2; Clarke 5–0–41–0; D. J. Hussey 3–0–9–1; White 2–0–10–2.

Umpires: S. A. Bucknor and S. J. A. Taufel.
Third umpire: R. J. Tucker. Referee: R. S. Mahanama.

AUSTRALIA v NEW ZEALAND

Fourth One-Day International

At Adelaide, February 10, 2009 (day/night). Australia won by six wickets. Toss: New Zealand.

Perhaps thrown off balance by his side's failure to chase in Sydney, Vettori now batted first on an Adelaide Oval pitch that had rewarded the team batting second all summer – and so it proved again after some judicious Australian bowling kept the target down to modest dimensions. Taylor played his shots with the wristy power of a minor genius. However, in the face of a disciplined spell by Hopes, he was unable to summon enough support to snap the frayed nerves of a side desperate to avoid a hat-trick of home series defeats. Despite an undemanding target, Australia's reply teetered at 101 for three: Clarke fell bunting to short cover, Ponting skyed an extremely ambitious (even for him) pull, and Haddin was run out by his scratchy partner David Hussey. Another wicket might have brought the lot down, but Guptill dropped a catch in the deep to reprieve Mike Hussey on five, and together he and his brother ensured victory with a stand of 115.

Man of the Match: D. J. Hussey.

New Zealand

†B. B. McCullum b Clarke	33	*D. L. Vettori not out		6
M. J. Guptill c Bracken b Johnson	45	T. G. Southee not out		7
P. G. Fulton c Bracken b Hopes	5	L-b 2, w 10		12
L. R. P. L. Taylor c Haddin b Johnson	76			
G. D. Elliott c D. J. Hussey b Johnson	26	1/69 (2) 2/83 (3)	(8 wkts, 50 overs)	244
C. D. Cumming c Johnson b Hopes	0	3/86 (1) 4/141 (5)		
N. T. Broom c Hopes b Hilfenhaus	11	5/141 (6) 6/173 (7)		
K. D. Mills b Bracken	23	7/226 (4) 8/235 (8)	10 overs: 32-0	

I. E. O'Brien did not bat.

Bracken 10–0–51–1; Hilfenhaus 10–0–56–1; Johnson 10–0–51–3; Hopes 10–1–37–2; Clarke 8–0–23–1; White 2–0–24–0.

Australia

†B. J. Haddin run out	43	C. J. Ferguson not out		13
M. J. Clarke c Fulton b O'Brien	14	L-b 1, w 6, n-b 1		8
*R. T. Ponting c Guptill b Southee	15			
D. J. Hussey b O'Brien	79	1/29 (2) 2/57 (3)	(4 wkts, 48.2 overs)	247
M. E. K. Hussey not out	75	3/101 (1) 4/216 (4)	10 overs: 40-1	

C. L. White, J. R. Hopes, M. G. Johnson, N. W. Bracken and B. W. Hilfenhaus did not bat.

Mills 9.2–2–30–0; Southee 10–0–61–1; O'Brien 10–0–54–2; Vettori 10–0–54–0; Elliott 9–0–47–0.

Umpires: S. A. Bucknor and S. J. Davis.
Third umpire: P. R. Reiffel.   Referee: R. S. Mahanama.

AUSTRALIA v NEW ZEALAND

Fifth One-Day International

At Brisbane, February 13, 2009 (day/night). No result. Toss: New Zealand. One-day international debuts: P. M. Siddle; B. J. Diamanti.

Rain first shortened then ruined this match, robbing New Zealand of a probable series win. When the final showers struck they needed only 33 more from six overs, with Guptill and the debutant Brendon Diamanti in almost total control. Just before this, Ponting could be seen offering angry directives to his wayward bowlers as the Chappell–Hadlee Trophy appeared to be slipping from his grasp. Earlier, Australia had done exceptionally well to score 168 from the 22 overs they were allowed. Quick wickets again stunted their progress, but Ferguson showed real invention and composure to make 55, including most of the 30 runs reaped from the two-over batting powerplay, while Haddin unleashed three sixes to send a soggy crowd into raptures. They were sat back in their seats when New Zealand (whose target was reduced by a brief shower in the innings break to 156 off 20) replied in kind, through the impressively clean-hitting Guptill, a brief cameo by Fulton, and a longer one from Diamanti, a 28-year-old one-day specialist from Central Districts.

Man of the Series: M. E. K. Hussey.

Australia

J. R. Hopes c Vettori b Mills	5	C. J. Ferguson not out		55
†B. J. Haddin not out	88	W 3		3
*R. T. Ponting c McCullum b Mills	2			
D. J. Hussey b O'Brien	6	1/9 (1) 2/20 (3)	(4 wkts, 22 overs)	168
M. E. K. Hussey c Diamanti b Vettori	9	3/30 (4) 4/70 (5)	4 overs: 20-1	

C. L. White, M. G. Johnson, P. M. Siddle, N. W. Bracken and B. W. Hilfenhaus did not bat.

Mills 4–0–22–2; Southee 5–0–49–0; O'Brien 5–0–40–1; Diamanti 2–0–25–0; Vettori 4–0–24–1; Elliott 2–0–8–0.

New Zealand

†B. B. McCullum b Hilfenhaus	2	K. D. Mills c M. E. K. Hussey b Siddle		1
M. J. Guptill not out	64	B. J. Diamanti not out		26
P. G. Fulton c Ferguson b Bracken	22	L-b 1, w 3		4
L. R. P. L. Taylor c M. E. K. Hussey b Johnson	4	1/2 (1) 2/40 (3)	(6 wkts, 14 overs)	123
G. D. Elliott c Haddin b Bracken	0	3/56 (4) 4/68 (5)		
N. T. Broom run out	0	5/68 (6) 6/73 (7)	4 overs: 45-2	

*D. L. Vettori, T. G. Southee and I. E. O'Brien did not bat.

Hilfenhaus 3–0–28–1; Bracken 3–0–33–2; Johnson 3–0–28–1; Siddle 3–0–13–1; Hopes 2–0–20–0.

Umpires: S. A. Bucknor and R. J. Tucker.
Third umpire: B. N. J. Oxenford.   Referee: R. S. Mahanama.

AUSTRALIA v NEW ZEALAND

Twenty20 International

At Sydney, February 15. 2009 (floodlit). Australia won by one run. Toss: Australia. Twenty20 international debuts: C. J. Ferguson, M. C. Henriques, P. M. Siddle; N. T. Broom, I. G. Butler, G. D. Elliott, M. J. Guptill, I. E. O'Brien.

The Australians snatched some optimism and pride from their final match of the home summer by just keeping out New Zealand. Fielding a team with an even more pronounced accent on youth than in the 50-over games, Australia were led with some verve by Haddin, after both Ponting and Clarke were rested ahead of the South African tour. Australia needed to be sharp in the field after setting a mediocre target, due to several batsmen getting out after a start. David Hussey spent 39 balls over 41, and Vettori was satisfied both with his own contribution – a parsimonious one for 23 – and the chase his men had to undertake. But Siddle and Bracken produced opening spells that shaped the final outcome. Siddle's pace and lift did for Guptill and Fulton, while Bracken's line was immaculate enough to result in ten consecutive dot-balls at the start of his spell. McCullum hit out intelligently against the change bowlers, before he fell to a brilliant catch by Voges, who made the interception on the boundary's edge, threw the ball aloft as he was about to overbalance, then dived forward to complete the catch inside the rope. Bracken's final over was almost as tight as his earlier ones, and he was given the match award despite not scoring a run, taking a catch or claiming a wicket.

Man of the Match: N. W. Bracken.

Australia

		B	4	6
D. A. Warner c 9 b 11	23	15	4	0
*†B. J. Haddin c and b 10	15	10	2	0
C. J. Ferguson b 8	8	9	1	0
D. J. Hussey c 4 b 9	41	39	1	1
A. C. Voges lbw b 5	26	24	2	0
C. L. White c 9 b 11	16	11	0	1
J. R. Hopes not out	16	10	1	0
M. C. Henriques run out	1	2	0	0
P. M. Siddle not out	1	1	0	0
L-b 1, w 1, n-b 1	3			

6 overs: 47-2   (20 overs) 150-7

1/34 2/38 3/52 4/104 5/128 6/135 7/138

N. W. Bracken and B. W. Hilfenhaus did not bat.

Franklin 1–0–6–0; Southee 4–0–31–1; O'Brien 4–0–34–2; Butler 4–0–30–1; Vettori 4–0–23–1; N. L. McCullum 2–0–14–0; Elliott 1–0–11–1.

New Zealand

		B	4	6
†B. B. McCullum c 5 b 11	61	47	5	2
M. J. Guptill lbw b 9	0	2	0	0
P. G. Fulton c 2 b 9	1	8	0	0
N. T. Broom c 3 b 7	36	26	6	0
G. D. Elliott not out	23	30	1	0
J. E. C. Franklin run out	3	3	0	0
N. L. McCullum not out	10	4	1	1
B 3, l-b 10, w 2	15			

6 overs: 43-2   (20 overs) 149-5

1/5 2/12 3/73 4/131 5/137

*D. L. Vettori, I. G. Butler, T. G. Southee and I. E. O'Brien did not bat.

Siddle 4–0–24–2; Bracken 4–1–16–0; Hilfenhaus 4–0–32–1; Hopes 4–0–40–1; Hussey 4–0–24–0.

Umpires: B. N. J. Oxenford and P. R. Reiffel.
Third umpire: R. J. Tucker.   Referee: R. S. Mahanama.

AUSTRALIA v WEST INDIES, 2009-10

JOHN TOWNSEND

Test matches (3): Australia 2, West Indies 0

A series that started with a whimper of West Indian woes ended with the alleged basket-case of world cricket getting within 36 runs of squaring the three-Test rubber against an Australian team whose behaviour deteriorated the more they were placed under pressure.

In a month of contradictions, supposed Test cricket sceptic Chris Gayle proved the five-day format's brightest star, with centuries as contrasting as they were substantial and a rare capacity to inspire his troops to become greater than their collective parts. But for ill-conceived strokes from Ramnaresh Sarwan and Dwayne Bravo at the WACA on the second-last day of the series, West Indies might even have earned a share of the Frank Worrell Trophy after being set the stiff challenge of chasing down 359 to win.

South Africa made 414 to triumph at the same ground a year earlier and West Indies, without several key players, nearly pulled off a similarly remarkable victory. Instead Doug Bollinger, briefly eschewing his self-proclaimed "loud and obnoxious" tag, and grabbing his opportunity in the absence of injured first-choice bowlers Ben Hilfenhaus and Peter Siddle, collected the final scalp – and eight in the match – to give Australia the series 2–0, and start their climb towards regaining the No. 1 position in the ICC rankings.

The result flattered Australia, who dominated the early going in the series when their opponents were reeling from a limited and disrupted preparation, were run over in the middle stages, and came back in stuttering bursts at the end. And it took a questionable decision from third umpire Asad Rauf, already a contentious figure for overruling Mark Benson at Adelaide with what he himself described as "common sense" and a "gut feeling" rather than any technological clarification, to get the home team over the line.

West Indies had not won a Test in Australia since February 1997, suffering nine straight defeats along the way, and it looked like a third consecutive series clean sweep after they lost by an innings in three days at the Gabba. But Gayle found something within himself and his ragtag collection of veterans, novices, recalled discards and journeymen that offers considerable optimism to those many people who believe a strong and vibrant West Indies team is essential for the well-being of world cricket.

Kemar Roach was just 21 at the start of the series, but bowled with extreme pace and hostility from a short and muscular action that harried Australia's best batsman Ricky Ponting to the point of distraction. Roach dismissed him three times in five innings, crushed his elbow tendon with a brutal delivery at Perth, and generally asked questions of Ponting that he has not been required to answer for some considerable time.

Opening batsman Adrian Barath shared Roach's diminutive stature and was two years younger, but hardly lacked impact by comparison. He produced a

Ryan Pierse, Getty Images

Leaping at the chance: Adrian Barath reaches a hundred on debut, in the Brisbane Test.

century on debut, the ninth teenager to do so, and his enforced absence from the final match was to prove costly for the visitors. It may come as some surprise to critics of a West Indian cricket system often considered beyond repair and populated by slothful opportunists that Barath's hamstring tear came from his eagerness to do extra training sessions between Tests. His attitude surely offers hope for the future.

Just as Australia did in the Ashes series, West Indies scored more runs and hundreds than their opponents, but were not able to win the crucial points at which momentum changed and victories were inspired. The West Indians collected four centuries – including Gayle's monolithic unbeaten 165 at Adelaide and his 70-ball blitzkrieg at the WACA – while eight Australians reached half-centuries, none of whom could go on to three figures. Only England, with 16 in five Tests against West Indies in 1963, managed more fifties in a series without a century than the 15 produced by this Australian combination.

There were no officially expressed concerns from the Australian camp about the stopped starts, just regular homilies about the positives that attach to having so many batsmen in outstanding form. The opening pair both had moments of heartache: Simon Katich fell for 99 for the second time in his career, while the ever-improving Shane Watson was skittled attempting to heave the boundary that would have brought up his maiden century.

That lack of discipline continued as the series proceeded, with Bollinger reprimanded in Adelaide and three Australians found guilty of disciplinary breaches in the final Test at Perth, where the provocative West Indies spinner Sulieman Benn was banned for two one-day internationals after a heated and ugly altercation with Brad Haddin and Mitchell Johnson. West Indies were not alone in being mystified that their player was suspended while the Australians received minor fines, but it was not the only issue that promoted significantly more speculation than clarity. The new umpire referral system left plenty shaking their heads – including Ponting several times in Adelaide – while Mark Benson abandoned that Test to fly home, pleading illness, after Asad Rauf overruled his seemingly correct on-field decision.

West Indies returned to Australia in February 2010 for several limited-overs matches; scores and reports of these games will appear in Wisden 2011.

WEST INDIAN TOURING PARTY

C. H. Gayle (*captain*), A. B. Barath, S. J. Benn, D. J. Bravo, S. Chanderpaul, N. Deonarine, T. M. Dowlin, B. P. Nash, D. Ramdin, R. Rampaul, K. A. J. Roach, D. J. G. Sammy, R. R. Sarwan, J. E. Taylor, G. C. Tonge. *Coach:* D. Williams.
    Taylor returned home after the First Test with hip trouble, but was not replaced.

TEST MATCH AVERAGES

AUSTRALIA – BATTING AND FIELDING

	T	I	NO	R	HS	100s	50s	Avge	Ct
B. J. Haddin............	3	5	2	225	88	0	2	75.00	14
†S. M. Katich...........	3	5	0	302	99	0	3	60.40	2
S. R. Watson	3	5	0	263	96	0	2	52.60	5
M. J. Clarke...........	3	5	1	209	71	0	2	52.25	4
†M. E. K. Hussey	3	5	0	235	82	0	2	47.00	5
N. M. Hauritz	3	4	2	80	50*	0	1	40.00	1
R. T. Ponting	3	5	1	136	55	0	1	34.00	2
†M. J. North...........	3	5	0	166	79	0	2	33.20	1
†M. G. Johnson.........	3	4	0	54	35	0	0	13.50	0

Played in two Tests: †D. E. Bollinger 0, 2*; P. M. Siddle 20*, 0 (2 ct). Played in one Test: B. W. Hilfenhaus did not bat (2 ct); C. J. McKay 10 (1 ct).

† *Left-handed batsman.*

BOWLING

	Style	O	M	R	W	BB	5W/i	Avge
B. W. Hilfenhaus.......	RFM	23	9	70	5	3-20	0	14.00
D. E. Bollinger	LFM	83.2	12	258	13	5-70	1	19.84
S. R. Watson	RFM	68	15	211	8	2-30	0	26.37
M. G. Johnson	LF	110.2	17	477	17	5-103	1	28.05
N. M. Hauritz	OB	123	21	363	11	3-17	0	33.00
P. M. Siddle..........	RFM	56	15	212	3	1-41	0	70.66

Also bowled: M. E. K. Hussey (RM) 2–0–3–1; C. J. McKay (RFM) 28–5–101–1; M. J. North (OB) 21–3–62–0.

WEST INDIES – BATTING AND FIELDING

	T	I	NO	R	HS	100s	50s	Avge	Ct
†C. H. Gayle............	3	6	1	346	165*	2	0	69.20	3
†B. P. Nash............	3	6	0	250	92	0	2	41.66	1
T. M. Dowlin	2	4	0	143	62	0	2	35.75	2
A. B. Barath	2	4	0	139	104	1	0	34.75	2
D. J. Bravo	3	6	0	176	104	1	0	29.33	5
†S. Chanderpaul	2	4	0	93	62	0	1	23.25	0
R. R. Sarwan..........	2	4	0	88	42	0	0	22.00	3
†S. J. Benn	3	6	1	101	33	0	0	20.20	2
†R. Rampaul............	3	6	2	65	40*	0	0	16.25	0
D. Ramdin	3	6	0	96	54	0	1	16.00	13
K. A. J. Roach	3	6	1	32	17	0	0	6.40	1

Played in one Test: †N. Deonarine 18, 82 (2 ct); D. J. G. Sammy 44, 10; J. E. Taylor 8, 0; G. C. Tonge 2, 23*.

† *Left-handed batsman.*

BOWLING

	Style	O	M	R	W	BB	5W/i	Avge
D. J. Bravo............	RFM	94.1	16	319	11	4-42	0	29.00
S. J. Benn.............	SLA	153	29	408	11	5-155	1	37.09
K. A. J. Roach	RF	94.1	12	357	7	3-93	0	51.00
R. Rampaul	RFM	77	14	290	4	1-21	0	72.50

Also bowled: A. B. Barath (OB) 1–0–4–0; N. Deonarine (OB) 24–4–75–2; C. H. Gayle (OB) 21–2–59–0; D. J. G. Sammy (RM) 23–2–100–2; J. E. Taylor (RF) 9–2–43–1; G. C. Tonge (RFM) 28–3–113–1.

At Allan Border Field, Brisbane, November 18, 19, 20, 21, 2009. **Drawn.** Toss: West Indians. **West Indians 271** (R. R. Sarwan 73, S. Chanderpaul 41, D. J. Bravo 49; D. J. Doran 3-107) **and 357-6** (A. B. Barath 74, T. M. Dowlin 53, S. Chanderpaul 69, R. R. Sarwan 66, B. P. Nash 36*); **Queensland 617-7 dec** (N. J. Kruger 172, W. J. Townsend 100, N. J. Reardon 147, C. P. Simpson 73, D. J. Doran 31*; K. A. J. Roach 3-135).

The tourists' modest first innings was put into perspective by Queensland's massive score, which featured maiden first-class hundreds from Nick Kruger (20 fours and five sixes) and Wade Townsend, who together added 243 for the second wicket, and also by Nathan Reardon, who hit 15 fours and seven sixes and put on 156 for the sixth wicket with his captain Chris Simpson. Sulieman Benn took 1-151 in 34 overs. Starting their second innings 346 behind, the West Indians had a day plus 40 overs to survive – and did so with relative ease. Still there at the end were Denesh Ramdin, captaining because Chris Gayle had returned to Jamaica as his mother was ill, and the former Queensland player Brendan Nash.

AUSTRALIA v WEST INDIES

First Test Match

At Brisbane, November 26, 27, 28, 2009. Australia won by an innings and 65 runs. Toss: Australia. Test debuts: A. B. Barath, R. Rampaul.

Australia went into the First Test seeking redemption after the comprehensive defeat at The Oval which led to the loss of the Ashes. West Indies, meanwhile, back to something like full strength after a bitter contracts dispute had led to a threadbare replacement team losing twice to Bangladesh, were simply looking to be competitive. Still, few observers gave them any chance of wresting back the Frank Worrell Trophy, or even winning their first Test in Australia in 12 years.

The visitors' task was made even more difficult by a series of hammer-blows in the lead-up to the series opener. Captain Chris Gayle, after providing only lukewarm rebuttals to his comments earlier in the year that he would not be too unhappy if Test cricket were to die, was called back to Jamaica after the sudden illness of his mother. He was in doubt for this Test and even the series, but his mother's rapid improvement allowed Gayle to return just 24 hours before the start, somewhat jet-lagged but with his mind considerably clearer.

Then Ramnaresh Sarwan suffered severe back spasms during a training session, and was ruled out of the Test. Further bad news came early in the match itself, when the leading fast bowler Jerome Taylor broke down with a hip injury that soon forced his return

---

YOUNGEST TO SCORE A TEST CENTURY FOR WEST INDIES

Years	Days			
19	**228**	**A. B. Barath (104)**	**v Australia at Brisbane**................	**2009-10**
20	230	G. A. Headley (176)	v England at Bridgetown............	1929-30
20	269	D. R. Smith (105*)	v South Africa at Cape Town............	2003-04
21	12	C. L. Hooper (100*)	v India at Calcutta.....................	1987-88
21	208	D. J. Bravo (107)	v South Africa at St John's.............	2004-05
21	215	G. S. Sobers (365*)	v Pakistan at Kingston	1957-58
21	285	B. H. Pairaudeau (115)	v India at Port-of-Spain	1952-53
21	301	M. N. Samuels (104)	v India at Kolkata	2002-03
21	302	C. H. Gayle (175)	v Zimbabwe at Bulawayo...............	2001
21	330	O. G. Smith (104)	v Australia at Kingston.................	1954-55

Note: Only the first hundred for each player is shown: Headley scored six centuries and Sobers three before the age of 22. Barath, Headley, Pairaudeau and both Smiths were making their Test debuts.

home. Taylor had missed the sole warm-up game with what was variously described as hip, back and general soreness, but, whatever the ailment, his absence was keenly felt after his early dismissal of Watson. Although Roach, still only 21, underlined his considerable promise by unfurling a barrage of 90mph questions that the Australians were mostly uncomfortable answering, his development would only have benefited from having a senior bowler at the other end.

Australia recalled the steady off-spinner Hauritz, whose absence at The Oval was seen as a critical reason for defeat, although the man himself was bemused that a career spent fending off criticism of his apparent lack of impact had given way to a new status as a match-winner *in absentia*. Fittingly, Hauritz was to produce his finest performance in his eighth Test, spread over more than five years, clipping a maiden half-century and bowling such incisive drifting and gripping off-breaks that he claimed five cheap wickets and was on a hat-trick.

ONLY HUNDRED IN A TEST FOR SIDE LOSING BY AN INNINGS

R. H. Catterall (120)	South Africa v England at Birmingham..................	1924
G. M. Wood (100)	Australia v Pakistan at Melbourne......................	1981-82
K. R. Rutherford (102)	New Zealand v Australia at Christchurch	1992-93
M. Azharuddin (102)	India v South Africa at Bangalore	1999-2000
A. B. Barath (104)	**West Indies v Australia at Brisbane**	**2009-10**

Each Australian contributed, five gathering half-centuries before an enterprising first-innings declaration from the usually conservative Ponting, while West Indies produced only modest resistance against an attack that was penetrating, persistent and varied. Swing bowler Hilfenhaus put aside the discomfort of knee tendinitis to collect five wickets, including Gayle lbw twice, while the seldom-used Hussey had an even rarer success, taking only his second Test wicket when Bravo, hooking a very medium-paced bouncer, fell for the sucker punch on the final day. Gayle stayed and called for a video review each time he was dismissed, and each time was shown to be comprehensively adjacent, indicating that greater understanding of the system was needed.

Journeyman Travis Dowlin, a Stanford beneficiary and a survivor of the Bangladesh shambles, was a revelation with a fighting 62, but it was the performance of the 19-year-old Trinidadian Adrian Barath that was to provide the greatest hope for the future. Ponting enforced the follow-on for just the third time in his 62-match tenure as captain (there had been seven further occasions when he had declined to do so, and an eighth followed at Perth), and it proved a wise decision as his bowlers scythed through the feeble batting to end the game on the third day. But Barath did his best to turn back the tide. Buoyed by his international exposure at the Champions League Twenty20 only a few weeks earlier, the diminutive Barath stood tall with 104 from just 138 deliveries with 19 fours, cutting and driving powerfully. He became only the ninth teenager to score a century on Test debut, following Pakistan's Umar Akmal by a day or two, and for a significant period was on track to produce the highest percentage of runs in a completed innings before he was finally dismissed for 104 out of 154. He was the youngest West Indian to score a Test century, beating the great George Headley by a year, and became just the fifth batsman to have hit the only century of a Test his side lost by an innings.

Nonetheless, the innings victory was Australia's ninth consecutive win against West Indies at home, equalling their record against any opponent, and was an emphatic step towards Ponting's goal of regaining the No. 1 Test ranking. It was also their 16th win in 21 Tests at the Gabba since their last defeat there, to West Indies in 1988-89.

Man of the Match: B. W. Hilfenhaus.

Close of play: First day, Australia 322-5 (North 42, Haddin 9); Second day, West Indies 134-5 (Dowlin 40, Ramdin 22).

Australia

S. R. Watson lbw b Taylor	0	N. M. Hauritz not out	50
S. M. Katich c Ramdin b Bravo	92	P. M. Siddle not out	20
*R. T. Ponting c Ramdin b Roach	55		
M. E. K. Hussey c and b Benn	66	B 2, l-b 9, w 1, n-b 20	32
M. J. Clarke c Gayle b Bravo	41		
M. J. North c Ramdin b Bravo	79	1/0 (1) 2/126 (3) (8 wkts dec, 135 overs) 480	
†B. J. Haddin c Ramdin b Rampaul	38	3/200 (2) 4/253 (4)	
M. G. Johnson c Ramdin b Benn	7	5/287 (5) 6/371 (7) 7/386 (8) 8/444 (6)	

B. W. Hilfenhaus did not bat.

Taylor 9–2–43–1; Roach 25–4–76–1; Rampaul 26–4–110–1; Bravo 32–4–118–3; Benn 34–5–86–2; Gayle 9–0–36–0.

West Indies

*C. H. Gayle lbw b Hilfenhaus	31	– lbw b Hilfenhaus	1
A. B. Barath c Watson b Johnson	15	– lbw b Watson	104
T. M. Dowlin c Watson b Hauritz	62	– b Hilfenhaus	4
S. Chanderpaul lbw b Siddle	2	– c Katich b Hilfenhaus	2
D. J. Bravo c Watson b Johnson	0	– c Hilfenhaus b Hussey	23
B. P. Nash c Haddin b Watson	18	– lbw b Hauritz	7
†D. Ramdin c North b Johnson	54	– c Haddin b Hauritz	16
S. J. Benn c Siddle b Hilfenhaus	28	– (9) not out	15
J. E. Taylor c Katich b Hauritz	8	– (8) c Hilfenhaus b Watson	0
K. A. J. Roach c Clarke b Hauritz	0	– c Hussey b Siddle	5
R. Rampaul not out	1	– c Haddin b Johnson	0
B 1, l-b 3, n-b 5	9	L-b 4, n-b 6	10

1/49 (1) 2/49 (2) 3/58 (4) 4/63 (5)   (63 overs) 228   1/6 (1) 2/18 (3)   (52.1 overs) 187
5/96 (6) 6/174 (7) 7/212 (8) 8/221 (9)   3/39 (4) 4/105 (5)
9/221 (10) 10/228 (3)   5/141 (6) 6/154 (2) 7/158 (8)
    8/170 (7) 9/187 (10) 10/187 (11)

Hilfenhaus 16–6–50–2; Siddle 13–4–51–1; Johnson 19–4–75–3; Watson 9–0–31–1; Hauritz 6–3–17–3. *Second Innings*—Hilfenhaus 7–3–20–3; Siddle 10–3–41–1; Johnson 9.1–1–35–1; Watson 10–0–44–2; Hauritz 14–1–40–2; Hussey 2–0–3–1.

Umpires: Asad Rauf and I. J. Gould.
Third umpire: M. R. Benson.   Referee: B. C. Broad.

AUSTRALIA v WEST INDIES

Second Test Match

At Adelaide, December 4, 5, 6, 7, 8, 2009. Drawn. Toss: West Indies.

What a difference a week makes. Reeling from a three-day shellacking at the Gabba that gave rise to a slew of "Worst Indies" headlines, the tourists outplayed their recent conquerors. And it was the much-maligned Gayle who led the way, with an innings of such substance and commitment that he single-handedly did more to sustain Test cricket than some players might achieve in a career.

A day after the South Australian government announced $A500m plans to convert the country's most graceful cricket ground into a multi-purpose stadium primarily for Australian football, the national cricket team appeared to go out in sympathy with the loss of the Adelaide Oval's 19th-century grandeur. Their batsmen could make little headway against an enthusiastic West Indies attack; their bowlers were stymied by dogged defence and audacious attack; and they had limited luck with the umpire review system.

Yet a pitch that deteriorated rapidly to start with, but then stayed the same for much of the final three days, ultimately aided Australia in their bid to save the match and protect

Mark Kolbe, Getty Images

Final verdict: umpire Mark Benson chats with Brad Haddin moments before his decision to give Shivnarine Chanderpaul (*extreme left*) not out is overturned by third umpire Asad Rauf.

their series lead. Seeking a record tenth consecutive home win against West Indies, Australia were dealt a tough blow when Hilfenhaus was declared unfit with deteriorating knee tendinitis. He had been one of the few bowlers not sent back from the recent one-day series in India although, as a key member of the Test attack, he more than almost anyone else would have benefited from time at home preparing for the summer.

West Indies regained Sarwan, who showed his experience with a valuable attempt to blunt the Australian pacemen, but it was the middle order that set up West Indies' control. Chanderpaul was the cornerstone, with a four-hour 62 that ended in controversial circumstances when the third umpire Asad Rauf ruled in favour of Australia after a referral, claiming that "common sense" enabled him to deduce the faintest of edges when the technology was not able to pick up the contact. The on-field umpire Mark Benson withdrew from the match that night and flew straight home to England, many observers speculating that his decision was driven by Rauf overruling him, although Benson later released a statement claiming he was ill and unable to see out the Test.

Bravo was certainly in the rudest health and, aided by the former Queenslander and transplanted Jamaican Nash (who completed a fighting 92 against his former countrymen), travelled comfortably to his third Test century, inspiring his team to a formidable 451. Australia went close in reply, but the batsmen continued their new-found habit of passing 50 without going on to three figures. Watson's attempt was the most poignant, the remade opener reaching 96 before losing his middle stump to the crafty Benn as he attempted to heave the boundary that would have brought his maiden Test century.

Soon Gayle entered the fray. A lead of just 12 left West Indies vulnerable, but their captain was to stand like a colossus between his sometimes fragile charges and an Australian attack nourished by regular wickets. He found allies who stayed in for an hour or so while he resisted his natural instinct to attack on the way to carrying his bat for a splendid, chanceless 165 out of 317. He remained in the middle throughout the 441-minute innings, saw off 285 deliveries and ten partners and struck 16 fours and a six. No West Indies captain had ever carried his bat in a Test before; indeed, only three other openers had ever managed it for them – Desmond Haynes (three times), Conrad Hunte and Frank Worrell.

A team with greater recent winning experience might have decided to bowl earlier than West Indies, who batted well into the last day for a lead of 329, but they remained the only side capable of winning the match. Australia were rarely troubled, although Bravo jangled their nerves with three quick strikes before Clarke eased them to safety.

Even so, Gayle revealed that a proud heart still beats below the maroon cap, and that West Indies' darkest hour – or decade – may be drawing to a close.

Man of the Match: C. H. Gayle.

Close of play: First day, West Indies 336-6 (Sammy 44, Nash 44); Second day, Australia 174-0 (Watson 96, Katich 71); Third day, West Indies 23-0 (Gayle 12, Barath 10); Fourth day, West Indies 284-8 (Gayle 155, Rampaul 0).

West Indies

*C. H. Gayle c Haddin b Bollinger	26	– not out	165
A. B. Barath c Hussey b Bollinger	3	– run out	17
R. R. Sarwan c Clarke b Johnson	28	– c Haddin b Johnson	7
S. Chanderpaul c Haddin b Watson	62	– lbw b Bollinger	27
B. P. Nash b Johnson	92	– b Watson	24
D. J. Bravo b Hauritz	104	– c Hauritz b Johnson	22
†D. Ramdin b Watson	4	– b Johnson	0
D. J. G. Sammy lbw b Siddle	44	– c Ponting b Bollinger	10
S. J. Benn lbw b Hauritz	17	– c Siddle b Johnson	5
K. A. J. Roach c Haddin b Johnson	2	– (11) c Ponting b Bollinger	8
R. Rampaul not out	40	– (10) b Johnson	14
B 5, l-b 14, w 5, n-b 5	29	B 8, l-b 3, w 1, n-b 6	18

1/26 (2) 2/39 (1) 3/84 (3) (124.1 overs) 451
4/235 (4) 5/239 (7) 6/273 (6)
7/336 (8) 8/380 (9) 9/383 (10) 10/451 (5)

1/45 (2) 2/61 (3) (99.5 overs) 317
3/133 (4) 4/194 (5)
5/251 (6) 6/251 (7) 7/277 (8)
8/284 (9) 9/302 (10) 10/317 (11)

In the first innings Nash, when 20, retired hurt at 119 and resumed at 273.

Bollinger 25-3-67-2; Siddle 25-6-92-1; Johnson 26.1-3-105-3; Hauritz 36-5-111-2; Watson 12-2-57-2. *Second Innings*—Johnson 22-1-103-5; Bollinger 17.5-3-50-3; Hauritz 27-4-68-0; Siddle 8-2-28-0; North 14-2-42-0; Watson 11-5-15-1.

Australia

S. R. Watson b Benn	96	– c Bravo b Sammy	48
S. M. Katich c Barath b Benn	80	– c Barath b Bravo	21
*R. T. Ponting c Bravo b Roach	36	– b Rampaul	20
M. E. K. Hussey c Ramdin b Roach	41	– c Ramdin b Bravo	29
M. J. Clarke c Sarwan b Benn	71	– not out	61
M. J. North c Bravo b Benn	16	– c Sarwan b Bravo	2
†B. J. Haddin not out	55	– not out	21
M. G. Johnson c Gayle b Sammy	7		
N. M. Hauritz c Ramdin b Roach	17		
P. M. Siddle c Bravo b Benn	0		
D. E. Bollinger run out	0		
L-b 2, n-b 18	20	B 1, l-b 2, n-b 7	10

1/174 (1) 2/193 (2) 3/233 (3) (131.1 overs) 439
4/312 (4) 5/353 (6) 6/370 (5)
7/377 (8) 8/418 (9) 9/419 (10) 10/439 (11)

1/33 (2) (5 wkts, 76 overs) 212
2/68 (3) 3/114 (1)
4/133 (4) 5/139 (6)

Roach 25.1-3-93-3; Rampaul 14-1-52-0; Bravo 12-1-43-0; Sammy 18-2-79-1; Benn 53-8-155-5; Gayle 9-1-15-0. *Second Innings*—Roach 16-3-66-0; Rampaul 9-2-22-1; Benn 27-10-51-0; Bravo 15-4-37-3; Gayle 3-1-8-0; Sammy 5-0-21-1; Barath 1-0-4-0.

Umpires: M. R. Benson and I. J. Gould.
Third umpire: Asad Rauf.   Referee: B. C. Broad.
Asad Rauf replaced Benson from the 2nd day, and B. N. J. Oxenford took over as third umpire.

AUSTRALIA v WEST INDIES

Third Test Match

At Perth, December 16, 17, 18, 19, 20, 2009. Australia won by 35 runs. Toss: Australia.
Test debuts: C. J. McKay; G. C. Tonge.

Having played the tortoise with such solidity and impact in Adelaide, Gayle was straining
to release the hare at the WACA little more than a week later. And what a release it was:
Gayle, the owner of the sole Twenty20 international century, hit an equally destructive Test
hundred. His 70-ball assault meant he reached three figures one delivery faster than the
furiously explosive century by Roy Fredericks at the same ground in 1975-76, and just 13
slower than home-town hero Adam Gilchrist in the 2006-07 Ashes series at Perth.

Yet for all the drama during Gayle's remarkable innings, which included a blow off
Hauritz that landed on the roof of the five-storey Lillee–Marsh Stand a full 110 metres
away, his effort and the fact that his team ran Australia to within 36 runs of victory was
overshadowed by a series of ugly confrontations between the players. Four of them were
disciplined, including the Barbadian spinner Benn, who was banned for two one-day
internationals after a protracted clash on the second day with the batsmen Johnson and
Haddin, for which the two Australians received relatively minor fines from referee Chris
Broad. Watson also received a fine after a spectacular reaction, likened by former
Australian bowler Geoff Lawson to a four-year-old's temper tantrum, to his dismissal of
Gayle in the second innings. Watson claimed he had been taunted by the batsman: "He
definitely let me know that he was keen for me to come on to bowl, so it was very nice to
get him out first ball."

Australia have struggled for impact in recent seasons at Perth, the ground where once
they dominated as bowlers used the pace and steepling bounce to their advantage while
batsmen made the most of the true but confronting surface and rapid outfield. Roach
relished the helpful conditions, producing a display of dynamic high-speed bowling that,
more than anything during the summer, posed questions about Ponting's longevity at the
highest level. Ponting was forced to retire hurt for the first time in his career when Roach
slammed a bumper into his left elbow, causing a tendon injury that the Australian
physiotherapist Alex Kountouris said was akin to "a piece of meat bashed by a mallet",
and which would trouble Ponting for the rest of the summer.

Australia looked impregnable after their early declaration at 520, Katich suffering the
chagrin of his second Test dismissal for 99 as the team's half-century tally escalated to 15,
while West Indies looked to be out of the contest after their middling reply of 312. The
highlight was Gayle's rampage, which started in Bollinger's first over and concluded only
when he ran out of ammunition 102 minutes later. Six of Gayle's shots flew over the fence,
several of them over the crowd and one on to the top of the stand. It was breathtaking
batting, and a display of such clean and brutal hitting that even the Australian players were
awestruck by the big Jamaican's power and fury.

Seemingly inspired by their captain's carnage, West Indies found Australia rattled by
Ponting's absence and vulnerable to the searching combination of Roach's pace and
Bravo's probing late swing. The innings failed to survive four hours as Bravo snared four
cheap wickets and Benn had a token of revenge with three, including his tormentor
Haddin. Ponting entered at 125 for seven – shortly after it had been announced that he
would not bat except in an emergency – but lasted only six balls.

West Indies required 359 to secure their sixth victory at the WACA – they won their
first five Tests there before losing the most recent one in 2000-01 – but the absence of cool
head Chanderpaul (forced to withdraw because of a finger damaged at Adelaide) and
teenage revelation Adrian Barath, who had torn a hamstring doing extra fitness sessions,
proved crucial. Sarwan fell trying an ambitious cut to the last ball before lunch on the
fourth day, and later Bravo's loose drive was snapped up in the gully. In between,
Chanderpaul's replacement Narsingh Deonarine – another Guyanese left-hander – and

Nash threatened the target with a dogged 128-run stand, then Benn and Roach hoicked and hammered at better than a run a ball during the closing stages, but it was to no avail.

The game had a dramatic finale – albeit with the participants motionless as they waited for several long minutes for video confirmation of the result – with the last wicket being eventually upheld on Asad Rauf's review despite no evidence to support the on-field umpire Billy Bowden's finding that Roach had feathered a catch behind.

Man of the Match: C. H. Gayle.   *Man of the Series:* C. H. Gayle.

Close of play: First day, Australia 339-3 (Hussey 81, North 23); Second day, West Indies 214-2 (Sarwan 42, Deonarine 10); Third day, Australia 137-8 (Hauritz 11, McKay 1); Fourth day, West Indies 308-9 (Roach 13, Tonge 12).

Australia

S. R. Watson c Ramdin b Roach	89	– lbw b Tonge	30
S. M. Katich c Roach b Benn	99	– b Rampaul	10
*R. T. Ponting retired hurt	23	– (9) c Dowlin b Roach	2
M. E. K. Hussey c Ramdin b Rampaul	82	– c Dowlin b Benn	17
M. J. Clarke c Gayle b Deonarine	11	– (3) c Ramdin b Bravo	25
M. J. North c and b Deonarine	68	– (5) c Ramdin b Bravo	1
†B. J. Haddin c Ramdin b Roach	88	– (6) c Bravo b Benn	23
M. G. Johnson c Benn b Bravo	35	– (7) c Nash b Bravo	5
N. M. Hauritz not out	2	– (8) c Sarwan b Bravo	11
C. J. McKay (did not bat)		– c Deonarine b Benn	10
D. E. Bollinger (did not bat)		– not out	2
B 4, l-b 2, w 1, n-b 16	23	B 9, l-b 2, w 1, n-b 2	14

1/132 (1) 2/260 (2)	(7 wkts dec, 130.4 overs) 520	1/15 (2) 2/66 (1)	(51.3 overs) 150
3/277 (5) 4/355 (4)		3/81 (3) 4/89 (4)	
5/444 (6) 6/510 (7) 7/520 (8)		5/109 (5) 6/117 (6) 7/125 (7)	
		8/134 (9) 9/146 (10) 10/150 (8)	

In the first innings Ponting retired hurt at 175.

Roach 22-2-104-2; Rampaul 22-6-85-1; Tonge 18-1-85-0; Bravo 17.4-1-79-1; Benn 28-4-87-1; Deonarine 23-4-74-2. *Second Innings*—Roach 6-0-18-1; Rampaul 6-1-21-1; Tonge 10-2-28-1; Deonarine 1-0-1-0; Bravo 17.3-6-42-4; Benn 11-2-29-3.

West Indies

*C. H. Gayle c Watson b Bollinger	102	– c Haddin b Watson	21
T. M. Dowlin c Hussey b Johnson	55	– c Clarke b Bollinger	22
R. R. Sarwan c Hussey b Bollinger	42	– c Haddin b Hauritz	11
N. Deonarine c Watson b Johnson	18	– b Watson	82
B. P. Nash c Clarke b Hauritz	44	– b Bollinger	65
D. J. Bravo c Haddin b Bollinger	26	– c Hussey b Johnson	1
†D. Ramdin b Bollinger	8	– b McKay	14
S. J. Benn c Haddin b Hauritz	3	– c sub (T. P. Doropoulos) b Johnson	33
R. Rampaul c Haddin b Hauritz	0	– c McKay b Johnson	10
K. A. J. Roach not out	0	– c Haddin b Bollinger	17
G. C. Tonge c Haddin b Bollinger	2	– not out	23
L-b 5, w 1, n-b 6	12	B 9, l-b 9, w 1, n-b 5	24

1/136 (1) 2/175 (2) 3/214 (3)	(81 overs) 312	1/35 (2) 2/52 (1)	(94.3 overs) 323
4/239 (4) 5/285 (6) 6/295 (5) 7/310 (8)		3/68 (3) 4/196 (4)	
8/310 (9) 9/310 (7) 10/312 (11)		5/197 (6) 6/231 (7) 7/245 (5)	
		8/279 (8) 9/279 (9) 10/323 (10)	

Bollinger 20-3-70-5; Johnson 18-3-92-2; McKay 14-3-45-0; Hauritz 17-1-66-3; Watson 12-3-34-0. *Second Innings*—Bollinger 20.3-3-71-3; Johnson 16-5-67-3; McKay 14-2-56-1; Watson 14-5-30-2; Hauritz 23-7-61-1; North 7-1-20-0.

Umpires: B. F. Bowden and I. J. Gould.
Third umpire: Asad Rauf.   Referee: B. C. Broad.

AUSTRALIA v PAKISTAN, 2009-10

Chloe Saltau

Test matches (3): Australia 3, Pakistan 0
One-day internationals (5): Australia 5, Pakistan 0
Twenty20 internationals (1): Australia 1, Pakistan 0

By the time Australia had completed their fourth consecutive 3–0 sweep against Pakistan, most of the pieces in their Test jigsaw had fallen into place. Shane Watson, who had seemed an odd fit when he replaced Phillip Hughes at the top of the order during the Ashes less than six months earlier, suddenly looked and performed like a Test opener. Nathan Hauritz, another player previously maligned in his own country, also emerged as a consistent Test performer in the seat that many had presumed he was simply warming until a more authentic spinner came along.

With the exception of Doug Bollinger, the energetic left-armer who seized his chance in the absence of the injured Ben Hilfenhaus, Australia won the series with the same players who had lost the Ashes, as the selectors forged ahead with their plan to build a settled and established team capable of winning them back.

Hauritz provided a perfect example of reward for perseverance. On the eve of the series, selection chairman Andrew Hilditch publicly challenged the off-spinner to show he could bowl Australia to victory, making note of his bloated fourth-innings bowling average in the forties. By the end of it, Hauritz was front and centre in the team victory photo, dragged into the foreground by his appreciative captain, having collected five-wicket hauls in back-to-back Tests and helped bowl Australia to wins on three consecutive occasions for a series-high 18 wickets at 23.05.

Just as the blossoming of Hauritz imbued the self-deprecating spinner with a new sense of belonging, Watson's man-of-the-series performance gave the team's top-order batting the punch it had missed since the decline and retirement of Matthew Hayden. The Australians were still prone to occasional collapses – the impressive left-armer Mohammad Aamer flattened the middle order in Melbourne, and the other Pakistani seamers exploited favourable conditions to roll the home side for 127 in Sydney – but Watson held them together with 346 runs at 69.20, and the home side were able to declare in four out of six innings. Watson's contribution was a major breakthrough for a driven cricketer who, because of his constant battles with injury, until now had not completed a home summer and so struggled to convince a sceptical Australian public of his credibility as a Test all-rounder. Only Marcus North at No. 6 failed to nail down his place in the side.

The visitors were as puzzling at the end of the series as they were at the beginning. Ricky Ponting made no secret of his hunch that Pakistan would be classier opponents than Australia's previous conquests, West Indies, and for more than a few fleeting moments, especially in Sydney, the captain's instincts

Mark Nolan, Getty Images

Acid drop: Danish Kaneria cannot look after Kamran Akmal (*left*) drops Mike Hussey at Sydney.

proved correct. But Pakistan lost the key moments: the first session of the series when both Australian openers were dropped; the fifth morning in Melbourne again when Mitchell Johnson struck twice in an over; on several occasions in Sydney; and the first morning in Hobart when Ponting was dropped on nought. Their fielding was inept from start to finish, and the number of dropped catches reached a silly 16. Still, officials resisted calls for a specialist fielding coach, instead pointing to a "grassroots" problem in Pakistan.

The campaign was also undermined by a stunning lack of communication between the Pakistan Cricket Board and team management in Australia, who sent an SOS for the former captain Younis Khan to strengthen the middle order after two modest batting displays in Melbourne. The request was ignored and, to the frustration of the captain, Mohammad Yousuf, his predecessor's arrival was delayed until the one-day series.

Then, after Kamran Akmal's unfortunate display with the gloves in Sydney, the board sent a new wicketkeeper, Sarfraz Ahmed, to Australia without initially informing the captain or team manager. The selection crisis that followed was damaging and incoherent. Kamran, a veteran of 48 Tests and whose presence as vice-captain on the on-tour selection committee complicated matters further, insisted out of pride that he would play in the Third Test, a dead-rubber game, while coach Intikhab Alam insisted he would not. Sadly, Pakistan's problems were exacerbated by their desperate lack of Test cricket in the preceding two years, and the team lacked the killer instinct to force home their commanding position after gaining a 206-run lead in the captivating Second Test in Sydney.

Yousuf argued that Pakistan's batting malaise, manifesting itself in his side's inability to pass 350 in any of the Tests, was a direct consequence of the nation's seduction by Twenty20, the form of the game in which Pakistan had recently become champions of the world. "Twenty20 is easy for Pakistanis because they know how to hit; nobody knows how to defend," Yousuf said. "Until players… play with discipline and play ball to ball and leave balls they are supposed to, we will struggle in ODIs, let alone Tests." His point was well made with respect to the precociously talented 19-year-old Umar Akmal, who took the breath away in Melbourne with his audacious 51, but was infuriating as well as impressive, and twice stumbled just short of half-centuries later in the tour. In Khurram Manzoor, though, the tourists appeared to have unearthed a batsman capable of patience, his 77 from 239 balls delaying the completion of the clean sweep at Hobart.

Yousuf's leadership style was gentle rather than inspirational. His tactics were later described by Shane Warne as "horrendous", in specific reference to the nine men stationed on the fence for the eventual match-winner, Mike Hussey, on the fourth morning of the Sydney Test. The visitors went on to blow a golden chance to level the series and crumbled for 139 in pursuit of 176. The result meant Ponting escaped further condemnation for his contentious decision to bat first on an SCG greentop, and by series end had also reminded the cricket world of his brilliance as a batsman with a supreme double-century. Along the way, Ponting became the most prolific winner of Test matches in the game's history, breaking the record for Test victories held by Steve Waugh as a leader and Warne as a player.

These achievements were brushed aside by Ponting, who derived much greater satisfaction from the progress of Watson and Hauritz, and Mitchell Johnson's returned confidence. Johnson insisted his technical and emotional struggles in England in mid-2009 had made him stronger, and during the home summer figured out he could lead the attack without taking the new ball. In Melbourne, he capped a tumultuous 12 months by joining such all-round greats as Ian Botham and Kapil Dev in the elite group to have taken 50 Test wickets and made 500 runs in a calendar year.

After winning five of the summer's six home Tests, and with short series against Pakistan and New Zealand to come before the return Ashes bout, Ponting believed he had taken another significant step towards moulding his crew of largely inexperienced cricketers into a consistently competitive team. He cast a keen eye across the Indian Ocean to South Africa, where England had just drawn the four-Test series 1–1. "I don't see a weak link in our side at the moment," Ponting said, and he hoped Andrew Strauss was listening.

Daniel Brettig writes on the limited-overs matches: Twelve months on from the loss of home Test and limited-overs series to South Africa, the Australians returned to the pattern of most recent home summers, by pummelling a Pakistan team that lurched from disaster to disaster. The contest began amid some of the bleakest headlines for limited-overs cricket yet written, and the Gabba at Brisbane was less than half-full for the first match. But crowds picked up later on, even when it become clear only one result was possible each time the two sides took to the field.

Australia had won their previous one-day series, in India, in great adversity: this one seemed a doddle by comparison. But such a view would undersell the achievements of a squad that played firm cricket irrespective of the eleven that took the field. All the batsmen played at least one significant innings: Mike Hussey and Cameron White were the stand-outs, although Ricky Ponting struggled for much of the series, a reminder of the captain's waning powers. Among the bowlers, Ryan Harris was given a chance by injury in the third match and proceeded to make himself undroppable, snatching no fewer than 13 wickets in three games, including successive five-fors. Clint McKay was only a little less impressive, showing the benefits of his time in India, and of the rest only Nathan Hauritz did not feature prominently. Peter Siddle was regrettably laid low by back stress fractures after he had been oddly persisted with, while Doug Bollinger and Shane Watson were sent home to rest.

Pakistan's tour seemingly collapsed after their batting did likewise in the final innings of a Sydney Test they should have won. Thereafter the captain Mohammad Yousuf, courteous though he was in public, looked incapable of doing anything to help. He suffered the ignominy of being told, via Pakistan television, that he would be relieved of his job after the tour, and while the PCB chairman Ijaz Butt subsequently denied this there seemed no way to stop the team sinking. Their best bowling prospect, Mohammad Aamer, was sidelined by a recurring groin problem, and the belated arrival of Younis Khan was of little measurable consequence.

The merest glimmer of hope was provided by the youthful middle-order duo of Umar Akmal and Fawad Alam, both of whom showed intelligence and grit whenever their turn came to bat. But Shahid Afridi's moments of brilliance were obscured by the bizarre sight of him biting the ball during the final 50-over match (he was banned for the Twenty20 game that followed) when he was supposed to be acting as captain, and an unhappy tour ended with the resignation of chief selector Iqbal Qasim. His conclusion that the Pakistan side needed "major surgery" seemed almost an understatement.

PAKISTAN TOURING PARTY

Mohammad Yousuf (*captain*), Kamran Akmal (*vice-captain*), Abdur Rauf, Danish Kaneria, Faisal Iqbal, Fawad Alam, Imran Farhat, Khurram Manzoor, Misbah-ul-Haq, Mohammad Aamer, Mohammad Asif, Mohammad Sami, Saeed Ajmal, Salman Butt, Shoaib Malik, Umar Akmal, Umar Gul. *Coach*: Intikhab Alam.

Mohammad Sami was added to the squad before the Test series when the team management requested an extra fast bowler. Pakistan's management sent for Younis Khan to join the squad during the First Test, but he did not arrive until the subsequent one-day series. Fawad Alam and Abdur Rauf were sent home after the First Test to reduce the size of the squad. Sarfraz Ahmed arrived as an alternative wicketkeeper before the Third Test.

For the one-day international series that followed the Tests, Iftikhar Anjum, Khalid Latif, Naved-ul-Hasan, Shahid Afridi and Younis Khan replaced Danish Kaneria, Faisal Iqbal, Khurram Manzoor, Misbah-ul-Haq and Mohammad Sami, while Fawad Alam returned. For the concluding Twenty20 international, Imran Nazir replaced Mohammad Yousuf and Younis Khan; Shahid Afridi was originally named to captain, but was banned, and replaced by Shoaib Malik.

TEST MATCH AVERAGES

AUSTRALIA – BATTING AND FIELDING

	T	I	NO	R	HS	100s	50s	Avge	Ct/St
S. R. Watson	3	6	1	346	120*	1	2	69.20	6
†M. E. K. Hussey	3	6	2	267	134*	1	1	66.75	3
M. J. Clarke	3	5	1	255	166	1	0	63.75	5
R. T. Ponting	3	6	0	378	209	1	2	63.00	3
†S. M. Katich	2	4	0	211	100	1	1	52.75	2
N. M. Hauritz	3	5	1	120	75	0	1	30.00	1
†M. G. Johnson	3	5	0	71	38	0	0	14.20	2
B. J. Haddin	3	5	0	70	41	0	0	14.00	17/1
†M. J. North	3	4	0	41	21	0	0	10.25	2

Played in three Tests: †D. E. Bollinger 9, 0 (2 ct); P. M. Siddle 1*, 38 (1 ct). Played in one Test: †P. J. Hughes 0, 37.

† *Left-handed batsman.*

BOWLING

	Style	O	M	R	W	BB	5W/i	Avge
S. M. Katich	SLC	15	4	57	3	3-34	0	19.00
D. E. Bollinger	LFM	96.5	29	262	12	4-72	0	21.83
N. M. Hauritz	OB	122.4	26	415	18	5-53	2	23.05
S. R. Watson	RFM	54	13	125	5	2-38	0	25.00
M. G. Johnson	LF	111	26	308	12	3-27	0	25.66
P. M. Siddle	RFM	98.2	32	262	8	3-25	0	32.75

PAKISTAN – BATTING AND FIELDING

	T	I	NO	R	HS	100s	50s	Avge	Ct/St
†Salman Butt	3	6	0	280	102	1	1	46.66	2
Umar Akmal	3	6	0	199	51	0	1	33.16	0
Mohammad Yousuf	3	6	0	178	61	0	1	29.66	3
Misbah-ul-Haq	2	4	1	76	65*	0	1	25.33	4
†Imran Farhat	3	6	0	148	53	0	1	24.66	3
Faisal Iqbal	2	4	0	97	48	0	0	24.25	4
Umar Gul	2	4	1	56	38*	0	0	18.66	2
Kamran Akmal	2	4	0	67	30	0	0	16.75	5/1
†Mohammad Aamer	2	4	1	49	30*	0	0	16.33	0
Mohammad Asif	3	6	3	30	29	0	0	10.00	0
Danish Kaneria	2	4	0	13	8	0	0	3.25	1

Played in one Test: Abdur Rauf 3, 5; Khurram Manzoor 0, 77; Mohammad Sami 13, 2; Saeed Ajmal 4, 10; Sarfraz Ahmed 1, 5 (4 ct); Shoaib Malik 58, 19 (1 ct).

† *Left-handed batsman.*

BOWLING

	Style	O	M	R	W	BB	5W/i	Avge
Mohammad Asif	RFM	135	30	370	13	6-41	1	28.46
Mohammad Sami	RFM	31.5	8	101	3	3-27	0	33.66
Mohammad Aamer	LFM	94	22	323	8	5-79	1	40.37
Danish Kaneria	LBG	106.4	9	414	9	5-151	1	46.00
Umar Gul	RFM	73.2	8	264	5	3-83	0	52.80

Also bowled: Abdur Rauf (RFM) 33–7–119–1; Imran Farhat (LB) 8–0–26–0; Saeed Ajmal (OB) 69.1–4–223–2; Shoaib Malik (OB) 11.4–0–43–2.

Note: Matches in this section which were not first-class are denoted by a dagger.

At Hobart, December 19, 20, 21, 2009. **Drawn**. Toss: Tasmania. **Pakistanis 437** (Imran Farhat 32, Salman Butt 153, Misbah-ul-Haq 43, Fawad Alam 33, Kamran Akmal 109; J. J. Krejza 3-162) **and 141-4** (Imran Farhat 40, Faisal Iqbal 32*, Umar Akmal 55); **Tasmania 193** (G. J. Bailey 50, B. Geeves 31; Saeed Ajmal 4-84).

Kamran Akmal smashed 109 from just 81 balls at No. 7, building on the opener Salman Butt's more patient hundred. Off-spinner Saeed Ajmal pressed his case for inclusion in the First Test with four cheap wickets. He said during the game that "these days the Australian spinners are just off-spinners, and it's not like they are taking five or six wickets every match"; unfortunately for Saeed, Nathan Hauritz would do precisely that in the opening two Tests.

AUSTRALIA v PAKISTAN

First Test Match

At Melbourne, December 26, 27, 28, 29, 30, 2009. Australia won by 170 runs. Toss: Australia.

The Boxing Day Test produced a tragicomic hero in Shane Watson and a killer trivia question, the answer to which is Abdur Rauf. And although Australia's most complete bowling performance of the year delivered a comfortable win, Pakistan could take encouragement from the efforts of two daring teenagers, Mohammad Aamer and Umar Akmal, who introduced themselves to the Australians in unforgettable fashion.

Pakistan first encountered problems at selection, when Danish Kaneria was ruled out with a hand injury and Umar Gul was omitted because of poor recent form rather than the vague leg injury later mentioned by captain Mohammad Yousuf. Gul's replacement, Rauf, will be remembered as the man who dropped Watson on 99 to hand the Australian all-rounder-turned-opener his long-awaited maiden Test century – an achievement some of the more excitable local media ranked alongside the conquering of Mount Everest and man's first visit to the moon.

Watson's personal breakthrough of 120 not out in the second innings of his 15th Test was also a watershed for his team: he broke a century-drought dating back to the Fifth Ashes Test in August and ended a run of 20 unconverted fifties, a trend that reached ridiculous proportions as Watson, Katich, Ponting, Hussey and the night-watchman Hauritz all fell between 50 and 100 in the first innings. Rauf's performance was notable for little except his drop at backward point, and afterwards he was thanked for his time and put on a plane back to Lahore.

Unfortunately Rauf's lapse was part of a wider malaise among the Pakistan fielders. They set the tone for a clumsy series when they dropped Katich on eight and Watson on 43 before their opening stand of 182 laid the foundations of an intimidating first-innings score. The partnership was broken in heartbreaking fashion for Watson, who was on 93 and stranded at the same end as Katich when Imran Farhat rejoiced in removing the bails at the other. Katich took the blame, but there was an uncomfortable wait while the TV umpire determined that Watson had to go. In an example of cricketing karma, Katich later slashed a catch to point and also fell agonisingly short of a century, on 98. Australia eventually declared at 454 for five; never before had Ponting called in batsmen with so few first-innings runs in the bank, a move calculated to give his attack more time to break through.

Pakistan's reply was unremarkable except for an incredible cameo from the 19-year-old Umar, who stirred into action when he ducked into a Siddle bouncer. "I just smiled and said to him: 'Good ball, give me one more to the helmet.'" Soon afterwards Umar unleashed an over of power that produced 19 runs, including a brutal pull for six, against the aggressive Siddle.

Having seized a first-innings lead of 196 the Australians attempted to bat Pakistan out of the match, and Watson resumed his quest for the elusive hundred. His nervous passage through the nineties lasted more than an hour and had the suspense of a Hitchcock film. The tourists stacked the off side and bowled wide, tempting Watson into some dangerous slices, but he was determined not to blow his summer's fourth serious pursuit of triple figures and blocked out an over of spin from Saeed Ajmal before lunch. Rauf's fateful fumble on 99 allowed him to steal a single and raise his arms in triumph and relief.

He had shared an absorbing battle with the 17-year-old Aamer, who was fearless enough to clap his hands in Watson's face and blow him a kiss down the pitch. For once Watson, usually easily provoked, did not take the bait. But Aamer later seduced Ponting into a poorly executed pull, then wiped out the middle order of Hussey, Clarke, North and Haddin for a combined total of 61 runs, so becoming the youngest fast bowler in Test history to grab a five-for.

It was the discipline of the Australian bowlers, though, that dashed Pakistan's hopes of making 252 on the final day for an improbable win. Johnson's brilliant first over did the trick – Umar was out edging a ball angled across his body for the second time, and Misbah-ul-Haq went the same way next delivery. Hauritz sacrificed some accuracy for more aggressive lines and finally proved he could bowl Australia to victory. His five-for was a first, not only in Tests but in all top-level cricket.

Man of the Match: S. R. Watson.

Close of play: First day, Australia 305-3 (Hussey 37, Hauritz 5); Second day, Pakistan 109-4 (Umar Akmal 10, Mohammad Aamer 0); Third day, Australia 111-3 (Watson 64, Clarke 21); Fourth day, Pakistan 170-3 (Mohammad Yousuf 45, Umar Akmal 27).

Australia

S. R. Watson run out	93	– not out	120
S. M. Katich c Salman Butt b Mohammad Asif	98	– c Kamran Akmal b Mohammad Asif	2
*R. T. Ponting c Misbah-ul-Haq b Mohammad Asif	57	– c Salman Butt b Mohammad Aamer	12
M. E. K. Hussey lbw b Saeed Ajmal	82	– lbw b Mohammad Aamer	4
N. M. Hauritz lbw b Abdur Rauf	75	– (9) st Kamran Akmal b Saeed Ajmal	8
M. J. Clarke not out	28	– (5) c Kamran Akmal b Mohammad Aamer	37
M. J. North (did not bat)		– (6) b Mohammad Aamer	8
†B. J. Haddin (did not bat)		– (7) c Kamran Akmal b Mohammad Aamer	0
M. G. Johnson (did not bat)		– (8) run out	22
B 2, l-b 12, n-b 7	21	L-b 2, w 3, n-b 7	12

1/182 (1) 2/233 (2)   (5 wkts dec, 128 overs) 454   1/15 (2)   (8 wkts dec, 73.1 overs) 225
3/291 (3) 4/382 (4) 5/454 (5)   2/32 (3) 3/40 (4) 4/143 (5)
5/161 (6) 6/161 (7) 7/198 (8) 8/225 (9)

P. M. Siddle and D. E. Bollinger did not bat.

Mohammad Asif 27–5–86–2; Mohammad Aamer 27–7–101–0; Abdur Rauf 23–4–86–1; Saeed Ajmal 46–3–150–1; Imran Farhat 5–0–17–0. *Second Innings*—Mohammad Asif 16–3–38–1; Mohammad Aamer 24–6–79–5; Saeed Ajmal 23.1–1–73–1; Abdur Rauf 10–3–33–0.

Pakistan

Imran Farhat lbw b Johnson	9	– lbw b Bollinger	12
Salman Butt lbw b Watson	45	– lbw b Johnson	33
Faisal Iqbal c Clarke b Hauritz	15	– b Hauritz	48
*Mohammad Yousuf c Haddin b Siddle	22	– c Katich b Hauritz	61
Umar Akmal c Ponting b Johnson	51	– c Haddin b Johnson	27
Mohammad Aamer c North b Bollinger	15	– (8) c Katich b Hauritz	0
Misbah-ul-Haq not out	65	– (6) c Haddin b Johnson	0
†Kamran Akmal c Haddin b Bollinger	12	– (7) st Haddin b Hauritz	30
Abdur Rauf c North b Bollinger	3	– b Bollinger	5
Mohammad Asif c Watson b Siddle	0	– (11) not out	1
Saeed Ajmal b Johnson	4	– (10) c Watson b Hauritz	10
B 4, l-b 3, w 1, n-b 9	17	B 13, l-b 4, w 2, n-b 5	24

1/26 (1) 2/59 (3) 3/84 (2) 4/109 (4)   (99 overs) 258   1/18 (1) 2/80 (2)   (72 overs) 251
5/159 (5) 6/203 (6) 7/215 (8) 8/219 (9)   3/116 (3) 4/171 (5) 5/171 (6)
9/220 (10) 10/258 (11)   6/214 (7) 7/214 (8) 8/221 (9)
9/250 (4) 10/251 (10)

Bollinger 20–6–50–3; Siddle 24–7–77–2; Hauritz 20–3–58–1; Johnson 22–10–36–3; Watson 13–3–30–1. *Second Innings*—Bollinger 15–5–42–2; Siddle 13–5–32–0; Hauritz 24–4–101–5; Johnson 18–6–46–3; Katich 2–0–13–0.

Umpires: B. R. Doctrove and R. E. Koertzen.
Third umpire: E. A. R. de Silva.   Referee: R. S. Madugalle.

AUSTRALIA v PAKISTAN

Second Test Match

At Sydney, January 3, 4, 5, 6, 2010. Australia won by 36 runs. Toss: Australia.

Waqar Younis, the Pakistan bowling coach, stood on the SCG at sunset on day two and turned up the heat on Australia. His old adversary Ponting was vulnerable, Waqar said, and had handed Pakistan a gift-wrapped advantage by choosing to bat first on the greenest Sydney Test pitch in recent memory. "They are 200 runs behind but they will come hard," said Waqar, who had been part of the attack that inflicted Australia's most recent Test defeat by Pakistan, at the same ground 14 years earlier. "We have to stick to our plans and keep picking up wickets at regular intervals, and if we do that the game should be ours."

It was a confident statement, but not an outrageous one given events of the first two days. Only five times in the history of Test cricket had teams come back from a first-innings deficit of more than 200 to win, and the classy Pakistan seam attack was brimming with confidence after bowling the Australians out for 127 inside 45 overs. It was Australia's lowest total at home since 1996, and Waqar was right: Ponting *had* looked vulnerable since he was struck on the elbow by West Indies' Kemar Roach earlier in the summer, a theory that grew legs when the Australian captain was caught playing a half-hearted pull shot for the second time in the series.

What Waqar had not taken into account was Pakistan's seemingly insatiable appetite for self-destruction, or the perseverance of Australia's ninth-wicket pair. Hussey and Siddle capitalised on the tourists' lapses in a match-winning partnership of 123, setting Pakistan a tricky fourth-innings target of 176.

Afterwards, Mohammad Yousuf blamed his own dismissal, a catch smashed back to Hauritz that took the spinner's thumbnail clean off, but was clutched to his chest as he crashed to the pitch. But that was a harsh self-assessment from the captain, for it did not take account of four catches dropped by the hapless wicketkeeper Kamran Akmal, three of which allowed Hussey to progress to one of the most significant centuries of his career. The other fluffed chance – arguably the easiest – spared Siddle on his way to a restrained but priceless 38.

Yousuf's greatest mistake was to set overly defensive fields to Hussey on the fourth morning. After raising his hundred (only his second in his last 22 Tests) with an emphatic straight drive off Umar Gul, the resilient Hussey celebrated by punching the air, recognising that he had not only dispelled lingering doubts about his form, but given his team a sniff of victory.

Not even the most optimistic Australians could have sensed such a possibility after the first innings. Mohammad Aamer had been forced out of the team with a groin problem, but Mohammad Sami stepped seamlessly into the breach after a two-year absence. He exploited the atmospheric conditions to demolish the top order with a potent mix of pace and swing, before Mohammad Asif's rare ability to move the ball both ways off the seam earned him a career-best six for 41.

Katich, out with a sore elbow inflicted by Aamer at Melbourne, proved much more difficult to replace. He had formed the spine of the Australian order since returning as an opener in 2008, and Hughes cut an anxious figure by comparison in his first appearance in five months, flailing around outside his off stump for a ten-ball duck. The wisdom of

First blood: despite wincing in pain after losing a thumbnail holding a return catch, Nathan Hauritz took four more wickets to bowl Australia to victory.

Ponting's decision to bat first was vigorously questioned, but few of the batsmen could blame the conditions. The same was true for Pakistan, who from a position of 205 for two in reply should have batted Australia out of the match. But the rest of the batting seemed to forget they were playing a Test – two were caught on the boundary – and the tourists were bowled out for 333, a lead of 206.

Seam gave way to spin in the second innings, and the charismatic leggie Danish Kaneria reprised his excellent SCG adventure of five years earlier to spin Pakistan into a commanding position with five wickets, none better than the googly that removed Johnson's middle stump. Had Kamran displayed a safer pair of hands, the game might have been over in three days, but he developed a severe case of the yips. "He said 'Sorry, mate' three times," Kaneria lamented later. Watson carried on his imperious form, only to fall agonisingly short of a century for the third time in the summer, while North must have envied the opener his problems in the nineties. He was having enough trouble getting to double figures; on this occasion he prodded a catch to short leg on just two.

Hussey and Siddle steadied Australia from an uncomfortable 257 for eight, batting until after lunch on the fourth day to present Pakistan with a tense chase. The scene was set for the long-awaited but still somehow unexpected arrival of Hauritz as a match-winning spinner. He had fewer runs to play with than in Melbourne, and was belted for three fours in an over just before tea, but held his nerve to dismiss Yousuf and Misbah-ul-Haq in three balls, reducing Pakistan to 77 for five. He went on to wipe out the tail and hold the ball aloft for the second time in two Tests. That night, as Yousuf accepted the blame for Pakistan's defeat and Ponting declared his contentious decision at the toss had been vindicated, the Australians toasted Nathan "Hard as Nails" Hauritz every time they cracked open a drink to celebrate an improbable victory.

Man of the Match: M. E. K. Hussey.

Close of play: First day, Pakistan 14-0 (Imran Farhat 9, Salman Butt 3); Second day, Pakistan 331-9 (Danish Kaneria 2, Mohammad Asif 0); Third day, Australia 286-8 (Hussey 73, Siddle 10).

Australia

S. R. Watson c Kamran Akmal b Mohammad Sami	6	– c Faisal Iqbal b Umar Gul	97
P. J. Hughes c Faisal Iqbal b Mohammad Sami....	0	– c and b Danish Kaneria	37
*R. T. Ponting c Umar Gul b Mohammad Sami	0	– c Faisal Iqbal b Umar Gul	11
M. E. K. Hussey c Misbah-ul-Haq			
b Mohammad Asif.	28	– not out	134
M. J. Clarke b Mohammad Asif.	3	– lbw b Mohammad Asif	21
M. J. North c Kamran Akmal b Mohammad Asif ..	10	– c Faisal Iqbal b Danish Kaneria.....	2
†B. J. Haddin c Mohammad Yousuf			
b Mohammad Asif.	6	– lbw b Danish Kaneria.	15
M. G. Johnson c Imran Farhat b Mohammad Asif .	38	– b Danish Kaneria	3
N. M. Hauritz b Mohammad Asif	21	– c Misbah-ul-Haq b Umar Gul	4
P. M. Siddle not out	1	– c Misbah-ul-Haq b Mohammad Asif .	38
D. E. Bollinger b Umar Gul	9	– b Danish Kaneria	0
B 1, l-b 2, w 1, n-b 1	5	B 6, l-b 5, w 3, n-b 5	19

1/2 (2) 2/2 (3) 3/10 (1) 4/36 (5)   (44.2 overs) 127   1/105 (2) 2/144 (3)   (125.4 overs) 381
5/51 (4) 6/51 (6) 7/62 (7) 8/106 (9)   3/159 (1) 4/217 (5)
9/117 (8) 10/127 (11)   5/226 (6) 6/246 (7) 7/252 (8)
    8/257 (9) 9/380 (10) 10/381 (11)

Mohammad Asif 20–6–41–6; Mohammad Sami 12–4–27–3; Umar Gul 10.2–0–38–1; Danish Kaneria 2–0–18–0. *Second Innings*—Mohammad Asif 27–8–53–2; Mohammad Sami 19.5–4–74–0; Umar Gul 28–4–83–3; Danish Kaneria 47.5–3–151–5; Imran Farhat 3–0–9–0.

Pakistan

Imran Farhat c Haddin b Hauritz	53	– c Johnson b Bollinger.	22
Salman Butt c Haddin b Johnson	71	– c Haddin b Johnson	21
Faisal Iqbal c Watson b Siddle.	27	– c Haddin b Johnson	7
*Mohammad Yousuf c Haddin b Johnson	46	– c and b Hauritz	19
Umar Akmal lbw b Bollinger.	49	– c Johnson b Bollinger.	49
Misbah-ul-Haq c Haddin b Bollinger.	11	– c Hussey b Hauritz	0
†Kamran Akmal c Watson b Bollinger	14	– c Haddin b Johnson	11
Mohammad Sami c Haddin b Watson	13	– c Haddin b Hauritz	2
Umar Gul c Bollinger b Watson.	12	– c Siddle b Hauritz.	6
Danish Kaneria c Hussey b Bollinger	4	– c Watson b Hauritz.	0
Mohammad Asif not out	0	– not out	0
B 2, l-b 16, w 5, n-b 10	33	W 1, n-b 1	2

1/109 (1) 2/144 (2) 3/205 (3)   (96.5 overs) 333   1/34 (1) 2/50 (3)   (38 overs) 139
4/237 (4) 5/277 (5) 6/286 (6)   3/51 (2) 4/77 (4) 5/77 (6)
7/295 (7) 8/323 (9) 9/331 (8) 10/333 (10)   6/103 (7) 7/133 (8) 8/133 (5)
    9/135 (10) 10/139 (9)

Bollinger 21.5–5–72–4; Siddle 22–4–62–1; Johnson 20–2–64–2; Watson 17–4–40–2; Hauritz 16–3–77–1. *Second Innings*—Bollinger 12–3–32–2; Siddle 4–1–27–0; Hauritz 12–1–53–5; Johnson 10–2–27–3.

Umpires: E. A. R. de Silva and B. R. Doctrove.
Third umpire: R. E. Koertzen.   Referee: R. S. Madugalle.

AUSTRALIA v PAKISTAN

Third Test Match

At Hobart, January 14, 15, 16, 17, 18, 2010. Australia won by 231 runs. Toss: Australia. Test debut: Sarfraz Ahmed.

    Pakistan's implosion in Sydney replicated itself off the field before the final Test, and at the heart of the selection crisis was Kamran Akmal. Wicketkeeper, vice-captain and member of the on-tour selection team, he refused to concede his place after a shocker with the gloves at the SCG, even after the Pakistan Cricket Board put a replacement, 22-year-old Sarfraz Ahmed, on a plane to Hobart and the coach Intikhab Alam said Sarfraz was certain to make his debut.

The plot thickened when Umar Akmal complained of a sore back, giving rise to a conspiracy theory, denied strenuously by management, that he intended to pull out in protest at the treatment of his older brother. In the end Umar did play and Kamran did not. The tourists also made three other changes: Faisal Iqbal, after failing to reach 50 in his first four innings, was replaced at No. 3 by Khurram Manzoor. Misbah-ul-Haq, whose mindless slice to point hastened the Sydney collapse, made way for the former captain Shoaib Malik. And the return to fitness of Mohammad Aamer meant Pakistan fielded a full-strength attack for the first time in the series.

Before long, Aamer must have wished the Bellerive Oval would open up and swallow him whole, such was the gravity of his mistake at deep backward square leg in the first hour, before Ponting had scored. All had been relatively quiet in the Australian camp before the dead-rubber game: Katich had recovered from his elbow problem, and a renewed self-belief was born of the dramatic turnaround at the SCG. Still, questions hovered over the Australian captain. Would the outstanding batsman of the past decade be forced to shelve his once-imperious pull shot, which had malfunctioned since he was injured in Perth and cost him his wicket in Melbourne and Sydney? Had he simply been restricted by the aching elbow, or was his summer average of 27 the sign that his powers were fraying like the baggy green cap that had to be stitched back together between Tests?

The answers would have been very different had Aamer held the catch Ponting served up four balls into his innings, when he swivelled into a pull shot just as Pakistan had hoped he would. Aamer fumbled the catch and sank to his knees, and from that moment the champion made it his mission to torment his dispirited opponents. Far from putting away the pull and hook, Ponting kept playing them as if to prove he still could. For a while it was a dangerous game – he wore an Umar Gul bouncer on the helmet and glanced another attempt into his hip – but soon enough the old timing and command returned. To celebrate his 39th Test century Ponting kissed the crest on his helmet for the first time in his great career, a reflection of the milestone's significance, before converting it into a magnificent 209 – his fifth double-century.

Along the way, Ponting and Clarke shared the second-biggest fourth-wicket partnership by an Australian pair – 352 in just over a day's play. Only Bradman and Ponsford, with 388 at Leeds in 1934, had scored more. Clarke's return to form brought 166 sweetly accumulated runs, eclipsing his previous career-best 151 on debut in Bangalore.

By stumps on day two the contrast between the triumphant Australian captain and his despairing Pakistan counterpart, Mohammad Yousuf, could not have been more pronounced. Yousuf stood with hands on hips in disbelief and glared at his opening batsman, Salman Butt, after the first of two diabolical run-outs that robbed the visitors of their most gifted batsmen. "We're not playing for self, we're playing for country," the captain fumed after Butt ignored his call for an easy third run. "I just stopped here, [didn't] say anything. [It's] just very sad because he's 25 years old and he can't run." Moments later, when the hard-hitting Umar Akmal took off for a single, Butt could not find his way around the bowler and Umar could not make it back before Haddin had again whipped off the bails in delight. "I'm not sure on this run because when I saw the replay Hauritz was in front of him," Yousuf said. "But he is a little lazy runner, everyone knows." So chilly was the atmosphere in the dressing-room that Butt thought it safest to stay in the middle and seek redemption with 102, a companion for his maiden Test century in Sydney five years earlier.

A rare appearance at the bowling crease from Katich instigated a dramatic collapse, but with a defiant last-wicket stand of 53 Gul and Mohammad Asif forced Ponting to abandon his preferred plan to enforce the follow-on. The Australians still seized a first-innings lead of 218, and only the threatening Hobart weather could have prevented them from completing a clean sweep after a fluent 100 from Katich and 89 from Ponting in the second innings stretched the advantage to an unassailable 437.

This time Watson, bowling from stump to stump with dangerous reverse swing, accounted for the middle-order duo of Yousuf and Umar, and the rain held off long enough for Hauritz to live up to his new-found reputation as a fourth-innings finisher.

Man of the Match: R. T. Ponting. *Man of the Series:* S. R. Watson.

Close of play: First day, Australia 302-3 (Ponting 137, Clarke 111); Second day, Pakistan 94-4 (Salman Butt 34, Shoaib Malik 4); Third day, Australia 59-1 (Katich 33, Ponting 25); Fourth day, Pakistan 103-4 (Khurram Manzoor 23, Shoaib Malik 18).

Australia

S. R. Watson c Imran Farhat b Umar Gul	29	– c Mohammad Yousuf b Mohammad Aamer	1
S. M. Katich lbw b Mohammad Asif	11	– c Shoaib Malik b Danish Kaneria	100
*R. T. Ponting c Mohammad Yousuf b Mohammad Aamer	209	– c Sarfraz Ahmed b Shoaib Malik	89
M. E. K. Hussey c Sarfraz Ahmed b Mohammad Aamer	6	– not out	13
M. J. Clarke b Danish Kaneria	166		
M. J. North c Sarfraz Ahmed b Mohammad Asif	21		
†B. J. Haddin c Umar Gul b Danish Kaneria	41	– (5) run out	8
M. G. Johnson c Sarfraz Ahmed b Danish Kaneria	8	– (6) c Imran Farhat b Shoaib Malik	0
N. M. Hauritz not out	12		
B 1, l-b 3, w 5, n-b 7	16	B 4, l-b 4	8

1/28 (2) 2/52 (1)   (8 wkts dec, 142.5 overs) 519   1/1 (1)   (5 wkts dec, 48.4 overs) 219
3/71 (4) 4/423 (5) 5/443 (3)   2/192 (2) 3/202 (3)
6/498 (7) 7/499 (6) 8/519 (8)   4/213 (5) 5/219 (6)

P. M. Siddle and D. E. Bollinger did not bat.

Mohammad Asif 36–8–104–2; Mohammad Aamer 31–7–97–2; Umar Gul 25–4–98–1; Danish Kaneria 42.5–2–189–3; Shoaib Malik 8–0–27–0. *Second Innings*—Mohammad Asif 9–0–48–0; Mohammad Aamer 12–2–46–1; Umar Gul 10–0–45–0; Danish Kaneria 14–2–56–1; Shoaib Malik 3.4–0–16–2.

Pakistan

Imran Farhat c Haddin b Siddle	38	– c Haddin b Siddle	14
Salman Butt c Clarke b Katich	102	– b Bollinger	8
Khurram Manzoor c Ponting b Siddle	0	– c Haddin b Hauritz	77
*Mohammad Yousuf run out	7	– lbw b Watson	23
Umar Akmal run out	8	– lbw b Watson	15
Shoaib Malik c Bollinger b Hauritz	58	– c Haddin b Siddle	19
†Sarfraz Ahmed c Clarke b Katich	1	– c Clarke b Hauritz	5
Mohammad Aamer c Watson b Katich	4	– not out	30
Umar Gul not out	38	– c Clarke b Hauritz	0
Danish Kaneria c Ponting b Hauritz	8	– (11) b Siddle	1
Mohammad Asif c Hussey b Hauritz	29	– (10) b Johnson	0
B 2, l-b 2, w 2, n-b 2	8	B 10, l-b 3, n-b 1	14

1/63 (1) 2/63 (3) 3/74 (4)   (105.4 overs) 301   1/11 (2) 2/29 (1)   (86.2 overs) 206
4/84 (5) 5/213 (2) 6/215 (7) 7/219 (6)   3/61 (4) 4/83 (5)
8/227 (8) 9/248 (10) 10/301 (11)   5/104 (6) 6/123 (7) 7/189 (3)
8/191 (9) 9/192 (10) 10/206 (11)

Bollinger 15–6–35–0; Siddle 20–8–39–2; Johnson 20–2–76–0; Hauritz 33.4–9–96–3; Watson 7–2–17–0; Katich 10–3–34–3. *Second Innings*—Bollinger 13–4–31–1; Siddle 15.2–7–25–3; Johnson 21–4–59–1; Watson 17–4–38–2; Hauritz 17–6–30–3; Katich 3–1–10–0.

Umpires: E. A. R. de Silva and R. E. Koertzen.
Third umpire: B. R. Doctrove. Referee: R. S. Madugalle.

LIMITED-OVERS INTERNATIONAL REPORTS
BY DANIEL BRETTIG

†AUSTRALIA v PAKISTAN

First One-Day International

At Brisbane, January 22, 2010 (day/night). Australia won by five wickets. Toss: Pakistan.

A match in which Pakistan mostly held the upper hand was ultimately snatched away with a flourish by Cameron White. His emergence as a middle-order batsman of quality to go with his natural power had begun in England during the one-day postscript to the Ashes, but a first international century at home was both significant and arresting. He hit one coruscating cover-drive off Naved-ul-Hasan to go with the usual leg-side heaves, and in his 88-ball innings White struck eight fours and four sixes (three of them in succession off Shahid Afridi); his fluency contrasted with Pakistan's more halting efforts earlier in the day. Salman Butt and Kamran Akmal had given them the ideal start as Australia's pacemen found little of the swing so common at the Gabba. Butt was particularly elegant, lifting Pakistan to 117 for one in the 23rd over. However, Bollinger, as he had for much of the summer, then whirred down a pair of fast and awkward short balls to have Butt caught behind and Mohammad Yousuf bowled off his body, the ball landing directly on top of the bails. Shahid Afridi offered some fireworks during a 26-ball stay, but Younis Khan was becalmed in his first innings of the tour, facing 74 balls, and the eventual total was competitive rather than intimidating. Watson was the victim of a swift spell by Mohammad Aamer that also troubled Ponting, whose exit for an uncertain 27 appeared to open the door for Pakistan. But it was soon to be slammed shut by White, in the company of the inconspicuously effective Clarke.

Man of the Match: C. L. White.

Pakistan

Salman Butt c Haddin b Bollinger	72		Saeed Ajmal c Clarke b Watson	2	
†Kamran Akmal c Clarke b Watson	34		Mohammad Asif run out	0	
Younis Khan c Marsh b McKay	46				
*Mohammad Yousuf b Bollinger	2		L-b 4, w 5, n-b 2	11	
Umar Akmal c Haddin b McKay	23				
Shoaib Malik c Haddin b Watson	28		1/62 (2) 2/117 (1)	(49.4 overs)	274
Shahid Afridi c Hussey b Watson	48		3/123 (4)4/156 (5) 5/205 (6)		
Mohammad Aamer c Haddin b McKay	0		6/221 (3) 7/227 (8) 8/269 (7)		
Naved-ul-Hasan not out	8		9/274 (10) 10/274 (11)	10 overs: 54-0	

Bollinger 9.4–0–37–2; Siddle 8–1–48–0; McKay 9–0–61–3; Watson 10–0–36–4; Hauritz 9–0–68–0; Clarke 2–0–8–0; Hussey 2–0–12–0.

Australia

S. R. Watson c Saeed Ajmal b Mohammad Aamer	5		M. E. K. Hussey not out	35
S. E. Marsh c Naved-ul-Hasan b Mohammad Asif	15		†B. J. Haddin not out	7
*R. T. Ponting c sub (Khalid Latif) b Shahid Afridi	27		B 4, l-b 10, w 9	23
M. J. Clarke run out	58		1/16 (1) 2/37 (2) (5 wkts, 48.3 overs)	275
C. L. White b Naved-ul-Hasan	105		3/84 (3) 4/186 (4)	
			5/260 (5)	10 overs: 44-2

N. M. Hauritz, C. J. McKay, P. M. Siddle and D. E. Bollinger did not bat.

Mohammad Asif 10–1–44–1; Mohammad Aamer 9–0–29–1; Naved-ul-Hasan 10–0–61–1; Shahid Afridi 10–0–66–1; Saeed Ajmal 9.3–0–61–0.

Umpires: E. A. R. de Silva and R. J. Tucker.
Third umpire: P. R. Reiffel. Referee: R. S. Madugalle.

†AUSTRALIA v PAKISTAN

Second One-Day International

At Sydney, January 24, 2010 (day/night). Australia won by 140 runs. Toss: Pakistan.

A muggy day and a green-tinged pitch encouraged Mohammad Yousuf to bowl first. It was a decision he would regret. The Australians batted intelligently, then ripped out the Pakistanis batting with all the ease of a gardener uprooting a carrot. They owed much to Watson and Marsh, who forged a stand of 100 under testing conditions. In roles that were becoming well grooved, Marsh played straight and true while Watson flexed his cross-batted muscle, preventing Umar Gul from finding rhythm in the process. Shahid Afridi and Saeed Ajmal slowed down the run-rate and coaxed the openers into error, and a mid-innings decline to 166 for four gave Pakistan some chance. But White reprised his Gabba effort, in terms of impact if not volume, and the final tally soon looked distant as the ball zipped around in the early evening. Bollinger and McKay found bounce to their liking, while Siddle defeated Umar Akmal with one that straightened to kiss the top of off stump. There would be no recovery from 32 for four, and Yousuf had time to ponder his decision at the toss during a fruitless 94-ball 58.

Man of the Match: S. R. Watson.

Australia

S. R. Watson c Shoaib Malik b Shahid Afridi	69	†B. J. Haddin not out...................	27
S. E. Marsh c Umar Gul b Shahid Afridi...	41	N. M. Hauritz not out	1
*R. T. Ponting c Mohammad Yousuf b Mohammad Aamer.	13		
M. J. Clarke c Shahid Afridi b Umar Gul ..	25	B 1, l-b 3, w 2, n-b 1	7
C. L. White c Mohammad Yousuf b Mohammad Aamer.	55	1/100 (1) 2/114 (2) (6 wkts, 50 overs) 267
M. E. K. Hussey c Shoaib Malik b Mohammad Aamer.	29	3/138 (3) 4/166 (4) 5/221 (6) 6/261 (5) 10 overs: 65-0

C. J. McKay, P. M. Siddle and D. E. Bollinger did not bat.

Mohammad Aamer 9–0–53–3; Umar Gul 10–0–70–1; Naved-ul-Hasan 7–0–47–0; Shahid Afridi 10–0–35–2; Saeed Ajmal 10–1–41–0; Shoaib Malik 4–0–17–0.

Pakistan

Salman Butt c White b Bollinger	2	Umar Gul not out....................	1
†Kamran Akmal run out	16	Saeed Ajmal c Haddin b McKay.........	3
Younis Khan c White b Bollinger........	0		
*Mohammad Yousuf c Hauritz b McKay ...	58	L-b 1, w 4	5
Umar Akmal b Siddle	0		
Shoaib Malik c Ponting b McKay	2	1/7 (1) 2/7 (3) 3/32 (2) (37.3 overs) 127
Shahid Afridi c and b Watson	9	4/32 (5) 5/42 (6) 6/58 (7)
Mohammad Aamer c and b Hauritz	4	7/71 (8) 8/117 (9) 9/123 (4)
Naved-ul-Hasan st Haddin b Hauritz......	27	10/127 (11) 10 overs: 31-2

Bollinger 9–1–19–2; Siddle 8–1–23–1; McKay 7.3–0–15–3; Watson 3–0–10–1; Hauritz 7–0–45–2; Clarke 3–0–14–0.

Umpires: E. A. R. de Silva and R. J. Tucker.
Third umpire: P. R. Reiffel.   Referee: R. S. Madugalle.

" The courageous Dutch filched an overthrow – and thousands of orange supporters were tickled pink.**"**
England v The Netherlands, World Twenty20, page 537

†AUSTRALIA v PAKISTAN

Third One-Day International

At Adelaide, January 26, 2010 (day/night). Australia won by 40 runs. Toss: Australia.

Pakistan shaved 100 runs from the margin inflicted in Sydney, but remained little more than Australia Day fodder for a side energised by Queensland fast bowler Ryan Harris's five wickets. Marsh and Watson again got off to a striking start – 63 in 13 overs this time – and despite Ponting's third-ball duck there was enough momentum to take the final total near 300, with the help of some pyrotechnics from Hussey, who faced only 28 balls for 49. Clarke continued his run of high scores with low boundary tallies (three fours here, after only one in his 58 at the Gabba), hinting that he was growing into a Javed Miandad-like scrounger of runs. Harris, 30, had waited a year and two major injuries to add to his solitary one-day cap, and he zipped one through Kamran Akmal for the first wicket of Pakistan's reply. Salman Butt was duplicating the serenity of his Brisbane innings until scythed down by a horrid lbw from Asoka de Silva – the ball pitched outside leg, and was bouncing over the stumps as well – and the seniors Younis Khan and Mohammad Yousuf contributed little. It was left to Umar Akmal and Fawad Alam to grind out some sort of partnership, and after they put on 85 Shahid Afridi and Naved-ul-Hasan hinted at a dramatic finish. But Harris returned to nip out four of the last six wickets and clinch the series at the earliest opportunity. The crowd figure of 15,521 compared badly with the 17,722 who attended the domestic Twenty20 final at the same ground three days before.

Man of the Match: R. J. Harris.

Australia

S. R. Watson b Mohammad Asif	33	†B. J. Haddin not out		1
S. E. Marsh st Kamran Akmal b Saeed Ajmal	83	N. M. Hauritz not out		0
*R. T. Ponting lbw b Naved-ul-Hasan	0	B 1, l-b 1, w 5, n-b 5		12
M. J. Clarke b Umar Gul	80			
C. L. White c Kamran Akmal		1/63 (1) 2/64 (3)	(6 wkts, 50 overs)	286
b Naved-ul-Hasan	28	3/149 (2) 4/204 (5)		
M. E. K. Hussey c Younis Khan b Umar Gul	49	5/284 (6) 6/284 (4)		10 overs: 44-0

R. J. Harris, C. J. McKay and D. E. Bollinger did not bat.

Mohammad Asif 10–0–51–1; Umar Gul 10–1–80–2; Naved-ul-Hasan 10–0–57–2; Shahid Afridi 10–0–55–0; Saeed Ajmal 10–0–41–1.

Pakistan

Salman Butt lbw b McKay	34	Saeed Ajmal not out		8
†Kamran Akmal lbw b Harris	1	Mohammad Asif c Haddin b Hauritz		1
Younis Khan c Haddin b McKay	12			
*Mohammad Yousuf b Watson	11	L-b 11, w 3		14
Umar Akmal c Haddin b Harris	59			
Fawad Alam b McKay	33	1/14 (2) 2/47 (1) 3/58 (4)	(47.4 overs)	246
Shahid Afridi b Harris	40	4/60 (3) 5/145 (5) 6/168 (6)		
Naved-ul-Hasan c White b Harris	33	7/226 (7) 8/226 (9) 9/238 (8)		
Umar Gul c Haddin b Harris	0	10/246 (11)		10 overs: 42-1

Bollinger 9–0–35–0; Harris 10–0–43–5; Watson 9–0–66–1; McKay 10–1–48–3; Hauritz 7.4–0–37–1; Clarke 2–0–6–0.

Umpires: E. A. R. de Silva and S. J. A. Taufel.
Third umpire: R. J. Tucker.   Referee: R. S. Madugalle.

†AUSTRALIA v PAKISTAN

Fourth One-Day International

At Perth, January 29, 2010 (day/night). Australia won by 135 runs. Toss: Australia.

Australia were made to sweat for much of their innings, as Pakistan applied themselves well before showing signs of frailty in the field. Then they crumbled once more with the bat, finding no answer to the irrepressible Harris. He swung the ball at speed to grab a second five-wicket haul in two matches. It was the second high-class display of seam and swing of the day, after Mohammad Asif had led some of Pakistan's best bowling of the tour to have Australia in some bother at 190 for six. They wriggled out of it via the steady hand of Hussey and the rather more manic hitting of Hauritz, who spent only 39 balls over 53, his maiden one-day half-century, with four sixes. Chasing around 50 more runs than they would have liked, the Pakistanis were utterly defeated by Harris's away movement at a slippery pace, while Siddle charged in at the other end in what turned out to be his last appearance of the summer. Harris's first spell was 4–2–6–2, and his second included two wickets in two balls. He was the first bowler to take two five-fors in his first three one-day internationals, edging a record previously held by another Australian, Gary Gilmour, who did it in his third and fourth matches, during the 1975 World Cup. Having delved deeper than ever before into his pace resources, Ponting enthused: "Ryan has been spectacular. It just shows you the depth we have with the bowling." Australia had never before defeated Pakistan in a one-day international at the WACA, having lost the previous four encounters.

Man of the Match: R. J. Harris.

Australia

S. E. Marsh c Kamran Akmal		N. M. Hauritz not out	53
b Mohammad Asif.	12	R. J. Harris c Shahid Afridi	
†B. J. Haddin b Naved-ul-Hasan	32	b Mohammad Asif.	4
*R. T. Ponting c Kamran Akmal		C. J. McKay not out	0
b Shahid Afridi.	30		
M. J. Clarke run out	10	L-b 2, w 6, n-b 1	9
C. L. White c Mohammad Asif			
b Saeed Ajmal.	44	1/30 (1) 2/55 (2) (8 wkts, 50 overs) 277	
M. E. K. Hussey c Mohammad Yousuf		3/77 (4) 4/110 (3)	
b Saeed Ajmal.	67	5/159 (5) 6/190 (7)	
J. R. Hopes b Mohammad Asif	16	7/270 (6) 8/275 (9) 10 overs: 40-1	

P. M. Siddle did not bat.

Mohammad Asif 10–1–42–3; Naved-ul-Hasan 10–0–70–1; Iftikhar Anjum 10–0–64–0; Shahid Afridi 10–1–44–1; Saeed Ajmal 10–0–55–2.

Pakistan

Salman Butt c White b Harris	0	Saeed Ajmal b Hauritz.	7
†Kamran Akmal c Haddin b Siddle	17	Mohammad Asif not out	0
Younis Khan c Haddin b Harris	6		
*Mohammad Yousuf c Haddin b Siddle	10	L-b 5, w 3, n-b 1	9
Umar Akmal b Harris	38		
Fawad Alam run out	21	1/2 (1) 2/14 (3) 3/38 (2) (37.5 overs) 142	
Shahid Afridi c Hauritz b McKay	29	4/39 (4) 5/99 (6) 6/125 (5)	
Naved-ul-Hasan c Haddin b Harris	0	7/125 (8) 8/131 (7) 9/140 (10)	
Iftikhar Anjum c Haddin b Harris	5	10/142 (9) 10 overs: 39-4	

Harris 9.5–3–19–5; Siddle 6–0–31–2; McKay 7–2–16–1; Hopes 7–0–23–0; Hauritz 8–0–48–1.

Umpires: E. A. R. de Silva and R. J. Tucker.
Third umpire: P. R. Reiffel. Referee: R. S. Madugalle.

†AUSTRALIA v PAKISTAN

Fifth One-Day International

At Perth, January 31, 2010 (day/night). Australia won by two wickets. Toss: Pakistan.

A drunken spectator's frightening tackle of Pakistan fielder Khalid Latif and the ball-biting antics of Shahid Afridi completely overshadowed the most competitive match of the series. In the closing overs Afridi – captain for the day after Mohammad Yousuf pulled out pleading knee trouble – was captured on television biting the ball as if it were an apple. After this footage was shown, the umpires immediately replaced the ball, and Afridi was subsequently banned for two Twenty20 internationals for ball-tampering. His initial explanation was, "I tried to smell it, how it's feeling. There was something on it so I tried to move it." Later he added: "There is no team in the world that doesn't tamper with the ball." It was a bizarre sight, but was less significant than the fact that a spectator managed to evade the security staff and bring Latif to the ground at the end of the 46th over. In the stands, radio summariser Terry Alderman winced as he recalled his own shoulder-wrecking clash with a spectator at the WACA in 1982-83. Observers mused over the

Shahid Afridi bites the ball.

ramifications of such an invader carrying a weapon, and from Pakistan there were calls to install fences and ban alcohol on Australian grounds – the second contention was immediately rejected by a flustered Cricket Australia. Away from the madness, the Australians eked out a two-wicket victory after again restricting Pakistan to a mediocre total. At 16 for three the contest looked destined for an early finish, but Umar Akmal and the punchy Fawad Alam demonstrated their considerable promise in contrasting innings during a stand of 82. The Australian chase had regular hiccoughs, despite Ponting's only half-century of the series, and they required all of Hussey's resourcefulness, plus some fortunate hitting by Hauritz and Harris, who collected the winning run from a high no-ball caught by Afridi at mid-off.

Man of the Match: C. J. McKay.   *Man of the Series:* R. J. Harris.

Pakistan

Salman Butt c Haddin b Harris	0
Khalid Latif c and b Johnson	0
Younis Khan c Haddin b McKay	3
Shoaib Malik run out	36
Umar Akmal b McKay	67
Fawad Alam c Hauritz b McKay	63
*Shahid Afridi c Hauritz b Harris	1
†Sarfraz Ahmed c White b Johnson	6
Naved-ul-Hasan b Harris	8
Iftikhar Anjum c Ponting b McKay	16
Mohammad Asif not out	0
B 5, l-b 3, w 4	12

1/0 (1) 2/0 (2) 3/16 (3)   (49.3 overs) 212
4/76 (4) 5/158 (5) 6/162 (7)
7/180 (8) 8/189 (9) 9/212 (10)
10/212 (6)   10 overs: 17-3

Harris 10–1–44–3; Johnson 10–1–42–2; McKay 9.3–3–35–4; Hopes 10–1–45–0; Hauritz 10–0–38–0.

Australia

S. E. Marsh c Fawad Alam b Mohammad Asif	25
†B. J. Haddin c Shoaib Malik b Naved-ul-Hasan	7
*R. T. Ponting c Umar Akmal b Shoaib Malik	55
C. L. White b Shahid Afridi	13
A. C. Voges c Younis Khan b Shoaib Malik	24
M. E. K. Hussey not out	40
J. R. Hopes c Younis Khan b Shahid Afridi	6
M. G. Johnson c Sarfraz Ahmed b Naved-ul-Hasan	13
N. M. Hauritz lbw b Iftikhar Anjum	18
R. J. Harris not out	2
W 9, n-b 1	10

1/21 (2) 2/54 (1)   (8 wkts, 49.2 overs) 213
3/73 (4) 4/122 (3) 5/139 (5)
6/150 (7) 7/178 (8) 8/210 (9)   10 overs: 53-1

C. J. McKay did not bat.

Mohammad Asif 10–0–40–1; Naved-ul-Hasan 10–0–55–2; Iftikhar Anjum 9.2–1–39–1; Shahid Afridi 10–0–31–2; Shoaib Malik 10–0–48–2.

Umpires: E. A. R. de Silva and P. R. Reiffel.
Third umpire: R. J. Tucker.   Referee: R. S. Madugalle.

†AUSTRALIA v PAKISTAN

Only Twenty20 International

At Melbourne, February 5, 2010 (floodlit). Australia won by two runs. Toss: Australia. Twenty20 international debuts: T. R. Birt, S. P. D. Smith; Imran Farhat.

Australia consigned Pakistan to a 9–0 defeat in the international matches of their tour by squeaking to the narrowest of victories. A crowd of 60,054 was subdued by Australia's poor showing with the bat, as Pakistan demonstrated some of the bowling and fielding prowess that had taken them to the World Twenty20 title in England the previous year. Three Australians were run out, and the final total owed much to the invention of David Hussey. A score of 127 looked inadequate, but the slinger Shaun Tait (recalled for his first international match in more than a year) was used to defending slim scores for South Australia, and he soon had Pakistan off balance with a ferocious spell during which he broke the 160kph barrier; his third ball was measured at 160.7, or 99.8mph. Kamran Akmal's response was to hurtle to 64 at almost two runs a ball, and while he was there the chase looked well in hand. But Tait returned to induce a drive to mid-on, and the rest departed at dizzying speed, hastened by some sharp captaincy from Clarke and the hard-spun leg-breaks of the debutant Steve Smith. Shoaib Malik resumed the Pakistan captaincy in the absence of the banned Shahid Afridi.

Man of the Match: S. W. Tait.

Australia		B	4	6
S. R. Watson *run out*		8	8	1	0
D. A. Warner *c 2 b 11*	24	14	1	1
*M. J. Clarke *c 7 b 9*	32	26	2	0
D. J. Hussey *not out*	40	31	1	2
C. L. White *run out*	4	8	0	0
T. R. Birt *b 5*	1	2	0	0
†B. J. Haddin *st 3 b 5*	1	3	0	0
S. P. D. Smith *b 8*	8	8	1	0
M. G. Johnson *c 3 b 9*	2	7	0	0
D. P. Nannes *run out*	4	3	0	0
S. W. Tait *c 7 b 9*	1	2	0	0
L-b	2			

6 overs: 50-1   (18.4 overs) 127

1/14 2/54 3/68 4/77 5/78 6/81 7/102 8/106 9/119 10/127

Mohammad Asif 4–0–31–1; Naved-ul-Hasan 4–0–27–1; Shoaib Malik 4–0–31–2; Umar Gul 3.4–0–20–3; Saeed Ajmal 3–0–18–0.

Pakistan		B	4	6
Imran Farhat *c 1 b 11*	8	10	1	0
Imran Nazir *run out*	0	5	0	0
†Kamran Akmal *c 4 b 11*	64	33	7	2
Khalid Latif *lbw b 1*	6	8	1	0
*Shoaib Malik *c 6 b 11*	3	11	0	0
Umar Akmal *c 2 b 1*	21	25	0	0
Fawad Alam *c 5 b 8*	1	5	0	0
Naved-ul-Hasan *st 7 b 8*	1	9	0	0
Umar Gul *b 10*	10	9	0	1
Saeed Ajmal *not out*	1	3	0	0
Mohammad Asif *not out*	5	2	1	0
L-b 3, w 2	5			

6 overs: 44-3   (20 overs) 125-9

1/5 2/10 3/44 4/59 5/98 6/103 7/107 8/118 9/118

Tait 4–0–13–3; Nannes 4–1–27–1; Johnson 4–1–24–0; Watson 4–1–24–2; Smith 4–0–34–2.

Umpires: P. R. Reiffel and R. J. Tucker.
Third umpire: B. N. J. Oxenford.   Referee: R. S. Madugalle.

DOMESTIC CRICKET IN AUSTRALIA, 2008-09

PETER ENGLISH

Victoria dominated the season, reaching all three finals, yet had to wait until the last match to secure a trophy and erase doubts about their performances in deciding contests. Since their previous first-class triumph in 2003-04, the Bushrangers had been runners-up to Queensland and New South Wales, and their fear of failure increased when the same teams inflicted narrow defeats at the climax of the Twenty20 and one-day competitions in early 2009. When it came to the five-day

CRICKET VICTORIA

final against Queensland, however, a first-innings total of 510 and a day and a half lost to rain eased the threat. Victoria had much the better of the draw, which allowed them to collect the Sheffield Shield – refurbished when new sponsor Weet-Bix restored the first-class tournament's traditional name, after nine seasons of the Pura Cup.

Victoria were so strong in the Shield that no opponent could take a point from them in the ten qualifying games. Opener Chris Rogers was outstanding in his first season after leaving Western Australia, picking up 1,195 runs and five centuries, including 105 in his maiden first-class final, though it was not enough to interest the national selectors. Brad Hodge was another strong contributor: his highlight was 261 when Victoria piled on 806 for eight declared, the ninth-highest total in Australian history, at home to Queensland a week before meeting them in the decider. The only bright spot for the visitors was that wicketkeeper Chris Hartley set a world record for the largest total without a single bye conceded.

Bradley Kanaris, Getty Images

Chris Hartley

By then **Queensland** had already upset Victoria by stealing the one-day Ford Ranger Cup at the MCG. The hosts were on target to overhaul the Bulls' 187 until Nathan Rimmington and Ben Laughlin brought about a dramatic collapse and they fell 12 short. The young Queensland side had also performed strongly in the Twenty20 competition, a satisfying set of results for Chris Simpson's first year as leader, though they lost five as well as winning four in reaching the Shield final. Lee Carseldine continued his remarkable development after back surgery and septicaemia to score heavily in all forms, but Andrew Symonds, suspended from the national side for large parts of the season, managed only 197 runs at 15 in eight Shield appearances. The state bade farewell to two stalwarts when Andy Bichel gave up his attempt to come back after shoulder surgery and Martin Love joined him in retirement after a century in the final, while Ashley Noffke departed in June after receiving a two-year offer from Western Australia.

The third trophy went to **New South Wales**, who were last in the Shield and one-day tournaments but won the Twenty20 title, ending Victoria's stranglehold in the competition's first three seasons. Hiring Brendon McCullum, the New Zealand wicketkeeper-batsman, for the final ensured a controversial build-up, though he fell in the fourth over of New South Wales's chase and it was left to Ben Rohrer's brutal 20-ball 44 to seal success off the last delivery. There were flashes of brilliance from the young batting trio of Phillip Hughes (four first-class hundreds), David Warner and Usman Khawaja. Fast bowler Aaron Bird was suspended for a suspect action after dominating both limited-overs arenas.

Life was rosier in **South Australia** as they improved from fifth to third in the Shield, although to develop further they must start winning while the season is still alive. A late surge of three consecutive victories was helped by the recall of Mark Cosgrove, who scored two hundreds in those games, and leg-spinner Cullen Bailey. Michael Klinger, who had moved west from Victoria, started the summer in style and was the Shield's leading run-scorer with 1,203 at 70. His four centuries included 255 against Western Australia, and he made another 469 runs in the one-day competition, in which the Redbacks also finished third.

Tasmania had a chance of reaching the Shield final until the last round. While team glory was ultimately missing, the state was able to watch the international promotions of the bowlers Brett Geeves and Ben Hilfenhaus. A new captain was to lead them into 2009-10: George Bailey, who led their Shield run-list with 673, took over from Dan Marsh in a planned succession.

There were few highs in **Western Australia**, with Tom Moody's squad finishing fifth in all three competitions. Brett Dorey's 42 Shield wickets were the most by any bowler, and Steve Magoffin was briefly elevated to Australia's squad as injury cover in South Africa, where his state captain Marcus North scored a hundred on Test debut, but the campaign ended with more talk of dressing-room fractures and the need for rebuilding.

FIRST-CLASS AVERAGES, 2008-09

BATTING

(Qualification: 500 runs)

	M	I	NO	R	HS	100s	Avge	Ct/St
M. J. Clarke (*Australia*)	5	9	1	600	138	2	75.00	4
†C. J. L. Rogers (*Victoria*)	11	19	3	1,195	159	5	74.68	9
M. Klinger (*South Australia*)	10	19	2	1,203	255	4	70.76	14
†P. J. Hughes (*New South Wales*)	8	15	1	963	198	4	68.78	6
†S. M. Katich (*New South Wales & Australia*)	6	11	1	626	143	2	62.60	5
B. J. Hodge (*Victoria*)	9	14	1	803	261	2	61.76	2
M. L. Love (*Queensland*)	10	18	2	842	219*	3	52.62	11
†M. S. Wade (*Victoria*)	11	15	4	545	100*	2	49.54	57
G. A. Manou (*South Australia*)	10	17	3	647	124	2	46.21	32/2

	M	I	NO	R	HS	100s	Avge	Ct/St
†L. A. Carseldine (*Queensland*)	8	14	1	595	152	1	45.76	5
D. J. Harris (*South Australia*)	9	18	0	813	124	2	45.16	8
N. Jewell (*Victoria*)	11	19	2	737	164	2	43.35	9
C. J. Ferguson (*South Australia*)	9	16	1	644	132	2	42.93	4
†U. T. Khawaja (*New South Wales*)	8	14	1	554	172*	2	42.61	4
D. J. Thornely (*New South Wales*)	11	18	2	680	110*	1	42.50	3
D. J. Hussey (*Victoria*)	9	14	1	522	113	1	40.15	11
R. A. Broad (*Queensland*)	11	21	2	743	118	3	39.10	7
†M. J. North (*Western Australia*)	7	14	1	505	141	2	38.84	11
†R. J. Quiney (*Victoria*)	10	15	2	503	127	1	38.69	8
†W. M. Robinson (*Western Australia*)	7	14	0	531	141	1	37.92	3
G. J. Bailey (*Tasmania*)	10	20	2	673	130*	2	37.38	6
†C. D. Hartley (*Queensland*)	11	18	3	524	121	2	34.93	52/2
†L. A. Pomersbach (*Western Australia*)	10	20	2	621	144	2	34.50	8

† *Left-handed batsman.*

BOWLING

(Qualification: 20 wickets)

	Style	O	M	R	W	BB	5W/i	Avge
B. W. Hilfenhaus (*Tasmania*)	RFM	173.2	54	448	24	5-14	2	18.66
M. G. Johnson (*Australia*)	LF	225.2	50	594	31	8-61	2	19.16
D. P. Nannes (*Victoria*)	LF	235	52	798	38	7-50	1	21.00
C. J. McKay (*Victoria*)	RFM	287.4	87	707	33	5-78	1	21.42
A. B. McDonald (*Victoria and Australia*) . .	RM	213.1	58	542	25	6-68	1	21.68
B. T. Cockley (*New South Wales*)	RFM	191.2	43	599	27	5-76	2	22.18
J. R. Hopes (*Queensland*)	RFM	307.1	85	771	34	5-34	1	22.67
L. R. Butterworth (*Tasmania*)	RM	233.2	74	681	30	5-13	2	22.70
S. J. Magoffin (*Western Australia*)	RFM	331.3	99	869	38	6-66	1	22.86
B. Geeves (*Tasmania*)	RFM	276.1	64	883	37	6-47	2	23.86
B. R. Dorey (*Western Australia*)	RFM	365.3	102	1,013	42	6-28	4	24.11
D. T. Christian (*South Australia*)	RFM	181.3	24	706	27	5-62	1	26.14
R. J. Harris (*Queensland*)	RFM	279.5	64	874	33	4-59	0	26.48
T. P. Macdonald (*Tasmania*)	RFM	191.2	34	639	23	6-40	1	27.78
D. E. Bollinger (*NSW & Australia*)	LFM	189.2	43	558	20	6-47	1	27.90
D. G. Wright (*Victoria*)	RFM	295.2	90	684	24	5-53	1	28.50
C. R. Swan (*Queensland*)	RFM	275.1	90	689	24	4-21	0	28.70
M. F. Cleary (*South Australia*)	RFM	343.2	90	999	32	7-91	1	31.21
P. R. George (*South Australia*)	RFM	217.5	51	643	20	4-56	0	32.15
N. M. Hauritz (*NSW and Australia*)	OB	403.1	104	972	25	4-86	0	38.88
G. M. Lambert (*New South Wales*)	RFM	209	22	811	20	5-74	2	40.55

Full scores of the 2008-09 Australian season can be found at www.cricinfo.com/db/ARCHIVE/2008-09/AUS_LOCAL/ and www.cricketarchive.co.uk/Archive/Seasons/2008-09_AUS.html and in the *ACS Overseas First-Class Annual 2009.*

SHEFFIELD SHIELD, 2008-09

	Played	Won	Lost	Drawn	1st-inns points	Points	Quotient
Victoria	10	6	0	4	8	44	1.520
Queensland	10	4	5	1	4	28	0.949
South Australia	10	4	3	3	2	26	1.064
Tasmania	10	4	5	1	2	26	0.881
Western Australia.	10	3	5	2	2	20	0.836
New South Wales.	10	2	5	3	6	18	0.878

Final: Victoria drew with Queensland but won the Sheffield Shield by virtue of heading the table.

Outright win = 6 pts; lead on first-innings in a drawn or lost game = 2 pts.

Quotient = runs per wicket scored divided by runs per wicket conceded.

At Brisbane, October 10, 11, 12, 2008. **Queensland won by 48 runs.** Toss: Tasmania. **Queensland 236** (C. D. Hartley 55, C. R. Swan 76*; T. P. Macdonald 4-42) **and 62** (B. W. Hilfenhaus 5-14); **Tasmania 106 and 144** (J. R. Hopes 4-24). *Queensland 6 pts.*

Despite two disastrous collapses – they were 91-8 in their first innings before Chris Hartley and Chris Swan added 135 for the ninth wicket, and 34-8 in their second – Queensland pulled off a three-day win.

At Perth, October 10, 11, 12, 13, 2008. **Western Australia won by eight wickets.** Toss: Western Australia. **New South Wales 177** (N. W. Bracken 63; S. J. Magoffin 4-36) **and 310** (G. J. Mail 77, D. J. Thornely 97; S. J. Magoffin 6-66); **Western Australia 265** (G. M. Lambert 5-82) **and 224-2** (S. E. Marsh 74*, L. A. Pomersbach 78). *Western Australia 6 pts.*

Defending champions New South Wales slumped to 97-8 before Nathan Bracken scored a maiden fifty, but Steve Magoffin set up a home victory with 10-102 in the match.

At Adelaide, October 14, 15, 16, 17, 2008. **Drawn.** Toss: Victoria. **Victoria 473-6 dec** (C. J. L. Rogers 63, N. Jewell 164, B. J. Hodge 104, A. B. McDonald 60) **and 151; South Australia 357-7 dec** (M. Klinger 150*) **and 176-7** (D. J. Harris 62). *Victoria 2 pts.*

Michael Klinger scored a career-best 150 on his debut for South Australia against his old team.*

At Perth, October 19, 20, 21, 22, 2008. **Western Australia won by four wickets.** Toss: Western Australia. **Tasmania 187** (G. J. Bailey 71) **and 292** (R. J. G. Lockyear 77, T. D. Paine 54); **Western Australia 283** (A. C. Voges 69, S. J. Magoffin 79; B. Geeves 5-76) **and 197-6** (T. P. Doropoulos 58*; B. Geeves 4-62). *Western Australia 6 pts.*

Western Australia made it two wins in two matches. Fourteen wickets fell on the opening day, but nightwatchman Steve Magoffin batted four hours for a maiden half-century to rescue them from 33-4.

At Brisbane, October 21, 22, 23, 2008. **Victoria won by nine wickets.** Toss: Victoria. **Queensland 245** (R. A. Broad 96, M. L. Love 54; D. G. Wright 4-64, D. P. Nannes 4-45) **and 150** (D. P. Nannes 7-50); **Victoria 353** (C. J. L. Rogers 51, R. J. Quiney 127) **and 45-1.** *Victoria 6 pts.*

Dirk Nannes's career-best bowling and a maiden century from Rob Quiney steered Victoria to their opening win of the campaign in their first encounter with Queensland. Brad Hodge overtook Dean Jones's 10,412 to become Victoria's leading first-class run-scorer as he helped to knock off the target on the third day.

At Adelaide, October 24, 25, 26, 27, 2008. **Drawn.** Toss: South Australia. **South Australia 313** (G. A. Manou 80, A. W. O'Brien 63) **and 300-5** (D. J. Harris 63, M. Klinger 74, Younis Khan 71*); **New South Wales 576** (P. J. Hughes 198, P. J. Forrest 135, B. Casson 70, N. M. Hauritz 66). *New South Wales 2 pts.*

Phillip Hughes, who narrowly missed a maiden double-hundred, and Peter Forrest, who arrived in New South Wales's second over, added 253 for the second wicket. Pakistan batsman Younis Khan, engaged for two months by South Australia, made a first-ball duck on Shield debut but later ensured the draw with 71.*

At Perth, October 31, November 1, 2, 3, 2008. **Queensland won by 127 runs.** Toss: Western Australia. **Queensland 208** (C. T. Perren 58) **and 321-8 dec** (R. A. Broad 118, L. A. Carseldine 67, C. D. Hartley 50*; B. R. Dorey 4-75); **Western Australia 206** (M. J. North 94; R. J. Harris 4-67) **and 196** (L. A. Pomersbach 104; A. A. Noffke 4-27). *Queensland 6 pts.*

Early on the second day, Western Australia were 33-4 – 32 scored by Liam Davis, one leg-bye and three ducks. Captain Marcus North revived the innings but was last out in sight of a century, and Ryan Broad's career-best 118 set up victory for Queensland.

At Hobart, November 3, 4, 5, 6, 2008. **Tasmania won by three wickets.** Toss: Tasmania. **South Australia 232** (M. Klinger 65, C. J. Ferguson 65; T. P. Macdonald 6-40) **and 200** (B. W. Hilfenhaus 5-53); **Tasmania 252** (P. R. George 4-56) **and 184-7** (T. D. Paine 69*). *Tasmania 6 pts.*

Tasmania were 76-6 chasing 181 in the final innings before wicketkeeper Tim Paine saw them home. South Australia remained without a point after three matches.

At Sydney, November 4, 5, 6, 7, 2008. **Drawn.** Toss: New South Wales. **New South Wales 261** (U. T. Khawaja 66, D. L. R. Smith 56; D. P. Nannes 4-57, C. J. McKay 4-33) **and 340-8** (P. J.

Hughes 86, P. J. Forrest 55, D. J. Thornely 58); **Victoria 440** (C. J. L. Rogers 159, B. J. Hodge 66, D. J. Hussey 63, A. B. McDonald 53; B. T. Cockley 5-84). *Victoria 2 pts.*

Darren Pattinson took only one wicket on his return to Victoria after his unexpected Test appearance for England in 2008. Chris Rogers secured first-innings points with his maiden hundred for Victoria.

At Adelaide, November 10, 11, 12, 13, 2008. **Drawn.** Toss: Western Australia. **Western Australia 309** (W. M. Robinson 141) **and 247-6** (L. A. Pomersbach 144, M. J. North 50); **South Australia 479-9 dec** (M. Klinger 255, C. J. Borgas 105). *South Australia 2 pts.*

Michael Klinger and Cameron Borgas added 265 for the third wicket; Klinger batted for ten hours 12 minutes in all and hit 33 fours in a career-best 255 which ensured South Australia's first points of the season.

At Melbourne, November 15, 16, 17, 18, 2008. **Victoria won by ten wickets.** Toss: Tasmania. **Tasmania 218** (G. J. Bailey 73) **and 300** (D. J. Marsh 75, B. Geeves 99*; C. J. McKay 5-78); **Victoria 484** (N. Jewell 92, D. J. Hussey 76, R. J. Quiney 88, D. G. Wright 84; B. Geeves 4-103) **and 35-0.** *Victoria 6 pts.*

*The first day started at 1 p.m. because several players had to fly back from Brisbane, where they had taken part in a Twenty20 game between an Australian Cricketers' Association All*Stars XI and an Australian XI the previous night. One of them was Brad Hodge, who overtook Darren Berry's record of 138 first-class games for Victoria but made only three runs. Victoria went top of the Shield table for the first time in the season.*

At Sydney, November 21, 22, 23, 24, 2008. **Queensland won by ten wickets.** Toss: New South Wales. **New South Wales 210** (B. Casson 63; C. R. Swan 4-21) **and 262** (D. L. R. Smith 70; C. P. Simpson 5-68); **Queensland 354** (N. J. Kruger 78, M. L. Love 110; B. T. Cockley 5-76) **and 119-0** (R. A. Broad 51*, N. J. Kruger 61*). *Queensland 6 pts.*

Martin Love scored his 43rd century but his first since January 2007, and Queensland wicketkeeper Chris Hartley made ten dismissals in the match.

At Perth, November 21, 22, 23, 24, 2008. **Victoria won by six wickets.** Toss: Victoria. **Western Australia 239** (M. J. North 103) **and 404-8 dec** (M. J. North 141, A. C. Voges 52, S. J. Magoffin 66*; D. G. Wright 5-53); **Victoria 326** (C. J. L. Rogers 115, M. S. Wade 68; B. R. Dorey 5-104) **and 321-4** (C. J. L. Rogers 147*, D. J. Hussey 87, A. B. McDonald 60*). *Victoria 6 pts.*

On the first morning, Dirk Nannes was ordered out of Victoria's attack in the second over after bowling three full tosses – one dismissing Shaun Marsh, the other two called as no-balls – for figures of 0.1–0–2–1. Marcus North scored twin hundreds for Western Australia, only for his former team-mate Chris Rogers to match his feat and steer Victoria home with seven balls to spare.

At Brisbane, November 28, 29, 30, December 1, 2008. **South Australia won by three wickets.** Toss: South Australia. **Queensland 352** (L. A. Carseldine 152, R. J. Harris 51) **and 392** (M. L. Love 50, S. R. Watson 81, C. D. Hartley 75*; D. T. Christian 4-89); **South Australia 411** (Younis Khan 118, C. J. Ferguson 132; S. R. Watson 7-69) **and 334-7** (M. Klinger 137, C. J. Borgas 60). *South Australia 6 pts.*

Lee Carseldine rescued Queensland from 78-5 with 152, his first century for six years, and Shane Watson followed up his career-best 7-69 with 81 runs, but Michael Klinger's third century of the season put South Australia on course for their first win.

At Hobart, December 2, 3, 4, 2008. **Tasmania won by three wickets.** Toss: Tasmania. **New South Wales 172** (P. J. Hughes 93; G. J. Denton 5-18) **and 173** (P. J. Hughes 108); **Tasmania 127** (N. W. Bracken 5-28) **and 221-7** (D. J. Marsh 58, T. D. Paine 59*). *Tasmania 6 pts, New South Wales 2 pts.*

Phillip Hughes scored more than half New South Wales's runs in each innings. Asked to score 219, the highest total of the game, to win, Tasmania were 90-5 before Jonathan Wells (46) and Dan Marsh added 82 to set up victory. There were 12 ducks in the match, equalling the Shield record.

At Melbourne, December 15, 16, 17, 2008. **Victoria won by eight wickets.** Toss: Victoria. **Western Australia 211** (D. C. Bandy 66; D. G. Wright 4-42) **and 140** (A. B. McDonald 4-38); **Victoria 296** (C. L. White 51, A. B. McDonald 60, D. G. Wright 60) **and 58-2.** *Victoria 6 pts.*

Victoria completed their third successive win on the third afternoon after taking Western Australia's last nine wickets for 77.

At Hobart, December 16, 17, 18, 19, 2008. **Tasmania won by six wickets.** Toss: Tasmania. **Queensland 230 and 93** (L. R. Butterworth 5-13); **Tasmania 214** (R. J. Harris 4-59) **and 111-4.** *Tasmania 6 pts, Queensland 2 pts.*

Luke Butterworth caused a Queensland collapse of nine for 63 on the third day, and Tasmania would have completed a second successive three-day win but for rain; they needed only five balls on the final morning.

At Sydney, December 18, 19, 20, 21, 2008. **New South Wales won by 75 runs.** Toss: New South Wales. **New South Wales 483-6 dec** (P. J. Hughes 114, B. J. Rohrer 109, D. J. Thornely 87*, D. L. R. Smith 96) **and 120-2 dec** (B. J. Rohrer 57*); **South Australia 304-3 dec** (M. Klinger 125, C. J. Borgas 90*) **and 224** (Younis Khan 90; D. E. Bollinger 6-47). *New South Wales 6 pts.*

Michael Klinger scored his fourth century of the season – and third in successive first-class matches – before South Australia declared behind in the hope of chasing a target on the last day. But Doug Bollinger's career-best 6-47 earned New South Wales victory and himself a Test debut against South Africa. Younis Khan passed 10,000 first-class runs.

At Newcastle, January 30, 31, February 1, 2, 2009. **New South Wales won by 114 runs.** Toss: New South Wales. **New South Wales 521-4 dec** (P. J. Hughes 151, S. M. Katich 143, D. J. Thornely 110*, B. J. Rohrer 53*) **and 157-5 dec** (P. J. Hughes 82*); **Tasmania 328** (R. J. G. Lockyear 52, T. D. Paine 63, B. Geeves 99*; N. M. Hauritz 4-86) **and 236** (J. W. Wells 85; M. A. Cameron 4-51). *New South Wales 6 pts.*

New South Wales's 521-4 featured three centuries, including Phillip Hughes's third in three games and fourth of the season, and Simon Katich's 143 in 150 balls, with six sixes, in his only Shield match of 2008-09.

At Brisbane, January 30, 31, February 1, 2009. **Western Australia won by six wickets.** Toss: Western Australia. **Queensland 247** (M. L. Love 96; B. R. Dorey 6-28) **and 179** (L. A. Carseldine 55; B. R. Dorey 5-60, S. J. Magoffin 4-62); **Western Australia 236** (W. M. Robinson 78, L. A. Pomersbach 79; R. J. Harris 4-60) **and 193-4** (A. C. Voges 80*). *Western Australia 6 pts, Queensland 2 pts.*

Andrew Symonds returned for his first game of 2009 after knee surgery; he lasted seven balls in the first innings and eight in the second. Brett Dorey claimed 11-88 in the match, while Adam Voges held seven catches, five of them in Queensland's first innings – equalling both Shield records for catches in the field.

At Melbourne, January 30, 31, February 1, 2, 2009. **Victoria won by 25 runs.** Toss: Victoria. **Victoria 400** (N. Jewell 105, L. R. Mash 63, D. G. Wright 56, C. J. McKay 54) **and 262-6 dec** (N. Jewell 60, C. J. L. Rogers 93; D. T. Christian 5-62); **South Australia 348-9 dec** (D. J. Harris 58, C. J. Ferguson 81, G. A. Manou 124; A. B. McDonald 6-68) **and 289** (M. Klinger 59, C. J. Ferguson 115; B. E. McGain 5-104). *Victoria 6 pts.*

Victoria went 12 points clear at the top of the table with three rounds to go after South Australia, chasing 315, subsided from 162-3. Michael Klinger passed 1,000 first-class runs for the season.

At Adelaide, February 13, 14, 15, 16, 2009. **South Australia won by 19 runs.** Toss: South Australia. **South Australia 489-6 dec** (D. J. Harris 117, M. J. Cosgrove 133, G. A. Manou 108) **and 143-7 dec** (M. Klinger 57); **Queensland 300-8 dec** (R. A. Broad 84, L. A. Carseldine 51; C. B. Bailey 5-90) **and 313** (L. A. Carseldine 86, C. D. Hartley 102; J. A. Haberfield 4-60). *South Australia 6 pts.*

Mark Cosgrove and Cullen Bailey were recalled for their first Shield game of the season, and helped to inflict Queensland's fourth successive defeat with a century and career-best bowling figures respectively.

At Melbourne, February 15, 16, 17, 2009. **Victoria won by an innings and two runs.** Toss: New South Wales. **New South Wales 227** (G. J. Mail 101) **and 218** (C. J. McKay 4-56, J. W. Hastings 5-61); **Victoria 447** (C. J. L. Rogers 61, B. J. Hodge 98, M. S. Wade 62; B. T. Cockley 4-65). *Victoria 6 pts.*

Even with Dirk Nannes and Shane Harwood injured and unable to bowl for much of the match, Victoria completed their fifth successive win to ensure their place in the final.

At Hobart, February 16, 17, 18, 2009. **Tasmania won by five wickets.** Toss: Tasmania. **Western Australia 189** (W. M. Robinson 84; L. R. Butterworth 4-16) **and 168** (S. J. Magoffin 59*; C. J.

Duval 4-29); **Tasmania 163** (D. J. Marsh 64; B. R. Dorey 5-37) **and 197-5** (D. J. Marsh 58*). *Tasmania 6 pts, Western Australia 2 pts.*

Tasmania's fourth win, like the previous three, came at Hobart after they put the visitors in and successfully chased a fourth-innings target. It lifted them to second place with two rounds to go.

At Brisbane, February 26, 27, 28, March 1, 2009. **Queensland won by an innings and 129 runs.** Toss: New South Wales. **New South Wales 269** (U. T. Khawaja 112; J. R. Hopes 4-80) **and 149** (J. R. Hopes 5-34); **Queensland 547-7 dec** (M. L. Love 219*, A. Symonds 52, J. R. Hopes 55, C. D. Hartley 121). *Queensland 6 pts.*

Queensland ended their losing streak and regained second place. In his final home match before retirement, Martin Love batted nine hours five minutes for his ninth double-hundred (but his first for five years), and added 233, a sixth-wicket Shield record for Queensland, with Chris Hartley, who scored a career-best and also made ten New South Wales dismissals for the second time in the season.

At Hobart, February 26, 27, 28, March 1, 2009. **Drawn.** Toss: Tasmania. **Victoria 535** (C. J. L. Rogers 82, N. Jewell 83, B. J. Hodge 79, M. S. Wade 100) **and 158** (B. Geeves 6-47); **Tasmania 300** (J. W. Wells 98, G. J. Bailey 130*; D. J. Pattinson 5-38) **and 155-5.** *Victoria 2 pts.*

Tasmania's home strategy finally came unstuck after they conceded a 235-run lead to the leaders; even Brett Geeves's career-best 6-47 was not enough to earn them an achievable target. Wicketkeeper Tim Paine made five catches and a stumping in Victoria's first innings.

At Perth, February 26, 27, 28, March 1, 2009. **South Australia won by nine wickets.** Toss: South Australia. **Western Australia 243** (L. A. Pomersbach 51; M. F. Cleary 4-70) **and 228** (L. A. Pomersbach 57; D. T. Christian 4-52); **South Australia 457-9 dec** (D. J. Harris 124, G. A. Manou 85, A. W. O'Brien 55; A. C. Voges 4-97) **and 17-1.** *South Australia 6 pts.*

South Australia's revival continued thanks to Daniel Harris's highest score and their captain, Graham Manou, who narrowly missed his third hundred in as many matches.

At Sydney, March 5, 6, 7, 8, 2009. **Drawn.** Toss: Western Australia. **Western Australia 210** (A. K. Heal 66; B. T. Cockley 4-37) **and 248-4** (W. M. Robinson 51, D. C. Bandy 87*); **New South Wales 526-8 dec** (E. J. M. Cowan 58, G. J. Mail 59, D. J. Thornely 56, U. T. Khawaja 172*). *New South Wales 2 pts.*

First-innings points were not enough to save New South Wales from the wooden spoon. David Warner, who had already played Twenty20 international cricket for Australia, scored 42 in 48 balls on first-class debut, but was outshone by Usman Khawaja's five-and-a-half-hour career-best 172.*

At Adelaide, March 5, 6, 7, 8, 2009. **South Australia won by five wickets.** Toss: Tasmania. **Tasmania 301** (G. J. Bailey 123, C. J. Duval 61; M. F. Cleary 7-91) **and 289-9 dec** (L. R. Butterworth 77, J. J. Krejza 59*; D. T. Christian 4-76); **South Australia 253** (J. D. Smith 50, C. J. Ferguson 54; L. R. Butterworth 5-43) **and 338-5** (D. J. Harris 82, M. J. Cosgrove 118, G. A. Manou 55*). *South Australia 6 pts, Tasmania 2 pts.*

Tasmania recovered from 82-7 on the opening day, thanks to an eighth-wicket stand of 139 between George Bailey and Chris Duval. But Mark Cosgrove led South Australia's successful pursuit of 338 on the final day to achieve their third consecutive win and deny Tasmania a place in the Shield final.

At Melbourne, March 5, 6, 7, 8, 2009. **Drawn.** Toss: Queensland. **Queensland 302** (S. R. Watson 145; J. W. Hastings 4-56) **and 187-1** (M. L. Love 77, R. A. Broad 100*); **Victoria 806-8 dec** (C. J. L. Rogers 123, B. J. Hodge 261, D. J. Hussey 62, C. L. White 124, R. J. Quiney 94, M. S. Wade 100*; C. P. Simpson 4-194). *Victoria 2 pts.*

Victoria's 806-8 declared was the ninth-highest total in Australian first-class cricket and the seventh-highest in the Sheffield Shield. It was a world record for a total in which the opposing wicketkeeper (Chris Hartley) did not concede a bye. Had Robert Quiney scored six more runs, Victoria would have equalled the Australian record of five centuries in an innings. Brad Hodge's 261 was his 50th first-class century and his tenth double, and made him the sixth player to reach 10,000 Shield runs; he added 244 for the second wicket with Chris Rogers, who passed 1,000 runs for the season.

HIGHEST TOTALS IN WHICH WICKETKEEPER DID NOT CONCEDE A BYE

806-8 dec	**C. D. Hartley, Queensland v Victoria at Melbourne**	**2008-09**
746-9 dec	R. C. Russell, Gloucestershire v Northamptonshire at Bristol	2002
726-9 dec	**H. A. P. W. Jayawardene, Sri Lanka v India at Mumbai**	**2009-10**
717	C. M. Gazzard, Somerset v Surrey at Guildford	2006
716	R. Paul, Tamil Nadu v Karnataka at Bhadravati	1995-96
713-3 dec	T. Taibu, Zimbabwe v Sri Lanka at Bulawayo	2003-04
700-9 dec	C. M. W. Read, Nottinghamshire v Essex at Chelmsford	2007
686-6 dec	C. A. McWatt, British Guiana v Barbados at Bridgetown	1949-50
675-5 dec	P. A. Nixon, Leicestershire v Somerset at Taunton	2007
672-7 dec	A. P. Wickham, Somerset v Hampshire at Taunton	1899

FINAL

VICTORIA v QUEENSLAND

At St Kilda, March 13, 14, 15, 16, 17, 2009. Drawn. Victoria won the Sheffield Shield by virtue of leading the qualifying table. Toss: Victoria.

In a final played at St Kilda because the MCG was staging a charity concert for bushfire victims, Victoria showed no charity to Queensland. After a wobble on the first evening, against the second new ball, they regained their footing to reach a formidable 510 and were not challenged again. Wet weather made this the first final to be drawn in nine years, but Victoria needed only a draw to lift their 27th first-class trophy. White, who was dropped on 45 and 46, rebuilt the innings from 277 for six, adding 135 with Wade and batting into the fourth day for his 135. He made sure there was no waste of the groundwork from Rogers and Hussey, who had registered centuries (the fifth of the season for Rogers) during a stand of 181. Rain washed out the second day and the third was restricted to 49 overs; in addition to the weather, there were short delays to shoo away pigeons attracted by grass seed around the square. Queensland were all out for 200 in their first innings, with Nannes taking four, and were soon back in the field watching rapid half-centuries from Hodge, Jewell and White before being set a nominal target of 593 on the final day. There was time for Wade to make his 57th dismissal of the season, one short of the Shield record set by Wade Seccombe. Love's last match – his unbeaten 104 took him past 10,000 Shield runs a week after Hodge – mirrored his debut, in the 1992-93 final, as he bowed out watching the opposition lift the Sheffield Shield.

Man of the Match: C. L. White.   *Attendance:* 6,331.

Close of play: First day, Victoria 281-6 (White 21, Wade 2); Second day, No play; Third day, Victoria 423-8 (White 84, McKay 4); Fourth day, Victoria 82-1 (Jewell 31, Hodge 7).

Victoria

C. J. L. Rogers c Broad b Doran	105	– (2) b Cutting	42
N. Jewell lbw b Hopes	6	– (1) b Simpson	75
B. J. Hodge c Watson b Symonds	17	– c Carseldine b Laughlin	90
D. J. Hussey lbw b Symonds	113	– b Simpson	4
*C. L. White c Hartley b Hopes	135	– c Cutting b Laughlin	61
R. J. Quiney c Hartley b Hopes	4	– not out	6
D. P. Nannes lbw b Symonds	1		
†M. S. Wade hit wkt b Laughlin	70	– (7) not out	0
D. G. Wright b Laughlin	0		
C. J. McKay not out	39		
S. M. Harwood c Hartley b Symonds	1		
B 1, l-b 13, n-b 5	19	B 1, l-b 2, n-b 1	4

1/15 (2) 2/55 (3) 3/236 (1)   (166 overs) 510
4/265 (4) 5/272 (6) 6/277 (7) 7/412 (8)
8/412 (9) 9/505 (5) 10/510 (11)

1/57 (2)   (5 wkts dec, 51 overs) 282
2/151 (1) 3/165 (4)
4/267 (3) 5/276 (5)

Hopes 44–12–119–3; Laughlin 26–5–93–2; Cutting 20–4–81–0; Doran 35–6–120–1; Symonds 24–8–48–4; Simpson 17–3–35–0. *Second Innings*—Hopes 4–0–28–0; Cutting 13–0–76–1; Laughlin 11–0–55–2; Simpson 13–2–49–2; Doran 10–2–71–0.

Queensland

M. L. Love b Harwood	41	– (2) not out	104
R. A. Broad c Wade b Harwood	27	– (1) c Wade b Harwood	109
L. A. Carseldine b McKay	12	– not out	5
S. R. Watson c Wade b Nannes	13		
A. Symonds b McKay	14		
†C. D. Hartley lbw b Nannes	0		
J. R. Hopes c Rogers b McKay	25		
*C. P. Simpson b White	27		
B. C. J. Cutting b Nannes	21		
D. J. Doran not out	3		
B. Laughlin b Nannes	0		
B 7, l-b 10	17	B 1, l-b 1, w 1	3

1/65 (2) 2/70 (1) 3/98 (4) 4/102 (3) (61 overs) **200** 1/199 (1) (1 wkt, 52 overs) **221**
5/113 (5) 6/117 (6) 7/153 (7) 8/194 (8)
9/194 (9) 10/200 (11)

Nannes 17–5–65–4; Wright 13–2–31–0; Harwood 14–5–38–2; McKay 13–4–35–3; White 4–0–14–1. *Second Innings*—Nannes 8–1–30–0; Wright 11–2–48–0; Harwood 8–1–47–1; McKay 9–1–37–0; White 9–0–40–0; Hussey 5–1–11–0; Quiney 2–0–6–0.

Umpires: B. N. J. Oxenford and P. R. Reiffel
Third umpire: I. H. Lock.   Referee: R. W. Stratford.

CHAMPIONS

Sheffield Shield					
1892-93	Victoria	1926-27	South Australia	1963-64	South Australia
1893-94	South Australia	1927-28	Victoria	1964-65	New South Wales
1894-95	Victoria	1928-29	New South Wales	1965-66	New South Wales
1895-96	New South Wales	1929-30	Victoria	1966-67	Victoria
1896-97	New South Wales	1930-31	Victoria	1967-68	Western Australia
1897-98	Victoria	1931-32	New South Wales	1968-69	South Australia
1898-99	Victoria	1932-33	New South Wales	1969-70	Victoria
1899-1900	New South Wales	1933-34	Victoria	1970-71	South Australia
1900-01	Victoria	1934-35	Victoria	1971-72	Western Australia
1901-02	New South Wales	1935-36	South Australia	1972-73	Western Australia
1902-03	New South Wales	1936-37	Victoria	1973-74	Victoria
1903-04	New South Wales	1937-38	New South Wales	1974-75	Western Australia
1904-05	New South Wales	1938-39	South Australia	1975-76	South Australia
1905-06	New South Wales	1939-40	New South Wales	1976-77	Western Australia
1906-07	New South Wales	1940–46	No competition	1977-78	Western Australia
1907-08	Victoria	1946-47	Victoria	1978-79	Victoria
1908-09	New South Wales	1947-48	Western Australia	1979-80	Victoria
1909-10	South Australia	1948-49	New South Wales	1980-81	Western Australia
1910-11	New South Wales	1949-50	New South Wales	1981-82	South Australia
1911-12	New South Wales	1950-51	Victoria	1982-83	New South Wales*
1912-13	South Australia	1951-52	New South Wales	1983-84	Western Australia
1913-14	New South Wales	1952-53	South Australia	1984-85	New South Wales
1914-15	Victoria	1953-54	New South Wales	1985-86	New South Wales
1915–19	No competition	1954-55	New South Wales	1986-87	Western Australia
1919-20	New South Wales	1955-56	New South Wales	1987-88	Western Australia
1920-21	New South Wales	1956-57	New South Wales	1988-89	Western Australia
1921-22	Victoria	1957-58	New South Wales	1989-90	New South Wales
1922-23	New South Wales	1958-59	New South Wales	1990-91	Victoria
1923-24	Victoria	1959-60	New South Wales	1991-92	Western Australia
1924-25	Victoria	1960-61	New South Wales	1992-93	New South Wales
1925-26	New South Wales	1961-62	New South Wales	1993-94	New South Wales
		1962-63	Victoria	1994-95	Queensland

1995-96	South Australia	*Pura Cup*	2006-07 Tasmania
1996-97	Queensland*	2000-01 Queensland	2007-08 New South Wales
1997-98	Western Australia	2001-02 Queensland	
1998-99	Western Australia*	2002-03 New South Wales*	*Sheffield Shield*
		2003-04 Victoria	2008-09 Victoria
Pura Milk Cup		2004-05 New South Wales*	
1999-2000 Queensland		2005-06 Queensland	

New South Wales have won the title 45 times, Victoria 27, Western Australia 15, South Australia 13, Queensland 6, Tasmania 1.

* Second in table but won final. Finals were introduced in 1982-83.

Note: Matches in the following sections were not first-class.

FORD RANGER CUP, 2008-09

50-over league plus final

	Played	Won	Lost	Tied	Bonus points	Points	Net run-rate
Victoria	10	7	3	0	2	30	0.10
Queensland	10	6	4	0	6	30	0.84
South Australia	10	5	5	0	3	23	0.04
Tasmania	10	4	5	1	2	20	0.07
Western Australia	10	4	6	0	0	16	−0.34
New South Wales	10	3	6	1	1	15	−0.64

Victoria finished above Queensland, earning the right to host the final, having won more matches.

Final

At Melbourne, February 22, 2009 (day/night). **Queensland won by 12 runs.** Toss: Queensland. **Queensland 187-8** (50 overs); **Victoria 175** (48 overs) (R. J. Quiney 52) (N. J. Rimmington 4-40).
    Victoria were 72-1 in the 17th over, then lost four wickets in eight overs; Queensland seamer Nathan Rimmington picked up four as they suffered their third successive 50-over final defeat.

KFC TWENTY20 BIG BASH, 2008-09

20-over league plus final

	Played	Won	Lost	Points	Net run-rate
New South Wales.	5	3	2	6	−0.16
Queensland.	5	3	2	6	0.62
Victoria	5	3	2	6	1.09
South Australia.	5	2	3	4	0.54
Western Australia.	5	2	3	4	−1.68
Tasmania	5	2	3	4	−0.46

Teams tied on points were separated on points in head-to-head matches (for instance, New South Wales beat Queensland and Victoria, and Queensland beat Victoria).

Play-off

At Brisbane, January 21, 2009 (floodlit). **Victoria won by six wickets.** Toss: Queensland. **Queensland 112-6** (20 overs) (L. A. Carseldine 52); **Victoria 113-4** (18 overs) (B. J. Hodge 59*).
    Victoria were 7-3 in the third over, but Brad Hodge and Adam Crosthwaite (40) added 83 in 12 overs to secure a place in the final – and in the Champions League in India.*

Final

At Olympic Park, Sydney, January 24, 2009 (floodlit). **New South Wales won by five wickets.** Toss: Victoria. **Victoria 166-4** (20 overs) (R. J. Quiney 91); **New South Wales 167-5** (20 overs).
    The final was dominated by two left-hand batsmen. First, Victorian opener Rob Quiney hit 91 from 56 balls, with eight sixes; then Ben Rohrer, coming in when New South Wales were 92-4 in the 13th over, struck 44 from 20 balls, with four sixes, and ran a bye off the game's final ball.

BANGLADESH CRICKET, 2009

A statistical success

UTPAL SHUVRO

For a Bangladeshi cricket fan talking about 2009, the obvious temptation would be to refer to statistics. They show that Bangladesh were the most successful Test team in 2009. And it doesn't stop there: even in one-day internationals, their win percentage was the highest among the Test-playing nations.

Oh, statistics! Lies! Damn lies! you might say. But that would not deter the Tigers' supporters from celebrating 2009 as the team's most successful year. Bangladesh won two of the three Tests they played, a 66.66% success rate, comfortably ahead of Australia (53.84%).

In the one-day arena, their record was even more impressive – on paper, anyway. Bangladesh won 14 of 19 matches for a success rate of 73.68%, which is even more outstanding if you compare it with the previous year, when they won only five out of 26. It will be argued that Bangladesh hardly faced any

BANGLADESH IN 2009

	Played	Won	Lost	Drawn/No result
Tests	3	2	1	–
One-day internationals	19	14	5	–
Twenty20 internationals	3	–	3	–

DECEMBER / JANUARY	2 Tests (h) v Sri Lanka	(see *Wisden 2009*, page 1062)
	Triangular ODI tournament (h) v Sri Lanka and Zimbabwe	(page 1086)
	3 ODIs (h) v Zimbabwe	(page 1089)
FEBRUARY		
MARCH		
APRIL		
MAY		
JUNE	World Twenty20 (in England)	(page 527)
JULY / AUGUST	2 Tests, 3 ODIs and 1 T20I (a) v West Indies	(page 1421)
	5 ODIs (a) v Zimbabwe	(page 1445)
SEPTEMBER / OCTOBER	Champions Trophy (in South Africa)	(page 1015)
NOVEMBER	5 ODIs (h) v Zimbabwe	(page 1090)
DECEMBER		

For a review of Bangladesh domestic cricket from the 2008-09 season, see page 1097.

Jewel Samad, AFP/Getty Images

Centre of attention: Shakib Al Hasan – batsman, bowler, captain, inspiration – enjoyed an outstanding year in 2009, and signed for Worcestershire.

top-ranked opposition: 14 of those 19 one-day internationals were against Zimbabwe, and their two Test wins (and three more in one-dayers) came against a seriously under-strength West Indies team. However, Zimbabwe fielded their strongest side since the Heath Streak era (and Streak himself was back as a coach). By making the scoreline 10–4 overall, and winning both the home and away series 4–1, Bangladesh proved themselves a notch above their former arch-rivals, and ready to challenge the higher-ranked teams.

Proof of that came at the beginning of the year, when Bangladesh walloped Sri Lanka to book their ticket for the final of a home triangular series also involving Zimbabwe. They almost repeated the feat in the final, when after making a paltry 152 they took the first five Sri Lankan wickets for only six runs, easily the lowest score at the fall of the fifth wicket in any one-day international. It took Muttiah Muralitharan's late hitting to get Sri Lanka home and deny Bangladesh a first major trophy.

The highlight of the year was undoubtedly the tour of the West Indies, where Bangladesh swept away a depleted home side in both the Test and one-day series. When Bangladesh embarked on the trip, they had only one Test win to show from 59 matches, a solitary victory against Zimbabwe in January 2005. But after the two Tests in the Caribbean, that number had tripled: a first overseas series victory followed the first win abroad, to give long-suffering supporters a lot to cheer.

Admittedly, the glory days of West Indies cricket became a sepia-tinted picture long ago, and they were in a complete shambles when Bangladesh arrived. The first-choice players boycotted the series on the eve of the First Test in the latest round of a long-running dispute over contracts. A second-string team was hastily cobbled together, but that doesn't make Bangladesh's achievement discreditable.

They had to contend with losing their captain and premier pace bowler Mashrafe bin Mortaza with a serious knee injury on the third morning of the First Test. They also found themselves saddled with the unusual tag of favourites, which put enormous pressure on the young side. To make things worse, even on the morning of the First Test Bangladesh were in the dark about the make-up of the opposition team.

That Bangladesh came out of these difficulties with flying colours, remaining unbeaten until the final day of the tour when they lost a Twenty20 international, was laudable, and much of the credit should go to Shakib Al Hasan. He led from the front with bat and ball, besides coping with the unexpected burden of captaincy. Only in his third year in international cricket, and appointed vice-captain before this tour, Shakib responded superbly, turning out to be an inspirational leader. He continued to dazzle throughout the year, becoming the new poster boy of Bangladesh cricket. He was adjudged the Test player of the year by the *Wisden Cricketer* magazine, and ranked top of the ICC's list of one-day all-rounders. Later he was signed by Worcestershire for 2010, becoming the first Bangladeshi to be contracted by an English first-class county.

The year saw other changes at the helm in the cricket team as well as the board. Mohammad Ashraful was sacked after the debacle of the World Twenty20 in England, where Bangladesh fell at the first fence after losing to Ireland. A. H. M. Mostafa Kamal, a ruling party MP, was nominated as the new Bangladesh Cricket Board president, replacing Lt-General Sina Ibne Jamali. Although all the board directors are elected, the president continued to be nominated by the government.

TRI-NATION TOURNAMENT, 2008-09

1. Sri Lanka   2. Bangladesh   3. Zimbabwe

For a thrilling period in the final of this low-key tournament Bangladesh looked set to pull off a stunning victory over one of one-day cricket's leading lights: Sri Lanka, chasing 153, slumped to a scarcely believable six for five. Later still they were 114 for eight, only for Muttiah Muralitharan, so often a bowling thorn in Bangladeshi sides, to turn batting hero. In the end Sri Lanka got home by two wickets.

None of this had looked likely after the first match, when unfancied Zimbabwe stunned the hosts with a victory that threatened to knock them out of their own party – but then Zimbabwe's heavy defeat by Sri Lanka, followed by Bangladesh's upset victory over Sri Lanka (complete with a vital bonus point), set up the intriguing finale.

NATIONAL SQUADS

Bangladesh *Mohammad Ashraful, Enamul Haque, jun., Junaid Siddique, Mahbubul Alam, Mahmudullah, Mashrafe bin Mortaza, Mehrab Hossain, jun., Mushfiqur Rahim, Naeem Islam, Nazmul Hossain, Raqibul Hasan, Rubel Hossain, Shakib Al Hasan, Tamim Iqbal. *Coach:* J. D. Siddons.

Sri Lanka *D. P. M. D. Jayawardene, C. R. D. Fernando, S. T. Jayasuriya, S. H. T. Kandamby, C. K. Kapugedera, K. M. D. N. Kulasekara, M. F. Maharoof, A. D. Mathews, B. A. W. Mendis, M. T. T. Mirando, J. Mubarak, M. Muralitharan, K. T. G. D. Prasad, K. C. Sangakkara, W. U. Tharanga. *Coach:* T. H. Bayliss.

Zimbabwe *P. Utseya, E. Chigumbura, A. G. Cremer, K. M. Dabengwa, H. Masakadza, S. Matsikenyeri, C. B. Mpofu, T. Mupariwa, F. Mutizwa, R. W. Price, E. C. Rainsford, V. Sibanda, T. Taibu, M. N. Waller, S. C. Williams. *Coach:* W. R. Chawaguta.

* *Captain.*

Note: Matches in this section were not first-class.

At Mirpur, January 10, 2009. **Zimbabwe won by 38 runs.** Toss: Bangladesh. **Zimbabwe 205-9** (50 overs) (S. Matsikenyeri 39, E. Chigumbura 64; Shakib Al Hasan 3-23, Naeem Islam 3-32); **Bangladesh 167** (46.2 overs) (Shakib Al Hasan 52). *Zimbabwe 4 pts. One-day international debut:* Mahbubul Alam (Bangladesh). *Man of the Match:* E. Chigumbura.

Bangladesh were never really in the hunt once Junaid Siddique and Mushfiqur Rahim both departed for ducks, leaving them 10-2. Three run-outs hindered their cause. Zimbabwe had earlier been 94-5 before Chigumbura's responsible 95-ball innings. It was Zimbabwe's first one-day win over a Test-playing nation since they beat West Indies in November 2007.

At Mirpur, January 12, 2009. **Sri Lanka won by 130 runs.** Toss: Zimbabwe. **Sri Lanka 210-6** (50 overs) (W. U. Tharanga 43, J. Mubarak 31, A. D. Mathews 52*; E. C. Rainsford 3-41); **Zimbabwe 80** (28.2 overs) (K. M. D. N. Kulasekara 3-13, B. A. W. Mendis 3-15). *Sri Lanka 5 pts. Man of the Match:* A. D. Mathews.

After early problems against Kulasekara, who reduced them to 27-3, Zimbabwe collapsed completely against the spin of Mendis and Muralitharan (3–1–4–2). Only Stuart Matsikenyeri (15) reached double figures, although there were 16 extras. When he dismissed Ray Price, Mendis took his 50th wicket in his 19th one-day international, beating the previous record of 23 by India's Ajit Agarkar. Earlier Sri Lanka had encountered problems of their own, slipping from 73-1 to 97-5, but Mathews put on 69 with Mubarak and 44 with Thilan Thushara Mirando (28*). Sri Lanka's big victory earned them a bonus point.*

BANGLADESH v SRI LANKA

At Mirpur, January 14, 2009. Bangladesh won by five wickets. Bangladesh 5 pts. Toss: Bangladesh. One-day international debut: Rubel Hossain.

Bangladesh recorded only their second victory over Sri Lanka in 25 one-day internationals, and did so by a wide enough margin to claim the bonus point which propelled them past Zimbabwe and into the final. In a match reduced by bad light to 31 overs a side, the home team were indebted to Shakib Al Hasan, who steadied them after a nervous start. Needing only 148 to win after Sri Lanka's batting misfired again, two run-outs helped reduce Bangladesh to 11 for three. But Shakib took charge, hitting ten fours and two sixes in a forthright 69-ball innings that hurried them over the line. Mohammad Ashraful called it his side's "best victory".

Man of the Match: Shakib Al Hasan.

Sri Lanka

W. U. Tharanga lbw b Mashrafe bin Mortaza	0	K. M. D. N. Kulasekara c Naeem Islam	
S. T. Jayasuriya		b Rubel Hossain .	5
c and b Mashrafe bin Mortaza .	54	M. Muralitharan not out	6
†K. C. Sangakkara b Mashrafe bin Mortaza .	0	B. A. W. Mendis c Mohammad Ashraful	
*D. P. M. D. Jayawardene c Rubel Hossain		b Rubel Hossain .	0
b Naeem Islam .	28		
C. K. Kapugedera b Mahbubul Alam	28	L-b 3, w 10, n-b 1	14
J. Mubarak run out	10		
A. D. Mathews c Mashrafe bin Mortaza		1/0 (1) 2/4 (3) 3/75 (4) (30.3 overs)	147
b Rubel Hossain .	2	4/95 (2) 5/124 (6) 6/128 (7)	
M. T. T. Mirando c Mushfiqur Rahim		7/130 (5) 8/135 (9) 9/141 (8)	
b Rubel Hossain .	0	10/147 (11)	6 overs: 27-2

Mashrafe bin Mortaza 7–1–25–3; Mahbubul Alam 4–0–25–1; Rubel Hossain 5.3–0–33–4; Shakib Al Hasan 6–0–24–0; Naeem Islam 6–0–24–1; Mahmudullah 2–0–13–0.

Bangladesh

Tamim Iqbal run out	9	Naeem Islam not out	12
Junaid Siddique run out	0		
†Mushfiqur Rahim c Sangakkara b Mirando	1	L-b 5, w 3	8
*Mohammad Ashraful c Jayasuriya			
b Kulasekara .	26	1/0 (2) 2/10 (3) (5 wkts, 23.5 overs)	151
Shakib Al Hasan not out	92	3/11 (1) 4/102 (4)	
Raqibul Hasan c Muralitharan b Mendis . . .	3	5/126 (6)	6 overs: 29-3

Mahmudullah, Mashrafe bin Mortaza, Mahbubul Alam and Rubel Hossain did not bat.

Kulasekara 6–1–45–1; Mirando 4–1–12–1; Mendis 6.5–0–37–1; Mathews 1–0–12–0; Muralitharan 6–0–40–0.

Umpires: B. R. Doctrove and Nadir Shah.
Third umpire: A. F. M. Akhtaruddin. Referee: A. G. Hurst

QUALIFYING TABLE

	Played	Won	Lost	Bonus Points	Points	Net run-rate
Sri Lanka	2	1	1	1	5	1.27
Bangladesh	2	1	1	1	5	-0.03
Zimbabwe	2	1	1	0	4	-0.92

Win = 4 pts. One bonus point awarded for achieving victory with a run-rate 1.25 times that of the opposition. Net run-rate is calculated by subtracting runs conceded per over from runs scored per over.

FINAL

BANGLADESH v SRI LANKA

At Mirpur, January 16, 2009. Sri Lanka won by two wickets. Toss: Sri Lanka.

When Sri Lanka were reeling at six for five, the Bangladesh nation was dreaming of glory in a significant one-day tournament. The beginning of the Sri Lankan reply certainly proved the perfect start for Bangladesh: Jayasuriya was run out from the first ball of the innings, then Nazmul Hossain took three quick wickets. The dream remained alive despite Sangakkara's obdurate 133-ball innings and, when he and Kulasekara departed in the space of three balls in a double-wicket maiden from Shakib Al Hasan, leaving Sri Lanka 114 for eight in the 44th over, it really did look all over. But Muralitharan marched in, and flailed away while Maharoof watched approvingly. Murali spanked four fours and two sixes from just 16 balls – all but two of his runs came off two overs from Rubel Hossain – and Bangladesh's hearts were finally broken with 11 balls remaining. "It is tough on them, especially after trying so hard," said Sangakkara afterwards, "but it was not to be. I guess our experience in finals won us the game."

Man of the Match: K. C. Sangakkara.   *Man of the Series:* Shakib Al Hasan.

Bangladesh

Tamim Iqbal c Sangakkara b Kulasekara . .	18	Nazmul Hossain lbw b Muralitharan		0
Junaid Siddique c Sangakkara b Kulasekara	1	Rubel Hossain c Kapugedera b Mendis		0
†Mushfiqur Rahim b Kulasekara	4			
*Mohammad Ashraful c Sangakkara				
b Maharoof .	13			
Shakib Al Hasan c Sangakkara b Mirando .	9	B 4, l-b 2, w 10, n-b 1		17
Raqibul Hasan not out	43			
Mahmudullah b Muralitharan	26	1/8 (2) 2/12 (3) 3/34 (4) (49.4 overs)		152
Naeem Islam c Mubarak b Mendis	21	4/42 (1) 5/54 (5) 6/98 (7)		
Mashrafe bin Mortaza c Kapugedera		7/151 (8) 8/151 (9) 9/151 (10)		
b Mendis .	0	10/152 (11)	10 overs: 29-2	

Kulasekara 8–1–19–3; Mirando 7–2–20–1; Maharoof 8–0–33–1; Mendis 9.4–0–24–3; Muralitharan 10–1–33–2; Jayasuriya 7–1–17–0.

Sri Lanka

W. U. Tharanga c Mushfiqur Rahim		J. Mubarak run out		16
b Nazmul Hossain .	2	M. F. Maharoof not out		38
S. T. Jayasuriya run out	0	K. M. D. N. Kulasekara b Shakib Al Hasan		0
†K. C. Sangakkara c and b Shakib Al Hasan	59	M. Muralitharan not out		33
*D. P. M. D. Jayawardene c Mushfiqur		L-b 2, w 1		3
Rahim b Nazmul Hossain .	0			
C. K. Kapugedera c Junaid Siddique		1/0 (2) 2/4 (1) (8 wkts, 48.1 overs)		153
b Mashrafe bin Mortaza .	1	3/4 (4) 4/5 (5) 5/6 (6)		
M. T. T. Mirando b Nazmul Hossain	1	6/51 (7) 7/114 (3) 8/114 (9)	10 overs: 15-5	

B. A. W. Mendis did not bat.

Mashrafe bin Mortaza 10–1–18–1; Nazmul Hossain 10–3–30–3; Shakib Al Hasan 10–2–22–2; Rubel Hossain 9–2–52–0; Naeem Islam 9.1–2–29–0.

Umpires: B. R. Doctrove and Enamul Haque, sen.
Third umpire: A. F. M. Akhtaruddin.   Referee: A. G. Hurst.

BANGLADESH v ZIMBABWE, 2008-09

One-day internationals (3): Bangladesh 2, Zimbabwe 1

After the tri-nation tournament also involving Sri Lanka, the Zimbabweans stayed on in Bangladesh to contest three more one-day internationals, and pulled off another surprise by winning the first. Bangladesh recovered their composure to take the other two, and with them a series in which neither side threatened to reach 200. The squads remained the same as for the preceding triangular tournament.

Note: Matches in this section which were not first-class are signified by a dagger.

At Bogra, January 6, 7, 8, 2009. **Zimbabweans won by 195 runs.** Toss: Zimbabweans. **Zimbabweans 89** (Sajidul Islam 5-14, Nazmul Hossain 4-28) **and 273** (H. Masakadza 66, S. Matsikenyeri 42, T. Taibu 70; Nazmul Hossain 4-49, Saqlain Sajib 3-62); **Bangladesh Cricket Board Academy 59** (E. C. Rainsford 3-27, E. Chigumbura 3-7) **and 108** (Kamrul Islam 31, Naeem Islam 36; T. Mupariwa 3-21, R. W. Price 6-21).

Twenty-two wickets fell on the opening day, when both first innings combined lasted only 45.1 overs. Acting-captain Masakadza and Taibu led the Zimbabweans to a more respectable 273 second time round, despite Nazmul Hossain claiming four wickets for the second time in the match, but the Academy collapsed again and Price completed victory 15 balls into the third day.

†At Mirpur, January 19, 2009. **First one-day international: Zimbabwe won by two wickets.** Toss: Bangladesh. **Bangladesh 124** (48.1 overs) (R. W. Price 4-22, K. M. Dabengwa 3-15); **Zimbabwe 127-8** (49.2 overs) (Mashrafe bin Mortaza 3-21, Shakib Al Hasan 3-11). *One-day international debut:* M. N. Waller (Zimbabwe). *Man of the Match:* R. W. Price.

In a low-scoring match, Zimbabwe completed their second successive defeat of Bangladesh. Price and Dabengwa throttled the home side's innings, but Zimbabwe also struggled on a slow, low pitch. They slumped to 44-6, and later 92-8, when Bangladesh looked favourites – but Price (23* from 52 balls) and Tawanda Mupariwa (10* from 22) survived until the end. Price won the match with successive fours off Nazmul Hossain from the first two balls of the final over. Debutant Malcolm Waller is the son of the former Zimbabwe Test player Andy.

†At Mirpur, January 21, 2009. **Second one-day international: Bangladesh won by six wickets.** Toss: Bangladesh. **Zimbabwe 160-9** (50 overs) (S. C. Williams 59, P. Utseya 38; Nazmul Hossain 3-28); **Bangladesh 164-4** (44.5 overs) (Mehrab Hossain 43, Raqibul Hasan 52*). *Man of the Match:* Raqibul Hasan.

Bangladesh levelled the series with a relatively simple victory on another bowler-friendly surface. Zimbabwe were reeling at 47-6 before a stand of 96 in almost 30 overs between Williams (who faced 89 balls and hit only four boundaries) and Utseya (101 balls, three singles). Mehrab Hossain jun. (85 balls) and Raqibul Hasan (seven fours from 100 balls) held the Bangladesh reply together.

†At Mirpur, January 23, 2009. **Third one-day international: Bangladesh won by six wickets.** Reduced to 37 overs a side. Toss: Bangladesh. **Zimbabwe 119-9** (37 overs) (S. C. Williams 38; Mashrafe bin Mortaza 3-26, Shakib Al Hasan 3-15); **Bangladesh 121-4** (32.3 overs) (Tamim Iqbal 34, Shakib Al Hasan 33*). *Man of the Match:* Mashrafe bin Mortaza. *Man of the Series:* Shakib Al Hasan.

Bangladesh came from behind to pinch the series with victory in a match which started late after thick morning fog. Zimbabwe were set back by Mashrafe bin Mortaza's fine opening spell of 6–0–16–3, and struggled to reach a competitive total. Bangladesh were never in much trouble, despite another accurate spell from slow left-armer Ray Price (7–2–9–2).

BANGLADESH v ZIMBABWE, 2009-10

One-day internationals (5): Bangladesh 4, Zimbabwe 1

Bangladesh had toured Zimbabwe for five one-day internationals earlier in 2009, and now returned the favour. In the end, the scoreline was the same, although this time Zimbabwe won the first match, which meant that interest was sustained for a little longer. On spin-friendly pitches, though, the overall result was never really in doubt: Bangladesh's assorted spinners took 37 of the 44 wickets to fall to their bowlers. The best match was the last, which the home side sneaked by the skin of their teeth with their last pair at the crease – but that followed an embarrassing fourth game, when Zimbabwe chose to bat first but were skittled for 44.

Neither side were led by the original choice as captain. Bangladesh's selectors had reappointed Mashrafe bin Mortaza, but he had not fully recovered from the knee surgery that had followed his early return from the Caribbean after just one Test: Shakib Al Hasan continued as stand-in skipper. For Zimbabwe, Prosper Utseya injured his ankle in the first one-day international, and Hamilton Masakadza deputised for the rest of the series. Zimbabwe suffered an even more crucial injury blow when Tatenda Taibu tweaked a hamstring in the second game, and missed the last three matches.

ZIMBABWEAN SQUAD

P. Utseya *(captain)*, C. J. Chibhabha, E. Chigumbura, C. K. Coventry, A. G. Cremer, K. M. Jarvis, H. Masakadza, S. Matsikenyeri, C. B. Mpofu, F. Mutizwa, R. W. Price, T. Taibu, B. R. M. Taylor, M. A. Vermeulen, M. N. Waller. *Coach:* H. H. Streak.

Note: Matches in this section were not first-class.

At Fatullah, October 23, 2009. **Bangladesh Cricket Board XI won by four wickets.** Toss: Zimbabweans. **Zimbabweans 206** (42 overs) (B. R. M. Taylor 36, T. Taibu 62; Tareq Aziz 3-40, Talha Jubair 3-45); **Bangladesh Cricket Board XI 207-6** (44.5 overs) (Faisal Hossain 81*, Saghir Hossain 35*; C. J. Chibhabha 3-32).

The Zimbabweans were 128-3, but lost their last seven wickets for 78 in 15 overs. Then the Board XI were 122-6 in the 33rd over before Faisal Hossain, who hit nine fours and two sixes, carried his team over the line in an unbroken partnership of 85 with wicketkeeper Saghir Hossain.

At Fatullah, October 25, 2009. **Zimbabweans won by 192 runs.** Toss: Bangladesh Cricket Board XI. **Zimbabweans 335-5** (50 overs) (B. R. M. Taylor 139, T. Taibu 68, E. Chigumbura 45, M. N. Waller 37*); **Bangladesh Cricket Board XI 143** (36.4 overs) (Faisal Hossain 30; C. J. Chibhabha 3-29).

Taylor, who hit nine fours and six sixes, put on 188 for the second wicket with Taibu as the Zimbabweans racked up a huge score. Imrul Kayes fell to the first ball of the Board XI's reply, and regular wickets tumbled after that.

At Mirpur, October 27, 2009 (day/night). **First one-day international: Zimbabwe won by five wickets.** Toss: Zimbabwe. **Bangladesh 186** (46.5 overs) (Mushfiqur Rahim 56, Dolar Mahmud 41; E. Chigumbura 3-27); **Zimbabwe 189-5** (34.4 overs) (C. K. Coventry 32, S. Matsikenyeri 47*, E. Chigumbura 60*; Abdur Razzak 3-36). *Man of the Match:* E. Chigumbura.

Zimbabwe upset the odds with a straightforward victory in the first match. It might have been even easier: Bangladesh were 124-8 before No. 10 Dolar Mahmud hit 41 from 30 balls and put on 54 with Mushfiqur Rahim, who collected five fours from 77 balls. Zimbabwe made a decent start, then lost three wickets at 39 in the eighth over, Abdur Razzak's first, which would have been a triple-wicket maiden had the first delivery not gone for five wides. Matsikenyeri helped Coventry add 36, then put on 99 for the sixth wicket with Chigumbura, whose 60 came from 50 balls. Play was briefly held up when a section of the crowd threw plastic bottles on to the field. Prosper Utseya suffered an ankle injury, which kept him out of the rest of the series: Hamilton Masakadza took over as captain.

At Mirpur, October 29, 2009 (day/night). **Second one-day international: Bangladesh won by seven wickets.** Toss: Zimbabwe. **Zimbabwe 219** (47.2 overs) (H. Masakadza 34, C. J. Chibhabha 39, T. Taibu 38, M. N. Waller 40; Abdur Razzak 5-29); **Bangladesh 221-3** (29.3 overs) (Raqibul Hasan 39*, Shakib Al Hasan 105*). *Man of the Match:* Abdur Razzak.

Bangladesh levelled the series with an emphatic victory, completed when Shakib Al Hasan hit Chibhabha for two fours, the first to reach his century in just 68 balls: Shakib, who hit 15 fours and three sixes in all, dominated a fourth-wicket stand of 165 with Raqibul Hasan, who faced 75 deliveries. Earlier, Zimbabwe's batsmen tended to get out when set: five men passed 20, but none made more than 40 as all ten wickets fell to the spinners.

At Mirpur, October 31, 2009 (day/night). **Third one-day international: Bangladesh won by four wickets.** Toss: Bangladesh. **Zimbabwe 196** (41.1 overs) (H. Masakadza 84; Nazmul Hossain 3-13, Enamul Haque, jun. 3-45); **Bangladesh 198-6** (40.4 overs) (Tamim Iqbal 80, Mohammad Ashraful 63; K. M. Jarvis 3-38). *Man of the Match:* Tamim Iqbal.

Masakadza led from the front with 84 from 79 balls, hitting 12 fours and a six and passing 1,000 runs in one-day internationals in 2009, but no one could stay with him for long. Bangladesh seemed to be hurtling to victory while Tamim Iqbal (who hit ten fours and two sixes) and Mohammad Ashraful were putting on 98 for the second wicket, then Ashraful and Raqibul Hasan added 53, but from 175-2 four wickets tumbled for 19 runs, making the scoreline appear more respectable for the visitors. The win put Bangladesh ahead of Zimbabwe 23–22 in ODIs between the two countries.

BANGLADESH v ZIMBABWE

Fourth One-Day International

At Chittagong, November 3, 2009. Bangladesh won by six wickets. Toss: Zimbabwe.

Rarely has a captain misread a pitch so spectacularly: Zimbabwe won the toss, chose to bat... and were rolled over for 44 as the ball bounced or skidded through on a surface taking a lot of turn. "It looked like a good batting track, but it was too slow for a one-day wicket," said stand-in captain Masakadza afterwards. "Some guys gave their wickets away but, having said that, the wicket did play quite a big role. The ball was holding up and there was too much spin on it." There had been only four lower totals in one-day internationals, two of them by Zimbabwe, but it was the first time Bangladesh had bowled anyone out for less than 100. Zimbabwe were soon floundering at eight for four, then after some brief resistance from Waller and Matsikenyeri – the only players to reach

LOWEST ONE-DAY INTERNATIONAL TOTALS AGAINST BANGLADESH

44	by Zimbabwe at Chittagong	2009-10	146	by Zimbabwe at Mirpur.....	2006-07
105	by Hong Kong at Colombo ..	2004	**147**	**by Sri Lanka at Mirpur....**	**2008-09**
118	by Kenya at Nairobi........	2006	153	by Scotland at Chittagong ...	2006-07
130	by Zimbabwe at Jaipur......	2006-07	161	by Pakistan at Northampton .	1999
132	by Scotland at Mirpur	2006-07	161	by Kenya at Khulna........	2005-06

Completed (all-out) innings only.

double figures – the last six wickets folded for 12 runs. Bangladesh themselves lost four wickets to the spinners in the space of 17 balls, but it was never going to change the outcome. The match was over before the scheduled mid-innings break at the ground now called the Zohur Ahmed Chowdhury Stadium, but formerly known as the Chittagong Divisional Stadium.

Man of the Match: Nazmul Hossain.

Zimbabwe

*H. Masakadza c Mohammad Ashraful b Nazmul Hossain	2	E. Chigumbura c and b Enamul Haque	4	
M. A. Vermeulen lbw b Abdur Razzak	3	A. G. Cremer not out	7	
†B. R. M. Taylor c and b Abdur Razzak	0	R. W. Price lbw b Shakib Al Hasan	0	
C. K. Coventry c Mushfiqur Rahim b Nazmul Hossain	1	K. M. Jarvis c and b Shakib Al Hasan	0	
M. N. Waller c Nazmul Hossain b Shakib Al Hasan	13	W 3	3	
S. Matsikenyeri c Mohammad Ashraful b Enamul Haque	11			
C. J. Chibhabha b Enamul Haque	0			

1/2 (1) 2/3 (3) 3/4 (4)   (24.5 overs)   44
4/8 (2) 5/32 (6) 6/32 (7)
7/36 (5) 8/36 (8) 9/39 (10)
10/44 (11)   10 overs: 19-4

Nazmul Hossain 6–2–10–2; Abdur Razzak 5–0–10–2; Enamul Haque 7–2–16–3; Shakib Al Hasan 6.5–1–8–3.

Bangladesh

Tamim Iqbal c Cremer b Price	22	†Mushfiqur Rahim not out	2
Junaid Siddique c Vermeulen b Cremer	8	L-b 2, w 4, n-b 2	8
Mohammad Ashraful lbw b Price	0		
Raqibul Hasan not out	9	1/33 (1) 2/33 (3) (4 wkts, 11.5 overs) 49	
Naeem Islam c Chibhabha b Cremer	0	3/36 (2) 4/38 (5) 10 overs: 40-4	

*Shakib Al Hasan, Mahmudullah, Abdur Razzak, Enamul Haque jun. and Nazmul Hossain did not bat.

Jarvis 2–0–21–0; Chigumbura 1–0–1–0; Matsikenyeri 2–0–9–0; Price 4–2–5–2; Cremer 2.5–0–11–2.

Umpires: Aleem Dar and Nadir Shah.
Third umpire: Sharfuddoula. Referee: R. S. Madugalle.

At Chittagong, November 5, 2009. **Fifth one-day international: Bangladesh won by one wicket.** Toss: Bangladesh. **Zimbabwe 221-9** (50 overs) (B. R. M. Taylor 118*, E. Chigumbura 38; Abdur Razzak 3-56, Shakib Al Hasan 3-29, Mahmudullah 3-52); **Bangladesh 222-9** (49 overs) (Raqibul Hasan 31, Mahmudullah 33, Naeem Islam 73*). *Man of the Match:* Naeem Islam. *Man of the Series:* Abdur Razzak.

Bangladesh took the series 4–1, but the final match was a close-run affair: after reaching 174-5 in their chase for 222, Bangladesh lost four wickets for 13, and it was left to the last pair to take them over the line. Naeem Islam led the way, and No. 11 Nazmul Hossain faced just four balls – and contributed a single – as the last 35 runs came from 25 balls. Naeem hit four fours and four sixes. Earlier, Taylor finally reached his first one-day international century, in his 90th match, after being out three times in the nineties, but a middle-order collapse from 80-2 to 113-7 compromised Zimbabwe's chances. Abdur Razzak finished with 15 wickets in the series at 11.46: no one else took more than seven.

BANGLADESH U-19 v ENGLAND U-19, 2009-10

Paul Edwards

Under-19 Test: Bangladesh 1, England 0
Under-19 one-day internationals (7): Bangladesh 5, England 2

England's Under-19 tour of Bangladesh late in 2009 was as tough as John Abrahams hoped it would be. Abrahams, the ECB's elite player development manager, opted to take the country's brightest young talents to the subcontinent precisely because the conditions would be so different from those they were used to in England, or those they would encounter during the Under-19 World Cup in New Zealand early in 2010. Abrahams wanted to make sure his charges would be extended and tested. He achieved his aim.

Playing cricket in Bangladesh offers the ambitious young cricketer some challenges: an unfamiliar climate, a different culture, and slow, turning wickets with battalions of spinners eager to bowl on them. Given that eight of England's players were making their Under-19 Test debuts at Chittagong, and that nine of them played their first youth one-day internationals on the tour, it was not surprising that they struggled. A batting collapse on the final day of the Test went a long way towards explaining England's two-wicket defeat, and two further collective failures in the 50-over games played a large part in Azeem Rafiq's side losing four one-day internationals inside a week.

"We played pretty good cricket in the Test, and we were disappointed to lose that game on the last day when we deserved better," said Mick Newell, the coach, after the fourth limited-overs international. "But in the one-dayers, apart from the first game where we lost by one run, we've been outplayed." Yet some of Newell's charges rose to the challenge, not least slow left-arm Danny Briggs, whose 42 overs on the last two days at Chittagong nearly secured a famous victory instead of a gut-wrenching defeat.

Yorkshire's Joe Root scored two of the four half-centuries England mustered in the long-winded seven-match one-day series, and his 194 runs earned him the series award, even though Bangladesh's Tasamul Haque scored more runs (210). Off-spinner and captain Azeem Rafiq took 13 wickets at 19.07 apiece in the 50-over matches, although he was just pipped by slow left-armer Shaker Ahmed (15 at 15.06) as the leading wicket-taker. Yet even after Michael Bates's doughty resistance is acknowledged and the debilitating virus that forced James Goodman home early is taken into account, no rational critic could deny the superiority of the hosts or the effect of the vice-like grip in which their four or five spinners frequently held the English batsmen. If players of the quality of Mahmudul Hasan, Anamul Haque and Shaker Ahmed can mature, the prospects for Bangladesh cricket are pleasingly bright.

ENGLAND UNDER-19 TOURING PARTY

Azeem Rafiq (*captain*), A. M. Bates, P. M. Best, S. W. Billings, D. R. Briggs, N. L. Buck, J. C. Buttler, C. D. J. Dent, M. P. Dunn, J. E. Goodman, C. J. Haggett, A. Javid, D. A. Payne, C. G. Roebuck, J. E. Root, B. A. Stokes, J. M. Vince. *Coach:* M. Newell. *Manager:* J. Abrahams.

Note: Matches in this section were not first-class.

At Narayanganj Osmani Stadium, Fatullah, October 12, 13, 2009. **Bangladesh Cricket Board XI v England Under-19. Abandoned.**
   No play was possible on a saturated ground, and the teams decamped to Mirpur to play a 50-over game on the scheduled second day instead.

At Shere Bangla National Stadium, Mirpur, October 13, 2009. **Bangladesh Cricket Board XI won by four wickets.** Toss: England Under-19. **England Under-19 213** (50 overs) (B. A. Stokes 53, Azeem Rafiq 51, P. M. Best 57; Sabbir Rahman 3-51); **Bangladesh Cricket Board XI 214-6** (46 overs) (Mominul Haque 93*; N. L. Buck 3-17).
   Each side named 12 players, of whom 11 could bat and 11 field.

BANGLADESH v ENGLAND

Only Under-19 Test

At Zohur Ahmed Chowdhury Stadium, Chittagong, October 16, 17, 18, 19, 2009. Bangladesh Under-19 won by two wickets. Toss: England Under-19.
   Sixteen wickets fell on the last day at Chittagong as a hitherto slow, rain-interrupted match produced a finish to test teenage temperaments. Going into the final morning England led by 87 with eight second-innings wickets in hand, and fancied their chances of forcing a victory. But a batting order lacking the ill James Goodman collapsed to 107 all out in the face of some fine bowling by the spin-dominated Bangladesh attack, and only some resolute lower-order resistance stretched the target to a modest 157. However, the hosts found the road to victory littered with difficulties as Hampshire slow left-armer Danny Briggs took five wickets, giving him excellent match figures of eight for 96. Reduced to 118 for six, Bangladesh nevertheless found a match-winner in wicketkeeper/batsman Anamul Haque, whose unbeaten 58 was both the highest innings of the match and the best. All this excitement probably came as something of a surprise to anyone who had watched the match from the start. England's batsmen treated both the pitch and the opposition attack with respect in the first two days, grinding out a total of 201 for seven in the 108 overs allowed by the rain. The captain, Azeem Rafiq, occupied the crease for 169 minutes for 53. Bangladesh found the conditions scarcely more conducive to fluent strokeplay on the third day, when Nathan Buck made early inroads before Briggs tied down the middle order. Haque's 66-ball 48 was a portent of his later heroics.
   Man of the Match: Anamul Haque.
   Close of play: First day, England Under-19 125-5 (Azeem Rafiq 11, Best 16); Second day, England Under-19 201-7 (Bates 18, Haggett 6); Third day, England Under-19 38-2 (Root 13, Roebuck 0).

England Under-19

J. E. Root c Anamul Haque b Sabbir Rahman	21	– c Mominul Haque b Shaker Ahmed . 13
C. D. J. Dent b Mahmudul Hasan	45	– c Mominul Haque b Mahmudul Hasan 25
J. E. Goodman c Imamul Hossain b Noor Hossain .	8	– absent ill
C. G. Roebuck st Anamul Haque b Noor Hossain	2	– b Alauddin Babu 0
B. A. Stokes c Anamul Haque b Noor Hossain	11	– c Anamul Haque b Alauddin Babu . . 0
*Azeem Rafiq lbw b Alauddin Babu	53	– c Sabbir Rahman b Shaker Ahmed . . 4
P. M. Best c Anamul Haque b Shaker Ahmed.	24	– (3) lbw b Mahmudul Hasan 0
†M. D. Bates c Amit Majumder b Shaker Ahmed . . .	22	– (7) b Sabbir Rahman 27
C. J. Haggett c Anamul Haque b Shaker Ahmed . .	14	– (8) b Sabbir Rahman 18
D. R. Briggs not out	4	– (9) c Shaker Ahmed b Mominul Haque 11
N. L. Buck c Mahmudul Hasan b Shaker Ahmed . .	0	– (10) not out 2
B 9, l-b 5, n-b 3	17	B 1, l-b 2, w 1, n-b 3 7

1/64 (1) 2/72 (2) 3/81 (4) 4/90 (3) (118.5 overs) 221   1/37 (2) 2/37 (3)   (68.4 overs) 107
5/97 (5) 6/147 (7) 7/182 (6)   3/38 (1) 4/38 (4)
8/208 (8) 9/221 (9) 10/221 (11)   5/42 (5) 6/46 (6) 7/85 (7) 8/95 (8)
                                     9/107 (9)

Abul Hasan 15–6–32–0; Alauddin Babu 14–4–22–1; Shaker Ahmed 27.5–7–47–4; Noor Hossain 25–3–46–3; Mahmudul Hasan 22–8–37–1; Sabbir Rahman 12–6–21–1; Mominul Haque 3–1–2–0. *Second Innings*—Alauddin Babu 9–2–18–2; Saikat Ali 3–0–5–0; Shaker Ahmed

22–11–32–2; Mahmudul Hasan 12–3–20–2; Noor Hossain 13–4–22–0; Sabbir Rahman 8–4–7–2; Mominul Haque 1.4–1–0–1.

Bangladesh Under 19

Amit Majumder lbw b Buck	1	– c and b Briggs	20
Saikat Ali b Best	45	– b Briggs	29
Imamul Hossain b Buck	4	– c sub b Best	9
Mominul Haque c Stokes b Azeem Rafiq	18	– c sub b Briggs	1
†Anamul Haque run out	46	– not out	58
*Mahmudul Hasan lbw b Briggs	21	– c Bates b Buck	17
Sabbir Rahman c Roebuck b Briggs	12	– lbw b Briggs	0
Noor Hossain c Azeem Rafiq b Briggs	1	– (9) c Dent b Buck	5
Alauddin Babu c Bates b Stokes	3	– (8) c and b Briggs	4
Abul Hasan c Bates b Buck	7	– not out	9
Shaker Ahmed not out	3		
L-b 2, n-b 9	11	L-b 4, n-b 1	5

1/14 (1) 2/20 (3) 3/45 (4) 4/111 (5) (74 overs) 172
5/137 (2) 6/149 (6) 7/153 (8) 8/160 (9)
9/162 (7) 10/172 (10)

1/50 (1) (8 wkts, 47.1 overs) 157
2/55 (2) 3/57 (4)
4/91 (3) 5/113 (6) 6/118 (7) 7/128 (8)
8/142 (9)

Buck 13–5–23–3; Haggett 4–1–7–0; Azeem Rafiq 24–4–75–1; Stokes 7–5–8–1; Briggs 22–6–46–3; Best 4–0–11–1. *Second Innings*—Buck 11.1–0–52–2; Stokes 3–0–14–0; Azeem Rafiq 8–1–23–0; Briggs 20–1–50–5; Best 5–1–14–1.

Umpires: Mahbubur Rahman and Mizanur Rahman.
Referee: Raqibul Hasan.

At Zohur Ahmed Chowdhury Stadium, Chittagong. October 21, 2009. **England Under-19 won by 117 runs.** Toss: England Under-19. **England Under-19 258-8** (50 overs) (J. E. Root 65, J. M. Vince 87, B. A Stokes 47; Mominul Haque 3-22); **Bangladesh Cricket Board XI 141** (45.3 overs) (B. A. Stokes 3-21).
Each side named 12 players, of whom 11 could bat and 11 field.

At Zohur Ahmed Chowdhury Stadium, Chittagong, October 23, 2009. **First one-day international: Bangladesh Under-19 won by one run.** Toss: England Under-19. **Bangladesh Under-19 212-9** (50 overs) (Mominul Haque 31, Mahmudul Hasan 31, Noor Hossain 34, Abul Hasan 32*; N. L. Buck 3-38, Azeem Rafiq 3-18); **England Under-19 211-9** (50 overs) (J. E. Root 54, B. A. Stokes 45; Shaker Ahmed 4-43). *Man of the Match:* Shaker Ahmed.
Noor Hossain and Abul Hasan's ninth-wicket partnership of 56 proved vital in helping Bangladesh secure a thrilling victory in the first match of the series. Nevertheless, England needed only 53 off 14.1 overs with six wickets in hand when opener Joe Root was run out. Slow left-armer Shaker Ahmed was easily the pick of the Bangladeshi attack.

At Narayanganj Osmani Stadium, Fatullah, October 26, 2009. **Second one-day international: Bangladesh Under-19 won by seven wickets.** Toss: Bangladesh Under-19. **England Under-19 97** (35.4 overs) (Saikat Ali 3-11); **Bangladesh Under-19 100-3** (22.1 overs) (Anamul Haque 56). *Man of the Match:* Saikat Ali.
England collapsed from 41-0 to 73-9 in 19.4 overs, and their paltry total was overhauled with ease, Anamul Haque facing 65 balls and hitting seven fours and two sixes.

At Narayanganj Osmani Stadium, Fatullah, October 27, 2009. **Third one-day international: Bangladesh Under-19 won by 87 runs.** Toss: England Under-19. **Bangladesh Under-19 251-8** (50 overs) (Nurul Hasan 40, Tasamul Haque 66, Mahmudul Hasan 35; C. J. Haggett 4-32, Azeem Rafiq 3-64); **England Under-19 164** (43.1 overs) (A. M. Bates 33; Mahmudul Hasan 3-46, Sabbir Rahman 3-22). *Man of the Match:* Mahmudul Hasan.
Somerset seamer Calum Haggett bowled well to take four wickets, but his efforts were not enough to save England from a third successive defeat. Uninhibited hitting by Bangladesh's lower order

helped them to set a target of five an over, but England subsided from 46-0 to 86-6, their second meek capitulation in as many days.

At Narayanganj Osmani Stadium, Fatullah, October 29, 2009. **Fourth one-day international: Bangladesh Under-19 won by four wickets.** Toss: England Under-19. **England Under-19 151** (44.4 overs) (J. E. Root 54, D. R Briggs 41; Shaker Ahmed 3-26); **Bangladesh Under-19 152-6** (34.2 overs) (Saikat Ali 46, Tasamul Haque 50*). *Man of the Match:* Saikat Ali.

Bangladesh clinched the seven-match series at the earliest opportunity, going four up with three games to play. England failed to use up their 50 overs, and were then given another lesson in how to bat on slow pitches. However, Joe Root collected his second fifty of the series and Danny Briggs had an outstanding match, hitting 41 off 40 balls then returning figures of 10–4–14–2, a contribution which delayed Bangladesh's triumph, without impairing its sweetness.

At Narayanganj Osmani Stadium, Fatullah, October 31, 2009. **Fifth one-day international: England Under-19 won by five wickets.** Toss: Bangladesh Under-19. **Bangladesh Under-19 196** (49.5 overs) (Tasamul Haque 36, Mahmudul Hasan 48, Noor Hussain 39; D. A. Payne 4-56, Azeem Rafiq 3-36); **England Under-19 197-5** (48.5 overs) (J. M. Vince 71, A. Javid 34*, A. M. Bates 31*). *Man of the Match:* J. M. Vince.

England's first victory in the seven-match one-day series amounted to something more than consolation; it reflected well on the character of the tourists, for whom Gloucestershire left-arm seamer David Payne bowled well to prevent the Bangladesh tail boosting their side's total. Hampshire's James Vince then played a polished 87-ball innings, with 11 fours, to set up a deserved win.

At Shere Bangla National Stadium, Mirpur, November 2, 2009. **Sixth one-day international: England Under-19 won by three wickets.** Toss: England Under-19. **Bangladesh Under-19 224-9** (50 overs) (Anamul Haque 74, Sabbir Rahman 53, Abul Hasan 34; C. J. Haggett 3-21); **England Under-19 225-7** (48.4 overs) (J. E. Root 48, A. M. Bates 35, A. Javid 63; Mahmudul Hasan 3-33). *Man of the Match:* A. Javid.

England's batsmen maintained their improvement by chasing down 225 with eight balls to spare. Warwickshire's Ateeq Javid played the best innings for the tourists, who provided further evidence that they were finally adjusting to the unfamiliar pitches.

At Shere Bangla National Stadium, Mirpur, November 4, 2009. **Seventh one-day international: Bangladesh Under-19 won by eight runs.** Toss: Bangladesh Under-19. **Bangladesh Under-19 206** (49.5 overs) (Saikat Ali 52, Amit Majumder 32; N. L. Buck 3-43, M. P. Dunn 3-42); **England Under-19 198** (49.1 overs) (C. G. Roebuck 40, J. C. Buttler 42, B. A. Stokes 39, Azeem Rafiq 31; Mahmudul Hasan 3-45). *Man of the Match:* Mahmudul Hasan. *Man of the Series:* J. E. Root.

Bangladesh's victory meant they won the one-day series 5–2, which was probably an accurate reflection of the overall balance of play. Saikat Ali's half-century gave his colleagues a good platform for a large total, but the English attack stuck to their task well. Despite a determined pursuit by the tourists, the home bowlers kept their nerve.

DOMESTIC CRICKET IN BANGLADESH, 2008-09

UTPAL SHUVRO

The unavailability of Bangladesh's international players for most of the season, plus the defection of 14 players to the unofficial Indian Cricket League in September 2008, created the most open National Cricket League in recent history.

Dhaka and Khulna, who had won six of the eight titles between them since the competition became first-class, were badly hit, with defending champions **Khulna** finishing third and **Dhaka** fourth.

In fact, it turned into a two-horse race between Rajshahi and Barisal. Rajshahi, who were runners-up the previous season and winners in 2005-06, were always fancied, but Barisal were the surprise package. Their best finish in eight seasons had been third, the year Rajshahi won, and they were largely written off in advance. Their young brigade played with such enthusiasm and vigour, however, that they could have won both the four-day and the one-day leagues.

Amazingly, Rajshahi and Barisal finished tied on points in both competitions. **Rajshahi** won the first-class title, having five outright wins to Barisal's four;

Mahmudullah

the one-day tournament, played in January, was even closer, as they had identical playing records, but **Barisal** pipped Rajshahi to the trophy because they had won both their head-to-head encounters.

The first-class race was a thrilling drama decided in the final session of the final day. Barisal started the last round with one point more than Rajshahi, and at lunch on the fourth day it seemed they were on their way to victory and the title, as they had reduced Dhaka to 95 for eight chasing a target of 216. But in-form batsman Mahmudullah, dropped at gully on three, found an ally in Elias

Sunny, and their unbroken ninth-wicket stand of 124 took Dhaka home. Rajshahi also lost, but had one more bonus point, enough to give them the title by a whisker.

Mahmudullah's unbeaten 116 in that final round was his fourth century in four matches – an unprecedented feat in the competition's history – and the highlight of the season; it earned him a recall to the national side. He headed the batting averages and was the second-highest run-scorer, with 710. Faisal Hossain, who played five times for Bangladesh in 2004, scored 775 runs including three centuries in successive games, although his team, **Chittagong**, finished fifth with a single outright win.

Sylhet, who failed to win at all for the second season running, finished last again, but they too had an outstanding performer in Nabil Samad. The left-arm spinner twice collected eight wickets in an innings and 13 in the match (though he lost both games) and finished with 41 wickets in all, surpassed only by fellow left-arm spinner Suhrawadi Shuvo of Rajshahi, who took 59, and Robiul Islam of Khulna, with 48.

Arguably the best-prepared team of the competition, Rajshahi were buoyed by tremendous team spirit and the inspirational presence of former Bangladesh captain Khaled Mashud, but had only two batsmen in the top 25 run-scorers: Jahurul Islam and Anisur Rahman, who took over the captaincy from Mashud after two rounds. Suhrawadi Shuvo played a vital role, though; besides taking his 59 wickets, he scored 361 runs – easily the leading first-class all-rounder.

Overall, the first-class standard was not high enough to cure the major defect of Bangladesh's Test players: their inability to bat for long periods.

In the Dhaka Premier League, international bowler Mashrafe bin Mortaza led Abahani to their third consecutive title, with Surjotorun runners-up.

FIRST-CLASS AVERAGES, 2008-09

BATTING

(Qualification: 400 runs, average 30.00)

	M	I	NO	R	HS	100s	Avge	Ct/St
Mahmudullah (*Dhaka*)	9	15	2	710	152	4	54.61	10
†Shakib Al Hasan (*Khulna and Bangladesh*)	5	9	0	481	129	1	53.44	3
†Faisal Hossain (*Chittagong*)	9	15	0	775	129	3	51.66	9
Tushar Imran (*Khulna*)	9	17	2	692	137	1	46.13	4
Nadif Chowdhury (*Dhaka*)	10	15	2	516	101*	1	39.69	5
Jahurul Islam (*Rajshahi & BCB Academy*)	11	20	4	604	130	1	37.75	9
Masumud Dowla (*Chittagong*)	7	13	2	409	120*	2	37.18	4
Javed Omar (*Dhaka*)	10	17	2	554	112*	1	36.93	6
Anisur Rahman (*Rajshahi*)	10	15	0	533	142	1	35.53	5
Rajin Saleh (*Sylhet and Bangladesh*)	9	16	1	508	135	1	33.86	8
Rony Talukder (*Barisal*)	8	14	0	472	176	1	33.71	8
Raihan Anas (*Khulna*)	9	16	3	414	90	0	31.84	12
†Rezaul Karim (*Chittagong*)	8	14	1	407	128	1	31.30	0
†Nasiruddin Faruque (*Barisal & BCB Acad.*)	11	20	1	590	109	2	31.05	9

† *Left-handed batsman.*

BOWLING

(Qualification: 20 wickets, average 25.00)

	Style	O	M	R	W	BB	5W/i	Avge
Ziaur Rahman (*Khulna*)	RFM	229.5	53	639	38	5-36	2	16.81
Elias Sunny (*Dhaka*)	SLA	277.3	73	641	37	7-79	3	17.32
Suhrawadi Shuvo (*Rajshahi*)	SLA	460.1	127	1,045	59	6-71	4	17.71
Talha Jubair (*Barisal*)	RM	232.4	57	696	37	5-35	2	18.81

	Style	O	M	R	W	BB	5Wli	Avge
Arafat Salahuddin (*Barisal*)	RFM	180	55	437	23	5-44	1	19.00
Robiul Islam (*Khulna*)	RFM	271.1	33	927	48	5-60	3	19.31
Sajidul Islam (*Barisal & BCB Academy*) . .	LM	169	30	467	24	6-51	2	19.45
Tareq Aziz (*Chittagong*)	RFM	237.5	61	718	35	5-69	1	20.51
Arafat Sunny (*Dhaka*)	SLA	396	123	854	40	7-50	3	21.35
Alamgir Kabir (*Rajshahi*)	RM	169	42	485	22	7-76	1	22.04
Nabil Samad (*Sylhet*)	SLA	357.1	81	912	41	8-61	5	22.24
Shafiul Islam (*Rajshahi*)	RFM	193.1	50	513	23	4-38	0	22.30
Subashis Roy (*Sylhet*)	RFM	168.5	46	481	21	5-18	2	22.90
Kamrul Islam (*Chittagong*)	LFM	200	57	536	23	5-21	2	23.30

Full scores of the 2008-09 Bangladeshi season can be found at www.cricinfo.com/db/ARCHIVE/ 2008-09/BDESH_LOCAL/, www.cricketarchive.co.uk/Archive/Seasons/2008-09_BDESH.html and in the *ACS Overseas First-Class Annual 2009.*

ISPAHANI MIRZAPORE TEA NATIONAL CRICKET LEAGUE, 2008-09

					1st-inns	Bonus points			Net
	Played	Won	Lost	Drawn	points	Batting	Bowling	Points	run-rate
Rajshahi	10	5	2	3	3	17	35	101	0.27
Barisal	10	4	1	5	6	15	38	101	−0.22
Khulna	10	4	3	3	3	15	34	90	0.01
Dhaka	10	3	3	4	5	13	35	85	0.21
Chittagong	10	1	3	6	7	14	32	73	−0.12
Sylhet	10	0	5	5	2	16	36	64	−0.09

Win = 8 pts; draw = 2 pts; first-innings lead in a drawn match = 2 pts; no result on first innings = 1 pt each.
First-innings bonus points were awarded as follows: one point for the first 200 runs and then for 251, 301 and 351; one point for the fifth wicket taken and then for the sixth, eighth and tenth.

At Narayanganj Osmani Stadium, Fatullah, October 10, 11, 12, 13, 2008. **Drawn.** Toss: Dhaka. **Dhaka 210** (Tareq Aziz 4-44, Mohammad Younus 5-59) **and 64-2;** Chittagong 212-9 dec (Tariq Ahmed 73; Arafat Sunny 5-46). *Dhaka 6 pts, Chittagong 9 pts.*
  Rain and a waterlogged pitch prevented any play on the first two days.

At Khulna Divisional Stadium, Khulna, October 10, 11, 12, 2008. **Khulna won by 35 runs.** Toss: Sylhet. **Khulna 178** (Nabil Samad 8-61) **and 187** (Subashis Roy 5-43, Nabil Samad 5-73); **Sylhet 74 and 256** (Rajin Saleh 135; Ziaur Rahman 4-63, Robiul Islam 5-60). *Khulna 12 pts, Sylhet 4 pts.*
  Left-arm spinner Nabil Samad took a career-best 8-61 and 13-134 in the match (the other seven Khulna wickets all went to Subashis Roy), but finished on the losing side after Sylhet collapsed to 18-5 and then 43-7 on their way to a first-innings 74.

At Rajshahi Stadium, Rajshahi, October 10, 11, 12, 13, 2008. **Drawn.** Toss: Rajshahi. **Barisal 273** (Imran Ahmed 110, Sajidul Islam 50; Alamgir Kabir 7-76) **and 204** (Farhad Hossain 4-74); **Rajshahi 215** (Sajidul Islam 6-51) **and 135-3** (Farhad Hossain 56*). *Rajshahi 7 pts, Barisal 10 pts.*

At Narayanganj Osmani Stadium, Fatullah, October 18, 19, 20, 21, 2008. **Drawn.** Toss: Barisal. **Barisal 288** (Nasir Hossain 67, Shahin Hossain 52; Sajidul Islam 75; Robiul Islam 5-86) **and 181** (Robiul Islam 4-40); **Khulna 210** (Talha Jubair 4-43) **and 207-8** (Tushar Imran 56; Tariqul Islam 5-83). *Barisal 10 pts, Khulna 7 pts.*
  Shahin Hossain and Sajidul Islam added 127 for Barisal's eighth wicket on the opening day.

At Rajshahi Stadium, Rajshahi, October 18, 19, 20, 21, 2008. **Rajshahi won by an innings and 22 runs.** Toss: Rajshahi. **Rajshahi 438-9 dec** (Farhad Hossain 88, Anisur Rahman 142, Khaled Mashud 72; Mohammad Younus 4-110); **Chittagong 120** (Suhrawadi Shuvo 5-34) **and 296** (Gazi Salahuddin 78, Tariq Ahmed 54; Suhrawadi Shuvo 5-122, Farhad Hossain 4-100). *Rajshahi 16 pts, Chittagong 3 pts.*

At Sylhet Stadium, Sylhet, October 18, 19, 20, 21, 2008. **Dhaka won by six wickets.** Toss: Sylhet. **Sylhet 343** (Golam Rahman 71, Mithun Ali 69, Kamrul Islam 62, Ezaz Ahmed 88; Elias Sunny 7-79) **and 113** (Elias Sunny 6-28); **Dhaka 254** (Shamsur Rahman 78, Marshall Ayub 59, Nazmul Hossain 54; Rashedur Rahman 5-38) **and 205-4** (Mahmudullah 56*). *Dhaka 14 pts, Sylhet 7 pts.*

Dhaka's left-arm spinner, Elias Sunny, took a hat-trick in his career-best 7-79, and finished with 13-107 in the match. It was only the second hat-trick in the competition's history, following Dolar Mahmud's the previous season.

At Shaheed Chandu Stadium, Bogra, October 26, 27, 28, 29, 2008. **Barisal were awarded the match when Sylhet refused to play.** Toss: Barisal. **Sylhet 163; Barisal 160-5.** *Barisal 12 pts.*

The first two days of all three matches in this round were washed out by a cyclone. As Barisal approached a first-innings lead on the fourth, Sylhet captain Imtiaz Hossain claimed the light was too bad to continue. This was interpreted as refusal to play; Barisal were awarded the game, and Imtiaz was fined 75% of his match fee.

At Chittagong Divisional Stadium, Chittagong, October 26, 27, 28, 29, 2008. **Drawn.** Toss: Khulna. **Chittagong 302-5 dec** (Nafis Iqbal 122*, Faisal Hossain 96); **Khulna 113-5.** *Chittagong 3 pts, Khulna 3 pts.*

No first-innings bonus points were awarded in this or the next match.

At Rajshahi Stadium, Rajshahi, October 26, 27, 28, 29, 2008. **Drawn.** Toss: Dhaka. **Dhaka 179** (Javed Omar 82, Nadif Chowdhury 64; Farhad Hossain 4-19); **Rajshahi 117-6.** *Rajshahi 3 pts, Dhaka 3 pts.*

At Narayanganj Osmani Stadium, Fatullah, November 2, 3, 4, 5, 2008. **Drawn.** Toss: Chittagong. **Barisal 385** (Rony Talukder 176, Tariqul Islam 55; Tareq Aziz 4-99, Kamrul Islam 5-62) **and 182-4 dec** (Nasiruddin Faruque 100*); **Chittagong 392-9 dec** (Gazi Salahuddin 51, Faisal Hossain 127). *Barisal 9 pts, Chittagong 12 pts.*

At Shere Bangla National Stadium, Mirpur, November 2, 3, 4, 5, 2008. **Dhaka won by 176 runs.** Toss: Khulna. **Dhaka 251-9 dec** (Shamsur Rahman 53, Nadif Chowdhury 54) **and 266-7 dec** (Nadif Chowdhury 101*); **Khulna 110** (Tushar Imran 50*; Arafat Sunny 4-45) **and 231** (Nazmus Sadat 50, Tushar Imran 70, Ziaur Rahman 65; Elias Sunny 4-44). *Dhaka 14 pts, Khulna 3 pts.*

Robiul Islam of Khulna and Dhaka's Mahmudullah were fined for an altercation on the last day.

At Sylhet Stadium, Sylhet, November 2, 3, 4, 5, 2008. **Rajshahi won by 40 runs.** Toss: Rajshahi. **Rajshahi 117** (Subashis Roy 5-18) **and 253** (Monir Hossain 5-78); **Sylhet 172** (Suhrawadi Shuvo 4-27) **and 158.** *Rajshahi 12 pts, Sylhet 4 pts.*

At Shaheed Chandu Stadium, Bogra, November 9, 10, 11, 12, 2008. **Barisal won by 118 runs.** Toss: Barisal. **Barisal 274** (Nasiruddin Faruque 109, Imran Ahmed 54; Elias Sunny 5-63) **and 146** (Elias Sunny 4-51); **Dhaka 116** (Talha Jubair 4-30) **and 186** (Shamsur Rahman 53, Marshall Ayub 58; Saju Datta 4-53). *Barisal 14 pts, Dhaka 4 pts.*

At Chittagong Divisional Stadium, Chittagong, November 9, 10, 11, 12, 2008. **Chittagong won by 53 runs.** Toss: Chittagong. **Chittagong 293** (Gazi Salahuddin 50, Faisal Hossain 129; Nabil Samad 8-69) **and 140** (Faisal Hossain 69; Nabil Samad 5-47, Monir Hossain 5-35); **Sylhet 201-9 dec and 179.** *Chittagong 13 pts, Sylhet 5 pts.*

For the second time in a month, Nabil Samad finished on the losing side after claiming eight wickets in an innings and 13 in the match.

At Khulna Divisional Stadium, Khulna, November 9, 10, 11, 12, 2008. **Rajshahi won by eight wickets.** Toss: Rajshahi. **Khulna 229** (Tushar Imran 137; Suhrawadi Shuvo 4-56) **and 213** (Saghir Hossain 56; Shafiul Islam 4-38); **Rajshahi 390** (Jahurul Islam 130, Farhad Hossain 51, Anisur Rahman 67; Ziaur Rahman 4-64) **and 53-2.** *Rajshahi 16 pts, Khulna 5 pts.*

At Shaheed Chandu Stadium, Bogra, November 17, 18, 19, 20, 2008. **Barisal won by 222 runs.** Toss: Barisal. **Barisal 166** (Hannan Sarkar 77) **and 342** (Hannan Sarkar 99, Nasir Hossain 92; Suhrawadi Shuvo 4-119, Farhad Hossain 4-33); **Rajshahi 204** (Talha Jubair 5-41) **and 82** (Tariqul Islam 5-21). *Barisal 12 pts, Rajshahi 5 pts.*

Barisal reduced Rajshahi to 48-7 on the third day, and completed victory in this top-of-the-table clash to hold the advantage with four rounds to go.

At Chittagong Divisional Stadium, Chittagong, November 17, 18, 19, 20, 2008. **Drawn.** Toss: Chittagong. **Chittagong 314** (Tariq Ahmed 83, Faisal Hossain 102) **and 314-7** (Nafis Iqbal 77, Rezaul Karim 59, Masumud Dowla 102*); **Dhaka 366-9 dec** (Anwar Hossain 65, Marshall Ayub 181; Tareq Aziz 4-61). *Chittagong 8 pts, Dhaka 12 pts.*

Faisal Hossain scored his third hundred in three matches. It was almost four: he was out for 96 in the game preceding the sequence.

At Sylhet Stadium, Sylhet, November 18, 19, 20, 21, 2008. **Drawn.** Toss: Sylhet. **Sylhet 300** (Saikat Ali 88, Mithun Ali 106) **and 198** (Kamrul Islam 89*; Atiqur Rahman 5-37); **Khulna 364** (Ashraful Aziz 105, Raihan Anas 73; Nabil Samad 5-81) **and 78-4.** *Sylhet 8 pts, Khulna 12 pts.*

At Chittagong Divisional Stadium, Chittagong, November 24, 25, 26, 2008. **Rajshahi won by eight wickets.** Toss: Rajshahi. **Rajshahi 240** (Suhrawadi Shuvo 56) **and 73-2;** **Chittagong 80 and 227** (Masumud Dowla 53; Mohammad Shahzada 4-80). *Rajshahi 13 pts, Chittagong 4 pts.*

Chittagong recovered from 45-8 in their first innings, but their eventual 80 was still their lowest first-class total.

At Shere Bangla National Stadium, Mirpur, November 24, 25, 26, 27, 2008. **Drawn.** Toss: Dhaka. **Sylhet 363** (Imtiaz Hossain 58, Rajin Saleh 94, Kamrul Islam 77, Rezaul Haque 73; Arafat Sunny 5-73) **and 153-7** (Arafat Sunny 4-22); **Dhaka 438** (Mahmudullah 103, Nadif Chowdhury 81, Javed Omar 112*). *Dhaka 12 pts, Sylhet 10 pts.*

At Khulna Divisional Stadium, Khulna, November 24, 25, 2008. **Barisal won by an innings and 52 runs.** Toss: Barisal. **Barisal 252** (Nasiruddin Faruque 61, Shahin Hossain 58; Robiul Islam 4-58); **Khulna 69** (Talha Jubair 5-35) **and 131** (Arafat Salahuddin 5-44). *Barisal 14 pts, Khulna 4 pts.*

Khulna succumbed for 69 in only 19.1 overs in their first innings.

At Shere Bangla National Stadium, Mirpur, December 1, 2, 3, 4, 2008. **Rajshahi won by nine wickets.** Toss: Rajshahi. **Dhaka 142** (Delwar Hossain 5-45) **and 256** (Mahmudullah 105; Delwar Hossain 5-60); **Rajshahi 283** (Jahurul Islam 83, Suhrawadi Shuvo 85) **and 117-1** (Jahurul Islam 68*). *Rajshahi 14 pts, Dhaka 4 pts.*

At Khulna Divisional Stadium, Khulna, December 1, 2, 3, 2008. **Khulna won by 35 runs.** Toss: Khulna. **Khulna 301-9 dec** (Raihan Anas 63, Nahidul Haque 67; Tareq Aziz 5-69) **and 54** (Kamrul Islam 5-21); **Chittagong 121** (Ziaur Rahman 5-36) **and 199** (Faisal Hossain 79; Dolar Mahmud 4-57). *Khulna 15 pts, Chittagong 3 pts.*

Khulna won the match despite being bowled out for 54, the lowest total in Bangladeshi first-class cricket, in their second innings, when only Raihan Anas (12) reached double figures. It was the second time in successive matches they had been dismissed for less than 70.

At Sylhet Stadium, Sylhet, December 1, 2, 3, 4, 2008. **Drawn.** Toss: Sylhet. **Sylhet 366-9 dec** (Saikat Ali 111, Golam Rahman 116; Tariqul Islam 4-78) **and 251-7 dec** (Imtiaz Hossain 82, Rajin Saleh 71); **Barisal 270** (Nasiruddin Faruque 66, Hannan Sarkar 50) **and 178-6** (Nasir Hossain 60). *Sylhet 12 pts, Barisal 7 pts.*

At Chittagong Divisional Stadium, Chittagong, December 14, 15, 16, 17, 2008. **Drawn.** Toss: Barisal. **Barisal 244 and 266** (Raqibul Hasan 77; Tareq Aziz 4-86, Mohammad Younus 4-51); **Chittagong 198 and 290-8** (Rezaul Karim 128, Tariq Ahmed 54). *Chittagong 6 pts, Barisal 9 pts.*

At Khulna Divisional Stadium, Khulna, December 14, 15, 16, 17, 2008. **Khulna won by 170 runs.** Toss: Khulna. **Khulna 355** (Imrul Kayes 58, Tushar Imran 54, Shakib Al Hasan 59; Mahbubul Alam 4-82, Marshall Ayub 4-36) **and 352** (Shakib Al Hasan 129, Raihan Anas 90); **Dhaka 181-9 dec and 356** (Javed Omar 76, Mahmudullah 152; Ziaur Rahman 5-82, Robiul Islam 4-115). *Khulna 15 pts, Dhaka 4 pts.*

Shakib Al Hasan, one of several Bangladesh internationals who returned from South Africa to reinforce these two sides, added 202 for the sixth wicket with Raihan Anas in Khulna's second innings; both scored career-bests. Another returning international, Dhaka's Shahadat Hossain, was fined for verbally abusing Robiul Islam.

At Rajshahi Stadium, Rajshahi, December 14, 15, 16, 17, 2008. **Drawn.** Toss: Sylhet. **Rajshahi 264** (Naeem Islam 87; Sumon Saha 4-55) **and 101-2 dec** (Jahurul Islam 53*); **Sylhet 127** (Mithun Ali 57; Delwar Hossain 5-33) **and 67-2.** *Rajshahi 10 pts, Sylhet 6 pts.*

Rajshahi were 56-5 at the end of the first day, which was reduced to 30.3 overs by fog, until Naeem Islam fought back; more fog wiped out the third day to ensure the draw.

At Narayanganj Osmani Stadium, Fatullah, December 21, 22, 23, 24, 2008. **Dhaka won by two wickets.** Toss: Dhaka. **Barisal 125** (Arafat Sunny 7-50) **and 265** (Rony Talukder 67, Imran Ahmed 56; Ashraful Haque 5-71); **Dhaka 175** (Javed Omar 62) **and 219-8** (Mahmudullah 116*; Monowar Hossain 4-69). *Dhaka 12 pts, Barisal 4 pts.*

Barisal seemed to have the league title in the bag when they reduced Dhaka to 95-8 chasing 216 on the final day, but Mahmudullah denied them, adding 124* for the ninth wicket with Elias Sunny and completing his fourth century in as many matches.

At Rajshahi Stadium, Rajshahi, December 21, 22, 23, 24, 2008. **Khulna won by 28 runs.** Toss: Khulna. **Khulna 255-9 dec** (Nazmus Sadat 59; Suhrawadi Shuvo 6-71) **and 347** (Fariduddin 57, Dolar Mahmud 65; Suhrawadi Shuvo 6-124); **Rajshahi 251** (Suhrawadi Shuvo 55; Robiul Islam 5-68) **and 323** (Anisur Rahman 71, Hamidul Islam 53, Sabbir Rahman 72; Dolar Mahmud 4-82). *Khulna 14 pts, Rajshahi 5 pts.*

Dolar Mahmud hit 65 – his highest score – in 52 balls, including seven sixes and four fours, out of 77 runs scored while he was at the crease. Slow left-armer Suhrawadi Shuvo took a career-best 6-71 in Khulna's first innings, and another six in the second to finish with 12-195. Rajshahi's bonus points were enough to secure them the title, despite their defeat.

At Sylhet Stadium, Sylhet, December 21, 22, 23, 24, 2008. **Drawn.** Toss: Chittagong. **Chittagong 382** (Rezaul Karim 81, Masumud Dowla 120*) **and 185-7 dec** (Arman Hossain 61*); **Sylhet 268** (Golam Rahman 55, Imtiaz Hossain 95; Rubel Hossain 5-60) **and 65-4.** *Sylhet 8 pts, Chittagong 12 pts.*

Sylhet wicketkeeper Lablur Rahman made five catches and a stumping in Chittagong's second innings.

NATIONAL CRICKET LEAGUE WINNERS

1999-2000	Chittagong	2002-03	Khulna	2006-07	Dhaka
2000-01	Biman Bangladesh Airlines	2003-04	Dhaka	2007-08	Khulna
2001-02	Dhaka	2004-05	Dhaka	2008-09	Rajshahi
		2005-06	Rajshahi		

Dhaka have won the title four times, Khulna and Rajshahi twice, Biman Bangladesh Airlines and Chittagong once each. In 1999-2000, the competition was not first-class.

Note: Matches in the following section were not first-class.

ISPAHANI MIRZAPORE TEA ONE-DAY LEAGUE, 2008-09

	Played	Won	Lost	Points	Net run-rate
Barisal	10	7	3	14	−0.02
Rajshahi	10	7	3	14	0.57
Chittagong	10	6	4	12	0.13
Khulna	10	4	6	8	−0.80
Dhaka	10	3	7	6	−0.05
Sylhet	10	3	7	6	0.03

Barisal won the league because they won both their matches against Rajshahi, with whom they tied on points. Similarly, Dhaka won both their matches against Sylhet.

INDIAN CRICKET, 2009

The view from the summit

ANAND VASU

For years – no, decades – the complaint India's players endured from their overseas peers was that the country produced brilliant individuals but few world-beating teams. In the meantime, Indian cricket administrators were traditionally never accused of brilliance, but it was said that they were worried only about votes or money. Against that backdrop, 2009 was a crucial year for Indian cricket. The team rose to the top of the ICC's Test rankings for the first time – yet this only sharpened the criticism of administrators.

If cricket's biggest challenge is asserting the primacy of Test matches, three specific areas require addressing: the need for a careful balance between bat and ball, only ensured by sporting pitches; thoughtful scheduling of matches in all formats; and a quality experience at grounds for the paying public.

On all these counts, the Board of Control for Cricket in India abdicated its substantial responsibility. The board's attitude to pitches was exposed when the final one-day international of the year, against Sri Lanka at Delhi on December 27, was called off after just 23.3 overs. Alan Hurst, the match referee, called the pitch "unfit" and "totally unsuitable for one-day international cricket" in his report following the abandonment. The BCCI promptly

INDIA IN 2009

	Played	Won	Lost	Drawn/No result
Tests	6	3	–	3
One-day internationals	31	17	10	4
Twenty20 internationals	10	4	6	–

disbanded its grounds and pitches committee, something many argued they should have done before. Eventually Delhi managed to keep its chances of hosting matches in the 2011 World Cup alive, as the BCCI agreed to stage no matches at the Feroz Shah Kotla ground in 2010 and allow an ICC-appointed specialist to supervise work on the pitch.

Essentially, pitch preparation had been left to each state association, with a zonal representative of the grounds and pitches committee overseeing the work. This led to frequent disagreements as confused groundsmen received multiple instructions in a situation where no one was accountable. What happened at the Kotla was an aberration but underlined the system's failings.

In the recent past, plenty of lip service was paid to the need for sporting wickets. This resulted in a tinkering with pitches that left the country without a single genuinely quick track. Chennai is the one venue that is usually still capable of producing a surface with some bounce and carry. Mohali was once hard and pacy, and Mumbai encouraging, but repeated relaying of their pitches has robbed them of any life.

The effect of playing domestic cricket solely on two types of wicket – rank bad ones when a home side is desperate for points, or batting beauties – has left many young batsmen with genuine problems adjusting to extra bounce overseas. Suresh Raina and Rohit Sharma, two batsmen thought to be successors of the likes of Rahul Dravid and Sachin Tendulkar, have been in and out of the national team after persistent problems against short balls.

Local problems, though, are not limited to pitches. Shortly before the abandonment, there was more embarrassment at the Kotla, when the Australians turned up to practise a day before their one-day international in October, and found that all the pitches had been watered. While Ricky Ponting and his team, the local media, and even a few hundred fans all knew that the Aussies would be practising, the groundsman apparently did not.

Even as the Sri Lanka one-dayer was abandoned, the quarter-finals of the Ranji Trophy, the premier first-class competition, took place on small grounds completely unsuited to staging matches of that stature. The Delhi–Tamil Nadu game was played at the Palam Grounds, on the outskirts of Delhi near the airport, making it almost impossible for fans to attend. The match between Haryana and Mumbai took place in the village of Lahli, in bitingly cold conditions, at a ground in the middle of sugar-cane fields. There wasn't a hotel that could accommodate a full team, and there was no mobile-phone signal at the ground. In Guwahati, Assam's match against Uttar Pradesh was played at the North East Frontier Railways ground rather than the Nehru Stadium where one-day internationals are played, as that was being used for a football tournament. The Karnataka–Punjab match was played in the picturesque Gangotri Glades ground in Mysore, and here at least some spectators gathered. But, incredibly, none of these matches was broadcast live, as none of the grounds had the minimum facilities needed for the production of TV pictures.

If the Ranji quarter-finals not being on TV was scarcely credible, equally ridiculous was the scheduling of the seven rounds of league games that preceded them. Every match was played from Tuesday to Friday, making it as difficult as possible for spectators to attend.

Net gain: Sachin Tendulkar and India coach Gary Kirsten at the training ground.

While the domestic competition received second-rate treatment, the marquee Tests did not do much better. India played only six in 2009, three in New Zealand, where they won a series for the first time since 1967-68, and three at home against Sri Lanka, where a 2–0 win took them up to No. 1.

Contrast this to 2008, when India played 15 Tests, including home series against Australia and England. If the problem was paucity in 2009, the previous year smacked of poor planning, with England's first tour fixture beginning on November 9, the fourth day of the final Test against Australia. There was no chance for spectators to savour either series, and the traditional build-up that precedes a major tour was wholly absent.

The rise to No. 1 in the Test rankings prompted many players to state publicly the need for more Tests in 2010 (the BCCI had originally scheduled only two away against Bangladesh in January and three against South Africa at the year's end). This resulted in February's home five-match one-day series against South Africa being converted into two Tests and three one-dayers. This happened in January, leaving no time for travelling supporters to make plans to visit and support the team, or indeed for home associations to market the event properly.

While there was hope that India's No. 1 ranking would force administrators to schedule more Test matches, this was balanced by the fact that Lalit Modi headed the board's tour programmes and fixtures committee. Modi's involvement with franchise-based Twenty20 cricket, its expansion, and the desire for a long and international "natural window" for the IPL, led to scepticism over whether he would actually try to schedule more Tests.

In the two ICC tournaments of 2009 – the World Twenty20 in England and the 50-over Champions Trophy in South Africa – India were knocked out in the group stage. They had gone to England as defending champions, yet defeated only Bangladesh and Ireland. India were unable to make good the loss of Sehwag, injured in the IPL, and found that opposing pace bowlers bounced out their top order – notably Raina and Sharma – in his absence.

The year was also marked by the board's directive to state associations to acquire land and build cricket grounds of their own rather than use stadiums that belonged to the municipal corporation or trusts on long leases. The board's sizeable annual infrastructure subsidy (in the region of 30m rupees, or more than £400,000) to states led some of them – notably Vidarbha, the home of BCCI president Shashank Manohar – following through on developing their own facilities. The new stadium at Jamtha, outside Nagpur, seats 50,000 and boasts state-of-the-art facilities that prompted the ICC to call it "a blueprint for all future grounds internationally" after a routine inspection ahead of the World Cup. The problem was that it lies more than 12 miles outside Nagpur, with no reliable public transport, making it excessively expensive for spectators to attend. The Vidarbha Cricket Association made matters worse by selling only season tickets for the Test against Australia, further deterring spectators from making the trip. In the end, approximately 50,000 people – a fifth of the total capacity – watched that game over its five days.

The other shocking instance of spectator neglect came in Sri Lanka's fourth one-day international at Eden Gardens in Kolkata on December 24. The famous venue was allotted a match after Jagmohan Dalmiya's shrill cries that his state was being denied their due by the BCCI. The Cricket Association of Bengal then took the amazing decision of staging the game without putting a single ticket up for sale to the general public. Because of development work on the ground several stands had been torn down, reducing the capacity by more than half to approximately 40,000. The CAB distributed tickets to its members, sponsors and state government agencies, ensuring that members of the public could not buy a ticket, even if they wanted to.

The recurring story during Sri Lanka's visit, at a time when the world was debating the place Test cricket would occupy in the coming years, was the pitches. In the First Test at Ahmedabad the ball barely beat bat on a surface that reduced bowlers to tears: 1,598 runs were scored for the loss of only 21 wickets, with the game not even nearing completion in five days. The pitch at Kanpur was not much better, but a Sri Lankan collapse triggered a result. With the Board having disbanded its grounds and pitches committee, it was not clear just how they proposed to address the tricky task of preparing sporting tracks that restore the balance between bat and ball.

India's climb to No. 1 – the dominant theme as the year ended – came on the back of strong performances by the Test team, but it did not come without collateral damage. The board sacked former internationals Venkatesh Prasad (the bowling coach) and Robin Singh (fielding coach) without any notice in October. The team's poor one-day fielding and the lack of improvement in the bowling group were cited as reasons. Both had been working without long-term contracts, and were paid on a series-by-series basis. If anything, 2009 was a year when cricket, in all forms, thrived in India, despite what the administrators did.

INDIA v AUSTRALIA, 2009-10

DANIEL BRETTIG

One-day internationals (7): India 2, Australia 4

A series that began under clouds of meaninglessness ended up being rightfully acclaimed as one of the more arresting limited-overs contests. The weeks leading up to the tour had been filled so completely by Twenty20 games and the Champions Trophy that the arrival of the Australians in India was accompanied by a cover of India's *Open Magazine* that blared "Your wife was right, cricket is boring." But there was nothing dull about Australia's come-from-behind triumph, which was completed in the far western provincial centre of Guwahati despite a surfeit of injuries and only after they had emerged victorious in tight circumstances at Vadodara and Chandigarh, and then at Hyderabad in one of the great matches.

Ricky Ponting described the success of his team, which was thrown haphazardly together by a vast collection of physical ailments that could be largely attributed to the horribly bloated international schedule, as among the finest he had enjoyed in 50-over cricket. His Indian counterpart, the agile Mahendra Singh Dhoni, was left to bemoan a lost opportunity to reach the top of the one-day rankings, and to puzzle over how his team had managed to lose by a clear margin at home to injury-hit opponents. Indian administrators had conceded before the tour that there was too much cricket being played, even for a public as ravenous as the subcontinent's, and it was significant that the capacity crowds and substantial television ratings for the six matches (the seventh game in Mumbai was washed out) were greeted with relief by both the Indian board and the players.

If the series had a turning point it was in the selection of the left-arm fast bowler Doug Bollinger, a long way back in pre-tour calculations. He added an element of danger and heart to the Australian attack, and his wickets led to a fighting win at Chandigarh. From there it was on to Hyderabad for the flattest of pitches and the most entertaining of matches, with fine innings by Shane Watson and Shaun Marsh completely overshadowed by a Sachin Tendulkar masterpiece which, like many of his others, had the unhappy post-script of an Indian defeat. Guwahati produced the most sporting pitch of the tour, and Bollinger and Mitchell Johnson broke the back of India's batting inside ten overs.

The Australians sent home James Hopes (hamstring), Brett Lee (elbow), Tim Paine (broken finger), Peter Siddle (side stiffness) and Hopes's replacement Moises Henriques (hamstring) as the series went on, while Johnson (ankle) and Ben Hilfenhaus (knee) fought niggling complaints. Hilfenhaus's tendinitis was later to flare up badly enough to keep him out of all but one Test of the home summer, calling into question why he made this tour in the first place.

When added to pre-existing injuries that ruled out Nathan Bracken, Michael Clarke, Callum Ferguson and Brad Haddin, the roster of wounded made up a full eleven. This, of course, provided openings for others, and Bollinger and Clint McKay took the fullest advantage. Bollinger's efforts made him the bowler of the series and began an upward curve that had him well entrenched in the Test team by summer's end, while McKay was able to continue his graduation from fringe Victorian seamer to Test representative.

Mike Hussey spent most of the tour answering questions about his Test place, and responded with his most assertive batting in more than a year. He was the only batsman on either side to make more than 300 runs, and he finished with an average of 104.33. Another to enhance his reputation was Shane Watson, the player of the series, who cheerfully acknowledged the irony that the most injury-prone Australian of recent years had made it through not only unscathed but as the most consistent performer in his team. Apart from his 256 runs he also took ten wickets, more than anyone else in the six matches.

India's performances, an improvement on their rapid elimination from the Champions Trophy, were nonetheless bedevilled by inconsistency. They might have snatched the first match at Vadodara with a couple more big hits from Harbhajan Singh, and they did win the next two games – after which they might have expected to take advantage of ramshackle opposition. However, the inability of their batsmen to make use of a start proved critical, with Virender Sehwag particularly guilty. Of the bowlers, Ishant Sharma maintained his struggle to regain the rhythm of 2008, and no one was able to better Harbhajan's modest haul of eight wickets at nearly 34. Gary Kirsten's assistant coaches Venkatesh Prasad (bowling) and Robin Singh (fielding) had been relieved of their duties before the series, and there seemed no greater direction in their absence.

AUSTRALIAN TOURING PARTY

R. T. Ponting (*captain*), M. E. K. Hussey (*vice-captain*), D. E. Bollinger, N. M. Hauritz, B. W. Hilfenhaus, J. M. Holland, J. R. Hopes, M. G. Johnson, B. Lee, S. E. Marsh, T. D. Paine, P. M. Siddle, A. C. Voges, S. R. Watson, C. L. White. *Coach:* T. J. Nielsen.

G. A. Manou joined the side after Paine broke a finger. M. C. Henriques flew in when Hopes went home with a hamstring injury, but soon pulled his own right hamstring and was replaced by A. B. McDonald. C. J. McKay replaced Lee (elbow), while B. T. Cockley replaced Siddle when he went home with a sore left side.

Note: Matches in this section were not first-class.

INDIA v AUSTRALIA

First One-Day International

At Vadodara, October 25, 2009. Australia won by four runs. Toss: Australia.

Australia began with a victory, though not before their old adversary Harbhajan Singh had once again managed to rile them. Until he and Kumar joined forces the Indians had scarcely fired a shot, first allowing the Australians to build a decent total then offering little of substance with the bat. This contrasted with the diligence of Ponting and Paine, who negotiated some testing overs against the new ball after Watson fell to a well-pitched inswinger from Nehra. Their platform allowed Hussey to play with some extravagance in the closing overs and take the total near 300. In reply Sehwag was out to a good one, and Gambhir was the only batsman to offer security in the face of tidy work by Hauritz in particular. With India 201 for seven, the match seemed to have run its course, but Harbhajan's slaps and Kumar's relatively correct approach made headway against bowling that was suddenly ragged: Watson especially seemed unable to pitch the ball where he wanted, and the eighth-wicket pair added 84 in less than ten overs. Only nine runs were needed from the final over, and there was much Australian relief when Siddle disturbed Harbhajan's stumps with the second ball: Nehra proved unable to hit the six required from the final delivery. Hopes and Lee suffered injuries in the field which soon saw them go home, while Johnson also hurt his ankle. This match (and the next two) was umpired by two local officials after Mark Benson fell ill shortly before the start.

Man of the Match: M. E. K. Hussey.

Australia

S. R. Watson lbw b Nehra	5		B. Lee b Sharma		0
†T. D. Paine c Dhoni b Sharma	50				
*R. T. Ponting lbw b Jadeja	74		L-b 2, w 4, n-b 2		8
C. L. White c Raina b Nehra	51				
M. E. K. Hussey c Kohli b Sharma	73		1/5 (1) 2/102 (2)	(8 wkts, 50 overs)	292
A. C. Voges c Gambhir b Harbhajan Singh	3		3/151 (3) 4/227 (4)		
J. R. Hopes run out	14		5/233 (6) 6/256 (7)		
M. G. Johnson not out	14		7/291 (5) 8/292 (9)	10 overs: 56-1	

N. M. Hauritz and P. M. Siddle did not bat.

Kumar 10–0–77–0; Nehra 10–0–58–2; Sharma 10–0–50–3; Harbhajan Singh 10–0–57–1; Jadeja 9–0–39–1; Raina 1–0–9–0.

India

V. Sehwag c Paine b Lee	13		P. Kumar not out		40
S. R. Tendulkar c Ponting b Watson	14		A. Nehra not out		2
G. Gambhir lbw b Johnson	68		L-b 10, w 14		24
V. Kohli c Watson b Voges	30				
*†M. S. Dhoni c Lee b Watson	34		1/25 (1) 2/45 (2)	(8 wkts, 50 overs)	288
S. K. Raina c and b Johnson	9		3/103 (4) 4/167 (3)		
R. A. Jadeja lbw b Hauritz	5		5/183 (6) 6/186 (5)		
Harbhajan Singh b Siddle	49		7/201 (7) 8/285 (8)	10 overs: 49-2	

I. Sharma did not bat.

Lee 6–0–28–1; Siddle 9–0–55–1; Watson 10–0–70–2; Johnson 10–0–59–2; Hopes 2–0–10–0; Voges 4–0–22–1; Hauritz 9–1–34–1.

Umpires: A. M. Saheba and S. K. Tarapore.
Third umpire: S. Asnani.   Referee: B. C. Broad.

INDIA v AUSTRALIA

Second One-Day International

At Jamtha, Nagpur, October 28, 2009 (day/night). India won by 99 runs. Toss: Australia.

It is hard to imagine any Australian cricketer choosing Nagpur as a holiday destination after this hiding in the second match made it two hefty losses to India in as many years at the home of the Indian board's president Shashank Manohar. After the Test here in November 2008, Ponting was heavily criticised for addressing the problem of a slow over-rate when a possible win beckoned, and this time he was left rueful about his decision to bowl. Dew had been expected to play a significant role in the second innings, but such concerns were made moot by an utterly benign surface that offered enough pace for batsmen to play their shots. While the Australians were able to claim regular wickets through the first half of the innings, the Indians continued to rumble along at six an over, a rate that was likely to increase if a partnership could be formed. Dhoni, in irresistible touch, and Raina did just that: carnage ensued. Only Siddle and Hauritz escaped total domination, 87 came from the last seven overs, and India's final score was their highest against Australia. Dhoni faced 107 balls, hitting nine fours and three sixes, one a remarkable flat crack over midwicket off Hilfenhaus. Paine had fractured a finger when trying to clasp a Siddle bouncer, and his frustrated heave at Kumar set the pattern for a despairing chase.

Man of the Match: M. S. Dhoni.

India

V. Sehwag c Hilfenhaus b Johnson	40	P. Kumar run out		1
S. R. Tendulkar c White b Siddle	4			
G. Gambhir run out	76	B 1, l-b 6, w 14, n-b 2		23
Yuvraj Singh c and b Hilfenhaus	23			
*†M. S. Dhoni c Paine b Johnson	124	1/21 (2) 2/67 (1) (7 wkts, 50 overs)		354
S. K. Raina c Paine b Johnson	62	3/97 (4) 4/216 (3)		
Harbhajan Singh not out	1	5/352 (5) 6/353 (6) 7/354 (8) 10 overs: 67-1		

R. A. Jadeja, A. Nehra and I. Sharma did not bat.

Hilfenhaus 10–0–83–1; Siddle 10–0–55–1; Johnson 10–0–75–3; Hauritz 10–0–54–0; Voges 5–0–33–0; Watson 5–0–47–0.

Australia

S. R. Watson c Tendulkar b Sharma	19	P. M. Siddle c Dhoni b Sharma		3
†T. D. Paine b Kumar	8	B. W. Hilfenhaus run out		16
*R. T. Ponting lbw b Kumar	12			
C. L. White c Raina b Harbhajan Singh	23	L-b 5, w 8		13
M. E. K. Hussey b Jadeja	53			
A. C. Voges b Jadeja	36	1/20 (2) 2/41 (1) 3/45 (3) (48.3 overs)		255
S. E. Marsh st Dhoni b Jadeja	21	4/93 (4) 5/140 (5) 6/180 (7)		
M. G. Johnson b Nehra	21	7/194 (6) 8/223 (8) 9/230 (10)		
N. M. Hauritz not out	30	10/255 (11) 10 overs: 45-2		

Kumar 8–1–37–2; Nehra 7–0–40–1; Sharma 8–0–34–2; Harbhajan Singh 10–0–62–1; Yuvraj Singh 8–0–39–0; Jadeja 6.3–0–35–3; Raina 1–0–3–0.

Umpires: A. M. Saheba and S. K. Tarapore.
Third umpire: S. S. Hazare.   Referee: B. C. Broad.

INDIA v AUSTRALIA

Third One-Day International

At Delhi, October 31, 2009 (day/night). India won by six wickets. Toss: Australia. One-day international debuts: M. C. Henriques, G. A. Manou.

A Feroz Shah Kotla surface that was more pudding than pitch had bedevilled batsmen during the Champions League Twenty20, and now did so again. It took an expert partnership between Dhoni and Yuvraj Singh to steady India's chase and hand their side a 2–1 series lead. Australia's preparations were hampered when they arrived for a training session the day before the match to find the practice pitches watered and unusable, an oversight that caused Ponting to fume that "it seems everybody in the world other than the groundsman knew that we were training at nine this morning". Heads full of Kotla horror stories from their Twenty20 participants, the Australians batted in a circumspect manner, Ponting – opening for only the second time in his 327 one-day internationals – playing with genuine grit that would go unrewarded when he was lbw to a full delivery from Jadeja. Hussey again showed real verve to pick up the rate, and 230 appeared a decent target. It was looking distant when Johnson shattered the stumps of Sehwag (bowled) and Tendulkar (run out from mid-off), but Dhoni and Yuvraj built patiently. They took full toll of the debutant Moises Henriques (the first international cricketer to have been born in Portugal) and part-timer Voges at the right time, grabbing 24 runs from the 34th and 35th overs, a spike that left the rest of the pursuit to be carried out in some comfort. Players on both sides commented that they had never played on a slower limited-overs surface, and the trouble hinted at here would bloom regrettably against Sri Lanka in December, when the match had to be abandoned midway through the first innings.

Man of the Match: Yuvraj Singh.

Australia

S. R. Watson st Dhoni b Yuvraj Singh	41	M. G. Johnson not out	9
*R. T. Ponting lbw b Jadeja	59	B 4, l-b 3, w 3	10
M. E. K. Hussey not out	81		
C. L. White c Dhoni b Raina	0	1/72 (1) 2/128 (2) (5 wkts, 50 overs)	229
A. C. Voges c Kumar b Harbhajan Singh	17	3/129 (4) 4/172 (5)	
M. C. Henriques b Jadeja	12	5/200 (6) 10 overs: 40-0	

†G. A. Manou, N. M. Hauritz, P. M. Siddle and D. E. Bollinger did not bat.

Kumar 5–1–16–0; Nehra 9–0–51–0; Sharma 5–0–24–0; Jadeja 9–1–41–2; Harbhajan Singh 10–0–37–1; Yuvraj Singh 8–0–30–1; Raina 4–0–23–1.

India

V. Sehwag b Johnson	11	S. K. Raina not out	9
S. R. Tendulkar run out	32	B 4, l-b 4, w 14, n-b 1	23
G. Gambhir b Hauritz	6		
Yuvraj Singh lbw b Henriques	78	1/37 (1) 2/51 (2) (4 wkts, 48.2 overs)	230
*†M. S. Dhoni not out	71	3/53 (3) 4/201 (4) 10 overs: 39-1	

R. A. Jadeja, Harbhajan Singh, P. Kumar, A. Nehra and I. Sharma did not bat.

Johnson 9.2–2–43–1; Siddle 10–0–41–0; Bollinger 10–0–26–0; Henriques 8–0–51–1; Hauritz 10–0–48–1; Voges 1–0–13–0.

Umpires: S. S. Hazare and A. M. Saheba.
Third umpire: S. K. Tarapore.   Referee: B. C. Broad.

INDIA v AUSTRALIA

Fourth One-Day International

At Mohali, November 2, 2009 (day/night). Australia won by 24 runs. Toss: India.
To this point India had been the better side, but they now lost their way in a manageable chase against an undermanned team that summoned great spirit in adversity. Dhoni's decision to field first was based on the liveliest pitch of the series, and the new ball did seam in the opening overs, accounting for Marsh and forcing Watson and Ponting into Test-match mode. But the bounce was true and the outfield fast, and as the ball aged the score mounted to reach a promising 217 for four by the 43rd over. Some improved bowling and wasteful batting – four players were run out – hastened a late-innings slide, and 250 seemed barely adequate. As had been his habit, Sehwag gave India a rollicking start – 30 from 19 balls with seven fours – before giving his wicket away. With Gambhir nursing a sore neck (he was hit while fielding close in to Ponting in the previous match), the No. 3 spot was taken by Virat Kohli, and his cheap dismissal opened up the middle order. Tendulkar fell to a doubtful lbw decision by Asoka de Silva, but Yuvraj Singh was brilliantly thrown out from short cover by the predatory Ponting, and the others could not stand up to the speed of Bollinger, the thrift of Hauritz and the improved rhythm of Watson.
Man of the Match: S. R. Watson.

Australia

S. R. Watson c Dhoni b Harbhajan Singh	49	P. M. Siddle c Jadeja b Nehra	1
S. E. Marsh lbw b Nehra	5	D. E. Bollinger run out	0
*R. T. Ponting run out	52		
C. L. White run out	62	L-b 1, w 9, n-b 1	11
M. E. K. Hussey c Sharma b Yuvraj Singh	40		
M. C. Henriques st Dhoni b Harbhajan Singh	6	1/24 (2) 2/88 (1) 3/123 (3) (49.2 overs)	250
M. G. Johnson b Nehra	8	4/196 (5) 5/217 (6) 6/226 (4)	
†G. A. Manou run out	7	7/236 (7) 8/241 (8) 9/247 (10)	
N. M. Hauritz not out	9	10/250 (11) 10 overs: 37-1	

Kumar 9.2–0–41–0; Nehra 8–0–37–3; Sharma 5–0–42–0; Jadeja 7–0–27–0; Harbhajan Singh 10–0–48–2; Yuvraj Singh 10–0–54–1.

India

V. Sehwag c Watson b Bollinger	30	A. Nehra c Hauritz b Watson	7
S. R. Tendulkar lbw b Hauritz	40	I. Sharma not out	3
V. Kohli c Manou b Bollinger	10		
Yuvraj Singh run out	12	B 1, l-b 5, w 20, n-b 1	27
*†M. S. Dhoni c Manou b Bollinger	26		
S. K. Raina b Hauritz	17	1/40 (1) 2/78 (3) 3/94 (2) (46.4 overs)	226
R. A. Jadeja run out	7	4/113 (4) 5/145 (5) 6/156 (6)	
Harbhajan Singh c and b Watson	31	7/177 (7) 8/204 (8) 9/217 (9)	
P. Kumar c Manou b Watson	16	10/226 (10) 10 overs: 54-1	

Johnson 9–0–74–0; Siddle 5–2–15–0; Bollinger 9–2–38–3; Henriques 7–0–33–0; Hauritz 9–1–31–2; Watson 7.4–1–29–3.

Umpires: E. A. R. de Silva and A. M. Saheba.

Third umpire: S. S. Hazare. Referee: B. C. Broad.

INDIA v AUSTRALIA

Fifth One-Day International

At Uppal, Hyderabad, November 5, 2009 (day/night). Australia won by three runs. Toss: Australia. One-day international debut: C. J. McKay.

One of the most bewitching limited-overs matches yet played saw Australian composure win out despite the majesty of Tendulkar. It was clear after only a few overs that the pitch was of the highest quality for batting, as Watson struck crisply through the line to get Australia off to a powerful start. Marsh was more reserved, but gathered momentum as he went on, and once Watson had perished within sight of a century Marsh anchored the innings in a manner reminiscent of his father, Geoff, who also scored his first one-day hundred against India, 23 years previously. Late hammer blows by White (who hit five sixes from just 33 balls) and Hussey took Australia as far as 350, a total India had never successfully chased. Knowing the required rate did not allow for a moment's hesitation, and again losing Sehwag after a start of unfulfilled promise, Tendulkar – who passed 17,000 runs in one-day internationals early on – took it upon himself to scale the mountain. Taking an approach reminiscent of his younger self, he was audacious in the manner of Sharjah 1998 (when he scored 80, 143 and 134 in successive matches against Australia in the Coca-Cola Cup), and for some time the Siddle-less attack had no answer. Raina provided the support to take India within sight, and the last three overs began with just 19 required and four wickets left. Ponting had been counselling his battered bowlers to change their pace in the absence of any help from the surface, and it was a slower ball, from the debutant Clint McKay, that Tendulkar scooped fatefully to short fine leg. A chaotically panicked end followed, as Australia salvaged a meritorious victory at the last gasp. But memories of Tendulkar's effort will live longer than those of the result. His superb innings, which occupied 141 balls and contained 19 fours and four sixes, was his 45th one-day hundred – and the 12th that failed to secure victory.

Man of the Match: S. R. Tendulkar.

Australia

S. R. Watson c Jadeja b Harbhajan Singh	93	
S. E. Marsh c Gambhir b Nehra	112	
*R. T. Ponting b Kumar	45	
C. L. White c Tendulkar b Kumar	57	
M. E. K. Hussey not out	31	
L-b 6, w 5, n-b 1	12	
1/145 (1) 2/236 (3) (4 wkts, 50 overs)	350	
3/270 (2) 4/350 (4) 10 overs: 56-0		

A. C. Voges, †G. A. Manou, N. M. Hauritz, B. W. Hilfenhaus, D. E. Bollinger and C. J. McKay did not bat.

Kumar 9–0–68–2; Nehra 10–0–79–1; Patel 9–0–73–0; Jadeja 5–0–44–0; Harbhajan Singh 10–0–44–1; Yuvraj Singh 7–0–36–0.

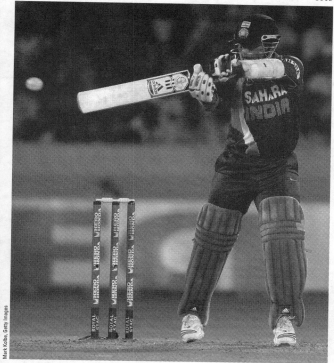

Mark Kolbe, Getty Images

Going down in style: Sachin Tendulkar hits out, but his fireworks came in a losing cause.

India

V. Sehwag c Bollinger b Hilfenhaus	38
S. R. Tendulkar c Hauritz b McKay	175
G. Gambhir c Hilfenhaus b McKay	8
Yuvraj Singh c and b Watson	9
*†M. S. Dhoni c Voges b McKay	6
S. K. Raina c Manou b Watson	59
Harbhajan Singh c Manou b Watson	0
R. A. Jadeja run out	23
P. Kumar run out	9

A. Nehra c Hussey b Bollinger	1
M. M. Patel not out	2
B 1, l-b 5, w 8, n-b 3	17

1/66 (1) 2/92 (3) 3/126 (4) (49.4 overs) 347
4/162 (5) 5/299 (6) 6/300 (7)
7/332 (2) 8/333 (8) 9/335 (10)
10/347 (9)

10 overs: 68-1

Hilfenhaus 10–0–72–1; Bollinger 10–0–75–1; McKay 10–0–59–3; Watson 8.4–0–47–3; Hauritz 5–0–43–0; Voges 3–0–19–0; Hussey 3–0–26–0.

Umpires: E. A. R. de Silva and S. K. Tarapore.
Third umpire: S. S. Hazare.   Referee: B. C. Broad.

INDIA v AUSTRALIA

Sixth One-Day International

At Guwahati, November 8, 2009. Australia won by six wickets. Toss: India.

Australia secured a laudable series victory in the space of around 45 minutes. In that time Johnson (back after missing the previous match with his ankle injury) and Bollinger delivered high-class spells of speed and swing in helpful morning conditions to reduce India to 27 for five after nine overs, depths from which they were unable to recover. Dhoni had predicted a difficult first few overs against the new ball, given the 8.30 a.m. start which was designed to counterbalance Guwahati's early twilight. But it was worse than he expected: gaining swing and bounce unseen virtually all series, Johnson bent the ball through Sehwag and around Gambhir in the first over, while Bollinger cramped Tendulkar into a return catch and had some luck when Yuvraj Singh saw the ball spin from his body on to the stumps. Given such a wretched start, 170 was a creditable recovery, but it was not enough to trouble the Australians despite increasing amounts of turn in the afternoon. After his side mopped up the required runs, Ponting declared this series win, in considerable adversity, the equal of anything he had achieved in 50-over matches.

Man of the Match: D. E. Bollinger.

India

V. Sehwag b Johnson	6	A. Nehra b Watson	4
S. R. Tendulkar c and b Bollinger	10	M. M. Patel b Watson	0
G. Gambhir b Johnson	0		
Yuvraj Singh b Bollinger	6	B 1, l-b 1, w 4, n-b 3	9
*†M. S. Dhoni lbw b Bollinger	24		
S. K. Raina c Hauritz b Johnson	0	1/7 (1) 2/7 (3) 3/23 (2) (48 overs)	170
R. A. Jadeja c White b Bollinger	57	4/24 (4) 5/27 (6) 6/75 (5)	
Harbhajan Singh b Bollinger	0	7/75 (8) 8/149 (7) 9/170 (10)	
P. Kumar not out	54	10/170 (11)	10 overs: 27-5

Johnson 9–1–39–3; Bollinger 10–4–35–5; McKay 10–1–44–0; Hauritz 9–2–19–0; Watson 8–0–27–2; Voges 2–0–4–0.

Australia

S. R. Watson c Sehwag b Harbhajan Singh	49	A. C. Voges not out	23
S. E. Marsh lbw b Patel	6	B 6, l-b 2, w 1	9
*R. T. Ponting c Raina b Harbhajan Singh	25		
C. L. White lbw b Raina	25	1/24 (2) 2/85 (1) (4 wkts, 41.5 overs)	172
M. E. K. Hussey not out	35	3/90 (3) 4/143 (4)	10 overs: 41-1

M. G. Johnson, †G. A. Manou, N. M. Hauritz, D. E. Bollinger and C. J. McKay did not bat.

Kumar 2–0–10–0; Nehra 3–0–21–0; Patel 4–1–13–1; Jadeja 10–1–36–0; Harbhajan Singh 10–1–23–2; Yuvraj Singh 7–1–29–0; Raina 3–0–13–1; Sehwag 2–0–8–0; Tendulkar 0.5–0–11–0.

Umpires: E. A. R. de Silva and S. K. Tarapore.
Third umpire: S. S. Hazare.   Referee: B. C. Broad.

INDIA v AUSTRALIA

Seventh One-Day International

At Dr D. Y. Patil Sports Academy, Mumbai, November 11, 2009 (day/night). Abandoned.

A cyclone in the Arabian Sea led to the game being called off without either team travelling to the ground, and the trophy was handed to Ponting in the team hotel after Australia's 4–2 series victory. This was to have been the first international match at the new ground inside the Dr D. Y. Patil University campus in Nerul, about 30 miles east of central Mumbai, where the first IPL final was played in June 2008.

Man of the Series: S. R. Watson.

INDIA v SRI LANKA, 2009-10

NAGRAJ GOLLAPUDI

Test matches (3): India 2, Sri Lanka 0
One-day internationals (5): India 3, Sri Lanka 1
Twenty20 internationals (2): India 1, Sri Lanka 1

The Sri Lankans slipped into India while the country was busy gushing over their most celebrated son, Sachin Tendulkar, completing 20 years in international cricket. It was a happy distraction, as the visitors did not mind being left alone to prepare for their series. But Kumar Sangakkara did get peeved when the media harassed him at every opportunity for a quote on Tendulkar. Reluctantly, rolling his eyes, and nodding in disbelief, the Sri Lankan captain doled out some clichéd compliments. His irritation had much to do with the fact that the media seemed to have forgotten that Sri Lanka were the world's second-ranked Test team, only a touch behind South Africa.

But Sangakkara understood well enough that the tour would test his side's mettle. India had lost only two Test series at home in the 21st century. Since losing to South Africa early in 2000, they had played 15 further series, with 11 victories, four draws and one loss. The only defeat came against one of the best of all Australian sides, in 2004-05, when Ricky Ponting's men captured the "final frontier". Sri Lanka themselves had toured India six times over the previous 27 years, playing 14 Tests – and had yet to win one.

Sangakkara, who has studied law, knew the best way to relieve the pressure would be to divert attention. Asked if the pressure was on his young team, he countered that India had just lost a one-day series to an under-strength Australian side. Obviously he knew he was up against it, leading a mostly young and inexperienced squad. Only four of the others had played Tests in India: Tillekeratne Dilshan, Mahela Jayawardene, Muttiah Muralitharan and Thilan Samaraweera. None of them had made a Test century there, while Murali's bowling average of 39.58 in India was his second-worst overseas, after Australia (75.41).

Without the long-serving Chaminda Vaas to lead their fast bowling, Sri Lanka's attack looked unfamiliar, but nonetheless it had variety. Even if they were short on experience, Thilan Thushara Mirando, Nuwan Kulasekara, Dammika Prasad, Chanaka Welagedara and the burgeoning all-rounder Angelo Mathews constituted a healthy pace battery, while the spin trio of Muralitharan, Ajantha Mendis and slow left-armer Rangana Herath was full of variety and promise on paper.

To add to the tension, this was also Sri Lanka's first Test series abroad since the tragic events in Lahore in March. So they remained alert, and let it be known when they felt they did not have adequate security on their way to training during the warm-up game in Mumbai.

But by the time they arrived in Ahmedabad for the First Test any insecurity had moved to the field of play, after injuries to the first-choice new-ball pair of

Mirando and Kulasekara. However, Welagedara answered his captain's call after being drafted in at the last minute, and immediately had the Indians under the cosh at 32 for four, until Rahul Dravid audaciously plucked them out of danger. That first hour was the only eventful one in the entire game, the rest of which was played out on an unresponsive pitch.

For the Second Test at Kanpur, the Sri Lankan think tank opted for a three-pronged spin attack, which backfired miserably as Sreesanth and Zaheer Khan showed that even if the Green Park pitch was slow and low, seamers were still a better bet. In Mumbai, Mendis was replaced by Kulasekara, but on a captivating second day, the magic of Virender Sehwag would have spelled doom for the best.

The most important revelation for Sri Lanka was that they came to understand what life would be like without their talisman, Muralitharan, who entered the series needing a further 17 wickets to become the first bowler to take 800 in Tests. By the end Murali was reduced to a net bowler, and managed just nine wickets at a forgettable average of 65. Herath was the best of the visiting bowlers, daring to flight the ball even on placid tracks and teasing the batsmen. Despite the decline of Murali, Sri Lanka have in Herath and Mendis – if he can find his mojo again – two spinners who could carry forward the legacy that Muralitharan established over some 15 years.

Two other players emerged from the series with reputations enhanced. Dilshan and Mathews have the potential and positive intent that could form the backbone of Sri Lanka's batting over the next few years. The experienced Dilshan showed his skills were more varied and higher than just his scoop-shot, a raging Twenty20 hit. His two hundreds in Ahmedabad and Mumbai strengthened the opinion that he had successfully filled the gap left by the retirement of Sanath Jayasuriya. Mathews showed that he was hungry to learn, and even cried when he missed his maiden century in Mumbai by just one run. He bounced back with some lively spells of pace bowling and, if groomed properly, has the potential to become a top-class batting all-rounder.

If Sri Lanka were trying to find their feet on shifting sands, India had a more settled outlook. It was no surprise that they climbed to the top of the rankings through this series win. As Gary Kirsten later declared, India had been rehearsing for the occasion for the previous 21 months, ever since he took charge as head coach. Victories, both home and away, have allowed India to build a battle-hardened side that can take care of any situation. Hence Murali Vijay, who was brought back for his second Test a year after his debut, charged Muralitharan confidently and hit him for six to reach a maiden half-century in Mumbai.

Sehwag and Gautam Gambhir were hailed during 2009 as the best opening combination India have ever had. Even more than that, though, they have proved consistently that they are individual match-winners first. Gambhir started 2009 with his Napier marathon, and continued to build on that with four centuries in successive matches in which he played (he added a fifth against Bangladesh early in 2010). Sehwag finished the year with two memorable innings; not only his tour de force in Mumbai, where he nearly became only the second man to score 300 in a day's play in a Test, but also his spectacular century at Kanpur, which helped India breach the 400-mark in a day. Ian Chappell has already called him the new Bradman and Sehwag is not blushing yet.

The one-day series, which ended in farce on a dreadful pitch at Delhi, proved little beyond the fact that both sides still had a lot of work to do to challenge for top spot in the 50-over format. The most obvious area where India and Sri Lanka currently trailed Australia and South Africa was in the fielding. It could prove to be one of the most important factors in determining the outcome of the 2011 World Cup, but these games showed that neither of these South Asian neighbours was yet fit enough.

SRI LANKAN TOURING PARTY

K. C. Sangakkara (*captain*), T. M. Dilshan, H. M. R. K. B. Herath, D. P. M. D. Jayawardene, H. A. P. W. Jayawardene, S. H. T. Kandamby, K. M. D. N. Kulasekara, A. D. Mathews, B. A. W. Mendis, M. T. T. Mirando, M. Muralitharan, N. T. Paranavitana, K. T. G. D. Prasad, T. T. Samaraweera, J. K. Silva, U. W. M. B. C. A. Welagedara. *Coach:* T. H. Bayliss.

Mirando returned home with a shoulder injury early in the tour and was replaced by C. R. D. Fernando. For the Twenty20 matches that followed the Tests, C. U. Jayasinghe, S. T. Jayasuriya, C. K. Kapugedera, S. L. Malinga, M. Pushpakumara and K. Weeraratne replaced Herath, H. A. P. W. Jayawardene, Kandamby, Paranavitana, Prasad, Samaraweera and Silva. For the subsequent one-day international series Kandamby, Samaraweera and W. U. Tharanga came in for Jayasinghe, Pushpakumara and Weeraratne. Fernando and Muralitharan returned home with finger injuries, and were replaced by R. A. S. Lakmal, Pushpakumara and S. Randiv. Mathews injured his arm during the second match, and was replaced by N. L. T. C. Perera.

TEST MATCH AVERAGES

INDIA – BATTING AND FIELDING

	T	I	NO	R	HS	100s	50s	Avge	Ct
V. Sehwag	3	4	0	491	293	2	1	122.75	1
R. Dravid	3	4	0	433	177	2	1	108.25	4
M. S. Dhoni	3	3	1	214	110	2	0	107.00	10
†G. Gambhir	2	3	0	282	167	2	0	94.00	1
S. R. Tendulkar	3	4	1	197	100*	1	1	65.66	2
V. V. S. Laxman	3	4	1	176	63	0	3	58.66	2
†Yuvraj Singh	3	3	0	158	68	0	2	52.66	1
Harbhajan Singh	3	3	0	28	22	0	0	9.33	1
Zaheer Khan	3	3	0	20	12	0	0	6.66	0

Played in two Tests: †P. P. Ojha 1*, 5* (3 ct); S. Sreesanth 0, 8. Played in one Test: A. Mishra 7*, 24 (1 ct); I. Sharma 0; M. Vijay 87 (2 ct).

† *Left-handed batsman.*

BOWLING

	Style	O	M	R	W	BB	5W/i	Avge
P. P. Ojha	SLA	85.1	21	258	9	3-101	0	28.66
S. Sreesanth	RFM	62	13	240	8	5-75	1	30.00
Zaheer Khan	LFM	104	18	365	10	5-72	1	36.50
Harbhajan Singh	OB	158.2	19	533	13	4-112	0	41.00

Also bowled: A. Mishra (LBG) 58–6–203–1; V. Sehwag (OB) 16–3–47–1; I. Sharma (RFM) 33–0–135–2; S. R. Tendulkar (RM/OB/LB) 8–0–26–0; Yuvraj Singh (SLA) 23–1–90–1.

SRI LANKA – BATTING AND FIELDING

	T	I	NO	R	HS	100s	50s	Avge	Ct/St
D. P. M. D. Jayawardene	3	5	0	373	275	1	0	74.60	1
H. A. P. W. Jayawardene	3	5	1	297	154*	1	0	74.25	2/1
T. M. Dilshan	3	5	0	248	112	2	0	49.60	4
†K. C. Sangakkara	3	5	0	241	137	1	0	48.20	1
†N. T. Paranavitana.	3	5	0	200	54	0	2	40.00	0
T. T. Samaraweera	3	5	1	151	78*	0	2	37.75	1
A. D. Mathews	3	5	0	149	99	0	1	29.80	2
M. Muralitharan	3	4	1	53	29	0	0	17.66	2
†H. M. R. K. B. Herath	3	4	0	28	13	0	0	7.00	0
U. W. M. B. C. A. Welagedara. . .	3	4	1	19	8	0	0	6.33	0

Played in one Test: K. M. D. N. Kulasekara 12, 19 (2 ct); B. A. W. Mendis 6*, 27; K. T. G. D. Prasad 21 (1 ct).

† *Left-handed batsman.*

BOWLING

	Style	O	M	R	W	BB	5W/i	Avge
H. M. R. K. B. Herath	SLA	148.3	12	537	11	5-121	1	48.81
M. Muralitharan.	OB	151.5	14	591	9	4-195	0	65.66
U. W. M. B. C. A. Welagedara	LFM	99	12	397	6	4-87	0	66.16

Also bowled: T. M. Dilshan (OB) 8–0–38–0; K. M. D. N. Kulasekara (RFM) 20–1–105–1; A. D. Mathews (RFM) 50–9–164–1; B. A. W. Mendis (OB/LBG) 38–3–162–2; N. T. Paranavitana (OB) 1–0–7–0; K. T. G. D. Prasad (RFM) 35–1–162–2.

Note: Matches in this section which were not first-class are denoted by a dagger.

At Bandra Kurla Complex, Mumbai, November 11, 12, 13, 2009. **Indian Board President's XI v Sri Lankans. Abandoned.**
    Heavy rain, and finally a damp pitch, washed out the Sri Lankans' only pre-Test warm-up.

INDIA v SRI LANKA

First Test Match

At Ahmedabad, November 16, 17, 18, 19, 20, 2009. Drawn. Toss: India.
    The contrast between the start and end of the match was striking. Inside the first hour Sri Lanka, led by Welagedara's probing left-arm swing, knocked off four top-order wickets. A result seemed certain. But what unfolded over the better part of the next five days was nothing short of a snooze-fest as the pitch remained hard as granite on which champion bowlers were rendered useless and batsmen prospered.
    At the start, the visitors would not have imagined they would wrest control of the match so quickly. Their first-choice fast bowlers – Thilan Thushara Mirando and Nuwan Kulasekara – were both declared unfit minutes before the toss, and Welagedara had hurried into his whites five minutes before the start. He was playing his first Test since his debut against England in December 2007. Dammika Prasad, three Tests under his belt, was included for his big heart and the ability to reverse-swing the ball.
    The raw new-ball pair were surprisingly nerveless, and it was the Indians who found trouble early on, as the bowlers made full use of the morning moisture. At 32 for four,

Natural partners: Jayawardenes Prasanna (*left*) and Mahela head for the highest sixth-wicket stand in Tests.

India were wobbling dangerously, and without an uncharacteristic 27th Test century from Dravid they might have ceded control completely of the game. Dravid's future had been in question after he was dropped from the preceding one-day series against Australia. But now he retrieved the situation yet again for India – this time with belligerent strokeplay, as he added positive intent to his famed mental strength.

Even in the company of aggressors such as Dhoni and Yuvraj Singh, Dravid never relented. He opened gateways when none seemed to exist. When Sangakkara packed the off side with deep point, short extra cover and mid-off, Dravid still managed to find gaps in the field. Little wonder then that, out of his unbeaten 177 by the end of the first day – the most he had ever scored in a day in a Test – Dravid had collected 110 in boundaries. During his innings he became only the fifth man to score 11,000 runs in Tests. Dhoni also reached his century, his second in Tests, scampering ones and twos.

Dravid's aggression left his team-mates gasping: at lunch Laxman, who had taken a nap to try to forget his early dismissal, woke up to find India in a strong position. He was told that Dravid was leading the fightback, and had hit the slow left-armer Herath for six just before lunch. Laxman had to pinch Dravid to confirm that.

However, on the second morning Welagedara bowled Dravid without addition, and the Sri Lankans wasted no time wrapping up the Indian tail. Their batsmen then retaliated strongly, building a mammoth total of 760, the highest in a Test in India. Dilshan and Sangakkara led the initial assault, laying a strong platform for the two Jayawardenes. Mahela, Sri Lanka's most reliable batsman, assumed control on the second afternoon, after Dilshan and Sangakkara fell in quick succession. Showing amazing focus for the next two days, Jayawardene reached his sixth Test double-century, passing 9,000 runs, and put on 351 for the sixth wicket with his namesake Prasanna, a new Test record, eclipsing the 346 of Jack Fingleton and Don Bradman for Australia against England at Melbourne in 1936-37 (Bradman dropped to No. 7 in that innings, promoting some expendable tailenders while the wicket was wet, and scored 270).

The Indian bowlers were inconsistent, with the exception of Zaheer Khan, returning to international cricket after a four-month lay-off with a shoulder injury sustained in the IPL.

Harbhajan Singh, leading the spin attack, had a miserable match, while leg-spinner Mishra became only the sixth Indian to concede more than 200 runs in a Test innings.

Sri Lanka possibly missed the chance of forcing a result when they failed to accelerate on the third evening and the first session on the fourth day. They eventually left themselves 135 overs to bowl India out a second time, but solid resistance – notably in the form of hundreds by Gambhir and Tendulkar – quelled their hopes. Tendulkar's century was the 43rd of a Test career that had begun 20 years and one day before this match started.

Muralitharan was the big disappointment and, as Sangakkara admitted, a concern. The unrelenting surface could be blamed to an extent, but good batsmen were beginning to find a way to counter Murali as his powers waned. Here, he managed only three wickets in the match, including a solitary top-order batsman, while the last time he had bowled more than 20 overs in any Test innings without taking a wicket – as happened in the second innings here – was almost ten years previously, against Zimbabwe at Harare in December 1999.

In the end the main culprit was the dead pitch. Sunil Gavaskar felt that the groundsman could work on Gujarat's roads, so flat was the pitch, while Sourav Ganguly, another former captain, said that another Test could have been played on the same track.

Man of the Match: D. P. M. D. Jayawardene.

Close of play: First day, India 385-6 (Dravid 177, Harbhajan Singh 2); Second day, Sri Lanka 275-3 (D. P. M. D. Jayawardene 36, Samaraweera 45); Third day, Sri Lanka 591-5 (D. P. M. D. Jayawardene 204, H. A. P. W. Jayawardene 84); Fourth day, India 190-2 (Gambhir 74, Mishra 12).

India

G. Gambhir b Welagedara	1	– c Prasad b Herath	114
V. Sehwag lbw b Welagedara	16	– c Mathews b Herath	51
R. Dravid b Welagedara	177	– lbw b Welagedara	38
S. R. Tendulkar b Welagedara	4	– (5) not out	100
V. V. S. Laxman b Prasad	0	– (6) not out	51
Yuvraj Singh c Dilshan b Muralitharan	68		
*†M. S. Dhoni c H. A. P. W. Jayawardene b Prasad	110		
Harbhajan Singh b Muralitharan	22		
Zaheer Khan lbw b Herath	12		
A. Mishra not out	7	– (4) c Dilshan b Mathews	24
I. Sharma st H. A. P. W. Jayawardene b Muralitharan	0		
B 2, l-b 2, w 1, n-b 4	9	B 12, l-b 9, w 2, n-b 11	34

1/14 (1) 2/27 (2) 3/31 (4)   (104.5 overs) 426   1/81 (2)   (4 wkts, 129 overs) 412
4/32 (5) 5/157 (6) 6/381 (7) 7/389 (3)   2/169 (3) 3/209 (4)
8/414 (9) 9/426 (8) 10/426 (11)   4/275 (1)

Welagedara 22–4–87–4; Prasad 22–1–106–2; Mathews 12–1–50–0; Muralitharan 25.5–4–97–3; Herath 22–2–79–1; Dilshan 1–0–3–0. *Second Innings*—Welagedara 21–1–76–1; Prasad 13–0–56–0; Herath 40–6–97–2; Muralitharan 38–6–124–0; Mathews 15–6–29–1; Dilshan 1–0–2–0; Paranavitana 1–0–7–0.

Sri Lanka

T. M. Dilshan c Dravid b Zaheer Khan	112	K. T. G. D. Prasad c Mishra	
N. T. Paranavitana c Dhoni b Sharma	35	b Harbhajan Singh	21
*K. C. Sangakkara c Tendulkar			
b Zaheer Khan	31	B 5, l-b 16, w 4, n-b 20	45
D. P. M. D. Jayawardene b Mishra	275		
T. T. Samaraweera c Yuvraj Singh b Sharma	70	1/74 (2) (7 wkts dec, 202.4 overs) 760	
A. D. Mathews c Gambhir		2/189 (1) 3/194 (3)	
b Harbhajan Singh	17	4/332 (5) 5/375 (6)	
†H. A. P. W. Jayawardene not out	154	6/726 (4) 7/760 (8)	

H. M. R. K. B. Herath, M. Muralitharan and U. W. M. B. C. A. Welagedara did not bat.

Zaheer Khan 36–6–109–2; Sharma 33–0–135–2; Harbhajan Singh 48.4–4–189–2; Mishra 58–6–203–1; Yuvraj Singh 16–1–64–0; Tendulkar 7–0–20–0; Sehwag 4–1–19–0.

Umpires: D. J. Harper and A. L. Hill.
Third umpire: A. M. Saheba.   Referee: J. J. Crowe.

INDIA v SRI LANKA

Second Test Match

At Kanpur, November 24, 25, 26, 27, 2009. India won by an innings and 144 runs. Toss: India. Test debut: P. P. Ojha.

By the end of the first day, India had piled up more runs – 417 – than they had ever managed in a day before. By the end of the second, Gambhir, after completing back-to-back centuries, was confident the Test could have only one winner. And by the end of the third Sreesanth had all but ensured that Gambhir would be right, with a comeback performance that forced Sri Lanka to follow on. An hour after lunch on the fourth day, India completed their 100th Test victory.

India were the sixth team to complete a century of Test wins, and although they arrived at the milestone the slowest – it took them 432 matches – they had been improving at a steady rate since the turn of the millennium. In the first decade of the 21st century (and including the Third Test of this series) India won 40 of their 103 matches. Various protagonists have been involved in their surge to the summit, but none has had the chutzpah of Virender Sehwag. This was the 26th win in which he had featured, and he had gone in first in 25 of them, easily passing Sunil Gavaskar's previous record of 22 for an Indian opener, from far more Tests.

Once again Sehwag left an enormous imprint on this Test. At Ahmedabad his swift, streaky half-century had doused Sri Lanka's soaring hopes of a positive result. But on a dry pitch, with a light green stubble that promised more movement than it delivered, Sehwag spread panic among the Sri Lankans with a clinical dissection of their bowlers. He had the patient Gambhir on hand to help, and they set about shredding the attack with relish. They are both aggressive by nature, but their most important quality has been to tailor their play to the situation. In Sehwag's case it has sometimes been easy to forget this, as he always seems to be in attacking mode. The reality is different. Sehwag did not hit a boundary from his first 26 deliveries; after 11 overs on the first morning, India were 31 without loss.

But by lunch they had added a further 100 runs, with 73 plundered from nine overs of spin before the break. Just as they had in helping India bounce back at Galle in 2008 after defeat in the First Test in Sri Lanka, Sehwag and Gambhir split the responsibilities. Gambhir drove Herath out of the attack as soon as he was introduced, while Sehwag took charge of Mendis, the third spinner who had been included after much deliberation. Gambhir also used his feet and the crease smartly to neutralise Muralitharan, who finally found some confidence on a more encouraging pitch.

The Sehwag effect was so emphatic that by the time he departed in the 42nd over, to a brilliant diving catch at extra cover by Dilshan, India had already scored 233. The rest of the day was more sedate: 184 from 48.4 overs. Sehwag's century was his first in 16 months since his majestic 201 in that match at Galle. But it had hardly been a drought, since he had scored some valuable fifties in the interim, including an important one at Chennai to set up victory over England, an innings overshadowed by Tendulkar's emotional century. Gambhir also reached three figures, his fourth century in as many Tests.

Sri Lanka were also to blame for their own plight. With the fourth ball of the match Welagedara induced a thick edge off Sehwag that was travelling to Mahela Jayawardene at first slip. But Prasanna Jayawardene intercepted – and fumbled. It proved the turning point of the match. Sri Lanka's situation worsened as Dravid recorded another hundred, following his Ahmedabad blitz, and half-centuries from Laxman and Yuvraj Singh ensured

India would bat just once. The only blot was that the last six wickets fell for only 29 runs; Herath, who dared to flight the ball in the face of the assault, was rewarded with his first overseas five-for, but Muralitharan and Mendis were expensive.

Replying to a total of more than 600 was always a daunting prospect on a pitch taking turn. Sri Lanka were immediately in trouble, when Dilshan top-edged the first ball, a harmless leg-side loosener from Zaheer Khan, to mid-on, where the debutant Pragyan Ojha took the catch from his first possible delivery in a Test. Further fissures appeared as Sreesanth – whose previous Test, 19 months before, had also been at Green Park – capped a successful return with two spectacular spells to ensure that Sri Lanka had to follow on. In the morning Sreesanth made use of the early moisture to get the ball to swing, and destroyed the top order with a spell of 9–2–28–3. In the afternoon, he stormed back, finding appreciable reverse swing in addition to cutting the ball off the seam, for a spell of 7–2–18–2.

Sri Lanka were clearly oppressed by a deficit of 413, and Mahela Jayawardene, the top-scorer in the first innings, was embarrassingly run out by his captain in the second. Sangakkara himself played on four balls later. They were 57 for four (still 356 behind) on the third evening and, although Samaraweera resisted in spirited fashion, by midway through the following day the Indians could celebrate their century of wins, and start focusing on the next goal: becoming the No. 1 team in the world rankings. For that, they needed to win the final Test in Mumbai.

Man of the Match: S. Sreesanth.

Close of play: First day, India 417-2 (Dravid 85, Tendulkar 20); Second day, Sri Lanka 66-1 (Paranavitana 30, Sangakkara 30); Third day, Sri Lanka 57-4 (Samaraweera 1, Mathews 2).

India

G. Gambhir c and b Muralitharan	167	S. Sreesanth lbw b Herath	0
V. Sehwag c Dilshan b Muralitharan	131	P. P. Ojha not out	1
R. Dravid run out	144		
S. R. Tendulkar c Samaraweera b Mendis	40		
V. V. S. Laxman c Dilshan b Herath	63	B 4, l-b 11, n-b 4	19
Yuvraj Singh c Sangakkara b Mendis	67		
*†M. S. Dhoni b Herath	4	1/233 (2) 2/370 (1) (154 overs)	642
Harbhajan Singh b Herath	5	3/464 (4) 4/511 (5) 5/613 (5)	
Zaheer Khan c D. P. M. D. Jayawardene		6/619 (7) 7/639 (8) 8/641 (6)	
b Herath	1	9/641 (9) 10/642 (10)	

Welagedara 26–4–103–0; Mathews 17–2–49–0; Herath 33–2–121–5; Mendis 38–3–162–2; Muralitharan 37–0–175–2; Dilshan 3–0–17–0.

Sri Lanka

T. M. Dilshan c Ojha b Zaheer Khan	0	– (2) c Dhoni b Sreesanth	11
N. T. Paranavitana c Dhoni b Sreesanth	38	– (1) lbw b Sehwag	20
*K. C. Sangakkara b Sreesanth	44	– b Harbhajan Singh	11
D. P. M. D. Jayawardene c Tendulkar b Ojha	47	– run out	10
T. T. Samaraweera b Sreesanth	2	– not out	78
A. D. Mathews b Harbhajan Singh	13	– c Dravid b Zaheer Khan	15
†H. A. P. W. Jayawardene c Dhoni b Sreesanth	39	– b Harbhajan Singh	29
H. M. R. K. B. Herath b Sreesanth	11	– lbw b Harbhajan Singh	13
M. Muralitharan lbw b Ojha	6	– b Ojha	29
U. W. M. B. C. A. Welagedara			
lbw b Harbhajan Singh	7	– (11) c and b Ojha	4
B. A. W. Mendis not out	6	– (10) lbw b Yuvraj Singh	27
B 9, l-b 2, n-b 5	16	B 7, l-b 1, n-b 14	22

1/0 (1) 2/82 (2) 3/101 (3) 4/111 (5)   (84 overs) 229   1/13 (2) 2/37 (1)   (65.3 overs) 269
5/134 (6) 6/194 (7) 7/204 (4) 8/216 (8)   3/54 (4) 4/54 (3)
9/219 (9) 10/229 (10)   5/79 (6) 6/140 (7) 7/154 (8)
                                                             8/191 (9) 9/264 (10) 10/269 (11)

Zaheer Khan 17–5–51–1; Sreesanth 22–4–75–5; Harbhajan Singh 21–5–54–2; Ojha 23–12–37–2; Yuvraj Singh 1–0–1–0. *Second Innings*—Zaheer Khan 11–0–63–1; Sreesanth 11–4–47–1; Harbhajan Singh 22–2–98–3; Sehwag 3–0–4–1; Ojha 15.3–4–36–2; Tendulkar 1–0–6–0; Yuvraj Singh 2–0–7–1.

Umpires: A. L. Hill and N. J. Llong.
Third umpire: S. S. Hazare.   Referee: J. J. Crowe.

INDIA v SRI LANKA

Third Test Match

At Brabourne Stadium, Mumbai, December 2, 3, 4, 5, 6, 2009. India won by an innings and 24 runs. Toss: Sri Lanka.

Sri Lanka tried everything they could to avert Hurricane Sehwag, but were swept aside for the second time in a fortnight. India broke their own national record for runs in a day, surpassing the 417 on the first day of the previous Test with 443 on the second day here, made from just 79 overs. By the end of the run-glut, India had taken an important lead, even though Sri Lanka had fallen only just short of 400 themselves in the first innings of the match.

Once again Sehwag was in no rush to start with. He said later that Gary Kirsten, India's coach, had impressed upon him that if he could survive the first ten overs, he had the potential to do the unimaginable. In the first 45 minutes, Sehwag had hit just one boundary; by the eighth over he had scored only 15 from 31 balls. But he was soon to take off, Usain Bolt-style, and leave the opposition gasping in his wake.

By the end of the day, Sehwag was only 16 short of becoming the first man to make three triple-centuries in Tests. On the way, he became the Indian with most double-centuries (six, one more than Dravid), and broke his own Indian record for runs in a day. It was only the second time in Test cricket that a player had been involved in double-century stands for each of the first two wickets – and on each occasion that player was Sehwag. The first time was against South Africa at Chennai in 2007-08, when his 319 included stands of 213 with Wasim Jaffer and 268 with Dravid.

The pitch for the Brabourne Stadium's first Test since February 1973 was not the lame slab of Ahmedabad nor the slower variant at Kanpur, with its low bounce. Here, the wicket started taking turn from the first hour, when Harbhajan Singh bowled the 12th over. So Muralitharan and Herath were operating in favourable conditions – but they were rendered impotent by Sehwag, who dominated them before they could even begin to hatch any plans.

Sehwag forced the bowlers into panic. Even a master like Muralitharan fell into the trap, trying too many variations. When Sehwag had 248, Murali pitched one on middle stump; Sehwag instantly turned the bat-face and hit an incredible reverse paddle-sweep through the empty slip region for four, to reach his fourth score of 250-plus in Tests (only Bradman, with five, had made more). Sehwag has always cleared milestones with nonchalant ease: earlier he had cut, flicked, glanced and slogged boundaries in the same Kulasekara over, hurrying from 184 to 202 in the space of five balls, with four of his eventual 40 fours (there were also seven sixes).

"The guys tried most things," said Sri Lanka's coach Trevor Bayliss. "Different fields, bowling different sides of the wicket – but no matter where they put the ball he was skilful enough to put it away into the gaps. It was one of those days you needed 20 fielders out there."

But it all ended in anticlimax. Early on the third morning, after adding only nine to his overnight score, Sehwag scooped a simple return catch to Murali, who clutched the ball

There goes another four: Virender Sehwag treats Prasanna Jayawardene to an extended lesson in the art of batting.

dearly to his bosom at the second attempt. Sehwag departed seven short of 300, but remained upbeat: "Not many people have got two triple-centuries and followed that with 293. So there is nothing to be disappointed about." He faced just 254 balls and batted for 366 minutes.

The scoring-rate returned to something like normal after Sehwag's departure and, although Dhoni hit six sixes, his third Test century came up in the sedate time of 154 minutes. In all, India scored 283 runs on the third day – one fewer than Sehwag had managed on his own the day before. Still, Dhoni was able to declare at India's highest Test total, beating 705 for seven at Sydney in 2003-04.

Sehwag's blitz was all the more meritorious as it had followed a bright start from Sri Lanka, who racked up 366 for eight themselves on an entertaining first day. Dilshan's mature century, his 11th in Tests, had given the visitors a strong start in a match they needed to win to square the series. After putting on 93 for the first wicket with Paranavitana, Dilshan sensibly snuffed out the challenge posed by a lively pitch, easily the best of the series, and probing spells from Sreesanth and Harbhajan in the second session. Unfortunately, he was defeated by an umpiring error, given out caught bat-pad even though there was daylight between the two (the new umpiring review system was not in use in this series).

Mathews finally showed why he was seen as a promising all-rounder, leading a late surge before stumps, but he was unlucky to be run out next morning, by Tendulkar's return from deep square, stretching for the run that would have brought up his maiden Test century. He departed in tears. But worse was to follow as Sehwag came in to deliver his knockout punches.

Sri Lanka had learned harsh lessons in the previous Test by fielding three spinners. This time they left out Ajantha Mendis and brought back their leading fast bowler, the fit-again Kulasekara. India, too, were forced to make a change after Gambhir opted to attend his sister's wedding. Murali Vijay returned to open with Sehwag, having made an impressive debut against Australia a year before at Nagpur when Gambhir was banned.

When Sri Lanka batted again, 333 runs in arrears, things soon started going wrong. Early on the fourth day Dilshan was given out wrongly for the second time in the match, umpire Harper upholding an lbw appeal after he had padded up to one from Harbhajan that pitched on off stump but turned: Hawk-Eye indicated that it was easily missing leg. If there was any hope, it came in the form of Sangakkara, who finally scored his first Test century in India, on his second Test tour. He played a fine innings, accelerating in the final session, but his side were still 59 behind at the end of the fourth day, with only four wickets remaining.

Zaheer returned next morning to subdue the challenge, removing Sangakkara with the third ball of the day. India soon completed their second successive innings victory, one which put them on top of the Test rankings for the first time since the ICC introduced them in 2003.

Man of the Match: V. Sehwag. *Man of the Series:* V. Sehwag.

Close of play: First day, Sri Lanka 366-8 (Mathews 86, Muralitharan 0); Second day, India 443-1 (Sehwag 284, Dravid 62); Third day, Sri Lanka 11-0 (Paranavitana 8, Dilshan 3); Fourth day, Sri Lanka 274-6 (Sangakkara 133, Kulasekara 9).

Sri Lanka

N. T. Paranavitana c Dravid b Harbhajan Singh	53	– lbw b Sreesanth	54
T. M. Dilshan c Vijay b Harbhajan Singh	109	– lbw b Harbhajan Singh	16
*K. C. Sangakkara c Dhoni b Ojha	18	– c Dhoni b Zaheer Khan	137
D. P. M. D. Jayawardene c Sehwag b Sreesanth	29	– c Dhoni b Zaheer Khan	12
T. T. Samaraweera c Vijay b Harbhajan Singh	1	– c Laxman b Zaheer Khan	0
A. D. Mathews run out	99	– c Dhoni b Ojha	5
†H. A. P. W. Jayawardene c Harbhajan Singh b Ojha	43	– lbw b Ojha	32
K. M. D. N. Kulasekara c Dhoni b Zaheer Khan	12	– c Laxman b Zaheer Khan	19
H. M. R. K. B. Herath c Dravid b Harbhajan Singh	1	– c Ojha b Zaheer Khan	3
M. Muralitharan not out	4	– c Dhoni b Harbhajan Singh	14
U. W. M. B. C. A. Welagedara lbw b Ojha	8	– not out	0
B 4, l-b 6, w 2, n-b 4	16	B 12, l-b 1, w 1, n-b 3	17

1/93 (1) 2/128 (3) 3/187 (4) (94.4 overs) 393
4/188 (5) 5/262 (2) 6/329 (7)
7/359 (8) 8/362 (9) 9/379 (6)
10/393 (11)

1/29 (2) 2/119 (1) (100.4 overs) 309
3/135 (4) 4/137 (5)
5/144 (6) 6/208 (7) 7/278 (3)
8/282 (9) 9/307 (8) 10/309 (10)

Zaheer Khan 19–2–70–1; Sreesanth 16–1–82–1; Harbhajan Singh 32–3–112–4; Ojha 23.4–1–101–3; Yuvraj Singh 4–0–18–0. *Second Innings*—Harbhajan Singh 34.4–5–80–2; Ojha 23–4–84–2; Zaheer Khan 21–5–72–5; Sreesanth 13–4–36–1; Sehwag 9–2–24–0.

India

M. Vijay lbw b Herath	87
V. Sehwag c and b Muralitharan	293
R. Dravid c H. A. P. W. Jayawardene b Welagedara	74
S. R. Tendulkar b Kulasekara	53
V. V. S. Laxman c Kulasekara b Muralitharan	62
Yuvraj Singh c Mathews b Herath	23
*†M. S. Dhoni not out	100
Harbhajan Singh b Muralitharan	1

Zaheer Khan c Kulasekara b Muralitharan	7
S. Sreesanth lbw b Herath	8
P. P. Ojha not out	5
L-b 3, n-b 10	13

1/221 (1) (9 wkts dec, 163.3 overs) 726
2/458 (2) 3/487 (3)
4/558 (4) 5/591 (5) 6/610 (6)
7/615 (8) 8/647 (9) 9/670 (10)

Welagedara 30–3–131–1; Kulasekara 20–1–105–1; Herath 53.3–2–240–3; Muralitharan 51–4–195–4; Mathews 6–0–36–0; Dilshan 3–0–16–0.

Umpires: D. J. Harper and N. J. Llong.
Third umpire: S. K. Tarapore. Referee: J. J. Crowe.

†INDIA v SRI LANKA

First Twenty20 International

At Jamtha, Nagpur, December 9, 2009 (floodlit). Sri Lanka won by 29 runs. Toss: India. Twenty20 international debuts: A. B. Dinda, A. Nehra; C. U. Jayasinghe, M. Pushpakumara.

After four overs, when Sri Lanka had made only 17, Dhoni's decision to bowl first seemed wise. But five spilled catches allowed Sri Lanka to surge. The first to take advantage were the swashbuckling duo of Jayasuriya and Dilshan, after which Sangakkara made his highest score in Twenty20 internationals to lift his side past 200. Sehwag, Sri Lanka's nemesis in the Tests, vanished quickly, but Gambhir played some bold strokes as 77 came from the first powerplay. However, after Gambhir was bowled, attempting to sweep Mathews, no one could sustain the momentum. The relieved tourists finally celebrated their first win of the trip in animated fashion.

Man of the Match: K. C. Sangakkara.

Sri Lanka		B	4	6
T. M. Dilshan *b 5*	34	33	5	0
S. T. Jayasuriya *c 11 b 8*	26	20	5	0
*K. C. Sangakkara *run out* ...	78	37	11	2
D. P. M. D. Jayawardene *b 7* ...	9	6	1	0
C. K. Kapugedera *b 9*	47	20	7	1
A. D. Mathews *not out*	15	4	0	2
B 1, l-b 3, w 2	6			

6 overs: 43-0   (20 overs) 215-5

1/43 2/117 3/126 4/195 5/215

C. U. Jayasinghe, M. Pushpakumara, K. M. D. N. Kulasekara, C. R. D. Fernando and S. L. Malinga did not bat.

Nehra 4–0–52–1; I. Sharma 4–0–22–0; Dinda 3–0–34–1; Pathan 4–0–54–1; Ojha 2–0–27–0; R. G. Sharma 3–0–22–1.

India		B	4	6
G. Gambhir *b 6*	55	26	11	0
V. Sehwag *c 6 b 9*	26	14	3	1
*†M. S. Dhoni *c 8 b 2*	9	12	0	0
Yuvraj Singh *c 9 b 6*	6	8	0	0
R. G. Sharma *run out*	3	4	0	0
S. K. Raina *c 1 b 8*	21	13	1	1
Y. K. Pathan *c 11 b 2*	0	2	0	0
A. B. Dinda *b 1*	19	20	1	0
A. Nehra *run out*	22	13	1	2
P. P. Ojha *not out*	10	6	0	1
I. Sharma *not out*	5	2	1	0
B 2, l-b 3, w 5	10			

6 overs: 77-1   (20 overs) 186-9

1/32 2/93 3/99 4/104 5/105 6/115 7/129 8/167 9/173

Kulasekara 3–0–36–1; Fernando 3–0–26–0; Malinga 2–0–29–0; Mathews 4–0–30–2; Jayasuriya 4–0–19–2; Pushpakumara 3–0–27–1; Dilshan 1–0–14–1.

Umpires: A. M. Saheba and S. K. Tarapore.   Third umpire: S. S. Hazare.   Referee: J. J. Crowe.

†INDIA v SRI LANKA

Second Twenty20 International

At Mohali, December 12, 2009 (floodlit). India won by six wickets. Toss: Sri Lanka. Twenty20 international debut: S. Tyagi.

Yuvraj Singh celebrated his 28th birthday with a fine all-round performance, first picking up three wickets then clouting a belligerent half-century, from just 20 balls, as India pulled off the highest successful chase in Twenty20 internationals, surpassing South Africa's 208 against West Indies in 2007-08. The victory ended India's four-match losing Twenty20 streak, but they were lucky as this time the opposition matched them for poor fielding. The Indians again contrived to drop five catchable chances, as Sangakkara once more helped the visitors past 200 with a 31-ball half-century. But Jayasuriya dropped Sehwag at mid-on when he had 14, and he zoomed to 64. Yuvraj turned the game in India's favour, scoring 19 of the 21 runs that leaked from the 13th over, bowled by Weeraratne, and 22 in the 16th, bowled by Kulasekara, being dropped by Dilshan at long-off in mid-assault. Dhoni, put down by Kapugedera when one, helped Yuvraj put on 80 in six overs as India squared the series.

Man of the Match: Yuvraj Singh.   *Man of the Series:* K. C. Sangakkara.

Sri Lanka

		B	4	6
T. M. Dilshan *b* 10	1	3	0	0
S. T. Jayasuriya *lbw b* 7	31	21	5	1
*†K. C. Sangakkara *c* 9 *b* 4	59	31	8	2
C. U. Jayasinghe *c* 8 *b* 4	38	28	3	1
D. P. M. D. Jayawardene *c* 11 *b* 10	12	6	1	1
C. K. Kapugedera *c* 6 *b* 4	2	4	0	0
K. Weeraratne *run out*	3	4	0	0
A. D. Mathews *not out*	26	13	1	2
K. M. D. N. Kulasekara *not out* . .	10	10	0	0
L-b 7, w 17	24			

6 overs: 73-1   (20 overs) 206-7

1/10 2/91 3/121 4/141 5/155 6/167 7/167

C. R. D. Fernando and S. L. Malinga did not bat.

Nehra 3–0–44–0; Sharma 4–0–42–2; Tyagi 2–0–21–0; Pathan 3–0–29–1; Raina 1–0–10–0; Jadeja 4–0–30–0; Yuvraj Singh 3–0–23–3.

India

		B	4	6
G. Gambhir *run out*	21	18	1	0
V. Sehwag *c* 7 *b* 11	64	36	7	3
*M. S. Dhoni *b* 10	46	28	3	2
Yuvraj Singh *not out*	60	25	3	5
S. K. Raina *run out*	9	7	2	0
†K. D. Karthik *not out*	4	1	1	0
L-b 2, w 5	7			

6 overs: 58-1   (19.1 overs) 211-4

1/58 2/108 3/188 4/200

Y. K. Pathan, R. A. Jadeja, A. Nehra, I. Sharma and S. Tyagi did not bat.

Weeraratne 3–0–43–0; Kulasekara 4–0–50–0; Malinga 4–0–28–1; Fernando 4–0–29–1; Mathews 3.1–0–49–0; Dilshan 1–0–10–0.

Umpires: S. S. Hazare and S. K. Tarapore.   Third umpire: S. Asnani.   Referee: J. J. Crowe.

†INDIA v SRI LANKA

First One-Day International

At Rajkot, December 15, 2009. India won by three runs. Toss: Sri Lanka. One-day international debut: U. W. M. B. C. A. Welagedara.

When India roared past 400 for only the second time in one-day internationals – minnows Bermuda were the others on the receiving end, during the 2007 World Cup – victory seemed a formality, even though the pitch was as flat as a pancake. It seemed impossible that the Sri Lankans could match the audacity of Sehwag, who had hurtled to the highest of his 12 one-day centuries, facing only 102 balls and slamming 17 fours and six sixes. But the visitors came out bristling with intent, and Dilshan produced a calculated assault to silence a partisan full house. He and Tharanga started by piling on 188 in 24 overs, before Sangakkara produced a blistering 90 from just 43 balls, hitting ten fours and five sixes. Suddenly the target was no longer far over the horizon: 164 were needed in the last 20 overs, and 124 from 15 when the batting powerplay was taken. But just as India had lost focus at the same point, Sri Lanka were also distracted – and, though they managed 52 runs to India's 33, they lost three crucial wickets, including Sangakkara and Dilshan, who hit a superb 160 from 124 balls with 20 fours and three sixes. Eventually it boiled down to 11 from the final over. Mathews was looking dangerous, but with six needed from Nehra's last three deliveries Tendulkar clasped a superb catch at widish mid-on to end Sri Lanka's dramatic fightback. The match aggregate of 825 runs has only ever been surpassed by the 872 of the South Africa–Australia classic at Johannesburg in March 2006.

Man of the Match: V. Sehwag.

India

V. Sehwag *c* Dilshan *b* Welagedara	146	R. A. Jadeja *not out*	30
S. R. Tendulkar *b* Fernando	69	P. Kumar *not out*	5
*†M. S. Dhoni *c* Mathews *b* Fernando	72	B 5, l-b 4, w 12, n-b 6	27
S. K. Raina *c* Jayasuriya *b* Kulasekara . .	16		
G. Gambhir *c* Sangakkara *b* Kulasekara . . .	11	1/153 (2) 2/309 (1) (7 wkts, 50 overs) 414
Harbhajan Singh *c* Kulasekara *b* Mathews .	1	3/311 (3) 4/325 (5)
V. Kohli *b* Welagedara	27	5/347 (4) 6/352 (6) 7/386 (7) 10 overs: 71-0

Zaheer Khan and A. Nehra did not bat.

Kulasekara 10–0–65–2; Welagedara 10–0–63–2; Fernando 9–0–66–2; Mathews 7–0–60–1; Jayasuriya 7–0–76–0; Kandamby 5–0–49–0; Dilshan 2–0–26–0.

Sri Lanka

W. U. Tharanga st Dhoni b Raina	67		K. M. D. N. Kulasekara not out	2
T. M. Dilshan b Harbhajan Singh	160		U. W. M. B. C. A. Welagedara not out	1
*†K. C. Sangakkara c Jadeja b Kumar	90		L-b 7, w 13, n-b 1	21
S. T. Jayasuriya st Dhoni b Harbhajan Singh	5			
D. P. M. D. Jayawardene run out	3		1/188 (1) 2/316 (3) (8 wkts, 50 overs)	411
S. H. T. Kandamby run out	24		3/328 (4) 4/339 (2)	
A. D. Mathews c Tendulkar b Nehra	38		5/345 (5) 6/401 (6)	
T. T. Samaraweera run out	0		7/404 (8) 8/409 (7) 10 overs: 81-0	

C. R. D. Fernando did not bat.

Kumar 9–0–67–1; Nehra 10–0–81–1; Zaheer Khan 10–0–88–0; Jadeja 8–0–73–0; Harbhajan Singh 10–0–58–2; Raina 3–0–37–1.

Umpires: M. Erasmus and S. K. Tarapore.
Third umpire: S. S. Hazare.   Referee: J. J. Crowe.

†INDIA v SRI LANKA

Second One-Day International

At Jamtha, Nagpur, December 18, 2009 (day/night). Sri Lanka won by three wickets. Toss: India. One-day international debuts: R. A. S. Lakmal, S. Randiv (formerly known as M. M. M. Suraj).

This venue continued to be a good-luck charm for Sri Lanka, who had won the Twenty20 game here: now they squared this series. Though India lost their top order quickly Dhoni led the fightback with a hard-working hundred, his sixth in one-day internationals: he and Raina put on 126 for the fifth wicket in 20 overs. Off-spinner Suraj Randiv, a replacement for Muralitharan who had gone home with a finger injury, finished with three wickets on his debut. Dilshan again provided the initial thrust of Sri Lanka's reply, scoring his second successive century, a more serene and clinical one than his Rajkot rampage. Mathews, batting virtually on one leg after pulling a thigh muscle, stood tall in the face of the rising pressure after Sri Lanka lost three quick wickets. With eight wanted from the last nine deliveries he drove a Nehra full toss straight to mid-on, but the ball squeezed through Zaheer Khan's legs and went for four, hugely easing Sri Lanka's task. India's over-rate sagged during the final stages – they managed only eight in the last hour – and afterwards Dhoni was banned for two one-day internationals for allowing the tempo to slip so much. This match was originally scheduled for Visakhapatnam, in the south Indian state of Andhra Pradesh, but a volatile political climate meant that a move was deemed prudent.

Man of the Match: T. M. Dilshan.

India

V. Sehwag c Sangakkara b Welagedara	4		Harbhajan Singh st Sangakkara b Randiv	0
S. R. Tendulkar st Sangakkara b Mendis	43			
G. Gambhir run out	2		L-b 7, w 4	11
V. Kohli lbw b Randiv	54			
*†M. S. Dhoni c Dilshan b Randiv	107		1/4 (1) 2/19 (3) (7 wkts, 50 overs)	301
S. K. Raina c Randiv b Mathews	68		3/81 (2) 4/132 (4) 5/258 (6)	
R. A. Jadeja not out	12		6/300 (5) 7/301 (8) 10 overs: 45-2	

P. Kumar, Zaheer Khan and A. Nehra did not bat.

Welagedara 9–0–53–1; Mathews 10–1–60–1; Lakmal 8–0–57–0; Mendis 10–0–57–1; Randiv 10–0–51–3; Dilshan 3–0–16–0.

Sri Lanka

W. U. Tharanga c Sehwag	C. K. Kapugedera b Zaheer Khan 2
b Harbhajan Singh . 37	S. Randiv run out. 5
T. M. Dilshan b Nehra. 123	B. A. W. Mendis not out 2
*†K. C. Sangakkara run out. 21	B 1, l-b 5, w 3 9
D. P. M. D. Jayawardene c Dhoni	
b Zaheer Khan . 39	1/102 (1) 2/147 (3) (7 wkts, 49.1 overs) 302
S. H. T. Kandamby c Kohli b Zaheer Khan 27	3/213 (2) 4/232 (4)
A. D. Mathews not out 37	5/264 (5) 6/267 (7) 7/285 (8) 10 overs: 81-0

R. A. S. Lakmal and U. W. M. B. C. A. Welagedara did not bat.

Kumar 8–0–48–0; Zaheer Khan 10–0–63–3; Nehra 10–0–74–1; Harbhajan Singh 10–0–58–1; Jadeja 9.1–0–42–0; Raina 2–0–11–0.

Umpires: M. Erasmus and S. K. Tarapore.
Third umpire: S. S. Hazare. Referee: J. J. Crowe.

†INDIA v SRI LANKA

Third One-Day International

At Cuttack, December 21, 2009 (day/night). India won by seven wickets. Toss: Sri Lanka.

For the third match in a row Sri Lanka got off the blocks smoothly and maintained the momentum to the middle overs, but this time they failed to build for a final surge. From 165 for one in the 23rd over they declined to 239 all out, with the slow left-armer Ravindra Jadeja maintaining a tight line. Sharma, whose first three overs had disappeared for 46, returned to put the brakes on, and dismissed Kandamby and Randiv with consecutive balls. For India – captained by Sehwag in place of the banned Dhoni – there was no such panic, Tendulkar playing an innings of controlled aggression and accumulation as his side reclaimed the series lead. Tendulkar, who hit 13 fours, ended undefeated but just short of his 46th century in one-day internationals. He might have got there but for Karthik's six off Randiv in the 42nd over; a few balls later the match ended when a loose one from Malinga shot down the leg side for five wides.

Man of the Match: R. A. Jadeja.

Sri Lanka

W. U. Tharanga b Jadeja 73	S. L. Malinga b Nehra. 13
T. M. Dilshan c Karthik b Nehra. 41	B. A. W. Mendis b Jadeja 6
*†K. C. Sangakkara st Karthik b Sehwag . . . 46	U. W. M. B. C. A. Welagedara not out 2
D. P. M. D. Jayawardene c Raina	B 1, l-b 2, w 6 9
b Harbhajan Singh . 2	
S. H. T. Kandamby b Sharma 22	1/65 (2) 2/165 (3) (44.2 overs) 239
C. K. Kapugedera b Jadeja 15	3/169 (1) 4/173 (4) 5/204 (6)
K. M. D. N. Kulasekara lbw b Jadeja 10	6/210 (5) 7/210 (8) 8/218 (7)
S. Randiv c Karthik b Sharma. 0	9/236 (10) 10/239 (9) 10 overs: 86-1

Zaheer Khan 7–0–49–0; Sharma 7–0–63–2; Nehra 6.2–0–32–2; Harbhajan Singh 9–0–29–1; Sehwag 4–0–26–1; Jadeja 10–0–32–4; Yuvraj Singh 1–0–5–0.

India

*V. Sehwag c Dilshan b Welagedara 44	
S. R. Tendulkar not out 96	
G. Gambhir c and b Randiv. 32	
Yuvraj Singh c Sangakkara b Welagedara . 23	
†K. D. Karthik not out. 32	
L-b 5, w 11 16	

1/55 (1) 2/127 (3) (3 wkts, 42.3 overs) 243
3/169 (4) 10 overs: 66-1

S. K. Raina, R. A. Jadeja, Harbhajan Singh, Zaheer Khan, A. Nehra and I. Sharma did not bat.

Welagedara 8–1–35–2; Kulasekara 8–0–47–0; Malinga 9.3–1–56–0; Mendis 9–0–67–0; Randiv 8–1–33–1.

Umpires: M. Erasmus and S. S. Hazare.
Third umpire: S. K. Tarapore.   Referee: A. G. Hurst.

†INDIA v SRI LANKA

Fourth One-Day International

At Kolkata, December 24, 2009 (day/night). India won by seven wickets. Toss: Sri Lanka. One-day international debut: N. L. T. C. Perera.

In a decision that would backfire, Sangakkara decided to bat first on an Eden Gardens pitch that was slow with low bounce. He was influenced by his bowlers' inexperience, but his decision took no account of the notorious Kolkata evening dew, and his bowlers duly struggled to grip the ball later on. Gambhir and Kohli took full advantage as India comfortably overhauled Sri Lanka's handy total of 315. That included Tharanga's first one-day international century for three years and 53 innings, while Sangakkara continued his good form with another brisk half-century. When Suranga Lakmal claimed the prized scalps of Sehwag and Tendulkar in the space of seven balls – his first international wickets – things looked bright for Sri Lanka, but Gambhir, who hit 14 fours in equalling his highest one-day score (he had also made 150 in Colombo in February), turned the tide. He and Kohli, who completed his first one-day international hundred from 110 balls, rotated the strike with the speedy efficiency of a London cab driver during peak hours to get India home and seal the series 3–1. They kept pace with each other throughout their stand of 224, and reached their hundreds from consecutive deliveries in the 38th over of the innings, from Dilshan.

Man of the Match: G. Gambhir.

Sri Lanka

W. U. Tharanga b Zaheer Khan	118	S. H. T. Kandamby not out	23
T. M. Dilshan c Kohli b Nehra	9	T. T. Samaraweera not out	13
S. T. Jayasuriya c Tendulkar b Zaheer Khan	15	L-b 3, w 10	13
*†K. C. Sangakkara st Karthik b Harbhajan Singh	60		
D. P. M. D. Jayawardene run out	33	1/31 (2) 2/72 (3) (6 wkts, 50 overs)	315
N. L. T. C. Perera c Jadeja b Nehra	31	3/198 (4) 4/234 (1)	
		5/271 (6) 6/287 (5) 10 overs: 45-1	

S. Randiv, R. A. S. Lakmal and S. L. Malinga did not bat.

Zaheer Khan 10–0–49–2; Nehra 9–1–68–2; Sharma 7–0–67–0; Harbhajan Singh 10–0–53–1; Jadeja 9–1–51–0; Sehwag 3–0–15–0; Raina 2–0–9–0.

India

*V. Sehwag c Dilshan b Lakmal	10
S. R. Tendulkar c Randiv b Lakmal	8
G. Gambhir not out	150
V. Kohli c sub (M. Pushpakumara) b Randiv	107
†K. D. Karthik not out	19
L-b 5, w 16, n-b 2	23

1/13 (1) 2/23 (2)   (3 wkts, 48.1 overs)   317
3/247 (4)   10 overs: 74-2

S. K. Raina, R. A. Jadeja, Harbhajan Singh, Zaheer Khan, A. Nehra and I. Sharma did not bat.

Perera 9–0–66–0; Lakmal 10–0–55–2; Malinga 9.1–0–75–0; Randiv 10–0–57–1; Jayasuriya 7–0–42–0; Dilshan 3–0–17–0.

Umpires: M. Erasmus and S. S. Hazare.
Third umpire: S. K. Tarapore.   Referee: A. G. Hurst.

†INDIA v SRI LANKA

Fifth One-Day International

At Delhi, December 27, 2009. No result. Toss: India. One-day international debuts: S. Tyagi; M. Pushpakumara.

Play was abandoned after 23.3 overs on a relaid Feroz Shah Kotla pitch that, referee Alan Hurst concluded, was "dangerous with variable bounce". Most of those who batted were hit on the body – mainly fingers, arms and toes – while Dilshan, Sri Lanka's best batsman on the tour, threw the bat away in disgust after being struck on the left elbow by one from Nehra that rose from a good length. Jayasuriya, who had made his one-day international debut 20 years and one day earlier, applied himself well for 31. Tharanga was probably not too upset to fall to the first ball of the match, and it was a dream pitch for the debutant Sudeep Tyagi, a fast bowler from Uttar Pradesh, who dismissed Sangakkara in his third over. Later a ball from Tyagi pitched just short of a length but reared wide of off stump, and Dhoni collected it in front of first slip (remarkably on such an untrustworthy pitch, he did not concede any byes). The Sri Lankan management gestured to their batsmen to walk off, and after lengthy deliberations between the match officials and board administrators the game was abandoned. The embarrassed Indian board instantly dissolved the five-man grounds and pitches committee headed by Daljit Singh, who had been overseeing the relaying of the Delhi pitch. The ICC later banned the venue – one of those earmarked for the 2011 World Cup – for the whole of 2010.

Man of the Series: T. M. Dilshan.

Sri Lanka

W. U. Tharanga b Zaheer Khan	0	M. Pushpakumara not out		7
T. M. Dilshan c Dhoni b Zaheer Khan	20	L-b 1, w 8, n-b 1		10
S. T. Jayasuriya lbw b Harbhajan Singh	31			
*†K. C. Sangakkara c Raina b Tyagi	1	1/0 (1) 2/39 (2)	(5 wkts, 23.3 overs)	83
T. T. Samaraweera run out	2	3/58 (4) 4/60 (3)		
S. H. T. Kandamby not out	12	5/63 (5)	10 overs: 39-1	

N. L. T. C. Perera, S. Randiv, R. A. S. Lakmal and U. W. M. B. C. A. Welagedara did not bat.

Zaheer Khan 8–1–31–2; Nehra 5–0–24–0; Tyagi 6.3–1–15–1; Harbhajan Singh 4–0–12–1.

India

G. Gambhir, V. Sehwag, *†M. S. Dhoni, V. Kohli, K. D. Karthik, S. K. Raina, R. A. Jadeja, Harbhajan Singh, Zaheer Khan, S. Tyagi and A. Nehra.

Umpires: M. Erasmus and S. K. Tarapore.
Third umpire: S. S. Hazare. Referee: A. G. Hurst.

AIRTEL CHAMPIONS LEAGUE TWENTY20, 2009-10

Nick Hoult

The inaugural Champions League Twenty20, won by the Australian domestic champions New South Wales, never attracted the hype and media interest of its sister tournament, the Indian Premier League. But as the competition progresses over the next few years its growth may well have a greater bearing on the Twenty20 format in other countries than the money and movie-star image of the IPL.

Qualification for the tournament will no doubt increase the competitiveness of domestic Twenty20 competitions around the world. That will in turn improve standards and create new paydays for those players gifted at the game's shortest format.

Somerset and Sussex were the English participants in this long-delayed new tournament – the first, originally planned for September 2008, was initially postponed by three months over a disagreement about dates, then cancelled just before the rescheduled start in December after a terrorist attack on Mumbai. Both counties returned from India in no doubt about the growing gulf, on and off the field, between Twenty20 cricket at home and other leading cricketing nations. Somerset's solitary victory, a one-wicket win off the last ball against the Deccan Chargers, was the only meaningful contribution either county made to the tournament. Only Sussex's Luke Wright managed to hit more than one six, and only Wes Durston – subsequently released by Somerset – managed a half-century.

The Champions League truly reflected the fact that England's weaknesses at international level are a product of the flaws of the domestic game. Somerset, admittedly, were weakened by the loss of Marcus Trescothick, who flew home after the opening group stage, sensing a recurrence of his stress-related illness. But even with him in the side they were outclassed by Trinidad & Tobago. When the Somerset chairman, Andy Nash, conceded that India had shown the ECB a "clean pair of heels" in terms of managing Twenty20 cricket, it was the first acceptance of an unpalatable truth for English cricket's administrators.

When both Mark Robinson and Brian Rose, Sussex and Somerset's respective directors of cricket, admitted they left India with much work to do, it was the coaches' turn to swallow a difficult fact. Both teams could only look on their fellow competitors with envy, since the counties have to battle an annual numerical disadvantage – beating 16 other sides to qualify – which makes prolonged exposure to the tournament unlikely. For English teams the Champions League may well remain a mere end-of-season salary bonus.

The prize pool of US$6.5m was the highest for any cricket tournament, bar the Stanford Super Series, as domestic teams from around the world were pitched against each other for the first time. The unfamiliarity of many of the players to Indian audiences was always going to be its weak point. Crowds for matches not involving Indian teams were generally very low, and the organisers were stung by early media reports of poor TV ratings. For a tournament propped up by a rights deal worth $1billion over ten years with the broadcaster, ESPN, the ratings are as important as fours and sixes.

The performances of the three Indian teams – Delhi Daredevils, Royal Challengers Bangalore and Deccan Chargers – did not help. All had exited before the end of the second phase, with the Deccan Chargers, the IPL champions, losing both their opening group games.

Whereas the English sides looked tired after a long summer of county cricket, the IPL teams played like strangers, proving that star names – each side could choose four overseas players – do not guarantee team harmony.

The two finalists, New South Wales and Trinidad & Tobago, were the best organised and most motivated teams – and neither had an overseas player. Both flew to India after lengthy training camps, and it showed, particularly in their fielding. In the absence of Indian interest, Trinidad became the adopted team for most of the supporters, but NSW, with their plethora of Australian internationals, were the strongest team and worthy winners of the $2.5m first prize. Their star performer was Brett Lee, whose eight wickets cost just 9.87 runs apiece, while his economy-rate of 3.76 over was probably even more impressive. Lee's team-mates David Warner (207) and Phillip Hughes (202) were two of only three batsmen to make more than 200 runs in the tournament, although the leading scorer was the Cape Cobras' J-P. Duminy, with 224. The highest strike-rate, for anyone with more than 50 runs, was 197.29 by T&T's Kieron Pollard, whose 146 runs in the tournament needed just 74 balls.

CHAMPIONS LEAGUE TWENTY20, 2009-10

Group A

	Played	Won	Lost	No result	Points	Net run-rate
TRINIDAD & TOBAGO	2	2	0	0	4	1.17
SOMERSET SABRES	2	1	1	0	2	–1.00
Deccan Chargers	2	0	2	0	0	–0.17

Group B

	Played	Won	Lost	No result	Points	Net run-rate
NEW SOUTH WALES BLUES	2	2	0	0	4	2.20
DIAMOND EAGLES	2	1	1	0	2	–1.32
Sussex Sharks	2	0	2	0	0	–0.87

Group C

	Played	Won	Lost	No result	Points	Net run-rate
CAPE COBRAS	2	2	0	0	4	1.52
ROYAL CHALLENGERS BANGALORE	2	1	1	0	2	1.83
Otago Volts	2	0	2	0	0	–3.35

Group D

	Played	Won	Lost	No result	Points	Net run-rate
DELHI DAREDEVILS............	2	1	1	0	2	0.70
VICTORIA BUSHRANGERS	2	1	1	0	2	0.13
Wayamba Elevens................	2	1	1	0	2	–0.87

League A

	Played	Won	Lost	No result	Points	Net run-rate
TRINIDAD & TOBAGO	3	3	0	0	6	1.37
NEW SOUTH WALES BLUES	3	2	1	0	4	1.84
Diamond Eagles	3	1	2	0	2	–1.11
Somerset Sabres.	3	0	3	0	0	–2.00

League B

	Played	Won	Lost	No result	Points	Net run-rate
VICTORIA BUSHRANGERS	3	2	1	0	4	0.91
CAPE COBRAS	3	2	1	0	4	−0.21
Royal Challengers Bangalore	3	1	2	0	2	−0.11
Delhi Daredevils	3	1	2	0	2	−0.39

Win = 2 pts. No result = 1 pt.

The top two teams from each group progressed to the League stage, where they played the teams they had not met before, while the winner of the match between teams from the same group carried those points forward.

Semi-finals New South Wales Blues beat Victoria Bushrangers by 79 runs; Trinidad & Tobago beat Cape Cobras by seven wickets.

Final New South Wales Blues beat Trinidad & Tobago by 41 runs.

Note: Matches in this section were not first-class.

Full scores of the games that follow can be found at www.cricinfo.com and www.cricketarchive.co.uk.

Group A

At Uppal, Hyderabad, October 10, 2009 (floodlit). **Somerset Sabres won by one wicket.** Toss: Somerset Sabres. **Deccan Chargers 153-9** (20 overs) (V. V. S. Laxman 46; B. J. Phillips 3-31); **Somerset Sabres 157-9** (20 overs) (A. C. Thomas 30*; R. P. Singh 3-23). *Somerset Sabres 2 pts. Man of the Match: A. C. Thomas.*

Somerset defeated the IPL champions on their home ground from the final ball of a thrilling match. Alfonso Thomas hit two of the last three deliveries (from Scott Styris, one of nine bowlers tried by Adam Gilchrist) for four, after putting on 50 for the eighth wicket with James Hildreth (25) to rescue his side from 99-7. This was the third defeat in as many matches for the tournament's Indian sides.

At Bangalore, October 12, 2009. **Trinidad & Tobago won by 44 runs.** Toss: Trinidad & Tobago. **Trinidad & Tobago 150-9** (20 overs) (D. Ramdin 39; C. M. Willoughby 3-35); **Somerset Sabres 106** (20 overs) (Z. de Bruyn 43*; D. J. Bravo 4-23). *Trinidad & Tobago 2 pts. Man of the Match: S. Ganga.*

A listless-looking Marcus Trescothick was out fifth ball for three, before his early return home three days later, as Somerset were outclassed in all areas by an energised Trinidad & Tobago side. The match award went to T&T's Sherwin Ganga, who followed 18* with 3–0–16–2.

At Uppal, Hyderabad, October 14, 2009 (floodlit). **Trinidad & Tobago won by three runs.** Toss: Deccan Chargers. **Trinidad & Tobago 149-7** (20 overs) (W. K. D. Perkins 38, K. A. Pollard 31; F. H. Edwards 3-32); **Deccan Chargers 146** (20 overs) (A. C. Gilchrist 51, Y. Venugopal Rao 30; D. J. Bravo 3-24). *Trinidad & Tobago 2 pts. Man of the Match: D. J. Bravo.*

Victory for the Chargers would have eliminated Somerset and ended English interest. After Gilchrist's 31-ball half-century that looked likely – until the final over when, with eight runs needed, Dwayne Bravo bowled R. P. Singh and ran out Fidel Edwards to eliminate the IPL champions.

Group B

At Delhi, October 9, 2009. **New South Wales Blues won by 53 runs.** Toss: New South Wales Blues. **New South Wales Blues 144-6** (20 overs) (S. M. Katich 53); **Diamond Eagles 91-9** (20 overs) (R. McLaren 40; S. R. Clark 3-12). *New South Wales Blues 2 pts. Man of the Match: S. M. Katich.*

A sluggish Delhi pitch could not prevent Brett Lee (4–1–14–1) and Stuart Clark from blowing away the Diamond Eagles, who reached 91 only thanks to Ryan McLaren. His defiant innings was the first sign of the fighting spirit that ran through this South African side.

At Delhi, October 11, 2009. **New South Wales Blues won by 35 runs.** Toss: New South Wales Blues. **New South Wales Blues 130-2** (20 overs) (P. J. Hughes 62*, M. C. Henriques 51*); **Sussex**

Sharks 95-8 (20 overs) (M. C. Henriques 3-23). *New South Wales Blues 2 pts. Man of the Match: M. C. Henriques.*

The seven lowest scores of the tournament were recorded at Delhi, and Sussex became the third team to fail to reach three figures there. A partnership of 90* in 11.2 overs between Phillip Hughes and Moises Henriques set Sussex a total that proved beyond their reach at an empty Feroz Shah Kotla stadium.

At Delhi, October 13, 2009 (floodlit). **Diamond Eagles won after an eliminator over, following a tie.** Toss: Sussex Sharks. **Sussex Sharks 119-7** (20 overs); **Diamond Eagles 119-4** (20 overs) (R. R. Rossouw 65). *Diamond Eagles 2 pts. Man of the Match: R. R. Rossouw.*

The tournament's only "super over" ended with Sussex eliminated. They had pulled themselves back into contention thanks to their slow bowlers, who restricted the Eagles' batsmen when they had needed 48 off 54 balls with all ten wickets in hand. In the end a desperate last-ball swish for four by Ryan McLaren off Yasir Arafat (the only Pakistani player on view in the tournament) forced the one-over tie-breaker. Arafat was trusted again: the Eagles managed only nine runs, but Cornelius de Villiers took two wickets with the first two balls to send his side through.

Group C

At Bangalore, October 8, 2009 (floodlit). **Cape Cobras won by five wickets.** Toss: Royal Challengers Bangalore. **Royal Challengers Bangalore 180-4** (20 overs) (R. V. Uthappa 51, L. R. P. L. Taylor 53*); **Cape Cobras 184-5** (19.4 overs) (J-P. Duminy 99*; P. Kumar 3-32). *Cape Cobras 2 pts. Man of the Match: J-P. Duminy.*

Duminy followed a spectacular opening ceremony with a show-stopping performance of his own in the first match of the tournament, scoring an unbeaten 99 off 52 balls with eight fours and five sixes as the Cobras won a high-scoring match in the final over. Earlier, Ross Taylor had spanked 53* from 24 balls, with four fours and four sixes.

At Uppal, Hyderabad, October 10, 2009. **Cape Cobras won by 54 runs.** Toss: Otago Volts. **Cape Cobras 193-4** (20 overs) (A. G. Puttick 104*, J-P. Duminy 32, J. L. Ontong 39*); **Otago Volts 139** (17.1 overs) (N. L. McCullum 38; R. K. Kleinveldt 3-24). *Cape Cobras 2 pts. Man of the Match: A. G. Puttick.*

Cape Cobras became the first team to qualify for the second phase as Andrew Puttick hit the only hundred of the tournament. A sparse crowd gave a glimpse of what was to follow when Indian sides were not involved. After Puttick's 104, scored off 62 balls with 12 fours and three sixes, Otago faded quickly.

At Bangalore, October 12, 2009 (floodlit). **Royal Challengers Bangalore won by 80 runs.** Toss: Royal Challengers Bangalore. **Royal Challengers Bangalore 188-2** (20 overs) (J. H. Kallis 73*, R. V. Uthappa 42, V. Kohli 32, L. R. P. L. Taylor 32*); **Otago Volts 108** (17.5 overs) (J. H. Kallis 3-18). *Royal Challengers Bangalore 2 pts. Man of the Match: J. H. Kallis.*

The winners would progress to the next round, and Bangalore delivered exactly what the Indian organisers required amid a fevered atmosphere at the Chinnaswamy Stadium. Kallis followed up his 59-ball 73 with three wickets with the new ball to floor Otago, who became the first side to be eliminated.

Group D

At Delhi, October 9, 2009 (floodlit). **Victoria Bushrangers won by seven wickets.** Toss: Delhi Daredevils. **Delhi Daredevils 98-8** (20 overs) (C. J. McKay 3-17); **Victoria Bushrangers 100-3** (16.4 overs) (R. J. Quiney 40). *Victoria Bushrangers 2 pts. Man of the Match: C. J. McKay.*

A large crowd were left disappointed by an insipid display from Delhi, who failed to reach three figures on another pudding of a pitch. Victoria looked a well-drilled team as they won with 20 balls to spare.

At Delhi, October 11, 2009 (floodlit). **Delhi Daredevils won by 50 runs.** Toss: Delhi Daredevils. **Delhi Daredevils 170-5** (20 overs) (V. Sehwag 66, K. D. Karthik 61); **Wayamba Elevens 120-7** (20 overs) (D. P. M. D. Jayawardene 53; D. P. Nannes 4-24). *Delhi Daredevils 2 pts. Man of the Match: V. Sehwag.*

A large and very noisy Delhi crowd lifted the home team, who recorded the first victory by an Indian side. The pitch could not stifle the explosive talents of Virender Sehwag, who struck ten fours and a six, or Dinesh Karthik, who hit Ajantha Mendis for three consecutive sixes, as Delhi recorded what would be the tournament's highest score on this ground.

At Delhi, October 13, 2009. **Wayamba Elevens won by 15 runs.** Toss: Wayamba Elevens. **Wayamba Elevens 118-9** (20 overs) (H. G. J. M. Kulatunga 41, M. G. Vandort 42; S. M. Harwood 3-14); **Victoria Bushrangers 103-4** (20 overs) (B. J. Hodge 44*). *Wayamba Elevens 2 pts. Man of the Match:* S. M. Harwood.

A desperately dull affair saw Victoria qualify for the next phase despite defeat. Once Wayamba had made 118 from their 20 overs Victoria knew they could lose and still qualify on run-rate ahead of their opponents if they managed to score 84, a total it took them 18 laborious overs to reach.

League A

At Uppal, Hyderabad, October 16, 2009. **Diamond Eagles won by five wickets.** Toss: Somerset Sabres. **Somerset Sabres 132-8** (20 overs) (J. C. Hildreth 31, W. J. Durston 57; C. J. D. de Villiers 4-17); **Diamond Eagles 133-5** (18.4 overs) (M. N. van Wyk 47). *Diamond Eagles 2 pts. Man of the Match:* C. J. D. de Villiers.

Without Marcus Trescothick, who had returned home on the eve of the match, Somerset looked flat as they compiled a modest total on the fastest pitch in the tournament. Trescothick's replacement Wes Durston hit a gutsy half-century, but only after some accurate seam bowling by Cornelius de Villiers had seen Somerset slump to 52-5 in a virtually deserted stadium.

At Uppal, Hyderabad, October 16, 2009 (floodlit). **Trinidad & Tobago won by four wickets.** Toss: New South Wales Blues. **New South Wales Blues 170-4** (20 overs) (P. J. Hughes 83, D. A. Warner 63; D. J. Bravo 3-31); **Trinidad & Tobago 171-6** (18.3 overs) (D. Ganga 32, K. A. Pollard 54*). *Trinidad & Tobago 2 pts. Man of the Match:* K. A. Pollard.

Two teams who emerged as crowd favourites in Hyderabad in place of the home team delivered a stunning match. Needing 80 from 42 balls, T&T appeared a beaten side until some tremendous hitting from Kieron Pollard, whose 54 came from only 18 balls and included five fours and five sixes. He destroyed Moises Henriques, hitting him for 27 in an over; then, after Simon Katich entrusted Henriques with the ball again, Pollard thumped two more sixes to complete an extraordinary turnaround.*

At Uppal, Hyderabad, October 18, 2009 (floodlit). **New South Wales Blues won by six wickets.** Toss: New South Wales Blues. **Somerset Sabres 111-7** (20 overs) (S. R. Clark 3-15); **New South Wales Blues 112-4** (11.5 overs) (D. A. Warner 40). *New South Wales Blues 2 pts. Man of the Match:* S. R. Clark.

Somerset could manage only a sorry 111 after a feeble batting performance against NSW, who cruised into the semi-finals. Clark's accuracy and Lee's fire were too much for Somerset, whose captain Justin Langer retired after this match. Phillip Hughes and David Warner set off at a gallop, and NSW took less than 12 overs to send Somerset home.

At Uppal, Hyderabad, October 18, 2009 (floodlit). **Trinidad & Tobago won by 24 runs.** Toss: Trinidad & Tobago. **Trinidad & Tobago 213-4** (20 overs) (W. K. D. Perkins 35, A. B. Barath 63, L. M. P. Simmons 40, N. D. Stewart 33*); **Diamond Eagles 189-5** (20 overs) (R. R. Rossouw 44, D. du Preez 35, H. H. Dippenaar 33). *Trinidad & Tobago 2 pts. Man of the Match:* A. B. Barath.

By now, T&T had become firm favourites with the Hyderabad crowds, and the stadium was three-quarters full as they recorded the tournament's highest total, the only one in excess of 200. Adrian Barath marked his Twenty20 debut with some stunning strokeplay (and the match award) as T&T's batsmen collected 13 sixes and 18 fours.

League B

At Bangalore, October 15, 2009 (floodlit). **Victoria Bushrangers won by seven wickets.** Toss: Royal Challengers Bangalore. **Royal Challengers Bangalore 127-6** (20 overs) (M. K. Pandey 39, R. Dravid 33; A. B. McDonald 4-21); **Victoria Bushrangers 133-3** (15.5 overs) (D. J. Hussey 31*). *Victoria Bushrangers 2 pts. Man of the Match:* A. B. McDonald.

Victoria completed another relatively comfortable victory over an Indian side, finishing the match off with more than four overs in hand after restricting Bangalore to a modest total on their home turf. Andrew McDonald, something of a spare part during Australia's Ashes tour earlier in the year, showed the value of bowling straight, dismissing Manish Pandey (the only Indian to score an IPL century), Rahul Dravid, Virat Kohli and Ross Taylor.

At Bangalore, October 17, 2009. **Cape Cobras won by eight wickets.** Reduced to 17 overs a side. Toss: Victoria Bushrangers. **Victoria Bushrangers 125-5** (17 overs); **Cape Cobras 129-2** (16 overs) (H. Davids 69*). *Cape Cobras 2 pts. Man of the Match:* H. Davids.

   A bomb scare delayed the match by more than 90 minutes after police discovered traces of explosive in a bag carried by a young cricketer from Kashmir, who was staying in the Chinnaswamy Stadium academy. He was arrested but later released without charge. Herschelle Gibbs was so rattled he skipped the match, and the Eagles captain, Andrew Puttick, admitted he did not know his line-up at the toss because he wasn't sure which players had agreed to play. His side showed admirable steel to recover from the scare to win, mainly thanks to the powerful hitting of Henry Davids, who clouted seven fours and two sixes. Victoria never really overcame losing Rob Quiney and Brad Hodge for ducks to the first and third balls of the match, from Monde Zondeki.

At Bangalore, October 17, 2009 (floodlit). **Royal Challengers Bangalore won by eight wickets.** Toss: Royal Challengers Bangalore. **Delhi Daredevils 138-6** (20 overs) (V. Sehwag 47; A. Kumble 3-20); **Royal Challengers Bangalore 139-2** (15.1 overs) (R. Dravid 32*, L. R. P. L. Taylor 65). *Royal Challengers Bangalore 2 pts. Man of the Match:* L. R. P. L. Taylor.

   It was billed as "Saturday Night Diwali Fever" and, despite the earlier bomb scare, there was a cracking atmosphere in Bangalore as the home team, who had been eliminated by Cape Cobras' earlier victory, rubber-stamped Delhi's exit too, to end Indian interest in the competition. Ross Taylor hit six fours and four sixes as Bangalore romped home with 29 balls to spare.

At Delhi, October 19, 2009 (floodlit). **Delhi Daredevils won by 30 runs.** Toss: Cape Cobras. **Delhi Daredevils 114-6** (20 overs) (O. A. Shah 39*); **Cape Cobras 84** (18.3 overs) (D. P. Nannes 3-19). *Delhi Daredevils 2 pts. Man of the Match:* O. A. Shah.

   Cape Cobras recorded the tournament's lowest total – but, bizarrely, did not mind. They had already qualified, and this result meant they would avoid the sluggish Delhi pitch in the semi-finals. Dirk Nannes managed to ratchet up the pace to take three wickets – all bowled – as Delhi completed a consolation victory in front of their home fans.

Semi-finals

At Delhi, October 21, 2009 (floodlit). **New South Wales Blues won by 79 runs.** Toss: New South Wales Blues. **New South Wales Blues 169-7** (20 overs) (P. J. Hughes 35, D. A. Warner 48; C. J. McKay 3-27); **Victoria Bushrangers 90-9** (20 overs) (M. C. Henriques 3-11). *Man of the Match:* D. A. Warner.

   A sparsely populated Feroz Shah Kotla witnessed a one-sided match between two teams who were again forced to toil for runs on a substandard pitch. David Warner and Phillip Hughes opted to attack, and some straight hitting down the ground helped them post an opening stand of 62 inside seven overs. It would be a match-winning burst. NSW opened the bowling with spinner Nathan Hauritz and the fiery Brett Lee, a yin-and-yang combination that stifled Victoria who, at the end of the six-over powerplay, were 17-3. They had lost both openers for ducks in Hauritz's first over after Lee started with a maiden.

At Uppal, Hyderabad, October 22, 2009 (floodlit). **Trinidad & Tobago won by seven wickets.** Toss: Cape Cobras. **Cape Cobras 175-5** (20 overs) (H. H. Gibbs 42, J-P. Duminy 61*); **Trinidad & Tobago 178-3** (19.2 overs) (D. Ganga 44*, D. J. Bravo 58*). *Man of the Match:* D. J. Bravo.

   A decent crowd showed up to lend their support to the West Indian side. They were rewarded with a thrilling contest. Herschelle Gibbs finally made an impression, hitting four boundaries in one Dwayne Bravo over as the Cobras managed 52 in their first six overs: they raced along at nine an over for the majority of their innings. T&T's magnificent fielding pegged them back, and Ravi Rampaul's final over cost only two runs. Typically, T&T set off at a rattling pace, with Adrian Barath and William Perkins flailing the ball to all parts, but a run-out set them on their heels, and the slow bowlers brought the Cobras back into the match. T&T needed 73 from the last 42 balls, a tall order – but then catches started going down as the pressure mounted. Justin Ontong dropped a straightforward chance off Bravo at long-on, and the next ball disappeared for six. Two further sixes from Bravo in the next over saw the asking-rate drop dramatically: Bravo and Daren Ganga grew in confidence and took their side home in a stand of 93.*

FINAL

NEW SOUTH WALES BLUES v TRINIDAD & TOBAGO

At Uppal, Hyderabad, October 23, 2009 (floodlit). New South Wales Blues won by 41 runs. Toss:
Trinidad & Tobago.

It had taken a one-man show from Kieron Pollard to settle the earlier match between these two
sides, and it was a similarly solo performance that won the final. Sadly for Trinidad and their noisy
supporters, the party could not last. New South Wales, inspired with both bat and ball by Brett Lee,
took the final with cold, Australian professionalism to inflict on Trinidad their only defeat of the
tournament. The Rajiv Gandhi Stadium was full – which no doubt settled a few nerves among the
organisers – and loud, as Trinidad took early control. The decision to start with speed and spin paid
off, as the dangerous opening partnership of Hughes and Warner failed. Some tidy bowling drew
mistakes from nervous-looking Australian batsmen: Lee was their last hope. He started slowly,
sensing the importance of staying in. But once he felt confident and attuned to the pitch – this was
only his third innings of the tournament – the bottom-handed boundaries started to flow. He struck

Brutally, Brett Lee: he swings another six to steer New South Wales towards a match-winning total.

three sixes in the 16th over before being the last man out, but by then a defendable total had been reached. Lee fed off his batting. He bowled Perkins with his second ball, and took a smart return catch off Simmons. With Bollinger and Clark accounting for the middle order, Trinidad were again looking to Pollard for a miracle. He nearly pulled it off. Sixes off Hauritz and Bollinger brought the asking-rate down to 47 from 31 balls, but another desperate attempt to clear the ropes ended with a skier to long-on, where Lee – it had to be – took it comfortably.

Man of the Match: B. Lee.   *Man of the Series:* B. Lee.

New South Wales

		B	4	6
D. A. Warner *c 10 b 5*	19	16	4	0
P. J. Hughes *b 11*	3	5	0	0
*S. M. Katich *c 2 b 5*	16	14	0	2
M. C. Henriques *c 8 b 7*	4	7	0	0
B. J. Rohrer *c 8 b 10*	16	12	1	1
S. P. D. Smith *c 3 b 8*	33	26	2	1
†D. L. R. Smith *b 11*	3	3	0	0
B. Lee *c 1 b 11*	48	31	1	5
N. M. Hauritz *run out*	10	6	1	0
S. R. Clark *not out*	0	0	0	0
L-b 5, w 2	7			

6 overs: 42-2   (20 overs)   159-9

1/24 2/32 3/45 4/47 5/75 6/83 7/132 8/159 9/159

D. E. Bollinger did not bat.

S. Ganga 4–0–29–1; Rampaul 4–0–20–3; Bravo 3–0–27–2; Pollard 3–0–27–0; Mohammed 3–0–19–1; Simmons 2–0–23–0; Stewart 1–0–9–0.

Trinidad & Tobago

		B	4	6
W. K. D. Perkins *b 8*	0	2	0	0
A. B. Barath *c 7 b 6*	14	6	2	1
L. M. P. Simmons *c and b 8*	4	7	1	0
*D. Ganga *c 1 b 6*	19	20	1	1
D. J. Bravo *b 11*	17	13	2	1
†D. Ramdin *c 6 b 10*	16	23	1	0
K. A. Pollard *c 8 b 9*	26	15	0	3
S. Ganga *c 4 b 9*	5	7	0	0
N. D. Stewart *c 4 b 10*	4	3	1	0
D. Mohammed *c 2 b 10*	1	2	0	0
R. Rampaul *not out*	0	0	0	0
L-b 5, w 4, n-b 3	12			

6 overs: 47-4   (15.5 overs)   118

1/1 2/21 3/21 4/45 5/68 6/93 7/107 8/113 9/118

Lee 2–0–10–2; S. P. D. Smith 4–0–32–2; Bollinger 4–0–27–1; Clark 3.5–0–21–3; Hauritz 2–0–23–2.

Umpires: D. J. Harper and R. E. Koertzen.
Third umpire: A. M. Saheba.   Referee: S. Venkataraghavan.

DOMESTIC CRICKET IN INDIA, 2008-09

R. MOHAN

India's love affair with Twenty20, specifically the IPL, has had the unexpected effect of lifting the national team's cricket in all forms of the game, including Tests. But its effects have spread into domestic cricket, too. Not only has the

IPL transformed personal fortunes, it has injected a hefty dose of confidence into the average Indian cricketer. Those lucky enough to get IPL contracts virtually double their income from the game, which now offers real scope as a career. Bolstered by the Indian board's income from television rights, domestic pay has risen fivefold over the past six years, so that a regular first-class player can now earn about two million rupees (about £25,000) for a full home season, and as much again from the IPL. Indian cricket, bolstered by the national team's performances, is in the pink of health.

The 2008-09 domestic season saw a swing back to the traditional powerhouses, Mumbai and West Zone. **Mumbai** claimed their 38th Ranji Trophy, more than

Mumbai captain Wasim Jaffer holds the Ranji Trophy.

half the 75 tournaments played to date. They had a bit of the rub of the green, especially with the umpiring, and might have been knocked out in the semi-final, despite a triple-hundred from captain Wasim Jaffer. If **Saurashtra**, who got the rough end of the stick when they were hanging on in the face of threatening weather in Chennai, had kept one or two wickets intact to deny Mumbai a decision on first-innings lead, they would have gone through on their net run-rate throughout the tournament.

No team plays knockouts better than Mumbai, however, and the intimidating atmosphere of their home stadium could not be held responsible as the quarter-finals onwards were staged at neutral venues. The final in Hyderabad saw **Uttar Pradesh** finish runners-up for the second successive

year, after Mumbai's Rohit Sharma scored twin hundreds. Uttar Pradesh put down four catches and missed two run-outs and a stumping, but such ineptitude may have owed something to the lack of full professional support; while all first-class teams are well served by raw talent, and only a few have not had the wherewithal or inclination to modernise their game, the more prosperous associations such as Mumbai have put in the best back-room support possible.

Jaffer might have surrendered his Test place to Gautam Gambhir, but his appetite for runs was intact; he finished with 1,260 Ranji runs, closely followed by his colleague Ajinkya Rahane's 1,089. He also led **West Zone** to wins in the Duleep and Deodhar Trophy finals, a memorable treble. West's 17th Duleep Trophy (including three shared titles) matched North's record. They beat **South Zone** in the final after going in first and batting well enough to set a massive target of 678 in the fourth innings; South managed 403.

No overseas team played in the Duleep Trophy, as in recent seasons, but a Zimbabwean side took part in the one-day Deodhar Trophy, without winning a match. **Tamil Nadu** won the 50-over Vijay Hazare Trophy. In the Ranji Trophy, **Himachal Pradesh** and **Bengal** earned promotion from the Plate to the Elite groups – and also took part in the Elite quarter-finals rather than contesting their own final.

Back in September 2008 the Mohammad Nissar Trophy, for the champions of India and Pakistan, went to Pakistan for the first time in its three seasons, when **Sui Northern Gas** beat **Delhi** on first innings in a rain-ruined match. A week later Delhi lost to the Rest of India in the traditional season opener, the Irani Cup, which gave the Rest's Test stars the ideal preparation for October's series against Australia. Rahul Dravid batted himself into form while Anil Kumble and Harbhajan Singh exploited a wearing pitch to dismiss Delhi cheaply.

Statistics suggested a suspected tilt in balance towards bowlers over the last few seasons had swung back towards batsmen. Jaffer and Rahane were the first to score 1,000 Ranji runs since 2003-04, though the feat has been achieved nine times since 1996-97, after two instances in the previous 62 seasons (admittedly from fewer games). On the other hand, Bishan Bedi's Ranji record of 64 wickets remains unmatched since 1974-75; the highest total in 2008-09 was 42, by Mumbai newcomer Dhawal Kulkarni and Saurashtra's Ravi Jadeja.

A rising star was 20-year-old Cheteshwar Pujara of Saurashtra, who set the season alight by following two triple-hundreds in the Under-22 tournament with 302 not out against Orissa in the Ranji Trophy, then run-a-ball centuries against Punjab and Mumbai. The prolific Pujara was the Ranji's third-highest scorer and should enter the Test team in the near future.

One talking point was the quality of the SG balls used in most domestic cricket, which lost shape so quickly that the BCCI took it up with the manufacturers. Captains also complained about inconsistency in the use of television umpires within tournaments.

FIRST-CLASS AVERAGES, 2008-09

BATTING

(Qualification: 600 runs)

	M	I	NO	R	HS	100s	Avge	Ct/St
R. G. Sharma (*Mumbai*)	8	13	2	881	141	4	80.09	5
B. D. Thaker (*Gujarat and West Zone*)	10	15	4	830	192	3	75.45	13
Wasim Jaffer (*Mumbai and West Zone*)	14	24	1	1,549	301	4	67.34	28
A. M. Rahane (*Mumbai, West Zone & India A*) . .	13	22	1	1,390	201	5	66.19	15
†G. Gambhir (*Delhi and India*)	7	14	0	920	206	3	65.71	6

	M	I	NO	R	HS	100s	Avge	Ct/St
C. A. Pujara (*Saurashtra, West Zone & India A*) .	12	19	3	1,049	302*	4	65.56	5
†A. Mukund (*Tamil Nadu and South Zone*)......	10	15	1	911	300*	4	65.07	4
K. D. Karthik (*Tamil Nadu and South Zone*)	11	17	1	1,026	213	5	64.12	39/1
Sangram Singh (*Himachal Pradesh*)	7	12	1	703	215*	2	63.90	7
K. M. Jadhav (*Maharashtra and West Zone*)....	8	14	2	759	114*	1	63.25	7
S. Badrinath (*Tamil Nadu, S. Zone & India A*)...	12	16	2	876	200	4	62.57	10
V. V. S. Laxman (*Hyderabad, S. Zone & India*) .	9	15	3	718	224	2	59.83	7
†R. A. Jadeja (*Saurashtra and India A*)	10	15	2	776	232*	2	59.69	5
S. R. Tendulkar (*Mumbai and India*)	8	15	3	678	122*	3	56.50	3
M. Vijay (*T. Nadu, S. Zone, India & Ind A*).....	8	13	0	733	243	1	56.38	7
B. J. Thakkar (*Himachal Pradesh*)...........	7	11	0	619	166	4	56.27	6
V. Kohli (*Delhi, North Zone and India A*)......	10	12	1	613	197	2	55.72	7
†P. A. Patel (*Gujarat, West Zone & India A*).....	13	17	1	818	206	2	51.12	27/3
S. Sohal (*Punjab and North Zone*)	8	15	2	663	110	3	51.00	1
M. Kaif (*Uttar Pradesh, C. Zone and India A*)...	12	17	1	812	144	2	50.75	8
R. V. Uthappa (*Karnataka, S. Zone & India A*) ..	12	20	1	946	160	4	49.78	6
A. Chopra (*Delhi and North Zone*)	11	17	1	789	210	2	49.31	15
†T. M. Srivastava (*Uttar Pradesh & C. Zone*)	10	17	1	735	159	2	45.93	6
W. P. Saha (*Bengal, East Zone & India A*).....	10	16	1	632	159	1	42.13	23/1
R. Dravid (*Karnataka, South Zone & India*)	13	23	0	896	138	3	38.95	18

† *Left-handed batsman.*

BOWLING

(Qualification: 25 wickets, average 25.00)

	Style	O	M	R	W	BB	5W/i	Avge
R. R. Bose (*Bengal and East Zone*)	RFM	237	79	577	37	6-62	3	15.59
D. S. Mohanty (*Orissa*)	RM	235.2	79	463	28	5-72	1	16.53
A. K. Thakur (*Himachal Pradesh*)	LM	212	59	492	29	6-30	2	16.96
U. Yadav (*Vidarbha and Central Zone*).....	RFM	168.5	43	456	26	6-105	2	17.53
Sarandeep Singh (*Himachal Pradesh*)	OB	206.1	46	538	29	4-37	0	18.55
I. K. Pathan (*Baroda*)	LFM	202	50	508	27	7-35	3	18.81
L. Balaji (*Tamil Nadu and South Zone*)....	RFM	306.3	83	820	43	6-24	4	19.06
A. Katti (*Assam and East Zone*)...........	SLA	191.1	52	477	25	7-93	1	19.08
I. Sharma (*Delhi and India*)	RFM	267.4	57	747	39	7-24	1	19.15
M. B. Parmar (*Gujarat and India A*)	OB	433.3	127	1,010	52	6-51	4	19.42
V. Malik (*Himachal Pradesh & N. Zone*) ...	RM	283.2	73	783	39	7-29	2	20.07
R. A. Jadeja (*Saurashtra and India A*)......	SLA	409.3	116	923	45	7-31	4	20.51
S. B. Joshi (*Karnataka*)	SLA	302.2	95	694	33	7-29	3	21.03
S. K. Trivedi (*Gujarat and West Zone*)	RM	333	103	844	40	5-43	2	21.10
S. S. Bandekar (*Goa and South Zone*)	RFM	225.1	50	698	33	6-75	3	21.15
A. B. Dinda (*Bengal, E. Zone & India A*) ...	RFM	304.3	66	915	43	5-28	4	21.27
S. P. Pandey (*Madhya Pradesh*)...........	RM	218.3	57	533	25	4-50	0	21.32
D. S. Kulkarni (*Mumbai, W. Zone & India A*)	RM	366.3	89	1,079	49	7-50	4	22.02
J. Billa (*Haryana*).....................	RM	193	41	557	25	6-58	2	22.28
B. C. Mohanty (*Orissa and East Zone*)	RFM	254.2	57	655	29	7-27	2	22.58
P. Awana (*Delhi and North Zone*)	RM	218	40	679	28	5-60	2	24.25
S. M. Fallah (*Maharashtra & West Zone*) ...	LM	269	51	853	35	6-102	4	24.37
R. R. Powar (*Mumbai and West Zone*)......	OB	323.3	52	1,076	44	7-140	3	24.45

Full scores of the 2008-09 Indian season can be found at www.cricinfo.com/db/ARCHIVE/2008-09/
IND_LOCAL/ and www.cricketarchive.co.uk/Archive/Seasons/2008-09_IND.html and in the *ACS
Overseas First-Class Annual 2009.*

MOHAMMAD NISSAR TROPHY, 2008-09

Ranji Trophy Champions v Quaid-e-Azam Trophy Champions

At Feroz Shah Kotla, Delhi, September 15, 16, 17, 18, 2008. **Drawn.** Sui Northern Gas won the Mohammad Nissar Trophy by virtue of their first-innings lead. Toss: Delhi. **Delhi 134** (V. Kohli 52; Imran Ali 6-52) **and 516-4** (A. Chopra 182, V. Kohli 197); **Sui Northern Gas 266** (Umar Akmal 58, Khurram Shehzad 66).

Delhi captain Virender Sehwag elected to bat, but was one of five ducks in their first innings; his team collapsed from 90-2 on the opening day, when Imran Ali took a hat-trick. They fought back as Aakash Chopra and Virat Kohli added 385 for their second wicket, and Delhi led by 384 on the third evening. But a last-day washout made Sui Northern Gas the first Pakistani champions to claim the Mohammad Nissar Trophy, in its third season, thanks to their first-innings lead.

IRANI CUP, 2008-09

Ranji Trophy Champions (Delhi) v Rest of India

At Reliance Stadium, Vadodara, September 24, 25, 26, 27, 2008. **Rest of India won by 187 runs.** Toss: Rest of India. **Rest of India 252** (Wasim Jaffer 50) **and 302** (R. Dravid 69, M. S. Dhoni 84; C. Nanda 5-48); **Delhi 177** (M. M. Patel 4-31) **and 190** (G. Gambhir 91; Harbhajan Singh 4-31).

The Rest fielded ten Test players (to Delhi's five) plus a one-day international and were led by Test captain Anil Kumble. Rahul Dravid batted for nearly five hours in the second innings, while Mahendra Singh Dhoni hit a more forceful half-century, striking 12 fours and a six in 113 balls. Delhi captain Virender Sehwag left Vadodara on the third day, citing a migraine; he was already out in the second innings. Harbhajan Singh wrapped up the Rest's win with a day to spare.

RANJI TROPHY, 2008-09

Elite League
Group A

	Played	Won	Lost	Drawn	1st-inns points	Bonus points	Points	Quotient
Mumbai	7	5	0	2	4	2	31	1.741
Gujarat	7	4	1	2	6	3	29	1.593
Saurashtra	7	3	2	2	6	2	23	1.401
Delhi	7	2	0	5	9	1	20	1.094
Punjab	7	2	3	2	2	0	12	0.800
Hyderabad	7	0	3	4	10	0	10	0.809
Orissa	7	1	4	2	4	0	9	0.640
Rajasthan	7	0	4	3	3	0	3	0.538

Elite League
Group B

	Played	Won	Lost	Drawn	1st-inns points	Bonus points	Points	Quotient
Tamil Nadu	6	2	0	4	12	1	23	2.110
Karnataka	6	3	0	3	3	1	19	1.126
Uttar Pradesh	6	1	1	4	12	0	17	0.970
Baroda	6	2	2	2	4	1	15	1.019
Railways	6	1	0	5	7	0	12	0.863
Maharashtra	6	0	3	3	7	0	7	0.731
Andhra	6	0	3	3	3	0	3	0.704

The top three teams from each Group were joined in the quarter-finals by the Plate semi-final winners.

Quarter-finals: Tamil Nadu beat Bengal by eight wickets; Uttar Pradesh drew with Gujarat but reached the semi-final by virtue of their first-innings lead; Mumbai beat Himachal Pradesh by nine wickets; Saurashtra beat Karnataka by five wickets.

Semi-finals: Mumbai drew with Saurashtra but reached the final by virtue of their first-innings lead; Uttar Pradesh drew with Tamil Nadu but reached the final by virtue of their first-innings lead.

Final: Mumbai beat Uttar Pradesh by 243 runs.

Plate League
Group A

	Played	Won	Lost	Drawn	1st-inns points	Bonus points	Points	Quotient
Himachal Pradesh	5	3	1	1	3	1	19	1.881
Goa	5	3	1	1	1	0	15*	1.058
Haryana	5	2	2	1	3	1	14	1.388
Kerala.	5	2	1	2	4	0	14	0.970
Jammu and Kashmir	5	1	3	1	1	0	6	0.633
Jharkhand	5	0	3	2	4	0	4	0.657

Plate League
Group B

	Played	Won	Lost	Drawn	1st-inns points	Bonus points	Points	Quotient
Bengal	5	3	0	2	4	2	21	1.857
Madhya Pradesh	5	2	0	3	9	2	21	1.664
Assam	5	3	2	0	0	0	15	0.894
Vidarbha	5	2	2	1	1	0	11	0.986
Tripura	5	1	3	1	1	0	6	0.760
Services	5	0	4	1	1	0	1	0.550

* 1 point deducted for fielding too many players from outside Goa against Kerala in the opening round.

Semi-finals: Bengal drew with Goa but advanced by virtue of their first-innings lead; Himachal Pradesh beat Madhya Pradesh by an innings and 175 runs.

No final was held, as Bengal and Himachal Pradesh advanced to the Elite League quarter-finals; they were also promoted to the Elite League in 2009-10 (replacing Andhra and Rajasthan).

Outright win = 5 pts; lead on first innings in a drawn match = 3 pts; deficit on first innings in a drawn match = 1 pt; win by an innings or ten wickets = 1 bonus pt. Quotient = runs scored per wicket divided by runs conceded per wicket.

Elite League Group A

At Roshanara Club Ground, Delhi, November 3, 4, 5, 6, 2008. **Drawn.** Toss: Delhi. **Punjab 391** (S. Sohal 110, U. Kaul 95, A. Kakkar 56; P. Sangwan 4-102) **and 140-3; Delhi 519** (A. Chopra 76, S. Dhawan 72, M. Manhas 58, R. Bhatia 99, P. Bisht 76, C. Nanda 56). *Delhi 3 pts, Punjab 1 pt.*
    Delhi's 519 included six individual fifties.

At Brabourne Stadium, Mumbai, November 3, 4, 5, 6, 2008. **Mumbai won by 237 runs.** Toss: Mumbai. **Mumbai 307** (Wasim Jaffer 60, A. M. Rahane 73, R. G. Sharma 62) **and 305-7 dec** (S. O. Kukreja 83, R. G. Sharma 128; Pankaj Singh 4-83); **Rajasthan 204** (V. A. Saxena 76; D. S. Kulkarni 5-40, R. R. Powar 5-44) **and 171** (D. S. Kulkarni 4-48). *Mumbai 5 pts.*
    Dhawal Kulkarni took nine wickets in his third first-class game, his first in the Ranji Trophy.

At Barabati Stadium, Cuttack, November 3, 4, 5, 6, 2008. **Drawn.** Toss: Orissa. **Hyderabad 296** (D. B. Ravi Teja 71, S. A. Pai 78, Abhinav Kumar 99*) **and 263-5** (D. Rushi Raj 56, S. A. Pai 53); **Orissa 269** (S. S. Das 80). *Orissa 1 pt, Hyderabad 3 pts.*
    Abhinav Kumar was one short of a maiden hundred when No. 11 Ashwin Yadav was run out.

At Madhavrao Scindia Ground, Rajkot, November 3, 4, 5, 6, 2008. **Gujarat won by an innings and 227 runs.** Toss: Saurashtra. **Gujarat 581-6 dec** (B. D. Thaker 192, S. J. Patel 90, T. K. Patel 104*); **Saurashtra 153** (S. K. Trivedi 5-44) **and 201** (R. V. Dhruve 52*; M. B. Parmar 4-30). *Gujarat 6 pts.*
    Bhavik Thaker and Timil Patel took Gujarat past 500 by adding 200 for the sixth wicket. Siddharth Trivedi reduced Saurashtra to 7-4 in the seventh over of their first innings; in their second, off-spinner Mohnish Parmar's analysis was 29–16–30–4.

At Lalabhai Contractor Stadium, Surat, November 10, 11, 12, 2008. **Mumbai won by an innings and 239 runs.** Toss: Gujarat. **Mumbai 486** (Wasim Jaffer 172, A. M. Rahane 104, A. A. Muzumdar 61; M. B. Parmar 6-143); **Gujarat 203** (A. M. Makda 73; D. S. Kulkarni 4-70) and **44.** *Mumbai 6 pts.*

Gujarat's 44 was only one run above their all-time low, against the same opposition (then Bombay) in 1958-59. Only No. 10 Amit Singh reached double figures. In the first innings, he and No. 9 Ashraf Makda had added 100 to rescue Gujarat from 101-8. Wasim Jaffer had set Mumbai on the way to their three-day win by adding 218 for the second wicket with Ajinkya Rahane and another 109 for the third with Amol Muzumdar.

At Rajiv Gandhi Stadium, Uppal, Hyderabad, November 10, 11, 12, 13, 2008. **Drawn.** Toss: Hyderabad. **Hyderabad 334** (S. A. Pai 130, Abhinav Kumar 76; P. Sangwan 4-86) and **230-3** (T. L. Suman 52, D. B. Ravi Teja 113*, A. S. Yadav 54*); **Delhi 284** (A. Chopra 51, P. Bisht 78; A. D. Yadav 6-52). *Hyderabad 3 pts, Delhi 1 pt.*

At PCA Ground, Mohali, November 10, 11, 12, 2008. **Punjab won by nine wickets.** Toss: Rajasthan. **Rajasthan 133** (Gagandeep Singh 4-37, M. S. Gony 4-39) and **169** (V. A. Saxena 83); **Punjab 262** (S. Sohal 106; Gajendra Singh 4-67) and **41-1.** *Punjab 5 pts.*

Gagandeep Singh reduced Rajasthan to 22-7 by the 13th over of the match.

At Khandheri Stadium, Rajkot, November 10, 11, 12, 13, 2008. **Saurashtra won by an innings and 84 runs.** Toss: Saurashtra. **Saurashtra 620-4 dec** (C. A. Pujara 302*, R. A. Jadeja 232*); **Orissa 302** (S. S. Das 76, S. S. Biswal 62, S. V. Sehgal 64*; S. P. Jobanputra 4-56, K. R. Makwana 4-142) and **234** (R. A. Jadeja 5-44). *Saurashtra 6 pts.*

This was the first first-class match at the Khandheri Stadium. Cheteshwar Pujara and Ravi Jadeja joined forces at 100-4 and added 520, a world record for the fifth wicket (beating the Waugh twins' 464* for New South Wales against Western Australia in 1990-91) and the eighth-highest stand for any wicket. Pujara scored his maiden first-class triple-hundred, batting ten hours three minutes and 423 balls and hitting 33 fours and three sixes; Jadeja's 232* was his maiden century, and he batted for eight hours before taking a career-best 5-44 to complete the innings victory. Saurashtra's total was their first of 600; Pujara and Jadeja scored the highest and third-highest individual innings for the team.*

At Feroz Shah Kotla, Delhi, November 16, 17, 18, 19, 2008. **Drawn.** Toss: Mumbai. **Mumbai 330** (A. M. Rahane 160, A. A. Muzumdar 83; S. Narwal 4-43) and **468-4** (S. O. Kukreja 229*, Wasim Jaffer 98, A. M. Rahane 78, V. R. Samant 53*); **Delhi 295** (M. Manhas 98, R. Bhatia 81). *Delhi 1 pt, Mumbai 3 pts.*

Amol Muzumdar's 61st Ranji half-century beat Amarjit Kaypee's record of 60; he added 223 for Mumbai's third wicket with Ajinkya Rahane. Sahil Kukreja batted throughout Mumbai's second innings for his maiden double-hundred, having missed it by one run in his previous match against Delhi a year earlier, and shared three century partnerships. Kukreja's was the last of five double-centuries scored during this round of Ranji cricket.

At Sardar Patel Stadium, Ahmedabad, November 16, 17, 18, 19, 2008. **Drawn.** Toss: Gujarat. **Gujarat 520-9 dec** (N. D. Modi 250*, N. K. Patel 76); **Hyderabad 225** (S. A. Quadri 57; S. K. Trivedi 4-44) and **287-7** (A. S. Yadav 117*). *Gujarat 3 pts, Hyderabad 1 pt.*

Nilesh Modi batted throughout Gujarat's innings for 11 hours 31 minutes (163.1 overs) and a career-best 250 – the second-highest individual score for Gujarat.*

At Veer Surendra Sai Stadium, Sambalpur, November 16, 17, 18, 19, 2008. **Drawn.** Toss: Rajasthan. **Orissa 281** (B. S. Pati 72, S. S. Das 74, H. M. Das 59*; V. Yadav 4-45) and **209** (S. S. Das 61, N. J. Behera 54; V. Yadav 4-38); **Rajasthan 270** (G. K. Khoda 127; Dhiraj Kumar 7-83) and **131-4** (R. D. Bist 60*). *Orissa 3 pts, Rajasthan 1 pt.*

Left-arm spinner Dhiraj Kumar took 7-83 on debut, in the first first-class match at Sambalpur for 17 years.

At Madhavrao Scindia Ground, Rajkot, November 16, 17, 18, 19, 2008. **Drawn.** Toss: Punjab. **Punjab 482** (R. Inder Singh 114, S. Sohal 103, T. Kohli 79, A. Kakkar 67; R. A. Jadeja 5-106); **Saurashtra 679-8** (S. H. Kotak 102, C. A. Pujara 189, R. A. Jadeja 56, J. N. Shah 178). *Saurashtra 3 pts, Punjab 1 pt.*

Saurashtra raised their highest total for the second time in a week. Shitanshu Kotak and Cheteshwar Pujara – who scored 189 in 182 balls – added 258 for the third wicket. All 11 of the Punjab team bowled, and off-spinner Charanjeet Singh conceded 220 in 59 overs.

At Sardar Vallabhai Patel Stadium, Valsad, November 23, 24, 25, 26, 2008. **Drawn.** Toss: Gujarat. **Gujarat 350** (P. A. Patel 55, B. D. Thaker 151) **and 259-6** (P. A. Patel 71); **Delhi 314** (G. Chhabra 63, Y. Nagar 79; M. B. Parmar 4-104). *Gujarat 3 pts, Delhi 1 pt.*

At Rajiv Gandhi Stadium, Uppal, Hyderabad, November 23, 24, 25, 26, 2008. **Drawn.** Toss: Hyderabad. **Hyderabad 553-6 dec** (T. L. Suman 50, S. A. Pai 85, V. V. S. Laxman 224, S. A. Quadri 100*) **and 33-0; Rajasthan 405** (R. D. Bist 136, R. K. Bishnoi 97, V. A. Deshpande 73*; A. D. Yadav 4-67). *Hyderabad 3 pts, Rajasthan 1 pt.*

Hyderabad captain Laxman scored his eighth double-hundred, four weeks after the seventh, against Australia in the Delhi Test. He added 215 for the sixth wicket with Ahmed Quadri, who reached a maiden century in his third first-class match.

At East Coast Railway SA Ground, Bhubaneswar, November 23, 24, 25, 26, 2008. **Orissa won by nine wickets.** Toss: Orissa. **Punjab 60** (B. C. Mohanty 7-27) **and 378** (K. Goel 58, U. Kaul 71, A. Kakkar 117; D. S. Mohanty 5-72); **Orissa 352** (N. J. Behera 74, S. S. Biswal 54, P. M. Mullick 100*, H. M. Das 80; Gagandeep Singh 4-45) **and 87-1.** *Orissa 5 pts.*

This was the first first-class match at the East Coast Railway Sports Association Ground. Basant Mohanty's career-best 9.2–1–27–7 dismissed Punjab for 60, their second-lowest first-class total, before lunch on the opening day; only captain Pankaj Dharmani (23*) reached double figures. In Orissa's reply, Pravanjan Mullick and Halhadar Das added 143 for the seventh wicket.

At Madhavrao Scindia Ground, Rajkot, November 23, 24, 25, 26, 2008. **Drawn.** Toss: Saurashtra. **Saurashtra 643-4 dec** (C. R. Pathak 170, B. M. Chauhan 104, S. H. Kotak 78, C. A. Pujara 176); **Mumbai 214** (U. R. Malvi 56; B. N. Jadeja 4-41) **and 157-7.** *Saurashtra 3 pts, Mumbai 1 pt.*

Saurashtra passed 600 for the third time in their history – all in the last three matches. Chirag Pathak, a 21-year-old left-hander who scored 170 on first-class debut, and Bhushan Chauhan, with a maiden century, set them off with 275 for the first wicket, then Cheteshwar Pujara scored his third successive hundred, 176 from 173 balls. Balkrishna Jadeja took 4-41 on first-class debut to force Mumbai to follow on.

At Feroz Shah Kotla, Delhi, November 29, 30, 2008. **Delhi won by 52 runs.** Toss: Orissa. **Delhi 78 and 150** (S. Narwal 66*; D. S. Mohanty 4-31, S. P. Khatua 4-58); **Orissa 80** (I. Sharma 7-24) **and 96** (I. Sharma 4-27). *Delhi 5 pts.*

Test fast bowler Ishant Sharma claimed a career-best 8.3–2–24–7 and went on to his best match figures as Delhi completed a two-day win; only one innings out of four reached 100 and only three batsmen reached 20.

At Sardar Patel Stadium, Ahmedabad, November 29, 30, December 1, 2008. **Gujarat won by ten wickets.** Toss: Gujarat. **Gujarat 300** (P. A. Patel 84, B. D. Thaker 158; Gagandeep Singh 5-59) **and 34-0; Punjab 137** (M. S. Gony 69; S. K. Trivedi 4-53, A. M. Makda 5-20) **and 192** (U. Kaul 56*; S. K. Trivedi 5-43). *Gujarat 6 pts.*

Five men fell without scoring as Gujarat lost their first three wickets for four runs, and their last six for nine; two century partnerships in between the collapses gave them a match-winning total. Punjab's reply featured four ducks as they slumped to 16-7, but No. 10 Manpreet Gony scored 69 from 50 balls with five sixes and six fours.

At Madhavrao Scindia Ground, Rajkot, November 29, 30, December 1, 2008. **Saurashtra won by an innings and 74 runs.** Toss: Saurashtra. **Saurashtra 344** (C. R. Pathak 88, B. M. Chauhan 114; Pankaj Singh 5-59, Gajendra Singh 4-119); **Rajasthan 185** (R. K. Bishnoi 67*; K. R. Makwana 4-74) **and 85** (K. R. Makwana 4-31). *Saurashtra 6 pts.*

At Bandra Kurla Complex, Mumbai, December 2, 3, 4, 5, 2008. **Mumbai won by an innings and 108 runs.** Toss: Mumbai. **Mumbai 602-6 dec** (Wasim Jaffer 256, A. M. Rahane 137, A. B. Agarkar 77*; M. P. Arjun 4-99); **Hyderabad 251** (T. L. Suman 67, S. A. Pai 66, S. A. Quadri 50*; R. R. Powar 5-67) **and 243** (D. B. Ravi Teja 107, Abhinav Kumar 62; D. S. Kulkarni 7-50). *Mumbai 6 pts.*

This was the first first-class match at the Bandra Kurla Complex. Wasim Jaffer, who scored his sixth double-hundred, and Ajinkya Rahane added 335 in 79 overs for Mumbai's second wicket.

Hyderabad's entire team failed to match Jaffer's individual score in either innings; in their second, Dhawal Kulkarni claimed a career-best 7-50, and Jaffer took four catches in the field.

At Rajiv Gandhi Stadium, Uppal, Hyderabad, December 12, 13, 14, 15, 2008. **Punjab won by nine wickets.** Toss: Hyderabad. **Hyderabad 335** (T. L. Suman 131, A. J. Shinde 57, S. A. Quadri 80; Sarabjit Singh 4-72) **and 164** (S. A. Pai 50; Sarabjit Singh 5-39); **Punjab 291** (U. Kaul 106) **and 211-1** (S. Sohal 91*, R. Inder Singh 112*). *Punjab 5 pts.*

At Barabati Stadium, Cuttack, December 12, 13, 14, 2008. **Mumbai won by 315 runs.** Toss: Mumbai. **Mumbai 180** (B. C. Mohanty 5-50) **and 361-5 dec** (S. O. Kukreja 53, A. M. Rahane 201, Wasim Jaffer 66); **Orissa 108** (H. M. Das 62*; D. S. Kulkarni 5-27) **and 118** (P. Jayachandra 72). *Mumbai 5 pts.*

Orissa were 26-8 in their first innings until Halhadar Das and Basant Mohanty added 82 in a last-wicket partnership (their captain Shiv Sunder Das was unable to bat). Ajinkya Rahane scored a maiden double-hundred to set up Mumbai's crushing victory, which secured their place in the quarter-finals with a round to go.

At K. L. Saini Ground, Jaipur, December 12, 13, 14, 2008. **Gujarat won by seven wickets.** Toss: Gujarat. **Rajasthan 136** (Amit Singh 4-31) **and 186** (V. S. Chanwaria 88; Amit Singh 7-31); **Gujarat 227** (N. K. Patel 51, B. D. Thaker 52; Mohammad Aslam 4-22) **and 99-3.** *Gujarat 5 pts.*
Amit Singh equalled his best bowling figures in the first innings and outstripped them in the second.

At Madhavrao Scindia Ground, Rajkot, December 12, 13, 14, 15, 2008. **Delhi won by six wickets.** Toss: Saurashtra. **Saurashtra 241** (B. M. Chauhan 61, R. A. Jadeja 56; P. Awana 5-60) **and 274** (R. A. Jadeja 143; P. Awana 5-77); **Delhi 384** (A. Chopra 58, S. Dhawan 93, V. Kohli 69) **and 132-0** (S. Dhawan 84*). *Delhi 6 pts.*
Delhi wicketkeeper Punit Bisht made nine dismissals in the match, including six catches in Saurashtra's second innings.

At Brabourne Stadium, Mumbai, December 18, 19, 20, 21, 2008. **Mumbai won by nine wickets.** Toss: Punjab. **Punjab 202** (A. Kakkar 67; R. A. Shaikh 4-50) **and 382** (S. Sohal 51, U. Kaul 136*, A. Kakkar 58); **Mumbai 436-9 dec** (V. R. Samant 65, A. M. Rahane 80, A. A. Muzumdar 113, R. G. Sharma 85, A. M. Nayar 61) **and 151-1** (Wasim Jaffer 52*, A. M. Rahane 82*). *Mumbai 5 pts.*
There were 11 individual fifties in the match, five of them in Mumbai's first innings. Mumbai ended the group stage with their third consecutive win, and their fifth in seven games, with no defeats.

At East Coast Railway SA Ground, Bhubaneswar, December 18, 19, 20, 21, 2008. **Gujarat won by an innings and 78 runs.** Toss: Orissa. **Orissa 162** (M. B. Parmar 6-53) **and 154** (N. J. Behera 50; M. B. Parmar 6-51); **Gujarat 394** (P. K. Parmar 206; P. A. Patel 206). *Gujarat 6 pts.*
Parthiv Patel scored his maiden double-century, batting four minutes short of nine hours, and his team-mate Mohnish Parmar claimed a career-best 12-104.

At Sawai Mansingh Stadium, Jaipur, December 18, 19, 20, 21, 2008. **Drawn.** Toss: Delhi. **Rajasthan 295** (V. A. Saxena 71, Kuldeep Singh 77) **and 55-3; Delhi 688** (A. Chopra 210, S. Dhawan 118, V. Kohli 83, R. Bhatia 112; P. Sangwan 52; Pankaj Singh 4-125). *Rajasthan 1 pt, Delhi 3 pts.*
Aakash Chopra hit his fifth double-hundred, sharing an opening stand of 280 with Shikhar Dhawan.

At Madhavrao Scindia Ground, Rajkot, December 18, 19, 20, 2008. **Saurashtra won by 105 runs.** Toss: Saurashtra. **Saurashtra 133 and 183** (A. J. Shinde 4-13); **Hyderabad 140** (B. N. Jadeja 6-29) **and 71** (R. A. Jadeja 7-31). *Saurashtra 5 pts.*
Left-arm spinner Ravi Jadeja's career-best 7-31 wound up Hyderabad for 71, only two runs more than their lowest-ever total of 69 against Mysore in 1959-60, to complete a three-day win. His namesake Balkrishna Jadeja's 6-29 in the first innings was also a career-best.

Elite League Group B

At M. Chinnaswamy Stadium, Bangalore, November 3, 4, 5, 6, 2008. **Drawn.** Toss: Karnataka. **Karnataka 365** (K. B. Pawan 54, R. V. Uthappa 131, M. K. Pandey 64; M. Kartik 5-83) **and 127** (K. Anureet Singh 6-49); **Railways 389** (S. B. Bangar 84, Y. K. T. Goud 122*, Raja Ali 52) **and 17-2.** *Karnataka 1 pt, Railways 3 pts.*

At Hutatma Anant Kanhere Maidan, Golf Club Ground, Nasik, November 3, 4, 5, 6, 2008. **Drawn.** Toss: Tamil Nadu. **Tamil Nadu 648-3 dec** (M. Vijay 243, A. Mukund 300*, V. Sivaramakrishnan 59); **Maharashtra 457** (A. J. Shrikhande 195, K. M. Jadhav 63; C. Suresh 5-122) **and 250-6** (K. M. Jadhav 95, N. S. Paradkar 92). *Maharashtra 1 pt, Tamil Nadu 3 pts.*

Abhinav Mukund and Murali Vijay put on 462 together, the sixth-highest first-wicket partnership in first-class history and two runs short of the Indian record. At 18 years 303 days, Mukund was the third-youngest player to score a triple-hundred; it was the third-highest score for Tamil Nadu, and he batted nine hours 28 minutes and 383 balls, hitting 33 fours and five sixes. After scoring the second double-century of his career, Vijay was called up by India and made his Test debut against Australia at Nagpur on the final day of this game. Bangladesh Test spinner Enamul Haque, who was playing for Maharashtra, had figures of 31–1–171–0.

YOUNGEST PLAYERS TO SCORE A FIRST-CLASS TRIPLE-HUNDRED

Years	Days				
17	311	Javed Miandad	311	Karachi Whites v National Bank at Karachi .	1974-75
18	265	Wasim Jaffer	314*	Mumbai v Saurashtra at Rajkot	1996-97
18	**303**	**A. Mukund**	**300***	**Tamil Nadu v Maharashtra at Nasik**	**2008-09**
19	164	Raqibul Hasan	313*	Barisal v Sylhet at Fatullah	2006-07
19	199	F. M. M. Worrell	308*	Barbados v Trinidad at Bridgetown	1943-44
19	344	Arjan Kripal Singh	302*	Tamil Nadu v Goa at Panaji	1988-89

Research: Philip Bailey

At Sports Stadium, Civil Lines, Meerut, November 3, 4, 5, 6, 2008. **Drawn.** Toss: Andhra. **Andhra 349** (L. N. P. Reddy 94, A. G. Pradeep 102*; Bhuvneshwar Singh 5-58) **and 130-2** (H. H. Watekar 69); **Uttar Pradesh 412** (T. M. Srivastava 154, M. Kaif 144; M. Suresh 5-80). *Uttar Pradesh 3 pts, Andhra 1 pt.*

Tanmay Srivastava and Mohammad Kaif added 285 for Uttar Pradesh's third wicket (before eight wickets fell for 79).

At Moti Bagh Stadium, Vadodara, November 10, 11, 12, 13, 2008. **Drawn.** Toss: Uttar Pradesh. **Baroda 235** (R. K. Solanki 71; P. Kumar 5-71) **and 314** (S. S. Parab 67, R. K. Solanki 71; P. P. Chawla 4-122); **Uttar Pradesh 286** (T. M. Srivastava 79, M. Kaif 51, P. Kumar 50; I. K. Pathan 6-85) **and 151-6.** *Baroda 1 pt, Uttar Pradesh 3 pts.*

At M. Chinnaswamy Stadium, Bangalore, November 10, 11, 12, 13, 2008. **Drawn.** Toss: Tamil Nadu. **Tamil Nadu 531** (K. B. Arun Karthik 149, V. Sivaramakrishnan 193, S. Suresh Kumar 90; S. B. Joshi 4-136); **Karnataka 267** (C. Raghu 76; C. Suresh 4-58) **and 269-4** (K. B. Pawan 84, M. K. Pandey 57*). *Karnataka 1 pt, Tamil Nadu 3 pts.*

Opening batsman Konda Bhaskar Arun Karthik made 149 on first-class debut, and rescued Tamil Nadu from 51-3 by adding 246 with Vidyut Sivaramakrishnan, who narrowly missed a maiden double-hundred.

At Hutatma Anant Kanhere Maidan, Golf Club Ground, Nasik, November 10, 11, 12, 13, 2008. **Drawn.** Toss: Andhra. **Andhra 348** (H. H. Watekar 142; S. M. Fallah 6-102) **and 210-5 dec** (L. N. P. Reddy 53, B. A. Sumanth 58*); **Maharashtra 393** (H. H. Khadiwale 103, R. U. Bhosale 77, A. J. Shrikhande 59, K. M. Jadhav 63; M. Suresh 4-75) **and 27-1.** *Maharashtra 3 pts, Andhra 1 pt.*

At Gangothri Glades Ground, Mysore, November 16, 17, 18, 19, 2008. **Karnataka won by 202 runs.** Toss: Karnataka. **Karnataka 366** (R. V. Uthappa 133, S. B. Joshi 65; D. Kalyankrishna 4-85) **and 171** (R. Dravid 50; P. D. Vijaykumar 6-51); **Andhra 218** (V. M. Sai 70, M. Suresh 54; S. B. Joshi 5-41) **and 117** (K. P. Appanna 4-24). *Karnataka 5 pts.*

Karnataka wicketkeeper Thilak Naidu made nine dismissals in the match, including five catches and a stumping in Andhra's second innings.

At Karnail Singh Stadium, Delhi, November 16, 17, 18, 19, 2008. **Drawn.** Toss: Railways. **Railways 224** (K. V. Sharma 79, M. Rawat 67; I. K. Pathan 4-42) **and 240-5** (A. A. Pagnis 67, S. B. Bangar 55, M. Rawat 57*); **Baroda 460-8 dec** (C. C. Williams 137, A. A. Bilakhia 157). *Railways 1 pt, Baroda 3 pts.*

Connor Williams and Azhar Bilakhia added 278 for Baroda's second wicket. Test bowler Irfan Pathan was fined the whole of his match fee for throwing the ball at Railways' Sanjay Bangar, rather than the stumps, after fielding it in his follow-through.

At Jawaharlal Nehru Stadium, Ghaziabad, November 16, 17, 18, 2008. **Tamil Nadu won by an innings and 238 runs.** Toss: Tamil Nadu. **Uttar Pradesh 150** (L. Balaji 4-38, P. Amarnath 4-53) **and 119** (L. Balaji 5-42, C. Ganapathy 4-21); **Tamil Nadu 507** (S. Badrinath 123, K. D. Karthik 213; P. P. Gupta 4-123). *Tamil Nadu 6 pts.*

Dinesh Karthik scored a maiden double-century and added 213 for Tamil Nadu's third wicket with Subramaniam Badrinath.

At Rajinder Singh Institute Ground, Bangalore, November 23, 24, 25, 26, 2008. **Karnataka won by ten wickets.** Toss: Karnataka. **Baroda 169** (R. K. Solanki 53; S. N. Raju 4-30) **and 285** (C. C. Williams 137, R. K. Solanki 66; S. B. Joshi 6-48); **Karnataka 395** (R. Dravid 83, V. S. T. Naidu 90, S. B. Joshi 55, B. Akhil 66; A. K. Argal 4-93) **and 60-0.** *Karnataka 6 pts.*

Sunil Joshi's 55 included six sixes and three fours.

At Karnail Singh Stadium, Delhi, November 23, 24, 25, 26, 2008. **Railways won by seven wickets.** Toss: Andhra. **Andhra 208** (Y. Gnaneswara Rao 50, M. Suresh 51*; K. V. Sharma 4-37) **and 108** (K. Anureet Singh 4-29, K. S. Parida 4-10); **Railways 227** (S. C. Sanyal 70) **and 90-3.** *Railways 5 pts.*

At Modi Stadium, Kanpur, November 23, 24, 25, 26, 2008. **Uttar Pradesh won by eight wickets.** Toss: Maharashtra. **Maharashtra 221** (H. H. Khadiwale 56, K. M. Jadhav 93*) **and 230** (K. M. Jadhav 65, D. V. Shilamkar 56); **Uttar Pradesh 315** (S. S. Shukla 131, Parvinder Singh 68; S. M. Fallah 5-93) **and 140-2** (T. M. Srivastava 65*, Parvinder Singh 60). *Uttar Pradesh 5 pts.*

At Indira Gandhi Stadium, Vijayawada, November 29, 30, December 1, 2, 2008. **Drawn.** Toss: Tamil Nadu. **Andhra 283** (B. A. Sumanth 90, Y. Gnaneswara Rao 62) **and 95-3; Tamil Nadu 286-4 dec** (A. Mukund 150, S. Badrinath 121). *Andhra 1 pt, Tamil Nadu 3 pts.*

Abhinav Mukund and Subramaniam Badrinath added 244 for Tamil Nadu's second wicket.

At Moti Bagh Stadium, Vadodara, November 29, 30, December 1, 2, 2008. **Baroda won by four wickets.** Toss: Baroda. **Maharashtra 228** (K. M. Jadhav 80; I. K. Pathan 5-54) **and 303** (R. U. Bhosale 69, A. J. Shrikhande 114; M. M. Patel 4-40, R. V. Pawar 4-46); **Baroda 305** (Y. K. Pathan 58, P. R. Shah 56, I. K. Pathan 51; S. M. Fallah 5-104) **and 229-6** (Y. K. Pathan 100, I. K. Pathan 50*). *Baroda 5 pts.*

At Karnail Singh Stadium, Delhi, November 29, 30, December 1, 2, 2008. **Drawn.** Toss: Uttar Pradesh. **Uttar Pradesh 346** (S. K. Raina 66, P. Kumar 98) **and 150-6 dec** (T. M. Srivastava 62); **Railways 200** (Y. K. T. Goud 78*; P. P. Chawla 5-33) **and 215-8** (S. B. Bangar 70*, M. Rawat 80; Bhuvneshwar Singh 5-35). *Railways 1 pt, Uttar Pradesh 3 pts.*

In Uttar Pradesh's second innings, off-spinner Kulamani Parida had figures of 13–8–7–2.

At Moti Bagh Stadium, Vadodara, December 12, 13, 14, 2008. **Tamil Nadu won by 259 runs.** Toss: Tamil Nadu. **Tamil Nadu 117** (S. Y. Veragi 5-24) **and 402** (R. Prasanna 92, K. D. Karthik 123; A. K. Argal 4-59); **Baroda 166** (P. Amarnath 5-60) **and 94** (L. Balaji 5-47, C. Ganapathy 4-24). *Tamil Nadu 5 pts.*

Medium-pacer Salim Veragi's career-best 5-24 included a hat-trick to wind up Tamil Nadu's first innings; in their second, Ramaswamy Prasanna and Dinesh Karthik added 200 for the third wicket. Victory saw them through to the quarter-finals with a round to spare.

At M. Chinnaswamy Stadium, Bangalore, December 12, 13, 14, 15, 2008. **Drawn.** Toss: Uttar Pradesh. **Karnataka 511** (R. V. Uthappa 65, C. Raghu 64, B. Akhil 135, S. B. Joshi 64); **Uttar Pradesh 567** (T. M. Srivastava 159, M. Kaif 112, Bhuvneshwar Singh 55, P. P. Chawla 96). *Karnataka 1 pt, Uttar Pradesh 3 pts.*

Tanmay Srivastava and Mohammad Kaif added 247, their second double-century partnership for Uttar Pradesh's third wicket in this tournament. This was Uttar Pradesh's last group game, and they had to wait for results in the final round to find out whether they would reach the quarter-finals.

At Hutatma Anant Kanhere Maidan, Golf Club Ground, Nasik, December 12, 13, 14, 15, 2008. **Drawn.** Toss: Maharashtra. **Railways 212** (Y. K. T. Goud 75, S. C. Sanyal 70; S. M. Fallah 5-49) **and 334-6 dec** (Y. K. T. Goud 89, S. C. Sanyal 82, M. Kartik 56); **Maharashtra 244** (A. J. Shrikhande 113; S. C. Sanyal 4-26) **and 251-5** (K. M. Jadhav 114*, A. R. Bawne 52). *Maharashtra 3 pts, Railways 1 pt.*

At Moti Bagh Stadium, Vadodara, December 18, 19, 20, 2008. **Baroda won by an innings and 60 runs.** Toss: Baroda. **Baroda 400** (S. S. Parab 130, A. A. Bilakhia 73, R. K. Solanki 64, P. R. Shah 72; T. Atchuti Rao 5-66); **Andhra 77** (I. K. Pathan 7-35) **and 263** (M. Suresh 54, D. Prabhu Kiran 65*; Y. K. Pathan 4-72). *Baroda 6 pts.*

Irfan Pathan collected a career-best 10–1–35–7 as Andhra folded for 77 on the second day, a slight recovery from 24-4.

At Rajinder Singh Institute Ground, Bangalore, December 18, 19, 20, 2008. **Karnataka won by 155 runs.** Toss: Karnataka. **Karnataka 252** (C. M. Gautam 108; S. M. Fallah 4-47) **and 229** (B. Akhil 62; S. A. Agharkar 4-56); **Maharashtra 210** (H. H. Khadiwale 70; S. B. Joshi 6-62, K. P. Appanna 4-40) **and 116** (S. B. Joshi 7-29). *Karnataka 5 pts.*

On his 100th Ranji appearance, former Test spinner Sunil Joshi took a career-best 7-29 and 11-91 in all – his fifth ten-in-a-match – in a three-day win which saw Karnataka into the quarter-finals.

At M. A. Chidambaram Stadium, Chennai, December 18, 19, 20, 21, 2008. **Drawn.** Toss: Tamil Nadu. **Tamil Nadu 475-6 dec** (A. Mukund 162, K. D. Karthik 113, R. Ashwin 103*) **and 389-7 dec** (K. B. Arun Karthik 107, S. Suresh Kumar 90, C. Ganapathy 53*); **Railways 314** (V. Cheluvaraj 65, Y. K. T. Goud 97; V. Y. Mahesh 4-90). *Tamil Nadu 3 pts, Railways 1 pt.*

Dinesh Karthik scored his third hundred for Tamil Nadu in five weeks while adding 210 for the third wicket with Abhinav Mukund.

Quarter-finals

At M. Chinnaswamy Stadium, Bangalore, December 26, 27, 28, 29, 2008. **Tamil Nadu won by eight wickets.** Toss: Bengal. **Bengal 345** (W. P. Saha 53, M. K. Tiwary 144, D. P. Chakrabarty 57; C. Ganapathy 5-59) **and 187** (L. Balaji 6-24); **Tamil Nadu 306** (S. Suresh Kumar 75) **and 227-2** (M. Vijay 73, S. Badrinath 92*).

Bengal took first-innings lead, but their second innings foundered. Both openers were ill, and batted down the order, as Lakshmipathy Balaji took five wickets for seven runs and gave Tamil Nadu time to chase a target of 227.

At Moti Bagh Stadium, Vadodara, December 26, 27, 28, 29, 2008. **Drawn.** Uttar Pradesh qualified for the semi-final by virtue of their first-innings lead. Toss: Gujarat. **Uttar Pradesh 305** (S. K. Raina 93, Parvinder Singh 64) **and 375** (T. M. Srivastava 67, Amir Khan 56*, P. P. Gupta 74; M. B. Parmar 5-113); **Gujarat 117** (P. Kumar 5-29) **and 106-3** (N. D. Modi 57*).

Gujarat collapsed to 48-7 on the second day before Timil Patel steered them to three figures with 43. But Amir Khan and Praveen Gupta added 125 for the ninth wicket in Uttar Pradesh's second innings to bat them out of the game.*

At Sardar Patel Stadium, Ahmedabad, December 26, 27, 28, 29, 2008. **Mumbai won by nine wickets.** Toss: Mumbai. **Himachal Pradesh 250** (A. Mannu 61, Sarandeep Singh 75; A. M. Nayyar 6-45) **and 287** (Sangram Singh 58, P. Dogra 90; A. B. Agarkar 5-78); **Mumbai 495** (Wasim Jaffer 108, R. G. Sharma 98, A. B. Agarkar 50, Extras 54) **and 43-1.**

Wasim Jaffer's third hundred of the tournament took him past 1,000 first-class runs for the season.

At Brabourne Stadium, Mumbai, December 26, 27, 28, 29, 2008. **Saurashtra won by five wickets.** Toss: Saurashtra. **Karnataka 305** (R. V. Uthappa 139; R. A. Jadeja 5-82) **and 208** (R. Dravid 52, B. Akhil 56; S. P. Jobanputra 5-54, R. A. Jadeja 4-58); **Saurashtra 189 and 327-5** (S. H. Kotak 87, C. A. Pujara 112*, R. A. Jadeja 55, J. N. Shah 55*).

Ravi Jadeja took five in an innings for the fourth time in this tournament, but Saurashtra looked like going out when they conceded a 116-run lead and slid to 13-3 on the third morning chasing 325. Cheteshwar Pujara saw them through with his fourth hundred of the tournament, adding 163 for the fourth wicket with Shitanshu Kotak.

Semi-finals

At M. A. Chidambaram Stadium, Chennai, January 4, 5, 6, 7, 2009. **Drawn.** Mumbai qualified for the final by virtue of their first-innings lead. Toss: Mumbai. **Mumbai 637-6 dec** (Wasim Jaffer 301, A. M. Rahane 85, S. R. Tendulkar 122*) **and 42-1;** Saurashtra 379 (S. H. Kotak 89, K. R. Makwana 56*; R. R. Powar 4-108).

Wasim Jaffer scored his second triple-century, his fourth hundred and second double in this Ranji Trophy, batting ten hours 35 minutes and 459 balls, with 27 fours. He added 241 for the second wicket with Ajinkya Rahane (who passed 1,000 for the season), their third double-century partnership in the 2008-09 tournament, and 226 for the third with Sachin Tendulkar, a stand broken only when Tendulkar retired hurt. Saurashtra might yet have reached the final on overall net run-rate had they avoided being bowled out and denied Mumbai a decision on first innings, but they were all out on the final day.

At VCA Stadium, Nagpur, January 4, 5, 6, 7, 2009. **Drawn.** Uttar Pradesh qualified for the final by virtue of their first-innings lead. Toss: Tamil Nadu. **Tamil Nadu 445** (A. Mukund 100, M. Vijay 69, S. Badrinath 65, K. D. Karthik 72, C. Ganapathy 67*); **Uttar Pradesh 447-8** (S. S. Shukla 178*, Parvinder Singh 138; L. Balaji 5-114).

Uttar Pradesh wicketkeeper Amir Khan made six catches in Tamil Nadu's innings, including Abhinav Mukund, who scored his fourth hundred of the tournament (and sixth in all) two days before his 19th birthday. In reply, Shivakant Shukla and Parvinder Singh added 272 for the fourth wicket; Shukla batted for 13 hours 41 minutes, the fourth-longest recorded innings in first-class cricket, and Parvinder completed a maiden century, to enable Uttar Pradesh to claim first-innings lead and reach their third final in four years.

Final

At Rajiv Gandhi Stadium, Uppal, Hyderabad, January 12, 13, 14, 15, 16, 2009. **Mumbai won by 243 runs.** Toss: Uttar Pradesh. **Mumbai 402** (R. G. Sharma 141, A. M. Nayar 99; Bhuvneshwar Singh 5-78) **and 367** (V. R. Samant 113, Wasim Jaffer 85, R. G. Sharma 108; P. P. Chawla 4-94); **Uttar Pradesh 245** (S. S. Shukla 99; Zaheer Khan 7-54) **and 281** (M. Kaif 72, Bhuvneshwar Singh 80; D. S. Kulkarni 5-76).

Mumbai were 55-4 after being put in on the first day, with Sachin Tendulkar dismissed for his first-ever duck in Ranji cricket. Rohit Sharma and Abhishek Nayar rescued them with 207 for the fifth wicket, then Zaheer Khan claimed his best figures on Indian soil – 27.2–14–54–7 – which took him past 500 first-class wickets. Thanks to international duties, it was only his third Ranji game for Mumbai since he joined them in 2006-07. Shivakant Shukla followed his semi-final marathon by batting another six hours 35 minutes before Zaheer finally dismissed him. In Mumbai's second innings, Vinayak Samant scored his maiden hundred and Sharma his second of the match. Uttar Pradesh needed 525 on the last day, but were never in it after slumping to 58-4. Dhawal Kulkarni's 5-76 made him this tournament's joint-leading wicket-taker in his first first-class season. Wasim Jaffer finished the tournament with 1,260 runs, the third-highest total in Ranji history, as well as 20 catches, three short of his own Ranji record of 2003-04.

RANJI TROPHY WINNERS

1934-35	Bombay	1944-45	Bombay	1954-55	Madras
1935-36	Bombay	1945-46	Holkar	1955-56	Bombay
1936-37	Nawanagar	1946-47	Baroda	1956-57	Bombay
1937-38	Hyderabad	1947-48	Holkar	1957-58	Baroda
1938-39	Bengal	1948-49	Bombay	1958-59	Bombay
1939-40	Maharashtra	1949-50	Baroda	1959-60	Bombay
1940-41	Maharashtra	1950-51	Holkar	1960-61	Bombay
1941-42	Bombay	1951-52	Bombay	1961-62	Bombay
1942-43	Baroda	1952-53	Holkar	1962-63	Bombay
1943-44	Western India	1953-54	Bombay	1963-64	Bombay

1964-65	Bombay	1979-80	Delhi	1994-95	Bombay
1965-66	Bombay	1980-81	Bombay	1995-96	Karnataka
1966-67	Bombay	1981-82	Delhi	1996-97	Mumbai
1967-68	Bombay	1982-83	Karnataka	1997-98	Karnataka
1968-69	Bombay	1983-84	Bombay	1998-99	Karnataka
1969-70	Bombay	1984-85	Bombay	1999-2000	Mumbai
1970-71	Bombay	1985-86	Delhi	2000-01	Baroda
1971-72	Bombay	1986-87	Hyderabad	2001-02	Railways
1972-73	Bombay	1987-88	Tamil Nadu	2002-03	Mumbai
1973-74	Karnataka	1988-89	Delhi	2003-04	Mumbai
1974-75	Bombay	1989-90	Bengal	2004-05	Railways
1975-76	Bombay	1990-91	Haryana	2005-06	Uttar Pradesh
1976-77	Bombay	1991-92	Delhi	2006-07	Mumbai
1977-78	Karnataka	1992-93	Punjab	2007-08	Delhi
1978-79	Delhi	1993-94	Bombay	2008-09	Mumbai

Bombay/Mumbai have won the Ranji Trophy 38 times, Delhi 7, Karnataka 6, Baroda 5, Holkar 4, Bengal, Hyderabad, Madras/Tamil Nadu, Maharashtra and Railways 2, Haryana, Nawanagar, Punjab, Uttar Pradesh and Western India 1.

Plate League Group A

At Chaudhary Bansi Lal Stadium, Rohtak, November 3, 4, 5, 2008. **Himachal Pradesh won by 103 runs.** Toss: Himachal Pradesh. **Himachal Pradesh 113** (S. Badhwar 5-30) **and 238** (P. Dogra 64); **Haryana 98** (V. Malik 6-43) **and 150** (R. Dewan 66; V. Malik 7-29). *Himachal Pradesh 5 pts.*
  Vikramjeet Malik took 7-29 and 13-72 in the match, both records for Himachal Pradesh as well as career-bests for him, to complete a three-day win.

At Mecon Sail Stadium, Ranchi, November 3, 4, 5, 6, 2008. **Drawn.** Toss: Jharkhand. **Jammu and Kashmir 225** (M. V. Joglekar 77, Aditya Pratap Singh 56) **and 366** (M. V. Joglekar 58, Shafiq Khan 143; S. S. Rao 4-99); **Jharkhand 301** (I. R. Jaggi 58, S. S. Tiwary 89) **and 167-3** (S. Ghosh 83, I. R. Jaggi 71*). *Jharkhand 3 pts, Jammu and Kashmir 1 pt.*

At Fort Maidan, Palakkad, November 3, 4, 5, 6, 2008. **Drawn.** Toss: Goa. **Goa 460** (S. K. Kamat 52, S. A. Asnodkar 191, A. Ratra 136; S. K. Cheruvathur 6-96) **and 69-3; Kerala 486** (S. R. Nair 155, P. Rohan Prem 138; S. B. Jakati 4-139). *Kerala 3 pts.*
  Swapnil Asnodkar and Ajay Ratra added 253 for Goa's fourth wicket; Sreekumar Nair and Rohan Prem retaliated with 241 for Kerala's fourth. Goa's one point was deducted for fielding too many players from outside their territory.

At Dr Rajendra Prasad Stadium, Margao, November 10, 11, 12, 13, 2008. **Goa won by 110 runs.** Toss: Jammu and Kashmir. **Goa 337** (S. A. Asnodkar 93, R. R. D'Souza 65, R. Ninan 58) **and 180; Jammu and Kashmir 267** (M. V. Joglekar 120, S. Beigh 61; S. S. Bandekar 4-69) **and 140** (S. B. Jakati 5-39). *Goa 5 pts.*

At Chaudhary Bansi Lal Stadium, Rohtak, November 10, 11, 12, 13, 2008. **Haryana won by an innings and 61 runs.** Toss: Jharkhand. **Haryana 500-9 dec** (N. Saini 125, Sunny Singh 127, Sumeet Sharma 82, A. Lavasa 51; S. S. Rao 4-108); **Jharkhand 113** (S. Rana 5-32) **and 326** (S. Ghosh 89, I. R. Jaggi 101; Dhruv Singh 5-56). *Haryana 6 pts.*
  Nitin Saini and Sunny Singh set up Haryana's match-winning total with 201 for the third wicket. Nineteen-year-old Ishank Jaggi scored a maiden hundred on the final day of his second first-class match.

At HPCA Stadium, Dharmasala, November 10, 11, 12, 2008. **Himachal Pradesh won by an innings and 56 runs.** Toss: Kerala. **Himachal Pradesh 370** (Sangram Singh 72, Mukesh Sharma 88; T. Yohannan 6-89); **Kerala 135** (A. K. Thakur 5-26) **and 179** (V. Malik 4-17). *Himachal Pradesh 6 pts.*
  Himachal Pradesh wicketkeeper Manish Gupta made nine catches in the match, four of them as Kerala slipped to 59-8 in their first innings.

At Dr Rajendra Prasad Stadium, Margao, November 16, 17, 18, 19, 2008. **Goa won by 161 runs.** Toss: Goa. **Goa 190** (S. B. Jakati 68; S. S. Rao 5-51) **and 256** (A. N. Katkar 76; S. R. Roy 4-75); **Jharkhand 147 and 138** (S. S. Tiwary 72; S. S. Bandekar 5-53, R. R. D'Souza 4-40). *Goa 5 pts.*
Goa eventually won despite being reduced to 26-5 on the first day after choosing to bat.

At HPCA Stadium, Dharmasala, November 16, 17, 18, 2008. **Himachal Pradesh won by 480 runs.** Toss: Himachal Pradesh. **Himachal Pradesh 295** (B. J. Thakkar 122, A. Mannu 50; S. Beigh 6-94) **and 449-1 dec** (B. J. Thakkar 104, Sangram Singh 215*, V. A. Indulkar 109*); **Jammu and Kashmir 120** (Sarandeep Singh 4-37) **and 144** (Sarandeep Singh 4-49). *Himachal Pradesh 5 pts.*
Sangram Singh scored his third double-hundred, equalling his career-best. He put on 254 for Himachal Pradesh's first wicket with Bhavin Thakkar, who scored his second century of the match, and 195 for the second with Vinit Indulkar, whose 88-ball 109 ensured that all three second-innings batsmen reached three figures. This was Himachal's third successive victory, and their biggest-ever in terms of runs.*

At Fort Maidan, Palakkad, November 16, 17, 18, 19, 2008. **Drawn.** Toss: Kerala. **Kerala 334** (S. K. Sarma 103, V. G. Nair 65; J. Billa 6-58) **and 236-2** (S. K. Sarma 111*); **Haryana 581-4 dec** (R. Dewan 254*, Sunny Singh 124, Sumeet Sharma 114). *Kerala 1 pt, Haryana 3 pts.*
In his third first-class match, Rahul Dewan converted a maiden century into 254, the second-highest individual score for Haryana, batting for nine hours 17 minutes – throughout the 133 overs of the innings. He added 256 for the second wicket with Sunny Singh and 234 for the third with Sumeet Sharma. For Kerala, Sambasiva Sarma scored the first two hundreds of his career in his fourth match.*

At Chaudhary Bansi Lal Stadium, Rohtak, November 29, 30, December 1, 2, 2008. **Haryana won by 198 runs.** Toss: Haryana. **Haryana 287** (R. Dewan 52, Sunny Singh 50; S. S. Bandekar 5-72) **and 263-7 dec** (Dhruv Singh 74*, A. Mishra 58*); **Goa 190** (A. Ratra 51; J. Billa 5-72) **and 162** (R. R. D'Souza 54*; S. Rana 5-60). *Haryana 5 pts.*
Goa lost their first three wickets to Jitender Billa without a run on the board; in their second innings, they lost their top eight to Billa and Sachin Rana for 41 before the tail rallied, adding 121 for the last two wickets. In Haryana's second innings, Dhruv Singh and Amit Mishra added 134 for the eighth wicket.*

At Mecon Sail Stadium, Ranchi, November 29, 30, December 1, 2, 2008. **Drawn.** Toss: Jharkhand. **Himachal Pradesh 551-8 dec** (Sangram Singh 210, B. J. Thakkar 166, Mukesh Sharma 56*) **and 181-2** (M. Gupta 75, Sangram Singh 91); **Jharkhand 431** (M. S. Vardhan 66, S. S. Tiwary 169; Mohinderraj Sharma 4-68). *Jharkhand 1 pt, Himachal Pradesh 3 pts.*
Sangram Singh made his fourth double-hundred, and his second in successive innings, adding 353, an all-wicket Himachal Pradesh record, for their second wicket with Bhavin Thakkar – to follow their 254 opening against Jammu and Kashmir a fortnight earlier. Sangram has scored all but one of Himachal's five double-hundreds: Rajeev Nayyar retains their all-time record with 271 against Jammu and Kashmir in 1999-2000.

At Fort Maidan, Palakkad, November 29, 30, December 1, 2008. **Kerala won by eight wickets.** Toss: Jammu and Kashmir. **Jammu and Kashmir 184** (Shafiq Khan 50; T. Yohannan 5-43) **and 199** (I. Dev Singh 61); **Kerala 299** (P. Rohan Prem 124*; Ahmed Nizam 4-47) **and 87-2.** *Kerala 5 pts.*
Kerala were 176-9 before Rohan Prem and Tinu Yohannan added 123 for their last wicket.

At Chaudhary Bansi Lal Stadium, Rohtak, December 12, 13, 14, 15, 2008. **Jammu and Kashmir won by 44 runs.** Toss: Jammu and Kashmir. **Jammu and Kashmir 314** (Javed Ahmed 55, I. Dev Singh 71; S. Badhwar 5-69) **and 173** (I. Dev Singh 78; J. Billa 4-67, S. Badhwar 4-36); **Haryana 285** (Manav Sharma 98; S. Beigh 6-89) **and 158.** *Jammu and Kashmir 5 pts.*
Jammu and Kashmir's first win of the season kept Haryana out of the Plate semi-finals.

At HPCA Stadium, Dharmasala, December 12, 13, 14, 2008. **Goa won by six wickets.** Toss: Goa. **Himachal Pradesh 218** (P. Dogra 53, A. Mannu 56*; R. R. D'Souza 4-52) **and 108; Goa 134** (R. D. Asnodkar 53*; A. K. Thakur 6-30) **and 196-4** (S. A. Asnodkar 84). *Goa 5 pts.*

At Keenan Stadium, Jamshedpur, December 12, 13, 14, 15, 2008. **Kerala won by eight wickets.** Toss: Jharkhand. **Jharkhand 301** (S. S. Tiwary 125; S. Sreesanth 4-64) **and 212** (S. K. Cheruvathur 4-40); **Kerala 376** (R. M. Fernandez 124, P. Rohan Prem 109; S. R. Roy 5-128) **and 138-2** (R. M. Fernandez 59*). *Kerala 5 pts.*

Plate League Group B

At Emerald High School Ground, Indore, November 3, 4, 5, 2008. **Madhya Pradesh won by ten wickets.** Toss: Vidarbha. **Vidarbha 217** (F. Y. Fazal 77; S. M. Dholpure 7-37) **and 162** (S. P. Pandey 4-66, S. M. Dholpure 5-50); **Madhya Pradesh 353** (H. H. Kanitkar 75, D. S. Bundela 59; U. Yadav 4-72) **and 29-0.** *Madhya Pradesh 6 pts.*
   This was the first first-class match at the Emerald High School; Vidarbha elected to bat but were sunk as Sunil Dholpure took a career-best 7-37 on the opening day, and 12-87 in all.

At Model Sports Complex, Delhi, November 3, 4, 5, 6, 2008. **Tripura won by 54 runs.** Toss: Tripura. **Tripura 223** (R. H. Saha 58; Rakesh Kumar 5-79, S. S. Karmakar 5-44) **and 230** (V. Jain 58*); **Services 138** (Tahir Khan 52) **and 261** (A. K. Mohanty 52, Jasvir Singh 67; J. S. Debnath 4-55). *Tripura 5 pts.*
   This was Tripura's fourth first-class victory in four seasons, and their first away from Agartala, after none at all in their first two decades.

At Captain Roop Singh Stadium, Gwalior, November 10, 11, 12, 13, 2008. **Drawn.** Toss: Madhya Pradesh. **Bengal 210** (R. R. Kundu 66) **and 227** (A. S. Chowdhury 60, W. P. Saha 83; S. K. Pitre 5-50); **Madhya Pradesh 278** (H. H. Kanitkar 76, B. R. Tomar 62, J. S. Saxena 50; A. B. Dinda 5-85) **and 63-6.** *Madhya Pradesh 3 pts, Bengal 1 pt.*

At Model Sports Complex, Delhi, November 10, 11, 12, 13, 2008. **Vidarbha won by 135 runs.** Toss: Services. **Vidarbha 151** (Rakesh Kumar 5-45) **and 346-5 dec** (F. Y. Fazal 200*, R. S. Paradkar 58; Pankaj Kumar 4-94); **Services 77** (S. R. Singh 5-27) **and 285** (S. S. Tomar 63, D. S. Israni 53*). *Vidarbha 5 pts.*
   Faiz Fazal batted throughout Vidarbha's second innings for his maiden double-hundred in eight hours 44 minutes and 122.5 overs, after the first two innings added together lasted only 90.2 overs. Vidarbha off-spinner Pritam Gandhi took a hat-trick on the final day.

At Maharaja Bir Bikram College Stadium, Agartala, November 10, 11, 12, 2008. **Assam won by five wickets.** Toss: Assam. **Tripura 215** (R. K. Dutta 54; A. Konwar 5-59) **and 192** (N. S. Shetty 55; A. Katti 4-63); **Assam 195** (S. P. Purkayastha 77) **and 213-5** (R. R. Parida 79; J. S. Debnath 4-69). *Assam 5 pts.*

At Eden Gardens, Kolkata, November 16, 17, 18, 2008. **Bengal won by an innings and 226 runs.** Toss: Bengal. **Services 107** (S. S. Sarkar 5-21) **and 109** (A. B. Dinda 4-28); **Bengal 442-6 dec** (A. P. Majumdar 80, R. B. Banerjee 176, L. R. Shukla 101). *Bengal 6 pts.*
   Laxmi Shukla had figures of 9–4–8–3 in Services' first innings (all middle-order wickets). Rohan Banerjee scored 176 on first-class debut, easily outscoring either Services innings single-handed.

At Maharaja Bir Bikram College Stadium, Agartala, November 16, 17, 18, 19, 2008. **Vidarbha won by 73 runs.** Toss: Tripura. **Vidarbha 224** (R. S. Paradkar 75; T. S. Saha 6-51) **and 203** (R. S. Paradkar 50; J. S. Debnath 4-54, T. S. Saha 4-65); **Tripura 150** (M. S. Acharya 4-23) **and 204** (B. S. Dey 75; P. V. Gandhe 4-58). *Vidarbha 5 pts.*

At Emerald High School Ground, Indore, November 20, 21, 22, 2008. **Madhya Pradesh won by an innings and 59 runs.** Toss: Madhya Pradesh. **Assam 96** (S. K. Pitre 5-35) **and 177** (S. P. Pandey 4-50); **Madhya Pradesh 332** (D. S. Bundela 64, N. V. Ojha 116; K. S. Das 6-61). *Madhya Pradesh 6 pts.*
   Madhya Pradesh wicketkeeper Naman Ojha made nine dismissals in the match to go with his second first-class century.

At Eden Gardens, Kolkata, November 29, 30, December 1, 2008. **Bengal won by an innings and 11 runs.** Toss: Tripura. **Tripura 88** (R. R. Bose 5-19) **and 208** (N. S. Shetty 73, R. K. Dutta 58); **Bengal 307** (A. N. Ghosh 50, M. K. Tiwary 109). *Bengal 6 pts.*
   Ranadeb Bose wrecked Tripura's first innings with figures of 9–4–19–5, and Bengal won in seven sessions.

At Model Sports Complex, Delhi, November 29, 30, December 1, 2, 2008. **Drawn.** Toss: Services. **Madhya Pradesh 223** (S. M. Dholpure 59) **and 240-2 dec** (J. S. Saxena 100*); **Services 140** (Y. A. Golwalkar 4-30) **and 248-8** (Jasvir Singh 103*). *Services 1 pt, Madhya Pradesh 3 pts.*

At VCA Ground, Nagpur, November 29, 30, December 1, 2, 2008. **Assam won by 71 runs.** Toss: Vidarbha. **Assam 299** (J. J. Martin 71, S. P. Purkayastha 51) **and 193** (R. R. Parida 89; U. Yadav 4-11); **Vidarbha 324-9 dec** (S. U. Shrivastava 68, S. B. Wagh 110*; K. S. Das 5-83) **and 97.** *Assam 5 pts.*

Debutant Pritam Debnath was lbw to the first ball of the match; he made seven second time round.

At North-East Frontier Railway Stadium, Guwahati, December 5, 6, 7, 2008. **Bengal won by nine wickets.** Toss: Assam. **Assam 86** (R. R. Bose 5-10) **and 139** (A. B. Dinda 5-28); **Bengal 207** (M. K. Tiwary 101; A. Katti 7-93) **and 19-1.** *Bengal 5 pts.*

Slow left-armer Anand Katti took a career-best 7-93, but it was not enough to save Assam from defeat – Bengal's third successive three-day victory – after seamer Ranadeb Bose reduced them to 15-5 on the first morning, earning figures of 9–5–10–5. In their second innings another left-arm spinner, Iresh Saxena, tied them down with 27–17–27–2.

At Model Sports Complex, Delhi, December 12, 13, 14, 15, 2008. **Assam won by six wickets.** Toss: Assam. **Services 244** (S. Chatarjee 118; D. S. Goswami 4-86) **and 304-9 dec** (S. Chatarjee 71, Pankaj Kumar 54*); **Assam 178** (D. S. Goswami 79; Rakesh Kumar 6-36) **and 371-4** (Tarjinder Singh 80, R. R. Parida 136, J. J. Martin 80*). *Assam 5 pts.*

Services looked to have a chance of their first first-class win for two years when they set Assam a target of 371 on the final day. But Assam, led by captain Rashmi Parida, who scored 136 in 160 balls, achieved the highest successful run-chase in Ranji history, beating 360-4 by Rajasthan against Vidarbha in 1989-90.

At Maharaja Bir Bikram College Stadium, Agartala, December 12, 13, 14, 15, 2008. **Drawn.** Toss: Tripura. **Madhya Pradesh 453-7 dec** (J. S. Saxena 129, D. S. Bundela 94, N. V. Ojha 51, B. R. Tomar 65, J. S. Saxena 74) **and 136-5 dec** (S. M. Dholpure 63); **Tripura 305** (N. S. Shetty 118; S. P. Pandey 4-60) **and 223-7** (S. D. Chowdhury 118; Y. A. Golwalkar 4-85). *Tripura 1 pt, Madhya Pradesh 3 pts.*

At VCA Ground, Nagpur, December 12, 13, 14, 15, 2008. **Drawn.** Toss: Bengal. **Vidarbha 403** (M. S. Acharya 51, S. U. Shrivastava 63, V. P. Gonnade 78) **and 134-7** (A. B. Dinda 5-46); **Bengal 426** (W. P. Saha 159, D. P. Chakrabarty 56; U. Yadav 6-105). *Vidarbha 1 pt, Bengal 3 pts.*

Plate League Semi-finals

At Karnail Singh Stadium, Delhi, December 18, 19, 20, 21, 2008. **Drawn.** Bengal advanced by virtue of their first-innings lead. Toss: Goa. **Bengal 337** (W. P. Saha 54, S. C. Ganguly 69, D. P. Chakrabarty 82, S. S. Sarkar 60; S. S. Bandekar 6-75) **and 193-5** (M. K. Tiwary 80); **Goa 230** (R. Ninan 88*; R. R. Bose 6-62).

Former Test captain Sourav Ganguly helped Bengal into the Elite quarter-finals in his only Ranji game of the season, which he said would be his last first-class match. He had scored 14,933 runs at 43.92 since his debut in March 1990. Ranadeb Bose effectively settled the first-innings lead by reducing Goa to 34-5.

At VCA Ground, Nagpur, December 18, 19, 20, 21, 2008. **Himachal Pradesh won by an innings and 175 runs.** Toss: Madhya Pradesh. **Madhya Pradesh 228** (J. S. Saxena 107; A. K. Thakur 4-41, V. Malik 4-73) **and 176** (H. H. Kanitkar 66; Mohinderraj Sharma 5-45, Sarandeep Singh 4-52); **Himachal Pradesh 579** (B. J. Thakkar 111, V. A. Indulkar 80, Mukesh Sharma 161, A. Mannu 93).

Himachal Pradesh won on the back of 579, their highest first-class total, thanks to a fifth-wicket stand of 218 between Mukesh Sharma, whose 161 was a career-best, and Ajay Mannu.

Bengal and Himachal Pradesh advanced to the quarter-finals of the Ranji Elite League.

DULEEP TROPHY, 2008-09

Four-day knockout for five zonal teams

Quarter-final

At M. Chinnaswamy Stadium, Bangalore, January 22, 23, 24, 25, 2009. **Drawn.** South Zone advanced by virtue of their first-innings lead. Toss: South Zone. **South Zone 329** (K. D. Karthik 153, M. Suresh 58*; U. Yadav 5-76) **and 377** (R. Dravid 118, A. S. Yadav 68, K. D. Karthik 103; Pankaj Singh 5-90); **Central Zone 326** (M. Kaif 73, N. V. Ojha 85) **and 255-9** (M. Kaif 87; M. Suresh 6-84).

Dinesh Karthik scored twin hundreds, which gave him five in the season, after his previous six seasons had brought him a total of four centuries. He hit 153 in 113 balls, with 24 fours and four sixes, followed by 103 in 121 balls, with 17 fours. In the first innings, Karthik and Maripuri Suresh more than doubled South Zone's score, joining forces at 144-7 to add 146, and they turned out to have done just enough for the decisive first-innings lead. Central Zone wicketkeeper Naman Ojha made eight dismissals in the match, including five catches and a stumping in South Zone's second innings. Suresh followed his highest score with his best bowling figures.

Semi-finals

At Madhavrao Scindia Ground, Rajkot, January 29, 30, 31, February 1, 2009. **South Zone won by 411 runs.** Toss: South Zone. **South Zone 548** (S. Badrinath 200, R. Dravid 138, A. S. Yadav 70) **and 319-3 dec** (R. V. Uthappa 160, R. Ashwin 66*); **North Zone 300** (R. Dewan 81, S. Sohal 94) **and 156** (S. Dhawan 61).

South Zone captain Subramaniam Badrinath scored his third double-hundred and added 312 for their third wicket with Rahul Dravid, while in their second innings Robin Uthappa hit 160 in 159 balls with 19 fours and three sixes. Defending champions North Zone had two men injured and unable to bat in either innings.

At Brabourne Stadium, Mumbai, January 29, 30, 31, 2009. **West Zone won by eight wickets.** Toss: West Zone. **East Zone 171** (R. R. Parida 63; R. V. Pawar 6-34) **and 200** (S. S. Das 56); **West Zone 282** (R. V. Pawar 56; R. R. Bose 4-70) **and 90-2** (P. A. Patel 54*).

Slow left-armer Rajesh Pawar's first-innings analysis was 9.3–3–34–6, and he later scored a fifty to build West Zone's lead in a low-scoring game they won with a day to spare.

Final

At M. A. Chidambaram Stadium, Chennai, February 5, 6, 7, 8, 9, 2009. **West Zone won by 274 runs.** Toss: West Zone. **West Zone 459** (Wasim Jaffer 69, A. M. Rahane 165, B. D. Thaker 73) **and 417-8 dec** (P. A. Patel 131, A. M. Rahane 98, R. V. Pawar 50*); **South Zone 199** (S. Badrinath 100*) **and 403** (M. Vijay 63, R. V. Uthappa 94, S. Badrinath 59, K. D. Karthik 75; R. R. Powar 7-140).

Ajinkya Rahane scored his fifth hundred of the season, and almost made it six in the second innings, when Parthiv Patel retired with cramps but resumed to complete his own century. For South Zone, only their captain Subramaniam Badrinath thrived against the spinners, Rajesh Pawar and Ramesh Powar, in the first innings. But they batted bravely to reach 403 in pursuit of 678 in the final innings, when Powar's off-spin claimed seven wickets to give West Zone the title and him 10-187 in the match.

Note: Matches in the following sections were not first-class.

DEODHAR TROPHY, 2008-09

50-over league plus final

Group A

	Played	Won	Lost	Bonus points	Points	Net run-rate
East Zone.....................	2	2	0	1	9	0.84
North Zone	2	1	1	0	3	−0.53
Central Zone	2	0	2	2	0	−0.31

Group B

	Played	Won	Lost	Bonus points	Points	Net run-rate
West Zone	2	2	0	2	10	1.25
South Zone	2	1	1	1	4	–0.31
ZCU President's XI	2	0	2	0	–2	–1.05

Win = 4 pts; loss = –1 pt; no result = 2 pts. One bonus point awarded for achieving victory with a run-rate 1.25 times that of the opposition, and one for losing without conceding a bonus point.

Final

At Barabati Stadium, Cuttack, March 18, 2009. **West Zone won by 218 runs.** Toss: West Zone. **West Zone 362-5** (50 overs) (Wasim Jaffer 116, C. A. Pujara 94, R. A. Jadeja 61*, A. M. Nayar 54*); **East Zone 144** (39.4 overs).

Wasim Jaffer lifted his third trophy of the season after he and Cheteshwar Pujara added 158 for West Zone's fourth wicket, while Ravi Jadeja and Abhishek Nayar smashed 99 off the last 46 balls of the innings. East Zone sank to 49-6 and there was no way back.

N. K. P. SALVE CHALLENGER TROPHY, 2008-09

50-over mini-league plus final

Final

At Barabati Stadium, Cuttack, October 26, 2008 (day/night). **India Blue won by eight wickets.** Toss: India Red. **India Red 151** (43 overs) (S. Badrinath 56); **India Blue 152-2** (25.4 overs) (A. M. Rahane 53).

VIJAY HAZARE TROPHY, 2008-09

50-over league plus knockout

Semi-finals

At Maharaja Bir Bikram College Stadium, Agartala, March 6, 2009. **Bengal won by 81 runs.** Toss: Bengal. **Bengal 227** (49.5 overs); **Baroda 146** (40.2 overs).

At Polytechnic Institute Ground, Agartala, March 6, 2009. **Tamil Nadu won by 35 runs.** Toss: Tamil Nadu. **Tamil Nadu 197** (49.5 overs) (S. Suresh Kumar 94); **Uttar Pradesh 162** (44.5 overs) (R. U. Shukla 56*).

Final

At Maharaja Bir Bikram College Stadium, Agartala, March 9, 2009. **Tamil Nadu won by 66 runs.** Toss: Tamil Nadu. **Tamil Nadu 284-6** (50 overs) (A. Mukund 118); **Bengal 218** (45.2 overs) (M. K. Tiwary 76).

The Indian Premier League, which was relocated to South Africa for security reasons, can be found in South African Cricket, page 1299.

INDIAN CRICKET LEAGUE, 2008-09

The unofficial Indian Cricket League, founded by a disgruntled television company which had failed to win the rights to cover the Indian national team, entered its second season, but the prospects of a third seemed to be fading. The wealth and glamour of the Indian Premier League, the official response from the Board of Control for Cricket in India, left the ICL, like much of the international circuit, trailing in its wake. Negotiations aimed at securing recognition from the International Cricket Council repeatedly failed. And, after the BCCI had wielded the stick by attempting to ban all ICL-contracted players, whether Indian or overseas, from playing in officially sanctioned cricket anywhere, there came the carrot: in early 2009, various national boards which had followed the official line offered amnesties to players renouncing the ICL. The grandest gesture came from the BCCI itself, which welcomed back 79 of the 84 Indian ICL players into domestic cricket, though they would have to wait a further 12 months before being considered for international duty.

Few new overseas names had signed up for 2008-09 – Graeme Hick, who had just retired from county cricket, joined Chandigarh – though the ICL did sign up an entire squad of Bangladeshis, led by former Test captain Habibul Bashar, who formed the second foreign team in the league alongside Inzamam-ul-Haq's Pakistanis.

Three tournaments were staged in 2008-09, all in the Twenty20 format, on grounds no longer used by BCCI-affiliated associations. The warm-up, in September, was for Indian players only. Chandigarh Lions won the final against Chennai Superstars – the previous domestic champions, though then they had played 50 overs a side.

The main event was the Indian Championship, contested by the same seven Indian sides (now mixing native and overseas players), the Lahore Badshahs and the Dhaka Warriors. The tournament, which ran from October to November, followed a remarkably similar course to the one seven months earlier, producing the same semi-finalists and finalists. This time, however, it was Lahore Badshahs who beat title-holders Hyderabad Heroes in the best-of-three finals; they clinched the trophy when Imran Nazir hit 111 from 44 balls, including 11 sixes and seven fours, in the third game. His team-mate, Naved-ul-Hasan, was the tournament's leading wicket-taker, with 22, and the Man of the Series.

Halfway through the competition the Chandigarh captain, New Zealander Chris Cairns, and his team-mate Dinesh Mongia, one of the best-known Indians in the ICL, were suspended on "disciplinary grounds". Apparently Cairns had failed to disclose he was carrying an ankle injury, and Mongia had known this but not informed officials. Both denied these reports.

Rumours about the Badshahs – there were allegations that they had thrown the previous year's final, and eyebrows raised when Inzamam bowled for the first time in six years during a defeat by Delhi Giants (though he did take a wicket) – were also denied.

The Indian Championship was followed by the World Series, expanded to four teams with the addition of a Bangladesh XI (almost identical to the Dhaka Warriors). Held in late November, it was abandoned with three games to go because of the terrorist attacks on Mumbai. The fall-out of the attacks, which made it difficult for Pakistanis to visit India, led to the cancellation of another tournament planned for March 2009.

The ICL insisted it was still in business for 2009-10. "A few domestic and overseas players and support staff have approached us with an application to be released," it said. "The ICL has been set up for the development of cricket, to unearth and nurture young talent for the game, and if certain players do wish to go back to the BCCI fold we will not stop them, nor would we ever wish to exercise contractual authority to stall their dreams." This sounded, at least for the time being, like the end.

ICL 20-20 DOMESTIC CHAMPIONSHIP, 2008-09

	Played	Won	Lost	Points	Net run-rate
Chandigarh Lions	6	5	1	10	0.79
Chennai Superstars	6	5	1	10	0.52
Royal Bengal Tigers	6	3	3	6	0.70
Delhi Giants	6	3	3	6	−0.61
Mumbai Champs	6	2	4	4	−0.04
Hyderabad Heroes	6	2	4	4	−0.78
Ahmedabad Rockets	6	1	5	2	−0.75

Final: Chandigarh Lions beat Chennai Superstars by six wickets.

ICL 20-20 INDIAN CHAMPIONSHIP, 2008-09

	Played	Won	Lost	Points	Net run-rate
Hyderabad Heroes	8	6	2	12	0.99
Lahore Badshahs	8	5	3	10	0.83
Chennai Superstars	8	5	3	10	0.81
Royal Bengal Tigers	8	5	3	10	−0.27
Dhaka Warriors	8	4	4	8	0.21
Delhi Giants	8	4*	4	8	−0.83
Ahmedabad Rockets	8	3	5	6	0.26
Chandigarh Lions	8	3	5*	6	−0.47
Mumbai Champs	8	1	7	2	−1.34

* Delhi Giants tied with Chandigarh Lions, but beat them in a bowl-out.

Semi-finals: Lahore Badshahs beat Chennai Superstars by six wickets; Hyderabad Heroes beat Royal Bengal Tigers by three wickets.

Final: Lahore Badshahs beat Hyderabad Heroes 2–1 in the best-of-three finals: they won the first final by four wickets, lost the second by eight runs, and won the third by eight wickets.

ICL 20s WORLD SERIES, 2008-09

	Played	Won	Lost	Abandoned	Points	Net run-rate
ICL Pakistan XI	3	1	1	1	3	0.34
ICL India XI	3	1	1	1	3	0.09
ICL Bangladesh XI	3	1	1	1	3	−0.17
ICL World XI	3	1	1	1	3	−0.27

The last round of matches and the final were cancelled because of the terrorist attacks on Mumbai in November 2008.

NEW ZEALAND CRICKET, 2009

Vettori's one-man band

DON CAMERON

The 2009 international season opened with all the spirit and thunder of Tchaikovsky's *1812 Overture*. Sachin Tendulkar conducted victory in the First Test; in the Second, New Zealand returned with a three-century blast from Ross Taylor, Jesse Ryder and Brendon McCullum, before India built a score high enough to secure a draw. Then, in the third, Harbhajan Singh's subtle grip strangled New Zealand before last-day rain ensured a stalemate.

At the end of 2009 there was more subcontinental splendour, when the touring Pakistanis provided a full share of the old-fashioned beauties of Test cricket – three highly competitive matches, with no spite or bite to spoil the midsummer charm. New Zealand won the first, Pakistan the second and just as New Zealand were bustling toward victory in the third, rain cut 90 vital minutes. Pakistan conceded that Allah had not been on New Zealand's side.

NEW ZEALAND IN 2009

	Played	Won	Lost	Drawn / No result
Tests	8	1	4	3
One-day internationals	24	10	11	3
Twenty20 internationals	12	6	6	–

DECEMBER JANUARY	} 2 Tests, 5 ODIs and 2 T20Is (h) v West Indies	(see *Wisden 2009*, page 1187)
FEBRUARY	5 ODIs and 1 Twenty20I (a) v Australia	(page 1037)
MARCH APRIL	} 3 Tests, 5 ODIs and 2 T20Is (h) v India	(page 1163)
MAY		
JUNE	World Twenty20 (in England)	(page 527)
JULY		
AUGUST	} 2 Tests and 2 T20Is (a) v Sri Lanka	(page 1353)
SEPTEMBER	Triangular ODI series (a) in Sri Lanka	(page 1361)
OCTOBER	Champions Trophy (in South Africa)	(page 1015)
NOVEMBER	5 ODIs (in UAE) v Pakistan	(page 1222)
DECEMBER	} 3 Tests (h) v Pakistan	(page 1178)

For a review of New Zealand domestic cricket from the 2008-09 season, see page 1193.

Between these two splendid adverts for the five-day Test match, New Zealand had plenty of humdrum mischief and mystery, several moments close to triumph, and old heroes departing as new hopes emerged.

Their playing record was patchy. In June's World Twenty20 affair they could beat only Scotland and Ireland. In September, they lost their first Champions Trophy one-dayer in South Africa, but surprised everyone by beating Sri Lanka, England and Pakistan – only to lose to Australia in the final.

Sandwiched between those events, a short trip to Sri Lanka brought two Test defeats, two Twenty20 wins and two one-day defeats. This tour projected Daniel Vettori, the captain, into the role of his team's most effective all-rounder. In four Test innings he scored 42, 67, 23 and 140. He was to follow up with 99, 8, 6, 40 and 134 in three home Tests against Pakistan, taking his century count to five and rocketing him into the select group with 300 Test wickets and 3,000 runs.

What made this progress more astonishing was that it came when his team was in disarray. When John Bracewell left as national coach in late 2008, Andy Moles, who had previous success coaching Northern Districts, was the last credible candidate; experienced international coaches such as Steve Rixon and Tom Moody were not interested. So Moles – an amiable man – took over.

Rumours that Moles was not effective began to circulate; then a group of senior players reportedly told New Zealand Cricket they no longer wanted him. They maintained the coach was not having the necessary impact or contact with the players. Whether Moles was invited to resign or told to, his time was up by October – but not before his lawyer had gained him a very large pay-off, rather more than NZC expected.

There was a strong push to hire John Wright, the opening batsman and former coach of Kent and India, but for the moment he prefers to play a minor innings. That left the burden of running the team temporarily with Vettori – captain, top bowler, leading batsman and member of the coaching team.

Vettori's first big parade was the opening Test against Pakistan at Dunedin's spruced-up University Oval in November. Afterwards his smile was wide. Although he had hurt his bowling shoulder, it did not prevent him batting in his own special style – mixing strokes classical with mowing sweeps. He may have been dismissed at 99, but by that stage the New Zealand first innings was past 400. And the man who finished off the 32-run win was Shane Bond, released from his ICL chains, who ripped out eight wickets. Bond was man of the match and looked every inch the champion he had been five years before.

New Zealand rejoiced. Their attack had regained Bond's sharp edge, and Iain O'Brien, while not so muscularly aggressive as Bond, had developed into a very able back-up man. But it was a false dawn. Bond missed the remaining two Tests with a torn abdominal muscle and O'Brien announced after the Second that he would soon join his wife in England. Soon after came the desperately sad news that Bond would play only one-day matches in future.

So New Zealand must rebuild an attack around Chris Martin, big of heart but short of pace, Tim Southee, who needs serious coaching if he is to be sharp, James Franklin, with more promise than performance, plus Jeetan Patel, Vettori's only spinning partner. Some ten years after he started as a burly

Hannah Johnston, Getty Images

A brief return: Shane Bond is welcomed back to Test cricket by Daniel Vettori.

youngster, Daryl Tuffey is now back in the front line. He actually looked sharper at 31, and took four for 32 to go with a swaggering 80 not out in the Third Test against Pakistan.

Tuffey is a mystery. So, too, is Ryder, but at least he is a survivor. After several alcohol-influenced infractions Ryder was told he had received his last warning. However, at the Champions Trophy he was so annoyed at being dismissed that he whacked a dressing-room chair with his bat. The New Zealand manager, Dave Currie (who has no considerable cricket background but comes with a gee-whizz reputation as manager of the national Olympic teams), told him to stop. Twice Ryder gave Currie what Australians call a "verbal spray". However, Ryder remained with the team, at least until a series of injuries kept him out for the rest of 2009.

If, or when, he returns he will join Ross Taylor, Brendon McCullum, Vettori, Martin Guptill and, provided his footwork improves, Tim McIntosh among the senior batsmen. Of those, only Ryder and Taylor have Test averages better than 40. Waiting in the wings are the South African-born Grant Elliott and B. J. Watling, who moved to New Zealand when he was ten.

NEW ZEALAND v INDIA, 2008-09

Anand Vasu

Test matches (3): New Zealand 0, India 1
One-day internationals (5): New Zealand 1, India 3
Twenty20 internationals (2): New Zealand 2, India 0

"The rock stars of cricket are here," screamed New Zealand Cricket's enthusiastic marketing campaign even before the Indian team arrived. The home board did not seem to worry that their adverts might dent the egos of their own players, and instead focused on just how big India's visit would be. It mattered little that India had not won a Test series in New Zealand in 41 years. What mattered was that this tour provided NZC with their biggest earning possibility in more than a decade.

To be fair, this was one of the strongest Indian teams to visit. Previously New Zealand's formula had been simple: serve up seaming pitches and India would have neither the bowling nor, crucially, the batting to provide serious resistance. But this side were different. Not only had they graduated from winning just the odd Test abroad, but Mahendra Singh Dhoni's team were one to reckon with in all conditions. The usual problem in New Zealand had been a lack of fast bowling – but India arrived with Zaheer Khan, who, if not quite the new Wasim Akram, was the one bowler who could make the ball do things in all conditions. Zaheer was partnered by Ishant Sharma, who had opened up Ricky Ponting like a can of sardines: surely New Zealand's batsmen wouldn't be a problem? But cricket beats to its own rhythm, and India promptly lost the Twenty20 internationals. In a format where they were expected to wallop New Zealand, India's brightest were cheaply bested.

However, when the 50-over matches started (although New Zealand's weather rarely allows these games to span their full duration), the gap in skills became more apparent. India easily won the series before New Zealand made a dent at the end.

But the real test was the Tests, and here New Zealand fluffed their lines. They allowed India's Test specialists – including Rahul Dravid and V. V. S. Laxman – to appear in the local first-class competition while the one-day series was in progress, as a return favour after India agreed to play a third Test and second Twenty20. Big mistake. Traditionally, New Zealand had thrived on exposing Indian batsmen's inability to adapt quickly to conditions. This time they rolled out the red carpet, and it didn't help.

India's previous tour to New Zealand, in 2002-03, was a nightmare of poor pitches, with batsmen from both sides struggling. India never reached 200 in the Tests (both of which they lost) and only twice in seven one-day internationals. The home batsmen did not do much better. New Zealand's pitches of that vintage were of no benefit to anyone, except mediocre seam bowlers.

That NZC were accused of bending over backwards to ensure there were no objectionable pitches this time shows how deep ran the scars of 2002-03.

Actually, the home groundsmen would have struggled to serve up wickets that favoured their team in any way: India's batting was too imposing, their lone spinner Harbhajan Singh was the equal of Daniel Vettori on a fair pitch and much superior on a dustbowl, and Zaheer and Sharma far more penetrative than any quick bowlers New Zealand had, as Shane Bond was still excluded because of his association with the unauthorised Indian Cricket League.

Prior to this series Dhoni, despite all his initial fireworks with the bat, had proved to be a defensive captain. But as soon as he realised he had the ammunition to do the job, and the opportunity to go where no Indian captain since the Nawab of Pataudi in 1967-68 had been, Dhoni sealed the deal. Pataudi is considered India's most cerebral captain, and even the all-conquering Sourav Ganguly could not conjure a series win in New Zealand. However, Dhoni delivered a package that few Indian fans thought possible. He may not realise it yet, as he was barely forced to struggle, but New Zealand might be the win that begins to separate Dhoni from India's best.

INDIAN TOURING PARTY

M. S. Dhoni (*captain*), L. Balaji, R. Dravid, G. Gambhir, Harbhajan Singh, K. D. Karthik, D. S. Kulkarni, V. V. S. Laxman, A. Mishra, M. M. Patel, V. Sehwag, I. Sharma, R. G. Sharma, S. R. Tendulkar, M. Vijay, Yuvraj Singh, Zaheer Khan. *Coach:* G. Kirsten.

For the limited-overs internationals which preceded the Tests, P. Kumar, P. P. Ojha, I. K. Pathan, Y. K. Pathan and S. K. Raina replaced Balaji, Dravid, Kulkarni, Laxman, Mishra and Vijay. Tendulkar joined the team after the Twenty20 internationals, for which R. A. Jadeja took his place in the squad.

TEST MATCH AVERAGES
NEW ZEALAND – BATTING AND FIELDING

	T	I	NO	R	HS	100s	50s	Avge	Ct
†J. D. Ryder............	3	5	0	327	201	2	0	65.40	2
L. R. P. L. Taylor.......	3	5	0	322	151	2	0	64.40	6
†D. L. Vettori...........	3	5	1	220	118	1	1	55.00	3
B. B. McCullum........	3	5	0	232	115	1	1	46.40	11
M. J. Guptill...........	3	5	0	136	49	0	0	27.20	0
†J. E. C. Franklin.......	3	5	0	130	52	0	1	26.00	1
I. E. O'Brien.........	3	5	2	61	19*	0	0	20.33	1
†D. R. Flynn..........	2	4	0	79	67	0	1	19.75	0
†T. G. McIntosh.........	3	5	0	60	32	0	0	12.00	3
C. S. Martin............	3	3	3	4	4*	0	0	–	2

Played in one Test: J. M. How 1 (1 ct); K. D. Mills 0, 2; J. S. Patel 1; T. G. Southee 16, 3 (1 ct).

† *Left-handed batsman.*

BOWLING

	Style	O	M	R	W	BB	5W/i	Avge
C. S. Martin........	RFM	134.1	32	458	14	4-98	0	32.71
J. S. Patel........	OB	64	12	180	4	2-60	0	45.00
I. E. O'Brien.......	RFM	125.5	29	452	9	3-103	0	50.22
D. L. Vettori.......	SLA	136.4	32	366	7	2-45	0	52.28

Also bowled: J. E. C. Franklin (LFM) 89–17–290–1; J. M. How (OB) 1–1–0–0; K. D. Mills (RFM) 24.2–4–119–1; J. D. Ryder (RM) 33–14–89–2; T. G. Southee (RFM) 30–3–152–2; L. R. P. L. Taylor (OB) 2–1–4–0.

INDIA – BATTING AND FIELDING

	T	I	NO	R	HS	100s	50s	Avge	Ct/St
†G. Gambhir	3	6	1	445	167	2	1	89.00	1
M. S. Dhoni	2	3	1	155	56*	0	2	77.50	11/1
V. V. S. Laxman	3	5	1	295	124*	1	2	73.75	4
S. R. Tendulkar	3	5	0	344	160	1	2	68.80	2
R. Dravid	3	6	1	314	83	0	4	62.80	4
Zaheer Khan	3	4	2	110	51*	0	1	55.00	1
†Yuvraj Singh	3	5	1	125	54*	0	1	31.25	2
V. Sehwag	3	5	0	140	48	0	0	28.00	5
M. M. Patel	3	3	2	24	15*	0	0	24.00	1
Harbhajan Singh	3	4	0	94	60	0	1	23.50	0
I. Sharma	3	3	0	24	18	0	0	8.00	1

Played in one Test: K. D. Karthik 6 (1 ct).

† *Left-handed batsman.*

BOWLING

	Style	O	M	R	W	BB	5W/i	Avge
Harbhajan Singh	OB	147.4	28	342	16	6-63	1	21.37
Zaheer Khan	LFM	115.3	24	400	13	5-65	1	30.76
I. Sharma	RFM	94.2	21	334	8	4-73	0	41.75
M. M. Patel	RFM	84	15	290	6	3-60	0	48.33

Also bowled: V. Sehwag (OB) 22-0-116-0; S. R. Tendulkar (RM/OB/LB) 9-0-45-2; Yuvraj Singh (SLA) 22.3-2-84-1.

Note: Matches in this section which were not first-class are signified by a dagger.

†NEW ZEALAND v INDIA

First Twenty20 International

At Christchurch, February 25, 2009 (floodlit). New Zealand won by seven wickets. Toss: New Zealand.

India were strong favourites in the shortest version of the game, but their batsmen, possibly too anxious to show off their skills, went too hard at the bowlers and often perished trying to clear the small square boundaries. Sehwag's ten-ball 26 included four sixes, three of them off the first three balls he received, in Southee's first over, but Raina – who hit five sixes of his own – was the only top-order batsman to get going properly. Yusuf Pathan later emulated Sehwag by swinging Nathan McCullum for three successive sixes. The home batsmen clobbered 11 sixes between them to India's 13: the match total of 24 was a Twenty20 international record, beating 20 in India's game against Australia at Durban in September 2007. Anchored by Brendon McCullum, New Zealand weathered a good opening burst from Zaheer Khan, and strolled home in the end.

Man of the Match: B. B. McCullum.

India

	B	*4*	*6*
G. Gambhir *b 11*	6	7	1	0
V. Sehwag *b 11*	26	10	0	4
S. K. Raina *not out*	61	43	2	5
R. G. Sharma *c 2 b 9*	7	7	0	1
Yuvraj Singh *lbw b 8*	1	3	0	0
*†M. S. Dhoni *b 9*	2	6	0	0
Y. K. Pathan *c 5 b 7*	20	8	0	3
I. K. Pathan *c 7 b 1*	12	14	1	0
Harbhajan Singh *b 10*	21	22	2	0
L-b 3, w 3	6			

6 overs: 56-3   (20 overs) 162-8

1/25 2/32 3/54 4/56 5/61 6/82 7/101 8/162

Zaheer Khan and I. Sharma did not bat.

Southee 4–0–42–1; O'Brien 4–0–36–2; Butler 4–0–29–2; Vettori 4–0–18–1; N. L. McCullum 2–0–27–1; Ryder 2–0–7–1.

New Zealand

	B	*4*	*6*
J. D. Ryder *lbw b 11*	1	4	0	0
†B. B. McCullum *not out*	56	49	2	3
M. J. Guptill *lbw b 9*	41	28	4	3
L. R. P. L. Taylor *b 10*	31	20	1	3
J. D. P. Oram *not out*	29	15	3	2
W 5, n-b 3	8			

6 overs: 54-1   (18.5 overs) 166-3

1/2 2/56 3/106

N. T. Broom, N. L. McCullum, *D. L. Vettori, I. G. Butler, T. G. Southee and I. E. O'Brien did not bat.

Zaheer Khan 4–0–20–1; I. Sharma 4–0–35–1; I. K. Pathan 3–0–38–0; Harbhajan Singh 4–0–19–1; Y. K. Pathan 2.5–0–37–0; Yuvraj Singh 1–0–17–0.

Umpires: G. A. V. Baxter and E. A. Watkin.   Third umpire: A. L. Hill.   Referee: R. S. Madugalle.

†NEW ZEALAND v INDIA

Second Twenty20 International

At Westpac Stadium, Wellington, February 27, 2009 (floodlit). New Zealand won by five wickets. Toss: New Zealand.

For the second time in three days India's batting went for broke… and came out bankrupt. They insisted there was no complacency involved, but there was no denying the shot selection was poor. Too many batsmen tried to do too much too early, and the result was wickets for any bowler who was disciplined and stuck to a plan. Yuvraj Singh's 34-ball 50 included four sixes, but he was lucky to survive the first one, as Broom at square leg dropped a skyed pull off Butler while his foot was touching the rope. For the second match running Brendon McCullum guided his side home, although this was a close-run thing: needing nine from the last three balls he belted Irfan Pathan for two fours, to midwicket and long-off, then collected the winning run off the last ball with an uppish waft that just cleared Rohit Sharma at mid-off.

Man of the Match: B. B. McCullum.

India

	B	*4*	*6*
G. Gambhir *c 2 b 9*	10	13	0	1
V. Sehwag *c 8 b 11*	24	11	5	0
S. K. Raina *c 10 b 9*	0	4	0	0
Yuvraj Singh *c 5 b 11*	50	34	3	4
*†M. S. Dhoni *not out*	28	30	2	0
Y. K. Pathan *b 8*	0	2	0	0
R. A. Jadeja *c 3 b 10*	19	16	1	1
I. K. Pathan *not out*	15	10	0	1
L-b 2, w 1	3			

6 overs: 47-2   (20 overs) 149-6

1/29 2/36 3/47 4/92 5/94 6/121

Harbhajan Singh, Zaheer Khan and I. Sharma did not bat.

New Zealand

	B	*4*	*6*
J. D. Ryder *b 10*	26	15	3	2
†B. B. McCullum *not out*	69	55	8	1
M. J. Guptill *lbw b 9*	10	19	1	0
L. R. P. L. Taylor *b 8*	27	25	2	0
J. D. P. Oram *c 5 b 8*	0	1	0	0
N. T. Broom *c 8 b 4*	5	3	1	0
N. L. McCullum *not out*	1	2	0	0
B 1, l-b 6, w 5	12			

6 overs: 60-1   (20 overs) 150-5

1/53 2/69 3/125 4/125 5/134

*D. L. Vettori, I. G. Butler, T. G. Southee and I. E. O'Brien did not bat.

Southee 4–0–36–1; O'Brien 4–0–30–2; Butler 4–0–42–2; Vettori 4–0–21–1; Ryder 4–0–18–0.

I. K. Pathan 4–0–41–2; Zaheer Khan 4–0–30–1; Sharma 2–0–19–0; Harbhajan Singh 4–0–15–1; Jadeja 4–0–21–0; Yuvraj Singh 2–0–17–1.

Umpires: G. A. V. Baxter and A. L. Hill.   Third umpire: E. A. Watkin.   Referee: R. S. Madugalle.

†NEW ZEALAND v INDIA

First One-Day International

At Napier, March 3, 2009 (day/night). India won by 53 runs (D/L method). Toss: India.

On the day the horrific attack on Sri Lanka's cricketers in Lahore shocked the sporting world, India began their 50-over campaign with a comfortable win. Two rain-breaks and a typically powerful batting performance sealed New Zealand's fate. Learning from his side's mistakes in the Twenty20s, Sehwag took a few moments to size up the bowling before cutting loose. He attacked everyone, but picked the deliveries to hit judiciously, and still ended up scoring 77 from just 56 balls, with 11 fours and a six. Dhoni played in two gears, holding the innings together while occasionally unveiling an unorthodox earthy heave to the ropes. Raina again demonstrated his improvement with a flurry of late strokes that lifted India to 273 from 38 overs. Rain in the 21st over of New Zealand's reply meant the target was adjusted to 216 from 28: already struggling at 111 for four, they were never in the hunt once Harbhajan Singh grabbed three wickets in four balls, starting with top-scorer Guptill, whose 64 occupied 70 deliveries.

Man of the Match: M. S. Dhoni.

India

V. Sehwag c Taylor b Vettori	77	Y. K. Pathan not out		20
S. R. Tendulkar c McCullum b Butler	20	B 1, l-b 1, n-b 2		4
*†M. S. Dhoni not out	84			
Yuvraj Singh run out	2	1/69 (2) 2/121 (1)	(4 wkts, 38 overs)	273
S. K. Raina c O'Brien b Elliott	66	3/131 (4) 4/241 (5)	8 overs: 49-0	

G. Gambhir, Harbhajan Singh, Zaheer Khan, P. Kumar and M. M. Patel did not bat.

Mills 7–0–69–0; O'Brien 8–1–52–0; Butler 8–1–42–1; Oram 2–0–19–0; Vettori 8–0–42–1; Ryder 3–0–27–0; Elliott 2–0–20–1.

New Zealand

J. D. Ryder c Sehwag b Kumar	11	*D. L. Vettori not out		26
†B. B. McCullum c Harbhajan Singh b Kumar	0	I. E. O'Brien not out		3
M. J. Guptill c Gambhir b Harbhajan Singh	64			
L. R. P. L. Taylor c Tendulkar b Pathan	31	L-b 10, w 3, n-b 1		14
G. D. Elliott run out	11			
J. D. P. Oram c Dhoni b Yuvraj Singh	0	1/0 (2) 2/23 (1)	(9 wkts, 28 overs)	162
N. T. Broom st Dhoni b Harbhajan Singh	2	3/81 (4) 4/111 (5)		
I. G. Butler c Patel b Zaheer Khan	0	5/111 (6) 6/132 (3) 7/132 (7)		
K. D. Mills c Sehwag b Harbhajan Singh	0	8/132 (9) 9/132 (8)	8 overs: 23-2	

Zaheer Khan 6–1–19–1; Kumar 6–1–28–2; Patel 2–0–14–0; Yuvraj Singh 6–0–42–1; Pathan 4–0–22–1; Harbhajan Singh 4–0–27–3.

Umpires: A. L. Hill and R. E. Koertzen.
Third umpire: G. A. V. Baxter.   Referee: R. S. Madugalle.

†NEW ZEALAND v INDIA

Second One-Day International

At Westpac Stadium, Wellington, March 6, 2009 (day/night). No result. Toss: India. One-day international debut: P. D. McGlashan.

India's hopes of building some momentum after winning the first one-dayer were quickly cut short, as a series of downpours ensured that only 28.4 overs of play were possible, even on a ground that drains well. The rain could not have come at a worse time for the visitors. Sehwag had continued in blistering form before falling to an umpiring blunder – replays suggested the ball clipped his pad-flap, not his bat, on its way to the debutant wicketkeeper Peter McGlashan – while Tendulkar played himself back into form, making 61 from 69 balls before missing a sweep. Play was interrupted after 19 and 24 overs, so the match was already reduced to 34 a side before the heavens finally opened.

India

V. Sehwag c McGlashan b Butler	54		S. K. Raina not out		13
S. R. Tendulkar lbw b Vettori	61		L-b 3, w 4		7
G. Gambhir c Elliott b O'Brien	30				
Yuvraj Singh c Taylor b Mills	0		1/76 (1) 2/139 (2)	(4 wkts, 28.4 overs)	188
*†M. S. Dhoni not out	23		3/142 (4) 4/166 (3)	10 overs: 65-0	

Y. K. Pathan, Harbhajan Singh, Zaheer Khan, P. Kumar and M. M. Patel did not bat.

Mills 7–0–46–1; O'Brien 6–0–44–1; Butler 7–0–38–1; Oram 4–0–29–0; Vettori 3–0–14–1; Ryder 1.4–0–14–0.

New Zealand

J. D. Ryder, B. B. McCullum, M. J. Guptill, L. R. P. L. Taylor, G. D. Elliott, J. D. P. Oram, †P. D. McGlashan, K. D. Mills, I. G. Butler, *D. L. Vettori and I. E. O'Brien.

Umpires: R. E. Koertzen and E. A. Watkin.
Third umpire: G. A. V. Baxter. Referee: R. S. Madugalle.

†NEW ZEALAND v INDIA

Third One-Day International

At Christchurch, March 8, 2009 (day/night). India won by 58 runs. Toss: New Zealand.

While Tendulkar gave a masterclass in innings construction, building his first one-day international hundred in New Zealand in perfect blocks, Yuvraj Singh finished with strokes of such power and brutality that the home side did well eventually to respond in kind. Tendulkar's 163 (his 43rd and, at the time, second-highest one-day hundred) included straight-driving of the utmost quality, but what caught the eye was his innovation – inside-out hits over cover, and paddle-sweeps off the faster bowlers – before he retired at the end of the 45th over with an injured stomach muscle. Yuvraj freed his arms spectacularly in his 60-ball 87, clearing the fence six times and collecting ten fours as well. India's 392 was easily the highest total in any one-day international in New Zealand, surpassing the home side's 350 for nine to beat Australia at Hamilton in 2006-07, but Ryder's maiden one-day international century, which came up in just 72 balls, turned what looked like a mismatch into a contest. He started by putting on 166 in 22 overs with McCullum, and although Ryder's cutting, thrusting, punching, counter-attacking innings still left his side well short, the day's run-aggregate was 726, second only to the 872 of the epic South Africa–Australia match at Johannesburg in March 2006.

Man of the Match: S. R. Tendulkar.

India

V. Sehwag b Mills	3	Y. K. Pathan not out	1
S. R. Tendulkar retired hurt	163		
G. Gambhir c McGlashan b Butler	15	L-b 5, w 8, n-b 4	17
Yuvraj Singh c McGlashan b Elliott	87		
*†M. S. Dhoni c McGlashan b Mills	68	1/15 (1) 2/65 (3) (4 wkts, 50 overs)	392
S. K. Raina not out	38	3/203 (4) 4/382 (5) 10 overs: 58-1	

Harbhajan Singh, Zaheer Khan, P. Kumar and M. M. Patel did not bat.

Tendulkar retired hurt at 338.

Mills 10–0–58–2; Southee 10–0–105–0; Butler 5–0–37–1; Oram 8–1–34–0; Patel 5–0–37–0; Ryder 5–0–56–0; Elliott 7–0–60–1.

New Zealand

J. D. Ryder c Zaheer Khan b Harbhajan Singh	105	K. D. Mills c Zaheer Khan b Pathan	54
*B. B. McCullum run out	71	T. G. Southee c and b Kumar	32
L. R. P. L. Taylor run out	7	J. S. Patel not out	0
M. J. Guptill lbw b Yuvraj Singh	1	L-b 2, w 4, n-b 2	8
G. D. Elliott b Zaheer Khan	18	1/166 (2) 2/179 (3) (45.1 overs)	334
J. D. P. Oram b Harbhajan Singh	7	3/182 (4) 4/188 (1) 5/203 (6)	
†P. D. McGlashan b Zaheer Khan	7	6/217 (5) 7/218 (7) 8/251 (8)	
I. G. Butler b Yuvraj Singh	24	9/334 (9) 10/334 (10) 10 overs: 67-0	

Zaheer Khan 9–0–65–2; Kumar 8.1–0–60–1; Patel 7.2–0–79–0; Yuvraj Singh 10–0–71–2; Harbhajan Singh 10–0–56–2; Pathan 0.4–0–1–1.

Umpires: G. A. V. Baxter and R. E. Koertzen.
Third umpire: E. A. Watkin. Referee: R. S. Madugalle.

†NEW ZEALAND v INDIA

Fourth One-Day International

At Hamilton, March 11, 2009 (day/night). India won by 84 runs (D/L method). Toss: New Zealand. One-day international debut: E. P. Thompson.

This time it was Sehwag's turn to show what India's batsmen could do. Batting first on another rain-interrupted day, New Zealand did well to reach 270 from 47 overs, McCullum leading the way with 77 from 95 balls before Elliott and McGlashan piled on 95 in the last 10.1 overs. But Sehwag, with one eye on the clouds, came out swinging. Advancing down the track and lifting the ball effortlessly over mid-on and mid-off when the field restrictions were in force, Sehwag hit four fours in O'Brien's first over, while Ewen Thompson, in his first one-day international, was thrashed out of the attack. After rain interrupted the chase at ten overs, Sehwag only pushed harder, sprinting from 51 to 92 in only 19 balls. He clattered Vettori for six over long-off to reach his hundred from 60 balls, the fastest by an Indian, two quicker than Mohammad Azharuddin at Baroda in 1988-89, also against New Zealand. Two more showers interrupted play, trimming the overs available to 33 and India's target to 197 – and, since they had already scored 201, the match was declared over without a resumption (the winning margin is derived from New Zealand's Duckworth/Lewis par score of 117 at 23.3 overs). India thus took a 3–0 winning lead in the series.

Man of the Match: V. Sehwag.

New Zealand

J. D. Ryder c Raina b Yuvraj Singh	46	G. D. Elliott not out	35
B. B. McCullum lbw b Zaheer Khan	77		
L. R. P. L. Taylor c R. G. Sharma b Pathan	5	L-b 9, w 13, n-b 3	25
M. J. Guptill c sub (K. D. Karthik) b I. Sharma	25		
J. D. P. Oram c Dhoni b I. Sharma	1	1/102 (1) 2/114 (3) (5 wkts, 47 overs)	270
†P. D. McGlashan not out	56	3/155 (2) 4/156 (5)	
		5/175 (4) 10 overs: 43-0	

K. D. Mills, *D. L. Vettori, E. P. Thompson and I. E. O'Brien did not bat.

Zaheer Khan 10–0–49–1; Kumar 7–0–51–0; I. Sharma 8–0–57–2; Yuvraj Singh 9–0–40–1; Pathan 5–0–14–1; Harbhajan Singh 8–0–50–0.

India

G. Gambhir not out	63
V. Sehwag not out	125
L-b 9, w 4	13
(no wkt, 23.3 overs)	201
9 overs: 75-0	

S. K. Raina, R. G. Sharma, Yuvraj Singh, *†M. S. Dhoni, Y. K. Pathan, Harbhajan Singh, Zaheer Khan, P. Kumar and I. Sharma did not bat.

Mills 5–0–29–0; Thompson 4–0–42–0; O'Brien 3–0–37–0; Vettori 5–0–32–0; Oram 4.3–0–43–0; Elliott 2–0–9–0.

Umpires: G. A. V. Baxter and R. E. Koertzen.
Third umpire: E. A. Watkin.   Referee: R. S. Madugalle.

†NEW ZEALAND v INDIA

Fifth One-Day International

At Auckland, March 14, 2009 (day/night). New Zealand won by eight wickets. Toss: India.

New Zealand managed a consolation win that had little impact on the Indians' morale. The intensity of the first four games was noticeably absent, and it took a fine all-round display from Ryder to breathe life into a 43-over contest. His military-mediums extracted the kind of consistent swing that had been missing in the earlier matches, and winkled out the power-hitting trio of Yuvraj Singh, Dhoni and Yusuf Pathan cheaply as India were skittled for a lowly 149: Rohit Sharma was left high and dry with 43 from 74 balls. With no pressure from the scoreboard Ryder then made quick work of the target, pulling repeatedly as the bowlers dropped short: three of his four sixes came off Ishant Sharma, and he also collected six fours. Then Guptill helped himself to an entertaining half-century, his second of a promising series, as New Zealand won at a canter with nearly 20 overs to spare.

Man of the Match: J. D. Ryder.

India

G. Gambhir c McGlashan b Mills	5	P. Kumar c McGlashan b O'Brien	6
V. Sehwag c McCullum b Oram	40	I. Sharma c Taylor b O'Brien	3
S. K. Raina c Styris b Oram	8		
R. G. Sharma not out	43	L-b 9, w 9	18
Yuvraj Singh c McGlashan b Ryder	11		
*†M. S. Dhoni b Ryder	9	1/30 (1) 2/65 (3) 3/69 (2) (36.3 overs)	149
Y. K. Pathan b Ryder	0	4/88 (5) 5/110 (6) 6/111 (7)	
Harbhajan Singh run out	1	7/116 (8) 8/131 (9) 9/143 (10)	
Zaheer Khan run out	5	10/149 (11) 9 overs: 64-1	

Mills 7–0–27–1; O'Brien 7.3–0–43–2; Oram 9–0–22–2; Ryder 9–0–29–3; Vettori 4–0–19–0.

New Zealand

J. D. Ryder b I. Sharma	63
B. B. McCullum b Kumar	2
M. J. Guptill not out	57
L. R. P. L. Taylor not out	28
W 1	1

1/9 (2) 2/93 (1)   (2 wkts, 23.2 overs) 151
                       9 overs: 48-1

S. B. Styris, G. D. Elliott, J. D. P. Oram, †P. D. McGlashan, K. D. Mills, *D. L. Vettori and I. E. O'Brien did not bat.

Kumar 4–0–22–1; Zaheer Khan 8–1–51–0; I. Sharma 7.2–1–63–1; Harbhajan Singh 4–0–15–0.

Umpires: G. A. V. Baxter and R. E. Koertzen.
Third umpire: E. A. Watkin.   Referee: R. S. Madugalle.

NEW ZEALAND v INDIA

First Test Match

Don Cameron

At Hamilton, March 18, 19, 20, 21, 2009. India won by ten wickets. Toss: India. Test debut: M. J. Guptill.

India were quick off the blocks in the Test series, cruising to a comfortable victory at Seddon Park. Six of their side – Dravid, Harbhajan Singh, Laxman, Sehwag, Tendulkar and Zaheer Khan – had lost here in 2002-03, when an extravagantly lively pitch allowed an aggregate of only 507 runs for 36 wickets, but this time India had a steely backbone, recently forged in a tough home series win over Australia. Most of the batsmen had found their form during the preceding one-day series, which India won easily. And above all they had a clever captain in Dhoni, who was unscarred by the earlier disaster and justifiably confident about India's all-round technical strength.

The bland pitch had a hint of early moisture, but presented no obvious help to the bowlers or danger to the batsmen. However, Dhoni looked beyond that – at a New Zealand batting line-up that started with Martin Guptill in his first Test and Tim McIntosh in his third. Flynn was a novice No. 3, Taylor was out of form at No. 4, while the big-hitting one-day openers Ryder and McCullum were now in the middle of the batting order. Dhoni sensed that there might be enough in the pitch to cause some early mischief, and let his four-man bowling attack loose when he won the toss.

It was the first masterstroke that led to India's four-day win. Ishant Sharma had the speed and lift, Zaheer Khan the subtle movement in the air and off the pitch. It took six overs before they made the ball rear or move late, but Zaheer had Guptill caught in his fourth over, and Flynn (for a duck) in his fifth. Then Sharma struck, removing McIntosh for 12 off 52 balls, bowling Taylor, and having Franklin caught behind for another duck; next Patel had McCullum caught at second slip. The New Zealanders ate a tasteless lunch at 61 for six.

Fortunately for them, the pitch lost its early life under the hot afternoon sun. Ryder put away his usual booming strokes, patiently and skilfully picking up ones and twos. Vettori, never likely to pose for a coaching manual, drove strongly, showed new skill pulling through midwicket, and frustrated the bowlers with the way he blithely accepted the boundaries as unplanned edges evaded the catchers and raced to the fence.

They quietly assembled a half-century partnership before Vettori increased the pace, driving well and reaching his own fifty from 85 deliveries. Ryder and Vettori added 101 between lunch and tea, and afterwards Vettori raced to his century, his third in Tests (and second on his home ground), needing only 54 balls for the second half. The stand was worth 186 – a seventh-wicket record for New Zealand against India, beating the 163 of Bert Sutcliffe and Bruce Taylor at Calcutta in 1964-65 – when at last a Vettori edge found Dhoni's gloves.

Ryder had 77 at the time, and his chances of reaching his first Test century were not helped when Mills fell first ball. Ryder changed patience to power and went for his shots, but he lost O'Brien (charging down the wicket) at 98, and watched anxiously as last man Martin (Test batting average: 2.17) coolly survived the next five balls from Harbhajan. Then Ryder joyfully whacked his 14th four to reach three figures, and cared not a whit when he was caught after skying the next ball.

The last four wickets had lifted the score from 60 to an almost-respectable 279 – the lowest all-out total in Tests to include two centuries. India took 29 runs without trouble before stumps and, after losing 15 minutes to rain on the second morning, set out to profit from the inoffensive pitch. Sehwag wasted an opportunity to feast by dawdling to be run out by Franklin's direct hit from the covers, but Gambhir and Dravid produced a pleasant flow of runs that took India to 108 for one at lunch. They rather lost their way in the afternoon: Gambhir was undone by Martin, and David bowled by one of the few tricks the ball performed all day. Even Tendulkar seemed slightly out of sorts, his strokes out of harmony with the gentle pace of the pitch. At 13 he sent a weird swish toward midwicket, but Flynn could not latch on to a difficult catch.

Between lunch and tea India managed only 89, ending the session still 82 behind, but afterwards Tendulkar, who had been pecking away for runs like a farmyard fowl, changed to the soaring eagle that is Sachin at his sublime best. By stumps he had surged to 70, with a range of sumptuous shots, and on the third morning he was simply magnificent as he threaded stroke after stroke through the gaps, often to the fence. His eventual 160, which contained 26 fours from 260 balls, was the perfect counter-point of classic charm to his brutal 163 in the one-dayer at Christchurch 12 days previously. This was his 42nd Test century, his fourth against New Zealand.

New Zealand's bowling was limp, conceding a deficit of 241, and by the end of the third day the batting was looking none too healthy either, at 75 for three. Only Flynn, with 67 from 183 balls, offered serious fourth-day resistance as Harbhajan Singh's probing spin proved too much for the rest. At 199 for eight the bowlers relaxed a little, allowing McCullum to hit 11 fours in a quickfire 84: he and O'Brien put on 76 before India completed their first Test win in New Zealand for 33 years.

Man of the Match: S. R. Tendulkar.

Close of play: First day, India 29-0 (Gambhir 6, Sehwag 22); Second day, India 278-4 (Tendulkar 70, Yuvraj Singh 8); Third day, New Zealand 75-3 (Flynn 24).

New Zealand

T. G. McIntosh c Sehwag b Sharma	12	– c Tendulkar b Zaheer Khan	0
M. J. Guptill c Dravid b Zaheer Khan	14	– c Sehwag b Harbhajan Singh	48
D. R. Flynn c Dhoni b Zaheer Khan	0	– c Gambhir b Harbhajan Singh	67
L. R. P. L. Taylor b Sharma	18	– (5) c Sehwag b Patel	4
J. D. Ryder c Laxman b Sharma	102	– (6) lbw b Harbhajan Singh	21
J. E. C. Franklin c Dhoni b Sharma	0	– (7) c Patel b Harbhajan Singh	14
†B. B. McCullum c Laxman b Patel	3	– (8) c Laxman b Yuvraj Singh	84
*D. L. Vettori c Dhoni b Patel	118	– (9) c Dhoni b Harbhajan Singh	21
K. D. Mills b Patel	0	– (4) lbw b Patel	2
I. E. O'Brien st Dhoni b Harbhajan Singh	8	– c Laxman b Harbhajan Singh	14
C. S. Martin not out	0	– not out	0
L-b 1, n-b 3	4	B 1, l-b 3	4

1/17 (2) 2/17 (3) 3/40 (1) 4/51 (4)   (78.2 overs) 279
5/51 (6) 6/60 (7) 7/246 (8) 8/246 (9)
9/275 (10) 10/279 (5)

1/0 (1) 2/68 (2)   (102.3 overs) 279
3/75 (4) 4/110 (5)
5/132 (6) 6/154 (7) 7/161 (3)
8/199 (9) 9/275 (10) 10/279 (8)

Zaheer Khan 16–3–70–2; Sharma 19.2–4–73–4; Patel 18–4–60–3; Harbhajan Singh 22–7–57–1; Sehwag 3–0–18–0. *Second Innings*—Zaheer Khan 28–7–79–1; Sharma 22–7–62–0; Patel 17–2–60–2; Harbhajan Singh 28–2–63–6; Yuvraj Singh 7.3–2–11–1.

India

G. Gambhir c McCullum b Martin	72	– not out	30
V. Sehwag run out	24		
R. Dravid b O'Brien	66	– (2) not out	8
S. R. Tendulkar c Taylor b O'Brien	160		
V. V. S. Laxman c Taylor b Martin	30		
Yuvraj Singh b Martin	22		
*†M. S. Dhoni c McCullum b O'Brien	47		
Harbhajan Singh c Vettori b Mills	16		
Zaheer Khan not out	51		
I. Sharma c McCullum b Vettori	6		
M. M. Patel c Martin b Vettori	9		
B 6, l-b 3, n-b 8	17	B 1	1

1/37 (2) 2/142 (1) 3/177 (3)   (152.4 overs) 520   (no wkt, 5.2 overs) 39
4/238 (5) 5/314 (6) 6/429 (7)
7/443 (4) 8/457 (8) 9/492 (10) 10/520 (11)

Martin 30–9–98–3; Mills 22–4–98–1; O'Brien 33–7–103–3; Franklin 23–1–98–0; Vettori 35.4–8–90–2; Ryder 9–5–24–0. *Second Innings*—Martin 3–0–17–0; Mills 2.2–0–21–0.

Umpires: I. J. Gould and S. J. A. Taufel.
Third umpire: G. A. V. Baxter. Referee: A. G. Hurst.

NEW ZEALAND v INDIA

Second Test Match

At Napier, March 26, 27, 28, 29, 30, 2009. Drawn. Toss: New Zealand.

India came out to wine country in Napier on a high, in the rare position of leading a Test series in New Zealand. Perhaps it was that advantage which allowed them to breeze into town just a day before the Second Test, choosing instead to practise in Auckland after the First Test in Hamilton. Dhoni turned unusually philosophical when asked about his team's approach: "It depends on what you're feeding into the mind. The mind doesn't know if it's Napier or some other place, it's about how you treat the mind." Dhoni eventually missed the game anyway, with a strained back, and Sehwag led the side.

Talk beforehand centred on how the groundsman might somehow produce a green seamer which would blunt the visiting batsmen while giving New Zealand's seam bowlers the shot in the arm they would need to level the series. When the pitch was unveiled, though, it was clear that McLean Park was not about to lose its reputation as a batting paradise. The track was dry and hard, the square boundaries short, and the outfield lightning-quick. Vettori expressed confidence that the surface would stay true for all five days, leaving the tourists wondering if he was trying to bluff them – but as it turned out he was on the money, although India's batsmen tried their hardest to prove him wrong.

Vettori chose to bat after winning an important toss and, although New Zealand stumbled to 23 for three in the 11th over, they put up a batting performance that would have done India's star-studded line-up proud. Ryder, better known for his brushes with authority and alcohol than his authoritative cover-drives, set the record straight. The shift from one-day to five-day cricket suited him perfectly, as he demonstrated why shot selection remains one of the most important aspects of batting. Leaving alone anything remotely dangerous, Ryder waited well, and feasted on anything in his zone. Reminding observers of Inzamam-ul-Haq – not just in build – he clinically took apart India's bowlers. He got well on top of the ball when driving through the off side, and always had

The Walls of India: Rahul Dravid and Gautam Gambhir head for lunch on day four.

plenty of time to deal with anything short or on the pads. His pulls bore the stamp of someone who knew how to transfer weight from one foot to the other, and the manner in which he tucked the ball off his hips showed off his ability to score runs while expending the least energy.

Ryder's polar opposite was Taylor, whose game is more conventional, yet frustrating for fans who seek consistency. On this day Taylor got away with plenty – he was dropped twice – but showed just why many in New Zealand rate him their most exciting batsman since Martin Crowe. He and Ryder picked off India's bowlers with minimum fanfare, and it became clear that something special was in the offing when New Zealand ended the first day at 351 for four, having scored at nearly four an over throughout. Taylor clattered 151 before chancing his arm once too often against a Harbhajan Singh *doosra* to be caught at square leg. Optimistic Indian hopes of a collapse receded as Ryder controlled the game like a veteran, reaching 201 before a lapse in concentration allowed a flashing drive off Zaheer Khan to end up in the stumps via a thick inside edge. He had exactly matched the score of another J. Ryder – Jack of Australia – against England at Adelaide in 1924-25 (although he was not out). McCullum played within himself to reach his third Test century, and New Zealand passed 600 for only the third time in Tests – the second against India – before Vettori declared.

After a promising start, India lost both openers and the night-watchman Sharma, to end a painful second day 540 behind. More horrors followed next morning as Tendulkar tried to run a ball to third man and was beaten when it held its line, and later Dravid shaped to cut a wide one from Ryder and was caught behind after 282 minutes. Even Laxman's 76 pushed the total to only 305, and the follow-on was inevitable.

What followed, however, was a rearguard action that can scarcely be praised enough. Gambhir, blocking as if his life depended on it, wore down the bowlers to the point where the match as a contest ended. India's most prolific Twenty20 player showed he had the wherewithal to bat long when there was no need for quick runs. Dravid and Tendulkar departed soon after reaching half-centuries, but Gambhir soldiered on, never once attempting to do anything but occupy the crease. His 137 came from 17 minutes short of 11 hours (only five batsmen had batted longer in Tests for India) and took his side into the

LONGEST TEST INNINGS FOR INDIA

Mins			
740	R. Dravid (270)	v Pakistan at Rawalpindi	2003-04
708	S. M. Gavaskar (172)	v England at Bangalore	1981-82
673	N. S. Sidhu (201)	v West Indies at Port-of-Spain	1996-97
671	A. D. Gaekwad (201)	v Pakistan at Jullundur	1983-84
644	S. M. Gavaskar (236*)	v West Indies at Madras	1983-84
643	G. R. Viswanath (222)	v England at Madras	1981-82
643	**G. Gambhir (137)**	**v New Zealand at Napier**	**2008-09**
631	V. V. S. Laxman (281)	v Australia at Kolkata	2000-01
629	R. Dravid (217)	v England at The Oval	2002
613	S. R. Tendulkar (241*)	v Australia at Sydney	2003-04

The longest Test innings of all is Hanif Mohammad's 337 in 970 minutes for Pakistan v West Indies at Bridgetown in 1957-58.

lead. Sehwag, captaining for only the second time in Tests, dubbed him the "Second Wall of India, this time from the North" in a reference to Dravid's nickname. And when Gambhir finally left, to a borderline leg-before decision, Laxman (who made his 14th Test century) and Yuvraj Singh ensured the draw.

Man of the Match: J. D. Ryder.

Close of play: First day, New Zealand 351-4 (Ryder 137, Franklin 26); Second day, India 79-3 (Dravid 21, Tendulkar 0); Third day, India 47-1 (Gambhir 14, Dravid 11); Fourth day, India 252-2 (Gambhir 102, Tendulkar 58).

New Zealand

T. G. McIntosh c Karthik b Sharma	12	
M. J. Guptill c Sehwag b Zaheer Khan	8	
J. M. How b Zaheer Khan	1	
L. R. P. L. Taylor c Yuvraj Singh b Harbhajan Singh	151	
J. D. Ryder b Zaheer Khan	201	
J. E. C. Franklin run out	52	
†B. B. McCullum c Tendulkar b Sharma	115	
*D. L. Vettori b Sharma	55	
J. S. Patel c Sharma b Harbhajan Singh	1	
I. E. O'Brien not out	1	
B 7, l-b 8, n-b 7	22	

C. S. Martin did not bat.

1/21 (1)   (9 wkts dec, 154.4 overs) 619
2/22 (3) 3/23 (2)
4/294 (4) 5/415 (6) 6/477 (5) 7/605 (8)
8/618 (7) 9/619 (9)

Zaheer Khan 34–6–129–3; Sharma 27–5–95–3; Patel 28–3–128–0; Harbhajan Singh 41.4–7–120–2; Sehwag 12–0–73–0; Yuvraj Singh 12–0–59–0.

India

G. Gambhir c Vettori b Patel	16	– lbw b Patel	137	
*V. Sehwag c McCullum b Vettori	34	– lbw b Patel	22	
R. Dravid c McCullum b Ryder	83	– c How b Vettori	62	
I. Sharma lbw b Vettori	0			
S. R. Tendulkar c Taylor b Patel	49	– (4) c McCullum b Martin	64	
V. V. S. Laxman c McIntosh b Martin	76	– (5) not out	124	
Yuvraj Singh c McIntosh b Martin	0	– (6) not out	54	
†K. D. Karthik c Ryder b Martin	6			
Harbhajan Singh c Martin b O'Brien	18			
Zaheer Khan c Ryder b O'Brien	8			
M. M. Patel not out	0			
B 1, l-b 7, n-b 7	15	B 9, l-b 1, n-b 3	13	

1/48 (2) 2/73 (1) 3/78 (4)   (93.5 overs) 305
4/165 (5) 5/246 (3) 6/253 (7)
7/270 (8) 8/291 (6) 9/305 (9) 10/305 (10)

1/30 (2)   (4 wkts dec, 180 overs) 476
2/163 (3)
3/260 (4) 4/356 (1)

Martin 24–5–89–3; Franklin 15–4–34–0; Vettori 19–5–45–2; O'Brien 13.5–4–66–2; Patel 19–2–60–2; Ryder 3–1–3–1. *Second Innings*—Martin 30–8–86–1; O'Brien 32–9–94–0; Franklin 21–5–48–0; Patel 45–10–120–2; Ryder 11–5–38–0; Vettori 38–13–76–1; Taylor 2–1–4–0; How 1–1–0–0.

Umpires: B. R. Doctrove and I. J. Gould. E. A. Watkin replaced Doctrove from the third day.
Third umpire: E. A. Watkin – replaced by C. B. Gaffaney.   Referee: A. G. Hurst.

NEW ZEALAND v INDIA

Third Test Match

At Basin Reserve, Wellington, April 3, 4, 5, 6, 7, 2009. Drawn. Toss: New Zealand.

At the end of a long campaign, India had the option to go for glory and risk everything, but instead they chose to hold fire and defend their hard-fought series lead in the worst weather of the tour. They had enjoyed the best of a hospitable New Zealand summer, but now they were forced to adapt to a windy and witheringly cold Wellington, as the warm season's last embers faded away. Greeted by conditions best suited to kite-flying, India's batsmen and bowlers were forced to rethink their strategy in weather that finally began to resemble what they had been warned about before leaving for the Land of the Long White Cloud.

The New Zealanders hoped familiarity with the windy conditions would give them the edge, even if the pitch was uncharacteristically devoid of live grass. But sincerely as the bowlers worked with the swirling breeze, toiling against it manfully when required, the elements refused to yield to any one team.

Dhoni, restored to health, lost the toss, and Vettori decided to bowl, aiming for quick wickets: nine did go down on the first day, but India rattled along at almost 4.2 an over with contributions down the order: 185 runs came in 35 overs in the final session. Then Zaheer Khan showed that most observations about the wind had been academic, as he moved the ball both ways in the air and off the pitch to finish with five wickets. New Zealand flirted with the follow-on at 160 for eight, just saving it before they were dismissed in the last session of the second day.

India bedded down again. Gambhir, keen to remind spectators that he was not merely a blocker, allowed himself the freedom to attack. After Sehwag departed for 12 (characteristically made up of three fours), he shared a 170-run stand with Dravid, whose contribution was only 60. Gambhir then found additional allies as he accumulated 167; eventually he walked across his stumps and missed a straight one from the tireless O'Brien. Still, India's imposing total left New Zealand an improbable 617 to win, or, more realistically, to bat five and a half sessions and deny the visitors their 100th Test victory.

Gambhir headed off suggestions that India had sat on their lead and left it too late. "With the kind of bowling that we have, we can easily get New Zealand out in five sessions. If we can't do that, then we don't deserve to win," he said, refusing to take the weather into account. As it turned out, the rain did have a part to play: intermittent showers ultimately saved New Zealand, who had reached 281 for eight by the (literally) bitter end, which came shortly after lunch on the final day. Another century from Taylor and 49 from the ever-improving Guptill were the main contributions. McIntosh provided Dravid with his 182nd catch, breaking Mark Waugh's Test record for an outfielder.

Dhoni still copped some criticism for not declaring earlier, but given India's series lead he could hardly be blamed for not worrying about the weather. New Zealand needed to force the pace, but they could not do so at any stage; after 41 long years they finally lost a home series to India.

Man of the Match: G. Gambhir.

Close of play: First day, India 375-9 (Sharma 15, Patel 14); Second day, India 51-1 (Gambhir 28, Dravid 9); Third day, India 349-5 (Yuvraj Singh 15, Dhoni 16); Fourth day, New Zealand 167-4 (Taylor 69, Franklin 26).

India

G. Gambhir lbw b Franklin	23	– lbw b O'Brien	167
V. Sehwag c McCullum b O'Brien	48	– c Taylor b Martin	12
R. Dravid c Franklin b Martin	35	– c McCullum b Vettori	60
S. R. Tendulkar c McCullum b Martin	62	– c Taylor b Vettori	9
V. V. S. Laxman c McIntosh b Southee	4	– b O'Brien	61
Yuvraj Singh lbw b Ryder	9	– c Taylor b Martin	40
*†M. S. Dhoni c O'Brien b Southee	52	– not out	56
Harbhajan Singh c Vettori b Martin	60	– c Southee b Martin	0
Zaheer Khan c McCullum b O'Brien	33	– not out	18
I. Sharma c McCullum b Martin	18		
M. M. Patel not out	15		
B 2, l-b 8, w 3, n-b 7	20	L-b 5, w 1, n-b 5	11

1/73 (2) 2/75 (1) 3/165 (4)　　　(92.1 overs) 379　　1/14 (2)　(7 wkts dec, 116 overs) 434
4/173 (5) 5/182 (6) 6/204 (3)　　　　　　　　　　　2/184 (3)
7/283 (7) 8/315 (8) 9/347 (9) 10/379 (10)　　　　3/208 (4) 4/314 (1) 5/319 (5)
　　　　　　　　　　　　　　　　　　　　　　　　　6/397 (6) 7/397 (8)

Martin 25.1–3–98–4; Southee 18–1–94–2; O'Brien 22–3–89–2; Franklin 14–4–38–1; Vettori 9–1–47–0; Ryder 4–2–3–1. *Second Innings*—Southee 12–2–58–0; Martin 22–7–70–3; O'Brien 25–6–100–2; Franklin 16–3–72–0; Ryder 6–1–21–0; Vettori 35–5–108–2.

New Zealand

T. G. McIntosh c Yuvraj Singh b Zaheer Khan	32	– c Dravid b Zaheer Khan	4
M. J. Guptill b Zaheer Khan	17	– lbw b Harbhajan Singh	49
D. R. Flynn c Dhoni b Zaheer Khan	2	– b Zaheer Khan	10
L. R. P. L. Taylor c Dhoni b Harbhajan Singh	42	– b Harbhajan Singh	107
J. D. Ryder c Dhoni b Zaheer Khan	3	– c Dravid b Harbhajan Singh	0
J. E. C. Franklin c Sehwag b Harbhajan Singh	15	– lbw b Tendulkar	49
†B. B. McCullum c Dhoni b Harbhajan Singh	24	– c Dravid b Tendulkar	6
*D. L. Vettori c Dhoni b Sharma	11	– not out	15
T. G. Southee c and b Zaheer Khan	16	– c Dhoni b Harbhajan Singh	3
I. E. O'Brien c Dhoni b Patel	19	– not out	19
C. S. Martin not out	4		
B 9, l-b 3	12	B 10, l-b 2, w 1, n-b 6	19

1/21 (2) 2/31 (3) 3/80 (1) 4/98 (5)　　(65 overs) 197　　1/30 (1)　(8 wkts, 94.3 overs) 281
5/120 (4) 6/125 (6) 7/138 (8) 8/160 (9)　　　　　　　　　2/54 (3) 3/84 (2)
9/181 (7) 10/197 (10)　　　　　　　　　　　　　　　　　4/84 (5) 5/226 (4) 6/244 (7)
　　　　　　　　　　　　　　　　　　　　　　　　　　　7/253 (6) 8/258 (9)

Zaheer Khan 18–2–65–5; Sharma 14–3–47–1; Patel 8–2–20–1; Harbhajan Singh 23–4–43–3; Yuvraj Singh 2–0–10–0. *Second Innings*—Zaheer Khan 19.3–6–57–2; Patel 13–4–22–0; Sharma 12–2–57–0; Harbhajan Singh 33–8–59–4; Yuvraj Singh 1–0–4–0; Sehwag 7–0–25–0; Tendulkar 9–0–45–2.

Umpires: D. J. Harper and S. J. A. Taufel.
Third umpire: A. L. Hill.　Referee: A. G. Hurst.

NEW ZEALAND v PAKISTAN, 2009-10

Lynn McConnell

Test matches (3): New Zealand 1, Pakistan 1

New Zealand were in the unusual position of officially being "visitors" on their own grounds when this series, supposed to be staged in Pakistan, had to be relocated because of continuing security fears. After contesting three one-day internationals in Abu Dhabi and two Twenty20 games in Dubai (see page 1222), the teams arrived in New Zealand in mid-November to play three Tests. Pakistan had a new captain, Mohammad Yousuf, as Younis Khan had stepped down after losing the one-day series and requested a sabbatical; New Zealand were also in flux, having parted with their coach, Andy Moles, before the trip to the United Arab Emirates when the players indicated they had lost faith in him.

The Tests proved neither side deserved to be ranked among the upper echelons of cricket's order (Pakistan stood at sixth and New Zealand seventh in the ICC Test rankings). Pakistan's fielding was lamentable – they dropped 17 chances during the series – while New Zealand's batting, the top order especially, was too flaky. Their weaknesses meant they were well matched, however, and produced a stimulating lack of certainty from day to day. The first and last matches went to the final session, with both sides having a chance. New Zealand won the opening Test, at Dunedin's University Oval, by 32 runs, while the weather in usually clement Napier had the final say, forcing the players off as New Zealand were attempting to chase 208 in 43 overs. But Pakistan easily won the Second Test, the 50th at the Basin Reserve in Wellington, after dismissing New Zealand for 99 in their first innings.

Pakistan fielded two young stars. Left-arm bowler Mohammad Aamer demonstrated his potential from the first ball of the series, which bowled Tim McIntosh. With a style reminiscent of Wasim Akram on his debut, also against New Zealand almost a quarter of a century earlier, Aamer proved competitive, although the toll of playing three matches in quick succession had its effect on a 17-year-old; he clearly struggled with his workload in Napier's heat and was forced from the field in distress. Series figures of seven wickets at an average of 43 did not do justice to his influence, especially in Dunedin. But an unbeaten 73 in the last one-day match in Abu Dhabi had demonstrated a fierce capability with the bat that should see him emerge as a genuine all-rounder.

Umar Akmal, aged 19, already had a one-day international century to his name, and marked his Test debut with an outstanding hundred at Dunedin, a demonstration of talent, confidence and innovation against the superior pace of Shane Bond which made compelling watching. Nothing seemed too much trouble to Umar, and he maintained that spirit throughout the series without quite managing to repeat that century. He was the leading batsman on either side, with 379 runs at 63, and the mainstay of Pakistan's batting; while he and his brother Kamran were at the wicket, there was every chance they would run

Oh brother! Kamran Akmal looks on in admiration at his brother Umar, who has just reached his century on debut in the First Test at Dunedin.

down their target in Dunedin. But Bond dismissed him for the second time in the match, allowing his colleagues to set about the Pakistan tail.

Of the old guard, Yousuf never produced the dominant display New Zealand feared from him, although he managed a couple of eighties. Leg-spinner Danish Kaneria was not wanted for the First Test but picked up 13 cheap wickets in the remaining two, and regularly flummoxed lower-order batsmen.

While Aamer offered promise, it was Mohammad Asif who provided performance. He had not played a Test for two years after drugs-related offences; though his comeback began in the Champions Trophy in September, he had not played in the games in the UAE, as he was banned from there. Asif bolstered the young side with his consistent nagging off-stump line and a little away movement to the right-hander. His 19 wickets, including nine for 107 in the Wellington victory, made him the series' leading wicket-taker.

New Zealand were also boosted at the start of the series by a fast bowler enjoying a comeback: like Asif, Shane Bond was playing his first Test in two years, reprieved from exile after his involvement in the Indian Cricket League. Bond dominated the First Test, demanding constant respect from batsmen, and the match award reflected his worth. Injury continued to haunt his career, however, and an abdominal strain kept him out of the last two games. By Christmas, he had announced he was retiring from Test cricket, though he hoped to be fit enough to play one-day and Twenty20 internationals. Seamer

Iain O'Brien had already revealed he would be retiring from Test cricket after the series, to live in England with his English wife and play for Middlesex. These twin blows hit New Zealand hard; O'Brien took 15 wickets in the series, and it was he and Bond who had turned the First Test on the final afternoon.

New Zealand's failure to secure consistent runs from their top order meant the load fell on Ross Taylor and captain Daniel Vettori again, with McCullum as back-up. Taylor hit 301 runs and averaged 60, narrowly missing a hundred twice; Vettori was out for 99 in Dunedin before securing his fifth Test century in Napier when he moved up the order to No. 6. Vettori's 287 runs and ten wickets showed the responsibility of captaincy had not reduced his effectiveness. But remedial action was clearly needed by New Zealand's batsmen for them to become a competitive unit at Test level.

PAKISTAN TOURING PARTY

Mohammad Yousuf (*captain*), Kamran Akmal (*vice-captain*), Abdur Rauf, Danish Kaneria, Faisal Iqbal, Fawad Alam, Imran Farhat, Khurram Manzoor, Misbah-ul-Haq, Mohammad Aamer, Mohammad Asif, Saeed Ajmal, Salman Butt, Sarfraz Ahmed, Shoaib Malik, Umar Akmal, Umar Gul, Yasir Arafat. *Coach:* Intikhab Alam.

Younis Khan was originally selected as captain, but stepped down after the preceding limited-overs matches in the United Arab Emirates and asked for a break from cricket; he was replaced by Misbah-ul-Haq.

TEST MATCH AVERAGES

NEW ZEALAND – BATTING AND FIELDING

	T	I	NO	R	HS	100s	50s	Avge	Ct/St
L. R. P. L. Taylor	3	5	0	301	97	0	3	60.20	7
†D. L. Vettori	3	5	0	287	134	1	1	57.40	7
D. R. Tuffey	2	3	1	86	80*	0	1	43.00	1
B. B. McCullum	3	5	0	191	89	0	2	38.20	15/1
†T. G. McIntosh	3	6	1	134	74	0	1	26.80	3
M. J. Guptill	3	5	0	88	60	0	1	17.60	6
I. E. O'Brien	3	5	1	67	31	0	0	16.75	1
G. D. Elliott	2	4	0	59	25	0	0	14.75	0
†D. R. Flynn	3	5	0	62	29	0	0	12.40	1
P. G. Fulton	2	4	0	42	29	0	0	10.50	4
C. S. Martin	3	5	3	1	1*	0	0	0.50	1

Played in one Test: S. E. Bond 22, 7 (2 ct); T. G. Southee 0; B. J. Watling 18, 60*.

† *Left-handed batsman.*

BOWLING

	Style	O	M	R	W	BB	5W/i	Avge
M. J. Guptill	OB	13.2	2	37	3	3-37	0	12.33
S. E. Bond	RF	48.5	9	153	8	5-107	1	19.12
D. R. Tuffey	RFM	75.5	14	222	8	4-52	0	27.75
I. E. O'Brien	RFM	143.3	25	448	15	4-35	0	29.86
C. S. Martin	RFM	117	24	343	11	4-52	0	31.18
D. L. Vettori	SLA	152	50	364	10	4-58	0	36.40
T. G. Southee	RFM	48	12	126	3	2-64	0	42.00

Also bowled: G. D. Elliott (RM) 7–1–11–2.

PAKISTAN – BATTING AND FIELDING

	T	I	NO	R	HS	100s	50s	Avge	Ct/St
Umar Akmal	3	6	0	379	129	1	3	63.16	3
†Imran Farhat	3	6	1	268	117*	1	1	53.60	2
Kamran Akmal	3	6	1	257	82	0	3	51.40	12/1
Mohammad Yousuf.	3	6	0	230	89	0	2	38.33	2
†Salman Butt.	2	4	0	122	66	0	1	30.50	1
†Mohammad Aamer	3	6	0	101	26	0	0	16.83	0
Misbah-ul-Haq	2	4	0	61	33	0	0	15.25	2
Shoaib Malik.	2	4	0	46	32	0	0	11.50	2
Umar Gul.	3	6	0	66	31	0	0	11.00	0
Danish Kaneria	2	4	1	27	16	0	0	9.00	1
Mohammad Asif	3	6	1	14	10	0	0	2.80	0

Played in one Test: Faisal Iqbal 6, 67 (1 ct); †Fawad Alam 29, 5 (2 ct); Khurram Manzoor 6, 4; Saeed Ajmal 1*, 1*.

† *Left-handed batsman.*

BOWLING

	Style	O	M	R	W	BB	5W/i	Avge
Mohammad Asif	RFM	126.4	33	376	19	5-67	1	19.78
Danish Kaneria.	LBG	95	18	269	13	7-168	1	20.69
Mohammad Aamer	LFM	95	22	306	7	2-29	0	43.71
Umar Gul	RFM	104	22	370	8	3-41	0	46.25

Also bowled: Saeed Ajmal (OB) 54.5–15–117–2; Shoaib Malik (OB) 1–0–5–0.

Note: Matches in this section which were not first-class are signified by a dagger.

†At Queenstown, November 18, 19, 20, 2009. **Drawn.** Toss: New Zealand Invitation XI. **New Zealand Invitation XI 234** (D. R. Flynn 49, J. E. C. Franklin 43, R. A. Young 75; Abdur Rauf 4-43) **and 231-2** (T. G. McIntosh 131*, D. R. Flynn 56); **Pakistanis 286** (Imran Farhat 52, Fawad Alam 77, Sarfraz Ahmed 37).

Each side named 12 players, of whom 11 could bat and 11 field. On the opening day, four bowlers who had not been part of Pakistan's squad in the UAE – Mohammad Asif, Abdur Rauf, Yasir Arafat and Danish Kaneria – all chipped in to dismiss the Invitation XI for a moderate total. But few of their batting colleagues made the same good use of their opportunities. Though the Pakistanis took a 52-run lead, the Invitation XI easily batted out the final day, with opener Tim McIntosh, one of seven New Zealand players who would feature in the Test series, occupying almost five hours and striking 16 fours in an unbeaten century.

PAKISTAN v NEW ZEALAND

First Test Match

At University Oval, Dunedin, November 24, 25, 26, 27, 28, 2009. New Zealand won by 32 runs. Toss: Pakistan. Test debut: Umar Akmal.

During the match, a magazine profile of Daniel Vettori quoted him as saying that one of his goals in Test cricket was to have New Zealand's batsmen score enough runs to bowl opposing sides out on the fifth afternoon of a match. Little did he realise what lay ahead in this immensely entertaining Test.

From the very first ball, with which Mohammad Aamer bowled McIntosh, there was always something happening on a pitch offering assistance to bowlers prepared to work hard. What looked like becoming a typical New Zealand top-order collapse was stemmed initially by Guptill and Taylor, who added 117 for the third wicket. But as so often it took Vettori, batting nearly four hours before he was caught behind for 99, and McCullum, who was reprieved by third umpire Rudi Koertzen after Simon Taufel gave him lbw to Mohammad Asif in the first day's final over, to provide what proved a match-winning advantage. They shared a seventh-wicket stand of 164, and New Zealand batted throughout the first two days (the second cut to 36 overs by rain) for a first-innings total of 429.

It was Asif's consistent line, on or around off stump, that most troubled the batsmen, especially those lacking the technique to keep him out. He collected four wickets, and was delighted with how quickly he fitted back into Test cricket after serving a suspension for drugs offences. Pakistan paid the price for dreadful catching lapses, however – something they could not shake off throughout the match.

They were not immune from batting problems, either. Martin made the early breakthroughs, removing both openers, before the long-awaited return of Shane Bond bore fruit in his second spell. Not long after lunch on day three, he unleashed a burst of three wickets in ten balls. Mohammad Yousuf, like him a rehabilitated Indian Cricket League player, was his first victim, offering a low caught and bowled chance which the hungry Bond snaffled with ease. Yousuf said afterwards that Bond was one of the most difficult bowlers he had faced.

Pakistan's recovery was led by 19-year-old Umar Akmal, who seemed completely unaffected by the circumstances. He hit his first ball in Test cricket to the third-man boundary and went on to become the 11th Pakistani to reach a century on debut – and the second in five months, after Fawad Alam. A disregard for convention allowed him to race to his hundred by taking four, six and four in four balls from O'Brien. His older brother Kamran was evidently overwhelmed by emotion, as he fell to Vettori in the next over after they had added 176 in three hours. Vettori quickly brought Bond back, and he removed the younger Akmal on the way to his fifth five-wicket bag in Tests. But Umar's 129, from 160 balls in 219 minutes with 21 fours and two sixes, was the innings of the series.

New Zealand's runs in the bank proved vital, as they collapsed again in the third innings; only Taylor's fifty showed the desire necessary to ensure Pakistan were set a tough chase. Asif took four wickets again as the home side were all out for 153 early on the last morning. As a result of the overs added on to compensate for bad light and rain on the previous three days, Pakistan had 91 overs to score 251.

Bond was soon among the top order as they slumped to 24 for three, but Yousuf and Umar Akmal, who batted another 222 minutes for 75 and revealed a defensive quality as impressive as his earlier attacking efforts, rebuilt the innings. Martin eventually separated them, getting the ball to lift sharply on Yousuf, who edged behind. As long as Umar was at the crease, however, Pakistan's hopes were alive. It was Bond who got him again, caught and bowled, to make it 195 for six. Two runs later, O'Brien exposed the tail when he trapped Kamran lbw. Vettori had his wish when he claimed the last two wickets. An exciting final day had ended in victory for New Zealand with 15 overs to spare.

MOST RUNS BY A TEST DEBUTANT IN A LOSING CAUSE

216 (62, 154*)	K. S. Ranjitsinhji	England v Australia at Manchester..........	1896
204 (129, 75)	**Umar Akmal**.......	**Pakistan v New Zealand at Dunedin**.......	**2009-10**
200 (164, 36)	A. A. Jackson.......	Australia v England at Adelaide............	1928-29
193 (119, 74)	G. Gunn	England v Australia at Sydney	1907-08
184 (16, 168)	**Fawad Alam**.......	**Pakistan v Sri Lanka at Colombo (PSS)**....	**2009**
163 (163, 0)	A. C. Hudson.......	South Africa v West Indies at Bridgetown....	1991-92
157 (93, 64)	N. S. Harford	New Zealand v Pakistan at Lahore..........	1955-56
156 (38, 118)	L. Amarnath.......	India v England at Bombay	1933-34
151 (145, 6)	Aminul Islam	Bangladesh v India at Dhaka	2000-01

Research: Philip Bailey

Bond, who claimed eight for 153 in the match and bowled with undiminished speed, said: "It was a perfect comeback – this is the way you want to play Test cricket. It was the first time I had bowled with only four bowlers. I just wanted to bowl well and take wickets." Sadly, it was to be his Test swansong.

Man of the Match: S. E. Bond.

Close of play: First day, New Zealand 276-6 (McCullum 25, Vettori 40); Second day, New Zealand 404-8 (Bond 8, O'Brien 2); Third day, Pakistan 307-8 (Mohammad Aamer 12, Mohammad Asif 0); Fourth day, New Zealand 147-8 (Elliott 20, O'Brien 4).

New Zealand

T. G. McIntosh b Mohammad Aamer	0	– (2) lbw b Mohammad Asif	31
M. J. Guptill c Fawad Alam b Mohammad Aamer	60	– (1) b Mohammad Aamer	0
D. R. Flynn c Kamran Akmal b Mohammad Asif	8	– lbw b Mohammad Aamer	0
L. R. P. L. Taylor c Imran Farhat b Saeed Ajmal	94	– run out	59
P. G. Fulton b Mohammad Asif	29	– lbw b Umar Gul	0
G. D. Elliott c Kamran Akmal b Mohammad Asif	8	– c Kamran Akmal b Umar Gul	25
†B. B. McCullum b Umar Gul	78	– c Kamran Akmal b Mohammad Asif	0
*D. L. Vettori c Kamran Akmal b Umar Gul	99	– c Fawad Alam b Mohammad Asif	8
S. E. Bond c Kamran Akmal b Mohammad Asif	22	– b Mohammad Asif	7
I. E. O'Brien not out	13	– lbw b Umar Gul	4
C. S. Martin lbw b Saeed Ajmal	0	– not out	1
L-b 14, w 1, n-b 3	18	B 4, l-b 5, w 1, n-b 3, p 5	18

1/0 (1) 2/27 (3) 3/144 (2)   (131.5 overs)   429
4/192 (4) 5/210 (5) 6/211 (6)
7/375 (7) 8/402 (8) 9/428 (9) 10/429 (11)

1/0 (1) 2/0 (3) 3/87 (4)   (67 overs)   153
4/91 (5) 5/112 (2)
6/115 (7) 7/123 (8) 8/143 (9)
9/150 (10) 10/153 (6)

Mohammad Aamer 24–3–87–2; Mohammad Asif 34–6–108–4; Umar Gul 36–10–129–2; Saeed Ajmal 37.5–10–91–2. *Second Innings*—Mohammad Aamer 16–7–29–2; Mohammad Asif 20–6–43–4; Umar Gul 14–3–41–3; Saeed Ajmal 17–5–26–0.

Pakistan

Khurram Manzoor b Martin	6	– c McCullum b Bond	4
Imran Farhat lbw b Martin	22	– c McIntosh b Martin	1
Fawad Alam c McCullum b Bond	29	– c Fulton b Bond	5
*Mohammad Yousuf c and b Bond	17	– c McCullum b Martin	41
Umar Akmal c Fulton b Bond	129	– c and b Bond	75
Shoaib Malik b Bond	2	– c McCullum b O'Brien	32
†Kamran Akmal c Taylor b Vettori	82	– lbw b O'Brien	27
Mohammad Aamer c Vettori b Bond	26	– c and b Vettori	15
Umar Gul lbw b Vettori	6	– c Vettori b O'Brien	4
Mohammad Asif c McIntosh b Martin	10	– c Taylor b Vettori	0
Saeed Ajmal not out	1	– not out	1
N-b 2	2	B 9, l-b 1, w 2, n-b 1	13

1/11 (1) 2/43 (2) 3/74 (4) 4/79 (3)   (96.5 overs)   332
5/85 (6) 6/261 (7) 7/293 (5)
8/302 (9) 9/320 (10) 10/332 (8)

1/4 (1) 2/6 (2) 3/24 (3)   (76 overs)   218
4/95 (4) 5/161 (6)
6/195 (5) 7/197 (7) 8/203 (9)
9/213 (10) 10/218 (8)

Bond 27.5–4–107–5; Martin 21–8–63–3; O'Brien 21–3–98–0; Vettori 27–7–64–2. *Second Innings*—Bond 21–5–46–3; Martin 16–4–45–2; O'Brien 23–3–63–3; Vettori 14–1–51–2; Elliott 2–0–3–0.

Umpires: B. R. Doctrove and S. J. A. Taufel.
Third umpire: R. E. Koertzen. Referee: A. G. Hurst.

PAKISTAN v NEW ZEALAND

Second Test Match

At Basin Reserve, Wellington, December 3, 4, 5, 6, 2009. Pakistan won by 141 runs. Toss: New Zealand.

New Zealand suffered a severe blow when an abdominal strain forced Bond to withdraw. His place was taken by Daryl Tuffey, playing his first Test in five and a half years, while Pakistan made three changes. They swapped opener Salman Butt for Khurram Manzoor and brought in Misbah-ul-Haq for Fawad Alam, ostensibly to exploit his slip-catching ability, while Umar Akmal moved up to No. 3; meanwhile leg-spinner Danish Kaneria replaced Saeed Ajmal. But Pakistan's hopes that their catching would improve were unfounded; New Zealand's misfortune would have been even greater had the fielding been anywhere close to adequate.

The Test was the 50th at the Basin Reserve. A wet outfield meant no play until the first afternoon, and it seemed New Zealand were in for a long haul after they invited Pakistan to bat and saw the revamped opening pair, Butt and Imran Farhat, raise 60. But once the breakthrough came, three wickets fell in four overs, including Mohammad Yousuf for a second-ball duck. Again, the Akmal brothers did the most productive scoring, though this time not in tandem. Umar smashed 46 in 48 balls, a 57-minute spectacular, while Kamran hit 70 in 85, though he survived two reviews of lbw decisions – one when Vettori pressed his appeal, the other in the next over, when Rudi Koertzen gave him out to O'Brien and Kamran himself referred the verdict. Both Akmals fell to Tuffey, who like Vettori finished with four wickets. Yousuf claimed he was happy with a total of 264; locals chortled at the thought.

He was even happier by the end of the second day, however, as New Zealand batted abysmally. Their eventual total was only 99, and eight men contributed 13 between them: Taylor was the top scorer with 30. Pakistan's bowling was accurate but hardly deadly, and most of the batsmen were undone by a lack of technique and application. Mohammad Asif led the way again with nagging fast-medium bowling which netted four for 40; Kaneria's leg-spin exposed New Zealand's failings as he took three for six.

Yousuf stepped back into the No. 3 berth in the second innings and hit 83 in a demonstration of application for the cause. He occupied 283 minutes before he was lbw on review after Koertzen had given him not out. Umar Akmal wafted, knowing he had the freedom of a substantial lead, to make 52 from 33 balls, but was caught off Martin just as he was threatening to explode. Two wickets in successive balls from Elliott gave New Zealand hope but, while the final six wickets fell for 29 runs, their target was still an improbable 405. O'Brien, who announced he would retire at the end of the series, and Martin had four wickets each.

With New Zealand's top order failing again, miracles were going to be required for them to clinch the series, and Asif was in no mood to allow that. His accuracy forced them to capitulate. They did have the advantage of a benign pitch, but only Taylor, who narrowly missed a century for the second match running in an innings featuring five sixes and nine fours, and Vettori, who knocked up 40 in 57 balls when the issue was almost beyond doubt, batted with anything like the expected purpose.

Asif took five more wickets to claim the match award, while Kaneria, who was required to bowl all but one of his 31 overs into Wellington's breeze, claimed another three. Yet again, New Zealand had been unable to build on the advantage of winning the First Test.

Man of the Match: Mohammad Asif.

Close of play: First day, Pakistan 161-6 (Kamran Akmal 21, Mohammad Aamer 2); Second day, Pakistan 64-2 (Mohammad Yousuf 10, Misbah-ul-Haq 1); Third day, New Zealand 70-3 (Taylor 15, Fulton 12).

Pakistan

Imran Farhat c Taylor b Vettori	32	– c Fulton b O'Brien	35
Salman Butt c Tuffey b O'Brien	29	– c Taylor b O'Brien	18
Umar Akmal b Tuffey	46	– (5) c Vettori b Martin	52
*Mohammad Yousuf lbw b Vettori	0	– (3) lbw b Martin	83
Misbah-ul-Haq lbw b Vettori	21	– (4) c McCullum b O'Brien	33
Shoaib Malik c Vettori b Tuffey	9	– b McCullum b Elliott	3
†Kamran Akmal c Vettori b Tuffey	70	– c McCullum b Elliott	0
Mohammad Aamer c Taylor b O'Brien	21	– c Guptill b Martin	9
Umar Gul c O'Brien b Tuffey	31	– c Fulton b O'Brien	1
Mohammad Asif c and b Vettori	4	– (11) not out	0
Danish Kaneria not out	0	– (10) c Taylor b Martin	0
W 1	1	B 4, l-b 1	5

1/60 (2) 2/66 (1) 3/66 (4) 4/119 (3) (88.2 overs) 264
5/131 (6) 6/156 (5) 7/193 (8)
8/257 (7) 9/264 (10) 10/264 (9)

1/49 (2) 2/54 (1) (86.3 overs) 239
3/131 (4) 4/197 (5) 5/210 (6) 6/210 (7)
7/230 (8) 8/239 (3) 9/239 (10) 10/239 (9)

Martin 20–2–64–0; Tuffey 23.2–5–64–4; O'Brien 23–4–78–2; Vettori 22–6–58–4. *Second Innings*—Martin 19–4–52–4; Tuffey 16–3–45–0; Vettori 25–11–63–0; O'Brien 21.3–4–66–4; Elliott 5–1–8–2.

New Zealand

T. G. McIntosh c Salman Butt b Mohammad Asif	4	– (2) lbw b Mohammad Asif	2
M. J. Guptill c Kamran Akmal b Mohammad Aamer	0	– (1) b Mohammad Asif	15
D. R. Flynn lbw b Mohammad Asif	29	– c Kamran Akmal b Mohammad Asif	20
L. R. P. L. Taylor b Umar Gul	30	– c Misbah-ul-Haq b Mohammad Aamer	97
P. G. Fulton lbw b Umar Gul	0	– c Kamran Akmal b Mohammad Aamer	13
G. D. Elliott c and b Danish Kaneria	20	– b Danish Kaneria	6
†B. B. McCullum c Shoaib Malik b Mohammad Asif	0	– c Kamran Akmal b Danish Kaneria	24
*D. L. Vettori c Misbah-ul-Haq b Danish Kaneria	6	– c Umar Akmal b Mohammad Asif	40
D. R. Tuffey c Mohammad Yousuf b Mohammad Asif	3	– lbw b Danish Kaneria	3
I. E. O'Brien c Imran Farhat b Danish Kaneria	0	– c Shoaib Malik b Mohammad Asif	31
C. S. Martin not out	0	– not out	0
L-b 7	7	B 6, l-b 6	12

1/1 (2) 2/5 (1) 3/48 (4) 4/52 (5) (36.5 overs) 99
5/85 (3) 6/85 (7) 7/95 (6) 8/96 (8)
9/96 (10) 10/99 (9)

1/4 (2) 2/36 (1) (82.5 overs) 263
3/37 (3) 4/80 (5) 5/108 (6) 6/186 (4)
7/206 (7) 8/212 (9) 9/252 (8) 10/263 (10)

Mohammad Aamer 11–2–25–1; Mohammad Asif 12.5–2–40–4; Umar Gul 7–2–21–2; Danish Kaneria 6–2–6–3. *Second Innings*—Mohammad Aamer 16–3–64–2; Mohammad Asif 23.5–9–67–5; Danish Kaneria 31–6–74–3; Umar Gul 11–2–41–0; Shoaib Malik 1–0–5–0.

Umpires: R. E. Koertzen and S. J. A. Taufel.
Third umpire: B. R. Doctrove. Referee: A. G. Hurst.

NEW ZEALAND v PAKISTAN

Third Test Match

Don Cameron

At Napier, December 11, 12, 13, 14, 15, 2009. Drawn. Toss: Pakistan. Test debut: B. J. Watling.

Well might Mohammad Yousuf, Pakistan's deeply religious captain, tug at his considerable beard and concede that Allah had smiled on his team as they escaped defeat in a dramatic, dogged and sometimes brilliantly exciting match. When heavy rain stopped New Zealand's second-innings victory charge at 90 without loss – with another 118 needed from 24 overs at a very similar scoring-rate – Yousuf readily agreed that something beyond natural causes might well have saved his side.

In fact, millions of Pakistanis may have had a distant hand in it. Because the threat of terrorism had forced Pakistan to play what should have been a home series on their opponents' soil, they had asked to start the Tests at noon in New Zealand, so that viewers back home could switch on at 4 a.m. rather than 2.30. Though the number of overs was unaffected, it had been a sunny morning, so New Zealanders might have won before the rain arrived had they kept to their usual hours.

This Test – and the whole series – displayed all the competitiveness and incident, the charm and tradition, that produce variety and intrigue impossible in the one-day game. Seven of the nine Tests on the rock-hard McLean Park pitch have been drawn. But groundsman Phil Stoyanoff told a press huddle he was sure this one would produce an outright result – not so much through a change in preparation, but because the batsmen had been "hopeless" in the first two Tests. The spin doctors were in a tizzy trying to soften this criticism, so the fact that Stoyanoff had changed his pre-Test ritual slightly, leaving a little more moisture in the smooth, hard strip, was ignored.

Vettori was spared a tricky decision when Yousuf won the toss and, knowing the pitch's reputation, batted. Salman Butt was bowled by a nasty seamer from Southee, making his first appearance of the series. Then O'Brien found the little bits of swing and seam (predicted by Stoyanoff) that had lain dormant for years and removed four top-order batsmen, three of them for ducks. At one stage, he had the staggering figures of 5–4–3–4 as Pakistan slumped to 51 for five in 19 overs.

Slowly, the sun mopped up the mischief in the pitch but, though Imran Farhat soldiered on, carrying his bat for 117 with 14 fours and a six, his team-mates returned to the suicidal swishing and nicking of the panic before lunch. Tuffey, an earnest and honest trundler, finished them off, his four victims all caught behind.

On the second day Danish Kaneria's leg-spin quickly took four wickets, and New Zealand were struggling. As so often happened during his golden summer, Vettori came to the rescue. He promoted himself to No. 6. McCullum played a steadier than usual, and their stand of 176 lifted the team to 321 for six. A blistering counter-attack had Vettori collecting his fifth Test century and Tuffey striking eight fours and two sixes. As the score raced past 400, only the faithful Kaneria showed any pluck. He finished with seven wickets from 53 overs.

With the Test half over and any vice drained from the pitch, Farhat and Butt calmly clipped 128 off arrears of 248 without mishap on the third day. But next morning Guptill, a very occasional provider of hopeful off-spin, was given the ball for the first over. He caught and bowled Butt off his third delivery and Farhat shortly afterwards. With 102 still needed to make New Zealand bat again, Pakistan had to rebuild. Yousuf took command, Umar Akmal scored another half-century and they toiled to 347 for four by the close. By now the pitch totally favoured the batsmen, but Vettori and the ghostly-pale O'Brien, who was plainly unwell, chipped out the occasional wicket and tried to avoid being mauled by Kamran Akmal. Pakistan's lead eased past 200 before Guptill returned to winkle out the last man.

New Zealand needed 208 in the 43 overs that might be possible if the weather held. Rather than start with his power-hitters, Taylor and McCullum, Vettori bravely retained the dogged McIntosh and the novice B. J. Watling to start the chase. They started carefully, with six runs from five overs, then stepped up to 35 from ten before Kaneria arrived to stifle the charge. But Pakistan reckoned without Watling, a newcomer with good one-day form. His inventive strokes had boundaries flowing, and New Zealand were close to a winning recipe as the rate reached 4.7 an over.

With another 118 needed at 4.9, and all ten wickets standing, they were poised to hurtle to victory – when the heavens had mercy on Pakistan. What might have been a brilliant win to either side, or even a tie, turned into a damp but unforgettable draw between two brave teams, neither of them top class, but on almost every day of the series paying tribute to the noble traditions of Test cricket.

Man of the Match: D. L. Vettori.

Close of play: First day, New Zealand 47-0 (McIntosh 31, Watling 13); Second day, New Zealand 346-6 (Vettori 100, Tuffey 13); Third day, Pakistan 128-0 (Imran Farhat 55, Salman Butt 66); Fourth day, Pakistan 347-4 (Umar Akmal 48, Misbah-ul-Haq 4).

Pakistan

Imran Farhat not out	117	– c and b Guptill	61
Salman Butt b Southee	9	– c and b Guptill	66
Faisal Iqbal c Guptill b O'Brien	6	– c Taylor b Martin	67
*Mohammad Yousuf c McIntosh b O'Brien	0	– c McCullum b O'Brien	89
Umar Akmal c Guptill b O'Brien	0	– c McCullum b Southee	77
Misbah-ul-Haq c McCullum b O'Brien	0	– st McCullum b Vettori	7
†Kamran Akmal c Guptill b Martin	22	– not out	56
Mohammad Aamer c McCullum b Tuffey	23	– c Martin b Vettori	7
Umar Gul c McCullum b Tuffey	24	– c Flynn b O'Brien	0
Mohammad Asif c McCullum b Tuffey	0	– (11) lbw b Guptill	0
Danish Kaneria c McCullum b Tuffey	16	– (10) c McCullum b Southee	11
L-b 2, n-b 4	6	B 3, l-b 2, w 1, n-b 3, p 5	14

1/14 (2) 2/39 (3) 3/43 (4) 4/51 (5)   (64.3 overs) 223   1/129 (2) 2/146 (1)   (193.2 overs) 455
5/51 (6) 6/90 (7) 7/159 (8) 8/194 (9)   3/274 (3) 4/333 (4)
9/194 (10) 10/223 (11)   5/361 (6) 6/397 (5) 7/421 (8)
                                        8/423 (9) 9/449 (10) 10/455 (11)

Martin 9–0–37–1; Southee 17–4–62–1; O'Brien 15.3–4–52–4; Tuffey 15.3–4–52–4; Vettori 8–0–35–0. *Second Innings*—Martin 32–6–82–1; Southee 31–8–64–2; O'Brien 40–6–108–2; Tuffey 21–2–61–0; Vettori 56–25–93–2; Guptill 13.2–2–37–3.

New Zealand

T. G. McIntosh c Kamran Akmal b Danish Kaneria	74	– not out	23
B. J. Watling c Umar Akmal b Mohammad Asif	18	– not out	60
M. J. Guptill lbw b Danish Kaneria	13		
L. R. P. L. Taylor c Mohammad Yousuf b Danish Kaneria	21		
D. R. Flynn c Kamran Akmal b Danish Kaneria	5		
*D. L. Vettori c Umar Akmal b Mohammad Asif	134		
†B. B. McCullum c Faisal Iqbal b Umar Gul	89		
D. R. Tuffey not out	80		
T. G. Southee lbw b Danish Kaneria	0		
I. E. O'Brien st Kamran Akmal b Danish Kaneria	19		
C. S. Martin lbw b Danish Kaneria	0		
B 8, l-b 4, w 2, n-b 4	18	B 2, l-b 1, n-b 4	7

1/60 (2) 2/82 (3) 3/118 (4)   (139 overs) 471   (no wkt, 19 overs) 90
4/136 (1) 5/145 (5) 6/321 (7)
7/408 (6) 8/409 (9) 9/471 (10) 10/471 (11)

Mohammad Aamer 22–6–74–0; Mohammad Asif 31–10–103–2; Umar Gul 33–5–114–1; Danish Kaneria 53–10–168–7. *Second Innings*—Mohammad Asif 5–0–15–0; Mohammad Aamer 6–1–27–0; Danish Kaneria 5–0–21–0; Umar Gul 3–0–24–0.

Umpires: B. R. Doctrove and R. E. Koertzen.
Third umpire: S. J. A. Taufel.   Referee: A. G. Hurst.

ENGLAND LIONS IN NEW ZEALAND, 2008-09

CHARLES RANDALL

A-Team Test matches (2): New Zealand A 0, England Lions 0
One-day matches (2): New Zealand A 2, England Lions 0
Twenty20 match (1): New Zealand A 1, England Lions 0

The value of the England A tour to New Zealand under the captaincy of Robert Key was belatedly made apparent in the following 2009 season at home, when Jonathan Trott scored a century on his Test debut at The Oval to help win the Ashes.

Trott, well known in New Zealand for a successful season with Otago in 2005-06, showed impressive all-round form for the Lions, though if the players assumed they would stand or fall by their figures, Samit Patel came in for a rude shock. His figure was too big for his own good.

Patel was prevented from joining the England one-day series in the West Indies because he failed to meet basic fitness tests. He was publicly admonished in a statement from the ECB, and his tour colleague Gareth Batty was sent in his place. This humiliation was regrettable because when the news broke Patel had just hit a magnificent century in the four-day match against New Zealand A at Queenstown. Patel himself felt the decision to be unjustified, though all he could say publicly was that he would work harder. His Championship runs for Nottinghamshire dried up in the following summer, as he scored just four fifties.

Trott's advance and the subsequent introduction of Joe Denly to the England one-day side gave the Lions tour some justification. Some benefit simply had to be seen in order to save face: in a top-heavy party, no fewer than eight management and coaching staff travelled to New Zealand for at least the first few weeks, all for the benefit of 15 players. In addition, the former Australia coach John Buchanan flew over from Queensland as a consultant for the first couple of days.

The most impressive bowler proved to be the accurate Mark Davies, such a consistent wicket-taker for Durham. He caused more problems on the slowish pitches than the faster, more direct Test men Sajid Mahmood and Liam Plunkett. Behind the stumps, Ben Scott relished his chance to play every match after the early departure of Steve Davies to the West Indies. Key, while an authoritative leader, failed to drive home his Test case in the way Trott did. Stephen Moore and especially Luke Wright advanced their batting reputations significantly.

The two four-day matches against New Zealand A at Queenstown and Christchurch resulted in draws full of interest, but the depleted Lions were outclassed in the two one-dayers at Palmerston North and the 20-over finale at New Plymouth. Even the presence of Graham Napier, a replacement already successful in New Zealand with Wellington, could not lift their performances.

The Events Centre ground at Queenstown near Lake Wakatipu made a deep impression on the players, as with all visiting teams, because the sawtooth crags of the Remarkables mountain range provided such an awe-inspiring backdrop. The tour party landed in a small plane at the adjacent Frankton airport, having had a low-level first sight of the cricket ground. Here was the country's bungee-jumping and rapids-shooting capital, activities not permitted for the cricketers, in theory at least.

New Zealand A, coached by Mark O'Neill, son of the former Australia batsman Norm, proved hard to crack, with the captain Jamie How carrying his bat for 190 at Queenstown after Trott's anchoring century and Patel's more exciting 101 for the Lions. The second four-dayer at Lincoln University ended in an unlikely draw thanks to a century for the New Zealanders by their so-called invisible man, Iain Robertson, who took no part in the series until flourishing as a late substitute on the final windswept afternoon. A mature hundred by Wright had put the Lions in charge.

Davies and Wright had to rest ankle injuries for the one-day matches, and their absence was most keenly felt in the 20-over game, a thumping 84-run defeat at Pukekura Park in front of 2,000 spectators.

ENGLAND LIONS TOURING PARTY

R. W. T. Key (Kent) (*captain*), G. J. Batty (Worcestershire), M. Davies (Durham), L. A. Dawson (Hampshire), J. L. Denly (Kent), R. H. Joseph (Kent), S. I. Mahmood (Lancashire), S. C. Moore (Worcestershire), E. J. G. Morgan (Middlesex), G. R. Napier (Essex), S. R. Patel (Nottinghamshire), L. E. Plunkett (Durham), B. J. M. Scott (Middlesex), I. J. L. Trott (Warwickshire), L. J. Wright (Sussex).

R. S. Bopara (Essex), S. M. Davies (Worcestershire) and A. Khan (Kent) were promoted to the senior England party in the West Indies within the first week. T. R. Ambrose (Warwickshire), originally due to join the Lions after the Tests, remained in the Caribbean. Batty left for the senior tour after the second four-day game. The replacements were Joseph for the full tour, and Napier and Dawson for the one-day series.

Coach: D. Parsons. *Manager:* G. A. M. Jackson. *Assistant coaches:* K. J. Shine, D. F. Hills, R. G. Halsall. *Media relations manager:* M. Ward. *Physiotherapist:* S. McCaig. *Physiologist:* M. Spivey.

Note: Matches in this section which were not first-class are signified by a dagger.

†At Bert Sutcliffe Oval, Lincoln, February 22, 23, 2009. **Drawn.** Toss: England Lions. **New Zealand Emerging Players 321-7 dec** (T. G. McIntosh 43, J. M. Brodie 124, S. R. Allen 35; I. J. L. Trott 3-31); **England Lions 277** (S. C. Moore 75, R. W. T. Key 31, E. J. G. Morgan 31, B. J. M. Scott 53*, G. J. Batty 35; T. T. Davis 3-61).

Both sides chose 12 players, of whom 11 could bat and 11 field. Jonathan Trott showed useful ability with his part-time seam bowling, though the Lions were surprised by the tenacity of the Wellington left-hander Josh Brodie. An intriguing scorebook entry failed to materialise when a skyed chance from Te Ahu Davis was dropped by Steve Davies off Mark Davies.

†At Bert Sutcliffe Oval, Lincoln, February 25, 26, 2009. **Drawn.** Toss: England Lions. **England Lions 278** (S. C. Moore 54, S. R. Patel 31, E. J. G. Morgan 38, G. J. Batty 66; M. J. McClenaghan 5-36, L. J. Shaw 3-71) and **86-2** (I. J. L. Trott 41*, S. R. Patel 41*); **New Zealand Emerging Players 277** (J. M. Brodie 57, B. M. K. Patton 30, G. R. Hay 60*; S. I. Mahmood 3-58, L. E. Plunkett 4-76).

Both sides chose 13 players, of whom 11 could bat and 11 field. A last-wicket stand of 64 by Gareth Batty and Sajid Mahmood bolstered the Lions total, and Mahmood ran out the last man Nick Beard to give them a first-innings "victory" by one run. There was time left for Joe Denly to be bowled by the left-armer Mitchell McClenaghan for his second first-over duck of the game.

NEW ZEALAND A v ENGLAND LIONS

First A-Team Test

At Queenstown, March 1, 2, 3, 4, 2009. Drawn. Toss: New Zealand A.

Fielders on both sides admitted that the stunning mountain scenery could be distracting, with the temptation to gaze up at the Remarkables. Though the pitch permitted seam movement, the batsmen rather surprisingly finished on top as Trott compiled a chanceless 138 not out in six hours 20 minutes, and Patel drove his way to a 136-ball hundred. The openers Key and Moore survived competently through the crucial rain-shortened first day. Seam bowlers continued to beat the bat, but the New Zealand A captain Jamie How, who carried his bat for a career-best, ensured his side saved the game. How had been dropped from the Test side for lack of form, and he had to survive hair-raising moments against Joseph and Davies before entrenching himself for more than nine hours. Among the spectators was the former England all-rounder Dermot Reeve, coach of Central Districts.

Close of play: First day, England Lions 123-0 (Key 79, Moore 42); Second day, New Zealand A 22-1 (How 5, Ingram 12); Third day, New Zealand A 375-3 (How 161, Franklin 83).

England Lions

*R. W. T. Key c Young b McClenaghan	90	– (2) not out	66
S. C. Moore c How b Arnel	43	– (1) c Arnel b McClenaghan	11
I. J. L. Trott not out	138	– not out	75
S. R. Patel c Ingram b Arnel	101		
E. J. G. Morgan b McClenaghan	18		
L. J. Wright c Young b Williamson	55		
†B. J. M. Scott not out	34		
B 4, l-b 5, w 3, n-b 2	14	L-b 2, n-b 4	6

1/130 (2) 2/140 (1)   (5 wkts dec, 133 overs) 493   1/18 (1)   (1 wkt, 41 overs) 158
3/304 (4) 4/356 (5)
5/437 (6)

G. J. Batty, L. E. Plunkett, M. Davies and R. H. Joseph did not bat.

Boult 21–3–62–0; Franklin 25–1–113–0; Arnel 27–7–56–2; McClenaghan 24–1–100–2; Woodcock 22–1–90–0; Williamson 14–0–63–1. *Second Innings*—Franklin 9–0–33–0; McClenaghan 8–0–35–1; Arnel 12–0–38–0; Woodcock 9–2–35–0; Williamson 3–0–15–0.

New Zealand A

T. G. McIntosh c Patel b Davies	3	B. J. Arnel b Wright	0
*J. M. How not out	190	T. A. Boult c Scott b Joseph	8
P. J. Ingram c Scott b Davies	73	B. J. Watling absent hurt	
K. S. Williamson b Batty	22	L-b 5, w 11, n-b 18	34
J. E. C. Franklin c Moore b Plunkett	92		
†R. A. Young c Joseph b Davies	1	1/4 (1) 2/181 (3) 3/236 (4) (133.2 overs)	430
L. J. Woodcock c Morgan b Davies	6	4/385 (5) 5/386 (6) 6/392 (7)	
M. J. McClenaghan b Batty	1	7/399 (8) 8/400 (9) 9/430 (10)	

Joseph 17.2–4–67–1; Davies 29–13–54–4; Plunkett 26–2–96–1; Wright 21–2–83–1; Batty 26–7–78–2; Trott 7–3–21–0; Patel 7–1–26–0.

Umpires: C. B. Gaffaney and D. M. Quested.

NEW ZEALAND A v ENGLAND LIONS

Second A-Team Test

At Bert Sutcliffe Oval, Lincoln, March 7, 8, 9, 10, 2009. Drawn. Toss: New Zealand A.

England Lions walked off the Bert Sutcliffe Oval with a mixture of emotions – angry disappointment, bafflement and admiration – after they had been denied a seemingly certain win by

Iain Robertson's supreme 110-ball century from No. 8. The local fringe-Canterbury batsman had been drafted in for the final afternoon when all-rounder Ewen Thompson was unexpectedly called up for New Zealand's one-day series against India. Six wickets down with 47 overs remaining, all looked lost for the outplayed New Zealanders when Robertson arrived at the crease with only one first-class hundred to his name. The tension reached its peak as the last pair survived the final 20 balls. Splendidly fluent innings of 69 and 105 by Wright had guaranteed Lions dominance, though an ankle injury to Davies blunted their attack.

Close of play: First day, England Lions 331-9 (Mahmood 40, Davies 5); Second day, England Lions 56-0 (Moore 29, Key 25); Third day, New Zealand A 72-1 (Redmond 27, Flynn 28).

England Lions

S. C. Moore c Redmond b Thompson	22	–	c Young b Franklin	41
*R. W. T. Key c Young b Franklin	4	–	lbw b Arnel	38
I. J. L. Trott c Flynn b Thompson	7	–	c Williamson b Thompson	51
S. R. Patel c Young b Arnel	64	–	c and b Thompson	16
J. L. Denly c B. P. Martin b Arnel	12	–	b B. P. Martin	7
L. J. Wright lbw b Arnel	69	–	c Redmond b B. P. Martin	105
†B. J. M. Scott c Williamson b B. P. Martin	1	–	b Franklin	47
G. J. Batty b Thompson	64	–	c Young b Franklin	2
L. E. Plunkett b C. S. Martin	29	–	c Williamson b Arnel	22
S. I. Mahmood b Thompson	52	–	not out	7
M. Davies not out	6			
B 2, l-b 6, n-b 8	16		B 1, l-b 8, w 4, n-b 4	17
	346		(9 wkts dec, 89 overs)	353

1/8 (2) 2/24 (3) 3/51 (1) 4/103 (5) (93.4 overs) 346   1/82 (2) (9 wkts dec, 89 overs) 353
5/112 (4) 6/154 (7) 7/219 (6)   2/102 (1) 3/149 (4)
8/276 (8) 9/299 (9) 10/346 (10)   4/162 (5) 5/165 (3) 6/282 (7)
7/291 (8) 8/342 (9) 9/353 (6)

C. S. Martin 19–4–58–1; Franklin 16–2–54–1; Thompson 18.4–2–98–4; B. P. Martin 17–1–63–1; Arnel 20–8–47–3; Williamson 3–0–18–0. *Second Innings*—C. S. Martin 16–2–64–0; Thompson 14–1–72–2; Arnel 16–5–39–2; Franklin 16–2–56–3; B. P. Martin 27–2–113–2.

New Zealand A

A. J. Redmond c Wright b Davies	0	–	lbw b Plunkett	55
*J. M. How c Mahmood b Davies	4	–	lbw b Davies	8
D. R. Flynn c Batty b Plunkett	33	–	c Moore b Plunkett	45
P. G. Fulton c Scott b Davies	9	–	c Trott b Batty	45
K. S. Williamson lbw b Davies	35	–	c Scott b Mahmood	48
J. E. C. Franklin c Key b Davies	2	–	c Key b Mahmood	1
†R. A. Young b Batty	71	–	b Trott	59
E. P. Thompson lbw b Batty	60			
B. P. Martin c Trott b Mahmood	0	–	c Patel b Mahmood	0
B. J. Arnel lbw b Mahmood	0	–	lbw b Trott	5
C. S. Martin not out	0	–	not out	0
I. A. Robertson (did not bat)		–	(8) not out	107
B 5, l-b 8, w 2, n-b 14	29		L-b 19, w 1	20
	243		(9 wkts, 109 overs)	393

1/1 (1) 2/27 (2) 3/43 (4) 4/57 (3) (59.4 overs) 243   1/15 (2) (9 wkts, 109 overs) 393
5/59 (6) 6/142 (5) 7/225 (7)   2/107 (1) 3/124 (3)
8/226 (9) 9/226 (10) 10/243 (8)   4/211 (4) 5/217 (6) 6/223 (4)
7/370 (7) 8/371 (9) 9/393 (10)

Robertson replaced Thompson, who had been called up by New Zealand.

Mahmood 16–2–77–2; Davies 13–2–47–4; Plunkett 8–2–23–1; Trott 1–0–1–0; Wright 7–0–33–0; Batty 14.4–4–49–3. *Second Innings*—Davies 13–1–59–1; Mahmood 28–4–118–3; Plunkett 21–4–78–2; Trott 16.5–5–33–2; Batty 24–6–77–1; Patel 3–0–7–0; Wright 4–2–2–0.

Umpires: E. J. Gray and T. J. Parlane.

†At Palmerston North, March 13, 14, 2009. **New Zealand A won by 35 runs.** Toss: England Lions. **New Zealand A 373-6** (50 overs) (P. J. Ingram 135, J. A. H. Marshall 34, S. L. Stewart 59, N. L. McCullum 50*, B. J. Diamanti 39*; G. R. Napier 3-74); **England Lions 338** (48.1 overs) (R. W. T. Key 44, I. J. L. Trott 94, E. J. G. Morgan 74, G. R. Napier 77; M. J. Mason 3-61, B. J. Diamanti 3-74).

An innings of 77 in 41 balls by Graham Napier led a lively reply to a formidable total. Jonathan Trott's 94 took 97 balls and Eoin Morgan's 74 only 60, but the damage had been done. The mature New Zealanders, captained by Craig Cumming, pulverised a weakened Lions attack, with Robbie Joseph conceding 89 off his ten overs. Rain ruled out any play on the scheduled day, but the game was rearranged.

†At Palmerston North, March 16, 2009. **New Zealand A won by six wickets.** Toss: England Lions. **England Lions 284-9** (50 overs) (J. L. Denly 68, I. J. L. Trott 48, B. J. M. Scott 31); **New Zealand A 285-4** (46.1 overs) (P. J. Ingram 38, J. A. H. Marshall 125*, G. J. Hopkins 66*).

New Zealand won with almost four overs spare, taking the one-day series 2–0. Joe Denly scored 68 off 78 balls, his only significant innings of the tour, but too many batsmen gave up their wickets. The seemingly impressive total of 284 proved nowhere near enough as Jamie Marshall's 125 off 112 balls secured a comfortable New Zealand win.

†At New Plymouth, March 19, 2009. **New Zealand A won by 84 runs.** Toss: New Zealand A. **New Zealand A 227-6** (20 overs) (S. L. Stewart 88*, G. J. Hopkins 41); **England Lions 143** (16.4 overs) (S. R. Patel 64; E. P. Thompson 3-23).

The narrow Pukekara Park, always full of runs, provided a humiliating send-off for the Lions as they conceded 227 off their 20 overs in front of a 2,000 crowd. Shanan Stewart hoisted seven sixes in his 88 from 39 balls. Only Samit Patel, with 64 from 36, emerged with credit in a shambolic Lions reply that featured the early run-outs of openers Joe Denly and Rob Key.

DOMESTIC CRICKET IN NEW ZEALAND, 2008-09

Don Cameron

A curious feature of the southern summer of 2008-09 was the prominence of a man who never played a first-class match. In 2007, fast bowler Shane Bond had gained clearance from New Zealand Cricket to play in the unofficial Indian Cricket League, only to have it withdrawn after heavy pressure from the Indian board on the ICC. Fulfilling his ICL agreement meant Bond was banned from the New Zealand team, and he also lost his first-class contract with Canterbury as he could not guarantee his availability for the full programme.

He did, however, appear in most of Canterbury's 50-over and Twenty20 games, looking the highly efficient wicket-taking technician of his glorious past. Then the good news came: an amnesty for ICL players. There was a joyful surge in the mood of New Zealand cricket as Bond was quickly readmitted to NZC's official contract list. Then the bad news: Bond announced his retirement from Test cricket because of unceasing injuries.

The season witnessed a continuing improvement in playing and practice facilities. Whangarei has a fine new ground at Okara Park, whose pavilion is a twin-towered facsimile of Lord's. Hamilton's Seddon Park is now a splendid Test-quality ground. Wellington already has established Test and one-day venues, and McLean Park in Napier will have new stands built for the 2011 Rugby World Cup. The downside of that tournament is that rebuilding at Eden Park in Auckland and Lancaster Park in Christchurch has downgraded first-class cricket facilities, though the rebuilt Eden Park will suit one-day and Twenty20 internationals. The University Oval in Dunedin has a pitch of Test quality, but the outfield will not be of proper dimensions until a solid blockhouse at the east end is removed.

Rebecca Naden, PA Photos

Mathew Sinclair

Domestic pitches overwhelmingly favoured batsmen in 2008-09, with 62 centuries in the first-class State Championship, up from 37 the previous season, though the number of matches remained the same at 25. There were eight totals over 500 (compared with one in 2007-08), and only seven all-out totals under 200.

State Championship winners **Auckland** passed 500 three times – four including a game against the West Indians. They were almost unstoppable in March, when a run of three wins was ended only by a high-scoring draw against **Central Districts**, when Auckland's 662 for five was the sixth-highest total on New Zealand soil. Central Districts had inflicted their only defeat, in November. But when they met for a third time, in the final, Central Districts were bowled out cheaply in the final's first innings and, despite a recovery, failed to halt Auckland's charge to the title.

Central Districts did have the tournament's two leading run-scorers, Mathew Sinclair (also the top scorer in the 50-over Shield and second-highest in the Twenty20, and winner of the inaugural award for the domestic season's Most Valuable Player) and Peter Ingram; both passed 800 runs. Auckland could claim the three most successful bowlers, Daryl Tuffey, Lance Shaw and leg-spinner Tarun Nethula, who took 81 wickets between them.

Wellington's first-class campaign fell away after they lost James Franklin to international duties; he scored 631 at 157 in only four games. **Northern Districts** found a potential star in 18-year-old Kane Williamson, who contributed 707 at 54 in the four-day tournament and 320 at 45 to help them win the State Shield. Southern hearts were happy when **Otago** were declared Twenty20 champions as league-leaders when the final was washed out.

The previous season's first-class title-holders, **Canterbury**, finished bottom, without a win. Their only success came when their women won the 50-over final against Wellington, who beat them in the Twenty20 final the following day.

NZC were boosted by a $NZ50m Sony contract at the start of the season, but the State Insurance company which had sponsored cricket since 2001 decided not to renew. The 2009-10 season began with no sponsor for the first-class competition, which reverted to its traditional name, the Plunket Shield.

FIRST-CLASS AVERAGES, 2008-09

BATTING

(Qualification: 500 runs)

	M	I	NO	R	HS	100s	Avge	Ct/St
G. J. Hopkins (*Auckland*)	8	11	4	554	132*	3	79.14	23/2
†J. D. Ryder (*New Zealand*)	5	8	1	532	201	2	76.00	5
M. S. Sinclair (*Central Districts*)	9	15	3	904	164	4	75.33	18
C. D. Cumming (*Otago*)	7	12	0	784	173	4	65.33	2
P. J. Ingram (*Central Districts & NZ A*)	9	15	0	957	247	2	63.80	5
†J. E. C. Franklin (*Wellington, NZ & NZ A*)	11	16	2	865	219	3	61.78	4
J. G. Myburgh (*Canterbury*)	7	14	2	739	199	3	61.58	6
M. H. W. Papps (*Canterbury*)	7	14	2	719	128	3	59.91	5
M. D. Bell (*Wellington*)	8	11	0	591	146	3	53.72	6
†B. M. K. Patton (*Central Districts*)	7	12	2	521	142	2	52.10	5
C. de Grandhomme (*Auckland*)	10	14	3	566	104	2	51.45	13
K. S. Williamson (*Northern Districts & NZ A*)	9	16	0	812	111	2	50.75	12
N. T. Broom (*Otago*)	7	12	2	501	140*	1	50.10	4
R. A. Young (*Auckland & New Zealand A*)	11	16	1	749	100*	2	49.93	17
R. A. Jones (*Auckland*)	10	15	0	703	201	3	46.86	3
M. E. Parlane (*Northern Districts*)	8	16	3	599	103	1	46.07	5
P. G. Fulton (*Canterbury & New Zealand A*)	6	12	0	536	122	1	44.66	4
†T. G. McIntosh (*Auckland, NZ & NZ A*)	12	19	1	792	191	3	44.00	9
J. M. How (*N. Zealand, NZ A & C. Districts*)	8	14	2	513	190*	2	42.75	10

† *Left-handed batsman.*

BOWLING

(Qualification: 15 wickets, average 40.00)

	Style	O	M	R	W	BB	5W/i	Avge
Harbhajan Singh (*India*)	OB	147.4	28	342	16	6-63	1	21.37
D. R. Tuffey (*Auckland*)	RFM	267.1	86	604	27	6-33	1	22.37
A. M. Ellis (*Canterbury*)	RFM	201.2	66	547	23	4-39	0	23.78
L. J. Shaw (*Auckland*)	RFM	180.2	26	666	28	5-59	1	23.78
C. de Grandhomme (*Auckland*)	RFM	185	49	516	21	3-12	0	24.57
B. J. Arnel (*Northern Districts & NZ A*)	RFM	219.4	72	522	20	4-38	0	26.10
H. K. Bennett (*Canterbury*)	RFM	206.5	40	761	26	4-48	0	29.26
M. J. Harvie (*Otago*)	RFM	183.5	41	589	19	4-73	0	31.00
E. P. Thompson (*Central Districts & NZ A*)	LFM	306	72	905	29	5-57	1	31.20
N. Wagner (*Otago*)	LFM	219	42	700	21	3-32	0	33.33
T. G. Southee (*Northern Districts & NZ*)	RFM	172	48	545	16	5-43	1	34.06
A. J. McKay (*Auckland*)	LFM	229.2	37	790	23	4-37	0	34.34
D. L. Vettori (*New Zealand*)	SLA	235.4	64	584	17	6-56	1	34.35
G. W. Aldridge (*Northern Districts*)	RFM	146.4	26	525	15	3-46	0	35.00
J. S. Patel (*Wellington & New Zealand*)	OB	290	68	751	21	5-65	2	35.76
D. J. Bowden (*Wellington*)	LFM	161.1	20	595	16	4-55	0	37.18
N. L. McCullum (*Otago*)	OB	270.3	64	724	19	3-46	0	38.10
T. S. Nethula (*Auckland*)	LB	299.2	29	1,127	29	4-39	0	38.86
I. E. O'Brien (*New Zealand*)	RFM	190.5	42	663	17	6-75	1	39.00

Full scores of the 2008-09 New Zealand season can be found at www.cricinfo.com/db/ARCHIVE/
2008-09/NZ_LOCAL/, www.cricketarchive.co.uk/Archive/Seasons/2008-09_NZ.html and in the
ACS Overseas First-Class Annual 2009.

STATE CHAMPIONSHIP, 2008-09

	Played	Won	Lost	Drawn	1st-inns points	Points	Net avge runs per wkt
Auckland	8	4	1	3	13	37	11.57
Central Districts	8	4	0	4	7	31	0.52
Wellington	8	2	1	5	10	22	10.03
Northern Districts	8	2	4	2	6	18	−4.96
Otago	8	0	2	6	8	8	−8.44
Canterbury	8	0	4	4	4	4	−4.76

*Teams played each other once in a round robin (five matches each); then the top three from the
2007-08 table played each of the bottom three a second time (three matches each).*

Final: Auckland beat Central Districts by five wickets.

*Outright win = 6 pts; lead on first innings = 2 pts; no result or tie on first innings = 1 pt each.
Net average runs per wicket is calculated by subtracting average runs conceded per wicket from
average runs scored per wicket.*

At MainPower Oval, Rangiora, November 10, 11, 12, 13, 2008. **Auckland won by 73 runs.** Toss:
Canterbury. **Auckland 398** (T. G. McIntosh 140, R. A. Young 100) **and 175** (B. C. Hiini 4-47);
Canterbury 169 (A. J. McKay 4-37) **and 331** (P. G. Fulton 64, J. G. Myburgh 67, C. J. Anderson
88*). Auckland 8 pts.
   Auckland made a winning start to their campaign, as defending champions Canterbury fell short
of a 405-run target. Johann Myburgh made five catches in the field in Auckland's second innings.

At Nelson Park, Napier, November 17, 18, 19, 20, 2008. **Central Districts won by 138 runs.** Toss:
Auckland. **Central Districts 213** (B. M. K. Patton 57) **and 335** (B. M. K. Patton 142, T. I. Weston
66, M. S. Sinclair 58; A. J. McKay 4-57); **Auckland 207** (S. J. Croft 59; E. P. Thompson 5-57) **and
203** (S. B. Styris 71). *Central Districts 8 pts.*

Auckland crashed back to earth when Ewen Thompson reduced them to 42-6, and a maiden century from Brad Patton helped Central Districts to victory. Central Districts' 18-year-old seamer Doug Bracewell, son of Test bowler Brendon and nephew of John (who was about to step down as New Zealand coach), became the fifth member of his family to play first-class cricket.

At University Oval, Dunedin, November 17, 18, 19, 20, 2008. **Drawn.** Toss: Otago. **Northern Districts 275** (K. S. Williamson 82) **and 181-7; Otago 277-9 dec** (C. D. Cumming 85, N. T. Broom 54; T. A. Boult 5-58). *Otago 2 pts.*

At Basin Reserve, Wellington, November 17, 18, 19, 20, 2008. **Wellington won by an innings and 42 runs.** Toss: Wellington. **Wellington 428-8 dec** (M. D. Bell 146, J. E. C. Franklin 69, L. J. Woodcock 58*); **Canterbury 162 and 224** (L. J. Woodcock 4-40). *Wellington 8 pts.*
    Canterbury lost again after following on against Wellington, the team they beat in the previous season's final.

At Eden Park Outer Oval, Auckland, November 24, 25, 26, 27, 2008. **Drawn.** Toss: Auckland. **Wellington 533-5 dec** (M. D. Bell 122, J. E. C. Franklin 219, L. J. Woodcock 102*); **Auckland 441-7** (T. G. McIntosh 191, R. A. Jones 69; G. R. Napier 4-52). *Auckland 1 pt, Wellington 1 pt.*
    After a first-day washout, James Franklin scored his second double-hundred, a career-best, with eight sixes and 28 fours in 290 balls. He added 282 for Wellington's fifth wicket with Luke Woodcock, mostly on the extended third day which saw 419 runs scored and only Franklin dismissed.

At Seddon Park, Hamilton, November 24, 25, 26, 27, 2008. **Central Districts won by eight wickets.** Toss: Central Districts. **Northern Districts 325** (C. J. Merchant 89, K. S. Williamson 73, G. W. Aldridge 73*) **and 249** (B. J. Watling 111); **Central Districts 479-9 dec** (P. J. Ingram 247, M. S. Sinclair 101; B. P. Martin 4-145) **and 99-2.** *Central Districts 8 pts.*
    Peter Ingram scored a maiden double-hundred, with 31 fours and four sixes. His 247 was the highest individual score for Central Districts, beating 243 by Mathew Sinclair the previous season; Sinclair helped him add 264 for the third wicket to set up their second straight win.*

At Queenstown Events Centre, Queenstown, November 24, 25, 26, 27, 2008. **Drawn.** Toss: Otago. **Otago 352** (S. B. Haig 52, N. T. Broom 140*; L. M. Burtt 5-119) **and 113-5 dec; Canterbury 174-5 dec** (M. H. W. Papps 53) **and 285-7** (A. M. Ellis 71, S. L. Stewart 69*). *Otago 2 pts.*
    Despite 69 in 68 balls from Shanan Stewart, Canterbury finished seven runs short of a target of 292.*

At Basin Reserve, Wellington, December 1, 2, 3, 4, 2008. **Wellington won by an innings and 12 runs.** Toss: Northern Districts. **Northern Districts 310** (G. W. Aldridge 67*; M. R. Gillespie 4-81) **and 198** (J. A. H. Marshall 105*; M. R. Gillespie 4-43); **Wellington 520-7 dec** (J. M. Brodie 110, G. D. Elliott 78, J. E. C. Franklin 160, L. J. Woodcock 53, C. J. Nevin 71*). *Wellington 8 pts.*
    James Franklin added 121 for Wellington's sixth wicket with Luke Woodcock followed by 164 for the seventh with Chris Nevin. Northern Districts wicketkeeper Peter McGlashan did not concede a bye in Wellington's total of 520-7.

At McLean Park, Napier, December 5, 6, 7, 8, 2008. **Central Districts won by eight wickets.** Toss: Central Districts. **Otago 357** (C. D. Cumming 133, N. T. Broom 60; E. P. Thompson 4-64) **and 281** (G. R. Todd 74, D. C. de Boorder 73*); **Central Districts 378** (P. J. Ingram 51, M. S. Sinclair 108; M. J. Harvie 4-73) **and 261-2** (B. M. K. Patton 100*, M. S. Sinclair 52*). *Central Districts 8 pts.*

At Seddon Park, Hamilton, December 12, 13, 14, 15, 2008. **Drawn.** Toss: Northern Districts. **Northern Districts 430** (K. S. Williamson 98, J. A. F. Yovich 65, P. D. McGlashan 91, G. W. Aldridge 75) **and 152-5 dec** (J. G. Myburgh 61) **dec; Canterbury 265** (P. G. Fulton 84, J. G. Myburgh 61) **and 294-8** (T. D. Astle 101, P. G. Fulton 56). *Northern Districts 2 pts.*
    In Northern Districts' first innings, Peter McGlashan and Graeme Aldridge put on 163 for the eighth wicket. Canterbury reached 238-2 chasing 318 but could not complete the task, and entered the midsummer break without a single point.

At Basin Reserve, Wellington, December 12, 13, 14, 15, 2008. **Drawn.** Toss: Wellington. **Central Districts 523** (M. S. Sinclair 164, B. B. J. Griggs 143); **Wellington 376-7** (M. D. Bell 75, N. R. Parlane 54, G. D. Elliott 63, L. J. Woodcock 59). *Wellington 1 pt, Central Districts 1 pt.*

Mathew Sinclair scored his third hundred in successive matches and Bevan Griggs made a career-best as they added 235 for Central Districts' sixth wicket in a top-of-the-table clash.

At Eden Park Outer Oval, Auckland, December 13, 14, 15, 16, 2008. **Drawn.** Toss: Auckland. **Otago 418** (C. D. Cumming 105, A. J. Redmond 50, G. R. Todd 98, N. T. Broom 60) **and 343-7** (C. D. Cumming 58, S. B. Haig 108, D. C. de Boorder 68*; T. S. Nethula 4-100); **Auckland 430-8 dec** (M. J. Guptill 148, R. A. Young 54, S. B. Styris 94, S. J. Croft 53; M. J. Harvie 4-89). *Auckland 2 pts.*

Martin Guptill scored a maiden hundred in his only State Championship innings of the season.

At MainPower Oval, Rangiora, March 6, 7, 8, 9, 2009. **Drawn.** Toss: Canterbury. **Canterbury 543** (M. H. W. Papps 127, R. Dravid 102, J. G. Myburgh 107, C. F. K. van Wyk 92; B. J. Diamanti 5-74) **and 19-3; Central Districts 263** (G. H. Worker 50, M. S. Sinclair 56; A. M. Ellis 4-39) **and 468-6 dec** (T. I. Weston 78, G. R. Hay 131*, B. J. Diamanti 135*). *Canterbury 2 pts.*

Rahul Dravid, making a one-off appearance as a warm-up for India's Test series with New Zealand, was one of three century-makers for Canterbury on the first day, with Kruger van Wyk falling just short of becoming a fourth. Central Districts followed on 280 behind and lost six wickets clearing the deficit, but were rescued by Greg Hay and Brendon Diamanti, who added 205 for the seventh wicket. Left-arm fast bowler Mitchell McClenaghan took a hat-trick before Canterbury had a run on the board in their brief second innings.*

At Cobham Oval (New), Whangarei, March 6, 7, 8, 9, 2009. **Auckland won by 22 runs.** Toss: Auckland. **Auckland 388** (S. B. Styris 95, C. de Grandhomme 63) **and 259** (G. J. Hopkins 100, D. R. Tuffey 53; J. J. Boult 4-78); **Northern Districts 268** (B. S. Wilson 62, M. E. Parlane 75; T. S. Nethula 4-72) **and 246.** *Auckland 8 pts.*

This was the first first-class match at the new Cobham Oval, which had superseded the old ground of the same name. In the second innings, Gareth Hopkins and Daryl Tuffey added 106 for the ninth wicket to give Auckland what proved a decisive advantage.

At University Oval, Dunedin, March 6, 7, 8, 9, 2009. **Drawn.** Toss: Wellington. **Otago 174** (M. Burns 4-41) **and 286** (G. R. Todd 73; L. J. Woodcock 4-70); **Wellington 139** (W. C. McSkimming 4-40) **and 283-6** (N. R. Parlane 59, B. J. Crook 101*, L. J. Woodcock 69). *Otago 2 pts.*

At Village Green, Christchurch, March 13, 14, 15, 16, 2009. **Northern Districts won by six wickets.** Toss: Northern Districts. **Canterbury 246** (J. G. Myburgh 50, I. A. Robertson 61, C. F. K. van Wyk 67; T. G. Southee 5-43, B. J. Arnel 4-38) **and 309** (M. H. W. Papps 128, P. G. Fulton 122; K. S. Williamson 5-75); **Northern Districts 383** (B. S. Wilson 109, D. R. Flynn 104, K. S. Williamson 53) **and 173-4.** *Northern Districts 8 pts.*

In Northern Districts' first innings, Brad Wilson and Daniel Flynn put on 209 for the second wicket; when Canterbury batted again, Michael Papps and Peter Fulton, who hit eight sixes and 12 fours in 196 balls, countered with 259 for their third wicket. But their last eight wickets fell for 42, and Northern Districts won with nearly two sessions to spare.

At McLean Park, Napier, March 13, 14, 15, 16, 2009. **Drawn.** Toss: Wellington. **Wellington 410** (N. R. Parlane 59, J. E. C. Franklin 76, C. J. Nevin 134) **and 299-5 dec** (M. D. Bell 60, J. E. C. Franklin 107*); **Central Districts 296** (M. Vijay 93, M. S. Sinclair 62; D. J. Bowden 4-55) **and 174-1** (J. M. How 101*, G. H. Worker 63*). *Wellington 2 pts.*

Another of the Indian tourists seeking match practice, Murali Vijay, was the leading scorer in Central Districts' first innings.

At Queenstown Events Centre, Queenstown, March 13, 14, 15, 2009. **Auckland won by an innings and 84 runs.** Toss: Auckland. **Otago 210** (L. J. Morgan 54; D. R. Tuffey 4-32, T. S. Nethula 4-39) **and 240** (N. T. Broom 79; A. J. McKay 4-58); **Auckland 534-7 dec** (T. G. McIntosh 74, R. A. Jones 102, A. K. Kitchen 125, R. A. Young 100*). *Auckland 8 pts.*

Three centuries helped Auckland to an innings win, which put them on top of the table.

At Eden Park Outer Oval, Auckland, March 20, 21, 22, 2009. **Auckland won by an innings and 16 runs.** Toss: Auckland. **Northern Districts 306** (K. S. Williamson 111) **and 218** (M. E. Parlane 72, K. S. Williamson 95; D. R. Tuffey 6-33); **Auckland 540** (R. A. Jones 62, A. K. Kitchen 132, R. A. Young 78, C. de Grandhomme 104; J. A. F. Yovich 4-136). *Auckland 8 pts.*

*Kane Williamson, aged 18, hit a maiden century and almost made it two in Northern Districts'
second innings, but had little support as Daryl Tuffey cleaned up with 6-33, the best return of the
tournament. Auckland's third successive win guaranteed their place in the final with a round to go.*

At Basin Reserve, Wellington, March 20, 21, 22, 23, 2009. **Drawn.** Toss: Wellington. **Otago 270**
(A. J. Redmond 76, L. J. Morgan 64; J. S. Patel 5-65) **and 257-2** (C. D. Cumming 118, G. R. Todd
94*); **Wellington 325-9 dec** (C. J. Nevin 93, D. J. Bowden 85). *Wellington 2 pts.*
*Joshua Brodie made five catches in the field in Otago's first innings. Wellington slumped to 98-6
before Chris Nevin and Dewayne Bowden added 148 to put them on the way to first-innings points.*

At Pukekura Park, New Plymouth, March 21, 22, 23, 24, 2009. **Central Districts won by three
wickets.** Toss: Canterbury. **Canterbury 493** (M. H. W. Papps 54, P. G. Fulton 64, J. G. Myburgh
199, S. L. Stewart 67; M. J. Mason 5-83) **and 169-2 dec** (M. H. W. Papps 63*, J. G. Myburgh 101*);
Central Districts 215 (E. P. Thompson 51; L. M. Burtt 4-48, H. K. Bennett 4-48) **and 450-7** (P. J.
Ingram 166, J. M. How 93, G. H. Worker 55, T. I. Weston 89*). *Central Districts 6 pts, Canterbury
2 pts.*
*Johann Myburgh hit a century in each innings, but finished on the losing side after Central
Districts rose to the challenge set by Canterbury's declaration, which asked them to score 448 in a
day plus 20 overs. Peter Ingram batted more than six hours to bring the target in sight, and Tim
Weston finished the job. Victory secured Central Districts a place in the final.*

At Village Green, Christchurch, March 28, 29, 30, 31, 2009. **Drawn.** Toss: Otago. **Canterbury 315**
(C. F. K. van Wyk 105, R. J. McCone 102) **and 289** (M. H. W. Papps 103, P. G. Fulton 61, J. G.
Myburgh 50*); **Otago 320** (C. D. Cumming 173, A. J. Redmond 58; J. G. Myburgh 4-84). *Otago
2 pts.*
*After a first-day washout, Canterbury were 101-7 before No. 9 Ryan McCone scored 102 on first-
class debut. He hit 17 fours in 173 balls and added 167 for the eighth wicket with Kruger van Wyk.*

At Cobham Oval (New), Whangarei, March 28, 29, 30, 31, 2009. **Northern Districts won by eight
wickets.** Toss: Wellington. **Wellington 321** (M. D. Bell 100, N. R. Parlane 62, C. J. Nevin 72; B. P.
Martin 6-73) **and 289** (J. M. Brodie 56, G. D. Elliott 84); **Northern Districts 546** (B. S. Wilson 94,
M. E. Parlane 103, K. S. Williamson 100, P. McGlashan 56, B. E. Scott 55*; M. Burns 4-61) **and
65-2.** *Northern Districts 8 pts.*
*Following his 111 and 95 in the previous game, Kane Williamson scored his second first-class
hundred to help Northern Districts reach their highest total.*

At Eden Park Outer Oval, Auckland, March 29, 30, 31, April 1, 2009. **Drawn.** Toss: Central Districts.
Auckland 662-5 dec (J. A. Raval 256, R. A. Young 74, G. J. Hopkins 132*, C. de Grandhomme
103*) **and 198-3** (R. J. Nicol 104*, G. J. Hopkins 70*); **Central Districts 318** (P. J. Ingram 54,
M. S. Sinclair 131*; M. D. Bates 4-82). *Auckland 2 pts.*
*Jeet Raval, a 20-year-old Indian-born left-handed opener, scored 256 in his third first-class match,
and only his second innings. He took ten hours three minutes, hit 43 fours and two sixes in 483 balls,
and equalled Auckland's third-highest individual score. Gareth Hopkins added 228 for Auckland's
fifth wicket with Raval and 151* for the sixth wicket with Colin de Grandhomme, who hit eight sixes and
eight fours in 92 balls. It was the fourth time Auckland had passed 500 in the season (including one
match against the West Indians). Their 662-5 dec was the sixth-highest first-class total on New
Zealand soil, and the third-highest in the domestic competition, beaten only by Canterbury's 777 v
Otago in 1996-97 and their own 693-9 dec v Canterbury in 1939-40. With both teams already
assured of their places in the final, Auckland waived the follow-on and the match was drawn.*

Final

At Bert Sutcliffe Oval, Lincoln, April 6, 7, 8, 9, 10, 2009. **Auckland won by five wickets.** Toss:
Auckland. **Central Districts 180** (L. J. Shaw 5-59) **and 349** (P. J. Ingram 90, E. P. Thompson 54*);
Auckland 342 (R. A. Jones 109, A. K. Kitchen 115) **and 188-5** (C. de Grandhomme 54*).
*Lance Shaw undermined Central Districts with a career-best 5-59 on the opening day, and
centuries from Richard Jones and Anaru Kitchen set up a first-innings lead of 162. But Central
batted far better next time, to leave a fifth-day target of 188. Despite a shaky start by the top order,
Colin de Grandhomme saw Auckland home with 54* in 59 balls.*

CHAMPIONS

Plunket Shield					
1921-22	Auckland	1954-55	Wellington	1982-83	Wellington
1922-23	Canterbury	1955-56	Canterbury	1983-84	Canterbury
1923-24	Wellington	1956-57	Wellington	1984-85	Wellington
1924-25	Otago	1957-58	Otago	1985-86	Otago
1925-26	Wellington	1958-59	Auckland	1986-87	Central Districts
1926-27	Auckland	1959-60	Canterbury	1987-88	Otago
1927-28	Wellington	1960-61	Wellington	1988-89	Auckland
1928-29	Auckland	1961-62	Wellington	1989-90	Wellington
1929-30	Wellington	1962-63	Northern Districts	1990-91	Auckland
1930-31	Canterbury	1963-64	Auckland	1991-92	{ Central Districts / Northern Districts
1931-32	Wellington	1964-65	Canterbury		
1932-33	Otago	1965-66	Wellington	1992-93	Northern Districts
1933-34	Auckland	1966-67	Central Districts	1993-94	Canterbury
1934-35	Canterbury	1967-68	Central Districts	1994-95	Auckland
1935-36	Wellington	1968-69	Auckland	1995-96	Auckland
1936-37	Auckland	1969-70	Otago	1996-97	Canterbury
1937-38	Auckland	1970-71	Central Districts	1997-98	Canterbury
1938-39	Auckland	1971-72	Otago	1998-99	Central Districts
1939-40	Auckland	1972-73	Wellington	1999-2000	Northern Districts
1940–45	No competition	1973-74	Wellington	2000-01	Wellington
1945-46	Canterbury	1974-75	Otago		
1946-47	Auckland			*State Championship*	
1947-48	Otago	*Shell Trophy*		2001-02	Auckland
1948-49	Canterbury	1975-76	Canterbury	2002-03	Auckland
1949-50	Wellington	1976-77	Otago	2003-04	Wellington
1950-51	Otago	1977-78	Auckland	2004-05	Auckland
1951-52	Canterbury	1978-79	Otago	2005-06	Central Districts
1952-53	Otago	1979-80	Northern Districts	2006-07	Northern Districts
1953-54	Central Districts	1980-81	Auckland	2007-08	Canterbury
		1981-82	Wellington	2008-09	Auckland

Auckland have won the title outright 22 times, Wellington 20, Canterbury 15, Otago 13, Central Districts 7, Northern Districts 5. Central Districts and Northern Districts also shared the title once.

Note: Matches in the following sections were not first-class.

STATE SHIELD, 2008-09

50-over league plus knockout

	Played	Won	Lost	No result	Bonus points	Points	Net run-rate
Northern Districts	10	7	3	0	1	29	0.29
Canterbury	10	5	4	1	2	24	0.17
Otago	10	4	4	2	4	24	0.57
Central Districts	10	5	5	0	2	22	−0.22
Wellington	10	4	6	0	0	16	−0.39
Auckland	10	3	6	1	0	14	−0.31

Play-off

At Village Green, Christchurch, January 28, 2009. **Otago won by eight wickets.** Toss: Otago. **Canterbury 86** (39 overs); **Otago 90-2** (14 overs).
   South African Neil Wagner reduced Canterbury to 14-3 by the ninth over, and they never recovered.

Final

At Seddon Park, Hamilton, January 31, 2009. **Northern Districts won by 49 runs.** Toss: Otago. **Northern Districts 238-9** (50 overs) (J. A. F. Yovich 78*; I. G. Butler 5-55); **Otago 189** (45.4 overs) (G. W. Aldridge 5-39).

Joseph Yovich came in at 94-5 and hit 78 in 76 balls, a one-day best. Graeme Aldridge struck twice in his first four overs, then returned to claim three in eight deliveries, including Dimitri Mascarenhas for 17 in 70 balls.*

STATE TWENTY20, 2008-09

	Played	Won	Lost	No result	Points	Net run-rate
Otago.	8	6	1	1	26	1.74
Canterbury	8	5	2	1	22	−0.02
Auckland.	8	5	2	1	22	−0.06
Wellington	8	4	3	1	18	−0.36
Central Districts	8	1	6	1	6	−0.72
Northern Districts	8	0	7	1	2	−0.73

Canterbury qualified for the final ahead of Auckland because they won their first head-to-head match (the second was abandoned).

Final

At University Oval, Dunedin, March 1, 2009. **Otago v Canterbury. Abandoned.**

Otago won the State Twenty20 title by virtue of a superior league record when the final was washed out.

PAKISTAN CRICKET, 2009

Despite everything, cricket struggles on…

OSMAN SAMIUDDIN

In shocking hindsight, it had to happen. Indeed, how had it not already happened? Cricket and life have for so long been one and the same thing in Pakistan, wrapped in such an embrace of love, disgust, hate and ecstasy, that the terrorist attacks on the Sri Lankan cricket team in Lahore on March 3, 2009, had all the morbid inevitability of death.

The two years building up to it had existed to the blasts of suicide bombs – well over 100 of them. Thousands upon thousands had been killed, including a larger-than-life former prime minister, institutions had been attacked, the economy crashed, and war raged in northern parts of the country.

Cricket paralleled it: misery piled upon misery, each time bringing the belief that it couldn't get worse; and each time it did. But on that morning the barrel

PAKISTAN IN 2009

	Played	Won	Lost	Drawn/No result
Tests	9	1	4	4
One-day internationals	20	8	12	–
Twenty20 internationals	11	9	2	–

JANUARY	3 ODIs (h) v Sri Lanka	(page 1205)
FEBRUARY MARCH	2 Tests (h) v Sri Lanka	(page 1205)
APRIL MAY	5 ODIs and 1 T20I (in UAE) v Australia	(page 1215)
JUNE JULY	World Twenty20 (in England)	(page 527)
AUGUST		
SEPTEMBER OCTOBER	Champions Trophy (in South Africa)	(page 1015)
NOVEMBER	3 ODIs and 2 T20Is (in UAE) v New Zealand	(page 1222)
DECEMBER	3 Tests (a) v New Zealand	(page 1178)
JANUARY FEBRUARY	3 Tests, 5 ODIs and 1 T20I (a) v Australia	(page 1055)

For a review of Pakistan domestic cricket from the 2008-09 season, see page 1228.

was surely scraped; country and cricket collapsed into each other, leaving one great scary heap of a mess behind. Sri Lanka's cricketers, halfway through a hideously dull Test series, were on their way to the Gaddafi Stadium from their hotel for the third day of the Second Test. As they approached Liberty Market, in up-scale Lahore, a white car cut them off at a roundabout, a few hundred yards from the entrance to the stadium.

Gunmen suddenly appeared from behind trees, some in traditional *shalwar kameez*, some in trousers and shirts. They pelted the team bus with bullets, aiming first for the tyres. The driver, Mohammad Khalil, at the urging of the Sri Lankan players, drove on and eventually made it into the stadium and safety. Lucky he did, for a rocket and grenades just missed the bus.

At the end of the attack, six security officials and two civilians were dead. Seven Sri Lankan players were hurt, mostly by shrapnel, though Thilan Samaraweera – who had just scored two consecutive double-centuries – and Tharanga Paranavitana sustained more serious injuries. The third umpire, Ahsan Raza, in a separate van following the bus, was shot, his lung and liver heavily damaged. Other officials, such as Chris Broad, Simon Taufel and Steve Davis, escaped unhurt physically, perhaps not mentally.

On TV, it all seemed eerily lifeless, an airless chamber in which went on the soundless ferocity of modern life. There were no big explosions, little visible blood or any real mayhem. The gunmen were engaged in a shootout with commandos, but all 12 soon disappeared into nearby back streets as if they owned the morning.

The fallout was ugly, and Pakistani. The PCB shed themselves swiftly of all blame, accusing Broad of lying when he said, rightly, that the security had left them for sitting ducks; even in the board's wretched history, nothing has been as shameful, not even the match-fixing crisis. The local government said they had given warnings of such an attack, and the federal government did what it always does: call for an inquiry. A circle of ineptitude and blamelessness was thus created.

But the deeper implications could not be washed away and thus, after years of teetering on the brink, international cricket finally came to an end in Pakistan. David Morgan, the ICC president, said he could not see it returning there before 2011. In any case, there had been little enough in preceding years. The 2011 World Cup, to be held jointly across India, Pakistan, Sri Lanka and Bangladesh, was taken away. The board pursued an expensive legal fight, ostensibly to keep their share of the World Cup, but actually to try to ensure that roughly US$10m could be kept, as a "hosting" fee and some more compensation. It was.

Publicly, officials such as Wasim Bari – who was appointed the PCB's chief operations officer in September, after his former Test team-mate Salim Altaf was sacked – spoke confidently of drawing up plans for international cricket to return to Pakistan. Those plans were not as nonsensical as chairman Ijaz Butt's claims, immediately after the attacks, that cricket would return within "six to nine months". But privately, everyone knew that, with war still going on, timetables were meaningless. Anything, anyone is a target, and international cricket will only return when international cricket returns.

World champions: Younis Khan (*centre*) and his triumphant team at the World Twenty20, the highlight of a traumatic year.

The real costs will emerge in coming years: cancelled tours by India, the lost World Cup, and no tours at home until 2011 – at the earliest – have left the administration near financial ruin. In 2009, estimated the PCB, they lost up to 71% of their total revenues, nearly US$125m; Butt inherited an already pillaged administration, and the austerity drive he launched thereafter was as admirable as it was necessary.

How bad are things? The board, it is believed, have been unable to buy Kookaburra balls for domestic cricket because they were too expensive. Hosting "home" series in the Middle East and in England will not be cheap either, and so working with the ICC task force to ensure ways are found to keep the board afloat has become doubly crucial. Finding ways to restart ties with India might be even more vital.

That there was an on-field aspect to Pakistan's cricket was some cause for good cheer. The team went through 2008 without playing a single Test, so managing nine in 2009 was a giant step forward, even if they only won once. Unsurprisingly, they played much of it as if unused to the format. Pakistan were on top at times in Sri Lanka and New Zealand, and even sparkled occasionally in Australia, where they have now lost their last nine Tests. Pakistan should probably have beaten both Sri Lanka and New Zealand, but too often the batting fell apart, mostly through trying to play in Tests (and 50-over matches, in which no series was won in 2009) as if it were Twenty20.

The shortest format, in fact, provided Pakistan with their brightest moment of 2009. The World Twenty20 triumph in England was, arguably, the sport's most charming, feel-good moment of the year; a team without a home, having played so little, coming together at just the right time, in just the right way, to win a world title. Briefly, after many months, an entire country smiled and rejoiced, and the format be damned.

Pakistan had four different captains in this most depressing of years, and in a way that was a comforting throwback to more successful, brighter, fractious times in the 1990s, when the captaincy seemingly changed as often as day became night. Shoaib Malik began the year as captain in all three formats, but ended it as twelfth man in the Test side… and not many complained, not even Malik. Younis Khan, brave and solid, was supposed to have been the man for it all along, and when he won the World Twenty20 title, things seemed bright.

But such is the self-defeating way in which Pakistan works that he stepped down from the post twice over the next few months, claiming the second time that he had lost command of his players. Mohammad Yousuf took up what nobody wanted, and brought calm to a mischievous dressing-room. But on the field he was timid, inert and tactically meek; what Pakistan needed was someone with Younis's gusto and Yousuf's calm. Shahid Afridi, ever the maverick, seemed to have matured and took over as the Twenty20 captain. Then he was caught biting the ball and was slapped with a ban.

Ultimately, however, the year progressed for cricket as it did for country: at every turn questions were being asked of its very existence and future. The arrivals of Umar Akmal and Mohammad Aamer allayed at least one fear: talent not only remained in Pakistan, but it would find its way to the very top. Another promising Under-19 batch, from the team that reached the final of the youth World Cup in New Zealand early in 2010, will do much the same.

How will an absence of international cricket in Pakistan play out? Cricket here had long become a lounge experience. Tests have attracted abysmal numbers for much of the last decade, especially in the bigger centres. More recently, even one-day internationals have been very poorly attended. Simply, Pakistanis experience cricket differently now – on TV sets in living-rooms – but not necessarily in any lessened or reduced way.

Domestic cricket goes on, children still take to the streets regularly with taped tennis ball in hand, and people were still getting up at ungodly hours to follow Pakistan around New Zealand and Australia. The game remains as embedded in the country's fabric as anything else and, in most places, discussion of the fortunes of the sport remains only just behind that of the political situation. Displaced it is, but alive as well, for now.

PAKISTAN v SRI LANKA, 2008-09

REVIEW BY QAMAR AHMED

Test matches (2): Pakistan 0, Sri Lanka 0
One-day internationals (3): Pakistan 1, Sri Lanka 2

The fear of terrorist attack, insurgencies and suicide bombers in a politically unstable country had already caused Australia and India to pull out of their scheduled tours of Pakistan. Tragically, it turned out to be fully justified when the Sri Lankan players were attacked by extremists before the start of the third day's play in the Lahore Test.

The series had been hastily organised after India declined to come. Some of their politicians accused Pakistan of involvement in the Mumbai terror attacks of November 2008, which killed more than 170 people (and led to the temporary suspension of England's tour of India). Friendly relations between Pakistan and Sri Lanka came to the rescue, though there was an extra hurdle to clear when Arjuna Ranatunga, the chairman of the Sri Lankan cricket board, was sacked by sports minister Gamini Lokuge just after the tour had been agreed in December. But Lokuge and president Mahinda Rajapakse soon gave it the green light, with Rajapakse declaring that "the players are sent to Pakistan as ambassadors of goodwill". It was the first international cricket played in Pakistan since the Asia Cup in July.

The tour was split into two halves, as Sri Lanka had arranged an additional one-day series with the Indians, who also found themselves with a gap in their programme after cancelling their visit to Pakistan. In January, there were three one-day internationals, which the Sri Lankans won 2–1 before going home to play India. Pakistan lost the third game so heavily that the captain, Shoaib Malik, was sacked, and Younis Khan, the preferred choice ever since Inzamam-ul-Haq stepped down in 2007, was finally persuaded to take on the job.

By the time Sri Lanka returned in February their own captain, Mahela Jayawardene, had announced that he would return to the ranks after the two Test matches. He and Thilan Samaraweera scored double-centuries in the First Test at Karachi, while Younis responded with a triple-hundred in a high-scoring draw. Like the one-day series, the match passed without any security-related incident.

As the First Test ended, however, the provincial government of Punjab was dismissed and president Asif Ali Zardari imposed federal rule through its governor. This prompted officials of the Pakistan Cricket Board to consider whether it was safe to play a Test in Punjab's troubled capital, Lahore, while agitators ruled the streets. Their decision to continue with the original schedule was to cost the country dearly.

The Sri Lankans had been promised "presidential" security by the interior ministry and the PCB, but in Lahore, Trevor Bayliss, their coach, noticed that the trucks bearing soldiers with fixed machine-guns which had flanked the team bus in Karachi had disappeared. After two days of the match, during which Samaraweera scored a second double-hundred, the bus came under attack by terrorists as it approached the ground on the third morning.

It had reached the Liberty Roundabout and was about to turn right for the Gaddafi Stadium when a rocket launcher was fired (luckily, it missed), followed by grenades and then gunfire from every direction. The shocked Sri Lankans immediately dived to the floor of the bus, but even so some of them were hit

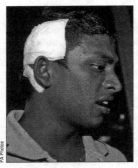

by shrapnel and bullets. The bus driver, Mehar Mohammad Khalil, had the presence of mind to drive off, and kept his foot on the accelerator until the team reached the safety of the stadium 500 metres away. He was feted as a hero and later decorated by the PCB, the Pakistan government and the Sri Lankan government, who invited him and his family to a ceremony in Colombo. But his friend Zafar Khan, who was driving the umpires' minibus, was killed instantly as a bullet lodged in his heart. Fourth umpire Ahsan Raza and liaison officer Abdul Sami Khan were wounded, but survived; a policeman managed to drive their bus away as referee Chris Broad attempted to comfort Raza, whose lung and liver had been damaged. Six policemen died, including a traffic warden.

Ajantha Mendis arrives back at Colombo airport after being injured in the Lahore terrorist attack.

Several Sri Lankan players were injured, most seriously Samaraweera, who was hit by a bullet in his left thigh, near the knee joint, and Tharanga Paranavitana, who was struck in the chest. Spinner Ajantha Mendis suffered shrapnel wounds in the head and back; there were also injuries to Jayawardene, Kumar Sangakkara, Suranga Lakmal, Thilan Thushara Mirando and assistant coach Paul Farbrace. Samaraweera and Paranavitana were rushed to the nearby Services Hospital. Then the entire party was flown back to Colombo overnight, in a chartered plane sent by the Sri Lankan president, as the tour was abandoned. All have played again.

Eyewitnesses said there were 12 gunmen involved in the attack; all of them escaped. Suspicion fell on various extremist groups, including Lashkar-e-Jhangvi, Lashkar-e-Taiba, Al-Qaeda and the Taliban; Pakistanis unwilling to believe the terrorism could be home-grown even accused the Indian intelligence forces. A number of men were later arrested, and three months later the police apprehended a man who they claimed was the head of the gang and a member of the "Punjabi Taliban".

The tour organised to show other nations that Pakistan was a safe place to play cricket thus ended in catastrophe, with the country's future as an international venue in even greater doubt. It will not be remembered for Younis's triple-century, or for Samaraweera becoming the seventh batsman in history to score double-hundreds in back-to-back Tests, or for the fact that 1,553 runs were scored in the First Test for the loss of only 18 wickets. Instead, it will be remembered as the first time a cricket team were attacked by a group of terrorists.

"It has completely changed the landscape, not just in the subcontinent. On many occasions we have been told that cricketers would not be targeted in Pakistan. This morning, events have proved that to be incorrect," said ICC president David Morgan.

Wisden correspondent's narrow escape

Qamar Ahmed was on his way to the Gaddafi Stadium when the attack took place:

"For the first two days of the Test, I walked from the Lahore Gymkhana to the ground through the Liberty Roundabout, the scene of the incident. On the third morning I was delayed by a late breakfast, but I had left my nearby lodgings for my usual walk to the ground when the team coach passed me at about 8.40 a.m. Five minutes later, I heard a bang, which I later found out was the rocket launcher, and then gunfire, which lasted about 12 minutes, and I witnessed people running for cover. I took shelter behind a tree. My sixth sense told me it could be nothing else but an attack on the team coach, but I did not know whether it was the Sri Lankan or the Pakistan bus. If it had not been for my late breakfast, I would have been at the Liberty Roundabout when it happened."

SRI LANKAN TOURING PARTY

D. P. M. D. Jayawardene (*captain*), T. M. Dilshan, C. R. D. Fernando, H. A. P. W. Jayawardene, C. K. Kapugedera, R. A. S. Lakmal, M. F. Maharoof, B. A. W. Mendis, M. T. T. Mirando, M. Muralitharan, N. T. Paranavitana, T. T. Samaraweera, K. C. Sangakkara, W. P. U. J. C. Vaas, B. S. M. Warnapura. Coach: T. H. Bayliss.

H. A. P. W. Jayawardene, Lakmal, Paranavitana, Samaraweera, Vaas and Warnapura replaced S. T. Jayasuriya, S. H. T. Kandamby, K. M. D. N. Kulasekara, A. D. Mathews, J. Mubarak and W. U. Tharanga who were in the one-day squad for the first half of the tour in January. Maharoof withdrew with an injury during the Test series.

Note: Matches in this section which were not first-class are signified by a dagger.

ONE-DAY INTERNATIONAL REPORTS
BY OSMAN SAMIUDDIN

†PAKISTAN v SRI LANKA

First One-Day International

At Karachi, January 20, 2009 (day/night). Pakistan won by eight wickets. Toss: Sri Lanka.

Pakistan talked bullishly of plans to neutralise Ajantha Mendis, Sri Lanka's "other" unusual spinner – the *doosra* to Muralitharan, so to speak. For once talk wasn't cheap, as many of their batsmen had grown up playing similar finger-spinners in tape-ball cricket. Salman Butt and Khurram Manzoor did not take Mendis apart in an opening stand of 168; instead, they played him as a medium-pacer and milked him, never letting up on singles and rarely missing a boundary-ball. Butt cover-drove and cut to give the innings some shape, before settling down to bat through to his eighth one-day hundred. That Pakistan had no more than 220 to chase was down to the unheralded Iftikhar Anjum. Brisk, accurate and finding some swerve, he picked up four wickets, including the big two of Sangakkara and Jayawardene, to reel in Sri Lanka from 81 for one in their first ten overs. This being a batsman's age, Butt edged him for the match award.

Man of the Match: Salman Butt.

Sri Lanka

T. M. Dilshan c Salman Butt b Umar Gul . .	42
S. T. Jayasuriya lbw b Umar Gul	38
†K. C. Sangakkara c Salman Butt	
b Iftikhar Anjum .	49
*D. P. M. D. Jayawardene c Kamran Akmal	
b Iftikhar Anjum .	1
C. K. Kapugedera b Shahid Afridi	27
J. Mubarak run out	8
M. F. Maharoof c Misbah-ul-Haq	
b Shoaib Malik .	11
M. T. T. Mirando c Kamran Akmal	
b Iftikhar Anjum .	0

K. M. D. N. Kulasekara c Kamran Akmal	
b Umar Gul .	24
M. Muralitharan not out	7
B. A. W. Mendis b Iftikhar Anjum	1
L-b 3, w 6, n-b 2	11

1/71 (1) 2/86 (2) 3/89 (4)   (45.2 overs) 219
4/143 (5) 5/170 (6) 6/176 (3)
7/176 (8) 8/209 (7) 9/211 (9)
10/219 (11)   10 overs: 81-1

Shoaib Akhtar 7–0–43–0; Sohail Tanvir 5–0–35–0; Iftikhar Anjum 8.2–1–42–4; Umar Gul 9–0–30–3; Shahid Afridi 10–1–47–1; Shoaib Malik 6–0–19–1.

Pakistan

Khurram Manzoor c and b Muralitharan . . .	83
Salman Butt not out.	100
Younis Khan c Mendis b Maharoof	20
*Shoaib Malik not out.	11
L-b 4, w 1, n-b 1	6

1/168 (1) 2/205 (3)   (2 wkts, 45.5 overs) 220
                        10 overs: 32-0

Misbah-ul-Haq, Shahid Afridi, †Kamran Akmal, Sohail Tanvir, Umar Gul, Iftikhar Anjum and Shoaib Akhtar did not bat.

Kulasekara 8–1–35–0; Mirando 8–0–31–0; Maharoof 7.5–0–44–1; Muralitharan 10–1–42–1; Mendis 7–0–41–0; Jayasuriya 3–0–16–0; Dilshan 2–0–7–0.

Umpires: N. J. Llong and Nadeem Ghauri.
Third umpire: Ahsan Raza.   Referee: B. C. Broad.

†PAKISTAN v SRI LANKA

Second One-Day International

At Karachi, January 21, 2009 (day/night). Sri Lanka won by 129 runs. Toss: Pakistan.

Dilshan had opened the batting in only three one-day internationals before this series, but was promoted in Pakistan because of an injury to Tharanga. The move paid dividends – even more so when he went to England for the World Twenty20 – as he got Sri Lanka off to another flier. He was severe on Shoaib Akhtar, hooking, cutting and driving without any doubt on a true pitch. Handy contributions, especially from Kandamby and Kapugedera, lifted Sri Lanka to 290, and it could have been more but for Umar Gul's expertise when he bowled at the death. Pakistan's reply was a forlorn thing, with three wickets in their first four overs. Butt and Shoaib Malik counter-punched briefly but, once Malik fell, Mendis and Muralitharan gobbled up the lower order. To deflect criticism, Malik used his post-match press conference to rip apart the listless-looking Akhtar, questioning his commitment, fitness and international future.

Man of the Match: T. M. Dilshan.

Sri Lanka

T. M. Dilshan c Misbah-ul-Haq b Shoaib Akhtar	76		M. T. T. Mirando c Kamran Akmal b Umar Gul	8	
S. T. Jayasuriya hit wkt b Umar Gul	19		M. Muralitharan not out	11	
†K. C. Sangakkara run out	16		K. M. D. N. Kulasekara not out	0	
S. H. T. Kandamby c Shoaib Malik b Iftikhar Anjum	59				
*D. P. M. D. Jayawardene c Kamran Akmal b Umar Gul	24		L-b 1, w 9, n-b 6	16	
C. K. Kapugedera c Younis Khan b Umar Gul	44		1/43 (2) 2/66 (3) (8 wkts, 50 overs)	290	
M. F. Maharoof b Sohail Tanvir	17		3/165 (1) 4/190 (4)		
			5/231 (5) 6/253 (7) 7/269 (8)		
B. A. W. Mendis did not bat.			8/289 (6)		
			10 overs: 58-1		

Shoaib Akhtar 6–0–45–1; Sohail Tanvir 7–0–50–1; Iftikhar Anjum 10–1–43–1; Umar Gul 9–0–58–4; Shahid Afridi 10–0–42–0; Shoaib Malik 8–0–51–0.

Pakistan

Khurram Manzoor lbw b Kulasekara	1		Iftikhar Anjum lbw b Mendis	5	
Salman Butt c Jayawardene b Jayasuriya	62		Shoaib Akhtar not out	1	
Younis Khan b Kulasekara	4		B 1, l-b 3, w 8	12	
Misbah-ul-Haq c Sangakkara b Mirando	1				
*Shoaib Malik c Sangakkara b Muralitharan	54		1/6 (1) 2/14 (3) 3/17 (4) (34.5 overs)	161	
†Kamran Akmal c Sangakkara b Mendis	6		4/125 (5) 5/125 (2) 6/145 (6)		
Shahid Afridi c Kulasekara b Muralitharan	14		7/150 (8) 8/151 (9) 9/153 (7)		
Sohail Tanvir c Dilshan b Muralitharan	1		10/161 (10)		
Umar Gul lbw b Mendis	0		10 overs: 39-3		

Kulasekara 7–0–31–2; Mirando 5–0–24–1; Maharoof 5–0–31–0; Mendis 6.5–1–29–3; Jayasuriya 4–1–23–1; Muralitharan 7–1–19–3.

Umpires: Asad Rauf and N. J. Llong.
Third umpire: Ahsan Raza.   Referee: B. C. Broad.

†PAKISTAN v SRI LANKA

Third One-Day International

At Lahore, January 24, 2009 (day/night). Sri Lanka won by 234 runs. Toss: Sri Lanka.

Kulasekara and Thushara Mirando swung and seamed their way through Pakistan under the floodlights, reducing them to 22 for six, which became 75 all out, Pakistan's lowest total on home soil, inside 23 overs. The six wickets they shared highlighted a startling depth in Sri Lankan pace – with better-known bowlers such as Chaminda Vaas and Lasith Malinga absent – hitherto hidden by the fuss over their spinners, though Muralitharan completed the series victory with his 500th wicket in one-day internationals. Dilshan had ensured they bowled without pressure, taking his good form to its logical conclusion with a fine hundred, only his second at this level. The top order extracted full value from a benign pitch that came to life, like a vampire, in the night. Thus the original themes, that Pakistani pace and Sri Lankan spin would decide the series, were subverted. A few days after Pakistan's heaviest one-day defeat in terms of runs, Malik was ousted as captain, his coach and management calling him a "loner" and "aloof"; he was replaced by Younis Khan.

Man of the Match: T. M. Dilshan.   *Man of the Series:* T. M. Dilshan.

Sri Lanka

T. M. Dilshan not out 137	M. F. Maharoof not out 8
S. T. Jayasuriya c Saeed Ajmal b Umar Gul 45	
†K. C. Sangakkara run out 50	
S. H. T. Kandamby c Khurram Manzoor	
b Sohail Khan . 32	L-b 5, w 13, n-b 1 19
*D. P. M. D. Jayawardene c Kamran Akmal	
b Umar Gul . 18	1/76 (2) 2/180 (3)　　(5 wkts, 50 overs) 309
C. K. Kapugedera c Kamran Akmal	3/237 (4) 4/284 (5)
b Umar Gul . 0	5/284 (6)　　　　　　　　10 overs: 29-0

M. T. T. Mirando, K. M. D. N. Kulasekara, M. Muralitharan and B. A. W. Mendis did not bat.

Umar Gul 9–2–45–3; Sohail Khan 10–1–52–1; Iftikhar Anjum 5–0–53–0; Saeed Ajmal 9–0–51–0; Shahid Afridi 10–0–60–0; Shoaib Malik 7–0–43–0.

Pakistan

Khurram Manzoor c Maharoof b Kulasekara 3	Sohail Khan b Muralitharan 4
Younis Khan lbw b Mirando 4	Saeed Ajmal not out 2
Salman Butt c Kandamby b Kulasekara . . . 0	
†Kamran Akmal lbw b Mirando 9	L-b 1, w 6 7
*Shoaib Malik c Jayawardene b Maharoof . . 19	
Misbah-ul-Haq c Sangakkara b Mirando . . . 0	1/4 (2) 2/5 (3) 3/17 (4)　　(22.5 overs) 75
Shahid Afridi b Kulasekara 0	4/17 (1) 5/18 (6) 6/22 (7)
Umar Gul lbw b Mendis 27	7/68 (8) 8/68 (5) 9/72 (9)
Iftikhar Anjum lbw b Muralitharan 0	10/75 (10)　　　　　　　10 overs: 30-6

Kulasekara 7–2–17–3; Mirando 7–1–33–3; Mendis 3–0–10–1; Maharoof 4–1–12–1; Muralitharan 1.5–0–2–2.

Umpires: Asad Rauf and N. J. Llong.
Third umpire: Nadeem Ghauri.　　Referee: B. C. Broad.

†At Southend CC, Karachi, February 17, 18, 2009. **PCB Patron's XI won by 112 runs.** Toss: PCB Patron's XI. **PCB Patron's XI 395-4** (90 overs) (Azhar Ali 100, Ahmed Shehzad 146*, Saeed Bin Nasir 41, Shahid Afridi 49); **Sri Lankans 283-5** (90 overs) (K. C. Sangakkara 100*, D. P. M. D. Jayawardene 49, T. T. Samaraweera 45, H. A. P. W. Jayawardene 46*).
　　Each side named 14 players, of whom 11 could bat and 11 field (in fact 11 Pakistanis bowled on the second day). The teams were allocated one day (90 overs) each to bat. Sangakkara retired to allow his team-mates batting practice.

TEST REPORTS BY QAMAR AHMED

PAKISTAN v SRI LANKA

First Test Match

At Karachi, February 21, 22, 23, 24, 25, 2009. Drawn. Toss: Sri Lanka. Test debuts: Khurram Manzoor, Sohail Khan; N. T. Paranavitana.

Pakistan's first Test in 14 months produced a surfeit of runs and records. In front of almost empty stands, batsmen plundered hapless bowlers who could not extract any life from the placid pitch.

The tone was set by double-centuries from Sri Lanka's Mahela Jayawardene and Thilan Samaraweera. Then it was the turn of Pakistan's new captain, Younis Khan, to haunt the bowlers, with a triple-century which helped his side reach their highest Test total. Briefly on the last day it looked as if there might be an upset, when Sri Lanka lost five second-innings wickets clearing a deficit of 121. But there was too little time for Pakistan to drive home their advantage, and Samaraweera steered the tourists to the close without further loss.

The Test produced 1,553 runs and only 18 wickets, but the first wicket fell in the opening over, from Umar Gul: Tharanga Paranavitana, caught by second slip Misbah-ul-Haq off his first ball in Test cricket. Warnapura batted sedately until he too edged to second slip, and Misbah picked up a third catch, this time at midwicket, when Sangakkara charged wrist-spinner Danish Kaneria after scoring 70, studded with nine fours.

For the rest of the day it was the Jayawardene and Samaraweera show, as they hurried on to 406 for three. Jayawardene, who had announced he would resign the captaincy after this series, continued to tick off batting landmarks. His innings was not without blemish: he was dropped three times, at 17, 43 (a rare miss by Misbah at slip) and 123. But his seventh four made him the first Sri Lankan to amass 8,000 Test runs, in his 101st match, and his 15th four, to point off Kaneria, completed his 25th Test century. His first against Pakistan, it gave him a full set of hundreds against the other nine Test sides. Samaraweera reached his own century with a flourish, stroking off-spinner Shoaib Malik to mid-off for his 17th four just before the new ball was taken.

On the second day, Jayawardene and Samaraweera extended their stand to 437, a fourth-wicket Test record, passing 411 by Peter May and Colin Cowdrey against West Indies in 1957. Jayawardene advanced to his fifth Test double and Samaraweera to his first, reaching 3,000 Test runs from the same shot. The tide finally turned when Jayawardene was caught behind, sweeping at Malik, for 240, after 531 minutes and 423 balls, and 32 fours. As often happens after a massive stand, his partner Samaraweera departed in the next over, deceived by Kaneria's wrong 'un after 454 minutes, 318 deliveries and 31 fours. With the loss of Dilshan at the same score, three wickets had gone down in ten balls just before tea. After the interval, Sri Lanka declared at 644 for seven – their fourth-highest total and biggest against Pakistan, beating 528 at Lahore in 2001-02.

BOTH CAPTAINS SCORING 150-PLUS IN THE SAME TEST

R. B. Simpson (A)	311	E. R. Dexter (E)	174	at Manchester	1964
S. M. Gavaskar (I)	205	A. I. Kallicharran (WI)	187	at Bombay	1978-79
S. R. Waugh (A)	199	B. C. Lara (WI)	153*	at Bridgetown	1998-99
M. P. Vaughan (E)	166	R. T. Ponting (A)	156	at Manchester	2005
D. P. M. D. Jayawardene (SL)	**240**	**Younis Khan (P)**	**313**	**at Karachi**	**2008-09**

Muralitharan claimed his 770th Test wicket, Salman Butt, before the close, but Pakistan lost only two more batsmen on the third day. Their scoring-rate was lethargic, however; in the first session they made 79, in the second 90, in the last 83 – a total of 252 in 90 overs, compared with Sri Lanka's 406 on the opening day. Younis was dropped on 92 and survived an appeal for caught behind on 98 but reached three figures just before tea, with two to point off Fernando. Malik was run out by a direct throw from Murali, but the new ball, taken in the 97th over, had little effect, and Pakistan finished the third day at 296 for three. Even so, they needed 149 more to avoid the follow-on.

They finally achieved that feat on the fourth afternoon. With well-executed shots all round, Younis progressed to his second Test double-hundred, becoming the sixth Pakistani to score 5,000 runs on the way. This was only the second Test in which three batsmen scored double-centuries, after Bill Lawry and Bob Simpson did it for Australia and Seymour Nurse for West Indies at Bridgetown in 1964-65, and the first in which both captains reached 200. By the close, Younis had made it 300, with a reverse sweep of Muralitharan. It was only the third triple-century for Pakistan, after Hanif Mohammad's 337 against West Indies at Bridgetown in 1957-58, and Inzamam-ul-Haq's 329 against New Zealand at Lahore in 2002. Younis had also shared three consecutive century partnerships: 149 with Malik, 130 with Misbah, and 174 with Faisal Iqbal.

HIGHEST SCORES BY TEST CAPTAINS

400*	B. C. Lara	West Indies v England at St John's	2003-04
374	D. P. M. D. Jayawardene	Sri Lanka v South Africa at Colombo (SSC) . . .	2006
334*	M. A. Taylor	Australia v Pakistan at Peshawar	1998-99
333	G. A. Gooch	England v India at Lord's	1990
313	**Younis Khan**	**Pakistan v Sri Lanka at Karachi**	**2008-09**
311	R. B. Simpson	Australia v England at Manchester	1964
299	M. D. Crowe	New Zealand v Sri Lanka at Wellington	1990-91
285*	P. B. H. May	England v West Indies at Birmingham	1957
277	G. C. Smith	South Africa v England at Birmingham	2003
274*	S. P. Fleming	New Zealand v Sri Lanka at Colombo (PSS) . . .	2003
270	D. G. Bradman	Australia v England at Melbourne	1936-37
262	S. P. Fleming	New Zealand v South Africa at Cape Town	2005-06
259	G. C. Smith	South Africa v England at Lord's	2003
257*	Wasim Akram	Pakistan v Zimbabwe at Sheikhupura	1996-97
249	M. S. Atapattu	Sri Lanka v Zimbabwe at Bulawayo	2003-04
242*	C. H. Lloyd	West Indies v India at Bombay	1974-75
240	W. R. Hammond	England v Australia at Lord's	1938
240	**D. P. M. D. Jayawardene** . . .	**Sri Lanka v Pakistan at Karachi**	**2008-09**

Hopes were growing that he might overtake Brian Lara's Test record of 400 not out on the final day. But that was a tough ask, and Younis added only seven to his overnight score before he was bowled by a gem from Fernando which cut back in. His vigil had lasted 12 hours 40 minutes, in which he faced 568 balls and hit 27 fours and six sixes.

Pakistan finally stepped up a gear. They pushed on from 574 for five to 765 for six, their highest total, overtaking 708 at The Oval in 1987, and the fifth-highest by any Test side. The declaration came late – an hour after lunch – after Kamran Akmal had reached a career-best 158, making this the first Test ever to include four scores of 150-plus. He hit five sixes, out of 12 in the innings; curiously, despite their faster run-rate, Sri Lanka never cleared the boundary.

It looked as if there might be a final twist when Sri Lanka slid to 120 for five, still one run behind, despite responsible batting by Sangakkara and Jayawardene. But time was running out, and Samaraweera remained defiant.

Man of the Match: Younis Khan.

Close of play: First day, Sri Lanka 406-3 (D. P. M. D. Jayawardene 136, Samaraweera 130); Second day, Pakistan 44-1 (Khurram Manzoor 18, Younis Khan 0); Third day, Pakistan 296-3 (Younis Khan 149, Misbah-ul-Haq 20); Fourth day, Pakistan 574-5 (Younis Khan 306, Kamran Akmal 27).

Sri Lanka

B. S. M. Warnapura c Misbah-ul-Haq b Yasir Arafat	59	– c Kamran Akmal b Umar Gul	2
N. T. Paranavitana c Misbah-ul-Haq b Umar Gul . .	0	– run out	9
K. C. Sangakkara c Misbah-ul-Haq b Danish Maneria	70	– lbw b Danish Kaneria	65
*D. P. M. D. Jayawardene c Kamran Akmal b Shoaib Malik	240	– (5) c Faisal Iqbal b Danish Kaneria . .	22
T. T. Samaraweera b Danish Kaneria	231	– (6) not out	24
T. M. Dilshan c Kamran Akmal b Shoaib Malik . .	0	– (4) c Faisal Iqbal b Umar Gul	8
†H. A. P. W. Jayawardene b Danish Kaneria	18	– not out	7
W. P. U. J. C. Vaas not out	12		
L-b 4, w 1, n-b 9	14	N-b 7	7

1/3 (2) 2/93 (1)	(7 wkts dec, 155.2 overs) 644	1/2 (1) 2/32 (2) (5 wkts, 31 overs) 144
3/177 (3) 4/614 (4)		3/45 (4) 4/103 (5)
5/614 (5) 6/614 (6) 7/644 (7)		5/120 (3)

M. Muralitharan, B. A. W. Mendis and C. R. D. Fernando did not bat.

Umar Gul 24–2–92–1; Sohail Khan 21–2–131–0; Yasir Arafat 26–2–90–1; Shoaib Malik 36–3–140–2; Danish Kaneria 46.2–5–170–3; Younis Khan 1–0–6–0; Salman Butt 1–0–11–0. *Second Innings*—Umar Gul 9–1–41–2; Sohail Khan 6–0–33–0; Yasir Arafat 6–0–32–0; Danish Kaneria 9–1–35–2; Shoaib Malik 1–0–3–0.

Pakistan

Khurram Manzoor		
c H. A. P. W. Jayawardene b Mendis .	27	†Kamran Akmal not out 158
Salman Butt c D. P. M. D. Jayawardene		Yasir Arafat not out 50
b Muralitharan .	23	
*Younis Khan b Fernando	313	B 4, l-b 12, w 5, n-b 18 39
Shoaib Malik run out	56	
Misbah-ul-Haq lbw b Fernando	42	1/44 (2) (6 wkts dec, 248.5 overs) 765
Faisal Iqbal lbw b D. P. M. D. Jayawardene	57	2/78 (1) 3/227 (4)
		4/357 (5) 5/531 (6) 6/596 (3)

Sohail Khan, Umar Gul and Danish Kaneria did not bat.

Vaas 36–10–66–0; Fernando 39–2–124–2; Mendis 59–14–157–1; Muralitharan 65–14–172–1; Dilshan 19–3–82–0; Paranavitana 5–0–33–0; Sangakkara 10–0–34–0; D. P. M. D. Jayawardene 6.5–0–41–1; Warnapura 9–0–40–0.

Umpires: S. J. Davis and S. J. A. Taufel.
Third umpire: Zameer Haider. Referee: B. C. Broad.

PAKISTAN v SRI LANKA

Second Test Match

At Lahore, March 1, 2, 3, 2009. Drawn. Toss: Pakistan. Test debut: Mohammad Talha.
    The final Test of the short series was abandoned on the third morning, after a terrorist attack on the Sri Lankan team's bus as it drove to the Gaddafi Stadium. A dozen gunmen ambushed them at the nearby Liberty Roundabout; six policemen were killed, as was the driver of the umpires' bus. Fourth umpire Ahsan Raza was badly wounded and several Sri Lankan players were hit, though most escaped with minor shrapnel injuries.
    The two days of play before the outrage were dominated by the Sri Lankan batsmen, who were put in but soon resumed their mauling of the bowlers. Samaraweera scored his second double-hundred in successive Tests, the seventh player to do so, and shared double-century partnerships with Sangakkara and Dilshan.
    It did not all go Sri Lanka's way. Umar Gul claimed two wickets in the first nine overs, Warnapura caught at slip and Paranavitana at point, and after lunch he added the captain, Mahela Jayawardene, caught at the wicket. Later, both Sangakkara and Samaraweera were

DOUBLE-HUNDREDS IN SUCCESSIVE TESTS

D. G. Bradman (Australia)	⎰ 254 & 334 v England 1930
	⎱ 304 & 244 v England 1934
	⎰ 270 & 212 v England 1936-37
W. R. Hammond (England)	⎰ 251 & 200 v Australia 1928-29
	⎱ 227 & 336* v New Zealand 1932-33
V. G. Kambli (India)	224 v England 1992-93; 227 v Zimbabwe 1992-93
G. C. Smith (South Africa)	277 & 259 v England 2003
R. T. Ponting (Australia)	242 & 257 v India 2003-04
K. C. Sangakkara (Sri Lanka)	200* & 222* v Bangladesh 2007
T. T. Samaraweera (Sri Lanka)	**231 & 214 v Pakistan 2008-09**

dropped. But they reached their centuries in consecutive overs after tea. It was the new ball which caused Sangakkara's downfall; he edged a catch off Yasir Arafat, after they had put on 204 in 55 overs. But Samaraweera survived, and added 135 on the second morning with Dilshan, reaching lunch at 452 for four. Soon afterwards, Samaraweera completed his second double-century of the series. Once Dilshan had notched up his hundred, however, with their partnership standing at 207 from 45 overs, he called Samaraweera for a single, then changed his mind; Samaraweera was stranded as Kamran Akmal removed the bails. He had struck 32 fours in 338 balls, and batted six minutes short of seven hours.

Dilshan was also run out, for a delightful 145 full of meaty strokes through the covers and the on side. Sri Lanka were all out for 606 seven overs after tea, with Umar Gul claiming six wickets in a Test innings for the first time. In the 24 overs remaining Pakistan scored a brisk 110 until Mahela Jayawardene threw down the stumps from short fine leg to dismiss Salman Butt. His opening partner, Khurram Manzoor, had hit a maiden fifty with 11 fours in his second Test. But events at the Liberty Roundabout meant that Khurram never resumed his innings, while Samaraweera, a likely candidate for player of the series, was flown back to Colombo with a bullet in his leg.

Close of play: First day, Sri Lanka 317-4 (Samaraweera 133, Dilshan 3); Second day, Pakistan 110-1 (Khurram Manzoor 59).

Sri Lanka

B. S. M. Warnapura c Misbah-ul-Haq b Umar Gul	8	
N. T. Paranavitana c Shoaib Malik b Umar Gul	21	
K. C. Sangakkara c Kamran Akmal b Yasir Arafat	104	
*D. P. M. D. Jayawardene c Kamran Akmal b Umar Gul	30	
T. T. Samaraweera run out	214	
T. M. Dilshan run out	145	
†H. A. P. W. Jayawardene c Kamran Akmal b Umar Gul	15	
M. T. T. Mirando b Umar Gul	10	
M. Muralitharan b Mohammad Talha	22	
B. A. W. Mendis b Umar Gul	0	
C. R. D. Fernando not out	14	
B 4, l-b 1, w 5, n-b 13	23	
1/16 (1) **2/35** (2) **3/96** (4) (151 overs)	**606**	
4/300 (3) **5/507** (5) **6/542** (7)		
7/566 (8) **8/572** (6) **9/572** (10) **10/606** (9)		

Umar Gul 37–2–135–6; Mohammad Talha 17–0–88–1; Yasir Arafat 20–2–106–1; Danish Kaneria 47–5–183–0; Shoaib Malik 28–3–80–0; Younis Khan 2–0–9–0.

Pakistan

Khurram Manzoor not out	59	
Salman Butt run out	48	
N-b 3	3	
1/110 (2) (1 wkt, 23.4 overs)	**110**	

*Younis Khan, Shoaib Malik, Misbah-ul-Haq, Faisal Iqbal, †Kamran Akmal, Yasir Arafat, Mohammad Talha, Umar Gul and Danish Kaneria did not bat.

Mirando 8–0–46–0; Fernando 2–0–20–0; Mendis 8–2–21–0; Muralitharan 4.4–0–23–0; Dilshan 1–1–0–0.

Umpires: S. J. Davis and S. J. A. Taufel.
Third umpire: Nadeem Ghauri.   Referee: B. C. Broad.

PAKISTAN v AUSTRALIA, 2008-09

Andrew Stevenson

One-day internationals (5): Pakistan 2, Australia 3
Twenty20 international (1): Pakistan 1, Australia 0

Even before the Sri Lankan team was attacked by terrorists in March 2009, Pakistan had conceded that their held-over series against Australia would have to be played in the United Arab Emirates, a choice which seemed wiser still after the events of Lahore.

While their government attempted to grapple with the Taliban insurgency, the pressing concern for Pakistan cricket was to return to the field of play. This one-day series then became a test of whether the UAE might prove a suitable home for as long as the Pakistan team is forced to wander the world. Crowd support was of no concern: enough of the three million expatriates in the Emirates are from Pakistan to guarantee strong crowds, with numbers and exuberance rising towards evening, especially if Pakistan are doing well.

But while a return to the field was an enormous fillip for Pakistan's supporters and players – even before Lahore, they had not faced a team from outside Asia for more than a year – moving to the neutral venue cut heavily into sponsorship revenues. It also forced the Pakistan Cricket Board to swallow huge security costs, provide accommodation in some of the most expensive cities in the world, and negotiate gate-sharing agreements with local promoters. PCB estimates put the cost at around $US2m more than playing at home.

The notional home side were also affected by bans on players who had participated in the unauthorised Indian Cricket League. Bold selections paid off, however, with off-spinner Saeed Ajmal, 31, but with only five one-day internationals under his belt, appearing as if from another planet to stun Australia in the first game with his *doosra*. Shahid Afridi, too, opened the series with a showman's aplomb, capturing six wickets and igniting a frenzy of adulation from the crowd.

Australia had squeezed in this tour between a one-day series in South Africa and the World Twenty20 in England in June. Ricky Ponting, the captain, Mike Hussey and Mitchell Johnson were rested, so Michael Clarke led his first overseas tour. Returns after injury (Brett Lee, Shane Watson and Stuart Clark) or personal indiscretion (Andrew Symonds) meant that most of the squad were on trial in one way or another.

After the first match, embarrassment for Australia seemed a distinct possibility, with a successful trap apparently laid to exploit what Pakistan's coach Intikhab Alam perceived to be a weakness against spin. Australia's response reflected the nature of their cricket: they returned to their hotel, to their laptops and video analysis, and proceeded to seek a way to bat the spinners out of the game or, if that was not possible, survive against them in order to deprive Pakistan of the rush of adrenalin that infuses their game when they sniff victory.

Ultimately, discretion was revealed as the better part of valour. The Australians decided to work the spinners for singles in what became a low-scoring series. Ajmal, Afridi and Shoaib Malik kept hounding, but didn't regain the ascendancy until the last match, a Twenty20 game. The Australians were also helped when Ajmal's action was reported after the second match: although he played on, the incident undoubtedly shook his confidence to bowl the *doosra*.

All the on-trial Australians passed – some only just. Symonds had one solid innings, hitting 58 to secure victory in the second match, but failed elsewhere; Lee's return was delayed until the final game; Watson did not bowl, but topped the batting figures (271 runs at 90.33 in the 50-over matches) to underline his all-round potential; and Clarke was impressive as captain, batsman and part-time spinner.

Pakistan's moment of destiny arrived in the third match, in Abu Dhabi. With the series tied at 1–1 and Australia despatched for 198, the openers Salman Butt and Ahmed Shehzad, only 17 years old, had their side rolling comfortably to victory – only for the later batting to collapse in an unseemly heap. Intikhab called it a nightmare, while their captain Younis Khan said his side's performance was so bad it had reduced him to laughter, an attitude that was not taken as a joke in Pakistan.

NATIONAL SQUADS

Pakistan *Younis Khan, Fawad Alam, Iftikhar Anjum, Kamran Akmal, Misbah-ul-Haq, Nasir Jamshed, Saeed Ajmal, Salman Butt, Shahid Afridi, Shoaib Akhtar, Shoaib Malik, Sohail Tanvir, Umar Gul, Yasir Arafat. *Coach:* Intikhab Alam.

Nasir Jamshed pulled a hamstring in the first match, and was replaced by Ahmed Shehzad.

Australia *M. J. Clarke, D. E. Bollinger, N. W. Bracken, S. R. Clark, C. J. Ferguson, B. J. Haddin, N. M. Hauritz, B. W. Hilfenhaus, J. R. Hopes, D. J. Hussey, B. Laughlin, S. E. Marsh, A. Symonds, S. R. Watson. *Coach:* T. J. Nielsen.

B. Lee was originally selected, but had not recovered from ankle surgery and was replaced by Bollinger. B. Geeves, another original selection, broke his foot late in the preceding South African tour, and was replaced by Clark. Marsh injured his hamstring during the first match, and was replaced by M. J. North.

* *Captain.*

Note: Matches in this section were not first-class.

PAKISTAN v AUSTRALIA

First One-Day International

At Dubai, April 22, 2009 (day/night). Pakistan won by four wickets. Toss: Australia.

Before the series Pakistan believed they had an ace in the pack. The Australians were worried about the fast bowlers Umar Gul and Shoaib Akhtar, but Pakistan's management knew their best chance of victory lay with their spinners. After Australia started strongly, reaching 95 for the loss of Marsh, the spinners arrived, and the wickets tumbled, to the delight of the pro-Pakistan crowd for the first official one-day international at the Dubai International Stadium, and to the consternation of Australia's batsmen who, with the exception of Hopes, offered no resistance as eight wickets fell for 27 in 12.1 overs. Shahid Afridi's six wickets grabbed the headlines, but it was Saeed Ajmal, playing only his sixth one-day international, who caused the most confusion with his mixture of off-spin and *doosras*. In reply, Pakistan ground their way to their modest target, although the time taken and the loss of six wickets in the process instilled little confidence about their capacity to carry on for a series victory.

Man of the Match: Shahid Afridi.

Australia

S. E. Marsh run out	16	N. W. Bracken b Shahid Afridi		1
†B. J. Haddin c Younis Khan b Shahid Afridi	40	S. R. Clark b Shahid Afridi		2
S. R. Watson b Shahid Afridi	40	B. W. Hilfenhaus b Umar Gul		4
*M. J. Clarke c Kamran Akmal b Saeed Ajmal	4			
A. Symonds c Kamran Akmal		L-b 1, w 7		8
b Shahid Afridi	2			
C. J. Ferguson c Misbah-ul-Haq		1/41 (1) 2/95 (2) 3/100 (4) (38.5 overs)		168
b Shahid Afridi	2	4/107 (5) 5/108 (3) 6/109 (6)		
J. R. Hopes not out	48	7/110 (8) 8/118 (9) 9/122 (10)		
N. M. Hauritz b Saeed Ajmal	1	10/168 (11)	10 overs: 49-1	

Umar Gul 9.5–0–48–1; Shoaib Akhtar 6–0–35–0; Iftikhar Anjum 2–0–18–0; Shahid Afridi 10–0–38–6; Saeed Ajmal 10–1–19–2; Shoaib Malik 1–0–9–0.

Pakistan

Salman Butt lbw b Hilfenhaus	5	Umar Gul not out		8
†Kamran Akmal c Haddin b Clark	48			
*Younis Khan c Bracken b Hopes	11	L-b 5, w 1, n-b 6		12
Shoaib Malik c Haddin b Hopes	24			
Misbah-ul-Haq not out	30	1/5 (1) 2/33 (3) (6 wkts, 44.1 overs)		171
Shahid Afridi c Bracken b Hilfenhaus	24	3/81 (2) 4/99 (4)		
Nasir Jamshed b Symonds	9	5/138 (6) 6/152 (7)	10 overs: 33-1	

Shoaib Akhtar, Iftikhar Anjum and Saeed Ajmal did not bat.

Bracken 9.1–2–25–0; Hilfenhaus 10–3–42–2; Hopes 8–1–22–2; Clark 8–1–32–1; Hauritz 6–0–27–0; Symonds 3–0–18–1.

Umpires: B. F. Bowden and Nadeem Ghauri.
Third umpire: Asad Rauf.   Referee: J. J. Crowe.

PAKISTAN v AUSTRALIA

Second One-Day International

At Dubai, April 24, 2009 (day/night). Australia won by six wickets. Toss: Pakistan. One-day international debuts: Ahmed Shehzad; D. E. Bollinger.

Younis Khan decided to bat first, apparently to save his pacemen – notably the ageing and unfit Shoaib Akhtar – from having to bowl in the oppressive afternoon heat. Salman Butt again top-scored, but also ran out the 17-year-old debutant Ahmed Shehzad in the first over, and it was only some lower-order slugging from Shahid Afridi and Shoaib Akhtar that lifted Pakistan past 200. Haddin went cheaply in reply, then Watson and Hopes pushed the score to 93 before both fell in the space of three balls. This exposed the new batsmen, Clarke and Symonds, to the spinners – and they responded with the defining partnership of the series, working the ball for singles and sweeping when possible. There were some anxious moments during a stand of 90 in less than 18 overs, but victory was all but assured by the time Afridi torpedoed Symonds with one that kept low and evaded his attempted pull.

Man of the Match: A. Symonds.

Pakistan

Salman Butt c Symonds b Hauritz	57	Iftikhar Anjum not out		1
Ahmed Shehzad run out	4	Saeed Ajmal run out		0
*Younis Khan c Haddin b Laughlin	28			
Shoaib Malik c Haddin b Hauritz	7	L-b 2, n-b 1		3
Misbah-ul-Haq c Hussey b Hauritz	12			
Shahid Afridi c Haddin b Hopes	41	1/5 (2) 2/58 (3) 3/71 (4) (46.2 overs)		207
†Kamran Akmal c Hussey b Hopes	19	4/103 (5) 5/122 (1) 6/161 (7)		
Umar Gul c Hauritz b Symonds	10	7/176 (6) 8/206 (8) 9/206 (9)		
Shoaib Akhtar c Clarke b Symonds	25	10/207 (11)	10 overs: 34-1	

Bracken 8.2–1–24–0; Bollinger 10–1–26–0; Hopes 7–0–45–2; Hauritz 10–1–41–3; Laughlin 9–0–57–1; Symonds 2–0–12–2.

Australia

†B. J. Haddin b Umar Gul	8	C. J. Ferguson not out		10
J. R. Hopes lbw b Shahid Afridi	48			
S. R. Watson c Misbah-ul-Haq		L-b 4, w 8, n-b 3		15
b Saeed Ajmal	30			
*M. J. Clarke not out	39	1/16 (1) 2/93 (3) (4 wkts, 45.1 overs)		208
A. Symonds b Shahid Afridi	58	3/93 (2) 4/183 (5)	10 overs: 54-1	

D. J. Hussey, N. M. Hauritz, N. W. Bracken, D. E. Bollinger and B. Laughlin did not bat.

Shoaib Akhtar 7–1–32–0; Umar Gul 10–0–51–1; Iftikhar Anjum 9–0–32–0; Shahid Afridi 10–0–38–2; Saeed Ajmal 7–0–37–1; Shoaib Malik 2.1–0–14–0.

Umpires: Asad Rauf and B. F. Bowden.
Third umpire: Zameer Haider.   Referee: J. J. Crowe.

PAKISTAN v AUSTRALIA

Third One-Day International

At Abu Dhabi, April 27, 2009 (day/night). Australia won by 27 runs. Toss: Australia.

Play moved to the Sheikh Zayed Stadium in Abu Dhabi for the third match, on which the series swung. On a dead, flat pitch the Australians struggled to hit the ball off the square, managing only 19 fours and a six (by Hauritz) in their 50 overs. Pakistan bowled 29 overs of spin: Shoaib Malik and Shahid Afridi were both very tight, but Saeed Ajmal – whose bowling action had been reported after the previous game – was less effective. Pakistan needed only 199, and seemed to be coasting at 95 without loss after 22 overs. But Hauritz sent back Salman Butt and Younis Khan with successive balls, and Clarke claimed three quick wickets as Pakistan collapsed. "It was a nightmare, really," said their coach Intikhab Alam. "I think that will remain in my mind for a long time."

Man of the Match: M. J. Clarke.

Australia

J. R. Hopes run out	15	N. M. Hauritz not out		19
†B. J. Haddin b Shoaib Malik	26	N. W. Bracken not out		2
S. R. Watson b Umar Gul	0	B 3, l-b 3, w 4, n-b 2		12
*M. J. Clarke c and b Shahid Afridi	66			
A. Symonds lbw b Shahid Afridi	7	1/28 (1) 2/28 (3) (7 wkts, 50 overs)		198
C. J. Ferguson c Sohail Tanvir b Umar Gul	41	3/74 (2) 4/91 (5)		
D. J. Hussey c Yasir Arafat b Umar Gul	10	5/145 (4) 6/168 (6) 7/188 (7)	10 overs: 40-2	

S. R. Clark and B. W. Hilfenhaus did not bat.

Umar Gul 8–0–38–3; Sohail Tanvir 6–1–28–0; Yasir Arafat 7–1–31–0; Shahid Afridi 10–2–31–2; Shoaib Malik 10–2–22–1; Saeed Ajmal 9–0–42–0.

Pakistan

Salman Butt c Clarke b Hauritz	48		Umar Gul b Clark	0
Ahmed Shehzad b Clarke	40		Saeed Ajmal not out	0
*Younis Khan c Symonds b Hauritz	0			
Misbah-ul-Haq c Hauritz b Clarke	9		B 4, l-b 3, w 9	16
Shoaib Malik run out	30			
Shahid Afridi c Hussey b Clarke	6		1/95 (1) 2/95 (3) 3/107 (4) (47.1 overs)	171
†Kamran Akmal c Hopes b Bracken	8		4/107 (2) 5/123 (6) 6/141 (7)	
Yasir Arafat b Symonds	3		7/148 (8) 8/170 (9) 9/170 (5)	
Sohail Tanvir c Hussey b Hilfenhaus	11		10/171 (10)	10 overs: 40-0

Bracken 10–1–37–1; Hilfenhaus 6–0–20–1; Clark 3.1–0–15–1; Hauritz 10–3–25–2; Hopes 2–0–11–0; Symonds 10–1–41–1; Clarke 6–2–15–3.

Umpires: Asad Rauf and B. F. Bowden.
Third umpire: Nadeem Ghauri. Referee: J. J. Crowe.

PAKISTAN v AUSTRALIA

Fourth One-Day International

At Abu Dhabi, May 1, 2009 (day/night). Australia won by eight wickets. Toss: Pakistan. One-day international debut: M. J. North.

Runs were again hard to come by as ball dominated bat. Pakistan, apparently shaken by their failure to win the pivotal third match, struggled from the start after winning the toss: Salman Butt fell to the third ball of the day, and Younis Khan again went cheaply, in the fourth over. The left-arm fast bowler Doug Bollinger, in only his second one-day international, started by tempting Butt into an expansive drive, and later wrapped up the innings with two wickets in three balls to finish with a maiden five-for. Then Australia produced the first compelling batting performance of the series. Shoaib Akhtar began with a full head of steam, firing out Haddin and the debutant Marcus North in his first two overs, but Umar Gul had surprisingly been rested, and that was the extent of the damage. Watson and Clarke took stock, and batted calmly towards the modest target under the lights. Watson played the support role, eventually facing 140 balls, while Clarke led from the front, using his feet skilfully to counter the spinners. Watson swept the winning boundary shortly after Clarke reached his fourth one-day century, from 122 balls, with his 14th four.

Man of the Match: D. E. Bollinger.

Pakistan

Salman Butt c Haddin b Bollinger	2		Shoaib Akhtar c Clarke b Bollinger	2
Ahmed Shehzad c Ferguson b Hauritz	43		Saeed Ajmal b Bollinger	0
*Younis Khan b Bracken	7			
Misbah-ul-Haq lbw b Clarke	34		B 3, l-b 4, w 1, n-b 1	9
Shoaib Malik lbw b Bollinger	27			
Shahid Afridi c North b Bollinger	40		1/2 (1) 2/12 (3) 3/80 (4) (48.4 overs)	197
†Kamran Akmal b Clark	1		4/116 (2) 5/140 (5) 6/145 (7)	
Yasir Arafat not out	23		7/174 (6) 8/190 (9) 9/196 (10)	
Sohail Tanvir c Hauritz b Bracken	9		10/197 (11)	10 overs: 30-2

Bollinger 7.4–0–35–5; Bracken 10–1–31–2; Clark 10–1–39–1; Hopes 3–0–5–0; Hauritz 10–0–34–1; North 3–0–16–0; Clarke 4–0–21–1; Symonds 1–0–9–0.

Australia

```
S. R. Watson not out . . . . . . . . . . . . . . . . .  85
†B. J. Haddin c Kamran Akmal
               b Shoaib Akhtar .   0
M. J. North lbw b Shoaib Akhtar . . . . . . . .   1
*M. J. Clarke not out . . . . . . . . . . . . . . . . . 100
      L-b 6, w 7, n-b 1 . . . . . . . . . . . . . .  14

1/1 (2)  2/3 (3)       (2 wkts, 44.2 overs) 200
                          10 overs: 38-2
```

J. R. Hopes, A. Symonds, C. J. Ferguson, N. M. Hauritz, N. W. Bracken, S. R. Clark and D. E. Bollinger did not bat.

Shoaib Akhtar 7–0–42–2; Sohail Tanvir 7–1–41–0; Yasir Arafat 8–1–30–0; Shahid Afridi 7–0–31–0; Saeed Ajmal 10–1–20–0; Shoaib Malik 5.2–0–30–0.

Umpires: Aleem Dar and B. F. Bowden.
Third umpire: Zameer Haider.   Referee: J. J. Crowe.

PAKISTAN v AUSTRALIA

Fifth One-Day International

At Abu Dhabi, May 3, 2009 (day/night). Pakistan won by seven wickets. Toss: Australia.

Watson finally delivered the innings he had been threatening all series: a fine unbeaten century, built on his natural aggression and power. Pakistan's fast bowlers were the main victims of his assault, as the spinners again proved hard to get away, putting the brakes on after 71 came from the first ten overs. Australia's total was the highest of the series but, well as Watson played, Kamran Akmal was even better: he too scored 116, but from 115 balls to Watson's 146, mixing some powerful blows square of the wicket with boundaries stolen by beating the field with clever tickles and sweeps. Akmal, who hit 13 fours in all, received solid support from Misbah-ul-Haq after they had come together with their side dawdling at 56 for three from 16 overs. Salman Butt was run out without facing in the first over. Australia tried seven different bowlers, but only Hauritz registered a wicket as Pakistan cruised to victory.

Man of the Match: Kamran Akmal. *Man of the Series:* M. J. Clarke.

Australia

S. R. Watson not out 116	C. J. Ferguson not out 41	
†B. J. Haddin c Younis Khan b Shoaib Akhtar 36	L-b 3, w 7, n-b 1 11	
M. J. North st Kamran Akmal b Saeed Ajmal 5		
*M. J. Clarke c Kamran Akmal b Umar Gul 26	1/58 (2) 2/83 (3) (4 wkts, 50 overs) 250	
A. Symonds b Shoaib Malik 15	3/140 (4) 4/166 (5) 10 overs: 71-1	

J. R. Hopes, N. M. Hauritz, D. E. Bollinger, B. W. Hilfenhaus and B. Laughlin did not bat.

Shoaib Akhtar 7–1–43–1; Umar Gul 8–0–44–1; Yasir Arafat 5–0–38–0; Saeed Ajmal 10–0–40–1; Shahid Afridi 10–0–36–0; Shoaib Malik 10–0–46–1.

Pakistan

```
Ahmed Shehzad lbw b Hauritz . . . . . . . . . .  19
Salman Butt run out . . . . . . . . . . . . . . . . .   0
*Younis Khan c Hilfenhaus b Hauritz . . . . . .  27
†Kamran Akmal not out . . . . . . . . . . . . . . . 116
Misbah-ul-Haq not out . . . . . . . . . . . . . . .  76
       B 4, l-b 2, w 7, n-b 3 . . . . . . . . . . . .  16

1/2 (2)  2/46 (3)       (3 wkts, 47 overs) 254
3/56 (1)                   10 overs: 30-1
```

Shoaib Malik, Shahid Afridi, Yasir Arafat, Umar Gul, Shoaib Akhtar and Saeed Ajmal did not bat.

Bollinger 8–0–40–0; Hilfenhaus 8–1–43–0; Laughlin 7–0–48–0; Hauritz 10–0–44–2; Clarke 4–1–27–0; Hopes 8–0–32–0; Symonds 2–0–14–0.

Umpires: Aleem Dar and B. F. Bowden.
Third umpire: Nadeem Ghauri. Referee: J. J. Crowe.

PAKISTAN v AUSTRALIA

Only Twenty20 International

At Dubai, May 7, 2009. Pakistan won by seven wickets. Toss: Pakistan. Twenty20 international debuts: Ahmed Shehzad, Saeed Ajmal; N. M. Hauritz, M. J. North.

Australia made a bright start, racing along at ten an over until the in-form Watson was adjudged lbw by Aleem Dar from Umar Gul's first delivery. Watson immediately hit his bat with his hand and made his displeasure clear as he left the field. Haddin, captaining as Clarke had returned home early to rest ahead of the England tour, also objected when Symonds was lbw: both Haddin and Watson were later fined for dissent. Symonds was out first ball in what seemed likely to be his last innings for Australia, after the latest in a long line of indiscretions saw him sent home from the World Twenty20 the following month. Shahid Afridi then dismantled the top order, before Gul returned to complete a remarkable analysis. Haddin later accused his team of having one foot on the plane after an inept batting display. Lee, back after four months out with an ankle injury, sent down his first ball at 149kph (92.5mph): he soon dismissed the teenager Ahmed Shehzad, but no bowler in world cricket could have hoped to defend a total this small. Another wicket did tickle Pakistani nerves a little, but Kamran Akmal smacked three sixes, and his partnership with Misbah-ul-Haq (captaining after Younis Khan stepped down to allow Fawad Alam to play) was ended only when the scores were level.

Men of the Match: Shahid Afridi and Umar Gul.

Australia

		B	4	6
S. R. Watson *lbw b 7*	33	14	5	0
*†B. J. Haddin *c 7 b 5*	24	27	2	0
J. R. Hopes *lbw b 6*	6	9	0	0
A. Symonds *lbw b 6*	0	1	0	0
D. J. Hussey *b 6*	4	11	0	0
C. J. Ferguson *st 3 b 5*	8	9	0	0
M. J. North *b 7*	20	21	1	0
N. M. Hauritz *c 5 b 7*	2	7	0	0
B. Lee *b 7*	0	3	0	0
N. W. Bracken *not out*	3	11	0	0
B. W. Hilfenhaus *c 6 b 11*	2	8	0	0
L-b 3, w 1, n-b 2	6			

6 overs: 53-1   (19.5 overs)   108

1/42 2/61 3/61 4/69 5/73 6/85 7/94 8/94 9/105

Shoaib Akhtar 2–0–18–0; Sohail Tanvir 3–0–32–0; Umar Gul 4–0–8–4; Saeed Ajmal 3.5–0–19–1; Shahid Afridi 4–1–14–3; Shoaib Malik 3–0–14–2.

Pakistan

		B	4	6
Salman Butt *c 3 b 11*	16	12	3	0
Ahmed Shehzad *c 12 b 9*	4	12	1	0
†Kamran Akmal *not out*	59	42	5	3
*Misbah-ul-Haq *c 10 b 8*	24	32	1	0
Shoaib Malik *not out*	0	1	0	0
W 5, n-b 1	6			

6 overs: 37-2   (16.2 overs)   109-3

1/17 2/23 3/108

Shahid Afridi, Umar Gul, Fawad Alam, Shoaib Akhtar, Sohail Tanvir and Saeed Ajmal did not bat.

Lee 4–0–22–1; Bracken 3–0–24–0; Hilfenhaus 4–0–20–1; Hauritz 3.2–0–20–1; Hopes 2–0–23–0.

Umpires: Aleem Dar and Zameer Haider. Third umpire: Nadeem Ghauri. Referee: J. J. Crowe.

PAKISTAN v NEW ZEALAND, 2009-10

One-day internationals (3): Pakistan 1, New Zealand 2
Twenty20 internationals (2): Pakistan 2, New Zealand 0

This short one-day series – played in the United Arab Emirates as Pakistan remained off-limits to touring sides – was overshadowed by the seemingly endless saga of who should captain Pakistan. Younis Khan had resigned after the Champions Trophy in the wake of unproven match-fixing claims, but was persuaded to return. Now, though, rumours that senior players were unhappy at his approach resurfaced, and Younis finally stepped down, presumably for good, after a narrow defeat in the one-day series in Abu Dhabi.

Younis told the Pakistan board that he felt he had "no command" over his team. "And if a leadership has no command over its players, what is the point of continuing to lead?" Mohammad Yousuf stepped up to captain the Test and 50-over sides, while Shahid Afridi continued to lead in Twenty20 games (he won both of the matches against New Zealand, in Dubai).

New Zealand won the 50-over series despite being weakened by the absence of Grant Elliott, Jesse Ryder and Daryl Tuffey, all injured during the Champions Trophy. They also travelled without a coach: Andy Moles resigned three days before the team departed. Some reports suggested Moles had been forced out by senior players unhappy at his technical input, but this was denied by New Zealand Cricket, which claimed the decision came after a review of recent performances.

NATIONAL SQUADS

Pakistan *Younis Khan, Abdul Razzaq, Iftikhar Anjum, Imran Farhat, Kamran Akmal, Khalid Latif, Mohammad Aamer, Mohammad Yousuf, Naved-ul-Hasan, Saeed Ajmal, Salman Butt, Shahid Afridi, Shoaib Malik, Umar Akmal, Umar Gul, Wahab Riaz. *Coach:* Intikhab Alam.

For the Twenty20 internationals Fawad Alam, Imran Nazir and Sohail Tanvir replaced Khalid Latif, Mohammad Yousuf, Salman Butt and Younis Khan, with Shahid Afridi taking over as captain.

New Zealand *D. L. Vettori, S. E. Bond, N. T. Broom, I. G. Butler, J. E. C. Franklin, M. J. Guptill, B. B. McCullum, N. L. McCullum, K. D. Mills, J. D. P. Oram, A. J. Redmond, T. G. Southee, S. B. Styris, L. R. P. L. Taylor, B. J. Watling. *Coach:* none.

* *Captain.*

Note: Matches in this section were not first-class.

Full scores of the games that follow can be found at: www.cricinfo.com/pakvnz2009/content/series/426717.html and www.cricketarchive.co.uk/Archive/Seasons/UAE/2009-10_UAE_New_Zealand_in_United_Arab_Emirates_2009-10.html.

PAKISTAN v NEW ZEALAND

First One-Day International

At Abu Dhabi, November 3, 2009 (day/night). Pakistan won by 138 runs. Toss: Pakistan.

Pakistan recovered from a terrible start – losing Salman Butt in the first over and Younis Khan in the third, both to Bond before a run had been scored – to reach a total that proved far beyond New Zealand's powers, despite a good pitch. Khalid Latif dropped anchor for 112 balls, but the impetus was provided by Shahid Afridi, who cracked 70 from 50 deliveries, with three sixes. Kamran Akmal took up the cudgels, hitting four sixes of his own in a 43-ball onslaught as Pakistan, 81 for four at halfway, piled on 206 runs from their second 25 overs: Bond, whose first five-over spell brought him two for 11, went for 50 in his last five as the floodgates opened. After a decent start New Zealand stumbled, losing three wickets in 17 balls, and, although Redmond hung around for 91 deliveries, only Vettori of the others resisted for long. Afridi, at the centre of gossip about his supposed captaincy ambitions, did his cause no harm with two wickets in successive balls with his skiddy leg-spin, missing a hat-trick when an impassioned lbw appeal against Butler was denied.

Man of the Match: Shahid Afridi.

Pakistan

Salman Butt c B. B. McCullum b Bond	0	Mohammad Aamer c B. B. McCullum		
Khalid Latif b Vettori	64		b Southee	0
*Younis Khan c B. B. McCullum b Bond	0	Saeed Ajmal not out		0
Mohammad Yousuf run out	30	L-b 8, w 11, n-b 2		21
Umar Akmal b Vettori	9			
Shahid Afridi c Butler b Oram	70	1/0 (1) 2/0 (3) (9 wkts, 50 overs) 287		
†Kamran Akmal not out	67	3/57 (4) 4/75 (5)		
Abdul Razzaq c Styris b Butler	26	5/176 (6) 6/184 (2) 7/270 (8)		
Umar Gul run out	0	8/271 (9) 9/277 (10)		

Bond 10-2-61-2; Southee 10-2-54-1; Butler 7-0-54-1; Oram 10-0-47-1; Vettori 10-1-34-2; N. L. McCullum 3-0-29-0.   10 overs: 25-2

New Zealand

†B. B. McCullum b Umar Gul	21	I. G. Butler run out		4
A. J. Redmond lbw b Saeed Ajmal	52	S. E. Bond not out		4
M. J. Guptill b Umar Gul	4	T. G. Southee lbw b Saeed Ajmal		1
L. R. P. L. Taylor c Kamran Akmal		L-b 8, w 2, n-b 1		11
b Mohammad Aamer	0			
S. B. Styris c sub (Imran Farhat)		1/30 (1) 2/34 (3) 3/35 (4) (39.2 overs) 149		
b Abdul Razzaq	5	4/50 (5) 5/119 (2) 6/139 (6)		
*D. L. Vettori b Shahid Afridi	38	7/139 (8) 8/139 (7) 9/144 (9)		
J. D. P. Oram b Abdul Razzaq	9	10/149 (11)		
N. L. McCullum lbw b Shahid Afridi	0			

Mohammad Aamer 7-1-15-1; Umar Gul 6-3-24-2; Abdul Razzaq 9-1-38-2; Shahid Afridi 10-0-46-2; Saeed Ajmal 7.2-0-18-2.   10 overs: 34-2

Umpires: Asad Rauf and B. N. J. Oxenford.
Third umpire: Zameer Haider. Referee: A. J. Pycroft.

PAKISTAN v NEW ZEALAND

Second One-Day International

At Abu Dhabi, November 6, 2009 (day/night). New Zealand won by 64 runs. Toss: New Zealand.

New Zealand levelled the series with a comprehensive victory of their own, inspired by Brendon McCullum's stunning return to form. McCullum had made only two half-centuries in 27 one-day internationals since hammering an under-strength Ireland for 166 in July 2008, but now he collected his second one-day hundred, hitting 14 fours and three sixes – the pick a superbly timed short-arm pull over the square-leg boundary off Mohammad Aamer – from 129 balls before departing with a total of 300 in sight. Guptill helped him add 126, and finally Oram made sure Pakistan had a mountain to climb. The openers started circumspectly, and their useful stand of 77 occupied 16.2 overs; then Salman Butt and the out-of-form Younis Khan (whose 19 took 37 balls) lifted the score to 124 for one after 27.1. Three wickets in 11 deliveries for Styris – including the crucial one of Shahid Afridi, to his first legal ball after a wide – left the other batsmen with too much to do.

Man of the Match: B. B. McCullum.

New Zealand

†B. B. McCullum b Umar Gul	131	J. D. P. Oram not out	33
A. J. Redmond c Younis Khan b Mohammad Aamer	6	K. D. Mills c Khalid Latif b Umar Gul	4
M. J. Guptill c Mohammad Aamer b Abdul Razzaq	62	S. E. Bond not out	10
L. R. P. L. Taylor b Shahid Afridi	0	B 1, l-b 11, w 3, n-b 3	18
S. B. Styris run out	9		
*D. L. Vettori c Kamran Akmal b Abdul Razzaq	30	1/21 (2) 2/147 (3) (8 wkts, 50 overs) 303	
N. T. Broom lbw b Shahid Afridi	0	3/147 (4) 4/160 (5)	
		5/214 (6) 6/218 (7)	
		7/274 (1) 8/287 (9)	

T. G. Southee did not bat.

10 overs: 55-1

Mohammad Aamer 10–0–64–1; Umar Gul 10–0–59–2; Abdul Razzaq 10–0–60–2; Saeed Ajmal 10–0–59–0; Shahid Afridi 10–0–49–2.

Pakistan

Salman Butt run out	59	Mohammad Aamer c Guptill b Bond	12
Khalid Latif lbw b Vettori	45	Saeed Ajmal not out	3
*Younis Khan c Taylor b Styris	19	B 2, l-b 3, w 8, n-b 1	14
Shahid Afridi c Taylor b Styris	0		
†Kamran Akmal c Guptill b Styris	4	1/77 (2) 2/124 (3) 3/125 (4) (47.2 overs) 239	
Mohammad Yousuf lbw b Vettori	18	4/133 (5) 5/134 (1) 6/158 (6)	
Shoaib Malik c Southee b Mills	26	7/194 (7) 8/209 (9) 9/231 (8)	
Abdul Razzaq c Guptill b Southee	35	10/239 (10)	
Umar Gul c Oram b Mills	4		10 overs: 47-0

Mills 10–1–57–2; Bond 9.2–1–43–1; Southee 8–0–48–1; Oram 6–0–26–0; Vettori 10–0–37–2; Styris 4–0–23–3.

Umpires: B. N. J. Oxenford and Zameer Haider.
Third umpire: Asad Rauf. Referee: A. J. Pycroft.

PAKISTAN v NEW ZEALAND

Third One-Day International

At Abu Dhabi, November 9, 2009 (day/night). New Zealand won by seven runs. Toss: New Zealand.
New Zealand stole the series with a narrow victory, increasing the pressure on Younis Khan, who resigned the captaincy two days later. For most of Pakistan's chase of 212, though, it looked like a rout: an inexplicable collapse after a decent start eventually left them reeling at 101 for nine in the 34th over on a placid pitch. Younis, struggling for form, scratched three from 15 balls before perishing the ball after Salman Butt was run out. Shoaib Malik, usually a calming influence, hoicked straight to deep square, then Umar Akmal, rather surprisingly preferred to Mohammad Yousuf, edged a catch behind. Abdul Razzaq was run out after playing out a maiden from Oram, and although Umar Gul hung around for ten overs a disappointed crowd was streaming out before he eventually

LAST PAIR DOUBLING THE SCORE IN LIST A MATCH

51-9 to 132	S. Turner and R. E. East	Essex v Yorkshire at Leeds	1982
20-9 to 56	J. Burger and A. J. Swanepoel	Griqual'd W. v N. T'vaal at Kimberley .	1995-96
42-9 to 84	B. L. Kotze and R. J. van Vuuren	Namibia v Pakistan at Kimberley.	2002-03
41-9 to 82	L. D. Sutton and D. B. Powell	Derbys v Durham at Chester-le-Street . .	2004
70-9 to 147	D. M. Benkenstein and N. Killeen	Durham v Warks at Chester-le-Street. . .	2005
55-9 to 111	Tahir Khan and Pankaj Kumar	Services v Delhi at Chandigarh	2006-07
101-9 to 204	**Moh'd Aamer and Saeed Ajmal**	**Pak v NZ at Abu Dhabi . . . .**	**2009-10**

Research: Philip Bailey

clipped Oram to deep midwicket. But the unheralded last pair of Mohammad Aamer and Saeed Ajmal batted intelligently, and scared the New Zealanders – and the bookmakers, who were offering 1,000-1 against Pakistan when the ninth wicket fell – by more than doubling the score, only the second such instance in one-day internationals after Namibia managed it during the 2002-03 World Cup. Aamer, whose 73 not out was the highest by a No. 10 in a one-dayer (beating Dougie Marillier's 56 not out for Zimbabwe v India at Faridabad in 2001-02), took the lead role, slog-sweeping three sixes in a Vettori over and also hitting seven fours from 81 balls, while Ajmal lasted 44 deliveries before Oram finally ended the fun with the first ball of the final over. It was only the second century partnership for the last wicket in one-day internationals, and the first featuring two genuine tailenders: in 1984 West Indies' last pair put on 106 against England at Old Trafford, but Michael Holding's share was just 12 as Viv Richards marauded to 189. Earlier, Brendon McCullum was again the New Zealand batting star, making 76 from 78 balls before Ajmal – whose career-best bowling preceded his batting best – worked his way through the middle order.

Man of the Match: Mohammad Aamer. *Man of the Series:* B. B. McCullum.

New Zealand

†B. B. McCullum c and b Shoaib Malik	76	S. E. Bond not out	11
A. J. Redmond c Mohammad Aamer		T. G. Southee c Abdul Razzaq	
b Umar Gul .	21	b Mohammad Aamer .	4
M. J. Guptill c Younis Khan b Saeed Ajmal	8		
L. R. P. L. Taylor lbw b Saeed Ajmal	44		
S. B. Styris run out	14	L-b 6, w 6	12
*D. L. Vettori lbw b Saeed Ajmal	15		
N. T. Broom lbw b Shahid Afridi	0	1/72 (2) 2/88 (3) 3/138 (1) (46.3 overs)	211
J. D. P. Oram lbw b Saeed Ajmal	2	4/164 (5) 5/187 (4) 6/188 (7)	
K. D. Mills c Saeed Ajmal		7/190 (6) 8/194 (8) 9/198 (9)	
b Mohammad Aamer .	4	10/211 (11) 10 overs: 65-0	

Mohammad Aamer 8.3–0–41–2; Umar Gul 8–1–47–1; Abdul Razzaq 3–0–19–0; Saeed Ajmal 10–0–33–4; Shahid Afridi 10–0–33–1; Shoaib Malik 7–0–32–1.

Pakistan

Salman Butt run out.	25	Mohammad Aamer not out	73
Khalid Latif lbw b Vettori	19	Saeed Ajmal c Mills b Oram	33
*Younis Khan c Taylor b Bond.	3		
Shoaib Malik c Styris b Mills	11	B 4, l-b 4, w 4, n-b 1	13
Umar Akmal c McCullum b Southee	12		
Shahid Afridi c McCullum b Oram	5	1/47 (2) 2/51 (1) 3/51 (3) (49.1 overs)	204
†Kamran Akmal c Vettori b Southee	4	4/74 (4) 5/82 (5) 6/84 (6)	
Abdul Razzaq run out	0	7/86 (7) 8/86 (8) 9/101 (9)	
Umar Gul c Redmond b Oram.	6	10/204 (11) 10 overs: 50-1	

Mills 10–1–62–1; Bond 10–1–46–1; Vettori 10–2–42–1; Southee 10–0–26–2; Oram 9.1–2–20–3.

Umpires: Nadeem Ghauri and B. N. J. Oxenford.
Third umpire: Zameer Haider. Referee: A. J. Pycroft.

PAKISTAN v NEW ZEALAND

First Twenty20 International

At Dubai, November 12, 2009 (floodlit). Pakistan won by 49 runs. Toss: New Zealand. Twenty20 international debut: B. J. Watling.

Pakistan reinforced their standing as Twenty20 kings with an emphatic victory as the action shifted to the Dubai Sports City stadium. Imran Nazir kick-started their innings, lacing successive balls from Butler over long-on and long-off for six, then going after him again, collecting two fours and another six in his next over. A late burst from Abdul Razzaq propelled the total to 161, and New Zealand were never in the hunt once Brendon McCullum (captaining in place of Vettori, resting after being hit on the head in the second 50-over game) sliced to backward point. New Zealand were also without the injured Franklin and Mills, while Oram had returned home on paternity leave, and were further handicapped when Redmond was unable to bat after straining his groin while bowling.

Man of the Match: Imran Nazir.

Pakistan

		B	4	6
Imran Nazir c 11 b 9	58	38	5	4
†Kamran Akmal c 9 b 10	13	15	2	0
Umar Akmal c 5 b 4	3	6	0	0
*Shahid Afridi c 10 b 11	24	16	2	1
Shoaib Malik c and b 11	6	7	0	0
Fawad Alam c 8 b 9	15	14	0	0
Abdul Razzaq not out	26	15	3	1
Sohail Tanvir c 7 b 10	12	8	1	1
Mohammad Aamer c 12 b 10	2	2	0	0
W 1, n-b 1	2			

6 overs: 35-1   (20 overs) 161-8

1/34 2/56 3/92 4/101 5/116 6/134 7/158 8/161

Umar Gul and Saeed Ajmal did not bat.

Bond 4–1–17–2; Southee 4–0–28–3; Butler 3–0–42–0; Styris 4–0–32–1; N. L. McCullum 2.1–0–18–0; Redmond 2.5–0–24–2.

New Zealand

		B	4	6
*B. B. McCullum c 6 b 9	19	13	3	0
M. J. Guptill c 2 b 8	8	4	2	0
L. R. P. L. Taylor c 2 b 9	5	8	1	0
S. B. Styris c 3 b 7	4	5	1	0
†B. J. Watling st 2 b 11	22	36	1	0
N. T. Broom c 10 b 7	14	16	0	1
N. L. McCullum c 10 b 11	22	21	0	0
I. G. Butler b 4	1	4	0	0
S. E. Bond not out	1	1	0	0
T. G. Southee c 5 b 4	6	3	0	1
L-b 8, w 2	10			

6 overs: 40-3   (18.3 overs) 112-9

1/25 2/33 3/34 4/41 5/67 6/95 7/98 8/106 9/112

A. J. Redmond did not bat.

Mohammad Aamer 3–1–21–2; Sohail Tanvir 4–0–22–1; Abdul Razzaq 3–0–9–2; Umar Gul 2–0–13–0; Shahid Afridi 3.3–0–21–2; Saeed Ajmal 3–0–18–2.

Umpires: Nadeem Ghauri and Zameer Haider.   Third umpire: Ahsan Raza.   Referee: A. J. Pycroft.

PAKISTAN v NEW ZEALAND

Second Twenty20 International

At Dubai, November 13, 2009 (floodlit). Pakistan won by seven runs. Toss: Pakistan.

This was a much closer game, though Pakistan won again, which cheered a large, partisan crowd. Umar Akmal led the way as Pakistan reached a respectable total, then Brendon McCullum anchored New Zealand's chase. He finally fell in the 19th over, leaving an unlikely requirement of 18 from the last, to be bowled by Umar Gul. Styris spanked the first ball over long-on for six, then Franklin lofted the third delivery to long-on, where Shoaib Malik (who had earlier caught McCullum there) claimed a good low catch. The New Zealanders asked for TV replays, which as so often were inconclusive, and Franklin survived, to the Pakistanis' chagrin. There was still too much to do, though, and Styris really was caught by Malik off the last ball. Earlier, a Shahid Afridi six had almost hit Geoff Allott, the former New Zealand fast bowler who is now an administrator.

Man of the Match: Umar Akmal.   *Man of the Series:* Shahid Afridi.

Pakistan

		B	4	6
Imran Nazir *b 8*	19	12	3	1
†Kamran Akmal *lbw b 8*	26	22	4	1
Umar Akmal *not out*	56	49	5	1
*Shahid Afridi *c 9 b 7*	22	17	1	1
Shoaib Malik *c 5 b 8*	7	7	1	0
Abdul Razzaq *c 2 b 6*	0	1	0	0
Fawad Alam *not out*	17	13	0	1
W 5, n-b 1	6			

6 overs: 48-1   (20 overs)   153-5

1/40 2/51 3/96 4/114 5/114

Sohail Tanvir, Mohammad Aamer, Umar Gul and Saeed Ajmal did not bat.

Bond 4–0–33–0; Southee 4–0–31–0; Butler 4–0–28–3; Franklin 3–0–26–1; Styris 2–0–19–0; N. L. McCullum 3–0–16–1.

Umpires: Nadeem Ghauri and Zameer Haider.

New Zealand

		B	4	6
*B. B. McCullum *c 5 b 11*	47	41	3	1
†B. J. Watling *c 2 b 8*	7	9	1	0
M. J. Guptill *b 10*	17	21	3	0
L. R. P. L. Taylor *lbw b 4*	13	12	0	1
S. B. Styris *c 5 b 10*	43	33	2	2
J. E. C. Franklin *not out*	5	4	0	0
L-b 6, w 8	14			

6 overs: 34-1   (20 overs)   146-5

1/20 2/46 3/66 4/132 5/146

N. T. Broom, N. L. McCullum, T. G. Southee, I. G. Butler and S. E. Bond did not bat.

Mohammad Aamer 4–0–33–0; Sohail Tanvir 3–0–14–1; Umar Gul 4–0–29–2; Saeed Ajmal 4–0–24–1; Shahid Afridi 3–0–21–1; Shoaib Malik 2–0–19–0.

Third umpire: Ahsan Raza.   Referee: A. J. Pycroft.

DOMESTIC CRICKET IN PAKISTAN, 2008-09

ABID ALI KAZI

Sialkot proved their strength in both first-class and 20-over cricket when they won the Quaid-e-Azam Trophy in between a brace of Twenty20 titles. The Twenty20 competition had not been staged in 2007-08, so the PCB held one in October 2008 and another in May 2009. Sialkot won both, which meant they had triumphed in all but the first of Pakistan's five Twenty20 tournaments.

Sialkot also won the five-day Quaid-e-Azam final on their home ground in March, though the victory was overshadowed by the terrorist attack on the Sri Lankan team in Lahore on the first day of the game. In a match devoid of international players, Sialkot beat **Khan Research Laboratories** after Kamran Younis and Naeemuddin shared an opening stand of 150 to help secure a first-innings lead of 90, and Naved Arif took six wickets in KRL's second innings to restrict the target to 158, which they achieved despite a few alarms.

Unusually, the format of Pakistan's domestic season was barely changed from the previous year. The significant difference was that all nine departmental sides were bundled into Group A of the Quaid-e-Azam, along with second teams from Karachi and Lahore, while Group B contained only regional sides.

Abdur Rauf

This ensured that the final would include a regional team; normally, the departmental sides dominate domestic cricket because they can have first choice of players. The segregation for most of the tournament certainly benefited Sialkot.

Even a change which had been announced failed to take place. Contrary to earlier statements, no Quaid-e-Azam teams were relegated to the non-first-class circuit before or after the 2008-09 season. The original plan had been to relegate six teams from the 2007-08 competition, to reduce an unwieldy 22 sides to 16. Then it was decided that only Hyderabad and Quetta would be demoted. In fact, even these two were allowed to stay, resulting in a number of one-sided matches: Quetta alone made five totals under 100, the lowest being 41.

The first-class season opened in October with the Pentangular Cup. For the second year running, this was contested only by provincial teams and no departments, but the 2008-09 edition added a final between the top two. **Punjab** and **Sind**, traditionally the strongest provinces, suffered most from the call-up of players for a one-day international series in Abu Dhabi; **North West Frontier Province** dominated the tournament from start to finish, winning all four league games plus a low-scoring final against **Baluchistan**. Winless the previous season, Baluchistan were the surprise success, though they were bolstered by players from other provinces.

Once the international players returned, Punjab won all their one-day Pentangular games, including the final against the fifth team, **Federal Areas**. The Royal Bank of Scotland One-Day Cup (whose name was changed after sponsor ABN Amro was taken over) was won by **Pakistan International Airlines**, who beat National Bank in the final.

Despite the volume of cricket, only one batsman crossed the 1,000-run mark in 2008-09: Saeed Bin Nasir, one of Baluchistan's guest players and the Pentangular Cup's leading run-scorer with 419, to which he added 590 for Sui Southern Gas. The averages were headed by Fawad Alam, with 977 at 97.70, including 296 not out (his only century) for National Bank against PIA, the highest score of the domestic season. Abdur Rauf, aged 30, was the leading wicket-taker, with 72 wickets for Baluchistan and Multan, while 16-year-old Mohammad Aamer topped the averages with 56 at 15.26 in his first season. Rauf, Aamer and Fawad all made their Test debuts during Pakistan's tour of Sri Lanka in July; Fawad scored a century on debut, the first Pakistani to do so on foreign soil.

FIRST-CLASS AVERAGES, 2008-09

BATTING

(Qualification: 700 runs)

	M	I	NO	R	HS	100s	Avge	Ct/St
†Fawad Alam (*Sind & National Bank*)	9	16	6	977	296*	1	97.70	7
Ashraf Ali (*Lahore Ravi*)	10	15	4	767	124*	3	69.72	5
Khurram Manzoor (*Sind, PIA & Pakistan*)	11	15	3	772	201*	2	64.33	7
†Haris Sohail (*Sialkot*)	11	16	3	794	155	1	61.07	10
†Sheharyar Ghani (*Karachi Blues*)	10	16	1	820	181*	2	54.66	5
†Nasir Jamshed (*National Bank*)	9	16	1	802	156*	4	53.46	10
†Adnan Raees (*NWFP & Abbottabad*)	15	20	1	995	205	3	52.36	16
Azeem Ghumman (*Hyderabad*)	9	14	0	728	199	3	52.00	6
Mohammad Ayub (*Punjab & Sialkot*)	13	21	3	909	146	3	50.50	12
Usman Saeed (*Federal Areas & Rawalpindi*)	14	22	5	841	144	3	49.47	4
†Bilal Khilji (*Baluchistan & WAPDA*)	12	18	3	740	130*	3	49.33	8
Khalid Latif (*Sind & Karachi Whites*)	12	22	2	972	123*	3	48.60	7
Sarfraz Ahmed (*Sind & PIA*)	14	20	2	869	115	1	48.27	45/3
†Naeemuddin (*Sialkot*)	11	16	0	754	173	3	47.12	7
†Kashif Siddiq (*Lahore Ravi*)	10	15	0	706	117	2	47.06	11
†Ali Asad (*Karachi Whites*)	10	18	1	789	172	3	46.41	8
†Umar Amin (*Federal Areas & National Bank*)	12	22	1	967	127	2	46.04	9
Saeed Bin Nasir (*Baluchistan & Sui S. Gas*)	13	24	2	1,009	119	2	45.86	13
Abid Ali (*Lahore Shalimar*)	10	18	1	731	141	3	43.00	9
Zahoor Elahi (*Pakistan Customs*)	10	19	2	712	102*	1	41.88	5
†Saeed Anwar (*Baluchistan & KRL*)	16	29	2	969	130	3	35.88	7
Azhar Ali (*Punjab & KRL*)	13	24	2	788	135	3	35.81	12
Umar Akmal (*Punjab & Sui Northern Gas*)	14	23	1	714	130	1	32.45	15

† *Left-handed batsman.*

BOWLING

(Qualification: 35 wickets, average 25.00)

	Style	O	M	R	W	BB	5W/i	Avge
Mohammad Aamer (*Fed Areas & Nat Bank*)	LFM	274.1	50	855	56	7-61	3	15.26
Shakeel-ur-Rehman (*NWFP & Sui S. Gas*) ..	RM	174.1	35	535	35	6-72	2	15.28
Junaid Nadir (*ZTBL*).	RFM	215.4	48	605	37	6-30	3	16.35
Saad Altaf (*Islamabad*)	LFM	319.5	58	1,033	61	6-29	5	16.93
Abdur Rauf (*Baluchistan & Multan*)	RFM	406.2	91	1,237	72	7-84	9	17.18
Mohammad Rameez (*Rawalpindi*).	RFM	266.2	70	724	41	6-17	2	17.65
Rizwan Akbar (*Rawalpindi*).	RFM	263.2	64	786	44	7-39	4	17.86
Sohail Tanvir (*Federal Areas & KRL*)	LFM/							
	SLA	310.1	54	955	53	8-54	5	18.01
Junaid Khan (*NWFP & KRL*).	LFM	267.5	46	810	43	6-56	2	18.83
Rauf Akbar (*Islamabad*).	RFM	269.2	48	785	40	6-64	1	19.62
Nayyer Abbas (*Sialkot*)	SLA	308.2	57	872	44	5-53	1	19.81
Najaf Shah (*PIA*)	LFM	406.4	101	1,061	52	6-39	4	20.40
Samiullah Khan (*Sui Northern Gas*)	LFM	316.2	59	900	44	5-46	1	20.45
Nazar Hussain (*Baluchistan & Quetta*)	LFM	250	53	754	36	6-54	2	20.94
Waqas Ahmed (*Lahore Ravi*).	RFM	266.3	52	740	35	6-36	2	21.14
Imran Ali (*Punjab & Sui Northern Gas*)	RFM	336	75	978	45	5-31	2	21.73
Nauman Habib (*NWFP & Peshawar*)	RM	305.5	49	1,142	52	7-57	3	21.96
Kamran Hussain (*Baluchistan & Habib Bank*)	LFM	295	74	799	36	5-58	2	22.19
Naved Arif (*Sialkot*).	LFM	396.5	76	1,388	62	6-33	5	22.38
Waqar Ahmed (*NWFP & Peshawar*).	LFM	334.3	46	1,293	57	7-114	5	22.68
Yasir Arafat (*Federal Areas, KRL & Pakistan*)	RFM	280.2	41	980	43	9-35	4	22.79
Mohammad Talha (*Punjab, Nat Bank & Pak*)	RFM	294.4	30	1,216	51	6-59	4	23.84
Danish Kaneria (*Habib Bank & Pakistan*). . .	LBG	315.5	58	1,060	43	8-59	3	24.65

Full scores of the 2008-09 Pakistani season can be found at www.cricinfo.com/db/ARCHIVE/2008-09/PAK_LOCAL/, www.cricketarchive.co.uk/Archive/Seasons/2008-09_PAK.html and in the *ACS Overseas First-Class Annual 2009.*

RBS PENTANGULAR CUP, 2008-09

	Played	Won	Lost	Drawn	1st-inns Points	Points	Net run-rate
North West Frontier Province . . .	4	4	0	0	9	33	0.24
Baluchistan	4	2	1	1	3	15	0.09
Federal Areas	4	1	2	1	0	6	−0.61
Sind	4	0	2	2	6	6	0.14
Punjab	4	0	2	2	3	3	0.18

Final: North West Frontier Province beat Baluchistan by 28 runs.

Outright win = 6 pts; lead on first innings in a won or drawn game = 3 pts. Net run-rate is calculated by subtracting runs conceded per over from runs scored per over.

At Bugti Stadium, Quetta, October 25, 26, 27, 2008. **North West Frontier Province won by an innings and 236 runs.** Toss: North West Frontier Province. **North West Frontier Province 550-5 dec** (Yasir Hameed 72, Adnan Raees 205, Wajid Ali 82, Shoaib Khan 81*); **Baluchistan 93** (Umar Gul 6-39) **and 221** (Yasir Shah 4-96). *North West Frontier Province 9 pts.*

 Adnan Raees batted ten minutes short of ten hours for his maiden double-hundred. Baluchistan's last seven first-innings wickets tumbled for 27, five of them to NWFP captain Umar Gul, who enforced the follow-on.

At National Stadium, Karachi, October 25, 26, 27, 28, 2008. **Drawn.** Toss: Sind. **Federal Areas 322** (Usman Saeed 136*; Tanvir Ahmed 5-62) **and 411-3 dec** (Raheel Majeed 66, Umair Khan 64*, Umar Amin 115, Bazid Khan 91, Naved Ashraf 54*); **Sind 367** (Khurram Manzoor 96; Sohail Tanvir 5-100) **and 247-4** (Khalid Latif 123*, Shahid Afridi 59). *Sind 3 pts.*

At Diamond Club Ground, Islamabad, October 31, November 1, 2, 3, 2008. **Federal Areas won by four wickets.** Toss: Federal Areas. **Punjab 306** (Salman Butt 155) **and 144** (Shoaib Akhtar 4-14); **Federal Areas 213** (Naved Ashraf 55; Imran Ali 4-64) **and 238-6** (Umar Amin 76*; Mohammad Talha 4-96). *Federal Areas 6 pts.*

On first-class debut, Federal Areas' 17-year-old stand-in wicketkeeper Jamal Anwar made seven catches in Punjab's second innings and ten in the match – despite a finger injury.

At National Stadium, Karachi, October 31, November 1, 2, 3, 2008. **Baluchistan won by six wickets.** Toss: Baluchistan. **Sind 126** (Azharullah 4-32) **and 380** (Khalid Latif 78, Fawad Alam 68, Shahid Afridi 81, Sarfraz Ahmed 57; Kamran Hussain 5-83); **Baluchistan 362** (Usman Tariq 50, Saeed Bin Nasir 89, Gulraiz Sadaf 84; Sohail Khan 4-66, Shahid Afridi 4-113) **and 147-4.** *Baluchistan 9 pts.*

Saeed Bin Nasir and Gulraiz Sadaf added 181 for Baluchistan's eighth wicket.

At Arbab Niaz Stadium, Peshawar, November 6, 7, 8, 2008. **North West Frontier Province won by ten wickets.** Toss: North West Frontier Province. **Federal Areas 236** (Usman Saeed 73; Shakeel-ur-Rehman 6-72) **and 103** (Shakeel-ur-Rehman 5-38); **North West Frontier Province 261** (Yasir Hameed 76, Zulfiqar Jan 60; Yasir Arafat 5-97) **and 82-0** (Rafatullah Mohmand 52*). *North West Frontier Province 9 pts.*

At Gaddafi Stadium, Lahore, November 6, 7, 8, 9, 2008. **Drawn.** Toss: Sind. **Punjab 400-9 dec** (Mohammad Hafeez 78, Azhar Ali 135, Umar Akmal 52) **and 80-3** (Mohammad Hafeez 61*); **Sind 509-7 dec** (Khurram Manzoor 201*, Afsar Nawaz 66, Sarfraz Ahmed 115). *Sind 3 pts.*

Khurram Manzoor batted for 708 minutes, throughout Sind's 153-over innings, for his second double-hundred, and earned a call-up from Pakistan in their one-day series against West Indies.

At Arbab Niaz Stadium, Peshawar, November 12, 13, 14, 2008. **North West Frontier Province won by an innings and 85 runs.** Toss: North West Frontier Province. **Sind 96 and 137** (Nauman Habib 5-45, Shakeel-ur-Rehman 4-63); **North West Frontier Province 318** (Rafatullah Mohmand 93, Shoaib Khan 56; Anwar Ali 5-95). *North West Frontier Province 9 pts.*

At Gaddafi Stadium, Lahore, November 12, 13, 14, 15, 2008. **Drawn.** Toss: Baluchistan. **Punjab 526-8 dec** (Azhar Ali 104, Adnan Raza 113, Mohammad Ayub 117, Khurram Shehzad 93*) **and 17-5;** **Baluchistan 271** (Bilal Khilji 70; Abdur Rehman 4-85) **and 330** (Saeed Bin Nasir 119, Kamran Hussain 52). *Punjab 3 pts.*

Azhar Ali and Adnan Raza added 218 for Punjab's third wicket in their first innings, and Baluchistan were made to follow on; but Asad Ali struck back with a hat-trick in Punjab's disastrous second innings, when they slid to 17-5 chasing 76 in 18 overs before bad light stopped play in the fourth over.

At Diamond Club Ground, Islamabad, November 18, 19, 20, 21, 2008. **Baluchistan won by two wickets.** Toss: Baluchistan. **Federal Areas 146** (Bilal Khilji 4-13) **and 303** (Umar Amin 51, Usman Saeed 87*; Kamran Hussain 5-58); **Baluchistan 57** (Sohail Tanvir 7-21) **and 393-6** (Shoaib Khan 64, Saeed Anwar 130, Saeed Bin Nasir 58). *Baluchistan 6 pts.*

Baluchistan unexpectedly won through to the final despite being all out for 57 in their first innings, when Sohail Tanvir took a career-best 7-21; they fought back to reach a target of 393.

At Gaddafi Stadium, Lahore, November 18, 19, 20, 21, 2008. **North West Frontier Province won by six wickets.** Toss: North West Frontier Province. **Punjab 265** (Azhar Ali 116; Shakeel-ur-Rehman 4-60) **and 134** (Junaid Khan 6-56); **North West Frontier Province 228** (Younis Khan 75*; Mohammad Talha 6-59) **and 172-4** (Rafatullah Mohmand 75*). *North West Frontier Province 6 pts.*

NWFP dropped their only points of the tournament when they failed to take first-innings lead.

Final

At Gaddafi Stadium, Lahore, November 24, 25, 26, 27, 28, 2008. **North West Frontier Province won by 28 runs.** Toss: Baluchistan. **North West Frontier Province 222** (Zulfiqar Jan 83; Abdur Rauf 5-72) **and 223** (Adnan Raees 98; Abdur Rauf 5-63); **Baluchistan 174** (Kamran Hussain 61; Shakeel-ur-Rehman 4-41) **and 243** (Usman Tariq 63; Yasir Shah 6-87).

Abdur Rauf gave Baluchistan a chance of the title with five wickets in each innings; they needed 272 to win, but leg-spinner Yasir Shah reduced them to 217-9. Their last pair batted into the final morning, when they needed 38 more runs, but NWFP completed their fifth straight win to claim the trophy in the fifth over of the day.

PENTANGULAR CUP WINNERS

The competition has been held fitfully, and in some seasons featured more than five teams. It was called the PACO Cup between 1980-81 and 1986-87, after sponsors Pakistan Automobile Corporation.

1973-74	PIA	1982-83	Habib Bank	1995-96	United Bank
1974-75	National Bank	1984-85	United Bank	2005-06	National Bank
1975-76	PIA	1985-86	PACO	2006-07	Habib Bank
1976-77	PIA	1986-87	PIA	2007-08	Sind
1980-81	PIA	1990-91	United Bank	2008-09	North West FP
1981-82	Habib Bank	1994-95	National Bank		

QUAID-E-AZAM TROPHY, 2008-09

Group A	Played	Won	Lost	Drawn	1st-inns Points	Points	Net run-rate
KRL	10	5	0	5	21	51	0.489
National Bank	10	5	0	5	21	51	0.462
PIA	10	4	2	4	18	42	0.747
Sui Northern Gas	10	4	2	4	12	36	0.161
ZTBL	10	3	1	6	15	33	−0.256
Habib Bank	10	3	2	5	9	27	0.146
WAPDA	10	2	0	8	9	21	0.263
Sui Southern Gas	10	0	4	6	15	15	−0.698
Karachi Whites	10	0	4	6	9	9	−0.227
Lahore Shalimar	10	0	4	6	6	6	−0.507
Pakistan Customs	10	0	7	3	0	0	−0.321

Group B	Played	Won	Lost	Drawn	1st-inns Points	Points	Net run-rate
Sialkot	10	6	2	2	24	60	0.508
Rawalpindi	10	6	0	4	18	54	1.036
Islamabad	10	4	2	4	21	45	0.509
Abbottabad	10	3	2	5	9	27	−0.109
Multan	10	3	3	4	9	27	0.041
Lahore Ravi	10	1	0	9	21	27	−0.106
Faisalabad	10	2	1	7	12	24	−0.103
Karachi Blues	10	2	3	5	12	24	0.251
Peshawar	10	2	4	4	6	18	−0.513
Quetta	10	1	8	1	0	6	−0.826
Hyderabad	10	0	5	5	6	6	−0.561

WAPDA = Water and Power Development Authority; PIA = Pakistan International Airlines; ZTBL = Zarai Taraqiati Bank Limited (formerly ADBP); KRL = Khan Research Laboratories.

Final: Sialkot beat KRL by four wickets.

Outright win = 6 pts; lead on first innings in a won or drawn game = 3 pts. Net run-rate is calculated by subtracting runs conceded per over from runs scored per over.
KRL qualified for the final ahead of National Bank on net run-rate (runs scored per over minus runs conceded per over).

Group A

At National Stadium, Karachi, December 28, 29, 30, 2008. **PIA won by an innings and 193 runs.** Toss: PIA. **Karachi Whites 65** (Najaf Shah 4-30, Anwar Ali 5-17) **and 161** (Anwar Ali 5-43); **PIA 419** (Khurram Manzoor 51, Yasir Hameed 78, Fahad Iqbal 53, Kamran Sajid 57). *PIA 9 pts.*
Karachi Whites were all out for 65 on the opening day, the lowest first-class total by a Karachi team since January 2001; PIA were 173-1 by the close, on their way to a crushing win.

At KRL Ground, Rawalpindi, December 28, 29, 30, 31, 2008. **Drawn.** Toss: ZTBL. **KRL 249** (Rizwan Ahmed 101; Mohammad Khalil 4-61) **and 265-5 dec** (Azhar Ali 81, Saeed Anwar 102); **ZTBL 255** (Afaq Raheem 76; Saeed Ajmal 7-63) **and 187-4** (Umar Javed 74*, Wajahatullah Wasti 58). *ZTBL 3 pts.*
KRL opener Azhar Ali made five catches in the field in ZTBL's first innings.

At National Bank Sports Complex, Karachi, December 28, 29, 30, 2008. **National Bank won by 171 runs.** Toss: Habib Bank. **National Bank 209** (Fawad Alam 54, Qaiser Abbas 50*; Kamran Hussain 4-34) **and 130** (Danish Kaneria 5-43); **Habib Bank 80** (Mohammad Aamer 4-20) **and 88** (Mohammad Talha 5-37). *National Bank 9 pts.*
Twenty-one wickets fell on the second day, which the previous season's finalists Habib Bank began on 11-2 and finished on 10-3; they failed to reach 90 in either innings. National Bank's captain, Test wicketkeeper Kamran Akmal, made seven catches in Habib Bank's first innings and nine in the match.

At Quaid-e-Azam Park, Karachi, December 28, 29, 30, 31, 2008. **Drawn.** Toss: Pakistan Customs. **Sui Southern Gas 346** (Saeed Bin Nasir 52, Ahmed Zeeshan 104*) **and 189-7**; **Pakistan Customs 302** (M. Q. Sheikh 103; Mohammad Kashif 4-63). *Sui Southern Gas 3 pts.*

At Sheikhupura Stadium, Sheikhupura, December 28, 29, 30, 31, 2008. **Drawn.** Toss: WAPDA. **Sui Northern Gas 134-9 dec** (Kashif Raza 5-55); **WAPDA 30-4.**

At UBL Sports Complex, Karachi, January 2, 3, 4, 2009. **Habib Bank won by an innings and 98 runs.** Toss: Pakistan Customs. **Habib Bank 314** (Younis Khan 71, Kamran Hussain 86; Murtaza Hussain 4-88); **Pakistan Customs 87 and 129** (Zahoor Elahi 81). *Habib Bank 9 pts.*

At Quaid-e-Azam Park, Karachi, January 2, 3, 4, 5, 2009. **Drawn.** Toss: Karachi Whites. **Karachi Whites 278** (Asim Kamal 71, Javed Mansoor 51; Mohammad Kashif 4-96) **and 292** (Afsar Nawaz 62, Asim Kamal 76, Shahzaib Ahmed 51*; Haaris Ayaz 4-63); **Sui Southern Gas 311** (Wajid Ali 81, Saeed Bin Nasir 94; Tanvir Ahmed 5-61, Azam Hussain 4-92) **and 64-2.** *Sui Southern Gas 3 pts.*

At KRL Ground, Rawalpindi, January 2, 3, 4, 5, 2009. **Drawn.** Toss: KRL. **WAPDA 302** (Atiq-ur-Rehman 51, Aamer Sajjad 78, Bilal Khilji 100*; Yasir Ali 4-84); **KRL 18-1.**

At LCCA Ground, Lahore, January 2, 3, 4, 5, 2009. **Drawn.** Toss: ZTBL. **Lahore Shalimar 376-7 dec** (Junaid Malik 85, Suleman Khan 83); **ZTBL 364-7** (Afaq Raheem 151, Inam-ul-Haq 104; Ghulam Mustafa 4-91).
Afaq Raheem and Inam-ul-Haq put on 257 for ZTBL's first wicket.

At National Bank Sports Complex, Karachi, January 2, 3, 4, 5, 2009. **National Bank won by 112 runs.** Toss: PIA. **National Bank 213** (Nasir Jamshed 63; Anwar Ali 4-81) **and 322** (Nasir Jamshed 115, Fawad Alam 86*; Tahir Khan 5-62); **PIA 215** (Khurram Manzoor 86*; Mohammad Aamer 6-48) **and 208** (Faisal Iqbal 52; Wahab Riaz 4-42). *National Bank 6 pts.*
Khurram Manzoor carried his bat through PIA's first innings as 16-year-old Mohammad Aamer took 6-48 in his third first-class match.

At UBL Sports Complex, Karachi, January 9, 10, 11, 12, 2009. **Drawn.** Toss: Habib Bank. **PIA 200** (Shoaib Malik 63) **and 355-5 dec** (Khurram Manzoor 151, Faisal Iqbal 50, Shoaib Malik 100*); **Habib Bank 171** (Shahid Afridi 73; Aizaz Cheema 6-52) **and 249-5** (Ahmed Shehzad 73, Khaqan Arsal 104*). *PIA 3 pts.*
All-rounder Shahid Afridi denied slapping an autograph-hunter while fielding for Habib Bank on the opening day. PIA wicketkeeper Sarfraz Ahmed made seven catches in Habib Bank's first innings,

plus a stumping in their second. Pakistan captain Shoaib Malik hit 100* in 100 balls, with four sixes and 12 fours.

At Quaid-e-Azam Park, Karachi, January 9, 10, 11, 12, 2009. **Drawn.** Toss: Pakistan Customs. **Pakistan Customs 186** (Misbah Khan 4-72) **and 312-8** (Mohammad Sami 96; Misbah Khan 4-111); **Karachi Whites 368** (Asad Shafiq 73, Ali Asad 70, Khalid Latif 73, Tanvir Ahmed 56*; Fawad Ahmed 6-109). *Karachi Whites 3 pts.*

At KRL Ground, Rawalpindi, January 9, 10, 11, 2009. **KRL won by two wickets.** Toss: KRL. **Sui Northern Gas 145** (Misbah-ul-Haq 50; Shoaib Akhtar 4-24, Yasir Arafat 4-54) **and 114** (Yasir Arafat 7-45); **KRL 133** (Asad Ali 5-51) **and 127-8** (Asad Ali 4-49). *KRL 6 pts.*

At Gaddafi Stadium, Lahore, January 9, 10, 11, 12, 2009. **Drawn.** Toss: Lahore Shalimar. **WAPDA 330** (Nawaz Sardar 147, Aamer Sajjad 53; Mohammad Naved 8-128) **and 303-6** (Aamer Sajjad 118, Bilal Khilji 116*); **Lahore Shalimar 477-7 dec** (Abid Ali 141, Raza Ali Dar 183, Zulqarnain Haider 50*). *Lahore Shalimar 3 pts.*
    Mohammad Naved took a career-best 8-128 in WAPDA's first innings.

At National Bank Sports Complex, Karachi, January 9, 10, 11, 12, 2009. **Drawn.** Toss: National Bank. **Sui Southern Gas 390** (Wajid Ali 101, Saeed Bin Nasir 70, Haaris Ayaz 57) **and 201** (Saeed Bin Nasir 65; Uzair-ul-Haq 4-27); **National Bank 204** (Umar Amin 63, Fawad Alam 53; Sohail Khan 5-90) **and 204-3** (Umar Amin 52, Naumanullah 75*). *Sui Southern Gas 3 pts.*

At Quaid-e-Azam Park, Karachi, January 14, 15, 16, 17, 2009. **Habib Bank won by an innings and 217 runs.** Toss: Habib Bank. **Habib Bank 501-8 dec** (Ahmed Shehzad 153, Khaqan Arsal 76, Aftab Alam 76, Kamran Hussain 67); **Sui Southern Gas 162** (Danish Kaneria 8-59) **and 122** (Fahad Masood 5-38, Danish Kaneria 5-22). *Habib Bank 9 pts.*
    Test leg-spinner Danish Kaneria took a career-best 8-59 in Sui Southern's first innings, and 13-81 in the match.

At Southend Club Stadium, Karachi, January 14, 15, 16, 17, 2009. **Drawn.** Toss: National Bank. **National Bank 386** (Nasir Jamshed 62, Naumanullah 66, Fawad Alam 87, Qaiser Abbas 98; Fahad Khan 4-98, Malik Aftab 5-73) **and 264-2 dec** (Nasir Jamshed 51, Rashid Riaz 100*, Fawad Alam 79*); **Karachi Whites 279** (Khalid Latif 56, Afsar Nawaz 66; Irfanuddin 5-59) **and 292-8** (Ali Asad 85). *National Bank 3 pts.*
    This was the first domestic first-class game at this ground, formerly the Defence Housing Authority Stadium, for nine years.

At Lahore Country Club, Muridke, January 14, 15, 2009. **KRL won by ten wickets.** Toss: KRL. **Lahore Shalimar 103** (Jaffar Nazir 4-44) **and 118** (Jaffar Nazir 4-43); **KRL 193** (Saeed Anwar 65; Mohammad Naved 7-90) **and 29-0.** *KRL 9 pts.*

At National Bank Sports Complex, Karachi, January 14, 15, 16, 17, 2009. **PIA won by seven wickets.** Toss: PIA. **Pakistan Customs 310** (Rameez Aziz 141, Zahoor Elahi 54; Najaf Shah 4-74) **and 284** (Rameez Raja 117; Najaf Shah 6-66); **PIA 443-7 dec** (Agha Sabir 160, Fahad Iqbal 61, Faisal Iqbal 61) **and 152-3** (Kamran Sajid 52, Sarfraz Ahmed 60*). *PIA 9 pts.*
    The final day started with Customs 127-1, six runs behind with nine second-innings wickets standing; but Najaf Shah bowled them out for 284, and PIA scored at more than eight an over to reach a target of 152.

At Sports Stadium, Sargodha, January 14, 15, 16, 17, 2009. **Drawn.** Toss: ZTBL. **Sui Northern Gas 156** (Mohammad Khalil 4-32, Junaid Nadir 4-29) **and 75-4;** **ZTBL 241-4 dec** (Aamer Bashir 51, Wajahatullah Wasti 56*). *ZTBL 3 pts.*

At Southend Club Stadium, Karachi, January 20, 21, 22, 23, 2009. **Drawn.** Toss: Habib Bank. **Habib Bank 176** (Ahmed Shehzad 50; Misbah Khan 5-49) **and 353-6** (Ahmed Shehzad 175, Farhan Iqbal 63*); **Karachi Whites 498-8 dec** (Ali Asad 108, Asim Kamal 125, Tanvir Ahmed 75). *Karachi Whites 3 pts.*

At LCCA Ground, Lahore, January 20, 21, 22, 23, 2009. **Sui Northern Gas won by nine wickets.** Toss: Sui Northern Gas. **Lahore Shalimar 207** (Mohammad Saeed 59*) **and 199;** **Sui Northern**

Gas 288 (Umar Akmal 70, Azhar Shafiq 55, Khurram Shehzad 57; Mohammad Naved 5-86) **and** 120-1 (Ali Waqas 50*, Umar Akmal 58*). *Sui Northern Gas 9 pts.*

At National Bank Sports Complex, Karachi, January 20, 21, 22, 2009. **National Bank won by an innings and 310 runs.** Toss: Pakistan Customs. **Pakistan Customs 130** (Rameez Aziz 52; Mohammad Talha 5-44) **and 187** (Zahoor Elahi 102*; Mohammad Talha 5-75, Mohammad Aamer 4-48); **National Bank 627** (Nasir Jamshed 105, Fawad Alam 296*, Qaiser Abbas 52). *National Bank 9 pts.*
  National Bank's 627 was their highest first-class total. Fawad Alam was stranded four short of converting his maiden double-hundred into a triple, after hitting 35 fours and two sixes in 294 balls and 443 minutes. He scored more in one innings than Customs' batsmen in 22 (disregarding their 30 extras). Mohammad Talha took five wickets in each innings.

At Quaid-e-Azam Park, Karachi, January 20, 21, 22, 23, 2009. **PIA won by an innings and 18 runs.** Toss: Sui Southern Gas. **Sui Southern Gas 278** (Imran Abbas 90) **and 191** (Wajid Ali 68*, Haaris Ayaz 50; Tahir Khan 4-63); **PIA 487-6 dec** (Fahad Iqbal 75, Faisal Iqbal 200*, Sarfraz Ahmed 82). *PIA 9 pts.*
  PIA captain Faisal Iqbal scored his second double-hundred to set up victory.

At Sheikhupura Stadium, Sheikhupura, January 20, 21, 22, 23, 2009. **Drawn.** Toss: ZTBL. **WAPDA 199** (Azhar Attari 4-47) **and 333-8 dec** (Bilal Khilji 130*, Nawaz Sardar 51, Imranullah Aslam 77; Azhar Attari 4-77); **ZTBL 242** (Afaq Raheem 82, Junaid Nadir 60; Mustafa Iqbal 4-39) **and 139-4** (Aamer Bashir 61*). *ZTBL 3 pts.*

At National Stadium, Karachi, January 26, 27, 28, 2009. **ZTBL won by two wickets.** Toss: ZTBL. **Karachi Whites 232** (Murtaza Majeed 67; Junaid Nadir 5-64) **and 80** (Junaid Nadir 6-30); **ZTBL 224** (Shakeel Ansar 54, Mohammad Khalil 55*; Tariq Haroon 5-81) **and 92-8.** *ZTBL 6 pts.*
  Karachi Whites succumbed for 80 on the third day, the second time in the season they had been dismissed in double figures; ZTBL made heavy weather of chasing 89, sliding to 81 for eight before victory.

At KRL Ground, Rawalpindi, January 26, 27, 28, 29, 2009. **KRL won by 131 runs.** Toss: Sui Southern Gas. **KRL 191** (Shehzad Butt 4-47) **and 229-7 dec** (Mohammad Wasim 101*); **Sui Southern Gas 79** (Yasir Arafat 9-35) **and 210** (Wajid Ali 69; Junaid Khan 4-40). *KRL 9 pts.*
  Yasir Arafat bowled unchanged throughout Sui Southern's first innings of 79 for career-best figures of 12.4–3–35–9 (interrupted by a second-day washout), which took him past 600 first-class wickets. Mohammad Wasim scored 101 in 101 balls.*

At Gaddafi Stadium, Lahore, January 26, 27, 28, 29, 2009. **Habib Bank won by six wickets.** Toss: Habib Bank. **Lahore Shalimar 252** (Zulqarnain Haider 67*, Muzaffar Mahboob 54; Fahad Masood 4-53) **and 109; Habib Bank 257** (Imran Nazir 55, Younis Khan 99; Mohammad Naved 7-129) **and 108-4.** *Habib Bank 9 pts.*
  On the second day, Younis Khan was summoned to an emergency meeting by the PCB, which appointed him Pakistan captain.

At Jinnah Stadium, Gujranwala, January 26, 27, 28, 29, 2009. **Sui Northern Gas won by 177 runs.** Toss: Pakistan Customs. **Sui Northern Gas 196** (Azhar Shafiq 98*; Aamer Yousuf 5-68) **and 224-8 dec** (Azhar Shafiq 50); **Pakistan Customs 140** (Samiullah Khan 4-61, Imran Ali 4-37) **and 103** (Samiullah Khan 5-46, Imran Ali 5-56). *Sui Northern Gas 9 pts.*

At Jinnah Stadium, Sialkot, January 26, 27, 28, 29, 2009. **Drawn.** Toss: PIA. **WAPDA 274-7** (Ali Azmat 52*, Imranullah Aslam 50) **v PIA.**

At National Stadium, Karachi, February 1, 2, 3, 4, 2009. **WAPDA won by one wicket.** Toss: Karachi Whites. **Karachi Whites 133** (Ali Asad 67*; Kashif Raza 5-44) **and 262** (Khalid Latif 81; Azharullah 4-83); **WAPDA 226** (Ahmed Said 63, Jahangir Mirza 77; Tanvir Ahmed 6-77) **and 173-9** (Malik Aftab 4-42). *WAPDA 9 pts.*
  WAPDA were 73-7 and then 135-9 chasing 170 before their final pair saw them home.

At Mirpur Cricket Stadium, Mirpur, February 1, 2, 3, 4, 2009. **KRL won by seven wickets.** Toss: KRL. **PIA 152** (Sohail Tanvir 8-54) **and 248** (Fahad Iqbal 52; Sohail Tanvir 7-120); **KRL 275** (Saeed Anwar 89, Sohail Tanvir 52*; Najaf Shah 5-103) **and 126-3.** *KRL 9 pts.*

Sohail Tanvir bowled continuously throughout both PIA innings for analyses of 27–10–54–8 and 42–9–120–7; his first-innings 8-54 and match return of 15-174 were career-bests.

At LCCA Ground, Lahore, February 1, 2, 3, 4, 2009. **Drawn.** Toss: Pakistan Customs. **Pakistan Customs 325** (Rameez Raja 87, Zahoor Elahi 81; Mohammad Naved 4-120, Ghulam Mustafa 6-97) **and 310** (Mohammad Hussain 87; Ghulam Mustafa 5-128); **Lahore Shalimar 360** (Ahmed Dar 73, Abid Ali 114, Raza Ali Dar 80; Yasir Hussain 7-91) **and 131-2** (Abid Ali 69, Saadullah Ghauri 58*). *Lahore Shalimar 3 pts.*

At Gaddafi Stadium, Lahore, February 1, 2, 3, 4, 2009. **National Bank won by 283 runs.** Toss: National Bank. **National Bank 225** (Naumanullah 56, Qaiser Abbas 55; Iftikhar Anjum 4-56) **and 358-6 dec** (Salman Butt 202, Fawad Alam 58); **ZTBL 147** (Mohammad Talha 4-53, Mohammad Aamer 4-44) **and 153** (Mohammad Talha 4-60, Wahab Riaz 4-24). *National Bank 9 pts.*

Naumanullah made five catches in the field in ZTBL's first innings. Salman Butt scored his third double-hundred, hitting 24 fours in 226 balls.

At Sheikhupura Stadium, Sheikhupura, February 1, 2, 3, 2009. **Sui Northern Gas won by an innings and 199 runs.** Toss: Sui Northern Gas. **Sui Southern Gas 135** (Imran Ali 5-31) **and 160** (Ahmed Zeeshan 52); **Sui Northern Gas 494-6 dec** (Mohammad Hafeez 142, Misbah-ul-Haq 247, Khurram Shehzad 50). *Sui Northern Gas 9 pts.*

Mohammad Hafeez and Misbah-ul-Haq (who scored his fifth and highest double-hundred, containing 23 fours and seven sixes) added 293 for Sui Northern's fourth wicket.

At Gaddafi Stadium, Lahore, February 7, 8, 9, 10, 2009. **Drawn.** Toss: Habib Bank. **Sui Northern Gas 410** (Umar Akmal 63, Azhar Shafiq 105, Misbah-ul-Haq 58, Yasir Shah 71; Abdur Rehman 4-83); **Habib Bank 307-8** (Rehan Rafiq 56, Kamran Hussain 50, Abdur Rehman 79*; Imran Ali 4-80).

At National Bank Sports Complex, Karachi, February 7, 8, 9, 10, 2009. **Drawn.** Toss: Karachi Whites. **Karachi Whites 268** (Khalid Latif 87, Tanvir Ahmed 58; Yasir Arafat 6-53) **and 455-7** (Ali Asad 107, Asad Shafiq 117, Khalid Latif 58, Ahmed Iqbal 59*); **KRL 353** (Saeed Anwar 125; Khalid Mahmood 6-65). *KRL 3 pts.*

In Karachi Whites' second innings, Ali Asad and Asad Sharif added 209 for the second wicket.

At LCCA Ground, Lahore, February 7, 8, 9, 10, 2009. **Drawn.** Toss: Lahore Shalimar. **Lahore Shalimar 148** (Fazl-e-Akbar 4-46, Najaf Shah 6-39) **and 142-5** (Abid Ali 71*); **PIA 440-9 dec** (Yasir Hameed 100, Fahad Iqbal 67, Faisal Iqbal 52, Shoaib Khan 102; Mohammad Naved 4-154). *PIA 3 pts.*

At Lahore Country Club, Muridke, February 7, 8, 9, 10, 2009. **Drawn.** Toss: ZTBL. **ZTBL 150** (Rajesh Ramesh 5-37) **and 229** (Sohail Khan 6-82); **Sui Southern Gas 159** (Saeed Bin Nasir 52) **and 89-5.** *Sui Southern Gas 3 pts.*

Rajesh Ramesh reduced ZTBL to 7-5 on the first morning.

At Mirpur Cricket Stadium, Mirpur, February 8, 9, 10, 11, 2009. **Drawn.** Toss: National Bank. **WAPDA 280** (Bilal Khilji 86, Aamer Sajjad 68); **National Bank 363-1** (Nasir Jamshed 156*, Umar Amin 127, Fawad Alam 51*). *National Bank 3 pts.*

Nasir Jamshed and Umar Amin put on 285 for National Bank's first wicket.

At National Bank Sports Complex, Karachi, February 13, 14, 15, 2009. **Sui Northern Gas won by an innings and 90 runs.** Toss: Sui Northern Gas. **Karachi Whites 121** (Adnan Baig 50*; Imran Ali 4-48) **and 177** (Khalid Latif 71); **Sui Northern Gas 388-8 dec** (Mohammad Hafeez 60, Umar Akmal 53, Khurram Shehzad 124, Ali Raza 59). *Sui Northern Gas 9 pts.*

At KRL Ground, Rawalpindi, February 13, 14, 15, 16, 2009. **Drawn.** Toss: KRL. **Habib Bank 241** (Aftab Alam 120*); **KRL 258-8** (Mohammad Wasim 91; Mohammad Aslam 4-57). *KRL 3 pts.*

At Gaddafi Stadium, Lahore, February 13, 14, 15, 2009. **National Bank won by an innings and 90 runs.** Toss: National Bank. **Lahore Shalimar 134** (Wahab Riaz 5-36) **and 153** (Zulqarnain Haider 60; Mohammad Aamer 7-61); **National Bank 377-4 dec** (Umar Amin 73, Anwaar Hafeez 71, Qaiser Abbas 104*). *National Bank 9 pts.*

At Sheikhupura Stadium, Sheikhupura, February 13, 14, 15, 16, 2009. **ZTBL won by ten wickets.** Toss: Pakistan Customs. **Pakistan Customs 280** (B. M. Shafayat 55, Zeeshan Ali 50*; Iftikhar Anjum 4-85) **and 237** (Zohaib Khan 5-72, Junaid Nadir 4-8); **ZTBL 517** (Inam-ul-Haq 110, Aamer Bashir 99, Abdul Razzaq 98, Faisal Naved 72; Mohammad Hussain 4-156) **and 4-0.** *ZTBL 9 pts.*
   Abdul Razzaq just missed a century on his return to official Pakistani cricket from his ICL exile.

At Lahore Country Club, Muridke, February 13, 14, 15, 16, 2009. **Drawn.** Toss: Sui Southern Gas. **WAPDA 460-9 dec** (Aamer Sajjad 86, Ali Azmat 102, Jahangir Mirza 72, Naved-ul-Hasan 110) **and 98-6; Sui Southern Gas 179** (Ahmed Zeeshan 67; Naved-ul-Hasan 5-37, Nawaz Sardar 4-33). *WAPDA 3 pts.*
   In WAPDA's first innings, Jahangir Mirza and Naved-ul-Hasan added 165 for the seventh wicket.

At Sheikhupura Stadium, Sheikhupura, February 19, 20, 21, 22, 2009. **ZTBL won by 158 runs.** Toss: Habib Bank. **ZTBL 290** (Wajahatullah Wasti 85) **and 256** (Inam-ul-Haq 74, Abdul Razzaq 74; Mohammad Aslam 4-61); **Habib Bank 85** (Abdul Razzaq 5-38, Junaid Nadir 5-34) **and 303** (Hasan Raza 62; Abdul Razzaq 4-48). *ZTBL 9 pts.*

At KRL Ground, Rawalpindi, February 19, 20, 21, 22, 2009. **Drawn.** Toss: KRL. **National Bank 184** (Rashid Riaz 61; Sohail Tanvir 4-87) **and 357-4 dec** (Nasir Jamshed 107, Umar Amin 85, Naumanullah 80, Qaiser Abbas 63*); **KRL 237** (Mohammad Aamer 6-95) **and 152-7** (Mohammad Wasim 72*). *KRL 3 pts.*

At Lahore Country Club, Muridke, February 19, 20, 21, 22, 2009. **Drawn.** Toss: Lahore Shalimar. **Karachi Whites 501-7 dec** (Ali Asad 172, Khalid Latif 123, Afsar Nawaz 101*) **and 194-4 dec** (Khalid Latif 105*); **Lahore Shalimar 384** (Mohammad Asim 64, Suleman Khan 58, Asif Raza 55) **and 112-3.** *Karachi Whites 3 pts.*
   Khalid Latif scored a century in each innings, sharing an opening stand of 249 with Ali Asad on the first day.

At Jinnah Stadium, Sialkot, February 19, 20, 21, 22, 2009. **WAPDA won by eight wickets.** Toss: Pakistan Customs. **Pakistan Customs 303** (Rameez Aziz 85, M. Q. Sheikh 60, Zahoor Elahi 52; Shabbir Ahmed 6-65) **and 144; WAPDA 244** (Jahangir Mirza 135*) **and 206-2** (Jahangir Mirza 101*). *WAPDA 6 pts.*
   Jahangir Mirza scored a century in each innings, the first two of his career; no one else in WAPDA's first innings reached 30.

At Iqbal Stadium, Faisalabad, February 19, 20, 21, 22, 2009. **PIA won by two wickets.** Toss: PIA. **Sui Northern Gas 325** (Umar Akmal 93; Tahir Khan 4-48) **and 183** (Najaf Shah 5-51); **PIA 223** (Sarfraz Ahmed 88) **and 286-8** (Yasir Hameed 73, Sarfraz Ahmed 61; Yasir Shah 4-83). *PIA 6 pts.*

At Sheikhupura Stadium, Sheikhupura, February 25, 26, 27, 28, 2009. **Drawn.** Toss: WAPDA. **Habib Bank 202** (Imran Farhat 100) **and 317** (Rehan Rafiq 94, Hasan Raza 63); **WAPDA 264** (Aamer Sajjad 61, Nawaz Sardar 52; Abdur Rehman 4-75) **and 83-4.** *WAPDA 3 pts.*

At Mirpur Cricket Stadium, Mirpur, February 25, 26, 27, 2009. **KRL won by 320 runs.** Toss: Pakistan Customs. **KRL 208** (Ali Naqvi 64; Farhan Ayub 5-86) **and 370-8 dec** (Mohammad Wasim 165, Ali Naqvi 82; Farhan Ayub 5-103); **Pakistan Customs 179** (Zahoor Elahi 64; Sohail Tanvir 7-91) **and 79** (Junaid Khan 5-4). *KRL 9 pts.*
   Nineteen-year-old left-armer Junaid Khan's full figures in the second innings were 4–0–4–5; he helped KRL to a three-day victory which proved enough to see them into the final when National Bank drew.

At LCCA Ground, Lahore, February 25, 26, 27, 28, 2009. **Drawn.** Toss: Lahore Shalimar. **Lahore Shalimar 456** (Abid Ali 114, Sheraz Butt 96, Zulqarnain Haider 72; Adnan Malik 4-105) **and 120-3** (Ahmed Dar 52); **Sui Southern Gas 459** (Wajid Ali 119, Ahmed Zeeshan 91, Saeed Bin Nasir 119; Sheraz Butt 5-65). *Sui Southern Gas 3 pts.*
   Saeed Bin Nasir reached 1,000 first-class runs for the season.

At Multan Cricket Stadium, Multan, February 25, 26, 27, 28, 2009. **Drawn.** Toss: Sui Northern Gas. **National Bank 326** (Nasir Jamshed 51, Umar Amin 84, Naumanullah 55; Samiullah Khan 4-60) **and 242** (Naumanullah 60, Qaiser Abbas 55; Adnan Rasool 5-77); **Sui Northern Gas 292** (Umar Akmal 130; Wahab Riaz 4-74) **and 162-2** (Mohammad Hafeez 100*). *National Bank 3 pts.*

National Bank needed a win to be sure of reaching the final, but failed to dismiss Sui Northern twice.

At Iqbal Stadium, Faisalabad, February 25, 26, 27, 28, 2009. **Drawn.** Toss: ZTBL. **PIA 459-9 dec** (Fahad Iqbal 200*, Sarfraz Ahmed 65, Ali Imran 69) **and 269-3** (Shoaib Khan 114*, Sarfraz Ahmed 62*); **ZTBL 345** (Afaq Raheem 61, Inam-ul-Haq 145). *PIA 3 pts.*

Fahad Iqbal scored his maiden double-hundred and added 170 for PIA's eighth wicket with Ali Imran.

Group B

At Diamond Club Ground, Islamabad, December 28, 29, 30, 31, 2008. **Rawalpindi won by three wickets.** Toss: Rawalpindi. **Islamabad 252** (Ali Sarfraz 64; Nasir Malik 4-80) **and 124** (Haseeb Azam 6-64); **Rawalpindi 288** (Fawad Hussain 108; Rauf Akbar 4-46) **and 139-7** (Hammad Azam 62; Rauf Akbar 4-46). *Rawalpindi 6 pts.*

Nineteen-year-old Fawad Hussain scored 108 in his second first-class match, to follow 103 in his only previous innings, 12 months earlier.*

At UBL Sports Complex, Karachi, December 28, 29, 30, 31, 2008. **Karachi Blues won by ten wickets.** Toss: Quetta. **Karachi Blues 289** (Shadab Kabir 91, Mohammad Faheem 50; Nazar Hussain 5-55) **and 99-0** (Shahzaib Hasan 59*); **Quetta 129** (Tabish Khan 4-50) **and 258** (Nasim Khan 62). *Karachi Blues 9 pts.*

At Gaddafi Stadium, Lahore, December 28, 29, 30, 31, 2008. **Drawn.** Toss: Faisalabad. **Lahore Ravi 327** (Kashif Siddiq 114); **Faisalabad 290** (Imran Ali 83, Usman Arshad 71; Waqas Ahmed 4-70). *Lahore Ravi 3 pts.*

At Multan Cricket Stadium, Multan, December 28, 29, 30, 31, 2008. **Drawn.** Toss: Hyderabad. **Multan 234-8 dec** (Naved Yasin 54); **Hyderabad 132-3** (Faisal Athar 83*).

At Arbab Niaz Stadium, Peshawar, December 28, 29, 30, 2008. **Abbottabad won by nine wickets.** Toss: Abbottabad. **Peshawar 66** (Armaghan Elahi 9-38) **and 247** (Sajjad Ahmed 84, Mohammad Rizwan 60; Rashid Mansoor 5-45); **Abbottabad 292** (Ghulam Mohammad 94, Fawad Khan 69) **and 22-1.** *Abbottabad 9 pts.*

Left-armer Armaghan Elahi bowled unchanged for career-best figures of 13.5–4–38–9, dismissing Peshawar for 66 with only one man reaching double figures.

At Diamond Club Ground, Islamabad, January 2, 3, 4, 5, 2009. **Drawn.** Toss: Abbottabad. **Rawalpindi 325** (Awais Zia 80, Jamal Anwar 52, Rashid Latif 82; Noor-ul-Amin 4-71) **v Abbottabad.**

At Iqbal Stadium, Faisalabad, January 2, 3, 4, 5, 2009. **Faisalabad won by an innings and 69 runs.** Toss: Faisalabad. **Hyderabad 179** (Zulqarnain 4-66) **and 106** (Saadat Munir 4-20); **Faisalabad 354-3 dec** (Imran Ali 103, Zeeshan Butt 133*, Usman Arshad 52*). *Faisalabad 9 pts.*

At National Stadium, Karachi, January 2, 3, 4, 5, 2009. **Sialkot won by seven wickets.** Toss: Sialkot. **Karachi Blues 226** (Shadab Kabir 52, Mohammad Hasan 62; Nayyer Abbas 4-41) **and 219** (Shahzaib Hasan 51, Babar Rehman 59); **Sialkot 238** (Haris Sohail 74*; Babar Rehman 5-73) **and 211-3** (Kamran Younis 55, Haris Sohail 63*, Mohammad Ayub 69*). *Sialkot 9 pts.*

At Marghzar Cricket Ground, Islamabad, January 3, 4, 5, 6, 2009. **Drawn.** Toss: Peshawar. **Islamabad 47-2 v Peshawar.**

At Multan Cricket Stadium, Multan, January 3, 4, 5, 6, 2009. **Multan won by eight wickets.** Toss: Multan. **Quetta 210** (Nasim Khan 54; Abdur Rauf 5-50) **and 137** (Nasim Khan 71; Zulfiqar Babar 4-24); **Multan 193** (Rameez Alam 82*; Nazar Hussain 6-54) **and 155-2** (Usman Tariq 68*). *Multan 6 pts.*

At Diamond Club Ground, Islamabad, January 9, 10, 11, 2009. **Islamabad won by eight wickets.** Toss: Islamabad. **Abbottabad 163** (Rauf Akbar 4-35) **and 189** (Saad Altaf 5-52); **Islamabad 243** (Raheel Majeed 57) **and 110-2** (Umair Khan 51*). *Islamabad 9 pts.*

The highest contributor to Abbottabad's first-innings 163 was 46 from Extras, including 35 no-balls, 25 of them conceded by Shehzad Azam in nine overs.

At Iqbal Stadium, Faisalabad, January 9, 10, 11, 2009. **Faisalabad won by an innings and 167 runs.** Toss: Quetta. **Faisalabad 447-8 dec** (Ijaz Ahmed 229*, Mohammad Salman 90; Mohammad Aslam 4-82); **Quetta 173 and 107.** *Faisalabad 9 pts.*

Ijaz Ahmed scored his second double-hundred, and added 203 for Faisalabad's sixth wicket with Mohammad Salman.

At National Stadium, Karachi, January 9, 10, 11, 12, 2009. **Drawn.** Toss: Karachi Blues. **Lahore Ravi 222** (Shahnawaz Malik 104*; Babar Rehman 4-79) **and 374-8** (Kashif Siddiq 91, Ashraf Ali 124*, Rana Adnan 63); **Karachi Blues 450** (Shahzaib Hasan 156, Tabish Khan 57; Azam Khan 5-89). *Karachi Blues 3 pts.*

At Marghzar Cricket Ground, Islamabad, January 9, 10, 11, 2009. **Rawalpindi won by seven wickets.** Toss: Rawalpindi. **Multan 187** (Rizwan Akbar 5-59) **and 93** (Rizwan Akbar 7-39); **Rawalpindi 121** (Abdur Rauf 5-39) **and 160-3.** *Rawalpindi 6 pts.*

Rizwan Akbar took 12-98 in the match.

At Jinnah Stadium, Sialkot, January 9, 10, 11, 12, 2009. **Sialkot won by an innings and 186 runs.** Toss: Sialkot. **Hyderabad 252** (Aqeel Anjum 104) **and 102** (Sarmad Anwar 4-32, Nadeem Javed 5-23); **Sialkot 540-9 dec** (Kamran Younis 89, Naeemuddin 173, Nadeem Javed 61, Mohammad Ayub 53; Naeem-ur-Rehman 4-120). *Sialkot 9 pts.*

At Mirpur Cricket Stadium, Mirpur, January 14, 15, 16, 17, 2009. **Drawn.** Toss: Rawalpindi. **Faisalabad 252** (Mohammad Salman 65; Rizwan Akbar 4-94) **and 196-7** (Ammar Mahmood 51; Mohammad Rameez 4-56); **Rawalpindi 379** (Babar Naeem 143, Usman Saeed 130; Saadat Munir 5-101). *Rawalpindi 3 pts.*

At Diamond Club Ground, Islamabad, January 14, 15, 16, 17, 2009. **Drawn.** Toss: Islamabad. **Multan 118** (Shehzad Azam 5-45) **and 247-8** (Rameez Alam 50, Kashif Naved 56*); **Islamabad 159** (Abdur Rauf 5-75). *Islamabad 3 pts.*

At UBL Sports Complex, Karachi, January 14, 15, 16, 17, 2009. **Drawn.** Toss: Peshawar. **Peshawar 290** (Israrullah 88, Sajjad Ahmed 68; Abdul Ameer 5-74) **and 313-5** (Sajjad Ahmed 53, Mahfooz Sabri 56, Akbar Badshah 72*, Mohammad Rizwan 53*); **Karachi Blues 302** (Sheharyar Ghani 78, Akbar-ur-Rehman 84*; Imran Khan 4-43). *Karachi Blues 3 pts.*

At Jinnah Stadium, Sialkot, January 14, 15, 16, 2009. **Sialkot won by an innings and 137 runs.** Toss: Sialkot. **Quetta 92** (Naved Arif 4-45, Nadeem Javed 5-18) **and 158** (Tariq Mahmood 4-26); **Sialkot 387-6 dec** (Kamran Younis 50, Naeemuddin 53, Mohammad Ayub 103, Haris Sohail 51). *Sialkot 9 pts.*

At LCCA Ground, Lahore, January 15, 16, 17, 18, 2009. **Drawn.** Toss: Hyderabad. **Lahore Ravi 218** (Ali Raza 68, Waqas Ahmed 50; Naeem-ur-Rehman 4-54) **and 34-4; Hyderabad 172** (Waqas Ahmed 6-36). *Lahore Ravi 3 pts.*

At Gymkhana Ground, Okara, January 20, 21, 22, 23, 2009. **Drawn.** Toss: Faisalabad. **Multan 332-9 dec** (Usman Tariq 75, Naved Yasin 92, Majid Majeed 75; Zahoor Khan 5-100) **and 137-3; Faisalabad 105** (Abdur Rauf 4-51, Sajjad Hussain 5-20) **and 400-8 dec** (Imran Ali 135, Mohammad Salman 67, Ijaz Ahmed 60). *Multan 3 pts.*

At UBL Sports Complex, Karachi, January 20, 21, 22, 2009. **Abbottabad won by ten wickets.** Toss: Abbottabad. **Karachi Blues 149** (Rashid Mansoor 6-76) **and 154** (Sheharyar Ghani 55; Rashid Mansoor 4-94, Armaghan Elahi 6-42); **Abbottabad 294** (Fawad Khan 62, Riaz Kail 87; Tabish Khan 4-99, Abdul Ameer 5-55) **and 10-0.** *Abbottabad 9 pts.*

At Lahore Country Club, Muridke, January 20, 21, 22, 23, 2009. **Drawn.** Toss: Quetta. **Quetta 256** (Mohammad Aslam 52) **and 214** (Mohammad Aslam 60, Ata-ur-Rehman 51; Waqas Ahmed 5-41); **Lahore Ravi 279** (Ashraf Ali 51; Nazar Hussain 4-73). *Lahore Ravi 3 pts.*

At Diamond Club Ground, Islamabad, January 20, 21, 22, 23, 2009. **Rawalpindi won by 218 runs.** Toss: Sialkot. **Rawalpindi 297** (Babar Naeem 79, Naved Ashraf 74, Fawad Hussain 51; Naved Arif 6-63) **and 239-8 dec** (Awais Zia 86, Naved Ashraf 58); **Sialkot 155** (Haris Sohail 56; Mohammad Rameez 4-45) **and 163** (Mohammad Rameez 5-63). *Rawalpindi 9 pts.*

At Niaz Stadium, Hyderabad, January 21, 22, 23, 24, 2009. **Peshawar won by six wickets.** Toss: Peshawar. **Hyderabad 292** (Azeem Ghumman 100; Imran Khan 4-53) **and 192** (Waqar Ahmed 4-42); **Peshawar 360** (Adil Amin 93, Sajjad Ahmed 60, Mahfooz Sabri 52, Mohammad Rizwan 68*; Lal Kumar 4-60) **and 125-4** (Mohammad Rizwan 50*). *Peshawar 9 pts.*

At Iqbal Stadium, Faisalabad, January 26, 27, 28, 29, 2009. **Drawn.** Toss: Faisalabad. **Faisalabad 151** (Ijaz Ahmed 61*; Saad Altaf 5-75) **and 246-6 dec** (Zeeshan Butt 75*, Usman Arshad 75); **Islamabad 158** (Saadat Munir 6-39) **and 164-7.** *Islamabad 3 pts.*

At Niaz Stadium, Hyderabad, January 26, 27, 28, 29, 2009. **Drawn.** Toss: Abbottabad. **Hyderabad 471-9 dec** (Azeem Ghumman 147, Faisal Athar 140, Hanif Malik 73; Armaghan Elahi 5-69) **and 23-1; Abbottabad 429** (Hammad Ali 100, Mohammad Kashif 53, Adnan Raees 76, Riaz Kail 65, Extras 60; Lal Kumar 4-81). *Hyderabad 3 pts.*
  Azeem Ghumman and Faisal Athar added 237 for Hyderabad's third wicket.

At LCCA Ground, Lahore, January 26, 27, 28, 29, 2009. **Drawn.** Toss: Lahore Ravi. **Rawalpindi 304** (Naved Ashraf 105, Fawad Hussain 106) **and 321-3** (Babar Naeem 96, Awais Zia 125*, Usman Saeed 85); **Lahore Ravi 267** (Babar Manzoor 53, Ashraf Ali 97; Yasim Murtaza 5-52). *Rawalpindi 3 pts.*

At Gymkhana Ground, Okara, January 26, 27, 28, 29, 2009. **Sialkot won by 239 runs.** Toss: Multan. **Sialkot 339** (Naeemuddin 65, Ayaz Tasawwar 100*) **and 241-6 dec; Multan 241** (Rameez Alam 67, Rizwan Haider 55*) **and 100** (Naved Arif 6-33, Nayyer Abbas 4-22). *Sialkot 9 pts.*

At Arbab Niaz Stadium, Peshawar, January 27, 28, 29, 30, 2009. **Peshawar won by an innings and 45 runs.** Toss: Quetta. **Quetta 51** (Nauman Habib 4-20, Waqar Ahmed 6-29) **and 207** (Nauman Habib 7-57); **Peshawar 303-7 dec** (Mahfooz Sabri 95, Mohammad Rizwan 51*). *Peshawar 9 pts.*
  Only opener Taimur Ali reached double figures as Quetta were all out in the 18th over after a first-day washout. Nauman Habib took 11-77 in the match and Waqar Ahmed 9-129.

At Diamond Club Ground, Islamabad, February 1, 2, 3, 2009. **Abbottabad won by ten wickets.** Toss: Abbottabad. **Quetta 164** (Noor-ul-Amin 4-58) **and 173** (Noor-ul-Amin 4-56); **Abbottabad 255** (Riaz Kail 90*; Imran Khan 4-72) **and 84-0.** *Abbottabad 9 pts.*

At Niaz Stadium, Hyderabad, February 1, 2, 3, 4, 2009. **Islamabad won by 280 runs.** Toss: Islamabad. **Islamabad 258** (Rauf Akbar 116; Lal Kumar 4-52) **and 332-8 dec** (Umair Khan 70, Rauf Akbar 77, Imad Wasim 56*; Lal Kumar 4-83); **Hyderabad 173** (Kamran Hussain 4-34) **and 137** (Saad Altaf 5-51, Kamran Hussain 5-41). *Islamabad 9 pts.*
  Rauf Akbar rescued Islamabad on the first day, coming in at 73-7 to score a maiden century from No. 9.

At Multan Cricket Stadium, Multan, February 1, 2, 3, 4, 2009. **Multan won by ten wickets.** Toss: Multan. **Peshawar 341** (Naved Khan 70, Mohammad Idrees 63, Mahfooz Sabri 62; Abdur Rauf 7-84) **and 124** (Abdur Rauf 5-63); **Multan 451** (Usman Tariq 171, Naved Yasin 130, Gulraiz Sadaf 60*) **and 17-0.** *Multan 9 pts.*
  Abdur Rauf took 12-147 in the match, including a hat-trick to wind up Peshawar's first innings. Usman Tariq and Naved Yasin added 283 for Multan's fourth wicket.

At KRL Ground, Rawalpindi, February 1, 2, 3, 4, 2009. **Rawalpindi won by eight wickets.** Toss: Karachi Blues. **Rawalpindi 289** (Awais Zia 147*; Tabish Khan 5-57) **and 171-2** (Babar Naeem 56); **Karachi Blues 134** (Rizwan Akbar 5-46) **and 324** (Shahzaib Hasan 95, Sheharyar Ghani 74; Mohammad Rameez 4-101). *Rawalpindi 9 pts.*

At Jinnah Stadium, Sialkot, February 1, 2, 3, 4, 2009. **Drawn.** Toss: Sialkot. **Lahore Ravi 287** (Sohail Ahmed 68, Ali Raza 57*; Bilawal Bhatti 4-87) **and 327-6** (Shahnawaz Malik 56, Ashraf Ali 103*, Ali Haider 61); **Sialkot 385** (Naeemuddin 64, Ayaz Tasawwar 93; Sohail Ahmed 4-67). *Sialkot 3 pts.*

At Sheikhupura Stadium, Sheikhupura, February 7, 8, 9, 10, 2009. **Drawn.** Toss: Sialkot. **Abbottabad 243** (Rashid Mansoor 68) **and 177-5** (Hammad Ali 85*); **Sialkot 385** (Naeemuddin 112, Mohammad Ayub 73). *Sialkot 3 pts.*

At Sports Stadium, Sargodha, February 7, 8, 9, 10, 2009. **Drawn.** Toss: Faisalabad. **Faisalabad 388** (Imran Ali 55, Usman Arshad 81, Zeeshan Butt 80, Mohammad Salman 93); **Karachi Blues 158** (Shahzaib Hasan 63; Zahoor Khan 5-31) **and 412-9** (Sheharyar Ghani 181*, Faraz Patel 54, Owais Rehmani 54; Zahoor Khan 7-86). *Faisalabad 3 pts.*
    Zahoor Khan took 12-117 in the match.

At Niaz Stadium, Hyderabad, February 7, 8, 9, 10, 2009. **Drawn.** Toss: Hyderabad. **Rawalpindi 481** (Zahid Mansoor 146, Usman Saeed 144, Yasim Murtaza 75) **and 90-0** (Babar Naeem 52*); **Hyderabad 422** (Azeem Ghumman 199; Qamar Abbas 4-76). *Rawalpindi 3 pts.*
    Zahid Mansoor and Usman Saeed added 279 for Rawalpindi's fourth wicket. In reply, 18-year-old Azeem Ghumman scored a fourth hundred in his 11th first-class match, and his third in three weeks, narrowly missing a maiden double.

At Diamond Club Ground, Islamabad, February 7, 8, 9, 2009. **Islamabad won by an innings and 415 runs.** Toss: Islamabad. **Quetta 94** (Rauf Akbar 6-64, Saad Altaf 4-30) **and 96** (Saad Altaf 6-29); **Islamabad 605-9 dec** (Raheel Majeed 87, Zeeshan Mushtaq 230, Ashar Zaidi 97, Rauf Akbar 76). *Islamabad 9 pts.*
    Zeeshan Mushtaq, in his third first-class match, added 204 for Islamabad's fourth wicket with Ashar Zaidi and converted his maiden hundred into a double, with 28 fours and four sixes in 274 balls; he had scored 12 runs in his previous four innings. Islamabad reached 600 for the first time, while Quetta failed to achieve three figures in either innings.

At Arbab Niaz Stadium, Peshawar, February 7, 8, 9, 10, 2009. **Drawn.** Toss: Peshawar. **Lahore Ravi 362** (Sohail Ahmed 73, Kashif Siddiq 66, Ashraf Ali 77, Ali Haider 53; Waqar Ahmed 6-120) **and 205-6 dec** (Kashif Siddiq 66, Mohammad Sohail 71; Waqar Ahmed 4-76); **Peshawar 348** (Mohammad Idrees 91, Jamaluddin 96; Junaid Zia 5-87) **and 87-2.** *Lahore Ravi 3 pts.*

At Sports Stadium, Sargodha, February 13, 14, 15, 16, 2009. **Drawn.** Toss: Abbottabad. **Faisalabad 297-4 dec** (Zeeshan Butt 142*, Usman Arshad 55); **Abbottabad 25-1.**

At Diamond Club Ground, Islamabad, February 13, 14, 15, 16, 2009. **Drawn.** Toss: Islamabad. **Karachi Blues 249** (Owais Rehmani 53*; Saad Altaf 4-82) **and 34-3; Islamabad 300-3 dec** (Umair Khan 80, Zeeshan Mushtaq 121*). *Islamabad 3 pts.*
    Zeeshan Mushtaq followed up his 230 the previous week with 121* in his fourth first-class match.

At LCCA Ground, Lahore, February 13, 14, 15, 16, 2009. **Drawn.** Toss: Lahore Ravi. **Multan 306** (Naved Yasin 125*; Kashif Siddiq 4-33, Sohail Ahmed 4-38) **and 79-2; Lahore Ravi 361** (Raza Ali 56, Kashif Siddiq 79, Ashraf Ali 80; Zulfiqar Babar 7-98). *Lahore Ravi 3 pts.*

At Arbab Niaz Stadium, Peshawar, February 13, 14, 15, 16, 2009. **Sialkot won by an innings and 20 runs.** Toss: Peshawar. **Sialkot 369-9 dec** (Haris Sohail 155, Mohammad Ayub 146; Nauman Habib 4-116, Waqar Ahmed 5-107); **Peshawar 178** (Nayyer Abbas 5-53) **and 171** (Mahfooz Sabri 89, Nauman Habib 50; Naved Arif 6-73). *Sialkot 9 pts.*
    Haris Sohail and Mohammad Ayub added 273 for Sialkot's fifth wicket.

At Marghzar Cricket Ground, Islamabad, February 13, 14, 15, 2009. **Rawalpindi won by nine wickets.** Toss: Rawalpindi. **Quetta forfeited first innings and 41** (Mohammad Rameez 6-17); **Rawalpindi forfeited first innings and 44-1.** *Rawalpindi 9 pts.*
    The entire game lasted only 20.1 overs, the shortest completed match in first-class cricket; 85 was the lowest aggregate. After the first two days were washed out, both sides forfeited their first innings; Quetta were bowled out in 13.3 overs, and Rawalpindi knocked off a target of 42 in 40 balls, losing only one wicket in the match.

At Sports Stadium, Sargodha, February 19, 20, 21, 22, 2009. **Drawn.** Toss: Peshawar. **Faisalabad 399** (Usman Arshad 134, Ijaz Ahmed 118; Waqar Ahmed 7-114) **and 396** (Qaiser Iqbal 69, Usman Arshad 88, Naved Latif 81, Zulqarnain 50; Nauman Habib 7-119); **Peshawar 279** (Jamaluddin 102*; Saadat Munir 4-57) **and 153-1** (Naved Khan 66, Israrullah 75*). *Faisalabad 3 pts.*
Usman Arshad and Ijaz Ahmed added 258 for Faisalabad's fourth wicket in the first innings.

At Municipal Sports Complex, Mirpur Khas, February 19, 20, 21, 22, 2009. **Quetta won by three runs.** Toss: Hyderabad. **Quetta 163** (Taimur Ali 50; Pir Zulfiqar 4-50) **and 359** (Taimur Ali 60, Jalat Khan 170); **Hyderabad 249** (Azeem Ghumman 68; Nazar Hussain 4-78) **and 270** (Lal Kumar 63, Hanif Malik 75; Gauhar Faiz 4-86, Nazar Hussain 4-74). *Quetta 6 pts.*
This was the first first-class match at this ground; Mirpur Khas had last staged first-class cricket at the Gama Stadium in February 1977. Visitors Quetta scraped through to their only victory of the season when Hyderabad, also without a win, were bowled out four short of a target of 274 after reaching 236-6.

At Diamond Club Ground, Islamabad, February 19, 20, 21, 22, 2009. **Islamabad won by five wickets.** Toss: Sialkot. **Sialkot 268** (Kamran Younis 63, Mohammad Ayub 60; Rauf Akbar 4-69, Saad Altaf 4-70) **and 185** (Haris Sohail 60, Mohammad Ayub 65; Saad Altaf 4-62); **Islamabad 361** (Raheel Majeed 62, Ashar Zaidi 124, Imad Wasim 57; Naved Arif 4-108) **and 93-5.** *Islamabad 9 pts.*

At UBL Sports Complex, Karachi, February 19, 20, 21, 22, 2009. **Karachi Blues won by 202 runs.** Toss: Multan. **Karachi Blues 326** (Sheharyar Ghani 135; Abdur Rauf 7-108) **and 194-9 dec** (Sheharyar Ghani 76, Akbar-ur-Rehman 54; Zulfiqar Babar 5-69); **Multan 185** (Kashif Naved 55; Tabish Nawab 6-74) **and 133** (Tabish Khan 4-34, Tabish Nawab 4-55). *Karachi Blues 9 pts.*

At LCCA Ground, Lahore, February 19, 20, 21, 22, 2009. **Drawn.** Toss: Abbottabad. **Abbottabad 287** (Ghulam Mohammad 133) **and 378-5** (Adnan Raees 159, Rahimbaz Khan 96); **Lahore Ravi 437** (Raza Ali 111, Sohail Ahmed 126, Ashraf Ali 53; Inam Khan 4-99). *Lahore Ravi 3 pts.*
Raza Ali and Sohail Ahmed added 202 for Lahore Ravi's third wicket; Abbottabad's own third-wicket pair, Adnan Raees and Rahimbaz Khan, responded by adding 240 in the second innings.

At Nawabshah Cricket Stadium, February 25, 26, 27, 28, 2009. **Drawn.** Toss: Hyderabad. **Hyderabad 278** (Nasrullah Memon 70; Tabish Khan 4-64) **and 302-9 dec** (Azeem Ghumman 51, Aqeel Anjum 78; Adnan Kaleem 4-90); **Karachi Blues 206** (Lal Kumar 5-77) **and 219-6** (Shadab Kabir 64). *Hyderabad 3 pts.*
This was the first first-class match at Nawabshah; home side Hyderabad held the advantage but still ended the season without a win.

At Diamond Club Ground, Islamabad, February 25, 26, 27, 28, 2009. **Lahore Ravi won by 220 runs.** Toss: Islamabad. **Lahore Ravi 387** (Sohail Ahmed 102, Ashraf Ali 113; Saad Altaf 5-93) **and 314-9 dec** (Kashif Siddiq 117, Waqas Ahmed 58*); **Islamabad 264** (Ali Sarfraz 72; Waqas Ahmed 4-53, Usman Malik 4-63) **and 217** (Kamran Hussain 61; Usman Malik 6-84). *Lahore Ravi 9 pts.*
Lahore Ravi won their final game after drawing the previous nine.

At Gymkhana Ground, Okara, February 25, 26, 27, 28, 2009. **Multan won by nine wickets.** Toss: Multan. **Abbottabad 333** (Ghulam Mohammad 64, Fawad Khan 111; Ansar Javed 5-50) **and 248** (Adnan Raees 142; Abdur Rauf 5-44); **Multan 550-6 dec** (Mohammad Yasir 71, Kashif Naved 193, Naved Yasin 80, Gulraiz Sadaf 50*, Rizwan Haider 73) **and 32-1.** *Multan 9 pts.*
Kashif Naved and Naved Yasin added 223 for Multan's fourth wicket.

At Arbab Niaz Stadium, Peshawar, February 25, 26, 2009. **Rawalpindi won by six wickets.** Toss: Peshawar. **Peshawar 156** (Riaz Afridi 66; Rizwan Akbar 4-26) **and 145** (Riaz Afridi 50; Rizwan Akbar 5-61); **Rawalpindi 157** (Waqar Ahmed 5-80, Riaz Afridi 4-31) **and 148-4** (Hamid Riaz 73). *Rawalpindi 9 pts.*

At Jinnah Stadium, Sialkot, February 25, 26, 27, 2009. **Sialkot won by ten wickets.** Toss: Sialkot. **Faisalabad 122 and 309** (Imran Ali 128; Naved Arif 5-120); **Sialkot 379** (Haris Sohail 86, Bilal Azmat 100; Qaiser Iqbal 4-66) **and 53-0.** *Sialkot 9 pts.*
Sialkot's three-day victory confirmed their place in the final.

Final

At Jinnah Stadium, Sialkot, March 3, 4, 5, 6, 7, 2009. **Sialkot won by four wickets.** Toss: Sialkot. **KRL 296** (Azhar Ali 99) **and 247** (Zulfiqar Jan 56, Ali Naqvi 86; Naved Arif 6-58); **Sialkot 386** (Kamran Younis 86, Naeemuddin 135; Saeed Ajmal 5-105) **and 158-6** (Ayaz Tasawwar 53; Yasir Ali 4-64).

Sialkot secured their second Quaid-e-Azam Trophy in four seasons, despite slipping to 89-5 in pursuit of a straightforward target of 158. Their left-armer Naved Arif had claimed eight wickets in the match, finishing as the tournament's leading wicket-taker with 62.

QUAID-E-AZAM TROPHY WINNERS

1953-54	Bahawalpur	1975-76	National Bank	1992-93	Karachi Whites
1954-55	Karachi	1976-77	United Bank	1993-94	Lahore City
1956-57	Punjab	1977-78	Habib Bank	1994-95	Karachi Blues
1957-58	Bahawalpur	1978-79	National Bank	1995-96	Karachi Blues
1958-59	Karachi	1979-80	PIA	1996-97	Lahore City
1959-60	Karachi	1980-81	United Bank	1997-98	Karachi Blues
1961-62	Karachi Blues	1981-82	National Bank	1998-99	Peshawar
1962-63	Karachi A	1982-83	United Bank	1999-2000	PIA
1963-64	Karachi Blues	1983-84	National Bank	2000-01	Lahore City Blues
1964-65	Karachi Blues	1984-85	United Bank	2001-02	Karachi Whites
1966-67	Karachi	1985-86	Karachi	2002-03	PIA
1968-69	Lahore	1986-87	National Bank	2003-04	Faisalabad
1969-70	PIA	1987-88	PIA	2004-05	Peshawar
1970-71	Karachi Blues	1988-89	ADBP	2005-06	Sialkot
1972-73	Railways	1989-90	PIA	2006-07	Karachi Urban
1973-74	Railways	1990-91	Karachi Whites	2007-08	Sui Northern Gas
1974-75	Punjab A	1991-92	Karachi Whites	2008-09	Sialkot

The competition has been contested sometimes by regional teams, sometimes by departments, and sometimes by a mixture of the two. Karachi teams have won the Quaid-e-Azam Trophy 18 times, PIA 6, National Bank 5, Lahore teams and United Bank 4, Bahawalpur, Peshawar, Punjab, Railways and Sialkot 2, ADBP, Faisalabad, Habib Bank and Sui Northern Gas 1.

Note: Matches in the following sections were not first-class.

RBS PENTANGULAR ONE-DAY CUP, 2008-09

50-over league plus final

	Played	Won	Lost	No Result	Points	Net run-rate
Punjab Stallions	4	4	0	0	16	1.26
Federal Areas Leopards	4	2	1	1	10	−0.48
Sind Dolphins	4	1	2	1	6	−0.67
NWFP Panthers	4	1	3	0	4	0.19
Baluchistan Bears.	4	1	3	0	4	−0.68

Final

At National Stadium, Karachi, December 24, 2008. **Punjab Stallions won by eight wickets.** Toss: Punjab Stallions. **Federal Areas Leopards 218** (48.1 overs) (Umar Amin 77; Wahab Riaz 5-44); **Punjab Stallions 219-2** (41.5 overs) (Nasir Jamshed 63, Azhar Ali 87*, Salman Butt 51).

Punjab galloped home with eight overs to spare after left-armer Wahab Riaz ensured an easy target.

RBS CUP, 2008-09

Four 50-over leagues plus knockout

Semi-finals

At Iqbal Stadium, Faisalabad, March 30, 2009. **National Bank won by four wickets.** Toss: National Bank. **Lahore Lions 267-9** (50 overs) (Kashif Siddiq 55, Junaid Zia 50); **National Bank 271-6** (48.5 overs) (Qaiser Abbas 93*).

At Gaddafi Stadium, Lahore, March 30, 2009. **PIA won by six wickets.** Toss: PIA. **Multan Tigers 171** (35.2 overs) (Rizwan Haider 51); **PIA 175-4** (30.1 overs) (Khurram Manzoor 62, Sarfraz Ahmed 50).

Final

At Gaddafi Stadium, Lahore, April 1, 2009. **PIA won by 59 runs.** Toss: National Bank. **PIA 315-6** (50 overs) (Sarfraz Ahmed 56, Yasir Hameed 91, Shoaib Malik 96); **National Bank 256** (45.5 overs) (Umar Amin 68, Fawad Alam 74; Aizaz Cheema 5-37).

RBS TWENTY20 CUP, 2008-09

Four 20-over leagues plus knockout

Semi-finals

At Gaddafi Stadium, Lahore, October 7, 2008 (floodlit). **Karachi Dolphins won by nine wickets.** Toss: Islamabad Leopards. **Islamabad Leopards 68** (15.5 overs); **Karachi Dolphins 69-1** (10.4 overs).

At Gaddafi Stadium, Lahore, October 7, 2008 (floodlit). **Sialkot Stallions won by six runs.** Toss: Sialkot Stallions. **Sialkot Stallions 117-6** (20 overs); **Lahore Lions 111-6** (20 overs).

Final

At Gaddafi Stadium, Lahore, October 8, 2008 (floodlit). **Sialkot Stallions won by seven wickets.** Toss: Karachi Dolphins. **Karachi Dolphins 125-9** (20 overs); **Sialkot Stallions 126-3** (19.4 overs).

RBS TWENTY20 CUP, 2009

Four 20-over leagues plus knockout

Semi-finals

At Gaddafi Stadium, Lahore, May 28, 2009 (floodlit). **Lahore Lions won by three wickets.** Toss: Lahore Lions. **Islamabad Leopards 123-7** (20 overs); **Lahore Lions 125-7** (19.3 overs).

At Gaddafi Stadium, Lahore, May 28, 2009 (floodlit). **Sialkot Stallions won by 55 runs.** Toss: Lahore Eagles. **Sialkot Stallions 181** (19.5 overs); **Lahore Eagles 126** (19.2 overs).

Final

At Gaddafi Stadium, Lahore, May 29, 2009 (floodlit). **Sialkot Stallions won by four wickets.** Toss: Lahore Lions. **Lahore Lions 150-8** (20 overs); **Sialkot Stallions 151-6** (19.1 overs) (Imran Nazir 57).
Sialkot captain Imran Nazir hit 57 in 26 balls to steer his side to their fourth successive Twenty20 title.

SOUTH AFRICAN CRICKET, 2009

The busiest schedule yet

COLIN BRYDEN

More high-profile cricket was played in South Africa in 2009 than ever before, with the Republic playing host to the Indian Premier League and the Champions Trophy as well as staging home series against Australia, Zimbabwe and England. South Africa also hosted the 12-team World Cup qualifying tournament, from which Ireland, Canada, Kenya and the Netherlands booked their places for the 2011 event in Asia.

For the national team it was a disappointing year, falling short of the triumphs of 2008 when they won Test series in England and Australia. Staying at the top of the mountain proved every bit as difficult as reaching the summit. After clinching the series in Australia in December 2008, the South Africans were quickly brought back to earth in their first match of 2009 when they lost

SOUTH AFRICA IN 2009

	Played	Won	Lost	Drawn/No result
Tests	6	1	4	1
One-day internationals	18	11	7	–
Twenty20 internationals	12	8	4	–

DECEMBER / JANUARY	3 Tests, 5 ODIs and 2 T20Is (a) v Australia	(see *Wisden 2009*, page 1005)
FEBRUARY / MARCH / APRIL	3 Tests, 5 ODIs and 1 T20I (h) v Australia	(page 1250)
MAY		
JUNE / JULY	World Twenty20 (in England)	(page 527)
AUGUST		
SEPTEMBER / OCTOBER	Champions Trophy (in South Africa)	(page 1015)
NOVEMBER	2 ODIs (h) v Zimbabwe	(page 1268)
DECEMBER / JANUARY	4 Tests, 5 ODIs and 2 T20Is (h) v England	(page 1269)

For a review of South African domestic cricket from the 2008-09 season, see page 1313.

the final "dead rubber" Test at Sydney. It set the pattern for a year of inconsistent results, during which South Africa reached and then relinquished the No. 1 position in both the Test and one-day international rankings.

The highlights came in the one-day game. South Africa vanquished Australia both away and at home to become the official champions at the ICC's cut-off date of April 1. The 50-over crown did not rest easily, however. As they had done in the 2003 World Cup and, to a lesser extent, in the inaugural World Twenty20 in 2007, South Africa failed in a big event on home soil, losing two out of three matches in the Champions Trophy and being eliminated in the first phase.

One of the Champions Trophy defeats was against England. That form, or lack of it, continued when England won a rain-affected one-day series 2–1 at the start of their tour towards the end of the year, with two matches washed out by some unseasonably wet weather.

In Test cricket, South Africa were defeated in the first two matches of their home series against Australia, but came back with a thoroughly convincing innings win in the final game. It could be argued that the home Test series against Australia happened too soon after the away triumph. Not only was there hardly any time to savour the success, but South Africa went into the home series underprepared, against opponents who lifted their game after being badly stung by what had happened in their own country. The announcement that there would be no more back-to-back tours between South Africa and Australia was to be welcomed. Instead, there will be annual encounters between the two countries, with Test and one-day series being separated, so that every two years one country will host either Tests or one-day games.

At year's end, after what was by modern standards an inordinately long break from Test cricket of more than eight months, South Africa drew the First Test against England, but suffered an innings defeat at Durban in their final match of a year in which they won one, lost four and drew one of their six Test matches. South Africa squared the England series early in 2010 when, after another nail-biting draw in the Third Test, they won the Fourth by an innings, but the late rally was not enough to save Mickey Arthur's job as coach.

In statistical terms, the only regular members of the Test side who could objectively be claimed to have improved in 2009 were A. B. de Villiers, who was the leading run-scorer with 572 at an average of 57.20, and the slow left-armer Paul Harris, who took more wickets than anyone else (26 at 33.15).

The fast-bowling triumvirate of Dale Steyn, Morne Morkel and Makhaya Ntini largely lacked potency, Steyn doing best with 22 wickets at 32.86. Morkel's 15 wickets cost 40.66 runs apiece, while Ntini's 13 at 57.00 was a statistic which pointed to a player whose best days had passed.

An issue which was happily uncontroversial during the year was the racial composition of South African teams, with the likes of Ntini, Hashim Amla and J-P. Duminy ensuring a representative blend. Ntini's 100th Test match, against England at Centurion, was celebrated in appropriate fashion, although it was clear that, at 32, he was not the player he was in his pomp.

A black African presence in the national team is regarded as being important, and the search for Ntini's successor assumed some urgency. Lonwabo

Tsotsobe, a tall 25-year-old left-arm fast bowler with one-day and Twenty20 international experience, was the most obvious candidate, but his performances in domestic cricket during the first half of the 2009-10 season were modest.

In the medium term there were reasonable prospects of a more equable demographic representation, with no fewer than 13 Africans having played at franchise level by the end of December, and increasing numbers coming through at junior level. There were four in the South African Schools team, and it was encouraging that the indigenous talent went beyond the stereotype of black fast bowlers. One of the most promising African players was Mangaliso Mosehle, a wicketkeeper and top-order batsman who shone for the national Under-19 team in a series against England early in the year. Soweto-born Omphile Ramela, the captain of Stellenbosch University, was a capable batsman who made 87 on his SuperSport Series debut for the Cape Cobras.

In one-day cricket, it seemed that South Africa had mixed an excellent cocktail of bowlers, with Steyn and Wayne Parnell providing right-arm and left-arm pace, and Johan Botha and Roelof van der Merwe the equivalent in spin. The Champions Trophy and the series against England showed, however, that it had not taken long for opponents to work out ways to attack this combination.

South Africa's Twenty20 team was similar in composition to the 50-overs side, and performed impressively in reaching the semi-finals of the World Twenty20 in England before being outplayed by a Pakistan side inspired by Shahid Afridi.

You beauty! South Africa's leading run-scorer in Tests in 2009, A. B. de Villiers, congratulates Paul Harris, their leading wicket-taker.

Thamba Hadebe, APPA

Domestically, there was some debate about increasing the number of professional franchises from six to eight but, probably wisely, it was decided to stick at six. Despite the infrequent participation of the national representatives, the standard was regarded as good enough to provide a reasonable assessment of the readiness of players for the step up to international level.

A by-product of the amount of high-level cricket played was a dwindling of interest in the domestic game. Even on those rare occasions when the national stars were in action, attendances for the four-day SuperSport Series were negligible (despite free admission) and media coverage minimal.

Limited-overs matches continued to be televised, however, and the 20-over Standard Bank Pro20 remained popular. Because of poor crowds, the domestic one-day competition was rebranded as the MTN40, with matches reduced to 40 overs a side, teams allowed to name 12 players (only 11 to bat or field), and the batting team having two five-over powerplays. This led to higher scores than were the norm in 45-over innings. Initially, though, spectator numbers did not increase.

The amateur competition, nominally first-class, was ignored almost totally by the media to the extent that even brief scores were seldom seen in print. One of the proclaimed objectives of this competition was to provide a bridge between club and provincial cricket, but with rare exceptions this became almost impossible. With 14 teams playing a full round-robin of 13 three-day matches, and each three-day game followed by a one-day encounter, it effectively limited participation to students or those earning a living from cricket through coaching or some similar endeavour.

In South Africa, it seems, a year cannot go by without some sort of administrative contretemps, and what had been a relatively tranquil period was ended with an unseemly dispute between Cricket South Africa and the Gauteng Cricket Board, whose home ground is Johannesburg's Wanderers Stadium, the biggest in the country.

It started with the GCB requesting CSA's audit committee to conduct an urgent inquiry into the manner in which business had been done with the Indian Premier League, suggesting that CSA had been reckless and had exposed themselves to financial risk, and that Gerald Majola, the chief executive, "repeatedly acted in flagrant disregard of his duties". The GCB asked for a copy of the contract, alleging that the IPL had been promised rights by CSA which they did not have the power to deliver. The GCB, which staged the IPL final, felt they had been placed in an untenable position with regards to their arrangements with existing sponsors and suite-holders.

Instead of responding directly to the GCB's request, CSA called a meeting of the Members Forum, comprising the body's affiliates, which issued a statement in which it rejected the complaints "with contempt" and gave a full vote of confidence to Majola. An apology was demanded, together with the GCB's terms for staging international matches at the Wanderers, failing which they would not be staged by CSA at the stadium. The threat excluded matches in the Champions Trophy, which fell under the aegis of the ICC.

In response, CSA revealed for the first time the financial details of hosting the second season of the IPL. They said a hosting fee of R30m was negotiated by Majola, which because of foreign-exchange fluctuations was some R6m better than the US$3m originally offered. In addition, each host union received R125,000 a match to cover costs. CSA claimed that 800,000 spectators had watched the 59 matches, and that the tournament had been a resounding success.

A week later it was announced that no apology had been received and that the Wanderers had lost the three fixtures allocated to it for England's tour. There was another shock for the GCB when the fixtures for the Champions Trophy were announced three days later, with virtually all the most attractive fixtures – including the opening game, South Africa's group fixtures and the final – allocated to Centurion, despite its smaller capacity.

CSA claimed that the fixtures were decided by the ICC. This might have been technically correct, but an ICC spokesman confirmed that it acted on the host country's recommendations. A clue to the apparent willingness of the national body to sacrifice potential gate takings was the ICC's explanation that the host country was guaranteed US$2m in attendance revenue so that it would not be tempted to charge too much for tickets.

While the dispute was raging a group claiming to represent clubs from black areas alleged that there had been a lack of racial transformation by the Gauteng board. Mediators were appointed by the sports ministry, and the issue was resolved with a compromise – 18 years after the formation of a united national board – whereby a new board would be elected with an even split of white and black members, with Lazarus Zim, a prominent black businessman, as chairman.

Throughout the unpleasantness, the interests of the paying public appeared of secondary importance to the administrators, both in the allocation of fixtures for the Champions Trophy and the original decision to take England tour matches away from the Wanderers.

In the circumstances, there should hardly have been surprise when attendances for the Champions Trophy were no more than moderate, and public disillusion seemed to be confirmed when the Wanderers and Centurion were barely half-full two months later for Twenty20 internationals at the start of the England tour.

SOUTH AFRICA v AUSTRALIA, 2008-09

Neil Manthorp

Test matches (3): South Africa 1, Australia 2
One-day internationals (5): South Africa 3, Australia 2
Twenty20 internationals (2): South Africa 2, Australia 0

Not a single member of the South African team would be happy offering the emotional hangover of their country's first series win in Australia as an excuse for their below-par performance in the ensuing home series. But, though it might be a weak excuse, it is a fact. Fortified by their triumphs in the Tests and one-day games, and moved by the consistent and concerted physical efforts of so many senior players, the South African management were sufficiently emboldened to order everyone to treat the majority of the three weeks between series as a well-earned vacation.

Originally, they were not due to reconvene until three days before the First Test – but ten days after the squad's return, the coach Mickey Arthur began to have doubts about his own plan and told his charges that the new term was starting two days earlier (still only five days before the Test).

There was nothing wrong with the principle of rewarding the players with time off, nor the idea of preserving hard-working bodies for a new challenge, but it was the idea of a complete break from the game, for so long, which was flawed. Dale Steyn headed to the country for two weeks and never bowled a ball, and he wasn't the only one. No wonder they were rusty. Courtney Walsh, the most relentless fast-bowling machine of recent times, was a TV commentator during the series. He was gobsmacked by Steyn's preparation: "For 20 years I never went three days without bowling a ball," he said. "If he was going hunting and wanted to get away from it all, then he should have taken a ball with him, scratched out 22 yards in the dirt, and bowled an over at a thorn tree. That's all it takes to keep the rhythm."

None of this should detract from the achievement of Ricky Ponting and his very new team in claiming a revenge 2–1 victory in the Test series. When he was asked how it felt winning with a side he had built rather than inherited, Ponting's chest visibly swelled with pride: "Very, very special. It's up among the best achievements of my career. The new guys we brought into the squad have risen to the challenges presented to them, and I'm extremely proud of every single one of them."

For the first time in Ponting's life, let alone his career as captain, he had started a series as the underdog. The experience not only galled him, but galvanised his ambition and his ability to formulate game plans very different and more imaginative than the "Well, we have Warne and McGrath" strategy with which he had grown up as a leader.

The resources at Ponting's disposal were less than those at Graeme Smith's, but he gave each player a very specific role to perform, and they responded.

Hughes this? Phillip Hughes steps out of the shadows with twin hundreds at Durban.

Mitchell Johnson needed to be magnificent for the plan to come together – and he was. Peter Siddle, suddenly an automatic choice, needed to be as strong as an ox – and he was. Another fast bowler, Ben Hilfenhaus, surprisingly preferred to Doug Bollinger, also showed he was up to the task.

The fourth-seamer role, so often the doing and undoing of touring teams, was left in the hands of the medium-paced trundler Andrew McDonald, an all-rounder so underappreciated when he was first called up for the final Test at Sydney in January that it was likened to "raising the white flag" by some newspapers. Yet Ponting now had cards he had dealt himself, and one of them was the relentlessly accurate but otherwise largely unthreatening McDonald who, by dint of his red hair and slightly larger than average ears, was inevitably known as "Ronnie" McDonald, after the clown mascot of the world's biggest burger chain.

Ronnie's job was to bowl metronomic maidens while Johnson, Siddle and Hilfenhaus took wickets. Without a spinner he trusted, Ponting opted for Marcus North, the 29-year-old Western Australian captain, as a No. 6 batsman who could do a tidy job with the ball. And North, who had seemingly been destined for an entire career as a good first-class journeyman, responded with a century on debut and more than a couple of decent overs of off-spin. But it was McDonald's ability to frustrate South Africa's batsmen with his maddeningly straight, maddeningly medium-paced deliveries which really represented the "new" Australia, the world champions who had to graft at the coal-face for the first time in a decade and a half, rather than rely upon half a dozen or more champions to get the job done.

There were more unsung heroes for Australia but, naturally, the big-name players also responded. Ponting had his moments, and Johnson was quite phenomenal not only as a fast bowler but as an all-rounder, but the other star was a kid nobody in South Africa had heard of – Phillip Hughes. The 20-year-old opener looked, technically and aesthetically, like a club No. 9. Maybe No. 10. Yet his idiosyncratic style earned him 415 runs in the series, and played a vital part in winning it. He will either threaten every batting record ever set, or fade quickly after a couple of years once bowlers work him out. It almost seemed as though he had started out with the idea of doing everything the opposite way round from the coaching manual – but those who had known him best and for longest were betting on 10,000 Test runs even before he had faced a ball. It's not how that matters, it's how many.

South Africa finally did themselves justice and showed what might have been with the most comprehensive victory of all the season's six Tests when the teams reached Cape Town. It wasn't quite enough to earn them the ICC's No. 1 ranking, but it was proof that they were still a team on the rise and that Australia would have a far harder job hanging on to the top spot than they had had for the previous six years.

There was some compensation for the hosts in the limited-overs games, where they maintained their recent superiority and also unearthed a new starlet in Roelof van der Merwe, a hard-hitting slow left-armer from the Titans, whose instant success earned him an IPL contract with the Bangalore Royal Challengers.

AUSTRALIAN TOURING PARTY

R. T. Ponting (*captain*), M. J. Clarke (*vice-captain*), D. E. Bollinger, B. J. Haddin, N. M. Hauritz, B. W. Hilfenhaus, P. J. Hughes, M. E. K. Hussey, M. G. Johnson, S. M. Katich, A. B. McDonald, B. E. McGain, M. J. North, P. M. Siddle. *Coach:* T. J. Nielsen.

  B. Geeves and S. J. Magoffin reinforced the Test squad after injuries and illness. For the limited-overs internationals which followed the Tests, Geeves, N. W. Bracken, C. J. Ferguson, S. M. Harwood, J. R. Hopes, D. J. Hussey, B. Laughlin, D. A. Warner and C. L. White replaced Bollinger, Hilfenhaus, Hughes, Katich, McDonald, McGain and Siddle. A. C. Voges was originally selected for the one-day matches, but withdrew because he would not have been allowed to fly home for his wedding and was replaced by North. S. R. Clark was called up later when Geeves broke his foot.

TEST MATCH AVERAGES

SOUTH AFRICA – BATTING AND FIELDING

	T	I	NO	R	HS	100s	50s	Avge	Ct/St
A. B. de Villiers	3	5	1	357	163	2	1	89.25	7
J. H. Kallis	3	5	0	289	102	1	1	57.80	8
†J-P. Duminy	3	5	1	143	73*	0	1	35.75	3
†G. C. Smith	2	3	0	71	69	0	1	35.50	2
H. M. Amla	3	5	0	147	57	0	1	29.40	2

	T	I	NO	R	HS	100s	50s	Avge	Ct/St
N. D. McKenzie	2	4	0	102	36	0	0	25.50	4
M. V. Boucher..........	3	5	0	62	25	0	0	12.40	8/1
P. L. Harris	3	5	0	45	27	0	0	9.00	2
D. W. Steyn	3	5	0	38	17	0	0	7.60	1
†M. Morkel	2	4	0	30	24	0	0	7.50	1
M. Ntini	3	5	3	9	4*	0	0	4.50	1

Played in one Test: †I. Khan 20 (1 ct); †J. A. Morkel 58; †A. G. Prince 150 (2 ct).

† *Left-handed batsman.*

BOWLING

	Style	O	M	R	W	BB	5W/i	Avge
P. L. Harris	SLA	140.5	29	395	14	6-127	1	28.21
J. H. Kallis..........	RFM	56	10	177	6	3-22	0	29.50
D. W. Steyn........	RF	131	23	474	16	4-56	0	29.62
M. Ntini...........	RFM	108	28	340	10	3-52	0	34.00
M. Morkel	RF	76.4	9	299	6	3-117	0	49.83

Also bowled: J-P. Duminy (OB) 31–5–111–1; J. A. Morkel (RFM) 32–4–132–1.

AUSTRALIA – BATTING AND FIELDING

	T	I	NO	R	HS	100s	50s	Avge	Ct/St
†M. G. Johnson	3	5	2	255	123*	1	1	85.00	1
†P. J. Hughes.............	3	6	0	415	160	2	1	69.16	2
†S. M. Katich............	3	6	0	260	108	1	2	43.33	1
†M. J. North.............	2	4	0	160	117	1	0	40.00	2
R. T. Ponting	3	6	0	210	83	0	2	35.00	6
B. J. Haddin	3	5	0	165	63	0	1	33.00	13/1
M. J. Clarke	3	6	1	141	68	0	1	28.20	1
A. B. McDonald	3	5	1	92	68	0	1	23.00	1
†M. E. K. Hussey	3	6	0	132	50	0	1	22.00	1
P. M. Siddle	3	5	1	31	22*	0	0	7.75	3
B. W. Hilfenhaus	3	5	1	28	16	0	0	7.00	1

Played in one Test: B. E. McGain 2, 0.

† *Left-handed batsman.*

BOWLING

	Style	O	M	R	W	BB	5W/i	Avge
S. M. Katich........	SLC	14.2	2	54	5	3-45	0	10.80
P. M. Siddle........	RFM	122.3	42	270	12	3-46	0	22.50
M. G. Johnson	LF	139	28	400	16	4-25	0	25.00
A. B. McDonald	RM	87	26	227	6	3-25	0	37.83
B. W. Hilfenhaus ...	RFM	125	26	366	7	2-68	0	52.28

Also bowled: M. J. Clarke (SLA) 1–1–0–0; B. E. McGain (LBG) 18–2–149–0; M. J. North (OB) 38–9–98–2.

Note: Matches in this section which were not first-class are signified by a dagger.

At Potchefstroom, February 20, 21, 22, 2009. **Drawn. Toss:** Australians. **Cricket South Africa President's XI 403-7 dec** (I. Khan 100, A. N. Petersen 31, V. B. van Jaarsveld 49, G. H. Bodi 48, H. G. Kuhn 99, D. Wiese 50*) **and 182** (A. N. Petersen 36, H. G. Kuhn 47; D. E. Bollinger 3-29,

M. J. North 6-69); **Australians 360-5 dec** (S. M. Katich 124, R. T. Ponting 93, M. J. North 52*) **and 171-4** (P. J. Hughes 53, M. J. North 50).

The President's XI scored 393-5 on the first day after being put in, with Imraan Khan hitting 18 fours in his 100. The Australians were set 226 to win, and were 55 short when the captains agreed to end the match 25 minutes early. Openers Hughes and North (who had earlier taken his maiden first-class five-for – 11–0–69–6 – with his off-spin) both retired out in the second innings, as did Katich in the first. With several players suffering from stomach trouble Australia's fitness coach, Stuart Karppinen, fielded as substitute on the last day.

TEST MATCH REPORTS BY GEOFFREY DEAN

SOUTH AFRICA v AUSTRALIA

First Test Match

At Johannesburg, February 26, 27, 28, March 1, 2, 2009. Australia won by 162 runs. Toss: Australia. Test debuts: B. W. Hilfenhaus, P. J. Hughes, M. J. North.

Australia's fourth consecutive Test victory at the Wanderers was also the sixth in their last seven Tests in South Africa. The key to their success was a large first-innings total, a remarkable 466 on a sporting pitch where swing, seam movement and extra bounce offered pace bowlers encouragement throughout. While six Australians failed to make double figures, notably Phillip Hughes who was out fourth ball on debut, the other five batted extremely well, especially Marcus North, who became the 18th Australian to make a century in his first Test.

While the tourists had had the benefit of a first-class warm-up match at Potchefstroom, the South Africans had played only a few Twenty20 games since returning from their successful tour of Australia. This imbalance showed in the first three days when the home side (in particular their batsmen) looked underprepared. Even though they fought back to dismiss Australia for 207 in the second innings, a target of 454 was always likely to be unattainable on a surface whose cracks allowed some uneven bounce on the final day. South Africa were bowled out shortly after tea with 33 overs still remaining, the equivalent of half a day's play having been lost to bad light and rain earlier in the match.

A dropped catch on the first morning was undeniably significant, Smith missing Ponting when 40 at slip off Steyn. Had this straightforward chance been held, Australia would have been 67 for four with every chance of being bundled out for under 200 in bowler-friendly conditions. But by the time Ponting – who celebrated by hooking the next ball for six – was eventually fourth out for an excellent 83, offering no shot to a huge breakback from Ntini, the ball was 41 overs old and 151 was on the board. It was a much more comfortable time for North to come in and, after a nervy start, he dug in to reach 50 from 104 balls and his hundred from 207. Although he soon lost Clarke, whose positive 68 contained some sparkling off-side strokes, the pugnacious Haddin gave some valuable support.

Equally important assistance came from Johnson, who came in at 296 for seven just after the second new ball had been taken. Poorly though South Africa bowled with it, North and Johnson batted with application and skill to add a crucial 117 for the eighth wicket in 36 overs. Johnson, having advanced carefully to a third Test fifty from 100 balls, then demoralised the South Africans with a calculated assault on Harris, hitting 26 off one over with three sixes and two fours. He also struck two sixes off Duminy, who was pressed into service because a back strain restricted Kallis to just eight overs in the innings. That proved another piece of good fortune for the Australians, for in their second innings Kallis's three-wicket burst in seven balls precipitated their collapse from 99 for one to 147 for eight.

Punched out: Mitchell Johnson relishes the departure of Graeme Smith for a second-ball duck.

Australia had taken a big gamble in selecting only three front-line pace bowlers and no specialist spinner. Their raw attack could muster only 23 caps between them, 18 of those Johnson's. They nevertheless did an admirable job in helpful conditions, backed up by fine catching and undistinguished batting. While Johnson probed with remorseless accuracy, Siddle's pace and aggression unsettled the home side. Hilfenhaus dismissed Amla with his second ball in Test cricket, and shouldered a heavy workload manfully; McDonald gave nothing away at a tidy military medium. Protracted resistance came only from McKenzie, who batted for nearly three hours, and de Villiers, who celebrated his 50th Test with a fine hundred, his eighth, reached in 181 balls. Kallis became the first South African to pass 10,000 Test runs (83 of them for the World XI).

Mindful that his attack was both tired and inexperienced, Ponting understandably declined to enforce the follow-on, wary also of uneven bounce on the last day. Apart from Hughes, who this time cut and carved his way to 75 from 121 balls, the Australian top order batted with uncharacteristic ineptitude against some improved bowling. At one point, South Africa looked as if they might need fewer than the 414 they had needed to win in Perth ten weeks earlier, but some audacious strokes from Haddin and Siddle helped burgle a psychologically important 60 for the last two wickets.

With the ball not swinging, and the bounce still true enough on the fourth afternoon, South Africa batted well to reach 178 for two with a day (and 98 overs) remaining. Smith's departure for an ebullient 69 nonetheless proved crucial for, deprived of their talisman, the others found batting very hard work on the fifth morning against some disciplined bowling. The Australians' pressure brought mistakes, with Amla, de Villiers and Kallis all getting themselves out. Duminy and Boucher both held on for more than two hours, but the tail was brushed aside. The splendid Johnson, with four wickets in each innings to go with an unbeaten 96, then his highest Test score, was an automatic choice for the match award.

Man of the Match: M. G. Johnson.

Close of play: First day, Australia 254-5 (North 47, Haddin 37); Second day, South Africa 85-3 (McKenzie 35, de Villiers 13); Third day, Australia 51-1 (Hughes 36, Ponting 1); Fourth day, South Africa 178-2 (Amla 43, Kallis 26).

Australia

P. J. Hughes c Boucher b Steyn	0	– c de Villiers b Harris	75
S. M. Katich c McKenzie b Steyn	3	– c Boucher b Morkel	10
*R. T. Ponting b Ntini	83	– c Amla b Kallis	25
M. E. K. Hussey c Kallis b Morkel	4	– c Ntini b Kallis	0
M. J. Clarke c Boucher b Steyn	68	– c Kallis b Harris	0
M. J. North st Boucher b Harris	117	– b Kallis	5
†B. J. Haddin c Harris b Ntini	63	– c Boucher b Ntini	37
A. B. McDonald c Kallis b Steyn	0	– c Boucher b Ntini	7
M. G. Johnson not out	96	– c Kallis b Ntini	1
P. M. Siddle c Kallis b Morkel	9	– not out	22
B. W. Hilfenhaus c de Villiers b Morkel	0	– b Steyn	16
B 6, l-b 8, w 2, n-b 7	23	L-b 5, w 1, n-b 3	9

1/0 (1) 2/18 (2) 3/38 (4) (125.4 overs) 466   1/38 (2) 2/99 (3) (53.4 overs) 207
4/151 (5) 5/182 (5) 6/295 (7)   3/99 (4) 4/99 (5)
7/296 (8) 8/413 (6)   5/104 (6) 6/138 (1) 7/145 (8)
9/466 (10) 10/466 (11)   8/147 (9) 9/174 (7) 10/207 (11)

Steyn 30–4–113–4; Ntini 27–6–71–2; Morkel 28.4–3–117–3; Kallis 8–0–33–0; Harris 18–2–64–1; Duminy 14–2–54–0. *Second Innings*—Steyn 16.4–5–51–1; Ntini 11–3–52–3; Morkel 10–1–41–1; Harris 11–0–36–2; Kallis 5–0–22–3.

South Africa

N. D. McKenzie lbw b Siddle	36	– c Haddin b Johnson	35
*G. C. Smith c Haddin b Johnson	0	– c Johnson b Hilfenhaus	69
H. M. Amla c Ponting b Hilfenhaus	1	– c Hughes b Siddle	57
J. H. Kallis c Hussey b Siddle	27	– b Johnson	45
A. B. de Villiers not out	104	– lbw b McDonald	3
J-P. Duminy c Haddin b Johnson	17	– c Ponting b Siddle	29
†M. V. Boucher c Haddin b Johnson	0	– b Hilfenhaus	24
M. Morkel c and b Siddle	2	– c Hughes b Johnson	2
P. L. Harris lbw b North	1	– c Katich b Siddle	8
D. W. Steyn c North b McDonald	17	– b Johnson	6
M. Ntini b Johnson	1	– not out	0
B 4, l-b 6, n-b 4	14	B 1, l-b 6, w 2, n-b 4	13

1/1 (2) 2/2 (3) 3/49 (4) 4/93 (1) (81.1 overs) 220   1/76 (1) 2/130 (2) (119.2 overs) 291
5/138 (6) 6/138 (7) 7/154 (8)   3/206 (3) 4/211 (5)
8/156 (9) 9/208 (10) 10/220 (11)   5/229 (4) 6/268 (6) 7/272 (8)
                                                            8/284 (7) 9/289 (9) 10/291 (10)

Johnson 18.1–7–75–4; Hilfenhaus 25–9–58–1; Siddle 21–1–76–3; McDonald 10–4–22–1; North 7–0–29–1. *Second Innings*—Johnson 34.2–2–112–4; Hilfenhaus 31–7–68–2; Siddle 25–8–46–3; McDonald 22–8–31–1; North 7–0–27–0.

Umpires: B. F. Bowden and S. A. Bucknor.
Third umpire: Asad Rauf.   Referee: J. J. Crowe.

SOUTH AFRICA v AUSTRALIA

Second Test Match

At Durban, March 6, 7, 8, 9, 10, 2009. Australia won by 175 runs. Toss: Australia.

A match that followed a similar pattern to the First Test ended in emphatic victory for Australia 15 minutes before tea on the final day, giving them their fourth consecutive series win in South Africa. The key architects of their success were Phillip Hughes and

Mitchell Johnson. The left-hander Hughes, the son of a banana farmer from near Macksville in northern New South Wales, became the youngest batsman to score two hundreds in the same Test; at 20 years 98 days, he was nearly six months younger than George Headley when he achieved the feat for West Indies against England in 1929-30.

YOUNGEST AUSTRALIAN PLAYERS TO HIT A TEST HUNDRED

Years	Days				
19	122	R. N. Harvey	153	v India at Melbourne	1947-48
19	152	†A. Jackson	164	v England at Adelaide	1928-29
19	357	†K. D. Walters	155	v England at Brisbane	1965-66
20	**96**	**P. J. Hughes**	**115**	**v South Africa at Durban**	**2008-09**
20	129	D. G. Bradman	112	v England at Melbourne	1928-29
20	240	†J. W. Burke	101*	v England at Adelaide	1950-51
20	317	C. Hill	188	v England at Melbourne	1897-98
21	149	G. M. Wood	126	v West Indies at Georgetown	1977-78
21	226	V. T. Trumper	135*	v England at Lord's	1899
21	233	R. G. Archer	128	v West Indies at Kingston	1954-55
21	327	W. A. Brown	105	v England at Lord's	1934

Only the maiden century is given for each player.

† *Jackson, Walters and Burke were making their Test debuts.*

Research: Philip Bailey

YOUNGEST BATSMEN TO HIT TWO HUNDREDS IN A TEST

Years	Days					
20	**98**	**P. J. Hughes**	**115**	**160**	**Australia v South Africa at Durban**	**2008-09**
20	271	G. A. Headley	114	112	West Indies v England at Georgetown	1929-30
21	234	G. S. Sobers	125	109*	West Indies v Pakistan at Georgetown	1957-58
21	282	S. M. Gavaskar	124	220	India v West Indies at Port-of-Spain	1970-71
23	44	†L. G. Rowe	214	100*	West Indies v New Zealand at Kingston	1971-72
23	59	K. D. Walters	242	103	Australia v West Indies at Sydney	1968-69

† *Rowe was making his Test debut.*

Research: Philip Bailey

Hughes's often violent assault on some particularly poor bowling on the opening morning helped provide the springboard for Australia's triumph. He raced to 75 out of 119 by lunch, capitalising on the generous width he was given, as well as a surfeit of over-pitched deliveries. Some of his powerful driving down the ground showed he possessed more than just a devastating cut shot. Morne Morkel suffered particularly badly, conceding six fours to Hughes in his first two overs.

Hughes went from 93 to 105 with successive sixes off Harris, reaching his hundred from 132 balls. In doing so, he became the fourth-youngest Australian to make a Test hundred. His domination of a first-wicket stand of 184 in 44 overs was such that Katich's contribution was only 59, although he did have less of the strike. Katich, badly dropped when 55, went on to complete his own hundred from 177 balls, two-thirds of his runs scored through the off side.

Although Australia contrived to lose their last six wickets for just 23 in seven overs on the second morning, Johnson quickly wrecked the South African top order with some devastating new-ball bowling as he found some inswing. McKenzie, surprised by extra bounce, fell to the third ball of the innings and Amla to the fifth, playing across a rapid full-length ball which pitched on middle and would have hit leg stump. In his second over, Johnson, hitting the deck hard at around 90mph, extracted spiteful bounce from back of a length and hit Smith on the top hand as he tried to fend off. The knuckle above his right little finger was broken, forcing him not just out of this match but also the rest of the series. It was the second time in three Tests that Johnson had inflicted a fracture on Smith, whose left hand was damaged at Sydney in January.

When de Villiers was beaten by a Hilfenhaus off-cutter in the sixth over, South Africa were effectively six for four. Kallis and Duminy put on 50 before Johnson, returning for a second spell, also forced Kallis to retire hurt, hitting him under the grille with a nasty bouncer. While Kallis went off for three stitches in a bloody chin wound, Boucher had his off stump flattened by a Johnson yorker. Kallis returned when Harris was fifth out, but lasted only two balls before clipping McDonald to short midwicket. The innings was beyond repair, South Africa finding themselves 214 adrift, although Ponting again declined to enforce the follow-on. He had good reasons for his decision, primarily niggles that his three pace bowlers had carried into the match, as well as the fact that so much time still remained.

South Africa could match neither the excellence nor the hostility of Johnson's bowling when Australia batted again. Hughes galloped to his first fifty from 78 balls, but then showed his adaptability by grafting hard over his second, which took him a further 169 deliveries. Harris, bowling into the rough outside off stump, tied him down. Ponting, however, could not be restrained, playing some fine attacking strokes, including a dozen fours, in his 106-ball 81. Once past his twin-ton landmark, Hughes accelerated to score his third fifty from 65 balls. When he was finally out, sacrificing his wicket with a declaration imminent, he had batted for six and a quarter hours, faced 323 balls and hit 15 fours and three sixes.

Left with 170 overs to survive, and a notional target of 546, South Africa battled hard, reaching 244 for two after 80 overs by the end of the fourth day on a pitch offering little to the pace bowlers once the ball lost its hardness. The second new ball, however, brought Australia the breakthroughs they needed. Kallis was undone by Johnson's extra bounce, his 93 having come from 175 balls, and de Villiers fell soon afterwards to the impressive Siddle. With his seamers sore and tired, Ponting was grateful to his part-time spinners for mopping up, North taking a brilliant two-handed return catch to dismiss Boucher to atone for dropping Kallis before he had scored.

Man of the Match: P. J. Hughes.

Close of play: First day, Australia 303-4 (Hussey 37, North 17); Second day, South Africa 138-7 (Duminy 73, Steyn 8); Third day, Australia 292-3 (Hughes 136, Clark 14); Fourth day, South Africa 244-2 (Kallis 84, de Villiers 68).

Australia

P. J. Hughes c McKenzie b Kallis	115	– c Morkel b Ntini	160
S. M. Katich c Smith b Steyn	108	– c Harris b Kallis	30
*R. T. Ponting c McKenzie b Harris	9	– c McKenzie b Morkel	81
M. E. K. Hussey b Morkel	50	– c Kallis b Duminy	19
M. J. Clarke b Harris	3	– not out	23
M. J. North c Steyn b Kallis	38	– c de Villiers b Steyn	0
†B. J. Haddin c Amla b Ntini	5		
A. B. McDonald not out	4		
M. G. Johnson lbw b Ntini	0		
P. M. Siddle c Boucher b Steyn	0		
B. W. Hilfenhaus c Smith b Steyn	0		
B 6, l-b 4, w 2, n-b 8	20	B 12, l-b 2, n-b 4	18

1/184 (1) 2/208 (3) 3/259 (2)   (107.4 overs) 352
4/266 (5) 5/329 (4) 6/348 (6)
7/348 (7) 8/348 (9) 9/352 (10) 10/352 (11)

1/55 (2)   (5 wkts dec, 94.4 overs) 331
2/219 (3) 3/260 (4)
4/330 (1) 5/331 (6)

Steyn 25.4–3–83–3; Ntini 19–4–58–2; Morkel 24–4–81–1; Kallis 15–4–49–2; Harris 21–5–66–2; Duminy 3–1–5–0. *Second Innings*—Steyn 15.4–1–75–1; Ntini 15–2–55–1; Morkel 14–1–60–1; Kallis 8–0–21–1; Harris 31–8–68–0; Duminy 11–1–38–1.

South Africa

N. D. McKenzie c Haddin b Johnson	0	– (2) c Haddin b Siddle	31
*G. C. Smith retired hurt	2	– absent hurt	
H. M. Amla lbw b Johnson	0	– (1) c Ponting b Siddle	43
J. H. Kallis c Ponting b McDonald	22	– (3) c Ponting b Johnson	93
A. B. de Villiers lbw b Hilfenhaus	3	– (4) c Haddin b Siddle	84
J-P. Duminy not out	73	– (5) c Haddin b Hilfenhaus	17
†M. V. Boucher b Johnson	1	– (6) c and b North	25
P. L. Harris b McDonald	4	– (7) c Siddle b Katich	5
M. Morkel b McDonald	2	– (8) c Haddin b Katich	24
D. W. Steyn c Haddin b Siddle	8	– (9) st Haddin b Katich	7
M. Ntini lbw b Siddle	0	– (10) not out	4
B 10, l-b 12, n-b 1	23	B 13, l-b 11, w 3, n-b 10	37

1/0 (1) 2/0 (3) 3/6 (5) 4/62 (7)   (57.3 overs) 138   1/63 (2) 2/80 (1)   (132.2 overs) 370
5/104 (8) 6/104 (4) 7/106 (9)   3/267 (3) 4/279 (4)
8/138 (10) 9/138 (11)   5/299 (5) 6/307 (7) 7/345 (6)
                                       8/363 (8) 9/370 (9)

In the first innings Smith retired hurt at 3; Kallis, when 22, retired hurt at 56 and resumed at 104-5.

Johnson 16–5–37–3; Hilfenhaus 11–2–28–1; McDonald 12–4–25–3; Siddle 13.3–6–20–2; North 4–3–6–0; Clarke 1–1–0–0. *Second Innings*—Johnson 33–9–78–1; Hilfenhaus 24–4–79–1; Siddle 28–12–61–3; McDonald 16–3–47–0; North 20–6–36–1; Katich 11.2–1–45–3.

Umpires: Asad Rauf and B. F. Bowden.
Third umpire: S. A. Bucknor.   Referee: J. J. Crowe.

SOUTH AFRICA v AUSTRALIA

Third Test Match

At Cape Town, March 19, 20, 21, 22, 2009. South Africa won by an innings and 20 runs. Toss: Australia. Test debuts: I. Khan, J. A. Morkel; B. E. McGain.

After a four-day break for all their players when wives and girlfriends flew in, the Australians played, in Ponting's view, as poorly as they had for some time. South Africa, by contrast, at last reproduced the sort of form that had won them the previous series in December, inflicting Australia's first innings defeat since they lost to India at Calcutta in March 1998. The result also ended a long sequence of success for Australia at Newlands, where they had been victorious in nine of their ten previous Tests, losing only in 1969-70. South Africa dithered over their choice of captain to replace the injured Smith, initially naming Prince, who had not played a Test since November, only to backtrack and allow Kallis to lead for the second time (his other taste of Test leadership came in the final game of the previous home series against Australia).

After winning his sixth consecutive toss against South Africa, Ponting soon became a maiden Test victim for Albie Morkel, who had replaced his brother Morne in the side. It was Morkel's only wicket of the match, but a vital one nonetheless; Australia had been obliged to go in with only five specialist batsmen as they had no replacement for Marcus North, who had been admitted to hospital with gastroenteritis. Bryce McGain, a week short of his 37th birthday – the oldest debutant for Australia since his fellow leg-spinner Bob Holland in 1984-85 – came in, but the match was nothing less than a nightmare for him. McGain's tour portents had hardly been auspicious: he missed the flight out with the rest of the party.

Against some much improved bowling, no Australian batsman looked convincing on a good pitch. Katich, badly dropped at point by the debutant Imraan Khan when nine, scratched his way to 55 in nearly four hours before falling to a sweep shot off Harris, just as Hughes had done. Harris, skilfully using the breeze, tied up an end, allowing the pace

Hamish Blair, Getty Images

Scenting success: Paul Harris takes his fifth wicket (Peter Siddle) in Australia's second innings, to the delight of Imraan Khan, Ashwell Prince and Mark Boucher.

bowlers to attack downwind. Steyn exploited a weak defensive shot from Hussey and a misjudgment by Clarke to bowl both in successive overs. Haddin spoilt a good start by poking across a straight one from Harris, whereupon the lower order folded meekly.

South Africa scored quickly from the outset, taking 20 off Johnson's third over. Although the disciplined Siddle finally made a breakthrough in the 18th over, the others were quite unable to contain the home side in excellent batting conditions. McGain had his second ball in Test cricket struck back over his head for six by Prince, who batted beautifully on his return to the side. McGain's tendency to drop short repeatedly proved very costly, as his first ten overs were ravaged for 93. His final return – none for 149 from 18 overs – represented the second-worst economy-rate by a Test debutant bowling at least ten overs (Shahadat Hossain of Bangladesh conceded 101 from 12 overs in his first Test, at Lord's in 2005), as many as eight sixes and 17 fours being crashed off him. Clearly, South Africa had targeted McGain, refusing to let him settle.

Prince, allowed to concentrate on the unfamiliar role of opener after being relieved of the captaincy the day after being given it, reached his 11th Test hundred in the course of hitting McGain for three successive fours. With Kallis, he added 160 in 38 overs for the third wicket to take the game away from Australia. Kallis played with equal freedom, completing his fourth century against Australia with 14 fours, as well as two sixes, almost inevitably off McGain. When both were out, de Villiers flogged a wilting attack in brilliant fashion, surging to 163. A calculated assault on McDonald brought him four (all to leg) sixes off consecutive balls, making him the third batsman to achieve this feat in Test cricket after Kapil Dev and Shahid Afridi. De Villiers's two previous scoring shots had been sixes off McGain; he hit seven in all, as well as 12 fours. His buccaneering seventh-wicket stand of 124 with Morkel took only 20 overs, and ensured South Africa would reach 651, their biggest total against Australia (previously 622 for nine declared at Durban in 1969-70). The 62 extras were also the most conceded by Australia in any Test innings.

Needing 442 to make South Africa bat again, they were a beaten side by the time they lost their top six batsmen for 218 by the 89th over. Once again Harris dismissed both openers, Hughes edging an arm ball to slip and Katich, beaten in the flight, driving to mid-off. Later, Haddin miscued to deep mid-on. Steyn, back to his best, filleted the middle order – Ponting edging a drive, Hussey caught in the gully and Clarke playing on with no footwork.

Johnson and McDonald threatened to extend the match into the fifth day with well-executed and at times piratical stroke play in a seventh-wicket stand of 163 in 26 overs, but it was in a lost cause. While McDonald played positively to canter to his first Test fifty from 56 balls, Johnson thundered to a maiden first-class hundred from 86 with what was his fourth six, a pull off Steyn. His unbeaten 123 came from 103 balls with 11 fours and five sixes. Of more significance as far as the match was concerned was the unsung Harris's return of six for 127, the first five-wicket haul in a home Test by a South African slow bowler since off-spinner Harry Bromfield, also at Newlands, against England in 1964-65.

Man of the Match: P. L. Harris. *Man of the Series:* M. G. Johnson.

Close of play: First day, South Africa 57-0 (Khan 15, Prince 37); Second day, South Africa 404-3 (Kallis 102, de Villiers 39); Third day, Australia 102-2 (Katich 44, Hussey 13).

Australia

P. J. Hughes lbw b Harris	33	– c Kallis b Harris	32
S. M. Katich c Khan b Harris	55	– c Duminy b Harris	54
*R. T. Ponting c Boucher b Morkel	0	– c Boucher b Steyn	12
M. E. K. Hussey b Steyn	20	– c Duminy b Steyn	39
M. J. Clarke b Steyn	0	– b Steyn	47
†B. J. Haddin lbw b Harris	42	– c Duminy b Harris	18
A. B. McDonald c Kallis b Ntini	13	– c de Villiers b Harris	68
M. G. Johnson c Prince b Steyn	35	– not out	123
P. M. Siddle c de Villiers b Ntini	0	– c de Villiers b Harris	0
B. E. McGain c de Villiers b Steyn	2	– run out	0
B. W. Hilfenhaus not out	0	– c Prince b Harris	12
L-b 6, w 1, n-b 2	9	B 8, l-b 2, w 2, n-b 5	17

1/58 (1) 2/59 (3) 3/81 (4) 4/81 (5)   (72 overs) **209**   1/57 (1) 2/76 (3)   (121.5 overs) **422**
5/152 (2) 6/158 (6) 7/190 (7)   3/138 (2) 4/146 (4)
8/190 (9) 9/209 (8) 10/209 (10)   5/191 (6) 6/218 (5) 7/381 (7)
                                            8/381 (9) 9/388 (10) 10/422 (11)

Steyn 16-5-56-4; Ntini 17-7-38-2; Kallis 10-2-31-0; Morkel 12-3-44-1; Harris 17-5-34-3.
Second Innings—Steyn 27-5-96-3; Ntini 19-6-66-0; Morkel 20-1-88-0; Harris 42.5-9-127-6; Kallis 10-4-21-0; Duminy 3-1-14-0.

South Africa

I. Khan c and b Siddle	20	D. W. Steyn c Clarke b Katich	0
A. G. Prince c Haddin b Hilfenhaus	150	M. Ntini not out	4
H. M. Amla b Haddin b Johnson	46		
*J. H. Kallis c and b Hilfenhaus	102	B 19, l-b 24, w 9, n-b 10	62
A. B. de Villiers c McDonald b Katich	163		
J-P. Duminy b Johnson	7	1/65 (1) 2/162 (3) (154.3 overs) **651**
†M. V. Boucher c Ponting b Johnson	12	3/322 (2) 4/415 (4)
J. A. Morkel b McDonald	58	5/443 (6) 6/467 (7) 7/591 (8)
P. L. Harris c Haddin b Johnson	27	8/637 (5) 9/637 (10) 10/651 (9)

Johnson 37.3-5-148-4; Hilfenhaus 34-4-133-2; Siddle 35-15-67-1; McGain 18-2-149-0; McDonald 27-7-102-1; Katich 3-1-9-2.

Umpires: Asad Rauf and S. A. Bucknor.
Third umpire: B. F. Bowden. Referee: J. J. Crowe.

LIMITED-OVERS INTERNATIONAL REPORTS
BY NEIL MANTHORP

†SOUTH AFRICA v AUSTRALIA

First Twenty20 International

At Johannesburg, March 27, 2009 (floodlit). South Africa won by four wickets. Toss: South Africa. Twenty20 international debut: B. Geeves.

Australia's one-day team had become sick of the sight of Albie Morkel and his match-winning boundary-hitting in the preceding series back at home, but there was more to come. South Africa were not quite halfway to their target when the fifth wicket fell at the start of the 13th over, leaving them requiring another 84 from 47 balls. Morkel walloped 37 of those from just 19 deliveries, adding 58 with Boucher, no slouch himself with 36 from 22. But it was the Australian bowlers' inability to prevent Morkel from getting under the ball so often which rendered David Hussey's fine unbeaten 88, containing half a dozen sixes, a futile effort.

Man of the Match: D. J. Hussey.

Australia		B	4	6
D. A. Warner *c and b 9*	38	29	4	1
M. J. Clarke *b 11*	2	6	0	0
*R. T. Ponting *c 8 b 7*	1	5	0	0
D. J. Hussey *not out*	88	44	5	6
M. E. K. Hussey *run out*	0	1	0	0
†B. J. Haddin *c 7 b 9*	0	3	0	0
C. L. White *c 4 b 9*	16	20	0	1
M. G. Johnson *b 11*	10	10	1	0
J. R. Hopes *not out*	5	2	1	0
L-b 2, w 4	6			

6 overs: 40-2   (20 overs) 166-7

1/5 2/16 3/70 4/70 5/71 6/116 7/149

S. M. Harwood and B. Geeves did not bat.

Steyn 4–0–44–0; Parnell 4–0–29–2; Morkel 4–0–36–1; Botha 4–0–25–0; Peterson 4–0–30–3.

South Africa		B	4	6
H. M. Amla *b 4*	26	24	3	0
H. H. Gibbs *c 3 b 11*	19	12	2	1
A. B. de Villiers *b 11*	7	7	1	0
J-P. Duminy *b 9*	21	21	2	0
V. B. van Jaarsveld *b 4*	3	7	0	0
†M. V. Boucher *not out*	36	22	5	0
J. A. Morkel *c 4 b 8*	37	19	4	2
*J. Botha *not out*	7	5	1	0
L-b 3, w 8, n-b 1	12			

6 overs: 48-2   (19.2 overs) 168-6

1/26 2/46 3/64 4/81 5/83 6/141

R. J. Peterson, D. W. Steyn and W. D. Parnell did not bat.

Johnson 4–0–20–1; Harwood 4–0–48–0; Geeves 3.2–0–35–2; D. J. Hussey 4–0–21–2; Hopes 4–0–41–1.

Umpires: M. Erasmus and R. E. Koertzen.   Third umpire: B. G. Jerling.   Referee: J. J. Crowe.

†SOUTH AFRICA v AUSTRALIA

Second Twenty20 International

At Centurion, March 29, 2009 (floodlit). South Africa won by 17 runs. Toss: Australia. Twenty20 international debuts: Y. A. Abdulla, R. E. van der Merwe; B. Laughlin.

Roelof van der Merwe is about as subtle as a blacksmith shaping a crowbar, and bats with a very similar action. His "hit every ball for six" approach earned him 48 from 30 balls on debut in front of his home crowd – with four sixes, one of which was aimed at cow corner but actually flew over backward point. South Africa's 156 was competitive but not intimidating, although their other debutant, Dolphins left-arm seamer Yusuf Abdulla, quickly made it more daunting with the early wicket of Ponting in a clever spell with the new ball. But it was Botha who really strangled the tourists out of the game, conceding only 16 runs in his four overs. Ben Laughlin, Australia's debutant, is the son of Trevor, who played three Tests and six one-day internationals in the late 1970s.

Man of the Match: R. E. van der Merwe.

South Africa

		B	4	6
R. J. Peterson *b* 8	34	27	3	2
H. H. Gibbs *b* 9	20	13	1	1
A. B. de Villiers *c* 6 *b* 11	0	5	0	0
J-P. Duminy *b* 10	23	28	1	0
R. E. van der Merwe *c* 7 *b* 10	48	30	2	4
J. A. Morkel *not out*	14	10	1	1
†M. V. Boucher *not out*	9	8	0	1
B 1, l-b 2, w 4, n-b 1	8			

6 overs: 36-2   (20 overs) 156-5

1/22 2/24 3/71 4/96 5/133

*J. Botha, J. L. Ontong, Y. A. Abdulla and J. Louw did not bat.

Bracken 4–0–44–1; Harwood 4–0–21–2; Laughlin 4–0–32–1; Hopes 4–0–26–1; Hussey 3–0–24–0; White 1–0–6–0.

Australia

		B	4	6
M. J. Clarke *b* 8	27	33	2	0
D. A. Warner *b* 6	20	15	2	1
*R. T. Ponting *c* 7 *b* 10	1	3	0	0
D. J. Hussey *c* 2 *b* 5	27	18	3	1
C. J. Ferguson *run out*	0	1	0	0
C. L. White *c* 4 *b* 8	23	22	2	1
†B. J. Haddin *not out*	16	13	0	1
J. R. Hopes *c* 6 *b* 11	18	15	0	1
N. W. Bracken *c* 3 *b* 11	0	1	0	0
S. M. Harwood *not out*	0	0	0	0
L-b 1, w 5, n-b 1	7			

6 overs: 42-2   (20 overs) 139-8

1/37 2/38 3/63 4/63 5/101 6/106 7/131 8/138

B. Laughlin did not bat.

Louw 4–0–36–2; Abdulla 3–0–16–1; Morkel 3–0–24–1; van der Merwe 4–0–30–1; Botha 4–0–16–2; Peterson 2–0–16–0.

Umpires: M. Erasmus and B. G. Jerling.   Third umpire: R. E. Koertzen.   Referee: J. J. Crowe.

†SOUTH AFRICA v AUSTRALIA

First One-Day International

At Durban, April 3, 2009 (day/night). Australia won by 141 runs. Toss: Australia. One-day international debut: B. Laughlin.

The real Mike Hussey finally made an appearance, having been missing for most of the summer against South Africa. His unbeaten 83 from 79 balls built handily on Haddin's punchy fifty, and it was typical of Hussey, and the effect he has on an innings when in top form, that Australia suddenly had a very good score without ever appearing to accelerate, let alone hit top gear. Ntini was the only bowler to be really clobbered, when Hussey and Hauritz collected 18 from the final over. Having been dropped from the limited-overs team at the start of the season, Ntini had forced his way back only to be saddled with the responsibility of bowling at the death, something he had never succeeded with at any stage of his career. It mattered not: even Smith's half-century could not prevent his team feeling shamed by their ineptitude in reply, although Johnson and the rest of the attack had a very good evening. Off-spinner Hauritz finished with four wickets, but admitted afterwards that slow bowling can often be rewarding when you are facing a struggling team as their target climbs to seven an over.

Man of the Match: M. E. K. Hussey.

Australia

†B. J. Haddin *run out*	53	M. G. Johnson *c* Boucher *b* Steyn	1
M. J. Clarke *c* Duminy *b* Ntini	1	N. M. Hauritz *not out*	20
*R. T. Ponting *c* J. A. Morkel *b* M. Morkel	37	L-b 2, w 7, n-b 1	10
D. J. Hussey *run out*	18		
M. E. K. Hussey *not out*	83	1/2 (2) 2/79 (3)	(7 wkts, 50 overs) 286
C. J. Ferguson *c* Botha *b* Steyn	25	3/107 (4) 4/115 (1)	
J. R. Hopes *c* Steyn *b* M. Morkel	38	5/168 (6) 6/235 (7) 7/243 (8) 10 overs: 41-1	

N. W. Bracken and B. Laughlin did not bat.

Steyn 9–0–45–2; Ntini 9–1–67–1; M. Morkel 10–0–61–2; J. A. Morkel 8–0–51–0; Botha 10–0–38–0; Duminy 4–0–22–0.

South Africa

H. M. Amla c Haddin b Bracken	7	D. W. Steyn c M. E. K. Hussey b Laughlin		1
*G. C. Smith c and b Hauritz	52	M. Ntini not out		2
H. H. Gibbs c Clarke b Hopes	33			
A. B. de Villiers lbw b Johnson	2	L-b 4, w 5		9
J-P. Duminy c Johnson b Hopes	15			
†M. V. Boucher c Haddin b Hauritz	0	1/17 (1) 2/91 (3) 3/94 (4)	(33.1 overs)	145
J. Botha c M. E. K. Hussey b Johnson	8	4/110 (2) 5/112 (6) 6/125 (5)		
J. A. Morkel st Haddin b Hauritz	14	7/132 (7) 8/142 (8)		
M. Morkel c Laughlin b Hauritz	2	9/143 (10) 10/145 (9)	10 overs: 50-1	

Johnson 7–0–24–2; Bracken 6–0–36–1; Laughlin 5–0–28–1; Hopes 7–1–24–2; Hauritz 8.1–1–29–4.

Umpires: E. A. R. de Silva and R. E. Koertzen.
Third umpire: B. G. Jerling. Referee: R. S. Madugalle.

†SOUTH AFRICA v AUSTRALIA

Second One-Day International

At Centurion, April 5, 2009. South Africa won by seven wickets. Toss: Australia. One-day international debut: R. E. van der Merwe.

Australia's coach Tim Nielsen persuaded Ponting that it was a bat-first day despite the 10 a.m. start and the likelihood of early moisture in what admittedly looked a good batting pitch. Not only was there seam movement, but swing, too, and Australia were 19 for five before they could say "What was that, Tim?" In only his sixth one-day international, Ferguson did a commendable job with a mature 50 in hopeless circumstances, but there is only so long anyone can keep their finger in the dyke. Steyn shared the new ball with 19-year-old left-armer Wayne Parnell and, if it was a glimpse of South Africa's future, that looked very bright indeed as they shared eight wickets for 52 runs. Parnell can be on the slippery side of fast-medium but, apart from the ability to swing the ball, it was his reading of conditions and subsequent adjustment of pace which was so impressive. There was never a doubt about South Africa levelling the series once they reached lunch at 33 for one from seven overs.

Man of the Match: W. D. Parnell.

Australia

†B. J. Haddin b Steyn	1	N. W. Bracken c Gibbs b Parnell		5
M. J. Clarke lbw b Parnell	5	B. Laughlin not out		1
*R. T. Ponting c Boucher b Parnell	8			
D. J. Hussey c Boucher b Steyn	1	L-b 2, w 6, n-b 1		9
M. E. K. Hussey lbw b Parnell	3			
C. J. Ferguson c de Villiers b Steyn	50	1/2 (1) 2/11 (3) 3/14 (2)	(40.2 overs)	131
J. R. Hopes c Botha b Kallis	8	4/19 (4) 5/19 (5) 6/40 (7)		
M. G. Johnson lbw b Botha	30	7/103 (8) 8/124 (6)		
N. M. Hauritz c Boucher b Steyn	10	9/129 (10) 10/131 (9)	10 overs: 29-5	

Steyn 9.2–0–27–4; Parnell 8–4–25–4; Kallis 4–1–11–1; Morkel 5–0–15–0; Botha 9–0–29–1; van der Merwe 5–0–22–0.

South Africa

*G. C. Smith c Clarke b Laughlin	40
H. H. Gibbs c Hauritz b Johnson	2
J. H. Kallis c Haddin b Johnson	31
A. B. de Villiers not out	36
J-P. Duminy not out	11
L-b 6, w 6	12

1/7 (2) 2/76 (1)   (3 wkts, 26.2 overs) 132
3/93 (3)   10 overs: 49-1

†M. V. Boucher, J. A. Morkel, R. E. van der Merwe, J. Botha, D. W. Steyn and W. D. Parnell did not bat.

Johnson 10–0–47–2; Bracken 4–0–23–0; Laughlin 7.2–1–30–1; Hauritz 5–0–26–0.

Umpires: E. A. R. de Silva and B. G. Jerling.
Third umpire: R. E. Koertzen.   Referee: R. S. Madugalle.

†SOUTH AFRICA v AUSTRALIA

Third One-Day International

At Cape Town, April 9, 2009 (day/night). South Africa won by 25 runs. Toss: South Africa.

Kallis and de Villiers added a composed and chanceless 114 for the third wicket in 22 overs, to provide the bedrock for some highly effective late thrashing from Boucher and Morkel, which propelled South Africa close to 300 on a pitch where the par score looked about 250. Given the difficulties of batting under lights at Newlands, particularly at the extreme ends of the season, Australia were always up against it. They would have been completely out of the contest had Johnson not kept South Africa in check with a couple of fine spells, as clever as they were hostile. Van der Merwe's slow left-armers are a great deal more subtle than his slogging, and he was responsible for two of the first four wickets to fall by actually spinning the ball as well as varying his pace. At 114 for five the contest died, and was never resuscitated. Attractive half-centuries from Ferguson (his second in a row) and Hopes hauled Australia to within 25 runs – but it might as well have been 125.

Man of the Match: J. H. Kallis.

South Africa

H. H. Gibbs c Hopes b Bracken	26	R. E. van der Merwe not out	6
*G. C. Smith c Haddin b Johnson	8		
J. H. Kallis c Hopes b Geeves	70	L-b 4, w 2, n-b 4	10
A. B. de Villiers c Hauritz b Johnson	80		
J-P. Duminy c M. E. K. Hussey b Johnson	32	1/28 (2) 2/50 (1) (6 wkts, 50 overs)	289
J. A. Morkel b Johnson	29	3/164 (3) 4/198 (4)	
†M. V. Boucher not out	28	5/230 (5) 6/283 (6) 10 overs: 32-1	

J. Botha, D. W. Steyn and W. D. Parnell did not bat.

Johnson 10–2–34–4; Bracken 10–0–58–1; Geeves 10–0–67–1; Hauritz 8–0–37–0; Hopes 8–0–64–0; D. J. Hussey 4–0–25–0.

Australia

†B. J. Haddin run out	15	M. G. Johnson run out	9
M. J. Clarke b van der Merwe	35	B. Geeves not out	10
*R. T. Ponting c and b Botha	20	B 5, l-b 14, w 9	28
D. J. Hussey c Steyn b Duminy	20		
M. E. K. Hussey lbw b van der Merwe	1	1/30 (1) 2/66 (3) (7 wkts, 50 overs)	264
C. J. Ferguson c de Villiers b van der Merwe	63	3/80 (2) 4/83 (5)	
J. R. Hopes not out	63	5/114 (4) 6/211 (6) 7/226 (8) 10 overs: 30-1	

N. M. Hauritz and N. W. Bracken did not bat.

Steyn 10–0–44–0; Parnell 9–0–47–0; Kallis 4–0–19–0; Morkel 5–0–33–0; Botha 10–1–59–1; van der Merwe 10–0–37–3; Duminy 2–0–6–1.

Umpires: E. A. R. de Silva and R. E. Koertzen.
Third umpire: B. G. Jerling.   Referee: R. S. Madugalle.

†SOUTH AFRICA v AUSTRALIA

Fourth One-Day International

At Port Elizabeth, April 13, 2009. South Africa won by 61 runs. Toss: Australia. One-day international debut: S. M. Harwood.

Herschelle Gibbs completed his lengthy recovery with a magnificent century four months after starting an alcohol-rehabilitation course following disciplinary problems. He had scored just one half-century (admittedly a brilliant one, at Sydney) in eight one-day and four Twenty20 innings since his return, but this was the confirmation everyone wanted to see that Gibbs could still cut it aged 35. His 110 from 116 balls – his 21st one-day international century, 14 months and 19 matches after his 20th – thrilled a capacity crowd at one of his favourite grounds, but it was his partnership of 136 with de Villiers which did so much to take the game away from Australia. Victoria's Shane Harwood, a fast bowler making his 50-over international debut at 35, took two wickets, but proved expensive late on. Nonetheless, a win looked within Australia's reach after an opening stand of 129 between the blazing Haddin (78 from 61 balls) and a more restrained Clarke (50 from 68). Ponting, having publicly berated himself the day before for not scoring a one-day hundred for over a year, was in determined mood, grafting to 53 from 67 balls. But only two more batsmen reached double figures, handing the match, the series and a reinforced No. 1 ranking to South Africa.

Man of the Match: H. H. Gibbs.

South Africa

*G. C. Smith c Haddin b Hopes	20	J-P. Duminy c M. E. K. Hussey b Harwood	40
H. H. Gibbs c Clarke b Bracken	110	L-b 7, w 6	13
J. H. Kallis c Ferguson b Harwood	17		
A. B. de Villiers c Ferguson b Johnson	84	1/46 (1) 2/87 (3)	(6 wkts, 50 overs) 317
J. A. Morkel b Johnson	4	3/223 (4) 4/240 (5)	
†M. V. Boucher not out	29	5/252 (4) 6/317 (7)	10 overs: 46-0

R. E. van der Merwe, J. Botha, D. W. Steyn and W. D. Parnell did not bat.

Bracken 10–0–64–1; Johnson 10–0–59–2; Hopes 10–0–57–1; Harwood 10–0–57–2; Hauritz 7–0–51–0; Clarke 3–0–22–0.

Australia

†B. J. Haddin c Parnell b Botha	78	N. W. Bracken not out	0
M. J. Clarke b van der Merwe	50	S. M. Harwood b Steyn	0
*R. T. Ponting c Morkel b Steyn	53		
C. J. Ferguson st Boucher b van der Merwe	3	L-b 4, w 7	11
M. E. K. Hussey lbw b van der Merwe	2		
D. J. Hussey c and b Steyn	20	1/129 (1) 2/137 (2)	(45.5 overs) 256
J. R. Hopes c Gibbs b Parnell	31	3/145 (4) 4/151 (5) 5/188 (6)	
M. G. Johnson b Morkel	5	6/226 (3) 7/245 (8) 8/255 (7)	
N. M. Hauritz b Steyn	3	9/256 (9) 10/256 (11)	10 overs: 46-0

Steyn 7.5–1–44–4; Parnell 9–0–64–1; Kallis 4–0–25–0; Morkel 5–0–25–1; Botha 10–0–48–1; van der Merwe 10–0–46–3.

Umpires: E. A. R. de Silva and B. G. Jerling.
Third umpire: R. E. Koertzen.   Referee: R. S. Madugalle.

†SOUTH AFRICA v AUSTRALIA

Fifth One-Day International

At Johannesburg, April 17, 2009 (day/night). Australia won by 47 runs. Toss: South Africa.

At several stages of Australia's innings in their first one-day international at the Wanderers since the famous 872-run match of March 2006, it looked as if they might get close to their 434 that day: at 192 for two after 31 overs, 400 seemed distinctly possible. The top five all reached 40 at around a run a ball, but it was the inability of anyone to manage more than 66 that led to the total being only a touch over 300. It might have been even lower, as they lost five wickets for 54, but Mike Hussey and Hauritz again did a fine job, putting on 57 for the eighth wicket in the last nine overs. Gibbs led the chase with a delightful 82 until he missed a sweep against Hauritz and was lbw, and the South African innings began to decline from the heights of 150 for one. Kallis made 64 from just 69 balls – unusually well paced for him – but Hauritz and Johnson completed successful series by taking five wickets between them, and Australia secured a consolation victory.

Man of the Match: N. M. Hauritz. *Man of the Series:* A. B. de Villiers.

Australia

†B. J. Haddin c Duminy b J. A. Morkel	62	M. G. Johnson c and b Duminy	2	
M. J. Clarke c Duminy b van der Merwe	66	N. M. Hauritz not out	24	
*R. T. Ponting c van der Merwe b Duminy	40	B 1, l-b 3, w 9	13	
C. J. Ferguson c de Villiers b van der Merwe	41			
M. E. K. Hussey not out	49	1/127 (1) 2/138 (2) (7 wkts, 50 overs)	303	
D. J. Hussey st Boucher b Duminy	3	3/192 (4) 4/223 (3)		
J. R. Hopes run out	3	5/231 (6) 6/238 (7) 7/246 (8) 10 overs: 70-0		

N. W. Bracken and B. Laughlin did not bat.

Steyn 10–0–73–0; Ntini 6–0–48–0; M. Morkel 8–1–41–0; Kallis 2–0–21–0; J. A. Morkel 4–0–24–1; van der Merwe 10–0–44–2; Duminy 10–0–48–3.

South Africa

H. H. Gibbs lbw b Hauritz	82	D. W. Steyn run out	0	
*G. C. Smith c Haddin b Bracken	20	M. Ntini not out	9	
J. H. Kallis c Haddin b Bracken	64			
A. B. de Villiers b Laughlin	38	B 2, l-b 1, w 5	8	
J-P. Duminy c Haddin b Johnson	3			
†M. V. Boucher c Hauritz b Hopes	9	1/46 (2) 2/150 (1) 3/188 (3) (45.5 overs)	256	
J. A. Morkel c Laughlin b Hauritz	5	4/191 (5) 5/213 (6) 6/226 (7)		
R. E. van der Merwe c Bracken b Johnson	3	7/229 (4) 8/238 (8)		
M. Morkel c D. J. Hussey b Johnson	15	9/238 (10) 10/256 (9) 10 overs: 57-1		

Johnson 8.5–0–58–3; Bracken 10–1–54–2; Laughlin 9–0–56–1; Hauritz 9–0–34–2; Hopes 6–0–31–1; Clarke 2–0–16–0; D. J. Hussey 1–0–4–0.

Umpires: E. A. R. de Silva and R. E. Koertzen.
Third umpire: B. G. Jerling. Referee: R. S. Madugalle.

SOUTH AFRICA v ZIMBABWE, 2009-10

One-day internationals (2): South Africa 2, Zimbabwe 0

South Africa warmed up for their home series against England with two matches against their neighbours, and won them easily. The short series included the first appearance in South African colours of Ryan McLaren, who had abandoned his status as a Kolpak player with Kent to return to his homeland.

ZIMBABWEAN TOURING PARTY

P. Utseya (*captain*), C. J. Chibhabha, E. Chigumbura, C. K. Coventry, A. G. Cremer, K. M. Jarvis, H. Masakadza, S. Matsikenyeri, C. B. Mpofu, F. Mutizwa, R. W. Price, T. Taibu, B. R. M. Taylor, M. A. Vermeulen, M. N. Waller. *Coach:* H. H. Streak.

Full scores of these matches are available at: www.cricinfo.com/ci/content/series/430503.html and www.cricket archive.co.uk/archive/season/rsa/2009-10_rsa_zimbabwe_in_south_africa_2009-10.html

At Benoni, November 8, 2009. **First one-day international: South Africa won by 45 runs.** Toss: Zimbabwe. **South Africa 295-5** (50 overs) (H. M. Amla 80, G. C. Smith 35, A. B. de Villiers 51, A. N. Petersen 39, J. A. Morkel 50*; R. W. Price 3-44); **Zimbabwe 250-6** (50 overs) (T. Taibu 103*, S. Matsikenyeri 86; R. McLaren 3-51). *One-day international debut:* R. McLaren. *Man of the Match:* T. Taibu.

South Africa were grateful to Albie Morkel's late fireworks – 50 from 39 balls, with three fours and three sixes – which took them to an imposing total. Zimbabwe crashed to 48-5 before Taibu and Matsikenyeri put on 188, a national record for the sixth wicket in one-day internationals. Taibu reached his second one-day hundred (both against South Africa), but his side were never realistically in touch with the asking-rate. Charl Langeveldt returned to the South African side after 20 months.

At Centurion, November 10, 2009 (day/night). **Second one-day international: South Africa won by 212 runs.** Toss: Zimbabwe. **South Africa 331-5** (50 overs) (G. C. Smith 53, J. H. Kallis 81, J-P. Duminy 111*, M. V. Boucher 31*; R. W. Price 3-55); **Zimbabwe 119** (34.3 overs) (T. Taibu 52; C. K. Langeveldt 3-36, J. A. Morkel 3-20, R. E. van der Merwe 3-27). *Man of the Match:* J-P. Duminy. *Man of the Series:* T. Taibu.

Zimbabwe's top order imploded again – both openers went for ducks – and this time there was no significant recovery, despite another defiant innings from Taibu (the next-best score was 13). Earlier Duminy's maiden one-day international hundred came up from just 82 balls as South Africa hastened past 300.

SOUTH AFRICA v ENGLAND, 2009-10

Colin Bateman

Test matches (4): South Africa 1, England 1
One-day internationals (5): South Africa 1, England 2
Twenty20 internationals (2): South Africa 1, England 1

At the end of another winter tour, another England captain stood down. This time, though, Andrew Strauss did it with the blessing of the selectors, the ECB and the coaching staff. His departure was to be only temporary. A day after the heavy defeat in the final Test that had seen South Africa level the series, Strauss confirmed what had been rumoured for some time: he was taking a four-month break and handing over the reins for the forthcoming tour of Bangladesh to his young deputy Alastair Cook.

Ignoring a chorus of disapproval from former captains, Strauss said he felt "jaded" after the 12 months he had had since taking charge amid the turmoil caused by the forced resignation of Kevin Pietersen and the sacking of head coach Peter Moores. "The notion that a captain continues until he is mentally and physically exhausted doesn't seem in the best interest of the side," said Strauss. "The Ashes and the World Cup next winter are two big priorities for this side, and I would never forgive myself if I turned up in Australia feeling exhausted and not giving myself the best chance of performing my job as a captain and a batsman, and not having the energy to keep the players going in some pretty stressful situations."

Strauss had gone to South Africa determined that his England team, having regained the Ashes the previous summer, would not fall into the same trap as the 2005 side, which basked in the glory of beating Australia far too long and failed to build on their success. There could have been few tougher challenges than going to South Africa to test that resolve. The home side were top of the ICC Test rankings when England arrived in early November, but Strauss and team director Andy Flower quietly felt their squad, strong on team ethics and resilience if a little short of star quality, could cause an upset.

South Africa undoubtedly had world-class batsmen and bowlers to call upon, but their penchant for faltering under pressure was exposed again, certainly early in the tour as England won the 50-over series. The tourists then took a lead in a Test series that was full of drama – two cliffhanging finishes in which England's No. 11 Graham Onions was the batting hero – and a fair dash of controversy, before the home side levelled it at 1–1 in the Fourth Test to retain the Basil D'Oliveira Trophy.

It was also a battle between two immensely strong and mature leaders, Strauss and Graeme Smith, equally impressive in their contrasting styles. The two kept their distance all series but, while there was clearly no love lost between them, there was respect. Strauss refused to be drawn into the mind games that South Africa indulged in before a ball was bowled in anger, but when two of his players, Stuart Broad and James Anderson, had a finger of

Well-armed: South Africa's pace attack, led by Dale Steyn (*left*) and Morne Morkel, had the edge over England's.

suspicion pointed at them over ball-tampering during the Third Test, Strauss fiercely defended them, describing South Africa's accusations as "a little bit malicious".

Strauss's form as an opener deserted him, and he finished last among the specialist batsmen in England's Test averages with 24.28, while Smith averaged 61, boosted by centuries in the last two Tests. In the end, South Africa got their star players fit, picked the right side, and finally crushed England's defiance in a Johannesburg Test that was mired in a row about the Umpire Decision Review System (or UDRS, as the ICC rather clumsily called it).

It seemed initially that the system, which allowed teams to ask for a review of decisions made by the on-field umpires from the third official watching a TV monitor, was not going to be used for the series. Both teams were sceptical, and not all the high-tech pieces of equipment such as Hot Spot – an infra-red view which detects the heat generated by ball hitting bat (or batsman) – and the Snickometer were available. A few weeks earlier, India had refused to use the new system for their series against Sri Lanka, and the ICC, desperate for their new baby not to be smothered at birth, sent their cricket manager Dave Richardson to South Africa to bang a few heads together.

Both sides did finally agree to UDRS being used, but it was not long before there were complaints, particularly from the England camp. In the First Test, Flower questioned referee Roshan Mahanama about the length of time South

Africa had taken before asking for a review of a decision involving Broad, who complained to the on-field umpires after being given out. There were insinuations that signals had come from the South African dressing-room, which were flatly denied.

The confrontational Broad had a chequered series, and was lucky to walk away from it without a reprimand from Mahanama for his at-times petulant behaviour. As well as stepping on the ball in the Cape Town Test, which sparked the suggestion of ball-tampering, he again showed dissent when given out after a review in the final Test.

England's loudest moan about the system came during that Test at the Wanderers, and led in part to their downfall, as they became distracted by a sense of injustice over a decision early on which could have changed the course of the match. Smith was given not out after England called for a review when they thought he had been caught behind for 15. The players on the field and some television viewers – including those in the England dressing-room – heard a snick as ball passed bat. Smith conceded there had been a noise, but said he had felt nothing on his bat. The third umpire Daryl Harper, however, heard and saw nothing to suggest to him that Smith should have been given out, which led to complaints from Flower that Harper had not turned up the volume on his monitor.

"Snickogate" ensued, with conspiracy theories about the host broadcaster, SABC, not supplying the required technology to Harper. In a complete overreaction, the ECB's Hugh Morris demanded that the team should have their lost referral reinstated, while the chairman Giles Clarke, who was at the match, called the system "a shambles" and hinted that the ECB would refuse to use it in the future unless it was overhauled. The fact that Smith went on to make a century that set up his side's innings victory may have had something to do with England's outrage.

The tour had started serenely enough for England, with Strauss announcing he had "never seen a squad so motivated". After early victories in the warm-up games, the party was boosted by the arrival of Pietersen, who had been out of action since July because of surgery on his right Achilles tendon. The tour meant a great deal to Pietersen, being his first Test series in the country of his birth, but it was to become one of frustration for England's most gifted batsman, who reached 50 only once and averaged a modest 25.28 in the four Test matches.

Much was made of England's South African-born players – Strauss, Pietersen, Matt Prior and Jonathan Trott. They were christened "The Boer Four", and TV adverts building up to the series poked fun at the Afrikaans accents in the England huddle. Possibly the mockery worked, because all four had disappointing tours.

After sharing the Twenty20 series, during which Cook made his bow as an England captain when Paul Collingwood suffered a back injury, England shocked the home side in the one-day internationals by becoming the only team other than Australia to win a bilateral 50-over series in South Africa. The weather ruined two of the five games, but they played impressive, well-organised cricket to take the trophy. Collingwood, who became England's

Graham Morris

Not tempted: Paul Collingwood lets a short ball pass by during his second innings at Cape Town.

most capped one-day player (171 appearances) in the first match staged, was named Man of the Series to launch what became a highly successful tour for him.

Under Flower, England took a more strategic approach to the 50-over game rather than regarding it as a sideshow, and the outcome was encouraging. The emphasis was on athletic fielders, and batsmen prepared to hit over the top, notably Eoin Morgan, whose performances later earned him an IPL contract, and Collingwood, who hit five sixes in the three matches played. England had also started the tour a few days earlier than originally planned, to put in some extra practice. They were taking this seriously.

There were no plodders in the field, and the omission of Owais Shah and Ravi Bopara also greatly improved the running between the wickets. Trott made a success of opening the batting, England's two victories coming when he was Strauss's partner at the start of the innings; and Broad, who had been out for three weeks with a right shoulder injury suffered in the first warm-up match, teamed up with Anderson to form an effective new-ball pairing.

South Africa were handicapped by injuries to Jacques Kallis (rib) and Dale Steyn (hamstring), which not only affected their one-day performances but were to have an impact on the first half of the Test series. As in the 20-over games, England won the first 50-over contest only for South Africa to hit back emphatically in the second. Anderson destroyed the home side with five for 23, his best one-day international figures, in the third match, which proved decisive. The Durban weather ruined the last scheduled game, to give England the series 2–1 and an impressive 7–1 winning sequence against South Africa in one-day internationals.

One casualty of the one-day games was Adil Rashid, who had been picked as the second-choice spinner to Graeme Swann. Rashid's leg-breaks came in for heavy punishment in the two international games he played – his four overs cost 52 – and he rapidly faded from England's plans. Kent off-spinner James Tredwell, ostensibly added to the squad as cover for Swann (who had been suffering from a sore side), became a permanent member of the touring party. Rashid was then dropped for the following tour of Bangladesh, Tredwell taking his place.

The start of the Test series at Centurion was all about another landmark: Makhaya Ntini, the first black South African to play for his country, was to win his 100th cap. There was never any question that Ntini would play, although his fast bowling had gone into terminal decline and there were doubts that he was worth his place. An iconic figure in South African sport, Ntini was feted by the good and the great, the plaudits including a handwritten letter from Nelson Mandela, and, when it came to the final over of the Test, Smith lobbed him the ball in the hope that he might dislodge England's last wicket to win the match – but there was to be no fairytale.

Onions navigated that final over successfully to give England a draw they just about deserved. Astonishingly, Onions was to do exactly the same thing at Cape Town to save the Third Test, but this time the bowler was Morne Morkel, Ntini having been dropped after the innings defeat at Durban, in which he was ineffectual. Ntini was left out of the squad altogether for the final Test, and out of South Africa's tour party for India which was named after the series ended. A wonderful sporting story had seemingly come to an end.

While all eyes had been on the fast bowlers in Centurion, Swann slipped under the radar to earn the match award for his all-round performance. After taking five wickets in South Africa's first innings, he hit a lusty 85 when England batted to keep his side in touch during a match in which they were always second-best. Swann added a second match award to his collection in the Boxing Day Test at Durban, where his match figures of nine for 164 propelled his side to a crushing innings victory in a performance Strauss described as the best he had seen by any England team on tour.

Swann went on to be England's Man of the Series, and was probably the most effective finger-spinner seen in South Africa since Hugh Tayfield's 1950s heyday. Swann had a penchant for taking a wicket in the first over of a spell (he had done it 17 times in 16 Tests by the end of the series) and for left-handers. Of his first 50 wickets (he brought up his half-century in the First Test) 33 were left-handers, an unrivalled percentage. His hold over Ashwell Prince was complete: he bowled five balls to Prince in the series, and dismissed him three times. It completed a remarkable year for Swann, who had started 2009 carrying the drinks in Jamaica as understudy to first-choice spinner Monty Panesar.

Panesar was in South Africa too, but he was trying to rebuild his career with the local franchise team Highveld Lions, while Swann, who had made his Test debut only the previous December in India, was making a case for being the player of the year. He took 54 Test wickets in 2009, second in the world only to Australia's Mitchell Johnson, who took 63.

THE UMPIRE DECISION REVIEW SYSTEM

A qualified success

STEVE JAMES

It was all going so well. Acceptance seemed nearer, understanding had increased, and the Umpire Decision Review System was showing itself to be an enhancement, not a hindrance. Then came the Graeme Smith blunder in the final Test at Johannesburg and all hell broke loose. Smith survived an edge on 15 before making a crucial century, and all because third umpire Daryl Harper could not hear the noise as Smith attempted to cut.

This highlighted the system's greatest failing in this series: the absence of Hot Spot, owing to the local broadcasters' penury. As a result, to review an edged caught-behind decision became pointless, because cast-iron evidence could never be found. Harper was castigated, but no other decision in the series had been made on noise alone.

There were other problems, such as the time sometimes taken to call for a review. In the First Test, after J-P. Duminy's original appeal for lbw against Stuart Broad was denied, it took Smith 35 seconds to decide upon a review. Broad, hardly a shrinking violet, voiced his concerns to the umpires. But the review stood, and eventually the correct decision was made: Broad was plumb lbw. Just as importantly, it was almost the only display of dissent in the series. But this timeframe had to be addressed: 20 seconds should be long enough. It could be the responsibility of the third umpire to begin his stopwatch the moment a decision is made. He could then, say, flash a red light when time was up.

Another severe drawback is that the crowd is kept in the dark as the review is considered. They simply do not know what is happening as the review is considered. They should be informed via the big screen; they have as much right as the TV viewer, who gets to see the evidence.

Overall, the new directives for lbws were much improved, taking pressure off the third umpire, and producing automated responses to three questions (Pitching in line? Hitting in line? Hitting the wickets?) via the predictive tool of Hawk-Eye. The benefit of the doubt went to the on-field umpire: good, because he didn't become a mere hat-stand and, as at all lower levels, he still had to make a decision.

There were anomalies, though. At Centurion, A. B. de Villiers was given not out: Hawk-Eye suggested that the ball would have hit the stumps – but not with the middle-of-the-ball-on-middle-of-the-stump certainty which the regulations demanded for the decision to be overturned. Later Duminy was given out: this time the review showed less of the ball was hitting than in de Villiers's case, but the decision had to stand and Duminy had to go.

England did not like the system, and whined rather too strongly at Johannesburg. But it had saved them at Cape Town: without it the heroic rearguard between Ian Bell and Paul Collingwood would never have started. Collingwood was given out first ball, caught at slip off Paul Harris, but a review showed the ball hit hip not bat.

Crucially, however, the system rectified the howlers – for instance Harper adjudging Ashwell Prince caught down the leg side at Cape Town when he wasn't within a country mile of it – and surely that is its purpose.

In the First Test, there were 15 reviews, three of which resulted in the original decision being overturned; in the Second Test 12 (four); Third Test 13 (four); Fourth Test eight (three).

Swann's importance to the team had been amplified by England's decision to go into the series with six specialist batsmen. His control and wickets allowed Strauss to rotate three pace bowlers at the other end. Anderson, who carried a knee injury into the series, was the most successful of the pace attack, but again England looked worryingly blunt when the conditions did not help the faster bowlers. Onions posed as many problems as anyone for the batsmen, but found himself dropped for the final Test despite his heroic efforts with the bat.

South Africa had their fast-bowling problems too. Their strike bowler Steyn missed the First Test with a hamstring injury, and was not fully fit until the Third. Kallis, who had suffered a rib injury, was not able to bowl at full pace until the Third Test either, while in the same match, Friedel de Wet, who had

Graham Morris

The great survivor: Graham Onions celebrates England's Cape escape.

made his debut in the First Test and then replaced Ntini in the Third, broke down with a stress fracture of the back. Not simply with the wisdom of hindsight, England could have benefited from a more attacking selection for the First Test so as to hit South Africa, still smarting from the one-day loss, when they were down and distracted by the Ntini issue.

Smith's rampaging 183 at Newlands had left England needing to bat for a day and a half to save the Third Test, and they looked doomed when they were five wickets down before lunch on the last day. Collingwood, however, an old hand at rearguard actions, revelled in the situation and found an unlikely ally in Ian Bell, who was one of the few success stories of the series for England.

Bell, given his chance as England's sixth batsman, had a miserable First Test, but then scored a fluent 140 at Durban. At Cape Town he was required to show a

much grittier side to his personality – a side many felt he did not have. In adversity, Bell played an innings of great character as he and Collingwood held out for almost four hours to give England a chance of escaping with a draw. Bell was ninth out for 78 and the last pair, Onions and Swann, had to survive 17 balls, which they did – to the disbelief of the South Africans, who had once again failed to deliver the knockout blow.

Desperate for a victory, South Africa "had a word" with the Wanderers groundsman, Chris Scott, who assured them there would be a result pitch for the last Test unless the weather intervened. As it turned out, the game was over before lunch on the fourth day, in around two and a half days' actual playing time. England were bowled out twice, neither innings lasting 50 overs, as Steyn and Morkel took 14 wickets between them.

South Africa deserved their share of the spoils. In Steyn and Morkel they had the two outstanding fast bowlers of the series. They had scored five centuries in the four Tests to England's two, and the only department in which England could claim superiority was spin. Strauss, however, could rightly point to the fact that mattered most: a 1–1 drawn series, a result that suggested his team were heading in the right direction. Even if they would have to do without him in Bangladesh.

ENGLAND TOURING PARTY

A. J. Strauss (Middlesex) (*captain*), A. N. Cook (Essex) (*vice-captain*), J. M. Anderson (Lancashire), I. R. Bell (Warwickshire), S. C. J. Broad (Nottinghamshire), P. D. Collingwood (Durham), S. M. Davies (Surrey), G. Onions (Durham), K. P. Pietersen (Hampshire), L. E. Plunkett (Durham), M. J. Prior (Sussex), A. U. Rashid (Yorkshire), R. J. Sidebottom (Nottinghamshire), G. P. Swann (Nottinghamshire), I. J. L. Trott (Warwickshire), L. J. Wright (Sussex).

For the limited-overs internationals that preceded the Tests, T. T. Bresnan, J. E. Denly, S. I. Mahmood and E. J. G. Morgan replaced Bell, Davies, Plunkett and Sidebottom, although Plunkett was later added to the one-day squad as injury cover. J. C. Tredwell also joined the party for the first two one-day internationals while Swann was injured. Collingwood (and Cook when Collingwood was injured) led England in the Twenty20 matches. M. A. Carberry, M. Davies and J. C. Tredwell reinforced the Test party after various injuries.

Coach: A. Flower. *Assistant coaches:* O. D. Gibson and R. G. Halsall. *Team operations manager:* P. A. Neale. *Team analyst (one-day squad):* G. Broad. *Team analyst (Test squad):* N. A. Leamon. *Physiotherapist:* K. A. Russell. *Physiologist:* H. R. Bevan. *Team doctor (one-day squad):* Dr M. G. Wotherspoon. *Team doctor (Test squad):* Dr S. H. Till. *Massage therapist:* M. E. S. Saxby. *Security officer:* R. C. Dickason. *Media relations manager (one-day squad):* J. D. Avery. *Media relations manager (Test squad):* A. J. Walpole.

TEST MATCH AVERAGES

SOUTH AFRICA – BATTING AND FIELDING

	T	I	NO	R	HS	100s	50s	Avge	Ct
†G. C. Smith	4	7	0	427	183	2	1	61.00	7
M. V. Boucher	4	7	1	341	95	0	3	56.83	16
J. H. Kallis	4	7	0	363	120	2	1	51.85	5
H. M. Amla	4	7	0	311	100	1	2	44.42	2
A. B. de Villiers	4	7	0	276	64	0	3	39.42	5
D. W. Steyn	3	5	2	78	47	0	0	26.00	1
P. L. Harris	3	5	1	97	38	0	0	24.25	0
†M. Morkel	4	5	1	73	23	0	0	18.25	3
†J-P. Duminy	4	7	0	114	56	0	1	16.28	2
†A. G. Prince	4	7	0	97	45	0	0	13.85	3
M. Ntini	2	3	3	11	6*	0	0	–	0

Played in two Tests: F. de Wet 20, 0 (1 ct). Played in one Test: †R. McLaren 33*; †W. D. Parnell did not bat (1 ct).

† *Left-handed batsman.*

BOWLING

	Style	O	M	R	W	BB	5W/i	Avge
J-P. Duminy	OB	53.5	6	169	8	3-89	0	21.12
M. Morkel	RF	147	28	408	19	5-75	1	21.47
D. W. Steyn	RF	118.5	24	357	15	5-51	1	23.80
F. de Wet	RFM	71	19	186	6	4-55	0	31.00
P. L. Harris	SLA	150	39	444	11	5-123	1	40.36

Also bowled: J. H. Kallis (RFM) 55–11–143–2; R. McLaren (RFM) 13–4–43–1; M. Ntini (RFM) 70–15–233–2; W. D. Parnell (LFM) 11–1–35–2.

ENGLAND – BATTING AND FIELDING

	T	I	NO	R	HS	100s	50s	Avge	Ct
P. D. Collingwood	4	7	1	344	91	0	3	57.33	8
I. R. Bell.	4	7	0	313	140	1	1	44.71	3
†A. N. Cook	4	7	0	287	118	1	2	41.00	4
G. P. Swann	4	7	1	171	85	0	1	28.50	3
I. J. L. Trott.	4	7	0	190	69	0	1	27.14	2
K. P. Pietersen	4	7	0	177	81	0	1	25.28	0
†A. J. Strauss	4	7	0	170	54	0	1	24.28	2
M. J. Prior.	4	7	0	158	76	0	2	22.57	12
†J. M. Anderson	4	7	3	56	29	0	0	14.00	1
†S. C. J. Broad	4	7	0	76	25	0	0	10.85	2
G. Onions	3	5	5	11	4*	0	0	–	0

Played in one Test: †R. J. Sidebottom 0, 15.

† *Left-handed batsman.*

BOWLING

	Style	O	M	R	W	BB	5W/i	Avge
G. P. Swann	OB	210.2	25	659	21	5-54	2	31.38
S. C. J. Broad	RFM	155	36	435	13	4-43	0	33.46
J. M. Anderson	RFM	162.5	29	548	16	5-63	1	34.25
G. Onions	RFM	115	23	366	8	3-86	0	45.75

Also bowled: P. D. Collingwood (RM) 20–3–66–0; K. P. Pietersen (OB) 9–0–30–0; R. J. Sidebottom (LFM) 31–6–98–2; I. J. L. Trott (RM) 11–0–58–0.

Note: Matches in this section which were not first-class are signified by a dagger.

LIMITED-OVERS MATCH REPORTS BY SCYLD BERRY

†At Bloemfontein, November 6, 2009. **England XI won by 185 runs.** Toss: Eagles. **England XI 294-7** (50 overs) (A. J. Strauss 72, I. J. L. Trott 85, E. J. G. Morgan 67*); **Eagles 109** (26.4 overs).
England set the tone for their 50-over cricket to come as they made sure they did not lose too many early wickets, which they had been doing, then accelerated. On a slow pitch, Strauss led the way with 72 from 85 balls, including 12 runs from five reverse sweeps, the stroke which had recently got him into trouble against Australia's Nathan Hauritz. Trott was bounced first ball on his first England appearance in his native country, but went on to an assured 85 from 104 balls; Morgan finished with 67 from 52 and helped add 57 in the batting powerplay, another improvement on recent England efforts. The only drawback came when Stuart Broad jarred his right shoulder diving on the boundary and put himself out for three weeks. He was still one of five bowlers to take two wickets apiece here as the Eagles failed to take flight.

†At Kimberley, November 8, 2009. **England XI won by eight wickets.** Toss: Warriors. **Warriors 254-5** (50 overs) (J. P. Kreusch 32, R. R. Jeggels 30, A. Jacobs 83*, D. J. Jacobs 50; G. P. Swann 3-26); **England XI 256-2** (40.5 overs) (A. J. Strauss 117*, J. L. Denly 82, A. N. Cook 34).
England won with eight wickets and 9.1 overs in hand against the Warriors franchise flown in from the Eastern Cape without their international players (Warriors had 12 players, of whom 11 could bat and 11 field). Denly hit the ball over the pad and shared a match-winning opening stand with Strauss, who attacked the new ball – one straight six – as 84 came from the first 15 overs (their eventual target was worth 175 in 29) to propel England ahead of the asking-rate on another grudging pitch that had prompted Paul Collingwood to bowl off-cutters. Strauss ended with an unbeaten 117 from 119 balls. The pick of the bowlers was Swann, who immediately found the right pace for his off-breaks, while Matt Prior supported him with another flawless display.

†At Bloemfontein, November 10, 2009 (floodlit). **South Africa A won by four wickets.** Toss: South Africa A. **England XI 89** (17.3 overs); **South Africa A 90-6** (17.3 overs). *Man of the Match:* T. Tshabalala.

England, without Andrew Strauss to guide them, were at their worst in their only 20-over warm-up. The experiment of opening with Alastair Cook was not a success, even though he top-scored with 22: of the 30 deliveries he faced, 13 were dot-balls, and when he was out in the 14th over – which made it 75-5 – he had hit only one four. Desperate to increase the run-rate, England lost three late wickets to pinpoint throwing. As a team England misread conditions that were highly favourable to spin: Paul Collingwood, bowled by a big off-break from Thandi Tshabalala's first ball, admitted they should have aimed for 120–130. After a penetrative opening spell by Swann – who had made his one-day international debut on this ground a decade earlier – South Africa A were always in control of their run-chase.

†SOUTH AFRICA v ENGLAND

First Twenty20 International

At Johannesburg, November 13, 2009 (floodlit). England won by one run (D/L method). Toss: South Africa. Twenty20 international debut: R. McLaren.

For their surprising win – only their ninth in this format – England were indebted to Collingwood, who hit four sixes (damaging his back in the process) and was far more relaxed as Twenty20 captain than hitherto; to Morgan, who made England's highest Twenty20 innings with some breathtaking strokeplay; and to South Africa's fourth-wicket pair, who seemed not to be alert to the Duckworth/Lewis target posted on the scoreboard as rain arrived. Thanks to Anderson conceding only six runs in the 13th over – which turned out to be the last – the home side fell one run short. Morgan's pull against Steyn had earlier sent the ball past a four-storey building outside the ground at roof height,

Full-blooded intent: Eoin Morgan strikes one of his five sixes into the Johannesburg night.

while his fine sweep for six off Langeveldt in the last over was further evidence of a skill which no England limited-overs side had enjoyed before: the ability not just to hit the ball to all corners but over the boundary for 360 degrees.

Man of the Match: E. J. G. Morgan.

England		*B*	*4*	*6*
J. L. Denly *lbw b 11*	0	1	0	0
A. N. Cook *lbw b 7*	11	8	1	0
I. J. L. Trott *run out*	33	25	5	0
*P. D. Collingwood *c 9 b 7*	57	32	3	4
E. J. G. Morgan *not out*	85	45	7	5
L. J. Wright *c 4 b 10*	2	5	0	0
†M. J. Prior *c 5 b 7*	0	1	0	0
T. T. Bresnan *not out*	3	3	0	0
L-b 5, w 6	11			

6 overs: 56-2   (20 overs)   202-6

1/0 2/25 3/61 4/159 5/167 6/169

G. P. Swann, S. I. Mahmood and J. M. Anderson did not bat.

Langeveldt 4–0–39–1; McLaren 4–0–33–3; Steyn 4–0–40–1; Morkel 2–0–32–0; van der Merwe 2–0–17–0; Botha 4–0–36–0.

South Africa		*B*	*4*	*6*
*G. C. Smith *c 5 b 6*	41	23	3	4
L. L. Bosman *c 4 b 9*	58	31	5	4
J-P. Duminy *lbw b 10*	6	5	1	0
A. B. de Villiers *not out*	10	10	1	0
J. A. Morkel *not out*	9	9	0	1
W 3	3			

6 overs: 67-0   (13 overs)   127-3

1/97 2/101 3/112

†M. V. Boucher, R. McLaren, R. E. van der Merwe, J. Botha, D. W. Steyn and C. K. Langeveldt did not bat.

Anderson 3–0–24–0; Bresnan 2–0–25–0; Mahmood 3–0–31–1; Wright 2–0–17–1; Swann 3–0–30–1.

Umpires: M. Erasmus and B. G. Jerling.   Third umpire: J. D. Cloete.   Referee: J. Srinath.

†SOUTH AFRICA v ENGLAND

Second Twenty20 International

At Centurion, November 15, 2009. South Africa won by 84 runs. Toss: South Africa. Twenty20 international debut: H. G. Kuhn.

The concession of a record opening stand for all Twenty20 internationals – beating the 145 of Chris Gayle and Devon Smith for West Indies against South Africa in the first World Twenty20 in September 2007 – marked Cook's first attempt at England captaincy since Under-19 level. Smith and Bosman, who between them hit 15 sixes, powered to 170 from just 13.1 overs. Smith, suffering from stomach cramps, favoured the leg side, as did Bosman, who was given less than a handful of balls outside off. Sticking to line and length or short balls, not yorkers and the odd bouncer, England's pace bowlers were all taken apart, except for Anderson. Wright's first over cost 18, and Mahmood's 21, while Rashid conceded four sixes – two to each opener – in his only over. England's senior players weighed in with well-meaning suggestions for Cook, but simply added to the impression of chaos… and contributed to him being fined 20% of his match fee for a slow over-rate (even then, the calculation of only one over short was very lenient). England were never in the chase – Pietersen was rusty in his first game for four months – and went down to their biggest Twenty20 defeat by runs.

Man of the Match: L. L. Bosman.

South Africa

		B	4	6
*G. C. Smith c 10 b 1	88	44	8	6
L. L. Bosman c 11 b 6	94	45	5	9
J. A. Morkel c 8 b 4	14	6	2	1
J-P. Duminy c 6 b 11	2	4	0	0
A. B. de Villiers run out	24	13	3	1
J. H. Kallis b 10	7	5	1	0
†H. G. Kuhn not out	5	4	0	0
R. McLaren not out	1	1	0	0
B 2, l-b 1, w 1, n-b 2	6			

6 overs: 69-0   (20 overs) 241-6

1/170 2/192 3/203 4/204 5/214 6/238

R. E. van der Merwe, D. W. Steyn and Y. A. Abdulla did not bat.

Anderson 4-0-28-1; Bresnan 4-0-48-0; Mahmood 4-0-61-1; Wright 4-0-40-1; Rashid 1-0-25-0; Pietersen 2-0-27-1; Denly 1-0-9-1.

12th man J. Botha.

England

		B	4	6
J. L. Denly b 11	14	14	2	0
*A. N. Cook c 9 b 3	26	21	5	0
I. J. L. Trott c 7 b 3	51	40	1	3
K. P. Pietersen b 9	29	19	1	2
E. J. G. Morgan b 10	10	7	2	0
L. J. Wright c 12 b 10	12	5	1	1
†M. J. Prior not out	10	8	1	0
T. T. Bresnan c 1 b 8	0	3	0	0
A. U. Rashid run out	1	2	0	0
S. I. Mahmood not out	1	1	0	0
W 3	3			

6 overs: 43-1   (20 overs) 157-8

1/20 2/65 3/117 4/132 5/144 6/146 7/146 8/150

J. M. Anderson did not bat.

Steyn 4-0-29-2; Abdulla 4-0-28-1; McLaren 4-0-26-1; van der Merwe 4-0-39-1; Morkel 4-0-35-2.

Umpires: M. Erasmus and B. G. Jerling.   Third umpire: J. D. Cloete.   Referee: J. Srinath.

†At Potchefstroom, November 17, 2009 (day/night). **England XI won by four wickets.** Toss: South Africa A. **South Africa A 279-9** (50 overs) (H. M. Amla 37, A. G. Puttick 62, H. G. Kuhn 42*); **England XI 281-6** (48.1 overs) (A. J. Strauss 65, I. J. L. Trott 78, M. J. Prior 54). *Man of the Match:* I. J. L. Trott.

Determined to reverse their trend of underperforming in warm-up games, England put in a very competent performance on their long day-trip from Johannesburg, as Strauss resumed the captaincy and hit 65 from 71 balls. Their inexperienced bowling attack – England had only 11 fit players when Alastair Cook was unable to walk after the two-hour coach journey (he was later found to have a bulging disc) – contained a strong South Africa A side with back-of-a-length pace on another pitch of tennis-ball bounce. Although Pietersen failed to clear mid-off when batting with Trott, his partner went on to 78 from 89 balls. When England needed 64 from the last seven overs, Trott, Prior and Wright "went aerial" to plunder 61 from the batting powerplay.

†SOUTH AFRICA v ENGLAND

First One-Day International

At Johannesburg, November 20, 2009 (day/night). Abandoned.

Play was never a possibility on the third consecutive day of continuous rain, as an unseasonal cold front sat over Johannesburg. The abandonment came as a relief to two key England players, Collingwood and Anderson, who had not recovered from back and knee injuries.

†SOUTH AFRICA v ENGLAND

Second One-Day International

At Centurion, November 22, 2009. England won by seven wickets. Toss: England.

England carried on from where they had left off against South Africa A: they contained their opponents with straight, back-of-a-length pace on a pitch where the ball didn't come on, then knocked off the runs with a flourish in the batting powerplay. The difference was that an influential toss allowed England to take two major wickets before the pitch dried out after a week of rain, while

South Africa also missed the technical excellence of the injured Jacques Kallis. A proud day for Collingwood, who set an England record with his 171st one-day international appearance, began with a diving catch to his left at point off a square cut, and two wickets. He then scored an unbeaten 105 from 110 balls, his fifth one-day century, and played the assertive, senior role in a stand of 162 with Trott, playing only his second one-day international (after making a duck in his first, against Ireland); Trott confidently scored 87 – with 71 on the leg side – from 119 balls. He was, however, officially warned for time-wasting when he took too long to settle into his stance. Strauss, perhaps preoccupied with planning England's sixth consecutive win over South Africa (excluding a no result in Cardiff and the abandonment in Johannesburg), dropped three catches of varying difficulty at short extra cover, a key position on a pitch where driving was difficult, but he aptly summed up Collingwood: "It was great to see him overtake the record because of all the hard work he has put in. He's playing better than he's ever played."

Man of the Match: P. D. Collingwood.

South Africa

H. M. Amla c Strauss b Collingwood	57
*G. C. Smith c Strauss b Bresnan	12
A. B. de Villiers c Collingwood b Anderson . .	2
J-P. Duminy c Prior b Wright	41
A. N. Petersen b Bresnan	64
R. McLaren c Prior b Anderson	5
J. A. Morkel c Morgan b Collingwood	6
†M. V. Boucher not out	30
R. E. van der Merwe c Bresnan b Anderson . .	5

D. W. Steyn c Trott b Mahmood 12
C. K. Langeveldt not out 6

L-b 3, w 6, n-b 1 10

1/27 (2) 2/38 (3)   (9 wkts, 50 overs) 250
3/111 (4) 4/131 (1)
5/155 (6) 6/165 (7) 7/205 (5)
8/222 (9) 9/242 (10)   10 overs: 46-2

Anderson 10–0–60–3; Bresnan 10–0–46–2; Mahmood 7–0–41–1; Wright 7–0–28–1; Rashid 3–0–27–0; Collingwood 6–0–24–2; Trott 7–0–21–0.

England

I. J. L. Trott c Amla b Langeveldt	87
*A. J. Strauss b de Villiers b Langeveldt	16
K. P. Pietersen b Morkel	4
P. D. Collingwood not out	105
E. J. G. Morgan not out	27
L-b 1, w 8, n-b 4	13

1/28 (2) 2/45 (3)   (3 wkts, 46 overs) 252
3/207 (1)   10 overs: 37-1

†M. J. Prior, L. J. Wright, T. T. Bresnan, A. U. Rashid, S. I. Mahmood and J. M. Anderson did not bat.

Steyn 10–0–64–0; Langeveldt 10–0–46–2; McLaren 8–0–43–0; Morkel 5–0–26–1; van der Merwe 9–0–55–0; Duminy 4–0–17–0.

Umpires: B. G. Jerling and R. J. Tucker.
Third umpire: M. Erasmus. Referee: J. Srinath.

†SOUTH AFRICA v ENGLAND

Third One-Day International

At Cape Town, November 27, 2009 (day/night). South Africa won by 112 runs. Toss: South Africa. England expected a South African backlash, and it came in the form of some power-packed batting that produced the second-highest one-day total made against England – the only bigger one was India's 387 at Rajkot just over a year before – and some bowling which was more varied than the tourists' on a batting pitch. These two areas of superiority had far more influence on the result than the fact that South Africa batted in daylight and England under floodlights (so early in the summer, dew played no part). Unable to take early wickets for once, even when Swann was tried for the 11th over, England were almost helpless as Smith hit 54 from 56 balls and Amla 86 off 92; then de Villiers drove even more powerfully, reaching his fourth one-day international century from 75 balls and lasting 85 in all. South Africa hit 34 fours but only one six; England managed five sixes (three by Collingwood), but too much haste, including the promotion of Wright, led to the loss of three wickets in their first ten overs. England were beaten by as large a margin as they won their other two games, but they played without inspiration rather than badly. As Strauss said of de Villiers's innings: it was "a really top-quality knock".

Man of the Match: A. B. de Villiers.

South Africa

H. M. Amla c Prior b Broad	86	R. McLaren b Broad		0
*G. C. Smith b Wright	54	B 2, l-b 4, w 8		14
A. B. de Villiers c Trott b Broad	121			
J-P. Duminy c Morgan b Wright	6	1/107 (2) 2/201 (1)	(6 wkts, 50 overs)	354
A. N. Petersen not out	51	3/217 (4) 4/312 (3)		
†M. V. Boucher c Wright b Broad	22	5/349 (6) 6/354 (7)	10 overs: 60-0	

R. E. van der Merwe, W. D. Parnell, M. Morkel and D. W. Steyn did not bat.

Anderson 7–0–55–0; Broad 10–0–71–4; Bresnan 10–0–61–0; Swann 9–0–49–0; Collingwood 5–0–38–0; Wright 8–0–66–2; Trott 1–0–8–0.

England

*A. J. Strauss c Boucher b Morkel	24	G. P. Swann not out		6
L. J. Wright c McLaren b Parnell	24	J. M. Anderson lbw b Parnell		1
I. J. L. Trott c Smith b Parnell	9			
K. P. Pietersen b Duminy	45	L-b 4, w 10		14
P. D. Collingwood c Amla b Parnell	86			
E. J. G. Morgan c sub (J. Botha) b Duminy	0	1/41 (2) 2/58 (1) 3/58 (3)	(41.3 overs)	242
†M. J. Prior c Smith b Morkel	16	4/142 (4) 5/150 (6) 6/214 (7)		
T. T. Bresnan c Smith b Morkel	7	7/223 (5) 8/227 (8) 9/236 (9)		
S. C. J. Broad b Parnell	10	10/242 (11)	10 overs: 58-3	

Steyn 6–0–42–0; Parnell 9.3–1–48–5; Morkel 9–1–39–3; McLaren 5–0–34–0; van der Merwe 6–0–50–0; Duminy 6–0–25–2.

Umpires: M. Erasmus and R. J. Tucker.
Third umpire: B. G. Jerling.   Referee: J. Srinath.

†SOUTH AFRICA v ENGLAND

Fourth One-Day International

At Port Elizabeth, November 29, 2009. England won by seven wickets. Toss: South Africa.

Although Smith chose to bat first, England's three main pace bowlers found just enough swing and seam under thin cloud to take eight wickets for 68 between them. Anderson took two in his opening spell, and returned to claim three more in his last four overs to finish with his first one-day five-for. However, he admitted that he had bowled better for less reward and that "the catches went to hand". This was partly by design: Anderson moved second slip to short midwicket the over before Amla clipped a catch there, while his best delivery seamed past Boucher's outside edge to hit off stump. England were assisted by some umpiring which saw the Australian Rod Tucker give three marginal lbws their way, while Brian Jerling reprieved Strauss for a catch behind. But Smith admitted that his batsmen – apart from the locally born Alviro Petersen, who calmly made his third consecutive fifty of the series – had been slow to appreciate that conditions were different from Newlands: they should have aimed for 220–240. Trott was massively assured for someone in only his fourth one-day international, and spoilt the party at St George's Park, which featured live trumpet music, by taking England to what turned out to be a decisive 2–1 lead.

Man of the Match: J. M. Anderson.

South Africa

H. M. Amla c Swann b Anderson	11	M. Morkel lbw b Collingwood	7
*G. C. Smith lbw b Broad	2	C. K. Langeveldt not out	0
A. B. de Villiers lbw b Bresnan	22		
J-P. Duminy c Prior b Anderson	6	W 5	5
A. N. Petersen c Wright b Broad	51		
†M. V. Boucher b Anderson	13	1/6 (2) 2/24 (1) 3/35 (4) (36.5 overs) 119	
R. McLaren c Collingwood b Anderson	0	4/55 (3) 5/78 (6) 6/78 (7)	
J. Botha c Prior b Anderson	1	7/84 (8) 8/92 (9) 9/112 (10)	
W. D. Parnell c Strauss b Collingwood	1	10/119 (5) 10 overs: 35-2	

Anderson 10–3–23–5; Broad 9.5–0–30–2; Wright 5–0–31–0; Bresnan 8–2–15–1; Collingwood 4–0–20–2.

England

I. J. L. Trott not out	52
*A. J. Strauss lbw b Botha	32
K. P. Pietersen c de Villiers b Botha	3
P. D. Collingwood c Boucher b McLaren	2
E. J. G. Morgan not out	28
L-b 1, w 3	4

1/74 (2) 2/80 (3)   (3 wkts, 31.2 overs) 121
3/83 (4)   10 overs: 39-0

†M. J. Prior, L. J. Wright, T. T. Bresnan, S. C. J. Broad, G. P. Swann and J. M. Anderson did not bat.

Parnell 6–0–30–0; Langeveldt 5–1–24–0; Morkel 6.2–1–19–0; McLaren 6–1–25–1; Botha 8–0–22–2.

Umpires: B. G. Jerling and R. J. Tucker.
Third umpire: J. D. Cloete.   Referee: J. Srinath.

†SOUTH AFRICA v ENGLAND

Fifth One-Day International

At Durban, December 4, 2009 (day/night). Abandoned.

A week of rain in Durban caused this match to be abandoned at 5 p.m., leaving England 2–1 winners of the series. It was their first one-day series victory in South Africa: only Australia had won a bilateral there before (twice). It was also the first time that Graeme Smith had lost a home one-day series.

Man of the Series: P. D. Collingwood.

WARM-UP MATCH REPORTS BY COLIN BATEMAN

†At East London, December 9, 10, 2009. **Drawn.** England XI batted first by arrangement. **England XI 329-8 dec** (A. N. Cook 81, P. D. Collingwood 33, I. R. Bell 48, M. J. Prior 44, G. P. Swann 39*; C. Pietersen 3-71); **South African Invitational XI 167-7** (S. E. Avontuur 68, W. Bossenger 35*; G. P. Swann 6-55).

With both matches in East London restricted to two days, they were only going to be glorified middle practice, with no attempt to forge meaningful contests. The first was further spoiled by rain, which allowed only 36.2 overs on the opening day. England batted first by agreement, and Cook – who had been away with the England Performance Programme – hit 12 fours after Strauss's early departure for a single. Later Bell and Prior both retired out to allow others a bat. For the Invitational XI, Sammy-Joe Avontuur hit ten fours from 111 balls before becoming the first of three wickets in four balls for Swann, who later said that his third victim, Mangaliso Mosehle, got out because he was still laughing after his fellow wicketkeeper, Prior, told him: "There are two things you should never do: cut a spinner and pat a burning dog." Durham's Mark Davies, a recent addition to the touring party, took none for 24 in ten overs.

†At East London, December 11, 12, 2009. **Drawn.** Toss: South African Invitational XI. **England XI 317-5 dec** (A. J. Strauss 100, A. N. Cook 52, I. J. L. Trott 50, K. P. Pietersen 71); **South African Invitational XI 263** (M. Y. Vallie 56, C. Pietersen 64, D. Wiese 80; R. J. Sidebottom 5-42).

Strauss (who hit 14 fours), Cook and Trott all retired out after useful knocks, but the most encouraging sight for England was Kevin Pietersen batting for two hours and returning to something like form, collecting 12 fours as he continued his rehabilitation after a long injury lay-off. When England bowled, all eyes were on James Anderson, who had not played competitively for two weeks after a knee injury. He came through 15 overs successfully, but it was Sidebottom who was the most impressive bowler. The Invitational XI slipped to 143-6 before Charl Pietersen (no relation) and David Wiese, a Titans all-rounder with a first-class double-century to his credit, put on 119 for the seventh wicket.

SOUTH AFRICA v ENGLAND

First Test Match

Neil Manthorp

At Centurion, December 16, 17, 18, 19, 20, 2009. Drawn. Toss: England. Test debut: F. de Wet.

For the second time in five months, England's last-wicket pair saved a Test amid high drama but, unlike the opening Ashes Test at Cardiff in July when James Anderson and Monty Panesar defied the odds to conclude a prolonged and proud rearguard action, this time it was more a tail-between-the-legs escape after an embarrassing, final-session collapse.

South Africa had slid to an ominous 46 for four in their second innings, a lead of just 108, so it was no surprise that a relieved Smith had opted for the luxury of batting England out of the game. Amla's studious century and his counter-attacking fifth-wicket partnership of 119 with de Villiers had permitted Boucher and Morkel to score rapidly towards the close of the fourth day. Any target in excess of 300 on a dry, slow and cracked pitch would almost certainly have been beyond England, but Smith pushed it to 364 in 96 overs – far in excess of the scoring-rate of the first three innings – so he could remain on the attack for the whole of the final day.

Strauss was caught behind off a round-the-wicket lifter from Morkel shortly before the end of the fourth day (following an impossible grubber in his first innings), and in the 13th over of the final morning England were 27 for three and facing likely defeat. The irony that what turned out to be – just – the match-saving partnership was staged between two converted South Africans was not lost on any of the unconverted, spectators or players.

Pietersen and Trott made the heavily tarnished surface look pristine in a stand of 145 and, more pertinently, more than 43 overs, until Pietersen ran himself out after tea in extraordinary fashion by pushing a delivery almost straight back to the debutant fast bowler Friedel de Wet and setting off like an Olympic sprinter with ear-plugs.

It escaped nobody's notice, however, that the feisty (and extremely confident) Trott waited until his senior and far more illustrious team-mate was within a foot of safety at his end before very consciously grounding his bat. He clearly had plenty of time to think of sacrificing himself before deciding against it. Pietersen later said his junior partner had "done the right thing".

De Wet, with the aid of the second new ball, then kicked the door down. Almost. The 29-year-old de Wet had talent to burn from an early age, but a brace of back operations limited his career to such an extent that he turned away from it for two years to seek sanctuary and a secure living in a nursery and landscaping business. His dream of Test

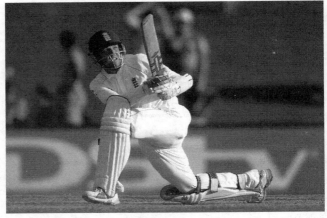

Swann on song: Graeme Swann's ebullient 85 helps snatch the initiative from South Africa.

cricket was relinquished. But when it was reignited, he wasn't about to let it go out. A seven-over spell of eyeballs-out intensity brought him three for 11 and, with a wicket each for Harris and Morkel in a madcap final 80 minutes, England lost five wickets in 11 overs.

Collingwood produced a smaller version of his Cardiff blockade with an unbeaten 26 from 99 balls, but was unable to prevent last man Onions from having to endure a dozen torturous deliveries. Collingwood admitted later that he should have rejected Onions's call for a single off the fourth ball of the penultimate over, which left the No. 11 to face the final six deliveries. But Onions survived with some aplomb, and topped it off with an inappropriate but nonetheless delightfully endearing fist-pump.

That final over was bowled by Ntini, who had earlier stolen much of the show after becoming the fifth South African to reach 100 Test caps. Naturally and rightly he was heralded more than the others for an extraordinary journey as a pioneer and ambassador for the young black cricketers who will have to carry the future of the game in the country.

The contest started, as many of the better ones do, with both captains unsure of what to do at the toss. It was a good one to lose. Strauss manfully chose to bowl – and then watched in protracted suffering as his four-man attack laboured in torrid heat for 153 overs. To be fair, Onions was fabulous in his first two spells and, with better fortune, might have vindicated the decision to bowl. Anderson, too, beat the edge often, and at 159 for four the innings was in the balance – but the bowling unit became desperate and Broad, in particular, bowled too short.

Kallis was at his belligerent best and most determined, knowing that he would be unable to bowl after picking up a rib injury (although he did try three exploratory overs on the final day at reduced pace). His 32nd Test century – only Tendulkar, Ponting, Gavaskar and Lara have made more – bore almost an air of inevitability about it, despite the uneven bounce and two-paced pitch, but the tone was set by the painstaking scoring-rate which was maintained for almost the entire match.

Swann produced the exceptional innings and, though he might not have thought it at the time, his exuberant 85 from 81 balls was a match-saver. He hooked Ntini for a thrilling six, eyes off the ball Ian Botham-style, then twice despatched Harris to the boundary using his own version of Pietersen's switch-hit. It reduced England's deficit from an unmanageable 197 when he came to the crease to just 62, but more importantly he prolonged the innings by at least a session that England might otherwise have had to face. Swann's ninth-wicket stand of 106 with Anderson was every bit as exciting as it was unlikely – and painful for South Africa.

Swann also bowled his off-spinners with such verve and zest in the first innings that it was hard for anybody to recall a more vigorous or attacking "traditional" finger-spinner for generations, and his five-wicket haul was richly deserved. It included his 50th Test wicket (de Villiers) 33 of his victims were left-handers, an unprecedented proportion.

MOST LEFT-HANDERS DISMISSED IN FIRST 50 TEST WICKETS

33	**G. P. Swann (England)**	21	S. L. Malinga (Sri Lanka)
26	N. Boje (South Africa)	21	C. R. Miller (Australia)
24	Abdul Razzaq (Pakistan)	21	Saqlain Mushtaq (Pakistan)
22	**M. Morkel (South Africa)**	20	A. Nel (South Africa)
22	J. E. C. Franklin (New Zealand)	20	Zaheer Khan (India)

Those in bold type took their 50th wicket during 2009. The fewest left-hand batsmen among a bowler's first 50 Test wickets is one, by W. W. Armstrong (Australia), W. Bates (England), G. A. Faulkner (South Africa), W. A. Johnston (Australia), E. Jones (Australia) and D. L. Underwood (England).

Research: Philip Bailey

South Africa's spinner, left-armer Harris, completed a first-innings five-for of his own, but it owed more to his accuracy and deceptive sliding deliveries than to spin or bounce. Nonetheless, each man celebrated the other's success because, in Swann's words, "bowling finger-spin is the hardest job in Test cricket".

Smith, by entrusting Ntini with the final over at what had been de Wet's end, displayed a hitherto unsuspected sense of theatre and belief in fairytales. The journey of Ntini – a former goat-herder from the tiny Eastern Cape town of Mdingi – to 100 Test caps was harder than even his closest team-mates could imagine, let alone the millions of his countrymen who had just voted him the country's most popular sportsman for the third time. If he had taken the final wicket to win the Test it would have provided an anecdote in South Africa's cricket history to rank alongside anything which had preceded it in the already colourful Rainbow Nation's return to international competition. But it was not to be, and that was a fair result.

South Africa's disappointment at the near miss was tempered by the knowledge that Dale Steyn was set to return to the attack for the Second Test, and that Kallis would also take a fuller place among the bowlers.

The Test was played with the use of the significantly revised Umpire Decision Review System and, although Andy Flower pronounced himself "not a fan" after England had wasted a couple of reviews which were at best 50/50 decisions, both teams were considerably less sceptical at the end of the match than they had been before. The only significant moment of controversy came when South Africa took 35 seconds to ask for a review of an lbw decision against Broad, given not out but subsequently overturned. The batsman stomped around the umpires in what looked like a petulant refusal to leave the crease. But while the time taken by the South Africans to ask for the review was excessive and should have been curbed by the umpires, there could be no doubt that the correct decision was reached.

Man of the Match: G. P. Swann.

Close of play: First day, South Africa 262-4 (Kallis 112, Duminy 38); Second day, England 88-1 (Strauss 44, Trott 18); Third day, South Africa 9-1 (Smith 6, Harris 2); Fourth day, England 11-1 (Cook 4, Anderson 6).

South Africa

*G. C. Smith c Prior b Broad	0	– (2) b Onions	12
A. G. Prince c Collingwood b Swann	45	– (1) b Anderson	0
H. M. Amla c Collingwood b Onions	19	– (4) b Anderson	100
J. H. Kallis c Collingwood b Anderson	120	– (5) c Cook b Broad	4
A. B. de Villiers c Cook b Swann	32	– (6) c Bell b Broad	64
J-P. Duminy c Collingwood b Swann	56	– (7) lbw b Anderson	11
†M. V. Boucher c Cook b Swann	49	– (8) not out	63
M. Morkel c Prior b Onions	13	– (9) not out	22
P. L. Harris b Onions	38	– (3) b Anderson	11
F. de Wet lbw b Swann	20		
M. Ntini not out	4		
B 2, l-b 15, w 5	22	L-b 10, w 4	14

1/1 (1) 2/51 (3) 3/93 (2)   (153.2 overs) 418   1/2 (1)   (7 wkts dec, 85.5 overs) 301
4/159 (5) 5/283 (4) 6/316 (6) 7/341 (8)   2/20 (3) 3/34 (2)
8/377 (7) 9/414 (9) 10/418 (10)   4/46 (5) 5/165 (6) 6/191 (7) 7/266 (4)

Anderson 37–9–104–1; Broad 32–8–74–1; Onions 30–5–86–3; Swann 45.2–10–110–5; Collingwood 7–1–18–0; Trott 2–0–9–0. *Second Innings*—Anderson 20.5–1–73–4; Onions 16–3–50–1; Broad 16–5–58–2; Swann 27–3–91–0; Collingwood 6–1–19–0.

England

*A. J. Strauss b Ntini	46	– c Boucher b Morkel	1
A. N. Cook c Boucher b de Wet	15	– c Smith b Harris	12
I. J. L. Trott b Harris	28	– (4) c de Villiers b de Wet	69
K. P. Pietersen b Morkel	40	– (5) run out	81
P. D. Collingwood c Kallis b Harris	50	– (6) not out	26
I. R. Bell b Harris	5	– (7) c Boucher b de Wet	2
†M. J. Prior c de Wet b Harris	4	– (8) c Boucher b de Wet	0
S. C. J. Broad lbw b Duminy	17	– (9) c Boucher b Harris	0
G. P. Swann c Smith b Harris	85	– (10) lbw b Morkel	2
J. M. Anderson c Morkel b Ntini	29	– (3) c Boucher b de Wet	10
G. Onions not out	4	– not out	1
B 8, l-b 8, w 5, n-b 12	33	B 10, l-b 3, n-b 11	24

1/25 (2) 2/98 (1) 3/119 (3)   (104 overs) 356   1/5 (1) 2/16 (3)   (9 wkts, 96 overs) 228
4/168 (4) 5/189 (6) 6/211 (7)   3/27 (2) 4/172 (5)
7/221 (5) 8/242 (8) 9/348 (10) 10/356 (9)   5/205 (4) 6/207 (7) 7/208 (8)
8/209 (9) 9/218 (10)

Ntini 23–4–78–2; de Wet 20–3–72–1; Morkel 21–0–60–1; Harris 37–10–123–5; Duminy 3–0–7–1. *Second Innings*—Ntini 18–7–41–0; Morkel 18–3–46–2; Harris 26–11–51–2; de Wet 23–8–55–4; Duminy 8–2–17–0; Kallis 3–1–5–0.

Umpires: Aleem Dar and S. J. Davis.
Third umpire: A. M. Saheba.   Referee: R. S. Mahanama.

SOUTH AFRICA v ENGLAND

Second Test Match

DEAN WILSON

At Durban, December 26, 27, 28, 29, 30, 2009. England won by an innings and 98 runs. Toss: South Africa.

The last Test match of 2009 began against the backdrop of Christmas celebrations on the South African coast, and ended in a humiliating defeat for the home team, while England could bask in a job clinically done and enjoy their New Year's Eve festivities in Cape Town with a 1–0 lead and two games to play.

England's victory provided Graeme Smith with an unwelcome first, since he had never previously been a part of a South African team which had lost by an innings. With it South Africa also lost any hopes of regaining the No. 1 Test ranking they had held as recently as November.

For all the anger and disappointment etched across Smith's face during what became a free afternoon on the fifth day, he could neither deny the excellence of England's batsmen – two of whom, Cook and Bell, collected their tenth and ninth Test centuries respectively – nor could he ignore the capitulation of his own side for just 133 in exactly 50 overs to finish the game.

Broad, a victim of some harsh criticism of his on-field behaviour in the run-up to the match, was South Africa's chief tormentor with the ball on the fourth evening, but another five-wicket haul for Swann earned him successive match awards to complete a remarkable year for England's laugh-a-minute off-spinner.

South Africa made one change from the side that came within a whisker of winning the First Test, with Steyn having recovered from a hamstring injury to replace Friedel de Wet, despite his final-day heroics at the end of his debut in the previous match. Many suggested that it should have been Ntini who made way, since he had looked out of sorts on the high-veld, but with 100 Test caps to his name he was given one more chance.

Smith's decision to bat first seemed the sensible thing to do, even though Prince departed in just the third over and Amla in the tenth. Smith and Kallis emphasised the point by making batting look a formality once they had taken the shine off the new ball. A feature of the series was the huge impact of the new Kookaburra ball; however, it tended to lose its sparkle after around 20 overs, so it became vital to strike early.

Throughout the afternoon Smith and Kallis provided an example of Test-match batting to sit back and enjoy, but within seven overs of the tea-break both had departed – Smith, after being called for a too-quick single, was just beaten back to the stumps by Cook coming in from cover – along with Duminy, to leave some work to be done on the second day.

A 63-run partnership between de Villiers and Boucher was ended only when England finally succeeded in having a verdict overturned. After Boucher was given not out following Swann's lbw appeal, third umpire Steve Davis was able to point out that the ball had actually hit pad first, not bat, so Boucher was indeed out. Improved usage of the review system in this Test was to be a welcome bonus for England.

A carousing 47 from Steyn lifted his team to a competitive, if unexceptional, 343. However, he appeared to give the normally stoic and sensible Strauss an idea: his 49-ball half-century was as out of character as it was thrilling, easily his fastest in Tests, though he could not extend it beyond 54.

The third day was all about a trio of English batsmen who have probably had more questions asked about their positions in the Test side than are posed in the average TV quiz show. Cook, with just one half-century in 11 innings, ground his way to the most disciplined hundred of his career, practically ignoring anything outside off stump to bind the innings together, while Collingwood came within nine of his own century before cutting Duminy's part-time off-spin to the wicketkeeper.

At the close Bell had 55, and had certainly been the most pleasing on the eye, following the sort of mistake in the First Test that will haunt him for many a year, when he let a ball from Harris pass unmolested to hit middle stump. He completed his hundred next morning, going on to 140 as England piled up a lead of 231. It was the sort of advantage that justified their selection policy of six specialist batsmen and just four bowlers – although Strauss happily pointed out that the difference between the right and the wrong decision is only apparent in hindsight when something either works or does not.

From this launchpad England were able to exert much greater pressure with the ball, and the now irrepressible Swann got them rolling towards victory with the first two wickets of Prince and Amla, bowled through the gate with a looping off-break, before tea. Even then, with four sessions left for South Africa to save the game, there was little indication of the drama to come before the day was out.

Philip Brown

It's that man again: Graeme Swann bowled England to victory with his fourth five-for of the year.

With less than 15 overs bowled with the new ball, Broad detected a hint of reverse swing, thanks to two incredibly hot days which had parched the pitch and the outfield. Using his height, accuracy and just enough movement to fool the batsman, he hit the top of Kallis's off stump with no shot offered. He then trapped de Villiers lbw as the ball zeroed in towards off stump – again, no shot was offered – and the next ball clattered into Duminy's stumps via the inside edge after he thought about playing a shot and then decided against it. Fifteen balls, one run, three wickets, and not a shot in sight – the game was as good as up.

When Swann dismissed Smith for 22 it meant England needed just four more wickets on the last day to complete the win, and it didn't take them long. At 10.42 a.m. a final lbw for Swann against Steyn completed his fourth five-wicket haul in just his 14th Test. Fittingly, it secured England's first innings win over South Africa since another off-spinner, Fred Titmus, bowled them to victory at the same ground in 1964-65.

The only concern for England afterwards was the dislocated left index finger suffered by Collingwood during fielding practice on the fourth morning, which left him unable to field and made him a doubt for the Third Test. The concerns for South Africa ran far deeper, and led to strong words in the dressing-room after the match, and later the axing of the iconic Ntini, whose opening spell of three overs for 25 had conceded the advantage to Strauss and England in the first place.

Man of the Match: G. P. Swann.

Close of play: First day, South Africa 175-5 (de Villiers 8, Boucher 1); Second day, England 103-1 (Cook 31, Trott 17); Third day, England 386-5 (Bell 55, Prior 11); Fourth day, South Africa 76-6 (Boucher 20, Morkel 7).

South Africa

*G. C. Smith run out	75	– (2) lbw b Swann			22
A. G. Prince c Swann b Anderson	2	– (1) c Bell b Swann			16
H. M. Amla lbw b Broad	2	– b Swann			6
J. H. Kallis c Collingwood b Swann	75	– b Broad			3
A. B. de Villiers c Prior b Broad	50	– lbw b Broad			2
J-P. Duminy lbw b Onions	4	– b Broad			0
†M. V. Boucher lbw b Swann	39	– c Prior b Broad			29
M. Morkel lbw b Swann	23	– lbw b Swann			15
P. L. Harris lbw b Swann	2	– c Broad b Anderson			36
D. W. Steyn c Prior b Anderson	47	– lbw b Swann			3
M. Ntini not out	6	– not out			1
B 1, l-b 17	18				

1/3 (2) 2/10 (3) 3/160 (4)　　　　(108.3 overs) 343　　1/27 (1) 2/37 (3)　　　(50 overs) 133
4/166 (1) 5/170 (6) 6/233 (7) 7/269 (5)　　　　　　　　3/40 (4) 4/44 (5) 5/44 (6)
8/280 (9) 9/285 (8) 10/343 (10)　　　　　　　　　　　6/50 (2) 7/86 (8) 8/108 (7)
　　　　　　　　　　　　　　　　　　　　　　　　　9/129 (9) 10/133 (10)

Anderson 23.3–4–75–2; Onions 23–6–62–1; Broad 20–6–44–2; Swann 35–3–110–4; Trott 4–0–19–0; Pietersen 2–0–7–0; Collingwood 1–0–8–0. *Second Innings*—Anderson 8–2–24–1; Onions 4–1–12–0; Swann 21–3–54–5; Broad 17–3–43–4.

England

*A. J. Strauss b Morkel	54	J. M. Anderson not out		1
A. N. Cook c Kallis b Morkel	118	G. Onions not out		2
I. J. L. Trott c Boucher b Morkel	18			
K. P. Pietersen lbw b Harris	31	L-b 10, w 6, n-b 1		17
P. D. Collingwood c Boucher b Duminy	91			
I. R. Bell c Boucher b Steyn	140	1/71 (1)　　(9 wkts dec, 170 overs)		574
†M. J. Prior b Duminy	60	2/104 (3) 3/155 (4)		
S. C. J. Broad c Kallis b Duminy	20	4/297 (2) 5/365 (5) 6/477 (7)		
G. P. Swann c Prince b Steyn	22	7/536 (8) 8/564 (9) 9/568 (6)		

Steyn 34–6–94–2; Ntini 29–4–114–0; Morkel 31–6–78–3; Kallis 14–1–43–0; Harris 38–4–146–1; Duminy 24–1–89–3.

Umpires: Aleem Dar and A. M. Saheba.
Third umpire: S. J. Davis.　Referee: R. S. Mahanama.

SOUTH AFRICA v ENGLAND

Third Test Match

GEOFFREY DEAN

At Cape Town, January 3, 4, 5, 6, 7, 2010. Drawn. Toss: England.

A match of high drama, as notable for its off-field controversy as for its gripping finish, ended at 5.59 p.m. when, for the second time in the series, Graham Onions survived the last over to salvage a draw for his side. The final day followed a remarkably similar pattern to that of the First Test, as England appeared to have made the game safe before collapsing in the final session.

This time, they had five wickets in hand at tea, and the last-wicket pair came together with 17 balls remaining, 11 of which Onions blocked out – all from Morkel. When the very last delivery of the match was directed harmlessly wide of off stump, Onions again held his right arm aloft to the team balcony, before being embraced by Swann. Hundreds of England supporters – and there were several thousand in the ground – danced and celebrated as if they had won a treasured victory. This latest great escape by England meant they could not lose the series.

Smith was left to reflect both on the timing of his declaration and his side's suggestions after play on the third day that England might have tampered with the ball in the second innings. He might easily have declared 20 or 30 minutes earlier with a lead of around 430, but he knew that de Wet's back complaint, which required an injection on the fourth afternoon, could restrict his use. In the end, he could manage only a dozen overs in the innings, and was later found to have a stress fracture.

If South Africa might have been overly cautious with their declaration, a strong case could be argued that the way in which they went about voicing their suspicions of ball-tampering was cynical, or even "a little bit malicious" as Strauss put it. They made no formal complaint to the match referee, but used the media to let everyone know they had asked him to inspect the ball's condition. That, of course, is the job of the umpires, who have the power to change it if they believe it has been deliberately tampered with. The umpires were perfectly happy with the state of the ball, a key factor in the case against England collapsing.

Smarting from the fact that England found reverse swing in Durban more quickly than their own bowlers, South Africa based their thinly veiled accusations against England on one incident when Broad put his boot on the ball, and another when Anderson was filmed working on it. The accusations of tampering, strongly denied by England, may well have stiffened their resolve when they were left with a day and a half to bat to save the match. To do so, even on a pitch that got slower and did not deteriorate as expected, was a fine achievement.

Strauss's decision to field first had stronger justification than in the First Test. A cool, cloudy first morning and a pitch with some grass left on it promised swing and seam movement. Prince gloved one that bounced in the first over, and Smith should also have departed in the second when he edged Onions's loosener to second slip. Swann, deputising for Collingwood (who had to field in the deep to protect the finger he had dislocated in Durban), dropped a regulation chance. As a result, Kallis was spared the most tricky batting conditions of the match – the first hour – and did not have to come in until the 17th over.

Kallis's wicket was the key, for although South Africa slipped to 127 for five when Duminy was out first ball for the second time running, he was there to lead the revival, first with Boucher, who counter-attacked gamely in a 79-ball fifty, and then with Steyn. Kallis played immaculately to reach his hundred from 173 balls: it was his third in successive Tests against England on his home ground, and his sixth there in all. Despite losing their last four wickets in 16 deliveries to the second new ball on the second morning, South Africa showed their total was a competitive one by reducing England to 73 for four, helped by some poor stroke execution from Strauss, Trott and Pietersen. Cook, with a solid 112-ball fifty, and Bell both batted adeptly before giving their wickets away, but Prior, with a well-constructed 76 from 118 balls, masterminded the extraction of 99 from the last four wickets. The last pair's stand of 32 proved significant, as it helped to delay Smith's declaration next day. Morkel bowled excellently to claim his second Test five-for, and was well supported by Steyn.

Although Prince fell in the 12th over, England's pace bowlers did not look like making further inroads on a pitch now playing at its best. England were further handicapped by the furnace-like heat of the third day, when temperatures reached 38°C without a breath of wind. Smith and, in particular, Amla profited from Strauss's refusal to post a third man. An unusually high percentage of the runs came there during an excellent stand of 230 in 54 overs, which easily eclipsed the old second-wicket record in a Test at Newlands: 172

Mass appeal: Paul Harris and most of his team-mates believe, wrongly, that Stuart Broad is out.

by Eddie Barlow and Tony Pithey against England in 1964-65. As the bowlers wilted in the stifling heat, South Africa upped the tempo in the final session, plundering 147 runs, of which Smith made 97.

That evening, South Africa made their accusations. Broad, who had stopped the ball under his boot in the 15th over, was effectively cited by the home management, as was Anderson for allegedly picking the quarter-seam. The fact that they were England's best exponents of reverse swing may not have been a coincidence. Neither was found to be culpable of changing the ball's state when the umpires examined TV footage. Nor had any reverse swing been obtained by England that day.

Smith, who fell for an outstanding 183 in six and a half hours with 25 fours, four of them in one Trott over, made his declaration 45 minutes after lunch, but had to wait until the 37th over for a breakthrough, when Cook top-edged a pull. After getting rid of both Strauss and Pietersen that evening, South Africa were strong favourites going into the final day. It took them 45 minutes next morning, however, to remove the night-watchman, Anderson, who perished to the generally disappointing Harris. Trott was the only other casualty before lunch, beaten by a fine off-cutter.

The second new ball was due within an over of the resumption but, crucially, Collingwood and Bell managed to survive it. Collingwood, reprieved by the third umpire on referral after being given out caught at slip first ball off the hip, was beaten outside off stump on more than half a dozen occasions by Steyn. It proved to be one of Collingwood's finest rearguards, his 40 using up 188 balls. His sixth-wicket alliance of 112 in 57 overs with Bell appeared to have saved the match, for only 13 overs remained when Collingwood was out. But after Prior and Broad were both caught at short leg, prodding nervously at the spinners, Bell was finally out the ninth, steering to first slip a ball he could have left, his excellent 78 having spanned 213 balls. South Africa scented victory, but Onions, showing admirable composure and back-foot defence, again could not be shifted. An entranced final-day crowd of 14,364 took the total attendance to 79,375, a Newlands record.

Man of the Match: G. C. Smith.

Close of play: First day, South Africa 279-6 (Kallis 108, Steyn 26); Second day, England 241-7 (Prior 52, Swann 5); Third day, South Africa 312-2 (Smith 162, Kallis 20); Fourth day, England 132-3 (Trott 24, Anderson 0).

South Africa

*G. C. Smith c Prior b Anderson	30	– (2) c Collingwood b Onions	183
A. G. Prince c Prior b Anderson	0	– (1) lbw b Swann	15
H. M. Amla lbw b Onions	14	– c Cook b Swann	95
J. H. Kallis c Prior b Onions	108	– c Prior b Anderson	46
A. B. de Villiers c Strauss b Swann	36	– c Broad b Anderson	34
J-P. Duminy c Prior b Swann	0	– c Prior b Anderson	36
†M. V. Boucher lbw b Broad	51	– c Bell b Swann	15
D. W. Steyn c Trott b Anderson	26	– not out	1
M. Morkel c Swann b Anderson	0		
P. L. Harris not out	10		
F. de Wet lbw b Anderson	0		
B 1, l-b 13, w 1, n-b 1	16	B 8, l-b 7, n-b 2, p 5	22

1/1 (2) 2/46 (3) 3/51 (1) 4/127 (5)   (86.1 overs) 291
5/127 (6) 6/216 (7) 7/280 (4)
8/280 (8) 9/281 (9) 10/291 (11)

1/31 (1)   (7 wkts dec, 111.2 overs) 447
2/261 (3) 3/346 (2)
4/376 (4) 5/401 (5) 6/442 (7) 7/447 (6)

Anderson 21.1–1–63–5; Onions 20–4–69–2; Broad 19–6–54–1; Swann 22–1–74–2; Pietersen 4–0–17–0. *Second Innings*—Anderson 22.2–1–98–3; Onions 22–4–87–1; Swann 37–5–127–3; Broad 22–4–79–0; Pietersen 3–0–6–0; Trott 5–0–30–0.

England

*A. J. Strauss c Boucher b Morkel	2	– c Amla b Harris	45
A. N. Cook c Prince b Morkel	65	– c Boucher b de Wet	55
I. J. L. Trott b Steyn	20	– b Steyn	42
K. P. Pietersen c and b Steyn	0	– lbw b Steyn	6
P. D. Collingwood lbw b Morkel	19	– (6) c Kallis b Duminy	40
I. R. Bell c Duminy b Kallis	48	– (7) c Smith b Morkel	78
†M. J. Prior b Steyn	76	– (8) c de Villiers b Duminy	4
S. C. J. Broad b Steyn	25	– (9) c de Villiers b Harris	0
G. P. Swann c Smith b Morkel	5	– (10) not out	10
J. M. Anderson c Smith b Morkel	0	– (5) c Prince b Harris	9
G. Onions not out	4	– not out	0
L-b 6, w 2, n-b 1	9	B 1, l-b 4, w 1, n-b 1	7

1/2 (1) 2/36 (3) 3/36 (4) 4/73 (5)   (88 overs) 273
5/133 (2) 6/174 (6) 7/225 (8) 8/241 (9)
9/241 (10) 10/273 (7)

1/101 (2)   (9 wkts, 141 overs) 296
2/107 (1) 3/129 (4)
4/153 (5) 5/160 (3) 6/272 (6)
7/278 (8) 8/286 (9) 9/290 (7)

Morkel 22–4–75–5; de Wet 16–3–36–0; Steyn 22–5–74–4; Kallis 14–2–27–1; Harris 9–0–39–0; Duminy 5–0–16–0. *Second Innings*—Morkel 28–9–51–1; Steyn 35–11–74–2; de Wet 12–5–23–1; Harris 40–14–85–3; Kallis 14–4–28–0; Duminy 12–3–30–2.

Umpires: D. J. Harper and A. L. Hill.
Third umpire: Aleem Dar.   Referee: R. S. Mahanama.

SOUTH AFRICA v ENGLAND

Fourth Test Match

Mike Atherton

At Johannesburg, January 14, 15, 16, 17, 2009. South Africa won by an innings and 74 runs. Toss: England. Test debuts: R. McLaren, W. D. Parnell.

Mickey Arthur, in what turned out to be his last game as South African coach, called his team's victory in the final Test a "hollow one". The ease of it, and the way in which

Philip Brown

In the thick of it: the combative Mark Boucher scores freely on the third day.

his team had dominated two out of the other three Tests meant that, although South Africa retained the Basil D'Oliveira Trophy, they regarded the drawn series as a missed opportunity.

It was hard not to see why. Over ten rounds (the match was finished in only 209.4 overs, or around two and a half days of playing time) in the Bullring, England were pulverised as surely as if they had been a welterweight contesting a heavyweight bout. When Ryan Sidebottom, strangely included in place of Graham Onions, had his stumps rearranged by Duminy on the point of lunch on the fourth day, the destruction was complete.

From the moment Strauss won a fateful toss and decided to bat first, it was hard to think of a session, or indeed part of a session, where England competed, so one-sided was the contest. The tourists, as they had been throughout the series, were never short of pluck or endeavour in the field or with the ball but, on a pitch that offered at times disconcerting bounce and pace, the batsmen's technique and stomach for the fight were brought into question.

The key difference was in pace bowling, where South Africa could boast two of the outstanding practitioners in a barren age. Morkel and Steyn were named as joint Men of the Match, which was fitting since they shared 14 wickets between them. England were twice bowled out for under 200, neither innings lasting more than 50 overs. They were blown away.

This was not a great Test because of its one-sidedness, but there were plenty of ingredients to make sure that it will remain in the memory. There was another marvellous hundred from Smith, who specialises – at least against England – in making runs that matter, and another street-fighting innings from Boucher who, along with Swann, shared the series award. Boucher is one of those cricketers who likes, to use one of Red Smith's phrases, to "get where the cabbage is cooking and catch the scents". He is always in the thick of it.

By the end of the first day, it was clear that Strauss would have regretted his decision to bat first. The pitch, while not as green as the mischief-makers wanted us to believe, had a decent covering of grass, and the day, if not overcast, had enough cloud cover to make a captain pause for thought. Strauss, though, explained that he was worried about the dents, which would have been created because the surface was dampish, later in the match – the reason that Smith gave for his admission that he, too, would have batted first.

It was a good toss to lose. By the end of a day shortened by 30 overs because of bad light, England had been bowled out for 180. No batsman reached 50, and nobody looked comfortable against the bounce of Morkel and the pace of Steyn, backed by two promising debutants in Wayne Parnell and Ryan McLaren. As at Headingley some months before, England looked destabilised by the early dismissal of their captain – brilliantly and instinctively caught by Amla at short leg – as Strauss turned the first ball of the match off his hip; and there were also worrying signs of lack of form emanating from Trott and Pietersen, occupying the key slots at Nos 3 and 4. (Strauss provided the 28th instance of a batsman falling to the opening delivery of a Test, but it was the first time it had happened to an England opener for more than 73 years, since Derbyshire's Stan Worthington was caught behind off the first ball of the 1936-37 Ashes series at Brisbane.)

It would be hard to assert that the game hinged on the controversy in the fourth over of the following morning, but it would be fair to say that a player of Smith's calibre needed no second invitation to take advantage of the reprieve given him when he seemingly edged Sidebottom into the wicketkeeper's gloves having scored just 15. Smith cut at a wide delivery and the ensuing edge was heard by all and sundry – except the on-field umpire, Tony Hill, and the third official, who was subsequently brought into action, Daryl Harper.

All kinds of conspiracy theories followed the resulting verdict of "not out" given by Harper, who failed to hear any noise. Harper, and subsequently the ICC, were adamant that he had been given a faulty feed by SABC, the host broadcaster. For their part, SABC put it about surreptitiously that they had given Harper the right feed, but that he had failed to turn up the volume to the requisite level. England harrumphed and made a formal complaint. Ridiculously, the ECB chairman Giles Clarke waded in to the debate and demanded a return of the wasted review.

When South Africa were 242 for five – a lead of only 62 – Harper overturned a decision against de Villiers off Swann, with minimal evidence to contradict the on-field umpire who thought he had gloved an attempted sweep to leg slip. Harper arrived at his decision too quickly, since close scrutiny seemed to suggest the ball kissed the back of the bat: de Villiers survived to add 120 with Boucher. England, clearly, had their minds on other things, and South Africa eventually waltzed to 423 before declaring with a lead of 243.

You cannot be serious! Graeme Smith, on 15, survives an appeal for caught behind; the body language of the England fielders is eloquent.

There was always the chance that weather might alter the course of events thereafter, but the game, to all intents and purposes, was up.

The Smith controversy highlighted a number of problems with the umpire review system. If technology is to be used (and those of us who wish it had not been expanded beyond line decisions accept that there is no going back now), then it is vital there is a standardisation across the board. If the ICC cannot afford Hot Spot, then caught-behind and bat-pad decisions should not be reviewed. Without Hot Spot, the third umpire is in a far worse position than the on-field umpire to make a decision.

More fundamentally, the Smith decision suggested that players find, and will find, it much more difficult to accept mistakes than before. It should not be forgotten that the on-field umpire also gave Smith not out, a decision that before the advent of the referral system would have been grumbled about but ultimately accepted. Now we had a situation where England and their administrators simply could not bring themselves to accept an umpiring decision – a regrettable development.

Indeed, the instances of petulance grew throughout the series – particularly from England – and it is clear that the ability of players to challenge umpiring decisions will have repercussions far beyond the scope of the ICC's sphere of control. One of the first principles of cricket – that the umpire's decision is final – has been fatally undermined. If decisions are to be reviewed, then the umpires should be the ones doing the reviewing. The umpire review system dominated much of what was otherwise a wonderful series – and that, too, was regrettable.

Smith timed his declaration perfectly, so that England lost three wickets on the third evening before bad light again curtailed play. On the fourth morning, only Collingwood showed any fight, the rest falling to a combination of poor strokes (Pietersen's drive and Prior's hook) and irresistible bowling and catching. Broad's dismissal on review, which provoked a peevish, head-shaking departure after a definite glove down the leg side, suggested that England harboured a clear grievance about the umpiring in this match.

As ever, this was a red herring. South Africa had outplayed them, a drawn series – ultimately – the least they deserved.

Men of the Match: M. Morkel and D. W. Steyn.
Men of the Series: M. V. Boucher and G. P. Swann.
Close of play: First day, South Africa 29-0 (Smith 12, Prince 15); Second day, South Africa 215-2 (Amla 73, Kallis 7); Third day, England 48-3 (Pietersen 9, Collingwood 0).

England

*A. J. Strauss c Amla b Steyn	0	– lbw b Parnell	22
A. N. Cook lbw b Morkel	21	– c Smith b Morkel	1
I. J. L. Trott lbw b Morkel	5	– c de Villiers b Steyn	8
K. P. Pietersen c Parnell b Morkel	7	– c Boucher b Parnell	12
P. D. Collingwood c Duminy b McLaren	47	– c Morkel b Duminy	71
I. R. Bell b Steyn	35	– c Kallis b Morkel	5
†M. J. Prior c Boucher b Steyn	14	– c Smith b Morkel	0
S. C. J. Broad c Morkel b Kallis	13	– c Boucher b Morkel	1
G. P. Swann c Boucher b Steyn	27	– c de Villiers b Steyn	20
R. J. Sidebottom c Boucher b Steyn	0	– b Duminy	15
J. M. Anderson not out	6	– not out	1
L-b 2, w 3	5	L-b 6, w 1, n-b 6	13

1/0 (1) 2/7 (3) 3/32 (4) 4/39 (2) (47.5 overs) 180
5/115 (5) 6/133 (6) 7/136 (7)
8/148 (8) 9/155 (10) 10/180 (9)

1/6 (2) 2/21 (3) (42.5 overs) 169
3/48 (1) 4/84 (4)
5/103 (6) 6/103 (7) 7/104 (8)
8/134 (9) 9/154 (5) 10/169 (10)

Steyn 13.5–1–51–5; Morkel 11–1–39–3; McLaren 10–3–30–1; Parnell 3–0–18–0; Kallis 10–3–40–1. *Second Innings*—Steyn 14–1–64–2; Morkel 16–5–59–4; Parnell 8–1–17–2; McLaren 3–1–13–0; Duminy 1.5–0–10–2.

South Africa

*G. C. Smith c Strauss b Sidebottom	105	R. McLaren not out	33
A. G. Prince c Swann b Broad	19	D. W. Steyn not out	1
H. M. Amla c Prior b Broad	75	B 8, l-b 9, w 5, n-b 1	23
J. H. Kallis c Anderson b Sidebottom	7		
A. B. de Villiers c Collingwood b Broad	58	(7 wkts dec, 119 overs)	423
J-P. Duminy c Collingwood b Swann	7		
†M. V. Boucher c Trott b Swann	95		

1/36 (2) 2/201 (1) 3/217 (3)
4/217 (4) 5/235 (6) 6/355 (5) 7/419 (7)

M. Morkel and W. D. Parnell did not bat.

Anderson 30–4–111–0; Sidebottom 31–6–98–2; Broad 29–4–83–3; Swann 23–0–93–2;
Collingwood 6–1–21–0.

Umpires: S. J. Davis and A. L. Hill.
Third umpire: D. J. Harper.   Referee: R. S. Mahanama.

INDIAN PREMIER LEAGUE, 2008-09

Neil Manthorp

The creators and owners of the Indian Premier League pulled off one of the greatest feats of logistical management in sports history by moving the entire tournament from India to South Africa at less than a month's notice. The self-styled IPL "commissioner" Lalit Modi and his team were impossibly brilliant, almost too clever to comprehend, in relocating rather than postponing or cancelling when the Indian government refused to guarantee security at certain venues because the dates coincided with national elections in the world's largest democracy.

It was pretty obvious, even to the diffident and disinterested, that moving the tournament en masse to South Africa was a big deal but, just in case anybody was in any doubt, Modi announced it and pronounced it. Over and over again.

The numbers were almost universally huge, from the 1,000-plus visas the South African government issued in 24 hours (as opposed to the customary ten working days) to more than 40,000 hotel-room nights, and the alleged $US50m by which South Africa's economy benefited.

One number which was conspicuously low in the greater scheme of things was the $1m paid to Cricket South Africa and its affiliates to bleach their stadiums of adverts, vacate their offices and leave behind their finest wines for the approaching hordes. "We took a very pragmatic view," said a CSA committee member just days after the Deccan Chargers had swapped the wooden spoon for the not-so-subtle winners trophy, encrusted with rubies and yellow and blue sapphires. "Was it worth our while as a cricket board, with member unions feeling trampled on and taken advantage of, with their own members marginalised and unable to make use of executive suites they have owned for 15 years? Probably not. But were we in a position to say no when so many other South Africans could benefit? And when future relations between our countries were considered? Definitely not."

So did South Africa bend over backwards to accommodate the IPL in order to curry favour in future years? "Everyone knows who butters the bread in world cricket these days, and it isn't necessarily us," said the CSA official.

Of more concern to the global game, however, especially given the millions of dollars so boastfully generated by the tournament, was the absence of the ICC's Anti Corruption and Security Unit. All the ingredients for temptation were there. Some mega-rich, egotistical team owners and their hundreds of hangers-on, a cavernous divergence in salaries between players and, crucially, no natural guard against impropriety in the form of national pride or a sense of history.

The IPL did, in fact, enquire about making use of the ACSU, but baulked at the quoted price-tag of more than $1m, even though that was a pittance in the context of the overall budget. Instead, they appointed a private South African security company, Nicholls Steyn & Associates to cover security arrangements.

An extraordinary 11th-hour about-turn saw the Indian board request the ACSU's involvement the day before the tournament began, but it was made clear that the job involved a lot more than standing in dressing-room doorways looking out for dodgy blokes in sunglasses. A minimum of six to eight weeks of research and preparation was required.

Consequently the tournament was awash with events and happenings regarded, more often than not, as peculiar, when they may have been innocent. Late-night franchise parties involved hundreds of guests, most seeking the attention of the eight or nine big-name Indian players and other internationals which every team boasted. It was simply not right and proper, although there was no evidence any of them was approached, that many of the world's best players were exposed to wealthy and influential "fans" at midnight.

The ACSU was not completely excluded, however. Its general manager and chief investigator, Ravi Sawani, along with one of his staff, briefed five of the eight teams, while a couple of the regional security managers supervised the locals hired to perform their usual role. But it was a lukewarm compromise.

While no doubt eyebrows were raised on the field, too, when they need not have been. Sudden promotions to open the bowling or a string of batting failures were innocent extremes of experimentation and form, some were open to misinterpretation and an official stamp from the game's most qualified authorities would have quelled the bar and bookie talk.

Common sense prevailed in the months after the tournament when IPL officials confirmed that ACSU surveillance had been commissioned for the third year of the IPL, when it will presumably be back on Indian soil.

For all the scars and scabs the tournament left behind, there can be no doubting the veracity of the vainglorious yells of success from the organisers. Thousands of tickets were given away, but so what – many stadiums were full, and even the ones that weren't were at 60% capacity. The enormous Indian population in Lenasia, a suburb of Johannesburg, ensured that the Wanderers had few empty seats, while Durban, home to the largest Indian diaspora outside the subcontinent, was positively humming with IPL fever.

The bling and glam of the Indian nouveau riche was obnoxious to many who were exposed to it, but to the majority of locals the tournament had a strong novelty value, the tickets were cheap, and it was never over-exposed in one region for too long. It was backed up with a preposterously huge advertising campaign (ten times greater than anything Cricket South Africa had ever been able to spend on a series) and the country was awash with the IPL to such an extent that even cricket-watching virgins felt compelled to see what all the fuss was about. Or some did, at least.

On the field Matthew Hayden and Adam Gilchrist shone like men a decade away from retirement, not in the first year of the slippers-and-pipe stage of their careers. Other "oldies" blossomed, too, such as Anil Kumble, while some of the "stars" who failed to shine first time around finally came good – like the locals Jacques Kallis and Mark Boucher.

The result was that the two teams who finished in the bottom two places in 2007-08 contested the final a year later: the Deccan Chargers (captained by Gilchrist) and the Royal Challengers from Bangalore. The Challengers were brought together by Anil Kumble after a poor start under Kevin Pietersen, one of several England players who failed to shine. Andrew Flintoff's bowling, and his lack of a slower ball, proved costly for Chennai before he was injured; Paul Collingwood and Owais Shah could not get a game for Delhi, and the only redemption came from Ravi Bopara in a matchwinning innings of 84 for Kings XI Punjab. The most expensive and glamorous of the franchises, however, the Kolkata Knight Riders, finished dead last and became the laughing stock of the league when an anonymous online blogger posted a series of embarrassingly accurate accounts of life inside the camp under the increasingly eccentric coaching of John Buchanan and philanthropic hedonism of owner Shah Rukh Khan. Buchanan was sacked a couple of months later.

As a sports and entertainment package, it was big. Very big. It was even good at times, too. As a cricket package, however, it was small. Sometimes very small. Modi has many of the elements which comprise genius, including an intractable belief in everything he does. One of his stated ambitions is for IPL franchises to become popular enough to challenge the world's great football teams for global following. Kings XI Punjab versus Real Madrid, Delhi Daredevils take on Manchester United…

It may even happen, but it will always be a superficial and fickle popularity because even the most fanatical sports following depends on the quality of the product, and so long as IPL teams are limited to playing just four internationals and a couple of Indian stars, the standard of cricket played will always be compromised.

The glass ceiling imposed on teams by the compulsory inclusion of four or five junior players in every starting XI may benefit certain aspects of Indian cricket, but the tournament – while that system remains in place – will never grow beyond the status of circus, albeit one with a bigger marquee and more clowns than any before. In cricket, anyway.

LEADING RUN-SCORERS

	M	I	NO	Runs	HS	Avge	50s	SR	4s	6s
†M. L. Hayden (*Chennai Super Kings*)	12	12	1	572	89	52.00	5	144.81	60	22
†A. C. Gilchrist (*Deccan Chargers*)	16	16	0	495	85	30.93	3	152.30	54	29
A. B. de Villiers (*Delhi Daredevils*)	15	13	4	465	105*	51.66	3	130.98	39	12
†S. K. Raina (*Chennai Super Kings*)	14	14	0	434	98	31.00	2	140.90	37	21
T. M. Dilshan (*Delhi Daredevils*)	14	13	3	418	67*	41.80	4	122.58	42	13
†J-P. Duminy (*Mumbai Indians*)	13	12	3	372	62	41.33	5	114.46	26	11
H. H. Gibbs (*Deccan Chargers*)	14	14	3	371	69*	33.72	4	112.08	32	12
B. J. Hodge (*Kolkata Knight Riders*)	12	12	3	365	73	40.55	3	117.74	34	9
S. R. Tendulkar (*Mumbai Indians*)	13	13	2	364	68	33.09	2	120.13	39	10
R. G. Sharma (*Deccan Chargers*)	16	16	3	362	52	27.84	1	114.92	22	18
J. H. Kallis (*Royal Challengers B'lore*)	15	15	4	361	69*	27.76	3	108.73	37	8
†Yuvraj Singh (*Kings XI Punjab*)	14	14	2	340	58*	28.33	2	115.64	25	16
M. S. Dhoni (*Chennai Super Kings*)	14	13	5	332	58*	41.50	2	127.20	22	9
†K. C. Sangakkara (*Kings XI Punjab*)	14	13	2	332	60	30.18	2	102.46	29	5

† *Left-hand batsman.*

There were two centuries in the tournament, by A. B. de Villiers and by M. K. Pandey (114, for Royal Challengers Bangalore), who finished with 168 runs from five matches. The highest strike-rate for anyone scoring more than 100 runs was 162.87 by D. R. Smith (215 runs for Deccan Chargers).*

LEADING WICKET-TAKERS

	Style	O	M	R	W	BB	4WIi	Avge	SR	ER
R. P. Singh (*Deccan Chargers*).......	LFM	59.4	1	417	23	4-22	1	18.13	15.5	6.98
A. Kumble (*Royal Challengers B'lore*) .	LBG	59.1	1	347	21	5-5	2	16.52	16.9	5.86
A. Nehra (*Delhi Daredevils*)...........	LFM	51	1	346	19	3-27	0	18.21	16.1	6.78
S. L. Malinga (*Mumbai Indians*).......	RF	49.3	2	312	18	3-11	0	17.33	16.5	6.30
P. P. Ojha (*Deccan Chargers*).........	SLA	53.3	0	348	18	3-21	0	19.33	17.8	6.50
I. K. Pathan (*Kings XI Punjab*).......	LFM	50.2	1	390	17	3-35	0	22.94	17.7	7.74
M. M. Patel (*Rajasthan Royals*).......	RFM	34.5	1	241	16	2-14	0	15.06	13.0	6.91
P. Sangwan (*Delhi Daredevils*)........	LM	46.4	1	360	15	3-18	0	24.00	18.6	7.71
D. P. Nannes (*Delhi Daredevils*)......	LF	49.3	0	372	15	3-27	0	24.80	19.8	7.51
Y. A. Abdulla (*Kings XI Punjab*)	LFM	28	1	241	14	4-31	2	17.21	12.0	8.60
M. Muralitharan (*Chennai Super Kings*)	OB	50	1	261	14	3-11	0	18.64	21.4	5.22
A. Mishra (*Delhi Daredevils*).........	LBG	42	0	294	14	3-14	0	21.00	18.0	7.00
S. K. Warne (*Rajasthan Royals*).......	LBG	50	0	365	14	3-24	0	26.07	21.4	7.30
S. B. Jakati (*Chennai Super Kings*)...	SLA	29	0	217	13	4-22	2	16.69	13.3	7.48
L. Balaji (*Chennai Super Kings*)......	RFM	37.2	0	316	13	4-21	1	24.30	17.2	8.46
J. A. Morkel (*Chennai Super Kings*)...	RFM	40	1	328	13	2-13	0	25.23	18.4	8.20
P. Kumar (*Royal Challengers B'lore*)...	RFM	49.4	1	394	13	3-30	0	30.30	22.9	7.93
Harbhajan Singh (*Mumbai Indians*)	OB	44	0	256	12	4-17	1	21.33	22.0	5.81
P. P. Chawla (*Kings XI Punjab*).......	LBG	44.5	1	308	12	2-22	0	25.66	22.4	6.86

Yuvraj Singh (Kings XI Punjab) took two hat-tricks, and R. G. Sharma (Deccan Chargers) one.

LEADING WICKETKEEPERS

Dis	M		Dis	M	
18 (10 ct, 8 st)	16	A. C. Gilchrist (*Deccan*)	8 (6 ct, 2 st)	14	K. C. Sangakkara (*Punjab*)
17 (12 ct, 5 st)	15	K. D. Karthik (*Delhi*)	8 (6 ct, 2 st)	9	P. R. Shah (*Mumbai*)

LEADING FIELDERS

Ct	M		Ct	M	
13	15	A. B. de Villiers (*Delhi*)	9	16	V. Kohli (*Bangalore*)
11	14	H. H. Gibbs (*Deccan*)	8	10	D. P. M. D. Jayawardene (*Punjab*)

INDIAN PREMIER LEAGUE, 2008-09

20-over league plus knockout

	Played	Won	Lost	No result	Points	Net run-rate
DELHI DAREDEVILS	14	10	4	0	20	0.31
CHENNAI SUPER KINGS	14	8	5	1	17	0.95
ROYAL CHALLENGERS BANGALORE ..	14	8	6	0	16	–0.19
DECCAN CHARGERS	14	7	7	0	14	0.20
Kings XI Punjab	14	7	7	0	14	–0.48
Rajasthan Royals......................	14	6	7	1	13	–0.35
Mumbai Indians.......................	14	5	8	1	11	0.29
Kolkata Knight Riders	14	3	10	1	7	–0.78

Semi-finals: Deccan Chargers beat Delhi Daredevils by six wickets; Royal Challengers Bangalore beat Chennai Super Kings by six wickets.

Final: Deccan Chargers beat Royal Challengers Bangalore by six runs.

Note: Matches in this section were not first-class.

Full scores of the games that follow can be found at www.cricinfo.com/ipl2009/content/series/ 374163.html and www.cricketarchive.co.uk/Archive/Seasons/RSA/2009_RSA_Indian_Premier_ League_2009.html.

Match Notes by Nagraj Gollapudi

At Cape Town, April 18, 2009. **Mumbai Indians won by 19 runs.** Toss: Chennai Super Kings. **Mumbai Indians 165-7** (20 overs) (S. R. Tendulkar 59*, A. M. Nayar 35); **Chennai Super Kings 146-7** (20 overs) (M. L. Hayden 44, M. S. Dhoni 36; S. L. Malinga 3-15). *Mumbai Indians 2 pts. Man of the Match:* S. R. Tendulkar.

Tendulkar was not distracted either by the drizzle or by a stray dog that eluded capture for 11 minutes: he batted through the innings, hitting seven fours, and was helped by Abhishek Nayar's dazzling 14-ball assault, which included three sixes. Despite Hayden's solid start, Chennai were rarely up with the rate, even before the hostile Malinga returned to dismiss Badrinath (second ball) and Dhoni.

At Cape Town, April 18, 2009 (floodlit). **Royal Challengers Bangalore won by 75 runs.** Toss: Royal Challengers Bangalore. **Royal Challengers Bangalore 133-8** (20 overs) (K. P. Pietersen 32, R. Dravid 66; A. D. Mascarenhas 3-20); **Rajasthan Royals 58** (15.1 overs) (A. Kumble 5-5). *Royal Challengers Bangalore 2 pts. Man of the Match:* R. Dravid.

Bangalore feared the worst when Mascarenhas took wickets with the first two balls of the match, but Dravid scored more than the other ten batsmen put together to push his side to a defendable total. Praveen Kumar took two quick wickets when defending champions Rajasthan batted, then Kumble treated a sizable Newlands crowd – which had flocked to watch the second of the opening day's matches – to a delightful (and penetrative) spell of leg-spin bowling.

At Cape Town, April 19, 2009. **Delhi Daredevils won by ten wickets** (D/L method). Reduced to 12 overs a side. Toss: Delhi Daredevils. **Kings XI Punjab 104-7** (12 overs) (K. Goel 33; D. L. Vettori 3-15); **Delhi Daredevils 58-0** (4.5 overs) (V. Sehwag 38*). *Delhi Daredevils 2 pts. Man of the Match:* D. L. Vettori.

After a delayed start, more rain early in Delhi's innings reduced their target to 54 from six overs, and they scooted home with seven balls to spare.

At Cape Town, April 19, 2009 (floodlit). **Deccan Chargers won by eight wickets.** Toss: Kolkata Knight Riders. **Kolkata Knight Riders 101** (19.4 overs) (B. J. Hodge 31; R. P. Singh 4-22); **Deccan Chargers 104-2** (13.1 overs) (H. H. Gibbs 43*, R. G. Sharma 36*). *Deccan Chargers 2 pts. Man of the Match:* R. P. Singh.

Having shelved their coach John Buchanan's original idea of having multiple captains – one each for batting, bowling and fielding – Kolkata seemed still to be in some disarray, especially after their sole captain turned out to be Brendon McCullum rather than Kolkata hero Sourav Ganguly. The batsmen failed to come to grips with the pace and swing of Fidel Edwards (4–1–6–0) and R. P. Singh, and only just reached three figures.

At Port Elizabeth, April 20, 2009 (floodlit). **Chennai Super Kings won by 92 runs.** Toss: Chennai Super Kings. **Chennai Super Kings 179-5** (20 overs) (P. A. Patel 30, M. L. Hayden 65); **Royal Challengers Bangalore 87** (15.2 overs) (M. Muralitharan 3-11). *Chennai Super Kings 2 pts. Man of the Match:* M. Muralitharan.

After defeat in the tournament opener, Chennai bounced back in style: first Hayden sprinted to 65 from 35 balls, with nine fours and two sixes, then Muralitharan and Flintoff (3–0–11–1) bowled with guile and pace.

At Durban, April 21, 2009. **Kolkata Knight Riders won by 11 runs** (D/L method). Toss: Kolkata Knight Riders. **Kings XI Punjab 158-6** (20 overs) (I. K. Pathan 32, Yuvraj Singh 38, D. P. M. D. Jayawardene 31*); **Kolkata Knight Riders 79-1** (9.2 overs) (C. H. Gayle 44*). *Kolkata Knight Riders 2 pts. Man of the Match:* C. H. Gayle.

For the second match running, rain spoiled Punjab's chances. This time they were held up by Ganguly (4–0–24–2), then Gayle (who faced only 26 balls and hit four sixes) took a liking to the left-armers Irfan Pathan and Yusuf Abdulla; Kolkata were ten ahead of the Duckworth/Lewis par score when rain stopped play.

At Durban, April 21, 2009 (floodlit). **Mumbai Indians v Rajasthan Royals. Abandoned.** *Mumbai Indians 1 pt, Rajasthan Royals 1 pt.*

At Cape Town, April 22, 2009 (floodlit). **Deccan Chargers won by 24 runs.** Toss: Deccan Chargers. **Deccan Chargers 184-6** (20 overs) (A. C. Gilchrist 71, R. G. Sharma 52); **Royal Challengers Bangalore 160-8** (20 overs) (R. Dravid 48, V. Kohli 50; S. B. Styris 3-32). *Deccan Chargers 2 pts. Man of the Match:* A. C. Gilchrist.

Blazing innings from Gilchrist (45 balls, five sixes, six fours) and Rohit Sharma (30 balls, five sixes) set an imposing target for Bangalore, who were already out of it when they tottered to 64-4 at halfway, with Pietersen gone for 11. Dravid and Kohli reduced the margin, but it was too late.

At Durban, April 23, 2009. **Delhi Daredevils won by nine runs.** Toss: Delhi Daredevils. **Delhi Daredevils 189-5** (20 overs) (A. B. de Villiers 105*, T. M. Dilshan 50; L. Balaji 3-19); **Chennai Super Kings 180-9** (20 overs) (M. L. Hayden 57, S. K. Raina 41; P. Sangwan 3-28). *Delhi Daredevils 2 pts. Man of the Match:* A. B. de Villiers.

At 8-2, with Gambhir and Sehwag both out, Delhi looked in trouble, but de Villiers took centre stage, racing to the tournament's first century, in just 51 balls, with five fours and six sixes. Flintoff's four overs cost 50. Hayden and Raina had kept Chennai in the frame by the time of the mid-innings strategic time-out (a new innovation this season), but immediately afterwards Delhi regained the initiative, as Raina and Dhoni fell quickly.

At Cape Town, April 23, 2009 (floodlit). **Rajasthan Royals won after an eliminator over, following a tie.** Toss: Kolkata Knight Riders. **Rajasthan Royals 150-6** (20 overs) (Y. K. Pathan 42); **Kolkata Knight Riders 150-8** (20 overs) (C. H. Gayle 41, S. C. Ganguly 46; Kamran Khan 3-18). *Rajasthan Royals 2 pts. Man of the Match:* Y. K. Pathan.

A Twenty20 classic, and the only match of this tournament to require the "super over" tie-breaker. It got that far only because the unheralded Kamran Khan, a left-arm fast bowler playing just his second match, kept Rajasthan alive with a superb final over – Kolkata had needed seven to win, but Ganguly was caught behind fifth ball, and Ishant Sharma run out going for the second that would have won the game. In the eliminator Gayle hit 15 of the 16 runs Kolkata made in Kamran's extra over, but Yusuf Pathan smashed 6264 off the first four balls from Ajantha Mendis.

At Durban, April 24, 2009 (floodlit). **Kings XI Punjab won by seven wickets.** Toss: Royal Challengers Bangalore. **Royal Challengers Bangalore 168-9** (20 overs) (J. D. Ryder 32, J. H. Kallis 62, L. R. P. L. Taylor 35; I. K. Pathan 3-35, Y. A. Abdulla 4-31); **Kings XI Punjab 173-3** (19 overs) (R. S. Bopara 84, Yuvraj Singh 30*). *Kings XI Punjab 2 pts. Man of the Match:* R. S. Bopara.

Bopara showed up Bangalore's lack of death bowlers with a well-paced innings containing four fours and five sixes. He was out just before the end, but Yuvraj Singh sealed victory with a six off Kallis, whose four overs cost 51.

At Durban, April 25, 2009. **Deccan Chargers won by 12 runs.** Toss: Deccan Chargers. **Deccan Chargers 168-9** (20 overs) (A. C. Gilchrist 35, H. H. Gibbs 58, D. R. Smith 35; S. L. Malinga 3-19, D. J. Bravo 3-34); **Mumbai Indians 156-7** (20 overs) (S. R. Tendulkar 36, J-P. Duminy 47; P. P. Ojha 3-21). *Deccan Chargers 2 pts. Man of the Match:* P. P. Ojha.

Pragyan Ojha showed why he was considered India's leading left-arm spinner, taking three wickets as many overs, including the prize scalps of Tendulkar and Duminy after a rousing start. Mumbai had needed 85 from ten overs after the mid-innings break, but the Chargers' bowlers made sure of a third straight victory. Earlier, Mumbai's attack had also done well at the end of the innings: only 43 runs came in the last seven overs, for the loss of seven wickets.

At Cape Town, April 25, 2009 (floodlit). **Chennai Super Kings v Kolkata Knight Riders. Abandoned.** *Chennai Super Kings 1 pt, Kolkata Knight Riders 1 pt.*

At Port Elizabeth, April 26, 2009. **Delhi Daredevils won by six wickets.** Toss: Royal Challengers Bangalore. **Royal Challengers Bangalore 149-7** (20 overs) (K. P. Pietersen 37, L. R. P. L. Taylor 31, M. V. Boucher 36); **Delhi Daredevils 150-4** (19.2 overs) (T. M. Dilshan 67*). *Delhi Daredevils 2 pts. Man of the Match:* T. M. Dilshan.

Although Rahul Dravid was back in India for the birth of his second child, and Kallis fell to the first ball of the match, Bangalore still looked set for a big score as Pietersen finally got going. But he fell trying an audacious switch-hit against Vettori, and the other batsmen failed to accelerate in the second half, scoring 75 in the last ten overs – one more than in the first ten. Then some poor out-cricket ensured Bangalore's third successive defeat: Delhi started the 17th over still needing 43, but in that over Robin Uthappa misjudged a catch at long-on – it went for four – then next ball Prabhu

Appanna failed to get behind a ball at deep midwicket, and it squeezed through his legs for another boundary to put Delhi back in charge.

At Cape Town, April 26, 2009 (floodlit). **Kings XI Punjab won by 27 runs.** Toss: Kings XI Punjab. **Kings XI Punjab 139-6** (20 overs) (K. C. Sangakkara 60, I. K. Pathan 39); **Rajasthan Royals 112-7** (20 overs) (R. A. Jadeja 37, S. K. Warne 34*; Y. A. Abdulla 3-21). *Kings XI Punjab 2 pts. Man of the Match:* K. C. Sangakkara.

The defending champions sorely missed the services of their other Shane – Watson – as their top order misfired again in the face of a modest total from Punjab, who themselves had looked in danger at 48-4, only to be rescued by a stand of 75 in ten overs between Sangakkara and Irfan Pathan.

At Durban, April 27, 2009. **Deccan Chargers won by six wickets.** Toss: Deccan Chargers. **Chennai Super Kings 165-6** (20 overs) (M. L. Hayden 49, J. D. P. Oram 41*); **Deccan Chargers 169-4** (19.3 overs) (A. C. Gilchrist 44, H. H. Gibbs 69*). *Deccan Chargers 2 pts. Man of the Match:* H. H. Gibbs.

Gilchrist's 19-ball firework display and a more restrained effort from Gibbs (56 balls) kept their side in charge despite some tight middle-overs bowling from spinners Muralitharan (4–0–17–1) and Raina (4–0–18–2). Chennai's total was around 20 short of par on a good batting pitch, despite some fierce striking from the tall and broad-shouldered pair of Hayden and Oram at either end of the innings.

At Port Elizabeth, April 27, 2009 (floodlit). **Mumbai Indians won by 92 runs.** Toss: Mumbai Indians. **Mumbai Indians 187-6** (20 overs) (S. T. Jayasuriya 52, S. R. Tendulkar 68; L. R. Shukla 3-25); **Kolkata Knight Riders 95** (15.2 overs) (S. C. Ganguly 34; S. L. Malinga 3-11, A. M. Nayar 3-13). *Mumbai Indians 2 pts. Man of the Match:* S. R. Tendulkar.

Tendulkar and Jayasuriya led a furious assault on some toothless bowling: the hundred partnership came up in just 52 balls, and they eventually put on 127 in 12.2 overs, setting the platform for a formidable total. Kolkata's batting fizzled out miserably as Malinga and Abhishek Nayar made smart use of pace and length.

At Centurion, April 28, 2009 (floodlit). **Rajasthan Royals won by five wickets.** Toss: Delhi Daredevils. **Delhi Daredevils 143-7** (20 overs) (A. B. de Villiers 50); **Rajasthan Royals 147-5** (18.3 overs) (G. C. Smith 44*, Y. K. Pathan 62*; A. Mishra 3-34). *Rajasthan Royals 2 pts. Man of the Match:* Y. K. Pathan.

At 64-5, needing a further 80 runs off the last nine overs, Shane Warne's team looked out of contention, but Yusuf Pathan clattered 62 from 30 balls, with six sixes and three fours, to inflict Delhi's first defeat after three victories.*

At Durban, April 29, 2009. **Royal Challengers Bangalore won by five wickets.** Toss: Kolkata Knight Riders. **Kolkata Knight Riders 139-6** (20 overs) (C. H. Gayle 40, M. N. van Wyk 43*); **Royal Challengers Bangalore 143-5** (19.5 overs) (S. P. Goswami 43; B. J. Hodge 3-29). *Royal Challengers Bangalore 2 pts. Man of the Match:* M. V. Boucher.

Kevin Pietersen returned to England for the Tests against West Indies with a smile after getting most of his decisions right: he included three spinners, surprised everyone by bowling the first over of the day himself, and proved it was a wise move by having his opposite number Brendon McCullum caught with the very first ball. He couldn't quite finish it off himself, falling to Hodge for 13; Shreevats Goswami anchored the innings, and Boucher supplied the necessary oomph at the end, slamming 25 from 13 balls.*

At Durban, April 29, 2009 (floodlit). **Kings XI Punjab won by three runs.** Toss: Kings XI Punjab. **Kings XI Punjab 119-8** (20 overs) (K. C. Sangakkara 45*); **Mumbai Indians 116-7** (20 overs) (J-P. Duminy 59). *Kings XI Punjab 2 pts. Man of the Match:* K. C. Sangakkara.

Tight bowling and athletic fielding – plus Yusuf Abdulla (4–0–19–2) staying calm in the pressure-cooker last over when 12 were needed – allowed Punjab to defend a modest total against Mumbai, whose later batsmen were again found wanting after the early departures of Jayasuriya (first ball) and Tendulkar (for one).

At Centurion, April 30, 2009. **Delhi Daredevils won by six wickets.** Toss: Delhi Daredevils. **Deccan Chargers 148-9** (20 overs) (D. R. Smith 48); **Delhi Daredevils 150-4** (18.4 overs) (T. M. Dilshan 52*, K. D. Karthik 41). *Delhi Daredevils 2 pts. Man of the Match:* D. P. Nannes.

Delhi left out the off-form V. V. S. Laxman, while Glenn McGrath spun yarns in the dugout as his replacement, Dirk Nannes, continued his sparkling form, dispatching the dangerous pair of Gilchrist and Gibbs early on to end the Chargers' unbeaten run after four straight victories. There were more changes of fortune to come, though none as dramatic as Fidel Edwards's loss of control in what became the final over of the match – Dilshan hit 4426 from the balls he could reach among a wide, a no-ball and a bouncer.

At Centurion, April 30, 2009 (floodlit). **Chennai Super Kings won by 38 runs.** Toss: Rajasthan Royals. **Chennai Super Kings 164-5** (20 overs) (S. K. Raina 98); **Rajasthan Royals 126** (19.3 overs) (R. A. Jadeja 37; L. Balaji 4-21). *Chennai Super Kings 2 pts. Man of the Match:* S. K. Raina.

   Suresh Raina celebrated after smacking his 54th ball, from Munaf Patel, through the covers in the final over to reach what the scoreboard said was his hundred. In reality, though, he had only 98 – and was out next ball. He hit ten fours and five sixes. But he had done enough to ensure a comfortable victory, Chennai's first in three attempts against Rajasthan, whose batting was again a disappointment.

At East London, May 1, 2009. **Mumbai Indians won by nine runs.** Toss: Mumbai Indians. **Mumbai Indians 148-6** (20 overs) (S. R. Tendulkar 34, J-P. Duminy 52*); **Kolkata Knight Riders 139-6** (20 overs) (B. J. Hodge 73, M. N. van Wyk 32; Z. Khan 3-31). *Mumbai Indians 2 pts. Man of the Match:* J-P. Duminy.

   Kolkata looked set for a rare victory after restricting Mumbai to 148, but none of their batsmen, Hodge excepted, showed much gumption against Zaheer Khan and company.

At Durban, May 1, 2009 (floodlit). **Royal Challengers Bangalore won by eight runs.** Toss: Royal Challengers Bangalore. **Royal Challengers Bangalore 145-9** (20 overs) (R. E. van der Merwe 35; Y. A. Abdulla 4-36, Yuvraj Singh 3-22); **Kings XI Punjab 137-7** (20 overs) (Yuvraj Singh 50). *Royal Challengers Bangalore 2 pts. Man of the Match:* Yuvraj Singh.

   Yuvraj Singh took a hat-trick, promoted himself to open as Ravi Bopara had returned to England, and scored a rapid half-century… but still could not stop his side imploding: from 70-0 in the tenth over Punjab's batting fell apart, and when 13 were needed from the final over Praveen Kumar took two wickets and conceded only four runs.

At Port Elizabeth, May 2, 2009. **Rajasthan Royals won by three wickets.** Toss: Deccan Chargers. **Deccan Chargers 141-5** (20 overs) (A. C. Gilchrist 39, R. G. Sharma 38, T. L. Suman 41*); **Rajasthan Royals 142-7** (19.4 overs) (L. A. Carseldine 39, A. S. Raut 36*). *Rajasthan Royals 2 pts. Man of the Match:* Y. K. Pathan.

   Two unsung Indians, Tirumalasetti Suman and Abhishek Raut, excelled in a see-saw battle. Suman top-scored for the Chargers with 41 from 30 balls and, after Yusuf Pathan had blasted 24 from 14 balls, Raut kept his nerve to ensure Rajasthan collected the 11 runs they needed from the last two overs.*

At Johannesburg, May 2, 2009 (floodlit). **Chennai Super Kings won by 18 runs.** Toss: Delhi Daredevils. **Chennai Super Kings 163** (20 overs) (M. L. Hayden 30, S. K. Raina 32, S. Badrinath 45; D. P. Nannes 3-27, A. Nehra 3-27); **Delhi Daredevils 145-8** (20 overs) (D. A. Warner 51, K. D. Karthik 52; S. B. Jakati 4-24). *Chennai Super Kings 2 pts. Man of the Match:* S. B. Jakati.

   Delhi looked likelier winners when they needed 36 from the last 26 balls with seven wickets left, but Dhoni cannily kept the spinners on: Muralitharan (4–0–22–1) and the Goan slow left-armer Shadab Jakati throttled the batsmen.

At Port Elizabeth, May 3, 2009. **Kings XI Punjab won by six wickets.** Toss: Kolkata Knight Riders. **Kolkata Knight Riders 153-3** (20 overs) (B. J. Hodge 70*); **Kings XI Punjab 154-4** (20 overs) (S. M. Katich 34, D. P. M. D. Jayawardene 52*). *Kings XI Punjab 2 pts. Man of the Match:* D. P. M. D. Jayawardene.

   Hodge continued his spectacular form with a fine 70 from 43 balls, with ten fours and a six, but Punjab's batsmen made the most of numerous fielding errors to secure a last-ball win.*

At Johannesburg, May 3, 2009 (floodlit). **Royal Challengers Bangalore won by nine wickets.** Toss: Mumbai Indians. **Mumbai Indians 149-4** (20 overs) (S. T. Jayasuriya 52, D. J. Bravo 50*; D. du Preez 3-32); **Royal Challengers Bangalore 150-1** (18.1 overs) (J. H. Kallis 69*, R. V. Uthappa 66*). *Royal Challengers Bangalore 2 pts. Man of the Match:* J. H. Kallis.

   Bangalore continued their recovery, breezing to their third successive victory thanks mainly to Kallis, one of the disappointments of the first IPL, and Uthappa, who had looked miserable in the first half of this one. They put on 126 in 15.1 overs, hitting 13 fours and four sixes between them.*

At East London, May 4, 2009 (floodlit). **Chennai Super Kings won by 78 runs.** Toss: Chennai Super Kings. **Chennai Super Kings 178-3** (20 overs) (M. Vijay 31, M. L. Hayden 43, M. S. Dhoni 58*, S. K. Raina 32); **Deccan Chargers 100** (14.4 overs) (D. R. Smith 49; S. B. Jakati 4-22). *Chennai Super Kings 2 pts. Man of the Match:* M. S. Dhoni.

Some ruthless power-hitting from Hayden (26 balls), Dhoni (37) and Raina (19) set up an imposing target, which the Chargers never threatened after the early departures of Gilchrist, Gibbs and Laxman for ducks. Dwayne Smith blasted five sixes in his 49 from 23 balls, but the other batsmen struggled against Shadab Jakati, who took his second four-for in only his third IPL match (he didn't bowl in the first one), as Chennai went top of the table.

At Durban, May 5, 2009. **Rajasthan Royals won by 78 runs.** Toss: Kings XI Punjab. **Rajasthan Royals 211-4** (20 overs) (N. V. Ojha 68, G. C. Smith 77, R. A. Jadeja 33); **Kings XI Punjab 133-8** (20 overs) (Yuvraj Singh 48; Amit Singh 3-9). *Rajasthan Royals 2 pts. Man of the Match:* G. C. Smith.

Graeme Smith, who had scored only 65 runs in his first six matches, returned to form with a blistering 77* from 44 balls, including 12 fours and a six. He put on 135 for the first wicket in 14.5 overs with Naman Ojha, who matched him for big hitting (five fours and five sixes), and the later batsmen made sure the total reached 200 – the only time that barrier was breached in this tournament (there were 11 scores of 200-plus in the first IPL, in India). Punjab lost two wickets in the first over, and never looked like climbing the mountain.

At Durban, May 5, 2009 (floodlit). **Delhi Daredevils won by nine wickets.** Toss: Kolkata Knight Riders. **Kolkata Knight Riders 154-3** (20 overs) (M. N. van Wyk 74, B. B. McCullum 35, M. C. Henriques 30*); **Delhi Daredevils 157-1** (19 overs) (G. Gambhir 71*, D. A. Warner 36, T. M. Dilshan 42*). *Delhi Daredevils 2 pts. Man of the Match:* G. Gambhir.

Morne van Wyk, who popped up to open after Chris Gayle left to captain West Indies in the Tests in England, came up with a superb 48-ball innings, studded with 11 fours, to take his side to a handy total. But Delhi, anchored by Gambhir, had little difficulty knocking off the runs, helped by some shoddy out-fielding.

At Centurion, May 6, 2009 (floodlit). **Deccan Chargers won by 19 runs.** Toss: Deccan Chargers. **Deccan Chargers 145-6** (20 overs) (R. G. Sharma 38); **Mumbai Indians 126-8** (20 overs) (J-P. Duminy 52; R. G. Sharma 4-6). *Deccan Chargers 2 pts. Man of the Match:* R. G. Sharma.

The victory which ended the Chargers' three-match losing streak looked certain from the moment R. P. Singh (4-0-19-2) dismissed Jayasuriya and Tendulkar with successive balls in the second over of Mumbai's reply. Duminy worked hard for a half-century, but any lingering hopes were killed off by Rohit Sharma's part-time off-breaks, which brought him four wickets in five balls, including a hat-trick.

At Centurion, May 7, 2009. **Rajasthan Royals won by seven wickets.** Toss: Rajasthan Royals. **Royal Challengers Bangalore 105** (20 overs) (Amit Singh 4-19, R. A. Jadeja 3-15); **Rajasthan Royals 107-3** (15 overs) (N. V. Ojha 52*). *Rajasthan Royals 2 pts. Man of the Match:* Amit Singh.

Bangalore's batsmen froze against the pace of the inexperienced Amit Singh from Gujarat. With Naman Ojha making his second successive half-century, Rajasthan romped home with as many as 30 balls remaining.

At Centurion, May 7, 2009 (floodlit). **Chennai Super Kings won by 12 runs** (D/L method). Toss: Chennai Super Kings. **Chennai Super Kings 185-3** (18 overs) (M. L. Hayden 89, S. K. Raina 32, M. S. Dhoni 56*); **Kings XI Punjab 174-3** (18 overs) (S. M. Katich 50, Yuvraj Singh 58*, D. P. M. D. Jayawardene 44*). *Chennai Super Kings 2 pts. Man of the Match:* M. L. Hayden.

A brief rain interruption early in Chennai's innings reduced this to a 18-overs match: Punjab's target was revised upwards slightly to 187. Hayden, who hit eight fours and six sixes from 58 balls, powered his side to a big total, but Jayawardene and Yuvraj Singh shared an unbroken partnership of 90, and looked set to clinch victory before Raina, bowling the 15th and 17th overs, conceded only eight runs (plus two leg-byes). That left Punjab needing an unlikely 25 from Lakshmipathy Balaji's final over of the match.

At East London, May 8, 2009 (floodlit). **Delhi Daredevils won by seven wickets.** Toss: Mumbai Indians. **Mumbai Indians 116** (20 overs) (D. J. Bravo 35; R. Bhatia 3-15); **Delhi Daredevils 118-3** (18.5 overs) (A. B. de Villiers 50*). *Delhi Daredevils 2 pts. Man of the Match:* A. Nehra.

Mumbai, the IPL's most expensive franchise, made changes in a bid to salvage their season: Jayasuriya was dropped, but his replacement, the Australian Luke Ronchi, was out second ball, and Duminy also departed for a duck in the first over. Tendulkar dropped to No. 4, but he was out for 15 as his side failed to sparkle: Delhi chased down their modest target with relative ease.

At Kimberley, May 9, 2009. **Kings XI Punjab won by three wickets.** Toss: Kings XI Punjab. **Deccan Chargers 168-5** (20 overs) (A. Symonds 60*, Y. Venugopal Rao 32); **Kings XI Punjab 169-7** (19.5 overs) (S. Sohal 30, D. P. M. D. Jayawardene 43). *Kings XI Punjab 2 pts. Man of the Match: D. P. M. D. Jayawardene.*

Playing his first game of the tournament, Andrew Symonds made an instant impact with a quickfire 60* from 36 balls, with four sixes and two fours, to set up a challenging target. Jayawardene looked to be taking Punjab home before he was run out with 20 still wanted – but Brett Lee swung Ryan Harris for a big six to settle any nerves.

At Kimberley, May 9, 2009 (floodlit). **Chennai Super Kings won by seven wickets.** Toss: Rajasthan Royals. **Rajasthan Royals 140-7** (20 overs) (G. C. Smith 30); **Chennai Super Kings 141-3** (18.2 overs) (M. L. Hayden 48, S. Badrinath 59*). *Chennai Super Kings 2 pts. Man of the Match: S. Badrinath.*

Warne said beforehand that Chennai were poor chasers, and was nearly proved right as he and Yusuf Pathan kept a tight leash on the scoring on a big-turning pitch. But Hayden would not be subdued, then Badrinath hit out, ignoring the opposition's sledging. He hit nine fours and a six, and in the end forced Warne to eat his words.

At Port Elizabeth, May 10, 2009. **Mumbai Indians won by 16 runs.** Toss: Mumbai Indians. **Mumbai Indians 157-2** (20 overs) (A. M. Rahane 62*, J-P. Duminy 59*); **Royal Challengers Bangalore 141-7** (20 overs) (M. V. Boucher 48*). *Mumbai Indians 2 pts. Man of the Match: J-P. Duminy.*

Desperate for a win after three straight defeats, Mumbai lost Tendulkar for a duck, but recovered thanks to a third-wicket stand of 104* between Duminy and Ajinkya Rahane. Bangalore struggled to 58-4 at halfway, and fell short in the end despite a typical innings from the resilient Boucher.

At Johannesburg, May 10, 2009 (floodlit). **Delhi Daredevils won by seven wickets.** Toss: Delhi Daredevils. **Kolkata Knight Riders 123-8** (20 overs) (S. C. Ganguly 44, A. B. Agarkar 39; A. Mishra 3-14); **Delhi Daredevils 125-3** (17.1 overs) (D. A. Warner 36, A. B. de Villiers 40*). *Delhi Daredevils 2 pts. Man of the Match: A. Mishra.*

Delhi underlined their standing as one of the tournament favourites, ending Kolkata's chances of reaching the semi-finals with relative ease after Nannes (4–0–15–2), Nehra (4–0–29–2) and Mishra helped restrict the Knight Riders to a modest total.

At Kimberley, May 11, 2009 (floodlit). **Deccan Chargers won by 53 runs.** Toss: Deccan Chargers. **Deccan Chargers 166-7** (20 overs) (A. Symonds 30, D. R. Smith 47; Y. K. Pathan 3-34); **Rajasthan Royals 113** (19.3 overs) (S. A. Asnodkar 44; R. G. Sharma 3-12). *Deccan Chargers 2 pts. Man of the Match: D. R. Smith.*

The Chargers completed their biggest victory in terms of runs thanks to significant contributions from two of their lower-key overseas signings: Dwayne Smith smashed four sixes (but no fours) from 32 balls to lift the total, then Chaminda Vaas, playing his first game of the tournament, bowled with great nous (if at a sedate pace) for 4–0–19–2 as Rajasthan were throttled early on.

At Centurion, May 12, 2009. **Royal Challengers Bangalore won by six wickets.** Toss: Royal Challengers Bangalore. **Kolkata Knight Riders 173-4** (20 overs) (B. B. McCullum 84*, D. J. Hussey 43); **Royal Challengers Bangalore 176-4** (19.2 overs) (J. H. Kallis 32, L. R. P. L. Taylor 81*). *Royal Challengers Bangalore 2 pts. Man of the Match: L. R. P. L. Taylor.*

McCullum batted through the innings, hitting ten fours and two sixes from 64 balls, and was helped by David Hussey's 27-ball blitz in setting up a daunting total: but still Kolkata couldn't win, as Ross Taylor hammered 81 from just 33 balls, with seven fours and five sixes of his own. It meant that the IPL's most glamorous franchise, could not now reach the semi-finals.

At Centurion, May 12, 2009 (floodlit). **Mumbai Indians won by eight wickets.** Toss: Kings XI Punjab. **Kings XI Punjab 119-9** (20 overs) (S. Sohal 43); **Mumbai Indians 122-2** (16.2 overs) (D. J. Bravo 70*, S. R. Tendulkar 41*). *Mumbai Indians 2 pts. Man of the Match: Harbhajan Singh.*

Mumbai's three off-spinners – Duminy (4–0–15–2), Harbhajan Singh (4–0–9–1) and Ajinkya Rahane (1–0–5–1) – stifled Punjab's eight left-handers, then Bravo knocked off the modest target almost single-handed.

At Durban, May 13, 2009 (floodlit). **Delhi Daredevils won by 12 runs.** Toss: Deccan Chargers. **Delhi Daredevils 173-7** (20 overs) (T. M. Dilshan 37, A. B. de Villiers 44, K. D. Karthik 44*); **Deccan Chargers 161** (19.4 overs) (A. C. Gilchrist 64, A. Symonds 41; P. Sangwan 3-18, R. Bhatia 4-15). *Delhi Daredevils 2 pts. Man of the Match: R. Bhatia.*

Sehwag returned to the Delhi fold after missing the previous four games due to injury, but he was hardly needed as the in-form trio of Dilshan, de Villiers and Karthik ensured a big total. Deccan's Aussie heavyweights Gilchrist and Symonds led the chase, but two little-known Indians, 18-year-old left-arm paceman Pradeep Sangwan and the medium-paced all-rounder Rajat Bhatia, dismissed them and went on to wrap up victory.

At Durban, May 14, 2009. **Royal Challengers Bangalore won by two wickets.** Toss: Chennai Super Kings. **Chennai Super Kings 129** (19.4 overs) (M. L. Hayden 60); **Royal Challengers Bangalore 132-8** (19.4 overs) (L. R. P. L. Taylor 46, V. Kohli 38). *Royal Challengers Bangalore 2 pts. Man of the Match: L. R. P. L. Taylor.*

Hayden punched another 60 runs from 38 balls, but had little support at the other end (the next-highest score was Dhoni's 18). Kumble opened the bowling and kept the runs down, finishing with 4–0–12–2, and Kallis (4–0–18–2) also ensured that the brakes remained on. Enterprising innings from Virat Kohli, who took calculated risks against Muralitharan, and Taylor ensured that Bangalore ended Chennai's five-match winning streak.

At Durban, May 14, 2009 (floodlit). **Rajasthan Royals won by two runs.** Toss: Rajasthan Royals. **Rajasthan Royals 145-7** (20 overs) (R. J. Quiney 51, R. A. Jadeja 42); **Mumbai Indians 143** (19.5 overs) (S. R. Tendulkar 40, A. M. Nayar 35; S. K. Warne 3-24). *Rajasthan Royals 2 pts. Man of the Match: S. K. Warne.*

Warne orchestrated a victory that had seemed to be slipping away when Abhishek Nayar was using the long handle to great effect: he hit four fours and a six from 18 balls, and while he and Tendulkar were together Mumbai were favourites. But Tendulkar was trapped in front by Warne, and the rest of the batsmen were like rabbits in the headlights. They entered the last over, bowled by Munaf Patel, needing just four runs with only seven wickets down, but three wickets in four balls, two of them run-outs, left them short.

At Bloemfontein, May 15, 2009 (floodlit). **Kings XI Punjab won by six wickets.** Toss: Kings XI Punjab. **Delhi Daredevils 120-9** (20 overs) (K. D. Karthik 32; B. Lee 3-15); **Kings XI Punjab 123-4** (19.1 overs) (K. C. Sangakkara 43*). *Kings XI Punjab 2 pts. Man of the Match: B. Lee.*

Punjab needed to win to keep their semi-final hopes alive, and did so in the end mainly thanks to their fast bowlers Lee and Sreesanth (4–0–20–2), who kept the Delhi total down. Punjab themselves stuttered to 35-3 before Sangakkara steadied the ship, and finally Irfan Pathan arrived to bludgeon three sixes in the last two overs, from the inexperienced Pradeep Sangwan and a rusty Farveez Maharoof.

At Port Elizabeth, May 16, 2009. **Chennai Super Kings won by seven wickets.** Toss: Mumbai Indians. **Mumbai Indians 147-5** (20 overs) (S. T. Jayasuriya 30, J-P. Duminy 62, A. M. Nayar 35*); **Chennai Super Kings 151-3** (19.1 overs) (M. L. Hayden 60*). *Chennai Super Kings 2 pts. Man of the Match: M. L. Hayden.*

Mumbai lost the plot – and their chances of making the semi-finals, barring improbable results elsewhere – in the final overs of either innings. When Mumbai batted they managed only 17 from their last 13 balls, whereas Chennai conjured up 30, to win with five balls to spare. The vital innings was played by Hayden, who eschewed his usual all-out attack to make 60 from 57 balls – his first boundary came from his 34th ball.*

At Johannesburg, May 16, 2009 (floodlit). **Deccan Chargers won by six wickets.** Toss: Deccan Chargers. **Kolkata Knight Riders 160-5** (20 overs) (S. C. Ganguly 33, B. J. Hodge 48, D. J. Hussey 43); **Deccan Chargers 166-4** (20 overs) (A. C. Gilchrist 43, T. L. Suman 31, R. G. Sharma 32*). *Deccan Chargers 2 pts. Man of the Match: R. G. Sharma.*

David Hussey did not arrive until the end of the 15th over, but he hammered 43 from 17 balls with four sixes to propel Kolkata to a big total; however, his sparkling display was trumped by the nerveless Rohit Sharma. Deccan needed 21 from the last over, bowled by Bangladesh's Mashrafe bin Mortaza, and Sharma got them. The first delivery was called a no-ball as there were only three fielders inside the circle: Sharma hit it for four. Three balls later he clouted a huge six over midwicket, then a wide, a two and a four left the scores level as the final ball was bowled: Sharma joyously pulled it for six.

At Johannesburg, May 17, 2009. **Kings XI Punjab won by one run.** Toss: Deccan Chargers. **Kings XI Punjab 134-7** (20 overs) (K. C. Sangakkara 56; R. P. Singh 3-26); **Deccan Chargers 133-8** (20 overs) (R. G. Sharma 42; Yuvraj Singh 3-13). *Kings XI Punjab 2 pts. Man of the Match:* Yuvraj Singh.

Gilchrist and his men were back on the field only a few hours after their last-ball win over Kolkata, and they were again involved in another thriller: this time Rohit Sharma could not quite conjure victory, falling in the last over for a 26-ball 42. Four needed from the last three balls from Irfan Pathan, but that proved beyond the tail. Earlier Yuvraj Singh had taken his second hat-trick of the tournament.

At Bloemfontein, May 17, 2009 (floodlit). **Delhi Daredevils won by 14 runs.** Toss: Delhi Daredevils. **Delhi Daredevils 150-3** (20 overs) (A. B. de Villiers 79*, T. M. Dilshan 33); **Rajasthan Royals 136-9** (20 overs) (J. Botha 37; A. Mishra 3-33). *Delhi Daredevils 2 pts. Man of the Match:* A. B. de Villiers.

Delhi made a poor start, losing India's Test openers Gambhir and Sehwag for single-figure scores – but de Villiers (55 balls) and Dilshan repaired the damage before a powerful final thrust from Karthik (23* from 11 balls) ensured a challenging target. Rajasthan also stumbled at the start – they were 24-3 in the seventh over – and were never really on terms after that as Delhi confirmed their semi-final place.

At Centurion, May 18, 2009 (floodlit). **Kolkata Knight Riders won by seven wickets.** Toss: Chennai Super Kings. **Chennai Super Kings 188-3** (20 overs) (G. J. Bailey 30, S. K. Raina 52, M. S. Dhoni 40*); **Kolkata Knight Riders 189-3** (20 overs) (B. B. McCullum 81, B. J. Hodge 71*). *Kolkata Knight Riders 2 pts. Man of the Match:* B. J. Hodge.

After almost a month of misery, controversy and failed strategies, Kolkata finally managed a victory, only their second in 13 games. Imperious strokeplay from McCullum kick-started their successful chase: he collected 11 fours and three sixes from 48 balls before handing the baton to Hodge, whose 71* came from 44 deliveries. Chennai's total owed much to a useful opening stand of 59 in six overs between Parthiv Patel (25) and George Bailey, then Raina and Dhoni put on 74 for the third wicket.

At Johannesburg, May 19, 2009 (floodlit). **Royal Challengers Bangalore won by seven wickets.** Toss: Delhi Daredevils. **Delhi Daredevils 134-7** (20 overs) (K. D. Karthik 31; P. Kumar 3-30); **Royal Challengers Bangalore 135-3** (19 overs) (J. H. Kallis 58*, R. Dravid 38). *Royal Challengers Bangalore 2 pts. Man of the Match:* J. H. Kallis.

Sehwag's horrendous form continued: he departed for a duck in Praveen Kumar's first over of the match, as did Mithun Manhas. Bangalore also started slowly, scoring only 27 in the first six overs, but Sehwag fatally delayed the introduction of spin until the ninth over, by which time Kallis and Dravid were well set.

At Durban, May 20, 2009. **Kolkata Knight Riders won by four wickets.** Toss: Kolkata Knight Riders. **Rajasthan Royals 101-9** (20 overs) (C. K. Langeveldt 3-15); **Kolkata Knight Riders 102-6** (19.3 overs) (L. R. Shukla 48*). *Kolkata Knight Riders 2 pts. Man of the Match:* L. R. Shukla.

Coach Buchanan's eccentric decision to pack his Kolkata team with batsmen had kept out local favourite Charl Langeveldt until now, but he made an instant impact with a first-ball wicket, and added two more in a four-over spell which never allowed Rajasthan to take off (Langeveldt did, however, pick up an injury which stopped him playing for Derbyshire later in the year). Rajasthan's eventual 101 equalled Kolkata's own score against Deccan Chargers as the lowest first-innings total of this tournament, but with Warne inspiring his men with tight lines and innovative field-placing, Kolkata still had trouble in chasing it, crashing to 45-6 before Laxmi Ratan Shukla and Ajit Agarkar (13*) dug in. Defeat for Rajasthan scuppered the holders' semi-final hopes.

At Durban, May 20, 2009 (floodlit). **Chennai Super Kings won by 24 runs.** Toss: Chennai Super Kings. **Chennai Super Kings 116-9** (20 overs) (P. A. Patel 32); **Kings XI Punjab 92-8** (20 overs). *Chennai Super Kings 2 pts. Man of the Match:* M. Muralitharan.

Sreesanth's ecstatic celebrations after dismissing Badrinath and Dhoni in the space of three balls were a highlight of Chennai's innings. Punjab's hopes were high after restricting their opponents to 116, but again there were twists in the plot: Dhoni had included an extra off-spinner to counter Punjab's many left-handers, and it paid off as Muralitharan (4–0–8–2), Raina (4–0–17–2) and Ravichandran Ashwin (4–0–13–2) choked the life out of the batsmen. Only Luke Pomersbach (26) and Irfan Pathan (14) reached double figures as Chennai confirmed their semi-final place.

At Centurion, May 21, 2009. Delhi Daredevils won by four wickets. Toss: Delhi Daredevils. **Mumbai Indians** 165-8 (20 overs) (S. R. Tendulkar 46, A. M. Rahane 56; D. P. Nannes 3-27); **Delhi Daredevils** 166-6 (17.3 overs) (G. Gambhir 47, V. Sehwag 50; Harbhajan Singh 4-17). *Delhi Daredevils 2 pts. Man of the Match:* V. Sehwag.

Sehwag finally made his first half-century of this tournament, from just 26 balls, to underpin his side's successful run-chase. Harbhajan Singh caused them some anxious moments, twice taking two wickets with successive balls, but by then Delhi were nearly home for the victory which confirmed their place at the top of the group table.

At Centurion, May 21, 2009 (floodlit). Royal Challengers Bangalore won by 12 runs. Toss: Royal Challengers Bangalore. **Royal Challengers Bangalore** 170-4 (20 overs) (M. K. Pandey 114*); **Deccan Chargers** 158-6 (20 overs) (H. H. Gibbs 60). *Royal Challengers Bangalore 2 pts. Man of the Match:* M. K. Pandey.

Manish Pandey made the final league game special by becoming the first Indian to make a century in the IPL – it was the second hundred of this tournament, after A. B. de Villiers's earlier one for Delhi, and the eighth overall in the IPL's two seasons. Pandey, a 19-year-old from Karnataka, started uncertainly and was dropped early on by R. P. Singh, but he came into his own after a few streaky shots to swat, cut, sweep and caress the bowlers to all parts. He finished with ten fours and four sixes from 73 balls. In reply, Gibbs made 60 from 43 balls, but the Chargers were rarely in the hunt, although their consolation was qualification for the semis, ahead of Punjab on run-rate.

Semi-finals

At Centurion, May 22, 2009 (floodlit). Deccan Chargers won by six wickets. Toss: Deccan Chargers. **Delhi Daredevils** 153-8 (20 overs) (V. Sehwag 39, T. M. Dilshan 65; R. J. Harris 3-27); **Deccan Chargers** 154-4 (17.4 overs) (A. C. Gilchrist 85; A. Mishra 3-19). *Man of the Match:* A. C. Gilchrist.

Adam Gilchrist's ruthless 35-ball assault will be long remembered: he battered a Delhi attack containing two of the tournament's best fast bowlers – the left-arm pair of Nannes and Nehra – to make a challenging target under lights look as simple as making scrambled eggs. He clattered ten fours and five sixes in his 85, putting fine innings by Sehwag and Dilshan for Delhi (who regrouped well after losing Gambhir and Warner for ducks in the first over) into the shade.

At Johannesburg, May 23, 2009 (floodlit). Royal Challengers Bangalore won by six wickets. Toss: Royal Challengers Bangalore. **Chennai Super Kings** 146-5 (20 overs) (P. A. Patel 36); **Royal Challengers Bangalore** 149-4 (18.5 overs) (M. K. Pandey 48, R. Dravid 44). *Man of the Match:* M. K. Pandey.

Mahendra Singh Dhoni is by nature an instinctive player, but he got it wrong this time: after promoting himself to No. 3, his 28 from 30 balls slowed Chennai down, and they fell around 20 short of a par score. Led by Pandey, who followed his century in the previous match with another mature innings containing some classical shots, Bangalore secured a place in the final. Pandey shared a crucial stand of 72 with the cool Dravid, and when they were out Virat Kohli (24) and Ross Taylor (17*) hit two sixes apiece to ensure victory with a cushion of seven balls to spare.*

FINAL

DECCAN CHARGERS v ROYAL CHALLENGERS BANGALORE

At Johannesburg, May 24, 2009 (floodlit). Deccan Chargers won by six runs. Toss: Royal Challengers Bangalore.

Kumble's decision to open the bowling was fully justified as he dismissed the dangerous Gilchrist third ball, but Gibbs took up the cudgels, helped by Symonds, who spanked 33 from 21 balls as his side posted a reasonable total. Bangalore also struggled at first, but fancied their chances at 99 for four after 14 overs... then lost Ross Taylor and Virat Kohli to successive balls from Symonds, who had a say in everything – batting, fielding, sledging, decision-making. The last over started with Bangalore needing 15, their last pair at the crease, and R. P. Singh ensured a fairytale victory for the Deccan Chargers, who came from last in the inaugural edition of the IPL to first in this.

Man of the Match: A. Kumble. *Man of the Series:* A. C. Gilchrist.

Deccan Chargers

		B	4	6
*†A. C. Gilchrist *b 11*	0	3	0	0
H. H. Gibbs *not out*	53	48	3	2
T. L. Suman *c 2 b 10*	10	11	1	0
A. Symonds *b 11*	33	21	4	1
R. G. Sharma *c 2 b 11*	24	23	1	1
Y. Venugopal Rao *c 5 b 11*	0	2	0	0
A. A. Bilakhia *lbw b 10*	6	7	0	0
R. J. Harris *not out*	9	5	0	0
L-b 2, w 6	8			

6 overs: 31-2   (20 overs) 143-6

1/0 2/18 3/58 4/110 5/115 6/134

R. P. Singh, P. P. Ojha and H. S. Bansal did not bat.

Kumble 4–0–16–4; Kallis 4–0–24–0; Vinay Kumar 4–0–30–2; van der Merwe 4–0–28–0;.

RC Bangalore

		B	4	6
J. H. Kallis *b 9*	15	17	3	0
M. K. Pandey *c 1 b 10*	4	8	0	0
R. E. van der Merwe *st 1 b 10*	32	21	1	3
R. Dravid *b 11*	9	13	0	0
L. R. P. L. Taylor *c 6 b 4*	27	20	3	1
V. Kohli *st 1 b 4*	7	8	1	0
†M. V. Boucher *c 2 b 11*	5	6	1	0
R. V. Uthappa *not out*	17	15	0	1
P. Kumar *c 9 b 10*	2	3	0	0
R. Vinay Kumar *c 11 b 8*	8	8	1	0
*A. Kumble *not out*	1	1	0	0
L-b 9, w 1	10			

6 overs: 36-1   (20 overs) 137-9

1/20 2/36 3/57 4/79 5/99 6/99 7/107 8/110 9/129

Harris 4–1–34–1; Singh 4–0–16–1; Symonds 3–0–18–2; Ojha 4–0–28–3; Bansal 4–0–23–2; Sharma 1–0–9–0.

Umpires: R. E. Koertzen and S. J. A. Taufel.   Third umpire: D. J. Harper.   Referee: J. Srinath.

IPL FINALS

2007-08 Rajasthan Royals beat Chennai Super Kings by three wickets in Mumbai.
2008-09 Deccan Chargers beat Royal Challengers Bangalore by six runs at Johannesburg.

DOMESTIC CRICKET IN SOUTH AFRICA, 2008-09

Colin Bryden

The **Titans** dominated South African domestic cricket in 2008-09, winning the four-day SuperSport Series and the 45-over MTN tournament. Their only failure was a costly one: they failed to defend their title in the crowd-pulling Standard Bank Pro20. Instead, the Cape Cobras and the Eagles went forward to the lucrative Indian-financed Champions League as Pro20 finalists. The Titans had qualified in 2007-08, only to be denied when it was cancelled after terrorist attacks in Mumbai.

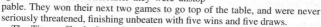

The Centurion-based Titans franchise, captained by Pierre Joubert and coached by Richard Pybus, made a slow start in the first-class competition. After a rain-ruined opening match in Durban, they held on for a draw, with only two wickets standing, against the Cobras. Thereafter they were unstoppable. They won their next two games to go top of the table, and were never seriously threatened, finishing unbeaten with five wins and five draws.

The Titans effectively settled their second first-class title in three seasons with a round to spare: they beat their nearest rivals, the Eagles, by ten wickets in Bloemfontein, thanks to an outstanding performance by Test fast bowler Morne Morkel, who took 12 for 91. This followed his 11 for 56 and career-best 82 not out as the Titans defeated the Warriors on a lively East London pitch in October. Morkel took 30 wickets at 17 in five SuperSport games.

Duif du Toit, Getty Images

Morne Morkel

With Morkel one of four or five players frequently absent on national duty, the Titans relied on strength in depth. Farhaan Behardien was their top scorer, with 588 at 49, but Blake Snijman, Francois du Plessis, Joubert and wicketkeeper Heino Kuhn all batted well, and Jacques Rudolph averaged 75 when he returned for the last four games. In a varied attack, their leading wicket-taker was leg-spinner Imran Tahir, with 32; when Test left-armer Paul Harris was available, they made a fine spin combination. Married to a South African, Tahir qualified for his adopted country in April 2009. Another left-arm spinner, Roelof van der Merwe, played only one four-day game but was the leading performer in the 45-over competition, with 30 wickets – almost double anyone else's total – in 12 matches. The Titans also had the one-day tournament's leading run-scorer in left-hander Gulam Bodi.

Once again punching above their weight from a low player base, defending SuperSport champions the **Eagles**, based in Bloemfontein, were runners-up in all three competitions. Well led by Boeta Dippenaar, who had another consistent season with the bat, they fielded one of South African cricket's rising stars in 19-year-old Rilee Rossouw, a left-hander who hit three first-class centuries and averaged around 40 in the four-day and 45-over formats.

The **Warriors**, based in the Eastern Cape, had two of the top four run-scorers in the first-class tournament in Ashwell Prince and Arno Jacobs, and headed the Pro20 table but failed to reach the final. The **Lions**, from Johannesburg, propped up both limited-overs leagues, but their batsman Alviro Petersen started and finished the SuperSport tournament by scoring two hundreds in a match; bolstered by a handful of games against touring teams and for the amateur side North West, he accumulated 1,376 first-class runs to beat the record for a South African player in the home season, set by H. D. Ackerman in 1997-98.

Despite winning the Pro20, in which Charl Langeveldt confirmed himself as one of the best 20-over bowlers in the world, the **Cape Cobras** were let down by inconsistent batting. Claude Henderson, the 36-year-old left-arm spinner who had joined the Cape Town franchise in August, worked valiantly, bowling an average 50 overs in each first-class match to finish the leading SuperSport wicket-taker with 39.

The **Dolphins** of KwaZulu-Natal finished bottom of the SuperSport table, without a win, though they had the tournament's highest scorer in Imraan Khan, the left-handed opener, who hit 835 runs at 55, including four centuries, and achieved the rare feat of forcing himself into the Test side through weight of runs in a single season.

In the amateur competitions, **Griqualand West** retained the first-class title, while **Boland** won the one-day tournament.

FIRST-CLASS AVERAGES, 2008-09

BATTING

(Qualification: 500 runs)

	M	I	NO	R	HS	100s	Avge	Ct/St
J. F. Mostert (*North West*)	6	11	4	544	126*	2	77.71	4
†A. G. Prince (*Warriors & South Africa*)	12	21	5	1,180	254	3	73.75	10
D. Wiese (*Easterns*)	6	11	3	564	208	2	70.50	8
P. de Bruyn (*Dolphins & KwaZulu-Natal*)	8	11	3	545	116*	1	68.12	9
A. N. Petersen (*Lions, North West & S. Africa A*)	15	27	3	1,376	152	6	57.33	6
C. Williams (*Namibia*)	6	11	0	614	134	2	55.81	8
F. Behardien (*Titans & Northerns*)	11	15	2	702	150*	3	54.00	7
†I. Khan (*Dolphins & South Africa*)	12	20	2	961	145	5	53.38	5
†A. G. Puttick (*Cape Cobras & South Africa A*)	13	24	1	1,206	174	4	52.43	15
†A. Jacobs (*Warriors & South Africa A*)	13	24	3	1,033	131	2	49.19	13
D. J. Vilas (*Lions & Gauteng*)	9	16	1	653	203	3	43.53	32/1

	M	I	NO	R	HS	100s	Avge	Ct/St
A. M. Amla (*Dolphins & South Africa A*)	13	20	1	819	164*	2	43.10	9
F. du Plessis (*Titans*)	9	14	1	536	176	1	41.23	13
H. G. Kuhn (*Titans, Northerns & South Africa A*).	14	23	1	903	203	2	41.04	32/2
†R. R. Rossouw (*Eagles & Free State*)	11	21	1	789	111	3	39.45	16
S. C. Cook (*Lions & Gauteng*)	12	22	1	826	132	1	39.33	2
†V. B. van Jaarsveld (*Lions*)	9	17	1	615	110	1	38.43	8
A. J. A. Gray (*Cape Cobras & W. Province*) . . .	12	23	1	838	188*	3	38.09	12
H. H. Dippenaar (*Eagles*)	10	20	2	673	106	1	37.38	25
†S. van Zyl (*Cape Cobras & Boland*)	9	18	1	618	103*	1	36.35	9
H. Davids (*Cape Cobras & South Africa A*)	10	16	0	580	113	2	36.25	8
N. D. McKenzie (*Lions & South Africa*)	11	19	3	563	110	1	35.18	16
†G. H. Bodi (*Titans*)	10	16	0	560	138	1	35.00	2
J. T. Smuts (*Warriors & Eastern Province*)	11	22	0	758	83	0	34.45	6
D. J. Jacobs (*Warriors*)	10	17	0	577	101	1	33.94	36/2
R. R. Hendricks (*Eagles & Griqualand West*). . .	12	22	3	644	151*	1	33.89	12
R. T. Bailey (*Eagles*)	10	19	1	553	150	1	30.72	0

† *Left-handed batsman.*

BOWLING

(Qualification: 20 wickets, average 30.00)

	Style	O	M	R	W	BB	5W/i	Avge
J. T. Mafa (*Gauteng*)	RFM	143.3	18	492	33	7-39	4	14.90
P. P. van den Berg (*Easterns*)	RM	127.4	35	344	22	6-28	2	15.63
C. Pietersen (*Eagles & Griqualand West*). . . .	LFM	359.4	88	1,025	58	5-47	1	17.67
N. G. Brouwers (*South Western Districts*) . . .	SLA	132.5	22	448	25	5-87	1	17.92
M. Ntini (*Warriors & South Africa*)	RFM	338	108	870	47	6-85	2	18.51
D. L. Brown (*Warriors & Border*)	RFM	160.1	39	503	27	4-14	0	18.62
L. L. Tsotsobe (*Warriors & South Africa A*) .	LFM	188.5	59	522	28	4-3	0	18.64
A. C. R. Birch (*Warriors & Eastern Province*) .	RFM	255.5	60	776	41	6-62	2	18.92
F. de Wet (*Lions*)	RFM	172.3	50	425	22	4-30	0	19.31
J. P. Bothma (*Cape Cobras & Boland*)	RFM	166.3	25	524	27	6-59	2	19.40
L. Mbane (*Border*)	RM	170.1	42	562	26	4-21	0	21.61
D. D. Carolus (*Eagles & Griqualand West*) . .	RM	190.2	36	651	30	5-40	2	21.70
M. Morkel (*Titans & South Africa*)	RF	282.2	46	996	44	6-43	4	22.63
C. K. Langeveldt (*Cape Cobras*)	RFM	182.5	34	510	22	3-24	0	23.18
V. Gobind (*Dolphins & KwaZulu-Natal*)	RFM	174.2	26	541	23	5-38	1	23.52
W. A. Deacon (*Lions & North West*)	LFM	307.1	76	872	37	6-45	2	23.56
P. Joubert (*Titans*)	RFM	183.4	63	477	20	7-38	1	23.85
D. du Preez (*Eagles*)	RFM	183.2	55	490	20	4-48	0	24.50
Imran Tahir (*Titans & Easterns*).	LBG	373.5	84	1,135	46	7-94	3	24.67
P. V. Mpitsang (*Eagles & Free State*)	RFM	225.5	57	575	23	4-36	0	25.00
Q. Friend (*Dolphins*)	RFM	206.3	40	581	22	3-33	0	26.40
P. L. Harris (*Titans & South Africa*)	SLA	310.5	69	865	32	7-94	3	27.03
U. Govender (*Dolphins & KwaZulu-Natal*) . .	RFM	282.2	70	787	29	4-36	0	27.13
C. W. Henderson (*Cape Cobras*)	SLA	463.4	117	1,059	39	7-64	3	27.15
J. Theron (*Warriors*)	RFM	261.5	64	755	27	7-46	2	27.96
D. W. Steyn (*South Africa*)	RF	183	35	676	24	5-63	1	28.16

Averages include South African Airways Three-Day Challenge matches played in Namibia.

Full scores of the 2008-09 South African season can be found at www.cricinfo.com/db/ARCHIVE/
2008-09/RSA_LOCAL/ and www.cricketarchive.co.uk/Archive/Seasons/2008-09_RSA.html and in
the *ACS Overseas First-Class Annual 2009.*

SUPERSPORT SERIES, 2008-09

	Played	Won	Lost	Drawn	Bonus points Batting	Bowling	Points
Titans	10	5	0	5	37.10	31	118.10
Eagles	10	5	4	1	23.94	36	109.94
Warriors	10	3	3	4	31.48	30	91.48
Lions	10	2	2	6	33.90	24	77.90
Cape Cobras	10	1	4	5	31.02	29	70.02
Dolphins	10	0	3	7	29.88	31	56.88*

* 4 pts deducted for slow over-rate.   Outright win = 10 pts.

Bonus points awarded for the first 100 overs of each team's first innings. One batting point was awarded for the first 150 runs and 0.02 of a point for every subsequent run. One bowling point was awarded for the third wicket taken and for every subsequent two.

At Durban, October 2, 3, 4, 5, 2008. **Drawn.** Toss: Dolphins. **Titans** 211 (M. van Jaarsveld 58, G. H. Bodi 62); **Dolphins** 292 (J. C. Kent 91, P. de Bruyn 73; Imran Tahir 5-103). *Dolphins 7.4 pts, Titans 5.22 pts.*

At Kimberley, October 2, 3, 4, 2008. **Eagles won by 86 runs.** Toss: Cape Cobras. **Eagles** 296 (H. H. Dippenaar 81, R. T. Bailey 91) **and** 129 (R. R. Rossouw 63*); **Cape Cobras** 125 (D. du Preez 4-48, C. J. D. de Villiers 4-32) **and** 214. *Eagles 16.42 pts, Cape Cobras 3 pts.*

At Johannesburg, October 2, 3, 4, 5, 2008. **Lions won by 37 runs.** Toss: Lions. **Lions** 255 (A. N. Petersen 131, V. B. van Jaarsveld 51) **and** 311 (A. N. Petersen 120; R. J. Peterson 5-60); **Warriors** 316 (A. Jacobs 50, D. J. Jacobs 59, J. P. Kreusch 85*) **and** 213 (A. Nel 4-51). *Lions 17.1 pts, Warriors 8.32 pts.*
    Twin hundreds from Alviro Petersen helped to put the Lions on top of the first-round table.

At Durban, October 9, 10, 11, 12, 2008. **Drawn.** Toss: Lions. **Dolphins** 459-5 dec (I. Khan 115, A. M. Amla 164*, P. de Bruyn 64, D. Smit 55*) **and** 266-5 dec (I. Khan 103, D. A. Miller 56, A. M. Amla 54); **Lions** 379-7 dec (N. D. McKenzie 110, J. D. Vandiar 172*) **and** 121-2 (A. N. Petersen 52). *Dolphins 7.42 pts, Lions 5.56 pts.*
    Imraan Khan hit two hundreds in the match; Ahmed Amla scored a career-best.

At Benoni, October 9, 10, 11, 12, 2008. **Drawn.** Toss: Cape Cobras. **Cape Cobras** 417 (A. G. Puttick 88, J-P. Duminy 124, J. L. Ontong 63; M. Morkel 4-111) **and** 281-7 dec (H. Davids 64, R. C. C. Canning 76*); **Titans** 413 (G. H. Bodi 138, F. Behardien 52, J. A. Morkel 55, M. Morkel 56; C. W. Henderson 5-105) **and** 185-8 (F. du Plessis 55). *Titans 8.32 pts, Cape Cobras 9.34 pts.*

At Port Elizabeth, October 9, 10, 11, 12, 2008. **Warriors won by 261 runs.** Toss: Warriors. **Warriors** 256 (A. Jacobs 77, A. G. Prince 51; P. V. Mpitsang 4-36) **and** 272-4 dec (Z. de Bruyn 81, A. Jacobs 80*); **Eagles** 28 (M. Ntini 5-9, L. L. Tsotsobe 4-3) **and** 239 (R. R. Rossouw 66, T. Tshabalala 51*; J. Theron 7-46). *Warriors 17.12 pts, Eagles 4 pts.*
    The Eagles were bowled out for 28, the fourth-lowest total in South African cricket and the lowest not by Border. Only Ryan Bailey reached ten. Makhaya Ntini's full figures were 10.5–5–9–5 and Lonwabo Tsotsobe's 8–6–3–4.

LOWEST FIRST-CLASS TOTALS IN SOUTH AFRICA

16	Border v Natal at East London (first innings)	1959-60
18	Border v Natal at East London (second innings)	1959-60
23	Border v Natal at East London	1920-21
28	**Eagles v Warriors at Port Elizabeth**	**2008-09**
29	Griqualand West v Transvaal at Johannesburg	1950-51
30	South Africa v England at Port Elizabeth	1895-96
31	Griqualand West v Natal at Johannesburg	1906-07

At Paarl, October 16, 17, 18, 19, 2008. **Drawn.** Toss: Dolphins. **Dolphins 435** (H. D. Ackerman 70, J. C. Kent 110, D. Smit 77; C. W. Henderson 5-126) **and 93-3; Cape Cobras 476** (H. Davids 80, J-P. Duminy 138, J. L. Ontong 51). *Cape Cobras 5.94 pts, Dolphins 4.68 pts.*

At Bloemfontein, October 16, 17, 18, 19, 2008. **Eagles won by 77 runs.** Toss: Eagles. **Eagles 329** (H. H. Dippenaar 93, M. N. van Wyk 53, T. Tshabalala 55; G. J-P. Kruger 4-74) **and 158** (W. A. Deacon 5-38); **Lions 171 and 239** (N. D. McKenzie 51, J. Symes 50; C. D. de Lange 4-64). *Eagles 17.76 pts, Lions 4.42 pts.*

At East London, October 16, 17, 18, 19, 2008. **Titans won by 196 runs.** Toss: Warriors. **Titans 190** (A. B. de Villiers 52) **and 202** (M. Morkel 82*); **Warriors 119** (M. Morkel 6-47) **and 77** (M. Morkel 5-9). *Titans 15.8 pts, Warriors 4 pts.*

Morne Morkel steered the Titans to victory with a career-best 6-47 followed by 8–3–9–5 which gave him ten in a match for the first time; he also rescued them from 91-8 by scoring 82*, another career-best, from No. 9.

At Paarl, October 30, 31, November 1, 2, 2008. **Drawn.** Toss: Cape Cobras. **Cape Cobras 348** (A. J. A. Gray 71, A. G. Puttick 59, S. van Zyl 71, R. E. Levi 69) **and 235-4 dec** (A. G. Puttick 74); **Lions 395** (S. C. Cook 132, V. B. van Jaarsveld 98, J. D. Vandiar 50; A. J. A. Gray 4-47) **and 107-4.** *Cape Cobras 3.88 pts, Lions 4.84 pts.*

Opening batsman Alistair Gray took a hat-trick in the Lions' first innings with his leg-spin.

At Durban, October 30, 31, November 1, 2, 2008. **Drawn.** Toss: Dolphins. **Warriors 375** (J. T. Smuts 50, D. J. Jacobs 74, J. P. Kreusch 72, J. Theron 58) **and 175-8 dec** (Z. de Bruyn 56; U. Govender 4-63); **Dolphins 277** (A. M. Amla 97, D. A. Miller 70; M. Ntini 6-85) **and 168-7** (I. Khan 66, D. Smit 68*). *Dolphins 6.54 pts, Warriors 8.54 pts.*

At Benoni, October 30, 31, November 1, 2, 2008. **Titans won by 139 runs.** Toss: Titans. **Titans 423-9 dec** (B. D. Snijman 70, F. Behardien 150*, P. Joubert 62) **and 214-5 dec** (B. D. Snijman 52); **Eagles 254** (D. Elgar 57, R. R. Rossouw 106; Imran Tahir 4-63, P. L. Harris 5-86) **and 244** (D. Elgar 155; P. L. Harris 7-94). *Titans 17.98 pts, Eagles 5.08 pts.*

Test left-arm spinner Paul Harris claimed 7-94 and 12-180 in the match, both career-bests, to lift the Titans to the top of the table for the first time in the season.

At Paarl, November 6, 7, 8, 9, 2008. **Drawn.** Toss: Cape Cobras. **Cape Cobras 340** (A. G. Puttick 105, S. van Zyl 65, R. E. Levi 53; J. Theron 5-51) **and 190-7 dec; Warriors 263** (A. Jacobs 92; F. C. Plaatjies 4-59) **and 206-8** (A. G. Prince 72*). *Cape Cobras 7.36 pts, Warriors 4.26 pts.*

Ashwell Prince, who had left the Cobras for the Warriors, saved them from 87-5 chasing 268.

At Durban, November 6, 7, 8, 9, 2008. **Drawn.** Toss: Dolphins. **Eagles 420** (D. Elgar 70, H. H. Dippenaar 106, R. T. Bailey 150) **and 26-5 dec; Dolphins 275** (I. Khan 56, A. M. Amla 72) **and 8-1.** *Dolphins 4.5 pts, Eagles 6.66 pts.*

In the Eagles' first innings, Boeta Dippenaar and Ryan Bailey added 217 for the fourth wicket; in their second innings, they slid to 6-4 before declaring to set a target of 172 in 35 overs, before bad light.

At Centurion, November 6, 7, 8, 9, 2008. **Drawn.** Toss: Titans. **Titans 417** (F. du Plessis 176, P. Joubert 61, P. L. Harris 53; C. J. Alexander 5-110); **Lions 382-6** (W. L. Coetsee 116*, M. J. Harris 65*). *Titans 7.3 pts, Lions 7.3 pts.*

Faf du Plessis's career-best 176 included 27 fours and two sixes. Werner Coetsee and Matthew Harris added 126* for the Lions' seventh wicket.

At Cape Town, February 26, 27, 28, March 1, 2009. **Eagles won by 80 runs.** Toss: Cape Cobras. **Eagles 256** (R. R. Rossouw 111; R. K. Kleinveldt 7-43) **and 355-7 dec** (R. R. Hendricks 151*, R. T. Bailey 75, A. J. Pienaar 60); **Cape Cobras 285** (A. G. Puttick 72, A. J. A. Gray 110; C. Pietersen 4-62) **and 246** (S. van Zyl 85, R. K. Kleinveldt 55; C. Pietersen 4-36). *Eagles 17.12 pts. Cape Cobras 7.7 pts.*

The Eagles completed victory despite missing four front-line bowlers (three of them suspended for misconduct). In their second innings, Herschelle Gibbs caught five of the seven wickets to fall; in the Cobras' second innings, Rory Kleinveldt reached 50 in 28 balls, finishing with eight fours and three sixes in 33 balls.

At Benoni, February 26, 27, 28, March 1, 2009. **Titans won by 220 runs.** Toss: Titans. **Titans 276** (G. H. Bodi 64) **and 272-6 dec** (B. D. Snijman 114, H. G. Kuhn 50, P. J. Malan 66*); **Dolphins 228** (D. A. Miller 62, A. M. Amla 88; Imran Tahir 5-65) **and 100** (J. A. Morkel 5-25). *Titans 17.52 pts, Dolphins 6.56 pts.*

At Port Elizabeth, February 26, 27, 28, March 1, 2009. **Drawn.** Toss: Warriors. **Warriors 219** (A. Jacobs 64*; F. de Wet 4-30, C. J. Alexander 4-80) **and 296** (A. Jacobs 76, A. G. Prince 77; R. Frylinck 4-48); **Lions 349** (A. N. Petersen 80, V. B. van Jaarsveld 110, A. M. Phangiso 53) **and 148-6** (J. Symes 65). *Warriors 4.38 pts, Lions 7.12 pts.*

Lions wicketkeeper Dane Vilas made ten catches in the match; his opposite number, Davey Jacobs, six catches and a stumping, including Vilas in both innings.

At Paarl, March 5, 6, 7, 2009. **Titans won by an innings and 41 runs.** Toss: Cape Cobras. **Cape Cobras 228** (R. C. C. Canning 122; P. Joubert 7-38) **and 91; Titans 360** (G. H. Bodi 63, F. du Plessis 57, F. Behardien 54; V. D. Philander 5-60). *Titans 17.5 pts, Cape Cobras 4.56 pts.*

The Cobras were 113-9 before Ryan Canning and Pepler Sandri added 115 for the last wicket; Sandri's contribution was 14. Pierre Joubert's 7-38 was the best return of this tournament.*

At Bloemfontein, March 5, 6, 7, 8, 2009. **Eagles won by three wickets.** Toss: Warriors. **Warriors 484** (C. A. Thyssen 65, Z. de Bruyn 53, A. G. Prince 56, D. J. Jacobs 66, L. Meyer 54*, Extras 52) **and 135-6 dec** (J. T. Smuts 50); **Eagles 335-7 dec** (R. R. Hendricks 51, H. H. Dippenaar 75, R. T. Bailey 59*, M. N. van Wyk 65*) **and 285-7** (R. R. Rossouw 80, M. N. van Wyk 100*). *Eagles 15.7 pts, Warriors 6.44 pts.*

In Warriors' first innings Lyall Meyer and Juan Theron (35) added 104 for the last wicket. Morne van Wyk took the Eagles to victory with seven balls to spare.

At Potchefstroom, March 5, 6, 7, 8, 2009. **Drawn.** Toss: Dolphins. **Dolphins 543-8 dec** (I. Khan 122, H. D. Ackerman 102, P. de Bruyn 116*, Q. Friend 78); **Lions 338** (J. Symes 52, S. C. Cook 93) **and 193-8** (V. B. van Jaarsveld 52). *Lions 3.88 pts, Dolphins 7.16 pts.*

Pierre de Bruyn and Quinton Friend added 178 for the Dolphins' eighth wicket.

At Pietermaritzburg, March 12, 13, 14, 15, 2009. **Drawn.** Toss: Cape Cobras. **Cape Cobras 281** (H. Davids 113, R. C. C. Canning 55; Y. A. Abdulla 5-63) **and 300-2** (A. J. A. Gray 131, S. van Zyl 103*); **Dolphins 366** (I. Khan 145, J. C. Kent 69; J-P. Duminy 5-108). *Dolphins 8.62 pts, Cape Cobras 5.62 pts.*

At Johannesburg, March 12, 13, 14, 15, 2009. **Lions won by nine runs.** Toss: Lions. **Lions 160 and 196** (V. B. van Jaarsveld 88; C. Pietersen 4-44); **Eagles 167** (R. R. Hendricks 51; G. J-P. Kruger 4-73) **and 180** (C. J. Alexander 4-28). *Lions 15.2 pts, Eagles 5.34 pts.*

Eagles wicketkeeper Morne van Wyk caught five in each Lions innings. On the final day, ninth-wicket pair Boeta Dippenaar and C. J. de Villiers added 49 to bring the Eagles within ten runs of victory before both fell in the space of four balls.

At Centurion, March 12, 13, 14, 15, 2009. **Drawn.** Toss: Warriors. **Warriors 548-6 dec** (A. G. Prince 254, M. V. Boucher 63, J. Botha 76*) **and 84-3; Titans 531** (H. G. Kuhn 203, J. A. Rudolph 58, A. B. de Villiers 64). *Titans 6.26 pts, Warriors 6.44 pts.*

This was the seventh first-class match in South African history to feature two double-hundreds. Ashwell Prince batted nine hours 14 minutes and 356 balls, hitting 28 fours and eight sixes in the highest innings of this tournament; Heino Kuhn batted nine hours ten minutes.

At Bloemfontein, March 26, 27, 28, 2009. **Titans won by ten wickets.** Toss: Eagles. **Eagles 178** (R. R. Rossouw 109; M. Morkel 6-43) **and 169** (M. Morkel 6-48); **Titans 210** (C. Pietersen 5-47) **and 139-0** (H. G. Kuhn 78*). *Titans 16.2 pts, Eagles 5.56 pts.*

The Titans defeated their closest rivals, the Eagles, to enter the final round with a lead of 18.46 points. The Eagles' 178 was the fourth-lowest total in South Africa to include a century – 109 by 19-year-old Rilee Rossouw, who added 67 for the last wicket with Victor Mpitsang. For the second time in the tournament, Morne Morkel improved on his best innings and match figures.

At Potchefstroom, March 26, 27, 28, 29, 2009. **Cape Cobras won by six wickets.** Toss: Cape Cobras. **Lions 296** (N. D. McKenzie 76, J. Symes 50, S. C. Cook 90; S. van Zyl 4-36) **and 242** (S. C. Cook 59, A. Nel 51; C. W. Henderson 4-64); **Cape Cobras 434** (A. G. Puttick 174, H. Davids 51, R. E. Levi 57) **and 107-4.** *Cape Cobras 18.62 pts, Lions 4.92 pts.*

Cobras opening bowler Rory Kleinveldt had figures of 23–9–34–3 in the Lions' second innings.

At Port Elizabeth, March 26, 27, 28, 29, 2009. **Warriors won by 231 runs.** Toss: Dolphins. **Warriors 162** (K. J. Abbott 5-18) **and 358-8 dec** (J. T. Smuts 77, A. Jacobs 64, D. J. Jacobs 64; D. Smit 4-88); **Dolphins 123** (M. W. Olivier 5-38) **and 166** (M. W. Olivier 6-59). *Warriors 15.24 pts, Dolphins 4 pts.*

Mario Olivier claimed 11-97 in his first game of the 2008-09 SuperSport tournament.

At Kimberley, April 2, 3, 2009. **Eagles won by eight wickets.** Toss: Dolphins. **Dolphins 132** (K. J. Abbott 50*; A. J. Pienaar 4-46) **and 175** (J. C. Kent 64*; A. J. Pienaar 4-40); **Eagles 215** (R. R. Rossouw 79; K. J. Abbott 4-40) **and 98-2.** *Eagles 16.3 pts, Dolphins 4 pts.*

A low-scoring victory was not enough for the Eagles to overtake the leaders Titans.

At Johannesburg, April 2, 3, 4, 5, 2009. **Drawn.** Toss: Lions. **Lions 526-9 dec** (A. N. Petersen 129, D. J. Vilas 203) **and 167-2 dec** (A. N. Petersen 105*); **Titans 360** (J. A. Rudolph 52, F. du Plessis 53, F. Behardien 114, P. Joubert 71) **and 250-3** (J. A. Rudolph 126*, F. du Plessis 65*). *Lions 7.56 pts, Titans 6 pts.*

Alviro Petersen ended the tournament as he began it, with twin hundreds; he and Dane Vilas added 228 for the fifth wicket in Lions' first innings. Petersen equalled the record of six hundreds in a South African season, and beat H. D. Ackerman's 1997-98 record of 1,373 runs by a South African player in the home season, reaching 1,376. Results elsewhere confirmed Titans as champions.

At East London, April 2, 3, 4, 2009. **Warriors won by 236 runs.** Toss: Cape Cobras. **Warriors 237** (A. Jacobs 59, Z. de Bruyn 54, D. J. Jacobs 52; C. W. Henderson 7-64) **and 197** (D. J. Jacobs 101); **Cape Cobras 124** (A. C. R. Birch 5-48) **and 74** (D. L. Brown 4-14, Z. de Bruyn 4-28). *Warriors 16.74 pts, Cape Cobras 4 pts.*

CHAMPIONS

Currie Cup

1889-90	Transvaal	1952-53	Western Province
1890-91	Kimberley	1954-55	Natal
1892-93	Western Province	1955-56	Western Province
1893-94	Western Province	1958-59	Transvaal
1894-95	Transvaal	1959-60	Natal
1896-97	Western Province	1960-61	Natal
1897-98	Western Province	1962-63	Natal
1902-03	Transvaal	1963-64	Natal
1903-04	Transvaal	1965-66	Natal
1904-05	Transvaal		Transvaal
1906-07	Transvaal	1966-67	Natal
1908-09	Western Province	1967-68	Natal
1910-11	Natal	1968-69	Transvaal
1912-13	Natal	1969-70	Transvaal
1920-21	Western Province		Western Province
1921-22	Transvaal	1970-71	Transvaal
	Natal	1971-72	Transvaal
	Western Province	1972-73	Transvaal
1923-24	Transvaal	1973-74	Natal
1925-26	Transvaal	1974-75	Western Province
1926-27	Transvaal	1975-76	Natal
1929-30	Transvaal	1976-77	Natal
1931-32	Western Province	1977-78	Western Province
1933-34	Natal	1978-79	Transvaal
1934-35	Transvaal	1979-80	Transvaal
1936-37	Natal	1980-81	Natal
1937-38	Natal	1981-82	Western Province
	Transvaal	1982-83	Transvaal
1946-47	Natal	1983-84	Transvaal
1947-48	Natal	1984-85	Transvaal
1950-51	Transvaal	1985-86	Western Province
1951-52	Natal	1986-87	Transvaal
		1987-88	Transvaal

1988-89	Eastern Province	1998-99	Western Province
1989-90	{ Eastern Province Western Province	1999-2000	Gauteng
		2000-01	Western Province
Castle Cup		2001-02	KwaZulu-Natal
1990-91	Western Province	2002-03	Easterns
1991-92	Eastern Province	2003-04	Western Province
1992-93	Orange Free State	2004-05	{ Dolphins Eagles
1993-94	Orange Free State		
1994-95	Natal	2005-06	{ Dolphins Titans
1995-96	Western Province		
		2006-07	Titans
SuperSport Series		2007-08	Eagles
1996-97	Natal	2008-09	Titans
1997-98	Free State		

Transvaal/Gauteng have won the title outright 25 times, Natal/KwaZulu-Natal 21, Western Province 18, Orange Free State/Free State 3, Eastern Province and Titans 2, Eagles, Easterns and Kimberley 1. The title has been shared seven times as follows: Transvaal 4, Natal and Western Province 3, Dolphins 2, Eagles, Eastern Province and Titans 1.

From 1971-72 to 1990-91, the non-white South African Cricket Board of Control (later the South African Cricket Board) organised its own three-day tournaments. These are now recognised as first-class (see *Wisden 2006*, pages 79–80). A list of winners appears in *Wisden 2007*, page 1346.

SOUTH AFRICAN AIRWAYS THREE-DAY CHALLENGE, 2008-09

Pool A	Played	Won	Lost	Drawn	Bonus points Batting	Bonus points Bowling	Points
Griqualand West	6	4	1	1	24.32	24	88.32
Gauteng	6	4	0	2	21.10	23	84.10
Easterns	6	3	1	2	27.10	23	80.10
Eastern Province	6	2	1	3	29.34	24	73.34
South Western Districts	6	1	4	1	24.94	22	56.94
KwaZulu-Natal	6	0	3	3	23.28	19	42.28
Boland	6	0	4	2	17.70	21	38.70

Pool B	Played	Won	Lost	Drawn	Bonus points Batting	Bonus points Bowling	Points
North West	6	3	0	3	32.24	24	86.24
Northerns	6	2	0	4	27.22	23	70.22
Border	6	2	3	1	20.28	23	63.28
Namibia	6	1	2	3	25.70	22	57.70
Free State	6	1	0	5	25.68	19	54.68
KwaZulu-Natal Inland	6	1	2	3	19.38	23	52.38
Western Province	6	0	3	3	21.48	22	43.48

Final: Griqualand West beat North West by 243 runs.

Outright win = 10 pts.
Bonus points awarded for the first 85 overs of each team's first innings. One bonus batting point was awarded for the first 100 runs and 0.02 of a point for every subsequent run. One bonus bowling point was awarded for the second wicket taken and for every subsequent two up to eight. Each team's first innings was restricted to 85 overs, except that, if the first team was bowled out inside 85 overs, their unused overs were added to the second team's allocation.

Pool A

At Port Elizabeth, October 2, 3, 4, 2008. **Drawn.** Toss: Gauteng. **Gauteng 327-9** (D. J. Vilas 166; M. B. Njoloza 4-75) **and 293-5 dec** (W. C. Swan 122*); **Eastern Province 314-7** (J. T. Smuts 83, C. Baxter 99, S. R. Adair 70; D. R. Deeb 4-89) **and 128-6** (E. O'Reilly 4-36). *Eastern Province 9.28 pts, Gauteng 8.54 pts.*

At Benoni, October 2, 3, 4, 2008. **Easterns won by seven wickets.** Toss: Easterns. **Griqualand West 290-8** (H. G. de Kock 72, W. Bossenger 81*) **and 169** (J. Brooker 68; P. P. van den Berg 5-61); **Easterns 388** (D. Wiese 208) **and 72-3.** *Easterns 20.76 pts, Griqualand West 8.8 pts.*
David Wiese scored 208 out of 303 after coming in at 85-3. He was last out after striking five sixes and 28 fours from 185 balls, having added 113 for the ninth wicket with Lee Coetzee (19).

At Johannesburg, October 16, 17, 18, 2008. **Gauteng won by one wicket.** Toss: Gauteng. **South Western Districts 301-8 dec** (J. G. Strydom 58, B. C. de Wett 128; J. T. Mafa 4-66) **and 71** (J. T. Mafa 5-17); **Gauteng 111** (D. J. Vilas 63; B. L. Fransman 5-31; T. A. Davis-Taylor 4-31) **and 262-9** (W. C. Swan 51, D. L. Makalima 56, D. R. Deeb 58). *Gauteng 15.22 pts, South Western Districts 9.02 pts.*

At Kimberley, October 16, 17, 18, 2008. **Griqualand West won by 166 runs.** Toss: Boland. **Griqualand West 224** (J. P. Bothma 4-52, H. W. de Wet 5-49) **and 307** (H. G. de Kock 91); **Boland 189** (L. R. Walters 54; D. D. Carolus 5-74) **and 176** (D. D. Carolus 4-18). *Griqualand West 17.48 pts, Boland 6.78 pts.*

At Benoni, October 23, 24, 25, 2008. **Drawn.** Toss: Eastern Province. **Easterns 246** (T. M. Bodibe 50, J. J. Pienaar 54; A. C. R. Birch 6-62) **and 278-7 dec** (M. R. Sekhoto 79, D. Wiese 58); **Eastern Province 271** (A. dos Santos 50, W. E. Bell 61, A. C. R. Birch 55) **and 164-5** (J. T. Smuts 68, C. A. Ingram 52). *Easterns 7.92 pts, Eastern Province 8.42 pts.*

At Chatsworth, October 23, 24, 25, 2008. **Drawn.** Toss: South Western Districts. **South Western Districts 295** (J. G. Strydom 64, R. E. Hillermann 107; S. Mlongo 6-65); **KwaZulu-Natal 190-7** (D. Govender 103). *KwaZulu-Natal 6.8 pts, South Western Districts 7.9 pts.*

At Paarl, November 13, 14, 15, 2008. **Drawn.** Toss: KwaZulu-Natal. **Boland 181** (B. C. Adams 56; V. Gobind 4-31); **KwaZulu-Natal 277-7** (M. Pillay 82, G. S. Fotheringham 65; J. P. Bothma 5-55). *Boland 5.62 pts, KwaZulu-Natal 8.54 pts.*

At Johannesburg, January 8, 9, 10, 2009. **Drawn.** Toss: Gauteng. **Gauteng 192** (M. J. Harris 58, R. Cameron 80; F. S. Holtzhausen 5-43) **and 115-4** (S. C. Cook 58*); **Griqualand West 166** (A. P. McLaren 73; J. T. Mafa 5-75). *Gauteng 6.84 pts, Griqualand West 6.32 pts.*
Richard Cameron took a hat-trick to end Griquas' innings.

At Oudtshoorn, January 8, 9, 10, 2009. **South Western Districts won by 225 runs.** Toss: Boland. **South Western Districts 303** (S. E. Avontuur 57, N. M. Murray 58; J. P. Bothma 4-45) **and 218-8 dec** (B. C. de Wett 58); **Boland 156** (R. G. Arendse 59*; N. G. Brouwers 4-40) **and 140** (B. L. Fransman 4-32). *South Western Districts 19.06 pts, Boland 6.12 pts.*

At Nelson Mandela Metropole University, Port Elizabeth, January 15, 16, 17, 2009. **Eastern Province won by 23 runs.** Toss: KwaZulu-Natal. **Eastern Province 375-4** (C. A. Ingram 190, S. R. Adair 101*) **and 177** (C. A. Ingram 78, S. R. Adair 56; U. Govender 4-36, V. Gobind 5-38); **KwaZulu-Natal 305-9** (G. S. Fotheringham 64, B. G. Barnes 60; J. T. Smuts 4-85) **and 224** (M. Bekker 86; J. T. Smuts 6-80). *Eastern Province 20.5 pts, KwaZulu-Natal 7.1 pts.*
Colin Ingram and Sean Adair added 257 for the fourth wicket in Eastern Province's first innings.

At Durban, January 22, 23, 24, 2009. **Drawn.** Toss: Easterns. **KwaZulu-Natal 317-7** (R. Gobind 78, C. Delport 77, G. S. Fotheringham 70*; I. C. Hlengani 4-75) **and 299-3 dec** (R. Gobind 130*, C. Delport 110, G. S. Fotheringham 52*); **Easterns 256-9** (T. M. Bodibe 76) **and 236-6** (T. M. Bodibe 60, J. Booysen 107). *KwaZulu-Natal 9.34 pts, Easterns 7.12 pts.*

At Oudtshoorn, January 22, 23, 24, 2009. **Griqualand West won by nine wickets.** Toss: South Western Districts. **South Western Districts 254** (S. E. Avontuur 68, P. A. Stuurman 85*; C. Pietersen 4-56, H. G. de Kock 4-45) **and 94** (D. D. Carolus 4-23); **Griqualand West 304** (A. K. Kruger 116,

C. Pietersen 50*; B. L. Fransman 4-41, N. G. Brouwers 5-87) **and 45-1.** *Griqualand West 18.86 pts, South Western Districts 8.08 pts.*

At Paarl, January 29, 30, 31, 2009. **Gauteng won by five wickets.** Toss: Boland. **Boland 237-9** (G. C. Stevens 51) **and 212** (R. Das Neves 4-60); **Gauteng 176** (J. P. Bothma 6-59) **and 274-5** (G. Mokoena 71, S. C. Cook 96). *Gauteng 16.52 pts, Boland 7.74 pts.*
   Gauteng wicketkeeper Matthew Harris made seven catches and two stumpings in the match.

At Benoni, February 5, 6, 2009. **Easterns won by an innings and 108 runs.** Toss: South Western Districts. **Easterns 412-8** (M. R. Sekhoto 59, D. Wiese 118, J. J. Pienaar 70, P. P. van den Berg 60*, G. C. Viljoen 59; N. G. Brouwers 4-97); **South Western Districts 121** (B. D. Walters 4-38, P. P. van den Berg 6-28) **and 183.** *Easterns 21.24 pts, South Western Districts 5.42 pts.*
   Paul van den Berg and G. C. Viljoen added 124 for Easterns' eighth wicket on the way to a two-day win.

At Kimberley, February 5, 6, 7, 2009. **Griqualand West won by one wicket.** Toss: Griqualand West. **Eastern Province 225** (J. T. Smuts 51, A. C. R. Birch 51) **and 299** (J. T. Smuts 53, M. B. A. Smith 70; D. D. Carolus 5-40); **Griqualand West 317** (W. Bossenger 96, J. Brooker 56; A. C. R. Birch 4-99) **and 208-9.** *Griqualand West 19.34 pts, Eastern Province 7.5 pts.*

At Paarl, February 12, 13, 14, 2009. **Easterns won by 130 runs.** Toss: Easterns. **Easterns 303** (R. Jappie 62, J. Booysen 76) **and 216-5 dec** (J. Booysen 56, D. Wiese 73*); **Boland 164** (O. A. Ramela 62; P. P. van den Berg 4-29) **and 225** (L. van Wyk 67, L. R. Walters 52; Imran Tahir 7-94). *Easterns 19.06 pts, Boland 6.28 pts.*

At Chatsworth, February 19, 20, 21, 2009. **Gauteng won by nine wickets.** Toss: Gauteng. **Gauteng 362-6** (W. C. Swan 52, D. J. Vilas 103*, M. J. Harris 90) **and 54-1;** **KwaZulu-Natal 200** (C. Delport 61; R. Frylinck 4-52) **and 213** (J. T. Mafa 5-62). *Gauteng 20.24 pts, KwaZulu-Natal 6 pts.*

At Oudtshoorn, February 19, 20, 21, 2009. **Eastern Province won by eight wickets.** Toss: Eastern Province. **South Western Districts 273** (B. C. de Wett 57, P. A. Stuurman 55; M. J. Kennedy 4-53) **and 113** (A. C. R. Birch 4-41); **Eastern Province 336-7** (C. Baxter 103, M. B. A. Smith 60, L. Meyer 68; N. G. Brouwers 4-97) **and 52-2.** *Eastern Province 19.48 pts, South Western Districts 7.46 pts.*

At Kimberley, February 26, 27, 28, 2009. **Griqualand West won by six wickets.** Toss: Griqualand West. **KwaZulu-Natal 175** (P. de Bruyn 82; R. A. Adams 5-19) **and 356** (K. Zondo 89, P. de Bruyn 54, B. G. Barnes 59, C. Chetty 61*; R. Pietersen 4-46); **Griqualand West 365-5** (A. P. McLaren 83, W. Bossenger 90*, J. Brooker 86*) **and 169-4** (A. P. McLaren 80*). *Griqualand West 17.52 pts, KwaZulu-Natal 4.5 pts.*
   Wendell Bossenger and Jason Brooker joined forces at 195-5 to add 170 for Griquas' sixth wicket. Adrian McLaren swept them to victory with 80* off 46 balls (ten fours, two sixes).*

At Port Elizabeth, March 5, 6, 7, 2009. **Drawn.** Toss: Eastern Province. **Boland 258-9** (L. van Wyk 57) **and 182** (R. G. Arendse 62; C. A. Ingram 4-32); **Eastern Province 258-4** (M. B. A. Smith 64, C. A. Ingram 102, S. R. Adair 70*) **and 172-9.** *Eastern Province 8.16 pts, Boland 6.16 pts.*

At Johannesburg, March 5, 6, 2009. **Gauteng won by 206 runs.** Toss: Easterns. **Gauteng 187** (J. J. Pienaar 5-39) **and 212** (R. G. Mutch 4-49); **Easterns 78** (J. T. Mafa 7-39) **and 115** (J. T. Mafa 4-51, E. O'Reilly 5-3). *Gauteng 16.74 pts, Easterns 4 pts.*
   Ethan O'Reilly's full analysis was 3-1-3-5.

Pool B

At Bloemfontein, October 2, 3, 4, 2008. **Drawn.** Toss: Northerns. **Free State 279-9** (D. J. van Wyk 62, H. O. von Rauenstein 116, G. N. Nieuwoudt 55) **and 261-9 dec** (D. J. van Wyk 93; S. W. Liebisch 4-43, R. E. van der Merwe 4-59); **Northerns 287** (P. J. Malan 115, A. J. Seymore 93; W. J. van Zyl 6-96) **and 71-3.** *Free State 8.58 pts, Northerns 8.74 pts.*

At Bellville, October 2, 3, 4, 2008. **Drawn.** Toss: KwaZulu-Natal Inland. **Western Province 197 and 73-1; KwaZulu-Natal Inland 244-9** (D. J. Watson 84; L. F. Simpson 4-25). *Western Province 6.94 pts, KwaZulu-Natal Inland 7.68 pts.*

At United Ground, East London, October 9, 10, 11, 2008. **North West won by 72 runs.** Toss: Border. **North West 285-6** (M. Akoojee 56, C. Jonker 89, B. J. Pelser 56*) **and 135** (P. Fojela 4-30); **Border 167** (L. Mbane 71; E. Gerber 5-37) **and 181** (M. F. Richardson 61). *North West 18.7 pts, Border 5.34 pts.*

This was the first first-class match on the United Cricket Club Ground.

At Windhoek, October 16, 17, 18, 2008. **Namibia won by 301 runs.** Toss: Namibia. **Namibia 328-9** (G. Snyman 84, L. J. Burger 125; G. R. Rabie 6-48) **and 287-8 dec** (A. J. Burger 79, T. Verwey 72); **Western Province 168** (R. E. Levi 51; K. B. Burger 5-69, S. F. Burger 4-22) **and 146** (M. D. Walters 75; K. B. Burger 5-47). *Namibia 19.56 pts, Western Province 6.36 pts.*

At L. C. de Villiers Oval, Pretoria, October 16, 17, 18, 2008. **Northerns won by ten wickets.** Toss: Northerns. **Northerns 250** (A. L. Ndlovu 64*; L. Mbane 4-57) **and 9-0; Border 52** (M. A. Mashimbyi 5-25) **and 203.** *Northerns 18 pts, Border 4 pts.*

Mandla Mashimbyi bowled unchanged in Border's first innings for a career-best 9–1–25–5.

At Pietermaritzburg, October 23, 24, 25, 2008. **Drawn.** Toss: KwaZulu-Natal Inland. **Free State 169** (A. van Vuuren 6-31) **and 67-1; KwaZulu-Natal Inland 268-9 dec** (R. D. McMillan 57, O. E. Humphries 60*). *KwaZulu-Natal Inland 7.16 pts, Free State 6.38 pts.*

At Potchefstroom, October 23, 24, 25, 2008. **North West won by ten wickets.** Toss: North West. **Namibia 230** (H. H. Paulse 4-62) **and 344** (S. T. Ackermann 57, C. Williams 134; E. Gerber 5-60); **North West 450-8** (M. Akoojee 96, C. Jonker 122, T. A. Bula 62) **and 125-0** (J. F. Mostert 60*, W. L. Coetsee 53*). *North West 21.18 pts, Namibia 6.6 pts.*

At Technikon, Bloemfontein, January 8, 9, 10, 2009. **Free State won by six wickets.** Toss: Free State. **Border 200** (D. L. Brown 57) **and 211** (C. A. Thyssen 66; S. C. van Schalkwyk 4-39); **Free State 244** (J. A. Beukes 53, C. J. D. de Villiers 84; P. Fojela 4-36) **and 168-4** (J. A. Beukes 54*). *Free State 17.88 pts, Border 7 pts.*

At Pietermaritzburg, January 15, 16, 17, 2009. **Drawn.** Toss: KwaZulu-Natal Inland. **North West 235-9** (J. F. Mostert 53, W. A. Deacon 57) **and 269-2** (J. F. Mostert 126*, L. J. Kgamadi 70, C. Jonker 70*); **KwaZulu-Natal Inland 235** (M. S. van Vuuren 99*, S. Dorasamy 52; W. A. Deacon 6-45). *KwaZulu-Natal Inland 7.7 pts, North West 7.7 pts.*

At L. C. de Villiers Oval, Pretoria, January 15, 16, 17, 2009. **Drawn.** Toss: Western Province. **Northerns 295-6** (P. J. Malan 60, H. E. van der Dussen 87, A. J. Seymore 62) **and 252-9 dec** (A. J. Seymore 56, J. R. Jumat 58*); **Western Province 287-8** (L. M. G. Masekela 6-46) **and 135-4.** *Northerns 8.9 pts, Western Province 7.74 pts.*

At Windhoek, January 22, 23, 24, 2009. **Drawn.** Toss: Namibia. **Northerns 246-8** (M. J. Mokonyama 60, A. L. Ndlovu 64); **Namibia 294** (A. J. Burger 70, L. P. van der Westhuizen 85*). *Namibia 8.88 pts, Northerns 7.92 pts.*

At Bloemfontein, January 29, 30, 31, 2009. **Drawn.** Toss: Free State. **Western Province 337-3** (A. J. A. Gray 188*, M. D. Walters 106) **and 19-1; Free State 398-7** (D. J. van Wyk 69, J. A. Beukes 117, H. O. von Rauenstein 63). *Free State 7.96 pts, Western Province 8.74 pts.*

Alistair Gray and Martin Walters added 255 for Western Province's third wicket.

At East London, February 5, 6, 7, 2009. **Border won by ten wickets.** Toss: KwaZulu-Natal Inland. **Border 329-8** (M. N. Ranger 61, D. L. Brown 112*) **and 59-0; KwaZulu-Natal Inland 111** (L. Mbane 4-21) **and 275** (G. N. Addicott 125; Y. Pangabantu 4-37). *Border 19.58 pts, KwaZulu-Natal Inland 5.22 pts.*

When KwaZulu-Natal Inland followed on, Glen Addicott's 125 included 25 fours.

At Windhoek, February 5, 6, 7, 2009. **Drawn.** Toss: Namibia. **Namibia 298-9** (R. van Schoor 57, N. R. P. Scholtz 50, C. Williams 75; G. A. Vries 4-42) **and 157-5** (R. van Schoor 60); **Free State 181** (R. K. Terblanche 64*; B. L. Kotze 5-41). *Namibia 8.96 pts, Free State 6.62 pts.*

At Potchefstroom, February 12, 13, 14, 2009. **Drawn.** Toss: North West. **Northerns 303-9 dec** (H. G. Kuhn 76, P. J. Malan 62, R. E. van der Merwe 81) **and 298** (H. G. Kuhn 70, M. J. Mokonyama

54; W. L. Coetsee 5-73); **North West 392-6** (A. N. Petersen 152, M. Akoojee 71, W. L. Coetsee 77) **and 97-2.** *North West 10.52 pts, Northerns 8.06 pts.*

Alviro Petersen (who hit 24 fours and two sixes) and Muhammad Akoojee added 206 for North West's second wicket.

At University of Cape Town Bowl, Cape Town, February 12, 13, 14, 2009. **Border won by 113 runs.** Toss: Western Province. **Border 218** (M. F. Richardson 70, K. D. Bennett 56; A. J. A. Gray 5-31) **and 278** (A. Z. M. Dyili 58); **Western Province 228** (E. P. van Wyk 86*; L. Mbane 4-73, D. L. Brown 4-65) **and 155** (S. de Kock 4-44). *Border 17.36 pts, Western Province 7.56 pts.*

At L. C. de Villiers Oval, Pretoria, February 19, 20, 21, 2009. **Northerns won by ten wickets.** Toss: Northerns. **KwaZulu-Natal Inland 159 and 182** (S. A. Nowak 4-39, T. P. Kaber 5-85); **Northerns 317** (H. E. van der Dussen 50, F. Behardien 114; R. T. Hlela 5-60) **and 29-0.** *Northerns 18.6 pts, KwaZulu-Natal Inland 5.18 pts.*

At East London, February 26, 27, 28, 2009. **Drawn.** Toss: Border. **Namibia 255-8** (D. B. Kotze 64, L. P. Vorster 58*; S. de Kock 4-46) **and 242** (G. Snyman 53, C. Williams 82; Y. Pangabantu 4-68, D. L. Brown 4-66); **Border 350-8** (M. F. Richardson 53, K. D. Bennett 176) **and 88-3.** *Border 10 pts, Namibia 8.1 pts.*

At Potchefstroom, February 26, 27, 28, 2009. **Drawn.** Toss: North West. **Free State 313-8** (D. J. van Wyk 63, J. A. Beukes 56, M. N. Erlank 105) **and 239-8 dec** (R. D. McMillan 105); **North West 370-5** (J. F. Mostert 99, L. J. Kgamadi 110; R. K. Terblanche 4-77). *North West 10.4 pts, Free State 7.26 pts.*

Johan Mostert and Jimmy Kgamadi opened with 210 for North West's first wicket.

At Pietermaritzburg, March 5, 6, 7, 2009. **KwaZulu-Natal Inland won by 85 runs.** Toss: Namibia. **KwaZulu-Natal Inland 322-6** (M. Olivier 89, R. D. McMillan 105) **and 239-8 dec** (R. D. McMillan 57, G. N. Addicott 57, M. S. van Vuuren 58; B. M. Scholtz 5-65); **Namibia 180** (C. Williams 103; O. E. Humphries 6-59, R. T. Hlela 4-51) **and 296** (G. J. Rudolph 74; M. S. van Vuuren 4-63). *KwaZulu-Natal Inland 19.44 pts, Namibia 5.6 pts.*

At Goodwood, March 5, 6, 7, 2009. **North West won by eight wickets.** Toss: Western Province. **Western Province 157** (R. Ramoo 65) **and 238** (B. L. Bennett 59, M. Abbas 50, E. P. van Wyk 79*; M. P. Siboto 5-56); **North West 244** (J. F. Mostert 105*, C. Jonker 51) **and 157-2** (J. F. Mostert 68*, W. L. Coetsee 63). *North West 17.74 pts, Western Province 6.14 pts.*

Johan Mostert carried his bat through North West's first innings.

Final

At Kimberley, March 19, 20, 21, 22, 2009. **Griqualand West won by 243 runs.** Toss: North West. **Griqualand West 482** (R. R. Hendricks 129, A. P. McLaren 131) **and 150-4 dec; North West 248** (A. N. Petersen 53, B. J. Pelser 65, C. F. J. Schoeman 63; J. Coetzee 5-41) **and 141** (B. J. Pelser 61*; R. A. Adams 4-30).

Note: Matches in the following sections were not first-class.

MTN DOMESTIC CHAMPIONSHIP, 2008-09

45-over league plus knockout

	Played	Won	Lost	Tied	No result	Bonus points	Points	Net run-rate
Eagles	10	7	2	0	1	4	34	0.84
Titans	10	6	2	0	2	1	29	0.06
Cape Cobras	10	5	3	0	2	2	26	0.24
Dolphins	10	4	4	0	2	1	21	−0.34
Warriors	10	2	7	0	1	1	11	−0.31
Lions	10	2	8	0	0	1	9	−0.36

Semi-finals

At Centurion, January 9, 2009 (day/night). **Titans won by nine wickets.** Reduced to 33 overs a side. Toss: Titans. **Cape Cobras 183-9** (33 overs) (R. E. van der Merwe 5-31); **Titans 186-1** (26 overs) (G. H. Bodi 84*, R. E. van der Merwe 64*).

Roelof van der Merwe followed up career-best bowling figures with 64* off 42 balls, including four sixes and six fours.

At Bloemfontein, January 11, 2009. **Eagles won by eight runs.** Toss: Dolphins. **Eagles 253-8** (45 overs) (L. L. Bosman 95, H. H. Dippenaar 71); **Dolphins 245-71** (45 overs) (D. Smit 55*).

Dolphins keeper Daryn Smit bowled three overs of leg-spin for 3-13, and later scored 55* in 35 balls.

Final

At Bloemfontein, January 16, 2009 (day/night). **Titans won by eight wickets.** Toss: Titans. **Eagles 138** (44 overs) (P. L. Harris 5-27); **Titans 141-2** (25.3 overs) (G. H. Bodi 69, B. D. Snijman 53*).

Paul Harris, the Test spinner who had just returned from Australia because South Africa did not require him for their limited-overs matches, returned his best one-day figures to help Titans retain their title.

STANDARD BANK PRO20 SERIES, 2008-09

	Played	Won	Lost	Tied	No result	Bonus points	Points	Net run-rate
Warriors	5	4	1	0	0	1	17	1.17
Dolphins	5	3	1	0	1	1	15	0.86
Cape Cobras	5	2	2	1	0	0	10	−0.69
Eagles	5	2	3	0	0	1	8*	0.00
Titans	5	1	2	0	2	0	8	−1.47
Lions	5	0	3	1	1	0	4	−0.34

* 1 pt deducted for slow over-rate.

Eagles were placed above Titans by virtue of having won more matches.

Semi-finals

Eagles won their three-leg semi-final against Warriors 2–1; Cape Cobras beat Dolphins 2–1. In both semi-finals, the third leg was tied; Eagles and Cape Cobras reached the final by winning an eliminator over.

Final

At Cape Town, February 21, 2009 (day/night). **Cape Cobras won by 22 runs.** Toss: Cape Cobras. **Cape Cobras 147-5** (20 overs) (H. H. Gibbs 87*); **Eagles 125-8** (20 overs).

Herschelle Gibbs hit 87* in 62 balls, with seven fours and four sixes.

SOUTH AFRICAN AIRWAYS ONE-DAY CHALLENGE, 2008-09

45-over league plus knockout

Semi-finals

At Paarl, March 28, 2009. **Boland won by five wickets.** Toss: Boland. **KwaZulu-Natal Inland 69** (19.2 overs) (J. M. van Wyk 4-29, J. P. Bothma 4-4); **Boland 70-5** (14.4 overs).

At Cape Town, March 28, 2009. **KwaZulu-Natal won by six wickets.** Toss: KwaZulu-Natal. **Western Province 187-9** (45 overs); **KwaZulu-Natal 188-4** (41.5 overs) (R. Gobind 51, C. Chetty 51*).

Final

At Paarl, April 4, 2009. **Boland won by six wickets.** Toss: Boland. **KwaZulu-Natal 204-9** (45 overs) (G. S. Fotheringham 70); **Boland 208-4** (41.5 overs) (O. A. Ramela 50).

SRI LANKAN CRICKET, 2009

A change of captaincy

CHARLIE AUSTIN

While the inner turmoil within Sri Lanka's cricket administration subsided in 2009, the year did not lack incident on or off the field. Sadly the year's most unforgettable event was the appalling terrorist attack on the Sri Lankan team bus in Lahore. The other key off-field events included the surprise resignation of Mahela Jayawardene as captain in February 2009, the subsequent appointment of Kumar Sangakkara as his successor, the retirement of Chaminda Vaas from Test cricket and his axing from the one-day team, and the government appointment of a new cricket board headed by chairman Somachandra de Silva, the former Test leg-spinner.

On the field, the year was marked by the batting exploits of Tillekeratne Dilshan, who rescued a flagging career with electric performances in all formats, a troubled time for spin twins Muttiah Muralitharan and Ajantha

SRI LANKA IN 2009

	Played	Won	Lost	Drawn/ No result
Tests	11	5	2	4
One-day internationals	27	12	14	1
Twenty20 internationals	13	7	6	–

DECEMBER	2 Tests (a) v Bangladesh	(see *Wisden 2009*, page 1062)
	Triangular ODI tournament (a) in Bangladesh	(page 1086)
JANUARY	3 ODIs (a) v Pakistan	(page 1205)
FEBRUARY	5 ODIs and 1 T20I (h) v India	(page 1331)
MARCH	2 Tests (a) v Pakistan	(page 1205)
APRIL		
MAY		
JUNE	World Twenty20 (in England)	(page 527)
JULY	3 Tests, 5 ODIs and 1 T20I (h) v Pakistan	(page 1338)
AUGUST	2 Tests and 2 T20Is (h) v New Zealand	(page 1353)
SEPTEMBER	Triangular ODI series (h) v India and New Zealand	(page 1361)
OCTOBER	Champions Trophy (in South Africa)	(page 1015)
NOVEMBER	3 Tests, 5 ODIs and 2 T20Is (a) v India	(page 1115)
DECEMBER		

For a review of Sri Lankan domestic cricket from the 2008-09 season, see page 1366.

Mendis, prolific Test batting from Jayawardene and Thilan Samaraweera, the emergence of Angelo Mathews as a world-class all-rounder, and the international renaissance of left-arm spinner Rangana Herath, who was whisked out of Staffordshire league cricket midway through the year and finished with more Test wickets than anyone else – 34 at 33.82.

As a team, Sri Lanka had mixed fortunes, faring better overall in Test cricket as they rose to No. 2 in the rankings after series wins over Pakistan and New Zealand at home. Sri Lanka won five of the 11 Tests they played, and three of their five series, although the year ended in great disappointment after a 0–2 series defeat scuttled high hopes of a maiden victory on Indian soil. The silver lining of that tough injury-plagued tour was the successful injection of new young players into the squad, a development that suggested the rockiest moments of Sri Lanka's post-2007 World Cup rebuilding phase might be over.

In one-day internationals the picture was bleaker: a disappointing win ratio of 46% from 26 matches. A rare highlight was the rise to No. 1 in the bowling rankings of Nuwan Kulasekara as he cemented his new-ball position. In Twenty20 cricket Sri Lanka fared moderately in general, but they did light up the World Twenty20 in England with a courageous and entertaining display. In their first tour since the Lahore attacks in March, the team rallied around Sangakkara in his first assignment as captain with the three Ms – Muralitharan, Malinga and Mendis – giving them unparalleled variety and unpredictability in the bowling, which proved especially useful on the subcontinent-like pitches at Trent Bridge and The Oval. However, the core weakness – a lack of batting depth – proved their undoing against Pakistan in the final.

The best decision of the year was undoubtedly Jayawardene's gamble with Dilshan as an opener. He had started the year fighting for his international career: axed from the one-day team late in 2008, he was facing increasingly stiff competition for his Test place. However, Dilshan hit form in the first week of January with 162 and 143 in the Second Test against Bangladesh at Chittagong. With Sri Lanka's batting struggling in the one-day tri-series that followed – they scraped the final against Bangladesh by two wickets thanks to an audacious 33 from 16 balls from Muralitharan, after they had been six for five – that form propelled Dilshan into the squad for a hastily arranged tour by Pakistan. Then, when Upul Tharanga was injured, Jayawardene gave Dilshan a chance at the top: he responded with 42, 76 and 137 not out. After a good IPL season for Delhi Daredevils, he top-scored in the World Twenty20 with 317 runs, and was named Player of the Tournament. Afterwards Sangakkara also put him up the order in Tests, to create room for Mathews as an all-rounder, and Dilshan finished the calendar year with 1,097 Test runs at 64, plus 980 in one-dayers at 57 and 471 Twenty20 runs: in all he made ten international centuries, a number only ever exceeded in a calendar year by Sachin Tendulkar (12 in 1998) and Ricky Ponting (11 in 2003).

While Jayawardene's decision to promote Dilshan was a masterstroke, his own year started badly, with poor form in one-day cricket. After a brutal year in 2008, during which he was at loggerheads with the board chairman Arjuna Ranatunga over player contracts and the IPL, Jayawardene looked increasingly

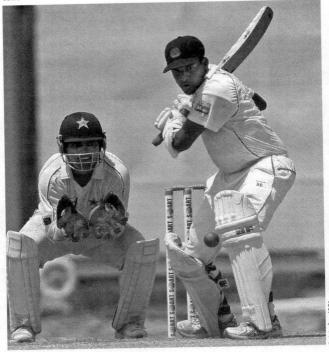

Revitalised: Thilan Samaraweera was 2009's highest run-scorer in Tests, with 1,234 at 72.58.

drained emotionally, and three days after his second home one-day series defeat by India in six months he announced that he would stand down after the tour of Pakistan, saying: "This is something I have been considering for some time as it has been my long-held belief that my successor should have at least 18 months in the job to imprint his vision on the team for the 2011 World Cup. I have concluded that the time has come for fresh leadership to take over. It was not an easy decision to make, because being the Sri Lanka captain has been the source of enormous pride. I hope to play a major part in the team's success as a batsman."

While Sangakkara appeared the obvious successor, no decision was officially made until after the aborted Pakistan series. There were wild-card candidates discussed in the corridors of power, including split-captaincy options to reduce the burden on Sangakkara, who already had the dual role of batting and wicketkeeping in limited-overs games. In the end, though, Sangakkara was appointed, with Muralitharan as his deputy. While Murali was initially reluctant, Sangakkara persuaded him to take on the responsibility. It turned out to be a canny choice, with Muralitharan offering pragmatic strategic advice and strong support within the dressing-room. The new leadership was also given increased input into team-related decisions by the new cricket board, and went on to form a solid working relationship with the selection committee, chaired by Ashantha de Mel.

Sangakkara enjoyed a honeymoon period: the World Twenty20 success was followed by a maiden home Test-series win over Pakistan. He quickly showed a willingness to take tough decisions, especially on selection. Those decisions were not universally acclaimed at the start – such as the dropping of Vaas in favour of Thilan Thushara Mirando, and the use of a makeshift wicketkeeper (Dilshan) after an injury to Prasanna Jayawardene – but they paid off against both Pakistan and New Zealand. Later in the year, though, Sangakkara's decision-making attracted greater scrutiny during a disappointing Champions Trophy and on the Indian tour. Encouragingly, the heightened pressure helped him grow as a leader, as he led from the front with the bat and looked increasingly composed on the field.

Sri Lanka's new cricket administration was appointed in February 2009, replacing the ad hoc Sports Ministry management committee that had taken over from Ranatunga. Notable decisions included a major expansion of central player contracts to 76, increased security for academy and development players, a record US$4.85million team-sponsorship deal with telecoms provider Mobitel, and an immediate improvement in bilateral ties with India. The board had faced possible bankruptcy in late 2008, but now found its financial position much healthier after lucrative tours by India in February and

Murali wanted to play in the World Cup

September, participation in the inaugural Champions League Twenty20, and more commitments from India in 2010. The new cricket committee decided to push ahead with the construction of international stadiums in Pallakelle (near Kandy) and Hambantota in the deep south, to be ready for matches in early 2010 and the following year's World Cup.

The team was also focused on the 2011 World Cup as the New Year started, and there was a clear shift in selection thinking after the Indian tour. The future of 40-year-old Sanath Jayasuriya within the one-day side was increasingly uncertain, although a possible role as a spin-bowling all-rounder in the middle order could keep him in the squad.

Vaas had not officially announced his retirement from one-dayers, but remained outside the selection radar after the emergence of Thushara Mirando and Chanaka Welegedara, two more left-armers. Muralitharan was also under pressure after a year of niggling injuries limited him to 16 one-day internationals (22 wickets at 29.45) and eight Tests (26 at 45.96). Now 37, he announced that he planned to retire from Test cricket at the end of West Indies' tour of Sri Lanka in November 2010, but said he wanted to play in the 2011 World Cup, form and fitness permitting.

Ajantha Mendis and Lasith Malinga also finished the year without guaranteed places. After his spectacular start in 2008, Mendis struggled in his second year of Test cricket, with 18 wickets at 45.55, as batsmen started to decode his different deliveries. Malinga also struggled to recapture his best form after returning from a long-term knee injury in time for the second IPL in South Africa. The major concern was his physical condition, and after a disappointing Indian tour he was dropped, with the team management putting him on a two-month crash course to get him fit for the World Twenty20 in April.

The 50-over team's composition changed dramatically, with Thilina Kandamby cementing a middle-order place with 674 runs at 42 from 20 matches, and Mathews securing a regular berth at No. 7. Tharanga returned in place of Jayasuriya at the top of the order, and also rediscovered his form after two lean years. Rising young stars such as off-spinner Suraj Randiv, all-rounder Tissara Perera, fast bowler Suranga Lakmal, wicketkeeper Dinesh Chandimal and middle-order batsman Lahiru Thirimanne broke into the national squad and pushed hard for places. The rise of several players from the development and youth squads created additional excitement about the future, with the Under-19 team – assisted by batting coach Aravinda de Silva – winning a maiden series in Australia and impressing many throughout the year.

The Sri Lanka team management was bolstered early in the year by the return of Tommy Simsek as head physiotherapist. Simsek was released by the previous administration because of his contract with Chennai Super Kings, but the new IPL-friendly board welcomed him back. Trevor Bayliss continued as head coach, but his position became vulnerable after the Champions Trophy, and he was nearly replaced. However, the departure of his assistant Paul Farbrace, back to Kent, and the non-availability of other senior coaches prompted a rethink, and Bayliss was given a contract extension until the 2011 World Cup. Stuart Law was appointed his assistant at the end of the year, alongside Chandika Hathurusinghe, the former A-team coach who is being groomed for the top job.

SRI LANKA v INDIA, 2008-09

SA'ADI THAWFEEQ

One-day internationals (5): Sri Lanka 1, India 4
Twenty20 international (1): Sri Lanka 0, India 1

This was a series that Sri Lanka simultaneously wanted and didn't want – and ultimately it proved disastrous. They staved off a whitewash only in the fifth match, after competing properly in only one of the first four.

India's tour to Pakistan was cancelled in the aftermath of the Mumbai terrorist attacks, leaving Sri Lanka caught in the middle, trying to appease both countries, which would otherwise have been without international cricket in January and February. Sri Lanka accepted a split tour to Pakistan consisting of three one-day matches and a later two-Test series. Sandwiched between them was this one-day series, which cash-strapped Sri Lanka Cricket embraced with an eye on the television rights, worth \$US6m.

India were on a high after thrashing England 5–0, and they continued in the same vein against a weary Sri Lankan team who had been on the road for two months touring Bangladesh, Zimbabwe and Pakistan. Sri Lanka had emerged victorious from all three countries, but against a strong side such as India they lacked the zest to extend that run.

Significantly, Sri Lanka lost the toss in the four matches they lost. At Dambulla they were inserted, but the pitch was a good one, and India could time their chase with ease; in the next three, India chose to bat, as teams at Colombo's R. Premadasa Stadium invariably do in day/night games, leaving Sri Lanka to cope with exacting conditions under the lights. When the coin finally favoured them, they won, though since it was a day game, the importance of the toss was less.

The pitches were better batting strips than against England two years earlier, when run-scoring was a constant problem. But it was the Indian batsmen who prospered most, partly because they seemed to have unravelled the mystery of Ajantha Mendis. Muttiah Muralitharan, meanwhile, who at the start of the series needed just three to overhaul Wasim Akram's record of 502 one-day international wickets, had to wait until the fourth match to claim his crown. Indeed, it was India's Pragyan Ojha who emerged as the most potent and niggardly slow bowler on either side.

Yuvraj Singh, Gautam Gambhir and Mahendra Singh Dhoni all averaged over 50, though Sachin Tendulkar missed out. After three dubious lbw decisions, he was rested for the last two 50-over games and returned home before the Twenty20 international.

Sri Lanka, however, did have problems with their batting, which failed to deliver until the final game. Kumar Sangakkara hit three fifties, but only the vastly experienced Sanath Jayasuriya reached three figures, becoming the oldest player to score a hundred in one-day internationals. Mahela Jayawardene struggled for runs, and at the end of the series stepped down from the captaincy to concentrate on his batting.

Up in lights: Muttiah Muralitharan moved past Wasim Akram's total of 502 ODI wickets by dismissing Gautam Gambhir in the fourth match. Kumar Sangakkara and Sanath Jayasuriya offer congratulations at Murali's second world record.

His side were beaten fair and square by an all-round Indian outfit that had an answer to everything the Sri Lankans could offer. Player for player, there was little to choose between the two sides, but India were increasingly confident, daring in their approach, and they took chances; Sri Lanka, their backs to the wall, were always second-best. The defeat was Sri Lanka's third in succession in a home bilateral series.

INDIAN TOURING PARTY

M. S. Dhoni (*captain*), L. Balaji, G. Gambhir, R. A. Jadeja, P. Kumar, P. P. Ojha, M. M. Patel, I. K. Pathan, Y. K. Pathan, S. K. Raina, V. Sehwag, I. Sharma, R. G. Sharma, S. R. Tendulkar, Yuvraj Singh, Zaheer Khan. *Coach:* G. Kirsten.

SRI LANKA v INDIA

First One-Day International

At Dambulla, January 28, 2009. India won by six wickets. Toss: India.

Sri Lanka may have been surprised by a Dambulla wicket that for once played true. Asked to bat, they made a cautious start after losing Dilshan to the third ball of the innings – run out after a misunderstanding with Jayasuriya, who went on to his 28th hundred in limited-overs internationals, from 108 balls. He also became only the second batsman, after Tendulkar, to pass 13,000 runs. Tendulkar himself departed to a doubtful lbw – the first player to be given out by Kumar Dharmasena, Sri Lanka's former World Cup-winning player, who was making his international umpiring debut. Thanks to three fifties and some fallible Sri Lankan catching, India had no difficulty reaching their target.

Man of the Match: S. T. Jayasuriya.

NOT ALWAYS A YOUNG MAN'S GAME

The oldest batsmen to hit a century in one-day internationals:

Years	days			
39	**212**	**S. T. Jayasuriya (107)**	**Sri Lanka v India at Dambulla**	**2008-09**
39	51	G. Boycott (105)	England v Australia at Sydney	1979-80
39	6	S. T. Jayasuriya (125)	Sri Lanka v India at Karachi	2008
39	0	S. T. Jayasuriya (130)	Sri Lanka v Bangladesh at Karachi	2008
38	149	D. L. Hemp (102*)	Bermuda v Kenya at Potchefstroom	2008-09
38	113	S. M. Gavaskar (103*)	India v New Zealand at Nagpur	1987-88
38	18	D. L. Haynes (115)	West Indies v England at Port-of-Spain	1993-94
37	321	C. G. Greenidge (117)	West Indies v India at St John's	1988-89

Research: Philip Bailey

Sri Lanka

T. M. Dilshan run out	0	
S. T. Jayasuriya c Patel b Zaheer Khan	107	
†K. C. Sangakkara c Raina b Ojha	44	
S. H. T. Kandamby c Zaheer Khan		
b I. Sharma . .	17	
M. F. Maharoof b I. Sharma	35	
*D. P. M. D. Jayawardene c R. G. Sharma		
b I. Sharma . .	11	

C. K. Kapugedera run out 15
M. T. T. Mirando not out 12
K. M. D. N. Kulasekara not out. 0
W 3, n-b 2 5

1/0 (1) 2/118 (3)   (7 wkts, 50 overs) 246
3/169 (4) 4/171 (2)
5/204 (6) 6/222 (5) 7/245 (7)   10 overs: 33-1

M. Muralitharan and B. A. W. Mendis did not bat.

Zaheer Khan 10–2–40–1; Patel 5–0–32–0; I. Sharma 10–1–52–3; Ojha 10–0–52–1; Pathan 7–0–32–0; Raina 4–0–16–0; R. G. Sharma 4–1–22–0.

India

G. Gambhir c Kandamby b Muralitharan . .	62	
S. R. Tendulkar lbw b Mirando	5	
S. K. Raina run out	54	
Yuvraj Singh c Muralitharan b Maharoof . .	23	
*†M. S. Dhoni not out	61	

R. G. Sharma not out. 25
L-b 8, w 8, n-b 1 17

1/13 (2) 2/126 (1)   (4 wkts, 48.1 overs) 247
3/137 (3) 4/181 (4)   10 overs: 54-1

Y. K. Pathan, Zaheer Khan, P. P. Ojha, I. Sharma and M. M. Patel did not bat.

Kulasekara 7–0–32–0; Mirando 8–0–44–1; Maharoof 8–0–35–1; Mendis 10–0–47–0; Muralitharan 10–0–52–1; Dilshan 5.1–0–29–0.

Umpires: H. D. P. K. Dharmasena and B. G. Jerling.
Third umpire: M. G. Silva.   Referee: B. C. Broad.

SRI LANKA v INDIA

Second One-Day International

At R. Premadasa Stadium, Colombo, January 31, 2009 (day/night). India won by 15 runs. Toss: India.

Kandamby's career-best unbeaten 93 took the match into the final over, but a third consecutive run-out spelled an Indian victory. He shared a partnership of 100 with Jayawardene after Sri Lanka were reduced to 36 for three, but no one else stayed for long. Maharoof failed to make the most of his luck after a Zaheer Khan yorker deflected off his leg stump without dislodging a bail and sped to the boundary for four byes. The innings was held up in the 24th over when Sharma, fielding at fine leg, was hit by a nut thrown from the crowd; he responded with three vital wickets. Earlier, Tendulkar and Yuvraj Singh both fell to two more dubious lbw decisions, Yuvraj off a thick inside edge on to his pads. He was slow to depart, but was later cleared of dissent by match referee Chris Broad.

Man of the Match: I. Sharma.

India

V. Sehwag run out	42	P. Kumar c Jayawardene b Mendis	15
S. R. Tendulkar lbw b Kulasekara	6	P. P. Ojha not out	0
G. Gambhir c Sangakkara b Maharoof	27	L-b 1, w 8, n-b 1	10
Yuvraj Singh lbw b Kulasekara	66		
S. K. Raina c Kapugedera b Dilshan	29	1/13 (2) 2/62 (3) (9 wkts, 50 overs) 256	
*†M. S. Dhoni c Sangakkara b Maharoof	23	3/83 (1) 4/168 (5)	
Y. K. Pathan run out	21	5/180 (4) 6/219 (7) 7/223 (6)	
Zaheer Khan c Dilshan b Mendis	17	8/256 (9) 9/256 (8)	

I. Sharma did not bat.

Kulasekara 9–0–61–2; Mirando 8–0–59–0; Maharoof 10–0–40–2; Mendis 10–0–44–2; Muralitharan 10–1–32–0; Dilshan 3–0–19–1.

Sri Lanka

T. M. Dilshan c Sharma b Zaheer Khan	8	K. M. D. N. Kulasekara run out	1
S. T. Jayasuriya b Ojha b Sharma	17	B. A. W. Mendis run out	0
†K. C. Sangakkara c Tendulkar b Kumar	4		
*D. P. M. D. Jayawardene c Pathan b Ojha	52	B 4, l-b 4, w 10	18
S. H. T. Kandamby not out	93		
C. K. Kapugedera c Dhoni b Sharma	31	1/15 (1) 2/33 (2) 3/36 (3) (49.2 overs) 241	
M. F. Maharoof b Sharma	7	4/136 (4) 5/187 (6) 6/206 (7)	
M. T. T. Mirando c Pathan b Sharma	7	7/228 (8) 8/236 (9) 9/237 (10)	
M. Muralitharan run out	3	10/241 (11) 10 overs: 47-3	

Zaheer Khan 10–0–56–1; Kumar 8.2–1–22–1; Sharma 10–1–57–4; Ojha 7–0–39–1; Pathan 5–0–21–0; Sehwag 5–0–19–0; Raina 4–0–19–0.

Umpires: B. G. Jerling and M. G. Silva.
Third umpire: H. D. P. K. Dharmasena.   Referee: B. C. Broad.

SRI LANKA v INDIA

Third One-Day International

At R. Premadasa Stadium, Colombo, February 3, 2009 (day/night). India won by 147 runs. Toss: India.

Despite losing two early wickets – Tendulkar on the receiving end of a third debatable lbw call in three innings – India dominated this game. Yuvraj Singh and Sehwag piled on 221 from 167 balls, Yuvraj reaching a century from 82 deliveries and Sehwag his from 75. Pathan weighed in with three sixes to take India – who were helped by more ragged fielding – to the ground's highest total in one-day internationals. Sri Lanka were strangled by the left-arm spin of Ojha as they tumbled to their biggest home defeat. India had won the series at the earliest opportunity. The only positive for Sri Lanka came when Muralitharan had Yuvraj caught at cover to break the huge stand; it took Murali level with Wasim Akram on 502 wickets.

Man of the Match: Yuvraj Singh.

India

V. Sehwag run out	116	Y. K. Pathan not out 59
S. R. Tendulkar lbw b Fernando	7	W 7, n-b 3 10
G. Gambhir run out	10	
Yuvraj Singh c Kapugedera b Muralitharan	117	1/9 (2) 2/24 (3) (5 wkts, 50 overs) 363
*†M. S. Dhoni not out	35	3/245 (4) 4/265 (1)
S. K. Raina st Sangakkara b Mendis	9	5/278 (6)
		10 overs: 68-2

Zaheer Khan, P. Kumar, P. P. Ojha and I. Sharma did not bat.

Kulasekara 10–0–68–0; Fernando 8–0–63–1; Maharoof 7–0–68–0; Mendis 9–0–64–1; Muralitharan 10–0–60–1; Jayasuriya 6–1–40–0.

Sri Lanka

T. M. Dilshan b Zaheer Khan	31	M. Muralitharan c Dhoni b Ojha	0
S. T. Jayasuriya b Kumar	0	B. A. W. Mendis not out	8
†K. C. Sangakkara c Yuvraj Singh b Ojha	83	C. R. D. Fernando run out	19
*D. P. M. D. Jayawardene c Sehwag b Kumar	30	
S. H. T. Kandamby c Yuvraj Singh b Sehwag	10	L-b 3, w 5 8
C. K. Kapugedera b Ojha	2	1/7 (2) 2/51 (1) 3/118 (4) (41.4 overs) 216
M. F. Maharoof c Gambhir b Ojha	22	4/132 (5) 5/139 (6) 6/184 (7)
K. M. D. N. Kulasekara c Tendulkar b Yuvraj Singh	3	7/189 (3) 8/189 (9) 9/189 (8)
		10/216 (11) 10 overs: 56-2

Zaheer Khan 8–1–44–1; Kumar 7–0–41–2; Sharma 5–0–35–0; Ojha 10–0–38–4; Sehwag 7–0–30–1; Yuvraj Singh 3.4–0–14–1; Tendulkar 1–0–11–0.

Umpires: B. G. Jerling and M. G. Silva.
Third umpire: H. D. P. K. Dharmasena.   Referee: B. C. Broad.

SRI LANKA v INDIA

Fourth One-Day International

At R. Premadasa Stadium, Colombo, February 5, 2009 (day/night). India won by 67 runs. Toss: India.

From the first ball of his tenth and last over, Muralitharan finally claimed the record for most wickets in limited-overs internationals – but not before Gambhir, his historic 503rd victim, had amassed 150. Gambhir's personal-best included a six and 14 fours from 147 deliveries as he and Dhoni, who promoted himself up the order, added 188 after the early loss of Sehwag. Sri Lanka began their assault on their steep target at speed, with Jayasuriya launching a couple of early off-side sixes. Both openers had gone, though, by the time play was interrupted in the 18th over when stones were thrown from the stands. Dhoni took his team off the field for nearly half an hour before the game resumed. Otherwise, India were unstoppable as they notched up their ninth successive victory in one-day internationals.

Man of the Match: G. Gambhir.

India

V. Sehwag c Jayasuriya b Kulasekara	5	R. G. Sharma not out	4
G. Gambhir c Sangakkara b Muralitharan	150	L-b 9, w 15, n-b 1 25
*†M. S. Dhoni c Fernando b Jayasuriya	94	
Yuvraj Singh b Kulasekara	5	1/14 (1) 2/202 (3) (5 wkts, 50 overs) 332
Y. K. Pathan b Kulasekara	0	3/207 (4) 4/207 (5)
S. K. Raina not out	49	5/310 (2)
		10 overs: 50-1

I. K. Pathan, P. Kumar, P. P. Ojha and I. Sharma did not bat.

Kulasekara 10–0–63–3; Maharoof 10–0–60–0; Fernando 9–0–64–0; Mathews 3–0–24–0; Muralitharan 10–0–66–1; Jayasuriya 8–0–46–1.

Sri Lanka

T. M. Dilshan c Yuvraj Singh b Kumar	... 38	K. M. D. N. Kulasekara not out	 39
S. T. Jayasuriya c R. G. Sharma		M. Muralitharan c Raina b I. K. Pathan	 0
	b I. K. Pathan. 27	C. R. D. Fernando b Kumar	 9
†K. C. Sangakkara c Gambhir b Sehwag	... 56		
*D. P. M. D. Jayawardene c Dhoni b Sehwag	28	L-b 3, w 5	 8
S. H. T. Kandamby lbw b Y. K. Pathan	... 10		
C. K. Kapugedera b Ojha	 16	1/55 (2) 2/79 (1) 3/140 (4) (48 overs) 265
A. D. Mathews c Dhoni b Yuvraj Singh	... 6	4/163 (5) 5/174 (3) 6/183 (7)
M. F. Maharoof c R. G. Sharma		7/207 (6) 8/220 (8) 9/220 (10)
	b I. K. Pathan. 28	10/265 (11) 10 overs: 73-1

Kumar 9–0–38–2; I. K. Pathan 7–0–58–3; I. Sharma 5–0–39–0; Ojha 10–0–34–1; Sehwag 9–0–43–2; Y. K. Pathan 3–0–13–1; Yuvraj Singh 5–0–37–1.

Umpires: H. D. P. K. Dharmasena and B. G. Jerling.
Third umpire: M. G. Silva. Referee: B. C. Broad.

SRI LANKA v INDIA

Fifth One-Day International

At R. Premadasa Stadium, Colombo, February 8, 2009. Sri Lanka won by 68 runs. Toss: Sri Lanka. One-day international debut: R. A. Jadeja.

At last, Sri Lanka turned their game around to prevent a whitewash. It started at the toss which, eventually, Jayawardene won. As so often, Jayasuriya provided the launch-pad: Dilshan and Sangakkara added 143 as Dhoni juggled nine bowlers. The innings juddered to a temporary halt when four wickets fell for one run in 12 deliveries, but took off again during the batting powerplay, which yielded 46 from the last five overs. India's recent form suggested they might make 321, but the departure of Yuvraj Singh for a 62-ball 73 left them struggling at 121 for five. They managed just the one fifty partnership: 55 for the seventh wicket between Dhoni and the debutant Ravindra Jadeja, a 20-year-old all-rounder whose left-arm spin had helped India win the Under-19 World Cup a year earlier. An overdue decent display in the field helped Sri Lanka to a consolation win.

Man of the Match: K. C. Sangakkara. *Man of the Series:* Yuvraj Singh.

Sri Lanka

T. M. Dilshan run out	 97	M. T. T. Mirando c and b I. Sharma	 11
S. T. Jayasuriya c Raina b I. K. Pathan	... 37	K. M. D. N. Kulasekara not out	 10
†K. C. Sangakkara c R. G. Sharma		M. Muralitharan not out	 3
	b Yuvraj Singh. 84	B 3, l-b 8, w 7, n-b 1	 19
S. H. T. Kandamby b I. Sharma	 26		
*D. P. M. D. Jayawardene c Raina		1/66 (2) 2/209 (3) (8 wkts, 50 overs) 320
	b Yuvraj Singh. 1	3/255 (4) 4/255 (1)
C. K. Kapugedera c Dhoni b I. Sharma	 0	5/256 (6) 6/256 (5)
M. F. Maharoof run out	 32	7/277 (8) 8/315 (7) 10 overs: 66-0

B. A. W. Mendis did not bat.

I. K. Pathan 9–0–55–1; I. Sharma 10–0–60–3; Balaji 5–0–32–0; Sehwag 3–0–26–0; Jadeja 6–0–40–0; Y. K. Pathan 3–0–20–0; Raina 6–0–24–0; Yuvraj Singh 6–0–39–2; R. G. Sharma 2–0–13–0.

India

G. Gambhir c Sangakkara b Kulasekara ...	13
V. Sehwag c Jayasuriya b Mirando	6
S. K. Raina c Sangakkara b Kulasekara ...	0
Yuvraj Singh c and b Muralitharan	73
R. G. Sharma c Kulasekara b Maharoof ...	15
*†M. S. Dhoni c Kulasekara b Jayasuriya ...	53
Y. K. Pathan b Muralitharan	3
R. A. Jadeja not out	60
I. K. Pathan c Kapugedera b Mendis	8

L. Balaji c Kulasekara b Mendis	7
I. Sharma b Maharoof	4
L-b 2, w 8	10

1/8 (2) 2/9 (3) 3/52 (1)   (48.5 overs) 252
4/85 (5) 5/121 (4) 6/138 (7)
7/193 (6) 8/217 (9) 9/243 (10)
10/252 (11)   10 overs: 60-3

Kulasekara 9–0–42–2; Mirando 6–0–34–1; Maharoof 5.5–0–46–2; Muralitharan 10–0–41–2; Mendis 10–0–44–2; Jayasuriya 6–0–28–1; Dilshan 2–0–15–0.

Umpires: B. G. Jerling and T. H. Wijewardene.
Third umpire: H. D. P. K. Dharmasena.   Referee: B. C. Broad.

SRI LANKA v INDIA

Twenty20 International

At R. Premadasa Stadium, Colombo, February 10, 2009 (day/night). India won by three wickets. Toss: Sri Lanka. Twenty20 international debuts: S. I. de Saram; R. A. Jadeja.

Victory seemed to be within Sri Lanka's grasp when it was snatched away by the Pathan brothers, who carried India to an exciting win in the first Twenty20 international played in Sri Lanka. India were in serious trouble at 115 for seven in the 16th over, but the Pathans added 59 from 25 deliveries to see them home with four balls to spare. In his first game as captain, Dilshan, who also kept wicket, won the toss and, after understudying Jayasuriya in an opening stand worth 59, accelerated to give his side a defendable total. But his wayward seamers, who conceded 13 wides, gave him a headache before the spinners exerted some control. Three wickets for the leg-spin of Malinga Bandara looked to have turned things round before the Pathans gained the last laugh.

Man of the Match: Y. K. Pathan.

Sri Lanka

		B	4	6
*†T. M. Dilshan c 3 b 11	61	47	7	1
S. T. Jayasuriya c 11 b 9	33	17	3	2
J. Mubarak c and b 8	13	19	1	0
C. K. Kapugedera c 2 b 8	16	9	3	0
L. P. C. Silva not out	21	18	2	1
K. Weeraratne not out	10	10	1	0
B 1, l-b 10, w 6	17			

6 overs: 59-1   (20 overs) 171-4

1/59 2/87 3/107 4/152

S. I. de Saram, M. T. T. Mirando, C. M. Bandara, C. R. D. Fernando and S. L. Malinga did not bat.

Zaheer Khan 4–0–34–0; I. Sharma 4–0–40–1; I. K. Pathan 4–0–34–1; Y. K. Pathan 4–0–23–2; Jadeja 4–0–29–0.

India

		B	4	6
G. Gambhir c 6 b 8	13	6	3	0
V. Sehwag run out	1	1	0	0
S. K. Raina c 7 b 9	35	27	5	1
Yuvraj Singh c 1 b 3	32	21	3	2
*†M. S. Dhoni b 9	13	17	1	0
R. G. Sharma c 3 b 2	4	11	0	0
R. A. Jadeja b 9	5	7	0	0
Y. K. Pathan not out	22	10	1	2
I. K. Pathan not out	33	16	2	2
L-b 2, w 14	16			

6 overs: 57-2   (19.2 overs) 174-7

1/14 2/14 3/81 4/99 5/108 6/110 7/115

Zaheer Khan and I. Sharma did not bat.

Malinga 3.2–0–38–0; Mirando 3–0–27–1; Fernando 4–0–44–0; Weeraratne 4–0–12–0; Mubarak 1–0–9–1; Bandara 4–0–32–3; Jayasuriya 3–0–10–1.

Umpires: M. G. Silva and T. H. Wijewardene.
Third umpire: H. D. P. K. Dharmasena.   Referee: B. C. Broad.

SRI LANKA v PAKISTAN, 2009

Sa'adi Thawfeeq

Test matches (3): Sri Lanka 2, Pakistan 0
One-day internationals (5): Sri Lanka 3, Pakistan 2
Twenty20 international (1): Sri Lanka 0, Pakistan 1

Four months after the harrowing experience of Lahore, when the Sri Lankan team touring Pakistan were targeted by terrorists, the two countries met in another Test series. The resumption was eagerly awaited, but few predicted the eventual outcome: Sri Lanka won the Test series 2–0, although that margin flatters them a little, while the reverse was true in the one-day series, which Sri Lanka clinched by winning the first three matches fairly comfortably, before Pakistan improved the look of the scoreline by taking the last two. It was the first time Sri Lanka had beaten Pakistan at home in either a Test series or a bilateral one-day series.

Pakistan's Test performances have long been unpredictable, and that quality was again to the fore as they wasted good positions in both the first two Tests, which they ended up losing. Their best form came right at the end of the tour: after winning the last two one-day internationals they confirmed their superiority in the shortest format of all by winning the one-off repeat of the World Twenty20 final at Lord's in June.

The way Younis Khan's team lost the first two Tests gave rise to whispers of match-fixing. *Express*, an Urdu newspaper in Pakistan, claimed that some of the players said they had been approached by suspicious people who were staying in the same hotel as the team. The Pakistan Cricket Board ordered an immediate investigation into the allegations, in consultation with the ICC, whose Anti-Corruption and Security Unit regional manager was present during the series. Following their investigations the ACSU reported that they were satisfied there was no substance to the suggestions, and that there was no evidence any such contacts existed.

Over the years Sri Lanka's top-order batting, and the bowling of Muttiah Muralitharan and Chaminda Vaas, have been major factors in their Test successes, but that was rather less the case this time. Pakistan managed a century in each Test, while Sri Lanka's only hundred was captain Kumar Sangakkara's fighting innings to ensure a draw in the Third Test. And while it was Sri Lanka's bowling which won the day, it was done without Muralitharan, who missed the Tests with a knee injury, while Vaas was not considered for the first two Tests, and played in the last only to allow him a fitting farewell before retirement. On top of that Prasanna Jayawardene, arguably the world's best wicketkeeper, damaged a finger and was ruled out of the First Test. In a surprise move the gloves went not to Sangakkara, who had enough on his plate captaining the side, but to Tillekeratne Dilshan, who began his first-class career as a keeper, but had never started a Test behind the stumps before. He performed so well that he retained the gloves throughout the series, but at some cost – in the final Test he broke his right index finger taking a catch and was ruled out of the one-dayers.

Sri Lanka's unfamiliar bowling attack featured a new-ball pairing of Nuwan Kulasekara – basking in the status of No. 1 in the ICC's one-day bowling rankings – and left-armer Thilan Thushara Mirando. When Murali was ruled out, the board sent out an SOS to the slow left-armer Rangana Herath, who was playing league cricket in Staffordshire. In the end this trio won the Test series through some excellent performances, which accounted for 44 of the 55 Pakistan wickets that fell to bowlers. They needed to perform, since Ajantha Mendis – the sensation of 2008 – bowled well only in patches, and proved to be largely ineffectual against batsmen who managed to play him freely: his five wickets cost 43.40 apiece.

Pakistan's side was a blend of youth and experience. Mohammad Yousuf and Abdul Razzaq were recalled after their bans for playing in the unauthorised Indian Cricket League were lifted, but neither made an outstanding contribution. Yousuf did make the first century of the series, but Razzaq was not seriously considered for any of the Tests. The finds for Pakistan were Mohammad Aamer, 17, a left-arm fast bowler in the Wasim Akram mould who had done well in the World Twenty20 in England not long before, and 19-year-old Umar Akmal (the younger brother of wicketkeeper Kamran Akmal), whose batting in the one-day internationals was sometimes reminiscent of the great Javed Miandad.

The Test series was plagued throughout by the Kookaburra balls going out of shape. Pakistan's veteran coach Intikhab Alam thought the home bowlers were trying to take advantage: "If you analyse the first two Test matches and this one," he said during the Third Test, "every time the ball was changed it has worked. Today they changed it twice, and I don't want to say anything about it, but it's just one of those things. The first ball they changed didn't do anything and then they certainly got the right ball and it did the trick. It's part and parcel of the game."

Security throughout the tour was extremely tight, despite the end of the Sri Lankan government's long conflict with the Tamil Tigers. Following the traumatic experience of Lahore, Sri Lanka Cricket appointed a consultant to oversee all security arrangements for the national team both at home and abroad. The Pakistan tour was handled by Major-General Lawrence Fernando, a former Sri Lankan Army chief of staff, who was first appointed for the World Twenty20.

PAKISTAN TOURING PARTY

Younis Khan (*captain*), Abdul Razzaq, Abdur Rauf, Danish Kaneria, Faisal Iqbal, Fawad Alam, Kamran Akmal, Khurram Manzoor, Misbah-ul-Haq, Mohammad Aamer, Mohammad Yousuf, Saeed Ajmal, Salman Butt, Shoaib Malik, Umar Gul. *Coach:* Intikhab Alam.

For the one-day matches that followed the Tests, Iftikhar Anjum, Imran Nazir, Nasir Jamshed, Naved-ul-Hasan, Shahid Afridi and Umar Akmal replaced Abdur Rauf, Danish Kaneria, Faisal Iqbal, Khurram Manzoor and Salman Butt.

TEST MATCH AVERAGES
SRI LANKA – BATTING AND FIELDING

	T	I	NO	R	HS	100s	50s	Avge	Ct
†K. C. Sangakkara........	3	6	1	331	130*	1	1	66.20	2
A. D. Mathews	3	5	1	191	64*	0	1	47.75	0
†N. T. Paranavitana.......	3	6	0	242	73	0	2	40.33	2
T. T. Samaraweera.......	3	6	1	171	73	0	1	34.20	1
D. P. M. D. Jayawardene .	3	6	1	167	79	0	1	33.40	5
T. M. Dilshan.........	3	4	0	114	44	0	0	28.50	11
K. M. D. N. Kulasekara..	3	4	0	75	38	0	0	18.75	0
†B. S. M. Warnapura......	3	6	0	98	54	0	1	16.33	1
†M. T. T. Mirando........	3	4	2	31	15*	0	0	15.50	2
†H. M. R. K. B. Herath	3	4	1	42	20*	0	0	14.00	1
B. A. W. Mendis	2	3	1	6	5	0	0	3.00	0

Played in one Test: †W. P. U. J. C. Vaas 4 (1 ct).

† *Left-handed batsman.*

BOWLING

	Style	O	M	R	W	BB	5W/i	Avge
K. M. D. N. Kulasekara.........	RFM	95.4	20	256	17	4-21	0	15.05
H. M. R. K. B. Herath...........	SLA	137.3	25	404	15	5-99	2	26.93
M. T. T. Mirando	LFM	102.4	14	373	12	5-83	1	31.08
A. D. Mathews	RFM	39	5	138	4	1-13	0	34.50
B. A. W. Mendis	OB/LBG	62	5	217	5	3-20	0	43.40

Also bowled: D. P. M. D. Jayawardene (RM) 2–0–9–0; N. T. Paranavitana (OB) 6–0–26–1; W. P. U. J. C. Vaas (LFM) 39–12–90–1.

PAKISTAN – BATTING AND FIELDING

	T	I	NO	R	HS	100s	50s	Avge	Ct/St
†Fawad Alam.............	2	4	0	216	168	1	0	54.00	2
Shoaib Malik............	3	6	1	262	134	1	0	52.40	3
Mohammad Yousuf......	3	6	0	253	112	1	1	42.16	1
Misbah-ul-Haq..........	3	6	0	158	65	0	2	26.33	6
Khurram Manzoor.......	3	6	0	153	93	0	1	25.50	3
Younis Khan	3	6	0	124	74	0	1	20.66	13/1
Kamran Akmal	3	6	0	131	82	0	1	21.83	1
†Mohammad Aamer	3	6	3	37	22*	0	0	12.33	0
Umar Gul..............	3	6	0	67	46	0	0	11.16	1
Abdur Rauf	2	4	0	44	31	0	0	11.00	0
Saeed Ajmal	3	6	3	13	8	0	0	4.33	0

Played in one Test: Danish Kaneria 1, 5; †Salman Butt 0, 28 (1 ct).

BOWLING

	Style	O	M	R	W	BB	5W/i	Avge
Younis Khan	LB	37	5	123	5	2-23	0	24.60
Danish Kaneria	LBG	56.3	6	176	7	5-62	0	25.14
Saeed Ajmal	OB	146.4	24	421	14	4-87	0	30.07
Abdur Rauf	RFM	42	4	159	5	2-59	0	31.80
Mohammad Aamer ..	LFM	80	14	261	6	3-38	0	43.50
Umar Gul..........	RFM	70	6	308	7	4-43	0	44.00

Also bowled: Shoaib Malik (OB) 18.5–2–59–2.

Note: Matches in this section which were not first-class are signified by a dagger.

†At Colts CC, Colombo, June 29, 30, July 1, 2009. **Drawn.** Toss: Sri Lanka Cricket XI. **Sri Lanka Cricket XI 345-5 dec** (W. U. Tharanga 50, H. D. R. L. Thirimanne 116, C. K. Kapugedera 115) **and 137-2 dec** (W. U. Tharanga 44, N. T. Paranavitana 48, J. K. Silva 34*); **Pakistanis 400-8 dec** (Khurram Manzoor 83, Salman Butt 82, Younis Khan 37, Faisal Iqbal 32, Fawad Alam 83*, Abdur Rauf 39*; M. Pushpakumara 3-100, S. Randiv 4-120) **and 54-4.**

  Both sides chose from 13 players, of whom 11 could bat and 11 field. Chamara Kapugedera, who hit 11 fours and three sixes and eventually retired out, put on 170 for the third wicket in 34 overs with Lahiru Thirimanne – but neither played in the First Test which followed. On the final afternoon the SLC XI captain Thilina Kandamby set a tempting target of 83 in 18 overs, but four quick wickets spoilt the tourists' chances.

SRI LANKA v PAKISTAN

First Test Match

At Galle, July 4, 5, 6, 7, 2009. Sri Lanka won by 50 runs. Toss: Pakistan. Test debuts: A. D. Mathews; Abdur Rauf, Mohammad Aamer, Saeed Ajmal.

  Before the fourth day started no one gave Sri Lanka a chance. Pakistan needed only 97 runs to win, with eight wickets in hand and opener Salman Butt and first-innings centurion Mohammad Yousuf to resume. But left-armers Thilan Thushara Mirando and Rangana Herath produced exceptional spells to remove those eight wickets for just 46 runs, bringing about a spectacular collapse that turned the match on its head.

  Pakistan's woes began from the seventh ball of the day, when left-arm spinner Herath trapped Yousuf lbw; in the same over he dismissed Butt, who rashly holed out at deep square. From then on it was all Sri Lanka. Thushara Mirando, long overshadowed by the absent Chaminda Vaas, offered not a single loose delivery in an eight-over spell during which he beat the batsmen frequently. He seamed the ball away and swung it in, which slowed down the run-rate, helped by Sangakkara's field settings, which forced the batsmen to take chances if they were to reach even the modest target of 168. The game was over before lunch, with Pakistan making what was then their lowest Test total against Sri Lanka (previously 132 in another defeat, at the Colombo Cricket Club in 1985-86). Thushara Mirando finished with only two wickets, but Herath, proving an ideal replacement for the injured Muttiah Muralitharan, claimed four, adding the last two to those vital early strikes.

  Pakistan also fielded a raw bowling attack, including three debutants, but although they all performed well – Mohammad Aamer took a wicket with his sixth ball in Test cricket, and another with his 13th – they were overshadowed by the poor batting in the second innings. Pakistan had dominated this Test right from the toss… but lost it in one session on the fourth morning. They didn't score enough in the first innings, either: with Yousuf (who had cut his ties with the unauthorised Indian Cricket League) scoring his 24th hundred on his return to Test cricket after 20 months, the lead could have been around 150, which would have shut Sri Lanka out of the game. But no one else exceeded Misbah-ul-Haq's 56, and the eventual lead of 50 proved insufficient – in fact, it was exactly the margin of defeat.

Seventh heaven: Sri Lankan fielders rejoice after Misbah-ul-Haq, given run out by the third umpire, is seventh out at 85.

Younis Khan blamed the second-innings collapse on his country's recent lack of competition. "It's very easy right now to write this team off," he said later, "but how many Tests have we played in the last 14 months? For one full year we didn't play at all. As and when we start playing more regularly, we will learn to adapt. I think it's not about the technique, not about the bowling, not about the weather. Give this team some time. The reality is, we haven't been playing any Test cricket."

Man of the Match: H. M. R. K. B. Herath.

Close of play: First day, Pakistan 15-2 (Younis Khan 7, Abdur Rauf 0); Second day, Sri Lanka 0-0 (Herath 0, Warnapura 0); Third day, Pakistan 71-2 (Salman Butt 28, Mohammad Yousuf 12).

Sri Lanka

B. S. M. Warnapura b Mohammad Aamer	2	– (2) c Younis Khan b Umar Gul	0
N. T. Paranavitana c Misbah-ul-Haq b Abdur Rauf	72	– (3) c Kamran Akmal b Mohammad Aamer	49
*K. C. Sangakkara c Shoaib Malik b Mohammad Aamer	9	– (4) c Kamran Akmal b Mohammad Aamer	14
D. P. M. D. Jayawardene c Kamran Akmal b Abdur Rauf	30	– (5) c Kamran Akmal b Mohammad Aamer	0
T. T. Samaraweera c Kamran Akmal b Younis Khan	31	– (6) c Misbah-ul-Haq b Saeed Ajmal	34
†T. M. Dilshan c Shoaib Malik b Mohammad Aamer	28	– (7) c Khurram Manzoor b Younis Khan	22
A. D. Mathews c Kamran Akmal b Umar Gul	42	– (8) c Salman Butt b Abdur Rauf	27
K. M. D. N. Kulasekara c Kamran Akmal b Younis Khan	38	– (9) lbw b Saeed Ajmal	25
H. M. R. K. B. Herath not out	20	– (1) lbw b Younis Khan	15
M. T. T. Mirando c Khurram Manzoor b Saeed Ajmal	10	– not out	15
B. A. W. Mendis st Kamran Akmal b Saeed Ajmal	5	– b Saeed Ajmal	1
B 1, l-b 3, n-b 1	5	L-b 7, w 1, n-b 7	15

1/3 (1) 2/21 (3) 3/96 (4) 4/139 (2) (80.2 overs) 292
5/160 (5) 6/194 (6) 7/241 (7)
8/271 (8) 9/282 (10) 10/292 (11)

1/0 (2) 2/68 (1)   (56.2 overs) 217
3/86 (4) 4/88 (5)
5/101 (4) 6/138 (7) 7/156 (6)
8/191 (8) 9/211 (9) 10/217 (11)

Umar Gul 14–3–45–1; Mohammad Aamer 19–3–74–3; Abdur Rauf 14–1–59–2; Younis Khan 7–2–23–2; Saeed Ajmal 23.2–4–79–2; Shoaib Malik 3–1–8–0. *Second Innings*—Mohammad Aamer 11–2–38–3; Umar Gul 10–2–62–1; Abdur Rauf 13–1–49–1; Younis Khan 10–1–27–2; Saeed Ajmal 12.2–0–34–3.

Pakistan

Khurram Manzoor lbw b Mirando	2	– c Jayawardene b Mendis	15
Salman Butt b Kulasekara	0	– c Paranavitana b Herath	28
*Younis Khan c Dilshan b Mathews	25	– lbw b Mathews	3
Abdur Rauf c Dilshan b Kulasekara	31	– (8) c Jayawardene b Herath	13
Mohammad Yousuf run out	112	– (4) lbw b Herath	12
Misbah-ul-Haq c Jayawardene b Herath	56	– (5) run out	7
Shoaib Malik b Kulasekara	38	– (6) c Dilshan b Mirando	0
†Kamran Akmal run out	31	– (7) lbw b Mirando	6
Umar Gul b Kulasekara	7	– b Mendis	9
Mohammad Aamer c Paranavitana b Mirando	4	– c Dilshan b Herath	6
Saeed Ajmal not out	1	– not out	1
B 12, l-b 15, w 1, n-b 7	35	B 13, l-b 3, w 1	17

1/1 (2) 2/5 (1) 3/55 (4) 4/80 (3)   (94 overs) 342   1/36 (1) 2/39 (3)   (44.3 overs) 117
5/219 (6) 6/294 (5) 7/303 (7)   3/71 (4) 4/72 (2)
8/329 (8) 9/339 (8) 10/342 (10)   5/72 (6) 6/80 (7) 7/85 (5)
    8/95 (9) 9/110 (10) 10/117 (8)

Kulasekara 24–3–71–4; Mirando 21–3–77–2; Mendis 25–2–89–0; Mathews 8–2–26–1; Herath 16–2–52–1. *Second Innings*—Kulasekara 7–1–25–0; Mirando 12–4–21–2; Mathews 4–0–13–1; Mendis 10–0–27–2; Herath 11.3–5–15–4.

Umpires: I. J. Gould and D. J. Harper.
Third umpire: H. D. P. K. Dharmasena. Referee: A. G. Hurst.

SRI LANKA v PAKISTAN

Second Test Match

At P. Sara Oval, Colombo, July 12, 13, 14, 2009. Sri Lanka won by seven wickets. Toss: Pakistan. Test debut: Fawad Alam.

In a roller-coaster of a match Pakistan were shot out for 90, but bounced back to grab the initiative – only to collapse again and allow Sri Lanka to take a winning 2–0 lead in the series. Pakistan's comeback, though, was a memorable one. They were bowled out midway between lunch and tea on the first day, with only Shoaib Malik lasting for long. Kulasekara was the pick of the bowlers, although Mendis nipped in at the end, taking three wickets in 15 balls. Pakistan's bowlers responded in kind, restricting Sri Lanka's lead to 150, before Fawad Alam, making his Test debut and opening for only the second time in first-class cricket, scored a remarkable 168. He had replaced Salman Butt, who paid for his foolhardiness at Galle with his place, and collected a six and 15 fours, many of them whipped off the legs as the bowlers zeroed in on a pronounced shuffle across the stumps. Afterwards Younis Khan presented Fawad with a ball on which he had inscribed "Fawad Alam... debut... 100". Younis said he had written it on a hunch before the Test, and kept the ball in his bag. Fawad was touched: "To know that the captain believed so much in me is an indescribable feeling."

Fawad and Younis put on 200 for the second wicket, stretching the lead to 135. The bowling seemed at their mercy, and a big target looked on the cards. But Sangakkara, desperate to break the partnership, tried the part-time off-spin of Tharanga Paranavitana. Younis was tempted by a full toss outside leg stump, and – just like Mike Gatting against Allan Border at a vital moment in the 1987-88 World Cup final – tried a reverse sweep. Just like Gatting's fateful effort, it took the shoulder of the bat and went straight up, giving the wicketkeeper an easy catch. After that Pakistan collapsed spectacularly: in all, the last nine wickets tumbled for just 35 runs. Younis's fatal reverse sweep will long be discussed, but this was the shot he had employed repeatedly and effectively against the same team during his Karachi triple-century five months before, and that attack *did* include Muttiah Muralitharan.

In fact, rather than Younis's reckless shot it was the second new ball, taken straight after lunch, that did the trick. At the interval Pakistan, even after the loss of their captain, were still strongly placed at 294 for two, with Fawad 164. However, the entire complexion of the game changed when Sangakkara tossed the new ball to Herath. He trapped Mohammad Yousuf lbw with his second delivery, and from then on it was a downward slide. "No matter who bowled we needed someone to stand up and do something special for us," said Sangakkara. On this occasion it was Herath, with his maiden Test five-for, and Kulasekara, who showed himself ready to assume the mantle of the soon-to-retire Chaminda Vaas as the bowling spearhead, taking four more wickets and eight in the match. Sri Lanka had little difficulty in reaching the 171 they needed for victory in the match and series, winning shortly before the end of the third day.

Just before the match started, the committee of the Tamil Union Cricket and Athletic Club announced that the ground (formerly known as the P. Saravanamuttu Stadium) was to be renamed the P. Sara Oval. This was done with the intention of keeping the traditional name of the ground – the Colombo Oval – while also continuing to commemorate Paikiasothy Saravanamuttu, the former Tamil Union president and a guiding hand behind the construction of the original stadium in the 1940s. It hosted matches against international sides for many years before Sri Lanka's first official Test was staged there in 1981-82.

Men of the Match: Fawad Alam and K. M. D. N. Kulasekara.

Close of play: First day, Sri Lanka 164-3 (Sangakkara 81, Samaraweera 13); Second day, Pakistan 178-1 (Fawad Alam 102, Younis Khan 35).

Pakistan

Khurram Manzoor c Dilshan b Kulasekara	3	– c Dilshan b Herath 38
Fawad Alam lbw b Mathews	16	– c Warnapura b Herath 168
*Younis Khan b Mirando	0	– c Dilshan b Paranavitana 82
Mohammad Yousuf c Herath b Kulasekara	10	– lbw b Herath 6
Misbah-ul-Haq c Dilshan b Kulasekara	0	– lbw b Kulasekara 3
Shoaib Malik not out	39	– b Herath 6
†Kamran Akmal c Dilshan b Mirando	9	– lbw b Kulasekara 3
Abdur Rauf lbw b Kulasekara	0	– lbw b Kulasekara 0
Umar Gul c Samaraweera b Mendis	1	– lbw b Herath 2
Mohammad Aamer lbw b Mendis	2	– not out 1
Saeed Ajmal lbw b Mendis	0	– lbw b Kulasekara 0
B 4, l-b 2, w 2, n-b 2	10	B 8, l-b 1, w 1, n-b 1 11

1/4 (1) 2/6 (3) 3/17 (4) 4/19 (5)   (36 overs) 90   1/85 (1) 2/285 (3)   (96.4 overs) 320
5/51 (2) 6/67 (7) 7/74 (8)   3/294 (4) 4/303 (5)
8/80 (9) 9/90 (10) 10/90 (11)   5/303 (2) 6/306 (7) 7/312 (6)
                                                       8/316 (8) 9/319 (9) 10/320 (11)

Kulasekara 9–3–21–4; Mirando 8–3–23–2; Mendis 10–3–20–3; Mathews 3–0–15–1; Herath 6–3–5–0. *Second Innings*—Kulasekara 19.4–6–37–4; Mirando 13–0–48–0; Mathews 6–0–20–0; Mendis 17–0–81–0; Herath 35–5–99–5; Paranavitana 6–0–26–1.

Sri Lanka

B. S. M. Warnapura lbw b Umar Gul	11	– c Kamran Akmal b Abdur Rauf	54
N. T. Paranavitana c Kamran Akmal b Saeed Ajmal	26	– b Saeed Ajmal	17
*K. C. Sangakkara b Umar Gul	87	– c Misbah-ul-Haq b Shoaib Malik	46
D. P. M. D. Jayawardene c Khurram Manzoor b Saeed Ajmal	19	– not out	37
T. T. Samaraweera run out	21	– not out	6
†T. M. Dilshan c Kamran Akmal b Saeed Ajmal	20		
A. D. Mathews c Mohammad Yousuf b Saeed Ajmal	27		
K. M. D. N. Kulasekara c Misbah-ul-Haq b Umar Gul	11		
H. M. R. K. B. Herath c and b Umar Gul	0		
M. T. T. Mirando lbw b Abdur Rauf	1		
B. A. W. Mendis not out	0		
B 8, l-b 1, n-b 8	17	L-b 7, n-b 4	11

1/28 (1) 2/82 (2) 3/133 (4) 4/177 (5) (80 overs) 240   1/60 (2)   (3 wkts, 31.5 overs) 171
5/188 (3) 6/203 (6) 7/220 (8)   2/100 (1)
8/220 (9) 9/227 (10) 10/240 (7)   3/160 (3)

Umar Gul 18–1–43–4; Mohammad Aamer 13–2–36–0; Abdur Rauf 11–1–38–1; Saeed Ajmal 31–5–87–4; Younis Khan 7–1–27–0. *Second Innings*—Umar Gul 6–0–38–0; Mohammad Aamer 6–0–33–0; Saeed Ajmal 12–1–56–1; Abdur Rauf 4–1–13–1; Younis Khan 2–0–11–0; Shoaib Malik 1.5–0–13–1.

Umpires: D. J. Harper and S. J. A. Taufel.
Third umpire: H. D. P. K. Dharmasena.   Referee: A. G. Hurst.

SRI LANKA v PAKISTAN

Third Test Match

At Sinhalese Sports Club, Colombo, July 20, 21, 22, 23, 24, 2009. Drawn. Toss: Sri Lanka.
A placid pitch not only ensured that this Test lasted the full five days, unlike the first two, but also produced a tame draw with neither side straining to win. Although 21 wickets went down on the opening two days, the next nine sessions yielded only 12. Despite the prospect of a whitewash Sri Lanka's batsmen could not summon up the courage for one final dash, while Pakistan trundled through the final day for just one wicket: Danish Kaneria, who had taken five in the first innings, could make little impression, and neither could Saeed Ajmal, whose off-spinners and *doosras* had brought him three wickets first time around.

When play was eventually called off with 15 overs remaining, Sri Lanka were 101 short of their target of 492, with Sangakkara still there after 471 minutes of defiance – he faced 303 balls in all, and hit just seven fours. During his innings he became only the second Sri Lankan to reach 7,000 runs in Tests, reaching the landmark in 83 matches compared to Mahela Jayawardene's 92.

There was a brief flurry after tea, with Mathews charging down the track to loft Ajmal over long-on for six shortly after reaching his maiden Test half-century, but Sangakkara ultimately decided to settle for the 2–0 series win. He admitted his decision not to continue the run-chase had a lot to do with an injury to Dilshan, who had fractured his right index finger while keeping wicket.

Earlier, Pakistan had looked in danger of subsiding to another defeat at 67 for four in their second innings – only 133 ahead – with their two senior batsmen Younis Khan and Mohammad Yousuf back in the pavilion, but two century partnerships shifted the balance in the final two sessions of the third day. The common factor was Shoaib Malik, the former captain, who put some indifferent form behind him to score a beautifully paced hundred, only his second in Tests, both scored on this ground. Misbah-ul-Haq and Kamran Akmal were perfect foils, scoring half-centuries, and by stumps Pakistan's lead had swelled to 366. Previously in the series Sri Lanka had sparked collapses with the second new ball, but after tea this time there came only a torrent of runs.

Pakistan's first-innings 299 owed much to Khurram Manzoor and Mohammad Yousuf, who added 167 for the third wicket after Thushara Mirando had taken two wickets in an over to snuff out a promising start. Both batsmen missed out on centuries: a clearly nervous Manzoor poked at one that left him, while Yousuf was run out following an overthrow after taking the single that lifted him too to 7,000 Test runs.

Pakistan managed a 66-run lead largely thanks to the efforts of Kaneria, whose five wickets included that of top-scorer Jayawardene, bowled with a flipper the ball after having treatment for cramps in his leg. Dilshan, down at No. 8 after breaking his finger catching Fawad Alam on the first morning, smashed sixes off Kaneria and Umar Gul, and also organised the tail well. Eventually he top-edged a sweep into his helmet, and it went through the grille and cut his eyebrow: next over he thick-edged an attempted cut to the wicketkeeper.

This Test was the 111th and last of Chaminda Vaas's distinguished career. He bowed out gracefully as Sri Lanka's second-highest wicket-taker – behind Muttiah Muralitharan – with 355 wickets in Tests and a round 400 in one-day internationals.

Man of the Match: K. C. Sangakkara. *Man of the Series:* K. M. D. N. Kulasekara.

Close of play: First day, Pakistan 289-7 (Kamran Akmal 1, Danish Kaneria 1); Second day, Pakistan 16-1 (Fawad Alam 14, Younis Khan 0); Third day, Pakistan 300-5 (Shoaib Malik 106, Kamran Akmal 60); Fourth day, Sri Lanka 183-3 (Sangakkara 50, Samaraweera 20).

Pakistan

Khurram Manzoor c Jayawardene b Vaas	93	– b Herath	2
Fawad Alam c Dilshan b Mirando	16	– c and b Mirando	16
*Younis Khan b Mirando	2	– lbw b Kulasekara	19
Mohammad Yousuf run out	90	– c Sangakkara b Herath	23
Misbah-ul-Haq c Dilshan b Kulasekara	27	– c Sangakkara b Mathews	65
Shoaib Malik lbw b Mirando	45	– c sub (R. A. S. Lakmal) b Herath	134
†Kamran Akmal b Mirando	1	– c Jayawardene b Kulasekara	74
Umar Gul b Kulasekara	2	– c Vaas b Herath	46
Danish Kaneria lbw b Kulasekara	1	– c Mirando b Herath	5
Mohammad Aamer not out	2	– not out	22
Saeed Ajmal b Mirando	8	– not out	3
B 10, n-b 2	12	B 10, l-b 2, w 2, n-b 2	16

1/34 (2) 2/36 (3) 3/203 (1)   (89.4 overs) 299   1/16 (1)   (9 wkts dec, 123 overs) 425
4/210 (4) 5/285 (6) 6/285 (5)   2/22 (2)
7/287 (8) 8/289 (9) 9/289 (7) 10/299 (11)   3/54 (3) 4/67 (4) 5/186 (5) 6/319 (7)
                                                                 7/371 (6) 8/399 (8) 9/405 (9)

Vaas 20–6–43–1; Kulasekara 16–2–47–3; Mirando 20.4–2–83–5; Herath 23–4–76–0; Mathews 8–2–31–0; Jayawardene 2–0–9–0. *Second Innings*—Kulasekara 20–5–55–2; Mirando 28–2–121–1; Herath 46–6–157–5; Vaas 19–6–47–0; Mathews 10–1–33–1.

Sri Lanka

B. S. M. Warnapura b Umar Gul	0	– (2) c Shoaib Malik b Danish Kaneria 31
N. T. Paranavitana b Younis Khan	5	– (1) c Fawad Alam b Shoaib Malik 73
*K. C. Sangakkara lbw b Saeed Ajmal	45	– not out 130
D. P. M. D. Jayawardene b Danish Kaneria	79	– c Kamran Akmal b Danish Kaneria 2
T. T. Samaraweera b Saeed Ajmal	6	– c Kamran Akmal b Saeed Ajmal 73
A. D. Mathews c Misbah-ul-Haq b Danish Kaneria	31	– not out 64
W. P. U. J. C. Vaas lbw b Danish Kaneria	4	
†T. M. Dilshan c Kamran Akmal b Danish Kaneria	44	
K. M. D. N. Kulasekara c Misbah-ul-Haq b Saeed Ajmal	1	
H. M. R. K. B. Herath lbw b Danish Kaneria	7	
M. T. T. Mirando not out	5	
L-b 2, n-b 4	6	B 1, l-b 7, w 1, n-b 9 18

1/0 (1) 2/23 (2) 3/63 (3) 4/82 (5) (68.3 overs) 233
5/153 (6) 6/171 (7) 7/174 (4)
8/181 (9) 9/204 (10) 10/233 (8)

1/83 (2) (4 wkts, 134 overs) 391
2/139 (1)
3/155 (4) 4/277 (5)

Umar Gul 10–0–55–1; Mohammad Aamer 10–2–34–0; Younis Khan 3–1–10–1; Saeed Ajmal 25–5–70–3; Danish Kaneria 20.3–3–62–5. *Second Innings*—Umar Gul 12–0–65–0; Mohammad Aamer 21–5–46–0; Younis Khan 8–0–25–0; Saeed Ajmal 43–9–95–1; Shoaib Malik 14–1–38–1; Danish Kaneria 36–3–114–2.

Umpires: I. J. Gould and S. J. A. Taufel.
Third umpire: M. G. Silva.   Referee: A. G. Hurst.

†At Kurunegala, July 27, 2009. **Sri Lanka A won by 15 runs.** Toss: Sri Lanka A. **Sri Lanka A 348-6** (50 overs) (M. L. Udawatte 161, S. H. T. Kandamby 59, C. K. Kapugedera 101; Abdul Razzaq 4-70); **Pakistanis 333** (50 overs) (Shahid Afridi 34, Fawad Alam 85, Umar Akmal 103*, Abdul Razzaq 56; C. R. D. Fernando 3-50, M. F. Maharoof 3-75).

Sri Lanka A made a remarkable recovery after losing wickets to the first two balls of the match, from Abdul Razzaq. Mahela Udawatte hit 19 fours and two sixes, putting on 114 with Thilina Kandamby then 222 with Chamara Kapugedera, whose innings lasted only 91 balls. The Pakistanis also lost a wicket in the first over, and were struggling at 129-6 in the 26th before Umar Akmal, who faced just 76 balls, put on 85 with Fawad Alam and 102 in 9.2 overs with Razzaq, whose 56 lasted only 29 balls and included four sixes.

†SRI LANKA v PAKISTAN

First One-Day International

At Dambulla, July 30, 2009. Sri Lanka won by 36 runs. Toss: Pakistan. One-day international debut: Mohammad Aamer.

A topsy-turvy match was dominated by tail-end contributions. Sri Lanka were struggling at 131 for six after being sent in on an awkward pitch, but Mathews put on 42 with Kulasekara, then Muralitharan – back after the knee injury which kept him out of the Tests – smashed 32 from just 15 balls, and the eventual total of 232 gave Sri Lanka something to bowl at. Pakistan also struggled at first: they were 95 for six in the 26th over, but Fawad Alam played the Mathews role while Umar Gul tried to emulate Murali. He collected six fours in making 33 from 21 balls, and put on 62 in seven overs with Mohammad Aamer, but in the end Pakistan fell short. Earlier, Jayasuriya was twice dropped off the bowling of Abdul Razzaq, who was playing his first one-day international for more than two years after a dalliance with the Indian Cricket League: first Kamran Akmal dropped him behind the wicket, then Razzaq spurned an embarrassingly simple return catch from a leading edge.

Man of the Match: M. Muralitharan.

Sri Lanka

W. U. Tharanga c Kamran Akmal		
b Abdul Razzaq .	17	
S. T. Jayasuriya c Mohammad Aamer		
b Umar Gul .	15	
*†K. C. Sangakkara c Shahid Afridi		
b Saeed Ajmal .	36	
D. P. M. D. Jayawardene run out	33	
C. K. Kapugedera c Kamran Akmal		
b Shahid Afridi .	8	
T. T. Samaraweera c Younis Khan		
b Abdul Razzaq .	10	
A. D. Mathews c and b Mohammad Aamer	43	

K. M. D. N. Kulasekara c Abdul Razzaq
            b Mohammad Aamer . 16
M. Muralitharan b Mohammad Aamer 32
M. T. T. Mirando not out 8
S. L. Malinga not out 4

    B 1, l-b 4, w 4, n-b 1 10

1/31 (2) 2/45 (1)   (9 wkts, 50 overs) 232
3/93 (3) 4/106 (5)
5/125 (6) 6/131 (4) 7/173 (8)
8/204 (7) 9/223 (9)   10 overs: 38-1

Mohammad Aamer 10–0–45–3; Abdul Razzaq 10–0–33–2; Umar Gul 8–0–46–1; Saeed Ajmal 10–0–40–1; Younis Khan 2–0–13–0; Shahid Afridi 10–1–50–1.

Pakistan

†Kamran Akmal b Mirando.	20
Shoaib Malik b Kulasekara	9
Shahid Afridi c Sangakkara b Mirando	27
Mohammad Yousuf c Sangakkara	
b Kulasekara .	4
*Younis Khan c Mathews b Mirando	12
Misbah-ul-Haq c and b Muralitharan	9
Fawad Alam c Sangakkara b Jayasuriya . . .	31
Abdul Razzaq lbw b Muralitharan	17

Umar Gul b Malinga 33
Mohammad Aamer run out 23
Saeed Ajmal not out 0
    L-b 5, w 5, n-b 1 11

1/29 (2) 2/41 (1) 3/48 (4)   (44.4 overs) 196
4/73 (3) 5/78 (5) 6/95 (6)
7/134 (7) 8/134 (8) 9/196 (10)
10/196 (9)   10 overs: 45-2

Kulasekara 7–1–30–2; Malinga 8.4–0–50–1; Mirando 8–0–29–3; Muralitharan 10–0–46–2; Mathews 5–0–22–0; Jayasuriya 6–0–14–1.

Umpires: S. J. Davis and E. A. R. de Silva.
Third umpire: H. D. P. K. Dharmasena.   Referee: A. G. Hurst.

†SRI LANKA v PAKISTAN

Second One-Day International

At Dambulla, August 1, 2009. Sri Lanka won by six wickets. Toss: Sri Lanka. One-day international debut: Umar Akmal.

Chamara Kapugedera, a gifted player who had long been something of an international underachiever, finally came good to steer Sri Lanka to victory with an unbeaten half-century – his first one-day score above 44 in 22 matches dating back nearly a year. His unbroken stand of 95 with Thilan Samaraweera – restored to the one-day side for this series after almost four years out of favour – settled the match after Sri Lanka had been rocking, losing both Sangakkara and Jayasuriya in three balls in the 11th over and looking unsteady at 74 for four in the 23rd. Kapugedera pulled Shahid Afridi for six before hammering Umar Gul through the covers to reach 50, while Samaraweera was especially strong square on the off side. Earlier, Thushara Mirando helped reduce Pakistan to 87 for seven on a pitch with a touch of green, but the tail did well to take the total to 168. Mohammad Aamer top-scored from No. 10, although Extras was the largest contributor (the 38th such instance in one-day internationals) as Sri Lanka's outcricket lost its keen edge late on.

Man of the Match: C. K. Kapugedera.

Pakistan

Nasir Jamshed c Jayawardene b Kulasekara	0	Mohammad Aamer not out 24
†Kamran Akmal c Samaraweera b Mirando	13	Saeed Ajmal run out 16
*Younis Khan c Kapugedera b Muralitharan	23	
Shoaib Malik lbw b Mirando	0	B 4, l-b 4, w 18 26
Umar Akmal c Sangakkara b Mathews . . .	18	
Fawad Alam c Sangakkara b Mirando	10	1/0 (1) 2/21 (2) 3/21 (4) (47 overs) 168
Shahid Afridi c Jayasuriya b Muralitharan	7	4/53 (5) 5/67 (6) 6/78 (3)
Abdul Razzaq c Mirando b Jayasuriya	17	7/87 (7) 8/125 (9) 9/128 (8)
Umar Gul run out	14	10/168 (11) 10 overs: 31-3

Kulasekara 8–2–17–1; Malinga 10–0–37–0; Mirando 9–2–33–3; Mathews 7–1–15–1; Muralitharan 10–0–42–2; Jayasuriya 3–0–17–1.

Sri Lanka

W. U. Tharanga c Nasir Jamshed		C. K. Kapugedera not out 67
b Mohammad Aamer.	10	T. T. Samaraweera not out 38
S. T. Jayasuriya c Umar Akmal		B 2, l-b 4, w 2, n-b 2 10
b Abdul Razzaq .	30	
*†K. C. Sangakkara run out	2	1/23 (1) 2/44 (3) (4 wkts, 43.4 overs) 169
D. P. M. D. Jayawardene c Younis Khan		3/44 (2) 4/74 (4)
b Shahid Afridi .	12	
		10 overs: 42-1

A. D. Mathews, K. M. D. N. Kulasekara, M. Muralitharan, M. T. T. Mirando and S. L. Malinga did not bat.

Mohammad Aamer 9.4–2–31–1; Abdul Razzaq 10–1–35–1; Umar Gul 8–0–30–0; Shahid Afridi 8–0–39–1; Saeed Ajmal 6–0–21–0; Shoaib Malik 2–0–7–0.

Umpires: S. J. Davis and H. D. P. K. Dharmasena.
Third umpire: E. A. R. de Silva.   Referee: A. G. Hurst.

†SRI LANKA v PAKISTAN

Third One-Day International

At Dambulla, August 3, 2009. Sri Lanka won by six wickets. Toss: Sri Lanka.

The late withdrawal of Sanath Jayasuriya with a stomach bug left Sri Lanka short of an opener. Facing a target of 289, Jayawardene offered to go in first, and made the most of his chance, dominating an opening stand of 202 with Tharanga, and completing his first one-day international hundred for two years. It helped Sri Lanka ease home with 21 balls to spare, and sealed the series at the earliest opportunity. Jayawardene's innings was superb: he was strong down the ground and also punished anything short with crisp pulls. Even cramp failed to slow him down, and he struck 14 fours and a six in all. Tharanga reached his own half-century from 55 balls, then throttled down a little as Jayawardene took control. Earlier, Pakistan's innings was a fraternal affair: Umar Akmal carried on where his brother left off. Kamran hit 45 from 46 balls before Umar made 66 from 65. That and some rapid lower-order contributions lifted Pakistan to an imposing 288 – but still it wasn't enough.

Man of the Match: D. P. M. D. Jayawardene.

Pakistan

†Kamran Akmal c Sangakkara b Mathews . .	45	Naved-ul-Hasan not out 30
Nasir Jamshed c Samaraweera b Mirando . .	1	Mohammad Aamer not out 4
*Younis Khan run out	44	L-b 1, w 10 11
Shoaib Malik c Sangakkara b Fernando . . .	12	
Umar Akmal b Muralitharan	66	1/9 (2) 2/80 (1) (8 wkts, 50 overs) 288
Fawad Alam c and b Mathews	13	3/101 (4) 4/107 (3)
Shahid Afridi b Muralitharan	32	5/149 (6) 6/190 (7) 7/226 (5)
Abdul Razzaq c Jayawardene b Kulasekara	30	8/266 (8)
		10 overs: 56-1

Saeed Ajmal did not bat.

Kulasekara 10–0–74–1; Mirando 10–0–46–1; Fernando 10–1–62–1; Mathews 10–0–41–2; Muralitharan 10–0–64–2.

Sri Lanka

W. U. Tharanga lbw b Saeed Ajmal 76	C. K. Kapugedera not out	8
D. P. M. D. Jayawardene c Fawad Alam	B 1, l-b 4, w 8	13
b Abdul Razzaq . 123		
*†K. C. Sangakkara not out 37	1/202 (1) 2/210 (2) (4 wkts, 46.3 overs) 289	
T. T. Samaraweera c and b Saeed Ajmal . . . 0	3/212 (4) 4/268 (5)	
S. H. T. Kandamby b Mohammad Aamer . 32		10 overs: 66-0

A. D. Mathews, K. M. D. N. Kulasekara, M. Muralitharan, M. T. T. Mirando and C. R. D. Fernando did not bat.

Mohammad Aamer 9.3–1–45–1; Abdul Razzaq 9–0–62–1; Naved-ul-Hasan 7–0–41–0; Shahid Afridi 6–0–45–0; Saeed Ajmal 9–0–54–2; Shoaib Malik 6–0–37–0.

Umpires: S. J. Davis and E. A. R. de Silva.
Third umpire: H. D. P. K. Dharmasena.   Referee: A. G. Hurst.

†SRI LANKA v PAKISTAN

Fourth One-Day International

At R. Premadasa Stadium, Colombo, August 7, 2009 (day/night). Pakistan won by 146 runs. Toss: Pakistan.

Pakistan's first win of the tour came courtesy of Umar Akmal's maiden international hundred and Younis Khan's first half-century in 14 one-day matches as captain. The Premadasa pitch often favours the team batting first, and so it proved again as Pakistan ran up a big score. Umar, 19 and in only his third one-day international, entered in the 26th over with the total an unremarkable 130 for four, but outscored Younis in a stand of 176. Umar's half-century came from 46 balls, after which he stepped up his assault, finishing with five fours and four sixes. Strong on the leg side, Umar hit consecutive fours off Mendis, collected 13 off the 46th over, bowled by Malinga, then smacked him straight back over his head for six in his next over. He finished unbeaten on 102, from just 72 balls. The total of 321 was always going to be a tall order to chase under lights: Tharanga tried to keep his side in the hunt, but he received little support. Iftikhar Anjum claimed career-best figures as the last seven wickets tumbled for just 18 runs in 6.3 overs, the first of them (Kapugedera) to a stunning one-handed catch by Naved-ul-Hasan, back-pedalling and diving at long-off. Sri Lanka's only heavier home defeat by runs (147) came at India's hands earlier in 2009.

Man of the Match: Umar Akmal.

Pakistan

†Kamran Akmal b Bandara 57	Shahid Afridi not out	2
Imran Nazir b Mirando 23		
*Younis Khan c Kapugedera b Mirando 89	B 4, w 29	33
Mohammad Yousuf c Jayawardene		
b Mendis . 6	1/61 (2) 2/106 (1) (5 wkts, 50 overs) 321	
Misbah-ul-Haq lbw b Bandara 9	3/115 (4) 4/130 (5)	
Umar Akmal not out 102	5/306 (3)	10 overs: 61-1

Naved-ul-Hasan, Iftikhar Anjum, Mohammad Aamer and Saeed Ajmal did not bat.

Malinga 10–0–79–0; Mirando 10–0–74–2; Mathews 8–0–48–0; Bandara 10–0–44–2; Mendis 10–0–56–1; Kandamby 2–0–16–0.

Sri Lanka

W. U. Tharanga c Kamran Akmal	
b Iftikhar Anjum .	80
D. P. M. D. Jayawardene c Mohammad	
Aamer b Naved-ul-Hasan .	19
*†K. C. Sangakkara c Imran Nazir	
b Iftikhar Anjum .	39
S. H. T. Kandamby c Younis Khan	
b Saeed Ajmal .	15
C. K. Kapugedera c Naved-ul-Hasan	
b Saeed Ajmal .	8
T. T. Samaraweera c Kamran Akmal	
b Iftikhar Anjum .	2
A. D. Mathews st Kamran Akmal	
b Shahid Afridi .	8
C. M. Bandara c Misbah-ul-Haq	
b Shahid Afridi .	0
M. T. T. Mirando b Iftikhar Anjum	0
S. L. Malinga c Misbah-ul-Haq	
b Iftikhar Anjum .	0
B. A. W. Mendis not out	0
L-b 1, w 3	4

1/36 (2) 2/101 (3) 3/130 (4) (36.1 overs) 175
4/157 (5) 5/159 (6) 6/166 (1)
7/167 (8) 8/171 (9) 9/175 (7)
10/175 (10)   10 overs: 64-1

Mohammad Aamer 5–0–34–0; Naved-ul-Hasan 7–0–46–1; Iftikhar Anjum 8.1–0–30–5; Shahid Afridi 9–0–40–2; Saeed Ajmal 7–0–24–2.

Umpires: S. J. Davis and M. G. Silva.
Third umpire: H. D. P. K. Dharmasena.   Referee: A. G. Hurst.

†SRI LANKA v PAKISTAN

Fifth One-Day International

At R. Premadasa Stadium, Colombo, August 9, 2009 (day/night). Pakistan won by 132 runs. Toss: Pakistan.

For the second match running Sri Lanka slumped to a big defeat, though it mattered little as the series was already safe. Naved-ul-Hasan, later to star with the ball, gave Pakistan's innings a boost after they had threatened to squander the hard work done by Younis Khan and Misbah-ul-Haq. Naved then took the ball, and blew Sri Lanka away in concert with Mohammad Aamer. Naved's fourth wicket was his 100th in one-day internationals, but it was Aamer who set the tone, whacking Tharanga on the finger first ball and inducing an edge two deliveries later. It was 74 for eight by the end of the 18th over, and although Kandamby and Bandara prevented complete humiliation the match was as good as over. This was the tenth successive one-day international on this ground won by the side batting first.

Man of the Match: Naved-ul-Hasan.   *Man of the Series:* M. T. T. Mirando.

Pakistan

†Kamran Akmal lbw b Kulasekara	0
Imran Nazir lbw b Mendis	35
*Younis Khan b Prasad	76
Mohammad Yousuf c Sangakkara	
b Jayasuriya .	43
Misbah-ul-Haq not out	73
Umar Akmal c Tharanga b Mathews	6
Shahid Afridi c Sangakkara b Kulasekara . .	5
Naved-ul-Hasan c Tharanga b Kulasekara .	33
Iftikhar Anjum run out	0
L-b 1, w 4, n-b 3	8

1/0 (1) 2/45 (2)   (8 wkts, 50 overs) 279
3/113 (4) 4/196 (3)
5/208 (6) 6/214 (7) 7/274 (8)
8/279 (9)   10 overs: 52-2

Mohammad Aamer and Saeed Ajmal did not bat.

Kulasekara 10–1–46–3; Prasad 9–0–61–1; Mendis 10–0–45–1; Mathews 6–0–30–1; Bandara 6–0–39–0; Jayasuriya 9–0–57–1.

Sri Lanka

W. U. Tharanga c Umar Akmal b Mohammad Aamer.	0
S. T. Jayasuriya c Misbah-ul-Haq b Naved-ul-Hasan.	6
D. P. M. D. Jayawardene c Kamran Akmal b Mohammad Aamer.	31
*†K. C. Sangakkara c Shahid Afridi b Naved-ul-Hasan.	16
C. K. Kapugedera c Misbah-ul-Haq b Mohammad Aamer.	1
S. H. T. Kandamby not out	42
A. D. Mathews c Kamran Akmal b Mohammad Aamer.	5
K. M. D. N. Kulasekara c Misbah-ul-Haq b Mohammad Aamer.	0
K. T. G. D. Prasad b Naved-ul-Hasan	1
C. M. Bandara st Kamran Akmal b Shahid Afridi .	31
B. A. W. Mendis c Misbah-ul-Haq b Shahid Afridi .	0
L-b 2, w 9, n-b 3	14

1/0 (1) 2/19 (2) 3/54 (4)   (34.2 overs) 147
4/58 (3) 5/59 (5) 6/69 (7)
7/70 (8) 8/74 (9) 9/145 (10)
10/147 (11)   10 overs: 54-3

Mohammad Aamer 9–1–28–4; Naved-ul-Hasan 8–0–44–4; Iftikhar Anjum 7–1–28–0; Saeed Ajmal 7–0–29–0; Shahid Afridi 3.2–0–16–2.

Umpires: S. J. Davis and M. G. Silva.
Third umpire: H. D. P. K. Dharmasena.   Referee: A. G. Hurst.

†SRI LANKA v PAKISTAN

Twenty20 International

At R. Premadasa Stadium, Colombo, August 12, 2009 (floodlit). Pakistan won by 52 runs. Twenty20 international debut: Umar Akmal.

Two months after contesting the World Twenty20 final at Lord's, the two sides met again, and the result was the same. The winner of the match award was the same too: Shahid Afridi, captaining Pakistan for the first time, slammed 50 from 37 balls before taking an important wicket during a tight spell. Kamran Akmal fell to the first ball of the match, but Pakistan regrouped with ease. Imran Nazir made a rapid 40 before Afridi and Umar Akmal put on 66 in seven overs. Sri Lanka started brightly, but Udawatte and Jayasuriya went in the space of three balls, and when Sangakkara departed – one of six wickets shared by Saeed Ajmal and Naved-ul-Hasan – the others were left with too much to do: in all the last eight wickets fell for 49.

Man of the Match: Shahid Afridi.

Pakistan

		B	4	6
†Kamran Akmal b 8	0	1	0	0
Imran Nazir c 11 b 10	40	28	5	1
Shoaib Malik b 11	14	10	3	0
*Shahid Afridi c 8 b 10	50	37	4	2
Umar Akmal c 4 b 6	30	20	4	0
Abdul Razzaq not out	25	17	3	0
Misbah-ul-Haq not out	5	7	0	0
B 4, l-b 2, w 2	8			

6 overs: 49-2   (20 overs)   172-5

1/0 2/35 3/59 4/125 5/139

Naved-ul-Hasan, Mohammad Aamer, Iftikhar Anjum and Saeed Ajmal did not bat.

Kulasekara 4–0–37–1; Mirando 4–0–37–2; Malinga 4–0–28–1; Muralitharan 4–0–30–0; Mathews 3–0–25–1; Jayasuriya 1–0–9–0.

Sri Lanka

		B	4	6
M. L. Udawatte lbw b 8	11	8	2	0
S. T. Jayasuriya c 5 b 9	23	17	1	2
D. P. M. D. Jayawardene c 6 b 10	12	13	0	1
*†K. C. Sangakkara b 11	38	31	2	1
C. K. Kapugedera c 8 b 4	10	15	0	0
A. D. Mathews run out	9	9	1	0
S. H. T. Kandamby c 2 b 11	2	3	0	0
K. M. D. N. Kulasekara b 8	1	3	0	0
M. Muralitharan c 5 b 11	1	4	0	0
M. T. T. Mirando b 8	3	6	0	0
S. L. Malinga not out	0	1	0	0
L-b 6, w 3, n-b 1	10			

6 overs: 55-2   (18.1 overs)   120

1/39 2/71 3/71 4/100 5/106 6/115 7/115 8/117 9/119

Mohammad Aamer 3–0–22–1; Naved-ul-Hasan 3.1–0–19–3; Iftikhar Anjum 4–0–34–1; Saeed Ajmal 4–0–18–3; Shahid Afridi 4–0–21–1.

Umpires: E. A. R. de Silva and T. H. Wijewardene.   Third umpire: M. G. Silva.   Referee: A. G. Hurst.

SRI LANKA v NEW ZEALAND, 2009

Sa'adi Thawfeeq

Test matches (2): Sri Lanka 2, New Zealand 0
Twenty20 internationals (2): Sri Lanka 0, New Zealand 2

Of all New Zealand Test squads to tour Sri Lanka since the first in 1984, Daniel Vettori's was the least experienced. Vettori, with 92 Tests, was by far the most experienced visitor, and more than half the squad had played 11 Tests or fewer.

From the outset, New Zealand looked like no-hopers to beat a confident Sri Lankan side who had just overcome a strong Pakistan in both Test and one-day series. As expected, Kumar Sangakkara's men had too much experience and too many match-winners: they won both Test matches quite comfortably. But what they didn't bargain for was the way New Zealand bounced back in the two Twenty20 Internationals to beat them pretty convincingly.

Vettori stood head and shoulders above his team-mates, not only as leader but as a fine all-rounder. Vettori himself said he was picked as a bowler, but his contributions with the bat marked him as a player who carried his country's destiny on his back.

He took ten wickets and scored 272 runs in the two Tests, topping both averages. He also became only the second New Zealand bowler after Sir Richard Hadlee to take 300 Test wickets, a feat he achieved in the Second Test at Colombo's Sinhalese Sports Club.

Carrying New Zealand: captain Daniel Vettori took most wickets and scored most runs for his side.

The biggest disappointment for New Zealand was the form of their explosive wicketkeeper-batsman Brendon McCullum. He struggled throughout, which put an extra burden on an inexperienced batting line-up that had to deal not only with two of the most potent spinners in the world – Muttiah Muralitharan and Ajantha Mendis – but a rejuvenated Rangana Herath and a seam-bowling attack that had just destroyed Pakistan.

New Zealand's inexperience was obvious as Sri Lanka amassed 400-plus in the first innings of each Test to beat them comprehensively, by 202 runs and by 96. The Sri Lankans scored five centuries and three nineties; Vettori was New Zealand's solitary centurion, his plucky career-best 140 pushing the SSC Test till tea on the final day. The New Zealand tail offered far more resistance than their top order thanks to Vettori, who proved a thorn for the Sri Lankan bowlers.

Most impressive for Sri Lanka were Thilan Samaraweera, who made big centuries in each of the Tests, their former captain Mahela Jayawardene, who continued his outstanding form at home with a century and twin nineties, and Tillekeratne Dilshan, who excelled in his new role as opener to pound the New Zealand bowlers into submission with his aggressive batting. He made it easy for the rest of the batsmen to continue the damage.

New Zealand had previously endured two harrowing tours of Sri Lanka during the height of the war with the Tamil Tiger rebels, but showed no reservations on this occasion. A tight security system was put in place, ensuring the visitors had a trouble free-tour. The long-running war seemed finally to have reached its end.

NEW ZEALAND TOURING PARTY

D. L. Vettori (*captain*), C. D. Cumming, G. D. Elliott, D. R. Flynn, M. J. Guptill, B. B. McCullum, T. G. McIntosh, C. S. Martin, I. E. O'Brien, J. D. P. Oram, J. S. Patel, J. D. Ryder, L. R. P. L. Taylor, D. R. Tuffey, R. A. Young. *Coach:* A. J. Moles.

For the limited-overs internationals that followed the Tests, S. E. Bond, N. T. Broom, I. G. Butler, B. J. Diamanti, G. J. Hopkins, N. L. McCullum, P. D. McGlashan and K. D. Mills replaced Cumming, Flynn, McIntosh, Martin, O'Brien and Young.

Note: Matches in this section which were not first-class are signified by a dagger.

At Colts CC, Colombo, August 7, 8, 9, 2009. **Drawn**. Toss: Sri Lanka Cricket Development XI. **Sri Lanka Cricket Development XI 159** (L. D. Chandimal 64; D. R. Tuffey 3-41) **and 257-6** (N. T. Paranavitana 51, M. L. Udawatte 47, N. M. N. P. Nawela 64*, S. M. S. M. Senanayake 30*; J. D. P. Oram 3-32); **New Zealanders 493** (D. R. Flynn 75, L. R. P. L. Taylor 93, B. B. McCullum 78, D. L. Vettori 106, J. S. Patel 39; A. B. T. Lakshitha 4-96, B. M. A. J. Mendis 4-91). First-class debut: L. D. Chandimal.

Daryl Tuffey took three wickets in his first game for the New Zealanders since defecting to the unsanctioned ICL Twenty20 tournament. Daniel Vettori's hundred, made from No. 8, was his sixth in first-class cricket.

At Nondescripts CC, Colombo, August 12, 13, 14, 2009. **Drawn**. Toss: New Zealanders. **New Zealanders 297** (M. J. Guptill 54, L. R. P. L. Taylor 75, J. D. P. Oram 42, J. S. Patel 72; S. Prasanna 3-66) **and 240-6** (T. G. McIntosh 43, L. R. P. L. Taylor 58, J. D. P. Oram 35*); **Sri Lanka Cricket Development XI 330** (T. M. Dilshan 68, L. D. Chandimal 109, K. T. G. D. Prasad 73; D. L. Vettori 3-87, J. S. Patel 3-81).

Tillekeratne Dilshan seized his chance to make an impression as an opener before the Test series. Ten of the 16 New Zealand wickets to fall were lbws. Nineteen-year-old Dinesh Chandimal, playing only his second first-class match, shared stands of 99 with Dilshan and 127 with Dammika Prasad.

SRI LANKA v NEW ZEALAND

First Test Match

At Galle, August 18, 19, 20, 21, 22, 2009. Sri Lanka won by 202 runs. Toss: New Zealand.

In his new role as Test opener Dilshan got the series off to an explosive start, racing to 92 off 72 balls in the first innings and following it up with an unbeaten century in the second, helping his team set New Zealand an improbable 413 for victory. That was well beyond Vettori's inexperienced side.

The manner in which Dilshan dominated exposed the desperation of New Zealand's bowlers. On the first day he was on course for the fastest Test hundred by a Sri Lankan when he finally chopped a ball from the expensive O'Brien back on to his stumps. Vettori admitted the uneven contest shut his team out of the match.

However, Sri Lanka's batting was a collective effort. Jayawardene and Samaraweera scored centuries in the first innings – their 26th and tenth respectively. And the middle order stepped up to get some quick runs in setting the target during the second innings.

It was not that New Zealand were without opportunities. They chose to bowl first on an overcast opening day, and made early inroads in both innings, only to be thwarted by Dilshan's remorseless strokeplay. "Dilshan took it away from us and played exceptionally well," said Vettori. "When you have a player like that it makes it very tough to captain."

New Zealand's worries were compounded when seven of their players were hit by a stomach bug. McCullum and Ryder were the worst affected, forced to return to the team hotel at the start of the third day. Though the illness had a bearing on the way New Zealand batted it was not an excuse. In reply to Sri Lanka's 452, five of their top batsmen got starts, but only one reached fifty, the opener McIntosh batting 75 overs for 69 before his luck against Muralitharan ran out.

By tea on the fourth day, when Sri Lanka's declaration came, the lead was 412 and New Zealand's chance of survival very much dependent on the weather. But though it rained for nearly an hour soon afterwards, their hopes of saving the game were dashed early on the last morning, when they lost three wickets for the addition of just 15 runs. After that setback, saving the game was beyond even Vettori. He led by example throughout, taking five wickets in the Test and contributing two defiant innings.

Muralitharan, after missing the preceding Pakistan series with a leg injury, now passed Shane Warne's record as the bowler with most maidens in Test cricket (1,761). But the disappointing aspect for New Zealand was not the way they handled the threat posed by Murali and Mendis – in fact the only encouragement they could take into the next Test was how their batsmen handled spin – but their lack of competitiveness against pace. Fast

1,000 MAIDENS IN TESTS

	Tests	Balls	Maidens	Runs	Wickets	Avge	Overs per maiden
M. Muralitharan (Sri Lanka) .	**132**	**43,669**	**1,786**	**17,989**	**792**	**22.21**	**4.07**
S. K. Warne (Australia)........	145	40,704	1,761	17,995	708	25.41	3.85
A. Kumble (India)...........	132	40,850	1,576	18,355	619	29.65	4.32
G. D. McGrath (Australia)	124	29,248	1,471	12,186	563	21.64	3.31
L. R. Gibbs (West Indies)	79	27,115	1,313	8,989	309	29.09	3.44
D. L. Underwood (England)	86	21,862	1,239	7,674	297	25.83	2.94
S. M. Pollock (South Africa)....	108	24,353	1,222	9,733	421	23.11	3.21
C. A. Walsh (West Indies)	132	30,019	1,144	12,688	519	24.44	4.37
B. S. Bedi (India)............	67	21,364	1,096	7,637	266	28.71	3.24
Kapil Dev (India)	131	27,740	1,060	12,867	434	29.64	4.36
D. L. Vettori...............	**97**	**24,037**	**1,004**	**10,520**	**313**	**33.61**	**3.99**
C. E. L. Ambrose (West Indies) .	98	22,103	1,001	8,501	405	20.99	3.68

Note: Figures to January 28, 2010.

bowlers Thushara Mirando and Kulasekara took eight of the 20 New Zealand wickets, and their success had a significant impact on the outcome.

Man of the Match: T. M. Dilshan.

Close of play: First day, Sri Lanka 293-3 (D. P. M. D. Jayawardene 108, Samaraweera 82); Second day, New Zealand 87-2 (McIntosh 36, Patel 6); Third day, New Zealand 281-8 (Vettori 33, O'Brien 3); Fourth day, New Zealand 30-1 (Guptill 17, Taylor 8).

Sri Lanka

N. T. Paranavitana c McCullum b Martin	0	– c Taylor b O'Brien	5
T. M. Dilshan b O'Brien	92	– not out	123
*K. C. Sangakkara c Flynn b Martin	8	– run out	46
D. P. M. D. Jayawardene c Taylor b O'Brien	114	– c and b Patel	27
T. T. Samaraweera c Patel b Vettori	159	– c Taylor b Vettori	20
A. D. Mathews c McCullum b Vettori	39		
†H. A. P. W. Jayawardene c Flynn b Vettori	7	– (6) not out	30
K. M. D. N. Kulasekara c McCullum b Martin	18		
M. T. T. Mirando c O'Brien b Vettori	1		
M. Muralitharan c McCullum b Martin	8		
B. A. W. Mendis not out	0		
B 1, l-b 2, w 2, n-b 2	7	B 5, l-b 3	8

1/0 (1) 2/16 (3) 3/134 (2)   (117.4 overs) 452   1/19 (1)   (4 wkts dec, 49 overs) 259
4/300 (4) 5/386 (6) 6/408 (7)   2/120 (3) 3/174 (4)
7/444 (5) 8/444 (8) 9/452 (10) 10/452 (9)   4/205 (5)

Martin 23–5–77–4; O'Brien 21–1–125–2; Oram 7–1–25–0; Vettori 37.4–9–78–4; Patel 24–3–120–0; Ryder 5–1–24–0. *Second Innings*—Martin 5–1–25–0; O'Brien 8–1–45–1; Oram 5–0–31–0; Vettori 19–3–81–1; Patel 12–0–69–1.

New Zealand

T. G. McIntosh lbw b Muralitharan	69	– (4) c Samaraweera b Mirando	0
M. J. Guptill b Mirando	24	– (1) b Mirando	18
D. R. Flynn b Mendis	14	– (2) c D. P. M. D. Jayawardene b Kulasekara	0
J. S. Patel lbw b Muralitharan	26	– (9) st H. A. P. W. Jayawardene b Muralitharan	22
L. R. P. L. Taylor c H. A. P. W. Jayawardene b Mirando	35	– (3) c H. A. P. W. Jayawardene b D. P. M. D. Jayawardene	16
J. D. Ryder b Kulasekara	42	– (7) c H. A. P. W. Jayawardene b Muralitharan	24
†B. B. McCullum b Mirando	1	– (8) run out	29
J. D. P. Oram c sub (B. S. M. Warnapura) b Muralitharan	12	– (5) lbw b Mendis	21
*D. L. Vettori b Mirando	42	– (6) c H. A. P. W. Jayawardene b Mendis	67
I. E. O'Brien c H. A. P. W. Jayawardene b Muralitharan	9	– c Paranavitana b Muralitharan	5
C. S. Martin not out	2	– not out	0
B 6, l-b 5, w 1, n-b 11	23	B 4, l-b 1, n-b 3	8

1/45 (2) 2/80 (3) 3/129 (4)   (116 overs) 299   1/1 (2) 2/37 (1)   (71.5 overs) 210
4/180 (5) 5/188 (1) 6/195 (7)   3/39 (4) 4/45 (3)
7/223 (8) 8/259 (6) 9/290 (10) 10/299 (9)   5/86 (5) 6/134 (7) 7/167 (6)
   8/204 (9) 9/210 (10) 10/210 (8)

Kulasekara 10–2–41–1; Mirando 23–2–81–4; Mendis 39–8–85–1; Muralitharan 42–10–73–4; Paranavitana 2–0–8–0. *Second Innings*—Kulasekara 8–2–20–1; Mirando 14–3–37–2; Mendis 18.5–4–50–2; Muralitharan 27–4–88–3; D. P. M. D. Jayawardene 4–1–10–1.

Umpires: D. J. Harper and N. J. Llong.
Third umpire: E. A. R. de Silva.   Referee: A. J. Pycroft.

SRI LANKA v NEW ZEALAND

Second Test Match

At Sinhalese Sports Club, Colombo, August 26, 27, 28, 29, 30, 2009. Sri Lanka won by 96 runs. Toss: Sri Lanka.

Vettori was left to carry a flagging team almost single-handed, and the 2–0 margin of New Zealand's defeat reflected the gulf between the sides. He ended the series as his side's highest wicket-taker and run-scorer.

In the last innings, New Zealand needed 494 to win or, more realistically, to bat almost five sessions for a draw. They lost early wickets on a pitch whose bounce and spin suited the Sri Lankan spinners, a failure which was put to shame by a stubborn late-order fightback. The tailenders made sure Sri Lanka were denied any early victory celebrations, and the hosts had to wait till the 68th over of the final day before they finally bowled out New Zealand for 397, the highest fourth-innings total in a Test at the SSC.

New Zealand had been 182 for six at stumps on day four, but then Sri Lanka came up against Vettori. He was determined not to let the Test slip away, although his effort was ultimately in a lost cause. He frustrated Sri Lanka in two partnerships – an excellent 124 with Oram and then 69 with No. 10 O'Brien.

Aptly enough, Vettori's was the last wicket to fall, when a fighting 140 from 189 balls was ended by an excellent tumbling catch at deep square leg by Herath, whose long spells of left-arm spin brought him five wickets in the innings.

The opening day was also significant for Vettori, who picked up the two wickets he needed for 300 in Tests. He reached the landmark in the 41st over of his 94th Test match, when Sangakkara attempted a slog-sweep and was caught at deep midwicket by Oram. Vettori became only the eighth Test player (and the second from New Zealand) to take 300 wickets and score 3,000 runs. "For a spin bowler from New Zealand, it's not something a lot of people would expect to happen," he said. "To play for that amount of time and to do so well is very special."

3,000 TEST RUNS AND 300 TEST WICKETS

	Tests	Runs	Avge	Wickets	Avge	Tests for double
I. T. Botham (England)	102	5,200	33.54	383	28.40	72
R. J. Hadlee (New Zealand)	86	3,124	27.16	431	22.29	83
Imran Khan (Pakistan).	88	3,807	37.69	362	22.81	75
Kapil Dev (India).	131	5,248	31.05	434	29.64	83
S. M. Pollock (South Africa).	108	3,781	32.31	421	23.11	87
W. P. U. J. C. Vaas (Sri Lanka). . .	111	3,089	24.32	355	29.58	108
D. L. Vettori (New Zealand). . . .	**97**	**3,779**	**30.72**	**313**	**33.61**	**94**
S. K. Warne (Australia).	145	3,154	17.32	708	25.41	142

However, Samaraweera, who passed 140 for the fourth time in 2009, guided Sri Lanka on past 400; at 389 for five, though, it had looked as if they would bat New Zealand out of the game. But Sri Lanka lost their last five wickets for just 27, before the home pace bowlers struck back quickly to regain the initiative. The New Zealand top order failed again, with the exception of Taylor, who defied for three hours to make 81. As in the First Test, New Zealand trailed by more than 150 on first innings, with Oram and Vettori having to ensure they avoided the follow-on.

Another remorseless accumulation of runs in the second innings by Sangakkara and Jayawardene deflated New Zealand's spirits. Sangakkara completed his first century of the series, and sixth at the SSC, extending his stand for the third wicket with Jayawardene to 173. Sangakkara's brisk 109 sported an array of shots that included his customary bent-knee drive past cover.

At the other end, Jayawardene, though generally more cautious, was in his element, caressing the ball through the covers. Sri Lanka pushed back the declaration until after lunch on the fourth day, to try to allow Jayawardene his customary hundred at the SSC. (Since 2006, his scores here have been 374, 127, 195, 136, 79, 2 and, in the first innings of this match, 92.) But it wasn't to be. After the break, O'Brien, for the second time in the match, dismissed him in the nineties. Sri Lanka declared at the fall of his wicket and, for the second time in successive Tests, New Zealand were left with an improbable target and too long to be able to survive.

Man of the Match: D. P. M. D. Jayawardene.   *Man of the Series:* T. T. Samaraweera.
Close of play: First day, Sri Lanka 262-3 (D. P. M. D. Jayawardene 79, Samaraweera 78); Second day, New Zealand 159-5 (Taylor 70, McCullum 5); Third day, Sri Lanka 157-2 (Sangakkara 64, D. P. M. D. Jayawardene 23); Fourth day, New Zealand 182-6 (Oram 7, Vettori 5).

Sri Lanka

N. T. Paranavitana c Taylor b Vettori	19	– (2) c McCullum b Vettori.......... 34
T. M. Dilshan c and b O'Brien.................	29	– (1) c Guptill b Patel 33
*K. C. Sangakkara c Oram b Vettori	50	– c Taylor b Patel.................109
D. P. M. D. Jayawardene c McCullum b O'Brien ..	92	– c Taylor b O'Brien.............. 96
T. T. Samaraweera c McCullum b Patel	143	– lbw b Vettori 25
C. K. Kapugedera c Vettori b Patel	35	– not out 7
†H. A. P. W. Jayawardene c O'Brien b Martin	17	
K. T. G. D. Prasad c Taylor b Patel	6	
H. M. R. K. B. Herath lbw b Patel	0	
M. Muralitharan not out	17	
M. T. T. Mirando c Patel b Vettori	0	
B 2, l-b 5, n-b 1	8	L-b 1, w 2, n-b 4.......... 7

1/34 (1) 2/75 (2) 3/115 (3)   (130.3 overs) 416
4/295 (4) 5/367 (6) 6/389 (7)
7/396 (8) 8/396 (9) 9/415 (5) 10/416 (11)

1/56 (1)   (5 wkts dec, 85.2 overs) 311
2/89 (2) 3/262 (3)
4/301 (5) 5/311 (4)

Martin 24–3–81–1; O'Brien 22–4–73–2; Vettori 40.3–12–104–3; Oram 21–7–56–0; Patel 20–3–78–4; Ryder 3–1–17–0. *Second Innings*—Vettori 24–4–62–2; O'Brien 15.2–1–77–1; Martin 9–0–34–0; Patel 34.2–2–122–2; Ryder 3–0–15–0.

New Zealand

T. G. McIntosh lbw b Prasad	5	– b Prasad 7
M. J. Guptill c Muralitharan b Mirando.........	35	– c H. A. P. W. Jayawardene b Herath . 28
D. R. Flynn c H. A. P. W. Jayawardene b Mirando.	13	– lbw b Herath.................. 50
L. R. P. L. Taylor c H. A. P. W. Jayawardene b Herath.	81	– c D. P. M. D. Jayawardene b Herath . 27
J. D. Ryder c Paranavitana b Herath	23	– lbw b Herath.................. 38
J. S. Patel c D. P. M. D. Jayawardene b Muralitharan.	1	– (9) c Kapugedera b Muralitharan 12
†B. B. McCullum c D. P. M. D. Jayawardene b Muralitharan.	18	– (6) b Muralitharan 13
J. D. P. Oram c Kapugedera b Herath	24	– (7) c Sangakkara b Dilshan 56
*D. L. Vettori c Kapugedera b Dilshan	23	– (8) c Herath b Muralitharan 140
I. E. O'Brien lbw b Muralitharan.................	4	– c H. A. P. W. Jayawardene b Herath . 12
C. S. Martin not out	0	– not out 0
L-b 3, w 2, n-b 2......................	7	L-b 13, n-b 1 14

1/14 (1) 2/49 (3) 3/63 (2)   (77.4 overs) 234
4/148 (5) 5/149 (6) 6/183 (7)
7/183 (4) 8/226 (9) 9/234 (8) 10/234 (10)

1/36 (1) 2/41 (2)   (123.5 overs) 397
3/97 (4) 4/131 (3)
5/158 (6) 6/176 (5) 7/300 (7)
8/318 (9) 9/387 (10) 10/397 (8)

Dilshan 3–0–12–1; Mirando 9–2–37–2; Prasad 6–0–41–1; Herath 34–11–70–3; Muralitharan 25.4–2–71–3. *Second Innings*—Paranavitana 1–0–2–0; Mirando 23.3–1–78–0; Prasad 15–1–56–1; Herath 48–9–139–5; Muralitharan 28.2–2–85–3; Dilshan 6–0–15–1; Kapugedera 2–0–9–0.

Umpires: D. J. Harper and N. J. Llong.
Third umpire: H. D. P. K. Dharmasena.   Referee: A. J. Pycroft.

†SRI LANKA v NEW ZEALAND

First Twenty20 International

At R. Premadasa Stadium, Colombo, September 2, 2009 (floodlit). New Zealand won by three runs. Toss: New Zealand. Twenty20 international debut: R. J. M. G. M. Rupasinghe.

New Zealand finally had something to smile about when they pulled off a narrow win thanks largely to the batting of Taylor (60 from 45 balls) and a hat-trick from Oram that left Sri Lanka agonisingly short. New Zealand's total of 141 did not look threatening as Dilshan blazed his way to 57 off 28 balls. In the first over, he welcomed Bond back to international cricket after two years of contract wrangles with four consecutive boundaries, driving the crowd to raptures. But his dismissal in the eighth over at 75 saw New Zealand crawl back into the game. Vettori tightened the screws with the most niggardly four-over spell by a New Zealand bowler in Twenty20 internationals, and Oram added the finishing touches. He took wickets with the first two balls of the last over, to add to that of Mathews, the last recognised batsman, with the final ball of his previous spell.

Man of the Match: D. L. Vettori.

New Zealand

		B	4	6
B. B. McCullum *run out*	9	9	0	1
J. D. Ryder *c 9 b 8*	13	14	2	0
M. J. Guptill *c 6 b 9*	29	25	2	1
L. R. P. L. Taylor *c 8 b 7*	60	45	5	1
J. D. P. Oram *c 8 b 11*	8	13	0	0
N. T. Broom *not out*	5	5	0	0
†P. D. McGlashan *run out*	1	1	0	0
K. D. Mills *b 10*	7	5	1	0
*D. L. Vettori *b 10*	0	1	0	0
I. G. Butler *not out*	0	2	0	0
B 3, l-b 3, w 3	9			

6 overs: 38-2   (20 overs) 141-8

1/14 2/26 3/79 4/117 5/126 6/127 7/136 8/136

S. E. Bond did not bat.

Kulasekara 4–0–21–1; Malinga 4–0–21–2; Mathews 2–0–19–1; Mendis 4–0–25–1; Bandara 4–0–25–1; Jayasuriya 2–0–24–0.

Sri Lanka

		B	4	6
T. M. Dilshan *c 2 b 10*	57	28	8	2
S. T. Jayasuriya *c 11 b 8*	1	3	0	0
D. P. M. D. Jayawardene *run out*	3	6	0	0
*†K. C. Sangakkara *c 1 b 9*	13	9	1	0
R. J. M. G. M. Rupasinghe				
lbw b 9	15	21	1	0
C. K. Kapugedera *b 10*	3	7	0	0
A. D. Mathews *c and b 5*	21	22	2	0
K. M. D. N. Kulasekara *c 6 b 5*	12	11	0	0
C. M. Bandara *c 1 b 5*	7	9	0	0
S. L. Malinga *not out*	4	3	0	0
B. A. W. Mendis *not out*	0	1	0	0
L-b 2	2			

6 overs: 64-2   (20 overs) 138-9

1/22 2/43 3/67 4/75 5/85 6/109 7/122 8/133 9/133

Bond 4–0–27–0; Mills 4–0–36–1; Butler 4–0–29–2; Oram 4–0–33–3; Vettori 4–0–11–2.

Umpires: E. A. R. de Silva and H. D. P. K. Dharmasena.
Third umpire: M. G. Silva.   Referee: A. J. Pycroft.

†SRI LANKA v NEW ZEALAND

Second Twenty20 International

At R. Premadasa Stadium, Colombo, September 4, 2009 (floodlit). New Zealand won by 22 runs. Toss: New Zealand.

Sri Lanka suffered their fourth Twenty20 defeat in a row when New Zealand secured back-to-back victories in the two-match series. Once again Vettori called correctly, though unlike the first game, his side ran up a decent total, powered by an opening stand of 84 off 62 balls by McCullum and Ryder. Bond then gained sweet revenge for the punishment he got in the previous game when he dismissed Dilshan off the fifth delivery to pick up his first wicket in international cricket since 2007. With Mills sending back Udawatte and Jayasuriya in successive overs Sri Lanka were sliding towards defeat at 11 for three. But Jayawardene and Sangakkara, two experienced batsmen, added 67 off 43 balls as the momentum picked up again. In the 11th over Nathan McCullum ensured New Zealand's deserved victory when he struck two fatal blows, sending back Jayawardene and Mathews. After that it was almost over, despite Sangakkara's 40-ball half-century.

Man of the Match: J. D. Ryder. Man of the Series: J. D. Ryder.

New Zealand

		B	4	6
†B. B. McCullum *c and b* 2	49	34	4	2
J. D. Ryder *c 7 b 11*	52	37	3	3
L. R. P. L. Taylor *lbw b* 2 ...	16	18	1	0
M. J. Guptill *b 10*	32	20	2	1
J. D. P. Oram *not out*	17	12	1	0
L-b 2, w 1, n-b 1	4			

6 overs: 49-0   (20 overs) 170-4

1/84 2/109 3/127 4/170

N. T. Broom, N. L. McCullum, *D. L. Vettori, K. D. Mills, I. G. Butler and S. E. Bond did not bat.

Kulasekara 4–0–40–0; Malinga 4–0–35–1; Mendis 4–0–21–1; Jayasuriya 4–0–22–1; Bandara 2–0–19–0; Dilshan 2–0–31–0.

Sri Lanka

		B	4	6
T. M. Dilshan *c 4 b 11*	1	3	0	0
S. T. Jayasuriya *c 3 b 9*	7	8	1	0
M. L. Udawatte *c 6 b 9*.......	0	1	0	0
D. P. M. D. Jayawardene *c 2 b 7*	41	30	5	1
**†K. C. Sangakkara *c and b 5*	69	50	7	0
A. D. Mathews *c 3 b 7*	1	2	0	0
R. J. M. G. M. Rupasinghe *c 8 b 11*	18	18	1	0
K. M. D. N. Kulasekara *c 3 b 11*	2	4	0	0
C. M. Bandara *not out*	4	4	0	0
S. L. Malinga *not out*	0	0	0	0
L-b 2, w 3	5			

6 overs: 37-3   (20 overs) 148-8

1/2 2/2 3/11 4/78 5/80 6/129 7/143 8/148

B. A. W. Mendis did not bat.

Bond 4–0–18–3; Mills 3–0–22–2; Butler 4–0–34–0; Vettori 3–0–27–0; N. L. McCullum 3–0–18–2; Oram 3–0–27–1.

Umpires: M. G. Silva and T. H. Wijewardene.
Third umpire: H. D. P. K. Dharmasena.   Referee: A. J. Pycroft.

†At Sinhalese Sports Club, Colombo, September 6, 2009. **Sri Lanka A won by 61 runs.** Toss: Sri Lanka A. **Sri Lanka A 234** (47.5 overs) (H. D. R. L. Thirimanne 51, R J. M. G. M. Rupasinghe 34, M. Pushpakumara 42; D. R. Tuffey 5-53); **New Zealanders 173** (41.5 overs) (B. B. McCullum 34, J. D. P. Oram 39; C. R. D. Fernando 3-40, M. Pushpakumara 3-36).

Sri Lanka and New Zealand's matches in the 50-over Compaq Cup (September 8–14, 2009) can be found on page 1361.

COMPAQ CUP, 2009

Anand Vasu

1. India   2. Sri Lanka   3. New Zealand

There was no disrespect intended to hosts Sri Lanka Cricket, but everyone who congregated in Colombo for the four-match Compaq Cup tri-series knew the tournament was little more than match practice ahead of the Champions Trophy. New Zealand, who had been here for over a month playing Tests and Twenty20s (see page 1353), seemed to have little choice in the matter as their scheduled five-match bilateral one-day series was turned into a triangular, also involving India.

For the Indians, one of the main draws was a chance to take the No. 1 spot in the ICC one-day rankings. This they achieved, with a win against New Zealand, but it lasted only 24 hours as a rout by Sri Lanka sent them slipping back down the table.

Since the matches were all day-nighters at the R. Premadasa Stadium, the toss was vital. In ten games leading into the tournament the team batting first had won every time. The pitch, slow and low to begin with, and the humidity, which caused the new ball to jag around under lights, meant chasing was a thankless task. The trend continued, with three of the four games won by the team batting first; the only exception was the second game, when New Zealand made just 155, and India won by six wickets.

The tournament was a forgettable one for New Zealand, who lost both their games, and it came down to a straight contest between India and Sri Lanka. While the home side looked comfortably the stronger team, largely because India were missing Zaheer Khan's left-arm pace and the power batting of Virender Sehwag, a Sachin Tendulkar classic saved them in the final. Tendulkar, whose nerveless 138 earned him his 59th match award in one-day internationals, said: "This is one of my best innings... considering the conditions and the ground."

The win was important for India, only their third from 26 in multi-team events since 2000. The tournament, though, will be remembered, if at all, for tough games of cricket where bowling was no fun – and batting even less. The usually cricket-crazy Colombo public voted with their feet and largely stayed away.

NATIONAL SQUADS

India *M. S. Dhoni, R. Dravid, Harbhajan Singh, K. D. Karthik, V. Kohli, P. Kumar, A. Mishra, A. M. Nayar, A. Nehra, Y. K. Pathan, S. K. Raina, I. Sharma, R. P. Singh, S. R. Tendulkar, Yuvraj Singh. *Coach:* G. Kirsten.

New Zealand *D. L. Vettori, S. E. Bond, N. T. Broom, I. G. Butler, B. J. Diamanti, G. D. Elliott, M. J. Guptill, G. J. Hopkins, B. B. McCullum, N. L. McCullum, K. D. Mills, J. D. P. Oram, J. S. Patel, J. D. Ryder, L. R. P. L. Taylor, D. R. Tuffey. *Coach:* A. J. Moles.

Sri Lanka *K. C. Sangakkara, C. M. Bandara, T. M. Dilshan, S. T. Jayasuriya, D. P. M. D. Jayawardene, S. H. T. Kandamby, C. K. Kapugedera, K. M. D. N. Kulasekara, S. L. Malinga, A. D. Mathews, B. A. W. Mendis, M. T. T. Mirando, M. Muralitharan, K. T. G. D. Prasad, T. T. Samaraweera, W. U. Tharanga. *Coach:* T. H. Bayliss.

* Captain.

Note: Matches in this section were not first-class.

SRI LANKA v NEW ZEALAND

At R. Premadasa Stadium, Colombo, September 8, 2009 (day/night). Sri Lanka won by 97 runs. Sri Lanka 5 pts. Toss: Sri Lanka. One-day international debut: N. L. McCullum.

After a disappointing Test series and short relief in two Twenty20 matches, which they won, New Zealand returned to their exasperating ways in the opener of the Compaq Cup. Batting first, Sri Lanka's top order did their best to implode; at 69 for five the game should have been over. But Samaraweera dug in and ignored the scoreboard, working ones and twos on a pitch that eased out nicely. Mathews provided sensible support, and Samaraweera's maiden one-day international century lifted the score to 216. New Zealand's batsmen then showed a collective lack of application. They handed Malinga four wickets, including three in the 19th over, to be shot out for a paltry 119. Batting under lights was always going to be a problem, but New Zealand's batsmen committed the most elementary mistakes. It was a particularly rotten day for the McCullum family: Brendon crawled to an unusually slow 14, and his older brother Nathan, an off-spinning all-rounder, was bowled for a golden duck on debut.

Man of the Match: T. T. Samaraweera.

Sri Lanka

T. M. Dilshan b Tuffey	4	K. M. D. N. Kulasekara not out.	6
S. T. Jayasuriya c Butler b Bond	7	M. T. T. Mirando not out	6
D. P. M. D. Jayawardene c Taylor b Bond	0	L-b 3, w 2	5
*†K. C. Sangakkara c Oram b Butler	18		
T. T. Samaraweera b Butler	104	1/4 (1) 2/5 (3) (7 wkts, 50 overs) 216	
S. H. T. Kandamby c Taylor b Vettori	15	3/22 (2) 4/38 (4) 5/69 (6)	
A. D. Mathews b Bond	51	6/196 (7) 7/204 (5) 10 overs: 26-3	

S. L. Malinga and B. A. W. Mendis did not bat.

Tuffey 9–0–35–1; Bond 10–2–43–3; Butler 10–1–55–2; Oram 6–0–22–0; Vettori 8–0–31–1; N. L. McCullum 7–1–27–0.

New Zealand

†B. B. McCullum b Malinga	14	D. R. Tuffey run out	2
J. D. Ryder lbw b Mirando	0	S. E. Bond not out	1
M. J. Guptill c Sangakkara b Kulasekara	3		
L. R. P. L. Taylor lbw b Kulasekara	2	B 6, l-b 1, w 10	17
G. D. Elliott b Jayasuriya	41		
J. D. P. Oram c Sangakkara b Malinga	4	1/2 (2) 2/5 (3) 3/7 (4) (36.1 overs) 119	
N. L. McCullum b Malinga	0	4/37 (1) 5/41 (6) 6/41 (7)	
*D. L. Vettori lbw b Jayasuriya	10	7/76 (8) 8/101 (5) 9/116 (10)	
I. G. Butler b Malinga	25	10/119 (9) 10 overs: 17-3	

Kulasekara 6–1–18–2; Mirando 6–1–5–1; Mendis 7–1–14–0; Malinga 6.1–0–28–4; Mathews 5–0–19–0; Jayasuriya 6–0–28–2.

Umpires: E. A. R. de Silva and B. R. Doctrove.
Third umpire: H. D. P. K. Dharmasena.   Referee: B. C. Broad.

INDIA v NEW ZEALAND

At R. Premadasa Stadium, Colombo, September 11, 2009 (day/night). India won by six wickets. India 4 pts. Toss: New Zealand.

India became the No. 1-ranked one-day team in the world for the first time, thanks to a hard-working win. Batting first, New Zealand found Nehra hitting perfect lengths and before long they had slumped to 66 for five, worse even than their feckless display in the first game. All out for 155, New Zealand gave themselves little chance of staying in the tournament. Tendulkar batted with purpose, and even a mini-collapse to 84 for four did not change the course of the game. Dhoni and Raina closed the match out, leaving India with a dead fixture against Sri Lanka before the final.

Man of the Match: A. Nehra.

New Zealand

†B. B. McCullum lbw b Nehra	3	I. G. Butler c Harbhajan Singh b Nehra	6
J. D. Ryder lbw b Nehra	0	S. E. Bond not out	10
M. J. Guptill c Dravid b Yuvraj Singh	22		
L. R. P. L. Taylor c Dhoni b R. P. Singh	11	L-b 4, w 1	5
G. D. Elliott c Dhoni b Yuvraj Singh	22		
J. D. P. Oram c and b Sharma	24	1/1 (2) 2/4 (1) 3/19 (4) (46.3 overs)	155
N. T. Broom c Raina b Yuvraj Singh	21	4/51 (3) 5/66 (5) 6/101 (6)	
*D. L. Vettori b Sharma	25	7/116 (7) 8/134 (9)	
K. D. Mills b R. P. Singh	6	9/142 (8) 10/155 (10) 10 overs: 30-3	

Nehra 8.3–0–24–3; R. P. Singh 8–2–22–2; Sharma 10–2–26–2; Yuvraj Singh 10–0–31–3; Harbhajan Singh 8–0–39–0; Raina 1–0–4–0; Pathan 1–0–5–0.

India

K. D. Karthik lbw b Mills	4	S. K. Raina not out	45
S. R. Tendulkar c Guptill b Vettori	46	L-b 3, w 1	4
R. Dravid lbw b Oram	14		
Yuvraj Singh c Guptill b Vettori	8	1/7 (1) 2/67 (3) (4 wkts, 40.3 overs)	156
*†M. S. Dhoni not out	35	3/71 (2) 4/84 (4) 10 overs: 34-1	

Y. K. Pathan, Harbhajan Singh, R. P. Singh, A. Nehra and I. Sharma did not bat.

Mills 5.3–1–25–1; Bond 10–3–30–0; Butler 4–0–25–0; Vettori 10–0–33–2; Oram 7–1–19–1; Elliott 2–0–9–0; Guptill 2–0–12–0.

Umpires: H. D. P. K. Dharmasena and B. R. Doctrove.
Third umpire: M. G. Silva.   Referee: B. C. Broad.

SRI LANKA v INDIA

At R. Premadasa Stadium, Colombo, September 12, 2009 (day/night). Sri Lanka won by 139 runs. Sri Lanka 5 pts. Toss: Sri Lanka.

India's reign as the No. 1 one-day side was cut rudely short by Sri Lanka, whose batsmen put together 307 batting first, a score never overhauled on this ground. Jayasuriya, under pressure to keep his place, answered his critics in characteristic fashion, cutting, driving and heaving his way to 98 at the top of the order. A bright start was given the perfect finish by the left-hander Kandamby, who also came close to a century. India needed a pacy start if they were to chase a substantial target, but lost both openers for just 67 inside 15 overs. A middle-order stumble made a heavy defeat inevitable, and only 47 from Dravid, back in the one-day team after nearly two years, reduced the margin to 139 runs. The all-rounder Mathews did most damage: through accuracy and changes of pace he took six for 20, the fifth-best one-day figures for Sri Lanka.

Man of the Match: A. D. Mathews.

Sri Lanka

T. M. Dilshan c Dhoni b Sharma	23	K. M. D. N. Kulasekara not out	3
S. T. Jayasuriya lbw b Nehra	98		
D. P. M. D. Jayawardene st Dhoni b Pathan	17	L-b 4, w 10, n-b 1	15
*†K. C. Sangakkara lbw b Harbhajan Singh	5		
A. D. Mathews st Dhoni b Raina	19	1/57 (1) 2/94 (3) (6 wkts, 50 overs)	307
S. H. T. Kandamby not out	91	3/102 (4) 4/172 (2)	
C. K. Kapugedera run out	36	5/176 (5) 6/259 (7) 10 overs: 72-1	

M. T. T. Mirando, S. L. Malinga and B. A. W. Mendis did not bat.

Nehra 9–0–62–1; R. P. Singh 8–0–58–0; Sharma 10–0–67–1; Harbhajan Singh 10–1–37–1; Pathan 7–0–45–1; Yuvraj Singh 3–0–20–0; Raina 3–0–14–1.

India

K. D. Karthik c Sangakkara b Mirando	16	A. Nehra b Mathews	1
S. R. Tendulkar c Mendis b Kulasekara	27	I. Sharma c sub (W. U. Tharanga) b Mendis	13
R. Dravid b Mathews	47		
Yuvraj Singh c Sangakkara b Malinga	16	B 1, l-b 1, w 14	16
S. K. Raina c Sangakkara b Mathews	0		
*†M. S. Dhoni b Mathews	8	1/32 (1) 2/67 (2) 3/105 (4) (37.2 overs)	168
Y. K. Pathan c Sangakkara b Mathews	1	4/108 (5) 5/126 (3) 6/129 (6)	
Harbhajan Singh b Mathews	4	7/130 (7) 8/135 (8) 9/139 (10)	
R. P. Singh not out	19	10/168 (11) 10 overs: 53-1	

Kulasekara 8–1–35–1; Mirando 6–0–34–1; Malinga 8–0–33–1; Dilshan 2–0–17–0; Mathews 6–0–20–6; Jayasuriya 2–0–5–0; Mendis 5.2–0–22–1.

Umpires: H. D. P. K. Dharmasena and B. R. Doctrove.
Third umpire: M. G. Silva.   Referee: B. C. Broad.

QUALIFYING TABLE

	Played	Won	Lost	Bonus points	Points	Net run-rate
SRI LANKA	2	2	0	2	10	2.36
INDIA	2	1	1	0	4	–1.04
New Zealand	2	0	2	0	0	–1.37

Win = 4pts. One bonus point awarded to the winning team for achieving victory with a run-rate 1.25 times that of the opposition. Net run-rate is calculated by subtracting runs conceded per over from runs scored per over.

" So delighted were his once cricket-apathetic family at his and his team's success that they sacrificed a lamb and gave it to the poor in his home village."
ICC World Cup Qualifier, page 1459

FINAL

SRI LANKA v INDIA

At R. Premadasa Stadium, Colombo, September 14, 2009 (day/night). India won by 46 runs. Toss: India.

A modern classic from Tendulkar, a thoroughly efficient half-century from Dhoni and a return to form for Yuvraj Singh ensured that India paid Sri Lanka back when it mattered most. Dhoni won an important toss, and once the batsmen put the runs on the board – 319 of them – the bowlers merely had to ensure they didn't throw it away. Tendulkar's chanceless innings, paced perfectly on a sluggish pitch in extreme heat and humidity, almost ended the game as a contest. But Sri Lanka's batsmen fought hard, initially through the openers Dilshan and Jayasuriya, who attacked relentlessly. Harbhajan, pressed into service early, responded to the heat of battle with a typically belligerent performance, picking up crucial wickets. The pressure on Sri Lanka to keep the scoring-rate up helped India chip away at the middle order. A 70-run seventh-wicket partnership between Kandamby and Kapugedera gave the Indians a scare, but they held their nerve.

Man of the Match: S. R. Tendulkar. *Man of the Series:* S. R. Tendulkar.

India

R. Dravid c Dilshan b Jayasuriya	39	V. Kohli not out	2
S. R. Tendulkar lbw b Mendis	138	B 1, w 18, n-b 1	20
*M. S. Dhoni c Kandamby b Malinga	56		
Yuvraj Singh not out	56	1/95 (1) 2/205 (3) (5 wkts, 50 overs)	319
Y. K. Pathan c Kapugedera b Mirando	0	3/276 (2) 4/277 (5)	
S. K. Raina c Kulasekara b Mirando	8	5/302 (4) 10 overs: 52-0	

Harbhajan Singh, R. P. Singh, A. Nehra and I. Sharma did not bat.

Kulasekara 8–0–38–0; Mirando 10–0–71–2; Malinga 10–0–81–1; Mendis 10–0–70–1; Jayasuriya 9–0–43–1; Mathews 3–0–15–0.

Sri Lanka

T. M. Dilshan b Harbhajan Singh	42	S. L. Malinga c and b Harbhajan Singh	0
S. T. Jayasuriya c Nehra b Pathan	36	B. A. W. Mendis st Dhoni	
D. P. M. D. Jayawardene		b Harbhajan Singh	7
c and b Harbhajan Singh	1		
*†K. C. Sangakkara hit wkt b R. P. Singh	33	L-b 3, w 11, n-b 1	15
M. T. T. Mirando b Sharma	5		
A. D. Mathews c Raina b Yuvraj Singh	14	1/64 (1) 2/76 (3) 3/85 (2) (46.4 overs)	273
S. H. T. Kandamby b Harbhajan Singh	66	4/108 (5) 5/131 (6) 6/182 (4)	
C. K. Kapugedera c Dhoni b Raina	35	7/252 (8) 8/264 (7) 9/264 (10)	
K. M. D. N. Kulasekara not out	9	10/273 (11) 10 overs: 79-2	

Nehra 7–0–43–0; Sharma 7–0–51–1; R. P. Singh 5–0–34–1; Harbhajan Singh 9.4–0–56–5; Pathan 4–0–36–1; Yuvraj Singh 6–0–24–1; Raina 8–0–26–1.

Umpires: E. A. R. de Silva and B. R. Doctrove.
Third umpire: H. D. P. K. Dharmasena. Referee: B. C. Broad.

DOMESTIC CRICKET IN SRI LANKA, 2008-09

SA'ADI THAWFEEQ

The 2008-09 season saw the return of the first-class Interprovincial Tournament after a three-year absence – and with it the emergence of a new Sri Lankan star, Angelo Mathews. The former Under-19 captain later shone in the World Twenty20 tournament, in England in June 2009, as Sri Lanka cruised to the final. Mathews could not round off the story by winning them the trophy, but back at home his devastating form with the bat had helped secure two first-class titles. Because of one-day international duties, he played only four games in the Premier League: in those he contributed 292 runs at 58 for the eventual champions, **Colts**, including 168 in an innings victory over **Colombo**.

Mathews then dominated the Interprovincial Tournament with 746 runs at 93 for **Basnahira North** (formerly Western Province North). Three more hundreds included 270 in another innings win, over **Kandurata** (formerly Central), and 152 in the final, when he fashioned Basnahira North's victory over **Wayamba** (North West) alongside Muthumudalige Pushpakumara, who made 103 and took five wickets. Overall, Mathews was the season's leading run-scorer with 1,038 from just nine matches; the only other player to reach four figures, his provincial team-mate Kaushal Silva, got there in 14.

Anthony Devlin, PA Photos

Angelo Mathews

In Tier A of the Premier League, Colts went into their final match needing less than four points to overtake defending champions **Sinhalese** and win the crown. They did it in style, rattling off 426 runs in 88.4 overs on the opening day against **Badureliya**. Colts were led from the front by Test opener Malinda Warnapura, who fell for 95 in that first innings but reached an unbeaten 100 before settling for the draw, with the points in the bag. Former Sri Lankan wicketkeeper and pinch-hitter Romesh Kaluwitharana, Colts' captain when they last won the title in 2004-05 and now their coach, put their success down to "sheer commitment and hard team work".

A highlight for Colts came when Jeevantha Kulatunga and Roshen Silva rescued them from a perilous 32 for four against **Ragama** by adding 353, a national fifth-wicket record. One of the previous record-holders – Hemantha Wickremaratne, who put on 317 with Arjuna Ranatunga for Sinhalese against

Sebastianites 12 years earlier – was fielding for Ragama as his landmark was wiped out. Kulatunga scored his first double-century in an 18-year first-class career, making 234 against Ragama.

The season had begun on a hesitant note, with 18 of the 21 Premier clubs threatening to pull out unless Sri Lanka Cricket enforced the relegation of Badureliya to the league's Tier B. Eventually sports minister Gamini Lokuge said that the tournament must not be abandoned and requested that Badureliya be allowed to remain in Tier A in 2008-09. Two tournament committee members resigned in protest over the issue. Badureliya celebrated with an innings win over **Nondescripts** in the tournament's opening weekend, but soon fell away again. They still finished above the **Army**, who had been promoted thanks to the outstanding performances of spinner Ajantha Mendis but could not manage a single win (Mendis played only one game for them because he was required by Sri Lanka). But Lokuge spared them from relegation too, and by 2009-10 Tier A had swollen from ten teams to 12.

The 12th team were **Saracens**, eventually declared the winners of Tier B. The outcome was in doubt when a crucial match between second-placed **Panadura** and **Sebastianites** was called off after a huge chunk of the pitch – about four and a half feet – came off at one end. Sebastianites were ordered to restage the fixture, but were awarded the game when Panadura arrived with a different eleven, which they argued was contrary to regulations. Another match, between the **Air Force** and **Seeduwa Raddoluwa** in January, was halted by a bomb explosion outside the ground and resumed a fortnight later.

In the limited-overs competitions, **Wayamba** won the Interprovincial Twenty20 final, with Isuru Udana, the 21-year-old left-arm fast bowler, accounting for four of Basnahira South's top five batsmen and earning a place in the World Twenty20 squad. **Bloomfield** won the Premier Tier A one-day final and **Sebastianites** took Tier B.

FIRST-CLASS AVERAGES, 2008-09

BATTING

(Qualification: 600 runs, average 30.00)

	M	I	NO	R	HS	100s	Avge	Ct/St
A. D. Mathews (*Colts and Basnahira North*)	9	13	0	1,038	270	4	79.84	7
†W. U. Tharanga (*Nondescripts and Ruhuna*).....	7	13	1	875	265*	3	72.91	3
J. K. Silva (*Sinhalese and Basnahira North*).....	15	21	3	1,012	133	3	56.22	35/4
†J. Mubarak (*Colombo and Wayamba*)...........	9	15	2	684	136	2	52.61	8
†R. J. M. G. M. Rupasinghe (*Tamil U and B Sth*)..	11	19	1	945	154*	3	52.50	8
†N. T. Paranavitana (*Sinhalese*).................	9	14	2	621	123*	3	51.75	8
†D. N. Hunukumbura (*Moors and Wayamba*).....	12	21	1	948	117	1	47.40	6
†P. K. Bodhisha (*Saracens*).....................	9	15	1	663	179	2	47.35	3
S. I. de Saram (*Ragama and Ruhuna*)	14	23	2	986	150*	4	46.95	16
W. M. B. Perera (*Colombo and Basnahira Nth*) ..	12	20	3	777	139	1	45.70	10
L. P. C. Silva (*Bloomfield and Basnahira Sth*)	14	22	1	957	132*	3	45.57	22
†S. I. Fernando (*Tamil Union and Kandurata*)	14	23	1	975	139	2	44.31	7
N. M. N. P. Nawela (*Moors and Kandurata*)	11	17	1	649	148*	3	40.56	6
G. I. Daniel (*Ragama and Basnahira North*)......	15	24	1	907	165	3	39.43	13
†M. Pushpakumara (*Tamil Union and Bas Nth*) ...	14	21	5	630	108*	2	39.37	19
H. G. J. M. Kulatunga (*Colts and Wayamba*)	15	23	2	822	234	2	39.14	17

	M	I	NO	R	HS	100s	Avge	Ct/St
†W. M. G. Ramyakumara (*Chilaw and Bas Nth*)	12	21	2	728	111*	2	38.31	1
S. M. A. Priyanjan (*Tamil Union and Ruhuna*)	13	22	1	767	99	0	36.52	13
L. J. P. Gunaratne (*Chilaw and Basnahira Sth*)	12	21	2	692	122*	1	36.42	3
†K. Y. de Silva (*Bloomfield and Basnahira Sth*)	14	23	0	737	116	1	32.04	14
†K. D. Gunawardene (*Nondescripts and Kand*)	13	22	1	654	137	3	31.14	6
S. K. L. de Silva (*Tamil Union and Wayamba*)	14	23	3	608	103	1	30.40	17/1

† *Left-handed batsman.*

BOWLING

(Qualification: 35 wickets)

	Style	O	M	R	W	BB	5W/i	Avge
A. A. C. E. Athukorala (*Sebastianites*)	RFM	175.2	43	493	35	7-21	2	14.08
D. M. G. S. Dissanayake (*Bloom and Bas Nth*)	SLA	220.5	33	639	38	4-31	0	16.81
S. Madanayake (*Air Force*)	SLA	249.4	34	858	50	7-15	3	17.16
D. G. R. Dhammika (*Seeduwa Raddoluwa*)	SLA	201.5	48	603	35	6-72	1	17.22
S. I. Vithana (*Singha*)	OB	239.4	37	747	43	6-78	3	17.37
C. A. M. Madusanka (*Burgher*)	SLA	210	29	678	39	6-40	2	17.38
P. M. Pushpakumara (*Saracens*)	SLA	348.1	80	987	56	6-65	4	17.62
R. S. R. de Zoysa (*Moratuwa*)	LB	217.4	34	717	40	7-43	5	17.92
T. M. U. S. Karunaratne (*Seeduwa Raddoluwa*)	OB	197.1	28	660	36	6-54	3	18.33
G. D. R. Eranga (*Burgher*)	LFM	184.5	29	739	38	6-82	2	19.44
A. B. T. Lakshitha (*Bloomfield & Ruhuna*)	RFM	272.4	43	950	47	7-59	4	20.21
S. Weerakoon (*Colts and Ruhuna*)	SLA	482.1	98	1,445	71	7-40	5	20.35
S. Prasanna (*Army and Kandurata*)	LB	430	70	1,470	71	8-59	5	20.70
S. M. Senanayake (*Sinhalese and Ruhuna*)	OB	508.5	102	1,349	64	6-61	4	21.07
D. T. Kottehewa (*Nondescripts and Bas South*)	RFM	272.5	44	840	39	4-33	0	21.53
T. D. D. Darshanpriya (*Ragama and Bas Nth*)	RFM	266.4	37	941	42	8-51	3	22.40
C. W. Vidanapathirana (*Colombo and Kandu*)	RFM	367.4	57	1,329	55	5-40	1	24.16
C. M. Bandara (*Ragama and Basnahira South*)	LBG	358.1	63	1,048	43	5-105	1	24.37
M. M. M. Suraj (*Bloomfield and Kandurata*)	OB	301.1	48	1,055	43	6-73	2	24.53
M. Pushpakumara (*Tamil Union and Bas Nth*)	OB	378.2	60	1,141	46	5-84	1	24.80
W. R. S. de Silva (*Colombo and Ruhuna*)	LFM	275.3	34	1,015	39	5-52	1	26.02
D. Hettiarachchi (*Chilaw and Basnahira South*)	SLA	423	77	1,348	47	7-187	5	28.68

Full scores of the 2008-09 Sri Lankan season can be found at www.cricinfo.com/db/ARCHIVE/
2008-09/SL_LOCAL/, www.cricketarchive.co.uk/Archive/Seasons/2008-09_SL.html and in the *ACS
Overseas First-Class Annual 2009.*

PREMIER LEAGUE, 2008-09

					1st-inns	Bonus points		
Tier A	Played	Won	Lost	Drawn	Points	Batting	Bowling	Points
Colts CC	10	5†	1	4	24	20.585	15.3	123.885
Sinhalese SC	10	3†	0	7	40	20.100	14.8	114.900
Ragama CC	10	4*	1	5	24	20.005	16.2	110.205
Bloomfield C & AC	10	4*	2	4	24	16.550	16.3	106.850
Colombo CC	10	2	2	6	24	19.895	15.1	82.995
Tamil Union C & AC	10	1	1	8	32	21.795	15.0	80.795
Chilaw Marians CC	10	1	1	8	24	21.475	12.7	70.175
Moors SC	10	1	2	7	24	19.220	13.7	68.920
Nondescripts CC	10	0	3	7	32	18.695	13.1	63.795
Badureliya SC	10	2*	3	5	0	16.815	13.1	55.915
Army SC	10	0	7	3	0	15.375	15.9	31.275

Tier B

	Played	Won	Lost	Drawn	1st-inns Points	Bonus points Batting	Bowling	Points
Saracens SC	9	4	1	4	32	17.105	16.4	113.505
Panadura SC	9	5*	1	3	8	15.520	14.1	99.620
Seeduwa Raddoluwa SC ...	9	4*	3	2	8	16.410	14.3	96.710
Burgher Recreation Club ...	9	3	2	4	16	16.335	14.5	82.835
Air Force SC..............	9	3*	2	4	0	16.240	15.6	69.840
Moratuwa SC	9	2	2	5	16	16.865	12.7	69.565
Singha SC	9	2	4	3	8	16.480	13.7	62.180
Sebastianites C & AC	9	2*	3	4	8	14.470	12.1	60.570
Police SC.................	9	1	5	3	16	15.110	14.2	57.310
Lankan CC	9	0	3	6	24	15.755	14.5	54.255

* *Includes one win by an innings.* † *Includes two wins by an innings.*

Saracens SC were promoted to Tier A, and Navy SC to Tier B.

Outright win = 12 pts; outright win by an innings = 14 pts; lead on first innings in a drawn game = 8 pts. Bonus points were awarded as follows: 0.1 pt for each wicket taken and 0.005 pt for each run scored, up to 400 runs per innings.

Tier A

At Bloomfield C & AC, Colombo, November 14, 15, 16, 2008. **Bloomfield won by 148 runs.** Toss: Bloomfield. **Bloomfield 148 and 276** (L. P. C. Silva 58); **Colombo 135** (A. B. T. Lakshitha 4-41) **and 141.** *Bloomfield 16.12 pts, Colombo 3.38 pts.*
    Colombo's left-armer Sujeewa de Silva took a hat-trick in Bloomfield's second innings.

At Colts CC, Colombo, November 14, 15, 16, 2008. **Colts won by an innings and 68 runs.** Toss: Colts. **Colts 502-7 dec** (B. S. M. Warnapura 61, D. N. Pathirana 150, M. D. K. Perera 94; P. N. Ranjith 4-119); **Moors 212** (D. N. Hunukumbura 54; S. Weerakoon 5-43, M. D. K. Perera 4-62) **and 222** (T. K. D. Sudarshana 82; S. Weerakoon 5-78). *Colts 18 pts, Moors 2.87 pts.*
    Colts scored 403-5 from 90 overs on the first day, and their slow left-armer Sajeewa Weerakoon took five wickets in each innings to start their campaign with an innings victory.

At Nondescripts CC, Colombo, November 14, 15, 16, 2008. **Badureliya won by an innings and two runs.** Toss: Badureliya. **Nondescripts 141 and 176** (G. D. D. Indika 69; U. M. A. Prasad 4-49); **Badureliya 319** (A. A. S. Silva 70, T. M. N. Sampath 82, B. A. R. S. Priyadarshana 63; D. T. Kottehewa 4-96). *Badureliya 17.595 pts, Nondescripts 2.585 pts.*

At Sinhalese SC, Colombo, November 14, 15, 16, 2008. **Drawn.** Toss: Chilaw Marians. **Sinhalese 319** (J. K. Silva 133, F. D. M. Karunaratne 63; D. Hettiarachchi 4-101, S. H. M. Silva 5-43) **and 233-5 dec** (T. T. Samaraweera 111, J. K. Silva 74); **Chilaw Marians 186** (S. M. Senanayake 4-37) **and 274-6** (W. A. S. Niroshan 112, L. J. P. Gunaratne 73*). *Sinhalese 12.36 pts, Chilaw Marians 3.8 pts.*

At P. Saravanamuttu Stadium, Colombo, November 14, 15, 16, 2008. **Drawn.** Toss: Ragama. **Tamil Union 207** (B. M. A. J. Mendis 52, S. K. L. de Silva 58) **and 358** (B. M. A. J. Mendis 61, S. K. L. de Silva 63, S. I. Fernando 94; K. Weeraratne 4-104); **Ragama 355** (G. I. Daniel 165; I. Udana 4-60) **and 191-8** (H. D. R. L. Thirimanne 54, S. I. de Saram 60; R. A. S. Lakmal 4-41). *Tamil Union 4.625 pts, Ragama 12.73 pts.*
    Lanka de Silva passed 10,000 first-class career runs in Tamil Union's first innings.

At FTZ Sports Complex, Katunayake, November 21, 22, 23, 2008. **Chilaw Marians won by one wicket.** Toss: Chilaw Marians. **Army 229** (K. C. Prasad 54; D. Hettiarachchi 6-48) **and 57** (W. M. G. Ramyakumara 6-23, D. Hettiarachchi 4-24); **Chilaw Marians 217** (T. A. M. Siriwardene 62; S. Prasanna 4-74) **and 72-9** (S. Prasanna 5-31). *Chilaw Marians 15.445 pts, Army 3.33 pts.*
    The Army slumped to 18-6 in their second innings; they eventually reached 57, matching their previous lowest first-class total and leaving a seemingly straightforward target of 70. Chilaw Marians only just made it after losing their ninth wicket at 50.

At Moors SC, Colombo, November 21, 22, 23, 2008. **Ragama won by an innings and 37 runs.** Toss: Badureliya. **Ragama 285** (R. S. S. S. de Zoysa 50, W. D. D. S. Perera 82, C. M. Bandara 50*); **Badureliya 54** (P. A. S. S. Jeewantha 5-18) **and 194** (K. R. N. U. Perera 68, P. S. Jayaprakashdaran 50*; K. Weeraratne 6-47). *Ragama 17.425 pts, Badureliya 2.24 pts.*

At Colombo CC, Colombo, November 21, 22, 23, 2008. **Drawn.** Toss: Nondescripts. **Colombo 168** (S. S. Pathirana 71; D. T. Kottehewa 4-33) **and 232-5** (D. K. Ranaweera 99, W. M. B. Perera 53, K. G. N. Randika 50*); **Nondescripts 254** (C. K. B. Kulasekara 83, D. T. Kottehewa 62*; C. W. Vidanapathirana 4-57, M. I. Ratnayake 4-65). *Colombo 3 pts, Nondescripts 10.77 pts.*

At Sinhalese SC, Colombo, November 21, 22, 23, 2008. **Drawn.** Toss: Sinhalese. **Sinhalese 378** (L. A. H. N. Perera 96, F. D. M. Karunaratne 55, D. N. T. Zoysa 67; M. D. K. Perera 5-120); **Colts 164** (D. N. T. Zoysa 5-22) **and 197-4** (T. M. I. Mutaliph 64, D. N. Pathirana 75). *Sinhalese 11.29 pts, Colts 2.805 pts.*

At P. Saravanamuttu Stadium, Colombo, November 21, 22, 23, 2008. **Drawn.** Toss: Bloomfield. **Tamil Union 299** (R. J. M. G. M. Rupasinghe 154*; A. B. T. Lakshitha 5-58) **and 32-0; Bloomfield 573** (K. Y. de Silva 81, T. M. Dilshan 112, L. P. C. Silva 61, H. A. P. W. Jayawardene 58, C. U. Jayasinghe 81, D. M. G. S. Dissanayake 92, Extras 53). *Tamil Union 2.655 pts, Bloomfield 11 pts.*
  Nos 3 to 8 in Bloomfield's batting line-up all passed 50, as did Extras, to give them their highest first-class total.

At Nondescripts CC, Colombo, November 28, 29, 30, 2008. **Drawn.** Toss: Chilaw Marians. **Badureliya 146** (D. Hettiarachchi 5-48) **and 250-4** (U. K. D. Aravinda 88, D. V. Gunawardene 98); **Chilaw Marians 234** (T. A. M. Siriwardene 81, L. J. P. Gunaratne 65). *Badureliya 2.98 pts, Chilaw Marians 10.57 pts.*

At Bloomfield C & AC, Colombo, November 28, 29, 30, 2008. **Drawn.** Toss: Moors. **Bloomfield 102** (K. H. R. K. Fernando 5-24); **Moors 206** (L. P. C. Silva 4-24). *Bloomfield 1.51 pts, Moors 10.03 pts.*

At Colombo CC, Colombo, November 28, 29, 30, 2008. **Drawn.** Toss: Colombo. **Colombo 252** (W. M. B. Perera 139; S. Prasanna 4-101) **and 89-0** (M. G. Vandort 53*); **Army 226** (B. A. D. Balasooriya 59; S. S. Pathirana 6-90). *Colombo 10.705 pts, Army 2.13 pts.*
  Nineteen-year-old left-arm spinner Sachith Pathirana took 6-90 in his second first-class match.

At Moors SC, Colombo, November 28, 29, 30, 2008. **Drawn.** Toss: Ragama. **Sinhalese 329-8** (L. A. H. N. Perera 93, K. P. S. P. Karunanayake 77; C. M. Bandara 5-105) **v Ragama.** *Ragama 0.8 pts, Sinhalese 1.645 pts.*

At P. Saravanamuttu Stadium, Colombo, November 28, 29, 30, 2008. **Drawn.** Toss: Nondescripts. **Tamil Union 277** (S. K. L. de Silva 51, I. Udana 75*; W. C. A. Ganegama 4-57); **Nondescripts 278-6** (M. K. Gajanayake 100*, C. K. B. Kulasekara 50). *Tamil Union 1.985 pts, Nondescripts 10.39 pts.*
  Malintha Gajanayake scored the second first-class hundred of his eight-year career, in his 88th match.

At Army Ground, Panagoda, December 5, 6, 7, 2008. **Drawn.** Toss: Tamil Union. **Army 179** (T. R. D. Mendis 68; S. D. C. Malinga 4-36) **and 200** (H. H. M. de Zoysa 67); **Tamil Union 223** (S. I. Fernando 113) **and 113-5** (S. M. A. Priyanjan 53; S. Prasanna 4-37). *Army 3.395 pts, Tamil Union 11.68 pts.*

At R. Premadasa Stadium, Colombo, December 5, 6, 7, 2008. **Drawn.** Toss: Colombo. **Badureliya 244** (M. R. C. N. Bandaratilleke 59); **Colombo 343-2** (M. G. Vandort 138, J. Mubarak 100*, W. M. B. Perera 51*). *Badureliya 1.42 pts, Colombo 10.715 pts.*

At Colts CC, Colombo, December 5, 6, 7, 2008. **Drawn.** Toss: Chilaw Marians. **Chilaw Marians 253** (W. M. G. Ramyakumara 111*; W. P. U. J. C. Vaas 4-35); **Colts 273-5** (B. S. M. Warnapura 133*, T. M. I. Mutaliph 65). *Colts 10.365 pts, Chilaw Marians 1.765 pts.*

At Nondescripts CC, Colombo, December 5, 6, 7, 2008. **Drawn.** Toss: Nondescripts. **Moors 36** (C. K. B. Kulasekara 6-13) **and 135-6; Nondescripts 287-9 dec** (K. D. Gunawardene 137; H. M. R. K. B. Herath 4-51). *Nondescripts 11.035 pts, Moors 1.755 pts.*

Kosala Kulasekara had career-best figures of 8–1–13–6 as Moors collapsed for their lowest first-class total (and the joint second-lowest in Sri Lankan first-class cricket) on the opening day. They were saved from almost certain defeat by a third-day washout.

At Sinhalese SC, Colombo, December 5, 6, 7, 2008. **Drawn.** Toss: Bloomfield. **Sinhalese 233** (N. T. Paranavitana 51, K. S. Lokuarachchi 83; T. P. Gamage 4-50) **and 1-0; Bloomfield 257** (L. P. C. Silva 106; S. M. Senanayake 5-84). *Sinhalese 2.17 pts, Bloomfield 10.285 pts.*

At Army Ground, Panagoda, December 12, 13, 14, 2008. **Moors won by 73 runs.** Toss: Army. **Moors 161 and 265** (D. N. Hunukumbura 61, H. M. R. K. B. Herath 55; S. Prasanna 5-93, B. A. D. Balasooriya 4-49); **Army 154** (H. M. R. K. B. Herath 6-28) **and 199** (K. C. Prasad 58*). *Moors 16.13 pts, Army 3.765 pts.*

At Moors SC, Colombo, December 12, 13, 14, 2008. **Drawn.** Toss: Chilaw Marians. **Chilaw Marians 214** (M. M. D. N. R. G. Perera 77; K. Weeraratne 4-79) **and 281-7** (M. L. Udawatte 109, N. H. G. Cooray 72; H. G. D. Nayanakantha 4-65); **Ragama 372** (H. E. Vithana 113, S. I. de Saram 53, C. M. Bandara 50; D. Hettiarachchi 5-133, L. J. P. Gunaratne 4-65). *Chilaw Marians 3.475 pts, Ragama 11.56 pts.*

At Colombo CC, Colombo, December 12, 13, 14, 2008. **Colts won by an innings and 31 runs.** Toss: Colts. **Colts 379** (A. D. Mathews 168); **Colombo 133** (K. M. D. N. Kulasekara 6-31) **and 215** (D. K. Ranaweera 87, S. S. Pathirana 58; S. Weerakoon 5-44). *Colts 17.895 pts, Colombo 2.74 pts.*

Angelo Mathews scored what was then his career-best, 168 from 259 balls.

At Sinhalese SC, Colombo, December 12, 13, 14, 2008. **Drawn.** Toss: Nondescripts. **Nondescripts 194** (S. M. Senanayake 4-61) **and 347-8** (W. U. Tharanga 118, W. L. P. Fernando 52, M. S. R. Wijeratne 51*); **Sinhalese 308-7 dec** (J. K. Silva 54, D. P. M. D. Jayawardene 60, K. S. Lokuarachchi 68). *Sinhalese 11.34 pts, Nondescripts 3.405 pts.*

At P. Saravanamuttu Stadium, Colombo, December 12, 13, 14, 2008. **Drawn.** Toss: Badureliya. **Tamil Union 349** (S. M. A. Priyanjan 74, R. J. M. G. M. Rupasinghe 84; D. F. Arnolda 5-79) **and 164-5 dec** (B. M. A. J. Mendis 61, S. I. Fernando 50); **Badureliya 203** (A. A. S. Silva 75*) **and 233-7** (R. M. A. R. Ratnayake 58, B. A. R. S. Priyadarshana 70*, M. R. C. N. Bandaratilleke 50*; M. Pushpakumara 4-84). *Tamil Union 12.265 pts, Badureliya 3.68 pts.*

At R. Premadasa Stadium, Colombo, December 19, 20, 21, 2008. **Bloomfield won by an innings and 23 runs.** Toss: Bloomfield. **Badureliya 63** (A. N. P. R. Fernando 4-19) **and 211** (D. W. A. N. D. Vitharana 114, C. M. Withanage 62; T. P. Gamage 5-43); **Bloomfield 297** (W. S. Jayantha 106, L. P. C. Silva 100). *Bloomfield 17.485 pts, Badureliya 2.37 pts.*

At Nondescripts CC, Colombo, December 19, 20, 21, 2008. **Drawn.** Toss: Moors. **Ragama 279** (S. I. de Saram 125; K. H. R. K. Fernando 4-67) **and 305-6 dec** (S. I. de Saram 150*, W. D. D. S. Perera 64); **Moors 206** (M. N. Mazahir 60; T. D. D. Darshanpriya 4-51) **and 132-2** (D. N. Hunukumbura 53*, M. N. Mazahir 50). *Moors 3.29 pts, Ragama 12.12 pts.*

Indika de Saram scored twin centuries; his second-innings 150 came from 145 balls, and included six sixes and eight fours.*

At Bloomfield C & AC, Colombo, December 26, 27, 28, 2008. **Ragama won by three wickets.** Toss: Ragama. **Bloomfield 218** (D. M. G. S. Dissanayake 67; T. D. D. Darshanpriya 8-51) **and 159; Ragama 142** (A. N. P. R. Fernando 5-36) **and 238-7** (S. I. de Saram 103*; A. B. T. Lakshitha 5-78). *Ragama 15.9 pts, Bloomfield 3.585 pts.*

Dinesh Daminda Darshanpriya took 8-51 as 20 wickets fell on the opening day and finished with 11-77 in the match, both career-bests. Indika de Saram scored his third hundred in four innings, and Ragama replaced Bloomfield at the top of the table.

At Colombo CC, Colombo, December 26, 27, 28, 2008. **Drawn.** Toss: Chilaw Marians. **Colombo 376** (C. S. Fernando 111, J. Mubarak 64; K. R. P. Silva 4-35) **and 200-3 dec** (W. M. B. Perera 104*,

K. G. N. Randika 54*); **Chilaw Marians 249** (M. M. D. N. R. G. Perera 62, D. M. Gunathilake 62) **and 211-5** (L. J. P. Gunaratne 122*). *Colombo 12.38 pts, Chilaw Marians 3.6 pts.*

At Colts CC, Colombo, December 26, 27, 28, 2008. **Tamil Union won by seven wickets.** Toss: Tamil Union. **Colts 277** (A. R. S. Silva 82) **and 203** (A. D. Mathews 53); **Tamil Union 289** (S. M. A. Priyanjan 88) **and 194-3** (S. M. A. Priyanjan 58*). *Tamil Union 16.415 pts, Colts 3.7 pts.*

At Moors SC, Colombo, December 26, 27, 28, 2008. **Drawn.** Toss: Badureliya. **Moors 401** (N. M. N. P. Nawela 142, W. R. Fernando 68, A. Rideegammanagedera 70; D. F. Arnolda 4-113) **and 179-7 dec** (T. K. D. Sudarshana 56); **Badureliya 320** (D. W. A. N. D. Vitharana 92, E. F. M. U. Fernando 84) **and 223-8** (B. A. R. S. Priyadarshana 53). *Moors 12.695 pts, Badureliya 4.415 pts.*

At Sinhalese SC, Colombo, December 26, 27, 28, 2008. **Sinhalese won by an innings and 32 runs.** Toss: Army. **Sinhalese 355** (N. T. Paranavitana 107, L. A. H. N. Perera 52, J. K. Silva 76; P. K. N. M. K. Rathnayake 5-47); **Army 193** (D. A. S. Gunaratne 58; S. H. T. Kandamby 4-36) **and 130** (K. P. S. P. Karunanayake 4-48, S. M. Senanayake 4-16). *Sinhalese 17.775 pts, Army 2.615 pts.*

At Colts CC, Colombo, January 2, 3, 4, 2009. **Colts won by eight wickets.** Toss: Colts. **Army 175** (R. D. I. A. Karunatilleke 51; S. Weerakoon 4-48) **and 123** (S. Weerakoon 4-43); **Colts 226** (D. R. F. Weerasinghe 60, N. L. T. C. Perera 52) **and 73-2.** *Colts 15.495 pts, Army 2.69 pts.*

At Moors SC, Colombo, January 2, 3, 4, 2009. **Drawn.** Toss: Moors. **Chilaw Marians 389** (D. N. A. Athulathmudali 93, K. R. P. Silva 78, W. M. G. Ramyakumara 110; U. W. M. B. C. A. Welagedara 4-107) **and 253-9** (W. M. G. Ramyakumara 78; C. R. B. Mudalige 7-102); **Moors 344** (D. N. Hunukumbura 52, M. N. Mazahir 53, A. Rideegammanagedera 69*; D. Hettiarachchi 5-109). *Moors 3.62 pts, Chilaw Marians 12.21 pts.*

At Nondescripts CC, Colombo, January 2, 3, 4, 2009. **Drawn.** Toss: Bloomfield. **Nondescripts 257** (W. U. Tharanga 119; A. B. T. Lakshitha 6-48) **and 244** (W. L. P. Fernando 86; M. M. M. Suraj 4-55); **Bloomfield 366** (K. Y. de Silva 116, L. P. C. Silva 60; D. T. Kottehewa 4-68). *Nondescripts 3.505 pts, Bloomfield 11.83 pts.*

At Sinhalese SC, Colombo, January 2, 3, 2009. **Sinhalese won by an innings and 177 runs.** Toss: Badureliya. **Sinhalese 436-9 dec** (S. H. T. Kandamby 184, D. N. T. Zoysa 79, K. P. S. P. Karunanayake 76; U. M. A. Prasad 4-112); **Badureliya 161 and 98** (S. M. Senanayake 4-37, K. S. Lokuarachchi 4-30). *Sinhalese 18 pts, Badureliya 2.195 pts.*

Sinhalese were 58-5 before Thilina Kandamby added 110 with Nuwan Zoysa for the sixth wicket and 165 with Shalika Karunanayake for the seventh, setting up a two-day victory, completed when Badureliya were bowled out in double figures for the third time in the season; they lost 19 wickets on the second day. Sinhalese's second successive innings win took them to the top of the table.

At P. Saravanamuttu Stadium, Colombo, January 2, 3, 4, 2009. **Colombo won by three wickets.** Toss: Colombo. **Tamil Union 309** (R. J. M. G. M. Rupasinghe 146, S. D. C. Malinga 59*) **and 195; Colombo 352** (D. K. Ranaweera 75, C. S. Fernando 55, M. P. N. L. Perera 50) **and 153-7** (J. Mubarak 56*). *Colombo 16.525 pts, Tamil Union 4.22 pts.*

On the opening day, Tamil Union were 62-7 before Gihan Rupasinghe added 105 for the eighth wicket with Omesh Wijesiriwardene (39) and 109 for the seventh with Surappulige Malinga.

At R. Premadasa Stadium, Colombo, January 9, 10, 11, 2009. **Badureliya won by four wickets.** Toss: Badureliya. **Army 140** (T. D. T. Soysa 59; M. R. C. N. Bandaratilleke 4-16) **and 155** (M. R. C. N. Bandaratilleke 6-45); **Badureliya 160** (D. W. A. N. D. Vitharana 85; P. K. N. M. K. Rathnayake 5-35, S. Prasanna 5-43) **and 137-6** (B. A. R. S. Priyadarshana 66). *Badureliya 15.485 pts, Army 3.075 pts.*

At Moors SC, Colombo, January 9, 10, 11, 2009. **Drawn.** Toss: Ragama. **Colts 448** (H. G. J. M. Kulatunga 234, A. R. S. Silva 147; S. A. D. U. Indrasiri 5-107) **and 149-5** (N. L. T. C. Perera 64; S. A. D. U. Indrasiri 4-55); **Ragama 400** (R. S. S. S. de Zoysa 104, W. D. D. S. Perera 135; N. L. T. C. Perera 4-49). *Colts 11.745 pts, Ragama 3.5 pts.*

Jeevantha Kulatunga scored 234 in 194 balls with 12 sixes and 23 fours – his maiden double-hundred nearly 18 years after first-class debut. He and Roshen Silva, who scored a maiden century, rescued Colts from 32-4 by adding 353, a national record for the fifth wicket. In reply, Ragama's fifth-wicket pair, Sameera de Zoysa and Duminda Perera, added 204.

At Nondescripts CC, Colombo, January 9, 10, 11, 2009. **Drawn.** Toss: Nondescripts. **Chilaw Marians 255** (M. M. D. N. R. G. Perera 79, W. M. G. Ramyakumara 50; D. R. G. Subasinghe 4-51) **and 204; Nondescripts 238** (C. K. B. Kulasekara 96; W. M. G. Ramyakumara 4-41) **and 104-7** (W. M. G. Ramyakumara 4-37). *Nondescripts 3.71 pts, Chilaw Marians 11.995 pts.*

At Sinhalese SC, Colombo, January 9, 10, 11, 2009. **Drawn.** Toss: Sinhalese. **Colombo 201** (K. G. N. Randika 52; D. N. T. Zoysa 4-58) **and 293** (S. S. Pathirana 83); **Sinhalese 248** (N. T. Paranavitana 117; S. S. Pathirana 5-41) **and 180-6** (L. A. H. N. Perera 55). *Sinhalese 12.14 pts, Colombo 4.07 pts.*

At P. Saravanamuttu Stadium, Colombo, January 9, 10, 11, 2009. **Drawn.** Toss: Moors. **Tamil Union 325** (S. C. Serasinghe 70, R. J. M. G. M. Rupasinghe 112) **and 239-5** (S. I. Fernando 52, S. K. L. de Silva 68*); **Moors 280** (T. K. D. Sudarshana 61). *Tamil Union 11.82 pts, Moors 2.9 pts.*

At Army Ground, Panagoda, January 16, 17, 18, 2009. **Drawn.** Toss: Nondescripts. **Nondescripts 411** (K. D. Gunawardene 103, M. S. R. Wijeratne 94, C. K. B. Kulasekara 66; S. Prasanna 5-162) **and 129-7** (S. Prasanna 4-63); **Army 282** (P. N. Kaluarachchi 113; N. C. Komasaru 4-91). *Army 3.11 pts, Nondescripts 11.645 pts.*

At Colombo CC, Colombo, January 16, 17, 18, 2009. **Colombo won by ten wickets.** Toss: Ragama. **Ragama 215** (T. D. D. Darshanpriya 64*; W. R. S. de Silva 5-52) **and 146** (S. S. Pathirana 5-41); **Colombo 341** (C. S. Fernando 64, W. M. B. Perera 113; H. G. D. Nayanakantha 4-58, S. A. D. U. Indrasiri 4-78) **and 23-0.** *Colombo 15.82 pts, Ragama 2.805 pts.*
    Ragama's Hemantha Wickremaratne passed 10,000 first-class runs.

At Colts CC, Colombo, January 16, 17, 2009. **Colts won by four wickets.** Toss: Bloomfield. **Bloomfield 159** (D. M. G. S. Dissanayake 66; S. Weerakoon 5-30) **and 119** (S. Weerakoon 7-40); **Colts 87** (D. M. G. S. Dissanayake 4-31, M. M. M. Suraj 5-12) **and 194-6.** *Colts 15.405 pts, Bloomfield 2.99 pts.*
    Slow left-armer Sajeewa Weerakoon set up Colts' two-day victory with 12-70 in the match.

At Sinhalese SC, Colombo, January 16, 17, 18, 2009. **Sinhalese won by eight wickets.** Toss: Sinhalese. **Moors 227** (D. N. Hunukumbura 60, K. H. R. K. Fernando 51; S. M. Senanayake 4-61) **and 205** (D. N. Hunukumbura 88, A. S. A. Perera 52; S. M. Senanayake 6-84); **Sinhalese 126** (L. H. D. Dilhara 4-46, H. M. R. K. B. Herath 4-21) **and 308-2** (N. T. Paranavitana 123*, T. T. Samaraweera 154*). *Sinhalese 16.17 pts, Moors 3.36 pts.*
    Tharanga Paranavitana and Thilan Samaraweera, who passed 10,000 first-class runs, added 283* for the third wicket in 52 overs to complete victory for Sinhalese, who had trailed by 101 on first innings.

At P. Saravanamuttu Stadium, Colombo, January 16, 17, 18, 2009. **Drawn.** Toss: Tamil Union. **Chilaw Marians 366** (W. A. S. Niroshan 138; S. D. C. Malinga 5-47) **and 216-8** (D. N. A. Athulathmudali 52, W. A. S. Niroshan 65; B. M. A. J. Mendis 4-46); **Tamil Union 463** (S. I. Fernando 78, S. M. A. Priyanjan 82, B. M. A. J. Mendis 125, I. Udana 88; D. Hettiarachchi 7-187). *Tamil Union 11.8 pts, Chilaw Marians 3.91 pts.*
    No. 8 Isuru Udana hit seven sixes and five fours in his career-best 88.

At Colombo CC, Colombo, January 23, 24, 25, 2009. **Ragama won by 196 runs.** Toss: Army. **Ragama 350** (G. I. Daniel 107, R. S. S. S. de Zoysa 64, R. P. A. H. Wickremaratne 75; P. K. N. M. K. Rathnayake 4-75, S. Prasanna 4-109) **and 222** (H. D. R. L. Thirimanne 55, C. M. Bandara 54); **Army 168 and 208** (T. D. D. Darshanpriya 5-27). *Ragama 16.86 pts, Army 3.88 pts.*

At Bloomfield C & AC, Colombo, January 23, 24, 25, 2009. **Bloomfield won by seven wickets.** Toss: Chilaw Marians. **Chilaw Marians 178** (M. L. Udawatte 69; M. M. M. Suraj 6-73) **and 243** (W. A. S. Niroshan 93); **Bloomfield 377** (K. Y. de Silva 69, D. M. G. S. Dissanayake 106, L. P. C. Silva 61, H. A. P. W. Jayawardene 51) **and 45-3.** *Bloomfield 16.11 pts, Chilaw Marians 3.405 pts.*

At Moors SC, Colombo, January 23, 24, 25, 2009. **Drawn.** Toss: Moors. **Moors 386** (D. N. Hunukumbura 79, L. H. D. Dilhara 142) **and 248** (A. Rideegammanagedera 65; C. W. Vidanapathirana 5-40); **Colombo 314** (D. K. Ranaweera 72, M. G. Vandort 71; L. H. D. Dilhara 5-40) **and 18-1.** *Moors 12.27 pts, Colombo 3.66 pts.*
    Dilhara Lokuhettige hit 142 in 134 balls, with five sixes and 17 fours, then took 5-40.

At Nondescripts CC, Colombo, January 23, 24, 2009. **Colts won by six wickets.** Toss: Nondescripts. **Nondescripts 161** (S. Weerakoon 4-73) **and 177** (C. G. Wijesinghe 66; S. Weerakoon 4-63); **Colts 166** (W. P. U. J. C. Vaas 56, A. R. S. Silva 56; D. T. Kottehewa 4-66, C. G. Wijesinghe 4-21) **and 175-4** (D. N. Pathirana 109). *Colts 15.705 pts, Nondescripts 3.09 pts.*

Colts owed their second successive two-day win to slow left-armer Sajeewa Weerakoon, who claimed four wickets in each innings, and Dhanuka Pathirana, who came in at 10-3 chasing 173 and hit 109 from 118 balls.

At Sinhalese SC, Colombo, January 23, 24, 25, 2009. **Drawn.** Toss: Sinhalese. **Sinhalese 454** (T. T. Samaraweera 140, J. K. Silva 78, K. Magage 76) **and 202-4** (N. T. Paranavitana 88, L. A. H. N. Perera 74); **Tamil Union 386** (S. I. Fernando 139, S. M. A. Priyanjan 79, R. J. M. G. M. Rupasinghe 74; S. M. Senanayake 6-136). *Sinhalese 12.01 pts, Tamil Union 3.33 pts.*

Reigning champions Sinhalese ended their programme on top of the table, but less than four points ahead of Colts, who had a game in hand.

At Army Ground, Panagoda, January 30, 31, 2009. **Bloomfield won by 130 runs.** Toss: Army. **Bloomfield 161** (P. K. N. M. K. Rathnayake 5-64, S. Prasanna 4-36) **and 226** (W. S. Jayantha 69; S. Prasanna 8-59); **Army 102 and 155.** *Bloomfield 15.935 pts, Army 3.285 pts.*

Leg-spinner Seekkuge Prasanna took 8-59 and 12-95 in the match, both career-bests, but his team still went down to their seventh defeat, inside two days.

At Colts CC, Colombo, January 30, 31, February 1, 2009. **Drawn.** Toss: Badureliya. **Colts 426** (B. S. M. Warnapura 95, H. G. J. M. Kulatunga 69, N. L. T. C. Perera 88; P. S. Jayaprakashdaran 4-73) **and 354-8 dec** (T. M. I. Mutaliph 55, B. S. M. Warnapura 100*); **Badureliya 347** (P. K. J. R. N. Nonis 73, D. F. Arnolda 62). *Colts 12.77 pts, Badureliya 3.535 pts.*

Colts ended the campaign as they had begun it, scoring 400-plus on the opening day, and made sure of the Premier title when they claimed the first-innings lead.

At Nondescripts CC, Colombo, January 30, 31, February 1, 2009. **Ragama won by 149 runs.** Toss: Nondescripts. **Ragama 155** (W. C. A. Ganegama 5-58) **and 346-9 dec** (G. I. Daniel 62, S. I. de Saram 147; D. T. Kottehewa 4-53); **Nondescripts 158** (K. Weeraratne 4-51) **and 194** (R. D. Dissanayake 4-41). *Ragama 16.505 pts, Nondescripts 3.66 pts.*

Ragama's victory confirmed they would finish third.

CHAMPIONS

Lakspray Trophy		1994-95	Bloomfield C & AC	2001-02	Colts CC
1988-89	Nondescripts CC		Sinhalese SC	2002-03	Moors SC
	Sinhalese SC	1995-96	Colombo CC	2003-04	Bloomfield C & AC
1989-90	Sinhalese SC	1996-97	Bloomfield C & AC	2004-05	Colts CC
		1997-98	Sinhalese SC	2005-06	Sinhalese SC
P. Saravanamuttu Trophy				2006-07	Colombo CC
1990-91	Sinhalese SC	*Premier League*		2007-08	Sinhalese SC
1991-92	Colts CC	1998-99	Bloomfield C & AC	2008-09	Colts CC
1992-93	Sinhalese SC	1999-2000	Colts CC		
1993-94	Nondescripts CC	2000-01	Nondescripts CC		

Sinhalese have won the title outright 6 times, Colts 5, Bloomfield 3, Colombo and Nondescripts 2, Moors 1. Sinhalese have also shared the title twice, and Bloomfield and Nondescripts once each.

Tier B

At Burgher RC, Colombo, November 14, 15, 16, 2008. **Burgher won by six wickets.** Toss: Burgher. **Saracens 222** (C. S. Pussegolla 98) **and 136** (W. R. D. Wimaladarma 7-34); **Burgher 222** (K. D. C. Pushpalal 51) **and 165-4** (B. M. P. D. Fernando 76). *Burgher 15.935 pts, Saracens 3.33 pts.*

At FTZ Sports Complex, Katunayake, November 14, 15, 16, 2008. **Drawn.** Toss: Lankan. **Sebastianites 143** (R. H. T. A. Perera 54) **and 333-9 dec** (G. R. P. Peiris 53, A. A. C. E. Athukorala 79*); **Lankan 221** (B. M. D. T. D. Ariyasinghe 54) **and 165-5.** *Lankan 11.83 pts, Sebastianites 3.88 pts.*

At Tyronne Fernando Stadium, Moratuwa, November 14, 15, 16, 2008. **Moratuwa won by two runs.** Toss: Police. **Moratuwa 162** (D. S. Wijemanne 52; K. P. W. M. Priyadarshana 4-38) **and 232; Police 167 and 225** (S. R. Kumar 82; R. S. R. de Zoysa 5-67). *Moratuwa 15.97 pts, Police 3.96 pts.*

Police were 211-7 chasing 228, but fell three runs short.

At R. Premadasa Stadium, Colombo, November 14, 15, 16, 2008. **Seeduwa Raddoluwa won by seven wickets.** Toss: Singha. **Singha 220** (T. M. U. S. Karunaratne 5-55) **and 229** (D. G. R. Dhammika 4-38); **Seeduwa Raddoluwa 332** (H. G. Kumara 76, T. M. U. S. Karunaratne 64; S. I. Vithana 5-90) **and 118-3** (P. M. Priyantha 69). *Seeduwa Raddoluwa 16.25 pts, Singha 3.545 pts.*

Newly promoted Seeduwa Raddoluwa's first first-class match ended in victory.

At Air Force Ground, Colombo, November 14, 15, 2008. **Panadura won by an innings and 160 runs.** Toss: Air Force. **Air Force 138** (W. M. P. N. Wanasinghe 4-28) **and 126; Panadura 424** (M. A. Sandaruwan 72, J. S. K. Peiris 100, K. A. D. M. Fernando 138; M. K. G. C. P. Lakshitha 4-105). *Panadura 18 pts, Air Force 2.32 pts.*

Primal Buddika Kularatne carried his bat through Air Force's second innings for 36* as Panadura crushed them in two days.

At Tyronne Fernando Stadium, Moratuwa, November 21, 22, 23, 2008. **Seeduwa Raddoluwa won by 47 runs.** Toss: Seeduwa Raddoluwa. **Seeduwa Raddoluwa 210** (T. M. U. S. Karunaratne 65; W. J. S. D. Perera 4-69) **and 157** (R. S. R. de Zoysa 7-43); **Moratuwa 168 and 152.** *Seeduwa Raddoluwa 15.835 pts, Moratuwa 3.6 pts.*

Seeduwa Raddoluwa's wicketkeeper, Chirantha de Silva, made six catches in Moratuwa's second innings.

At Panadura Esplanade, Panadura, November 21, 22, 23, 2008. **Panadura won by six wickets.** Toss: Panadura. **Singha 151** (A. S. Wewalwala 57; W. M. P. N. Wanasinghe 4-42) **and 170** (D. A. Faux 77; M. N. R. Cooray 4-40, G. A. S. Perera 4-35); **Panadura 168 and 156-4.** *Panadura 15.62 pts, Singha 3.005 pts.*

At Police Park, Colombo, November 21, 22, 23, 2008. **Drawn.** Toss: Lankan. **Police 213** (M. M. Rasmijinan 89) **and 262-8 dec** (P. R. Nirmal 59, K. P. W. M. Priyadarshana 53); **Lankan 102** (K. P. W. M. Priyadarshana 4-16) **and 80-5.** *Police 11.875 pts, Lankan 2.71 pts.*

At Bloomfield C & AC, Colombo, November 21, 22, 23, 2008. **Drawn.** Toss: Saracens. **Sebastianites 237** (H. P. G. Perera 65, J. M. P. C. Jayasundera 68; I. C. Soysa 4-39) **and 188-8** (G. R. P. Peiris 55*); **Saracens 321** (W. G. R. K. Alwis 144, P. K. Bodhisha 53). *Saracens 11.405 pts, Sebastianites 3.125 pts.*

Saracens wicketkeeper Rajitha Wickramarachchi made three catches and three stumpings in Sebastianites' first innings.

At Air Force Ground, Colombo, November 21, 22, 2008. **Air Force won by an innings and 72 runs.** Toss: Burgher. **Air Force 275** (M. S. Warnapura 50, S. Madanayake 86); **Burgher 45** (S. Madanayake 7-15) **and 158** (S. Madanayake 5-55). *Air Force 17.375 pts, Burgher 2.015 pts.*

Slow left-armer Suwanji Madanayake bowled unchanged for career-best figures of 9.1–2–15–7 to dismiss Burgher inside 20 overs for 45, their lowest-ever total. He took 12-70 in all, after scoring 86, to set up Air Force's two-day win.

At Burgher RC, Colombo, November 28, 29, 30, 2008. **Drawn.** Toss: Panadura. **Burgher 155** (W. M. P. N. Wanasinghe 4-42) **and 163** (M. N. R. Cooray 4-37); **Panadura 147** (P. U. M. Chanaka 4-29) **and 156-9** (C. A. M. Madusanka 5-19). *Burgher 11.49 pts, Panadura 3.515 pts.*

At Thurstan College, Colombo, November 28, 29, 30, 2008. **Drawn.** Toss: Seeduwa Raddoluwa. **Seeduwa Raddoluwa 173** (H. G. Kumara 63) **and 135** (P. C. Hewage 4-43); **Lankan 131** (W. K. G. Dilruk 4-10) **and 14-4.** *Lankan 2.725 pts, Seeduwa Raddoluwa 10.94 pts.*

At Royal College, Colombo, November 28, 29, 30, 2008. **Drawn.** Toss: Saracens. **Moratuwa 93** (L. T. A. de Silva 50) **and 180-7** (H. U. K. de Silva 56*; M. D. R. Prabath 4-38); **Saracens 234-6 dec** (W. G. R. K. Alwis 52, P. K. Bodhisha 66, W. S. D. Fernando 53). *Moratuwa 1.965 pts, Saracens 10.87 pts.*

Only one previous first-class match had been staged at Royal College, in March 1994.

At Police Park, Colombo, November 28, 29, 30, 2008. **Drawn.** Toss: Air Force. **Air Force 198 and 165-5** (K. A. Kumara 60*); **Police 213** (P. R. Nirmal 73; S. Madanayake 7-56). *Police 10.565 pts, Air Force 2.815 pts.*
Suwanji Madanayake took seven wickets in an innings for the second week running.

At Tyronne Fernando Stadium, Moratuwa, November 28, 29, 30, 2008. **Drawn.** Toss: Singha. **Singha 205** (D. T. M. Rajakaruna 66); **Sebastianites 122-6.** *Sebastianites 1.61 pts, Singha 1.625 pts.*

At Burgher RC, Colombo, December 5, 6, 7, 2008. **Drawn.** Toss: Seeduwa Raddoluwa. **Seeduwa Raddoluwa 359** (W. B. H. Samarawickrame 71, D. G. R. Dhammika 94; G. D. R. Eranga 6-82) **and 7-0; Burgher 245** (P. H. M. G. Fernando 50; D. G. R. Dhammika 6-72). *Burgher 2.225 pts, Seeduwa Raddoluwa 10.83 pts.*

At FTZ Sports Complex, Katunayake, December 5, 6, 7, 2008. **Saracens won by five wickets.** Toss: Saracens. **Lankan 204** (B. M. D. T. D. Ariyasinghe 66; P. M. Pushpakumara 5-58) **and 216** (H. A. H. U. Tillekeratne 56; R. K. P. Priyankara 4-65, P. M. Pushpakumara 6-65); **Saracens 302** (P. K. Bodhisha 112; M. D. S. Perera 6-54) **and 122-5** (K. Silva 50). *Saracens 16.12 pts, Lankan 3.6 pts.*

At Police Park, Colombo, December 5, 6, 7, 2008. **Police won by five wickets.** Toss: Police. **Singha 140** (M. M. Rasmijinan 4-26) **and 153; Police 248** (P. H. K. S. Nirmala 116; D. R. S. Perera 5-64) **and 46-5.** *Police 15.47 pts, Singha 2.965 pts.*

At Air Force Ground, Colombo, December 5, 6, 7, 2008. **Drawn.** Toss: Air Force. **Moratuwa 155 and 252** (W. J. S. D. Perera 61; D. P. L. M. Liyanage 4-55); **Air Force 113 and 170-6** (R. S. R. de Zoysa 5-56). *Air Force 3.415 pts, Moratuwa 11.635 pts.*

At Nondescripts CC, Colombo, December 12, 13, 2008. **Singha won by nine wickets.** Toss: Singha. **Moratuwa 126** (H. U. K. de Silva 50; N. C. K. Liyanage 5-48) **and 87** (N. C. K. Liyanage 4-26); **Singha 156** (A. S. Wewalwala 82*; A. B. L. D. Rodrigo 4-12) **and 59-1.** *Singha 15.075 pts, Moratuwa 2.165 pts.*
After three defeats and a draw, Singha completed their first win of the season in two days.

At Panadura Esplanade, Panadura, December 12, 13, 14, 2008. **Panadura won by 17 runs.** Toss: Police. **Panadura 101** (W. L. Manoj 5-35) **and 311** (G. Y. S. R. Perera 65, P. S. Liyanage 90, K. A. D. M. Fernando 51; K. P. W. M. Priyadarshana 6-41); **Police 167** (M. N. R. Cooray 6-34) **and 228** (P. H. K. S. Nirmala 60, M. M. Rasmijinan 57*). *Panadura 16.06 pts, Police 3.975 pts.*

At Royal College, Colombo, December 12, 13, 14, 2008. **Saracens won by two wickets.** Toss: Saracens. **Seeduwa Raddoluwa 129** (P. M. Pushpakumara 4-31) **and 180** (P. M. Pushpakumara 4-62); **Saracens 197** (C. S. Pussegolla 58, I. C. Soysa 68; D. G. R. Dhammika 4-66) **and 115-8** (T. M. U. S. Karunaratne 6-54). *Saracens 15.56 pts, Seeduwa Raddoluwa 3.345 pts.*
Saracens were 48-6 in their first innings, but recovered to lead by 68; they then slipped to 67-7 chasing 113, but managed a victory to go top of the table.

At Tyronne Fernando Stadium, Moratuwa, December 12, 13, 14, 2008. **Burgher won by 46 runs.** Toss: Sebastianites. **Burgher 230** (P. D. M. A. Cooray 52) **and 108; Sebastianites 144** (G. D. R. Eranga 4-45, C. A. M. Madusanka 4-26) **and 148** (P. B. Ediriweera 59, J. W. H. D. Boteju 53; C. A. M. Madusanka 6-40). *Burgher 15.69 pts, Sebastianites 3.46 pts.*

At Air Force Ground, Colombo, December 12, 13, 14, 2008. **Drawn.** Toss: Lankan. **Air Force 276** (M. S. Warnapura 51, E. K. Y. A. de Silva 64; M. D. S. Perera 5-90) **and 205** (S. Madanayake 53, M. D. S. Wanasinghe 54*); **Lankan 367** (W. M. J. Wannakuwatta 64, J. R. G. Namal 51, P. C. Hewage 51, K. M. P. Kumara 51*) **and 99-7** (S. Madanayake 4-44). *Air Force 4.105 pts, Lankan 12.33 pts.*

At Burgher RC, Colombo, December 19, 20, 21, 2008. **Drawn.** Toss: Burgher. **Burgher 295** (G. R. Perera 101*; S. I. Vithana 4-76) **and 257-9 dec** (P. H. M. G. Fernando 78, P. D. M. A. Cooray 66*; S. I. Vithana 6-78); **Singha 301** (H. H. R. Kavinga 79, N. C. K. Liyanage 58*; K. D. J. Nishantha 4-61) **and 198-5** (D. A. Faux 54, A. S. Wewalwala 76*). *Burgher 4.26 pts, Singha 12.395 pts.*

At FTZ Sports Complex, Katunayake, December 19, 20, 21, 2008. **Drawn.** Toss: Lankan. **Moratuwa 337** (R. C. Rupasinghe 54, H. U. K. de Silva 135; P. C. Hewage 5-60) **and 279-6** (W. J. S. D. Perera 76, L. T. A. de Silva 100*); **Lankan 261** (W. M. J. Wannakuwatta 59, J. R. G. Namal 64; P. C. M. Fernando 4-54). *Lankan 2.905 pts, Moratuwa 12.08 pts.*

At Panadura Esplanade, Panadura, December 19, 20, 21, 2008. **Panadura won by ten wickets.** Toss: Panadura. **Seeduwa Raddoluwa 104** (J. G. N. Priyantha 51) **and 105** (K. A. D. M. Fernando 4-18, M. N. R. Cooray 4-24); **Panadura 204** (J. S. K. Peiris 52, K. A. D. M. Fernando 67; J. D. M. de Silva 5-49) **and 6-0.** *Panadura 15.05 pts, Seeduwa Raddoluwa 2.045 pts.*

At Police Park, Colombo, December 19, 20, 21, 2008. **Saracens won by two wickets.** Toss: Saracens. **Police 165** (R. K. P. Priyankara 5-50) **and 112** (M. M. Rasmijinan 51; P. M. Pushpakumara 4-36); **Saracens 98 and 184-8.** *Saracens 15.41 pts, Police 3.185 pts.*

At Tyronne Fernando Stadium, Moratuwa, December 19, 20, 21, 2008. **Air Force won by seven wickets.** Toss: Sebastianites. **Sebastianites 179 and 148; Air Force 242** (M. S. Warnapura 72, S. Madanayake 57; J. M. P. C. Jayasundera 4-69) **and 87-3.** *Air Force 15.645 pts, Sebastianites 2.935 pts.*

At R. Premadasa Stadium, Colombo, December 26, 27, 28, 2008. **Drawn.** Toss: Singha. **Lankan 304** (H. A. H. U. Tillekeratne 101, W. M. J. Wannakuwatta 57; S. I. Vithana 6-83) **and 282-6 dec** (J. R. G. Namal 100*, M. D. S. Perera 51); **Singha 187** (H. H. R. Kavinga 56; N. A. C. T. Perera 5-74) **and 266-6** (D. A. Faux 62, S. I. Vithana 68*). *Lankan 12.53 pts, Singha 3.865 pts.*

At Tyronne Fernando Stadium, Moratuwa, December 26, 27, 28, 2008. **Drawn.** Toss: Panadura. **Panadura 347** (K. A. D. M. Fernando 75, C. P. Mapatuna 51, M. N. R. Cooray 57; R. S. R. de Zoysa 5-99) **and 219** (P. C. M. Fernando 4-44); **Moratuwa 194** (R. C. Rupasinghe 73; G. A. S. Perera 5-45) **and 195-5** (N. M. S. M. Sepala 98*, H. U. K. de Silva 55). *Moratuwa 3.945 pts, Panadura 12.33 pts.*

At Police Park, Colombo, December 26, 27, 28, 2008. **Drawn.** Toss: Police. **Burgher 331** (G. R. Perera 122, P. D. M. A. Cooray 67; W. N. M. Soysa 4-21) **and 221-4 dec** (B. M. P. D. Fernando 82, K. D. J. Nishantha 62*; W. N. M. Soysa 4-81); **Police 261** (R. G. D. Sanjeewa 73, Y. A. N. Mendis 53; D. C. B. Keerthisinghe 4-44) **and 151-8.** *Police 3.46 pts, Burgher 12.56 pts.*

At Thurstan College, Colombo, December 26, 27, 28, 2008. **Seeduwa Raddoluwa won by two wickets.** Toss: Sebastianites. **Sebastianites 209** (T. M. U. S. Karunaratne 6-62) **and 271-6 dec** (G. R. P. Peiris 114, J. W. H. D. Boteju 61); **Seeduwa Raddoluwa 281** (W. B. H. Samarawickrame 113; A. A. C. E. Athukorala 6-77) **and 200-8.** *Seeduwa Raddoluwa 16.005 pts, Sebastianites 4.2 pts.*

At Air Force Ground, Colombo, December 26, 27, 28, 2008. **Drawn.** Toss: Air Force. **Saracens 404-9 dec** (K. Silva 51, C. S. Pussegolla 71, R. S. Wickramarachchi 80; S. Madanayake 4-113) **and 191** (P. K. Bodhisha 56, K. Silva 54; A. Rizan 7-44); **Air Force 306** (W. A. Eranga 64, K. S. T. Perera 53, P. S. A. N. Shiroman 88) **and 191-8** (P. M. Pushpakumara 5-64). *Air Force 4.385 pts, Saracens 12.755 pts.*

At Tyronne Fernando Stadium, Moratuwa, January 2, 3, 4, 2009. **Moratuwa won by seven wickets.** Toss: Moratuwa. **Moratuwa 299** (N. M. S. M. Sepala 59, A. B. L. D. Rodrigo 59) **and 86-3** (R. C. Rupasinghe 57*); **Burgher 127** (W. J. S. D. Perera 6-59) **and 257** (P. H. M. G. Fernando 73, G. R. Perera 74; R. S. R. de Zoysa 5-94). *Moratuwa 15.925 pts, Burgher 3.22 pts.*

At Panadura Esplanade, Panadura, January 2, 3, 4, 2009. **Panadura won by ten wickets.** Toss: Panadura. **Lankan 219** (S. D. de Saram 99, J. R. G. Namal 52; K. A. D. M. Fernando 5-73) **and 203** (J. R. G. Namal 79; G. A. S. Perera 4-29); **Panadura 413** (M. M. D. R. Cooray 92, K. A. D. M. Fernando 64, M. N. R. Cooray 65) **and 10-0.** *Panadura 16.05 pts, Lankan 3.11 pts.*

At Police Park, Colombo, January 2, 3, 4, 2009. **Sebastianites won by an innings and 90 runs.** Toss: Sebastianites. **Sebastianites 372** (T. L. T. Peiris 104, A. A. C. E. Athukorala 59*; Y. A. N. Mendis 4-94); **Police 57** (A. A. C. E. Athukorala 7-21) **and 225** (H. M. Jayawardene 55; A. A. C. E. Athukorala 4-48). *Sebastianites 17.86 pts, Police 2.41 pts.*
  Chatura Athukorala hit 59 and took 11-69 in the match.*

At Bloomfield C & AC, Colombo, January 2, 3, 4, 2009. **Saracens won by six wickets.** Toss: Saracens. **Singha 164** (A. S. Wewalwala 71; R. K. P. Priyankara 6-71) **and 306** (K. N. C. Fernando

55, T. J. Madanayake 78*; P. M. Pushpakumara 6-95); **Saracens 223** (I. C. Soysa 58*, J. G. A. Janoda 53; N. C. K. Liyanage 4-67) **and 248-4** (K. Silva 69, W. G. R. K. Alwis 50*). *Saracens 16.355 pts, Singha 3.75 pts.*

At Air Force Ground, Colombo, January 2, 17, 18, 2009. **Air Force won by five wickets.** Toss: Air Force. **Seeduwa Raddoluwa 224** (H. G. Kumara 89; D. M. A. D. Karunaratne 4-72) **and 247** (J. G. N. Priyantha 54, T. M. U. S. Karunaratne 74*, D. G. R. Dhammika 51); **Air Force 258** (K. S. T. Perera 69; J. G. N. Priyantha 5-56) **and 214-5** (P. S. A. N. Shiroman 92*, K. S. T. Perera 57). *Air Force 16.36 pts, Seeduwa Raddoluwa 3.855 pts.*
   A bomb explosion near the ground on January 3 injured one Seeduwa player and damaged the eardrums of three others; there was a two-week delay before the match was resumed.

At Burgher RC, Colombo, January 9, 10, 2009. **Burgher won by nine wickets.** Toss: Burgher. **Lankan 137** (G. D. R. Eranga 5-41, W. H. L. D. Fernando 4-52) **and 146** (H. G. P. Ranaweera 62; G. D. R. Eranga 4-66); **Burgher 241** (C. A. M. Madusanka 51) **and 47-1.** *Burgher 15.44 pts, Lankan 2.515 pts.*

At Tyronne Fernando Stadium, Moratuwa, January 9, 10, 11, 2009. **Drawn.** Toss: Moratuwa. **Sebastianites 410-4 dec** (U. L. K. D. Fernando 101, P. B. Ediriweera 101, G. R. P. Peiris 77, J. W. H. D. Boteju 53*); **Moratuwa 258** (W. J. S. D. Perera 116*; J. W. H. D. Boteju 5-43) **and 118-5.** *Moratuwa 2.28 pts, Sebastianites 11.5 pts.*

At Panadura Esplanade, Panadura, January 9, 10, 11, 2009. **Drawn.** Toss: Saracens. **Panadura 184** (M. M. D. R. Cooray 80) **and 295-7** (G. S. U. Fernando 89, G. Y. S. R. Perera 94; P. M. Pushpakumara 4-88); **Saracens 437-6 dec** (P. K. Bodhisha 179, I. C. Soysa 121*). *Panadura 2.995 pts, Saracens 11.7 pts.*
   First-innings points extended Saracens' lead over second-placed Panadura, who had a match in hand.

At Police Park, Colombo, January 9, 10, 11, 2009. **Seeduwa Raddoluwa won by an innings and 39 runs.** Toss: Seeduwa Raddoluwa. **Police 129** (J. D. M. de Silva 4-37) **and 153** (J. D. M. de Silva 6-72); **Seeduwa Raddoluwa 321** (W. W. P. Taraka 127). *Seeduwa Raddoluwa 17.605 pts, Police 2.41 pts.*

At Colombo CC, Colombo, January 9, 10, 11, 2009. **Singha won by 107 runs.** Toss: Air Force. **Singha 155** (S. I. Vithana 52; D. M. A. D. Karunaratne 5-44) **and 236** (H. H. R. Kavinga 50); **Air Force 99** (N. C. K. Liyanage 7-36) **and 185** (S. M. Fernando 51; R. D. Abeydeera 5-50). *Singha 15.955 pts, Air Force 3.42 pts.*

At Tyronne Fernando Stadium, Moratuwa, January 16, 2009. **Drawn.** Toss: Panadura. **Panadura 175** (P. S. Liyanage 51; L. D. I. Perera 4-33); **Sebastianites 24-1.**
   The umpires called off the match after a large chunk of the pitch came loose on the first evening. The tournament committee ordered a replay to take place the following week, between the same elevens. Sebastianites protested that Panadura had changed their side and, after an enquiry, the committee awarded Sebastianites the 12 points for a win.

INTERPROVINCIAL TOURNAMENT, 2008-09

	Played	Won	Lost	Drawn	1st-inns Points	Batting	Bowling	Points
Wayamba	4	1	0	3	16	10.345	6.2	44.545
Basnahira North	4	2*	0	2	0	10.835	7.0	43.835
Basnahira South	4	1	1	2	8	12.230	5.7	37.930
Kandurata	4	1	2	1	8	8.460	6.5	34.960
Ruhuna	4	1	3	0	0	9.145	7.1	28.245

* Includes one win by an innings.

Final: Basnahira North beat Wayamba by ten wickets.

Outright win = 12 pts; outright win by an innings = 14 pts; lead on first innings in a drawn game = 8 pts. Bonus points were awarded as follows: 0.1 pt for each wicket taken and 0.005 pt for each run scored, up to 400 runs per innings.

At Sinhalese SC, Colombo, February 12, 13, 14, 15, 2009. **Basnahira North won by an innings and 56 runs.** Toss: Basnahira North. **Kandurata 262** (C. U. Jayasinghe 101*; D. M. G. S. Dissanayake 4-45) **and 245** (M. M. M. Suraj 64; W. L. Manoj 4-69, M. Pushpakumara 5-84); **Basnahira North 563-8 dec** (G. I. Daniel 116, A. D. Mathews 270, J. K. Silva 91). *Basnahira North 18 pts, Kandurata 3.335 pts.*

Angelo Mathews scored a maiden double-hundred, adding 214 for the third wicket with Ian Daniel and 204 for the fifth with Kaushal Silva. His 270 was the highest score of the season; Kandurata's eleven could not match it in either innings. In their first innings, slow left-armer Shanuka Dissanayake took a hat-trick.

At Rangiri Dambulla International Stadium, Dambulla, February 12, 13, 14, 15, 2009. **Drawn.** Toss: Basnahira South. **Basnahira South 402** (R. J. M. G. M. Rupasinghe 53, L. P. C. Silva 71, L. J. P. Gunaratne 78, D. N. T. Zoysa 114) **and 431-6 dec** (K. Y. de Silva 72, M. D. K. Perera 51, L. P. C. Silva 132*, C. M. Bandara 50*); **Wayamba 440** (D. N. Hunukumbura 69, J. Mubarak 94, K. S. Lokuarachchi 63, K. P. S. P. Karunanayake 92). *Basnahira South 5 pts, Wayamba 11.6 pts.*

All three innings topped 400. Nuwan Zoysa scored 114 in 117 balls, his maiden century, from No. 9.

At Sinhalese SC, Colombo, February 19, 20, 21, 22, 2009. **Basnahira North won by 251 runs.** Toss: Ruhuna. **Basnahira North 303** (L. A. H. N. Perera 58, A. D. Mathews 72) **and 348-5 dec** (J. K. Silva 112*, M. Pushpakumara 108*); **Ruhuna 221** (S. M. A. Priyanjan 99, A. Rideegammanagedera 56) **and 179** (M. Pushpakumara 4-36). *Basnahira North 17.255 pts, Ruhuna 3.5 pts.*

In Basnahira North's second innings, Kaushal Silva and Muthumudalige Pushpakumara added 205 for the sixth wicket to set Ruhuna a target of 431.*

At Rangiri Dambulla International Stadium, Dambulla, February 19, 20, 21, 2009. **Kandurata won by ten wickets.** Toss: Kandurata. **Kandurata 370** (S. I. Fernando 72, N. M. N. P. Nawela 104, K. Weeraratne 90*; C. M. Bandara 4-61) **and 21-0; Basnahira South 123** (R. J. M. G. M. Rupasinghe 55) **and 267** (R. J. M. G. M. Rupasinghe 54). *Kandurata 15.955 pts, Basnahira South 2.95 pts.*

Sajith Fernando passed 10,000 first-class runs.

At R. Premadasa Stadium, Colombo, February 26, 27, 28, March 1, 2009. **Drawn.** Toss: Basnahira North. **Basnahira South 405** (K. Y. de Silva 98, H. D. R. L. Thirimanne 145, T. A. M. Siriwardene 70; K. T. G. D. Prasad 4-56) **and 228** (K. H. R. K. Fernando 76, D. N. T. Zoysa 52; K. R. N. U. Perera 4-66); **Basnahira North 296** (G. I. Daniel 82, A. D. Mathews 64; P. D. R. L. Perera 4-61) **and 199-7** (J. K. Silva 64). *Basnahira North 4.475 pts, Basnahira South 12.84 pts.*

Yohan de Silva and Lahiru Thirimanne opened with 207 in Basnahira South's first innings.

At Rangiri Dambulla International Stadium, Dambulla, February 26, 27, 28, March 1, 2009. **Wayamba won by 140 runs.** Toss: Wayamba. **Wayamba 275** (M. L. Udawatte 85; S. Weerakoon 4-43) **and 236** (D. N. Hunukumbura 117; A. B. T. Lakshitha 7-59); **Ruhuna 215** (S. I. de Saram 66; U. W. M. B. C. A. Welagedara 4-51, H. M. R. K. B. Herath 5-68) **and 156** (J. Mubarak 6-11). *Wayamba 16.555 pts, Ruhuna 3.855 pts.*

Captain Jehan Mubarak's off-spin earned him career-best figures of 11.3–3–11–6 and helped Wayamba to a convincing win.

At Rangiri Dambulla International Stadium, Dambulla, March 5, 6, 7, 8, 2009. **Drawn.** Toss: Basnahira North. **Basnahira North 374** (A. D. Mathews 118, W. M. G. Ramyakumara 72; I. Udana 4-98) **and 247-6** (J. K. Silva 100, W. M. G. Ramyakumara 62*); **Wayamba 421** (D. N. Hunukumbura 55, J. Mubarak 136, S. K. L. de Silva 103). *Basnahira North 4.105 pts, Wayamba 11.6 pts.*

Jehan Mubarak and Lanka de Silva added 201 for Wayamba's fourth wicket. Kaushal Silva's century took him past 1,000 first-class runs for the season.

At R. Premadasa Stadium, Colombo, March 5, 6, 7, 2009. **Ruhuna won by 87 runs.** Toss: Ruhuna. **Ruhuna 268** (W. U. Tharanga 98, L. H. D. Dilhara 61*; C. W. Vidanapathirana 4-71) **and 213; Kandurata 206 and 188** (C. U. Jayasinghe 59). *Ruhuna 16.405 pts, Kandurata 3.97 pts.*

At Colts CC, Colombo, March 12, 13, 14, 15, 2009. **Basnahira South won by four wickets.** Toss: Ruhuna. **Ruhuna 450** (W. U. Tharanga 265*; U. M. A. Prasad 4-110, T. A. M. Siriwardene 4-31)

and 177 (G. A. C. R. Perera 4-49); **Basnahira South 383** (T. A. M. Siriwardene 135, L. P. C. Silva 86; S. Weerakoon 4-120) **and 247-6** (C. S. Fernando 61, H. D. R. L. Thirimanne 66*; S. M. Senanayake 4-70). *Basnahira South 17.15 pts, Ruhuna 4.485 pts.*

Upul Tharanga carried his bat through Ruhuna's first innings, completing a maiden double-hundred.

At Rangiri Dambulla International Stadium, Dambulla, March 12, 13, 14, 15, 2009. **Drawn.** Toss: Wayamba. **Wayamba 394** (M. G. Vandort 123, N. L. T. C. Perera 53*) **and 364-7** (D. N. Hunukumbura 73, R. S. S. S. de Zoysa 53, H. G. J. M. Kulatunga 102); **Kandurata 402** (K. D. Gunawardene 121, N. M. N. P. Nawela 148*, B. M. A. J. Mendis 73). *Kandurata 11.7 pts, Wayamba 4.79 pts.*

Kanchana Gunawardene and Nadeera Nawela added 234 for Kandurata's third wicket. Despite conceding first-innings lead, Wayamba headed the table.

Final

At R. Premadasa Stadium, Colombo, March 19, 20, 21, 2009. **Basnahira North won by ten wickets.** Toss: Wayamba. **Wayamba 223** (K. S. Lokuarachchi 70; T. D. D. Darshanpriya 5-55) **and 181** (M. G. Vandort 50; M. Pushpakumara 4-49); **Basnahira North 389** (A. D. Mathews 152, M. Pushpakumara 103) **and 16-0.**

Basnahira North were 96-5 early on the second day, before Angelo Mathews added 185 for the sixth wicket with Muthumudalige Pushpakumara. Mathews scored his third century of the tournament and fourth of 2008-09, passing 1,000 runs for the season. Pushpakumara went on to take four wickets with his off-spin, and Basnahira North won with a day to spare.

INTERPROVINCIAL CHAMPIONS

1989-90	Western Province	1994-95	Western Province City
1990-91	Western Province City	2003-04	Central Province
1991-92	Western Province North	2004-05	North Central Province
1993-94	Western Province City	2008-09	Basnahira North

Note: Matches in the following sections were not first-class.

PREMIER LIMITED-OVERS TOURNAMENT, 2008-09

50-over league plus knockout

Tier A Semi-finals

At R. Premadasa Stadium, Colombo, February 18, 2009. **Bloomfield won by 81 runs.** Toss: Bloomfield. **Bloomfield 276** (48.2 overs) (A. U. Katipiarachchi 64, C. U. Jayasinghe 69; S. H. M. Silva 5-43); **Chilaw Marians 195** (41.2 overs) (W. M. G. Ramyakumara 65; M. M. M. Suraj 4-41).

At Sinhalese SC, Colombo, February 25, 2009. **Tamil Union won by 36 runs.** Toss: Nondescripts. **Tamil Union 259-8** (50 overs) (S. C. Serasinghe 67); **Nondescripts 223** (46.3 overs) (W. U. Tharanga 84; B. M. A. J. Mendis 4-43).

Tier A Final

At R. Premadasa Stadium, Colombo, March 17, 2009. **Bloomfield won by 115 runs.** Toss: Bloomfield. **Bloomfield 244-9** (50 overs) (G. A. S. K. Gangodawila 70*); **Tamil Union 129** (34.3 overs).

Sanjaya Gangodawila scored 70 from 46 balls, with ten fours and two sixes, from No. 9.

Tier B Semi-finals

At FTZ Sports Complex, Katunayake, March 4, 2009. **Police won by 104 runs.** Toss: Seeduwa Raddoluwa. **Police 187** (47.2 overs) (M. S. Kamileen 4-36); **Seeduwa Raddoluwa 83** (29 overs).

At FTZ Sports Complex, Katunayake, March 11, 2009. **Sebastianites won by six wickets.** Toss: Sebastianites. **Panadura 131** (42.4 overs); **Sebastianites 136-4** (27.4 overs).

Tier B Final

At Colts CC, Colombo, March 18, 2009. **Sebastianites won by five wickets.** Toss: Sebastianites. **Police 255-7** (50 overs) (T. A. N. Weerasinghe 54, H. P. A. Priyantha 53*); **Sebastianites 256-5** (47.1 overs) (R. H. T. A. Perera 72).

INTERPROVINCIAL TWENTY20 TOURNAMENT, 2008-09

	Played	*Won*	*Lost*	*No Result*	*Bonus Points*	*Points*	*Net run-rate*
Basnahira South	5	5	0	0	1	21	1.37
Wayamba	5	4	1	0	2	18	0.73
Kandurata	5	3	2	0	1	13	0.09
Ruhuna	5	2	3	0	2	10	0.73
Basnahira North	5	1	4	0	0	4	−1.13
Sri Lanka Schools	5	0	5	0	0	0	−1.94

Semi-finals

At Sinhalese SC, Colombo, April 4, 2009. **Basnahira South won by 15 runs.** Toss: Kandurata. **Basnahira South 137-9** (20 overs); **Kandurata 122-8** (20 overs) (G. A. C. R. Perera 4-19).

At Sinhalese SC, Colombo, April 4, 2009. **No result.** Toss: Ruhuna. **Ruhuna 88-7** (15 overs) **v Wayamba.**

Wayamba advanced to the final after winning a bowling contest 3–2.

Final

At Sinhalese SC, Colombo, April 5, 2009. **Wayamba won by five wickets.** Toss: Basnahira South. **Basnahira South 144** (19.1 overs) (T. M. Dilshan 66; I. Udana 4-31); **Wayamba 149-5** (19 overs).

From 133-1 in 16 overs, Basnahira South lost their last nine wickets for 11 runs in 19 balls – a collapse triggered by Isuru Udana claiming three wickets in his third over, which concluded with a run-out.

WEST INDIAN CRICKET, 2009

Turbulent end to a turbulent decade

TONY COZIER

Another turbulent year marked the end of a decade during which West Indies cricket plummeted inexorably towards irrelevance, perhaps even towards its eventual demise.

Ironically, the year started and ended with encouraging performances on the field. After nine years, the Wisden Trophy was regained from England following a close, fiercely fought series in the Caribbean in February and March. Then in November and December heavy defeat in the First Test in Australia was transformed into spirited competitiveness in the next two that contrasted starkly with the 5–0 and 3–0 whitewashes of the two previous tours.

In between, there was the characteristic controversy and confrontation beyond the boundary that had long since shaped the failings within it. Yet again, the catalyst was the prolonged hostility between the West Indies Cricket

WEST INDIES IN 2009

	Played	Won	Lost	Drawn/No result
Tests	12	1	6	5
One-day internationals	21	4	15	2
Twenty20 internationals	8	5	3	–

DECEMBER — JANUARY	2 Tests, 5 ODIs and 2 T20Is (a) v New Zealand	(see *Wisden 2009*, page 1187)
FEBRUARY — MARCH — APRIL	5 Tests, 5 ODIs and 1 T20I (h) v England	(page 1386)
MAY	2 Tests and 3 ODIs (a) v England	(page 463)
JUNE	World Twenty20 (in England)	(page 527)
JULY	4 ODIs (h) v India	(page 1417)
AUGUST	2 Tests, 3 ODIs and 1 T20I (h) v Bangladesh	(page 1421)
SEPTEMBER — OCTOBER	Champions Trophy (in South Africa)	(page 1015)
NOVEMBER — DECEMBER	3 Tests (a) v Australia	(page 1044)

For a review of West Indian domestic cricket from the 2008-09 season, see page 1432.

Board and the West Indies Players Association, principally over retainer contracts. When Ottis Gibson was appointed head coach early in 2010, he could hardly have had a more daunting task.

There was disagreement as well over a brief, hastily arranged return series in England in May that the players felt had been foisted on them, prompting a virtual go-slow and the immediate surrender of the Wisden Trophy. By July, the issues had developed into a full-blown strike by the leading players, the second in four years, reducing the home rubber against Bangladesh to a farce. A team of unprepared and inexperienced reserves was quickly cobbled together but lost both Tests and all three one-day internationals; retained for the subsequent Champions Trophy, they predictably lost all three matches.

It took the intervention of the relevant governments of Caricom, the regional alliance, to secure a grudging, provisional agreement that ended the stand-off, returned the strikers to the fold, and allowed the selection of a full-strength team for the series in Australia. There were inevitable casualties from the fall-out. The board's chief executive, Donald Peters, jumped before he could be pushed, and was replaced by Ernest Hilaire, a close and well-credentialled associate of the president Julian Hunte, a fellow St Lucian. It was the fifth time the post had changed hands in the decade. Immediately following the Bangladesh series John Dyson, the former Australian opening batsman, was dismissed less than halfway through his three-year contract; he had been the ninth head coach in 15 years. Omar Khan, the senior team's manager for two years, was demoted to the Under-19s. Two eminent former players were appointed instead: Lance Gibbs took charge for the Bangladesh series and the Champions Trophy, while Joel Garner took over for the Australian tour.

The absence of key players offered unexpected opportunities to others. Travis Dowlin, a Guyanese batsman with a modest record whose dream of Test cricket had seemingly long passed at the age of 32, and the Barbadian fast bowler Kemar Roach, 21, capitalised on theirs. With his genuine pace and controlled hostility, Roach emerged as the find of the year.

Signs of the players' discontent had been growing for some time before the 13 originally chosen for the Bangladesh series, along with several others who might have taken their places, opted out. The team pointedly stayed away from an official function and covered the sponsor's logo on their shirts during the first one-day international against England in March, and were said to have been close to pulling out of the final match in St Lucia.

It would be three months until they made their move, two days before the First Test against Bangladesh in St Vincent. As the board raised its substitute side, mutual loathing was so deep that a settlement appeared out of the question. Hunte angrily accused the striking players of "the highest form of disregard and disdain for West Indies cricket". Keen to have his players back in international cricket, WIPA chief executive Dinanath Ramnarine sought the intervention of Caricom. The former Guyana foreign minister and Common-wealth secretary-general Sir Shridath Ramphal was appointed as mediator – but even he couldn't bring the sides together, blaming the failure on the board's intransigence. In the end, under pressure from the public – and, discreetly but

Give him a big hand: Kemar Roach appeals, unsuccessfully this time, for the wicket of Ricky Ponting during the Test series in Australia.

effectively, from Cricket Australia – Hunte and Ramnarine grudgingly signed an accord (in New York, of all places) put forward by Caricom.

Even then, the year ended with further disagreement over the board's decision to cut the 2010 first-class tournament to one round (according to Hilaire, based on its financial situation); the format in 2009 had been home-and-away for only the second time. The first item on WIPA's 15-point development plan, released only weeks earlier, had advocated a tournament of two rounds with a minimum of 12 matches per team "to better prepare the players for international Test cricket".

Even within the board itself there were misgivings about the decision to stage four of the matches under lights using the untested pink ball. Hilaire responded that the board had to be "brave and try new things and approaches"; this was an attempt "to breathe new life into West Indies cricket at all levels" and "to get fans coming back to the game they love".

The tenuous state of cricket in the region, already evident from West Indies' lowly position in the ICC's Test and one-day rankings, was accentuated in August when the Trinidad and Tobago Cricket Board boycotted the WICB's annual general meeting, an action unprecedented in the 87 years of the board's existence.

"Over the past few years the WICB, and its administrative arm, have not functioned effectively and have demonstrated little inclination to change, to meet the requirements of the modern cricket environment in which we operate," the TTCB stated. It explained that the decision was "to signal that it is not happy with this state of affairs", adding that for West Indies cricket "to survive and flourish… the status quo is not an option".

When its chief executive Forbes Persaud warned that, unless the WICB was properly restructured, "we will have no choice but to think about playing as an individual territory on the international scene", it seemed as if the sport that had united the disparate former colonies of the region for more than a century would go the way of the ill-fated political federation 50 years earlier and fragment into its several parts. The spirited achievement by the Trinidad & Tobago team in reaching the final of the inaugural Champions League Twenty20 tournament in India in October gave further credence to the premise.

Ernest Hilaire, chief executive of the WICB.

Even in the current circumstances such a proposal was too radical by far. It was one reason for the removal of the TTCB executive, headed by the former West Indies wicketkeeper Deryck Murray, after a vote at its annual general meeting, but it was another symptom of the general dissatisfaction with the way West Indies cricket was being administered.

It was reflected in the WICB's inability, for the second year running, to attract sponsors for its main tournaments, and in the stillborn plans for a central academy, first mooted as long as eight years earlier. The situation was exacerbated by the embarrassing downfall of the Texan financier Allen Stanford, which ended the US$3m he paid the board annually for his Twenty20 tournament franchise.

A large chunk of what financial resources the board did have was allocated to central contracts for 33 players, signed in November at an estimated cost of US$3.2m, and an increase in match fees for the first-class tournament from $300 to $1,400.

Throughout his time in Australia as team manager, Joel Garner stressed the need for the ICC to pay more economic attention to the impoverished West Indies, "a long-standing member of the cricketing family", than to so-called emerging markets like China and the United States. It was a valid position, but the lack of money is only one piece in a very complex puzzle.

WEST INDIES v ENGLAND, 2008-09

REVIEW BY JOHN ETHERIDGE

Test matches (5): West Indies 1, England 0
One-day internationals (5): West Indies 2, England 3
Twenty20 international (1): West Indies 1, England 0

England were engulfed in turmoil before they left for the West Indies in early 2009, and the team's performances were not good enough to allow the pre-tour conflict to be forgotten completely. Under a new captain, Andrew Strauss, and a makeshift coach, Andy Flower, England lost the Test series 1–0. The defining passage of play on the 11-week trip came on the fourth day of the First Test at Kingston in Jamaica, when Jerome Taylor produced a high-quality, high-velocity spell of swing bowling and England were blitzed for just 51, the third-lowest total in their history.

There was no coming back. Strauss himself scored three centuries as his team passed 500 in the first innings in each of the last three Tests but, on benign surfaces, and with West Indies showing more resilience and discipline than in recent years, England's bowling lacked the oomph to take 20 wickets. They managed 19 at St John's and 18 at Port-of-Spain, but all 20 proved beyond them. Three successive draws after Kingston – four if you count the ten-ball abandoned match in a sandpit at the Sir Vivian Richards Stadium in Antigua – allowed West Indies to regain the Wisden Trophy they surrendered in 2000 and secure their first Test series victory for five years, since they beat Bangladesh.

England were thrashed in the lone Twenty20 international but salvaged a measure of respect in the one-day matches, which they won 3–2. Their victory was based on aggressive bowling from James Anderson and Stuart Broad, fielding that was flawless by the end, and clever captaincy which lent an illusion of variety to an attack that was almost entirely right-arm pace. Even then, their successes came courtesy of a catastrophic misreading of the Duckworth/Lewis calculations by West Indies coach John Dyson and two other rain-affected games. They were the only three competitive matches England won throughout their winter of 2008-09 on their visits to Antigua, India and back to the Caribbean.

After England contrived to lose their head coach and captain – Peter Moores and Kevin Pietersen were sacked a fortnight before the squad departed – the first task of Strauss and Flower, the former Zimbabwe captain who had been batting coach under Moores, was to restore harmony. By and large, this was achieved. Strauss was imperious with the bat, and his captaincy and public pronouncements grew in stature. He showed he was not afraid to make awkward decisions: Ian Bell, Monty Panesar and Steve Harmison were all dropped at various times. He was articulate and clean-cut, and even those who believed he left his declarations too late in Antigua and Trinidad could not seriously doubt he was the right man for the job.

A few days after returning home, however, Strauss chose not to stand for the captaincy of England's World Twenty20 team, which meant England were looking for a fifth captain in nine months. He claimed his batting was not explosive enough for the shortest form of the game – before the tour, he had been out of the one-day side since the 2007 World Cup – although his 79 not out from 61 balls in the fourth one-day international, in a run-chase reduced by rain to 20 overs, belied his own theory. Strauss retained his leadership of the Test and 50-over sides.

Finding a replacement for Moores was a constant subplot. Strauss was unequivocal in his support for Flower, who decided mid-tour that he wanted the job. It was clear they had developed a close rapport, and Flower was duly confirmed as England team director (as the job was now called) less than two weeks after the tour ended. Despite a firm of head-hunters being engaged to scour the globe, the most likely man always seemed to be lurking on the ECB's own doorstep.

Flower impressed with his honesty and understated authority and was not fazed by the presence of his boss, England managing director Hugh Morris, for all but a week of the tour. Morris joined the squad initially in a firefighting capacity, to douse any glowing embers from the Moores–Pietersen fallout. Some senior players disapproved of Pietersen's attempt to overthrow Moores after just three Test matches as captain. Andrew Flintoff, for his part, was unhappy at being directly implicated in Pietersen's downfall. After some early unease Pietersen and Flintoff, the two biggest beasts in England's dressing-room, became comfortable in each other's company and united behind Strauss and Flower. Pietersen was angry at his perceived harsh treatment by the ECB rather than at his team-mates.

On probation: makeshift coach Andy Flower and new captain Andrew Strauss at Port-of-Spain.

Philip Brown

The relief in the England camp was almost tangible when Pietersen and Flintoff attracted identical bids – $1.55m (around £1.1m at the prevailing exchange rate) – in the Indian Premier League auction which took place during the First Test. Neither could feel envious of the other, although their colleagues might have turned a tinge of green. Some blamed the distraction of the IPL bidding as a factor in England's collapse in Jamaica, but that was too simplistic a view, and devalued Taylor's superb bowling.

Pietersen scored a century in the first practice match and showed instantly that his return to the ranks was not going to affect his batting, focusing on his own performances with customary professionalism and attention to detail. He scored a Test century in Trinidad and would have made another in Jamaica but for his attempt to reach three figures with a six – prompting the memorable headline "Dumbslog Millionaire" after the Oscar-winning film *Slumdog Millionaire* and his IPL price-tag.

> She was paid to appear on an ice-dancing TV show

Pietersen created a few ripples towards the end of the tour when he claimed in a newspaper interview that he was "at the end of my tether" because of England's defeats and the lengthy separation from his wife, the pop singer Jessica Taylor. His team-mates were quick to point out that Mrs Pietersen did not join her husband because she was being paid to appear on an ice-dancing TV show. Pietersen had actually asked to fly home for 48 hours between Tests, but was turned down by Strauss, who had the overall authority, and Flower.

Flintoff injured his side in the warm-ups and was later forced to return to England for treatment on a strained hip muscle that caused him to miss the final two Tests. He was out for a pair in the rearranged Test in Antigua and, as so often, failed to take as many wickets as his bowling appeared to merit. By the end of the series, Graeme Swann had as many five-wicket hauls – two – in his five Tests as Flintoff in 75. Yet Flintoff, when fit, was still a compelling cricketer, providing balance and power, and he came back to finish the tour with a hat-trick in the final one-day international. In St Lucia two years earlier, he had been suspended from a World Cup game after taking to the sea on a pedalo. Now he left the island on a wave of euphoria, only to injure himself again in the IPL in South Africa.

Flintoff did make one boat trip when he and Harmison spent a night with supporters and several former players on a cruise ship off Jamaica, hours after England were bowled out for 51. The boat chugged round the island and the pair flew back by helicopter to the team hotel the next morning. Their jolly raised some eyebrows but they were given permission by team management, apparently.

After the debacle at Kingston, runs were not a problem for England. They scored an aggregate of nine centuries in the Test series – plus three other scores in the nineties – but their bowling stumbled on the rock of flat surfaces and Ramnaresh Sarwan's bat. Sarwan totalled 626 runs in six innings in the series, matching Strauss's three hundreds. With further centuries from Chris Gayle, Denesh Ramdin, Shiv Chanderpaul and Brendan Nash, the Australian-born left-hander who added a steeliness to the middle and later order, there was plenty of frustration for England's bowlers. They were not helped, either, by the tendency for the Kookaburra balls to go soft after about 20 overs. In Barbados, England conceded the second-highest total in their history when West Indies racked up 749 for nine, with Sarwan contributing 291 and Ramdin 166. This was a determined West Indies side and, although they still had financial issues with their board, which prompted talk of a strike during the one-day series, they were devoted to their cool-as-you-like captain, Gayle.

Anderson was England's best bowler. He improved visibly and, by the end, was able to gain both orthodox and reverse swing almost at will – and with improved accuracy, too. Anderson deserved better returns than his nine wickets at 38. In Kingston, Broad claimed his first five-for in Test cricket. His self-belief and aggression marked him down as a fine prospect, especially when you threw in his batting. Broad was one who benefited from having Flintoff at the other end, and his figures were sure to improve as he gained strength. He received widespread acclaim for refusing to put his name forward to the IPL auction, preferring instead to rest and prepare for a busy summer, and reacted calmly when his father Chris, an ICC referee, was caught up in the terrorist attack on the Sri Lankan team and match officials' buses in Lahore.

Swann showed that finger spinners do not always need a *doosra* or so-called mystery ball to be effective at the highest level. Old-fashioned virtues such as flight and turn can suffice, particularly when combined with a gambler's mentality. Thirteen of his 19 wickets belonged to West Indies' numerous left-handed batsmen. Swann experienced pain from a long-standing elbow problem and, instead of playing in the one-day games, he flew to the USA for an operation which removed 29 fragments of bone. Spinning all-rounder Samit Patel was deselected from the one-day squad because he turned up overweight and unfit on the Lions tour of New Zealand; and Gareth Batty, who was called up from that tour to replace Swann, did not get enough work on the ball to keep his place throughout the one-day series.

Swann outbowled Panesar, who had responded to several disappointing performances during 2008 by working with bowling coach Mushtaq Ahmed on shortening his run and developing an arm-ball. By the second innings in Port-of-Spain, when Panesar took two for 34 from 19.5 overs, there were signs of progress.

Ryan Sidebottom laboured because of various injuries and went home early, while Harmison was in, out, in, out of the Test team without ever shaking it all about. Amjad Khan, a replacement, played in the final Test but was racked by nerves and looked a mess with his tight shirt, blue corset and falling-down trousers. Even the media officer, Andrew Walpole, went home after being tipped on his head by a wave in Barbados and breaking a vertebra.

Alastair Cook was appointed vice-captain at the start of the tour, and thus became Strauss's heir apparent. In Bridgetown, he reached his first century for England for 14 months. Collingwood was persuaded, somewhat reluctantly, to be Strauss's unofficial deputy for the one-day series, a harbinger of his later reappointment as England's captain for the World Twenty20 campaign.

Ravi Bopara, like Khan summoned from the Lions tour of New Zealand, scored his maiden Test hundred, although he looked vulnerable against the

Close encounters: England were one wicket from victory as Graeme Swann bowled the last over in Antigua, and two as Monty Panesar did the same in Trinidad.

short ball. Tim Ambrose made a rapid 76 not out in Bridgetown while Matt Prior was back in England with his wife, who had given birth to their first child. On his return, Prior himself registered a century in Port-of-Spain and presented a strong case to be promoted above Flintoff to No. 6 in England's batting order. His wicketkeeping, however, remained scrappy as he struggled to cure the basic flaw of not staying down long enough against the spinners, especially in Trinidad.

Owais Shah endured a miserable tour – he was a poor fielder, a terrible runner between the wickets, and so intense that he suffered from cramps in his arms because he gripped his bat so hard. Bell was dropped after the First Test, told to lose weight and gain mental toughness. His response was to train on the beach at 6 a.m. most mornings under the eye of the team's security officer, Reg Dickason; the management was impressed. Adil Rashid, Yorkshire's wrist-spinning all-rounder, hardly played and looked some way short of international readiness when he did.

As much as for the play this tour will be remembered for two major embarrassments in Antigua. When the Test at the stadium bearing his name was abandoned after ten balls because of an unfit outfield, Sir Vivian Richards was, not surprisingly, furious. But anybody at the ground 24 hours earlier could see the problem: Antigua, an island supposed to have 365 beaches, had produced a 366th. The match was switched to the Antigua Recreation Ground at St John's, scene of Brian Lara's two world record innings and Richards's fastest-ever Test century. Within 36 hours, the creaking venue was given a lick of paint, while two giant steamrollers flattened the outfield and strip. Half a dozen football matches had been played there each week since the ground's removal from the international rota, and the halfway line ran across the pitch.

In the event, the surface played remarkably well. Strauss illuminated day one with the first of his three centuries in the series, and Collingwood also reached three figures, as he would do again in Trinidad. Sarwan fought back with 94 and 106 and, in a thrilling climax, West Indies' last-wicket pair Daren Powell and Fidel Edwards survived for ten overs. It was a terrific match, and the old ground was pumping to a calypso beat. Why did cricket ever leave the Recreation Ground, everyone wondered? Not least of the game's charms

Fraud on an unimaginable scale

was that TV engineers did not have sufficient time to install the technology required for the experimental referral system, which was nothing short of a shambles in the other Tests. The system confused and annoyed the players, and did little to increase the accuracy of decisions.

Giles Clarke, the ECB chairman, had been a driving force behind the Antigua Test being rescheduled: he did not want to disappoint the thousands of travelling England supporters. Within the week, however, he was embarrassed when the American authorities accused Sir Allen Stanford, the Texan who had built an empire in Antigua and put up money for Twenty20 tournaments in the West Indies and England, of committing fraud on an almost unimaginable scale. Clarke was the man who had allowed Stanford to land a helicopter at Lord's in 2008, when they signed a five-year deal. Surrounded by journalists in a TV control room in Antigua, Clarke was for once flustered and unsure of himself. When his re-election as chairman was confirmed a week later he responded with a media blitz, insisting on one-to-one interviews so he could not be ambushed. Some found it amusing that Lord Marland, who had withdrawn from an ill-timed challenge for the ECB chairmanship just before the Tests began, was staying in the adjoining hotel to Clarke's in Barbados. Although their sunbeds were said to be just 20 yards apart, they never met.

ENGLAND TOURING PARTY

A. J. Strauss (Middlesex) (*captain*), A. N. Cook (Essex) (*vice-captain*), T. R. Ambrose (Warwickshire), J. M. Anderson (Lancashire), I. R. Bell (Warwickshire), S. C. J. Broad (Nottinghamshire), P. D. Collingwood (Durham), A. Flintoff (Lancashire), S. J. Harmison (Durham), M. S. Panesar (Northamptonshire), K. P. Pietersen (Hampshire), M. J. Prior (Sussex), A. U. Rashid (Yorkshire), O. A. Shah (Middlesex), R. J. Sidebottom (Nottinghamshire), G. P. Swann (Nottinghamshire).

R. S. Bopara (Essex) and A. Khan (Kent) were summoned from the England Lions tour of New Zealand when Flintoff returned home injured after the Third Test. Flintoff returned for the one-day series, when G. J. Batty (Worcestershire), S. M. Davies (Worcestershire) and A. D. Mascarenhas

(Hampshire) replaced Ambrose, Cook and Panesar. Sidebottom and Swann went home injured, and S. R. Patel (Nottinghamshire), who had been selected for the one-day party, was left at home for fitness reasons.

Team operations manager: P. A. Neale. *Assistant coaches:* A. Flower, O. D. Gibson, R. G. Halsall and Mushtaq Ahmed. *Team analyst:* M. Garaway. *Physiotherapist:* K. A. Russell. *Physiologist:* S. Bradley. *Team doctor (Test squad):* Dr M. Stone. *Team doctor (one-day squad):* Dr N. Peirce. *Massage therapist:* M. E. S. Saxby. *Security officer:* R. C. Dickason. *Media relations managers:* A. J. Walpole, C. R. Gibson and J. D. Avery.

TEST MATCH AVERAGES

WEST INDIES – BATTING AND FIELDING

	T	I	NO	R	HS	100s	50s	Avge	Ct
R. R. Sarwan	5	6	0	626	291	3	1	104.33	1
†S. Chanderpaul	5	6	1	299	147*	1	2	59.80	1
D. Ramdin	5	6	1	254	166	1	0	50.80	11
†C. H. Gayle	5	6	0	292	104	2	0	48.66	1
†B. P. Nash	5	6	0	239	109	1	1	39.83	2
†D. S. Smith	5	6	0	165	55	0	1	27.50	7
F. H. Edwards	5	5	4	25	10*	0	0	25.00	1
J. E. Taylor	4	4	0	91	53	0	1	22.75	1
†R. O. Hinds	4	5	0	91	27	0	0	18.20	3
D. B. Powell	5	6	2	66	22*	0	0	16.50	0
†S. J. Benn	4	4	0	58	23	0	0	14.50	2

Played in one Test: †L. S. Baker 0; X. M. Marshall 0 (1 ct); L. M. P. Simmons 24, 8 (1 ct).

† *Left-handed batsman.*

BOWLING

	Style	O	M	R	W	BB	5W/i	Avge
J. E. Taylor	RF	100.2	24	319	11	5-11	1	29.00
L. S. Baker	RFM	31	5	116	4	2-39	0	29.00
S. J. Benn	SLA	162.4	29	479	12	4-31	0	39.91
F. H. Edwards	RF	126.2	11	494	9	3-151	0	54.88
R. O. Hinds	SLA	109.1	10	432	7	2-45	0	61.71
C. H. Gayle	OB	100	21	252	4	1-16	0	63.00
D. B. Powell	RF	112	15	416	6	2-33	0	69.33

Also bowled: B. P. Nash (LM) 46–6–152–1; R. R. Sarwan (LBG) 5–0–27–0; L. M. P. Simmons (RM) 11–0–55–0; D. S. Smith (OB) 1–0–3–0.

ENGLAND – BATTING AND FIELDING

	T	I	NO	R	HS	100s	50s	Avge	Ct/St
M. J. Prior	4	6	2	310	131*	1	2	77.50	6/1
†A. J. Strauss	5	9	1	541	169	3	0	67.62	1
P. D. Collingwood	5	7	0	430	161	2	1	61.42	7
K. P. Pietersen	5	8	1	406	102	1	3	58.00	1
†A. N. Cook	5	9	2	384	139*	1	3	54.85	1
O. A. Shah	4	6	0	133	57	0	1	22.16	1
†S. C. J. Broad	5	7	2	94	44	0	0	18.80	0
A. Flintoff	3	4	0	67	43	0	0	16.75	2
S. J. Harmison	2	3	1	14	7*	0	0	7.00	0

Played in four Tests: †J. M. Anderson 4, 20 (1 ct). Played in three Tests: †M. S. Panesar 0, 0*; †R. J. Sidebottom 26*, 6; G. P. Swann 20*, 11* (1 ct). Played in one Test: T. R. Ambrose 76* (1 ct); I. R. Bell 28, 4; R. S. Bopara 104; A. Khan did not bat.

† *Left-handed batsman.*

BOWLING

	Style	O	M	R	W	BB	5W/i	Avge
G. P. Swann........	OB	180.2	52	457	19	5-57	2	24.05
A. Flintoff	RF	62.2	19	151	5	3-47	0	30.20
S. C. J. Broad......	RFM	131	32	367	12	5-85	1	30.58
S. J. Harmison	RF	54.4	10	147	4	2-49	0	36.75
J. M. Anderson	RFM	129	30	342	9	3-24	0	38.00
M. S. Panesar......	SLA	109.5	29	270	5	2-34	0	54.00

Also bowled: R. S. Bopara (RM) 13–0–66–0; P. D. Collingwood (RM) 20–1–73–0; A. Khan (RF) 29–1–122–1; K. P. Pietersen (OB) 21–2–87–0; O. A. Shah (OB) 5–0–31–0; R. J. Sidebottom (LFM) 59–9–181–1.

Note: Matches in this section which were not first-class are signified by a dagger.

†At Basseterre, St Kitts, January 25, 26, 27, 2009. **England XI won by 217 runs.** Toss: England XI. **England XI 424-8 dec** (A. N. Cook 52, I. R. Bell 36, K. P. Pietersen 103, O. A. Shah 125*, S. J. Harmison 58; A. E. Willett 5-118) **and 265-5 dec** (A. J. Strauss 103, A. N. Cook 50, I. R. Bell 52, S. C. J. Broad 35); **St Kitts and Nevis Invitation XI 251** (C. L. Rogers 63, A. E. Willett 36, J. M. Simmonds 48; M. S. Panesar 4-53) **and 221** (S. M. Jeffers 41, C. L. Rogers 79, J. A. Mitchum 30; M. S. Panesar 3-51).

St Kitts and Nevis named 14 players, of whom 11 could bat and 11 field; England started with 11, but were allowed to call up two more after Andrew Flintoff strained his side and Owais Shah scratched his cornea. Kevin Pietersen hit 103 from 90 balls with three sixes and 13 fours, while Shah's more sedate century included eight fours; in the second innings, Andrew Strauss hit 103 from 116 balls with one six and 12 fours before he retired out (as did Cook on completing his second fifty).

WEST INDIES A v ENGLAND XI

At Basseterre, St Kitts, January 29, 30, 31, 2009. Drawn. Toss: West Indies A.

On a flat pitch of rolled mud, two young Trinidadians tormented the bowlers competing to form England's attack. Lendl Simmons, nephew of former Test batsman Phil, and 18-year-old Adrian Barath added 262 on the opening day, and it was Pietersen's occasional off-spin that finally broke the stand. Both reached career-bests; Simmons went on to 282, hitting 26 fours, eight sixes and a seven (thanks to overthrows) in more than nine and a half hours. He fell at last to Sidebottom, playing his first first-class game for six months, whereupon Harmison found enough menace to collect four wickets. Sammy declared 15 minutes after tea on the second day at 574 for eight – the highest total by a non-Australian team against a touring England side in a first-class warm-up. Cook poked his first ball to gully, but Strauss dug in, sharing century partnerships with Bell and Pietersen, who hit leg-spinner Wallace for five fours in an over.

Close of play: First day, West Indies A 343-2 (Simmons 171, Chattergoon 24); Second day, England XI 134-2 (Strauss 59, Pietersen 12).

West Indies A

K. O. A. Powell c Bell b Anderson	14	– not out	1
A. B. Barath c Collingwood b Pietersen	132	– not out	13
L. M. P. Simmons lbw b Sidebottom.............	282		
S. Chattergoon c Prior b Anderson	37		
L. R. Johnson c Prior b Harmison	26		
*D. J. G. Sammy lbw b Harmison	14		
†D. C. Thomas c Prior b Harmison	38		
K. R. McClean b Harmison	10		
A. S. Jaggernauth not out	0		
B 6, l-b 10, w 1, n-b 4	21	B 1, n-b 1..................	2

1/28 (1) 2/290 (2)		(8 wkts dec, 149.5 overs)	574	
3/390 (4) 4/468 (5)				(no wkt, 5 overs) 16
5/490 (6) 6/547 (3) 7/570 (7) 8/574 (8)				

G. Wallace and B. J. Bess did not bat.

Anderson 29–5–92–2; Harmison 25.5–1–101–4; Sidebottom 23–8–61–1; Swann 41–2–160–0;
Collingwood 20–4–75–0; Pietersen 6–0–38–1; Bell 5–0–31–0. *Second Innings*—Sidebottom
2–0–5–0; Harmison 2–0–2–0; Swann 1–0–8–0.

England XI

*A. J. Strauss b Wallace	97	R. J. Sidebottom c and b Bess 18
A. N. Cook c Johnson b McClean	0	S. J. Harmison c and b McClean 1
I. R. Bell b Wallace	52	J. M. Anderson not out 1
K. P. Pietersen b Jaggernauth	90	B 6, l-b 2, w 2, n-b 6 16
P. D. Collingwood c Johnson b McClean . .	82	
O. A. Shah lbw b Jaggernauth	9	1/5 (2) 2/119 (3) 3/242 (1) (90.5 overs) 414
†M. J. Prior run out	36	4/252 (4) 5/270 (6) 6/350 (7)
G. P. Swann c Sammy b Wallace	12	7/364 (8) 8/407 (5) 9/410 (9) 10/414 (10)

Bess 10–0–50–1; McClean 14.5–1–56–3; Sammy 15–1–51–0; Jaggernauth 27–2–100–2; Wallace
24–1–149–3.

Umpires: A. L. Kelly and W. Mitchum.

WEST INDIES v ENGLAND

First Test Match

Tony Cozier

At Kingston, Jamaica, February 4, 5, 6, 7, 2009. West Indies won by an innings and 23
runs. Toss: England.

For the third time in England's last four series in the Caribbean, one brief and irresistible
spell by a fast bowler transformed a close, hard-fought Test match into a rout. Jerome
Taylor's burst of five for 11 from nine overs either side of lunch on the fourth day set off
the rapid disintegration of England's second innings to 51, their third-smallest Test total,
and a heavy and unlikely defeat. It echoed Curtly Ambrose's six for 24 at the Queen's
Park Oval in 1993-94, which despatched England for 46 all out (their second-lowest) in a
similar beating, and Steve Harmison's seven for 12 at Sabina Park in 2003-04, when West
Indies capitulated for 47, their own nadir, triggering a 3–0 series loss.

Taylor's dramatic intervention came out of the clear blue Kingston sky: as with Ambrose
and Harmison, there was no hint in the preceding play of what was to follow. Unusually
for Sabina, the pitch was slow and more favourable to spin than speed, seam or swing.
The left-arm spin of Benn, the 6ft 7in beanpole, and the gentle off-breaks of Gayle
accounted for 68.2 overs in England's first-innings 318; Panesar's 47 overs were the most
by any of the six touring bowlers as West Indies responded with 392.

When England set out on their second innings, 40 minutes before lunch on the fourth
day, their initial task seemed straightforward enough – to erase a deficit of 74. On the
assumption that West Indies would bat last on a worn, fifth-day surface, the contest was
evenly balanced. But a quarter of an hour before tea it was all over. Appropriately, the last
wicket to fall was that of Harmison, West Indies' tormentor five years earlier, bowled
round his legs by Benn.

Sprinting in from the northern end like one of his fellow-Jamaican Olympians and
generating pace in the high 80s mph, Taylor began the slide with his seventh ball, Cook's
outside edge diverting a catch to second slip. Conscious that his bowler was carrying a
sore calf muscle, Gayle removed him after three overs, but Bell's careless cut shot against
Benn yielded a second opportune wicket two balls before lunch.

After attention on the physio's table during the interval, Taylor set about his destruction
in earnest with his first delivery on resumption. Fast and of full length, it started its path
on a leg-stump line, and Pietersen, his strutting confidence enhanced by a first-innings 97,

High five: Jerome Taylor enjoys the wicket of Matt Prior, his fifth in England's catastrophic collapse.

shaped to drive it through midwicket, right leg in the air, his patented "flamingo" stroke. As he did so, the ball suddenly swung past the outside of the bat to remove the off stump, setting off raucous celebrations on the field and in the stands.

Six overs passed before Taylor struck again, when England's captain Strauss repeated his first-innings dismissal, a thin edge to the wicketkeeper as he drove. Collingwood was next: a dogged batsman not easily dislodged, he was so deceived by an off-cutter – for Taylor was, throughout, mixing finger-spun off-cutters with seam-up outswingers – that he was turning for a second run off an inside edge to fine leg when fielders drew his attention to the missing leg bail and he realised he had been bowled. For the next three balls of the over, Taylor offered Prior full-length outswingers that the batsman carefully kept out. For the fourth, he dragged his fingers down on the ball, and the off-cutter landed just where he wanted it. Prior's forward defence seemed copybook perfect, but the ball somehow breached it to uproot the off stump.

By now, Sabina was in an uproar. The last time it had witnessed such mayhem, it was cause for tears and despondency; now Taylor was doing to England what Harmison had done to West Indies. The outcome was only a matter of time; with the Second Test less than a week away, Gayle gave Taylor his leave after six successive overs, allowing others to complete the job. In his absence, Flintoff compiled the innings' only double-figure score before he missed a swing at Edwards and was bowled.

Benn collected the other three wickets to finish with four in the innings and eight in the match. It was the first time a spinner had taken as many for West Indies since Lance Gibbs's nine for 143 in Bombay in 1974-75; in his fourth Test, Benn palpably outbowled his counterpart, Panesar, whose return in his 36th Test was a solitary wicket for 122.

The eventual drama contrasted utterly with the attritional cricket of the first three days. On the sluggish pitch and outfield, the average rate during the two first innings was 2.5 runs an over; even free-scoring batsmen such as Pietersen (97 off 172 balls), Gayle (104 off 193) and Sarwan (107 off 290) were held in check.

After Strauss chose to bat, England were faltering at 94 for four, 40 minutes into the second session, before Pietersen and Flintoff consolidated in a partnership of 86. The two seemed entrenched when Pietersen's belligerence provided West Indies with a critical break. Two fours and a six over midwicket off successive balls from Benn carried him to 97, yet Gayle declined to station a protective fielder in the deep. It was a challenge Pietersen could not resist. Benn duly offered him the flighted bait and he took it, seeking a slog-sweep to raise his hundred. The ball spiralled off the top edge and Ramdin skipped forward to gather the catch.

ENGLAND'S LOWEST TEST TOTALS

45	v Australia at Sydney (England won by 13 runs)	1886-87
46	v West Indies at Port-of-Spain (West Indies won by 147 runs)	1993-94
51	**v West Indies at Kingston (West Indies won by an innings and 23 runs).......**	**2008-09**
52	v Australia at The Oval (Australia won by an innings and 149 runs)	1948
53	v Australia at Lord's (1st innings) (Australia won by 61 runs).................	1888
61	v Australia at Melbourne (Australia won by 229 runs)........................	1901-02
61	v Australia at Melbourne (Australia won by 218 runs)........................	1903-04
62	v Australia at Lord's (2nd innings) (Australia won by 61 runs)	1888
64	v New Zealand at Wellington (New Zealand won by 72 runs)..................	1977-78
65†	v Australia at Sydney (1st innings) (Australia won by an innings and 147 runs)....	1894-95
71	v West Indies at Manchester (West Indies won by 425 runs)..................	1976
72†	v Australia at Sydney (2nd innings) (Australia won by an innings and 147 runs) ...	1894-95

† *One man absent hurt.*

Flintoff and Prior stayed together to the close to carry England's hopes of a significant total into the second day, but Flintoff sliced a catch to point without adding to his overnight 43, leaving the forthright Prior and the bowlers to carry the score past 300. For the remainder of the day and most of the next morning, Gayle and Sarwan laid the foundations for a formidable reply by adding 202. While Gayle was assured from the start, greeting Flintoff's second ball and Harmison's fourth with sixes over mid-on and midwicket respectively, Sarwan began with the uncertainty of his preceding travails in New Zealand.

Each survived on the umpires' review, on trial for the first time in a series in the Caribbean. Sarwan was five and still scratchy when he challenged an lbw decision in Harmison's favour; he acknowledged afterwards that he might have been lucky to be reprieved, apparently on height. Gayle was already 85 when the TV evidence supported his objection that Prior's leg-side catch off Flintoff came off his thigh, rather than his bat. The standing umpire in each instance was New Zealand's Tony Hill, a late replacement for the original appointee, Asoka de Silva (who had visa problems).

Once settled, the pair asserted their dominance in contrasting ways. Gayle, powerful as always, smote Panesar for successive sixes followed by a deft deflection for three in the same over to beat Sarwan to a hundred. It was Gayle's ninth in Tests, but his first in nine games on his home ground. Sarwan was still one short of his 12th century when Broad bowled Gayle off the inside edge and claimed Marshall lbw in the same over. England continued to regain ground with the wickets of Sarwan, who dragged Flintoff back into his stumps after six hours of neat accumulation and steady concentration, and Chanderpaul, whose lbw provided Broad with his third deserved victim.

Still 64 in arrears with their main batsmen gone, West Indies were in need of a partnership; as in his debut Test series in New Zealand, Nash, the little Australian-born Jamaican, was one half of it. Ramdin was the other, their stand of 66 carrying West Indies past England's total. A few vigorous blows by Benn helped extend the lead to 74. Broad dismissed him and Nash, claiming five in an innings for the first time in his 11 Tests.

It seemed a useful but hardly intimidating advantage at the time. Taylor soon proved it was more than enough.

Man of the Match: J. E. Taylor.

Close of play: First day, England 236-5 (Flintoff 43, Prior 27); Second day, West Indies 160-1 (Gayle 71, Sarwan 74); Third day, West Indies 352-7 (Nash 47, Benn 10).

England

*A. J. Strauss c Ramdin b Taylor	7	– c Ramdin b Taylor	9
A. N. Cook c Sarwan b Powell	4	– c Smith b Taylor	0
I. R. Bell c Smith b Gayle	28	– c Ramdin b Benn	4
K. P. Pietersen c Ramdin b Benn	97	– b Taylor	1
P. D. Collingwood lbw b Benn	16	– b Taylor	1
A. Flintoff c Nash b Powell	43	– b Edwards	24
†M. J. Prior c and b Benn	64	– b Taylor	0
S. C. J. Broad c Benn b Taylor	4	– c Marshall b Benn	0
R. J. Sidebottom not out	26	– lbw b Benn	6
S. J. Harmison lbw b Taylor	7	– b Benn	0
M. S. Panesar lbw b Benn	0	– not out	0
B 7, l-b 8, n-b 7	22	B 2, n-b 4	6

1/8 (1) 2/31 (2) 3/71 (3) 4/94 (5)   (122.2 overs) 318
5/180 (4) 6/241 (6) 7/256 (8)
8/288 (7) 9/313 (10) 10/318 (11)

1/1 (2) 2/11 (3)   (33.2 overs) 51
3/12 (4) 4/20 (1)
5/23 (5) 6/23 (7) 7/26 (8)
8/50 (9) 9/51 (6) 10/51 (10)

Taylor 20–4–74–3; Edwards 14–1–58–0; Powell 20–5–54–2; Benn 44.2–13–77–4; Gayle 24–9–40–1. *Second Innings*—Taylor 9–4–11–5; Powell 7–3–5–0; Benn 14.2–2–31–4; Gayle 2–1–1–0; Edwards 1–0–1–1.

West Indies

*C. H. Gayle b Broad	104	D. B. Powell c Prior b Harmison	9
D. S. Smith lbw b Flintoff	6	F. H. Edwards not out	10
R. R. Sarwan b Flintoff	107		
X. M. Marshall lbw b Broad	0	B 6, l-b 8, w 1	15
S. Chanderpaul lbw b Broad	20		
B. P. Nash c Prior b Broad	55	1/18 (2) 2/220 (1) (157.4 overs) 392
†D. Ramdin c Collingwood b Panesar	35	3/220 (4) 4/235 (3)
J. E. Taylor lbw b Harmison	8	5/254 (5) 6/320 (7) 7/341 (8)
S. J. Benn c Cook b Broad	23	8/371 (9) 9/376 (6) 10/392 (10)

Sidebottom 24–5–35–0; Flintoff 33–11–72–2; Harmison 20.4–4–49–2; Broad 29–7–85–5; Panesar 47–14–122–1; Pietersen 4–1–15–0.

Umpires: A. L. Hill and R. E. Koertzen.
Third umpire: D. J. Harper.   Referee: A. G. Hurst.

> **"**
> Three years ago, *Wisden* wrote that New Zealand 'again punched above their weight' as they reached the semi-final. They went one round further this time; perhaps they are just heavier than they look."
> Champions Trophy, page 1016

First Test referrals

STEVE JAMES

Just like England's first domestic taste of the umpire review system, in the 2007 Friends Provident Trophy, their first international experience stirred controversy and criticism.

At the heart of the problem was a lack of understanding. The system was not designed for marginal decisions; it was designed to eradicate howlers. Neither the players nor the TV umpire, Daryl Harper, showed a true understanding of this basic principle.

The crucial directive from the ICC was: "The on-field umpire will reverse his decision if the nature of the supplementary information received from the TV umpire leads him to conclude with a *high degree of confidence* that his original decision was incorrect."

Harper's misreading of this was clear when he overturned umpire Tony Hill's decision to give Sarwan lbw to Harmison. He could not possibly have possessed a "high degree of confidence" that the ball would have passed over the stumps, so the decision should have stood.

This created both confusion and precedent for the remainder of the match. Referrals became arbitrary: because England still had two available in their first innings, both Harmison and Panesar speculatively tried their luck. And Harper's decisions took too long. The Sarwan decision required nearly four minutes, and spectators became understandably frustrated.

	Grounds for appeal	Batsman	Bowler	Original verdict	Review requested	Review verdict
Eng 1st	lbw	Collingwood		Not out	West Indies	Not out

Hit Collingwood outside the line of off stump, so decision correctly upheld.

Eng 1st	lbw	Harmison	Taylor	Out	England	Out

Rightly upheld.

Eng 1st	lbw	Panesar	Benn	Out	England	Out

Hit bat only after point of contact with pad.

WI 1st	lbw	Smith	Flintoff	Not out	England	Out

Looked as if the left-hander might have been hit outside the line of leg stump as he jumped, not having picked up the ball out of the background of the George Headley Stand. Umpire Hill's decision overturned as the ball had in fact hit Smith in line. Excellent use of technology.

WI 1st	lbw	Sarwan	Flintoff	Not out	England	Not out

Ball pitched outside leg stump.

WI 1st	lbw	Sarwan	Harmison	Out	West Indies	Not out

Overturned as TV umpire Harper deemed that the ball was going over the stumps. Poor decision, too marginal.

WI 1st	ct wicketkeeper	Gayle	Flintoff	Out	West Indies	Not out

Gayle given out on 85 caught down the leg side by Prior. Overturned as replays showed the ball had flicked his trouser leg rather than bat or glove. Technology again to the fore.

WI 1st	lbw	Chanderpaul	Panesar	Not out	England	Not out

Padding up outside off stump; the ball might well have gone on to hit the stumps but, spinning sharply out of the rough, it was too difficult to give.

WI 1st	lbw	Chanderpaul	Broad	Out	West Indies	Out

Clearly hitting the stumps.

WI 1st	ct wicketkeeper	Powell	Harmison	Out	West Indies	Out

Wrongly upheld: there was clearly daylight between bat and ball on the TV replays, so Harper should have had a "high degree of confidence" and given it not out.

Eng 2nd	lbw	Sidebottom	Benn	Out	England	Out

Attempting to pull – desperation from Sidebottom as England collapsed.

In all there were 11 reviews (nine lbws and two caught behind). Three decisions were overturned (1 out, in favour of England/the bowler, 2 not out, in favour of West Indies/the batsmen).

WEST INDIES v ENGLAND

Second Test Match

Vic Marks

At North Sound, Antigua, February 13, 2009. Drawn. Toss: West Indies.

This was the shortest Test in the history of the game, leaving aside those abandoned without a ball bowled. It was also one of the most ignominious for a quartet of guilty parties: in increasing order of self-importance, the Antigua Cricket Association, the Leeward Islands Cricket Association, the West Indies Cricket Board and the International Cricket Council.

It was the second time in 11 years that the Caribbean had suffered such a humiliation during an England tour. In Jamaica, in January 1998, the Kingston Test was called off after 10.1 overs because the pitch was too dangerous for batsmen. Here it did not take so long to establish that bowlers were at risk if they tried to propel the ball at full tilt.

Just ten balls had been bowled, either side of a rain-break, by the West Indies opening pair, Jerome Taylor and Fidel Edwards, when the two umpires, Daryl Harper and Tony Hill, accompanied by referee Alan Hurst, led the players from the field in front of a bewildered crowd, made up mostly of English tourists.

"The bowlers were having trouble with their footings," Hurst explained. "They were digging into the sand, and the turf was giving way. We considered it very dangerous and play was abandoned on the grounds of health and safety." Asked why no action had been taken before the Test began, he said, "There was no evidence to go on, but we knew there were problems after two overs."

In fact, there had been warning signs. England had not been allowed to practise at the Sir Vivian Richards Stadium until the eve of the match, and were so alarmed by the state of the outfield that the ECB's managing director of England cricket, Hugh Morris, had written to Hurst expressing those concerns before the start.

Grassroots problem: work on the North Sound outfield began soon after the Test was called off.

If a number of heads had been buried in the sand beforehand, there was, at least, an impressive resolve and decisiveness in evidence after the players left the field. By three o'clock, it was agreed that another Test match would take place at the ramshackle but charismatic old ground at St John's within 48 hours. Thus the Antigua Recreation Ground, abandoned by cricket when the new stadium was built for the 2007 World Cup, had an unexpected reprieve.

The decision was driven by the ECB's chairman, Giles Clarke, and forced by the presence of thousands of English tourists, who had paid many more thousands of pounds to be in Antigua for the cricket. Many of those spectators had already endured a dreadful morning, queuing for 40 minutes or more outside the ground amid scudding showers because there were insufficient staff to carry out the security checks.

The West Indies Board, who were primarily to blame, especially as their headquarters are only a couple of miles from the stadium, were hardly in a position to argue when the ECB insisted that a game must go ahead in Antigua. Nor could they complain at the decision, taken by the ICC in March, not to permit any international cricket at the ground for at least 12 months, giving them time to carry out "extensive remedial work".

England

*A. J. Strauss not out 6
A. N. Cook not out . . . . <u>1</u>

(no wkt, 1.4 overs) 7

O. A. Shah, K. P. Pietersen, P. D. Collingwood, A. Flintoff, †M. J. Prior, S. C. J. Broad, R. J. Sidebottom, J. M. Anderson and M. S. Panesar did not bat.

Taylor 1–0–5–0; Edwards 0.4–0–2–0.

West Indies

*C. H. Gayle, D. S. Smith, R. R. Sarwan, R. O. Hinds, S. Chanderpaul, B. P. Nash, †D. Ramdin, J. E. Taylor, S. J. Benn, D. B. Powell and F. H. Edwards.

Umpires: D. J. Harper and A. L. Hill.
Third umpire: R. E. Koertzen. Referee: A. G. Hurst.

WEST INDIES v ENGLAND

Third Test Match

VIC MARKS

At St John's, Antigua, February 15, 16, 17, 18, 19, 2009. Drawn. Toss: West Indies.

After the fall came the pride. The West Indies Board and the Antigua Cricket Association had been humiliated by the events of Friday 13 at the Sir Vivian Richards Stadium. Cricket in the Caribbean was a shambles again, and the folly of building all those white elephant stadiums for the 2007 World Cup had been highlighted with piercing clarity.

Yet out of this mess something special happened. The grassroots of West Indian cricket, unencumbered by missives from the ICC or their own board, set to work on the Antigua Recreation Ground, and within 36 hours the dilapidated old stadium was fit for purpose. Thus a Test was played back at cricket's spiritual home on the island. Viv Richards could be seen with a smile on his face again. A proud little nation had responded nobly to their crisis. Everyone from the prime minister downwards – it was election time – was determined that cricket should return to the Rec.

The lines of the football pitch, the ground's main function since the erection of the new stadium out in the wilderness at North Sound, were still visible even on the square; the

Passing the Test: on February 11 the Antigua Recreation Ground was hosting an England kickabout; four days later, it was staging international cricket.

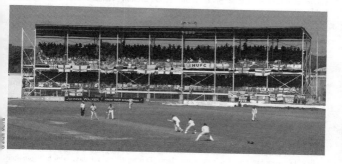

white paint on hastily erected sightscreens might have been damp. But the stands were swept, the pitch was flattened, and the outfield after heavy rolling was no worse than cricketers experienced a few decades ago at Northampton (where the long-leg boundary doubled as a football pitch) or Bath (rugby).

On the eve of the match, there was an uplifting buzz of activity: the clunk of hammers, the screech of saws, the swish of paintbrushes. The television crews entered into the spirit of it all, laying cables and erecting scaffolds at breakneck speed to ensure that the world could watch.

The sudden switch meant the technology required for the referral system could not be put into place in time, but there were no complaints from either side about that. And this underlined the view that a good old-fashioned Test match – no executive boxes, no suffocating security, no referrals – was under way, and a very good match it was, ending with the home side's last pair hanging on for a draw. In every sense, and against the odds, West Indies somehow managed to leave Antigua with their heads held high, though their achievement had to compete for media coverage with the breaking Stanford scandal. The English and West Indian boards hastily suspended their dealings with Texan financier Sir Allen Stanford as it emerged that the US Securities and Exchange Commission had charged him with an alleged $9.2 billion investment fraud. The news was a heavy economic blow for Antigua, as the Stanford Group was one of the island's biggest employers.

Back when Antigua's headaches centred on the state of a cricket ground, England had been keen on the switch to the Rec for two reasons. They had genuine sympathy for the thousands of supporters who had come to watch a Test; they also fancied a victory here. Earlier in the week they had practised on the pitch which was eventually used for the Test, and it had been spicy. Since they were 1–0 down, this relocation suited the tourists nicely.

So they made two changes to the side selected for the ten-ball Test. In anticipation of a lively wicket with some steep bounce, Harmison returned to the team at the expense of Ryan Sidebottom, while Swann replaced Monty Panesar as a more attacking spinner. And it would be Swann, rather than Harmison, who took England to the brink of victory.

West Indies seemed less enamoured by the sudden rearrangement. Having put England in to bat, they were lacklustre in the field, bowling with little purpose or pace on the first day, while Strauss, batting as assertively as he ever had for England, sped to a century. It soon became clear that the mammoth roller seconded to the Recreation Ground on the eve of the match had deadened the pitch.

All the batsmen, with the unusual exception of Pietersen, played fluently as England hurried to 566, declaring when Collingwood was out for 113. Then the early dismissal of Gayle, who was in frenetic mood on the second evening, enabled them to sustain their hold on the game. Swann, bowling with a shrewdness seldom seen from an English spinner in recent times, returned his best figures in Test cricket as West Indies were bowled out for 285. Sarwan had batted impeccably for 94 before losing concentration and his wicket against Swann, but he received modest support.

As is the modern way, Strauss declined to enforce the follow-on even though West Indies were 281 behind. There were good reasons for his decision – Harmison was sick, Swann's elbow was sore, and Flintoff's right hip was beginning to cause trouble – but this strategy wasted time. More culpably, so did the decision to use a night-watchman, Anderson, on the third evening to protect Shah, who had replaced Bell after the defeat in Jamaica.

The following morning Anderson, understandably for a tailender, was unable to take the attack to the West Indies bowlers as effectively as a front-line batsman, so more valuable minutes were squandered. Moreover, Strauss, no doubt mindful of the team's recent defeat after a declaration in Chennai, delayed bringing England's second innings to a close until the target was 503.

Even so, towards the end of an enthralling fifth day, England had ten overs at West Indies' last pair but could not dislodge them. During that final day, which began late because of squally showers, the balance of power shifted deliciously. When the Guyanese pair of Sarwan and Chanderpaul batted into the mid-afternoon, a draw seemed inevitable. But Strauss, galloping in with the new ball, removed both in swift succession – Sarwan bowled by a ball that came back and kept low just after he completed his second hundred of the series – and England seemed on course.

But every one of West Indies' lower-order batsmen resisted stoutly as the pitch grew ever more moribund. Harmison could wring no life from it, nor could Flintoff, who produced two sharp spells even though it was obvious that he was bowling in pain and in danger of causing himself lasting damage. So England had to depend on their next generation and, valiantly though Broad, Anderson and Swann tried, they could not extract Edwards or Powell as the sun set rapidly into the Caribbean sea.

Man of the Match: R. R. Sarwan.

Close of play: First day, England 301-3 (Pietersen 8, Anderson 3); Second day, West Indies 55-1 (Smith 10, Powell 2); Third day, England 31-1 (Cook 4, Anderson 4); Fourth day, West Indies 143-3 (Sarwan 47, Chanderpaul 18).

England

*A. J. Strauss c and b Edwards	169	– c Smith b Edwards	14
A. N. Cook c Smith b Gayle	52	– c Smith b Hinds	58
O. A. Shah run out	57	– (4) b Powell	14
K. P. Pietersen b Taylor	51	– (5) c Ramdin b Benn	32
J. M. Anderson c Ramdin b Edwards	4	– (3) c Ramdin b Powell	20
P. D. Collingwood c Smith b Hinds	113	– b Hinds	34
A. Flintoff b Taylor	0	– (9) c Hinds b Benn	0
†M. J. Prior c Chanderpaul b Nash	39	– (7) not out	15
S. C. J. Broad c Ramdin b Hinds	44	– (8) run out	1
G. P. Swann not out	20		
S. J. Harmison (did not bat)		– (10) not out	7
B 10, l-b 1, w 1, n-b 5	17	B 12, l-b 3, w 5, n-b 6	26

1/123 (2) 2/276 (3)   (9 wkts dec, 165.2 overs) 566   1/23 (1)   (8 wkts dec, 50 overs) 221
3/295 (1) 4/311 (5)   2/69 (3) 3/97 (4)
5/405 (4) 6/405 (7) 7/467 (8)   4/145 (2) 5/189 (5)
8/529 (9) 9/566 (6)   6/195 (6) 7/201 (8) 8/206 (9)

Taylor 28–7–73–2; Edwards 26–2–75–2; Powell 26–3–103–0; Gayle 13–1–41–1; Benn 39–5–143–0; Hinds 22.2–4–86–2; Nash 11–2–34–1. *Second Innings*—Edwards 9–1–36–1; Taylor 9–2–34–0; Powell 7–0–33–2; Benn 14–1–58–2; Hinds 11–1–45–2.

West Indies

*C. H. Gayle c Anderson b Harmison	30	– lbw b Swann	46
D. S. Smith b Swann	38	– lbw b Harmison	21
D. B. Powell c Collingwood b Swann	22	– (10) not out	22
R. R. Sarwan c Flintoff b Swann	94	– (3) b Broad	106
R. O. Hinds c Prior b Flintoff	27	– (4) c Shah b Broad	6
S. Chanderpaul c Prior b Broad	1	– (5) c Prior b Broad	55
B. P. Nash c Collingwood b Flintoff	18	– (6) lbw b Swann	23
†D. Ramdin c and b Swann	0	– (7) b Anderson	21
J. E. Taylor c and b Flintoff	19	– (8) c sub (I. R. Bell) b Anderson	11
S. J. Benn lbw b Swann	0	– (9) lbw b Swann	21
F. H. Edwards not out	1	– not out	5
B 17, l-b 5, w 2, n-b 11	35	B 21, l-b 7, w 1, n-b 4	33

1/45 (1) 2/109 (2) 3/130 (3)   (89.2 overs) 285   1/59 (2)   (9 wkts, 128 overs) 370
4/200 (5) 5/201 (6) 6/251 (4)   2/81 (1) 3/96 (4)
7/251 (8) 8/278 (7) 9/279 (10) 10/285 (9)   4/244 (3) 5/261 (5) 6/287 (6)
                                           7/313 (8) 8/322 (7) 9/353 (9)

Anderson 19–1–55–0; Flintoff 14.2–3–47–3; Harmison 12–3–44–1; Broad 14–4–24–1; Swann 24–7–57–5; Pietersen 2–0–14–0; Collingwood 4–0–22–0. *Second Innings*—Anderson 25–6–68–2; Broad 21–3–69–3; Swann 39–12–92–3; Harmison 22–3–54–1; Flintoff 15–5–32–0; Pietersen 3–0–15–0; Shah 3–0–12–0.

Umpires: D. J. Harper and R. E. Koertzen.
Third umpire: N. A. Malcolm.   Referee: A. G. Hurst.

---

†At Lucas Street, Barbados, February 22, 23, 2009. **Drawn.** Toss: Barbados CA President's XI. **England XI 351-8 dec** (A. J. Strauss 66, I. R. Bell 44, T. R. Ambrose 74, R. S. Bopara 124*; K. A. Stoute 4-67) **and 142-2** (A. N. Cook 52, I. R. Bell 72); **Barbados CA President's XI 245** (S. S. J. Brooks 69, K. A. Stoute 56, J. O. Holder 50; A. Khan 5-79).

Barbados CA President's XI named 13 players, of whom 11 could bat and 11 field. England picked only 11, including Ravi Bopara and Amjad Khan, who had been called up from the England Lions' tour of New Zealand as cover for Andrew Flintoff. After a 41-hour journey, they arrived in the Caribbean the afternoon before the game started, but Bopara beat the jetlag to hit 124 from 125 balls with three sixes and 17 fours, and Khan followed up with five wickets.

WEST INDIES v ENGLAND

Fourth Test Match

S C Y L D   B E R R Y

At Bridgetown, Barbados, February 26, 27, 28, March 1, 2, 2009. Drawn. Toss: England.

The Bridgetown Test was a dull, predictable, non-contest for the 10,000 or so England supporters who flew thousands of miles to see it and formed most of the crowd. West Indies made 749 for nine, the second-biggest total ever conceded by England: only their 751 at St John's five years earlier, by Brian Lara's 400 not out, was higher. Yet England scored even more runs for even fewer wickets – 879 for the loss of eight in all. It was a bad time for Test cricket. The Karachi match between Pakistan and Sri Lanka had just been built on the same statistical proportions, and the Lahore Test was abandoned when terrorists attacked the Sri Lankan team the day after this game finished.

It was a pitch with more pace and carry than Sabina Park or either of Antigua's tracks had provided: twice in one over Edwards made the ball fly above the wicketkeeper's grasp, and there were other instances. The trouble was that the ball never deviated off the seam and all too soon went soft. Less than a year before, the Bridgetown Test against Australia had been a lively affair, as the ball had carried through, but shortly after that a concert had been held on the square, and the stage had been left standing for too long. The result was too little live grass, no sideways deviation for the pace bowlers, and a lop-sided balance between bat and ball. As with the farce in Antigua, there were no resignations.

There might have been a conclusive outcome if the West Indian fielders had taken their chances, mostly off Edwards, in England's first innings: in theory, more than 300 runs could have been saved. Gayle, at first slip, dropped Strauss when he was on 58; Pietersen was missed by Taylor at fine leg on the first evening; Bopara too was dropped by Taylor when hooking at Edwards; and Ambrose, before he had scored, was dropped by Ramdin top-edging a cut at Hinds. All were chances that would be accepted more often than not at Test level.

England did not drop chances, if only because they did not create enough. Anderson was tidy throughout the ordeal but never found any reverse swing: the outfield, ironically, was in perfect shape, its grass well-sprinkled and immaculate, so the ball was not roughened. Sidebottom (brought back to replace Harmison) found some conventional swing, and bowled Sarwan with the new ball, but it was the third one, and off an inside edge, and overall he found it a strain to push his pace up to the early-to-mid-80s mph. Broad, like Taylor, laboured after his exertions earlier in the series, when they had been the best pace bowlers on their respective sides. Most wickets went to the bowler who spun it most, Swann, and he would have had more than five if England had not exhausted their allocation of referrals – two unsuccessful ones – long before Powell gave short leg a catch off pad and glove, only for umpire Tiffin to turn the appeal down. Again, both sides found the referral experiment unsatisfactory, as did their supporters, who were never informed of what was happening.

After a brief reconnaissance – six runs from 26 balls – Strauss launched into the width offered by Powell and scored his next 136 from only 184 balls. Sensing that England's bowlers would need a lot of time, Strauss soon left Cook in his wake and scored all round the wicket, no strokes better than his driving on the up past mid-off's right hand. He never allowed Benn to settle, either: the most economical West Indian bowler was Gayle, and he declined to turn his arm over on the second day. At tea, after 62 overs, England were 221 without loss, already their highest partnership on the ground, and their first-wicket record against West Indies anywhere (beating 212 by Reg Simpson and Cyril Washbrook at Trent Bridge in 1950). But Edwards with the second new ball slowed them a little – and, on the second morning, gave Bopara, who had replaced the injured Flintoff, an initiation ceremony in his fourth Test.

Powering on: Ramnaresh Sarwan caps a prolific series with a career-best 291.

Bopara went for his hooks, in the air initially. When four, he was dropped at deep square, and he only just cleared deep square leg with another hook. When 27, he was hit on the grille by Edwards and cut below his right eye, but still hooked the next ball for a single. As his maiden Test hundred unfolded, he kept the ball more on the ground, and even let one bouncer pass. When the ball was pitched up, the feature of Bopara's batting was how often he leg-glanced anything straight with a twist of his wrists. Collingwood played less sumptuously, more grittily, but still drove Nash – who had been allowed to bowl too much in the series – back over his head for successive fours.

When Bopara reached his century with a single, he celebrated in the style of Usain Bolt, the Jamaican sprinter, drawing an imaginary bow. Collingwood never got there because, after reaching 96, he tried to drive the next ball over the off side and was caught at wide third man (Strauss, on 99, had slog-swept Benn for six). Before the declaration, Ambrose took toll of the tiring attack as efficiently as Prior might have done if he had not gone home to see his wife following the birth of their first child.

West Indies, aiming to preserve their 1–0 lead, might have totalled 1,000 but for the referrals system. Five of their top six batsmen – the left-handers – were given out leg-before, all but Hinds after a referral. The system was designed to obviate blatant errors, and most of the decisions were marginal in any umpire's book, but the dismissal of Chanderpaul *was* a blatant error. When playing forward, he was hit well above the knee roll, and first given out by Tiffin; then TV umpire Harper failed to overturn the decision. As Sarwan lasted for 698 minutes on that pitch, and Ramdin for 424, Chanderpaul could have batted a week. "The most important thing for the TV umpire is to decide whether there is any conclusive evidence to change the decision," said the referee, Alan Hurst.

Sarwan, without being weak on the leg side, favoured the off in the course of his highest Test score: 184 runs, including 26 fours and an upper-cut six, on the off; 107 on the leg, with four fours and a six off Swann. His cover-driving in particular excited the supporters of both sides. The form of Sarwan's life rubbed off on Ramdin, who had never hit a Test century before, and had not reached 50 in his previous 27 innings. When he reached his

HIGHEST TEST TOTALS AGAINST ENGLAND

751-5 dec	West Indies at St John's (drew)	2003-04
749-9 dec	**West Indies at Bridgetown (drew)**	**2008-09**
729-6 dec	Australia at Lord's (Australia won by seven wickets)	1930
708	Pakistan at The Oval (drew)	1987
701	Australia at The Oval (Australia won by 562 runs)	1934
695	Australia at The Oval (Australia won by an innings and 39 runs)	1930
692-8 dec	West Indies at The Oval (drew)	1995
687-8 dec	West Indies at The Oval (West Indies won by 231 runs)	1976
682-6 dec	South Africa at Lord's (South Africa won by an innings and 92 runs)	2003
681-8 dec	West Indies at Port-of-Spain (drew)	1953-54
674-6 dec	**Australia at Cardiff (drew)**	**2009**
664	India at The Oval (drew)	2007
659-8 dec	Australia at Sydney (Australia won by an innings and 33 runs)	1946-47
656-8 dec	Australia at Manchester (drew)	1964
653-4 dec	Australia at Leeds (Australia won by an innings and 148 runs)	1993
652-8 dec	West Indies at Lord's (West Indies won by an innings and 226 runs)	1973

main landmark, Ramdin held up a note to thank three mentors – Sarwan, Ian Bishop and West Indies' assistant coach David Williams (who fielded as sub, aged 45, on the final day). Towards the end, as West Indies sought a lead, Ramdin accelerated with wristy aerial shots – one of them, off Swann, landing at deep midwicket where Sidebottom, who set off in the wrong direction, had been when the ball was hit.

After more than two days in the heat and the field, England would have been at their most vulnerable if Gayle had declared soon enough for Edwards to have had more than one over on the fourth evening. They batted out the last day comfortably enough as Cook reached his first Test hundred in 16 Tests since December 2007 and went on to his highest score. In all, on a pitch where the ball would not deviate, or go up and down, 1,628 runs were scored for the loss of only 17 wickets. Only four Tests ever had seen a higher number of runs per wicket than the 95.76 here.

Man of the Match: R. R. Sarwan.

Close of play: First day, England 301-3 (Pietersen 32, Collingwood 11); Second day, West Indies 85-1 (Smith 37, Sarwan 40); Third day, West Indies 398-5 (Sarwan 184, Ramdin 25); Fourth day, England 6-0 (Strauss 5, Cook 0).

England

*A. J. Strauss b Powell	142	– b Gayle	38
A. N. Cook c Hinds b Taylor	94	– not out	139
O. A. Shah c Smith b Benn	7	– lbw b Benn	21
K. P. Pietersen lbw b Edwards	41	– not out	72
P. D. Collingwood c Nash b Edwards	96		
R. S. Bopara c Taylor b Edwards	104		
†T. R. Ambrose not out	76		
S. C. J. Broad not out	13		
B 5, l-b 3, w 11, n-b 8	27	B 6, n-b 3	9

1/229 (1) 2/241 (2)   (6 wkts dec, 153.2 overs) 600   1/88 (1)   (2 wkts dec, 81 overs) 279
3/259 (3) 4/318 (4)   2/129 (3)
5/467 (5) 6/580 (6)

G. P. Swann, R. J. Sidebottom and J. M. Anderson did not bat.

Taylor 29.2-7-107-1; Edwards 30-0-151-3; Powell 24-3-107-1; Benn 30-7-106-1; Gayle 15-4-28-0; Hinds 14-2-62-0; Nash 9-1-20-0; Sarwan 2-0-11-0. *Second Innings*—Edwards 10-1-41-0; Powell 12-0-35-0; Benn 21-1-64-1; Taylor 4-0-15-0; Gayle 17-5-46-1; Hinds 14-1-56-0; Sarwan 3-0-16-0.

West Indies

D. S. Smith lbw b Swann 55	S. J. Benn c Ambrose b Anderson 14
*C. H. Gayle lbw b Anderson 6	D. B. Powell not out 13
R. R. Sarwan b Sidebottom 291	B 15, l-b 11, w 1, n-b 6 33
R. O. Hinds lbw b Swann 15	
S. Chanderpaul lbw b Anderson 70	1/13 (2) (9 wkts dec, 194.4 overs) 749
B. P. Nash lbw b Swann 33	2/121 (1)
†D. Ramdin b Swann. 166	3/159 (4) 4/281 (5) 5/334 (6) 6/595 (3)
J. E. Taylor b Swann 53	7/672 (8) 8/701 (9) 9/749 (7)

F. H. Edwards did not bat.

Anderson 37–9–125–3; Sidebottom 35–4–146–1; Broad 32–4–113–0; Swann 50.4–8–165–5; Pietersen 9–1–38–0; Bopara 13–0–66–0; Collingwood 16–1–51–0; Shah 2–0–19–0.

Umpires: Aleem Dar and R. B. Tiffin.
Third umpire: D. J. Harper.   Referee: A. G. Hurst.

WEST INDIES v ENGLAND

Fifth Test Match

Ian Bishop

At Port-of-Spain, Trinidad, March 6, 7, 8, 9, 10, 2009. Drawn. Toss: England. Test debuts: L. M. P. Simmons; A. Khan.

A largely mundane Test match culminated in a gripping contest, with Monty Panesar bowling the final over, and all of England's fielders except mid-off gathered within an arm's length of West Indian tailender Fidel Edwards. He safely negotiated the over in front of a crowd which, if not large, was hugely vocal and pro-West Indian; spectators had trickled in steadily as news spread of the exciting finish. When the players shook hands with one delivery remaining, West Indies were eight wickets down, still 126 adrift of the target, with only last man Baker – yet to score a run in a two-Test career – to come. A self-restraining and disciplined innings of 17 from 87 balls by Ramdin, a natural strokeplayer if ever there was one, had saved the Test and brought West Indies a 1–0 series victory.

On a last-day pitch belatedly offering assistance to spinners and – because of its cracked, abrasive soil – lots of reverse swing for the impressive Anderson, England set West Indies a target of 240 runs in 66 overs spanning two sessions, after Pietersen had bludgeoned his way to his first Test hundred of the tour, from only 88 balls: it was a marvel of sweeps and switch-hits, and hard running with Prior. The declaration proved conservative, in spite of Strauss's assertion that he was willing to lose the Test in order to win it. Seemingly lacking the ambition to play for anything but a draw from the moment they landed in Trinidad, Gayle's men gave no sign throughout their innings that they were going to rise to the challenge of chasing the target, or even put any pressure on England's bowlers and fielders, a dangerous ploy which could easily have borne regret.

Some of the most crucial moments in the match came via the controversial umpire referral system. En route to their first-innings hundreds, Nash was lucky that England had unwisely used up their referrals when an lbw shout from Panesar went in his favour, while Chanderpaul had a caught-behind decision overturned. Strauss was given not out after edging one to the keeper on day four. And when Chanderpaul was confirmed out lbw in the second innings, after requesting a review, he used up the last one available, which could have saved Hinds when he was wrongly given out caught at slip after battling for 94 balls; that made it 90 for six.

Immovable: Shivnarine Chanderpaul helps himself to his fourth unbeaten hundred against England.

Nine long and often frustrating years had passed since West Indies last held the Wisden Trophy, which had been a symbol of pride for a people who liked to claim a measure of superiority over their former colonial masters. That England, for all their problems off and on the field, travelled to the Caribbean ranked No. 5 in the world, while West Indies were No. 7 and without a Test series victory since Bangladesh in June 2004, emphasised the importance of seizing the moment and the series as they headed into the final Test at the Queen's Park Oval.

Against this backdrop, a team selected and hailed as "one for the conditions" by coach John Dyson perplexingly included a seventh batsman in debutant Lendl Simmons, and only three recognised front-line bowlers: Edwards, who had bowled with pace and hostility throughout the series for little reward on slow unresponsive pitches; Baker, playing his second Test; and the woefully underachieving Powell. (Taylor had an ankle injury.) Gayle's insistence that West Indies would be trying to win, even though they had left out their leading wicket-taker and sole specialist spinner Sulieman Benn, was a prevarication.

The team's mindset was epitomised by the droop of Edwards's shoulders when he failed to find even minimal assistance from the surface in his opening over; his damning stare at the pitch suggested he was ready to commit a heinous crime. His frustration that the series was played out on a succession of the most benign wickets produced in the Caribbean in recent memory was palpable. Two turgid days of less than spirited bowling to defensive field settings paved the way for England to eke out their third consecutive first-innings total of over 500. As in the previous two, the foundations were laid by a typically professional Strauss century. Collingwood continued his good run with 161, while Prior's 131 underlined his ability to counter-attack and dominate tiring bowlers. They added 218 together, a record for England's fifth wicket against West Indies, gradually increasing the tempo in pursuit of a declaration.

Rarely in recent memory has the Queen's Park Oval pitch started off so dry and so bereft of grass. Given that it had rained consistently for the preceding two months in Trinidad, this naturally sparked conspiracy theories that it was tailored to the request of the team management. Only a year earlier against Sri Lanka, West Indies chased 253 and won on a pitch with a liberal covering of grass which offered movement for the seamers early on and flattened out into a good batting surface towards the end. England's disappointment at the lack of spin and wear until day five (they had picked two spinners for the first time in the series) was evident in the mutterings of Broad, who vented his frustration to the media, saying he could not wait to get back to England where the conditions would allow for some movement off the pitch.

Comparatively patient hundreds from Gayle, who injured his hamstring when taking the quick single to bring it up, Chanderpaul, not one to miss out on such giftings, and the deserving Nash enabled West Indies to inch to within two runs of England's 546. They also had the help of 74 extras, two short of the Test record, including 35 byes, 16 off the bowling of Panesar as Prior kept coming up too soon. It was fitting that Chanderpaul accompanied Nash to his maiden Test hundred during a vital partnership of 234, a fifth-wicket record on this ground. Nash had made no secret of his reverence for Chanderpaul's approach to batting; not only did he incorporate some of those characteristics into his own game, he was slightly more fluent.

MOST EXTRAS IN A TEST INNINGS

	b	l-b	w	n-b		
76	35	26	0	15	Pakistan (537) v India at Bangalore	2007-08
74	**35**	**12**	**11**	**16**	**West Indies (544) v England at Port-of-Spain**	**2008-09**
71	21	8	4	38	Pakistan (435) v West Indies at Georgetown.	1987-88
68	29	11	0	28	Pakistan (291) v West Indies at Bridgetown.	1976-77
65	10	18	1	36	Zimbabwe (319-8) v Sri Lanka at Harare.	1994-95
64	12	25	0	27	India (565) v West Indies at Calcutta	1987-88
64	4	18	6	36	South Africa (460) v Pakistan at Johannesburg	1994-95
64	18	11	1	34	England (437) v West Indies at Manchester.	1995
64	25	21	5	13	South Africa (682-6 dec) v England at Lord's	2003

To England's enormous credit on this slow pitch, they dismissed Sarwan cheaply twice with thoughtful bowling and skilful catching. First, they exploited his propensity to play across the line early on with a full fast delivery from the enigmatic but brisk newcomer Amjad Khan, and in the second innings he fell to a smart catch by Collingwood at slip off Swann. Considering Sarwan's previous lowest score in the series was 94, this was a significant achievement.

Edwards, who had cut a forlorn figure and operated within himself over the opening rounds, suddenly sprang to life with his last ball on the fourth day. With time an issue in probing for a result, England had hustled to 76 for three in the 15th over when Edwards produced the most vicious bouncer of the series, at 92mph, which almost decapitated Pietersen and spiralled over the slips for four off his protecting glove. It showed what could be done with a willing intent, and was the precursor to an exciting final day after the long phoney war.

As in the Durban Test and Wellington one-day international which began the same day, players wore black armbands and observed a minute's silence before the start of the game for the victims of the terrorist attack on the Sri Lankan players and match officials in Lahore earlier in the week.

Man of the Match: M. J. Prior.   *Man of the Series:* R. R. Sarwan.

Close of play: First day, England 258-2 (Strauss 139, Collingwood 54); Second day, West Indies 92-1 (Gayle 49, Powell 0); Third day, West Indies 349-4 (Chanderpaul 52, Nash 70); Fourth day, England 80-3 (Pietersen 34, Collingwood 1).

England

*A. J. Strauss b Edwards	142	– c and b Gayle	14
A. N. Cook c Ramdin b Powell	12	– c Ramdin b Hinds	24
O. A. Shah run out	33	– c Ramdin b Baker	1
K. P. Pietersen b Hinds	10	– c sub (D. J. Bravo) b Edwards	102
P. D. Collingwood lbw b Baker	161	– c and b Hinds	9
†M. J. Prior not out	131	– b Baker	61
S. C. J. Broad c Simmons b Baker	19	– not out	13
G. P. Swann not out	11		
B 8, l-b 7, w 1, n-b 11	27	B 2, l-b 6, w 1, n-b 4	13

1/26 (2) 2/156 (4)   (6 wkts dec, 158.5 overs) 546   1/26 (1)   (6 wkts dec, 38.4 overs) 237
3/263 (1) 4/268 (3)   2/27 (3) 3/72 (2)
5/486 (5) 6/530 (7)   4/101 (5) 5/207 (6) 6/237 (4)

A. Khan, J. M. Anderson and M. S. Panesar did not bat.

In the first innings Shah, when 29, retired hurt at 133 and resumed at 263.

Edwards 24–5–63–1; Powell 16–1–79–1; Baker 23–4–77–2; Nash 23–3–77–0; Gayle 26–1–80–0; Hinds 39.5–2–126–1; Smith 1–0–3–0; Simmons 6–0–26–0. *Second Innings*—Edwards 11.4–1–67–1; Baker 8–1–39–2; Gayle 3–0–16–1; Hinds 8–0–57–2; Simmons 5–0–29–0; Nash 3–0–21–0.

West Indies

*C. H. Gayle c Strauss b Swann	102	– (8) lbw b Panesar	4
D. S. Smith b Panesar	28	– (1) lbw b Swann	17
D. B. Powell c Pietersen b Broad	0	– (9) b Anderson	0
R. R. Sarwan lbw b Khan	14	– (3) c Collingwood b Swann	14
L. M. P. Simmons lbw b Panesar	24	– (2) c Collingwood b Anderson	8
S. Chanderpaul not out	147	– (5) lbw b Swann	6
B. P. Nash c Collingwood b Broad	109	– (6) lbw b Anderson	1
R. O. Hinds st Prior b Swann	23	– (4) c Collingwood b Panesar	20
†D. Ramdin lbw b Anderson	15	– (7) not out	17
F. H. Edwards c Prior b Broad	8	– not out	1
L. S. Baker lbw b Swann	0		
B 35, l-b 12, w 11, n-b 16	74	B 17, l-b 6, w 1, n-b 2	26

1/90 (2) 2/96 (3) 3/118 (4)   (178.4 overs) 544   1/25 (2)   (8 wkts, 65.5 overs) 114
4/203 (5) 5/437 (7) 6/482 (8)   2/31 (1) 3/58 (3)
7/519 (9) 8/526 (1) 9/543 (10) 10/544 (11)   4/80 (5) 5/85 (6) 6/90 (4)
                                                   7/107 (8) 8/109 (9)

In the first innings Gayle, when 100, retired hurt at 195 and resumed at 519.

Anderson 32–7–70–1; Broad 30–11–67–3; Khan 25–1–111–1; Swann 45.4–12–130–3; Panesar 43–6–114–2; Pietersen 3–0–5–0. *Second Innings*—Anderson 16–7–24–3; Broad 5–3–9–0; Swann 21–13–13–3; Khan 4–0–11–0; Panesar 19.5–9–34–2.

Umpires: D. J. Harper and R. B. Tiffin.
Third umpire: Aleem Dar.   Referee: A. G. Hurst.

---

†At Pointe-à-Pierre, Trinidad, March 14, 2009. **England XI won by 51 runs.** Toss: England XI. **England XI 299-8** (50 overs) (R. S. Bopara 56, I. R. Bell 55, A. D. Mascarenhas 84*, A. K. Allert 3-59); **West Indies Players' Association President's Select XI 248** (43.4 overs) (L. M. P. Simmons 30, K. D. Williams 60, S. Badree 84*; J. M. Anderson 3-47, S. J. Harmison 4-59).

The WIPA President's Select XI named 13 players, of whom 11 could bat and 11 field; England stuck with 11, as they rested senior players (Ian Bell led the side). Dimitri Mascarenhas hit 84 from 54 balls with two sixes and nine fours, before James Anderson and Steve Harmison reduced the home side to 66-6. Kenroy Williams and Samuel Badree added 114 for the eighth wicket to restore some respectability.

TWENTY20 AND ONE-DAY INTERNATIONAL REPORTS
BY SCYLD BERRY

†WEST INDIES v ENGLAND

Twenty20 International

At Port-of-Spain, Trinidad, March 15, 2009. West Indies won by six wickets. Toss: West Indies. Twenty20 international debuts: G. J. Batty, S. M. Davies, A. Khan.

England underperformed almost as much as they had at the Stanford match in Antigua four months before, overwhelmed by an excited capacity crowd. They began all right, thanks to some cover-drives and clips from Steve Davies on his England debut, and reached 50 off 39 balls, one quicker than West Indies would manage, but could not adapt thereafter to a slow pitch. Shah and Collingwood offered leg-side skiers instead of working the ball around, and Pietersen was given out to a ludicrous decision after he had stepped back from leg stump. Sarwan, who had run out Batty with a direct hit from extra cover, helped to knock off the runs with two overs to spare. Ramdin, on his home ground, led West Indies for the first time because of Gayle's hamstring injury, while another Trinidadian, Bravo, returned after missing the Test series.

Man of the Match: R. R. Sarwan.

England		*B*	*4*	*6*
R. S. Bopara *b 9*	13	11	2	0
†S. M. Davies *b 5*	27	21	5	0
K. P. Pietersen *lbw b 11*	12	16	0	0
O. A. Shah *c 6 b 11*	6	12	0	0
P. D. Collingwood *c 4 b 10*	14	11	2	0
*A. J. Strauss *run out*	22	25	2	0
A. D. Mascarenhas *run out*	0	3	0	0
G. J. Batty *run out*	4	7	0	0
S. C. J. Broad *c 11 b 8*	2	5	0	0
A. Khan *b 11*	2	4	0	0
J. M. Anderson *not out*	0	0	0	0
L-b 7, w 12	19			

6 overs: 47-1   (19.1 overs) **121**

1/25 2/55 3/66 4/82 5/95 6/98 7/114 8/117 9/121

Edwards 3.1–0–18–1; Baker 2–0–12–1; Sammy 4–0–14–1; Bravo 4–0–34–1; Benn 4–0–24–3; Pollard 2–0–12–0.

West Indies		*B*	*4*	*6*
R. R. Sarwan *b 10*	59	46	4	2
A. D. S. Fletcher *c 7 b 9*	6	5	1	0
S. Chanderpaul *c 5 b 11*	12	13	3	0
L. M. P. Simmons *not out*	23	32	1	0
D. J. Bravo *c 3 b 10*	8	11	1	0
K. A. Pollard *not out*	4	1	1	0
B 1, l-b 1, w 9	11			

6 overs: 51-2   (18 overs) **123-4**

1/11 2/45 3/105 4/119

*†D. Ramdin, F. H. Edwards, L. S. Baker, D. J. G. Sammy and S. J. Benn did not bat.

Anderson 3–0–19–1; Broad 3–0–26–1; Khan 4–0–34–2; Batty 3–0–17–0; Mascarenhas 4–0–17–0; Collingwood 1–0–8–0.

Umpires: C. R. Duncan and N. A. Malcolm.   Third umpire: C. E. Mack.   Referee: J. Srinath.

†WEST INDIES v ENGLAND

First One-Day International

At Providence, Guyana, March 20, 2009. England won by one run (D/L method). Toss: England.

A mistake by West Indies coach John Dyson presented England with their first overseas one-day victory for more than a year. With his team one run behind the Duckworth/Lewis par score, he signalled to his batsmen to accept the umpires' offer of bad light, believing they were two runs ahead. "I went down the wrong column," Dyson said, referring to the D/L sheet. "It's my responsibility. I've apologised to the team, that's all I can do. It was a bad mistake." Gayle, charitably, commented: "I'm not going to kill him." On a turgid pitch England had batted well (except during the third powerplay which yielded 17 for two) by eschewing glory shots and running hard, notably Collingwood, who made 69 off 77 balls despite a migraine. During the West Indian powerplay, Chanderpaul predicted perfectly where his Durham team-mate Harmison was going to bowl: in one over he hit him for five fours, mostly by stepping back and carving over the off side, and a swivelling scoop for six. Harmison then dropped Pollard at long-on. But Broad took charge, Harmison recovered to catch Pollard at deep square, and England were saved by Dyson and darkness (although 45 minutes were lost to rain, only 15 minutes were deducted from the interval). The West Indians wore masking tape over the sponsor's logo on their sleeves, and the six domestic teams were boycotting the opening day of their first-class matches, in another round of player discontent with the board.

Man of the Match: P. D. Collingwood.

England

*A. J. Strauss c Bravo b Powell	15	S. C. J. Broad run out		8
R. S. Bopara lbw b Miller	43	G. J. Batty not out		2
K. P. Pietersen c Powell b Bravo	17	L-b 4, w 23, n-b 1		28
O. A. Shah c Ramdin b Bravo	62			
P. D. Collingwood c Bravo b Pollard	69	1/28 (1) 2/64 (3)	(7 wkts, 50 overs)	270
A. D. Mascarenhas lbw b Pollard	0	3/117 (2) 4/215 (4)		
†M. J. Prior not out	26	5/216 (6) 6/243 (5) 7/263 (8)	10 overs: 50-1	

S. J. Harmison and J. M. Anderson did not bat.

Powell 5–0–27–1; Edwards 5–0–23–0; Bravo 10–0–65–2; Sammy 10–0–43–0; Miller 9–0–48–1; Pollard 8–0–46–2; Gayle 3–0–14–0.

West Indies

*C. H. Gayle lbw b Broad	2	D. J. G. Sammy not out		0
L. M. P. Simmons c Anderson b Batty	62			
R. R. Sarwan c Strauss b Collingwood	57	B 5, l-b 4, w 14		23
S. Chanderpaul c Strauss b Broad	46			
K. A. Pollard c Harmison b Anderson	42	1/6 (1) 2/131 (3)	(7 wkts, 46.2 overs)	244
D. J. Bravo c Bopara b Anderson	1	3/152 (2) 4/212 (4)		
†D. Ramdin lbw b Broad	11	5/213 (6) 6/242 (5) 7/244 (7)	10 overs: 36-1	

D. B. Powell, N. O. Miller and F. H. Edwards did not bat.

Broad 9.2–2–41–3; Anderson 8–0–39–2; Harmison 7–0–51–0; Mascarenhas 8–0–33–0; Batty 7–0–34–1; Collingwood 7–0–37–1.

Umpires: Aleem Dar and C. R. Duncan.
Third umpire: C. E. Mack. Referee: J. Srinath.

†WEST INDIES v ENGLAND

Second One-Day International

At Providence, Guyana, March 22, 2009. West Indies won by 21 runs. Toss: West Indies.
England's men could not live up to the England Women, who won the World Cup earlier in the day. They were outbatted by the two Guyanese: Sarwan, who saw off a fine opening spell by Anderson (6–1–15–2) with 74 off 89 balls, and Chanderpaul, with 112 not out – his tenth one-day international century – off 134 balls. The previous day a street in Georgetown had been renamed Shiv Chanderpaul Drive, but he also deserved to have a second named after him as he flicked three of England's bowlers over what Strauss had intended to be short third man. Prior dropping Chanderpaul when he was 27, off a faint inside edge against Mascarenhas, was the turning point. England were nearly always behind the rate as Strauss could find no partner to match Sarwan, with Bopara and Pietersen dragging on. Relying on square-of-the-wicket shots, Strauss almost equalled Chanderpaul in scoring 105 from 129 balls – his third one-day international century, and second against West Indies (the other was against Bangladesh). Following the first match, the captains agreed to use the six floodlights, which allowed this game to be concluded in full.

Man of the Match: S. Chanderpaul.

West Indies

*C. H. Gayle b Anderson	20	N. O. Miller b Collingwood 0
L. M. P. Simmons c Prior b Anderson.....	0	F. H. Edwards not out 3
R. R. Sarwan c Collingwood b Anderson ..	74	B 2, l-b 6, w 7, n-b 1 16
S. Chanderpaul not out	112	
K. A. Pollard c Pietersen b Mascarenhas...	8	1/15 (2) 2/24 (1) (8 wkts, 50 overs) 264
D. J. Bravo c Collingwood b Mascarenhas .	19	3/157 (3) 4/206 (5)
†D. Ramdin c Harmison b Collingwood....	1	5/237 (6) 6/238 (7)
D. J. G. Sammy lbw b Collingwood	11	7/256 (8) 8/256 (9)

L. S. Baker did not bat.   10 overs: 41-2

Broad 7–0–48–0; Anderson 9–1–37–3; Harmison 7–0–29–0; Batty 6–0–38–0; Mascarenhas 10–0–53–2; Collingwood 10–0–49–3; Bopara 1–0–2–0.

England

*A. J. Strauss b Pollard	105	S. J. Harmison not out 18
R. S. Bopara b Baker..................	14	J. M. Anderson b Pollard 8
K. P. Pietersen b Edwards	12	
O. A. Shah lbw b Bravo	22	B 1, l-b 11, w 12 24
P. D. Collingwood b Bravo	1	
†M. J. Prior c Ramdin b Sammy	2	1/18 (2) 2/36 (3) 3/86 (4) (48.2 overs) 243
A. D. Mascarenhas run out	29	4/88 (5) 5/97 (6) 6/156 (7)
S. C. J. Broad c and b Miller............	3	7/168 (8) 8/185 (9) 9/229 (1)
G. J. Batty run out	5	10/243 (11) 10 overs: 55-2

Baker 6–0–31–1; Edwards 6–0–31–1; Bravo 9–0–40–2; Sammy 10–1–36–1; Miller 9–0–42–1; Pollard 7.2–0–46–2; Gayle 1–0–5–0.

Umpires: Aleem Dar and C. R. Duncan.
Third umpire: C. E. Mack.   Referee: J. Srinath.

†WEST INDIES v ENGLAND

Third One-Day International

At Bridgetown, Barbados, March 27, 2009. West Indies won by eight wickets (D/L method). Toss: West Indies.

In a replay of West Indian cricket of the 1980s, on the fastest pitch of the tour, England's batsmen were bounced out, then their bowlers blasted out of the ground. The top three plus Flintoff and Mascarenhas all fell to hooks, while Prior steered a short off-side ball to point. As Strauss was first to go, the team followed their captain's example all too precisely. Flower said afterwards: "You expect them to see the same thing, but maybe assuming things is dangerous." Strauss elaborated that they knew conditions would be "very, very different from Guyana", and it was pretty humiliating: "The way we batted, there wasn't enough thought." Rain, which might have freshened the pitch, reduced the game to 45 then 44 overs per side, but England were 68 for eight by the 25th over. They needed Mascarenhas to make 36 off 76 balls to pass their previous one-day low against West Indies, 114 on the same ground in 1985-86. Bravo won the match award, although it was Edwards who put the wind up England. Gayle then used the pitch's pace to hit eight sixes and five fours off 43 balls, pulling, clipping, upper-cutting and driving straight in pursuit of 117. West Indies went 2–1 up; the gap seemed rather bigger after they reached their target with 29 overs to spare.

Man of the Match: D. J. Bravo.

England

*A. J. Strauss c Gayle b Edwards	2	G. J. Batty c Sammy b Bravo	17
R. S. Bopara c Sarwan b Edwards	10	J. M. Anderson not out	0
K. P. Pietersen c Pollard b Bravo	3		
O. A. Shah c Sammy b Baker	17	B 8, l-b 1, w 10	19
P. D. Collingwood lbw b Bravo	6		
A. Flintoff c Edwards b Bravo	0	1/15 (1) 2/17 (2) 3/41 (3) (41.3 overs)	117
†M. J. Prior c Sammy b Pollard	7	4/42 (4) 5/43 (6) 6/54 (5)	
A. D. Mascarenhas c Bravo b Edwards	36	7/68 (7) 8/68 (9) 9/116 (10)	
S. C. J. Broad c Ramdin b Pollard	0	10/117 (8) 9 overs: 22-2	

Edwards 8.3–1–28–3; Baker 9–5–21–1; Bravo 7–1–19–4; Sammy 9–2–19–0; Pollard 6–0–16–2; Miller 2–0–5–0.

West Indies

*C. H. Gayle b Anderson	80
L. M. P. Simmons not out	14
R. R. Sarwan b Broad	10
S. Chanderpaul not out	3
B 4, n-b 6	10

1/98 (1) 2/114 (3)   (2 wkts, 14.4 overs) 117
9 overs: 91-0

K. A. Pollard, D. J. Bravo, D. J. G. Sammy, †D. Ramdin, N. O. Miller, F. H. Edwards and L. S. Baker did not bat.

Broad 3.4–1–31–1; Anderson 5–0–39–1; Flintoff 5–0–19–0; Mascarenhas 1–0–24–0.

Umpires: S. A. Bucknor and S. J. Davis.
Third umpire: N. A. Malcolm.   Referee: J. Srinath.

†WEST INDIES v ENGLAND

Fourth One-Day International

At Bridgetown, Barbados, March 29, 2009. England won by nine wickets (D/L method). Toss: England.

Rain and Duckworth/Lewis favoured England, but only after their bowlers and fielders had rallied admirably from the rout two days before. Conditions helped their all-seam attack, but Gayle still hit five sixes off 39 balls, and flawless fielding was needed to keep England in the game. Mascarenhas ran from mid-on to square leg to bring off a run-out, then conceded only two more runs in his ten-over spell than he had in six balls to Gayle in the previous match. Pietersen, who had just criticised Chanderpaul publicly for not being a team player, was bowling to him when his back went into spasm and he had to leave mid-over. Only Bravo evaded England's tightening grip, hitting 36 out of 50 added in the five overs of the West Indian powerplay. After rain had shortened the run-chase to 135 off 20 overs, Strauss enjoyed the belter of a pitch, striking four consecutive fours off Baker's second over and, after a brief mid-innings lull, 79 off 61 balls. Strauss and Bopara hit a six each, after England had managed only one in the first three games. Afterwards, Steve Bucknor walked round the ground to acknowledge applause for his distinguished career. He was the only umpire at the time of his retirement to have stood in 100 Tests, and only Rudi Koertzen had stood in more than Bucknor's 181 one-day internationals, which included five consecutive World Cup finals.

Man of the Match: A. J. Strauss.

West Indies

*C. H. Gayle c Prior b Broad	46	F. H. Edwards c Collingwood b Anderson	0
L. M. P. Simmons run out	29	L. S. Baker not out	11
R. R. Sarwan b Flintoff	6		
S. Chanderpaul c Prior b Mascarenhas	27	W 7, n-b 2	9
†D. Ramdin c Flintoff b Mascarenhas	26		
D. J. Bravo c sub (I. R. Bell) b Broad	69	1/72 (1) 2/76 (2) (9 wkts, 50 overs) 239
K. A. Pollard c Flintoff b Mascarenhas	0	3/83 (3) 4/126 (5)
D. J. G. Sammy b Broad	6	5/143 (4) 6/145 (7) 7/173 (8)
N. O. Miller not out	10	8/224 (10) 9/225 (6) 10 overs: 54-0

Miller, when 7, retired hurt at 203 and resumed at 225.

Anderson 10–1–41–1; Broad 10–0–62–3; Flintoff 9–0–58–1; Harmison 8–0–42–0; Mascarenhas 10–1–26–3; Pietersen 0.5–0–0–0; Shah 1.1–0–6–0; Collingwood 1–0–4–0.

England

*A. J. Strauss not out	79
R. S. Bopara c Miller b Pollard	35
†M. J. Prior not out	14
L-b 3, w 5	8
1/108 (2) (1 wkt, 18.3 overs) 136	
4 overs: 41-0	

K. P. Pietersen, O. A. Shah, P. D. Collingwood, A. Flintoff, A. D. Mascarenhas, S. C. J. Broad, S. J. Harmison and J. M. Anderson did not bat.

Baker 2–0–24–0; Edwards 3–0–24–0; Bravo 3.3–0–22–0; Sammy 4–0–31–0; Pollard 4–0–20–1; Miller 2–0–12–0.

Umpires: S. A. Bucknor and S. J. Davis.
Third umpire: N. A. Malcolm. Referee: J. Srinath.

†WEST INDIES v ENGLAND

Fifth One-Day International

At Gros Islet, St Lucia, April 3, 2009. England won by 26 runs. Toss: West Indies.

Inadequate drainage reduced this decider to 29 overs a side, but the home team were even worse at soaking up the pressure of chasing. On a slow, low and uneven pitch – also reflecting ill on the local administration – batsmen had to content themselves with working the ball into gaps, and England's were slightly more calculating and patient. Collingwood and Prior even added 23 in the two overs of their batting powerplay, more than the team had achieved in five in the first match in Guyana. England had no spinner of Benn's calibre, but their right-arm fast-to-medium bowling was backed by more error-free fielding and forced the required rate up. As naive a shot as any was Chanderpaul's slog-sweep into the prevailing wind. West Indies still had a chance while Bravo – whose back-foot six off Mascarenhas was the shot of the day – and Pollard were together, but they offered catches off consecutive balls. The match was effectively settled, with just Ramdin and the tailenders left to score 38 off three overs, even before Flintoff took only the third one-day hat-trick for England, bowling Ramdin behind his legs and following up with a full toss and a yorker. England's first one-day series victory in the Caribbean in seven attempts owed much to the batting and captaincy of Strauss, the player of the series, his opening bowlers Anderson and Broad, and the all-round fielding.

Man of the Match: A. Flintoff.   *Man of the Series:* A. J. Strauss.

And for my first trick… Andrew Flintoff takes the wicket of Sulieman Benn to complete his maiden hat-trick in international cricket.

England

*A. J. Strauss c Bravo b Rampaul	3	†M. J. Prior not out	25
R. S. Bopara c Ramdin b Pollard	44	L-b 3, w 4, n-b 1	8
K. P. Pietersen c Sammy b Benn	48		
O. A. Shah c Simmons b Benn	6	1/8 (1) 2/88 (3) (5 wkts, 29 overs) 172	
P. D. Collingwood not out	35	3/104 (2) 4/107 (4)	
A. Flintoff c Chanderpaul b Pollard	3	5/112 (6) 6 overs: 35-1	

A. D. Mascarenhas, S. C. J. Broad, S. J. Harmison and J. M. Anderson did not bat.

Edwards 2–0–17–0; Rampaul 4–0–19–1; Bravo 5–0–31–0; Pollard 5–0–31–2; Sammy 6–0–45–0; Benn 6–0–23–2; Gayle 1–0–3–0.

West Indies

*C. H. Gayle c Flintoff b Anderson	0	R. Rampaul lbw b Flintoff	0
L. M. P. Simmons c Broad b Flintoff	17	S. J. Benn b Flintoff	0
R. R. Sarwan c Prior b Flintoff	23	F. H. Edwards not out	2
S. Chanderpaul c sub (I. R. Bell) b Collingwood	13	B 1, l-b 3, w 5	9
D. J. Bravo c Flintoff b Broad	33	1/1 (1) 2/40 (3) 3/45 (2) (28 overs) 146	
K. A. Pollard c Collingwood b Anderson	30	4/69 (4) 5/124 (5) 6/124 (6)	
†D. Ramdin b Flintoff	12	7/140 (7) 8/140 (9) 9/140 (10)	
D. J. G. Sammy run out	7	10/146 (8) 6 overs: 32-1	

Anderson 6–0–34–2; Broad 6–0–32–1; Flintoff 5–0–19–5; Harmison 3–0–17–0; Mascarenhas 4–0–16–0; Collingwood 4–0–24–1.

Umpires: S. J. Davis and N. A. Malcolm.
Third umpire: G. E. Greaves.   Referee: J. Srinath.

WEST INDIES v INDIA, 2009

Tony Cozier

One-day internationals (4): West Indies 1, India 2

At a time when the game's leading players were openly complaining about the increasing surfeit of cricket of all types, only the administrators could appreciate the relevance of India's four one-day internationals at the start of the Caribbean hurricane season. It was a reciprocal arrangement, following West Indies' equally brief trip to India before the 2007 World Cup; if nothing else, it boosted the West Indies Cricket Board's coffers through a lucrative television contract.

For the West Indian players, it was yet another ride on the interminable merry-go-round that had taken them to Abu Dhabi and New Zealand, back to the Caribbean, and on to England over the previous seven months. The Indians had spent two months engaged in the IPL in South Africa and the World Twenty20 championship in England, after which both teams flew straight to Jamaica for the first two matches. India were without three leading players – Sachin Tendulkar, Virender Sehwag and Zaheer Khan – as much through fatigue as injury, appreciably diminishing their appeal. While West Indies were nominally at full strength, they were distracted by yet another of the seemingly never-ending disagreements between the board and the players' association, which originally put the two matches in St Lucia in doubt. A pointed no-show at an ICC function to launch ticket sales for the 2010 World Twenty20 in the Caribbean the night before the final match was the prelude to the refusal of the main players to take part in the subsequent series against Bangladesh.

It was soon clear there was little interest in this contest: Sabina Park was no more than half full for its matches; the Beausejour Stadium, usually packed to over-capacity, was even emptier, although the omission of local all-rounder Darren Sammy was a factor. Inevitably, it rained in St Lucia, reducing the third match to 27 overs a side and ending the fourth after little more than half an hour.

INDIAN TOURING PARTY

M. S. Dhoni (*captain*), Yuvraj Singh (*vice-captain*), S. Badrinath, G. Gambhir, Harbhajan Singh, R. A. Jadeja, K. D. Karthik, P. Kumar, A. M. Nayar, A. Nehra, P. P. Ojha, Y. K. Pathan, I. Sharma, R. G. Sharma, R. P. Singh, M. Vijay. *Coach:* G. Kirsten.

Note: Matches in this section were not first-class.

WEST INDIES v INDIA

First One-Day International

At Kingston, Jamaica, June 26, 2009. India won by 20 runs. Toss: India. One-day international debut: D. M. Bravo.

India won a high-scoring match thanks to an innings of breathtaking brilliance from Yuvraj Singh, whose 131 from 102 balls included ten fours and seven sixes, one of which – a pull off Gayle – disappeared into a car park. He also swatted Taylor for 26 from five balls (46466) as India collected

62 in their five-over batting powerplay. Pathan and Harbhajan Singh, who both hit two sixes of their own, ensured a total well over 300 and, although West Indies kept up with the required rate – 100 came up in the 16th over and 200 in the 34th – the later batsmen (who included Darren Bravo, making his debut alongside his older brother Dwayne) were eventually left with too much to do. Pakistan's 349 against Zimbabwe in the 2007 World Cup was the only previous total of 300 or more in a one-day international at Sabina Park, while the match aggregate of 658 runs had been surpassed only once in the Caribbean, by the 671 of Australia (377 for six) and South Africa (294) in St Kitts, also during the 2007 World Cup.

Man of the Match: Yuvraj Singh.

India

K. D. Karthik c Ramdin b Bernard	67	Harbhajan Singh not out 21
G. Gambhir c D. J. Bravo b Taylor	13	
R. G. Sharma c D. J. Bravo b Baker	4	B 1, l-b 8, w 10, n-b 3 22
Yuvraj Singh c Ramdin b D. J. Bravo.	131	
*†M. S. Dhoni run out	41	1/25 (2) 2/32 (3) (6 wkts, 50 overs) 339
R. A. Jadeja c Ramdin b D. J. Bravo.	0	3/167 (1) 4/253 (4)
Y. K. Pathan not out	40	5/253 (6) 6/298 (5) 10 overs: 43-2

R. P. Singh, I. Sharma and A. Nehra did not bat.

Taylor 10–1–74–1; Baker 9–0–62–1; D. J. Bravo 10–0–66–2; Bernard 8–0–50–1; Benn 10–0–50–0; Gayle 3–0–28–0.

West Indies

*C. H. Gayle c Harbhajan Singh b Nehra	37	S. J. Benn b R. P. Singh. 7
R. S. Morton c Dhoni b Pathan	42	L. S. Baker not out 0
R. R. Sarwan run out	45	
S. Chanderpaul c Jadeja b Pathan	63	B 4, l-b 4, w 19, n-b 2 29
D. J. Bravo c R. G. Sharma b I. Sharma	8	
D. M. Bravo c R. P. Singh b Harbhajan Singh	19	1/65 (1) 2/100 (2) (48.1 overs) 319
J. E. Taylor lbw b Pathan	21	3/151 (3) 4/188 (5) 5/224 (4)
†D. Ramdin c Harbhajan Singh b Nehra	29	6/241 (6) 7/250 (7) 8/294 (9)
D. E. Bernard c R. G. Sharma b Nehra	19	9/318 (10) 10/319 (8) 10 overs: 70-1

R. P. Singh 7–0–44–1; Nehra 7.1–1–49–3; I. Sharma 5–0–38–1; Jadeja 7–1–34–0; Pathan 8–0–56–3; Harbhajan Singh 10–0–56–1; Yuvraj Singh 4–0–34–0.

Umpires: N. J. Llong and N. A. Malcolm.
Third umpire: C. E. Mack.   Referee: B. C. Broad.

WEST INDIES v INDIA

Second One-Day International

At Kingston, Jamaica, June 28, 2009. West Indies won by eight wickets. Toss: India.

There was no repeat of the first match run-fest: by the 22nd over India were floundering at 82 for eight, most of the damage having been done by Rampaul, swinging the ball away. He was helped by attacking captaincy from Gayle, in his 200th one-day international for West Indies: he kept a second slip in, against Rampaul's wishes, and saw him catch Rohit Sharma after a deflection from the wicketkeeper. Yuvraj Singh briefly promised another big innings, only to fall to the first ball of the seventh over of Taylor's opening spell. It took a mature 130-ball innings from Dhoni – and his ninth-wicket partnership of 101 with R. P. Singh – to ensure any sort of target. But West Indies' openers tore into the Indian attack, and the match was all but decided by the time Gayle departed in the 16th over, for 64 from 46 balls. Morton took his side over the line with a six to level the series with 95 balls to spare.

Man of the Match: R. Rampaul.

India

K. D. Karthik c Ramdin b Taylor	4	
G. Gambhir c Ramdin b Rampaul	0	
R. G. Sharma c Morton b Rampaul	0	
Yuvraj Singh c Ramdin b Taylor	35	
*†M. S. Dhoni b Taylor	95	
Y. K. Pathan c Gayle b D. J. Bravo	0	
R. A. Jadeja c Ramdin b Rampaul	7	
Harbhajan Singh c Ramdin b D. J. Bravo	7	
P. Kumar c Gayle b Rampaul	1	

R. P. Singh c Benn b D. J. Bravo 23
A. Nehra not out 0

L-b 4, w 12 16

1/4 (1) 2/6 (2) 3/7 (3)   (48.2 overs) 188
4/54 (4) 5/57 (6) 6/70 (7)
7/81 (8) 8/82 (9) 9/183 (10)
10/188 (5)   10 overs: 48-3

Taylor 9.2–0–35–3; Rampaul 10–2–37–4; D. J. Bravo 9–0–26–3; Benn 10–1–37–0; Bernard 7–0–36–0; Gayle 3–0–13–0.

West Indies

*C. H. Gayle c Gambhir b Sharma	64
R. S. Morton not out	85
R. R. Sarwan st Dhoni b Sharma	15
S. Chanderpaul not out	18
L-b 5, w 4, n-b 1	10

1/101 (1) 2/132 (3)   (2 wkts, 34.1 overs) 192
10 overs: 69-0

D. J. Bravo, D. M. Bravo, †D. Ramdin, J. E. Taylor, D. E. Bernard, S. J. Benn and R. Rampaul did not bat.

Kumar 7–1–37–0; Nehra 4–0–36–0; R. P. Singh 3–0–15–0; Pathan 2–0–15–0; Harbhajan Singh 8.1–0–45–0; Sharma 8–0–27–2; Jadeja 2–0–12–0.

Umpires: N. J. Llong and N. A. Malcolm.
Third umpire: C. E. Mack.   Referee: B. C. Broad.

WEST INDIES v INDIA

Third One-Day International

At Gros Islet, St Lucia, July 3, 2009. India won by six wickets (D/L method). Toss: India. One-day international debut: A. M. Nayar.

India took an ultimately decisive lead in the series during a shortened game at the Beausejour Stadium. Rain briefly delayed the start, and interrupted West Indies' innings three times before they had completed ten overs: the eventual total, which owed much to Sarwan's unflustered 62, was a decent one in the circumstances. After another rain-break India's target was adjusted to 159 from 22 overs, and they scrambled home with one ball to spare. Karthik and Gambhir gave them a lively start, but nevertheless West Indies were marginal favourites going into the last over, with 11 still needed – before Dhoni effectively settled the issue by hoisting Taylor's second ball over deep midwicket for six. In a series with a barely discernible pulse, it was a genuinely pulsating moment.

Man of the Match: M. S. Dhoni.

West Indies

*C. H. Gayle c Dhoni b Nehra	27	
R. S. Morton st Dhoni b Harbhajan Singh	22	
R. R. Sarwan run out	62	
S. Chanderpaul c Nehra b Pathan	15	
D. J. Bravo c Dhoni b Nehra	14	
D. M. Bravo b Nehra	21	
†D. Ramdin not out	14	

J. E. Taylor c I. Sharma b Harbhajan Singh   1

L-b 7, w 2, n-b 1 10

1/27 (1) 2/78 (2)   (7 wkts, 27 overs) 186
3/125 (4) 4/135 (3)
5/170 (6) 6/173 (5) 7/186 (8)   8 overs: 49-1

D. E. Bernard, S. J. Benn and R. Rampaul did not bat.

I. Sharma 5–0–35–0; Nehra 5–1–21–3; R. P. Singh 5–0–34–0; Harbhajan Singh 5–0–35–2; Yuvraj Singh 2–0–19–0; R. G. Sharma 1–0–7–0; Pathan 4–0–28–1.

India

K. D. Karthik run out	47	Y. K. Pathan not out		1
G. Gambhir c Ramdin b Benn	44	L-b 4, w 3, n-b 1		8
*†M. S. Dhoni not out	46			
Yuvraj Singh c D. M. Bravo b Bernard	2	1/84 (1) 2/108 (2)	(4 wkts, 21.5 overs)	159
R. G. Sharma c Bernard b D. J. Bravo	11	3/117 (4) 4/148 (5)	5 overs: 36-0	

A. M. Nayar, Harbhajan Singh, R. P. Singh, I. Sharma and A. Nehra did not bat.

Taylor 3.5–0–39–0; Rampaul 4–0–26–0; D. J. Bravo 4–0–27–1; Bernard 3–0–21–1; Benn 5–0–31–1; Gayle 2–0–11–0.

Umpires: C. R. Duncan and N. J. Llong.
Third umpire: G. E. Greaves.   Referee: B. C. Broad.

WEST INDIES v INDIA

Fourth One-Day International

At Gros Islet, St Lucia, July 5, 2009. No result. Toss: India.
   Rain delayed the start and, after Gayle had fallen second ball, returned in earnest after little more than half an hour to prevent any further play: India thus took the series 2–1. Abhishek Nayar from Mumbai ended his second one-day international still not having batted, bowled or taken a catch.
   Man of the Series: M. S. Dhoni.

West Indies

*C. H. Gayle c Dhoni b I. Sharma		0
R. S. Morton not out		12
R. R. Sarwan not out		12
L-b 1, w 1, n-b 1		3
1/0 (1)	(1 wkt, 7.3 overs)	27

S. Chanderpaul, D. J. Bravo, D. M. Bravo, †D. Ramdin, J. E. Taylor, D. E. Bernard, S. J. Benn and R. Rampaul did not bat.

I. Sharma 4–0–17–1; Nehra 3.3–1–9–0.

India

K. D. Karthik, G. Gambhir, *†M. S. Dhoni, Yuvraj Singh, R. G. Sharma, Y. K. Pathan, A. M. Nayar, Harbhajan Singh, R. P. Singh, I. Sharma and A. Nehra.

Umpires: C. R. Duncan and N. J. Llong.
Third umpire: G. E. Greaves.   Referee: B. C. Broad.

WEST INDIES v BANGLADESH, 2009

TONY COZIER

Test matches (2): West Indies 0, Bangladesh 2
One-day internationals (3): West Indies 0, Bangladesh 3
Twenty20 international (1): West Indies 1, Bangladesh 0

On their second tour of the Caribbean, Bangladesh were inadvertently provided with all the circumstances to transform their habitual Test agony into historic success.

They arrived to find the perennial row between the West Indies Cricket Board and the West Indies Players' Association simmering ominously; it came to the boil a couple of days before the First Test when, under advice from the WIPA, all 13 players selected (captain Chris Gayle, Adrian Barath, Sulieman Benn, Dwayne Bravo, Shivnarine Chanderpaul, Narsingh Deonarine, Runako Morton, Brendan Nash, Denesh Ramdin, Ravi Rampaul, Andrew Richardson, Ramnaresh Sarwan and Jerome Taylor) declared themselves unavailable, as did several others who would have qualified as their replacements.

From the severely reduced residue, the selectors hurriedly assembled teams for the two Tests, three one-day internationals and one Twenty20 international. Most players had no international experience: there were seven debutants in the First Test at St Vincent – the most for West Indies since their inaugural match in England in 1928 – and only two of those had played one-day internationals before. The captain was Floyd Reifer, who turned 37 before the one-day series; he had played the last of his four previous Tests ten years earlier.

Bangladesh's unexpected advantage was further enhanced by pitches that favoured their strength in spin bowling and, conversely, confirmed West Indies' weakness against it. Coach John Dyson and captain Reifer hopped around the Caribbean imploring groundstaff to provide surfaces with pace and bounce; they were left fuming when, despite promises, they got the opposite.

The upshot was a clean sweep of Tests and one-day internationals by Bangladesh, a dramatic turnaround from their usual misfortunes. Their only previous Test win had come at home to Zimbabwe four years earlier, leading to their only previous Test series victory. They bettered this by winning 2–0 overseas, and followed up with their first 100% record in a one-day series against a Test side other than Zimbabwe. West Indies' consolation win came in the final match, a solitary Twenty20.

None of Bangladesh's victories was straightforward; they trailed by 69 on first innings at St Vincent, slid to 67 for four seeking 215 at Grenada, and had to amass their highest winning score chasing in the second one-day international. The principal difference was confidence. Bangladesh's grew by the day, while the ad hoc West Indies side lacked the experience to capitalise on promising positions. Unfairly, if not surprisingly, the board identified Dyson as their scapegoat, firing him from what was a hopeless job within two weeks of the tour's end.

It was impossible to make a proper assessment of either the results or individual performances. Bangladesh had to place their triumphs over little more than a third-choice line-up into perspective; West Indies' selectors needed to remember Bangladesh's previous record when deciding who to retain when they next had a full list of players available.

There was one indisputable individual advance for Bangladesh. Shakib Al Hasan brought with him a burgeoning reputation as a left-hand bat and slow left-armer; this was further enhanced, not least by his leadership qualities. The captaincy came to him by default on the third day of the First Test when Mashrafe bin Mortaza injured his knee. Mortaza himself was leading Bangladesh for the first time, after Mohammad Ashraful was sacked following the World Twenty20 campaign in June.

Shakib thrived with his new responsibility; he was Man of the Series in the Tests – in which he took 13 wickets and turned trouble into triumph with a counter-attacking, unbeaten 96 in Grenada – and again in the one-day

Plenty to smile about: Shakib Al Hasan shows off the trophy for the winners of the Test series.

internationals, with two fifties and an economy-rate of 3.4 an over. There was a calm, smiling assurance in whatever he did. Still 22, Shakib is sure to be vital to Bangladesh's long-term prospects. Left-hander Tamim Iqbal confirmed his position as the established opening batsman with a maiden Test hundred, setting up victory in St Vincent in a century stand with Junaid Siddique. Raqibul Hasan and the little wicketkeeper Mushfiqur Rahim also played important innings, but it was not until the limited-overs matches that Ashraful, perhaps unsettled by losing the captaincy, found his form. In his first Test series, Mahmudullah showed all-round promise.

By and large, the key to Bangladesh's achievement was spin; they will rarely find pitches and batting so co-operative. West Indies, on the other hand, relied on the contrasting pace of Kemar Roach and Darren Sammy. In spite of the slow surfaces, Roach, a trim 21-year-old, was genuinely fast and hostile, one for the future whoever else might be involved. He took to kissing the West Indies badge on his shirt after every wicket; he did so 23 times in all, six in the first innings at Grenada, five in the first one-day international. The experienced Sammy, several miles an hour slower, used control and movement off the seam for five-wicket innings returns in both Tests.

David Bernard, whose previous Test had been against Australia in 2003, was the only West Indian comfortable against the variations of flight and spin, passing 50 three times in the Tests. His useful medium-pace bowling and athletic fielding enhanced his value. Travis Dowlin, a 32-year-old journeyman in his 12th first-class season, made the most of his chance with 95 and 49 in the Second Test and an unbeaten 100 in the second one-day international – the only West Indian hundred of the tour. Omar Phillips, a limited left-handed opener and one of four players from the University of the West Indies, was within six of a century on Test debut, but the batting generally lacked quality.

Only in Dominica, hosting international cricket for the first time at the new Windsor Park Stadium (financed and constructed by the Chinese), was there more than a sprinkling of spectators. Given the widespread public dissatisfaction with the never-ending feud between board and players, and the quality of cricket between two teams effectively below Test standard, it was no surprise.

BANGLADESHI TOURING PARTY

Mashrafe bin Mortaza (*captain*), Shakib Al Hasan (*vice-captain*), Enamul Haque, jun., Imrul Kayes, Junaid Siddique, Mahbubul Alam, Mahmudullah, Mehrab Hossain, jun., Mohammad Ashraful, Mushfiqur Rahim, Raqibul Hasan, Rubel Hossain, Saghir Hossain, Shahadat Hossain, Tamim Iqbal. *Coach:* J. D. Siddons.

Mashrafe bin Mortaza was injured during the First Test; he was replaced in the squad by Nazmul Hossain, while Shakib Al Hasan took over the captaincy. Mushfiqur Rahim was promoted to the vice-captaincy for the one-day series which followed, when Abdur Razzak, Naeem Islam and Syed Rasel replaced Enamul Haque, Saghir Hossain and Shahadat Hossain.

Note: Matches in this section which were not first-class are signified by a dagger.

At Bridgetown, Barbados, July 3, 4, 5, 2009. **Drawn.** Toss: Bangladeshis. **Bangladeshis 195** (Mohammad Ashraful 50; K. A. J. Roach 5-62, R. A. Austin 5-71) **and 233-5** (Tamim Iqbal 72, Imrul Kayes 44, Raqibul Hasan 49*, Shakib Al Hasan 33; R. A. Austin 4-65; **West Indies A 248** (S. Chattergoon 50, D. C. Thomas 105; Shahadat Hossain 3-54, Shakib Al Hasan 3-72). *First-class debut:* A. S. Creary.

Trinidadian Adrian Barath was named in the Test squad after opening for West Indies A, but thanks to the player strike it was Kemar Roach, who claimed five in an innings for the first time, and off-spinner Ryan Austin, with match-best figures of 9-136, who eventually made their Test debuts. Devon Thomas batted four hours for a maiden first-class hundred. Tamim Iqbal and Imrul Kayes shared an opening stand of 123 in the Bangladeshis' improved second innings.

WEST INDIES v BANGLADESH

First Test Match

At Arnos Vale, St Vincent, July 9, 10, 11, 12, 13, 2009. Bangladesh won by 95 runs. Toss: Bangladesh. Test debuts: R. A. Austin, T. M. Dowlin, N. O. Miller, O. J. Phillips, D. M. Richards, K. A. J. Roach, C. A. K. Walton; Mahmudullah, Rubel Hossain.

The circumstances of Bangladesh's second Test victory, in their 60th match since gaining Test status nine years earlier, were not dissimilar to their first, over Zimbabwe at Chittagong in January 2005. Like Zimbabwe, West Indies were severely weakened after their leading players pulled out; and Bangladesh were further favoured by a slow pitch yielding to spin that might have been in the middle of Chittagong's M. A. Aziz Stadium, rather than the Arnos Vale Playing Fields in the heart of the Caribbean.

Not since their inaugural Test, in England in 1928, had West Indies fielded so many debutants. The belated withdrawal of the 13 players originally chosen, in the latest of their contract disputes with the West Indies Cricket Board, meant frantic telephone calls by selectors seeking out those still willing, and eager, to play in spite of a directive from the Players' Association. They finally announced a squad of 15. Four came from the Combined Campuses & Colleges team based at the University of the West Indies campus in Barbados

MOST TESTS MISSED BETWEEN APPEARANCES

Tests		Previous Test	Comeback Test
114	M. P. Bicknell (England)	5th Test v A, 1993	4th Test v SA, 2003
109	**F. L. Reifer (West Indies) . . . .**	**5th Test v SA, 1998-99**	**1st Test v B, 2009**
104	Younis Ahmed (Pakistan)	2nd Test v NZ, 1969-70	3rd Test v I, 1986-87
103	D. Shackleton (England)	1st Test v I, 1951-52	2nd Test v WI, 1963
96	H. L. Jackson (England)	3rd Test v NZ, 1949	3rd Test v A, 1961
86	P. I. Pocock (England)	3rd Test v WI, 1976	4th Test v WI, 1984

(whose principal, Sir Hilary Beckles, is a WICB director); among them was the captain, Floyd Reifer, who had played his last Test in South Africa ten years before. Also included, but eventually released to return to the annual regional Under-19 tournament, were 16-year-old opener Kraigg Brathwaite, a prolific scorer in schools and club cricket with two first-class games for Barbados behind him, and Jamaican Andre Creary, who had made his first-class debut a few days earlier for West Indies A. The home side counted 22 Tests in their starting eleven, Bangladesh 157.

Yet West Indies still held the advantage over the first three days, securing a first-innings lead of 69 that appeared crucial. Usually daunted by such an equation, Bangladesh took control once they recognised the limitations in class and experience of their makeshift opposition. The outcome was determined by the home team's weakness in spin, both bowling and batting, over the last two innings.

A maiden Test hundred from Tamim Iqbal and his second-wicket partnership of 146 with fellow left-hander Junaid Siddique were the basis of a match-winning total. And, despite a familiar collapse on the final morning, when Bangladesh's last five wickets tumbled for 18, Shakib Al Hasan, who had assumed the captaincy after a knee injury ended Mashrafe bin Mortaza's tour early on the third day, and debutant Mahmudullah exposed West Indies' incompetence against the turning ball. Only Bernard, with his second fifty in the match, was untroubled and unbeaten as Bangladesh completed a notable triumph, their first in a Test overseas, with 9.5 overs remaining.

Torrential downpours, not uncommon in the southern Caribbean at the start of the hurricane season, had restricted the first day to 18.5 overs; with further rain, only the efficient outfield drainage installed for the 2007 World Cup, when Arnos Vale was a venue for warm-up matches, prevented any more lengthy delays. When play resumed, Bangladesh never got going against disciplined bowling and fielding; it took the forthright late-order approach of Mushfiqur Rahim, Mortaza and Shahadat Hossain, who hit ten fours and three sixes between them, to raise 89 from the last three wickets.

The left-hander Omar Phillips, a second-year history undergraduate, shored up West Indies' top order for three and three-quarter hours, almost creating history himself until a loose drive to cover denied him a hundred on debut and provided another newcomer, Rubel Hossain, a 19-year-old fast bowler with a slingshot action, with the second of his three wickets. Bernard played pleasantly, Sammy attacked effectively, but West Indies' uncertainty against spin was evident as their last six wickets went for 80.

The result was all but settled by the end of the fourth day, when Bangladesh were ahead by 252. Tamim profited from chances to slip at 30, off Sammy, and to midwicket at 76, off Ryan Austin's off-spin, but was otherwise assured in becoming Bangladesh's ninth Test centurion. He struck 17 fours in five hours and 11 minutes before pulling a low catch to mid-on. Siddique was equally solid but, when he became the first of Sammy's five victims, the innings faltered. Bangladesh appeared unsure how to capitalise on their unaccustomed ascendancy, but their doubts were soon dispelled by the jittery West Indian batsmen. Dale Richards was run out in the third over, carelessly lingering out of his ground waiting for an umpiring decision on an lbw appeal, and only Bernard coped with the combination of Shakib's left-arm spin and Mahmudullah's off-breaks and straight balls.

The sprinkling of spectators, no more than a few hundred at any time, reflected the public's disenchantment with the continuing wrangling in West Indian cricket. Not that it mattered to the celebrating Bangladeshis – the eleven on the field and the millions back home watching on live television – when victory was achieved in the final hour.

Man of the Match: Tamim Iqbal.

Close of play: First day, Bangladesh 42-0 (Tamim Iqbal 14, Imrul Kayes 26); Second day, West Indies 17-1 (Phillips 0, Austin 1); Third day, Bangladesh 26-0 (Tamim Iqbal 11, Imrul Kayes 14); Fourth day, Bangladesh 321-5 (Shakib Al Hasan 26, Mushfiqur Rahim 28).

Bangladesh

Tamim Iqbal c Reifer b Best	14	– c Dowlin b Bernard	128
Imrul Kayes lbw b Sammy	33	– c Roach b Austin	24
Junaid Siddique c Dowlin b Bernard	27	– c Richards b Sammy	78
Raqibul Hasan c Sammy b Bernard	14	– b Sammy	18
Mohammad Ashraful c Walton b Best	6	– lbw b Roach	3
Shakib Al Hasan c Richards b Roach	17	– c Austin b Sammy	30
†Mushfiqur Rahim run out	36	– b Roach	37
Mahmudullah c Phillips b Roach	9	– lbw b Roach	8
*Mashrafe bin Mortaza c Walton b Roach	39	– c Roach b Sammy	0
Shahadat Hossain c Walton b Austin	33	– not out	0
Rubel Hossain not out	3	– lbw b Sammy	1
B 2, l-b 2, w 1, n-b 2	7	L-b 9, w 2, n-b 7	18

1/45 (1) 2/49 (2) 3/79 (4) 4/98 (3)   (88.2 overs) 238
5/100 (5) 6/121 (6) 7/149 (8)
8/172 (7) 9/207 (9) 10/238 (10)

1/82 (2) 2/228 (1)   (120.1 overs) 345
3/258 (3) 4/261 (5)
5/267 (4) 6/327 (6) 7/342 (8)
8/344 (9) 9/344 (7) 10/345 (11)

Best 17-4-58-2; Roach 23-11-46-3; Sammy 19-7-38-1; Bernard 11-2-30-2; Austin 13.2-5-35-1; Miller 5-1-27-0. *Second Innings*—Roach 26-4-67-3; Best 13-3-49-0; Austin 30-4-78-1; Sammy 30.1-6-70-5; Miller 17-4-40-0; Bernard 4-0-32-1.

West Indies

D. M. Richards lbw b Shakib Al Hasan	13	– run out	14
O. J. Phillips c Raqibul Hasan b Rubel Hossain	94	– lbw b Shakib Al Hasan	14
R. A. Austin c Imrul Kayes b Rubel Hossain	17	– (9) lbw b Mahmudullah	0
T. M. Dowlin lbw b Shakib Al Hasan	22	– (3) c Imrul Kayes b Mahmudullah	19
*F. L. Reifer c Shakib Al Hasan b Mahmudullah	25	– (4) lbw b Mahmudullah	19
D. E. Bernard c sub (Mehrab Hossain, jun.) b Shahadat Hossain	53	– (5) not out	52
†C. A. K. Walton c Shakib Al Hasan b Mahmudullah	0	– (6) lbw b Mahmudullah	10
D. J. G. Sammy b Mahmudullah	48	– (7) c Shahadat Hossain b Shakib Al Hasan	19
N. O. Miller c Mushfiqur Rahim b Rubel Hossain	0	– (8) c Mushfiqur Rahim b Mohammad Ashraful	5
K. A. J. Roach c sub (Mehrab Hossain, jun.) b Mohammad Ashraful	6	– c Mushfiqur Rahim b Mahmudullah	3
T. L. Best not out	1	– lbw b Shakib Al Hasan	9
B 4, l-b 3, w 2, n-b 19	28	B 5, l-b 5, w 2, n-b 5	17

1/15 (1) 2/94 (3) 3/142 (4)   (95.1 overs) 307
4/176 (2) 5/227 (5) 6/227 (7)
7/267 (6) 8/267 (9) 9/306 (10) 10/307 (8)

1/20 (1) 2/33 (2)   (70.1 overs) 181
3/69 (4) 4/72 (3)
5/82 (6) 6/119 (7) 7/151 (8)
8/164 (9) 9/172 (10) 10/181 (11)

Mashrafe bin Mortaza 6.3-0-26-0; Shahadat Hossain 13-2-48-1; Shakib Al Hasan 35-10-76-2; Rubel Hossain 15-1-76-3; Mahmudullah 19.4-2-59-3; Mohammad Ashraful 6-0-15-1. *Second Innings*—Shahadat Hossain 12-2-32-0; Rubel Hossain 10-1-45-0; Shakib Al Hasan 28.1-11-39-3; Mahmudullah 15-4-51-5; Mohammad Ashraful 5-1-4-1.

Umpires: E. A. R. de Silva and A. L. Hill.
Third umpire: C. R. Duncan.   Referee: A. J. Pycroft.

WEST INDIES v BANGLADESH

Second Test Match

At St George's, Grenada, July 17, 18, 19, 20, 2009. Bangladesh won by four wickets. Toss: Bangladesh.

When Bangladesh slipped to 67 for four midway through the fourth afternoon, in quest of a target of 215, it seemed West Indies had gained the momentum in a low-scoring contest typified by indifferent batting. But Shakib Al Hasan, his qualities as captain growing with every session and his influence on the match already immense, swung it irreversibly back to his team with a calculated offensive. When he formalised Bangladesh's third Test victory with two fours and a dismissive six over long-on in the same over off Kemar Roach, he was four short of his first Test hundred, having faced 97 balls; he had also taken eight for 129 in the match. Raqibul Hasan lent sensible support in a partnership of 106 that gradually undermined West Indies' confidence; Roach, physically drained by his efforts in the first innings, when he took six for 48, could not reignite his fire, and only the persistent Sammy, with his second return of five in an innings in successive Tests, kept the home side interested.

West Indies were livid to find another shorn pitch that suited Bangladesh's strengths, even more so since it lay alongside a well-grassed strip much more to their liking. Shakib chose to bowl: he and fellow-spinners Enamul Haque and Mahmudullah, who between them accounted for nine wickets and 58 of the 76 overs, enjoyed turn and bounce not usually on offer on the opening day of a Test. Yet West Indies began strongly, passing 100 with only one down. It was once Mahmudullah had removed the aggressive Richards and Hinds, through return catches in the penultimate over before lunch, that the rot set in. Travis Dowlin carried the fight for the remainder of the innings, joined for an hour and a half by Austin in an eighth-wicket stand of 59; when Dowlin was last out, to Tamim Iqbal's overhead catch at extra cover, he was five away from a hard-fought hundred after three and a half diligent hours.

If West Indies' downfall was again spin, Bangladesh's just as predictably was pace. Tamim, Raqibul, Mushfiqur Rahim and Mahmudullah were each in for an hour and a half or more, but never settled against Roach's controlled hostility; his figures over two spells on the second afternoon were 12.5–5–20–5. By the time he led the team off the ground, his shirt was soaked by his exertions in hot, humid weather, and the badge that he kissed after each wicket even more so.

With scores virtually level, second innings would determine the outcome. Until the partnership between Raqibul and Shakib, the result seemed to hang on more feeble batting. Once again, Dowlin and Bernard were the only West Indians to resist against the obligatory diet of spin. Dowlin, offering no stroke to Enamul, appeared unlucky to be ruled lbw one away from his second half-century of the match; Bernard advanced past his third in the series before he was ninth out to the 13th ball of a rain-delayed fourth day. No one else reached 30.

Bangladesh's stuttering start to the run-chase reflected an ingrained lack of self-belief. But that was not a condition afflicting Shakib, who quickly seized the initiative with his counter-attack. Within minutes of completing the job, he stepped forward to receive the trophy for Bangladesh's first Test series victory overseas, and personal awards for the match and the series.

As in St Vincent, the few spectators were lost in the vast stadium, constructed for the 2007 World Cup with a capacity of 16,000. The president of the Grenada Cricket Association, Cecil Greenidge, called the turn-out, estimated at 500 a day, a "great disappointment" and a "disaster". The causes were obvious.

Man of the Match: Shakib Al Hasan.   *Man of the Series:* Shakib Al Hasan.

Close of play: First day, Bangladesh 35-1 (Tamim Iqbal 14, Enamul Haque 5); Second day, West Indies 56-1 (Phillips 17, Dowlin 23); Third day, West Indies 192-8 (Bernard 61, Best 4).

West Indies

D. M. Richards c and b Mahmudullah	69	– lbw b Shakib Al Hasan	12
O. J. Phillips c Tamim Iqbal b Shakib Al Hasan	23	– c Mohammad Ashraful b Shakib Al Hasan	29
T. M. Dowlin c Tamim Iqbal b Shakib Al Hasan	95	– lbw b Enamul Haque	49
R. O. Hinds c and b Mahmudullah	2	– c Mahmudullah b Shakib Al Hasan	2
*F. L. Reifer lbw b Mahmudullah	1	– lbw b Mahmudullah	3
D. E. Bernard c Mohammad Ashraful b Shakib Al Hasan	17	– st Mushfiqur Rahim b Enamul Haque	69
D. J. G. Sammy lbw b Enamul Haque	1	– c Raqibul Hasan b Enamul Haque	22
†C. A. K. Walton c Mohammad Ashraful b Enamul Haque	2	– c Mahmudullah b Shakib Al Hasan	1
R. A. Austin hit wkt b Shahadat Hossain	19	– c Tamim Iqbal b Shahadat Hossain	3
T. L. Best b Enamul Haque	0	– c Mushfiqur Rahim b Shakib Al Hasan	12
K. A. J. Roach not out	4	– not out	1
L-b 1, n-b 3	4	L-b 2, n-b 4	6

1/60 (2) 2/104 (1) 3/106 (3)   (76.1 overs) 237
4/114 (5) 5/157 (6) 6/158 (7)
7/160 (8) 8/219 (9) 9/220 (10) 10/237 (3)

1/20 (1) 2/72 (2)   (70.5 overs) 209
3/84 (4) 4/95 (5)
5/110 (3) 6/166 (7) 7/167 (8)
8/187 (9) 9/201 (6) 10/209 (10)

Shahadat Hossain 9–2–30–1; Rubel Hossain 6–0–27–0; Enamul Haque 24–2–62–3; Shakib Al Hasan 21.1–7–59–3; Mahmudullah 13–2–44–3; Mohammad Ashraful 3–0–14–0. *Second Innings—* Rubel Hossain 9–1–34–0; Shahadat Hossain 4–0–18–1; Enamul Haque 17–3–48–3; Shakib Al Hasan 24.5–3–70–5; Mahmudullah 15–1–37–1; Mohammad Ashraful 1–1–0–0.

Bangladesh

Tamim Iqbal c Walton b Bernard	37	– c Walton b Sammy	18
Imrul Kayes c Walton b Sammy	14	– c Sammy b Roach	8
Enamul Haque, jun. c Walton b Roach	13		
Junaid Siddique b Austin	7	– (3) c Reifer b Sammy	5
Raqibul Hasan c Walton b Roach	44	– (4) c and b Sammy	65
Mohammad Ashraful c Sammy b Hinds	12	– (5) c Walton b Sammy	3
*Shakib Al Hasan c Austin b Roach	16	– (6) not out	96
†Mushfiqur Rahim c Walton b Roach	48	– (7) c and b Sammy	12
Mahmudullah c Austin b Roach	28	– (8) not out	0
Shahadat Hossain c Richards b Roach	0		
Rubel Hossain not out	1		
L-b 2, w 3, n-b 7	12	B 1, l-b 3, w 2, n-b 4	10

1/26 (2) 2/51 (3) 3/75 (1) 4/77 (4)   (79.5 overs) 232
5/106 (6) 6/150 (5) 7/157 (7)
8/219 (8) 9/223 (10) 10/232 (9)

1/27 (2)   (6 wkts, 54.4 overs) 217
2/29 (1) 3/49 (3)
4/67 (5) 5/173 (4) 6/201 (7)

Roach 23.5–8–48–6; Best 17–3–47–0; Sammy 15–3–45–1; Bernard 8–0–29–1; Austin 8–0–29–1; Hinds 8–1–32–1. *Second Innings—*Best 9–0–38–0; Bernard 9–1–33–0; Roach 13.4–4–68–1; Sammy 16–1–55–5; Austin 3–0–13–0; Hinds 4–0–6–0.

Umpires: E. A. R. de Silva and A. L. Hill.
Third umpire: N. A. Malcolm. Referee: A. J. Pycroft.

†At Benjamin's Park, Portsmouth, Dominica, July 24, 2009. **Bangladeshis won by 16 runs.** Toss: Bangladeshis. **Bangladeshis 167-6** (25 overs) (Raqibul Hasan 34, Mushfiqur Rahim 82*); **University of West Indies Vice-Chancellor's XI 151-8** (25 overs) (O. J. Phillips 49; Naeem Islam 3-19).
   The match was scheduled for 50 overs but reduced to 25 by rain. Acting-captain Mushfiqur Rahim rescued his side from 38-3 and set up their eventual victory with 82 in 59 balls, hitting four fours and three sixes.

†WEST INDIES v BANGLADESH

First One-Day International

At Roseau, Dominica, July 26, 2009. Bangladesh won by 52 runs. Toss: West Indies. One-day international debuts: T. M. Dowlin, N. T. Pascal, D. M. Richards.

This was the first international staged in Dominica, at the two-year-old Windsor Park stadium, and a wicket fell to the very first ball, from Roach, when Tamim Iqbal edged to the keeper. But though Roach bagged five victims, West Indies were rarely in contention. Mohammad Ashraful returned to the form that had eluded him in the Tests, Shakib Al Hasan retained his, and Mahmudullah hit the only two sixes in a challenging total. In response to home coach John Dyson's pleas, the head groundsman had promised a pitch with pace and bounce; in the event, it was little different to those in the two Tests, and West Indies were again undone by Bangladesh's four spinners. Handed the new ball, slow left-armer Abdur Razzak, who had joined the tourists for the one-day series, trapped Richards with his first legitimate delivery, and finished with four for 39. Only Devon Smith, recalled after his omission from the Tests, and Bernard batted with any confidence.

Man of the Match: Abdur Razzak.

Bangladesh

Tamim Iqbal c Fletcher b Roach	0	Syed Rasel b Roach	7
Junaid Siddique c Lewis b Bernard	36	Rubel Hossain not out	1
Mohammad Ashraful run out	57		
Raqibul Hasan b Roach	12	B 1, l-b 8, w 10	19
*Shakib Al Hasan c Dowlin b Roach	54		
†Mushfiqur Rahim c Sammy b Lewis	11	1/0 (1) 2/74 (2) (9 wkts, 50 overs) 246	
Mahmudullah c Bernard b Miller	42	3/97 (4) 4/128 (3)	
Naeem Islam not out	7	5/149 (6) 6/228 (7) 7/230 (5)	
Abdur Razzak lbw b Roach	0	8/231 (9) 9/241 (10) 10 overs: 50-1	

Roach 10–0–44–5; Pascal 4–0–29–0; Sammy 9–0–48–0; Bernard 10–1–31–1; Miller 9–0–50–1; Lewis 8–0–35–1.

West Indies

D. M. Richards lbw b Abdur Razzak	1	K. A. J. Roach run out	0
†A. D. S. Fletcher b Syed Rasel	5	N. T. Pascal lbw b Abdur Razzak	0
D. S. Smith lbw b Shakib Al Hasan	65		
*F. L. Reifer c Raqibul Hasan b Mahmudullah	3	B 4, l-b 1, w 2	7
T. M. Dowlin b Abdur Razzak	10		
D. E. Bernard c Tamim Iqbal b Naeem Islam	38	1/2 (1) 2/8 (2) 3/23 (4) (43.4 overs) 194	
D. J. G. Sammy lbw b Abdur Razzak	28	4/42 (5) 5/120 (3) 6/130 (6)	
R. N. Lewis b Rubel Hossain	21	7/171 (8) 8/188 (7) 9/191 (10)	
N. O. Miller not out	16	10/194 (11) 10 overs: 34-3	

Syed Rasel 8–0–30–1; Abdur Razzak 9.4–0–39–4; Mahmudullah 7–0–38–1; Shakib Al Hasan 8–0–26–1; Naeem Islam 7–0–28–1; Rubel Hossain 4–0–28–1.

Umpires: B. R. Doctrove and A. L. Hill.
Third umpire: C. R. Duncan. Referee: R. S. Mahanama.

†WEST INDIES v BANGLADESH

Second One-Day International

At Roseau, Dominica, July 28, 2009. Bangladesh won by three wickets. Toss: West Indies. One-day international debuts: D. C. Thomas, G. C. Tonge.

An extraordinary loss of control by Roach, until then West Indies' most effective bowler, proved decisive. With Bangladesh requiring 56 off eight overs to reach 275 – then their highest successful one-day run-chase – he conceded 18 in the 43rd over, with Mushfiqur Rahim thumping two fours and Shakib Al Hasan pulling what should have been the last ball of the over for six. Because it was

Roach's second full toss above waist height, it was called no-ball and forced his instant disqualification from the attack. With only five main bowlers, Reifer asked wicketkeeper Devon Thomas, making his international debut, to finish the over – and soon gave him another, in which he took two wickets. But by then the force was with Bangladesh, who clinched the series with an over to spare. West Indies owed their total mainly to Dowlin's innings of two halves; his first fifty took 88 balls, his second 29 as he, Lewis and Sammy plundered 98 off the last ten overs. Despite Mohammad Ashraful's second successive half-century and Shakib's consistent form, Bangladesh were well behind the required rate until Roach's meltdown. Fifteen wides were also significant.

Man of the Match: Shakib Al Hasan.

West Indies

D. M. Richards run out	20	R. N. Lewis b Syed Rasel		22
A. D. S. Fletcher c Naeem Islam		D. J. G. Sammy not out		24
b Shakib Al Hasan	22			
D. S. Smith run out	44			
T. M. Dowlin not out	100	L-b 3, w 10		13
*F. L. Reifer c Shakib Al Hasan				
b Naeem Islam	7	1/33 (2) 2/52 (1)	(6 wkts, 50 overs)	274
D. E. Bernard st Mushfiqur Rahim		3/118 (3) 4/134 (5)		
b Abdur Razzak	22	5/181 (6) 6/245 (7)	10 overs: 50-1	

†D. C. Thomas, K. A. J. Roach and G. C. Tonge did not bat.

Syed Rasel 8-0-61-1; Rubel Hossain 5-0-38-0; Shakib Al Hasan 10-2-42-1; Abdur Razzak 10-0-58-1; Naeem Islam 8-0-26-1; Mahmudullah 9-1-46-0.

Bangladesh

Tamim Iqbal c Bernard b Roach	29	Naeem Islam not out		3
Junaid Siddique c Roach b Bernard	22	Abdur Razzak not out		11
Mohammad Ashraful c Richards b Lewis	64	B 5, l-b 5, w 15, n-b 2		27
Raqibul Hasan c Reifer b Bernard	20			
*Shakib Al Hasan c Richards b Sammy	65	1/46 (2) 2/64 (1)	(7 wkts, 49 overs)	276
†Mushfiqur Rahim c Sammy b Thomas	31	3/116 (4) 4/190 (3)		
Mahmudullah c sub (N. O. Miller) b Thomas	3	5/238 (5) 6/251 (7) 7/261 (6)	10 overs: 45-0	

Syed Rasel and Rubel Hossain did not bat.

Roach 7.5-0-55-1; Tonge 10-0-49-0; Sammy 10-0-39-1; Bernard 10-0-59-2; Lewis 10-0-53-1; Thomas 1.1-0-11-2.

Umpires: B. R. Doctrove and A. L. Hill.
Third umpire: N. A. Malcolm. Referee: R. S. Mahanama.

†WEST INDIES v BANGLADESH

Third One-Day International

At Basseterre, St Kitts, July 31, 2009. Bangladesh won by three wickets. Toss: West Indies. One-day international debut: K. O. A. Powell.

For a change, West Indies were set back by two of Bangladesh's quicker bowlers, each in his first international of the tour. Mahbubul Alam's first ball was a wide, his second removed 19-year-old debutant left-hander Kieran Powell; at the other end, Nazmul Hossain bowled Smith with his seventh delivery. Fletcher responded with three sixes in 52 off 42 balls, but he was not the only West Indian seduced by the short boundaries and caught in the deep. Reifer spent 79 balls over 40, his only decent score of the series, and Sammy supplied late momentum with 40 off 33. Tamim Iqbal punched five fours in Roach's first two overs but, once he drove Sammy to mid-on, the balance swung back towards West Indies. It was even at 133 for five, when Roach bowled Junaid Siddique leg stump in the 28th over, but shifted moments later when he had Mahmudullah dropped at slip. Mahmudullah proceeded to an unbeaten 51, guiding Bangladesh to a series sweep with seven balls remaining.

Man of the Match: Mahmudullah.   *Man of the Series:* Shakib Al Hasan.

West Indies

K. O. A. Powell lbw b Mahbubul Alam . . .	0	N. O. Miller c Mahmudullah b Naeem Islam	13
A. D. S. Fletcher c Mohammad Ashraful		K. A. J. Roach c Tamim Iqbal	
b Abdur Razzak .	52	b Mahmudullah .	10
D. S. Smith b Nazmul Hossain	4	G. C. Tonge run out	1
T. M. Dowlin run out	38		
*F. L. Reifer c Shakib Al Hasan		L-b 2, w 18	20
b Mahbubul Alam .	40		
D. E. Bernard c Mohammad Ashraful		1/1 (1) 2/10 (3) 3/86 (2) (47.4 overs)	248
b Mahmudullah .	1	4/115 (4) 5/124 (6) 6/188 (5)	
D. J. G. Sammy c and b Abdur Razzak	40	7/190 (7) 8/221 (9) 9/244 (10)	
†D. C. Thomas not out	29	10/248 (11) 10 overs: 58-2	

Mahbubul Alam 6–0–42–2; Nazmul Hossain 5–0–27–1; Abdur Razzak 10–0–63–2; Shakib Al Hasan 9.4–2–28–0; Naeem Islam 10–1–48–1; Mahmudullah 7–0–38–2.

Bangladesh

Tamim Iqbal c Powell b Sammy	30	Naeem Islam c Thomas b Roach	26
Junaid Siddique b Roach	55	Abdur Razzak not out	6
Mohammad Ashraful c Thomas b Bernard .	19		
Raqibul Hasan c Reifer b Roach	5	L-b 2, w 8	10
*Shakib Al Hasan c sub (D. M. Richards)			
b Roach .	16	1/54 (1) 2/83 (3) (7 wkts, 48.5 overs)	249
†Mushfiqur Rahim c Thomas b Sammy	31	3/96 (4) 4/128 (5)	
Mahmudullah not out	51	5/133 (2) 6/183 (6) 7/232 (8) 10 overs: 56-1	

Mahbubul Alam and Nazmul Hossain did not bat.

Roach 9.5–1–63–4; Tonge 10–2–59–0; Sammy 10–1–37–2; Bernard 10–0–47–1; Miller 9–0–41–0.

Umpires: C. R. Duncan and A. L. Hill.
Third umpire: N. A. Malcolm.   Referee: R. S. Mahanama.

†WEST INDIES v BANGLADESH

Twenty20 International

At Basseterre, St Kitts, August 2, 2009. West Indies won by five wickets. Toss: Bangladesh. Twenty20 debut: D. C. Thomas. Twenty20 international debuts: D. E. Bernard, T. M. Dowlin, N. O. Miller, F. L. Reifer, D. M. Richards, G. C. Tonge; Nazmul Hossain.

West Indies made the most of Bangladesh's distinctly end-of-term approach to gain a consolation victory at the last. While the tourists squandered wickets with careless strokes and running, the home side were unusually sharp in the field. Their four run-outs were all from direct hits, two by Sammy, who also dismissed Junaid Siddique and Mohammad Ashraful with his fourth and fifth balls. At 66 for seven, Bangladesh were in danger of undercutting their lowest Twenty20 total (83 against Sri Lanka, in the 2007-08 world tournament in South Africa) before Mahmudullah guided them past 100. Shakib Al Hasan bowled Richards with the first ball of West Indies' reply, but Smith, Dowlin and the captain, Reifer, ensured they had something at least to show from a distressing series.

Man of the Match: D. J. G. Sammy.

Bangladesh

		B	4	6
Tamim Iqbal c 5 b 10	7	6	1	0
Junaid Siddique c 3 b 6	5	6	1	0
Mohammad Ashraful c 10 b 6	0	1	0	0
Naeem Islam run out	27	18	2	2
*Shakib Al Hasan b 11	17	16	3	0
†Mushfiqur Rahim run out	3	9	0	0
Mahmudullah run out	21	27	2	0
Raqibul Hasan lbw b 11	1	4	0	0
Mehrab Hossain, jun. run out	10	17	1	0
Nazmul Hossain not out	3	12	0	0
Rubel Hossain not out	8	5	1	0
L-b 6, w 5, n-b 5	16			

6 overs: 43-4   (20 overs) 118-9

1/12 2/12 3/12 4/43 5/57 6/62 7/66 8/92 9/103

Tonge 4–0–25–1; Sammy 4–0–33–2; Miller 4–0–22–2; Roach 4–0–15–0; Bernard 4–0–17–0.

West Indies

		B	4	6
D. M. Richards b 5	0	1	0	0
A. D. S. Fletcher lbw b 10	8	14	1	0
D. S. Smith c 6 b 11	37	27	3	2
T. M. Dowlin not out	37	37	5	0
*F. L. Reifer c 7 b 3	22	20	2	1
D. J. G. Sammy c 7 b 3	6	2	0	1
D. E. Bernard not out	1	1	0	0
L-b 4, w 3, n-b 1	8			

6 overs: 46-2   (16.5 overs) 119-5

1/0 2/46 3/67 4/107 5/114

†D. C. Thomas, K. A. J. Roach, G. C. Tonge and N. O. Miller did not bat.

Shakib Al Hasan 4–0–13–1; Naeem Islam 2–0–21–0; Mahmudullah 1–0–15–0; Nazmul Hossain 2–0–15–1; Mehrab Hossain 2.5–0–20–0; Rubel Hossain 3–0–13–1; Mohammad Ashraful 2–0–18–2.

Umpires: C. R. Duncan and N. A. Malcolm. Third umpire: C. E. Mack. Referee: R. S. Mahanama.

DOMESTIC CRICKET IN THE WEST INDIES, 2008-09

HAYDN GILL

The West Indian first-class competition of 2008-09 was the longest yet, with home and away rounds restored for the first time in four years, and a seventh team retained in addition to the usual six. There was no sponsor for this or the one-day tournament, as Carib Beer and KFC had both withdrawn.

Jamaica were in a class by themselves as they retained the first-class title: they were crowned champions with two rounds to play. Even with Chris Gayle and Jerome Taylor absent throughout, they were generally unstoppable. A whole-hearted team effort earned them seven victories from 12 matches.

Carlton Baugh, the dashing jockey-sized wicket-keeper-batsman, was surprisingly overlooked by the Jamaican selectors after returning from West Indies' tour of New Zealand, but made the most of his chance when finally recalled in March. He scored 484 at 60 in just five matches – the only Jamaican to average over 35 or score two centuries. The other batsmen, however, contributed when needed. Tamar Lambert was a respected leader, and enjoyed one of his better seasons with the bat, while all-rounder Dave Bernard's consistent form won him a place on the England tour. But much of Jamaica's progress centred on a varied bowling attack; other teams could not get their measure. Leg-spinner Odean Brown blossomed with 52 wickets, and combined with slow left-armer Nikita Miller, fellow leg-spinner Gavin Wallace and tall fast bowler Andrew Richardson to form a potent force.

Andres Leighton, AP/PA

Carlton Baugh

Windward Islands, so often the regional tournaments' whipping boys, finished second for the first time since 1982-83. They won six matches, but inconsistency meant they also lost five. The all-round efforts of captain Rawl Lewis and Darren Sammy, along with off-spinner Shane Shillingford's 56 wickets, were the principal factors in their improvement. Lewis resigned the captaincy after two heavy defeats in January, but an emergency meeting of the Windwards board persuaded him to carry on after resolving his differences with manager Lockhart Sebastien.

Leeward Islands also raised their game after three poor seasons to claim third place. Runako Morton, one of three men to scale 1,000 runs in the tournament, was their stand-out batsman, and Gavin Tonge grabbed 44 wickets, the most by a fast bowler (nine of the top ten wicket-takers were spinners).

Trinidad & Tobago, who defeated Barbados in the regional limited-overs final in November, a few weeks after beating Middlesex to win the Twenty20 Stanford Champions Cup, were badly affected by rain and finished fourth. Two youngsters appeared to be West Indies players in waiting: little opener Adrian Barath piled up 845 regional runs at 44, and left-hander Darren Bravo, brother of the international all-rounder Dwayne, 605 at 43. Each scored two centuries. Barath went on to score a hundred on Test debut in Australia.

Barbados started promisingly; four wins in six games, three of them by an innings, put them second, nine points behind Jamaica, at the halfway stage. Then they suffered an unexplained slump, losing four successive matches – all but one against opponents they had already beaten.

The **Combined Campuses & Colleges**, a team introduced the previous season, managed four wins but finished next to bottom. Two former Barbados players enjoyed notable success: off-spinner Ryan Austin, out of favour with the Barbados selectors, made an outstanding first-class comeback and was the leading wicket-taker with 60, while 36-year-old Floyd Reifer used his experience to gather 1,001 runs. Austin made an unexpected Test debut, and Reifer found himself leading West Indies ten years after his last Test, when the long-running dispute between the West Indies Cricket Board and the West Indies Players' Association resulted in the entire first-choice squad pulling out of a series with Bangladesh.

Guyana embarrassingly lost their first four matches (all away), never won, and predictably took the cellar position. They had the consolation of producing the leading run-scorer, Narsingh Deonarine, whose 1,068 runs from 11 matches easily beat the previous record for the first-class tournament, 974 from eight, by Stuart Williams for Leeward Islands in 2001-02.

FIRST-CLASS AVERAGES, 2008-09

BATTING

(Qualification: 500 runs, average 30.00)

	M	I	NO	R	HS	100s	Avge	Ct
R. R. Sarwan (*West Indies*)	5	6	0	626	291	3	104.33	1
†A. J. Strauss (*England XI*)	6	10	1	638	169	3	70.88	1
P. D. Collingwood (*England XI*)	6	8	0	512	161	2	64.00	8
L. M. P. Simmons (*T&T, West Indies & WI A*)	8	14	1	817	282	2	62.84	6
†N. Deonarine (*Guyana*)	11	20	2	1,068	198	2	59.33	7
R. S. Morton (*Leeward Islands*)	11	18	0	1,010	231	2	56.11	8
D. M. Richards (*Barbados*)	6	10	0	523	117	2	52.30	4
R. S. Smith (*Barbados*)	11	19	3	833	155	2	52.06	14
†R. O. Hinds (*Barbados & West Indies*)	12	17	0	883	240	3	51.94	9
A. B. Barath (*Trinidad & Tobago, WI A*)	12	22	2	990	192	3	49.50	10
†F. L. Reifer (*Campuses & Colleges*)	12	21	0	1,001	140	3	47.66	17
D. Ganga (*Trinidad & Tobago*)	12	21	5	739	96*	0	46.18	9
†D. M. Bravo (*Trinidad & Tobago*)	9	14	0	605	111	2	43.21	14
R. T. Crandon (*Guyana*)	8	16	3	561	136*	1	43.15	2
K. A. Edwards (*Barbados*)	7	14	2	504	107	1	42.00	2
†D. S. Smith (*Windward Islands & West Indies*)	9	13	0	524	212	1	40.30	10

	M	I	NO	R	HS	100s	Avge	Ct
R. N. Lewis (*Windward Islands*)............	12	22	4	720	85	0	40.00	3
K. A. Stoute (*Barbados*)...................	9	16	0	604	186	2	37.75	1
†K. O. A. Powell (*Leeward Islands & WI A*) ...	11	18	2	582	93	0	36.37	4
D. E. Bernard (*Jamaica*)..................	12	22	3	657	97	0	34.57	12
T. L. Lambert (*Jamaica*).................	12	22	0	759	143	1	34.50	13
O. J. Phillips (*Campuses & Colleges*)........	9	18	0	601	204	1	33.38	10
†W. M. Hinds (*Jamaica*)	10	18	2	527	75	0	32.93	2
T. M. Dowlin (*Guyana*)	11	19	0	580	87	0	30.52	4

† *Left-handed batsman.*

BOWLING

(Qualification: 20 wickets, average 30.00)

	Style	O	M	R	W	BB	5W/i	Avge
N. O. Miller (*Jamaica*)	SLA	365.1	110	621	38	8-41	2	16.34
R. Rampaul (*Trinidad & Tobago*)	RFM	184	30	579	33	6-44	3	17.54
K. R. McClean (*Campuses & Colleges, WI A*)	RF	182.1	33	577	31	5-49	1	18.61
S. Shillingford (*Windward Islands*)........	OB	456.4	107	1,067	56	6-57	2	19.05
I. Khan (*Trinidad & Tobago*)	SLA	273.4	50	729	38	5-33	2	19.18
G. Wallace (*Jamaica & West Indies A*).....	LBG	203.1	27	675	34	8-20	1	19.85
P. T. Collins (*Barbados*)	LFM	147.1	33	428	20	5-31	1	21.40
O. V. Brown (*Jamaica*)	LBG	426.3	82	1,143	52	6-85	3	21.98
D. K. Butler (*Windward Islands*)...........	LFM	262.5	59	728	32	5-29	1	22.75
A. Martin (*Leeward Islands*)	LBG	368.1	87	957	42	7-81	3	22.78
A. P. Richardson (*Jamaica*)...............	RFM	217.5	36	763	33	5-55	1	23.12
K. Catlin (*Campuses & Colleges*)	RFM	132.5	11	492	21	4-56	0	23.42
D. J. G. Sammy (*Windward Islands & WI A*)	RM	197.5	42	549	23	5-67	1	23.86
V. Permaul (*Guyana*)...................	OB	316.3	76	766	32	4-42	0	23.93
R. A. Austin (*Campuses & Colleges*)	OB	543.1	109	1,444	60	6-123	3	24.06
K. A. Stoute (*Barbados*)	RFM	146	23	530	22	4-41	0	24.09
C. D. Collymore (*Barbados*).............	RFM	234.3	62	629	26	4-67	0	24.19
D. E. Bernard (*Jamaica*)	RFM	217.5	33	778	32	4-31	0	24.31
G. C. Tonge (*Leeward Islands*)	RFM	302.1	46	1,104	44	7-58	4	25.09
S. Ganga (*Trinidad & Tobago*)	OB	280	71	671	26	5-40	1	25.80
T. L. Best (*Barbados*)	RF	131.1	23	518	20	5-44	1	25.90
R. O. Hinds (*Barbados & West Indies*)	SLA	424.3	84	1,148	43	6-89	1	26.69
R. N. Lewis (*Windward Islands*)	LBG	197.5	35	563	21	5-39	1	26.80
N. T. Pascal (*Windward Islands*)..........	RF	185.5	24	697	25	5-57	1	27.88

Note: Averages exclude Bangladesh's tour in July 2009.

Full scores of the 2008-09 West Indian season can be found at www.cricinfo.com/db/ARCHIVE/
2008-09/WI_LOCAL/, www.cricketarchive.co.uk/Archive/Seasons/2008-09_WI.html and in the
ACS Overseas First-Class Annual 2009.

WICB PRESIDENT'S TROPHY 2008-09

	Played	Won	Lost	Drawn	1st-inns points	Points
Jamaica..........................	12	7	2	3	13	106
Windward Islands.................	12	6	5	1	4	79
Leeward Islands	12	5	4	3	8	77
Trinidad & Tobago................	12	2	2	8	22	70
Barbados........................	12	4	5	3	3	60
Combined Campuses & Colleges.....	12	4	4	4	0	60
Guyana	12	0	6	6	15	33

Domestic Cricket in the West Indies, 2008-09 1435

Win = 12 pts; draw = 3 pts; first-innings lead in a drawn match = 3 pts; first-innings lead in a lost match = 4 pts; no first-innings lead in a drawn match = 1 pt each.

At Police Ground, Weymouth, Barbados, January 9, 10, 11, 12, 2009. **Drawn.** Toss: Trinidad & Tobago. **Trinidad & Tobago 264** (D. Ganga 56, D. M. Bravo 97; R. O. Hinds 4-50) **and 212-3 dec** (A. B. Barath 79, L. M. P. Simmons 74); **Barbados 199** (D. M. Richards 65; S. Ganga 5-40, A. S. Jaggernauth 4-64) **and 197-4** (D. M. Richards 113). *Barbados 3 pts, Trinidad & Tobago 6 pts.*
  This was the first first-class match in Weymouth.

At Warner Park, Basseterre, St Kitts, January 9, 10, 11, 2009. **Jamaica won by six wickets.** Toss: Leeward Islands. **Leeward Islands 298** (O. A. C. Banks 108; O. V. Brown 5-82) **and 91** (K. O. A. Powell 53; G. Wallace 8-20); **Jamaica 227** (D. J. Pagon 62; A. Martin 5-48) **and 163-4.** *Jamaica 12 pts, Leeward Islands 4 pts.*
  Leg-spinner Gavin Wallace took a career-best 10–2–20–8 to dismiss Leewards for 91, and 11-73 in the match, as Jamaica started their defence of the title with a three-day victory.

At Queen's Park, St George's, Grenada, January 9, 10, 11, 2009. **Windward Islands won by an innings and 147 runs.** Toss: Guyana. **Guyana 172** (T. M. Dowlin 50; S. Shillingford 4-43) **and 95** (D. K. Butler 5-29); **Windward Islands 414-9 dec** (D. S. Smith 212, D. J. G. Sammy 57, S. Shillingford 51). *Windward Islands 12 pts.*
  Devon Smith batted throughout Windwards' innings for a maiden double-hundred (they declared when he was ninth out in the 106th over). Overwhelmed, Guyana folded for 95 and lost on the third afternoon.

At Three Ws Oval, Bridgetown, Barbados, January 16, 17, 18, 19, 2009. **Combined Campuses & Colleges won by 96 runs.** Toss: Guyana. **Combined Campuses & Colleges 265 and 300-5 dec** (N. Parris 105, C. A. K. Walton 51*); **Guyana 247** (D. O. Christian 52; K. R. McClean 5-49) **and 222** (N. Deonarine 86, R. T. Crandon 67). *Combined Campuses & Colleges 12 pts.*

At Queen's Park Oval, Port-of-Spain, Trinidad, January 16, 17, 18, 19, 2009. **Drawn.** Toss: Jamaica. **Trinidad & Tobago 202** (D. Ganga 57; O. V. Brown 4-61) **and 98-3; Jamaica 355-7 dec** (B. A. Parchment 54, W. W. Hinds 52, D. E. Bernard 75, K. H. Hibbert 60*). *Trinidad & Tobago 3 pts, Jamaica 6 pts.*

At Progress Park, St Andrew's, Grenada, January 16, 17, 18, 19, 2009. **Barbados won by an innings and 66 runs.** Toss: Windward Islands. **Barbados 395-8 dec** (R. O. Hinds 89, J. L. Carter 52, S. J. Benn 79, K. A. J. Roach 52*; S. Shillingford 4-91); **Windward Islands 192** (R. N. Lewis 84; R. O. Hinds 4-36) **and 137** (S. J. Benn 4-38). *Barbados 12 pts.*
  This was the first first-class match in St Andrew's. Ryan Hinds passed 5,000 first-class runs.

At Three Ws Oval, Bridgetown, Barbados, January 23, 24, 25, 26, 2009. **Jamaica won by 51 runs.** Toss: Combined Campuses & Colleges. **Jamaica 161** (X. M. Marshall 74) **and 165; Combined Campuses & Colleges 106** (N. O. Miller 8-41) **and 169.** *Jamaica 12 pts.*
  Slow left-armer Nikita Miller took a career-best 8-41 as Combined Campuses & Colleges collapsed for 106 (a recovery from 59-5).

At Carib Lumber Park, Philipsburg, St Maarten, January 23, 24, 25, 2009. **Barbados won by an innings and 55 runs.** Toss: Barbados. **Barbados 507** (D. M. Richards 68, R. O. Hinds 240, R. R. Nurse 59; T. A. Willett 5-92); **Leeward Islands 204** (R. S. Morton 82, T. A. Willett 70; P. T. Collins 5-31) **and 248** (R. S. Morton 102). *Barbados 12 pts.*
  Ryan Hinds reached his maiden double-hundred in 192 balls, and faced 218 in all for 240, with 35 fours and four sixes, paving the way for Barbados's second successive innings win, despite 102 in 144 balls from Runako Morton.

At Guaracara Park, Pointe-à-Pierre, Trinidad, January 23, 24, 25, 26, 2009. **Trinidad & Tobago won by 166 runs.** Toss: Trinidad & Tobago. **Trinidad & Tobago 310** (D. M. Bravo 105, K. A. Pollard 57; D. J. G. Sammy 5-67) **and 243-5 dec** (L. M. P. Simmons 62, D. Ganga 78, D. Ramdin 52*); **Windward Islands 181** (A. K. Allert 4-57) **and 206** (D. J. G. Sammy 61; A. S. Jaggernauth 6-47). *Trinidad & Tobago 12 pts.*
  Windwards captain Rawl Lewis announced his resignation after this defeat, but was persuaded to carry on.

At Three Ws Oval, Bridgetown, Barbados, January 30, 31, February 1, 2009. **Windward Islands won by seven wickets.** Toss: Windward Islands. **Combined Campuses & Colleges** 227 (N. Parris 54, F. L. Reifer 92) **and** 186 (N. Parris 57; S. Shillingford 5-47); **Windward Islands** 323 (J. Charles 55, A. D. S. Fletcher 69; R. A. Austin 5-108) **and 91-3.** *Windward Islands 12 pts.*

At Kensington Park, Kingston, Jamaica, January 30, 31, February 1, 2, 2009. **Jamaica won by six wickets.** Toss: Barbados. **Barbados** 293 **and** 221 (P. A. Browne 57*); **Jamaica** 314 (W. W. Hinds 75) **and 203-4** (W. W. Hinds 59*, D. E. Bernard 60*). *Jamaica 12 pts.*

At Grove Park, Charlestown, Nevis, January 30, 31, February 1, 2, 2009. **Leeward Islands won by ten runs.** Toss: Leeward Islands. **Leeward Islands** 225 (O. A. C. Banks 65*; V. Permaul 4-42) **and** 245 (M. V. Hodge 78; D. Bishoo 6-64); **Guyana** 229 (T. M. Dowlin 61; T. A. Willett 4-54, A. Martin 4-39) **and 231** (N. Deonarine 56, R. T. Crandon 52; A. Martin 7-81). *Leeward Islands 12 pts, Guyana 4 pts.*
   This match was moved to Nevis from Antigua, with financial reasons cited. Antigua had not staged a regional first-class game since February 2004. Leg-spinner Anthony Martin took a career-best 7-81, and 11-120 in the match, to secure Leeward Islands' first win of the season.

At Windward Park, Lucas Street, Barbados, February 6, 7, 8, 2009. **Barbados won by an innings and 59 runs.** Toss: Guyana. **Barbados** 495-8 dec (J. A. M. Haynes 104, R. O. Hinds 134, D. R. Smith 80, P. A. Browne 66, N. G. R. Charles 54*); **Guyana** 288 (T. M. Dowlin 87, R. T. Crandon 69) **and 148** (L. R. Johnson 65). *Barbados 12 pts.*
   Guyana went down to their fourth successive defeat, all away from home, as Barbados completed their third innings victory in four games.

At National Cricket Centre, Couva, Trinidad, February 6, 7, 8, 9, 2009. **Drawn.** Toss: Trinidad & Tobago. **Combined Campuses & Colleges** 315 (N. Parris 58, F. L. Reifer 82) **and 71-2** (S. Jackson 52*); **Trinidad & Tobago** 362 (L. M. P. Simmons 78, S. Ganga 90; R. A. Austin 6-123). *Trinidad & Tobago 6 pts, Combined Campuses & Colleges 3 pts.*

At Beausejour Stadium, Gros Islet, St Lucia, February 6, 7, 8, 2009. **Windward Islands won by seven wickets.** Toss: Leeward Islands. **Leeward Islands** 75 **and 283** (K. O. A. Powell 93; K. A. James 4-38); **Windward Islands** 318 (D. B. Hector 67, D. K. Butler 51*; L. S. Baker 6-84) **and 47-3.** *Windward Islands 12 pts.*
   Only Shane Jeffers (34) managed double figures as Leewards struggled from 27-5 to be bowled out for less than 100 for the second time in the season.*

At Mount Gay North Stars, Crab Hill, Barbados, February 13, 14, 15, 2009. **Barbados won by six wickets.** Toss: Barbados. **Combined Campuses & Colleges** 198 (D. R. Smith 4-45) **and** 183 (R. K. Currency 56; K. A. J. Roach 4-57); **Barbados** 271 (D. R. Smith 155, K. A. Stoute 50; K. R. McClean 4-57) **and 112-4** (K. A. Edwards 59*). *Barbados 12 pts.*
   Barbados's fourth win in five matches took them to the top of the table.

At Providence Stadium, Guyana, February 13, 14, 15, 16, 2009. **Drawn.** Toss: Jamaica. **Jamaica** 441-8 dec (D. J. Pagon 105, D. E. Bernard 97) **and 132-8 dec** (T. L. Lambert 59); **Guyana** 302 (T. M. Dowlin 72, D. O. Christian 113) **and 159-4** (L. R. Johnson 58, N. Deonarine 51*). *Guyana 3 pts, Jamaica 6 pts.*
   Travis Dowlin and Derwin Christian – who reached a maiden hundred in 99 balls – added 163 for Guyana's seventh wicket to help them halt their losing streak.

At Sir Frank Worrell Ground, St Augustine, Trinidad, February 13, 14, 15, 16, 2009. **Drawn.** Toss: Leeward Islands. **Trinidad & Tobago** 349 (A. B. Barath 192; G. C. Tonge 6-86) **and 101-1 dec** (A. B. Barath 52*); **Leeward Islands** 221 (R. S. Morton 55, O. A. C. Banks 55; I. Khan 5-33) **and 36-0.** *Trinidad & Tobago 6 pts, Leeward Islands 3 pts.*
   Adrian Barath batted nearly seven hours, with 23 fours and three sixes, and fell just short of a maiden double-hundred.

At Windsor Park, Roseau, Dominica, February 19, 20, 21, 22, 2009. **Jamaica won by an innings and 13 runs.** Toss: Jamaica. **Windward Islands** 261 (K. Lesporis 50, A. D. S. Fletcher 61, K. A. James 55; O. V. Brown 6-85) **and 134** (O. V. Brown 5-27); **Jamaica** 408 (D. J. Pagon 81, T. L. Lambert 92, W. W. Hinds 53; S. Shillingford 5-90). *Jamaica 12 pts.*
   Jamaica regained the head of the table at the halfway stage of the tournament.

At Three Ws Oval, Bridgetown, Barbados, February 20, 21, 22, 23, 2009. **Leeward Islands won by 111 runs.** Toss: Combined Campuses & Colleges. **Leeward Islands 275** (M. V. Hodge 65; K. Kantasingh 4-93, R. A. Austin 5-75) **and 242-7 dec** (T. A. Willett 77, O. A. C. Banks 66*); **Combined Campuses & Colleges 190** (S. Jackson 71; L. S. Baker 4-47) **and 216** (F. L. Reifer 101; G. C. Tonge 4-56). *Leeward Islands 12 pts.*

At Providence Stadium, Guyana, February 20, 21, 22, 23, 2009. **Drawn.** Toss: Guyana. **Trinidad & Tobago 530-8 dec** (L. M. P. Simmons 167, D. Ganga 50, K. A. Pollard 94, G. Mohammed 53*) **and 178-8 dec; Guyana 402** (C. D. Barnwell 56, N. Deonarine 143; I. Khan 4-92) **and 133-4** (R. T. Crandon 55*). *Guyana 3 pts, Trinidad & Tobago 6 pts.*

At Providence Stadium, Guyana, February 27, 28, March 1, 2, 2009. **Windward Islands won by 151 runs.** Toss: Windward Islands. **Windward Islands 215** (A. D. S. Fletcher 53) **and 375-9 dec** (C. C. Alexander 62, D. J. G. Sammy 58, D. B. Hector 79*); **Guyana 280** (L. R. Johnson 73; N. T. Pascal 4-65, D. K. Butler 4-46) **and 159** (T. M. Dowlin 58; N. T. Pascal 4-62, R. N. Lewis 5-39). *Windward Islands 12 pts, Guyana 4 pts.*

At Sabina Park, Kingston, Jamaica, February 27, 28, March 1, 2, 2009. **Leeward Islands won by 28 runs.** Toss: Jamaica. **Leeward Islands 221** (S. S. W. Liburd 116*) **and 202** (W. W. Cornwall 102); **Jamaica 220** (B. A. Parchment 75, D. E. Bernard 51*; W. W. Cornwall 5-37) **and 175** (X. M. Marshall 61; G. C. Tonge 7-58). *Leeward Islands 12 pts.*
Leewards captain Steve Liburd rescued his side from 29-5 with a maiden hundred, and Gavin Tonge's career-best 7-58 completed Jamaica's first defeat of the season.

At Guaracara Park, Pointe-à-Pierre, Trinidad, February 27, 28, March 1, 2, 2009. **Drawn.** Toss: Trinidad & Tobago. **Trinidad & Tobago 505** (D. M. Bravo 111, K. A. Pollard 174, I. Khan 71*, Extras 56; C. D. Collymore 4-72) **and 99-3; Barbados 273** (D. R. Smith 71, P. A. Browne 72; R. Rampaul 5-49) **and 373** (J. A. Parris 67, K. A. Stoute 60, D. R. Smith 126*; R. Rampaul 6-76). *Trinidad & Tobago 6 pts, Barbados 3 pts.*
Darren Bravo and Kieron Pollard both scored career-bests as they put on 250 for Trinidad & Tobago's fourth wicket; Pollard went on to add 118 for the eighth with Imran Khan. In the same innings, Pedro Collins took his 400th first-class wicket and Corey Collymore his 300th, and Kemar Roach conceded 14 no-balls in 16 overs to boost Extras to 56. Barbados followed on, but Dwayne Smith's 144-ball 126 saved the game.*

At Kensington Oval, Bridgetown, Barbados, March 6, 7, 8, 9, 2009. **Windward Islands won by one wicket.** Toss: Barbados. **Barbados 192** (K. A. Edwards 64, P. A. Browne 58) **and 306** (J. A. M. Haynes 56, K. A. Edwards 107; S. Shillingford 6-57); **Windward Islands 303** (D. J. G. Sammy 121, R. N. Lewis 54; C. D. Collymore 4-67, T. L. Best 5-44) **and 200-9** (D. J. G. Sammy 70*). *Windward Islands 12 pts.*
Wicketkeeper Patrick Browne equalled two Barbados records for dismissals when he made seven catches in Windwards' first innings and ten in all, but could not remove Darren Sammy, who scored a maiden hundred and later steered his side home by a single wicket.

At Bourda, Georgetown, Guyana, March 6, 7, 8, 9, 2009. **Drawn.** Toss: Combined Campuses & Colleges. **Combined Campuses & Colleges 254** (F. L. Reifer 72, J. Smith 56; V. Permaul 4-72) **and 67-1; Guyana 497-7 dec** (N. Deonarine 198, T. M. Dowlin 51, A. B. Fudadin 93). *Guyana 6 pts, Combined Campuses & Colleges 3 pts.*
Narsingh Deonarine's career-best 198 gave Guyana a chance of their first win of the season, until rain seeped under the covers and wiped out the final day.

At Alpart Sports Club, St Elizabeth, Jamaica, March 6, 7, 8, 9, 2009. **Jamaica won by 124 runs.** Toss: Trinidad & Tobago. **Jamaica 275** (C. S. Baugh 129) **and 285** (D. J. Pagon 68, W. W. Hinds 59; A. S. Jaggernauth 5-43); **Trinidad & Tobago 190** (A. B. Barath 58) **and 246** (A. B. Barath 71, D. M. Bravo 70; A. P. Richardson 5-55). *Jamaica 12 pts.*
In his first first-class match for ten months, Carlton Baugh hit nine sixes and nine fours in 160 balls in Jamaica's first innings; in their second, Darren Bravo made five catches, equalling the Trinidadian record for a fielder.

At Kensington Oval, Bridgetown, Barbados, March 13, 14, 15, 16, 2009. **Jamaica won by 242 runs.** Toss: Barbados. **Jamaica 272** (T. L. Lambert 143; K. A. Stoute 4-41) **and 397-8 dec** (C. S. Baugh

108*, N. O. Miller 86, D. B. Powell 69); **Barbados 155** (N. O. Miller 5-33) **and 272** (D. M. Richards 117, K. A. Edwards 51; N. O. Miller 4-55, D. E. Bernard 4-42). *Jamaica 12 pts.*

In Jamaica's second innings, the seventh wicket contributed 252 runs in two separate century partnerships; Carlton Baugh retired hurt, for his second hundred in successive matches, after putting on 136* with Nikita Miller, who added another 116 with Daren Powell.

At Albion, Berbice, Guyana, March 13, 14, 15, 16, 2009. **Drawn.** Toss: Guyana. **Guyana 341** (N. Deonarine 94, A. B. Fudadin 82; A. Martin 5-79); **Leeward Islands 206-4** (R. S. Morton 87). *Guyana 4 pts, Leeward Islands 4 pts.*

At Arnos Vale, St Vincent, March 13, 14, 15, 16, 2009. **Combined Campuses & Colleges won by 155 runs.** Toss: Combined Campuses & Colleges. **Combined Campuses & Colleges 277** (F. L. Reifer 129; S. Shillingford 4-74) **and 183-8 dec** (O. J. Phillips 64, F. L. Reifer 53; S. Shillingford 4-39); **Windward Islands 160** (K. J. Wilkinson 4-45) **and 145** (K. R. McClean 4-31). *Combined Campuses & Colleges 12 pts.*

At Mount Gay North Stars, Crab Hill, Barbados, March 21, 22, 23, 2009. **Leeward Islands won by an innings and five runs.** Toss: Leeward Islands. **Leeward Islands 439** (R. S. Morton 210); **Barbados 241** (K. A. Edwards 54, D. R. Smith 62) **and 193** (K. A. Stoute 100; G. C. Tonge 5-62, T. A. Willett 4-51). *Leeward Islands 12 pts.*

All three matches due to begin on March 20 started a day late because of the dispute between the West Indies Players' Association and the West Indies Cricket Board. Runako Morton needed a runner after a groin injury, but the second double-hundred of his career spanned all but the first four balls of Leewards' innings and set up a three-day win.

At Sabina Park, Kingston, Jamaica, March 21, 22, 23, 24, 2009. **Drawn.** Toss: Combined Campuses & Colleges. **Combined Campuses & Colleges 171** (N. Parris 53) **and 369-8 dec** (F. L. Reifer 140; B. M. Brown 5-59); **Jamaica 229** (B. A. Parchment 52; K. Kantasingh 4-79) **and 190-7** (C. S. Baugh 58*). *Jamaica 6 pts, Combined Campuses & Colleges 3 pts.*

Combined Campuses & Colleges were 27-5 on the first day, but on the last reduced Jamaica to 45-4 chasing 312.

At Arnos Vale, St Vincent, March 21, 22, 23, 24, 2009. **Drawn.** Toss: Windward Islands. **Trinidad & Tobago 361** (J. N. Mohammed 80, S. Ganga 98) **and 168** (N. T. Pascal 5-57); **Windward Islands 257** (D. B. Hector 99, R. N. Lewis 85; R. Rampaul 4-47, S. Ganga 4-26) **and 165-7** (R. N. Lewis 66*; R. Rampaul 4-35). *Windward Islands 3 pts, Trinidad & Tobago 6 pts.*

At Trelawny Greenfields, Jamaica, March 27, 28, 29, 2009. **Windward Islands won by three wickets.** Toss: Jamaica. **Jamaica 229** (T. L. Lambert 93, C. S. Baugh 60; K. K. Peters 5-60) **and 107** (D. E. Bernard 50); **Windward Islands 222** (D. S. Smith 55; D. E. Bernard 4-31) **and 118-7** (O. V. Brown 4-44). *Windward Islands 12 pts, Jamaica 4 pts.*

Jamaica collapsed to 17-5 and suffered their second defeat of the tournament, but first-innings points proved enough to make them regional champions.

At Grove Park, Charlestown, Nevis, March 27, 28, 29, 30, 2009. **Drawn.** Toss: Combined Campuses & Colleges. **Combined Campuses & Colleges 519** (O. J. Phillips 204, K. A. M. Corbin 67, F. L. Reifer 92, C. A. K. Walton 50) **and 44-1;** **Leeward Islands 596** (M. V. Hodge 64, R. S. Morton 231; A. W. L. Sealy 4-170). *Leeward Islands 6 pts, Combined Campuses & Colleges 3 pts.*

Omar Phillips batted for more than eight and a half hours to convert his maiden century into a double; Runako Morton responded with his third and highest double-hundred, and his second in nine days.

At Queen's Park Oval, Port-of-Spain, Trinidad, March 27, 28, 29, 30, 2009. **Drawn.** Toss: Guyana. **Guyana 282** (S. Chattergoon 68, S. A. Jacobs 54; I. Khan 5-42) **and 213-7** (C. D. Barnwell 57, N. Deonarine 74); **Trinidad & Tobago 259** (D. Ganga 92; V. Permaul 4-54). *Trinidad & Tobago 3 pts, Guyana 6 pts.*

At Three Ws Oval, Bridgetown, Barbados, April 3, 4, 5, 6, 2009. **Combined Campuses & Colleges won by five wickets.** Toss: Combined Campuses & Colleges. **Barbados 235** (K. C. Brathwaite 73, R. O. Hinds 58; A. W. L. Sealy 4-66) **and 278** (D. R. Smith 87, K. A. Stoute 63, T. L. Best 51; R. A. Austin 4-93); **Combined Campuses & Colleges 377** (O. J. Phillips 89, C. A. K. Walton 87, K. R. McClean 50*; R. O. Hinds 6-89) **and 137-5.** *Combined Campuses & Colleges 12 pts.*

Chadwick Walton and Kevin McClean added 128 for Combined Campuses & Colleges' ninth wicket, giving them an advantage that resulted in Barbados's fourth consecutive defeat.

At Sabina Park, Kingston, Jamaica, April 3, 4, 5, 6, 2009. **Jamaica won by 139 runs.** Toss: Guyana. **Jamaica 389** (D. P. Hyatt 69, T. L. Lambert 90, C. S. Baugh 63; C. D. Barnwell 5-77) **and 248** (D. Bishoo 4-56); **Guyana 308** (S. Chattergoon 63, N. Deonarine 63; D. E. Bernard 4-85) **and 190** (N. Deonarine 55). *Jamaica 12 pts.*

Narsingh Deonarine became the first player to score 1,000 runs in the West Indian regional first-class tournament, passing Stuart Williams's record of 974 for Leeward Islands in 2001-02.

At Ronald Webster Park, The Valley, Anguilla, April 3, 4, 5, 6, 2009. **Trinidad & Tobago won by nine wickets.** Toss: Leeward Islands. **Leeward Islands 303** (K. O. A. Powell 57; A. S. Jaggernauth 5-81) **and 256** (R. S. Morton 72); **Trinidad & Tobago 433** (A. B. Barath 113, I. Khan 125, D. Ganga 96*; B. A. DeFreitas 5-88) **and 131-1** (I. Khan 68*). *Trinidad & Tobago 12 pts.*

Adrian Barath and Imran Khan opened with 239 in Trinidad & Tobago's first innings.

At Three Ws Oval, Bridgetown, Barbados, April 11, 12, 13, 2009. **Combined Campuses & Colleges won by 63 runs.** Toss: Trinidad & Tobago. **Combined Campuses & Colleges 153** (R. Rampaul 6-44) **and 174** (K. A. M. Corbin 70; I. Khan 4-36); **Trinidad & Tobago 154 and 110** (K. Catlin 4-56). *Combined Campuses & Colleges 12 pts, Trinidad & Tobago 4 pts.*

Floyd Reifer passed 1,000 runs in the tournament.

At Providence Stadium, Guyana, April 11, 12, 13, 14, 2009. **Drawn.** Toss: Guyana. **Guyana 334** (R. T. Crandon 136*) **and 360** (S. Chattergoon 111; N. G. R. Charles 5-99); **Barbados 396** (R. O. Hinds 100, K. A. Stoute 186; D. Bishoo 4-125) **and 67-1.** *Guyana 3 pts, Barbados 6 pts.*

Ryan Hinds and Kevin Stoute added 239 for Barbados's fourth wicket in their first innings.

At Addelita Cancryn Ground, Charlotte Amalie, St Thomas, April 11, 12, 13, 14, 2009. **Leeward Islands won by 28 runs.** Toss: Leeward Islands. **Leeward Islands 243** (K. O. A. Powell 88, R. S. Morton 53, T. A. Willett 61*) **and 276** (M. V. Hodge 58, D. C. Thomas 74); **Windward Islands 271** (R. N. Lewis 81*; A. Martin 4-54) **and 220** (L. O. D. James 50, S. Shillingford 57; G. C. Tonge 5-44). *Leeward Islands 12 pts, Windward Islands 4 pts.*

Runako Morton passed 1,000 runs in the tournament. Set a target of 249, Windwards subsided to 37-6 before Shane Shillingford added 63 for the seventh wicket with Lyndon James and 84 for the ninth with Deighton Butler; they finally fell only 29 short.

REGIONAL CHAMPIONS

Shell Shield			1982-83	Guyana	*President's Cup*	
1965-66	Barbados		1983-84	Barbados	1997-98	{ Leeward Islands
1966-67	Barbados		1984-85	Trinidad & Tobago		{ Guyana
1967-68	No competition		1985-86	Barbados		
1968-69	Jamaica		1986-87	Guyana	*Busta Cup*	
1969-70	Trinidad				1998-99	Barbados
1970-71	Trinidad				1999-2000	Jamaica
1971-72	Barbados		*Red Stripe Cup*		2000-01	Barbados
1972-73	Guyana		1987-88	Jamaica	2001-02	Jamaica
1973-74	Barbados		1988-89	Jamaica		
1974-75	Guyana		1989-90	Leeward Islands	*Carib Beer Cup*	
1975-76	{ Trinidad		1990-91	Barbados	2002-03	Barbados
	{ Barbados		1991-92	Jamaica	2003-04	Barbados
1976-77	Barbados		1992-93	Guyana	2004-05	Jamaica
1977-78	Barbados		1993-94	Leeward Islands	2005-06	Trinidad & Tobago
1978-79	Barbados		1994-95	Barbados	2006-07	Barbados
1979-80	Barbados		1995-96	Leeward Islands	2007-08	Barbados
1980-81	Combined Islands		1996-97	Barbados	*President's Trophy*	
1981-82	Barbados				2008-09	Jamaica

Barbados have won the title outright 19 times, Jamaica 9, Guyana 5, Trinidad/Trinidad & Tobago 4, Leeward Islands 3, Combined Islands 1. Barbados, Guyana, Leeward Islands and Trinidad have also shared the title.

Note: Matches in the following section were not first-class.

WEST INDIES CRICKET BOARD CUP, 2008-09

50-over league plus knockout

	Played	Won	Lost	No Result	Bonus Points	Points	Net run-rate
Trinidad & Tobago	4	3	0	1	3	16	1.50
Leeward Islands	4	3	1	0	4	16	1.44
Barbados	4	3	1	0	1	13	0.42
Jamaica	4	2	1	1	3	12	0.95
Guyana	4	2	2	0	1	9	0.18
Combined Campuses & Colleges	4	2	2	0	1	9	−0.06
Windward Islands	4	1	3	0	0	4	−0.83
USA	4	0	3	1	0	1	−1.60
Canada	4	0	3	1	0	1	−2.99

Semi-finals

At Providence Stadium, Guyana, November 21, 2008 (day/night). **Trinidad & Tobago won by three wickets.** Toss: Jamaica. **Jamaica 197-8** (50 overs) (T. L. Lambert 55); **Trinidad & Tobago 200-7** (47 overs) (K. A. Pollard 76).

Kieron Pollard scored 76 in 63 balls, with four fours and six sixes, to see Trinidad & Tobago within seven runs of victory.

At Providence Stadium, Guyana, November 22, 2008 (day/night). **Barbados won by 168 runs.** Toss: Barbados. **Barbados 295-5** (50 overs) (D. M. Richards 62, R. O. Hinds 75, D. R. Smith 82); **Leeward Islands 127** (37.4 overs) (T. A. Willett 51).

Dwayne Smith hit 82 in 65 balls, with four fours and three sixes.

Final

At Providence Stadium, Guyana, November 23, 2008 (day/night). **Trinidad & Tobago won by seven wickets.** Toss: Barbados. **Barbados 142** (45.5 overs); **Trinidad & Tobago 143-3** (27 overs).

Barbados managed less than half their total of the previous night's semi-final, and Trinidad & Tobago won with 23 overs to spare.

Matches in the Stanford Super Series in October–November 2008 can be found in Wisden 2009 *pages 1360-69.*

ZIMBABWE CRICKET, 2009

Recovery on the horizon?

MEHLULI SIBANDA

Zimbabwe played 27 one-day internationals during 2009, more than double the dozen they managed the previous year. Of those games, 13 were won, although nine of those victories came against Kenya, and the other four against Bangladesh. There was still no five-day cricket – Zimbabwe's last Test was in 2005 – and no Twenty20 internationals either, following the pragmatic decision to pull out of the World Twenty20 in England after the British government indicated that the players would not be granted visas.

With New Zealand postponing their planned tour until 2010 at least, Zimbabwe were forced to play four separate series against Bangladesh – one triangular and two bilateral away series, and one at home. They played only three matches against top-class opposition – one against Sri Lanka in that Bangladesh tri-series and two matches in South Africa, all of which they lost.

Off the field Zimbabwe Cricket spent most of 2009 trying to clean up its image after years of controversy. Managing director Ozias Bvute, whose arrival coincided with the start of the decline in 2004, courted several people

ZIMBABWE IN 2009

One-day internationals	Played 27	Won 13	Lost 14	Drawn/No result –
JANUARY	Triangular ODI tournament in Bangladesh			(page 1086)
	3 ODIs (a) v Bangladesh			(page 1089)
FEBRUARY	5 ODIs (a) v Kenya			(page 1476)
MARCH				
APRIL				
MAY				
JUNE				
JULY				
AUGUST	5 ODIs (h) v Bangladesh			(page 1445)
SEPTEMBER				
OCTOBER	5 ODIs (h) v Kenya			(page 1448)
	5 ODIs (a) v Bangladesh			(page 1090)
NOVEMBER	2 ODIs (a) v South Africa			(page 1268)
DECEMBER				

For a review of Zimbabwean domestic cricket from the 2008-09 season, see page 1449.

he had previously denounced, while the long-serving ZC chairman Peter Chingoka stayed largely out of the limelight. He had in recent years been banned from travelling to the European Union and to Australia, and remained closely associated with Robert Mugabe's regime. The new sports minister David Coltart – from the MDC party sharing power with Mugabe's ZANU-PF – has long been a cricket fan and privately stated his aim to clean up the game in Zimbabwe.

The improved atmosphere meant several of the players who had been deemed surplus to requirements in 2004 returned to the fold. Heath Streak, whose sacking as captain led to the player revolt in the first place, was brought in as the national team's bowling coach, a fitting honour for the only Zimbabwean to take 200 wickets in both Tests and one-day internationals. Alistair Campbell, another former captain, was appointed as head of the national selection panel, which also included former players David Mutendera and John Rennie. Campbell was also appointed chairman of ZC's cricket committee.

As Zimbabwe sought more credibility and a return to Test cricket, the former captain Andy Waller (whose son Malcolm played his first one-day internationals during 2009) was named as national coaching director, and another former captain, David Houghton, came in as a coaching consultant. Former England fast bowler Mike Hendrick conducted coaching seminars for the five new franchises.

The franchise system was introduced in June 2009 in line with a suggestion from the ICC. This saw the abolition of national contracts as players were now contracted to their respective franchises. The new teams were the Mashonaland Eagles (based in Harare), Matabeleland Tuskers (Bulawayo), Mountaineers (Mutare), Southern Rocks (Masvingo) and Midwest Rhinos (Kwekwe). There was some controversy over the appointment of the franchises' chief executives, but the system proved a success and persuaded several former internationals to return home along with some overseas players. The one-time national captain Terry Duffin came back and joined the Tuskers, along with former team-mates Dion Ebrahim, Keegan Meth and Gavin Ewing. Chris Silverwood, the former England fast bowler, signed up for the Mashonaland Eagles, where he was joined by Greg Lamb, who had returned home after a spell with Hampshire. Southern Rocks signed two Kenyans – Steve Tikolo and Thomas Odoyo – while the Midwest Rhinos secured the services of the Northamptonshire batsman/wicketkeeper Riki Wessels.

Prosper Utseya continued as Zimbabwe's captain despite the team's modest results. He was no longer the miserly off-spinner who at one stage had a better economy-rate than Muttiah Muralitharan, but Zimbabwe Cricket persisted with him. Hamilton Masakadza was by far Zimbabwe's best batsman, with 1,087 runs at 43.48 in the 27 matches, settling well in as an opener or No. 3. In the five-match home series against Kenya in October he scored 467 runs, to beat Chris Gayle's record for any bilateral one-day series. He was, however, found wanting when Zimbabwe toured Bangladesh, passing 50 only once; and his captaincy skills came under scrutiny when, given a chance after Utseya picked up an ankle injury in Bangladesh, he led Zimbabwe to four straight defeats.

Munir Uz Zaman, AFP/Getty Images

Survivor: Prosper Utseya saw out the year as captain.

Charles Coventry made his international return after more than three years, and in his fourth match back tied the record for the highest individual score in a one-day international. His unbeaten 194 against Bangladesh at Bulawayo matched Saeed Anwar's 194 for Pakistan against India in May 1997. But it seemed a one-off: ten further innings produced a highest score of only 32.

It was also a chastening year for Chamu Chibhabha, once seen as a promising all-rounder, who was given too many responsibilities, and buckled under the pressure. At home against Bangladesh, he was picked as opening batsman and opening bowler, and failed to deliver.

Tatenda Taibu, another former Zimbabwe captain, spent most of the year in dispute with board officials, and played only nine full internationals. It all started when his kit was left behind as the team returned from Bangladesh: he refused to play in another player's kit and missed the series against Kenya. Allegations that he had assaulted ZC's finance manager Esther Lupepe surfaced; the matter went to court and Taibu was acquitted – but it did not end there, as he confessed to ZC officials that he had lied in court. He was slapped with a ten-match ban and missed the home series against Bangladesh, although the late addition of the Kenyan series meant he was eligible for the later tours of Bangladesh and South Africa. He picked up a thigh injury and missed the last three matches in Bangladesh, but was fit to play against South Africa, scoring his second one-day hundred against them and picking up the series award.

Some other returnees bolstered the national side. After missing Zimbabwe's home matches against Sri Lanka at the end of the previous year and the early tours in 2009, preferring to play club cricket overseas, Brendan Taylor returned against Bangladesh and recorded two half-centuries despite having to keep wicket in Taibu's absence. After several near-misses he finally recorded his maiden one-day international century in Bangladesh, but failed to make an impact in South Africa.

Slow left-armer Ray Price, the oldest player in the team at 33, led by example, and was Zimbabwe's leading bowler in 2009 with 44 wickets at just 20.61. He rose to No. 3 in the ICC rankings for one-day bowlers – the highest ever by any Zimbabwean – after fruitful trips to Bangladesh and South Africa.

Kyle Jarvis, who represented Zimbabwe at the 2008 Under-19 World Cup, was fast-tracked into the national team when he returned home from South Africa. The son of the former Test fast bowler Malcolm Jarvis, Kyle is genuinely quick and, if carefully managed, could be a force to reckon with in Zimbabwe's bowling attack.

All in all, there were several encouraging signs for Zimbabwe's cricket in 2009. However, there is still a long way to go before the team can be considered ready for Test cricket again.

ZIMBABWE v BANGLADESH, 2009

MEHLULI SIBANDA

One-day internationals (5): Zimbabwe 1, Bangladesh 4

Zimbabwe had toured Bangladesh in January, and now Bangladesh returned the favour, contesting a five-match one-day series. To cut down on travel all the matches were played in Bulawayo (all the games in Zimbabwe's previous home series, against Sri Lanka, were played in Harare, as their next series against Kenya would be).

The main talking-points came in the fourth match, when Zimbabwe's Charles Coventry equalled the one-day international record with an innings of 194 not out, yet still finished on the losing side, as Bangladesh clinched the series with Tamim Iqbal hammering 154. Coventry had returned to the national team after three years, having been missing since falling out with the then coach Kevin Curran early in 2006. Back after an even longer gap was Mark Vermeulen, who had last played in December 2004, and in the interim had been convicted of arson after a fire destroyed Zimbabwe Cricket's academy. Forgiven now, he started with 92 in his first match, although his returns fell away after that and he missed the last game. One man absent from Zimbabwe's side was Tatenda Taibu, serving a ten-match ban after a heated argument with a board employee.

Bangladesh, fresh from their triumphant tour of the West Indies, relished Zimbabwe's friendly bowling, twice making more than 300 (which they had only ever done twice before) and recording their highest-ever total in the process. Three of their batsmen – Tamim, skipper Shakib Al Hasan and former captain Mohammad Ashraful – made centuries, while Mushfiqur Rahim was promoted to open in the final match and made 98.

BANGLADESH TOURING PARTY

Shakib Al Hasan (*captain*), Mushfiqur Rahim (*vice-captain*), Dolar Mahmud, Enamul Haque, jun., Imrul Kayes, Junaid Siddique, Mahbubul Alam, Mahmudullah, Mehrab Hossain, jun., Mohammad Ashraful, Naeem Islam, Raqibul Hasan, Shahadat Hossain, Syed Rasel, Tamim Iqbal. *Coach:* J. D. Siddons.

Abdur Razzak was originally selected, but withdrew with a leg injury and was replaced by Enamul Haque, while Rubel Hossain injured his side and was replaced by Dolar Mahmud.

Note: Matches in this section were not first-class.

Full scores of the games that follow can be found at: www.cricketarchive.co.uk/Archive/Seasons/ZIM/2009_ZIM_Bangladesh_in_Zimbabwe_2009.html and www.cricinfo.com/db/ARCHIVE/2009/BDESH_IN_ZIM/

At Bulawayo Athletic Club, August 7, 2009. **Zimbabwe A won by seven wickets.** Toss: Bangladeshis. **Bangladeshis 180** (49.3 overs) (Raqibul Hasan 55, Mushfiqur Rahim 32, Enamul Haque, jun. 37*; A. N. Manyuwma 3-32); **Zimbabwe A 181-3** (38.1 overs) (T. Taibu 66*, F. Mutizwa 78*).

Zimbabwe A made a poor start in response to a modest target, slipping to 31-3 in the tenth over, before Tatenda Taibu and Forster Mutizwa took them home with 71 balls to spare after an unbroken stand of 150. Bangladesh's coach Jamie Siddons claimed the result was not a true reflection of his side's ability, saying several of the players were distracted as their luggage had been delayed in transit from South Africa.

At Queens Club, Bulawayo, August 9, 2009. **First one-day international: Bangladesh won by eight wickets.** Toss: Bangladesh. **Zimbabwe 207** (47.5 overs) (M. A. Vermeulen 92; Nazmul Hossain 3-29); **Bangladesh 211-2** (34.3 overs) (Tamim Iqbal 63, Mohammad Ashraful 103*). *Man of the Match:* Mohammad Ashraful.

Mark Vermeulen, in his first one-day international for nearly five years, held Zimbabwe's innings together, hitting six fours from 128 balls, but Bangladesh had no difficulty in hurrying to victory. Mohammad Ashraful, who hit 12 fours and two sixes from 103 balls, hit his third one-day century, passing 3,000 runs in the process.

At Queens Club, Bulawayo, August 11, 2009. **Second one-day international: Bangladesh won by 49 runs.** Toss: Zimbabwe. **Bangladesh 320-8** (50 overs) (Tamim Iqbal 79, Shakib Al Hasan 104, Raqibul Hasan 35; E. Chigumbura 3-59); **Zimbabwe 271** (46.1 overs) (C. K. Coventry 61, S. C. Williams 75, S. Matsikenyeri 39, E. Chigumbura 31). *Man of the Match:* Shakib Al Hasan.

Shakib Al Hasan, who reached Bangladesh's fastest one-day international hundred from 63 balls and in all hit nine fours and four sixes, lifted his side to their highest one-day total (previously 301-7 v Kenya at Bogra in 2005-06). The innings included four run-outs, one short of the one-day international record. Led by Sean Williams, who made his highest score in one-dayers, Zimbabwe kept within touching distance of the asking-rate, but fell short in the end. Elton Chigumbura's 31 from 20 balls included three sixes, but no fours.

At Queens Club, Bulawayo, August 14, 2009. **Third one-day international: Zimbabwe won by 69 runs.** Toss: Bangladesh. **Zimbabwe 323-7** (50 overs) (H. Masakadza 102, B. R. M. Taylor 94, E. Chigumbura 61*); **Bangladesh 254** (44.2 overs) (Raqibul Hasan 78, Mushfiqur Rahim 33, Mahbubul Alam 59; T. Mupariwa 3-32, R. W. Price 3-34). *Man of the Match:* E. Chigumbura.

Now it was Zimbabwe's turn to run up a big total – their highest against a Test-playing country in one-day internationals. It was based on a fourth-wicket stand of 142 between Hamilton Masakadza, who made his maiden one-day international century more than eight years after scoring 119 in his first Test, and Brendan Taylor. Late impetus was provided by Elton Chigumbura, who blasted five sixes (and three fours) in a 33-ball innings during which he was dropped twice. Tamim Iqbal was out first ball: Bangladesh were 16-3 in the fifth over, and never recovered. Their total was boosted by a 43-ball onslaught from No. 9 by Mahbubul Alam, which made up in part for his nine overs earlier costing 84.

ZIMBABWE v BANGLADESH

Fourth One-Day International

At Queens Club, Bulawayo, August 16, 2009. Bangladesh won by four wickets. Toss: Zimbabwe.
The bespectacled right-hander Charles Coventry equalled the highest individual score in one-day internationals, matching Saeed Anwar's 194 for Pakistan against India at Chennai in May 1997 – but still ended up on the losing side, as his onslaught was trumped by a similar one from Tamim Iqbal, whose 154 left Bangladesh close to their series-clinching victory. Both scores were records for the countries concerned. Coventry was lucky to make as many: he was dropped twice at deep square leg, first by Syed Rasel when he had 13, and by Mahmudullah at 137. But he made the most of his escapes, interspersing powerful cover-drives with occasional heaves and slog-sweeps, and might have become the first man to make a one-day international double-century had he not lost the strike early in each of the last three overs. His innings, which lasted 156 balls and included 16 fours and seven sixes (three in succession over midwicket off Enamul Haque and Shakib Al Hasan), was still an eye-popping one for someone whose previous-best was 74 and who had walked out of the national team in 2006 after a disagreement with the then coach, Kevin Curran. Zimbabwe reached 300 against a Test-playing nation for the first time since making 300 for seven against New Zealand at Taupo in January 2001, but it wasn't enough on a docile pitch against a docile attack. While Tamim sealed up one end – he faced 138 balls, and hit seven fours and six sixes – Bangladesh crucially avoided losing wickets at the other, and entered the last ten overs needing just 67 more runs. They got home with 13 balls to spare, a comfortable margin in the circumstances.

Men of the Match: C. K. Coventry and Tamim Iqbal.

HIGHEST INDIVIDUAL SCORE FOR LOSING SIDE IN ONE-DAY INTERNATIONALS

194*	C. K. Coventry	**Zimbabwe v Bangladesh at Bulawayo**	**2009**
181*	M. L. Hayden	Australia v New Zealand at Hamilton	2006-07
175	**S. R. Tendulkar**	**India v Australia at Hyderabad**	**2009-10**
167*	R. A. Smith	England v Australia at Birmingham	1993
164	R. T. Ponting	Australia v South Africa at Johannesburg	2005-06
152*	C. H. Gayle	West Indies v South Africa at Johannesburg	2003-04
149*	S. Chanderpaul	West Indies v India at Nagpur	2006-07
146	S. R. Tendulkar	India v Zimbabwe at Jodhpur	2000-01
145	A. Flower	Zimbabwe v India at Colombo	2002-03
143	S. R. Tendulkar	India v Australia at Sharjah	1997-98
143	H. H. Gibbs	South Africa v New Zealand at Johannesburg	2002-03

Zimbabwe

M. A. Vermeulen c Junaid Siddique b Mahbubul Alam .	5
H. Masakadza c Raqibul Hasan b Mohammad Ashraful .	21
C. K. Coventry not out	194
†B. R. M. Taylor lbw b Enamul Haque	5
S. C. Williams b Naeem Islam	4
S. Matsikenyeri run out	37
E. Chigumbura c Naeem Islam b Enamul Haque .	15

R. W. Price did not bat.

M. N. Waller b Mahbubul Alam	3
T. Mupariwa lbw b Syed Rasel	0
*P. Utseya not out	7
B 1, l-b 3, w 12, n-b 1	17

1/5 (1) 2/87 (2) (8 wkts, 50 overs) 312
3/102 (4) 4/111 (5)
5/218 (6) 6/282 (7)
7/302 (8) 8/303 (9)

10 overs: 58-1

Syed Rasel 9–1–52–1; Mahbubul Alam 8–0–63–2; Shakib Al Hasan 9–0–70–0; Enamul Haque 9–0–51–2; Mahmudullah 6–0–32–0; Mohammad Ashraful 4–1–11–1; Naeem Islam 5–0–29–1.

Bangladesh

Tamim Iqbal c sub (V. Sibandra) b Price .	154
Junaid Siddique c Williams b Masakadza .	38
Mohammad Ashraful c Coventry b Price .	10
Raqibul Hasan b Price	35
*Shakib Al Hasan c Waller b Masakadza .	19
†Mushfiqur Rahim lbw b Utseya	15
Mahmudullah not out	21

Naeem Islam not out	4
L-b 1, w 15, n-b 1	17

1/68 (2) 2/94 (3) (6 wkts, 47.5 overs) 313
3/213 (4) 4/246 (5)
5/279 (1) 6/300 (6)

10 overs: 69-1

Mahbubul Alam, Enamul Haque, jun. and Syed Rasel did not bat.

Mupariwa 8.5–0–65–0; Chigumbura 9–0–63–0; Utseya 10–0–46–1; Masakadza 7–0–52–2; Price 10–0–60–3; Waller 3–0–26–0.

Umpires: K. C. Barbour and A. M. Saheba.
Third umpire: O. Chirombe. Referee: J. Srinath.

At Queens Club, Bulawayo, August 18, 2009. **Fifth one-day international: Bangladesh won by five wickets.** Toss: Zimbabwe. **Zimbabwe 209** (46.4 overs) (B. R. M. Taylor 61, R. W. Price 46; Dolar Mahmud 4-28); **Bangladesh 212-5** (47.5 overs) (Mushfiqur Rahim 98, Shakib Al Hasan 30). Man of the Match: Dolar Mahmud. *Man of the Series:* Tamim Iqbal.

Bangladesh took the series 4–1, their victory owing much to Mushfiqur Rahim, who opened for the first time in a one-day international and hit 11 fours in his highest score. Earlier, Zimbabwe's fate was all but sealed when they slipped to 69-6 in the 14th over. After their heroics in the previous match, Charles Coventry was out seventh ball for a duck, while Tamim Iqbal lasted 23 balls for four. Coventry later took over as wicketkeeper when Brendan Taylor went off with an ear infection after 15 overs, and stumped Mushfiqur off Ray Price.

ZIMBABWE v KENYA, 2009-10

Kenya made the short trip to Zimbabwe in October for an Intercontinental Cup match (see separate section) and five one-day internationals. Zimbabwe won the one-day series 4–1, as Kenya's bowlers struggled to contain the home batsmen, for whom Hamilton Masakadza made 467 runs in the five matches, a record for any bilateral one-day series.

KENYAN TOURING PARTY

M. A. Ouma (*captain*), J. K. Kamande (*vice-captain*), R. G. Aga, A. S. Luseno, A. Obanda, C. O. Obuya, D. O. Obuya, N. Odhiambo, T. M. Odoyo, P. J. Ongondo, L. N. Onyango, E. Otieno, R. R. Patel, S. O. Tikolo, H. A. Varaiya. *Coach:* E. A. E. Baptiste.

At Harare, October 12, 2009. **First one-day international: Zimbabwe won by 91 runs.** Toss: Zimbabwe. **Zimbabwe 313-4** (50 overs) (H. Masakadza 156, M. A. Vermeulen 49, B. R. M. Taylor 44*); **Kenya 222** (49.5 overs) (S. O. Tikolo 49; K. M. Jarvis 3-36, P. Utseya 3-36). *One-day international debut:* K. M. Jarvis. *Man of the Match:* H. Masakadza.
   Zimbabwe were propelled to a huge total by Masakadza, who hit 11 fours and six sixes from 151 balls, dominating an opening stand of 121 with Vermeulen. Lameck Onyango conceded 91 runs in ten overs, an unwanted Kenyan record. Kenya made a bright start, scoring 32 in five overs, but regular wickets meant they were never up with the rate, and nine Zimbabweans had a bowl.

At Harare, October 13, 2009. **Second one-day international: Zimbabwe won by 86 runs.** Toss: Zimbabwe. **Zimbabwe 263-7** (50 overs) (H. Masakadza 66, M. A. Vermeulen 32, S. C. Williams 33, S. Matsikenyeri 71*, A. G. Cremer 31*; H. A. Varaiya 3-38); **Kenya 177** (44.5 overs) (D. O. Obuya 49, M. A. Ouma 31; P. Utseya 3-29, A. G. Cremer 6-46). *Man of the Match:* A. G. Cremer.
   Zimbabwe controlled the match, Masakadza and Vermeulen leading off with an opening stand of 77 in 15 overs, before Matsikenyeri and Cremer (who faced only 19 balls) provided late impetus. After Kenya's openers David Obuya and Rakep Patel (17) had put on 49, Cremer demolished the innings with his leg-spin, following his career-best batting with easily his best bowling figures.

At Harare, October 15, 2009. **Third one-day international: Kenya won by 20 runs.** Toss: Kenya. **Kenya 266-9** (50 overs) (D. O. Obuya 56, A. Obanda 65, C. O. Obuya 52); **Zimbabwe 246** (49.5 overs) (H. Masakadza 44, B. R. M. Taylor 92, S. Matsikenyeri 58; N. Odhiambo 4-61). *Man of the Match:* N. Odhiambo.
   Kenya kept the series alive with a narrow victory, helped when Sean Williams was unable to bat after being injured in the field. Kenya's openers David Obuya and Alex Obanda put on 119 in 20 overs, and later David's brother Collins added 52 from 63 balls to swell the total. Zimbabwe dipped to 19-2, but Taylor and Matsikenyeri added 142 for the fourth wicket. However, both fell in the space of three balls from slow left-armer Hiren Varaiya.

At Harare, October 17, 2009. **Fourth one-day international: Zimbabwe won by six wickets.** Toss: Kenya. **Kenya 270-8** (50 overs) (D. O. Obuya 49, A. Obanda 33, R. R. Patel 47, M. A. Ouma 58, T. M. Odoyo 30; P. Utseya 4-46); **Zimbabwe 271-4** (48 overs) (M. A. Vermeulen 56, F. Mutizwa 79, B. R. M. Taylor 60*, S. Matsikenyeri 37). *Man of the Match:* F. Mutizwa.
   Zimbabwe clinched the series, overhauling Kenya's reasonable total with two overs to spare. Their star was Forster Mutizwa, whose highest score in one-day internationals took 97 balls.

At Harare, October 18, 2009. **Fifth one-day international: Zimbabwe won by 142 runs.** Toss: Zimbabwe. **Zimbabwe 329-3** (50 overs) (H. Masakadza 178*, F. Mutizwa 55, B. R. M. Taylor 52); **Kenya 187** (39.3 overs) (J. K. Kamande 37; C. B. Mpofu 3-44). *One-day international debut:* T. N. Garwe (Zimbabwe). *Man of the Match:* H. Masakadza. *Man of the Series:* H. Masakadza.
   Masakadza hit 17 fours and four sixes from 167 balls, sharing stands of 127 with Mutizwa (who made a third successive one-day half-century), 102 with Taylor, and 82 in 7.3 overs with Charles Coventry (25). Masakadza became the first batsman to hit 150 twice in the same one-day series, and finished with 467 runs overall, a record for any bilateral one-day series, beating Chris Gayle's 455 in seven matches for West Indies v India in 2002-03.

DOMESTIC CRICKET IN ZIMBABWE, 2008-09

Mehluli Sibanda

Zimbabwe Cricket revised their domestic structure again in 2008-09, cutting the five provincial teams back to four, and staging each of the three interprovincial tournaments in a single centre. The one-day Faithwear series and the first-class competition, the Logan Cup, were both held in Harare, and both were won by Easterns (formerly known as Manicaland). Then came a Twenty20 tournament in Bulawayo, won by the home team, Westerns (formerly Matabeleland).

Mark Vermeulen

But in June 2009, the format was shaken up yet again, as ZC adopted an ICC proposal and introduced a franchise system for 2009-10, hoping to attract corporate sponsorship as the country's economy slowly improved. The five franchises, set up to be independent of ZC, corresponded to the provincial teams (with Southerns making a swift return), each based in a major city: Mashonaland Eagles in Harare, Matabeleland Tuskers in Bulawayo, Mountaineers in Mutare, Midwest Rhinos in Kwekwe and Southern Rocks in Masvingo. Players were now contracted to their franchises, and national contracts were abolished. The new system encouraged several former internationals, such as Terrence Duffin, Dion Ebrahim and Gavin Ewing, to return home, and players from England and Kenya signed up too. First-class and 50-over games would be played in all five cities.

ZC had blamed logistics for the fact that, for the first time, in 2008-09 all Logan Cup matches were staged in Harare – though the four teams played each other twice, as if on a home and away basis, over its seven weeks. Easterns (the future Mountaineers) and Northerns (Mashonaland), who had the bulk of Zimbabwe's national and A-team players, were always favourites, while Centrals and Westerns struggled. In the end, the title was decided on the final day, when **Easterns** maintained their unbeaten record by edging past defending champions **Northerns** by one wicket, after off-spinner Prosper Utseya, the national captain, took ten wickets for Easterns for the second match running. **Centrals** finished third, with a single win over bottom-placed **Westerns**, who lost their first five games and drew the last.

Easterns, led by Zimbabwe batsman Hamilton Masakadza, thus claimed their second trophy of the season; they had been crowned champions in the Faithwear tournament in March, while Westerns were runners-up.

The Twenty20 brought down the curtain on the season; this time, ZC took the matches to Bulawayo. Playing in front of their own fans, Westerns put their disappointing show in the Logan Cup behind them to beat log-leaders Northerns by four runs in the final. It was a tournament full of thrills; had Zimbabwe not been forced to withdraw from the World Twenty20 in England in June, they could have caused a few upsets.

Westerns also emerged victorious in a women's tournament in Harare just after Easter.

The winners of the three provincial competitions each received $US1,000 in prize money, enough inspiration for the players to perform at their best; many also had their equipment subsidised, since most had appeared for Zimbabwe at some level. Much of the kit – balls, helmets and bats – was imported from Pakistan.

Club cricket was played only in Bulawayo and Harare, which have attracted many players away from the smaller centres. ZC ran a national league, won by Harare's Takashinga who beat Bulawayo Athletic Club in the final.

The unexpected comeback of the year was that of Mark Vermeulen, who fought his way back from a period of mental illness during which he had set fire to the national cricket academy. He had been cleared of arson in January 2008, after evidence of complex partial epilepsy and impulsive behaviour disorder following a head injury sustained on a tour of Australia. Vermeulen played all six one-day games for Westerns in March 2009, then toured Namibia with Zimbabwe A.

There was a setback when Vermeulen injured his hand fielding for Westerns in the second round of the Logan Cup – he missed the rest of the tournament – but he recovered in time for the Twenty20 competition, played in Bulawayo where he grew up. Opening for Westerns, Vermeulen struck two fifties and 108 in 54 balls in his first three innings, and was the tournament's leading scorer with 311 runs at an average of 44 and strike-rate of 175. He won himself $200 for that, and another $200 for hitting 15 sixes in his seven games. By August 2009, he was back in Zimbabwe's one-day side after an absence of nearly five years.

FIRST-CLASS AVERAGES, 2008-09

BATTING

(Qualification: 200 runs, average 20.00)

	M	I	NO	R	HS	100s	Avge	Ct/St
M. N. Waller (*Centrals*)	6	11	1	503	85	0	50.30	5
F. Mutizwa (*Easterns*)	6	10	1	447	124	1	49.66	19/2
H. Masakadza (*Easterns & Zim. Select XI*)	7	12	0	565	142	2	47.08	4
S. Matsikenyeri (*Easterns & Zim. Select XI*)	7	12	0	562	142	2	46.83	10
E. Chigumbura (*Northerns & Zim. Select XI*)	7	13	1	531	94	0	44.25	2
C. J. Chibhabha (*Centrals & Zim. Select XI*)	6	12	1	428	82	0	38.90	6
†B. Mlambo (*Easterns*)	6	10	0	350	158	1	35.00	4
S. K. Nyamuzinga (*Easterns*)	4	7	0	239	120	1	34.14	3
T. Taibu (*Northerns*)	6	11	0	374	92	0	34.00	16/4
T. Maruma (*Easterns & Zimbabwe Select XI*)	6	11	2	281	66*	0	31.22	5
C. K. Coventry (*Westerns*)	5	10	0	268	106	1	26.80	7
T. Ngulube (*Westerns*)	6	12	3	233	48*	0	25.88	14/2
R. W. Chakabva (*Northerns & Zim. Select XI*)	7	13	0	313	131	1	24.07	9

	M	I	NO	R	HS	100s	Avge	Ct/St
†K. M. Dabengwa (*Westerns & Zim. Select XI*) ...	6	11	1	232	57	0	23.20	7
A. G. Cremer (*Northerns & Zimbabwe Select XI*) .	7	12	1	255	74	0	23.18	2
R. W. Price (*Northerns*).................	6	11	0	240	77	0	21.81	7
T. Mupariwa (*Westerns*)	6	11	1	217	48	0	21.70	2

† *Left-handed batsman.*

BOWLING

(Qualification: 10 wickets)

	Style	O	M	R	W	BB	5W/i	Avge
E. C. Rainsford (*Centrals*)................	RFM	68.3	15	172	16	6-34	1	10.75
R. W. Price (*Northerns*).................	SLA	219.2	70	402	29	6-69	2	13.86
H. Masakadza (*Easterns*)................	LBG/RM	79.5	26	179	11	4-11	0	16.27
P. Utseya (*Easterns & Zimbabwe Select XI*) ..	OB	232.4	51	560	33	7-56	2	16.96
A. M. Manyumwa (*Northerns*)	RM	112.5	34	330	19	5-15	3	17.36
D. T. Hondo (*Easterns*)	RFM	87.4	20	251	12	5-59	1	20.91
E. Chigumbura (*Northerns & Zim. Select XI*) .	RM	192.2	52	542	24	5-71	1	22.58
N. Mushangwe (*Easterns*)................	LB	112	22	336	14	4-40	0	24.00
A. G. Cremer (*Northerns & Zim. Select XI*)...	LBG	239.1	52	674	27	5-53	1	24.96
S. W. Masakadza (*Easterns & Zim. Select XI*)	RM	181.2	38	623	24	5-102	1	25.95
K. M. Dabengwa (*Westerns & Zim. Select XI*)	SLA	160.2	40	414	14	3-58	0	29.57
T. Kamungozi (*Centrals*)..................	LB	189.1	39	525	17	5-130	1	30.88
J. Nyumbu (*Westerns*)	OB	163	32	535	17	5-78	1	31.47
B. Mugochi (*Centrals*)...................	SLA	139	28	441	14	5-115	1	31.50
C. J. Chibhabha (*Centrals*)...............	RM	82	9	325	10	3-25	0	32.50
C. B. Mpofu (*Westerns & Zim. Select XI*) ..	RFM	199	43	626	18	4-64	0	34.77
T. Mupariwa (*Westerns*).................	RFM	190.4	40	627	18	4-84	0	34.83
T. Muzarabani (*Centrals*)...............	RFM	118.3	13	455	11	4-46	0	41.36

Full scores of the 2008-09 Zimbabwean season can be found at www.cricinfo.com/db/ARCHIVE/2008-09/ZIM_LOCAL/, www.cricketarchive.co.uk/Archive/Seasons/2008-09_ZIM.html and in the *ACS Overseas First-Class Annual 2009.*

LOGAN CUP, 2008-09

	Played	Won	Lost	Drawn	Bonus points Batting	Bowling	Points	Net run-rate
Easterns..........	6	5	0	1	13	24	93	0.07
Northerns	6	4	2	0	13	24	77	0.88
Centrals........	6	1	3	2	10	24	77	0.88
Westerns........	6	0	5	1	5	20	45*	−0.37
							31	−0.55

* *6 points deducted for slow over-rate.*

Win = 10 pts; draw = 6 pts.
Bonus points awarded for the first 100 overs of each team's first innings. One bonus batting point was awarded for the first 175 runs and another point for each further 50. One bonus bowling point was awarded for the third wicket taken and every subsequent two.

At Country Club, Harare, March 24, 25, 26, 2009. **Easterns won by an innings and 275 runs.** Toss: Westerns. **Westerns 156 and 110** (H. Masakadza 4-11); **Easterns 541-9 dec** (H. Masakadza 107, S. Matsikenyeri 111, F. Mutizwa 124, S. K. Nyamuzinga 120). *Easterns 18 pts, Westerns 2 pts.*

 Hamilton Masakadza and Stuart Matsikenyeri added 169 for Easterns' third wicket; Forster Mutizwa and Steven Nyamuzinga 207 for the sixth. Nyamuzinga, who hit 14 fours and three sixes and reached 100 in 106 balls, had figures of 4–3–2–3 in Westerns' first innings, and Masakadza 5–1–11–4 in the second; both were career-bests.

At Harare Sports Club, Harare, March 24, 25, 26, 2009. **Northerns won by three wickets.** Toss: Centrals. **Centrals 184** (M. N. Waller 69; A. G. Cremer 4-81) **and 180** (M. N. Waller 73); **Northerns 184** (E. Chigumbura 82; T. Muzarabani 4-61) **and 181-7** (R. W. Price 58; E. C. Rainsford 4-20). *Northerns 15 pts, Centrals 5 pts.*
    Elton Chigumbura scored 82 from 67 balls out of 117 added before he was last out, hitting six sixes and seven fours. Ray Price had figures of 13–4–15–0 in Centrals' first innings and 17.5–4–20–3 in their second (30.5–8–35–3 in the match).

At Old Hararians, Harare, March 31, April 1, 2, 3, 2009. **Drawn.** Toss: Easterns. **Easterns 255** (F. Mutizwa 60) **and 331-7 dec** (T. Maruma 66*, F. Mutizwa 52*; B. Mugochi 5-115); **Centrals 252** (B. M. Chapungu 85; D. T. Hondo 5-59) **and 176-4** (M. N. Waller 68*). *Centrals 12 pts, Easterns 12 pts.*
    Timycen Maruma and Forster Mutizwa shared a stand of 111 for Easterns' eighth wicket.*

At Alexandra Sports Club, Harare, March 31, April 1, 2, 3, 2009. **Northerns won by 269 runs.** Toss: Northerns. **Northerns 300** (E. Chigumbura 53, A. G. Cremer 74) **and 267** (E. Chigumbura 94, R. W. Price 77); **Westerns 158** (A. M. Manyumwa 5-15) **and 140** (R. W. Price 6-69, A. G. Cremer 4-36). *Northerns 17 pts, Westerns 4 pts.*
    Medium-pacer Admire Manyumwa had career-best figures of 18.2–11–15–5 in Westerns' first innings. Elton Chigumbura and Ray Price added 160 to rescue Northerns from 96-7.

At Harare Sports Club, Harare, April 6, 7, 8, 2009. **Centrals won by nine wickets.** Toss: Centrals. **Westerns 145** (F. Takarusenga 65*; T. Muzarabani 4-46) **and 201** (E. C. Rainsford 6-34); **Centrals 325** (M. N. Waller 81, E. C. Rainsford 51; T. Mupariwa 4-84) **and 22-1.** *Centrals 17 pts, Westerns 4 pts.*
    Freedom Takarusenga carried his bat through Westerns' first innings for a maiden fifty.

At Country Club, Harare, April 6, 7, 8, 9, 2009. **Easterns won by two wickets.** Toss: Easterns. **Northerns 207** (N. Mushangwe 4-40) **and 267** (C. Zhuwawo 51; S. W. Masakadza 5-102); **Easterns 146** (F. Mutizwa 52; A. M. Manyumwa 5-19) **and 330-8** (S. Matsikenyeri 60, H. Masakadza 142). *Easterns 14 pts, Northerns 5 pts.*
    Hamilton Masakadza hit 20 fours and two sixes and equalled his highest first-class score as Easterns successfully chased a target of 329.

At Harare Sports Club, Harare, April 21, 22, 23, 24, 2009. **Easterns won by 56 runs.** Toss: Westerns. **Easterns 200** (F. Mutizwa 50; J. Nyumbu 5-78, F. Takarusenga 4-35) **and 276** (S. Matsikenyeri 142); **Westerns 265** (M. M. Mabuza 106) **and 155.** *Easterns 15 pts, Westerns 6 pts.*
    Zimbabwe captain Prosper Utseya had figures of 19.5–10–20–2 in Westerns' second innings.

At Alexandra Sports Club, Harare, April 21, 22, 23, 2009. **Northerns won by an innings and 290 runs.** Toss: Northerns. **Northerns 510-9 dec** (B. R. M. Taylor 95, T. Taibu 92, R. W. Chakabva 131); **Centrals 122** (R. W. Price 5-6) **and 98** (A. M. Manyumwa 5-25, R. W. Price 4-28). *Northerns 19 pts, Centrals 2 pts.*
    Regis Chakabva hit a career-best 131. In Central's first innings, Ray Price had figures of 8.5–6–6–5; in their second, Admire Manyumwa took five in an innings for the third match running.

At Old Hararians, Harare, April 27, 28, 29, 30, 2009. **Easterns won by an innings and nine runs.** Toss: Centrals. **Centrals 275** (C. J. Chibhabha 80, M. N. Waller 85, T. Mahlunge 50; P. Utseya 4-54) **and 169** (C. J. Chibhabha 82; P. Utseya 7-56); **Easterns 453** (B. Mlambo 158, H. Masakadza 51, S. Matsikenyeri 85, F. Mutizwa 51; T. Kamungozi 5-130). *Easterns 18 pts, Centrals 4 pts.*
    Bernard Mlambo's 158, his maiden century, was to be the highest score of the tournament; he batted almost seven hours. Prosper Utseya took 7-56 in Centrals' second innings and 11-110 in the match, which were likewise personal career-bests and the best returns of this tournament.

At Country Club, Harare, April 27, 28, 29, 30, 2009. **Northerns won by two wickets.** Toss: Northerns. **Westerns 220** (K. M. Dabenga 57, C. K. Coventry 76; A. G. Cremer 5-53) **and 332** (C. K. Coventry 106, S. C. Williams 102; E. Chigumbura 5-71); **Northerns 245 and 308-8** (P. Masvaure 90, T. N. Garwe 56*; C. B. Mpofu 4-64). *Northerns 16 pts, Westerns 5 pts.*
    Former Test captain Tatenda Taibu passed 5,000 first-class runs in Northerns' first innings. Charles Coventry, who scored a maiden hundred.

At Harare Sports Club, Harare, May 5, 6, 7, 8, 2009. **Drawn.** Toss: Westerns. **Centrals 299** (A. Tichana 65, M. N. Waller 61) **and 280-7 dec** (T. Mahlunge 66*, R. Nyathi 100); **Westerns 269 and 44-3.** *Centrals 11 pts, Westerns 10 pts.*

Tarisai Mahlunge and Remembrance Nyathi, who scored a maiden hundred, joined forces at 88-6 and added 165 for the seventh wicket.

At Alexandra Sports Club, Harare, May 5, 6, 7, 8, 2009. **Easterns won by one wicket.** Toss: Northerns. **Northerns 213** (T. Taibu 74; P. Utseya 4-38) **and 166** (P. Utseya 6-55); **Easterns 227** (B. Mlambo 60, T. Maruma 52) **and 155-9** (A. G. Cremer 4-57). *Easterns 16 pts, Northerns 5 pts.*

This match was effectively a final for the tournament's top two teams; Prosper Utseya took ten wickets for the second time in successive matches to reach 150 in his first-class career, but Graeme Cremer's leg-spin almost ended Easterns' unbeaten record for the season before their last pair saw them home to clinch the title.

LOGAN CUP WINNERS

1993-94	Mashonaland Under-24	1999-2000	Mashonaland	2005-06	No competition
1994-95	Mashonaland	2000-01	Mashonaland	2006-07	Easterns
1995-96	Matabeleland	2001-02	Mashonaland	2007-08	Northerns
1996-97	Mashonaland	2002-03	Mashonaland	2008-09	Easterns
1997-98	Mashonaland	2003-04	Mashonaland		
1998-99	Matabeleland	2004-05	Mashonaland		

Mashonaland have won the title nine times, Matabeleland and Easterns twice, Mashonaland Under-24 and Northerns once each.

The touring Sri Lankans' matches in 2008-09 appeared in Zimbabwe v Sri Lanka in Wisden 2009 *(page 1381).*

Note: Matches in the following sections were not first-class.

FAITHWEAR INTERPROVINCIAL ONE-DAY COMPETITION, 2008-09

50-over league

	Played	Won	Lost	No result	Bonus points	Points	Net run-rate
Easterns	6	5	0	1	2	24	1.12
Westerns....	6	3	3	0	0	12	-0.51
Northerns...	6	2	3	1	2	12	0.37
Centrals	6	1	5	0	0	4	-0.77

METROPOLITAN BANK TWENTY20, 2008-09

	Played	Won	Lost	Tied	Bonus points	Points	Net run-rate
Northerns ...	6	3	2	1	3	17	0.89
Westerns...	6	3	1	2	0	17	0.39
Centrals	6	2	3	1	0	14*	0.39
Easterns	6	2	4	0	0	8*	-0.54
						6*	-0.72

* 2 points deducted for slow over-rate.

Third-place play-off

At Queens Sports Club, Bulawayo, May 16, 2009. **Easterns won by 70 runs.** Toss: Centrals. **Easterns 239-3** (20 overs) (S. Matsikenyeri 65, H. Masakadza 62*); **Centrals 169** (16.3 overs) (B. M. Chapungu 75).

Final

At Queens Sports Club, Bulawayo, May 16, 2009. **Westerns won by four runs.** Toss: Northerns. **Westerns 116** (19.2 overs) (T. N. Garwe 4-23); **Northerns 112-9** (20 overs) (M. M. Mabuza 5-14).

Westerns were put in and collapsed to 68-7, but won the tournament after off-spinner Mbekezele Mabuza picked up five Northerns wickets in 17 balls.

OTHER A-TEAM TOURS

AUSTRALIA A v PAKISTAN A, 2009

Pakistan A toured Australia in June–July 2009. They lost their two-match first-class series with Australia A 1–0 and the one-day series 2–1, and also lost a Twenty20 game. The most striking success of the tour was 19-year-old Umar Akmal, brother of Test wicketkeeper Kamran Akmal, who hit two first-class hundreds and another in the one-day victory, when he smashed 104 in 70 balls with ten fours and five sixes. The squad of 14 was captained by Mohammad Hafeez and coached by Shahid Anwar.

At Townsville, June 26, 27, 28, 29, 2009. **Drawn.** Toss: Pakistan A. **Australia A 399** (M. Klinger 31, A. C. Voges 78, C. L. White 34, M. C. Henriques 76; J. J. Krejza 101*; Wahab Riaz 5-98) **and 256-5 dec** (R. A. Broad 43, C. L. White 77, T. D. Paine 54*); **Pakistan A 338** (Azhar Ali 78, Umar Akmal 54, Fahad Iqbal 42, Sarfraz Ahmed 56; C. J. McKay 6-75) **and 207-5** (Mohammad Hafeez 31, Umar Akmal 100*, Sarfraz Ahmed 50*).

No. 8 Jason Krejza reached a maiden hundred out of the 188 added by Australia A's last four wickets. Clint McKay took six in an innings for the first time to give the home side the advantage, and Pakistan A were set a target of 318. Umar Akmal ensured the draw with 100 in 110 balls.*

At Townsville, July 3, 4, 5, 6, 2009. **Australia A won by 101 runs.** Toss: Pakistan A. **Australia A 230** (R. A. Broad 32, C. J. Ferguson 60, T. D. Paine 31, M. C. Henriques 48; Mohammad Hafeez 3-20) **and 402-9 dec** (R. A. Broad 85, C. L. White 67, T. D. Paine 46, M. C. Henriques 82); **Pakistan A 333** (Umar Akmal 129, Fahad Iqbal 52, Sarfraz Ahmed 61, Abdur Rehman 36; D. E. Bollinger 5-82) **and 198** (Azhar Ali 73, Umar Amin 30; D. E. Bollinger 3-54, J. J. Krejza 4-54).

Doug Bollinger reduced Pakistan A's first innings to 41-5 on the first evening before Umar Akmal and Fahad Iqbal rescued them in a stand of 161. Akmal scored 129 in 145 balls with 14 fours and three sixes, his second century in successive innings, and paved the way for a first-innings lead of 103. But Australia A amassed 402 second time round to leave a target of 300 in 80 overs; Jason Krejza's off-spin demolished the middle order, Australia taking the series with three overs to spare.

SRI LANKA A v PAKISTAN A, 2009

Pakistan A toured Sri Lanka in August 2009. They won their two-match first-class series with Sri Lanka A 1–0 and lost the one-day series 3–2 (after leading 2–0). They also drew a two-day warm-up against an SLC Development XI and lost a one-day game against an SLC XI. The squad of 16 was captained by Faisal Iqbal and coached by Ijaz Ahmed.

At Dambulla, August 7, 8, 9, 10, 2009. **Drawn.** Toss: Sri Lanka A. **Sri Lanka A 417** (J. Mubarak 160, R. J. M. G. M. Rupasinghe 76, J. K. Silva 48; Wahab Riaz 3-95) **and 271-5 dec** (B. S. M. Warnapura 48, H. D. R. L. Thirimanne 62, J. Mubarak 33, R. J. M. G. M. Rupasinghe 59*); **Pakistan A 315** (Khurram Manzoor 65, Umar Amin 153; U. W. M. B. C. A. Welagedara 3-61, S. Randiv 4-90) **and 156-6** (Ahmed Shehzad 59, Azhar Ali 45*; S. Randiv 3-49).

Both first innings featured a big century, but Jehan Mubarak had more support than Umar Amin, and Sri Lanka A were able to set a target of 374 on the final day. Pakistan A made a disastrous start when their openers – who had put on 158 together on the second day – went for ducks. That brought in Azhar Ali, who held out for more than 70 overs to secure the draw. Wicketkeeper Sarfraz Ahmed made five catches and a stumping in Sri Lanka A's first innings, and nine dismissals in the match.

At R. Premadasa Stadium, Colombo, August 13, 14, 15, 16, 2009. **Pakistan A won by eight wickets.** Toss: Pakistan A. **Pakistan A 342** (Khurram Manzoor 35, Ahmed Shehzad 96, Faisal Iqbal 83, Fahad Iqbal 41; C. W. Vidanapathirana 3-43) **and 71-2** (Umar Amin 34*); **Sri Lanka A 180** (B. S. M. Warnapura 37, H. D. R. L. Thirimanne 51; Mohammad Talha 5-79, Wahab Riaz 4-52) **and 229** (J. K. Silva 79*, M. Pushpakumara 95; Wahab Riaz 3-52, Abdur Rehman 5-82).

Sri Lanka A reached 79-0 before losing all ten first-innings wickets for 101 and slumping to 30-5 in the follow-on. Kaushal Silva and Muthumudalige Pushpakumara averted an innings defeat, adding 161 for the sixth wicket, but Pakistan A charged to victory in the 23rd over of the final day. Eyebrows were raised when it emerged that the SLC Umpires Committee had appointed Upali Warnapura to referee the match, in which his son Malinda opened Sri Lanka A's batting.

ICC INTERCONTINENTAL CUP, 2009-10

The ICC's ambitious first-class tournament for the leading non-Test countries had a change of format for 2009-10, with the number of teams reduced by one. The competition was restricted to the six Associate sides with full one-day international status – a group that, after the World Cup qualifying tournament earlier in the year, now included the ever-improving Afghanistan – plus a representative team from Zimbabwe, as the ICC continued efforts to restore the standard of cricket there. This change was hard on Namibia, who had topped the table in the previous tournament, eventually losing in the final to Ireland. Instead they and Bermuda (who had lost their one-day status during 2009) took part in the new Intercontinental Shield (see below), along with Uganda and the United Arab Emirates.

Batting feats dominated the early games, with the Zimbabwean Test players Tatenda Taibu and Vusi Sibanda and the veteran Kenyan Steve Tikolo all scoring two hundreds in a match, a feat emulated by Noor Ali of Afghanistan, who was making his first-class debut.

Full scores of the matches that follow can be found at: www.cricinfo.com/icccont2010/engine/series/408325.html, and in the *ACS Overseas First-Class Annual 2009*.

At Aberdeen, July 2, 3, 4, 2009. **Scotland won by 29 runs.** Toss: Scotland. **Scotland 185** (G. D. Drummond 52; Khurram Chauhan 6-37) **and 199** (J. H. Stander 64); **Canada 142** (C. S. MacLeod 4-66) **and 213.** *Scotland 20 pts.*
   Scotland were struggling at 102-8 before Gordon Drummond, their new four-day captain (Gavin Hamilton continued in charge of the one-day side), hit 52 from 97 balls at No. 10. In the second innings, when Scotland batted one short as wicketkeeper Simon Smith had dislocated his shoulder in a game of football during the second-day warm-ups, Drummond did well again, making 34 in a stand of 69 for the eighth wicket with Jan Stander. Scotland's eventual lead of 242 proved just enough.

At Eglinton, July 3, 4, 5, 6, 2009. **Drawn.** Toss: Ireland. **Ireland 404** (J. P. Bray 89, P. R. Stirling 100, A. R. Cusack 63; S. O. Tikolo 6-80) **and 224-7 dec** (A. R. Cusack 55, A. R. White 59*); **Kenya 331** (D. O. Obuya 64, M. A. Ouma 52, J. K. Kamande 73; R. M. West 4-94) **and 245-8** (C. O. Obuya 84). *Ireland 9 pts, Kenya 3 pts.*
   A close match ended with Kenya 53 short of victory with two wickets left. Set 298, they had looked well set during a fifth-wicket partnership of 105 between new captain Maurice Ouma and Collins Obuya, who hit ten fours and two sixes, but after they fell the shutters went up. Earlier, Ireland had started with a fine opening stand of 128 between Jeremy Bray, who hit 14 fours, and 18-year-old Paul Stirling, whose maiden first-class hundred included 13 fours and a six, before Kenya's former skipper Steve Tikolo tweaked his way through the middle order.

At Hazelaarweg, Rotterdam, July 15, 16, 17, 18, 2009. **Drawn.** Toss: Canada. **Canada 177 and 419-9 dec** (Qaiser Ali 61, S. Dhaniram 144; B. A. Westdijk 4-85); **Netherlands 229** (N. A. Statham 57) **and 233-8** (D. L. S. van Bunge 98*; Umar Bhatti 4-32). *Netherlands 9 pts, Canada 3 pts.*
   The Netherlands, set an unlikely 368 to win, held on for a draw, mainly thanks to Daan van Bunge, who survived 294 balls and ended just short of a maiden first-class century. The Dutch began the final day at 120-5, and soon lost another wicket, but van Bunge dug in, helped by the tailenders and the weather, which lopped around 40 overs off the day's ration. He put on 31 in 27 overs with No. 9 Mark Jonkman, who scored 12 in 68 balls before finally falling to off-spinner Qaiser Ali, whose second-innings figures were 8–7–1–1. Canada owed their big lead largely to 40-year-old Sunil Dhaniram, who hit 17 fours and two sixes in the highest score of a first-class career that began for Guyana in 1992-93.

At King City, August 14, 15, 16, 17, 2009. **Kenya won by 247 runs.** Toss: Kenya. **Kenya 317** (S. O. Tikolo 158) **and 362-3 dec** (S. R. Waters 157*, S. O. Tikolo 169); **Canada 234** (M. Z. Zahir 57) **and 198** (A. M. Samad 87; H. A. Varaiya 6-45). *Kenya 20 pts.*

Steve Tikolo, freed of the cares of captaincy, hit two memorable centuries. In the first innings he struck 22 fours, and collected 21 more (plus two sixes) in the second, when he put on 330 for the third wicket with Seren Waters – half his age at 19 – who made his maiden first-class hundred. Canada had no answer, and slow left-armer Hiren Varaiya spun Kenya to victory. The only resistance came from opener Abdool Samad, who batted for 190 minutes and hit 17 fours.

At Mutare, August 16, 17, 18, 19, 2009. **Drawn.** Toss: Afghanistan. **Zimbabwe XI 350** (T. Taibu 172) **and 446-9 dec** (T. Taibu 120, F. Mutizwa 56, T. N. Garwe 117); **Afghanistan 427** (Noor Ali 130, Mohammad Shahzad 79, Mohammad Nabi 102; T. Maruma 6-106) **and 211-4** (Noor Ali 100*). *Zimbabwe XI 3 pts, Afghanistan 9 pts.*

Tatenda Taibu, leading a virtual Zimbabwe A side with only one other player (Chris Mpofu) of Test experience, showed his class with twin centuries. Taibu hit 26 fours in the first innings, and 16 in the second, when he shared a sixth-wicket stand of 165 with Forster Mutizwa before Trevor Garwe's maiden first-class century stretched the lead to 369. However, although their side contained nine men making their first-class debut, Afghanistan were not outclassed, and opener Noor Ali, a 21-year-old right-hander, became only the fourth man to score two centuries in his first first-class match. The previous three all became Test players: Arthur Morris (Australia), Nari Contractor (India) and Aamer Malik (Pakistan).

At Aberdeen, August 17, 18, 19, 20, 2009. **Drawn.** Toss: Scotland. **Ireland 202** (W. T. S. Porterfield 77; G. Goudie 4-58, R. M. Haq 5-30) **and 303** (W. T. S. Porterfield 118, A. R. White 55; G. Goudie 4-61, R. M. Haq 4-88); **Scotland 208** (M. Q. Sheikh 100*; R. M. West 7-88) **and 72-5.** *Scotland 9 pts, Ireland 3 pts.*

Ireland's hopes of a probable win were washed away when no play was possible on the final day at Mannofield. Scotland, needing 298, had declined to 50-5 on the third evening, but Irish optimism came to nothing – and the Scots took the lion's share of the points after grabbing a narrow first-innings lead thanks to Qasim Sheikh's first hundred for them, which included ten fours and a six.

At Amstelveen, August 24, 25, 26, 2009. **Afghanistan won by one wicket.** Toss: Netherlands. **Netherlands 181** (T. N. de Grooth 54; Hameed Hasan 4-45, Mohammad Nabi 4-52) **and 132** (P. W. Borren 63; Shapoor Zadran 4-28, Mirwais Ashraf 4-24); **Afghanistan 107 and 209-9** (Noor Ali 56; E. Schiferli 5-57). *Netherlands 6 pts, Afghanistan 14 pts.*

Afghanistan continued their remarkable rise with a narrow victory in a low-scoring game. Set 207, they reached 197-7 before two quick wickets left the last pair at the crease with six still wanted. But Samiullah Shenwari (25*) and last man Hameed Hasan (1*) proved equal to the task, Shenwari slashing the winning boundary over the slips off Mudassar Bukhari. Twenty wickets fell on the first day, and 12 in 56.1 overs on the rain-shortened second.

At Kwekwe, October 7, 8, 9, 10, 2009. **Zimbabwe XI won by five wickets.** Toss: Zimbabwe XI. **Kenya 333** (S. O. Tikolo 61, A. Obanda 51) **and 254** (M. A. Ouma 54); **Zimbabwe XI 352** (V. Sibanda 209, R. W. Chakabva 67) **and 238-5** (C. J. Chibhabha 64, V. Sibanda 116*). *Zimbabwe XI 20 pts.*

A fine double by Vusi Sibanda gave the Zimbabweans the upper hand, which they never relinquished. In the first innings Sibanda hit 26 fours and a six from 320 balls in nearly seven hours at the crease. He and Regis Chakabva added 161 for the eighth wicket, taking their side into the lead after they had been 178-7. Then, with the Zimbabwe XI facing a testing target of 236, Sibanda entered at 24-2 and made another century to ensure victory, this time adding 166 for the third wicket with Chamu Chibhabha.

QUALIFYING TABLE

(at December 31, 2009)

	Played	Won	Lost	Drawn	1st-inns Lead	Points
Scotland	2	1	0	1		29
Kenya	3	1	1	1	2	29
Zimbabwe XI	2	1	1	1	1	23
Afghanistan	2	1	0	1	1	23
Netherlands	2	0	1	1	1	23
Ireland	2	0	0	2	2	15
Canada	3	0	2	1	1	12
					0	3

Win = 14 pts. Tie = 7 pts. Draw with more than ten hours lost to weather = 7 pts. Draw with less than ten hours lost to the weather = 3 pts. First-innings lead = 6 pts. Tie on first innings = 3 pts. Abandoned = 10 pts. Teams finishing level on points separated by (a) most outright wins, and (b) the higher net runs-per-wicket ratio.

Remaining fixtures (scores will appear in *Wisden 2011*): Jan 23–26 Afghanistan v Ireland (at Dambulla, Sri Lanka); 25–28 Kenya v Scotland; Feb 20–23 Afghanistan v Canada (in the UAE); June 10–13 Netherlands v Scotland; August 11–14 Ireland v Netherlands, Scotland v Afghanistan; 21–24 Canada v Zimbabwe XI; September 1–4 Canada v Ireland, Netherlands v Zimbabwe XI; October 2–5 Kenya v Afghanistan; 6–9 Zimbabwe XI v Ireland, 13–16 Zimbabwe XI v Scotland; November 25–29 Final (Dubai).

ICC INTERCONTINENTAL CUP FINALS

2004	SCOTLAND beat Canada by an innings and 84 runs at Sharjah.
2005	IRELAND beat Kenya by six wickets at Windhoek.
2006-07	IRELAND beat Canada by an innings and 115 runs at Leicester.
2007-08	IRELAND beat Namibia by nine wickets at Port Elizabeth.

ICC INTERCONTINENTAL SHIELD, 2009-10

In 2009 the ICC introduced an additional first-class competition for second-tier nations. Bermuda, Namibia and the United Arab Emirates (who had previously played in the Intercontinental Cup) were joined by Uganda. Only two of the six matches had been played by the end of 2009.

Remaining fixtures (scores will appear in *Wisden 2011*): January 20–23 UAE v Uganda; April 2–5 Namibia v Bermuda; June 11–14 Bermuda v UAE; September 18–21 Uganda v Namibia; November 25–28 Final.

At Hamilton, August 17, 18, 19, 2009. **Uganda won by seven wickets.** Toss: Bermuda. **Bermuda 91** (F. Nsubuga 4-20) **and 138** (D. K. Arinaitwe 4-34); **Uganda 119** (R. J. Trott 5-39) **and 111-3.** *Uganda 20 pts.*

Bermuda, fielding a new-look side captained by David Hemp after several senior players announced their retirements, never recovered after losing their first three wickets for one run on the first morning. The highest individual innings of a low-scoring match was wicketkeeper Lawrence Sematimba's 39 in Uganda's second innings.

At Windhoek, December 5, 6, 7, 8, 2009. **United Arab Emirates won by four wickets.** Toss: United Arab Emirates. **Namibia 369** (S. F. Burger 65, W. van Vuuren 55, L. P. van der Westhuizen 70; Fayyaz Ahmed 4-75) **and 237** (R. van Schoor 87; Mohammad Tauqir 5-40); **United Arab Emirates 297** (Arfan Haider 84; L. Klazinga 5-61) **and 311-6** (Khurram Khan 109, Fayyaz Ahmed 52). *United Arab Emirates 14 pts, Namibia 6 pts.*

UAE overturned a first-innings deficit of 72 to win, chasing down their target of 310 in 64.1 overs. Khurram Khan hit 12 fours and a six from 144 balls. Namibia's second innings included ten penalty runs – five after the UAE bowlers changed the condition of the ball, and five more when the ball struck a helmet on the ground behind the wicketkeeper.

ICC WORLD CUP QUALIFIER, 2008-09

WILL LUKE

1. Ireland   2. Canada   3. Netherlands   4. Kenya   5. Afghanistan   6. Scotland

Cricket played by Associate nations rarely attracts global media attention, but then again it rarely warrants it. However, the World Cup Qualifier offered more of a spectacle than minnow tournaments of recent years, largely thanks to two nations geographically and politically poles apart. Ireland and Afghanistan ran away with the headlines and plaudits, as did the ICC, whose committed work among developing nations should be acclaimed.

Few tournaments involving the non-Test nations are begun without someone insisting it is wide open and anyone can win it. Not so in South Africa. **Ireland** were almost universally expected to triumph, unless Kenya – a fractious, fragile side these days – could gel themselves in time. They couldn't, and through William Porterfield's leadership and batting, as well as the wile and nous of their former captain, Trent Johnston, Ireland were deserved winners, far and away the most accomplished side on show.

Ireland came unstuck against Afghanistan and (in what was for them, though not their opponents, a dead match) against Kenya, but their march towards the final was never in doubt. The confidence they showed in that final, where they coasted to a nine-wicket victory, epitomised a team comfortable with its status as the top Associate dog. Johnston tore through Canada with five for 14 while Porterfield's magnificent, composed 104 revealed his growing stature as a batsman and a man thriving on leadership.

Porterfield has benefited from the English county system, though his allegiance lies squarely with Ireland for now. It has not been so straightforward for some of his compatriots. Midway through the tournament, Eoin Morgan was selected by England for their World Twenty20 squad. While that didn't rankle with the player himself, nor his team-mates – at least on the surface – the fact that their best players were poached by a rich England and her plump counties did irritate some in Irish cricket. The board, led by the enthusiastic and sharp Warren Deutrom, remain ambitious enough to aspire to Test status, but until then more players seem likely to follow Morgan (who was recalled by Middlesex and so missed the final). It may be scant consolation, but producing high-calibre cricketers such as Morgan, Ed Joyce, Kevin and Niall O'Brien, Boyd Rankin and Paul Stirling at least swells Irish hearts with pride.

Scotland, long Ireland's close rivals, were a disappointment, at times shambolic. They lost to Afghanistan and came close to losing their full one-day international status too. During the tournament, Paul Hoffmann, a former Scotland international, called for the resignation of Scotland's captain, the miserably out of form Ryan Watson. **Bermuda**, meanwhile, did their utmost to undermine the credibility of Associate cricket with a spate of woefully lazy performances, angering their coach but seemingly not the partying players. Rumours abounded of late nights at the bar. The coach, Gus Logie, gave his

AFGHANISTAN'S JOURNEY

"Cricket is our chance"

WILL LUKE

"I am an ambassador of my country. I will show my culture to the rest of the world that we are not warrior people." Raees Ahmadzai was waiting to bat at Senwes Park, Potchefstroom, in a country he never thought he would be fortunate enough to visit, after spending his childhood in the notorious Kacha Gari refugee camp near Peshawar in Pakistan.

Ahmadzai's family had crossed the border as they fled the Soviets in the 1980s, and he learned the game barefoot, fashioning balls out of shirt cloth and using shoes for stumps. Bats were begged, borrowed or made from sticks, and stripped tree bark was ingeniously used to give a truish surface to the "pitch". Rudimentary doesn't begin to describe his cricketing background, nor that of his team-mates from Afghanistan, for whom he plays with such chest-swelling, tearful pride.

Afghanistan's journey to the World Cup Qualifier felt like a dream for the players – and a wholly improbable tale for everyone else. It began in Division Five of the World Cricket League, held in Jersey in May 2008, when Taj Malik, the first national coach, made what then seemed a ludicrous prediction: "Not only are we going to bring the cup back from Jersey," he declared, "but we are also going to the World Cup." Afghanistan did indeed win in Jersey.

After winning Division Four in Tanzania five months later, each member of the team was rewarded with a trip to Mecca by the Afghan Ministry of Hajj. Their brazenly confident attitude bristled uncomfortably in the sometimes staid atmosphere of Affiliate and Associate cricket, and few opponents took them seriously. To their peril. Next came Division Three in Argentina in January 2009 and, unbelievably, another triumph that bought them entry to the World Cup Qualifier in South Africa, where they flicked aside the eventual champions Ireland, Scotland (twice), Bermuda, Namibia and Denmark. They could not quite reach the World Cup proper, but had the considerable consolation of full one-day international status.

To speak to Ahmadzai was to begin to understand a people wholly unconnected with the affluence of a rich sport. The loss of a wicket hurt – a duck was greeted in true Nasser Hussain bat-flinging style – though such is their background that all the members of the team realised their true position in the world: cricket is a game. Yet it can also be a passport to a better life. Hameed Hasan is, like so many fast bowlers before him, a nightmare to face on the pitch and as gentle as a feather off it. When Afghanistan looked to be crashing out of Division Three in Argentina – they were hugely fortunate to be reprieved by the weather – Hasan came off the pitch crying. "I have seen people die, and I have not shed a tear," he said, "but there is something about cricket that gets me here [pointing to his heart]. Cricket is our chance."

Over the years, cricket has changed all sorts of players' lives, from anonymous mining villages in England, vast outback farms in Australia or the slums of India, and the sport brings genuine opportunity for benevolence. Yet nothing twangs the heartstrings in the same way as seeing a team of refugees outplay – and outjoy – affluent nations through sheer willpower and belief. "I am the lucky man," says Ahmadzai, plonking on his helmet and stepping over his interviewer's feet. "I can do something special for my country."

side a verbal walloping via an interview on Cricinfo, and angered his players, who mistook honesty for treachery. Logie's outburst worked in one sense, though: a raft of drifting players retired or left the set-up in the wake of the tournament. An exhausted Logie – an honourable, hard-working and passionate coach – soon followed.

Afghanistan, too, had teenage tendencies, but in their joyful naivety rather than their careless attitude. Unlike Bermuda, the young Afghans took to the tournament with spirit, class, inventiveness and real ability. Ireland, Scotland and Bermuda were all beaten, and these successes were no flukes. Karim Sadiq, usually the wicketkeeper, broke a finger and so turned to off-spin, picking up 11 economical wickets; he batted beautifully too. Nowroz Mangal anchored many innings in calm fashion, while Hameed Hasan demonstrated the benefits of genuine pace, if not always the control he would wish for. Then again, he did not start wearing spikes until 2007. So delighted were his once cricket-apathetic family at his and the team's success that they sacrificed a lamb and gave it to the poor in his home village.

Success was born from adversity for Afghanistan, many of whose players grew up behind barbed wire in refugee camps, or lost family to war or disease. Some opponents, taken aback by their sudden impact, grumbled at the speed of their ascension, and suffered as a consequence. **Netherlands** always battled hard, and in Edgar Schiferli possessed the player of the tournament: his enthusiastic medium-pace claimed 24 wickets, six more than anyone else. The diminutive Alexei Kervezee was a remarkably mature batsman for a 19-year-old. But for all their individual excellence, Netherlands rarely threaten to dominate tournaments. This one was no exception.

The once-dominant **Kenya** were a side in transition. That they restricted their renowned tendency to implode to just two matches was almost remarkable, but a side bristling with raw natural ability should be challenging and beating teams such as Ireland more regularly. Off-pitch administrative wranglings did not help. **Namibia** did more than make up the numbers, but there was little likelihood of their qualifying for the 2011 World Cup, as they had for the 2003 version. The third African team was **Uganda**, who did enough to show they might yet be a force to be reckoned with.

Canada edged their way to the final, though in reality they, like the **United Arab Emirates**, promised much but only occasionally delivered. **Oman** and **Denmark** brought up the rear, with the Danes particularly feeble. The ICC remain committed to Associate and Affiliate cricket, and insist that professionalisation – to use that ugly word – is vital for the future. Ireland, indeed, provides convincing proof, but quite how countries such as the UAE – whose side, though amply talented, is filled with part-timers relying on generous employers to allow them time off – can be encouraged to professionalise their set-up is a battle which will be fought throughout the new decade.

Notes: Matches in this section were not first-class.

In the group stages, only those games between two teams with ODI status before the tournament began (Kenya, Scotland, Ireland, Canada, Bermuda and Netherlands) constituted official ODIs.

However, games played between these teams in the Super Eights were not official ODIs. The final, as well as the play-offs for third and fifth places, were official ODIs; the six sides contesting these three games (Ireland, Canada, Netherlands, Kenya, Afghanistan and Scotland) enjoy ODI status until the next World Cup Qualifier tournament.

In the matches that follow, official ODIs are marked with a double dagger.

Full scores of all these matches are available at www.cricketarchive.co.uk/Archive/Seasons/RSA/2008-09_RSA_ICC_World_Cup_Qualifier_2008-09.html and www.cricinfo.com/iccwcq2009/content/series/384067.html

Group A

At L. C. de Villiers Oval, Pretoria, April 1, 2009. **Canada won by 103 runs.** Toss: Oman. **Canada 247** (49.3 overs) (Rizwan Cheema 64, S. Dhaniram 100*; Awal Khan 3-19, Tariq Hussain 5-39); **Oman 144** (40 overs) (N. N. Parmar 38*, Farhan Khan 43; Khurram Chauhan 4-27). *Canada 2 pts.*
Sunil Dhaniram crushed Oman with a 91-ball hundred, despite an impressive five-for by Tariq Hussain. At one stage, Oman were 4-5.

‡At Benoni, April 1, 2009. **Ireland won by seven wickets.** Toss: Ireland. **Scotland 232-7** (50 overs) (N. F. I. McCallum 121*); **Ireland 233-3** (37.4 overs) (W. T. S. Porterfield 101, E. J. G. Morgan 60). *Ireland 2 pts.* One-day international debuts: M. M. Iqbal, J. H. Stander (Scotland).
Scotland were 24-4 when Neil McCallum reached the crease. Despite his 121* from 138 balls, they looked a side without direction, and bowled as such. William Porterfield hit a classy 101 from 89 balls, aided by Morgan's urgency between the wickets.

At Krugersdorp, April 1, 2009. **Uganda won by six runs.** Toss: Namibia. **Uganda 234-7** (50 overs) (R. G. Mukasa 51, J. Olwenyi 42, F. Nsubuga 45*); **Namibia 228-9** (50 overs) (R. van Schoor 59, S. F. Burger 50; D. K. Arinaitwe 4-53). *Uganda 2 pts.*
Uganda, an improving side, outplayed their more experienced African cousins. Impressive containment from left-arm spinner Davis Arinaitwe restricted Namibia when the push was on.

At University of Witwatersrand, Johannesburg, April 2, 2009. **Canada won by five wickets.** Toss: Uganda. **Uganda 231-8** (50 overs) (R. G. Mukasa 42, K. Kamyuka 85; Khurram Chauhan 3-31); **Canada 232-5** (47 overs) (G. E. F. Barnett 102*, A. Bagai 33, S. Dhaniram 39). *Canada 2 pts.*
Kenneth Kamyuka's 86-ball 85, with five fours and two sixes, pushed Uganda to a competitive total, but Canada's Geoff Barnett demonstrated his experience with a calm hundred in response.

At Krugersdorp, April 2, 2009. **Ireland won by 116 runs.** Toss: Ireland. **Ireland 285-4** (50 overs) (W. T. S. Porterfield 32, G. C. Wilson 46, A. R. White 71*, K. J. O'Brien 101*); **Oman 169** (37.3 overs) (Zeeshan Siddiqui 48, N. N. Parmar 41; P. Connell 3-24, R. M. West 5-26). *Ireland 2 pts.*
Ireland wobbled from 65-0 to 111-4, but Kevin O'Brien – one of Associate cricket's biggest hitters – thrashed 101 from 91 balls to quell Oman's hopes. Regan West, a deft left-arm spinner built like a prop forward, took five canny wickets.

At L. C. de Villiers Oval, Pretoria, April 2, 2009. **Scotland won by 73 runs.** Toss: Namibia. **Scotland 267-6** (50 overs) (K. J. Coetzer 68, N. F. I. McCallum 103, J. H. Stander 37*); **Namibia 194** (44.4 overs) (G. Snyman 95*; J. D. Nel 3-37, G. Goudie 3-24). *Scotland 2 pts.*
Neil McCallum's second consecutive hundred this time came in a winning cause. Gerrie Snyman's response was a long-handled 95*: thrilling to watch, but ultimately in vain.

At L. C. de Villiers Oval, Pretoria, April 4, 2009. **Canada won by 141 runs.** Toss: Namibia. **Canada 319** (49.5 overs) (J. M. Davison 131, G. E. F. Barnett 46, I. S. Billcliff 61; M. C. van Zyl 4-53); **Namibia 178** (48 overs) (S. F. Burger 75, M. C. van Zyl 48). *Canada 2 pts.*
Canada's powerful batting line-up demolished Namibia. John Davison sparkled with a typically brutal 131 from 99 balls.

At Krugersdorp, April 4, 2009. **Ireland won by six wickets.** Toss: Uganda. **Uganda 155** (44.2 overs) (J. Olwenyi 40, J. Z. Kwebiha 51; A. R. White 4-22); **Ireland 160-4** (31 overs) (W. T. S. Porterfield 44, G. C. Wilson 61). *Ireland 2 pts.*
Andrew White's off-breaks cut through Uganda, who were unable to cope with his spin. Ireland's clinical victory suggested they were content to be called favourites.

At University of Witwatersrand, Johannesburg, April 4, 2009. **Scotland won by nine runs.** Toss: Oman. **Scotland 274-9** (50 overs) (K. J. Coetzer 127, N. S. Poonia 79; Zeeshan Siddiqui 3-64); **Oman 265-9** (50 overs) (Maqsood Hussain 70, Zeeshan Siddiqui 50, N. N. Parmar 37, Aamer Ali 41*; J. H. Stander 4-41). *Scotland 2 pts.*

Scotland nearly slipped up against Oman as Maqsood Hussain blazed 70 from 30 balls in pursuit of 275. Inexperience and a shaky lower-order cost them a major upset.

‡At Benoni, April 6, 2009. **Ireland won by six wickets.** Toss: Ireland. **Canada 220** (48 overs) (J. M. Davison 41, G. E. F. Barnett 49, I. S. Billcliff 38); **Ireland 223-4** (41 overs) (E. J. G. Morgan 84*, N. J. O'Brien 32, K. J. O'Brien 89*; Umar Bhatti 3-28). *Ireland 2 pts.*

Morgan oozed class and calculation; Kevin O'Brien flayed and hammered with bravado, helping demonstrate Ireland's all-round professionalism. Canada were never in the chase once John Davison fell for 41 – a failure by his standards.

At Krugersdorp, April 6, 2009. **Namibia won by 119 runs.** Toss: Oman. **Namibia 291-9** (50 overs) (C. Williams 64, G. Snyman 76, N. R. P. Scholtz 64; Tariq Hussain 3-54); **Oman 172** (43.4 overs) (Adnan Ilyas 33, Awal Khan 62; S. F. Burger 5-44). *Namibia 2 pts.*

Oman slipped to 6-3, and there was little of great substance thereafter. Sarel Burger's tidy spell of seam earned him 5-44 in Namibia's first win.

At University of Witwatersrand, Johannesburg, April 6, 2009. **Scotland won by 45 runs.** Toss: Uganda. **Scotland 209-8** (50 overs) (G. M. Hamilton 56, N. F. I. McCallum 101*); **Uganda 164** (43.1 overs) (R. G. Mukasa 37, J. Z. Kwebiha 69). *Scotland 2 pts.*

A better performance from Scotland's bowlers – five took two wickets each – helped them book their Super Eight place.

‡At Benoni, April 8, 2009. **Canada won by 148 runs.** Toss: Scotland. **Canada 252-7** (50 overs) (J. M. Davison 32, A. Bagai 87, S. Dhaniram 41; C. M. Wright 3-23); **Scotland 104** (30.5 overs) (C. J. O. Smith 43; Umar Bhatti 3-31). *Canada 2 pts.*

Canada totally outplayed Scotland, whose top order was blitzed by Umar Bhatti and Henry Osinde. Ashish Bagai, temporarily away from the world of banking, hit a valuable 87.

At University of Witwatersrand, Johannesburg, April 8, 2009. **Ireland won by seven wickets.** Toss: Namibia. **Namibia 213-9** (50 overs) (N. R. P. Scholtz 62, D. B. Kotze 33, M. C. van Zyl 31, Extras 31); **Ireland 214-3** (45 overs) (W. T. S. Porterfield 84, E. J. G. Morgan 42, N. J. O'Brien 64*). *Ireland 2 pts.*

This made it five wins out of five for Ireland. Their experienced batsmen eased them home with five overs to spare; the gulf between them and other Associate nations was stark.

At L. C. de Villiers Oval, Pretoria, April 8, 2009. **Oman won by one wicket.** Toss: Uganda. **Uganda 298-5** (50 overs) (N. K. J. Bibodi 54, J. Olwenyi 85, F. Nsubuga 48, B. Musoke 44*; H. J. Mehta 3-55); **Oman 302-9** (37.1 overs) (Farhan Khan 95, H. J. Mehta 49, Aamer Ali 43; A. Seiga 3-79, F. Nsubuga 3-54). *Oman 2 pts.*

An extraordinary run-chase handed Oman their first win of the tournament in their last group match. Farhan Khan carved seven brave sixes in a thrilling 95 from 49 balls, as Oman scored at more than eight an over.

Group B

At Vanderbijlpark, April 1, 2009. **Afghanistan won by five wickets.** Toss: Afghanistan. **Denmark 204-9** (50 overs) (C. R. Pedersen 46, S. Vestergaard 39; Karim Sadiq 4-27); **Afghanistan 205-5** (46.2 overs) (Karim Sadiq 39, Mohammad Shahzad 55*, Mohammad Nabi 47, Extras 31). *Afghanistan 2 pts.*

Karim Sadiq, who would have been keeping but for a broken finger, grabbed 4-27 with his off-breaks. He also struck 39, though it was Mohammad Shahzad's bristling 55 that sealed the win.*

At Absa Puk Oval, Potchefstroom, April 1, 2009. **United Arab Emirates won by four wickets.** Toss: Bermuda. **Bermuda 187** (46.3 overs) (J. J. Tucker 66; Khurram Khan 3-40); **United Arab

Emirates 190-6 (47.1 overs) (Arshad Ali 41, Saqib Ali 31, Khurram Khan 40*). *United Arab Emirates 2 pts.*

UAE outplayed a complacent Bermuda, whose problems had only just begun. Khurram Khan took 3-40 and, although the talented Janeiro Tucker cracked 66, there was little other resistance.

‡At Senwes Park, Potchefstroom, April 1, 2009. **Netherlands won by seven wickets.** Toss: Kenya. **Kenya 247-8** (50 overs) (T. M. Odoyo 36, J. K. Kamande 58; E. Schiferli 4-49); **Netherlands 248-3** (46.2 overs) (R. N. ten Doeschate 106*, B. Zuiderent 64*). *Netherlands 2 pts.*

Arguably the finest Associate all-rounder, Ryan ten Doeschate showed his class with bat (106 from 84 deliveries) and ball (10–1–48–2) to ease Netherlands past Kenya.*

At Senwes Park, Potchefstroom, April 2, 2009. **Afghanistan won by 60 runs.** Toss: Afghanistan. **Afghanistan 239-9** (50 overs) (Karim Sadiq 83, Asghar Stanikzai 38, Nowroz Mangal 71); **Bermuda 179** (49.3 overs) (G. Blakeney 68, S. D. Outerbridge 62; Samiullah Shenwari 4-28). *Afghanistan 2 pts.*

This was a huge upset, justifying the hype surrounding Afghanistan and the concern for Bermuda. Karim Sadiq made 83 from 103 balls, but it was Afghanistan's bowlers – especially leg-spinner Samiullah Shenwari – who shone, tearing through a hapless Bermuda. Their captain, Irvine Romaine, was disconcertingly phlegmatic: "This is part of cricket. Sometimes you show up to play, sometimes you don't."

At Absa Puk Oval, Potchefstroom, April 2, 2009. **Netherlands won by seven wickets.** Toss: Netherlands. **Denmark 245-9** (50 overs) (M. R. Pedersen 121, C. R. Pedersen 41, A. B. Chawla 31; E. Schiferli 3-43); **Netherlands 246-3** (43 overs) (A. N. Kervezee 121*, E. S. Szwarczynski 64). *Netherlands 2 pts.*

An unbeaten 121 from the prodigiously talented Alexei Kervezee helped Netherlands crunch their near neighbours, despite a fine hundred from Michael Pedersen.

At Vanderbijlpark, April 2, 2009. **Kenya won by nine wickets.** Toss: Kenya. **United Arab Emirates 79** (30.1 overs) (Naeemuddin Aslam 34; L. N. Onyango 6-14); **Kenya 80-1** (12.2 overs) (M. A. Ouma 50). *Kenya 2 pts.*

Medium-pacer Lameck Onyango helped Kenya thrash UAE, who recovered slightly from 49-9.

At Absa Puk Oval, Potchefstroom, April 4, 2009. **Kenya won by 107 runs.** Toss: Kenya. **Kenya 282-5** (50 overs) (M. A. Ouma 35, K. O. Otieno 109*, A. Obanda 60); **Afghanistan 175** (47 overs) (Mohammad Nabi 56; T. M. Odoyo 3-29). *Kenya 2 pts.*

Kenya put Afghanistan back in their box with a commanding all-round display, exposing their inexperience. Thomas Odoyo's 3-29 cut a hole through Afghanistan's run-chase; only Mohammad Nabi offered resistance with a well-played 56.

At Vanderbijlpark, April 4, 2009. **Bermuda won by nine wickets.** Toss: Bermuda. **Denmark 157** (48.3 overs) (J. J. Tucker 3-29, R. J. Trott 4-30); **Bermuda 160-1** (38.1 overs) (F. S. Crockwell 36, D. L. Hemp 76*, S. D. Outerbridge 33*). *Bermuda 2 pts.*

David Hemp, a vital cog in the Bermudian machine, was instrumental in their convincing victory. Seamers Janeiro Tucker and Jacobi Robinson demolished Denmark's overawed middle order.

At Senwes Park, Potchefstroom, April 4, 2009. **United Arab Emirates won by two wickets.** Toss: UAE. **Netherlands 265** (49.3 overs) (E. S. Szwarczynski 56, B. Zuiderent 50, E. Schiferli 32, Extras 30; Zahid Shah 4-53, Arshad Ali 3-45); **United Arab Emirates 268-8** (49.1 overs) (N. Gopal 51, Saqib Ali 78; E. Schiferli 3-45). *United Arab Emirates 2 pts.*

UAE made light of a steep target, largely thanks to Saqib Ali's controlled 78, but also through their lower-order muscle as Zahid Shah crashed a run-a-ball 21 from No. 9.

At Vanderbijlpark, April 6, 2009. **Netherlands won by five wickets.** Toss: Netherlands. **Afghanistan 204-9** (50 overs) (Karim Sadiq 72, Mohammad Nabi 36; R. N. ten Doeschate 3-50, Mudassar Bukhari 3-41); **Netherlands 208-5** (46.2 overs) (D. L. S. van Bunge 65*, B. Zuiderent 30). *Netherlands 2 pts.*

Ryan ten Doeschate and Mudassar Bukhari shared six wickets in an easy win for the more experienced Netherlands. Karim Sadiq, however, continued to impress with 72 silky runs.

‡At Senwes Park, Potchefstroom, April 6, 2009. **Kenya won by seven wickets.** Toss: Kenya. **Bermuda 259-5** (50 overs) (F. S. Crockwell 45, D. L. Hemp 102*, S. D. Outerbridge 31, G. Blakeney 30); **Kenya 260-3** (45 overs) (M. A. Ouma 57, K. O. Otieno 63, S. O. Tikolo 60*, C. O. Obuya 43*). *Kenya 2 pts. One-day international debuts: G. Blakeney, F. S. Crockwell (Bermuda).*

An improved display from Bermuda's batsmen, if not their bowlers, but it still left them on the brink of elimination and, with it, the loss of their prized ODI status. David Hemp played with his usual authority and calmness for an unbeaten century, but Kenya eased home against tame bowling.

At Absa Puk Oval, Potchefstroom, April 6, 2009. **United Arab Emirates won by 112 runs.** Toss: Denmark. **United Arab Emirates 379-6** (50 overs) (Amjad Javed 164, Arshad Ali 35, Khurram Khan 56, N. Gopal 35); **Denmark 267** (44.4 overs) (M. R. Pedersen 60, C. R. Pedersen 58, F. A. Klokker 77, Extras 30). *United Arab Emirates 2 pts.*

Denmark again lost out against a team bristling with confidence – perhaps not all of it justified. But what raw ability: Amjad Javed's extraordinary 164 – 117 balls, with 17 fours and eight sixes – was laced with power and authority. In reply, Denmark folded from a respectable 233-4 to 267 all out in less than eight overs.

At Vanderbijlpark, April 8, 2009. **United Arab Emirates won by five wickets.** Toss: United Arab Emirates. **Afghanistan 251-8** (50 overs) (Mohammad Shahzad 30, Asghar Stanikzai 69, Nowroz Mangal 46, Samiullah Shenwari 31*; Zahid Shah 4-59); **United Arab Emirates 257-5** (47.2 overs) (Arshad Ali 41, N. Gopal 81, Saqib Ali 69, Naeemuddin Aslam 47*). *United Arab Emirates 2 pts.*

A fascinating clash between two ramshackle sides oozing raw talent promised much and duly delivered, yet it was the UAE – a team of bursars and baggage handlers – who emerged victorious over the romantics' choice. UAE lost two quick wickets late on while chasing 252, but Saqib Ali's controlled 69 had set them a fine platform. Afghanistan's dreams of reaching the Super Eights, however, were not over.

‡At Senwes Park, Potchefstroom, April 8, 2009. **Netherlands won by 63 runs.** Toss: Bermuda. **Netherlands 304-9** (50 overs) (D. J. Reekers 35, A. N. Kervezee 44, R. N. ten Doeschate 67, E. Schiferli 41, Extras 30); **Bermuda 241-9** (50 overs) (D. L. Hemp 81, G. Blakeney 42; R. N. ten Doeschate 3-51). *Netherlands 2 pts.*

Bermuda, in a must-win clash, failed to deliver, so losing their ODI status, not that many would lament them after another shambolic tournament. Ten Doeschate owned the game with a bruising 67 and three good wickets. David Hemp, as ever, fought a lone battle.

At Absa Puk Oval, Potchefstroom, April 8, 2009. **Kenya won by nine wickets.** Toss: Kenya. **Denmark 173-8** (50 overs) (M. Lund 45; E. Otieno 3-51); **Kenya 174-1** (33.1 overs) (K. O. Otieno 84*, S. R. Waters 61*). *Kenya 2 pts.*

Kennedy Otieno and Seren Waters shared an unbroken stand of 140 in 27 overs.

GROUP TABLES

Group A	Played	Won	Lost	Points	Net run-rate
IRELAND	5	5	0	10	1.49
CANADA	5	4	1	8	1.49
SCOTLAND	5	3	2	6	−0.31
NAMIBIA	5	1	4	2	−0.50
Uganda	5	1	4	2	−0.92
Oman	5	1	4	2	−1.14

Group B	Played	Won	Lost	Points	Net run-rate
KENYA	5	4	1	8	1.68
NETHERLANDS	5	4	1	8	0.55
UAE	5	4	1	8	−0.13
AFGHANISTAN	5	2	3	4	−0.27
Bermuda	5	1	4	2	−0.44
Denmark	5	0	5	0	−1.34

SUPER EIGHTS

At Krugersdorp, April 11, 2009. **Afghanistan won by 22 runs.** Toss: Ireland. **Afghanistan 218-7** (50 overs) (Mohammad Shahzad 46, Asghar Stanikzai 47, Raees Ahmadzai 50*); **Ireland 196** (47.3 overs) (A. R. White 56, K. J. O'Brien 52; Hameed Hasan 5-23). *Afghanistan 2 pts.*
  This was an astonishing upset for Ireland and for cricket. Ireland had bowled well to restrict Afghanistan to 218, but on a slightly corrugated pitch their batsmen couldn't cope with the pace and accuracy of 22-year-old Hameed Hasan, a highly regarded fast bowler who has represented MCC, and who began wearing spikes just 18 months before this game. No other team had come close to beating Ireland.

At Benoni, April 11, 2009. **Canada won by seven wickets.** Toss: Canada. **Kenya 181** (43.5 overs) (J. K. Kamande 61, N. Odhiambo 34*; H. Osinde 4-39); **Canada 185-3** (34.3 overs) (G. E. F. Barnett 38, Rizwan Cheema 49, I. S. Billcliff 36*, A. Bagai 40*). *Canada 2 pts.*
  A convincing win by Canada kept their hopes of reaching the final alive. Henry Osinde bustled in with verve to pick up four wickets; Kenya collapsed to 51-5 by the 11th over. It was game over, and Rizwan Cheema ensured they were dealt a hammering by striking 49 from 24 balls.

At L. C. de Villiers Oval, Pretoria, April 11, 2009. **Namibia won by 49 runs.** Toss: United Arab Emirates. **Namibia 280-7** (50 overs) (S. F. Burger 30, C. Williams 40, G. Snyman 32, L. J. Burger 61, N. R. P. Scholtz 57); **United Arab Emirates 231-9** (50 overs) (Naeemuddin Aslam 53, S. Nayak 42, Fayyaz Ahmed 53*; L. Klazinga 3-44). *Namibia 2 pts.*
  Namibia, unconvincing before now, surged into life. So impressive thus far, UAE looked tired in the field and complacent with the bat; the surprisingly slippery Louis Klazinga took 3-44. Louis Burger and Nicolaas Scholtz shared a stand of 115, helped by a bounty of gifts from UAE's sleepy bowlers.

At University of Witwatersrand, Johannesburg, April 11, 2009. **Scotland won by 26 runs.** Toss: Netherlands. **Scotland 216-8** (50 overs) (G. M. Hamilton 52, J. H. Stander 80*; E. Schiferli 4-37); **Netherlands 190** (48.4 overs) (A. N. Kervezee 36, B. Zuiderent 67; J. A. R. Blain 5-45, J. D. Nel 3-34). *Scotland 2 pts.*
  Scotland finally found the resolve and grit befitting their nation's stereotype, recovering from 59-5 to reach a respectable 216-8 before skittling Netherlands for 190. Jan Stander belted an unbeaten 80 while John Blain found a consistently nagging line in his five-for.

At L. C. de Villiers Oval, Pretoria, April 13, 2009. **Canada won by six wickets.** Toss: Canada. **Afghanistan 265-8** (50 overs) (Noor Ali 122, Nowroz Mangal 49; Rizwan Cheema 3-41); **Canada 268-4** (48.3 overs) (Rizwan Cheema 46, I. S. Billcliff 96*, A. Bagai 68). *Canada 2 pts.*
  Afghanistan's confidence got the better of them. Canada played with great determination and, though Afghanistan's ambitions remained cheerfully lofty, the defeat taught them that dreams are made and squashed on the pitch. Ian Billcliff's powerful 96 led Canada to their target. Despite a classy hundred from Noor Ali, Afghanistan had tottered against Rizwan Cheema's slow-medium.

At University of Witwatersrand, Johannesburg, April 13, 2009. **Ireland won by eight wickets.** Toss: United Arab Emirates. **United Arab Emirates 133** (39.5 overs) (Fayyaz Ahmed 63; R. M. West 3-39); **Ireland 134-2** (27.4 overs) (W. T. S. Porterfield 37, G. C. Wilson 49, E. J. G. Morgan 30*). *Ireland 2 pts.*
  Ireland all but booked their place in the 2011 World Cup in a convincing win. UAE slumped to 3-3 in the fourth over – Boyd Rankin taking two of the wickets – and collapsed to 38-6, from which they never fully recovered. William Porterfield and Gary Wilson carved 83 in 19.4 overs as Ireland romped towards their modest target.

At Krugersdorp, April 13, 2009. **Kenya won by 24 runs.** Toss: Kenya. **Kenya 178** (49.4 overs) (C. O. Obuya 32; J. A. R. Blain 4-59); **Scotland 154** (47.2 overs) (L. N. Onyango 4-26, N. Odhiambo 3-21). *Kenya 2 pts.*
  Both teams had blown hot and cold before this clash. Scotland restricted Kenya to 178, but reverted to type with the bat, slipping to 39-3, leaving the lower order far too much to do.

At Benoni, April 13, 2009. **Netherlands won by two wickets.** Toss: Netherlands. **Namibia 258-8** (50 overs) (R. van Schoor 50, S. F. Burger 51, C. Williams 43, N. R. P. Scholtz 33*; P. W. Borren

3-59); **Netherlands 262-8** (47.1 overs) (A. N. Kervezee 52, R. N. ten Doeschate 134*, P. W. Borren 33; G. Snyman 3-41, L. Klazinga 3-48). *Netherlands 2 pts.*

Another sublime innings from Ryan ten Doeschate sank Namibia, who had begun well. Fifties from Raymond van Schoor and Sarel Burger took Netherlands to 126-1 in the 33rd over, and though there was a mini-collapse, a total of 258 was more than respectable – particularly when Netherlands lost two early wickets. Then it was over to ten Doeschate who faced 121 balls and, with Alexei Kervezee, added 131.

At Benoni, April 15, 2009. **Afghanistan won by 42 runs.** Toss: Scotland. **Afghanistan 279** (50 overs) (Karim Sadiq 92, Nowroz Mangal 72); **Scotland 237** (47.1 overs) (K. J. Coetzer 91, G. M. Hamilton 71; Shapoor Zadran 3-36). *Afghanistan 2 pts.*

Afghanistan's victory left Scotland's ODI status hanging by a thread. Karim Sadiq's explosive batting continued, with 92 from 101 balls, though his dismissal sparked a collapse from 177-2 to 216-6 before the lower order made sure the start was not wasted. Scotland preserved their wickets, but could not score quickly enough: 187-2 seemed encouraging, but that was in the 40th over, and the pressure for runs had inevitable consequences. They lost their last eight wickets for 50 in 7.4 overs.

At Krugersdorp, April 15, 2009. **United Arab Emirates won by five wickets.** Toss: Canada. **Canada 194** (49.5 overs) (G. E. F. Barnett 39, S. Jyoti 43, W. D. Balaji Rao 39; Saqib Ali 3-20); **United Arab Emirates 200-5** (31.2 overs) (Amjad Javed 40, N. Gopal 37, Khurram Khan 53*, Saqib Ali 37). *United Arab Emirates 2 pts.*

UAE bounced back impressively to roll Canada over for just 194: they collapsed from 97-1 in the 17th over. Saqib Ali picked up 3-20 with his off-spin, and stroked 37 with the bat, but it was Khurram Khan's composed 53 which sealed the deal for UAE.

At L. C. de Villiers Oval, Pretoria, April 15, 2009. **Ireland won by six wickets.** Toss: Ireland. **Netherlands 222** (50 overs) (A. N. Kervezee 77; W. B. Rankin 3-48, A. R. Cusack 3-26); **Ireland 226-4** (44.3 overs) (W. T. S. Porterfield 78, E. J. G. Morgan 76). *Ireland 2 pts.*

Ireland secured their World Cup place, while Boyd Rankin proved that he was a genuine fast-bowling prospect. He and the other seamers struck regularly to damage Netherlands' efforts, though Kervezee compiled a steady 77. Two other seventies from the increasingly mature William Porterfield and Eoin Morgan put Ireland on track for a convincing win.

At University of Witwatersrand, Johannesburg, April 15, 2009. **Namibia won by 201 runs.** Toss: Kenya. **Namibia 305** (49.5 overs) (R. van Schoor 61, A. J. Burger 125, C. Williams 34; L. N. Onyango 3-68); **Kenya 104** (30 overs) (L. Klazinga 3-27, S. F. Burger 4-29). *Namibia 2 pts.*

Kenya have a history of imploding, and here, against bottom-of-the-table Namibia, was a spectacular addition to the collection. Raymond van Schoor and Jan-Berrie Burger put on 191 in 31 overs for the first wicket, which took the wind out of Kenya's sails. Kenya sped to 27 in 3.1 overs, but it was all downhill from there.

At Krugersdorp, April 17, 2009. **Afghanistan won by 21 runs.** Toss: Afghanistan. **Afghanistan 243-7** (50 overs) (Mohammad Shahzad 73, Nowroz Mangal 78); **Namibia 222** (48.3 overs) (G. Snyman 54, N. R. P. Scholtz 33; Hameed Hasan 3-37). *Afghanistan 2 pts.*

Victory gave Afghanistan, essentially a team of refugees desperate to show the world a positive side of their nation, one-day international status. The captain, Nowroz Mangal, stroked an effortless 78 while Mohammad Shahzad cracked 73. It was their bowlers, however, who stole the show. Hameed Hasan capped an impressive tournament with 3-37, and the brisk left-armer Shapoor Zadran helped reduce Namibia to 79-5. Gerrie Snyman briefly gave them hope, but this was Afghanistan's day.

At University of Witwatersrand, Johannesburg, April 17, 2009. **Netherlands won by six wickets.** Toss: Netherlands. **Canada 205-8** (50 overs) (S. Dhaniram 33, S. Jyoti 46, Umar Bhatti 39*); **Netherlands 206-4** (47.1 overs) (A. N. Kervezee 77, Mudassar Bukhari 84; S. Dhaniram 3-38). *Netherlands 2 pts.*

Alexei Kervezee and his fellow opener Mudassar Bukhari put on 167 to set up the victory that secured a place in the 2011 World Cup. Sunil Dhaniram's left-arm spin caused a few problems, but Bas Zuiderent and Paul Borren kept cool heads. Bukhari and Edgar Schiferli, later chosen as the player of the tournament, had earlier struck with the new ball, and Netherlands were a slick outfit in the field.

At L. C. de Villiers Oval, Pretoria, April 17, 2009. **Kenya won by six wickets.** Toss: Ireland. **Ireland 208-9** (50 overs) (N. J. O'Brien 59, J. F. Mooney 34; S. O. Tikolo 3-11); **Kenya 209-4** (48 overs) (K. O. Otieno 31, C. O. Obuya 66*, T. M. Odoyo 50*). *Kenya 2 pts.*

When it mattered, Kenya produced a performance that sealed their place in a fifth successive World Cup. They may have been fortunate in playing Ireland, the tournament's strongest team, after they had already guaranteed a berth in the final. In pursuit of 209, Kenya stumbled to 96-4, but Collins Obuya (66 from 73 balls) and Thomas Odoyo (50* from 68) combined beautifully to add 113* for the fifth wicket.*

At Benoni, April 17, 2009. **Scotland won by 122 runs.** Toss: Scotland. **Scotland 299-7** (50 overs) (G. M. Hamilton 127, K. J. Coetzer 35, N. F. I. McCallum 54, Extras 31; Qasim Zubair 3-62); **United Arab Emirates 177** (39.4 overs) (N. Gopal 50; C. M. Wright 4-41). *Scotland 2 pts.*

This was Scotland's most convincing display of a poor campaign. Gavin Hamilton used his experience – he would later be appointed Ryan Watson's successor as one-day captain – to make a terrific hundred, helping Scotland set a target of 300. UAE's performances were spectacularly good or woefully bad, and this tended to the woeful as Craig Wright's swing and seam made deep inroads. There was a lot riding on this game: the winners would enjoy ODI status, but not the losers.

SUPER EIGHTS TABLE

	Played	Won	Lost	Points	Net run-rate
IRELAND	7	5	2	10	0.68
CANADA	7	4	3	8	0.68
Kenya	7	4	3	8	0.03
Netherlands	7	4	3	8	0.02
Scotland	7	3	4	6	−0.14
Afghanistan	7	3	4	6	−0.20
UAE	7	3	4	6	−1.08
Namibia	7	2	5	4	−0.07

FINAL

‡CANADA v IRELAND

At Centurion, April 19, 2009. Ireland won by nine wickets. Toss: Ireland.

Although both teams had already bagged the important rewards – ODI status and a World Cup spot – Ireland maintained an unerring focus on winning this tournament. They had to cope without Eoin Morgan, recalled for county duty with Middlesex, while Canada had also lost their star, John Davison, with injury. Ireland saved their best for last, or certainly Trent Johnston did, as he tore through Canada's line-up to take five wickets. Athletic in the field, Ireland rolled Canada over for 185, and fittingly it was William Porterfield, the captain and second-highest run-scorer in the tournament (behind Bermuda's David Hemp), who led the charge with the bat. Ireland stormed towards victory – no hesitancy here – and reached their target in the 43rd over. No one could sensibly doubt that they were the best Associate nation, bar none.

Man of the Match: D. T. Johnston.   *Man of the tournament:* E. Schiferli (Netherlands).

Canada

G. E. F. Barnett c N. J. O'Brien b Connell . 19	H. S. Baidwan lbw b Rankin 14
A. A. Mulla lbw b Johnston 36	Khurram Chauhan run out. 26
Rizwan Cheema c K. J. O'Brien b Johnston 8	H. Osinde not out 0
I. S. Billcliff b Johnston. 10	B 1, l-b 9, w 5 15
A. Bagai c West b Johnston 4	
S. Dhaniram c Cusack b Johnston 7	1/36 (1) 2/61 (3) 3/69 (2) (48 overs) 185
S. Jyoti c Johnston b Rankin 0	4/78 (4) 5/88 (6) 6/88 (5) 7/92 (7)
Umar Bhatti run out. 46	8/131 (9) 9/185 (8) 10/185 (10) 10 overs: 61-2

Connell 8–0–55–1; Rankin 10–3–34–2; Johnston 10–4–14–5; Cusack 7–0–29–0; McCallan 8–0–25–0; West 5–0–18–0.

Ireland

*W. T. S. Porterfield not out	104
G. C. Wilson c Billcliff b Jyoti	38
†N. J. O'Brien not out	38
L-b 2, w 6	8

1/89 (2)   (1 wkt, 42.3 overs) 188
                  10 overs: 40-0

K. J. O'Brien, A. R. White, A. R. Cusack, D. T. Johnston, W. K. McCallan, R. M. West, P. Connell and W. B. Rankin did not bat.

Umar Bhatti 10–2–23–0; Osinde 6–1–20–0; Khurram Chauhan 7.3–0–56–0; Rizwan Cheema 5–0–21–0; Baidwan 3–0–14–0; Jyoti 7–1–26–1; Dhaniram 4–0–26–0.

Umpires: M. Erasmus and R. J. Tucker.
Referee: R. S. Mahanama.

Third-place Play-off

‡At Senwes Park, Potchefstroom, April 19, 2009. **Netherlands won by six wickets.** Toss: Netherlands. **Kenya 179** (43.1 overs) (S. O. Tikolo 45, R. L. Bhudia 47; E. Schiferli 4-23, R. G. Nijman 3-31); **Netherlands 183-4** (32.1 overs) (B. Zuiderent 57*, D. L. S. van Bunge 80). *One-day international debut:* R. G. Nijman.

Edgar Schiferli maintained his magnificent form to rip the heart out of the Kenyan batting: when he took his fourth wicket in the game's ninth over, Kenya were reeling at 28-5. Steve Tikolo oversaw a recovery, but although Netherlands slipped to 10-2, Bas Zuiderent and Daan van Bunge (who crashed 80 from 65 balls) had few problems in a third-wicket stand of 119.

Fifth-place Play-off

‡At Benoni, April 19, 2009. **Afghanistan won by 89 runs.** Toss: Afghanistan. **Afghanistan 295-8** (50 overs) (Noor Ali 45, Mohammad Nabi 58, Nowroz Mangal 32, Raees Ahmadzai 39, Samiullah Shenwari 52; J. A. R. Blain 3-62); **Scotland 206** (40 overs) (K. J. Coetzer 44, N. F. I. McCallum 36, J. A. R. Blain 41; Hameed Hasan 3-33). *One-day international debuts:* Asghar Stanikzai, Dawlat Ahmadzai, Hameed Hasan, Hasti Gul, Karim Sadiq, Khaliq Dad, Mohammad Nabi, Noor Ali, Nowroz Mangal, Raees Ahmadzai, Samiullah Shenwari (all Afghanistan).

Afghanistan, playing their first official ODI, defeated the Scots for the second time in four days. Noor Ali got the Afghanistan innings off to a flier with 45 from 28 balls, and Hasti Gul ensured it reached a rousing crescendo with 23 from 11. In between, there were plenty of runs from the middle order. Scotland crashed to 117-7, and a last-wicket stand of 63 between John Blain and Gordon Drummond simply saved a little face.

Seventh-place Play-off

At Krugersdorp, April 19, 2009. **United Arab Emirates won by four wickets.** Toss: Namibia. **Namibia 267-9** (50 overs) (A. J. Burger 42, G. Snyman 33, L. J. Burger 33, N. R. P. Scholtz 54; Fayyaz Ahmed 3-49); **United Arab Emirates 269-6** (41.3 overs) (Khurram Khan 124, S. Nayak 60, Saqib Ali 41).

A blistering 120-ball 124 from Khurram Khan ensured UAE sprinted home with oceans of time to spare.

Ninth-place Play-off Semi-finals

At Absa Puk Oval, Potchefstroom, April 11, 2009. **Bermuda won by eight wickets.** Toss: Oman. **Oman 254** (48.1 overs) (H. P. Desai 58, Zeeshan Siddiqui 41, Sultan Ahmed 62, Aamer Ali 53; R. J. Trott 4-43); **Bermuda 256-2** (48.2 overs) (D. L. Hemp 124*, S. D. Outerbridge 91).

Bermuda scarcely broke sweat in pursuit of a decent total thanks to a second-wicket partnership of 180 between David Hemp (124 from 125 balls) and Steven Outerbridge (91 from 126). Rodney Trott's off-breaks had earlier eviscerated the Omani middle order.*

At Senwes Park, Potchefstroom, April 11, 2009. **Uganda won by 62 runs.** Toss: Denmark. **Uganda 292-6** (50 overs) (A. S. Kyobe 32, N. K. J. Bibodi 104*, J. Olwenyi 57); **Denmark 230-8** (50 overs) (M. Lund 59, C. R. Pedersen 41, H. S. Hansen 45*, D. O. Borchersen 36*).

An innings of 104 at precisely a run a ball by Nehal Bibodi was the mainstay of the Ugandan innings. The result was inevitable before Denmark slipped to 149-8.

Ninth-place Play-off

At Senwes Park, Potchefstroom, April 13, 2009. **Bermuda won by eight wickets.** Toss: Uganda. **Uganda 352-7** (50 overs) (N. K. J. Bibodi 109, J. Olwenyi 45, F. Nsubuga 98); **Bermuda 356-2** (48.3 overs) (D. L. Hemp 170*, S. D. Outerbridge 107, L. O. B. Cann 32*).

A second hundred in 48 hours by Nehal Bibodi, supported by an explosive 98 in just 63 balls from Frank Nsubuga, was not enough to win a high-scoring game. Two days earlier, David Hemp and Steven Outerbridge had put on 180 together; now they combined to add 223 in 31 overs.

Eleventh-place Play-off

At Absa Puk Oval, Potchefstroom, April 13, 2009. **Oman won by five wickets.** Toss: Oman. **Denmark 220** (48.2 overs) (M. R. Pedersen 72; H. J. Mehta 5-29); **Oman 222-5** (41.4 overs) (Awal Khan 69, Adnan Ilyas 89*; D. O. Borchersen 4-43).

Denmark left South Africa winless after seven matches. After Hemal Mehta's left-arm spin had polished off five of the Danes' last six wickets, Oman needed only a modest 221, which they achieved with some ease, despite four wickets for David Borchersen's medium-pace.

WEST INDIES WOMEN v ENGLAND WOMEN, 2009-10

Alison Mitchell

One-day internationals (3): West Indies 2, England 1
Twenty20 internationals (3): West Indies 2, England 1

Double world champions England suffered two shock series defeats on their first tour of the West Indies in November 2009.

The primary motivation for the trip was to experience Caribbean conditions ahead of the World Twenty20 tournament the following May – all the matches were played at Basseterre in St Kitts, which was to host the group games in 2010. England left two senior players at home: batsman Claire Taylor, recently named ICC Women's Cricketer of the Year, took time out to focus on her job as a management consultant, while wicketkeeper and opening bat Sarah Taylor was rested. But little in the way of stiff opposition was expected from West Indies, an emerging side in the women's game.

This was only the third one-day series between these teams, and West Indies had won a single victory in 1979. It was a major upset, then, when England lost the first one-day international. In the absence of Sarah Taylor, captain Charlotte Edwards forged a new opening partnership with Ebony-Jewel Rainford-Brent, but England were dismissed for 195 chasing 236. Changes were made for the second match, when a career-best 72 from Rainford-Brent helped them level the series. In the deciding game, West Indies were set just 177 to win. Though England reduced them to 66 for six, the home team were saved by an 87-run stand between Stacy-Ann King and Deandra Dottin, and won by one wicket with 21 balls to spare.

There was more to come. The two sides had never met in a Twenty20 international before, but West Indies, enjoying vocal home support, inflicted further damage with another 2–1 series win. England gained a consolation victory in the final game, as West Indies rested three players.

The double triumph marked a significant improvement in an enthusiastic West Indian team, coached by former men's Test opener Sherwin Campbell. Their Player of the Series, Pamela Lavine, was already 40 years old, but there were youngsters who contributed to their success, too, including 18-year-old Stafanie Taylor.

"West Indies played with no fear," said England coach Mark Lane. "Whether that was because they were playing at home in front of a very knowledgeable cricket crowd, I don't know. They hit the ball hard, they bowled with discipline and they fielded with flair, throwing the ball in from 75 yards, right over the stumps, no relay throwing. Last time we played them, their fielding was a real weak spot."

ENGLAND TOURING PARTY

C. M. Edwards (Kent) (*captain*), C. M. G. Atkins (Sussex), T. T. Beaumont (Kent), K. H. Brunt (Yorkshire), H. L. Colvin (Sussex), L. S. Greenway (Kent), I. T. Guha (Berkshire), J. L. Gunn (Notts), D. Hazell (Yorkshire), L. A. Marsh (Sussex), B. L. Morgan (Middlesex), E-J. C-L. R. C. Rainford-Brent (Surrey), N. J. Shaw (Surrey), A. Shrubsole (Somerset). *Coach:* M. G. Lane.

Note: Matches in this section were not first-class.

At Basseterre, November 4, 2009. **First one-day international: West Indies won by 40 runs.** Toss: West Indies. **West Indies 235-6** (50 overs) (P. Y. Lavine 49, C. P. Jack 81*, M. R. Aguilleira 32); **England 195** (47.4 overs) (C. M. Edwards 58, L. S. Greenway 41; P. Y. Lavine 3-26, C. N. Nation 3-22). *One-day international debut:* T. T. Beaumont (England). *Player of the Match:* C. P. Jack.
Cordel Jack's maiden fifty for West Indies and Pamela Lavine's all-round form produced an upset.

At Basseterre, November 5, 2009. **Second one-day international: England won by 13 runs.** Toss: England. **England 232-5** (50 overs) (E-J. C-L. R. C. Rainford-Brent 72, J. L. Gunn 57, C. M. G. Atkins 44*; S. R. Taylor 3-29); **West Indies 219** (47.5 overs) (P. Y. Lavine 57, M. R. Aguilleira 44). *One-day international debut:* D. Hazell (England). *Player of the Match:* E-J. C-L. R. C. Rainford-Brent.
Ebony-Jewel Rainford-Brent scored a maiden international fifty and added 100 for the second wicket with Jenny Gunn to help England level the series.

At Basseterre, November 7, 2009. **Third one-day international: West Indies won by one wicket.** Toss: England. **England 176-9** (50 overs) (C. M. Edwards 30, L. S. Greenway 61; P. Y. Lavine 3-29; West Indies 179-9** (46.3 overs) (S. R. Taylor 43, S-A. C-A. King 40, D. J. S. Dottin 41, Extras 30; H. L. Colvin 4-24). *Player of the Match:* S-A. C-A. King.
West Indies slid to 66-6 chasing 177 before Stacy-Ann King and Deandra Dottin added 87; even so, it took the last-wicket pair to secure victory in the match and the series.

At Basseterre, November 9, 2009. **First Twenty20 international: West Indies won by four wickets.** Toss: West Indies. **England 112-8** (20 overs) (C. M. Edwards 34; S. R. Taylor 3-16); **West Indies 115-6** (19.5 overs) (C. P. Jack 39; I. T. Guha 3-21). *Twenty20 international debuts:* T. T. Beaumont, D. Hazell (England). *Player of the Match:* S. R. Taylor.
After a thunderstorm delayed the start, England recovered from 68-6, but West Indies scraped home with a ball to spare.

At Basseterre, November 10, 2009. **Second Twenty20 international: West Indies won by five wickets.** Toss: West Indies. **England 99** (19.4 overs) (C. M. Edwards 41; P. Y. Lavine 4-21); **West Indies 102-5** (19.1 overs) (P. Y. Lavine 37). *Player of the Match:* P. Y. Lavine.
Only Charlotte Edwards passed 14 for England, who lost their last eight for 29, and Pamela Lavine ensured West Indies took the Twenty20 series with four wickets and 37 in 40 balls.

At Basseterre, November 12, 2009. **Third Twenty20 international: England won by six wickets.** Toss: West Indies. **West Indies 119-6** (20 overs) (P. Y. Lavine 61); **England 120-4** (18.1 overs) (J. L. Gunn 35). *Player of the Match:* P. Y. Lavine. *Player of the Series:* P. Y. Lavine.
England ended the tour with a consolation victory, despite 61 in 49 balls from Pamela Lavine.

CRICKET IN AFGHANISTAN, 2009

Swapping Kalashnikovs for Kookaburras

SHAHID HASHMI

Afghanistan is in the midst of another revolution, one that has more to do with Kookaburras than Kalashnikovs. The most important date of the revolution, thus far, is April 17, 2009, when Afghanistan defeated Namibia by 21 runs in Krugersdorp, South Africa. Victory guaranteed Afghanistan a top-six finish in the World Cup Qualifier tournament; while that was not enough to gain entry to the World Cup itself, it did bring full one-day international status. For a team that, less than a year before, had been playing Japan in the ICC World Cricket League, Division Five Group B, the feat was astonishing. And they celebrated in style: their next game, the fifth-place play-off, was also their first official one-day international, and they beat Scotland at a canter. For once, this war-ravaged country, considered one of the world's most dangerous, had generated some unambiguously positive news.

Less than a month later, on May 11, President Hamid Karzai decreed the formation of the Afghanistan National Independent Cricket Board. This allowed the organised promotion of the game, which worked like magic on this passionate people. "We came so close to qualifying for the 2011 World Cup, but in the end gaining one-day status was a great achievement, and it brought about a new change in Afghanistan cricket," said Sayed Shah Aminzai, chief executive of the new board.

Until the board was set up, the promotion of the game was dependent upon dedicated individuals. One such was a currency dealer called Allahdad Noori, who played for the national team until 2004. A pioneer of the game in Afghanistan, he persuaded the Asian Cricket Council (ACC) and the ICC to provide support. Noor's infectious zeal for the game also won backing from the Pakistan Cricket Board, who allowed the use of their grounds by refugees from the Afghan war, and provided them with equipment. The refugee camps in Pakistan were where many Afghans gained their first taste of cricket, although the game was not totally unfamiliar: there is a distinct connection with *toop danda*, a game involving bat and ball that has been played in Afghanistan for centuries. Many in the camps took to cricket like a duck to water.

Noori is elated that his efforts have borne fruit: "With the president backing the game, we hope it will progress by leaps and bounds. The real thing now is money, and if sponsors come in, which didn't happen in the past, then the sky will be the limit for us." If Noori's enthusiasm has been vital in finding a route for cricket through Afghan politics, then the board's special task officer, Taj Malik, has played an equally important role. His meticulous promotional skills are ensuring that the cricket ball is beginning to replace the rocket and grenade in the psyche of a people scarred by so much violence.

"We have been assigned a target for 2013, and that is to have four international grounds, full ICC membership, a first-class structure in place and promotion of junior level cricket," said Malik, who was the country's first coach. "After the children watched our players creating history in South Africa last April, the game has spread like wildfire."

Cricket today is everywhere in Afghanistan – from Kabul to Jalalabad, Kandahar to Kunduz, Khost to Herat. There are nearly 200 registered clubs, with almost every province having at least one, and the number is growing. Boys playing cricket are now a common sight and, if they have the money, there is new equipment to be bought in the shops.

All of which explains the optimism of the current coach, Kabir Khan, who played Test cricket for Pakistan in the 1990s. "The signs are very positive," he said. "Cricket is now played in 20 of the 34 provinces in Afghanistan, and the World Cup Qualifier successes have given a new life to the game. The highlights are on television and, if security improves, the game will rise to new heights because players are eager to learn. They don't behave like scholars of cricket. They tell me that they don't know anything, they just want to learn and I am happy that they are learning fast."

Khan was concerned that his players might not have the temperament for four-day cricket, but he was delighted to be proved wrong when, in the Intercontinental Cup in August – Afghanistan's maiden first-class match – they took first-innings points in a draw against a Zimbabwe XI led by Tatenda Taibu. Noor Ali became the fourth batsman ever to score twin centuries on first-class debut. A week later, they made 209 for nine in the fourth innings to overcome the Netherlands on a tricky pitch at Amstelveen, after being dismissed for 107 on the first afternoon.

In February 2010, Afghanistan qualified for the third World Twenty20 in the West Indies. Nowhere is the popularity of cricket growing more rapidly than in the country of war and peace.

CRICKET IN CANADA, 2009

A few steps backwards

FARAZ SARWAT

Canada began its innings in 2009 by planting its front foot forward... and then shooting it. The previous year had seen many administrative triumphs, not least the securing of meaningful corporate sponsorship and visits from Test-playing countries – but, to the bafflement of many, Cricket Canada fired its chief executive officer, Atul Ahuja, in January. This precipitated much political wrangling within the board and its affiliated provincial bodies.

The acrimony resulted in two more high-profile casualties. In February Mike Kendall, the president of the largest provincial body, the Ontario Cricket Association, resigned as vice-president of the national board. Kendall's resignation and subsequent barbs about board mismanagement increased the pressure on Ben Sennik, Cricket Canada's beleaguered president, who also stepped down in May rather than face a no-confidence motion from the provinces. The infighting caught the attention of the main corporate sponsors, Scotiabank, who publicly continued to back Cricket Canada but by November had terminated their sponsorship agreement a year early.

Cricket Canada's response to the crisis was largely seen as bizarre, typified by the interim president Ranjit Saini being incredulous that Scotiabank expected exposure in the form of a national championship, something the board deemed cost-prohibitive, if not impossible. No national championship took place in 2009.

Increased funding from the ICC allowed Canada to sign seven players to central contracts, a move designed to regularise training sessions with a core group of cricketers. For the likes of Rizwan Cheema, who had been working in a fast-food restaurant called Popeyes Chicken and Biscuits, quitting the day job to play cricket was an easy decision; others, such as the investment banker Ashish Bagai, had to mull it over before signing, even with the global financial crisis raging.

In sharp contrast to 2008, when West Indies, Pakistan, Sri Lanka and Zimbabwe all visited Canada, there was disappointment that 2009 proved virtually barren. The only international visitors were Kenya, who won their Intercontinental Cup match after Steve Tikolo stole the show with twin hundreds to set up a 247-run victory.

The three-match one-day international series that followed against the same opponents ended 1–0 in favour of Canada, albeit in farcical circumstances when, after the second match was rained off, the third game also had to be cancelled owing to a wet outfield, this time because the sprinklers were left on. With little cricket staged at home, it was a minor triumph that a handful of players were placed with Sri Lankan first-class teams for a few matches.

In spite of an unstable cricket board, Canada qualified for its third consecutive World Cup (their fourth overall). To prepare for the World Cup Qualifier in South Africa, eight players were sent to Sri Lanka to train under Marvan Atapattu, although Canada's new batting coach might have been surprised that five of the eight turned out to be bowlers. By the end of the qualifying tournament in South Africa, Atapattu – who hit 15 sixes in 268 one-day internationals – was asking Rizwan Cheema (who hit 14 sixes in the tournament) whether you always need to try to hit the ball out of the park.

The high of World Cup qualification aside, it is difficult to lose the impression that Canadian cricket took a few steps backwards during 2009. Strengthening administrative weaknesses will need to be a priority in the year ahead.

ONE-DAY INTERNATIONALS IN CANADA IN 2009

At King City, August 19 (day/night). **First one-day international: Canada won by nine wickets.** Toss: Canada. **Kenya 113** (33.1 overs) (M. A. Ouma 43*; Khurram Chauhan 4-26); **Canada 117-1** (16.2 overs) (Rizwan Cheema 76*, A. M. Samad 30*). *One-day international debut:* H. Patel (Canada). *Man of the Match:* Khurram Chauhan.

Only three men reached double figures in Kenya's disappointing total, which Canada knocked off with all of 202 balls remaining. Rizwan Cheema's 76* came from just 38 deliveries, with ten fours and four sixes, but the match award went to another Pakistan-born player, seamer Khurram Chauhan, whose impressive bowling figures included a spell of three wickets in seven balls.

At King City, August 21, 22 (day/night). **Second one-day international: No result.** Toss: Kenya. **Canada 63-3** (17.1 overs) (T. M. Odoyo 3-11) **v Kenya**. *One-day international debut:* J. J. Dawood (Canada).

Violent storms left the outfield saturated, and no play was possible on the scheduled day. The teams tried again the following day, in a match reduced to 33 overs after a late start, but more rain forced an abandonment after Canada had regrouped from 14-3. Thomas Odoyo took all the wickets in the space of ten balls.

At King City, August 23. **Third one-day international: Canada v Kenya.** Abandoned.

A saturated ground meant no play was possible in the final match, so Canada took the series 1–0.

CRICKET IN KENYA, 2009

Failing to build

MARTIN WILLIAMSON

For Kenyan cricket, 2009 was marked by indifferent on-field performances and continuing troubles off it. They made it through the qualifying tournament in South Africa for the 2011 World Cup – the holy grail of the Associate world – but failed to build on that success.

As was the case for all the leading Associates, Cricket Kenya found it impossible to arrange fixtures against the leading Test-playing countries. The virtual impossibility of their task was highlighted by the revelation that South Africa had demanded almost US$100,000 to host two one-day internationals against Kenya in November, a sum that would have swallowed almost 20% of CK's annual income from the ICC.

Instead, Kenya had to make do with one-dayers against Zimbabwe (nine of the ten matches were lost) and other Associates, where results were equally poor – only one win, against the hapless Bermudians, in seven completed games.

The nadir came in December, when Kenya lost back-to-back Twenty20 matches against their up-and-coming neighbours Uganda. A 3–0 victory in the 50-over series that followed was not enough to stifle the discontent which had been close to the surface all year. With the World Twenty20 Qualifiers scheduled for February 2010, it seemed likely that Kenya's failure to play more than a smattering of 20-over games would count against them.

Once again, Kenya's best performances came in the Intercontinental Cup, where they battled to a draw against the dominant Irish and thrashed Canada. They also had the whip hand against a strong Zimbabwe team before being almost single-handedly defied by Vusi Sibanda.

There was some cause for guarded optimism with the emergence of some promising young players, as the old guard gradually began to fade from the scene. Maurice Ouma, who replaced Steve Tikolo as captain after the World Cup Qualifiers, proved a capable leader, while two young batsmen – Seren Waters and Rakep Patel – made good impressions.

Internally, the efforts of the board to revive development in schools and clubs bore fruit with success for the Under-17 and women's teams. There was an expansion of the game in the Rift Valley, and even the Maasai were introduced to cricket.

There was also a change of coach, as Andy Kirsten's one-year contract was not renewed. Capable technically, he too often appeared unable to exercise enough control over some strong factions within the national team. He was replaced by the former West Indies fast bowler Eldine Baptiste.

Off the field, Kenya were left bewildered and out of pocket by the ICC's decision to strip them of hosting rights for the 2010 Under-19 World Cup

It was claimed, some eight months before the scheduled start, that some of the grounds would not be ready. There was more than a suggestion that commercial pressures within the ICC had been a major factor, and CK's vociferous protests that preparations were on track proved accurate, as all the venues were ready before the year was out. The blow was even greater because, believing they would automatically be playing in the tournament as hosts, the board sent a weakened side to the African qualifying tournament. As a result, when the ICC switched the event to New Zealand, Kenya were not even invited to that.

In December came the biggest blow of all to a board still looking to shed the reputation for mismanagement it had acquired in the Sharad Ghai era. Tom Tikolo, a respected player and administrator, was forced to stand down as chief executive after US$10,000 paid to him as expenses for a junior tournament in the Caribbean was discovered to have gone missing. The board, to its credit, acted swiftly and was cleared of any involvement, but its critics wasted no time in pouncing.

Swamibapa broke Kanbis's six-year stranglehold on the Nairobi Provincial Cricket Association Super League, but the standard was again patchy and did little to help prepare players for international cricket. The ill-fated elite competition, which had made a low-key debut in 2008, failed to reappear.

ONE-DAY INTERNATIONALS IN KENYA IN 2009

At Mombasa, January 27. **First one-day international: Zimbabwe won by 109 runs.** Toss: Zimbabwe. **Zimbabwe 306-7** (50 overs) (H. Masakadza 71, V. Sibanda 77, E. Chigumbura 79); **Kenya 197** (46.2 overs) (S. R. Waters 32, S. O. Tikolo 37, J. K. Kamande 74, H. A. Varaiya 34). *One-day international debuts: A. G. Cremer, F. Mutizwa (Zimbabwe).*

Hamilton Masakadza made 71 from 61 balls to set up a big score, which was achieved when Elton Chigumbura blazed his highest one-day score of 79 from just 38 deliveries, with three fours and seven sixes. Kenya were never in the hunt after slipping to 93-6, although a seventh-wicket stand of 90 between Jimmy Kamande and Hiren Varaiya made the scores appear a little more respectable. No match awards were made in this series.

At Mombasa, January 29. **Second one-day international: Zimbabwe won by 151 runs.** Toss: Zimbabwe. **Zimbabwe 351-7** (50 overs) (V. Sibanda 41, S. Matsikenyeri 90, M. N. Waller 63, E. Chigumbura 68, Extras 30); **Kenya 200** (45.1 overs) (K. O. Otieno 37, S. O. Tikolo 56).

Zimbabwe sprinted to their highest score in one-day internationals, beating 340-2 against Namibia at Harare during the 2002-03 World Cup. Stuart Matsikenyeri improved his one-day best with 90 from 95 balls, putting on 105 in 14 overs with Malcolm Waller, but the real damage was done at the end by Elton Chigumbura, who replicated his pyrotechnics of the previous match, this time hurting to 68 from just 29 balls, with ten fours and three sixes. His onslaught included 25 (4640461) off a Peter Ongondo over which included a no-ball (the third four came off the resultant free hit); mainly thanks to Chigumbura, the last four overs produced 60 runs. Thomas Odoyo bowled only two overs before injuring a thigh muscle; he did not bat later. Kenya lost Seren Waters in the first over, and were never on terms, despite a stand of 87 between the veterans Kennedy Otieno and Steve Tikolo.

At Nairobi Gymkhana, January 31. **Third one-day international: Zimbabwe won by four wickets.** Toss: Kenya. **Kenya 234** (49.3 overs) (A. Obanda 49, M. A. Ouma 33, C. O. Obuya 55; A. G. Cremer 4-39); **Zimbabwe 236-6** (48.2 overs) (E. Chigumbura 43, P. Utseya 68*, F. Mutizwa 58*).

Zimbabwe clinched the series, although this win was in doubt when they dipped to 150-6 in the 39th over, chasing 235. But Prosper Utseya, who made his highest one-day score, and Forster Mutizwa batted sensibly, putting on 86 without being parted and sealing victory in the penultimate over. Earlier, Zimbabwe's spinners had restricted Kenya, taking eight of the ten wickets to fall. Seren Waters was caught behind off the first ball of the match for his second successive duck.

At Nairobi Gymkhana, February 1. **Fourth one-day international: Zimbabwe won by 66 runs.**
Toss: Zimbabwe. **Zimbabwe 285-8** (50 overs) (H. Masakadza 58, S. C. Williams 43, E. Chigumbura
36, P. Utseya 51*, F. Mutizwa 61; N. Odhiambo 3-56); **Kenya 219** (49 overs) (A. Obanda 96*;
E. Chigumbura 4-28, A. G. Cremer 3-34).

*This match returned to the script of the first two: Zimbabwe ran up a big score, helped by a late
flourish from Prosper Utseya and Forster Mutizwa, who added 107 for the seventh wicket in 13.3
overs, then Kenya failed to threaten an upset. Alex Obanda faced 93 balls, hitting seven fours and
five sixes (four of them off Ray Price, whose ten overs cost 58), before running out of partners.*

At Nairobi Gymkhana, February 4. **Fifth one-day international: Zimbabwe won by seven wickets.**
Toss: Kenya. **Kenya 199** (48.5 overs) (C. O. Obuya 75, R. L. Bhudia 40; A. G. Cremer 4-31);
Zimbabwe 203-3 (35 overs) (H. Masakadza 84*, S. Matsikenyeri 50, S. C. Williams 63*).

*Zimbabwe completed a 5–0 clean sweep with another facile victory, passing Kenya's modest total
with 15 overs to spare. They started badly, with Keith Dabengwa and Vusi Sibanda both out in the
first seven balls of the reply, but Hamilton Masakadza anchored the chase with a run-a-ball innings.
Earlier, Kenya were struggling at 92-6 before Collins Obuya (who hit four fours and four sixes) and
Rajesh Bhudia put on 75 in 18 overs. This win took Zimbabwe up past Ireland into tenth place in the
ICC's one-day rankings.*

CRICKET ROUND THE WORLD, 2010

<small>COMPILED BY TONY MUNRO</small>

ICC WORLD CRICKET LEAGUE

After hogging the headlines in 2008, the cricketers of Afghanistan did so again in 2009. Their fifth-place finish in the World Cup qualifying tournament in South Africa in April might not have been quite enough to ensure a fantastical passage to the 2011 event, but it elevated them, for the first time, to official one-day status – until 2013 at least. It secured a place at both the World Twenty20 qualifying tournament in the United Arab Emirates, which took place in February this year, and the ICC's Intercontinental Cup. For a team of former refugees, who as recently as 2008 had been languishing in Division Five of the World Cricket League, this was some story.

It could have been even better. Defeat by the UAE in the group stages of the 50-over qualifying tournament left the Afghanis with too much to do in the Super Eights, from which the top four sides – Ireland, the eventual winners, Canada, the Netherlands and Kenya – qualified for the World Cup. And although Afghanistan subsequently achieved memorable wins over Ireland, Namibia and Scotland (twice), they ended one win short of a top-four spot.

Their progress to the qualifying tournament had been surprisingly fraught. Needing only to beat the lowly Cayman Islands in their final World Cricket League Division Three game in Buenos Aires in January 2009, they found themselves facing probable defeat when, after they limped to 68 for five from 31 overs, rain interrupted the Islands' reply at 35 for two after only seven overs. Chastened, Afghanistan won the replay the following day by 82 runs to gain promotion along with Uganda, who pipped Papua New Guinea on net run-rate. The Cayman Islands were relegated to Division Four with hosts Argentina.

Lower down the ladder, Singapore, coached by the former Australia all-rounder Trevor Chappell, and Bahrain qualified for Division Five following a six-team tournament in Singapore in August and September, while Botswana and Norway went down to Division Seven. Earlier in the year in Guernsey, the hosts as well as Bahrain had made it through to Division Six. There are now eight divisions in total, with all but the lowest tier – which contains eight sides – comprising six teams.

BELGIUM

One evening in a Brussels park a cricket ball whistled from behind a bush past your correspondent's ear. I wasn't the only one. Belgian dog-walkers stopped and stared as balls zoomed past their pooches' noses, or had to be retrieved from the middle of the nearby – and rather more familiar – football kickaround. It turned out a group of lads were making the most of one of the park's white gravel paths to get some practice in after persuading the mayor to lend them the use of the local football stadium for a Saturday-evening, 12-team sixes competition. This endearingly make-do – but highly enthusiastic – moment captured the spirit of Belgian cricket in 2009 and the headlines told the story: "Thirty youngsters from the Gent region learn cricket at a five-day summer camp"… "De Wijze Eik School enrols in the schools programme with local club Arcadians"… "Sixty students from eight schools and clubs take part in ICC's 'Catch the Spirit' competition". The last event was particularly good, with two pitches at the British School of Brussels hosting games on a wonderful, sunny weekend in May. Much of this paid off, as Belgium won the European Under-19 Division Two Championship at Antwerp in August. Not only did they have to overhaul Italy's 161 in the final match of the round-robin format, they had to do so without losing a wicket to edge out the Isle of Man. To scenes of great celebration, openers Nirvam Shah and Jamie Farmiloe duly obliged with unbeaten half-centuries. At senior club level, Ostend CC, narrowly beaten in 2008, won the Belgian first division for the first time and were crowned champion club, receiving their award from the former Surrey and England wicketkeeper Jack Richards, who now lives in Belgium; he handed other divisional awards to Crescent CC, Gent CC and Antwerp Indians CC. Elsewhere, there was much to enjoy, including the former Zimbabwe Test seamer Brighton Watambwa's innings of 60 as Belgium beat Germany by two wickets in a high-scoring senior international in Bonn. Meanwhile, umpires Ted Vorzanger and Hector Doel hung up their Belgian league umpire coats for the last time. Both symbolise much of what is good about Belgian cricket and will be sorely missed. Lifetime achievement awards for people such as Marc Vanderiviere and Javaid Siddiqi recognise the behind-the-scenes efforts that make it all possible. COLIN WOLFE

BRAZIL

Cricket in Brazil cannot be taken for granted, with domestic games often requiring plane travel or all-day bus rides, plus an overnight stay or two, but 2009 was no less successful for all that. The senior men's season kicked off in March with São Paulo travelling to the HSBC ground in Curitiba, where the home team, Paraná, finally recorded consecutive victories against their long-time rivals. A month later, São Paulo hosted the eighth South American Championships, won by Argentina A, while in May the senior women's team headed for Florida to compete in its first ICC Americas tournament, finishing joint-fifth in a competition involving more experienced sides from Canada, USA, Argentina, Trinidad & Tobago and Bermuda. All-rounder Juliana Brito was named best fielder. Curitiba hosted the first South American Under-13 boys' championship in July, involving Brazil, Chile and Argentina, the eventual winners, and the following month São Paulo won the national Twenty20 tournament in Brasília. Perhaps the highlight of the year, however, came when the senior men's team, who had already won all three matches against Mexico in October, qualified for Division Two of the World Cricket League by going undefeated in the Division Three tournament in Chile. Thanks to tremendous efforts in Brasília to develop the sport among Brazilians, half the national team is now home-grown, including the opening bowler Rudyard Hartmann, and Guilherme Lefévre, voted the event's best wicketkeeper. The Brazilian Cricket Association's junior development programme took a big step forward in Curitiba, where it became partners with the city school board to teach cricket in public schools. A schools programme has also been started in Rio de Janeiro, where cricket began back in the mid-19th century. NORMAN BALDWIN

CHILE

When Simon Shalders, captain of the national side, hit an unbeaten 195 against Peru in an Americas Division Three match in Santiago, he might have done even better. Unaware he was in the 190s, Shalders played some fairly tame shots instead of going all out for a double-century. At least he ensured his game would not suffer when he came to Chile to set up a backpackers' hostel – thought to be the only one in the country to house a cricket net in its back garden. TONY MUNRO

HIGHEST SCORES IN MINOR ONE-DAY INTERNATIONALS

217	Moosa Kaleem	Maldives v Brunei at Bangkok.	2004-05
213*	Arshad Ali	UAE v Brunei at Kuala Lumpur.	2006
209*	Saeed Al-Saffar	UAE v Thailand at Kathmandu	1998-99
203*	A. N. French	Hong Kong v Maldives at Singapore	2002
200*	Shamazuddin Khan	Germany v Switzerland at Zuoz.	1997
197	S. S. Nadkarni	USA v Suriname at Fort Lauderdale.	2008-09
196	G. Snyman	Namibia v UAE at Windhoek.	2007-08
196	D. J. Reekers	Netherlands v Norway at Dublin	2008
195*	**S. Shalders**	**Chile v Peru at Santiago**.	**2009-10**
191	K. Mendis	Singapore v Thailand at Singapore.	2002
180*	S. Shalders	Chile v Turks & Caicos Islands at Paramaribo.	2005-06

Research: Roy Morgan

CHINA

China briefly overshadowed even Afghanistan as the most-hyped international cricket team in 2009 when it made its debut in January at a tournament for the lowest-ranked sides in Asia. However, fears of annihilation were realised when their fellow minnows, Iran, crushed them by 307 runs. The debacle continued when they were routed for 39 by Thailand, before the Maldives inflicted another heavy defeat, this time by 315 runs. They did manage one victory, though, in the play-off for last place, beating Myanmar by 118 runs. The Chinese Cricket Association (CCA) has chosen to bypass the traditional club structure by developing cricket in schools and universities, region by region, and by late 2009, the game had been introduced to seven regions in all. The champion schools and universities from each region play annually in a national tournament, and the CCA say girls and boys of all ages play the sport. There have been some signs of success in this approach, notably when China's Under-19s won two games in another tournament for the lowest-ranked Asian teams, only to go down to Kuwait by 403 runs in the third-place play-off. Its women's team finished fourth at an Asian Twenty20 tournament, although the men were last in their corresponding event in the Middle East, dismissed in one game for 27 by United Arab Emirates, with 13 of the runs coming from wides. Bizarrely, defence seemed to take priority over attack, although no team fielded more keenly than the Chinese. The ultimate gauge of their progress, however, will come in November this year, when Twenty20 cricket debuts at the Asian Games in Guangzhou, and China will be up against teams representing the continent's four Test-playing nations. TONY MUNRO

CHRISTMAS ISLAND

A crowd of around 200 looks on as an Afghan bowler sends down a delivery on the rolled dirt wicket to a Sri Lankan batsman, while the fielders – both Afghans and Sri Lankans – are ready to pounce. The scores are recorded studiously, for errors cannot be afforded in this vigorously contested limited-overs game. Behind the razor wire of the Christmas Island Detention Centre in the Indian Ocean, cricket provides a vital degree of normality for the lives of the detainees, who stay for around three months on this Australian territory while visa applications are processed. This game is not an isolated event: there are organised competitions contested by up to ten teams, usually of mixed nationalities. Neither is the sport confined to the detention centre. The staff take part in the occasional match against the Christmas Island Cricket and Sporting Club, whose eclectic civilian membership play up to six games a year. The club organises most of the sporting activity on this island of nearly 1,500 people, including Australian Rules, touch football, soccer and softball. But cricket remains the primary sport, and the Department of Immigration and SERCO (the security operators) work with the cricket club to ensure there are opportunities to play for those in detention. The multicultural nature of the population is reflected in the club's membership: Australian, English, Malay, Chinese – and even an Inuit. The Sri Lankans, meanwhile, bring flair. One has an action like the country's slingy Test bowler Lasith Malinga; another kisses the ball before each delivery. Last year the club, which recently celebrated its 50th anniversary, included matches against the staff of the detention centre, visiting Royal Australian Navy ships and teams from Cocos Island, 900km to the south-west. It also hosts the Coconut Ashes, an annual clash between "chalkies" (teachers) and the locals. The community oval has its own peculiar features: it is mostly surrounded by jungle, which makes losing balls something of a hazard, while fog and low cloud can get in the way too, as games take place on top of "The Rock", as the island is referred to, a full 300m above sea level. TONY MUNRO AND RHETT BOWDEN

CROATIA

Nepotism is an unlikely formula for the expansion of cricket, not least in a remote outpost in the Adriatic. But the efforts of Dorothy Burrows, an 84-year-old follower of the game on the island of Vis, may yet help the game flourish in Croatia. Burrows, a great-great-niece of the Royal Navy captain Sir

William Hoste, succeeded in persuading 28 of Hoste's descendants, some from as far away as Hong Kong, to travel to Vis to play against the cricket club that bears his name. A protégé of Admiral Horatio Nelson, Hoste established a garrison on Vis in 1809 during the Napoleonic Wars, and permitted his men to play cricket as a way of staving off boredom between skirmishes. "We have established a cricket club at this wretched place," he wrote to his mother. "And when we do get anchored for a few hours, it passes away an hour very well." Cricket did not really endure, but a revival towards the end of the 1990s, fuelled by expatriate and second-generation Croatian-Australians, has led to four cricket clubs springing up in Zagreb, Split and Vis. It took inclusion in the Croatian edition of *Playboy* to arouse cricket in Vis again. The club's co-founder, Rob Dumancic, stumbled across an interview with a local winemaker, Oliver Roki, in which he expressed a vague hope of resuscitating Hoste's sporting legacy. But his interest in the game was far from frivolous. "Apart from one expat and two guys from England, the rest of the team discovered the game seven years ago and had never played it before," said Roki. "We have six or seven kids who can really play, but they have no one to play against." Vis's story stirred the interest of the most famous club of all, MCC, who sent a touring side to face the national team and developmental XIs on Vis's Plisko Polje ground in August. A team boasting former first-class players Darren Bicknell and Rob Turner won all four matches, but they were not cakewalks. Lord's even bought into the spirit of the occasion, appointing Norfolk captain Steve Livermore to skipper MCC (Sir William, born in Ingoldisthorpe, came from the same county). MCC arrived bearing a grant of US$2,500 for the Croatian Cricket Federation, which, along with a donation of $1,250 from the ICC, will be channelled into ECB Level Two coaching courses in the country. A reciprocal visit of the national side to England would seem the next step, but an improvement in results may be required first. Croatia lost all six matches in their ICC European Championship tournament in 2008, and surrendered Division Two status when Israel beat them in a play-off at Zagreb's newly constructed Budenec Oval ground in October.   JAMES COYNE

DENMARK

Denmark's stock has fluctuated ever since it reached the semi-finals of the inaugural ICC Trophy in 1979, with new member nations entering the fray, often from large populations of paid professionals – no easy competition for a small, amateur country like ours. On the domestic scene, Glostrup clinched a second national championship, despite losing three times to the runners-up, Herning, who were less consistent in beating teams from below. Skanderborg were relegated, but Ishoj's bid for promotion failed against Esbjerg. Visitors last year included, for a ninth time, Bancroft's School from Essex, who again included the former England bowler John Lever in their party. To round off the year, an evening was held in late September for all those who had played in at least one of the official internationals which began in 1954. Some 65 turned up for a long night's memories.   PETER S. HARGREAVES

IRAQ

Cricket continued to be played at the heavily fortified British Embassy in Baghdad. To mark the withdrawal of the British troops from Iraq, an embassy team, captained by Christopher Prentice, Ambassador to Iraq and a former Oxford University batsman, met a team from the British Services Unit, led by Lt. Gen. Brown, the most senior British officer in Iraq, in an eight-a-side game on the embassy compound. The teams played for "The Dirt", a golden, metallic trophy about the size of a wine glass filled with Iraqi soil. The compound has a purpose-built all-weather pitch, as well as two "duck and covers" in the north-east and north-west corners, for fielders (and anyone else) to take cover from incoming mortars or rockets. Tennis balls were used, but retrieval of anything hit over the compound walls was not an option: since the departure of the Americans, the International Zone has been less well-protected. Local rules applied – six runs for a blow over the fence but within the compound; four for hitting the ball through a gap in the fence; and four overs to be bowled by every player. The embassy also staged a game of continuous cricket as part of its staff's sports day, and it was so well-received among the local nationals working within the office and the maintenance areas that it is being considered as a vehicle to encourage greater interaction between Iraqi and British staff. Both events were played against the hum of Baghdad. Not only was there the sound of the occasional mortar, but there were also helicopters, some used as a sort of bus service and others as ambulances for the local hospital, up and flying. The usual noises of traffic, beeping horns and sirens could also be heard, as well as the call to prayer. DILWYN GRIGGS

ISRAEL

It was one of the most exciting seasons Israeli cricket has experienced. In July we hosted the 18th Maccabi Games, with South Africa winning both the senior competition – Adam Bacher, playing in his last tournament, hit an undefeated 83 to rescue his side from 15 for three in pursuit of 146 against India – and the junior version. Israel won bronze in both, surprisingly beating Australia twice in the senior tournament. A new ground was opened in Lod, while on the last day of the games a new net facility at the Hadar Yosef sports complex in Tel Aviv was dedicated to the Ziff family: great contributors to Israeli cricket over the last decade. Later in the year, our Under-15 team went to Italy to gain experience, while the Under-19s travelled to Belgium for the World Cup qualifiers and finished in the top half of the table. Three members of that team subsequently joined the senior squad for the European third division competition in Spain and, under the superb leadership of Hershel Gutman – who was appointed the country's first national cricket development officer – emerged triumphant, vindication of the decision to select six players who had come through the youth programme. Victory there meant Israel qualified for a promotion play-off against Croatia in Zagreb on October 11. The result was a famous win, with Steven Shein claiming five for 27 to dismiss the hosts for double figures, before Gutman's unbeaten 45 completed a six-wicket victory. Success on the field, with seven wins out of ten, was complemented by the strides we made with our social project involving Bedouin and Arab children, who are now playing cricket on a regular basis in a region otherwise bereft of interaction between the various ethnic groups. The sport is fast becoming a unifying factor overriding class or economic considerations. STANLEY PERLMAN

JAPAN

In a year of several changes in Japanese cricket, some things stayed the same. The Tokyo Wombats won the Japan Cricket League, contested by both expatriate and indigenous teams, for the fourth successive year, while Paddy Foley CC lifted the Japan Cup knockout competition for the second time, and L-Dore won the national women's club competition for the second consecutive year. Yuichi Takano, the Adore CC middle-order batsman, hit two centuries and averaged 72 on his way to winning the Greg Chappell Cricket Centre men's player of the year award, and stable-mate Shizuku Mijayi averaged 124 with the bat, 12 with the ball, and took vital wickets for the national team to claim the women's award. The innovations came on the representative scene. The National Competition, incorporating regional branches for the first time, was held in November, with Hokkaido beating Sano in a closely fought final. Tohoku made their first appearance in the competition. Elsewhere, the inaugural Kanto Premier League was played in the greater Tokyo area and won by South West Kanto, and in the first-ever Women's Premier League, North Japan beat South Japan. The men's national team played in the ICC World Cricket League Division Seven, finishing fourth, the highlight being Patrick Giles-Jones's remarkable spell of seven for nine in ten overs against Suriname. Japan also played in the ICC EAP Cricket Trophy, finishing fourth in the Twenty20 tournament and third in the 50-over competition. The Japanese women's national team finished second in the first Shanghai International Women's Twenty20 event, beaten by a strong Zaheer Abbas Cricket Academy including six Pakistan national team players, but finishing ahead of Singapore. NAOKI MYAJI

KOSOVO

It may be surprising to learn that cricket was played in Kosovo, a country which declared its independence as recently as February 2008, by previous generations – or at least something resembling cricket. The pastime of *guxha* (pronounced "goojah") was a traditional game now largely replaced among young Kosovars' affections by football. But Dritan, a Kosovar living in Brighton, realised there was something familiar about the game being played down the road from his home at the County Ground in Hove. "I remember my father playing *guxha*, and I have since seen cricket being played here, and there are similarities between the skills and the way of scoring," he said. Inevitably, the more conventional version of the game arrived with the influx of armed forces during the conflict in Kosovo in the late 1990s, and expats of virtually every Test nation played in the UNMIK (United Nations Mission in Kosovo) gym in Pristina using a taped-up tennis ball and a home-made bat. Encouraged, perhaps, by the presence of Maj.-Gen. Garry Robison, who was on peacekeeping duties in the country and is the current chairman of combined services cricket, the ICC also ventured into Kosovo, staging a "Spirit of Cricket" weekend in February 2002 at the national stadium in Pristina – which was said to have been used to detain 10,000 Albanians during the height of the conflict. As well as introducing the game to Serbian and Albanian children as a means of breaking down barriers between the communities, there was a 15-over match between The Princess of Wales' Royal Regiment, the forces champions at the time, and the Indian personnel of UNMIK. More recently, a team of Gurkhas based in Pristina travelled to Skopje to take part in a three-team Twenty20 tournament along with a KFOR (Kosovo Force) side in June 2007. The Gurkhas began by putting on an excellent display of military prowess with the "presentation of the *kukri*", although they lost one of their star players, who managed to slash his own arm with a *kukri* (knife) during the pre-match ritual. It mattered little as the Gurkhas claimed victory thanks to the performance of Rifleman Chandrakumar Limbu-by-Prasad Chamarty, whose name troubled the scorers almost as much as his runs did. TIMOTHY ABRAHAM

MACEDONIA

The name of Leonard Stephen Durtanovich may not mean much to most of Skopje's inhabitants, but to an ambitious band of Macedonian cricketers in the country's capital he is a demigod. Known rather better by his adopted name, Len Pascoe, this son of Macedonian immigrants played 14 Tests and 29 one-day internationals for Australia. Almost three decades after he alarmed England's batsmen during the Centenary Test at Lord's, cricket has seen phenomenal developments in the country of his heritage. The game was first played in Macedonia in 2007, but a breakthrough came in 2009 when a village team from Wales – Carmel & District CC – became the first foreign side to play in Skopje. Live ball-by-ball coverage was beamed to the Balkans and beyond by state broadcaster MTV (Macedonian Television) – not bad for a non-ICC affiliate member. Such was the interest that TV station Skynet also produced a documentary on cricket's arrival in Macedonia. The match was played on a turf wicket prepared by Viktor Aleksoski, a local groundsman who spent a decade learning his trade in New Zealand – although 40°C temperatures ensured the baked track was more of an Indian featherbed than the artificial surfaces more typical of Europe. Despite a man-of-the-match performance from Dan Doncev, vice-president of the Obedineti za Makedonija (United for Macedonia) party, the hosts were beaten, but not dispirited. Ray Power, chairman of the British Business Group Macedonia, has since worked tirelessly to secure significant funding from local authorities in order to redevelop completely the site used for the game against Carmel and give the country's cricketers a permanent home. Registration of the Macedonian Cricket Association is ongoing and in the summer of 2010 the new ground will play host to an eight-team Twenty20 tournament featuring national sides from Bulgaria, Hungary, Croatia and Slovakia. The only matter dividing the players is whether to name the ground after Pascoe or one of Macedonia's slightly better-known ancestors, Alexander the Great, whose crest features in the national flag, unwittingly made up of MCC's egg and bacon colours. TIMOTHY ABRAHAM

NAMIBIA

It was a difficult year for cricket in Namibia. The national team missed out on World Cup qualification after winning only three games out of 12, and were then relegated by the ICC from the Intercontinental Cup, in which they had finished runners-up in 2007-08, to the newly created Intercontinental Shield, to make way for a Zimbabwe XI. The Shield meant Namibia could play only four matches, as opposed to the seven available in the Cup. Worse was to come when the ICC replaced Namibia in the ICC World Twenty20 Qualifier with the United States, who were deemed to have greater marketing potential. The national team again competed in Cricket South Africa's interprovincial competition, losing one game, winning two and drawing three in the three-day league. In the one-day league, Namibia won two, lost two, tied one and had one no-result. Perhaps anticipating a reduced playing schedule, a host of players retired, while the highly regarded all-rounder Gerrie Snyman opted to spend the 2009-10 season playing club cricket in New Zealand. It was unclear whether he would return. TONY MUNRO

RWANDA

Bob Bashir Songa became the pin-up boy of his country's development programme when he won the match award on his senior international debut in October. The 13-year-old Songa took four for 13 as Rwanda beat Gambia by seven wickets in Africa Division Three of the World Cricket League. Songa only began playing cricket at the age of ten after stumbling on a junior clinic when he and friends went to a park to play football. He liked what he saw, and was happy to walk the long distances necessary to continue at this strange new game. TONY MUNRO

SERBIA

Standing only a few inches over five feet, Vladimir Ninkovic is not exactly compelling evidence of a bold assertion that Serbia have the potential to become the West Indies of Europe. But what Ninkovic, an opening batsman, lacks in height he more than makes up for in ambition and canny cricket knowledge as he plots the future of the sport in Serbia – as well as attempting to unearth the country's answer to Curtly Ambrose. Serbia is one of the world's tallest nations and thus blessed with a stockpile of natural athletes who, in theory at least, possess the raw attributes to develop into fast-bowling talent. For the time being its giants are lured on to the basketball courts with dreams of following national hero Peja Stojakovic into the NBA, but such has been the rapid progress of Serbian cricket they may in future be perfecting bouncers rather than slam-dunks. Previously there had been a few unsuccessful attempts to get cricket off the ground in Belgrade, including the expat-dominated Red Star CC team founded in 2002: it has seemingly disappeared without trace. There was even speculation that the former captain of a cricket team in the ex-Yugoslav capital was an MI6 agent who helped mastermind the arrest of former president Slobodan Milosevic, then fled the country. Cricket's rebirth in Serbia is largely down to former rugby league team-mates Ninkovic and Haris Dajc, who started two clubs – Stari Grad and Mirijevo – in 2007 after being introduced to the game by friends from England and Australia. The growth in player numbers led to the establishment of the Belgrade Cricket Association in January 2009, with Twenty20 and 40-over domestic championships played in the summer. A BCA Select XI also hosted a touring team from Wales and, under the captaincy of Ninkovic, played their first game abroad, travelling to Slovenia to face Mezica CC. The Serbian Cricket Federation, whose membership is dominated by indigenous players, has since been officially recognised by the Serbian sports ministry. Finding a permanent ground and securing ICC Affiliate status will now dominate the cricket agenda, perhaps allowing the rest of Europe to breathe more easily: the Balkans' answer to Ambrose will not be unleashed just yet.   TIMOTHY ABRAHAM

SINGAPORE

Cricket arrived in Singapore when the British colonised the island in the early 19th century, with the first recorded match taking place on October 14, 1852. The British withdrawal in 1969 was a setback for a sport that had flourished since the 1930s, but after nearly three decades of hibernation it has recently shown signs of returning to life. The cricket complex at Kallang is on lease from the government, but the Singapore Cricket Association will soon move to new premises in Sengkang, and there are already plans for four grounds, two of international standard. The Singapore cricket community largely comprises expat South Asians, with a sprinkling of Chinese and Europeans, so to a degree the game suffers from an absence of local flavour as well as the lack of official support and the apathy of the media. But the players' enthusiasm is laudable, and Singapore celebrated a return to Division Five of the ICC's World Cricket League when they hosted the Division Six tournament in August and September and won all six matches, culminating in a 68-run victory over Bahrain in the final.

Even so, cricket remains a minority sport, a state of affairs not helped by national service, which takes potential players for two years in their late teens, after which they become career-oriented. Despite this, the SCA is committed to the promotion of cricket in the island, and the Asian Cricket Council's developmental programme provides useful, basic training to players, coaches and umpires. In 2007-08, the SCA received an award for the best administration and implementation of the ACC and the ICC development programmes, and in 2009 it organised 1,100 matches, a record. At times, the biggest challenge has been to arrange enough umpires and scorers, but the

SCA has prevailed upon the education ministry to make cricket part of the curriculum and is trying to repackage the game as a "thinking person's" sport in order to fit in with the country's emphasis on academic excellence. But the road ahead is rough and steep. The challenge for Singapore cricket is to project a new identity – one that moves the heart, stirs the soul and inspires the mind.   RAVI CHATURVEDI

Cricket with altitude

LAWRENCE BOOTH

To touch the heights is a cliché most sportsmen happily aspire to, yet few can have done so more literally than the Everest Test expedition, which in April 2009 beat the world record for high-altitude cricket by playing a game of Twenty20 cricket on the side of the planet's tallest peak. The match, between teams named Hillary and Tensing after the first men to reach the summit in 1953, was the centrepiece of the expedition's money-raising endeavours for the Lord's Taverners and the Himalayan Trust UK, and it took place on the Gorak Shep plateau, 5,165 metres above sea level. In 2007, a Kwik Cricket match involving a tennis ball, several sherpas and the Essex all-rounder Graham Napier had been staged at 5,400 metres, but failed to achieve official recognition.

This time there were no such obstacles and, following a gruelling nine-day hike – during which the teams delivered three bags of Lord's Taverners kit to local schools and led a training session, involving around 70 pupils, at one of them in Khumjung – a non-turf pitch was laid and battle commenced. Team Hillary, who could boast Alastair Cook as its honorary captain, defeated Team Tensing – skippered in spirit by Andrew Strauss – by 36 runs when Glen Lowis bowled his fellow New Zealander Mike Preston, and Charlie Campbell was presented with the match award by the Taverners' Shona Langridge. For more photographs and information, visit www.theeveresttest.com.

UNITED STATES

The complete lack of any matches for the national team in 2009 belied the suspicion that something always seemed to be happening in American cricket. Following the appointment in April of Don Lockerbie as the national board's first chief executive – a move that lent the USACA a degree of credibility – the Under-19 National Tournament in Brooklyn in May unearthed some hidden gems, most significantly the Johannesburg-born all-rounder Ryan Corns. At the Under-19 World Cup qualifying event in Toronto, Corns scored 230 runs and took 13 wickets, winning the player-of-the-tournament award and hitting 86 to help beat Ireland – their only defeat in the competition. The USA finished fifth to reach the final stages in New Zealand in January 2010, where they lost all three group games. The domestic scene threw up some bizarre scenarios. One game in July's Eastern Conference Tournament in Washington was decided when umpires awarded five penalty runs to the South East team – eight wickets down and still two runs short of victory – because the opposing wicketkeeper had used "obscene language". Two weeks later at the Western Conference Tournament in Minneapolis, the Central West squad took a page out of Pakistan's book by forfeiting a match because of what they felt was inconsistent enforcement of over-rate penalties. And at the National Championships in Fort Lauderdale in November, the third-place game between South West and South East was halted in the middle of the first innings, then stopped altogether during the second, when Central Broward Regional Park officials forced the teams off the field to allow a pair of community soccer games to be played. Hours later at the tournament banquet, USACA board member Ahmed Jeddy, the Central West team manager responsible for the Minneapolis forfeit, proclaimed with a straight face that it had been the best-run USACA tournament he had ever seen. Still, these shenanigans didn't stop the chief executive of New Zealand Cricket, Justin Vaughan, from pursuing a partnership with USACA, one that could see the New Zealanders playing matches on American soil as early as 2010.   PETER DELLA PENNA

TOURNAMENTS CONTESTED BY NON-TEST NATIONS, 2008-09 AND 2009

Competition	Winner	Runners-up	Others
WCL Division Three	Afghanistan	Uganda	PNG, Hong Kong, Cayman Islands, Argentina
World Cup Qualifier	Ireland	Canada	Netherlands, Kenya, Afghanistan, Scotland, UAE, Namibia, Bermuda, Uganda, Oman, Denmark
WCL Division Six	Singapore	Bahrain	Guernsey, Malaysia, Botswana, Norway
WCL Division Seven	Bahrain	Guernsey	Japan, Nigeria, Gibraltar, Suriname
WCL Africa Division Three	Malawi	Sierra Leone	Rwanda, Gambia, Lesotho
ACC Trophy Challenge	Oman	Bhutan	Maldives, Thailand, China, Myanmar
East Asia Pacific Trophy (1)	PNG	Fiji	Japan
East Asia Pacific Trophy (2)	Vanuatu	Samoa	Cook Islands, Tonga, Indonesia
WCL European Division Three	Israel	Isle of Man	Spain, Belgium, Portugal, Malta
WCL European Division Four	Cyprus	Switzerland	Austria, Luxembourg, Finland, Slovenia
WCL European Division Five	Greece	Sweden	Czech Republic, Bulgaria, Estonia, Turkey
Nordic Cup (Twenty20)	Norway	Denmark XI	Sweden, Finland
WCL Americas Division Three	Brazil	Belize	Chile, Peru
Central American Champ (T20)	Panama	Mexico	Belize, Costa Rica, El Salvador
South American Champ	Argentina A	Chile	Brazil, Peru

UMPIRES

PART FIVE

Law and
Administration

OFFICIAL BODIES

INTERNATIONAL CRICKET COUNCIL

The ICC are world cricket's governing body. They are responsible for managing the playing conditions and Code of Conduct for international fixtures, expanding the game and organising the major international tournaments, including the World Cup. Their mission statement says the ICC "will lead to promoting and protecting the game, and its unique spirit" and "optimising their commercial rights and properties for the benefit of their members".

Ten national governing bodies are currently Full Members of the ICC; full membership qualifies a nation (or geographic area) to play official Test matches. A candidate for full membership must meet a number of playing and administrative criteria, after which elevation is decided by a vote among existing Full Members. There are also currently 34 Associate Members (non-Test-playing nations or geographic areas where cricket is firmly established and organised) and 60 Affiliate Members (other countries or geographic areas where the ICC recognise that cricket is played in accordance with the Laws).

The ICC were founded in 1909 as the Imperial Cricket Conference by three Foundation Members: England, Australia and South Africa. Other countries (or geographic areas) became Full Members and thus acquired Test status as follows: India, New Zealand and West Indies in 1926, Pakistan in 1952, Sri Lanka in 1981, Zimbabwe in 1992 and Bangladesh in 2000. South Africa ceased to be a member on leaving the Commonwealth in 1961, but were re-elected as a Full Member in 1991.

In 1965, the Conference were renamed the International Cricket Conference and new rules permitted the election of countries from outside the Commonwealth for the first time. The first Associate Members (Fiji and USA), who had diluted voting rights, were admitted. However, Foundation Members retained a veto over all resolutions. In 1989, the Conference were again renamed without changing their initials. The new International Cricket Council adopted revised rules, aimed at producing an organisation which could make a larger number of binding decisions, rather than simply make recommendations to national governing bodies. In 1993, the Council, which had previously been administered by MCC, gained their own secretariat and chief executive, though their headquarters remained at Lord's. The category of Foundation Member was abolished.

In 1997, the Council became an incorporated body, with an executive board, and a president instead of a chairman. The ICC remained at Lord's, with a commercial base in Monaco, until August 2005, when after 96 years they moved to Dubai in the United Arab Emirates, which offered organisational and tax advantages.

Officers

President: F. D. Morgan. *Vice-President:* S. G. R. Pawar. *Chief Executive:* H. Lorgat.

Chairs of Committees – Chief Executives' Committee: H. Lorgat. *Cricket:* C. H. Lloyd. *Audit:* A. R. Isaac. *Governance Review:* J. R. Hunte. *Human Resources, Remuneration and Appointments:* S. Inamdar. *Development:* H. Lorgat. *Code of Conduct Commission:* M. J. Beloff QC. *Women's Committee:* B. Timmer. *Finance and Commercial Affairs:* S. G. R. Pawar. *Medical Committee:* Dr P. R. Harcourt.

Executive Board: The president, president-elect and chief executive sit on the board *ex officio*. They are joined by P. F. Chingoka (Zimbabwe), C. G. Clarke (England), J. J. Clarke (Australia), D. S. de Silva (Sri Lanka), J. R. Hunte (West Indies), Ijaz Butt (Pakistan), S. Inamdar (Kenya), A. R. Isaac (New Zealand), I. Khwaja (Singapore), S. V. Manohar (India), A. H. M. Mustafa Kamal (Bangladesh), M. Nyoka (South Africa), N. Speight (Bermuda). I. S. Bindra (ICC Principal Advisor) also attends board meetings.

Chief Executives' Committee: The chairman, president and cricket committee chairman sit on the Chief Executives' Committee *ex officio.* They are joined by the chief executives of the ten Full Member boards and three Associate Member boards: O. Bvute (Zimbabwe), D. G. Collier (England), J. A. Cribbin (Hong Kong), W. Deutrom (Ireland), F. Erasmus (Namibia), E. Hilaire (West Indies), M. G. Majola (South Africa), Nizam Uddin Chowdhury (Bangladesh), N. Ranatunga (Sri Lanka), N. Srinivasan (India), J. A. Sutherland (Australia), J. T. C. Vaughan (New Zealand), Wasim Bari (Pakistan).

General Manager – Cricket: D. J. Richardson. *General Manager – Commercial:* D. C. Jamieson. *Anti-Corruption and Security Unit General Manager:* R. Sawani. *Global Development Manager:* M. R. Kennedy. *Chief Financial Officer:* K. Das. *Head of Legal and Company Secretary:* D. Becker. *Member Services and Corporate Affairs Manager:* J. Long. *Human Resources and Administration Manager:* S. K. Banerjee. *Media and Communications Manager:* C. R. Gibson.

Constitution

President: F. D. Morgan of England became president in June 2008, and S. G. R. Pawar of India is due to succeed him in 2010.

Chief Executive: Appointed by the Council. In 2008, H. Lorgat succeeded M. W. Speed, who had served for seven years.

Membership

Full Members: Australia, Bangladesh, England, India, New Zealand, Pakistan, South Africa, Sri Lanka, West Indies and Zimbabwe.

Associate Members*: Argentina (1974), Belgium (2005), Bermuda (1966), Botswana (2005), Canada (1968), Cayman Islands (2002), Denmark (1966), Fiji (1965), France (1998), Germany (1999), Gibraltar (1969), Guernsey (2005), Hong Kong (1969), Ireland (1993), Israel (1974), Italy (1995), Japan (2005), Jersey (2007), Kenya (1981), Kuwait (2005), Malaysia (1967), Namibia (1992), Nepal (1996), Netherlands (1966), Nigeria (2002), Papua New Guinea (1973), Scotland (1994), Singapore (1974), Tanzania (2001), Thailand (2005), Uganda (1998), United Arab Emirates (1990), USA (1965), Vanuatu (1995), Zambia (2003).

Affiliate Members*: Afghanistan (2001), Austria (1992), Bahamas (1987), Bahrain (2001), Belize (1997), Bhutan (2001), Brazil (2002), Brunei (2002), Bulgaria (2008), Cameroon (2007), Chile (2002), China (2004), Cook Islands (2000), Costa Rica (2002), Croatia (2001), Cuba (2002), Cyprus (1999), Czech Republic (2000), Estonia (2008), Falkland Islands (2007), Finland (2000), Gambia (2002), Ghana (2002), Greece (1995), Indonesia (2001), Iran (2003), Isle of Man (2004), Lesotho (2001), Luxembourg (1998), Malawi (2003), Maldives (2001), Mali (2005), Malta (1998), Mexico (2004), Morocco (1999), Mozambique (2003), Myanmar (2006), Norway (2000), Oman (2000), Panama (2002), Peru (2007), Philippines (2000), Portugal (1996), Qatar (1999), Rwanda (2003), St Helena (2001), Samoa (2000), Saudi Arabia (2003), Sierra Leone (2002), Slovenia (2005), South Korea (2001), Spain (1992), Suriname (2002), Swaziland (2007), Sweden (1997), Switzerland (1985), Tonga (2000), Turkey (2008), Turks & Caicos Islands (2002).

* Year of election shown in parentheses.

Full Members: The governing body for cricket (recognised by the ICC) of a country, or countries associated for cricket purposes, or a geographical area, from which representative teams are qualified to play official Test matches.

Associate Members: The governing body for cricket (recognised by the ICC) of a country, or countries associated for cricket purposes, or a geographical area, which does not qualify as a Full Member but where cricket is firmly established and organised.

Affiliate Members: The governing body for cricket (recognised by the ICC) of a country, or countries associated for cricket purposes, or a geographical area (which is not part of one of those already constituted as a Full or Associate Member) where the ICC recognise that cricket is played in accordance with the Laws of Cricket. Five Affiliate Member representatives have the right to attend or vote at the ICC annual conference.

ENGLAND AND WALES CRICKET BOARD

The England and Wales Cricket Board (ECB) became responsible for the administration of all cricket – professional and recreational – in England and Wales on January 1, 1997. They took over the functions of the Cricket Council, the Test and County Cricket Board and the National Cricket Association which had run the game in England and Wales since 1968. At the AGM on May 31, 2005, a new constitution was approved which streamlined and modernised the governance of English cricket. The Management Board of 18 directors was replaced by a Board of Directors numbering 12, with three of them appointed by the first-class counties and two by the county boards.

Officers

Chairman: C. G. Clarke. *Deputy Chairman:* D. L. Amiss. *Chief Executive:* D. G. Collier.

Board of Directors: C. G. Clarke (*chairman*), D. L. Amiss, D. G. Collier, M. V. Fleming, B. W. Havill, N. R. A. Hilliard, R. Jackson, I. N. Lovett, Lord Morris of Handsworth, J. B. Pickup, J. Simmons, D. P. Stewart.

Chairmen of Committees – Cricket: P. G. Wright. *Commercial:* C. G. Clarke. *Recreational Assembly:* J. B. Pickup. *Audit:* D. P. Stewart. *Remuneration:* N. R. A. Hilliard. *Discipline:* G. Elias QC.

Managing Director, England Cricket: H. Morris. *Managing Director, Cricket Partnerships:* M. W. Gatting. *Finance Director:* B. W. Havill. *Director of England Cricket:* J. D. Carr. *Commercial Director:* J. Perera. *Head of Corporate Communications:* S. Elworthy. *Executive Director for Women's Cricket:* C. J. Connor. *Head of Operations (First-class cricket):* A. Fordham. *Cricket Operations Manager (Non-first-class cricket):* P. Bedford. *National Selector:* G. Miller.

ECB: D. G. Collier, Lord's Ground, London NW8 8QZ (020 7432 1200; fax 020 7289 5619/020 7286 5583; website www.ecb.co.uk).

THE MARYLEBONE CRICKET CLUB

The Marylebone Cricket Club evolved out of the White Conduit Club in 1787, when Thomas Lord laid out his first ground in Dorset Square. Their members revised the Laws in 1788 and gradually took responsibility for cricket throughout the world. However, they relinquished control of the game in the UK in 1968 and the International Cricket Council finally established their own secretariat in 1993. MCC still own Lord's and remain the guardian of the Laws. They call themselves "a private club with a public function" and aim to support cricket everywhere, especially at grassroots level and in countries where the game is least developed.

Patron: HER MAJESTY THE QUEEN

Officers

President: 2009-10 – J. R. T. Barclay. *Club Chairman:* O. H. J. Stocken. *Treasurer:* L. J. Dowley. *Trustees:* J. M. Brearley, Sir Timothy Rice, A. W. Wreford. *Hon. Life Vice-Presidents:* Sir Alec Bedser, Lord Bramall, D. G. Clark, E. R. Dexter, G. H. G. Doggart, Lord Griffiths, D. J. Insole, M. E. L. Melluish, D. R. W. Silk, J. J. Warr, J. C. Woodcock.

Secretary and Chief Executive: K. Bradshaw. *Deputy Secretary:* C. Maynard. *Assistant Secretaries – Cricket and Estates:* J. P. Stephenson. *Legal:* H. A-M. Roper-Curzon. *Finance:* S. J. M. Gibb. *Marketing:* J. D. Robinson. *Catering:* S. A. Swift. *Masterplan Project Director:* D. N. Batts.

MCC Committee: R. Q. Cake, P. R. Carroll, M. V. Fleming, C. A. Fry, C. M. Gupte, R. Heyhoe-Flint, P. L. O. Leaver, Sir John Major, C. D. A. Martin-Jenkins, N. M. Peters, A. J. Stewart, J. R. Wileman. The president, club chairman, treasurer and committee chairmen are on the committee *ex officio*.

Chairmen of Committees – Arts and Library: A. I. Lack. *Cricket:* M. G. Griffith. *Development:* W. R. Griffiths. *Estates:* B. N. Gorst. *Finance:* L. J. Dowley. *Membership and General Purposes:* J. A. F. Vallance. *World Cricket:* A. R. Lewis.

MCC: The Secretary and Chief Executive, Lord's Ground, London NW8 8QN (020 7616 8500; email reception@mcc.org.uk; website www.lords.org/mcc. Tickets 020 7432 1000; fax 020 7616 8700; email ticketing@mcc.org.uk).

PROFESSIONAL CRICKETERS' ASSOCIATION

The Professional Cricketers' Association were formed in 1967 (as the Cricketers' Association) to be the collective voice of first-class professional players and enhance and protect their interests. During the 1970s, they succeeded in establishing pension schemes and a minimum wage. In the last decade their strong commercial operations and increased funding from the ECB have ensured that services to current and past players have increased. In 2009 the PCA had a staff of ten and provided extensive education, legal, financial and benevolent help to members.

President: Sir Ian Botham. *Chief Executive:* A. Porter. *Chairman:* V. S. Solanki. *Assistant Chief Executive:* J. D. Ratcliffe. *Vice-President – Health Trust:* D. A. Graveney. *Events Director:* S. A. Marsh. *Legal Director:* I. T. Smith. *Commercial Director:* J. Grave. *Non-Executive Group Chairman:* A. W. Wreford. *Non-Executive Director:* M. Wheeler.

PCA: Unit 5, Utopia Village, 7 Chalcot Road, London NW1 8LH (020 7449 4221; fax 020 7586 8520; email events@thepca.co.uk; website www.thepca.co.uk).

FEDERATION OF INTERNATIONAL CRICKETERS' ASSOCIATIONS

The Federation of International Cricketers' Associations were established in 1998 to coordinate the activities of all national players' associations. They aim to protect the interests of professional cricketers throughout the world. In 2003 FICA were recognised as an official representative body by the ICC.

President: J. C. Adams. *Chief Executive:* T. B. A. May. *Secretary:* A. Irish. *Treasurer:* P. Marsh. *Senior Vice-President:* D. A. Graveney.

FICA: T. B. A. May, 1511 Rockcliff Road, Austin, Texas 78746. (email tbamay@gmail.com).

ADDRESSES

INTERNATIONAL CRICKET COUNCIL

ICC: H. Lorgat, Street 69, Dubai Sports City, Emirates Road, PO Box 500 070, Dubai, United Arab Emirates (+971 4382 8800; fax +971 4382 8600; website www.icc-cricket.yahoo.net; email enquiry@icc-cricket.com).

Full Members

Australia: Cricket Australia, J. A. Sutherland, 60 Jolimont Street, Jolimont, Victoria 3002 (+61 3 9653 9999; fax +61 3 9653 9900; website www.cricket.com.au; email penquiries@cricket.com.au).

Bangladesh: Bangladesh Cricket Board, Nizam Uddin Chowdhury, Sher-e-Bangla National Cricket Stadium, Mirpur, Dhaka 1216 (+880 2 803 1001; fax +880 2 803 1199; website www.tigercricket.com; email info@bcb-cricket.com).

England: England and Wales Cricket Board (see above).

India: Board of Control for Cricket in India, N. Srinivasan, Cricket Centre, 2nd Floor, Wankhede Stadium, D Road, Churchgate, Mumbai 400 020 (+91 22 2289 8800; fax +91 22 2289 8801; website www.bcci.tv and bccicricket.org; email bcci@vsnl.com).

New Zealand: New Zealand Cricket, J. T. C. Vaughan, PO Box 958, Level 6, 164 Hereford Street, Christchurch (+64 3 366 2964; fax +64 3 365 7491; website www.blackcaps.co.nz; email info@nzcricket.org.nz).

Pakistan: Pakistan Cricket Board, Wasim Bari, Gaddafi Stadium, Ferozpur Road, Lahore 54600 (+92 42 571 7231; fax +92 42 571 1860; website www.pcb.com.pk; email mail@pcb.com.pk).

South Africa: Cricket South Africa, M. G. Majola, Wanderers Club, PO Box 55009, 21 North Street, Illovo, Northlands 2116 (+27 11 880 2810; fax +27 11 880 6578; website www.cricket.co.za; email csa@cricket.co.za).

Sri Lanka: Sri Lanka Cricket, N. Ranatunga, 35 Maitland Place, Colombo 7 (+94 112 681 601; fax +94 112 697 405; website www.srilankacricket.lk; email info@srilankacricket.lk).

West Indies: West Indies Cricket Board, E. Hilaire, PO Box 616 W, Factory Road, St John's, Antigua (+1 268 481 2450; fax +1 268 481 2498; website www.windiescricket.com; email wicb@windiescricket.com).

Zimbabwe: Zimbabwe Cricket, O. Bvute, PO Box 2739, 28 Maiden Drive, Highlands, Harare (+263 4 788 092; fax +263 4 788 094; website www.zimcricket.org; email info@zimcricket.org).

Associate and Affiliate Members

Afghanistan Sayed Shah Aminzai, ceo@afghancricket.af.

Argentina G. Dugmore, www.cricketargentina.com, admin@cricketargentina.com.

Austria W. Tesar, aca.secretariat@gmail.com.

Bahamas G. T. Taylor, firstslip@hotmail.com.

Bahrain M. Hamed M. Sadeq, mhmsadeq@yahoo.com.

Belgium M. O'Connor, www.cricket-belgium.com, office@cricket-belgium.com.

Belize E. R. V. Wade, jun., ervwade@yahoo.com.

Bermuda N. Speight, www.bermudacricketboard.com, nspeight@cricket.bm.

Bhutan J. Norbu, www.bhutancricket.org, jigmenorbu@hotmail.com.

Botswana S. Damodar, sumod@mega.bw.

Brazil N. Baldwin, montrealconsultants@terra.com.br.

Brunei M. B. Ahmad, bruneicricket@gmail.com.

Bulgaria S. Vasileva, cricket_bg@abv.bg.

Cameroon B. N. Jacob, fecacricket@yahoo.com.

Canada I. Liburd, www.canadiancricket.org, ingletonl@gmail.com.

Cayman Islands T. Cuffy, cicaadmin@candw.ky.

Chile J. Fecci, www.cricketchile.cl, admin@cricketchile.cl.

China Zhang Tian, zhangterryzt@163.com.

Cook Islands A. Steric, alister@cookislandscricket.co.uk.

Costa Rica R. T. R. Illingworth, illings@racsa.co.cr.

Croatia J. Butkovic, www.croatia-cricket.hr, info@croatia-cricket.hr.

Cuba L. I. Ford-Miller, cecirafull@infomed.sld.cu.

Cyprus C. Klein, www.cypruscricket.com, cklein@ramnous.com.
Czech Republic H. Banks, www.czechcricket.cz, info@czechcricket.cz.
Denmark O. Roland, www.cricket.dk, dcf@cricket.dk.
Estonia J. Ramsden, james-tallinn@hotmail.com.
Falkland Islands R. Marlor, falklandscricket@horizon.co.fk.
Fiji M. Shaw, www.sportingpulse.com/assoc_page.cgi?assoc=1354&pID=2, fijicrick@connect. com.fj.
Finland A. Armitage, www.cricketfinland.com, fcachairman@cricketfinland.com.
France P. Townsend, www.ffbsc.org and www.icc-europe.org/FRANCE, francecricket.secretary@ orange.fr.
Gambia J. Kookorie, gambiacricketassociation@yahoo.com.
Germany B. Fell, www.cricket.de, brimarfell@t-online.de.
Ghana W. Ampofo, wampofo@noguchi.mimcom.net.
Gibraltar T. J. Finlayson, www.icc-europe.org/GIBRALTAR, gca@gibetelecom.net.
Greece E. Stefopoulou, crickadm@otenet.gr.
Guernsey M. Latter, www.guernseycricket.com, mark@guernseycricket.com.
Hong Kong D. Lai, www.hkca.cricket.org, hkca@hkabc.net.
Indonesia P. Vijaykumar, prakash@cricketindonesia.com.
Iran J. Sawhney, bsrc_iranf@yahoo.com.
Ireland W. Deutrom, www.irishcricket.org, info@irishcricket.org.
Isle of Man S. Davidson, www.icc-europe.org/ISLEOFMAN, iomca@manx.net.
Israel S. Perlman, www.israel.cricket.org, sperlman@zahav.net.il.
Italy L. Bruno, www.crickitalia.org, segreteria@crickitalia.org.
Japan N. A. Miyaji, www.cricket.or.jp/eng/, n-miyaji@cricket.or.jp.
Jersey C. Minty, www.jerseycricket.net, chris.minty@jerseycricket.net.
Kenya S. Inamdar, www.kenyacricket.org, inamdar@africaonline.co.ke.
Kuwait A. Baig, www.cricketkuwait.com, abaig@gulfconsult.net.
Lesotho P. Maliehe, admin@lsrc.org.ls.
Luxembourg M. Smith, www.cricket.lu, mark.smith@ec.europa.eu.
Malawi T. Tarmohammed, tariqmt@yahoo.com.
Malaysia S. Chinnadurai, www.malaysiacricket.com, siva_1946@yahoo.com.
Maldives I. Ismail, www.maldivescricket.org, imad@microtech.com.mv.
Mali S. Watson, femacrik@yahoo.fr.
Malta M. Caruana, www.maltacricket.biz, maltacricket@yahoo.co.uk.
Mexico D. Choudhuri, debchoudhuri@yahoo.com.
Morocco F. Boujoual, cricketmaroc@yahoo.com.
Mozambique D. Sengupta, debala.group@teledata.mz.
Myanmar A. Akhter, akhteradowath@gmail.com.
Namibia L. Pieters, www.cricketnamibia.com, cricket@iway.na.
Nepal T. P. Paneru, www.cricketnepal.org, tpaneru@gmail.com.
Netherlands J. Zwart, www.kncb.nl, cricket@kncb.nl.
Nigeria A. Dans, cricketnigfed@yahoo.com.
Norway B. Gibb, www.cricketforbundet.no, admin@cricketforbundet.no.
Oman Madhu Jesrani, Krwatchs@omantel.net.om.
Panama I. Patel, patel@cwpanama.net.
Papua New Guinea B. Leane, billleane@yahoo.com.au.
Peru H. Hildebrand, hildebra@markham.edu.pe.
Philippines I. Sinclair, www.philippinecricketassociation.com, philippinecricket@yahoo.com.au.
Portugal F. Buccimazza, www.icc-europe.org/PORTUGAL, sandyb@netcabo.pt.
Qatar Manzoor Ahmad, manzoor.ahmad@arup.com.
Rwanda M. M. Hussein, rwandacricket@yahoo.fr.
St Helena B. A. George, barbara@sainthelena.gov.sh.
Samoa T. Macumber, tina.macumber@cricketsamoa.ws.
Saudi Arabia N. A. Nadwi, date@zajil.net.
Scotland R. C. Smith, www.cricketscotland.com, roddysmith@cricketscotland.com.
Sierra Leone S. Benka, besiomak1@yahoo.co.uk.
Singapore D. Mulewa, www.cricket.org.sg, cricket@singnet.com.sg.
Slovenia M. Oman, www.ljcricket.com, mark_oman@hotmail.com.
South Korea S. Kennedy, daami@cricket.or.kr.
Spain J. Howden, jhowden999@yahoo.co.uk.
Suriname R. S. Narain, sdb.rsn@sr.net.

Swaziland Sohail Khan, sohail@swazi.net.
Sweden S. Forslund, www.swedishcricket.se, secretary@swedishcricket.se.
Switzerland P. Vijayadas, www.swisscricket.ch, pradeep.vijayadas@swisscricket.ch.
Tanzania Z. Rehemtulla, www.tanzaniacricket.com, wizards@cats-net.com.
Thailand M. A. Kader, kader@thailandcricket.com.
Tonga H. Tenisi, ceo.tongancricket@gmail.com.
Turkey S. Mahmud, syed@bilkent.edu.tr.
Turks & Caicos Islands R. Doughty, doughtyralph@yahoo.com.
Uganda C. M. Mpeka, ugandacricket@utonline.co.ug.
United Arab Emirates D. Mani, www.emiratescricket.com, dmani@eim.ae.
USA D. Lockerbie, www.usaca.org, dlockerbie@usaca.org.
Vanuatu P. Chilia, vanuatucricket@vanuatu.com.vu.
Zambia A. Shawa, drshawa@yahoo.com.

Note: Full contact details for all Associate and Affiliate Members may be found at the ICC website www.icc-cricket.yahoo.net/the-icc/icc_members/overview.php.

REGIONAL ORGANISATIONS

Asian Cricket Council: Syed Ashraful Huq, Level 20-2, CP Tower, No. 11 Jalan 16/11, 46350 Petaling Jaya, Selangor Darul Ehsan, Malaysia (+603 7956 9594; website www.asiancricket.org).
European Cricket Council: R. Holdsworth, Europe Office, The Clock Tower, Lord's Ground, London NW8 8QN (020 7616 8635; website www.icc-europe.org).
Americas Region: M. Vieira, ICC – Americas, 3 Concorde Gate, Suite 301, Toronto M3C 3N7, Canada (+1 416 426 7312; website www.icccricket. yahoo.net/the-icc/icc_members/americas/).
Africa Cricket Association: C. Suliman, Willowmoore Park, PO Box 596, Benoni 1500, South Africa (+27 11 845 4881; website www.africacricket.org).
East Asia-Pacific Region: M. Weisheit, c/o Cricket Australia, 60 Jolimont Street, Jolimont, Victoria 3002, Australia (+61 3 9653 9945; website www.icceap.com).

THE LAWS IN 2009

FRASER STEWART

In a year that featured an Ashes series, the World Twenty20, the Champions Trophy and a number of other games at the top level, it is unsurprising that several incidents left viewers and commentators searching for interpretations of those peculiar incidents that help make cricket so special.

Sometimes the ICC will ask MCC for a clarification of a particular matter, but the Laws are usually clear and, far more often than not, the umpires implement them correctly. Fans, players and umpires from all over the world contact MCC to check on particular events, from the Test arena to the village green; as well as answering these queries, MCC has been reacting to events at the top level and has been busy with a redraft of the Laws for 2010.

With fielders seemingly becoming ever more athletic, 2009 saw at least three examples of quick thinking by international players attempting catches on the boundary. Australia's Adam Voges and New Zealand's Jacob Oram both caught the ball inside the boundary but realised their momentum was going to take them over the rope. They threw the ball up before stepping over the boundary, quickly regained their balance and composure, then returned to the field to catch the ball they had tossed up a few moments earlier. The batsman was correctly given out on each occasion.

During the World Twenty20, Sri Lanka's Angelo Mathews raised eyebrows at Trent Bridge when he went further than Voges and Oram. His throw in the air (after "catching" the ball) went outside the boundary. He stepped outside the boundary and, to ensure he was not grounded while in contact with the ball, leapt in the air and parried it back inside the rope. The fielding was legal, as at no point was Mathews in contact with the ball and the ground beyond the boundary at the same time. (See Laws 19.3(a)(ii), 32.3 and 32.4.)

In the Third Ashes Test, Australia's first-choice wicketkeeper, Brad Haddin, broke his finger after the toss but before the start of play. The Australian team had been nominated in writing by Ricky Ponting before the toss, so a replacement could be allowed only with the England captain's consent. It was particularly relevant that a wicketkeeper was injured. A replacement player is different from a substitute: a replacement may take a full part in the game, but a substitute may not bat, bowl or act as wicketkeeper or captain. Andrew Strauss would have been within his rights under Law 1.2 to refuse Ponting's request, which would have meant that one of the ten remaining players had to keep wicket and that Australia could have batted with only ten men – a significant disadvantage in a five-day game. However, to widespread praise, Strauss allowed the request, and Graham Manou made his Test debut.

It should be noted that while the opposition captain has the sole authority to grant a replacement, the use of a substitute is solely at the discretion of the umpires and, acting within the limitation of the Laws, the opposing captain has no involvement in this matter. This part of the Law was brought into question during the Champions Trophy in South Africa, and again involved Strauss.

After fielding for 50 overs and batting for 40, South Africa's Graeme Smith, suffering from cramp, asked the umpires for a runner. The umpires felt that cramp was a fitness issue, rather than an illness or injury, and refused. Smith then asked Strauss (who legally had no say in the matter) for his permission, but met the same response, resulting in some labelling Strauss as unsporting.

Opinion is split on whether cramp is a matter of fitness and conditioning, and so an integral part of a physical sport, or an injury or illness that would qualify a player for a runner or substitute. The ICC's medical committee has stated the former opinion – a view shared by the vast playing experience of members of MCC's world cricket committee. However, others highlight inconsistent treatment of batsmen and bowlers. A batsman gets cramp and may not have a runner. Yet, if a fast bowler gets cramp mid-over and is unable to run, most umpires would allow him to leave the field, be replaced by a substitute fielder and permit another player to finish the over, rather than force him to hobble in for the last three balls. While this may be a rare concession to the bowler in a batsman-friendly game, is it fair that the two should be treated differently?

Take this a step further: if cramp does not qualify the batsman for a runner, then neither should he be able to retire hurt. He may retire but, unlike when a batsman retires after an injury, he may only resume his innings with the consent of the opposing captain – and if he does not resume his innings, he should be recorded as "Retired – out" (see Law 2.9). MCC is working closely with the ICC on the issue of cramp and, if necessary, will seek further medical opinion before formally stating its position.

In 2008, there was criticism of Paul Collingwood's refusal to withdraw an appeal in a one-day international against New Zealand after a collision between the batsman Grant Elliott and the bowler Ryan Sidebottom that saw Elliott knocked to the ground, injured, stranded, and run out. So it was pleasing that 2009 saw at least two incidents where captains took a more sporting approach: Strauss did not feel it would be right for Mathews to be run out after colliding with Graham Onions; then, in a twist of fate, Collingwood was batting against New Zealand when reprieved by their captain, Daniel Vettori, after he wandered out of his ground before the ball was dead at the end of an over.

In October 2010, a fourth edition of the 2000 Code of Laws is due to come into effect. Some proposed amendments are:

- A removal of the "offering of the light" to the batting side (umpires should keep the players on the field until it is unreasonable or dangerous).
- A tightening-up on batsmen damaging the pitch.
- A new restriction that a fielder must make his first contact with the ball after his last contact with the ground was inside the boundary – this is aimed at preventing fielders, seeing a ball clearly going for six, back-pedalling beyond the boundary and jumping in the air to parry it back.

Any amendments have to be approved by MCC's members at the club's AGM in May 2010 (see www.lords.org).

Fraser Stewart is laws manager at MCC.

THE LAWS OF CRICKET

(2000 CODE)

As updated in 2008.

World copyright of MCC and reprinted by permission of MCC. Copies of the "Laws of Cricket" are obtainable from Lord's Cricket Ground.

INDEX OF THE LAWS

THE PREAMBLE – THE SPIRIT OF CRICKET

Cricket is a game that owes much of its unique appeal to the fact that it should be played not only within its Laws, but also within the Spirit of the Game. Any action which is seen to abuse this spirit causes injury to the game itself. The major responsibility for ensuring the spirit of fair play rests with the captains.

1. There are two Laws which place the responsibility for the team's conduct firmly on the captain.

Responsibility of captains

The captains are responsible at all times for ensuring that play is conducted within the Spirit of the Game as well as within the Laws.

Player's conduct

In the event of a player failing to comply with instructions by an umpire, or criticising by word or action the decisions of an umpire, or showing dissent, or generally behaving in a manner which might bring the game into disrepute, the umpire concerned shall in the first place report the matter to the other umpire and to the player's captain, and instruct the latter to take action.

2. Fair and unfair play

According to the Laws the umpires are the sole judges of fair and unfair play. The umpires may intervene at any time, and it is the responsibility of the captain to take action where required.

3. The umpires are authorised to intervene in cases of

- Time-wasting.
- Damaging the pitch.
- Dangerous or unfair bowling.
- Tampering with the ball.
- Any other action that they consider to be unfair.

4. The Spirit of the Game involves respect for

- Your opponents.
- Your own captain and team.
- The role of the umpires.
- The game's traditional values.

5. It is against the Spirit of the Game

- To dispute an umpire's decision by word, action or gesture.
- To direct abusive language towards an opponent or umpire.
- To indulge in cheating or any sharp practice, for instance:

    (a) To appeal knowing that the batsman is not out.

    (b) To advance towards an umpire in an aggressive manner when appealing.

    (c) To seek to distract an opponent either verbally or by harassment with persistent clapping or unnecessary noise under the guise of enthusiasm and motivation of one's own side.

6. Violence

There is no place for any act of violence on the field of play.

7. Players

Captains and umpires together set the tone for the conduct of a cricket match. Every player is expected to make an important contribution to this.

The players, umpires and scorers in a game of cricket may be of either gender and the Laws apply equally to both. The use, throughout the text, of pronouns indicating the male gender is purely for brevity. Except where specifically stated otherwise, every provision of the Laws is to be read as applying to women and girls equally as to men and boys.

LAW 1. THE PLAYERS

1. Number of players

A match is played between two sides, each of 11 players, one of whom shall be captain. By agreement a match may be played between sides of more or less than 11 players, but not more than 11 players may field at any time.

2. Nomination of players

Each captain shall nominate his players in writing to one of the umpires before the toss. No player may be changed after the nomination without the consent of the opposing captain.

3. Captain

If at any time the captain is not available, a deputy shall act for him.

(a) If a captain is not available during the period in which the toss is to take place, then the deputy must be responsible for the nomination of the players, if this has not already been done, and for the toss. See 2 above and Law 12.4 (The toss).

(b) At any time after the toss, the deputy must be one of the nominated players.

4. Responsibility of captains

The captains are responsible at all times for ensuring that play is conducted within the spirit and traditions of the game as well as within the Laws. See The Preamble – The Spirit of Cricket and Law 42.1 (Fair and unfair play – responsibility of captains).

LAW 2. SUBSTITUTES AND RUNNERS; BATSMAN OR FIELDER LEAVING THE FIELD; BATSMAN RETIRING; BATSMAN COMMENCING INNINGS

1. Substitutes and runners

(a) If the umpires are satisfied that a player has been injured or become ill after the nomination of the players, they shall allow that player to have:

(i) A substitute acting instead of him in the field.

(ii) A runner when batting.

Any injury or illness that occurs at any time after the nomination of the players until the conclusion of the match shall be allowable, irrespective of whether play is in progress or not.

(b) The umpires shall have discretion, for other wholly acceptable reasons, to allow a substitute for a fielder, or a runner for a batsman, at the start of the match or at any subsequent time.

(c) A player wishing to change his shirt, boots, etc. must leave the field to do so. No substitute shall be allowed for him.

2. Objection to substitutes

The opposing captain shall have no right of objection to any player acting as a substitute on the field, nor as to where the substitute shall field. However, no substitute shall act as wicketkeeper. See 3 below.

3. Restrictions on the role of substitutes

A substitute shall not be allowed to bat or bowl nor to act as wicketkeeper or as captain on the field of play.

4. A player for whom a substitute has acted

A player is allowed to bat, bowl or field even though a substitute has previously acted for him.

5. Fielder absent or leaving the field

If a fielder fails to take the field with his side at the start of the match or at any later time, or leaves the field during a session of play:

    (a) The umpire shall be informed of the reason for his absence.

    (b) He shall not thereafter come on to the field during a session of play without the consent of the umpire. See 6 below. The umpire shall give such consent as soon as is practicable.

    (c) If he is absent for 15 minutes or longer, he shall not be permitted to bowl thereafter, subject to (i), (ii) or (iii) below, until he has been on the field for at least that length of playing time for which he was absent.

        (i) Absence or penalty for time absent shall not be carried over into a new day's play.

        (ii) If, in the case of a follow-on or forfeiture, a side fields for two consecutive innings, this restriction shall, subject to (i) above, continue as necessary into the second innings but shall not otherwise be carried over into a new innings.

        (iii) The time lost for an unscheduled break in play shall be counted as time on the field for any fielder who comes on to the field at the resumption of play. See Law 15.1 (An interval).

6. Player returning without permission

If a player comes on to the field of play in contravention of 5(b) above and comes into contact with the ball while it is in play:

    (i) The ball shall immediately become dead and the umpire shall award five penalty runs to the batting side. See Law 42.17 (Penalty runs). The ball shall not count as one of the over.

    (ii) The umpire shall inform the other umpire, the captain of the fielding side, the batsmen and, as soon as practicable, the captain of the batting side of the reason for this action.

    (iii) The umpires together shall report the occurrence as soon as possible to the executive of the fielding side and any governing body responsible for the match, who shall take such action as is considered appropriate against the captain and player concerned.

7. Runner

The player acting as a runner for a batsman shall be a member of the batting side and shall, if possible, have already batted in that innings. The runner shall wear external protective equipment equivalent to that worn by the batsman for whom he runs and shall carry a bat.

8. Transgression of the Laws by a batsman who has a runner

    (a) A batsman's runner is subject to the Laws. He will be regarded as a batsman except where there are specific provisions for his role as a runner. See 7 above and Law 29.2 (Which is a batsman's ground).

    (b) A batsman with a runner will suffer the penalty for any infringement of the Laws by his runner as though he had been himself responsible for the infringement. In particular he will be out if his runner is out under any of Laws 33 (Handled the ball), 37 (Obstructing the field) or 38 (Run out).

    (c) When a batsman with a runner is striker he remains himself subject to the Laws and will be liable to the penalties that any infringement of them demands.

    Additionally, if he is out of his ground when the wicket is put down at the wicketkeeper's end, he will be out in the circumstances of Law 38 (Run out) or Law 39 (Stumped) irrespective of the position of the non-striker or of the runner. If he is thus dismissed, runs completed by the runner and the other batsman before the dismissal shall not be scored. However, the penalty for a no-ball or a wide shall stand, together with any penalties to be awarded to either side when the ball is dead. See Law 42.17 (Penalty runs).

    (d) When a batsman with a runner is not the striker:

(i) He remains subject to Laws 33 (Handled the ball) and 37 (Obstructing the field) but is otherwise out of the game.

(ii) He shall stand where directed by the striker's end umpire so as not to interfere with play.

(iii) He will be liable, notwithstanding (i) above, to the penalty demanded by the Laws should he commit any act of unfair play.

9. Batsman leaving the field or retiring

A batsman may retire at any time during his innings. The umpires, before allowing play to proceed, shall be informed of the reason for a batsman retiring.

(a) If a batsman retires because of illness, injury or any other unavoidable cause, he is entitled to resume his innings subject to (c) below. If for any reason he does not do so, his innings is to be recorded as "Retired – not out".

(b) If a batsman retires for any reason other than as in (a) above, he may resume his innings only with the consent of the opposing captain. If for any reason he does not resume his innings it is to be recorded as "Retired – out".

(c) If after retiring a batsman resumes his innings, it shall be only at the fall of a wicket or the retirement of another batsman.

10. Commencement of a batsman's innings

Except at the start of a side's innings, a batsman shall be considered to have commenced his innings when he first steps on to the field of play, provided "Time" has not been called. The innings of the opening batsmen, and that of any new batsman at the resumption of play after a call of "Time", shall commence at the call of "Play".

LAW 3. THE UMPIRES

1. Appointment and attendance

Before the match, two umpires shall be appointed, one for each end to control the game as required by the Laws, with absolute impartiality. The umpires shall be present on the ground and report to the executive of the ground at least 45 minutes before the start of each day's play.

2. Change of umpire

An umpire shall not be changed during the match, other than in exceptional circumstances, unless he is injured or ill. If there has to be a change of umpire, the replacement shall act only as the striker's end umpire unless the captains agree that he should take full responsibility as an umpire.

3. Agreement with captains

Before the toss the umpires shall:

(a) Ascertain the hours of play and agree with the captains:

(i) The balls to be used during the match. See Law 5 (The ball).

(ii) Times and durations of intervals for meals and times for drinks intervals. See Law 15 (Intervals).

(iii) The boundary of the field of play and allowances for boundaries. See Law 19 (Boundaries).

(iv) Any special conditions of play affecting the conduct of the match.

(b) Inform the scorers of the agreements in (ii), (iii) and (iv) above.

4. To inform captains and scorers

Before the toss the umpires shall agree between themselves and inform both captains and both scorers:

(i) Which clock or watch and back-up timepiece is to be used during the match.

(ii) Whether or not any obstacle within the field of play is to be regarded as a boundary. See Law 19 (Boundaries).

5. The wickets, creases and boundaries

Before the toss and during the match, the umpires shall satisfy themselves that:

(i) The wickets are properly pitched. See Law 8 (The wickets).

(ii) The creases are correctly marked. See Law 9 (The bowling, popping and return creases).

(iii) The boundary of the field of play complies with the requirements of Law 19.2 (Defining the boundary – boundary marking).

6. Conduct of the game, implements and equipment

Before the toss and during the match, the umpires shall satisfy themselves that:

(a) The conduct of the game is strictly in accordance with the Laws.

(b) The implements of the game conform to the requirements of Laws 5 (The ball) and 6 (The bat), together with either Laws 8.2 (Size of stumps) and 8.3 (The bails) or, if appropriate, Law 8.4 (Junior cricket).

(c) (i) No player uses equipment other than that permitted.

(ii) The wicketkeeper's gloves comply with the requirements of Law 40.2 (Gloves).

7. Fair and unfair play

The umpires shall be the sole judges of fair and unfair play.

8. Fitness of ground, weather and light

The umpires shall be the final judges of the fitness of the ground, weather and light for play. See 9 below and Law 7.2 (Fitness of the pitch for play).

9. Suspension of play for adverse conditions of ground, weather or light

(a) (i) All references to ground include the pitch. See Law 7.1 (Area of pitch).

(ii) For the purpose of this Law the batsmen at the wicket may deputise for their captain at any appropriate time.

(b) If at any time the umpires together agree that the condition of the ground, weather or light is not suitable for play, they shall inform the captains and, unless

(i) in unsuitable ground or weather conditions both captains agree to continue, or to commence, or to restart play, or

(ii) in unsuitable light the batting side wish to continue, or to commence, or to restart play,

they shall suspend play, or not allow play to commence or to restart.

(c) (i) After agreeing to play in unsuitable ground or weather conditions, either captain may appeal against the conditions to the umpires before the next call of "Time". The umpires shall uphold the appeal only if, in their opinion, the factors taken into account when making their previous decision are the same or the conditions have further deteriorated.

(ii) After deciding to play in unsuitable light, the captain of the batting side may appeal against the light to the umpires before the next call of "Time". The umpires shall uphold the appeal only if, in their opinion, the factors taken into account when making their previous decision are the same or the condition of the light has further deteriorated.

(d) If at any time the umpires together agree that the conditions of ground, weather or light are so bad that there is obvious and foreseeable risk to the safety of any player or umpire, so that it would be unreasonable or dangerous for play to take place, then notwithstanding the provisions of 9(b)(i) and 9(b)(ii) above, they shall immediately suspend play, or not allow play to commence or to restart. The decision as to whether conditions are so bad as to warrant such action is one for the umpires alone to make.

Merely because the grass and the ball are wet and slippery does not warrant the ground conditions being regarded as unreasonable or dangerous. If the umpires consider the ground is so wet or slippery as to deprive the bowler of a reasonable foothold, the fielders of the power of free movement, or the batsmen of the ability to play their strokes or to run between the wickets, then these conditions shall be regarded as so bad that it would be unreasonable for play to take place.

(e) When there is a suspension of play it is the responsibility of the umpires to monitor the conditions. They shall make inspections as often as appropriate, unaccompanied by any of the players or officials. Immediately the umpires together agree that conditions are suitable for play they shall call upon the players to resume the game.

(f) If play is in progress up to the start of an agreed interval then it will resume after the interval unless the umpires together agree that conditions are or have become unsuitable or dangerous. If they do so agree, then they shall implement the procedure in (b) or (d) above, as appropriate, whether or not there had been any decision by the captains to continue, or any appeal against the conditions by either captain, prior to the commencement of the interval.

10. Exceptional circumstances

The umpires shall have the discretion to implement the procedures of 9 above for reasons other than ground, weather or light if they consider that exceptional circumstances warrant it.

11. Position of umpires

The umpires shall stand where they can best see any act upon which their decision may be required. Subject to this over-riding consideration the umpire at the bowler's end shall stand where he does not interfere with either the bowler's run-up or the striker's view.

The umpire at the striker's end may elect to stand on the off side instead of the on side of the pitch, provided he informs the captain of the fielding side, the striker and the other umpire of his intention to do so.

12. Umpires changing ends

The umpires shall change ends after each side has had one completed innings. See Law 14.2 (Forfeiture of an innings).

13. Consultation between umpires

All disputes shall be determined by the umpires. The umpires shall consult with each other whenever necessary. See also Law 27.6 (Consultation by umpires).

14. Signals

(a) The following code of signals shall be used by umpires.

(i) Signals made while the ball is in play:

Dead ball	– by crossing and re-crossing the wrists below the waist.
No-ball	– by extending one arm horizontally.
Out	– by raising the index finger above the head. (If not out the umpire shall call "Not out.")
Wide	– by extending both arms horizontally.

(ii) When the ball is dead, the signals above, with the exception of the signal for "Out", shall be repeated to the scorers. The signals listed below shall be made to the scorers only when the ball is dead.

Boundary 4	– by waving an arm from side to side finishing with the arm across the chest.
Boundary 6	– by raising both arms above the head.
Bye	– by raising an open hand above the head.
Commencement of last hour	– by pointing to a raised wrist with the other hand.

Five penalty runs awarded to the batting side	– by repeated tapping of one shoulder with the opposite hand.
Five penalty runs awarded to the fielding side	– by placing one hand on the opposite shoulder.
Leg-bye	– by touching a raised knee with the hand.
New ball	– by holding the ball above the head.
Revoke last signal	– by touching both shoulders, each with the opposite hand.
Short run	– By bending one arm upwards and touching the near shoulder with the tips of the fingers.

(b) The umpires shall wait until each signal to the scorers has been separately acknowledged by a scorer before allowing play to proceed.

15. Correctness of scores

Consultation between umpires and scorers on doubtful points is essential. The umpires shall satisfy themselves as to the correctness of the number of runs scored, the wickets that have fallen and, where appropriate, the number of overs bowled. They shall agree these with the scorers at least at every interval, other than a drinks interval, and at the conclusion of the match. See Laws 4.2 (Correctness of scores), 21.8 (Correctness of result) and 21.10 (Result not to be changed).

LAW 4.   THE SCORERS

1. Appointment of scorers

Two scorers shall be appointed to record all runs scored, all wickets taken and, where appropriate, number of overs bowled.

2. Correctness of scores

The scorers shall frequently check to ensure that their records agree. They shall agree with the umpires, at least at every interval, other than a drinks interval, and at the conclusion of the match, the runs scored, the wickets that have fallen and, where appropriate, the number of overs bowled. See Law 3.15 (Correctness of scores).

3. Acknowledging signals

The scorers shall accept all instructions and signals given to them by the umpires. They shall immediately acknowledge each separate signal.

LAW 5.   THE BALL

1. Weight and size

The ball, when new, shall weigh not less than $5^{1}/_{2}$oz/155.9g, nor more than $5^{3}/_{4}$oz/163g, and shall measure not less than $8^{13}/_{16}$in/22.4cm, nor more than 9in/22.9cm in circumference.

2. Approval and control of balls

(a) All balls to be used in the match, having been approved by the umpires and captains, shall be in the possession of the umpires before the toss and shall remain under their control throughout the match.

(b) The umpire shall take possession of the ball in use at the fall of each wicket, at the start of any interval and at any interruption of play.

3. New ball

Unless an agreement to the contrary has been made before the match, either captain may demand a new ball at the start of each innings.

4. New ball in match of more than one day's duration

In a match of more than one day's duration, the captain of the fielding side may demand a new ball after the prescribed number of overs has been bowled with the old one. The governing body for cricket in the country concerned shall decide the number of overs applicable in that country, which shall not be less than 75 overs.

The umpires shall indicate to the batsmen and the scorers whenever a new ball is taken into play.

5. Ball lost or becoming unfit for play

If, during play, the ball cannot be found or recovered or the umpires agree that it has become unfit for play through normal use, the umpires shall replace it with a ball which has had wear comparable with that which the previous ball had received before the need for its replacement. When the ball is replaced the umpires shall inform the batsmen and the fielding captain.

6. Specifications

The specifications as described in 1 above shall apply to men's cricket only. The following specifications will apply to:

    (i) *Women's cricket*
        Weight   – from $4^{15}/_{16}$oz/140g to $5^{5}/_{16}$oz/151g.
        Circumference – from $8^{1}/_{4}$in/21.0cm to $8^{7}/_{8}$in/22.5cm.

    (ii) *Junior cricket – Under-13*
        Weight   – from $4^{11}/_{16}$oz/133g to $5^{1}/_{16}$oz/144g.
        Circumference – from $8^{1}/_{16}$in/20.5cm to $8^{11}/_{16}$in/22.0cm.

LAW 6. THE BAT

1. The bat

The bat consists of two parts, a handle and a blade.

2. Measurements

All provisions in sections 3 to 6 below are subject to the measurements and restrictions stated in Appendix E.

3. The handle

    (a) One end of the handle is inserted into a recess in the blade as a means of joining the handle and the blade. The part of the handle that is then wholly outside the blade is defined to be the upper portion of the handle. It is a straight shaft for holding the bat. The remainder of the handle is its lower portion used purely for joining the blade and the handle together. It is not part of the blade but, solely in interpreting 5 and 6 below, references to the blade shall be considered to extend also to the lower portion of the handle where relevant.

    (b) The handle is to be made principally of cane and/or wood, glued where necessary and bound with twine along the upper portion.

    (c) Providing 7 below is not contravened, the upper portion may be covered with materials solely to provide a surface suitable for gripping. Such covering is an addition and is not part of the bat. Note, however, 8 below.

    (d) Notwithstanding 4(c) and 5 below, both the twine binding and the covering grip may extend beyond the junction of the upper and lower portions, to cover part of the shoulders as defined in Appendix E.

4. The blade

(a) The blade comprises the whole of the bat apart from the handle as defined above. The blade has a face, a back, a toe, sides and shoulders. See Appendix E.

(b) The blade shall consist solely of wood.

(c) No material may be placed on or inserted into either the blade or the lower portion of the handle other than as permitted in 3(d) above and 5 and 6 below, together with the minimal adhesives or adhesive tape used solely for fixing these items, or for fixing the handle to the blade.

5. Covering the blade

All bats may have commercial identifications on the blade.

Grade A and Grade B bats may have no other covering on the blade except as permitted in 6 below. Grade C bats may have a cloth covering on the blade. This may be treated as specified in 6(d) below. Such covering is additional to the blade and is not part of the bat. Note, however, 8 below.

6. Protection and repair

Providing neither 4 above nor 7 below is contravened,

(a) solely for the purposes of

either   (i) protection from surface damage to the face, sides and shoulders of the blade,

or   (ii) repair to the blade after damage

material that is not rigid, either at the time of its application to the blade or subsequently, may be placed on these surfaces.

Any such material shall not extend over any part of the back of the blade except in the case of (ii) above and then only when it is applied as a continuous wrapping covering the damaged area.

(b) solid material may be inserted into the blade for repair after damage other than surface damage. Additionally, for protection from damage for Grades B and C, material may be inserted at the toe and/or along the sides, parallel to the face of the blade.

The only material permitted for any insertion is wood with minimal essential adhesives.

(c) to prevent damage to the toe, material may be placed on that part of the blade but shall not extend over any part of the face, back or sides of the blade.

(d) the surface of the blade may be treated with non-solid materials to improve resistance to moisture penetration and/or mask natural blemishes in the appearance of the wood. Save for the purpose of giving a homogenous appearance by masking natural blemishes, such treatment must not materially alter the colour of the blade.

Any materials referred to in (a), (b), (c) or (d) are additional to the blade and not part of the bat. Note, however, 8 below.

7. Damage to the ball

(a) For any part of the bat, covered or uncovered, the hardness of the constituent materials and the surface texture thereof shall not be such that either or both could cause unacceptable damage to the ball.

(b) Any material placed on any part of the bat, for whatever purpose, shall similarly not be such that it could cause unacceptable damage to the ball.

(c) For the purposes of this Law, unacceptable damage is deterioration greater than normal wear and tear caused by the ball striking the uncovered wooden surface of the blade.

8. Contact with the ball

In these Laws,

(a) reference to the bat shall imply that the bat is held in the batsman's hand or a glove worn on his hand, unless stated otherwise.

(b) contact between the ball and

 either (i) the bat itself

 or (ii) the batsman's hand holding the bat

 or (iii) any part of a glove worn on the batsman's hand holding the bat

 or (iv) any additional materials permitted under 3, 5 or 6

shall be regarded as the ball striking or touching the bat, or being struck by the bat.

LAW 7. THE PITCH

1. Area of pitch

The pitch is a rectangular area of the ground 22yds/20.12m in length and 10ft/3.05m in width. It is bounded at either end by the bowling creases and on either side by imaginary lines, one each side of the imaginary line joining the centres of the two middle stumps, each parallel to it and 5ft/1.52m from it. See Laws 8.1 (Width and pitching) and 9.2 (The bowling crease).

2. Fitness of the pitch for play

The umpires shall be the final judges of the fitness of the pitch for play. See Laws 3.8 (Fitness of ground, weather and light) and 3.9 (Suspension of play for adverse conditions of ground, weather or light).

3. Selection and preparation

Before the toss the ground authority shall be responsible for the selection and preparation of the pitch. During the match the umpires shall control its use and maintenance.

4. Changing the pitch

The pitch shall not be changed during the match unless the umpires decide that it is unreasonable or dangerous for play to continue on it and then only with the consent of both captains.

5. Non-turf pitches

In the event of a non-turf pitch being used, the artificial surface shall conform to the following measurements:

 Length – a minimum of 58ft/17.68m.
 Width – a minimum of 6ft/1.83m.

See Law 10.8 (Non-turf pitches).

LAW 8. THE WICKETS

1. Width and pitching

Two sets of wickets shall be pitched opposite and parallel to each other at a distance of 22yds/20.12m between the centres of the two middle stumps. Each set shall be 9in/22.86cm wide and shall consist of three wooden stumps with two wooden bails on top.

2. Size of stumps

The tops of the stumps shall be 28in/71.1cm above the playing surface and shall be dome-shaped except for the bail grooves. The portion of a stump above the playing surface shall be cylindrical, apart from the domed top, with a circular section of diameter not less than 1³/₈in/3.49cm nor more than 1¹/₂in/3.81cm.

3. The bails

(a) The bails, when in position on the top of the stumps:

    (i) Shall not project more than $^1/_2$in/1.27cm above them.

    (ii) Shall fit between the stumps without forcing them out of the vertical.

(b) Each bail shall conform to the following specifications.

Overall length	– 4$^5/_{16}$in/10.95cm.
Length of barrel	– 2$^1/_8$in/5.40cm.
Longer spigot	– 1$^3/_8$in/3.49cm.
Shorter spigot	– $^{13}/_{16}$in/2.06cm.

4. Junior cricket

In junior cricket, the same definitions of the wickets shall apply subject to the following measurements being used:

Width	– 8in/20.32cm.
Pitched for Under-13	– 21yds/19.20m.
Pitched for Under-11	– 20yds/18.29m.
Pitched for Under-9	– 18yds/16.46m
Height above playing surface	– 27in/68.58cm.

Each stump

Diameter	– not less than 1$^1/_4$in/3.18cm
	– nor more than 1$^3/_8$in/3.49cm.

Each bail

Overall	– 3$^{13}/_{16}$in/9.68cm.
Barrel	– 1$^{13}/_{16}$in/4.60cm.
Longer Spigot	– 1$^1/_4$in/3.18cm.
Shorter Spigot	– $^3/_4$in/1.91cm.

5. Dispensing with bails

The umpires may agree to dispense with the use of bails, if necessary. If they so agree then no bails shall be used at either end. The use of bails shall be resumed as soon as conditions permit. See Law 28.4 (Dispensing with bails).

LAW 9.   THE BOWLING, POPPING AND RETURN CREASES

1. The creases

A bowling crease, a popping crease and two return creases shall be marked in white, as set out in 2, 3 and 4 below, at each end of the pitch.

2. The bowling crease

The bowling crease, which is the back edge of the crease marking, shall be the line through the centres of the three stumps at that end. It shall be 8ft 8in/2.64m in length, with the stumps in the centre.

3. The popping crease

The popping crease, which is the back edge of the crease marking, shall be in front of and parallel to the bowling crease and shall be 4ft/1.22m from it. The popping crease shall be marked to a minimum of 6ft/1.83m on either side of the imaginary line joining the centres of the middle stumps and shall be considered to be unlimited in length.

4. The return creases

The return creases, which are the inside edges of the crease markings, shall be at right angles to the popping crease at a distance of 4ft 4in/1.32m either side of the imaginary line joining the centres of the two middle stumps. Each return crease shall be marked from the popping crease to a minimum of 8ft/2.44m behind it and shall be considered to be unlimited in length.

LAW 10. PREPARATION AND MAINTENANCE OF THE PLAYING AREA

1. Rolling

The pitch shall not be rolled during the match except as permitted in (a) and (b) below.

(a) Frequency and duration of rolling

During the match the pitch may be rolled at the request of the captain of the batting side, for a period of not more than seven minutes, before the start of each innings, other than the first innings of the match, and before the start of each subsequent day's play. See (d) below.

(b) Rolling after a delayed start

In addition to the rolling permitted above, if, after the toss and before the first innings of the match, the start is delayed, the captain of the batting side may request to have the pitch rolled for not more than seven minutes. However, if the umpires together agree that the delay has had no significant effect on the state of the pitch, they shall refuse the request for the rolling of the pitch.

(c) Choice of rollers

If there is more than one roller available the captain of the batting side shall have the choice.

(d) Timing of permitted rolling

The rolling permitted (maximum seven minutes) before play begins on any day shall be started not more than 30 minutes before the time scheduled or rescheduled for play to begin. The captain of the batting side may, however, delay the start of such rolling until not less than ten minutes before the time scheduled or rescheduled for play to begin, should he so desire.

(e) Insufficient time to complete rolling

If a captain declares an innings closed, or forfeits an innings, or enforces the follow-on, and the other captain is prevented thereby from exercising his option of the rolling permitted (maximum seven minutes), or if he is so prevented for any other reason, the extra time required to complete the rolling shall be taken out of the normal playing time.

2. Sweeping

(a) If rolling is to take place the pitch shall first be swept to avoid any possible damage by rolling in debris. This sweeping shall be done so that the seven minutes allowed for rolling is not affected.

(b) The pitch shall be cleared of any debris at all intervals for meals, between innings and at the beginning of each day, not earlier than 30 minutes nor later than ten minutes before the time scheduled or rescheduled for play to begin. See Law 15.1 (An interval).

(c) Notwithstanding the provisions of (a) and (b) above, the umpires shall not allow sweeping to take place where they consider it may be detrimental to the surface of the pitch.

3. Mowing

(a) The pitch

The pitch shall be mown on each day of the match on which play is expected to take place, if ground and weather conditions allow.

(b) The outfield

In order to ensure that conditions are as similar as possible for both sides, the outfield shall be mown on each day of the match on which play is expected to take place, if ground and weather conditions allow.

If, for reasons other than ground and weather conditions, complete mowing of the outfield is not possible, the ground authority shall notify the captains and umpires of the procedure to be adopted for such mowing during the match.

(c) **Responsibility for mowing**

All mowings which are carried out before the match shall be the responsibility of the ground authority.

All subsequent mowings shall be carried out under the supervision of the umpires.

(d) **Time of mowing**

   (i) Mowing of the pitch on any day of the match shall be completed not later than 30 minutes before the time scheduled or rescheduled for play to begin on that day.

   (ii) Mowing of the outfield on any day of the match shall be completed not later than 15 minutes before the time scheduled or rescheduled for play to begin on that day.

4. Watering

The pitch shall not be watered during the match.

5. Re-marking creases

The creases shall be re-marked whenever either umpire considers it necessary.

6. Maintenance of footholes

The umpires shall ensure that the holes made by the bowlers and batsmen are cleaned out and dried whenever necessary to facilitate play. In matches of more than one day's duration, the umpires shall allow, if necessary, the re-turfing of footholes made by the bowler in his delivery stride, or the use of quick-setting fillings for the same purpose.

7. Securing of footholds and maintenance of pitch

During play, the umpires shall allow the players to secure their footholds by the use of sawdust provided that no damage to the pitch is caused and that Law 42 (Fair and unfair play) is not contravened.

8. Non-turf pitches

Wherever appropriate, the provisions set out in 1 to 7 above shall apply.

LAW 11.   COVERING THE PITCH

1. Before the match

The use of covers before the match is the responsibility of the ground authority and may include full covering if required. However, the ground authority shall grant suitable facility to the captains to inspect the pitch before the nomination of their players and to the umpires to discharge their duties as laid down in Laws 3 (The umpires), 7 (The pitch), 8 (The wickets), 9 (The bowling, popping and return creases) and 10 (Preparation and maintenance of the playing area).

2. During the match

The pitch shall not be completely covered during the match unless provided otherwise by regulations or by agreement before the toss.

3. Covering bowlers' run-ups

Whenever possible, the bowlers' run-ups shall be covered in inclement weather, in order to keep them dry. Unless there is agreement for full covering under 2 above the covers so used shall not extend further than 5ft/1.52m in front of each popping crease.

4. Removal of covers

(a) If after the toss the pitch is covered overnight, the covers shall be removed in the morning at the earliest possible moment on each day that play is expected to take place.

(b) If covers are used during the day as protection from inclement weather, or if inclement weather delays the removal of overnight covers, they shall be removed promptly as soon as conditions allow.

LAW 12.   INNINGS

1. Number of innings

(a) A match shall be one or two innings of each side according to agreement reached before the start of play.

(b) It may be agreed to limit any innings to a number of overs or by a period of time. If such an agreement is made then:

    (i) In a one-innings match it shall apply to both innings.

    (ii) In a two-innings match it shall apply to either
      the first innings of each side, or
      the second innings of each side, or
      both innings of each side.

2. Alternate innings

In a two-innings match each side shall take their innings alternately except in the cases provided for in Law 13 (The follow-on) or Law 14.2 (Forfeiture of an innings).

3. Completed innings

A side's innings is to be considered as completed if:

(a) The side is all out, or

(b) At the fall of a wicket, further balls remain to be bowled, but no further batsman is available to come in, or

(c) The captain declares the innings closed, or

(d) The captain forfeits the innings, or

(e) In the case of an agreement under 1(b) above, either

    (i) the prescribed number of overs has been bowled, or

    (ii) the prescribed time has expired.

4. The toss

The captains shall toss for the choice of innings on the field of play not earlier than 30 minutes, nor later than 15 minutes, before the scheduled or any rescheduled time for the match to start. Note, however, the provisions of Law 1.3 (Captain).

5. Decision to be notified

The captain of the side winning the toss shall notify the opposing captain of his decision to bat or to field, not later than ten minutes before the scheduled or any rescheduled time for the match to start. Once notified the decision may not be altered.

LAW 13.   THE FOLLOW-ON

1. Lead on first innings

(a) In a two-innings match of five days or more, the side which bats first and leads by at least 200 runs shall have the option of requiring the other side to follow their innings.

(b) The same option shall be available in two-innings matches of shorter duration with the minimum required leads as follows:

    (i) 150 runs in a match of three or four days.

    (ii) 100 runs in a two-day match.

    (iii) 75 runs in a one-day match.

2. Notification

A captain shall notify the opposing captain and the umpires of his intention to take up this option. Law 10.1 (e) (Insufficient time to complete rolling) shall apply.

3. First day's play lost

If no play takes place on the first day of a match of more than one day's duration, 1 above shall apply in accordance with the number of days remaining from the actual start of the match. The day on which play first commences shall count as a whole day for this purpose, irrespective of the time at which play starts.

Play will have taken place as soon as, after the call of "Play", the first over has started. See Law 22.2 (Start of an over).

LAW 14.   DECLARATION AND FORFEITURE

1. Time of declaration

The captain of the batting side may declare an innings closed, when the ball is dead, at any time during a match.

2. Forfeiture of an innings

A captain may forfeit either of his side's innings. A forfeited innings shall be considered as a completed innings.

3. Notification

A captain shall notify the opposing captain and the umpires of his decision to declare or to forfeit an innings. Law 10.1 (e) (Insufficient time to complete rolling) shall apply.

LAW 15.   INTERVALS

1. An interval

The following shall be classed as intervals:

     (i) The period between close of play on one day and the start of the next day's play.

     (ii) Intervals between innings.

     (iii) Intervals for meals.

     (iv) Intervals for drinks.

     (v) Any other agreed interval.

All these intervals shall be considered as scheduled breaks for the purposes of Law 2.5 (Fielder absent or leaving the field).

2. Agreement of intervals

    (a) Before the toss:

       (i) The hours of play shall be established.

       (ii) Except as in (b) below, the timing and duration of intervals for meals shall be agreed.

       (iii) The timing and duration of any other interval under 1(v) above shall be agreed.

    (b) In a one-day match no specific time need be agreed for the tea interval. It may be agreed instead to take this interval between the innings.

    (c) Intervals for drinks may not be taken during the last hour of the match, as defined in Law 16.6 (Last hour of match – number of overs). Subject to this limitation the captains and umpires shall agree the times for such intervals, if any, before the toss and on each subsequent day not later than ten minutes before play is scheduled to start. See also Law 3.3 (Agreement with captains).

3. Duration of intervals

(a) An interval for lunch or for tea shall be of the duration agreed under 2(a) above, taken from the call of "Time" before the interval until the call of "Play" on resumption after the interval.

(b) An interval between innings shall be ten minutes from the close of an innings to the call of "Play" for the start of the next innings, except as in 4, 6 and 7 below.

4. No allowance for interval between innings

In addition to the provisions of 6 and 7 below:

(a) If an innings ends when ten minutes or less remain before the time agreed for close of play on any day, there will be no further play on that day. No change will be made to the time for the start of play on the following day on account of the ten minutes between innings.

(b) If a captain declares an innings closed during an interruption in play of more than ten minutes duration, no adjustment shall be made to the time for resumption of play on account of the ten minutes between innings, which shall be considered as included in the interruption. Law 10.1(e) (Insufficient time to complete rolling) shall apply.

(c) If a captain declares an innings closed during any interval other than an interval for drinks, the interval shall be of the agreed duration and shall be considered to include the ten minutes between innings. Law 10.1(e) (Insufficient time to complete rolling) shall apply.

5. Changing agreed times for intervals

If for adverse conditions of ground, weather or light, or for any other reason, playing time is lost, the umpires and captains together may alter the time of the lunch interval or of the tea interval. See also 6, 7 and 9(c) below.

6. Changing agreed time for lunch interval

(a) If an innings ends when ten minutes or less remain before the agreed time for lunch, the interval shall be taken immediately. It shall be of the agreed length and shall be considered to include the ten minutes between innings.

(b) If, because of adverse conditions of ground, weather or light, or in exceptional circumstances, a stoppage occurs when ten minutes or less remain before the agreed time for lunch then, notwithstanding 5 above, the interval shall be taken immediately. It shall be of the agreed length. Play shall resume at the end of this interval or as soon after as conditions permit.

(c) If the players have occasion to leave the field for any reason when more than ten minutes remain before the agreed time for lunch then, unless the umpires and captains together agree to alter it, lunch will be taken at the agreed time.

7. Changing agreed time for tea interval

(a) (i) If an innings ends when 30 minutes or less remain before the agreed time for tea, then the interval shall be taken immediately. It shall be of the agreed length and shall be considered to include the ten minutes between innings.

(ii) If, when 30 minutes remain before the agreed time for tea, an interval between innings is already in progress, play will resume at the end of the ten-minute interval.

(b) (i) If, because of adverse conditions of ground, weather or light, or in exceptional circumstances, a stoppage occurs when 30 minutes or less remain before the agreed time for tea, then unless

either there is an agreement to change the time for tea, as permitted in 5 above, or the captains agree to forgo the tea interval, as permitted in 10 below,

the interval shall be taken immediately. The interval shall be of the agreed length. Play shall resume at the end of this interval or as soon after as conditions permit.

(ii) If a stoppage is already in progress when 30 minutes remain before the time agreed for tea, 5 above will apply.

8. Tea interval – nine wickets down

If either nine wickets are already down when two minutes remain to the agreed time for tea, or the ninth wicket falls within these two minutes or at any later time up to and including the final ball of the over in progress at the agreed time for tea, then not withstanding the provisions of Law 16.5 (b) (Completion of an over) tea will not be taken until the end of the over in progress 30 minutes after the originally agreed time for tea, unless the players have cause to leave the field of play or the innings is completed earlier.

9. Intervals for drinks

(a) If on any day the captains agree that there shall be intervals for drinks, the option to take such intervals shall be available to either side. Each interval shall be kept as short as possible and in any case shall not exceed five minutes.

(b) (i) Unless both captains agree to forgo any drinks interval, it shall be taken at the end of the over in progress when the agreed time is reached. If, however, a wicket falls within five minutes of the agreed time then drinks shall be taken immediately. No other variation in the timing of drinks intervals shall be permitted except as provided for in (c) below.

(ii) For the purpose of (i) above and Law 3.9(a)(ii) (Suspension of play for adverse conditions of ground, weather or light) only, the batsmen at the wicket may deputise for their captain.

(c) If an innings ends or the players have to leave the field of play for any other reason within 30 minutes of the agreed time for a drinks interval, the umpires and captains together may rearrange the timing of drinks intervals in that session.

10. Agreement to forgo intervals

At any time during the match, the captains may agree to forgo the tea interval or any of the drinks intervals. The umpires shall be informed of the decision.

11. Scorers to be informed

The umpires shall ensure that the scorers are informed of all agreements about hours of play and intervals, and of any changes made thereto as permitted under this Law.

LAW 16.   START OF PLAY; CESSATION OF PLAY

1. ll of "Play"

The umpire at the bowler's end shall call "Play" at the start of the match and on the resumption of play after any interval or interruption.

2. Call of "Time"

The umpire at the bowler's end shall call "Time" on the cessation of play before any interval or interruption of play and at the conclusion of the match. See Law 27 (Appeals).

3. Removal of bails

After the call of "Time", the bails shall be removed from both wickets.

4. Starting a new over

Another over shall always be started at any time during the match, unless an interval is to be taken in the circumstances set out in 5 below, if the umpire, after walking at his normal pace, has arrived at his position behind the stumps at the bowler's end before the time agreed for the next interval, or for the close of play, has been reached.

5. Completion of an over

Other than at the end of the match:

(a) If the agreed time for an interval is reached during an over, the over shall be completed before the interval is taken except as provided for in (b) below.

(b) When less than two minutes remain before the time agreed for the next interval, the interval will be taken immediately if either

(i) a batsman is out or retires, or

(ii) the players have occasion to leave the field

whether this occurs during an over or at the end of an over. Except at the end of an innings, if an over is thus interrupted it shall be completed on resumption of play.

6. Last hour of match – number of overs

When one hour of playing time of the match remains, according to the agreed hours of play, the over in progress shall be completed. The next over shall be the first of a minimum of 20 overs which must be bowled, provided that a result is not reached earlier and provided that there is no interval or interruption in play.

The umpire at the bowler's end shall indicate the commencement of this 20 overs to the players and the scorers. The period of play thereafter shall be referred to as the last hour, whatever its actual duration.

7. Last hour of match – interruptions of play

If there is an interruption in play during the last hour of the match, the minimum number of overs to be bowled shall be reduced from 20 as follows:

(a) The time lost for an interruption is counted from the call of "Time" until the time for resumption of play as decided by the umpires.

(b) One over shall be deducted for every complete three minutes of time lost.

(c) In the case of more than one such interruption, the minutes lost shall not be aggregated; the calculation shall be made for each interruption separately.

(d) If, when one hour of playing time remains, an interruption is already in progress:

(i) Only the time lost after this moment shall be counted in the calculation.

(ii) The over in progress at the start of the interruption shall be completed on resumption of play and shall not count as one of the minimum number of overs to be bowled.

(e) If, after the start of the last hour, an interruption occurs during an over, the over shall be completed on resumption of play. The two part-overs shall between them count as one over of the minimum number to be bowled.

8. Last hour of match – intervals between innings

If an innings ends so that a new innings is to be started during the last hour of the match, the interval starts with the end of the innings and is to end ten minutes later.

(a) If this interval is already in progress at the start of the last hour, then to determine the number of overs to be bowled in the new innings, calculations are to be made as set out in 7 above.

(b) If the innings ends after the last hour has started, two calculations are to be made, as set out in (c) and (d) below. The greater of the numbers yielded by these two calculations is to be the minimum number of overs to be bowled in the new innings.

(c) Calculation based on overs remaining:

(i) At the conclusion of the innings, the number of overs that remain to be bowled, of the minimum in the last hour, to be noted.

(ii) If this is not a whole number it is to be rounded up to the next whole number.

(iii) Three overs to be deducted from the result for the interval.

(d) Calculation based on time remaining:

(i) At the conclusion of the innings, the time remaining until the agreed time for close of play to be noted.

(ii) Ten minutes to be deducted from this time, for the interval, to determine the playing time remaining.

(iii) A calculation to be made of one over for every complete three minutes of the playing time remaining, plus one more over for any further part of three minutes remaining.

9. Conclusion of match

The match is concluded:

(a) As soon as a result, as defined in sections 1, 2, 3 or 4 of Law 21 (The result), is reached.

(b) As soon as both

(i) the minimum number of overs for the last hour are completed, and

(ii) the agreed time for close of play is reached

unless a result has been reached earlier.

(c) If, without the match being concluded either as in (a) or in (b) above, the players leave the field, either for adverse conditions of ground, weather or light, or in exceptional circumstances, and no further play is possible thereafter.

10. Completion of last over of match

The over in progress at the close of play on the final day shall be completed unless either

(i) a result has been reached, or

(ii) the players have occasion to leave the field. In this case there shall be no resumption of play except in the circumstances of Law 21.9 (Mistakes in scoring), and the match shall be at an end.

11. Bowler unable to complete an over during last hour of match

If, for any reason, a bowler is unable to complete an over during the last hour, Law 22.8 (Bowler incapacitated or suspended during an over) shall apply.

LAW 17. PRACTICE ON THE FIELD

1. Practice on the field

(a) There shall be no bowling or batting practice on the pitch, or on the area parallel and immediately adjacent to the pitch, at any time on any day of the match.

(b) There shall be no bowling or batting practice on any other part of the square on any day of the match, except before the start of play or after the close of play on that day. Practice before the start of play:

(i) Must not continue later than 30 minutes before the scheduled time or any rescheduled time for play to start on that day.

(ii) Shall not be allowed if the umpires consider that, in the prevailing conditions of ground and weather, it will be detrimental to the surface of the square.

(c) There shall be no practice on the field of play between the call of "Play" and the call of "Time", if the umpire considers that it could result in a waste of time. See Law 42.9 (Time-wasting by the fielding side).

(d) If a player contravenes (a) or (b) above he shall not be allowed to bowl until either at least one hour later than the contravention or until there has been at least 30 minutes of playing time since the contravention, whichever is sooner. If an over is in progress at the contravention he shall not be allowed to complete that over.

2. Trial run-up

No bowler shall have a trial run-up between the call of "Play" and the call of "Time" unless the umpire is satisfied that it will not cause any waste of time.

LAW 18. SCORING RUNS

1. A run

The score shall be reckoned by runs. A run is scored:

    (a) So often as the batsmen, at any time while the ball is in play, have crossed and made good their ground from end to end.

    (b) When a boundary is scored. See Law 19 (Boundaries).

    (c) When penalty runs are awarded. See 6 below.

    (d) When "Lost ball" is called. See Law 20 (Lost ball).

2. Runs disallowed

Notwithstanding 1 above, or any other provisions elsewhere in the Laws, the scoring of runs or awarding of penalties will be subject to any disallowance of runs provided for within the Laws that may be applicable.

3. Short runs

    (a) A run is short if a batsman fails to make good his ground on turning for a further run.

    (b) Although a short run shortens the succeeding one, the latter if completed shall not be regarded as short. A striker taking stance in front of his popping crease may run from that point also without penalty.

4. Unintentional short runs

Except in the circumstances of 5 below:

    (a) If either batsman runs a short run, unless a boundary is scored the umpire concerned shall call and signal "Short run" as soon as the ball becomes dead and that run shall not be scored.

    (b) If, after either or both batsmen run short, a boundary is scored, the umpire concerned shall disregard the short running and shall not call or signal "Short run".

    (c) If both batsmen run short in one and the same run, this shall be regarded as only one short run.

    (d) If more than one run is short then, subject to (b) and (c) above, all runs so called shall not be scored.

If there has been more than one short run the umpire shall inform the scorers as to the number of runs scored.

5. Deliberate short runs

Notwithstanding 4 above, if either umpire considers that either or both batsmen deliberately runs short at his end, the following procedure shall be adopted:

    (a) (i) The umpire concerned shall, when the ball is dead, warn the batsmen that the practice is unfair, indicate that this is a first and final warning and inform the other umpire of what has occurred. This warning shall continue to apply throughout the innings. The umpire shall so inform each incoming batsman.

       (ii) The batsmen shall return to their original ends.

       (iii) Whether a batsman is dismissed or not, the umpire at the bowler's end shall disallow all runs to the batting side from that delivery other than the penalty for a no-ball or wide, or penalties under Laws 42.5 (Deliberate distraction or obstruction of batsman) and 42.13 (Fielders damaging the pitch), if applicable.

       (iv) The umpire at the bowler's end shall inform the scorers as to the number of runs scored.

    (b) If there is any further instance of deliberate short running by any batsman in that innings, when the ball is dead the umpire concerned shall inform the other umpire of what has occurred and the procedure set out in (a)(ii) and (iii) above shall be repeated. Additionally, the umpire at the bowler's end shall:

       (i) Award five penalty runs to the fielding side. See Law 42.17 (Penalty runs).

(ii) Inform the scorers as to the number of runs scored.

(iii) Inform the batsmen, the captain of the fielding side and, as soon as practicable, the captain of the batting side of the reason for this action.

(iv) Report the occurrence, with the other umpire, to the executive of the batting side and any governing body responsible for the match, who shall take such action as is considered appropriate against the captain and player or players concerned.

6. Runs scored for penalties

Runs shall be scored for penalties under 5 above and Laws 2.6 (Player returning without permission), 24 (No-ball), 25 (Wide ball), 41.2 (Fielding the ball), 41.3 (Protective helmets belonging to the fielding side) and 42 (Fair and unfair play).

7. Runs scored for boundaries

Runs shall be scored for boundary allowances under Law 19 (Boundaries).

8. Runs scored for lost ball

Runs shall be scored when "Lost ball" is called under Law 20 (Lost ball).

9. Batsman dismissed

When either batsman is dismissed:

(a) Any penalties to either side that may be applicable shall stand but no other runs shall be scored, except as stated in 10 below.

(b) 12(a) below will apply if the method of dismissal is caught, handled the ball or obstructing the field. 12(a) will also apply if a batsman is run out, except in the circumstances of Law 2.8 (Transgression of the Laws by a batsman who has a runner) where 12(b) below will apply.

(c) The not out batsman shall return to his original end except as stated in (b) above.

10. Runs scored when a batsman is dismissed

In addition to any penalties to either side that may be applicable, if a batsman is:

(a) Dismissed handled the ball, the batting side shall score the runs completed before the offence.

(b) Dismissed obstructing the field, the batting side shall score the runs completed before the offence.

If, however, the obstruction prevents a catch from being made, no runs other than penalties shall be scored.

(c) Dismissed run out, the batting side shall score the runs completed before the dismissal. If however, a striker with a runner is himself dismissed run out, no runs other than penalties shall be scored. See Law 2.8 (Transgression of the Laws by a batsman who has a runner).

11. Runs scored when ball becomes dead

(a) When the ball becomes dead on the fall of a wicket, runs shall be scored as laid down in 9 and 10 above.

(b) When the ball becomes dead for any reason other than the fall of a wicket, or is called dead by an umpire, unless there is specific provision otherwise in the Laws, the batting side shall be credited with:

(i) All runs completed by the batsmen before the incident or call, and

(ii) the run in progress if the batsmen have crossed at the instant of the incident or call. Note specifically, however, the provisions of Law 34.4(c) (Runs permitted from a ball lawfully struck more than once) and 42.5(b)(iii) (Deliberate distraction or obstruction of batsman), and

(iii) any penalties that are applicable.

12. Batsman returning to wicket he has left

(a) If, while the ball is in play, the batsmen have crossed in running, neither shall return to the wicket he has left, except as in (b) below.

(b) The batsmen shall return to the wickets they originally left in the cases of, and only in the cases of:

    (i) A boundary.

    (ii) Disallowance of runs for any reason.

    (iii) The dismissal of a batsman, except as in 9(b) above.

LAW 19. BOUNDARIES

1. The boundary of the field of play

(a) Before the toss, the umpires shall agree the boundary of the field of play with both captains. The boundary shall if possible be marked along its whole length.

(b) The boundary shall be agreed so that no part of any sightscreen is within the field of play.

(c) An obstacle or person within the field of play shall not be regarded as a boundary unless so decided by the umpires before the toss. See Law 3.4(ii) (To inform captains and scorers).

2. Defining the boundary – boundary marking

(a) Wherever practicable the boundary shall be marked by means of a white line or a rope laid along the ground.

(b) If the boundary is marked by a white line:

    (i) The inside edge of the line shall be the boundary edge.

    (ii) A flag, post or board used merely to highlight the position of a line marked on the ground must be placed outside the boundary edge and is not itself to be regarded as defining or marking the boundary. Note, however, the provisions of (c) below.

(c) If a solid object is used to mark the boundary, it must have an edge or a line to constitute the boundary edge.

    (i) For a rope, which includes any similar object of curved cross section lying on the ground, the boundary edge will be the line formed by the innermost points of the rope along its length.

    (ii) For a fence, which includes any similar object in contact with the ground, but with a flat surface projecting above the ground, the boundary edge will be the base line of the fence.

(d) If the boundary edge is not defined as in (b) or (c) above, the umpires and captains must agree, before the toss, what line will be the boundary edge. Where there is no physical marker for a section of boundary, the boundary edge shall be the imaginary straight line joining the two nearest marked points of the boundary edge.

(e) If a solid object used to mark the boundary is disturbed for any reason during play, then if possible it shall be restored to its original position as soon as the ball is dead. If this is not possible, then:

    (i) If some part of the fence or other marker has come within the field of play, that portion is to be removed from the field of play as soon as the ball is dead.

    (ii) The line where the base of the fence or marker originally stood shall define the boundary edge.

3. Scoring a boundary

(a) A boundary shall be scored and signalled by the umpire at the bowler's end whenever, while the ball is in play, in his opinion:

    (i) The ball touches the boundary, or is grounded beyond the boundary.

    (ii) A fielder, with some part of his person in contact with the ball, touches the boundary or has some part of his person grounded beyond the boundary.

(b) The phrases "touches the boundary" and "touching the boundary" shall mean contact with either

    (i) the boundary edge as defined in 2 above, or

    (ii) any person or obstacle within the field of play which has been designated a boundary by the umpires before the toss.

(c) The phrase "grounded beyond the boundary" shall mean contact with either

    (i) any part of a line or a solid object marking the boundary, except its boundary edge, or

    (ii) the ground outside the boundary edge, or

    (iii) any object in contact with the ground outside the boundary edge.

4. Runs allowed for boundaries

(a) Before the toss, the umpires shall agree with both captains the runs to be allowed for boundaries. In deciding the allowances, the umpires and captains shall be guided by the prevailing custom of the ground.

(b) Unless agreed differently under (a) above, the allowances for boundaries shall be six runs if the ball having been struck by the bat pitches beyond the boundary, but otherwise four runs. These allowances shall still apply even though the ball has previously touched a fielder. See also (c) below.

(c) The ball shall be regarded as pitching beyond the boundary and six runs shall be scored if a fielder:

    (i) Has any part of his person touching the boundary or grounded beyond the boundary when he catches the ball.

    (ii) Catches the ball and subsequently touches the boundary or grounds some part of his person beyond the boundary while carrying the ball but before completing the catch. See Law 32 (Caught).

5. Runs scored

When a boundary is scored:

(a) The penalty for a no-ball or a wide, if applicable, shall stand together with any penalties under any of Laws 2.6 (Player returning without permission), 18.5(b) (Deliberate short runs) or Law 42 (Fair and unfair play) that apply before the boundary is scored.

(b) The batting side, except in the circumstances of 6 below, shall additionally be awarded whichever is the greater of:

    (i) The allowance for the boundary.

    (ii) The runs completed by the batsmen, together with the run in progress if they have crossed at the instant the boundary is scored. When these runs exceed the boundary allowance, they shall replace the boundary for the purposes of Law 18.12 (Batsman returning to wicket he has left).

6. Overthrow or wilful act of fielder

If the boundary results either from an overthrow or from the wilful act of a fielder the runs scored shall be:

    (i) The penalty for a no-ball or a wide, if applicable, and any penalties under Laws 2.6 (Player returning without permission), 18.5(b) (Deliberate short runs) or Law 42 (Fair and unfair play) that are applicable before the boundary is scored, and

    (ii) the allowance for the boundary, and

    (iii) the runs completed by the batsmen, together with the run in progress if they have crossed at the instant of the throw or act.

Law 18.12(a) (Batsman returning to the wicket he has left) shall apply as from the instant of the throw or act.

LAW 20. LOST BALL

1. Fielder to call "Lost ball"

If a ball in play cannot be found or recovered, any fielder may call "Lost ball". The ball shall then become dead. See Law 23.1 (Ball is dead). Law 18.12(a) (Batsman returning to wicket he has left) shall apply as from the instant of the call.

2. Ball to be replaced

The umpires shall replace the ball with one which has had wear comparable with that which the previous ball had received before it was lost or became irrecoverable. See Law 5.5 (Ball lost or becoming unfit for play).

3. Runs scored

(a) The penalty for a no-ball or a wide, if applicable, shall stand, together with any penalties under any of Laws 2.6 (Player returning without permission), 18.5(b) (Deliberate short runs) or Law 42 (Fair and unfair play) that are applicable before the call of "Lost ball".

(b) The batting side shall additionally be awarded either

    (i) the runs completed by the batsmen, together with the run in progress if they have crossed at the instant of the call, or

    (ii) six runs,

whichever is the greater.

4. How scored

If there is a one-run penalty for a no-ball or for a wide, it shall be scored as a no-ball extra or as a wide as appropriate. See Laws 24.13 (Runs resulting from a no-ball – how scored) and 25.6 (Runs resulting from a wide – how scored). If any other penalties have been awarded to either side, they shall be scored as penalty extras. See Law 42.17 (Penalty runs).

Runs to the batting side in 3(b) above shall be credited to the striker if the ball has been struck by the bat, but otherwise to the total of byes, leg-byes, no-balls or wides as the case may be.

LAW 21. THE RESULT

1. A win – two-innings match

The side which has scored a total of runs in excess of that scored in the two completed innings of the opposing side shall win the match. Note also 6 below.

A forfeited innings is to count as a completed innings. See Law 14 (Declaration and forfeiture).

2. A win – one-innings match

The side which has scored in its one innings a total of runs in excess of that scored by the opposing side in its one completed innings shall win the match. Note also 6 below.

3. Umpires awarding a match

(a) A match shall be lost by a side which either

    (i) concedes defeat, or

    (ii) in the opinion of the umpires, refuses to play

and the umpires shall award the match to the other side.

(b) If an umpire considers that an action by any player or players might constitute a refusal by either side to play then the umpires together shall ascertain the cause of the action. If they then decide together that this action does constitute a refusal to play by one side, they shall so inform the captain of that side. If the captain persists in the action the umpires shall award the match in accordance with (a)(ii) above.

(c) If action as in (b) above takes place after play has started and does not constitute a refusal to play:

  (i) Playing time lost shall be counted from the start of the action until play recommences, subject to Law 15.5 (Changing agreed times for intervals).

  (ii) The time for close of play on that day shall be extended by this length of time, subject to Law 3.9 (Suspension of play for adverse conditions of ground, weather or light).

  (iii) If applicable, no overs shall be deducted during the last hour of the match solely on account of this time.

4. A tie

The result of a match shall be a tie when the scores are equal at the conclusion of play, but only if the side batting last has completed its innings.

5. A draw

A match which is concluded, as defined in Law 16.9 (Conclusion of a match), without being determined in any of the ways stated in 1, 2, 3 or 4 above, shall count as a draw.

6. Winning hit or extras

(a) As soon as a result is reached, as defined in 1, 2, 3 or 4 above, the match is at an end. Nothing that happens thereafter, except as in Law 42.17(b), shall be regarded as part of it. Note also 9 below.

(b) The side batting last will have scored enough runs to win only if its total of runs is sufficient without including any runs completed before the dismissal of the striker by the completion of a catch or by the obstruction of a catch.

(c) If a boundary is scored before the batsmen have completed sufficient runs to win the match, then the whole of the boundary allowance shall be credited to the side's total and, in the case of a hit by the bat, to the striker's score.

7. Statement of result

If the side batting last wins the match without losing all its wickets, the result shall be stated as a win by the number of wickets still then to fall. If the side batting last has lost all its wickets but, as the result of an award of five penalty runs at the end of the match, has scored a total of runs in excess of the total scored by the opposing side, the result shall be stated as a win to that side by penalty runs. If the side fielding last wins the match, the result shall be stated as a win by runs.

If the match is decided by one side conceding defeat or refusing to play, the result shall be stated as "Match conceded" or "Match awarded" as the case may be.

8. Correctness of result

Any decision as to the correctness of the scores shall be the responsibility of the umpires. See Law 3.15 (Correctness of scores).

9. Mistakes in scoring

If, after the umpires and players have left the field in the belief that the match has been concluded, the umpires discover that a mistake in scoring has occurred which affects the result, then, subject to 10 below, they shall adopt the following procedure.

(a) If, when the players leave the field, the side batting last has not completed its innings, and either

  (i) the number of overs to be bowled in the last hour has not been completed, or

  (ii) the agreed finishing time has not been reached,

then unless one side concedes defeat the umpires shall order play to resume.

If conditions permit, play will then continue until the prescribed number of overs has been completed and the time remaining has elapsed, unless a result is reached earlier. The number of overs and/or the time remaining shall be taken as they were when the players left the field; no account shall be taken of the time between that moment and the resumption of play.

(b) If, when the players leave the field, the overs have been completed and time has been reached, or if the side batting last has completed its innings, the umpires shall immediately inform both captains of the necessary corrections to the scores and to the result.

10. Result not to be changed

Once the umpires have agreed with the scorers the correctness of the scores at the conclusion of the match – see Laws 3.15 (Correctness of scores) and 4.2 (Correctness of scores) – the result cannot thereafter be changed.

LAW 22. THE OVER

1. Number of balls

The ball shall be bowled from each wicket alternately in overs of six balls.

2. Start of an over

An over has started when the bowler starts his run-up or, if he has no run-up, his delivery action for the first delivery of that over.

3. Call of "Over"

When six balls have been bowled other than those which are not to count in the over and as the ball becomes dead – see Law 23 (Dead ball) – the umpire shall call "Over" before leaving the wicket.

4. Balls not to count in the over

(a) A ball shall not count as one of the six balls of the over unless it is delivered, even though a batsman may be dismissed or some other incident occurs before the ball is delivered.

(b) A ball which is delivered by the bowler shall not count as one of the six balls of the over:

(i) If it is called dead, or is to be considered dead, before the striker has had an opportunity to play it. See Law 23 (Dead ball).

(ii) If it is a no-ball. See Law 24 (No-ball).

(iii) If it is a wide. See Law 25 (Wide ball).

(iv) If it is called dead in the circumstances of Law 23.3(b)(vi) (Umpire calling and signalling "Dead ball").

(v) When five penalty runs are awarded to the batting side under any of Laws 2.6 (Player returning without permission), 41.2 (Fielding the ball), 42.4 (Deliberate attempt to distract striker) or 42.5 (Deliberate distraction or obstruction of batsman).

5. Umpire miscounting

If an umpire miscounts the number of balls, the over as counted by the umpire shall stand.

6. Bowler changing ends

A bowler shall be allowed to change ends as often as desired, provided only that he does not bowl two overs, or parts thereof, consecutively in the same innings.

7. Finishing an over

(a) Other than at the end of an innings, a bowler shall finish an over in progress unless he is incapacitated, or he is suspended under any of Laws 17.1 (Practice on the field), 42.7 (Dangerous and unfair bowling – action by the umpire), 42.9 (Time-wasting by the fielding side), or 42.12 (Bowler running on the protected area after delivering the ball).

(b) If for any reason, other than the end of an innings, an over is left uncompleted at the start of an interval or interruption of play, it shall be completed on resumption of play.

8. Bowler incapacitated or suspended during an over

If for any reason a bowler is incapacitated while running up to bowl the first ball of an over, or is incapacitated or suspended during an over, the umpire shall call and signal "Dead ball". Another bowler shall complete the over from the same end, provided that he does not bowl two overs, or parts thereof, consecutively in one innings.

LAW 23. DEAD BALL

1. Ball is dead

(a) The ball becomes dead when:
  (i) It is finally settled in the hands of the wicketkeeper or the bowler.
  (ii) A boundary is scored. See Law 19.3 (Scoring a boundary).
  (iii) A batsman is dismissed.
  (iv) Whether played or not it becomes trapped between the bat and person of a batsman or between items of his clothing or equipment.
  (v) Whether played or not it lodges in the clothing or equipment of a batsman or the clothing of an umpire.
  (vi) It lodges in a protective helmet worn by a member of the fielding side.
  (vii) There is a contravention of Law 41.2 (Fielding the ball) or Law 41.3 (Protective helmets belonging to the fielding side).
  (viii) This is an award of penalty runs under Law 2.6 (Player returning without permission).
  (ix) "Lost ball" is called. See Law 20 (Lost ball).
  (x) The umpire calls "Over" or "Time".

(b) The ball shall be considered to be dead when it is clear to the umpire at the bowler's end that the fielding side and both batsmen at the wicket have ceased to regard it as in play.

2. Ball finally settled

Whether the ball is finally settled or not is a matter for the umpire alone to decide.

3. Umpire calling and signalling "Dead ball"

(a) When the ball has become dead under 1 above, the bowler's end umpire may call "Dead ball", if it is necessary to inform the players.

(b) Either umpire shall call and signal "Dead ball" when:
  (i) He intervenes in a case of unfair play.
  (ii) A serious injury to a player or umpire occurs.
  (iii) He leaves his normal position for consultation.
  (iv) One or both bails fall from the striker's wicket before he has the opportunity of playing the ball.
  (v) He is satisfied that for an adequate reason the striker is not ready for the delivery of the ball and, if the ball is delivered, makes no attempt to play it.
  (vi) The striker is distracted by any noise or movement or in any other way while he is preparing to receive or receiving a delivery. This shall apply whether the source of the distraction is within the game or outside it. Note, however, the provisions of Law 42.4 (Deliberate attempt to distract the striker).
      The ball shall not count as one of the over.
  (vii) The bowler drops the ball accidentally before delivery.

(viii) The ball does not leave the bowler's hand for any reason other than an attempt to run out the non-striker before entering his delivery stride. See Law 42.15 (Bowler attempting to run out non-striker before delivery).

(ix) He is required to do so under any of the Laws.

4. Ball ceases to be dead

The ball ceases to be dead – that is, it comes into play – when the bowler starts his run-up or, if he has no run-up, his bowling action.

5. Action on call of "Dead ball"

(a) A ball is not to count as one of the over if it becomes dead or is to be considered dead before the striker has had an opportunity to play it.

(b) If the ball becomes dead or is to be considered dead after the striker has had an opportunity to play the ball, except in the circumstances of 3(b)(vi) above and Law 42.4 (Deliberate attempt to distract striker), no additional delivery shall be allowed unless "No-ball"; or "Wide" has been called.

LAW 24.   NO-BALL

1. Mode of delivery

(a) The umpire shall ascertain whether the bowler intends to bowl right-handed or left-handed, and whether over or round the wicket, and shall so inform the striker.

It is unfair if the bowler fails to notify the umpire of a change in his mode of delivery. In this case the umpire shall call and signal "No-ball".

(b) Underarm bowling shall not be permitted except by special agreement before the match.

2. Fair delivery – the arm

For a delivery to be fair in respect of the arm the ball must not be thrown. See 3 below.

Although it is the primary responsibility of the striker's end umpire to ensure the fairness of a delivery in this respect, there is nothing in this Law to debar the bowler's end umpire from calling and signalling "No-ball" if he considers that the ball has been thrown.

(a) If, in the opinion of either umpire, the ball has been thrown, he shall:

(i) Call and signal "No-ball".

(ii) Caution the bowler, when the ball is dead. This caution shall apply throughout the innings.

(iii) Inform the other umpire, the batsmen at the wicket, the captain of the fielding side and, as soon as practicable, the captain of the batting side of what has occurred.

(b) If either umpire considers that after such caution, a further delivery by the same bowler in that innings is thrown, the umpire concerned shall repeat the procedure set out in (a) above, indicating to the bowler that this is a final warning. This warning shall also apply throughout the innings.

(c) If either umpire considers that a further delivery by the same bowler in that innings is thrown:

(i) The umpire concerned shall call and signal "No-ball". When the ball is dead he shall inform the other umpire, the batsmen at the wicket and, as soon as practicable, the captain of the batting side of what has occurred.

(ii) The umpire at the bowler's end shall direct the captain of the fielding side to take the bowler off forthwith. The over shall be completed by another bowler, who shall neither have bowled the previous over nor be allowed to bowl the next over. The bowler thus taken off shall not bowl again in that innings.

(iii) The umpires together shall report the occurrence as soon as possible to the executive of the fielding side and any governing body responsible for the match, who shall take such action as is considered appropriate against the captain and bowler concerned.

3. Definition of fair delivery – the arm

A ball is fairly delivered in respect of the arm if, once the bowler's arm has reached the level of the shoulder in the delivery swing, the elbow joint is not straightened partially or completely from that point until the ball has left the hand. This definition shall not debar a bowler from flexing or rotating the wrist in the delivery swing.

4. Bowler throwing towards striker's end before delivery

If the bowler throws the ball towards the striker's end before entering his delivery stride, either umpire shall instantly call and signal "No-ball". See Law 42.16 (Batsmen stealing a run). However, the procedure stated in 2 above of caution, informing, final warning, action against the bowler and reporting shall not apply.

5. Fair delivery – the feet

For a delivery to be fair in respect of the feet, in the delivery stride:

    (i) The bowler's back foot must land within and not touching the return crease.

    (ii) The bowler's front foot must land with some part of the foot, whether grounded or raised, behind the popping crease.

If the umpire at the bowler's end is not satisfied that both these conditions have been met, he shall call and signal "No-ball".

6. Ball bouncing more than twice or rolling along the ground

The umpire at the bowler's end shall call and signal "No-ball" if a ball which he considers to have been delivered, without having previously touched the bat or person of the striker, either

    (i) bounces more than twice, or

    (ii) rolls along the ground

before it reaches the popping crease.

7. Ball coming to rest in front of striker's wicket

If a ball delivered by the bowler comes to rest in front of the line of the striker's wicket, without having touched the bat or person of the striker, the umpire shall call and signal "No-ball" and immediately call and signal "Dead ball".

8. Call of "No-ball" for infringement of other Laws

In addition to the instances above, an umpire shall call and signal "No-ball" as required by the following Laws.

Law 40.3	– Position of wicketkeeper.
Law 41.5	– Limitation of on-side fielders.
Law 41.6	– Fielders not to encroach on the pitch.
Law 42.6	– Dangerous and unfair bowling.
Law 42.7	– Dangerous and unfair bowling – action by the umpire.
Law 42.8	– Deliberate bowling of high full-pitched balls.

9. Revoking a call of "No-ball"

An umpire shall revoke the call of "No-ball" if the ball does not leave the bowler's hand for any reason.

10. No-ball to over-ride wide

A call of "No-ball" shall over-ride the call of "Wide ball" at any time. See Law 25.1 (Judging a wide) and 25.3 (Call and signal of "Wide ball").

11. Ball not dead

The ball does not become dead on the call of "No-ball".

12. Penalty for a No-ball

A penalty of one run shall be awarded instantly on the call of "No-ball". Unless the call is revoked this penalty shall stand even if a batsman is dismissed. It shall be in addition to any other runs scored, any boundary allowance and any other penalties awarded.

13. Runs resulting from a no-ball – how scored

The one-run penalty for a no-ball shall be scored as a no-ball extra. If other penalty runs have been awarded to either side, these shall be scored as in Law 42.17 (Penalty runs). Any runs completed by the batsmen or a boundary allowance shall be credited to the striker if the ball has been struck by the bat; otherwise they also shall be scored as no-ball extras.

Apart from any award of a five-run penalty, all runs resulting from a no-ball, whether as no-ball extras or credited to the striker, shall be debited against the bowler.

14. No-ball not to count

A no-ball shall not count as one of the over. See Law 22.4 (Balls not to count in the over).

15. Out from a no-ball

When "No-ball" has been called, neither batsman shall be out under any of the Laws except Laws 33 (Handled the ball), 34 (Hit the ball twice), 37 (Obstructing the field) or 38 (Run out).

LAW 25. WIDE BALL

1. Judging a wide

(a) If a bowler bowls a ball, not being a no-ball, the umpire shall adjudge it a wide if, according to the definition in (b) below, in his opinion the ball passes wide of the striker where he is standing and would also have passed wide of him in a normal guard position.

(b) The ball will be considered as passing wide of the striker unless it is sufficiently within his reach for him to be able to hit it with his bat by means of a normal cricket stroke.

2. Delivery not a wide

The umpire shall not adjudge a delivery as being a wide:

(a) If the striker, by moving, either

(i) causes the ball to pass wide of him, as defined in 1(b) above, or

(ii) brings the ball sufficiently within his reach to be able to hit it with his bat by means of a normal cricket stroke.

(b) If the ball touches the striker's bat or person.

3. Call and signal of "Wide ball"

(a) If the umpire adjudges a delivery to be a wide he shall call and signal "Wide ball" as soon as the ball passes the striker's wicket. It shall, however, be considered to have been a wide from the instant of delivery, even though it cannot be called wide until it passes the striker's wicket.

(b) The umpire shall revoke the call of "Wide ball" if there is then any contact between the ball and the striker's bat or person.

(c) The umpire shall revoke the call of "Wide ball" if a delivery is called a "No-ball". See Law 24.10 (No-ball to over-ride wide).

4. Ball not dead

The ball does not become dead on the call of "Wide ball".

5. Penalty for a wide

A penalty of one run shall be awarded instantly on the call of "Wide ball". Unless the call is revoked (see 3 above), this penalty shall stand even if a batsman is dismissed, and shall be in addition to any other runs scored, any boundary allowance and any other penalties awarded.

6. Runs resulting from a wide – how scored

All runs completed by the batsmen or a boundary allowance, together with the penalty for the wide, shall be scored as wide balls. Apart from any award of a five-run penalty, all runs resulting from a wide shall be debited against the bowler.

7. Wide not to count

A wide shall not count as one of the over. See Law 22.4 (Balls not to count in the over).

8. Out from a wide

When "Wide ball" has been called, neither batsman shall be out under any of the Laws except Laws 33 (Handled the ball), 35 (Hit wicket), 37 (Obstructing the field), 38 (Run out) or 39 (Stumped).

LAW 26.   BYE AND LEG-BYE

1. Byes

If the ball, not being a no-ball or a wide, passes the striker without touching his bat or person, any runs completed by the batsmen or a boundary allowance shall be credited as byes to the batting side.

2. Leg-byes

(a) If a ball delivered by the bowler first strikes the person of the striker, runs shall be scored only if the umpire is satisfied that the striker has either

  (i) attempted to play the ball with his bat, or

  (ii) tried to avoid being hit by the ball.

If the umpire is satisfied that either of these conditions has been met, and the ball makes no subsequent contact with the bat, runs completed by the batsmen or a boundary allowance shall be credited to the batting side as in (b). Note, however, the provisions of Laws 34.3 (Ball lawfully struck more than once) and 34.4 (Runs permitted from ball lawfully struck more than once).

(b) The runs in (a) above shall

  (i) if the delivery is not a no-ball, be scored as leg-byes.

  (ii) if no-ball has been called, be scored together with the penalty for the no-ball as no-ball extras.

3. Leg-byes not to be awarded

If in the circumstances of 2(a) above the umpire considers that neither of the conditions (i) and (ii) therein has been met, then leg-byes will not be awarded. The batting side shall not be credited with any runs from that delivery apart from the one run penalty for a no-ball if applicable. Moreover, no other penalties shall be awarded to the batting side when the ball is dead. See Law 42.17 (Penalty runs). The following procedure shall be adopted.

(a) If no run is attempted but the ball reaches the boundary, the umpire shall call and signal "Dead ball", and disallow the boundary.

(b) If runs are attempted and if:

  (i) Neither batsman is dismissed and the ball does not become dead for any other reason, the umpire shall call and signal "Dead ball" as soon as one run is completed or the ball reaches the boundary. The batsmen shall return to their original ends. The run or boundary shall be disallowed.

(ii) Before one run is completed or the ball reaches the boundary, a batsman is dismissed, or the ball becomes dead for any other reason, all the provisions of the Laws will apply, except that no runs and no penalties shall be credited to the batting side, other than the penalty for a no-ball if applicable.

LAW 27. APPEALS

1. Umpire not to give batsman out without an appeal

Neither umpire shall give a batsman out, even though he may be out under the Laws, unless appealed to by the fielding side. This shall not debar a batsman who is out under any of the Laws from leaving his wicket without an appeal having been made. Note, however, the provisions of 7 below.

2. Batsman dismissed

A batsman is dismissed if either

(a) he is given out by an umpire, on appeal, or

(b) he is out under any of the Laws and leaves his wicket as in 1 above.

3. Timing of appeals

For an appeal to be valid it must be made before the bowler begins his run-up or, if he has no run-up, his bowling action to deliver the next ball, and before "Time" has been called.

The call of "Over" does not invalidate an appeal made prior to the start of the following over provided "Time" has not been called. See Laws 16.2 (Call of "Time") and 22.2 (Start of an over).

4. Appeal "How's that?"

An appeal "How's that?" covers all ways of being out.

5. Answering appeals

The umpire at the bowler's end shall answer all appeals except those arising out of any of Laws 35 (Hit wicket), 39 (Stumped) or 38 (Run out) when this occurs at the striker's wicket. A decision "Not out" by one umpire shall not prevent the other umpire from giving a decision, provided that each is considering only matters within his jurisdiction.

When a batsman has been given not out, either umpire may, within his jurisdiction, answer a further appeal provided that it is made in accordance with 3 above.

6. Consultation by umpires

Each umpire shall answer appeals on matters within his own jurisdiction. If an umpire is doubtful about any point that the other umpire may have been in a better position to see, he shall consult the latter on this point of fact and shall then give his decision. If, after consultation, there is still doubt remaining the decision shall be "Not out".

7. Batsman leaving his wicket under a misapprehension

An umpire shall intervene if satisfied that a batsman, not having been given out, has left his wicket under a misapprehension that he is out. The umpire intervening shall call and signal "Dead ball" to prevent any further action by the fielding side and shall recall the batsman.

8. Withdrawal of an appeal

The captain of the fielding side may withdraw an appeal only with the consent of the umpire within whose jurisdiction the appeal falls and before the outgoing batsman has left the field of play. If such consent is given the umpire concerned shall, if applicable, revoke his decision and recall the batsman.

9. Umpire's decision

An umpire may alter his decision provided that such alteration is made promptly. This apart, the umpire's decision, once made, is final.

LAW 28. THE WICKET IS DOWN

1. Wicket put down

(a) The wicket is put down if a bail is completely removed from the top of the stumps, or a stump is struck out of the ground by:

   (i) The ball.

   (ii) The striker's bat, whether he is holding it or has let go of it.

   (iii) The striker's person or by any part of his clothing or equipment becoming detached from his person.

   (iv) A fielder, with his hand or arm, provided that the ball is held in the hand or hands so used, or in the hand of the arm so used.
   The wicket is also put down if a fielder pulls a stump out of the ground in the same manner.

(b) The disturbance of a bail, whether temporary or not, shall not constitute its complete removal from the top of the stumps, but if a bail in falling lodges between two of the stumps this shall be regarded as complete removal.

2. One bail off

If one bail is off, it shall be sufficient for the purpose of putting the wicket down to remove the remaining bail, or to strike or pull any of the three stumps out of the ground, in any of the ways stated in 1 above.

3. Remaking the wicket

If the wicket is broken or put down while the ball is in play, the umpire shall not remake the wicket until the ball is dead. See Law 23 (Dead ball). Any fielder, however, may:

   (i) Replace a bail or bails on top of the stumps.

   (ii) Put back one or more stumps into the ground where the wicket originally stood.

4. Dispensing with bails

If the umpires have agreed to dispense with bails, in accordance with Law 8.5 (Dispensing with bails), the decision as to whether the wicket has been put down is one for the umpire concerned to decide.

(a) After a decision to play without bails, the wicket has been put down if the umpire concerned is satisfied that the wicket has been struck by the ball, by the striker's bat, person, or items of his clothing or equipment separated from his person as described in 1(a)(ii) or 1(a)(iii) above, or by a fielder with the hand holding the ball or with the arm of the hand holding the ball.

(b) If the wicket has already been broken or put down, (a) above shall apply to any stump or stumps still in the ground. Any fielder may replace a stump or stumps, in accordance with 3 above, in order to have an opportunity of putting the wicket down.

LAW 29. BATSMAN OUT OF HIS GROUND

1. When out of his ground

A batsman shall be considered to be out of his ground unless his bat or some part of his person is grounded behind the popping crease at that end.

2. Which is a batsman's ground?

(a) If only one batsman is within a ground:

   (i) It is his ground.

   (ii) It remains his ground even if he is later joined there by the other batsman.

(b) If both batsmen are in the same ground and one of them subsequently leaves it, (a)(i) above applies.

(c) If there is no batsman in either ground, then each ground belongs to whichever of the batsmen is nearer to it, or, if the batsmen are level, to whichever was nearer to it immediately prior to their drawing level.

(d) If a ground belongs to one batsman, then, unless there is a striker with a runner, the other ground belongs to the other batsman irrespective of his position.

(e) When a batsman with a runner is striker, his ground is always that at the wicketkeeper's end. However, (a), (b), (c) and (d) above will still apply, but only to the runner and the non-striker, so that that ground will also belong to either the non-striker or the runner, as the case may be.

3. Position of non-striker

The non-striker, when standing at the bowler's end, should be positioned on the opposite side of the wicket to that from which the ball is being delivered, unless a request to do otherwise is granted by the umpire.

LAW 30.   BOWLED

1. Out Bowled

(a) The striker is out *Bowled* if his wicket is put down by a ball delivered by the bowler, not being a no-ball, even if it first touches his bat or person.

(b) Notwithstanding (a) above he shall not be out bowled if before striking the wicket the ball has been in contact with any other player or with an umpire. He will, however, be subject to Laws 33 (Handled the ball), 37 (Obstructing the field), 38 (Run out) and 39 (Stumped).

2. Bowled to take precedence

The striker is out bowled if his wicket is put down as in 1 above, even though a decision against him for any other method of dismissal would be justified.

LAW 31.   TIMED OUT

1. Out Timed out

(a) Unless "Time" has been called, the incoming batsman must be in position to take guard or for his partner to be ready to receive the next ball within three minutes of the fall of the previous wicket. If this requirement is not met, the incoming batsman will be out, *Timed out*.

(b) In the event of protracted delay in which no batsman comes to the wicket, the umpires shall adopt the procedure of Law 21.3 (Umpires awarding a match). For the purposes of that Law the start of the action shall be taken as the expiry of the three minutes referred to above.

2. Bowler does not get credit

The bowler does not get credit for the wicket.

LAW 32.   CAUGHT

1. Out Caught

The striker is out *Caught* if a ball delivered by the bowler, not being a no-ball, touches his bat without having previously been in contact with any member of the fielding side and is subsequently held by a fielder as a fair catch before it touches the ground.

2. Caught to take precedence

If the criteria of 1 above are met and the striker is not out bowled, then he is out caught even though a decision against either batsman for another method of dismissal would be justified. Runs completed by the batsmen before the completion of the catch will not be scored. Note also Laws 21.6 (Winning hit or extras) and 42.17(b) (Penalty runs).

3. A fair catch

A catch shall be considered to have been fairly made if:

    (a) Throughout the act of making the catch:

        (i) Any fielder in contact with the ball is within the field of play. See 4 below.

        (ii) The ball is at no time in contact with any object grounded beyond the boundary.

    The act of making the catch shall start from the time when a fielder first handles the ball and shall end when a fielder obtains complete control both over the ball and over his own movement.

    (b) The ball is hugged to the body of the catcher or accidentally lodges in his clothing or, in the case of the wicketkeeper, in his pads. However, it is not a fair catch if the ball lodges in a protective helmet worn by a fielder. See Law 23 (Dead ball).

    (c) The ball does not touch the ground, even though the hand holding it does so in effecting the catch.

    (d) A fielder catches the ball after it has been lawfully struck more than once by the striker, but only if the ball has not touched the ground since first being struck.

    (e) A fielder catches the ball after it has touched an umpire, another fielder or the other batsman. However, it is not a fair catch if the ball has touched a protective helmet worn by a fielder, although the ball remains in play.

    (f) A fielder catches the ball in the air after it has crossed the boundary provided that:

        (i) He has no part of his person touching, or grounded beyond, the boundary at any time when he is in contact with the ball.

        (ii) The ball has not been grounded beyond the boundary.

    See Law 19.3 (Scoring a boundary).

    (g) The ball is caught off an obstruction within the boundary, provided it has not previously been decided to regard the obstruction as a boundary.

4. Fielder within the field of play

    (a) A fielder is not within the field of play if he touches the boundary or has any part of his person grounded beyond the boundary. See Law 19.3 (Scoring a boundary).

    (b) Six runs shall be scored if a fielder:

        (i) Has any part of his person touching, or grounded beyond, the boundary when he catches the ball.

        (ii) Catches the ball and subsequently touches the boundary or grounds some part of his person over the boundary while carrying the ball but before completing the catch.

    See Laws 19.3 (Scoring a boundary) and 19.4 (Runs allowed for boundaries).

5. No runs to be scored

If the striker is dismissed caught, runs from that delivery completed by the batsmen before the completion of the catch shall not be scored, but any penalties awarded to either side when the ball is dead, if applicable, will stand. Law 18.12(a) (Batsman returning to wicket he has left) shall apply from the instant of the catch.

LAW 33.   HANDLED THE BALL

1. Out Handled the ball

Either batsman is out *Handled the ball* if he wilfully touches the ball while in play with a hand or hands not holding the bat unless he does so with the consent of the opposing side.

2. Not out Handled the ball

Notwithstanding 1 above, a batsman will not be out under this Law if:

    (i) He handles the ball in order to avoid injury.

(ii) He uses his hand or hands to return the ball to any member of the fielding side without the consent of that side. Note, however, the provisions of Law 37.4 (Returning the ball to a member of the fielding side).

3. Runs scored

If either batsman is dismissed under this Law, any runs completed before the offence, together with any penalty extras and the penalty for a no-ball or wide, if applicable, shall be scored. See Laws 18.10 (Runs scored when a batsman is dismissed) and 42.17 (Penalty runs).

4. Bowler does not get credit

The bowler does not get credit for the wicket.

LAW 34. HIT THE BALL TWICE

1. Out Hit the ball twice

(a) The striker is out *Hit the ball twice* if, while the ball is in play and it strikes any part of his person or is struck by his bat and, before the ball has been touched by a fielder, he wilfully strikes it again with his bat or person, other than a hand not holding the bat, except for the sole purpose of guarding his wicket. See 3 below and Laws 33 (Handled the ball) and 37 (Obstructing the field).

(b) For the purpose of this Law, "struck" or "strike" shall include contact with the person of the striker.

2. Not out Hit the ball twice

Notwithstanding 1(a) above, the striker will not be out under this Law if:

(i) He makes a second or subsequent stroke in order to return the ball to any member of the fielding side. Note, however, the provisions of Law 37.4 (Returning the ball to a member of the fielding side).

(ii) He wilfully strikes the ball after it has touched a fielder. Note, however, the provisions of Law 37.1 (Out obstructing the field).

3. Ball lawfully struck more than once

Solely in order to guard his wicket and before the ball has been touched by a fielder, the striker may lawfully strike the ball more than once with his bat or with any part of his person other than a hand not holding the bat.

Notwithstanding this provision, the striker may not prevent the ball from being caught by making more than one stroke in defence of his wicket. See Law 37.3 (Obstructing a ball from being caught).

4. Runs permitted from ball lawfully struck more than once

When the ball is lawfully struck more than once, as permitted in 3 above, only the first strike is to be considered in determining whether runs are to be allowed and how they are to be scored.

(a) If on the first strike the umpire is satisfied that either

(i) the ball first struck the bat, or

(ii) the striker attempted to play the ball with his bat, or

(iii) the striker tried to avoid being hit by the ball,

then any penalties to the batting side that are applicable shall be allowed.

(b) If the conditions in (a) above are met then, if they result from overthrows, and only if they result from overthrows, runs completed by the batsmen or a boundary will be allowed in addition to any penalties that are applicable. They shall be credited to the striker if the first strike was with the bat. If the first strike was on the person of the striker they shall be scored as leg-byes or no-ball extras, as appropriate. See Law 26.2 (Leg-byes).

(c) If the conditions of (a) above are met and there is no overthrow until after the batsmen have started to run, but before one run is completed:

    (i) Only subsequent completed runs or a boundary shall be allowed. The first run shall count as a completed run for this purpose only if the batsmen have not crossed at the instant of the throw.

    (ii) If in these circumstances the ball goes to the boundary from the throw then, notwithstanding the provisions of Law 19.6 (Overthrow or wilful act of fielder), only the boundary allowance shall be scored.

    (iii) If the ball goes to the boundary as the result of a further overthrow, then runs completed by the batsmen after the first throw and before this final throw shall be added to the boundary allowance. The run in progress at the first throw will count only if they have not crossed at that moment; the run in progress at the final throw shall count only if they have crossed at that moment. Law 18.12 (Batsman returning to wicket he has left) shall apply as from the moment of the final throw.

(d) If, in the opinion of the umpire, none of the conditions in (a) above has been met then, whether there is an overthrow or not, the batting side shall not be credited with any runs from that delivery apart from the penalty for a no-ball if applicable. Moreover, no other penalties shall be awarded to the batting side when the ball is dead. See Law 42.17 (Penalty runs).

5. Ball lawfully struck more than once – action by the umpire

If no runs are to be allowed, either in the circumstances of 4(d) above, or because there has been no overthrow and:

    (a) If no run is attempted but the ball reaches the boundary, the umpire shall call and signal "Dead ball" and disallow the boundary.

    (b) If the batsmen run and:

        (i) Neither batsman is dismissed and the ball does not become dead for any other reason, the umpire shall call and signal "Dead ball" as soon as one run is completed or the ball reaches the boundary. The batsmen shall return to their original ends. The run or boundary shall be disallowed.

        (ii) A batsman is dismissed, or if for any other reason the ball becomes dead before one run is completed or the ball reaches the boundary, all the provisions of the Laws will apply except that the award of penalties to the batting side shall be as laid down in 4(a) or 4(d) above as appropriate.

6. Bowler does not get credit

The bowler does not get credit for the wicket.

LAW 35. HIT WICKET

1. Out Hit wicket

(a) The striker is out *Hit wicket* if, after the bowler has entered his delivery stride and while the ball is in play, his wicket is put down either by the striker's bat or person as described in Law 28.1(a)(ii) and (iii) (Wicket put down) either

    (i) in the course of any action taken by him in preparing to receive or in receiving a delivery, or

    (ii) in setting off for his first run immediately after playing, or playing at, the ball, or

    (iii) if he makes no attempt to play the ball, in setting off for his first run, provided that in the opinion of the umpire this is immediately after he has had the opportunity of playing the ball, or

    (iv) in lawfully making a second or further stroke for the purpose of guarding his wicket within the provisions of Law 34.3 (Ball lawfully struck more than once).

(b) If the striker puts his wicket down in any of the ways described in Law 28.1(a)(ii) and (iii) (Wicket put down) before the bowler has entered his delivery stride, either umpire shall call and signal "Dead ball".

2. Not out Hit wicket

Notwithstanding 1 above, the batsman is not out under this Law should his wicket be put down in any of the ways referred to in 1 above if:

(a) It occurs after he has completed any action in receiving the delivery, other than as in 1(a)(ii), (iii) or (iv) above.

(b) It occurs when he is in the act of running, other than in setting off immediately for his first run.

(c) It occurs when he is trying to avoid being run out or stumped.

(d) It occurs while he is trying to avoid a throw-in at any time.

(e) The bowler, after entering his delivery stride, does not deliver the ball. In this case either umpire shall immediately call and signal "Dead ball". See Law 23.3 (Umpire calling and signalling "Dead ball").

(f) The delivery is a no-ball.

LAW 36.   LEG BEFORE WICKET

1. Out LBW

The striker is out *LBW* in the circumstances set out below.

(a) The bowler delivers a ball, not being a no-ball, and

(b) the ball, if it is not intercepted full pitch, pitches in line between wicket and wicket or on the off side of the striker's wicket, and

(c) the ball not having previously touched his bat, the striker intercepts the ball, either full pitch or after pitching, with any part of his person, and

(d) the point of impact, even if above the level of the bails, either

(i) is between wicket and wicket, or

(ii) is either between wicket and wicket or outside the line of the off stump, if the striker has made no genuine attempt to play the ball with his bat, and

(e) but for the interception, the ball would have hit the wicket.

2. Interception of the ball

(a) In assessing points (c), (d) and (e) in 1 above, only the first interception is to be considered.

(b) In assessing point (e) in 1 above, it is to be assumed that the path of the ball before interception would have continued after interception, irrespective of whether the ball might have pitched subsequently or not.

3. Off side of wicket

The off side of the striker's wicket shall be determined by the striker's stance at the moment the ball comes into play for that delivery.

LAW 37.   OBSTRUCTING THE FIELD

1. Out Obstructing the field

Either batsman is out *Obstructing the field* if he wilfully obstructs or distracts the opposing side by word or action. It shall be regarded as obstruction if either batsman wilfully, and without the consent of the fielding side, strikes the ball with his bat or person, other than a hand not holding the bat, after the ball has touched a fielder. See 4 below.

2. Accidental obstruction

It is for either umpire to decide whether any obstruction or distraction is wilful or not. He shall consult the other umpire if he has any doubt.

3. Obstructing a ball from being caught

The striker is out should wilful obstruction or distraction by either batsman prevent a catch being made.

This shall apply even though the striker causes the obstruction in lawfully guarding his wicket under the provisions of Law 34.3 (Ball lawfully struck more than once).

4. Returning the ball to a member of the fielding side

Either batsman is out under this Law if, without the consent of the fielding side and while the ball is in play, he uses his bat or person to return the ball to any member of that side.

5. Runs scored

If a batsman is dismissed under this Law, runs completed by the batsmen before the offence shall be scored, together with the penalty for a no-ball or a wide, if applicable. Other penalties that may be awarded to either side when the ball is dead shall also stand. See Law 42.17(b) (Penalty runs).

If, however, the obstruction prevents a catch from being made, runs completed by the batsmen before the offence shall not be scored, but other penalties that may be awarded to either side when the ball is dead shall stand. See Law 42.17(b) (Penalty runs).

6. Bowler does not get credit

The bowler does not get credit for the wicket.

LAW 38.   RUN OUT

1. Out Run out

 (a) Either batsman is out *Run out*, except as in 2 below, if at any time while the ball is in play

   (i) he is out of his ground and

   (ii) his wicket is fairly put down by the opposing side.

 (b) (a) above shall apply even though "No-ball" has been called and whether or not a run is being attempted, except in the circumstances of Law 39.3(b) (Not out Stumped).

2. Batsman not Run out

Notwithstanding 1 above, a batsman is not out run out if:

 (a) He has been within his ground and has subsequently left it to avoid injury, when the wicket is put down.

 (b) The ball has not subsequently been touched again by a fielder, after the bowler has entered his delivery stride, before the wicket is put down.

 (c) The ball, having been played by the striker, or having come off his person, directly strikes a helmet worn by a fielder and without further contact with him or any other fielder rebounds directly on to the wicket. However, the ball remains in play and either batsman may be run out in the circumstances of 1 above if a wicket is subsequently put down.

 (d) He is out stumped. See Law 39.1(b) (Out Stumped).

 (e) He is out of his ground, not attempting a run and his wicket is fairly put down by the wicketkeeper without the intervention of another member of the fielding side, if "No-ball" has been called. See Law 39.3(b) (Not out Stumped).

3. Which batsman is out

The batsman out in the circumstances of 1 above is the one whose ground is at the end where the wicket is put down. See Laws 2.8 (Transgression of the Laws by a batsman who has a runner) and 29.2 (Which is a batsman's ground).

4. Runs scored

If a batsman is dismissed run out, the batting side shall score the runs completed before the dismissal together with the penalty for a no-ball or wide, if applicable. Other penalties to either side that may be awarded when the ball is dead shall also stand. See Law 42.17 (Penalty runs).

If, however, a striker with a runner is himself dismissed run out, runs completed by the runner and the other batsman before the dismissal shall not be scored. The penalty for a no-ball or a wide and any other penalties to either side that may be awarded when the ball is dead shall stand. See Laws 2.8 (Transgression of the Laws by a batsman who has a runner) and 42.17(b) (Penalty runs).

5. Bowler does not get credit

The bowler does not get credit for the wicket.

LAW 39.   STUMPED

1. Out Stumped

     (a) The striker is out *Stumped* if

         (i) he is out of his ground, and

         (ii) he is receiving a ball which is not a no-ball, and

         (iii) he is not attempting a run, and

         (iv) his wicket is fairly put down by the wicketkeeper without the intervention of another member of the fielding side. Note Law 40.3 (Position of wicketkeeper).

     (b) The striker is out stumped if all the conditions of (a) above are satisfied, even though a decision of run out would be justified.

2. Ball rebounding from wicketkeeper's person

     (a) If the wicket is put down by the ball, it shall be regarded as having been put down by the wicketkeeper, if the ball

         (i) rebounds on to the stumps from any part of his person, other than a protective helmet, or

         (ii) has been kicked or thrown on to the stumps by the wicketkeeper.

     (b) If the ball touches a helmet worn by the wicketkeeper, the ball is still in play but the striker shall not be stumped. He will, however, be liable to be run out in these circumstances if there is subsequent contact between the ball and any member of the fielding side. Note, however, 3 below.

3. Not out Stumped

     (a) If the striker is not out stumped, he is liable to be out run out if the conditions of Law 38 (Run out) apply, except as set out in (b) below.

     (b) The striker shall not be out run out if he is out of his ground, not attempting a run, and his wicket is fairly put down by the wicketkeeper without the intervention of another member of the fielding side, if "No-ball" has been called.

LAW 40.   THE WICKETKEEPER

1. Protective equipment

The wicketkeeper is the only member of the fielding side permitted to wear gloves and external leg guards. If he does so, these are to be regarded as part of his person for the purposes of Law 41.2 (Fielding the ball). If by his actions and positioning it is apparent to the umpires that he will not be able to discharge his duties as a wicketkeeper, he shall forfeit this right and also the right to be recognised as a wicketkeeper for the purposes of Laws 32.3 (A fair catch), 39 (Stumped), 41.1 (Protective equipment), 41.5 (Limitation of on-side fielders) and 41.6 (Fielders not to encroach on the pitch).

2. Gloves

If, as permitted under 1 above, the wicketkeeper wears gloves, they shall have no webbing between fingers except joining index finger and thumb, where webbing may be inserted as a means of support. If used, the webbing shall be

(a) a single piece of non-stretch material which, although it may have facing material attached, shall have no reinforcement or tucks.

(b) such that the top edge of the webbing.

(i) does not protrude beyond the straight line joining the top of the index finger to the top of the thumb.

(ii) is taut when a hand wearing the glove has the thumb fully extended.

3. Position of wicketkeeper

The wicketkeeper shall remain wholly behind the wicket at the striker's end from the moment the ball comes into play until

(a) a ball delivered by the bowler either

(i) touches the bat or person of the striker, or

(ii) passes the wicket at the striker's end, or

(b) the striker attempts a run.

In the event of the wicketkeeper contravening this Law, the umpire at the striker's end shall call and signal "No-ball" as soon as possible after the delivery of the ball.

4. Movement by wicketkeeper

It is unfair if the wicketkeeper standing back makes a significant movement towards the wicket after the ball comes into play and before it reaches the striker. In the event of such unfair movement by the wicketkeeper, either umpire shall call and signal "Dead ball". It will not be considered a significant movement if the wicketkeeper moves a few paces forward for a slower delivery.

5. Restriction on actions of wicketkeeper

If in the opinion of either umpire the wicketkeeper interferes with the striker's right to play the ball and to guard his wicket, Law 23.3(b)(vi) (Umpire calling and signalling "Dead Ball") shall apply. If, however, the umpire concerned considers that the interference by the wicketkeeper was wilful, then Law 42.4 (Deliberate attempt to distract striker) shall apply.

6. Interference with wicketkeeper by striker

If, in playing at the ball or in the legitimate defence of his wicket, the striker interferes with the wicketkeeper, he shall not be out, except as provided for in Law 37.3 (Obstructing a ball from being caught).

LAW 41. THE FIELDER

1. Protective equipment

No member of the fielding side other than the wicketkeeper shall be permitted to wear gloves or external leg guards. In addition, protection for the hand or fingers may be worn only with the consent of the umpires.

2. Fielding the ball

A fielder may field the ball with any part of his person but if, while the ball is in play, he wilfully fields it otherwise:

(a) The ball shall become dead and five penalty runs shall be awarded to the batting side. See Law 42.17 (Penalty runs). The ball shall not count as one of the over.

(b) The umpire shall inform the other umpire, the captain of the fielding side, the batsmen and, as soon as practicable, the captain of the batting side of what has occurred.

(c) The umpires together shall report the occurrence as soon as possible to the executive of the fielding side and any governing body responsible for the match who shall take such action as is considered appropriate against the captain and player concerned.

3. Protective helmets belonging to the fielding side

Protective helmets, when not in use by fielders, shall only be placed, if above the surface, on the ground behind the wicketkeeper and in line with both sets of stumps. If a helmet belonging to the fielding side is on the ground within the field of play, and the ball while in play strikes it, the ball shall become dead. Five penalty runs shall then be awarded to the batting side. See Laws 18.11 (Runs scored when ball becomes dead) and 42.17 (Penalty runs).

4. Penalty runs not to be awarded

Notwithstanding 2 and 3 above, if from the delivery by the bowler the ball first struck the person of the striker and if, in the opinion of the umpire, the striker neither

(i) attempted to play the ball with his bat, nor

(ii) tried to avoid being hit by the ball,

then no award of five penalty runs shall be made and no other runs or penalties shall be credited to the batting side except the penalty for a no-ball if applicable. See Law 26.3 (Leg-byes not to be awarded).

5. Limitation of on-side fielders

At the instant of the bowler's delivery there shall not be more than two fielders, other than the wicketkeeper, behind the popping crease on the on side. A fielder will be considered to be behind the popping crease unless the whole of his person, whether grounded or in the air, is in front of this line.

In the event of infringement of this Law by the fielding side the umpire at the striker's end shall call and signal "No-ball".

6. Fielders not to encroach on the pitch

While the ball is in play and until the ball has made contact with the bat or person of the striker, or has passed the striker's bat, no fielder, other than the bowler, may have any part of his person grounded on or extended over the pitch.

In the event of infringement of this Law by any fielder other than the wicketkeeper, the umpire at the bowler's end shall call and signal "No-ball" as soon as possible after the delivery of the ball. Note, however, Law 40.3 (Position of wicketkeeper).

7. Movement by fielders

Any significant movement by any fielder after the ball comes into play and before the ball reaches the striker is unfair. In the event of such unfair movement, either umpire shall call and signal "Dead ball". Note also the provisions of Law 42.4 (Deliberate attempt to distract striker).

8. Definition of significant movement

(a) For close fielders anything other than minor adjustments to stance or position in relation to the striker is significant.

(b) In the outfield, fielders are permitted to move in towards the striker or striker's wicket, provided that 5 above is not contravened. Anything other than slight movement off line or away from the striker is to be considered significant.

(c) For restrictions on movement by the wicketkeeper see Law 40.4 (Movement by wicketkeeper).

LAW 42. FAIR AND UNFAIR PLAY

1. Fair and unfair play – responsibility of captains

The responsibility lies with the captains for ensuring that play is conducted within the spirit and traditions of the game, as described in The Preamble – The Spirit of Cricket, as well as within the Laws.

2. Fair and unfair play – responsibility of umpires

The umpires shall be sole judges of fair and unfair play. If either umpire considers an action, not covered by the Laws, to be unfair, he shall intervene without appeal and, if the ball is in play, shall call and signal "Dead ball" and implement the procedure as set out in 18 below. Otherwise the umpires shall not interfere with the progress of play, except as required to do so by the Laws.

3. The match ball – changing its condition

(a) Any fielder may:

    (i) Polish the ball provided that no artificial substance is used and that such polishing wastes no time.

    (ii) Remove mud from the ball under the supervision of the umpire.

    (iii) Dry a wet ball on a towel.

(b) It is unfair for anyone to rub the ball on the ground for any reason, interfere with any of the seams or the surface of the ball, use any implement, or take any other action whatsoever which is likely to alter the condition of the ball, except as permitted in (a) above.

(c) The umpires shall make frequent and irregular inspections of the ball.

(d) In the event of any fielder changing the condition of the ball unfairly, as set out in (b) above, the umpires after consultation shall:

    (i) Change the ball forthwith. It shall be for the umpires to decide on the replacement ball, which shall, in their opinion, have had wear comparable with that which the previous ball had received immediately prior to the contravention.

    (ii) Inform the batsmen that the ball has been changed.

    (iii) Award five penalty runs to the batting side. See 17 below.

    (iv) Inform the captain of the fielding side that the reason for the action was the unfair interference with the ball.

    (v) Inform the captain of the batting side as soon as practicable of what has occurred.

    (vi) Report the occurrence as soon as possible to the executive of the fielding side and any governing body responsible for the match, who shall take such action as is considered appropriate against the captain and team concerned.

(e) If there is any further instance of unfairly changing the condition of the ball in that innings, the umpires after consultation shall:

    (i) Repeat the procedure in (d)(i), (ii) and (iii) above.

    (ii) Inform the captain of the fielding side of the reason for the action taken and direct him to take off forthwith the bowler who delivered the immediately preceding ball. The bowler thus taken off shall not be allowed to bowl again in that innings.

    (iii) Inform the captain of the batting side as soon as practicable of what has occurred.

    (iv) Report the occurrence as soon as possible to the executive of the fielding side and any governing body responsible for the match, who shall take such action as is considered appropriate against the captain and team concerned.

4. Deliberate attempt to distract striker

It is unfair for any member of the fielding side deliberately to attempt to distract the striker while he is preparing to receive or receiving a delivery.

(a) If either umpire considers that any action by a member of the fielding side is such an attempt, at the first instance he shall:

    (i) Immediately call and signal "Dead ball".

    (ii) Warn the captain of the fielding side that the action is unfair and indicate that this is a first and final warning.

    (iii) Inform the other umpire and the batsmen of what has occurred.

Neither batsman shall be dismissed from that delivery and the ball shall not count as one of the over.

(b) If there is any further such deliberate attempt in that innings, by any member of the fielding side, the procedures, other than warning, as set out in (a) above shall apply. Additionally, the umpire at the bowler's end shall:

   (i) Award five penalty runs to the batting side. See 17 below.

   (ii) Inform the captain of the fielding side of the reason for this action and, as soon as practicable, inform the captain of the batting side.

   (iii) Report the occurrence, together with the other umpire, as soon as possible to the executive of the fielding side and any governing body responsible for the match, who shall take such action as is considered appropriate against the captain and player or players concerned.

5. Deliberate distraction or obstruction of batsman

In addition to 4 above, it is unfair for any member of the fielding side, by word or action, wilfully to attempt to distract or to obstruct either batsman after the striker has received the ball.

   (a) It is for either one of the umpires to decide whether any distraction or obstruction is wilful or not.

   (b) If either umpire considers that a member of the fielding side has wilfully caused or attempted to cause such a distraction or obstruction he shall:

   (i) Immediately call and signal "Dead ball".

   (ii) Inform the captain of the fielding side and the other umpire of the reason for the call.

Additionally:

   (iii) Neither batsman shall be dismissed from that delivery.

   (iv) Five penalty runs shall be awarded to the batting side. See 17 below. In this instance, the run in progress shall be scored, whether or not the batsmen had crossed at the instant of the call. See Law 18.11 (Runs scored when ball becomes dead).

   (v) The umpire at the bowler's end shall inform the captain of the fielding side of the reason for this action and, as soon as practicable, inform the captain of the batting side.

   (vi) The ball shall not count as one of the over.

   (vii) The batsmen at the wicket shall decide which of them is to face the next delivery.

   (viii) The umpires shall report the occurrence as soon as possible to the executive of the fielding side and any governing body responsible for the match, who shall take such action as is considered appropriate against the captain and player or players concerned.

6. Dangerous and unfair bowling

(a) Bowling of fast short-pitched balls

   (i) The bowling of fast short-pitched balls is dangerous and unfair if the umpire at the bowler's end considers that by their repetition and taking into account their length, height and direction they are likely to inflict physical injury on the striker, irrespective of the protective equipment he may be wearing. The relative skill of the striker shall be taken into consideration.

   (ii) Any delivery which, after pitching, passes or would have passed over head height of the striker standing upright at the crease, although not threatening physical injury, shall be included with bowling under (i) when the umpire is considering whether the bowling of fast short-pitched balls has become dangerous and unfair and after he has so decided. The umpire shall call and signal "No-ball" for each such delivery.

(b) Bowling of high full-pitched balls

   (i) Any delivery, other than a slow-paced one, which passes or would have passed on the full above waist height of the striker standing upright at the crease is to be deemed dangerous and unfair, whether or not it is likely to inflict physical injury on the striker.

   (ii) A slow delivery which passes or would have passed on the full above shoulder height of the striker standing upright at the crease is to be deemed dangerous and unfair, whether or not it is likely to inflict physical injury on the striker.

7. Dangerous and unfair bowling – action by the umpire

(a) As soon as the umpire at the bowler's end decides under 6(a) above that the bowling of fast short-pitched balls has become dangerous and unfair, or, except as in 8 below, there is an instance of dangerous and unfair bowling as defined in 6(b) above, he shall call and signal "No-ball" and, when the ball is dead, caution the bowler, inform the other umpire, the captain of the fielding side and the batsmen of what has occurred. This caution shall continue to apply throughout the innings.

(b) If there is any further instance of such dangerous and unfair bowling by the same bowler in the same innings, the umpire at the bowler's end shall repeat the above procedure and indicate to the bowler that this is a final warning.

Both the above caution and final warning shall continue to apply even though the bowler may later change ends.

(c) Should there be any further repetition by the same bowler in that innings, the umpire shall:

  (i) call and signal "No-ball".

  (ii) Direct the captain, when the ball is dead, to take the bowler off forthwith. The over shall be completed by another bowler, who shall neither have bowled the previous over nor be allowed to bowl the next over.

  The bowler thus taken off shall not be allowed to bowl again in that innings.

  (iii) Report the occurrence to the other umpire, the batsmen and, as soon as practicable, the captain of the batting side.

  (iv) Report the occurrence, with the other umpire, as soon as possible to the executive of the fielding side and to any governing body responsible for the match, who shall take such action as is considered appropriate against the captain and bowler concerned.

8. Deliberate bowling of high full-pitched balls

If the umpire considers that a high full pitch which is deemed to be dangerous and unfair, as defined in 6(b) above, was deliberately bowled, then the caution and warning prescribed in 7 above shall be dispensed with. The umpire shall:

  (a) Call and signal "No-ball".

  (b) Direct the captain, when the ball is dead, to take the bowler off forthwith.

  (c) Implement the remainder of the procedure as laid down in 7(c) above.

9. Time-wasting by the fielding side

It is unfair for any member of the fielding side to waste time.

(a) If the captain of the fielding side wastes time, or allows any member of his side to waste time, or if the progress of an over is unnecessarily slow, at the first instance the umpire shall call and signal "Dead ball" if necessary and:

  (i) Warn the captain, and indicate that this is a first and final warning.

  (ii) Inform the other umpire and the batsmen of what has occurred.

(b) If there is any further waste of time in that innings, by any member of the fielding side, the umpire shall either

  (i) if the waste of time is not during the course of an over, award five penalty runs to the batting side (See 17 below), or

  (ii) if the waste of time is during the course of an over, when the ball is dead, direct the captain to take the bowler off forthwith. If applicable, the over shall be completed by another bowler, who shall neither have bowled the previous over nor be allowed to bowl the next over. The bowler thus taken off shall not be allowed to bowl again in that innings.

  (iii) Inform the other umpire, the batsmen and, as soon as practicable, the captain of the batting side, of what has occurred.

  (iv) Report the occurrence, with the other umpire, as soon as possible to the executive of the fielding side and to any governing body responsible for the match, who shall take such action as is considered appropriate against the captain and team concerned.

10. Batsman wasting time

It is unfair for a batsman to waste time. In normal circumstances the striker should always be ready to take strike when the bowler is ready to start his run-up.

(a) Should either batsman waste time by failing to meet this requirement, or in any other way, the following procedure shall be adopted. At the first instance, either before the bowler starts his run-up or when the ball is dead, as appropriate, the umpire shall:

  (i) Warn the batsman and indicate that this is a first and final warning. This warning shall continue to apply throughout that innings. The umpire shall so inform each incoming batsman.

  (ii) Inform the other umpire, the other batsman and the captain of the fielding side of what has occurred.

  (iii) Inform the captain of the batting side as soon as practicable.

(b) If there is any further time-wasting by any batsman in that innings, the umpire shall, at the appropriate time while the ball is dead:

  (i) Award five penalty runs to the fielding side. See 17 below.

  (ii) Inform the other umpire, the other batsman, the captain of the fielding side and, as soon as practicable, the captain of the batting side, of what has occurred.

  (iii) Report the occurrence, with the other umpire, as soon as possible to the executive of the batting side and to any governing body responsible for the match, who shall take such action as is considered appropriate against the captain and player or players, or, if appropriate, the team concerned.

11. Damaging the pitch – area to be protected

(a) It is incumbent on all players to avoid unnecessary damage to the pitch. It is unfair for any player to cause deliberate damage to the pitch.

(b) An area of the pitch, to be referred to as "the protected area", is defined as that area contained within a rectangle bounded at each end by imaginary lines parallel to the popping creases and 5ft/1.52m in front of each and on the sides by imaginary lines, one each side of the imaginary line joining the centres of the two middle stumps, each parallel to it and 1ft/30.48cm from it.

12. Bowler running on the protected area after delivering the ball

(a) If the bowler, after delivering the ball, runs on the protected area as defined in 11(b) above, the umpire shall at the first instance, and when the ball is dead:

  (i) Caution the bowler. This caution shall continue to apply throughout the innings.

  (ii) Inform the other umpire, the captain of the fielding side and the batsmen of what has occurred.

(b) If, in that innings, the same bowler runs on the protected area again after delivering the ball, the umpire shall repeat the above procedure, indicating that this is a final warning.

(c) If, in that innings, the same bowler runs on the protected area a third time after delivering the ball, when the ball is dead the umpire shall:

  (i) Direct the captain of the fielding side to take the bowler off forthwith. If applicable, the over shall be completed by another bowler, who shall neither have bowled the previous over nor be allowed to bowl the next over. The bowler thus taken off shall not be allowed to bowl again in that innings.

  (ii) Inform the other umpire, the batsmen and, as soon as practicable, the captain of the batting side of what has occurred.

  (iii) Report the occurrence, with the other umpire, as soon as possible to the executive of the fielding side and to any governing body responsible for the match, who shall take such action as is considered appropriate against the captain and bowler concerned.

13. Fielders damaging the pitch

(a) If any fielder causes avoidable damage to the pitch, other than as in 12(a) above, at the first instance the umpire shall, when the ball is dead:

    (i) Caution the captain of the fielding side, indicating that this is a first and final warning. This caution shall continue to apply throughout the innings.

    (ii) Inform the other umpire and the batsmen of what has occurred.

(b) If there is any further avoidable damage to the pitch by any fielder in that innings, the umpire shall, when the ball is dead:

    (i) Award five penalty runs to the batting side. See 17 below.

    (ii) Inform the other umpire, the batsmen, the captain of the fielding side and, as soon as practicable, the captain of the batting side of what has occurred.

    (iii) Report the occurrence, with the other umpire, as soon as possible to the executive of the fielding side and any governing body responsible for the match, who shall take such action as is considered appropriate against the captain and player or players concerned.

14. Batsman damaging the pitch

(a) If either batsman causes avoidable damage to the pitch, at the first instance the umpire shall, when the ball is dead:

    (i) Caution the batsman. This caution shall continue to apply throughout the innings. The umpire shall so inform each incoming batsman.

    (ii) Inform the other umpire, the other batsman, the captain of the fielding side and, as soon as practicable, the captain of the batting side.

(b) If there is a second instance of avoidable damage to the pitch by any batsman in that innings:

    (i) The umpire shall repeat the above procedure, indicating that this is a final warning.

    (ii) Additionally he shall disallow all runs to the batting side from that delivery other than the penalty for a no-ball or a wide, if applicable. The batsmen shall return to their original ends.

(c) If there is any further avoidable damage to the pitch by any batsman in that innings, the umpire shall, when the ball is dead:

    (i) Disallow all runs to the batting side from that delivery other than the penalty for a no-ball or a wide, if applicable.

    (ii) Additionally award five penalty runs to the fielding side. See 17 below.

    (iii) Inform the other umpire, the other batsman, the captain of the fielding side and, as soon as practicable, the captain of the batting side of what has occurred.

    (iv) Report the occurrence, with the other umpire, as soon as possible to the executive of the batting side and any governing body responsible for the match, who shall take such action as is considered appropriate against the captain and player or players concerned.

15. Bowler attempting to run out non-striker before delivery

The bowler is permitted, before entering his delivery stride, to attempt to run out the non-striker. The ball shall not count in the over.

The umpire shall call and signal "Dead ball" as soon as possible if the bowler fails in the attempt to run out the non-striker.

16. Batsmen stealing a run

It is unfair for the batsmen to attempt to steal a run during the bowler's run-up. Unless the bowler attempts to run out either batsman – see 15 above and Law 24.4 (Bowler throwing towards striker's end before delivery) – the umpire shall:

    (i) Call and signal "Dead ball" as soon as the batsmen cross in any such attempt.

    (ii) Return the batsmen to their original ends.

(iii) Award five penalty runs to the fielding side. See 17 below.

(iv) Inform the other umpire, the other batsman, the captain of the fielding side and, as soon as practicable, the captain of the batting side of the reason for the action taken.

(v) Report the occurrence, with the other umpire, as soon as possible to the executive of the batting side and any governing body responsible for the match, who shall take such action as is considered appropriate against the captain and player or players concerned.

17. Penalty runs

(a) When penalty runs are awarded to either side, when the ball is dead the umpire shall signal the penalty runs to the scorers as laid down in Law 3.14 (Signals).

(b) Notwithstanding the provisions of Law 21.6 (Winning hit or extras), penalty runs shall be awarded in each case where the Laws require the award. Note, however, that the restrictions on awarding penalty runs in Laws 26.3 (Leg-byes not to be awarded), 34.4(d) (Runs permitted from ball struck lawfully more than once) and Law 41.4 (Penalty runs not to be awarded) will apply.

(c) When five penalty runs are awarded to the batting side, under either Law 2.6 (Player returning without permission) or Law 41 (The fielder) or under 3, 4, 5, 9 or 13 above, then:

(i) They shall be scored as penalty extras and shall be in addition to any other penalties.

(ii) They shall not be regarded as runs scored from either the immediately preceding delivery or the following delivery and shall be in addition to any runs from those deliveries.

(iii) The batsmen shall not change ends solely by reason of the five-run penalty.

(d) When five penalty runs are awarded to the fielding side, under Law 18.5(b) (Deliberate short runs), or under 10, 14 or 16 above, they shall be added as penalty extras to that side's total of runs in its most recently completed innings. If the fielding side has not completed an innings, the five penalty extras shall be added to its next innings.

18. Players' conduct

If there is any breach of the Spirit of the Game by a player failing to comply with the instructions of an umpire, or criticising his decisions by word or action, or showing dissent, or generally behaving in a manner which might bring the game into disrepute, the umpire concerned shall immediately report the matter to the other umpire.

The umpires together shall:

(i) Inform the player's captain of the occurrence, instructing the latter to take action.

(ii) Warn him of the gravity of the offence, and tell him that it will be reported to higher authority.

(iii) Report the occurrence as soon as possible to the executive of the player's team and any governing body responsible for the match, who shall take such action as is considered appropriate against the captain and player or players, and, if appropriate, the team concerned.

Appendices A–D can be found at www.lords.org/laws-and-spirit/laws-of-cricket/laws

APPENDIX E – The bat

Grading of bats Grades A, B and C are bats conforming to Law 6 sections 1 to 8 inclusive. Any other bats are graded below C and are not recognised in the Laws. Grade A bats, the top grade, may be used at any level. Grades B, C and lower grades may be used only at or below levels determined by the governing body for cricket in the country concerned.

The blade The face of the blade is its main striking surface. The back is the opposite surface. The shoulders, sides and toe are the remaining surfaces, separating the face and the back.

The shoulders, one on each side of the handle, are along that portion of the blade between the first entry point of the handle and the point at which the blade first reaches its full width.

The toe is the surface opposite to the shoulders taken as a pair.

The sides, one on each side of the blade, are along the rest of the blade, between the toe and the shoulders.

Adhesives Throughout, adhesives are permitted only where essential and only minimal in quantity.

Materials in handle As a proportion of the total volume of the handle, materials other than cane, wood or twine are restricted to one-tenth for Grades A and B and one-fifth for Grade C. Such materials must not project more than 3.25 in/8.26cm into the lower portion of the handle.

Binding and covering of handle The permitted continuation beyond the junction of the upper and lower portions of the handle is restricted to a maximum, measured along the length of the handle, of

2.5 in/6.35 cm for the twine binding

2.75 in/6.99 cm for the covering grip.

Length and width

(a) The overall length of the bat, when the lower portion of the handle is inserted, shall not be more than 38 in/96.5 cm.

(b) The width of the bat shall not exceed 4.25 in/10.8 cm at its widest part.

(c) Permitted coverings, repair material and toe guards, not exceeding their specified thicknesses, may be additional to the dimensions above.

Length of handle Except for bats of size 6 and less, the handle shall not exceed 52% of the overall length of the bat.

Covering of blade The cloth covering permitted for Grade C bats shall be of thickness not exceeding 0.012 in/0.3 mm before treatment as in 6.6(d).

Protection and repair of blade The material permitted in 6.6(a) shall not exceed 0.04 in/1 mm in thickness. In 6.6(a)(ii), the repair material shall not extend along the length of the blade more than 0.79 in/2 cm in each direction beyond the limits of the damaged area. Where used as a continuous binding, any overlapping shall not breach the maximum of 0.04 in/1 mm in total thickness.

In 6.6(d), the use of non-solid material which when dry forms a hard layer more than 0.004 in/0.1 mm in thickness is not permitted.

Toe and side inserts The wood used must not be more than 0.3 in/0.89 cm in thickness.

The toe insert shall not extend from the toe more than 2.5 in/6.35 cm up the blade at any point.

Neither side insert may extend from the edge more than 1 in/2.54 cm across the blade at any point.

Toe protection The maximum permitted thickness of protective material placed on the toe of the blade is 0.12 in/3mm.

Commercial identifications These identifications must not exceed 0.008 in/0.2 mm in thickness. On the back of the blade they must cover no more than 50% of the surface. On the face of the blade, they must be confined within the top 9 in/22.86 cm, measured from the bottom of the grip.

REGULATIONS OF THE INTERNATIONAL CRICKET COUNCIL

Extracts

1. Standard playing conditions

The following playing conditions were in force from October 1, 2009:

Duration of Test Matches

Test matches shall be of five days' scheduled duration and of two innings per side. The two participating countries may:

(a) Provide for a rest day during the match, and/or a reserve day after the scheduled days of play.

(b) Play on any scheduled rest day, conditions and circumstances permitting, should a full day's play be lost on any day prior to the rest day.

(c) Play on any scheduled reserve day, conditions and circumstances permitting, should a full day's play not take place on more than five days.

(d) Make up time lost in excess of five minutes in each day's play due to circumstances outside the game, other than acts of God.

Hours of Play and Minimum Overs in the Day in Test Matches

A. Start and Cessation Times: The home board shall determine the hours of play, subject to there being six hours' scheduled playing time per day (Pakistan, a minimum of five hours).

1. Minimum Overs in the Day:

(a) On days other than the last day, play shall continue on each day until the completion of a minimum target of 90 overs (or 15 overs per hour) or the completion of the scheduled or rescheduled cessation time, whichever is the later, provided that play shall not continue for more than 30 minutes beyond the scheduled or rescheduled cessation time (permitted overtime). For the sake of clarity, if any of the minimum target number of overs have not been bowled at the completion of the permitted overtime, play shall cease upon completion of the over in progress. The overs not bowled shall not be made up on any subsequent day.

(b) On the last day, a minimum of 75 overs (or 15 overs per hour) shall be bowled during the playing time other than the last hour of the match where a minimum of 15 overs shall be bowled. All calculations with regard to suspensions of play or the start of a new innings shall be based on one over for each full four minutes. On the final day, if both captains (the batsmen at the wicket may act for their captain) accept that there is no prospect of either side achieving a victory, they may agree to finish the match after the start of the last hour or when a minimum of 15 overs remain to be bowled, whichever is the later. If any of the minimum of 75 overs (or as recalculated) have not been bowled when one hour's scheduled playing time remains, the last hour of the match shall be regarded as the hour immediately following the completion of these overs.

2. Reduction in minimum overs: except in the last hour of the match, if play is suspended due to adverse weather or light or any other reason (other than normal intervals) for more than one hour on any day, the minimum number of overs shall be reduced by one over for each full four minutes of the aggregate playing time lost. For the avoidance of doubt, the aggregate of one hour shall be inclusive of any time that may have been brought forward from previous days due to playing time lost on such previous days under clause 3(b) below.

3. Making up lost time:

(a) On the day: subject to weather and light, except in the last hour of the match, in the event of play being suspended for any reason other than normal intervals, the playing time on that day shall be extended by the amount of time lost up to a maximum of one hour. For the avoidance of doubt, the maximum of one hour shall be inclusive of any time that may have been added to the scheduled playing time due to playing time having been lost on previous days under clause 3(b) below.

(b) On subsequent days: if any time is lost and cannot be made up under clause 3(a) above, additional time of up to a maximum of 30 minutes per day shall be added to the scheduled playing hours for the next day, and subsequent day(s) as required (to make up as much lost time as possible). Where appropriate this additional time shall be added prior to the scheduled start of the first session. In circumstances where this is not possible, the additional time may be added to the second and/or the third sessions. When such time is added, the minimum overs for that day shall be increased by one over for each four minutes of additional time or part thereof.

(c) On the last day only: Clause 3(a) applies, but the definition of playing time shall be the time up to the most recently scheduled time for the start of the last hour. Should an interruption in play commence prior to the most recently scheduled time for the last hour and continue past this time:

    (i) Only the playing time lost prior to this last-hour start time will be made up (subject to the maximum of one hour described in (a) above), with the start time for the last hour rescheduled accordingly.

    (ii) The period between the scheduled last-hour start time at the start of the interruption and the time of the resumption of play will not be made up. The minimum number of overs to be bowled prior to the last hour at the start of the interruption will be reduced by one for each full four minutes of aggregate time lost.

    (iii) The start time for the last hour will thus be the later of the rescheduled time (as defined at the end of (i) above) and the time at which the minimum overs prior to the last hour have been completed, or reduced to zero by the formula in (ii) above.

    (iv) No time is made up in respect of any interruptions that commence after the start of the last hour.

B. Extra Time: The umpires may decide to play 30 minutes (a minimum of eight overs) extra time at the end of any day (other than the last day) if requested by either captain if, in the umpires' opinion, it would bring about a definite result on that day. If the umpires do not believe a result can be achieved no extra time shall be allowed. If it is decided to play such extra time, the whole period shall be played out even though the possibility of finishing the match may have disappeared before the full period has expired. Only the actual amount of playing time up to the maximum 30 minutes' extra time by which play is extended on any day shall be deducted from the total number of hours of play remaining, and the match shall end earlier on the final day by that amount of time.

Use of Artificial Lights:

If, in the opinion of the umpires, natural light is deteriorating to an unfit level, they shall authorise the ground authorities to use the available artificial lighting so that the match can continue in acceptable conditions.

    The lights are only to be used to enable a full day's play to be completed as provided for in Clause A above. In the event of power failure or lights malfunction, the existing provisions of Clause A shall apply.

Dangerous and Unfair Bowling: The Bowling of Fast, Short-Pitched Balls: Law 42.6(a)

1   (a) A bowler shall be limited to two fast, short-pitched deliveries per over.

    (b) A fast, short-pitched delivery is defined as a ball which passes or would have passed above the shoulder height of the striker standing upright at the crease.

    (c) The umpire at the bowler's end shall advise the bowler and the batsman on strike when each fast, short-pitched ball has been bowled.

    (d) For the purpose of this regulation, a ball that passes above head height of the batsman that prevents him from being able to hit it with his bat by means of a normal cricket stroke shall be called a wide.

    (e) Any fast, short-pitched delivery called a wide under this condition shall count as one of the allowable short-pitched deliveries in that over.

    (f) In the event of a bowler bowling more than two fast, short-pitched deliveries in an over, the umpire at the bowler's end shall call and signal "no-ball" on each occasion. The umpire shall call and signal "no-ball" and then tap the head with the other hand.

    (g) If a bowler delivers a third fast, short-pitched ball in an over, the umpire must call no-ball and then invoke the procedures of caution, final warning, action against the bowler and reporting as set out in Law 42.7. The umpires will report the matter to the ICC referee who shall take such action as is considered appropriate against the captain and bowler concerned.

The above Regulation is not a substitute for Law 42.6 (as amended below), which umpires are able to apply at any time:

The bowling of fast, short-pitched balls is unfair if the umpire at the bowler's end considers that, by their repetition and taking into account their length, height and direction, they are likely to inflict physical injury on the striker, irrespective of the protective clothing and equipment he may be wearing. The relative skill of the striker shall also be taken into consideration.

The umpire at the bowler's end shall adopt the procedures of caution, final warning, action against the bowler and reporting as set out in Law 42.7. The ICC referee shall take any further action considered appropriate against the captain and bowler concerned.

New Ball: Law 5.4

The captain of the fielding side shall have the choice of taking a new ball at any time after 80 overs have been bowled with the previous ball. The umpires shall indicate to the batsmen and the scorers whenever a new ball is taken into play.

Ball Lost or Becoming Unfit for Play: Law 5.5

The following shall apply in addition to Law 5.5

However, if the ball needs to be replaced after 110 overs for any of the reasons above, it shall be replaced by a new ball. If the ball is to be replaced, the umpires shall inform the batsmen.

Judging a Wide: Law 25.1

Law 25.1 will apply, but in addition

For bowlers attempting to utilise the rough outside a batsman's leg stump, not necessarily as a negative tactic, and for bowlers whom umpires consider to be bowling down the leg side as a negative tactic, the strict limited-overs wide interpretation shall be applied.

Practice on the Field: Law 17

In addition to Law 17.1:

The use of the square for practice on any day of any match will be restricted to any netted practice area or bowling strips specifically prepared on the edge of the square for that purpose.

Bowling practice on such strips shall also be permitted during the interval or change of innings unless the umpires consider that it will be detrimental to the surface of the square.

Fielder Absent or Leaving the Field: Law 2.5

If a fielder fails to take the field with his side at the start of the match or at any later time, or leaves the field during a session of play, the umpire shall be informed of the reason for his absence, and he shall not thereafter come on to the field during a session without the consent of the umpire. The umpire shall give such consent as soon as practicable. If the player is absent from the field longer than eight minutes, he shall not be permitted to bowl in that innings after his return until he has been on the field for at least that length of playing time for which he was absent. This restriction will, if necessary, be carried over into a new day's play, and in the event of a follow-on or a forfeiture, it will continue into the second innings. Nor shall he be permitted to bat unless or until, in the aggregate, he has returned to the field and/or his side's innings has been in progress for at least that length of playing time for which he has been absent or, if earlier, when his side has lost five wickets. The restrictions shall not apply if he has suffered an external blow (as opposed to an internal injury such as a pulled muscle) while participating earlier in the match and consequently been forced to leave the field, nor if he has been absent for very exceptional and wholly acceptable reasons (other than injury or illness).

2. Classification of Official Cricket

A. Test matches

Test matches are those which:

(a) are played in accordance with the ICC standard Test match playing conditions and other ICC regulations pertaining to Test matches; and

(b) are between

(i) teams selected by Full Members of the ICC as representative of the member countries (Full Member teams).

(ii) a Full Member team and a composite team selected by the ICC as representative of the best players from the rest of the world.

B. One-day internationals

One-day international matches are those which:

(a) are played in accordance with the ICC standard one-day international playing conditions and other ICC regulations pertaining to one-day internationals; and

(b) are between

(i) any teams participating in and as part of the World Cup or Champions Trophy.

(ii) Full Member teams.

(iii) a Full Member team and any of the top six Associate/Affiliates.

(iv) any of the top six Associate/Affiliates.

(v) a Full Member team (or top six Associate/Affiliate) and a composite team selected by the ICC as representative of the best players from the rest of the world.

Note: The identity of the top six Associate/Affiliate teams will be determined through the ICC World Cup Qualifier tournament. The ICC will determine the precise point during the tournament at which the new top six shall take effect.

C. Twenty20 international matches

Twenty20 international matches are those which:

(a) are played in accordance with the ICC standard Twenty20 international playing conditions and other ICC regulations pertaining to Twenty20 matches; and

(b) are between

(i) any teams participating in and as part of the ICC World Twenty20 Championship.

(ii) Full Member teams.

(iii) a Full Member team and any of the Associate/Affiliate Member teams whose matches have been granted one-day international status (i.e. the top six Associates/ Affiliates).

(iv) any of the top six Associates/Affiliates.

D. Other Official Internationals

Any one-day match between Associate/Affiliate international teams other than those already classified as one-day internationals.

E. First-class matches

First-class matches are those matches of three or more days' duration between two sides of 11 players played on natural turf pitches and substantially conforming to ICC standard playing conditions.

Full Members may, if they wish, introduce playing regulations allowing the 11 playing members of a side to be changed after the start of a match without the match forgoing its first-class status, provided any such changes relate solely to a player's call-up to or release from international duty. However, no playing members of a side in a first-class match may be replaced for reasons of tactics or injury.

(a) The status of all matches in an official ICC competition shall be decided by the ICC. For matches outside official ICC competitions (b) and (c) shall apply.

(b) Full Members of the ICC shall decide the status of matches of three or more days' duration played in their countries.

(c) in matches of three or more days' duration played in countries which are not Full Members of the ICC

    (i) if only one team comes from a Full Member country or both teams come from the same Full Member country then that country shall decide the status; otherwise

    (ii) if both teams come from different Full Member countries then the status shall be decided by agreement between those countries if possible; otherwise

    (iii) the ICC shall decide.

Notes: Governing bodies agree that the interest of first-class cricket will be served by ensuring that first-class status is not accorded to any match in which one or other of the teams taking part cannot on a strict interpretation of the definitions be adjudged first-class.

Decisions regarding awarding a match first-class status should whenever possible be taken prior to its commencement, failing which as soon as possible thereafter. Where a decision regarding first-class status has already been made, including in respect of all matches played prior to these classifications taking effect, any subsequent reversal of a decision (i.e. to upgrade a match to first-class status or downgrade it from first-class status) shall be permitted only in exceptional circumstances, and then only with the approval of the ICC.

First-Class Status

The following matches of three or more days' duration shall be regarded as first-class, subject to the provisions of the first-class match definition being complied with. The list below is not exhaustive and is merely indicative of the matches which would fall into the first-class definition.

    (a) Test matches.

    (b) ICC Intercontinental Cup matches.

    (c) Matches played by A-teams of Full Member countries against teams and judged first-class (including other A-teams).

    (d) **In all Full Member Countries:** Matches against teams adjudged first-class played by official touring teams.

    (e) **In England and Wales:** (i) County Championship matches between counties; (ii) MCC v any first-class county; (iii) Oxford University v Cambridge University; (iv) Cambridge, Durham, Loughborough and Oxford UCCEs v any first-class county.

    (f) **In Australia:** Sheffield Shield matches between states.

    (g) **In South Africa:** (i) SuperSport Series matches between franchises; (ii) Provincial three-day competition matches between provinces.

    (h) **In West Indies:** Regional four-day competition matches between countries and Combined Campuses & Colleges.

    (i) **In New Zealand:** State Championship/Plunket Shield matches between provinces.

    (j) **In India:** (i) Ranji Trophy matches between states; (ii) Duleep Trophy matches between zones; (iii) Irani Trophy match (winner of previous Ranji Trophy against Rest of India).

    (k) **In Pakistan:** (i) Quaid-e-Azam Trophy (Grade I) matches between regions and departments; (ii) Pentangular Cup matches between leading teams from the other first-class tournaments.

    (l) **In Sri Lanka:** (i) Premier League Division I matches between clubs; (ii) Interprovincial Tournament matches between provinces.

    (m) **In Zimbabwe:** Logan Cup matches between areas.

    (n) **In Bangladesh:** National Cricket League matches between divisions.

F. List A limited-overs matches

Any one-day international or limited-overs match scheduled for one day's duration and of one innings of a minimum 40 overs per side, played at least at state, county or provincial level in a Full Member country or as an official match of a touring Test team against at least state, county or provincial level teams and accorded List A limited-overs status by the relevant governing bodies. A match will still be regarded as List A limited-overs even if reduced by bad weather or for other reasons to fewer than 40 overs per side.

G. List A Twenty20 matches

Any Twenty20 international or limited-overs match scheduled for one day's duration and of one innings with a limit of 20 overs per side played at least at state, county or provincial level in a Full Member country or as an official match of a touring Test team against at least state, county or provincial level teams and accorded List A Twenty20 status by the relevant governing bodies.

Rules: The rules on who should decide the status of matches of one day's duration are the same as those for first-class matches (above).

Note: List A matches should be those one-day matches played at the highest domestic level. Matches that are primarily arranged as festival, friendly or practice matches and outside of any competitive structure should not qualify as List A matches.

H. Other matches

Other cricket played under the auspices of a Member country may be classified by such Member country as Official Cricket, including but not limited to:

(a) matches between the A-teams, National Academy or age-group teams of member countries.

(b) all other matches played as part of a competition or tournament held under the auspices of a member including club cricket, schools, age groups and university cricket.

Notes: Matches involving an A-team or age-group team shall not be classified as Test matches, one-day internationals or Twenty20 internationals. Matches involving age-group teams up to and including Under-19 shall not be classified as first-class cricket.

In case of any disputes arising from these Rules, failing unanimous agreement being reached between the disputing parties, the chief executive of the ICC shall refer the matter to the ICC disputes resolution committee for its final and binding determination.

3. Player eligibility qualification criteria

A. Core Nationality Criteria

To be eligible to represent an ICC Member at Under-19 level or above, a player must meet at least one of the following core nationality criteria:

(a) A national of the country (as defined by the country).

(b) Born in the country.

(c) Resident in the country for at least 183 days in each of the immediately preceding seven years

(d) Resident in the country for at least 183 days in each of the immediately preceding four years (some restrictions for Associates and Affiliates detailed below).

B. Restrictions

(a) The player must not have represented another ICC Member at Under-19 level or above in an ICC-sanctioned match in the immediately preceding four years.

(b) For Associate and Affiliate Members, a player must also meet at least one of the following development criteria:

(i) he shall have played 50% of games in the country's national/domestic competition in any three of the five preceding years.

(ii) he shall have spent a cumulative total of 100 days over the preceding five years doing cricket work in the country.

(iii) he shall have represented that country at Under-19 level or above in the past, either under previous ICC rules (prior to 2006) or where the current ICC development criteria had applied.

(iv) he shall have done enough to convince the chairman of the ICC cricket committee that he has genuine commitment to the development of cricket in that country.

(c) Associate and Affiliate Members are limited to a maximum of two players in any team who qualify under A(d).

(d) Associates and Affiliates are limited to a maximum of two players in any team who have formerly represented a Full Member at Under-19 level or above.

C. Notes

(a) The restriction at B(a) does not apply for a player progressing from representing an Associate or Affiliate Member to representing a Full Member.

(b) For Associate and Affiliate members, when playing a Full Member or in a tournament involving Full Member(s), or when playing any one-day international, or when playing in the ICC World Cup Qualifier, the restrictions B(b), (c) and (d) do not apply.

(c) Upon application, the chairman of the ICC cricket committee may grant a player who is ineligible under these rules the ability to play due to exceptional circumstances.

(d) Countries may enforce stricter eligibility rules for their own selection processes.

ICC CODES OF CONDUCT

The ICC Code of Conduct, first introduced in 1991, was divided into three Codes in 2009. These are the Code of Conduct, the Anti-Corruption Code, and the Anti-Racism Code. There is also an Anti-Doping Code. Full details of their scope and application, offences under the Codes, disciplinary procedures, sanctions and appeals may be found on the ICC website at http://icc-cricket.yahoo.net/rules_and_regulations.php.

CRIME AND PUNISHMENT

ICC Code of Conduct – Breaches and Penalties in 2008-09 to 2009-10

M. S. Panesar   England v West Indies, Fifth Test at Port-of-Spain
Celebrated prospective dismissals before umpire's verdict. Fined 25% of match fee by A. G. Hurst.

A. Khan   England v West Indies, Fifth Test at Port-of-Spain
Celebrated prospective dismissal before umpire gave verdict. Severely reprimanded by A. G. Hurst.

Younis Khan   Pakistan v Australia, Second One-Day International at Dubai.
Failed to ensure his team met minimum over-rate. Fined 50% of match fee by J. J. Crowe.

S. R. Watson   Australia v Pakistan, Twenty20 International at Dubai.
Dissent at umpire's decision when given out. Fined 25% of match fee by J. J. Crowe.

B. J. Haddin   Australia v Pakistan, Twenty20 International at Dubai.
Dissent at umpire's decision when team-mate given out. Fined 15% of match fee by J. J. Crowe.

Shakib Al Hasan   Bangladesh v West Indies, First Test at St Vincent.
Excessive appealing. Fined 10% of match fee by A. J. Pycroft.

Shahadat Hossain   Bangladesh v West Indies, First Test at St Vincent.
Excessive appealing. Fined 5% of match fee by A. J. Pycroft.

Imrul Kayes   Bangladesh v West Indies, First Test at St Vincent.
Excessive appealing. Reprimanded by A. J. Pycroft.

Danish Kaneria   Pakistan v Sri Lanka, Third Test at Colombo (SSC).
Abusive language after taking wicket. Reprimanded by A. G. Hurst.

K. A. J. Roach   West Indies v Bangladesh, Second One-Day International at Roseau.
Bowled two high full-pitched balls. Fined 10% of match fee by R. S. Mahanama.

F. L. Reifer   West Indies v Bangladesh, Second One-Day International at Roseau.
Failed to ensure Roach did not not repeat high full-pitched ball. Reprimanded by R. S. Mahanama.

Saeed Ajmal   Pakistan v Sri Lanka, Twenty20 International at Colombo (RPS).
Aggressive gesture on dismissal of batsman. Fined 15% of match fee by A. G. Hurst.

N. T. Paranavitana   Sri Lanka v New Zealand, Second Test at Colombo (SSC).
Claimed and celebrated "catch" while umpires conferred. Fined 50% of match fee by A. J. Pycroft.

J. D. Ryder   New Zealand v Sri Lanka, One-Day International at Johannesburg.
Broke chair with bat after dismissal. Fined 15% of match fee by J. Srinath.

A. Obanda   Kenya v Zimbabwe, Fourth One-Day International at Harare.
Dissent at umpire's decision when given out. Fined 15% of match fee by A. G. Hurst.

Dolar Mahmud   Bangladesh v Zimbabwe, Second One-Day International at Mirpur.
Bowled two high full-pitched balls. Fined 15% of match fee by R. S. Madugalle.

K. D. Mills   New Zealand v Pakistan, Third One-Day International at Abu Dhabi.
Excessive appealing and obscene language. Fined 20% (10% for each) of match fee by A. J. Pycroft.

D. E. Bollinger   Australia v West Indies, Second Test at Adelaide.
Dissent at umpire's decision to reject appeal. Reprimanded by B. C. Broad.

S. J. Benn   West Indies v Australia, Third Test at Perth.
Altercation with opponents after collision. Banned for two one-day internationals by B. C. Broad.

B. J. Haddin   Australia v West Indies, Third Test at Perth.
Altercation with opponent. Fined 25% of match fee by B. C. Broad.

M. G. Johnson   Australia v West Indies, Third Test at Perth.
Altercation with opponent after collision. Fined 10% of match fee by B. C. Broad.

S. R. Watson   Australia v West Indies, Third Test at Perth.
Aggressive celebration of batsman's dismissal. Fined 15% of match fee by B. C. Broad.

M. S. Dhoni   India v Sri Lanka, Second One-Day International at Nagpur.
Failed to ensure team met minimum over-rate. Banned for two one-day internationals by J. J. Crowe.

Shahid Afridi   Pakistan v Australia, Fifth One-Day International at Perth.
Changing the condition of the ball – by biting it. Banned for two T20 internationals by R. S. Madugalle.

Note: Details of these and six further breaches which took place in Associate Member matches may be found at http://icc-cricket.yahoo.net/breaches-and-penalties.php?year=2009 and http://icc-cricket.yahoo.net/breaches-and-penalties.php?year=2010.

INTERNATIONAL UMPIRES' PANELS

In 1993, the International Cricket Council formed an international umpires' panel, containing at least two officials from each Full Member. A third-country umpire from this panel stood with a "home" umpire, not necessarily from the panel, in every Test from February 1994 onwards. In March 2002, an elite panel of umpires was appointed; two elite umpires were to stand in all Tests from April 2002, and at least one in every one-day international. A supporting panel of international umpires was created to provide cover at peak times in the Test schedule, and to provide a second umpire in one-day internationals. The ICC also appointed specialist third umpires to give rulings from TV replays. The panels are sponsored by Emirates Airlines.

At the end of 2009, the following umpires were on the elite panel: Aleem Dar (Pakistan), Asad Rauf (Pakistan), M. R. Benson (England), B. F. Bowden (New Zealand), S. J. Davis (Australia), E. A. R. de Silva (Sri Lanka), B. R. Doctrove (West Indies), I. J. Gould (England), D. J. Harper (Australia), A. L. Hill (New Zealand), R. E. Koertzen (South Africa) and S. J. A. Taufel (Australia). (*M. R. Benson stepped down in February 2010.*)

The international panel consisted of K. C. Barbour (Zimbabwe), G. A. V. Baxter (New Zealand), H. D. P. K. Dharmasena (Sri Lanka), C. R. Duncan (West Indies), Enamul Haque (Bangladesh), M. Erasmus (South Africa), C. B. Gaffaney (New Zealand), B. G. Jerling (South Africa), R. A. Kettleborough (England), N. J. Llong (England), N. A. Malcolm (West Indies), Nadeem Ghauri (Pakistan), Nadir Shah (Bangladesh), B. N. J. Oxenford (Australia), A. M. Saheba (India), S. K. Tarapore (India), R. B. Tiffin (Zimbabwe), R. J. Tucker (Australia), T. H. Wijewardene (Sri Lanka) and Zamir Haider (Pakistan).

The specialist third umpires were Ahsan Raza (Pakistan), O. Chirombe (Zimbabwe), J. D. Cloete (South Africa), G. E. Greaves (West Indies), S. S. Hazare (India), R. K. Illingworth (England), C. E. Mack (West Indies), R. Martinesz (Sri Lanka), P. R. Reiffel (Australia), Sharfuddoula (Bangladesh) and E. A. Watkin (New Zealand).

There is also an Associate and Affiliate international panel, consisting of N. G. Bagh (Denmark), P. K. Baldwin (Germany), K. Bayney (Canada), R. Dill (Bermuda), J. J. Luck (Namibia), S. R. Modi (Kenya), B. B. Pradhan (Nepal), S. S. Prasad (Singapore), I. N. Ramage (Scotland) and Shahul Hameed (Indonesia).

ICC REFEREES' PANEL

In 1991, the International Cricket Council formed a panel of referees to enforce their Code of Conduct for Tests and one-day internationals, to impose penalties for slow over-rates, breaches of the Code and other ICC regulations, and to support the umpires in upholding the conduct of the game. In March 2002, the ICC launched an elite panel of referees, on two-year full-time contracts, to act as their independent representatives in all international cricket. A supplementary panel, created to provide cover during busy periods, was dropped in April 2004 when the elite panel was expanded.

At the end of 2009, the panel consisted of B. C. Broad (England), J. J. Crowe (New Zealand), A. G. Hurst (Australia), R. S. Madugalle (Sri Lanka), R. S. Mahanama (Sri Lanka), A. J. Pycroft (Zimbabwe) and J. Srinath (India). The panel is sponsored by Emirates Airlines.

REGULATIONS FOR FIRST-CLASS MATCHES IN BRITAIN, 2009

Hours of play

Championship, tourist matches and MCC v Champions, all days. . . . . 11.00 a.m. to 6.00 p.m.
Other matches, 1st, 2nd [and 3rd in 4-day matches] days. . . . . 11.00 a.m. to 6.30 p.m.
Other matches, Final day. . . . . 11.00 a.m. to 6.00 p.m.

Intervals

Lunch: (Championship and Tourist matches) 1.00 p.m. to 1.40 p.m.
(Other Matches) 1.15 p.m. to 1.55 p.m. (1st, 2nd [3rd] days); 1.00 p.m. to 1.40 p.m. (final day)

Tea: (Championship matches) A tea interval of 20 minutes shall normally be taken at 3.40 p.m., or at the conclusion of the over in progress at that time, provided 32 overs or less remain to be bowled (except on the final day). The over in progress shall be completed unless a batsman is out or retires either within two minutes of, or after, the scheduled time for the interval. In the event of more than 32 overs remaining, the tea interval will be delayed.
　　If an innings ends or there is a stoppage caused by weather or light, or the players have cause to leave the field, within 30 minutes of the scheduled time, the tea interval shall be taken immediately.

(Tourist matches) 3.40 p.m. to 4.00 p.m.

(Other matches) 4.10 p.m. to 4.30 p.m. (1st, 2nd [3rd] days), 3.40 p.m. to 4.00 p.m. (final day).

Note: The hours of play, including intervals, are brought forward by half an hour for matches scheduled to start in September.

Minimum Overs in the Day – Championship matches

(i) Play shall continue on each day until the completion of a minimum number of overs or until the scheduled cessation time, whichever is the later. The minimum number of overs, unless an innings ends or an interruption occurs, shall be 96 on days other than the last day, and 80 on the last day before the last hour. Subject to weather and light, in the event of playing time being lost on the first three days, the scheduled close of play on that day shall be delayed by the amount of time lost up to a maximum of 30 minutes.

(ii) Where there is a change of innings during a day's play (except during an interval or suspension of play or exceptional circumstances or during the last hour), two overs will be deducted from the minimum number, plus any over in progress at the end of the completed innings.

(iii) If interruptions for ground, weather or light conditions occur, other than in the last hour of the match, the minimum number of overs shall be reduced by one over for each full $3^3/_4$ minutes of the aggregate playing time lost.

(iv) On the last day, if any of the minimum of 80 overs, or as recalculated, have not been bowled when one hour of scheduled playing time remains, the last hour of the match shall be the hour immediately following the completion of those overs.

(v) Law 16.6, 16.7 and 16.8 will apply except that a minimum of 16 overs shall be bowled in the last hour, and all calculations with regard to suspensions of play or the start of a new innings shall be based on one over for each full $3^3/_4$ minutes. If, however, both captains accept that there is no prospect of either side achieving victory, they may agree to finish the match after the time for the start of the last hour has been reached.

(vi) The captains may agree or, in the event of disagreement, the umpires may decide to play 30 minutes (a minimum eight overs) extra time at the end of any day other than the last day if, in their opinion, there is a reasonable prospect that it would bring about a definite result on that day. The whole period shall be played out even though the possibility of finishing the match may have disappeared before the full period has expired. The time by which play is extended on any day shall be deducted from the total number of hours remaining, and the match shall end earlier on the last day by the amount of time by which play was extended. If there is a change of innings immediately prior to the start of, or during the period of extra time, then two overs shall be deducted.

(vii) Notwithstanding any other provision, there shall be no further play on any day, other than the last day, if a wicket falls or a batsman retires, or if the players leave the field during the last minimum over within two minutes of the scheduled or rescheduled cessation time or thereafter.

(viii) An over completed on resumption of a new day's play shall be disregarded in calculating minimum overs for that day.

(ix) The scoreboard shall show the number of overs up to 120 in each side's first innings and subsequently the number bowled with the current ball, and the minimum remaining to be bowled. In addition it shall indicate the number of overs that the fielding side is ahead of or behind the over-rate.

Substitutes

(Domestic matches only) Law 2.1 will apply, but in addition:

No substitute may take the field until the player for whom he is to substitute has been absent from the field for two consecutive complete overs, with the exception that if a fieldsman sustains an obvious, serious injury or is obviously taken ill, a substitute shall be allowed immediately. A substitute shall be allowed immediately for all head or blood injuries. Substitutes shall be allowed at the sole discretion of the umpires.

The umpires shall have discretion, for other wholly acceptable reasons, to allow a substitute for a fielder, or a runner for a batsman, at the start of the match or at any subsequent time.

A substitute shall not be allowed to bat or bowl, or to act as captain. The opposing captain shall have no right of objection to any player acting as substitute, or to where the substitute shall field, with the exception of the position of wicketkeeper. However, with the agreement of both captains (not to be unreasonably withheld), any substitute may act as wicketkeeper. In the event of the captains' disagreement, the substitute shall not be allowed to act as wicketkeeper.

A replacement player shall be allowed by right immediately in the event of a cricketer currently playing in a Championship match being required to join the England team for a Test match or one-day international (either through a call-up after the start of the Championship match or through being placed on official stand-by beforehand). Such a replacement player may be permitted to bat or bowl in that match, subject to the approval of the ECB. If the cricketer is batting when he is required to leave, he shall retire "not out" and his replacement player may be permitted to bat later in that innings subject to the approval of the ECB. If the cricketer is subsequently not required by England then, subject to the approval of the ECB, he may return and resume a full part in the match, taking over from the player that replaced him. If the replacement player is batting, he shall complete his innings and the cricketer shall take over thereafter. If the replacement player is bowling when the cricketer is ready to take the field, the replacement player shall complete any unfinished over and the cricketer shall take the field thereafter.

If a player is released by England prior to the teams being named in his county match, his county may have a fielding-only substitute until the cricketer is able to join the match. If a player is released by England after the county teams have been named and before the scheduled start of the third scheduled day, then he may return to that match and take the place of a nominated player, who may or may not have already participated. Each county that has representation in the England squad must, if it wishes that a specified England player shall participate in a county match if released, specify which player will be replaced. This shall be done at the nomination of the teams to the umpires.

If the England player is released, then he must make all reasonable efforts to take his place in the county side at the earliest opportunity. Unless special dispensation is given by the ECB, no replacement will be allowed if the England player is released after the scheduled start of the third scheduled day. There is no option for the county to refuse the England player if they have nominated a player to be replaced.

If the nominated player is batting, he shall complete his innings and the England player shall take over thereafter. If the nominated player is bowling when the England player is ready to take the field, then the nominated player shall complete any unfinished over, and the England player shall take the field thereafter.

Fieldsman leaving the field

ICC regulations apply (see page 1553) but, in domestic matches, it is explained that "external blow" should include, but not be restricted to, collisions with boundary boards, clashes of heads, heavy falls etc.

New ball

The captain of the fielding side shall have the choice of taking the new ball after 80 overs have been bowled with the old one.

Covering of pitches and surrounding areas

The whole pitch shall be covered:

(a) The night before the match and, if necessary, until the first ball is bowled; and whenever necessary and possible at any time prior to that during the preparation of the pitch.

(b) On each night of the match and, if necessary, throughout any rest days.

(c) In the event of play being suspended on account of bad light or rain, during the specified hours of play, and at lunch, tea and between innings on account of rain.

The bowler's run-up shall be covered to a distance of at least ten yards, with a width of four yards, as will the areas 20 feet either side of the length of the pitch.

UMPIRES FOR 2010

FIRST-CLASS UMPIRES

R. J. Bailey, N. L. Bainton, M. R. Benson, M. J. D. Bodenham, N. G. B. Cook, N. G. Cowley, B. Dudleston, J. H. Evans, S. A. Garratt, M. A. Gough, I. J. Gould, P. J. Hartley, V. A. Holder, R. K. Illingworth, T. E. Jesty, R. A. Kettleborough, N. J. Llong, J. W. Lloyds, N. A. Mallender, D. J. Millns, R. T. Robinson, G. Sharp, J. F. Steele, P. Willey. *Reserves:* P. K. Baldwin, K. T. Coburn, I. Dawood, M. A. Eggleston, S. C. Gale, A. Hicks, G. D. Lloyd, S. J. Malone, M. J. Saggers, S. J. O'Shaughnessy.

MINOR COUNTIES UMPIRES

P. K. Baldwin, S. F. Bishopp, M. L. Brown, A. Bullock, D. L. Burden, A. Clark, K. T. Coburn, T. Cox, A. Davies, B. J. Debenham, M. Dixon, A. D'Leny, M. Dobbs, R. G. Eagleton, M. A. Eggleston, L. E. Elgar, H. Evans, R. Evans, S. C. Gale, A. Hicks, M. J. Izzard, J. H. James, D. Johnson, R. N. Johnson, P. W. Joy, J. C. Lofthouse, S. J. Malone, S. Z. Marszal, P. W. Matten, M. J. Miller, S. Nelson, G. Parker, C. T. Puckett, J. G. Reed, B. W. Reidy, I. Royle, P. A. Sadler, R. M. Sutton, R. W. Tolchard, B. S. Toombs, J. M. Tythcott, T. J. Urben, S. Waterhouse, C. Watts, M. C. White, J. Wilkinson.

THE DUCKWORTH/LEWIS METHOD

In 1997, the ECB's one-day competitions adopted a new method to revise targets in interrupted games, devised by Frank Duckworth of the Royal Statistical Society and Tony Lewis of the University of the West of England. The method was gradually taken up by other countries and, in 1999, the ICC decided to incorporate it into the standard playing conditions for one-day internationals.

The system aims to preserve any advantage that one team has established before the interruption. It uses the idea that teams have two resources from which they make runs – an allocated number of overs, and ten wickets. It also takes into account when the interruption occurs, because of the different scoring-rates typical of different stages of an innings. Traditional run-rate calculations relied only on the overs available, and ignored wickets lost.

After modifications, the system now uses one table with 50 rows, covering matches of any length up to 50 overs, and ten columns, from nought to nine wickets down. Each figure in the table gives the percentage of the total runs in an innings that would, on average, be scored with a certain number of overs left and wickets lost. If a match is shortened before it begins, for instance to 33 overs a side, the figure for 33 overs and ten wickets remaining would be the starting point. The same table is used for Twenty20 cricket, starting with the row for 20 overs remaining.

If overs are lost, the table is used to calculate the expected number of runs the team would be expected to score in those missing overs. This is obtained by reading off the figure for the number of overs left and wickets down when play stops and subtracting from it the corresponding figure for the number of overs remaining when it resumes. If the suspension of play occurs between innings, and the second team's allocation of overs is reduced, then their target is obtained by calculating the appropriate percentage for the reduced number of overs with all ten wickets standing. For instance, if the second team's innings halves from 50 overs to 25, the table shows that they still have 66.5% of their resources, so have to beat two-thirds of the first team's total, rather than half.

If the first innings is complete and the second innings is interrupted or prematurely terminated, the score to be beaten is reduced by the percentage of the innings lost. In the World Cup match between South Africa and Sri Lanka at Durban on March 3, 2003, South Africa's run-chase was ended by rain after 45 overs, when they were 229 for six. The Duckworth/Lewis tables showed that, with five overs left and four wickets standing, South Africa had used 85.7% of their run-scoring resources, and 14.3% remained unused. Multiplying Sri Lanka's 50-over total, 268, by 85.7% produced a figure of 229.67. This was rounded down to 229 to give the par score (the runs needed to tie), and the target to win became par plus one – 230 in 45 overs. Under old-fashioned average run-rate per over, the target would have been 242; South Africa benefited because they had preserved wickets into the final stages. (If they had lost one more wicket, par would have been 233; one fewer, 226.)

The system also covers interruptions to the first innings, multiple interruptions and innings terminated by rain. The tables were revised slightly in 2002, taking account of rising scoring-rates; the average 50-over total in a one-day international is now taken to be 235, rather than 225.

The version known as the "Professional Edition" was introduced into one-day internationals from October 1, 2003, and subsequently into several national one-day competitions. Based on a more advanced mathematical formula (it is entirely computerised), in effect it adjusts the tables to make allowance for the different scoring-rates that emerge in matches with above-average first-innings scores. The former version, now known as "Standard Edition", has been retained for use where computers are not available and at lower levels of the game.

POWERPLAYS

In the first ten "powerplay" overs of an uninterrupted one-day international innings (first six overs in a Twenty20 international), only two fieldsmen may be positioned outside the area marked by two semi-circles of 30-yard (27.43 metres) radius behind each set of stumps, joined by straight lines parallel to the pitch. In one-day internationals, there must also be two "close" (and stationary) fielders in this initial period.

After the first mandatory ten-over powerplay in an uninterrupted one-day international, two further blocks of five overs each must be claimed by the respective captains (or the batsmen at the crease in the case of the batting side). During these overs, a maximum of three players may be stationed outside the 30-yard area. If either team chooses not to take the powerplay available to them, the umpires will enforce it at the latest available point in the innings (so, in an uninterrupted innings, an unclaimed powerplay would begin at the start of the 46th over). At all other times no more than five fieldsmen are permitted outside the 30-yard area. In matches affected by the weather, the number of overs in each powerplay is reduced in proportion to the overall reduction of overs.

MEETINGS AND DECISIONS, 2009

ENGLAND CAPTAINCY AND TEAM DIRECTOR

On January 7, the England and Wales Cricket Board announced that they had accepted the resignation of Kevin Pietersen as England captain (though it later appeared that Pietersen had not actually offered it) and decided that England team director Peter Moores should relinquish his post. This followed an irretrievable breakdown in the relationship between the two since Pietersen was appointed captain in August 2008. Andrew Strauss was named to lead the tour of the West Indies, due to begin two weeks later; on January 8, he was confirmed as Test captain. The assistant coach, former Zimbabwean captain Andy Flower, took over Moores's role for the tour. On April 15, after the team returned from the Caribbean, the ECB appointed Flower England team director.

ICC EXECUTIVE BOARD

The ICC Executive Board met in Perth on January 31 and February 1. Dr Julian Hunte, president of the West Indies Cricket Board, presented an interim report on his visit to Zimbabwe with ICC chief executive Haroon Lorgat in November 2008. None of the stakeholders they had met believed Zimbabwe were ready to return to Test cricket; timeframes proposed ranged from six months to two years or more. The Board of Control for Cricket in India and Cricket South Africa had offered Zimbabwe Cricket playing and administrative support. With the BCCI and the ECB expressing reservations about an enhanced Test championship, the board agreed that ICC management and the Chief Executives' Committee should consult further on an acceptable model for the Future Tours Programme from 2012. They also endorsed the view that international over-rates were a key issue. After reconsidering the Oval Test between England and Pakistan in 2006, taking account of legal advice and input from MCC, the board reversed their decision of July 2008 to change the result to a draw and decided that the original umpires' decision to award the match to England should stand. Chief executive Haroon Lorgat said this ensured the integrity of the game and upheld the Laws of Cricket, and thanked the Pakistan Cricket Board for their understanding.

With several countries expressing reservations about touring Pakistan, it was decided to relocate the Champions Trophy, already postponed from 2008 and now scheduled for September–October 2009. The board agreed Pakistan would retain the revenue due for hosting the tournament. A task team would be formed to find ways to ensure that, wherever possible, international cricket was played in Pakistan in the future.

The WICB's recommendation that the World Twenty20 tournament in 2010 should be staged in Barbados, Guyana and St Lucia was accepted. A parallel women's tournament would be played in St Kitts, with the women's semi-finals and final taking place on the same days and at the same venues as the men's.

The board agreed new regulations for domestic cricket events and approved/disapproved cricket, following recommendations from a working party. They decided that a host member could determine if a match or tournament within its territory was approved or disapproved, while the ICC would determine this in a non-member territory. No foreign player should take part in domestic cricket without a no-objection certificate from his home board, and no ICC member countries, or their players, coaches or officials should participate in disapproved cricket. Regulations would be implemented from June 1, 2009.

STANFORD CONTRACTS TERMINATED

On February 20, the ECB served notice that, following the charges filed against Sir Allen Stanford and his organisation by the US Securities and Exchange Commission, they were terminating their contracts with the Stanford Group with immediate effect, and would not proceed with any further Stanford Twenty20 matches in Antigua or the Stanford international Quadrangular Twenty20 in England, scheduled for May 2010. The counties were assured this had no impact on projected fee payments to them or the Recreational Assembly.

ECB CHAIRMAN

On February 23, Giles Clarke was re-elected chairman of the ECB for a second term, running until March 31, 2011. Another candidate, Lord Marland of Odstock, had withdrawn from the nomination process; at that time, 16 votes had been cast from the 18 first-class counties and MCC, and Clarke led 14–2. The 21 county boards and the Minor Counties Cricket Association were also part of the electorate.

ICC CHIEF EXECUTIVES' COMMITTEE

The Chief Executives' Committee met in Johannesburg on February 24 and 25, 2009, and continued to consider options to replace the current Future Tours Programme after May 2012. A working group of Full Member representatives were discussing measures to promote Test cricket ahead of the South Africa–Australia series which would determine the top side in the Test championship table.

The meeting heard that the World Anti-Doping Agency had confirmed the ICC's 2009 Anti-Doping Code complied with its standards. Ravi Sawani, general manager and chief investigator of the Anti-Corruption and Security Unit, said that, although the ACSU was regarded as a world leader in the fight against corruption in sport, it could not be complacent if the previous decade's problems were to be avoided.

The committee discussed measures to avoid any repeat of the events surrounding the West Indies–England Test in Antigua, which was abandoned after ten balls because of an unfit outfield.

A strategy session aimed to establish key aims, objectives and challenges which would feed into other decision-making forums including the ICC Executive Board, and help all Members, as well as the ICC, to shape their long-term thinking and plans for international cricket in a cohesive and mutually beneficial way.

ICC EXECUTIVE BOARD

An ICC board teleconference on March 16 confirmed South Africa as the new host for the Champions Trophy, originally planned for Pakistan in September 2008 but cancelled for security reasons. The initial reserve venue was Sri Lanka, but there were concerns over the weather given that the tournament was to be staged in September and October 2009; it was felt that the South African weather would be more stable. There was a further offer from the United Arab Emirates. The teleconference also agreed the dates for the 2010 World Twenty20 in the West Indies as April 30 to May 16.

INDIAN PREMIER LEAGUE

On March 22, the BCCI decided to move the IPL overseas in 2009, amid security fears in the aftermath of the terrorist attack on the Sri Lankan team and match officials in Lahore on March 3. An Indian general election was due to take place in April and May, coinciding with the IPL, and the Indian government said they could not provide adequate security for the tournament as well. The ECB and CSA both volunteered to stage the IPL, but on March 24 the BCCI settled for South Africa, for logistical reasons including their climate and permanent floodlights.

ENGLAND PERFORMANCE SQUAD

On April 8, the ECB announced a 25-man England Performance Squad for the summer. The England coach would have the right to withdraw any of these players from domestic cricket. The squad consisted of 12 players already on 12-month ECB contracts running from October 2008: England captain Andrew Strauss, James Anderson, Ian Bell, Stuart Broad, Paul Collingwood, Alastair Cook, Andrew Flintoff, Steve Harmison, Monty Panesar, Kevin Pietersen, Ryan Sidebottom and Michael Vaughan; seven on increment contracts: Tim Ambrose, Ravi Bopara, Samit Patel, Matt Prior, Owais Shah, Graeme Swann and Luke Wright; and six others: James Foster, Robert Key, Amjad Khan, Dimitri Mascarenhas, Sajid Mahmood and Adil Rashid. All except Rashid had already appeared for England.

ICC EXECUTIVE BOARD

The ICC Executive Board met in Dubai on April 17 and 18 and resolved that, given uncertain security situation in Pakistan, the country should not host matches in the 2011 World Cup, which would now be hosted entirely by the other three countries sharing responsibility for the tournament, India, Sri Lanka and Bangladesh. The tournament secretariat would be moved from Lahore.

The board received a report on the terrorist attack on the Sri Lankan team and match officials in Lahore on March 3, and also heard from referee Chris Broad, one of the officials attacked, and Sri Lanka's then captain Mahela Jayawardene. Lord Condon, chairman of the ICC's Anti-Corruption and Security Unit, was asked to lead a task team to review security arrangements for all international cricket, assessing whether current protocols were adequate and, if not, how to improve them. ICC management should approach other sports to share information on how security was conducted. It was agreed international cricket should not take place in Pakistan in the immediate future, but Pakistan should maintain a full international programme and fellow Members of the ICC would do all they could to facilitate this.

The latest report on cricket in Zimbabwe from Dr Julian Hunte's task team stated that a return to Test cricket would be possible when Zimbabwe's national sides had satisfied performance criteria in first-class matches; various structures and processes had been updated, and domestic structures upgraded; and a more competitive first-class league introduced. There should be a partnership between ZC and the ICC member services department to track ZC's performance against their strategic plan.

The board agreed that former Indian all-rounder Ravi Shastri should be the new media representative on the ICC cricket committee, replacing Michael Holding who resigned in 2008. Former England Women's captain Clare Connor, now head of the women's game at the ECB, would be invited to join as women's representative.

The board considered an application from the Indian Cricket League to be approved as unofficial cricket, but decided it did not meet the criteria. In relation to ICL players returning to official cricket, the board said players could not swap between official and unofficial cricket at will, but the nature of sanctions was a matter for each individual member.

WORLD CUP PREPARATIONS

The Central Organising Committee for the 2011 World Cup met in Mumbai on April 28, their first meeting since the ICC Board resolved that Pakistan should not stage any matches given the security situation.

The committee decided that of the 14 matches originally scheduled for Pakistan, eight should go to India, four to Sri Lanka and two to Bangladesh. (This meant a total of 29 in India, 12 in Sri Lanka and eight in Bangladesh.) Each of the four co-hosts had been scheduled to stage one quarter-final; Bangladesh would now have two. The semi-finals would be held in India and Sri Lanka, and the final in India. Scheduling for the quarter and semi-finals would attempt to ensure a home game for any host country qualifying. The tournament secretariat would be based in Mumbai, rather than Lahore, and the tournament director was confirmed as Professor Ratnakar Shetty.

ECB BOARD AND MCC

On May 12, MCC secretary and chief executive Keith Bradshaw stepped down from the ECB board of directors, explaining that he felt there could be situations in which his loyalty as an ECB director conflicted with his executive duties at MCC. On September 2, MCC appointed committee member and former Kent player Matthew Fleming as their new representative on the ECB Board.

MCC ANNUAL GENERAL MEETING

The 222nd AGM of the Marylebone Cricket Club was held at Lord's on May 13, with the president, Derek Underwood, in the chair. He announced that his successor, from October, would be John Barclay, the former Sussex captain. Resolutions were passed increasing members' entrance fees and annual subscriptions and amending various Rules of the Club. Membership of the club on December 31, 2008, totalled 22,506, made up of 17,969 full members, 3,997 associate members, 302 honorary members, 170 senior members and 68 out-match members. There were 9,971 candidates awaiting election to full membership; in 2008, 437 vacancies arose.

MCC had also held a Special General Meeting on January 26, at which members approved a resolution to install retractable floodlights at Lord's. There were 9,971 candidates awaiting election to full membership; in 2008, 437 vacancies arose.

ICC ANNUAL MEETINGS

In the ICC's centenary year, their annual conference returned to Lord's, and ran from June 22 to 26.

The Chief Executives' Committee and the ICC Board received draft proposals for a new Future Tours Programme to run from 2012, and agreed on further consultation so that it could be finalised as soon as possible.

They also considered recommendations made by the cricket committee in May, and agreed that the Umpire Decision Review System should be rolled out in Test cricket from October 2009. An exploration of the opportunities of day/night Test cricket should include trials of an appropriate ball, experiments at first-class level, and research on whether or not it was wanted; if these were satisfactory, a day/night Test could be held as early as 2010. Stricter penalties should be imposed on boards and venues found guilty of producing poor and unfit pitches – and the term "poor" should include batsmen-friendly "featherbed" surfaces. Play should be suspended for bad light only when umpires considered conditions unreasonable or dangerous (rather than unsuitable), and umpires should make the decision rather than offering it to the batsmen. Slow over-rates should be tackled in several ways: fines would be doubled; the captain of a side guilty of three over-rate fines in the same format of the game over 12 months would be banned automatically for the team's next match in that format; delays should be minimised, especially from unscheduled drinks breaks and sightscreen issues; and team over-rates should be displayed on scoreboards. The current practice of appointing "neutral" umpires for international matches continued, but players and umpires would be surveyed for their opinions before further discussion in 2010.

The Pakistan Cricket Board had accepted the offer of an ICC task team, led by ECB chairman Giles Clarke, to help ensure Pakistan retained their position in international cricket.

The board decided that Kenya would not be ready to host the Under-19 World Cup in February 2010, so the event would be transferred to New Zealand.

Vanuatu were upgraded to associate membership of the ICC, becoming the 35th Associate.

ECB/SPORT ENGLAND FUNDING PLAN

On July 17, the ECB agreed a four-year funding plan for grassroots cricket with Sport England, who awarded a £37.8m grant running up to 2013. It was to be invested in projects which grow participation, sustain involvement, increase participants' satisfaction, create pathways from the playground to the Test arena, and improve opportunities for women, girls and disabled players. ECB chief executive David Collier said this was the largest grant made to any national governing body. Along with government funding, it would enable the Cricket Foundation's *Chance to shine* initiative's £20m four-year investment programme to move ahead.

ENGLISH DOMESTIC SEASON

On July 29, the ECB decided to change the current domestic structure of four competitions to three. The LV County Championship would remain as a 16-match two-division competition; there would also be a Twenty20 tournament, based on two pools of nine (split on north–south lines) and played in June and July with a finals day later in the season; and there would be a limited-overs Sunday afternoon competition. Earlier plans for a second Twenty20 competition in the later part of the season were dropped.

On August 27, the first-class counties voted 13–5 to confirm this format for 2010–2013, with the details of the Sunday afternoon competition as follows: there would be three pools of seven teams, playing 12 matches each throughout the season, leading to semi-finals and a final in September. (In September, the three non-county teams were confirmed as an ECB Recreational XI, Scotland and the Netherlands, after Ireland declined the invitation because of their growing international schedule.) Matches would be 40 overs a side, leaving England without a domestic 50-over competition to mirror the current one-day international format; the board argued that the strongest one-day international team, South Africa, did not play 50-over domestic cricket, and the ICC were to review the 50-over format after the 2011 World Cup. One overseas player would be allowed per team in the County Championship and 40-over competition, and two in the Twenty20.

ENGLAND HOME INTERNATIONAL SCHEDULE

On July 29, the ECB awarded Durham their first Ashes Test, to be staged at Chester-le-Street in 2013, on the recommendation of the independent Major Match Group. The Oval was also awarded an Ashes Test, and bids were invited to host the other three. It was announced that three of the four Tests against India in 2014 would be staged at Hampshire's Rose Bowl (already awarded its Test debut in 2011 against Sri Lanka), Old Trafford and The Oval. Durham were also to host a Test against Sri Lanka in 2016.

On September 10, the ECB decided to award the two Tests against Bangladesh in 2010 to Old Trafford and Lord's, and two Tests between Pakistan and Australia, transferred to England because of the security situation in Pakistan, to Headingley and Lord's. This meant that Lord's would stage three Tests in 2010, the third being between England and Pakistan. Originally, Headingley had been assigned a Test against Bangladesh, but once it was given Pakistan v Australia (because of the large Pakistani community in Yorkshire) this was transferred to Old Trafford, which previously had been told it would not stage another Test before 2012.

WORLD CUP DISPUTE RESOLVED

On August 27, ICC president David Morgan and PCB chairman Ijaz Butt met in Dubai to resolve their dispute over the staging of the 2011 World Cup, after the 14 games originally allocated to Pakistan, one of the four host countries, were reassigned because of the security crisis. It was agreed that the PCB should retain their host fees and receive additional compensation for the loss of hosting rights, but they would be free of the liabilities and obligations associated with hosting matches. The PCB agreed to withdraw legal proceedings against the ICC.

ENGLAND CENTRAL CONTRACTS

On September 11, the ECB awarded 11 England central contracts running for 12 months from October 1, 2009, to James Anderson, Ian Bell, Stuart Broad, Paul Collingwood, Alastair Cook, Graham Onions, Kevin Pietersen, Matt Prior, Ryan Sidebottom, Andrew Strauss and Graeme Swann. Compared with September 2008, Onions, Prior and Swann had replaced Michael Vaughan (who had retired), Andrew Flintoff, Stephen Harmison and Monty Panesar. Because Flintoff had retired from Test cricket, he was offered one of the England increment contracts introduced the previous year; players on increment contracts receive a one-off ECB payment on top of their county salary, whereas centrally contracted players are paid by the ECB rather than their county. Flintoff turned down the contract to increase his availability for non-England cricket such as the IPL. Increment contracts were awarded again to Ravi Bopara, Owais Shah and Luke Wright, and for the first time to Tim Bresnan, Adil Rashid and Jonathan Trott; since the previous year, Prior and Swann had been promoted from increments to central contracts, while Tim Ambrose and Samit Patel were dropped from the list. Non-contracted players can earn an increment contract by amassing 20 appearance points between October and September, with five points awarded for a Test and two for a Twenty20 or one-day international.

On September 28 the ECB announced that Bresnan and Eoin Morgan had been awarded increment contract payments for the year about to end after achieving 20 appearance points during recent one-day internationals. They were the third and fourth players to earn increment contracts by this method, following Dimitri Mascarenhas and Graham Onions.

ICC CHIEF EXECUTIVES' COMMITTEE

The Chief Executives' Committee met in Johannesburg on October 1 and 2 and received an update on preparations for the World Twenty20 tournament in the West Indies in May 2010. They continued work on the draft for the post-2012 Future Tours Programme. It was agreed to extend a project on promoting cricket to include research and analysis of the three formats of international cricket. A working group should carry out a competitive analysis of other sports and entertainment products, with further research on variations such as day/night Test matches. The committee enhanced the scope of the Test working group, looking at ways to promote Test cricket as the pinnacle of the game, to include all Full Member chief executives. Justin Vaughan from New Zealand Cricket joined the cricket committee, and Nishantha Ranatunga of Sri Lanka Cricket the development committee.

ICC EXECUTIVE BOARD

The ICC Executive Board met in Johannesburg on October 6 and 7, and approved in principle the Chief Executives' Committee's draft post-2012 Future Tours Programme, which would now be subject to a commercial evaluation. The board also approved the schedule for the Under-19 World Cup in New Zealand in January 2010, and the following groupings for the 2011 World Cup: Group A – Australia, Pakistan, New Zealand, Sri Lanka, Zimbabwe, Canada and Kenya; Group B – India, South Africa, England, West Indies, Bangladesh, Ireland and the Netherlands.

The board considered their planned Anti-Doping Code, and especially the issue of players filing information on their whereabouts to enable out-of-competition drug testing, because of Indian concerns about players' privacy; they agreed to continue testing of international cricketers in the meantime. They unanimously approved an enhanced ICC Code of Conduct, Anti-Corruption Code and Anti-Racism Code.

An update on the ICC Development Programme focused on work to promote cricket in the United States and China. There were reports from task teams charged with looking into the problems of Zimbabwe, Pakistan and general security around international cricket.

ECB SPONSORSHIP DEAL

The ECB announced on October 15 that life and pensions company Friends Provident would be the title sponsor for their new Twenty20 competition from 2010 to 2013. Friends Provident had sponsored the 50-over competition for the previous three seasons.

DAVIES REPORT

On November 13, an independent advisory panel chaired by David Davies, the former broadcaster and football administrator, reported on their review of listed sporting events to the secretary of state for Culture, Media and Sport. They recommended that "sporting events with a special national resonance should continue to be protected for the widest possible television audience." Currently, there were two lists, one of events which must be shown live on free-to-air television channels and one of events which must have free-to-air highlights coverage. The panel preferred a single list of live events and said that protecting highlights (the only coverage currently required for England's home Tests) was insufficient. They recommended that home Ashes Tests should be on the list for live, free-to-air broadcast; the 2009 series had been the first such to be shown live only on Sky Sports' subscription channels, with highlights on free-to-air Channel 5.

The ECB expressed alarm and called for further consultation, insisting that their finances and investment in grassroots cricket depended on their revenue from the Sky Sports deal, and that these would suffer if the Ashes, their most attractive asset, were to be withdrawn from that package. They argued that, instead, the list of highlights events should be strengthened, to ensure that all Test highlights were shown in peak family viewing time.

ICC CHIEF EXECUTIVES' COMMITTEE

The ICC Chief Executives' Committee met in Dubai on November 30 and December 1. They recommended that, in the 2011 World Cup to be staged in India, Sri Lanka and Bangladesh, host countries reaching the quarter-finals and semi-finals should where possible play them in their home country; should two co-hosts be involved, the higher-ranked side from the group stage would take priority. A committee was formed to draft a paper on the shape of the Future Tours Programme and create a context for Test and one-day international cricket. The chief executives approved the recommendation that the top four sides from the Women's World Twenty20 in the West Indies in 2010 should earn direct qualification for the 2012 event in Sri Lanka; the remaining four places would be subject to qualification. The committee granted one-day international status to the Olympic Stadium in Sydney, and temporary one-day international status to the Koninklijke UD ground in the Netherlands for the World Cricket League to be staged in July 2010. There was also an update on the Umpire Decision Review System as implemented in the recent Dunedin and Brisbane Tests.

ECB CHAMPIONSHIP REGULATIONS

An ECB board meeting on December 10 decided to revise the County Championship points system for 2010. Teams would receive 16 points for a win and three for a draw (rather than 14 and four, as in recent years), and the threshold for achieving bonus points would be reduced to 110 overs (from 120 in 2009, and 130 in 2008). The use of the heavy roller would be banned after the start of the match. The changes were intended to encourage positive cricket and the preparation of good pitches.

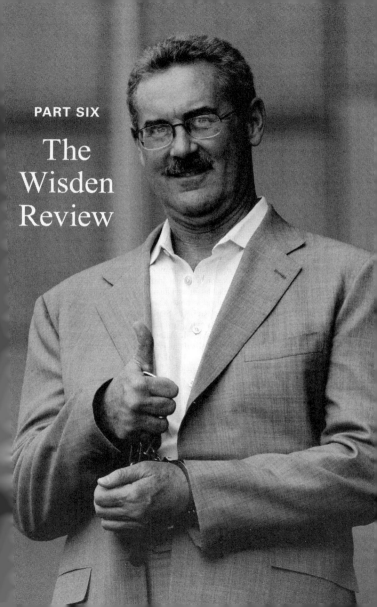

PART SIX

The
Wisden
Review

CHRONICLE OF 2009

JANUARY

6 Australia beat South Africa at Sydney; they lose the Test series 2–1, but stay top of the world rankings. **7 Kevin Pietersen sacked as England captain, Peter Moores removed as coach, after news of their disaffection becomes public. 8 Andrew Strauss is appointed captain. 11** David Warner, yet to play a first-class match, scores 89 from 43 balls in his first Twenty20 international for Australia. **13** Australia's Matthew Hayden announces his retirement. **16** Sri Lanka win final of tri-series against Bangladesh after recovering from six for five. **22** ECB agree deal to allow England players to participate in IPL for three weeks. **28** Younis Khan appointed Pakistan captain after Shoaib Malik is sacked. **30** BBC scorer Bill Frindall dies, aged 69.

FEBRUARY

1 The ICC reverse their earlier decision to declare the 2006 Oval Test a draw: it reverts to an England win (Pakistan forfeited the match by refusing to play on). **5** Muttiah Muralitharan takes his 503rd wicket in one-day internationals, passing Wasim Akram's record. **6** Andrew Flintoff and Kevin Pietersen each fetch $US1.55m at IPL auction. **7 West Indies bowl out England for 51 to win First Test in Jamaica. 9** Giles Clarke re-elected unopposed as ECB chairman. **11** Peter Moores appointed Lancashire coach. **13** West Indies–England Test at the Sir Vivian Richards Stadium in Antigua is abandoned after ten balls as the outfield is unfit; extra Test added at the old Antigua Recreation Ground. **17 US authorities allege Sir Allen Stanford's companies involved in "a fraud of shocking magnitude". 19** West Indies' last pair survive 11 overs to deny England victory in Third Test in Antigua. **25** Younis Khan makes 313 in drawn First Test against Sri Lanka at Karachi.

MARCH

1 Ramnaresh Sarwan scores 291 in drawn Fourth Test against England at Bridgetown. **3 Several Sri Lankan players are injured in a terrorist attack on their bus in Lahore during the Second Test; the tour is immediately abandoned. 4** Samit Patel is dropped from England's one-day squad in the West Indies for "unsatisfactory" fitness. **8** Phillip Hughes becomes the youngest player to score twin centuries in a Test; Australia go on to win the Second Test at Durban, and clinch the series in South Africa. **10** West Indies, eight wickets down, hang on to draw Fifth Test in Trinidad and take series against England 1–0. **21** India beat New Zealand by ten wickets at Hamilton, and go on to win three-match Test series 1–0. **22 England beat New Zealand to win women's World Cup final in Sydney.** Security issues surrounding national elections force the BCCI to relocate the second IPL season outside India; two days later it is announced it will be played in South Africa. **29** Steve Bucknor retires after umpiring 128 Tests and 181 one-day internationals.

APRIL

2 The ICC announce that the 2009 Champions Trophy (originally scheduled for 2008 in Pakistan) will be played in South Africa in September. **3** Andrew Flintoff's hat-trick in St Lucia helps England win one-day series against West Indies 3–2. **15 Andy Flower named as England's new "team director".** **17** The ICC confirm that no matches in the 2011 World Cup will be staged in Pakistan. **18** The ICC reject an application from the Indian Cricket League for official recognition. **19** Ireland beat Canada in the final of the World Cup qualifying tournament; Kenya and the Netherlands also qualify.

MAY

1 Dublin-born Eoin Morgan named in England's one-day squad, effectively ending his career with Ireland. **8** England complete three-day victory over West Indies in First Test at Lord's. **12** South African spinner Johan Botha's *doosra* ruled illegal by the ICC. **18 England beat West Indies by an innings at Chester-le-Street, regaining the Wisden Trophy 69 days after surrendering it.** **20** Former England all-rounder Chris Lewis jailed for 13 years after being found guilty of smuggling cocaine into Britain from St Lucia. **24** Deccan Chargers, captained by Adam Gilchrist, win the second IPL title, beating Royal Challengers Bangalore in the Johannesburg final.

JUNE

4 Andrew Symonds sent home from the World Twenty20 in England after flouting a ban on drinking in public. **5** The Netherlands defeat England after a last-ball overthrow in the opening match of the World Twenty20 at Lord's. **8** Australia's second defeat sends them out of the World Twenty20 after three days; Ireland reach Super Eight stage after beating Bangladesh. **10** Abdul Razzaq of Pakistan is the first to return to international cricket. **18** Pakistan beat South Africa, and Sri Lanka overwhelm West Indies, in the World Twenty20 semi-finals. Simon Jones ruled out of the rest of the season with another knee injury (he is later released by Worcestershire). **19** Sir Allen Stanford arrested in the USA. **21 Pakistan beat Sri Lanka to win the World Twenty20 at Lord's; England beat New Zealand in the women's final.** Younis Khan retires from Twenty20 cricket after leading his side to victory. **23** Mashrafe bin Mortaza named as Bangladesh's captain (replacing Mohammad Ashraful) for the tour of West Indies. **26** ECB announce two Pakistan–Australia Tests will be staged in England in 2010. **30 Michael Vaughan, troubled by knee injuries, announces his immediate retirement.**

JULY

8 The Ashes series starts at Cardiff, the world's 100th Test venue. West Indies' first-choice team withdraws from the First Test against Bangladesh the following day, as a contracts dispute rumbles on. **12** England's last pair hang on for 69 balls to scrape a draw in First Ashes Test. **13** Bangladesh win their first Test overseas, against a makeshift West Indian side in St Vincent. England's women retain their version of the Ashes, after a draw in a one-off Test against Australia at Worcester. **15** Andrew Flintoff announces his retirement from Test cricket at the end of the season. **20 England beat Australia at Lord's for the first time since 1934, to take 1–0 lead in Ashes series.** Bangladesh win their first overseas Test series after beating West Indies in Grenada. **22** Kevin Pietersen undergoes surgery on Achilles tendon injury, and misses rest of Ashes series. **23** Justin Langer passes Don Bradman's record first-class aggregate (28,067) by an Australian batsman. **24** Chaminda Vaas retires from Test cricket after Sri Lanka beat Pakistan 2–0 at home. **25** Hampshire beat Sussex in Friends Provident Trophy final at Lord's.

AUGUST

1 Pakistan board tells the ICC that its players were approached by "suspicious characters" during the preceding month's series in Sri Lanka. **2** Andy Caddick announces he will retire at the end of the season after 19 years with Somerset, and 62 Test caps. **6** Mark Butcher, who played 71 Tests for England, is forced to retire by a knee injury. **9** Australia square the Ashes series with an innings victory at Headingley. **13** John Dyson sacked as West Indies' coach after a depleted side lose Test and one-day series to Bangladesh. **15** Sussex win Twenty20 Cup final, beating Somerset at Edgbaston; both qualify for inaugural Champions League Twenty20. **16** Charles Coventry of Zimbabwe equals the highest score in one-day internationals with 194 not out, but finishes on the losing side against Bangladesh at Bulawayo. **17** West Indies name a depleted squad for the Champions Trophy. **23 England win the Fifth Test at The Oval by 197 runs, and regain the Ashes.** **24** Andrew Flintoff undergoes knee surgery. **26** Daniel Vettori becomes the first left-arm spinner to take 300 Test wickets, during New Zealand's Second Test against Sri Lanka in Colombo.

SEPTEMBER

7 Ricky Ponting announces retirement from Twenty20 internationals. **11 Durham retain the County Championship. 15** Six Uganda Under-19 players go missing during tour of Canada. **20** England win the final one-day international at Chester-le-Street, but Australia take series 6–1. **22** Sri Lanka beat hosts South Africa in first match of Champions Trophy. **27** Sussex win NatWest Pro40 title despite losing their last match.

OCTOBER

2 Australia beat England in Champions Trophy semi-final. **3** New Zealand beat Pakistan in second semi-final. **5** Australia retain Champions Trophy, beating New Zealand in final. **8** Simon Jones signs for Hampshire. The inaugural Champions League Twenty20 starts in Bangalore. **14** Organisers of the 2011 World Cup announce that the final will be at the Wankhede Stadium in Mumbai. **15** Somerset's Marcus Trescothick flies home from Champions League after recurrence of the stress-related illness. **23** New South Wales win the inaugural Champions League Twenty20, beating Trinidad & Tobago in the final at Hyderabad, India. **24** Andy Moles resigns as New Zealand's coach after less than a year. **25** Lions' Stephen Cook breaks South African domestic batting record with 390 against Warriors at East London. **27 Former Test umpire David Shepherd dies, aged 68.**

NOVEMBER

3 Chris Gayle reappointed West Indies captain in full-strength side to tour Australia. **4** New Zealand restore the Plunket Shield (last contested in 1974-75) as the prize for their domestic first-class competition after loss of sponsor. **9** Matthew Hoggard, released by Yorkshire, joins Leicestershire as captain. **11** Younis Khan resigns as Pakistan's captain, citing lack of support within the team; Mohammad Yousuf is appointed for tours of New Zealand and Australia. **13 Review panel recommends that Ashes series in England should be on free-to-air television. 16** Justin Langer named as Australia's batting coach and mentor. Monty Panesar joins Sussex from Northamptonshire. **19** Mahela Jayawardene scores 275 as Sri Lanka reach 760 for seven against India at Ahmedabad. Adam Gilchrist signs to play Twenty20 cricket for Middlesex in 2010. **27** India complete 100th Test victory, beating Sri Lanka by an innings at Kanpur. **28** Debutant Adrian Barath, 19, becomes youngest West Indian to score a Test century, but Australia win First Test by an innings.

DECEMBER

4 A washout at Durban means England win the one-day series in South Africa 2–1. In the first Test for 35 years at Mumbai's Brabourne Stadium, Virender Sehwag falls for 293, seven short of becoming the first to make three Test triple-centuries; **India go on to beat Sri Lanka 2–0 after another innings victory, going to the top of the ICC Test rankings for the first time. 5** Umpire Mark Benson flies home from Second Australia–West Indies Test at Adelaide, saying he is ill: suggestions that he is unhappy with the new umpire-referral system are denied. **8** Chris Gayle carries his bat for 165 out of 317 as West Indies draw Second Test. **11** Multan slow left-armer Zulfiqar Baba takes all ten Islamabad wickets for 143 in Pakistan domestic match. **16** Makhaya Ntini wins 100th cap as South Africa–England Test series starts at Centurion. **20** England's last pair hang on for a draw in First Test. At Perth, West Indies – chasing 359 – fall 36 short as Australia take series 2–0. **22** Andrew Gale is named Yorkshire captain after Anthony McGrath stands down. **23** New Zealand fast bowler Shane Bond announces retirement from Test cricket. **24** Surrey re-sign Rory Hamilton-Brown, 22, from Sussex and appoint him captain for 2010. **26** Arthur McIntyre, England's oldest Test player, dies at 91. **27** Final one-day international of Sri Lanka's tour of India is abandoned after 23.3 overs because of a dangerous pitch at Delhi; India win series 3–1. **30** England win Second Test at Durban – their first innings victory in South Africa since 1964-65 – to go 1–0 up in series.

The following items were also reported in the media during 2009:

DAILY LIBERAL, DUBBO   January 6

A two-year-old pied cock pigeon called "Tubby" (named after Mark Taylor) beat 11 other contenders also called after cricket commentators in the inaugural Great Betfair Pink Pigeon Race over a 30km course from the Glenn McGrath Oval in Narromine to Trangie. The event was held to raise money for the McGrath Foundation, in honour of Glenn's late wife Jane. "Tubby" finished just ahead of "Scoop" (Simon O'Donnell) and "Warnie".

INDO-ASIAN NEWS SERVICE   January 9

In Mahendra Singh Dhoni's home town of Ranchi, kite-maker Mohammad Talib said he was unable to meet demand from children wanting kites carrying the Indian captain's image: "Every day I prepare around 1,500 kites with photos of Dhoni. But I get over 2,000 young customers daily asking for them."

SUNDAY TIMES/THE TIMES   January 25/June 27

Two Irish musicians, Neil Hannon and Thomas Walsh, have linked up to record a cricket-themed album, called *The Duckworth Lewis Method*. Tracks include "Gentlemen and Players", "The Sweet Spot", "Jiggery Pokery" (about the Warne–Gatting ball) and the Indian-tinged tune "The Age of Revolution" that contained the lines: "Always denied entry by the English gentry / Now we're driving Bentleys / Playing Twenty20." *The Times* called it "barking mad, and brilliant".

WALTHAM FOREST GUARDIAN   February 12/May 26

Plans to build a school on the former Essex county ground at Leyton have provoked furious opposition from residents. The site, now used as a general sports amenity, was described by one neighbour, Lin Walton, as "a wonderful green oasis". More than 900 protest letters followed. Leyton, the Essex HQ for much of the club's history, was last used for county cricket in 1977.

NEW SCIENTIST   February 14
Scientists searching for possible new perfumes at Procter & Gamble have
distilled the essence of Lord's. They have captured the odours of freshly cut
grass, bats, laundered kit and the dressing-rooms (minus the players).
"Perfumers need inspiration," said spokesman Will Andrews, "and this can
come from people that surround them, places they've visited, or things that
they love in the world."

LORDS.ORG   February 18
MCC has had a record number of applications to work as stewards at Lord's.
Head steward Dave Juchau said the club had already received over 1,200
enquiries for the 2009 season, more than it had all year in 2008. Candidates
are expected to be over 18 and "physically fit".

REUTERS   February 23
Play in a one-day match between Himachal Pradesh and Punjab at Una was
halted when a helicopter landed on the field by mistake. The pilot thought the
H for Himachal painted on the pitch was a landing pad.

HERALD SUN, MELBOURNE   March 8
One man died and another was seriously injured after they waded into the surf
to fetch the ball during a game of beach cricket at Lake Tyers, Victoria. Police
said they were carried away by a rip on a dangerous stretch of shore.

ECONOMIC JOURNAL   March 19
Captains bat first too often in daytime one-day internationals, according to
Professor V. Bhaskar of University College, London. Professor Bhaskar found
that captains winning the toss and batting won only 43.7% of the matches –
although in day-night matches the figure rose to 55.5%. "In day matches,
commentators seem to overvalue the importance of runs on the board and the
'pressure of chasing'," he said.

HERALD SUN, MELBOURNE/AFP   April 1

A newspaper April Fool's Day joke suggesting a Chinese firm had bought naming rights to the Melbourne Cricket Ground sparked an angry online reaction. By midday there were more than 200 comments on the *Herald Sun* website after the paper said the MCG would now be the Mekong Cricket Ground. Many were not amused even though the story quoted spokeswoman April Fulton. "Let's just give up this whole country to the Asians and be done with it," posted Mister Master. "What did our diggers fight and die for in the past wars?"

DAILY MIRROR, COLOMBO   April 3

A 23-year-old man was reported after playing in a schools match for a Galle team at Pallekele. The match referee became suspicious when the player did not mingle with his team-mates. He then discovered the interloper was unable to name either the school principal or his class teacher.

REUTERS   April 20

About 500 prisoners went on hunger strike in a Kolkata jail after prison authorities refused to install cable TV so they could watch IPL matches.

CRICINFO   April 21

President Barack Obama did somewhat better than his predecessor, George W. Bush, when he met Brian Lara in Trinidad and attempted the traditionally embarrassing presidential ritual of trying to play cricket. Observers thought his forward defensive was respectable, though his driving less so. Obama said he had always wanted to meet the "Michael Jordan of cricket".

CHURCH TIMES   April 24

The Bishop of Wolverhampton, the Rt Rev. Clive Gregory, scored 103 not out for the diocese of Lichfield in a 16-run win over Birmingham in the *Church Times* Cup.

INDO-ASIAN NEWS SERVICE   May 4

President Obama told an interviewer that, after three months in the White House, he was sick of briefing books and had now begun a novel: the cricket-themed *Netherland* by Joseph O'Neill. Publishers Random House immediately printed extra copies to meet expected Obama-fuelled demand.

EAST ANGLIAN DAILY TIMES   May 6

The league match in Essex between Frinton and Abberton was abandoned after two Abberton fielders, Matt Gilray and Mark Copson, collided and were taken to hospital. Umpire Martin White said neither team wanted to continue: "Gilray was in a bad way and Copson didn't know what time of day it was."

THE SCOTSMAN   May 12

Perthshire, once the proudest county in Scottish cricket, can no longer field a senior team. "The Big County" won 20 county championships between 1953 and 1978 and later brought Adam Gilchrist and Justin Langer as pros to their ground at North Inch. However, the club has been in a lengthy decline, and plans to merge with fellow strugglers Perth Mayfield were thwarted by the trust document that governs the ground. The club still has a thriving junior section.

SRILANKANEWSTODAY.COM   May 16

A government official announced the news of the death of the rebel Tamil Tiger leader Prabhakaran with the following words: "Match over, series won, captain's wicket gone, stumps drawn, players heading for pavilion. That's all I can say for now."

BIRMINGHAM MAIL   May 18

Families near the Perry Hall playing fields have gathered 500 signatures for a petition urging the city council to allocate less land to the Birmingham Cricket League. Angelina Davies, who started the Playing Fields for All campaign, said: "It's not fair. The cricketers only meet once a week but for the remainder of the week local residents are not allowed to play on the squares. "The rest of the park is overgrown and covered in goose excrement." The league has been

granted 13 squares and wants two more. "This is our main ground," said league
vice-chairman Amjad Aziz. "We're being squeezed out all over the city."

ASIAN TRIBUNE   May 18
Three former Test cricketers have been elected to the new 543-member Indian
parliament at the 2009 election, all supporters of the victorious Congress Party:
Navjot Singh Sidhu, Kirti Azad and Mohammad Azharuddin.

DAWN   May 21
Organisers of veterans' cricket in Pakistan plan to offer fitness guidelines to
competitors following the death of two players this year. Javed Sheikh, 53,
collapsed after complaining of chest pains while bowling in Karachi only
weeks after Fakhr Khairi, a 60-year-old doctor, died while running between
the wickets. Officials are also contemplating a ban on players with a history of
heart trouble.

ALDERSHOT NEWS & MAIL   May 28
Lee Wood and Toby Harper shared a century opening stand for Hartley
Wintney in the club's traditional Bank Holiday fixture against a team fielded
by Harlequins rugby club. Of the first hundred, Wood scored 93, Extras seven
– and Harper nought. Harper had allowed his partner, known as a swashbuckler,
to farm the strike. Then, after Wood retired on scoring his century, he stayed
to reach double figures. "Toby got by far the biggest cheer of the day – far
louder than for Lee's hundred – when he finally scored a run," said Hartley
Wintney committee member Jonathan Rowe.

LOUGHBOROUGH ECHO   May 29
Australian Julian Saye appealed for lbw so enthusiastically in a Leicestershire
Senior League match that he dislocated his shoulder. Saye, playing for Birstall
Village against Bharat Sports, had the consolation of getting the verdict – and
returned to take two more wickets.

CRICINFO   May 29
Muttiah Muralitharan cancelled a visit to speak at the Oxford Union because
of fears for his security. ICC security experts advised him not to attend after a
report in *The Times* that 20,000 Tamil civilians had been killed in Sri Lanka.

TELEGRAPH & ARGUS, BRADFORD   June 3
Four players were banned by the Quaid-e-Azam League in Yorkshire for terms
ranging from three years to life after an attack on a teenage umpire. Fielders
from the Bradford-based Shimla Cricket Club hit 18-year-old Matt Lowson
with the stumps after a series of decisions they disliked.

CROYDON ADVERTISER   June 5
Dominic Sibley, 13-year-old son of former ECB commercial director Mark
Sibley, hit six sixes off the last over of Whitgift School Under-13's innings
against Harris School.

TIMES OF INDIA   June 7

The Slam Bang Ten-10 tournament, between corporate teams in Vadodara, was described as "a major hit". Normal fours were scored as sixes and sixes became eights.

COVER-POINT.COM   June 9

Twelve-year-old Mark Vincent took seven wickets in seven balls – in his first competitive game of cricket. Playing for Grosvenor Grammar School in Northern Ireland against Parkhall he took the wickets in his first two overs. His father Ivan said Mark had no idea that he had done anything remarkable: "He was a bit downbeat when we asked him how he got on, telling us he had only scored two. It was only when his brother Drew asked about the bowling that the story of the seven wickets came out."

MORPETH HERALD   June 12

Retail giant Tesco apologised after inviting senior members of Northumberland County Council to a corporate box at the Durham v Sussex match – weeks before the planning committee was due to rule on an application for a new supermarket outside Morpeth.

BBC SPORT   June 17

Indian international batsman Abhijit Kale hit 39 off an over in Division 3 of the Kent League. Improbably playing for Linden Park against Catford Wanderers, Kale took a single off the first ball; his partner took a single off the next; he then hit the third for two, and struck the next six for six. Balls 1, 2 and 5 were no-balls. The bowler, left-arm seamer Damion Grosscel, had conceded only 23 in 13 previous overs and had, said Kale, been bowling very well. However, Grosscel declined the suggestion of a commemorative photo.

LIVERPOOL DAILY POST   June 19

In North Wales, Cameron Edwards took four wickets in five balls for the Northop Hall Under-9 team against Chirk – then ran out another batsman with the final delivery. Cameron, a veteran of ten, had dispensation to play in the fixture. "I don't know how it happened," he said. "I just bowled the ball straight and it hit the wicket each time." "He's the next Freddie Flintoff," said his father.

READING POST   June 23

Newbury Under-11s had a total of 50 in their match against Mortimer West End – but none of their batsmen scored a run. Nine were bowled for ducks, and the tenth was run out. Their runs came from six no-balls and 19 wides, which all counted double under age group rules. West End won by ten wickets.

LIVERPOOL DAILY POST   June 24

The captain of Llandudno CC, Steve Smith, was originally banned for life after "unacceptable remarks" about other clubs and officials were found on the club's Facebook site. This was reduced on appeal to an eight-week suspension. Three other players were also punished.

BEXLEY TIMES   June 25

Jack Robertson of Eltham College Under-15s scored 44 in an over against Colfe's – four sixes and five fours. It was a ten-ball over containing four no-balls. Robertson plays for the college first team and has ambitions to play professionally. "I guess I just hit the first few and it seemed like fun, and just continued to try and hit the ball as far as possible," he said. "I don't think I'll ever get the chance to do this again."

TELEGRAPH.CO.UK   June 28

The historic pitch at Sheffield Park in Uckfield, Sussex, has been revived. The ground regularly hosted fixtures against the Australians in the late 19th century, watched by crowds of up to 25,000. Its owner, the Earl of Sheffield, was a cricket enthusiast and patron who put up the original £150 to fund the Sheffield Shield. But on his death in 1909 the estate was sold on and the square became a wheat field. It was briefly restored between the wars before the park was taken over by the Canadian armoured division. The present owners, the National Trust, allowed a local side, The Armadillos, to restore the ground, which was inaugurated with a match between old England and Australia players.

BIRMINGHAM MAIL   June 30

Mohammed Junaid Hussain, 17, died in hospital after being struck by lightning while sheltering under a tree with friends. They had all been playing cricket in Small Heath Park when the storm started. Five of the other players were detained in hospital.

ASIAN NEWS, MANCHESTER   July 1

The Heaton Muslims Community Trust beat the Northern Jewish Cricket League by 21 runs in an inter-communal match in Stockport.

EALING GAZETTE   July 24

The annual grudge match between opposing parties on Ealing Council was cancelled when the Conservatives refused to play in protest against Labour attacks on the Tory mayor. "It's a way of saying their behaviour is not acceptable," said Conservative leader Jason Stacey. The Labour MP for Ealing North, Steve Pound, said: "I suppose the fact we beat them last time doesn't have any bearing on it."

SYDNEY MORNING HERALD July 27

New York police officers have been organising regular cricket matches for Asian youngsters living in Brooklyn. The scheme was the brainchild of police commissioner Raymond Kelly and followed a successful scheme to engage with Arab youths through soccer. The competition co-ordinator, Jeff Thompson (no relation), is a Brooklyn-born cop who learned cricket after marrying an Australian.

MIRROR.CO.UK August 1

Twin brothers Nazim and Zahid Mohammad have been banned after successfully pulling off an identity switch during an inter-league match. Nazim was picked as a bowler for the Liverpool & District Competition against the Nottinghamshire Premier League, but brother Zahid, the better batsman, took his place at the crease when Nazim's turn came. Officials failed to notice at the time – since Zahid made nought, there was not much time to notice – but word leaked out later. The brothers have now left their club, New Brighton.

LAWYERSWEEKLY.COM.AU August 4

Australia beat defending champions India by two wickets in the final of the Lawyers' Cricket World Cup at The Oval.

YORKSHIRE EVENING POST August 4

The Dewsbury Young Stars turned out an all-Patel team against Warwick, who also included three Patels – leading to a dismissal reading Patel c Patel b Patel 27. "It's just a coincidence," insisted club secretary Yunus Patel.

SUNDAY INDEPENDENT, PLYMOUTH August 9

Chris Prestt, 21, of Stokeinteignhead took all the Dartington & Totnes wickets in a South Devon League fixture, even though it was a match in which he was restricted to nine overs. Prestt took ten for 20 in 52 balls, as the opposition crumbled to 39 all out.

HEMEL GAZETTE   August 11

In Hertfordshire, two cricketers broke the same club's bowling records on the same day. Brad Klosterman took nine for 15 for the Leverstock Green first team, only to hear later that Imran Iqbal had taken nine for 13 for the second team that afternoon.

BBC.CO.UK   August 18

In Pakistan, a team of eunuchs has beaten a team of "normal" male cricketers in what is thought to have been the first match of its kind. The Sanam (Beloved) XI easily beat a local club, the Olympians, before a large crowd in the city of Sukkur. Eunuchs have long been regarded as outcasts in Pakistan – earning a precarious living by dancing, begging or prostitution – but Pakistan's chief justice, Iftikhar Chaudhry, has been working hard to improve the eunuchs' status. After the players had done an impromptu celebratory dance, captain Sanam Khan dedicated the victory to Justice Chaudhry.

DORSET ECHO   August 26

Robbie Stammas took ten for 13 in 10.5 overs for Wayfarers in the Dorset League against Old Blandfordians, who were bowled out for 39.

TIMES OF INDIA   August 28

A shopkeeper from Uttar Pradesh sold his shop and its entire stock of CDs and cassettes to pay for a trip to Mahendra Singh Dhoni's home town of Ranchi after his fiancée said she would marry him only if he could offer proof that he had met Dhoni. He spent a month in Ranchi, sometimes sleeping rough, awaiting the return of the cricketer, who eventually heard the story, took pity, and posed for a picture.

PRIVATE EYE   September 4

Citizen watches ran a press ad featuring Kevin Pietersen the day after injury forced his withdrawal from the Ashes. The slogan was: "Unstoppable? Kevin Pietersen is."

MUMBAI MIRROR   September 8

Residents living near the Wankhede Stadium, which is being renovated to host the 2011 World Cup final, have complained that the building site has become a breeding ground for malaria.

DAILY TELEGRAPH   September 9

Researchers from Loughborough University found that the behaviour of disruptive children improved after being introduced to cricket, even if it was only for a few hours. The study also found that cricket helped girls overcome "restrictive gender beliefs". One 11-year-old girl told researchers that she would get kicked if she played football with boys but added: "With cricket no one really tries to trick you and cheat. And we clap when someone does well."

FREE PRESS JOURNAL, MUMBAI   September 16

About a hundred members of clubs affiliated to the Coimbatore District Cricket Association in Tamil Nadu have staged a one-day fast to protest against alleged irregularities and officials "doing nothing" for the game's development.

FREE PRESS JOURNAL, MUMBAI   September 23

Warring factions battling for control of the Rajasthan Cricket Association both locked the other side out of the Sawai Man Singh stadium in Jaipur. Association president Sanjay Dixit had locked the offices but rebels who claimed they had voted Dixit out of office broke through barricades and installed their own padlocks.

MIDDELBURG OBSERVER   September 25

Ten-year-old South African leg-spinner David Blenkinsop has taken a hat-trick of hat-tricks, achieving the feat in three consecutive matches. Playing for Middelburg Primary's Under-11s he stormed through the three matches with combined figures of ten for five in five overs. David, whose hero is Shane Warne, practises for an hour and a half every day.

THE WISDEN CRICKETER   October

Players in south-east England who have been finding over-60s cricket too strenuous have started arranging over-70s matches. "We have two types of players: those who can run and those who can't," says organiser Roger Hawkins.

BIRMINGHAM POST   October 2

Warwickshire captain Ian Westwood has apologised for making derogatory remarks at a club dinner about women's cricket. Westwood called it "pointless" and "a waste of time" and said he would watch only if the players wore short skirts.

LANCASHIRE TELEGRAPH   October 15

Bowler Dave Bonner, retiring after 49 years playing for Darwen, turned out for the second XI in his final match, against Blackpool – and took a wicket with his last ball.

SURREY ADVERTISER   October 16

TV personality Henry Kelly infuriated the audience as guest speaker at the Surrey Championship's annual dinner at Sandown Park, a night described by one diner as "desperately sad but absolutely riveting". Presenting the prizes, Kelly mispronounced team names and made remarks like "whoever you are". A question and answer session involving officials from The Oval had to be aborted and when Kelly began his "rambling" speech he was slow hand-clapped. One man rose to ask "Are you being paid for tonight?" and a vote was taken on whether Kelly should be heard. Those in favour failed to muster double figures.

REUTERS   October 18

Olympic sprint champion Usain Bolt, a schoolboy cricket star, played in a charity match in Jamaica and hit West Indian captain Chris Gayle for a straight six. He also bowled Gayle, having welcomed him to the crease with a bouncer which brought the crowd at the Kaiser Sports Ground to its feet. "It's all coming back now," said Bolt.

SBS.COM.AU   October 19

Sir Don Bradman has been dumped from the Australian citizenship test to make it more relevant. Instead, migrants will be asked about their understanding of civic duty. Applicants will still be expected to know that Bradman was the "greatest cricketer of all time". But immigration minister Chris Evans said: "The new test is not a general knowledge quiz about Australia."

THE SPIN   October 27

Following in the footsteps of Australian opener-turned-cook Matthew Hayden, Simon Katich won his heat in Australia's *Celebrity Masterchef*, offering crusted salmon with lemon wilted spinach and creamy potato mash. The programme was shown on the day Katich was in Hyderabad, achieving another victory: captaining New South Wales to the Twenty20 Champions League. Katich had to overcome the culinary handicap of having no sense of smell. "The only problem I have is I don't know when something is burning."

DAILY EXPRESS   October 30

The Barmy Army is thinking of changing its name to Balmy Army in an attempt to establish a new brand image, according to founder Paul Burnham. "The word barmy makes us a sitting duck for allegations of being troublemakers," he said.

AGENCE FRANCE-PRESSE   November 6

A 12-year-old has scored 439 in the tournament that propelled Sachin Tendulkar to fame. Twenty-one years after Tendulkar (as a 15-year-old) scored 329 in the Harris Shield, Sarfaraz Khan surpassed him, playing for Springfield Rizvi School against the Indian Education Society. Sarfaraz enjoyed hitting 12 sixes and 56 fours in 421 balls, but disliked the fuss afterwards. "I swear I will never hit another 400 in my life," he was quoted as saying. "Slogging on the field is way easier than posing."

DAILY MAIL   November 19

Despite optimistic expectations of London publishers, celebratory Ashes books have failed to repeat the high sales figures of 2005. With only six selling weeks left to Christmas, Andrew Flintoff's latest opus led a flagging pack with UK bookshop sales of just 12,926 copies. Books by Mike Atherton, Andrew Strauss and the full England team were doing worse, with a newly published book by Stuart Broad managing just 107. Booksellers blamed the series' absence from terrestrial TV.

THE ISLAND   November 19

In Sri Lanka, the Under-13 cricketers of Mayadunne Vidyalaya were bowled out for 15 and four in a two-innings match against Rajasinghe school. Kasun Heshan took 13 wickets.

DAILY MIRROR, COLOMBO   November 21

Prageeth Dankumbura of Ehaliyagoda school took two hat-tricks in an innings in an Under-13 match against Aloysius school. Dankumbura took nine for five in three overs and Aloysius were bowled out for 18.

SUNDAY ISLAND   November 22

An eight-year-old off-spinner, Samud Weerakoon, startled his seniors in Sri Lankan Under-13 cricket by taking six for one in three overs for St Joseph's College, Kuliyapitiya.

GUARDIAN.CO.UK   November 26

An advertising campaign for Advanced Hair Studio featuring Shane Warne
and Graham Gooch has been called misleading by the UK Advertising
Standards Authority. The national press ad featured Warne and the line "Hair
worries are out!" And a series of photographs showed Gooch's scalp before
and after treatment. The ASA agreed with a complainant who said the ad
wrongly implied that treatment could lead to hair growing back. This reversed
a previous decision on the subject. The company said it would continue to
consult with the authority over its campaigns.

BBC NEWS   November 28

An art exhibition displaying the work of former England captain Michael
Vaughan has opened in Cardiff. Vaughan, first introduced to art galleries in
London by his team-mate Ashley Giles, has developed an abstract expressionist
technique he calls "artballing". Using painted cricket balls, Vaughan bats them
at the canvas and exhibits the results. He says the technique also relieved his
frustration after retirement.

MARKETING   November 30

England batsman Kevin Pietersen has emulated Denis Compton by becoming a poster boy for Brylcreem. Using the slogan "It's amazing where good hair gets you", the campaign shows Pietersen making himself at home in the Oval Office of the White House. The photos were shot on the set of the TV drama *The West Wing*.

THE GUARDIAN   November 30

The BBC apologised after an off-air comment by Geoff Boycott was picked up by a live microphone in the commentary box at the Port Elizabeth one-day international. Boycott shouted "effing tosser" when Ryan McLaren was dismissed.

THE TIMES   December 3

Cricket has been banned from Marina Beach, the stretch of sand near Chennai famous for thousands of informal games. The move, part of a "beautification project" to make the beaches more attractive to tourists, attracted furious local criticism, and special police units were dispatched to the beach to keep order. Youngsters have been spotted playing football instead.

BRAND REPUBLIC   December 10

Michael Vaughan has become the latest follically challenged cricketer to sign up for an advertising campaign with the Advanced Hair Studio.

SYDNEY SUN-HERALD   December 13

Anthony Karam of Parramatta took two hat-tricks in an innings in a third-grade fixture against North Sydney, who were bowled out for eight, thought to be the lowest score in the 116-year history of Sydney grade cricket. Eight players were out for ducks and Karam finished with seven for three.

THE SPIN   December 15

Andrew Flintoff and Shane Warne have become rivals as celebrity endorsers of socks, aimed at the Christmas present market. Flintoff has teamed up with artist Duncan Cargill to produce three "unique and exclusive" sock motifs. Two days later Warne's "Spinners" range is available in a "funky palette of colours and stripes in trendy fitted trunks and hipster briefs". Flintoff's profits were going to charity.

THE TOP-SPIN   December 22

Chris Hollins has become the third first-class cricketer to win the BBC contest *Strictly Come Dancing* in its five years, following Darren Gough and Mark Ramprakash. Hollins is best known as a BBC sports reporter and the son of

England footballer John Hollins. But he also scored 131 for Oxford in the 1994 University Match.

AUSTRALIAN ASSOCIATED PRESS   December 28

Hazel Smith of Melbourne has been awarded the ICC Centenary Volunteer Medal after providing about 27,000 sandwiches and 20,000 scones to cricketers over the past 68 years. Mrs Smith, 88, has made the teas at the Cameron Cricket Club since she married and gave up playing herself when she was 20.

DAILY EXPRESS   December 31

British taxpayers are being forced to pay almost £3m to teach criminals in Jamaica to play cricket. The cash is being provided from the Returns and Reintegration Fund, set up to support the repatriation of failed asylum seekers and foreign prisoners. "The initiative combines cricket training with instruction in life skills," said a Foreign Office spokesman. Shadow Justice Secretary Dominic Grieve described the scheme as "astonishing".

We welcome contributions from readers, especially items from local or non-UK media. Please send newspaper cuttings to Matthew Engel at Fair Oak, Bacton, Herefordshire HR2 0AT (always including the paper's name and date) and weblinks to almanack@wisdengroup.com.

RETIREMENTS IN 2009

Vaughan goes quietly

STEVE JAMES

Although he desperately wanted it, there was to be no Ashes-winning sequel involving **Michael Vaughan**. The Oval Test of 2005 was his last against Australia, and just over a week before the 2009 battle began Vaughan took his leave from the game.

His timing was spot on. Thoughts of one last crack at the ultimate enemy as England's No. 3 were not as fanciful as some suggested (he was still on a central contract, after all), but his body – especially his wonky right knee – was ailing and his mind becoming numbed in the anonymity of the shires. He did not get through one day of Championship cricket without going off for repairs before announcing his retirement at the end of June.

Vaughan departed with his reputation intact, though. The captain of that glorious 2005 winning series, he will be for ever remembered as one of England's shrewdest tacticians. He wasn't a bad batsman either. Indeed, in Australia in 2002-03 he was a great batsman, scoring 633 runs in the series, with three centuries, and almost single-handedly laying the foundations for the 2005 success with his fearless response to those perennial stabbers of English hearts, Glenn McGrath and Shane Warne.

That series in Australia was **Andrew Caddick's** last as a Test cricketer. In fact in its final innings the Somerset beanpole took seven for 94 to usher England to victory. It was a dead rubber and, of course, the second innings. And therein lay the great conundrum about Caddick: why was there such a huge difference between his first-innings bowling average (37.06) and second (20.81) in Tests?

To attribute this wholly to mental weakness is too simplistic. Caddick is, after all, currently eighth in England's all-time list of Test wicket-takers with 234, and he took 1,180 first-class wickets. He was a giant in the county game. While his bowling was simple – a high, smooth action modelled on compatriot Richard Hadlee – his character was anything but. Widely disliked by opponents (his "sledging" was often puerile), he endeared himself more easily to team-mates, who always averred that "he would do anything for you". Repairing TVs in Pakistan was, apparently, a speciality.

He required sympathetic handling, and was at his best for England under skipper Nasser Hussain and coach Duncan Fletcher. That he was not selected under a previous regime for the 1998-99 Ashes tour, despite having just taken 105 first-class wickets in the season, must rank as one of the most glaring omissions of all time.

Mark Butcher's match-winning 173 not out at Headingley in the 2001 Ashes said everything about his suitability at the top table, especially against the quicker men. His off-side play off the back foot was often sublime, but a

Michael Vaughan moved easily from player to pundit. *Right:* John Crawley, "an unfulfilled talent at international level".

short period batting with him at The Oval in 1998 against Muttiah Muralitharan revealed to me serious shortcomings against spin. Charging down the pitch with the ball turning so sharply away was not a good idea.

John Crawley was a better player of spin, and demonstrated as much in that Oval match with a classy 156 not out. But he was also an unfulfilled talent at international level, despite his coruscating county record at Lancashire and Hampshire. Considered too fond of the leg side early in his career, he worked at that. Considered a little too well-fed, he also worked at that (although taking up smoking was a curious beginning).

Truth be told, he was probably more deeply affected by being beaten up in Cairns early on the 1998-99 Ashes tour than he cared to admit. Confidence waned, inconsistency loomed at Test level. But a penchant for monstrous scores at the lower level remained. He made seven scores of 250 or more, including two unbeaten triple-centuries (both against Nottinghamshire).

Crawley's opposing captain in the 1993 Varsity match was **Jason Gallian,** later of Lancashire, Nottinghamshire and Essex. Educated at Oxford University (and an Australian Under-19 captain) he may have been, but Gallian was essentially from the old school. The modern fitness requirements were never to his liking. He played sumptuous off-drives on both front foot and back with a smile on his face, and then made friends with everyone. Apart from Kevin Pietersen, of course, whose kit he once threw over the balcony at Trent Bridge. Gallian was the only opponent ever to advise me to "get my head down" on a flat pitch.

Martin Saggers was another jolly fellow and, like Gallian, won three Test caps. As a bustling swing bowler he liked to get you out, though. And he often did. His was a heart-warming story of a late developer, a product of Minor

JUSTIN LANGER

A worker and a battler

Batting is hard work. And to watch Justin Langer bat was to understand its true extent. He was a worker, a battler. Elegance and fashion belonged elsewhere, residing with those not forever fretting about one's head falling over and succumbing lbw.

But the unfashionableness never affected the productivity. Langer might have often walked in the wake of the greats of his time, but his figures always talked as loudly as any Shane Warne or Glenn McGrath sledge. He made 7,696 Test runs at 45, with 23 centuries. He scored 28,382 first-class runs, more than any Australian, more even than Sir Donald Bradman.

The baggy green has surely never perched on a prouder pate. Crouched over his bat, the little left-hander was a picture of determination, passion and intensity. To Langer, batting was footwork and a sharp eye. In him cricket met pugilism, his favoured training method – he was also a martial-arts expert – and home to his all-time hero, Muhammad Ali.

So little wonder Langer was brave. He was hit everywhere on his debut against West Indies, still with a fearsome attack in 1992-93, and copped particularly nasty blows on the head from Andrew Caddick at The Oval in 2001 and Makhaya Ntini at Johannesburg in 2005-06. The second one (from the first ball he faced) rendered him horribly concussed and he took no further part in what was his 100th Test. But he was ready to. Against all advice ("another blow and you could die", the medics warned), he was padded up as Australia crept past South Africa by two wickets.

It is easily forgotten that Langer reinvented himself. Having been dropped after his initial foray into Test cricket and a pair against New Zealand, he returned with a resolve to attack. Australia had just initiated a policy to up their scoring-rate, and Langer recognised his duty. In one of the most fruitful opening partnerships of all time, he often outscored his towering ally and great mate Matthew Hayden, setting the tone with boundaries square of the wicket before Hayden had sized up the straighter extremes. It always irked Langer that he played only eight one-day internationals.

He finished his first-class career as captain of Somerset, after an earlier fruitful spell with Middlesex. He was not universally popular, but the best leaders often aren't. He wanted his charges to match his fanatical work ethic. Many could not. Some did not want to. But county cricket would be much the better for a few more injections of this steeliness.

He also finished amid some controversy. A pre-Ashes email sent to Australia's coach Tim Nielsen, detailing some unflattering thoughts about the England players, was leaked – to me, as it happens – and a brouhaha ensued. Langer was distraught, but he need not have been. Hardly anyone disagreed with him. He will now make a shrewd batting coach for Australia.   STEVE JAMES

Justin Langer's thoughts on English cricket appear on page 47.

Counties cricket discarded by Durham who then found remarkable success at Kent. In 2002 he was the joint leading wicket-taker in the country with 83. He is now becoming an umpire.

So too is **Alex Wharf**. He thrived at his third county, Glamorgan (after spells with Yorkshire and Nottinghamshire), and won 13 one-day international caps while there. He won the match award for his three for 30 on debut against India at Trent Bridge in 2004, an occasion still remembered light-heartedly by all journalists present for his painfully monosyllabic answers afterwards. At

Mark Ealham, dealer in consistency.

his best and fittest, Wharf was quick – a scar below my right eye after an eventful pre-season net session bears ample testimony to that. But too often he wasn't.

On the other hand **Mark Ealham** dealt in consistency. Here was a dependable, unspectacular all-rounder, a Falstaffian figure of voracious appetite also with a curiously modern predilection for fast, flashy cars. He could transcend his middling image on the field too – he did play 64 one-day internationals and eight Tests, after all – as when taking five for 15 against Zimbabwe in 1999-2000 (all lbw, still a one-day international record), and striking the season's fastest first-class century (45 balls) in 2006. For a man steeped in Kent history – his father Alan was a stalwart too – it was a surprise when he left for Nottinghamshire in 2004. But he did not let them down either.

Neither did **Jason Lewry** at Sussex. Indeed, he should have played for England, but the thought of the big stage (even televised county matches) unnerved him. A gentle, amiable soul, he was quicker than all of his contemporary English left-arm bowlers, and waspish late swing made him an awkward proposition.

Three wicketkeepers also left the game in 2009. Middlesex's **David Nash** was a chirpy, competitive scrapper who, despite premature promotion to England A in the winter of 1997-98, proved dependable at county level. **Jamie Pipe** was a better gloveman but could not establish himself fully at Worcestershire; he was beginning to do so at Derbyshire when the opportunity arose to become their physiotherapist. And Somerset's **Carl Gazzard** would have hoped for a lengthy career after Rob Turner's retirement in 2005, but unfortunately for him Craig Kieswetter arrived.

CAREER FIGURES

Players not expected to appear in county cricket in 2010
(minimum 40 first-class appearances)

BATTING

	M	I	NO	R	HS	100s	Avge	1,000r/ season
S. J. Adshead	73	118	18	3,179	156*	3	31.79	–
J. F. Brown	130	147	59	655	38	0	7.44	–
M. A. Butcher.........	280	478	39	17,870	259	38	40.70	8
A. R. Caddick.........	275	356	70	4,259	92	0	14.89	–
J. P. Crawley	351	584	60	24,361	311*	54	46.49	10
M. A. Ealham	281	422	67	11,349	153*	13	31.96	1
I. D. Fisher	80	119	19	2,201	103*	1	22.01	–
T. Frost	120	175	28	4,779	242*	6	32.51	1
J. E. R. Gallian	259	443	36	15,266	312	38	37.50	6
M. Hayward	133	150	55	1,074	55*	0	11.30	–
T. Henderson	86	137	17	1,897	81	0	15.80	–
C. B. Keegan	47	57	6	607	44	0	11.90	–
G. J. Kruis...........	130	180	58	1,849	59	0	15.15	–
J. L. Langer..........	360	622	57	28,382	342	86	50.23	5+6
S. G. Law	367	601	65	27,080	263	79	50.52	9+2
J. D. Lewry...........	187	247	66	1,834	72	0	10.13	–
Murtaza Hussain.......	148	211	40	3,571	117	1	20.88	–
D. C. Nash	140	203	43	5,684	114	11	35.52	–
J. Ormond...........	137	165	39	1,911	64*	0	15.16	–
D. J. Pipe...........	82	121	22	2,870	133*	4	28.98	–
M. J. Saggers	119	147	43	1,165	64	0	11.20	–
C. E. W. Silverwood...	183	242	48	3,075	80	0	15.85	–
C. M. Spearman	201	360	16	13,021	341	30	37.85	3
S. D. Stubbings........	139	251	14	7,557	151	12	31.88	3
B. V. Taylor..........	54	68	26	431	40	0	10.26	–
A. J. Tudor	129	169	34	2,960	144	2	21.92	–
M. P. Vaughan	268	468	27	16,295	197	42	36.95	4
A. G. Wharf	121	184	29	3,570	128*	6	23.03	–
P. J. Wiseman.........	186	254	51	4,254	130	2	20.95	–

Note: 5+6 indicates five seasons in England and six overseas.

BOWLING AND FIELDING

	R	W	BB	Avge	5W/i	10W/m	Ct/St
S. J. Adshead	–	–	–	–	–	–	192/15
J. F. Brown.............	14,039	414	7-69	33.91	22	5	26
M. A. Butcher..........	4,237	125	5-86	33.89	1	–	263
A. R. Caddick	31,387	1,180	9-32	26.59	78	17	88
J. P. Crawley	283	2	1-7	141.50	–	–	222/1
M. A. Ealham...........	17,962	643	8-36	27.93	24	2	158
I. D. Fisher.............	6,728	157	5-30	42.85	7	1	27
T. Frost................	30	1	1-12	30.00	–	–	259/18
J. E. R. Gallian.........	4,164	96	6-115	43.37	1	–	231
M. Hayward............	12,735	442	6-31	28.81	9	2	36
T. Henderson	7,024	262	7-67	26.80	10	1	31
C. B. Keegan	4,887	140	6-114	34.90	6	–	14
G. J. Kruis	12,804	406	7-58	31.53	19	1	45
J. L. Langer	210	5	2-17	42.00	–	–	324
S. G. Law..............	4,236	83	5-39	51.03	1	–	408

	R	W	BB	Avge	5W/i	10W/m	Ct/St
J. D. Lewry	16,834	621	8-106	27.10	31	4	52
Murtaza Hussain	14,305	573	9-54	24.96	36	7	70
D. C. Nash	105	2	1-8	52.50	–	–	297/23
J. Ormond	13,479	448	7-63	30.08	20	1	31
D. J. Pipe	5	0	–	–	–	–	226/21
M. J. Saggers	10,513	415	7-79	25.33	18	–	27
C. E. W. Silverwood	15,749	574	7-93	27.43	25	1	43
C. M. Spearman	55	1	1-37	55.00	–	–	197
S. D. Stubbings	121	0	–	–	–	–	64
B. V. Taylor	4,535	136	6-32	33.34	4	–	6
A. J. Tudor	11,023	351	7-48	31.40	14	–	36
M. P. Vaughan	5,245	114	4-39	46.00	–	–	117
A. G. Wharf	10,941	293	6-59	37.34	5	1	63
P. J. Wiseman	15,727	466	9-13	33.74	18	4	79

CRICKET BOOKS, 2009

One long ululation

ROBIN MARTIN-JENKINS

England's 2005 Ashes series sparked mania in the publishing world. A barrage of books hit the shops before it began, and again, following England's victory, in time for the Christmas rush. Some were excellent, many were awful. But it appears publishers have learnt their lesson this time round. Or it could be that the England players, determined not to make such a Trafalgar Square-induced embarrassment of themselves, decided to keep their laptops closed.

The best, appropriately, came from two of the most highly rated young(ish) cricket writers from either side of the world, Mike Atherton and Gideon Haigh. They have gone head-to-head with collections of their newspaper columns and Ashes reports. **Atherton's Ashes** may be an ironic title considering how close the author ever came to winning the urn as a player, but one of the joys of Atherton's writing is the eloquent ability to reveal an informed, experiential touch alongside his calculated analysis, and the 33 Ashes Tests he played lend this body of work much clout. "It's the quiet of those opening seconds that gets you," he says of the first ball of an Ashes series, and you can almost hear his mind whirr with recollection. "The bowler thundering in and the crowd utterly engrossed, more than a hundred years of gripping narrative distilled into one silent moment."

Haigh did not play a Test match, but his writing has much power in itself, and he is quickly establishing himself as the finest cricket writer to emerge from Australia. In **The Ultimate Test** he tells the story of the Ashes objectively – he was born in England – but with an Australian lilt that makes for refreshingly honest scrutiny. His wit and turn of phrase are so sharp that these pieces, while inevitably contemporaneous, will stand the test of time and be as enjoyable to read in 20 years. Speaking about Jimmy Anderson's knack of running in to bowl under helpful cloud cover when it had been sunny 20 minutes before, he remarks: "It's getting to the point where you wouldn't ask him to a barbeque."

Pit these two books against each other in a five-match series and the result would probably be 2–2. But, of course, there's no need to make it a competition. Buy them both and revel in some wonderful writing.

If interest at my local bookshop was anything to go by, however, the title that outsold these two at Christmas was **England's Ashes – The exclusive and official story of the npower Ashes Series 2009.** A catchy title you'd have to not agree. It is an amalgamation of interviews with the England players that is expertly woven together into a narrative by Peter Hayter, following the success of a similar ECB project in 2005. But while sanctioned time in the company of the players garnering their opinions might make the book "official" and "exclusive", it does not make it interesting – you would only have to listen to post-match TV interviews with the players to know that.

And what of the books brought out to whet the pre-Ashes appetite? There is an excellent publication of editorial work by Edward Craig in which he brings together the best pieces of writing on the Ashes that have appeared in *The Cricketer, Wisden Cricket Monthly* and the magazine progeny of their union, *The Wisden Cricketer*. **Story of the Ashes** covers the history of cricket's

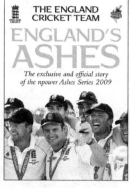

greatest rivalry in a vivid, magazine-style layout full of superb photos, drawings and charts. Alongside the eyewitness reports and analysis of matches are several fine essays on Ashes "heroes", from Jack Hobbs to Michael Vaughan. Most of the great cricket writers appear: R. C. Robertson-Glasgow, Neville Cardus, E. W. Swanton and, latterly, Atherton, Haigh and, dare it be said, CMJ. Such content deserves to be treasured for many years, and so its appearance, in a floppy "bookazine" format suggesting transience, is a shame.

The grown-up, big brother companion piece to this is **Wisden on the Ashes**, the history of the contest as told by this publication. Steven Lynch has painstakingly filtered through a vast, brooding collection of writing representing over 130 years of Ashes chronicle. The resulting 600 pages must be the most comprehensive and authoritative biography of the Ashes ever produced. For cricket lovers who don't have the complete set of yellow books this will be a vital addition to their library.

In **Bradman and the Summer that Changed Cricket** Christopher Hilton details the 1930 Australian tour of England, on which Bradman announced himself to the cricketing world with the small matter of 3,396 runs in 34 matches. That the touring team played so many games is one of the many delightful anachronisms to appear in a book that describes almost every step the Australian players took on their trip, bringing a lost world to life. The travel on slow, chugging trains between games, rarely with any days off, must have been exhausting for the players. Indeed, once the Ashes had been secured after six days of cricket in a timeless deciding Test at The Oval, the Australians hopped on a train early next morning for a two o'clock start against Gloucestershire. No wonder the Australian captain returned to the dressing-room after inspecting the pitch to find his whole team asleep. And there were five more games after that.

The book's USP is a description of every one of the 974 runs Bradman scored in the Test series. Yes, you read correctly: every run. Using a host of sources, from hitherto unseen reports, eyewitness accounts from players and pundits, scorecards and newspapers, Hilton details every turn off the hip for one, every cover drive and hook for four. It is a remarkable feat of research from a veteran of more than 60 books. It does make for a dry page or two, and the reader is left feeling rather like the England fielders must have done when

Bradman was scoring 334 at Headingley. But there is a running narrative about the friction that built up between Bradman, his team-mates and the tour manager, and this, together with the snippets of history interspersed with the match descriptions, keeps the book's head above water. Above all it gives a unique insight into how the most prolific batsman of all time went about building an innings.

Jack Fingleton was just too young for the 1930 tour, making his Australian debut two years later, but his life was to intertwine with Bradman's for 50 years until his death in 1981. The Australian journalist Greg Growden has used the long-running feud between the two as the overriding theme in his excellent biography **Jack Fingleton: The Man who Stood Up to Bradman**.

It appears Fingleton's relationship with the Don was strained from their first meeting when, as teenagers, Bradman had corrected him on his pronunciation of the word tetanus, with apparent scorn in his voice. Fingleton filed away the thought that the young Bradman's self-assuredness marked him out from his peers. As they became team-mates, first for New South Wales and then for their country, their differences became irreconcilable, and incident after incident opened up a chasm of loathing between them. Fingleton was envious of Bradman's prolificacy, undoubtedly. But there was envy on both sides, for Bradman took his newspaper work very seriously, and Fingleton was clearly the more gifted writer. Things came to a head during the Bodyline series when the now infamous conversation between Bill Woodfull, the Australian captain, and Pelham Warner, the MCC manager ("there are two teams out there; one is trying to play cricket and the other is not") was leaked to the press, causing a volcano of emotion to spill out into a full-blown diplomatic crisis. Fingleton was convinced it was Bradman who disclosed the story, and wrote about it many times in his later career as a journalist. Bradman always countered the claims by insinuating Fingleton was the culprit. All the actors in this drama have now died, taking their secrets to the grave, but Growden collates enough evidence to support Fingleton's allegations, and the rest of his life is played out with bitterness towards Bradman.

This is not an especially balanced memoir. Despite admitting that his subject could be "abrasive, petulant and infuriatingly forthright", the author clearly takes sides against Bradman. It is a shame, too, that only snippets of Fingleton's writing appear throughout the book. He was probably the most respected Australian cricket writer of his time, and this book would seem the ideal platform to showcase his talent. It is, nonetheless, a well-researched, smoothly written and fascinating read that goes some way towards redressing the balance of the endless volumes of hagiography dedicated to Bradman.

Books can reach out to different people in so many ways. Imaginations are captured by brilliant stories; or ordinary stories brilliantly told. Sometimes the story is inconsequential; it is the quality of the writing that entertains. The life and times of Neville Cardus would make a good tale in itself but in **Cardus, Celebrant of Beauty** Robin Daniels has illustrated a personal memoir of the iconic writer with countless quotes and passages from Cardus's lifetime body of work, thus guaranteeing each page is permeated with grace and eloquence in equal measure.

Much is made of the fact that Cardus's genius sprang from the most unlikely of circumstances: his mother was a prostitute, part of a sprawling family fighting to float above the poverty line in Victorian Manchester. He never knew his father. Forced to leave school at 13 to help contribute to the family coffers, Cardus nevertheless educated himself at local libraries, "directed," he says, "by forces born within me – I indulged those forces."

Falling into the world of cricket almost by chance, he quickly established himself as the foremost commentator on the game, revelling in column-inch space that would make the modern hack swoon. Take this description of a Bradman innings: "In the forge of his batsmanship, molten history was being beaten into shape... Spirit lived in every stroke. Beauty that comes out of life at the crown of manhood." His style might appear florid to us now, but Daniels points out that many of today's breed of cricket writers owe their existence to Cardus, John Arlott calling him "the father of literate sports writing".

It is a comprehensive and wide-ranging memoir in which Cardus's life in cricket plays out as just one act. He was, of course, equally revered in the music world. Daniels portrays his subject as a kindly writer, a "celebrant of beauty" indeed, whose music reviews and musings on cricket were quick to focus on individual personality; they were "hymns of praise" to the artists he watched. Daniels's own hymn of praise to his friend is one of the most engaging reads of the year.

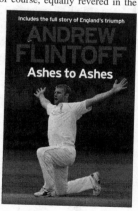

Includes the full story of England's triumph

ANDREW FLINTOFF

Ashes to Ashes

The book is blemished slightly by a peculiar piece of miscasting that sees Andrew Flintoff as one of four (yes, four) introducers. Reading Flintoff's contribution is like seeing Jean-Claude Van Damme appear on stage beside Sir Laurence Olivier.

Fortunately, Freddie has made amends with a book of his own (introduced by no one) where he plays the Van Damme role in a more natural setting. **Ashes to Ashes** (how do they come up with those titles?) is a straight-talking account of the four years since the 2005 Ashes series. Myles Hodgson worked with Flintoff on his previous title (*Being Freddie*), which was the biggest-selling sports book of 2005, partly as a result of that Ashes-induced euphoria that swept the nation, and he has again captured Flintoff's voice well. But this book has a more serious air than its predecessor, reflecting perhaps both a more mature Flintoff and what the all-rounder has been through since the high drama of 2005.

Flintoff recalls the 0–5 return-series drubbing in Australia, "Fredalo" in the West Indies, friction with Duncan Fletcher, a loss of batting form, a range of career-threatening injuries... The controversies are handled with trademark Flintoff unfussiness. Things didn't work out as England captain? No matter, I wasn't cut out for it anyway. Fletcher slagged me off in his book? I didn't read

it. He has a commendably straightforward approach to life, and that is one of the reasons he has remained a darling of the nation for so long. Transcribe this attitude to the page, however, and the result is slight tedium for any reader hoping for a juicy warts-and-all revelation.

If it's scandalous gossip you're after, you should probably avoid anything by a current cricketer, let alone one who is captain of his country and enjoying the job too much to compromise his position with salacious comment. So you'll find none of that in Andrew Strauss's book **Testing Times – in Pursuit of The Ashes**, written with Scyld Berry, which, according to the cover sleeve, is the "Ashes-winning captain's personal account of a remarkable and tumultuous two-year period in world cricket". It has to be said there is not much tumult in the book, although the Mumbai bombings are discussed, as are the relative debacles the Stanford 20/20 and the Peter Moores/KP saga.

Strauss, of course, was a major beneficiary of the latter cock-up, and reading his shiningly simple captaincy philosophy, it's difficult to see why he wasn't chosen ahead of KP in the first place. Most of the book covers the 2009 Ashes series and, unlike some, this reviewer sees no problem with the fact that it appeared on the shelves only three weeks after Graeme Swann took the final wicket at The Oval. This immediacy lends the book an energy that more considered post-mortems can lack. There may be no point criticising the book too much anyway because the ghost writer might have used his executive power as *Wisden* editor to scrub these comments out but, as it happens, Berry has made a superior job of eliciting the excitement and mania an Ashes series brings to the England players and in particular their captain. Strauss's insights into the demands of the job are most revealing and, overall, this is a pleasing book: intelligent, level-headed, although perhaps lacking a little pizzazz. Rather like Strauss's batting, really.

Freed from the shackles of an ECB contract, Michael Vaughan has been somewhat spicier in his autobiography, **Time to Declare**, written with Mike Dickson. Serialised in *The Times* during the summer, it caused quite a stir, particularly with his hitherto unknown, trenchant views on Peter Moores and the England selectors. These are sometimes revealed in a "secret diary" format that permeates the book at strangely inconsistent intervals. That Vaughan was the most successful England Test captain of all time lends his opinions much credence, and this book does a fine job of revealing why he thrived in one of the most high-profile positions in sport. From an early age he seems to have been imbued with a natural phlegm (of the un-sticky kind) which was to serve him well in the pressurised environment of Test match captaincy. It also came in handy dealing with a senior England team whose ego sizes varied from the quite large upwards.

But the merit of this book really lies in Vaughan's candid admission of mental frailty, particularly towards the end of his career. The turmoil in his head during his last few months of captaincy may not compare with Marcus Trescothick's breakdown, but in revealing his problems so frankly in his autobiography last year, Trescothick has paved the way for other cricketers to pour out their hearts. Vaughan certainly follows suit. Struggling with batting form and confidence… worried about dropping catches… believing his luck

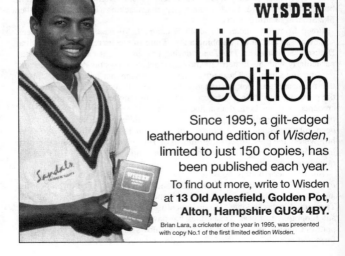

had run out as captain... a lack of confidence in Moores and the selectors (Geoff Miller in particular is painted in an underwhelming light)... increasing impatience with the press and other off-field aspects of the job... tension in his home life... It may have been a bombshell to the general public when he resigned, but reading the book and seeing what the job of England captain really entails, the only surprise is that it took so long for the strain and anxiety to reach boiling point.

One player who hasn't waited for his retirement before spilling the beans is Matthew Hoggard. **Hoggy – welcome to my world** is the most original cricket autobiography to be produced for many years. It's an eccentric book, as befits an eccentric character, which begins with a foreword written by his two dogs (renamed paw-word) and then takes you through his life accompanied by a series of doodles, puzzles, "Hogfacts" (such as "when flies take off, they jump backwards"), various bits by his wife, Sarah, and even some by his two-year-old son, Ernie. It's all presented in a variety of typefaces with passages of text punctuated by lists, such as the top five messiest England cricketers, and sometimes his attempt at showing just how much of a madcap, straight-talking Yorkshireman he is grates. But cut through all the wackiness, and there is an entertaining, informative and revealing story to be read.

Hoggard clearly possesses an able mind, and his eye picks out some of the more interesting aspects of life on tour with England or in a county dressing-room; the descriptions of on-field action are kept mercifully brief. There is a lot of humour in the book – especially enjoyable is his discussion of the strange concept that is the night-watchman: "Is there any other sport where somebody gets promoted specifically because they're not very good at doing something?" But there is also plenty of pathos: the difficulties his marriage went through when they were trying to conceive, and the depression suffered by his wife, are both told with agonising honesty (thanks again, perhaps, to Trescothick).

The main bean-spilling revolves around the ECB and their poor treatment of Hoggard when he was dropped from the England team, losing his central contract in the process. Almost a whole summer went by without any contact between the two, and Hoggard is scathing about the ECB's lack of man-management skills. Geoff Miller is again implied with the complaint: "And these are people given highly paid jobs because of their supposed ability to manage people." Hoggard may have signed his England death warrant with some of his comments, but this is not an acerbic book on the whole. It is a bawdy romp through the career of one of England's most unusual cricketers of recent times.

Another of England's biggest "characters" of recent times (note the deliberate inverted commas), Ronnie Irani, has written the year's biggest stinker. In **No Boundaries**, Irani is at great pains to tell everyone just how hard he plays life, both on and off the pitch. It may appeal to those who tune in to his raucous talkSport radio show, but it reminded me of the autobiography of Dave Podmore, a fictional county cricketer who appeared in a column in *The Guardian* a few years ago. "Pod", as he liked to be known, played for various counties, always gave 110%, and was forever hoping for "the nod" from the selectors. Pod's book was an extremely funny send-up of just the sort of autobiography Irani has written. Like one of his out-swingers on a good length, it should be left well alone.

Of the many autobiographical works to have appeared this year, the most enlightening is Mark Wagh's **Pavilion to Crease… and Back**. This is the Mark Wagh without the "u", from Birmingham rather than Sydney. No tales about batting in the back garden with Tugga then, but rather an intelligent diary of a county season in which Wagh's team, Nottinghamshire, came within a sliver of winning two trophies. We are taken, sans ghost writer, deep into the psyche of the journeyman county cricketer; a place full of fear, paranoia, self-loathing and, just occasionally, joy. All of which is unsurprising coming from an Oxford psychology graduate.

Wagh intersperses the short accounts of the matches and practice days that make up the body of the season with longer reflections on the psychology of the game – What is mental strength? What makes a good captain? – and these are interesting enough, if a little studied. There are moments of fun in the dressing-room too: a banana-eating contest to stave off boredom on a rainy day; coach Mick Newell's almost schizophrenic strops; any event involving Mark Ealham. But it is the refreshing candour with which Wagh analyses his own performances and his interaction with his team-mates that is the real heartbeat of the piece. He is a one-man testament to the widely held theory that cricket is played 90% with the mind and only 10% with the body. Time and again the reader is transported into the mind of Wagh, the batsman, as he takes guard with myriad negative thoughts thundering past. His description of batting as a "mental ordeal" seems apt.

Wagh's skill as a writer is to take you on this journey of self-discovery with disarming honesty. Accounts of seemingly innocent events on and off the pitch are laced with self-reproach: a misdirected throw that costs his team a run during a comfortable victory haunts him for three days; a visit to a children's orphanage on a pre-season tour of Uganda leaves him feeling awkward when he finds he has "virtually no ability to relate to kids". His humility leaves you rooting for the man as he wades through the mire of a long county season.

Anyone who has ever played sport to any degree of seriousness will at some point have tasted defeat, and have someone say: "No matter. It's not the winning that counts, but the taking part." What rot!

Or so I thought until reading Max Davidson's book, **It's Not the Winning That Counts:** The Most Inspiring Moments of Sporting Chivalry. Inspired by the iconic photograph of Andrew Flintoff consoling Brett Lee after the epic Edgbaston Test in 2005, Davidson set out to discover more tales of sporting gallantry, and pondered the question of whether these individual moments of grace and chivalry can transcend the meaning of two people, or teams, battling to beat each other.

The 50 or so short tales are impeccably researched and elegantly framed into a convincing narrative that takes you all over the globe, across many different sports, and even millennia. We see how the Roman Emperor Titus, chucking out the rule book, awarded a draw to the gladiators contesting the Colosseum's opening games, much against the wishes of a crowd baying for blood. Two thousand years later Mark Taylor, the Australia cricket captain, declared with his own score on 334 so he would not surpass the record of the great Don Bradman, instinctively realising, says Davidson, that: "Records are just numbers on a page. It is the grace notes, the flashes of underlying humanity, that make professional sport so enthralling."

This is a book for those who like to spread open and devour the sports pages of the weekend broadsheets, a breath of fresh air for those who lament the age of highly paid sportsmen hitting the headlines for all the wrong reasons. Davidson is warm, erudite and a joy to read. There is plenty of cricket in the book (he is clearly a cricket nut), justifying its inclusion here, and there are also familiar anecdotes from other mainstream sports. But the book also takes the reader into the less widespread worlds of chess, round the world yachting and women's Olympic fencing, to name but a few, and it is here that the true heroes emerge.

Take the Australian sculler, Bobby Pearce who, in the 1928 Olympics in Amsterdam, stopped rowing in the quarter-final to allow a family of ducks to cross his path. He still won the race, but in that moment: "Olympic gold no longer mattered. Ducks did matter. How stupid. How sublime."

One person who would no doubt have enjoyed Davidson's book was the late cricket writer Alan Gibson. For 20 years from 1967 Gibson wrote for *The Times* and *The Cricketer*, mainly reporting on county cricket, developing a unique style that gathered a cult-like readership. Those unfamiliar with his work can join that cult thanks to his son Anthony, who has collected his father's best pieces into an anthology: **Of Didcot and the Demon**.

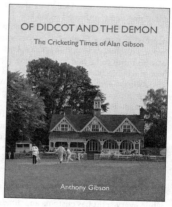

OF DIDCOT AND THE DEMON

The Cricketing Times of Alan Gibson

Anthony Gibson

Possessed of a brilliant mind and a breathtaking wit, Gibson painted vibrant pictures of the cricket he watched. It was the players he was interested in, more so than the play. While watching Boycott make a double-hundred at Colchester, Gibson was fascinated by Yorkshire's running between the wickets: "The present Yorkshire system is for both batsmen to shout simultaneously, pause and then shout again. If, as happens about once an over, this has not cleared the situation up, it is considered wise to keep shouting. This is especially the policy of Boycott, whose progress down the pitch is often one long ululation."

Later, Gibson sums up Boycott's innings: "On only 45 occasions, I estimate, did Boycott give Essex the slightest hope. Just before lunch he played and missed at Boyce; at 84 he popped a ball which had checked just short of cover; there was one appeal for leg-before which may not have been too far away, and on 42 occasions he might have been run out."

At another match, on hearing Trevor Jesty was unfit to bowl, he found out why: "He was, I heard him explain, suffering from 'a strain on the inner wall of the lower abdomen'. There is your modern cricketer. Tom Goddard would have said: 'Oy dun me gut.'"

Some of his favourite cricketers acquired whimsically god-like status, such as the Somerset stalwart, Colin Dredge, whom he nicknamed the Demon of Frome. On first seeing him play, Gibson included this tribute: "The authors of Methuen's *Little Guide to Somerset* once wrote that 'Frome has never helped to make history' and that 'the visitor would do well to make his way at once to the church, which is practically the only thing in Frome worth seeing.' The next edition will have to have a footnote for our lanky and enthusiastic Demon."

Such digressions coloured all of his writing. Indeed he was at his best when there was no play to watch, his pen always quick to find inspiration in the characters around the ground, or in the ground itself. John Woodcock summed up his style with the line: "I wrote about the cricket; Alan wrote about a day at the cricket." He was the P. G. Wodehouse of cricket writers. Although he had an encyclopaedic knowledge of the game, his simple elegant prose always entertained first, informed second.

Unfortunately, Gibson's private life was rather more complicated. A manic depressive with a fondness for the bottle, he littered his writing with light-hearted references to public houses, bars and barmaids, but for his family there was no mirth to be had from reading them. His self-destructive streak landed him in trouble more than once and, in 1975, resulted in his sacking from the *Test Match Special* commentary team. We learn all this from his son, who has written introductions to each, chronologically laid out, chapter. They serve as a poignant account of his father's descent into alcoholism that damaged his family, his work and eventually his life. But while the book quite rightly tackles these issues, they are but a footnote: this is a collection of works, not a biography. Above all, it is a celebration of one of the most amusing cricket writers of all time, and undoubtedly one of the best books of the year.

Another of the year's "collected works" of note comes from Gideon Haigh. Not content with a collection of his Ashes columns (see above), he has gathered together articles written for various publications over the past decade under the rather loose theme of "cricket culture". In **Inside Out**, Haigh explains that while every sport has customs and dimensions that distinguish itself from other games, in cricket these processes seem "peculiarly sophisticated and evolved, being commingled with notions of class, race, nation, empire, past and future".

Hence the essays are wide-ranging: from a discussion of Bodyline to the Packer revolution or the art of the leave in batting. Cricket's future is discussed, in particular the role of Twenty20, and there is a section of reviews of cricket's most "meaningful" books. Inevitably from an Australian writer, there is an Aussie slant to the pieces. In a comprehensive segment on Bradman, he assesses the man and the phenomenon more successfully than any biography has ever done and, in an outstanding dissection of what it means to Australian cricketers to wear the "baggy green", Haigh notes how it has only been seen as a national icon since Steve Waugh's reign. The fast bowler Frank Misson thought the cap "a little unfashionable", and Bill Brown said: "In my day they were just cricket caps and flung into our bags. We didn't look after them." Bradman and Richie Benaud gave all of theirs away. The myth that the cap has always been part of the national consciousness is eroded gently with allusion to the Marxist historian Eric Hobsbawm and his concept of "invented tradition". Such erudite references litter Haigh's copy, colouring it with an intelligence unparalleled in current cricket writing. And yet his writing is never dry. His pen drips with the purest of cricketing prose, making each page a delight to read.

Only the most devoted listeners of *Test Match Special* could cite the name of its producer of 34 years: Peter Baxter. But anyone who has enjoyed even five minutes of *TMS's* legendary *joie de vivre* will gain pleasure from **Inside the Box**, Baxter's account of his life with the BBC institution. Working with some of cricket's greatest characters has given him a rich seam of material, and warm stories spring from every page. Many of the best involve the troubles of broadcasting in the cricket-mad but chaotic subcontinent. There are also familiar tales told with a new slant from the producer's all-seeing eye. Thus we learn that Jonathan Agnew's famous line in the "leg-over incident" was premeditated, fed to him by a press-box colleague before he went on air. He knew exactly the reaction it would cause in his fellow commentator, Brian Johnston. Even 18 years later, having been recounted numerous times, the episode can't fail to raise a smile. This is indeed a life-affirming book that envelops the reader, rather as the *TMS* listener, tuned in on a rainy day, is enveloped in a warm fug of gently humorous anecdotes.

Several of those stories involve the time-keeping issues and general absent-mindedness of Christopher Martin-Jenkins, whom Baxter has dubbed "the late CMJ". But even though he once mistook his mobile phone for a TV remote control, CMJ is one of the game's most respected and distinguished voices. In his latest book, **The Top 100 Cricketers of All Time**, he has leant on his experience to profile the greatest players who have graced the game. It is a mammoth task, which he accomplishes with consummate skill, the essays being revealing, clear and concise. With the exception of Adam Gilchrist, perhaps, there are few surprises in his top ten, Bradman coming top, of course. Some will inevitably disagree with his other choices, and the order in which they come, and in his introduction and conclusion he names a hundred more players that might have made the list on another day. Joel Garner, Mike Procter and Anil Kumble would probably have made this reviewer's list, but who is he to argue with the author's 40 years of experience in cricket, especially as his inheritance has yet to be divvied out.

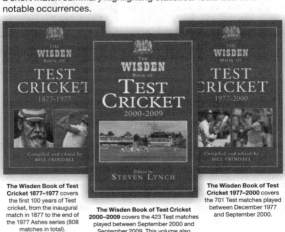

The year's most visually arresting book is **Cricket Grounds from the Air**. Ian Hay has taken astonishing aerial photos of every county headquarters and many of the outgrounds too; Zaki Cooper and Daniel Lightman have provided descriptions and potted histories of the counties. There is something about the aerial photo that appeals to the eye, rooted as it usually is to terra firma, and here each photo holds and challenges the viewer, even when you think you know the ground inside out. Only an aerial photo can show the perfect symmetry of the Rose Bowl, or how recent stand remodelling has cruelly cut corners off Trent Bridge and The Oval (rendering the latter distinctly un-oval in shape). Headingley looks resplendent in Leeds sunshine, but no amount of sun can hide the harsh ugliness of Old Trafford or Edgbaston. And did you realise how close Chester-le-Street is to the sea? It is a fabulous book. No coffee table should be without it.

The subtitle to Simon Hughes's book **And God Created Cricket** is so clunky it is enough to put anyone off. The publishers haven't helped his cause either by including a quote from a cricket commentator called "Richie Bernard" in their press release. But this "irreverent history of the English game and how other people (like Australians) got annoyingly good at it" has its moments, and Hughes's attempt to reach out to younger generations who might not have the concentration to devour the seminal work that is Derek Birley's *A Social History of English Cricket* is laudable. The text skips along at a happy rate, forever defaulting to humour, even when tackling some of cricketing history's weightier subjects.

Mostly the irreverence is fun, although sometimes the jokes misfire, as when he blames C. B. Fry for starting the Second World War: "He once spent an hour chatting to Hitler, trying, and failing, to persuade him to form a cricket team. He spent so long explaining the lbw law that it drove Germany into invading Poland." This book somehow just misses the mark, as if 500 years of cricket history should deserve a more formal analysis. It also deserves an index and some photographs – glaring omissions in a book of this kind.

Another conspicuous exclusion, apart from half a page of reference, is any description of the rebel tours to South Africa undertaken by various international teams in the 1980s. This period of cricketing controversy has been neatly swept under the carpet for too long. Peter May has tried to redress the balance with a well-crafted account of the six tours. **Rebel Tours** reads very well, and the descriptions of the cricket are excellent. Unfortunately, however, while there is plenty of first-hand comment from the South African players involved, the author has persuaded only two English "rebels" to talk. May claims he attempted to speak to all those involved, but one wonders how hard he tried, and his failure to gather the recollections and opinions of any of the main figures in the touring parties strips this book of much authority. So we are left to speculate about why Graham Gooch and Mike Gatting (among others) put their careers at great risk for such a controversial venture.

Another of cricket's greatest controversies, Bodyline, has never suffered from a lack of coverage. If anything, the impact of the story, revisited every Ashes year, is in danger of being diminished by overexposure. The effect it had on the players involved, however, should never be underestimated.

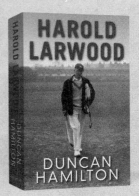

Reputations were made and lost, and lives for ever altered. And none was more affected than Harold Larwood, one of England's greatest fast bowlers. His life has finally been properly told in an outstanding authorised biography by Duncan Hamilton.

In **Harold Larwood**, Hamilton tenderly recounts a life full of pathos. Bowling was Larwood's escape from the twin drudgeries of coal mining and Methodism in working-class Nottinghamshire. The remarkable speed he produced from a scrawny 5ft 4in frame quickly became legend. The author is perhaps prone to exaggerate the extent of that speed, or at least the regularity with which he hit batsmen and broke stumps, but it is clear Larwood was a phenomenon of his time.

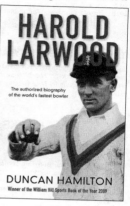

Used as Bodyline's chief weapon by England captain Douglas Jardine, whose obsession with humiliating Don Bradman was the genesis of leg theory, Larwood was then exploited as a scapegoat during the ensuing diplomatic crisis. Asked to apologise by an elitist MCC, he refused, was condemned, and never played for England again. His county career petered out unhappily too, his body, broken on the hard pitches of Australia, unable to reproduce the demon speed that had scythed through the Australian batting and tamed the great Bradman. He retired to run a sweet shop in Blackpool, though bitter resentment filled his veins, and then, less than 20 years after the Bodyline series and having had enough of the mother country, he emigrated to Australia. The irony of his final resting place was not lost on Larwood, and the hitherto unfamiliar account of his life in Australia is immaculately researched and narrated.

Hamilton won the William Hill Sports Book of the Year award in 2007 for his biography of Brian Clough, and here again he effortlessly employs his skills as a fine storyteller. The book is a biographical tour de force, reading like a great, sweeping historical novel. Moreover, it is beautifully produced, scattered with lovely, previously unpublished photographs and other documents from Larwood's own collection. However big a media event the modern-day Ashes series has become – and 2009 was no exception – there will never be another story to emerge from them as poignant, or important, as this. *Harold Larwood*, by Duncan Hamilton, is the *Wisden* Book of the Year.

Robin Martin-Jenkins has played first-class cricket for Sussex since 1995.

WISDEN BOOK OF THE YEAR

Since 2003, *Wisden's* reviewer has selected a Book of the Year. The winners have been:

2003 *Bodyline Autopsy* by David Frith
2004 *No Coward Soul* by Stephen Chalke and Derek Hodgson
2005 *On and Off the Field* by Ed Smith
2006 *Ashes 2005* by Gideon Haigh
2007 *Brim Full of Passion* by Wasim Khan
2008 *Tom Cartwright: The Flame Still Burns* by Stephen Chalke
2009 *Sweet Summers: The Classic Cricket Writing of JM Kilburn* edited by Duncan Hamilton
2010 *Harold Larwood: The authorized biography of the world's fastest bowler* by Duncan Hamilton

THE CRICKET SOCIETY AND MCC BOOK OF THE YEAR AWARD

The Cricket Society Literary Award has been presented since 1970 to the author of the cricket book judged best of the year. The 2009 award, the first to be made by the Cricket Society in association with MCC, was won by John Barclay for **Life Beyond the Airing Cupboard** (Fairfield Books); he received £3,000.

BOOKS RECEIVED IN 2009

GENERAL

Arnold, Michael **The Bodyline Hypocrisy** Conversations with Harold Larwood (Know the Score Books, £12.99, paperback)

Atherton, Mike **Atherton's Ashes** How England Won the 2009 Ashes (Simon & Schuster, £18.99)

Barker, Tony **Cricket's Wartime Sanctuary** The First-Class Flight to Bradford Foreword by Bob Appleyard (Association of Cricket Statisticians – ACS Sales, Blue Bell House, 2–4 Main Street, Scredington, Sleaford, Lincolnshire NG34 0AE, email: sales@acscricket.com, £20)

Baxter, Peter **Inside the Box** My life with Test Match Special Foreword by Jonathan Agnew (Quiller, £18.99)

Berkmann, Marcus **Ashes to Ashes** 35 Years of Humiliation (and About 20 Minutes of Ecstasy) Watching England v Australia (Little, Brown, £16.99)

Botham, Sir Ian **My Sporting Heroes** Botham: His 50 Greatest from Britain and Ireland (Mainstream, £18.99)

Chaturvedi, Ravi **Legendary Indian Cricketers** (Men, Moments and Memories) Foreword by Sharad Pawar (Ocean Books, Rs 500)

cricketwithballs.com (Jarrod Kimber) **The year of the balls 2008: a disrespective** Foreword by Gideon Haigh (Lulu, £7, paperback)

Davidson, Max **It's Not the Winning that Counts** The most inspiring moments of sporting chivalry (Little, Brown, £12.99)

England Cricket Team, The **England's Ashes** The exclusive and official story of the npower Ashes Series 2009 (Orion, £18.99)

Evans, Colin **Mods & Blockers** Lancashire's Rock 'n' Roll Summer (Max Books, £9.99)
    Former Wisden correspondent's account of the summer of 1965.

Ezekiel, Gulu **The Penguin Book of Cricket Lists** (Penguin India, paperback, Rs 200)

Firth, Grenville **Yorkshire's Cricketing Legends** Foreword by Ray Illingworth (Breedon Books, £16.99)

Frindall, Bill **Ask Bearders** Answers to the World's Most Challenging Cricket Questions Foreword by Jonathan Agnew (BBC Books, £9.99)

Gibson, Anthony **Of Didcot and the Demon** The Cricketing Times of Alan Gibson Foreword by John Woodcock (Fairfield Books, £20)

Haigh, Gideon **Inside Out** Writings on Cricket (Aurum, £8.99, paperback)

Haigh, Gideon **The Ultimate Test** The Full Story of the 2009 Ashes Series (Aurum, £12.99)

Hignell, Andrew **From Sophia to Swalec** A History of Cricket in Cardiff (The History Press, £20)

Hilton, Bob ed. **The Elusive Mr Cardus** Letters and Other Writings of Neville Cardus, 1916–1975 (limited edition of 500, from Rev. Malcolm Lorimer, 4 The Willows, Manor Avenue, Sale, Cheshire M33 4NA, £15, paperback)

Hilton, Christopher **Bradman and the Summer that Changed Cricket** The Amazing 1930 Australian Tour of England (JR Books, £18.99)

Hughes, Simon **And God Created Cricket** An Irreverent History of the English Game and How Other People (like Australians) Got Annoyingly Good at It (Doubleday, £20)

Martin-Jenkins, Christopher **The Top 100 Cricketers of All Time** (Corinthian, £14.99)

Maun, Ian comp. **From Commons to Lord's: A Chronology of Cricket 1700–1799** Volume I: 1700–1750 Foreword by the Duke of Richmond and Gordon (limited edition of 220, from Roger Heavens, 2 Lowfields, Little Eversden, Cambridgeshire CB23 1HJ, www.booksoncricket.net, £12, inc CD)

May, Peter **The Rebel Tours** Cricket's Crisis of Conscience (SportsBooks, £17.99)

Murphy, Patrick **The Centurions** from Grace to Ramprakash (Fairfield Books, £18)

Murray, Bruce and Vahed Goolam, eds **Empire & Cricket** The South African Experience 1884–1914 Foreword by André Odendaal (University of South Africa Press, £30, paperback)

Norridge, Julian **Can We Have Our Balls Back, Please?** How The British Invented Sport (And then almost forgot how to play it) (Penguin, £9.99, paperback)

Oxborrow, Ian and Pritchard, Rob **Fletcher's Aces and Jokers** Essex – County Cricket Champions 1979 (Desert Island Books, £12.99, paperback)

Perry, Roland **Bradman's Invincibles** The story of the 1948 Ashes tour (Aurum, £20)

Stewart, Alec **My Cricket Companion** (Corinthian, £16.99)

Tennant, Andy **Cricket Manual** The official guide to playing the game Foreword by Michael Vaughan (Haynes, £17.99)

Wellock, Tim **Summers with Durham** A Celebration of Durham County Cricket Club Foreword by Stephen Harmison (Caboodle Books, paperback, £9.99)

BIOGRAPHY

Barker, Tony **Ric Charlesworth** This Sporting, Medical and Political Life (Association of Cricket Statisticians – ACS Sales, Blue Bell House, 2–4 Main Street, Scredington, Sleaford, Lincolnshire NG34 0AE, email: sales@acscricket.com, paperback, £11)

Briggs, Paddy **John Shepherd** The Loyal Cavalier (ACS, paperback, £12)

Daniels, Robin **Cardus, Celebrant of Beauty** (Palatine, £25)

Growden, Greg **Jack Fingleton** The Man who Stood Up to Bradman (Allen & Unwin, £20.00)

Hamilton, Duncan **Harold Larwood** The authorized biography of the world's fastest bowler (Quercus, £20)

Harragan, Bob and Hignell, Andrew **C. P. Lewis** The Champion Cricketer of South Wales (ACS, paperback, £11)

Pracy, David **A. P. 'Bunny' Lucas** The Best of All My Boys (ACS, paperback, £12)

Ryan, Christian **Golden Boy** Kim Hughes and the bad old days of Australian cricket (Allen & Unwin, £10.99, paperback)

Sandford, Christopher **Imran Khan The Cricketer, The Celebrity, The Politician** (HarperCollins, £20)

Veysey, Wayne **KP: Cricket Genius?** The Biography of Kevin Pietersen (Know the Score, £14.99)

AUTOBIOGRAPHY

Broad, Stuart **Bowled Over** An Ashes Celebration – My Side of the Story (Hodder & Stoughton, £18.99)

Flintoff, Andrew **Ashes to Ashes** (Hodder & Stoughton, £19.99)

Hoggard, Matthew **Hoggy** Welcome to my world (HarperSport, £18.99)

Irani, Ronnie **No Boundaries** Passion and Pain On and Off the Pitch (John Blake, £18.99)

Ramprakash, Mark **Strictly Me** My Life Under the Spotlight Forewords by Karen Hardy and Darren Gough (Mainstream, £18.99)

Strauss, Andrew **Testing Times** In Pursuit of the Ashes (Hodder & Stoughton, £19.99)

Vaughan, Michael **Time to Declare** My Autobiography (Hodder & Stoughton, £19.99)

Wagh, Mark **Pavilion to Crease… and Back** Photographs by Sam Bowles, Foreword by Stephen Fleming (Fairfield Books, £15)

ANTHOLOGY

Booth, Lawrence, ed. **"What Are The Butchers For?"** And Other Splendid Cricket Quotations (John Wisden, £9.99)

Craig, Edward, ed. **Story of the Ashes** Cricket's greatest rivalry as told by the writers who were there Foreword by Christopher Martin-Jenkins (The Wisden Cricketer, £7.99, paperback)

Lynch, Steven ed. **Wisden on the Ashes** The Authoritative Story of Cricket's Greatest Rivalry Foreword by Sir Alec Bedser (John Wisden, £40)

ILLUSTRATED

Cooper, Zaki and Lightman, Daniel, with photographs by Ian Hay **Cricket Grounds from the air** Introduction by Geoffrey Boycott (Myriad, £9.99)

Murphy, Janet **Cricket in Chesterfield** A Century of Club and County Matches at Queen's Park (Merton Priory Press, paperback, £12.95)

Sydney, Albert **Postmarks from Paradise** The Philatelic & Numismatic History of West Indies Cricket Photographs by Patrick Eagar (privately published)

Trevillion, Paul and Holder, John **You Are The Umpire** The ultimate illustrated guide to the laws of cricket Foreword by Shane Warne (The Observer, £12.99)

FICTION

Rae, Simon **Unplayable** Foreword by Mike Gatting (Top Edge Press, paperback, £9.99)

TECHNICAL

ECB **Cricket** Know the Game (A&C Black, paperback, £6.99)

STATISTICAL

Bailey, Philip comp. **First-Class Cricket Matches 1920** and **1921** (ACS Sales, Blue Bell House, 2–4 Main Street, Scredington, Sleaford, Lincolnshire NG34 0AE, email: sales@acscricket.com, (£18 and £20 respectively)

Isaacs, Richard comp. **Minor Counties List A Cricketers** (ACS, £10)

Ledbetter, Jim comp. **First-Class Cricket – A Complete Record 1926** (ACS, £26)

Webb, Tony ed. **The Minor Counties Championship 1903** (ACS, £11)

HANDBOOKS AND ANNUALS

Agnew, Jonathan **Cricket Year 2009** 28th edition (A&C Black, £24.99)

Bailey, Philip ed. **ACS International Cricket Year Book 2009** (ACS Sales, Blue Bell House, 2–4 Main Street, Scredington, Sleaford, Lincolnshire NG34 0AE, email: sales@acscricket.com, £16)

Bryant, John ed. **ACS Overseas First-Class Annual 2009** (ACS, £35)
First edition of new series containing full scorecards for all first-class matches outside England in 2008 and 2008-09.

Bryden, Colin ed. **Mutual & Federal SA Cricket Annual 2009** (CSA, fromcricket@mf.co.za, R170 plus p&p)

Frindall, Bill ed. **Playfair Cricket Annual 2009** (Headline, £6.99, paperback)

Gerrish, Keith ed. **First-Class Counties Second Eleven Annual 2009** (ACS, £7)

Heatley, Michael ed. **The Cricketers' Who's Who 2009** (Green Umbrella, £18.99)

Irish Cricket Annual 2009 (from Cricket Ireland, Sport HQ, 13 Joyce Way, Parkwest, Dublin 12, £4/Euros 7)

Lynch, Steven ed. **The Cricinfo Guide to International Cricket 2010** (A&C Black, £8.99)

Payne, Francis and Smith, Ian ed. **2009 New Zealand Cricket Almanack** (Hodder Moa, $NZ45)

All first-class counties produce handbooks of varying quality. Details available from each club.

REPRINTS AND UPDATES

John Wisden's Cricketers' Almanack for 1931, 1932 and 1933 (facsimile editions, Willows Publishing, 17 The Willows, Stone, Staffordshire ST15 0DE, tel: 01785 814700, email: jenkins.willows@ntlworld.com. £61 for 1931, £62 for 1932 (tan binding); also available in original hard cloth cover for £5 extra; all editions plus £4 p&p, or £7 p&p overseas)

Warne, Shane **Shane Warne's Century** My top 100 Test cricketers (Mainstream, paperback, £7.99)

Tebay, K. Martin **Charlie Hallows** 80 Years On – 1,000 Runs in May, 1928 (limited edition of 125, Red Rose Books, email: info@redrosebooks.co.uk, standard edition £9.95, de luxe hardback edition £49.95)

Tebay, K. Martin **Four in Four and Plenty More** Lancashire v Somerset, played on the Old Trafford cricket ground, Manchester on the 3rd and 4th July, 1905 (limited edition of 137, Red Rose Books, email: info@redrosebooks.co.uk, standard edition £9.95, de luxe hardback edition £49.95)

Tebay, K. Martin **"No Native Er'e Did That Before** Jimmy Hallows' Championship Double, 1904 (limited edition of 108, Red Rose Books, email: info@redrosebooks.co.uk, standard edition £9.95, de luxe hardback edition £49.95)

CATALOGUES

Down, Michael, ed. **Boundary Books Catalogue 38** Twentieth anniversary edition (free from Boundary Books, The Haven, West Street, Childrey OX12 9UL)

PERIODICALS

All Out Cricket ed. Andy Afford (PCA Management/TriNorth, £3.95. Subscriptions: 0844 322 1229, www.alloutcricket.com/subs)

SPIN World Cricket Monthly ed. Duncan Steer (WW Magazines, £3.95. Subscription details from: www.wwmagazines.com/spin/)

The Cricket Statistician (quarterly) ed. Simon Sweetman (ACS, £3 to non-members)

The Journal of the Cricket Society (twice yearly) ed. Andrew Hignell (from D. Seymour, 13 Ewhurst Road, Crofton Park, London, SE4 1AG, £5 to non-members)

The Wisden Cricketer (monthly) ed. John Stern (Wisden Cricketer Publishing, £3.95. Subscriptions: Dovetail Services, 800 Guillat Avenue, Kent Science Park, Sittingbourne, Kent ME9 8GU, 0844 815 0864, email: twc@servicehelpline.co.uk)

CRICKET IN THE MEDIA, 2009

Farewell concerts and phoney bylines

MICHAEL HENDERSON

Unlike the summer of 2005, to which people alluded whenever they had the opportunity, and sometimes when they hadn't, the Ashes contest of 2009 was not a vintage year. It was decent enough, but it fell short of greatness. Two moderate sides, was the general view, and England were luckier. Yet, despite the absence of abundant class on the field, there was just as much to write about. The appalling treatment by English crowds of Ricky Ponting, the one genuinely great player on view, roused the commentariat, and Andrew Flintoff's prolonged farewell used up a few more barrels of ink. Then there were the travails of Kevin Pietersen, the first Test to be staged (successfully, as it happens) in Cardiff, the World Twenty20, the palsied fumblings of the ECB, and Steve Harmison's weekly use of the *Mail on Sunday* as a personal noticeboard – "come and get me, skipper!" Not a vintage harvest, perhaps, but there were a few grapes to press.

The Flintoff factor became an issue the moment the all-rounder stated, on the eve of the Second Test at Lord's, in a bulletin that achieved almost ministerial significance, that he would play his final Test at The Oval. After that declaration, every week, every day it seemed at times, brought forth stories about his fitness. He bowled beautifully on the final morning at Lord's, to set up a victory, but it was plain as day that every appearance was a considerable act of will. Finally, at Leeds, Andrew Strauss took the view that his best bowler was not up to the task of playing for five days. This was the cue for Andrew "Chubby" Chandler, Flintoff's manager, to wield the willow on his client's behalf. Flintoff, he told Mike Atherton, as England subsided to a miserable defeat, had wanted to play at Leeds, and was bitterly disappointed to have been stood down. Whether Chandler was saying this in a professional capacity or, as he said later, a personal one, was lost in translation, as *The Times* ran their correspondent's story on the back page. It was a good summer for Atherton, whose clear-eyed reporting throughout the season was matched by the equally outstanding Mike Selvey in *The Guardian*.

Jim Lawton, *The Independent's* brilliant chief sports writer, put Flintoff's exclusion at Headingley into perspective. "What's it all about, Freddie?" he asked. "Is it about England regaining the urn won so gloriously with the help of your inspiration in 2005, and then a year later squandered so grievously under your captaincy – or a series of Flintoff farewell concerts as stagey as any produced by the late Mr Frank Sinatra? Anyone with one eye open at Edgbaston three days earlier would surely have had to accuse England of dereliction of duty had they not considered this vital issue. Even in the middle of his brilliant innings Flintoff looked like a man worn down to the last of his physical resources."

As Lawton suggested, the Flintoff farewell was stage-managed carefully by his handlers, ever mindful of their man's commercial value. Whether or not he was a great cricketer (Atherton thought not: Simon Barnes, his colleague, thought otherwise), he was undoubtedly a star. At Lord's he went down on one knee, to hog the spotlight, and there was a touch of the thespian (as opposed to showman) about his performance that threatened to undo much of the noble work he had done on the team's behalf. Martin Samuel, the *Daily Mail's* chief sports writer, excelled on the Test beat. "Despite statistics that demonstrate Flintoff was often not as influential on the pitch as he was in the minds of his supporters, his team-mates have grown used to having him as their security blanket. The situation is never as bleak as it seems because Freddie might save the day; the fact he seldom did grew to be one of the great frailties of English cricket." Nevertheless, Flintoff came back for a final fling at The Oval, where his dramatic running-out of Ponting supplied what Atherton called "a scene-stealing effort of which Marlon Brando would have been proud". The gods, wrote his former Lancashire team-mate, "had granted him, out of recognition for a remarkable career, the day's defining image". At long last, his race was finally run, and he could take his leave as an Ashes victor with everybody's blessing.

Tabloid euphoria greets the recapture of the urn.

Naturally, it wouldn't be an Ashes summer without a columnist on the opinion pages declaring a love for cricket that had hitherto been taken on trust. This time it was the turn of Jonathan Freedland in *The Guardian*, who simply couldn't resist checking the Test scores on his Blackberry while enjoying his French holiday. "On match days it required acts of monastic willpower not to hit refresh at five-minute intervals to find out what new ordeal fate had meted out to the England cricket team." Right! "I might be faced with a stunning Albigensian castle, or the gorgeous, sparkling Canal du Midi, but still my thumb itched to find out if Anderson had broken through on the last day at Edgbaston or if Bopara had held firm in Headingley (they hadn't)."

Why Freedland hadn't written this column in 2005, when England really was gripped by the Ashes contest, was a bit of a puzzle. Nor did he cover himself in glory with what he went on to say. "Snobbish followers of cricket will boast that theirs is the cerebral sport, human chess." Whoa! Hold it there. It was John Arlott, the cricket correspondent for the paper in which Freedland opines so freely, who made the comparison with chess. Is there anything "snobbish" about that? As for "cerebral", cricket is a sport that has traditionally appealed to the mind as well as the senses. Why else was an intelligent man like Freedland drawn to it in the first place? "Sport," he went on, "offers what the news cannot. It promises clarity and resolution to a world short of both… gives us a certainty we rarely know." And with that less than gripping observation the philosopher went back to those stunning castles.

Another *Guardian* writer, Richard Williams, also favours the longer view. In the course of the summer Williams brought out a book, *The Blue Moment*, about the making of Miles Davis's classic jazz recording, *Kind of Blue*, but it was the Twenty20 World Cup that caught his eye in June. Swimming against the tide of received opinion, he liked what he saw, and wasn't afraid to say so. "Cricket-lovers who grew up with cable-knit woollen sweaters, sausage-roll batting gloves, proper leather boots and the beauty of a slow-motion Ken Barrington century have found it hard to come to terms with a game so utterly different in its superficial aspects. The studious patience inculcated in generations of young cricketers is of minimal value in a form of the game that depends on rapid reaction and in which the outcome of virtually every ball provokes an instant reassessment of the state of play."

This was good stuff, as one would expect from so fair-minded an observer, though he had harsher words for those MCC members who stayed away from Lord's throughout the tournament. "Some sort of arrangement should be made to ensure that, if they are not interested in attending, their places go to cricket-lovers not hidebound by joyless prejudice." Prejudice, of course, does not always wear an egg-and-bacon tie. Later in the summer, it was loosed in the most vocal and vulgar way by the mob whenever the Australian captain walked to the crease – at least, until the final Test, when The Oval, in an attempt to make amends, rose to salute a gallant loser. Ponting's cheerful acceptance of his disgraceful treatment was almost as impressive as his batting, which, without reaching Alpine peaks, nevertheless provided an exquisite innings on the first afternoon of the Headingley Test. From a cricketing point of view, that was the finest hour of the summer. His point may even have been taken by Chris Gayle, the captain of West Indies, who told *The Guardian* earlier in the summer that he "wouldn't be so sad" if Test cricket withered on the vine. Gayle later tried to claw back some ground, saying that his own career was now better suited to crash and bash than a five-day labour, but the damage had been done – to his reputation.

Patrick Collins, writing as well as ever in the *Mail on Sunday*, has often taken his cudgels to the rabble-rousers, and he showed the Barmy Army the maker's name in a column that sought to regain the good name of the game. "Cricket, by its very nature, is more reflective, more subtle [than football]. Schemes are laid, and plots unravel." The oikish behaviour of too many spectators, "the chanting, the loutishness, the arrogance" offended the aesthetic sense of all who truly loved cricket. "Season by season, they are demeaning a marvellous game" … "Chants which would seem only mildly malicious in a football ground acquire a more sinister resonance in a Test arena." He spoke for many, though not everybody within the lucre-fixated ECB would agree. As Philip Larkin, a cricket-lover, wrote in another context: "All we can hope to leave them now is money."

Collins is right, but the tide is shifting in all kinds of ways. In the newspaper world, for instance, the coverage of county cricket has changed out of all recognition. The modern tabloid has little use for cricket, unless it involves a handful of recognisable names, and the broadsheets (by tradition, if not page size) are less keen on the summer game than they were. By tradition the most comprehensive, as opposed to the best, coverage could be found in the *Telegraph*, but in 2009 that paper was stung in the most embarrassing manner when *Private Eye*, home to that enterprising sports columnist, Miss Sally Jockstrap, revealed secrets that left it defending its wicket without bat or pads.

All papers use cod names to cover sports events. Usually the disguised correspondents are reporters on other papers, taking on a spot of additional work. However, the *Telegraph's* blunder was to pretend that the imaginary reporters at Championship fixtures were actually present in flesh and blood, taking notes, and scribbling their match reports at twilight. As the *Eye* disclosed, the reporters included such notable penmen as Oliver Clive, Perry Crooke and Dan Harbles, an anagram of "Handlebars". "Without all those phoney bylines", the story concluded, "readers would know what they already suspect, that the paper's once-famous cricket coverage has become, quite literally, a charade."

One man really was still at it, though. In the year he turned 80, David Foot continued to contribute elegant essays to *The Guardian* that kept the county game alive in the hearts of all those who remembered those happy days when county cricket was the foundation stone of the summer game; indeed, of summer itself. On the first day of July, as the smoke of the Twenty20 bash began to clear, and thoughts turned towards the five Tests against Australia, Foot, who grew up in East Coker, recalled his first glimpse of the fabled tourists, back in 1948. "It was the best railway journey I ever made," he began, and in the next 600 words this much-loved reporter, who has been a professional journalist man and boy, supplied the most evocative essay of the year.

He remembered the varied cargo on the train, the coal-smeared driver and fireman, who were thrown a few rabbits for assisting the local farmers with their crates, and the young cricket-lovers with "eyes dreamy and distant, virgin scorebooks and jam sandwiches in their hands". All our yesterdays, brought vividly to life by the kind of wordsmith that modern newspapers feel they can do without. Who wants to staff a County Championship game when there is football to appease? "Soccer's brash re-arrival before the series is over," wrote Foot, "will have the statistics of popularity undeniably on its side. But where is the real comparison when it comes to soul? I would never have taken that bone-shaking ride on a single-track railway to see a ball being belted into the opposing penalty area." A game that claims the love of men like David Foot is still worth celebrating. So, until they make 20-over cricket compulsory, and turn the lights out, celebrate it we must.

Michael Henderson is a freelance writer on sport and music, and a former cricket correspondent of the Daily Telegraph.

CRICKET AND BLOGS, 2009

Without fear, favour… or money

JARROD KIMBER

"I am back guys! Things have been pretty tight lately. There's been a crackdown. Every player is looking over his shoulder. Nobody knows who I am. But I exist, right within them, right next to them. Every breath they take, every move they make. I am watching! And they know it. And they are scared. They are worried."

That was the word from the funny, overdramatic, controversial, mendacious, famous and eventually disappointing blogger known as the Fake IPL Player (**fakeiplplayer.blogspot.com**). Blogging had been around for years, but generally cricket blogs were still in the dark underbelly of the internet. There were the odd standouts like **leftarmchinaman.blogspot.com**, **kingcricket.co.uk**, **wellpitched.com** and the cricket watcher's journal (**tcwj.blogspot.com**) that had been well known on the internet for a long time, but they were hardly mentioned in the mainstream media. The Corridor (**cricket.mailliw.com**), written by Will Luke, was so popular during the 2005 Ashes that Will ended up working for Cricinfo, but this was very rare.

The Fake IPL Player made the news, not because of the quality of the writing, but because he was purporting to be a player with the Kolkata Knight Riders. His information was seemingly valid and, with the KKR imploding on every level, the story had more credence. Everyone seemed to want to know who he was; every blog post received hundreds of comments, the media in India were frenetically trying to identify him, English newspapers mentioned him, he was getting reportedly 100,000 hits a day, and the other blogs were ablaze with stories, rumours and mockery of him.

The chances of him being a real cricket player were very slim, but it was a dare-to-dream situation. Dileep Premachandran on *The Guardian's* website was a believer: "If anything, it's the vehemence of the denial that makes you almost certain he exists." The denial he referred to came from the KKR official website: "poison pen writing of the dirtiest variety, but far too many factual errors". The more you publicly deny something, the more people can believe it is true.

A far better blog, **Amy-cricket.blogspot.com**, sprung up during the IPL, written by the very talented Amy Sanders. Amy was an Australian cricket writer, who in her own words was born with the ability to dislike Australian cricketers. Her blog was everything a blog should be. Rapidly updated, completely insane, fanatic, vitriolic, inventive, educational and amusing. In a short time Amy had gathered hundreds of devout followers with her Albie Morkel love and her goading of A. B. de Villiers fans.

Quickly she became a must-read for blog fans. Unfortunately for her readers, she was also a star at her day job, and was hired by Australian Prime Minister

Amy-cricket.blogspot.com

Kevin Rudd in his media relations team. It took up a lot of her time, and her blogging output suffered dramatically. During this period Amy also contracted swine flu, and her health deteriorated. During early July when she should have been entertaining people with her coverage of the Ashes she died in a car accident coming back from Canberra Hospital. It was a massive loss for the cricket blogging community.

At least that was the story, written by a grieving friend, that appeared on her blog. However, in the months that followed, *Wisden* was unable to come up with any proof that someone by the name of Amy Sanders ever existed, let alone worked for Kevin Rudd or died in an accident. *Wisden* tried contacting the friend who wrote the obituary post on Amy's site, but there has been no response. Either a talented writer died tragically young in an accident, or a hoax has been perpetrated by a blogger who burnt out. Whatever the truth, it was a dramatic end for the blog.

Like Amy, the Fake IPL player also knew how blogs worked. He courted controversy brilliantly, calling many cricket characters by outrageous nicknames, such as the Little Monster for Sachin Tendulkar. There are many more nicknames with explanations at New Zealand sports blog

The Wisden Review

Cricket on twitter

Phillip Hughes is an innovative cricketer, not just for his batting technique: he also became the first Test cricketer to tweet his omission from a team. Hughes brought the micro-blogging social network platform, twitter, into the mainstream by posting: "Disappointed not to be on the field with the lads today. Will be supporting the guys, it's a BIG test match 4 us. Thanks 4 all the support." He actually didn't tweet it, his manager's IT guy did, which makes it worse. It sent the press box at Edgbaston into a fluster as the older generation of cricket writers were trying to get a crash course in what twitter actually was. Cricket Australia were less than impressed, warning Hughes for the breach in protocol.

This didn't stop other players from taking to twitter. Graeme Swann entertains thousands of people there, whether talking about Swedish porn films he has accidentally watched or calling James Anderson mono-browed. Swann, Anderson and all-rounder Tim Bresnan were tweeting their nightly activities in South Africa during the Champions Trophy until Bresnan got in trouble. When a fan edited a photo to make him look much rounder than usual, Bresnan retorted with: "don't mind my mates dishing it out, but who the fuck are you. Crawl out off your mums basement U KNOB." The English players were not banned from twitter, but Andy Flower was less than happy to be dealing with twitter nonsense.

There are also older cricket identities on twitter who have many followers. Sky announced David "Bumble" Lloyd was on twitter during the First Ashes Test; within days thousands were following his wisdom, and his bad jokes. BBC stars were also following suit, with Alison Mitchell and Jonathan Agnew proving incredibly popular. Agnew even used twitter to gain support when an article was written in *The Observer* claiming that an interview that Agnew did with singer Lily Allen was a bit pervy. Agnew interviewed Allen only because she showed her love for cricket – including Graham Onions's penchant for long bowling spells – on twitter.

sportsfreak.co.nz/show-column.asp?ID=653. He spent a great deal of his blog talking about the after-hours work of famous players.

Almost daily, rumours surfaced of people being outed as the fake, from IPL players such as Anureet Singh and Ranadeb Bose, to the more improbable Harsha Bhogle and several prominent bloggers (including Anand Ramachandran of **bosey.co.in**). Then, on April 26, two players from the Kolkata Knight Riders were sent home: Aakash Chopra (himself a very accomplished writer) and Sanjay Bangar. Sending home two players mid-tournament led to people jumping to conclusions.

All players denied involvement. In the seven days from April 19–26, the fake IPL Player wrote 26 times, but from then on he never wrote more than four times a week. The blog seemed to have run out of insights, and its popularity waned. Towards the end of the IPL, the writer said he would retire from cricket and out himself.

Instead, the FIP (as he was now calling himself) decided not to show his face, or own up to who he was, but instead make a video of his shadow talking nonsense for four minutes. He claimed he was an insider, but he could have been a sock puppet for all that people cared. It was an appropriate finish to a gimmicky website.

In late 2008 a real cricketer, New Zealand's Iain O'Brien, started blogging about cricket. The blog (**iainobrien.co.nz**) was the first unedited non-ghost-written unpaid blog that any current Test cricketer had written. The blog was soon in the news when O'Brien wrote about being called a "fagot" (*sic*) by the fans at the Gabba. After some media training on what to say and what not to say, O'Brien continued unedited. The blog is a gold mine for cricket lovers. O'Brien gives in-depth coverage of his life on the cricket field as it happens. Let us hope he is equally uncensored when he reports on the Middlesex dressing-room in 2010.

O'Brien was not the only player educating and entertaining people with his blogs in 2009. Brett Geeves, the Tasmanian and occasional one-day player for Australia, was writing a blog for Cricket Tasmania and Cricket Australia. While edited by Tasmania cricket officials – and not updated as much as O'Brien's blog – it has become quite popular. The highlight, or lowlight, has to be when, for the second time in the 2008-09 season, Tim Macdonald was last out, leaving Geeves stranded on 99. Geeves had this to say: "In conclusion, I would like to thank you for doing your best. It's unfortunate that it's not good enough and you have caused me much heartbreak Macdonald. I would like to explain to you Macdonald why I am referring to you by your last name only. A teacher of mine in primary school once taught us that it is disrespectful to call people by their last names. In all honesty, I will be calling you Macdonald for the rest of your time in Tasmania." Geeves is still searching for a first-class hundred.

During the 2009 Ashes, the blogging community was much quieter than had been the case in either the 2006-07 or 2005 series. There were no wars between blogs, and generally the blogs were just another place to read about the cricket rather than a fan v fan argument, as they can be for some series. There was, however, a bloggers' Ashes match: **thevillagecricketer.com** captained an English team against the **cricketwithballs.com** Australian team. In a sign of things to come, the English team won by 28 runs. Highlights of the game were Cricinfo's Andrew Miller swinging the Mongoose bat, Patrick Kidd of *The Times* (**timesonline.typepad.com/line_and_length**) playing for time with the Mongoose, and Suave from **republiquecricket.com** taking a wicket with a nipple-high full toss.

In the real Ashes, some of the best blogging came from a new boy on the block, **theoldbatsman.blogspot.com**. He covered the Ashes, and also some of the worst writing of the mainstream media. His writing prose is quite exceptional: "Ravi Bopara went to an old-school slower ball yesterday, one that seduced and then mugged him, one that fooled his senses. It's not good for the self-image that sort of failure, with your bat in the air, your guts lurching queasily."

One of the highlights of the blogging year was the blog **getahundred.com/**. This didn't talk about international or domestic cricket, but was instead about the blogger's own quest to make the perfect maiden hundred (from 50 balls or fewer), with videos showing his many, many failures. The site was so good you hoped he wouldn't succeed so that the journey could keep going. The best of the county blogs was **lastofthesummerwhine.com** by Yorkshire Len: full of top-ten lists and satirical reviews of his favourite team.

Cricket blogging is still not a medium respected by everyone, and when it is poor, it can be very poor. But at its best it can be as good as any cricket media, and in Gideon Haigh it has a high-profile supporter. In a speech, delivered in Oxford, about cricket and media, he said: "I do know that a lot of the toughest, cleverest, funniest and best-informed writing about cricket these days is to be found in the blogosphere, where the writers are without fear or favour, and also, of course, money. Alas, the number of bloggers accredited by the ECB this summer: zero. Can't we do better? Avid viewers, curious readers, discriminating consumers – they are out there in vast numbers, and it is up to cricket and the media to deserve them."

Jarrod Kimber blogs on cricketwithballs.com.

CRICKETANA IN 2009

Shaken and most definitely stirred

DAVID RAYVERN ALLEN

Whatever next? "Ian Fleming's *Diamonds Are Forever* and *Wisden's Cricketing* (sic) *Almanacks* make top prices," stated the press release after the Bonham's auction in November 2009. Fleming's final revised typescript, "peppered with authorial tweaks", more than doubled its estimate to fetch £62,400, while a set of *Wisdens* from 1864 to 1984, handsomely bound and in fine condition, which was estimated to sell for £50–70,000, actually made £90,000.

If you believe that James Bond and John Wisden have no connection whatsoever, think again. Among the obituaries in last year's *Wisden* was that of Robert Harling, who died at the great age of 98. He had been a close friend of Fleming's – and was also a brilliant typographer, responsible for the redesign of *Wisden* to mark the 75th edition in 1938. The resulting engraving of two top-hatted cricketers by Eric Ravilious endures to this day. Harling was even fondly depicted as the typeface make-up man on the *Chelsea Clarion* in the Bond novel *The Spy Who Loved Me*. Incidentally, Fleming's nephew Matthew was briefly a member of the board of John Wisden & Co. And for readers who prefer a more hands-on 007, see page 894 of the 2009 Almanack.

The Bonham's *Wisden* set – which came from a private vendor in the Midlands (having been a collection of the vendor's father, now deceased) – was not an absolute top price in comparison to recent years. In the current financial climate, however, it was a reasonable return. The general consensus among auctioneers and bookdealers is that, in effect, a two-tier system is now operating. John Mullock, who holds his sporting auctions at the picturesque Ludlow racecourse in south Shropshire, and whose catchphrase "moving along nicely" is an engaging feature of the sales, agrees: "The good items will sell, whereas the bottom end of the market is struggling. *Wisdens* are holding up remarkably well, especially compared, say, with golf, which has largely died a death."

Aside from the Almanacks, there was an unusual Wisden artefact on offer in Mullock's autumn auction: a hinged two-ring brass cricket-ball gauge giving both maximum and minimum size circumference that had been manufactured by John Wisden & Co. at their Mortlake and Tonbridge factories during the Edwardian era. It could have fetched considerably more than the hammer price of £70, an outcome which delighted the successful bidder.

There was widespread surprise when the precious first four volumes (1864–1867) of the Almanack were found in the Hertford branch of an Oxfam charity shop. Donated by an unknown visitor and found among a pile of run-of-the-mill books, the Almanacks were sent for auction to Trevor Vennett-Smith at his new location in Gotham, just outside Nottingham. They failed to reach the reserve of £18,000, but it is highly likely they will be re-auctioned. Vennett-Smith, who runs two postal and two general sporting auctions a year, found the market "very volatile and spasmodic. *Vanity Fairs* [caricatures] and modern books are not selling at the moment. Middle-period books – first part of the 20th century – are so-so, but if they have a dust-wrapper they'll fetch four or five times as much. Pamphlets, cricket postcards, tremendous: I can't get enough of them."

A little way down the M1 at Leicester, Tim Knight held five sporting auctions, with two of them devoted solely to *Wisdens*: "The recession hasn't bitten too hard, especially for the right item, though it's difficult to find an outlet for limited-edition prints and 1970 cricket bats even if they have all the signatures." Two "right items" in his sales included a large Australian 1879 calendar-cum-advertising-poster with caricatures of the players, which attracted £6,800, and a one-page typed statement from Greg Chappell apologising for the infamous incident when he instructed his brother Trevor to bowl underarm during the one-day international between Australia and New Zealand at Melbourne in 1980-81. With premium, this unique piece of paper made just under £1,000.

In November 2009, Christie's included a select and attractive cricket section within a sale of fine printed books, manuscripts and traditional-sports items. An exquisite 1862 menu of the sumptuous banquet given by the Sydney Cricket Association in honour of the Melbourne Eleven, printed in blue on white paper with a perforated silk-pattern border, and of which this was the only known copy, went (with an extortionate 25% premium) for £1,125.

Graham Budd at Sotheby's, using their quarters on both sides of Bond Street, sold the Bill Frindall Collection – or at least some of it – together with other cricketana. Frankly, the sale was somewhat disappointing. As usual, Budd had produced a beautifully illustrated catalogue, but too many items became a prisoner of the auction-house's high minimum estimated price-per-lot policy. Consequently, for example, some desirable personalised drawings and caricatures – which were likely to have found buyers if offered individually or as part of a small assortment – were bundled together as a very large group in a single lot, and unsurprisingly remained unsold. One could not escape the conclusion that a less prestigious and more specialist auction-house might have better served the late Bearded Wonder's legatees.

Finally, a find with a future. The *John Wisden Cricketer's Notebooks* are the scarcest of all cricket annuals, at least according to that legendary cricket polymath Irving Rosenwater. Produced from 1900 to 1913 in pocket-diary form, the *Notebooks* contain fascinating information on the curiosities of cricket, gathered together by another great student of the game, F. S. Ashley-Cooper. As far as is known, there are only two complete sets in existence. One of those recently resurfaced from the bowels of the Lord's archive after a seven-year search. As a result, there are now plans to reproduce all the volumes, as well as the manuscript *Notebooks* for 1914 and 1915 – the First World War interrupted the printing process.

The mongoose and the pink herring

NORMAN HARRIS

Spare a thought for the bat inventor, and the marketing representatives, who attend the baptism of a revolutionary new product. May 26, 2009, at the Riverside was just such an occasion, as a small entourage stood anxiously awaiting the first use anywhere of the new Mongoose bat. Everything depended on "their" man, Derbyshire's Stuart Law, who had started his Twenty20 innings against Durham with eight overs remaining, and was playing himself in with a conventional bat before switching to the revolutionary new blade.

The inventor, Marcus Codrington Fernandez, later said he had never been more nervous at any of life's great events, such as marriage or the arrival of a first-born. All watching were fearful that Law would get out just before sending for the Mongoose. But all was well: with 12 balls remaining and his score 32, Law made the call.

The eye-catching new bat has a short, stubby blade which, instead of being twice the length of the handle as with regular bats, has handle and blade in roughly equal proportion. It looks rather like a kayak paddle, and offers great bat speed – about 20% more, it is claimed. Its advocates say it represents "the single most radical change to cricket equipment since 1771". That is a very big claim, but not necessarily an over-hyped one. A counter-claim can be made for the Gray-Nicolls "Scoop", which appeared in the 1970s and had a dramatic and lasting impact with its perimeter-weighting principle. And yet, the Mongoose *is* revolutionary: despite a lot of tinkering over the years, it seems that no bat-maker had ever tried a short blade and a long handle.

Law played a couple of unexceptional drives for singles with his new bat, and then delivered the one stroke that spelt success. He seemed to dip underneath the ball, and lifted it like a drop-kick, very high, over midwicket for six. It was the style as much as the outcome that was eye-catching, and it certainly did convey the impression of great bat speed. Up in the media centre there was delight among Law's backers. "I had looked up and seen them there," said Law. "The timing was perfect pantomime, really."

The Mongoose seems destined to be labelled a Twenty20 bat, yet Law argues for its use by "Joe Club Cricketer, who hasn't the strength to hit the ball hard – this will give him the bat speed, and leverage, he lacks". That is, if Joe can dismiss those natural feelings of self-consciousness: Law's own caution in not using the bat until he had played himself in perhaps also had something to do with the avoidance of egg on face. Cricketers – especially professionals – are generally a conservative lot.

Pink cricket balls seemed another radical step in modern cricket equipment when they were first mooted, although as trials continue the shock has faded. The only issue remaining is whether pink really is the right colour for night cricket. One brief trial in 2009 came after a televised floodlit match at Hove finished early, allowing a few players to bowl and hit pink balls, primarily to see how they looked on the TV screen. The commentators' verdict was that they looked fine against the dark sky, less good against the pale grass of the pitch. But why, one wondered, wasn't a white ball – and, indeed, orange and yellow ones – also tried, for comparison?

The answer seemed to be that MCC is focused on trying to make the pink ball work. An MCC spokesman said "it ticks most of the boxes" – those boxes embracing, as well as visibility, the need for resilience on hard, abrasive pitches that tend to wear away the thin coating of colour quickly. Whereas the red colour can be dyed into the leather of the traditional ball, white and other colours can only be applied as a relatively thin outer coat (white ones are then given a polyurethane finish to help "fix" it).

Can the boffins really succeed, as they hope, in dying the pink further into the leather? Some ball-makers say this is impossible. One, however, is aiming to develop a better outer coating, including a rubber-like ingredient. In a trial match in Australia in November, a state side found these balls lasted well on a hard surface, allowed spin and were extremely visible. Those balls were orange, as used in many limited-overs competitions (especially evening ones) in English club cricket. And so the future may yet be orange, at least at grass-roots level.

Merlyn can replicate a Murali over

On the other hand, it could be yellow, a colour said to avoid problems for cricketers who are red–green colour-blind. Dukes, who supply balls for England's home Tests and for the first division of the County Championship, have even supplied the Hong Kong Sixes with a yellow ball with a rough finish, to prevent swing. But what shade of yellow to use – lemon, or so bright that it verges on orange? And should coloured balls be fluorescent?

Clearly there are many boxes still to tick, and arguments to win. Some in the ball-making business refer to "the pink herring" and, while the authorities continue to encourage them to keep trying new ideas, there is a limit to how many they can afford to invest in. "I just don't know what they want," said one frustrated ball-maker. "There's no clear indication."

In *Wisden 2006* there was mention (page 1563) of a prototype bowling machine called "Merlyn", which had been invented by Welshman Henry Pryor and his cricket-writer son Matthew. Four years on, Merlyn hit the big time when a new model, capable of multiple spin variations, was used extensively by the England team to prepare for their forthcoming matches in the UAE and Bangladesh early in 2010. One was also tried by the England High Performance Programme in South Africa earlier in the winter, and the players loved it – so much so that the ECB ordered 20 of the machines, one for each of the first-class counties and two for the Academy at Loughborough. They are now being manufactured by Stuart & Williams, the Bristol company which has long made the Bola bowling machine. Software is being developed which will enable Merlyn's operator to replicate an over from the likes of Muttiah Muralitharan on a big-turning Sri Lankan "bunsen".

CRICKET AND THE WEATHER, 2009

Monsoon summer redeemed by September sun

PHILIP EDEN

The summer of 2009 will long be remembered, ironically, as the "barbecue summer". Whether it slips into the folk memory as effectively as that other public relations disaster, British Rail's "wrong kind of snow" – 19 years old and counting – remains to be seen, but it looks as if it might. There is a difference, though: the "wrong kind of snow" was a slip by BR's operations director during a live television interview. The Met Office's "barbecue summer" tag was a disaster of their own making. As their chief forecaster subsequently admitted: "We were trying to help the newspapers by suggesting a headline." Surely we all know tabloid newspapers are perfectly able to concoct their own inane headlines without any help from the Met Office, thank you very much.

All this came to the fore at the end of July, a particularly wet month throughout the UK, when long-range forecasters, fully decked out in hair shirts, felt the need to amend their forecast for the summer quarter because it seemed to be going so badly wrong. Murphy's Law then kicked in and, at least in eastern and southern counties of England, August turned out to be a dry, bright and warm month.

In fact, the main characteristic, meteorologically speaking, of summer 2009 was the contrast between a tolerably dry and warm season in the south-eastern segment of England, and a third consecutive dull and wet one in Wales and north-west England. For those who play their cricket in Scotland or in Ireland it was even worse, with rainfall records broken in both countries.

The cricket season began under leaden skies over the Easter weekend at Lord's, but there were lengthy spells of fine weather in April and May, interspersed with cooler, showery, interludes. Sadly, these cooler episodes coincided with the two Tests against West Indies, on May 6–8 and May 14–18; the Second Test at Chester-le-Street suffered poor attendances as afternoon temperatures struggled to reach 13 or 14°C. The best of the summer weather came in two spells, the first in late May and early June, and the second in late June and early July, when the temperature exceeded 30°C on four consecutive days.

But by the time the first Ashes Test started in Cardiff, the July monsoon was already well established, and it was fortunate that rain seriously affected only two of the five matches of the series. July was a wet month nationwide: between two and three times the normal amount of rain fell in northern, western, and some midland counties, but Kent and Essex were only marginally wetter than average. August was similarly wet in north-west England, but it was a very dry month in London and the South-East. September continued the act of redemption, with hazy blue skies and a soft warmth lasting until the final Pro40 matches were completed on September 27, the latest the English season had ever ended.

The meteorological statistics, averaged over England and Wales, for the 2009 season, are as follows:

	Average max temperature (°C)	Difference from normal for 1971–2000	Total rainfall (mm)	% of normal	Total sunshine (hours)	% of normal
April	14.7	+2.5	47	75	185	118
May...........	16.5	+0.5	56	92	229	113
June..........	19.8	+0.9	54	79	218	115
July	20.2	−1.1	133	232	192	96
August.........	20.5	−0.5	66	91	179	91
September.....	18.0	+0.1	33	40	158	109
2009 season ...	**18.3**	**+0.4**	**389**	**101**	**1,161**	**107**

Each summer has slightly different regional variations, although in most years northern and western counties are cooler, cloudier and damper than those in the east and south. The *Wisden Summer Index* allows us to compare the summer county by county (the formula for the index is explained in *Wisden 2004*, page 1597). Broadly speaking, an index over 650 indicates a good summer whereas one below 500 clearly describes a poor one. Values for each county for the summer of 2009 against the average for standard reference period of 1971–2000 are given below:

	2009	Normal	Difference		2009	Normal	Difference
Derbyshire......	556	580	−24	Middlesex........	699	670	+29
Durham	485	525	−40	Northamptonshire .	642	615	+27
Essex..........	738	640	+98	Nottinghamshire...	565	590	−25
Glamorgan	488	555	−67	Somerset........	592	620	−28
Gloucestershire ..	598	595	+3	Surrey...........	702	675	+27
Hampshire......	670	645	+25	Sussex...........	676	665	+11
Kent	733	655	+78	Warwickshire	573	555	+18
Lancashire......	465	530	−65	Worcestershire	595	615	−20
Leicestershire ...	600	585	+15	Yorkshire	585	560	+25

Rarely can there have been a bigger contrast between the North and West on the one hand, and the South-East on the other. Both Lancashire and Glamorgan had another dire summer, with the index over 60 points below average, while Kent and especially Essex were particularly well favoured. As in 2008, Durham could reasonably claim that they won the County Championship in spite of the poor hand dealt them by the clerk of the weather.

Taking a national view, 2009's index of 568 was 43 points higher than 2008, but it was still 22 below the long-term average. It has to be said, though, that July was the only month of the entire season which was in negative territory (when averaged nationally).

1998	565	2001	632	2004	541	2007	503
1999	637	2002	506	2005	623	2008	525
2000	559	2003	647	2006	633	2009	568

Highest: 812 in 1976   Lowest: 309 in 1879

As the administrators attempt to shoehorn more and more cricket into a packed schedule, the start and finish dates of the season gradually head winterwards.

In recent years, the game has been comparatively fortunate in the weather experienced during April and September, but it is worth remembering just how bad these months can be. Cricket on the margins may bring in extra money when the weather is good, but costs will outweigh income if players cannot get out of the pavilion. The April of 1917 was the coldest of the 20th century: much of England was snow-covered for about a week, and on several days temperatures struggled to climb much above freezing. September 1918 was the wettest on record: rain fell on 29 of the 30 days; crops were abandoned in flooded fields; and afternoon highs were typically around 14–16°C. Changing climate or no, such months shall, in all probability, come again.

Rain men: umpires Nigel Llong and Nick Cook see the funnier side of a shower at Southgate.

CRICKET GROUNDS IN 2009

Still building after all these years

IVO TENNANT

Bolstered by ECB grants for new floodlights and drainage systems, and undeterred by the recession, most counties continued to redevelop their main grounds in 2009. No venture was more ambitious than at **Lord's**, where MCC were intent on making sweeping changes over a ten-year period at a cost of £400m. The plans drawn up by the architects, Herzog & de Meuron, depicted stands with lectern-style blocks of seats, an underground academy, food outlets and a sports clinic, as well as apartments which would be sold to finance the project. The scheme envisages almost every existing building, with the exception of the Pavilion, the relatively new Mound and Grand Stands and the media centre, being replaced. The museum, MCC, Middlesex and ECB offices will move, while MCC hope that in due course the ICC will return from Dubai.

These plans were to go before the club's 18,000 members, Westminster City Council and the mayor of London, Boris Johnson. There was a caveat: Keith Bradshaw, MCC's chief executive, said redevelopment was conditional on a guarantee of two Tests a year at Lord's. He also stated he would seek funding from multinational companies in India.

Redevelopment elsewhere was inevitably on a smaller scale. At **The Oval**, where the OCS Stand was refurbished during the winter, Surrey postponed work on their new hotel until late 2011, although planning permission has been granted after an inquiry into the safety of the adjacent gasometers. Work at **Trent Bridge**, where £8.2m was spent in 2008, is complete – for the time being. At **Old Trafford**, Lancashire's determination to put in a strong bid for an Ashes Test in 2013 necessitated an update to facilities. A glass-fronted conference and events suite, holding up to 1,000 people, is due to be finished before the one-day international on June 27. At the end of the 2010 season, Lancashire plan to rotate the square 90° to avoid difficulties with the setting sun. Further rebuilding of the ground will cost around £50m – all subject to planning permission. Work at **Chester-le-Street** was limited to a new drainage system.

Yorkshire have three partners investing in the £21m Carnegie Pavilion at **Headingley** which, it is expected, will be opened by a member of the Royal Family during the Pakistan–Australia Test in June. Not by Geoffrey Boycott? "Well, he is royalty," quipped a Yorkshire spokesman. This building will be five storeys high, and the facilities shared with Leeds Metropolitan University. The redevelopment of **Edgbaston** – originally due to be completed by the winter of 2011 – should include a state-of-the-art pavilion, conference and banqueting suites, club offices, improved drainage and practice facilities, and will take in the area from the corner of the Hollies Stand to the Priory/Raglan

Stand. However, the start of work was delayed by the objection of local residents. Capacity should be increased from 21,000 to 25,000.

Cardiff's **Swalec Stadium** was finished in time for its inaugural Test in July 2009, and only some touching up of the paintwork was required. At the **Rose Bowl**, a competitor for international fixtures, Hampshire were confident they would complete the £49m redevelopment in time for their first Test in 2011. Two new stands with covered seating for 5,000 should be ready for the 2010 season. A second access road, a hotel and a relaid car park are the other main projects. However, a £32m investment from Eastleigh Council was challenged by another hotel group, who claimed the scheme was of little benefit to the wider community.

Elsewhere on the south coast, Sussex pulled down the Gilligan Stand. The remainder of the redevelopment of the southern end at **Hove** should be carried out in the winter of 2010-11. Two more floodlights have been erected, making six in all. The groundstaff are moving to a different site, as the area they occupied for many years, adjacent to the pavilion, has become a restaurant.

Kent are having a second stab at redeveloping the **St Lawrence Ground**. A £4m loan was obtained from Canterbury City Council to help build a hotel, a conference facility, health and fitness centre, hospitality boxes, retail units and to refurbish their stands, at a total cost of £8.2m. Chief executive Paul Millman took early retirement before work started, but his acting successor, Jamie Clifford, said he was "totally committed" to the project, though he could not say when it would start.

Work at **Chelmsford**, incorporating flats, business and retail outlets, plus 1,500 extra seats, is expected to start at the end of this 2010 season. Essex still expect to play most matches in 2011 at the County Ground, and have no plans yet to return to Ilford and Leyton. Extra seating is a priority, too, at **Bristol**: after the coming season Gloucestershire hope to rebuild the Mound Stand in front of the old orphanage, adding around 2,000 seats to take the capacity above 5,000. At **Taunton**, a long room and viewing gallery were created in the Colin Atkinson Pavilion (the players have decamped to the Andrew Caddick Pavilion), and the museum, created in 1989, benefited from a £250,000 bequest by a committee member from Bath.

In the Midlands, Leicestershire largely left **Grace Road** alone. Work on rotating the **Derby** square, also suffering problems caused by the setting sun in the late season, has now been completed. They also added 2,000 seats on the northern side of the ground, taking the total seating to just under 4,500; a permanent marquee holds 300 people. Later this year they hope to modernise facilities for players and umpires.

At **Northampton**, the club paid £150,000 towards the cost of six floodlights, with the other £500,000 coming from the ECB. They are a distinct improvement on the Meccano-like pylons that dominated the old adjacent Northampton Town football pitch, where George Best once scored six goals. Worcestershire, who remain determined to stay at **New Road** despite the frequency of winter floods, severely reduced their cricket budget, but hoped to find £9m to build a 120-bedroom hotel, and restaurant, later in 2010.

CRICKET PEOPLE

Plenty of room on the sofa

LAWRENCE BOOTH AND SIDDARTHA VAIDYANATHAN

TMS has traditionally meant only one thing in cricket broadcasting, but a much sat-upon armchair in Tooting Bec is providing an entertaining twist. *Test Match Sofa*, the brainchild of former internet project manager and City worker **Daniel Norcross**, is a simple enough idea: a group of friends sit in his south London front room and commentate on England's matches off the TV for an online audience that grew from 120 at the start of the South Africa tour to 2,500 by its end. It's off-beat, impassioned and not for the easily offended. As Norcross explains: "It's never going to appeal to the standard MCC member."

The sofa was dreamed up after the 40-year-old Norcross was made redundant during the credit crunch. With the 2009 Ashes looming, he decided it was now or never, indulged the inner commentator every cricket fanatic believes lurks within, and enlisted the help of four fellow obsessives. As the weeks passed, the commentary team ballooned to 15: "all either unemployed, unemployable, retired or teachers". And although the overused tag of "internet phenomenon" may not have been earned just yet, *Test Match Sofa* (www.testmatchsofa.com) is very much a product of its times: twitter has helped spread the word.

Norcross's credentials will strike a chord with plenty of amateur enthusiasts. Ignoring his mother's attempts to wean him on Jane Austen, he preferred the 1958 *Wisden*. Cricket commentary was practised in his boyhood mirror, and he regularly turns out these days for Alleyn and Honor Oak CC in Dulwich. When he says his attraction to his partner, Catherine, was confirmed upon learning she once sent Graham Gooch a lump of Stilton when on tour in India, you suspect he's only half-joking. Stoically, she has so far tolerated the early-morning knocks on the door as the merry band of commentators, summarisers and stattos arrive for another shift.

Passion is the key. "We were motivated originally by bringing the game to relatives who live outside the BBC's jurisdiction – my brother has lived in America for 25 years – and are thus unable to tune into the more conventional *TMS*," he says. "But it's not really competition for the BBC and in a sense without *Test Match Special* we wouldn't be able to do what we do. It's wonderful fun."

Swami Parathasarathy may just be the perfect man for a crisis. His on-field skills certainly help: he plays regularly, even in his early eighties, and a couple of years ago took a hat-trick against the Calcutta Cricket and Football Club. But it's the calm he derives from his own view of life that makes him unusual. Parathasarathy is the world's foremost exponent of Vedanta, an ancient Hindu philosophy that means "culmination of knowledge". In 1988 he established his own Vedanta academy in the hills of Malavali, near Mumbai, and leads his acolytes on the field too. But what's the relevance to cricket?

Lean, alert and with a twinkle in his eye, Parathasarathy – who played the game in his youth before giving it up for nearly three decades to concentrate on his studies – explains that Vedanta is all about self-realisation through the use of reason and the development of the intellect. "The relative theme is to find peace wherever you are, whatever you do," he says. "And to be able to progress successfully in what you do." His standing in India is such that cricketers from the national side have sought him out for advice.

"I told one of them that he lacks concentration," says Parathasarathy. "He nearly jumped out of his seat. He said: 'The whole world thinks I'm concentrating.' But what happens is, the mind has a tendency to slip into the past or the future. You're worrying all the time about what happened in the past and what's going to happen. So you've got to hold the mind in the present."

Parathasarathy's Vedanta Institute team play a dozen games a year, including a few on tour in England and South Africa, and his steadying influence on his players – some of them a quarter his age – is reflected in his role as an opening batsman. "I played a Twenty20 game recently and carried my bat for about 20," he smiles. "But runs were not the point. I was the anchor. I hit the first ball for the single then the others hit all over the place. Almost every over I just give the other fellow a chance. I'm a tactical batsman. Otherwise it gets confusing and you get all out."

Few cricketers in North America will have heard of **Nawshad "Chubby" Bedessee**, let alone visited his 50,000 sq ft storeroom in Brooklyn, New York. But there's a fair chance their cricket equipment once rested in his warehouse. Cricketers may purchase gear from outlets such as Dick's Sporting Goods, Modell's Sporting Goods, Fogdog Sports, Dreamcricket and Amazon, but it is the 41-year-old Bedessee and his ten staff who ship most of the orders.

His clients are an eclectic bunch. Bedessee has sent equipment to the North Pole and Alaska, an infantry tank in Kasik, Iraq ("to play in their free time"), army sergeants in Illesheim, Germany, and, intriguingly, the San Francisco 49ers American football team, who are thought to use stumps to practise throwing. His database includes addresses in Japan, Belize and Athens.

Bedessee, who doesn't play cricket but funds a successful local side in Brooklyn, is the chief distributor for more than 20 brands of cricket equipment in the western hemisphere. In 2009 he imported 6,200 bats and 62,500 balls, not to mention innumerable pads, helmets, stumps, kitbags, gloves, trousers, pitch mats, shirts – and four bowling machines. He found more than 150 vendors to sell his stockpile.

Cricket accounted for $5m of his revenues last year, but that was a fraction of his thriving $50m food-importing enterprise. The family-run business began in 1977, when Chubby's father, Lionel, migrated from the Guyanese town of Berbice to Toronto and imported fish and sorrel syrup.

Over the years his son expanded the Bedessee influence by setting up storehouses in Montreal, New York and Florida, importing items as varied as sardines from Scotland, Dettol from England, Lalah's curry powder from India and corned beef from Australia. Their primary focus remains Caribbean specialities such as indigenous burnt sugar, almond essence and sorrel syrup.

CRICKET AND THE LAW, 2009

STANFORD FACES 250-YEAR SENTENCE

The man who in 2008 was being hailed as saviour of both English and West Indian cricket ended 2009 in the federal detention centre in Houston, Texas, awaiting trial for an alleged $7 billion fraud. Sir Allen Stanford's pre-Christmas request to be released on bail after six months incarceration was rejected by a judge with the single word "denied". The trial has been scheduled for January 2011. Stanford fell from grace on February 17, 2009 when the US Securities and Exchange Commission (SEC) accused him of a fraud of "shocking magnitude". "Stanford and the close circle of family and friends with whom he runs his businesses perpetuated a massive fraud based on false promises," said Linda Chatman Thomsen, director of enforcement at the commission.

In June 2008, he had appeared at Lord's in a helicopter with a chest purportedly containing $20m to fund his so-called Super Series (see *Wisden 2009*, page 1360) to much public derision but wide-eyed delight from the players and administrators: ECB chairman Giles Clarke called him "a legendary entrepreneur".

A year after that, and four months after the charges, Stanford was indicted by a federal grand jury and surrendered to FBI agents in Virginia. He was led into court wearing leg irons. His lawyer, Christina Sarchio, said Stanford was "confident that a fair jury will find him not guilty of any criminal wrongdoing", and blamed the SEC for the collapse of his companies. If convicted, Stanford, 59, could be jailed for a notional 250 years.

CHRIS LEWIS JAILED FOR 13 YEARS

The former England cricketer Chris Lewis, who played 32 Tests and 53 one-day internationals, was sentenced to 13 years imprisonment after being convicted of smuggling cocaine into Britain.

Lewis, 41, had been arrested at Gatwick Airport in December 2008 after flying in from St Lucia with five cans purporting to be fruit and vegetable juice in his cricket bag. The cans contained a brown liquid that turned out to be dissolved cocaine. After evaporation, Croydon Crown Court was told, it would yield 3.75kg of pure cocaine with a value of about £140,000.

On May 20, the jury found both Lewis and his accomplice Chad Kirnon guilty. The two men originally claimed to be travelling alone, but prosecuting counsel Tom Wilkins said that the cricket bag was labelled with Kirnon's name, one link of several between the defendants. During the eight-day trial, both Lewis and Kirnon denied conspiring to import cocaine, each blaming the other. Lewis said he was carrying the cans for Kirnon and believed they were simply juice. He added: "Throughout my life, my cricket career, when things have gone wrong, they have gone wrong very publicly."

Lewis played for Leicestershire, Nottinghamshire and Surrey between 1987 and 2000. He made a brief comeback for Surrey in two one-day games in 2008, aged 40.

MATTHEWS SENTENCED TO COMMUNITY SERVICE

A Sydney local court ordered former Australian Test player Greg Matthews, 49, to 200 hours community service after he admitted his third drink-driving offence in eight years. He pleaded guilty on April 27 to a "mid-range" offence with a blood-alcohol reading of 0.113. "To my mind it is a crime of selfishness," said magistrate Sharon Freund. She noted the representations made to the court about Matthews's charity work.

FORMER ENGLAND OPENER CLEARED OF ASSAULT

David Smith, who played twice for England on the 1985-86 tour of West Indies, was cleared on August 26 of assaulting a fellow guest at a charity event to celebrate Sir Ian Botham's knighthood.

Smith, 53, was accused at Southwark Crown Court of punching Stephen Best and breaking his nose. Best had intervened in a row between Smith and his girlfriend at the Grosvenor House Hotel. Smith, who played for Surrey, Worcestershire and Sussex, said he had been drinking and had little memory of the incident.

IF YOU DON'T LIKE SIXES, MOVE

A county court judge in Guildford threw out an application for an injunction against Shamley Green CC in Surrey from a neighbour who complained about sixes being hit into his garden.

Judge Robert Reid QC said on May 15 that Mike Burgess had known that cricket was played next to his bungalow when he moved into the property in 2005. Burgess had demanded the club erect a 25ft safety net and, when it refused, he went to court. He said he had been unfairly made out to be a Victor Meldrew figure. "Anyone who doesn't like the sound of a klaxon shouldn't buy a house next to a fire station," said club president Jim Drummond.

CRICKET BAT USED TO STIR CURRY

Chung-Hung Cheung of the Mandarin House restaurant in Knighton, mid-Wales, admitted a series of food hygiene offences, which included using a cricket bat to stir a curry. Cheung was fined £2,515 by Brecon magistrates in January. He said the bat – which had been gnawed by rats – was used for stirring only once.

DISABILITY CRICKET 2009

Change and opportunity

PAUL EDWARDS

None of England's disability teams played international cricket last summer, yet 2009 may still be seen as a crucial year in the growth of the disabled game. In March, memoranda of understanding were signed by the ECB and the organisations representing disabled players. The significance of the documents is that they bring these cricketers within the remit of the governing body in several ways: the ECB are now responsible for the preparation, performance and funding of the national disability teams; each impairment group knows what it needs to deliver to receive financial help; and disability organisations are now able to develop the domestic element of their game in partnership with professional staff from county boards. The ECB are the first governing body in the cricket world to reach such an agreement with its disabled groups.

Ian Martin, the ECB's national disability cricket manager, described the agreements as a "major step forward" and expressed the hope that there would be 80 disability focus clubs in place by 2013. Symbolising this optimism, blind cricketer Nathan Foy was named as the first Disabled Player of the Year, and in May he stood proudly alongside senior award-winners Andrew Strauss and Claire Taylor in the Lord's Long Room. These are times of rapid change and unparalleled opportunity for disabled cricketers.

The ICC are also taking a closer interest in the development of the disabled game. In June, Martin gave a presentation to the Heads of Development of each Test-playing nation, and he was later charged with carrying out a worldwide audit of disability cricket activity and reporting back. "I felt the weight of every disabled cricketer on my shoulders when I spoke at that conference," he said.

But if 2009 saw domestic disabled cricketers brought within the overall care of the ECB and begin to make their voices heard on the international stage, it did not prevent them feeling the unwelcome impact of political volatility and economic weakness. In August, the Test series between England's and Pakistan's blind teams was cancelled after the British High Commission refused to grant visas to the prospective tourists. In the same month, fears about the viability of the Deaf World Cup were confirmed when the event was postponed for a year because of lack of sponsorship. It is now scheduled to take place in Auckland, running from December 2010 into January 2011.

That served to focus even more attention on the third Learning Disability Tri-Nations tournament, contested by teams from England, Australia and South Africa and held in Melbourne in early December. Thanks to a victory against South Africa and the abandonment of one of their games against Australia, England reached the final, but lost by eight wickets to the host country, who maintained their supremacy in this form of the game.

UMPIRING IN 2009

The system under review

CHARLES RANDALL

The move by the ICC to implement the Umpire Decision Review System in the international game with a guarded reaction when the use of electronic back-up was declared mandatory from October 1, 2009. Initial objections focused on the high cost to the home boards, and it was almost two months before the system was used for New Zealand's Test against Pakistan at Dunedin and for Australia v West Indies at Brisbane the same week.

The ICC used four earlier series for fine-tuning the UDRS, also known as DRS. The stated intention was to eliminate umpiring clangers rather than place all decision-making under intensive analysis. After a few third-umpire gaffes in trials, general accuracy improved naturally, though there was a human price when Mark Benson dramatically stood down and flew home to England after the first day of West Indies' Test at Adelaide in December. Indifferent health was officially given as the reason for his sudden departure, but Benson had apparently been exasperated by a third-umpire reversal, and he later stood down from the elite panel.

Television broadcasters had long enjoyed scrutinising decisions from on high in the name of entertainment, but now devices such as Hawk-Eye and Hot Spot could no longer be regarded as toys. Careers and international matches were at stake. The ICC had sanctioned third-umpire assistance for line decisions through video replay since November 1992, and significant electronic advances eased the progression to DRS. It is now only a short step towards on-field decisions through, say, a Hawk-Eye monitor strapped to the umpire's wrist.

At the ICC's trials the batsmen and fielding captain were allowed up to three failed attempts each per innings at overturning an umpiring decision, though this was soon reduced to two when players were tempted to waste time with unexpired referrals without a realistic chance of success. The four series selected for testing were Sri Lanka v India (August 2008), New Zealand v West Indies (December 2008), West Indies v England (February–March 2009) and South Africa v Australia (February–March 2009).

The ICC's first list of approved aids included slow-motion replays, super-slow-motion replays, ultra-motion replays, the infra-red detector Hot Spot, ball-tracking technology, stump-microphone sound (at normal speed and slow motion) and the "pitch mat". Ball-tracking usually featured Hawk-Eye, which used sophisticated software and several high-speed cameras to predict the path of the ball. ICC policy stated that umpires should receive the benefit of the doubt on DRS. This was logical, if at times a little hard on batsmen.

To doubters, the system was a moral mishmash of electronics, "T" signs and the raised finger. The Indian board expressed their scepticism, joining

South Africa and New Zealand in concerns about costs. It seemed that justice came at too high a price, until sponsors stepped in.

The ICC could subsequently argue that, with better accuracy of decision-making, player behaviour improved, and one unexpected benefit was to create a much more fertile environment for finger-spinners. Bat-pad catches could usually be nailed, and there were probably more lbw dismissals than ever before. Graeme Swann, the England off-spinner, enjoyed a surge in his career as a direct result.

The ICC's general manager Dave Richardson said that during final trials correct decisions rose from 93% to 98%. Players began to appreciate the new accuracy once they had adjusted to the philosophy of referral. The dismissal of Mitchell Johnson at Brisbane in November seemed controversial, owing to the balance of doubt. Ian Gould gave the left-handed Johnson out caught behind as he pushed forward against the spin of the West Indian slow left-armer Sulieman Benn. The batsman called for a review, but third umpire Benson could see no compelling reason to overrule the decision even though Hot Spot did not show a snick. Gould thought he heard a sound as the ball passed the outside edge.

At Dunedin, the Pakistan seamer Mohammad Asif's referral confirmed that umpire Billy Doctrove should give Grant Elliott out lbw, but Elliott survived because the third umpire noticed that Asif had overstepped, so Pakistan's appeal failed on the no-ball. That escape created a new routine duty for non-strikers – to check for overstepping.

Referrals were required to be made within "a few seconds", and the South Africans delayed one appeal for more than half a minute during their Test against England at Centurion in December. Relatively little was made of this incident, although it highlighted the possibility of influence from people watching television.

The DRS reduced on-field dissent noticeably, a trend suggesting that the concept of neutral officials could become redundant. This would reduce the burn-out from constant travelling, which in the recent past has persuaded respected officials such as Peter Willey, Jeremy Lloyds and Neil Mallender to withdraw from the international panel at a relatively young age.

In England, the former Premier League and FIFA referee Martin Bodenham completed his first season on the ECB's first-class list, although at 59 he was probably too late to emulate another former FIFA referee, Steve Bucknor, by joining the ICC's elite panel.

The death of Alcwyn Jenkins from an accident on the field cast a shadow over club cricket. The incident, during a South Wales Cricket Association match between Swansea and Llangennech at St Helen's in July, was an all too vivid reminder of the physical dangers facing umpires. Jenkins, 72, had positioned himself to adjudicate a quick single as mid-off ran in, and he was struck on the back of the head by the throw. He died in an air ambulance on the way to hospital. For safety reasons umpires are encouraged to take position on the far side of the crease for in-field incidents, but Jenkins's misfortune showed that errors could be made in the heat of the moment.

CRICKET AND THE BRAIN

KP and the case for neural plasticity

MICHAEL ARMSTRONG-JAMES

In February 2010, in a Twenty20 international against Pakistan at Melbourne, Australia's Shaun Tait released a ball at 160.7kph. Tait therefore came within a whisker of being the third bowler to clock 100mph, after Shoaib Akhtar and Brett Lee.

From the moment that Tait released the ball, to the instant that it reached Pakistan's batsman Imran Farhat, was about 400 milliseconds. However, the batsman had to go through five stages of neural processing, taking a minimum of 550 milliseconds, before he could *start* to hit the ball.

The five stages are: (1) the visual information was processed in the retina; (2) this information was relayed to the visual areas of the brain to be interpreted; (3) from there it was further relayed to motor areas to generate a response plan; (4) the plan was then sent via the spinal cord to the body's motor nerves which control the muscles; (5) finally, the movement was executed by the muscles to make the shot.

So how did the batsman find the extra time needed to hit the ball? Fortunately, the brain provides a way. As you may have guessed, it is done by anticipation. The start of the shot can be initiated around half a second before the release of a fast ball from cues provided by the bowler, such as changes in his body and limb angles before release of the ball; others could be cumulative knowledge of the finer (and sometimes coarser) points of the bowler's previous behaviour and body language.

In modern cricket, the use of trigger movements has been adopted: quick shuffles of the feet, just prior to delivery of the ball. Behavioural neuroscientists call these "priming movements". There is some evidence that these pre-select the precise memory circuits in the brain required for an immediate forthcoming action – in this case the stroke. Priming by trigger movements reduces the time between decision and action, giving the batsman a critical edge in time to strike a ball. The better the batsman, the earlier he evaluates the different cues that betray intended ball speed, bounce and trajectory. The best are able to predict such finesses as the probable length of the ball, enabling the critical decision between playing a cross-bat or vertical stroke.

You might think from all this that executing a stroke is a very tedious process needing continuous thought, but that is not the case. Skilled movements are perfected for timing, form, speed and sequence by repeated trial and error; they are automatically and unconsciously improved by repetitive use.

Learning processes for skilled movement are not unique to man, but work in a similar way throughout the entire animal kingdom. An intriguing example is provided by the archer fish, which traps insects by spitting at them. However, since its prey is above the water line, it has to compensate for the bending of light through the water interface to strike the insect. The fish has no way of calculating this and learns to make all the corrections according to experience, good attempts being reinforced by success. Entirely unconsciously, like the batsman, it also builds in an early start to the movement (i.e. anticipation), allowing for the neural processing times the brain needs to make the movement.

When we strike a ball, we do not think about which parts of our body to move in which sequence; we just do it, selecting the pre-wired connections from brain to the spinal cord, and then to muscles. To get a sequence of movements needs millions, if not billions, of nerve cells (neurones) firing in the right sequences. Not only that, but we need many circuits firing together in parallel. To make only the right movement needs a way of blocking unwanted circuits in the brain and the spinal cord. Very cleverly, this is done by specialised inhibitory neurones, which reduce or block output from the excitatory neurones, which relay messages forward. For example, when you flex your arm – perhaps to play a pull shot – the extensors are automatically inhibited.

There is no such thing as muscle memory, as some coaches assert, but we can train the brain. As we learn progressively from experience, brain circuits generating a skill become strengthened and better selected by repetitive use. Skill-learning circuitry is created by use-dependent strengthening of circuits.

On the other hand, rarely used connections get less powerful. Modification of the operation of both the excitatory *and* inhibitory neurones is required to mould these learning circuits. Hence, with repeated practice of a stroke not only are successful patterns of output for movement strengthened, but useless patterns are inhibited and weakened for economy of action: thus a batsman learns to drop his hands when he ducks the 99mph bouncer rather than lift them in front of his face.

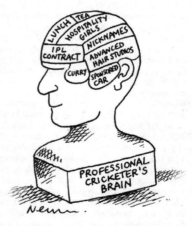

Skill-learning occurs almost exclusively by an increase in the conduction power of synapses, the nerve-fibre junctions between neurones. It does not occur by an increase in the number of neurones or by significant growth of nerve fibres. Otherwise, our heads would increase in size!

There still remains the question of how the brain processes visual cues to produce skilled learned movements such as a cricket stroke. Many brain areas contribute, but three areas of the cerebral cortex are critical. Visual information, including cues, is received and analysed in the visual areas of cortex, whereas movement plans are delivered by the motor cortex. Linking the two, to interpret the visual cues and design the correct movement, is an extraordinary sensori-motor command area: the posterior parietal cortex, or PPX. Repeated sensory experiences stimulate the PPX to learn, speeding up and refining movement plans in proportion to practice. Not only does the PPX play a crucial role in generating and perfecting movement patterns specific to cues, but it routinely stores these movement patterns for years, and sometimes for a lifetime.

Learning a successful stroke benefits from being remembered within the context of the delivery, tying visual recognition of cues to memory. This is called context-dependent learning, and is essential for choosing a shot. For example, a major problem for a batsman is to identify and practise playing the uncommon balls – the full toss perhaps – that tend to dismiss him, and finally recall how he dealt with those deliveries for future practice.

However, there is a potential down side to refinement of neural circuitry patterns for repetitive tasks. Curiously, the perfection of skills can lead to a reduced repertoire of shots, and hence stereotyped responses. Similarly, rationalisation of cue interpretation can cause rationalisation of strokes. A further problem is that plasticity of the brain, i.e. the process of circuit modification, decreases rapidly with age as adulthood is approached. Varied and extensive early experiences will make the batsman much better equipped to detect a wide range of cues to survive dismissal.

So, in general, the earlier in life that we learn our skills, the better we execute them at maturity. A wonderful example is Lewis Hamilton, who learned his early skills in motor racing in go-karts from the age of six. He built on his skills formidably as he progressed to adulthood, with progressively faster circuits and more complex machinery. However, for batsmen who rapidly achieve stardom at a very early age there is a down side. Those who exclusively play on excellent and predictable pitches against good opposition when they are very young will have much less capability later in life in dealing with uneven pitches and unconventional bowlers.

So far we have discussed skill learning that arises from practice and experience, a process which is common throughout the animal kingdom. However, mankind is unique in being able to communicate through language. This provides the opportunity for declarative learning – learning from verbal instruction, providing us with the capacity to benefit from the knowledge and experiences of others. It is entirely independent of skill learning. Declarative learning cannot develop a skill, but it can speed up the process of understanding what is required to perfect that skill or introduce new ideas and attitudes. The areas of the brain which store this type of knowledge are entirely different from those used for learning skills, and people with poor declarative memories can still have phenomenal physical skills: one example, by all accounts, is Andrew Flintoff.

Once a cricketer has reached full maturity, it is exceptionally difficult for him to retrain. The process of learning is powerfully embedded in the modified synapses and hence in the development of preferred neural circuits. To change a run-up, a bowler has to practise the change a thousand times or more to allow progressive resetting of the same circuits. For a batsman it is even more difficult. Marcus Trescothick in his recent book states how he spent a winter in Perth leaving the ball outside off stump instead of automatically playing the shot and often nicking it. But, sadly, even mature cricketers often relapse into old habits under pressure, when the old neural circuitry flips back into action.

One coaching axiom is "keep your eye on the ball and you won't get hit". The reason, of course, is to prevent avoidance behaviour, part of which is shutting the eyes, which is an instinctive movement. Instinctive movements differ from skills, being faster, life-preserving reactions, and have no place in creative batting strokes or learning, only in survival.

A person's attitude to survival profoundly influences his or her physical behaviour. Mammals are broadly divided into carnivores and herbivores. Humans are somewhere between the two – omnivores. Just how close we are to a herbivore or a carnivore indexes our whole response pattern to threatening experiences. Essentially, herbivores either take avoidance or freeze when challenged, whereas carnivores act or fight. It follows that naturally aggressive carnivore-like batsmen are liable to take greater risks: Viv Richards and Kevin Pietersen are examples. It is possible that coaches in future could use psychological profiling to choose a perfectly balanced batting team against known opposition.

Bowlers' skills are fundamentally different from those of batsmen, and personality is not such a big factor. A major difference is that bowlers do not have to react rapidly to cues or danger. This is because the bowler chooses his movements well in advance of delivery. He knows what he will do and does not have to be immediately responsive to a batsman's movements. Unlike the batsman, a bowler's repertoire of movements will have been learned without excessive attention to cues. When he releases the ball, the whole plan of delivery has been thought out a few seconds earlier. So, in contrast to the batsman, cognitive thought is a more significant factor for the bowler. Since thought processes are undiminished at maturity, this may explain why good bowlers are able to further exploit their skills from their late teens onwards, whereas a good batsman has to establish them much earlier.

We have concentrated on how a batsman learns to deliver a perfect stroke. Through experience and teaching, the range and quality of skills improve, but they risk becoming stereotyped. The ultimate answer to stereotyped batting is to use all the skills you have learned, but be able to use them also in an unconventional way – he who dares wins. Pietersen did just that by turning from a right-handed to left-handed stance and developing the outrageous switch-hit. Other adventurous shots no doubt will follow. Long live neural plasticity!

Michael Armstrong-James is Emeritus Professor of Neurophysiology at the University of London.

OBITUARIES

ACKERMAN, HYLTON MICHAEL, who died on September 2, 2009, aged 62, was an exuberantly gifted member of the lost generation of white South African cricketers. He was a thrilling left-hand bat who announced himself as a 17-year-old with a century in two and a half hours for Border against M. J. K. Smith's MCC team in 1964-65. But by the time he reached maturity, South Africa were out of the international game. There were

Patrick Eagar

Hylton Ackerman: part of South Africa's lost generation.

those who thought he never did reach maturity. The Northamptonshire coach Percy Davis had seen the Border match and recommended this exciting new talent to the county. When he became eligible for the Championship in 1968, Ackerman immediately teamed up with Colin Milburn, both on the field and off it. Both were rumbustious hitters, and both gave life a bit of welly after nightfall. The on-field partnership was wrecked when Milburn lost his eye a year later, and Ackerman had to take his place at the top of the order. But the carousing continued, even after Ackerman was diagnosed with sugar diabetes. Some critics believe this explains a career average of 32. "He was a wonderful player when he was in the mood," said his more serious-minded team-mate David Steele, "but he wasn't in the mood often enough." Sometimes everything would click, as with his 112 for the Sobers-led World XI against Australia at Brisbane in 1971-72, an innings of which he could remember

little – he told friends – owing to a heavy night. "He had a magnificent talent," recalled Geoff Cook, who briefly opened with him for Northamptonshire. "Brilliant hand–eye co-ordination, not a lot of footwork. Behind that, there was a cricket brain that was not exploited enough by a fairly dour Northamptonshire side." Ackerman left county cricket after 1971 but played on another decade for Western Province. He also became a successful coach – full of enthusiasm when he spotted a real talent – and an idiosyncratic TV commentator until illness eventually took its toll. He was famously shaky on details, always referring, for instance, to "one-day Tests". On one detail, though, he was pernickety. He always referred to his son Hylton Deon Ackerman, who did play Test cricket, with grave formality, as "H. D. Ackerman".

AGASHE, DAYANESHWAR CHANDRASEKHAR, who died on January 2, 2009, aged 66, was a wicketkeeper and unorthodox batsman, with a penchant for lofted shots. He played 13 matches, mostly for Maharashtra, in the 1960s and later became vice-president of the Board of Control for Cricket in India. Son of a rich industrialist, Agashe himself had widespread business interests and founded the Shree Suvarna Sahakari Bank in 1969: this failed in 2006, and police contended it was not only his strokeplay that was unorthodox. Six weeks before his death, from diabetes-related complications, he was arrested along with one of his sons, and was in custody facing fraud charges when he died. Despite his downfall, many people paid tribute to his philanthropy.

AIRD, SIR ALASTAIR STURGIS, GCVO, who died on September 30, 2009, aged 78, served Queen Elizabeth the Queen Mother as a courtier for 42 years and was her private secretary for the decade before her death in 2002. He was the nephew of Ronny Aird, the former secretary of MCC, and himself opened the bowling for Eton against Harrow at Lord's in 1948 and 1949.

ALLINGHAM, HENRY WILLIAM, was considered to be the oldest man in the world when he died on July 18, 2009, aged 113. He was also the last survivor – on either side – of the Battle of Jutland, in which he served on *HMS Kingfisher*, and, beyond reasonable doubt, the last person alive to have watched W. G. Grace bat. As a child, Allingham was taken to watch Grace at The Oval, evidently in the London County v Surrey match in 1903. "He walked like an elderly person because his pads were too long for him," Allingham recalled. Since WG would have been 54 at the time, he might have seemed elderly to a child, but Allingham set new benchmarks in this regard. During and after a working life spent largely at Ford in Dagenham, he followed cricket from a distance. But in 2006, when he was 109, one of his carers, Simon Massey, who also coaches at The Oval, took him back to the ground after 103 years. Allingham charmed everyone and the publicity helped turn him into a national celebrity. He came back twice more, in 2007 and 2008. Although deaf and wheelchair-bound, he was still sharp and humorous: he called 90-year-old Sir Alec Bedser a "spring chicken" and attributed his own longevity to "cigarettes, whisky and wild, wild women".

ANDERSON, DOUGLAS IAN EVANS, who died on December 19, 2009, a month short of his 100th birthday, was a batsman who played five matches for Transvaal before the Second World War, scoring 63 in the second one, against Rhodesia at Johannesburg in 1931-32. But his third and fourth games produced three ducks, and his only other match came five years later.

ASIM BUTT died suddenly in his sleep on November 30, 2009, while visiting relatives in Lahore. He was 42, and thought to be in good health, although some years previously he had needed an operation to remove a blood clot from his brain. A strongly built left-arm swing bowler and occasional tail-end hitter, Butt played 21 first-class matches in his native Pakistan, taking nine for 88 in the match for Lahore City Blues against Lahore Division in 1984-85. In the 1990s he moved to Scotland, where he combined non-cricket work and weekend club pro-ing. Butt made his debut for the full Scotland team in 1998, and took 106 wickets in 71 games for them before his international career ended under a cloud in 2005, when he was banned from all cricket for a year after failing a drugs test. He claimed he had been given a cigarette laced with Ecstasy, but accepted his suspension stoically, keeping fit by running around the grounds where he was now banned even from practising. Butt had played in all Scotland's matches in the 1999 World Cup, starting with their first wicket in official one-day internationals – Australia's Adam Gilchrist, for six at Worcester.

Asim Butt in full flow for Scotland in 1998.

Mike Hewitt, Getty Images

He finished the day with figures of one for 21 from his ten overs. "Asim was one of the best bowlers I ever played with, and a superb bloke," said his former Scotland new-ball partner John Blain.

BAILEY, Sir DERRICK THOMAS LOUIS, Bt, DFC, who died on June 19, 2009, aged 90, was a surprise choice as Gloucestershire's amateur captain in 1951 after a handful of matches over the previous two years: he lasted for two seasons before seven of the senior professionals wrote to the committee complaining about his rather eccentric leadership. "I don't think I have met another man whose head was so full of theories," said Tom Graveney, one of the signatories. "His enthusiasm for the game was equalled only by the number of theories he had about it." Ideas ran in the family: his father, the

South African industrialist Sir Abe Bailey, came up with the original proposal for what is now the International Cricket Council. The son, meanwhile, was a better batsman than some of those amateurs promoted blinking into county cricket around this time: he passed 1,000 runs in 1951, scoring centuries from No. 3 against Sussex and Northamptonshire. The following year, when bowlers were wiser to his forthright approach, he still managed 864 runs. By then, though, his team-mates were terminally irritated by his habit of asking them what to do – and doing the opposite. Sam Cook, who had won an England cap in 1947, lost rhythm, apparently as a result of Bailey's meddling, while "Bomber" Wells had a number of clashes with him, many of them to do with Wells's comically short run-up. After finishing with Gloucestershire, Bailey continued to run the family farm in Herefordshire, combining that with club cricket and hunting. Later he moved to the Channel Islands, where he founded an airline, Aurigny, which now serves 22 routes to and round the islands. During the Second World War, Bailey was decorated after flying more than 50 operational sorties during the Italian campaign. His family was impeccably connected: his godfathers were Louis Botha, South Africa's first prime minister, and Earl Haig, while his half-brother was briefly married to Winston Churchill's daughter Diana.

PA Photos

Derrick Bailey in 1952: "His enthusiasm for the game was equalled only by the number of theories he had about it."

BALA, RAJAN, died of kidney failure on October 9, 2009, aged 63. Bala (born Natarajan Balasubramaniam) was a journalist who worked for several of India's leading newspapers, most recently the *Deccan Chronicle* and *Asian Age*. "He had strong opinions and was fearless in expressing them," said the Australian writer Mike Coward. Several of the gifted new generation of Indian cricket writers are his protégés. Bala's books included biographies of Sachin Tendulkar and Bhagwat Chandrasekhar, and a look at the political history of Indian cricket. His final work, *Time Well Spent*, was about to be released when he died.

BASHIR MIANDAD died on December 3, 2009, of head injuries sustained in a car crash the previous month. He was 59, and the older brother and mentor of Pakistan's leading Test batsman Javed Miandad. Writing in his autobiography about their marathon childhood cricket sessions, Javed said: "I credit him with taking away my fear of the ball, probably the single most important contribution anyone has ever made towards the evolution of my batsmanship." Bashir himself played five uneventful first-class matches, mostly for Habib Bank.

BATES, TERENCE NORMAN, died of a heart attack on January 5, 2009, aged 72. Terry Bates was one of the new breed of administrators who emerged at Lord's in the 1990s as the game's organisation expanded. He had spent most of his career in local government, with forays into football, running the youth teams at Wrexham and Peterborough. But Bates was also the voluntary general secretary of the National Association of Young Cricketers, and this led to an offer of a post as No. 2 to Keith Andrew at the National Cricket Association, which was then in charge of the recreational game; he became national development manager when the ECB assumed control in 1997, and later ran the Cricket Foundation. "Terry was a bit gruff in committee and he spoke as he found," said Tim Lamb, the ECB's first chief executive. "But he was a very good organiser – someone who got things done."

BAXTER, DAVID ANDERSON, who died on February 7, 2009, aged 75, was a wicketkeeper for the Ferguslie club who played twice for Scotland against the 1956 Australians, when he stumped Ray Lindwall and his opposite number Gil Langley. He also kept goal for St Mirren and Queen's Park. He spent much of his working life with Esso, and was in charge of their advertising division at the time of their famous "tiger in your tank" campaign.

BEGBIE, DENIS WARBURTON, who died on March 10, 2009, aged 94, was a South African batsman who lost his best cricketing years to the Second World War. He still won five caps, all at home, against England in 1948-49 and Australia the following season. Begbie ensured selection with a six-hour 154 for Transvaal against George Mann's MCC side a week before the First Test, but did little of note in his international appearances. A good domestic season had earned him a place on the 1947 tour of England, but he could not break into the Test side. "A quiet, business-like cricketer," John Arlott called him after watching him score a century against Essex. "He knew his limitations and worked within them busily but unobtrusively." Arlott thought Begbie's flattish leg-spin, which brought him only one Test wicket (Neil Harvey), harmed his cause, though he took 13 for 174 in one pre-war Currie Cup match. Begbie was also a scratch golfer in his time, and was a member of the Royal Johannesburg club for 80 years.

BILLOT, JOHN DAVID, who died on September 28, 2009, six days short of his 80th birthday, was a Welsh rugby and cricket journalist. He served the Cardiff paper, the *Western Mail*, for 43 years, the last seven before retirement as sports editor. Billot's most lasting contribution will be his 1970 *History of Welsh International Rugby*, which put the national obsession's records on a proper footing. He was also a long-standing presence on Welsh grounds, a genial, knowledgeable press box companion, and *Wisden's* Glamorgan correspondent from 1985 to 1990.

BOSHIER, BRIAN STANLEY, who died on September 2, 2009, aged 77, was a fast-medium bowler who did a lot with the ball, and took 108 wickets in both 1958 (earning his Leicestershire cap) and 1961. He was tall and solid and not terribly flexible: Terry Spencer, who often shared the new ball with Boshier, remembered that he had a lot of problems with his knees and back. "His thigh muscles were rock hard – he was just not supple," he said. "It's amazing he played as much as he did. But he was a great bloke, he enjoyed his cricket tremendously and we had some great days together." One of those

MOST SUCCESSIVE FIRST-CLASS INNINGS WITHOUT SCORING A RUN

12	M. A. Robinson (Northamptonshire).............................	1990
10	B. J. Griffiths (Northamptonshire).............................	1974 to 1977
10	P. J. Visser (Central Districts)	1984-85–1985-86
10	M. H. A. Jabbar (Singha, Sebastianites and Galle)	1997-98–2001-02
9	J. P. Candler (Cambridge University)	1894–1895
9	T. W. J. Goddard (Gloucestershire).............................	1923
9	A. H. S. Clark (Somerset)	1930
9	B. S. Boshier (Leicestershire)	1955
9	O. S. Wheatley (Glamorgan)	1966
9	M. W. W. Selvey (Middlesex).................................	1972
9	P. L. Garlick (Cambridge University)	1984
9	G. Jayakumar (Kerala)......................................	1990-91
9	D. Ramnarine (West Indies and Trinidad & Tobago)	2001-02
9	C. S. Martin (New Zealand and Warwickshire).....................	2008–2008-09

Notes: Table includes not-out innings. Seymour Clark's nine scoreless innings comprised his entire first-class career. John Candler scored his only runs (8*) in his seventh and final first-class match.

days came at Brentwood in 1957 when Spencer dismissed the Essex openers and Boshier cleaned up the next eight for 45. And, on a damp pitch against Lancashire at Grace Road in 1960, he took ten wickets in the match for 85: unfortunately, Lancashire had Brian Statham, who shot Leicestershire out for 37. Boshier was an infamously hopeless batsman (career average: 4.32), and he started the 1955 season with nine scoreless innings, equalling the record at the time. He wrote the details of this sequence on the bat he was using, and it was placed on the coffin at his funeral. After leaving Leicestershire in 1964, Boshier ran a pub in Yorkshire before that inflexible body started rebelling: he ended his days in a wheelchair.

CAREY, PAUL ALEXANDER HUNTLY DOBRÉE, died on November 13, 2009, aged 89. Horsham-born fast bowler Paul Carey (also known as Dobrée-Carey) played 42 matches for Sussex in the three immediate post-war seasons, taking 115 wickets. Fifty-four of them came in 1947, including a hat-trick against Glamorgan. But his output halved in 1948, and he left the staff, moving to Durham where he combined teaching with running a sports shop, occasional appearances in the Minor Counties Championship, and acting as pro at Darlington. In 1964 he emigrated to Australia, and remained there. During the war Carey had played ten first-class matches in India, and was on the winning side, Baroda, in the 1942-43 Ranji Trophy final.

CHATRAPALSINHJI, KUMAR SHRI, who died on April 29, 2009, aged 72, was a great-nephew of Ranjitsinhji, a nephew of Duleepsinhji, and the uncle of the Indian Test batsman Ajay Jadeja. He played for four Indian states (and East Zone) in a first-class career that stretched over 15 seasons from 1957-58, when he started with Delhi in the Ranji Trophy. He never made a century but missed out by only two runs for Saurashtra against Gujarat in 1962-63.

COLLINS, ROY, who died suddenly on November 5, 2009, aged 75, was a well-built all-rounder and a Lancashire regular, if not an automatic choice, for nine years. Collins enlivened many games with big hitting – his 449 runs in his final season included 25 sixes – but that was 1962, the year before one-day cricket started, and he then, perhaps prematurely, decided to quit. He later became a successful insurance broker. Collins had an eventful debut for Lancashire's first team, entering at 60 for five in reply to Hampshire's 59 and steadying the innings with 33. But he scored only two first-class hundreds, both in August 1961: that year he scored 858 runs and took 52 wickets with his off-spin, including six for 63 against Sussex in between his centuries. This purple patch earned him his county cap. After leaving Lancashire, Collins played on in the leagues, and for Cheshire. He was the brother-in-law of Jim Cumbes, now Lancashire's chief executive. "To this day I don't think I've seen a cleaner hitter," said Cumbes. "I saw him strike two sixes on to the railway station when the pitch was on the pavilion side of the ground. Then he smashed the pavilion clock."

CORBOYS, JACK, who died in March 2009, aged 93, played and umpired cricket in and around Halifax in Yorkshire for 66 years until his retirement at 80. He once said that he got through the Second World War thanks to cricket: "I got introduced to a lot of important people and they helped me stay out of trouble." He still needed luck: he was in one of the leading tanks at Arnhem when it was hit by a shell. "Everything was on fire, but the sergeant and I survived."

CRAWFORD, WILLIAM PATRICK ANTHONY, died on January 21, 2009, aged 75. For two seasons in the mid-1950s, it seemed as though Pat Crawford would be the natural successor to the ageing Keith Miller and Ray Lindwall as Australia's pace spearhead. After watching Crawford's first-class debut in 1954-55, Lindsay Hassett picked him as one to watch. He did indeed make the Australian side within two years – but at 25 he was out of first-class cricket. A mixture of personal impetuosity and the stiff-necked attitudes

Lancashire in 1960, before the Roses Match. *Standing:* Geoff Pullar, Ken Higgs, Roy Collins (who died in 2009), Peter Marner, Jack Dyson and Geoff Clayton. *Seated:* Tommy Greenhough (who also died in 2009), Alan Wharton, Bob Barber, Brian Statham and Ken Grieves.

of cricket officialdom blighted his early promise, leading the writer Gideon Haigh to comment later: "Rarely has a cricketer made such a striking impression as this strapping young paceman… Rarely, too, has one suffered such an undignified fall from grace." Ian Craig, a state colleague, remembered Crawford warmly: "Pat had undoubted ability, and his combination of speed and movement made him an uncomfortable proposition for most batsmen."

Crawford came from distant Dubbo, but made a rapid impression when he arrived in Sydney. He generated pace, lift and movement from a high action, and a run of about 30 yards, which meant his (eight-ball) overs often lasted five minutes, an almost Wagnerian length by the standards of the time. In November 1954, he marked his New South Wales debut, against the MCC tourists, by having both Bill Edrich and Reg Simpson taken in the slips during one over early on the first morning, and finished with seven wickets in the match. He had 34 wickets at 16.02 that season, and maintained his form and his fire to earn selection for the 1956 Ashes tour. His English wife (they had met when he spent the 1955 season with East Lancashire) was pregnant by then, but the Australian board ruled that she could neither travel on the same ship as her husband, nor stay with him on tour. Ultimately, they travelled separately: Richie Benaud noted that "Crawford could have had a mistress on board but not his wife, and the board would have said nothing."

He replaced the injured Alan Davidson for the Second Test, at Lord's. However, he pulled a muscle and limped out of the match after bowling only five overs. He struggled for the rest of the tour but did play in the three Tests against India on the way home, his best performance coming at Madras, where he took four for 50 from 38 overs in the match and scored an important 34 from No. 10. During this time, though, his personal life unravelled. His wife decided to remain in England with their child, and the board invoked a clause in his Ashes contract which prevented him accepting an offer from Kent in 1957. Instead he wandered round the bush doing odd jobs until he got together with Nona Hayes in 1963, a partnership that restored stability to his life. Haigh met him in 1996, and wrote that "he recalled the charisma of Keith Miller and the kindness of Arthur Morris with great pleasure. But he had no mementoes of his career, save a few faded newspaper clippings in a small envelope marked 'Cricket'."

CROSSAN, ERNEST ERIC, who died on August 10, 2009, aged 94, was the last man alive who had played for New South Wales before the Second World War. Ern Crossan was a genuine all-rounder: a powerful batsman who once scored an even-time 217 in a grade match, and an English-style seamer reliant on accuracy and movement. The war meant that he played only four first-class matches, two before and two afterwards, and he had little chance to make an impression. He was an engineer, and spent the war installing and maintaining Australia's coastal guns.

CULL, DAVID WALTER, who died on February 14, 2009, aged 66, was on the MCC cricket staff before turning to real tennis, ending up as the head professional at the court behind the Lord's pavilion. Cull was among the leading players of his time, winning the British Open doubles title, and a fine coach with a chirpy-Cockney approach: he often regaled fellow players with tales of his pet parrot and his racing greyhounds (several MCC members joined him in ownership syndicates). After retirement, Cull – as his predecessor Henry Johns had done – continued to hand-stitch real-tennis balls for use at Lord's and elsewhere.

DIEDRICKS, WILFRED ANDREW, died on August 18, 2009, aged 64. Wilf Diedricks emerged from the vibrant, largely Indian, Bharat club in Durban to become one of South Africa's leading umpires. He stood in Howa Bowl matches (later declared first-class) under apartheid, before being chosen to umpire the Port Elizabeth Test against India in the country's first post-isolation series, in 1992-93. This came during a short-lived experiment in which two home umpires took turns on the field and in the TV-replay box, while an overseas umpire stayed outside throughout. Diedricks never stood in another Test, but was a regular in one-day internationals until 2001. Dave Richardson, who took nine catches in that Test said: "He came across as a modest and dedicated man, with a great respect for the game."

DILDAR AHMED MALIK, who died on September 10, 2009, aged 41, was a Pakistani wicketkeeper who played 22 matches, all but one for Multan. He made his debut in 1987-88 alongside another newcomer, Waqar Younis, and the following season against Faisalabad made six catches and a stumping in the first innings.

DIMBLEBY, DESMOND EDGAR, MC, who died on March 21, 2008, aged 88, played for both South Africa's Eastern and Western Provinces in a career that spanned the Second World War. He scored 87 for EP against George Mann's MCC team at Port Elizabeth in 1948-49 as well as a century for WP against Border a year earlier. He often played alongside his brother Ken (who died in 2006), and they shared two century stands. Des Dimbleby won his MC at Minturno Creek during the Italian campaign in 1944, while seconded to the King's Own Yorkshire Light Infantry. Later, he became a journalist and covered the 1955 South African tour of England.

DINWIDDY, HUGH POCHIN, OBE, who died on October 31, 2009, aged 97, was Kent's oldest player at the time of his death. He had played ten matches for the county in the 1930s – as well as five for Cambridge University, without winning a Blue – after making 218 for the Second Eleven against Devon at Blackheath in July 1933. He was also the last man who played against both Jack Hobbs ("he was very kind to me and wished me luck") and Don Bradman ("he was all right – he didn't say much"). Dinwiddy was a useful batsman, but in first-class cricket never passed 45. He later became a teacher, at Ampleforth

College and also in Uganda. According to his cousin Rachel Lewin, he would cry "Hooray! All joy! All joy!" when he arrived at a family gathering. She also described him as "distinguished, erudite, fascinating".

DUFTY, ROSS, died on August 4, 2009, aged 81. A pugnacious batsman and lively seamer, he played two first-class matches for Tasmania in their pre-Shield days. In the second of them, he made a face-saving 39 as a makeshift opener against the Australian team on their way to the 1961 Ashes series. In 1955-56, he took all ten wickets, nine clean bowled, for 41 in a Hobart grade match.

EDRICH, BRIAN ROBERT, who died on May 31, 2009, aged 86, was the youngest and last survivor of the remarkable quartet of Norfolk cricketing brothers. Bill Edrich of Middlesex and England was the most famous, while Eric and Geoff also played county cricket – John Edrich was their cousin. Brian turned out for Kent's Second Eleven in 1939, but the war delayed his first-class debut until he was almost 25. He was a left-hand batsman, described by brother Bill as "a powerful driver, but with a fatal inclination to hit everything round the corner". Someone with a less distinguished pedigree might never have survived his start with Kent: he had not reached 50 in 36 matches before facing Sussex at Tunbridge Wells in June 1949. But then, after making 60 in the first innings, he hammered 193 not out as Kent followed on, adding 161 for the ninth wicket with Fred Ridgway, a stand which included "the biggest hitting seen on a Kent ground for years", according to one local paper. "Though the ball often turned quickly and rose nastily," reported *Wisden*, "he mastered the attack in great style." Even though Kent lost, this earned Edrich his county cap. Earlier that month he had taken seven for 41 against Hampshire with his off-breaks, and he took seven Gloucestershire wickets for 64 immediately after his Tunbridge Wells heroics. However, he never quite hit such heights again. Three more

Brian Edrich in 1949.

centuries followed, two of them in 1951 when he scored 1,000 runs for the only time, but he was released in 1953 after suffering an injury that affected his bowling and throwing. He moved to Glamorgan for three unexceptional seasons, before becoming their assistant coach and captaining the Second Eleven. Edrich was a popular coach at St Edward's School in Oxford for 20 years from 1964, and played for Oxfordshire.

EDWARDS, JOHN HILEY, died of a brain tumour on November 8, 2009, aged 58. Hiley Edwards was a stylish left-hand batsman who played for Devon for 18 years, captaining them between 1985 and 1991. His last game was the one-day Holt Cup final at Lord's in 1991 – Devon's first cup-final appearance there – when they lost narrowly to Staffordshire. His brother and his two sons also played for Devon.

EDWARDS, THOMAS WILLIAM MUIR McKINNELL, OBE, died on October 25, 2009, aged 87. Bill Edwards was a small, chatty Welshman who was never more than a sociable club tailender, but he became one of the best-known and most influential figures in Welsh cricket. In 1947, after leaving the RAF, he set up Bill Edwards County Sports Shop, just by the St Helen's ground in Swansea, and from this poky and chaotic base ran an improbable international business, supplying sports goods all over the world, including – for many years – all the equipment for the West Indies Cricket Board. But he was a man

Glamorgan Cricket Archives

Bill Edwards (*second from right*) with three of his many contacts: Gilbert Parkhouse, Trevor Bailey and Tony Lewis.

of phenomenal range, resourcefulness, energy and generosity with his time. Edwards was the honorary secretary of Glamorgan's western area, which meant he effectively ran the St Helen's matches on behalf of the club in an era when Swansea was considered a more important venue than Cardiff. He would organise the gatemen, spend the day scoring for BBC Wales, then come down and count the often considerable takings. He was also president (from its formation in 1973 until its death) of the South Wales Junior League, the biggest in the country, chairman of the Welsh Cricket Association, and father-figure and secretary of the Wales Minor Counties side from its formation in 1988. As a Glamorgan character, perhaps only Wilf Wooller surpassed him, and there is an endless supply of Bill Edwards stories, mostly about his extraordinary contacts. "He was a man of considerable charm," said former Glamorgan captain Ossie Wheatley. "He had this ability to ring up captains of industry or whoever and talk them into being sponsors." Somehow he managed to get the prisoners from the local prison to paint the seats at St Helen's, and he also seemed to have a hotline to Buckingham Palace whereby Prince Philip (the unlikely patron of Wales Minor Counties) would regularly appear at Bill's events. Once Edwards rang the chief executive of British Airways to get a consignment of cricket balls sent on the next flight to the West Indies "because the Test match could not start without them". He is said to have missed his own wedding reception because he had to blow up some rugby balls for Swansea RFC. The sign on his shop door usually said "Back in five minutes" – except, so the local joke ran, when he went abroad. Then it said "Back in ten minutes".

FENNER, DESMOND, died on August 31, 2009, aged 80. Des "Jacko" Fenner was a tall, orthodox left-hander who scored more than 2,000 runs in 52 matches for Border, with one century – 132 against North-Eastern Transvaal (including the future Test opening bowler Peter Heine) at Benoni in 1952-53. His first-class career looked to have ended in 1960, but he reappeared after more than six years against the 1966-67 Australian tourists, and hit 54. Fenner was also an accurate but flat left-arm spinner: exactly half his 18 first-class wickets came during a fortnight in January 1953. He later worked for the East London council.

FORBES, CARLTON, who died of cancer in Jamaica on May 28, 2009, aged 72, was a famously laid-back left-arm pace bowler who took 100 wickets in three successive seasons for Nottinghamshire from 1965: worse bowlers have played for West Indies. Forbes started with the Lucas club in east Kingston, but could not break into the Jamaican side, and tried his luck in England as Middlesbrough's professional. He was soon scouted by Nottinghamshire, who signed him in 1959, although he had to wait until 1961 before he qualified to play in the County Championship. He responded with 1,020 runs, which he never approached again. But with the ball he was often a handful, taking two cheap seven-fors at Trent Bridge in 1966. Against Hampshire at Worksop in July 1968, Forbes took six for 51, outshining his new-ball partner, Garry Sobers (none for 24). The rather more celebrated West Indian rated Forbes highly, and remembered: "I never met anyone in cricket who laughed as much as Carlton. Even in the most serious situations he would be smiling." Sobers was also struck by Forbes's feet. "The soles of my feet are white, like those of most black men," he said. "But Carlton's were black. He was a very black man." Forbes declined a new contract in 1970, preferring club cricket, although he did play a few games before returning to the county staff in 1973, his final season. His nickname, "Cha-Cha," derived from his dancing skills and his ownership of the New Calypso Club, a Nottingham nightspot. He had eight children.

FREUD, Sir CLEMENT RAPHAEL, who died on April 15, 2009, aged 84, was a versatile and sometimes almost ubiquitous figure in British public life. He was best known as a radio and TV personality, Liberal MP and gourmet, a range that meant his sports writing was often overlooked. Freud wrote beautifully over the years for various newspapers, and was one of three writers *Wisden* despatched to sample the early days of Twenty20 in 2005. He used a trip to Middlesex v Hampshire at Richmond to reminisce engagingly: "Price kept wicket for Middlesex; I was a wicketkeeper at school and very much admired the fact that Price kept without a long-stop. My long-stop won the fielding cup." He also contributed a savage denunciation of the non-communication with spectators at the Oval Test forfeited by Pakistan a year later.

FRINDALL, WILLIAM HOWARD, MBE, died of Legionnaires' disease on January 30, 2009, aged 69. Bill Frindall was the most famous of all scorers and statisticians. His reputation and celebrity, which spread to those who knew little of cricket, derived from his 43 seasons (1966–2008) scoring for BBC Radio's *Test Match Special*. The reputation came from the excellence of his work; his celebrity came from his mellow microphone voice and a high level of confidence and self-regard, which he used to build up a considerable sideline as an author and speaker. Sometimes he gave the impression that brain surgery and world peace might be trivialities in comparison to the great issues of leg-byes and first-class status. But he single-handedly elevated an obscure corner of an arcane sport: he made it matter because he insisted that it did matter.

Frindall got the *TMS* job in the course of a sequence in which five BBC scorers either died or resigned in rapid succession. In his autobiography, he denied this was a rerun of *Kind Hearts and Coronets*. Nonetheless, fresh out of the RAF – he had stayed on after national service – and with minimal scoring experience, he faced surprisingly little competition. The BBC were doubtless impressed by his application letter, written in his trademark copperplate hand. If so, it was a shrewd judgment: the handwriting was the key to the man. His scoring – using the linear method pioneered, though not invented, by the Australian Bill Ferguson – was astoundingly accurate, as well as neat. Above all, it was based on phenomenal powers of concentration, which he believed he mastered serving in a NATO war-room: "The handwriting was a bonus," said Peter Baxter, *TMS* producer almost throughout the Frindall era, "but it was his concentration that made him the master." From his debut at Old Trafford, aged 27, until his death, Frindall scored every Test in England for *TMS*. Indeed, he never missed a day – except for the Saturdays during the

Few who disturbed Bill Frindall at work were given even half a smile, but at Chesterfield in 1975 photographer Patrick Eagar was honoured. *Right:* the zestful club cricketer in 2008.

brief period when he was horribly miscast as the cricket correspondent of the *Mail on Sunday*. Quite possibly, he never missed a ball, since he believed that toilets were places to be used only during intervals.

Over the years, *Test Match Special* changed little, but Frindall seemed to change hardly at all: the beard grew greyer and the tone gruffer, as he corrected the errors of the more chaotic members of the commentary team with the air of an exasperated schoolmaster, but he always sounded good-humoured. This could be misleading. His first stint as *Wisden's* chief statistician ended in 1978 amid fearsome acrimony, partly over editor Norman Preston's insistence that the England v Rest of the World fixtures in 1970 should be regarded as Tests. There was another horrendous spat with the even more obsessive Irving Rosenwater, then scoring for TV. And his personal life was torrid – he was divorced twice – until he settled down in Wiltshire with his third wife Debbie and new daughter Alice in the 1990s.

Frindall happily adapted to new technology, but computerisation eroded his competitive advantage because his matchless accuracy mattered less: he never cared for the more obscure stats that became popular after the construction of cricketing databases. Ever consistent and inflexible, he rejected the ICC's insistence on regarding the Australia–World XI fiasco of 2005-06 as a Test, and thereafter his records differed from almost everyone else's. But his dedication ensured that he remained pre-eminent. He edited *Playfair Cricket Annual* for 23 years, five editions of *The Wisden Book of Test Cricket* and four of *The Wisden Book of Cricket Records*. He was the president of British Blind Sport. In his youth, he bowled quite fast for teams such as the RAF and Hampshire Seconds, and remained a zestful club cricketer until he died. Indeed, Frindall had just returned from tours of Malta and Dubai when he became ill, but characteristically insisted on fulfilling an engagement to address the Herefordshire Cricket Society. His audience assumed he had flu, but his condition rapidly deteriorated over the next week. After he died, the England players wore black armbands for the Test in Kingston. Frindall revelled in having been born on the opening day of the longest Test – the ten-day "timeless" match in Durban; he was buried the same day as the shortest, the ten-ball abandoned match in Antigua.

GAGANDEEP SINGH died on October 9, 2009, aged 18, after being caught up in a shooting incident outside a kebab shop in Meerut. Gagandeep, a slow left-armer, was about to represent Uttar Pradesh in the C. K. Nayudu Under-22 tournament. Earlier in the year he had toured Australia with India's Under-19s, and he was on the verge of making his Ranji Trophy debut. "His death is a huge loss not just to Uttar Pradesh cricket but also Indian cricket as a whole," said Gyanendra Pandey, UP's coach. "We have lost a potential star." When the news came out, some TV channels pictured another Gagandeep Singh, who plays for Punjab and then had to reassure his family and friends that he was fine.

GARNER, PHILLIP JOHN, who died on September 2, 2009, aged 63, captained Oxfordshire to two of their four Minor Counties Championship titles, in 1982 and 1989. A diminutive batsman with a penchant for slog-sweeping the spinners, Phil Garner scored more than 9,000 runs for Oxfordshire in 24 seasons, 12 of them as a thoughtful captain: team-mate Alan Crossley called him "the Mike Brearley of Oxfordshire cricket". Garner later played for Shipton-under-Wychwood, helping them win the National Village Championship at Lord's in 2002.

GREENHOUGH, THOMAS, died on September 15, 2009, aged 77. An accurate, big-spinning leg-break bowler with a longish run-up, a distinctive whirling action and a well-disguised googly, Tommy Greenhough had two memorable seasons for Lancashire – 1959 and 1960 – taking more than 100 wickets in both and earning all four of his England caps. He was lucky still to be playing, as in 1950 he had badly injured both feet after falling 30 feet in an accident while working at a cotton mill. Lancashire, cautious about his fitness, re-engaged him on a weekly basis (he had first signed for them at 16 in 1948), but eventually he rejoined the staff full-time. However, Old Trafford was well endowed with slow bowlers – off-spinner Roy Tattersall and left-armer Malcolm Hilton had both played for England – and he made little headway (and kept breaking fingers) until 1956, when his 62 wickets included six for 64 against Derbyshire and 11 in the match at Bournemouth. After a poor season in 1958, he seriously considered giving up. He was persuaded to carry on by his captain, Cyril Washbrook, and it paid off the next season – a much drier summer – when Greenhough took 122 wickets at 22, and played for England for the first time. In his second Test, at Lord's, he took five Indian wickets for 12 runs in 31 balls, and might have had more had Godfrey Evans not missed four stumpings in two overs – errors which ended Evans's own Test career after 91 matches. However, in *The Times*, John Woodcock made the point that India's batting was "lamentable".

Tommy Greenhough in 1961, after the last of his four Tests.

Problems with following through down the pitch drove Greenhough out of first-class cricket for a few weeks, but he was back for the Oval Test and took four more wickets. In the West Indies that winter, Greenhough could not force his way past spinners who were better batsmen, but he played once more for England, back at The Oval the following summer against South Africa, finishing with 16 Test wickets at the fine average of 22.31 – and the remarkable economy-rate, for a leg-spinner, of 1.89 an over. Greenhough's 121 wickets at 18.91 that summer helped Lancashire finish second in the Championship, but injuries began to impinge more and more afterwards, and he never again managed a full season. The England selectors, never terribly trusting of leg-spin, looked elsewhere too; Greenhough slipped quietly away and finished his county career in 1966, by which time his always low-slung action had dipped so much that Ray Illingworth told him "I don't know if you realise, but you're bowling on your knees."

GROVE, BRIAN PERCIVAL, who died on May 1, 2009, aged 88, was an exciting but impetuous strokeplayer who represented South Australia three times in 1952-53, his 93 runs including 43 against a mighty New South Wales attack. After he took three wickets on debut against Victoria, including a surprised Sam Loxton for a duck, his lively pace bowling earned him the new ball in his next two games – but with no further success. Following injuries to both Lindwall and Miller during the Adelaide Test against South Africa, he joined Ian Craig in spending two days in the field as a substitute.

HALE, SAMUEL STANLEY, died on January 11, 2009, aged 83. Former toolmaker Sam Hale was Worcestershire's first-team scorer from 1998 to 2001, when he returned to the Second Eleven after struggling with the then novel laptops which were starting to supplant the traditional scorebook. Hale had previously been an umpire, standing in several Second Eleven and Minor Counties Championship matches, as well as the ICC Trophy final between Canada and Sri Lanka at Worcester in 1979.

HALL, GEOFFREY HAROLD, died on November 1, 2009, aged 68. Fast-medium swing bowler Geoff Hall played 48 matches for Somerset in the early 1960s, after being a consistent wicket-taker in the Lancashire League for his home-town club Colne. Hall had problems with control – Peter Roebuck's Somerset history noted that he "wore horn-rimmed glasses, notwithstanding which he seldom delivered two balls on the same portion of the pitch" – and never quite nailed down a regular county place, despite taking six for 60 against Nottinghamshire in 1965, which turned out to be his final season. He also claimed five for 34 in the 1964 Gillette Cup quarter-final in a losing cause against Sussex.

HAMID, ABID, died on March 29, 2009, aged 51, after feeling unwell while playing for Old Hararians, the prominent Zimbabwean club of which he was the cricket section's chairman. "Abi" Hamid had also been a match referee in Zimbabwe, and managed both the Mashonaland Logan Cup squad and Zimbabwe A.

HARRIS, LESLIE FITZROY, who died on May 20, 2007, aged 86, became a popular broadcaster on Barbadian radio, after representing the island at both football and cricket. Widely known as "Shell", a nickname of inexplicable origin, Harris captivated listeners with his thick Bajan brogue and idioms in commentaries on cricket, football and, especially, boxing. He was a contemporary of Frank Worrell's at Combermere School, where he first came to notice as a flighty leg-spinner and dogged lower-order batsman. He played five first-class matches for Barbados in the 1940s, all against Trinidad, taking four for 55 in the second one, in July 1942.

HASLAM, Rear-Admiral Sir DAVID WILLIAM, KBE, CB, who died in August 2009, aged 86, was Hydrographer of the Navy from 1975 to 1985. He was also a notably active and enthusiastic president of Derbyshire in 1991-92.

HAY, Sir DAVID OSBORNE, CBE, DSO, who died on May 18, 2009, aged 92, was a career diplomat who rose to become Australia's ambassador to the United Nations in 1964 before being appointed Administrator of Papua New Guinea (then an Australian territory) late in 1966. A renowned schoolboy batsman, he played four first-class matches while at Oxford in the 1930s without winning a Blue, scoring 96 against Lancashire in 1938. Hay's grandfather, William Moule, represented Australia in the first Test ever played in England, at The Oval in 1880.

HETHERINGTON, MICHAEL ANDREW, was presumed dead after disappearing while climbing in the Drakensberg mountains in South Africa in February 2008. He was 73. Hetherington was a long-standing teacher at Aldenham School and took the Dragons team of public schoolboys – including Derek Pringle and Mark Nicholas – to South Africa in 1977, an early, low-key, boycott-busting tour. After retirement, he was baggage master to the 1996 Indians, a job which involved scouring Worcester for hand-warmers. "He was gentle and gentlemanly," recalled Pringle, "and never failed to sparkle when the talk turned to cricket."

HOLMES, GEOFFREY CLARKE, died of a brain haemorrhage on March 23, 2009, aged 50. Geoff Holmes was a busy Geordie all-rounder who became a mainstay of the usually struggling Glamorgan team of the 1980s, and played one season for Border. He made 209 first-class appearances between 1978 and 1991, passing 1,000 runs three times with two near misses. Although never a star, he was regarded as an ideal team man: an adaptable batsman who could find the gaps and turn ones into twos; a fine fielder; and a defensive seamer in the Championship, who was sometimes more than that in the one-day game – in 1984 he took five for two in 14 balls in a Sunday League match against Derbyshire at Ebbw Vale. "He was the cricketer every side needs," said Matthew Maynard, his room-mate and later his neighbour. "Above all, he was very professional at a time when a lot of players weren't. He studied the game and would think how to deal with a particular player." Holmes once told Maynard that his hero was Geoff Boycott. Maynard, astonished, asked why. "Because he worked out his own game so well," was the answer. After retiring, Holmes became an area manager of the Principality Building Society until returning to the game in 2005 as director of the Cricket Board of Wales, a job he did with character-

Geoff Holmes: "the cricketer every side needs".

istic energy and effectiveness until his sudden death. His brother revealed at the funeral that Holmes had invented his middle name when he joined the MCC groundstaff; he thought the extra initial would be helpful. Some team-mates commented that another one would have been even better.

HOUGH, KENNETH WILLIAM, died on September 20, 2009, aged 80. A strapping Australian-born fast bowler – his captain John Reid remembered his "tremendous torso and incongruously dainty bowling action" – Ken Hough played two Tests for New Zealand against England in 1958-59. A whole-hearted performer who had previously kept goal in soccer internationals for both Australia and New Zealand and later represented Papua New Guinea at rugby league, Hough took six Test wickets, including Colin Cowdrey in both matches, swinging the ball at a lively pace. He did not need the help of a fielder for any of them, five being bowled and one lbw – no one has taken more Test wickets without the help of a fielder. Hough also smote Fred Trueman back over his head into the stands at Christchurch for one of the biggest sixes seen there: "Freddie was too dazed either to cuss or follow up with a bouncer," said Reid. The following season Hough took seven for 43 (and five for 103) for Auckland against Central Districts a fortnight after scoring a career-best 91 against Otago. However, the leading New Zealand batsman Bert Sutcliffe wrote that "officialdom decided that Hough wasn't quite one of us", and he returned to Australia shortly afterwards: he played for the New South Wales Country XI against the 1965-66 England tourists at Bathurst.

HOWARD-DOBSON, General Sir PATRICK JOHN, GCB, who died on November 8, 2009, aged 88, was an outstanding schoolboy batsman at Framlingham. The cricket master's pre-season worry, according to *Wisden 1941*, was who could stay with him. Howard-Dobson later became president of the Hong Kong Cricket Club, and played for the Free Foresters and I Zingari. He was awarded the US Silver Star and Poland's Virtuti Militari for gallantry in Italy in 1944, and a long military career culminated with his appointment as a vice-chief of the defence staff from 1979 to 1981.

HOYOS, WENCESLAUS FREDERICK, died on December 3, 2009, aged 96. "Ben" Hoyos was an accountant, and honorary secretary of the Barbados Cricket Association from 1946 to 1985, during which time the island produced a host of illustrious players and was the dominant team in regional cricket. Within two years of taking office, Hoyos was at the heart of organising the first post-war Test match in the Caribbean, against England. His responsibilities became ever greater as the amount of cricket grew. "It is to his greatest credit that the BCA was highly regarded as the best-run sporting association, not only in Barbados but the whole of the West Indies," said Peter Short, who was president for the last 13 years of Hoyos's term. The post has been since filled by a paid, full-time chief executive.

IMLAH, MICHAEL OGILVIE, died of motor neurone disease on January 12, 2009, aged 52. Mick Imlah, born in Aberdeen, was one of the most admired British poets of his generation. His career peaked with his final collection, *The Lost Leader*, an exploration of Scottish history and legend. He was also poetry editor of the *Times Literary Supplement* for 16 years and a star turn in the now-defunct annual match between the *TLS* and the publishers. Imlah was a combative, charismatic all-rounder who played to a good standard. "He was a big-hearted bowler with a bounding delivery stride who could work up a bit of pace," recalled the author Simon Rae. "With his flowing locks, there was something Truemanesque about him."

JACKSON, EDWARD OLIVER, CBE, died on October 5, 2009, aged 86. Ted Jackson was a tireless worker for youth cricket in Middlesex, especially at his own club, Brondesbury, where one of the talents he helped unearth was Mike Gatting. As a fast bowler, he represented Cambridge in a one-day wartime Varsity Match, claiming three wickets, and played one first-class game, taking five wickets for Delhi in the Ranji Trophy while stationed in India after the war. Jackson remained passionate about the game as both player and coach, even while leading a busy life as a tax barrister, usually representing the Inland Revenue. "Like others, I would get long, typed letters from him, highlighted by diagrams and coloured inks," wrote Mike Brearley. "He was particularly keen on what he called 'gapping' – adjusting the angle of the bat to play the ball into spaces, and introduced a 'red dot' elaboration to scorebooks, indicating a failure to attend to this possibility." Ted, he added, "enriched people's lives".

JAVED AKHTAR SIDDIQUI, who died of liver cancer on January 28, 2009, aged 58, was a former Indian basketball player who turned to journalism, covering several cricket tours by India and Pakistan. He was the media liaison officer for Pakistan's visit to India in 2007-08, and was later a consultant for the company which handled media accreditation for the IPL.

JENKINS, ALCWYN, who died after being hit by a ball on July 4, 2009, aged 72, was a well-known and much-loved umpire in Welsh club cricket. He was struck on the head by a fielder's return during Swansea's match against Llangennech at St Helen's, which was then abandoned. Jenkins was airlifted to hospital, but to no avail. Neil Hobbs, the league's chairman, said: "The throw would have been from about 40 yards away. Umpires do get hit by the ball occasionally, but the chances of it being a fatality must be less than one in a million." Jenkins died performing a role he adored; he would umpire almost every day in summer. "The only law he wasn't *au fait* with was that tea should be no more than 20 minutes," said the Welsh cricket writer Bob Harragan. "Tea was over when Alcwyn had finished."

JOHNSON, Air Vice-Marshal FRANK SIDNEY ROLAND, CB, OBE, died on May 10, 2009, aged 91. "Johnnie" Johnson joined the RAF at 17, starting as a wireless mechanic and rising to become director-general of supply in 1971, fighting hard in Whitehall to maintain manpower levels at a time of cuts. While in India during the Second World War he played four first-class matches, three for Sind (scoring 39 against Bombay) and one for Delhi. He played a final first-class match back in England in 1947, for Combined Services.

JONES, FRED ALAN, died on August 14, 2009, aged 82. Alan Jones played only 16 first-class matches, but had an unusually varied career. A forcing bat who could also keep wicket, he made his debut while at Oxford in 1951, but failed to win a Blue. He then played for Scotland, making 88 against the 1959 Indian tourists at Paisley, and 52 in a non-first-class match (after coming in at 16 for three) against Richie Benaud's Australians at the Grange, his home club, two years later. Shortly after that Jones went to teach in Pakistan, where he represented Hyderabad in the Quaid-e-Azam Trophy, after the future journalist Qamar Ahmed saw him watching the side in the nets and asked him to join in. "I found that he was a good keeper despite a rather portly figure," remembered Qamar. "There were no qualification rules for playing in domestic cricket at the time, and he was selected to keep wicket. He was a fluent player, good on the back foot, and a very safe keeper."

KAPLICKÝ, JAN, died on January 14, 2009, aged 71, hours after the birth of a daughter. Kaplický was the Czech architect responsible for the media centre at Lord's, as well as the largely windowless branch of Selfridges in Birmingham. The Lord's commission almost bankrupted his practice but secured his reputation when it won the 1999 Stirling Prize. It also gained MCC unexpected cachet in avant-garde architectural circles. Much praised by critics ("an otherworldly, entirely unboxy, glossy white disc"), the media centre is, like most prize-winning buildings, widely disliked by those who have to use it, since it renders the cricket partly invisible and wholly inaudible.

KEMP, LEONARD DENTON, died on January 21, 2009, four months short of his 100th birthday. Dinnie Kemp was a gifted schoolboy batsman at Melbourne's Scotch College, and subsequently played five matches for Victoria, only one of them in the Sheffield Shield. His best innings was 114 from No. 7 against Tasmania at Hobart in 1932-33. As captain of Prahran in the Melbourne grade competition, Kemp won 21 out of 24 tosses in the mid-1930s. Two of his nephews, David and Rod Kemp, served as ministers in the Australian government at the turn of the 21st century, Rod as minister for sport.

KHAN MOHAMMAD, who died on July 4, 2009, aged 81, formed half of a potent new-ball pairing for Pakistan in their early Tests. His partner, Fazal Mahmood, is remembered as one of the greatest exponents of seam and cut, but there were those who preferred to face him than the waspish Khan, who was quicker and also made the ball move around or lift awkwardly. Khan bowled the first ball in Pakistan's inaugural Test – at Delhi in October 1952 – and took their first wicket, India's opener Pankaj Roy: "It was an outswinger pitched outside leg stump," explained Khan. "Roy tried to glance it and was bowled round his legs." After this promising start he encountered problems with fitness, and with Pakistan's autocratic captain Abdul Hafeez Kardar, but still took 54 wickets in just 13 Tests, including five for 61 in Pakistan's first Test in England, at Lord's in 1954. All five victims were bowled, as England slipped to 117 for nine, and among the victims was Len Hutton, beaten by a swinging yorker: "I sent his middle stump cartwheeling 15 yards back on the very first ball he faced from me. It lifted our spirits and made us believe the English were also mortal." Then he took six for 21 as New Zealand were shot out for

Khan Mohammad at Lord's in 1971, imparting his knowledge to another generation.

70 at Dacca in 1955-56. But perhaps his most famous analysis featured no wickets at all: at Kingston in 1957-58, after Mahmood Hussain broke down in his first over on a Sabina Park belter, Khan had to toil through 54 overs (Fazal bowled 85.2) as Garry Sobers made 365 not out and West Indies 790 for three. Khan finished with none for 259, still the most expensive wicketless figures in Test history: when reminded of this in later years, he would smile ruefully and say, "Everyone always wants to talk about my none for 259. They never want to know about the time I bowled Len Hutton for a duck at Lord's." His final first-class game was for his native Lahore in 1960-61. He then settled in England and turned to coaching, as well as running a travel agency.

KIRTON, KEITH NORMAN, who died on August 3, 2009, aged 81, captained both Border and Eastern Province in a long career which stretched over 16 years from 1947. He came close to a South African cap, particularly after 1954-55, his best season. He made three of his ten centuries that summer, and in a remarkable match against Rhodesia at East London both he and Ossie Dawson scored centuries before lunch on New Year's Day. It was still not enough to secure Kirton a place on the 1955 tour of England. His brother Cecil captained North-Eastern Transvaal, and in that eventful 1954-55 season they led their respective teams against each other in the Currie Cup. "They beat us in Pretoria," recalled Keith, "but we thrashed them in East London."

LAMBERT, OSWALD, died on April 13, 2009, aged 82. Ossie Lambert was a safe and unshowy wicketkeeper who was, unusually, selected for New South Wales straight from the provincial city of Newcastle to succeed Ron Saggers and Stan Sismey in 1950-51. He won a permanent place for three seasons from 1954-55. In club cricket, he was a competent nudger of the ball, but in first-class cricket he averaged just five. He played for the Lambton club for 20 years from 1944, his 170 catches and 168 stumpings telling of the different skills required of keepers in his time.

LEWIS, VICTOR JOSEPH, MBE, died on February 9, 2009, aged 89. Vic Lewis was a musician, bandleader and impresario who managed Cilla Black and arranged American tours for the Beatles and Elton John. Probably his proudest achievement, however, was to found a charity cricket team which raised millions of pounds. Lewis also represented the United States at ICC meetings in London for many years from 1980, and served on the Middlesex committee. His peculiar passion was his vast collection of cricket ties, and he compiled a book about them in 1984, although his enthusiasm waned after a thief disturbed all the name tags, making identification almost impossible. In 1987 he produced an autobiography, *Music & Maiden Overs*, which featured among other celebrities on its cover the buxom Hollywood actress Jayne Mansfield, wearing a Cross Arrows cricket cap. "To me, cricket is not just another sport," Lewis wrote inside. "Cricket is a religion, a way of life, a brotherhood. If only the politicians would keep their noses out of cricket, I believe the world would be a more peaceful place."

LUCAS, NOEL STEPHEN, died in Toronto, Canada, on July 4, 2009, aged 82. An attacking right-hand batsman, "Brickie" Lucas played three matches for Barbados in the mid-1950s, making his debut against Len Hutton's 1953-54 MCC touring team. His final innings was his only one of note, 91 against British Guiana, when he shared a 178-run stand with Garry Sobers. He also represented Barbados at football. His elder brother, Johnny, who played for Barbados and Canada, predeceased him by a year.

McCORQUODALE, ALASTAIR, who died on February 27, 2009, aged 83, was a fast bowler who took three wickets in three matches for Middlesex in 1951, and toured Canada with a strong MCC side later that year. Scottish-born, Harrow-educated, McCorquodale was best known as a sprinter, despite a training regime which was said to include stubbing out a cigarette just before going to the blocks. At the London Olympics in 1948 he was involved in a blanket finish in the 100 metres final. The photo-finish camera – in use for the first time at those Games – eventually placed him fourth, although he was given the same time as the silver and bronze medallists. He did, however, help the British team to a silver medal in the sprint relay before retiring from the track. McCorquodale then devoted his life to the family printing firm, eventually becoming its chairman, and was involved in the company's decision to buy half of John Wisden, publishers of *Wisden*, in 1984, which it retained until it was itself taken over three years later. His son, Neil, married Lady Sarah Spencer, the sister of Princess Diana.

McINTYRE, ARTHUR JOHN WILLIAM, who died on December 26, 2009, aged 91, was the oldest surviving England Test cricketer. He played only three Tests and in one of those was picked as a batsman. But in a first-class career spanning 25 years, he built up a reputation as one of the best – maybe *the* best – day-in, day-out wicketkeeper of his generation. The flamboyant Godfrey Evans won the applause, the headlines and the caps; McIntyre, along with the much younger Keith Andrew, won almost as much respect from his peers.

"Mac" was a Surrey boy from the start. Born almost within earshot of the Oval crowd and educated at Kennington Road School, he would watch Jack Hobbs bat and, aged 18,

Vic Lewis, bandleader and collector, in 1991.

Surrey boy: Arthur McIntyre keeps in the 1953 MCC v Champion County game; Doug Insole bats, before being caught by McIntyre for 64, while Peter May is at slip.

was put in charge of the cycle shed. His destiny as a keeper was by no means assured: he kept for London Schools (sharing a century stand with Denis Compton) but made his Surrey debut, in 1938, as a leg-spinner who batted. He played 11 pre-war matches and, after being wounded during the Anzio landings, was active in the makeshift military cricket the British played in Italy. There he linked up with the Bedser twins whom he credited with pointing out that, at 5ft 5in, he might have more future keeping than bowling. After coaching from Herbert Strudwick, the Surrey job became his in 1947. He made progress as a batsman too, passing 1,000 each year from 1948 to 1950.

The story goes that in 1950 Evans, the established England keeper, was having dinner with McIntyre and his wife Dorothy, who suggested he should get injured to give her husband a chance. Evans promptly broke his finger and McIntyre made his debut at The Oval against West Indies. "You witch!" Godders told her next time they met. Both men went to Australia that winter, and McIntyre was – eccentrically – picked ahead of Gilbert Parkhouse as a batsman for the First Test. In the final innings, with England still hopeful of victory, he was run out attempting a fourth. Andrew was preferred as No. 2 on the 1954-55 Ashes tour and McIntyre did not play another Test until 1955, against South Africa at Headingley, when Evans was again injured. But the two were not far apart as batsmen (seven centuries each; McIntyre's career average – 22 v 21 – fractionally better) and some preferred the less obtrusive style of keeping. "Mac had very strong hands, but at the same time he was velvety," recalled his team-mate Micky Stewart. "Most of all, he was quick on his feet, and so smooth that people didn't see how fast he could go."

Off the field, McIntyre was as quiet as Evans was boisterous, but he was a Londoner through and through: "If something needed saying, he'd be the first to say it," said Stewart. He was a fixture in the Surrey team through their seven Championship years of the 1950s, and in 1958 *Wisden* chose him in the Five. However, at the end of that season he effectively retired, some thought prematurely, to allow Roy Swetman – who had been earmarked as an England keeper – to claim a regular county place. McIntyre succeeded Andy Sandham as Surrey coach, a job he held until 1976; he insisted on rigorous respect for the old values, but was a kindly mentor. However, he made a brief comeback in 1963 in Arnold Long's absence, playing at Bramall Lane against a Yorkshire side including the young Geoff Boycott, who was his 795th and final first-class victim. Since McIntyre had played against Woolley, and Boycott was to play one of his last matches against Graeme Hick, the four players form a chain of first-class cricket stretching from 1906 to 2008. Add in Lord Hawke, who played against Woolley, and the five-man chain stretches back to 1881. Sir Alec Bedser, 51 days his junior, succeeded McIntyre as the senior England player.

FROM HAWKE TO HICK

The links of a chain connecting first-class careers from 1881 to 2008:

Lord Hawke
(Yorkshire, 1881–1911)

At Dover,
August 23, 24, 25, 1909.
Kent drew with Yorkshire.

Frank Woolley
(Kent, 1906–1938)

At Blackheath,
July 9, 11, 1938.
Kent lost to Surrey by nine wickets.

Arthur McIntyre
(Surrey, 1938–1963)

At Sheffield,
July 20, 22, 23, 1963.
Yorkshire drew with Surrey.

Geoffrey Boycott
(Yorkshire, 1962–1986)

At Worcester,
June 18, 19, 20, 1986.
Worcestershire drew with Yorkshire.

Graeme Hick
(Worcestershire, 1984–2008)

MADRAY, IVAN SAMUEL, who died on April 23, 2009, aged 74, played only six first-class matches – but the fourth and sixth of them were Tests. The hope was that his leg-spin would provide a counterpart to Lance Gibbs's off-breaks against Pakistan in 1957-58 – but he failed to take a wicket. The pair had shared eight for British Guiana (now Guyana) against Jamaica at Georgetown in October 1956, Madray's victims including the Test players Allan Rae, John Holt and Collie Smith. Soon after his two Tests, he moved to England, where he turned out for Lincolnshire, and he later lived in America. Madray was one of several promising young players to emerge from the sugar-growing area around Port Mourant – contemporaries included Rohan Kanhai, Basil Butcher and Joe Solomon – during a training programme instituted by Clyde Walcott.

MARMENT, ARTHUR VERRIOUR, MC and bar, TD, who died on January 17, 2009, aged 91, was twice decorated for gallantry during the Burma campaigns in the Second World War. A useful cricketer who kept wicket for Oundle School and played for Young Amateurs at Lord's in 1935 against a Young Professionals side including Denis Compton and Jack Robertson, he captained the St Fagans club in Glamorgan, and also played for the county's Second Eleven.

MATTHEWS, JOHN DUNCAN, who died on January 22, 2009, aged 87, captained the 1942 Cambridge University team to victory over Oxford at Lord's in one of the most dramatic finishes to any Varsity Match: four wickets fell in the last ten minutes. Matthews had scored 68 himself and then shown leadership that *Wisden* called both "bold" and "astute" when he finally recalled the spinner Frank Austin to bowl the last over and take the crucial wicket. Matthews had also played the previous year, but these were wartime one-day fixtures for which full Blues were not awarded, and his first-class cricket was confined to five matches for Scotland in the 1950s after he qualified as a doctor. He later became a fine golfer although, according to *The Scotsman*, "his swing always showed the characteristics of a glorious left-handed cover-drive". His older brother, Dudley, played a few matches for Lancashire.

MISCHLER, NORMAN MARTIN, who died on September 10, 2009, aged 88, won Blues at Cambridge in 1946 and 1947. He also played three first-class matches in India during the war. A wicketkeeper, he was also a handy batsman, hitting 76 against Somerset at Bath in 1947. He later became chairman of the pharmaceutical company Hoechst UK.

MONTEITH, JAMES DERMOTT, died on December 6, 2009, aged 66. Dermott Monteith was almost ever-present in the Ireland side from his debut in 1965 to 1984, captaining them from 1978. His career was effectively ended by a hit-and-run driver who left him with a fractured skull and a shattered pelvis. Before that, he took 326 wickets, a national record, with his flattish left-arm spin, delivered at almost medium-pace with an arm increasingly more horizontal than vertical. That included eight for 44 – 13 for 93 in the match – against MCC at Lord's in 1973. The same year he took seven for 38 in the annual first-class game against Scotland, and scored 78 into the bargain. Monteith (at least half-joking) liked to call himself the world's third-best left-arm spinner, after Bishan Bedi and Dilip Doshi – and said that he changed his mind about Doshi when he actually saw him bowl. Middlesex also rated him and signed him, as a greying 38-year-old, in 1981 as cover for the expected absence of John Emburey and Phil Edmonds with England. He took 24 wickets in eight matches at 24.83, including five-fors against Essex and Northampton-shire, and played once more in 1982 before his brief county career was over, although as Middlesex won the Championship that qualified him for a trip to Buckingham Palace, where the trophy was presented by the Duke of Edinburgh. Mike Brearley introduced Monteith as "our Irishman", whereupon the Duke remarked "You're the second Irishman we have had in the Palace this year," referring to Michael Fagan, who had broken in and made it as far as the Queen's bedroom. Monteith, who played most of his club cricket for

Lisburn in Northern Ireland, later became an administrator, serving as president of the Irish Cricket Union in 1999, and a national selector. "He was quite simply a magnificent cricketer, and a pioneer in many ways, being one of the first Irishmen in the modern era to make a mark in county cricket," remembered Roy Torrens, now Ireland's manager. "He was also an innovative captain, who had no fear of failure." Brearley described him as "a poor man's Derek Underwood", adding: "On damp and slow Irish pitches in particular he must have been a real handful." Monteith stood up to Brearley, too, complaining that he was being given over-attacking fields at first when he was bound to be nervous. Brearley replied that the batsman, facing an unfamiliar bowler, would be nervous too.

Baron **MOORE** of WOLVERCOTE, GCB, GCVO, CMG, QSO, PC, who died on April 7, 2009, the day after his 88th birthday, was the Queen's private secretary between 1977 and 1986. Philip Moore was an outstanding sportsman in his youth, playing rugby for England and cricket for Oxfordshire. He was top of both the batting and bowling averages at Cheltenham College in 1940 and, on being ennobled, he chose to include cricket and rugby balls in his coat of arms. In 1930 Moore had been one of a bunch of schoolboys who asked Don Bradman for his autograph during the Australians' match at Canterbury, only to be brusquely turned down just after The Don had been dismissed for 18 by Tich Freeman. At a lunch in Adelaide in 1986, Moore – accompanying the Queen on a Royal Tour – asked Bradman if he remembered the incident. Typically, he did: "I was very angry, I really was. He diddled me with that top-spinner… I'm awfully sorry. I must make amends." And he promptly signed the menu.

MOORHOUSE, GEOFFREY, who died on November 26, 2009, aged 77, was an eclectic travel writer and historian whose 29 books ranged from monasticism to rugby league. They were all written with great craftsmanship and integrity. Most famous of all was *Calcutta*, written 40 years ago, but still the definitive portrait of the city. His books also included *The Best Loved Game*, a superb evocation of the 1978 English cricket season: he sat quietly on grounds as different as Lord's and Lanehead (Bacup), listened and observed. Graham Gooch, he noted, "is built like a guardsman, and that expressionless face… surely saw service in England's old imperial wars, defending Rorke's Drift and marching up the Khyber Pass". Shortly afterwards, MCC agreed to give Moorhouse unprecedented access to the archives to write a portrait of the club, called simply *Lord's*. He wrote the book reviews in the 1994 *Wisden* and a cool appraisal of W. G. Grace for his 150th anniversary in 1998. Moorhouse came from Bolton and, under Matthew Engel's editorship, there was an understanding that he would write the celebratory *Wisden* article if and when Lancashire finally became champions again – a piece that never did get written.

MUDDIAH, VENATAPPA MUSANDRA, who died on October 1, 2009, aged 80, was an off-spinner who made a remarkable entry to first-class cricket, taking eight for 54 (and adding all four wickets to fall in the second innings) for Services against Southern Punjab at Patiala in 1949-50. But at a time when India's spin resources were plentiful, it was almost a decade before the national selectors chose him – for the ill-starred 1959 tour of England. Unused to turf pitches, he tried to bowl too quickly, struggled, and was never in serious contention for a Test place – which might have been a blessing, as India were whitewashed 5–0. Muddiah did play against Australia at Delhi in December 1959, but failed to take a wicket or score a run in an innings defeat, and was overlooked for a year until he was recalled to face Pakistan at Kanpur. This time at least he achieved something, dismissing three top batsmen, but he never reappeared. He played most of his domestic cricket for Services (and rose to become a wing commander in the Indian air force), although he also represented Mysore and Hyderabad early in his career.

MUKHERJEE, RABINRANATH, died on March 14, 2009, aged 65. Robin Mukherjee scored almost 3,000 runs in a 15-year career in Indian domestic cricket. He was a regular for Bihar for most of the 1970s after earlier representing Railways and Bengal. After retirement Mukherjee became chief curator for the East Zone, and also served as a Bengal selector. His younger brother, Avinash Kumar, also had a long career for Bihar.

MURRAY, GEORGE, who died on September 8, 2009, aged 75, was a prominent Scottish coach who did much work with children with special needs. He was a mainstay of the Aberdeenshire club as player, coach and, for 50 years, committee man.

NICHOLLS, PAUL ALLEN, died of liver cancer on January 17, 2009, aged 62. A tall, slim off-spinner, Nicholls made an auspicious debut for Western Australia against South Australia at Adelaide in 1971-72, taking eight wickets in the match for 128 before surviving 114 minutes for four runs in a vain attempt to stave off defeat. Thereafter, his state's traditional suspicion of spin asserted itself, and his bowling was used only grudgingly, although he was given an extended opportunity to translate his effective club batting to state level; Nicholls looked the part, but in 19 matches never passed 38. He was a talented Australian Rules footballer, kicking four crucial goals in East Fremantle's 1974 victory in the WA state competition. Nicholls spent a decade practising as a solicitor at Albany, on the state's south coast, before becoming a magistrate, an appointment which curtailed a promising umpiring career.

NOLAN, FRANK EDWARD, who died on October 12, 2009, aged 89, was one of the cavalcade of opening bowlers tried by Queensland in the late 1940s. He dismissed three Test players on debut, including Lindsay Hassett, but played only twice more before being transferred to work in South Australia, which marked the end of his first-class career. In Adelaide grade cricket, he had a spectacular day for Woodville against Prospect in which he transformed figures of nought for 16 into nine for 22. In December 1942, Nolan, a gunner on an RAAF bomber, was mentioned in despatches after helping fight off a Japanese attack.

NORMAN, JOHN, who died on July 29, 2008, aged 79, has a small but significant niche in cricket history. He was the BBC producer who gave the instruction for the tape to be left running at Swansea in 1968, thus enabling perhaps the most famous over in cricket – Garry Sobers's six sixes off Malcolm Nash – to be recorded for posterity. A BBC Wales team was at the game but was officially stood down when *Grandstand* concluded that Saturday afternoon. The cameraman was a keen cricket fan and wanted to watch Sobers bat through the lens, so Norman let him keep filming. It was a fluke, but Norman was prone to such moments of inspiration: a year earlier he had given a similar instruction at the Dunlop Masters golf tournament at Sandwich, so ensuring the first televised hole-in-one – by Tony Jacklin.

NUSRAT AZEEM, who died on July 4, 2009, aged 81, was – at almost 22 years – the longest-serving president of the Karachi Cricket Association. During his tenure Karachi teams won the Quaid-e-Azam Trophy seven times.

OWEN, TOMOS BEFAN, who died of leukaemia on January 4, 2009, aged 31, was the producer and mainstay of the cricket output on BBC Radio Wales. He was a fine club batsman for Aberystwyth and adored the game. Edward Bevan, the BBC Wales cricket correspondent, said: "He would have got to the very top in his profession. And as a player, he'd have been very close to county standard if the job hadn't been so demanding. He was a lovely bloke too." A memorial plaque (in Welsh) has been unveiled in the new Sophia Gardens media centre.

PARRIS, STANTON ELLIOT, who died on January 5, 2009, aged 78, was a Barbadian umpire whose first-class career stretched almost 20 years from 1971-72 and included five Test matches. Lawrence Rowe scored 302 in his first, against England at Bridgetown in 1973-74. That Test also produced an appeal against Keith Fletcher for caught behind, turned down by Parris as West Indies pressed for victory. It was, said Tony Cozier, the only time he had ever seen Garry Sobers react angrily to a decision.

PEARMAN, ROGER, who died suddenly on April 9, 2009, aged 66, was chief executive of Derbyshire from 1981 to 1987. Pearman was a batsman who played briefly for Middlesex (as did his brother Hugh), topping their Championship batting averages in his debut year, 1962, with 244 runs at 40.66 – mainly thanks to an unbeaten 72 in a rain-ruined match against Nottinghamshire. He was also a prolific run-getter for Hornsey and helped found the Middlesex County League. Pearman was recruited from business to take over Derbyshire. A relaxed, gregarious man, his style belied his efficiency. "He made a success of the new pavilion and took the club into profit," said Gerald Mortimer, *Wisden's* Derbyshire correspondent, "and in his own way ran it very successfully." Not everyone on the committee appreciated the Pearman way; he was sacked and went off to make a success of running a local hotel.

PICKETT, EDWARD ARTHUR, OAM, died on January 29, 2009, two months short of his century, having been in excellent health until shortly before his death. Ted Pickett was a wicketkeeper who played 11 times for Tasmania between 1928-29 and 1935-36 in the days when opportunities for its players were sparse. His keeping was both agile and secure, but first-class cricket exposed the flaws in his explosive club-level batting. There was, however, a renaissance quality to his sporting skills: he was a professional sprinter, Australian snooker champion (1955) and a high-class player of Australian Rules football, tennis, badminton and golf.

RAJ SINGH DUNGARPUR, who died on September 12, 2009, aged 73, was a significant figure in Indian cricket for half a century: as a player, administrator, selector, commentator, and centre of attention. Raj Singh was the son of a prince and had a long-standing

relationship with "India's Nightingale", Lata Mangeshkar, which made him doubly glamorous in Indian eyes. He was also tall, voluble and very sociable, with an anecdote for every occasion, which made him popular with those around him. And with no urgent need to make a living, he put his energies into the game. His father was the last Maharawal of Dungarpur, a 15-gun state in Rajasthan. At Daly College in Indore, Raj learned to swing the ball, and he had a long career in the Ranji Trophy, mainly with Rajasthan, playing 86 first-class matches without making the Indian team. But he soon established himself as a power off the field, firstly in the Cricket Club of India, the national equivalent of MCC, where his aristocratic lineage, bearing, and reputation for integrity enabled him to establish some authority in a body full of warring factions. He became a regular tour manager, most successfully on the 1986 tour of England, and a selector with a penchant for youth. Raj propelled a reluctant

"All the graces of a maharaja": Raj Singh Dungarpur in 1982.

Mohammad Azharuddin into the captaincy and quickly recognised the talent of the young Sachin Tendulkar, getting the CCI rules changed so he could enter the dressing-rooms at 14, and picking him for the Test team at 16. In 1996 he achieved Indian cricket's highest office, the presidency of the Board of Control, serving three years, but was still acting as a tour manager as late as 2005-06, when – perhaps already suffering the early stages of mental decline – he feuded with another strong character, coach Greg Chappell. At the height of his powers, he was a shrewd operator: "Despite the image of a man who always played straight," noted

Pradeep Magazine of the *Hindustan Times*, "he was not immune to changing his stand or loyalties according to the needs of the power structure." Above all, though, Raj Singh was a man who loved the game more than he loved himself, which has not been true of every modern Indian administrator. "He had all the graces of a maharaja," said Raman Subba Row, the former chairman of the English Test and County Cricket Board, "but he always understood that cricket had to keep moving forward."

RAJESH, SUBRAMANIAM, who died on May 7, 2009, aged 49, played 27 matches for Kerala in the 1980s, captaining them in 1988-89 before being forced to retire by injury. He scored over 1,100 runs, with a highest score of 70 against Karnataka at Raichur in December 1987. He later became a state selector. Two of his brothers also played for Kerala.

RAYMOND, KIT ARTHURINE, who died on January 25, 2009, aged 78, played for the Australian women's team against New Zealand twice: at Adelaide in 1956-57 and four years later at Dunedin. Her three innings produced only 11 runs, but her quality was better reflected in an 11-year career in domestic cricket during which she scored 704 runs at 29.33. Born in rural Queensland, Raymond grew up in Sydney and excelled in many sports, particularly hockey. Her influence as a coach in both cricket and hockey was incalculable; for over 30 years she taught PE at Sydney's Abbotsleigh School, where her headmistress for 12 years was the former England captain Betty Archdale. One of Raymond's protégées there was the gifted Australian batsman Denise Annetts.

RICHARDSON, EDWARD NOEL, who died on July 29, 2009, aged 79, was a member of one of Tasmania's most prominent cricketing families. His father played for the state in the 1920s, as later did four of his brothers. Ted Richardson was an aggressive left-hander and a right-arm medium-pacer who was both persistent and effective. He played six times for Tasmania and its Combined XIs between 1958-59 and 1963-64; in his second game, against Peter May's MCC tourists at Launceston, his four wickets included May, Tom Graveney and Ted Dexter. Richardson was a schoolteacher who was president of the Tasmanian Schools Cricket Association from its inception in 1970, and oversaw the state's Under-19 side for nearly 30 years.

RILSTONE, THOMAS MELVILLE, died on March 3, 2009, aged 91. Mel Rilstone was born in South Australia, but spent most of his adult life in Canada after becoming a pilot there during the Second World War. He played cricket for Canada for many years, including three first-class matches, two of them on tour in England in 1954. A handy batsman and a leg-spinner, he was hit for 34 in an over (664666) during a club match in Montreal in 1953. The batsman, Dr Bruce Lang, had taken 19 off his previous over (446041), and Rilstone was left nursing sorry figures of 5.4–0–81–3.

ROBINSON, ALBERT GEORGE, died on July 31, 2009, aged 92. Bert Robinson was a brisk seam bowler with a modest record for struggling Northamptonshire just before and after the Second World War. He made his reputation, however, as the seemingly eternal cricket coach at Radley College in Oxfordshire. He held the job officially from 1949 to 1982, during which time he most famously nurtured Ted Dexter. But he stayed on unofficially, supporting his similarly durable successor Andy Wagner, and thus helped develop such talents as Jamie Dalrymple, Robin Martin-Jenkins, Ben Hutton and Andrew Strauss. When Strauss scored his Test century on debut at Lord's in 2004, Robinson called it "the best day of my life". At that time, as *Wisden 2005* reported (page 1708), little had changed for Robinson since he notionally retired. "He still lives in the same house, in the same village, with the same wife (Doris) and, wearing the same tie, does the same job, if at a slightly more leisurely pace… and still has the same touch." He was in evidence even during the early part of the 2009 season, and Radley summers will now never be the same again. "Bert was an outstanding school coach and an outstanding human being," said

"…and they just worshipped him": Bert Robinson at the Radley College bowling machine.

Dennis Silk, the former college warden who later became chairman of the TCCB. "He bowled about two bad balls a year and was still bowling in the nets at 85. He treated everyone with respect, even the smallest boy, and they just worshipped him."

ROBSON, Sir ROBERT WILLIAM, CBE, died on July 31, 2009, aged 76. Bobby Robson was manager of the England football team at the 1986 and 1990 World Cups, widely reviled for his tactics until England reached the 1990 semi-finals and lost on penalties. After that, he gradually ascended to national treasure status. He was also a great enthusiast for cricket. In his first autobiography, *Time on the Grass*, he described his childhood as "Utopia – football in the winter, cricket in the summer and marbles when we had time to play". In his playing days for Fulham, Robson was a fine batsman in benefit matches, good enough, according to his friend Micky Stewart, to have played for a top Surrey league club. One unfulfilled ambition was to watch an Ashes series in Australia: he was planning to go in 2006-07 but had to withdraw when his cancer returned.

SARRE, RONALD BASIL, died on September 3, 2009, aged 77. Ron Sarre was given an extended trial as an opener for Western Australia in the 1950s, impressing Alec Bedser with the soundness of his technique. In 15 matches, however, he had limited success except when he made 103 against the 1953 Australian team en route to England. His off-breaks were handy partnership-breakers.

SAXENA, DALJIT SINGH, who died on August 5, 2009, aged 74, was a tall off-spinner who had a long Ranji Trophy career, with Southern Punjab and then Delhi for ten years from 1967-68. Bishan Bedi, a Delhi team-mate, remembered him as "a crafty bowler who could always be relied upon for a breakthrough". In all, Daljit Singh took 187 wickets at just 20.78. As a youngster, he was a useful batsman, making his only century in his fourth match for Southern Punjab.

SHAKESPEAR, Lt-Col. HENRY GORDON WYNDHAM, MC, died on April 13, 2009, aged 88. Gordon Shakespear was a fine schoolboy sportsman who played cricket, soccer and rackets for Malvern College, where he was head boy. Later in life he turned to golf. He played at Lord's in 1937, taking four wickets for Young Amateurs in a two-innings match against Young Professionals. He was decorated during the Second World War after being severely wounded in Italy: "Hell of a name, hell of an officer," wrote a contributor to the Rogue Gunner military website.

SHEPHERD, DAVID ROBERT, MBE, died of cancer on October 27, 2009, aged 68. David Shepherd made his name in two separate cricketing incarnations: first as a highly distinctive if never outstanding county cricketer; and then as an umpire, in which capacity he rose to be, by common consent, the best in the world. In both roles he remained "Shep" to everyone in cricket, and without an enemy. He was placid, friendly, humorous and devoted to the game, its players and its best traditions. The authorities struggle for a definition of The Spirit of Cricket. Perhaps the best answer is simply "David Shepherd".

His secret lay in his roots. They were always in the Devon village of Instow, where his mother and then his brother, Bill, kept the post office. Instow was home to North Devon CC and he naturally gravitated towards the ground. Even as a youngster David was ruddy-cheeked and rotund but still nifty enough to be a serviceable scrum-half for South Molton. And at Barnstaple Grammar School he developed into a formidable run-getter, which took him into the Devon minor counties team and – after a brief stint as a teacher – on to the Gloucestershire staff. On his debut at Oxford in 1965, he made 108 out of 139 while he was at the crease, though it took a year to establish himself in the team and four before he began to live up to expectations. Then in 1969 he ran into form before succumbing to a back injury which hampered the county's assault on the title. Shepherd won his cap and his reputation.

The crowds loved him, and he became "Good old Shep" by the time he was 30. The affection came partly from his build which, after a car accident robbed the game of Colin Milburn in 1969, was unique in professional cricket; partly from his obviously sunny disposition; and partly because he was a typical burly batsman, and whacked the ball. "He could play all the shots," said his captain, Tony Brown. "He could late cut and hit off the back foot, but he did love the aerial route. He was brave too: I remember him taking on Butch White, who was very quick. And he was surprisingly nimble on the field, very light on his feet. He was as fast over 22 yards as anyone."

Writers loved him too: he was such an obvious countryman that even the best of them could not resist the bucolic imagery. "Any film producer making *The Farmer's Wife* or *Lorna Doone* on location would seize upon him as an extra, with double rate and free cider," wrote Alan Gibson. "His bottom hand is clamped massively just above the shoulder of his bat," observed Geoffrey Moorhouse in *The Best Loved Game*, "as some ancestor probably held a scythe, or possibly a blacksmith's maul. He stands, ready to back up, with a bunch of knuckles on one hip, head scanning the field of play the way men do by gates when they are contemplating their crops... When he runs down the pitch in response to the striker's call, he does so with shoulders squared and arms heavily round, as though he were chivvying bullocks out of a field and into the yard."

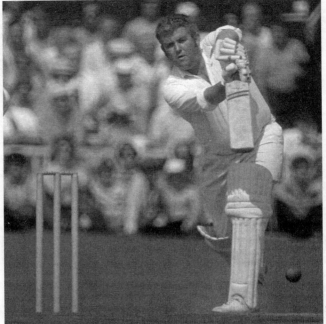

Shep on the front foot, 1973.

He had regular failures and he would return to the pavilion, as Gibson noted, purple-faced rather than red. But his triumphs could be lustrous, like his wonderful unbeaten 72 against Surrey that rescued Gloucestershire from 24 for five early in their triumphant march towards Lord's in the 1973 Gillette Cup. The club did try to persuade him to lose weight: his friend and team-mate Jack Davey has a story about him being booked into a health farm which was, unfortunately, dangerously close to one of the players' favourite pubs. A ground-floor room... a large sash window offering an escape route... and a landlord not averse to making late-night fry-ups for his regulars. Shep liked a pint, without being an uncontrolled drinker, but he really did like his grub, and would often have dinner with his team-mates and then nip out for a solitary curry.

Shepherd played on through the 1970s but never troubled the heights of the averages or the England selectors. He then began to contemplate a move into umpiring, which surprised Davey, since – beneath the *bonhomie* – he knew Shep to be a worrier. But Dickie Bird made a success of umpiring on that basis. And Tony Brown says that Shep worried about getting things right, which is what umpires close to do. His second debut (almost wholly rained-off) was again in the Parks, 15 years after his first appearance there. A year later he was on the full first-class list. In 1985 he was umpiring his first Test; before 1987 was out, he was in charge of a World Cup semi-final, disqualified from the final because England were in it.

He umpired 92 Tests, spread out over 20 years, and 172 one-day internationals, and these did include three successive World Cup finals: 1996, 1999 and 2003. There never was any doubt about his skill as an umpire: his decision-making was excellent – but it was not the only consideration. "What doesn't get highlighted is man-management skills: creating a happy environment for players to play in. And Shep was magnificent at that," said his colleague Simon Taufel. "The players had this enormous respect for him as a

Shep on Nelson, 1998.

person. He put them at their ease and forged relationships that crossed all cultural and political divides."

Shepherd stood in at least one Test in England – nearly always more – every year between 1985 and 2001. But as the pattern of umpiring changed, he increasingly worked abroad, a regime that became particularly tough, almost oppressive, when the elite panel was set up in 2002 and neutral-country umpiring became the fixed pattern. Then the Shepherd temperament would stand him in even better stead, and his younger colleagues were more grateful than ever for his calm sagacity, and his endurance. As Taufel put it: "He wasn't the fittest bloke in the world, but he was match fit. He could get through five days in Multan or Mumbai as well as anyone." He was certainly still a trencherman: there was a deal with Taufel, who would do an extra lap of the gym for him, and he would have Taufel's scoop of ice cream in return.

Spectators will remember him best for his one affectation: the superstitious hops and skips that came whenever the score reached Nelson or its multiples: 111, 222, 333... This seems to have been his own invention, dating back to his Devonian club days, and went little-noticed when he was playing. At Old Trafford in 2001, Shepherd had a rare bad match against Pakistan, missing at least two no-balls that took wickets. He was so upset he tried to resign, and also forgot to skip on 333. That, he concluded, was responsible for a small earthquake off the North Devon coast.

Generally, though, he disliked fuss, and turned down an offer from the ICC to subvert modern practice and let him have a farewell appearance at Lord's in the 2005 Ashes. Instead, he retired quietly and returned to Instow, as he always had done – to Jenny (his partner for 36 years but not his wife until 2008), his dog, and brother Bill at the post office, whom he liked to help with the paper round. Shortly afterwards, however, Shepherd was diagnosed with cancer, and his last two years were sad and painful. But he leaves a legacy of happy memories far richer than those of many greater cricketers. He will always be good old Shep.

SHILLINGFORD, GRAYSON CLEOPHAS, died of cancer on December 23, 2009, aged 65. A bowler of lively, if not express, pace, with out-swing delivered from a bounding, angled run-in, Shillingford was the first of Dominica's four West Indian Test cricketers, preceding his cousin, the batsman Irvine Shillingford, by eight years. He was picked for the 1969 West Indies tour of England following the dramatic dropping of all four fast bowlers, Wes Hall and Charlie Griffith included, after the tour of Australia and New Zealand five weeks earlier that marked the end of the glory days under Frank Worrell and Garry Sobers. Shillingford had taken only three wickets in three first-class matches for the Windward Islands at the time, but was the leading wicket-taker on tour with 36 at 18.58 runs apiece. He took six for 63 at Worcester and made his debut in the Second Test at Lord's. But Shillingford and others were unable to meet the unrealistic expectations created by their predecessors. He played in seven Tests in all but West Indies failed to win any of them. Shillingford toured England again in 1973, by which time a new generation was establishing itself that would lead Caribbean cricket to new peaks. Keith Boyce and Bernard Julien kept Shillingford out of the Test team and, although he continued to take wickets in regional cricket for six years, he did not play another Test. His quick wit often lifted the mood in the dressing-room during the lean period. As off-spinner Jack Noreiga was motioned to lead the team off after his nine for 95 against India at Port-of-Spain early in 1971, Shillingford, who had taken the first wicket, rushed to his side, put his arm around him and remarked: "Ah, we wrecked 'em, Jack." He subsequently emigrated to Canada, returning home shortly before his death. He received one of Dominica's highest decorations, the Sisserou Award of Honour, in the 2009 Independence Day list.

SISMEY, STANLEY GEORGE, OAM, died on June 19, 2009, aged 92. A promising young wicketkeeper for New South Wales before the Second World War, Stan Sismey was superseded after it by the artistic Ron Saggers. But Saggers's absence on tour in South

A spring day: Grayson Shillingford bowls at Arundel against the Duke of Norfolk's XI, April 1969.

Africa, followed by his retirement in 1950-51, permitted Sismey a brief Indian summer in the state side. His work behind the stumps reflected the man: understated yet reliable. And he was one of the last of his kind regularly able and willing to stand up to the quick bowlers. Sismey is best remembered in England as a member of the popular Australian Services team which enlivened the victory summer of 1945. He was seconded to an RAF squadron operating Catalina flying boats out of Gibraltar, and badly wounded by shrapnel when his plane was brought down in 1942. After convalescence, he became a test pilot in Scotland: he claimed that the shrapnel still in his body caused compass malfunction. Sismey still achieved the rank of squadron-leader, and was appointed commanding officer of that Australian Services team, making fifties in two of the matches against England at Lord's, and 78 in a Scarborough festival match. He spent 43 years working for the Bank of New South Wales (now Westpac), latterly as a branch manager, while also serving 20 years as a state selector. The bank gave him a year off in 1951-52, and he returned to Scotland, playing for Clydesdale and representing Scotland in a fixture against Yorkshire, making him Scotland's oldest surviving player before he died.

SIVASANKARIAH, M. S., who died on December 29, 2009, aged 82, was an Indian umpire who stood in 34 first-class matches in a long career that stretched from 1955-56 to 1981-82 and included three Tests in the 1970s.

SIZIBA, WISDOM THOMAS, died on April 17, 2009, of an apparent heart attack while doing his laundry at home in Gauteng. He was only 28, and an epileptic. A wicketkeeper, and a batsman with a good eye, if limited footwork, Siziba made a notable first-class debut in his native Zimbabwe: he carried his bat through Matabeleland's second innings against Manicaland at Harare in March 2000. Siziba made 40 not out in four hours. Two years later, he scored his only century, 103 against Midlands in Bulawayo. He opened and kept wicket for Zimbabwe A in an unofficial Test against Bangladesh A at Kwekwe in February 2005 – but that turned out to be his last first-class appearance, as shortly afterwards, with the economic and political situation at home worsening, he moved to South Africa.

SMITH, CYRIL ROBERT, died on January 1, 2009, aged 82. In the years after the Second World War, many opening bowlers were tried for Queensland, but few remained chosen. Smith was one of the exceptions, taking 71 wickets in 27 matches between 1947-48 and 1953-54. Fair-haired, tall and powerfully built, he had genuine pace and used his height to make the ball kick disconcertingly, as when he took seven for 58 against Victoria at Melbourne in 1951-52. He was, however, an archetypal No. 11, reaching double figures only six times. Smith also represented Queensland at Australian Rules football. In 1955 he moved to Melbourne, where he became a director of his family's tyre business and turned out for the Melbourne club.

SNELLGROVE, KENNETH LESLIE, died on March 8, 2009, aged 67. Ken Snellgrove was an unsung member of the powerful Lancashire side of the 1960s and '70s: a powerful back-foot batsman and a fine strong-armed fielder. After several seasons in the Second Eleven he made his county debut in 1965, and two years later made his maiden century against Glamorgan at Old Trafford, in an innings in which no one else managed more than 22. But he made only one further hundred, although that too came from an unpromising position at Old Trafford: against Middlesex in 1970 Lancashire were 57 for five before Snellgrove entered and made 138. The following year he fell just nine short of 1,000 runs and won his county cap, but he faded away after three more modest seasons. He played in half the games when Lancashire won the Sunday League in 1970, but missed out on all their Lord's cup final appearances. Farokh Engineer, Lancashire's wicketkeeper, remembered him as "a fine batsman – and an extremely skilful three-card-brag player". He once took a fair sum off umpire Cec Pepper: "I warned Snelly not to let the ball so much as touch his pads," Engineer recalled. Snellgrove emerged from the Bootle club, and still watched their matches; his son David started his first season as Bootle's captain a few weeks after his father's death.

STEELE, HOWARD KEITH CHILLINGWORTH, died suddenly on June 7, 2009, aged 58. Keith Steele was a New Zealander who won Blues at Cambridge in 1971 and 1972, when his team-mates included Majid Khan and Phil Edmonds. A middle-order batsman and seamer, Steele scored a century for Cambridge against Sussex in 1972, although his performances in his two Varsity Matches were unspectacular. Back home, he briefly played for Auckland – bagging pairs in successive matches in December 1974 – before moving to Australia, where he became a successful lawyer, rising to be head of litigation at the large national firm, Freehills, where he also established the firm's *pro bono* programme. "Keith was a modern colossus in this firm," said managing partner Peter Butler. "He was its conscience and a brilliant lawyer."

Baron **STEINBERG** of BELFAST, who died on November 2, 2009, aged 73, was the founder of the Stanley Leisure Group (mainly betting-shops and casinos), which he established in Belfast in the 1950s. Leonard Steinberg moved himself and the company to England after he was shot on his doorstep by the Provisional IRA early in 1977, having refused to pay protection money. He became deputy treasurer of the Conservative Party and, at the time of his death, was president of Lancashire, whose chief executive Jim Cumbes remembered: "Len was a keen and passionate cricket fan. On one occasion I invited him to a Test match as a guest of the club, and halfway through lunch he asked if he could be excused as he wanted to get back to watching the cricket. When he was first asked about becoming president, he described it as the greatest honour he could ever have bestowed on him."

SYMINGTON, STUART JOHNSTON, who died on December 11, 2009, aged 83, was Leicestershire's amateur captain in 1949, when he was only 22. He had first played for them in a wartime match at 17. Symington made his first-class debut in 1948, scoring 40 against Essex in his second match, as well as opening the bowling. That proved enough for him to be offered the captaincy the following season, even though he was still in the army and not always available. In the event he did reasonably well with the bat – averaging 21 – but his enthusiastic medium-pace proved expensive. Leicestershire finished a distant 17th and last in the table, and Major Symington returned full-time to the army, where he eventually became ADC to the Governor of the Bahamas.

TAYLOR, ALFRED MAURICE, committed suicide in his native Barbados on June 16, 2009, aged 65. An aggressive batsman and stylish wicketkeeper, Taylor played for Barbados in the 1966-67 Shell Shield tournament and against the Rest of the World in the match to mark the nation's independence. As Barbados collapsed to defeat in their second innings, Taylor counter-attacked for 46. He continued to play club cricket, but his job as a hotel manager – which included a stint as president of the Caribbean Hotel Association – effectively ended his first-class career. His father, "Charlie", was an opening batsman who played 16 matches for Barbados.

THORPE, LINSLEY JAMES, OAM, died on June 19, 2009, aged 86. Wicketkeeper "Lindsay" Thorpe faced several hurdles in making the Queensland side in the 1950s: his career coincided with those of Don Tallon and Wally Grout, and he also played in the regional city of Toowoomba, 75 miles from Brisbane. His chance came at the age of 34 in 1957-58, while Grout was touring South Africa; he also played twice while Grout was involved in the Ashes series a year later. Thorpe could not reproduce his consistent club batting, but his keeping was secure and unostentatious. He gave long administrative service to country cricket, and captained the Queensland Country XI against the 1960-61 West Indians. He was also chairman of Toowoomba Turf Club.

TRIBE, GEORGE EDWARD, who died on April 5, 2009, aged 88, played three Tests for Australia in the first post-war Ashes series. He took just two wickets for 330, and that was the start and finish of his Test career. Instead he turned into a county cricket legend, becoming a major factor – arguably *the* major factor – in making the once-laughable Northamptonshire team one of the most formidable sides in England throughout the 1950s. In his eight full seasons at Northampton, he did the 1,000 runs–100 wickets double seven times, and in 1955 took 176 wickets. That year, he was named one of *Wisden's* Five. The Almanack's correspondent, Eb Eden, called him a "noteworthy personality" who had enjoyed "high success". His team-mates put it more strongly than that. Wicketkeeper Keith Andrew called him "probably the best cricketer I ever played with"; Frank Tyson described Australia's neglect of him as "criminal".

As a teenager, Tribe had been a traditional left-arm finger-spinner but took a conscious decision to change his style to take advantage of the 1937 change in the lbw law, which abolished the requirement that the ball had to pitch straight. He switched to left-arm wrist-spin, his stock ball being the chinaman, coming in to the right-hander – if one can use a phrase as mundane as "stock ball". Some reckoned he had six or seven different deliveries, including an off-cutter. There was also a sort of top-spinner he called a "squibber", whose trajectory depended on how it hit

John Watson

George Tribe: his neglect by Australia was "criminal".

the seam. Tribe grew up in Melbourne, and played Australian Rules for Footscray; he was briefly called up during the war and then discharged, because he had qualified as an engineer, a reserved occupation. He was the top wicket-taker in 1945-46, and the top Australian the following season: 13 of his 48 wickets came for 153 in one match for Victoria against South Australia, which secured his Test place.

After his disappointing series, he accepted an offer to play for Milnrow in the Central Lancashire League, a contract that could then be worth more to an Australian than an Ashes tour. It was assumed Tribe would return to Test cricket: Don Bradman had hinted as much. But family circumstances – his wife gave birth to twins after they arrived in Lancashire – led him to stay, and Australian selectors tended to ignore the growing band of exiles playing in England. There was also a theory that the Australian keeper Don Tallon was among those unable to read Tribe's bowling.

Still, Tribe was hugely successful over five years with Milnrow and Rawtenstall. This qualified him for county cricket, and Lancashire were interested. But his friend Jock Livingston was already connected with Northamptonshire, and recommended him; the local engineering firm of British Timken, then controlled by the cricket-loving John Pascoe, happily subsidised Tribe's salary by offering him winter work. He started his Championship career with 40 wickets in the first four matches, and his form hardly wavered from that moment. The best batsmen in England consistently struggled against him (Tom Graveney was among the rare exceptions). The Northamptonshire opener Peter Arnold remembers a match at Tunbridge Wells in 1955 when Colin Cowdrey, in prime form, played and missed six times in an over. Tribe's skill was matched by low cunning – players like Graveney would be given a single to get them down the other end, so he could bowl at the innocents. His batting was effective, if unorthodox: his team-mates called him "Tripod" because he could drag the ball with perfect control to the cow-corner boundary, ending up with bat splayed on the ground like a third leg. There was a hint of cunning in his fielding too: "He would run under a bus to take a catch," said Richie Benaud, pausing theatrically, "...off his own bowling."

He was also a charming, almost courtly man, and a great enthusiast: he would stop his car to coach kids playing by the roadside. But he never lost his competitive streak: when he returned to Australia after the 1959 season (working for the Australian branch of Timken), he captained Yarraville, the club where he had started as a 15-year-old. Playing for a knockabout team called The Owls in his fifties, he took five for eight against a media team and was taken off. "I was in danger of making you blokes look farcical," he said. And, as he lay dying – so a carer reported – he was asked what he would like to do. He replied: "I want to play cricket with the boys on the hill."

UNDERDOWN, DAVID EDWARD, who died on September 26, 2009, aged 84, was a well-known historian, born in Somerset. He specialised in 17th-century England but spent his academic life in the US, finishing his career with a professorship at Yale. Underdown remained a lifelong Somerset supporter and his final book, in 2000, was about cricket – *Start of Play: Cricket and Culture in Eighteenth-Century England*. Gillian Reynolds, the reviewer in *Wisden 2001*, was thrilled by it, saying it "bubbles with scholarly glee". She concluded: "Lucky Yale to have had him as a teacher. Lucky us to have this book."

VYFHUIS, COMPTON F., who died on January 23, 2009, aged 76, was a Guyanese umpire who stood in six Tests in the 1970s. These included the famous one at Port-of-Spain in 1975-76 when India scored 406 for four to win. He also umpired two one-day internationals, including the first ever played in the Caribbean: at Berbice in March 1977.

WALLING, Sir SYDNEY LEOPOLD SYLVANUS, who died on October 8, 2009, aged 102, was Antigua's most celebrated cricketer until the emergence of Viv Richards and Andy Roberts in the 1970s. He first played for Antigua in 1927, but the island was seen as a cricketing backwater, and even 154 in a trial match could not earn him selection to tour

England. Some commentators felt that Walling could have been West Indies' first W, preceding the famous three, Weekes, Worrell and Walcott. In 1933 Walling became the first black player to captain Antigua, in itself a significant breakthrough. Described by the Antiguan writer Tim Hector as "all wrists and elegance", Walling continued to score consistently into his fifties, and as late as 1953-54 (when he was 46) represented the fledgling Leeward Islands side against Len Hutton's MCC tourists. Walling was knighted by the Antigua & Barbuda government in 2004, not only for his cricketing feats but also for his off-field career, during which he rose from post office clerk to become the first black postmaster-general. A stand at the Antigua Recreation Ground was named in his honour in 1988, as was one of the roads leading to the new Sir Vivian Richards Stadium when it opened for the 2007 World Cup.

WHITE, MALCOLM FRANK, who died in January 2009, aged 84, was a wicketkeeper who would have won a Blue at Cambridge but for the Second World War – he played twice against Oxford at Lord's, in 1943 and 1944, taking three catches in a six-wicket victory in the second game, but these were one-day matches and full Blues were not awarded. He played once for Warwickshire in 1946, bagging a pair against Derbyshire.

WHITING, HAIG HERBERT, who died on November 16, 2009, aged 91, was a batsman who captained Upper Hutt to victory in New Zealand's senior club championship, before a ball from the Test fast bowler Bob Blair broke his jaw in three places. Whiting, a teacher, turned to administration, combining umpiring with youth development. He managed two youth tours of Australia, and eventually became an honorary life member of New Zealand Cricket. "In a strange way, New Zealand cricketers can be grateful to Bob Blair," said historian Don Neely.

WILKIN, CALVIN, who died on August 22, 2009, aged 84, was a stalwart of Leeward Islands cricket: he captained his native St Kitts, and later became a West Indian selector. He was assistant manager of the West Indian team which beat England 4–0 in 1988. His son, Charles, was a Cambridge Blue in 1970.

WILTSHIRE, COLIN FRANCIS, who died on December 18, 2009, aged 74, was, physically and technically, a solid right-hand opener for British Guiana. He played eight matches between 1959 and 1964, usually preceding a formidable middle order of Test batsmen, and made 197 against Combined Islands in 1961-62. He later served for several years as honorary secretary of the Guyana Cricket Board.

WINTER, Dr JOHN, who died in November 2009, aged 90, held the record for runs in a season in the Liverpool Competition for 52 years. His 1955 total of 1,423 for Northern was not beaten until Carl Hey surpassed him, also for Northern, in 2007; Winter was on the ground to congratulate him. In his vintage summer, Winter scored eight centuries and averaged 88. He was a legend at the club over a 25-year playing career and had an 11-year sequence in which he topped the league averages eight times and came second once – the other two seasons he was playing for Somerset Second Eleven. He was a consultant radiologist at Walton Hospital.

WOOLRIDGE, RANDOLPH JOSEPH, who died of bone cancer on May 9, 2009, aged 53, was an Australian umpire who stood in 12 first-class matches between 1998-99 and 2001-02; in the first of them, Shane Warne was fined $A2,400 for his public criticism of Woolridge's lbw decision against Warne's Victorian team-mate Graeme Vimpani. During 2000-01, Woolridge was the third umpire for the Perth Test between Australia and West Indies. Born in India, he emigrated to Perth and was talked into becoming an umpire when his son began playing junior cricket.

Four Wrights: Carleton (*second left*) is joined by son David (*far left*) and nephews Nick (current chairman, *second right*) and Peter (*far right*) at the Essex Show, 1967.

WRIGHT, CARLETON NEVILLE, who died aged 96, on March 3, 2009, was chairman of J. S. Wright & Sons, the Essex-based company which is said to be the largest supplier of English cricket bat willow. His father Jessie founded the firm in 1894 and (war service aside) Carleton was in the business from leaving school until he was 85. The company is still family-run, supplying "hundreds of thousands" of blades a year. His grandson Jeremy Ruggles, now the managing director, attributes this to Carleton's decision to plant thousands of extra trees after he took control in 1963, even though it was not obvious there would be sufficient demand.

ZACHARIAH, HARRY, who died on March 15, 2009, aged 97, was a versatile Australian left-arm bowler who was equally adept at swinging the new ball or spinning the old one out of the back of his hand. Aged 19, he took five for 74, including George Headley and Learie Constantine, for the Victorian Country XI against the 1930-31 West Indian tourists. Six years later, he dismissed both Wally Hammond and Maurice Leyland for Australian Universities against the 1936-37 MCC tourists. Yet, despite a long and productive career in club cricket, he played only twice for Victoria, both games against Tasmania in 1935-36, taking eight wickets.

He became a teacher, coaching the adolescent Keith Miller at Melbourne High School, and then joining Brighton Grammar School in 1942, beginning a 60-year association, including 28 years as vice-principal and 15, after retirement, as archivist. On his last day of "official" service in 1988, he was greeted by a guard of honour of boys whose grandfathers he had taught.

BRIEFLY NOTED

The following, whose deaths were noted during 2009, played in ten or fewer first-class (fc) matches. Further details can be found on www.cricinfo.com (enter the player's name in the search box on the home page) or at www.cricketarchive.co.uk.

	Died	*Age*	*Main team*

Abbott, Alan Wesley   28.11.2008   82   Leicestershire
Opening bowler who failed to take a wicket in his solitary Championship appearance in 1946.

Aitchison, John Edward   2.4.2009   80   Kent
Slow left-armer who took three wickets on fc debut in 1949, but none in his other two matches.

Anwar Sheikh   3.8.2007   81   Sind (Pakistan)
Five fc matches in Pakistan in 1950s, including 1954-55 Indian tourists and 1955-56 MCC A team.

Asquith, John Patrick Kenyon   10.9.2009   77   Cambridge University
Wicketkeeper who played five fc matches in 1953 and 1954 without winning a Blue.

Brockett, Walter Blyth   13.8.2009   74   Transvaal B
Also played once for Transvaal. Five for 53 v Orange Free State in 1963-64.

Carmody, Kevin Joseph   9.9.2009   84   Umpire
Stood in two one-day internationals in Australia in 1979-80, and 19 fc matches all at the MCG.

Copelin, Stanley Arthur   15.6.2009   82   Umpire
Australian-born umpire who stood in eight fc matches in Central Districts, New Zealand.

Forbes, John Henry Vivian   16.4.2009   85   Orange Free State
Batsman, born in Cambridge, who scored 80 against Western Province at Cape Town in 1954-55.

Kalia, Rajesh   20.6.2009   58   Haryana
Opening bowler who took 13 wickets but never reached double figures in nine fc matches.

Mohan, Janardhanan   19.11.2009   66   Kerala
Batsman who had little success in five fc matches, usually as opener.

Narayan, Pratik   9.1.2009   60   Bihar
Scored 17* in an innings victory over Assam in his only Ranji Trophy match, in 1976-77.

Nathanielsz, Eustace Basil "Tita"   12.1.2009   89   Ceylon
Fast bowler from the Colts Club who played three fc matches; later a noted golf writer.

Nayyar, Sham Sunder   21.3.09   76   Eastern Punjab
Two Ranji Trophy matches in 1951-52. In England, won 1974 National Club Knockout with Sunbury.

Raw, Charles Denver   15.3.2009   61   Orange Free State
Left-hander who played two Currie Cup matches in 1975-76, scoring 45 in the first.

Rowe, Leonard Charles   1.4.2009   71   Oxford University
On Northants staff but his five fc matches were for Oxford; reached double figures only once.

Saheed, Burlin   15.4.2009   67   British Guiana/Berbice
Slow left-armer nicknamed "The Little Magician" who played only one Shell Shield match.

	Died	Age	Main team
Shyam, Lulla Pinomal	27.11.2009	68	Mysore

Scored 14 in his only fc match, an innings victory over Kerala in 1961-62.

Varadaraj, Chanchikotti Malkote	24.4.2009	75	Mysore

Slow left-armer who took 22 wickets at 19.86 in eight fc matches between 1952-53 and 1960-61.

Witherden, Errol Ferris	7.7.2009	86	Border

Fast-medium bowler who took 18 wickets in seven fc matches in the 1950s.

Wyatt, Ivan Edgar	26.3.2009	85	Auckland

Wicketkeeper in three matches in 1947-48; 11 years later scored 202 for Nelson in the Hawke Cup.

CAREER FIGURES OF TEST CRICKETERS

	Tests				First-class			
	Runs	Avge	Wkts	Avge	Runs	Avge	Wkts	Avge
D. W. Begbie	138	19.71	1	130.00	2,727	35.88	88	23.69
W. P. A. Crawford	53	17.66	7	15.28	424	19.27	110	21.02
T. Greenhough	4	1.33	16	22.31	1,913	8.39	751	22.37
K. W. Hough	62	62.00	6	29.16	624	16.42	119	20.87
Khan Mohammad	100	10.00	54	23.92	544	11.57	214	23.22
A. J. W. McIntyre	19	3.16	–	–	11,145	22.83	4	45.00
I. S. Madray	3	1.00	0	–	73	9.12	16	38.87
V. M. Muddiah	11	5.50	3	44.66	805	13.87	175	23.76
G. C. Shillingford	57	8.14	15	35.80	791	10.14	217	26.54
G. E. Tribe	35	17.50	2	165.00	10,177	27.35	1,378	20.55

McIntyre took 638 catches and 157 stumpings in first-class cricket, including eight catches in three Tests.

The obituaries section comprises those who died, or whose deaths were notified, in 2009. Wisden always welcomes information about those who might be included. Please send details to almanack@wisden.com, or to John Wisden & Co, 13 Old Aylesfield, Golden Pot, Alton, Hampshire GU34 4BY.

DATES IN CRICKET HISTORY

c. **1550**	Evidence of cricket being played in Guildford, Surrey.
1610	Reference to "cricketing" between Weald and Upland and North Downs near Chevening, Kent.
1611	Randle Cotgrave's French–English dictionary translates the French word "crosse" as a cricket staff. Two youths fined for playing cricket at Sidlesham, Sussex.
1624	Jasper Vinall becomes first man known to be killed playing cricket: hit by a bat while trying to catch the ball – at Horsted Green, Sussex.
1676	First reference to cricket being played abroad, by British residents in Aleppo, Syria.
1694	Two shillings and sixpence paid for a "wagger" (wager) about a cricket match at Lewes.
1697	First reference to "a great match" with 11 players a side for fifty guineas, in Sussex.
1700	Cricket match announced on Clapham Common.
1709	First recorded inter-county match: Kent v Surrey.
1710	First reference to cricket at Cambridge University.
1727	Articles of Agreement written governing the conduct of matches between the teams of the Duke of Richmond and Mr Brodrick of Peperharow, Surrey.
1729	Date of earliest surviving bat, belonging to John Chitty, now in the pavilion at The Oval.
1730	First recorded match at the Artillery Ground, off City Road, central London, still the cricketing home of the Honourable Artillery Company.
1744	Kent beat All England by one wicket at the Artillery Ground. First known version of the Laws of Cricket, issued by the London Club, formalising the pitch as 22 yards long.
c. **1767**	Foundation of the Hambledon Club in Hampshire, the leading club in England for the next 30 years.
1769	First recorded century, by John Minshull for Duke of Dorset's XI v Wrotham.
1771	Width of bat limited to $4\frac{1}{4}$ inches, where it has remained ever since.
1774	LBW law devised.
1776	Earliest known scorecards, at the Vine Club, Sevenoaks, Kent.
1780	The first six-seamed cricket ball, manufactured by Dukes of Penshurst, Kent.
1787	First match at Thomas Lord's first ground, Dorset Square, Marylebone – White Conduit Club v Middlesex. Formation of Marylebone Cricket Club by members of the White Conduit Club.
1788	First revision of the Laws of Cricket by MCC.
1794	First recorded inter-schools match: Charterhouse v Westminster.
1795	First recorded case of a dismissal "leg before wicket".
1806	First Gentlemen v Players match at Lord's.
1807	First mention of "straight-armed" (i.e. round-arm) bowling: by John Willes of Kent.

1809	Thomas Lord's second ground opened at North Bank, St John's Wood.
1811	First recorded women's county match: Surrey v Hampshire at Ball's Pond, London.
1814	Lord's third ground opened on its present site, also in St John's Wood.
1827	First Oxford v Cambridge match, at Lord's. A draw.
1828	MCC authorise the bowler to raise his hand level with the elbow.
1833	John Nyren publishes his classic *Young Cricketer's Tutor* and *The Cricketers of My Time.*
1836	First North v South match, for many years regarded as the principal fixture of the season.
c. 1836	Batting pads invented.
1841	General Lord Hill, commander-in-chief of the British Army, orders that a cricket ground be made an adjunct of every military barracks.
1844	First official international match: Canada v United States.
1845	First match played at The Oval.
1846	The All-England XI, organised by William Clarke, begins playing matches, often against odds, throughout the country.
1849	First Yorkshire v Lancashire match.
c. 1850	Wicketkeeping gloves first used.
1850	John Wisden bowls all ten batsmen in an innings for North v South.
1853	First mention of a champion county: Nottinghamshire.
1858	First recorded instance of a hat being awarded to a bowler taking three wickets with consecutive balls.
1859	First touring team to leave England, captained by George Parr, draws enthusiastic crowds in the US and Canada.
1864	"Overhand bowling" authorised by MCC. John Wisden's *The Cricketer's Almanack* first published.
1868	Team of Australian aborigines tour England.
1873	W. G. Grace becomes the first player to record 1,000 runs and 100 wickets in a season. First regulations restricting county qualifications, often regarded as the official start of the County Championship.
1877	First Test match: Australia beat England by 45 runs in Melbourne.
1880	First Test in England: a five-wicket win against Australia at The Oval.
1882	Following England's first defeat by Australia in England, an "obituary notice" to English cricket in the *Sporting Times* leads to the tradition of The Ashes.
1889	Present Lord's pavilion begun. South Africa's first Test match. Declarations first authorised, but only on the third day, or in a one-day match.
1890	County Championship officially constituted.
1895	W. G. Grace scores 1,000 runs in May, and reaches his 100th hundred.
1899	A. E. J. Collins scores 628 not out in a junior house match at Clifton College, the highest individual score in any match. Selectors choose England team for home Tests, instead of host club issuing invitations.

1900   Six-ball over becomes the norm, instead of five.

1909   Imperial Cricket Conference (ICC – now the International Cricket Council) set up, with England, Australia and South Africa the original members.

1910   Six runs given for any hit over the boundary, instead of only for a hit out of the ground.

1912   First and only triangular Test series played in England, involving England, Australia and South Africa.

1915   W. G. Grace dies, aged 67.

1926   Victoria score 1,107 v New South Wales at Melbourne, the record total for a first-class innings.

1928   West Indies' first Test match.
              A. P. Freeman of Kent and England becomes the only player to take more than 300 first-class wickets in a season: 304.

1930   New Zealand's first Test match.
              Donald Bradman's first tour of England: he scores 974 runs in the five Ashes Tests, still a record for any Test series.

1931   Stumps made higher (28 inches not 27) and wider (nine inches not eight – this was optional until 1947).

1932   India's first Test match.
              Hedley Verity of Yorkshire takes ten wickets for ten runs v Nottinghamshire, the best innings analysis in first-class cricket.

1932-33 The Bodyline tour of Australia in which England bowl at batsmen's bodies with a packed leg-side field to neutralise Bradman's scoring.

1934   Jack Hobbs retires, with 197 centuries and 61,237 runs, both records.
              First women's Test: Australia v England at Brisbane.

1935   MCC condemn and outlaw Bodyline.

1947   Denis Compton of Middlesex and England scores a record 3,816 runs in an English season.

1948   First five-day Tests in England.
              Bradman concludes Test career with a second-ball duck at The Oval and a batting average of 99.94 – four runs short of 100.

1952   Pakistan's first Test match.

1953   England regain the Ashes after a 19-year gap, the longest ever.

1956   Jim Laker of England takes 19 wickets for 90 v Australia at Manchester, the best match analysis in first-class cricket.

1960   First tied Test, Australia v West Indies at Brisbane.

1963   The first major one-day tournament begins in England: the Gillette Cup.
              Distinction between amateurs and professionals abolished in English cricket.

1969   Limited-over Sunday League inaugurated for first-class counties.

1970   Proposed South African tour of England cancelled: South Africa excluded from international cricket because of their government's apartheid policies.

1971   First one-day international: Australia v England at Melbourne.

1975   First World Cup: West Indies beat Australia in final at Lord's.

1976   First women's match at Lord's, England v Australia.

1977   Centenary Test at Melbourne, with identical result to the first match: Australia beat England by 45 runs.

Australian media tycoon Kerry Packer signs 51 of the world's leading players in defiance of the cricketing authorities.

1978   Graham Yallop of Australia wears a protective helmet to bat in a Test match, the first player to do so.

1979   Packer and official cricket agree peace deal.

1981   England beat Australia in Leeds Test, after following on with bookmakers offering odds of 500–1 against them winning.

1982   Sri Lanka's first Test match.

1991   South Africa return, with a one-day international in India.

1992   Zimbabwe's first Test match.

Durham become first county since Glamorgan in 1921 to attain first-class status.

1993   The ICC ceases to be administered by MCC, becoming an independent organisation with its own chief executive.

1994   Brian Lara becomes the first player to pass 500 in a first-class innings: 501 not out for Warwickshire v Durham.

2000   South Africa's captain Hansie Cronje banned from cricket for life after admitting receiving bribes from bookmakers in match-fixing scandal.

Bangladesh's first Test match.

County Championship split into two divisions, with promotion and relegation.

The Laws of Cricket revised and rewritten.

2001   Sir Donald Bradman dies, aged 92.

2003   Twenty20 Cup, a 20-over-per-side evening tournament, inaugurated in England.

2004   Lara becomes the first man to score 400 in a Test innings, against England.

2005   England regain the Ashes after 16 years.

2006   Pakistan become first team to forfeit a Test, for refusing to resume at The Oval.

England lose the Ashes after 462 days, the shortest tenure in history.

Shane Warne becomes the first man to take 700 Test wickets.

2007   Australia complete 5–0 Ashes whitewash for the first time since 1920-21.

Australia win the World Cup for the third time running.

India beat Pakistan in the final of the inaugural World Twenty20 tournament.

Muttiah Muralitharan passes Warne's record to end the year on 723 Test wickets.

2008   Indian Premier League of 20-over matches launched, featuring many international players on lucrative contracts.

Durham win the County Championship for the first time.

Sachin Tendulkar becomes the leading scorer in Tests, passing Brian Lara.

England lose a $US20m winner-takes-all Twenty20 match in Antigua.

2009   Terrorists attack Sri Lankan team bus in Lahore.

Umpire Decision Review System implemented by the ICC.

ANNIVERSARIES IN 2010-11

COMPILED BY STEVEN LYNCH

2010

May 19   Alan Melville (South Africa) born, 1910.
Stylish batsman who made four centuries in successive Test innings either side of World War Two.

June 15   Kent beat Worcestershire inside a day, 1960.
The last such instance in first-class cricket, on a drying pitch at Tunbridge Wells.

June 24   Geoff Griffin (South Africa) takes the first Test hat-trick at Lord's, 1960.
Controversial fast bowler also no-balled for throwing 11 times, and never played another Test.

July 3   Charles Barnett (England) born, 1910.
Stylish Gloucestershire opener who scored 98* before lunch in the 1938 Trent Bridge Ashes Test.

July 16   Stan McCabe (Australia) born, 1910.
Attacking batsman who hit a thrilling 187 not out in the first Bodyline Test in 1932-33.

August 1   Mahomed Nissar (India) born, 1910.
Tall fast bowler who took 5-93 on India's first day of Test cricket, at Lord's in 1932.

August 16   Lord Hawke (England) born, 1860.
Aristocrat who captained Yorkshire to eight Championships during 28 seasons in charge.

August 28   Allen Hill (England) dies, 1910.
Yorkshire roundarm bowler who took the first wicket in the first Test of all, in 1877.

October 15   Xenophon Balaskas (South Africa) born, 1910.
Leg-spinner of Greek descent who took nine wickets at Lord's in SA's first Test win in England.

November 12   Dudley Nourse (South Africa) born, 1910.
Captained the 1951 team in England, scoring 208 at Nottingham despite a broken thumb.

December 2   C. T. Studd (England) born, 1860.
One of Ivo Bligh's side who recaptured the new Ashes urn in 1882-83; later a famous missionary.

December 14   Test cricket's first tie, 1960.
Australia and West Indies finish all square in a cliffhanger at Brisbane.

December 16   Freddie Brown (England) born, 1910.
Toured Australia with the Bodyline team in 1932-33, and returned there as captain in 1950-51.

December 18   Eric Tindill (New Zealand) born, 1910.
Double international (also rugby) who during 2009 became the longest-lived Test player of all.

December 29   David Boon (Australia) born, 1960.
Tasmanian batsman who scored 7,422 runs in 107 Test matches.

2011

February 7   Harry Graham (Australia) dies, 1911.
Victoria's "Little Dasher", who scored a century on Test debut at Lord's in 1893.

February 18   Billy Murdoch (Australia and England) dies, 1911.
Captained Australia in England in 1880, 1882 (the match that inspired the Ashes), 1884 and 1890.

March 7   Aubrey Faulkner (South Africa) finishes Test series with 732 runs, 1911.
He passed 50 seven times – with 204 at Melbourne – but Australia still won the series 4–1.

ONE HUNDRED YEARS AGO

From Wisden Cricketers' Almanack 1911

ETON v HARROW, AT LORD'S, JULY 8, 9 [1910]   Eton and Harrow have been meeting on the cricket field for over a hundred years, but they have never played a match quite so remarkable as that of 1910. Indeed in the whole history of cricket there has been nothing more sensational. After following their innings Eton were only four ahead with nine wickets down, and yet in the end they won the game by nine runs... The struggle between the two public schools last season will be known for all time as Fowler's match. Never has a school cricketer risen to the occasion in more astonishing fashion. When Harrow went in with only 55 to get, Fowler took command of the game, secured eight wickets – five of them bowled down – for 23 runs and brought off what might fairly be described as a forty to one chance... On Saturday morning, Eton's first innings was soon finished off for 67, and a follow-on against a balance of 165 was involved... Despite Fowler's heroic efforts – his 64 was the highest innings in the match – the position was reached of Eton being only four runs ahead with a wicket to fall. Then began the cricket which will for ever make the match memorable. Kaye joined Manners, and so finely and fearlessly did Manners hit that in less than twenty-five minutes 50 runs were put on, the total being carried from 169 to 219... In the case of any ordinary match the ground would have been half empty before the Eton innings closed, but an Eton and Harrow crowd is a law to itself and when Harrow went in with 55 to get about 10,000 people watched the cricket. Whatever their feelings, they must have been glad they stayed as they may never see such a finish again... The scene of enthusiasm at the finish was quite indescribable.

THE LEADING COUNTIES IN 1910   The County Championship in 1910 was fought out under a new system of reckoning points, the result being determined by the percentage of wins to matches played. This method was proposed by Lancashire, and adopted for one season at least as an experiment. Its defects were obvious, but as things turned out some exceptionally interesting cricket was seen. Curiously enough Lancashire suffered most from the change. They finished fourth, but under the old system they would have been second. Kent carried off the Championship for the second year in succession and would have won according to any method of scoring... Deducting one fixture abandoned owing to the death of King Edward and five curtailed on account of the funeral, 176 matches were played in the Championship.

OBITUARIES IN 1910   H. M. King Edward VII died at Buckingham Palace on May 6th. As a small boy he received tuition at Windsor from F. Bell, of Cambridge, but it cannot be said that he ever showed much aptitude for the game. He played occasionally during his Oxford days, however, and, while he was staying at Madingley Hall, a special wicket was reserved for his use at Fenner's.

FIFTY YEARS AGO

From Wisden Cricketers' Almanack 1962

WEST INDIES IN AUSTRALIA, 1960–61   Never has it been more apparent that the game is greater than the result than in Melbourne on February 17, 1961. Commerce in this Australian city stood almost still as the smiling cricketers from the West Indies, the vanquished not the victors, were given a send-off the like of which is normally reserved for royalty and national heroes. Open cars paraded the happy players from the Caribbean among hundreds of thousands of Australians who had been sentimentalised through the media of cricket as it should be played. Worrell, the handsome West Indies captain, Hall, a bowler big in heart as well as stature, Kanhai, a fleet-footed batsman in the best tradition, and the suave Ramadhin, who had come a long way since he was introduced to cricket at the Canadian Mission School in Trinidad, were among those whom it was said, were moved to tears by the enthusiasm of the farewell.

From Wisden Cricketers' Almanack 1961

THE GREATEST TEST MATCH [by E. M. Wellings]   I was there. I saw it all. That is something that countless thousands would give much to be able to say. For it was The Greatest Test Match, The Greatest Cricket Match and surely The Greatest Game ever played with a ball. Australia v West Indies at Brisbane from December 9 to December 14 was already a great match before it bounded explosively to its amazing climax to produce the only tie in the history of Test cricket... That final over lasted nine minutes and ended four minutes after the appointed time... But for a comparatively recent law amendment, which provided for the last over being played out whatever the time, we lucky spectators would not have palpitated to the last tremendous thrill of that last tremendous over. Nor perhaps would spectators, bounding with excitement no less than the fielders, have raced across the ground to cheer and call for the heroes of the day, and repeat their cheers again and again in front of the players' pavilion... Davidson... had a great match. He had taken 11 wickets and scored 44 [and 80]... Such was his all-round success that in normal circumstances the Test would rightly go down to history as Davidson's Match. As it is, this is to be known as The Greatest Test Match, but it was big enough to carry also a sub-title recognising Davidson's performance.

NOTES BY THE EDITOR [Norman Preston]   Most lovers of cricket will look back on 1960 as "The Sad Season." It will be remembered for the rain which spoiled so many matches, for the alarming fall in attendances and for its bitter controversies – the throwing of Griffin, the sacking of Buller as a Test umpire, the withdrawal by MCC and Surrey of privileges to Laker following the publication of his book, *Over to Me*, and the Graveney dispute over the Gloucestershire captaincy.

Compiled by Christopher Lane

HONOURS AND AWARDS 2009-10

In 2009-10, the following were decorated for their services to cricket:

Queen's Birthday Honours, 2009: C. M. Edwards (England Women; services to sport) MBE; G. A. Hick (Worcestershire and England; services to sport) MBE; R. Torrens (Ireland cricketer, later Ireland team manager; services to cricket and football in Northern Ireland) OBE; D. L. Waters (services to underprivileged young people and cricket in Kenya) MBE.

Queen's Birthday Honours (Australia), 2009: G. K. Harinath (Chairman of Cricket NSW; services to cricket and the community) OAM.

Queen's Birthday Honours (New Zealand), 2009: J. F. M. Morrison (Wellington and New Zealand; services to cricket and the community) MNZM.

New Year's Honours, 2010: J. A. Jameson (Warwickshire and England, later coach and administrator; services to cricket) MBE; K. H. Moss (president of Bradford Cricket League; voluntary services to sport) MBE; S. C. Taylor (England Women; services to cricket) MBE.

Australia Day Honours, 2010: S. R. Bernard (New South Wales: services to cricket as player, selector and Australian team manager) OAM; M. L. Hayden (Queensland and Australia; services to cricket and the community) AM; T. V. Hohns (Queensland and Australia; services to cricket as player and selector) OAM; T. H. Iceton (Sutherland CC; services to cricket in New South Wales) OAM; D. K. Lillee (Western Australia and Australia; services to cricket as player, coach and administrator and to charities supporting children with special needs) AM; D. E. Meiklejohn (president of Melbourne CC; services to business and sport) AM.

ICC AWARDS

The International Cricket Council's sixth annual award ceremony, presented in association with the Federation of International Cricketers' Associations, was held in Johannesburg in October 2009, during the Champions Trophy. The following awards were voted for by a panel of players, journalists and officials:

Sir Garfield Sobers Trophy (Cricketer of the Year)	**Mitchell Johnson**
Test Player of the Year	**Gautam Gambhir**
One-day International Player of the Year	**Mahendra Singh Dhoni**
Women's Cricketer of the Year	**Claire Taylor**
Emerging Player of the Year	**Peter Siddle**
Associate/Affiliate Player of the Year	**William Porterfield**
Twenty20 International Performance of the Year	**Tillekeratne Dilshan**
Umpire of the Year	**Aleem Dar**
Team Best Exemplifying the Spirit of Cricket	**New Zealand**

ALLAN BORDER MEDAL

For the first time in its ten-year history the Allan Border Medal, for the best Australian international player of the past 12 months, was shared, by Test captain **Ricky Ponting** and his deputy **Michael Clarke**. Both had won the medal before, Ponting three times; other previous winners were Glenn McGrath, Steve Waugh, Matthew Hayden, Adam Gilchrist and Brett Lee. At a ceremony in February 2009, Ponting and Clarke were declared to have won 41 votes each from team-mates, umpires and journalists, three ahead of Michael Hussey. Clarke was also named Test Cricketer of the Year, while **Nathan Bracken** was One-Day International Player of the Year. **Michael Klinger**, who had refreshed his career by moving to South Australia for the 2008-09 season, was State Player of the Year, and **Phillip Hughes** of New South Wales was Bradman Young Player of the Year. The award for the Women's International Cricketer of the Year went to **Shelley Nitschke**.

VODAFONE ENGLAND PLAYER OF THE YEAR AWARDS

England captain **Andrew Strauss** won the men's Vodafone England Cricketer of the Year Award in May 2009, after scoring six Test hundreds in the previous 12 months, including two in Chennai and then three in successive matches in the West Indies. He had previously won the award in 2005. For the second year running, the women's award went to **Claire Taylor**, whose 324 runs at 64.80 made her the leading run-scorer in the Women's World Cup won by England in March.

PROFESSIONAL CRICKETERS' ASSOCIATION AWARDS

The following awards were announced at the PCA's annual dinner in October 2009.

Reg Hayter Cup (NatWest PCA Player of the Year)	**Marcus Trescothick**
John Arlott Cup (NatWest PCA Young Player of the Year)	**James Taylor**
ECB Special Award	**Michael Vaughan**
PCA Special Merit Award	**Andrew Strauss**
PCA Umpire of the Year	**Richard Kettleborough**
Sky Sports Sixes League	**Dwayne Smith**
Impossible is Nothing Award	**Graham Stevenson**

WALTER LAWRENCE TROPHY

The Walter Lawrence Trophy for the fastest century in 2009 was won by Worcestershire captain **Vikram Solanki**, who reached his maiden Twenty20 hundred in 47 balls against Glamorgan at Worcester on June 24. This was the second time in the Trophy's 75-year history that the competition was extended to cover all senior cricket in England; traditionally, it was reserved for the fastest first-class hundred against authentic bowling (in 2009, this was Peter Trego's 54-ball hundred which hustled Somerset to a fourth-innings 479 inside 86 overs to beat Yorkshire at Taunton on July 3). Solanki received £5,000 along with the trophy at a lunch at Lord's. **Anand Ashok** of Cambridge won the Walter Lawrence award for the highest score by a batsman from the University/UCCE teams against a first-class county or another university side; he made 164* against Oxford in an MCC Universities Championship match at Cambridge in June, and received a silver medallion and £1,000.

CRICKET WRITERS' CLUB AWARDS

The Young Cricketer of the Year was **James Taylor** of Leicestershire, who beat the 2006 winner Stuart Broad into second place. The Peter Smith Memorial Award "for services to the presentation of cricket to the public" went to **Geoff Cook**, the former Northamptonshire batsman, who had just coached Durham to their second successive County Championship.

A list of Young Cricketers from 1950 to 2004 appears in Wisden 2005, *page 995. A list of Peter Smith Award winners from 1992 to 2004 appears in* Wisden 2005, *page 745.*

UK COACHING AWARDS

The England Women's coach **Mark Lane** was named UK Coach of the Year and High Performance Coach of the Year at the UK Coaching Awards in December. The initiative whereby eight members of the women's team were given jobs as coaching ambassadors for the Chance to shine scheme won the Coaching Intervention of the Year Award.

DENIS COMPTON SCHOLAR

The Compton Scholar is the overall winner of an award given to the most promising player at each county, organised by NBC Sports Management since 1997. The winner in 2009 was Leicestershire batsman **James Taylor**.

SECOND ELEVEN PLAYER OF THE YEAR

The Association of Cricket Statisticians and Historians named **Andrew Carter** of Nottinghamshire the Les Hatton Second Eleven Player of the Year for 2009. A seam bowler, he took 54 wickets at 12.16 in eight Second Eleven Championship matches for Nottinghamshire, including 13-99 in their victory over Warwickshire, all before his 21st birthday.

GROUNDSMEN OF THE YEAR

The Oval's seven-year monopoly of the Groundsman of the Year award was finally broken by **Matt Merchant**, in his first season as head groundsman at Old Trafford after a long apprenticeship under Peter Marron. Merchant won the four-day category, with Mick Hunt of Lord's as runner-up. The one-day title also left Surrey, going to Derby's **Neil Godrich**, with Sean Williams of Bristol and Phil Frost of Taunton sharing second place. Bill Gordon of The Oval had to be content with a commendation for his one-day pitches. **Ross Spry** of Cheltenham won the prize for the best outground, ahead of previous winners Micky Stewart and Christian Dunkerley of Scarborough, while **John Moden** at Fenner's in Cambridge pulled ahead of Oxford's Richard Sula at the Parks to win the UCCE award.

CRICKET SOCIETY AWARDS

Wetherell Award Leading First-class All-rounder	**Ian Blackwell** (Durham)
Wetherell Award for Leading Schools All-rounder	**Aaron West** (Brentwood School)
Most Promising Young Cricketer	**James Taylor** (Leicestershire)
Most Promising Young Woman Cricketer	**Beth MacGregor** (Essex)
Sir John Hobbs Silver Jubilee Memorial Prize	**Wilf Marriott** (Radley)
A. A. Thomson Fielding Prize for Best Schoolboy Fielder	**Ruaidhri Smith** (Glamorgan)
Christopher Box-Grainger Memorial Trophy	**Highshore School** (Peckham)
Don Rowan Memorial Trophy	**Gosden House School** (Surrey)
Ian Jackson Award for Services to Cricket	**Stephen Chalke** (Fairfield Books)

The Perry-Lewis/Kershaw Trophy for contribution to the Cricket Society XI went to **Charles Noakes**, who died in November 2009.

WOMBWELL CRICKET LOVERS' SOCIETY AWARDS

George Spofforth Cricketer of the Year	**Marcus Trescothick** (Somerset)
Brian Sellers Captain of the Year	**Will Smith** (Durham)
C. B. Fry Young Cricketer of the Year	**James Taylor** (Leicestershire)
Arthur Wood Wicketkeeper of the Year	**Geraint Jones** (Kent)
Learie Constantine Fielder of the Year	**Marcus Trescothick** (Somerset)
Dr Taylor Award (best performance in Yorks–Lancs matches)	**Adil Rashid** (Yorkshire)
Les Bailey Most Promising Young Yorkshire Player	**Jonathan Bairstow**
Ted Umbers Services to Yorkshire Cricket	**Mollie Staines***
J. M. Kilburn Cricket Writer of the Year	**Duncan Hamilton**

* Mollie Staines was the first woman to serve on the Yorkshire committee.

VEUVE CLICQUOT ENGLAND CRICKET PHOTOGRAPHY AWARDS

Freelance sports photographer **Philip Brown** won the inaugural Veuve Clicquot England Cricket Photography Award in May 2009 for a picture of Ravi Bopara during England's tour of the Caribbean earlier in the year. He received £5,000 and a Veuve Clicquot Yellow Label Methuselah engraved with his name. Paul Thomas was awarded second place and Richard Heathcote third place, while Stuart Robinson was highly commended.

ECB OSCAs

The ECB presented the 2009 NatWest Outstanding Service to Cricket Awards to volunteers from recreational cricket in October. The winners were:

Young Volunteer Award (for under-25s)   **Niall Holmes** (Cumbria)
   Helps Haverigg CC with scoring, the website and pitch management, and acts as DJ as social functions.

Building Partnerships Award   **Mohammed Razaq** (Gloucestershire)
  *Pak Bristolians and Bristol Under-13 coach who works on co-ordinating inner-city clubs, the
  Chance to shine project and the Citi Cricket Week which provided coaching for 75 youngsters in
  2009.*
Behind the Scenes Award   **Paul Fletcher** (Leicestershire) **and Nazir Ahmed** (Yorkshire)
  *Fletcher acts as Kirby Muxloe's treasurer, groundsman, kit organiser and membership secretary;
  Ormesby Hall chairman Nazir Ahmed used his joinery and painting skills to rebuild the club from
  scratch after a fire.*
Leagues and Boards Award   **Ruth Prideaux** (Sussex)
  *Former England player and coach of the 1993 World Cup winners, recently retired as chair of the
  Sussex Women's Cricket Association. One of the first women to be awarded an MCC Advanced
  Coaching Certificate.*
Outside the Scorebox   **David Edwards** (Surrey)
  *Set up the Surrey Cricket Board Association of Cricket Officials in 2007, which was responsible
  for training 100 new umpires last year, and as secretary of the Surrey Championship co-ordinates
  the activities of 70 clubs.*
NatWest CricketForce Award   **Richard Butler** (Devon)
  *Organised Exmouth CC's CricketForce weekend, when he enlisted more than 70 volunteers who
  carried out work valued at over £10,000 before the start of the 2009 season.*
Lifetime Achiever   **Malcolm Pratt** (Durham)
  *More than fifty years with Philadelphia CC, serving as secretary, chairman and president; as a
  Chester-le-Street councillor helped to steer through the development of Durham's Riverside
  Ground.*

ACS STATISTICIAN OF THE YEAR

In March 2010, the Association of Cricket Statisticians and Historians awarded the Statistician of the
Year trophy to **Ian Maun** for his book from *From Commons to Lord's*, a chronology of 18th-century
cricket.

2010 FIXTURES

np Test	npower Test match
LV=CC D1/2	LV= County Championship Division 1/Division 2
CB40	Clydesdale Bank 40-over one-day league
FP T20	Friends Provident Twenty20 Cup
FP Twenty20I	Friends Provident Twenty20 international
FP WT20I	Friends Provident Women's Twenty20 international
Univs	University matches
♀	Day/night or floodlit game

Note: All matches of three days or more are first-class, except those involving England Women, England Under-19 or Leeds/Bradford or Cardiff UCCEs.

Mon Mar 29–Thu Apr 1	**Friendly**	MCC	v Durham	Abu Dhabi
Sat Apr 3–Mon 5	**Univs**	Cambridge UCCE	v Surrey	Cambridge
		Derbyshire	v Loughboro UCCE	Derby
		Durham UCCE	v Lancashire	Durham
		Essex	v Leeds/Brad UCCE	Chelmsford
		Gloucestershire	v Cardiff UCCE	Bristol
		Oxford UCCE	v Northamptonshire	Oxford
Fri Apr 9–Mon 12	**LV=CC D1**	Essex	v Hampshire	Chelmsford
		Warwickshire	v Yorkshire	Birmingham
	LV=CC D2	Glamorgan	v Sussex	Cardiff
		Leicestershire	v Northamptonshire	Leicester
		Surrey	v Derbyshire	The Oval
		Worcestershire	v Middlesex	Worcester
Sat Apr 10–Mon 12	**Univs**	Durham UCCE	v Nottinghamshire	Durham
		Kent	v Loughboro UCCE	Canterbury
		Somerset	v Cardiff UCCE	Taunton Vale
Thu Apr 15–Sun 18	**LV=CC D1**	Durham	v Essex	Chester-le-St
		Lancashire	v Warwickshire	Manchester
		Nottinghamshire	v Kent	Nottingham
		Yorkshire	v Somerset	Leeds
	LV=CC D2	Derbyshire	v Leicestershire	Derby
		Gloucestershire	v Northamptonshire	Bristol
		Middlesex	v Glamorgan	Lord's
		Sussex	v Surrey	Hove
Thu Apr 15–Sat 17	**Univs**	Oxford UCCE	v Hampshire	Oxford
		Worcestershire	v Leeds/Brad UCCE	Kidderminster
Wed Apr 21–Sat 24	**LV=CC D1**	Durham	v Hampshire	Chester-le-St
		Essex	v Lancashire	Chelmsford
		Kent	v Yorkshire	Canterbury
		Nottinghamshire	v Somerset	Nottingham
	LV=CC D2	Derbyshire	v Glamorgan	Derby
		Gloucestershire	v Sussex	Bristol
		Northamptonshire	v Middlesex	Northampton
		Surrey	v Worcestershire	Whitgift School
Wed Apr 21–Fri 23	**Univs**	Cambridge UCCE	v Leicestershire	Cambridge
Sun Apr 25	**CB40**	Durham	v Hampshire	Chester-le-St
		Essex	v Yorkshire	Chelmsford
		Glamorgan	v Somerset	Cardiff
		Gloucestershire	v Derbyshire	Bristol
		Kent	v Warwickshire	Canterbury
		Leicestershire	v Nottinghamshire	Leicester

Sun Apr 25	**CB40**	Northamptonshire	v Middlesex	Northampton
		Surrey	v Lancashire	Whitgift School
		Worcestershire	v Sussex	Worcester
Tue Apr 27–Fri 30	**LV=CC D1**	Lancashire	v Kent	Manchester
		Somerset	v Essex	Taunton
		Warwickshire	v Hampshire	Birmingham
		Yorkshire	v Durham	Leeds
	LV=CC D2	Middlesex	v Gloucestershire	Lord's
		Northamptonshire	v Derbyshire	Northampton
		Sussex	v Leicestershire	Hove
		Worcestershire	v Glamorgan	Worcester
Sun May 2	**CB40**	Hampshire	v Nottinghamshire	Southampton
		Kent	v Durham	Canterbury
		Lancashire	v Glamorgan	Manchester
		Middlesex	v Essex	Lord's
		Surrey	v Unicorns	The Oval
		Warwickshire	v Leicestershire	Birmingham
		Yorkshire	v Northamptonshire	Scarborough
Mon May 3	**CB40**	Derbyshire	v Essex	Leek
		Lancashire	v Somerset	Manchester
		Leicestershire	v Durham	Leicester
		Sussex	v Unicorns	Hove
		Worcestershire	v Surrey	Worcester
Tue May 4–Fri 7	**LV=CC D1**	Hampshire	v Nottinghamshire	Southampton
		Kent	v Warwickshire	Canterbury
		Lancashire	v Somerset	Manchester
		Yorkshire	v Essex	Scarborough
	LV=CC D2	Leicestershire	v Worcestershire	Leicester
		Surrey	v Gloucestershire	The Oval
Wed May 5–Sat 8	**LV=CC D2**	Sussex	v Middlesex	Hove
Wed May 5–Fri 7	**Univs**	Durham UCCE	v Durham	Durham
		Glamorgan	v Cardiff UCCE	Cardiff
Fri May 7	**CB40**	Northamptonshire	v Derbyshire	Northampton
Sat May 8	**CB40**	Nottinghamshire	v Kent	Nottingham
Sun May 9	**CB40**	Essex	v Gloucestershire	Chelmsford
		Glamorgan	v Worcestershire	Cardiff
		Somerset	v Unicorns	Taunton
		Sussex	v Lancashire	Hove
		Warwickshire	v Durham	Birmingham
		Yorkshire	v Derbyshire	Leeds
Sun May 9–Tue 11	**Tour match**	Surrey	v Bangladeshis	The Oval
Mon May 10–Thu 13	**LV=CC D1**	Essex	v Kent	Chelmsford
		Hampshire	v Somerset	Southampton
		Nottinghamshire	v Durham	Nottingham
	LV=CC D2	Glamorgan	v Northamptonshire	Cardiff
		Gloucestershire	v Leicestershire	Bristol
		Middlesex	v Derbyshire	Lord's
Mon May 10–Wed 12	**Univs**	Leeds/Brad UCCE	v Warwickshire	Weetwood
		Yorkshire	v Loughboro UCCE	Leeds
Wed May 12–Fri 14	**Univs**	Cambridge UCCE	v Sussex	Cambridge
Fri May 14	**CB40**	Hampshire	v Warwickshire	Southampton
		Middlesex	v Gloucestershire	Lord's

Fri May 14–Sun 16	Tour match	Essex	v Bangladeshis	Chelmsford
Sat May 15	CB40	Somerset	v Sussex	Taunton
		Yorkshire	v Netherlands	Leeds
Sun May 16	CB40	Leicestershire	v Scotland	Leicester
		Middlesex	v Netherlands	Lord's
		Nottinghamshire	v Hampshire	Nottingham
		Unicorns	v Glamorgan	Bournemouth
		Warwickshire	v Kent	Birmingham
		Worcestershire	v Lancashire	Worcester
Mon May 17–Thu 20	LV=CC D1	Kent	v Durham	Canterbury
		Nottinghamshire	v Hampshire	Nottingham
		Somerset	v Yorkshire	Taunton
		Warwickshire	v Lancashire	Birmingham
	LV=CC D2	Glamorgan	v Gloucestershire	Cardiff
		Surrey	v Middlesex	The Oval
		Worcestershire	v Derbyshire	Worcester
Tue May 18–Fri 21	LV=CC D2	Northamptonshire	v Sussex	Northampton
Wed May 19–Sat 22	Tour match	England Lions	v Bangladeshis	Derby
Fri May 21	CB40	Glamorgan	v Surrey	Cardiff ♀
		Netherlands	v Essex	Amstelveen
Sat May 22	CB40	Scotland	v Kent	Edinburgh
		Warwickshire	v Hampshire	Birmingham
Sun May 23	CB40	Durham	v Leicestershire	Chester-le-St
		Gloucestershire	v Northamptonshire	Bristol
		Lancashire	v Surrey	Manchester
		Netherlands	v Middlesex	Amstelveen
		Unicorns	v Sussex	Arundel
		Scotland	v Nottinghamshire	Edinburgh
		Somerset	v Worcestershire	Bath
Mon May 24–Thu 27	LV=CC D1	Durham	v Kent	Chester-le-St
		Hampshire	v Yorkshire	Southampton
		Lancashire	v Essex	Manchester
		Somerset	v Warwickshire	Taunton
	LV=CC D2	Derbyshire	v Gloucestershire	Derby
		Leicestershire	v Glamorgan	Leicester
		Northamptonshire	v Surrey	Northampton
		Sussex	v Worcestershire	Hove
Tue May 25–Thu 27	Univs	Oxford UCCE	v Middlesex	Oxford
Thu May 27–Mon 31	1st np Test	**ENGLAND**	**v BANGLADESH**	**Lord's**
Sat May 29–Tue Jun 1	LV=CC D1	Nottinghamshire	v Essex	Nottingham
		Warwickshire	v Durham	Birmingham
		Yorkshire	v Lancashire	Leeds
	LV=CC D2	Glamorgan	v Surrey	Cardiff
		Leicestershire	v Middlesex	Leicester
		Worcestershire	v Gloucestershire	Worcester
Sun May 30	CB40	Derbyshire	v Netherlands	Derby
		Hampshire	v Scotland	Southampton
Mon May 31	CB40	Kent	v Scotland	Canterbury
		Northamptonshire	v Netherlands	Northampton
Tue Jun 1	FP T20	Sussex	v Somerset	Hove ♀

Wed Jun 2	FP T20	Essex	v Kent	Chelmsford ♀
		Leicestershire	v Derbyshire	Leicester
Thu Jun 3	FP T20	Hampshire	v Kent	Southampton ♀
		Middlesex	v Sussex	Lord's ♀
		Warwickshire	v Northamptonshire	Birmingham
		Yorkshire	v Derbyshire	Leeds
Fri Jun 4	FP T20	Durham	v Lancashire	Chester-le-St
		Glamorgan	v Gloucestershire	Cardiff ♀
		Worcestershire	v Yorkshire	Worcester
Fri Jun 4–Mon 7	LV=CC D1	Hampshire	v Essex	Southampton
		Kent	v Nottinghamshire	Tunbridge Wells
		Warwickshire	v Somerset	Birmingham
	LV=CC D2	Middlesex	v Northamptonshire	Lord's
		Surrey	v Leicestershire	The Oval
Fri Jun 4–Tue 8	2nd np Test	**ENGLAND**	**v BANGLADESH**	**Manchester**
Sat Jun 5–Tue 8	LV=CC D2	Derbyshire	v Sussex	Derby
Sun Jun 6	FP T20	Durham	v Worcestershire	Chester-le-St
Tue Jun 8	FP T20	Glamorgan	v Hampshire	Cardiff ♀
		Northamptonshire	v Leicestershire	Northampton ♀
		Surrey	v Gloucestershire	The Oval
Wed Jun 9	FP T20	Derbyshire	v Warwickshire	Derby ♀
		Kent	v Sussex	Tunbridge Wells
		Lancashire	v Northamptonshire	Manchester
		Middlesex	v Somerset	Lord's ♀
Thu Jun 10	FP T20	Surrey	v Essex	The Oval ♀
		Worcestershire	v Nottinghamshire	Worcester
		Yorkshire	v Durham	Leeds
Fri Jun 11	FP T20	Essex	v Glamorgan	Chelmsford ♀
		Gloucestershire	v Sussex	TBC
		Hampshire	v Somerset	Southampton ♀
		Kent	v Middlesex	Canterbury
		Lancashire	v Leicestershire	Manchester
		Northamptonshire	v Worcestershire	Northampton ♀
		Nottinghamshire	v Derbyshire	Nottingham
		Warwickshire	v Durham	Birmingham
Sat Jun 12	FP T20	Glamorgan	v Sussex	Cardiff ♀
		Somerset	v Surrey	Taunton
Sun Jun 13	FP T20	Derbyshire	v Durham	Derby
		Gloucestershire	v Kent	TBC
		Hampshire	v Surrey	Southampton
		Middlesex	v Essex	Lord's
		Nottinghamshire	v Worcestershire	Nottingham
		Warwickshire	v Lancashire	Birmingham
		Yorkshire	v Northamptonshire	Leeds
Mon Jun 14	FP T20	Durham	v Leicestershire	Chester-le-St
Tue Jun 15	FP T20	Middlesex	v Glamorgan	Richmond
		Nottinghamshire	v Lancashire	Nottingham
Wed Jun 16	FP T20	Somerset	v Essex	Taunton
		Sussex	v Gloucestershire	Hove ♀
		Warwickshire	v Nottinghamshire	Birmingham

Thu Jun 17	Tour match	Ireland	v Australians	Clontarf
	FP T20	Derbyshire	v Nottinghamshire	Derby �...
		Middlesex	v Surrey	Lord's ♀
		Yorkshire	v Lancashire	Leeds
Fri Jun 18	FP T20	Durham	v Yorkshire	Chester-le-St
		Leicestershire	v Northamptonshire	Leicester
		Somerset	v Gloucestershire	Taunton
		Surrey	v Kent	The Oval ♀
		Sussex	v Hampshire	Hove
		Worcestershire	v Warwickshire	Worcester
Sat Jun 19	ODI	**SCOTLAND**	**v ENGLAND**	**Edinburgh**
	Tour match	Middlesex	v Australians	Lord's
	FP T20	Glamorgan	v Essex	Cardiff ♀
		Gloucestershire	v Hampshire	Bristol
Sun Jun 20	FP T20	Durham	v Nottinghamshire	Chester-le-St
		Kent	v Somerset	Beckenham
		Lancashire	v Warwickshire	Manchester
		Leicestershire	v Yorkshire	Leicester
		Northamptonshire	v Derbyshire	Northampton
		Surrey	v Sussex	The Oval
Mon Jun 21	FP T20	Derbyshire	v Worcestershire	Derby ♀
Tue Jun 22	ODI	**ENGLAND**	**v AUSTRALIA**	**Southampton ♀**
	FP T20	Lancashire	v Durham	Manchester
		Nottinghamshire	v Northamptonshire	Nottingham
		Surrey	v Hampshire	The Oval
		Yorkshire	v Worcestershire	Leeds
Wed Jun 23	Tour match	Ireland	v New Zealand A	Belfast
		Scotland	v India A	Glasgow
	FP T20	Gloucestershire	v Essex	Bristol
		Kent	v Surrey	Beckenham
		Sussex	v Glamorgan	Hove ♀
		Warwickshire	v Leicestershire	Birmingham
Thu Jun 24	ODI	**ENGLAND**	**v AUSTRALIA**	**Cardiff ♀**
	FP T20	Middlesex	v Kent	Lord's ♀
		Yorkshire	v Nottinghamshire	Leeds
Fri Jun 25	Tour match	Ireland	v New Zealand A	Belfast
		Scotland	v India A	Glasgow
	FP T20	Essex	v Surrey	Chelmsford ♀
		Hampshire	v Gloucestershire	Southampton ♀
		Leicestershire	v Lancashire	Leicester
		Nottinghamshire	v Durham	Nottingham
		Somerset	v Sussex	Taunton
		Warwickshire	v Derbyshire	Birmingham
		Worcestershire	v Northamptonshire	Worcester
Sat Jun 26	FP T20	Glamorgan	v Middlesex	Cardiff ♀
		Northamptonshire	v Durham	Northampton

Sun Jun 27	ODI	**ENGLAND**	**v AUSTRALIA**	**Manchester**
	FP T20	Gloucestershire	v Middlesex	Bristol
		Hampshire	v Essex	Southampton
		Nottinghamshire	v Warwickshire	Nottingham
		Sussex	v Kent	Hove
		Worcestershire	v Derbyshire	Worcester
		Yorkshire	v Leicestershire	Leeds
Mon Jun 28	Tour match	India A	v New Zealand A	Northampton
	FP T20	Somerset	v Glamorgan	Taunton
Mon Jun 28–Wed 30	Tour match	Kent	v Pakistanis	Canterbury
Mon Jun 28–Thu Jul 1	LV=CC D1	Durham	v Warwickshire	Chester-le-St
		Lancashire	v Yorkshire	Manchester
	LV=CC D2	Derbyshire	v Surrey	Chesterfield
		Gloucestershire	v Middlesex	Bristol
		Worcestershire	v Leicestershire	Worcester
Tue Jun 29	FP WT20I	**England Women**	**v NZ Women**	**Chelmsford**
	Tour match	England Lions	v New Zealand A	Northampton
	FP T20	Essex	v Sussex	Chelmsford ♀
Wed Jun 30	ODI	**ENGLAND**	**v AUSTRALIA**	**The Oval** ♀
Thu Jul 1	FP WT20I	**England Women**	**v NZ Women**	**Southampton**
	Tour match	England Lions	v India A	Leicester
	FP T20	Hampshire	v Glamorgan	Southampton ♀
Fri Jul 2	Tour (T20)	**Essex**	**v Pakistanis**	**Chelmsford**
	FP WT20I	**England Women**	**v NZ Women**	**Hove**
	Tour match	India A	v New Zealand A	Leicester
	FP T20	Derbyshire	v Leicestershire	Chesterfield
		Durham	v Warwickshire	Chester-le-St
		Gloucestershire	v Glamorgan	Bristol
		Kent	v Hampshire	Canterbury
		Northamptonshire	v Yorkshire	Northampton ♀
		Surrey	v Somerset	The Oval ♀
		Sussex	v Middlesex	Hove ♀
Sat Jul 3	ODI	**ENGLAND**	**v AUSTRALIA**	**Lord's**
	Tour (T20)	Northamptonshire	v Pakistanis	Northampton
	Tour match	Sussex	v Bangladeshis	Hove
Sun Jul 4	Univs	Oxford Univ.	v Cambridge Univ.	Lord's
	Tour match	England Lions	v New Zealand A	Worcester
	FP T20	Derbyshire	v Lancashire	Chesterfield
		Essex	v Hampshire	Chelmsford
		Kent	v Gloucestershire	Canterbury
		Leicestershire	v Nottinghamshire	Leicester
Sun Jul 4	FP T20	Somerset	v Middlesex	Taunton
		Surrey	v Glamorgan	The Oval
		Yorkshire	v Warwickshire	Leeds
Mon Jul 5	FP T20I	**PAKISTAN**	**v AUSTRALIA**	**Birmingham**
	Tour match	Middlesex	v Bangladeshis	Lord's
	FP T20	Lancashire	v Worcestershire	Manchester

Mon Jul 5–Thu 8	LV=CC D1	Essex	v Nottinghamshire	Chelmsford
		Hampshire	v Kent	Southampton
		Yorkshire	v Warwickshire	Leeds
	LV=CC D2	Northamptonshire	v Glamorgan	Northampton
Tue Jul 6	FP T20I	**PAKISTAN**	**v AUSTRALIA**	**Birmingham**
	Tour match	England Lions	v India A	Worcester
Tue Jul 6–Fri 9	Univs	Oxford Univ.	v Cambridge Univ.	Oxford
Wed Jul 7	FP T20	Leicestershire	v Worcestershire	Leicester
Wed Jul 7–Sat 10	LV=CC D2	Sussex	v Gloucestershire	Arundel
Thu Jul 8	ODI	**ENGLAND**	**v BANGLADESH**	**Nottingham** ♀
	Tour match	Lancashire	v TBC	Manchester
	A-team triangular final			Worcester
	FP T20	Surrey	v Middlesex	The Oval ♀
Thu Jul 8–Fri 9	Tour match	Derbyshire	v Australians	Derby
		Leicestershire	v Pakistanis	Leicester
Fri Jul 9	FP T20	Glamorgan	v Surrey	Cardiff ♀
		Kent	v Essex	The Oval
		Lancashire	v Yorkshire	Manchester
		Northamptonshire	v Warwickshire	Northampton ♀
		Somerset	v Hampshire	Taunton
		Worcestershire	v Durham	Worcester
Sat Jul 10	ODI	**ENGLAND**	**v BANGLADESH**	**Bristol**
	Women's ODI	**England Women**	**v NZ Women**	**Taunton**
	FP T20	Middlesex	v Hampshire	Uxbridge
Sun Jul 11	FP T20	Essex	v Somerset	Chelmsford
		Kent	v Glamorgan	Canterbury
		Lancashire	v Derbyshire	Manchester
		Middlesex	v Gloucestershire	Uxbridge
		Northamptonshire	v Nottinghamshire	Northampton
		Sussex	v Surrey	Arundel
		Worcestershire	v Leicestershire	Worcester
Sun Jul 11–Tue 13	Tour match	Durham	v New Zealand A	Chester-le-St
		Yorkshire	v India A	Leeds
Mon Jul 12	ODI	**ENGLAND**	**v BANGLADESH**	**Birmingham**
	Women's ODI	**England Women**	**v NZ Women**	**Taunton**
Tue Jul 13–Sat 17	1st Test	**PAKISTAN**	**v AUSTRALIA**	**Lord's**
Wed Jul 14	FP T20	Durham	v Derbyshire	Chester-le-St
		Glamorgan	v Somerset	Cardiff ♀
Wed Jul 14	FP T20	Lancashire	v Nottinghamshire	Manchester
		Warwickshire	v Yorkshire	Birmingham
Thu Jul 15	Women's ODI	**England Women**	**v NZ Women**	**Derby** ♀
	FP T20	Essex	v Gloucestershire	Chelmsford ♀
		Northamptonshire	v Lancashire	Northampton ♀
		Nottinghamshire	v Leicestershire	Nottingham ♀

Fri Jul 16	FP T20	Derbyshire	v Northamptonshire	Derby ☂
		Glamorgan	v Kent	Cardiff ☂
		Gloucestershire	v Somerset	Bristol
		Hampshire	v Middlesex	Southampton ☂
		Leicestershire	v Durham	Leicester
		Sussex	v Essex	Hove ☂
		Warwickshire	v Worcestershire	Birmingham
Fri Jul 16–Mon 19	Tour match	India A	v New Zealand A	Manchester
Sat Jul 17	**Women's ODI**	**England Women**	**v NZ Women**	**Barnsley**
	FP T20	Nottinghamshire	v Yorkshire	Nottingham
Sun Jul 18	FP T20	Derbyshire	v Yorkshire	Derby
		Durham	v Northamptonshire	Chester-le-St
		Essex	v Middlesex	Chelmsford
		Gloucestershire	v Surrey	Bristol
		Hampshire	v Sussex	Southampton
		Leicestershire	v Warwickshire	Leicester
		Somerset	v Kent	Taunton
		Worcestershire	v Lancashire	Worcester
Mon Jul 19	CB40	Sussex	v Worcestershire	Hove ☂
Tue Jul 20	**Women's ODI**	**England Women**	**v NZ Women**	**Lord's**
	CB40	Derbyshire	v Gloucestershire	Derby ☂
Tue Jul 20–Fri 23	LV=CC D1	Durham	v Lancashire	Chester-le-St
		Essex	v Yorkshire	Chelmsford
		Somerset	v Kent	Taunton
		Warwickshire	v Nottinghamshire	Birmingham
	LV=CC D2	Surrey	v Northamptonshire	The Oval
Wed Jul 21–Sat 24	U19 Test	England U19	v Australia U19	Northampton
	LV=CC D2	Derbyshire	v Worcestershire	Derby
		Glamorgan	v Leicestershire	Swansea
		Middlesex	v Sussex	Uxbridge
Wed Jul 21–Sun 25	**2nd Test**	**PAKISTAN**	**v AUSTRALIA**	**Leeds**
Fri Jul 23–Mon 26	Tour match	India A	v New Zealand A	Southampton
Sat Jul 24	CB40	Lancashire	v Unicorns	Manchester
Sun Jul 25	CB40	Durham	v Nottinghamshire	Chester-le-St
		Glamorgan	v Sussex	Swansea
		Kent	v Hampshire	Canterbury
		Leicestershire	v Warwickshire	Leicester
		Middlesex	v Yorkshire	Lord's
		Northamptonshire	v Essex	Northampton
		Unicorns	v Worcestershire	Kidderminster
		Surrey	v Somerset	The Oval
Mon Jul 26	FP T20 Quarter-Finals			
Tue Jul 27	FP T20 Quarter-Finals			
Tue Jul 27–Fri 30	U19 Test	England U19	v Australia U19	Scarborough
Thu Jul 29	CB40	Gloucestershire	v Yorkshire	Cheltenham

Thu Jul 29–Sun Aug 1	LV=CC D1	Hampshire	v Lancashire	Southampton
		Kent	v Essex	Canterbury
		Somerset	v Nottinghamshire	Taunton
	LV=CC D2	Leicestershire	v Sussex	Leicester
		Middlesex	v Surrey	Lord's
		Worcestershire	v Northamptonshire	Worcester
Thu Jul 29–Mon Aug 2	1st np Test	**ENGLAND**	**v PAKISTAN**	**Nottingham**
Fri Jul 30–Mon Aug 2	LV=CC D2	Gloucestershire	v Glamorgan	Cheltenham
Fri Jul 30	CB40	Netherlands	v Derbyshire	Schiedam
Sat Jul 31	CB40	Scotland	v Durham	Glasgow
Sun Aug 1	CB40	Netherlands	v Yorkshire	Schiedam
		Scotland	v Warwickshire	Glasgow
Mon Aug 2	FP U19 T20	England U19	v Australia U19	Chester-le-St
Tue Aug 3	CB40	Lancashire	v Sussex	Manchester ☂
	FP U19 T20	England U19	v Australia U19	Chester-le-St
Tue Aug 3–Fri 6	LV=CC D1	Hampshire	v Durham	Basingstoke
		Kent	v Somerset	Canterbury
		Yorkshire	v Nottinghamshire	Leeds
	LV=CC D2	Leicestershire	v Derbyshire	Leicester
Wed Aug 4	CB40	Surrey	v Glamorgan	The Oval ☂
Wed Aug 4–Sat 7	LV=CC D1	Essex	v Warwickshire	Southend
	LV=CC D2	Gloucestershire	v Worcestershire	Cheltenham
Thu Aug 5	CB40	Middlesex	v Northamptonshire	Lord's ☂
Fri Aug 6–Tue 10	2nd np Test	**ENGLAND**	**v PAKISTAN**	**Birmingham**
Sat Aug 7	U19 ODI	England U19	v Australia U19	Cambridge
Sun Aug 8	CB40	Derbyshire	v Yorkshire	Chesterfield
		Essex	v Northamptonshire	Southend
		Glamorgan	v Lancashire	Colwyn Bay
		Gloucestershire	v Middlesex	Cheltenham
		Hampshire	v Durham	Southampton
		Kent	v Leicestershire	Canterbury
		Nottinghamshire	v Scotland	Nottingham
		Unicorns	v Somerset	Exmouth
		Surrey	v Sussex	Guildford
Mon Aug 9	U19 ODI	England U19	v Australia U19	Arundel
Mon Aug 9–Thu 12	LV=CC D1	Lancashire	v Durham	Manchester
		Somerset	v Hampshire	Taunton
	LV=CC D2	Derbyshire	v Northamptonshire	Chesterfield
		Glamorgan	v Worcestershire	Colwyn Bay
Mon Aug 9–Thu 12	LV=CC D2	Middlesex	v Leicestershire	Lord's
		Surrey	v Sussex	Guildford
Tue Aug 10	U19 ODI	England U19	v Australia U19	Arundel
Wed Aug 11	CB40	Yorkshire	v Gloucestershire	Leeds ☂
Thu Aug 12	U19 ODI	England U19	v Australia U19	Canterbury
	CB40	Nottinghamshire	v Warwickshire	Nottingham ☂

Fri Aug 13	U19 ODI	England U19	v Australia U19	Canterbury
Fri Aug 13–Sat 14	Tour match	Worcestershire	v Pakistanis	Worcester
Sat Aug 14	FP T20 Semi-Finals and Final			Southampton
Mon Aug 16	CB40	Somerset	v Lancashire	Taunton ☙
Mon Aug 16–Thu 19	LV=CC D1	Durham	v Yorkshire	Chester-le-St
		Nottinghamshire	v Warwickshire	Nottingham
	LV=CC D2	Glamorgan	v Middlesex	Cardiff
		Northamptonshire	v Gloucestershire	Northampton
		Worcestershire	v Surrey	Worcester
Tue Aug 17	CB40	Hampshire	v Leicestershire	Southampton ☙
Wed Aug 18–Sat 21	LV=CC D1	Essex	v Somerset	Colchester
		Kent	v Lancashire	Canterbury
	LV=CC D2	Sussex	v Derbyshire	Horsham
Wed Aug 18–Sun 22	3rd np Test	**ENGLAND**	**v PAKISTAN**	**The Oval**
Fri Aug 20	CB40	Glamorgan	v Unicorns	Cardiff ☙
Sat Aug 21	CB40	Scotland	v Hampshire	Aberdeen
Sun Aug 22	CB40	Durham	v Warwickshire	Chester-le-St
		Essex	v Derbyshire	Colchester
		Kent	v Nottinghamshire	Canterbury
		Netherlands	v Northamptonshire	Rotterdam
		Unicorns	v Surrey	Wormsley
		Scotland	v Leicestershire	Aberdeen
		Sussex	v Somerset	Horsham
		Worcestershire	v Glamorgan	Worcester
		Yorkshire	v Middlesex	Scarborough
Mon Aug 23	CB40	Gloucestershire	v Essex	Bristol ☙
Mon Aug 23–Thu 26	LV=CC D1	Yorkshire	v Hampshire	Scarborough
Tue Aug 24	CB40	Derbyshire	v Middlesex	Derby ☙
Tue Aug 24–Fri 27	LV=CC D1	Nottinghamshire	v Lancashire	Nottingham
		Somerset	v Durham	Taunton
	LV=CC D2	Leicestershire	v Surrey	Leicester
Wed Aug 25	CB40	Sussex	v Glamorgan	Hove ☙
Wed Aug 25–Sat 28	LV=CC D1	Warwickshire	v Essex	Birmingham
	LV=CC D2	Derbyshire	v Middlesex	Derby
		Northamptonshire	v Worcestershire	Northampton
Thu Aug 26	CB40	Netherlands	v Gloucestershire	Rotterdam
Thu Aug 26–Mon 30	4th np Test	**ENGLAND**	**v PAKISTAN**	**Lord's**
Fri Aug 27–Mon 30	LV=CC D2	Sussex	v Glamorgan	Hove
Sun Aug 29	CB40	Durham	v Scotland	Chester-le-St
		Essex	v Netherlands	Chelmsford
		Hampshire	v Kent	Southampton
		Nottinghamshire	v Leicestershire	Nottingham
		Somerset	v Surrey	Taunton
		Worcestershire	v Unicorns	Worcester

Mon Aug 30	**CB40**	Derbyshire	v Northamptonshire	Derby
		Gloucestershire	v Netherlands	Bristol
		Leicestershire	v Kent	Leicester
		Nottinghamshire	v Durham	Nottingham
		Unicorns	v Lancashire	Colwyn Bay
		Warwickshire	v Scotland	Birmingham
		Worcestershire	v Somerset	Worcester
Tue Aug 31	**CB40**	Northamptonshire	v Yorkshire	Northampton ♜
Tue Aug 31–Fri Sep 3	**LV=CC D1**	Durham	v Nottinghamshire	Chester-le-St
		Lancashire	v Hampshire	Liverpool
		Warwickshire	v Kent	Birmingham
	LV=CC D2	Gloucestershire	v Derbyshire	Bristol
Wed Sep 1	**CB40**	Surrey	v Worcestershire	The Oval ♜
Thu Sep 2	**Tour match**	Somerset	v Pakistanis	Taunton
	CB40	Essex	v Middlesex	Chelmsford ♜
Sat Sep 4	**CB40**	Durham	v Kent	Chester-le-St
		Lancashire	v Worcestershire	Liverpool
		Leicestershire	v Hampshire	Leicester
		Middlesex	v Derbyshire	Lord's
		Northamptonshire	v Gloucestershire	Northampton
		Somerset	v Glamorgan	Taunton
		Sussex	v Surrey	Hove
		Warwickshire	v Nottinghamshire	Birmingham
		Yorkshire	v Essex	Leeds
Sun Sep 5	**FP T20I**	**ENGLAND**	**v PAKISTAN**	**Cardiff**
Tue Sep 7	**FP T20I**	**ENGLAND**	**v PAKISTAN**	**Cardiff** ♜
Tue Sep 7–Fri 10	**LV=CC D1**	Essex	v Durham	Chelmsford
		Kent	v Hampshire	Canterbury
		Nottinghamshire	v Yorkshire	Nottingham
		Somerset	v Lancashire	Taunton
	LV=CC D2	Leicestershire	v Gloucestershire	Leicester
		Middlesex	v Worcestershire	Lord's
		Surrey	v Glamorgan	The Oval
		Sussex	v Northamptonshire	Hove
Fri Sep 10	**ODI**	**ENGLAND**	**v PAKISTAN**	**Chester-le-St**
Sat Sep 11	**CB40 Semi-Finals**			
Sun Sep 12	**ODI**	**ENGLAND**	**v PAKISTAN**	**Leeds**
Mon Sep 13–Thu 16	**LV=CC D1**	Durham	v Somerset	Chester-le-St
		Hampshire	v Warwickshire	Southampton
		Lancashire	v Nottinghamshire	Manchester
		Yorkshire	v Kent	Leeds
Mon Sep 13–Thu 16	**LV=CC D2**	Glamorgan	v Derbyshire	Cardiff
		Gloucestershire	v Surrey	Bristol
		Northamptonshire	v Leicestershire	Northampton
		Worcestershire	v Sussex	Worcester
Fri Sep 17	**ODI**	**ENGLAND**	**v PAKISTAN**	**The Oval** ♜
Sat Sep 18	**CB40 Final**			Lord's ♜
Mon Sep 20	**ODI**	**ENGLAND**	**v PAKISTAN**	**Lord's** ♜
Wed Sep 22	**ODI**	**ENGLAND**	**v PAKISTAN**	**Southampton** ♜

TEST MATCHES, 2009-10

Full details of these series, and others too late for inclusion, will appear in *Wisden 2011*.

BANGLADESH v INDIA, 2009-10

First Test At Chittagong, January 17, 18, 19, 20, 21, 2010. **India won by 113 runs.** Toss: Bangladesh. **India 243** (V. Sehwag 52, S. R. Tendulkar 105*; Shahadat Hossain 5-71, Shakib Al Hasan 5-62) **and 413-8 dec** (G. Gambhir 116, V. Sehwag 45, A. Mishra 50, V. V. S. Laxman 69*); **Bangladesh 242** (Tamim Iqbal 31, Mushfiqur Rahim 44, Mahmudullah 69; Zaheer Khan 3-54, A. Mishra 3-66) **and 301** (Tamim Iqbal 52, Mushfiqur Rahim 101; I. Sharma 3-48, A. Mishra 4-92).

Shahadat Hossain's pace and Shakib Al Hasan's left-arm spin reduced India to 150-6 on the opening day, but they were saved by Sachin Tendulkar's 44th Test century, which took him past 13,000 Test runs – both extending his own records, and he added a new one as his 266th Test innings beat Allan Border's 265. A seventh-wicket stand of 108 between Mushfiqur Rahim and Mahmudullah helped to keep Bangladesh's first-innings deficit to one run. But India batted far less complacently second time round, when Gautam Gambhir scored his fifth century in successive Tests. Mushfiqur's maiden Test hundred – the fastest of the match, reached in 112 balls – only delayed India's victory.

Second Test At Mirpur, January 24, 25, 26, 27, 2010. **India won by ten wickets.** Toss: Bangladesh. **Bangladesh 233** (Mohammad Ashraful 39, Shakib Al Hasan 34, Mushfiqur Rahim 30, Mahmudullah 96*; Zaheer Khan 3-62, I. Sharma 4-66) **and 312** (Tamim Iqbal 151, Junaid Siddique 55, Shahadat Hossain 40; Zaheer Khan 7-87); **India 544-8 dec** (G. Gambhir 68, V. Sehwag 56, R. Dravid 111 retired hurt, S. R. Tendulkar 143, M. Vijay 30, M. S. Dhoni 89; Shafiul Islam 3-86) **and 2-0.**

Bangladesh collapsed to 51-5 on the first morning, though Mahmudullah restored some respectability before he was stranded just short of a maiden Test century. Gautam Gambhir matched Viv Richards's record of scoring at least one fifty in 11 successive Tests. But the heart of India's huge total was a 222-run third-wicket partnership between Rahul Dravid and Sachin Tendulkar – their 17th century stand together, a Test record – which ended when Dravid's jaw was fractured by a bouncer from Shahadat Hossain. In reply, Tamim Iqbal, who reached 100 in 101 balls (Bangladesh's fastest Test century, beating Mushfiqur Rahim's 112 balls the previous week) and Junaid Siddique put on 200 for the second wicket. Both fell to Zaheer Khan, who took a Test-best 7-87, including the last four for nought in eight deliveries, despite a bad back. India needed only two runs for victory; they came from byes. It was their fifth consecutive Test series win.

INDIA v SOUTH AFRICA, 2009-10

First Test At Nagpur, February 6, 7, 8, 9, 2010. **South Africa won by an innings and six runs.** Toss: South Africa. **South Africa 558-6 dec** (H. M. Amla 253*, J. H. Kallis 173, A. B. de Villiers 53, M. V. Boucher 39; Zaheer Khan 3-96); **India 233** (G. Gambhir 109, S. Badrinath 56; D. W. Steyn 7-51) **and 319** (M. Vijay 32, S. R. Tendulkar 100, W. P. Saha 36, Harbhajan Singh 39, Zaheer Khan 33, Extras 31; D. W. Steyn 3-57, P. L. Harris 3-76).

South Africa lost both openers to Zaheer Khan for six runs, but the next wicket did not fall for 107 overs as Hashim Amla, who batted 11 hours 15 minutes for a career-best 253, and Jacques Kallis, with his 34th Test century, added 340 together. Virender Sehwag scored more than half of India's runs off the bat, and their last six wickets fell for 12 as Dale Steyn with reverse swing took a Test-best 7-51, including a final spell of 3.4–2–3–5, which forced them to follow on 325 behind. Sachin Tendulkar's hundred ensured a better second innings but could not make South Africa bat again.*

Second Test At Kolkata, February 14, 15, 16, 17, 18, 2010. **India won by an innings and 57 runs.** Toss: South Africa. **South Africa 296** (A. N. Petersen 100, H. M. Amla 114; Zaheer Khan 4-90, Harbhajan Singh 3-64) **and 290** (H. M. Amla 123*, Extras 35; Harbhajan Singh 5-59, A. Mishra 3-78); **India 643-6 dec** (V. Sehwag 165, S. R. Tendulkar 106, V. V. S. Laxman 143*, M. S. Dhoni 132*, Extras 36).

Alviro Petersen scored a hundred on Test debut and shared a second-wicket stand of 209 with Hashim Amla, before South Africa's last nine wickets fell for 78. There were four centuries in India's innings; Sachin Tendulkar, with his 47th Test hundred and fourth in successive matches, added 249 for the third wicket with Virender Sehwag, before V. V. S. Laxman and Mahendra Singh Dhoni put

Feeling at home: Hashim Amla moves towards his double-hundred at Nagpur. S. Badrinath takes evasive action.

on 259*, the third-highest seventh-wicket stand in Tests, to establish a lead of 347. The seventh century of the match (one short of the Test record) was Amla's third in successive innings. It gave him 490 runs for once out – the second-highest series average in Test history, after Wally Hammond's 563.00 in two Tests for England against New Zealand in 1932-33. None of Amla's team-mates passed 23, but the last three wickets used up 53.3 overs and more than three and a half hours before Harbhajan Singh finally trapped Morne Morkel with nine balls, plus several minutes, to spare. This was only the fourth instance of teams beating each other by an innings in consecutive Tests in the same series. The 1–1 draw enabled India to retain first place in the ICC Test championship, four points ahead of South Africa.

NEW ZEALAND v BANGLADESH, 2009-10

Only Test At Hamilton, February 15, 16, 17, 18, 19, 2010. **New Zealand won by 121 runs.** Toss: Bangladesh. **New Zealand 553-7 dec** (P. J. Ingram 42, L. R. P. L. Taylor 40, M. J. Guptill 189, B. B. McCullum 185, D. R. Tuffey 31*; Rubel Hossain 5-166) **and 258-5 dec** (T. G. McIntosh 89, L. R. P. L. Taylor 51, M. J. Guptill 56*); **Bangladesh 408** (Tamim Iqbal 68, Aftab Ahmed 33, Shakib Al Hasan 87, Mahmudullah 115; C. S. Martin 3-116, D. L. Vettori 3-88) **and 282** (Tamim Iqbal 30, Shakib Al Hasan 100, Mahmudullah 42; T. G. Southee 3-41).

Putting New Zealand in looked justified when they were 158-5, but Martin Guptill, with a maiden Test century, and Brendon McCullum, with the highest score by a New Zealand wicketkeeper, added 339, the third-highest sixth-wicket stand in Test cricket. For Bangladesh, Mahmudullah reached the maiden hundred he had missed a few weeks earlier, adding 145 for the seventh wicket with Shakib Al Hasan and avoiding the follow-on as Bangladesh reached their fifth-highest Test total. They needed almost as much again, however, when New Zealand set a target of 404. The top order collapsed a second time, to 78-5, but Shakib Al Hasan hit his own maiden century as the last five wickets added 204.

1718

ERRATA

WISDEN, 1940

Page 215   Wright did not take part in the defeat of Australia at The Oval in 1938, although he was selected for the match; injury forced him out before the Test started.

WISDEN, 1965

Page 402   R. B. Nicholls's Championship bowling figures should read 11–4–27–2–13.50.

WISDEN, 1974

Page 1029   England Women scored 279 for three, not 273, to beat Australia by 92 runs.

WISDEN, 1982

Page 960   In the Third Test v India, Australia's J. D. Higgs was lbw b Kapil Dev.

WISDEN, 1987

Page 926   In England's first innings v West Indies, the sixth wicket fell at 223 not 213.
Page 1018   The second final of the Benson and Hedges World Series Cup on February 9, 1986, was not a day/night game.

WISDEN, 1990

Page 674   MCC's planned fixture with France, cancelled because of the Revolution, would have been in 1789, not 1779.

WISDEN, 2004

Page 1257   The Zimbabwean fielder who dropped Matthew Hayden on 335 was Mark Vermeulen, at long-on, not Trevor Gripper.

WISDEN, 2009

Page 99   Kolkata Knight Riders signed C. H. Gayle for $800,000 in 2008, but he was injured and unable to play for them until the second tournament, played in South Africa in 2009.
Page 588   In Worcestershire's first innings, Masters's figures should be 17.5–4–50–2.
Page 619   Dimitri Mascarenhas was born in London to Sri Lankan parents.
Page 622   In Hampshire's first innings, Collins's figures should be 18.5–3–57–2.
Page 653   In Sussex's second innings, Cork's figures should be 4–1–13–0 and du Plessis bowled 1–0–1–0.
Page 689   In Warwickshire's first innings, Klusener's figures should be 16.2–4–63–1.
Page 695   In Essex's second innings, Foster walked halfway to the wicket before rain stopped play, and therefore, under Law 2.10, should be recorded as not out 0.
Page 718   In Somerset's second innings, Bresnan's figures should be 19.1–5–25–3 and Patterson's 16–1–56–2.
Page 732   In Surrey's second innings, Afzaal was caught by Langer, not de Bruyn.
Page 760   In Middlesex's first innings, Tahir's figures should be 22–7–65–1.
Page 762   In Northamptonshire's innings, Trott's figures should be 7.5–1–22–0.
Page 985   In the match between India and Sri Lanka on February 12, Sharma's figures should be 4–0–27–1 and Pathan's 4–0–29–0.
Page 1402   The ICC Intercontinental Cup final was between Ireland and Namibia.
Page 1515   Jack Simmons was elected the ECB's chairman of cricket, not chairman of the ECB itself, on February 5.
Page 1643   Archie Jackson was born on September 5, not December 5.

CHARITIES IN 2009

ARUNDEL CASTLE CRICKET FOUNDATION: more than 250,000 youngsters, mainly from inner-city areas and those with special needs, have received instruction and encouragement at Arundel since 1986; in 2009, over 5,000 benefited. Director of cricket: John Barclay, Arundel Park, Sussex BN18 9LH. Tel: 01903 882602; website: www.arundelcastlecricketfoundation.co.uk

THE BRIAN JOHNSTON MEMORIAL TRUST supports cricket for the blind, and aims to ease the financial worries of talented young cricketers through scholarships. The Johnners Dinner in October 2009 was a tribute to Bill Frindall. Trust administrator: Richard Anstey, 10 Buckingham Place, London SW1E 6HX. Tel: 020 7821 2828; website: www.lordstaverners.org

BRITISH ASSOCIATION FOR CRICKETERS WITH DISABILITIES was formed in 1991 to promote cricket to people with disabilities. It administers the national county championship for cricketers with physical and learning disabilities on behalf of the ECB. Hon. secretary: Richard Hill, 25 Nutfield, Welwyn Garden City, Hertfordshire AL7 1UL. Tel: 01707 882236; website: www.bacd.co.uk

BUNBURY CRICKET CLUB not a registered charity, although has raised more than £13m for national charities and local good causes. The Bunbury-sponsored ESCA Under-15 regional festival – which has produced many England players over the last 24 years – was held at Charterhouse School, Surrey, in 2009. Founder: Dr David English MBE, 1 Highwood Cottages, Nan Clark's Lane, London NW7 4HJ. Website: www.bunburycricket.com

CAPITAL KIDS CRICKET, formed in 1990, delivers cricket tuition to state schools throughout the 16 inner London boroughs, assists emerging clubs and organises competitions and festivals in local centres and parks, including its headquarters in Regent's Park, as well as residential courses during school holidays. William Greaves, 13 Canonbury Grove, London N1 2HR. Tel: 020 7226 2705; website: www.capitalkidscricket.co.uk

CHASE BEN HOLLIOAKE FUND was established in 2002 by the family of Ben Hollioake, the Surrey and England all-rounder killed in a car crash. The aim is to raise money for CHASE hospice care for children, which supports families with life-limited children. Fund manager: Diana de Moura Stewart, CHASE, Loseley Park, Guildford, Surrey GU3 1HS. Tel: 01483 454213; website: www.chasecare.org.uk/benhollioakefund

CRICKET FOR CHANGE uses cricket to change the lives of disadvantaged young people, employing its "Street 20" version of the game with the Metropolitan Police and *Chance to shine;* helps disability groups through its "Hit the Top" programme with Sport England and the Lord's Taverners; and runs youth training courses at its indoor facility. Overseas initiatives took place in 2009 in Israel, Jamaica and Sri Lanka. Chief executive: Tom Rodwell, The Cricket Centre, Plough Lane, Wallington, Surrey SM6 8JQ. Tel: 020 8669 2177; website: www.cricketforchange.org.uk

THE CRICKET FOUNDATION: *Chance to shine*, the foundation's campaign to regenerate competitive cricket in state schools, was launched in 2005 with a commitment to raise £25m from private sources, which the Government pledged to match. By the end of 2009, the Foundation had raised some £20m. Chief executive: Wasim Khan, Lord's Cricket Ground, London NW8 8QZ. Tel: 020 7432 1259; website: www.chancetoshine.org

THE CRICKET SOCIETY TRUST's principal aim is to support schools and organisations to encourage enjoyment of the game and to develop skills. Particular effort and concentration is given to special-needs children through a programme arranged with Arundel Castle Cricket Foundation. Hon. secretary: Ken Merchant, 16 Louise Road, Rayleigh, Essex SS6 8LW. Tel: 01268 747414; website: www.cricketsocietytrust.org.uk

THE DICKIE BIRD FOUNDATION, set up by the former umpire in 2004, helps financially disadvantaged young people under 18 to participate in the sport of their choice. Grants are made towards the cost of equipment, clothing and travel. Chairman of the trustees: Les Smith, 47 Ripon Road, Earlsheaton, Dewsbury, West Yorkshire WF12 7LG. Tel: 01924 430593 or 07904 440367; website: www.thedickiebirdfoundation.co.uk

ENGLAND AND WALES CRICKET TRUST was established in 2005 to aid community participation in cricket, with a fund from which to make interest-free loans to amateur cricket clubs. In its latest financial year it incurred costs on charitable activities of £9.5m – primarily grants to county cricket boards to support their programmes. Trustee: Brian Havill, Lord's Cricket Ground, London NW8 8QZ. Tel: 020 7432 1201; email: brian.havill@ecb.co.uk

FIELDS IN TRUST, the operating name of the National Playing Fields Association, helps local communities protect and manage their playing fields, and seeks to influence government to ensure that remaining fields are not sold. It offers a range of technical and consultancy services. Chief executive: Alison Moore-Gwyn, Ground Floor South, 100 Christian Street, London E1 1RS. Tel: 020 7264 2400; website: www.fieldsintrust.org

THE HORNSBY PROFESSIONAL CRICKETERS' FUND, established in 1928 from a bequest from the estate of J. H. J. Hornsby (Middlesex, MCC and the Gentlemen), supports former professionals and their families, both through regular financial help or one-off grants towards healthcare or similar essential needs. Secretary of trust: The Rev. Prebendary Mike Vockins OBE, Birchwood Lodge, Birchwood, Storridge, Malvern, Worcestershire WR13 5EZ. Tel: 01886 884366.

THE LORD'S TAVERNERS is one of the UK's leading youth sports charities and the official charity of recreational cricket. Its mission is "to give young people, particularly those with special needs, a sporting chance". In 2009, the Taverners donated nearly £3m to help young people of all abilities and backgrounds participate in cricket and other sporting activities. The Lord's Taverners, 10 Buckingham Place, London SW1E 6HX. Tel: 020 7821 2828; website: www.lordstaverners.org

THE OVAL CRICKET RELIEF TRUST assists in areas affected by natural disasters. The Surrey Cricket Village at Maggona in tsunami-stricken Sri Lanka provided 45 new houses and a cricket field; five grounds were restored following the earthquake in north-west Pakistan; and the St Moritz pavilion in Grenada was rebuilt after a hurricane. Chairman of trustees: Paul Sheldon, The Oval, Kennington, London SE11 5SS. Tel: 020 7582 6660; website: www.britoval.com/about/csr/charity

PCA BENEVOLENT FUND is part of the commitment of the Professional Cricketers' Association to aid current and former players and their dependants in times of hardship and upheaval, or to help them readjust to the world beyond the game. Player services executive: Rachel Newnham, 5 Utopia Village, 7 Chalcot Road, Primrose Hill, London NW1 8LH. Tel: 020 7449 4229; website: www.thepca.co.uk

THE PRIMARY CLUB provides sporting and recreational facilities for the blind and partially sighted. Membership is nominally restricted to those dismissed first ball in any form of cricket; almost 10,000 belong. In total, the club has raised £3m, helped by sales of its tie, popularised by *Test Match Special*. Andrew Strauss is president of the Primary Club Juniors. Hon. Secretary: Chris Larlham, PO Box 12121, Saffron Walden, Essex CB10 2ZF. Tel: 01799 586507; website: www.primaryclub.org

THE PRINCE'S TRUST CRICKET INITIATIVE harnesses the power of the game to help unemployed 16–25-year-olds on the trust's 12-week personal development course, building key workplace skills. Through county clubs, they have access to coaching sessions, motivational talks, workshops on healthy lifestyles and work placements. Sport development manager: Mark Newby, The Prince's Trust, 18 Park Square East, London NW1 4LH. Tel: 020 7543 1303; website: www.princes-trust.org.uk/cricket

THE PROFESSIONAL CRICKETERS' ASSOCIATION CHARITY: there are many worthy and needy cases among cricketers (and their dependants) who played in the era before the PCA came into being; the trustees work tirelessly to visit beneficiaries of the charity to ensure they are in good health. Chairman of trustees: David Graveney OBE, PCA, 5 Utopia Village, 7 Chalcot Road, Primrose Hill, London NW1 8LH. Website: www.thepca.co.uk

TCT LAURIE ENGEL FUND, which works with the Teenage Cancer Trust, was set up after the death in 2005 of 13-year-old Laurie Engel, son of former *Wisden* editor Matthew Engel. More than £900,000 has been raised towards a new £2.5m teenage cancer unit at Birmingham Children's Hospital, completed in 2009. TCT Laurie Engel Fund, Fair Oak, Bacton, Herefordshire HR2 0AT. Email: tctlaurie1@aol.com; website: www.laurieengelfund.org

CRICKET TRADE DIRECTORY

BOOKSELLERS

AARDVARK BOOKS, 19 Vanwall Drive, Waddington, Lincoln, Lincolnshire LN5 9LT. Tel: 01522 722671; email: pete@aardvarkcricketbooks.co.uk. Peter Taylor specialises in *Wisdens*, including rare hardbacks and early editions. Quarterly catalogues sent on request. *Wisdens* purchased. Cleaning, gilding and restoration undertaken.

ACUMEN BOOKS, Nantwich Road, Audley, Staffordshire ST7 8DL. Tel: 01782 720753; fax: 01782 720798; email: wca@acumenbooks.co.uk; website: www.acumenbooks.co.uk. Everything for umpires, scorers, officials, etc. Lawbooks, Tom Smith, open-learning manuals and other textbooks, Duckworth/Lewis, scorebooks, equipment, counters, gauges, heavy and Hi-Vis bails, etc; import/export.

BOUNDARY BOOKS, The Haven, West Street, Childrey OX12 9UL. Tel: 01235 751021; email: boundarybooks@btinternet.com. Rare and second-hand books, autographs and memorabilia bought and sold. Catalogues issued. Limited-editions published. Unusual and scarce items always available.

CHRISTOPHER SAUNDERS, Kingston House, High Street, Newnham-on-Severn, Gloucestershire GL14 1BB. Tel: 01594 516030; fax: 01594 517273; email: chrisbooks@ aol.com; website: www.cricket-books.com. Office/bookroom open by appointment. Second-hand/antiquarian cricket books and memorabilia bought and sold. Regular catalogues issued containing selections from over 12,000 items in stock.

GRACE BOOKS AND CARDS (TED KIRWAN), 3 Pine Tree Garden, Oadby, Leicester LE2 5UT. Tel: 0116 271 6363 (weekdays) and 0116 271 4267 (evenings and weekends). Second-hand and antiquarian cricket books, *Wisdens*, autographed material and cricket ephemera of all kinds. Now also modern postcards.

IAN DYER CRICKET BOOKS, 29 High Street, Gilling West, Richmond, North Yorkshire DL10 5JG. Tel: 01748 822786; email: iandyer@cricketbooks.co.uk; website: www.cricket-books.co.uk (keyword search & postage calculator). *Wisdens*, annuals (English/overseas), new/used/ antiquarian books, programmes/scorecards, tour guides, benefit brochures, videos/DVDs, memorabilia. Payment by Paypal or CC with SagePay security. Visit by appointment.

JOHN JEFFERS, The Old Mill, Aylesbury Road, Wing, Leighton Buzzard LU7 0PG. Tel: (044) (0)1296 688543 Mobile: 07846 537 692; e-mail: edgwarerover@live.co.uk. *Wisden* specialist. Immediate decision and top settlement for purchase of *Wisden* collections. Why wait for the next auction? Why pay the auctioneer's commission anyway?

J. W. McKENZIE, 12 Stoneleigh Park Road, Ewell, Epsom, Surrey KT19 0QT. Tel: 020 8393 7700; fax: 020 8393 1694; email: mckenziecricket@btconnect.com; website: www.mckenziecricket.co.uk. Specialist since 1971 in antiquarian and second-hand books, particularly *Wisdens* and cricket memorabilia. Regular catalogues issued. Cricket book publisher. Large shop premises open regular business hours, 30 minutes from London.

K & J BOOKS. Tel: 01689 835426; email: Keithparker88440@aol.com; website: www.keithandjuliescricketbooks.co.uk. *Wisden Cricketers' Almanacks* and *Lillywhite's* purchased.

KEN FAULKNER, 65 Brookside, Wokingham, Berkshire RG41 2ST. Tel: 0118 978 5255. Email: kfaulkner@bowmore.demon.co.uk; website: www.bowmore.demon.co.uk. My stall, with a strong *Wisden* stock, will be operating at the Cheltenham Cricket Festival in July/August 2010. Collections which include pre-1946 *Wisdens* wanted.

MARTIN WOOD CRICKET BOOKS, 1c Wickenden Road, Sevenoaks, Kent TN13 3PJ. Tel: 01732 457205; email: martin@martinwoodcricketbooks.co.uk; website: www.martinwoodcricketbooks.co.uk. Established 1970.

ROGER HEAVENS, 125 Keddington Road, Louth, Lincolnshire LN11 0BL. Tel: 01507 606102; mobile: 07967 096924; email: roger.heavens@btinternet.com; website: www.booksoncricket.net. Cricket publisher specialising in the works of Arthur Haygarth and early history of cricket. Send for free catalogue. Order direct – all major credit cards accepted.

ROGER PAGE, 10 Ekari Court, Yallambie, Victoria 3085, Australia. Tel: (+61) 3 9435 6332; fax: (+61) 3 9432 2050; email: rpcricketbooks@unite.com.au. Dealer in new and second-hand cricket books. Distributor of overseas cricket annuals and magazines. Agent for Association of Cricket Statisticians and Cricket Memorabilia Society.

ST MARY'S BOOKS & PRINTS, 9 St Mary's Hill, Stamford, Lincolnshire PE9 2DP. Tel: 01780 763033; email: info@stmarysbooks.com; website: www.stmarysbooks.com. Dealers in *Wisdens* 1864–2009, second-hand, rare cricket books and *Vanity Fair* prints. Book-search service offered.

SPORTSPAGES, The Oast House, Park Row, Farnham, Surrey GU9 7JH. Tel: 01252 727222; email: info@sportspages.com; website: www.sportspages.com. Large stock of *Wisdens*, fine cricket books, scorecards, autograph material, tour brochures. Books and memorabilia also purchased, please offer.

STUART TOPPS, 25 Ramsker Drive, Armthorpe, Doncaster DN3 3SE. Tel: 01302 300906. Our 120-page-plus catalogue of cricket books, *Wisdens*, booklets, brochures and county yearbooks is always available.

TIM BEDDOW, 66 Oak Road, Oldbury, West Midlands B68 0BD. Tel: 0121 421 7117; mobile: 07956 456112; email: wisden1864@hotmail.com. Wanted: cash paid for football, cricket, speedway and rugby union memorabilia, badges, books, programmes (amateur and professional), autographed items, match tickets, yearbooks and photographs – anything considered.

WILLIAM H. ROBERTS, The Crease, 113 Hill Grove, Salendine Nook, Huddersfield, West Yorkshire HD3 3TL. Tel/fax: 01484 654463; email: william.roberts2@virgin.net; website: www.williamroberts-cricket.com. Second-hand/antiquarian cricket books, *Wisdens*, autographs and memorabilia bought and sold.

WILLOWS PUBLISHING, 17 The Willows, Stone, Staffordshire ST15 0DE. Tel: 01785 814700; email: jenkins.willows@ntlworld.com. *Wisden* reprints 1880–1935 and 1940–1945. Send SAE for prices.

WISDEN DIRECT, website: www.wisden.com. Various editions of *Wisden Cricketers' Almanack* since 1997 and other Wisden publications, all at discounted prices.

WISDENWORLD. Tel: 01480 819272; email info@wisdenworld.com; website: www.wisdenworld.com. A unique and friendly service; quality *Wisdens* bought and sold at fair prices, along with free advice on the value of your collection. Other cricket memorabilia available.

WWW.WISDENS.ORG. Tel: 07793 060706; email: wisdens@cridler.com. The unofficial *Wisden* collectors' website. Valuations, guide, discussion forum, all free to use. We also buy and sell *Wisdens* for our members. Email us for free advice, especially around the pitfalls of collecting *Wisdens*.

AUCTIONEERS

ANTHEMION AUCTIONS, 15 Norwich Road, Cardiff CF23 9AB. Tel: 029 2047 2444; email: anthemions@aol.com; website: www.anthemionauctions.com. Sporting memorabilia specialists with an international clientele and extensive dedicated database of buyers.

BONHAMS AUCTIONEERS, New House, 150 Christleton Road, Chester CH3 5TD. Tel: 01244 313936; email: dan.davies@bonhams.com; website: www.bonhams.com. The world's leading auctioneer of sporting memorabilia.

CHRISTIE'S, 8 King Street, London SW1Y 6QT. Tel: 020 7389 2674; email: rneelands@christies.com. Christie's have held regular cricket auctions since the inaugural MCC Bicentenary sale in 1987, and recently sold the E. D. R. Eagar and Guy Curry libraries. For free valuations and other enquiries, contact Rupert Neelands.

DOMINIC WINTER BOOK AUCTIONS, Specialist Auctioneers & Valuers, Mallard House, Broadway Lane, South Cerney, Gloucestershire GL7 5UQ. Tel: 01285 860006; website: www.dominicwinter.co.uk. Check our website for forthcoming specialist sales.

GRAHAM BUDD AUCTIONS in association with Sotheby's, PO Box 47519, London N14 6XD. Tel: 020 8366 2525; website: www.grahambuddauctions.co.uk. Specialist auctioneer of sporting memorabilia.

KNIGHTS WISDEN, Norfolk. Tel: 01263 768488; email: tim@knights.co.uk; website: www.knightswisden.co.uk. Established and respected auctioneers; two specialist *Wisden* auctions and three major cricket/sporting memorabilia auctions per year. World-record *Wisden* prices achieved in 2007. *Wisden* auctions: April and September. Entries invited.

MULLOCK'S SPECIALIST AUCTIONEERS & VALUERS, The Old Shippon, Wall under Heywood, Church Stretton, Shropshire SY6 7DS. Tel: 01694 771771; website: www.mullocksauctions.com. For worldwide exposure, contact Europe's No. 1 sporting auction specialists. Regular cricket sales are held throughout the year and are fully illustrated on our website.

T. VENNETT-SMITH, 11 Nottingham Road, Gotham, Nottinghamshire NG11 0HE. Tel: 0115 983 0541; email: info@vennett-smith.com; website: www.vennett-smith.com. Auctioneers and valuers. Regular sales of cricket and sports memorabilia. The cricket auction is run by cricketers for cricket-lovers worldwide.

WWW.WISDENAUCTION.COM. Tel: 07793 060706; email: wisdenauction@cridler.com. A specially designed auction website for buying and selling *Wisdens*. List your spares today and bid live for that missing year. No sale, no fee. Many books ending daily. Built by collectors for collectors, with the best descriptions on the internet. See advert on page 1634.

CRICKET ART

DD DESIGNS, 62 St Catherine's Grove, Lincoln, Lincolnshire LN5 8NA. Tel: 01522 800298; email: denise@dd-designs.co.uk; website: www.dd-designs.co.uk. Specialists in genuinely signed limited-edition prints. Official producers of *Wisden's* "Five Cricketers of the Year" sets, and other signed cricket portfolios. Free information leaflet available.

CRICKET COACHING AND ACADEMIES

ACE CRICKET COACHING, P O Box 417, Scarborough, Perth, Western Australia. Tel: (61 8) 9445 3565; email: info@acecricketcoaching.com; website: www.acecricketcoaching.com. The Australian Cricket Experience offers cricket coaching, fitness development, sports psychology, life skills training and the opportunity to play league cricket. World class coaches and facilities.

CAPE CRICKET. Email: info@capecricket.com; website: www.capecricket.com. Professional cricket academy offering opportunities for gap-year, school, university or career-break cricketers who want to spend some time playing league cricket and coaching in Cape Town.

IN-TOUCH CRICKET ACADEMY, based at Epsom College, College Road, Epsom, Surrey KT17 4JQ. Tel: 0844 2492805; email: matt@intouchcricket.co.uk; Website: www.intouchcricket.co.uk. Various levels of coaching for club, district and county age-group cricketers from development to elite academy squads, ranging from Under-8 to Under-19 age groups.

WWW.TEAMER.NET, Unit 4 Minehill Business Centre, Kilternan, Co Dublin. Email: help@teamer.net; website: www.teamer.net. Taking the hassle out of team organisation. Teamer is a FREE to use online team management system which includes FREE text messaging to notify team events to players.

CRICKET EQUIPMENT

CRAZY CATCH, Walltree House Farm, Steane, Brackley, Northamptonshire NN13 5NS. Tel: 01295 816765; fax: 01295 810298; email: flicxuk@flicx.com; websites: www.crazycatch.com/uk, www.flicx.co.uk. Crazy Catch, distributed in the UK and Europe by Flicx UK Ltd.

CRICKET DIRECT, 4 Metro Centre, Ronsons Way, St Albans Road, Sandridge, St Albans, Hertfordshire AL4 9QT. Tel: 08452 303052; Fax: 01727 736969; email: info@cricketdirect.com; website: www.cricketdirect.com. Cricket Direct is the world's finest online cricket store, offering the very best and latest cricket equipment to cricketers of all levels. Visit our website for the most up-to-date prices.

DUKE SPORTSWEAR, Unit 4, Magdalene Road, Torquay, Devon TQ1 4AF. Tel/fax: 01803 292012. Test-standard sweaters to order in your club colours, using the finest yarns.

EXITO SPORTS COMPANY, Unit C1, Burley Heyes, Arley Road, Appleton Thorn, Warrington, Cheshire WA4 4RS. Tel: 01565 777300; email: info@exitosports.com; website: www.exitosports.com. Manufacturers and suppliers of quality cricket clothing and leisurewear to first-class and minor counties, amateur clubs, schools and colleges.

FORDHAM SPORTS, 81/85 Robin Hood Way, Kingston Vale, London SW15 3PW. Tel: 020 8974 5654; email: fordham@fordhamsports.co.uk; website: www.fordhamsports.co.uk. Cricket and rugby equipment specialist with largest range of branded stock in London at discounted prices. Mail order available. Free catalogue.

SERIOUS CRICKET, The Dummer Cricket Centre, Dummer, Basingstoke, Hampshire RG25 2AR. Tel: 01256 398633; email: sales@seriouscricket.co.uk; websites: www.seriouscricket.co.uk, www.seriouscricketcoaching.com. Serious Cricket stock the biggest range of cricket equipment from all manufacturers and offer a wide range of team clothing solutions. With the largest commercial coaching department in the UK, Serious Cricket is your complete one-stop shop for all things cricket!

SOMERSET COUNTY SPORTS, The County Ground, St James Street, Taunton, Somerset TA1 1JT. Tel/fax: 01823 337597; email: sales@somerset-countysports.com; website: www.somerset-countysports.com. Somerset County Sports is probably the leading cricket specialist in the south-west of England, stocking an even more extensive range for the 2009 season.

STUART & WILLIAMS (BOLA), 6 Brookfield Road, Cotham, Bristol BS6 5PQ. Tel: 0117 924 3569; email: info@bola.co.uk; website: www.bola.co.uk. Manufacturer of bowling machines and ball-throwing machines for all sports. Machines for recreational and commercial application for sale to the UK and overseas.

CRICKET TOURS

GULLIVERS SPORTS TRAVEL, Fiddington Manor, Tewkesbury, Gloucestershire GL20 7BJ. Tel: 01684 293175; email: gullivers@gulliverstravel.co.uk; website: www.gulliverstravel.co.uk. The UK's longest established and leading cricket tour operator – supporters' tours and playing tours for schools, clubs and universities. Official travel and tour provider for the International Cricket Council.

HOWZAT TRAVEL, The Pavilion, Burrough Court, Burrough-on-the-Hill, Leicestershire LE14 2QS. Tel: 0800 840 7288; email: info@howzattravel.co.uk; website: www.howzattravel.co.uk. Specialist cricket tour operator. England supporters' tours and playing tours for clubs and schools. Official operator for the Ashes 2010-11 and ICC World Twenty20.

SHIRE SPORTS TOURS. Tel: 0800 9121619 / 01270 524555; email: tours@shiresports.co.uk; website: www.shiresports.co.uk. ATOL-licensed sports tour operator established 1993 specialising in UK, Europe and worldwide cricket tours for clubs, schools and universities. FREE online fixture bureau www.efixtures.co.uk (500+ fixtures against touring sides available annually throughout the UK).

SPORT ABROAD, King's Place, 12–42 Wood Street, Kingston-upon-Thames, Surrey KT1 1JF. Tel: 08456 803 086; email: cricket@sportabroad.co.uk; website: www.sportabroad.co.uk. Established 1984 – one of the UK's leading cricket and sport tour operators. Sport Abroad, a Cricket Australia Travel Office-endorsed travel operator for the *3mobile* Ashes series 2010-11. Licence No: CATO1011/020/SA1.

SPORTING GETAWAYS. Tel: 0208 966 7124; email: reservations@sportinggetaways.co.uk; website: www.sportinggetaways.co.uk. Specialist tour operators to the Caribbean, Sri Lanka, South Africa and Australia. Schools, club sides, benefit tours, testimonials, intensive coaching academy – founders of Sir Garry Sobers Seniors and School Tournament in Barbados.

WISDEN CRICKETER SUPPORTERS' TOUR, ITC Sports, Concorde House, Canal Street, Chester, Cheshire CH1 4EJ. Tel: 01244 355494; email: info@itcsports.co.uk; website: www.itcsports.co.uk. Official tour operator for *The Wisden Cricketer* Supporters' Tour to Australia 2010-11. See the final two *3mobile* Test matches, and experience the country through a range of luxury touring options.

PITCHES AND GROUND EQUIPMENT

FLICX UK, Walltree House Farm, Steane, Brackley, Northamptonshire NN13 5NS. Tel: 01295 816765; fax: 01295 810298; email: flicxuk@flicx.com; websites: www.flicx.co.uk, www.crazycatch.com/uk. Manufacturers and suppliers of portable cricketing equipment, including Flicx pitches, Flicx bowling machines, portable nets and coaching equipment. Brochure and video available. UK distributors of Crazy Catch.

JMS SPORT UK, Parkside Works, Parkwood Street, Keighley, West Yorkshire BD21 4PJ. Tel; 01535 604777; email: info@jmssportuk.com; website: www.jmssportuk.com. Buy direct from the manufacturer. Mobile covers, flat sheets, sightscreens, mobile nets, slip cradles, plus much, much more. We've got cricket covered.

NOTTS SPORT, Innovation House, Magna Park, Lutterworth, LE17 4XH. Tel: 01455 883730; fax: 01455 883755; email: info@nottssport.com; website: www.nottssport.com. With over 25 years' experience, Notts Sport is the world's leading supplier of non-turf cricket pitch systems for coaching, practice and matchplay.

PLUVIUS, King Henry VIII Farm, Myton Road, Warwick CV34 6SB Tel: 01926 311324; email: pluviusltd@aol.com; website: www.pluvius.uk.com. Manufacturers of value-for-money pitch covers and sightscreens, currently used on Test, county, school and club grounds throughout the UK.

POWER PRECISION & FABRICATION, Gunnislake, Cornwall PL18 9AS. Tel: 01822 832608; fax: 01822 834796; email: sales@poweroll.com; website: www.poweroll.com. Poweroll wicket rollers. The largest range of purpose-built ride-on grass-rolling machines available, to suit most budgets.

STADIA SPORTS INTERNATIONAL, 19/20 Lancaster Way Business Park, Ely, Cambridge-shire CB6 3NW. Tel: 01353 668686; fax: 01353 669444; email: sales@stadiasports.co.uk; website: www.stadia-sports.co.uk. Stadia Sports sells screens, cages, netting, scoreboards, stumps, balls, bowling-machines, matting and grounds equipment for indoor and outdoor matchplay and practice. Buy online.

TECHNICAL SURFACES LTD, Standards House, Meridian East, Meridian Business Park, Leicester LE19 1WZ. Tel: 08702 400 700; fax: 08702 400 701; email: sales@technicalsurfaces. co.uk; website: www.technicalsurfaces.co.uk. Installation and refurbishment of artificial cricket pitches. Save money. Top quality carpets supplied and installed direct from the manufacturer. Over 20 years' experience. Nationwide service.

TILDENET, Hartcliffe Way, Bristol BS3 5RJ. Tel: 0117 966 9684; fax 0117 923 1251; email: enquiries@tildenet.co.uk; website: www.tildenet.co.uk. Extensive range of equipment – grass germination sheets, ball-stop fencing, mobile practice nets, fixed nets and frames, new all-weather outdoor practice nets, sightscreens, layflat and mobile rain covers, boundary ropes and practice netting.

SCOREBOARDS AND SCOREBOOKS

FSL SCOREBOARDS. Tel: 0288 676 6131; website: www.fslelectronics.com. UK-designed and manufactured. FSL offer complete range of electronic scoreboards in portable and self-install kits. The range of scoreboards includes one suitable for every club and budget.

WISDEN SCOREBOOKS, Specials Ltd, Nyewood House, Main Road, East Boldre, Brockenhurst, Hampshire SO42 7WL. Tel: 01590 612778; email: info@specialsgifts.com; website: www.specialsgifts.com. Official producers of *Wisden* Scorebooks.

SPEAKERS AND SOCIETIES

CRICKET MEMORABILIA SOCIETY. Honorary Secretary: Steve Cashmore, 4 Stoke Park Court, Stoke Road, Bishops Cleeve, Cheltenham, Gloucestershire GL52 8US. Email: cms87@btinternet.com; website: www.cricketmemorabilia.org. For collectors worldwide: magazines, meetings, auctions, speakers, and – most of all – friendship.

LOOK WHO'S TALKING (Ian Holroyd), PO Box 3257, Ufton, Leamington Spa CV33 9YZ. Tel: 01926 614443; email: ian@look-whos-talking.co.uk; website: www.look-whos-talking. co.uk. A company specialising in providing first-class public speakers for cricket and other sporting events. Contact us to discuss the event and type of speaker. All budgets catered for.

THE CRICKET SOCIETY, c/o David Wood, Hon Secretary, PO Box 6024, Leighton Buzzard, LU7 2ZS. Email: davidwood@cricketsociety.com; website: www.cricketsociety.com. A society that promotes a love of cricket in all its spheres for all ages and interests – playing, watching, reading and listening.

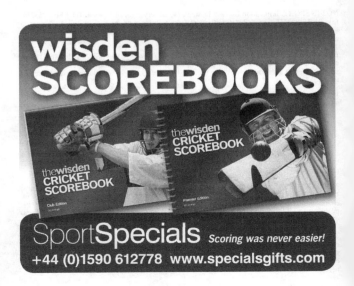

THE WISDEN QUIZ, 2010

All the answers to these questions can be found in this almanack. The winner will receive a collection of books with a recommended retail price of over £330: the three new volumes of *The Wisden Book of Test Cricket*, *Wisden on the Ashes*, *Whitaker's Almanack 2011*, *Schott's Almanack 2011*, and a leatherbound limited-edition copy of *The Wisden Anthology 1978–2006*. Five runners-up will receive a year's subscription to *The Wisden Cricketer* magazine.

1. Who during 2009 became only the second batsman to score more than 200 runs in his first Test match, yet finish on the losing side?

2. In which country was interest in cricket aroused by mention of it in the local edition of *Playboy*?

3. Who once took nine for 23 the day after watching *Gone With the Wind*?

4. Whose hat was blown off on National Wind Day, delaying play?

5. Where were original copies of the first four *Wisdens* (1864–1867) discovered in 2009?

6. Which current first-class player was born in Mesopotamia?

7. Who obtained Don Bradman's autograph 56 years after he asked for it?

8. Which team were coached by a passenger?

9. Who invented a middle name when he joined the MCC cricket staff, as he thought an extra initial might come in useful at Lord's?

10. Against whom did Jordan Price take a hat-trick?

11. Who made his first-class debut in a match between the two counties for which his father played?

12. Who took 13 wickets in a first-class match twice in a month – and finished on the losing side both times?

Please send your answers – which should include the page numbers where they are to be found – together with your name, postal address, phone number and email address to Wisden Quiz (SKS), PO Box 230, Plymouth PL1 2ZR or by email to Quiz@wisden.com. All entries must be received by December 31, 2010. Only one entry per person. In the event of a tie, there will be a draw to establish the prize-winners, whose names will be announced on www.wisden.com in January 2011, along with the answers. In all matters concerning this quiz, the editor's decision is final; no correspondence will be entered into.

The answers to last year's Wisden Quiz (*see page 1679 of Wisden 2009*) were: 1. Dimitri Mascarenhas (*see page 99 of Wisden 2009 and elsewhere*). 2. Vidarbha C. A. Stadium, Jamtha, Nagpur (*page 301*). 3. Ewen Thompson (*page 1194*). 4. Seren Waters; 63.71 (*pages 1393 and 917*). 5. Reg Harris (*page 1605*). 6. Josh Cobb (*page 681*). 7. Jerome Taylor (*page 1190*). 8. Sourav Ganguly (*page 97*). 9. Geoff Boycott (*page 53*). 10. West Indies (*page 1228*). 11. Ghana (*page 1425*). 12. Shivnarine Chanderpaul (*page 1375*). 13. 35 (*page 432*). 14. Akbar Ansari (*page 868*). 15. Daniel Vettori (*page 1058*). The winner of the first prize of £500 was Leslie Hopkin of Old Skellow, near Doncaster. The five runners-up, who each received a year's subscription to *The Wisden Cricketer* magazine, were: Nick Berentzen of Stockport; Chris Walmsley of East Grinstead; Anne Williams of Barnet; J. R. Charters of Chester-le-Street; and Marc Dumat of Nararayama-Shi, Japan.

INDEX OF UNUSUAL OCCURRENCES

INDEX OF ADVERTISEMENTS

PART TITLES

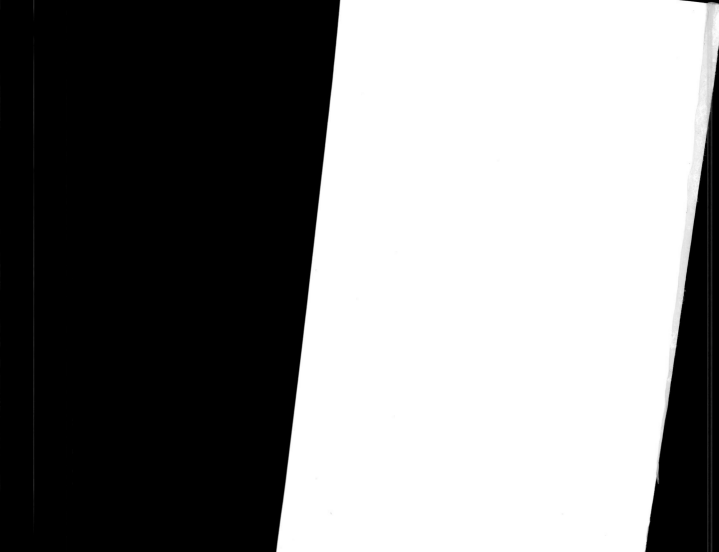